THE OXFORD UNIVERSITY PRESS

SECOND EDITION

DICTIONARY OF QUOTATIONS

THE OXFORD UNIVERSITY PRESS
SECOND EDITION
DICTIONARY OF
QUOTATIONS

UNIV.
OXONIENSIS

DOMI MINA
NUS· TIO·
ILLU MEA

CHANCELLOR
PRESS

Oxford University Press under the title
The Oxford Dictionary of Quotations
This revised second edition was first published
in Great Britain in 1953.

This edition published in 1985 by
Chancellor Press
59 Grosvenor Street
London W1

ISBN 0 907486 95 9

Printed in Great Britain

NOTE TO THE SECOND EDITION
(1953)

DURING the twelve years that have passed since the publication of the first edition the compilers have received a great many suggestions for quotations to be added to the *Dictionary*. These have now been considered in committee, *familiarity* being the criterion as in the first edition, and some 1,300 of them now appear. About 250 quotations originally included seemed no longer familiar and have been omitted. A number of errors have been corrected during the resetting of the type, and it has been possible to give many sources more precisely. The compilers wish to thank, among many others, Dr. R. W. Chapman for innumerable suggestions; Mr. S. H. Moore, who has enlarged the French, German, and Spanish entries; and Sir Humphrey Milford, who, before his death, read the proofs.

The arrangement has also been modified; foreign quotations and those under the headings Anonymous, Ballads, Holy Bible, Nursery Rhymes, Prayer Book, Scottish Psalter, and *Punch,* which in the first edition were to be found in separate sections at the end of the main body of the book, are now incorporated in the general alphabetical scheme. Under every author the arrangement of the quotations remains alphabetical according to the title of the poem or work from which the extract is taken, but where authors have written both poetry and prose, that medium is now given first in which the bulk of the quoted work appears. It is hoped that these alterations will assist quicker reference, toward which end also we have numbered each quotation, the first quotation on each page appearing as 1. An index reference therefore reads 163:15 (page number: quotation number).

The Oxford Dictionary of Nursery Rhymes (1951), edited by Iona and Peter Opie, has made it possible to give earlier sources than hitherto for many rhymes. While the text given below (pp. 366–369) represents the most generally familiar version of each rhyme, the source quoted indicates the place of its earliest known written appearance, often in a form greatly different from that now current.

The index has been entirely remade and is somewhat fuller than that to the first edition. Greek quotations are indexed separately.

THE COMPILERS TO THE READER

(1941)

'CLASSICAL quotation', said Johnson, 'is the *parole* of literary men all over the world.' Although this is no longer strictly true the habit of quoting, both in speech and writing, has steadily increased since his day, and Johnson would undoubtedly be surprised to find here eight and a half pages of his own work that have become part of the *parole* of the reading public. Small dictionaries of quotations have been published for many years—in 1799 D. E. Macdonnel brought out a *Dictionary of Quotations chiefly from Latin and French translated into English*—and during comparatively recent years several large works of American editorship have been produced. In this book the Oxford Press publishes what it is hoped will be a valuable addition to the Oxford Books of Reference already in existence.

The work remained in contemplation for some time before it first began to take shape under the general editorship of Miss Alice Mary Smyth, who worked, for purposes of selection, with a small committee formed of members of the Press itself. The existing dictionaries were taken as a foundation and the entries, pasted on separate cards, considered individually for rejection or inclusion. With these as a basis the most important authors were again dealt with either by the expert, or in committee, or by both. The Press is indebted for a great deal of work to the late Charles Fletcher, who among others made the original selections from Shakespeare, Milton, Pope, Tennyson, and Dryden: among those who dealt with single authors were Lady Charnwood and Mr. Bernard Darwin, who did the Dickens entries, Professor Dewar the Burns, Professor Ernest de Selincourt the Wordsworth: Mr. Colin Ellis did the Surtees, Sterne, and Whyte-Melville, Mr. E. Latham contributed the French quotations, and Mr. Harold Child made many valuable suggestions. A great many people, whom it is impossible to name individually, sent in one or more quotations.

During the whole work of selection a great effort was made to restrict the entries to actual current quotations and not to include phrases which the various editors or contributors believed to be quotable or wanted to be quoted: the work is primarily intended to be a dictionary of *familiar* quotations and not an anthology of every author good and bad; popularity and not merit being the password to inclusion. The selections from the Bible and Shakespeare were the most difficult because a great part of both are familiar to most people; but as concordances of both the Bible and Shakespeare are in print the quotations here included are meant to be the most well known where all is well known.

It has been found very difficult to put into precise words the standard of familiarity that has been aimed at or to imagine one man who might be asked whether or not the particular words were known to him. But it is believed that any of the quotations here printed might be found at some time in one or other of the leading articles of the daily

and weekly papers with their wide range of matter—political, literary, descriptive, humorous, &c. So much for the very elastic standard to which the quotations conform. No one person having been imagined to whom everything included in this book would be familiar, the committee have tried to keep in mind that a number of different kinds of readers would be likely to use the book: these are the 'professionals', such as journalists, writers, public speakers, &c.; the cross-word devotee, since this form of intellectual amusement appears to have come to stay; the man who has in his mind either a few or many half-completed or unidentified quotations which he would like to complete or verify; and (since, as Emerson wrote—'By necessity, by proclivity—and by delight, we all quote') everyone who has found joy and beauty in the words of the writers and wishes to renew that pleasure by using the words again—he whom perhaps Johnson meant by 'the literary man'. The book is not intended as a substitute for the complete works nor as an excuse to anyone not to drink deep of the Pierian spring. But it *is* hoped that the lover of Dickens, for instance, may find pleasure in reading through his entries and that even his detractors will have to admit how good he is in quotation: that the man who has always regarded Milton as a heavy and dull poet may here come across some lovely line and be inclined to read *Paradise Lost*. If the book serves to start people reading the poets it will have accomplished a great deal besides being a work of reference.

It is interesting to observe that the following are the most quoted writers (arranged in the order in which they appear here): Browning, Byron, Cowper, Dickens, Johnson, Kipling, Milton, Shakespeare, Shelley, Tennyson, Wordsworth, the Bible, and the Book of Common Prayer. On the other hand, certain authors of accepted merit or favour such as Trollope, Henry James, Jane Austen, and P. G. Wodehouse have none of them as much as one page to their credit: it would seem that their charm depends on character and atmosphere and that quotability is no real criterion of either popularity or merit in a writer.

The arrangement of authors is alphabetical and not chronological. Under each author the arrangement of the extracts is alphabetical according to the title of the poem or work from which the quotation is taken. The text is, wherever possible, the acknowledged authoritative text and the source of the quotation is always given as fully as possible. Some quotations have had to be omitted because every effort to trace their source has failed—e.g. 'Home, James, and don't spare the horses'. Proverbs and phrases are not included, since these have been dealt with fully in the *Oxford Dictionary of English Proverbs*.

It is to be expected that almost every reader will be shocked by what he considers obvious omissions. Should the reader's indignation be strong enough to prompt him to write pointing these out it is to be hoped that he will give the source of all his suggestions. It is not possible to give all the quotations familiar to every reader; almost all households have favourite books and authors from whom they frequently quote: to one family Stevenson is known and quoted by heart, to another the whole of the *Beggar's Opera* is as familiar as the extracts given here. Nor must the user expect

to find here every quotation given in cross-word puzzles: compilers of these often seek to be obscure rather than familiar.

Latin is no longer a normal part of the language of educated people as it was in the eighteenth century; but from that age certain classical phrases have survived to become part of contemporary speech and writing. It is these 'survivals' that have been included here together with a few of the sayings or writings of the Schoolmen and early theologians. In many places more of the context of the actual familiar phrase has been given than is strictly necessary; but this has been a practice throughout the book, and one which it was thought would add to its value and charm. The translations are usually taken from the works of the better-known translators. Some one or two of the Greek quotations may be known to the general reader in their English versions—e.g. 'The half is better than the whole' or 'Call no man happy till he dies'; but no apology is needed for the inclusion of two pages of matter most of which cannot pretend to be familiar to any but classical scholars.

The foreign quotations are not intended to satisfy the foreigner: they include such things as have become part of the speech and writings of English-speaking people either in their own language, such as 'les enfants terribles', or in an English translation, such as 'We will not go to Canossa'. As hardly any Spanish and no Russian or Swedish quotations are familiar to English readers most of these have been given only in translation.

The index occupies approximately one-third of the total bulk of the book. A separate note will be found at the beginning of the index explaining the arrangement that has been adopted. Of the Latin quotations only those phrases that are familiar to the reader have been indexed; the unfamiliar context has not. In the English translations much the same principle has been followed: where the quotation is known to the reader in its English equivalent it has been indexed; where only the Latin is familiar and a translation is merely supplied to assist the reader it is left unindexed. A great deal of care has been spent on the index and the compilers look at it with some pride, believing that unless the searcher has to say 'Iddy tiddity' for every important word in the quotation he is looking for he will be able to find it; if, like Pig-wig (in Beatrix Potter's *Pigling Bland*), he has only forgotten some of the words, the index is full enough for him to trace it.

CONTENTS

NOTE TO THE SECOND EDITION (1953)   v

THE COMPILERS TO THE READER (1941)   vii

INTRODUCTION   xiii

CORRIGENDA   xix

QUOTATIONS   1

INDEX   589

GREEK INDEX   1002

INTRODUCTION

By BERNARD DARWIN

QUOTATION brings to many people one of the intensest joys of living. If they need any encouragement they have lately received it from the most distinguished quarters. Mr. Roosevelt quoted Longfellow to Mr. Churchill; Mr. Churchill passed on the quotation to us and subsequently quoted Clough on his own account. Thousands of listeners to that broadcast speech must have experienced the same series of emotions. When the Prime Minister said that there were some lines that he deemed appropriate we sat up rigid, waiting in mingled pleasure and apprehension. How agreeable it would be if we were acquainted with them and approved the choice! How flat and disappointing should they be unknown to us! A moment later we heard 'For while the tired waves, vainly breaking' and sank back in a pleasant agony of relief. We whispered the lines affectionately to ourselves, following the speaker, or even kept a word or two ahead of him in order to show our familiarity with the text. We were if possible more sure than ever that Mr. Churchill was the man for our money. He had given his ultimate proofs by flattering our vanity. He had chosen what we knew and what, if we had thought of it, we could have quoted ourselves. This innocent vanity often helps us over the hard places in life; it gives us a warm little glow against the coldness of the world and keeps us snug and happy. It certainly does its full share in the matter of quotations. We are puffed up with pride over those that we know and, a little illogically, we think that everyone else must know them too. As to those which lie outside our line of country we say, with Jowett as pictured by some anonymous genius[1] at Balliol, 'What I don't know isn't knowledge.' Yet here again we are illogical and unreasonable, for we allow ourselves to be annoyed by those who quote from outside our own small preserves. We accuse them in our hearts, as we do other people's children at a party, of 'showing off'. There are some departments of life in which we are ready to strike a bargain of mutual accommodation. The golfer is prepared to listen to his friend's story of missed putts, in which he takes no faintest interest, on the understanding that he may in turn impart his own heart-rending tale, and the bargain is honourably kept by both parties. The same rule does not apply to other people's quotations, which are not merely tedious but wound us in our tenderest spot. And the part played by vanity is perhaps worth pointing out because everybody, when he first plunges adventurously into this great work, ought in justice to the compilers to bear it in mind.

It is safe to say that there is no single reader who will not have a mild grievance or two, both as to what has been put in and what has been left out. In particular he will 'murmur a little sadly' over some favourite that is not there. I, for instance, have a

---

[1] Since identified as H. C. Beeching.

small grievance. William Hepworth Thompson, sometime Master of Trinity, the author of many famous and mordant sayings on which I have been brought up, is represented by but a single one. Can it be, I ask myself, that this is due to the fact that an Oxford Scholar put several of the Master's sayings into his Greek exercise book but attributed them to one Talirantes? Down, base thought! I only mention this momentary and most unworthy suspicion to show other readers the sort of thing they should avoid as they would the very devil. It is not that of which any one of us is fondest that is entitled as of right to a place. As often as he feels ever so slightly aggrieved, the reader should say to himself, if need be over and over again, that this is not a private anthology, but a collection of the quotations which the public knows best. In this fact, moreover, if properly appreciated, there ought to be much comfort. 'My head', said Charles Lamb, 'has not many mansions nor spacious',[1] and is that not true of most of us? If in this book there are a great many quotations that we do not know, there are also a great many that we do. There is that example of Clough with which I began. We may have to admit under cross-examination that we have only a rather vague acquaintance with Clough's poems, but we do know 'Say not the struggle'; and there on page so-and-so it is. Both we and the dictionary's compilers are thereupon seen to be persons of taste and discrimination.

If I may be allowed to harp a little longer on this string of vanity, it is rather amusing to fancy the varied reception given to the book by those who are quoted in it. They will consist largely of more or less illustrious shades, and we may picture them looking over one another's pale shoulders at the first copy of the dictionary to reach the asphodel. What jealousies there will be as they compare the number of pages respectively allotted to them! What indignation at finding themselves in such mixed company! Alphabetical order makes strange bedfellows. Dickens and Dibdin must get on capitally and convivially together, but what an ill-assorted couple are Mrs. Humphry Ward and the beloved Artemus of the same name! George Borrow may ask, 'Pray, who is this John Collins Bossidy?' Many readers may incidentally echo his question, and yet no man better merits his niche, for Mr. Bossidy wrote the lines ending 'And the Cabots talk only to God', which have told the whole world of the blue blood of Boston. John Hookham Frere, singing of the mailed lobster clapping his broad wings, must feel his frivolity uncomfortably hushed for a moment by his next-door neighbour, Charles Frohman, on the point of going down with the *Lusitania*. And apropos of Frere, there rises before me the portentous figure of my great-great-grandfather, Erasmus Darwin. He was thought a vastly fine poet in his day and there is a family legend that he was paid a guinea a line for his too fluent verses. And yet he is deservedly forgotten, while those who parodied him in the *Anti-Jacobin* attain an equally well-deserved immortality. He was a formidable old gentleman, with something of the Johnson touch, but not without a sense of humour, and I do not think he will be greatly hurt.

The most famous poets must be presumed to be above these petty vanities, though

---

[1] *Elia*, 'The Old and the New Schoolmaster'.

it would be agreeable to think of Horace contemplating his array of columns and saying, 'I told you so—Exegi monumentum'. In any case the number of columns or pages does not constitute the only test. Another is the number of words in each line by which any particular quotation can be identified, and this gives me a chance of making my compliments to the ingenuity and fullness of the index. The searcher need never despair and should he draw blank under 'swings' he is pretty sure to find what he wants under 'roundabouts'. There is a little game to be played (one of the many fascinating games which the reader can devise for himself) by counting the number of 'key words' in each line and working out the average of fame to which any passage is entitled. Even a short time so spent shows unexpected results, likely to spread envy and malice among the shades. It might be imagined that Shakespeare would be an easy winner. It has been said that every drop of the Thames is liquid history and almost every line of certain passages in Shakespeare is solid quotation. Let us fancy that his pre-eminence is challenged, that a sweepstake is suggested, and that he agrees to be judged by 'To be or not to be'. It seems a sufficiently sound choice and is found to produce fifty-five key words in thirty-three lines. All the other poets are ready to give in at once; they cannot stand against such scoring as that and Shakespeare is about to pocket the money when up sidles Mr. Alexander Pope. What, he asks, about that bitter little thing of his which he sent to Mr. Addison? And he proves to be right, for in those two and twenty lines to Atticus there are fifty-two key words. I have not played this game nearly long enough to pronounce Pope the winner. Very likely Shakespeare or someone else can produce a passage with a still higher average, but here at any rate is enough to show that it is a good game and as full of uncertainties as cricket itself.

   Though the great poets may wrangle a little amongst themselves, they do not stand in need of anything that the dictionary can do for them. Very different is the case of the small ones, whose whole fame depends upon a single happy line or even a single absurd one. To them exclusion from these pages may virtually mean annihilation, while inclusion makes them only a little lower than the angels. Their anxiety therefore must be pitiful and their joy when they find themselves safe in the haven proportionately great. Sometimes that joy may be short-lived. Think of Mr. Robert Montgomery, who was highly esteemed till the ruthless Macaulay fell upon him. With trembling hand he turns the pages and finds no less than four extracts from 'The Omnipresence of the Deity'. Alas! under his own letter M the traducer is waiting for him, and by a peculiar refinement of cruelty there are quoted no less than five of Lord Macaulay's criticisms on that very poem. This is a sad case; let us take a more cheerful one and still among the M's. Thomas Osbert Mordaunt has full recognition as the author of 'Sound, sound the clarion, fill the fife', after having for years had to endure the attribution of his lines to Sir Walter Scott, who in pure innocency put them at the head of a chapter. This to be sure was known already, but whoever heard before the name of the author of 'We don't want to fight', the man who gave the word 'Jingo' to the world? We know that the Great McDermott sang it, but even he may not have

INTRODUCTION

known who wrote it, just as Miss Fotheringay did not know who wrote 'The Stranger'. Now G. W. Hunt comes into his kingdom and with him another who helped many thousands of soldiers on their way during the last war. Mr. George H. Powell[1] is fortunately still alive to enjoy the celebrity of 'Pack up your troubles in your old kit bag'. How many thousands, too, have sung 'Wrap me up in my tarpaulin jacket' without realizing that it was by Whyte-Melville? To him, however, recognition is of less account. His place was already secure.

Among the utterers of famous sayings some seem to have been more fortunate than others. Lord Westbury, for instance, has always had the rather brutal credit of telling some wretched little attorney to turn the matter over 'in what you are pleased to call your mind'; but how many of us knew who first spoke of a 'blazing indiscretion' or called the parks 'the lungs of London'? We may rejoice with all these who, having for years been wronged, have come into their rights at last, but there are others with whom we can only sympathize. They must be contented with the fact that their sayings or their verses have been deemed worth recording, even though their names 'shall be lost for evermoe'. The Rugby boy who called his headmaster 'a beast but a just beast' sleeps unknown, while through him Temple lives. He can only enjoy what the dynamiter Zero called 'an anonymous infernal glory'. So do the authors of many admirable limericks, though some of the best are attributed to a living divine of great distinction, who has not disclaimed such juvenile frolics. So again do those who have given us many household words from the advertisement hoardings, the beloved old jingle of 'the Pickwick, the Owl, and the Waverley pen', the alluring alliteration of 'Pink Pills for Pale People'. Let us hope that it is enough for them that they did their duty and sent the sales leaping upward.

So much for the authors without whom this book could never have been. Now for the readers and some of the happy uses to which they will put it. 'Hand me over the Burton's *Anatomy*', said Captain Shandon, 'and leave me to my abominable devices.' It was Greek and Latin quotations that he sought for his article, but fashion has changed and today it would rather be English ones. Here is one of the most obvious purposes for which the dictionary will be used. It cannot accomplish impossibilities. It will not prevent many an honest journalist from referring to 'fresh fields and pastures new' nor from describing a cup-tie as an example of 'Greek meeting Greek'. There is a fine old crusted tradition of misquoting not lightly to be broken and it might almost seem pedantry to deck these ancient friends in their true but unfamiliar colours. Misquoting may even be deemed an amiable weakness, since Dickens in one of his letters misquoted Sam Weller; but here at least is a good chance of avoiding it. There is likewise a chance of replenishing a stock grown somewhat threadbare. 'Well, you're a boss word', exclaimed Jim Pinkerton,[2] when he lighted on 'hebdomadary' in a dictionary. 'Before you're very much older I'll have you in type as long as yourself.' So the hard-pressed writer in turning over these pages may find and note many excellent phrases against future contingencies, whether to give a

[1] George Asaf. [2] *The Wrecker*, ch. vii.

pleasing touch of erudition or to save the trouble of thinking for himself. These, however, are sordid considerations, and the mind loves rather to dwell on fireside quoting-matches between two friends, each of whom thinks his own visual memory the more accurate. There are certain writers well adapted to this form of contest and among the moderns Conan Doyle must, with all respect to Mr. Wodehouse, be assigned the first place. Sherlock Holmes scholars are both numerous and formidable; they set themselves and demand of others a high standard. It is one very difficult to attain since there often seems no reason why any particular remark should have been made on any particular occasion. This is especially true of Dr. Watson. He was constantly saying that his practice was not very absorbing or that he had an accommodating neighbour, but when did he say which? Even the most learned might by a momentary blunder confuse 'A Case of Identity' with 'The Final Problem'. It would be dry work to plough through all the stories, even though the supreme satisfaction of being right should reward the search. Now a glance at the dictionary will dispose of an argument which would otherwise 'end only with the visit'.

It is incidentally curious and interesting to observe that two authors may each have the same power of inspiring devotion and the competitive spirit, and yet one may be, from the dictionary point of view, infinitely more quotable than the other. Hardly any prose writer, for instance, produces a more fanatical adoration than Miss Austen, and there are doubtless those who can recite pages of her with scarce a slip; but it is perhaps pages rather than sentences that they quote. Mr. Bennet provides an exception, but generally speaking she is not very amenable to the treatment by scissors and paste. George Eliot, if we leave out Mrs. Poyser, a professed wit and coiner of aphorisms, is in much poorer case. Another and a very different writer, Borrow, can rouse us to a frantic pitch of romantic excitement, but it is the whole scene and atmosphere that possess this magic and we cannot take atmosphere to pieces. These are but three examples of writers who do not seem to lend themselves to brief and familiar quotations. They have jewels in plenty, but these form part of a piece of elaborate ornament from which they cannot be detached without irreparable damage. The works of some other writers may by contrast be said to consist of separate stones, each of which needs no setting and can sparkle on its own account. Dickens is an obvious and unique instance. Stevenson, too, has the gift of producing characters such as Prince Florizel and Alan Breck, John Silver and Michael Finsbury, whose words can stand memorable by themselves, apart from context or atmosphere. Those who share my love for Florizel will rejoice to observe that he has had some faithful friend among the compilers. As for Michael I cannot help feeling that he has been rather scurvily used, for *The Wrong Box* is admirably suited to competition and even learned Judges of the Court of Appeal have been known, all unsuspected by their ignorant auditors, to bandy quotations from it on the Bench. Here, however, I take leave to give any indignant reader a hint. Let him not cry too loudly before he is hurt! It is true that 'nothing like a little judicious levity' is not in the main body of the dictionary, but someone awoke just in time and it is among the addenda.

To return to those friends by the fireside whom I pictured indulging in a heated quoting-match, it may be that they will presently become allies and unite to use the dictionary over a cross-word puzzle. It is hardly too much to say that the setters of these problems should not use a quotation unless it is to be found in the dictionary. A cross-word quotation should not be too simple, but it should be such that that hypothetical personage, the reasonable man, might have heard of it. The solver demands fair play, and the setter who takes a volume of verse at haphazard, finds a word that fits, and substitutes a blank for it, is not playing the game. There are solvers whose standard of sportsmanship is so high that they would as soon allow themselves to cheat at patience as have recourse to a book. We may admire though we cannot emulate this fine austere arrogance. It is the best fun to win unaided, but there is good fun too in ferreting out a quotation. It well repays the ardours of the chase. Moreover a setter of puzzles who oversteps honourable limits should be fought with his own weapons. He has palpably used books and this is an epoch of reprisals. Then let us use books too and hoist him with his own petard.

It is difficult today not to deal in warlike metaphors, but perhaps the truest and most perfect use of the dictionary is essentially peaceful. Reviewers are apt to say of a detective story that it is 'impossible to lay it down till the last page is reached'. It is rather for books of reference that such praise should be reserved. No others are comparable with them for the purposes of eternal browsing. They suggest all manner of lovely, lazy things, in particular the watching of a cricket match on a sunshiny day. We have only dropped in for half an hour, but the temptation to see just one more over before we go is irresistible. Evening draws on, the shadows of the fielders lengthen on the grass, nothing much is happening, a draw becomes every minute more inevitable, and still we cannot tear ourselves away. So it is with works of reference, even with the most arid, even with Bradshaw, whose vocabulary, as Sherlock Holmes remarked, is 'nervous and terse but limited'. Over the very next page of Bradshaw there may be hidden a Framlingham Admiral; adventure may always be in wait a little farther down the line. So, but a thousand times more so, is some exciting treasure-trove awaiting us over the next page of this dictionary. What it is we cannot guess, but it is for ever calling in our ears to turn over just one more. We have only taken down the book to look up one special passage, but it is likely enough that we shall never get so far. Long before we have reached the appropriate letter we shall have been waylaid by an earlier one, and shall have clean forgotten our original quest. Nor is this all, for, if our mood changes as we browse, it is so fatally, beautifully easy to change our pasture. We can play a game akin to that 'dabbing' cricket, so popular in private-school days, in which the batsman's destiny depended or was supposed to depend—for we were not always honest—on a pencil delivered with eyes tightly shut. We can close the book and open it again at random, sure of something that shall set us off again on a fresh and enchanting voyage of not too strenuous discovery.

Under this enchantment I have fallen deep. I have pored over the proofs so that only by a supreme effort of will could I lay them down and embark on the impertinent

task of trying to write about them. I now send them back to their home with a sense of privation and loneliness. Here seems to me a great book. Then

Deem it not all a too presumptuous folly,

this humble tribute to Oxford from another establishment over the way.

B. D.

May 1941

CORRIGENDA

6: 13, 125: 15, 250: 14 *A detailed history of this song, which has appeared in many versions, is given in Percy A. Scholes,* God Save the Queen! *(1954).*

7: 18 *A more precise source is given at 254:2.*

13: 13 *The literal translation of the Latin is,* Christ is risen today for the salvation of man.

64: 8 *The Latin,* Noli me tangere, *is more familiar* (Vulgate).

73: 14 *For an earlier history of this rhyme see* The Oxford Dictionary of Nursery Rhymes *(1951).*

144: 15 *An early instance of use of the phrase* iron curtain *in relation to the Soviet Union occurs in Ethel Snowden's* Through Bolshevik Russia *(1920), where she wrote of her arrival in Petrograd with an official Labour Party Delegation:* We were behind the 'iron curtain' at last! *Its wider application to countries within the Soviet sphere of influence originates with Dr. Goebbels's leading article in the issue of the weekly,* Das Reich, *dated 25 February, 1945:* Wenn das deutsche Volk die Waffen niederlegte, würden die Sowjets, auch nach den Abmachungen zwischen Roosevelt, Churchill und Stalin, ganz Ost- und Südosteuropa zuzüglich des größten Teiles des Reiches besetzen. Vor diesem einschließlich der Sowjetunion riesigen Territorium würde sich sofort ein eiserner Vorhang heruntersenken. . . . (Should the German people lay down its arms, the agreement between Roosevelt, Churchill and Stalin would allow the Soviets to occupy all Eastern and South-eastern Europe together with the major part of the Reich. An iron curtain would at once descend on this territory which, including the Soviet Union, would be of enormous dimensions.) *This article was reported in* The Times *and the* Manchester Guardian *ON 23.2.45. Churchill's first recorded use of the phrase was in a cable to Truman on 4 June, 1945:* I view with profound misgivings . . . the descent of an iron curtain between us and everything to the eastward (The Second World War, *vol. vi,* Triumph and Tragedy *(1954) p. 523).*

195: 25 *This remark in the form* We are all Socialists now *was first made by Sir William Harcourt (1827–1904). See* Fabian Essays *(1889), ed. Shaw (p. 194 in 1948 edition).*

210: 5 *An earlier source for these words is given at 10: 20.*

223: 12 *This remark in the version* Wenn ich Kultur höre . . . entsichere ich meinen Browning (Whenever I hear the word culture I release the safety catch of my revolver) *is made by one of the characters, a storm trooper, in* Schlageter *(1934), Act I, sc. i, by the Nazi writer Hanns Johst.*

228: 6 Apple-tree in 1899 edition, though illustration shows a willow.

273: 17 This has been circulated as if actually said by Johnson; when the truth is, it was only supposed by me. *Boswell's note,* Life of Johnson, 15 May 1776.

273: 19 *The correct translation of* nullum *should be* none. *As a proverbial expression the line is usually quoted with* nothing, *perhaps because in another part of the* Life *Boswell misquotes the Latin as* nihil *(Vol. I p. 412).*

277: 18 *The correct version is:* The only end of writing is to enable the readers better to enjoy life or better to endure it. *Johnson's review of Soame Jenyns,* The Enquiry into the Nature and Origin of Evil.

277: 19 *This occurs in Boswell's* Life, *vol. ii, p. 13. 15 February 1766:* So far is it from being true that men are naturally equal, that no two people can be half an hour together, but one shall acquire an evident superiority over the other.

CORRIGENDA

310: 22   . . . the statement of Herbert Spencer that the first thing necessary for success in life is 'to be a good animal'. *Lafcadio Hearn in a lecture on George Meredith delivered in 1900 and published in his* Life and Literature (1917, p. 168).

327: 8   *Dr. Magee's actual words were* I declare . . . that I should say it would be better that England should be free than that England should be compulsorily sober. *From his speech, as Bishop of Peterborough, in the Lords' Debate on the Intoxicating Liquor Bill, 2 May, 1872.*

327: 15, 328: 1   *The author of these passages is William Caxton (1422?–91).*

329: 18   *Louis XVIII in his* Relation d'un Voyage à Bruxelles à Coblentz en 1791 (1823, p. 59) *attributes this remark in the form* Que ne mangent-ils de la croûte de pâté? (Why don't they eat pastry?) *to Marie Thérèse (1638–83) wife of Louis XIV. A letter to* The Times *of 30 April, 1959, states that John Peckham (c. 1225–92) Archbishop of Canterbury, tells a similar anecdote in his Latin letters.*

403: 4   *This quotation is derived from what appears to have been a peep-show rhyme:*

> Whichever you please my little dears:
> You pays your money and you takes your choice.
> You pays your money and what you sees is
> A cow or a donkey just as you pleases.
>
> V. S. Lean, Collectanea (1902–4)

415: 6–10   *None of these hymns was written by Sankey. The authors are as follows: 6 & 10, Philip Bliss (1838–76); see also 77:23: 7, F. J. Crosby (Mrs. Van Alstyne) (1823–1915): 8, R. Lowry (1826–99): 9, S. R. Bennett (1836–98).*

420: 24   *These lines are quoted by Scott: Burns is their author.* My Heart's in the Highlands *was first published in vol. 3 of Johnson's* Scots Musical Museum (1790). *Burns noted in his copy of the* Museum . . . The first half stanza of this song is old, the rest is mine, *presumably referring to the beginning of the chorus.*

512: 5   *A pun on 368: 20 referring to a royal birthday ode 'full of allusions to "vocal groves and the feathered choirs" ' written by Henry James Pye (1745–1813), Poet Laureate from 1790. See* The Oxford Dictionary of Nursery Rhymes, *p. 394.*

547: 15   *John Poynder in* Literary Extracts from English and Other Works, 1844, vol. i, *gives this version:* Lord Chancellor Thurlow said that corporations have neither bodies to be punished, nor souls to be condemned, they therefore do as they like. *Wilberforce's Life of Thurlow has been given as the source for the remark but there is no such book. The mistake arises from a misreading of Poynder who quotes an extract from the Life of Wilberforce by his Sons immediately above the quotation about Thurlow.*

552: 15   *The version of Vaux's lines given in the* Fuller Worthies Library Miscellanies *vol. iv (1872), ed. Grosart, runs:*

> Ffor Age with stealing steps
> hath claude mee with his cruch.

See also Hamlet, v. i [77].

578: 27   *This stanza appeared in the MS. of 1819, in Part First, between lines 515 and 516 (Oxford English Texts edition) and was later omitted.*

DICTIONARY OF QUOTATIONS

PETER ABELARD

1079–1142

1 O quanta qualia sunt illa sabbata,
Quae semper celebrat superna curia.

O what their joy and their glory must be,
Those endless sabbaths the blessed ones see!
Hymnus Paraclitensis. Trans. by Neale in *Hymnal Noted,* 1858

**SIR J. E. E. DALBERG,
FIRST BARON ACTON**

1834–1902

2 Power tends to corrupt and absolute power corrupts absolutely.
Letter in Life of Mandell Creighton (1904), i. 372

CHARLES FOLLEN ADAMS

1842–1918

3 But ven he vash asleep in ped,
So quiet as a mouse,
I prays der Lord, 'Dake anyding,
But leaf dot Yawcob Strauss.'
Yawcob Strauss

CHARLES FRANCIS ADAMS

1807–1886

4 It would be superfluous in me to point out to your lordship that this is war.
Dispatch to Earl Russell, 5 Sept. 1863. C. F. Adams's Charles Francis Adams, p. 342

JOHN QUINCY ADAMS

1767–1848

5 Think of your forefathers! Think of your posterity!
Speech, 22 Dec. 1802

SAMUEL ADAMS

1722–1803

6 A Nation of shop-keepers are very seldom so disinterested.
Oration said to have been delivered at Philadelphia, 1776, p. 10. (See also 360:22, 503:11)

JOSEPH ADDISON

1672–1719

7 Pray consider what a figure a man would make in the republic of letters. *Ancient Medals,* 1

8 There is nothing more requisite in business than dispatch. *Ib.* 5

9 'Twas then great Marlbro's mighty soul was prov'd.
The Campaign, l. 279

10 In peaceful thought the field of death survey'd,
To fainting squadrons sent the timely aid,
Inspir'd repuls'd Battalions to engage,
And taught the doubtful battle where to rage.
Ib. l. 283

11 And, pleas'd th' Almighty's orders to perform,
Rides in the whirl-wind, and directs the storm.
The Campaign, l. 291

12 And those who paint 'em truest praise 'em most.
Ib. l. 476

13 The dawn is overcast, the morning lowers,
And heavily in clouds brings on the day,
The great, the important day, big with the fate
Of Cato and of Rome. *Cato,* I. i. 1

14 'Tis not in mortals to command success,
But we'll do more, Sempronius; we'll deserve it.
Ib. ii. 43

15 Blesses his stars, and thinks it luxury. *Ib.* iv. 70

16 'Tis pride, rank pride, and haughtiness of soul;
I think the Romans call it stoicism. *Ib.* 82

17 Were you with these, my prince, you'd soon forget
The pale, unripened beauties of the north. *Ib.* 134

18 Am I distinguished from you but by toils,
Superior toils, and heavier weight of cares?
Painful pre-eminence! *Ib.* III. v. 23

19 The woman that deliberates is lost. *Ib.* IV. i. 31

20 Curse on his virtues! they've undone his country.
Such popular humanity is treason. *Ib.* iv. 35

21 Content thyself to be obscurely good.
When vice prevails, and impious men bear sway,
The post of honour is a private station. *Ib.* 139

22 It must be so—Plato, thou reason'st well!—
Else whence this pleasing hope, this fond desire,
This longing after immortality?
Or whence this secret dread, and inward horror,
Of falling into naught? Why shrinks the soul
Back on herself, and startles at destruction?
'Tis the divinity that stirs within us;
'Tis heaven itself, that points out an hereafter,
And intimates eternity to man.
Eternity! thou pleasing, dreadful thought! *Ib.* v. i. 1

23 If there's a power above us,
(And that there is all nature cries aloud
Through all her works) he must delight in virtue.
Ib. 15

24 But thou shalt flourish in immortal youth,
Unhurt amidst the wars of elements,
The wrecks of matter, and the crash of worlds.
Ib. 28

25 From hence, let fierce contending nations know
What dire effects from civil discord flow.
Ib. iv. 111

26 Music, the greatest good that mortals know,
And all of heaven we have below.
Song for St. Cecilia's Day, st. 3

27 Round-heads and Wooden-shoes are standing jokes.
Prologue to The Drummer

28 I should think my self a very bad woman, if I had done what I do, for a farthing less.
The Drummer, Act 1

1 He more had pleas'd us, had he pleas'd us less.
English Poets (referring to Cowley)

2 For wheresoe'er I turn my ravished eyes,
Gay gilded scenes and shining prospects rise,
Poetic fields encompass me around,
And still I seem to tread on classic ground.
Letter from Italy

3 A painted meadow, or a purling stream. *Ib.*

4 A reader seldom peruses a book with pleasure until he knows whether the writer of it be a black man or a fair man, of a mild or choleric disposition, married or a bachelor. *The Spectator*, No. 1

5 Thus I live in the world rather as a spectator of mankind than as one of the species. *Ib.*

6 When I am in a serious humour, I very often walk by myself in Westminster Abbey. *Ib.* No. 26

7 A perfect tragedy is the noblest production of human nature. *Ib.* No. 39

8 In all thy humours, whether grave or mellow,
Thou'rt such a touchy, testy, pleasant fellow;
Hast so much wit, and mirth, and spleen about thee,
There is no living with thee, nor without thee.
Ib. No. 68

9 There is no place in the town which I so much love to frequent as the Royal Exchange. *Ib.* No. 69

10 The infusion of a China plant sweetened with the pith of an Indian cane. *Ib.*

11 Sir Roger . . . will suffer nobody to sleep in it [the church] besides himself; . . . if he sees anybody else nodding, either wakes them himself, or sends his servants to them. *Ib.* No. 112

12 Sir Roger told them, with the air of a man who would not give his judgment rashly, that much might be said on both sides. *Ib.* No. 122

13 My friends Sir Roger de Coverley and Sir Andrew Freeport are of different principles, the first of them inclined to the *landed* and the other to the *monied* interest. *Ib.* No. 126

14 It was a saying of an ancient philosopher, which I find some of our writers have ascribed to Queen Elizabeth, who perhaps might have taken occasion to repeat it, that a good face is a letter of recommendation. *Ib.* No. 221

15 I have often thought, says Sir Roger, it happens very well that Christmas should fall out in the Middle of Winter. *Ib.* No. 269

16 . . launched out into the praise of the late act of parliament for securing the Church of England, and told me with great satisfaction, that he believed it already began to take effect; for that a rigid dissenter, who chanced to dine at his house on Christmas day, had been observed to eat very plentifully of his plum-porridge. *Ib.*

17 Dr. Busby, a great man! he whipped my grandfather; a very great man! I should have gone to him myself, if I had not been a blockhead; a very great man! *Ib.* No. 329

18 These widows, Sir, are the most perverse creatures in the world. *Ib.* No. 335

19 The Knight in the triumph of his heart made several reflections on the greatness of the *British* Nation; as, that one *Englishman* could beat three *Frenchmen*; that we cou'd never be in danger of Popery so long as we took care of our fleet; that the *Thames* was the noblest river in *Europe*; that *London Bridge* was a greater piece of work than any of the Seven Wonders of the World; with many other honest prejudices which naturally cleave to the heart of a true *Englishman*.
The Spectator, No. 383

20 This Mr. Dryden calls 'the fairy way of writing'. *Ib.* No. 419

21 The Lord my Pasture shall prepare,
And feed me with a Shepherd's Care;
His Presence shall my wants supply,
And guard me with a watchful Eye.
Ib. No. 441

22 When all thy Mercies, O my God,
My rising Soul surveys;
Transported with the View, I'm lost
In Wonder, Love, and Praise.
Ib. No. 453

23 Through all Eternity to Thee
A joyful Song I'll raise,
For oh! Eternity's too short
To utter all thy Praise. *Ib.*

24 We have in England a particular bashfulness in every thing that regards religion. *Ib.* No. 458

25 The spacious firmament on high,
With all the blue ethereal sky.
Ib. No. 465. *Ode*

26 Soon as the evening shades prevail,
The moon takes up the wondrous tale,
And nightly to the listening Earth
Repeats the story of her birth. *Ib.*

27 Whilst all the stars that round her burn,
And all the planets, in their turn,
Confirm the tidings as they roll,
And spread the truth from pole to pole. *Ib.*

28 In Reason's ear they all rejoice,
And utter forth a glorious Voice,
For ever singing as they shine,
'The Hand that made us is Divine.' *Ib.*

29 A woman seldom asks advice before she has bought her wedding clothes. *Ib.* No. 475

30 Our disputants put me in mind of the skuttle fish, that when he is unable to extricate himself, blackens all the water about him, till he becomes invisible. *Ib.* No. 476

31 I value my garden more for being full of blackbirds than of cherries, and very frankly give them fruit for their songs. *Ib.* No. 477

32 If we may believe our logicians, man is distinguished from all other creatures by the faculty of laughter. *Ib.* No. 494

33 'We are always doing', says he, 'something for Posterity, but I would fain see Posterity do something for us.' *Ib.* No. 583

34 I remember when our whole island was shaken with an earthquake some years ago, there was an impudent mountebank who sold pills which (as he told the country people) were very good against an earthquake. *The Tatler*, No. 240

35 I have but ninepence in ready money, but I can draw for a thousand pounds. [On his deficiency in conversation.] Boswell's *Life of Johnson*, 7 May 1773

1 See in what peace a christian can die.
Dying words to his stepson Lord Warwick.
Young's *Conjectures on Original Composition*, 1759

2 Should the whole frame of nature round him break,
In ruin and confusion hurled,
He, unconcerned, would hear the mighty crack,
And stand secure amidst a falling world.
Translation of Horace, Odes, bk. III. iii

THOMAS ADY
c. 1655

3 Matthew, Mark, Luke, and John,
The Bed be blest that I lie on.
Four angels to my bed,
Four angels round my head,
One to watch, and one to pray,
And two to bear my soul away.
Quoted in part by Ady in *A Candle in the Dark* (1656)

AESCHYLUS
525–456 B.C.

ποντίων τε κυμάτων ἀνήριθμον γέλασμα.

4 Multitudinous laughter of the waves of ocean.
Prometheus Bound, 88. Trans. by Herbert Weir Smyth (Loeb edition).

AGATHON
447?–401 B.C.

5 Even God cannot change the past.
Attributed by Aristotle *in* The Nicomachean Ethics, vi.

CHARLES HAMILTON AÏDÉ
1830–1906

6 I sit beside my lonely fire,
And pray for wisdom yet—
For calmness to remember
Or courage to forget.   *Remember or Forget*

ALFRED AINGER
1837–1904

7 No flowers, by request.
At a dinner given to the contributors to the Dict. of Nat. Biog., *8 July 1897: his summary of their editor's instructions*

ARTHUR CAMPBELL AINGER
1841–1919

8 God is working His purpose out as year succeeds to year,
God is working His purpose out and the time is drawing near;
Nearer and nearer draws the time, the time that shall surely be,
When the earth shall be fill'd with the glory of God as the waters cover the sea.
God is Working His Purpose Out (1894)

MARK AKENSIDE
1721–1770

9 Such and so various are the tastes of men.
Pleasures of Imagination, bk. iii, l. 567

ALCUIN
735–804

10 Vox populi, vox dei.
The voice of the people is the voice of God.
Letter to Charlemagne, A.D. 800. *Works, Epis.* **127**

HENRY ALDRICH
1648–1710

11 If all be true that I do think,
There are five reasons we should drink;
Good wine—a friend—or being dry—
Or lest we should be by and by—
Or any other reason why.   *Reasons for Drinking*

THOMAS BAILEY ALDRICH
1836–1907

12 The fair, frail palaces,
The fading alps and archipelagoes,
And great cloud-continents of sunset-seas.
Sonnet: Miracles

ALEXANDER
356–323 B.C.

εἰ μὴ 'Αλέξανδρος ἤμην, Διογένης ἂν ἤμην.

13 If I were not Alexander, I would be Diogenes.
Plutarch, *Life of Alexander*, xiv. 3

CECIL FRANCES ALEXANDER
1818–1895

14 All things bright and beautiful,
All creatures great and small,
All things wise and wonderful,
The Lord God made them all.
All Things Bright and Beautiful (1848)

15 The rich man in his castle,
The poor man at his gate,
God made them, high or lowly,
And order'd their estate.   *Ib.*

16 By Nebo's lonely mountain,
On this side Jordan's wave,
In a vale in the land of Moab
There lies a lonely grave. *The Burial of Moses* (1854)

17 Do no sinful action,
Speak no angry word;
Ye belong to Jesus,
Children of the Lord. *Do No Sinful Action* (1848)

18 There's a wicked spirit
Watching round you still,
And he tries to tempt you
To all harm and ill.

But ye must not hear him,
Though 'tis hard for you
To resist the evil,
And the good to do.   *Ib.*

19 Jesus calls us; o'er the tumult
Of our life's wild restless sea. *Jesus Calls Us* (1852)

20 Once in royal David's city
Stood a lowly cattle shed,
Where a Mother laid her Baby
In a manger for His bed:
Mary was that Mother mild
Jesus Christ her little Child.
Once in Royal David's City (1848)

1 With the poor, and mean, and lowly,
Lived on earth our Saviour Holy.
Once in Royal David's City (1848)

2 Christian children all must be
Mild, obedient, good as He. *Ib.*

3 For He is our childhood's pattern,
Day by day like us He grew,
He was little, weak, and helpless,
Tears and smiles like us He knew;
And He feeleth for our sadness,
And He shareth in our gladness. *Ib.*

4 There is a green hill far away,
Without a city wall,
Where the dear Lord was crucified,
Who died to save us all.
There is a Green Hill (1848)

5 He only could unlock the gate
Of Heav'n, and let us in. *Ib.*

6 The roseate hues of early dawn,
The brightness of the day,
The crimson of the sunset sky,
How fast they fade away!
The Roseate Hues of Early Dawn (1852)

7 We are but little children weak
Nor born in any high estate.
We are but Little Children Weak (1850)

8 There's not a child so small and weak
But has his little cross to take,
His little work of love and praise
That he may do for Jesus' sake. *Ib.*

SIR WILLIAM ALEXANDER,
EARL OF STIRLING
1567?–1640

9 The weaker sex, to piety more prone.
Doomsday, Hour v, lv

10 Yet with great toil all that I can attain
By long experience, and in learned schools,
Is for to know my knowledge is but vain,
And those that think them wise, are greatest fools.
The Tragedy of Crœsus, II. i

HENRY ALFORD
1810–1871

11 Come, ye thankful people, come,
Raise the song of Harvest-home:
All is safely gathered in,
Ere the winter storms begin.
Come, Ye Thankful People, Come (1844)

12 Ten thousand times ten thousand,
In sparkling raiment bright.
Ten Thousand Times Ten Thousand (1867)

CYRIL ARGENTINE ALINGTON
1872–1955

13 As swift to scent the sophist as to praise
The honest worker or the well turned phrase.
Bishop Henson. The Times, 4 Oct. 1947

RICHARD ALISON
fl. c. 1606

14 There cherries grow, that none can buy
Till cherry ripe themselves do cry.
An Hour's Recreation in Music

ABBÉ D'ALLAINVAL
1700–1753

15 L'embarras des richesses.
The more alternatives, the more difficult the choice.
Title of Comedy, 1726

ELIZABETH AKERS ALLEN
1832–1911

16 Backward, turn backward, O Time, in your flight,
Make me a child again, just for to-night!
Rock Me To Sleep, Mother

GRANT ALLEN
1848–1899

17 The Woman who Did. *Title of Novel, 1895*

WILLIAM ALLINGHAM
1828–1889

18 Up the airy mountain,
Down the rushy glen,
We daren't go a-hunting,
For fear of little men. *The Fairies*

19 Four ducks on a pond,
A grass-bank beyond,
A blue sky of spring,
White clouds on the wing:
What a little thing
To remember for years—
To remember with tears! *A Memory*

ST. AMBROSE
c. 340–397

20 Si fueris Romae, Romano vivito more;
Si fueris alibi, vivito sicut ibi.
If you are at Rome live in the Roman style; if you
are elsewhere live as they live elsewhere.
Quoted by Jeremy Taylor, Ductor Dubitantium,
I. i. 5

FISHER AMES
1758–1808

21 A monarchy is a merchantman which sails well, but
will sometimes strike on a rock, and go to the bottom; a republic is a raft which will never sink, but
then your feet are always in the water.
Speech in the House of Representatives, 1795

MAXWELL ANDERSON
1888–

22 What Price Glory. *Title of Play, 1924*

BISHOP LANCELOT ANDREWES
1555–1626

23 The nearer the Church the further from God.
Sermon on the Nativity before James I (1622)

NORMAN ANGELL
1874–

24 The Great Illusion.
Title of book on the futility of war

ARCHIBALD DOUGLAS, FIFTH EARL OF ANGUS
1449?–1514

1 I shall bell the cat.
  Attr. by J. Man in Buchanan's Rerum Scoticarum
  Historia, *1762, bk. xii, § 41, note*

ANONYMOUS
English

2 A beast, but a just beast.
  Of Dr. Temple, Headmaster of Rugby, 1857–69

3 Absence makes the heart grow fonder.
  Davison, *Poetical Rhapsody, 1602 (see 36:28)*

4 Adam
  Had 'em.
  On the Antiquity of Microbes. (Said to be the shortest poem.)

5 All present and correct.
  King's Regulations (Army). Report of the Orderly Sergeant to the Officer of the Day

6 An abomination unto the Lord, but a very present help in time of trouble. [A lie.]
  (Cf. Proverbs xii. 22; the second half is from Psalms xlvi. 1)

7 An Austrian army, awfully arrayed,
  Boldly by battery besieged Belgrade;
  Cossack commanders cannonading come,
  Dealing destruction's devastating doom.
  Siege of Belgrade. The Trifler, 1817

8 And when with envy Time, transported,
    Shall think to rob us of our joys;
  You'll in your girls again be courted,
    And I'll go wooing in my boys.
  Winifreda. D. Lewis, Miscellaneous Poems, 1726

9 An old Soldier of the Queen's,
  And the Queen's old Soldier.
  Merry Drollery, 1661–9. An Old Soldier of The Queen's. Oxford Book of 17th Cent. Verse

10 An old song made by an aged old pate,
  Of an old worshipful gentleman who had a great estate. *The Old Courtier*

11 A place within the meaning of the Act.
  The Betting Act

12 Appeal from Philip drunk to Philip sober.
  See Valerius Maximus, Facta et Dicta Memorabilia (c. A.D. 15), bk. vi, ch. ii

13 Are we downhearted? No!
  Expression much used by British soldiers in War of 1914–18, probably based on remark of Joseph Chamberlain, q.v.

14 As I sat on a sunny bank,
  On Christmas Day in the morning,
  I spied three ships come sailing by.
  Carol: As I Sat on a Sunny Bank. Oxford Book of Carols

15 As Joseph was a-walking,
  He heard an angel sing:
  'This night shall be born
    Our heavenly king.'
  As Joseph was a-walking. Oxford Book of Carols

16 He neither shall be clothed
    In purple nor in pall,
  But all in fair linen.
    As were babies all.

  He neither shall be rock'd
    In silver nor in gold,
  But in a wooden cradle
    That rocks on the mould. *As Joseph was a-walking*

17 A swarm of bees in May
  Is worth a load of hay;
  A swarm of bees in June
  Is worth a silver spoon;
  A swarm of bees in July
  Is not worth a fly. *Old Rhyme*

18 A willing foe and sea room.
  Naval toast in the time of Nelson. Beckett, A Few Naval Customs, Expressions, Traditions, and Superstitions (1931)

19 Begone, dull care! I prithee begone from me!
  Begone, dull care, you and I shall never agree.
  Begone Dull Care

20 Be happy while y'er leevin,
  For y'er a lang time deid.
  Scottish Motto for a house. Notes and Queries, 7 Dec. 1901, p. 469

21 Born 1820, still going strong.
  Advertisement for Johnnie Walker Whisky

22 Bovril prevents that sinking feeling. *Advertisement*

23 Christmas is coming, the geese are getting fat,
  Please to put a penny in the old man's hat;
  If you haven't got a penny, a ha'penny will do,
  If you haven't got a ha'penny, God bless you!
  Beggar's Rhyme

24 Come, landlord, fill the flowing bowl
  Until it doth run over. . . .
    For to-night we'll merry be,
    To-morrow we'll be sober.
  Come, Landlord, Fill the Flowing Bowl. Oxford Song Book

25 Come lasses and lads, get leave of your dads,
  And away to the Maypole hie,
  For every he has got him a she,
  And the fiddler's standing by.
  For Willie shall dance with Jane,
  And Johnny has got his Joan,
  To trip it, trip it, trip it, trip it, trip it up and down.
  Come Lasses and Lads (c. 1670). Oxford Song Book

26 Conduct . . . to the prejudice of good order and military discipline. *Army Act, § 40*

27 Dear Sir, Your astonishment's odd:
  I am always about in the Quad.
    And that's why the tree
    Will continue to be,
  Since observed by Yours faithfully, God.
  Reply to limerick on Idealism, 'There was once a man who said "God . . ." ' (see 305:10)

28 Defence, not defiance.
  Motto of the Volunteers Movement, in 1859

29 Dollar Diplomacy.
  Term applied to Secretary Knox's activities in securing opportunities for the investment of American capital abroad, particularly in Latin America and China. See Harper's Weekly, 23 Apr. 1910, p. 8

ANONYMOUS

1 Dr. Williams' pink pills for pale people.
Advertisement

2 Early one morning, just as the sun was rising,
I heard a maid sing in the valley below:
'Oh, don't deceive me; Oh, never leave me!
How could you use a poor maiden so?'
Early One Morning. Oxford Song Book

3 Earned a precarious living by taking in one another's
washing.
In The Commonweal, 6 Aug. 1887, *William
Morris suggested that this was an invention of
Mark Twain's*

4 Esau selleth his birthright for a mess of potage.
Genevan Bible: chapter heading to Genesis, ch. 25

5 An intelligent Russian once remarked to us, 'Every
country has its own constitution; ours is absolutism
moderated by assassination.'
Georg Herbert, Count Münster, *Political
Sketches of the State of Europe, 1814–1867,* ed.
1868, p. 19

6 Every minute dies a man,
And one and one-sixteenth is born.
Parody by a Statistician of Tennyson's Vision of
Sin, pt. iv, st. 9. *(See 541:13)*

7 Father of his Country [George Washington].
Francis Bailey, *Nord Americanische Kalender,*
1779

8 Frankie and Johnny were lovers, my gawd, how they
could love,
Swore to be true to each other, true as the stars above;
He was her man, but he done her wrong.
Frankie and Johnny, st. 1

9 From ghoulies and ghosties and long-leggety beasties
And things that go bump in the night,
Good Lord, deliver us!   *Cornish*

10 God be in my head,
And in my understanding;

God be in my eyes,
And in my looking;

God be in my mouth,
And in my speaking;

God be in my heart,
And in my thinking;

God be at my end,
And at my departing.   *Sarum Missal*

11 God rest you merry, gentlemen,
Let nothing you dismay.
*Carol: God Rest You Merry. Oxford Book of
Carols*

12 O tidings of comfort and joy.   *Ib.*

13 God save great *George* our King.
Harmonia Anglicana. The Gentleman's Magazine,
Oct. 1745. *But see* 125:15, 250:14, *and Corri-
genda.*

14 God's own country.
Sir St. V. Troubridge *(Notes and Queries, 26 Sept.
1942) quotes from Sir W. Craigie's Dictionary of
American English:*
'A special part of the U.S. or the country as a
whole, viewed nostalgically as almost a paradise.'
*The earliest example without 'own' given is 1865, the
earliest with 'own' is 1921*

15 Good-morning! Have you used Pears' Soap?
Advertisement

16 Great Chatham with his sabre drawn
Stood waiting for Sir Richard Strachan;
Sir Richard, longing to be at 'em,
Stood waiting for the Earl of Chatham.
At Walcheren, 1809

17 Great God, what do I see and hear?
The end of things created.
Great God, What do I see. Collyer's *Hymns:
Partly Collected and Partly Original,* 1812

18 Greensleeves was all my joy,
Greensleeves was my delight,
Greensleeves was my heart of gold,
And who but Lady Greensleeves?
*A new Courtly Sonnet of the Lady Greensleeves,
to the new tune of 'Greensleeves'. From A Hand-
ful of Pleasant Delites* (1584)

19 Ha-ha-ha, you and me,
Little brown jug, don't I love thee.
The Little Brown Jug. Oxford Song Book

20 Here lies Fred,
Who was alive and is dead:
Had it been his father,
I had much rather;
Had it been his brother,
Still better than another;
Had it been his sister,
No one would have missed her;
Had it been the whole generation,
Still better for the nation:
But since 'tis only Fred,
Who was alive and is dead,—
There's no more to be said.
Horace Walpole, *Memoirs of George II* (1847),
vol. i, p. 436

21 Here's a health to all those that we love,
Here's a health to all those that love us,
Here's a health to all those that love them that love
those
That love them that love those that love us.
Old Toast

22 Here we come a-wassailing.   *Old Song*

23 Here we come gathering nuts in May
Nuts in May,
On a cold and frosty morning.   *Children's Song*

24 He talked shop like a tenth muse.
Of Gladstone's Budget speeches. G. W. E.
Russell's *Collections and Recollections,* ch. 12

25 He that fights and runs away
May live to fight another day.
*Musarum Deliciae, collected by Sir John Mennes
and Dr. James Smith,* 1656

26 He was a wight of high renown,
And thou's but of low degree.
It's pride that puts this country down:
Man, put thy old cloak about thee!
The Old Cloak. Oxford Book of 16th Cent. Verse

27 He won't be happy till he gets it.
Advertisement for Pears' Soap

28 Hierusalem, my happy home,
When shall I come to thee?
When shall my sorrows have an end,
Thy joys when shall I see?
Hierusalem. See Songs of Praise Discussed

1 Homocea touches the spot.　　　　*Advertisement*

2 'How different, how very different from the home life
of our own dear Queen!'
　　　　Irvin S. Cobb, *A Laugh a Day*

*As Cleopatra, Sarah Bernhardt stabbed the slave who
bore to her the tidings of Mark Antony's defeat at
Actium; she stormed, raved, wrecked some of the
scenery in her frenzy and finally, as the curtain
fell, dropped in a shuddering, convulsive heap.*

*As the applause died, a middle-aged British
matron was heard to say to her neighbour: 'How
different, how very different from the home life of
our own dear Queen!' (Victoria).*

3 I feel no pain dear mother now
But oh, I am so dry!
O take me to a brewery
And leave me there to die.
　　　　C. Fox-Smith's *Book of Shanties*, 1927

4 If he only knew a little of law, he would know a little
of everything.
　　　　Of Lord Brougham. Emerson, *Quotation and
Originality*, 1877

5 If you your lips would keep from slips
Of five things have a care:
To whom you speak, of whom you speak,
And how, and when, and where.
　　　　Quoted in Augustus Hare, *Story of My Life*

6 I know two things about the horse,
And one of them is rather coarse.
　　　　The Week-End Book

7 I'm arm'd with more than complete steel—The justice
of my quarrel.
　　　　Lust's Dominion (1657), IV. iii (*See 331:9*)

8 In Dublin s fair city, where girls are so pretty,
I first set my eyes on sweet Molly Malone,
As she wheeled her wheelbarrow through streets
broad and narrow,
Crying, Cockles and mussels! alive, alive, oh!
　　　　Cockles and Mussels. Oxford Song Book

9 In good King Charles's golden days,
When loyalty no harm meant;
A furious High-Churchman I was,
And so I gain'd preferment.
Unto my flock I daily preach'd,
Kings are by God appointed,
And damned are those who dare resist,
Or touch the Lord's Anointed.
And this is law, I will maintain,
Unto my dying day, Sir,
That whatsoever King shall reign,
I will be the Vicar of Bray, Sir!
　　　　The Vicar of Bray. Brit. Musical Miscellany
(1734), i

10 The Church of Rome I found would suit
Full well my constitution.　　　　*Ib.*

11 I turned the cat in pan again,
And swore to him allegiance.　　　　*Ib.*

12 When George in pudding time came o'er,
And moderate men look'd big, Sir.　　　　*Ib.*

13 　　I saw my lady weep,
And Sorrow proud to be exalted so
In those fair eyes where all perfections keep.
　　Her face was full of woe;

But such a woe, believe me, as wins more hearts,
Than Mirth can do with her enticing parts.
　　　　Songs set by John Dowland, iii. *Oxford Book of
16th Cent. Verse*

14 I saw three ships a-sailing there,
—A-sailing there, a-sailing there,
Jesu, Mary and Joseph they bare
On Christ's Sunday at morn.
Joseph did whistle and Mary did sing,
—Mary did sing, Mary did sing,
And all the bells on earth did ring
For joy Our Lord was born.
O they sail'd in to Bethlehem!
—To Bethlehem, to Bethlehem;
Saint Michael was the steresman,
Saint John sate in the horn.
　　　　I saw three ships. Oxford Book of Carols

15 I sing of a maiden
　　That is makeless;
King of all kings
　　To her son she ches.
　　　　Carol: I Sing of a Maiden (15th cent.). *Oxford
Book of Carols*

16 He came all so still
　　Where His mother was,
As dew in April
　　That falleth on the grass.　　　　*Ib.*

17 Mother and maiden
　　Was never none but she!
Well may such a lady
　　God's mother be.　　　　*Ib.*

18 I slept and dreamed that life was beauty;
I woke and found that life was duty.
　　　　Duty, c. 1850. *But see* Corrigenda

19 Is that Mr. Reilly, can anyone tell?
Is that Mr. Reilly that owns the hotel?
Well, if that's Mr. Reilly, they speak of so highly,
Upon me soul, Reilly, you're doin' quite well.
　　　　Is that Mr. Reilly? (1882). *Chorus*

20 The children of Lord Lytton organized a charade.
The scene displayed a Crusader knight returning
from the wars. At his gate he was welcomed by his
wife to whom he recounted his triumphs and the
number of heathen he had slain. His wife, pointing
to a row of dolls of various sizes, replied with pride,
'And I too, my lord, have not been idle'.
　　　　G. W. E. Russell's *Collections and Recollections,*
ch. 31

21 It's a long time between drinks.
　　　　*The Governor of South Carolina required the
return of a fugitive slave. The Governor of North
Carolina hesitated because of powerful friends of the
fugitive. He gave a banquet to his official brother.
The Governor of South Carolina in a speech demanded the return of the slave and ended with 'What
do you say?' The Governor of North Carolina
replied as above*

22 It is good to be merry and wise,
It is good to be honest and true,
It is best to be off with the old love,
Before you are on with the new.
　　　　Songs of England and Scotland. London, 1835,
vol. ii , p. 73

23 It's love, it's love that makes the world go round.
　　　　Chansons Nationales et Populaires de France,
vol. ii, p. 180

ANONYMOUS

1 I wish I were single again.
> *I Married a Wife* (19th century)

2 Jesus Christ is risen to-day,
Our triumphant holy day;
Who did once upon the cross
Suffer to redeem our loss.
Hallelujah!
> *Jesus Christ is Risen To-day. From a Latin Hymn of the 15th cent. Translator unknown*

3 King Charles the First walked and talked
Half an hour after his head was cut off.
> *See Peter Puzzlewell, A Choice Collection of Riddles, Charades and Rebusses (1792)*

4 Know all men by these presents, that I John Griffin make the aforementioned my last will and testament.
> *Cruise, Digest, 1752*

5 Like a fine old English gentleman,
All of the olden time.
> *The Fine Old English Gentleman. Oxford Song Book*

6 The newly-elected mayor who . . . said that during his year of office he should lay aside all his political prepossessions and be, 'like Caesar's wife, all things to all men'.
> *G. W. E. Russell's Collections and Recollections, ch. 29*

7 Lizzie Borden took an axe
And gave her mother forty whacks;
When she saw what she had done
She gave her father forty-one!
> *After an American murder trial of the 1890's in which Miss Borden was acquitted of murdering her father and stepmother*

8 Love me little, love me long,
Is the burden of my song.
> *Love me Little, Love me Long (1569-70)*

9 March winds and April showers
Bringeth vo'th May flowers.
> *West Somerset Word-Book, ed. Frederick Thomas Elworthy (1886), March*

10 Miss Buss and Miss Beale
Cupid's darts do not feel.
How different from us,
Miss Beale and Miss Buss.
> *Of the Headmistress of the North London Collegiate School and the Principal of the Ladies' College, Cheltenham. 19th cent.*

11 Most Gracious Queen, we thee implore
To go away and sin no more,
But if that effort be too great,
To go away at any rate.
> *Epigram on Queen Caroline, 1820. Quoted in Lord Colchester's Diary, 15 Nov. 1820; sent to him by Francis Burton*

12 Multiplication is vexation,
Division is as bad;
The Rule of three doth puzzle me,
And Practice drives me mad.
> *Elizabethan MS. dated 1570*

13 My anvil and hammer lies declined,
My bellows have quite lost their wind,
My fire's extinct, my forge decay'd,
My vice is in the dust all laid,
My coals is spent, my iron gone,
My nails are drove, my work is done,
My mortal part rests nigh this stone,
My soul to heaven I hope is gone.
> *Epitaph on John Hunter, a blacksmith, d. 10 Apr. 1792. Found in St. Andrew's Chapel, Shotley, and on other blacksmiths elsewhere*

14 My Love in her attire doth show her wit,
It doth so well become her:
For every season she hath dressings fit,
For winter, spring, and summer.
No beauty she doth miss,
When all her robes are on;
But beauty's self she is,
When all her robes are gone. *Madrigal*

15 My name is George Nathaniel Curzon,
I am a most superior person.
> *The Masque of Balliol, composed by and current among members of Balliol College in the late 1870's (see also 39:5, 511:5 and 6)*

16 My face is pink, my hair is sleek,
I dine at Blenheim once a week.
> *Ib. (a later addition)*

17 I am rather tall and stately,
And I care not very greatly
What you say, or what you do.
I'm Mackail,—and who are you? *Ib.*

18 Now I lay me down to sleep;
I pray the Lord my soul to keep.
If I should die before I wake,
I pray the Lord my soul to take.
> *First printed in a late edition of the* New England Primer, 1781

19 O Death, where is thy sting-a-ling-a-ling,
O Grave, thy victoree?
The bells of Hell go ting-a-ling-a-ling
For you but not for me.
> *Song popular in the British Army, 1914-18*

20 O God, if there be a God, save my soul, if I have a soul!
> *Prayer of a common soldier before the battle of Blenheim (see Notes and Queries, clxxiii. 264). Quoted in Newman's Apologia*

21 Oh, Shenandoah, I long to hear you.
Away, you rolling river,
Oh Shenandoah, I long to hear you.
Away, I'm bound to go
'Cross the wide Missouri. *Oxford Song Book*

22 Oh! the oak, and the ash, and the bonny ivy-tree,
They flourish at home in my own country.
> *O The Oak and The Ash (c. 1650). Oxford Song Book*

23 Oh, 'tis my delight on a shining night, in the season of the year.
> *The Lincolnshire Poacher. Oxford Song Book*

24 Oh, 'twas in the broad Atlantic,
'Mid the equinoctial gales,
That a young fellow fell overboard
Among the sharks and whales.
And down he went like a streak of light,
So quickly down went he,
Until he came to a mer-ma-id
At the bottom of the deep blue sea.
Singing, Rule Britannia, Britannia, rule the waves!
Britons never, never, never shall be mar-ri-ed to a mer-ma-id
At the bottom of the deep blue sea.
> *Oh! 'Twas in the Broad Atlantic. Oxford Song Book*

1 Oh! where is my wandering boy to-night?
The boy who was bravest of all.
Oh! Where is My Boy To-night?

2 Old soldiers never die;
They only fade away!
War Song of the British Soldiers, 1914–18

3 One Friday morn when we set sail,
And our ship not far from land,
We there did espy a fair pretty maid,
With a comb and a glass in her hand.
While the raging seas did roar,
And the stormy winds did blow,
And we jolly sailor-boys were all up aloft
And the land-lubbers lying down below.
The Mermaid. Oxford Song Book

4 O No John! No John! No John! No!
O No, John. Oxford Song Book

5 On Waterloo's ensanguined plain
Full many a gallant man was slain,
But none, by sabre or by shot,
Fell half so flat as Walter Scott.
On Scott's Field of Waterloo. 1815

6 O Paddy dear, an' did ye hear the news that's goin'
round?
The shamrock is by law forbid to grow on Irish
ground!
No more St. Patrick's Day we'll keep, his colour can't
be seen,
For there's a cruel law agin the wearin' o' the Green!
I met wid Napper Tandy, and he took me by the
hand,
And he said, 'How's poor ould Ireland, and how does
she stand?'
She's the most disthressful country that iver yet was
seen,
For they're hangin' men an' women there for the
wearin' o' the Green.
*The Wearin' o' the Green. (Famous street ballad,
later added to by Boucicault.)*

7 O ye'll tak' the high road, and I'll tak' the low road,
And I'll be in Scotland afore ye,
But me and my true love will never meet again,
On the bonnie, bonnie banks o' Loch Lomon'.
The Bonnie Banks o' Loch Lomon'. Oxford Song Book

8 But the broken heart it kens nae second spring again,
Tho' the waefu' may cease frae their greeting.   *Ib.*

9 Please her the best you may,
She looks another way.
Alas and well a day!
Phillida flouts me.
*The Disdainful Shepherdess. Oxford Book of 16th
Cent. Verse*

10 But she did all disdain,
And threw them back again;
Therefore it's flat and plain
Phillida flouts me.   *Ib.*

11 Please to remember the Fifth of November,
Gunpowder Treason and Plot.
Traditional since 17th cent. (See also 368:13)

12 Raise the stone, and there thou shalt find me, cleave
the wood and there am I.
*Oxyrhynchus Sayings of Christ. Sayings of Our
Lord, Logion 5, l. 23 (1897), p. 12*

13 Remember the Maine!
Slogan of the Spanish-American War

14 See the happy moron,
He doesn't give a damn.
I wish I were a moron.
My God! Perhaps I am!
Eugenics Review, July 1929, 86/2

15 Seven wealthy Towns contend for HOMER Dead
Through which the Living HOMER begged his Bread.
*Epilogue to Aesop at Tunbridge; or, a Few
Selected Fables in Verse. By No Person of
Quality, 1698*

16 She has kilted her coats o' green satin,
She has kilted them up to the knee,
And she's aff wi' Lord Ronald Macdonald,
His bride and his darling to be.   *Lizzy Lindsay*

17 Will ye gang wi' me, Lizzy Lindsay,
Will ye gang to the Highlands wi' me?
Will ye gang wi' me, Lizzy Lindsay,
My bride and my darling to be?   *Ib.*

18 She was poor but she was honest,
And her parents was the same,
Till she met a city feller,
And she lost her honest name.
1914–18 War Song. There are many versions

19 In a village in the country,
There her people now do live,
Drinking port wine that she sends 'em,
But they never can forgive.   *Ib.*

20 Its the same the whole world over,
Its the poor wot gets the blame,
Its the rich wot gets the pleasure,
Ain't it all a blooming shame.   *Ib.*

21 Since first I saw your face, I resolved to honour and
renown ye;
If now I be disdained, I wish my heart had never
known ye.
What? I that loved and you that liked, shall we begin
to wrangle?
No, no, no, my heart is fast, and cannot disentangle.
*Songs set by Thomas Ford, ii. Oxford Book of
16th Cent. Verse (Music of Sundry Kinds, 1607).*

22 Since wars begin in the minds of men, it is in the
minds of men that the defences of peace must be
constructed.
*Constitution of the United Nations Educational,
Scientific and Cultural Organisation (1946)*

23 So I wish him joy where'er he dwell,
That first found out the leather bottel.
The Leather Bottel

24 Some talk of Alexander, and some of Hercules;
Of Hector and Lysander, and such great names as
these;
But of all the world's brave heroes, there's none that
can compare
With a tow, row, row, row, row, row, for the British
Grenadier.   *The British Grenadiers*

25 Spheres of influence.
*'Spheres of action', found in Earl Granville's
letter to Count Münster, 29 Apr. 1885. Hertslet's
Map of Africa by Treaty, 3rd edn., p. 868. (See
313:21)*

26 Sumer is icumen in,
Lhude sing cuccu!
Groweth sed, and bloweth med,
And springth the wude nu.
Cuckoo Song, c. 1250

ANONYMOUS

1 Cuccu, cuccu, well singes thu, cuccu:
   Ne swike thu never nu;
Sing cuccu, nu, sing cuccu,
   Sing cuccu, sing cuccu, nu! *Cuckoo Song, c. 1250*

2 Swing low, sweet chariot—
Comin' for to carry me home;
I looked over Jordan and what did I see?
A band of angels comin' after me—
Comin' for to carry me home.
   American Negro Spiritual, c. 1850

3 That Kruschen feeling.
   Advertisement for Kruschen Salts

4 That schoolgirl complexion.
   Advertisement for Palmolive Soap

5 That we spent, we had:
That we gave, we have:
That we left, we lost.
   Epitaph of the Earl of Devonshire, as quoted by Spenser in The Shepherd's Calendar, May, l. 70 *(see 11:17)*

6 The almighty dollar is the only object of worship.
   Philadelphia Public Ledger, 2 Dec. 1836

7 The animals went in one by one,
There's one more river to cross.
   One More River. Oxford Song Book

8 The animals went in four by four,
The big hippopotamus stuck in the door. *Ib.*

9 The Campbells are comin', oho, oho.
   The Campbells are Comin' (c. 1715). Oxford Song Book

10 The children in Holland take pleasure in making What the children in England take pleasure in breaking. *Nursery Rhyme*

11 The eternal triangle.
   Book review in The Daily Chronicle, 5 Dec. 1907

12 The fault is great in man or woman
Who steals a goose from off a common;
But what can plead that man's excuse
Who steals a common from a goose?
   The Tickler Magazine, 1 Feb. 1821

13 The girl I left behind me.
   Title of song, c. 1759. Oxford Song Book

14 The holly and the ivy,
When they are both full grown,
Of all the trees that are in the wood,
The holly bears the crown:
The rising of the sun
And the running of the deer,
The playing of the merry organ,
Sweet singing in the choir.
   The Holly and the Ivy. Oxford Book of Carols

15 The King over the Water. *Jacobite Toast, 18th cent.*

16 The ministry of all the talents.
   A name given ironically to Grenville's coalition of 1806; also applied to later coalitions

17 The nature of God is a circle of which the centre is everywhere and the circumference is nowhere.
   Origin unknown; said to have been traced to a lost treatise of Empedocles. Quoted in the Roman de la Rose, and by S. Bonaventura in Itinerarius Mentis in Deum, cap. v. ad fin.

18 Then he kissed her cold corpus
A thousand times o'er,
He called her his Dinah—
Though she was no more!
He swallowed the pison
Like a true lovier brave,
And Vilikins and his Dinah
Lie a-buried in one grave.
   In Henry Mayhew's The Wandering Minstrels, 1834

19 The noble Duke of York,
He had ten thousand men,
He marched them up to the top of the hill,
And he marched them down again.
And when they were up, they were up,
And when they were down, they were down,
And when they were only half way up,
   They were neither up nor down.
   The Noble Duke of York, first printed in A. Rackham, Mother Goose (1913)

20 There is a lady sweet and kind,
Was never face so pleased my mind;
I did but see her passing by,
And yet I love her till I die.
   Found on back of leaf 53 of 'Popish Kingdome or reigne of Antichrist', in Latin verse by Thomas Naogeorgus, and Englished by Barnabe Googe. Printed 1570. See Notes and Queries, 9th series, x. 427

21 There is a tavern in the town,
  And there my dear love sits him down,
And drinks his wine 'mid laughter free,
And never, never thinks of me.
   Fare thee well, for I must leave thee,
   Do not let this parting grieve thee,
   And remember that the best of friends must part.

   Adieu, adieu, kind friends, adieu, adieu, adieu,
   I can no longer stay with you.
   I'll hang my harp on a weeping willow-tree,
   And may the world go well with thee.
   There is a Tavern in the Town. Oxford Song Book

22 There's nae luck about the house,
   There's nae luck at a',
There's nae luck about the house
   When our gudeman's awa'.
   The Mariner's Wife

23 There was an old Fellow of Trinity,
A Doctor well versed in Divinity;
But he took to free-thinking,
And then to deep drinking,
And so had to leave the vicinity.
   A. C. Hilton, in The Light Green, No. II, 1872

24 There was an old man of Boulogne,
Who sang a most topical song.
   It wasn't the words
   Which frightened the birds,
But the horrible double entendre.
   Langford Reed, The Limerick Book, p. 51

25 There was a young lady of Kent,
Who said that she knew what it meant
   When men asked her to dine,
   Gave her cocktails and wine,
She knew what it meant—but she went! *Ib. p. 49*

ANONYMOUS

1 There was a young lady of Lynn
Who was so uncommonly thin
   That when she essayed
   To drink lemonade,
She slipped through the straw and fell in.
> Langford Reed, *The Limerick Book*, p. 150

2 There was a young lady of Riga,
Who rode with a smile on a tiger;
   They returned from the ride
   With the lady inside,
And the smile on the face of the tiger. *Ib.* p. 103

3 The Sun himself cannot forget
His fellow traveller.
> On Sir Francis Drake. *Wit's Recreations (1640), Epigrams, No. 146*

4 They come as a boon and a blessing to men,
The Pickwick, the Owl, and the Waverley pen.
> *Advertisement*

5 They that wash on Monday
Have all the week to dry;
They that wash on Tuesday
Are not so much awry;
They that wash on Wednesday
Are not so much to blame;
They that wash on Thursday
Wash for shame;
They that wash on Friday
Wash in need;
And they that wash on Saturday,
Oh! they're sluts indeed.
> See Robert Hunt, *Popular Romances of the West of England* (1865), p. 430

6 To change the name, and not the letter,
Is a change for the worse, and not for the better.
> *Book of Days* (ed. Robert Chambers, 1802–71), vol. i, June, p. 723

7 Two men wrote a lexicon, Liddell and Scott;
Some parts were clever, but some parts were not.
Hear, all ye learned, and read me this riddle,
How the wrong part wrote Scott, and the right part
   wrote Liddell.
> On Henry Liddell (*1811–98*) and Robert Scott (*1811–87*), *co-authors of the Greek Lexicon, 1843*

8 Wash me in the water
That you washed the colonel's daughter
And I shall be whiter
Than the whitewash on the wall.
> *Song popular among the British troops in France, 1914–18*

9 We don't want to fight; but, by Jingo, if we do,
We won't go to the front ourselves, but we'll send the
   mild Hindoo.
> *1878 parody, on hearing that Indian troops were being sent to Malta to help the English.* G. W. E. Russell's *Collections and Recollections*, ch. 28

10 Weep you no more, sad fountains;
   What need you flow so fast?
> *Songs set by John Dowland*, viii. *Oxford Book of 16th Cent. Verse*

11 We hold these truths to be self-evident, that all men
are created equal, that they are endowed by their
Creator with certain unalienable rights, that among
these are life, liberty, and the pursuit of happiness.
> *The American Declaration of Independence, 4 July 1776.* (See 268:19)

12 'Well, what sort of sport has Lord — had?'
'Oh, the young Sahib shot divinely, but God was very
   merciful to the birds.'
> G. W. E. Russell's *Collections and Recollections*, ch. 30

13 We're here because we're here because we're here
   because we're here.
> *Refrain of an American folk-song, popular in the British Army, 1914–18*

14 Western wind, when wilt thou blow,
   The small rain down can rain?
Christ, if my love were in my arms
   And I in my bed again!
> *Oxford Book of 16th Cent. Verse*

15 What did you do in the Great War, daddy?
> *Recruiting placard, 1914–18 war*

16 What shall we do with the drunken sailor?
Early in the morning?
Hoo-ray and up she rises
Early in the morning.
> *What shall we do with the Drunken Sailor? Oxford Song Book*

17 What wee gave, we have;
What wee spent, wee had;
What wee kept, wee lost.
> *Epitaph on Edward Courtenay, Earl of Devon (d. 1419) and his wife, at Tiverton.* (See 10:5)

18 When Adam delved, and Eve span,
Who was then a gentleman?
> *Text of Ball's revolutionary sermon at Blackheath in Wat Tyler's Rebellion, 1381.* See J. R. Green, *Short Hist.* (1893), ii. 484. *(See 235:7)*

19 When Johnny Comes Marching Home Again.
> *Title of Song. Oxford Song Book*

20 When Molly smiles beneath her cow,
   I feel my heart—I can't tell how.
> *When Molly smiles, 1732*

21 When the wind is in the east,
'Tis neither good for man nor beast;
When the wind is in the north,
The skilful fisher goes not forth;
When the wind is in the south,
It blows the bait in the fishes' mouth;
When the wind is in the west,
Then 'tis at the very best.
> See J. O. Halliwell, *Popular Rhymes* (1849)

22 Where is the man who has the power and skill
To stem the torrent of a woman's will?
For if she will, she will, you may depend on't;
And if she won't, she won't; so there's an end on't.
> *From the Pillar Erected on the Mount in the Dane John Field, Canterbury. Examiner, 31 May 1829*

23 Whilst Adam slept, Eve from his side arose:
Strange his first sleep should be his last repose.
> *The Consequence*

24 Who passes by this road so late?
   Compagnon de la Majolaine!
Who passes by this road so late?
   Always gay!
Of all the king's knights 'tis the flower,
   Compagnon de la Majolaine,
Of all the king's knights 'tis the flower,
   Always gay!
> *Old French Song quoted by* Dickens, *Little Dorrit*, ch. 1

ANONYMOUS

1 Will you hear a Spanish lady
   How she woo'd an Englishman?
   Garments gay and rich as may be,
   Decked with jewels had she on.
                          The Spanish Lady's Love

2 With a heart of furious fancies,
   Whereof I am commander;
   With a burning spear,
   And a horse of air,
   To the wilderness I wander.   *Tom o' Bedlam*

3 Woo'd and married and a',
   Woo'd and married and a'
   Was she nae very weel aff,
   Was woo'd and married and a'.
                          Woo'd and Married and a'

4 Workers of the world, unite!
   Common form of 'Working men of all countries,
   unite!' *This is the English Translation* (1888)
   by Samuel Moore, revised by Engels, of 'Proletarier aller Länder, vereinigt euch!' *which con-
   cludes* The Communist Manifesto (1848), *by
   Marx and Engels, and is quoted as the final words
   of the programme of the Communist International*
   (1928). *Another common form is* 'Proletarians of
   the world, unite!'

5 Worth a guinea a box.
                  Advertisement for Beecham's Pills

6 Yet, if his majesty our sovereign lord
   Should of his own accord
   Friendly himself invite,
   And say 'I'll be your guest tomorrow night',
   How should we stir ourselves, call and command
   All hands to work!
                          From Christ Church MS.

7 'tis a duteous thing
   To show all honour to an earthly king,
   And after all our travail and our cost,
   So he be pleased, to think no labour lost.
   But at the coming of the King of Heaven
   All's set at six and seven:
   We wallow in our sin.
   Christ cannot find a chamber in the inn.
   We entertain Him always like a stranger,
   And as at first still lodge Him in the manger.   *Ib.*

8 You should see me on Sunday.
       Advertisement for Knight's Family Health Soap

9 You press the button, and we'll do the rest.
      Advertisement for the first Kodak cameras, c. 1888

French

10 An army marches on its stomach.
     Attrib. to Napoleon in, e.g., Windsor Magazine,
     1904, *p. 268*

     *Probably condensed from a long passage in Las
     Cases,* Mémorial de Ste-Hélène *(Nov. 1816)*

11 Ça ira.
    Untranslatable phrase, meaning 'That will certainly
    happen'.   *Refrain of French Revolutionary Song*

12 Cet animal est très méchant,
    Quand on l'attaque il se défend.
    This animal is very mischievous; when it is attacked
    it defends itself.
                     La Ménagerie, by Théodore P. K., *1828*

13 Chevalier sans peur et sans reproche.
    Knight without fear and without blemish.
      *Description in contemporary chronicles of Pierre
      Bayard, 1476–1524*

14 Il ne faut pas être plus royaliste que le roi.
    One must not be more royalist than the king.
      Phrase originated under Louis XVI. Chateau-
      briand, La Monarchie selon la Charte, *ed. 1876,
      p. 94*

15 Le monde est plein de fous, et qui n'en veut pas voir
    Doit se tenir tout seul, et casser son miroir.
      The world is full of fools, and he who would not
      see it
      Should live alone and smash his mirror.
        *An adaptation from an original form attributed to
        Claude Le Petit (1640–1665) in* Discours Sati-
        riques, *1686*

16 Liberté! Égalité! Fraternité!
    Liberty! Equality! Fraternity!
      *Phrase of unknown origin dating from before the
      French Revolution. Aulard in* Études et Leçons
      sur la Révolution Française *(6ᵉ série) gives the
      first official use of the phrase in the motion
      passed by the Club des Cordeliers (30 June
      1793): 'que les propriétaires seront invités, . . .
      de faire peindre sur la façade de leurs maisons,
      en gros caractères, ces mots: Unité, indivi-
      sibilité de la République, Liberté, Égalité,
      Fraternité ou la mort.'*
                          (*Journal de Paris, No. 182*)

17 L'ordre règne à Varsovie.
    Order reigns in Warsaw.
      *On 16 Sept. 1831, the Comte Horace Sebastiani,
      minister of foreign affairs, said that* 'La tran-
      quillité règne à Varsovie'. *The newspaper* Moni-
      teur *took it up*

18 Revenons à ces moutons.
      Let us return to our sheep. (Let us get back to the
      subject.)   *Maistre Pierre Pathelin (line 1191)
      Often quoted as* 'Retournons à nos moutons'

19 Taisez-vous! Méfiez-vous! Les oreilles ennemies
    vous écoutent.
      Be quiet! Be on your guard! Enemy ears are listen-
      ing to you.   *Official Notice in France in 1915*

20 Toujours perdrix!
    Always partridge!
      *Said to originate in a story of Henri IV's having
      ordered that nothing but partridge should be served
      to his confessor, who had rebuked the king for his
      liaisons.*

21 Tout passe, tout casse, tout lasse.
      Everything passes, everything perishes, everything
      palls.   Cahier, *Quelques six mille proverbes*

Greek

22 μηδὲν ἄγαν.
    Nothing in excess.
      *Written up in the temple at Delphi by Cleobulus,
      according to some accounts.* Quoted by Plato in
      Protagoras, 343 b

23 γνῶθι σεαυτόν.
    From the gods comes the saying 'Know thyself'.
      Juvenal, Satires, xi. 27. *The saying was written
      up in the temple of Delphi*

Italian

1 Se non è vero, è molto ben trovato.

If it is not true, it is a happy invention.
Apparently a common saying in the sixteenth century. Found in Giordano Bruno (1585) in the above form, and in Antonio Doni (1552) as 'Se non è vero, egli è stato un bel trovato'

Latin

2 Adeste, fideles,
Laeti triumphantes;
Venite, venite in Bethlehem.

O come, all ye faithful,
Joyful and triumphant,
O come, ye, O come ye to Bethlehem.
French or German hymn of 18th Cent. Trans. by Oakeley in *Murray's Hymnal*, 1852. See *Songs of Praise Discussed*

3 Ad majorem Dei gloriam.

To the greater glory of God.
Motto of the Society of Jesus

4 Ave Caesar, morituri te salutant.

Hail Caesar; those who are about to die salute you.
Salutation of Roman gladiators on entering the arena

5 Cras amet qui nunquam amavit, quique amavit cras amet!

Let those love now, who never lov'd before:
Let those who always lov'd, now love the more.
Pervigilium Veneris, 1. Trans. by Parnell

6 De non apparentibus et de non existentibus eadem est ratio.

It is presumed that what does not appear does not exist.
Law Maxim

7 Et in Arcadia ego.
Inscription on a tomb, frequently reproduced in paintings, e.g. by Guercino, Poussin, and Reynolds

Usually translated : 'And I too [the occupant of the tomb] was in Arcadia.' But perhaps rather, 'I too [the tomb itself] am in Arcadia': even in Arcadia there am I (Death). (See E. Panofsky in *Philosophy and History*: essays presented to E. Cassirer, 1936.)

8 Gaudeamus igitur,
Juvenes dum sumus
Post jucundam juventutem,
Post molestam senectutem,
Nos habebit humus.

Let us live then and be glad
While young life's before us
After youthful pastime had,
After old age hard and sad,
Earth will slumber o'er us.
Medieval students' song, traced to 1267, but revised in the 18th cent.

9 Meum est propositum in taberna mori,
Uinum sit appositum sitienti ori:
Ut dicant cum uenerint angelorum chori
'Deus sit propitius isti potatori.'

I desire to end my days in a tavern drinking,
May some Christian hold for me the glass when I am shrinking;
That the Cherubim may cry, when they see me sinking,
'God be merciful to a soul of this gentleman's way of thinking.'
The '*Archipoeta*'. Trans. by Leigh Hunt

10 Nemo me impune lacessit.

No one provokes me with impunity.
Motto of the Crown of Scotland and of all Scottish regiments

11 Orare est laborare, laborare est orare.

To pray is to work, to work is to pray.
See *Notes and Queries*, 6th series, vol. xi, p. 477

12 Quidquid agas, prudenter agas, et respice finem.

Whatever you do, do cautiously, and look to the end. *Gesta Romanorum*, cap. 103. init.

13 Surrexit Christus hodie
Humano pro solamine:
Alleluia.

Jesus Christ is risen to-day,
Alleluia!
Our triumphant holy day!
Alleluia!
German Easter Carol of 14th cent. Translation in *Lyra Davidica*, 1708. See *Songs of Praise Discussed; also* Corrigenda

14 Te Deum laudamus.

We praise thee, O God.
First words and title of Canticle attr. to S. Ambrose

15 Tempora mutantur, et nos mutamur in illis.

Times change, and we change with them.
Harrison, *Description of Britain* (1577), Pt. III, ch. iii, p. 99

CHRISTOPHER ANSTEY
1724–1805

16 If ever I ate a good supper at night,
I dream'd of the devil, and wak'd in a fright.
The New Bath Guide. Letter 4. A Consultation of the Physicians

17 You may go to Carlisle's, and to Almack's too;
And I'll give you my head if you find such a host,
For coffee, tea, chocolate, butter, and toast:
How he welcomes at once all the world and his wife,
And how civil to folk he ne'er saw in his life.
Ib. (1766), *letter* 13, *A Public Breakfast*

18 Hearken, Lady Betty, hearken,
To the dismal news I tell,
How your friends are all embarking
For the fiery gulf of hell. *Ib. letter* 14

CHARLES JAMES APPERLEY
see
NIMROD

THOMAS APPLETON
1812–1884

19 A Boston man is the east wind made flesh. *Attr.*

1 Good Americans, when they die, go to Paris.
O. W. Holmes, *Autocrat of the Breakfast Table*,
ch. 6

ARABIAN NIGHTS

2 Who will change old lamps for new ones? . . . new
lamps for old ones?   *The History of Aladdin*

3 Open Sesame!   *The History of Ali Baba*

WILLIAM ARABIN
1773–1841

4 Prisoner, God has given you good abilities, instead
of which you go about the country stealing ducks.
Attributed. See Notes and Queries, clxx. 310

JOHN ARBUTHNOT
1667–1735

5 He warns the heads of parties against believing their
own lies.   *The Art of Political Lying*, 1712

6 Law is a bottomless pit.
The History of John Bull (1712), ch. xxiv

7 Hame's hame, be it never so hamely.
Law is a Bottomless Pit

8 One of the new terrors of death.
Of Edmund Curll's biographies. R. Carru-
thers's *Life of Pope* (1857), p. 199

ARCHIMEDES
287–212 B.C.

9 εὕρηκα.
Eureka! (I have found!)
Vitruvius Pollio, *De Architectura*, ix. 215

10 δός μοι ποῦ στῶ καὶ κινῶ τὴν γῆν..
Give me but one firm spot on which to stand, and
I will move the earth.
Pappus Alexandr., Collectio, lib. viii, prop. 10,
§ xi (ed. Hultsch, Berlin 1878)

COMTE D'ARGENSON
1652–1721

11 L'ABBÉ GUYOT DESFONTAINES: Il faut que je vive.
D'ARGENSON: Je n'en vois pas la nécessité.
DESFONTAINES: I must live.
D'ARGENSON: I do not see the necessity.
Voltaire, *Alzire, Discours Préliminaire.* (*See 412 : 3*)

GEORGE DOUGLAS CAMPBELL,
EIGHTH DUKE OF ARGYLL
1823–1900

12 The Reign of Law.   *Title of a book*, 1867

ARISTOPHANES
c. 444–c. 380 B.C.

13 ὁ δ' εὔκολος μὲν ἐνθάδ', εὔκολος δ' ἐκεῖ.
'But he was easy there, is easy here' (Sophocles)
Frogs, 82. Trans. by Rogers

ARISTOTLE
384–322 B.C.

14 ἄνθρωπος φύσει πολιτικὸν ζῷον.
Man is by nature a political animal.
Politics, i. 2. 9. 1253 *a* (ed. W. L. Newman)

15 ἢ θηρίον ἢ θεός.
Either a beast or a god.   *Politics*, i. 14. 1253 *a*

16 ἔστιν οὖν τραγῳδία μίμησις πράξεως σπουδαίας καὶ τελείας
μέγεθος ἐχούσης . . . δι' ἐλέου καὶ φόβου περαίνουσα
τὴν τῶν τοιούτων παθημάτων κάθαρσιν.
A tragedy is the imitation of an action that is
serious and also, as having magnitude, complete
in itself . . . with incidents arousing pity and fear,
wherewith to accomplish its purgation of such
emotions.   *Poetics*, 6. 1449 *b*. Trans. by Bywater

17 διὸ καὶ φιλοσοφώτερον καὶ σπουδαιότερον ποίησις ἱστορίας
ἐστίν.
Poetry is something more philosophic and of graver
import than history.   *Ib.* 9. 1451 *b*

18 προαιρεῖσθαί τε δεῖ ἀδύνατα εἰκότα μᾶλλον ἢ δυνατὰ ἀπίθανα.
A likely impossibility is always preferable to an
unconvincing possibility.   *Ib.* 24. 1460 *a*

19 Amicus Plato, sed magis amica veritas
Plato is dear to me, but dearer still is truth.
Original ascribed to Aristotle

SIR JOHN ARKWRIGHT
1872–1954

20 O valiant hearts who to your glory came.   *Hymn*

ROBERT ARMIN
fl. 1610

21 A flea in his ear.   *Foole upon Foole*, 1605, c. 3

LEWIS ADDISON ARMISTEAD
1817–1863

22 Give them the cold steel, boys!
Attr. remark during Amer. Civil War, 1863

JOHN ARMSTRONG
1709–1779

23 Virtuous and wise he was, but not severe;
He still remember'd that he once was young.
Art of Preserving Health, 1744, bk. iv, l. 226

24   Much had he read,
Much more had seen; he studied from the life,
And in th' original perus'd mankind.   *Ib.* l. 231

25 'Tis not for mortals always to be blest.   *Ib.* l. 260

26 Of right and wrong he taught
Truths as refin'd as ever Athens heard;
And (strange to tell!) he practis'd what he preach'd.
Ib. l. 303

27 'Tis not too late to-morrow to be brave.   *Ib.* l. 460

SIR EDWIN ARNOLD
1832–1904

28 Veil after veil will lift—but there must be
Veil upon veil behind.   *The Light of Asia*, bk. viii

29 Lord! make us just, that we may be
A little justified with Thee.
Pearls of the Faith, No. 47

30   Nor ever once ashamed
So we be named
Press-men; Slaves of the Lamp; Servants of Light.
The Tenth Muse, st. 18

GEORGE ARNOLD
1834–1865

1 The living need charity more than the dead.
The Jolly Old Pedagogue

MATTHEW ARNOLD
1822–1888

2 And we forget because we must
And not because we will. *Absence*

3 Their ineffectual feuds and feeble hates,
Shadows of hates, but they distress them still.
Balder Dead, iii. 466

4 Hath man no second life?—Pitch this one high!

Was Christ a man like us?—Ah! let us try
If we then, too, can be such men as he!
The Better Part

5 The same heart beats in every human breast.
The Buried Life, l. 23

6 A bolt is shot back somewhere in our breast,
And a lost pulse of feeling stirs again.

A man becomes aware of his life's flow . . .
And there arrives a lull in the hot race

And then he thinks he knows
The hills where his life rose,
And the sea where it goes. *Ib.* l. 84

7 The Sea of Faith
Was once, too, at the full, and round earth's shore
Lay like the folds of a bright girdle furl'd.
But now I only hear
Its melancholy, long, withdrawing roar,
Retreating, to the breath
Of the night-wind, down the vast edges drear
And naked shingles of the world. *Dover Beach*, l. 21

8 And we are here as on a darkling plain
Swept with confused alarms of struggle and flight,
Where ignorant armies clash by night. *Ib.* l. 35

9 The will is free;
Strong is the soul, and wise, and beautiful;
The seeds of godlike power are in us still;
Gods are we, bards, saints, heroes, if we will!
Written in a copy of Emerson's Essays

10 Be neither saint nor sophist-led, but be a man.
Empedocles on Etna, I. ii. 136

11 We do not what we ought;
What we ought not, we do;
And lean upon the thought
That chance will bring us through;
But our own acts, for good or ill, are mightier powers.
Ib. 237

12 Nature, with equal mind,
Sees all her sons at play,
Sees man control the wind,
The wind sweep man away. *Ib.* 257

13 Is it so small a thing
To have enjoy'd the sun,
To have lived light in the spring,
To have loved, to have thought, to have done;
To have advanced true friends, and beat down baffling
foes? *Ib.* 397

14 Far, far from here,
The Adriatic breaks in a warm bay
Among the green Illyrian hills;

And there, they say, two bright and aged snakes,
Who once were Cadmus and Harmonia,
Bask in the glens or on the warm sea-shore,
In breathless quiet, after all their ills.
Empedocles on Etna, I. ii. 427

15 Not here, O Apollo!
Are haunts meet for thee.
But, where Helicon breaks down
In cliff to the sea. *Ib.* II. 421

16 'Tis Apollo comes leading
His choir, the Nine.
—The leader is fairest,
But all are divine. *Ib.* 445

17 The day in his hotness,
The strife with the palm;
The night in her silence,
The stars in their calm. *Ib.* 465

18 I must not say that thou wast true,
Yet let me say that thou wast fair;
And they, that lovely face who view,
Why should they ask if truth be there?
Euphrosyne, 1

19 Eyes too expressive to be blue,
Too lovely to be grey. *Faded Leaves*, 4. *On the Rhine*

20 This heart, I know,
To be long lov'd was never framed;
For something in its depths doth glow
Too strange, too restless, too untamed.
A Farewell, st. 5

21 I too have long'd for trenchant force,
And will like a dividing spear;
Have prais'd the keen, unscrupulous course,
Which knows no doubt, which feels no fear.
Ib. st. 9

22 Come, dear children, let us away;
Down and away below. *The Forsaken Merman*, l. 1

23 Now the great winds shoreward blow;
Now the salt tides seaward flow;
Now the wild white horses play,
Champ and chafe and toss in the spray. *Ib.* l. 4

24 Sand-strewn caverns, cool and deep,
Where the winds are all asleep;
Where the spent lights quiver and gleam;
Where the salt weed sways in the stream;
Where the sea-beasts rang'd all round
Feed in the ooze of their pasture-ground;

Where great whales came sailing by,
Sail and sail, with unshut eye,
Round the world for ever and aye. *Ib.* l. 35

25 Children dear, was it yesterday
(Call yet once) that she went away? *Ib.* l. 48

26 Children dear, were we long alone?
'The sea grows stormy, the little ones moan.
Long prayers', I said, 'in the world they say.'
Ib. l. 64

27 But, ah, she gave me never a look,
For her eyes were seal'd to the holy book.
Loud prays the priest; shut stands the door.
Come away, children, call no more.
Come away, come down, call no more. *Ib.* l. 80

ARNOLD

1 She will start from her slumber
When gusts shake the door;
She will hear the winds howling,
Will hear the waves roar.
We shall see, while above us
The waves roar and whirl,
A ceiling of amber,
A pavement of pearl.
Singing, 'Here came a mortal,
But faithless was she!
And alone dwell for ever
The kings of the sea.'   *The Forsaken Merman*, l. 112

2 Who saw life steadily, and saw it whole:
The mellow glory of the Attic stage;
Singer of sweet Colonus, and its child.
    Sonnet to a Friend: 'Who prop, thou ask'st.'

3 A wanderer is man from his birth.
He was born in a ship
On the breast of the river of Time. *The Future*, l. 1

4 And the width of the waters, the hush
Of the grey expanse where he floats,
Freshening its current and spotted with foam
As it draws to the Ocean, may strike
Peace to the soul of the man on its breast:
As the pale waste widens around him—
As the banks fade dimmer away—
As the stars come out, and the night-wind
Brings up the stream
Murmurs and scents of the infinite Sea. *Ib.* l. 78

5 Ah! not the nectarous poppy lovers use,
Not daily labour's dull, Lethaean spring,
Oblivion in lost angels can infuse
Of the soil'd glory, and the trailing wing.
    To a Gipsy Child by the Sea-shore

6 Not as their friend or child I speak!
But as on some far northern strand,
Thinking of his own Gods, a Greek
In pity and mournful awe might stand
Before some fallen Runic stone—
For both were faiths, and both are gone.
    The Grande Chartreuse, l. 79

7 Wandering between two worlds, one dead,
The other powerless to be born. *Ib.* l. 85

8 What helps it now, that Byron bore,
With haughty scorn which mock'd the smart,
Through Europe to the Aetolian shore
The pageant of his bleeding heart?
That thousands counted every groan,
And Europe made his woe her own? *Ib.* l. 133

9 Years hence, perhaps, may dawn an age,
More fortunate, alas! than we,
Which without hardness will be sage,
And gay without frivolity. *Ib.* l. 157

10 It is—last stage of all—
When we are frozen up within, and quite
The phantom of ourselves,
To hear the world applaud the hollow ghost
Which blamed the living man. *Growing Old*

11 So thou arraign'st her, her foe;
So we arraign her, her sons.
Yes, we arraign her! but she,
The weary Titan! with deaf
Ears, and labour-dimmed eyes,
. . . goes passively by,
Staggering on to her goal;

Bearing on shoulders immense,
Atlanteän, the load . . .
Of the too vast orb of her fate. *Heine's Grave*, l. 85

12 Who, Goethe said,
'Had every other gift, but wanted love.' *Ib.* l. 99

13 Only he,
His soul well-knit, and all his battles won,
Mounts, and that hardly, to eternal life. *Immortality*

14 The solemn peaks but to the stars are known,
But to the stars, and the cold lunar beams:
Alone the sun arises, and alone
Spring the great streams. *In Utrumque Paratus*

15 This truth—to prove, and make thine own:
'Thou hast been, shalt be, art, alone.'
    Isolation. To Marguerite, l. 29

16 The unplumb'd, salt, estranging sea.
    To Marguerite (contd.), l. 24

17 Calm soul of all things! make it mine
To feel, amid the city's jar,
That there abides a peace of thine,
Man did not make, and cannot mar!
    Lines written in Kensington Gardens, l. 37

18 Calm, calm me more! nor let me die
Before I have begun to live. *Ib.* l. 43

19 Let the long contention cease!
Geese are swans, and swans are geese.
    The Last Word, l. 5

20 Let the victors, when they come,
When the forts of folly fall,
Find thy body by the wall. *Ib.* l. 14

21 When Byron's eyes were shut in death,
We bow'd our head and held our breath.
He taught us little: but our soul
Had *felt* him like the thunder's roll.

We watch'd the fount of fiery life
Which serv'd for that Titanic strife.
    Memorial Verses, l. 6

22 He spoke, and loos'd our heart in tears.
He laid us as we lay at birth
On the cool flowery lap of earth. [Wordsworth]
    Ib. l. 47

23 Time may restore us in his course
Goethe's sage mind and Byron's force:
But where will Europe's latter hour
Again find Wordsworth's healing power? *Ib.* l. 60

24 Ere the parting hour go by,
Quick, thy tablets, Memory! *A Memory Picture*

25 All this I bear, for, what I seek, I know:
Peace, peace is what I seek, and public calm:
Endless extinction of unhappy hates. *Merope*, l. 100

26 With women the heart argues, not the mind.
    Ib. l. 341

27 He bears the seed of ruin in himself. *Ib.* l. 856

28 For this is the true strength of guilty kings,
When they corrupt the souls of those they rule.
    Ib. l. 1436

29 We cannot kindle when we will
The fire which in the heart resides,
The spirit bloweth and is still,
In mystery our soul abides:
But tasks in hours of insight will'd
Can be through hours of gloom fulfill'd.
    Morality, st. 1

[16]

1 With aching hands and bleeding feet
   We dig and heap, lay stone on stone;
We bear the burden and the heat
   Of the long day, and wish 'twere done.
Not till the hours of light return,
All we have built do we discern.   *Morality*, st. 2

2 Strew no more red roses, maidens,
Leave the lilies in their dew:
Pluck, pluck cypress, O pale maidens:
Dusk, O dusk the hall with yew!
                The New Sirens, l. 267

3 But Wordsworth's eyes avert their ken
From half of human fate.
   In Memory of the Author of Obermann, l. 53

4 What shelter to grow ripe is ours?
What leisure to grow wise?   *Ib.* l. 71

5 Too fast we live, too much are tried,
Too harass'd, to attain
Wordsworth's sweet calm, or Goethe's wide
And luminous view to gain.   *Ib.* l. 77

6 We, in some unknown Power's employ,
Move on a rigorous line:
Can neither, when we will, enjoy;
Nor, when we will, resign.   *Ib.* l. 133

7 On that hard Pagan world disgust
And secret loathing fell.
Deep weariness and sated lust
Made human life a hell.   *Obermann Once More*, l. 93

8 The East bow'd low before the blast,
In patient, deep disdain.
She let the legions thunder past,
And plunged in thought again.   *Ib.* l. 109

9 That gracious Child, that thorn-crown'd Man!
He lived while we believed.

Now he is dead. Far hence he lies
In the lorn Syrian town,
And on his grave, with shining eyes,
The Syrian stars look down.   *Ib.* l. 167

10 Say, has some wet bird-haunted English lawn
Lent it the music of its trees at dawn? *Parting*, l. 19

11 Hark! ah, the Nightingale!
The tawny-throated!
Hark! from that moonlit cedar what a burst!
What triumph! hark—what pain!   *Philomela*, l. 1

12 Listen, Eugenia—
How thick the bursts come crowding through the
    leaves!
Again—thou hearest!
Eternal Passion!
Eternal Pain!   *Ib.* l. 28

13 Cruel, but composed and bland,
Dumb, inscrutable and grand,
So Tiberius might have sat,
Had Tiberius been a cat.   *Poor Matthias*, l. 40

14 Nature's great law, and law of all men's minds?
To its own impulse every creature stirs:
Live by thy light, and Earth will live by hers.
          Religious Isolation, l. 12

15 Strew on her roses, roses,
   And never a spray of yew.
In quiet she reposes:
   Ah! would that I did too.

Her cabin'd ample Spirit,
   It flutter'd and fail'd for breath.
To-night it doth inherit
   The vasty hall of death.   *Requiescat*

16 Coldly, sadly descends
The autumn evening. The Field
Strewn with its dank yellow drifts
Of wither'd leaves, and the elms,
Fade into dimness apace,
Silent.   *Rugby Chapel*, l. 1

17 Somewhere, surely, afar,
In the sounding labour-house vast
Of being, is practised that strength,
Zealous, beneficent, firm.   *Ib.* l. 40

18 Friends who set forth at our side,
Falter, are lost in the storm.
We, we only, are left!   *Ib.* l. 102

19 Therefore to thee it was given
Many to save with thyself;
And, at the end of thy day,
O faithful shepherd! to come,
Bringing thy sheep in thy hand.   *Ib.* l. 140

20 Then, in such hour of need
Of your fainting, dispirited race,
Ye, like angels, appear,
Radiant with ardour divine!
Beacons of hope, ye appear!
Languor is not in your heart,
Weakness is not in your word,
Weariness not on your brow.   *Ib.* l. 188

21 Ye fill up the gaps in our files,
Strengthen the wavering line,
Stablish, continue our march,
On, to the bound of the waste,
On, to the City of God.   *Ib.* l. 204

22 But so many books thou readest,
But so many schemes thou breedest,
But so many wishes feedest,
   That thy poor head almost turns. *The Second Best*

23 Others abide our question. Thou art free.
We ask and ask: Thou smilest and art still,
Out-topping knowledge.   *Shakespeare*

24 And thou, who didst the stars and sunbeams know,
Self-school'd, self-scann'd, self-honour'd, self-secure,
Didst tread on Earth unguess'd at.—Better so!
All pains the immortal spirit must endure,
All weakness which impairs, all griefs which bow,
Find their sole speech in that victorious brow.   *Ib.*

25 Curl'd minion, dancer, coiner of sweet words!
          Sohrab and Rustum, l. 458

26   and Ruksh, the horse,
Who stood at hand, utter'd a dreadful cry:
No horse's cry was that, most like the roar
Of some pain'd desert lion, who all day
Hath trail'd the hunter's javelin in his side,
And comes at night to die upon the sand. *Ib.* l. 501

27 Truth sits upon the lips of dying men.   *Ib.* l. 656

28 But the majestic River floated on,
Out of the mist and hum of that low land,
Into the frosty starlight, and there mov'd,
Rejoicing, through the hush'd Chorasmian waste,
Under the solitary moon: he flow'd
Right for the Polar Star, past Orgunjè,
Brimming, and bright, and large: then sands begin

To hem his watery march, and dam his streams,
And split his currents; that for many a league
The shorn and parcell'd Oxus strains along
Through beds of sand and matted rushy isles—
Oxus, forgetting the bright speed he had
In his high mountain cradle in Pamere,
A foil'd circuitous wanderer—till at last
The long'd-for dash of waves is heard, and wide
His luminous home of waters opens, bright
And tranquil, from whose floor the new-bathed stars
Emerge, and shine upon the Aral Sea.
Sohrab and Rustum, l. 875

1 France, fam'd in all great arts, in none supreme.
To a Republican Friend (contd.)

2   The high
Uno'erleap'd Mountains of Necessity.   *Ib.*

3 Not deep the Poet sees, but wide.   *Resignation*, l. 214

4 Yet they, believe me, who await
No gifts from Chance, have conquer'd Fate.
Ib. l. 247

5 Go, for they call you, Shepherd, from the hill.
The Scholar-Gipsy, l. 1

6 All the live murmur of a summer's day.   *Ib.* l. 20

7 Tired of knocking at Preferment's door.   *Ib.* l. 35

8 In hat of antique shape, and cloak of grey,
The same the Gipsies wore.   *Ib.* l. 55

9 Crossing the stripling Thames at Bab-lock-hithe,
Trailing in the cool stream thy fingers wet,
As the slow punt swings round.   *Ib.* l. 74

10 Rapt, twirling in thy hand a wither'd spray,
And waiting for the spark from heaven to fall.
Ib. l. 119

11 The line of festal light in Christ-Church hall.
Ib. l. 129

12 Thou waitest for the spark from heaven! and we,
Light half-believers in our casual creeds

Who hesitate and falter life away,
And lose to-morrow the ground won to-day—
Ah, do not we, Wanderer, await it too?   *Ib.* l. 171

13 With close-lipp'd Patience for our only friend,
Sad Patience, too near neighbour to Despair.
Ib. l. 194

14 This strange disease of modern life.   *Ib.* l. 203

15 Still nursing the unconquerable hope,
Still clutching the inviolable shade.   *Ib.* l. 211

16 As some grave Tyrian trader, from the sea,
Descried at sunrise an emerging prow
Lifting the cool-hair'd creepers stealthily,
The fringes of a southward-facing brow
Among the Aegean isles;
And saw the merry Grecian coaster come,
Freighted with amber grapes, and Chian wine,
Green bursting figs, and tunnies steep'd in brine;
And knew the intruders on his ancient home,

The young light-hearted Masters of the waves;
And snatch'd his rudder, and shook out more sail,
And day and night held on indignantly
O'er the blue Midland waters with the gale,
Betwixt the Syrtes and soft Sicily,
To where the Atlantic raves
Outside the Western Straits, and unbent sails

There, where down cloudy cliffs, through sheets
of foam,
Shy traffickers, the dark Iberians come;
And on the beach undid his corded bales.
The Scholar-Gipsy, l. 232

17 Resolve to be thyself: and know, that he
Who finds himself, loses his misery.
Self-Dependence, l. 31

18 And see all sights from pole to pole,
And glance, and nod, and bustle by;
And never once possess our soul
Before we die.   *A Southern Night*, l. 69

19 Mild o'er her grave, ye mountains, shine!
Gently by his, ye waters, glide!
To that in you which is divine
They were allied.   *Ib.* l. 137

20 Still bent to make some port he knows not where,
Still standing for some false impossible shore.
A Summer Night, l. 68

21 The signal-elm, that looks on Ilsley downs,
The Vale, the three lone weirs, the youthful
Thames.   *Thyrsis*, l. 14

22 And that sweet City with her dreaming spires,
She needs not June for beauty's heightening.
Ib. l. 19

23 But Thyrsis of his own will went away.   *Ib.* l. 40

24 It irk'd him to be here, he could not rest.

He went ; his piping took a troubled sound
Of storms that rage outside our happy ground;
He could not wait their passing, he is dead!   *Ib.* l. 41

25 So have I heard the cuckoo's parting cry,
From the wet field, through the vext garden-trees,
Come with the volleying rain and tossing breeze:
'The bloom is gone, and with the bloom go I.'
Ib. l. 57

26 Too quick despairer, wherefore wilt thou go?
Soon will the high Midsummer pomps come on,
Soon will the musk carnations break and swell,
Soon shall we have gold-dusted snapdragon,
Sweet-William with his homely cottage-smell,
And stocks in fragrant blow.   *Ib.* l. 61

27 For Time, not Corydon, hath conquer'd thee.
Ib. l. 80

28 She loved the Dorian pipe, the Dorian strain.
But ah, of our poor Thames she never heard!
Her foot the Cumner cowslips never stirr'd;
And we should tease her with our plaint in vain.
Ib. l. 97

29 I know what white, what purple fritillaries
The grassy harvest of the river-fields,
Above by Ensham, down by Sandford, yields,
And what sedg'd brooks are Thames's tributaries.
Ib. l. 107

30 The foot less prompt to meet the morning dew,
The heart less bounding at emotion new,
And hope, once crushed, less quick to spring again.
Ib. l. 138

31 Hear it, O Thyrsis, still our Tree is there!—
Ah, vain! These English fields, this upland dim,
These brambles pale with mist engarlanded,
That lone, sky-pointing tree, are not for him.

ARNOLD

To a boon southern country he is fled,
And now in happier air,
Wandering with the great Mother's train divine
. . . .
Within a folding of the Apennine. *Thyrsis*, l. 171

1 Why faintest thou? I wander'd till I died,
Roam on! the light we sought is shining still.
Dost thou ask proof? Our Tree yet crowns the hill,
Our Scholar travels yet the loved hill-side. *Ib.* l. 237

2 Know, man hath all which Nature hath, but more,
And in that *more* lie all his hopes of good.
To an Independent Preacher

3 Philip's peerless son,
Who carried the great war from Macedon
Into the Soudan's realm, and thunder'd on
To die at thirty-five in Babylon.
Tristram and Iseult, iii. 147

4 For this and that way swings
The flux of mortal things,
Though moving inly to one far-set goal.—
After light's term, a term of cecity.
Westminster Abbey, l. 151

5 Nor bring, to see me cease to live,
Some doctor full of phrase and fame,
To shake his sapient head and give
The ill he cannot cure a name. *A Wish*

6 Calm's not life's crown, though calm is well.
'Tis all perhaps which man acquires,
But 'tis not what our youth desires. *Youth and Calm*

7 And sigh that one thing only has been lent
To youth and age in common—discontent.
Youth's Agitations

8 The magnificent roaring of the young lions of the *Daily Telegraph*.
Essays in Criticism, First Series, preface.

9 Passionate, absorbing, almost blood-thirsty clinging to life. *Ib.*

10 [Oxford] Beautiful city! so venerable, so lovely, so unravaged by the fierce intellectual life of our century, so serene! . . . whispering from her towers the last enchantments of the Middle Age. . . . Home of lost causes, and forsaken beliefs, and unpopular names, and impossible loyalties! *Ib.*

11 Wragg is in custody.
Ib. Functions of Criticism at the Present Time

12 I am bound by my own definition of criticism: a disinterested endeavour to learn and propagate the best that is known and thought in the world. *Ib.*

13 It always seems to me that the right sphere for Shelley's genius was the sphere of music, not of poetry. *Ib. Maurice de Guérin*, footnote

14 Philistine must have originally meant, in the mind of those who invented the nickname, a strong, dogged, unenlightened opponent of the chosen people, of the children of the light. *Ib. Heinrich Heine*

15 Philistinism!—We have not the expression in English. Perhaps we have not the word because we have so much of the thing. *Ib.*

16 The absence, in this country, of any force of educated literary and scientific opinion.
Ib. Literary Influence of Academies

17 The great apostle of the Philistines, Lord Macaulay.
Ib. Joubert

18 His expression may often be called bald . . . but it is bald as the bare mountain tops are bald, with a baldness full of grandeur.
Ib. Second Series, preface to *Poems of Wordsworth*

19 Nature herself seems, I say, to take the pen out of his hand, and to write for him with her own bare, sheer, penetrating power. *Ib.*

20 The difference between genuine poetry and the poetry of Dryden, Pope, and all their school, is briefly this: their poetry is conceived and composed in their wits, genuine poetry is conceived and composed in the soul. *Ib. Thomas Gray*

21 In poetry, no less than in life, he is 'a beautiful and ineffectual angel, beating in the void his luminous wings in vain'. *Ib. Shelley*
[Quoting his own sentence in his essay on Byron, *Essays on Criticism, Second Series*]

22 [Poetry] a criticism of life under the conditions fixed for such a criticism by the laws of poetic truth and poetic beauty. *Ib. The Study of Poetry*

23 Our society distributes itself into Barbarians, Philistines, and Populace; and America is just ourselves, with the Barbarians quite left out, and the Populace nearly. *Culture and Anarchy*, preface

24 The great aim of culture [is] the aim of setting ourselves to ascertain what perfection is and to make it prevail. *Ib. p.* 12

25 The pursuit of perfection, then, is the pursuit of sweetness and light . . . He who works for sweetness and light united, works to make reason and the will of God prevail. *Ib. p.* 47

26 The men of culture are the true apostles of equality. *Ib. p.* 49

27 One has often wondered whether upon the whole earth there is anything so unintelligent, so unapt to perceive how the world is really going, as an ordinary young Englishman of our upper class. *Ib. pp.* 70–1

28 For this [Middle] class we have a designation which now has become pretty well known, and which we may as well still keep for them, the designation of Philistines. *Ib. p.* 97

29 But that vast portion, lastly, of the working-class which . . . is now issuing from its hiding-place to assert an Englishman's heaven-born privilege of doing as he likes, and is beginning to perplex us by marching where it likes, meeting where it likes, bawling what it likes, breaking what it likes—to this vast residuum we may with great propriety give the name of Populace.
Thus we have got three distinct terms, Barbarians, Philistines, Populace, to denote roughly the three great classes into which our society is divided.
Ib. pp. 104–5

30 Hebraism and Hellenism—between these two points of influence moves our World. . . . Hebraism and Hellenism are, neither of them, the law of human development . . .; they are, each of them, contributions to human development. *Ib. pp.* 143, 157

31 'He knows', says Hebraism, 'his Bible!'—whenever we hear this said, we may, without any elaborate defence of culture, content ourselves with answering simply: 'No man, who knows nothing else, knows even his Bible.' *Ib. pp.* 181–2

1 The grand, old, fortifying, classical curriculum.
Friendship's Garland

2 The translator of Homer should above all be penetrated by a sense of four qualities of his author:—that he is eminently rapid; that he is eminently plain and direct both in the evolution of his thought and in the expression of it, that is, both in his syntax and in his words; that he is eminently plain and direct in the substance of his thought, that is, in his matter and ideas; and, finally, that he is eminently noble. *On Translating Homer*, i

3 Wordsworth says somewhere that wherever Virgil seems to have composed 'with his eye on the object', Dryden fails to render him. Homer invariably composes 'with his eye on the object', whether the object be a moral or a material one: Pope composes with his eye on his style, into which he translates his object, whatever it is. *Ib.*

4 He [the Translator] will find one English book and one only, where, as in the *Iliad* itself, perfect plainness of speech is allied with perfect nobleness; and that book is the Bible. *Ib.* iii

5 Nothing has raised more questioning among my critics than these words—noble, the grand style. ... I think it will be found that the grand style arises in poetry, when a noble nature, poetically gifted, treats with simplicity or with severity a serious subject. *Ib.* Last words

6 The theatre is irresistible; organise the theatre!
Irish Essays. The French Play in London

7 Miracles do not happen.
Literature and Dogma, preface to 1883 edition, last words

8 Culture, the acquainting ourselves with the best that has been known and said in the world, and thus with the history of the human spirit.
Ib. preface to 1873 edition

9 Terms like grace, new birth, justification ...: terms, in short, which with St. Paul are literary terms, theologians have employed as if they were scientific terms. *Ib.* ch. i, § 1

10 When we are asked further, what is conduct?—let us answer: Three-fourths of life. *Ib.*

11 The true meaning of religion is thus not simply morality, but morality touched by emotion.
Ib. § 2

12 Conduct is three-fourths of our life and its largest concern. *Ib.* § 3

13 For science, God is simply *the stream of tendency by which all things seek to fulfil the law of their being.*
Ib. § 4. (See 524:27)

14 Let us put into their 'Eternal' and 'God' no more science than they [the Hebrew writers] did:—the enduring power, not ourselves, which makes for righteousness. *Ib.* § 5

15 For it is what we call the Time-Spirit that is sapping the proof from miracles. ... The human mind, as its experience widens, is turning away from them.
Ib. ch. v, § 3

16 What is called 'orthodox divinity' is, in fact, an immense literary misapprehension. *Ib.* ch. vi, § 3

17 The eternal not ourselves which makes for righteousness. *Ib.* ch. viii, § 1

18 But there remains the question: what righteousness really is. The method and secret and sweet reasonableness of Jesus. *Literature and Dogma*, ch. xii, § 2

19 So we have the Philistine of genius in religion—Luther; the Philistine of genius in politics—Cromwell; the Philistine of genius in literature—Bunyan. *Mixed Essays, Lord Falkland*

SAMUEL JAMES ARNOLD
1774–1852

20 Our ships were British oak,
And hearts of oak our men. *Death of Nelson*

THOMAS ARNOLD
1795–1842

21 What we must look for here is, 1st, religious and moral principles: 2ndly, gentlemanly conduct: 3rdly, intellectual ability.
Arnold of Rugby (ed. J. J. Findlay), p. 65

22 My object will be, if possible, to form Christian men, for Christian boys I can scarcely hope to make.
Letter, in 1828, on appointment to Headmastership of Rugby

GEORGE ASAF
[GEORGE H. POWELL]
1880–1951

23 What's the use of worrying?
It never was worth while,
So, pack up your troubles in your old kit-bag,
And smile, smile, smile.
Pack Up Your Troubles In Your Old Kit-Bag

JOHN DUNNING, BARON ASHBURTON
1731–1783

24 The power of the Crown has increased, is increasing, and ought to be diminished.
Motion passed in the House of Commons, 1780

THOMAS ASHE
1836–1889

25 Meet we no angels, Pansie? *At Altenahr*, ii. *Poems*

DAISY ASHFORD
contemporary

26 Mr. Salteena was an elderly man of 42 and was fond of asking peaple to stay with him.
The Young Visiters (1919), ch. i

27 I do hope I shall enjoy myself with you ... I am parshial to ladies if they are nice I suppose it is my nature. I am not quite a gentleman but you would hardly notice it. *Ib.*

28 You look rather rash my dear your colors dont quite match your face. *Ib.* ch. 2

29 Bernard always had a few prayers in the hall and some whiskey afterwards as he was rarther pious
Ib. ch. 3

30 Oh this is most kind said Mr. Salteena.
Minnit closed his eyes with a tired smile.
Not kind sir he muttered quite usual. *Ib.* ch. 5

31 It was a sumpshous spot all done up in gold with plenty of looking glasses. *Ib.*

1 Oh I see said the Earl but my own idear is that these things are as piffle before the wind.
The Young Visiters, ch. 5

2 Ethel patted her hair and looked very sneery.
Ib. ch. 8

3 My life will be sour grapes and ashes without you.
Ib.

4 Take me back to the Gaierty hotel. *Ib. ch. 9*

**HERBERT HENRY ASQUITH,
EARL OF OXFORD
1852–1928**

5 Wait and see.
Phrase used repeatedly in speeches in 1910. Spender and Cyril Asquith's *Life of Lord Oxford and Asquith*, vol. i, p. 275

6 We shall never sheathe the sword which we have not lightly drawn until Belgium receives in full measure all and more than all that she has sacrificed, until France is adequately secured against the menace of aggression, until the rights of the smaller nationalities of Europe are placed upon an unassailable foundation, and until the military domination of Prussia is wholly and finally destroyed. *Speech at the Guildhall, 9 Nov. 1914*

**SIR JACOB ASTLEY
1579–1652**

7 O Lord! thou knowest how busy I must be this day: if I forget thee, do not thou forget me.
Prayer before the Battle of Edgehill (Sir Philip Warwick, *Memoires*, 1701, p. 229)

**EDWARD L. ATKINSON
and
APSLEY CHERRY-GARRARD**

8 A very gallant gentleman.
Inscription on the burial place of Capt. L. E. G. Oates *in the Antarctic, Nov. 1912. Being almost crippled, he walked to his death in a blizzard to enable his companions to proceed on their journey more quickly.*

**HARRIET AUBER
1773–1862**

9 And His that gentle voice we hear,
Soft as the breath of even,
That checks each fault, that calms each fear,
And speaks of heaven.
Spirit of the Psalms (1829), *Our Blest Redeemer, ere He breathed*

**JOHN AUBREY
1626–1697**

10 He was so fair that they called him *the lady of* Christ's College. *Brief Lives. John Milton*

11 Sir Walter, being strangely surprised and put out of his countenance at so great a table, gives his son a damned blow over the face. His son, as rude as he was, would not strike his father, but strikes over the face the gentleman that sat next to him and said 'Box about: 'twill come to my father anon'.
Ib. Sir Walter Raleigh

12 When he killed a calf he would do it in a high style, and make a speech. *Ib. William Shakespeare*

13 He was a handsome, well-shaped man: very good company, and of a very ready and pleasant smooth wit. *Brief Lives. William Shakespeare*

**ALEXANDER BOSWELL,
LORD AUCHINLECK
1706–1782**

14 He [Cromwell] gart kings ken they had a *lith* in their neck.
gart ken = made to know; lith = joint.
Boswell, v. 382, n. 2

**ÉMILE AUGIER
1820–1889**

15 La nostalgie de la boue.
Homesickness for the gutter.
Le Mariage d'Olympe, I. i

**ST. AUGUSTINE
354–430**

16 Fecisti nos ad te et inquietum est cor nostrum, donec requiescat in te.
Thou hast created us for thyself, and our heart cannot be quieted till it may find repose in thee.
Confessions, bk. i, ch. 1. Trans. by Watts

17 Nondum amabam, et amare amabam . . . quaerebam quid amarem, amans amare.
I loved not yet, yet I loved to love . . . I sought what I might love, in love with loving.
Ib. bk. iii, ch. 1

18 Et illa erant fercula, in quibus mihi esurienti te inferebatur sol et luna.
And these were the dishes wherein to me, hunger-starven for thee, they served up the sun and moon. *Ib.* ch. 6

19 Fieri non potest, ut filius istarum lacrimarum pereat.
It is not possible that the son of these tears should be lost. *Ib.* ch. 12

20 Da mihi castitatem et continentiam, sed noli modo.
Give me chastity and continency, but do not give it yet. *Ib.* bk. viii, ch. 7

21 Tolle lege, tolle lege.
Take up and read, take up and read. *Ib.* ch. 12

22 Sero te amavi, pulchritudo tam antiqua et tam nova, sero te amavi! et ecce intus eras et ego foris, et ibi te quaerebam.
Too late came I to love thee, O thou Beauty both so ancient and so fresh, yea too late came I to love thee. And behold, thou wert within me, and I out of myself, where I made search for thee. *Ib.* bk. x, ch. 27

23 Da quod iubes et iube quod vis. Imperas nobis continentiam.
Give what thou commandest, and command what thou wilt.
Thou imposest continency upon us. *Ib.* ch. 29

24 Securus iudicat orbis terrarum.
The verdict of the world is conclusive.
Contra Epist. Parmen. iii. 24

1 Salus extra ecclesiam non est.

No salvation exists outside the church.
De Bapt. IV, c. xvii. 24, referring back to St. Cyprian's 'Habere non potest Deum patrem qui ecclesiam non habet matrem' (He cannot have God for his Father who has not the church for his mother), *De Cath. Eccl. Unitate.* vi

2 Audi partem alteram.

Hear the other side. *De Duabus Animabus,* XIV. ii

3 Ama et fac quod vis.

Love and do what you will.
Popular version of St. Augustine's 'Dilige et quod vis fac' (Love and do what you will), *In Epist. Joann.* Hom. vii. 8

4 Multi quidem facilius se abstinent ut non utantur, quam temperent ut bene utantur.

To many, total abstinence is easier than perfect moderation. *On the Good of Marriage,* xxi.

5 Roma locuta est; causa finita est.

Rome has spoken; the case is concluded.
Sermons, bk. i

6 De vitiis nostris scalam nobis facimus, si vitia ipsa calcamus.

We make a ladder of our vices, if we trample those same vices underfoot. *Ib.* iii. *De Ascensione*

JANE AUSTEN
1775–1817

7 An egg boiled very soft is not unwholesome. [*Mr. Woodhouse.*] *Emma,* ch. 3

8 One half of the world cannot understand the pleasures of the other. [*Emma.*] *Ib.* ch. 9

9 A basin of nice smooth gruel, thin, but not too thin. *Ib.* ch. 12

10 With men he can be rational and unaffected, but when he has ladies to please, every feature works. [*Mr. Knightley of Mr. Elton.*] *Ib.* ch. 13

11 She believed he had been drinking too much of Mr. Weston's good wine. *Ib.* ch. 15

12 My mother's deafness is very trifling, you see, just nothing at all. By only raising my voice, and saying anything two or three times over, she is sure to hear. [*Miss Bates.*] *Ib.* ch. 19

13 'But, my dear sir,' cried Mr. Weston, 'if Emma comes away early, it will be breaking up the party.' 'And no great harm if it does,' said Mr. Woodhouse. 'The sooner every party breaks up the better.' *Ib.* ch. 25

14 That young man . . . is very thoughtless. Do not tell his father, but that young man is not quite the thing. He has been opening the doors very often this evening and keeping them open very inconsiderately. He does not think of the draught. I do not mean to set you against him, but indeed he is not quite the thing. [*Mr. Woodhouse.*] *Ib.* ch. 29

15 Open the windows! But, surely Mr. Churchill, nobody would think of opening the windows at Randalls. Nobody could be so imprudent. [*Mr. Woodhouse.*] *Ib.*

16 So extremely like Maple Grove. [*Mrs. Elton.*] *Emma,* ch. 32

17 They will have their barouche-landau, of course. [*Mrs. Elton.*] *Ib.*

18 Young ladies should take care of themselves. Young ladies are delicate plants. They should take care of their health and their complexion. My dear, did you change your stockings? [*Mr. Woodhouse.*] *Ib.* ch. 34

19 One has no great hopes from Birmingham. I always say there is something direful in the sound. [*Mrs. Elton.*] *Ib.* ch. 36

20 How shall we ever recollect half the dishes for grandmamma? [*Miss Bates.*] *Ib.* ch. 38

21 Let other pens dwell on guilt and misery. *Mansfield Park,* ch. 48

22 'And what are you reading, Miss —?' 'Oh! it is only a novel!' replies the young lady: while she lays down her book with affected indifference, or momentary shame.—'It is only Cecilia, or Camilla, or Belinda:' or, in short, only some work in which the most thorough knowledge of human nature, the happiest delineation of its varieties, the liveliest effusions of wit and humour are conveyed to the world in the best chosen language. *Northanger Abbey,* ch. 5

23 But are they all horrid, are you sure they are all horrid? [*Catherine.*] *Ib.* ch. 6

24 Oh, Lord! not I; I never read much; I have something else to do. [*John Thorpe.*] *Ib.* ch. 7

25 Sir Walter Elliot, of Kellynch-hall, in Somersetshire, was a man who, for his own amusement, never took up any book but the Baronetage; there he found occupation for an idle hour, and consolation in a distressed one; . . . this was the page at which the favourite volume always opened: ELLIOT OF KELLYNCH-HALL. *Persuasion,* ch. 1

26 My sore throats are always worse than anyone's. [*Mary Musgrove.*] *Ib.* ch. 18

27 All the privilege I claim for my own sex . . . is that of loving longest, when existence or when hope is gone. [*Anne.*] *Ib.* ch. 23

28 It is a truth universally acknowledged, that a single man in possession of a good fortune, must be in want of a wife. *Pride and Prejudice,* ch. 1

29 'Kitty has no discretion in her coughs,' said her father: 'she times them ill.' 'I do not cough for my own amusement,' replied Kitty fretfully. *Ib.* ch. 2

30 How can you contrive to write so even? [*Miss Bingley.*] *Ib.* ch. 10

31 Mr. Collins had only to change from Jane to Elizabeth—and it was soon done—done while Mrs. Bennet was stirring the fire. *Ib.* ch. 15

32 You have delighted us long enough. [*Mr. Bennet.*] *Ib.* ch. 18

33 An unhappy alternative is before you, Elizabeth. From this day you must be a stranger to one of your parents.—Your mother will never see you again if you do *not* marry Mr. Collins, and I will never see you again if you *do*. [*Mr. Bennet.*] *Ib.* ch. 20

1 Nobody is on my side, nobody takes part with me: I am cruelly used, nobody feels for my poor nerves. [*Mrs. Bennet.*] *Pride and Prejudice*, ch. 20

2 '... It is very hard to think that Charlotte Lucas should ever be mistress of this house, that *I* should be forced to make way for *her*, and live to see her take my place in it.'
'My dear, do not give way to such gloomy thoughts. Let us hope for better things. Let us flatter ourselves that *I* may be the survivor.' *Ib.* ch. 23

3 No arguments shall be wanting on my part, that can alleviate so severe a misfortune: or that may comfort you, under a circumstance that must be of all others most afflicting to a parent's mind. The death of your daughter would have been a blessing in comparison of this. [*Mr. Collins.*] *Ib.* ch. 48

4 You ought certainly to forgive them as a christian, but never to admit them in your sight, or allow their names to be mentioned in your hearing. [*Mr. Collins.*] *Ib.* ch. 57

5 For what do we live, but to make sport for our neighbours, and laugh at them in our turn? [*Mr. Bennet.*] *Ib.*

6 I have been a selfish being all my life, in practice, though not in principle. [*Mr. Darcy.*] *Ib.* ch. 58

7 If any young men come for Mary or Kitty, send them in, for I am quite at leisure. [*Mr. Bennet.*] *Ib.* ch. 59

8 An annuity is a very serious business. [*Mrs. Dashwood.*] *Sense and Sensibility*, ch. 2

9 Only conceive how comfortable they will be. Five hundred a year! I am sure I cannot imagine how they will spend half of it. [*Mrs. J. Dashwood.*] *Ib.*

10 'I am afraid,' replied Elinor, 'that the pleasantness of an employment does not always evince its propriety.' *Ib.* ch. 13

11 Lady Middleton . . . exerted herself to ask Mr. Palmer if there was any news in the paper. 'No, none at all,' he replied, and read on. *Ib.* ch. 19

12 'The little bit (two inches wide) of ivory on which I work with so fine a brush as produces little effect after much labour.' *Letter, 16 Dec. 1816*

ALFRED AUSTIN
1835–1913

13 An earl by right, by courtesy a man. *The Season*

14 Across the wires the electric message came: 'He is no better, he is much the same.'
On the Illness of the Prince of Wales, afterwards Edward VII. Attr. to Austin, but probably not his. *See* J. Lewis May in the *Dublin Review*, July 1937

SIR ROBERT AYTOUN
1570–1638

15 I loved thee once, I'll love no more,
Thine be the grief, as is the blame;
Thou art not what thou wast before,
What reason I should be the same?
To an Inconstant Mistress

WILLIAM EDMONDSTOUNE AYTOUN
1813–1865

16 Take away that star and garter—
Hide them from my aching sight!
Neither king nor prince shall tempt me
From my lonely room this night.
Charles Edward at Versailles on the Anniversary of Culloden

17 Nowhere beats the heart so kindly
As beneath the tartan plaid! *Ib.* l. 219

18 Sound the fife, and cry the slogan—
Let the pibroch shake the air.
The Burial-march of Dundee, l. 1

19 On the heights of Killiecrankie
Yester-morn our army lay. *Ib.* l. 49

20 Like a tempest down the ridges
Swept the hurricane of steel,
Rose the slogan of Macdonald—
Flashed the broadsword of Locheill! *Ib.* l. 137

21 So, amidst the battle's thunder,
Shot and steel, and scorching flame,
In the glory of his manhood
Passed the spirit of the Graeme! *Ib.* l. 165

22 News of battle!—news of battle!
Hark! 'tis ringing down the street:
And the archways and the pavement
Bear the clang of hurrying feet.
Edinburgh after Flodden, st. 1

23 Warder—warder! open quickly!
Man—is this a time to wait? *Ib.* st. 2

24 Do not lift him from the bracken,
Leave him lying where he fell—
Better bier ye cannot fashion:
None beseems him half so well
As the bare and broken heather,
And the hard and trampled sod,
Whence his angry soul ascended
To the judgement-seat of God!
The Widow of Glencoe, st. 1

25 They bore within their breasts the grief
That fame can never heal—
The deep, unutterable woe
Which none save exiles feel.
The Island of the Scots, xii

26 Fhairshon swore a feud
Against the clan M'Tavish;
Marched into their land
To murder and to rafish;
For he did resolve
To extirpate the vipers,
With four-and-twenty men
And five-and-thirty pipers.
The Massacre of the Macpherson, i

27 Fharshon had a son,
Who married Noah's daughter,
And nearly spoiled ta Flood,
By trinking up ta water:

28 Which he would have done,
I at least pelieve it,
Had the mixture peen
Only half Glenlivet. *Ib.* vii, viii

29 Come hither, Evan Cameron!
Come, stand beside my knee.
The Execution of Montrose, i

1 And some that came to scoff at him
  Now turned aside and wept.
  The Execution of Montrose, vi

2 But onwards—always onwards,
  In silence and in gloom,
  The dreary pageant laboured,
  Till it reached the house of doom. *Ib.* vii

3 The master-fiend Argyle! *Ib.*

4 The Marquis gazed a moment,
  And nothing did he say. *Ib.* viii

5 Then nail my head on yonder tower—
  Give every town a limb—
  And God who made shall gather them:
  I go from you to Him! *Ib.* xii

6 'He is coming! he is coming!'
  Like a bridegroom from his room,
  Came the hero from his prison
  To the scaffold and the doom. *Ib.* xiv

7 The grim Geneva ministers
  With anxious scowl drew near,
  As you have seen the ravens flock
  Around the dying deer. *Ib.* xvii

8 Like a brave old Scottish Cavalier,
  All of the olden time! *The Old Scottish Cavalier*

9 Have you heard of Philip Slingsby,
  Slingsby of the manly chest;
  How he slew the Snapping Turtle
  In the regions of the West?
  The Fight with the Snapping Turtle

10 The earth is all the home I have,
  The heavens my wide roof-tree.
  The Wandering Jew, l. 49

FRANCIS BACON
1561–1626

11 For all knowledge and wonder (which is the seed
  of knowledge) is an impression of pleasure in itself.
  Advancement of Learning, bk. I. i. 3 (ed. 1605)

12 Time, which is the author of authors. *Ib.* iv. 12

13 If a man will begin with certainties, he shall end in
  doubts; but if he will be content to begin with
  doubts, he shall end in certainties. *Ib.* v. 8

14 [Knowledge is] a rich storehouse for the glory of the
  Creator and the relief of man's estate. *Ib.* 11

15 Antiquities are history defaced, or some remnants of
  history which have casually escaped the shipwreck
  of time. *Ib.* bk. II. ii. 1

16 Poesy was ever thought to have some participation of
  divineness, because it doth raise and erect the mind,
  by submitting the shows of things to the desires of
  the mind; whereas reason doth buckle and bow the
  mind unto the nature of things. *Ib.* iv. 2

17 The knowledge of man is as the waters, some descending from above, and some springing from beneath;
  the one informed by the light of nature, the other
  inspired by divine revelation. *Ib.* v. 1

18 There was never miracle wrought by God to convert
  an atheist, because the light of nature might have
  led him to confess a God. *Ib.* vi. 1

19 They are ill discoverers that think there is no land,
  when they can see nothing but sea. *Ib.* vii. 5

20 Words are the tokens current and accepted for conceits, as moneys are for values. *Ib.* xvi. 3

21 A dance is a measured pace, as a verse is a measured
  speech. *Advancement of Learning,* II. xvi. 5

22 But men must know, that in this theatre of man's life
  it is reserved only for God and angels to be lookers
  on. *Ib.* xx. 8

23 We are much beholden to Machiavel and others, that
  write what men do, and not what they ought to do.
  Ib. xxi. 9

24 Men must pursue things which are just in present,
  and leave the future to the divine Providence.
  Ib. 11

25 Did not one of the fathers in great indignation call
  poesy *vinum dæmonum?* *Ib.* xxii. 13

26 All good moral philosophy is but an handmaid to
  religion. *Ib.* 14

27 Man seeketh in society comfort, use, and protection.
  Ib. xxiii. 2

28 A man must make his opportunity, as oft as find it.
  Ib. 3

29 Caesar, when he went first into Gaul, made no scruple
  to profess 'That he had rather be first in a village
  than second at Rome'. *Ib.* 36

30 Fortunes . . . come tumbling into some men's laps.
  Ib. 43

31 That other principle of Lysander, 'That children are
  to be deceived with comfits, and men with oaths.'
  Ib. 45

32 It is in life as it is in ways, the shortest way is commonly the foulest, and surely the fairer way is not
  much about. *Ib.*

33 There are in nature certain fountains of justice,
  whence all civil laws are derived but as streams.
  Ib. 49

34 The inseparable propriety of time, which is ever more
  and more to disclose truth. *Ib.* xxiv

35 Books must follow sciences, and not sciences books.
  Proposition touching Amendment of Laws

36 Anger makes dull men witty, but it keeps them poor.
  Related as a remark of Queen Elizabeth.
  Apothegms, 5

37 A beautiful face is a silent commendation. *Ib.* 12

38 Wise nature did never put her precious jewels into
  a garret four stories high: and therefore . . .
  exceeding tall men had ever very empty heads.
  Ib. 17

39 Hope is a good breakfast, but it is a bad supper.
  Ib. 36

40 Like strawberry wives, that laid two or three great
  strawberries at the mouth of their pot, and all the
  rest were little ones.
  A saying of Queen Elizabeth. Ib. 54

41 Sir Henry Wotton used to say, 'That critics are like
  brushers of noblemen's clothes.' *Ib.* 64

42 Mr. Savill was asked by my lord of Essex his opinion
  touching poets; who answered my lord; 'He thought
  them the best writers, next to those that write
  prose.' *Ib.* 66

43 Demosthenes when he fled from the battle, and that
  it was reproached to him, said; 'That he that flies
  mought fight again.' *Ib.* 169

1 One of the Seven was wont to say; "That laws were like cobwebs; where the small flies were caught, and the great brake through.' *Apothegms*, 181

2 Pyrrhus, when his friends congratulated to him his victory over the Romans, under the conduct of Fabricius, but with great slaughter of his own side, said to them again; 'Yes, but if we have such another victory, we are undone.' *Ib.* 193

3 Cosmus duke of Florence was wont to say of perfidious friends; 'That we read that we ought to forgive our enemies; but we do not read that we ought to forgive our friends.' *Ib.* 206

4 One of the fathers saith . . . that old men go to death, and death comes to young men. *Ib.* 270

5 Diogenes said of a young man that danced daintily, and was much commended: 'The better, the worse.' *Ib.* 266

6 Riches are a good handmaid, but the worst mistress. *De Dignitate et Augmentis Scientiarium*, pt. 1, bk. vi, ch. 3. *Antitheta*, 6 (ed. 1640, trans. Gilbert Watts)

7 Antiquitas saeculi juventus mundi.
The age of the centuries is the youth of the world. *Ib.* bk. vii, ch. 81

8 The voice of the people hath some divineness in it, else how should so many men agree to be of one mind? *Ib.* 9

9 Envy never makes holiday. *Ib.* 16

10 No terms of moderation takes place with the vulgar. *Ib.* 30

11 Silence is the virtue of fools. *Ib.* 31

12 The worst solitude is to be destitute of sincere friendship. *Ib.* 37

13 Omnia mutari, et nil vere interire, ac summam materiae prorsus eandem manere, satis constat.
That all things are changed, and that nothing really perishes, and that the sum of matter remains exactly the same, is sufficiently certain. *Cogitationes de Natura Rerum*, v. Trans. Spedding

14 I hold every man a debtor to his profession. *The Elements of the Common Law*, preface

15 My essays . . . come home, to men's business, and bosoms. *Essays*. Dedication of 1625 edition

16 It was a high speech of Seneca (after the manner of the Stoics) that, 'the good things which belong to prosperity are to be wished, but the good things that belong to adversity are to be admired.' *Ib.* 5 *Of Adversity*

17 It is yet a higher speech of his than the other, . . . 'It is true greatness to have in one the frailty of a man, and the security of a God.' *Ib.*

18 Prosperity is the blessing of the Old Testament, adversity is the blessing of the New. *Ib.*

19 The pencil of the Holy Ghost hath laboured more in describing the afflictions of Job than the felicities of Solomon. *Ib.*

20 Prosperity is not without many fears and distastes; and adversity is not without comforts and hopes. *Ib.*

21 Prosperity doth best discover vice, but adversity doth best discover virtue. *Ib.*

22 He that plots to be the only figure among ciphers, is the decay of the whole age. *Essays*, 36. *Of Ambition*

23 I had rather believe all the fables in the legend, and the Talmud, and the Alcoran, than that this universal frame is without a mind. *Ib.* 16. *Atheism*

24 God never wrought miracle to convince atheism, because his ordinary works convince it. *Ib.*

25 A little philosophy inclineth man's mind to atheism, but depth in philosophy bringeth men's minds about to religion. *Ib.*

26 They that deny a God destroy man's nobility; for certainly man is of kin to the beasts by his body; and, if he be not of kin to God by his spirit, he is a base and ignoble creature. *Ib.*

27 Virtue is like a rich stone, best plain set. *Ib.* 43. *Of Beauty*

28 That is the best part of beauty, which a picture cannot express. *Ib.*

29 There is no excellent beauty that hath not some strangeness in the proportion. *Ib.*

30 There is in human nature generally more of the fool than of the wise. *Ib.* 12. *Boldness*

31 He said it that knew it best. *Ib.*

32 In civil business; what first? boldness; what second and third? boldness: and yet boldness is a child of ignorance and baseness. *Ib.*

33 Boldness is an ill keeper of promise. *Ib.*

34 Mahomet made the people believe that he would call a hill to him, and from the top of it offer up his prayers for the observers of his law. The people assembled: Mahomet called the hill to come to him again and again; and when the hill stood still, he was never a whit abashed, but said, 'If the hill will not come to Mahomet, Mahomet will go to the hill.' *Ib.*

35 Houses are built to live in and not to look on; therefore let use be preferred before uniformity, except where both may be had. *Ib.* 45. *Of Building*

36 Light gains make heavy purses. *Ib.* 52. *Of Ceremonies and Respects*

37 Small matters win great commendation. *Ib.*

38 He that . . . giveth another occasion of satiety, maketh himself cheap. *Ib.*

39 A wise man will make more opportunities than he finds. *Ib.*

40 Books will speak plain when counsellors blanch. *Ib.* 20. *Of Counsel*

41 There be that can pack the cards and yet cannot play well; so there are some that are good in canvasses and factions, that are otherwise weak men. *Ib.* 22. *Of Cunning*

42 In things that are tender and unpleasing, it is good to break the ice by some whose words are of less weight, and to reserve the more weighty voice to come in as by chance. *Ib.*

43 I knew one that when he wrote a letter he would put that which was most material in the postscript, as if it had been a bymatter. *Ib.*

44 Nothing doth more hurt in a state than that cunning men pass for wise. *Ib.*

1 Men fear death as children fear to go in the dark; and as that natural fear in children is increased with tales, so is the other. *Essays, 2. Of Death*

2 There is no passion in the mind of man so weak, but it mates and masters the fear of death . . . Revenge triumphs over death; love slights it; honour aspireth to it; grief flieth to it. *Ib.*

3 It is as natural to die as to be born; and to a little infant, perhaps, the one is as painful as the other. *Ib.*

4 Above all, believe it, the sweetest canticle is *Nunc dimittis*, when a man hath obtained worthy ends and expectations. Death hath this also, that it openeth the gate to good fame, and extinguisheth envy. *Ib.*

5 Intermingle . . . jest with earnest. *Ib. 32. Of Discourse*

6 If you dissemble sometimes your knowledge of that you are thought to know, you shall be thought, another time, to know that you know not. *Ib.*

7 I knew a wise man that had it for a by-word, when he saw men hasten to a conclusion, 'Stay a little, that we may make an end the sooner.' *Ib. 25. Of Dispatch*

8 To choose time is to save time. *Ib.*

9 It is a miserable state of mind to have few things to desire and many things to fear. *Ib. 19. Of Empire*

10 Riches are for spending. *Ib. 28. Of Expense*

11 A man ought warily to begin charges which once begun will continue. *Ib.*

12 Lookers-on many times see more than gamesters. *Ib. 48. Of Followers and Friends*

13 There is little friendship in the world, and least of all between equals. *Ib.*

14 Chiefly the mould of a man's fortune is in his own hands. *Ib. 40. Of Fortune*

15 It had been hard for him that spake it to have put more truth and untruth together, in a few words, than in that speech: 'Whosoever is delighted in solitude is either a wild beast, or a god.' *Ib. 27. Of Friendship. (See 14:15)*

16 A crowd is not company, and faces are but a gallery of pictures, and talk but a tinkling cymbal, where there is no love. *Ib.*

17 It [friendship] redoubleth joys, and cutteth griefs in halves. *Ib.*

18 Cure the disease and kill the patient. *Ib.*

19 God Almighty first planted a garden; and, indeed, it is the purest of human pleasures. *Ib. 46. Of Gardens*

20 The inclination to goodness is imprinted deeply in the nature of man: insomuch, that if it issue not towards men, it will take unto other living creatures. *Ib. 13. Goodness, and Goodness of Nature*

21 If a man be gracious and courteous to strangers, it shows he is a citizen of the world. *Ib.*

22 Men in great place are thrice servants: servants of the sovereign or state, servants of fame, and servants of business. *Ib. 11. Of Great Place*

23 It is a strange desire to seek power and to lose liberty. *Ib.*

24 The rising unto place is laborious, and by pains men come to greater pains; and it is sometimes base, and by indignities men come to dignities. The standing is slippery, and the regress is either a downfall, or at least an eclipse. *Essays, 11. Of Great Place*

25 Set it down to thyself, as well to create good precedents as to follow them. *Ib.*

26 Severity breedeth fear, but roughness breedeth hate. Even reproofs from authority ought to be grave, and not taunting. *Ib.*

27 As in nature things move violently to their place and calmly in their place, so virtue in ambition is violent, in authority settled and calm. *Ib.*

28 All rising to great place is by a winding stair. *Ib.*

29 As the births of living creatures at first are ill-shapen, so are all innovations, which are the births of time. *Ib. 24. Of Innovations*

30 He that will not apply new remedies must expect new evils; for time is the greatest innovator. *Ib.*

31 The place of justice is a hallowed place. *Ib. 56. Of Judicature*

32 The speaking in a perpetual hyperbole is comely in nothing but in love. *Ib. 10. Of Love*

33 It has been well said that 'the arch-flatterer with whom all the petty flatterers have intelligence is a man's self.' *Ib.*

34 He that hath wife and children hath given hostages to fortune; for they are impediments to great enterprises, either of virtue or mischief. *Ib. 8. Of Marriage and Single Life*

35 There are some other that account wife and children but as bills of charges. *Ib.*

36 A single life doth well with churchmen, for charity will hardly water the ground where it must first fill a pool. *Ib.*

37 Wives are young men's mistresses, companions for middle age, and old men's nurses. *Ib.*

38 He was reputed one of the wise men that made answer to the question when a man should marry? 'A young man not yet, an elder man not at all.' *Ib.*

39 Nature is often hidden, sometimes overcome, seldom extinguished. *Ib. 38. Of Nature in Men*

40 It is generally better to deal by speech than by letter. *Ib. 47. Of Negotiating*

41 It is a reverend thing to see an ancient castle or building not in decay. *Ib. 14. Of Nobility*

42 New nobility is but the act of power, but ancient nobility is the act of time. *Ib.*

43 Nobility of birth commonly abateth industry. *Ib.*

44 The joys of parents are secret, and so are their griefs and fears. *Ib. 7. Of Parents and Children*

45 Children sweeten labours, but they make misfortunes more bitter. *Ib.*

46 The noblest works and foundations have proceeded from childless men, which have sought to express the images of their minds where those of their bodies have failed. *Ib.*

1 Fame is like a river, that beareth up things light and swollen, and drowns things weighty and solid.
Essays, 53. *Of Praise*

2 [Dreams and predictions] ought to serve but for winter talk by the fireside. *Ib.* 35. *Of Prophecies*

3 Age will not be defied. *Ib.* 30. *Of Regimen of Health*

4 Revenge is a kind of wild justice, which the more man's nature runs to, the more ought law to weed it out. *Ib.* 4. *Of Revenge*

5 Why should I be angry with a man for loving himself better than me? *Ib.*

6 A man that studieth revenge keeps his own wounds green. *Ib.*

7 Defer not charities till death; for certainly, if a man weigh it rightly, he that doth so is rather liberal of another man's than of his own. *Ib.* 34. *Of Riches*

8 The four pillars of government . . . (which are religion, justice, counsel, and treasure).
Ib. 15. *Of Seditions and Troubles*

9 The surest way to prevent seditions (if the times do bear it) is to take away the matter of them. *Ib.*

10 Money is like muck, not good except it be spread. *Ib.*

11 The remedy is worse than the disease. *Ib.*

12 The French are wiser than they seem, and the Spaniards seem wiser than they are.
Ib. 26. *Of Seeming Wise*

13 Studies serve for delight, for ornament, and for ability. *Ib.* 50. *Of Studies*

14 To spend too much time in studies is sloth. *Ib.*

15 They perfect nature and are perfected by experience. *Ib.*

16 Read not to contradict and confute, nor to believe and take for granted, nor to find talk and discourse, but to weigh and consider. *Ib.*

17 Some books are to be tasted, others to be swallowed, and some few to be chewed and digested; that is, some books are to be read only in parts; others to be read but not curiously; and some few to be read wholly, and with diligence and attention. Some books also may be read by deputy, and extracts made of them by others. *Ib.*

18 Reading maketh a full man; conference a ready man and writing an exact man. *Ib.*

19 Histories make men wise; poets, witty; the mathematics, subtile; natural philosophy, deep; moral, grave; logic and rhetoric, able to contend. *Ib.*

20 It were better to have no opinion of God at all than such an opinion as is unworthy of him; for the one is unbelief, the other is contumely.
Ib. 17. *Of Superstition*

21 There is a superstition in avoiding superstition. *Ib.*

22 Suspicions amongst thoughts are like bats amongst birds, they ever fly by twilight. *Ib.* 31. *Of Suspicion*

23 There is nothing makes a man suspect much, more than to know little. *Ib.*

24 Neither is money the sinews of war (as it is trivially said). *Ib.* 29. *Of The True Greatness of Kingdoms*

25 Neither will it be, that a people overlaid with taxes should ever become valiant and martial. *Ib.*

26 Thus much is certain; that he that commands the sea is at great liberty, and may take as much and as little of the war as he will.
Essays, 29. *Of The True Greatness of Kingdoms*

27 Travel, in the younger sort, is a part of education; in the elder, a part of experience. He that travelleth into a country before he hath some entrance into the language, goeth to school, and not to travel.
Ib. 18. *Of Travel*

28 Let diaries, therefore, be brought in use. *Ib.*

29 What is truth? said jesting Pilate; and would not stay for an answer. *Ib.* 1. *Of Truth*

30 A mixture of a lie doth ever add pleasure. *Ib.*

31 It is not the lie that passeth through the mind, but the lie that sinketh in, and settleth in it, that doth the hurt. *Ib.*

32 The inquiry of truth, which is the love-making, or wooing of it, the knowledge of truth, which is the presence of it, and the belief of truth, which is the enjoying of it, is the sovereign good of human nature. *Ib.*

33 Certainly, it is heaven upon earth, to have a man's mind . . . turn upon the poles of truth. *Ib.*

34 All colours will agree in the dark.
Ib. 3. *Of Unity in Religion*

35 It was prettily devised of Aesop, 'The fly sat upon the axletree of the chariot-wheel and said, what a dust do I raise.' *Ib.* 54. *Of Vain-Glory*

36 In the youth of a state arms do flourish; in the middle age of a state, learning; and then both of them together for a time; in the declining age of a state, mechanical arts and merchandise.
Ib. 58. *Of Vicissitude of Things*

37 Be so true to thyself as thou be not false to others.
Ib. 23. *Of Wisdom for a Man's Self*

38 It is a poor centre of a man's actions, himself. *Ib.*

39 It is the nature of extreme self-lovers, as they will set a house on fire, and it were but to roast their eggs. *Ib.*

40 It is the wisdom of the crocodiles, that shed tears when they would devour. *Ib.*

41 Young men are fitter to invent than to judge, fitter for execution than for counsel, and fitter for new projects than for settled business.
Ib. 42. *Of Youth and Age*

42 I have often thought upon death, and I find it the least of all evils. *An Essay on Death.* § 1

43 I do not believe that any man fears to be dead, but only the stroke of death. *Ib.* 3

44 Why should a man be in love with his fetters, though of gold? *Ib.* 4

45 He is the fountain of honour. *Essay of a King*

46 Lucid intervals and happy pauses.
History of King Henry VII, par. 3

47 Quare videmus araneam aut muscam aut formicam, in electro, monumento plus quam regio, sepultas, aeternizari.

Whence we see spiders, flies, or ants, entombed and preserved for ever in amber, a more than royal tomb.
Historia Vitae et Mortis, Provisional Rules Concerning the Duration of Life and the Form of Death, rule 1, Explanation. Trans. Spedding

1 I have taken all knowledge to be my province.
Letter to Lord Burleigh, 1592

2 Opportunity makes a thief.
Letter to the Earl of Essex, 1598

3 I am too old, and the seas are too long, for me to double the Cape of Good Hope.
Memorial of Access

4 I would live to study, and not study to live. *Ib.*

5 God's first Creature, which was Light. *New Atlantis*

6 Quatuor sunt genera Idolorum quae mentes humanas obsident. Iis (docendi gratia) nomina imposuimus; ut primum genus, Idola Tribus; secundum, Idola Specus; tertium, Idola Fori; quartum, Idola Theatri vocentur.

There are four classes of Idols which beset men's minds. To these for distinction's sake I have assigned names—calling the first class, Idols of the Tribe; the second, Idols of the Cave; the third, Idols of the Market-place; the fourth, Idols of the Theatre.
Novum Organon, Aphor. xxxix. Trans. Spedding

7 Quod enim mavult homo verum esse, id potius credit.

For what a man had rather were true he more readily believes. *Ib.* xlix. Trans. Spedding

8 Magna ista scientiarum mater.

This great mother of the sciences [natural philosophy]. *Ib.* lxxx. Trans. Spedding

9 Naturae enim non imperatur, nisi parendo.

We cannot command nature except by obeying her. *Ib.* cxxix. Trans. Spedding

10 Nam et ipsa scientia potestas est.

Knowledge itself is power.
Religious Meditations. Of Heresies

11 De Sapientia Veterum.

The wisdom of the ancients.
Title of Work. Tr. Sir Arthur Gorges, 1619

12 Praecipue autem lignum, sive virga, versus superiorem partem curva est.

Every rod or staff of empire is truly crooked at the top. *Ib.* 6, *Pan, sive Natura*

13 Universities incline wits to sophistry and affectation.
Valerius Terminus of the Interpretation of Nature, ch. 26

14 I have rather studied books than men.
Advice to Sir Geo. Villiers, Works, ed. 1765, vol. ii, p. 258

15 For my name and memory, I leave it to men's charitable speeches, and to foreign nations, and the next ages. *Last Will* (19 Dec. 1625). *Ib.* vol. iii, p. 677

16 The world's a bubble; and the life of man
Less than a span. *The World*

17 Who then to frail mortality shall trust,
But limns the water, or but writes in dust. *Ib.*

18 What is it then to have or have no wife,
But single thraldom, or a double strife? *Ib.*

19 What then remains, but that we still should cry,
Not to be born, or being born, to die? *Ib.*

CARL BAEDEKER
1801–1859

20 Oxford is on the whole more attractive than Cambridge to the ordinary visitor; and the traveller is therefore recommended to visit Cambridge first, or to omit it altogether if he cannot visit both.
Baedeker's Great Britain (1887), 30. *From London to Oxford*

WALTER BAGEHOT
1826–1877

21 The mystic reverence, the religious allegiance, which are essential to a true monarchy, are imaginative sentiments that no legislature can manufacture in any people.
The English Constitution, ch. 1. *The Cabinet*

22 The Crown is, according to the saying, the 'fountain of honour'; but the Treasury is the spring of business. *Ib.* (*See* 27: 45)

23 It has been said that England invented the phrase, 'Her Majesty's Opposition'; that it was the first government which made a criticism of adminstration as much a part of the polity as administration itself. This critical opposition is the consequence of cabinet government. *Ib.*

24 The *Times* has made many ministries. *Ib.*

25 We turned out the Quaker (Lord Aberdeen), and put in the pugilist (Lord Palmerston). (Change of Ministry, 1855). *Ib.*

26 The best reason why Monarchy is a strong government is, that it is an intelligible government. The mass of mankind understand it, and they hardly anywhere in the world understand any other.
Ib. ch. 2. *The Monarchy*

27 The characteristic of the English Monarchy is that it retains the feelings by which the heroic kings governed their rude age, and has added the feelings by which the constitutions of later Greece ruled in more refined ages. *Ib.*

28 Women—one half the human race at least—care fifty times more for a marriage than a ministry. *Ib.*

29 Royalty is a government in which the attention of the nation is concentrated on one person doing interesting actions. A Republic is a government in which that attention is divided between many, who are all doing uninteresting actions. Accordingly, so long as the human heart is strong and the human reason weak, Royalty will be strong because it appeals to diffused feeling, and Republics weak because they appeal to the understanding. *Ib.*

30 An Englishman whose heart is in a matter is not easily baffled. *Ib.*

31 Throughout the greater part of his life George III was a kind of 'consecrated obstruction'. *Ib.*

32 But of all nations in the world the English are perhaps the least a nation of pure philosophers. *Ib.*

33 The order of nobility is of great use, too, not only in what it creates, but in what it prevents. It prevents the rule of wealth—the religion of gold. This is the obvious and natural idol of the Anglo-Saxon.
Ib. ch. 4. *The House of Lords*

34 The House of Peers has never been a House where the most important peers were most important. *Ib.*

1 A severe though not unfriendly critic of our institutions said that 'the *cure* for admiring the House of Lords was to go and look at it.'
The English Constitution, ch. 4. *The House of Lords*

2 Nations touch at their summits. *Ib.*

3 Years ago Mr. Disraeli called Sir Robert Peel's Ministry—the last Conservative Ministry that had real power—'an organized hypocrisy', so much did the ideas of its 'head' differ from the sensations of its 'tail'. *Ib.*

4 It has been said, not truly, but with a possible approximation to truth, 'that in 1802 every hereditary monarch was insane'. *Ib.*

5 Queen Anne was one of the smallest people ever set in a great place. *Ib. ch. 7. Checks and Balances*

6 The soldier—that is, the great soldier—of to-day is not a romantic animal, dashing at forlorn hopes, animated by frantic sentiment, full of fancies as to a love-lady or a sovereign; but a quiet, grave man, busied in charts, exact in sums, master of the art of tactics, occupied in trivial detail; thinking, as the Duke of Wellington was said to do, *most* of the shoes of his soldiers; despising all manner of *éclat* and eloquence; perhaps, like Count Moltke, 'silent in seven languages'. *Ib.*

7 The most melancholy of human reflections, perhaps, is that, on the whole, it is a question whether the benevolence of mankind does most good or harm. *Physics and Politics*, No. v

8 Wordsworth, Tennyson, and Browning; or, Pure, Ornate, and Grotesque Art in English Poetry. *Title of Essay, National Review*, Nov. 1864

PHILIP JAMES BAILEY
1816–1902

9 We live in deeds, not years; in thoughts, not breaths; In feelings, not in figures on a dial. We should count time by heart-throbs. He most lives Who thinks most—feels the noblest—acts the best. *Festus*, v

10 America, thou half-brother of the world; With something good and bad of every land. *Ib.* x

CHARLES BRUCE BAIRNSFATHER
1888–1959

11 Well, if you knows of a better 'ole, go to it. *Fragments from France*, No. 1 (1915)

HENRY WILLIAMS BAKER
1821–1877

12 The King of Love my Shepherd is, Whose goodness faileth never. *Hymns Ancient and Modern. The King of Love my Shepherd is* (1868)

13 There is a blessed home Beyond this land of woe. *Ib. There is a Blessed Home* (1861)

MICHAEL BAKUNIN
1814–1876

14 We wish, in a word, equality—equality in fact as corollary, or, rather, as primordial condition of liberty. From each according to his faculties, to each according to his needs; that is what we wish sincerely and energetically. *Declaration signed by forty-seven anarchists on trial after the failure of their uprising at Lyons in 1870. See J. Morrison Davidson, The Old Order and the New, 1890. (See 333:12)*

STANLEY BALDWIN, EARL BALDWIN
1867–1947

15 When you think about the defence of England you no longer think of the chalk cliffs of Dover. You think of the Rhine. That is where our frontier lies to-day. *Speech, House of Commons, 30 July 1934*

BISHOP JOHN BALE
1495–1563

16 Though it be a foul great lie: Set upon it a good face. *King John*, l. 1978

ARTHUR JAMES BALFOUR
1848–1930

17 Defence of philosophic doubt. **Article in *Mind*, 1878**

18 Do not hesitate to shoot. *Attrib. to Balfour, actually part of a telegram sent by the Divisional Magistrate for Cork district in 1888: 'Deal very summarily with any organized resistance to lawful authority. If necessary do not hesitate to shoot. Plunkett.'*

19 The energies of our system will decay, the glory of the sun will be dimmed, and the earth, tideless and inert, will no longer tolerate the race which has for a moment disturbed its solitude. Man will go down into the pit, and all his thoughts will perish. *The Foundations of Belief*, pt. i, ch. 1

20 It is unfortunate, considering that enthusiasm moves the world, that so few enthusiasts can be trusted to speak the truth. *Letter to Mrs. Drew*, 1918

21 Frank Harris . . . said . . .: 'The fact is, Mr. Balfour, all the faults of the age come from Christianity and journalism.' 'Christianity, of course, but why journalism?' *Autobiography of Margot Asquith*, vol. i, ch. 10

BALLADS

22 There was a youth, and a well-beloved youth, And he was an esquire's son, He loved the bailiff's daughter dear, That lived in Islington. *The Oxford Book of Ballads. The Bailiff's Daughter of Islington*

23 But when his friends did understand His fond and foolish mind, They sent him up to fair London, An apprentice for to bind. *Ib.*

24 She stept to him, as red as any rose, And took him by the bridle-ring: 'I pray you, kind sir, give me one penny, To ease my weary limb.'
'I prithee, sweetheart, canst thou tell me, Where that thou wast born?'
'At Islington, kind sir,' said she, 'Where I have had many a scorn.'

'I prithee, sweetheart, canst thou tell me
  Whether thou dost know
The bailiff's daughter of Islington?'
  'She's dead, sir, long ago.'

'Then will I sell my goodly steed,
  My saddle and my bow;
I will into some far countrey,
  Where no man doth me know.'

'O stay, O stay, thou goodly youth!
  She's alive, she is not dead;
Here she standeth by thy side,
  And is ready to be thy bride.'
  The Oxford Book of Ballads. The Bailiff's Daugh-
  ter of Islington

1 In Scarlet town, where I was born,
  There was a fair maid dwellin',
  Made every youth cry *Well-a-way!*
  Her name was Barbara Allen.

  All in the merry month of May,
  When green buds they were swellin',
  Young Jemmy Grove on his death-bed lay,
  For love of Barbara Allen. *Ib. Barbara Allen's Cruelty*

2 So slowly, slowly rase she up,
  And slowly she came nigh him,
  And when she drew the curtain by—
  'Young man, I think you're dyin'!'. *Ib.*

3 'O mother, mother, make my bed,
  O make it soft and narrow:
  My love has died for me to-day,
  I'll die for him to-morrow.' *Ib.*

4 'Farewell,' she said, 'ye virgins all,
  And shun the fault I fell in:
  Henceforth take warning by the fall
  Of cruel Barbara Allen.' *Ib.*

5 It fell about the Lammas tide
  When husbands win their hay,
  The doughty Douglas bound him to ride
  In England to take a prey.
  Ib. The Battle of Otterburn, i

6 My wound is deep: I am fayn to sleep,
  Take thou the vaward of me,
  And hide me by the bracken bush
  Grows on yonder lilye-lee. *Ib.* lvii

7 There were twa sisters sat in a bour;
  Binnorie, O Binnorie!
  There came a knight to be their wooer,
  By the bonnie milldams o' Binnorie. *Ib. Binnorie*

8 Ye Highlands and ye Lawlands,
  O where hae ye been?
  They hae slain the Earl of Murray,
  And hae laid him on the green.
  Ib. The Bonny Earl of Murray

9 He was a braw gallant,
  And he rid at the ring;
  And the bonny Earl of Murray,
  O he might hae been a king! *Ib.*

10 He was a braw gallant,
  And he play'd at the gluve;
  And the bonny Earl of Murray,
  O he was the Queen's luve!

  O lang will his Lady
  Look owre the Castle Downe,
  Ere she see the Earl of Murray
  Come sounding through the town! *Ib.*

11 The Percy out of Northumberland,
  An avow to God made he
  That he would hunt in the mountains
  Of Cheviot within days three,
  In the maugre of doughty Douglas,
  And all that e'er with him be.
  The Oxford Book of Ballads. Chevy Chase, I. i

12 This began on a Monday at morn,
  In Cheviot the hills so hye;
  The child may rue that is unborn,
  It was the more pitye. *Ib.* iv

13 ['But I hae dream'd a dreary dream,
  Beyond the Isle of Sky;
  I saw a dead man win a fight,
  And I think that man was I.'
  Ib. The Battle of Otterbourne (xix in the Scottish
  version, but not included in the Oxford Book version)]

14 For Witherington my heart was woe
  That ever he slain should be:
  For when both his legs were hewn in two
  Yet he kneel'd and fought on his knee. *Ib. Chevy*
  Chase, II. i

15 Clerk Saunders and may Margaret
  Walk'd owre yon garden green;
  And deep and heavy was the love
  That fell thir twa between.

  'A bed, a bed,' Clerk Saunders said,
  'A bed for you and me!'
  'Fye na, fye na,' said may Margaret,
  'Till anes we married be!' *Ib. Clerk Saunders*

16 There's nae room at my head, Marg'ret,
  There's nae room at my feet;
  My bed it is fu' lowly now,
  Among the hungry worms I sleep. *Ib.*

17 He turn'd him round and round about,
  And the tear blinded his e'e:
  'I wad never hae trodden on Irish ground
  If it hadna been for thee'. *Ib. The Daemon Lover*

18 She hadna sail'd a league, a league,
  A league but barely three,
  Till grim, grim grew his countenance
  And gurly grew the sea.

  'What hills are yon, yon pleasant hills,
  The sun shines sweetly on?'—
  'O yon are the hills o' Heaven,' he said,
  'Where you will never won.' *Ib.*

19 He strack the top-mast wi' his hand,
  The fore-mast wi' his knee;
  And he brake that gallant ship in twain,
  And sank her in the sea. *Ib.*

20 O well's me o' my gay goss-hawk,
  That he can speak and flee!
  He'll carry a letter to my love,
  Bring another back to me. *Ib. The Gay Gosshawk*

21 But ne'er a word wad ane o' them speak,
  For barring of the door.
  Ib. Get Up and Bar the Door

22 Goodman, you've spoken the foremost word!
  Get up and bar the door. *Ib.*

23 A ship I have got in the North Country
  And she goes by the name of the *Golden Vanity*,
  O I fear she will be taken by a Spanish Ga-la-lee,
  As she sails by the Low-lands low.
  Ib. The Golden Vanity

1 He bored with his augur, he bored once and twice,
And some were playing cards, and some were playing
  dice,
When the water flowed in it dazzled their eyes,
And she sank by the Low-lands low.

So the Cabin-boy did swim all to the larboard side,
Saying 'Captain! take me in, I am drifting with the
  tide!'
'I will shoot you! I will kill you!' the cruel Captain
  cried,
'You may sink by the Low-lands low.'
    The Oxford Book of Ballads. The Golden Vanity

2 Then they laid him on the deck, and he closed his eyes
  and died,
As they sailed by the Low-lands low.   *Ib.*

3 I wish I were where Helen lies,
  Night and day on me she cries;
O that I were where Helen lies,
  On fair Kirkconnell lea!

Curst be the heart that thought the thought,
And curst the hand that fired the shot,
When in my arms burd Helen dropt,
  And died to succour me! *Ib. Helen of Kirkconnell*

4 And when we came through Glasgow toun,
  We were a comely sight to see;
My gude lord in the black velvet,
  And I mysel' in cramasie.   *Ib. Jamie Douglas*

5 O come ye here to fight, young lord,
  Or come ye here to play?
Or come ye here to drink good wine
  Upon the weddin'-day? *Ib. Katharine Johnstone*

6 O is my basnet a widow's curch?
  Or my lance a wand of the willow-tree?
Or my arm a ladye's lilye hand,
  That an English lord should lightly me!
    Ib. Kinmont Willie, x

7 He is either himself a devil frae hell,
  Or else his mother a witch maun be;
I wadna have ridden that wan water
  For a' the gowd in Christentie.   *Ib. xlvi*

8 O he's gart build a bonny ship,
  To sail on the salt sea;
The mast was o' the beaten gold,
  The sails o' cramoisie. *Ib. The Lass of Lochroyan*

9 Lady Nancy she died out of pure, pure grief,
  Lord Lovel he died out of sorrow. *Ib. Lord Lovel*

10 'What gat ye to your dinner, Lord Randal, my Son?
  What gat ye to your dinner, my handsome young
  man?'
'I gat eels boil'd in broo'; mother, make my bed soon,
  For I'm weary wi' hunting, and fain wald lie down.'
    Ib. Lord Randal

11 And the Lowlands o' Holland has twin'd my love and
  me.   *Ib. The Lowlands o' Holland*

12 This ae nighte, this ae nighte,
  —*Every nighte and alle,*
Fire and fleet[1] and candle-lighte,
  And Christe receive thy saule. Ib. Lyke-Wake Dirge

13 From Brig o' Dread when thou may'st pass,
  —*Every nighte and alle,*
To Purgatory fire thou com'st at last;
  And Christe receive thy saule.

    [1] —floor. Other readings are 'sleet' and 'salt'.

If ever thou gavest meat or drink,
  —*Every nighte and alle,*
The fire sall never make thee shrink;
  And Christe receive thy saule.
    The Oxford Book of Ballads. Lyke-Wake Dirge

14 When captains courageous, whom death could not
  daunt,
Did march to the siege of the city of Gaunt,
They mustered their soldiers by two and by three,
And the foremost in battle was Mary Ambree.
    Mary Ambree

15 For in my mind, of all mankind
  I love but you alone.   *Ib. The Nut Brown Maid*

16 For I must to the greenwood go
  Alone, a banished man.   *Ib.*

17 Marie Hamilton's to the kirk gane
  Wi' ribbons on her breast;
The King thought mair o' Marie Hamilton
  Than he listen'd to the priest.
    Ib. The Queen's Maries

18 Yestreen the Queen had four Maries,
  The night she'll hae but three;
There was Marie Seaton, and Marie Beaton,
  And Marie Carmichael, and me.   *Ib.*

19 O little did my mother ken,
  The day she cradled me,
The lands I was to travel in
  Or the death I was to die!   *Ib.*

20 'O pardon, O pardon', said the Bishop,
  'O pardon, I thee pray!
For if I had known it had been you,
  I'd have gone some other way.'
    Ib. Robin Hood and the Bishop of Hereford

21 There are twelve months in all the year,
  As I hear many men say,
But the merriest month in all the year
  Is the merry month of May.
    Ib. Robin Hood and the Widow's Three Sons

22 'Let me have length and breadth enough,
  And under my head a sod;
That they may say when I am dead,
  —*Here lies bold Robin Hood!*'
    Ib. The Death of Robin Hood

23 The king sits in Dunfermline town
  Drinking the blude-red wine.
    Ib. Sir Patrick Spens

24 Our king has written a braid letter,
  And seal'd it with his hand,
And sent it to Sir Patrick Spens,
  Was walking on the strand.

'To Noroway, to Noroway,
  To Noroway o'er the faem;
The king's daughter o' Noroway,
  'Tis thou must bring her hame.'

The first word that Sir Patrick read
  So loud, loud laughed he;
The neist word that Sir Patrick read
  The tear blinded his e'e.   *Ib.*

25 I saw the new moon late yestreen
  Wi' the auld moon in her arm;
And if we gang to sea, master,
  I fear we'll come to harm.'

Go fetch a web o' the silken claith,
  Another o' the twine,
And wap[1] them into our ship's side,
  And let nae the sea come in.
  The Oxford Book of Ballads. Sir Patrick Spens

1 O laith, laith were our gude Scots lords
  To wat their cork-heel'd shoon;
But lang or a' the play was play'd
  They wat their hats aboon.   *Ib.*

2 O lang, lang may the ladies sit,
  Wi' their fans into their hand,
Before they see Sir Patrick Spens
  Come sailing to the strand!

And lang, lang may the maidens sit
  Wi' their gowd kames in their hair,
A-waiting for their ain dear loves!
  For them they'll see nae mair.

Half-owre, half-owre to Aberdour,
  'Tis fifty fathoms deep;
And there lies gude Sir Patrick Spens,
  Wi' the Scots lords at his feet!   *Ib.*

3 And she has kilted her green kirtle
  A little abune her knee,
And she has braided her yellow hair
  A little abune her bree.   *Ib. Tam Lin.* v

4 About the dead hour of the night
  She heard the bridles ring;
And Janet was as glad at that
  As any earthly thing.   *Ib.* xli

5 'But what I ken this night, Tam Lin,
  Gin I had kent yestreen,
I wad ta'en out thy heart o' flesh,
  And put in a heart o' stane.'   *Ib.* l

6 True Thomas lay on Huntlie bank;
  A ferlie he spied wi' his e'e;
And there he saw a ladye bright
  Come riding down by the Eildon Tree.
  Ib. Thomas the Rhymer, i.

7 True Thomas he pu'd aff his cap,
  And louted low down on his knee.   *Ib.* iii

8 She's mounted on her milk-white steed,
  She's ta'en true Thomas up behind.   *Ib.* viii

9 'And see ye not yon braid, braid road,
  That lies across the lily leven?
That is the Path of Wickedness,
  Though some call it the Road to Heaven.' *Ib.* xii

10 That is the Road to fair Elfland,
  Where thou and I this night maun gae.   *Ib.* xiii

11 It was mirk, mirk night, there was nae starlight,
  They waded thro' red blude to the knee;
For a' the blude that's shed on the earth
  Rins through the springs o' that countrie. *Ib.* xvi

12 And till seven years were gane and past,
  True Thomas on earth was never seen.   *Ib.* xx

13 There were three ravens sat on a tree,
They were as black as they might be.
The one of them said to his make,
'Where shall we our breakfast take?'
  Ib. The Three Ravens

14 All the trees they are so high,
  The leaves they are so green,
  The day is past and gone, sweet-heart,

[1] wap = wrap.

That you and I have seen.
It is cold winter's night,
You and I must bide alone:
Whilst my pretty lad is young
And is growing.
  The Oxford Book of Ballads. The Trees so High

15 As I was walking all alane,
I heard twa corbies[2] making a mane:
The tane unto the tither did say,
'Where sall we gang and dine the day?'

'—In behint yon auld fail[3] dyke
I wot there lies a new-slain knight;
And naebody kens that he lies there
But his hawk, his hound, and his lady fair.

'His hound is to the hunting gane,
His hawk to fetch the wild-fowl hame,
His lady's ta'en anither mate,
So we may make our dinner sweet.

'Ye'll sit on his white hause-bane,[4]
And I'll pike out his bonny blue e'en:
Wi' ae lock o' his gowden hair
We'll theek[5] our nest when it grows bare.
  Ib. The Twa Corbies

[2] corbies = ravens.   [3] fail = turf.
[4] hause = neck.   [5] theek = thatch.

16 'The wind doth blow to-day, my love,
  And a few small drops of rain;
I never had but one true love;
  In cold grave she was lain.

'I'll do as much for my true-love
  As any young man may;
I'll sit and mourn all at her grave
  For a twelvemonth and a day.'
  Ib. The Unquiet Grave

17 ''Tis down in yonder garden green,
  Love, where we used to walk,
The finest flower that ere was seen
  Is wither'd to a stalk.

'The stalk is wither'd dry, my love,
  So will our hearts decay;
So make yourself content my love,
  Till God calls you away.'   *Ib.*

18 O waly, waly, up the bank,
  And waly, waly, doun the brae,
And waly, waly, yon burn-side,
  Where I and my Love wont to gae!

I lean'd my back unto an aik,
  I thocht it was a trustie tree;
But first it bow'd and syne it brake—
  Sae my true love did lichtlie me.

O waly, waly, gin love be bonnie
  A little time while it is new!
But when 'tis auld it waxeth cauld,
  And fades awa' like morning dew.

O wherefore should I busk my heid,
  Or wherefore should I kame my hair?
For my true Love has me forsook,
  And says he'll never lo'e me mair.
  Ib. Waly, Waly

19 But had I wist, before I kist,
  That love had been sae ill to win,
I had lock'd my heart in a case o' gowd,
  And pinn'd it wi' a siller pin.

And O! if my young babe were born,
And set upon the nurse's knee;
And I mysel' were dead and gane,
And the green grass growing over me!
The Oxford Book of Ballads. Waly, Waly

1 'Tom Pearse, Tom Pearse, lend me your grey mare,
All along, down along, out along, lee.
For I want for to go to Widdicombe Fair,
Wi' Bill Brewer, Jan Stewer, Peter Gurney, Peter
Davey, Dan'l Whiddon, Harry Hawk,
Old Uncle Tom Cobbleigh and all.
Old Uncle Tom Cobbleigh and all.'
Ib. Widdicombe Fair

2 It fell about the Martinmass,
When nights are lang and mirk,
The carline wife's three sons came hame,
And their hats were o' the birk.

It neither grew in dike nor ditch,
Nor yet in any sheugh;
But at the gates o' Paradise
That birk grew fair eneugh.
Ib. The Wife of Usher's Well

JOHN CODRINGTON BAMPFYLDE
1754–1796
3 Rugged the breast that beauty cannot tame.
Sonnet in Praise of Delia

GEORGE BANCROFT
fl. 1548
4 Where Christ erecteth his church, the devil in the
same churchyard will have his chapel.
Sermon preached at Paul's Cross, 9 Feb. 1588

GEORGE BANCROFT
1800–1891
5 It [Calvinism in Switzerland] established a religion
without a prelate, a government without a king.
History of the United States, vol. iii, ch. 6

EDWARD BANGS
fl. 1775
6 Yankee Doodle, keep it up,
Yankee Doodle dandy;
Mind the music and the step,
And with the girls be handy.
Yankee Doodle; or Father's Return to Camp. See
Nicholas Smith, *Stories of Great National Songs*

7 Yankee Doodle came to town
Riding on a pony;
Stuck a feather in his cap
And called it Macaroni.   *Ib.*

GEORGE LINNÆUS BANKS
1821–1881
8 For the cause that lacks assistance,
For the wrong that needs resistance,
For the future in the distance,
And the good that I can do.
Daisies in the Grass. What I Live For

THÉODORE DE BANVILLE
1823–1891
9 Nous n'irons plus aux bois, les lauriers sont coupés.
We will go no more to the woods, the laurel-trees
are cut. *Les Cariatides, Les Stalactites*
(*Nursery rhyme, earlier than Banville*)

ANNA LETITIA BARBAULD
1743–1825
10 So fades a summer cloud away;
So sinks the gale when storms are o'er;
So gently shuts the eye of day;
So dies a wave along the shore. *The Death of the Virtuous*

11 The world has little to bestow
Where two fond hearts in equal love are joined. *Delia*

12 And when midst fallen London, they survey
The stone where Alexander's ashes lay,
Shall own with humbled pride the lesson just
By Time's slow finger written in the dust.
Eighteen Hundred and Eleven

13 Of her scorn the maid repented,
And the shepherd—of his love.
Leave Me, Simple Shepherd

14 Life! we've been long together,
Through pleasant and through cloudy weather;
'Tis hard to part when friends are dear,
Perhaps 'twill cost a sigh, a tear;
Then steal away, give little warning;
Choose thine own time;
Say not 'Good-night'; but in some brighter clime
Bid me 'Good-morning'. *Ode to Life*

15 Society than solitude is worse,
And man to man is still the greatest curse.
Ovid to His Wife

JOHN BARBOUR
1316?–1395
16 Storys to rede ar delitabill,
Suppos that thai be nocht bot fabill.
The Bruce, bk. i, l. 1

17 A! fredome is a noble thing!
Fredome mayse man to haiff liking. *Ib. l. 225*

REV. RICHARD HARRIS BARHAM
1788–1845
18 Like a blue-bottle fly on a rather large scale,
With a rather large corking-pin stuck through his tail.
The Ingoldsby Legends. The Auto-da-Fé

19 Be kind to those dear little folks
When our toes are turned up to the daisies!
Ib. The Babes in the Wood

20 She help'd him to lean, and she help'd him to fat,
And it look'd like hare—but it might have been cat.
Ib. The Bagman's Dog

21 There was cakes and apples in all the Chapels,
With fine polonies, and rich mellow pears.
Ib. Barney Maguire's Account of the Coronation

22 Take a suck at the lemon, and at him again!
Ib. The Black Mousquetaire

23 Though I've always considered Sir Christopher
Wren,
As an architect, one of the greatest of men;
And, talking of Epitaphs,—much I admire his,
'Circumspice, si Monumentum requiris';
Which an erudite Verger translated to me,
'If you ask for his Monument, Sir-come-spy-see!'
Ib. The Cynotaph

1 What Horace says is,
Eheu fugaces
Anni labuntur, Postume, Postume!
Years glide away, and are lost to me, lost to me!
The Ingoldsby Legends. Epigram: Eheu fugaces

2 There, too, full many an Aldermanic nose
Roll'd its loud diapason after dinner.
Ib. The Ghost

3 'He won't—won't he? Then bring me my boots!' said
the Baron. *Ib. Grey Dolphin*

4 Tallest of boys, or shortest of men,
He stood in his stockings, just four foot ten.
Ib. Hon. Mr. Sucklethumbkin's Story

5 Tiger Tim, come tell me true,
What may a Nobleman find to do? *Ib.*

6 What *was* to be done?—'twas perfectly plain
That they could not well hang the man over again;
What *was* to be done?—The man was dead!
Nought *could* be done—nought could be said;
So—my Lord Tomnoddy went home to bed! *Ib.*

7 A servant's too often a negligent elf;
—If it's business of consequence, *do it yourself!*
Ib. The Ingoldsby Penance. Moral

8 The Jackdaw sat on the Cardinal's chair!
Bishop, and abbot, and prior were there;
Many a monk, and many a friar,
Many a knight, and many a squire,
With a great many more of lesser degree,—
In sooth a goodly company;
And they served the Lord Primate on bended knee.
Never, I ween,
Was a prouder seen,
Read of in books, or dreamt of in dreams,
Than the Cardinal Lord Archbishop of Rheims!
Ib. The Jackdaw of Rheims

9 And six little Singing-boys,—dear little souls!
In nice clean faces, and nice white stoles. *Ib.*

10 He cursed him in sleeping, that every night
He should dream of the devil, and wake in a fright.
Ib.

11 Never was heard such a terrible curse!
But what gave rise to no little surprise,
Nobody seem'd one penny the worse! *Ib.*

12 Heedless of grammar, they all cried, 'That's him!' *Ib.*

13 The Lady Jane was tall and slim,
The Lady Jane was fair.
Ib. The Knight and the Lady

14 He would pore by the hour, o'er a weed or a flower,
Or the slugs that come crawling out after a shower.
Ib.

15 Or great ugly things, all legs and wings,
With nasty long tails arm'd with nasty long stings.
Ib.

16 Go—pop Sir Thomas again in the pond—
Poor dear!—he'll catch us some more!! *Ib.*

17 Though his cassock was swarming
With all sorts of vermin,
He'd not take the life of a flea!
Ib. The Lay of St. Aloys

18 Ah, ha! my good friend!—Don't you wish you may
get it? *Ib.*

19 Here's a corpse in the case with a sad swell'd face,
And a Medical Crowner's a queer sort of thing!
The Ingoldsby Legends. A Lay of St. Gengulphus

20 And her bosom went in, and her tail came out.
Ib. A Lay of St. Nicholas

21 A German,
Who smoked like a chimney. *Ib. Lay of St. Odille*

22 So put that in your pipe, my Lord Otto, and smoke
it! *Ib.*

23 'Twas in Margate last July, I walk'd upon the pier,
I saw a little vulgar Boy—I said, 'What make you
here?' *Ib. Misadventures at Margate*

24 He had no little handkerchief to wipe his little nose!
Ib.

25 And now I'm here, from this here pier it is my fixed
intent
To jump, as Mr. Levi did from off the Monu-ment!
Ib.

26 I could not see my little friend—because he was not
there! *Ib.*

27 But when the Crier cried, 'O Yes!' the people cried.
'O No!' *Ib.*

28 It's very odd that Sailor-men should talk so very
queer—
And then he hitch'd his trousers up, as is, I'm told,
their use,
It's very odd that Sailor-men should wear those things
so loose. *Ib.*

29 He smiled and said, 'Sir, does your mother know that
you are out?' *Ib.*

30 You intoxified brute!—you insensible block!—
Look at the clock!—Do! —Look at the clock!
Ib. Patty Morgan. Fytte i.

31 They were a little less than 'kin', and rather more than
'kind'. *Ib. Nell Cook*

32 She drank Prussic acid without any water,
And died like a Duke-and-a-Duchess's daughter!
Ib. The Tragedy

33 *Cob* was the strongest, *Mob* was the wrongest,
Chittabob's tail was the finest and longest!
Ib. The Truants

34 Though port should have age,
Yet I don't think it sage
To entomb it, as some of your *connoisseurs* do,
Till it's losing its flavour, and body, and hue;
—I question if keeping it does it much good
After ten years in bottle and three in the wood.
Ib. The Wedding-Day. Moral

SABINE BARING-GOULD
1834–1924

35 Now the day is over,
Night is drawing nigh,
Shadows of the evening
Steal across the sky.
Hymns Ancient and Modern. Now the Day is Over

36 Birds and beasts and flowers
Soon will be asleep. *Ib.*

37 Guard the sailors tossing
On the deep blue sea. *Ib.*

1 Onward, Christian soldiers,
　　Marching as to war,
With the Cross of Jesus
　　Going on before.
　　*Hymns Ancient and Modern. Onward, Christian
　　Soldiers*

2 Hell's foundations quiver
　　At the shout of praise;
Brothers, lift your voices,
　　Loud your anthems raise. 　　　　　　　*Ib.*

3 Gates of hell can never
　　'Gainst that Church prevail;
We have Christ's own promise,
　　And that cannot fail. 　　　　　　　　*Ib.*

4 Through the night of doubt and sorrow
Onward goes the pilgrim band,
Singing songs of expectation,
Marching to the Promised Land.
　　Ib. Tr. from the Danish of B. S. Ingemann,
　　*1789–1862. Through the Night of Doubt and
　　Sorrow*

5 Brother clasps the hand of brother,
Stepping fearless through the night. 　　*Ib.*

6 Soon shall come the great awaking,
Soon the rending of the tomb,
Then, the scattering of all shadows
And the end of toil and gloom. 　　　　　*Ib.*

LADY ANNE BARNARD
1750–1825

7 When the sheep are in the fauld, when the cows come
　　hame,
When a' the weary world to quiet rest are gane.
　　　　　　　　　　　　　　Auld Robin Gray

8 My mither she fell sick—my Jamie was at sea—
And Auld Robin Gray, oh! he came a-courting me.
　　　　　　　　　　　　　　　　　　　Ib.

9 My father argued sair—my mother didna speak,
But she look'd in my face till my heart was like to
　　break. 　　　　　　　　　　　　　　*Ib.*

10 I hadna been his wife, a week but only four,
When mournfu' as I sat on the stane at my door,
I saw my Jamie's ghaist—I cou'dna think it he,
Till he said, 'I'm come hame, my love, to marry thee!'
　　　　　　　　　　　　　　　　　　　Ib.

CHARLOTTE ALINGTON BARNARD
1840–1869

11 I cannot sing the old songs
I sang long years ago,
For heart and voice would fail me,
And foolish tears would flow.
　　Fireside Thoughts. I Cannot Sing the Old Songs

BARNABE BARNES
1569?–1609

12 Ah, sweet Content! where doth thine harbour hold?
　　Parthenophil and Parthenophe, Sonnet lxvi

WILLIAM BARNES
1801–1886

13 An' there vor me the apple tree
Do leän down low in Linden Lea.
　　　　　　　　　My Orcha'd in Linden Lea

14 But still the neäme do bide the seäme—
'Tis Pentridge—Pentridge by the river.
　　　　　　　　　　Pentridge by the River

15 My love is the maïd ov all maïdens,
Though all mid be comely. 　　　*In the Spring*

16 Since I noo mwore do zee your feäce.
　　　　　　　　　　　　The Wife A-Lost

RICHARD BARNFIELD
1574–1627

17 As it fell upon a day,
In the merry month of May,
Sitting in a pleasant shade,
Which a grove of myrtles made.
Beasts did leap and birds did sing,
Trees did grow and plants did spring,
Everything did banish moan,
Save the nightingale alone.
She, poor bird, as all forlorn,
Lean'd her breast up-till a thorn,
And there sung the dolefull'st ditty
That to hear it was great pity.
Fie, fie, fie, now would she cry;
Tereu, Tereu, by and by.
　　　　　　Poems: in Divers Humors, An Ode

18 King Pandion, he is dead,
All thy friends are lapp'd in lead. 　　*Ib.*

19 If Music and sweet Poetry agree,
As they must needs (the Sister and the Brother)
Then must the love be great, 'twixt thee and me,
Because thou lov'st the one, and I the other.
　　　　　　　　　　　　Ib. Sonnet 1

20 Nothing more certain than incertainties;
Fortune is full of fresh variety:
Constant in nothing but inconstancy.
　　　　　　　The Shepherd's Content, xi

21 My flocks feed not,
My ewes breed not,
My rams speed not,
　　All is amiss.
Love is dying,
Faith's defying,
Heart's denying,
　　Causer of this. 　　*A Shepherd's Complaint*

22 She [Pecunia] is the sovereign queen, of all delights:
For her the lawyer pleads; the soldier fights.
　　　　　　Encomion of Lady Pecunia, xvi

23 The waters were his winding sheet, the sea was made
　　his tomb;
Yet for his fame the ocean sea, was not sufficient
　　room.
　　Ib. To the Gentlemen Readers. (On the death of
　　Hawkins.)

PHINEAS T. BARNUM
1810–1891

24 There's a sucker born every minute. 　　*Attrib.*

EATON STANNARD BARRETT
1786–1820

25 She, while Apostles shrank, could dangers brave,
Last at His cross and earliest at His grave.
　　　　　　　　　Woman, pt. i, l. 143

SIR JAMES MATTHEW BARRIE

1860–1937

1 His lordship may compel us to be equal upstairs, but there will never be equality in the servants' hall.
The Admirable Crichton, Act I

2 I'm a second eleven sort of chap. *Ib.* Act III

3 Never ascribe to an opponent motives meaner than your own.
'*Courage*', *Rectorial Address, St. Andrews*, 3 May 1922

4 Courage is the thing. All goes if courage goes. *Ib.*

5 Facts were never pleasing to him. He acquired them with reluctance and got rid of them with relief. He was never on terms with them until he had stood them on their heads.
Love Me Never or For Ever

6 I do loathe explanations.
My Lady Nicotine, ch. 16

7 When the first baby laughed for the first time, the laugh broke into a thousand pieces and they all went skipping about, and that was the beginning of fairies. *Peter Pan*, Act I

8 Every time a child says 'I don't believe in fairies' there is a little fairy somewhere that falls down dead. *Ib.*

9 To die will be an awfully big adventure. *Ib.* Act III

10 Do you believe in fairies? ... If you believe, clap your hands! *Ib.* Act IV

11 That is ever the way. 'Tis all jealousy to the bride and good wishes to the corpse. *Quality Street*, Act I

12 Oh the gladness of her gladness when she's glad,
And the sadness of her sadness when she's sad,
But the gladness of her gladness
And the sadness of her sadness
Are as nothing, Charles,
To the badness of her badness when she's bad.
Rosalind

13 The Twelve-pound Look. *Title of Play*

14 Have you ever noticed, Harry, that many jewels make women either incredibly fat or incredibly thin?
The Twelve-pound Look

15 It's a sort of bloom on a woman. If you have it [charm], you don't need to have anything else; and if you don't have it, it doesn't much matter what else you have. *What Every Woman Knows*, Act I

16 A young Scotsman of your ability let loose upon the world with £300, what could he not do? It's almost appalling to think of; especially if he went among the English. *Ib.*

17 You've forgotten the grandest moral attribute of a Scotsman, Maggie, that he'll do nothing which might damage his career. *Ib.* Act II

18 There are few more impressive sights in the world than a Scotsman on the make. *Ib.*

19 Every man who is high up loves to think that he has done it all himself; and the wife smiles, and lets it go at that. It's our only joke. Every woman knows that. *Ib.* Act IV

GEORGE BARRINGTON

b. 1755

20 True patriots we; for be it understood,
We left our country for our country's good.
Prologue for the opening of the Playhouse, Sydney, New South Wales, 16 Jan. 1796. The company was composed of convicts.

WILLIAM BASSE

d. 1653?

21 Renowned Spenser, lie a thought more nigh
To learned Chaucer, and rare Beaumont lie,
A little nearer Spenser, to make room
For Shakespeare, in your threefold, fourfold tomb.
Poetical Works. On Shakespeare

EDGAR BATEMAN

nineteenth century

22 Wiv a ladder and some glasses,
You could see to 'Ackney Marshes,
If it wasn't for the 'ouses in between.
If it wasn't for the 'Ouses in between

KATHERINE LEE BATES

1859–1929

23 America! America!
God shed His grace on thee
And crown thy good with brotherhood
From sea to shining sea! *America the Beautiful*

RICHARD BAXTER

1615–1691

24 I preach'd as never sure to preach again,
And as a dying man to dying men!
Love Breathing Thanks and Praise, pt. ii

25 In necessary things, unity; in doubtful things, liberty; in all things, charity. *Motto*

THOMAS HAYNES BAYLY

1797–1839

26 I'd be a butterfly born in a bower,
Where roses and lilies and violets meet.
I'd be a Butterfly

27 I'm saddest when I sing. *Title of poem*

28 Absence makes the heart grow fonder,
Isle of Beauty, Fare thee well!
Isle of Beauty (see 5:3)

29 It was a dream of perfect bliss,
Too beautiful to last. *It was a Dream*

30 The mistletoe hung in the castle hall,
The holly branch shone on the old oak wall.
The Mistletoe Bough

31 Oh! no! we never mention her,
Her name is never heard;
My lips are now forbid to speak
That once familiar word.
Oh! No! We Never Mention Her

32 Oh, Pilot! 'tis a fearful night,
There's danger on the deep. *The Pilot*

33 Fear not, but trust in Providence
Wherever thou may'st be. *Ib.*

1 She wore a wreath of roses,
The night that first we met.
She Wore a Wreath of Roses

2 Gaily the Troubadour
Touch'd his guitar. *Welcome Me Home*

3 We met, 'twas in a crowd, And I thought he would
shun me. *We Met, 'twas in a Crowd*

4 Why don't the men propose, mamma,
Why don't the men propose? *Why Don't the Men Propose?*

JAMES BEATTIE
1735–1803

5 His harp, the sole companion of his way.
The Minstrel, bk. I. iii

6 In truth, he was a strange and wayward wight,
Fond of each gentle and each dreadful scene.
In darkness and in storm he found delight. *Ib.* xxii

DAVID BEATTY, EARL BEATTY
1871–1936

7 There's something wrong with our bloody ships
to-day, Chatfield.
Remark during the Battle of Jutland, 1916: Winston Churchill, The World Crisis (1927), Pt. I, p. 129. The additional words commonly attributed: 'Steer two points nearer the enemy' are denied by Lord Chatfield

TOPHAM BEAUCLERK
1739–1780

8 [On Boswell saying that a certain man had good principles.] Then he does not wear them out in practice. *Boswell's Life of Johnson, 14 Apr. 1778*

PIERRE-AUGUSTIN DE BEAUMARCHAIS
1732–1799

9 Je me presse de rire de tout, de peur d'être obligé d'en pleurer.

I make myself laugh at everything, for fear of having to weep. *Le Barbier de Séville*, I. ii

10 (Figaro, to the Count Almaviva)
Est-ce qu'un homme comme vous ignore quelque chose?

Can anything be beyond the knowledge of a man like you? *Ib.* vi.

11 Parce que vous êtes un grand seigneur, vous vous croyez un grand génie! . . . Vous vous êtes donné la peine de naître, et rien de plus.

Because you are a great lord, you believe yourself to be a great genius! . . . You took the trouble to be born, but no more. *Mariage de Figaro*, v. iii

FRANCIS BEAUMONT
1584–1616

12 What things have we seen,
Done at the Mermaid! heard words that have been
So nimble, and so full of subtil flame,
As if that every one from whence they came,
Had meant to put his whole wit in a jest,
And had resolv'd to live a fool, the rest
Of his dull life. *Letter to Ben Jonson*

13 Here are sands, ignoble things,
Dropt from the ruin'd sides of Kings;
Here's a world of pomp and state,
Buried in dust, once dead by fate.
On the Tombs in Westminster Abbey

FRANCIS BEAUMONT
1584–1616
and
JOHN FLETCHER
1579–1625

14 There is no drinking after death.
The Bloody Brother, II. ii

15 And he that will to bed go sober,
Falls with the leaf still in October. *Ib.*

16 Three merry boys, and three merry boys,
And three merry boys are we,
As ever did sing in a hempen string
Under the gallows-tree. *Ib.* III. ii

17 Bad's the best of us. *Ib.* IV. ii

18 You are no better than you should be.
The Coxcomb, IV. iii

19 I care not two-pence. *Ib.* V. i

20 Death hath so many doors to let out life.
The Custom of the Country, II. ii

21 But what is past my help, is past my care.
The Double Marriage, I. i

22 It is always good
When a man has two irons in the fire.
The Faithful Friends, I. ii

23 Our acts our angels are, or good or ill,
Our fatal shadows that walk by us still.
Upon an Honest Man's Fortune, v

24 Let's meet, and either do, or die.
The Island Princess, II. ii

25 Nose, nose, jolly red nose,
And who gave thee this jolly red nose? . . .
Nutmegs and ginger, cinamon and cloves,
And they gave me this jolly red nose.
Knight of the Burning Pestle, I. iii

26 This is a pretty flim-flam. *Ib.* II. iii

27 Go to grass. *Ib.* IV. vi

28 Something given that way.
The Lovers' Progress, I. i

29 Deeds, not words shall speak me. *Ib.* III. vi

30 Thou wilt scarce be a man before thy mother. *Ib.* ii

31 I find the medicine worse than the malady. *Ib.*

32 Faith, Sir, he went away with a flea in 's ear. *Ib.* IV. iii

33 I'll put on my considering cap.
The Loyal Subject, II. i

34 I'll put a spoke among your wheels.
The Mad Lover, III. vi

35 Upon my buried body lie
Lightly, gentle earth. *The Maid's Tragedy*, II. i

36 Those have most power to hurt us that we love.
Ib. V. iv

37 Fountain heads, and pathless groves,
Places which pale passion loves.
The Nice Valour, Song, III. iii

1 Nothing's so dainty sweet, as lovely melancholy.
The Nice Valour, Song, III. iii

2   All your better deeds
Shall be in water writ, but this in marble. *Ib.* v. iii

3 'Tis virtue, and not birth that makes us noble:
Great actions speak great minds, and such should
govern.   *The Prophetess*, II. iii

4 I'll have a fling.
Rule a Wife and have a Wife, III. v

5 Kiss till the cow comes home. *Scornful Lady*, II. ii

6 There is no other purgatory but a woman. *Ib.* III. i

7 It would talk:
Lord how it talk't!   *Ib.* IV. i

8 Daisies smell-less, yet most quaint,
    And sweet thyme true,
Primrose first born child of Ver,
Merry Spring-time's Harbinger.
Two Noble Kinsmen, I. i

9 Care-charming Sleep, thou easer of all woes,
Brother to Death.   *Valentinian*, v. ii

10 God Lyæus ever young,
Ever honour'd, ever sung.   *Ib.* viii

11 Come sing now, sing; for I know ye sing well,
I see ye have a singing face.
The Wild Goose Chase, II. ii

12 Though I say't, that should not say't.
Wit at Several Weapons, II. ii

13 Whistle and she'll come to you.
Wit Without Money, IV. iv

14 Let the world slide.   *Ib.* v. ii

15 Have not you maggots in your brains?
Women Pleased, III. iv

CARL BECKER
1873-1945

16 Twice tricked by the British into a European war in
order to pull their chestnuts out of the fire.
Progress and Power (1935)

PETER BECKFORD
1740-1811

17 The colour I think of little moment; and am of
opinion with our friend Foote, respecting his negro
friend, that a good dog, like a good candidate,
cannot be of a bad colour.
Thoughts upon Hare and Fox Hunting, letter 3

WILLIAM BECKFORD
1759-1844

18 When he was angry, one of his eyes became so terrible,
that no person could bear to behold it; and the
wretch upon whom it was fixed instantly fell backward, and sometimes expired. For fear, however,
of depopulating his dominions, and making his
palace desolate, he but rarely gave way to his anger.
Vathek (1893), p. 1

19 He did not think, with the Caliph Omar Ben Adalaziz,
that it was necessary to make a hell of this world to
enjoy paradise in the next.   *Ib.* p. 2

20 Your presence I condescend to accept and beg you
will let me be quiet, for I am not over-fond of resisting temptation.   *Ib.* p. 134

THOMAS BECON
1512-1567

21 For when the wine is in, the wit is out.
Catechism, 375

THOMAS LOVELL BEDDOES
1798-1851

22 If thou wilt ease thine heart
Of love and all its smart,
Then sleep, dear, sleep.   *Death's Jest Book*, II. ii

23 But wilt thou cure thine heart
Of love and all its smart,
Then die, dear, die.   *Ib.*

24   If man could see
The perils and diseases that he elbows,
Each day he walks a mile; which catch at him,
Which fall behind and graze him as he passes;
Then would he know that Life's a single pilgrim,
Fighting unarmed amongst a thousand soldiers.
Ib. IV. i. (MS. III)

25 I have a bit of FIAT in my soul,
And can myself create my little world.   *Ib.* v. i

26 Old Adam, the carrion crow.   *Ib.* iv

27 King Death hath asses' ears.   *Ib.*

28 If there were dreams to sell,
    What would you buy?
Some cost a passing bell;
    Some a light sigh,
That shakes from Life's fresh crown
Only a roseleaf down.
If there were dreams to sell,
Merry and sad to tell,
And the crier rung the bell,
    What would you buy?   *Dream-Pedlary*

29   Him
Who was the planet's tyrant, dotard Death.
Letter from Göttingen

30 How many times do I love thee, dear?
Tell me how many thoughts there be
    In the atmosphere
Of a new-fal'n year,
Whose white and sable hours appear
The latest flakes of Eternity:
So many times do I love thee, dear.
Torrismond, I. iii

BEDE
673-735

31 Talis, inquiens, mihi videtur, rex, vita hominum
praesens in terris, ad conparationem eius, quod
nobis incertum est, temporis, quale cum te resi-
dente ad caenam cum ducibus ac ministris tuis
tempore brumali, . . . adveniens unus passerum domum citissime pervolaverit; qui cum per unum
ostium ingrediens, mox per aliud exierit. Ipso quidem tempore, quo intus est, hiemis tempestate non
tangitur, sed tamen parvissimo spatio serenitatis ad
momentum excurso, mox de hieme in hiemem re-
grediens, tuis oculis elabitur. Ita haec vita hominum ad modicum apparet; quid autem sequatur,
quidve praecesserit, prorsus ignoramus.

'Such,' he said, 'O King, seems to me the present life of men on earth, in comparison with
that time which to us is uncertain, as if when

on a winter's night you sit feasting with your ealdormen and thegns,—a single sparrow should fly swiftly into the hall, and coming in at one door, instantly fly out through another. In that time in which it is indoors it is indeed not touched by the fury of the winter, but yet, this smallest space of calmness being passed almost in a flash, from winter going into winter again, it is lost to your eyes. Somewhat like this appears the life of man; but of what follows or what went before, we are utterly ignorant.'
Ecclesiastical History, bk. ii, ch. 13

1 Scio, inquiens, quia ubi navem ascenderitis, tempestas vobis et ventus contrarius superveniet: sed tu memento ut hoc oleum quod tibi do, mittas in mare; et statim quiescentibus ventis, serenitas maris vos læta prosequetur.
I know, he said, that when you go on board ship, a storm and contrary wind will come upon you: but remember to pour this oil that I give you, on the water; and immediately with the winds dropping happy calm of ocean will ensue.
Ib. bk. iii, ch. 15

BERNARD ELLIOTT BEE
1823–1861

2 Let us determine to die here, and we will conquer. There is Jackson standing like a stone wall. Rally behind the Virginians.
First Battle of Bull Run, 1861. Poore, *Reminiscences of Metropolis*, ii. 85

HENRY CHARLES BEECHING
1859–1919

3 With lifted feet, hands still,
I am poised, and down the hill
Dart, with heedful mind;
The air goes by in a wind.
Going Down Hill on a Bicycle

4 Alas, that the longest hill
Must end in a vale; but still,
Who climbs with toil, wheresoe'er
Shall find wings waiting there. *Ib.*

5 First come I; my name is Jowett.
There's no knowledge but I know it.
I am Master of this college:
What I don't know isn't knowledge.
The Masque of Balliol, composed by and current among members of Balliol College in the late 1870s (see also 8:15, 511:5 and 6)

6 Not when the sense is dim,
But now from the heart of joy,
I would remember Him:
Take the thanks of a boy. *Prayers*

SIR MAX BEERBOHM
1872–1956

7 Most women are not so young as they are painted.
A Defence of Cosmetics

8 I belong to the Beardsley period. *Diminuendo*

9 There is always something rather absurd about the past. *1880*

10 To give an accurate and exhaustive account of that period would need a far less brilliant pen than mine. *Ib.*

11 She swam to the bell-rope and grasped it for a tinkle.
(*Parody of Meredith.*) *Euphemia Clashthought*

12 A swear-word in a rustic slum
A simple swear-word is to some,
To Masefield something more.
(*Caption to a cartoon.*) *Fifty Caricatures, 1913*

13 Not that I had any special reason for hating school. Strange as it may seem to my readers, I was not unpopular there. I was a modest, good-humoured boy. It is Oxford that has made me insufferable.
Going Back to School

14 None, it is said, of all who revelled with the Regent, was half so wicked as Lord George Hell.
The Happy Hypocrite, ch. 1

15 Mankind is divisible into two great classes: hosts and guests. *Hosts and Guests*

16 I maintain that though you would often in the fifteenth century have heard the snobbish Roman say, in a would-be off-hand tone, 'I am dining with the Borgias to-night,' no Roman ever was able to say, 'I dined last night with the Borgias.' *Ib.*

17 The Nonconformist Conscience makes cowards of us all. *King George the Fourth*

18 Fate wrote her [Queen Caroline] a most tremendous tragedy, and she played it in tights. *Ib.*

19 They so very indubitably *are*, you know! (*Parody of Henry James.*) *Mote in the Middle Distance*

20 'After all', as a pretty girl once said to me, 'women are a sex by themselves, so to speak.'
The Pervasion of Rouge

21 Savonarola love-sick! Ha, ha, ha!
Love-sick? He, love-sick? 'Tis a goodly jest!
The confirm'd misogyn a ladies' man!
Savonarola Brown, Act 1

22 Had Sav'narola spoken less than thus,
Methinks me, the less Sav'narola he. *Ib.*

23 LUCREZIA BORGIA. And what name gave he?
PORTER. Something-arola—
LUC. Savon?—show him up. *Ib.* Act II

24 Enter Michael Angelo. Andrea del Sarto appears for a moment at a window. Pippa passes. *Ib.* Act III

25 O the disgrace of it!—
The scandal, the incredible come-down! *Ib.* Act IV

26 A pretty sort of prison I have come to,
In which a self-respecting lady's cell
Is treated as a lounge. *Ib.*

27 Zuleika, on a desert island, would have spent most of her time in looking for a man's foot-print.
Zuleika Dobson, ch. 2

28 Your mentality, too, is bully, as we all predicate.
Ib. ch. 8

29 Deeply regret inform your grace last night two black owls came and perched on battlements remained there through night hooting at dawn flew away none knows whither awaiting instructions Jellings.
Ib. ch. 14

30 Prepare vault for funeral Monday Dorset. *Ib.*

31 The Socratic manner is not a game at which two can play. *Ib.* ch. 15

1 'Ah, say that again,' she murmured. 'Your voice is music.'
He repeated his question.
'Music!' she said dreamily; and such is the force of habit that 'I don't', she added, 'know anything about music, really. But I know what I like.'
Zuleika Dobson, ch. 16

ETHEL LYNN BEERS
1827–1879

2 All quiet along the Potomac to-night,
No sound save the rush of the river,
While soft falls the dew on the face of the dead—
The picket's off duty forever.
All Quiet along the Potomac

APHRA BEHN
1640–1689

3 Oh, what a dear ravishing thing is the beginning of an Amour! *The Emperor of the Moon*, I. i

4 Of all that writ, he was the wisest bard, who spoke this mighty truth—
He that knew all that ever learning writ,
Knew only this—that he knew nothing yet. *Ib.* iii

5 Love ceases to be a pleasure, when it ceases to be a secret. *The Lover's Watch, Four o'clock*

6 Faith, Sir, we are here to-day, and gone to-morrow.
The Lucky Chance, IV

7 I owe a duty, where I cannot love.
The Moor's Revenge, III. iii

8 A brave world, Sir, full of religion, knavery, and change: we shall shortly see better days.
The Roundheads, I. i

9 Variety is the soul of pleasure.
The Rover, Part II, Act I

10 Come away; poverty's catching. *Ib.*

11 Money speaks sense in a language all nations understand. *Ib.* III. i

12 Beauty unadorn'd. *Ib.* IV. ii

13 'Sure, I rose the wrong way to-day, I have had such damn'd ill luck every way.' *The Town Fop*, v. i

14 The soft, unhappy sex. *The Wandering Beauty*

W. H. BELLAMY
nineteenth century

15 Old Simon the Cellarer keeps a rare store
Of Malmsey and Malvoisie.
Song: Simon the Cellarer

JOACHIM DU BELLAY
1515–1560

16 France, mère des arts, des armes et des loix.

France, mother of arts, of warriors, and of laws.
Sonnets

17 Heureux qui comme Ulysse a fait un beau voyage.

Happy the wanderer, like Ulysses, who has come happily home at last. *Ib.*

HILAIRE BELLOC
1870–1953

18 The road went up, the road went down,
And there the matter ended it.
He broke his heart in Clermont town,
At Pontgibaud they mended it. *Auvergnat*

19 Child! do not throw this book about;
Refrain from the unholy pleasure
Of cutting all the pictures out!
Preserve it as your chiefest treasure.
Bad Child's Book of Beasts, dedication

20 Your little hands were made to take
The better things and leave the worse ones:
They also may be used to shake
The massive paws of elder persons. *Ib.*

21 A manner rude and wild
Is common at your age. *Ib.* introduction

22 Who take their manners from the Ape,
Their habits from the Bear,
Indulge the loud unseemly jape,
And never brush their hair. *Ib.*

23 Yet may you see his bones and beak
All in the Mu-se-um. *Ib. The Dodo*

24 The Dromedary is a cheerful bird:
I cannot say the same about the Kurd.
Ib. The Dromedary

25 When people call this beast to mind,
They marvel more and more
At such a little tail behind,
So large a trunk before. *Ib. The Elephant*

26 The Frog is justly sensitive
To epithets like these. *Ib. The Frog*

27 I shoot the Hippopotamus
With bullets made of platinum,
Because if I use leaden ones
His hide is sure to flatten 'em.
Ib. The Hippopotamus

28 You have a horn where other brutes have none:
Rhinoceros, you are an ugly beast.
Ib. The Rhinoceros

29 Mothers of large families, who claim to common sense,
Will find a Tiger well repay the trouble and expense.
Ib. The Tiger

30 The Whale that wanders round the Pole
Is not a table fish.
You cannot bake or boil him whole
Nor serve him in a dish. *Ib. The Whale*

31 Here is a House that armours a man
With the eyes of a boy and the heart of a ranger.
To the Balliol Men still in Africa

32 Balliol made me, Balliol fed me,
Whatever I had she gave me again;
And the best of Balliol loved and led me,
God be with you, Balliol men. *Ib.*

33 The nicest child I ever knew
Was Charles Augustus Fortescue.
Cautionary Tales. Charles Augustus Fortescue

34 Children in ordinary dress
May always play with sand. *Ib. Franklin Hyde*

35 Godolphin Horne was nobly born;
He held the human race in scorn.
Ib. Godolphin Horne

1 The chief defect of Henry King
Was chewing little bits of string.
Cautionary Tales. Henry King

2 Physicians of the utmost fame
Were called at once; but when they came
They answered, as they took their fees,
'There is no cure for this disease.' *Ib.*

3 'Oh, my friends, be warned by me,
That breakfast, dinner, lunch, and tea
Are all the human frame requires . . .'
With that, the wretched child expires. *Ib.*

4 'Ponto!' he cried, with angry frown,
'Let go, Sir! Down, Sir! Put it down!' *Ib. Jim*

5 Lord Lundy from his earliest years
Was far too freely moved to tears. *Ib. Lord Lundy*

6 In my opinion Butlers ought
To know their place, and not to play
The Old Retainer night and day. *Ib.*

7 Towards the age of twenty-six,
They shoved him into politics. *Ib.*

8 We had intended you to be
The next Prime Minister but three:
The stocks were sold; the Press was squared;
The Middle Class was quite prepared.
But as it is! . . . My language fails!
Go out and govern New South Wales! *Ib.*

9 Matilda told such Dreadful Lies,
It made one Gasp and Stretch one's Eyes;
Her Aunt, who, from her Earliest Youth,
Had kept a Strict Regard for Truth,
Attempted to Believe Matilda:
The effort very nearly killed her. *Ib. Matilda*

10 Summoned the Immediate Aid
Of London's Noble Fire Brigade. *Ib.*

11 Until Matilda's Aunt succeeded
In showing them they were not needed;
And even then she had to pay
To get the Men to go away! *Ib.*

12 For every time she shouted 'Fire!'
They only answered 'Little liar!' *Ib.*

13 It happened that a few Weeks later
Her Aunt was off to the Theatre
To see that Interesting Play
The Second Mrs. Tanqueray. *Ib.*

14 She was not really bad at heart,
But only rather rude and wild;
She was an aggravating child. *Ib. Rebecca*

15 Her funeral sermon (which was long
And followed by a sacred song)
Mentioned her virtues, it is true,
But dwelt upon her vices too. *Ib.*

16 Of Courtesy—it is much less
Than courage of heart or holiness;
Yet in my walks it seems to me
That the Grace of God is in Courtesy. *Courtesy*

17 From quiet homes and first beginning,
Out to the undiscovered ends,
There's nothing worth the wear of winning,
But laughter and the love of friends.
Dedicatory Ode

18 But I will sit beside the fire,
And put my hand before my eyes,
And trace, to fill my heart's desire,
The last of all our Odysseys. *Ib.*

19 We were? Why then, by God, we *are*—
Order! I call the Club to session! *Dedicatory Ode*

20 The moon on the one hand, the dawn on the other:
The moon is my sister, the dawn is my brother.
The moon on my left and the dawn on my right.
My brother, good morning: my sister, good night.
The Early Morning

21 The hundred little lands within one little land that lie
Where Severn seeks the sunset isles or Sussex scales
the sky. *The English Graves*

22 They died to save their country and they only saved
the world. *Ib.*

23 When I am dead, I hope it may be said:
'His sins were scarlet, but his books were read.'
Epigrams. On his Books

24 Of this bad world the loveliest and the best
Has smiled and said 'Good Night,' and gone to rest.
Ib. On a Dead Hostess

25 I said to Heart, 'How goes it?' Heart replied:
'Right as a Ribstone Pippin!' But it lied.
Ib. The False Heart

26 The accursed power which stands on Privilege
(And goes with Women, and Champagne, and Bridge)
Broke—and Democracy resumed her reign:
(Which goes with Bridge, and Women and Cham-
pagne). *Ib. On a Great Election*

27 The Devil, having nothing else to do,
Went off to tempt my Lady Poltagrue.
My Lady, tempted by a private whim,
To his extreme annoyance, tempted him.
Ib. On Lady Poltagrue, a Public Peril

28 Dear Mr. Noman, does it ever strike you,
The more we see of you, the less we like you?
Ib. On Noman, A Guest

29 Sally is gone that was so kindly,
Sally is gone from Ha'nacker Hill. *Ha'nacker Mill*

30 But Catholic men that live upon wine
Are deep in the water, and frank, and fine;
Wherever I travel I find it so,
Benedicamus Domino. *Heretics All*

31 Remote and ineffectual Don
That dared attack my Chesterton. *Lines to a Don*

32 Don different from those regal Dons!
With hearts of gold and lungs of bronze,
Who shout and bang and roar and bawl
The Absolute across the hall,
Or sail in amply billowing gown.
Enormous through the Sacred Town. *Ib.*

33 The Llama is a woolly sort of fleecy hairy goat,
With an indolent expression and an undulating throat
Like an unsuccessful literary man.
More Beasts for Worse Children. The Llama

34 I had an aunt in Yucatan
Who bought a Python from a man
And kept it for a pet.
She died, because she never knew
These simple little rules and few;—
The Snake is living yet. *Ib. The Python*

35 Birds in their little nests agree
With Chinamen, but not with me.
New Cautionary Tales. On Food

36 A smell of burning fills the startled air—
The Electrician is no longer there! *Newdigate Poem*

1 To praise, revere, establish and defend;
To welcome home mankind's mysterious friend
Wine, true begetter of all arts that be;
Wine, privilege of the completely free;
Wine, the foundation, wine the sagely strong;
Wine, bright avenger of sly-dealing wrong.
*Short Talks With The Dead. The Good Poet and
the Bad Poet. Heroic Poem on Wine.* (An adaptation from the *Heroic Poem in Praise of Wine.*)

2 Strong Brother in God, and last Companion: Wine.
Ib.

3 When I am living in the Midlands
That are sodden and unkind

the great hills of the South Country
Come back into my mind. *The South Country*

4 The faith in their happy eyes
Comes surely from our Sister the Spring
When over the sea she flies;
The violets suddenly bloom at her feet,
She blesses us with surprise. *Ib.*

5 I never get between the pines
But I smell the Sussex air. *Ib.*

6 A lost thing could I never find,
Nor a broken thing mend. *Ib.*

7 If I ever become a rich man,
Or if ever I grow to be old,
I will build a house with deep thatch
To shelter me from the cold,
And there shall the Sussex songs be sung
And the story of Sussex told.
I will hold my house in the high wood
Within a walk of the sea,
And the men that were boys when I was a boy
Shall sit and drink with me. *Ib.*

8 Do you remember an Inn,
Miranda? *Tarantella*

9 The fleas that tease in the high Pyrenees. *Ib.*

10 We also know the sacred height
Up on Tugela side,
Where those three hundred fought with Beit
And fair young Wernher died.
*Verses to a Lord who said that those who opposed
the South African adventure confused soldiers with
money-grubbers*

11 Tall Goltman, silent on his horse,
Superb against the dawn.
The little mound where Eckstein stood
And gallant Albu fell,
And Oppenheim, half blind with blood
Went fording through the rising flood—
My Lord, we know them well. *Ib.*

12 They sell good beer at Haslemere
And under Guildford Hill.
At Little Cowfold as I've been told
A beggar may drink his fill:
There is a good brew in Amberley too,
And by the bridge also;
But the swipes they take in at Washington Inn
Is the very best Beer I know.
West Sussex Drinking Song

13 It is the best of all trades, to make songs, and the
second best to sing them.
On Everything. On Song

14 From the towns all Inns have been driven: from the
villages most. . . . Change your hearts or you will
lose your Inns and you will deserve to have lost
them. But when you have lost your Inns drown
your empty selves, for you will have lost the last of
England. *This and That. On Inns*

JULIEN BENDA
1868–

15 La trahison des clercs.
The treason of the educated classes. *Attrib.*

ENOCH ARNOLD BENNETT
1867–1931

16 'Ye can call it influenza if ye like,' said Mrs. Machin.
'There was no influenza in my young days. We called
a cold a cold.' *The Card*, ch. 8

17 Being a husband is a whole-time job.
The Title, Act I

18 Journalists say a thing that they know isn't true, in
the hope that if they keep on saying it long enough
it *will* be true. *Ib.* Act II

HENRY BENNETT
1785–?

19 Oh, St. Patrick was a gentleman,
Who came of decent people;
He built a church in Dublin town,
And on it put a steeple.
St. Patrick was a Gentleman (*Oxford Song Book*)

ARTHUR CHRISTOPHER BENSON
1862–1925

20 Land of Hope and Glory, Mother of the Free,
How shall we extol thee, who are born of thee?
Wider still and wider shall thy bounds be set;
God who made thee mighty, make thee mightier yet.
Song from Pomp and Circumstance *by* Elgar, op.
39, No. 1

JEREMY BENTHAM
1748–1832

21 The greatest happiness of the greatest number is the
foundation of morals and legislation. (*See* 266:11)
The Commonplace Book (*Works*, vol. x. 142)

22 All punishment is mischief: all punishment in itself is
evil. *Principles of Morals and Legislation*, ch. 13, § 2

EDMUND CLERIHEW BENTLEY
1875–1956

23 The art of Biography
Is different from Geography.
Geography is about maps,
But Biography is about chaps.
Biography for Beginners

24 Chapman and Hall
Swore not at all.
Mr. Chapman's yea was yea,
And Mr. Hall's nay was nay.
Ib. Mr. Chapman and Mr. Hall

25 What I like about Clive
Is that he is no longer alive.
There is a great deal to be said
For being dead. *Ib. Clive*

1 Edward the Confessor
Slept under the dresser.
When that began to pall
He slept in the hall.
Biography for Beginners. Edward the Confessor

2 John Stuart Mill
By a mighty effort of will
Overcame his natural bonhomie
And wrote 'Principles of Political Economy'.
Ib. John Stuart Mill

3 Sir Christopher Wren
Said, 'I am going to dine with some men.
If anybody calls
Say I am designing St. Paul's.'
Ib. Sir Christopher Wren

4 George the Third
Ought never to have occurred.
One can only wonder
At so grotesque a blunder.
More Biographies. George the Third

RICHARD BENTLEY
1662–1742

5 He is believed to have liked port, but to have said of claret that 'it would be port if it could'.
R. C. Jebb, *Bentley*, p. 200

6 It is a pretty poem, Mr. Pope, but you must not call it Homer. *In* Johnson's *Life of Pope*

7 I hold it as certain, that no man was ever written out of reputation but by himself.
William Warburton, *The Works of Alexander Pope*, iv. 159

THOMAS BENTLEY
1693?–1742

8 No man is demolished but by himself.
A Letter to Mr. Pope, 1735

PIERRE-JEAN DE BÉRANGER
1780–1857

9 Il était un roi d'Yvetot
Peu connu dans l'histoire.

There was a king of Yvetot
Little known to history.
Œuvres, i, Le Roi d'Yvetot

10 Nos amis, les ennemis.
Our friends, the enemy.
L'Opinion de ces demoiselles

LORD CHARLES BERESFORD
1846–1919

11 The idea of a Commercial Alliance with England based on the integrity of China and the open door for all nations' trade.
The Break-Up of China, a Report to the British Associated Chambers of Commerce, from Shanghai, 20 Nov. 1898

BISHOP GEORGE BERKELEY
1685–1753

12 All the choir of heaven and furniture of earth—in a word, all those bodies which compose the mighty frame of the world—have not any subsistence without a mind. *Principles of Human Knowledge*

13 Westward the course of empire takes its way;
The four first acts already past,
A fifth shall close the drama with the day:
Time's noblest offspring is the last.
On the Prospect of Planting Arts and Learning in America

14 [Tar water] is of a nature so mild and benign and proportioned to the human constitution, as to warm without heating, to cheer but not inebriate.
Siris, par. 217

15 Truth is the cry of all, but the game of the few.
Ib. par. 368

IRVING BERLIN
1888–

16 Come on and hear, come on and hear, Alexander's Ragtime Band. *Alexander's Ragtime Band*

ST. BERNARD
1091–1153

17 Liberavi animam meam.
I have freed my soul. *Epistle 371*

WILLIAM BAYLE BERNARD
1807–1875

18 A Storm in a Teacup. *Title of farce*, 1854

SIR WALTER BESANT
1836–1901

19 The World went very well then. *Title*

RICHARD BETHELL, BARON WESTBURY
1800–1873

20 Deprive mankind of their hope of eternal damnation.
Attrib.

21 His Lordship says he will turn it over in what he is pleased to call his mind.
Nash, *Life of Westbury*, i. 158

THEOBALD VON BETHMANN HOLLWEG
1856–1921

22 Just for a word—'neutrality', a word which in war-time has so often been disregarded, just for a scrap of paper—Great Britain is going to make war.
To Sir Edward Goschen, 4 Aug. 1914. Dispatch by Sir Edward Goschen to the British Foreign Office

JACOB BEULER
nineteenth century

23 If I had a donkey wot wouldn't go,
D'ye think I'd wollop him? no, no, no.
Music Hall Song (c. 1822)

HOLY BIBLE

24 Upon the setting of that bright Occidental *Star*, Queen *Elizabeth* of most happy memory.
Holy Bible, Authorized Version, Epistle Dedicatory

25 The appearance of Your Majesty, as of the *Sun* in his strength. *Ib.*

Old Testament

26 In the beginning God created the heaven and the earth.

[43]

And the earth was without form, and void; and darkness was upon the face of the deep. And the Spirit of God moved upon the face of the waters.
And God said, Let there be light: and there was light.
Genesis i. 1

2 Fiat lux.
Let there be light. *Ib.* 3 (Vulgate)

3 And the evening and the morning were the first day.
Ib. 5

4 And God saw that it was good. *Ib.* 10

5 And God made two great lights; the greater light to rule the day, and the lesser light to rule the night: he made the stars also. *Ib.* 16

6 And God said, Let us make man in our image, after our likeness. *Ib.* 26

7 Dominion . . . over every creeping thing that creepeth upon the earth. *Ib.*

8 Male and female created he them. *Ib.* 27

9 Be fruitful, and multiply, and replenish the earth, and subdue it: and have dominion over the fish of the sea, and over the fowl of the air, and over every living thing that moveth upon the earth. *Ib.* 28

10 But there went up a mist from the earth, and watered the whole face of the ground. *Ib.* ii. 6

11 And the Lord God formed man of the dust of the ground, and breathed into his nostrils the breath of life; and man became a living soul.
And the Lord God planted a garden eastward in Eden. *Ib.* 7

12 The tree of life also in the midst of the garden. *Ib.* 9

13 But of the tree of the knowledge of good and evil, thou shalt not eat of it: for in the day that thou eatest thereof thou shalt surely die. *Ib.* 17

14 It is not good that the man should be alone; I will make him an help meet for him. *Ib.* 18

15 The Lord God . . . brought them unto Adam to see what he would call them. *Ib.* 19

16 And the Lord God caused a deep sleep to fall upon Adam, and he slept: and he took one of his ribs, and closed up the flesh instead thereof;
And the rib, which the Lord God had taken from man, made he a woman. *Ib.* 21

17 Bone of my bones, and flesh of my flesh. *Ib.* 23

18 Therefore shall a man leave his father and his mother, and shall cleave unto his wife: and they shall be one flesh. *Ib.* 24

19 Now the serpent was more subtil than any beast of the field. *Ib.* iii. 1

20 Ye shall be as gods, knowing good and evil. *Ib.* 5

21 And they sewed fig leaves together, and made themselves aprons [breeches *in Genevan Bible,* 1560].
And they heard the voice of the Lord God walking in the garden in the cool of the day. *Ib.* 7

22 The woman whom thou gavest to be with me, she gave me of the tree, and I did eat. *Ib.* 12

23 What is this that thou hast done? *Ib.* 13

24 The serpent beguiled me, and I did eat. *Ib.*

25 It shall bruise thy head, and thou shalt bruise his heel.
Genesis iii. 15

26 In sorrow thou shalt bring forth children. *Ib.* 16

27 In the sweat of thy face shalt thou eat bread. *Ib.* 19

28 For dust thou art, and unto dust shalt thou return.
Ib.

29 The mother of all living. *Ib.* 20

30 Am I my brother's keeper? *Ib.* iv. 9

31 The voice of thy brother's blood crieth unto me from the ground. *Ib.* 10

32 My punishment is greater than I can bear. *Ib.* 13

33 Dwelt in the land of Nod. *Ib.* 16

34 The father of such as dwell in tents. *Ib.* 20

35 And Enoch walked with God: and he was not; for God took him. *Ib.* v. 24

36 And Noah begat Shem, Ham, and Japheth. *Ib.* 32

37 There were giants in the earth in those days.
Ib. vi. 4

38 Mighty men which were of old, men of renown. *Ib.*

39 But the dove found no rest for the sole of her foot.
Ib. viii. 9

40 For the imagination of man's heart is evil from his youth. *Ib.* 21

41 While the earth remaineth, seedtime and harvest, and cold and heat, and summer and winter, and day and night shall not cease. *Ib.* 22

42 At the hand of every man's brother will I require the life of man. *Ib.* ix. 5

43 Whoso sheddeth man's blood, by man shall his blood be shed. *Ib.* 6

44 I do set my bow in the cloud. *Ib.* 13

45 Even as Nimrod the mighty hunter before the Lord.
Ib. x. 9

46 Let there be no strife, I pray thee, between thee and me . . . for we be brethren. *Ib.* xiii. 8

47 An horror of great darkness fell upon him. *Ib.* xv. 12

48 In a good old age. *Ib.* 15

49 His [Ishmael's] hand will be against every man, and every man's hand against him. *Ib.* xvi. 12

50 Old and well stricken in age. *Ib.* xviii. 11

51 And the Lord said unto Abraham, Wherefore did Sarah laugh? *Ib.* 13

52 Shall not the Judge of all the earth do right? *Ib.* 25

53 But his wife looked back from behind him, and she became a pillar of salt. *Ib.* xix. 26

54 Take now thy son, thine only son Isaac, whom thou lovest. *Ib.* xxii. 2

55 My son, God will provide himself a lamb. *Ib.* 8

56 Behold behind him a ram caught in a thicket by his horns. *Ib.* 13

57 Esau was a cunning hunter, a man of the field; and Jacob was a plain man, dwelling in tents.
Ib. xxv. 27

58 And he sold his birthright unto Jacob. *Ib.* 33

59 Behold, Esau my brother is a hairy man, and I am a smooth man. *Ib.* xxvii. 11

1 The voice is Jacob's voice, but the hands are the hands of Esau. *Genesis* xxvii. 22

2 Thy brother came with subtilty, and hath taken away thy blessing. *Ib.* 35

3 And he dreamed, and behold a ladder set up on the earth, and the top of it reached to heaven: and behold the angels of God ascending and descending on it. *Ib.* xxviii. 12

4 Surely the Lord is in this place; and I knew it not. *Ib.* 16

5 This is none other but the house of God, and this is the gate of heaven. *Ib.* 17

6 And Jacob served seven years for Rachel; and they seemed unto him but a few days, for the love he had to her. *Ib.* xxix. 20

7 A troop cometh: and she called his name Gad. *Ib.* xxx. 11

8 Mizpah; for he said, The Lord watch between me and thee, when we are absent one from another. *Ib.* xxxi. 49

9 There wrestled a man with him until the breaking of the day.
And when he saw that he prevailed not against him, he touched the hollow of his thigh; and the hollow of Jacob's thigh was out of joint, as he wrestled with him. *Ib.* xxxii. 24

10 I will not let thee go, except thou bless me. *Ib.* 26

11 For I have seen God face to face, and my life is preserved. *Ib.* 30

12 Now Israel loved Joseph more than all his children, because he was the son of his old age; and he made him a coat of many colours. *Ib.* xxxvii. 3

13 Behold, your sheaves stood round about, and made obeisance to my sheaf. *Ib.* 7

14 Behold, this dreamer cometh. *Ib.* 19

15 Some evil beast hath devoured him. *Ib.* 20

16 And she caught him by his garment, saying, Lie with me; and he left his garment in her hand, and fled. *Ib.* xxxix. 12

17 And the lean and the ill favoured kine did eat up the first seven fat kine. *Ib.* xli. 20

18 And the thin ears devoured the seven good ears. *Ib.* 24

19 Jacob saw that there was corn in Egypt. *Ib.* xlii. 1

20 Ye are spies; to see the nakedness of the land ye are come. *Ib.* 9

21 Bring down my gray hairs with sorrow to the grave. *Ib.* 38

22 Benjamin's mess was five times so much as any of their's. *Ib.* xliii. 34

23 Ye shall eat the fat of the land. *Ib.* xlv. 18

24 See that ye fall not out by the way. *Ib.* 24

25 Few and evil have the days of the years of my life been. *Ib.* xlvii. 9

26 Unstable as water, thou shalt not excel. *Ib.* xlix. 4

27 Issachar is a strong ass couching down between two burdens. *Ib.* 14

28 Unto the utmost bound of the everlasting hills. *Ib.* 26

29 Now there arose up a new king over Egypt, which knew not Joseph. *Exodus* i. 8

30 She took for him an ark of bulrushes, and daubed it with slime. *Ib.* ii. 3

31 Who made thee a prince and a judge over us? *Ib.* 14

32 I have been a stranger in a strange land. *Ib.* 22

33 Behold, the bush burned with fire, and the bush was not consumed. *Ib.* iii. 2

34 Put off thy shoes from off thy feet, for the place whereon thou standest is holy ground. *Ib.* 5

35 And Moses hid his face; for he was afraid to look upon God. *Ib.* 6

36 A land flowing with milk and honey; unto the place of the Canaanites, and the Hittites, and the Amorites, and the Perizzites, and the Hivites, and the Jebusites. *Ib.* 8

37 I AM THAT I AM. *Ib.* 14

38 The Lord God of your fathers, the God of Abraham, the God of Isaac, and the God of Jacob. *Ib.* 15

39 But I am slow of speech, and of a slow tongue. *Ib.* iv. 10

40 I know not the Lord, neither will I let Israel go. *Ib.* v. 2

41 My signs and my wonders in the land of Egypt. *Ib.* vii. 3

42 Aaron's rod swallowed up their rods.
And he hardened Pharaoh's heart, that he hearkened not. *Ib.* 12

43 A boil breaking forth with blains. *Ib.* ix. 10

44 Darkness which may be felt. *Ib.* x. 21

45 Your lamb shall be without blemish. *Ib.* xii. 5

46 Roast with fire, and unleavened bread; and with bitter herbs they shall eat it.
Eat not of it raw, nor sodden at all with water, but roast with fire; his head with his legs, and with the purtenance thereof. *Ib.* 8

47 With your loins girded, your shoes on your feet, and your staff in your hand; and ye shall eat it in haste; it is the Lord's passover.
For I will pass through the land of Egypt this night, and will smite all the firstborn in the land of Egypt, both man and beast. *Ib.* 11

48 And there was a great cry in Egypt. *Ib.* 30

49 And they spoiled the Egyptians. *Ib.* 36

50 And the Lord went before them by day in a pillar of a cloud, to lead them the way; and by night in a pillar of fire, to give them light. *Ib.* xiii. 21

51 The Lord is a man of war. *Ib.* xv. 3

52 Would to God we had died by the hand of the Lord in the land of Egypt, when we sat by the flesh pots, and when we did eat bread to the full. *Ib.* xvi. 3

53 But let not God speak with us, lest we die. *Ib.* xx. 19

54 Life for life,
Eye for eye, tooth for tooth, hand for hand, foot for foot,
Burning for burning, wound for wound, stripe for stripe. *Ib.* xxi. 23

55 Thou shalt not suffer a witch to live. *Ib.* xxii. 18

1 Thou shalt not seethe a kid in his mother's milk.
Exodus xxiii. 19

2 The Urim and the Thummim. *Ib.* xxviii. 30

3 And the people sat down to eat and to drink, and rose up to play. *Ib.* xxxii. 6

4 If not, blot me, I pray thee, out of thy book which thou hast written. *Ib.* 32

5 A stiffnecked people. *Ib.* xxxiii. 3

6 Joshua the son of Nun. *Ib.* 11

7 There shall no man see me, and live. *Ib.* 20

8 Let him go for a scapegoat into the wilderness.
Leviticus xvi. 10

9 Thou shalt love thy neighbour as thyself.
Ib. xix. 18; *St. Matthew* xix. 19

10 The Lord bless thee, and keep thee:
The Lord make his face shine upon thee, and be gracious unto thee:
The Lord lift up his countenance upon thee, and give thee peace. *Numbers* vi. 24

11 Would God that all the Lord's people were prophets.
Ib. xi. 29

12 Now the man Moses was very meek, above all the men which were upon the face of the earth.
Ib. xii. 3

13 Sent to spy out the land. *Ib.* xiii. 16

14 The giants, the sons of Anak. *Ib.* 33

15 Hear now, ye rebels; must we fetch you water out of this rock? *Ib.* xx. 10

16 Smote him with the edge of the sword. *Ib.* xxi. 24

17 He whom thou blessest is blessed, and he whom thou cursest is cursed. *Ib.* xxii. 6

18 Let me die the death of the righteous, and let my last end be like his! *Ib.* xxiii. 10

19 God is not a man, that he should lie. *Ib.* 19

20 I called thee to curse mine enemies, and, behold, thou hast altogether blessed them these three times.
Ib. xxiv. 10

21 Be sure your sin will find you out. *Ib.* xxxii. 23

22 I call heaven and earth to witness against you this day. *Deuteronomy* iv. 26

23 Man doth not live by bread only, but by every word that proceedeth out of the mouth of the Lord doth man live. *Ib.* viii. 3

24 A dreamer of dreams. *Ib.* xiii. 1

25 The wife of thy bosom. *Ib.* 6

26 Thou shalt not muzzle the ox when he treadeth out the corn. *Ib.* xxv. 4

27 Cursed be he that removeth his neighbour's landmark.
Ib. xxvii. 17

28 In the morning thou shalt say, Would God it were even! and at even thou shalt say, Would God it were morning! *Ib.* xxviii. 67

29 The secret things belong unto the Lord our God.
Ib. xxix. 29

30 I have set before you life and death, blessing and cursing: therefore choose life, that both thou and thy seed may live. *Ib.* xxx. 19

31 In the waste howling wilderness.
Deuteronomy xxxii. 10

32 Jeshurun waxed fat, and kicked. *Ib.* 15

33 As thy days, so shall thy strength be. *Ib.* xxxiii. 25

34 The eternal God is thy refuge, and underneath are the everlasting arms. *Ib.* 27

35 No man knoweth of his sepulchre unto this day.
Ib. xxxiv. 6

36 As I was with Moses, so I will be with thee: I will not fail thee, nor forsake thee. *Joshua* i. 5

37 Be strong and of a good courage; be not afraid, neither be thou dismayed: for the Lord thy God is with thee, whithersoever thou goest. *Ib.* 9

38 This line of scarlet thread. *Ib.* ii. 18

39 All the Israelites passed over on dry ground.
Ib. iii. 17

40 When the people heard the sound of the trumpet, and the people shouted with a great shout, that the wall fell down flat, so that the people went up into the city. *Ib.* vi. 20

41 Hewers of wood and drawers of water. *Ib.* ix. 21

42 Sun, stand thou still upon Gibeon; and thou, Moon, in the valley of Ajalon. *Ib.* x. 12

43 Is not this written in the book of Jasher? *Ib.* 13

44 I am going the way of all the earth. *Ib.* xxiii. 14

45 He delivered them into the hands of spoilers.
Judges ii. 14

46 Then Jael Heber's wife took a nail of the tent, and took an hammer in her hand, and went softly unto him, and smote the nail into his temples, and fastened it into the ground: for he was fast asleep and weary. *Ib.* iv. 21

47 I arose a mother in Israel. *Ib.* v. 7

48 The stars in their courses fought against Sisera.
Ib. 20

49 She brought forth butter in a lordly dish. *Ib.* 25

50 At her feet he bowed, he fell, he lay down. *Ib.* 27

51 The mother of Sisera looked out at a window, and cried through the lattice, Why is his chariot so long in coming? why tarry the wheels of his chariots?
Ib. 28

52 Have they not divided the prey; to every man a damsel or two? *Ib.* 30

53 Is not the gleaning of the grapes of Ephraim better than the vintage of Abi-ezer? *Ib.* viii. 2

54 Faint, yet pursuing. *Ib.* 4

55 Out of the eater came forth meat, and out of the strong came forth sweetness. *Ib.* xiv. 14

56 If ye had not plowed with my heifer, ye had not found out my riddle. *Ib.* 18

57 He smote them hip and thigh. *Ib.* xv. 8

58 The Philistines be upon thee, Samson. *Ib.* xvi. 9

59 He wist not that the Lord was departed from him.
Ib. 20

60 He did grind in the prison house. *Ib.* 21

61 From Dan even to Beer-sheba. *Ib.* xx. 1

62 The people arose as one man. *Ib.* 8

1 Intreat me not to leave thee, or to return from following after thee: for whither thou goest, I will go; and where thou lodgest, I will lodge: thy people shall be my people, and thy God my God:
Where thou diest, will I die, and there will I be buried: the Lord do so to me, and more also, if ought but death part thee and me. *Ruth* i. 16

2 Girded with a linen ephod. *I Samuel* ii. 18

3 The flower of their age. *Ib.* 33

4 The Lord called Samuel: and he answered, Here am I. *Ib.* iii. 4

5 Here am I; for thou calledst me. And he said, I called not; lie down again. *Ib.* 5

6 Speak, Lord; for thy servant heareth. *Ib.* 9

7 The ears of every one that heareth it shall tingle. *Ib.* 11

8 Quit yourselves like men. *Ib.* iv. 9

9 He fell from off the seat backward by the side of the gate, and his neck brake. *Ib.* 18

10 I-chabod, saying, The glory is departed from Israel. *Ib.* 21

11 Is Saul also among the prophets? *Ib.* x. 11

12 God save the king. *Ib.* 24

13 A man after his own heart. *Ib.* xiii. 14

14 I did but taste a little honey with the end of the rod that was in mine hand, and, lo, I must die. *Ib.* xiv. 43

15 What meaneth then this bleating of the sheep in mine ears, and the lowing of the oxen which I hear? *Ib.* xv. 14

16 To obey is better than sacrifice, and to hearken than the fat of rams.
For rebellion is as the sin of witchcraft. *Ib.* 22

17 Agag came unto him delicately. And Agag said, Surely the bitterness of death is past. *Ib.* 32

18 For the Lord seeth not as man seeth: for man looketh on the outward appearance, but the Lord looketh on the heart. *Ib.* xvi. 7

19 Now he was ruddy, and withal of a beautiful countenance, and goodly to look to. *Ib.* 12

20 I know thy pride, and the naughtiness of thine heart. *Ib.* xvii. 28

21 Let no man's heart fail because of him [Goliath]. *Ib.* 32

22 Go, and the Lord be with thee. *Ib.* 37

23 Five smooth stones out of the brook. *Ib.* 40

24 Am I a dog, that thou comest to me with staves? *Ib.* 43

25 Saul hath slain his thousands, and David his ten thousands. *Ib.* xviii. 7

26 And Jonathan gave his artillery unto his lad. *Ib.* xx. 40

27 As saith the proverb of the ancients, Wickedness proceedeth from the wicked. *Ib.* xxiv. 13

28 I have played the fool. *Ib.* xxvi. 21

29 The beauty of Israel is slain upon thy high places: how are the mighty fallen!
Tell it not in Gath, publish it not in the streets of Askelon; lest the daughters of the Philistines rejoice, lest the daughters of the uncircumcised triumph.
Ye mountains of Gilboa, let there be no dew, neither let there be rain, upon you, nor fields of offerings: for there the shield of the mighty is vilely cast away. *2 Samuel* i. 19

30 Saul and Jonathan were lovely and pleasant in their lives, and in their death they were not divided: they were swifter than eagles, they were stronger than lions.
Ye daughters of Israel, weep over Saul, who clothed you in scarlet, with other delights, who put on ornaments of gold upon your apparel.
How are the mighty fallen in the midst of the battle! O Jonathan, thou wast slain in thine high places.
I am distressed for thee, my brother Jonathan: very pleasant hast thou been unto me: thy love to me was wonderful, passing the love of women.
How are the mighty fallen, and the weapons of war perished! *Ib.* 23

31 Smote him under the fifth rib. *Ib.* ii. 23

32 Set ye Uriah in the forefront of the hottest battle. *Ib.* xi. 15

33 The poor man had nothing, save one little ewe lamb. *Ib.* xii. 3

34 Thou art the man. *Ib.* 7

35 As water spilt on the ground, which cannot be gathered up again. *Ib.* xiv. 14

36 Come out, come out, thou bloody man, thou son of Belial. *Ib.* xvi. 7

37 Would God I had died for thee, O Absalom, my son, my son! *Ib.* xviii. 33

38 The sweet psalmist of Israel. *Ib.* xxiii. 1

39 Went in jeopardy of their lives. *Ib.* 17

40 I have somewhat to say unto thee. And she said, Say on. *I Kings* ii. 14

41 A proverb and a byword among all people. *Ib.* ix. 7

42 And when the queen of Sheba had seen all Solomon's wisdom . . . there was no more spirit in her. *Ib.* x. 4

43 Behold, the half was not told me. *Ib.* 7

44 Ivory, and apes, and peacocks. *Ib.* 22

45 But king Solomon loved many strange women. *Ib.* xi. 1

46 My little finger shall be thicker than my father's loins. *Ib.* xii. 10

47 My father hath chastised you with whips, but I will chastise you with scorpions. *Ib.* 11

48 To your tents, O Israel: now see to thine own house, David. *Ib.* 16

49 He slept with his fathers. *Ib.* xiv. 20

50 Nevertheless in the time of his old age he was diseased in his feet. *Ib.* xv. 23

51 He went and dwelt by the brook Cherith, that is before Jordan.
And the ravens brought him bread and flesh in the morning, and bread and flesh in the evening; and he drank of the brook. *Ib.* xvii. 5

1 An handful of meal in a barrel, and a little oil in a cruse. *1 Kings* xvii. 12

2 How long halt ye between two opinions? *Ib.* xviii. 21

3 He is talking, or he is pursuing, or he is in a journey, or peradventure he sleepeth, and must be awaked. *Ib.* 27

4 There is a sound of abundance of rain. *Ib.* 41

5 There ariseth a little cloud out of the sea, like a man's hand. *Ib.* 44

6 He girded up his loins, and ran before Ahab. *Ib.* 46

7 Sat down under a juniper tree. *Ib.* xix. 4

8 But the Lord was not in the wind: and after the wind an earthquake; but the Lord was not in the earthquake:
And after the earthquake a fire: but the Lord was not in the fire: and after the fire a still small voice. *Ib.* 11

9 And it shall come to pass, that him that escapeth the sword of Hazael shall Jehu slay: and him that escapeth from the sword of Jehu shall Elisha slay. *Ib.* 17

10 Elijah passed by him, and cast his mantle upon him. *Ib.* 19

11 Let not him that girdeth on his harness boast himself as he that putteth it off. *Ib.* xx. 11

12 Hast thou found me, O mine enemy? *Ib.* xxi. 20

13 I saw all Israel scattered upon the hills, as sheep that have not a shepherd. *Ib.* xxii. 17

14 Feed him with bread of affliction and with water of affliction, until I come in peace.
And Micaiah said, If thou return at all in peace, the Lord hath not spoken by me. *Ib.* 27

15 And a certain man drew a bow at a venture, and smote the king of Israel between the joints of the harness. *Ib.* 34

16 The chariot of Israel, and the horsemen thereof. *2 Kings* ii. 12

17 The spirit of Elijah doth rest on Elisha. *Ib.* 15

18 Go up, thou bald head. *Ib.* 23

19 Is it well with the child? And she answered, It is well. *Ib.* iv. 26

20 There is death in the pot. *Ib.* 40

21 He shall know that there is a prophet in Israel. *Ib.* v. 8

22 Are not Abana and Pharpar, rivers of Damascus, better than all the waters of Israel? *Ib.* 12

23 I bow myself in the house of Rimmon. *Ib.* 18

24 Whence comest thou, Gehazi? *Ib.* 25

25 Is thy servant a dog, that he should do this great thing? *Ib.* viii. 13

26 Is it peace? And Jehu said, What hast thou to do with peace? turn thee behind me. *Ib.* ix. 18

27 The driving is like the driving of Jehu, the son of Nimshi; for he driveth furiously. *Ib.* 20

28 She painted her face, and tired her head, and looked out at a window. *Ib.* 30

29 Had Zimri peace, who slew his master? *Ib.* 31

30 Who is on my side? who? *Ib.* 32

31 And he said, Throw her down. So they threw her down. *2 Kings* ix. 33

32 They found no more of her than the skull, and the feet, and the palms of her hands. *Ib.* 35

33 Thou trustest upon the staff of this bruised reed, even upon Egypt, on which if a man lean, it will go into his hand, and pierce it. *Ib.* xviii. 21

34 He died in a good old age, full of days, riches, and honour. *1 Chronicles* xxix. 28

35 Every one with one of his hands wrought in the work, and with the other hand held a weapon. *Nehemiah* iv. 17

36 The man whom the king delighteth to honour. *Esther* vi. 9

37 Behold also, the gallows fifty cubits high. *Ib.* vii. 9

38 The sons of God came to present themselves before the Lord, and Satan came also among them.
And the Lord said unto Satan, Whence comest thou? Then Satan answered the Lord, and said, From going to and fro in the earth, and from walking up and down in it. *Job* i. 6

39 Doth Job fear God for naught? *Ib.* 9

40 The Lord gave, and the Lord hath taken away; blessed be the name of the Lord. *Ib.* 21

41 All that a man hath will he give for his life. *Ib.* ii. 4

42 And he took him a potsherd to scrape himself withal. *Ib.* 8

43 Curse God, and die. *Ib.* 9

44 Let the day perish wherein I was born, and the night in which it was said, There is a man child conceived. *Ib.* iii. 3

45 For now should I have lain still and been quiet, I should have slept: then had I been at rest,
With kings and counsellors of the earth, which built desolate places for themselves. *Ib.* 13

46 There the wicked cease from troubling, and there the weary be at rest. *Ib.* 17

47 Wherefore is light given to him that is in misery, and life unto the bitter in soul? *Ib.* 20

48 Then a spirit passed before my face; the hair of my flesh stood up. *Ib.* iv. 15

49 Shall mortal man be more just than God? shall a man be more pure than his maker? *Ib.* 17

50 Man is born unto trouble, as the sparks fly upward. *Ib.* v. 7

51 He taketh the wise in their own craftiness. *Ib.* 13

52 My days are swifter than a weaver's shuttle. *Ib.* vii. 6

53 He shall return no more to his house, neither shall his place know him any more. *Ib.* 10

54 The land of darkness and the shadow of death. *Ib.* x. 21

55 A land . . . where the light is as darkness. *Ib.* 22

56 Canst thou by searching find out God? *Ib.* xi. 7

57 No doubt but ye are the people, and wisdom shall die with you. *Ib.* xii. 2

58 With the ancient is wisdom; and in length of days understanding. *Ib.* 12

1 Man that is born of a woman is of few days, and full of trouble. *Job* xiv. 1

2 Miserable comforters are ye all. *Ib.* xvi. 2

3 The king of terrors. *Ib.* xviii. 14

4 I am escaped with the skin of my teeth. *Ib.* xix. 20

5 Oh that my words were now written! oh that they were printed in a book! *Ib.* 23

6 I know that my redeemer liveth, and that he shall stand at the latter day upon the earth:
And though after my skin worms destroy this body, yet in my flesh shall I see God. *Ib.* 25

7 Seeing the root of the matter is found in me. *Ib.* 28

8 The price of wisdom is above rubies. *Ib.* xxviii. 18

9 I was eyes to the blind, and feet was I to the lame. *Ib.* xxix. 15

10 The house appointed for all living. *Ib.* xxx. 23

11 My desire is . . . that mine adversary had written a book. *Ib.* xxxi. 35

12 Great men are not always wise. *Ib.* xxxii. 9

13 For I am full of matter, the spirit within me constraineth me. *Ib.* 18

14 One among a thousand. *Ib.* xxxiii. 23

15 Far be it from God, that he should do wickedness. *Ib.* xxxiv. 10

16 He multiplieth words without knowledge. *Ib.* xxxv. 16

17 Who is this that darkeneth counsel by words without knowledge? *Ib.* xxxviii. 2

18 Gird up now thy loins like a man. *Ib.* 3

19 Where wast thou when I laid the foundations of the earth? declare, if thou hast understanding. *Ib.* 4

20 When the morning stars sang together, and all the sons of God shouted for joy. *Ib.* 7

21 Hitherto shalt thou come, but no further: and here shall thy proud waves be stayed. *Ib.* 11

22 Hast thou entered into the springs of the sea? or hast thou walked in the search of the depth? *Ib.* 16

23 Hath the rain a father? or who hath begotten the drops of dew? *Ib.* 28

24 Canst thou bind the sweet influences of Pleiades, or loose the bands of Orion? *Ib.* 31

25 Canst thou guide Arcturus with his sons? *Ib.* 32

26 He paweth in the valley, and rejoiceth in his strength: he goeth on to meet the armed men. *Ib.* xxxix. 21

27 He swalloweth the ground with fierceness and rage: neither believeth he that it is the sound of the trumpet.
He saith among the trumpets, Ha, ha; and he smelleth the battle afar off, the thunder of the captains, and the shouting. *Ib.* 24

28 Behold now behemoth, which I made with thee; he eateth grass as an ox. *Ib.* xl. 15

29 Canst thou draw out leviathan with an hook? *Ib.* xli. 1

30 Wilt thou play with him as with a bird? or wilt thou bind him for thy maidens? *Ib.* 5

31 Hard as a piece of the nether millstone. *Ib.* 24

32 He maketh the deep to boil like a pot. *Ib.* 31

33 I have heard of thee by the hearing of the ear: but now mine eye seeth thee. *Job* xlii. 5

34 So the Lord blessed the latter end of Job more than his beginning. *Ib.* 12

35 Dominus illuminatio mea.
The Lord is my light. *Psalms* xxvii. 1 (Vulgate)

36 Nisi dominus frustra.
Except the Lord keep the city the watchman waketh but in vain. *Ib.* cxxvii. 1 (Vulgate) abridged
(*Motto of the City of Edinburgh*)

For psalms in the Book of Common Prayer see Prayer Book

37 My son, if sinners entice thee, consent thou not. *Proverbs* i. 10

38 Surely in vain the net is spread in the sight of any bird. *Ib.* 17

39 Wisdom crieth without; she uttereth her voice in the streets. *Ib.* 20

40 Length of days is in her right hand; and in her left hand riches and honour. *Ib.* iii. 16

41 Her ways are ways of pleasantness, and all her paths are peace. *Ib.* 17

42 Wisdom is the principal thing; therefore get wisdom: and with all thy getting get understanding. *Ib.* iv. 7

43 The path of the just is as the shining light, that shineth more and more unto the perfect day. *Ib.* 18

44 For the lips of a strange woman drop as an honeycomb, and her mouth is smoother than oil:
But her end is bitter as wormwood, sharp as a two-edged sword. *Ib.* v. 3

45 Go to the ant, thou sluggard; consider her ways, and be wise. *Ib.* vi. 6

46 Yet a little sleep, a little slumber, a little folding of the hands to sleep. *Ib.* 10

47 So shall thy poverty come as one that travelleth, and thy want as an armed man. *Ib.* 11

48 Neither let her take thee with her eyelids. *Ib.* 25

49 Can a man take fire in his bosom, and his clothes not be burned? *Ib.* 27

50 Come, let us take our fill of love until the morning: let us solace ourselves with loves.
For the goodman is not at home, he is gone a long journey. *Ib.* vii. 18

51 As an ox goeth to the slaughter. *Ib.* 22

52 Wisdom is better than rubies. *Ib.* viii. 11

53 Stolen waters are sweet, and bread eaten in secret is pleasant. *Ib.* ix. 17

54 A wise son maketh a glad father: but a foolish son is the heaviness of his mother. *Ib.* x. 1

55 The destruction of the poor is their poverty. *Ib.* 15

56 In the multitude of counsellors there is safety. *Ib.* xi. 14

57 He that is surety for a stranger shall smart for it. *Ib.* 15

58 As a jewel of gold in a swine's snout, so is a fair woman which is without discretion. *Ib.* 22

BIBLE

1 A virtuous woman is a crown to her husband.
Proverbs xii. 4

2 A righteous man regardeth the life of his beast: but the tender mercies of the wicked are cruel. *Ib.* 10

3 Hope deferred maketh the heart sick. *Ib.* xiii. 12

4 The way of transgressors is hard. *Ib.* 15

5 The desire accomplished is sweet to the soul. *Ib.* 19

6 He that spareth his rod hateth his son. *Ib.* 24

7 The heart knoweth his own bitterness; and a stranger doth not intermeddle with his joy. *Ib.* xiv. 10

8 In all labour there is profit. *Ib.* 23

9 Righteousness exalteth a nation. *Ib.* 34

10 A soft answer turneth away wrath. *Ib.* xv. 1

11 A merry heart maketh a cheerful countenance. *Ib.* 13

12 Better is a dinner of herbs where love is, than a stalled ox and hatred therewith. *Ib.* 17

13 Better is a mess of pottage with love, than a fat ox with evil will. *Ib.* (Matthew's Bible, 1535)

14 A word spoken in due season, how good is it! *Ib.* 23

15 Pride goeth before destruction, and an haughty spirit before a fall. *Ib.* xvi. 18

16 The hoary head is a crown of glory. *Ib.* 31

17 He that is slow to anger is better than the mighty; and he that ruleth his spirit than he that taketh a city. *Ib.* 32

18 He that repeateth a matter separateth very friends. *Ib.* xvii. 9

19 He that begetteth a fool doeth it to his sorrow. *Ib.* 21

20 A merry heart doeth good like a medicine. *Ib.* 22

21 A wounded spirit who can bear? *Ib.* xviii. 14

22 There is a friend that sticketh closer than a brother. *Ib.* 24

23 Wine is a mocker, strong drink is raging. *Ib.* xx. 1

24 Every fool will be meddling. *Ib.* 3

25 Even a child is known by his doings. *Ib.* 11

26 The hearing ear, and the seeing eye. *Ib.* 12

27 It is naught, it is naught, saith the buyer: but when he is gone his way, then he boasteth. *Ib.* 14

28 It is better to dwell in a corner of the housetop, than with a brawling woman in a wide house. *Ib.* xxi. 9

29 A good name is rather to be chosen than great riches. *Ib.* xxii. 1

30 Train up a child in the way he should go: and when he is old, he will not depart from it. *Ib.* 6

31 Riches certainly make themselves wings. *Ib.* xxiii. 5

32 Look not thou upon the wine when it is red, when it giveth his colour in the cup, . . .
At the last it biteth like a serpent, and stingeth like an adder. *Ib.* 31

33 The heart of kings is unsearchable. *Ib.* xxv. 3

34 A word fitly spoken is like apples of gold in pictures of silver. *Ib.* 11

35 Heap coals of fire upon his head. *Ib.* 22

36 As cold waters to a thirsty soul, so is good news from a far country. *Ib.* 25

37 As the bird by wandering, as the swallow by flying, so the curse causeless shall not come.
Proverbs xxvi. 2

38 Answer a fool according to his folly. *Ib.* 5

39 As a dog returneth to his vomit, so a fool returneth to his folly. *Ib.* 11

40 Seest thou a man wise in his own conceit? There is more hope of a fool than of him. *Ib.* 12

41 The slothful man saith, There is a lion in the way: a lion is in the streets. *Ib.* 13

42 The sluggard is wiser in his own conceit than seven men that can render a reason. *Ib.* 16

43 Boast not thyself of to morrow; for thou knowest not what a day may bring forth. *Ib.* xxvii. 1

44 Open rebuke is better than secret love. *Ib.* 5

45 Faithful are the wounds of a friend. *Ib.* 6

46 A continual dropping in a very rainy day and a contentious woman are alike. *Ib.* 15

47 Iron sharpeneth iron; so a man sharpeneth the countenance of his friend. *Ib.* 17

48 Though thou shouldest bray a fool in a mortar among wheat with a pestle, yet will not his foolishness depart from him. *Ib.* 22

49 The wicked flee when no man pursueth: but the righteous are bold as a lion. *Ib.* xxviii. 1

50 He that maketh haste to be rich shall not be innocent. *Ib.* 20

51 A fool uttereth all his mind. *Ib.* xxix. 11

52 Where there is no vision, the people perish. *Ib.* 18

53 Give me neither poverty nor riches. *Ib.* xxx. 8

54 The horseleach hath two daughters, crying, Give, give. *Ib.* 15

55 There are three things that are never satisfied, yea, four things say not, It is enough:
The grave; and the barren womb; the earth that is not filled with water; and the fire that saith not, It is enough. *Ib.*

56 The way of an eagle in the air; the way of a serpent upon a rock; the way of a ship in the midst of the sea; and the way of a man with a maid. *Ib.* 19

57 Who can find a virtuous woman? for her price is far above rubies. *Ib.* xxxi. 10

58 Her children arise up, and call her blessed. *Ib.* 28

59 Vanity of vanities, saith the Preacher, vanity of vanities; all is vanity.
What profit hath a man of all his labour which he taketh under the sun?
One generation passeth away, and another generation cometh. *Ecclesiastes* i. 2

60 All the rivers run into the sea; yet the sea is not full. *Ib.* 7

61 All things are full of labour; man cannot utter it: the eye is not satisfied with seeing, nor the ear filled with hearing.
The thing that hath been, it is that which shall be; and that which is done is that which shall be done: and there is no new thing under the sun. *Ib.* 8

62 All is vanity and vexation of spirit. *Ib.* 14

63 He that increaseth knowledge increaseth sorrow. *Ib.* 18

1 Wisdom excelleth folly, as far as light excelleth dark-ness. *Ecclesiastes* ii. 13

2 One event happeneth to them all. *Ib.* 14

3 To every thing there is a season, and a time to every purpose under the heaven:
A time to be born, and a time to die. *Ib.* iii. 1

4 Wherefore I praised the dead which are already dead more than the living which are yet alive. *Ib.* iv. 2

5 A threefold cord is not quickly broken. *Ib.* 12

6 God is in heaven, and thou upon earth: therefore let thy words be few. *Ib.* v. 2

7 Better is it that thou shouldest not vow, than that thou shouldest vow and not pay. *Ib.* 5

8 The sleep of a labouring man is sweet. *Ib.* 12

9 A good name is better than precious ointment; and the day of death than the day of one's birth.
It is better to go to the house of mourning, than to go to the house of feasting. *Ib.* vii. 1

10 As the crackling of thorns under a pot, so is the laughter of a fool. *Ib.* 6

11 Better is the end of a thing than the beginning thereof. *Ib.* 8

12 Say not thou, What is the cause that the former days were better than these? for thou dost not enquire wisely concerning this. *Ib.* 10

13 In the day of prosperity be joyful, but in the day of adversity consider. *Ib.* 14

14 Be not righteous over much. *Ib.* 16

15 One man among a thousand have I found; but a woman among all those have I not found. *Ib.* 28

16 God hath made man upright; but they have sought out many inventions. *Ib.* 29

17 There is no discharge in that war. *Ib.* viii. 8

18 A man hath no better thing under the sun, than to eat, and to drink, and to be merry. *Ib.* 15

19 A living dog is better than a dead lion. *Ib.* ix. 4

20 Go thy way, eat thy bread with joy, and drink thy wine with a merry heart; for God now accepteth thy works. *Ib.* 7

21 Whatsoever thy hand findeth to do, do it with thy might; for there is no work, nor device, nor know-ledge, nor wisdom, in the grave, whither thou goest. *Ib.* 10

22 The race is not to the swift, nor the battle to the strong. *Ib.* 11

23 Dead flies cause the ointment of the apothecary to send forth a stinking savour. *Ib.* x. 1

24 He that diggeth a pit shall fall into it. *Ib.* 8

25 Wine maketh merry: but money answereth all things. *Ib.* 19

26 For a bird of the air shall carry the voice, and that which hath wings shall tell the matter. *Ib.* 20

27 Cast thy bread upon the waters: for thou shalt find it after many days. *Ib.* xi. 1

28 In the place where the tree falleth, there it shall be. *Ib.* 3

29 He that observeth the wind shall not sow; and he that regardeth the clouds shall not reap. *Ib.* 4

30 In the morning sow thy seed, and in the evening withhold not thine hand. *Ecclesiastes* xi. 6

31 Truly the light is sweet, and a pleasant thing it is for the eyes to behold the sun. *Ib.* 7

32 Rejoice, O young man, in thy youth; and let thy heart cheer thee in the days of thy youth. *Ib.* 9

33 Remember now thy Creator in the days of thy youth, while the evil days come not, nor the years draw nigh, when thou shalt say, I have no pleasure in them;
While the sun, or the light, or the moon, or the stars, be not darkened, nor the clouds return after the rain:
In the day when the keepers of the house shall tremble, and the strong men shall bow themselves, and the grinders cease because they are few, and those that look out of the windows be darkened,
And the doors shall be shut in the streets, when the sound of the grinding is low, and he shall rise up at the voice of the bird, and all the daughters of musick shall be brought low;
Also when they shall be afraid of that which is high, and fears shall be in the way, and the almond tree shall flourish, and the grasshopper shall be a burden, and desire shall fail: because man goeth to his long home, and the mourners go about the streets:
Or ever the silver cord be loosed, or the golden bowl be broken, or the pitcher be broken at the fountain, or the wheel broken at the cistern.
Then shall the dust return to the earth as it was: and the spirit shall return unto God who gave it. *Ib.* xii. 1

34 The words of the wise are as goads. *Ib.* 11

35 Of making many books there is no end; and much study is a weariness of the flesh. *Ib.* 12

36 Fear God, and keep his commandments: for this is the whole duty of man.
For God shall bring every work into judgment, with every secret thing, whether it be good, or whether it be evil. *Ib.* 13

37 The song of songs, which is Solomon's.
Let him kiss me with the kisses of his mouth: for thy love is better than wine. *The Song of Solomon* i. 1

38 Thy name is an ointment poured forth, therefore do the virgins love thee. *Ib.* 3

39 I am black, but comely, O ye daughters of Jerusalem, as the tents of Kedar, as the curtains of Solomon. *Ib.* 5

40 Tell me, O thou whom my soul loveth, where thou feedest, where thou makest thy flock to rest at noon. *Ib.* 7

41 O thou fairest among women. *Ib.* 8

42 A bundle of myrrh is my wellbeloved unto me; he shall lie all night betwixt my breasts. *Ib.* 13

43 I am the rose of Sharon, and the lily of the valleys. *Ib.* ii. 1

44 His banner over me was love. *Ib.* 4

45 Stay me with flagons, comfort me with apples: for I am sick of love.
His left hand is under my head, and his right hand doth embrace me. *Ib.* 5

1 Rise up, my love, my fair one, and come away.
For, lo, the winter is past, the rain is over and gone;
The flowers appear on the earth; the time of the singing of birds is come, and the voice of the turtle is heard in our land. *The Song of Solomon* ii. 10

2 Take us the foxes, the little foxes, that spoil the vines. *Ib.* 15

3 My beloved is mine, and I am his: he feedeth among the lilies.
Until the day break, and the shadows flee away. *Ib.* 16

4 By night on my bed I sought him whom my soul loveth. *Ib.* iii. 1

5 Behold, thou art fair, my love; behold, thou art fair; thou hast doves' eyes within thy locks: thy hair is as a flock of goats, that appear from mount Gilead.
Thy teeth are like a flock of sheep that are even shorn, which came up from the washing; whereof every one bear twins, and none is barren among them.
Thy lips are like a thread of scarlet, and thy speech is comely: thy temples are like a piece of a pomegranate within thy locks.
Thy neck is like the tower of David builded for an armoury, whereon there hang a thousand bucklers, all shields of mighty men.
Thy breasts are like two young roes that are twins, which feed among the lilies. *Ib.* iv. 1

6 Thou art all fair, my love; there is no spot in thee. *Ib.* 7

7 A garden inclosed is my sister, my spouse; a spring shut up, a fountain sealed. *Ib.* 12

8 Awake, O north wind; and come, thou south; blow upon my garden, that the spices thereof may flow out. Let my beloved come into his garden, and eat his pleasant fruits. *Ib.* 16

9 I sleep, but my heart waketh: it is the voice of my beloved that knocketh, saying, Open to me, my sister, my love, my dove, my undefiled. *Ib.* v. 2

10 My beloved put in his hand by the hole of the door, and my bowels were moved for him. *Ib.* 4

11 I opened to my beloved; but my beloved had withdrawn himself. *Ib.* 6

12 The watchmen that went about the city found me, they smote me, they wounded me; the keepers of the walls took away my veil from me.
I charge you, O daughters of Jerusalem, if ye find my beloved, that ye tell him, that I am sick of love.
What is thy beloved more than another beloved, O thou fairest among women? *Ib.* 7

13 My beloved is white and ruddy, the chiefest among ten thousand. *Ib.* 10

14 His hands are as gold rings set with the beryl: his belly is as bright ivory overlaid with sapphires.
His legs are as pillars of marble, set upon sockets of fine gold: his countenance is as Lebanon, excellent as the cedars.
His mouth is most sweet: yea, he is altogether lovely. This is my beloved, and this is my friend, O daughters of Jerusalem. *Ib.* 14

15 Who is she that looketh forth as the morning, fair as the moon, clear as the sun, and terrible as an army with banners? *Ib.* vi. 10

16 Return, return, O Shulamite; return, return, that we may look upon thee. *The Song of Solomon* vi. 13

17 How beautiful are thy feet with shoes, O prince's daughter! *Ib.* vii. 1

18 Thy navel is like a round goblet, which wanteth not liquor: thy belly is like an heap of wheat set about with lilies. *Ib.* 2

19 Thy neck is as a tower of ivory; thine eyes like the fishpools in Heshbon, by the gate of Bath-rabbim: thy nose is as the tower of Lebanon which looketh toward Damascus. *Ib.* 4

20 Like the best wine, for my beloved, that goeth down sweetly, causing the lips of those that are asleep to speak. *Ib.* 9

21 O that thou wert as my brother, that sucked the breasts of my mother! when I should find thee without, I would kiss thee; yea, I should not be despised.
I would lead thee, and bring thee into my mother's house. *Ib.* viii. 1

22 Who is this that cometh up from the wilderness, leaning upon her beloved? I raised thee up under the apple tree: there thy mother brought thee forth: there she brought thee forth that bare thee.
Set me as a seal upon thine heart, as a seal upon thine arm: for love is strong as death; jealousy is cruel as the grave. *Ib.* 5

23 Many waters cannot quench love, neither can the floods drown it: if a man would give all the substance of his house for love, it would utterly be contemned. *Ib.* 7

24 We have a little sister, and she hath no breasts. *Ib.* 8

25 Make haste, my beloved, and be thou like to a roe or to a young hart upon the mountain of spices. *Ib.* 14

26 The ox knoweth his owner, and the ass his master's crib. *Isaiah* i. 3

27 The whole head is sick, and the whole heart faint. *Ib.* 5

28 As a lodge in a garden of cucumbers. *Ib.* 8

29 Bring no more vain oblations; incense is an abomination unto me; the new moons and sabbaths, the calling of assemblies, I cannot away with. *Ib.* 13

30 Though your sins be as scarlet, they shall be as white as snow. *Ib.* 18

31 They shall beat their swords into plowshares, and their spears into pruninghooks: nation shall not lift up sword against nation, neither shall they learn war any more. *Ib.* ii. 4

32 Cease ye from man, whose breath is in his nostrils. *Ib.* 22

33 The stay and the staff, the whole stay of bread, and the whole stay of water. *Ib.* iii. 1

34 Grind the faces of the poor. *Ib.* 15

35 Walk with stretched forth necks and wanton eyes, walking and mincing as they go, and making a tinkling with their feet. *Ib.* 16

36 In that day seven women shall take hold of one man. *Ib.* iv. 1

37 My wellbeloved hath a vineyard in a very fruitful hill. *Ib.* v. 1

1 And he looked that it should bring forth grapes, and it brought forth wild grapes. *Isaiah* v. 2

2 And he looked for judgment, but behold oppression; for righteousness, but behold a cry. *Ib.* 7

3 Woe unto them that join house to house, that lay field to field, till there be no place. *Ib.* 8

4 Woe unto them that rise up early in the morning, that they may follow strong drink. *Ib.* 11

5 Woe, woe unto them that draw iniquity with cords of vanity, and sin as it were with a cart rope. *Ib.* 18

6 Woe unto them that call evil good, and good evil. *Ib.* 20

7 For all this his anger is not turned away, but his hand is stretched out still. *Ib.* 25

8 In the year that king Uzziah died I saw also the Lord sitting upon a throne, high and lifted up, and his train filled the temple.
Above it stood the seraphims: each one had six wings; with twain he covered his face, and with twain he covered his feet, and with twain he did fly.
And one cried unto another, and said, Holy, holy, holy, is the Lord of hosts: the whole earth is full of his glory.
And the posts of the door moved at the voice of him that cried, and the house was filled with smoke.
Then said I, Woe is me! for I am undone; because I am a man of unclean lips, and I dwell in the midst of a people of unclean lips. *Ib.* vi. 1

9 Whom shall I send, and who will go for us? Then said I, Here am I; send me. *Ib.* 8

10 Make the heart of this people fat, and make their ears heavy, and shut their eyes; lest they see with their eyes, and hear with their ears, and understand with their heart, and convert, and be healed. *Ib.* 10.

11 Then said I, Lord, how long? *Ib.* 11

12 Behold, a virgin shall conceive, and bear a son, and shall call his name Immanuel.
Butter and honey shall he eat, that he may know to refuse the evil, and choose the good. *Ib.* vii. 14

13 For a stone of stumbling and for a rock of offence. *Ib.* viii. 14

14 The people that walked in darkness have seen a great light: they that dwell in the land of the shadow of death, upon them hath the light shined.
Thou hast multiplied the nation, and not increased the joy: they joy before thee according to the joy in harvest, and as men rejoice when they divide the spoil. *Ib.* ix. 2

15 For unto us a child is born, unto us a son is given: and the government shall be upon his shoulder: and his name shall be called Wonderful, Counsellor, The mighty God, The everlasting Father, The Prince of Peace.
Of the increase of his government and peace there shall be no end. *Ib.* 6

16 The zeal of the Lord of hosts will perform this. *Ib.* 7

17 And there shall come forth a rod out of the stem of Jesse, and a Branch shall grow out of his roots:
And the spirit of the Lord shall rest upon him, the spirit of wisdom and understanding, the spirit of counsel and might, the spirit of knowledge and of the fear of the Lord. *Isaiah* xi. 1

18 The wolf also shall dwell with the lamb, and the leopard shall lie down with the kid; and the calf and the young lion and the fatling together; and a little child shall lead them. *Ib.* 6

19 And the lion shall eat straw like the ox.
And the sucking child shall play on the hole of the asp, and the weaned child shall put his hand on the cockatrice' den.
They shall not hurt nor destroy in all my holy mountain: for the earth shall be full of the knowledge of the Lord, as the waters cover the sea. *Ib.* 7

20 Dragons in their pleasant palaces. *Ib.* xiii. 22

21 Hell from beneath is moved for thee to meet thee at thy coming. *Ib.* xiv. 9

22 How art thou fallen from heaven, O Lucifer, son of the morning! *Ib.* 12

23 I will also make it a possession for the bittern, and pools of water: and I will sweep it with the besom of destruction. *Ib.* 23

24 And in mercy shall the throne be established. *Ib.* xvi. 5

25 The burden of the desert of the sea. *Ib.* xxi. 1

26 Watchman, what of the night? Watchman, what of the night?
The watchman said, The morning cometh, and also the night. *Ib.* 11

27 Let us eat and drink; for to morrow we shall die. *Ib.* xxii. 13

28 Fasten him as a nail in a sure place. *Ib.* 23

29 Whose merchants are princes. *Ib.* xxiii. 8

30 Howl, ye ships of Tarshish. *Ib.* 14

31 A feast of fat things, a feast of wines on the lees. *Ib.* xxv. 6

32 We have as it were brought forth wind. *Ib.* xxvi. 18

33 For precept must be upon precept, precept upon precept; line upon line, line upon line; here a little, and there a little. *Ib.* xxviii. 10

34 We have made a covenant with death, and with hell are we at agreement. *Ib.* 15

35 They are drunken, but not with wine. *Ib.* xxix. 9

36 Their strength is to sit still. *Ib.* xxx. 7

37 Now go, write it before them in a table, and note it in a book. *Ib.* 8

38 Speak unto us smooth things, prophesy deceits. *Ib.* 10

39 In quietness and in confidence shall be your strength. *Ib.* 15

40 One thousand shall flee at the rebuke of one. *Ib.* 17

41 The bread of adversity. *Ib.* 20

42 This is the way, walk ye in it. *Ib.* 21

43 And a man shall be as an hiding place from the wind, and a covert from the tempest; as rivers of water in a dry place, as the shadow of a great rock in a weary land. *Ib.* xxxii. 2

44 The liberal deviseth liberal things. *Ib.* 8

45 An habitation of dragons, and a court for owls. *Ib.* xxxiv. 13

1 The wilderness and the solitary place shall be glad for them; and the desert shall rejoice, and blossom as the rose. *Isaiah xxxv. 1*

2 Strengthen ye the weak hands, and confirm the feeble knees. *Ib. 3*

3 Then shall the lame man leap as an hart, and the tongue of the dumb sing: for in the wilderness shall waters break out, and streams in the desert. *Ib. 6*

4 The wayfaring men, though fools, shall not err therein. *Ib. 8*

5 Sorrow and sighing shall flee away. *Ib. 10*

6 Set thine house in order. *Ib. xxxviii. 1*

7 I shall go softly all my years in the bitterness of my soul. *Ib. 15*

8 Comfort ye, comfort ye my people, saith your God. Speak ye comfortably to Jerusalem, and cry unto her, that her warfare is accomplished. *Ib. xl. 1*

9 The voice of him that crieth in the wilderness, Prepare ye the way of the Lord, make straight in the desert a highway for our God.
Every valley shall be exalted, and every mountain and hill shall be made low: and the crooked shall be made straight, and the rough places plain:
And the glory of the Lord shall be revealed, and all flesh shall see it together: for the mouth of the Lord hath spoken it. *Ib. 3*

10 The voice said, Cry. And he said, What shall I cry? All flesh is grass, and all the goodliness thereof is as the flower of the field:
The grass withereth, the flower fadeth: because the spirit of the Lord bloweth upon it: surely the people is grass. *Ib. 6*

11 He shall feed his flock like a shepherd: he shall gather the lambs with his arm, and carry them in his bosom, and shall gently lead those that are with young. *Ib. 11*

12 The nations are as a drop of a bucket, and are counted as the small dust of the balance: behold, he taketh up the isles as a very little thing. *Ib. 15*

13 Have ye not known? have ye not heard? hath it not been told you from the beginning? *Ib. 21*

14 But they that wait upon the Lord shall renew their strength: they shall mount up with wings as eagles; they shall run, and not be weary; and they shall walk, and not faint. *Ib. 31*

15 A bruised reed shall he not break, and the smoking flax shall he not quench. *Ib. xlii. 3*

16 He warmeth himself, and saith, Aha, I am warm, I have seen the fire. *Ib. xliv. 16*

17 Shall the clay say to him that fashioneth it, What makest thou? *Ib. xlv. 9*

18 Verily thou art a God that hidest thyself. *Ib. 15*

19 I have chosen thee in the furnace of affliction. *Ib. xlviii. 10*

20 O that thou hadst hearkened to my commandments! then had thy peace been as a river, and thy righteousness as the waves of the sea. *Ib. 18*

21 There is no peace, saith the Lord, unto the wicked. *Ib. 22*

22 How beautiful upon the mountains are the feet of him that bringeth good tidings, that publisheth peace; that bringeth good tidings of good, that publisheth salvation; that saith unto Zion, Thy God reigneth! *Isaiah lii. 7*

23 For they shall see eye to eye, when the Lord shall bring again Zion.
Break forth into joy, sing together, ye waste places of Jerusalem: for the Lord hath comforted his people, he hath redeemed Jerusalem. *Ib. 8*

24 Who hath believed our report? and to whom is the arm of the Lord revealed? *Ib. liii. 1*

25 He hath no form nor comeliness; and when we shall see him, there is no beauty that we should desire him.
He is despised and rejected of men; a man of sorrows, and acquainted with grief: and we hid as it were our faces from him; he was despised, and we esteemed him not.
Surely he hath borne our griefs, and carried our sorrows. *Ib. 2*

26 But he was wounded for our transgressions, he was bruised for our iniquities: the chastisement of our peace was upon him; and with his stripes we are healed.
All we like sheep have gone astray; we have turned every one to his own way; and the Lord hath laid on him the iniquity of us all.
He was oppressed, and he was afflicted, yet he opened not his mouth: he is brought as a lamb to the slaughter, and as a sheep before her shearers is dumb, so he openeth not his mouth. *Ib. 5*

27 He was cut off out of the land of the living. *Ib. 8*

28 He was numbered with the transgressors; and he bare the sin of many, and made intercession for the transgressors. *Ib. 12*

29 Ho, every one that thirsteth, come ye to the waters, and he that hath no money; come ye, buy, and eat; yea, come, buy wine and milk without money and without price.
Wherefore do ye spend money for that which is not bread? and your labour for that which satisfieth not? *Ib. lv. 1*

30 Seek ye the Lord while he may be found, call ye upon him while he is near. *Ib. 6*

31 For my thoughts are not your thoughts, neither are your ways my ways, saith the Lord. *Ib. 8*

32 Instead of the thorn shall come up the fir tree, and instead of the brier shall come up the myrtle tree. *Ib. 13*

33 I will give them an everlasting name, that shall not be cut off. *Ib. lvi. 5*

34 Peace to him that is far off, and to him that is near. *Ib. lvii. 19*

35 Is it such a fast that I have chosen? a day for a man to afflict his soul? *Ib. lviii. 5*

36 Is not this the fast that I have chosen? to loose the bands of wickedness, to undo the heavy burdens, and to let the oppressed go free, and that ye break every yoke? *Ib. 6*

37 Then shall thy light break forth as the morning, and thine health shall spring forth speedily. *Ib. 8*

38 They make haste to shed innocent blood. *Ib. lix. 7*

39 Arise, shine; for thy light is come, and the glory of the Lord is risen upon thee. *Ib. lx. 1*

1 A little one shall become a thousand, and a small one a strong nation. *Isaiah* lx. 22

2 The Spirit of the Lord God is upon me. *Ib.* lxi. 1

3 To bind up the brokenhearted, to proclaim liberty to the captives, and the opening of the prison to them that are bound;
To proclaim the acceptable year of the Lord, and the day of vengeance of our God; to comfort all that mourn. *Ib.* 1

4 To give unto them beauty for ashes, the oil of joy for mourning, the garment of praise for the spirit of heaviness. *Ib.* 3

5 Who is this that cometh from Edom, with dyed garments from Bozrah? *Ib.* lxiii. 1

6 I have trodden the winepress alone. *Ib.* 3

7 In all their affliction he was afflicted. *Ib.* 9

8 All our righteousnesses are as filthy rags; and we all do fade as a leaf. *Ib.* lxiv. 6

9 For, behold, I create new heavens and a new earth. *Ib.* lxv. 17

10 As one whom his mother comforteth, so will I comfort you. *Ib.* lxvi. 13

11 They were as fed horses in the morning: every one neighed after his neighbour's wife. *Jeremiah* v. 8

12 This people hath a revolting and a rebellious heart. *Ib.* 23

13 The prophets prophesy falsely, and the priests bear rule by their means; and my people love to have it so: and what will ye do in the end thereof? *Ib.* 31

14 Saying, Peace, peace; when there is no peace. *Ib.* vi. 14

15 Do they provoke me to anger? saith the Lord: do they not provoke themselves to the confusion of their own faces? *Ib.* vii. 19

16 The harvest is past, the summer is ended, and we are not saved. *Ib.* viii. 20

17 Is there no balm in Gilead? *Ib.* 22

18 Can the Ethiopian change his skin, or the leopard his spots? *Ib.* xiii. 23

19 A man of strife and a man of contention. *Ib.* xv. 10

20 The heart is deceitful above all things, and desperately wicked. *Ib.* xvii. 9

21 As the partridge sitteth on eggs, and hatcheth them not. *Ib.* 11

22 And seekest thou great things for thyself? seek them not. *Ib.* xlv. 5

23 Is it nothing to you, all ye that pass by? behold, and see if there be any sorrow like unto my sorrow. *Lamentations* i. 12

24 The wormwood and the gall. *Ib.* iii. 19

25 It is good for a man that he bear the yoke in his youth. *Ib.* 27

26 He giveth his cheek to him that smiteth him. *Ib.* 30

27 As if a wheel had been in the midst of a wheel. *Ezekiel* x. 10

28 As is the mother, so is her daughter. *Ib.* xvi. 44

29 The fathers have eaten sour grapes, and the children's teeth are set on edge. *Ib.* xviii. 2

30 When the wicked man turneth away from his wickedness that he hath committed, and doeth that which is lawful and right, he shall save his soul alive. *Ezekiel* xviii. 27

31 The king of Babylon stood at the parting of the way. *Ib.* xxi. 21

32 She doted upon the Assyrians her neighbours, captains and rulers clothed most gorgeously, horsemen riding upon horses, all of them desirable young men. *Ib.* xxiii. 12

33 The valley which was full of bones. *Ib.* xxxvii. 1

34 Can these bones live? *Ib.* 3

35 The image that Nebuchadnezzar the king had set up. *Daniel* iii. 3

36 The sound of the cornet, flute, harp, sackbut, psaltery, dulcimer, and all kinds of musick. *Ib.* 5

37 Cast into the midst of a burning fiery furnace. *Ib.* 6

38 We are not careful to answer thee in this matter. *Ib.* 16

39 Commanded that they should heat the furnace one seven times more than it was wont to be heated. *Ib.* 19

40 Then these men were bound in their coats, their hosen, and their hats, and their other garments, and were cast into the midst of the burning fiery furnace. *Ib.* 21

41 Shadrach, Meshach, and Abed-nego, ye servants of the most high God, come forth, and come hither. *Ib.* 26

42 MENE, MENE, TEKEL, UPHARSIN.
This is the interpretation of the thing: MENE; God hath numbered thy kingdom, and finished it.
TEKEL; Thou art weighed in the balances, and art found wanting.
PERES; Thy kingdom is divided, and given to the Medes and Persians. *Ib.* v. 25

43 The Ancient of days. *Ib.* vii. 9

44 O Daniel, a man greatly beloved. *Ib.* x. 11

45 Many shall run to and fro, and knowledge shall be increased. *Ib.* xii. 4

46 They have sown the wind, and they shall reap the whirlwind. *Hosea* viii. 7

47 Ye have plowed wickedness, ye have reaped iniquity. *Ib.* x. 13

48 I drew them . . . with bands of love. *Ib.* xi. 4

49 I have multiplied visions, and used similitudes. *Ib.* xii. 10

50 That which the palmerworm hath left hath the locust eaten. *Joel* i. 4

51 I will restore to you the years that the locust hath eaten. *Ib.* ii. 25

52 And it shall come to pass afterward, that I will pour out my spirit upon all flesh; and your sons and your daughters shall prophesy, your old men shall dream dreams, your young men shall see visions. *Ib.* 28

53 Multitudes in the valley of decision. *Ib.* iii. 14

54 Can two walk together, except they be agreed? *Amos* iii. 3

55 Shall there be evil in a city, and the Lord hath not done it? *Ib.* 6

1 A firebrand plucked out of the burning. *Amos* iv. 11

2 Woe to them that are at ease in Zion. *Ib.* vi. 1

3 The Lord stood upon a wall made by a plumbline, with a plumbline in his hand.
And the Lord said unto me, Amos, what seest thou? And I said, A plumbline. *Ib.* vii. 7

4 Come, and let us cast lots, that we may know for whose cause this evil is upon us. So they cast lots, and the lot fell upon Jonah. *Jonah* i. 7

5 Jonah was in the belly of the fish three days and three nights. *Ib.* 17

6 They shall sit every man under his vine and under his fig tree. *Micah* iv. 4

7 But thou, Beth-lehem Ephratah, though thou be little among the thousands of Judah, yet out of thee shall he come forth unto me that is to be ruler in Israel. *Ib.* v. 2

8 What doth the Lord require of thee, but to do justly, and to love mercy, and to walk humbly with thy God? *Ib.* vi. 8

9 Write the vision, and make it plain upon tables, that he may run that readeth it. *Habakkuk* ii. 2

10 Your fathers, where are they? And the prophets, do they live for ever? *Zechariah* i. 5

11 For who hath despised the day of small things? *Ib.* iv. 10

12 Turn you to the strong hold, ye prisoners of hope. *Ib.* ix. 12

13 I was wounded in the house of my friends. *Ib.* xiii. 6

14 Have we not all one father? hath not one God created us? *Malachi* ii. 10

15 But unto you that fear my name shall the Sun of righteousness arise with healing in his wings. *Ib.* iv. 2

Apocrypha

16 The first wrote, Wine is the strongest.
The second wrote, The king is strongest.
The third wrote, Women are strongest: but above all things Truth beareth away the victory. *I Esdras* iii. 10

17 Great is Truth, and mighty above all things. *Ib.* iv. 41

18 I shall light a candle of understanding in thine heart, which shall not be put out. *2 Esdras* xiv. 25

19 Magna est veritas et praevalet.
Great is truth and it prevails. *3 Esdras* iv. 41 (Vulgate)

20 The holy spirit of discipline. *The Wisdom of Solomon* i. 5

21 The ear of jealousy heareth all things. *Ib.* 10

22 Through envy of the devil came death into the world. *Ib.* ii. 24

23 But the souls of the righteous are in the hand of God, and there shall no torment touch them.
In the sight of the unwise they seemed to die: and their departure is taken for misery,
And their going from us to be utter destruction: but they are in peace.

For though they be punished in the sight of men, yet is their hope full of immortality.
And having been a little chastised, they shall be greatly rewarded: for God proved them, and found them worthy for himself. *The Wisdom of Solomon* iii. 1

24 And in the time of their visitation they shall shine, and run to and fro like sparks among the stubble. *Ib.* 7

25 Even so we in like manner, as soon as we were born, began to draw to our end. *Ib.* v. 13

26 Passeth away as the remembrance of a guest that tarrieth but a day. *Ib.* 14

27 O Lord, thou lover of souls. *Ib.* xi. 26

28 For men, serving either calamity or tyranny, did ascribe unto stones and stocks the incommunicable name. *Ib.* xiv. 21

29 My son, if thou come to serve the Lord, prepare thy soul for temptation. *Ecclesiasticus* ii. 1

30 For the Lord is full of compassion and mercy, long-suffering, and very pitiful, and forgiveth sins, and saveth in time of affliction. *Ib.* 11

31 We will fall into the hands of the Lord, and not into the hands of men: for as his majesty is, so is his mercy. *Ib.* 18

32 Be not curious in unnecessary matters: for more things are shewed unto thee than men understand. *Ib.* iii. 23

33 For if he curse thee in the bitterness of his soul, his prayer shall be heard of him that made him. *Ib.* iv. 6

34 Woe to him that is alone when he falleth, for he hath not another to help him up. *Ib.* 10

35 Be not ignorant of any thing in a great matter or a small. *Ib.* v. 15

36 A faithful friend is the medicine of life. *Ib.* vi. 16

37 Miss not the discourse of the elders. *Ib.* viii. 9

38 Open not thine heart to every man. *Ib.* 19

39 Give not thy soul unto a woman. *Ib.* ix. 2

40 Forsake not an old friend; for the new is not comparable to him; a new friend is as new wine; when it is old, thou shalt drink it with pleasure. *Ib.* 10

41 Many kings have sat down upon the ground; and one that was never thought of hath worn the crown. *Ib.* xi. 5

42 Judge none blessed before his death. *Ib.* 28

43 He that toucheth pitch shall be defiled therewith. *Ib.* xiii. 1

44 For how agree the kettle and the earthen pot together? *Ib.* 2

45 They received the use of the five operations of the Lord, and in the sixth place he imparted them understanding, and in the seventh speech, an interpreter of the cogitations thereof. *Ib.* xvii. 5

46 Be not made a beggar by banqueting upon borrowing. *Ib.* xviii. 33

47 He that contemneth small things shall fall by little and little. *Ib.* xix. 1

48 If thou hast heard a word, let it die with thee; and be bold, it will not burst thee. *Ib.* 10

1 All wickedness is but little to the wickedness of a woman. *Ecclesiasticus* xxv. 19

2 Neither [give] a wicked woman liberty to gad abroad. *Ib.* 25

3 The stroke of the tongue breaketh the bones. Many have fallen by the edge of the sword: but not so many as have fallen by the tongue. *Ib.* xxviii. 17

4 And weigh thy words in a balance, and make a door and bar for thy mouth. *Ib.* 25

5 Envy and wrath shorten the life. *Ib.* xxx. 24

6 Leave off first for manners' sake. *Ib.* xxxi. 17

7 Let thy speech be short, comprehending much in few words. *Ib.* xxxii. 8

8 Leave not a stain in thine honour. *Ib.* xxxiii. 22

9 Honour a physician with the honour due unto him for the uses which ye may have of him: for the Lord hath created him. *Ib.* xxxviii. 1

10 For of the most High cometh healing. *Ib.* 2

11 The wisdom of a learned man cometh by opportunity of leisure: and he that hath little business shall become wise. *Ib.* 24

12 How can he get wisdom . . . whose talk is of bullocks. *Ib.* 25

13 They will maintain the state of the world, and all their desire is in the work of their craft. *Ib.* 34

14 Let us now praise famous men, and our fathers that begat us. *Ib.* xliv. 1

15 Such as did bear rule in their kingdoms. *Ib.* 3

16 Such as found out musical tunes, and recited verses in writing: Rich men furnished with ability, living peaceably in their habitations. *Ib.* 5

17 There be of them, that have left a name behind them. *Ib.* 8

18 And some there be, which have no memorial. *Ib.* 9

19 Their bodies are buried in peace; but their name liveth for evermore. *Ib.* 14

20 It is a foolish thing to make a long prologue, and to be short in the story itself. *2 Maccabees* ii. 32

21 When he was at the last gasp. *Ib.* vii. 9

22 It was an holy and good thought. *Ib.* xii. 45

New Testament

23 There came wise men from the east to Jerusalem, Saying, Where is he that is born King of the Jews? for we have seen his star in the east, and are come to worship him. *St. Matthew* ii. 1

24 They presented unto him gifts; gold, and frankincense, and myrrh. *Ib.* 11

25 They departed into their own country another way. *Ib.* 12

26 Rachel weeping for her children, and would not be comforted, because they are not. *Ib.* 18

27 Repent ye: for the kingdom of heaven is at hand. *Ib.* iii. 2

28 The voice of one crying in the wilderness, Prepare ye the way of the Lord, make his paths straight. *Ib.* 3

29 Raiment of camel's hair, and a leathern girdle about his loins; and his meat was locusts and wild honey. *St. Matthew* iii. 4

30 O generation of vipers, who hath warned you to flee from the wrath to come? *Ib.* 7

31 And now also the axe is laid unto the root of the trees. *Ib.* 10

32 Suffer it to be so now: for thus it becometh us to fulfil all righteousness. *Ib.* 15

33 This is my beloved Son, in whom I am well pleased. *Ib.* 17

34 Man shall not live by bread alone, but by every word that proceedeth out of the mouth of God. *Ib.* iv. 4

35 Thou shalt not tempt the Lord thy God. *Ib.* 7

36 The devil taketh him up into an exceeding high mountain, and sheweth him all the kingdoms of the world, and the glory of them. *Ib.* 8

37 Angels came and ministered unto him. *Ib.* 11

38 Fishers of men. *Ib.* 19

39 Blessed are the poor in spirit: for their's is the kingdom of heaven.
Blessed are they that mourn: for they shall be comforted.
Blessed are the meek: for they shall inherit the earth.
Blessed are they which do hunger and thirst after righteousness: for they shall be filled.
Blessed are the merciful: for they shall obtain mercy.
Blessed are the pure in heart: for they shall see God.
Blessed are the peacemakers: for they shall be called the children of God. *Ib.* v. 3

40 Ye are the salt of the earth: but if the salt have lost his savour, wherewith shall it be salted? *Ib.* 13

41 Ye are the light of the world. A city that is set on an hill cannot be hid. *Ib.* 14

42 Let your light so shine before men, that they may see your good works. *Ib.* 16

43 Think not that I am come to destroy the law, or the prophets: I am come not to destroy, but to fulfil. *Ib.* 17

44 Except your righteousness shall exceed the righteousness of the scribes and Pharisees. *Ib.* 20

45 Whosoever shall say, Thou fool, shall be in danger of hell fire. *Ib.* 22

46 Agree with thine adversary quickly, whiles thou art in the way with him. *Ib.* 25

47 Till thou hast paid the uttermost farthing. *Ib.* 26

48 Swear not at all; neither by heaven; for it is God's throne:
Nor by the earth; for it is his footstool. *Ib.* 34

49 Let your communication be, Yea, yea; Nay, nay. *Ib.* 37

50 Resist not evil: but whosoever shall smite thee on thy right cheek, turn to him the other also. *Ib.* 39

51 Whosoever shall compel thee to go a mile, go with him twain. *Ib.* 41

52 He maketh his sun to rise on the evil and on the good, and sendeth rain on the just and on the unjust. *Ib.* 45

53 Do not even the publicans the same? *Ib.* 46

1 Be ye therefore perfect.   *St. Matthew* v. 48

2 When thou doest alms, let not thy left hand know what thy right hand doeth.   *Ib.* vi. 3

3 Use not vain repetitions, as the heathen do: for they think that they shall be heard for their much speaking.   *Ib.* 7

4 After this manner therefore pray ye: Our Father which art in heaven, Hallowed be thy name.
Thy kingdom come. Thy will be done in earth, as it is in heaven.
Give us this day our daily bread.
And forgive us our debts, as we forgive our debtors.
And lead us not into temptation, but deliver us from evil: For thine is the kingdom, and the power, and the glory, for ever. Amen.   *Ib.* 9

5 Lay not up for yourselves treasures upon earth, where moth and rust doth corrupt, and where thieves break through and steal.   *Ib.* 19

6 Lay up for yourselves treasures in heaven.   *Ib.* 20

7 Where your treasure is, there will your heart be also.   *Ib.* 21

8 If therefore the light that is in thee be darkness, how great is that darkness!   *Ib.* 23

9 No man can serve two masters.   *Ib.* 24

10 Ye cannot serve God and mammon.   *Ib.*

11 Is not the life more than meat, and the body than raiment?
Behold the fowls of the air: for they sow not, neither do they reap, nor gather into barns.   *Ib.* 25

12 Which of you by taking thought can add one cubit unto his stature?   *Ib.* 27

13 Consider the lilies of the field, how they grow; they toil not, neither do they spin:
And yet I say unto you, That even Solomon in all his glory was not arrayed like one of these.   *Ib.* 28

14 Seek ye first the kingdom of God, and his righteousness; and all these things shall be added unto you.   *Ib.* 33

15 Take therefore no thought for the morrow: for the morrow shall take thought for the things of itself. Sufficient unto the day is the evil thereof.   *Ib.* 34

16 Judge not, that ye be not judged.   *Ib.* vii: 1

17 Why beholdest thou the mote that is in thy brother's eye, but considerest not the beam that is in thine own eye?   *Ib.* 3

18 Neither cast ye your pearls before swine.   *Ib.* 6

19 Ask, and it shall be given you; seek, and ye shall find; knock, and it shall be opened unto you.   *Ib.* 7

20 Every one that asketh receiveth; and he that seeketh findeth.   *Ib.* 8

21 Or what man is there of you, whom if his son ask bread, will he give him a stone?   *Ib.* 9

22 Therefore all things whatsoever ye would that men should do to you, do ye even so to them: for this is the law and the prophets.   *Ib.* 12

23 Wide is the gate, and broad is the way, that leadeth to destruction, and many there be that go in thereat.   *Ib.* 13

24 Strait is the gate, and narrow is the way, which leadeth unto life, and few there be that find it.   *Ib.* 14

25 Beware of false prophets, which come to you in sheep's clothing, but inwardly they are ravening wolves.   *St. Matthew* vii. 15

26 Do men gather grapes of thorns, or figs of thistles?   *Ib.* 16

27 By their fruits ye shall know them.   *Ib.* 20

28 And great was the fall of it.   *Ib.* 27

29 For he taught them as one having authority, and not as the scribes.   *Ib.* 29

30 Lord, I am not worthy that thou shouldest come under my roof.   *Ib.* viii. 8

31 I am a man under authority, having soldiers under me: and I say to this man, Go, and he goeth; and to another, Come, and he cometh; and to my servant, Do this, and he doeth it.   *Ib.* 9

32 I have not found so great faith, no, not in Israel.   *Ib.* 10

33 But the children of the kingdom shall be cast out into outer darkness: there shall be weeping and gnashing of teeth.   *Ib.* 12

34 The foxes have holes, and the birds of the air have nests; but the Son of man hath not where to lay his head.   *Ib.* 20

35 Let the dead bury their dead.   *Ib.* 22

36 The whole herd of swine ran violently down a steep place into the sea, and perished in the waters.   *Ib.* 32

37 Sitting at the receipt of custom.   *Ib.* ix. 9

38 Why eateth your Master with publicans and sinners?   *Ib.* 11

39 They that be whole need not a physician, but they that are sick.   *Ib.* 12

40 I am not come to call the righteous, but sinners to repentance.   *Ib.* 13

41 Can the children of the bridechamber mourn, as long as the bridegroom is with them?   *Ib.* 15

42 Neither do men put new wine into old bottles.   *Ib.* 17

43 The maid is not dead, but sleepeth.   *Ib.* 24

44 He casteth out devils through the prince of the devils.   *Ib.* 34

45 The harvest truly is plenteous, but the labourers are few.   *Ib.* 37

46 Go rather to the lost sheep of the house of Israel.   *Ib.* x. 6

47 Freely ye have received, freely give.   *Ib.* 8

48 When ye depart out of that house or city, shake off the dust of your feet.   *Ib.* 14

49 Be ye therefore wise as serpents, and harmless as doves.   *Ib.* 16

50 He that endureth to the end shall be saved.   *Ib.* 22

51 The disciple is not above his master, nor the servant above his lord.   *Ib.* 24

52 Are not two sparrows sold for a farthing? and one of them shall not fall on the ground without your Father.   *Ib.* 29

53 The very hairs of your head are all numbered.   *Ib.* 30

54 Fear ye not therefore, ye are of more value than many sparrows.   *Ib.* 31

1 I came not to send peace, but a sword.
St. Matthew x. 34

2 A man's foes shall be they of his own household.
Ib. 36

3 He that findeth his life shall lose it: and he that loseth his life for my sake shall find it. *Ib.* 39

4 Whosoever shall give to drink unto one of these little ones a cup of cold water only in the name of a disciple, verily I say unto you, he shall in no wise lose his reward. *Ib.* 42

5 Art thou he that should come, **or do we look for** another? *Ib.* xi. 3

6 What went ye out into the wilderness to see? A reed shaken with the wind?
But what went ye out for to see? A man clothed in soft raiment? . . .
But what went ye out for to see? A prophet? yea, I say unto you, and more than a prophet. *Ib.* 7

7 The kingdom of heaven suffereth violence, and the violent take it by force. *Ib.* 12

8 We have piped unto you, and ye have not danced; we have mourned unto you, and ye have not lamented. *Ib.* 17

9 Wisdom is justified of her children. *Ib.* 19

10 Come unto me, all ye that labour and are heavy laden, and I will give you rest.
Take my yoke upon you, and learn of me; for I am meek and lowly in heart: and ye shall find rest unto your souls.
For my yoke is easy, and my burden is light. *Ib.* 28

11 He that is not with me is against me. Ib. xii. 30

12 The blasphemy against the Holy Ghost shall not be forgiven unto men. *Ib.* 31

13 The tree is known by his fruit. *Ib.* 33

14 Out of the abundance of the heart the mouth speaketh. *Ib.* 34

15 Every idle word that men shall speak, they shall give account thereof in the day of judgment. *Ib.* 36

16 An evil and adulterous generation seeketh after a sign. *Ib.* 39

17 Behold, a greater than Solomon is here. *Ib.* 42

18 Empty, swept, and garnished. *Ib.* 44

19 Then goeth he, and taketh with himself seven other spirits more wicked than himself, and they enter in and dwell there: and the last state of that man is worse than the first. *Ib.* 45

20 Behold my mother and my brethren! *Ib.* 49

21 Some seeds fell by the wayside. *Ib.* xiii. 4

22 Because they had no root, they withered away. *Ib.* 6

23 But other fell into good ground, and brought forth fruit, some an hundredfold, some sixtyfold, some thirtyfold. *Ib.* 8

24 The care of this world, and the deceitfulness of riches. *Ib.* 22

25 His enemy came and sowed tares. *Ib.* 25

26 An enemy hath done this. *Ib.* 28

27 Let both grow together until the harvest. *Ib.* 30

28 The kingdom of heaven is like to a grain of mustard seed. *Ib.* 31

29 So that the birds of the air come and lodge in the branches thereof. *St. Matthew* xiii. 32

30 One pearl of great price. *Ib.* 46

31 An householder, which bringeth forth out of his treasure things new and old. *Ib.* 52

32 Is not this the carpenter's son? *Ib.* 55

33 A prophet is not without honour, save in his own country, and in his own house. *Ib.* 57

34 They took up of the fragments that remained twelve baskets full. *Ib.* xiv. 20

35 In the fourth watch of the night Jesus went unto them, walking on the sea. *Ib.* 25

36 Be of good cheer; it is I; be not afraid. *Ib.* 27

37 O thou of little faith, wherefore didst thou doubt? *Ib.* 31

38 Not that which goeth into the mouth defileth a man; but that which cometh out of the mouth, this defileth a man. *Ib.* xv. 11

39 They be blind leaders of the blind. And if the blind lead the blind, both shall fall into the ditch. *Ib.* 14

40 The dogs eat of the crumbs which fall from their masters' table. *Ib.* 27

41 When it is evening, ye say, It will be fair weather: for the sky is red. *Ib.* xvi. 2

42 The signs of the times. *Ib.* 3

43 Thou art Peter, and upon this rock I will build my church; and the gates of hell shall not prevail against it. *Ib.* 18

44 Get thee behind me, Satan. *Ib.* 23

45 What is a man profited, if he shall gain the whole world, and lose his own soul? *Ib.* 26

46 It is good for us to be here. *Ib.* xvii. 4

47 If ye have faith as a grain of mustard seed, ye shall say unto this mountain, Remove hence to yonder place; and it shall remove. *Ib.* 20

48 Except ye be converted, and become as little children, ye shall not enter into the kingdom of heaven. *Ib.* xviii. 3

49 But whoso shall offend one of these little ones which believe in me, it were better for him that a millstone were hanged about his neck, and that he were drowned in the depth of the sea. *Ib.* 6

50 It must needs be that offences come; but woe to that man by whom the offence cometh! *Ib.* 7

51 If thine eye offend thee, pluck it out, and cast it from thee: it is better for thee to enter into life with one eye, rather than having two eyes to be cast into hell fire. *Ib.* 9

52 For where two or three are gathered together in my name, there am I in the midst of them. *Ib.* 20

53 Until seventy times seven. *Ib.* 22

54 Lord, have patience with me, and I will pay thee all. *Ib.* 26

55 Pay me that thou owest. *Ib.* 28

56 What therefore God hath joined together, let not man put asunder. *Ib.* xix. 6

57 Thou shalt love thy neighbour as thyself. *Ib.* 19

BIBLE

1 If thou wilt be perfect, go and sell that thou hast, and give to the poor, and thou shalt have treasure in heaven. *St. Matthew* xix. 21

2 He went away sorrowful: for he had great possessions. *Ib.* 22

3 It is easier for a camel to go through the eye of a needle, than for a rich man to enter into the kingdom of God. *Ib.* 24

4 With men this is impossible; but with God all things are possible. *Ib.* 26

5 But many that are first shall be last; and the last shall be first. *Ib.* 30

6 Why stand ye here all the day idle? *Ib.* xx. 6

7 Borne the burden and heat of the day. *Ib.* 12

8 I will give unto this last, even as unto thee.
Is it not lawful for me to do what I will with mine own? *Ib.* 14

9 It is written, My house shall be called the house of prayer; but ye have made it a den of thieves. *Ib.* xxi. 13

10 For many are called, but few are chosen. *Ib.* xxii. 14

11 Whose is this image and superscription? *Ib.* 20

12 Render therefore unto Cæsar the things which are Cæsar's. *Ib.* 21

13 Last of all the woman died also. *Ib.* 27

14 For in the resurrection they neither marry, nor are given in marriage. *Ib.* 30

15 They make broad their phylacteries, and enlarge the borders of their garments,
And love the uppermost rooms at feasts, and the chief seats in the synagogues. *Ib.* xxiii. 5

16 Whosoever shall exalt himself shall be abased; and he that shall humble himself shall be exalted. *Ib.* 12

17 Woe unto you, . . . for ye pay tithe of mint and anise and cummin. *Ib.* 23

18 Blind guides, which strain at a gnat, and swallow a camel. *Ib.* 24

19 Whited sepulchres, which indeed appear beautiful outward, but are within full of dead men's bones. *Ib.* 27

20 O Jerusalem, Jerusalem, thou that killest the prophets, and stonest them which are sent unto thee, how often would I have gathered thy children together, even as a hen gathereth her chickens under her wings, and ye would not! *Ib.* 37

21 Wars and rumours of wars. *Ib.* xxiv. 6

22 But the end is not yet. *Ib.*

23 For nation shall rise against nation, and kingdom against kingdom. *Ib.* 7

24 Abomination of desolation. *Ib.* 15

25 Wheresoever the carcase is, there will the eagles be gathered together. *Ib.* 28

26 Eating and drinking, marrying and giving in marriage. *Ib.* 38

27 One shall be taken, and the other left. *Ib.* 40

28 Unto one he gave five talents, to another two, and to another one; to every man according to his several ability. *Ib.* xxv. 15

29 Well done, thou good and faithful servant. *Ib.* 21

30 Enter thou into the joy of thy lord. *St. Matthew* xxv. 21

31 Lord, I knew thee that thou art an hard man, reaping where thou hast not sown, and gathering where thou hast not strawed. *Ib.* 24

32 Unto every one that hath shall be given, and he shall have abundance: but from him that hath not shall be taken away even that which he hath. *Ib.* 29

33 I was a stranger, and ye took me in:
Naked, and ye clothed me: I was sick, and ye visited me: I was in prison, and ye came unto me. *Ib.* 35

34 Inasmuch as ye have done it unto one of the least of these my brethren, ye have done it unto me. *Ib.* 40

35 A woman having an alabaster box of very precious ointment. *Ib.* xxvi. 7

36 To what purpose is this waste? *Ib.* 8

37 What will ye give me, and I will deliver him unto you? And they covenanted with him for thirty pieces of silver. *Ib.* 15

38 It had been good for that man if he had not been born. *Ib.* 24

39 This night, before the cock crow, thou shalt deny me thrice. *Ib.* 34

40 Though I should die with thee, yet will I not deny thee. *Ib.* 35

41 If it be possible, let this cup pass from me. *Ib.* 39

42 What, could ye not watch with me one hour? *Ib.* 40

43 The spirit indeed is willing, but the flesh is weak. *Ib.* 41

44 Hail, master; and kissed him. *Ib.* 49

45 Friend, wherefore art thou come? *Ib.* 50

46 All they that take the sword shall perish with the sword. *Ib.* 52

47 Thy speech bewrayeth thee.
Then began he to curse and to swear, saying, I know not the man. And immediately the cock crew. *Ib.* 73

48 Have thou nothing to do with that just man. *Ib.* xxvii. 19

49 He took water, and washed his hands before the multitude, saying, I am innocent of the blood of this just person: see ye to it. *Ib.* 24

50 His blood be on us, and on our children. *Ib.* 25

51 He saved others; himself he cannot save. *Ib.* 42

52 Eli, Eli, lama sabachthani? . . . My God, my God, why hast thou forsaken me? *Ib.* 46

53 The sabbath was made for man, and not man for the sabbath. *St. Mark* ii. 27

54 If a house be divided against itself, that house cannot stand. *Ib.* iii. 25

55 He that hath ears to hear, let him hear. *Ib.* iv. 9

56 With what measure ye mete, it shall be measured to you. *Ib.* 24

57 My name is Legion: for we are many. *Ib.* v. 9

58 Clothed, and in his right mind. *Ib.* 15

59 My little daughter lieth at the point of death. *Ib.* 23

60 Had suffered many things of many physicians, and had spent all that she had, and was nothing bettered, but rather grew worse. *Ib.* 26

[60]

1 Knowing in himself that virtue had gone out of him.
St. Mark v. 30

2 I see men as trees, walking. *Ib.* viii. 24

3 For what shall it profit a man, if he shall gain the whole world, and lose his own soul? *Ib.* 36

4 Lord, I believe; help thou mine unbelief. *Ib.* ix. 24

5 Where their worm dieth not, and the fire is not quenched. *Ib.* 44

6 Suffer the little children to come unto me, and forbid them not: for of such is the kingdom of God.
Ib. x. 14

7 Which devour widows' houses, and for a pretence make long prayers. *Ib.* xii. 40

8 And there came a certain poor widow, and she threw in two mites. *Ib.* 42

9 Go ye into all the world, and preach the gospel to every creature. *Ib.* xvi. 15

10 It seemed good to me also . . . to write unto thee . . . most excellent Theophilus. *St. Luke* i. 3

11 To turn the hearts of . . . the disobedient to the wisdom of the just. *Ib.* 17

12 Hail, thou that art highly favoured, the Lord is with thee: blessed art thou among women. *Ib.* 28

13 My soul doth magnify the Lord,
And my spirit hath rejoiced in God my Saviour.
For he hath regarded the low estate of his handmaiden: for, behold, from henceforth all generations shall call me blessed. *Ib.* 46

14 He hath shewed strength with his arm; he hath scattered the proud in the imagination of their hearts.
He hath put down the mighty from their seats, and exalted them of low degree.
He hath filled the hungry with good things; and the rich he hath sent empty away. *Ib.* 51

15 To give light to them that sit in darkness and in the shadow of death, to guide our feet into the way of peace. *Ib.* 79

16 And it came to pass in those days, that there went out a decree from Cæsar Augustus, that all the world should be taxed. *Ib.* ii. 1

17 Because there was no room for them in the inn. *Ib.* 7

18 And, lo, the angel of the Lord came upon them, and the glory of the Lord shone round about them: and they were sore afraid. *Ib.* 9

19 Glory to God in the highest, and on earth peace, good will toward men. *Ib.* 14

20 Lord, now lettest thou thy servant depart in peace, according to thy word. *Ib.* 29

21 Wist ye not that I must be about my Father's business? *Ib.* 49

22 Jesus increased in wisdom and stature, and in favour with God and man. *Ib.* 52

23 Be content with your wages. *Ib.* iii. 14

24 Shewed unto him all the kingdoms of the world in a moment of time. *Ib.* iv. 5

25 Physician, heal thyself. *Ib.* 23

26 Many widows were in Israel in the days of Elias . . .
But unto none of them was Elias sent. *Ib.* 25

27 Master, we have toiled all the night, and have taken nothing: nevertheless at thy word I will let down the net. *St. Luke* v. 5

28 No man . . . having drunk old wine straightway desireth new: for he saith, The old is better. *Ib.* 39

29 Woe unto you, when all men shall speak well of you! *Ib.* vi. 26

30 Judge not, and ye shall not be judged. *Ib.* 37

31 Give, and it shall be given unto you; good measure, pressed down, and shaken together, and running over, shall men give into your bosom. *Ib.* 38

32 The only son of his mother, and she was a widow. *Ib.* vii. 12

33 Simon, I have somewhat to say unto thee. And he saith, Master, say on. *Ib.* 40

34 Peace be to this house. *Ib.* x. 5

35 For the labourer is worthy of his hire. *Ib.* 7

36 I beheld Satan as lightning fall from heaven. *Ib.* 18

37 I thank thee, O Father, Lord of heaven and earth, that thou hast hid these things from the wise and prudent, and hast revealed them unto babes: even so, Father; for so it seemed good in thy sight. *Ib.* 21

38 For I tell you, that many prophets and kings have desired to see those things which you see, and have not seen them; and to hear those things which ye hear, and have not heard them. *Ib.* 24

39 Fell among thieves. *Ib.* 30

40 He passed by on the other side. *Ib.* 31

41 He took out two pence, and gave them to the host. *Ib.* 35

42 Whatsoever thou spendest more, when I come again, I will repay thee. *Ib.*

43 Go, and do thou likewise. *Ib.* 37

44 But Martha was cumbered about much serving. *Ib.* 40

45 But one thing is needful: and Mary hath chosen that good part, which shall not be taken away from her. *Ib.* 42

46 When a strong man armed keepeth his palace, his goods are in peace. *Ib.* xi. 21

47 All his armour wherein he trusted. *Ib.* 22

48 He that is not with me is against me. *Ib.* 23

49 Take heed therefore that the light which is in thee be not darkness. *Ib.* 35

50 Woe unto you, lawyers! for ye have taken away the key of knowledge. *Ib.* 52

51 Are not five sparrows sold for two farthings, and not one of them is forgotten before God? *Ib.* xii. 6

52 Soul, thou hast much goods laid up for many years; take thine ease, eat, drink, and be merry. *Ib.* 19

53 Thou fool, this night thy soul shall be required of thee. *Ib.* 20

54 Let your loins be girded about, and your lights burning. *Ib.* 35

55 But he that knew not, and did commit things worthy of stripes, shall be beaten with few stripes. *Ib.* 48

BIBLE

1 Cut it down; why cumbereth it the ground?
St. Luke xiii. 7

2 Begin with shame to take the lowest room. *Ib.* xiv. 9

3 Friend, go up higher. *Ib.* 10

4 For whosoever exalteth himself shall be abased; and he that humbleth himself shall be exalted. *Ib.* 11

5 They all with one consent began to make excuse.
Ib. 18

6 I pray thee have me excused. *Ib.*

7 I have married a wife, and therefore I cannot come.
Ib. 20

8 The poor, and the maimed, and the halt, and the blind. *Ib.* 21

9 Go out into the highways and hedges, and compel them to come in. *Ib.* 23

10 Leave the ninety and nine in the wilderness.
Ib. xv. 4

11 Rejoice with me; for I have found my sheep which was lost. *Ib.* 6

12 Joy shall be in heaven over one sinner that repenteth, more than over ninety and nine just persons, which need no repentance. *Ib.* 7

13 Wasted his substance with riotous living. *Ib.* 13

14 He would fain have filled his belly with the husks that the swine did eat: and no man gave unto him.
And when he came to himself, he said, How many hired servants of my father's have bread enough and to spare, and I perish with hunger!
I will arise and go to my father, and will say unto him, Father, I have sinned against heaven, and before thee,
And am no more worthy to be called thy son: make me as one of thy hired servants. *Ib.* 16

15 Bring hither the fatted calf, and kill it. *Ib.* 23

16 This my son was dead, and is alive again; he was lost, and is found. *Ib.* 24

17 Which hath devoured thy living with harlots. *Ib.* 30

18 I cannot dig; to beg I am ashamed. *Ib.* xvi. 3

19 Take thy bill, and sit down quickly, and write fifty.
Ib. 6

20 And the Lord commended the unjust steward, because he had done wisely: for the children of this world are in their generation wiser than the children of light. *Ib.* 8

21 Make to yourselves friends of the mammon of unrighteousness. *Ib.* 9

22 He that is faithful in that which is least is faithful also in much. *Ib.* 10

23 There was a certain rich man, which was clothed in purple and fine linen, and fared sumptuously every day. *Ib.* 19

24 The crumbs which fell from the rich man's table.
Ib. 21

25 Carried by the angels into Abraham's bosom. *Ib.* 22

26 Between us and you there is a great gulf fixed. *Ib.* 26

27 It were better for him that a millstone were hanged about his neck, and he cast into the sea. *Ib.* xvii. 2

28 Say, We are unprofitable servants: we have done that which was our duty to do. *Ib.* 10

29 Were there not ten cleansed? but where are the nine?
St. Luke xvii. 17

30 The kingdom of God is within you. *Ib.* 21

31 Remember Lot's wife. *Ib.* 32

32 Men ought always to pray, and not to faint.
Ib. xviii. 1

33 God, I thank thee, that I am not as other men are.
Ib. 11

34 God be merciful to me a sinner. *Ib.* 13

35 How hardly shall they that have riches enter into the kingdom of God! *Ib.* 24

36 Have thou authority over ten cities. *Ib.* xix. 17

37 Out of thine own mouth will I judge thee. *Ib.* 22

38 Thou knewest that I was an austere man. *Ib.*

39 If these should hold their peace, the stones would immediately cry out. *Ib.* 40

40 The things which belong unto thy peace. *Ib.* 42

41 And when they heard it, they said, God forbid.
Ib. xx. 16

42 In your patience possess ye your souls. *Ib.* xxi. 19

43 He shall shew you a large upper room furnished.
Ib. xxii. 12

44 I am among you as he that serveth. *Ib.* 27

45 Nevertheless, not my will, but thine, be done. *Ib.* 42

46 And the Lord turned, and looked upon Peter. *Ib.* 61

47 For if they do these things in a green tree, what shall be done in the dry? *Ib.* xxiii. 31

48 Father, forgive them; for they know not what they do. *Ib.* 34

49 Lord, remember me when thou comest into thy kingdom. *Ib.* 42

50 To day shalt thou be with me in paradise. *Ib.* 43

51 Father, into thy hands I commend my spirit. *Ib.* 46

52 He was a good man, and a just. *Ib.* 50

53 Why seek ye the living among the dead? *Ib.* xxiv. 5

54 Their words seemed to them as idle tales. *Ib.* 11

55 Did not our heart burn within us, while he talked with us by the way? *Ib.* 32

56 He was known of them in breaking of bread. *Ib.* 35

57 A piece of a broiled fish, and of an honeycomb. *Ib.* 42

58 In the beginning was the Word, and the Word was with God, and the Word was God. *St. John* i. 1

59 All things were made by him; and without him was not any thing made that was made. *Ib.* 3

60 And the light shineth in darkness; and the darkness comprehended it not. *Ib.* 5

61 There was a man sent from God, whose name was John. *Ib.* 6

62 The true Light, which lighteth every man that cometh into the world. *Ib.* 9

63 He came unto his own, and his own received him not.
Ib. 11

64 And the Word was made flesh, and dwelt among us, (and we beheld his glory, the glory as of the only begotten of the Father,) full of grace and truth.
Ib. 14

1 No man hath seen God at any time. *St. John* i. 18

2 Who coming after me is preferred before me, whose shoe's latchet I am not worthy to unloose. *Ib.* 27

3 Can there any good thing come out of Nazareth? *Ib.* 46

4 Behold an Israelite indeed, in whom is no guile! *Ib.* 47

5 Woman, what have I to do with thee? mine hour is not yet come. *Ib.* ii. 4

6 When he had made a scourge of small cords, he drove them all out of the temple. *Ib.* 15

7 The wind bloweth where it listeth, and thou hearest the sound thereof, but canst not tell whence it cometh, and whither it goeth. *Ib.* iii. 8

8 How can these things be? *Ib.* 9

9 God so loved the world, that he gave his only begotten Son, that whosoever believeth in him should not perish, but have everlasting life. *Ib.* 16

10 Men loved darkness rather than light, because their deeds were evil. *Ib.* 19

11 The friend of the bridegroom . . . rejoiceth greatly because of the bridegroom's voice. *Ib.* 29

12 He must increase, but I must decrease. *Ib.* 30

13 God is a Spirit: and they that worship him must worship him in spirit and in truth. *Ib.* iv. 24

14 They are white already to harvest. *Ib.* 35

15 Other men laboured, and ye are entered into their labours. *Ib.* 38

16 Rise, take up thy bed, and walk. *Ib.* v. 8

17 Passed from death unto life. *Ib.* 24

18 He was a burning and a shining light. *Ib.* 35

19 Search the scriptures. *Ib.* 39

20 What are they among so many? *Ib.* vi. 9

21 Gather up the fragments that remain, that nothing be lost. *Ib.* 12

22 Him that cometh to me I will in no wise cast out. *Ib.* 37

23 It is the spirit that quickeneth. *Ib.* 63

24 Never man spake like this man. *Ib.* vii. 46

25 Are ye also deceived? *Ib.* 47

26 He that is without sin among you, let him first cast a stone at her. *Ib.* viii. 7

27 Neither do I condemn thee: go, and sin no more. *Ib.* 11

28 The truth shall make you free. *Ib.* 32

29 Ye are of your father the devil. *Ib.* 44

30 There is no truth in him. *Ib.*

31 He is a liar, and the father of it. *Ib.*

32 Which of you convinceth me of sin? *Ib.* 46

33 The night cometh, when no man can work. *Ib.* ix. 4

34 He is of age; ask him: he shall speak for himself. *Ib.* 21

35 One thing I know, that, whereas I was blind, now I see. *Ib.* 25

36 I am the door. *Ib.* x. 9

37 The good shepherd giveth his life for the sheep. *St. John* x. 11

38 The hireling fleeth, because he is an hireling, and careth not for the sheep. *Ib.* 13

39 Other sheep I have, which are not of this fold. *Ib.* 16

40 I am the resurrection, and the life. *Ib.* xi. 25

41 Jesus wept. *Ib.* 35

42 It is expedient for us, that one man should die for the people. *Ib.* 50

43 Why was not this ointment sold for three hundred pence, and given to the poor? *Ib.* xii. 5

44 The poor always ye have with you. *Ib.* 8

45 Sir, we would see Jesus. *Ib.* 21

46 Walk while ye have the light, lest darkness come upon you. *Ib.* 35

47 Lord, dost thou wash my feet? *Ib.* xiii. 6

48 Now there was leaning on Jesus' bosom one of his disciples, whom Jesus loved. *Ib.* 23

49 That thou doest, do quickly. *Ib.* 27

50 Let not your heart be troubled: ye believe in God, believe also in me. *Ib.* xiv. 1

51 In my Father's house are many mansions. *Ib.* 2

52 I go to prepare a place for you. *Ib.*

53 I am the way, the truth, and the life: no man cometh unto the Father, but by me. *Ib.* 6

54 Lord, shew us the Father, and it sufficeth us. *Ib.* 8

55 Have I been so long time with you, and yet hast thou not known me, Philip? *Ib.* 9

56 Judas saith unto him, not Iscariot. *Ib.* 22

57 Greater love hath no man than this, that a man lay down his life for his friends. *Ib.* xv. 13

58 Ye have not chosen me, but I have chosen you. *Ib.* 16

59 Quo vadis? Whither goest thou? *Ib.* xvi. 5 (Vulgate) and the Apocryphal *Acts of Peter*

60 It is expedient for you that I go away: for if I go not away, the Comforter will not come unto you. *Ib.* 7

61 I have yet many things to say unto you, but ye cannot bear them now. *Ib.* 12

62 A little while, and ye shall not see me: and again, a little while, and ye shall see me, because I go to the Father. *Ib.* 16

63 Do ye now believe? *Ib.* 31

64 In the world ye shall have tribulation: but be of good cheer; I have overcome the world. *Ib.* 33

65 The son of perdition. *Ib.* xvii. 12

66 Put up thy sword into the sheath. *Ib.* xviii. 11

67 Answerest thou the high priest so? *Ib.* 22

68 Pilate saith unto him, What is truth? *Ib.* 38

69 Now Barabbas was a robber. *Ib.* 40

70 Ecce homo.
Behold the man. *Ib.* xix. 5 (Vulgate)

71 What I have written I have written. *Ib.* 22

72 Woman, behold thy son! . . .
Behold thy mother! *Ib.* 26

1 I thirst. *St. John* xix. 28

2 It is finished. *Ib.* 30

3 A new sepulchre, wherein was never man yet laid. *Ib.* 41

4 The first day of the week cometh Mary Magdalene early, when it was yet dark, unto the sepulchre, and seeth the stone taken away from the sepulchre. *Ib.* xx. 1

5 So they ran both together: and the other disciple did outrun Peter, and came first to the sepulchre. *Ib.* 4

6 She, supposing him to be the gardener. *Ib.* 15

7 She turned herself and saith unto him, Rabboni. *Ib.* 16

8 Touch me not. *Ib.* 17. *See also* Corrigenda

9 Except I shall see in his hands the print of the nails, and put my finger into the print of the nails, and thrust my hand into his side, I will not believe. *Ib.* 25

10 Be not faithless, but believing. *Ib.* 27

11 Thomas, because thou hast seen me, thou hast believed: blessed are they that have not seen, and yet have believed. *Ib.* 29

12 Simon Peter saith unto them, I go a fishing. *Ib.* xxi. 3

13 Children, have ye any meat? *Ib.* 5

14 Simon, son of Jonas, lovest thou me more than these? *Ib.* 15

15 Feed my lambs. *Ib.*

16 Feed my sheep. *Ib.* 16

17 Lord, thou knowest all things; thou knowest that I love thee. *Ib.* 17

18 When thou wast young, thou girdedst thyself, and walkedst whither thou wouldest: but when thou shalt be old, thou shalt stretch forth thy hands, and another shall gird thee, and carry thee whither thou wouldest not. *Ib.* 18

19 The disciple whom Jesus loved. *Ib.* 20

20 What shall this man do?
Jesus saith unto him, If I will that he tarry till I come, what is that to thee? *Ib.* 21

21 The former treatise have I made, O Theophilus. *The Acts of the Apostles* i. 1

22 Ye men of Galilee, why stand ye gazing up into heaven? *Ib.* 11

23 His bishoprick let another take. *Ib.* 20

24 A rushing mighty wind. *Ib.* ii. 2

25 Cloven tongues like as of fire. *Ib.* 3

26 Parthians, and Medes, and Elamites, and the dwellers in Mesopotamia, and in Judæa, and Cappadocia, in Pontus, and Asia.
Phrygia, and Pamphylia, in Egypt, and in the parts of Libya about Cyrene, and strangers of Rome, Jews and proselytes,
Cretes and Arabians, we do hear them speak in our tongues the wonderful works of God. *Ib.* 9

27 Silver and gold have I none; but such as I have give I thee. *Ib.* iii. 6

28 I wot that through ignorance ye did it. *Ib.* 17

29 They took knowledge of them, that they had been with Jesus. *The Acts of the Apostles* iv. 13

30 Barnabas, . . . The son of consolation. *Ib.* 36

31 We ought to obey God rather than men. *Ib.* v. 29

32 If this counsel or this work be of men, it will come to nought:
But if it be of God, ye cannot overthrow it; lest haply ye be found even to fight against God. *Ib.* 38

33 It is not reason that we should leave the word of God, and serve tables. *Ib.* vi. 2

34 The witnesses laid down their clothes at a young man's feet, whose name was Saul. *Ib.* vii. 58

35 Saul was consenting unto his death. *Ib.* viii. 1

36 Thy money perish with thee. *Ib.* 20

37 Thou hast neither part nor lot in this matter. *Ib.* 21

38 In the gall of bitterness, and in the bond of iniquity. *Ib.* 23

39 Understandest thou what thou readest? . . .
How can I, except some man should guide me? *Ib.* 30

40 Breathing out threatenings and slaughter. *Ib.* ix. 1

41 Saul, Saul, why persecutest thou me? *Ib.* 4

42 It is hard for thee to kick against the pricks. *Ib.* 5

43 The street which is called Straight. *Ib.* 11

44 Full of good works. *Ib.* 36

45 One Simon a tanner. *Ib.* 43

46 As it had been a great sheet knit at the four corners, and let down to the earth. *Ib.* x. 11

47 What God hath cleansed, that call not thou common. *Ib.* 15

48 God is no respecter of persons. *Ib.* 34

49 It is the voice of a god, and not of a man. *Ib.* xii. 22

50 He was eaten of worms, and gave up the ghost. *Ib.* 23

51 The gods are come down to us in the likeness of men. *Ib.* xiv. 11

52 We also are men of like passions with you. *Ib.* 15

53 Come over into Macedonia, and help us. *Ib.* xvi. 9

54 Lydia, a seller of purple, of the city of Thyatira. *Ib.* 14

55 A certain damsel possessed with a spirit of divination. *Ib.* 16

56 Certain lewd fellows of the baser sort. *Ib.* xvii. 5

57 These that have turned the world upside down. *Ib.* 6

58 What will this babbler say? *Ib.* 18

59 For all the Athenians and strangers which were there spent their time in nothing else, but either to tell, or to hear some new thing. *Ib.* 21

60 Ye men of Athens, I perceive that in all things ye are too superstitious.
For as I passed by, and beheld your devotions, I found an altar with this inscription, TO THE UNKNOWN GOD. Whom therefore ye ignorantly worship, him declare I unto you. *Ib.* 22

BIBLE

1 For in him we live, and move, and have our being.
The Acts of the Apostles xvii. 28

2 As certain also of your own poets have said. *Ib.*

3 Gallio cared for none of those things. *Ib.* xviii. 17

4 Mighty in the scriptures. *Ib.* 24

5 We have not so much as heard whether there be any Holy Ghost. *Ib.* xix. 2

6 Demetrius, a silversmith. *Ib.* 24

7 Some therefore cried one thing, and some another: for the assembly was confused; and the more part knew not wherefore they were come together. *Ib.* 32

8 All with one voice about the space of two hours cried out, Great is Diana of the Ephesians. *Ib.* 34

9 For we are in danger to be called in question for this day's uproar. *Ib.* 40

10 I go bound in the spirit unto Jerusalem. *Ib.* xx. 22

11 It is more blessed to give than to receive. *Ib.* 35

12 A citizen of no mean city. *Ib.* xxi. 39

13 Brought up in this city at the feet of Gamaliel. *Ib.* xxii. 3

14 And the chief captain answered, With a great sum obtained I this freedom. And Paul said, But I was free born. *Ib.* 28

15 God shall smite thee, thou whited wall. *Ib.* xxiii. 3

16 Revilest thou God's high priest? *Ib.* 4

17 I am a Pharisee, the son of a Pharisee. *Ib.* 6

18 A conscience void of offence toward God, and toward men. *Ib.* xxiv. 16

19 I appeal unto Cæsar. *Ib.* xxv. 11

20 Hast thou appealed unto Cæsar? unto Cæsar shalt thou go. *Ib.* 12

21 I think myself happy, king Agrippa. *Ib.* xxvi. 2

22 After the most straitest sect of our religion I lived a Pharisee. *Ib.* 5

23 Paul, thou art beside thyself; much learning doth make thee mad. *Ib.* 24

24 Words of truth and soberness. *Ib.* 25

25 For this thing was not done in a corner. *Ib.* 26

26 Almost thou persuadest me to be a Christian. *Ib.* 28

27 I would to God, that not only thou, but also all that hear me this day, were both almost, and altogether such as I am, except these bonds. *Ib.* 29

28 They used helps, undergirding the ship. *Ib.* xxvii. 17

29 They cast four anchors out of the stern, and wished for the day. *Ib.* 29

30 Without ceasing I make mention of you always in my prayers. *The Epistle of Paul to the Romans* i. 9

31 The just shall live by faith. *Ib.* 17

32 Worshipped and served the creature more than the Creator. *Ib.* 25

33 Patient continuance in well doing. *Ib.* ii. 7

34 For there is no respect of persons with God. *Ib.* 11

35 These . . . are a law unto themselves. *Ib.* 14

36 Let God be true, but every man a liar. *Ib.* iii. 4

37 Let us do evil, that good may come. *Romans* iii. 8

38 For all have sinned, and come short of the glory of God. *Ib.* 23

39 For where no law is, there is no transgression. *Ib.* iv. 15

40 Who against hope believed in hope. *Ib.* 18

41 Hope maketh not ashamed. *Ib.* v. 5

42 Where sin abounded, grace did much more abound. *Ib.* 20

43 Shall we continue in sin, that grace may abound? *Ib.* vi. 1

44 We also should walk in newness of life. *Ib.* 4

45 Christ being raised from the dead dieth no more; death hath no more dominion over him.
For in that he died, he died unto sin once: but in that he liveth, he liveth unto God. *Ib.* 9

46 The wages of sin is death. *Ib.* 23

47 Is the law sin? God forbid. Nay, I had not known sin, but by the law. *Ib.* vii. 7

48 Now then it is no more I that do it, but sin that dwelleth in me. *Ib.* 17

49 For the good that I would I do not: but the evil which I would not, that I do. *Ib.* 19

50 I find then a law, that, when I would do good, evil is present with me. *Ib.* 21

51 O wretched man that I am! who shall deliver me from the body of this death? *Ib.* 24

52 They that are after the flesh do mind the things of the flesh; but they that are after the Spirit the things of the Spirit.
For to be carnally minded is death. *Ib.* viii. 5

53 For ye have not received the spirit of bondage again to fear; but ye have received the Spirit of adoption, whereby we cry, Abba, Father. *Ib.* 15

54 We are the children of God:
And if children, then heirs; heirs of God, and joint-heirs with Christ. *Ib.* 16

55 For we know that the whole creation groaneth and travaileth in pain together until now. *Ib.* 22

56 All things work together for good to them that love God. *Ib.* 28

57 If God be for us, who can be against us? *Ib.* 31

58 For I am persuaded, that neither death, nor life, nor angels, nor principalities, nor powers, nor things present, nor things to come,
Nor height, nor depth, nor any other creature, shall be able to separate us from the love of God, which is in Christ Jesus our Lord. *Ib.* 38

59 I could wish that myself were accursed from Christ for my brethren, my kinsmen according to the flesh. *Ib.* ix. 3

60 Hath not the potter power over the clay, of the same lump to make one vessel unto honour, and another unto dishonour? *Ib.* 21

61 A zeal of God, but not according to knowledge. *Ib.* x. 2

62 I beseech you therefore, brethren, by the mercies of God, that ye present your bodies a living sacrifice, holy, acceptable unto God. *Ib.* xii. 1

[65]

1 Let love be without dissimulation.
The Epistle of Paul to the Romans xii. 9

2 Be kindly affectioned one to another with brotherly love; in honour preferring one another;
Not slothful in business; fervent in spirit; serving the Lord. *Ib.* 10

3 Given to hospitality. *Ib.* 13

4 Rejoice with them that do rejoice, and weep with them that weep. *Ib.* 15

5 Mind not high things, but condescend to men of low estate. Be not wise in your own conceits. *Ib.* 16

6 Vengeance is mine; I will repay, saith the Lord. *Ib.* 19

7 Be not overcome of evil, but overcome evil with good. *Ib.* 21

8 Let every soul be subject unto the higher powers. *Ib.* xiii. 1

9 The powers that be are ordained of God. *Ib.*

10 For rulers are not a terror to good works, but to the evil. *Ib.* 3

11 Render therefore to all their dues: tribute to whom tribute is due; custom to whom custom; fear to whom fear; honour to whom honour.
Owe no man anything, but to love one another: for he that loveth another hath fulfilled the law. *Ib.* 7

12 Love is the fulfilling of the law. *Ib.* 10

13 Now it is high time to awake out of sleep: for now is our salvation nearer than when we believed.
The night is far spent, the day is at hand: let us therefore cast off the works of darkness, and let us put on the armour of light. *Ib.* 11

14 Make not provision for the flesh, to fulfil the lusts thereof. *Ib.* 14

15 Doubtful disputations. *Ib.* xiv. 1

16 Let every man be fully persuaded in his own mind. *Ib.* 5

17 We then that are strong ought to bear the infirmities of the weak, and not to please ourselves. *Ib.* xv. 1

18 Salute one another with an holy kiss. *Ib.* xvi. 16

19 The foolishness of preaching.
The First Epistle of Paul to the Corinthians i. 21

20 God hath chosen the foolish things of the world to confound the wise; and God hath chosen the weak things of the world to confound the things which are mighty. *Ib.* 27

21 I determined not to know any thing among you, save Jesus Christ, and him crucified. *Ib.* ii. 2

22 I have planted, Apollos watered; but God gave the increase. *Ib.* iii. 6

23 Every man's work shall be made manifest. *Ib.* 13

24 Stewards of the mysteries of God. *Ib.* iv. 1

25 A spectacle unto the world, and to angels. *Ib.* 9

26 Absent in body, but present in spirit. *Ib.* v. 3

27 Know ye not that a little leaven leaveneth the whole lump? *Ib.* 6

28 Christ our passover is sacrificed for us:
Therefore let us keep the feast, not with the old leaven, neither with the leaven of malice and wickedness; but with the unleavened bread of sincerity and truth. *Ib.* 7

29 Your body is the temple of the Holy Ghost.
I *Corinthians* vi. 19

30 It is better to marry than to burn. *Ib.* vii. 9

31 The unbelieving husband is sanctified by the wife. *Ib.* 14

32 The fashion of this world passeth away. *Ib.* 31

33 Knowledge puffeth up, but charity edifieth. *Ib.* viii. 1

34 Who goeth a warfare any time at his own charges? who planteth a vineyard, and eateth not of the fruit thereof? *Ib.* ix. 7

35 I am made all things to all men. *Ib.* 22

36 Know ye not that they which run in a race run all, but one receiveth the prize? *Ib.* 24

37 Now they do it to obtain a corruptible crown; but we an incorruptible.
I therefore so run, not as uncertainly; so fight I, not as one that beateth the air:
But I keep under my body, and bring it into subjection: lest that by any means, when I have preached to others, I myself should be a castaway. *Ib.* 25

38 Let him that thinketh he standeth take heed lest he fall.
There hath no temptation taken you but such as is common to man: but God is faithful, who will not suffer you to be tempted above that ye are able; but will with the temptation also make a way to escape, that ye may be able to bear it. *Ib.* x. 12

39 All things are lawful for me, but all things are not expedient. *Ib.* 23

40 For the earth is the Lord's, and the fulness thereof. *Ib.* 26

41 Whether therefore ye eat, or drink, or whatsoever ye do, do all to the glory of God. *Ib.* 31

42 If a woman have long hair, it is a glory to her. *Ib.* xi. 15

43 Now there are diversities of gifts, but the same Spirit. *Ib.* xii. 4

44 Though I speak with the tongues of men and of angels, and have not charity, I am become as sounding brass, or a tinkling cymbal. *Ib.* xiii. 1

45 Though I have all faith, so that I could remove mountains, and have not charity, I am nothing.
And though I bestow all my goods to feed the poor, and though I give my body to be burned, and have not charity, it profiteth me nothing.
Charity suffereth long, and is kind; charity envieth not; charity vaunteth not itself, is not puffed up,
Doth not behave itself unseemly, seeketh not her own, is not easily provoked, thinketh no evil;
Rejoiceth not in iniquity, but rejoiceth in the truth;
Beareth all things, believeth all things, hopeth all things, endureth all things.
Charity never faileth: but whether there be prophecies, they shall fail; whether there be tongues, they shall cease; whether there be knowledge, it shall vanish away.
For we know in part, and we prophesy in part. *Ib.* 2

46 When I was a child, I spake as a child, I understood as a child, I thought as a child: but when I became a man, I put away childish things.

For now we see through a glass, darkly; but then face to face: now I know in part; but then shall I know even as also I am known.

And now abideth faith, hope, charity, these three; but the greatest of these is charity.
The First Epistle of Paul to the Corinthians xiii. 11

1 If the trumpet give an uncertain sound, who shall prepare himself to the battle? *Ib*. xiv. 8

2 Let your women keep silence in the churches: for it is not permitted unto them to speak. *Ib*. 34

3 If they will learn any thing, let them ask their husbands at home: for it is a shame for women to speak in the church. *Ib*. 35

4 Let all things be done decently and in order. *Ib*. 40

5 Last of all he was seen of me also, as of one born out of due time.
For I am the least of the apostles, that am not meet to be called an apostle, because I persecuted the church of God.
But by the grace of God I am what I am. *Ib*. xv. 8

6 I laboured more abundantly than they all: yet not I, but the grace of God which was with me. *Ib*. 10

7 We are of all men most miserable. *Ib*. 19

8 But now is Christ risen from the dead, and become the firstfruits of them that slept.
For since by man came death, by man came also the resurrection of the dead.
For as in Adam all die, even so in Christ shall all be made alive. *Ib*. 20

9 The last enemy that shall be destroyed is death. *Ib*. 26

10 If after the manner of men I have fought with beasts at Ephesus. *Ib*. 32

11 Let us eat and drink; for to morrow we die. *Ib*.

12 Evil communications corrupt good manners. *Ib*. 33

13 One star differeth from another star in glory. *Ib*. 41

14 It is sown in corruption; it is raised in incorruption. *Ib*. 42

15 The first man is of the earth, earthy. *Ib*. 47

16 Behold, I shew you a mystery; We shall not all sleep, but we shall all be changed,
In a moment, in the twinkling of an eye, at the last trump. *Ib*. 51

17 For this corruptible must put on incorruption, and this mortal must put on immortality. *Ib*. 53

18 O death, where is thy sting? O grave, where is thy victory? *Ib*. 55

19 Quit you like men, be strong. *Ib*. xvi. 13

20 Let him be Anathema Maran-atha. *Ib*. 22

21 Fleshy tables of the heart.
The Second Epistle of Paul to the Corinthians iii. 3

22 Not of the letter, but of the spirit: for the letter killeth, but the spirit giveth life. *Ib*. 6

23 We have this treasure in earthen vessels. *Ib*. iv. 7

24 An house not made with hands, eternal in the heavens. *Ib*. v. 1

25 We walk by faith, not by sight. *Ib*. 7

26 The love of Christ constraineth us. *Ib*. 14

27 Now is the accepted time. *Ib*. vi. 2

28 By honour and dishonour, by evil report and good report. II *Corinthians* vi. 8

29 As having nothing, and yet possessing all things. *Ib*. 10

30 Without were fightings, within were fears. *Ib*. vii. 5

31 God loveth a cheerful giver. *Ib*. ix. 7

32 For ye suffer fools gladly, seeing ye yourselves are wise. *Ib*. xi. 19

33 Are they Hebrews? so am I. Are they Israelites? so am I. Are they the seed of Abraham? so am I.
Are they ministers of Christ? (I speak as a fool) I am more. *Ib*. 22

34 Five times received I forty stripes save one. *Ib*. 24

35 In perils in the city, in perils in the wilderness, in perils in the sea, in perils among false brethren. *Ib*. 26

36 Whether in the body, I cannot tell; or whether out of the body, I cannot tell: God knoweth. *Ib*. xii. 2

37 There was given to me a thorn in the flesh, the messenger of Satan to buffet me. *Ib*. 7

38 My strength is made perfect in weakness. *Ib*. 9

39 In the mouth of two or three witnesses shall every word be established. *Ib*. xiii. 1

40 The right hands of fellowship.
The Epistle of Paul to the Galatians ii. 9

41 O foolish Galatians, who hath bewitched you? *Ib*. iii. 1

42 Weak and beggarly elements. *Ib*. iv. 9

43 Which things are an allegory. *Ib*. 24

44 Ye are fallen from grace. *Ib*. v. 4

45 For the flesh lusteth against the Spirit, and the Spirit against the flesh . . . so that ye cannot do the things that ye would. *Ib*. 17

46 But the fruit of the Spirit is love, joy, peace, longsuffering, gentleness, goodness, faith,
Meekness, temperance. *Ib*. 22

47 Be not deceived; God is not mocked: for whatsoever a man soweth, that shall he also reap. *Ib*. vi. 7

48 Let us not be weary in well doing: for in due season we shall reap, if we faint not. *Ib*. 9

49 Ye see how large a letter I have written unto you with mine own hand. *Ib*. 11

50 You hath he quickened, who were dead in trespasses and sins. *The Epistle of Paul to the Ephesians* ii. 1

51 Preached peace to you which were afar off, and to them that were nigh. *Ib*. 17

52 The unsearchable riches of Christ. *Ib*. iii. 8

53 To be strengthened with might by his Spirit in the inner man. *Ib*. 16

54 The love of Christ, which passeth knowledge. *Ib*. 19

55 Him that is able to do exceeding abundantly above all that we ask or think. *Ib*. 20

56 Worthy of the vocation wherewith ye are called. *Ib*. iv. 1

57 Carried about with every wind of doctrine. *Ib*. 14

58 We are members one of another. *Ib*. 25

1 Be ye angry, and sin not: let not the sun go down upon your wrath.
The Epistle of Paul to the Ephesians iv. 26

2 Nor foolish talking, nor jesting, which are not convenient. *Ib.* v. 4

3 Let no man deceive you with vain words: for because of these things cometh the wrath of God upon the children of disobedience. *Ib.* 6

4 Redeeming the time, because the days are evil. *Ib.* 16

5 Psalms and hymns and spiritual songs. *Ib.* 19

6 Wives, submit yourselves unto your own husbands, as unto the Lord. *Ib.* 22

7 The first commandment with promise. *Ib.* vi. 2

8 Ye fathers, provoke not your children to wrath. *Ib.* 4

9 Not with eyeservice, as menpleasers. *Ib.* 6

10 Put on the whole armour of God. *Ib.* 11

11 For we wrestle not against flesh and blood, but against principalities, against powers, against the rulers of the darkness of this world, against spiritual wickedness in high places.
Wherefore take unto you the whole armour of God, that ye may be able to withstand in the evil day, and having done all, to stand. *Ib.* 12

12 Your feet shod with the preparation of the gospel of peace. *Ib.* 15

13 The shield of faith, wherewith ye shall be able to quench all the fiery darts of the wicked. *Ib.* 16

14 I thank my God upon every remembrance of you.
The Epistle of Paul to the Philippians i. 3.

15 For to me to live is Christ, and to die is gain. *Ib.* 21

16 Having a desire to depart, and to be with Christ; which is far better. *Ib.* 23

17 But made himself of no reputation, and took upon him the form of a servant, and was made in the likeness of men. *Ib.* ii. 7

18 Given him a name which is above every name: That at the name of Jesus every knee should bow. *Ib.* 9

19 Work out your own salvation with fear and trembling. *Ib.* 12

20 An Hebrew of the Hebrews; as touching the law, a Pharisee. *Ib.* iii. 5

21 But what things were gain to me, those I counted loss for Christ. *Ib.* 7

22 If by any means I might attain unto the resurrection of the dead. *Ib.* 11

23 Forgetting those things which are behind, and reaching forth unto those things which are before, I press toward the mark. *Ib.* 13

24 Whose God is their belly, and whose glory is in their shame. *Ib.* 19

25 Rejoice in the Lord alway: and again I say, Rejoice. *Ib.* iv. 4

26 The peace of God, which passeth all understanding. *Ib.* 7

27 Whatsoever things are true, whatsoever things are honest, whatsoever things are just, whatsoever things are pure, whatsoever things are lovely, whatsoever things are of good report; if there be any

virtue, and if there be any praise, think on these things. *Philippians* iv. 8

28 I can do all things through Christ which strengtheneth me. *Ib.* 13

29 Touch not; taste not; handle not.
The Epistle of Paul to the Colossians ii. 21

30 Set your affection on things above, not on things on the earth. *Ib.* iii. 2

31 Where there is neither Greek nor Jew, circumcision nor uncircumcision, Barbarian, Scythian, bond nor free: but Christ is all, and in all. *Ib.* 11

32 Husbands, love your wives, and be not bitter against them. *Ib.* 19

33 Let your speech be alway with grace, seasoned with salt. *Ib.* iv. 6

34 Luke, the beloved physician. *Ib.* 14

35 Labour of love.
The First Epistle of Paul to the Thessalonians i. 3

36 Study to be quiet, and to do your own business. *Ib.* iv. 11

37 Pray without ceasing. *Ib.* v. 17

38 Prove all things; hold fast that which is good. *Ib.* 21

39 If any would not work, neither should he eat.
The Second Epistle of Paul to the Thessalonians iii. 10

40 Be not weary in well doing. *Ib.* 13

41 Fables and endless genealogies.
The First Epistle of Paul to Timothy i. 4

42 I did it ignorantly in unbelief. *Ib.* 13

43 Sinners; of whom I am chief. *Ib.* 15

44 If a man desire the office of a bishop, he desireth a good work. *Ib.* iii. 1

45 Not greedy of filthy lucre. *Ib.* 3

46 For every creature of God is good, and nothing to be refused, if it be received with thanksgiving. *Ib.* iv. 4

47 Old wives' fables. *Ib.* 7

48 Worse than an infidel. *Ib.* v. 8

49 Tattlers also and busybodies, speaking things which they ought not. *Ib.* 13

50 Drink no longer water, but use a little wine for thy stomach's sake and thine often infirmities. *Ib.* 23

51 For we brought nothing into this world, and it is certain we can carry nothing out. *Ib.* vi. 7

52 The love of money is the root of all evil. *Ib.* 10

53 Fight the good fight of faith, lay hold on eternal life. *Ib.* 12

54 Rich in good works. *Ib.* 18

55 Science falsely so called. *Ib.* 20

56 For God hath not given us the spirit of fear; but of power, and of love, and of a sound mind.
The Second Epistle of Paul to Timothy i. 7

57 Hold fast the form of sound words. *Ib.* 13

58 From a child thou hast known the holy scriptures. *Ib.* iii. 15

59 Be instant in season, out of season. *Ib.* iv. 2

60 I have fought a good fight, I have finished my course, I have kept the faith. *Ib.* 7

1 For Demas hath forsaken me, having loved this present world.
The Second Epistle of Paul to Timothy iv. 10

2 Only Luke is with me. *Ib.* 11

3 Alexander the coppersmith did me much evil: the Lord reward him according to his works. *Ib.* 14

4 Unto the pure all things are pure.
The Epistle of Paul to Titus i. 15

5 Being such an one as Paul the aged, and now also a prisoner of Jesus Christ.
The Epistle of Paul to Philemon 9

6 At sundry times and in divers manners.
The Epistle of Paul to the Hebrews i. 1

7 The brightness of his glory, and the express image of his person. *Ib.* 3

8 For the word of God is quick, and powerful, and sharper than any twoedged sword, piercing even to the dividing asunder of soul and spirit.
Ib. iv. 12

9 They crucify to themselves the Son of God afresh, and put him to an open shame. *Ib.* vi. 6

10 Without shedding of blood is no remission.
Ib. ix. 22

11 Not forsaking the assembling of ourselves together, as the manner of some is. *Ib.* x. 25

12 It is a fearful thing to fall into the hands of the living God. *Ib.* 31

13 Faith is the substance of things hoped for, the evidence of things not seen. *Ib.* xi. 1

14 For he looked for a city which hath foundations.
Ib. 10

15 These all died in faith. *Ib.* 13

16 Esteeming the reproach of Christ greater riches than the treasures in Egypt. *Ib.* 26

17 Of whom the world was not worthy. *Ib.* 38

18 Wherefore seeing we also are compassed about with so great a cloud of witnesses, let us lay aside every weight, and the sin which doth so easily beset us, and let us run with patience the race that is set before us,
Looking unto Jesus the author and finisher of our faith. *Ib.* xii. 1

19 Whom the Lord loveth he chasteneth. *Ib.* 6

20 He found no place of repentance, though he sought it carefully with tears. *Ib.* 17

21 The spirits of just men made perfect. *Ib.* 23

22 Let brotherly love continue.
Be not forgetful to entertain strangers: for thereby some have entertained angels unawares. *Ib.* xiii. 1

23 Jesus Christ the same yesterday, and to day, and for ever. *Ib.* 8

24 For here have we no continuing city, but we seek one to come. *Ib.* 14

25 To do good and to communicate forget not. *Ib.* 16

26 Let patience have her perfect work.
The General Epistle of James i. 4

27 If any of you lack wisdom, let him ask of God, that giveth to all men liberally, and upbraideth not. *Ib.* 5

28 Blessed is the man that endureth temptation: for when he is tried, he shall receive the crown of life.
James i. 12

29 Every good gift and every perfect gift is from above, and cometh down from the Father of lights, with whom is no variableness, neither shadow of turning.
Ib. 17

30 Be swift to hear, slow to speak, slow to wrath:
For the wrath of man worketh not the righteousness of God. *Ib.* 19

31 Superfluity of naughtiness. *Ib.* 21

32 Be ye doers of the word, and not hearers only.
Ib. 22

33 If any be a hearer of the word, and not a doer, he is like unto a man beholding his natural face in a glass:
For he beholdeth himself, and goeth his way, and straightway forgetteth what manner of man he was.
Ib. 23

34 If any man among you seem to be religious, and bridleth not his tongue, but deceiveth his own heart, this man's religion is vain.
Pure religion and undefiled before God and the Father is this, To visit the fatherless and widows in their affliction, and to keep himself unspotted from the world. *Ib.* 26

35 Faith without works is dead. *Ib.* ii. 20

36 How great a matter a little fire kindleth! *Ib.* iii. 5

37 The tongue can no man tame; it is an unruly evil.
Ib. 8

38 Doth a fountain send forth at the same place sweet water and bitter? *Ib.* 11

39 This wisdom descendeth not from above, but is earthly, sensual, devilish. *Ib.* 15

40 Resist the devil, and he will flee from you. *Ib.* iv. 7

41 For what is your life? It is even a vapour, that appeareth for a little time, and then vanisheth away. *Ib.* 14

42 Ye have heard of the patience of Job. *Ib.* v. 11

43 Let your yea be yea; and your nay, nay. *Ib.* 12

44 The effectual fervent prayer of a righteous man availeth much. *Ib.* 16

45 Whom having not seen, ye love.
The First Epistle General of Peter i. 8

46 All flesh is as grass, and all the glory of man as the flower of grass. The grass withereth, and the flower thereof falleth away. *Ib.* 24

47 As newborn babes, desire the sincere milk of the word.
Ib. ii. 2

48 But ye are a chosen generation, a royal priesthood, an holy nation, a peculiar people. *Ib.* 9

49 Abstain from fleshly lusts, which war against the soul.
Ib. 11

50 Honour all men. Love the brotherhood. Fear God. Honour the king. *Ib.* 17

51 For what glory is it, if, when ye be buffeted for your faults, ye shall take it patiently? but if, when ye do well, and suffer for it, ye take it patiently, this is acceptable with God. *Ib.* 20

52 The Shepherd and Bishop of your souls. *Ib.* 25

1 Ornament of a meek and quiet spirit.
The First Epistle General of Peter iii. 4

2 Giving honour unto the wife, as unto the weaker vessel. *Ib.* 7

3 Not rendering evil for evil, or railing for railing: but contrariwise blessing. *Ib.* 9

4 The end of all things is at hand. *Ib.* iv. 7

5 Charity shall cover the multitude of sins. *Ib.* 8

6 Be sober, be vigilant; because your adversary the devil, as a roaring lion, walketh about, seeking whom he may devour. *Ib.* v. 8

7 And the day star arise in your hearts.
The Second Epistle General of Peter i. 19

8 Not afraid to speak evil of dignities. *Ib.* ii. 10

9 The dog is turned to his own vomit again. *Ib.* 22

10 If we say that we have no sin, we deceive ourselves, and the truth is not in us.
The First Epistle General of John i. 8

11 But whoso hath this world's good, and seeth his brother have need, and shutteth up his bowels of compassion from him, how dwelleth the love of God in him? *Ib.* iii. 17

12 He that loveth not knoweth not God; for God is love. *Ib.* iv. 8

13 No man hath seen God at any time. *Ib.* 12

14 There is no fear in love; but perfect love casteth out fear. *Ib.* 18

15 If a man say, I love God, and hateth his brother, he is a liar: for he that loveth not his brother whom he hath seen, how can he love God whom he hath not seen? *Ib.* 20

16 The elder unto the elect lady.
The Second Epistle of John 1

17 Yet Michael the archangel, when contending with the devil he disputed about the body of Moses, durst not bring against him a railing accusation.
The General Epistle of Jude 9

18 Spots in your feasts of charity. *Ib.* 12

19 Clouds they are without water, carried about of winds. *Ib.*

20 Raging waves of the sea, foaming out their own shame; wandering stars, to whom is reserved the blackness of darkness for ever. *Ib.* 13

21 John to the seven churches which are in Asia: Grace be unto you, and peace, from him which is, and which was, and which is to come.
The Revelation of St. John the Divine i. 4

22 Behold, he cometh with clouds; and every eye shall see him, and they also which pierced him: and all kindreds of the earth shall wail because of him. Even so, Amen.
I am Alpha and Omega, the beginning and the ending, saith the Lord. *Ib.* 7

23 I John, who also am your brother, and companion in tribulation, and in the kingdom and patience of Jesus Christ, was in the isle that is called Patmos, for the word of God, and for the testimony of Jesus Christ.
I was in the Spirit on the Lord's day, and heard behind me a great voice, as of a trumpet. *Ib.* 9

24 What thou seest, write in a book, and send it unto the seven churches which are in Asia. *Revelation* i. 11

25 Being turned, I saw seven golden candlesticks. *Ib.* 12

26 Clothed with a garment down to the foot, and girt about the paps with a golden girdle. *Ib.* 13

27 His head and his hairs were white like wool, as white as snow; and his eyes were as a flame of fire;
And his feet like unto fine brass, as if they burned in a furnace; and his voice as the sound of many waters.
And he had in his right hand seven stars: and out of his mouth went a sharp twoedged sword: and his countenance was as the sun shineth in his strength.
And when I saw him, I fell at his feet as dead. *Ib.* 14

28 I am he that liveth, and was dead; and, behold, I am alive for evermore, Amen; and have the keys of hell and of death. *Ib.* 18

29 I have somewhat against thee, because thou hast left thy first love. *Ib.* ii. 4

30 Be thou faithful unto death, and I will give thee a crown of life. *Ib.* 10

31 I . . . will give him a white stone, and in the stone a new name written, which no man knoweth saving he that receiveth it. *Ib.* 17

32 I will not blot out his name out of the book of life. *Ib.* iii. 5

33 I will write upon him my new name. *Ib.* 12

34 I know thy works, that thou art neither cold nor hot: I would thou wert cold or hot.
So then because thou art lukewarm, and neither cold nor hot, I will spue thee out of my mouth. *Ib.* 15

35 Behold, I stand at the door, and knock. *Ib.* 20

36 And he that sat was to look upon like a jasper and a sardine stone: and there was a rainbow round about the throne, in sight like unto an emerald. *Ib.* iv. 3

37 And before the throne there was a sea of glass like unto crystal: and in the midst of the throne, and round about the throne, were four beasts full of eyes before and behind. *Ib.* 6

38 They were full of eyes within: and they rest not day and night, saying, Holy, holy, holy, Lord God Almighty, which was, and is, and is to come. *Ib.* 8

39 Thou hast created all things, and for thy pleasure they are and were created. *Ib.* 11

40 Who is worthy to open the book, and to loose the seals thereof? *Ib.* v. 2

41 A Lamb as it had been slain, having seven horns and seven eyes. *Ib.* 6

42 Golden vials full of odours, which are the prayers of saints. *Ib.* 8

43 He went forth conquering, and to conquer. *Ib.* vi. 2

44 A measure of wheat for a penny, and three measures of barley for a penny; and see thou hurt not the oil and the wine. *Ib.* 6

45 And I looked, and behold a pale horse: and his name that sat on him was Death. *Ib.* 8

46 How long, O Lord, holy and true, dost thou not judge and avenge our blood on them that dwell on the earth? *Ib.* 10

1 And the stars of heaven fell unto the earth, even as a fig tree casteth her untimely figs, when she is shaken of a mighty wind.
The Revelation of St. John the Divine vi. 13

2 Said to the mountains and rocks, Fall on us, and hide us from the face of him that sitteth on the throne, and from the wrath of the Lamb. *Ib.* 16

3 A great multitude, which no man could number, of all nations, and kindreds, and people, and tongues. *Ib.* vii. 9

4 And all the angels stood round about the throne, and about the elders and the four beasts, and fell before the throne on their faces, and worshipped God. *Ib.* 11

5 And one of the elders answered, saying unto me, What are these which are arrayed in white robes? and whence came they? *Ib.* 13

6 These are they which came out of great tribulation, and have washed their robes, and made them white in the blood of the Lamb. *Ib.* 14

7 They shall hunger no more, neither thirst any more; neither shall the sun light on them, nor any heat. *Ib.* 16

8 God shall wipe away all tears from their eyes. *Ib.* 17

9 There was silence in heaven about the space of half an hour. *Ib.* viii. 1

10 And the name of the star is called Wormwood. *Ib.* 11

11 Those men which have not the seal of God in their foreheads. *Ib.* ix. 4

12 And in those days shall men seek death, and shall not find it; and shall desire to die, and death shall flee from them. *Ib.* 6

13 And there were stings in their tails. *Ib.* 10

14 It was in my mouth sweet as honey: and as soon as I had eaten it, my belly was bitter. *Ib.* x. 10

15 The kingdoms of this world are become the kingdoms of our Lord, and of his Christ. *Ib.* xi. 15

16 And there appeared a great wonder in heaven; a woman clothed with the sun, and the moon under her feet, and upon her head a crown of twelve stars. *Ib.* xii. 1

17 And there was war in heaven: Michael and his angels fought against the dragon; and the dragon fought and his angels. *Ib.* 7

18 The devil is come down unto you, having great wrath, because he knoweth that he hath but a short time. *Ib.* 12

19 A time, and times, and half a time. *Ib.* 14

20 Who is like unto the beast? who is able to make war with him? *Ib.* xiii. 4

21 And that no man might buy or sell, save he that had the mark, or the name of the beast, or the number of his name. *Ib.* 17

22 The number of the beast: for it is the number of a man; and his number is Six hundred threescore and six. *Ib.* 18

23 They sung as it were a new song . . . and no man could learn that song but the hundred and forty and four thousand, which were redeemed from the earth. *Ib.* xiv. 3

24 And in their mouth was found no guile: for they are without fault before the throne of God. *Ib.* 5

25 Babylon is fallen, is fallen, that great city.
Revelation xiv. 8

26 And the smoke of their torment ascendeth up for ever and ever: and they have no rest day nor night, who worship the beast and his image. *Ib.* 11

27 Blessed are the dead which die in the Lord from henceforth: Yea, saith the Spirit, that they may rest from their labours; and their works do follow them. *Ib.* 13

28 And I saw as it were a sea of glass mingled with fire. *Ib.* xv. 2

29 Behold, I come as a thief. *Ib.* xvi. 15

30 And he gathered them together into a place called in the Hebrew tongue Armageddon. *Ib.* 16

31 I will shew unto thee the judgment of the great whore that sitteth upon many waters. *Ib.* xvii. 1

32 MYSTERY, BABYLON THE GREAT, THE MOTHER OF HARLOTS AND ABOMINATIONS OF THE EARTH.
And I saw the woman drunken with the blood of the saints. *Ib.* 5

33 And a mighty angel took up a stone like a great millstone, and cast it into the sea, saying, Thus with violence shall that great city Babylon be thrown down, and shall be found no more at all. *Ib.* xviii. 21

34 Blessed are they which are called unto the marriage supper of the Lamb. *Ib.* xix. 9

35 And I fell at his feet to worship him. And he said unto me, See thou do it not: I am thy fellow-servant. *Ib.* 10

36 And I saw heaven opened, and behold a white horse; and he that sat upon him was called Faithful and True. *Ib.* 11

37 And he hath on his vesture and on his thigh a name written, KING OF KINGS, AND LORD OF LORDS. *Ib.* 16

38 The key of the bottomless pit. *Ib.* xx. 1

39 And he laid hold on the dragon, that old serpent, which is the Devil, and Satan, and bound him a thousand years. *Ib.* 2

40 On such the second death hath no power. *Ib.* 6

41 And I saw a great white throne. *Ib.* 11

42 And I saw the dead, small and great, stand before God; and the books were opened. *Ib.* 12

43 And the sea gave up the dead which were in it. *Ib.* 13

44 And I saw a new heaven and a new earth: for the first heaven and the first earth were passed away; and there was no more sea.
And I John saw the holy city, new Jerusalem, coming down from God out of heaven, prepared as a bride adorned for her husband. *Ib.* xxi. 1

45 And God shall wipe away all tears from their eyes; and there shall be no more death, neither sorrow, nor crying, neither shall there be any more pain: for the former things are passed away.
And he that sat upon the throne said, Behold, I make all things new. And he said unto me, Write: for these words are true and faithful. *Ib.* 4

46 I will give unto him that is athirst of the fountain of the water of life freely. *Ib.* 6

47 The city was pure gold, like unto clear glass. *Ib.* 18

1 The first foundation was jasper; the second, sapphire;
the third, a chalcedony; the fourth, an emerald;
The fifth, sardonyx; the sixth, sardius; the seventh,
chrysolyte; the eighth, beryl; the ninth, a topaz;
the tenth, a chrysoprasus; the eleventh, a jacinth;
the twelfth, an amethyst.
The Revelation of St. John the Divine xxi. 19

2 The twelve gates were twelve pearls.   *Ib.* 21

3 The street of the city was pure gold.   *Ib.*

4 And I saw no temple therein.   *Ib.* 22

5 And the city had no need of the sun, neither of the
moon, to shine in it: for the glory of God did
lighten it, and the Lamb is the light thereof. *Ib.* 23

6 And he shewed me a pure river of water of life, clear
as crystal, proceeding out of the throne of God and
of the Lamb.   *Ib.* xxii. 1

7 And the leaves of the tree were for the healing of the
nations.   *Ib.* 2

8 He that is unjust, let him be unjust still: and he which
is filthy, let him be filthy still: and he that is righteous, let him be righteous still: and he that is holy,
let him be holy still.
And, behold, I come quickly.   *Ib.* 11

9 Whosoever loveth and maketh a lie.   *Ib.* 15

10 I am the root and the offspring of David, and the
bright and morning star.
And the Spirit and the bride say, Come. And let him
that heareth say, Come. And let him that is athirst
come. And whosoever will, let him take the water
of life freely.   *Ib.* 16

11 If any man shall add unto these things, God shall add
unto him the plagues that are written in this book.
Ib. 18

12 God shall take away his part out of the book of life,
and out of the holy city, and from the things which
are written in this book.   *Ib.* 19

13 Amen. Even so, come, Lord Jesus.   *Ib.* 20

ISAAC BICKERSTAFFE
1735?–1812?

14 Perhaps it was right to dissemble your love,
But—why did you kick me downstairs?
An Expostulation

15 There was a jolly miller once,
Lived on the river Dee;
He worked and sang from morn till night;
No lark more blithe than he.
Love in a Village, I. v

16 And this the burthen of his song,
For ever us'd to be,
I care for nobody, not I,
If no one cares for me.   *Ib.*

17 We all love a pretty girl—under the rose. *Ib.* II. ii

18 In every port he finds a wife.
Thomas and Sally (1761), ii

EDWARD HENRY BICKERSTETH
1825–1906

19 Peace, perfect peace, in this dark world of sin?
The Blood of Jesus whispers peace within.
Songs in the House of Pilgrimage (1875)

ROGER BIGOD
EARL OF NORFOLK
1245–1306

20 (Edward I: 'By God, earl, you shall either go or
hang!')
'O King, I will neither go nor hang!'
Hemingburgh's Chronicle, ii. 121

JOSH BILLINGS
see
HENRY WHEELER SHAW

LAURENCE BINYON
1869–1943

21 Now is the time for the burning of the leaves.
The Burning of the Leaves

22 With proud thanksgiving, a mother for her children,
England mourns for her dead across the sea.
Poems For the Fallen

23 They shall grow not old, as we that are left grow old:
Age shall not weary them, nor the years condemn.
At the going down of the sun and in the morning
We will remember them.   *Ib.*

24 That many-memoried name.   *Tristram's End*

FREDERICK EDWIN SMITH,
EARL OF BIRKENHEAD
1872–1930

25 The world continues to offer glittering prizes to those
who have stout hearts and sharp swords.
Rectorial Address, Glasgow University, 7 Nov. 1923

AUGUSTINE BIRRELL
1850–1933

26 That great dust-heap called 'history'.
Obiter Dicta. Carlyle

27 In the name of the Bodleian.   *Ib. Dr. Johnson*

28 What then did happen at the Reformation?
Title of Essay

OTTO VON BISMARCK
1815–1898

29 Die Politik ist keine exakte Wissenschaft.
Politics are not an exact science.
Speech, Prussian Chamber, 18 Dec. 1863

30 Nach Canossa gehen wir nicht.
We will not go to Canossa.
Speech, Reichstag, 14 May 1872

31 Die gesunden Knochen eines einzigen pommerschen
Musketiers.
The healthy bones of a single Pomeranian grenadier.
Ib. 5 Dec. 1876

32 Ehrlicher Makler.
An honest broker.   *Ib. 19 Feb. 1878*

33 Blut und Eisen.
Blood and iron.
Speech, Prussian House of Deputies, 28 Jan. 1886
(Legt eine möglichst starke militärische Kraft . . . in
die Hand des Königs von Preussen, dann wird er
die Politik machen können, die Ihr wünscht; mit

Reden und Schützenfesten und Liedern macht sie sich nicht, sie macht sich nur durch Blut und Eisen.

Place in the hands of the King of Prussia the strongest possible military power, then he will be able to carry out the policy you wish; this policy cannot succeed through speeches, and shooting-matches, and songs; it can only be carried out through blood and iron.)

1 I may avail myself of the opportunity of denying once more the truth of the story that Prince Bismarck had ever likened Lord Salisbury to a lath of wood painted to look like iron.
Sidney Whitman, *Personal Reminiscences of Prince Bismarck* (1902), p. 252.

VALENTINE BLACKER
1778–1823

2 'Put your trust in God, my boys, and keep your powder dry.'   *Oliver's Advice*

SIR WILLIAM BLACKSTONE
1723–1780

3 Man was formed for society.
Commentaries on the Laws of England, introd. § 2

4 Mankind will not be reasoned out of the feelings of humanity.   *Ib.* bk. i. 5

5 The king never dies.   *Ib.* 7

6 The royal navy of England hath ever been its greatest defence and ornament; it is its ancient and natural strength; the floating bulwark of the island.
Ib. 13

7 Time whereof the memory of man runneth not to the contrary.   *Ib.* 18

8 That the king can do no wrong, is a necessary and fundamental principle of the English constitution.
Ib. iii. 17

9 It is better that ten guilty persons escape than one innocent suffer.   *Ib.* iv. 27

HELEN SELINA BLACKWOOD,
LADY DUFFERIN
1807–1867

10 I'm sitting on the stile, Mary,
Where we sat, side by side.
Lament of the Irish Emigrant

11 The corn was springing fresh and green,
And the lark sang loud and high,
And the red was on your lip, Mary,
The love-light in your eye.   *Ib.*

12 They say there's bread and work for all,
And the sun shines always there:
But I'll not forget old Ireland,
Were it fifty times as fair.   *Ib.*

ROBERT BLAIR
1699–1746

13   The good he scorn'd
Stalk'd off reluctant, like an ill-us'd ghost,
Not to return; or if it did, its visits
Like those of angels, short, and far between.
The Grave, l. 586

CHARLES DUPEE BLAKE
1846–1903

14 Rock-a-bye-baby on the tree top,
When the wind blows the cradle will rock,
When the bough bends the cradle will fall,
Down comes the baby, cradle and all.
Attr., but see Corrigenda.

WILLIAM BLAKE
1757–1827

15 The errors of a wise man make your rule,
Rather than the perfections of a fool.
On Art and Artists, viii

16 When Sir Joshua Reynolds died
All Nature was degraded:
The King dropped a tear into the Queen's ear,
And all his pictures faded.   *Ib.* xxi

17 I understood Christ was a carpenter
And not a brewer's servant, my good Sir.   *Ib.* xxvi

18 To see a World in a Grain of Sand,
And a Heaven in a Wild Flower,
Hold Infinity in the palm of your hand,
And Eternity in an hour.   *Auguries of Innocence*

19 A Robin Redbreast in a Cage
Puts all Heaven in a Rage.   *Ib*

20 A dog starv'd at his master's gate
Predicts the ruin of the State,
A horse misus'd upon the road
Calls to Heaven for human blood.
Each outcry of the hunted hare
A fibre from the brain does tear,
A skylark wounded in the wing,
A cherubim does cease to sing.   *Ib.*

21 The bat that flits at close of eve
Has left the brain that won't believe.   *Ib.*

22 He who shall hurt the little wren
Shall never be belov'd by men.
He who the ox to wrath has mov'd
Shall never be by woman lov'd.   *Ib.*

23 The caterpillar on the leaf
Repeats to thee thy mother's grief.
Kill not the moth nor butterfly,
For the Last Judgement draweth nigh.   *Io.*

24 A truth that's told with bad intent
Beats all the lies you can invent.
It is right it should be so;
Man was made for Joy and Woe;
And when this we rightly know,
Thro' the World we safely go,
Joy and woe are woven fine,
A clothing for the soul divine.   *Ib.*

25 Every tear from every eye
Becomes a babe in Eternity.   *Ib.*

26 The bleat, the bark, bellow, and roar
Are waves that beat on Heaven's shore.   *Ib.*

27 The strongest poison ever known
Came from Caesar's laurel crown.   *Ib.*

28 He who doubts from what he sees
Will ne'er believe, do what you please.
If the Sun and Moon should doubt,
They'd immediately go out.
To be in a passion you good may do,
But no good if a passion is in you.

The whore and gambler, by the state
Licensed, build that nation's fate.
The harlot's cry from street to street
Shall weave old England's winding sheet.

Auguries of Innocence

1 God appears, and God is Light,
To those poor souls who dwell in Night;
But does a Human Form display
To those who dwell in realms of Day.   *Ib.*

2 Does the Eagle know what is in the pit
Or wilt thou go ask the Mole?
Can Wisdom be put in a silver rod,
Or Love in a golden bowl?

Book of Thel, Thel's motto.

3 Everything that lives,
Lives not alone, nor for itself.   *Ib.* 11

4 My brother John, the evil one.
*To Thomas Butts. 'With Happiness stretch'd
across the Hills', l. 15*

5 For double the vision my eyes do see,
And a double vision is always with me.
With my inward eye 'tis an Old Man grey,
With my outward, a Thistle across my way.
Ib. l. 27

6 'What,' it will be questioned, 'when the sun rises, do
you not see a round disc of fire somewhat like a
guinea?' 'O no, no, I see an innumerable company
of the heavenly host crying, "Holy, Holy, Holy is
the Lord God Almighty!"'
Descriptive Catalogue, 1810. *The Vision of
Judgment*

7 He has observ'd the golden rule,
Till he's become the golden fool.
Miscellaneous Epigrams, ii

8 Wondrous the gods, more wondrous are the men,
More wondrous, wondrous still the cock and hen,
More wondrous still the table, stool and chair;
But oh! more wondrous still the charming fair.
Ib. xiii. Imitation of Pope

9 To Chloe's breast young Cupid slyly stole,
But he crept in at Myra's pocket-hole.   *Ib.* xv

10 The Vision of Christ that thou dost see
Is my vision's greatest enemy.
Thine has a great hook nose like thine,
Mine has a snub nose like to mine.
The Everlasting Gospel. a

11 Both read the Bible day and night,
But thou read'st black where I read white.   *Ib.*

12 This life's five windows of the soul
Distorts the Heavens from pole to pole,
And leads you to believe a lie
When you see with, not thro', the eye.   *Ib.* γ

13 Jesus was sitting in Moses' chair.
They brought the trembling woman there.
Moses commands she be ston'd to death.
What was the sound of Jesus' breath?
He laid His hand on Moses' law;
The ancient Heavens, in silent awe,
Writ with curses from pole to pole,
All away began to roll.   *Ib.* ξ

14 I am sure this Jesus will not do,
Either for Englishman or Jew.   *Ib. Epilogue*

15 [Of Hayley's birth]
Of H—'s birth this was the happy lot:
His mother on his father him begot.
On Friends and Foes, iv

16 [On Hayley]
To forgive enemies H— does pretend,
Who never in his life forgave a friend,
And when he could not act upon my wife
Hired a villain to bereave my life.   *Ib.* v

17 To H[ayley]
Thy friendship oft has made my heart to ache:
Do be my enemy—for friendship's sake.   *Ib.* vi

18 On H[ayle]y's Friendship.
When H—y finds out what you cannot do,
That is the very thing he'll set you to.   *Ib.* vii

19 [On Cromek]
A petty sneaking knave I knew—
O! Mr. Cr—, how do ye do?   *Ib.* xxi

20 [On William Haines]
The Sussex men are noted fools,
And weak is their brain-pan;
I wonder if H— the painter
Is not a Sussex man?   *Ib.* xxiii

21 Mutual Forgiveness of each vice,
Such are the Gates of Paradise.
The Gates of Paradise, prologue

22 Truly, my Satan, thou art but a dunce,
And dost not know the garment from the man;
Every harlot was a virgin once,
Nor canst thou ever change Kate into Nan.

Tho' thou art worshipp'd by the names divine
Of Jesus and Jehovah, thou art still
The Son of Morn in weary Night's decline,
The lost traveller's dream under the hill.
Ib. epilogue

23 Great things are done when men and mountains meet;
This is not done by jostling in the street.
Gnomic Verses, i

24 If you have form'd a circle to go into,
Go into it yourself, and see how you would do.
Ib. ii. *To God*

25 Abstinence sows sand all over
The ruddy limbs and flaming hair,
But Desire gratified
Plants fruits of life and beauty there.   *Ib.* x

26 The sword sung on the barren heath,
The sickle in the fruitful field:
The sword he sung a song of death,
But could not make the sickle yield.   *Ib.* xiv

27 He who bends to himself a Joy
Doth the winged life destroy;
But he who kisses the Joy as it flies
Lives in Eternity's sunrise.   *Ib.* xvii. 1

28 What is it men in women do require?
The lineaments of gratified desire.
What is it women do in men require?
The lineaments of gratified desire.   *Ib.* xvii. 4

29 Since all the riches of this world
May be gifts from the Devil and earthly kings,
I should suspect that I worshipp'd the Devil
If I thank'd my God for worldly things.   *Ib.* xix

1 The Angel that presided o'er my birth
Said 'Little creature, form'd of joy and mirth,
Go, love without the help of anything on earth.'
Gnomic Verses, xxi

2 I must Create a System, or be enslav'd by another Man's;
I will not Reason and Compare: my business is to Create. *Jerusalem,* f. 10, l. 20

3 Near mournful
Ever-weeping Paddington. *Ib.* f. 12, l. 27

4 The fields from Islington to Marybone,
To Primrose Hill and Saint John's Wood,
Were builded over with pillars of gold;
And there Jerusalem's pillars stood. *Ib.* f. 27

5 Pancras and Kentish Town repose
Among her golden pillars high,
Among her golden arches which
Shine upon the starry sky. *Ib.*

6 For a tear is an intellectual thing,
And a sigh is the sword of an Angel King,
And the bitter groan of the martyr's woe
Is an arrow from the Almighty's bow. *Ib.* f. 52

7 He who would do good to another must do it in Minute Particulars.
General Good is the plea of the scoundrel, hypocrite, and flatterer;
For Art and Science cannot exist but in minutely organized Particulars. *Ib.* f. 55, l. 54

8 I give you the end of a golden string;
Only wind it into a ball,
It will lead you in at Heaven's gate,
Built in Jerusalem's wall. *Ib.* f. 77

9 O ye Religious, discountenance every one among you who shall pretend to despise Art and Science! *Ib.*

10 Let every Christian, as much as in him lies, engage himself openly and publicly, before all the World, in some mental pursuit for the Building up of Jerusalem. *Ib.*

11 England! awake! awake! awake!
Jerusalem thy sister calls!
Why wilt thou sleep the sleep of death,
And close her from thy ancient walls? *Ib.*

12 And now the time returns again:
Our souls exult, and London's towers
Receive the Lamb of God to dwell
In England's green and pleasant bowers. *Ib.*

13 I care not whether a man is Good or Evil; all that I care
Is whether he is a Wise man or a Fool. Go! put off Holiness,
And put on Intellect. *Ib.* f. 91

14 Father, O father! what do we here
In this land of unbelief and fear?
The Land of Dreams is better far,
Above the light of the morning star.
The Land of Dreams

15 Little Mary Bell had a Fairy in a nut,
Long John Brown had the Devil in his gut.
Long John Brown and Little Mary Bell

16 And did those feet in ancient time
Walk upon England's mountains green?
And was the holy Lamb of God
On England's pleasant pastures seen?

And did the Countenance Divine
Shine forth upon our clouded hills?
And was Jerusalem builded here
Among these dark Satanic mills?

Bring me my bow of burning gold!
Bring me my arrows of desire!
Bring me my spear! O clouds, unfold!
Bring me my chariot of fire!

I will not cease from Mental Fight,
Nor shall my Sword sleep in my hand,
Till we have built Jerusalem,
In England's green & pleasant Land.
Milton, preface

17 Mock on, mock on, Voltaire, Rousseau;
Mock on, mock on, 'tis all in vain!
You throw the sand against the wind,
And the wind blows it back again.
Mock on, mock on, Voltaire

18 Whether on Ida's shady brow,
Or in the chambers of the East,
The chambers of the sun, that now
From ancient melody have ceas'd;

Whether in Heaven ye wander fair,
Or the green corners of the earth,
Or the blue regions of the air
Where the melodious winds have birth;

Whether on crystal rocks ye rove,
Beneath the bosom of the sea
Wand'ring in many a coral grove,
Fair Nine, forsaking Poetry!

How have you left the ancient love
That bards of old enjoy'd in you!
The languid strings do scarcely move!
The sound is forc'd, the notes are few!
To the Muses

19 My Spectre around me night and day
Like a wild beast guards my way;
My Emanation far within
Weeps incessantly for my sin.
My Spectre around Me Night and Day, i

20 And throughout all Eternity
I forgive you, you forgive me.
As our dear Redeemer said:
'This the Wine, and this the Bread.' *Ib.* xiv

21 Never seek to tell thy love,
Love that never told can be;
For the gentle wind does move
Silently, invisibly. *Never Seek to Tell Thy Love*

22 Soon as she was gone from me,
A traveller came by,
Silently, invisibly:
He took her with a sigh. *Ib.*

23 Hear the voice of the Bard!
Who present, past, and future sees.
Songs of Experience, introduction

24 Tyger! Tyger! burning bright
In the forests of the night,
What immortal hand or eye
Could frame thy fearful symmetry?

In what distant deeps or skies
Burnt the fire of thine eyes?
On what wings dare he aspire?
What the hand dare seize the fire?

And what shoulder, and what art,
Could twist the sinews of thy heart?
And when thy heart began to beat,
What dread hand? and what dread feet?

What the hammer? What the chain?
In what furnace was thy brain?
What the anvil? what dread grasp
Dare its deadly terrors clasp?

When the stars threw down their spears,
And water'd heaven with their tears,
Did he smile his work to see?
Did he who made the Lamb make thee?

Tyger! Tyger! burning bright
In the forests of the night,
What immortal hand or eye,
Dare frame thy fearful symmetry?
Songs of Experience. The Tyger

1 Children of the future age,
Reading this indignant page,
Know that in a former time,
Love, sweet love, was thought a crime.
Ib. A Little Girl Lost

2 Love seeketh not itself to please,
Nor for itself hath any care,
But for another gives its ease,
And builds a Heaven in Hell's despair.
Ib. The Clod and the Pebble

3 Love seeketh only Self to please,
To bind another to its delight,
Joys in another's loss of ease,
And builds a Hell in Heaven's despite. *Ib.*

4 Then the Parson might preach, and drink, and sing,
And we'd be as happy as birds in the spring;
And modest Dame Lurch, who is always at church,
Would not have bandy children, nor fasting, nor
   birch. *Ib. The Little Vagabond*

5 I was angry with my friend
I told my wrath, my wrath did end.
I was angry with my foe:
I told it not, my wrath did grow.
Ib. A Poison Tree

6 Youth of delight, come hither,
And see the opening morn,
Image of truth new-born.
Ib. Voice of the Ancient Bard

7 Ah, Sun-flower! weary of time,
Who countest the steps of the Sun;
Seeking after that sweet golden clime,
Where the traveller's journey is done;

Where the Youth pined away with desire,
And the pale Virgin shrouded in snow,
Arise from their graves and aspire
Where my Sun-flower wishes to go.
Ib. Ah, Sun-Flower!

8 My mother groan'd, my father wept,
Into the dangerous world I leapt;
Helpless, naked, piping loud,
Like a fiend hid in a cloud. *Ib. Infant Sorrow*

9 Piping down the valleys wild,
Piping songs of pleasant glee,
On a cloud I saw a child,
And he laughing said to me:

'Pipe a song about a Lamb!'
So I piped with merry cheer.
'Piper, pipe that song again;'
So I piped: he wept to hear.

'Drop thy pipe, thy happy pipe;
Sing thy songs of happy cheer:'
So I sang the same again,
While he wept with joy to hear.

'Piper, sit thee down and write
In a book, that all may read.'
So he vanish'd from my sight,
And I pluck'd a hollow reed.

And I made a rural pen,
And I stain'd the water clear,
And I wrote my happy songs
Every child may joy to hear.
Songs of Innocence introduction

10 Little Lamb, who made thee?
Dost thou know who made thee?
Gave thee life, and bid thee feed,
By the stream and o'er the mead;
Gave thee clothing of delight,
Softest clothing, woolly, bright;
Gave thee such a tender voice,
Making all the vales rejoice?
Little Lamb, who made thee?
Dost thou know who made thee?

Little Lamb, I'll tell thee,
Little Lamb, I'll tell thee:
He is callèd by thy name,
For He calls Himself a Lamb,
He is meek, and He is mild;
He became a little child.
I a child, and thou a lamb,
We are callèd by His name.
Little Lamb, God bless thee!
Little Lamb, God bless thee! *Ib. The Lamb*

11 How sweet is the Shepherd's sweet lot!
Ib. The Shepherd

12 'I have no name:
I am but two days old.'
What shall I call thee?
'I happy am,
Joy is my name.'
Sweet joy befall thee! *Ib. Infant Joy*

13 My mother bore me in the southern wild,
And I am black, but O! my soul is white;
White as an angel is the English child,
But I am black, as if bereav'd of light.
Ib. The Little Black Boy

14 When the voices of children are heard on the green,
And laughing is heard on the hill. *Ib. Nurse's Song*

15 'Twas on a Holy Thursday, their innocent faces clean,
The children walking two and two, in red and blue
and green. *Ib. Holy Thursday*

16 Then cherish pity, lest you drive an angel from your
door. *Ib.*

17 When my mother died I was very young,
And my father sold me while yet my tongue
Could scarcely cry, "weep! 'weep! 'weep! 'weep!'
So your chimneys I sweep, and in soot I sleep.
Ib. The Chimney Sweeper

18 To Mercy, Pity, Peace, and Love
All pray in their distress. *Ib. The Divine Image*

1 For Mercy has a human heart,
Pity a human face,
And Love, the human form divine,
And Peace, the human dress.
Songs of Innocence. The Divine Image

2 And there the lion's ruddy eyes
Shall flow with tears of gold,
And pitying the tender cries,
And walking round the fold,
Saying, 'Wrath, by His meekness,
And, by His health, sickness,
Is driven away
From our immortal day.' *Ib. Night*

3 Can I see another's woe,
And not be in sorrow too?
Can I see another's grief,
And not seek for kind relief?
Ib. On Another's Sorrow

4 Cruelty has a human heart,
And Jealousy a human face;
Terror the human form divine,
And Secrecy the human dress.
Appendix to Songs of Innocence and of Experience. A Divine Image

5 Good English hospitality, O then it did not fail!
Songs from an Island in the Moon, xi

6 Energy is Eternal Delight.
Marriage of Heaven and Hell: The Voice of the Devil

7 The reason Milton wrote in fetters when he wrote of Angels and God, and at liberty when of Devils and Hell, is because he was a true Poet, and of the Devil's party without knowing it. *Ib. note*

8 The road of excess leads to the palace of wisdom.
Ib. Proverbs of Hell

9 Prudence is a rich, ugly, old maid courted by Incapacity. *Ib.*

10 He who desires but acts not, breeds pestilence. *Ib.*

11 A fool sees not the same tree that a wise man sees. *Ib.*

12 Eternity is in love with the productions of time. *Ib.*

13 Bring out number, weight, and measure in a year of dearth. *Ib.*

14 If the fool would persist in his folly he would become wise. *Ib.*

15 Prisons are built with stones of Law, brothels with bricks of Religion. *Ib.*

16 The pride of the peacock is the glory of God.
The lust of the goat is the bounty of God.
The wrath of the lion is the wisdom of God.
The nakedness of woman is the work of God. *Ib.*

17 The tigers of wrath are wiser than the horses of instruction. *Ib.*

18 Damn braces. Bless relaxes. *Ib.*

19 Sooner murder an infant in its cradle than nurse unacted desires. *Ib.*

20 Truth can never be told so as to be understood, and not be believ'd. *Ib.*

21 Then I asked: 'Does a firm persuasion that a thing is so, make it so?'
He replied: 'All Poets believe that it does, and in ages of imagination this firm persuasion removed mountains; but many are not capable of a firm persuasion of anything.' *Ib. A Memorable Fancy*

SUSANNA BLAMIRE
1747–1794

22 And ye shall walk in silk attire,
And siller ha'e to spare. *The Siller Crown*

PHILIPP BLISS
1838–1876

23 Hold the fort, for I am coming.
The Charm. Ho, My Comrades, See the Signal!

ROBERT BLOOMFIELD
1766–1823

24 Strange to the world, he wore a bashful look,
The Fields his study, Nature was his book.
Farmer's Boy. Spring, l. 31

HENRY BLOSSOM
1866–1919

25 I want what I want when I want it.
Title of song in Mlle. Modiste

GEBHARD LEBERECHT BLÜCHER
1742–1819

26 Was für plündern!
What a place to plunder!
On his visit to London in 1814. Attributed

EDMUND BLUNDEN
1896–

27 All things they have in common being so poor,
And their one fear, Death's shadow at the door.
Each sundown makes them mournful, each sunrise
Brings back the brightness in their failing eyes.
Almswomen

28 These were men of pith and thew,
Whom the city never called;
Scarce could read or hold a quill,
Built the barn, the forge, the mill. *Forefathers*

29 I am for the woods against the world,
But are the woods for me? *The Kiss*

30 How shines your tower, the only one
Of that especial site and stone!
And even the dream's confusion can
Sustain to-morrow's road. *The Survival*

WILFRID SCAWEN BLUNT
1840–1922

31 God! to hear the shrill
Sweet treble of her fifes upon the breeze,
And at the summons of the rock gun's roar
To see her red coats marching from the hill!
Gibraltar

32 I would not, if I could, be called a poet.
I have no natural love of the 'chaste muse'.
If aught be worth the doing I would do it;
And others, if they will, may tell the news.
Love Sonnets of Proteus, xcv

33 I like the hunting of the hare
Better than that of the fox. *The Old Squire*

34 I like to be as my fathers were,
In the days ere I was born. *Ib.*

1 To-day, all day, I rode upon the Down,
With hounds and horsemen, a brave company.
St. Valentine's Day

2 Your face my quarry was. For it I rode,
My horse a thing of wings, myself a god. *Ib.*

JOHN ERNEST BODE
1816–1874

3 I see the sights that dazzle.
The tempting sounds I hear.
*Hymns from the Gospel for the Day. O Jesus,
I Have Promised*

BOETHIUS
?480–524

4 Nam in omni adversitate fortunae infelicissimum
genus est infortunii, fuisse felicem.

For truly in adverse fortune the worst sting of
misery is to *have been* happy.
Consolation of Philosophy, bk. ii, prose 4 (H. R.
James's translation). (*See 138:35, 168:22*)

NICOLAS BOILEAU
1636–1711

5 Enfin Malherbe vint, et, le premier en France,
Fit sentir dans les vers une juste cadence.

At last comes Malherbe, and, the first to do so in
France, makes verse run smoothly.
L'Art Poétique, i. 131–2

6 Qu'en un lieu, qu'en un jour, un seul fait accompli
Tienne jusqu'à la fin le théâtre rempli.

One action, in one place, one day perpend
And you will hold your audience till the end.
Ib. iii. 45–6

7 Si j'écris quatre mots, j'en effacerai trois.

Of every four words I write, I strike out three.
Satires, ii

HENRY ST. JOHN, VISCOUNT BOLINGBROKE
1678–1751

8 The Idea of a Patriot King. *Title of Book*

9 What a world is this, and how does fortune banter us!
Letter, 3 Aug. 1714

10 Pests of society; because their endeavours are
directed to loosen the bands of it, and to take at least
one curb out of the mouth of that wild beast man.
Ib. 12 Sept. 1724

11 Truth lies within a little and certain compass, but
error is immense. *Reflections upon Exile*

12 They make truth serve as a stalking-horse to error.
On the Study of History, letter 1

13 I have read somewhere or other—in Dionysius of
Halicarnassus, I think—that History is Philosophy
teaching by examples. *Ib.* letter 2

14 Nations, like men, have their infancy. *Ib.* letter 4

15 They [Thucydides and Xenophon] maintained the
dignity of history. *Ib.* letter 5

HORATIUS BONAR
1808–1889

16 A few more years shall roll,
A few more seasons come,
And we shall be with those that rest,
Asleep within the tomb.
Songs for the Wilderness. A Few More Years

CARRIE JACOBS BOND
1862–1946

17 And we find at the end of a perfect day
The soul of a friend we've made.
A Perfect Day, st. 2

BARTON BOOTH
1681–1733

18 True as the needle to the pole,
Or as the dial to the sun. *Song*

'GENERAL' WILLIAM BOOTH
1829–1912

19 This Submerged Tenth—is it, then, beyond the reach
of the nine-tenths in the midst of whom they live.
In Darkest England (1890), I. ii. 23

GEORGE BORROW
1803–1881

20 The author of 'Amelia', the most singular genius
which their island ever produced, whose works it
has long been the fashion to abuse in public and to
read in secret. *The Bible in Spain*, ch. 1

21 My favourite, I might say, my only study, is man.
Ib. ch. 5

22 The genuine spirit of localism. *Ib.* ch. 31

23 There are no countries in the world less known by
the British than these selfsame British Islands.
Lavengro, preface

24 There's night and day, brother, both sweet things;
sun, moon, and stars, brother, all sweet things;
there's likewise a wind on the heath. Life is very
sweet, brother; who would wish to die? *Ib.* ch. 25

25 There's the wind on the heath, brother; if I could only
feel that, I would gladly live for ever. *Ib.*

26 Let no one sneer at the bruisers of England. What
were the gladiators of Rome, or the bull-fighters of
Spain, in its palmiest days, compared to England's
bruisers? *Ib.* ch. 26

27 A losing trade, I assure you, sir: literature is a drug.
Ib. ch. 30

28 Good ale, the true and proper drink of Englishmen.
He is not deserving of the name of Englishman who
speaketh against ale, that is good ale. *Ib.* ch. 48

29 Youth will be served, every dog has his day, and mine
has been a fine one. *Ib.* ch. 92

30 Fear God, and take your own part.
The Romany Rye, ch. 16

31 Tip them Long Melford. *Ib.*

MARÉCHAL BOSQUET
1810–1861

1 C'est magnifique, mais ce n'est pas la guerre.
   It is magnificent, but it is not war.
   Remark on the Charge of the Light Brigade, 1854

JOHN COLLINS BOSSIDY
1860–1928

2 And this is good old Boston,
   The home of the bean and the cod,
   Where the Lowells talk to the Cabots,
   And the Cabots talk only to God.
   On the Aristocracy of Harvard

GORDON BOTTOMLEY
1874–1948

3 When you destroy a blade of grass
   You poison England at her roots:
   Remember no man's foot can pass
   Where evermore no green life shoots.
   To Ironfounders and Others

BOULAY DE LA MEURTHE
1761–1840

4 C'est pire qu'un crime, c'est une faute.
   It is worse than a crime, it is a blunder.
   On hearing of the execution of the Duc d'Enghien,
   1804

FRANCIS WILLIAM BOURDILLON
1852–1921

5 The night has a thousand eyes,
   And the day but one;
   Yet the light of the bright world dies,
   With the dying sun.

   The mind has a thousand eyes,
   And the heart but one;
   Yet the light of a whole life dies,
   When love is done.   *Light*

W. ST. HILL BOURNE
1846–1929

6 The sower went forth sowing,
   The seed in secret slept.
   Church Bells. The Sower Went Forth Sowing

CHARLES, BARON BOWEN
1835–1894

7 The rain it raineth on the just
   And also on the unjust fella:
   But chiefly on the just, because
   The unjust steals the just's umbrella.
   Walter Sichel, Sands of Time

8 *On a metaphysician:* A blind man in a dark room
   —looking for a black hat—which isn't there.
   Attr. See Notes and Queries, clxxxii. 153

EDWARD ERNEST BOWEN
1836–1901

9 Forty years on, when afar and asunder
   Parted are those who are singing to-day.
   Forty Years On. Harrow School Song

10 Follow up! Follow up! Follow up! Follow up!
   Follow up!
   Till the field ring again and again,
   With the tramp of the twenty-two men,
   Follow up!   *Ib.*

WILLIAM LISLE BOWLES
1762–1850

11 The cause of Freedom is the cause of God!
   Edmund Burke, l. 78

JOHN BRADFORD
1510?–1555

12 But for the grace of God there goes John Bradford.
   Exclamation on seeing some criminals taken to
   execution. Dict. of Nat. Biog.

F. H. BRADLEY
1846–1924

13 Unearthly ballet of bloodless categories.
   Logic III. II. iv.

JOHN BRADSHAW
1602–1659

14 Rebellion to tyrants is obedience to God.
   Suppositious epitaph. Randall's *Life of Jeffer-*
   son, vol. iii, appendix No. IV, p. 585

JOHN BRAHAM
1774?–1856

15 England, home and beauty.
   The Americans (1811). Song, *The Death of*
   Nelson

HARRY BRAISTED
nineteenth century

16 If you want to win her hand,
   Let the maiden understand
   That she's not the only pebble on the beach.
   You're Not the Only Pebble on the Beach

REV. JAMES BRAMSTON
1694?–1744

17 What's not destroy'd by Time's devouring hand?
   Where's Troy, and where's the Maypole in the
   Strand?   *Art of Politics, l. 71*

RICHARD BRATHWAITE
1588?–1673

18 To Banbury came I, O profane one!
   Where I saw a Puritane-one
   Hanging of his cat on Monday,
   For killing of a mouse on Sunday.
   Barnabee's Journal, pt. i

JANE BRERETON
1685-1740

1 The picture plac'd the busts between,
  Adds to the thought much strength,
Wisdom, and wit are little seen,
  But folly's at full length.
  *Poems. On Mr. Nash's Picture at full Length
  between the Busts of Sir Isaac Newton and
  Mr. Pope. (Attr. also to Lord Chesterfield)*

NICHOLAS BRETON
1545?-1626?

2 We rise with the lark and go to bed with the lamb.
  The Court and Country, par. 8

3 I wish my deadly foe, no worse
Than want of friends, and empty purse.
  A Farewell to Town

4 Who can live in heart so glad
As the merry country lad. *The Happy Countryman*

5 A Mad World, My Masters. *Title of Dialogue*, 1635

6 He is as deaf as a door. *Miseries of Mavillia*, v.

7 In the merry month of May,
In a morn by break of day,
Forth I walked by the wood side,
Whenas May was in his pride:
There I spied all alone,
Phillida and Coridon.
Much ado there was, God wot,
He would love, and she would not.

She said never man was true,
He said, none was false to you.
He said, he had lov'd her long,
She said, Love should have no wrong.
Coridon would kiss her then,
She said, Maids must kiss no men,
Till they did for good and all. *Phillida and Coridon*

8 Come little babe, come silly soul,
Thy father's shame, thy mother's grief,
Born as I doubt to all our dole,
And to thy self unhappy chief:
  Sing lullaby and lap it warm,
  Poor soul that thinks no creature harm.
  A Sweet Lullaby

ROBERT BRIDGES
1844-1930

9 All women born are so perverse
No man need boast their love possessing.
  All Women Born Are So Perverse

10 Wanton with long delay the gay spring leaping
  cometh;
The blackthorn starreth now his bough on the eve of
  May. *April 1885*

11 Awake, my heart, to be loved, awake, awake!
  Awake, My Heart, To Be Loved

12 Awake, the land is scattered with light, and see,
Uncanopied sleep is flying from field and tree:
And blossoming boughs of April in laughter shake.
  Ib.

13 Clear and gentle stream!
Known and loved so long. *Clear and Gentle Stream*

14 The cliff-top has a carpet
Of lilac, gold and green:
The blue sky bounds the ocean,
The white clouds scud between. *The Cliff-Top*

15 Above my head the heaven,
The sea beneath my feet. *Ib.*

16 Were I a cloud I'd gather
My skirts up in the air,
And fly I well know whither,
And rest I well know where. *Ib. The Ocean*

17 Wherefore to-night so full of care,
My soul, revolving hopeless strife,
Pointing at hindrance, and the bare
Painful escapes of fitful life? *Dejection*

18 O soul, be patient: thou shalt find
A little matter mend all this;
Some strain of music to thy mind,
Some praise for skill not spent amiss. *Ib.*

19 O bold majestic downs, smooth, fair and lonely;
O still solitude, only matched in the skies.
Perilous in steep places,
Soft in the level races. *The Downs*

20 Gay Robin is seen no more:
He is gone with the snow.
  Gay Robin Is Seen No More

21 The whole world now is but the minister
Of thee to me. *Growth of Love*, 3

22   That old feud
'Twixt things and me is quash'd in our new truce.
  Ib.

23 The very names of things belov'd are dear,
And sounds will gather beauty from their sense,
As many a face thro' love's long residence
Groweth to fair instead of plain and sere. *Ib. 4*

24 Thus may I think the adopting Muses chose
Their sons by name, knowing none would be heard
Or writ so oft in all the world as those,—
Dan Chaucer, mighty Shakespeare, then for third
The classic Milton, and to us arose
Shelley with liquid music in the word. *Ib.*

25 And hither tempt the pilgrim steps of spring. *Ib. 6*

26   Beauty being the best of all we know
Sums up the unsearchable and secret aims
Of nature. *Ib. 8*

27 Winter was not unkind because uncouth;
His prison'd time made me a closer guest,
And gave thy graciousness a warmer zest,
Biting all else with keen and angry tooth. *Ib. 10*

28 There's many a would-be poet at this hour,
Rhymes of a love that he hath never woo'd,
And o'er his lamp-lit desk in solitude
Deems that he sitteth in the Muses' bower. *Ib. 11*

29 Lo, Shakespeare, since thy time nature is loth
To yield to art her fair supremacy;
In conquering one thou hast so enrichèd both.
What shall I say? for God—whose wise decree
Confirmeth all He did by all He doth—
Doubled His whole creation making thee. *Ib. 21*

30 I would be a bird, and straight on wings I arise,
And carry purpose up to the ends of the air. *Ib. 22*

31 The dark and serious angel, who so long
Vex'd his immortal strength in charge of me. *Ib. 61*

BRIDGES

1 What make ye and what strive for? keep ye thought
Of us, or in new excellence divine
Is old forgot? or do ye count for nought
What the Greek did and what the Florentine?
Growth of Love, 64

2 Ah heavenly joy! But who hath ever heard,
Who hath seen joy, or who shall ever find
Joy's language? There is neither speech nor word;
Nought but itself to teach it to mankind. *Ib.* 65

3 Eternal Father, who didst all create,
In whom we live, and to whose bosom move,
To all men be Thy name known, which is Love,
Till its loud praises sound at heaven's high gate.
Ib. 69

4 Christ with His lamp of truth
Sitteth upon the hill
Of everlasting youth,
And calls His saints around. *Hymn of Nature*, v

5 Gird on thy sword, O man, thy strength endue,
In fair desire thine earth-born joy renew.
Live thou thy life beneath the making sun
Till Beauty, Truth, and Love in thee are one.
Ib. vii

6 And every eve I say,
Noting my step in bliss,
That I have known no day
In all my life like this. *The Idle Life I Lead*

7 I have loved flowers that fade,
Within whose magic tents
Rich hues have marriage made
With sweet unmemoried scents.
I Have Loved Flowers That Fade

8 I heard a linnet courting
His lady in the spring:
His mates were idly sporting,
Nor stayed to hear him sing
His song of love.—
I fear my speech distorting
His tender love. *I Heard a Linnet Courting*

9 I love all beauteous things,
I seek and adore them;
God hath no better praise,
And man in his hasty days
Is honoured for them.

I too will something make
And joy in the making;
Altho' to-morrow it seem
Like the empty words of a dream
Remembered on waking.
I Love All Beauteous Things

10 I made another song,
In likeness of my love:
And sang it all day long,
Around, beneath, above:
I told my secret out,
That none might be in doubt. *I Made Another Song*

11 I never shall love the snow again
Since Maurice died.
I Never Shall Love the Snow Again

12 I will not let thee go.
Ends all our month-long love in this?
Can it be summed up so,
Quit in a single kiss?
I will not let thee go.
I Will Not Let Thee Go

13 I will not let thee go.
Had not the great sun seen, I might;
Or were he reckoned slow
To bring the false to light,
Then might I let thee go. *I Will Not Let Thee Go*

14 Thou sayest farewell, and lo!
I have thee by the hands,
And will not let thee go. *Ib.*

15 When men were all asleep the snow came flying,
In large white flakes falling on the city brown,
Stealthily and perpetually settling and loosely lying.
London Snow

16 'O look at the trees!' they cried, 'O look at the trees!'
Ib.

17 My delight and thy delight
Walking, like two angels white,
In the gardens of the night.
My Delight and Thy Delight

18 Beautiful must be the mountains whence ye come,
And bright in the fruitful valleys the streams, where-
from
Ye learn your song:
Where are those starry woods? O might I wander
there,
Among the flowers, which in that heavenly air
Bloom the year long! *Nightingales*

19 Nay, barren are those mountains and spent the
streams:
Our song is the voice of desire, that haunts our
dreams.
A throe of the heart. *Ib.*

20 As night is withdrawn
From these sweet-springing meads and bursting
boughs of May,
Dream, while the innumerable choir of day
Welcome the dawn. *Ib.*

21 Rejoice ye dead, where'er your spirits dwell,
Rejoice that yet on earth your fame is bright,
And that your names, remembered day and night,
Live on the lips of those who love you well.
Ode to Music

22 Perfect little body, without fault or stain on thee,
With promise of strength and manhood full and fair!
On a Dead Child

23 He
Must gather his faith together, and his strength make
stronger. *Ib.*

24 O youth whose hope is high,
Who dost to Truth aspire,
Whether thou live or die,
O look not back nor tire.
O Youth Whose Hope is High

25 If thou canst Death defy,
If thy Faith is entire,
Press onward, for thine eye
Shall see thy heart's desire. *Ib.*

26 Whither, O splendid ship, thy white sails crowding,
Leaning across the bosom of the urgent West,
That fearest nor sea rising, nor sky clouding,
Whither away, fair rover, and what thy quest?
A Passer-By

[81]

1 Since to be loved endures,
 To love is wise:
Earth hath no good but yours,
 Brave, joyful eyes:
Earth hath no sin but thine,
 Dull eye of scorn:
O'er thee the sun doth pine
 And angels mourn.   *Since to be Loved Endures*

2 So sweet love seemed that April morn,
When first we kissed beside the thorn,
So strangely sweet, it was not strange
We thought that love could never change.

But I can tell—let truth be told—
That love will change in growing old;
Though day by day is nought to see,
So delicate his motions be.   *So Sweet Love Seemed*

3 I wonder, bathed in joy complete,
How love so young could be so sweet.   *Ib.*

4 Back on budding boughs
Come birds, to court and pair,
Whose rival amorous vows
Amaze the scented air.   *Spring*, ode i. 1

5 And country life I praise,
And lead, because I find
The philosophic mind
Can take no middle ways.   *Ib.* 7

6 With ecstasies so sweet
As none can even guess,
Who walk not with the feet
Of joy in idleness.   *Ib.* 10

7 Spring goeth all in white,
Crowned with milk-white may:
In fleecy flocks of light
O'er heaven the white clouds stray:

White butterflies in the air;
White daisies prank the ground:
The cherry and hoary pear
Scatter their snow around.
    Spring Goeth All in White

8 Now will the Orientals make hither in return
Outlandish pilgrimage: their wiseacres have seen
The electric light i' the West, and come to worship.
    The Testament of Beauty, l. 592

9 There is a hill beside the silver Thames,
Shady with birch and beech and odorous pine:
And brilliant underfoot with thousand gems
Steeply the thickets to his floods decline.
    There is a Hill

10 Fight, to be found fighting: nor far away
Deem, nor strange thy doom.
Like this sorrow 'twill come,
And the day will be to-day.   *Weep Not To-Day*

11 When Death to either shall come,—
 I pray it be first to me,—
Be happy as ever at home,
 If so, as I wish, it be.
Possess thy heart, my own;
 And sing to the child on thy knee,
Or read to thyself alone
 The songs that I made for thee.
    When Death to Either Shall Come

12 When first we met we did not guess
That Love would prove so hard a master.
    When First We Met We Did Not Guess

13 When June is come, then all the day
I'll sit with my love in the scented hay:
And watch the sunshot palaces high,
That the white clouds build in the breezy sky.
    When June is Come

14 That
Sheep-worry of Europe. [Napoleon]
    Wintry Delights, l. 121

JOHN BRIGHT
1811–1889

15 My opinion is that the Northern States will manage
somehow to muddle through.
    During the American Civil War. Quoted in Justin
    McCarthy: *Reminiscences* (1899)

16 The knowledge of the ancient languages is mainly a
luxury.   *Letter in* Pall Mall Gaz., 30 Nov. 1886

17 The angel of death has been abroad throughout the
land; you may almost hear the beating of his wings.
    Speech, House of Commons, 23 Feb. 1855

18 I am for 'Peace, retrenchment, and reform', the
watchword of the great Liberal party 30 years ago.
    Ib. Birmingham, 28 Apr. 1859

19 England is the mother of Parliaments.
    Ib. 18 Jan. 1865

20 The right hon. Gentleman . . . has retired into what
may be called his political Cave of Adullam—and he
has called about him every one that was in distress
and every one that was discontented.
    Ib. House of Commons, 13 Mar. 1866

21 This party of two is like the Scotch terrier that was
so covered with hair that you could not tell which
was the head and which was the tail.   *Ib.*

22 Force is not a remedy. *Ib. Birmingham, 16 Nov. 1880*

ALEXANDER BROME
1620–1666

23 Something there is moves me to love, and I
Do know I love, but know not how, nor why.
    Love's without Reason, v

24 I have been in love, and in debt, and in drink,
This many and many a year.   *The Mad Lover*, l. 1

RICHARD BROME
d. 1652?

25 You rose o' the wrong side to-day.
    The Court-Beggar, Act II

26 I am a gentleman, though spoiled i' the breeding.
The Buzzards are all gentlemen. We came in with
the Conqueror.   *English Moor*, III. ii

J. BROMFIELD
fl. 1840

27 'Tis a very good world we live in,
To spend, and to lend, and to give in;
But to beg, or to borrow, or ask for our own,
'Tis the very worst world that ever was known.
    The Gatherer, The Mirror, 12 Sept. 1840

ISAAC HILL BROMLEY
1833-1898

1 Conductor, when you receive a fare,
Punch in the presence of the passenjare!—
Punch, brothers! Punch with care!
Punch in the presence of the passenjare!
Punch, Brother, Punch. N. G. Osborn's *Isaac H. Bromley*

2 John A. Logan is the Head Centre, the Hub, the King Pin, the Main Spring, Mogul, and Mugwump of the final plot.
New York Tribune, 16 Feb. 1877

ANNE BRONTË
1820-1849

3 Oh, I am very weary,
Though tears no longer flow;
My eyes are tired of weeping,
My heart is sick of woe. *Appeal*

4 Because the road is rough and long,
Shall we despise the skylark's song? *Views of Life*

CHARLOTTE BRONTË
1816-1855

5 Reader, I married him. *Jane Eyre, ch.* 38

6 Alfred and I intended to be married in this way almost from the first; we never meant to be spliced in the humdrum way of other people. *Villette, ch.* 42

EMILY BRONTË
1818-1848

7 No coward soul is mine,
No trembler in the world's storm-troubled sphere:
I see Heaven's glories shine,
And faith shines equal, arming me from fear.
Last Lines

8 O God within my breast,
Almighty! ever-present Deity!
Life—that in me has rest,
As I—undying Life—have power in Thee! *Ib.*

9 Vain are the thousand creeds
That move men's hearts: unutterably vain;
Worthless as withered weeds,
Or idlest froth amid the boundless main. *Ib.*

10 So surely anchor'd on
The steadfast rock of immortality. *Ib.*

11 Though earth and man were gone,
And suns and universes ceased to be,
And Thou wert left alone,
Every existence would exist in Thee. *Ib.*

12 There is not room for Death,
Nor atom that his might could render void:
Thou—THOU art Being and Breath,
And what THOU art may never be destroy'd. *Ib.*

13 Oh! dreadful is the check—intense the agony—
When the ear begins to hear, and the eye begins to see;
When the pulse begins to throb, the brain to think again;
The soul to feel the flesh, and the flesh to feel the chain. *The Prisoner*

14 Cold in the earth—and fifteen wild Decembers,
From those brown hills, have melted into spring.
Remembrance

15 I lingered round them, under that benign sky: watched the moths fluttering among the heath and hare-bells; listened to the soft wind breathing through the grass; and wondered how any one could ever imagine unquiet slumbers for the sleepers in that quiet earth.
Wuthering Heights. Last Words

HENRY BROOKE
1703?-1783

16 For righteous monarchs,
Justly to judge, with their own eyes should see;
To rule o'er freemen, should themselves be free.
Earl of Essex, 1

RUPERT BROOKE
1887-1915

17 The hawthorn hedge puts forth its buds,
And my heart puts forth its pain.
All Suddenly the Spring Comes Soft

18 And I shall find some girl perhaps,
And a better one than you,
With eyes as wise, but kindlier,
And lips as soft, but true.
And I daresay she will do. *The Chilterns*

19 Blow out, you bugles, over the rich Dead!
There's none of these so lonely and poor of old,
But, dying, has made us rarer gifts than gold.
These laid the world away; poured out the red
Sweet wine of youth; gave up the years to be
Of work and joy, and that unhoped serene,
That men call age; and those who would have been,
Their sons, they gave, their immortality. *The Dead*

20 Honour has come back, as a king, to earth,
And paid his subjects with a royal wage;
And Nobleness walks in our ways again;
And we have come into our heritage. *Ib.*

21 The cool kindliness of sheets, that soon
Smooth away trouble; and the rough male kiss of blankets. *The Great Lover*

22 The benison of hot water. *Ib.*

23 Fish say, they have their stream and pond;
But is there anything beyond? *Heaven*

24 One may not doubt that, somehow, good
Shall come of water and of mud;
And, sure, the reverent eye must see
A purpose in liquidity. *Ib.*

25 But somewhere, beyond space and time,
Is wetter water, slimier slime! *Ib.*

26 Immense, of fishy form and mind,
Squamous, omnipotent, and kind;
And under that Almighty Fin,
The littlest fish may enter in. *Ib.*

27 Oh! never fly conceals a hook,
Fish say, in the Eternal Brook,
But more than mundane weeds are there,
And mud, celestially fair. *Ib.*

1 Unfading moths, immortal flies,
And the worm that never dies.
And in that Heaven of all their wish,
There shall be no more land, say fish.   *Heaven*

2 Breathless, we flung us on the windy hill,
Laughed in the sun, and kissed the lovely grass.
The Hill

3 'We are Earth's best, that learnt her lesson here.
Life is our cry. We have kept the faith!' we said;
'We shall go down with unreluctant tread
Rose-crowned into the darkness!'   *Ib.*

4 —And then you suddenly cried, and turned away.
Ib.

5 With snuffle and sniff and handkerchief,
And dim and decorous mirth,
With ham and sherry, they'll meet to bury
The lordliest lass of earth.
*Lines Written in the Belief that the Ancient
Roman Festival of the Dead was called Ambar-
valia*

6 Spend in pure converse our eternal day;
Think each in each, immediately wise;
Learn all we lacked before; hear, know, and say
What this tumultuous body now denies;
And feel, who have laid our groping hands away;
And see, no longer blinded by our eyes.
Not With Vain Tears

7 Oh! Death will find me, long before I tire
Of watching you; and swing me suddenly
Into the shade and loneliness and mire
Of the last land!   *Oh! Death Will Find Me*

8 Oh! there the chestnuts, summer through,
Beside the river make for you
A tunnel of green gloom, and sleep
Deeply above.   *The Old Vicarage, Grantchester*

9 Here tulips bloom as they are told;
Unkempt about those hedges blows
An English unofficial rose.   *Ib.*

10 And there the unregulated sun
Slopes down to rest when day is done,
And wakes a vague unpunctual star,
A slippered Hesper.   *Ib.*

11 Curates, long dust, will come and go
On lissom, clerical, printless toe;
And oft between the boughs is seen
The sly shade of a Rural Dean.   *Ib.*

12 God! I will pack, and take a train,
And get me to England once again!
For England's the one land, I know,
Where men with splendid hearts may go;
And Cambridgeshire, of all England,
The shire for men who understand;
And of *that* district I prefer
The lovely hamlet Grantchester.   *Ib.*

13 For Cambridge people rarely smile,
Being urban, squat, and packed with guile.   *Ib.*

14 They love the Good; they worship Truth;
They laugh uproariously in youth;
(And when they get to feeling old,
They up and shoot themselves, I'm told.)   *Ib.*

15 Stands the Church clock at ten to three?
And is there honey still for tea?   *Ib.*

16 Now, God be thanked Who has matched us with His
hour,
And caught our youth, and wakened us from sleeping.
Peace

17 Leave the sick hearts that honour could not move,
And half-men, and their dirty songs and dreary,
And all the little emptiness of love.   *Ib.*

18 Naught broken save this body, lost but breath;
Nothing to shake the laughing heart's long peace
there
But only agony, and that has ending;
And the worst friend and enemy is but Death.   *Ib.*

19   Safe shall be my going,
Secretly armed against all death's endeavour;
Safe though all safety's lost; safe where men fall;
And if these poor limbs die, safest of all.   *Safety*

20 Some white tremendous daybreak.   *Second Best*

21 If I should die, think only this of me:
That there's some corner of a foreign field
That is for ever England. There shall be
In that rich earth a richer dust concealed;
A dust whom England bore, shaped, made aware,
Gave, once, her flowers to love, her ways to roam,
A body of England's, breathing English air,
Washed by the rivers, blest by suns of home.
And think, this heart, all evil shed away,
A pulse in the eternal mind, no less
Gives somewhere back the thoughts by England
given.
Her sights and sounds; dreams happy as her day;
And laughter, learnt of friends; and gentleness,
In hearts at peace, under an English heaven.
The Soldier

22 But there's wisdom in women, of more than they
have known,
And thoughts go blowing through them, are wiser
than their own.   *There's Wisdom in Women*

23 And there's an end, I think, of kissing,
When our mouths are one with Mouth.
Tiare Tahiti

PHILLIPS BROOKS
1835–1893

24 O little town of Bethlehem,
How still we see thee lie;
Above thy deep and dreamless sleep
The silent stars go by.
The Church Porch. O Little Town of Bethlehem

25 Yet in thy dark streets shineth
The everlasting light;
The hopes and fears of all the years
Are met in thee to-night.   *Ib.*

THOMAS BROOKS
1608–1680

26 For (magna est veritas et prævalebit) great is truth,
and shall prevail.
The Crown and Glory of Christianity (1662), p. 407

ROBERT BARNABAS BROUGH
1828–1860

27 My Lord Tomnoddy is thirty-four;
The Earl can last but a few years more.

My Lord in the Peers will take his place:
Her Majesty's councils his words will grace.
Office he'll hold and patronage sway;
Fortunes and lives he will vote away;
And what are his qualifications?—ONE!
He's the Earl of Fitzdotterel's eldest son.
My Lord Tomnoddy

HENRY, BARON BROUGHAM
1778-1868

1 In my mind, he was guilty of no error,—he was chargeable with no exaggeration,—he was betrayed by his fancy into no metaphor, who once said, that all we see about us, Kings, Lords, and Commons, the whole machinery of the State, all the apparatus of the system, and its varied workings, end in simply bringing twelve good men into a box.
Speech on the Present State of the Law, 7 Feb. 1828, p. 5

2 Look out, gentlemen, the schoolmaster is abroad!
Attr. to Speech, London Mechanics' Institute, 1825

3 Education makes a people easy to lead, but difficult to drive; easy to govern, but impossible to enslave.
Attr.

JOHN BROWN
1715-1766

4 Truth's sacred Fort th' exploded laugh shall win;
And Coxcombs vanquish Berkley by a grin.
Essay on Satire. On the Death of Pope, l. 223

5 Altogether upon the high horse.
Letter to Garrick, 27 Oct. 1765. Correspondence of Garrick (1831), vol. 1, p. 205

JOHN BROWN
1800-1859

6 I, John Brown, am now quite certain that the crimes of this guilty land will never be purged away but with blood.
Last Statement, 2 Dec. 1859. R. J. Hinton, John Brown and His Men

JOHN BROWN
1810-1882

7 'Dish or no dish', rejoined the Caledonian [to an Englishman,] 'there's a deal of fine confused feedin' about it, [a singed sheep's-head,] let me tell you.'
Horae Subsecivae ('With brains, Sir')

THOMAS BROWN
1663-1704

8 In the reign of King Charles the Second, a certain worthy Divine at Whitehall, thus address'd himself to the auditory at the conclusion of his sermon: 'In short, if you don't live up to the precepts of the Gospel, but abandon your selves to your irregular appetites, you must expect to receive your reward in a certain place, which 'tis not good manners to mention here.'
Laconics

9 A little before you made a leap into the dark.
Letters from the Dead

10 I do not love you, Dr. Fell,
But why I cannot tell;
But this I know full well,
I do not love you, Dr. Fell.
(trans. of *Martial, Epigrams*, i. 32.) *Works* (1719), vol. iv, p. 113

THOMAS EDWARD BROWN
1830-1897

11 O blackbird, what a boy you are!
How you do go it. *The Blackbird*

12 A garden is a lovesome thing, God wot! *My Garden*

13 Not God! in gardens! when the eve is cool?
Nay, but I have a sign;
'Tis very sure God walks in mine. *Ib.*

CHARLES FARRAR BROWNE
see
ARTEMUS WARD

SIR THOMAS BROWNE
1605-1682

14 He who discommendeth others obliquely commendeth himself. *Christian Morals*, pt. i, § xxxiv

15 That unextinguishable laugh in heaven.
The Garden of Cyrus, ch. 2

16 Life itself is but the shadow of death, and souls departed but the shadows of the living. All things fall under this name. The sun itself is but the dark *simulacrum*, and light but the shadow of God.
Ib. ch. 4

17 Flat and flexible truths are beat out by every hammer; but Vulcan and his whole forge sweat to work out Achilles his armour. *Ib.* ch. 5

18 But the quincunx of heaven runs low, and 'tis time to close the five ports of knowledge. *Ib.*

19 All things began in order, so shall they end, and so shall they begin again; according to the ordainer of order and mystical mathematics of the city of heaven. *Ib.*

20 Nor will the sweetest delight of gardens afford much comfort in sleep; wherein the dullness of that sense shakes hands with delectable odours; and though in the bed of Cleopatra, can hardly with any delight raise up the ghost of a rose. *Ib.*

21 Though Somnus in Homer be sent to rouse up Agamemnon, I find no such effects in these drowsy approaches of sleep. To keep our eyes open longer were but to act our Antipodes. The huntsmen are up in America, and they are already past their first sleep in Persia. But who can be drowsy at that hour which freed us from everlasting sleep? or have slumbering thoughts at that time, when sleep itself must end, and, as some conjecture, all shall awake again? *Ib.*

22 Dreams out of the ivory gate, and visions before midnight. *On Dreams* (*Works* [1835], vol. iv, p. 359)

23 Half our days we pass in the shadow of the earth; and the brother of death exacteth a third part of our lives. *Ib.*

1 I dare, without usurpation, assume the honourable style of a Christian. *Religio Medici*, pt. i, § 1

2 At my devotion I love to use the civility of my knee, my hat, and hand. *Ib.* § 3

3 I could never divide my self from any man upon the difference of an opinion, or be angry with his judgment for not agreeing with me in that, from which perhaps within a few days I should dissent my self. *Ib.* § 6

4 Many . . . have too rashly charged the troops of error, and remain as trophies unto the enemies of truth. *Ib.*

5 A man may be in as just possession of truth as of a city, and yet be forced to surrender. *Ib.*

6 Methinks there be not impossibilities enough in Religion for an active faith. *Ib.* § 9

7 As for those wingy mysteries in divinity, and airy subtleties in religion, which have unhinged the brains of better heads, they never stretched the *pia mater* of mine. *Ib.*

8 I love to lose myself in a mystery; to pursue my reason to an *O altitudo!* *Ib.* § 10

9 Who can speak of eternity without a solecism, or think thereof without an ecstasy? Time we may comprehend, 'tis but five days elder than ourselves. *Ib.* § 11

10 I have often admired the mystical way of Pythagoras, and the secret magic of numbers. *Ib.* § 12

11 We carry within us the wonders we seek without us: There is all Africa and her prodigies in us. *Ib.* § 15

12 All things are artificial, for nature is the art of God. *Ib.* § 16

13 'Twill be hard to find one that deserves to carry the buckler unto Samson. *Ib.* § 21

14 Obstinacy in a bad cause, is but constancy in a good. *Ib.* § 25

15 Persecution is a bad and indirect way to plant religion. *Ib.*

16 There are many (questionless) canonized on earth, that shall never be Saints in Heaven. *Ib.* § 26

17 Not pickt from the leaves of any author, but bred amongst the weeds and tares of mine own brain. *Ib.* § 35

18 This reasonable moderator and equal piece of justice, Death. *Ib.* § 37

19 I am not so much afraid of death, as ashamed thereof; 'tis the very disgrace and ignominy of our natures. *Ib.* § 39

20 Certainly there is no happiness within this circle of flesh, nor is it in the optics of these eyes to behold felicity; the first day of our Jubilee is death. *Ib.* § 43

21 I have tried if I could reach that great resolution . . . to be honest without a thought of Heaven or Hell. *Ib.* § 46

22 To believe only possibilities, is not faith, but mere Philosophy. *Ib.*

23 There is no road or ready way to virtue. *Ib.* § 53

24 My desires only are, and I shall be happy therein, to be but the last man, and bring up the rear in heaven. *Religio Medici*, pt. i, § 57

25 I am of a constitution so general, that it consorts and sympathiseth with all things. I have no antipathy, or rather idiosyncrasy, in diet, humour, air, any thing. *Ib.* pt. ii, § 1

26 If there be any among those common objects of hatred I do contemn and laugh at, it is that great enemy of reason, virtue, and religion, the multitude; that numerous piece of monstrosity, which, taken asunder, seem men, and the reasonable creatures of God, but, confused together, make but one great beast, and a monstrosity more prodigious than Hydra. *Ib.*

27 I feel not in myself those common antipathies that I can discover in others; those national repugnances do not touch me, nor do I behold with prejudice the French, Italian, Spaniard, or Dutch; but where I find their actions in balance with my countrymen's, I honour, love and embrace them in the same degree. *Ib.*

28 All places, all airs make unto me one country; I am in England, everywhere, and under any meridian. *Ib.*

29 It is the common wonder of all men, how among so many millions of faces, there should be none alike. *Ib.* § 2

30 No man can justly censure or condemn another, because indeed no man truly knows another. *Ib.* § 4

31 Charity begins at home, is the voice of the world. *Ib.*

32 Sure there is music even in the beauty, and the silent note which Cupid strikes, far sweeter than the sound of an instrument. For there is a music wherever there is a harmony, order or proportion; and thus far we may maintain the music of the spheres; for those well ordered motions, and regular paces, though they give no sound unto the ear, yet to the understanding they strike a note most full of harmony. *Ib.* § 9

33 For even that vulgar and tavern music, which makes one man merry, another mad, strikes in me a deep fit of devotion, and a profound contemplation of the first Composer, there is something in it of divinity more than the ear discovers. *Ib.*

34 I could be content that we might procreate like trees, without conjunction, or that there were any way to perpetuate the World without this trivial and vulgar way of coition: it is the foolishest act a wise man commits in all his life; nor is there any thing that will more deject his cool'd imagination, when he shall consider what an odd and unworthy piece of folly he hath committed. *Ib.*

35 We all labour against our own cure, for death is the cure of all diseases. *Ib.*

36 For the world, I count it not an inn, but an hospital, and a place, not to live, but to die in. *Ib.* § 12

37 There is surely a piece of divinity in us, something that was before the elements, and owes no homage unto the sun. *Ib.*

38 [Sleep is] in fine, so like death, I dare not trust it without my prayers. *Ib.* § 13

1 Sleep is a death, O make me try,
By sleeping what it is to die.
And as gently lay my head
On my grave, as now my bed. *Religio Medici*, pt. ii, § 31

2 Conclude in a moist relentment. *Urn Burial*, ch. 1

3 With rich flames, and hired tears, they solemnized
their obsequies. *Ib.* ch. 3

4 Hercules is not only known by his foot. *Ib.*

5 Men have lost their reason in nothing so much as their
religion, wherein stones and clouts make martyrs.
Ib. ch. 4

6 They carried them out of the world with their feet
forward. *Ib.*

7 Were the happiness of the next world as closely
apprehended as the felicities of this, it were a
martyrdom to live.

8 These dead bones have . . . quietly rested under the
drums and tramplings of three conquests. *Ib.* ch. 5

9 Time, which antiquates antiquities, and hath an art
to make dust of all things, hath yet spared these
minor monuments. *Ib.*

10 The long habit of living indisposeth us for dying. *Ib.*

11 Misery makes Alcmena's nights. *Ib.*

12 What song the Syrens sang, or what name Achilles
assumed when he hid himself among women,
though puzzling questions, are not beyond all
conjecture. *Ib.*

13 Circles and right lines limit and close all bodies, and
the mortal right-lined circle, must conclude and
shut up all. *Ib.*

14 Old families last not three oaks. *Ib.*

15 To be nameless in worthy deeds exceeds an infamous
history. *Ib.*

16 But the iniquity of oblivion blindly scattereth her
poppy, and deals with the memory of men without
distinction to merit of perpetuity. *Ib.*

17 Herostratus lives that burnt the Temple of Diana—
he is almost lost that built it. *Ib.*

18 The night of time far surpasseth the day, and who
knows when was the equinox? *Ib.*

19 Mummy is become merchandise, Mizraim cures
wounds, and Pharaoh is sold for balsams. *Ib.*

20 Man is a noble animal, splendid in ashes, and pompous in the grave. *Ib.*

21 Ready to be any thing, in the ecstasy of being ever,
and as content with six foot as the *moles* of Adrianus.
Ib.

WILLIAM BROWNE
1591–1643

22 And all the former causes of her moan
Did therewith bury in oblivion.
Britannia's Pastorals, bk. i, Song 2

23 Well languag'd Daniel. *Ib.* bk. ii, Song 2

24 Underneath this sable hearse
Lies the subject of all verse,
Sidney's sister, Pembroke's mother;
Death! ere thou hast slain another,
Fair and learn'd, and good as she,
Time shall throw a dart at thee.
Epitaph. On the Countess of Pembroke

25 May! Be thou never grac'd with birds that sing,
Nor Flora's pride!
In thee all flowers and roses spring,
Mine only died. *In Obitum M.S. xº. Maij*

SIR WILLIAM BROWNE
1692–1774

26 The King to Oxford sent a troop of horse,
For Tories own no argument but force:
With equal skill to Cambridge books he sent,
For Whigs admit no force but argument.
Reply to Trapp's epigram 'The King, observing
with judicious eyes' (*see 548:20*)
Nichols' Literary Anecdotes, vol. iii, p. 330

ELIZABETH BARRETT BROWNING
1806–1861

27 Here's God down on us! what are you about?
How all those workers start amid their work,
Look round, look up, and feel, a moment's space,
That carpet-dusting, though a pretty trade,
Is not the imperative labour after all.
Aurora Leigh, bk. i

28 Near all the birds
Will sing at dawn,—and yet we do not take
The chaffering swallow for the holy lark. *Ib.*

29 God answers sharp and sudden on some prayers,
And thrusts the thing we have prayed for in our face,
A gauntlet with a gift in't. *Ib.* bk. ii

30 The music soars within the little lark,
And the lark soars. *Ib.* bk. iii

31 I think it frets the saints in heaven to see
How many desolate creatures on the earth
Have learnt the simple dues of fellowship
And social comfort, in a hospital. *Ib.*

32 Now may the good God pardon all good men!
Ib. bk. iv

33 Since when was genius found respectable? *Ib.* bk. vi

34 The devil's most devilish when respectable.
Ib. bk. vii

35 Earth's crammed with heaven,
And every common bush afire with God;
But only he who sees, takes off his shoes,
The rest sit round it and pluck blackberries,
And daub their natural faces unaware
More and more from the first similitude. *Ib.*

36 'Jasper first,' I said,
'And second sapphire; third chalcedony;
The rest in order,—last an amethyst.' *Ib.* bk. ix

37 Speak low to me, my Saviour, low and sweet
From out the hallelujahs, sweet and low,
Lest I should fear and fall, and miss Thee so
Who art not missed by any that entreat. *Comfort*

38 O poets, from a maniac's tongue was poured the
deathless singing!
O Christians, at your cross of hope, a hopeless hand
was clinging!
O men, this man in brotherhood your weary paths
beguiling,
Groaned inly while he taught you peace, and died
while ye were smiling. *Cowper's Grave*

39 And kings crept out again to feel the sun.
Crowned and Buried

1 Do ye hear the children weeping, O my brothers,
  Ere the sorrow comes with years?
  The Cry of the Children

2 But the young, young children, O my brothers,
  They are weeping bitterly!
  They are weeping in the playtime of the others,
  In the country of the free. *Ib.*

3 And lips say, 'God be pitiful,'
  Who ne'er said, 'God be praised.'
  Cry of the Human

4 And that dismal cry rose slowly
  And sank slowly through the air,
  Full of spirit's melancholy
  And eternity's despair!
  And they heard the words it said—
  Pan is dead! great Pan is dead!
  Pan, Pan is dead! *The Dead Pan*

5 Oh, the little birds sang east, and the little birds sang
  west, *Toll slowly*.
  And I smiled to think God's greatness flowed around
  our incompleteness,—
  Round our restlessness, His rest.
  Rime of the Duchess May, last stanza

6 Thou large-brained woman and large-hearted man.
  To George Sand. A Desire

7 Or from Browning some 'Pomegranate', which, if
  cut deep down the middle,
  Shows a heart within blood-tinctured, of a veined
  humanity. *Lady Geraldine's Courtship*, xli

8 By thunders of white silence, overthrown.
  Hiram Power's Greek Slave

9 'Yes,' I answered you last night;
  'No,' this morning, sir, I say.
  Colours seen by candle-light
  Will not look the same by day. *The Lady's Yes*

10 In the pleasant orchard closes,
  'God bless all our gains,' say we;
  But 'May God bless all our losses,'
  Better suits with our degree. *The Lost Bower*

11 What was he doing, the great god Pan,
  Down in the reeds by the river?
  Spreading ruin and scattering ban,
  Splashing and paddling with hoofs of a goat,
  And breaking the golden lilies afloat
  With the dragon-fly on the river.
  A Musical Instrument

12 Yet half a beast is the great god Pan,
  To laugh as he sits by the river,
  Making a poet out of a man:
  The true gods sigh for the cost and pain,—
  For the reed which grows nevermore again
  As a reed with the reeds in the river. *Ib.*

13 And her smile, it seems half holy,
  As if drawn from thoughts more far
  Than our common jestings are.

  And if any poet knew her,
  He would sing of her with falls
  Used in lovely madrigals. *A Portrait*

14 God keeps a niche
  In Heaven, to hold our idols: and albeit
  He brake them to our faces, and denied
  That our close kisses should impair their white,—

I know we shall behold them raised, complete,
The dust swept from their beauty,—glorified,
New Memnons singing in the great God-light.
  Sonnets. Futurity

15 I tell you, hopeless grief is passionless.
  Sonnets. Grief

16 Straightway I was 'ware,
  So weeping, how a mystic shape did move
  Behind me, and drew me backward by the hair
  And a voice said in mastery while I strove, . . .
  'Guess now who holds thee?'—'Death', I said, but
  there
  The silver answer rang, . . . 'Not Death, but Love.'
  Sonnets from the Portuguese, 1

17 The face of all the world is changed, I think,
  Since first I heard the footsteps of thy soul
  Move still, oh, still, beside me, as they stole
  Betwixt me and the dreadful outer brink
  Of obvious death, where I, who thought to sink,
  Was caught up into love, and taught the whole
  Of a new rhythm. *Ib.* 7

18 If thou must love me, let it be for naught
  Except for love's sake only. *Ib.* 14

19 When our two souls stand up erect and strong
  Face to face, silent, drawing nigh and nigher.
  Ib. 22

20 Let us stay
  Rather on earth, Beloved—where the unfit
  Contrarious moods of men recoil away
  And isolate pure spirits, and permit
  A place to stand and love in for a day,
  With darkness and the death-hour rounding it. *Ib.*

21 God's gifts put man's best dreams to shame. *Ib.* 26

22 First time he kissed me, he but only kissed
  The fingers of this hand wherewith I write;
  And, ever since, it grew more clean and white. *Ib.* 38

23 And think it soon when others cry, 'Too late'. *Ib.* 40

24 How do I love thee? Let me count the ways.
  I love thee to the depth and breadth and height
  My soul can reach, when feeling out of sight
  For the ends of Being and ideal Grace.
  I love thee to the level of every day's
  Most quiet need, by sun and candle light.
  I love thee freely, as men strive for Right;
  I love thee purely, as they turn from Praise.
  I love thee with the passion put to use
  In my old griefs, and with my childhood's faith.
  I love thee with a love I seemed to lose
  With my lost saints—I love thee with the breath,
  Smiles, tears, of all my life!—and, if God choose,
  I shall but love thee better after death. *Ib.* 43

25 Of all the thoughts of God that are
  Borne inward unto souls afar,
  Along the Psalmist's music deep,
  Now tell me if that any is,
  For gift or grace, surpassing this—
  'He giveth His beloved, sleep.' *The Sleep*

26 O earth, so full of dreary noises!
  O men, with wailing in your voices!
  O delvèd gold, the wailers heap!
  O strife, O curse, that o'er it fall!
  God strikes a silence through you all,
  And giveth His belovèd, sleep. *Ib.*

1 Let One, most loving of you all,
Say, 'Not a tear must o'er her fall;
He giveth His belovèd, sleep.'   *The Sleep*

2 There Shakespeare, on whose forehead climb
The crowns o' the world. Oh, eyes sublime,
With tears and laughters for all time!
          A Vision of Poets, verse 100

3 Life treads on life, and heart on heart:
We press too close in church and mart
To keep a dream or grave apart.   *Ib.* (conclusion)

4 Knowledge by suffering entereth;
And Life is perfected by Death.   *Ib.*

5 And the rolling anapaestic
Curled like vapour over shrines!
          Wine of Cyprus, x

6 Our Euripides, the human,
With his droppings of warm tears,
And his touches of things common
Till they rose to touch the spheres!   *Ib.* xii

ROBERT BROWNING
1812–1889

7 Burrow awhile and build, broad on the roots of things.
          Abt Vogler, ii

8 On the earth the broken arcs; in the heaven, a perfect
round.   *Ib.* ix

9 All we have willed or hoped or dreamed of good shall
exist.   *Ib.* x

10 The high that proved too high, the heroic for earth too
hard,
The passion that left the ground to lose itself in the
sky,
Are music sent up to God by the lover and the bard;
Enough that he heard it once: we shall hear it by and
by.   *Ib.*

11 But God has a few of us whom he whispers in the
ear;
The rest may reason and welcome; 'tis we musicians
know.   *Ib.* xi

12 The C Major of this life.   *Ib.* xii

13 How he lies in his rights of a man!
Death has done all death can.   *After*

14 So free we seem, so fettered fast we are!
          Andrea del Sarto

15 Ah, but a man's reach should exceed his grasp,
Or what's a heaven for?   *Ib.*

16 Four great walls in the New Jerusalem,
Meted on each side by the angel's reed,
For Leonard, Rafael, Agnolo and me
To cover.   *Ib.*

17 Again the Cousin's whistle! Go, my Love.   *Ib.*

18 It all comes to the same thing at the end.
          Any Wife to Any Husband

19 Why need the other women know so much?   *Ib.*

20 A minute's success pays the failure of years.
          Apollo and the Fates, prologue

21 The Doric little Morgue!   *Apparent Failure*

22 It's wiser being good than bad;
It's safer being meek than fierce:
It's fitter being sane than mad.
My own hope is, a sun will pierce

The thickest cloud earth ever stretched;
That, after Last, returns the First,
Though a wide compass round be fetched;
That what began best can't end worst,
Nor what God blessed once, prove accurst.
          Apparent Failure

23 But, thanks to wine-lees and democracy,
We've still our stage where truth calls spade a spade!
          Aristophanes' Apology, l. 392

24 He lies now in the little valley, laughed
And moaned about by those mysterious streams.
          Ib. l. 5679

25 There up spoke a brisk little somebody,
Critic and whippersnapper, in a rage
To set things right.
          Balaustion's Adventure, pt. i, l. 308

26 A man can have but one life and one death,
One heaven, one hell.   *In a Balcony*, l. 13

27 I count life just a stuff
To try the soul's strength on.   *Ib.* l. 651

28 Truth that peeps
Over the glass's edge when dinner's done,
And body gets its sop and holds its noise
And leaves soul free a little.
          Bishop Blougram's Apology

29 A piano-forte is a fine resource,
All Balzac's novels occupy one shelf,
The new edition fifty volumes long.   *Ib.*

30 The funny type
They get up well at Leipsic.   *Ib.*

31 Just when we're safest, there's a sunset-touch,
A fancy from a flower-bell, some one's death,
A chorus-ending from Euripides,
And that's enough for fifty hopes and fears,—
The grand Perhaps.   *Ib.*

32 All we have gained then by our unbelief
Is a life of doubt diversified by faith,
For one of faith diversified by doubt:
We called the chess-board white—we call it black. *Ib.*

33 Demireps
That love and save their souls in new French books.
          Ib.

34 You, for example, clever to a fault,
The rough and ready man that write apace,
Read somewhat seldomer, think perhaps even less.
          Ib.

35 Be a Napoleon and yet disbelieve!
Why, the man's mad, friend, take his light away. *Ib.*

36 And that's what all the blessed Evil's for.   *Ib.*

37 Set you square with Genesis again.   *Ib.*

38 No, when the fight begins within himself,
A man's worth something.   *Ib.*

39 Gigadibs the literary man.   *Ib.*

40 He said true things, but called them by wrong names.
          Ib.

41 By this time he has tested his first plough,
And studied his last chapter of St. John.   *Ib.*

42 Saint Praxed's ever was the church for peace.
          The Bishop Orders His Tomb

43 Mistresses with great smooth marbly limbs.   *Ib.*

44 See God made and eaten all day long.   *Ib.*

45 Good, strong, thick, stupefying incense-smoke.   *Ib.*

1 Aha, ELUCESCEBAT quoth our friend?
No Tully, said I, Ulpian at the best.
The Bishop Orders His Tomb

2 There's a woman like a dew-drop, she's so purer than
the purest.   *A Blot in the 'Scutcheon,* I. iii

3 Morning, evening, noon and night,
'Praise God!' sang Theocrite.
The Boy and the Angel

4 How well I know what I mean to do
When the long dark autumn-evenings come.
By the Fireside, i

5 Not verse now, only prose!   *Ib.* ii

6 O woman-country, wooed not wed.   *Ib.* vi

7   That great brow
And the spirit-small hand propping it.   *Ib.* xxiii

8 We two stood there with never a third.   *Ib.* xxxviii

9 Oh, the little more, and how much it is!
And the little less, and what worlds away!
Ib. xxxix

10 If you join two lives, there is oft a scar.
They are one and one, with a shadowy third;
One near one is too far.   *Ib.* xlvi

11 One born to love you, sweet!   *Ib.* li

12 Letting the rank tongue blossom into speech.
Caliban upon Setebos, l. 23

13 Setebos, Setebos, and Setebos!
'Thinketh, He dwelleth i' the cold o' the moon.
'Thinketh He made it, with the sun to match,
But not the stars; the stars came otherwise. *Ib.* l. 24

14 'Let twenty pass, and stone the twenty-first.
Loving not, hating not, just choosing so. *Ib.* l. 103

15 A bitter heart that bides its time and bites. *Ib.* l. 167

16 Kentish Sir Byng stood for his King,
Bidding the crop-headed Parliament swing:
And, pressing a troop unable to stoop
And see the rogues flourish and honest folk droop,
Marched them along, fifty-score strong,
Great-hearted gentlemen, singing this song.

God for King Charles! Pym and such carles
To the Devil that prompts 'em their treasonous parles!
Cavalier Tunes, i. *Marching Along*

17 King Charles, and who'll do him right now?
King Charles, and who's ripe for fight now?
Give a rouse: here's, in Hell's despite now,
King Charles!   *Ib.* 2. *Give a Rouse*

18 To whom used my boy George quaff else,
By the old fool's side that begot him?
For whom did he cheer and laugh else,
While Noll's damned troopers shot him?   *Ib.*

19 Boot, saddle, to horse, and away!
Ib. 3. *Boot and Saddle*

20 'Tis the Last Judgment's fire must cure this place,
Calcine its clods and set my prisoners free.
Childe Roland, xi

21 One stiff blind horse, his every bone a-stare. *Ib.* xiii

22 I never saw a brute I hated so;
He must be wicked to deserve such pain.   *Ib.* xiv

23 Dauntless the slug-horn to my lips I set,
And blew. *Childe Roland to the Dark Tower came.*
Ib. xxxiv

24 Out of the little chapel I burst
Into the fresh night-air again.   *Christmas Eve,* i

25 The preaching man's immense stupidity.   *Ib.* iii

26 In the natural fog of the good man's mind.   *Ib.* iv

27 He was there.
He himself with his human air.   *Ib.* viii

28 Our best is bad, nor bears Thy test;
Still, it should be our very best.   *Ib.*

29 Some thrilling view of the surplice-question. *Ib.* xiv

30 The exhausted air-bell of the Critic.   *Ib.* xvi

31 While I watched my foolish heart expand
In the lazy glow of benevolence,
O'er the various modes of man's belief.   *Ib.* xx

32 The raree-show of Peter's successor.   *Ib.* xxii

33 For the preacher's merit or demerit,
It were to be wished the flaws were fewer
In the earthen vessel, holding treasure,
Which lies as safe in a golden ewer;
But the main thing is, does it hold good measure?
Heaven soon sets right all other matters!   *Ib.*

34   The sprinkled isles,
Lily on lily, that o'erlace the sea.
And laugh their pride when the light wave lisps
'Greece'.   *Cleon,* l. 1

35 I have written three books on the soul,
Proving absurd all written hitherto,
And putting us to ignorance again.   *Ib.* l. 57

36 What is he buzzing in my ears?
'Now that I come to die,
Do I view the world as a vale of tears?'
Ah, reverend sir, not I!   *Confessions*

37 To mine, it serves for the old June weather
Blue above lane and wall;
And that farthest bottle labelled 'Ether'
Is the house o'ertopping all.   *Ib.*

38 How sad and bad and mad it was—
But then, how it was sweet!   *Ib.*

39 There are flashes struck from midnights,
There are fire-flames noondays kindle,
Whereby piled-up honours perish,
Whereby swollen ambitions dwindle,
While just this or that poor impulse,
Which for once had play unstifled,
Seems the sole work of a life-time
That away the rest have trifled.   *Cristina,* 4

40 Stung by the splendour of a sudden thought.
A Death in the Desert, l. 59

41 Such ever was love's way: to rise, it stoops. *Ib.* l. 134

42 For life, with all it yields of joy and woe,
And hope and fear,—believe the aged friend—
Is just a chance o' the prize of learning love.
Ib. l. 245

43 I say, the acknowledgement of God in Christ
Accepted by thy reason, solves for thee
All questions in the earth and out of it.   *Ib.* l. 474

44 For I say, this is death and the sole death,
When a man's loss comes to him from his gain,
Darkness from light, from knowledge ignorance,
And lack of love from love made manifest. *Ib.* l. 482

1 Progress, man's distinctive mark alone,
Not God's, and not the beasts': God is, they are,
Man partly is and wholly hopes to be.
A Death in the Desert, l. 586

2 But 'twas Cerinthus that is lost. *Ib.* last line

3 Your ghost will walk, you lover of trees,
(If our loves remain)
In an English lane. *De Gustibus*

4 The bean-flowers' boon. *Ib.*

5 A castle, precipice-encurled,
In a gash of the wind-grieved Apennine. *Ib.*

6 Italy, my Italy!
Queen Mary's saying serves for me—
(When fortune's malice
Lost her—Calais)—
Open my heart and you will see
Graved inside of it, 'Italy'. *Ib.*

7 Reads verse and thinks she understands.
Dis aliter visum, iv

8 Schumann's our music-maker now. *Ib.* viii

9 Ingres's the modern man who paints. *Ib.*

10 Heine for songs; for kisses, how? *Ib.*

11 Sure of the Fortieth spare Arm-chair
When gout and glory seat me there. *Ib.* xii

12 With loves and doves, at all events
With money in the Three per Cents. *Ib.* xiii

13 Here comes my husband from his whist. *Ib.* xxx

14 That one Face, far from vanish, rather grows,
Or decomposes but to recompose,
Become my universe that feels and knows.
Dramatis Personae, epilogue, third speaker, xii

15 How very hard it is to be
A Christian! *Easter Day*, i

16 'Tis well averred,
A scientific faith's absurd. *Ib.* vi

17 A fierce vindictive scribble of red. *Ib.* xv

18 'Condemned to earth for ever, shut
From heaven!'
But Easter-Day breaks! But
Christ rises! Mercy every way
Is infinite—and who can say? *Ib.* xxxiii

19 Karshish, the picker-up of learning's crumbs.
An Epistle

20 Beautiful Evelyn Hope is dead! *Evelyn Hope*

21 Your mouth of your own geranium's red. *Ib.*

22 You will wake, and remember, and understand. *Ib.*

23 What if this friend happen to be—God?
Fears and Scruples, xii

24 Truth never hurts the teller.
Fifine at the Fair, xxxii

25 'What, and is it really you again?' quoth I:
'I again, what else did you expect?' quoth she.
Ib. epilogue, i

26 I chanced upon a new book yesterday:
I opened it, and where my finger lay
'Twixt page and uncut page those words I read,
Some six or seven at most, and learned thereby
That you, FitzGerald, whom by ear and eye
She never knew, 'thanked God my wife was dead.'

Ay, dead! and were yourself alive, good Fitz,
How to return your thanks would pass my wits.
Kicking you seems the common lot of curs—
While more appropriate greeting lends you grace:
Surely to spit there glorifies your face—
Spitting from lips once sanctified by Hers.
Rejoinder to a remark (see 207 : 33) by Edward FitzGerald on the death of E. B. Browning.
Athenaeum, No. 3220 (*13 July 1889*), p. 64

27 When the liquor's out why clink the cannikin?
The Flight of the Duchess, xvi

28 You're my friend—
What a thing friendship is, world without end!
Ib. xvii

29 I must learn Spanish, one of these days,
Only for that slow sweet name's sake.
The Flower's Name

30 Is there no method to tell her in Spanish
June's twice June since she breathed it with me? *Ib.*

31 If you get simple beauty and nought else,
You get about the best thing God invents.
Fra Lippo Lippi, l. 217

32 You should not take a fellow eight years old
And make him swear to never kiss the girls. *Ib.* l. 224

33 This world's no blot for us,
Nor blank; it means intensely, and means good:
To find its meaning is my meat and drink. *Ib.* l. 313

34 [*Christianity*]
'Tis the faith that launched point-blank her dart
At the head of a lie—taught Original Sin,
The corruption of Man's Heart. *Gold Hair*

35 The moth's kiss, first!
Kiss me as if you made believe
You were not sure, this eve,
How my face, your flower, had pursed
Its petals up. . . .
The bee's kiss, now!
Kiss me as if you entered gay
My heart at some noonday. *In a Gondola*

36 Let us begin and carry up this corpse,
Singing together. *A Grammarian's Funeral*, l. 1

37 He's for the morning. *Ib.* l. 24

38 This is our master, famous, calm, and dead,
Borne on our shoulders. *Ib.* l. 27

39 Yea, this in him was the peculiar grace . . .
That before living he'd learn how to live. *Ib.* l. 75

40 He said, 'What's time? leave Now for dogs and apes!
Man has Forever.' *Ib.* l. 83

41 That low man seeks a little thing to do,
Sees it and does it:
This high man, with a great thing to pursue,
Dies ere he knows it.
That low man goes on adding one to one,
His hundred's soon hit:
This high man, aiming at a million,
Misses an unit.
That, has the world here—should he need the next,
Let the world mind him!
This, throws himself on God, and unperplext
Seeking shall find Him. *Ib.* l. 113

42 He settled *Hoti's* business—let it be!—
Properly based *Oun*—
Gave us the doctrine of the enclitic *De*,
Dead from the waist down. *Ib.* l. 129

1 Lofty designs must close in like effects.
A Grammarian's Funeral, l. 145

2 O, world, as God has made it! all is beauty.
The Guardian Angel

3 This is Ancona, yonder is the sea. *Ib.*

4 Infinite mercy, but, I wis,
As infinite a justice too.
The Heretic's Tragedy, i

5 (And wanteth there grace of lute or clavicithern, ye
shall say to confirm him who singeth—)
We bring John now to be burned alive. *Ib.* ii

6 Forth John's soul flared into the dark. *Ib.* x

7 God help all poor souls lost in the dark! *Ib.*

8 I liken his Grace to an acorned hog.
Holy-Cross Day, iv

9 The Lord will have mercy on Jacob yet,
And again in his border see Israel set. *Ib.* xiii

10 Thou! if thou wast He, who at mid-watch came,
By the starlight, naming a dubious name! *Ib.* xvi

11 We gave the Cross, when we owed the Throne. *Ib.*

12 We withstood Christ then? Be mindful how
At least we withstand Barabbas now! *Ib.* xviii

13   We march, thy band,
South, East, and on to the Pleasant Land. *Ib.* xx

14 Oh, to be in England
   Now that April's there,
And whoever wakes in England
   Sees, some morning, unaware,
That the lowest boughs and the brushwood sheaf
   Round the elm-tree bole are in tiny leaf,
While the chaffinch sings on the orchard bough
   In England—now! *Home-thoughts, from Abroad*

15 That's the wise thrush; he sings each song twice over,
Lest you should think he never could recapture
The first fine careless rapture! *Ib.*

16 All will be gay when noontide wakes anew
The buttercups, the little children's dower
—Far brighter than this gaudy melon-flower! *Ib.*

17 Nobly, nobly Cape St. Vincent to the North-west
died away;
Sunset ran, one glorious blood-red, reeking into
Cadiz Bay.
Home-thoughts, from the Sea

18 'Here and here did England help me: how can I help
England?'—say,
Whoso turns as I, this evening, turn to God to praise
and pray,
While Jove's planet rises yonder, silent over Africa.
Ib

19   'With this same key
Shakespeare unlocked his heart' once more!
Did Shakespeare? If so, the less Shakespeare he!
House, x

20 How it strikes a Contemporary. *Title*

21 He took such cognizance of men and things.
How it Strikes a Contemporary, l. 30

22 I sprang to the stirrup, and Joris, and he;
I galloped, Dirck galloped, we galloped all three.
How they brought the Good News from Ghent to Aix

23 You know, we French stormed Ratisbon.
Incident of the French Camp

24 'You're wounded!' 'Nay,' the soldier's pride
Touched to the quick, he said:
'I'm killed, Sire!' And his chief beside
Smiling the boy fell dead. *Incident of the French Camp*

25 Ignorance is not innocence but sin.
The Inn Album, v

26 Just my vengeance complete,
   The man sprang to his feet,
Stood erect, caught at God's skirts, and prayed!
—So, *I* was afraid! *Instans Tyrannus*

27 The swallow has set her six young on the rail,
   And looks seaward. *James Lee*, III. i

28 Oh, good gigantic smile o' the brown old earth.
Ib. VII. i

29 I should be dead of joy, James Lee.
Ib. IX. viii

30 There's heaven above, and night by night
I look right through its gorgeous roof.
Johannes Agricola in Meditation

31 I said—Then, dearest, since 'tis so,
Since now at length my fate I know,
Since nothing all my love avails,
Since all, my life seemed meant for, fails,
Since this was written and needs must be—
My whole heart rises up to bless
Your name in pride and thankfulness!
Take back the hope you gave,—I claim
Only a memory of the same.
The Last Ride Together, i

32 Who knows but the world may end to-night? *Ib.* ii

33 Hush! if you saw some western cloud
All billowy-bosomed, over-bowed
By many benedictions—sun's
And moon's and evening-star's at once. *Ib.* iii

34   My soul
Smoothed itself out, a long-cramped scroll
Freshening and fluttering in the wind. *Ib.* iv

35 Might she have loved me? just as well
She might have hated, who can tell! *Ib.*

36 The petty done, the undone vast. *Ib.* v

37 What hand and brain went ever paired? *Ib.* vi

38 They scratch his name on the Abbey-stones.
My riding is better, by their leave. *Ib.*

39 Sing, riding's a joy! For me, I ride. *Ib.* vii

40 Ride, ride together, for ever ride? *Ib.* x

41 Escape me?
Never—
Beloved! *Life in a Love*

42 To dry one's eyes and laugh at a fall,
And, baffled, get up and begin again. *Ib.*

43 No sooner the old hope goes to ground
Than a new one, straight to the self-same mark,
I shape me—
Ever
Removed! *Ib.*

44 So I gave her eyes my own eyes to take,
   My hand sought hers as in earnest need,
And round she turned for my noble sake,
   And gave me herself indeed. *A Light Woman*

45 'Tis an awkward thing to play with souls,
And matter enough to save one's own. *Ib.*

46 And, Robert Browning, you writer of plays,
Here's a subject made to your hand! *Ib.*

1 A face to lose youth for, to occupy age
With the dream of, meet death with. *A Likeness*

2 Just for a handful of silver he left us,
Just for a riband to stick in his coat.
The Lost Leader

3 We that had loved him so, followed him, honoured him,
Lived in his mild and magnificent eye,
Learned his great language, caught his clear accents,
Made him our pattern to live and to die! *Ib.*

4 Shakespeare was of us, Milton was for us,
Burns, Shelley, were with us—they watch from their graves! *Ib.*

5 We shall march prospering,—not thro' his presence;
Songs may inspirit us,—not from his lyre;
Deeds will be done,—while he boasts his quiescence,
Still bidding crouch whom the rest bade aspire. *Ib.*

6 One more devils'-triumph and sorrow for angels,
One wrong more to man, one more insult to God! *Ib.*

7 Never glad confident morning again! *Ib.*

8 All's over, then; does truth sound bitter
As one at first believes? *The Lost Mistress*

9 I will hold your hand but as long as all may,
Or so very little longer! *Ib.*

10 Where the quiet-coloured end of evening smiles.
Love among the Ruins

11 Earth's returns
For whole centuries of folly, noise and sin! *Ib.*

12 Love is best. *Ib.*

13 How the March sun feels like May! *A Lovers' Quarrel*

14 Oppression makes the wise man mad. *Luria*, iv

15 But a bird's weight can break the infant tree
Which after holds an aery in its arms. *Ib.*

16 The only fault's with time;
All men become good creatures: but so slow! *Ib.* v

17 Argument's hot to the close.
Master Hugues of Saxe-Gotha, xiii

18 One dissertates, he is candid;
Two must discept,—has distinguished. *Ib.* xiv

19 A poor devil has ended his cares
At the foot of your rotten-runged rat-riddled stairs?
Do I carry the moon in my pocket? *Ib.* xxix

20 As I gain the cove with pushing prow,
And quench its speed i' the slushy sand.
Meeting at Night

21 A mile of warm sea-scented beach. *Ib.*

22 A tap at the pane, the quick sharp scratch
And blue spurt of a lighted match,
And a voice less loud, thro' its joys and fears,
Than the two hearts beating each to each! *Ib.*

23 Ah, did you once see Shelley plain,
And did he stop and speak to you
And did you speak to him again?
How strange it seems, and new! *Memorabilia*

24 A moulted feather, an eagle-feather!
Well, I forget the rest. *Ib.*

25 Have you found your life distasteful?
My life did, and does, smack sweet.
Was your youth of pleasure wasteful?
Mine I saved and hold complete.

Do your joys with age diminish?
When mine fail me, I'll complain.
Must in death your daylight finish?
My sun sets to rise again. *At the 'Mermaid'*

26 I find earth not grey but rosy,
Heaven not grim but fair of hue.
Do I stoop? I pluck a posy.
Do I stand and stare? All's blue. *Ib.*

27 'Next Poet'—(Manners, Ben!) *Ib.*

28 If such as came for wool, sir, went home shorn,
Where is the wrong I did them?
Mr. Sludge, 'The Medium', l. 630

29 Solomon of saloons
And philosophic diner-out. *Ib.* l. 773

30 This trade of mine—I don't know, can't be sure
But there was something in it, tricks and all!
Really, I want to light up my own mind. *Ib.* l. 809

31 Boston's a hole, the herring-pond is wide,
V-notes are something, liberty still more.
Beside, is he the only fool in the world?
Ib. last lines

32 This is a spray the bird clung to. *Misconceptions*

33 This is a heart the Queen leant on. *Ib.*

34 That's my last Duchess painted on the wall.
My Last Duchess, l. i

35 What matter to me if their star is a world?
Mine has opened its soul to me; therefore I love it.
My Star

36 Give me of Nelson only a touch.
Nationality in Drinks

37 All I can say is—I saw it! *Natural Magic*

38 Never the time and the place
And the loved one all together!
Never the Time and the Place

39 A lion who dies of an ass's kick,
The wronged great soul of an ancient Master
Old Pictures in Florence, vi

40 What's come to perfection perishes.
Things learned on earth, we shall practise in heaven.
Works done least rapidly, Art most cherishes.
Ib. xvii

41 There remaineth a rest for the people of God:
And I have had troubles enough, for one. *Ib.* xxii

42 All June I bound the rose in sheaves.
One Way of Love

43 Lose who may—I still can say,
Those who win heaven, blest are they! *Ib.*

44 There they are, my fifty men and women.
One Word More, i

45 Rafael made a century of sonnets,
Made and wrote them in a certain volume
Dinted with the silver-pointed pencil
Else he only used to draw Madonnas. *Ib.* ii

46 Suddenly, as rare things will, it vanished. *Ib.* iv

47 Dante once prepared to paint an angel:
Whom to please? You whisper 'Beatrice'. *Ib.* v

48 Dante, who loved well because he hated,
Hated wickedness that hinders loving. *Ib.*

49 Does he paint? he fain would write a poem—
Does he write? he fain would paint a picture.
Ib. viii

BROWNING

1 Heaven's gift takes earth's abatement.
One Word More, ix

2 Even he, the minute makes immortal,
Proves, perchance, but mortal in the minute. *Ib.*

3 Never dares the man put off the prophet. *Ib.* x

4 Other heights in other lives, God willing:
All the gifts from all the heights, your own, Love!
Ib. xii

5 He who blows thro' bronze, may breathe thro' silver.
Ib. xiii

6 I am mine and yours—the rest be all men's. *Ib.* xiv

7 Where my heart lies, let my brain lie also. *Ib.*

8   Lo, the moon's self!
Here in London, yonder late in Florence,
Still we find her face, the thrice-transfigured.
Curving on a sky imbrued with colour,
Drifted over Fiesole by twilight,
Came she, our new crescent of a hair's-breadth.
Full she flared it, lamping Samminiato,
Rounder 'twixt the cypresses and rounder,
Perfect till the nightingales applauded. *Ib.* xv

9 Blank to Zoroaster on his terrace,
Blind to Galileo on his turret,
Dumb to Homer, dumb to Keats—him, even!
Ib. xvi

10 God be thanked, the meanest of his creatures
Boasts two soul-sides, one to face the world with,
One to show a woman when he loves her! *Ib.* xvii

11 Silent silver lights and darks undreamed of,
Where I hush and bless myself with silence. *Ib.* xviii

12 Oh, their Rafael of the dear Madonnas,
Oh, their Dante of the dread Inferno,
Wrote one song—and in my brain I sing it,
Drew one angel—borne, see, on my bosom! *Ib.* xix

13 I see my way as birds their trackless way,
I shall arrive! what time, what circuit first,
I ask not: but unless God send his hail
Or blinding fireballs, sleet or stifling snow,
In some time, his good time, I shall arrive:
He guides me and the bird. In His good time!
Paracelsus, pt. I

14 Truth is within ourselves. *Ib.*

15 PARACELSUS:
I am he that aspired to *know*: and thou?
APRILE:
I would *love* infinitely, and be loved! *Ib.* pt. II

16   God is the perfect poet,
Who in his person acts his own creations. *Ib.*

17 Measure your mind's height by the shade it casts!
Ib. pt. III

18 Heap cassia, sandal-buds and stripes
Of labdanum, and aloe-balls. *Ib.* pt. IV

19 As when a queen, long dead, was young. *Ib.*

20 Over the sea our galleys went. *Ib.*

21 All at once they leave you, and you know them!
Ib. pt. V

22 I give the fight up: let there be an end,
A privacy, an obscure nook for me.
I want to be forgotten even by God. *Ib.*

23   Progress is
The law of life, man is not man as yet. *Ib.*

24 Thus the Mayne glideth
Where my Love abideth.
Sleep's no softer. *Paracelsus*, pt. v

25 Like plants in mines which never saw the sun,
But dream of him, and guess where he may be,
And do their best to climb and get to him. *Ib.*

26   If I stoop
Into a dark tremendous sea of cloud,
It is but for a time; I press God's lamp
Close to my breast; its splendour, soon or late,
Will pierce the gloom: I shall emerge one day. *Ib.*

27 Round the Cape of a sudden came the sea,
And the sun looked over the mountain's rim;
And straight was a path of gold for him,
And the need of a world of men for me.
Parting at Morning

28 It was roses, roses, all the way. *The Patriot*

29 The air broke into a mist with bells. *Ib.*

30 Sun-treader, life and light be thine for ever!
(*Shelley*) *Pauline*, l. 148

31 Ah, thought which saddens while it soothes!
Pictor Ignotus

32 Hamelin Town's in Brunswick,
By famous Hanover city;
The river Weser, deep and wide,
Washes its walls on the southern side.
The Pied Piper of Hamelin, st. i

33 Shrieking and squeaking
In fifty different sharps and flats. *Ib.* ii

34 A plate of turtle green and glutinous. *Ib.* iv

35 Anything like the sound of a rat
Makes my heart go pit-a-pat! *Ib.*

36 In did come the strangest figure! *Ib.* v

37 So munch on, crunch on, take your nuncheon,
Breakfast, supper, dinner, luncheon. *Ib.* vii

38 So, Willy, let me and you be wipers
Of scores out with all men, especially pipers! *Ib.* xv

39 Day! Faster and more fast,
O'er night's brim, day boils at last.
Pippa Passes, introduction

40 The year's at the spring,
And day's at the morn;
Morning's at seven;
The hill-side's dew-pearled;
The lark's on the wing;
The snail's on the thorn:
God's in his heaven—
All's right with the world! *Ib.* pt. I

41 God must be glad one loves His world so much!
Ib. pt. III

42 Some unsuspected isle in the far seas!
Some unsuspected isle in far-off seas! *Ib.*

43 In the morning of the world,
When earth was nigher heaven than now. *Ib.*

44 No need that sort of king should ever die! *Ib.*

45 You'll look at least on love's remains,
A grave's one violet:
Your look?—that pays a thousand pains.
What's death? You'll love me yet! *Ib.*

46 All service ranks the same with God—
With God, whose puppets, best and worst,
Are we; there is no last nor first. *Ib.* pt. iv

[94]

1 Stand still, true poet that you are!
  I know you; let me try and draw you.
  Some night you'll fail us: when afar
  You rise, remember one man saw you,
  Knew you, and named a star!   *Popularity*

2   With ardours manifold,
  The bee goes singing to her groom,
  Drunken and overbold.   *Ib.*

3   Who fished the murex up?
  What porridge had John Keats?   *Ib.*

4 The rain set early in to-night.   *Porphyria's Lover*

5   All her hair
  In one long yellow string I wound
  Three times her little throat around,
  And strangled her. No pain felt she;
  I am quite sure she felt no pain.   *Ib.*

6 And all night long we have not stirred,
  And yet God has not said a word!   *Ib.*

7 But flame? The bush is bare.   *Prologue (Asolando)*

8 Fear death?—to feel the fog in my throat,
  The mist in my face.   *Prospice*

9 Where he stands, the Arch Fear in a visible form.
  Ib.

10 I was ever a fighter, so—one fight more,
  The best and the last!
  I would hate that death bandaged my eyes, and for-
  bore,
  And bade me creep past.   *Ib.*

11 No! let me taste the whole of it, fare like my peers
  The heroes of old,
  Bear the brunt, in a minute pay glad life's arrears
  Of pain, darkness and cold.   *Ib.*

12 O thou soul of my soul! I shall clasp thee again,
  And with God be the rest!   *Ib.*

13 Grow old along with me!
  The best is yet to be,
  The last of life, for which the first was made:
  Our times are in His hand
  Who saith, 'A whole I planned,
  Youth shows but half; trust God: see all, nor be
  afraid!'   *Rabbi ben Ezra, i*

14 Irks care the crop-full bird? Frets doubt the maw-
  crammed beast?   *Ib. iv*

15 Then, welcome each rebuff
  That turns earth's smoothness rough,
  Each sting that bids nor sit nor stand but go!
  Be our joys three-parts pain!
  Strive, and hold cheap the strain;
  Learn, nor account the pang; dare, never grudge the
  throe!   *Ib. vi*

16 For thence,—a paradox
  Which comforts while it mocks,—
  Shall life succeed in that it seems to fail:
  What I aspired to be,
  And was not, comforts me.
  A brute I might have been, but would not sink i' the
  scale.   *Ib. vii*

17 Let us not always say
  'Spite of this flesh to-day
  I strove, made head, gained ground upon the whole!'
  As the bird wings and sings,
  Let us cry 'All good things
  Are ours, nor soul helps flesh more, now, than flesh
  helps soul.'   *Ib. xii*

18 Once more on my adventure brave and new.
  Rabbi ben Ezra, xiv

19   When evening shuts,
  A certain moment cuts
  The deed off, calls the glory from the grey.   *Ib.* xvi

20   Now, who shall arbitrate?
  Ten men love what I hate,
  Shun what I follow, slight what I receive:
  Ten, who in ears and eyes
  Match me: we all surmise,
  They, this thing, and I, that: whom shall my soul
  believe?   *Ib.* xxii

21 Fancies that broke through language and escaped.
  Ib. xxv

22   All that is, at all,
  Lasts ever, past recall;
  Earth changes, but thy soul and God stand sure.
  Ib. xxvii

23 Time's wheel runs back or stops: potter and clay
  endure.   *Ib.*

24 He fixed thee mid this dance
  Of plastic circumstance.   *Ib.* xxviii

25 Look not thou down but up!
  To uses of a cup.   *Ib.* xxx

26 My times be in Thy hand!
  Perfect the cup as planned!
  Let age approve of youth, and death complete the
  same!   *Ib.* xxxii

27 Do you see this square old yellow Book, I toss
  I' the air, and catch again.
  The Ring and the Book, bk. i, l. 33

28 The Life, Death, Miracles of Saint Somebody,
  Saint Somebody Else, his Miracles, Death and Life.
  Ib. l. 80

29 Well, British Public, ye who like me not,
  (God love you!).   *Ib.* l. 410

30 'Go get you manned by Manning and new-manned
  By Newman and, mayhap, wise-manned to boot
  By Wiseman.'   *Ib.* l. 444

31   A dusk mis-featured messenger,
  No other than the angel of this life,
  Whose care is lest men see too much at once.
  Ib. l. 593

32 Let this old woe step on the stage again!   *Ib.* l. 824

33   Youth means love,
  Vows can't change nature, priests are only men.
  Ib. l. 1056

34 O lyric Love, half angel and half bird
  And all a wonder and a wild desire.   *Ib.* l. 1391

35 Boldest of hearts that ever braved the sun,
  Took sanctuary within the holier blue,
  And sang a kindred soul out to his face,—
  Yet human at the red-ripe of the heart.   *Ib.* l. 1393

36 This is the same voice: can thy soul know change?
  Ib. l. 1401

37 Never may I commence my song, my due
  To God who best taught song by gift of thee,
  Except with bent head and beseeching hand.
  Ib. l. 1403

38 Their utmost up and on.   *Ib.* l. 1413

39 The story always old and always new.
  Ib. bk. ii, l. 214

1 But facts are facts and flinch not.
The Ring and the Book, bk. ii, l. 1049

2 Go practise if you please
With men and women: leave a child alone
For Christ's particular love's sake!—so I say.
Ib. bk. iii. l. 88

3 In the great right of an excessive wrong. *Ib.* l. 1055

4 Everyone soon or late comes round by Rome.
Ib. bk. v, l. 296

5 'Twas a thief said the last kind word to Christ:
Christ took the kindness and forgave the theft.
Ib. bk. vi, l. 869

6 O great, just, good God! Miserable me! *Ib.* l. 2105

7 The uncomfortableness of it all. *Ib.* bk. vii, l. 400

8 True life is only love, love only bliss. *Ib.* l. 960

9 O lover of my life, O soldier-saint. *Ib.* l. 1786

10 Through such souls alone
God stooping shows sufficient of His light
For us i' the dark to rise by. And I rise. *Ib.* l. 1843

11 Faultless to a fault. *Ib.* bk. ix, l. 1177

12 Of what I call God,
And fools call Nature. *Ib.* bk. x, l. 1073

13 Why comes temptation but for man to meet
And master and make crouch beneath his foot,
And so be pedestalled in triumph? *Ib.* l. 1185

14 White shall not neutralize the black, nor good
Compensate bad in man, absolve him so:
Life's business being just the terrible choice.
Ib. l. 1236

15 There's a new tribunal now,
Higher than God's—the educated man's! *Ib.* l. 1976

16 That sad obscure sequestered state
Where God unmakes but to remake the soul
He else made first in vain; which must not be.
Ib. l. 2130

17 Abate,—Cardinal,—Christ,—Maria,—God, . . .
Pompilia, will you let them murder me?
Ib. bk. xi, l. 2424

18 It is the glory and good of Art,
That Art remains the one way possible
Of speaking truths, to mouths like mine at least.
Ib. bk. xii, l. 842

19 Thy rare gold ring of verse (the poet praised)
Linking our England to his Italy. *Ib.* l. 873

20 Good, to forgive;
Best, to forget!
Living, we fret;
Dying, we live. *La Saisiaz*, dedication

21 How good is man's life, the mere living! how fit to employ
All the heart and the soul and the senses, for ever in joy! *Saul*, ix

22 All's love, yet all's law. *Ib.* xvii

23 'Tis not what man does which exalts him, but what man would do! *Ib.* xviii

24 It is by no breath,
Turn of eye, wave of hand, that salvation joins issue with death!
As thy Love is discovered almighty, almighty be proved
Thy power, that exists with and for it, of being beloved! *Ib.*

25 O Saul, it shall be
A Face like my face that receives thee; a Man like to me,
Thou shalt love and be loved by, for ever: a Hand like this hand
Shall throw open the gates of new life to thee! See the Christ stand! *Saul*, xviii

26 Because a man has shop to mind
In time and place, since flesh must live,
Needs spirit lack all life behind,
All stray thoughts, fancies fugitive,
All loves except what trade can give? *Shop*, xx

27 I want to know a butcher paints,
A baker rhymes for his pursuit,
Candlestick-maker much acquaints
His soul with song, or, haply mute,
Blows out his brains upon the flute. *Ib.* xxi

28 Nay but you, who do not love her,
Is she not pure gold, my mistress? *Song*

29 Who will, may hear Sordello's story told.
Sordello, bk. i

30 Sidney's self, the starry paladin. *Ib.*

31 whence the grieved and obscure waters slope
Into a darkness quieted by hope;
Plucker of amaranths grown beneath God's eye
In gracious twilights where his chosen lie. *Ib.*

32 Still more labyrinthine buds the rose. *Ib.*

33 A touch divine—
And the scaled eyeball owns the mystic rod;
Visibly through his garden walketh God. *Ib.*

34 Any nose
May ravage with impunity a rose. *Ib.* bk. vi

35 Who would has heard Sordello's story told. *Ib.*

36 You are not going to marry your old friend's love, after all? *A Soul's Tragedy*, Act II

37 I have known *Four*-and-twenty leaders of revolts.
Ib. last words

38 Gr-r-r- there go, my heart's abhorrence!
Water your damned flower-pots, do!
Soliloquy of the Spanish Cloister

39 I the Trinity illustrate,
Drinking watered orange-pulp—
In three sips the Arian frustrate;
While he drains his at one gulp. *Ib.*

40 There's a great text in Galatians,
Once you trip on it, entails
Twenty-nine distinct damnations,
One sure, if another fails. *Ib.*

41 My scrofulous French novel
On grey paper with blunt type! *Ib.*

42 'St, there's Vespers! Plena gratiâ
Ave, Virgo! Gr-r-r—you swine! *Ib.*

43 The glory dropped from their youth and love,
And both perceived they had dreamed a dream.
The Statue and the Bust

44 The world and its ways have a certain worth. *Ib.*

45 The soldier-saints, who row on row,
Burn upward each to his point of bliss. *Ib.*

46 The sin I impute to each frustrate ghost
Is—the unlit lamp and the ungirt loin,
Though the end in sight was a vice, I say. *Ib.*

1 All the breath and the bloom of the year in the bag of one bee. *Summum Bonum (Asolando)*

2 At the midnight in the silence of the sleep-time, When you set your fancies free. *Ib.* epilogue

3 Greet the unseen with a cheer. *Ib.*

4 One who never turned his back but marched breast forward,
Never doubted clouds would break,
Never dreamed, though right were worsted, wrong would triumph,
Held we fall to rise, are baffled to fight better,
Sleep to wake. *Ib.*

5 I've a Friend, over the sea;
I like him, but he loves me.
It all grew out of the books I write; *Time's Revenges*

6 There may be heaven; there must be hell;
Meantime, there is our earth here—well! *Ib.*

7 Hark, the dominant's persistence till it must be answered to! *A Toccata of Galuppi's*, viii

8 What of soul was left, I wonder, when the kissing had to stop? *Ib.* xiv

9 Dear dead women, with such hair, too—what's become of all the gold
Used to hang and brush their bosoms? I feel chilly and grown old. *Ib.* xv

10 As I ride, as I ride. *Through the Metidja to Abd-el-kadr*

11 Grand rough old Martin Luther
Bloomed fables—flowers on furze,
The better the uncouther:
Do roses stick like burrs? *The Twins*

12 Only I discern—
Infinite passion, and the pain
Of finite hearts that yearn. *Two in the Campagna*

13 Sky—what a scowl of cloud
Till, near and far,
Ray on ray split the shroud
Splendid, a star! *The Two Poets of Croisic*

14 Bang-whang-whang goes the drum, tootle-te-tootle the fife. *Up at a Villa—Down in the City*

15 Wanting is—what?
Summer redundant,
Blueness abundant,
—Where is the blot? *Wanting—is what?*

16 What's become of Waring
Since he gave us all the slip? *Waring*, I. i

17 Monstr'-inform'-ingens-horrend-ous
Demoniaco-seraphic
Penman's latest piece of graphic. *Ib.* iv

18 Some lost lady of old years. *Ib.*

19 In Vishnu-land what Avatar? *Ib.* vi

20 'When I last saw Waring . . .'
(How all turned to him who spoke!
You saw Waring? Truth or joke?
In land-travel or sea-faring?) *Ib.* II. i

21 Oh, never star
Was lost here but it rose afar! *Ib.* iii

22 But little do or can the best of us:
That little is achieved through Liberty.
In Andrew Reid's *Why I am a Liberal*

23 Let's contend no more, Love,
Strive nor weep:
All be as before, Love,
—Only sleep! *A Woman's Last Word*

24 What so wild as words are? *Ib.*

25 Where the apple reddens,
Never pry—
Lest we lose our Edens,
Eve and I. *Ib.*

26 That shall be to-morrow
Not to-night!
I must bury sorrow
Out of sight. *Ib.*

27 I knew you once: but in Paradise,
If we meet, I will pass nor turn my face. *The Worst of It*, xix

28 We have not sighed deep, laughed free,
Starved, feasted, despaired,—been happy. *Youth and Art*

29 And nobody calls you a dunce,
And people suppose me clever:
This could but have happened once,
And we missed it, lost it for ever. *Ib.*

MICHAEL BRUCE
1746–1767

30 Sweet bird! thy bower is ever green,
Thy sky is ever clear:
Thou hast no sorrow in thy song,
No winter in thy year! *To the Cuckoo. (Also attr. to John Logan)*

GEORGE BRYAN BRUMMELL
1778–1840

31 Who's your fat friend? [Of the Prince of Wales.]
Gronow, *Reminiscences* (1862), p. 63

JEAN DE LA BRUYÈRE
1645–1696

32 Tout est dit et l'on vient trop tard depuis plus de sept mille ans qu'il y a des hommes et qui pensent.
Everything has been said, and we are more than seven thousand years of human thought too late. *Les Caractères (Ouvrages de l'Esprit)*

33 Le peuple n'a guère d'esprit et les grands n'ont point d'âme . . . faut-il opter, je ne balance pas, je veux être peuple.
The people have little intelligence, the great no heart . . . if I had to choose I should have no hesitation in choosing the people. *Ib. (Des Grands)*

34 Entre le bon sens et le bon goût il y a la différence de la cause et son effet.
Between good sense and good taste there is the same difference as between cause and effect. *Ib. (Des Jugements)*

ALFRED BRYAN
nineteenth century

35 Who paid the rent for Mrs. Rip Van Winkle
When Rip Van Winkle went away? *Who Paid the Rent for Mrs. Rip Van Winkle?*

WILLIAM JENNINGS BRYAN
1860–1925

1 The humblest citizen of all the land, when clad in the armor of a righteous cause, is stronger than all the hosts of error.
Speech at the National Democratic Convention, Chicago, 1896

2 You shall not press down upon the brow of labor this crown of thorns, you shall not crucify mankind upon a cross of gold. *Ib.*

WILLIAM CULLEN BRYANT
1794–1878

3 So live, that when thy summons comes to join
The innumerable caravan, which moves
To that mysterious realm, where each shall take
His chamber in the silent halls of death,
Thou go not, like the quarry-slave at night,
Scourged to his dungeon, but, sustained and soothed
By an unfaltering trust, approach thy grave
Like one who wraps the drapery of his couch
About him, and lies down to pleasant dreams.
Thanatopsis, l. 73

4 They seemed
Like old companions in adversity.
A Winter Piece, l. 26

ROBERT WILLIAMS BUCHANAN
1841–1901

5 The Fleshly School of Poetry.
Title of article in The Contemporary Review, *Oct. 1871. (Applied to Swinburne, William Morris, D. G. Rossetti, and others.)*

6 She just wore
Enough for modesty—no more.
White Rose and Red, I. v, l. 60

7 The sweet post-prandial cigar. *De Berny*

GEORGE VILLIERS, SECOND DUKE OF BUCKINGHAM
1628–1687

8 The world is made up for the most part of fools and knaves. *To Mr. Clifford, on his Humane Reason*

9 What the devil does the plot signify, except to bring in fine things? *The Rehearsal*, III. i

10 Ay, now the plot thickens very much upon us. *Ib.* ii

JOHN SHEFFIELD, FIRST DUKE OF BUCKINGHAM AND NORMANBY
1648–1721

11 Read Homer once, and you can read no more,
For all books else appear so mean, so poor,
Verse will seem prose; but still persist to read,
And Homer will be all the books you need.
An Essay on Poetry

12 A faultless monster which the world ne'er saw. *Ib.*

HENRY J. BUCKOLL
1803–1871

13 Lord, behold us with Thy blessing
Once again assembled here.
Psalms and Hymns for the Use of Rugby School Chapel. Lord, Behold us with Thy Blessing

14 Lord, dismiss us with Thy blessing,
Thanks for mercies past receive.
Ib. Lord, Dismiss us with Thy Blessing

JOHN BALDWIN BUCKSTONE
1802–1879

15 On such an occasion as this,
All time and nonsense scorning,
Nothing shall come amiss,
And we won't go home till morning.
Billy Taylor, I. ii

EUSTACE BUDGELL
1686–1737

16 What Cato did, and Addison approved
Cannot be wrong.
Lines found on his desk after his suicide, 4 May 1737

GEORGES-LOUIS LECLERC DE BUFFON
1707–1788

17 Le style est l'homme même.
Style is the man himself. *Discours sur le Style*

18 Le génie n'est qu'une grande aptitude à la patience.
Genius is only a great aptitude for patience.
Attr. to Buffon by Hérault de Séchelles in Voyage à Montbard

ARTHUR BULLER
1874–1944

19 There was a young lady named Bright,
Whose speed was far faster than light;
She set out one day
In a relative way,
And returned home the previous night.
Limerick in Punch, *19 Dec. 1923*

EDWARD GEORGE BULWER-LYTTON
see
BARON LYTTON

EDWARD ROBERT BULWER, EARL OF LYTTON
see
OWEN MEREDITH

ALFRED BUNN
1796?–1860

20 Alice, where art thou? *Title of Song*

21 I dreamt that I dwelt in marble halls,
With vassals and serfs at my side.
Bohemian Girl, Act II

22 When other lips, and other hearts,
Their tales of love shall tell. *Ib.* Act III

1 The light of other days is faded,
And all their glory past.
The Maid of Artois, Act II

JOHN BUNYAN
1628–1688

2 Mr. Badman died . . . as they call it, like a Chrisom-child, quietly and without fear.
Life and Death of Mr. Badman

3 As I walk'd through the wilderness of this world.
Pilgrim's Progress, pt. i

4 The name of the one was Obstinate and the name of the other Pliable. *Ib.*

5 The name of the slough was Despond. *Ib.*

6 The gentleman's name was Mr. Worldly-Wise-Man. *Ib.*

7 Set down my name, Sir. *Ib.*

8 Come in, come in;
Eternal glory thou shalt win. *Ib.*

9 And behold there was a very stately palace before him, the name of which was Beautiful. *Ib.*

10 The valley of Humiliation. *Ib.*

11 A foul Fiend coming over the field to meet him; his name is Apollyon. *Ib.*

12 Then Apollyon straddled quite over the whole breadth of the way. *Ib.*

13 Set your faces like a flint. *Ib.*

14 It beareth the name of Vanity-Fair, because the town where 'tis kept, is lighter than vanity. *Ib.*

15 So soon as the man overtook me, he was but a word and a blow. *Ib.*

16 Hanging is too good for him, said Mr. Cruelty. *Ib.*

17 Yet my great-grandfather was but a water-man, looking one way, and rowing another: and I got most of my estate by the same occupation.
[Mr. By-Ends.] *Ib.*

18 They came at a delicate plain, called Ease, where they went with much content; but that plain was but narrow, so they went quickly over it. *Ib.*

19 A castle, called Doubting-Castle, the owner whereof was Giant Despair. *Ib.*

20 Now Giant Despair had a wife, and her name was Diffidence. *Ib.*

21 A grievous crab-tree cudgel. *Ib.*

22 They came to the Delectable Mountains. *Ib.*

23 Sleep is sweet to the labouring man. *Ib.*

24 A great horror and darkness fell upon Christian. *Ib.*

25 Then I saw that there was a way to hell, even from the gates of heaven. *Ib.*

26 So I awoke, and behold it was a dream. *Ib.*

27 A man that could look no way but downwards, with a muckrake in his hand. *Ib.* pt. ii

28 One leak will sink a ship, and one sin will destroy a sinner. *Ib.*

29 A young Woman her name was Dull. *Ib.*

30 One Great-heart. *Ib.*

31 He that is down needs fear no fall,
He that is low no pride.
He that is humble ever shall
Have God to be his guide.
I am content with what I have,
Little be it, or much:
And, Lord, contentment still I crave,
Because Thou savest such.
Fulness to such, a burden is,
That go on pilgrimage;
Here little, and hereafter bliss,
Is best from age to age.
Pilgrim's Progress, pt. ii. *Shepherd Boy's Song in the Valley of Humiliation*

32 A man there was, tho' some did count him mad,
The more he cast away, the more he had. *Ib.*

33 An ornament to her profession. *Ib.*

34 Whose name is Valiant-for-Truth. *Ib.*

35 Who would true valour see,
Let him come hither;
One here will constant be,
Come wind, come weather.
There's no discouragement
Shall make him once relent
His first avow'd intent
To be a pilgrim.

[*Altered version in 'English Hymnal':*
He who would valiant be
'Gainst all disaster,
Let him in constancy
Follow the Master. &c.] *Ib.*

36 Who so beset him round
With dismal stories,
Do but themselves confound—
His strength the more is. *Ib.*

37 Then fancies flee away!
I'll fear not what men say,
I'll labour night and day
To be a pilgrim. *Ib.*

38 Mr. Standfast. *Ib.*

39 My sword, I give to him that shall succeed me in my pilgrimage, and my courage and skill to him that can get it. [*Mr. Valiant-for-Truth.*] *Ib.*

40 I have formerly lived by hearsay, and faith, but now I go where I shall live by sight, and shall be with Him in whose company I delight myself. [*Mr. Standfast.*] *Ib.*

41 So he passed over, and all the trumpets sounded for him on the other side. *Ib.*

SAMUEL DICKINSON BURCHARD
1812–1891

42 We are Republicans and don't propose to leave our party and identify ourselves with the party whose antecedents are rum, Romanism, and rebellion.
Speech, New York City, 29 Oct. 1884

GELETT BURGESS
1866–1951

43 Are you a bromide?
Title of Essay in Smart Set, *1906*

1 I never saw a Purple Cow,
  I never hope to see one;
  But I can tell you, anyhow,
  I'd rather see than be one!
     Burgess Nonsense Book. The Purple Cow

2 Ah, yes! I wrote the 'Purple Cow'—
  I'm sorry, now, I wrote it!
  But I can tell you anyhow,
  I'll kill you if you quote it!   *Ib.*

REV. JOHN WILLIAM BURGON
1813–1888

3 A rose-red city—'half as old as Time'! *Petra, l. 132*

JOHN BURGOYNE
1722–1792

4 You have only, when before your glass, to keep pronouncing to yourself nimini-pimini—the lips cannot fail of taking their plie.   *The Heiress, III. ii*

EDMUND BURKE
1729–1797

5 Would twenty shillings have ruined Mr. Hampden's fortune? No! but the payment of half twenty shillings, on the principle it was demanded, would have made him a slave.
     Speech on American Taxation, 1774

6 It is the nature of all greatness not to be exact. *Ib.*

7 Falsehood has a perennial spring.   *Ib.*

8 It did so happen that persons had a single office divided between them, who had never spoken to each other in their lives; until they found themselves, they knew not how, pigging together, heads and points, in the same truckle-bed.   *Ib.*

9 For even then, sir, even before this splendid orb was entirely set, and while the western horizon was in a blaze with his descending glory, on the opposite quarter of the heavens arose another luminary, and, for his hour, became lord of the ascendant. *Ib.*

10 Great men are the guide-posts and landmarks in the state.   *Ib.*

11 Passion for fame; a passion which is the instinct of all great souls.   *Ib.*

12 To tax and to please, no more than to love and to be wise, is not given to men.   *Ib.*

13 The only liberty I mean, is a liberty connected with order; that not only exists along with order and virtue, but which cannot exist at all without them.
     Speech at his arrival at Bristol, 13 Oct. 1774

14 Parliament is not a *congress* of ambassadors from different and hostile interests; which interests each must maintain, as an agent and advocate, against other agents and advocates; but parliament is a *deliberative* assembly of *one* nation, with *one* interest, that of the whole; where, not local purposes, not local prejudices ought to guide, but the general good, resulting from the general reason of the whole. You choose a member indeed; but when you have chosen him, he is not member of Bristol, but he is a member of *parliament*.
     Speech to the Electors of Bristol, 3 Nov. 1774

15 Applaud us when we run; console us when we fall; cheer us when we recover: but let us pass on—for God's sake, let us pass on!
     Speech at Bristol previous to the Election, 1780

16 Bad laws are the worst sort of tyranny.   *Ib.*

17 The worthy gentleman [Mr. Coombe], who has been snatched from us at the moment of the election, and in the middle of the contest, whilst his desires were as warm, and his hopes as eager as ours, has feelingly told us, what shadows we are, and what shadows we pursue.
     Speech at Bristol on Declining the Poll, 1780

18 The cold neutrality of an impartial judge.
     Preface to the Address of M. Brissot, 1794

19 I have in general no very exalted opinion of the virtue of paper government.
     Speech on Conciliation with America, 22 Mar. 1775

20 The noble lord in the blue riband. [Lord North, the Prime Minister.]
     Ib. (the 'blue riband' being the badge of the Order of the Garter)

21 The concessions of the weak are the concessions of fear.   *Ib.*

22 Young man, there is America—which at this day serves for little more than to amuse you with stories of savage men, and uncouth manners; yet shall, before you taste of death, show itself equal to the whole of that commerce which now attracts the envy of the world.   *Ib.*

23 When we speak of the commerce with our colonies, fiction lags after truth; invention is unfruitful, and imagination cold and barren.   *Ib.*

24 A people who are still, as it were, but in the gristle and not yet hardened into the bone of manhood. *Ib.*

25 Through a wise and salutary neglect [of the colonies], a generous nature has been suffered to take her own way to perfection; when I reflect upon these effects, when I see how profitable they have been to us, I feel all the pride of power sink and all presumption in the wisdom of human contrivances melt and die away within me. My rigour relents. I pardon something to the spirit of liberty.   *Ib.*

26 The use of force alone is but *temporary*. It may subdue for a moment; but it does not remove the necessity of subduing again: and a nation is not governed, which is perpetually to be conquered.
     Ib.

27 Nothing less will content me, than *whole America*.
     Ib.

28 Abstract liberty, like other mere abstractions, is not to be found.   *Ib.*

29 All protestantism, even the most cold and passive, is a sort of dissent. But the religion most prevalent in our northern colonies is a refinement on the principle of resistance: it is the dissidence of dissent, and the protestantism of the Protestant religion.
     Ib.

30 In no country perhaps in the world is the law so general a study. . . . This study renders men acute, inquisitive, dexterous, prompt in attack, ready in defence, full of resources. . . . They augur misgovernment at a distance, and snuff the approach of tyranny in every tainted breeze.   *Ib.*

BURKE

1 The mysterious virtue of wax and parchment.
Speech on Conciliation with America, 22 Mar. 1775.

2 I do not know the method of drawing up an indictment against an whole people. *Ib.*

3 It is not, what a lawyer tells me I *may* do; but what humanity, reason, and justice, tell me I ought to do. *Ib.*

4 Govern two millions of men, impatient of servitude, on the principles of freedom. *Ib.*

5 I am not determining a point of law; I am restoring tranquillity. *Ib.*

6 The march of the human mind is slow. *Ib.*

7 Freedom and not servitude is the cure of anarchy; as religion, and not atheism, is the true remedy for superstition. *Ib.*

8 Instead of a standing revenue, you will have therefore a perpetual quarrel. *Ib.*

9 Parties must ever exist in a free country. *Ib.*

10 My hold of the colonies is in the close affection which grows from common names, from kindred blood, from similar privileges, and equal protection. These are ties which, though light as air, are as strong as links of iron. *Ib.*

11 Slavery they can have anywhere. It is a weed that grows in every soil. *Ib.*

12 Deny them this participation of freedom, and you break that sole bond, which originally made, and must still preserve the unity of the empire. *Ib.*

13 It is the love of the people; it is their attachment to their government, from the sense of the deep stake they have in such a glorious institution, which gives your army and your navy, and infuses into both that liberal obedience, without which your army would be a base rabble, and your navy nothing but rotten timber. *Ib.*

14 Magnanimity in politics is not seldom the truest wisdom; and a great empire and little minds go ill together. *Ib.*

15 By adverting to the dignity of this high calling, our ancestors have turned a savage wilderness into a glorious empire: and have made the most extensive, and the only honourable conquests, not by destroying, but by promoting the wealth, the number, the happiness of the human race. *Ib.*

16 The people never give up their liberties but under some delusion.
Speech at County Meeting of Buckinghamshire, 1784

17 Corrupt influence, which is itself the perennial spring of all prodigality, and of all disorder; which loads us, more than millions of debt; which takes away vigour from our arms, wisdom from our councils, and every shadow of authority and credit from the most venerable parts of our constitution.
Speech on the Economical Reform, 1780

18 Individuals pass like shadows; but the commonwealth is fixed and stable. *Ib.*

19 The people are the masters. *Ib.*

20 A rapacious and licentious soldiery.
Speech on Fox's East India Bill, 1783

21 He has put to hazard his ease, his security, his interest, his power, even his darling popularity, for the benefit of a people whom he has never seen. *Ib.*

22 What the greatest inquest of the nation has begun, its highest Tribunal [the British House of Commons] will accomplish.
Impeachment of Warren Hastings, 15 Feb. 1788

23 Religious persecution may shield itself under the guise of a mistaken and over-zealous piety.
Ib. 17 Feb. 1788

24 An event has happened, upon which it is difficult to speak, and impossible to be silent.
Ib. 5 May 1789

25 Resolved to die in the last dyke of prevarication.
Ib. 7 May 1789

26 There is but one law for all, namely, that law which governs all law, the law of our Creator, the law of humanity, justice, equity—the law of nature, and of nations. *Ib. 28 May 1794*

27 I impeach him in the name of the people of India, whose rights he has trodden under foot, and whose country he has turned into a desert. Lastly, in the name of human nature itself, in the name of both sexes, in the name of every age, in the name of every rank, I impeach the common enemy and oppressor of all!
Impeachment of Warren Hastings, as recorded by Macaulay in his essay on Warren Hastings

28 His virtues were his arts.
Inscription on the statue of the Marquis of Rockingham in Wentworth Park

29 The greater the power, the more dangerous the abuse.
Speech on the Middlesex Election, 1771

30 It is not a predilection to mean, sordid, home-bred cares, that will avert the consequences of a false estimation of our interest, or prevent the shameful dilapidation, into which a great empire must fall, by mean reparations upon mighty ruins.
Speech on the Nabob of Arcot's Debts

31 Old religious factions are volcanoes burnt out.
Speech on the Petition of the Unitarians, 1792

32 Dangers by being despised grow great. *Ib.*

33 To complain of the age we live in, to murmur at the present possessors of power, to lament the past, to conceive extravagant hopes of the future, are the common dispositions of the greatest part of mankind.
Thoughts on the Cause of the Present Discontents

34 The power of the crown, almost dead and rotten as Prerogative, has grown up anew, with much more strength, and far less odium, under the name of Influence. *Ib.*

35 The wisdom of our ancestors. *Ib.*

36 When bad men combine, the good must associate; else they will fall, one by one, an unpitied sacrifice in a contemptible struggle. *Ib.*

37 Of this stamp is the cant of *Not men, but measures*; a sort of charm by which many people get loose from every honourable engagement. *Ib.*

38 There is, however, a limit at which forbearance ceases to be a virtue.
Observations on a Publication, 'The present state of the nation'

[101]

1 Well stored with pious frauds, and, like most discourses of the sort, much better calculated for the private advantage of the preacher than the edification of the hearers.

Observations on a Publication, 'The present state of the nation'

2 It is a general popular error to imagine the loudest complainers for the public to be the most anxious for its welfare. *Ib.*

3 I flatter myself that I love a manly, moral, regulated liberty as well as any gentleman.

Reflections on the Revolution in France

4 Whenever our neighbour's house is on fire, it cannot be amiss for the engines to play a little on our own. *Ib.*

5 Politics and the pulpit are terms that have little agreement. No sound ought to be heard in the church but the healing voice of Christian charity. . . . Surely the church is a place where one day's truce ought to be allowed to the dissensions and animosities of mankind. *Ib.*

6 A state without the means of some change is without the means of its conservation. *Ib.*

7 Make the Revolution a parent of settlement, and not a nursery of future revolutions. *Ib.*

8 The confused jargon of their Babylonian pulpits. *Ib.*

9 People will not look forward to posterity, who never look backward to their ancestors. *Ib.*

10 Government is a contrivance of human wisdom to provide for human *wants*. Men have a right that these wants should be provided for by this wisdom. *Ib.*

11 It is now sixteen or seventeen years since I saw the Queen of France, then the Dauphiness, at Versailles; and surely never lighted on this orb, which she hardly seemed to touch, a more delightful vision. I saw her just above the horizon, decorating and cheering the elevated sphere she just began to move in,—glittering like the morning star, full of life, and splendour, and joy. . . . Little did I dream that I should have lived to see disasters fallen upon her in a nation of gallant men, in a nation of men of honour, and of cavaliers. I thought ten thousand swords must have leaped from their scabbards to avenge even a look that threatened her with insult. But the age of chivalry is gone. That of sophisters, economists, and calculators, has succeeded; and the glory of Europe is extinguished for ever. *Ib.*

12 The unbought grace of life, the cheap defence of nations, the nurse of manly sentiment and heroic enterprise is gone! *Ib.*

13 It is gone, that sensibility of principle, that chastity of honour, which felt a stain like a wound. *Ib.*

14 Vice itself lost half its evil, by losing all its grossness. *Ib.*

15 The offspring of cold hearts and muddy understandings. *Ib.*

16 In the groves of *their* academy, at the end of every vista, you see nothing but the gallows. *Ib.*

17 Kings will be tyrants from policy, when subjects are rebels from principle. *Ib.*

18 Learning will be cast into the mire, and trodden down under the hoofs of a swinish multitude. *Ib.*

19 France has always more or less influenced manners in England: and when your fountain is choked up and polluted, the stream will not run long, or will not run clear with us, or perhaps with any nation.

Reflections on the Revolution in France

20 Because half a dozen grasshoppers under a fern make the field ring with their importunate chink, whilst thousands of great cattle, reposed beneath the shadow of the British oak, chew the cud and are silent, pray do not imagine that those who make the noise are the only inhabitants of the field; that, of course, they are many in number; or that, after all, they are other than the little, shrivelled, meagre, hopping, though loud and troublesome *insects* of the hour. *Ib.*

21 Who now reads Bolingbroke? Who ever read him through? Ask the booksellers of London what is become of all these lights of the world. *Ib.*

22 Man is by his constitution a religious animal. *Ib.*

23 A perfect democracy is therefore the most shameless thing in the world. *Ib.*

24 The men of England, the men, I mean, of light and leading in England. *Ib.*

25 Nobility is a graceful ornament to the civil order. It is the Corinthian capital of polished society. *Ib.*

26 Superstition is the religion of feeble minds. *Ib.*

27 He that wrestles with us strengthens our nerves, and sharpens our skill. Our antagonist is our helper. *Ib.*

28 Our patience will achieve more than our force. *Ib.*

29 Good order is the foundation of all good things. *Ib.*

30 The delicate and refined play of the imagination.

On the Sublime and Beautiful, introduction

31 I am convinced that we have a degree of delight, and that no small one, in the real misfortunes and pains of others. *Ib.* pt. i, § xiv

32 No passion so effectually robs the mind of all its powers of acting and reasoning as fear.

Ib. pt. ii, § ii

33 Custom reconciles us to everything.

Ib. pt. iv, § xviii

34 Laws, like houses, lean on one another.

Tracts on the Popery Laws, ch. 3, pt. i

35 In all forms of Government the people is the true legislator. *Ib.*

36 And having looked to government for bread, on the very first scarcity they will turn and bite the hand that fed them. *Thoughts and Details on Scarcity*

37 The writers against religion, whilst they oppose every system, are wisely careful never to set up any of their own.

A Vindication of Natural Society, preface

38 The fabric of superstition has in our age and nation received much ruder shocks than it had ever felt before; and through the chinks and breaches of our prison we see such glimmerings of light, and feel such refreshing airs of liberty, as daily raise our ardour for more.

A Vindication of Natural Society

39 A good parson once said, that where mystery begins, religion ends. Cannot I say, as truly at least, of human laws, that where mystery begins, justice ends? *Ib.*

1 The lucrative business of mystery.
A Vindication of Natural Society

2 The only infallible criterion of wisdom to vulgar judgments—success.
Letter to a Member of the National Assembly

3 Those who have been once intoxicated with power, and have derived any kind of emolument from it, even though but for one year, can never willingly abandon it. *Ib.*

4 Cromwell was a man in whom ambition had not wholly suppressed, but only suspended the sentiments of religion. *Ib.*

5 Tyrants seldom want pretexts. *Ib.*

6 You can never plan the future by the past. *Ib.*

7 To innovate is not to reform.
A Letter to a Noble Lord, 1796

8 These gentle historians, on the contrary, dip their pens in nothing but the milk of human kindness. *Ib.*

9 The king, and his faithful subjects, the lords and commons of this realm,—the triple cord, which no man can break. *Ib.*

10 The coquetry of public opinion, which has her caprices, and must have her way.
Letter to Thos. Burgh, New Year's Day, 1780

11 The arrogance of age must submit to be taught by youth. *Letter to Fanny Burney, 29 July 1782*

12 People crushed by law have no hopes but from power. If laws are their enemies, they will be enemies to laws; and those, who have much to hope and nothing to lose, will always be dangerous, more or less. *Letter to the Hon. C. J. Fox, 8 Oct. 1777*

13 The grand Instructor, Time.
Letter to Sir H. Langrishe, 26 May 1795

14 All men that are ruined are ruined on the side of their natural propensities.
Letters on a Regicide Peace, letter 1

15 Example is the school of mankind, and they will learn at no other. *Ib.*

16 Never, no, never, did Nature say one thing and Wisdom say another. *Ib. No. 3*

17 Well is it known that ambition can creep as well as soar. *Ib.*

18 He [the Duke of Richmond] was a host of debaters in himself.
Letter to the Marquis of Rockingham, 10 Jan. 1773

19 I know many have been taught to think that moderation, in a case like this, is a sort of treason.
Letter to the Sheriffs of Bristol

20 Between craft and credulity, the voice of reason is stifled. *Ib.*

21 If any ask me what a free government is, I answer, that for any practical purpose, it is what the people think so. *Ib.*

22 Liberty, too, must be limited in order to be possessed. *Ib.*

23 Nothing in progression can rest on its original plan. We may as well think of rocking a grown man in the cradle of an infant. *Ib.*

24 Among a people generally corrupt, liberty cannot long exist. *Ib.*

25 Nothing is so fatal to religion as indifference, which is, at least, half infidelity.
Letter to Wm. Smith, 29 Jan. 1795

26 The silent touches of time. *Ib.*

27 Somebody has said, that a king may make a nobleman, but he cannot make a gentleman. *Ib.*

28 Not merely a chip of the old 'block', but the old block itself. *On Pitt's First Speech, 1781*

29 Mr. Burke observed that Johnson had been very great that night; Mr. Langton ... could have wished to hear more from another person; (plainly intimating that he meant Mr. Burke). 'O, no (said Mr. Burke), it is enough for me to have rung the bell to him.' *Boswell's Life of Johnson, vol. iv, p. 26*

30 'No, no,' said he, 'it is not a good imitation of Johnson; it has all his pomp, without his force; it has all the nodosities of the oak without its strength; it has all the contortions of the Sibyl without the inspiration.'
Remark to Boswell who had spoken of Croft's Life of Dr. Young as a good imitation of Johnson's style. Boswell's Life of Johnson, vol. iv, p. 59

WILLIAM CECIL, LORD BURLEIGH
1520–1598

31 What! all this for a song?
To Queen Elizabeth (when ordered to give a pension of £100 to Spenser). Birch, Life of Spenser, p. xiii

SIR FRANCIS COWLEY BURNAND
1836–1917

32 It's no matter what you do
If your heart be only true,
And his heart *was* true to Poll. *True to Poll*

BISHOP GILBERT BURNET
1643–1715

33 There was a sure way never to see it lost, and that was to die in the last ditch.
History of his own Times (1715), i. 457 (1766)

34 He [Halifax] had said he had known many kicked down stairs, but he never knew any kicked up stairs before. *Original Memoirs, c. 1697*

FANNY BURNEY [MME D'ARBLAY]
1752–1840

35 In the bosom of her respectable family resided Camilla. *Camilla, bk. i, ch. 1*

36 Travelling is the ruin of all happiness! There's no looking at a building here after seeing Italy. [*Mr. Meadows.*] *Cecilia, ed. 1904, bk. iv, ch. 2*

37 'True, very true, ma'am,' said he [Mr. Meadows], yawning, 'one really lives no where; one does but vegetate, and wish it all at an end.'
Ib. bk. vii, ch. 5

38 Indeed, the freedom with which Dr. Johnson condemns whatever he disapproves is astonishing.
Diary, 23 Aug. 1778

1 All the delusive seduction of martial music.
Diary, Ce 4 florial, 1802

2 'Do you come to the play without knowing what it is?' [*Mr. Lovell*]. 'O yes, Sir, yes, very frequently: I have no time to read play-bills; one merely comes to meet one's friends, and show that one's alive.'
Evelina, letter 20

JOHN BURNS
1858–1943

3 Every drop of the Thames is liquid 'istory.
Attrib. by Sir Frederick Whyte, K.C.S.I.

ROBERT BURNS
1759–1796

4 O thou! whatever title suit thee,
Auld Hornie, Satan, Nick, or Clootie.
Address to the Deil

5 But fare you weel, auld Nickie-ben!
O wad ye tak a thought an' men'!
Ye aiblins might—I dinna ken—
Still hae a stake:
I'm wae to think upo' yon den,
Ev'n for your sake!
Ib.

6 Ye're aiblins nae temptation.
Address To the Unco Guid

7 Then gently scan your brother man,
Still gentler sister woman;
Tho' they may gang a kennin wrang,
To step aside is human.
Ib.

8 Then at the balance let's be mute,
We never can adjust it;
What's done we partly may compute,
But know not what's resisted.
Ib.

9 Ae fond kiss, and then we sever.
Ae Fond Kiss

10 But to see her was to love her,
Love but her, and love for ever.
Ib.

11 Had we never lov'd sae kindly,
Had we never lov'd sae blindly,
Never met—or never parted,
We had ne'er been broken-hearted.
Ib.

12 Should auld acquaintance be forgot,
And never brought to mind?
Auld Lang Syne

13 We twa hae run about the braes,
And pu'd the gowans fine.
Ib.

14 We'll tak' a right gude-willie waught
For auld lang syne.
Ib.

15 We'll tak a cup o' kindness yet,
For auld lang syne.
Ib.

16 And there's a hand, my trusty fiere,
And gie's a hand o' thine.
Ib.

17 But tell me whisky's name in Greek,
I'll tell the reason.
The Author's Earnest Cry and Prayer, xxx

18 Freedom and Whisky gang thegither!
Ib. xxxi

19 Sleep I can get nane
For thinking on my dearie.
Ay Waukin O

20 The poor inhabitant below
Was quick to learn and wise to know
And keenly felt the friendly glow

And softer flame;
But thoughtless follies laid him low,
And stain'd his name!
A Bard's Epitaph

21 Know prudent cautious self-control
Is wisdom's root.
Ib.

22 Come, Firm Resolve, take thou the van,
Thou stalk o' carl-hemp in man!
And let us mind, faint heart ne'er wan
A lady fair;
Wha does the utmost that he can,
Will whyles do mair.
To Dr. Blacklock

23 To make a happy fire-side clime
To weans and wife,
That's the true pathos and sublime
Of human life.
Ib.

24 But aye the tear comes in my ee,
To think on him that's far awa.
The Bonnie Lad that's far awa

25 O saw ye bonnie Lesley
As she gaed o'er the border?
She's gane, like Alexander,
To spread her conquests farther.
To see her is to love her,
And love but her for ever,
For Nature made her what she is,
And ne'er made anither!
Bonnie Lesley

26 The Deil he could na scaith thee,
Or aught that wad belang thee;
He'd look into thy bonnie face,
And say, 'I canna wrang thee'.
Ib.

27 Bonnie wee thing, cannie wee thing,
Lovely wee thing, wert thou mine,
I wad wear thee in my bosom,
Lest my jewel it should tine.
The Bonnie Wee Thing

28 Your poor narrow foot-path of a street,
Where twa wheel-barrows tremble when they meet.
The Brigs of Ayr

29 Hark! the mavis' evening sang
Sounding Clouden's woods amang;
Then a-faulding let us gang,
My bonnie dearie.
Ca' the Yowes

30 She draiglet a' her petticoatie,
Coming through the rye
Coming through the Rye (taken from an old song, The Bob-tailed Lass).

31 Gin a body meet a body
Coming through the rye;
Gin a body kiss a body,
Need a body cry?
Ib.

32 Contented wi' little and cantie wi' mair.
Contented wi' Little

33 Th' expectant wee-things, toddlin', stacher through
To meet their Dad, wi' flichterin' noise an' glee.
His wee bit ingle, blinkin bonnilie,
His clean hearth-stane, his thrifty wifie's smile,
The lisping infant prattling on his knee,
Does a' his weary kiaugh and care beguile,
An' makes him quite forget his labour an' his toil.
The Cotter's Saturday Night, iii

34 The mother, wi' her needle an' her sheers,
Gars auld claes look amaist as weel's the new. *Ib.* v

35 They never sought in vain that sought the Lord aright! *Ib.* vi

BURNS

1 A wretch, a villain, lost to love and truth.
The Cotter's Saturday Night, x

2 The halesome parritch, chief of Scotia's food. *Ib.* xi

3 The sire turns o'er, wi' patriarchal grace,
The big ha'-Bible, ance his father's pride. *Ib.* xii

4 He wales a portion with judicious care,
And 'Let us worship God!' he says with solemn air.
Ib.

5 From scenes like these old Scotia's grandeur springs,
That makes her loved at home, revered abroad:
Princes and lords are but the breath of kings,
'An honest man's the noblest work of God.' *Ib.* xix

6 Ev'n ministers, they hae been kenn'd,
In holy rapture,
A rousing whid at times to vend,
And nail't wi' Scripture.
Death and Dr. Hornbook, i

7 I wasna fou, but just had plenty. *Ib.* iii

8 The auld kirk-hammer strak the bell
Some wee short hour ayont the twal. *Ib.* xxxi

9 On ev'ry hand it will allow'd be,
He's just—nae better than he should be.
A Dedication to Gavin Hamilton, l. 25

10 The De'il's Awa' Wi' the Exciseman. *Title of Song*

11 But Facts are chiels that winna ding,
An' downa be disputed. *A Dream*

12 Yet aft a ragged cowt's been known
To mak a noble aiver. *Ib.*

13 Duncan Gray cam here to woo,
Ha, ha, the wooing o't,
On blithe Yule-nicht when we were fou,
Ha, ha, the wooing o't,
Maggie coost her head fu' high,
Look'd asklent and unco skeigh,
Gart poor Duncan stand abeigh;
Ha, ha, the wooing o't. *Duncan Gray*

14 Meg was deaf as Ailsa Craig,
Ha, ha, the wooing o't.
Duncan sighed baith out and in,
Grat his een baith bleer't and blin',
Spak o' lowpin o'er a linn;
Ha, ha, the wooing o't; *Ib.*

15 How it comes let doctors tell,
Ha, ha, the wooing o't,
Meg grew sick as he grew haill,
Ha, ha, the wooing o't. *Ib.*

16 A Gentleman who held the patent for his honours
immediately from Almighty God.
Elegy on Capt. Matthew Henderson: from the title

17 Perhaps it may turn out a sang,
Perhaps turn out a sermon.
Epistle to a Young Friend, 1786

18 But still keep something to yoursel
Ye scarcely tell to ony. *Ib.*

19 I wa[i]ve the quantum o' the sin,
The hazard of concealing;
But och! it hardens a' within,
And petrifies the feeling! *Ib.*

20 An atheist-laugh's a poor exchange
For Deity offended. *Ib.*

21 And may ye better reck the rede
Than ever did th' adviser! *Ib.*

22 The heart aye's the part aye
That makes us right or wrang. *Epistle to Davie*

23 What's a' your jargon o' your schools,
Your Latin names for horns and stools;
If honest Nature made you fools,
What sairs your grammars?
First Epistle to John Lapraik

24 Gie me ae spark o' Nature's fire,
That's a' the learning I desire. *Ib.*

25 For thus the royal mandate ran,
When first the human race began,
'The social, friendly, honest man,
Whate'er he be,
'Tis he fulfils great Nature's plan,
And none but he!'
Second Epistle to Lapraik

26 My barmie noddle's working prime.
Epistle to James Smith

27 Some rhyme a neebor's name to lash;
Some rhyme (vain thought!) for needfu' cash;
Some rhyme to court the country clash,
An' raise a din;
For me, an aim I never fash;
I rhyme for fun. *Ib.*

28 Farewell dear, deluding Woman,
The joy of joys! *Ib.*

29 Flow gently, sweet Afton, among thy green braes,
Flow gently, I'll sing thee a song in thy praise.
My Mary's asleep by thy murmuring stream,
Flow gently, sweet Afton, disturb not her dream.
Flow gently, sweet Afton

30 The rank is but the guinea's stamp;
The man's the gowd for a' that!
For a' that and a' that

31 A man's a man for a' that. *Ib.*

32 A prince can mak a belted knight,
A marquis, duke, and a' that;
But an honest man's aboon his might,
Guid faith he mauna fa' that! *Ib.*

33 It's coming yet, for a' that,
That man to man the warld o'er
Shall brothers be for a' that. *Ib.*

34 My heart is sair, I daur na tell,
My heart is sair for Somebody.
For the Sake of Somebody

35 There's Death in the cup—so beware! *On a Goblet*

36 Go fetch to me a pint o' wine,
An' fill it in a silver tassie. *Go Fetch to Me a Pint*

37 Green grow the rashes O,
Green grow the rashes O;
The sweetest hours that e'er I spend,
Are spent amang the lasses O!

There's nought but care on ev'ry han',
In ev'ry hour that passes O;
What signifies the life o' man,
An 'twere na for the lasses O.
Green Grow the Rashes

38 But gie me a canny hour at e'en,
My arms about my dearie O;
An' warly cares, an' warly men,
May a' gae tapsalteerie O! *Ib.*

1 The wisest man the warl' saw,
   He dearly lov'd the lasses O.
   Green Grow the Rashes

2 Auld nature swears, the lovely dears
   Her noblest work she classes O;
   Her prentice han' she tried on man,
   An' then she made the lasses O. *Ib.*

3 That I for poor auld Scotland's sake,
   Some usefu' plan or beuk could make,
   Or sing a sang at least.
   To the Guidwife of Wauchope-House

4 Fair fa' your honest sonsie face,
   Great chieftain o' the puddin'-race!
   Aboon them a' ye tak your place,
   Painch, tripe, or thairm:
   Weel are ye wordy o' a grace
   As lang's my arm. *To a Haggis*

5 His spindle shank a guid whip-lash,
   His nieve a nit. *Ib.*

6 It's guid to be merry and wise,
   It's guid to be honest and true,
   It's guid to support Caledonia's cause,
   And bide by the buff and the blue.
   Here's a Health to Them that's Awa'

7 O, gie me the lass that has acres o' charms,
   O, gie me the lass wi' the weel-stockit farms.
   Hey for a Lass wi' a Tocher

8 Then hey, for a lass wi' a tocher—
   The nice yellow guineas for me! *Ib.*

9 The golden hours on angel wings
   Flew o'er me and my dearie;
   For dear to me as light and life
   Was my sweet Highland Mary. *Highland Mary*

10 But oh! fell death's untimely frost,
   That nipt my flower sae early! *Ib.*

11 Here some are thinkin' on their sins,
   An' some upo' their claes. *The Holy Fair*, x

12 Leeze me on drink! it gi'es us mair
   Than either school or college. *Ib.* xix

13 There's some are fou o' love divine,
   There's some are fou o' brandy. *Ib.* xxvii

14 I hae a wife o' my ain. *I Hae a Wife o' My Ain*

15 Naebody cares for me,
   I care for naebody. *Ib.*

16 It was a' for our rightfu' King
   We left fair Scotland's strand.
   It was a' for our Rightfu' King

17 Now a' is done that men can do,
   And a' is done in vain. *Ib.*

18 He turn'd him right and round about
   Upon the Irish shore;
   And gae his bridle-reins a shake,
   With adieu for evermore, My dear,
   Adieu for evermore. *Ib.*

19 John Anderson my jo, John,
   When we were first acquent,
   Your locks were like the raven,
   Your bonny brow was brent.
   John Anderson My Jo

20 John Anderson my jo, John,
   We clamb the hill thegither;
   And mony a canty day, John,
   We've had wi' ane anither:

Now we maun totter down, John,
   And hand in hand we'll go,
   And sleep thegither at the foot,
   John Anderson, my jo. *John Anderson My Jo*

21 There were three kings into the east,
   Three kings both great and high;
   And they hae sworn a solemn oath
   John Barleycorn should die. *John Barleycorn*

22 Partly wi' love o'ercome sae sair,
   And partly she was drunk.
   The Jolly Beggars, l. 221

23 Their tricks an' craft hae put me daft,
   They've ta'en me in, an' a' that,
   But clear your decks, an' '*here's the Sex*!'
   I like the jads for a' that. *Ib.* l. 266

24 A fig for those by law protected!
   Liberty's a glorious feast!
   Courts for cowards were erected,
   Churches built to please the priest. *Ib.* l. 292

25 Life is all a variorum,
   We regard not how it goes;
   Let them cant about decorum
   Who have characters to lose. *Ib.* l. 308

26 As cauld a wind as ever blew,
   A caulder kirk, and in't but few;
   A caulder preacher never spak;—
   Ye'se a' be het ere I come back.
   The Kirk of Lamington

27 I've seen sae mony changefu' years,
   On earth I am a stranger grown;
   I wander in the ways of men,
   Alike unknowing and unknown.
   Lament for James, Earl of Glencairn

28 The mother may forget the child
   That smiles sae sweetly on her knee;
   But I'll remember thee, Glencairn,
   And a' that thou hast done for me. *Ib.*

29 O had she been a country maid,
   And I the happy country swain.
   The Lass of Ballochmyle

30 When o'er the hill the eastern star
   Tells bughtin-time is near, my jo;
   I'll meet thee on the lea-rig,
   My ain kind dearie O. *The Lea-Rig*

31 True it is, she had one failing,
   Had a woman ever less?
   Lines written under the Picture of Miss Burns

32 Ha! whare ye gaun, ye crowlin' ferlie!
   Your impudence protects you sairly:
   I canna say but ye strunt rarely,
   Owre gauze and lace;
   Tho' faith! I fear ye dine but sparely
   On sic a place. *To a Louse*

33 O wad some Pow'r the giftie gie us
   To see oursels as others see us!
   It wad frae mony a blunder free us,
   And foolish notion. *Ib.*

34 Their sighin', cantin', grace-proud faces,
   Their three-mile prayers, and half-mile graces.
   To the Rev. John M'Math

35 May coward shame distain his name,
   The wretch that dares not die!
   Macpherson's Farewell

1   Nature's law,
That man was made to mourn.
Man was made to Mourn

2 Man's inhumanity to man
Makes countless thousands mourn!   *Ib.*

3 O Death, the poor man's dearest friend,
The kindest and the best!   *Ib.*

4 Thou lingering star, with lessening ray,
That lov'st to greet the early morn,
Again thou usherest in the day
My Mary from my soul was torn.
To Mary in Heaven

5 Time but the impression deeper makes,
As streams their channels deeper wear.   *Ib.*

6 I sigh'd, and said amang them a',
'Ye are na Mary Morison.'   *Mary Morison*

7 Wee modest crimson-tippèd flow'r.
To a Mountain Daisy

8 Ev'n thou who mourn'st the Daisy's fate,
That fate is thine—no distant date;
Stern Ruin's ploughshare drives elate
Full on thy bloom,
Till crush'd beneath the furrow's weight
Shall be thy doom!   *Ib.*

9 Wee, sleekit, cow'rin', tim'rous beastie,
O what a panic's in thy breastie!
Thou need na start awa sae hasty,
        Wi' bickering brattle!
I wad be laith to rin an' chase thee,
        Wi' murd'ring pattle!   *To a Mouse*

10 I'm truly sorry Man's dominion
Has broken Nature's social union,
An' justifies th' ill opinion
Which makes thee startle
At me, thy poor, earth-born companion
An' fellow-mortal!   *Ib.*

11 The best laid schemes o' mice an' men
Gang aft a-gley.   *Ib.*

12 My heart's in the Highlands, my heart is not here;
My heart's in the Highlands a-chasing the deer;
Chasing the wild deer, and following the roe,
My heart's in the Highlands, wherever I go.
My Heart's in the Highlands. But see 420:24 in
Corrigenda, *p. xx.*

13 Farewell to the Highlands, farewell to the North,
The birth-place of valour, the country of worth. *Ib.*

14 O, my Luve's like a red red rose
That's newly sprung in June:
O my Luve's like the melodie
That's sweetly play'd in tune.
My Love is like a Red Red Rose

15 The minister kiss'd the fiddler's wife,
An' could na preach for thinkin' o't.
My Love she's but a Lassie yet

16 She is a winsome wee thing,
She is a handsome wee thing,
She is a lo'esome wee thing,
This sweet wee wife o' mine.
My Wife's a Winsome Wee Thing

17 Of a' the airts the wind can blaw,
I dearly like the west.   *Of a' the Airts*

18 If there's another world, he lives in bliss;
If there is none, he made the best of this.
On a Friend. Epitaph on Wm. Muir

19 He ne'er was gi'en to great misguidin',
Yet coin his pouches wad na bide in.
On a Scotch Bard

20 Hear, Land o' Cakes, and brither Scots.
On Captain Grose's Peregrinations

21 If there's a hole in a' your coats,
       I rede you tent it:
A chield's amang you taking notes,
       And, faith, he'll prent it.   *Ib.*

22 He has a fouth o' auld nick-nackets.   *Ib.*

23 An idiot race to honour lost,
Who know them best, despise them most.
On Seeing Stirling Palace in Ruins

24 O, wert thou in the cauld blast,
    On yonder lea, on yonder lea,
My plaidie to the angry airt,
    I'd shelter thee, I'd shelter thee.
O, Wert Thou in the Cauld Blast

25 Thy bield should be my bosom,
To share it a', to share it a'.   *Ib.*

26 Or were I in the wildest waste,
    Sae black and bare, sae black and bare,
The desert were a paradise,
    If thou wert there, if thou wert there.   *Ib.*

27 The teeth o' Time may gnaw Tantallan,
    But thou's for ever!   *To Pastoral Poetry*

28 The mair they talk I'm kent the better.
E'en Let Them Clash

29 O Luve will venture in, where it daur na weel be
    seen.   *The Posie*

30 And I will pu' the pink, the emblem o' my dear,
For she's the pink o' womankind, and blooms without a peer.   *Ib.*

31 It's aye the cheapest lawyer's fee,
    To taste the barrel.   *Scotch Drink*

32 Scots, wha hae wi' Wallace bled,
Scots, wham Bruce has aften led,
Welcome to your gory bed,
    Or to victorie.
Now's the day, and now's the hour;
See the front o' battle lour!
See approach proud Edward's power—
    Chains and slaverie!   *Scots, Wha Hae*

33 Liberty's in every blow!
    Let us do or die!   *Ib.*

34 Some hae meat, and canna eat,
    And some wad eat that want it;
But we hae meat and we can eat,
    And sae the Lord be thankit.
The Selkirk Grace. As attributed to Burns

35 The Muse, nae poet ever fand her,
Till by himself he learned to wander
Adown some trotting burn's meander,
    An' no think lang:
To William Simpson

36 Good Lord, what is man! for as simple he looks,
Do but try to develop his hooks and his crooks,
With his depths and his shallows, his good and his evil,
All in all, he's a problem must puzzle the devil.
Sketch: inscribed to C. J. Fox

1 Tho' poor in gear, we're rich in love.
The Soldier's Return

2 Whare sits our sulky sullen dame,
Gathering her brows like gathering storm,
Nursing her wrath to keep it warm.
Tam o' Shanter, l. 10

3 Auld Ayr, wham ne'er a town surpasses
For honest men and bonnie lasses. *Ib. l. 15*

4 Ah, gentle dames! It gars me greet
To think how mony counsels sweet,
How mony lengthen'd sage advices,
The husband frae the wife despises! *Ib. l. 33*

5 His ancient, trusty, drouthy crony;
Tam lo'ed him like a vera brither;
They had been fou for weeks thegither. *Ib. l. 43*

6 Kings may be blest, but Tam was glorious,
O'er a' the ills o' life victorious! *Ib. l. 57*

7 But pleasures are like poppies spread—
You seize the flow'r, its bloom is shed;
Or like the snow falls in the river—
A moment white—then melts for ever. *Ib. l. 59*

8 Nae man can tether time or tide. *Ib. l. 67*

9 That hour, o' night's black arch the key-stane.
Ib. l. 69

10 Inspiring bold John Barleycorn!
What dangers thou canst make us scorn!
Wi' tippenny, we fear nae evil;
Wi' usquebae, we'll face the devil! *Ib. l. 105*

11 The mirth and fun grew fast and furious. *Ib. l. 143*

12 But Tam kent what was what fu' brawlie. *Ib. l. 163*

13 Ev'n Satan glowr'd, and fidg'd fu' fain,
An' hotched an' blew wi' might an' main:
Till first ae caper, syne anither,
Tam tint his reason a' thegither,
And roars out, 'Weel done, Cutty-sark!' *Ib. l. 185*

14 Ah, Tam! ah, Tam! thou'll get thy fairin'!
In hell they'll roast thee like a herrin'! *Ib. l. 201*

15 He'll hae misfortunes great and sma',
But aye a heart aboon them a'; *There was a Lad*

16 A man may drink and no be drunk;
A man may fight and no be slain;
A man may kiss a bonnie lass,
And aye be welcome back again.
There was a Lass, they ca'd her Meg

17 We labour soon, we labour late,
To feed the titled knave, man,
And a' the comfort we're to get,
Is that ayont the grave, man.
The Tree of Liberty, attributed to Burns

18 His lockèd, lettered, braw brass collar,
Shew'd him the gentleman and scholar.
The Twa Dogs, l. 13

19 The fient a pride na pride had he. *Ib. l. 16*

20 And there began a lang digression
About the lords of the creation. *Ib. l. 45*

21 But human bodies are sic fools,
For a' their colleges and schools,
That when nae real ills perplex them,
They mak enow themsels to vex them. *Ib. l. 195*

22 But hear their absent thoughts o' ither,
They're a' run deils an' jads thegither.
The Twa Dogs, l. 221

23 Rejoiced they were na men but dogs. *Ib. l. 236*

24 Up in the morning's no' for me,
Up in the morning early. *Up in the Morning*

25 Misled by fancy's meteor ray,
By passion driven;
But yet the light that led astray
Was light from Heaven. *The Vision, Duan II, xviii*

26 What can a young lassie, what shall a young lassie,
What can a young lassie do wi' an auld man?
What can a Young Lassie

27 And then his auld brass 'ill buy me a new pan. *Ib.*

28 O whistle, and I'll come to you, my lad:
O whistle, and I'll come to you, my lad:
Tho' father and mither and a' should gae mad,
O whistle, and I'll come to you, my lad.
Whistle, and I'll come to you, my Lad

29 Now we're married—speir nae mair—
Whistle owre the lave o't. *Whistle owre the lave o't*

30 We are na fou, we're nae that fou,
But just a drappie in our ee.
Willie Brewed a Peck o' Maut

31 It is the moon, I ken her horn,
That's blinkin' in the lift sae hie;
She shines sae bright to wyle us hame,
But, by my sooth! she'll wait a wee. *Ib.*

32 Sic a wife as Willie had,
I wad na gie a button for her! *Willie's Wife*

33 Her nose and chin they threaten ither. *Ib.*

34 Her face wad fyle the Logan-water. *Ib.*

35 The heart benevolent and kind
The most resembles God. *A Winter Night*

36 Ye banks and braes o' bonny Doon,
How can ye bloom sae fresh and fair?
How can ye chant, ye little birds,
And I sae weary fu' o' care?
Ye Banks and Braes o' Bonny Doon

37 Thou minds me o' departed joys,
Departed never to return. *Ib.*

38 And ilka bird sang of its love,
And fondly sae did I o' mine. *Ib.*

39 And my fause lover stole my rose,
But ah! he left the thorn wi' me. *Ib.*

40 Don't let the awkward squad fire over me.
A. Cunningham's *Works of Burns; with his Life*,
1834, vol. i, p. 344

JEREMIAH BURROUGHS
1599–1646

41 We use to say, it's a woman's reason to say, I will do
such a thing, because I will do it.
On Hosea, vol. iv, p. 80

BENJAMIN HAPGOOD BURT
nineteenth century

42 When you're all dressed up and no place to go.
Title of Song

HENRY BURTON
fl. 1886

1 Have you had a kindness shown?
  Pass it on!
'Twas not given for thee alone,
  Pass it on!
Let it travel down the years,
Let it wipe another's tears,
Till in Heaven the deed appears—
  Pass it on!   *Pass It On*

ROBERT BURTON
1577-1640

2 All my joys to this are folly,
  Naught so sweet as Melancholy.
  Anatomy of Melancholy. Author's Abstract of Melancholy

3 They lard their lean books with the fat of others' works.   *Ib. Democritus to the Reader*

4 We can say nothing but what hath been said. . . . Our poets steal from Homer. . . . Divines use Austin's words *verbatim* still, and our story-dressers do as much, he that comes last is commonly best. *Ib.*

5 I had no time to lick it into form, as she [a bear] doth her young ones.   *Ib.*

6 Like watermen, that row one way and look another. *Ib.*

7 Him that makes shoes go barefoot himself.   *Ib.*

8 All poets are mad.   *Ib.*

9 A loose, plain, rude writer.   *Ib.*

10 Cookery is become an art, a noble science: cooks are gentlemen.   *Ib. pt. i, § 2, memb. 2, subsect. 2*

11 Die to save charges.   *Ib. memb. 3, subsect. 12*

12 I may not here omit those two main plagues, and common dotages of human kind, wine and women, which have infatuated and besotted myriads of people. They go commonly together. *Ib. subsect. 13*

13 Hinc quam sit calamus sævior ense patet.
  From this it is clear how much the pen is worse than the sword.   *Ib. memb. 4, subsect. 4*

14 One was never married, and that's his hell; another is, and that's his plague.   *Ib. subsect. 7*

15 [Fabricius] finds certain spots and clouds in the sun. *Ib. pt. ii, § 2, memb. 3*

16 Seneca thinks he takes delight in seeing thee. The gods are well pleased when they see great men contending with adversity. *Ib. § 3, memb. 1, subsect. 1*

17 Every thing, saith Epictetus, hath two handles, the one to be held by, the other not.   *Ib. memb. 3*

18 Who cannot give good counsel? 'tis cheap, it costs them nothing.   *Ib.*

19 What is a ship but a prison?   *Ib. memb. 4*

20 All places are distant from Heaven alike.   *Ib.*

21 The Commonwealth of Venice in their armoury have this inscription, 'Happy is that city which in time of peace thinks of war.'   *Ib. memb. 6*

22 Tobacco, divine, rare, superexcellent tobacco, which goes far beyond all their panaceas, potable gold, and philosopher's stones, a sovereign remedy to all diseases. . . . But, as it is commonly abused by most men, which take it as tinkers do ale, 'tis a plague, a mischief, a violent purger of goods, lands, health, hellish, devilish, and damned tobacco, the ruin and overthrow of body and soul.
Anatomy of Melancholy, pt. ii, § 4, memb. 2, subsect. 1

23 Let me not live, saith Aretine's Antonia, if I had not rather hear thy discourse than see a play! *Ib. pt. iii, § 1, memb. 1, subsect. 1*

24 And this is that Homer's golden chain, which reacheth down from Heaven to earth, by which every creature is annexed, and depends on his Creator. *Ib. subsect. 2*

25 To enlarge or illustrate this—is to set a candle in the sun.   *Ib. § 2, memb. 1, subsect. 2*

26 Cornelia kept her in talk till her children came from school, and these, said she, are my jewels. *Ib. memb. 2, subsect. 3*

27 To these crocodile's tears, they will add sobs, fiery sighs, and sorrowful countenance.   *Ib. subsect. 4*

28 Diogenes struck the father when the son swore. *Ib.*

29 England is a paradise for women, and hell for horses: Italy a paradise for horses, hell for women, as the diverb goes.   *Ib. § 3, memb. 1, subsect. 2*

30 The miller sees not all the water that goes by his mill.   *Ib. memb. 4, subsect. 1*

31 The fear of some divine and supreme powers, keeps men in obedience. *Ib. § 4, memb. 1, subsect. 2*

32 One religion is as true as another.
  Ib. memb. 2, subsect. 1

33 Be not solitary, be not idle.   *Ib.* Last words

COMTE DE BUSSY-RABUTIN
1618-1693

34 L'absence est à l'amour ce qu'est au feu le vent; il éteint le petit, il allume le grand.
  Absence is to love what wind is to fire; it extinguishes the small, it enkindles the great.
  Histoire amoureuse des Gaules, Maximes d'Amours

BISHOP JOSEPH BUTLER
1692-1752

35 It has come, I know not how, to be taken for granted, by many persons, that Christianity is not so much as a subject of inquiry; but that it is, now at length, discovered to be fictitious.
  The Analogy of Religion (1756), *Advertisement*

36 But to *us*, probability is the very guide of life.
  Ib. Introduction

37 Things and actions are what they are, and the consequences of them will be what they will be: why then should we desire to be deceived?
  Fifteen Sermons. No. 7, § 16

38 Sir, the pretending to extraordinary revelations and gifts of the Holy Ghost is a horrid thing, a very horrid thing. [To John Wesley.]
  Wesley, *Works*, xiii. 449

NICHOLAS MURRAY BUTLER
1862–1947

1 ... a society like ours [U.S.A.] of which it is truly said
to be often but three generations 'from shirt-
sleeves to shirt-sleeves'. *True and False Democracy*

SAMUEL BUTLER
1612–1680

2 When civil fury first grew high,
And men fell out they knew not why.
Hudibras, pt. i, c. 1, l. 1

3 And pulpit, drum ecclesiastic,
Was beat with fist, instead of a stick. *Ib.* l. 11

4 Beside, 'tis known he could speak Greek,
As naturally as pigs squeak:
That Latin was no more difficile,
Than to a black-bird 'tis to whistle. *Ib.* l. 51

5 He was in logic a great critic,
Profoundly skill'd in analytic.
He could distinguish, and divide
A hair 'twixt south and south-west side.
On either which he would dispute,
Confute, change hands, and still confute. *Ib.* l. 65

6 He'd run in debt by disputation,
And pay with ratiocination. *Ib.* l. 77

7 For rhetoric he could not ope
His mouth, but out there flew a trope. *Ib.* l. 81

8 For all a rhetorician's rules
Teach nothing but to name his tools. *Ib.* l. 89

9 A Babylonish dialect
Which learned pedants much affect. *Ib.* l. 93

10 For he, by geometric scale,
Could take the size of pots of ale; ...
And wisely tell what hour o' th' day
The clock doth strike, by algebra. *Ib.* l. 121

11 Beside, he was a shrewd philosopher,
And had read ev'ry text and gloss over. *Ib.* l. 127

12 What ever sceptic could inquire for;
For every why he had a wherefore. *Ib.* l. 131

13 He knew what's what, and that's as high
As metaphysic wit can fly. *Ib.* l. 149

14 Such as take lodgings in a head
That's to be let unfurnished. *Ib.* l. 160

15 He could raise scruples dark and nice,
And after solve 'em in a trice:
As if Divinity had catch'd
The itch, of purpose to be scratch'd. *Ib.* l. 163

16 'T was Presbyterian true blue. *Ib.* l. 189

17 Such as do build their faith upon
The holy text of pike and gun. *Ib.* l. 193

18 And prove their doctrine orthodox
By apostolic blows and knocks. *Ib.* l. 197

19 And still be doing, never done:
As if Religion were intended
For nothing else but to be mended. *Ib.* l. 202

20 Compound for sins, they are inclin'd to
By damning those they have no mind to. *Ib.* l. 213

21 The trenchant blade, Toledo trusty,
For want of fighting was grown rusty,
And eat into it self, for lack
Of some body to hew and hack. *Ib.* l. 357

22 For rhyme the rudder is of verses,
With which like ships they steer their courses.
Hudibras, pt. i, c. 1, l. 457

23 For what is Worth in anything,
But so much Money as 'twill bring. *Ib.* l. 465

24 He ne'er consider'd it, as loth
To look a gift-horse in the mouth. *Ib.* l. 483

25 Quoth Hudibras, I smell a rat;
Ralpho, thou dost prevaricate. *Ib.* l. 815

26 Great actions are not always true sons
Of great and mighty resolutions. *Ib.* l. 885

27 There was an ancient sage philosopher,
That had read Alexander Ross over. *Ib.* c. 2, l. 1

28 Through perils both of wind and limb,
Through thick and thin she follow'd him. *Ib.* l. 369

29 Ay me! what perils do environ
The man that meddles with cold iron! *Ib.* c. 3, l. 1

30 I'll make the fur
Fly 'bout the ears of the old cur. *Ib.* l. 277

31 These reasons made his mouth to water. *Ib.* l. 379

32 Then while the honour thou hast got
Is spick and span-new, piping hot. *Ib.* l. 398

33 Cheer'd up himself with ends of verse,
And sayings of philosophers. *Ib.* l. 1011

34 Cleric before, and Lay behind;
A lawless linsy-woolsy brother,
Half of one order, half another. *Ib.* l. 1226

35 Learning, that cobweb of the brain,
Profane, erroneous, and vain. *Ib.* l. 1339

36 For nothing goes for sense, or light,
That will not with old rules jump right;
As if rules were not in the schools
Derived from truth, but truth from rules. *Ib.* l. 1353

37 Quoth Hudibras, Friend Ralph, thou hast
Outrun the constable at last. *Ib.* l. 1367

38 Not by your individual whiskers,
But by your dialect and discourse.
Ib. pt. ii, c. 1, l. 155

39 Some have been beaten till they know
What wood a cudgel's of by th' blow;
Some kick'd, until they can feel whether
A shoe be Spanish or neats-leather. *Ib.* l. 221

40 Such great achievements cannot fail,
To cast salt on a woman's tail. *Ib.* l. 277

41 She that with poetry is won
Is but a desk to write upon. *Ib.* l. 591

42 Love is a boy, by poets styl'd,
Then spare the rod, and spoil the child. *Ib.* l. 844

43 The sun had long since in the lap
Of Thetis, taken out his nap,
And like a lobster boil'd, the morn
From black to red began to turn. *Ib.* c. 2, l. 29

44 And after many circumstances,
Which vulgar authors in romances
Do use to spend their time and wits on,
To make impertinent description. *Ib.* l. 41

45 Have always been at daggers-drawing,
And one another clapper-clawing. *Ib.* l. 79

46 Oaths are but words, and words but wind. *Ib.* l. 107

1 For saints may do the same things by
The Spirit, in sincerity,
Which other men are tempted to.
Hudibras, pt. ii, c. 2. l. 235

2 As the ancients
Say wisely, Have a care o' th' main chance,
And look before you ere you leap;
For, as you sow, you are like to reap.   *Ib. l. 501*

3 Doubtless the pleasure is as great
Of being cheated, as to cheat.
As lookers-on feel most delight,
That least perceive a juggler's sleight,
And still the less they understand,
The more th' admire his sleight of hand.
Ib. c. 3, l. 1

4 He made an instrument to know
If the moon shine at full or no   *Ib. l. 261*

5 And fire a mine in China, here,
With sympathetic gunpowder.   *Ib. l. 295*

6 To swallow gudgeons ere th'are catch'd,
And count their chickens ere th'are hatch'd.
Ib. l. 923

7 T'enforce a desperate amour.   *Ib. pt. iii, c. 1, l. 2*

8 Still amorous, and fond, and billing,
Like Philip and Mary on a shilling.   *Ib. l. 687*

9 For in what stupid age or nation
Was marriage ever out of fashion?   *Ib. l. 817*

10 Discords make the sweetest airs.   *Ib. l. 919*

11 What makes all doctrines plain and clear?
About two hundred pounds a year.
And that which was prov'd true before,
Prove false again? Two hundred more.   *Ib. l. 1277*

12 With crosses, relics, crucifixes,
Beads, pictures, rosaries, and pixes,
The tools of working out salvation
By mere mechanic operation.   *Ib. l. 1495*

13 The saints engage in fierce contests
About their carnal interests.   *Ib. c. 2, introd.*

14 Both parties join'd to do their best
To damn the public interest.   *Ib. l. 147*

15 Neither have the hearts to stay,
Nor wit enough to run away.   *Ib. l. 569*

16 For if it be but half denied,
'Tis half as good as justified.   *Ib. l. 803*

17 For, those that fly, may fight again,
Which he can never do that's slain.   *Ib. c. 3, l. 243*

18 He that complies against his will,
Is of his own opinion still.   *Ib. l. 547*

19 For Justice, though she's painted blind,
Is to the weaker side inclin'd.   *Ib. l. 709*

20 For money has a power above
The stars and fate, to manage love.   *Ib. l. 1279*

21 And counted *breaking Priscian's head* a thing
More capital than to behead a king.
*Genuine Remains: Satire on the Imperfection of
Human Learning, pt. 2, l. 149*

22 The best of all our actions tend
To the preposterousest end.
*Ib. Satire upon the Weakness and Misery of
Man, l. 41*

23 The greatest saints and sinners have been made
The proselytes of one another's trade.
Miscellaneous Thoughts

24 All love at first, like generous wine,
Ferments and frets until 'tis fine;
But when 'tis settled on the lee,
And from th' impurer matter free,
Becomes the richer still the older,
And proves the pleasanter the colder.   *Ib.*

25 The souls of women are so small,
That some believe they've none at all.   *Ib.*

26 The law can take a purse in open court,
While it condemns a less delinquent for't.   *Ib.*

27 For trouts are tickled best in muddy water.
On a Hypocritical Nonconformist, iv

SAMUEL BUTLER
1835–1902

28 It has been said that though God cannot alter the past,
historians can; it is perhaps because they can be
useful to Him in this respect that He tolerates their
existence.   *Erewhon Revisited, ch. 14*

29 A wound in the solicitor is a very serious thing.
The Humour of Homer. Ramblings in Cheapside

30 I keep my books at the British Museum and at
Mudie's.   *Ib.*

31 The most perfect humour and irony is generally quite
unconscious.   *Life and Habit, ch. 2*

32 Life is one long process of getting tired.
Note Books. Life, vii

33 Life is the art of drawing sufficient conclusions from
insufficient premises.   *Ib. ix*

34 All progress is based upon a universal innate desire
on the part of every organism to live beyond its
income.   *Ib. xvi*

35 When the righteous man turneth away from his
righteousness that he hath committed and doeth
that which is neither quite lawful nor quite right,
he will generally be found to have gained in
amiability what he has lost in holiness.
Ib. Elementary Morality. Counsels of Imperfection

36 It costs a lot of money to die comfortably.
Ib. A Luxurious Death

37 The healthy stomach is nothing if not conservative.
Few radicals have good digestions.
Ib. Mind and Matter. Indigestion

38 The history of art is the history of revivals.
Ib. Handel and Music. Anachronism

39 Though wisdom cannot be gotten for gold, still less
can it be gotten without it. Gold, or the value of
what is equivalent to gold, lies at the root of wisdom,
and enters so largely into the very essence of the
Holy Ghost that 'no gold, no Holy Ghost' may pass
as an axiom.   *Ib. Cash and Credit. Modern Simony*

40 Genius . . . has been defined as a supreme capacity
for taking trouble. . . . It might be more fitly
described as a supreme capacity for getting its
possessors into trouble of all kinds and keeping
them therein so long as the genius remains.
Ib. Genius, i

1 The phrase 'unconscious humour' is the one contribution I have made to the current literature of the day.

Note Books. The Position of a Homo Unius Libri. Myself and 'Unconscious Humour'

2 We were saying what a delightful dispensation of providence it was that prosperous people will write their memoirs. We hoped Tennyson was writing his. (1890.)

P.S. We think his son has done nearly as well. (1898.)

Ib. The Enfant Terrible of Literature

3 An apology for the Devil: It must be remembered that we have only heard one side of the case. God has written all the books.

Ib. Higgledy-Piggledy. An Apology for the Devil

4 God is Love, I dare say. But what a mischievous devil Love is. *Ib. God is Love*

5 To live is like love, all reason is against it, and all healthy instinct for it. *Ib. Life and Love*

6 The public buys its opinions as it buys its meat, or takes in its milk, on the principle that it is cheaper to do this than to keep a cow. So it is, but the milk is more likely to be watered.

Ib. Material for a Projected Sequel to Alps and Sanctuaries. Public Opinion

7 I do not mind lying, but I hate inaccuracy.

Ib. Truth and Convenience. Falsehood, iv

8 The world will, in the end, follow only those who have despised as well as served it.

Ib. Life of the World to Come. The World

9 An honest God's the noblest work of man.

Further Extracts from the Note-Books (1934), p. 26. *See also Festing Jones, Memoir* (1919), vol. i, p. 212. *(See also* 267:16)

10 'Man wants but little here below' but likes that little good—and not too long in coming. *Ib. p. 61*

11 Dulce et decorum est desipere in loco.

Ib. p. 92. (Horace, *Odes*, III. ii. 14, and IV. xii. 28.)

12 Jesus! with all thy faults I love thee still. *Ib. p. 117*

13 Taking numbers into account, I should think more mental suffering had been undergone in the streets leading from St. George's, Hanover Square, than in the condemned cells of Newgate.

The Way of All Flesh, ch. 13

14 The advantage of doing one's praising for oneself is that one can lay it on so thick and exactly in the right places. *Ib. ch. 34*

15 There's many a good tune played on an old fiddle.

Ib. ch. 61

16 'Tis better to have loved and lost, than never to have lost at all. *Ib. ch. 77, cf.* 532: 20

17 O God! Oh Montreal! *Psalm of Montreal*

18 Preferrest thou the gospel of Montreal to the gospel of Hellas,

The gospel of thy connexion with Mr. Spurgeon's haberdasher to the gospel of the Discobolus?

Yet none the less blasphemed he beauty saying,

'The Discobolus hath no gospel,

But my brother-in-law is haberdasher to Mr. Spurgeon.' *Ib.*

19 Yet meet we shall, and part, and meet again,
Where dead men meet on lips of living men.

Poems. Life after Death

20 I would not be—not quite—so pure as you.

Ib. A Prayer

WILLIAM BUTLER
1535–1618

21 Doubtless God could have made a better berry [strawberry], but doubtless God never did.

Walton, *Compleat Angler*, pt. i, ch. 5

JOHN BYROM
1692–1763

22 Some say, that Signor Bononcini,
Compar'd to Handel's a mere ninny;
Others aver, to him, that Handel
Is scarcely fit to hold a candle.
Strange! that such high dispute shou'd be
'Twixt Tweedledum and Tweedledee.

Epigram on the Feuds between Handel and Bononcini

23 I shall prove it—as clear as a whistle.

Epistle to Lloyd, I. xii

24 Christians awake, salute the happy morn,
Whereon the Saviour of the world was born.

Hymn for Christmas Day

25 God bless the King, I mean the Faith's Defender;
God bless—no harm in blessing—the Pretender;
But who Pretender is, or who is King,
God bless us all—that's quite another thing.

To an Officer in the Army

GEORGE GORDON BYRON, LORD BYRON
1788–1824

26 The 'good old times'—all times when old are good—
Are gone. *The Age of Bronze, i*

27 For what were all these country patriots born?
To hunt, and vote, and raise the price of corn?

Ib. xiv

28 Year after year they voted cent. per cent.,
Blood, sweat, and tear-wrung millions—why? for rent! *Ib.*

29 Woe is me, Alhama! *Siege and Conquest of Alhama, i*

30 And thou art dead, as young and fair
As aught of mortal birth. *And Thou Art Dead*

31 And wilt thou weep when I am low?

And Wilt Thou Weep?

32 Like the lost Pleiad seen no more below.

Beppo, xiv

33 Just like a coffin clapt in a canoe. [A gondola.] *Ib. xix*

34 In short, he was a perfect cavaliero,
And to his very valet seem'd a hero. *Ib. xxxiii*

35 His heart was one of those which most enamour us,
Wax to receive, and marble to retain. *Ib. xxxiv*

36 Besides, they always smell of bread and butter.

Ib. xxxix

37 I am ashes where once I was fire.

To the Countess of Blessington

1 Know ye the land where the cypress and myrtle
　Are emblems of deeds that are done in their clime?
Where the rage of the vulture, the love of the turtle,
　Now melt into sorrow, now madden to crime!
　　　　　　　Bride of Abydos, c. I. i

2 Where the virgins are soft as the roses they twine,
And all, save the spirit of man, is divine? *Ib.*

3 The blind old man of Scio's rocky isle. *Ib.* c. II. ii

4 Mark! where his carnage and his conquests cease!
He makes a solitude, and calls it—peace! *Ib.* xx

5 Hark! to the hurried question of Despair:
'Where is my child?'—an echo answers—
　　　'Where?' *Ib.* xxvii

6 Adieu, adieu! my native shore
　Fades o'er the waters blue.
　　　　　　　Childe Harold, c. I. xiii

7 My native land—Good Night! *Ib.*

8 In Biscay's sleepless bay. *Ib.* xiv

9 Here all were noble, save Nobility. *Ib.* lxxxv

10 War, war is still the cry, 'War even to the knife!'
　　　　　　　Ib. lxxxvi

11 A schoolboy's tale, the wonder of an hour! *Ib.* c. II. ii

12 The dome of Thought, the palace of the Soul. *Ib.* vi

13 Well didst thou speak, Athena's wisest son!
'All that we know is, nothing can be known.' *Ib.* vii

14 Ah! happy years! once more who would not be a boy?
　　　　　　　Ib. xxiii

15 None are so desolate but something dear,
　Dearer than self, possesses or possess'd
A thought, and claims the homage of a tear. *Ib.* xxiv

16 　The joys and sorrows sailors find,
Coop'd in their winged sea-girt citadel. *Ib.* xxviii

17 Fair Greece! sad relic of departed worth!
Immortal, though no more; though fallen, great!
　　　　　　　Ib. lxxiii

18 Hereditary bondsmen! know ye not
Who would be free themselves must strike the blow?
　　　　　　　Ib. lxxvi

19 Where'er we tread 'tis haunted, holy ground.
　　　　　　　Ib. lxxxviii

20 What is the worst of woes that wait on age?
　What stamps the wrinkle deeper on the brow?
To view each loved one blotted from life's page,
And be alone on earth, as I am now. *Ib.* xcviii

21 Ada! sole daughter of my house and heart. *Ib.* c. III. i

22 Once more upon the waters! yet once more!
And the waves bound beneath me as a steed
That knows his rider. *Ib.* ii

23 　　　Years steal
Fire from the mind as vigour from the limb;
And life's enchanted cup but sparkles near the brim.
　　　　　　　Ib. viii

24 Stop!—for thy tread is on an Empire's dust!
An earthquake's spoil is sepulchred below! *Ib.* xvii

25 There was a sound of revelry by night,
　And Belgium's capital had gather'd then
Her beauty and her chivalry, and bright
　The lamps shone o'er fair women and brave men;
A thousand hearts beat happily; and when

Music arose with its voluptuous swell,
Soft eyes look'd love to eyes which spake again,
　And all went merry as a marriage bell;
But hush! hark! a deep sound strikes like a rising knell!
　　　　　　　Childe Harold, c. III. xxi

26 Did ye not hear it?—No; 'twas but the wind,
　Or the car rattling o'er the stony street;
On with the dance! let joy be unconfined;
　No sleep till morn, when Youth and Pleasure meet
To chase the glowing Hours with flying feet. *Ib.* xxii

27 Arm! Arm! it is—it is—the cannon's opening roar!
　　　　　　　Ib.

28 Within a window'd niche of that high hall
Sate Brunswick's fated chieftain. *Ib.* xxiii

29 He rush'd into the field, and, foremost fighting, fell.
　　　　　　　Ib.

30 And there was mounting in hot haste. *Ib.* xxv

31 　Swiftly forming in the ranks of war;
And the deep thunder peal on peal afar. *Ib.*

32 Or whispering, with white lips—'The foe! they come!
　they come!' *Ib.*

33 Grieving, if aught inanimate e'er grieves,
Over the unreturning brave,—alas! *Ib.* xxvii

34 Burning with high hope, shall moulder cold and low.
　　　　　　　Ib.

35 Battle's magnificently stern array! *Ib.* xxviii

36 Rider and horse,—friend, foe,—in one red burial
　blent! *Ib.*

37 Bright names will hallow song. *Ib.* xxix

38 The tree will wither long before it fall. *Ib.* xxxii

39 Like to the apples on the Dead Sea's shore,
All ashes to the taste. *Ib.* xxxiv

40 There sunk the greatest, nor the worst of men,
Whose spirit, antithetically mixt,
One moment of the mightiest, and again
On little objects with like firmness fixt. [Napoleon.]
　　　　　　　Ib. xxxvi

41 That untaught innate philosophy. *Ib.* xxxix

42 Quiet to quick bosoms is a hell. *Ib.* xlii

43 The castled crag of Drachenfels
Frowns o'er the wide and winding Rhine. *Ib.* lv.

44 But these are deeds which should not pass away,
And names that must not wither. *Ib.* lxvii

45 Lake Leman woos me with its crystal face. *Ib.* lxviii

46 To fly from, need not be to hate, mankind. *Ib.* lxix

47 I live not in myself, but I become
Portion of that around me; and to me
High mountains are a feeling, but the hum
Of human cities torture. *Ib.* lxxii

48 The self-torturing sophist, wild Rousseau. *Ib.* lxxvii

49 Sapping a solemn creed with solemn sneer. [Gibbon.]
　　　　　　　Ib. cvii

50 I have not loved the world, nor the world me;
　I have not flatter'd its rank breath, nor bow'd
To its idolatries a patient knee. *Ib.* cxiii

51 　　　I stood
Among them, but not of them; in a shroud
Of thoughts which were not their thoughts. *Ib.*

BYRON

1 I stood in Venice, on the Bridge of Sighs;
A palace and a prison on each hand.
Childe Harold, c. IV. i

2 Where Venice sate in state, throned on her hundred
isles! *Ib.*

3 The spouseless Adriatic mourns her lord. *Ib.* xi

4 Oh for an hour of blind old Dandolo. *Ib.* xii

5   It may be a sound—
A tone of music—summer's eve—or spring—
A flower—the wind—the Ocean—which shall wound,
Striking the electric chain wherewith we are darkly
bound. *Ib.* xxiii

6 The moon is up, and yet it is not night;
Sunset divides the sky with her; a sea
Of glory streams along the Alpine height
Of blue Friuli's mountains; Heaven is free
From clouds, but of all colours seems to be,—
Melted to one vast Iris of the West,—
Where the day joins the past Eternity. *Ib.* xxvii

7 The Ariosto of the North. [Scott.] *Ib.* xl

8 Italia! oh Italia! thou who hast
The fatal gift of beauty. *Ib.* xlii

9 Let these describe the undescribable. *Ib.* liii

10 Love watching Madness with unalterable mien.
Ib. lxxii

11 Then farewell, Horace; whom I hated so,
Not for thy faults, but mine. *Ib.* lxxvii

12 Oh Rome! my country! city of the soul! *Ib.* lxxviii

13 The Niobe of nations! there she stands,
Childless and crownless, in her voiceless woe.
Ib. lxxix

14 Yet, Freedom! yet thy banner, torn, but flying,
Streams like the thunder-storm *against* the wind.
Ib. xcviii

15 Alas! our young affections run to waste,
Or water but the desert. *Ib.* cxx

16 Of its own beauty is the mind diseased. *Ib.* cxxii

17 Time, the avenger! *Ib.* cxxx

18 The arena swims around him—he is gone,
Ere ceased the inhuman shout which hail'd the wretch
who won. *Ib.* cxl

19 He heard it, but he heeded not—his eyes
Were with his heart, and that was far away;
He reck'd not of the life he lost nor prize,
But where his rude hut by the Danube lay,
There were his young barbarians all at play,
There was their Dacian mother—he, their sire,
Butcher'd to make a Roman holiday. *Ib.* cxli

20 A ruin—yet what ruin! from its mass
Walls, palaces, half-cities, have been rear'd.
Ib. cxliii

21 While stands the Coliseum, Rome shall stand;
When falls the Coliseum, Rome shall fall;
And when Rome falls—the World. *Ib.* cxlv

22   Spared and blest by time;
Looking tranquillity. *Ib.* cxlvi

23 The Lord of the unerring bow,
The God of life, and poesy, and light. *Ib.* clxi

24   So young, so fair,
Good without effort, great without a foe. *Ib.* clxxii

25 Oh! that the desert were my dwelling-place,
With one fair spirit for my minister,
That I might all forget the human race,
And, hating no one, love but only her!
Childe Harold, c. IV. clxxvii

26 There is a pleasure in the pathless woods,
There is a rapture on the lonely shore,
There is society, where none intrudes,
By the deep sea, and music in its roar:
I love not man the less, but Nature more,
From these our interviews, in which I steal
From all I may be, or have been before,
To mingle with the Universe, and feel
What I can ne'er express, yet cannot all conceal.
Ib. clxxviii

27 Roll on, thou deep and dark blue Ocean—roll!
Ten thousand fleets sweep over thee in vain;
Man marks the earth with ruin—his control
Stops with the shore. *Ib.* clxxix

28 He sinks into thy depths with bubbling groan,
Without a grave, unknell'd, uncoffin'd, and unknown.
Ib.

29 Time writes no wrinkle on thine azure brow:
Such as creation's dawn beheld, thou rollest now.
Ib. clxxxii

30 Thou glorious mirror, where the Almighty's form
Glasses itself in tempests. *Ib.* clxxxiii

31 Dark-heaving—boundless, endless, and sublime,
The image of eternity. *Ib.*

32 And I have loved thee, Ocean! and my joy
Of youthful sports was on thy breast to be
Borne, like thy bubbles, onward: from a boy
I wanton'd with thy breakers, . . .
And trusted to thy billows far and near,
And laid my hand upon thy mane—as I do here.
Ib. clxxxiv

33 Eternal spirit of the chainless mind!
Brightest in dungeons, Liberty! thou art.
Sonnet on Chillon

34 Chillon! thy prison is a holy place,
   And thy sad floor an altar—for 'twas trod,
Until his very steps have left a trace
   Worn, as if thy cold pavement were a sod,
By Bonnivard! May none those marks efface!
   For they appeal from tyranny to God. *Ib.*

35 My hair is grey, but not with years,
       Nor grew it white
       In a single night,
As men's have grown from sudden fears.
The Prisoner of Chillon, i

36 Regain'd my freedom with a sigh. *Ib.* xiv

37 The comet of a season. *Churchill's Grave*

38 The glory and the nothing of a name. *Ib.*

39 We were a gallant company,
Riding o'er land, and sailing o'er sea.
Oh! but we went merrily! *Siege of Corinth*, prologue

40 Thus was Corinth lost and won! *Ib.* xxxiii

41 The fatal facility of the octo-syllabic verse.
The Corsair, preface

42 O'er the glad waters of the dark blue sea,
Our thoughts as boundless, and our souls as free.
Ib. c. I. i

43 She walks the waters like a thing of life. *Ib.* iii

1 Such hath it been—shall be—beneath the sun
The many still must labour for the one.
The Corsair, c. I. viii

2 There was a laughing devil in his sneer. *Ib.* ix

3 Much hath been done, but more remains to do—
Their galleys blaze—why not their city too?
Ib. c. II. iv

4 The weak alone repent. *Ib.* x

5 Oh! too convincing—dangerously dear—
In woman's eye the unanswerable tear!
Ib. xv

6 She for him had given
Her all on earth, and more than all in heaven!
Ib. c. III. xvii

7 He left a Corsair's name to other times,
Link'd with one virtue, and a thousand crimes.
Ib. xxiv

8 Slow sinks, more lovely ere his race be run,
Along Morea's hills the setting sun;
Not, as in northern climes, obscurely bright,
But one unclouded blaze of living light.
Curse of Minerva, I. I, and *The Corsair*, III. i

9 I had a dream, which was not all a dream. *Darkness*

10 I tell thee, be not rash; a golden bridge
Is for a flying enemy.
The Deformed Transformed, pt. II, sc. ii

11 Through life's road, so dim and dirty,
I have dragg'd to three-and-thirty.
What have these years left to me?
Nothing—except thirty-three.
Diary, 21 Jan. 1821. In Moore's *Life of Byron*,
vol. ii, p. 414 (1st ed.).

12 I wish he would explain his explanation.
Don Juan, c. I, dedication ii

13 The intellectual eunuch Castlereagh. *Ib.* xi

14 My way is to begin with the beginning. *Ib.* vii

15 In virtues nothing earthly could surpass her,
Save thine 'incomparable oil', Macassar! *Ib.* xvii

16 But—Oh! ye lords of ladies intellectual,
Inform us truly, have they not hen-peck'd you all?
Ib. xxii

17 She
Was married, charming, chaste, and twenty-three.
Ib. lix

18 Her stature tall—I hate a dumpy woman. *Ib.* lxi

19 What men call gallantry, and gods adultery,
Is much more common where the climate's sultry.
Ib. lxiii

20 Christians have burnt each other, quite persuaded
That all the Apostles would have done as they did.
Ib. lxxxiii

21 A little still she strove, and much repented,
And whispering 'I will ne'er consent'—consented.
Ib. cxvii

22 'Tis sweet to hear the watch-dog's honest bark
Bay deep-mouth'd welcome as we draw near home;
'Tis sweet to know there is an eye will mark
Our coming, and look brighter when we come.
Ib. cxxiii

23 Sweet is revenge—especially to women. *Ib.* cxxiv

24 Pleasure's a sin, and sometimes sin's a pleasure.
Ib. cxxxiii

25 Man's love is of man's life a thing apart,
'Tis woman's whole existence.
Don Juan, c. I. cxciv

26 My grandmother's review—the British. *Ib.* ccix

27 So for a good old-gentlemanly vice,
I think I must take up with avarice. *Ib.* ccxvi

28 There's nought, no doubt, so much the spirit calms
As rum and true religion. *Ib.* c. II. xxxiv

29 'Twas twilight, and the sunless day went down
Over the waste of waters. *Ib.* xlix

30 A solitary shriek, the bubbling cry
Of some strong swimmer in his agony. *Ib.* liii

31 If this be true, indeed,
Some Christians have a comfortable creed. *Ib.* lxxxvi

32 He could, perhaps, have pass'd the Hellespont,
As once (a feat on which ourselves we prided)
Leander, Mr. Ekenhead, and I did. *Ib.* cv

33 Let us have wine and women, mirth and laughter,
Sermons and soda-water the day after. *Ib.* clxxviii

34 Man, being reasonable, must get drunk;
The best of life is but intoxication. *Ib.* clxxix

35 Alas! they were so young, so beautiful,
So lonely, loving, helpless. *Ib.* cxcii

36 A group that's quite antique,
Half naked, loving, natural, and Greek. *Ib.* cxciv

37 Alas! the love of women! it is known
To be a lovely and a fearful thing! *Ib.* cxcix

38 In her first passion woman loves her lover,
In all the others all she loves is love. *Ib.* c. III. iii

39 Romances paint at full length people's wooings,
But only give a bust of marriages:
For no one cares for matrimonial cooings,
There's nothing wrong in a connubial kiss:
Think you, if Laura had been Petrarch's wife,
He would have written sonnets all his life? *Ib.* viii

40 Dreading that climax of all human ills,
The inflammation of his weekly bills. *Ib.* xxxv

41 He was the mildest manner'd man
That ever scuttled ship or cut a throat,
With such true breeding of a gentleman,
You never could divine his real thought. *Ib.* xli

42 But Shakspeare also says, 'tis very silly
'To gild refined gold, or paint the lily.' *Ib.* lxxvi

43 The isles of Greece, the isles of Greece!
Where burning Sappho loved and sung,
Where grew the arts of war and peace,
Where Delos rose, and Phœbus sprung!
Eternal summer gilds them yet,
But all, except their sun, is set. *Ib.* lxxxvi. I

44 The mountains look on Marathon—
And Marathon looks on the sea;
And musing there an hour alone,
I dream'd that Greece might still be free. *Ib.* 3

45 A king sate on the rocky brow
Which looks o'er sea-born Salamis;
And ships, by thousands, lay below,
And men in nations;—all were his!
He counted them at break of day—
And when the sun set where were they? *Ib.* 4

46 Earth! render back from out thy breast
A remnant of our Spartan dead!
Of the three hundred grant but three,
To make a new Thermopylæ! *Ib.* 7

1 Fill high the cup with Samian wine!
Don Juan, c. III. lxxxvi. 9

2 You have the Pyrrhic dance as yet;
  Where is the Pyrrhic phalanx gone!
Of two such lessons, why forget
  The nobler and the manlier one?
You have the letters Cadmus gave—
Think ye he meant them for a slave? *Ib.* 10

3 Place me on Sunium's marbled steep,
  Where nothing, save the waves and I,
May hear our mutual murmurs sweep;
  There, swan-like, let me sing and die:
A land of slaves shall ne'er be mine—
Dash down yon cup of Samian wine! *Ib.* 16

4 Milton's the prince of poets—so we say;
  A little heavy, but no less divine. *Ib.* xci

5 A drowsy frowzy poem, call'd the 'Excursion',
  Writ in a manner which is my aversion. *Ib.* xciv

6 We learn from Horace, 'Homer sometimes sleeps';
  We feel without him, Wordsworth sometimes wakes.
Ib. xcviii

7 Ave Maria! 'tis the hour of prayer!
  Ave Maria! 'tis the hour of love! *Ib.* ciii

8 Imagination droops her pinion. *Ib.* c. IV. iii

9 And if I laugh at any mortal thing,
  'Tis that I may not weep. *Ib.* iv

10 'Whom the gods love die young' was said of yore.
Ib. xii

11 'Arcades ambo', *id est*—blackguards both. *Ib.* xciii

12 I've stood upon Achilles' tomb,
  And heard Troy doubted; time will doubt of Rome.
Ib. ci

13 Oh! 'darkly, deeply, beautifully blue',
  As some one somewhere sings about the sky. *Ib.* cx

14 When amatory poets sing their loves
  In liquid lines mellifluously bland,
And pair their rhymes as Venus yokes her doves.
Ib. c. V. i

15 I have a passion for the name of 'Mary',
  For once it was a magic sound to me:
And still it half calls up the realms of fairy,
  Where I beheld what never was to be. *Ib.* iv

16 A lady in the case. *Ib.* xix

17 And put himself upon his good behaviour. *Ib.* xlvii

18 That all-softening, overpowering knell,
  The tocsin of the soul—the dinner-bell. *Ib.* xlix

19 Not to admire is all the art I know. *Ib.* ci
(*See 257:1, 386:33*)

20 Why don't they knead two virtuous souls for life
Into that moral centaur, man and wife? *Ib.* clviii

21 There is a tide in the affairs of women,
  Which, taken at the flood, leads—God knows
where. *Ib.* c. VI. ii

22 A lady of a 'certain age', which means
Certainly aged. *Ib.* lxix

23 A 'strange coincidence', to use a phrase
By which such things are settled now-a-days.
Ib. lxxviii

24 'Let there be light!' said God, 'and there was light!'
'Let there be blood!' says man, and there's a sea!
Ib. c. VII. xli

25 'Carnage, (so Wordsworth tells you), is God's
daughter.' *Don Juan*, c. VIII. ix

26 Oh, Wellington! (or 'Villainton')—for Fame
Sounds the heroic syllables both ways. *Ib.* c. IX. i

27 Call'd 'Saviour of the Nations'—not yet saved,
And 'Europe's Liberator'—still enslaved. [Welling-
ton.] *Ib.* v

28 Never had mortal man such opportunity,
Except Napoleon, or abused it more. *Ib.* ix

29 That water-land of Dutchmen and of ditches.
Ib. c. X. lxiii

30 When Bishop Berkeley said 'there was no matter',
And proved it—'twas no matter what he said.
Ib. c. XI. i

31 But Tom's no more—and so no more of Tom.
Ib. xx

32 And, after all, what is a lie? 'Tis but
The truth in masquerade. *Ib.* xxxvii

33 I—albeit I'm sure I did not know it,
Nor sought of foolscap subjects to be king.—
Was reckon'd, a considerable time,
The grand Napoleon of the realms of rhyme. *Ib.* lv

34 But Juan was my Moscow, and Faliero
My Leipsic, and my Mont Saint Jean seems Cain.
Ib. lvi

35 John Keats, who was kill'd off by one critique,
Just as he really promised something great,
If not intelligible, without Greek
Contrived to talk about the Gods of late,
Much as they might have been supposed to speak.
Poor fellow! His was an untoward fate;
'Tis strange the mind, that very fiery particle,
Should let itself be snuff'd out by an article. *Ib.* lx

36 Nought's permanent among the human race,
Except the Whigs *not* getting into place. *Ib.* lxxxii

37 Love rules the camp, the court, the grove—for love
Is heaven, and heaven is love. *Ib.* c. XII. xiii

38 And hold up to the sun my little taper. *Ib.* xxi

39 For talk six times with the same single lady,
And you may get the wedding dresses ready. *Ib.* lix

40   Merely innocent flirtation,
Not quite adultery, but adulteration. *Ib.* lxiii

41 A Prince . . .
With fascination in his very bow. *Ib.* lxxxiv

42 A finish'd gentleman from top to toe. *Ib.*

43 Beauteous, even where beauties most abound.
Ib. c. XIII. ii

44 Now hatred is by far the longest pleasure;
Men love in haste, but they detest at leisure. *Ib.* vi

45 Cervantes smiled Spain's chivalry away. *Ib.* xi

46 I hate to hunt down a tired metaphor. *Ib.* xxxvi

47 The English winter—ending in July,
  To recommence in August. *Ib.* xlii

48 Society is now one polish'd horde,
Form'd of two mighty tribes, the *Bores* and *Bored*.
Ib. xcv

49 I for one venerate a petticoat. *Ib.* c. XIV. xxvi

50 Of all the horrid, hideous notes of woe,
Sadder than owl-songs or the midnight blast,
Is that portentous phrase, 'I told you so.' *Ib.* l.

BYRON

1 'Tis strange—but true; for truth is always strange; Stranger than fiction. *Don Juan*, c. XIV. ci

2 A lovely being, scarcely form'd or moulded, A rose with all its sweetest leaves yet folded. *Ib.* c. XV. xliii

3 The antique Persians taught three useful things, To draw the bow, to ride, and speak the truth. *Ib.* c. XVI. i

4 Not so her gracious, graceful, graceless Grace. *Ib.* xlix

5 The loudest wit I e'er was deafen'd with. *Ib.* lxxxi

6 And both were young, and one was beautiful. *The Dream*, ii

7 A change came o'er the spirit of my dream. *Ib.* v

8 Still must I hear?—shall hoarse Fitzgerald bawl His creaking couplets in a tavern hall. *English Bards and Scotch Reviewers*, l. 1

9   I'll publish, right or wrong: Fools are my theme, let satire be my song. *Ib.* l. 5

10 'Tis pleasant, sure, to see one's name in print; A book's a book, although there's nothing in 't. *Ib.* l. 51

11 A man must serve his time to every trade Save censure—critics all are ready made. *Ib.* l. 63

12 With just enough of learning to misquote. *Ib.* l. 66

13   As soon Seek roses in December—ice in June; Hope constancy in wind, or corn in chaff; Believe a woman or an epitaph, Or any other thing that's false, before You trust in critics, who themselves are sore. *Ib.* l. 75

14 Better to err with Pope, than shine with Pye. *Ib.* l. 102

15 Sense and wit with poesy allied. *Ib.* l. 105

16 Who both by precept and example, shows That prose is verse, and verse is merely prose. *Ib.* l. 241

17 Be warm, but pure: be amorous, but be chaste. *Ib.* l. 306

18 Perverts the Prophets, and purloins the Psalms. *Ib.* l. 326

19 Oh, Amos Cottle!—Phoebus! what a name To fill the speaking trump of future fame! *Ib.* l. 399

20 The petrifactions of a plodding brain. *Ib.* l. 416

21 To sanction Vice, and hunt Decorum down. *Ib.* l. 621

22 To live like Clodius, and like Falkland fall. *Ib.* l. 686

23 Lords too are bards, such things at times befall, And 'tis some praise in peers to write at all. *Ib.* l. 719

24 Forsook the labours of a servile state. Stemm'd the rude storm, and triumph'd over fate. *Ib.* l. 779

25 [*Kirke White*:] 'Twas thine own genius gave the final blow, And help'd to plant the wound that laid thee low: So the struck eagle, stretch'd upon the plain, No more through rolling clouds to soar again, View'd his own feather on the fatal dart, And wing'd the shaft that quiver'd in his heart;

Keen were his pangs, but keener far to feel He nursed the pinion which impell'd the steel; While the same plumage that had warm'd his nest Drank the last life-drop of his bleeding breast. *English Bards and Scotch Reviewers*, l. 839

26 Yet Truth sometimes will lend her noblest fires, And decorate the verse herself inspires: This fact in Virtue's name let Crabbe attest; Though nature's sternest painter, yet the best. *Ib.* l. 855

27 The mighty master of unmeaning rhyme. [Darwin.] *Ib.* l. 894

28 Let simple Wordsworth chime his childish verse, And brother Coleridge lull the babe at nurse. *Ib.* l. 917

29 Glory, like the phoenix 'midst her fires, Exhales her odours, blazes, and expires. *Ib.*

30 I too can hunt a poetaster down. *Ib.*

31 The world is a bundle of hay,   Mankind are the asses who pull; Each tugs it a different way,   And the greatest of all is John Bull. *Epigram.*

32 My sister! my sweet sister! if a name Dearer and purer were, it should be thine. *Epistle to Augusta*

33 And know, whatever thou hast been, 'Tis something better not to be. *Euthanasia*

34 Fare thee well! and if for ever,   Still for ever, fare thee well. *Fare Thee Well!*

35 I only know we loved in vain— I only feel—Farewell!—Farewell! *Farewell! if ever Fondest Prayer*

36 Nor be, what man should ever be,   The friend of Beauty in distress? *To Florence*

37 Clime of the unforgotten brave! *The Giaour*, l. 103

38 For Freedom's battle once begun, Bequeath'd by bleeding Sire to Son, Though baffled oft is ever won. *Ib.* l. 123

39 Dark tree, still sad when others' grief is fled, The only constant mourner o'er the dead! [A cypress.] *Ib.* l. 286

40 And lovelier things have mercy shown To every failing but their own, And every woe a tear can claim Except an erring sister's shame. *Ib.* l. 418

41 The harp the monarch minstrel swept. *Title*

42 Or lend fresh interest to a twice-told tale. *Hints from Horace*, l. 184

43 Friendship is Love without his wings! *Hours of Idleness. L'Amitié*

44 I have tasted the sweets and the bitters of love. *Ib.* To Rev. J. T. Becher

45 Though women are angels, yet wedlock's the devil. *Ib.* To Eliza

46 Then receive him as best such an advent becomes, With a legion of cooks, and an army of slaves! *The Irish Avatar*

47 More happy, if less wise. *The Island*, c. II. xi

[117]

1 Jack was embarrassed—never hero more,
And as he knew not what to say, he swore.
The Island, c. IV. v

2 Who killed John Keats?
'I,' says the Quarterly,
So savage and Tartarly,
''Twas one of my feats.'   *John Keats*

3 Weep, daughter of a royal line.
Lines to a Lady Weeping

4 Left by his sire, too young such loss to know,
Lord of himself—that heritage of woe.
Lara, c. I. ii

5 His madness was not of the head, but heart.
Ib. xviii

6 Maid of Athens, ere we part,
Give, oh give me back my heart!
Or, since that has left my breast,
Keep it now, and take the rest!   *Maid of Athens*

7 Mont Blanc is the monarch of mountains;
They crown'd him long ago
On a throne of rocks, in a robe of clouds,
With a diadem of snow.   *Manfred*, I. i

8 When the moon is on the wave,
And the glow-worm in the grass,
And the meteor on the grave,
And the wisp on the morass;
When the falling stars are shooting,
And the answer'd owls are hooting,
And the silent leaves are still
In the shadow of the hill.   *Ib.*

9 By that most seeming-virtuous eye.   *Ib.*

10 The heart ran o'er
With silent worship of the great of old—
The dead but sceptred sovereigns, who still rule
Our spirits from their urns.   *Ib.* III. iv

11 Old man! 'tis not so difficult to die.   *Ib.*

12 You have deeply ventured;
But all must do so who would greatly win.
Marino Faliero, I. ii

13 'Bring forth the horse!'—the horse was brought;
In truth, he was a noble steed.   *Mazeppa*, ix. 1

14 My boat is on the shore,
And my bark is on the sea;
But, before I go, Tom Moore,
Here's a double health to thee!   *To Thomas Moore*

15 Here's a sigh to those who love me,
And a smile to those who hate;
And, whatever sky 's above me,
Here's a heart for every fate.   *Ib.*

16 My Murray.   *To Mr. Murray*

17 There be none of Beauty's daughters
With a magic like thee.
Stanzas for Music. 'There be none of Beauty's daughters'

18 There's not a joy the world can give like that it takes
away.   *Ib. 'There's not a joy the world can give'*

19 'Tis done—but yesterday a King!
And arm'd with Kings to strive—
And now thou art a nameless thing:
So abject—yet alive!   *Ode to Napoleon Bonaparte*

20 The Arbiter of others' fate
A Suppliant for his own!   *Ib.*

21 The Cincinnatus of the West. [Washington.]
Ode to Napoleon Bonaparte

22 But the poor dog, in life the firmest friend,
The first to welcome, foremost to defend.
Inscription on a Newfoundland Dog

23 Oh! snatched away in beauty's bloom,
On thee shall press no ponderous tomb;
But on thy turf shall roses rear
Their leaves, the earliest of the year.
Oh! Snatched Away in Beauty's Bloom

24 It is not in the storm nor in the strife
We feel benumb'd, and wish to be no more,
But in the after-silence on the shore,
When all is lost, except a little life.
On Hearing Lady Byron was Ill

25 The moral Clytemnestra of thy lord.   *Ib.*

26 My days are in the yellow leaf;
The flowers and fruits of love are gone;
The worm, the canker, and the grief
Are mine alone!
On This Day I Complete my Thirty-Sixth Year

27 Seek out—less often sought than found—
A soldier's grave, for thee the best;
Then look around, and choose thy ground,
And take thy rest.   *Ib.*

28 It is the hour when from the boughs
The nightingale's high note is heard;
It is the hour when lovers' vows
Seem sweet in every whisper'd word.   *Parisina*

29 Yet in my lineaments they trace
Some features of my father's face.   *Ib.*

30 Thy Godlike crime was to be kind,
To render with thy precepts less
The sum of human wretchedness.   *Prometheus*

31 Man in portions can foresee
His own funereal destiny.   *Ib.*

32 Oh, talk not to me of a name great in story;
The days of our youth are the days of our glory;
And the myrtle and ivy of sweet two-and-twenty
Are worth all your laurels, though ever so plenty.
Stanzas Written on the Road between Florence and Pisa.

33 Oh Fame!—if I e'er took delight in thy praises,
'Twas less for the sake of thy high-sounding phrases,
Than to see the bright eyes of the dear one discover,
She thought that I was not unworthy to love her.   *Ib.*

34 I knew it was love, and I felt it was glory.   *Ib.*

35 By all that's good and glorious take this counsel.
Sardanapalus, I. ii

36 I am the very slave of circumstance
And impulse—borne away with every breath!
Ib. IV. i

37 The Assyrian came down like the wolf on the fold,
And his cohorts were gleaming in purple and gold;
And the sheen of their spears was like stars on the sea,
When the blue wave rolls nightly on deep Galilee.
Destruction of Sennacherib

38 For the Angel of Death spread his wings on the
blast.   *Ib.*

39 And the might of the Gentile, unsmote by the sword,
Hath melted like snow in the glance of the Lord!   *Ib.*

1 She walks in beauty, like the night
  Of cloudless climes and starry skies;
  And all that's best of dark and bright
  Meet in her aspect and her eyes:
  Thus mellow'd to that tender light
  Which heaven to gaudy day denies.
                    Hebrew Melodies. She Walks in Beauty

2 And on that cheek, and o'er that brow,
  So soft, so calm, yet eloquent,
  The smiles that win, the tints that glow
  But tell of days in goodness spent,
  A mind at peace with all below,
  A heart whose love is innocent!   *Ib.*

3 Born in the garret, in the kitchen bred,
  Promoted thence to deck her mistress' head.   *A Sketch*

4 So, we'll go no more a roving
  So late into the night,
  Though the heart be still as loving,
  And the moon be still as bright.
            So, We'll Go No More a Roving

5 For the sword outwears its sheath,
  And the soul wears out the breast.
  And the heart must pause to breathe,
  And love itself have rest.   *Ib.*

6 Though the night was made for loving,
  And the day returns too soon,
  Yet we'll go no more a-roving
  By the light of the moon.   *Ib.*

7 Could Love for ever
  Run like a river.   *Stanzas*

8 Part in friendship—and bid good-night.   *Ib.*

9 Though the day of my destiny's over,
  And the star of my fate hath declined.
                    Stanzas to Augusta

10 In the desert a fountain is springing,
   In the wide waste there still is a tree,
   And a bird in the solitude singing,
   Which speaks to my spirit of *thee*.   *Ib.*

11 And Freedom hallows with her tread
   The silent cities of the dead.
            On the Star of 'The Legion of Honour'

12 And when we think we lead, we are most led.
                    The Two Foscari, II. i

13 The Mede is at his gate!
   The Persian on his throne!   *Vision of Belshazzar*

14 Saint Peter sat by the celestial gate:
   His keys were rusty, and the lock was dull.
                    Vision of Judgement, i

15 The angels all were singing out of tune,
   And hoarse with having little else to do,
   Excepting to wind up the sun and moon,
   Or curb a runaway young star or two.   *Ib.* ii

16 Each day too slew its thousands six or seven
   Till at the crowning carnage, Waterloo,
   They threw their pens down in divine disgust—
   The page was so besmear'd with blood and dust.
                    Ib. v

17 A better farmer ne'er brushed dew from lawn,
   A worse king never left a realm undone.   *Ib.* viii

18 It seem'd the mockery of hell to fold
   The rottenness of eighty years in gold.   *Ib.* x

19 In whom his qualities are reigning still,
   Except that household virtue, most uncommon,
   Of constancy to a bad, ugly woman.
                    Vision of Judgement, xii

20 'Midst them an old man
   With an old soul, and both extremely blind.   *Ib.* xxiii

21 As he drew near, he gazed upon the gate
   Ne'er to be entered more by him or Sin,
   With such a glance of supernatural hate
   As made Saint Peter wish himself within;
   He patter'd with his keys at a great rate,
   And sweated through his apostolic skin:
   Of course his perspiration was but ichor,
   Or some such other spiritual liquor.
                    Ib. xxv

22 Yet still between his Darkness and his Brightness
   There pass'd a mutual glance of great politeness.
                    Ib. xxxv

23 The Archangel bow'd, not like a modern beau.
                    Ib. xxxvi

24   Satan met his ancient friend
   With more hauteur, as might an old Castilian
   Poor noble meet a mushroom rich civilian.   *Ib.*

25 When Michael saw this host, he first grew pale,
   As angels can; next, like Italian twilight,
   He turn'd all colours—as a peacock's tail,
   Or sunset streaming through a Gothic skylight
   In some old abbey, or a trout not stale,
   Or distant lightning on the horizon *by* night
   Or a fresh rainbow, or a grand review
   Of thirty regiments in red, green, and blue.   *Ib.* lxi

26 And when the tumult dwindled to a calm,
   I left him practising the hundredth psalm.   *Ib.* cvi

27 Seductive Waltz!   *The Waltz*

28 Voluptuous Waltz!   *Ib.*

29 When we two parted
   In silence and tears,
   Half broken-hearted
   To sever for years,
   Pale grew thy cheek and cold,
   Colder thy kiss.   *When We Two Parted*

30 If I should meet thee
   After long years,
   How should I greet thee?—
   With silence and tears.   *Ib.*

31 The fault was Nature's fault not thine,
   Which made thee fickle as thou art.
                    To a Youthful Friend

32 No *Manual*, no letters, no tooth-powder, no *extract*
   from Moore's *Italy* concerning Marino Falieri, no
   nothing—as a man hallooed out at one of Burdett's
   elections, after a long ululatus of No Bastille! No
   Governor Aris! No '—God knows what';—but his
   ne plus ultra was, 'no nothing!'
                    Letter to Murray, 4 June 1817

33 I am sure my bones would not rest in an English
   grave, or my clay mix with the earth of that country.
   I believe the thought would drive me mad on my
   deathbed, could I suppose that any of my friends
   would be base enough to convey my carcass back
   to your soil.   *Ib. 7 June 1819*

34 The Princess of Parallelograms.
   (*Speaking of Annabella Milbanke to Lady Melbourne*)

[119]

1 As he [Lord Byron] himself briefly described it in his Memoranda, 'I awoke one morning and found myself famous.'—Moore's *Life of Byron, 1830*, vol. i, p. 347 (referring to the instantaneous success of *Childe Harold*)

HENRY JAMES BYRON
1834–1884

2 Life's too short for chess.   *Our Boys*, Act I

3 He's up to these grand games, but one of these days I'll loore him on to skittles—and astonish him.
Ib. Act II

JAMES BRANCH CABELL
1879–

4 I am willing to taste any drink once. *Jurgen*, ch. I

5 A man possesses nothing certainly save a brief loan of his own body: and yet the body of man is capable of much curious pleasure. *Ib.* ch. 20

6 The optimist proclaims that we live in the best of all possible worlds; and the pessimist fears this is true.   *The Silver Stallion*, bk. iv, ch. 26

AUGUSTUS CAESAR
63 B.C.–A.D. 14

7 Quintili Vare, legiones redde.
Quintilius Varus, give me back my legions.
Suetonius, *Divus Augustus*, 23

8 Urbem . . . excoluit adeo, ut iure sit gloriatus marmoream se relinquere, quam latericiam accepisset.
He so improved the city that he justly boasted that he found it brick and left it marble. *Ib.* 28

9 Ad Graecas Kalendas soluturos.
They will pay at the Greek Kalends.   *Ib.* 87

JULIUS CAESAR
102?–44 B.C.

10 Gallia est omnis divisa in partes tres.
Gaul as a whole is divided into three parts.
De Bello Gallico, I. i

11 Fere libenter homines id quod volunt credunt.
Men willingly believe what they wish. *Ib.* iii. 18

12 Et tu, Brute?
You also, Brutus?
Of unknown origin. Quoted by Shakespeare, '*Julius Caesar*', III. i, *perhaps from the (lost) Latin play* '*Caesar Interfectus*', *probably from* '*The True Tragedie of Richard Duke of York*.' '*Some have written that as M. Brutus came running upon him, he said "καὶ σύ, τέκνον", "and you, my son."'* (Holland's *Suetonius*, p. 33)

13 Veni, vidi, vici.
I came, I saw, I conquered.
Suetonius, *Divus Julius*, xxxvii. 2.
(*Inscription displayed in Caesar's Pontic triumph, or, according to Plutarch, l. 2, written in a letter by Caesar, announcing the victory of Zela which concluded the Pontic campaign*)

14 Iacta alea est.
The die is cast.   *Ib.* xxxii
At the crossing of the Rubicon

15 Caesar's wife must be above suspicion.
Traditional, based on Plutarch, *Life of Julius Caesar*, x. 6

16 Thou hast Caesar and his fortune with thee.
Plutarch, *Life of Julius Caesar*, xxxviii. 3. Trans. by North.

PEDRO CALDERÓN DE LA BARCA
1600–1681

17 No se pierde
El hacer bien, aun en sueños.
Don't relinquish right-doing, even in dreams.
La Vida es Sueño, sc. iv

CALIGULA
A.D. 12–41

18 Utinam populus Romanus unam cervicem haberet!
Would that the Roman people had but one neck!
Suetonius, *Life of Caligula*, 30

CALLIMACHUS
fl. 250 B.C.

19 μέγα βιβλίον μέγα κακόν.
Great book, great evil.
Proverb derived from Callimachus, *Fragments*, 359

CHARLES STUART CALVERLEY
1831–1884

20 The auld wife sat at her ivied door,
(*Butter and eggs and a pound of cheese*)
A thing she had frequently done before;
And her spectacles lay on her apron'd knees. *Ballad*

21 The farmer's daughter hath soft brown hair;
(*Butter and eggs and a pound of cheese*)
And I met with a ballad, I can't say where,
Which wholly consisted of lines like these. *Ib.*

22 And this song is consider'd a perfect gem,
And as to the meaning, it's what you please. *Ib.*

23 O Beer! O Hodgson, Guinness, Allsopp, Bass!
Names that should be on every infant's tongue! *Beer*

24 When 'Dulce est desipere in loco'
Was written, real Falernian winged the pen. *Ib.*

25 I cannot sing the old songs now!
It is not that I deem them low;
'Tis that I can't remember how
They go.   *Changed*

26 Sikes, housebreaker, of Houndsditch,
Habitually swore;
But so surpassingly profane
He never was before.   *Charades*, vi

27 Aspect anything but bland.   *Ib.*

28 You see this pebble-stone? It's a thing I bought
Of a bit of a chit of a boy i' the mid o' the day—
I like to dock the smaller parts-o'-speech,
As we curtail the already curtail'd cur
(You catch the paronomasia, play 'po' words?). *The Cock and the Bull*

29 The basis or substratum—what you will—
Of the impending eighty thousand lines. *Ib.*

1 Donn'd galligaskins, antigropeloes.
The Cock and the Bull

2 Ombrifuge (Lord love you!), case o' rain. *Ib.*

3 A bare-legg'd beggarly son of a gun. *Ib.*

4 Fiddlepin's end! Get out, you blazing ass!
Gabble o' the goose. Don't bugaboo-baby *me*! *Ib.*

5 Pretty i' the Mantuan! *Ib.*

6 It takes up about eighty thousand lines,
A thing imagination boggles at:
And might, odds-bobs, sir! in judicious hands,
Extend from here to Mesopotamy. *Ib.*

7 Life is with such all beer and skittles;
They are not difficult to please
About their victuals. *Contentment*

8 'Twas ever thus from childhood's hour!
My fondest hopes would not decay:
I never loved a tree or flower
Which was the first to fade away! *Disaster*

9 For king-like rolls the Rhine,
And the scenery 's divine,
And the victuals and the wine
Rather good. *Dover to Munich*

10 Forever! 'Tis a single word!
Our rude forefathers deemed it two:
Can you imagine so absurd
A view? *Forever*

11 Wherefore bless ye, O beloved ones:—
Now unto mine inn must I,
Your 'poor moralist', betake me,
In my 'solitary fly'. *'Hic Vir, Hic Est'*

12 For I've read in many a novel that, unless they've
souls that grovel,
Folks *prefer* in fact a hovel to your dreary marble
halls. *In the Gloaming*

13 Grinder, who serenely grindest
At my door the Hundredth Psalm.
Lines on Hearing the Organ

14 Meaning, however, is no great matter.
Lovers, and a Reflection

15 Thro' the rare red heather we danced together,
(O love my Willie!) and smelt for flowers:
I must mention again it was gorgeous weather,
Rhymes are so scarce in this world of ours. *Ib.*

16 Study first propriety. *Of Propriety*

17 How Eugene Aram, though a thief, a liar, and a
murderer,
Yet, being intellectual, was amongst the noblest of
mankind. *Of Reading*

18 Thou, who when fears attack,
Bidst them avaunt, and Black
Care, at the horseman's back
Perching, unseatest;
Sweet, when the morn is grey;
Sweet, when they've cleared away
Lunch; and at close of day
Possibly sweetest. *Ode to Tobacco*

19 I have a liking old
For thee, though manifold
Stories, I know, are told
Not to thy credit. *Ib.*

20 How they who use fusees
All grow by slow degrees
Brainless as chimpanzees,
Meagre as lizards:
Go mad, and beat their wives;
Plunge (after shocking lives)
Razors and carving knives
Into their gizzards. *Ode to Tobacco*

21 Jones—(who, I'm glad to say,
Asked leave of Mrs. J.)—
Daily absorbs a clay
After his labours. *Ib.*

22 Cats may have had their goose
Cooked by tobacco-juice;
Still why deny its use
Thoughtfully taken?
We're not as tabbies are:
Smith, take a fresh cigar!
Jones, the tobacco-jar!
Here 's to thee, Bacon! *Ib.*

RICHARD OWEN CAMBRIDGE
1717–1802

23 What is the worth of anything,
But for the happiness 'twill bring? *Learning*, l. 23

PIERRE-JACQUES, BARON DE CAMBRONNE
1770–1842

24 La Garde meurt, mais ne se rend pas.
The Guards die but do not surrender.
*Attr. to Cambronne when called upon to sur-
render by Col. Halkett. Cambronne denied the
saying at a banquet at Nantes, 1835*

WILLIAM CAMDEN
1551–1623

25 My friend, judge not me,
Thou seest I judge not thee.
Betwixt the stirrup and the ground
Mercy I asked, mercy I found.
*Remains. Epitaph for a Man Killed by Falling
from His Horse*

HERBERT CAMPBELL

26 Now we sha'n't be long. *Title of Song*

JANE MONTGOMERY CAMPBELL
1817–1878

27 We plough the fields, and scatter
The good seed on the land,
But it is fed and watered
By God's Almighty Hand;
He sends the snow in winter,
The warmth to swell the grain,
The breezes and the sunshine,
And soft refreshing rain.
All good gifts around us
Are sent from Heaven above,
Then thank the Lord, O thank the Lord,
For all His love.
We Plough the Fields. Tr. from the German.
C. S. Bere's *Garland of Songs*

1 He paints the wayside flower,
He lights the evening star.
We Plough the Fields. Tr. from the German.
C. S. Bere's *Garland of Songs*

THOMAS CAMPBELL
1777–1844

2 'Tis Lethe's gloom, but not its quiet,—
The pain without the peace of death!   *Absence*

3 Of Nelson and the North
Sing the glorious day's renown,
When to battle fierce came forth
All the might of Denmark's crown,
And her arms along the deep proudly shone,—
By each gun the lighted brand
In a bold determined hand;
And the Prince of all the land
Led them on.   *Battle of the Baltic*

4 There was silence deep as death,
And the boldest held his breath
For a time.   *Ib.*

5 Again! again! again!
And the havoc did not slack,
Till a feeble cheer the Dane
To our cheering sent us back.   *Ib.*

6 Out spoke the victor then
As he hailed them o'er the wave,
'Ye are brothers! ye are men!
And we conquer but to save;
So peace instead of death let us bring:
But yield, proud foe, thy fleet
With the crews at England's feet,
And make submission meet
To our King.'   *Ib.*

7 Let us think of them that sleep,
Full many a fathom deep,
By thy wild and stormy steep,
Elsinore!   *Ib.*

8 O leave this barren spot to me!
Spare, woodman, spare the beechen tree.
     The Beech-Tree's Petition

9 The lordly, lovely Rhine.   *The Child and the Hind*

10 There came to the beach a poor Exile of Erin.
     Exile of Erin

11 He sang the bold anthem of 'Erin go bragh!'   *Ib.*

12 Gay lilied fields of France.
     Gertrude of Wyoming, pt. ii. 15

13 When Transatlantic Liberty arose.   *Ib.* pt. iii. 6

14 To-morrow let us do or die!   *Ib.* 37

15 To live in hearts we leave behind
Is not to die   *Hallowed Ground*

16 On the green banks of Shannon, when Sheelah was
nigh,
No blithe Irish lad was so happy as I;
No harp like my own could so cheerily play,
And wherever I went was my poor dog Tray.
     The Harper

17 On Linden, when the sun was low,
All bloodless lay the untrodden snow,
And dark as winter was the flow
Of Iser, rolling rapidly.   *Hohenlinden*

18 Then shook the hills with thunder riven,
Then rushed the steed to battle driven,
And louder than the bolts of heaven
Far flashed the red artillery.   *Hohenlinden*

19 The combat deepens. On, ye brave,
Who rush to glory, or the grave!
Wave, Munich! all thy banners wave,
And charge with all thy chivalry!   *Ib.*

20 Few, few shall part where many meet!
The snow shall be their winding-sheet,
And every turf beneath their feet
Shall be a soldier's sepulchre.   *Ib.*

21 Better be courted and jilted
Than never be courted at all.   *The Jilted Nymph*

22 'Tis the sunset of life gives me mystical lore,
And coming events cast their shadows before.
     Lochiel's Warning

23 A chieftain to the Highlands bound
Cries, 'Boatman, do not tarry!
And I'll give thee a silver pound
To row us o'er the ferry.'   *Lord Ullin's Daughter*

24 'O, I'm the chief of Ulva's isle,
And this Lord Ullin's daughter.'   *Ib.*

25 Then who will cheer my bonny bride
When they have slain her lover?   *Ib.*

26 I'll meet the raging of the skies,
But not an angry father.   *Ib.*

27 One lovely hand she stretched for aid,
And one was round her lover.   *Ib.*

28 'Come back! come back!' he cried in grief
Across the stormy water:
'And I'll forgive your Highland chief,
My daughter! oh my daughter!'   *Ib.*

29 The waters wild went o'er his child,
And he was left lamenting.   *Ib.*

30 With Freedom's lion-banner
Britannia rules the waves.   *Ode to the Germans*

31 'Tis distance lends enchantment to the view,
And robes the mountain in its azure hue.
     Pleasures of Hope, pt. i, l. 7

32 The proud, the cold untroubled heart of stone,
That never mused on sorrow but its own. *Ib.* l. 185

33 Hope, for a season, bade the world farewell,
And Freedom shrieked—as Kosciusko fell!
     Ib. l. 381

34 Who hath not owned, with rapture-smitten frame,
The power of grace, the magic of a name?
     Ib. pt. ii, l. 5

35 And muse on Nature with a poet's eye.   *Ib.* l. 98

36 What millions died—that Caesar might be great!
     Ib. l. 174

37 Who hail thee, Man! the pilgrim of a day,
Spouse of the worm, and brother of the clay.
     Ib. l. 305

38 Truth, ever lovely,—since the world began
The foe of tyrants, and the friend of man. *Ib.* l. 347

39 But, sad as angels for the good man's sin,
Weep to record, and blush to give it in!   *Ib.* l. 357

40 Cease, every joy, to glimmer on my mind,
But leave, oh! leave the light of Hope behind!

What though my wingèd hours of bliss have been,
Like angel-visits, few and far between?
Pleasures of Hope, pt. ii, l. 375

1 Well can ye mouth fair Freedom's classic line.
And talk of Constitutions o'er your wine.
On Poland, l. 65

2 One moment may with bliss repay
Unnumbered hours of pain;
Such was the throb and mutual sob
Of the knight embracing Jane.   *The Ritter Bann*

3 And the sentinel stars set their watch in the sky.
The Soldier's Dream

4 Drink ye to her that each loves best,
    And, if you nurse a flame
That's told but to her mutual breast,
    We will not ask her name.
Song. Drink Ye To Her

5 Can you keep the bee from ranging,
Or the ringdove's neck from changing?
No! nor fettered Love from dying
In the knot there's no untying.
Song. How Delicious is the Winning

6 Again to the battle, Achaians!
Our hearts bid the tyrants defiance;
Our land, the first garden of Liberty's tree—
It has been, and shall yet be, the land of the free!
Song of the Greeks

7 Her women fair; her men robust for toil;
Her vigorous souls, high-cultured as her soil:
Her towns, where civic independence flings
The gauntlet down to senates, courts, and kings.
Theodric, l. 160

8 It was not strange; for in the human breast
Two master-passions cannot co-exist.   *Ib. l. 488*

9 'Twas the hour when rites unholy
Called each Paynim voice to prayer.
The Turkish Lady

10 Ye Mariners of England
That guard our native seas,
Whose flag has braved, a thousand years,
The battle and the breeze—
Your glorious standard launch again
To match another foe!
And sweep through the deep,
While the stormy winds do blow,—
While the battle rages loud and long,
And the stormy winds do blow.
Ye Mariners of England

11 Britannia needs no bulwarks,
No towers along the steep;
Her march is o'er the mountain waves,
Her home is on the deep.   *Ib.*

12 The meteor flag of England
Shall yet terrific burn,
Till danger's troubled night depart
And the star of peace return.   *Ib.*

13 An original something, fair maid, you would win me
To write—but how shall I begin?
For I fear I have nothing original in me—
Excepting Original Sin.
*To a Young Lady, Who Asked Me to Write
Something Original for Her Album*

14 Now Barabbas was a publisher.
Often attributed to Byron

SIR HENRY CAMPBELL-BANNERMAN
1836–1908

15 When was a war not a war? When it was carried on
by methods of barbarism.
*Speech at Dinner of National Reform Union,
14 June 1901*

THOMAS CAMPION
d. 1620

16 Rose-cheeked Laura, come;
Sing thou smoothly with thy beauty's
Silent music, either other
    Sweetly gracing.
Observations in the Art of English Poesie. Laura

17 Lovely forms do flow
From conceit divinely framed;
Heaven is music, and thy beauty's
    Birth is heavenly.   *Ib.*

18 Only beauty purely loving
    Knows no discord,
    But still moves delight,
Like clear springs renewed by flowing,
Ever perfect, ever in them-
    selves eternal.   *Ib.*

19 My sweetest Lesbia let us live and love,
And though the sager sort our deeds reprove,
Let us not weigh them: Heav'n's great lamps do dive
Into their west, and straight again revive,
But soon as once set is our little light,
Then must we sleep one ever-during night.
A Book of Airs, i

20 Follow thy fair sun, unhappy shadow,
    Though thou be black as night,
    And she made all of light,
Yet follow thy fair sun, unhappy shadow.   *Ib. iv*

21 When to her lute Corinna sings,
Her voice revives the leaden strings,
And both in highest notes appear,
As any challeng'd echo clear.
But when she doth of mourning speak,
Ev'n with her sighs the strings do break.   *Ib. vi*

22 Follow your Saint, follow with accents sweet;
Haste you, sad notes, fall at her flying feet.   *Ib. x*

23 The man of life upright,
Whose guiltless heart is free
From all dishonest deeds
    Or thought of vanity   *Ib. xviii*

24 He only can behold
    With unaffrighted eyes
The horrors of the deep
    And terrors of the skies.   *Ib.*

25 Good thoughts his only friends,
    His wealth a well-spent age,
The earth his sober inn
    And quiet pilgrimage.   *Ib.*

26 Hark, all you ladies that do sleep;
The fairy Queen Proserpina
Bids you awake and pity them that weep.   *Ib. xix*

27 When thou must home to shades of under ground,
And there arriv'd, a new admired guest,
The beauteous spirits do ingirt thee round,
White Iope, blithe Helen, and the rest,
To hear the stories of thy finisht love
From that smooth tongue whose music hell can move.
Ib. xx

1 Never weather-beaten sail more willing bent to shore,
Never tired pilgrim's limbs affected slumber more.
Two Books of Airs. Divine and Moral Songs, xi.

2 Kind are her answers,
But her performance keeps no day;
  Breaks time, as dancers
From their own Music when they stray.
Third Book of Airs, vii

3 Lost is our freedom,
When we submit to women so:
  Why do we need them,
When in their best they work our woe? *Ib.*

4 There is a garden in her face,
Where roses and white lilies grow;
A heav'nly paradise is that place,
Wherein all pleasant fruits do flow.
There cherries grow, which none may buy
Till 'Cherry ripe' themselves do cry.
Fourth Book of Airs, vii

5 Those cherries fairly do enclose
Of orient pearl a double row;
Which when her lovely laughter shows,
They look like rosebuds fill'd with snow.
Yet them nor peer nor prince can buy,
Till 'Cherry ripe' themselves do cry. *Ib.*

GEORGE CANNING
1770–1827

6 In matters of commerce the fault of the Dutch
Is offering too little and asking too much.
The French are with equal advantage content,
So we clap on Dutch bottoms just twenty per cent.
*Dispatch, in Cipher, To Sir Charles Bagot,
English Ambassador at The Hague, 31 Jan. 1826*

7 Needy Knife-grinder! whither are you going?
Rough is the road, your wheel is out of order—
Bleak blows the blast;—your hat has got a hole in't.
  So have your breeches.
The Friend of Humanity and the Knife-Grinder

8 Story! God bless you! I have none to tell, Sir. *Ib.*

9 *I* give thee sixpence! I will see thee damn'd first—
Wretch! whom no sense of wrongs can rouse to ven-
  geance;
Sordid, unfeeling, reprobate, degraded,
  Spiritless outcast! *Ib.*

10 So down thy hill, romantic Ashbourne, glides
The Derby dilly, carrying *Three* Insides.
The Loves of the Triangles, l. 178

11 A steady patriot of the world alone,
The friend of every country but his own. [The Jacobin.]
New Morality, l. 113

12 And finds, with keen discriminating sight,
Black's not so black;—nor white so very white.
Ib. l. 199

13 Give me the avowed, erect and manly foe;
Firm I can meet, perhaps return the blow;
But of all plagues, good Heaven, thy wrath can send,
Save me, oh, save me, from the candid friend.
Ib. l. 207

14 Pitt is to Addington
As London is to Paddington.
The Oracle, c. 1803–4

[124]

15 Man, only—rash, refined, presumptuous man,
Starts from his rank, and mars creation's plan.
Progress of Man, l. 55

16 A sudden thought strikes me, let us swear an eternal
friendship. *The Rovers*, I. i

17 Whene'er with haggard eyes I view
This Dungeon, that I'm rotting in,
I think of those Companions true
Who studied with me at the U-
  -NIVERSITY of GOTTINGEN,-
  -NIVERSITY of GOTTINGEN. *Song*

18 Sun, moon, and thou vain world, adieu. *Ib.*

19 (*Pitt*:)
When our perils are past, shall our gratitude sleep?
No,—here's to the pilot that weathered the storm.
*Song for the inauguration of the Pitt Club,
25 May 1802.*

20 Away with the cant of 'Measures not men'!—the idle
supposition that it is the harness and not the horses
that draw the chariot along. If the comparison must
be made, if the distinction must be taken, men are
everything, measures comparatively nothing.
Speech, House of Commons, 1801

21 I called the New World into existence, to redress the
balance of the Old. *Speech, 12 Dec. 1826*

CANUTE
994?–1035

22 Merrily sang the monks in Ely
When Cnut, King, rowed thereby;
Row, my knights, near the land,
And hear we these monks' song.
Attr. *Song of the Monks of Ely, Historia Eliensis*
(1066). Green, *Conquest of England*, ix

FRANCESCO CARACCIOLI
1752–1799

23 Il y a en Angleterre soixante sectes religieuses dif-
férentes, et une seule sauce.

In England there are sixty different religions,
and only one sauce. *Attrib.*

RICHARD CAREW
1555–1620

24 Take the miracle of our age, Sir Philip Sidney.
An Epistle on the Excellency of the English Tongue

THOMAS CAREW
1595?–1639?

25 He that loves a rosy cheek,
  Or a coral lip admires,
Or, from star-like eyes, doth seek
  Fuel to maintain his fires;
As old Time makes these decay,
So his flames must waste away.
Disdain Returned

26 Here lies a King that rul'd, as he thought fit
The universal monarchy of wit;
Here lies two Flamens, and both those the best:
Apollo's first, at last the true God's priest.
Elegy on the Death of Donne

1 Know, Celia (since thou art so proud,)
'Twas I that gave thee thy renown.
Thou had'st in the forgotten crowd
Of common beauties liv'd unknown,
Had not my verse extoll'd thy name,
And with it imped the wings of fame.
Ingrateful Beauty Threatened

2 Wise poets that wrapt Truth in tales,
Knew her themselves through all her veils. *Ib.*

3 An untimely grave.
Inscription on Tomb of the Duke of Buckingham

4 Good to the poor, to kindred dear,
To servants kind, to friendship clear,
To nothing but herself severe.
Inscription on Tomb of Lady Mary Wentworth

5 So though a virgin, yet a bride
To every Grace, she justified
A chaste polygamy, and died. *Ib.*

6 The purest soul that e'er was sent
Into a clayey tenement.
On the Lady Mary Villiers

7 Give me more love or more disdain;
The torrid or the frozen zone:
Bring equal ease unto my pain;
The temperate affords me none.
Mediocrity in Love Rejected

8 When thou, poor excommunicate
From all the joys of love, shalt see
The full reward and glorious fate
Which my strong faith shall purchase me,
Then curse thine own inconstancy.
To My Inconstant Mistress

9 Ask me no more where Jove bestows,
When June is past, the fading rose;
For in your beauty's orient deep
These flowers, as in their causes, sleep. *A Song*

10 Ask me no more whither doth haste
The nightingale when May is past;
For in your sweet dividing throat
She winters and keeps warm her note. *Ib.*

11 Ask me no more if east or west
The Phoenix builds her spicy nest;
For unto you at last she flies,
And in your fragrant bosom dies. *Ib.*

HENRY CAREY
1693?–1743

12 Aldiborontiphoscophornio!
Where left you Chrononhotonthologos?
Chrononhotonthologos, I. i

13 His cogitative faculties immers'd
In cogibundity of cogitation. *Ib.*

14 To thee, and gentle Rigdum-Funnidos,
Our gratulations flow in streams unbounded. *Ib.* iii

15 God save our gracious king!
Long live our noble king!
God save the king! *God Save the King.* (*But
see* 6:13, 250:14, *and* Corrigenda)

16 Confound their politics,
Frustrate their knavish tricks. *Ib.*

17 Of all the girls that are so smart
There's none like pretty Sally,
She is the darling of my heart,
And she lives in our alley. *Sally in our Alley*

18 When she is by I leave my work,
(I love her so sincerely)
My master comes like any Turk,
And bangs me most severely. *Sally in our Alley*

19 Of all the days that's in the week
I dearly love but one day—
And that's the day that comes betwixt
A Saturday and Monday. *Ib.*

WILLIAM CARLETON
1794–1869

20 Things at home are crossways, and Betsey and I
are out. *Farm Ballads. Betsey and I Are Out*

21 We arg'ed the thing at breakfast, we arg'ed the thing
at tea,
And the more we arg'ed the question, the more we
didn't agree. *Ib.*

THOMAS CARLYLE
1795–1881

22 A well-written Life is almost as rare as a well-
spent one.
Critical and Miscellaneous Essays, vol. i. *Richter*

23 'Providence has given to the French the empire of
the land, to the English that of the sea, to the
Germans that of—the air!'
(*Quoting a remark of J. P. F. Richter.*) *Ib.*

24 The three great elements of modern civilization,
Gunpowder, Printing, and the Protestant Religion.
Ib. State of German Literature

25 The 'golden-calf of Self-love.' *Ib. Burns*

26 So here has been dawning
Another blue day. *Ib. To-day*

27 Out of Eternity
This new Day is born;
Into Eternity
At night, will return. *Ib.*

28 It is the Age of Machinery, in every outward and
inward sense of that word.
Ib. vol. ii. *Signs of the Times*

29 The Bible-Society . . . is found, on inquiry, to be . . .
a machine for converting the Heathen. *Ib.*

30 Thought, he [Dr. Cabanis] is inclined to hold, is
still secreted by the brain; but then Poetry and
Religion (and it is really worth knowing) are 'a
product of the smaller intestines'! *Ib.*

31 What is all knowledge too but recorded experience,
and a product of history; of which, therefore,
reasoning and belief, no less than action and
passion, are essential materials? *Ib. On History*

32 History is the essence of innumerable biographies. *Ib.*

33 The foul sluggard's comfort: 'It will last my time.'
Ib. vol. iii. *Count Cagliostro. Flight Last*

34 This Mirabeau's work, then, is done. He sleeps with
the primeval giants. He has gone over to the
majority: *Abiit ad plures. Ib. Mirabeau*

35 There is no life of a man, faithfully recorded, but is
a heroic poem of its sort, rhymed or unrhymed.
Ib. vol. iv. *Sir Walter Scott*

CARLYLE

1 Under all speech that is good for anything there lies a silence that is better. Silence is deep as Eternity; speech is shallow as Time.
Critical and Miscellaneous Essays, vol. iv. *Sir Walter Scott*

2 To the very last, he [Napoleon] had a kind of idea; that, namely, of *La carrière ouverte aux talents*, The tools to him that can handle them. *Ib.*

3 It can be said of him [Scott], When he departed, he took a man's life along with him. No sounder piece of British manhood was put together in that eighteenth century of Time. *Ib.*

4 A witty statesman said, you might prove anything by figures. *Ib. Chartism*, ch. 2

5 Surely of all 'rights of man', this right of the ignorant man to be guided by the wiser, to be, gently or forcibly, held in the true course by him, is the indisputablest. *Ib.* ch. 6

6 In epochs when cash payment has become the sole nexus of man to man. *Ib.*

7 Thou wretched fraction, wilt thou be the ninth part even of a tailor? *Ib. Francia*

8 This idle habit of 'accounting for the moral sense', as they phrase it. . . . The moral sense, thank God, is a thing you never will 'account for'. . . . By no greatest happiness principle, greatest nobleness principle, or any principle whatever, will you make that in the least clearer than it already is.
Ib. vol. v. *Shooting Niagara: and After?*

9 'Genius' (which means transcendent capacity of taking trouble, first of all).
Frederick the Great, bk. iv, ch. 3

10 If they could forget, for a moment, the correggiosity of Correggio, and the learned babble of the sale-room and varnishing auctioneer.
Ib. ch. 6. (*See 513:15*)

11 Happy the people whose annals are blank in history-books! *Ib.* bk. xvi, ch. 1

12 France was long a despotism tempered by epigrams.
History of the French Revolution, pt. 1, bk. i, ch. 1

13 Indeed it is well said, 'in every object there is inexhaustible meaning; the eye sees in it what the eye brings means of seeing'. *Ib.* ch. 2

14 Is not every meanest day 'the conflux of two eternities!' *Ib.* bk. iv, ch. 4

15 A whiff of grapeshot. *Ib.* bk. v, ch. 3

16 History a distillation of rumour. *Ib.* bk. vii, ch. 5

17 The gospel according to Jean Jacques.
Ib. pt. 11, bk. i, ch. 6

18 The difference between Orthodoxy or My-doxy and Heterodoxy or Thy-doxy. *Ib.* bk. iv, ch. 2

19 The seagreen Incorruptible. [Robespierre.] *Ib.* ch. 4

20 Aristocracy of the Moneybag. *Ib.* bk. vii, ch. 7

21 It is well said, in every sense, that a man's religion is the chief fact with regard to him.
Heroes and Hero-Worship, i. *The Hero as Divinity.*

22 Worship is transcendent wonder. *Ib.*

23 No sadder proof can be given by a man of his own littleness than disbelief in great men. *Ib.*

24 No great man lives in vain. The history of the world is but the biography of great men. *Ib.*

25 The greatest of faults, I should say, is to be conscious of none.
Heroes and Hero-Worship, ii. *The Hero as Prophet*

26 The Hero can be Poet, Prophet, King, Priest or what you will, according to the kind of world he finds himself born into. *Ib.* iii. *The Hero as Poet*

27 In books lies the *soul* of the whole Past Time; the articulate audible voice of the Past, when the body and material substance of it has altogether vanished like a dream. *Ib.* v. *The Hero as Man of Letters*

28 The true University of these days is a collection of books. *Ib.*

29 Burke said there were Three Estates in Parliament; but, in the Reporters' Gallery yonder, there sat a *Fourth Estate* more important far than they all. *Ib.*

30 Adversity is sometimes hard upon a man; but for one man who can stand prosperity, there are a hundred that will stand adversity. *Ib.*

31 I hope we English will long maintain our *grand talent pour le silence*. *Ib.* vi. *The Hero as King*

32 Maid-servants, I hear people complaining, are getting instructed in the 'ologies'.
Inaugural Address at Edinburgh, 1866

33 Speech is human, silence is divine, yet also brutish and dead: therefore we must learn both arts.
Journal

34 Respectable Professors of the Dismal Science. [Political Economy.]
Latter-Day Pamphlets, No. 1. *The Present Time*

35 Little other than a redtape Talking-machine, and unhappy Bag of Parliamentary Eloquence. *Ib.*

36 A healthy hatred of scoundrels.
Ib. No. 2. *Model Prisons*

37 Idlers, game-preservers and mere human clothes-horses. [Exodus from Houndsditch.]
Ib. No. 8. *Downing Street*

38 Nature admits no lie. *Ib.* No. 5. *Stump Orator*

39 A Parliament speaking through reporters to Buncombe and the twenty-seven millions mostly fools.
Ib. No. 6. *Parliaments*

40 'May the Devil fly away with the fine arts!' exclaimed . . . in my hearing, one of our most distinguished public men. *Ib.* No. 8

41 Mother of dead dogs.
Letter to John Carlyle, 11 Sept. 1840 (Froude's *Carlyle*, 1884, vol. i, p. 196)

42 The unspeakable Turk should be immediately struck out of the question.
Letter to G. Howard, 24 Nov. 1876

43 Transcendental moonshine.
Life of John Sterling, pt. i, ch. 15

44 The progress of human society consists . . . in . . . the better and better apportioning of wages to work.
Past and Present, bk. i, ch. 3

45 Brothers, I am sorry I have got no Morrison's Pill for curing the maladies of Society. *Ib.* ch. 4

46 Thou and I, my friend, can, in the most flunkey world, make, each of us, *one* non-flunkey, one hero, if we like: that will be two heroes to begin with.
Ib. ch. 6

1 Cash-payment is not the sole nexus of man with man. *Past and Present*, bk. iii, ch. 9

2 Blessed is he who has found his work; let him ask no other blessedness. *Ib*. ch. 11

3 Captains of industry. *Ib*. bk. iv, title of ch. 4

4 The sunny plains and deep indigo transparent skies of Italy are all indifferent to the great sick heart of a Sir Walter Scott: on the back of the Apennines, in wild spring weather, the sight of bleak Scotch firs, and snow-spotted heath and desolation, brings tears into his eyes. *Ib*. ch. 5

5 Upwards of five-hundred-thousand two-legged animals without feathers lie round us, in horizontal positions; their heads all in nightcaps, and full of the foolishest dreams. *Sartor Resartus*, bk. i, ch. 3

6 He who first shortened the labour of copyists by device of *Movable Types* was disbanding hired armies, and cashiering most Kings and Senates, and creating a whole new democratic world: he had invented the art of printing. *Ib*. ch. 5

7 Man is a tool-using animal. . . . Without tools he is nothing, with tools he is all. *Ib*.

8 Whoso has sixpence is sovereign (to the length of sixpence) over all men; commands cooks to feed him, philosophers to teach him, kings to mount guard over him,—to the length of sixpence. *Ib*.

9 Lives the man that can figure a naked Duke of Windlestraw addressing a naked House of Lords? *Ib*. ch. 9

10 Language is called the garment of thought: however, it should rather be, language is the flesh-garment, the body, of thought. *Ib*. ch. 11

11 What printed thing soever I could meet with I read. *Ib*. bk. ii, ch. 3

12 The end of man is an action, and not a thought, though it were the noblest. *Ib*. ch. 6

13 The everlasting No. *Ib*. ch. 7, title

14 The folly of that impossible precept, 'Know thyself'; till it be translated into this partially possible one, 'Know what thou canst work at'. *Ib*.

15 My spiritual new-birth, or Baphometic Fire-baptism. *Ib*.

16 Great men are the inspired [speaking and acting] texts of that divine Book of Revelations, whereof a chapter is completed from epoch to epoch, and by some named History. *Ib*. ch. 8

17 The everlasting Yea. *Ib*. ch. 9, title

18 Man's unhappiness, as I construe, comes of his greatness; it is because there is an Infinite in him, which with all his cunning he cannot quite bury under the Finite. *Ib*.

19 Close thy Byron; open thy Goethe. *Ib*.

20 'Do the duty which lies nearest thee', which thou knowest to be a duty! Thy second duty will already have become clearer. *Ib*.

21 Be no longer a chaos, but a world, or even worldkin. Produce! Produce! Were it but the pitifullest infinitesimal fraction of a product, produce it in God's name! 'Tis the utmost thou hast in thee: out with it, then. *Ib*.

22 As the Swiss Inscription says: *Sprechen ist silbern, Schweigen ist golden* (Speech is silvern, Silence is golden); or as I might rather express it: Speech is of Time, Silence is of Eternity. *Sartor Resartus*, bk. iii, ch. 3

23 Two men I honour, and no third. *Ib*. ch. 4

24 I don't pretend to understand the Universe—it's a great deal bigger than I am. . . . People ought to be modester. *Remark to Wm. Allingham*. D. A. Wilson's and D. Wilson MacArthur's *Carlyle in Old Age*

25 If Jesus Christ were to come to-day, people would not even crucify him. They would ask him to dinner, and hear what he had to say, and make fun of it. *Remark*. D. A. Wilson's *Carlyle at his Zenith*

26 It were better to perish than to continue schoolmastering. *Remark*. D. A. Wilson's *Carlyle Till Marriage*

27 Macaulay is well for a while, but one wouldn't *live* under Niagara. *Remark*. R. M. Milnes's *Notebook, 1838*

28 A good book is the purest essence of a human soul. *Speech in support of the London Library, 1840*. F. Harrison's *Carlyle and the London Library*

29 '"Thou's gey" [pretty, pronounced *gyei*] "ill to deal wi"—Mother's allocution to me once, in some unreasonable moment of mine', is Carlyle's note on this phrase (which, indeed, is an old-fashioned country formula), cited by his wife in a letter to his mother in Dec. 1835. . . . The readers of Mr. Froude's *Life of Carlyle* will remember that he harps upon this phrase, using it as a sort of refrain, but always with the significant change of the word 'deal' to 'live'—'gey ill to *live* wi'. C. Eliot Norton, *Letters of Thomas Carlyle* (1888), I. 44

30 Who never ate his bread in sorrow,
Who never spent the darksome hours
Weeping and watching for the morrow
He knows ye not, ye heavenly Powers.
Translation of Goethe's Wilhelm Meister's Apprenticeship, bk. ii, ch. 13

31 Carlyle and Milnes were talking . . . of the Administration just formed by Sir Robert Peel, and Milnes was evincing some disappointment . . . that he had not been offered a post in it. 'No, no,' said Carlyle, 'Peel knows what he is about; there is only one post fit for you, and that is the office of perpetual president of the Heaven and Hell Amalgamation Society.' T. E. Wemyss Reid, *The Life of Lord Houghton* (1890), p. 187

32 MARGARET FULLER:
I accept the universe.
CARLYLE:
Gad! she'd better! *Attrib.*

JULIA CARNEY
1823–1908

33 Little drops of water, little grains of sand,
Make the mighty ocean, and the pleasant land.
So the little minutes, humble though they be,
Make the mighty ages of eternity.
Little Things. (Attr. also to E. C. Brewer, D. C. Colesworthy, and F. S. Osgood)

1 Little deeds of kindness, little words of love,
Help to make earth happy, like the heaven above.
(Changed by later compilers to 'make this earth an
Eden'.)   *Little Things*

JOSEPH EDWARDS CARPENTER
1813–1885

2 What are the wild waves saying
Sister, the whole day long,
That ever amid our playing,
I hear but their low lone song?
What are the Wild Waves Saying?

3 Yes! but there's something greater,
That speaks to the heart alone;
The voice of the great Creator,
Dwells in that mighty tone!   *Ib.*

LEWIS CARROLL
[CHARLES LUTWIDGE DODGSON]
1832–1898

4 What I tell you three times is true.
Hunting of the Snark, Fit 1. *The Landing*

5 He had forty-two boxes, all carefully packed,
With his name painted clearly on each:
But, since he omitted to mention the fact,
They were all left behind on the beach.   *Ib.*

6 He would answer to 'Hi!' or to any loud cry,
Such as 'Fry me!' or 'Fritter-my-wig!'   *Ib.*

7 His intimate friends called him 'Candle-ends',
And his enemies, 'Toasted-cheese'.   *Ib.*

8 Then the bowsprit got mixed with the rudder sometimes.   *Ib.*

9 But the principal failing occurred in the sailing,
And the Bellman, perplexed and distressed,
Said he *had* hoped, at least, when the wind blew due
East,
That the ship would *not* travel due West!
Ib. Fit 2. *The Bellman's Speech*

10 But oh, beamish nephew, beware of the day,
If your Snark be a Boojum! For then
You will softly and suddenly vanish away,
And never be met with again!
Ib. Fit. 3. *The Baker's Tale*

11 They sought it with thimbles, they sought it with care;
They pursued it with forks and hope;
They threatened its life with a railway-share;
They charmed it with smiles and soap.
Ib. Fit 5. *The Beaver's Lesson*

12 Recollecting with tears how, in earlier years,
It had taken no pains with its sums.   *Ib.*

13 And in charity-meetings it stands at the door,
And collects—though it does not subscribe. *Ib.*

14 For the Snark *was* a Boojum, you see.
Ib. Fit 8. *The Vanishing*

15 He thought he saw an Elephant,
That practised on a fife:
He looked again, and found it was
A letter from his wife.
'At length I realize,' he said,
'The bitterness of life!'   *Sylvie and Bruno*, ch. 5

16 He thought he saw a Buffalo
Upon the chimney-piece:
He looked again, and found it was
His sister's husband's niece.
'Unless you leave this house,' he said,
'I'll send for the Police!'   *Sylvie and Bruno*, ch. 6

17 He thought he saw a Rattlesnake
That questioned him in Greek,
He looked again and found it was
The Middle of Next Week.
'The one thing I regret,' he said,
'Is that it cannot speak!'   *Ib.*

18 He thought he saw a Banker's Clerk
Descending from the bus:
He looked again, and found it was
A Hippopotamus:
'If this should stay to dine,' he said,
'There won't be much for us.'   *Ib.* ch. 7

19 He thought he saw an Albatross
That fluttered round the lamp:
He looked again, and found it was
A penny-postage-stamp.
'You'd best be getting home,' he said,
'The nights are very damp.'   *Ib.* ch. 12

20 'What is the use of a book', thought Alice, 'without
pictures or conversations?'
Alice in Wonderland, ch. 1

21 Do cats eat bats? . . . Do bats eat cats?   *Ib.*

22 'Curiouser and curiouser!' cried Alice.   *Ib.* ch. 2

23 How doth the little crocodile
Improve his shining tail,
And pour the waters of the Nile
On every golden scale!   *Ib.*

24 How cheerfully he seems to grin,
How neatly spreads his claws,
And welcomes little fishes in
With gently smiling jaws!   *Ib.*

25 'I'll be judge, I'll be jury,' said cunning old Fury;
'I'll try the whole cause, and condemn you to death.'
Ib. ch. 3

26 The Duchess! The Duchess!
O my dear paws! Oh my fur and whiskers! *Ib.* ch. 4

27 'I can't explain *myself*, I'm afraid, sir,' said Alice,
'because I'm not myself, you see.' 'I don't see,'
said the Caterpillar.   *Ib.* ch. 5

28 'You are old, Father William,' the young man said,
'And your hair has become very white;
And yet you incessantly stand on your head—
Do you think, at your age, it is right?'

'In my youth,' Father William replied to his son.
'I feared it might injure the brain;
But now that I'm perfectly sure I have none,
Why, I do it again and again.'   *Ib.*

29 'I have answered three questions, and that is enough,'
Said his father; 'don't give yourself airs!
Do you think I can listen all day to such stuff?
Be off, or I'll kick you downstairs!'   *Ib.*

30 'I shall sit here,' he said, 'on and off, for days and
days.'   *Ib.* ch. 6

31 'If everybody minded their own business,' said the
Duchess in a hoarse growl, 'the world would go
round a deal faster than it does.'   *Ib.*

1 Speak roughly to your little boy,
    And beat him when he sneezes;
He only does it to annoy,
    Because he knows it teases.
                Alice in Wonderland, ch. 6

2 For he can thoroughly enjoy
    The pepper when he pleases!   *Ib.*

3 'Did you say pig, or fig?' said the Cat.   *Ib.*

4 This time it vanished quite slowly, beginning with the end of the tail, and ending with the grin, which remained some time after the rest of it had gone. [The Cheshire Cat.]   *Ib.*

5 'Have some wine,' the March Hare said in an encouraging tone. Alice looked all round the table, but there was nothing on it but tea. 'I don't see any wine,' she remarked. 'There isn't any,' said the March Hare.   *Ib.* ch. 7

6 'Then you should say what you mean,' the March Hare went on. 'I do,' Alice hastily replied; 'at least —at least I mean what I say—that's the same thing, you know.'
'Not the same thing a bit!' said the Hatter. 'Why, you might just as well say that "I see what I eat" is the same thing as "I eat what I see!"'   *Ib.*

7 'It was the *best* butter,' the March Hare meekly replied.   *Ib.*

8 Twinkle, twinkle, little bat!
How I wonder what you're at!
Up above the world you fly!
Like a teatray in the sky.   *Ib.*

9 'Take some more tea,' the March Hare said to Alice, very earnestly.
'I've had nothing yet,' Alice replied in an offended tone, 'so I can't take more.'
'You mean you can't take *less*,' said the Hatter: 'it's very easy to take *more* than nothing.'   *Ib.*

10 Let's all move one place on.   *Ib.*

11 'But they were *in* the well,' Alice said to the Dormouse. . . . 'Of course they were,' said the Dormouse,—'well in.'   *Ib.*

12 'They drew all manner of things—everything that begins with an M——' 'Why with an M?' said Alice. 'Why not?' said the March Hare.   *Ib.*

13 The Queen was in a furious passion, and went stamping about, and shouting, 'Off with his head!' or 'Off with her head!' about once in a minute.
                           Ib. ch. 8

14 'A cat may look at a king,' said Alice.   *Ib.*

15 And the moral of that is—'Oh, 'tis love, 'tis love, that makes the world go round!'   *Ib.* ch. 9

16 Everything's got a moral, if you can only find it. *Ib.*

17 Take care of the sense, and the sounds will take care of themselves.   *Ib.*

18 'That's nothing to what I could say if I chose,' the Duchess replied.   *Ib.*

19 'Just about as much right,' said the Duchess, 'as pigs have to fly.'   *Ib.*

20 I only took the regular course . . . the different branches of Arithmetic—Ambition, Distraction, Uglification, and Derision.   *Ib.*

21 'That's the reason they're called lessons,' the Gryphon remarked: 'because they lessen from day to day.'   *Ib.*

22 'Will you walk a little faster?' said a whiting to a snail, 'There's a porpoise close behind us, and he's treading on my tail.'   *Alice in Wonderland*, ch. 10

23 Will you, won't you, will you, won't you, will you join the dance?   *Ib.*

24 The further off from England the nearer is to France—
Then turn not pale, beloved snail, but come and join the dance.   *Ib.*

25 'Tis the voice of the lobster; I heard him declare, 'You have baked me too brown, I must sugar my hair.'   *Ib.*

26 Soup of the evening, beautiful Soup!   *Ib.*

27 The Queen of Hearts, she made some tarts,
    All on a summer day:
The Knave of Hearts, he stole those tarts,
    And took them quite away!   *Ib.* ch. 11

28 'Write that down,' the King said to the jury, and the jury eagerly wrote down all three dates on their slates, and then added them up, and reduced the answer to shillings and pence.   *Ib.*

29 Here one of the guinea-pigs cheered, and was immediately suppressed by the officers of the court. *Ib.*

30 'Where shall I begin, please your Majesty?' he asked. 'Begin at the beginning,' the King said, gravely, 'and go on till you come to the end: then stop.'   *Ib.*

31 '*Un*important, of course, I meant,' the King hastily said, and went on to himself in an undertone, 'important— unimportant— unimportant— important—' as if he were trying which word sounded best.   *Ib.* ch. 12

32 'That's not a regular rule: you invented it just now.' 'It's the oldest rule in the book,' said the King. 'Then it ought to be Number One,' said Alice.
                                 Ib.

33 They told me you had been to her,
    And mentioned me to him:
She gave me a good character,
    But said I could not swim.   *Ib.*

34 The jury all wrote down on their slates, '*She* doesn't believe there's an atom of meaning in it.'   *Ib.*

35 No! No! Sentence first—verdict afterwards.   *Ib.*

36 'Do I look like it?' said the Knave. (Which he certainly did *not*, being made entirely of cardboard.)
                                 Ib.

37 'The horror of that moment,' the King went on, 'I shall never, *never* forget!' 'You will, though,' the Queen said, 'if you don't make a memorandum of it.'   *Through the Looking-Glass*, ch. 1

38 'My precious Lily! My imperial kitten!'—
'Imperial fiddlestick!'   *Ib.*

39 'Twas brillig, and the slithy toves
    Did gyre and gimble in the wabe;
All mimsy were the borogoves,
    And the mome raths outgrabe.
'Beware the Jabberwock, my son!
    The jaws that bite, the claws that catch!
Beware the Jubjub bird, and shun
    The frumious Bandersnatch!'

He took his vorpal sword in hand:
    Long time the manxome foe he sought—
So rested he by the Tumtum tree,
    And stood awhile in thought.

And as in uffish thought he stood,
    The Jabberwock, with eyes of flame,
Came whiffling through the tulgey wood,
    And burbled as it came!

One, two! One, two! And through and through
    The vorpal blade went snicker-snack!
He left it dead, and with its head
    He went galumphing back.

'And hast thou slain the Jabberwock?
    Come to my arms, my beamish boy!
O frabjous day! Callooh! Callay!'
    He chortled in his joy.

Through the Looking-Glass, ch. 1

1 Curtsey while you're thinking what to say. It saves time. *Ib.* ch. 2

2 Speak in French when you can't think of the English for a thing. *Ib.*

3 'Now! Now!' cried the Queen. 'Faster! Faster!' *Ib.*

4 Now, *here*, you see, it takes all the running *you* can do, to keep in the same place. If you want to get somewhere else, you must run at least twice as fast as that! *Ib.*

5 'Sap and sawdust,' said the Gnat. *Ib.* ch. 3

6 Tweedledum and Tweedledee
    Agreed to have a battle;
For Tweedledum said Tweedledee
    Had spoiled his nice new rattle.

Just then flew down a monstrous crow,
    As black as a tar-barrel;
Which frightened both the heroes so,
    They quite forgot their quarrel. *Ib.* ch. 4

7 If you think we're wax-works, you ought to pay, you know. Wax-works weren't made to be looked at for nothing. Nohow! *Ib.*

8 'Contrariwise,' continued Tweedledee, 'if it was so, it might be; and if it were so, it would be: but as it isn't, it ain't. That's logic.' *Ib.*

9 The sun was shining on the sea,
    Shining with all his might:
He did his very best to make
    The billows smooth and bright—
And this was odd, because it was
    The middle of the night.
Ib. The Walrus and the Carpenter

10 'It's very rude of him,' she said
    'To come and spoil the fun!' *Ib.*

11 You could not see a cloud, because
    No cloud was in the sky:
No birds were flying overhead—
    There were no birds to fly. *Ib.*

12 The Walrus and the Carpenter
    Were walking close at hand;
They wept like anything to see
    Such quantities of sand:
'If this were only cleared away,'
    They said, 'it would be grand!'

'If seven maids with seven mops
    Swept it for half a year,
Do you suppose,' the Walrus said,
    'That they could get it clear?'
'I doubt it,' said the Carpenter,
    And shed a bitter tear.
Through the Looking-Glass, ch. 4. *The Walrus and the Carpenter*

13 But four young Oysters hurried up,
    All eager for the treat:
Their coats were brushed, their faces washed,
    Their shoes were clean and neat—
And this was odd, because, you know,
    They hadn't any feet. *Ib.*

14 And thick and fast they came at last,
    And more, and more, and more. *Ib.*

15 The Walrus and the Carpenter
    Walked on a mile or so,
And then they rested on a rock
    Conveniently low:
And all the little Oysters stood
    And waited in a row.

'The time has come,' the Walrus said,
    'To talk of many things:
Of shoes—and ships—and sealing wax—
    Of cabbages—and kings—
And why the sea is boiling hot—
    And whether pigs have wings.' *Ib.*

16 'For some of us are out of breath,
    And all of us are fat!' *Ib.*

17 'A loaf of bread,' the Walrus said,
    'Is what we chiefly need:
Pepper and vinegar besides
    Are very good indeed—
Now if you're ready, Oysters dear,
    We can begin to feed.' *Ib.*

18 'The night is fine,' the Walrus said.
    'Do you admire the view?' *Ib.*

19 The Carpenter said nothing but
    'The butter's spread too thick!' *Ib.*

20 'I weep for you,' the Walrus said:
    'I deeply sympathize.'
With sobs and tears he sorted out
    Those of the largest size,
Holding his pocket-handkerchief
    Before his streaming eyes. *Ib.*

21 But answer came there none—
    And this was scarcely odd because
    They'd eaten every one. *Ib.*

22 'Fit to snore his head off!' as Tweedledum remarked. *Ib.*

23 'Let's fight till six, and then have dinner,' said Tweedledum. *Ib.*

24 'You know,' he said very gravely, 'it's one of the most serious things that can possibly happen to one in a battle—to get one's head cut off.' *Ib.*

25 'I'm very brave generally,' he went on in a low voice: 'only to-day I happen to have a headache.' *Ib.*

26 Twopence a week, and jam every other day. *Ib.* ch. 5

27 The rule is, jam to-morrow and jam yesterday—but never jam to-day. *Ib.*

28 'It's a poor sort of memory that only works backwards,' the Queen remarked. *Ib.*

1 Consider anything, only don't cry!
Through the Looking-Glass, ch. 5

2 'I can't believe *that*!' said Alice. 'Can't you?' the Queen said in a pitying tone. 'Try again: draw a long breath, and shut your eyes.' Alice laughed. 'There's no use trying,' she said: 'one *can't* believe impossible things.' 'I daresay you haven't had much practice,' said the Queen. 'When I was your age, I always did it for half-an-hour a day. Why, sometimes I've believed as many as six impossible things before breakfast.' *Ib.*

3 'It's very provoking,' Humpty Dumpty said after a long silence,—'to be called an egg—*very*!' *Ib*. ch. 6

4 With a name like yours, you might be any shape, almost. *Ib.*

5 They gave it me,—for an un-birthday present. *Ib.*

6 'There's glory for you!' 'I don't know what you mean by "glory",' Alice said. 'I meant, "there's a nice knock-down argument for you!"' 'But "glory" doesn't mean "a nice knock-down argument",' Alice objected. 'When *I* use a word,' Humpty Dumpty said in a rather scornful tone, 'it means just what I choose it to mean,—neither more nor less.' *Ib.*

7 'The question is,' said Humpty Dumpty, 'which is to be master—that's all.' *Ib.*

8 I can explain all the poems that ever were invented—and a good many that haven't been invented just yet. *Ib.*

9 '*I* can repeat poetry as well as other folk if it comes to that—' 'Oh, it needn't come to that!' Alice hastily said. *Ib.*

10 The little fishes of the sea,
They sent an answer back to me.

The little fishes' answer was
'We cannot do it, Sir, because——' *Ib.*

11 I took a kettle large and new,
Fit for the deed I had to do. *Ib.*

12 I said it very loud and clear;
I went and shouted in his ear.

But he was very stiff and proud;
He said 'You needn't shout so loud!'

And he was very proud and stiff;
He said 'I'd go and wake them, if——' *Ib.*

13 You see it's like a portmanteau—there are two meanings packed up into one word. *Ib.*

14 He's an Anglo-Saxon Messenger—and those are Anglo-Saxon attitudes. *Ib*. ch. 7

15 The other Messenger's called Hatta. I must have *two* you know—to come and go. One to come, and one to go. *Ib.*

16 'There's nothing like eating hay when you're faint.' . . . 'I didn't say there was nothing *better*,' the King replied, 'I said there was nothing *like* it.' *Ib.*

17 'I'm sure nobody walks much faster than I do!' 'He can't do that,' said the King, 'or else he'd have been here first.' *Ib.*

18 It's as large as life, and twice as natural! *Ib.*

19 If you'll believe in me, I'll believe in you. *Ib.*

20 The [White] Knight said . . . 'It's my own invention.' *Ib*. ch. 8

21 But you've no idea what a difference it makes, mixing it with other things—such as gunpowder and sealing-wax. *Through the Looking-Glass*, ch. 8

22 I'll tell thee everything I can:
There's little to relate.
I saw an aged, aged man,
A-sitting on a gate.

'Who are you, aged man?' I said.
'And how is it you live?'
And his answer trickled through my head
Like water through a sieve.

He said, 'I look for butterflies
That sleep among the wheat:
I make them into mutton-pies,
And sell them in the street.' *Ib.*

23 I cried, 'Come, tell me how you live!'
And thumped him on the head. *Ib.*

24 He said, 'I hunt for haddocks' eyes
Among the heather bright,
And work them into waistcoat-buttons
In the silent night.

And these I do not sell for gold
Or coin of silvery shine,
But for a copper halfpenny,
And that will purchase nine.

I sometimes dig for buttered rolls,
Or set limed twigs for crabs;
I sometimes search the grassy knolls
For wheels of hansom-cabs.' *Ib.*

25 Or madly squeeze a right-hand foot
Into a left-hand shoe. *Ib.*

26 'Speak when you're spoken to!' the Red Queen sharply interrupted her. *Ib*. ch. 9

27 No admittance till the week after next! *Ib.*

28 It isn't etiquette to cut any one you've been introduced to. Remove the joint. *Ib.*

29 Un-dish-cover the fish, or dishcover the riddle. *Ib.*

WILLIAM HERBERT CARRUTH
1859–1924

30 Some call it evolution,
And others call it God.
Each In His Own Tongue, and Other Poems,
1908

PHOEBE CARY
1824–1871

31 And though hard be the task,
'Keep a stiff upper lip'. *Keep a Stiff Upper Lip*

32 Nearer my Father's house,
Where the many mansions be,
Nearer the great white throne,
Nearer the crystal sea. *Nearer Home*

HARRY CASTLING

33 What-Ho! She bumps! *Title of Song*

34 Let's all go down the Strand. *Title of Song*

REV. EDWARD CASWALL
1814–1878

1 Come, Thou Holy Spirit, come;
  And from Thy celestial home
    Shed a ray of light Divine;
  Come, Thou Father of the poor,
  Come, Thou source of all our store,
    Come, within our bosoms shine.
      Hymns and Poems. Come, Thou Holy Spirit, Come
      (*trans. from Latin*)

2 In our labour rest most sweet,
  Grateful coolness in the heat,
    Solace in the midst of woe.   *Ib.*

(*As adapted in 'Hymns Ancient and Modern'*):
3 Days and moments quickly flying,
  Blend the living with the dead;
    Soon will you and I be lying
    Each within our narrow bed.
          Ib. Days and Moments Quickly Flying

4 Earth has many a noble city;
  Bethlehem, thou dost all excel.
          Ib. Earth Has Many a Noble City

5 Hark! a thrilling voice is sounding;
  'Christ is nigh,' it seems to say.
          Ib. Hark! A Thrilling Voice is Sounding

6 Jesu, the very thought of Thee
  With sweetness fills the breast.
  Ib. Jesu, The Very Thought of Thee (*trans. from Latin*)

7 My God, I love Thee; not because
  I hope for heaven thereby.
  Ib. My God, I Love Thee (*trans. from Latin*)

CATO THE ELDER
234–149 B.C.

8 Delenda est Carthago.
  Carthage must be destroyed.
          Plutarch, *Life of Cato*

CATULLUS
87–54? B.C.

9 Cui dono lepidum novum libellum
  Arido modo pumice expolitum?

  Here's my small book out, nice and new,
  Fresh-bound—whom shall I give it to?
          Carmina, i, trans. by Sir W. Marris

10   Namque tu solebas
  Meas esse aliquid putare nugas.

  To you [Cornelius], who of yore
  Upon my trifles set some store.   *Ib.*

11 Plus uno maneat perenne saeclo.
  May it outlive an hundred year.   *Ib.*

12 Lugete, O Veneres Cupidinesque,
  Et quantum est hominum venustiorum.
  Passer mortuus est meae puellae,
  Passer, deliciae meae puellae.

  Come, all ye Loves and Cupids, haste
  To mourn, and all ye men of taste;
  My lady's sparrow, O, he's sped,
  The bird my lady loved is dead!   *Ib. iii*

13 Qui nunc it per iter tenebricosum
  Illuc, unde negant redire quenquam.

And now he treads the gloomy track
Whence no one, so they say, comes back.
          Carmina, iii

14 Sed haec prius fuere.
  All this is over now.   *Ib. iv*

15 Vivamus, mea Lesbia, atque amemus,
  Rumoresque senum severiorum
  Omnes unius aestimemus assis.
  Soles occidere et redire possunt:
  Nobis cum semel occidit brevis lux
  Nox est perpetua una dormienda.

  Lesbia mine, let's live and love!
  Give no doit for tattle of
  Crabbed old censorious men;
  Suns may set and rise again,
  But when our short day takes flight
  Sleep we must one endless night.   *Ib. v*

16 Da mi basia mille.
  Kiss me times a thousand o'er.   *Ib.*

17 Miser Catulle, desinas ineptire.
  Forgo your dream, poor fool of love.   *Ib. viii*

18 At tu, Catulle, destinatus obdura.
  But bide, Catullus, firm and set.   *Ib.*

19 Nec meum respectet, ut ante, amorem,
  Qui illius culpa cecidit velut prati
  Ultimi flos, praetereunte postquam
  Tactus aratro est.

  But ne'er look back again to find my love,
  My love, which for her fault has wilted now,
  Like meadow flower, upon the marge thereof,
  Touched by a passing plough.   *Ib. xi*

20 Totum ut te faciant, Fabulle, nasum.
  To make you nose and only nose.   *Ib. xiii*

21 O quid solutis est beatius curis?
  Cum mens onus reponit, ac peregrino
  Labore fessi venimus larem ad nostrum,
  Desideratoque acquiescimus lecto.
  Hoc est quod unum est pro laboribus tantis.
  Salve O venusta Sirmio atque hero gaude;
  Gaudete vosque O Lydiae lacus undae;
  Ridete quidquid est domi cachinnorum.

  What joy is like it? to be quit of care
  And drop my load, and after weary miles
  Come home, and sink upon the bed that so
  I used to dream of: this one thing is worth
  All that long service. Hail, sweet Sirmio!
  Welcome thy lord with laughter, and give back
  Your laughter, waters of the Lydian lake:
  Laugh, home of mine, with all your maddest mirth.
          Ib. xxxi

22   Quidquid est, ubicumque est,
  Quodcumque agit, renidet: hunc habet morbum,
  Neque elegantem, ut arbitror, neque urbanum.

      Whate'er the case, where'er he be,
  Or does, he smiles; with him it is a vice,
  And not, I think, a pretty one, nor nice. *Ib. xxxix*

23 Nam risu inepto res ineptior nulla est.
  Untimely grinning is the silliest sin.   *Ib.*

24 Iam ver egelidos refert tepores.
  Now Spring restores the balmy days.   *Ib. xlvi*

CATULLUS

1 Gratias tibi maximas Catullus
Agit pessimus omnium poeta,
Tanto pessimus omnium poeta,
Quanto tu optimus omnium's patronum.

    Catullus gives you warmest thanks,
    And he the worst of poets ranks;
    As much the worst of bards confessed,
    As you of advocates the best.   *Carmina*, xlix

2 Ille mi par esse deo videtur,
Ille, si fas est, superare divos,
Qui sedens adversus identidem **te**
    Spectat et audit
Dulce ridentem, misero quod omnis
Eripit sensus mihi.

    Like to a god he seems to me,
    Above the gods, if so may be,
    Who sitting often close to thee
        May see and hear
    Thy lovely laugh: ah, luckless man!   *Ib.* li

3 Quid est, Catulle? quid moraris emori?

    How now? why not be quick and die?   *Ib.* lii

4 Salaputium disertum!

    He can talk, that little cuss!   *Ib.* liii

5 Caeli, Lesbia nostra, Lesbia illa,
Illa Lesbia, quam Catullus unam
Plus quam se atque suos amavit omnes,
Nunc in quadruviis et angiportis
Glubit magnanimis Remi nepotes.

    My Lesbia,—Lesbia, whom once
    Catullus loved of girls alone
    Above himself and all his own—
    Now into lanes and corners runs
    To traffic with proud Remus' sons.   *Ib.* lviii

6 Torquatus volo parvulus
Matris e gremio suae
Porrigens teneras manus,
Dulce rideat ad patrem
Semihiante labello.

    Sit suo similis patri
    Manlio et facile inscieis
    Noscitetur ab omnibus,
    Et pudicitiam suo
    Matris indicet ore.

    I'd a wee Torquatus see
    Stretch soft finger-tips
    From his mother's lap, and smile
    Sweetly at his sire the while
        With half-parted lips;

    To his father Manlius so
    Very like, in sooth
    Even strangers him shall know,
    And his face alone shall show
        Forth his mother's truth.   *Ib.* lxi. 209

7 Vesper adest, iuvenes, consurgite: Vesper Olympo
Exspectata diu vix tandem lumina tollit.

    Up, lads! 'tis Eve at last: to longing eyes
    Upon Olympus Hesper lifts his ray.   *Ib.* lxii. 1

8 Quid datur a divis felici optatius hora?

    What gift hath heaven to match thy happy hour?
                Ib. 30

9 Ut flos in saeptis secretus nascitur hortis,
Ignotus pecori, nullo contusus aratro,
Quem mulcent aurae, firmat sol, educat imber;
Multi illum pueri, multae optavere puellae.

    As grows a flower within a garden close,
    Known to no cattle, by no ploughshare smit,
    Suns give it strength, rain growth, and air repose,
    And many lads and lasses long for it.
              Carmina, lxii. 39

10 Omnia fanda nefanda malo permixta furore,
Iustificam nobis mentem avertere deorum.

    Then right and wrong confused and all at odds
    Turned from us the just judgment of the gods.
              Ib. lxiv. 406

11   Sed mulier cupido quod dicit amanti,
In vento et rapida scribere oportet aqua.

    But a woman's sayings to her lover,
    Should be in wind and running water writ. *Ib.* lxx

12 Desine de quoquam quicquam bene velle mereri,
Aut aliquem fieri posse putare pium.

    Cease to expect to win men's gratitude,
    To think that human beings can be grateful.
              Ib. lxxiii

13 Siqua recordanti benefacta priora voluptas
Est homini.

    If it be good to mind each kindly act.   *Ib.* lxxvi

14 Difficile est longum subito deponere amorem.

    'Tis hard to drop at once old-standing love.   *Ib.*

15 Si vitam puriter egi.

    If my life be fair.   *Ib.*

16 O di, reddite mi hoc pro pietate mea.

    Gods, grant me this thing for my piety.   *Ib.*

17 Chommoda dicebat, si quando commoda vellet
Dicere.

    'Hallowances' said Arrius (meaning 'allowances').
              Ib. lxxxiv

18 Odi et amo: quare id faciam, fortasse requiris.
Nescio, sed fieri sentio et excrucior.

    I hate, I love—the cause thereof
    Belike you ask of me:
    I do not know, but feel 'tis so,
    And I'm in agony.   *Ib.* lxxxv

19 Si quicquam mutis gratum acceptumve sepulcris
Accidere a nostro, Calve, dolore potest.

    If the dumb grave, my Calvus, can receive
    Aught that is dear or grateful from our grief.
              Ib. xcvi

20 Multas per gentes et multa per aequora vectus
Advenio has miseras, frater, ad inferias,
Ut te postremo donarem munere mortis
Et mutam nequiquam alloquerer cinerem.
Quandoquidem fortuna mihi tete abstulit ipsum,
Heu miser indigne frater adempte mihi,
Nunc tamen interea haec prisco quae more parentum
Tradita sunt tristi munere ad inferias,
Accipe fraterno multum manantia fletu,
Atque in perpetuum, frater, ave atque vale.

    By many lands and over many a wave
    I come, my brother, to your piteous grave,
    To bring you the last offering in death
    And o'er dumb dust expend an idle breath;

For fate has torn your living self from me,
And snatched you, brother, O, how cruelly!
Yet take these gifts, brought as our fathers bade
For sorrow's tribute to the passing shade;
A brother's tears have wet them o'er and o'er;
And so, my brother, hail, and farewell evermore!
Carmina, ci

1 At non effugies meos iambos.

You shan't evade
These rhymes I've made.
Fragments, trans. Sir W. Marris

EDITH CAVELL
1865–1915

2 I realize that patriotism is not enough. I must have
no hatred or bitterness towards anyone.
Last Words, 12 Oct. 1915. The Times, 23 Oct.
1915

CAMILLO BENSO CAVOUR
1810–1861

3 Noi siamo pronti a proclamare nell' Italia questo gran
principio: Libera Chiesa in libero Stato.

We are ready to proclaim throughout Italy the great
principle of a free church in a free state.
Speech, 27 Mar. 1861. William de la Rive,
Remin. of Life and Character of Count Cavour
(1862), ch. 13, p. 276

ROBERT CECIL
see
SALISBURY

THOMAS OF CELANO
c. 1250

4 Dies irae, dies illa
Solvet saeclum in favilla,
Teste David cum Sibylla.

Day of wrath and doom impending,
David's word with Sibyl's blending
Heaven and earth in ashes ending!
Analecta Hymnica, liv, p. 269. (Trans. by Dr.
W. J. Irons in *The English Hymnal*)

SUSANNAH CENTLIVRE
1667?–1723

5 The real Simon Pure.   *Bold Stroke for a Wife,* v. i.

6 And lash the vice and follies of the age.
The Man's Bewitched, prologue

7 He is as melancholy as an unbrac'd drum.
Wonder, II. i

MIGUEL DE CERVANTES
1547–1616

8 El Caballero de la Triste Figura.

The Knight of the Sorrowful Countenance.
Don Quixote, pt. i, ch. 19. *Trans. by* Smollett

9 La mejor salsa del mundo es el hambre.

The best sauce in the world is hunger.
Ib. pt. ii, ch. 5

10 El pan comido y la compañía deshecha.

Where there's no more bread, boon companions
melt away.   *Don Quixote,* pt. ii, ch. 7

11 Muchos pocos hacen un mucho.

Many a pickle makes a mickle.   *Ib.*

12 [*Sancho asks whether, to get to heaven, we ought not
all to become monks.*]

No todos podemos ser frailes y muchos son los caminos por donde lleva Dios a los suyos al cielo.
Religión *es la caballería.*

We cannot all be friars, and many are the ways by
which God leads His children home. Religion *is*
knight-errantry.   *Ib.* ch. 8

13 [*Sancho, on his master*]

Es un entreverado loco, lleno de lúcidos intervalos.

He's a muddled fool, full of lucid intervals.
Ib. ch. 18

14 Dos linages sólos hay en el mundo, como decía una
abuela mia, que son el tenir y el no tenir.

There are but two families in the world, as my
grandmother used to say, the Haves and the
Have-nots.   *Ib.* ch. 20

15 Digo, paciencia y barajar.

Patience, and shuffle the cards.   *Ib.* ch. 23

16 Del dicho al hecho hay gran trecho.

It's a far cry from speech to deed.   *Ib.* ch. 34

17 La diligencia es madre de la buena ventura y la pereza,
su contrario, jamás llegó al término que pide un
buen deseo.

Diligence is the mother of good fortune, and idleness, its opposite, never brought a man to the
goal of any of his best wishes.   *Ib.*

18 Bien haya el que inventó el sueño, capa que cubre
todos los humanos pensamientos, manjar que quita
la hambre, agua que ahuyenta la sed, fuego que
calienta el frío, frío que templa el ardor, y, final-
mente, moneda general con que todas las cosas se
compran, balanza y peso que iguala al pastor con
el rey y al simple con el discreto.

Blessings on him who invented sleep, the mantle
that covers all human thoughts, the food that
appeases hunger, the drink that quenches thirst,
the fire that warms cold, the cold that moderates
heat, and, lastly, the general coin that purchases
all things, the balance and weight that equals the
shepherd with the king, and the simple with the
wise.   *Ib.* ch. 68. Trans. by Jervas

19 Los buenos pintores imitan la naturaleza, pero los
malos la vomitan.

Good painters imitate nature, bad ones vomit it.
El Licenciado Vidriera

20 Puesto ya el pie en el estribo.

With one foot already in the stirrup.
Preface to 'Persiles y Sigismunda' (4 days before his death.)

JOHN CHALKHILL
fl. 1600

21 Oh, the sweet contentment
The countryman doth find.
Coridon's Song

PATRICK REGINALD CHALMERS
1872–1942

1 'I find,' said 'e, 'things very much as 'ow I've always
found,
For mostly they goes up and down or else goes round
and round.'
*Green Days and Blue Days: Roundabouts and
Swings*

2 What's lost upon the roundabouts we pulls up on the
swings!   *Ib.*

JOSEPH CHAMBERLAIN
1836–1914

3 But the cup is nearly full. The career of high-handed
wrong is coming to an end.   *Speech, 20 Oct. 1884*

4 Provided that the City of London remains as it is at
present, the clearing-house of the world.
Ib. Guildhall, London, 19 Jan. 1904

5 Learn to think Imperially.   *Ib.*

6 The day of small nations has long passed away. The
day of Empires has come.
Ib. Birmingham, 12 May 1904

7 We are not downhearted. The only trouble is, we
cannot understand what is happening to our neighbours.   *Ib. Smethwick, 18 Jan. 1906*

NEVILLE CHAMBERLAIN
1869–1940

8 In war, whichever side may call itself the victor, there
are no winners, but all are losers.
Speech at Kettering, 3 July 1938

9 I believe it is peace for our time . . . peace with
honour.
*Radio Speech after Munich Agreement. 1 Oct.
1938*

10 Hitler has missed the bus.
*Speech to Central Council of the National Union of
Conservative and Unionist Associations, 4 April 1940*

CHARLES HADDON CHAMBERS
1860–1921

11 The long arm of coincidence.   *Captain Swift*, Act II

JOHN CHANDLER
1806–1876

12 Conquering kings their titles take
From the foes they captive make:
Jesu, by a nobler deed,
From the thousands He hath freed.
As in Hymns Ancient and Modern. *Conquering
Kings Their Titles Take*, trans. from Latin

ARTHUR CHAPMAN
1873–1935

13 Out where the handclasp's a little stronger,
Out where the smile dwells a little longer,
That's where the West begins.
Out where the West Begins

GEORGE CHAPMAN
1559?–1634?

14 I know an Englishman,
Being flatter'd, is a lamb; threaten'd, a lion;
Alphonsus, Emperor of Germany, I. ii

15 Berenice's ever-burning hair.
Blind Beggar of Alexandria

16 Speed his plough.   *Bussy D'Ambois*, I. i

17 Who to himself is law, no law doth need,
Offends no law, and is a king indeed.   *Ib.* II. i

18 Terror of darkness! O, thou king of flames!   *Ib.* v. i

19 Give me a spirit that on this life's rough sea
Loves t'have his sails fill'd with a lusty wind,
Even till his sail-yards tremble, his masts crack,
And his rapt ship run on her side so low
That she drinks water, and her keel ploughs air;
There is no danger to a man, that knows
What life and death is; there's not any law,
Exceeds his knowledge; neither is it lawful
That he should stoop to any other law.
He goes before them, and commands them all,
That to himself is a law rational.
Byron's Conspiracy, III. i

20 O incredulity! the wit of fools,
That slovenly will spit on all things fair,
The coward's castle, and the sluggard's cradle.
De Guiana, l. 82

21 We have watered our horses in Helicon.
May-Day, III. iii

22 For one heat, all know, doth drive out another,
One passion doth expel another still.
Monsieur D'Olive, v. i

23 They're only truly great who are truly good.
Revenge for Honour, v. ii

24 A poem, whose subject is not truth, but things like
truth.   *Revenge of Bussy D'Ambois*, dedication

25 Danger, the spur of all great minds.   *Ib.* v. i

26 And let a scholar all Earth's volumes carry,
He will be but a walking dictionary.
Tears of Peace, l. 266

CHARLES I OF GREAT BRITAIN
1600–1649

27 Never make a defence of apology before you be
accused.   *Letter to Lord Wentworth, 3 Sept. 1636*

28 As to the King, the Laws of the Land will clearly
instruct you for that. . . . For the People; and truly
I desire their Liberty and Freedom, as much as
any Body: but I must tell you, that their Liberty
and Freedom consists in having the Government
of those Laws, by which their Life and their Goods
may be most their own; 'tis not for having share in
Government [Sirs] that is nothing pertaining to
'em. A Subject and a Sovereign are clean different
things. . . . If I would have given way to an arbitrary
way, for to have all Laws chang'd according to the
Power of the Sword, I needed not to have come
here; and therefore I tell you (and I pray God it be
not laid to your Charge) that I am the Martyr of
the People.
Speech on the scaffold, 30 Jan. 1649. Rushworth's
Historical Collections (1703–8), vol. vi

1 I die a Christian, according to the Profession of the Church of England, as I found it left me by my Father.
Speech on the scaffold, 30 Jan. 1649. Rushworth's *Historical Collections* (1703–8), vol. vi

CHARLES II OF GREAT BRITAIN
1630–1685

2 It is upon the navy under the Providence of God that the safety, honour, and welfare of this realm do chiefly attend. *Articles of War.* Preamble

3 Better than a play.
(*On the Debates in the House of Lords on Lord Ross's Divorce Bill, 1670.*) A. Bryant, *King Charles II*

4 This is very true: for my words are my own, and my actions are my ministers'.
Reply to Lord Rochester's Epitaph on him [q.v.]

5 He [Charles II] said once to myself, he was no atheist, but he could not think God would make a man miserable only for taking a little pleasure out of the way.
Burnet, *History of My Own Time*, vol. i, bk. ii, ch. i

6 He [Lauderdale] told me, the king spoke to him to let that [Presbytery] go, for it was not a religion for gentlemen. *Ib.* ch. 2

7 King Charles gave him [Godolphin] a short character when he was page, which he maintained to his life's end, of being never *in* the way, nor *out* of the way.
Ib. vol. ii, bk. iii, ch. ii, n. (*The Earl of Dartmouth*)

8 Let not poor Nelly starve. *Ib.* ch. 17

9 Brother, I am too old to go again to my travels.
Hume's *History of Great Britain*, vol. ii, 1757, ch. 7

10 I am sure no man in England will take away my life to make you King. [To his brother James.]
W. King's *Political & Lit. Anecdotes*

11 He had been, he said, an unconscionable time dying; but he hoped that they would excuse it.
Macaulay's *Hist. England*, 1849, vol. i, ch. 4, p. 437

12 His nonsense suits their nonsense.
On a certain preacher

CHARLES V
1500–1558

13 Je parle espagnol à Dieu, italien aux femmes, français aux hommes et allemand à mon cheval.

To God I speak Spanish, to women Italian, to men French, and to my horse—German. *Attrib.*

SALMON PORTLAND CHASE
1808–1873

14 No more slave States: no slave Territories.
Platform of the Free Soil National Convention, 1848

15 The Constitution, in all its provisions, looks to an indestructible Union composed of indestructible States. *Decision in Texas v. White*, 7 Wallace, 725

16 The way to resumption is to resume.
Letter to Horace Greeley, 17 May 1866

EARL OF CHATHAM
see
WILLIAM PITT

THOMAS CHATTERTON
1752–1770

17 O! synge untoe mie roundelaie,
O! droppe the brynie teare wythe mee,
Daunce ne moe atte hallie daie,
Lycke a reynynge ryver bee;
Mie love ys dedde,
Gon to hys death-bedde,
Al under the wyllowe-tree. *Mynstrelles Songe*

FRANÇOIS-RENÉ DE CHATEAUBRIAND
1768–1848

18 L'écrivain original n'est pas celui qui n'imite personne, mais celui que personne ne peut imiter.

The original writer is not he who refrains from imitating others, but he who can be imitated by none. *Génie du Christianisme*

GEOFFREY CHAUCER
1340?–1400

19 Singest with vois memorial in the shade.
Anelida and Arcite, proem

20 Flee fro the prees, and dwelle with sothfastnesse...
Forth, pilgrim, forth! Forth, beste, out of thy stal!
Know thy contree, look up, thank God of al!
Hold the hye wey, and lat thy gost thee lede;
And trouthe shal delivere, hit is no drede.
Balade de Bon Conseyl

21 Whanne that Aprille with his shoures sote
The droghte of Marche hath perced to the rote.
Canterbury Tales. Prologue, l. 1

22 And smale fowles maken melodye,
That slepen al the night with open yë,
(So priketh hem nature in hir corages):
Than longen folk to goon on pilgrimages. *Ib.* l. 9

23   He loved chivalrye,
Trouthe and honour, freedom and curteisye. *Ib.* l. 45

24 He was a verray parfit gentil knight. *Ib.* l. 72

25 He was as fresh as is the month of May. *Ib.* l. 92

26 He coude songes make and wel endyte. *Ib.* l. 95

27 Curteys he was, lowly, and servisable,
And carf biforn his fader at the table. *Ib.* l. 99

28 Hir gretteste ooth was but by sëynt Loy. *Ib.* l. 120

29 Ful wel she song the service divyne,
Entuned in hir nose ful semely;
And Frensh she spak ful faire and fetisly,
After the scole of Stratford atte Bowe,
For Frensh of Paris was to hir unknowe. *Ib.* l. 122

30 She wolde wepe, if that she sawe a mous
Caught in a trappe, if it were deed or bledde.
Of smale houndes had she, that she fedde
With rosted flesh, or milk and wastel-breed.
But sore weep she if oon of hem were deed.
Ib. l. 144

31 He yaf nat of that text a pulled hen,
That seith, that hunters been nat holy men.
Ib. l. 177

1 A Frere ther was, a wantown and a merye.
Canterbury Tales. Prologue, l. 208

2 He knew the tavernes wel in every toun. *Ib*. l. 240

3 He was the best beggere in his hous. *Ib*. l. 252

4 Somwhat he lipsed, for his wantownesse,
To make his English swete up-on his tonge.
Ib. l. 264

5 A Clerk ther was of Oxenford also. *Ib*. l. 285

6 For him was lever have at his beddes heed
Twenty bokes, clad in blak or reed,
Of Aristotle and his philosophye,
Than robes riche, or fithele, or gay sautrye.
But al be that he was a philosophre,
Yet hadde he but litel gold in cofre. *Ib*. l. 293

7 And gladly wolde he lerne, and gladly teche.
Ib. l. 308

8 No-wher so bisy a man as he ther nas,
And yet he semed bisier than he was. *Ib*. l. 321

9 For he was Epicurus owne sone. *Ib*. l. 336

10 It snewed in his hous of mete and drinke. *Ib*. l. 345

11 A Shipman was ther, woning fer by weste:
For aught I woot, he was of Dertemouthe. *Ib*. l. 388

12 And, certeinly, he was a good felawe. *Ib*. l. 395

13 Of nyce conscience took he no keep.
If that he faught, and hadde the hyer hond,
By water he sente hem hoom to every lond.
Ib. l. 398

14 His studie was but litel on the bible. *Ib*. l. 438

15 She was a worthy womman al hir lyve,
Housbondes at chirche-dore she hadde fyve,
Withouten other companye in youthe;
But therof nedeth nat to speke as nouthe.
And thryes hadde she been at Jerusalem;
She hadde passed many a straunge streem;
At Rome she hadde been, and at Boloigne,
In Galice at seint Jame, and at Cologne. *Ib*. l. 459

16 A good man was ther of religioun,
And was a povre Persoun of a toun. *Ib*. l. 477

17 This noble ensample to his sheep he yaf,
That first he wroghte, and afterward he taughte.
Ib. l. 496

18 But Cristes lore, and his apostles twelve,
He taughte, but first he folwed it him-selve.
Ib. l. 527

19 That hadde a fyr-reed cherubinnes face. *Ib*. l. 624

20 Wel loved he garleek, oynons, and eek lekes,
And for to drinken strong wyn, reed as blood.
Ib. l. 634

21 His walet lay biforn him in his lappe,
Bret-ful of pardoun come from Rome al hoot.
Ib. l. 686

22 He hadde a croys of latoun, ful of stones,
And in a glas he hadde pigges bones.
But with thise relikes, whan that he fond
A povre person dwelling up-on lond,
Up-on a day he gat him more moneye
Than that the person gat in monthes tweye.
And thus, with feyned flaterye and japes,
He made the person and the peple his apes.
Ib. l. 699

23 Who-so shal telle a tale after a man,
He moot reherce, as ny as ever he can,
Everich a word, if it be in his charge,
Al speke he never so rudeliche and large;
Or elles he moot telle his tale untrewe,
Or feyne thing, or finde wordes newe.
Canterbury Tales. Prologue, l. 731

24 Thus with hir fader, for a certeyn space,
Dwelleth this flour of wyfly pacience,
That neither by hir wordes ne hir face
Biforn the folk, ne eek in hir absence,
Ne shewed she that hir was doon offence.
Ib. The Clerkes Tale, l. 862

25 O stormy peple! unsad and ever untrewe. *Ib.* l. 939

26 Trouthe is the hyeste thing that man may kepe.
Ib. The Frankeleyns Tale, l. 751

27 The carl spak oo thing, but he thoghte another.
Ib. The Freres Tale, l. 270

28 And therfore, at the kinges court, my brother,
Ech man for him-self, ther is non other.
Ib. Knightes Tale, l. 323

29 And whan a beest is deed, he hath no peyne;
But man after his deeth moot wepe and pleyne.
Ib. l. 461

30 The bisy larke, messager of day. *Ib.* l. 633

31 For pitee renneth sone in gentile herte. *Ib.* l. 903

32 The smyler with the knyf under the cloke.
Ib. l. 1141

33 Up roos the sonne, and up roos Emelye. *Ib.* l. 1415

34 What is this world? what asketh men to have?
Now with his love, now in his colde grave
Allone, with-outen any companye. *Ib.* l. 1919

35 She is mirour of alle curteisye.
Ib. Tale of the Man of Lawe, l. 68

36 Lat take a cat, and fostre him wel with milk,
And tendre flesh, and make his couche of silk,
And lat him seen a mous go by the wal;
Anon he weyveth milk, and flesh, and al,
And every deyntee that is in that hous,
Swich appetyt hath he to ete a mous.
Ib. The Maunciples Tale, l. 71

37 What is bettre than wisdom? Womman. And what is
bettre than a good womman? No-thing.
Ib. The Tale of Melibeus, § 15

38 Ful wys is he that can him-selven knowe.
Ib. The Monkes Tale, l. 149

39 Redeth the grete poete of Itaille,
That highte Dant, for he can al devyse
Fro point to point, nat o word wol he faille.
Ib. l. 470

40 The month in which the world bigan,
That highte March, whan god first maked man.
Ib. The Nonne Preestes Tale, l. 367

41 Daun Russel the fox sterte up at ones. *Ib.* l. 514

42 And on a Friday fil al this meschaunce. *Ib.* l. 521

43 And lightly as it comth, so wol we spende.
Ib. Pardoners Tale, l. 453

44 He can nat stinte of singing by the weye.
Ib. The Prioresses Tale, l. 105

45 Yet in our asshen olde is fyr y-reke.
Ib. The Reves Prologue, l. 28

1 The gretteste clerkes been noght the wysest men.
    Canterbury Tales. The Reves Tale, l. 134

2 So was hir joly whistle wel y-wet.   *Ib.* l. 235

3 He wolde sowen som difficultee,
Or springen cokkel in our clene corn.
    Ib. The Shipmannes Prologue, l. 20

4 A doghter hadde this worthy king also,
That yongest was, and highte Canacee.
    Ib. The Squieres Tale, l. 24

5 'Thou lokest as thou woldest finde an hare,
For ever up-on the ground I see thee stare.'
    Ib. Prologue to Sir Thopas, l. 6

6 The bacoun was nat fet for hem, I trowe,
That som men han in Essex at Dunmowe.
    Ib. The Prologue of the Wyves' Tale of Bathe, l. 217

7 And for to see, and eek for to be seye.   *Ib.* l. 552

8 But yet I hadde alwey a coltes tooth.
Gat-tothed I was, and that bicam me weel.
    Ib. l. 602

9 This is a long preamble of a tale.   *Ib.* l. 831

10 As thikke as motes in the sonne-beem.
    Ib. Tale of the Wyf of Bathe, l. 12

11 'My lige lady, generally,' quod he,
'Wommen desyren to have sovereyntee
As well over hir housbond as hir love.'
    Ib. l. 181

12 He is gentil that doth gentil dedis   *Ib.* l. 314

13 Ful craftier to pley she was
Than Athalus, that made the game
First of the ches: so was his name.
    The Book of the Duchesse, l. 662

14 O litel book, thou art so unconning,
How darst thou put thy-self in prees for drede?
    The Flower and the Leaf, l. 591

15   Venus clerk, Ovyde,
That hath y-sowen wonder wyde
The grete god of Loves name.
    The Hous of Fame, iii, l. 397

16 And as for me, thogh that I can but lyte,
On bokes for to rede I me delyte,
And to hem yeve I feyth and ful credence,
And in myn herte have hem in reverence
So hertely, that ther is game noon,
That fro my bokes maketh me to goon,
But hit be seldom, on the holyday;
Save, certeynly, whan that the month of May
Is comen, and that I here the foules singe,
And that the floures ginnen for to springe,
Farwel my book and my devocioun.
    Legend of Good Women. Prologue, l. 29

17   Of alle the floures in the mede,
Than love I most these floures whyte and rede,
Swiche as men callen daysies in our toun.   *Ib.* l. 41

18 Til that myn herte dye.   *Ib.* l. 57

19 That wel by reson men hit calle may
The 'dayesye' or elles the 'ye of day,'
The emperice and flour of floures alle.
I pray to god that faire mot she falle,
And alle that loven floures, for hir sake!   *Ib.* l. 183

20 Fo lo, the gentil kind of the lioun!
For whan a flye offendeth him or byteth,
He with his tayl awey the flye smyteth

Al esily; for, of his genterye,
Him deyneth nat to wreke him on a flye,
As doth a curre or elles another beste.
    Legend of Good Women. Prologue, l. 377

21 And she was fair as is the rose in May.
    Ib. Legend of Cleopatra, l. 34

22 The lyf so short, the craft so long to lerne,
Thassay so hard, so sharp the conquering.
    The Parlement of Foules, l. 1

23 For out of olde feldes, as men seith,
Cometh al this newe corn fro yeer to yere;
And out of olde bokes, in good feith,
Cometh al this newe science that men lere.   *Ib.* l. 22

24 Thou shalt make castels than in Spayne,
And dreme of joye, al but in vayne.
    Romaunt of the Rose, B. l. 2573

25 But the Troyane gestes, as they felle,
In Omer, or in Dares, or in Dyte,
Who-so that can, may rede hem as they wryte.
    Troilus and Criseyde, i, l. 145

26 For it is seyd, 'man maketh ofte a yerde
With which the maker is him-self y-beten.' *Ib.* l. 740

27 Unknowe, unkist, and lost that is unsought.
    Ib. l. 809

28 O wind, O wind, the weder ginneth clere. *Ib.* ii, l. 2

29 Til crowes feet be growe under your yë.   *Ib.* l. 403

30 And we shal speke of thee som-what, I trowe,
Whan thou art goon, to do thyne eres glowe!
    Ib. l. 1021

31 It is nought good a sleping hound to wake.
    Ib. iii, l. 764

32 For I have seyn, of a ful misty morwe,
Folwen ful ofte a mery someres day.   *Ib.* l. 1060

33 Right as an aspes leef she gan to quake.   *Ib.* l. 1200

34 And as the newe abaysshed nightingale,
That stinteth first whan she biginneth singe.
    Ib. l. 1233

35 For of fortunes sharp adversitee
The worst kinde of infortune is this,   *Ib.* l. 1625
A man to have ben in prosperitee,   (*See* 78:4,
And it remembren, when it passed is.   534:21)

36 Oon ere it herde, at the other out it wente.
    Ib. iv, l. 434

37 But manly set the world on sixe and sevene;
And, if thou deye a martir, go to hevene.   *Ib.* l. 622

38 For tyme y-lost may not recovered be.   *Ib.* l. 1283

39 Ye, fare-wel al the snow of ferne yere! *Ib.* v, l. 1176

40 Eek greet effect men wryte in place lyte. [i.e. little space]
Th'entente is al, and nought the lettres space.
    Ib. l. 1629

41 Go, litel book, go litel myn tragedie.   *Ib.* l. 1786

42 O yonge fresshe folkes, he or she.   *Ib.* l. 1835

43 O moral Gower, this book I directe
To thee.
    Ib. l. 1856

NIVELLE DE LA CHAUSSÉE
1692–1754

44 Quand tout le monde a tort, tout le monde a raison.
  When every one is wrong, every one is right.
    La Gouvernante, I. iii

ANDREW CHERRY
1762–1812

1 Loud roar'd the dreadful thunder,
The rain a deluge show'rd. *The Bay of Biscay*

2 Till next day,
There she lay,
In the Bay of Biscay, O! *Ib.*

PHILIP DORMER STANHOPE, EARL OF CHESTERFIELD
1694–1773

3 The dews of the evening most carefully shun,
Those tears of the sky for the loss of the sun.
Advice to a Lady in Autumn

4 Unlike my subject will I frame my song,
It shall be witty and it sha'n't be long.
Epigram on 'Long' Sir Thomas Robinson. D.N.B.

5 The picture plac'd the busts between,
Adds to the thought much strength;
Wisdom and Wit are little seen,
But Folly's at full length.
Wit and Wisdom of Lord Chesterfield. Epigrams. On the Picture of Richard Nash . . . between the Busts of . . . Newton and . . . Pope . . . at Bath. (Attr. also to Mrs. Jane Brereton)

6 In scandal, as in robbery, the receiver is always thought as bad as the thief.
Advice to his Son. Rules for Conversation, Scandal

7 In my mind, there is nothing so illiberal and so ill-bred, as audible laughter. *Ib. Graces, Laughter*

8 In my opinion, parsons are very like other men, and neither the better nor the worse for wearing a black gown. *Letter to his Son, 5 Apr. 1746*

9 The knowledge of the world is only to be acquired in the world, and not in a closet. *Ib. 4 Oct. 1746*

10 An injury is much sooner forgotten than an insult.
Ib. 9 Oct. 1746

11 Courts and camps are the only places to learn the world in. *Ib. 2 Oct. 1747*

12 There is a Spanish proverb, which says very justly, Tell me whom you live with, and I will tell you who you are. *Ib. 9 Oct. 1747*

13 Take the tone of the company that you are in. *Ib.*

14 Do as you would be done by is the surest method that I know of pleasing. *Ib. 16 Oct. 1747*

15 I recommend you to take care of the minutes: for hours will take care of themselves. *Ib. 6 Nov. 1747*

16 Advice is seldom welcome; and those who want it the most always like it the least. *Ib. 29 Jan. 1748*

17 Speak of the moderns without contempt, and of the ancients without idolatry. *Ib. 22 Feb. 1748*

18 Wear your learning, like your watch, in a private pocket: and do not merely pull it out and strike it; merely to show that you have one. *Ib.*

19 Sacrifice to the Graces. *Ib. 9 Mar. 1748*

20 I am neither of a melancholy nor a cynical disposition, and am as willing and as apt to be pleased as anybody; but I am sure that, since I have had the full use of my reason, nobody has ever heard me laugh. *Ib.*

21 If Shakespeare's genius had been cultivated, those beauties, which we so justly admire in him, would have been undisgraced by those extravagancies, and that nonsense, with which they are so frequently accompanied. *Letter to his Son, 1 Apr. 1748*

22 Women, then, are only children of a larger growth: they have an entertaining tattle, and sometimes wit; but for solid, reasoning good-sense, I never knew in my life one that had it, or who reasoned or acted consequentially for four and twenty hours together. *Ib. 5 Sept. 1748*

23 A man of sense only trifles with them [women], plays with them, humours and flatters them, as he does with a sprightly and forward child; but he neither consults them about, nor trusts them with, serious matters. *Ib.*

24 It must be owned, that the Graces do not seem to be natives of Great Britain; and I doubt, the best of us here have more of rough than polished diamond. *Ib. 18 Nov. 1748*

25 Idleness is only the refuge of weak minds. *Ib. 20 July 1749*

26 Women are much more like each other than men: they have, in truth, but two passions, vanity and love; these are their universal characteristics. *Ib. 19 Dec. 1749*

27 Knowledge may give weight, but accomplishments give lustre, and many more people see than weigh. *Ib. 8 May 1750*

28 Is it possible to love such a man? No. The utmost I can do for him is to consider him as a respectable Hottentot. [Lord Lyttelton.] *Ib. 28 Feb. 1751*

29 It is commonly said, and more particularly by Lord Shaftesbury, that ridicule is the best test of truth. *Ib. 6 Feb. 1752*

30 Every woman is infallibly to be gained by every sort of flattery, and every man by one sort or other. *Ib. 16 Mar. 1752*

31 A chapter of accidents. *Ib. 16 Feb. 1753*

32 In matters of religion and matrimony I never give any advice; because I will not have anybody's torments in this world or the next laid to my charge. *Letter to A. C. Stanhope, 12 Oct. 1765*

33 Religion is by no means a proper subject of conversation in a mixed company.
Undated Letter to his Godson, No. 112

34 I assisted at the birth of that most significant word, *flirtation*, which dropped from the most beautiful mouth in the world. *The World, No. 101*

35 Tyrawley and I have been dead these two years; but we don't choose to have it known.
Boswell's Johnson, 3 Apr. 1773

36 He once exclaimed to Anstis, Garter King at Arms, 'You foolish man, you do not even know your own foolish business.'
Jesse's Memoirs of the Court of England from 1688 to Geo. II, vol. ii

37 Give Dayrolles a chair.
Last Words. W. H. Craig, Life of Chesterfield

GILBERT KEITH CHESTERTON
1874–1936

1 Are they clinging to their crosses,
  F. E. Smith?
          Antichrist, or the Reunion of Christendom

2 Talk about the pews and steeples
  And the cash that goes therewith!
  But the souls of Christian peoples . . .
          Chuck it, Smith!   *Ib.*

3 Heaven shall forgive you Bridge at dawn,
  The clothes you wear—or do not wear—
          Ballade d'une Grande Dame

4 But for the virtuous things you do,
  The righteous work, the public care,
  It shall not be forgiven you.   *Ib.*

5 They spoke of progress spiring round,
  Of Light and Mrs. Humphry Ward—
  It is not true to say I frowned,
  Or ran about the room and roared;
  I might have simply sat and snored—
  I rose politely in the club
  And said, 'I feel a little bored;
  Will some one take me to a pub?'
          A Ballade of an Anti-Puritan

6 I'll read 'Jack Redskin on the Quest'
  And feed my brain with better things.
          A Ballade of a Book Reviewer

7 Prince, Prince-Elective on the modern plan,
  Fulfilling such a lot of people's Wills,
  You take the Chiltern Hundreds while you can—
  A storm is coming on the Chiltern Hills.
          A Ballade of the First Rain

8 The gallows in my garden, people say,
  Is new and neat and adequately tall.
          A Ballade of Suicide

9 The strangest whim has seized me. . . . After all
  I think I will not hang myself to-day.   *Ib.*

10 Prince, I can hear the trumpet of Germinal,
  The tumbrils toiling up the terrible way;
  Even to-day your royal head may fall—
  I think I will not hang myself to-day.   *Ib.*

11 Before the gods that made the gods
  Had seen their sunrise pass,
  The White Horse of the White Horse Vale
  Was cut out of the grass.
          Ballad of the White Horse, bk. i

12 There was not English armour left,
  Nor any English thing,
  When Alfred came to Athelney
  To be an English king.   *Ib.*

13 I tell you naught for your comfort,
  Yea, naught for your desire,
  Save that the sky grows darker yet
  And the sea rises higher.   *Ib.*

14 Last of a race in ruin—
  He spoke the speech of the Gaels.   *Ib.* bk. ii

15 For the great Gaels of Ireland
  Are the men that God made mad,
  For all their wars are merry,
  And all their songs are sad.   *Ib.*

16 The thing on the blind side of the heart,
  On the wrong side of the door,
  The green plant groweth, menacing
  Almighty lovers in the spring;
  There is always a forgotten thing,
  And love is not secure.
          Ballad of the White Horse, bk. iii

17 We have more lust again to lose
  Than you to win again.   *Ib.*

18 And when the last arrow
  Was fitted and was flown,
  When the broken shield was hung on the breast,
  And the hopeless lance was laid in rest,
  And the hopeless horn blown,
  The King looked up.   *Ib.* bk. vii

19 Nelson turned his blindest eye
  On Naples and on liberty.
          Blessed are the Peacemakers

20 The Christ-child stood at Mary's knee,
  His hair was like a crown,
  And all the flowers looked up at Him,
  And all the stars looked down. *A Christmas Carol*

21 When fishes flew and forests walked
  And figs grew upon thorn,
  Some moment when the moon was blood
  Then surely I was born.

  With monstrous head and sickening cry
  And ears like errant wings,
  The devil's walking parody
  On all four-footed things.   *The Donkey*

22 Fools! For I also had my hour;
  One far fierce hour and sweet:
  There was a shout about my ears,
  And palms before my feet.   *Ib.*

23 There is one creed: 'neath no world-terror's wing
  Apples forget to grow on apple-trees. *Ecclesiastes*

24 The men that worked for England
  They have their graves at home:

  And they that rule in England,
  In stately conclave met,
  Alas, alas for England
  They have no graves as yet.
          Elegy in a Country Churchyard

25 But since he stood for England
  And knew what England means,
  Unless you give him bacon
  You must not give him beans.   *The Englishman*

26 Lady, the stars are falling pale and small,
  Lady, we will not live if life be all,
  Forgetting those good stars in heaven hung;
  When all the world was young.
  For more than gold was in a ring, and love was not a
      little thing
  Between the trees in Ivywood, when all the world was
      young.   *The Flying Inn*, ch. 24

27 Mr. Mandragon, the Millionaire.
          The Good Rich Man

28 When Man is the Turk, and the Atheist,
  Essene, Erastian Whig,
  And the Thug and the Druse and the Catholic
  And the crew of the Captain's gig.
          The Higher Unity

1 But our rest is as far as the fire-drake swings
 And our peace is put in impossible things
 Where clashed and thundered unthinkable wings
  Round an incredible star. *The House of Christmas*

2 Or must Fate act the same grey farce again,
  And wait, till one, amid Time's wrecks and scars,
 Speaks to a ruin here, 'What poet-race
  Shot such Cyclopean arches at the stars?'
   King's Cross Station

3 White founts falling in the courts of the sun,
 And the Soldan of Byzantium is smiling as they run.
  Lepanto

4 The cold queen of England is looking in the glass;
 The shadow of the Valois is yawning at the Mass.
  Ib.

5 Strong gongs groaning as the guns boom far. *Ib.*

6 Don John of Austria is going to the war. *Ib.*

7 It is he that saith not 'Kismet'; it is he that knows
  not fate;
 It is Richard, it is Raymond, it is Godfrey in the gate!
  Ib.

8 Cervantes on his galley sets the sword back in the
  sheath,
 (Don John of Austria rides homeward with a wreath.)
  Ib.

9 And he smiles, but not as Sultans smile, and settles
  back the blade. . . .
 (But Don John of Austria rides home from the
  Crusade.) *Ib.*

10 For I come from Castlepatrick, and me heart is on me
  sleeve,
 But a lady stole it from me on St. Gallowglass's Eve.
  Me Heart

11 The folk that live in Liverpool, their heart is in their
  boots;
 They go to hell like lambs, they do, because the
  hooter hoots. *Ib.*

12 And they think we're burning witches when we're
  only burning weeds. *Ib.*

13 You saw the moon from Sussex Downs,
  A Sussex moon, untravelled still,
 I saw a moon that was the town's,
  The largest lamp on Campden Hill.
   The Napoleon of Notting Hill, dedication

14 This did not end by Nelson's urn
  Where an immortal England sits—
 Nor where your tall young men in turn
  Drank death like wine at Austerlitz. *Ib.*

15 Yes, Heaven is everywhere at home,
  The big blue cap that always fits. *Ib.*

16 The legend of an epic hour
  A child I dreamed, and dream it still,
 Under the great grey water-tower
  That strikes the stars on Campden Hill. *Ib.*

17 John Grubby, who was short and stout
 And troubled with religious doubt,
 Refused about the age of three
 To sit upon the curate's knee. *The New Freethinker*

18 From all the easy speeches
  That comfort cruel men. *O God of Earth and Altar*

19 'What of vile dust?' the preacher said.
  Methought the whole world woke.
   The Praise of Dust

20 Walter, be wise, avoid the wild and new!
 The Constitution is the game for you.
  The Revolutionary, or Lines to a Statesman (Rt.
  Hon. Walter Long)

21 Before the Roman came to Rye or out to Severn
  strode,
 The rolling English drunkard made the rolling
  English road. *The Rolling English Road*

22 That night we went to Birmingham by way of Beachy
  Head. *Ib.*

23 My friends, we will not go again or ape an ancient rage,
 Or stretch the folly of our youth to be the shame of
  age. *Ib.*

24 For there is good news yet to hear and fine things to
  be seen.
 Before we go to Paradise by way of Kensal Green. *Ib.*

25 And a few men talked of freedom, while England
  talked of ale. *The Secret People*

26 But the squire seemed struck in the saddle; he was
  foolish, as if in pain.
 He leaned on a staggering lawyer, he clutched a
  cringing Jew,
 He was stricken; it may be, after all, he was stricken
  at Waterloo. *Ib.*

27 We only know the last sad squires ride slowly towards
  the sea,
 And a new people takes the land: and still it is not
  we. *Ib.*

28 Smile at us, pay us, pass us; but do not quite forget.
 For we are the people of England, that never have
  spoken yet. *Ib.*

29 Lord Lilac thought it rather rotten
 That Shakespeare should be quite forgotten,
 And therefore got on a Committee
 With several chaps out of the City.
  The Shakespeare Memorial

30 The souls most fed with Shakespeare's flame
 Still sat unconquered in a ring,
 Remembering him like anything. *Ib.*

31 But not with that grand constancy
 Of Clement Shorter, Herbert Tree,
 Lord Rosebery and Comyns Carr
 And all the other names there are;
 Who stuck like limpets to the spot,
 Lest they forgot, lest they forgot.

 Lord Lilac was of slighter stuff;
 Lord Lilac had had quite enough. *Ib.*

32 God made the wicked Grocer
  For a mystery and a sign,
 That men might shun the awful shop
  And go to inns to dine. *Song Against Grocers*

33 The evil-hearted Grocer
  Would call his mother 'Ma'am,'
 And bow at her and bob at her,
  Her aged soul to damn. *Ib.*

34 He crams with cans of poisoned meat
  The subjects of the King,
 And when they die by thousands
  Why, he laughs like anything. *Ib.*

35 He keeps a lady in a cage
  Most cruelly all day,
 And makes her count and calls her 'Miss'
  Until she fades away. *Ib.*

1 The righteous minds of innkeepers
  Induce them now and then
To crack a bottle with a friend
  Or treat unmoneyed men,

But who hath seen the Grocer
  Treat housemaids to his teas
Or crack a bottle of fish-sauce
  Or stand a man a cheese? *Song Against Grocers*

2 And I dream of the days when work was scrappy,
  And rare in our pockets the mark of the mint,
And we were angry and poor and happy,
  And proud of seeing our names in print.
  A Song of Defeat

3 And sword in hand upon Afric's passes
  Her last republic cried to God. *Ib.*

4 And the faith of the poor is faint and partial,
  And the pride of the rich is all for sale,
And the chosen heralds of England's Marshal
  Are the sandwich-men of the *Daily Mail*. *Ib.*

5 They haven't got no noses,
  The fallen sons of Eve. *The Song of Quoodle*

6 And goodness only knowses
  The Noselessness of Man. *Ib.*

7 But I, I cannot read it
  (Although I run and run)
Of them that do not have the faith,
  And will not have the fun.
  The Song of the Strange Ascetic

8 Where his aunts, who are not married,
  Demand to be divorced. *Ib.*

9 Tea, although an Oriental,
  Is a gentleman at least;
Cocoa is a cad and coward,
  Cocoa is a vulgar beast.
  The Song of Right and Wrong

10 When old unbroken Pickwick walked
  Among the broken men.
  When I Came Back to Fleet Street

11 Still he that scorns and struggles
  Sees, frightful and afar,
All that they leave of rebels
  Rot high on Temple Bar. *Ib.*

12 And Noah he often said to his wife when he sat down
    to dine,
  'I don't care where the water goes if it doesn't get
    into the wine.' *Wine and Water*

13 Step softly, under snow or rain,
  To find the place where men can pray;
The way is all so very plain
  That we may lose the way. *The Wise Men*

14 Call upon the wheels, master, call upon the wheels;
  We are taking rest, master, finding how it feels.
  Song of the Wheels

15 And that is the meaning of Empire Day.
  Songs of Education. Geography

16 All slang is metaphor, and all metaphor is poetry.
  The Defendant. A Defence of Slang

17 The human race, to which so many of my readers
  belong... *The Napoleon of Notting Hill*, ch. 1

18 There is nothing the matter with Americans except
  their ideals. The real American is all right; it is
  the ideal American who is all wrong.
  New York Times, 1 Feb. 1931. Reprinted in
  Sidelights

19 Hardy went down to botanize in the swamp, while
  Meredith climbed towards the sun. Meredith
  became, at his best, a sort of daintily dressed Walt
  Whitman: Hardy became a sort of village atheist
  brooding and blaspheming over the village idiot.
  The Victorian Age in Literature, ch. 2

20 He [Tennyson] could not think up to the height of
  his own towering style. *Ib.* ch. 3

ALBERT CHEVALIER
1861–1923

21 'Wot's the good of Hanyfink? Why—Nuffink!'
  Cockney Complaint

22 We've been together now for forty years,
  An' it don't seem a day too much;
There ain't a lady livin' in the land
  As I'd 'swop' for my dear old Dutch! *My Old Dutch*

23 Knocked 'em in the Old Kent Road. *Title of Song*

WILLIAM CHILLINGWORTH
1602–1644

24 The Bible and the Bible only is the religion of Protestants. *The Religion of Protestants*

RUFUS CHOATE
1799–1859

25 Its constitution the glittering and sounding generalities of natural right which make up the Declaration
  of Independence.
  *Letter to the Maine Whig State Central Com-
  mittee, 9 Aug. 1856 (see 201:21)*

HENRY FOTHERGILL CHORLEY
1808–1872

26 God the All-terrible! King, Who ordainest
  Great winds Thy clarions, the lightnings Thy sword.
  Hullah's Part Music. God The All-Terrible!

DAVID CHRISTY
1802–?

27 Cotton is King. *Title of Book, 1855*

CHARLES CHURCHILL
1731–1764

28 Greatly his foes he dreads, but more his friends;
  He hurts me most who lavishly commends.
  The Apology, l. 19

29 Though by whim, envy, or resentment led,
  They damn those authors whom they never read.
  The Candidate, l. 57

30 The only difference, after all their rout,
  Is, that the one is in, the other out.
  The Conference, l. 165

31 If all, if all alas! were well at home. *Ib.* l. 226

32   Be England what she will,
  With all her faults, she is my country still.
  The Farewell, l. 27

33 It can't be Nature, for it is not sense. *Ib.* l. 200

1 England—a happy land we know,
Where follies naturally grow. *The Ghost*, bk. i, l. 111

2 Fame
Is nothing but an empty name. *Ib.* l. 229

3 And adepts in the speaking trade
Keep a cough by them ready made. *Ib.* bk. ii, l. 545

4 Who wit with jealous eye surveys,
And sickens at another's praise. *Ib.* l. 663

5 Just to the windward of the law. *Ib.* bk. iii, l. 56

6 [*Johnson:*] He for subscribers baits his hook,
And takes your cash; but where's the book?
No matter where; wise fear, you know,
Forbids the robbing of a foe;
But what, to serve our private ends,
Forbids the cheating of our friends? *Ib.* l. 801

7 A joke's a very serious thing. *Ib.* bk. iv, l. 1386

8 Railing at life, and yet afraid of death.
Gotham, i, l. 215

9 The danger chiefly lies in acting well;
No crime's so great as daring to excel.
Epistle to William Hogarth, l. 51

10 Candour, who, with the charity of Paul,
Still thinks the best, whene'er she thinks at all,
With the sweet milk of human kindness bless'd,
The furious ardour of my zeal repress'd. *Ib.* l. 55

11 By different methods different men excel;
But where is he who can do all things well?
Ib. l. 573

12 Keep up appearances; there lies the test;
The world will give thee credit for the rest.
Outward be fair, however foul within;
Sin if thou wilt, but then in secret sin. *Night*, l. 311

13 As one with watching and with study faint,
Reel in a drunkard, and reel out a saint. *Ib.* l. 323

14 Who often, but without success, have pray'd
For apt Alliteration's artful aid.
The Prophecy of Famine, l. 85

15 A heart to pity, and a hand to bless. *Ib.* l. 178

16 He sicken'd at all triumphs but his own.
The Rosciad, l. 64

17 Ne'er blush'd unless, in spreading Vice's snares,
She blunder'd on some virtue unawares. *Ib.* l. 137

18 Genius is of no country. *Ib.* l. 207

19 He mouths a sentence, as curs mouth a bone.
Ib. l. 322

20 Fashion!—a word which knaves and fools may use,
Their knavery and folly to excuse. *Ib.* l. 455

21 So much they talk'd, so very little said. *Ib.* l. 550

22 Learn'd without sense, and venerably dull. *Ib.* l. 572

23 Not without art, but yet to nature true. *Ib.* l. 699

24 But, spite of all the criticizing elves,
Those who would make us feel, must feel themselves.
Ib. l. 961

25 The two extremes appear like man and wife,
Coupled together for the sake of strife. *Ib.* l. 1005

26 Where he falls short, 'tis Nature's fault alone;
Where he succeeds, the merit's all his own.
Ib. l. 1025

27 The best things carried to excess are wrong.
Ib. l. 1039

28 With the persuasive language of a tear.
The Times, l. 308

LORD RANDOLPH SPENCER CHURCHILL
1849–1894

29 Ulster will fight; Ulster will be right.
Letter, 7 May 1886

30 The old gang. [Members of the Conservative Government.]
Speech, House of Commons, 7 Mar. 1878

31 He [Gladstone] told them that he would give them and all other subjects of the Queen much legislation, great prosperity, and universal peace, and he has given them nothing but chips. Chips to the faithful allies in Afghanistan, chips to the trusting native races of South Africa, chips to the Egyptian fellah, chips to the British farmer, chips to the manufacturer and the artisan, chips to the agricultural labourer, chips to the House of Commons itself. *Ib. 24 Jan. 1884*

32 An old man in a hurry. [Gladstone.]
Ib. To the Electors of South Paddington, June 1886

33 All great men make mistakes. Napoleon forgot Blücher, I forgot Goschen.
Leaves from the Notebooks of Lady Dorothy Nevill, p. 21

34 The duty of an Opposition is to oppose.
1830. Quoted (1882) by Lord Randolph Churchill.
W. S. Churchill, *Lord Randolph Churchill*, vol. i, ch 5

35 (*Decimal points:*) I never could make out what those damned dots meant. *Ib.* (1906), vol. ii, p. 184

WINSTON LEONARD SPENCER CHURCHILL
1874–1965

36 It cannot in the opinion of His Majesty's Government be classified as slavery in the extreme acceptance of the word without some risk of terminological inexactitude.
Speech, House of Commons, 22 Feb. 1906

37 The maxim of the British people is 'Business as usual'. *Speech at Guildhall, 9 Nov. 1914*

38 I would say to the House, as I said to those who have joined this Government, 'I have nothing to offer but blood, toil, tears and sweat'.
Speech, House of Commons, 13 May 1940

39 Victory at all costs, victory in spite of all terror, victory however long and hard the road may be; for without victory there is no survival. *Ib.*

40 We shall not flag or fail. We shall fight in France, we shall fight on the seas and oceans, we shall fight with growing confidence and growing strength in the air, we shall defend our island, whatever the cost may be, we shall fight on the beaches, we shall fight on the landing grounds, we shall fight in the fields and in the streets, we shall fight in the hills; we shall never surrender. *Ib. 4 June 1940*

41 Let us therefore brace ourselves to our duty and so bear ourselves that if the British Commonwealth and Empire lasts for a thousand years men will still say, 'This was their finest hour'.
Ib. 18 June 1940

1 Never in the field of human conflict was so much owed by so many to so few.
Speech, House of Commons, 20 Aug. 1940

2 The British Empire and the United States will have to be somewhat mixed up together in some of their affairs for the mutual and general advantage. For my own part, looking out upon the future, I do not view the process with any misgivings. I could not stop it if I wished; no one can stop it. Like the Mississippi, it just keeps rolling along. Let it roll. Let it roll on full flood, inexorable, irresistible, benignant, to broader lands and better days. *Ib.*

3 We are waiting for the long-promised invasion. So are the fishes.
Radio Broadcast to the French people, 21 Oct. 1940

4 I do not resent criticism, even when, for the sake of emphasis, it parts for the time with reality.
Speech, House of Commons, 22 Jan. 1941

5 Give us the tools, and we will finish the job.
Radio Broadcast. (Addressing President Roosevelt.) 9 Feb. 1941

6 This whipped jackal [Mussolini], who, to save his own skin, has made of Italy a vassal state of Hitler's Empire, is frisking up by the side of the German tiger with yelps not only of appetite—that could be understood—but even of triumph.
Speech, House of Commons, Apr. 1941

7 Do not let us speak of darker days; let us rather speak of sterner days. These are not dark days: these are great days—the greatest days our country has ever lived; and we must all thank God that we have been allowed, each of us according to our stations, to play a part in making these days memorable in the history of our race.
Address to the boys of Harrow School, 29 Oct. 1941

8 What kind of people do they [the Japanese] think we are? *Speech to U.S. Congress, 24 Dec. 1941*

9 When I warned them [the French Government] that Britain would fight on alone whatever they did, their Generals told their Prime Minister and his divided Cabinet: 'In three weeks England will have her neck wrung like a chicken.' Some chicken! Some neck!
Speech to the Canadian Parliament, 30 Dec. 1941

10 This is not the end. It is not even the beginning of the end. But it is, perhaps, the end of the beginning.
Speech at the Mansion House, 10 Nov. 1942. (Of the Battle of Egypt)

11 I have not become the King's First Minister in order to preside over the liquidation of the British Empire. *Ib.*

12 The soft under-belly of the Axis.
Report on the War Situation, House of Commons, 11 Nov. 1942

13 Not a seat but a springboard.
Radio Broadcast, 29 Nov. 1942. (On North Africa)

14 There is no finer investment for any community than putting milk into babies. *Ib. 21 Mar. 1943*

15 An iron curtain has descended across the Continent.
Address at Westminster College, Fulton, U.S.A., 5 Mar. 1946. But see Corrigenda

16 By being so long in the lowest form [at Harrow] I gained an immense advantage over the cleverer boys ... I got into my bones the essential structure of the normal British sentence—which is a noble thing. Naturally I am biased in favour of boys learning English; and then I would let the clever ones learn Latin as an honour, and Greek as a treat.
My Early Life (1930), Roving Commission

17 On the night of the tenth of May [1940], at the outset of this mighty battle, I acquired the chief power in the State, which henceforth I wielded in ever-growing measure for five years and three months of world war, at the end of which time, all our enemies having surrendered unconditionally or being about to do so, I was immediately dismissed by the British electorate from all further conduct of their affairs.
The Second World War, vol. i, The Gathering Storm (1948), p. 526

18 No one can guarantee success in war, but only deserve it. *Ib. vol. ii, Their Finest Hour (1949), p. 484.*

19 Dictators ride to and fro upon tigers which they dare not dismount. And the tigers are getting hungry.
While England Slept (1936)

20 I have watched this famous island descending incontinently, fecklessly, the stairway which leads to a dark gulf. It is a fine broad stairway at the beginning, but after a bit the carpet ends. A little farther on there are only flagstones, and a little farther on still these break beneath your feet. *Ib.*

COLLEY CIBBER
1671–1757

21 O say! What is that thing called Light, Which I can ne'er enjoy. *The Blind Boy*

22 Whilst thus I sing, I am a King, Altho' a poor blind boy. *Ib.*

23 Oh! how many torments lie in the small circle of a wedding-ring! *The Double Gallant, I. ii*

24 Dumb's a sly dog. *Love Makes a Man, IV. i*

25 One had as good be out of the world, as out of the fashion. *Love's Last Shift, Act II*

26 Off with his head—so much for Buckingham.
Richard III, altered, IV. iii

27 A weak invention of the enemy. *Ib. V. iii*

28 Conscience avaunt, *Richard's* himself again: Hark! the shrill trumpet sounds, to horse, away, My soul's in arms, and eager for the fray. *Ib.*

29 Perish the thought! *Ib. v*

30 Losers must have leave to speak.
The Rival Fools, Act I

31 Stolen sweets are best. *Ib.*

32 This business will never hold water.
She Would and She Would Not, Act IV

33 Persuasion tips his tongue whene'er he talks, And he has chambers in the King's Bench Walks.
Parody of Pope's lines on William Murray, Lord Mansfield, in Satires and Epistles of Horace Imitated, bk. i, Ep. vi (see 386:11)

MARCUS TULLIUS CICERO
106–43 B.C.

1 In Romuli faece.
Among the dregs of Romulus. *Ad Atticum*, II. i. 8

2 Spartam nactus es: hanc (ex)orna.
Sparta is your inheritance: make the best of her.
Ib. IV. vi. 2

3 Nihil tam absurde dici potest, quod non dicatur ab aliquo philosophorum.
There is nothing so absurd but some philosopher has said it. *De Divinatione*, ii. 58

4 Vulgo enim dicitur: Iucundi acti labores.
For it is commonly said: accomplished labours are pleasant. *De Finibus*, ii. 105

5 Salus populi suprema est lex.
The good of the people is the chief law.
De Legibus, III. iii. 8

6 'Ipse dixit.' 'Ipse' autem erat Pythagoras.
'He himself said it', and this 'he himself', it seems, was Pythagoras. *De Natura Deorum*, I. v.10

7 Summum bonum.
The highest good. *De Officiis*, I. ii. 5

8 Cedant arma togae, concedant laurea laudi.
Let wars yield to peace, laurels to paeans.
Ib. I. xxii. 82

9 Numquam se minus otiosum esse quam cum otiosus, nec minus solum quam cum solus esset.
Never less idle than when wholly idle, nor less alone than when wholly alone. *Ib.* III. i. 1

10 Mens cuiusque is est quisque.
The mind of each man is the man himself.
De Republica, vi. 26

11 Quousque tandem abutere, Catilina, patientia nostra?
How long will you abuse our patience, Catiline?
In Catilinam, I. i. 1

12 O tempora, O mores!
O what times, O what habits! *Ib.*

13 Abiit, excessit, evasit, erupit.
He departed, he withdrew, he strode off, he broke forth. *Ib.* II. i. 1

14 Civis Romanus sum.
I am a Roman citizen. *In Verrem*, v. lvii. 147

15 Omnes artes quae ad humanitatem pertinent habent quoddam commune vinclum et quasi cognatione quadam inter se continentur.
All arts which have anything to do with man have a common bond and as it were contain within themselves a certain affinity. *Pro Archia*, I. ii

16 Haec studia adulescentiam acuunt, senectutem oblectant, secundas res ornant, adversis perfugium ac solacium praebent, delectant domi, non impediunt foris, pernoctant nobiscum, peregrinantur, rusticantur.
These studies are an impetus to youth, and a delight to age; they are an adornment to good fortune, refuge and relief in trouble; they enrich private and do not hamper public life; they are with us by night, they are with us on long journeys, they are with us in the depths of the country.
Ib. VII. xvi

17 Oderint, dum metuant.
Let them hate so long as they fear.
Philippic, I. 14 (*quoted from the tragedian Accius*)

18 Quod di omen avertant.
May the gods avert this omen. *Ib.* III. xiv. 35

19 Silent enim leges inter arma.
Laws are inoperative in war. *Pro Milone*, IV. xi

20 Cui bono.
To whose profit. *Ib.* XII. xxxii

21 Ne quid res publica detrimenti caperet.
That no harm come to the state.
Ib. XXVI. lxx, *quoting the senatorial 'ultimate decree', beginning 'caveant consules' (let the consuls see to it).*

22 Id quod est praestantissimum maximeque optabile omnibus sanis et bonis et beatis, cum dignitate otium.
The thing which is the most outstanding and the most desirable to all healthy and good and well-off persons, is a peaceful life with honour.
Pro Sestio, xlv. 98

23 Errare, mehercule, malo cum Platone . . . quam cum istis vera sentire.
I would rather be wrong with Plato than right with such men as these [the Pythagoreans].
Tusculanae disputationes, I. xvii. 39

24 O fortunatam natam me consule Romam!
O happy Rome, born when I was consul!
Quoted in Juvenal, x. 122

EDWARD HYDE, EARL OF CLARENDON
1609–1674

25 Without question, when he [Hampden] first drew the sword, he threw away the scabbard.
History of the Rebellion, ed. W. Dunn Macray (1888), III. vii. 84

26 He [Hampden] had a head to contrive, a tongue to persuade, and a hand to execute any mischief. *Ib.*

27 He [Falkland] . . . would, with a shrill and sad accent, ingeminate the word *Peace, Peace.* *Ib.* 233

28 So enamoured on peace that he would have been glad the King should have bought it at any price.
Ib.

29 He [Cromwell] will be looked upon by posterity as a brave bad man. *Ib.* xv. last line

JAMES STANIER CLARKE
1765?–1834

30 Perhaps when you again appear in print you may choose to dedicate your volumes to Prince Leopold: any historical romance, illustrative of the history of the august House of Cobourg, would just now be very interesting.
Letter to Jane Austen, 27 March 1816. *Jane Austen's Letters*, ed. R. W. Chapman (1932), p. 451

JOHN CLARKE
fl. 1639

31 He that would thrive
Must rise at five;
He that hath thriven
May lie till seven.
Parœmiologia Anglo-Latina (1639)

1 Home is home, though it be never so homely.
Parœmiologia Anglo-Latina (1639)

HENRY CLAY
1777-1852

2 I had rather be right than be President.
To Senator Preston of South Carolina, 1839

3 The gentleman [Josiah Quincy] can not have forgotten his own sentiments, uttered even on the floor of this House, 'peaceably if we can, forcibly if we must'.
Speech, 8 Jan. 1813

SAMUEL LANGHORNE CLEMENS
see
MARK TWAIN

JOHN CLEVELAND
1613-1658

4 Had Cain been Scot, God would have changed his doom,
Nor forced him wander, but confined him home.
The Rebel Scot

STEPHEN GROVER CLEVELAND
1837-1908

5 I have considered the pension list of the republic a roll of honour.
Veto of Dependent Pension Bill, 5 July 1888

ROBERT CLIVE, LORD CLIVE
1725-1774

6 By God, Mr. Chairman, at this moment I stand astonished at my own moderation!
Reply during Parliamentary cross-examination, 1773

7 I feel that I am reserved for some end or other.
Words when his pistol failed to go off twice, in his attempt to commit suicide. G. R. Gleig, Life, ch. 1

ARTHUR HUGH CLOUGH
1819-1861

8 Rome, believe me, my friend, is like its own Monte Testaceo,
Merely a marvellous mass of broken and castaway wine-pots.
Amours de Voyage, c. 1. ii

9 The horrible pleasure of pleasing inferior people.
Ib. xi

10 Juxtaposition, in short; and what is juxtaposition?
Ib.

11 Allah is great, no doubt, and Juxtaposition his prophet.
Ib. iii. vi

12 Mild monastic faces in quiet collegiate cloisters.
Ib. ix

13 Tibur is beautiful, too, and the orchard slopes, and the Anio
Falling, falling yet, to the ancient lyrical cadence.
Ib. xi

14 Whither depart the souls of the brave that die in the battle,
Die in the lost, lost fight, for the cause that perishes with them?
Amours de Voyage, v. vi

15 Say, 'I am flitting about many years from brain unto brain of
Feeble and restless youths born to inglorious days:
But,' so finish the word, 'I was writ in a Roman chamber,
When from Janiculan heights thundered the cannon of France.'
Ib. end

16 The grave man, nicknamed Adam.
The Bothie of Tober-na-Vuolich, i

17 Over a ledge of granite
Into a granite bason the amber torrent descended.
Ib.

18 Good, too, Logic, of course; in itself, but not in fine weather.
Ib. ii

19 Petticoats up to the knees, or even, it might be, above them.
Ib.

20 Hope an Antinoüs mere, Hyperion of calves the Piper.
Ib.

21 Sesquipedalian blackguard.
Ib.

22 *Thicksides* and *hairy* Aldrich.
Ib.

23 Gay in the mazy
Moving, imbibing the rosy, and pointing a gun at the horny!
Ib. iii

24 Grace is given of God, but knowledge is bought in the market.
Ib. iv

25 Bright October was come, the misty-bright October.
Ib. vi

26 Dangerous Corryvreckan.
Ib. ix

27 This Rachel-and-Leah is marriage.
Ib.

28 They are married, and gone to New Zealand.
Ib.

29 Delicious. Ah!
What else is like the gondola?
Dipsychus, pt. 1. iv

30 How pleasant it is to have money, heigh-ho!
How pleasant it is to have money.
Ib.

31 'There is no God,' the wicked saith,
'And truly it's a blessing,
For what he might have done with us
It's better only guessing.'
Ib. v

32 But country folks who live beneath
The shadow of the steeple;
The parson and the parson's wife,
And mostly married people;

Youths green and happy in first love,
So thankful for illusion;
And men caught out in what the world
Calls guilt, in first confusion;

And almost every one when age,
Disease, or sorrows strike him,
Inclines to think there is a God,
Or something very like Him.
Ib.

33 Home, Rose, and home, Provence and La Palie.
Les Vaches

34 Thou shalt have one God only; who
Would be at the expense of two?
The Latest Decalogue

35 Thou shalt not kill; but need'st not strive
Officiously to keep alive.
Ib.

1 Do not **adultery commit**;
Advantage rarely comes of it. *The Latest Decalogue*

2 Thou shalt not steal; an empty feat,
When it's so lucrative to cheat. *Ib.*

3 Thou shalt not covet; but tradition
Approves all forms of competition. *Ib.*

4 Lo, here is God, and there is God!
Believe it not, O Man. *When Israel came out of Egypt*

5 What voice did on my spirit fall,
Peschiera, when thy bridge I crost?
''Tis better to have fought and lost,
Than never to have fought at all.' *Peschiera*

6 As ships, becalmed at eve, that lay
With canvas drooping, side by side,
Two towers of sail at dawn of day
Are scarce long leagues apart descried. *Qua Cursum Ventus*

7 O bounding breeze, O rushing seas!
At last, at last, unite them there! *Ib.*

8 Say not the struggle naught availeth,
The labour and the wounds are vain,
The enemy faints not, nor faileth,
And as things have been, things remain.

If hopes were dupes, fears may be liars;
It may be, in yon smoke concealed,
Your comrades chase e'en now the fliers,
And, but for you, possess the field.

For while the tired waves, vainly breaking,
Seem here no painful inch to gain,
Far back through creeks and inlets making
Comes silent, flooding in, the main.

And not by eastern windows only,
When daylight comes, comes in the light,
In front the sun climbs slow, how slowly,
But westward, look, the land is bright. *Say Not the Struggle Naught Availeth*

9 To finger idly some old Gordian knot,
Unskilled to sunder, and too weak to cleave,
And with much toil attain to half-believe. *Songs in Absence, Come back, Come back*

10 Green fields of England! whereso'er
Across this watery waste we fare,
Your image at our hearts we bear,
Green fields of England, everywhere. *Ib. Green Fields of England!*

11 Some future day when what is now is not,
When all old faults and follies are forgot. *Ib. Some Future Day*

12 That out of sight is out of mind
Is true of most we leave behind. *Ib. That Out of Sight*

13 Where lies the land to which the ship would go?
Far, far ahead, is all her seamen know.
And where the land she travels from? Away,
Far, far behind, is all that they can say. *Ib. Where Lies the Land*

14 It fortifies my soul to know
That, though I perish, Truth is so:
That, howsoe'er I stray and range,
Whate'er I do, Thou dost not change.
I steadier step when I recall
That, if I slip, Thou dost not fall. *With Whom Is No Variableness*

SIR WILLIAM LAIRD CLOWES
1856–1905

15 The Glorious First of June.
Page-heading in The Royal Navy: a History (1899), vol. iv, p. 225. Taken from explanatory pamphlet accompanying Cleveley's prints of the action: *Two prints . . . representing the Glorious and Memorable Action of the First of June 1794*

WILLIAM COBBETT
1762–1835

16 The slavery of the tea and coffee and other slop-kettle. *Advice to Young Men, letter i, 31*

17 Nouns of number, or multitude, such as *Mob*, Parliament, Rabble, House of Commons, Regiment, Court of King's Bench, Den of Thieves, and the like.
English Grammar, letter xvii, *Syntax as Relating to Pronouns*

18 All is vulgar, all clumsy, all dull, all torpid inanity.
Ib. letter xxiv, Six Lessons, Lesson 4

19 From a very early age, I had imbibed the opinion, that it was every man's duty to do all that lay in his power to leave his country as good as he had found it. *Political Register, 22 Dec. 1832*

20 But what is to be the fate of the great wen [London] of all? The monster, called . . . 'the metropolis of the empire'? *Rural Rides, 1821*

RICHARD COBDEN
1804–1865

21 I believe it has been said that one copy of *The Times* contains more useful information than the whole of the historical works of Thucydides.
Speech, Manchester, 27 Dec. 1850

CHARLES COBORN [C. W. McCALLUM]
1852–1945

22 Two lovely black eyes,
Oh! what a surprise!
Only for telling a man he was wrong,
Two lovely black eyes! *Two Lovely Black Eyes*

ALISON COCKBURN
1713–1794

23 I've seen the smiling of Fortune beguiling,
I've felt all its favours and found its decay. *The Flowers of the Forest*

24 I've seen the forest adorn'd the foremost,
With flowers of the fairest, most pleasant and gay:
Sae bonny was their blooming, their scent the air perfuming;
But now they are wither'd and weeded away. *Ib.*

25 For the flowers of the forest are withered away. *Ib.*

SIR ASTON COKAYNE
1608–1684

26 Sydney, whom we yet admire
Lighting our little torches at his fire.
Funeral Elegy on Mr. Michael Drayton

DESMOND F. T. COKE
1879–1931

1 His blade struck the water a full second before any other . . . until . . . as the boats began to near the winning-post, his own was dipping into the water *twice* as often as any other.

> *Sandford of Merton* (1903), ch. xii. *Often quoted as 'All rowed fast but none so fast as stroke', and attrib. to Ouida.*

SIR EDWARD COKE
1552–1634

2 Magna Charta is such a fellow, that he will have no sovereign.

> *On the Lords' Amendment to the Petition of Right, 17 May 1628.* Rushworth's *Hist. Coll.,* 1659, i

3 How long soever it hath continued, if it be against reason, it is of no force in law.

> *Institutes: Commentary upon Littleton. First Institute,* § 62a

4 Reason is the life of the law, nay the common law itself is nothing else but reason. . . . The law, which is the perfection of reason. *Ib.* § 97b

5 The gladsome light of Jurisprudence. *Ib. epilogus*

6 Syllables govern the world. *Ib.*

7 For a man's house is his castle, *et domus sua cuique est tutissimum refugium.* *Ib. Third Institute,* cap. 73

8 Six hours in sleep, in law's grave study six,
Four spend in prayer, the rest on Nature fix.
> *Pandects,* lib. ii, tit. iv, *De in Jus vocando*

9 The house of every one is to him as his castle and fortress. *Semayne's Case,* 5 Rep. 91b

10 They [corporations] cannot commit treason, nor be outlawed, nor excommunicate, for they have no souls. *Sutton's Hospital Case,* 10 Rep. 32b

HARTLEY COLERIDGE
1796–1849

11 But what is Freedom? Rightly understood,
A universal licence to be good. *Liberty*

12 She is not fair to outward view
As many maidens be;
Her loveliness I never knew
Until she smiled on me.
Oh! then I saw her eye was bright,
A well of love, a spring of light. *Song. She is not Fair*

13 Her very frowns are fairer far,
Than smiles of other maidens are. *Ib.*

14 Old times unqueen thee, and old loves endear thee.
> *To a Lofty Beauty, from her Poor Kinsman*

SIR JOHN COLERIDGE, BARON COLERIDGE
1820–1894

15 I speak not of this college or of that, but of the University as a whole; and, gentlemen, what a *whole* Oxford is!
> G. W. E. Russell's *Collections and Recollections,* ch. 29

MARY ELIZABETH COLERIDGE
1861–1907

16 Mother of God! no lady thou:
Common woman of common earth! *Our Lady*

17 We were young, we were merry, we were very, very wise,
And the door stood open at our feast,
When there passed us a woman with the West in her eyes,
And a man with his back to the East. *Unwelcome*

SAMUEL TAYLOR COLERIDGE
1772–1834

18 It is an ancient Mariner,
And he stoppeth one of three.
'By thy long grey beard and glittering eye,
Now wherefore stopp'st thou me?'
> *The Ancient Mariner,* pt. i

19 The guests are met, the feast is set:
May'st hear the merry din. *Ib.*

20 He holds him with his skinny hand,
'There was a ship,' quoth he.
'Hold off! unhand me, grey-beard loon!'
Eftsoons his hand dropt he.

He holds him with his glittering eye—
The Wedding-Guest stood still,
And listens like a three years' child:
The Mariner hath his will.

The Wedding-Guest sat on a stone:
He cannot choose but hear;
And thus spake on that ancient man,
The bright-eyed Mariner. *Ib.*

21 The ship was cheered, the harbour cleared,
Merrily did we drop
Below the kirk, below the hill,
Below the lighthouse top.

The Sun came up upon the left,
Out of the sea came he!
And he shone bright, and on the right
Went down into the sea. *Ib.*

22 The Wedding-Guest here beat his breast,
For he heard the loud bassoon. *Ib.*

23 The bride hath paced into the hall,
Red as a rose is she. *Ib.*

24 As who pursued with yell and blow
Still treads the shadow of his foe,
And forward bends his head. *Ib.*

25 And ice, mast-high, came floating by,
As green as emerald. *Ib.*

26 The ice was here, the ice was there,
The ice was all around:
It cracked and growled, and roared and howled,
Like noises in a swound! *Ib.*

27 It ate the food it ne'er had eat,
And round and round it flew.

The ice did split with a thunder-fit;
The helmsman steered us through! *Ib.*

28 And a good south wind sprung up behind;
The Albatross did follow,
And every day, for food or play,
Came to the mariner's hollo! *Ib.*

COLERIDGE

1 'God save thee, ancient Mariner!
  From the fiends that plague thee thus!—
  Why look'st thou so?'—With my cross-bow
  I shot the Albatross.   *The Ancient Mariner*, pt. i

2 Nor dim nor red, like God's own head,
  The glorious Sun uprist.   *Ib.* pt. ii

3 We were the first that ever burst
  Into that silent sea.   *Ib.*

4 All in a hot and copper sky,
  The bloody Sun, at noon,
  Right up above the mast did stand,
  No bigger than the Moon.   *Ib.*

5 As idle as a painted ship
  Upon a painted ocean.   *Ib.*

6 Water, water, every where,
  And all the boards did shrink;
  Water, water, every where.
  Nor any drop to drink.

  The very deep did rot: O Christ!
  That ever this should be!
  Yea, slimy things did crawl with legs
  Upon the slimy sea.

  About, about, in reel and rout
  The death-fires danced at night;
  The water, like a witch's oils,
  Burnt green, and blue and white.   *Ib.*

7 Nine fathom deep he had followed us
  From the land of mist and snow.   *Ib.*

8 There passed a weary time. Each throat
  Was parched, and glazed each eye.
  A weary time! a weary time!
  How glazed each weary eye.   *Ib.* pt. iii

9 I bit my arm, I sucked the blood,
  And cried, A sail! a sail!   *Ib.*

10 Gramercy! they for joy did grin,
   And all at once their breath drew in,
   As they were drinking all.   *Ib.*

11 When that strange shape drove suddenly
   Betwixt us and the Sun.   *Ib.*

12 And straight the Sun was flecked with bars,
   (Heaven's Mother send us grace!)
   As if through a dungeon-grate he peered
   With broad and burning face.   *Ib.*

13 *Her* lips were red, *her* looks were free,
   Her locks were yellow as gold:
   Her skin was white as leprosy,
   The Night-mare LIFE-IN-DEATH was she,
   Who thicks man's blood with cold.

   The naked hulk alongside came,
   And the twain were casting dice;
   'The game is done! I've won! I've won!'
   Quoth she, and whistles thrice.   *Ib.*

14 The Sun's rim dips; the stars rush out:
   At one stride comes the dark;
   With far-heard whisper, o'er the sea,
   Off shot the spectre-bark.   *Ib.*

15 We listened and looked sideways up!   *Ib.*

16 The hornèd Moon, with one bright star
   Within the nether tip.   *Ib.*

17 Each turned his face with a ghastly pang,
   And cursed me with his eye.   *Ib.*

18 And every soul, it passed me by,
   Like the whizz of my cross-bow!   *The Ancient Mariner*, pt. iii

19 'I fear thee, ancient Mariner!
   I fear thy skinny hand!
   And thou art long, and lank, and brown,
   As is the ribbed sea-sand.'   *Ib.* pt. iv

20 Alone, alone, all, all alone,
   Alone on a wide wide sea!
   And never a saint took pity on
   My soul in agony.   *Ib.*

21 And a thousand thousand slimy things
   Lived on; and so did I.   *Ib.*

22 An orphan's curse would drag to hell
   A spirit from on high;
   But oh! more horrible than that
   Is the curse in a dead man's eye.   *Ib.*

23 The moving Moon went up the sky,
   And no where did abide:
   Softly she was going up,
   And a star or two beside.   *Ib.*

24 And everywhere the blue sky belongs to them, and
   is their appointed rest and their native country
   and their own natural homes, which they enter unannounced, as lords that are certainly expected,
   and yet there is a silent joy at their arrival [the
   stars].   *Ib.* (*gloss*)

25 But where the ship's huge shadow lay,
   The charmed water burned alway
   A still and awful red.   *Ib.*

26 A spring of love gushed from my heart,
   And I blessed them unaware.   *Ib.*

27 Oh Sleep! it is a gentle thing,
   Beloved from pole to pole,
   To Mary Queen the praise be given!
   She sent the gentle sleep from Heaven,
   That slid into my soul.   *Ib.* pt. v

28 The silly buckets on the deck,
   That had so long remained,
   I dreamt that they were filled with dew;
   And when I awoke, it rained.   *Ib.*

29 Sure I had drunken in my dreams,
   And still my body drank.   *Ib.*

30 Beneath the lightning and the Moon
   The dead men gave a groan.   *Ib.*

31 It had been strange, even in a dream,
   To have seen those dead men rise.   *Ib.*

32 We were a ghastly crew.   *Ib.*

33 The body of my brother's son
   Stood by me, knee to knee:
   The body and I pulled at one rope,
   But he said nought to me.   *Ib.*

34 How they seemed to fill the sea and air
   With their sweet jargoning!   *Ib.*

35 It ceased; yet still the sails made on
   A pleasant noise till noon,
   A noise like of a hidden brook
   In the leafy month of June,
   That to the sleeping woods all night
   Singeth a quiet tune.   *Ib.*

36 With a short uneasy motion.   *Ib.*

37 Quoth he, 'The man hath penance done,
   And penance more will do.'   *Ib.*

[149]

COLERIDGE

1 The air is cut away before,
And closes from behind. *The Ancient Mariner*, pt. vi

2 Like one, that on a lonesome road
Doth walk in fear and dread,
And having once turned round walks on,
And turns no more his head;
Because he knows, a frightful fiend
Doth close behind him tread. *Ib.*

3 It raised my hair, it fanned my cheek
Like a meadow-gale of spring. *Ib.*

4 Oh! dream of joy! is this indeed
The lighthouse top I see?
Is this the hill? is this the kirk?
Is this mine own countree? *Ib.*

5 O let me be awake, my God!
Or let me sleep alway. *Ib.*

6 A man all light, a seraph-man,
On every corse there stood.

This seraph-band, each waved his hand:
It was a heavenly sight!
They stood as signals to the land,
Each one a lovely light. *Ib.*

7 No voice; but oh! the silence sank
Like music on my heart. *Ib.*

8 This Hermit good lives in that wood
Which slopes down to the sea.
How loudly his sweet voice he rears!
He loves to talk with marineres
That come from a far countree.

He kneels at morn, and noon, and eve—
He hath a cushion plump:
It is the moss that wholly hides
The rotted old oak-stump. *Ib. pt. vii*

9 Brown skeletons of leaves that lag
My forest-brook along;
When the ivy-tod is heavy with snow,
And the owlet whoops to the wolf below,
That eats the she-wolf's young. *Ib.*

10 Under the water it rumbled on,
Still louder and more dread:
It reached the ship, it split the bay;
The ship went down like lead. *Ib.*

11 I moved my lips—the Pilot shrieked
And fell down in a fit;
The holy Hermit raised his eyes,
And prayed where he did sit.

I took the oars: the Pilot's boy,
Who now doth crazy go,
Laughed loud and long, and all the while
His eyes went to and fro.
'Ha! ha!' quoth he, 'full plain I see,
The Devil knows how to row'. *Ib.*

12 I pass, like night, from land to land;
I have strange power of speech;
That moment that his face I see,
I know the man that must hear me:
To him my tale I teach. *Ib.*

13 And hark the little vesper-bell,
Which biddeth me to prayer! *Ib.*

14 O Wedding-Guest! this soul hath been
Alone on a wide wide sea:
So lonely 'twas, that God himself
Scarce seemed there to be. *Ib.*

15 O sweeter than the marriage-feast,
'Tis sweeter far to me,
To walk together to the kirk
With a goodly company.
To walk together to the kirk,
And all together pray,
While each to his great Father bends,
Old men, and babes, and loving friends
And youths and maidens gay!
The Ancient Mariner, pt. vii

16 He prayeth well, who loveth well
Both man and bird and beast.

He prayeth best, who loveth best
All things both great and small;
For the dear God who loveth us,
He made and loveth all. *Ib.*

17 He went like one that hath been stunned,
And is of sense forlorn:
A sadder and a wiser man,
He rose the morrow morn. *Ib.*

18 That he sings, and he sings; and for ever sings he—
'I love my Love, and my Love loves me!'
Answer to a Child's Question

19 And the Spring comes slowly up this way,
Christabel, pt. i

20 I guess, 'twas frightful there to see
A lady so richly clad as she—
Beautiful exceedingly! *Ib.*

21 Carved with figures strange and sweet,
All made out of the carver's brain. *Ib.*

22 A sight to dream of, not to tell! *Ib.*

23 But this she knows, in joys and woes,
That saints will aid if men will call:
For the blue sky bends over all! *Ib.*

24 Each matin bell, the Baron saith,
Knells us back to a world of death. *Ib. pt. ii*

25 Alas! they had been friends in youth;
But whispering tongues can poison truth. *Ib.*

26 And constancy lives in realms above;
And life is thorny; and youth is vain;
And to be wroth with one we love
Doth work like madness in the brain. *Ib.*

27 They stood aloof, the scars remaining,
Like cliffs which had been rent asunder;
A dreary sea now flows between. *Ib.*

28 In Köhln, a town of monks and bones,
And pavements fang'd with murderous stones
And rags, and hags, and hideous wenches;
I counted two and seventy stenches,
All well defined, and several stinks!
Ye Nymphs that reign o'er sewers and sinks,
The river Rhine, it is well known,
Doth wash your city of Cologne;
But tell me, Nymphs, what power divine
Shall henceforth wash the river Rhine? *Cologne*

29 My eyes make pictures, when they are shut.
A Day-Dream

30 Well! If the Bard was weatherwise, who made
The grand old ballad of Sir Patrick Spence.
Dejection: an Ode

31 A grief without a pang, void, dark and drear,
A stifled, drowsy, unimpassioned grief,
Which finds no natural outlet, no relief,
In word, or sigh, or tear. *Ib.*

COLERIDGE

1 And those thin clouds above, in flakes and bars,
That give away their motion to the stars.
Dejection: an Ode

2 I see them all so excellently fair,
I see, not feel, how beautiful they are!

3 I may not hope from outward forms to win
The passion and the life, whose fountains are within. *Ib.*

4 O Lady! we receive but what we give,
And in our life alone does Nature live. *Ib.*

5 A light, a glory, a fair luminous cloud
Enveloping the Earth. *Ib.*

6 Joy is the sweet voice, joy the luminous cloud—
We in ourselves rejoice!
And thence flows all that charms or ear or sight,
All melodies the echoes of that voice,
All colours a suffusion from that light. *Ib.*

7 From his brimstone bed at break of day
A walking the Devil is gone,
To visit his snug little farm the earth,
And see how his stock goes on.
The Devil's Thoughts. (See 507: 19–22)

8 And backward and forward he switched his long tail
As a gentleman switches his cane. *Ib.*

9 His jacket was red and his breeches were blue,
And there was a hole where the tail came through. *Ib.*

10 He saw a Lawyer killing a viper
On a dunghill hard by his own stable;
And the Devil smiled, for it put him in mind
Of Cain and his brother, Abel. *Ib.*

11 He saw a cottage with a double coach-house,
A cottage of gentility;
And the Devil did grin, for his darling sin
Is pride that apes humility. *Ib.*

12 As he went through Cold-Bath Fields he saw
A solitary cell;
And the Devil was pleased, for it gave him a hint
For improving his prisons in Hell. *Ib.*

13 With Donne, whose muse on dromedary trots,
Wreathe iron pokers into true-love knots.
On Donne's Poetry

14 What is an Epigram? a dwarfish whole,
Its body brevity, and wit its soul. *Epigram*

15 Swans sing before they die—'twere no bad thing
Did certain persons die before they sing.
Epigram on a Volunteer Singer

16 Stop, Christian passer-by!—Stop, child of God.
Epitaph for Himself

17 That he who many a year with toil of breath
Found death in life, may here find life in death. *Ib.*

18 Ere sin could blight or sorrow fade,
Death came with friendly care:
The opening bud to Heaven convey'd,
And bade it blossom *there*. *Epitaph on an Infant*

19 Forth from his dark and lonely hiding-place
(Portentous sight!) the owlet Atheism,
Sailing on obscene wings athwart the noon,
Drops his blue-fringèd lids, and holds them close,
And hooting at the glorious sun in Heaven,
Cries out, 'Where is it?' *Fears in Solitude*

20 Letters four do form his name. [Pitt.]
Fire, Famine and Slaughter

21 With what deep worship I have still adored
The spirit of divinest Liberty. *France*

22 So for the mother's sake the child was dear,
And dearer was the mother for the child.
*Sonnet to a Friend Who Asked How I Felt When
the Nurse First Presented My Infant to Me*

23 The frost performs its secret ministry,
Unhelped by any wind. *Frost at Midnight*

24 Only that film, which fluttered on the grate,
Still flutters there, the sole unquiet thing. *Ib.*

25 Therefore all seasons shall be sweet to thee,
Whether the summer clothe the general earth
With greenness, or the redbreast sit and sing
Betwixt the tufts of snow on the bare branch
Of mossy apple-tree, while the nigh thatch
Smokes in the sun-thaw; whether the eave-drops
fall
Heard only in the trances of the blast,
Or if the secret ministry of frost
Shall hang them up in silent icicles,
Quietly shining to the quiet moon. *Ib.*

26 It sounds like stories from the land of spirits
If any man obtain that which he merits
Or any merit that which he obtains.
The Good, Great Man

27 'Tis sweet to him who all the week
Through city-crowds must push his way,
To stroll alone through fields and woods,
And hallow thus the Sabbath-day. *Home-Sick*

28 Hast thou a charm to stay the morning-star
In his steep course?
Hymn before Sun-rise, in the Vale of Chamouni

29 And visited all night by troops of stars. *Ib.*

30 Earth, with her thousand voices, praises God. *Ib.*

31 The Knight's bones are dust,
And his good sword rust;—
His soul is with the saints, I trust.
The Knight's Tomb

32 In Xanadu did Kubla Khan
A stately pleasure-dome decree:
Where Alph, the sacred river, ran
Through caverns measureless to man
Down to a sunless sea.
So twice five miles of fertile ground
With walls and towers were girdled round:
And there were gardens bright with sinuous rills,
Where blossomed many an incense-bearing tree;
And here were forests ancient as the hills,
Enfolding sunny spots of greenery.
But oh! that deep romantic chasm which slanted
Down the green hill athwart a cedarn cover!
A savage place! as holy and enchanted
As e'er beneath a waning moon was haunted
By woman wailing for her demon-lover!
And from this chasm, with ceaseless turmoil seething,
As if this earth in fast thick pants were breathing,
A mighty fountain momently was forced.
Kubla Khan

33 And 'mid these dancing rocks at once and ever
It flung up momently the sacred river.
Five miles meandering with a mazy motion
Through wood and dale the sacred river ran,
Then reached the caverns measureless to man,
And sank in tumult to a lifeless ocean:

COLERIDGE

And 'mid this tumult Kubla heard from far
Ancestral voices prophesying war!

  The shadow of the dome of pleasure
  Floated midway on the waves;
  Where was heard the mingled measure
  From the fountain and the caves.
It was a miracle of rare device,
A sunny pleasure-dome with caves of ice!

  A damsel with a dulcimer
  In a vision once I saw:
  It was an Abyssinian maid,
  And on her dulcimer she played,
  Singing of Mount Abora.
  Could I revive within me
  Her symphony and song,
  To such a deep delight 'twould win me,
That with music loud and long,
I would build that dome in air,
That sunny dome! those caves of ice!
And all who heard should see them there,
And all should cry, Beware! Beware!
His flashing eyes, his floating hair!
Weave a circle round him thrice,
And close your eyes with holy dread,
For he on honey-dew hath fed,
And drunk the milk of Paradise.　　*Kubla Khan*

1 This Lime-Tree Bower my Prison.　　*Title*

2 　　　A charm
For thee, my gentle-hearted Charles, to whom
No sound is dissonant which tells of Life.　*Ib. l. 74*

3 All thoughts, all passions, all delights,
　Whatever stirs this mortal frame,
All are but ministers of Love,
　And feed his sacred flame.　　*Love*

4 Trochee trips from long to short.　　*Metrical Feet*

5 Iambics march from short to long;—
With a leap and a bound the swift Anapaests throng.
　　　　Ib.

6 Choose thou whatever suits the line;
Call me Sappho, call me Chloris,
Call me Lalage or Doris,
Only, only call me thine.　　*Names*

7 'Most musical, most melancholy' bird!
A melancholy bird? Oh! idle thought!
In Nature there is nothing melancholy.
　　　　The Nightingale

8 In the hexameter rises the fountain's silvery column;
In the pentameter aye falling in melody back.
　　　　Ovidian Elegiac Metre

9 The fair humanities of old religion.
　　　　Piccolomini, II. iv

10 But still the heart doth need a language, still
Doth the old instinct bring back the old names. *Ib.*

11 Something childish, but very natural.　　*Title*

12 O! I do love thee, meek *Simplicity!*
Sonnets Attempted in the Manner of Contemporary Writers. 2. To Simplicity.

13 And this reft house is that the which he built,
Lamented Jack!
Ib. 3. On a Ruined House in a Romantic Country

14 A mother is a mother still,
The holiest thing alive. *The Three Graves,* pt. III. x

15 We ne'er can be
　Made happy by compulsion.
　　　　The Three Graves, pt. IV. xii

16 Never, believe me,
　Appear the Immortals,
　　Never alone.
　　Visit of the Gods (Imit. from Schiller)

17 All Nature seems at work. Slugs leave their lair—
　The bees are stirring—birds are on the wing—
And Winter slumbering in the open air,
　Wears on his smiling face a dream of Spring!
And I the while, the sole unbusy thing,
Nor honey make, nor pair, nor build, nor sing.
　　　　Work Without Hope

18 Work without hope draws nectar in a sieve,
And hope without an object cannot live.　*Ib.*

19 Poor little Foal of an oppressed race!
I love the languid patience of thy face.
　　　　To a Young Ass

20 Verse, a breeze mid blossoms straying,
Where Hope clung feeding, like a bee—
Both were mine! Life went a-maying
　With Nature, Hope, and Poesy,
　　When I was young!　　*Youth and Age*

21 Like some poor nigh-related guest,
That may not rudely be dismist;
Yet hath outstay'd his welcome while,
And tells the jest without the smile.　　*Ib.*

22 He who begins by loving Christianity better than
Truth will proceed by loving his own sect or church
better than Christianity, and end by loving himself
better than all.
　Aids to Reflection: Moral and Religious Aphorisms, xxv

23 The most happy marriage I can picture or imagine to
myself would be the union of a deaf man to a blind
woman.　　*T. Allsop's Recollections* (1836)

24 If men could learn from history, what lessons it might
teach us! But passion and party blind our eyes,
and the light which experience gives is a lantern on
the stern, which shines only on the waves behind
us!　　*Ib.* (18 Dec. 1831)

25 Until you understand a writer's ignorance, presume
yourself ignorant of his understanding.
　　　Biographia Literaria, ch. 12

26 That willing suspension of disbelief for the moment,
which constitutes poetic faith.　　*Ib.* ch. 14

27 Our *myriad-minded* Shakespeare. Note Ἀνὴρ μυριόνους,
a phrase which I have borrowed from a Greek
monk, who applies it to a Patriarch of Constantinople.　　*Ib.* ch. 15

28 No man was ever yet a great poet, without being at the
same time a profound philosopher.　　*Ib.*

29 The dwarf sees farther than the giant, when he has the
giant's shoulder to mount on.
　　　The Friend, § i, Essay 8

30 Reviewers are usually people who would have been
poets, historians, biographers, &c., if they could;
they have tried their talents at one or at the other,
and have failed; therefore they turn critics.
　　Lectures on Shakespeare and Milton, i

31 Summer has set in with its usual severity.
　*Remark quoted in Lamb's Letter to V. Novello,
　9 May 1826*

1 The last speech, [Iago's soliloquy] the motive-hunting of motiveless malignity—how awful!
Notes on the Tragedies of Shakespeare, Othello

2 From whatever place I write you will expect that part of my 'Travels' will consist of excursions in my own mind.
Satyrane's Letters, ii. [The Friend, 7 Dec. 1809 No. 16. Biographia Literaria]

3 Schiller has the material sublime.
Table Talk, 29 Dec. 1822

4 You abuse snuff! Perhaps it is the final cause of the human nose. *Ib. 4 Jan. 1823*

5 To see him [Kean] act, is like reading Shakespeare by flashes of lightning. *Ib. 27 Apr. 1823*

6 I wish our clever young poets would remember my homely definitions of prose and poetry; that is, prose = words in their best order;—poetry = the *best* words in the best order. *Ib. 12 July 1827*

7 The man's desire is for the woman; but the woman's desire is rarely other than for the desire of the man. *Ib. 23 July 1827*

8 My mind is in a state of philosophical doubt as to animal magnetism. *Ib. 30 Apr. 1830*

9 Poetry is certainly something more than good sense, but it must be good sense at all events; just as a palace is more than a house, but it must be a house, at least. *Ib. 9 May 1830*

10 Swift was *anima Rabelaisii habitans in sicco*—the soul of Rabelais dwelling in a dry place. *Ib. 15 June 1830*

11 The misfortune is, that he [Tennyson] has begun to write verses without very well understanding what metre is. *Ib. 24 Apr. 1833*

12 When I was a boy, I was fondest of Æschylus; in youth and middle-age I preferred Euripides; now in my declining years I prefer Sophocles. I can now at length see that Sophocles is the most perfect. Yet he never rises to the sublime simplicity of Æschylus—a simplicity of design, I mean—nor diffuses himself in the passionate outpourings of Euripides. *Ib. 1 July 1833*

13 That passage is what I call the sublime dashed to pieces by cutting too close with the fiery four-in-hand round the corner of nonsense. *Ib. 20 Jan. 1834*

14 I believe Shakespeare was not a whit more intelligible in his own day than he is now to an educated man, except for a few local allusions of no consequence. He is of no age—nor of any religion, or party or profession. The body and substance of his works came out of the unfathomable depths of his own oceanic mind: his observation and reading, which was considerable, supplied him with the drapery of his figures. *Ib. 15 Mar. 1834*

15 This dark frieze-coated, hoarse, teeth-chattering Month. *Watchman, No. 6. Apr. 1796*

16 Poor Lamb, if he wants any *knowledge*, he may apply to me.
Ascribed by Lamb in a Letter to Southey, 28 July 1798

JESSE COLLINGS
1831–1920

17 Three acres and a cow.
Phrase used in his land-reform propaganda of 1885. (See 339:2)

JOHN CHURTON COLLINS
1848–1908

18 To ask advice is in nine cases out of ten to tout for flattery. *Maxims and Reflections, No. 59*

MORTIMER COLLINS
1827–1876

19 A man is as old as he's feeling,
A woman as old as she looks.
The Unknown Quantity

WILLIAM COLLINS
1721–1759

20 Fair Fidele's grassy tomb. *Dirge in Cymbeline*

21 And rifle all the breathing Spring. *Ib.*

22 Each lonely scene shall thee restore,
For thee the tear be duly shed;
Belov'd till life can charm no more,
And mourn'd, till Pity's self be dead. *Ib.*

23 If aught of oaten stop, or pastoral song,
May hope, O pensive Eve, to soothe thine ear.
Ode to Evening

24 While now the bright-haired sun
Sits in yon western tent, whose cloudy skirts,
With brede ethereal wove,
O'erhang his wavy bed:
Now air is hush'd, save where the weak-ey'd bat,
With short shrill shriek flits by on leathern wing,
Or where the beetle winds
His small but sullen horn,
As oft he rises 'midst the twilight path,
Against the pilgrim borne in heedless hum. *Ib.*

25 Hamlets brown, and dim-discover'd spires. *Ib.*

26 Bathe thy breathing tresses, meekest Eve! *Ib.*

27 Round the moist marge of each cold Hebrid isle.
Ode on the Popular Superstitions of the Highlands

28 Tho' taste, tho' genius bless,
To some divine excess,
Faints the cold work till thou inspire the whole.
Ode to Simplicity

29 How sleep the brave, who sink to rest,
By all their country's wishes blest!
Ode Written in the Year 1746

30 By fairy hands their knell is rung,
By forms unseen their dirge is sung;
There Honour comes, a pilgrim grey,
To bless the turf that wraps their clay,
And Freedom shall awhile repair,
To dwell a weeping hermit there! *Ib.*

31 When Music, heav'nly maid, was young.
The Passions, an Ode for Music

1 With eyes up-rais'd, as one inspir'd,
Pale Melancholy sate retir'd,
And from her wild sequester'd seat,
In notes by distance made more sweet,
Pour'd thro' the mellow horn her pensive soul.
The Passions, an Ode for Music

2 In hollow murmurs died away. *Ib.*

3 O Music, sphere-descended maid. *Ib.*

4 Too nicely Jonson knew the critic's part,
Nature in him was almost lost in Art.
Verses to Sir Thomas Hanmer

GEORGE COLMAN
1732–1794

5 Love and a cottage! Eh, Fanny! Ah, give me indifference and a coach and six!
The Clandestine Marriage, I. ii

GEORGE COLMAN
1762–1836

6 Mum's the word. *Battle of Hexham*, II. i

7 Praise the bridge that carried you over.
Heir-at-Law, I. i

8 Lord help you! Tell 'em Queen Anne's dead. *Ib.*

9 Oh, London is a fine town,
A very famous city,
Where all the streets are paved with gold,
And all the maidens pretty. *Ib.* ii

10 Not to be sneezed at. *Ib.* II. i

11 Oh, Miss Bailey! Unfortunate Miss Bailey!
Love Laughs at Locksmiths, Act II, *Song*

12 Says he, 'I am a handsome man, but I'm a gay
deceiver.' *Ib.*

13 Johnson's style was grand and Gibbon's elegant; the
stateliness of the former was sometimes pedantic,
and the polish of the latter was occasionally finical.
Johnson marched to kettle-drums and trumpets;
Gibbon moved to flutes and hautboys: Johnson
hewed passages through the Alps, while Gibbon
levelled walks through parks and gardens.
Random Records (1830), i. 121

14 My father was an eminent button maker—but I had
a soul above buttons—I panted for a liberal profession. *Sylvester Daggerwood*, I. x

15 His heart runs away with his head.
Who Wants a Guinea?, I. i

16 Impaling worms to torture fish.
Lady of the Wreck, c. II. l. 18

17 Mynheer Vandunck, though he never was drunk,
Sipped brandy and water gayly.
Mynheer Vandunck

18 Like two single gentlemen roll'd into one.
*My Nightgown and Slippers. Lodgings for Single
Gentlemen*

19 When taken, To be well shaken.
Ib. Newcastle Apothecary

CHARLES CALEB COLTON
1780?–1832

20 When you have nothing to say, say nothing.
Lacon, vol. i, No. 183

21 Examinations are formidable even to the best prepared, for the greatest fool may ask more than the
wisest man can answer. *Ib.* No. 322

22 If you would be known, and not know, vegetate in
a village; if you would know, and not be known,
live in a city. *Lacon*, vol. i, No. 334

23 Man is an embodied paradox, a bundle of contradictions. *Ib.* No. 408

24 The debt which cancels all others. *Ib.* vol. ii, No. 66

PRINCE DE CONDÉ
1621–1686

25 Silence! Voilà l'ennemi!
Hush! Here comes the enemy!
As Bourdaloue mounted the pulpit at St. Sulpice

WILLIAM CONGREVE
1670–1729

26 Is there in the world a climate more uncertain than
our own? And, which is a natural consequence,
is there any where a people more unsteady, more
apt to discontent, more *saturnine, dark*, and *melancholic* than our selves? Are we not of all people
the most unfit to be alone, and most unsafe to be
trusted with our selves? . . .'
*Amendments of Mr. Collier's False and Im-
perfect Citations*

27 Careless she is with artful care,
Affecting to seem unaffected. *Amoret*

28 She likes her self, yet others hates
For that which in herself she prizes;
And while she laughs at them, forgets
She is the thing that she despises. *Ib.*

29 It is the business of a comic poet to paint the vices
and follies of human kind.
The Double Dealer, Epistle Dedicatory

30 Retired to their tea and scandal, according to their
ancient custom. *Ib.* I. i

31 There is nothing more unbecoming a man of quality
than to laugh; Jesu, 'tis such a vulgar expression
of the passion! *Ib.* iv

32 Tho' marriage makes man and wife one flesh, it leaves
'em still two fools. *Ib.* II. iii

33 She lays it on with a trowel. *Ib.* III. x

34 When people walk hand in hand there's neither over-
taking nor meeting. *Ib.* IV. ii

35 See how love and murder will out. *Ib.* vi

36 No mask like open truth to cover lies,
As to go naked is the best disguise. *Ib.* v. iv

37 I cannot help it, if I am naturally more delighted
with any thing that is amiable, than with any thing
that is wonderful. *Preface to Dryden*

38 What he [Dryden] has done in any one species, or
distinct kind, would have been sufficient to have
acquired him a great name. If he had written
nothing but his Prefaces, or nothing but his Songs,
or his Prologues, each of them would have intituled
him to the preference and distinction of excelling
in his kind. *Ib.*

39 O Sleep! thou flatterer of happy minds.
Elegy to Sleep

40 The good receiv'd, the giver is forgot.
Epistle to Lord Halifax, l. 40

CONGREVE

1 Music alone with sudden charms can bind
The wand'ring sense, and calm the troubled mind.
Hymn to Harmony

2 Ah! Madam, . . . you know every thing in the world
but your perfections, and you only know not
those, because 'tis the top of perfection not to
know them. *Incognita*

3 I am always of the opinion with the learned, if they
speak first. *Ib.*

4 For 'tis some virtue, virtue to commend.
To Sir Godfrey Kneller

5 But soon as e'er the beauteous idiot spoke,
Forth from her coral lips such folly broke,
Like balm the trickling nonsense heal'd my wound,
And what her eyes enthral'd, her tongue unbound.
Lesbia

6 I confess freely to you, I could never look long upon
a monkey, without very mortifying reflections.
*Letter to Dennis, concerning Humour in Comedy,
1695*

7 If I can give that Cerberus a sop, I shall be at rest
for one day. *Love for Love*, I. iv

8 I warrant you, if he danced till doomsday, he thought
I was to pay the piper. *Ib.* II. v

9 Ferdinand Mendez Pinto was but a type of thee, thou
liar of the first magnitude. *Ib.*

10 Has he not a rogue's face? . . . a hanging-look
to me . . . has a damn'd Tyburn-face, without the
benefit o' the Clergy. . . . *Ib.* vii

11 I came upstairs into the world; for I was born in a
cellar. *Ib.*

12 What, wouldst thou have me turn pelican, and feed
thee out of my own vitals? *Ib.*

13 Oh fie, Miss, you must not kiss and tell. *Ib.* x

14 He that first cries out stop thief, is often he that has
stoln the treasure. *Ib.* III. xiv

15 Women are like tricks by slight of hand,
Which, to admire, we should not understand.
Ib. IV. xxi

16 A branch of one of your antediluvian families,
fellows that the flood could not wash away.
Ib. v. ii

17 To find a young fellow that is neither a wit in his
own eye, nor a fool in the eye of the world, is a
very hard task. *Ib.*

18 Music has charms to sooth a savage breast.
The Mourning Bride, I. i

19 How reverend is the face of this tall pile,
Whose ancient pillars rear their marble heads,
To bear aloft its arch'd and pond'rous roof,
By its own weight made stedfast and immoveable,
Looking tranquillity. It strikes an awe
And terror on my aching sight. *Ib.* II. iii

20 Heav'n has no rage, like love to hatred turn'd,
Nor Hell a fury, like a woman scorn'd. *Ib.* III. viii

21 ⸻⸻ Is he then dead?
What, dead at last, quite, quite for ever dead!
Ib. v. xi

22 In my conscience I believe the baggage loves me,
for she never speaks well of me her self, nor
suffers any body else to rail at me.
The Old Bachelor, I. i

23 One of love's April-fools. *Ib.*

24 The Devil watches all opportunities. *Ib.* vi

25 Man was by Nature Woman's cully made:
We never are, but by ourselves, betrayed. *Ib.* III. i

26 Bilbo's the word, and slaughter will ensue.
Ib. vii

27 Ask all the tyrants of thy sex, if their fools are not
known by this party-coloured livery—I am
melancholy when thou art absent; look like an ass
when thou art present; wake for thee, when I
should sleep, and even dream of thee, when I am
awake; sigh much, drink little, eat less, court
solitude, am grown very entertaining to my self,
and (as I am informed) very troublesome to everybody else. If this be not love, it is madness, and
then it is pardonable—Nay yet a more certain sign
than all this; I give thee my money. *Ib.* x

28 Eternity was in that moment. *Ib.* IV. vii

29 You were about to tell me something, child—but
you left off before you began. *Ib.* viii

30 Now am I slap-dash down in the mouth. *Ib.* ix.

31 Well, Sir Joseph, you have such a winning way with
you. *Ib.* v. vii

32 SHARPER.
Thus grief still treads upon the heels of pleasure:
Marry'd in haste, we may repent at leisure.
SETTER.
Some by experience find those words mis-plac'd:
At leisure marry'd, they repent in haste.
Ib. viii *and* ix

33 I could find it in my heart to marry thee, purely to
be rid of thee. *Ib.* x

34 Courtship to marriage, as a very witty prologue to
a very dull Play. *Ib.*

35 O Sleep, why dost thou leave me?
Why thy visionary joys remove?
O Sleep, again deceive me,
To my arms restore my wand'ring Love.
Semele, II. ii

36 Whom she refuses, she treats still
With so much sweet behaviour,
That her refusal, through her skill,
Looks almost like a favour. *Song: Doris*

37 False though she be to me and love,
I'll ne'er pursue revenge;
For still the charmer I approve,
Tho' I deplore her change.
Song: False Though She Be

38 Wou'd I were free from this restraint,
Or else had hopes to win her;
Wou'd she cou'd make of me a saint,
Or I of her a sinner.
Song: Pious Selinda Goes to Prayers

39 Alack he's gone the way of all flesh.
'Squire Bickerstaff Detected. (Attr. to Congreve)

40 Say what you will, 'tis better to be left than never to
have been loved. *The Way of the World*, II. i

1 Here she comes i' faith full sail, with her fan spread and streamers out, and a shoal of fools for tenders.
The Way of the World, II. iv

2 O ay, letters—I had letters—I am persecuted with letters—I hate letters—no body knows how to write letters; and yet one has 'em, one does not know why—They serve one to pin up one's hair. . . .
Ib.

3 WITWOUD.
Pray, Madam, do you pin up your hair with all your letters: I find I must keep copies.
MILLAMANT.
Only with those in verse, Mr. Witwoud. I never pin up my hair with prose.
Ib.

4 MILLAMANT.
I believe I gave you some pain.
MIRABEL.
Does that please you?
MILLAMANT.
Infinitely; I love to give pain.
MIRABEL.
You wou'd affect a cruelty which is not in your nature; your true vanity is in the power of pleasing.
MILLAMANT.
O I ask your pardon for that—one's cruelty is one's power, and when one parts with one's cruelty, one parts with one's power; and when one has parted with that, I fancy one's old and ugly. *Ib.*

5 Beauty is the lover's gift. *Ib.*

6 Lord, what is a lover, that it can give? Why one makes lovers as fast as one pleases, and they live as long as one pleases, and they die as soon as one pleases: and then if one pleases one makes more.
Ib.

7 Fools never wear out—they are such *drap-de-berry* things.
Ib. III. x

8 Love's but a frailty of the mind
When 'tis not with ambition join'd. *Ib.* xii

9 O, nothing is more alluring than a levee from a couch in some confusion.
Ib. IV. i

10 I nauseate walking; 'tis a country diversion, I loathe the country.
Ib. iv

11 O, I hate a lover that can dare to think he draws a moment's air, independent on the bounty of his mistress. There is not so impudent a thing in Nature, as the saucy look of an assured man, confident of success.
Ib. v

12 My dear liberty, shall I leave thee? My faithful solitude, my darling contemplation, must I bid you then adieu? Ay-h adieu—My morning thoughts, agreeable wakings, indolent slumbers, all ye *douceurs*, ye *sommeils du matin*, adieu—I can't do't, 'tis more than impossible.
Ib.

13 Don't let us be familiar or fond, nor kiss before folks, like my Lady Fadler and Sir Francis: Nor go to Hyde-Park together the first Sunday in a new chariot, to provoke eyes and whispers, and then never be seen there together again; as if we were proud of one another the first week, and asham'd of one another ever after. . . . Let us be very strange and well-bred: Let us be as strange as if we had been married a great while, and as well-bred as if we were not married at all. *Ib.*

14 These articles subscrib'd, if I continue to endure you a little longer, I may by degrees dwindle into a wife.
The Way of the World, IV. v

15 O horrid provisos! *Ib.*

16 Wilfull will do't. *Ib.* x

17 I hope you do not think me prone to any iteration of nuptials.
Ib. xii

T. W. CONNOR
nineteenth century

18 She was one of the early birds,
And I was one of the worms.
She Was A Dear Little Dickie-bird

HENRY CONSTABLE
1562–1613

19 Diaphenia, like the daffadowndilly,
White as the sun, fair as the lily,
Heigh ho, how I do love thee!
I do love thee as my lambs
Are beloved of their dams;
How blest were I if thou wouldst prove me!
[*Damelus' Song to his*] *Diaphenia*

CONSTANTINE
288?–337

20 In hoc signo vinces.
In this sign shalt thou conquer.
Words of Constantine's vision. Eusebius, *Life of Constantine*, i. 28

ELIZA COOK
1818–1889

21 I love it, I love it; and who shall dare
To chide me for loving that old arm-chair?
The Old Arm-chair

22 Better build schoolrooms for 'the boy',
Than cells and gibbets for 'the man'.
A Song for the Ragged Schools

CALVIN COOLIDGE
1872–1933

23 I do not choose to run for President in 1928.
Announcement in 1927

24 He said he was against it.
On being asked what had been said by a clergyman who preached on sin

25 The business of America is business.
Speech before Society of American Newspaper Editors, 17 Jan. 1925

26 They hired the money, didn't they?
With reference to the war debts incurred by England and others (1925)

SIR A. DUFF COOPER (VISCOUNT NORWICH)
1890–1954

27 Not lust of conquest but love of order is at the basis of Empire.
United Empire (1948)

GEORGE COOPER
1840–1927

1 O Genevieve, sweet Genevieve,
The days may come, the days may go,
But still the hands of mem'ry weave
The blissful dreams of long ago.   *Sweet Genevieve*

JAMES FENIMORE COOPER
1789–1851

2 The Last of the Mohicans.   *Title of Novel*

BISHOP RICHARD CORBET
1582–1635

3 Farewell rewards and fairies.   *The Fairy's Farewell*

4   Who of late for cleanliness,
Finds sixpence in her shoe?   *Ib.*

5 Let others write for glory or reward,
Truth is well paid when she is sung and heard.
    Elegy on Lord Howard, Baron of Effingham

PIERRE CORNEILLE
1606–1684

6 À vaincre sans péril, on triomphe sans gloire.
    When there is no peril in the fight, there is no glory
    in the triumph.   *Le Cid,* ii. 2

7 Faites votre devoir et laissez faire aux dieux.
    Do your duty, and leave the issue to the Gods.
    Horace, ii. 8

FRANCES CROFTS CORNFORD
1886–1960

8 A young Apollo, golden-haired,
Stands dreaming on the verge of strife,
Magnificently unprepared
For the long littleness of life.   *Rupert Brooke*

9 O fat white woman whom nobody loves,
Why do you walk through the fields in gloves,
         .   .   .   .
Missing so much and so much?
    To a Fat Lady Seen from a Train

FRANCIS MACDONALD CORNFORD
1874–1943

10 Every public action which is not customary, either is
wrong or, if it is right, is a dangerous precedent.
It follows that nothing should ever be done for the
first time.   *Microcosmographia Academica,* vii

MME CORNUEL
1605–1694

11 Il n'y a point de héros pour son valet de chambre.
    No man is a hero to his valet.
    Lettres de Mlle Aïssé, xii, 13 août 1728

BARRY CORNWALL
[BRYAN WALLER PROCTER]
1787–1874

12 The sea! the sea! the open sea!
The blue, the fresh, the ever free!   *The Sea*

CORONATION SERVICE

13 We present you with this Book, the most valuable
thing that this world affords. Here is wisdom; this
is the royal Law; these are the lively Oracles of
God.   *The Presenting of the Holy Bible*

ANTONIO CORREGGIO
1494–1534

14 Anch' io sono pittore!
    I, too, am a painter.
    *On seeing Raphael's 'St. Cecilia' at Bologna, c.
    1525*

WILLIAM JOHNSON CORY
1823–1892

15 They told me, Heraclitus, they told me you were
dead,
They brought me bitter news to hear and bitter tears
to shed.   *Heraclitus*

16   How often you and I
Had tired the sun with talking and sent him down
the sky.   *Ib.*

17 A handful of grey ashes, long long ago at rest.   *Ib.*

18 You promise heavens free from strife.
    Mimnermus in Church

19 This warm kind world is all I know.   *Ib.*

20 But oh, the very reason why
I clasp them, is because they die.   *Ib.*

NATHANIEL COTTON
1705–1788

21 Yet still we hug the dear deceit.   *Visions,* iv, *Content*

ÉMILE COUÉ
1857–1926

22 Tous les jours, à tous points de vue, je vais de mieux
en mieux.
    Every day, in every way, I am getting better and
    better.   *Formula in his clinic at Nancy*

VICTOR COUSIN
1792–1867

23 L'art pour l'art.
    Art for art's sake.   *Lecture at the Sorbonne*

THOMAS COVENTRY, BARON COVENTRY
1578–1640

24 The wooden walls are the best walls of this kingdom.
    *Speech to the Judges, 17 June 1635, given in
    Rushworth's Hist. Coll.* (1680), *vol. ii, p. 297*

NOEL COWARD
1899–

25 Mad dogs and Englishmen go out in the mid-day sun;
The Japanese don't care to, the Chinese wouldn't
dare to;
Hindus and Argentines sleep firmly from twelve to
one,
But Englishmen detest a siesta.
    Mad Dogs and Englishmen

ABRAHAM COWLEY
1618–1667

1 Love in her sunny eyes does basking play;
Love walks the pleasant mazes of her hair;
Love does on both her lips for ever stray;
And sows and reaps a thousand kisses there.
In all her outward parts Love's always seen;
But, oh, he never went within. *The Change*

2 Nothing is there to come, and nothing past,
But an eternal Now does always last.
Davideis, bk. i, l. 361

3 Poet and Saint! to thee alone are given
The two most sacred names of earth and Heaven.
On the Death of Mr. Crashaw

4 Thou
Wert living the same poet which thou'rt now,
Whilst Angels sing to thee their airs dívine,
And joy in an applause so great as thine.
Equal society with them to hold,
Thou need'st not make new songs, but say the old.
Ib.

5 His faith perhaps, in some nice tenents might
Be wrong; his life, I'm sure, was in the right. *Ib.*

6 Hail, Bard triumphant! and some care bestow
On us, the Poets Militant below! *Ib.*

7 The thirsty earth soaks up the rain,
And drinks, and gapes for drink again.
The plants suck in the earth, and are
With constant drinking fresh and fair. *Drinking*

8 Fill all the glasses there, for why
Should every creature drink but I,
Why, man of morals, tell me why? *Ib.*

9 God the first garden made, and the first city Cain.
The Garden

10 Ye fields of Cambridge, our dear Cambridge, say,
Have ye not seen us walking every day?
Was there a tree about which did not know
The love betwixt us two? *On William Harvey*

11 The world's a scene of changes, and to be
Constant, in Nature were inconstancy. *Inconstancy*

12 Well then; I now do plainly see
This busy world and I shall ne'er agree;
The very honey of all earthly joy
Does of all meats the soonest cloy,
And they (methinks) deserve my pity,
Who for it can endure the stings,
The crowd, and buz, and murmurings
Of this great hive, the city.
The Mistress, or Love Verses

13 Ah, yet, e'er I descend to th' grave
May I a small house, and large garden have!
And a few friends, and many books, both true,
Both wise, and both delightful too!
And since Love ne'er will from me flee,
A Mistress moderately fair,
And good as guardian angels are,
Only belov'd, and loving me! *Ib.*

14 What shall I do to be for ever known,
And make the age to come my own? *The Motto*

15 This only grant me, that my means may lie
Too low for envy, for contempt too high.
Of Myself

16 Acquaintance I would have, but when't depends
Not on the number, but the choice of friends.
Of Myself

17 I would not fear nor wish my fate,
But boldly say each night,
To-morrow let my sun his beams display,
Or in clouds hide them; I have lived to-day. *Ib.*

18 Nothing so soon the drooping spirits can raise
As praises from the men, whom all men praise.
Ode upon a Copy of Verses of My Lord Broghill's

19 Who lets slip Fortune, her shall never find.
Occasion once pass'd by, is bald behind.
Pyramus and Thisbe, xv

20 Lukewarmness I account a sin
As great in love as in religion. *The Request*

21 Life is an incurable disease. *To Dr. Scarborough*, vi

22 Let but thy wicked men from out thee go,
And all the fools that crowd thee so,
Even thou, who dost thy millions boast,
A village less than Islington wilt grow,
A solitude almost. *Of Solitude*, xii

23 The Dangers of an Honest Man in much Company.
*Discourses by Way of Essays, in Verse and
Prose*, 8, title

24 Hence, ye profane; I hate ye all;
Both the great vulgar, and the small.
Trans. of Horace, bk. iii, ode 1

HANNAH COWLEY
1743–1809

25 Five minutes! Zounds! I have been five minutes too
late all my life-time! *The Belle's Stratagem*, 1. i

26 Vanity, like murder, will out. *Ib.* iv

27 But what is woman?—only one of Nature's agreeable
blunders. *Who's the Dupe?*, 11

WILLIAM COWPER
1731–1800

28 Let my obedience then excuse
My disobedience now. *Beau's Reply*

29 When the British warrior queen,
Bleeding from the Roman rods,
Sought with an indignant mien,
Counsel of her country's gods,

Sage beneath a spreading oak
Sat the Druid, hoary chief. *Boadicea*

30 Rome shall perish—write that word
In the blood that she has spilt. *Ib.*

31 Hark! the Gaul is at her gates! *Ib.*

32 Regions Caesar never knew
Thy posterity shall sway,
Where his eagles never flew,
None invincible as they. *Ib.*

33 Ruffians, pitiless as proud,
Heav'n awards the vengeance due;
Empire is on us bestow'd,
Shame and ruin wait for you. *Ib.*

COWPER

1 Obscurest night involv'd the sky,
  Th' Atlantic billows roar'd,
When such a destin'd wretch as I,
  Wash'd headlong from on board,
Of friends, of hope, of all bereft,
His floating home for ever left.   *The Castaway*

2 But misery still delights to trace
Its semblance in another's case.   *Ib.*

3   We perish'd, each alone:
But I beneath a rougher sea,
And whelm'd in deeper gulphs than he.   *Ib.*

4 Truth is the golden girdle of the globe.   *Charity*, l. 86

5 Grief is itself a med'cine.   *Ib.* l. 159

6 He found it inconvenient to be poor.   *Ib.* l. 189

7 India's spicy shores.   *Ib.* l. 442

8 Pelting each other for the public good.   *Ib.* l. 623

9 Spare the poet for his subject's sake.   *Ib.* l. 636

10 But strive to be a man before your mother.
  Motto to Connoisseur, No. 111

11 Not more distinct from harmony divine,
The constant creaking of a country sign.
  Conversation, l. 9

12 Though syllogisms hang not on my tongue,
I am not surely always in the wrong!
'Tis hard if all is false that I advance—
A fool must now and then be right, by chance.
  Ib. l. 93

13 But still remember, if you mean to please,
To press your point with modesty and ease.
  Ib. l. 103

14 A noisy man is always in the right.   *Ib.* l. 114

15 A moral, sensible, and well-bred man
Will not affront me, and no other can.   *Ib.* l. 193

16 A tale should be judicious, clear, succinct;
The language plain, and incidents well link'd;
Tell not as new what ev'ry body knows;
And, new or old, still hasten to a close.   *Ib.* l. 235

17 The pipe, with solemn interposing puff,
Makes half a sentence at a time enough;
The dozing sages drop the drowsy strain,
Then pause, and puff—and speak, and pause again.
  Ib. l. 245

18 Pernicious weed! whose scent the fair annoys,
Unfriendly to society's chief joys,
Thy worst effect is banishing for hours
The sex whose presence civilizes ours.   *Ib.* l. 251

19 A fine puss-gentleman that's all perfume.   *Ib.* l. 284

20 His wit invites you by his looks to come,
But when you knock it never is at home.   *Ib.* l. 303

21 Our wasted oil unprofitably burns,
Like hidden lamps in old sepulchral urns.   *Ib.* l. 357

22 Whose only fit companion is his horse.   *Ib.* l. 412

23 A poet does not work by square or line.   *Ib.* l. 789

24   What appears
In England's case to move the muse to tears?
  Expostulation, l. 1

25 Th' embroid'ry of poetic dreams.   *Ib.* l. 234

26 War lays a burden on the reeling state,
And peace does nothing to relieve the weight.
  Ib. l. 306

27 The busy trifler.   *Expostulation*, l. 322

28 A pick-lock to a place.   *Ib.* l. 379

29   Thousands ...
Kiss the book's outside who ne'er look within.
  Ib. l. 389

30 Religion, if in heav'nly truths attir'd,
Needs only to be seen to be admired.   *Ib.* l. 492

31 The man that hails you Tom or Jack,
And proves by thumps upon your back
  How he esteems your merit,
Is such a friend, that one had need
Be very much his friend indeed
  To pardon or to bear it.   *Friendship*

32 John Gilpin was a citizen
  Of credit and renown,
A train-band captain eke was he
  Of famous London town.

John Gilpin's spouse said to her dear—
  Though wedded we have been
These twice ten tedious years, yet we
  No holiday have seen.   *John Gilpin*

33 To-morrow is our wedding-day,
  And we will then repair
Unto the Bell at Edmonton
  All in a chaise and pair.

My sister and my sister's child,
  Myself and children three,
Will fill the chaise; so you must ride
  On horseback after we.   *Ib.*

34 He soon replied—I do admire
  Of womankind but one,
And you are she, my dearest dear,
  Therefore it shall be done.

I am a linen-draper bold,
  As all the world doth know,
And my good friend the calender
  Will lend his horse to go.   *Ib.*

35   O'erjoy'd was he to find
That, though on pleasure she was bent,
  She had a frugal mind.   *Ib.*

36   And all agog
To dash through thick and thin!   *Ib.*

37 John Gilpin at his horse's side
  Seiz'd fast the flowing mane,
And up he got, in haste to ride,
  But soon came down again.   *Ib.*

38 So down he came; for loss of time,
  Although it griev'd him sore,
Yet loss of pence, full well he knew,
  Would trouble him much more.   *Ib.*

39 Good lack! quoth he—yet bring it me,
  My leathern belt likewise,
In which I bear my trusty sword
  When I do exercise.   *Ib.*

40 So, fair and softly, John he cried,
  But John he cried in vain.   *Ib.*

41 So stooping down, as needs he must
  Who cannot sit upright,
He grasp'd the mane with both his hands,
  And eke with all his might.   *Ib.*

1 His horse, who never in that sort
  Had handled been before,
What thing upon his back had got
  Did wonder more and more.

Away went Gilpin, neck or nought,
  Away went hat and wig!   *John Gilpin*

2 The dogs did bark, the children scream'd.
  Up flew the windows all;
And ev'ry soul cried out—Well done!
  As loud as he could bawl.

Away went Gilpin—who but he?
  His fame soon spread around—
He carries weight! he rides a race!
  'Tis for a thousand pound!   *Ib.*

3 The dinner waits, and we are tired:
  Said Gilpin—So am I   *Ib.*

4   Which brings me to
The middle of my song.   *Ib.*

5 My hat and wig will soon be here—
  They are upon the road.   *Ib.*

6 The calender, right glad to find
  His friend in merry pin.   *Ib.*

7 My head is twice as big as yours,
  They therefore needs must fit.   *Ib.*

8 Said John—It is my wedding-day,
  And all the world would stare,
If wife should dine at Edmonton
  And I should dine at Ware.   *Ib.*

9 'Twas for your pleasure you came here,
  You shall go back for mine.   *Ib.*

10 Nor stopp'd till where he had got up
  He did again get down.   *Ib.*

11 Now let us sing—Long live the king,
  And Gilpin long live he;
And, when he next doth ride abroad,
  May I be there to see!   *Ib.*

12 An honest man, close-button'd to the chin,
Broad-cloth without, and a warm heart within.
          Epistle to Jos. Hill, l. 62

13 No dancing bear was so genteel,
  Or half so dégagé.   *Of Himself*

14 Painful passage o'er a restless flood.   *Hope*, l. 3

15 Men deal with life as children with their play,
Who first misuse, then cast their toys away.
          Ib. l. 127

16 Some eastward, and some westward, and all wrong.
          Ib. l. 281

17 Could he with reason murmur at his case,
Himself sole author of his own disgrace?   *Ib.* l. 316

18 And diff'ring judgements serve but to declare
That truth lies somewhere, if we knew but where.
          Ib. l. 423

19 Seek to delight, that they may mend mankind,
And, while they captivate, inform the mind.
          Ib. l. 758

20 Absence from whom we love is worse than death,
And frustrate hope severer than despair.
          'Hope, Like the Short-Liv'd Ray'

21 The twentieth year is well-nigh past,
Since first our sky was overcast;
Ah would that this might be the last!
          My Mary!   *To Mary*

22 Thy needles, once a shining store,
For my sake restless heretofore,
Now rust disus'd, and shine no more,
          My Mary!   *Ib.*

23 Partakers of thy sad decline,
Thy hands their little force resign;
Yet, gently prest, press gently mine,
          My Mary!   *Ib.*

24 Greece, sound thy Homer's, Rome thy Virgil's name,
But England's Milton equals both in fame.
          To John Milton

25 Oh that those lips had language! Life has pass'd
With me but roughly since I heard thee last.
Those lips are thine—thy own sweet smiles I see,
The same that oft in childhood solac'd me.
          On the Receipt of My Mother's Picture, l. 1

26 Blest be the art that can immortalize.   *Ib.* l. 8

27 Wretch even then, life's journey just begun.   *Ib.* l. 24

28 Perhaps thou gav'st me, though unseen, a kiss;
Perhaps a tear, if souls can weep in bliss.   *Ib.* l. 25

29 Disappointed still, was still deceiv'd.   *Ib.* l. 39

30 Where once we dwelt our name is heard no more,
Children not thine have trod my nursery floor;
And where the gard'ner Robin, day by day,
Drew me to school along the public way,
Delighted with my bauble coach, and wrapt
In scarlet mantle warm, and velvet capt,
'Tis now become a history little known.   *Ib.* l. 46

31 Thy morning bounties ere I left my home,
The biscuit, or confectionary plum.   *Ib.* l. 60

32 The fragrant waters on my cheek bestow'd.   *Ib.* l. 62

33 Not scorn'd in heaven, though little notic'd here.
          Ib. l. 73

34   I should ill requite thee to constrain
Thy unbound spirit into bonds again.   *Ib.* l. 86

35 Me howling winds drive devious, tempest toss'd,
Sails ript, seams op'ning wide, and compass lost.
          Ib. l. 102

36 Some people are more nice than wise.
          Mutual Forbearance, l. 20

37 Oh, fond attempt to give a deathless lot
To names ignoble, born to be forgot!
          *On Observing Some Names of Little Note
          Recorded in the Biographia Britannica*

38 There goes the parson, oh! illustrious spark,
And there, scarce less illustrious, goes the clerk! *Ib.*

39 Thought again—but knew not what to think.
          The Needless Alarm, l. 54

40 Beware of desp'rate steps. The darkest day
(Live till to-morrow) will have pass'd away.
          Ib. l. 132

41 Hence jarring sectaries may learn
Their real int'rest to discern;
That brother should not war with brother,
And worry and devour each other.
          The Nightingale and Glow-Worm

COWPER

1 Oh! for a closer walk with God,
  A calm and heav'nly frame;
A light to shine upon the road
  That leads me to the Lamb! *Olney Hymns, 1*

2 What peaceful hours I once enjoy'd!
  How sweet their mem'ry still!
But they have left an aching void,
  The world can never fill. *Ib.*

3 The dearest idol I have known,
  Whate'er that idol be;
Help me to tear it from thy Throne,
  And worship only thee. *Ib.*

4 Nor sword nor spear the stripling took,
But chose a pebble from the brook. *Ib. 4*

5 O make this heart rejoice, or ache;
  Decide this doubt for me;
And if it be not broken, break,
  And heal it, if it be. *Ib. 9*

6 So unaccustom'd to the yoke,
So backward to comply. *Ib. 12*

7 There is a fountain fill'd with blood. *Ib. 15*

8 When this poor lisping stammering tongue
Lies silent in the grave. *Ib.*

9 Hark, my soul! it is the Lord;
'Tis thy Saviour, hear his word;
Jesus speaks, and speaks to thee;
'Say, poor sinner, lov'st thou me?' *Ib. 18*

10 I deliver'd thee when bound,
And, when bleeding, heal'd thy wound;
Sought thee wand'ring, set thee right,
Turn'd thy darkness into light. *Ib.*

11 'Can a woman's tender care
Cease, towards the child she bare?
Yes, she may forgetful be,
Yet will I remember thee.' *Ib.*

12 Mine is an unchanging love,
Higher than the heights above;
Deeper than the depths beneath,
Free and faithful, strong as death. *Ib.*

13 Lord, it is my chief complaint,
That my love is weak and faint;
Yet I love thee and adore,
Oh for grace to love thee more! *Ib.*

14 What various hindrances we meet
In coming to a mercy-seat! *Ib. 29*

15 And Satan trembles, when he sees
The weakest saint upon his knees. *Ib.*

16 While Moses stood with arms spread wide,
Success was found on Israel's side;
But when thro' weariness they fail'd,
That moment Amalek prevail'd. *Ib.*

17 I seem forsaken and alone,
  I hear the lion roar;
And ev'ry door is shut but one,
  And that is mercy's door. *Ib. 33*

18 God moves in a mysterious way
  His wonders to perform;
He plants his footsteps in the sea,
  And rides upon the storm.

Deep in unfathomable mines
  Of never failing skill
He treasures up his bright designs,
  And works his sovereign will.

Ye fearful saints fresh courage take,
  The clouds ye so much dread
Are big with mercy, and shall break
  In blessings on your head.

Judge not the Lord by feeble sense,
  But trust him for his grace;
Behind a frowning providence
  He hides a smiling face. *Olney Hymns, 35*

19 The bud may have a bitter taste,
  But sweet will be the flow'r. *Ib.*

20 Blind unbelief is sure to err,
  And scan his work in vain;
God is his own interpreter,
  And he will make it plain. *Ib.*

21 Sometimes a light surprises
  The Christian while he sings;
It is the Lord who rises
  With healing in his wings;
When comforts are declining,
  He grants the soul again
A season of clear shining
  To cheer it after rain. *Ib. 44*

22 I shall not ask Jean Jacques Rousseau,
If birds confabulate or no. *Pairing Time Anticipated*

23 The poplars are fell'd, farewell to the shade
And the whispering sound of the cool colonnade.
  The Poplar-Field

24 Unmiss'd but by his dogs and by his groom.
  Progress of Error, l. 95

25 Oh, laugh or mourn with me the rueful jest,
A cassock'd huntsman and a fiddling priest!
  Ib. l. 110

26 Himself a wand'rer from the narrow way,
His silly sheep, what wonder if they stray? *Ib. l. 118*

27 Remorse, the fatal egg by pleasure laid. *Ib. l. 239*

28 Woman, lovely woman, does the same. *Ib. l. 274*

29 Caesar's image is effac'd at last. *Ib. l. 280*

30 As creeping ivy clings to wood or stone,
And hides the ruin that it feeds upon. *Ib. l. 285*

31 How much a dunce that has been sent to roam
Excels a dunce that has been kept at home. *Ib. l. 415*

32 Talks of darkness at noon-day. *Ib. l. 451*

33 Thou god of our idolatry, the press. *Ib. l. 461*

34 The nobler tenants of the flood. *Ib. l. 482*

35 Laugh at all you trembled at before. *Ib. l. 592*

36 Pleasure is labour too, and tires as much.
  Hope, l. 20

37 He blam'd and protested, but join'd in the plan;
He shar'd in the plunder, but pitied the man.
  Pity for Poor Africans

38 Then, shifting his side, (as a lawyer knows how).
  Report of an Adjudged Case

39 But vers'd in arts that, while they seem to stay
A falling empire, hasten its decay. *Retirement, l. 383*

40 The disencumber'd Atlas of the state. *Ib. l. 394*

41 Prison'd in a parlour snug and small,
Like bottled wasps upon a southern wall. *Ib. l. 493*

42 Play the fool, but at a cheaper rate. *Ib. l. 562*

1 He likes the country, but in truth must own,
Most likes it, when he studies it in town.
Retirement, l. 573

2   Philologists who chase
A panting syllable through time and space,
Start it at home, and hunt it in the dark,
To Gaul, to Greece, and into Noah's ark. *Ib.* l. 619

3 Absence of occupation is not rest,
A mind quite vacant is a mind distress'd. *Ib.* l. 623

4 [Voltaire:]
Built God a church, and laugh'd his word to scorn.
Ib. l. 688

5 Beggars invention and makes fancy lame. *Ib.* l. 709

6 I praise the Frenchman, his remark was shrewd—
How sweet, how passing sweet, is solitude!
But grant me still a friend in my retreat,
Whom I may whisper—solitude is sweet. *Ib.* l. 739

7 Fast by the banks of the slow winding Ouse.
Ib. l. 804

8 The tear that is wip'd with a little address,
May be follow'd perhaps by a smile. *The Rose*

9 Toll for the brave—
    The brave! that are no more:
All sunk beneath the wave,
    Fast by their native shore.
Loss of the Royal George

10 A land-breeze shook the shrouds,
    And she was overset;
Down went the Royal George,
    With all her crew complete. *Ib.*

11 Toll for the brave—
    Brave Kempenfelt is gone,
His last sea-fight is fought,
    His work of glory done.
It was not in the battle,
    No tempest gave the shock,
She sprang no fatal leak,
    She ran upon no rock;
His sword was in the sheath,
    His fingers held the pen,
When Kempenfelt went down
    With twice four hundred men. *Ib.*

12 Weigh the vessel up,
    Once dreaded by our foes. *Ib.*

13 He and his eight hundred
Must plough the wave no more. *Ib.*

14 Oh, happy shades—to me unblest!
Friendly to peace, but not to me! *The Shrubbery*

15 Chief monster that hast plagued the nations yet.
Table Talk, l. 38

16 The lie that flatters I abhor the most. *Ib.* l. 88

17 Th' unwashed artificer. *Ib.* l. 152

18 As if the world and they were hand and glove.
Ib. l. 173

19 Admirals, extoll'd for standing still,
Or doing nothing with a deal of skill. *Ib.* l. 192

20 The leathern ears of stock-jobbers and Jews.
Ib. l. 197

21 The Frenchman, easy, debonair, and brisk,
Give him his lass, his fiddle, and his frisk,
Is always happy, reign whoever may,
And laughs the sense of mis'ry far away. *Ib.* l. 236

22 Freedom has a thousand charms to show,
That slaves, howe'er contented, never know.
Table Talk, l. 260

23 Stamps God's own name upon a lie just made,
To turn a penny in the way of trade. *Ib.* l. 420

24 Suspend your mad career. *Ib.* l. 435

25 Feels himself spent, and fumbles for his brains.
Ib. l. 537

26 Ages elaps'd ere Homer's lamp appear'd,
And ages ere the Mantuan swan was heard:
To carry nature lengths unknown before,
To give a Milton birth, ask'd ages more. *Ib.* l. 556

27 By low ambition and the thirst of praise. *Ib.* l. 591

28 [Pope:]
But he (his musical finesse was such,
So nice his ear, so delicate his touch)
Made poetry a mere mechanic art;
And ev'ry warbler has his tune by heart. *Ib.* l. 654

29 Pity religion has so seldom found
A skilful guide into poetic ground! *Ib.* l. 716

30 Hail Sternhold, then; and Hopkins, hail! *Ib.* l. 759

31 I sing the Sofa. *The Task*, bk. i, *The Sofa*, l. 1

32 The Fair commands the song. *Ib.* l. 7

33 So sit two kings of Brentford on one throne.
Ib. l. 78

34 Thus first necessity invented stools,
Convenience next suggested elbow-chairs,
And luxury the accomplish'd Sofa last. *Ib.* l. 86

35 The nurse sleeps sweetly, hir'd to watch the sick,
Whom, snoring, she disturbs. *Ib.* l. 89

36 Nor rural sights alone, but rural sounds,
Exhilarate the spirit, and restore
The tone of languid Nature. *Ib.* l. 181

37 Toils much to earn a monumental pile,
That may record the mischiefs he has done.
Ib. l. 276

38 God made the country, and man made the town.
Ib. l. 749

39 There is a public mischief in your mirth. *Ib.* l. 769

40 Oh for a lodge in some vast wilderness,
Some boundless contiguity of shade,
Where rumour of oppression and deceit,
Of unsuccessful or successful war,
Might never reach me more.
Ib. bk. ii, *The Timepiece*, l. 1

41   Mountains interpos'd
Make enemies of nations, who had else,
Like kindred drops, been mingled into one. *Ib.* l. 17

42 Slaves cannot breathe in England, if their lungs
Receive our air, that moment they are free;
They touch our country, and their shackles fall.
Ib. l. 40

43 England, with all thy faults, I love thee still—
My country! *Ib.* l. 206

44 I would not yet exchange thy sullen skies,
And fields without a flow'r, for warmer France
With all her vines. *Ib.* l. 212

45 Presume to lay their hand upon the ark
Of her magnificent and awful cause. *Ib.* l. 231

COWPER

1   Praise enough
To fill th' ambition of a private man,
That Chatham's language was his mother tongue,
And Wolfe's great name compatriot with his own.
         The Task, bk. ii, *The Timepiece*, l. 235

2 Chatham heart-sick of his country's shame.
         Ib. l. 244

3 There is a pleasure in poetic pains
Which only poets know.   *Ib.* l. 285

4 Variety's the very spice of life,
That gives it all its flavour.   *Ib.* l. 606

5   His head,
Not yet by time completely silver'd o'er,
Bespoke him past the bounds of freakish youth,
But strong for service still, and unimpair'd. *Ib.* l. 702

6 Domestic happiness, thou only bliss
Of Paradise that has surviv'd the fall!
         Ib. bk. iii, *The Garden*, l. 41

7 Guilty splendour.   *Ib.* l. 70

8 I was a stricken deer, that left the herd
Long since.   *Ib.* l. 108

9   Charge
His mind with meanings that he never had.
         Ib. l. 148

10 Great contest follows, and much learned dust
Involves the combatants.   *Ib.* l. 161

11 From reveries so airy, from the toil
Of dropping buckets into empty wells,
And growing old in drawing nothing up! *Ib.* l. 188

12 Exercise all functions of a man.   *Ib.* l. 198

13   Newton, childlike sage!
Sagacious reader of the works of God.   *Ib.* l. 252

14 Riches have wings.   *Ib.* l. 263

15 The only amaranthine flower on earth
Is virtue.   *Ib.* l. 268

16   Detested sport,
That owes its pleasures to another's pain.   *Ib.* l. 326

17 Studious of laborious ease.   *Ib.* l. 361

18 Who loves a garden loves a greenhouse too.
         Ib. l. 566

19 To combat may be glorious, and success
Perhaps may crown us; but to fly is safe.   *Ib.* l. 686

20 He comes, the herald of a noisy world,
With spatter'd boots, strapp'd waist, and frozen locks;
News from all nations lumb'ring at his back.
         Ib. bk. iv, *The Winter Evening*, l. 5

21 Now stir the fire, and close the shutters fast,
Let fall the curtains, wheel the sofa round,
And, while the bubbling and loud-hissing urn
Throws up a steamy column, and the cups,
That cheer but not inebriate, wait on each,
So let us welcome peaceful ev'ning in.   *Ib.* l. 34

22 Katterfelto, with his hair on end
At his own wonders, wond'ring for his bread.
         Ib. l. 85

23 'Tis pleasant through the loopholes of retreat
To peep at such a world; to see the stir
Of the great Babel, and not feel the crowd. *Ib.* l. 88

24 O Winter, ruler of th' inverted year.   *Ib.* l. 120

25 I love thee, all unlovely as thou seem'st
And dreaded as thou art.
         The Task, bk. iv, *The Winter Evening*, l. 128

26 I crown thee king of intimate delights,
Fire-side enjoyments, home-born happiness.
         Ib. l. 139

27   A Roman meal;
. . . . . .
a radish and an egg.   *Ib.* ll. 168–73

28 The slope of faces, from the floor to th' roof,
(As if one master-spring controll'd them all),
Relax'd into a universal grin.   *Ib.* l. 202

29 With spots quadrangular of di'mond form,
Ensanguin'd hearts, clubs typical of strife,
And spades, the emblem of untimely graves.
         Ib. l. 217

30 In indolent vacuity of thought.   *Ib.* l. 297

31 It seems the part of wisdom.   *Ib.* l. 336

32 All learned, and all drunk!   *Ib.* l. 478

33 Gloriously drunk, obey th' important call! *Ib.* l. 510

34 Sidney, warbler of poetic prose.   *Ib.* l. 516

35 I never fram'd a wish, or form'd a plan,
That flatter'd me with hopes of earthly bliss,
But there I laid the scene.   *Ib.* l. 695

36 Entangled in the cobwebs of the schools.   *Ib.* l. 726

37   The fragrant weed,
The Frenchman's darling. [Mignonette.]   *Ib.* l. 764

38 Prepost'rous sight! the legs without the man.
         Ib. bk. v, *The Winter Morning Walk*, l. 20

39 Half lurcher and half cur.   *Ib.* l. 46

40 Silently as a dream the fabric rose;—
No sound of hammer or of saw was there. *Ib.* l. 144

41 Great princes have great playthings.   *Ib.* l. 175

42 But war's a game, which, were their subjects wise,
Kings would not play at.   *Ib.* l. 187

43 And the first smith was the first murd'rer's son.
         Ib. l. 219

44 The beggarly last doit.   *Ib.* l. 316

45   All constraint,
Except what wisdom lays on evil men,
Is evil.   *Ib.* l. 448

46 He is the freeman whom the truth makes free.
         Ib. l. 733

47 Give what thou canst, without thee we are poor;
And with thee rich, take what thou wilt away.
         Ib. l. 905

48 There is in souls a sympathy with sounds;
And, as the mind is pitch'd the ear is pleas'd
With melting airs, or martial, brisk, or grave:
Some chord in unison with what we hear,
Is touch'd within us, and the heart replies.
         Ib. bk. vi, *The Winter Walk at Noon*, l. 1

49   Knowledge dwells
In heads replete with thoughts of other men;
Wisdom in minds attentive to their own.   *Ib.* l. 89

50 Knowledge is proud that he has learn'd so much;
Wisdom is humble that he knows no more. *Ib.* l. 96

51 Books are not seldom talismans and spells. *Ib.* l. 98

52 Nature is but a name for an effect,
Whose cause is God.   *Ib.* l. 223

1 A cheap but wholesome salad from the brook.
   The Task, bk. vi, *The Winter Walk at Noon*, l. 304

2 Anger insignificantly fierce.   *Ib.* l. 320

3 I would not enter on my list of friends
   (Tho' grac'd with polish'd manners and fine sense,
   Yet wanting sensibility) the man
   Who needlessly sets foot upon a worm.   *Ib.* l. 560

4 The crested worm.   *Ib.* l. 780

5   Stillest streams
   Oft water fairest meadows, and the bird
   That flutters least is longest on the wing. *Ib.* l. 929

6 Public schools 'tis public folly feeds.
   Tirocinium, l. 250

7 We love the play-place of our early days. *Ib.* l. 297

8 The little ones, unbutton'd, glowing hot,
   Playing our games, and on the very spot;
   As happy as we once, to kneel and draw
   The chalky ring, and knuckle down at taw;
   To pitch the ball into the grounded hat,
   Or drive it devious with a dex'trous pat. *Ib.* l. 304

9 The parson knows enough who knows a duke.
   Ib. l. 403

10   As a priest,
   A piece of mere church furniture at best. *Ib.* l. 425

11 His fav'rite stand between his father's knees.
   Ib. l. 570

12   Tenants of life's middle state,
   Securely plac'd between the small and great.
   Ib. l. 807

13 If it chance, as sometimes chance it will,
   That, though school-bred, the boy be virtuous still.
   Ib. l. 839

14 Humility may clothe an English dean. *Truth*, l. 118

15 He has no hope who never had a fear.   *Ib.* l. 298

16 Just knows, and knows no more, her Bible true—
   A truth the brilliant Frenchman never knew. [Voltaire.]
   Ib. l. 327

17 Envy, ye great, the dull unletter'd small. *Ib.* l. 375

18 One who wears a coronet, and prays.   *Ib.* l. 378

19 His mind his kingdom, and his will his law.
   Ib. l. 406

20 Mary! I want a lyre with other strings.
   Sonnet to Mrs. Unwin

21 Verse, that immortalizes whom it sings!   *Ib.*

22 I am monarch of all I survey,
   My right there is none to dispute;
   From the centre all round to the sea
   I am lord of the fowl and the brute.
   Oh, solitude! where are the charms
   That sages have seen in thy face?
   Better dwell in the midst of alarms,
   Than reign in this horrible place.
   Verses Supposed to be Written by Alexander Selkirk

23 Never hear the sweet music of speech.   *Ib.*

24 Society, friendship, and love,
   Divinely bestow'd upon man.   *Ib.*

25 But the sound of the church-going bell
   These valleys and rocks never heard,
   Ne'er sigh'd at the sound of a knell,
   Or smil'd when a sabbath appear'd.   *Ib.*

26 [On Johnson's inadequate treatment of *Paradise Lost*]
   Oh! I could thresh his old jacket till I made his
   pension jingle in his pockets.
   Letters, To the Rev. W. Unwin, 31 Oct. 1779

27 Our severest winter, commonly called the spring.
   Ib. 8 June 1783

28 He kissed likewise the maid in the kitchen, and
   seemed upon the whole a most loving, kissing,
   kind-hearted gentleman.
   Ib. To the Rev. J. Newton, 29 Mar. 1784

GEORGE CRABBE
1754–1832

29 What is a church?—Our honest sexton tells,
   'Tis a tall building, with a tower and bells.
   The Borough, letter ii, The Church, l. 11

30 Virtues neglected then, adored become,
   And graces slighted, blossom on the tomb. *Ib.* l. 133

31 Intrigues half-gather'd, conversation-scraps,
   Kitchen-cabals, and nursery-mishaps.
   Ib. letter iii, The Vicar, l. 71

32 Habit with him was all the test of truth,
   'It must be right: I've done it from my youth.'
   Ib. l. 138

33 Lo! the poor toper whose untutor'd sense,
   Sees bliss in ale, and can with wine dispense;
   Whose head proud fancy never taught to steer,
   Beyond the muddy ecstasies of beer.
   Inebriety, l. 120 (*Imitation of Pope*)

34 This, books can do—nor this alone: they give
   New views to life, and teach us how to live;
   They soothe the grieved, the stubborn they chastise;
   Fools they admonish, and confirm the wise.
   Their aid they yield to all: they never shun
   The man of sorrow, nor the wretch undone;
   Unlike the hard, the selfish, and the proud,
   They fly not sullen from the suppliant crowd;
   Nor tell to various people various things,
   But show to subjects, what they show to kings.
   The Library, l. 41

35 Here come the grieved, a change of thought to find,
   The curious here, to feed a craving mind;
   Here the devout their peaceful temple choose;
   And here the poet meets his favouring muse.
   With awe around these silent walks I tread:
   These are the lasting mansions of the dead.
   Ib. l. 101

36 And mighty folios first, a lordly band,
   Then quartos, their well-order'd ranks maintain,
   And light octavos fill a spacious plain;
   See yonder, ranged in more frequented rows,
   A humbler band of duodecimos.   *Ib.* l. 128

37 Hence, in these times, untouch'd the pages lie,
   And slumber out their immortality.   *Ib.* l. 157

38 Fashion, though Folly's child, and guide of fools,
   Rules e'en the wisest, and in learning rules. *Ib.* l. 167

39 Against her foes Religion well defends
   Her sacred truths, but often fears her friends.
   Ib. l. 249

40 Coldly profane, and impiously gay.   *Ib.* l. 265

41 The murmuring poor, who will not fast in peace.
   The Newspaper, l. 158

1 A master passion is the love of news.
The Newspaper, l. 279

2 Hold their glimmering tapers to the sun.
The Parish Register, introd. to pt. 1, l. 92

3 Our farmers round, well pleased with constant gain,
Like other farmers, flourish and complain.
Ib. pt. i, *Baptisms*, l. 273

4 I preach for ever; but I preach in vain!
Ib. pt. ii, *Marriages*, l. 130

5 When from the cradle to the grave I look,
Mine I conceive a melancholy book.
Ib. pt. iii, *Burials*, l. 21

6 Grave Jonas Kindred, Sybil Kindred's sire,
Was six feet high, and look'd six inches higher.
Tales, vi, *The Frank Courtship*, l. 1

7 When the coarse cloth she saw, with many a stain,
Soil'd by rude hinds who cut and came again.
Ib. vii, *The Widow's Tale*, l. 25

8 Who often reads, will sometimes wish to write.
Ib. xi, *Edward Shore*, l. 109

9 The wife was pretty, trifling, childish, weak;
She could not think, but would not cease to speak.
Ib. xiv, *Struggles of Conscience*, l. 343

10 But 'twas a maxim he had often tried,
That right was right, and there he would abide.
Ib. xv, *The Squire and the Priest*, l. 365

11 That all was wrong because not all was right.
Ib. xix, *The Convert*, l. 313

12 He tried the luxury of doing good.
Tales of the Hall, iii, *Boys at School*, l. 139

13 Secrets with girls, like loaded guns with boys,
Are never valued till they make a noise.
Ib. xi, *The Maid's Story*, l. 84

14 'The game', he said, 'is never lost till won.'
Ib. xv, *Gretna Green*, l. 334

15 The face the index of a feeling mind.
Ib. xvi, *Lady Barbara*, l. 124

16 Love warps the mind a little from the right.
Ib. xxi, *Smugglers and Poachers*, l. 216

17 Lo! where the heath, with withering brake grown o'er,
Lends the light turf that warms the neighbouring
poor;
From thence a length of burning sand appears,
Where the thin harvest waves its wither'd ears;
Rank weeds, that every art and care defy,
Reign o'er the land, and rob the blighted rye:
There thistles stretch their prickly arms afar,
And to the ragged infant threaten war;
There poppies, nodding, mock the hope of toil;
There the blue bugloss paints the sterile soil;
Hardy and high, above the slender sheaf,
The slimy mallow waves her silky leaf;
O'er the young shoot the charlock throws a shade,
And clasping tares cling round the sickly blade.
The Village, bk. i, l. 63

18 I sought the simple life that Nature yields. *Ib.* l. 110

19 And the cold charities of man to man. *Ib.* l. 245

20 A potent quack, long versed in human ills,
Who first insults the victim whom he kills;
Whose murd'rous hand a drowsy Bench protect,
And whose most tender mercy is neglect. *Ib.* l. 282

21 The ring so worn, as you behold,
So thin, so pale, is yet of gold:
The passion such it was to prove;
Worn with life's cares, love yet was love.
His Mother's Wedding Ring

MRS. DINAH MARIA CRAIK
1826–1887

22 Douglas, Douglas, tender and true.
Songs of Our Youth, 'Douglas, Douglas, Tender and True'

STEPHEN CRANE
1871–1900

23 The Red Badge of Courage. *Title*

ARCHBISHOP THOMAS CRANMER
1489–1556

24 This hand hath offended.
Strype's *Memorials of Cranmer*, 1694, vol. iii

RICHARD CRASHAW
1612?–1649

25 Nympha pudica Deum vidit, et erubuit.
The conscious water saw its God, and blushed.
Epigrammata Sacra. Aquae in Vinum Versae
(*His own translation.*)

26 All those fair and flagrant things.
The Flaming Heart upon the Book of Saint Teresa, l. 34

27 Love's passives are his activ'st part.
The wounded is the wounding heart. *Ib.* l. 73

28 O thou undaunted daughter of desires! *Ib.* l. 93

29 By all the eagle in thee, all the dove. *Ib.* l. 95

30 By thy large draughts of intellectual day. *Ib.* l. 97

31 By the full kingdom of that final kiss
That seized thy parting soul, and seal'd thee His;
By all the Heavens thou hast in Him—
Fair sister of the Seraphim!—
By all of Him we have in thee;
Leave nothing of myself in me.
Let me so read thy life, that I
Unto all life of mine may die! *Ib.* l. 101

32 I would be married, but I'd have no wife,
I would be married to a single life. *On Marriage*

33 I sing the Name which none can say
But touch'd with an interior ray.
To the Name Above Every Name, l.

34 Narrow, and low, and infinitely less. *Ib.* l. 22

35 Come; and come strong,
To the conspiracy of our spacious song. *Ib.* l. 70

36 Gloomy night embrac'd the place
Where the noble Infant lay.
The Babe look't up and shew'd his face;
In spite of darkness, it was day.
It was Thy day, sweet! and did rise
Not from the East, but from thine eyes.
Hymn of the Nativity, l. 17

1 Poor World (said I) what wilt thou do
To entertain this starry stranger?
Is this the best thou canst bestow?
A cold, and not too cleanly, manger?
Contend, ye powers of heav'n and earth
To fit a bed for this huge birth.
Hymn of the Nativity, l. 37

2 Proud world, said I; cease your contest
And let the mighty Babe alone.
The phoenix builds the phoenix' nest.
Love's architecture is his own. *Ib.* l. 44

3 I saw the curl'd drops, soft and slow,
Come hovering o'er the place's head;
Off'ring their whitest sheets of snow
To furnish the fair Infant's bed.
Forbear, said I; be not too bold.
Your fleece is white but 'tis too cold. *Ib.* l. 50

4 I saw the obsequious Seraphims
Their rosy fleece of fire bestow.
For well they now can spare their wings
Since Heaven itself lies here below.
Well done, said I: but are you sure
Your down so warm, will pass for pure? *Ib.* l. 58

5 We saw thee in thy balmy nest,
Young dawn of our eternal day!
We saw thine eyes break from their East
And chase the trembling shades away.
We saw thee; and we blest the sight
We saw thee by thine own sweet light. *Ib.* l. 71

6 Welcome, all wonders in one sight!
Eternity shut in a span. *Ib.* l. 79

7 Love's great artillery. *Prayer,* l. 15

8 Lo here a little volume, but large book.
On a Prayer-Book Sent to Mrs. M. R.

9 Happy soul, she shall discover
What joy, what bliss,
How many heavens at once it is,
To have a God become her lover. *Ib.*

10 Two walking baths; two weeping motions;
Portable, and compendious oceans.
Saint Mary Magdalene, or The Weeper, xix

11 Love, thou art absolute sole Lord
Of life and death.
Hymn to the Name & Honour of the Admirable Saint Teresa, l. 1

12 Farewell house, and farewell home!
She's for the Moors, and martyrdom. *Ib.* l. 63

13 Two went to pray? O rather say
One went to brag, th'other to pray:

One nearer to God's Altar trod,
The other to the Altar's God.
Steps to the Temple, Two Went up into the Temple to Pray

14 All is Caesar's; and what odds
So long as Caesar's self is God's? *Ib. Mark* 12

15 And when life's sweet fable ends,
Soul and body part like friends;
No quarrels, murmurs, no delay;
A kiss, a sigh, and so away. *Temperance*

16 Why, 'tis a point of faith. Whate'er it be,
I'm sure it is no point of charity.
On a Treatise of Charity

17 Whoe'er she be,
That not impossible she
That shall command my heart and me;

Where'er she lie,
Lock'd up from mortal eye,
In shady leaves of destiny.
Wishes to His Supposed Mistress.

18 Meet you her my wishes,
Bespeak her to my blisses,
And be ye call'd my absent kisses.

I wish her beauty,
That owes not all his duty
To gaudy tire, or glist'ring shoe-tie. *Ib.*

19 Life, that dares send
A challenge to his end,
And when it comes say 'Welcome Friend'. *Ib.*

20 Sydnaean showers
Of sweet discourse, whose powers
Can crown old Winter's head with flowers. *Ib.*

21 'Tis she, and here
Lo I unclothe and clear,
My wishes' cloudy character. *Ib.*

22 Let her full Glory,
My fancies, fly before ye,
Be ye my fictions; but her story. *Ib.*

MRS. EDMUND CRASTER
d. 1874

23 The Centipede was happy quite,
Until the Toad in fun
Said 'Pray which leg goes after which?'
And worked her mind to such a pitch,
She lay distracted in the ditch
Considering how to run. *Attrib.*

JULIA CRAWFORD
fl. 1835

24 Kathleen Mavourneen! the grey dawn is breaking,
The horn of the hunter is heard on the hill;
The lark from her light wing the bright dew is shaking;
Kathleen Mavourneen! what, slumbering still?
Oh! hast thou forgotten how soon we must sever?
Oh! hast thou forgotten this day we must part?
It may be for years, and it may be for ever,
Oh! why art thou silent, thou voice of my heart?
Kathleen Mavourneen. Metropolitan Magazine,
London, 1835

BISHOP MANDELL CREIGHTON
1843–1901

25 No people do so much harm as those who go about
doing good. *Life* (1904), vol. ii, p. 503

JOHN WILSON CROKER
1780–1857

26 We now are, as we always have been, decidedly and
conscientiously attached to what is called the Tory,
and which might with more propriety be called the
Conservative, party.
Article, Quarterly Review, Jan. 1830, p. 276

1 A game which a sharper once played with a dupe, entitled, 'Heads I win, tails you lose.'
Croker Papers, iii. 59

OLIVER CROMWELL
1599–1658

2 A few honest men are better than numbers.
Letter to Sir W. Spring, Sept. 1643

3 Such men as had the fear of God before them and as made some conscience of what they did . . . the plain russet-coated captain that knows what he fights for and loves what he knows.
Letter of Sept. 1643. In Carlyle, Letters and Speeches of Oliver Cromwell

4 I beseech you, in the bowels of Christ, think it possible you may be mistaken.
Letter to the General Assembly of the Church of Scotland, 3 Aug. 1650

5 The dimensions of this mercy are above my thoughts. It is, for aught I know, a crowning mercy.
Letter for the Honourable William Lenthall, 4 Sept. 1651

6 Not what they want but what is good for them.
Attr. remark

7 Mr. Lely, I desire you would use all your skill to paint my picture truly like me, and not flatter me at all; but remark all these roughnesses, pimples, warts, and everything as you see me, otherwise I will never pay a farthing for it.
Remark, Walpole's Anecdotes of Painting, ch. 12

8 Take away these baubles.
Remark, Sydney Papers (1825), p. 141

9 It is not fit that you should sit here any longer! . . . you shall now give place to better men.
Speech to the Rump Parliament, 22 Jan. 1654

10 It's a maxim not to be despised, 'Though peace be made, yet it's interest that keeps peace.'
Speech to Parliament, 4 Sept. 1654

11 Necessity hath no law. Feigned necessities, imaginary necessities, . . . are the greatest cozenage that men can put upon the Providence of God, and make pretences to break known rules by.
Ib. 12 Sept. 1654

12 Your poor army, those poor contemptible men, came up hither.
Ib. 21 Apr. 1657

13 You have accounted yourselves happy on being environed with a great ditch from all the world beside.
Ib. 25 Jan. 1658

14 My design is to make what haste I can to be gone.
Last Words. Morley, Life, v, ch. 10

THOMAS W. H. CROSLAND
1868–1924

15 The Unspeakable Scot.
Title of satirical essay

RICHARD ASSHETON, VISCOUNT CROSS
1823–1914

16 [When the House of Lords laughed at his speech in favour of Spiritual Peers]
I hear a smile.
G. W. E. Russell's Collections and Recollections, ch. 29

JOHN CROWNE
1640?–1703?

17 River Thames, attended by two nymphs, representing Peace and Plenty.
Calisto, prologue, stage directions

JOHANN CRÜGER
1598–1662

18 Nun danket alle Gott.
Now thank we all our God.
Hymn

BISHOP RICHARD CUMBERLAND
1631–1718

19 It is better to wear out than to rust out.
G. Horne, The Duty of Contending for the Faith

ALLAN CUNNINGHAM
1784–1842

20 A wet sheet and a flowing sea,
A wind that follows fast
And fills the white and rustling sail
And bends the gallant mast.
A Wet Sheet and a Flowing Sea

21 While the hollow oak our palace is,
Our heritage the sea.
Ib.

22 It's hame and it's hame, hame fain wad I be,
O, hame, hame, hame to my ain countree!
It's hame and It's hame. Hogg includes this poem among his Jacobite Relics, i. 135. In his notes, i. 294, he says he took it from Cromek's Galloway and Nithsdale Relics, and supposes that it owed much to Allan Cunningham

23 The lark shall sing me hame in my ain countree. *Ib.*

24 But the sun through the mirk blinks blithe in my e'e,
'I'll shine on ye yet in your ain countree.' *Ib.*

WILL CUPPY
1884–

25 The Dodo never had a chance. He seems to have been invented for the sole purpose of becoming extinct and that was all he was good for.
How to Become Extinct

JOHN PHILPOT CURRAN
1750–1817

26 The condition upon which God hath given liberty to man is eternal vigilance; which condition if he break, servitude is at once the consequence of his crime, and the punishment of his guilt.
Speech on the Right of Election of Lord Mayor of Dublin, 10 July 1790

GEORGE NATHANIEL CURZON, MARQUESS CURZON OF KEDLESTON
1859–1925

27 I do not exclude the intelligent anticipation of facts even before they occur.
Speech, House of Commons, 29 Mar. 1898

HENRY CUST
1861–1917

1 Let Hell afford
  The pavement of her Heaven. *Non Nobis, Domine*

HARRY DACRE
fl. 1892

2 Daisy, Daisy, give me your answer, do!
  I'm half crazy, all for the love of you!
  It won't be a stylish marriage,
    I can't afford a carriage,
  But you'll look sweet upon the seat
  Of a bicycle made for two! *Daisy Bell*

CHARLES ANDERSON DANA
1819–1897

3 When a dog bites a man that is not news, but when
  a man bites a dog that is news.
  What is News? The New York Sun, 1882

SAMUEL DANIEL
1562–1619

4   Princes in this case
  Do hate the traitor, though they love the treason.
  Tragedy of Cleopatra, IV. i

5   Unless above himself he can
  Erect himself, how poor a thing is man!
  To the Lady Margaret, Countess of Cumberland,
  xii

6 Custom that is before all law, Nature that is above
  all art. *A Defence of Rhyme*

7 Love is a sickness full of woes,
    All remedies refusing:
  A plant that with most cutting grows,
    Most barren with best using.
            Why so?
  More we enjoy it, more it dies,
  If not enjoy'd, it sighing cries,
            Hey ho.
  Hymen's Triumph, I. v

8 This is the thing that I was born to do.
  Musophilus, l. 577

9 And who, in time, knows whither we may vent
  The treasure of our tongue, to what strange shores
  This gain of our best glory shall be sent,
  T'enrich unknowing nations with our stores?
  What worlds in th'yet unformed Occident
  May come refin'd with th'accents that are ours?
  Ib. l. 957

10 But years hath done this wrong,
  To make me write too much, and live too long.
  Philotas, [Ded.] *To the Prince*, l. 108

11 Pity is sworn servant unto love:
  And this be sure, wherever it begin
  To make the way, it lets your master in.
  The Queen's Arcadia, II. 1

12 Care-charmer Sleep, son of the sable Night,
  Brother to Death, in silent darkness born:
  Relieve my languish, and restore the light,
  With dark forgetting of my care return,
  And let the day be time enough to mourn

The shipwreck of my ill adventured youth:
Let waking eyes suffice to wail their scorn,
Without the torment of the night's untruth.
  Sonnets to Delia, liv

13 Come worthy Greek, Ulysses come
    Possess these shores with me:
  The winds and seas are troublesome,
    And here we may be free.
  Here may we sit, and view their toil
    That travail on the deep,
  And joy the day in mirth the while,
    And spend the night in sleep.
  Ulysses and the Siren

JOHN JEREMIAH DANIELL
1819–1898

14 Sing, boys, in joyful chorus
    Your hymn of praise to-day,
  And sing, ye gentle maidens,
    Your sweet responsive lay.
  Hymns Ancient & Modern, Come, Sing with]
  Holy Gladness.

DANTE ALIGHIERI
1265–1321

15 Nel mezzo del cammin di nostra vita.
  In the middle of the road of our life.
  Divine Comedy. Inferno, i. 1

16 Or se' tu quel Virgilio?
  Art thou then that Virgil? *Ib.* 79

17 Lasciate ogni speranza voi ch'entrate!
  All hope abandon, ye who enter here. *Ib.* iii. 9

18 Non ragioniam di lor, ma guarda, e passa.
  Let us not speak of them, but look, and pass on.
  Ib. 51

19 Il gran rifiuto.
  The great refusal. *Ib.* 60

20 Onorate l'altissimo poeta.
  Honour to the greatest poet. *Ib.* iv. 80

21 Il Maestro di color che sanno.
  The Master of them that know. [Aristotle.]
  Ib. 131

22   Nessun maggior dolore,
  Che ricordarsi del tempo felice
  Nella miseria.
  There is no greater sorrow than to recall a time of
    happiness in misery. *Ib.* v. 121. (*See* 78:4)

23 Galeotto fu il libro e chi lo scrisse:
  Quel giorno più non vi leggemmo avante.
  Galeotto was the book and writer too: that day
    therein we read no more. *Ib.* 137

24 E quindi uscimmo a riveder le stelle.
  Thence we came forth to rebehold the stars.
  Ib. xxxiv. 139

25 Puro e disposto a salire alle stelle.
  Pure and made apt for mounting to the stars.
  Ib. Purgatorio, xxxiii. 145

26 E'n la sua volontade è nostra pace.
  In His will is our peace. *Ib. Paradiso*, iii. 85

1 Tu proverai sì come sa di sale
Lo pane altrui, e com' è duro calle
Lo scendere e il salir per l'altrui scale.
    You shall find out how salt is the taste of another's
    bread, and how hard a path the going down and
    going up another's stairs.
        Divine Comedy. Paradiso, xvii. 58

2 L'amor che muove il sole e l'altre stelle.
    The love that moves the sun and the other stars.
        Ib. xxxiii. 145

GEORGES JACQUES DANTON
1759–1794

3 De l'audace, et encore de l'audace, et toujours de
l'audace!
    Boldness, and again boldness, and always boldness!
    *Speech to the Legislative Committee of General
    Defence, 2 Sept. 1792. Le Moniteur, 4 Sept.
    1792*

CHARLES ROBERT DARWIN
1809–1882

4 A hairy quadruped, furnished with a tail and pointed
ears, probably arboreal in its habits.
        Descent of Man, ch. 21

5 We must, however, acknowledge, as it seems to me,
that man with all his noble qualities, . . . still bears
in his bodily frame the indelible stamp of his lowly
origin.   *Ib.* last words

6 I have called this principle, by which each slight
variation, if useful, is preserved, by the term of
Natural Selection.   *The Origin of Species*, ch. 3

7 We will now discuss in a little more detail the struggle
for existence.   *Ib.*

8 The expression often used by Mr. Herbert Spencer
of the Survival of the Fittest is more accurate, and
is sometimes equally convenient.   *Ib.*

CHARLES DAVENANT
1656–1714

9 Custom, that unwritten law,
By which the people keep even kings in awe.
        Circe, ii. iii

SIR WILLIAM DAVENANT
1606–1668

10 Had laws not been, we never had been blam'd;
For not to know we sinn'd is innocence.
        Dryden Miscellany, vi. l. 226

11 I shall sleep like a top.   *The Rivals*, Act III

12 For I must go where lazy Peace
Will hide her drowsy head;
And, for the sport of kings, increase
The number of the dead.
        The Soldier Going to the Field

13 The lark now leaves his wat'ry nest,
And climbing, shakes his dewy wings;
He takes this window for the east;
And to implore your light, he sings,
Awake, awake, the morn will never rise,
Till she can dress her beauty at your eyes.   *Song*

JOHN DAVIDSON
1857–1909

14 When the pods went pop on the broom, green broom.
        A Runnable Stag

15 A runnable stag, a kingly crop.   *Ib.*

SIR JOHN DAVIES
1569–1626

16 Skill comes so slow, and life so fast doth fly,
We learn so little and forget so much.
        Nosce Teipsum, introduction, xix

17 Wit to persuade, and beauty to delight. *Orchestra*, v

18 Why should your fellowship a trouble be,
Since man's chief pleasure is society?   *Ib.* xxxii

19 Judge not the play before the play be done.
        Respice Finem

SCROPE BERDMORE DAVIES
c. 1783–1852

20 Babylon in all its desolation is a sight not so awful
as that of the human mind in ruins.
    Letter to Thomas Raikes, May 1835. See
    Journal of T. Raikes, 1831 to 1847, 1856, vol. ii

WILLIAM HENRY DAVIES
1870–1940

21 A rainbow and a cuckoo's song
May never come together again;
May never come
This side the tomb.   *A Great Time.*

22 The simple bird that thinks two notes a song.
        April's Charms

23 The little hunchback of the snow.   *In the Snow*

24 What is this life if, full of care,
We have no time to stand and stare?   *Leisure*

25 Sweet Stay-at-Home, sweet Well-content.
        Sweet Stay-at-Home

JEFFERSON DAVIS
1808–1889

26 All we ask is to be let alone.
    *Attr. Remark in Inaugural Address as President
    of the Confederate States of America, 18 Feb.
    1861*

THOMAS OSBORNE DAVIS
1814–1845

27 Come in the evening, or come in the morning,
Come when you're looked for, or come without
warning.   *The Welcome*

STEPHEN DECATUR
1779–1820

28 Our country! In her intercourse with foreign nations,
may she always be in the right; but our country,
right or wrong.
    A. S. Mackenzie, *Life of Decatur*, ch. xiv

MARQUISE DU DEFFAND
1697–1780

1 La distance n'y fait rien; il n'y a que le premier pas qui coûte.

The distance is nothing; it is only the first step that is difficult.
Remark on the legend that St. Denis, carrying his head in his hands, walked two leagues. Letter to d'Alembert, 7 July 1763

DANIEL DEFOE
1661?–1731

2 The best of men cannot suspend their fate:
The good die early, and the bad die late.
Character of the late Dr. S. Annesley

3 We lov'd the doctrine for the teacher's sake. *Ib.*

4 Nature has left this tincture in the blood,
That all men would be tyrants if they could.
The Kentish Petition, addenda, l. 11

5 I was born in the year 1632, in the city of York, of a good family, though not of that county, my father being a foreigner of Bremen, who settled first at Hull.
The Life and Adventures of Robinson Crusoe, pt. i

6 Robin, Robin, Robin Crusoe, poor Robin Crusoe!
Where are you, Robin Crusoe? Where are you?
Where have you been? [*The parrot.*] *Ib.*

7 It happened one day, about noon, going towards my boat, I was exceedingly surprised with the print of a man's naked foot on the shore, which was very plain to be seen in the sand. I stood like one thunderstruck, or as if I had seen an apparition. *Ib.*

8 I takes my man Friday with me. *Ib.*

9 In trouble to be troubl'd
Is to have your trouble doubl'd.
Robinson Crusoe, The Farther Adventures

10 Necessity makes an honest man a knave.
Serious Reflections of Robinson Crusoe, ch. 2

11 Wherever God erects a house of prayer,
The Devil always builds a chapel there;
And 'twill be found, upon examination,
The latter has the largest congregation.
The True-Born Englishman, pt. i, l. 1

12 From this amphibious ill-born mob began
That vain, ill-natur'd thing, an Englishman.
Ib. l. 132

13 Your Roman-Saxon-Danish-Norman English.
Ib. l. 139

14 Great families of yesterday we show,
And lords whose parents were the Lord knows who.
Ib. l. 374

15 In their religion they are so uneven,
That each man goes his own By-way to heaven.
Ib. l. 104

16 And of all plagues with which mankind are curst,
Ecclesiastic tyranny's the worst. *Ib.* pt. ii, l. 299

17 When kings the sword of justice first lay down,
They are no kings, though they possess the crown.
Titles are shadows, crowns are empty things,
The good of subjects is the end of kings. *Ib.* l. 313

THOMAS DEKKER
1570?–1641?

18   The best of men
That e'er wore earth about him, was a sufferer,
A soft, meek, patient, humble, tranquil spirit,
The first true gentleman that ever breath'd.
The Honest Whore, pt. i. 1. ii

19 That great fishpond. [The sea.] *Ib.*

20 This principle is old, but true as fate,
Kings may love treason, but the traitor hate.
Ib. pt. iv. IV

21 Art thou poor, yet hast thou golden slumbers?
    Oh sweet content!
Art thou rich, yet is thy mind perplexed?
    Oh, punishment!
Dost thou laugh to see how fools are vexed
To add to golden numbers, golden numbers?
O, sweet content, O, sweet, O, sweet content!
    Work apace, apace, apace, apace;
    Honest labour bears a lovely face;
Then hey nonny, nonny; hey nonny, nonny.
Patient Grissil, Act I

22 Canst drink the waters of the crisped spring?
    O sweet content!
Swim'st thou in wealth, yet sink'st in thine own tears?
    O punishment! *Ib.*

23 Golden slumbers kiss your eyes,
Smiles awake you when you rise:
Sleep, pretty wantons, do not cry,
And I will sing a lullaby:
Rock them, rock them, lullaby.

Care is heavy, therefore sleep you;
You are care, and care must keep you. *Ib.* IV. ii

24 Cold's the wind, and wet's the rain,
    Saint Hugh be our good speed:
Ill is the weather that bringeth no gain,
    Nor helps good hearts in need.

Trowle the bowl, the jolly nut-brown bowl,
    And here kind mate to thee:
Let's sing a dirge for Saint Hugh's soul,
    And down it merrily.
Shoemaker's Holiday, Second Three-man's Song

WALTER DE LA MARE
1873–1956

25 Ann, Ann!
    Come! quick as you can!
There's a fish that *talks*
    In the frying-pan.
Out of the fat,
    As clear as glass,
He put up his mouth
    And moaned 'Alas!'
Oh, most mournful,
    'Alas, alack!'
Then turned to his sizzling,
    And sank him back. *Alas, Alack*

26 Oh, no man knows
Through what wild centuries
Roves back the rose. *All That's Past*

1 **Very** old are we **men**;
Our dreams are tales
Told in dim Eden
By Eve's nightingales;
We wake and whisper awhile,
But, the day gone by,
Silence and sleep like fields
Of amaranth lie.   *All That's Past*

2 Far are the shades of Arabia,
Where the Princes ride at noon.   *Arabia*

3 He is crazed with the spell of far Arabia,
They have stolen his wits away.   *Ib.*

4 What can a tired heart say,
Which the wise of the world have made dumb?
Save to the lonely dreams of a child,
  'Return again, come!'   *Dreams*

5 Bright towers of silence. [Clouds.]   *England*

6 Here lies a most beautiful lady,
    Light of step and heart was she;
I think she was the most beautiful lady
    That ever was in the West Country.
But beauty vanishes; beauty passes;
    However rare—rare it be;
And when I crumble, who will remember
    This lady of the West Country?   *Epitaph*

7 When I lie where shades of darkness
Shall no more assail mine eyes.   *Fare Well*, i

8 Memory fades, must the remembered
Perishing be?   *Ib.*

9 Look thy last on all things lovely,
Every hour—let no night
Seal thy sense in deathly slumber
Till to delight
Thou hast paid thy utmost blessing;
Since that all things thou wouldst praise
Beauty took from those who loved them
In other days.   *Ib.* iii

10 In Hans' old Mill his three black cats
Watch the bins for the thieving rats.
Whisker and claw, they crouch in the night,
Their five eyes smouldering green and bright:

Jekkel, and Jessup, and one-eyed Jill. *Five Eyes*

11 Three jolly gentlemen,
In coats of red,
Rode their horses
Up to bed.   *The Huntsmen*

12 Do diddle di do,
Poor Jim Jay
Got stuck fast
In Yesterday.   *Jim Jay*

13 'Is there anybody there?' said the traveller,
Knocking on the moonlit door.   *The Listeners*

14 'Tell them I came, and no one answered,
That I kept my word,' he said.   *Ib.*

15 Never the least stir made the listeners.   *Ib.*

16 Ay, they heard his foot upon the stirrup,
And the sound of iron on stone,
And how the silence surged softly backward,
When the plunging hoofs were gone.   *Ib.*

17 It's a very odd thing—
As odd as can be—
That whatever Miss T. eats
Turns into Miss T.
Porridge and apples,
Mince, muffins and mutton,
Jam, junket, jumbles—
Not a rap, not a button
It matters; the moment
They're out of her plate,
Though shared by Miss Butcher
And sour Mr. Bate,
Tiny and cheerful,
And neat as can be,
Whatever Miss T. eats
Turns into Miss T.   *Miss T*

18 'Won't you look out of your window, Mrs. Gill?'
Quoth the Fairy, nidding, nodding in the garden.
                                The Mocking Fairy

19 Never more, Sailor,
Shalt thou be
Tossed on the wind-ridden
Restless sea.   *Never More, Sailor*

20 No robin ever
On the deep
Hopped with his song
To haunt thy sleep.   *Ib.*

21 Thistle and darnel and dock grew there,
    And a bush, in the corner, of may,
On the orchard wall I used to sprawl,
    In the blazing heat of the day;
Half asleep and half awake,
    While the birds went twittering by,
And nobody there my line to share
    But Nicholas Nye.

Nicholas Nye was lean and grey,
    Lame of a leg and old,
More than a score of donkey's years
    He had seen since he was foaled;
He munched the thistles, purple and spiked,
    Would sometimes stoop and sigh,
And turn his head, as if he said,
    'Poor Nicholas Nye!'

But dusk would come in the apple boughs,
    The green of the glow-worm shine,
The birds in nest would crouch to rest,
    And home I'd trudge to mine;
And there, in the moonlight, dark with dew,
    Asking not wherefore nor why,
Would brood like a ghost, and as still as a post,
    Old Nicholas Nye.   *Nicholas Nye*

22 Three jolly Farmers
Once bet a pound
Each dance the others would
Off the ground.   *Off the Ground*

23 Old Sallie Worm from her hole doth peep;
'Come!' said Old Shellover,
'Ay!' said Creep.   *Old Shellover*

24 Lone and alone she lies,
    Poor Miss 7,
Five steep flights from the earth,
    And one from heaven;
Dark hair and dark brown eyes,—
Not to be sad she tries,
Still—still it's lonely lies
Poor Miss 7.   *Poor 'Miss 7'*

1 And still would remain
    My wit to try—
My worn reeds broken,
    The dark tarn dry,
All words forgotten—
    Thou, Lord, and I.   *The Scribe*

2 Slowly, silently, now the moon
Walks the night in her silver shoon.   *Silver*

3 Some one came knocking
    At my wee, small door;
Some one came knocking,
    I'm sure—sure—sure.   *Some One*

4 Ages and ages have fallen on me—
On the wood and the pool and the elder tree.
                                Song of Enchantment

5 And quiet did quiet remain.   *The Song of Finis*

6 Of all the trees in England,
    Oak, Elder, Elm and Thorn,
The Yew alone burns lamps of peace
    For them that lie forlorn.   *Trees*

7 Of all the trees in England,
    Her sweet three corners in,
Only the Ash, the bonnie Ash
    Burns fierce while it is green.   *Ib.*

8 And not a single one can see
My tiny watching eye.   *The Window*

SIR JOHN DENHAM
1615-1669

9 Where, with like haste, though several ways they run;
Some to undo, and some to be undone.
                                Cooper's Hill, l. 31

10 Oh, could I flow like thee, and make thy stream
My great example, as it is my theme!
Though deep, yet clear; though gentle, yet not dull;
Strong without rage, without o'erflowing full.
                                Ib. l. 189

11 Youth, what man's age is like to be doth show;
We may our ends by our beginnings know.
                                Of Prudence, l. 225

THOMAS, LORD DENMAN
1779-1854

12 Trial by jury itself, instead of being a security to
persons who are accused, will be a delusion, a
mockery, and a snare.
    Judgement in O'Connell v. *the Queen, 4 Sept.
    1844*

CLARENCE JAMES DENNIS
1876-1938

13 Me name is Mud.
    The Sentimental Bloke: A Spring Song, st. 2
    (1916)

JOHN DENNIS
1657-1734

14 A man who could make so vile a pun would not
scruple to pick a pocket.
    The Gentleman's Magazine (1781), p. 324 (Edit.
    note)

15 Damn them! They will not let my play run, but they
steal my thunder!
    W. S. Walsh, *Handy-book of Literary Curiosi-
    ties*

THOMAS DE QUINCEY
1785-1859

16 Set up as a theatrical scarecrow for superstitious
terrors.
    Confessions of an English Opium Eater. Preface,
    (1856)

17 The burden of the incommunicable.   *Ib.* pt. i

18 So, then, Oxford Street, stony-hearted stepmother,
thou that listenest to the sighs of orphans, and
drinkest the tears of children, at length I was dismissed from thee.   *Ib.*

19 Thou hast the keys of Paradise, oh just, subtle, and
mighty opium! *Ib.* pt. ii, *The Pleasures of Opium*

20 An Iliad of woes.   *Ib.* pt. iii, *The Pains of Opium*

21 Everlasting farewells! and again, and yet again
reverberated—everlasting farewells!   *Ib.*

22 Murder Considered as One of the Fine Arts.
                                Title of Essay

23 If once a man indulges himself in murder, very soon
he comes to think little of robbing; and from robbing he comes next to drinking and sabbath-breaking, and from that to incivility and procrastination.
                                Ib. Supplementary Papers

24 There is first the literature of *knowledge*, and secondly,
the literature of *power*. *Essays on the Poets; Pope*

25 Books, we are told, propose to *instruct* or to *amuse*.
Indeed! . . . The true antithesis to knowledge, in
this case, is not *pleasure*, but *power*. All that is
literature seeks to communicate power; all that is
not literature, to communicate knowledge.
    Letters to a Young Man, letter iii. *De Quincey
    adds that he is indebted for this distinction to
    'many years' conversation with Mr. Words-
    worth'*

RENÉ DESCARTES
1596-1650

26 Cogito, ergo sum.
    I think, therefore I am. *Le Discours de la Méthode*

27 Le bon sens est la chose du monde la mieux partagée,
car chacun pense en être bien pourvu.
    Common sense is the most widely shared com-
    modity in the world, for every man is convinced
    that he is well supplied with it.   *Ib.*

CAMILLE DESMOULINS
1760-1794

28 My age is that of the *bon Sansculotte Jésus*; an age
fatal to Revolutionists.
    Answer at his trial. Carlyle, *French Revolution*,
    bk. vi, ch. 2

PHILIPPE NÉRICAULT dit DESTOUCHES
1680-1754

29 Les absents ont toujours tort.
    The absent are always in the wrong.
                                L'Obstacle imprévu, i. vi

EDWARD DE VERE, EARL OF OXFORD
1550-1604

1 If women could be fair and yet not fond.
Women's Changeableness

ROBERT DEVEREUX, EARL OF ESSEX
see
ESSEX

GEORGE DEWEY
1837-1917

2 You may fire when you are ready, Gridley.
Dewey's *Autobiography*

CHARLES DIBDIN
1745-1814

3 Did you ever hear of Captain Wattle?
He was all for love and a little for the bottle.
Captain Wattle and Miss Roe

4 For a soldier I listed, to grow great in fame,
And be shot at for sixpence a-day. *Charity*

5 In every mess I finds a friend,
In every port a wife. *Jack in his Element*

6 What argufies sniv'ling and piping your eye?
Poor Jack

7 For they say there's a Providence sits up aloft,
To keep watch for the life of poor Jack! *Ib.*

8 But the standing toast that pleased the most
Was—The wind that blows, the ship that goes,
And the lass that loves a sailor! *The Round Robin*

9 Spanking Jack was so comely, so pleasant, so jolly,
Though winds blew great guns, still he'd whistle
and sing;
Jack lov'd his friend, and was true to his Molly,
And if honour gives greatness, was great as a king.
The Sailor's Consolation

10 Here, a sheer hulk, lies poor Tom Bowling,
The darling of our crew. *Tom Bowling*

11 Faithful, below, he did his duty;
But now he's gone aloft. *Ib.*

12 And did you not hear of a jolly young waterman,
Who at Blackfriars Bridge used for to ply;
And he feather'd his oars with such skill and dexterity,
Winning each heart, and delighting each eye.
The Waterman

13 As he row'd along, thinking of nothing at all. *Ib.*

14 Then farewell, my trim-built wherry!
Oars, and coat, and badge, farewell. *Ib.*

THOMAS JOHN DIBDIN
1771-1841

15 Oh! what a snug little Island,
A right little, tight little Island!
The Snug Little Island

16 Then a very great war-man call'd Billy the Norman
Cried 'D—n it, I never lik'd *my* land.' *Ib.*

CHARLES DICKENS
1812-1870

17 Rather a tough customer in argeyment, Joe, if anybody
was to try and tackle him. [*Parkes.*]
Barnaby Rudge, ch. 1

18 Something will come of this. I hope it mayn't be
human gore. [*Simon Tappertit.*] *Ib.* ch. 4

19 Polly put the kettle on, we'll all have tea. [*Grip.*]
Ib. ch. 17

20 'There are strings,' said Mr. Tappertit, ' . . . in the
human heart that had better not be wibrated.'
Ib. ch. 22

21 Oh gracious, why wasn't I born old and ugly?
[*Miss Miggs.*] *Ib.* ch. 70

22 Jarndyce and Jarndyce still drags its dreary length
before the Court, perennially hopeless.
Bleak House, ch. 1

23 This is a London particular. . . . A fog, miss.
Ib. ch. 3

24 Educating the natives of Borrioboola-Gha, on the
left bank of the Niger. [*Mrs. Jellyby.*] *Ib.* ch. 4

25 The wind's in the east. . . . I am always conscious of
an uncomfortable sensation now and then when
the wind is blowing in the east. [*Mr. Jarndyce.*]
Ib. ch. 6

26 I only ask to be free. The butterflies are free. Mankind
will surely not deny to Harold Skimpole what it
concedes to the butterflies! *Ib.*

27 'Not to put too fine a point upon it'—a favourite
apology for plain-speaking with Mr. Snagsby.
Ib. ch. 11

28 He wos wery good to me, he wos! [*Jo.*] *Ib.*

29 He [Mr. Turveydrop] is celebrated, almost everywhere, for his Deportment. [*Caddy.*] *Ib.* ch. 14

30 'It was a maxim of Captain Swosser's', said Mrs.
Badger, 'speaking in his figurative naval manner,
that when you make pitch hot, you cannot make it
too hot; and that if you only have to swab a plank,
you should swab it as if Davy Jones were after
you.' *Ib.* ch. 17

31 The Professor made the same remark, Miss Summer-
son, in his last illness; when (his mind wandering)
he insisted on keeping his little hammer under the
pillow, and chipping at the countenances of the
attendants. The ruling passion! [*Mrs. Badger.*] *Ib.*

32 What is peace? Is it war? No. Is it strife? No.
[*Mr. Chadband.*] *Ib.* ch. 19

33 The Chadband style of oratory is widely received
and much admired. *Ib.*

34 You are a human boy, my young friend. A human
boy. O glorious to be a human boy! . . .
O running stream of sparkling joy
To be a soaring human boy! [*Mr. Chadband.*] *Ib.*

35 Jobling, there *are* chords in the human mind. [*Guppy.*]
Ib. ch. 20

36 'It is,' says Chadband, 'the ray of rays, the sun of
suns, the moon of moons, the star of stars. It is the
light of Terewth.' *Ib.* ch. 25

37 Lo, the city is barren, I have seen but an eel. *Ib.*

G

DICKENS

1 It's my old girl that advises. She has the head. But I never own to it before her. Discipline must be maintained. [*Mr. Bagnet.*] *Bleak House*, ch. 27

2 It is a melancholy truth that even great men have their poor relations. *Ib.* ch. 28

3 Never have a mission, my dear child. [*Mr. Jellyby.*] *Ib.* ch. 30

4 England has been in a dreadful state for some weeks. Lord Coodle would go out, and Sir Thomas Doodle wouldn't come in, and there being nobody in Great Britain (to speak of) except Coodle and Doodle, there has been no Government. *Ib.* ch. 40

5 She's Colour-Sergeant of the Nonpareil battalion. [*Mr. Bagnet.*] *Ib.* ch. 52

6 A smattering of everything, and a knowledge of nothing. [*Minerva House.*] *Sketches by Boz. Tales*, ch. 3. *Sentiment*

7 Grief never mended no broken bones, and as good people's wery scarce, what I says is, make the most on 'em. *Ib. Scenes*, ch. 22, *Gin-Shops*

8 O let us love our occupations,
Bless the squire and his relations ,
Live upon our daily rations,
And always know our proper stations.
 The Chimes, 2nd Quarter

9 In came a fiddler—and tuned like fifty stomach-aches. In came Mrs. Fezziwig, one vast substantial smile. *A Christmas Carol*, stave 2

10 'God bless us every one!' said Tiny Tim, the last of all. *Ib.* stave 3

11 It *was* a turkey! He could never have stood upon his legs, that bird. He would have snapped 'em off short in a minute, like sticks of sealing-wax. *Ib.* stave 5

12 'Somebody's sharp.' 'Who is?' asked the gentleman, laughing. I looked up quickly; being curious to know. 'Only Brooks of Sheffield,' said Mr. Murdstone. I was relieved to find that it was only Brooks of Sheffield; for, at first, I really thought it was I. *David Copperfield*, ch. 2

13 'I am a lone lorn creetur',' were Mrs. Gummidge's words, . . . 'and everythink goes contrairy with me.' *Ib.* ch. 3

14 'I feel it more than other people,' said Mrs. Gummidge. *Ib.*

15 I'd better go into the house, and die and be a riddance! [*Mrs. Gummidge.*] *Ib.*

16 She's been thinking of the old 'un! [*Mr. Peggotty, of Mrs. Gummidge.*] *Ib.*

17 Barkis is willin'. *Ib.* ch. 5

18 'There was a gentleman here yesterday,' he said—'a stout gentleman, by the name of Topsawyer . . . he came in here, . . . ordered a glass of this ale—*would* order it—I told him not—drank it, and fell dead. It was too old for him. It oughtn't to be drawn; that's the fact.' [*The Waiter.*] *Ib.*

19 I live on broken wittles—and I sleep on the coals. [*The Waiter.*] *Ib.*

20 'When a man says he's willin',' said Mr. Barkis, . . . 'it's as much as to say, that a man's waitin' for a answer.' *Ib.* ch. 8

21 Experientia does it—as papa used to say. [*Mrs. Micawber.*] *David Copperfield*, ch. 11

22 I have known him [Micawber] come home to supper with a flood of tears, and a declaration that nothing was now left but a jail; and go to bed making a calculation of the expense of putting bow-windows to the house, 'in case anything turned up,' which was his favourite expression. *Ib.*

23 I never will desert Mr. Micawber. [*Mrs. Micawber.*] *Ib.* ch. 12

24 Annual income twenty pounds, annual expenditure nineteen nineteen six, result happiness. Annual income twenty pounds, annual expenditure twenty pounds ought and six, result misery. [*Mr. Micawber.*] *Ib.*

25 Mr. Dick had been for upwards of ten years endeavouring to keep King Charles the First out of the Memorial; but he had been constantly getting into it, and was there now. *Ib.* ch. 14

26 I am well aware that I am the 'umblest person going. . . . My mother is likewise a very 'umble person. We live in a numble abode. [*Uriah Heep.*] *Ib.* ch. 16

27 The mistake was made of putting some of the trouble out of King Charles's head into my head. *Ib.* ch. 17

28 We are so very 'umble. [*Uriah Heep.*] *Ib.*

29 'Orses and dorgs is some men's fancy. They're wittles and drink to me—lodging, wife, and children—reading, writing and 'rithmetic—snuff, tobacker, and sleep. *Ib.* ch. 19

30 I only ask for information. [*Miss Rosa Dartle.*] *Ib.* ch. 20

31 'It was as true', said Mr. Barkis, '. . . as taxes is. And nothing's truer than them.' *Ib.* ch. 21

32 What a world of gammon and spinnage it is, though, ain't it! [*Miss Mowcher.*] *Ib.* ch. 22

33 The whole social system . . . is a system of Prince's nails. [*Miss Mowcher.*] *Ib.*

34 'Oh, surely! surely!' said Mr. Spenlow. . . . 'I should be happy, myself, to propose two months, . . . but I have a partner. Mr. Jorkins.' *Ib.* ch. 23

35 Other things are all very well in their way, but give me Blood! [*Mr. Waterbrook.*] *Ib.* ch. 25

36 I assure you she's the dearest girl. [*Traddles.*] *Ib.* ch. 27

37 Accidents will occur in the best-regulated families; and in families not regulated by that pervading influence which sanctifies while it enhances the —a—I would say, in short, by the influence of Woman, in the lofty character of Wife, they may be expected with confidence, and must be borne with philosophy. [*Mr. Micawber.*] *Ib.* ch. 28

38 He told me, only the other day, that it was provided for. That was Mr. Micawber's expression, 'Provided for.' [*Traddles.*] *Ib.*

39 'People can't die, along the coast,' said Mr. Peggotty, 'except when the tide's pretty nigh out. They can't be born, unless it's pretty nigh in—not properly born, till flood. He's a going out with the tide.' *Ib.* ch. 30

DICKENS

1 Mrs. Crupp had indignantly assured him that there wasn't room to swing a cat there; but, as Mr. Dick justly observed to me, sitting down on the foot of the bed, nursing his leg, 'You know, Trotwood, I don't want to swing a cat. I never do swing a cat. Therefore, what does that signify to *me!*'
David Copperfield, ch. 35

2 It's only my child-wife. [*Dora.*] *Ib.* ch. 44

3 Circumstances beyond my individual control. [*Mr. Micawber.*] *Ib.* ch. 49

4 I'm Gormed—and I can't say no fairer than that! [*Mr. Peggotty.*] *Ib.* ch. 63

5 He's tough, ma'am, tough, is J. B. Tough, and devilish sly! [*Major Bagstock.*] *Dombey and Son*, ch. 7

6 There was no light nonsense about Miss Blimber. . . . She was dry and sandy with working in the graves of deceased languages. None of your live languages for Miss Blimber. They must be dead—stone dead—and then Miss Blimber dug them up like a Ghoul. *Ib.* ch. 11

7 As to Mr. Feeder, B.A., Doctor Blimber's assistant, he was a kind of human barrel-organ, with a little list of tunes at which he was continually working, over and over again, without any variation. *Ib.*

8 If I could have known Cicero, and been his friend, and talked with him in his retirement at Tusculum (beautiful Tusculum), I could have died contented. [*Mrs. Blimber.*] *Ib.*

9 'Wal'r, my boy,' replied the Captain, 'in the Proverbs of Solomon you will find the following words, "May we never want a friend in need, nor a bottle to give him!" When found, make a note of.' [*Captain Cuttle.*] *Ib.* ch. 15

10 Train up a fig-tree in the way it should go, and when you are old sit under the shade of it. [*Captain Cuttle.*] *Ib.* ch. 19

11 Cows are my passion. [*Mrs. Skewton.*] *Ib.* ch. 21

12 Mr. Toots devoted himself to the cultivation of those gentle arts which refine and humanize existence, his chief instructor in which was an interesting character called the Game Chicken, who was always to be heard of at the bar of the Black Badger, wore a shaggy white great-coat in the warmest weather, and knocked Mr. Toots about the head three times a week. *Ib.* ch. 22

13 It's of no consequence. [*Mr. Toots.*] *Ib.*

14 The bearings of this observation lays in the application on it. [*Bunsby.*] *Ib.* ch. 23

15 Say, like those wicked Turks, there is no What's-his-name but Thingummy, and What-you-may-call-it is his prophet! [*Mrs. Skewton.*] *Ib.* ch. 27

16 I positively adore Miss Dombey;—I—I am perfectly sore with loving her. [*Mr. Toots.*] *Ib.* ch. 30

17 If you could see my legs when I take my boots off, you'd form some idea of what unrequited affection is. [*Mr. Toots.*] *Ib.* ch. 48

18 Stranger, pause and ask thyself the question, Canst thou do likewise? If not, with a blush retire.
Edwin Drood, ch. 4

19 'Dear me,' said Mr. Grewgious, peeping in, 'it's like looking down the throat of Old Time.' *Ib.* ch. 9

20 'Umps', said Mr. Grewgious. *Ib.* ch. 11

21 Your sister is given to government. [*Joe Gargery.*]
Great Expectations, ch. 7

22 I had cherished a profound conviction that her bringing me up by hand, gave her no right to bring me up by jerks. *Ib.* ch. 8

23 On the Rampage, Pip, and off the Rampage, Pip; such is Life! [*Joe Gargery.*] *Ib.* ch. 15

24 Get hold of portable property. [*Wemmick.*]
Ib. ch. 24

25 You don't object to an aged parent, I hope? [*Wemmick.*] *Ib.* ch. 25

26 'Have you seen anything of London, yet?' [*Herbert.*] 'Why, yes: Sir—but we didn't find that it come up to its likeness in the red bills—it is there drawd too architectooralooral.' [*Joe Gargery.*] *Ib.* ch. 27

27 'Halloa! Here's a church! . . . Let's go in! . . . Here's Miss Skiffins! Let's have a wedding.' [*Wemmick.*]
Ib. ch. 55

28 Now, what I want is, Facts. . . . Facts alone are wanted in life. [*Mr. Gradgrind.*]
Hard Times, bk. i, ch. 1

29 Whatever was required to be done, the Circumlocution Office was beforehand with all the public departments in the art of perceiving—HOW NOT TO DO IT. *Little Dorrit*, bk. i, ch. 10

30 Look here. Upon my soul you mustn't come into the place saying you want to know, you know. [*Barnacle Junior.*] *Ib.*

31 One remark . . . I wish to make, one explanation I wish to offer, when your Mama came and made a scene of it with my Papa and when I was called down into the little breakfast-room where they were looking at one another with your Mama's parasol between them seated on two chairs like mad bulls what was I to do? [*Flora Finching.*]
Ib. ch. 13

32 The Great Fire of London was not the fire in which your Uncle George's workshops was burned down. [*Mr. F.'s Aunt.*] *Ib.*

33 I hate a fool! [*Mr. F.'s Aunt.*] *Ib.*

34 Take a little time—count five-and-twenty, Tattycoram. [*Mr. Meagles.*] *Ib.* ch. 16

35 There's milestones on the Dover Road! [*Mr. F.'s Aunt.*] *Ib.* ch. 23

36 You can't make a head and brains out of a brass knob with nothing in it. You couldn't when your Uncle George was living; much less when he's dead. [*Mr. F.'s Aunt.*] *Ib.*

37 He [Mr. Finching] proposed seven times once in a hackney-coach once in a boat once in a pew once on a donkey at Tunbridge Wells and the rest on his knees. [*Flora Finching.*] *Ib.* ch. 24

38 I revere the memory of Mr. F. as an estimable man and most indulgent husband, only necessary to mention Asparagus and it appeared or to hint at any little delicate thing to drink and it came like magic in a pint bottle it was not ecstasy but it was comfort. [*Flora Finching.*] *Ib.*

39 E please. Double good! [*Mrs. Plornish.*] *Ib.* ch. 25

[175]

1 Father is rather vulgar, my dear. The word Papa, besides, gives a pretty form to the lips. Papa, potatoes, poultry, prunes and prism, are all very good words for the lips; especially prunes and prism. [*Mrs. General.*] *Little Dorrit*, bk. ii, ch. 5

2 Dante—known to that gentleman [Mr. Sparkler] as an eccentric man in the nature of an Old File, who used to put leaves round his head, and sit upon a stool for some unaccountable purpose, outside the cathedral at Florence. *Ib.* ch. 6

3 Once a gentleman, and always a gentleman. [*Rigaud.*] *Ib.* ch. 28

4 The Lord No Zoo. [*Toby Chuzzlewit.*] *Martin Chuzzlewit*, ch. 1

5 'The name of those fabulous animals (pagan, I regret to say) who used to sing in the water, has quite escaped me.' Mr. George Chuzzlewit suggested 'Swans.' 'No,' said Mr. Pecksniff. 'Not swans. Very like swans, too. Thank you.' The nephew . . . propounded 'Oysters.' 'No,' said Mr. Pecksniff, . . . 'nor oysters. But by no means unlike oysters; a very excellent idea; thank you, my dear sir, very much. Wait. Sirens! Dear me! sirens, of course.' *Ib.* ch. 4

6 Any man may be in good spirits and good temper when he's well dressed. There an't much credit in that. [*Mark Tapley.*] *Ib.* ch. 5

7 Some credit in being jolly. [*Mark Tapley.*] *Ib.*

8 A highly geological home-made cake. *Ib.*

9 'Let us be merry.' Here he took a captain's biscuit. [*Mr. Pecksniff.*] *Ib.*

10 With affection beaming in one eye, and calculation shining out of the other. [*Mrs. Todgers.*] *Ib.* ch. 8

11 Oh, Todgers' could do it when it chose! Mind that. *Ib.* ch. 9

12 Charity and Mercy. Not unholy names, I hope? [*Mr. Pecksniff.*] *Ib.*

13 'Do not repine, my friends,' said Mr. Pecksniff, tenderly. 'Do not weep for me. It is chronic.' *Ib.*

14 Let us be moral. Let us contemplate existence. [*Mr. Pecksniff.*] *Ib.*

15 Here's the rule for bargains: 'Do other men, for they would do you.' That's the true business precept. [*Jonas Chuzzlewit.*] *Ib.* ch. 11

16 'Mrs. Harris,' I says, 'leave the bottle on the chimley-piece, and don't ask me to take none, but let me put my lips to it when I am so dispoged.' [*Mrs. Gamp.*] *Ib.* ch. 19

17 Some people . . . may be Rooshans, and others may be Prooshans; they are born so, and will please themselves. Them which is of other naturs thinks different. [*Mrs. Gamp.*] *Ib.*

18 Therefore I *do* require it, which I makes confession, to be brought reg'lar and draw'd mild. [*Mrs. Gamp.*] *Ib.* ch. 25

19 'She's the sort of woman now,' said Mould, . . . 'one would almost feel disposed to bury for nothing: and do it neatly, too!' *Ib.*

20 He'd make a lovely corpse. [*Mrs. Gamp.*] *Ib.*

21 All the wickedness of the world is print to him. [*Mrs. Gamp.*] *Ib.* ch. 26

22 'Sairey,' says Mrs. Harris, 'sech is life. Vich likeways is the hend of all things!' [*Mrs. Gamp.*] *Martin Chuzzlewit*, ch. 29

23 Our backs is easy ris. We must be cracked-up, or they rises, and we snarls. . . . You'd better crack up, you had! [*Chollop.*] *Ib.* ch. 33

24 Our fellow-countryman is a model of a man, quite fresh from Natur's mould! . . . Rough he may be. So air our Barrs. Wild he may be. So air our Buffalers. [*Pogram.*] *Ib.* ch. 34

25 'To be presented to a Pogram,' said Miss Codger, 'by a Hominy, indeed, a thrilling moment is it in its impressiveness on what we call our feelings.' *Ib.*

26 'Mind and matter,' said the lady in the wig, 'glide swift into the vortex of immensity. Howls the sublime, and softly sleeps the calm Ideal, in the whispering chambers of Imagination.' *Ib.*

27 'The Ankworks package,' . . . 'I wish it was in Jonadge's belly, I do,' cried Mrs. Gamp; appearing to confound the prophet with the whale in this miraculous aspiration. *Ib.* ch. 40

28 Oh Sairey, Sairey, little do we know wot lays afore us! [*Mrs. Gamp.*] *Ib.*

29 I know'd she wouldn't have a cowcumber! [*Betsey Prig.*] *Ib.* ch. 49

30 'Who deniges of it?' Mrs. Gamp enquired. *Ib.*

31 Ever since afore her First, which Mr. Harris who was dreadful timid went and stopped his ears in a empty dog-kennel, and never took his hands away or come out once till he was showed the baby, wen bein' took with fits, the doctor collared him and laid him on his back upon the airy stones, and she was told to ease her mind, his owls was organs. [*Mrs. Gamp.*] *Ib.*

32 No, Betsey! Drink fair, wotever you do! [*Mrs. Gamp.*] *Ib.*

33 'Bother Mrs. Harris!' said Betsey Prig. . . . 'I don't believe there's no sich a person!' *Ib.*

34 The words she spoke of Mrs. Harris, lambs could not forgive . . . nor worms forget. [*Mrs. Gamp.*] *Ib.*

35 Which fiddle-strings is weakness to expredge my nerves this night! [*Mrs. Gamp.*] *Ib.* ch. 51

36 Farewell! Be the proud bride of a ducal coronet, and forget me! . . . Unalterably, never yours, Augustus. [*Augustus Moddle.*] *Ib.* ch. 54

37 United Metropolitan Improved Hot Muffin and Crumpet Baking and Punctual Delivery Company. *Nicholas Nickleby*, ch. 2

38 EDUCATION.—At Mr. Wackford Squeers's Academy, Dotheboys Hall, at the delightful village of Dotheboys, near Greta Bridge in Yorkshire, Youth are boarded, clothed, booked, furnished with pocket-money, provided with all necessaries, instructed in all languages living and dead, mathematics, orthography, geometry, astronomy, trigonometry, the use of the globes, algebra, single stick (if required), writing, arithmetic, fortification, and every other branch of classical literature. Terms, twenty guineas per annum. No extras, no vacations, and diet unparalleled. *Ib.* ch. 3

1 He had but one eye, and the popular prejudice runs in favour of two. [*Mr. Squeers.*]
Nicholas Nickleby, ch. 4

2 Serve it right for being so dear. [*Mr. Squeers.*]
Ib. ch. 5

3 Subdue your appetites, my dears, and you've conquered human natur. [*Mr. Squeers.*] *Ib.*

4 Here's richness! [*Mr. Squeers.*] *Ib.*

5 C-l-e-a-n, clean, verb active, to make bright, to scour. W-i-n, win, d-e-r, der, winder, a casement. When the boy knows this out of the book, he goes and does it. [*Mr. Squeers.*] *Ib.* ch. 8

6 As she frequently remarked when she made any such mistake, it would be all the same a hundred years hence. [*Mrs. Squeers.*] *Ib.* ch. 9

7 There are only two styles of portrait painting; the serious and the smirk. [*Miss La Creevy.*]
Ib. ch. 10

8 Oh! they're too beautiful to live, much too beautiful! [*Mrs. Kenwigs.*] *Ib.* ch. 14

9 Sir, My pa requests me to write to you, the doctors considering it doubtful whether he will ever recuvver the use of his legs which prevents his holding a pen. [*Fanny Squeers.*] *Ib.* ch. 15

10 One mask of brooses both blue and green. [*Fanny Squeers.*] *Ib.*

11 I am screaming out loud all the time I write and so is my brother which takes off my attention rather and I hope will excuse mistakes. [*Fanny Squeers.*] *Ib.*

12 I pity his ignorance and despise him. [*Fanny Squeers.*] *Ib.*

13 This is all very well, Mr. Nickleby, and very proper, so far as it goes—so far as it goes, but it doesn't go far enough. [*Mr. Gregsbury.*] *Ib.* ch. 16

14 We've got a private master comes to teach us at home, but we ain't proud, because ma says it's sinful. [*Mrs. Kenwigs.*] *Ib.*

15 'What's the water in French, sir?' '*L'eau*,' replied Nicholas. 'Ah!' said Mr. Lillywick, shaking his head mournfully. 'I thought as much. Lo, eh? I don't think anything of that language—nothing at all.' *Ib.*

16 'It's very easy to talk,' said Mrs. Mantalini. 'Not so easy when one is eating a demnition egg,' replied Mr. Mantalini; 'for the yolk runs down the waistcoat, and yolk of egg does not match any waistcoat but a yellow waistcoat, demmit.'
Ib. ch. 17

17 Language was not powerful enough to describe the infant phenomenon. *Ib.* ch. 23

18 'I hope you have preserved the unities, sir?' said Mr. Curdle. . . .
'The unities, sir, . . . are a completeness—a kind of a universal dovetailedness with regard to place and time.' *Ib.* ch. 24

19 She's the only sylph I ever saw, who could stand upon one leg, and play the tambourine on her other knee, like a sylph. [*Mr. Crummles.*] *Ib.* ch. 25

20 The two countesses had no outlines at all, and the dowager's was a demd outline. [*Mr. Mantalini.*]
Ib. ch. 34

21 I am a demd villain! I will fill my pockets with change for a sovereign in half-pence and drown myself in the Thames . . . I will become a demd, damp, moist, unpleasant body! [*Mr. Mantalini.*]
Nicholas Nickleby, ch. 34

22 In the absence of the planet Venus, who has gone on business to the Horse Guards. [*The Gentleman in the Small-clothes.*] *Ib.* ch. 41

23 Bring in the bottled lightning, a clean tumbler, and a corkscrew. [*The Gentleman in the Small-clothes.*]
Ib. ch. 49

24 All is gas and gaiters. [*The Gentleman in the Small-clothes.*] *Ib.*

25 My life is one demd horrid grind! [*Mr. Mantalini.*]
Ib. ch. 64

26 He has gone to the demnition bow-wows. [*Mr. Mantalini.*] *Ib.*

27 Is the old min agreeable? [*Dick Swiveller.*]
The Old Curiosity Shop, ch. 2

28 What is the odds so long as the fire of soul is kindled at the taper of conwiviality, and the wing of friendship never moults a feather! [*Dick Swiveller.*] *Ib.*

29 Fan the sinking flame of hilarity with the wing of friendship; and pass the rosy wine. [*Dick Swiveller.*] *Ib.* ch. 7

30 Codlin's the friend, not Short. [*Codlin.*] *Ib.* ch. 19

31 If I know'd a donkey wot wouldn't go
To see Mrs. Jarley's waxwork show,
Do you think I'd acknowledge him,
Oh no no! *Ib.* ch. 27

32 I believe, Sir, that you desire to look at these apartments. They are very charming apartments, Sir. They command an uninterrupted view of—of over the way, and they are within one minute's walk of—of the corner of the street. [*Dick Swiveller.*]
Ib. ch. 34

33 I never nursed a dear Gazelle, to glad me with its soft black eye, but when it came to know me well, and love me, it was sure to marry a market-gardener. [*Dick Swiveller.*] *Ib.* ch. 56

34 'Did you ever taste beer?' 'I had a sip of it once,' said the small servant. 'Here's a state of things!' cried Mr. Swiveller. . . . 'She *never* tasted it—it can't be tasted in a sip!' *Ib.* ch. 57

35 It was a maxim with Foxey—our revered father, gentlemen—'Always suspect everybody.' [*Sampson Brass.*] *Ib.* ch. 66

36 Oliver Twist has asked for more! [*Bumble.*]
Oliver Twist, ch. 2

37 Known by the *sobriquet* of 'The artful Dodger.'
Ib. ch. 8

38 'Hard,' replied the Dodger. 'As nails,' added Charley Bates. *Ib.* ch. 9

39 There is a passion for hunting something deeply implanted in the human breast. *Ib.* ch. 10

40 I'll eat my head. [*Mr. Grimwig.*] *Ib.* ch. 14

41 I only know two sorts of boys. Mealy boys, and beef-faced boys. [*Mr. Grimwig.*] *Ib.*

42 Oh, Mrs. Corney, what a prospect this opens! What a opportunity for a jining of hearts and housekeepings! [*Bumble.*] *Ib.* ch. 27

1 'If the law supposes that,' said Mr. Bumble . . . 'the law is a ass—a idiot.' *Oliver Twist*, ch. 51

2 A literary man—*with* a wooden leg. [*Mr. Boffin on Silas Wegg.*] *Our Mutual Friend*, bk. i, ch. 5

3 Professionally he declines and falls, and as a friend he drops into poetry. [*Mr. Boffin on Silas Wegg.*] *Ib.*

4 Why then we should drop into poetry. [*Boffin.*] *Ib.*

5 Decline-and-Fall-Off-The-Rooshan-Empire. [*Mr. Boffin.*] *Ib.*

6 'Mrs. Boffin, Wegg,' said Boffin, 'is a highflyer at Fashion.' *Ib.*

7 Meaty jelly, too, especially when a little salt, which is the case when there's ham, is mellering to the organ. [*Silas Wegg.*] *Ib.*

8 'It is Rooshan; ain't it, Wegg?'
'No, sir. Roman. Roman.'
'What's the difference, Wegg?'
'The difference, sir?—There you place me in a difficulty, Mr. Boffin. Suffice it to observe, that the difference is best postponed to some other occasion when Mrs. Boffin does not honour us with her company.' *Ib.*

9 I didn't think this morning there was half so many Scarers in Print. [*Boffin.*] *Ib.*

10 Mr. Podsnap settled that whatever he put behind him he put out of existence. . . . Mr. Podsnap had even acquired a peculiar flourish of his right arm in often clearing the world of its most difficult problems, by sweeping them behind him. *Ib.* ch. 11

11 The question [with Mr. Podsnap] about everything was, would it bring a blush into the cheek of the young person? *Ib.*

12 The gay, the gay and festive scene,
The halls, the halls of dazzling light. [*Mrs. Boffin.*] *Ib.* ch. 15

13 Oh! *I* know their tricks and their manners. [*Fanny Cleaver.*] *Ib.* bk. ii, ch. 1

14 I think . . . that it is the best club in London. [*Mr. Twemlow, on the House of Commons.*] *Ib.* ch. 3

15 I don't care whether I am a Minx, or a Sphinx. [*Lavvy.*] *Ib.* ch. 8

16 A slap-up gal in a bang-up chariot. *Ib.*

17 Queer Street is full of lodgers just at present. [*Fledgeby.*] *Ib.* bk. iii, ch. 1

18 O Mrs. Higden, Mrs. Higden, you was a woman and a mother, and a mangler in a million million. [*Sloppy.*] *Ib.* ch. 9

19 He'd be sharper than a serpent's tooth, if he wasn't as dull as ditch water. [*Fanny Cleaver.*] *Ib.* ch. 10

20 T'other governor. [*Mr. Riderhood.*] *Ib.* bk. iv, ch. 1

21 The dodgerest of the dodgers. [*Mr. Fledgeby.*] *Ib.* ch. 8

22 The Golden Dustman. *Ib.* ch. 11

23 He had used the word in its Pickwickian sense. . . . He had merely considered him a humbug in a Pickwickian point of view. [*Mr. Blotton.*] *Pickwick Papers*, ch. 1

24 Heads, heads . . .! . . . five children—mother—tall lady, eating sandwiches—forgot the arch—crash—knock—children look round—mother's head off—sandwich in her hand—no mouth to put it in—head of a family off—shocking, shocking! [*Jingle.*] *Pickwick Papers*, ch. 2

25 'I am ruminating,' said Mr. Pickwick, 'on the strange mutability of human affairs.'
'Ah! I see—in at the palace door one day, out at the window the next. Philosopher, sir?'
'An observer of human nature, sir,' said Mr. Pickwick. *Ib.*

26 Half-a-crown in the bill, if you look at the waiter.—Charge you more if you dine at a friend's than they would if you dined in the coffee-room. [*Jingle.*] *Ib.*

27 Not presume to dictate, but broiled fowl and mushrooms—capital thing! [*Jingle.*] *Ib.*

28 Kent, sir—everybody knows Kent—apples, cherries, hops, and women. [*Jingle.*] *Ib.*

29 'It wasn't the wine,' murmured Mr. Snodgrass, in a broken voice. 'It was the salmon.' *Ib.* ch. 8

30 I wants to make your flesh creep. [*The Fat Boy.*] *Ib.*

31 'It's always best on these occasions to do what the mob do.' 'But suppose there are two mobs?' suggested Mr. Snodgrass. 'Shout with the largest,' replied Mr. Pickwick. *Ib.* ch. 13

32 'Can I unmoved see thee dying
On a log,
Expiring frog!' [*Mrs. Leo Hunter.*] *Ib.* ch. 15

33 'Sir,' said Mr. Tupman, 'you're a fellow.' 'Sir,' said Mr. Pickwick, 'you're another!' *Ib.*

34 Tongue; well that's a wery good thing when it an't a woman's. [*Mr. Weller.*] *Ib.* ch. 19

35 Mr. Weller's knowledge of London was extensive and peculiar. *Ib.* ch. 20

36 Be wery careful o' vidders all your life. [*Mr. Weller.*] *Ib.*

37 The wictim o' connubiality, as Blue Beard's domestic chaplain said, with a tear of pity, ven he buried him. [*Mr. Weller.*] *Ib.*

38 'It's a wery remarkable circumstance, sir,' said Sam, 'that poverty and oysters always seem to go together.' *Ib.* ch. 22

39 It's over, and can't be helped, and that's one consolation, as they always says in Turkey, ven they cuts the wrong man's head off. [*Sam Weller.*] *Ib.* ch. 23

40 Dumb as a drum vith a hole in it, sir. [*Sam Weller.*] *Ib.* ch. 25

41 Wery glad to see you, indeed, and hope our acquaintance may be a long 'un, as the gen'l'm'n said to the fi' pun' note. [*Sam Weller.*] *Ib.*

42 Wen you're a married man, Samivel, you'll understand a good many things as you don't understand now; but vether it's worth while goin' through so much to learn so little, as the charity-boy said ven he got to the end of the alphabet, is a matter o' taste. [*Mr. Weller.*] *Ib.* ch. 27

43 Our noble society for providing the infant negroes in the West Indies with flannel waistcoats and moral pocket handkerchiefs. *Ib.* ch. 27

1 'Eccentricities of genius, Sam,' said Mr. Pickwick.
Pickwick Papers, ch. 30

2 Keep yourself *to* yourself. [*Mr. Raddle.*] *Ib.* ch. 32

3 Pursuit of knowledge under difficulties, Sammy? [*Mr. Weller.*] *Ib.* ch. 33

4 A double glass o' the inwariable. [*Mr. Weller.*] *Ib.*

5 Poetry's unnat'ral; no man ever talked poetry 'cept a beadle on boxin' day, or Warren's blackin' or Rowland's oil, or some o' them low fellows. [*Mr. Weller.*] *Ib.*

6 Wot's the good o' callin' a young 'ooman a Wenus or a angel, Sammy? [*Mr. Weller.*] *Ib.*

7 'That's rather a sudden pull up, ain't it, Sammy?' inquired Mr. Weller.
'Not a bit on it,' said Sam; 'she'll vish there wos more, and that's the great art o' letter writin'.' *Ib.*

8 If your governor don't prove a alleybi, he'll be what the Italians call reg'larly flummoxed. [*Mr. Weller.*] *Ib.*

9 She's a swellin' wisibly before my wery eyes. [*Mr. Weller.*] *Ib.*

10 It's my opinion, sir, that this meeting is drunk, sir! [*Mr. Stiggins.*] *Ib.*

11 A Being, erect upon two legs, and bearing all the outward semblance of a man, and not of a monster. [*Buzfuz.*] *Ib.* ch. 34

12 Chops and Tomata sauce. Yours, Pickwick. *Ib.*

13 'Do you spell it with a "V" or a "W"?' inquired the judge.
'That depends upon the taste and fancy of the speller, my Lord,' replied Sam. *Ib.*

14 Put it down a we, my Lord, put it down a we. [*Mr. Weller.*] *Ib.*

15 'Little to do, and plenty to get, I suppose?' said Sergeant Buzfuz, with jocularity.
'Oh, quite enough to get, sir, as the soldier said ven they ordered him three hundred and fifty lashes,' replied Sam.
'You must not tell us what the soldier, or any other man, said, sir,' interposed the judge; 'it's not evidence.' *Ib.*

16 'Yes, I have a pair of eyes,' replied Sam, 'and that's just it. If they wos a pair o' patent double million magnifyin' gas microscopes of hextra power, p'raps I might be able to see through a flight o' stairs and a deal door; but bein' only eyes, you see my wision's limited.' *Ib.*

17 Oh Sammy, Sammy, vy worn't there a alleybi! [*Mr. Weller.*] *Ib.*

18 Miss Bolo rose from the table considerably agitated, and went straight home, in a flood of tears and a Sedan chair. *Ib.* ch. 35

19 A friendly swarry, consisting of a boiled leg of mutton with the usual trimmings. *Ib.* ch. 37

20 'You disliked the killibeate taste, perhaps?'
'I don't know much about that 'ere,' said Sam. 'I thought they'd a wery strong flavour o' warm flat-irons.'
'That *is* the killibeate, Mr. Weller,' observed Mr. John Smauker, contemptuously. *Ib.*

21 'That 'ere young lady,' replied Sam. 'She knows wot's wot, she does.' *Pickwick Papers*, ch. 37

22 *We* know, Mr. Weller—we, who are men of the world —that a good uniform must work its way with the women, sooner or later. *Ib.*

23 You're a amiably-disposed young man, sir, I don't think. [*Sam Weller.*] *Ib.* ch. 38

24 'And a bird-cage, sir,' says Sam. 'Veels vithin veels, a prison in a prison.' *Ib.* ch. 40

25 'It would make anyone go to sleep, that bedstead would, whether they wanted to or not.' [*Mr. Roker.*]
'I should think,' said Sam, ... 'poppies was nothing to it.' *Ib.* ch. 41

26 *They* don't mind it; it's a regular holiday to them— all porter and skittles. [*Sam Weller.*] *Ib.*

27 The have-his-carcase, next to the perpetual motion, is vun of the blessedest things as wos ever made. [*Sam Weller.*] *Ib.* ch. 43

28 Anythin' for a quiet life, as the man said wen he took the sitivation at the lighthouse. [*Sam Weller.*] *Ib.*

29 Wich puts me in mind o' the man as killed hisself on principle, wich o' course you've heerd on, sir. [*Sam Weller.*] *Ib.* ch. 44

30 Which is your partickler wanity? Vich wanity do you like the flavour on best, sir? [*Sam Weller.*] *Ib.* ch. 45

31 You've got the key of the street, my friend. [*Lowten.*] *Ib.* ch. 47

32 'Never ... see ... a dead postboy, did you?' inquired Sam ... 'No,' rejoined Bob, 'I never did.' 'No!' rejoined Sam triumphantly. 'Nor never vill; and there's another thing that no man never see, and that's a dead donkey.' *Ib.* ch. 51

33 'Vell, gov'ner, ve must all come to it, one day or another.'
'So we must, Sammy,' said Mr. Weller the elder.
'There's a Providence in it all,' said Sam.
'O' course there is,' replied his father with a nod of grave approval. 'Wot 'ud become of the undertakers vithout it, Sammy?' *Ib.* ch. 52

34 ''Cos a coachman's a privileged indiwidual,' replied Mr. Weller, looking fixedly at his son. ''Cos a coachman may do vithout suspicion wot other men may not; 'cos a coachman may be on the wery amicablest terms with eighty mile o' females, and yet nobody think that he ever means to marry any vun among them.' *Ib.*

35 I pass my whole life, miss, in turning an immense pecuniary Mangle. [*Mr. Lorry.*]
A Tale of Two Cities, bk. 1, ch. 4

36 If you must go flopping yourself down, flop in favour of your husband and child, and not in opposition to 'em. [*Jerry Cruncher.*] *Ib.* bk. ii, ch. 1

37 'I tell thee,' said madame—'that although it is a long time on the road, it is on the road and coming. I tell thee it never retreats, and never stops.' [*Mme Defarge.*]

38 'It is possible—that it may not come, during our lives. ... We shall not see the triumph.' [*Defarge.*]
'We shall have helped it,' returned madame.
Ib. ch. 16

1 There might be medical doctors . . . a cocking their medical eyes. [*Jerry Cruncher*.]
A Tale of Two Cities, bk. iii, ch. 9

2 It is a far, far better thing that I do, than I have ever done; it is a far, far better rest that I go to, than I have ever known. [*Sydney Carton*.] *Ib.* ch. 15

EMILY DICKINSON
1830–1886

3 Parting is all we know of heaven,
And all we need of hell. *Poems. Parting*

JOHN DICKINSON
1732–1808

4 Our cause is just. Our union is perfect.
Declaration on Taking Up Arms in 1775

5 Then join in hand brave Americans all,
By uniting we stand, by dividing we fall.
The Liberty Song. Memoirs of the Historical Soc. of Pennsylvania, vol. xiv

DENIS DIDEROT
1713–1784

6 L'esprit de l'escalier.

Staircase wit.
An untranslatable phrase, the meaning of which is that one only thinks on one's way downstairs of the smart retort one might have made in the drawing-room. Paradoxe sur le Comédien

WENTWORTH DILLON, EARL OF ROSCOMMON
1633?–1685

7 But words once spoke can never be recall'd.
Art of Poetry, l. 438

8 Choose an author as you choose a friend.
Essay on Translated Verse, l. 96

9 Immodest words admit of no defence,
For want of decency is want of sense. *Ib.* l. 113

10 The multitude is always in the wrong. *Ib.* l. 183

DIOGENES
fl. c. 380 B.C.

11 "μικρόν", εἶπεν, "ἀπὸ τοῦ ἡλίου μετάστηθι."

Alexander . . . asked him if he lacked anything. 'Yea,' said he, 'that I do: that you stand out of my sun a little.'
Plutarch, *Life of Alexander*, 14 (*North's translation*)

DIONYSIUS OF HALICARNASSUS
c. 40–8 B.C.

12 History is philosophy teaching by examples.
Antiquities of Rome

BENJAMIN DISRAELI, EARL OF BEACONSFIELD
1804–1881

13 Though I sit down now, the time will come when you will hear me.
Maiden Speech, 7 *Dec. 1837*. Meynell, *Disraeli*, i. 43

14 The Continent will not suffer England to be the workshop of the world.
Speech, House of Commons, 15 Mar. 1838

15 The noble Lord [Lord Stanley] is the Rupert of Parliamentary discussion. *Ib. 24 Apr. 1844*

16 The right hon. Gentleman [Sir Robert Peel] caught the Whigs bathing, and walked away with their clothes. *Ib. 28 Feb. 1845*

17 Protection is not a principle, but an expedient.
Ib. 17 Mar. 1845

18 A Conservative Government is an organized hypocrisy. *Ib.*

19 He traces the steam-engine always back to the tea-kettle. *Ib. 11 Apr. 1845*

20 A precedent embalms a principle. *Ib. 22 Feb. 1848*

21 Justice is truth in action. *Ib. 11 Feb. 1851*

22 I read this morning an awful, though monotonous, manifesto in the great organ of public opinion, which always makes me tremble: Olympian bolts; and yet I could not help fancying amid their rumbling terrors I heard the plaintive treble of the Treasury Bench. *Ib. 13 Feb. 1851*

23 England does not love coalitions. *Ib. 16 Dec. 1852*

24 Finality is not the language of politics.
Ib. 28 Feb. 1859

25 This shows how much easier it is to be critical than to be correct. *Ib. 24 Jan. 1860*

26 The Church of England is not a mere depositary of doctrine. *Ib. 27 Feb. 1861*

27 To put an end to these bloated armaments.
Ib. 8 May 1862

28 He seems to think that posterity is a pack-horse, always ready to be loaded. *Ib. 3 June 1862*

29 Colonies do not cease to be colonies because they are independent. *Ib. 5 Feb. 1863*

30 You are not going, I hope, to leave the destinies of the British Empire to prigs and pedants. *Ib.*

31 Never take anything for granted.
Ib. at Salthill, 5 Oct. 1864

32 I hold that the characteristic of the present age is craving credulity.
Ib. at Meeting of Society for Increasing Endowments of Small Livings in the Diocese of Oxford, 25 Nov. 1864

33 Man, my Lord [Bishop Wilberforce], is a being born to believe. *Ib.*

34 Party is organized opinion. *Ib.*

35 Is man an ape or an angel? Now I am on the side of the angels. *Ib.*

36 Assassination has never changed the history of the world. *Ib. House of Commons, 1 May 1865*

37 Change is inevitable. In a progressive country change is constant. *Ib. Edinburgh, 29 Oct. 1867*

38 I had to prepare the mind of the country, and . . . to educate our party. *Ib.*

39 We have legalized confiscation, consecrated sacrilege, and condoned high treason.
Ib. House of Commons, 27 Feb. 1871

1 I believe that without party Parliamentary government is impossible. *Speech, Manchester, 3 Apr. 1872*

2 As I sat opposite the Treasury Bench the ministers reminded me of one of those marine landscapes not very unusual on the coasts of South America. You behold a range of exhausted volcanoes. *Ib.*

3 Increased means and increased leisure are the two civilizers of man. *Ib.*

4 A University should be a place of light, of liberty, and of learning. *Ib. House of Commons, 11 Mar. 1873*

5 An author who speaks about his own books is almost as bad as a mother who talks about her own children. *Ib. at Banquet given by Glasgow to Lord Rector, 19 Nov. 1873*

6 King Louis Philippe once said to me that he attributed the great success of the British nation in political life to their talking politics after dinner. *Ib.*

7 Upon the education of the people of this country the fate of this country depends. *Ib. House of Commons, 15 June 1874*

8 He is a great master of gibes and flouts and jeers. *Referring to his colleague, the Marquis of Salisbury. Ib. 5 Aug. 1874*

9 Cosmopolitan critics, men who are the friends of every country save their own. *Ib. Guildhall, 9 Nov. 1877*

10 Lord Salisbury and myself have brought you back peace—but a peace I hope with honour. *Ib. House of Commons, 16 July 1878*

11 A series of congratulatory regrets. [Lord Harrington's Resolution on the Berlin Treaty.] *Ib. at Banquet in Riding School, Knightsbridge, 27 July 1878*

12 A sophistical rhetorician, inebriated with the exuberance of his own verbosity. [Gladstone.] *Ib.*

13 The hare-brained chatter of irresponsible frivolity. *Ib. Guildhall, London, 9 Nov. 1878*

14 One of the greatest of Romans, when asked what were his politics, replied, *Imperium et Libertas.* That would not make a bad programme for a British Ministry. *Ib. Mansion House, London, 10 Nov. 1879*

15 The key of India is in London. *Ib. House of Lords, 5 Mar. 1881*

16 Damn your principles! Stick to your party. *Attr. Remark to Bulwer Lytton* (Latham, *Famous Sayings*)

17 Protection is not only dead, but damned. (c. 1850) Monypenny and Buckle, *Life of Disraeli*, iii. 241

18 Pray remember, Mr. Dean, no dogma, no Dean. *Ib. iv. 368*

19 There is no reason to doubt the story which represents him as using more than once, in conversation with Her Majesty on literary subjects, the words: 'We authors, Ma'am.' *Ib. v. 49*

20 'I am dead: dead, but in the Elysian fields,' was Benjamin's reply to an acquaintance among the peers, who, when welcoming him to the Lords, expressed a fear lest he should miss the excitement of the Commons. *Ib. 522*

21 When I want to read a novel I write one. Monypenny and Buckle, *Life of Disraeli*, vi. 636

22 Everyone likes flattery; and when you come to Royalty you should lay it on with a trowel. *Remark to Matthew Arnold.* G. W. E. Russell, *Collections and Recollections*, ch. 23.

23 She is an excellent creature, but she never can remember which came first, the Greeks or the Romans. [Of his wife.] *Ib.* ch. 1

24 Your Majesty is the head of the literary profession. *Remark to Queen Victoria. Ib.* ch. 23

25 Never complain and never explain. J. Morley, *Life of Gladstone*, i. 122

26 Between ourselves, I could floor them all. This *entre nous*: I was never more confident of anything than that I could carry everything before me in that House. The time will come. *Letters, 7 Feb. 1833*

27 In the 'Town' yesterday, I am told 'some one asked Disraeli, in offering himself for Marylebone, on what he intended *to stand.* "On my head," was the reply.' *Ib. 8 Apr. 1833*

28 There can be no economy where there is no efficiency. *Ib. To Constituents, 3 Oct. 1868*

29 Tadpole and Taper were great friends. Neither of them ever despaired of the Commonwealth. *Coningsby*, bk. i, ch. 1

30 No Government can be long secure without a formidable Opposition. *Ib.* bk. ii, ch. 1

31 . . . the Arch-Mediocrity who presided, rather than ruled, over this Cabinet of Mediocrities. *Ib.*

32 Conservatism discards Prescription, shrinks from Principle, disavows Progress; having rejected all respect for antiquity, it offers no redress for the present, and makes no preparation for the future. *Ib.* ch. 5

33 'A sound Conservative government,' said Taper, musingly. 'I understand: Tory men and Whig measures.' *Ib.* ch. 6

34 Adventures are to the adventurous. *Ib.* bk. iii, ch. 1

35 The still hissing bacon and the eggs that looked like tufts of primroses. *Ib.*

36 Almost everything that is great has been done by youth. *Ib.*

37 Youth is a blunder; Manhood a struggle; Old Age a regret. *Ib.*

38 It seems to me a barren thing this Conservatism—an unhappy cross-breed, the mule of politics that engenders nothing. *Ib.* ch. 5

39 I have been ever of opinion that revolutions are not to be evaded. *Ib.* bk. iv, ch. 11

40 The depositary of power is always unpopular. *Ib.*

41 Where can we find faith in a nation of sectaries? *Ib.* ch. 13

42 Man is only truly great when he acts from the passions. *Ib.*

43 I grew intoxicated with my own eloquence. *Contarini Fleming*, pt. i, ch. 7

44 Read no history: nothing but biography, for that is life without theory. *Ib.* ch. 23

1 The practice of politics in the East may be defined by one word—dissimulation.
Contarini Fleming, pt. v, ch. 10

2 He flits across the stage a transient and embarrassed phantom. *Endymion*, bk. i, ch. 3

3 His Christianity was muscular. *Ib*. ch. 14

4 The Athanasian Creed is the most splendid ecclesiastical lyric ever poured forth by the genius of man.
Ib. ch. 54

5 'As for that,' said Waldershare, 'sensible men are all of the same religion.' 'And pray, what is that?' inquired the prince. 'Sensible men never tell.'
Ib. ch. 81

6 The sweet simplicity of the three per cents.
Ib. ch. 91

7 I believe they went out, like all good things, with the Stuarts. *Ib*. ch. 99

8 What we anticipate seldom occurs; what we least expect generally happens. *Ib*. bk. ii, ch. 4

9 Time is the great physician. *Ib*. bk. vi, ch. 9

10 They [the Furies] mean well; their feelings are strong, but their hearts are in the right place.
The Infernal Marriage, pt. i, 1

11 The blue ribbon of the turf. [The Derby.]
Life of Lord George Bentinck, ch. 26

12 Every day when he looked into the glass, and gave the last touch to his consummate toilette, he offered his grateful thanks to Providence that his family was not unworthy of him. *Lothair*, ch. 1

13 'I could have brought you some primroses, but I do not like to mix violets with anything.'
'They say primroses make a capital salad,' said Lord St. Jerome. *Ib*. ch. 13

14 A Protestant, if he wants aid or advice on any matter, can only go to his solicitor. *Ib*. ch. 27

15 London; a nation, not a city. *Ib*.

16 The gondola of London. [A hansom.] *Ib*.

17 When a man fell into his anecdotage it was a sign for him to retire from the world. *Ib*. ch. 28

18 He was not an intellectual Crœsus, but his pockets were full of sixpences. *Ib*.

19 What I admire in the order to which you belong is that they do live in the air; that they excel in athletic sports; that they can only speak one language; and that they never read. This is not a complete education, but it is the highest education since the Greek. *Ib*. ch. 29

20 Every woman should marry—and no man.
Ib. ch. 30

21 You know who the critics are? The men who have failed in literature and art. *Ib*. ch. 35

22 'My idea of an agreeable person,' said Hugo Bohun, 'is a person who agrees with me.' *Ib*. ch. 41

23 St. Aldegonde had a taste for marriages and public executions. *Ib*. ch. 88

24 'I rather like bad wine,' said Mr. Mountchesney; 'one gets so bored with good wine.'
Sybil, bk. i, ch. 1

25 The Egremonts had never said anything that was remembered, or done anything that could be recalled. *Ib*. ch. 3

26 To do nothing and get something, formed a boy's ideal of a manly career. *Sybil*, bk. i, ch. 5

27 Little things affect little minds. *Ib*. bk. iii, ch. 2

28 Mr. Kremlin himself was distinguished for ignorance, for he had only one idea,—and that was wrong.
Ib. bk. iv, ch. 5

29 I was told that the Privileged and the People formed Two Nations. *Ib*. ch. 8

30 A public man of light and leading in the country.
Ib. bk. v, ch. 1

31 The Youth of a Nation are the trustees of Posterity.
Ib. bk. vi, ch. 13

32 Guanoed her mind by reading French novels.
Tancred, bk. ii, ch. 9

33 That fatal drollery called a representative government.
Ib. ch. 13

34 A majority is always the best repartee. *Ib*. ch. 14

35 All is race; there is no other truth. *Ib*.

36 The East is a career. *Ib*

37 London is a modern Babylon. *Ib*. bk. v, ch. 5

38 The microcosm of a public school.
Vivian Grey, bk. i, ch. 2

39 I hate definitions. *Ib*. bk. ii, ch. 6

40 Information upon points of practical politics.
Ib. ch. 1

41 Experience is the child of Thought, and Thought is the child of Action. We cannot learn men from books. *Ib*. bk. v, ch. 1

42 There is moderation even in excess.
Ib. bk. vi, ch. 1

43 I repeat . . . that all power is a trust—that we are accountable for its exercise—that, from the people, and for the people, all springs, and all must exist.
Ib. ch. 7

44 All Paradise opens! Let me die eating ortolans to the sound of soft music!
The Young Duke, bk. i, ch. 10

45 A *dark* horse, which had never been thought of, and which the careless St. James had never even observed in the list, rushed past the grand stand in sweeping triumph. *Ib*. bk. ii, ch. 5

46 'The age of chivalry is past,' said May Dacre. 'Bores have succeeded to dragons.' *Ib*

47 A man may speak very well in the House of Commons, and fail very completely in the House of Lords. There are two distinct styles requisite: I intend, in the course of my career, if I have time, to give a specimen of both. *Ib*. bk. v, ch. 6

ISAAC D'ISRAELI
1766-1848

48 He wreathed the rod of criticism with roses. [Bayle.]
Curiosities of Literature, 1834, vol. i, p. 20

49 There is an art of reading, as well as an art of thinking, and an art of writing. *Literary Character*, ch. 11

SYDNEY THOMPSON DOBELL
1824–1874

1 The murmur of the mourning ghost
  That keeps the shadowy kine,
'Oh, Keith of Ravelston,
  The sorrows of thy line!'   *A Nuptial Eve*

HENRIETTA OCTAVIA DE LISLE DOBREE
1831–1894

2 Safely, safely gather'd in,
  Far from sorrow, far from sin.
    Children's Hymn Book, 1881. *Safely, Safely
    Gather'd In.*

HENRY AUSTIN DOBSON
1840–1921

3 And I wove the thing to a random rhyme,
For the Rose is Beauty, the Gardener, Time.
              A Fancy from Fontenelle

4 It may be that he could not count
The sires and sons to Jesse's fount,—
He liked the 'Sermon on the Mount,'—
      And more, he read it.
              A Gentleman of the Old School

5 All passes. Art alone
    Enduring stays to us;
The Bust outlasts the throne,—
    The Coin, Tiberius.
      Ars Victrix. (See Théophile Gautier, 214:3)

6 And where are the galleons of Spain?
              Ballad to Queen Elizabeth

7 O, Love's but a dance,
    Where Time plays the fiddle!
See the couples advance,—
O, Love's but a dance!
A whisper, a glance,—
    'Shall we twirl down the middle?'
O, Love's but a dance,
    Where Time plays the fiddle!   *Cupid's Alley*

8 Ah, would but one might lay his lance in rest,
And charge in earnest . . . were it but a mill!
              Don Quixote

9 Fame is a food that dead men eat,—
I have no stomach for such meat.
      Fame is a Food that Dead Men Eat

10 He held his pen in trust
To Art, not serving shame or lust.   *In After Days*

11 The ladies of St. James's!
    They're painted to the eyes,
Their white it stays for ever,
    Their red it never dies:
But Phyllida, my Phyllida!
    Her colour comes and goes;
It trembles to a lily,—
    It wavers to a rose.   *The Ladies of St. James's*

12 The ladies of St. James's!
    They have their fits and freaks;
They smile on you—for seconds;
    They frown on you—for weeks.   *Ib.*

13 But Phyllida, my Phyllida!
    She takes her buckled shoon,
When we go out a-courting
    Beneath the harvest moon.   *Ib.*

14 For I respectfully decline
  To dignify the Serpentine,
And make *hors-d'œuvres* for fishes.
              To 'Lydia Languish'

15 Time goes, you say? Ah no!
Alas, Time stays, *we* go.   *The Paradox of Time*

16 I intended an Ode,
    And it turned to a Sonnet.
It began *à la mode*,
I intended an Ode;
But Rose crossed the road
    In her latest new bonnet;
I intended an Ode;
    And it turned to a Sonnet.   *Rose-Leaves*

17 Rose kissed me to-day.
Will she kiss me to-morrow?
Let it be as it may,
Rose kissed me to-day,
But the pleasure gives way
To a savour of sorrow;—
Rose kissed me to-day,—
Will she kiss me to-morrow?   *Ib.*

18 This was the Pompadour's Fan!
    *On a Fan that belonged to the Marquise de
    Pompadour*

PHILIP DODDRIDGE
1702–1751

19 Hark, the glad sound! The Saviour comes,
  The Saviour promised long.
              Hymns (1755). *Hark, The Glad Sound*

20 O God of Bethel, by whose hand
    Thy people still are fed,
Who through this weary pilgrimage
    Hast all our fathers led:

Our vows, our prayers, we now present
    Before thy throne of grace,
God of our fathers, be the God
    Of their succeeding race.   *Ib. O God of Bethel*

21 Ye servants of the Lord,
    Each in his office wait,
Observant of His heav'nly Word,
    And watchful at His Gate.
              Ib. Ye Servants of the Lord

MARY ABIGAIL DODGE
see
GAIL HAMILTON

CHARLES LUTWIDGE DODGSON
see
LEWIS CARROLL

GEORGE BUBB DODINGTON, BARON MELCOMBE
1691–1762

22 Love thy country, wish it well,
    Not with too intense a care,
'Tis enough, that when it fell,
    Thou its ruin didst not share.   Spence's *Anecdotes*

CHARLES FLETCHER DOLE
1845–?

1 Democracy is on trial in the world, on a more colossal scale than ever before. *The Spirit of Democracy*

ALFRED DOMETT
1811–1887

2 It was the calm and silent night!—
Seven hundred years and fifty-three
Had Rome been growing up to might,
And now was Queen of land and sea!
No sound was heard of clashing wars;
Peace brooded o'er the hushed domain;
Apollo, Pallas, Jove and Mars,
Held undisturbed their ancient reign,
In the solemn midnight
Centuries ago! *Christmas Hymn*

ÆLIUS DONATUS
fl. 4th cent. A.D.

3 Huic quid simile sententiae et Comicus ait: 'nihil est dictum, quod non est dictum prius.' (Terent. in *Prolog. Eunuchi.*) Unde preceptor meus Donatus, cum istum versiculum exponeret: Pereant, inquit, qui ante nos nostra dixerunt.

The same idea is said by the comic poet: 'Nothing is said which has not been said before.' Whence my teacher Donatus, when he was speaking of that verse, said, 'Confound those who have said our remarks before us.'
St. Jerome, *Commentary on Ecclesiastes*, cap. i. Migne's *Patrologiae Lat. Cursus*, xxiii. 390

JOHN DONNE
1571?–1631

4 Twice or thrice had I loved thee,
Before I knew thy face or name.
So in a voice, so in a shapeless flame,
Angels affect us oft, and worshipped be.
Air and Angels

5 Just such disparity
As is 'twixt air and Angels' purity,
'Twixt women's love, and men's will ever be. *Ib.*

6 All other things, to their destruction draw,
Only our love hath no decay;
This, no to-morrow hath, nor yesterday,
Running it never runs from us away,
But truly keeps his first, last, everlasting day.
The Anniversary

7 Let us love nobly, and live, and add again
Years and years unto years, till we attain
To write threescore: this is the second of our reign.
Ib.

8 Come live with me, and be my love,
And we will some new pleasures prove
Of golden sands, and crystal brooks,
With silken lines, and silver hooks. *The Bait*

9 A naked thinking heart, that makes no show,
Is to a woman, but a kind of ghost. *The Blossom*

10 The day breaks not, it is my heart.
Break of Day (Attr. also to John Dowland)

11 For God's sake hold your tongue, and let me love.
The Canonization

12 Dear love, for nothing less than thee
Would I have broke this happy dream,
It was a theme
For reason, much too strong for fantasy,
Therefore thou wak'd'st me wisely; yet
My dream thou brok'st not, but continued'st it.
The Dream

13 Love built on beauty, soon as beauty, dies.
Elegies, No. 2. The Anagram

14 The grim eight-foot-high iron-bound serving-man,
That oft names God in oaths, and only then.
Ib. No. 4. The Perfume

15 She, and comparisons are odious.
Ib. No. 8. The Comparison

16 No Spring, nor Summer beauty hath such grace,
As I have seen in one Autumnal face.
Ib. No. 9. The Autumnal

17 So, if I dream I have you, I have you,
For, all our joys are but fantastical.
Ib. No. 10. The Dream

18 By our first strange and fatal interview.
Ib. No. 16. On His Mistress

19 All will spy in thy face
A blushing womanly discovering grace. *Ib.*

20 Whoever loves, if he do not propose
The right true end of love, he's one that goes
To sea for nothing but to make him sick.
Ib. No. 18. Love's Progress

21 The straight Hellespont between
The Sestos and Abydos of her breasts. *Ib.*

22 Those set our hairs, but these our flesh upright.
Ib. No. 19. On Going to Bed

23 O my America! my new-found-land. *Ib.*

24 Where harmless fish monastic silence keep.
Epicedes and Obsequies. Elegy on Mrs. Boulstred l. 14

25 O strong and long-liv'd death, how cam'st thou in *Ib. l. 21*

26 Hail, Bishop Valentine, whose day this is,
All the air is thy Diocese.
Epithalamions. 1, On the Lady Elizabeth and Count Palatine being Married on St. Valentine's Day.

27 The household bird, with the red stomacher. *Ib.*

28 So, so, break off this last lamenting kiss,
Which sucks two souls, and vapours both away,
Turn thou ghost that way, and let me turn this,
And let our selves benight our happiest day.
The Expiration

29 Where, like a pillow on a bed,
A pregnant bank swelled up, to rest
The violet's reclining head,
Sat we two, one another's best. *The Extasy*

30 So to'entergraft our hands, as yet
Was all the means to make us one,
And pictures in our eyes to get
Was all our propagation. *Ib.*

31 And whilst our souls negotiate there,
We like sepulchral statues lay;
All day, the same our postures were,
And we said nothing, all the day. *Ib.*

DONNE

1 But O alas, so long, so far
Our bodies why do we forbear?
They're ours, though they're not we, we are
The intelligencies, they the sphere. *The Extasy*

2 So must pure lovers' souls descend
T' affections, and to faculties,
Which sense may reach and apprehend,
Else a great Prince in prison lies. *Ib.*

3 She, she is dead; she's dead; when thou know'st this,
Thou know'st how dry a cinder this world is.
The First Anniversary, l. 427

4 Who ever comes to shroud me, do not harm
Nor question much
That subtle wreath of hair, which crowns my arm;
The mystery, the sign you must not touch,
For 'tis my outward soul,
Viceroy to that, which then to heaven being gone,
Will leave this to control,
And keep these limbs, her Province, from dissolution.
The Funeral

5 What ere she meant by it, bury it with me,
For since I am
Love's martyr, it might breed idolatry,
If into other's hands these relics came;
As 'twas humility
To afford to it all that a soul can do,
So, 'tis some bravery,
That since you would save none of me, I bury some
of you. *Ib.*

6 I wonder by my troth, what thou, and I
Did, till we lov'd? were we not wean'd till then?
But suck'd on country pleasures, childishly?
The Good-Morrow

7 And now good morrow to our waking souls,
Which watch not one another out of fear. *Ib.*

8 Without sharp North, without declining West. *Ib.*

9 That All, which always is All everywhere.
Holy Sonnets. Annunciation

10 Immensity cloistered in thy dear womb. *Ib.*

11 As due by many titles I resign
My self to thee, O God, first I was made
By thee, and for thee, and when I decayed
Thy blood bought that, the which before was thine.
Ib. ii

12 I am a little world made cunningly
Of elements, and an angelic sprite. *Ib. v*

13 At the round earth's imagined corners, blow
Your trumpets, Angels, and arise, arise. *Ib. vii*

14 All whom war, dearth, age, agues, tyrannies,
Despair, law, chance, hath slain. *Ib.*

15 Death be not proud, though some have called thee
Mighty and dreadful, for, thou art not so,
For, those, whom thou think'st, thou dost overthrow,
Die not, poor death. *Ib. x*

16 One short sleep past, we wake eternally,
And death shall be no more; death, thou shalt die.
Ib.

17 What if this present were the world's last night?
Ib. xiii

18 Batter my heart, three person'd God; for, you
As yet but knock, breathe, shine, and seek to mend.
Ib. xiv

19 Take me to you, imprison me, for I
Except you enthrall me, never shall be free,
Nor ever chaste, except you ravish me.
Holy Sonnets, xiv

20 Show me, dear Christ, thy spouse, so bright and
clear. *Ib. xviii*

21 As thou
Art jealous, Lord, so I am jealous now,
Thou lov'st not, till from loving more, thou free
My soul: whoever gives, takes liberty:
O, if thou car'st not whom I love
Alas, thou lov'st not me.
*Hymn to Christ, at the author's last going into
Germany*

22 Seal then this bill of my Divorce to all. *Ib.*

23 To see God only, I go out of sight:
And to scape stormy days, I choose
An everlasting night. *Ib.*

24 Wilt thou forgive that sin, where I begun,
Which is my sin, though it were done before?
Wilt thou forgive those sins through which I run
And do them still, though still I do deplore?
When thou hast done, thou hast not done,
For I have more.

Wilt thou forgive that sin, by which I'have won
Others to sin, and made my sin their door?
Wilt thou forgive that sin which I did shun
A year or two, but wallowed in a score?
When thou hast done, thou hast not done,
For I have more.

I have a sin of fear that when I have spun
My last thread, I shall perish on the shore;
Swear by thy self that at my death, thy Sun
Shall shine as it shines now, and heretofore;
And having done that, thou hast done,
I have no more. *Hymn to God the Father*

25 Since I am coming to that holy room,
Where, with thy quire of Saints for evermore,
I shall be made thy Music; as I come
I tune the instrument here at the door,
And what I must do then, think here before.
Hymn to God in My Sickness

26 Will no other vice content you? *The Indifferent*

27 Rob me, but bind me not, and let me go. *Ib.*

28 And by Love's sweetest part, Variety, she swore. *Ib.*

29 And said, alas, some two or three
Poor heretics in love there be,
Which think to stablish dangerous constancy. *Ib.*

30 Stand still, and I will read to thee
A lecture, Love, in love's philosophy.
A Lecture upon the Shadow

31 Love is a growing or full constant light;
And his first minute, after noon, is night. *Ib.*

32 When I died last, and, Dear, I die
As often as from thee I go,
Though it be but an hour ago,
And lovers' hours be full eternity. *The Legacy*

33 If yet I have not all thy love,
Dear, I shall never have it all. *Lovers' Infiniteness*

34 I long to talk with some old lover's ghost,
Who died before the god of love was born.
Love's Deity

1 Rebel and Atheist too, why murmur I,
As though I felt the worst that love could do?
Love's Deity

2 'Tis the year's midnight, and it is the day's.
Nocturnal upon St. Lucy's Day

3 The world's whole sap is sunk:
The general balm th' hydroptic earth hath drunk. *Ib.*

4 I sing the progress of a deathless soul.
Progress of the Soul, i

5 Great Destiny the Commissary of God. *Ib. iv*

6 To my six lustres almost now outwore. *Ib. v*

7 This soul to whom Luther, and Mahomet were
Prisons of flesh. *Ib. vii*

8 When my grave is broke up again
Some second guest to entertain,
(For graves have learnt that woman-head
To be to more than one a bed). *The Relic*

9 A bracelet of bright hair about the bone. *Ib.*

10 On a huge hill,
Cragged, and steep, Truth stands, and he that will
Reach her, about must, and about must go.
Satyre iii. l. 79

11 As till God's great *Venite* change the song.
The Second Anniversary, l. 44

12 Think then, my soul, that death is but a groom,
Which brings a taper to the outward room. *Ib. l. 85*

13 Her pure and eloquent blood
Spoke in her cheeks, and so distinctly wrought,
That one might almost say, her body thought.
Ib. l. 244

14 Whose twilights were more clear, than our mid-day.
Ib. l. 463

15 Sweetest love, I do not go,
For weariness of thee,
Nor in hope the world can show
A fitter Love for me;
But since that I
Must die at last, 'tis best,
To use my self in jest
Thus by feigned deaths to die. *Song*

16 Go, and catch a falling star,
Get with child a mandrake root,
Tell me, where all past years are,
Or who cleft the Devil's foot.
Song, Go and Catch a Falling Star

17 And swear
No where
Lives a woman true and fair. *Ib.*

18 Though she were true, when you met her,
And last, till you write your letter,
Yet she
Will be
False, ere I come, to two, or three. *Ib.*

19 Busy old fool, unruly Sun,
Why dost thou thus,
Through windows, and through curtains call on us?
Must to thy motions lovers' seasons run?
The Sun Rising

20 Love, all alike, no season knows, nor clime,
Nor hours, days, months, which are the rags of time.
Ib.

21 I am two fools, I know,
For loving, and for saying so
In whining Poetry. *The Triple Fool*

22 Who are a little wise, the best fools be. *Ib.*

23 I have done one braver thing
Than all the Worthies did,
And yet a braver thence doth spring,
Which is, to keep that hid. *The Undertaking*

24 So let us melt, and make no noise,
No tear-floods, nor sigh-tempests move,
'Twere profanation of our joys
To tell the laity our love.
A Valediction Forbidding Mourning

25 Dull sublunary lovers' love
(Whose soul is sense) cannot admit
Absence, because it doth remove
Those things which elemented it.

But we, by a love so much refined,
That ourselves know not what it is,
Inter-assured of the mind,
Care less, eyes, lips, and hands to miss.

Our two souls therefore, which are one,
Though I must go, endure not yet
A breach, but an expansion,
Like gold to airy thinness beat.

If they be two, they are two so
As stiff twin compasses are two,
Thy soul the fixt foot, makes no show
To move, but doth, if the other do.

And though it in the centre sit,
Yet when the other far doth roam,
It leans, and hearkens after it,
And grows erect, as that comes home.

Such wilt thou be to me, who must
Like th' other foot, obliquely run;
Thy firmness makes my circle just,
And makes me end, where I begun. *Ib.*

26 But I do nothing upon my self, and yet I am mine
own *Executioner.* *Devotions*

27 No man is an *Island*, entire of it self. *Ib.*

28 Any man's *death* diminishes *me*, because I am involved
in *Mankind*; And therefore never send to know for
whom the *bell* tolls; It tolls for *thee.* *Ib.*

29 John Donne, Anne Donne, Un-done.
Letter to his Wife

30 Poor intricated soul! Riddling, perplexed, labyrinthical soul! *Sermons, i, p. 486, No. xlviii*

31 A Day that hath no *pridie*, nor *postridie*, yesterday
doth not usher it in, nor tomorrow shall not drive
it out. Methusalem, with all his hundreds of
years, was but a mushroom of a night's growth,
to this Day, and all the four Monarchies, with all
their thousands of years, and all the powerful
Kings and Queens of this world, were but as a
bed of flowers, some gathered at six, some at
seven, some at eight, all in one morning, in respect
of this Day. *Ib. p. 747, No. lxxiii. Eternity*

32 I throw myself down in my chamber, and I call in,
and invite God, and his Angels thither, and when
they are there, I neglect God and his Angels, for
the noise of a fly, for the rattling of a coach, for the
whining of a door.
*Ib. p. 800, No. lxxx. At the Funeral of Sir
William Cokayne*

JULIA CAROLINE RIPLEY DORR
1825-1913

1 O true, brave heart! God bless thee, wheresoe'er
In God's great universe thou art to-day!
Friar Anselm and other Poems. How Can I Cease to Pray for Thee?

CHARLES SACKVILLE, EARL OF DORSET
1638-1706

2 To all you ladies now at land,
We men, at sea, indite.
To All You Ladies Now at Land

SARAH DOUDNEY
1843-1926

3 But the waiting time, my brothers,
Is the hardest time of all.
Psalms of Life, The Hardest Time of All

BISHOP GAVIN DOUGLAS
1474?-1522

4 Dame naturis menstralis, on that other part,
Thar blysfull bay entonyng every art,
To beyt thir amorus of thar nychtis baill,
The merl, the mavys, and the nychtyngale,
With mery notis myrthfully furth brest,
Enforcying thame quha mycht do clynk it best.
Eneados, bk. xii, prol. l. 231

5 And all small fowlys singis on the spray:
Welcum the lord of lycht and lamp of day. *Ib. l. 251*

WILLIAM DOUGLAS
1672-1748

6 And for bonnie Annie Laurie
I'd lay me doun and dee. *Annie Laurie*

LORENZO DOW
1777-1834

7 Observing the doctrine of Particular Election . . . and those who preached it up to make the Bible clash and contradict itself, by preaching somewhat like this:
You can and you can't—You shall and you shan't—
You will and you won't—And you will be damned if you do—
And you will be damned if you don't.
Reflections on the Love of God, vi (1836), 30

ERNEST DOWSON
1867-1900

8 And I was desolate and sick of an old passion.
Non Sum Qualis Eram

9 I have been faithful to thee, Cynara! in my fashion. *Ib.*

10 I have forgot much, Cynara! gone with the wind,
Flung roses, roses, riotously, with the throng,
Dancing, to put thy pale, lost lilies out of mind. *Ib.*

11 They are not long, the weeping and the laughter,
Love and desire and hate;
I think they have no portion in us after
We pass the gate. *Vitae Summa Brevis*

SIR ARTHUR CONAN DOYLE
1859-1930

12 What of the bow?
The bow was made in England:
Of true wood, of yew-wood,
The wood of English bows. *Song of the Bow*

13 'It seems . . . to be one of those simple cases which are so extremely difficult.' 'That sounds a little paradoxical.' 'But it is profoundly true. Singularity is almost invariably a clue. The more featureless and commonplace a crime is, the more difficult is it to bring it home.'
The Adventures of Sherlock Holmes. The Boscombe Valley Mystery

14 A little monograph on the ashes of one hundred and forty different varieties of pipe, cigar, and cigarette tobacco. *Ib.*

15 The husband was a teetotaller, there was no other woman, and the conduct complained of was that he had drifted into the habit of winding up every meal by taking out his false teeth and hurling them at his wife. *Ib. A Case of Identity*

16 It has long been an axiom of mine that the little things are infinitely the most important. *Ib.*

17 It is my belief, Watson, founded upon my experience, that the lowest and vilest alleys of London do not present a more dreadful record of sin than does the smiling and beautiful countryside.
Ib. Copper Beeches

18 A man should keep his little brain attic stocked with all the furniture that he is likely to use, and the rest he can put away in the lumber-room of his library, where he can get it if he wants it.
Ib. Five Orange Pips

19 It is quite a three-pipe problem.
Ib. The Red-Headed League

20 I have nothing to do to-day. My practice is never very absorbing. *Ib.*

21 To Sherlock Holmes she [Irene Adler] is always *the* woman. *Ib. Scandal in Bohemia*

22 It is a capital mistake to theorize before one has data. *Ib.*

23 You know my methods, Watson.
The Memoirs of Sherlock Holmes. The Crooked Man

24 'Excellent!' I [Dr. Watson] cried. 'Elementary,' said he [Holmes]. *Ib.*

25 'It is my duty to warn you that it will be used against you,' cried the Inspector, with the magnificent fair play of the British criminal law.
Ib. Dancing Men

26 He [Professor Moriarty] is the Napoleon of crime.
Ib. The Final Problem

27 'The practice is quiet,' said I [Dr. Watson], 'and I have an accommodating neighbour.' *Ib.*

28 You know my methods in such cases, Watson.
Ib. The Musgrave Ritual

29 My practice could get along very well for a day or two. *Ib. The Naval Treaty*

1 You mentioned your name as if I should recognize it, but beyond the obvious facts that you are a bachelor, a solicitor, a Freemason, and an asthmatic, I know nothing whatever about you.
The Memoirs of Sherlock Holmes. The Norwood Builder

2 'Arrest you!' said Holmes. 'This is really most grati—most interesting!' *Ib.*

3 These are much deeper waters than I had thought.
Ib. Reigate Squires

4 A long shot, Watson; a very long shot!
Ib. Silver Blaze

5 'Is there any point to which you would wish to draw my attention?'
'To the curious incident of the dog in the night-time.'
'The dog did nothing in the night-time.'
'That was the curious incident,' remarked Sherlock Holmes. *Ib.*

6 We have not yet met our Waterloo, Watson, but this is our Marengo.
The Return of Sherlock Holmes. Abbey Grange

7 You will ruin no more lives as you ruined mine. You will wring no more hearts as you wrung mine. I will free the world of a poisonous thing. Take that, you hound, and that!—and that!—and that!—and that! *Ib. Charles Augustus Milverton*

8 Now, Watson, the fair sex is your department.
Ib. The Second Stain

9 There is a spirituality about the face, however . . . which the typewriter does not generate. The lady is a musician. *Ib. The Solitary Cyclist*

10 All other men are specialists, but his specialism is omniscience.
Hist Last Bow. Bruce-Partington Plans

11 I thought I knew my Watson. *Ib. The Devil's Foot*

12 'I [Sherlock Holmes] followed you—' 'I saw no one.' 'That is what you may expect to see when I follow you.' *Ib.*

13 Good old Watson! You are the one fixed point in a changing age. *Ib. His Last Bow*

14 But here, unless I am mistaken, is our client.
Ib. Wisteria Lodge

15 There is but one step from the grotesque to the horrible. *Ib.*

16 The giant rat of Sumatra, a story for which the world is not yet prepared.
The Case Book. Sussex Vampire

17 They were the footprints of a gigantic hound!
The Hound of the Baskervilles, ch. 2

18 Detection is, or ought to be, an exact science, and should be treated in the same cold and unemotional manner. You have attempted to tinge it with romanticism, which produces much the same effect as if you worked a love-story or an elopement into the fifth proposition of Euclid.
The Sign of Four

19 An experience of women which extends over many nations and three separate continents. *Ib.*

20 How often have I said to you that when you have eliminated the impossible, whatever remains, *however improbable*, must be the truth? *Ib.*

21 You know my methods. Apply them.
The Sign of Four

22 The Baker Street irregulars. *Ib.*

23 London, that great cesspool into which all the loungers of the Empire are irresistibly drained.
A Study in Scarlet

24 'Wonderful!' I [Dr. Watson] ejaculated. 'Commonplace,' said Holmes. *Ib.*

25 'I should have more faith,' he said; 'I ought to know by this time that when a fact appears opposed to a long train of deductions it invariably proves to be capable of bearing some other interpretation.' *Ib.*

26 'I am inclined to think—' said I [Dr. Watson]. 'I should do so,' Sherlock Holmes remarked, impatiently. *The Valley of Fear*

27 The vocabulary of 'Bradshaw' is nervous and terse, but limited. *Ib.*

28 Mediocrity knows nothing higher than itself, but talent instantly recognizes genius. *Ib.*

SIR FRANCIS HASTINGS CHARLES DOYLE
1810–1888

29 Last night, among his fellow roughs,
He jested, quaff'd, and swore.
The Private of the Buffs

30 *To-day*, beneath the foeman's frown,
He stands in Elgin's place,
Ambassador from Britain's crown
And type of all her race. *Ib.*

31 Poor, reckless, rude, low-born, untaught,
Bewilder'd, and alone,
A heart with English instinct fraught
He yet can call his own. *Ib.*

32 Vain, mightiest fleets of iron framed;
Vain, those all-shattering guns;
Unless proud England keep, untamed,
The strong heart of her sons. *Ib.*

33 A man of mean estate,
Who died, as firm as Sparta's king,
Because his soul was great. *Ib.*

34 His creed no parson ever knew,
For this was still his 'simple plan,'
To have with clergymen to do
As little as a Christian can.
The Unobtrusive Christian

SIR FRANCIS DRAKE
1540?–1596

35 There is plenty of time to win this game, and to thrash the Spaniards too. *Attr. in the Dict. of Nat. Biog.*

'The tradition goes, that Drake would needs see the game up; but was soon prevail'd on to go and play out the rubber with the Spaniards.' W. Oldys' *Life of Ralegh* in Ralegh's *Hist. of the World*, 1736.

36 I remember Drake, in the vaunting style of a soldier, would call the Enterprise [of Cadiz, 1587] the singeing of the King of Spain's Beard.
Bacon, *Considerations touching a War with Spain* (*Harleian Misc.* 1745, vol. v, p. 85, col. 1)

1 I must have the gentleman to haul and draw with the
mariner, and the mariner with the gentleman. . . .
I would know him, that would refuse to set his hand
to a rope, but I know there is not any such here.
                Corbett, *Drake and the Tudor Navy*, i. 249

MICHAEL DRAYTON
1563–1631

2 Ill news hath wings, and with the wind doth go,
Comfort's a cripple and comes ever slow.
                The Barrons' Wars, bk. II, xxviii

3 He was a man (then boldly dare to say)
In whose rich soul the virtues well did suit,
In whom so mix'd the elements all lay,
That none to one could sovereignty impute,
As all did govern yet all did obey;
He of a temper was so absolute,
As that it seem'd when Nature him began,
She meant to shew all, that might be in man.
                Ib. bk. III, xl

4 The mind is free, whate'er afflict the man,
A King's a King, do Fortune what she can.
                Ib. bk. V, xxxvi

5 Thus when we fondly flatter our desires,
Our best conceits do prove the greatest liars.
                Ib. bk. VI, xciv

6 Fair stood the wind for France
When we our sails advance,
Nor now to prove our chance
        Longer will tarry.
                To the Cambro-Britons. Agincourt

7 They now to fight are gone,
Armour on armour shone,
Drum now to drum did groan,
        To hear, was wonder;
That with the cries they make,
The very earth did shake,
Trumpet to trumpet spake,
        Thunder to thunder.   *Ib.*

8 Suffolk his axe did ply,
Beaumont and Willoughby
Bare them right doughtily,
        Ferrers and Fanhope.

Upon Saint Crispin's Day
Fought was this noble fray,
Which fame did not delay
        To England to carry.
O when shall English men
With such acts fill a pen?
Or England breed again
        Such a King Harry?   *Ib.*

9 Care draws on care, woe comforts woe again,
Sorrow breeds sorrow, one grief brings forth twain.
                *England's Heroical Epistles. Henry Howard, Earl
                of Surrey, to the Lady Geraldine*, l. 87

10 When Time shall turn those amber locks to grey,
My verse again shall gild and make them gay.
                Ib. l. 123

11 Had in him those brave translunary things,
That the first poets had. [Marlowe.]
                To Henry Reynolds, of Poets and Poesy, l. 106

12 For that fine madness still he did retain
Which rightly should possess a poet's brain.
                Ib. l. 109

13 Next these, learn'd Jonson, in this list I bring,
Who had drunk deep of the Pierian spring.
                To Henry Reynolds, of Poets and Poesy, l. 129

14 I pray thee leave, love me no more,
        Call home the heart you gave me,
I but in vain the saint adore,
        That can, but will not, save me.
                To His Coy Love

15 These poor half-kisses kill me quite.   *Ib.*

16 He made him turn and stop, and bound,
To gallop, and to trot the round,
He scarce could stand on any ground,
        He was so full of mettle.
                Nymphidia, The Court of Fairy, lxv

17 That shire which we the heart of England well may
call.   *Poly-olbion*, song xiii, l. 2

18 Crave the tuneful nightingale to help you with her lay,
The ousel and the throstlecock, chief music of our
May.   *Shepherd's Garland*, eclogue iii, 17–18

19 How many paltry, foolish, painted things,
That now in coaches trouble ev'ry street,
Shall be forgotten, whom no poet sings,
Ere they be well wrapped in their winding sheet?
Where I to thee Eternity shall give,
When nothing else remaineth of these days,
And Queens hereafter shall be glad to live
Upon the alms of thy superfluous praise.
                Sonnets. Idea, vi

20 Since there's no help, come let us kiss and part,
Nay, I have done: you get no more of me,
And I am glad, yea glad with all my heart,
That thus so cleanly, I myself can free,
Shake hands for ever, cancel all our vows,
And when we meet at any time again,
Be it not seen in either of our brows,
That we one jot of former love retain;
Now at the last gasp of Love's latest breath,
When his pulse failing, Passion speechless lies,
When Faith is kneeling by his bed of death,
And Innocence is closing up his eyes,
Now if thou wouldst, when all have given him over,
From death to life, thou might'st him yet recover.
                Ib. lxi

WILLIAM DRENNAN
1754–1820

21 The men of the Emerald Isle.   *Erin*

JOHN DRINKWATER
1882–1937

22 He comes on chosen evenings,
My blackbird bountiful.   *Blackbird*

23 Moon-washed apples of wonder.   *Moonlit Apples*

THOMAS DRUMMOND
1797–1840

24 Property has its duties as well as its rights.
                Letter to the Earl of Donoughmore, 22 May 1838

WILLIAM DRUMMOND
1585–1649

25 This fair volume which we World do name.
                The World. Flowers of Sion

1 Or if by chance our minds do muse on ought,
It is some picture on the margin wrought.
The World. Flowers of Sion

2 The last and greatest herald of Heaven's King.
Poems. For the Baptist

3 Only the echoes which he made relent,
Ring from their marble caves, repent, repent. *Ib.*

4 Phœbus, arise,
And paint the sable skies,
With azure, white, and red. *Ib. Song* (ii)

5 I long to kiss the image of my death.
Ib. sonnet ix, *Sleep, Silence Child*

6 A morn
Of bright carnations did o'erspread her face. *Ib.* xlvi

JOHN DRYDEN
1631–1700

7 In pious times, ere priestcraft did begin,
Before polygamy was made a sin.
Absalom and Achitophel, pt. i, l. 1

8 And, wide as his command,
Scatter'd his Maker's image through the land.
Ib. l. 9

9 Whate'er he did was done with so much ease,
In him alone, 'twas natural to please. *Ib.* l. 27

10 The Jews, a headstrong, moody, murmuring race
As ever tried the extent and stretch of grace,
God's pampered people, whom, debauched with ease,
No king could govern nor no God could please.
Ib. l. 45

11 Plots, true or false, are necessary things,
To raise up commonwealths and ruin kings.
Ib. l. 83

12 For priests of all religions are the same:
Of whatsoe'er descent their Godhead be,
Stock, stone, or other homely pedigree,
In his defence his servants are as bold,
As if he had been born of beaten gold. *Ib.* l. 99

13 Of these the false Achitophel was first,
A name to all succeeding ages curst.
For close designs and crooked counsels fit,
Sagacious, bold, and turbulent of wit,
Restless, unfixed in principles and place,
In power unpleas'd, impatient of disgrace;
A fiery soul, which working out its way,
Fretted the pigmy body to decay:
And o'er informed the tenement of clay.
A daring pilot in extremity;
Pleased with the danger, when the waves went high
He sought the storms; but for a calm unfit,
Would steer too nigh the sands to boast his wit.
Great wits are sure to madness near alli'd,
And thin partitions do their bounds divide.
Ib. l. 150

14 Bankrupt of life, yet prodigal of ease. *Ib.* l. 168

15 And all to leave what with his toil he won
To that unfeather'd two-legg'd thing, a son.
Ib. l. 169

16 Resolv'd to ruin or to rule the state. *Ib.* l. 174

17 And Heav'n had wanted one immortal song.
Ib. l. 197

18 The people's prayer, the glad diviner's theme,
The young men's vision and the old men's dream!
Absalom and Achitophel, pt. i, l. 238

19 All empire is no more than power in trust.
Ib. l. 411

20 Better one suffer, than a nation grieve. *Ib.* l. 416

21 But far more numerous was the herd of such
Who think too little and who talk too much.
Ib. l. 533

22 A man so various that he seem'd to be
Not one, but all mankind's epitome.
Stiff in opinions, always in the wrong;
Was everything by starts, and nothing long:
But, in the course of one revolving moon,
Was chemist, fiddler, statesman, and buffoon.
Ib. l. 545

23 So over violent, or over civil,
That every man, with him, was God or Devil.
Ib. l. 557

24 In squandering wealth was his peculiar art:
Nothing went unrewarded, but desert.
Beggar'd by fools, whom still he found too late:
He had his jest, and they had his estate. *Ib.* l. 559

25 During his office treason was no crime,
The sons of Belial had a glorious time. *Ib.* l. 597

26 His tribe were God Almighty's gentlemen.
Ib. l. 645

27 Youth, beauty, graceful action seldom fail:
But common interest always will prevail:
And pity never ceases to be shown
To him, who makes the people's wrongs his own.
Ib. l. 723

28 For who can be secure of private right,
If sovereign sway may be dissolv'd by might?
Nor is the people's judgement always true:
The most may err as grossly as the few. *Ib.* l. 779

29 Never was patriot yet, but was a fool. *Ib.* l. 968

30 Beware the fury of a patient man. *Ib.* l. 1005

31 Henceforth a series of new time began,
The mighty years in long procession ran:
Once more the God-like David was restored,
And willing nations knew their lawful lord.
Ib. l. 1028

32 Doeg, though without knowing how or why,
Made still a blund'ring kind of melody;
Spurr'd boldly on, and dash'd through thick and thin,
Through sense and nonsense, never out nor in;
Free from all meaning, whether good or bad,
And in one word, heroically mad. *Ib.* pt. ii, l. 412

33 Rhyme is the rock on which thou art to wreck.
Ib. l. 486

34 The god-like hero sate
On his imperial throne;
His valiant peers were plac'd around;
Their brows with roses and with myrtles bound.
(So should desert in arms be crowned:)
The lovely Thais by his side,
Sate like a blooming Eastern bride
In flow'r of youth and beauty's pride.
Happy, happy, happy pair!
None but the brave,
None but the brave,
None but the brave deserves the fair.
Alexander's Feast, l. 4

1 Assumes the god,
Affects to nod,
And seems to shake the spheres.
Alexander's Feast, l. 44

2 Bacchus ever fair, and ever young. *Ib.* l. 48

3 Sound the trumpets; beat the drums;
Flush'd with a purple grace
He shows his honest face:
Now give the hautboys breath; he comes, he comes.
Ib. l. 50

4 Drinking is the soldier's pleasure. *Ib.* l. 57

5 Rich the treasure;
Sweet the pleasure;
Sweet is pleasure after pain. *Ib.* l. 58

6 And thrice he routed all his foes, and thrice he slew
the slain. *Ib.* l. 68

7 Fallen from his high estate,
And welt'ring in his blood:
Deserted at his utmost need
By those his former bounty fed;
On the bare earth expos'd he lies,
With not a friend to close his eyes. *Ib.* l. 78

8 Revolving in his alter'd soul
The various turns of chance below. *Ib.* l. 85

9 Softly sweet, in Lydian measures,
Soon he sooth'd his soul to pleasures.
War, he sung, is toil and trouble;
Honour but an empty bubble.
Never ending, still beginning,
Fighting still, and still destroying,
If the world be worth thy winning,
Think, oh think, it worth enjoying.
Lovely Thais sits beside thee,
Take the good the gods provide thee. *Ib.* l. 97

10 Sigh'd and look'd, and sigh'd again. *Ib.* l. 120

11 And, like another Helen, fir'd another Troy.
Ib. l. 154

12 Could swell the soul to rage, or kindle soft desire.
Ib. l. 160

13 Let old Timotheus yield the prize,
Or both divide the crown:
He rais'd a mortal to the skies;
She drew an angel down. *Ib.* l. 177

14 All For Love, or the World Well Lost.
Title of Play

15 My love's a noble madness. *All For Love*, II. i

16 Fool that I was, upon my eagle's wings
I bore this wren, till I was tired with soaring,
And now he mounts above me. *Ib.*

17 Give, you gods,
Give to your boy, your Caesar,
The rattle of a globe to play withal,
This gewgaw world, and put him cheaply off:
I'll not be pleased with less than Cleopatra. *Ib.*

18 The wretched have no friends. *Ib.* III. i

19 Nature has cast me in so soft a mould,
That but to hear a story, feigned for pleasure,
Of some sad lover's death, moistens my eyes,
And robs me of my manhood. *Ib.* IV. i

20 Men are but children of a larger growth;
Our appetites as apt to change as theirs,
And full as craving too, and full as vain. *Ib.*

21 Your Cleopatra; Dolabella's Cleopatra; every man's
Cleopatra. *All For Love*, IV. i

22 Welcome, thou kind deceiver!
Thou best of thieves; who, with an easy key,
Dost open life, and, unperceived by us,
Even steal us from ourselves. *Ib.* V. i

23 A knock-down argument; 'tis but a word and a blow.
Amphitryon, I. i

24 I am devilishly afraid, that's certain; but ... I'll sing,
that I may seem valiant. *Ib.* II. i

25 Whistling to keep myself from being afraid. *Ib.* III. i

26 I never saw any good that came of telling truth. *Ib.*

27 I am the true Amphitryon. *Ib.* V. i

28 As one that neither seeks, nor shuns his foe.
Annus Mirabilis, xli

29 By viewing nature, nature's handmaid art,
Makes mighty things from small beginnings grow:
Thus fishes first to shipping did impart,
Their tail the rudder, and their head the prow.
Ib. clv

30 And on the lunar world securely pry. *Ib.* clxiv

31 An horrid stillness first invades the ear,
And in that silence we the tempest fear.
Astræa Redux, l. 7

32 He made all countries where he came his own.
Ib. l. 76

33 Death, in itself, is nothing; but we fear,
To be we know not what, we know not where.
Aureng-Zebe, IV. i

34 When I consider life, 'tis all a cheat;
Yet, fool'd with hope, men favour the deceit;
Trust on, and think to-morrow will repay:
To-morrow's falser than the former day;
Lies worse, and, while it says, we shall be blest
With some new joys, cuts off what we possest.
Strange cozenage! None would live past years again,
Yet all hope pleasure in what yet remain;
And, from the dregs of life, think to receive,
What the first sprightly running could not give. *Ib.*

35 From harmony, from heavenly harmony
This universal frame began:
From harmony to harmony
Through all the compass of the notes it ran,
The diapason closing full in Man. *St. Cecilia's Day*, i

36 What passion cannot Music raise and quell? *Ib.* ii

37 The trumpet's loud clangour
Excites us to arms. *Ib.* iii

38 The soft complaining flute. *Ib.* iv

39 The trumpet shall be heard on high,
The dead shall live, the living die,
And Music shall untune the sky. *Ib.* Grand Chorus

40 And made almost a sin of abstinence.
Character of a Good Parson, l. 11

41 I am as free as nature first made man,
Ere the base laws of servitude began,
When wild in woods the noble savage ran.
The Conquest of Granada, pt. i, I. i

42 Forgiveness to the injured does belong;
But they ne'er pardon, who have done the wrong.
Ib. pt. ii, I. ii

1 Thou strong seducer, opportunity!
  The Conquest of Granada, pt. i, IV. iii

2 For he was great, ere fortune made him so.
  Death of Oliver Cromwell, vi

3 Old as I am, for ladies' love unfit,
The power of beauty I remember yet.
  Cymon and Iphigenia, l. 1

4 When beauty fires the blood, how love exalts the mind.
  Ib. l. 41

5 He trudg'd along unknowing what he sought,
And whistled as he went, for want of thought.
  Ib. l. 84

6 She hugg'd th' offender, and forgave th' offence,
Sex to the last.
  Ib. l. 367

7 Ill fortune seldom comes alone.
  Ib. l. 392

8 Of seeming arms to make a short essay,
Then hasten to be drunk, the business of the day.
  Ib. l. 407

9 Theirs was the giant race before the flood.
  Epistles. To Mr. Congreve, l. 5

10 Our builders were with want of genius curst;
The second temple was not like the first;
Till you, the best Vitruvius, come at length,
Our beauties equal, but excel our strength.
  Ib. l. 13

11 For Tom the Second reigns like Tom the First.
  Ib. l. 48

12 Heav'n, that but once was prodigal before,
To Shakespeare gave as much; she could not give him more.
  Ib. l. 62

13 How blessed is he, who leads a country life,
Unvex'd with anxious cares, and void of strife!
Who studying peace, and shunning civil rage,
Enjoy'd his youth, and now enjoys his age:
All who deserve his love, he makes his own;
And, to be lov'd himself, needs only to be known.
  Ib. To John Driden of Chesterton, l. 1

14 Lord of yourself, uncumber'd with a wife. *Ib.* l. 18

15 Better to hunt in fields, for health unbought,
Than fee the doctor for a nauseous draught.
The wise, for cure, on exercise depend;
God never made his work, for man to mend.
  Ib. l. 92

16 Ev'n victors are by victories undone. *Ib.* l. 164

17 His colours laid so thick on every place,
As only showed the paint, but hid the face.
  Ib. To Sir R. Howard, l. 75

18 Here lies my wife: here let her lie!
Now she's at rest, and so am I.
  Epitaph Intended for Dryden's Wife

19 He had brought me to my last legs; I was fighting as low as ever was Squire Widdrington.
  An Evening's Love, II. i

20 She fear'd no danger, for she knew no sin.
  The Hind and the Panther, pt. i, l. 4

21 And doom'd to death, though fated not to die.
  Ib. l. 8

22 For truth has such a face and such a mien
As to be lov'd needs only to be seen. *Ib.* l. 33

23 My thoughtless youth was winged with vain desires,
My manhood, long misled by wandering fires,
Followed false lights; and when their glimpse was gone
My pride struck out new sparkles of her own.
Such was I, such by nature still I am;
Be Thine the glory, and be mine the shame!
Good life be now my task: my doubts are done;
(What more could fright my faith than Three in One?) *The Hind and the Panther*, pt. i, l. 72

24 Reason to rule, but mercy to forgive:
The first is law, the last prerogative. *Ib.* l. 261

25 For all have not the gift of martyrdom. *Ib.* pt. ii, l. 59

26 Either be wholly slaves or wholly free. *Ib.* l. 285

27 Much malice mingled with a little wit. *Ib.* pt. iii, l. 1

28 Think you your new French proselytes are come
To starve abroad, because they starv'd at home?
Your benefices twinkl'd from afar,
They found the new Messiah by the star. *Ib.* l. 173

29 For present joys are more to flesh and blood
Than a dull prospect of a distant good. *Ib.* l. 364

30 By education most have been misled;
So they believe, because they so were bred.
The priest continues what the nurse began,
And thus the child imposes on the man. *Ib.* l. 389

31 The wind was fair, but blew a mack'rel gale.
  Ib. l. 456

32 T' abhor the makers, and their laws approve,
Is to hate traitors and the treason love. *Ib.* l. 706

33 For those whom God to ruin has design'd,
He fits for fate, and first destroys their mind.
  Ib. l. 1093

34 And love's the noblest frailty of the mind.
  The Indian Emperor, II. ii

35 Repentance is the virtue of weak minds. *Ib.* III. i

36 For all the happiness mankind can gain
Is not in pleasure, but in rest from pain. *Ib.* IV. i

37 Thou youngest virgin-daughter of the skies,
Made in the last promotion of the blest.
  To the Memory of Mrs. Killigrew, l. 1

38 Since heav'n's eternal year is thine. *Ib.* l. 15

39 While yet a young probationer,
And candidate of heav'n. *Ib.* l. 21

40 When rattling bones together fly
From the four corners of the sky. *Ib.* l. 184

41 That fairy kind of writing which depends only upon the force of imagination.
  King Arthur, Dedication

42 All heiresses are beautiful. *Ib.* I. i

43 War is the trade of kings. *Ib.* II. ii

44 Fairest Isle, all isles excelling,
Seat of pleasures, and of loves;
Venus here will choose her dwelling,
And forsake her Cyprian groves.
  Ib. v. *Song of Venus*

45 Ovid, the soft philosopher of love.
  Love Triumphant, II. i

46 Thou tyrant, tyrant Jealousy,
Thou tyrant of the mind!
  Song of Jealousy. Love Triumphant

DRYDEN

1 All human things are subject to decay,
And, when fate summons, monarchs must obey.
Mac Flecknoe, l. 1

2 The rest to some faint meaning make pretence,
But Shadwell never deviates into sense.
Some beams of wit on other souls may fall,
Strike through and make a lucid interval;
But Shadwell's genuine night admits no ray,
His rising fogs prevail upon the day. *Ib.* l. 19

3 And torture one poor word ten thousand ways.
Ib. l. 208

4 I am resolved to grow fat and look young till forty,
and then slip out of the world with the first wrinkle
and the reputation of five-and-twenty.
The Maiden Queen, III. i

5 I am to be married within these three days; married
past redemption. *Marriage à la Mode*, I. i

6 For secrets are edged tools,
And must be kept from children and from fools.
Sir Martin Mar-All, II. ii

7 We loathe our manna, and we long for quails.
The Medal, l. 131

8 But treason is not own'd when 'tis descried;
Successful crimes alone are justified. *Ib.* l. 207

9 Three poets, in three distant ages born,
Greece, Italy and England did adorn.
The first in loftiness of thought surpass'd;
The next in majesty, in both the last:
The force of nature could no farther go;
To make a third she join'd the former two.
Lines Under Portrait of Milton

10 Whatever is, is in its causes just. *Oedipus*, III. i

11 Wit will shine
Through the harsh cadence of a rugged line.
To the Memory of Mr. Oldham

12 But love's a malady without a cure.
Palamon and Arcite, bk. ii, l. 110

13 Fool, not to know that love endures no tie,
And Jove but laughs at lovers' perjury. *Ib.* l. 148

14 And Antony, who lost the world for love. *Ib.* l. 607

15 Unsham'd, though foil'd he does the best he can.
Ib. bk. iii, l. 741

16 Repentance is but want of power to sin. *Ib.* l. 813

17 Since ev'ry man who lives is born to die,
And none can boast sincere felicity,
With equal mind, what happens, let us bear,
Nor joy nor grieve too much for things beyond our
care.
Like pilgrims to th' appointed place we tend;
The world's an inn, and death the journey's end.
Ib. l. 883

18 A virgin-widow and a *Mourning Bride*. *Ib.* l. 927

19 Happy who in his verse can gently steer,
From grave to light; from pleasant to severe.
The Art of Poetry, c. i, l. 75

20 Errors, like straws, upon the surface flow;
He who would search for pearls must dive below.
Prologues and Epilogues: Prologue, All For Love

21 Bold knaves thrive without one grain of sense,
But good men starve for want of impudence.
Ib. Epilogue, Constantine the Great

22 For, Heaven be thank'd we live in such an age,
When no man dies for love, but on the stage.
Prologues and Epilogues: Epilogue, Mithridates

23 But 'tis the talent of our English nation,
Still to be plotting some new reformation.
Ib. Prologue, Sophonisba, l. 9

24 So poetry, which is in Oxford made
An art, in London only is a trade.
Prologue to the University of Oxford

25 Oxford to him a dearer name shall be,
Than his own mother University.
Thebes did his green unknowing youth engage,
He chooses Athens in his riper age. *Ib.*

26 And this unpolished rugged verse I chose
As fittest for discourse and nearest prose.
Religio Laici, ad fin.

27 I strongly wish for what I faintly hope:
Like the day-dreams of melancholy men,
I think and think on things impossible,
Yet love to wander in that golden maze.
Rival Ladies, III. i

28 Learn to write well, or not to write at all.
Essay on Satire, l. 281

29 This is the porcelain of humankind.
Don Sebastian, I. i

30 Brutus and Cato might discharge their souls,
And give them furloughs for another world;
But we, like sentries, are obliged to stand
In starless nights, and wait the 'pointed hour.
Ib. II. i

31 A very merry, dancing, drinking,
Laughing, quaffing, and unthinking time.
Secular Masque, l. 39

32 Joy rul'd the day, and Love the night. *Ib.* l. 81

33 There is a pleasure sure,
In being mad, which none but madmen know!
The Spanish Friar I. i (*see also* 203:27)

34 Lord of humankind. *Ib.* II. ii

35 And, dying, bless the hand that gave the blow. *Ib.*

36 They say everything in the world is good for something. *Ib.* III. ii

37 Or break the eternal Sabbath of his rest. *Ib.* v. ii

38 The clouds dispell'd, the sky resum'd her light,
And Nature stood recover'd of her fright.
But fear, the last of ills, remain'd behind,
And horror heavy sat on ev'ry mind.
Theodore and Honoria, l. 336

39 And that one hunting which the Devil design'd,
For one fair female, lost him half the kind.
Ib. l. 427

40 Mute and magnificent, without a tear.
Threnodia Augustalis, ii

41 Men met each other with erected look,
The steps were higher that they took;
Friends to congratulate their friends made haste;
And long inveterate foes saluted as they passed.
Ib. iv

42 Freedom which in no other land will thrive,
Freedom an English subject's sole prerogative. *Ib.* x

43 And he, who servilely creeps after sense,
Is safe, but ne'er will reach an excellence.
Tyrannic Love, Prologue

1 All delays are dangerous in war.   *Tyrannic Love*, I. i

2 Pains of love be sweeter far
Than all other pleasures are.   *Ib.* IV. i

3 We must beat the iron while it is hot, but we may
polish it at leisure.   *Dedication of the Aeneis*

4 I trade both with the living and the dead, for the
enrichment of our native language.   *Ib.*

5 A thing well said will be wit in all languages.
Essay of Dramatic Poesy

6 He was the man who of all modern, and perhaps
ancient poets, had the largest and most comprehensive soul. . . . He was naturally learn'd; he
needed not the spectacles of books to read Nature;
he looked inwards, and found her there. . . . He
is many times flat, insipid; his comic wit degenerating into clenches, his serious swelling into bombast.
But he is always great, when some occasion is presented to him. [Shakespeare.]   *Ib.*

7 The consideration of this made Mr. Hales of Eaton
say, that there was no subject of which any poet
ever writ, but he would produce it much better
done in Shakespeare.   *Ib.*

8 He invades authors like a monarch; and what would
be theft in other poets, is only victory in him.
[Ben Jonson.]   *Ib.*

9 If by the people you understand the multitude, the
hoi polloi, 'tis no matter what they think; they
are sometimes in the right, sometimes in the wrong:
their judgement is a mere lottery.   *Ib.*

10 He [Shakespeare] is the very Janus of poets; he
wears almost everywhere two faces; and you have
scarce begun to admire the one, ere you despise
the other.
Essay on the Dramatic Poetry of the Last Age

11 One of the greatest, most noble, and most sublime
poems which either this age or nation has produced.
[Paradise Lost.]   *Essays, Apology for Heroic Poetry*

12 What judgment I had increases rather than diminishes; and thoughts, such as they are, come
crowding in so fast upon me, that my only difficulty is to choose or reject; to run them into verse
or to give them the other harmony of prose.
Preface to Fables

13 'Tis sufficient to say [of Chaucer], according to the
proverb, that here is God's plenty.   *Ib.*

14 It becomes not me to draw my pen in defence of a
bad cause, when I have so often drawn it for a
good one.   *Ib.*

15 He [Chaucer] is a perpetual fountain of good sense.
Ib.

16 One of our late great poets is sunk in his reputation,
because he could never forgive any conceit which
came in his way; but swept like a drag-net, great
and small. There was plenty enough, but the dishes
were ill-sorted; whole pyramids of sweetmeats, for
boys and women; but little of solid meat for men.
Ib.

17 How easy it is to call rogue and villain, and that
wittily! But how hard to make a man appear a fool,
a blockhead, or a knave, without using any of those
opprobrious terms! To spare the grossness of the
names, and to do the thing yet more severely, is to

draw a full face, and to make the nose and cheeks
stand out, and yet not to employ any depth of
shadowing.   *Of Satire*

18 Sure the poet . . . spewed up a good lump of clotted
nonsense at once.   *On Settle*

19 A man may be capable, as Jack Ketch's wife said of
his servant, of a plain piece of work, a bare hanging;
but to make a malefactor die sweetly was only
belonging to her husband.   *Ib.*

20 Happy the man, and happy he alone,
He, who can call to-day his own:
He who, secure within, can say,
To-morrow do thy worst, for I have lived to-day.
Trans. of Horace, bk. iii, ode **xxix**

21 Not Heav'n itself upon the past has pow'r;
But what has been, has been, and I have had my
hour.   *Ib.*

22 I can enjoy her while she's kind;
But when she dances in the wind,
And shakes the wings, and will not stay,
I puff the prostitute away. [Fortune.]   *Ib.*

23 Look round the habitable world! how few
Know their own good; or knowing it, pursue.
Trans. of Juvenal, x

24 To see and to be seen, in heaps they run;
Some to undo, and some to be undone.
Trans. of Ovid, Art of Love, I. 109

25 Thus, while the mute creation downward bend
Their sight, and to their earthly mother tend,
Man looks aloft; and with erected eyes
Beholds his own hereditary skies.
Trans. of Ovid, Metamorphoses, I. 107

26 Who, for false quantities, was whipt at school.
Trans. of Persius, Satires, I. 135

27 Swear, fool, or starve; for the dilemma's even;
A tradesman thou! and hope to go to heaven?
Ib. V. 204

28 She knows her man, and when you rant and swear,
Can draw you to her *with a single hair*.   *Ib.* 246

29 Arms, and the man I sing, who, forced by fate,
And haughty Juno's unrelenting hate. . . .
Trans. of Virgil, Æneid, I. i

30 Cousin Swift, you will never be a poet.
Johnson's *Lives of the Poets: Swift*

GEORGE DUFFIELD
1818–1888

31 Stand up!—stand up for Jesus!
The Psalmist. Stand Up, Stand Up for Jesus

ALEXANDRE DUMAS
1802–1870

32 Cherchons la femme.
Let us look for the woman.
Les Mohicans de Paris, vol. ii, ch. 2
(Cherchez la femme. Attributed to Joseph Fouche.)

33 Tous pour un, un pour tous.
All for one, one for all.
Les Trois Mousquetiers, passim

MARÉCHAL DUMOURIEZ
1739–1823

1 Les courtisans qui l'entourent n'ont rien oublié et n'ont rien appris.

The courtiers who surround him have forgotten nothing and learnt nothing.

Of Louis XVIII, at the time of the Declaration of Verona, Sept. 1795. Examen. See also Talleyrand

WILLIAM DUNBAR
1465?–1530?

2 Timor mortis conturbat me.

Lament for the Makaris

3 London, thou art of townes *A per se.*   *London,* l. 1

4 Thou lusty Troynovaunt.   *Ib.* l. 9

5 London, thou art the flower of cities all!
Gemme of all joy, jasper of jocunditie.   *Ib.* l. 16

6 Fair be their wives, right lovesom, white and small.   *Ib.* l. 46

7 Thy famous Maire, by pryncely governaunce,
With sword of justice thee ruleth prudently.
No Lord of Parys, Venyce, or Floraunce
In dignitye or honour goeth to hym nigh.   *Ib.* l. 49

8 All love is lost but upon God alone.
The Merle and the Nightingale, ii

FINLEY PETER DUNNE
1867–1936

9 'Th' American nation in th' Sixth Ward is a fine people,' he says. 'They love th' eagle,' he says, 'on th' back iv a dollar.' *Mr. Dooley in Peace and War. Oratory on Politics*

JAMES DUPORT
1606–1679

10 Quem Jupiter vult perdere, dementat prius.
Whom God would destroy He first sends mad.
Homeri Gnomologia (1660), p. 282.

THOMAS D'URFEY
1653–1723

11 Neighbours o'er the Herring Pond.
Pills to Purge Melancholy, 1719, vol. ii, p. 333. *Fable of the Lady, the Lurcher, and the Marrow-Puddings,* xiv

SIR EDWARD DYER
c. 1540–1607

12 My mind to me a kingdom is,
   Such present joys therein I find,
That it excels all other bliss
   That earth affords or grows by kind.
Though much I want which most would have,
Yet still my mind forbids to crave.
My Mind to Me a Kingdom Is

13 Some have too much, yet still do crave;
   I little have, and seek no more.
They are but poor, though much they have,
   And I am rich with little store.
They poor, I rich; they beg, I give;
They lack, I leave; they pine, I live.   *Ib.*

JOHN DYER
1700?–1758

14 A little rule, a little sway,
A sunbeam in a winter's day,
Is all the proud and mighty have
Between the cradle and the grave.
Grongar Hill, l. 89

15 There is a kindly mood of melancholy,
That wings the soul and points her to the skies.
The Ruins of Rome, l. 347

JOHN DYER
fl. 1714

16 And he that will this health deny,
Down among the dead men let him lie.
Toast: Here's a Health to the King

MARIA EDGEWORTH
1767–1849

17 Well! some people talk of morality, and some of religion, but give me a little snug property.
The Absentee, ch. 2

18 And all the young ladies . . . said . . . that to be sure a love match was the only thing for happiness, where the parties could any way afford it.
Castle Rackrent (Continuation of Memoirs)

19 I've a great fancy to see my own funeral afore I die.
Ib.

20 Come when you're called;
And do as you're bid;
Shut the door after you;
And you'll never be chid.   *The Contrast,* ch. 1

21 Business was his aversion; pleasure was his business.
Ib. ch. 2

THOMAS ALVA EDISON
1847–1931

22 Genius is one per cent. inspiration and ninety-nine per cent. perspiration.
Newspaper Interview. Life (1932), ch. 24

JAMES EDMESTON
1791–1867

23 Lead us, Heavenly Father, lead us
O'er the world's tempestuous sea;
Guard us, guide us, keep us, feed us,
For we have no help but Thee.
Sacred Lyrics, Set 2. Lead Us, Heavenly Father

EDWARD III OF ENGLAND
1312–1377

24 Let the boy win his spurs.
Of the Black Prince at Crécy, 1345

Also say to them, that they suffre hym this day to wynne his spurres, for if god be pleased, I woll this iourney be his, and the honoure therof.   [158.
Lord Berners, *Froissart's Chron.,* 1812, I. cxxx.

EDWARD VII OF GREAT BRITAIN
1841–1910

We are all Socialists now-a-days.
Speech at Mansion House, 5 Nov. 1895.

25 *But see* Corrigenda

EDWARD VIII OF GREAT BRITAIN

1894-

1 I have found it impossible to carry the heavy burden of responsibility and to discharge my duties as King as I would wish to do without the help and support of the woman I love. *Broadcast, 11 Dec. 1936*

RICHARD EDWARDES

1523?–1566

2 In going to my naked bed, as one that would have slept,

I heard a wife sing to her child, that long before had wept.

She sighed sore, and sang full sweet, to bring the babe to rest,

That would not cease, but cried still in sucking at her breast.

She was full weary of her watch and grieved with her child,

She rocked it, and rated it, till that on her it smiled.

Then did she say, 'Now have I found this proverb true to prove:

The falling out of faithful friends, renewing is of love.' *Amantium Irae, ed. 1580*

JONATHAN EDWARDS

1629–1712

3 The bodies of those that made such a noise and tumult when alive, when dead, lie as quietly among the graves of their neighbours as any others.
Procrastination

OLIVER EDWARDS

1711–1791

4 I have tried too in my time to be a philosopher; but, I don't know how, cheerfulness was always breaking in. *Boswell's Johnson, 17 Apr. 1778*

5 For my part, now, I consider supper as a turnpike through which one must pass, in order to get to bed. [Boswell's *Note*: I am not absolutely sure but this was my own suggestion, though it is truly in the character of Edwards.] *Ib.*

'GEORGE ELIOT'
[MARY ANN CROSS]

1819–1880

6 A prophetess? Yea, I say unto you, and more than a prophetess—a uncommon pretty young woman.
Adam Bede, ch. 1

7 It's but little good you'll do a-watering the last year's crop. *Ib. ch. 18*

8 It was a pity he couldna be hatched o'er again, an' hatched different. *Ib.*

9 Our deeds determine us, as much as we determine our deeds. *Ib. ch. 29*

10 Mrs. Poyser 'has her say out'. *Ib. title of ch. 32*

11 It's them as take advantage that get advantage i' this world. *Ib. ch. 32*

12 A maggot must be born i' the rotten cheese to like it. *Ib.*

13 He was like a cock who thought the sun had risen to hear him crow. *Adam Bede, ch. 33*

14 We hand folks over to God's mercy, and show none ourselves. *Ib. ch. 42*

15 I'm not one o' those as can see the cat i' the dairy, an' wonder what she's come after. *Ib. ch. 52*

16 I'm not denyin' the women are foolish: God Almighty made 'em to match the men. *Ib. ch. 53*

17 A difference of taste in jokes is a great strain on the affections. *Daniel Deronda, bk. ii, ch. 15*

18 Men's men: gentle or simple, they're much of a muchness. *Ib. bk. iv, ch. 31*

19 Friendships begin with liking or gratitude—roots that can be pulled up. *Ib. ch. 32*

20 Prophecy is the most gratuitous form of error.
Middlemarch, ch. 10

21 Our deeds still travel with us from afar,
And what we have been makes us what we are.
Ib. heading to ch. 70

22 The law's made to take care o' raskills.
The Mill on the Floss, bk. iii, ch. 4

23 This is a puzzling world, and Old Harry's got a finger in it. *Ib. ch. 9*

24 The small old-fashioned book, for which you need only pay sixpence at a bookstall, works miracles to this day, turning bitter waters into sweetness. . . . It was written down by a hand that waited for the heart's prompting: it is the chronicle of a solitary hidden anguish, struggle, trust and triumph. [*The Imitation of Christ.*] *Ib. bk. iv, ch. 3*

25 I've never any pity for conceited people, because I think they carry their comfort about with them.
Ib. bk. v, ch. 4

26 The happiest women, like the happiest nations, have no history. *Ib. bk. vi, ch. 3*

27 If you please to take the privilege o' sitting down.
Ib. ch. 4

28 I should like to know what is the proper function of women, if it is not to make reasons for husbands to stay at home, and still stronger reasons for bachelors to go out. *Ib. ch. 6*

29 'Character', says Novalis, in one of his questionable aphorisms—'character is destiny'. *Ib.*

30 In every parting there is an image of death.
Scenes of Clerical Life, Amos Barton, ch. 10

31 Animals are such agreeable friends—they ask no questions, they pass no criticisms.
Mr. Gilfil's Love-Story, ch. 7

32 Nothing is so good as it seems beforehand.
Silas Marner, ch. 18

33 Debasing the moral currency.
Title of essay in 'Theophrastus Such' (1879)

34 Oh may I join the choir invisible
Of those immortal dead who live again
In minds made better by their presence.
Poems: Oh May I Join the Choir Invisible

35 So shall I join the choir invisible
Whose music is the gladness of the world. *Ib.*

Wise books
36 For half the truths they hold are honoured tombs.
Ib. The Spanish Gypsy, bk. ii

1 'Tis God gives skill,
But not without men's hands: He could not make
Antonio Stradivari's violins
Without Antonio.   *Poems: Stradivarius*, l. 140

THOMAS STEARNS ELIOT
1888–1965

2 Because I do not hope to turn again
Because I do not hope
Because I do not hope to turn.   *Ash Wednesday*

3   Turning
Wearily, as one would turn to nod good-bye to
    Rochefoucauld,
If the street were time and he at the end of the street.
          The Boston Evening Transcript

4 Time present and time past
Are both perhaps present in time future,
And time future contained in time past.
          Burnt Norton

5   Human kind
Cannot bear very much reality.   *Ib.*

6 At the still point of the turning world.   *Ib.*

7 In my beginning is my end.   *East Coker*

8 That was a way of putting it—not very satisfactory:
A periphrastic study in a worn-out poetical fashion,
Leaving one still with the intolerable wrestle
With words and meanings.   *Ib.*

9   Each venture
Is a new beginning, a raid on the inarticulate
With shabby equipment always deteriorating
In the general mess of imprecision of feeling.   *Ib.*

10 We are the hollow men
We are the stuffed men
Leaning together.   *The Hollow Men*

11 Between the idea
And the reality
Between the motion
And the act
Falls the Shadow.   *Ib.*

12 This is the way the world ends
Not with a bang but a whimper.   *Ib.*

13 A cold coming we had of it,
Just the worst time of the year
For a journey, and such a long journey:
The ways deep and the weather sharp,
The very dead of winter.   *Journey of the Magi*

14   Last season's fruit is eaten
And the fullfed beast shall kick the empty pail.
For last year's words belong to last year's language
And next year's words await another voice.
          Little Gidding

15 When the evening is spread out against the sky
Like a patient etherized upon a table.
          Love Song of J. Alfred Prufrock

16 In the room the women come and go
Talking of Michelangelo.   *Ib.*

17 The yellow fog that rubs its back upon the window-
panes.   *Ib.*

18 I have measured out my life with coffee spoons. *Ib.*

19 I should have been a pair of ragged claws
Scuttling across the floors of silent seas.   *Ib.*

20 And I have seen the eternal Footman hold my coat
and snicker,
And in short, I was afraid.
          Love Song of J. Alfred Prufrock

21 I grow old . . . I grow old . . .
I shall wear the bottoms of my trousers rolled. *Ib.*

22 I have heard the mermaids singing, each to each;
I do not think that they will sing to me.   *Ib.*

23 I am aware of the damp souls of housemaids
Sprouting despondently at area gates.
          Morning at the Window

24 The sapient sutlers of the Lord.
          Mr. Eliot's Sunday Morning Service

25 The last temptation is the greatest treason:
To do the right deed for the wrong reason.
          Murder in the Cathedral, pt. 1

26 The nightingales are singing near
The Convent of the Sacred Heart
And sang within the bloody wood
When Agamemnon cried aloud.
          Sweeney Among the Nightingales

27 April is the cruellest month, breeding
Lilacs out of the dead land, mixing
Memory and desire, stirring
Dull roots with spring rain.
          The Waste Land, i. *The Burial of the Dead*

28 And I will show you something different from either
Your shadow at morning striding behind you,
Or your shadow at evening rising to meet you
I will show you fear in a handful of dust.   *Ib.*

29 'Jug Jug' to dirty ears.   *Ib.* ii. *A Game of Chess*

30 Musing upon the king my brother's wreck
And on the king my father's death before him.
          Ib. iii. *The Fire Sermon*

31 O the moon shone bright on Mrs. Porter
And on her daughter
They wash their feet in soda water.   *Ib.*

32 When lovely woman stoops to folly and
Paces about her room again, alone,
She smoothes her hair with automatic hand,
And puts a record on the gramophone.   *Ib.*

33 Webster was much possessed by death.
          Whispers of Immortality

34 Donne, I suppose, was such another
Who found no substitute for sense,
To seize and clutch and penetrate;
Expert beyond experience.   *Ib.*

QUEEN ELIZABETH I
1533–1603

35 'Twas God the word that spake it,
He took the Bread and brake it;
And what the word did make it;
That I believe, and take it.
          *Answer on being asked her opinion of Christ's
          presence in the Sacrament.* S. Clarke's *Marrow
          of Ecclesiastical History*, pt. ii, *Life of Queen
          Elizabeth*, ed. 1675

36 The queen of Scots is this day leichter of a fair son,
and I am but a barren stock.
          Memoirs of Sir James Melville (1549–93)

1 Good-morning, gentlemen both. [To a delegation of eighteen tailors.]
> Chamberlin, *Sayings of Queen Elizabeth*, p. 28

2 To your text, Mr. Dean! to your text!   *Ib.* p. 137

3 I am your anointed Queen. I will never be by violence constrained to do anything. I thank God I am endued with such qualities that if I were turned out of the Realm in my petticoat I were able to live in any place in Christome.   *Ib.* p. 142

4 I will make you shorter by the head.
> *Recueil des Dépôts*, trans. by Cooper, vol. ii, p. 169, *cit.* Chamberlin, p. 224

5 The daughter of debate, that eke discord doth sow. [Mary Queen of Scots.]
> Chamberlin, *Sayings of Queen Elizabeth*, p. 301

6 Madam I may not call you; mistress I am ashamed to call you; and so I know not what to call you; but howsoever, I thank you. [To the wife of the Archbishop of Canterbury. The Queen did not approve of married clergy.]
> Harington, *Brief View of the State of the Church*, 1607

7 God may forgive you, but I never can. [To the Countess of Nottingham.]
> The Queen . . . crying to her that God might pardon her, but she never could.
> Hume, *History of England under the House of Tudor*, vol. ii, ch. 7

8 If thy heart fails thee, climb not at all.
> *Lines written on a window after Sir Walter Ralegh's line* 'Fain would I climb, yet fear I to fall.' Fuller, *Worthies of England*, vol. i, p. 419

9 Semper eadem.   *Motto*

10 As for me, I see no such great cause why I should either be fond to live or fear to die. I have had good experience of this world, and I know what it is to be a subject and what to be a sovereign. Good neighbours I have had, and I have met with bad: and in trust I have found treason.
> *Speech to Parliament, 1586.* Camden's *Annals*, p. 98

11 I know I have the body of a weak and feeble woman, but I have the heart and stomach of a king, and of a king of England too; and think foul scorn that Parma or Spain, or any prince of Europe, should dare to invade the borders of my realm.
> *Speech to the Troops at Tilbury on the Approach of the Armada, 1588*

12 Though God hath raised me high, yet this I count the glory of my crown: that I have reigned with your loves.
> *The Golden Speech, 1601.* D'Ewes's *Journal*, p. 659

13 Must! Is *must* a word to be addressed to princes? Little man, little man! thy father, if he had been alive, durst not have used that word.
> *To Robert Cecil. On her death-bed.* J. R. Green, *A Short History of the English People*, ch. vii

JOHN ELLERTON
1826–1893

14 Now the labourer's task is o'er;
Now the battle-day is past;

Now upon the farther shore
Lands the voyager at last.
> *Hymns for the Society for Promoting Christian Knowledge. Now the Labourer's Task*

15 Father, in Thy gracious keeping
Leave we now Thy servant sleeping.   *Ib.*

16 We stand to bless Thee ere our worship cease;
Then, lowly kneeling, wait Thy word of peace.
> *Hymns Ancient and Modern. Saviour, Again to Thy Dear Name We Raise*

17 The day Thou gavest, Lord, is ended,
The darkness falls at Thy behest.
> *A Liturgy for Missionary Meetings. The Day Thou Gavest*

JANE ELLIOT
1727–1805

18 I've heard them lilting, at the ewe milking.
Lasses a' lilting, before dawn of day;
But now they are moaning, on ilka green loaning;
The flowers of the forest are a' wede away.
> *The Flowers of the Forest*

CHARLOTTE ELLIOTT
1789–1871

19 'Christian! seek not yet repose,'
Hear thy guardian angel say;
Thou art in the midst of foes—
'Watch and pray.'
> *Morning and Evening Hymns. Christian! Seek Not Yet Repose*

20 Just as I am, without one plea
But that Thy blood was shed for me,
And that Thou bidd'st me come to Thee,
O Lamb of God, I come!
> *Invalid's Hymn Book. Just As I Am*

EBENEZER ELLIOTT
1781–1849

21 What is a communist? One who hath yearnings
For equal division of unequal earnings.
> *Poetical Works. Epigram*

22 When wilt thou save the people?
Oh, God of Mercy! when?
The people, Lord, the people!
Not thrones and crowns, but men!
> *Ib. The People's Anthem*

GEORGE ELLIS
see
SIR GREGORY GANDER

HENRY HAVELOCK ELLIS
1859–1939

23 Every artist writes his own autobiography.
> *The New Spirit. Tolstoi II*

ELSTOW

24 Elstow ['One Elstow, a friar of the order of Observant Friars'] smiling said . . . 'With thanks to God we know the way to heaven, to be as ready by water as by land, and therefore we care not which way we go.'
> *When threatened with drowning by Henry VIII.* Stow, *Annales*, 1615, p. 543.

EMERSON

RALPH WALDO EMERSON
1803–1882

1 There is no great and no small
 To the Soul that maketh all:
And where it cometh, all things are;
 And it cometh everywhere. *The Absorbing Soul*

2 I am the owner of the sphere,
 Of the seven stars and the solar year,
Of Caesar's hand, and Plato's brain,
Of Lord Christ's heart, and Shakespeare's strain. *Ib.*

3 If the red slayer think he slays,
 Or if the slain think he is slain,
They know not well the subtle ways
 I keep, and pass, and turn again. *Brahma*

4 Far or forgot to me is near. *Ib.*

5 I am the doubter and the doubt,
 And I the hymn the Brahmin sings. *Ib.*

6 But thou, meek lover of the good!
 Find me, and turn thy back on heaven. *Ib.*

7 By the rude bridge that arched the flood,
 Their flag to April's breeze unfurled,
Here once the embattled farmers stood,
 And fired the shot heard round the world.
 Hymn Sung at the Completion of the Concord Monument

8 Knows he who tills this lonely field,
 To reap its scanty corn,
What mystic fruit his acres yield
 At midnight and at morn? *Dirge. Concord, 1838*

9 Nor knowest thou what argument
Thy life to thy neighbour's creed has lent.
All are needed by each one;
Nothing is fair or good alone. *Each and All*

10 O fair and stately maid, whose eyes
Were kindled in the upper skies
At the same torch that lighted mine. *To Eva*

11 Hast thou named all the birds without a gun?
 Forbearance

12 Give all to love:
 Obey thy heart;
Friends, kindred, days,
Estate, good fame,
Plans, credit, and the Muse,—
Nothing refuse. *Give All to Love*

13 Cling with life to the maid;
But when the surprise,
First vague shadow of surmise
Flits across her bosom young
Of a joy apart from thee,
Free be she, fancy-free. *Ib.*

14 Heartily know,
When half-gods go,
The gods arrive. *Ib.*

15 Good-bye, proud world! I'm going home:
Thou art not my friend, and I'm not thine. *Good-bye*

16 For what are they all in their high conceit,
When man in the bush with God may meet? *Ib.*

17 A subtle chain of countless rings
The next unto the farthest brings,
And, striving to be man, the worm
Mounts through all the spires of form. *May Day*

18 The mountain and the squirrel
Had a quarrel;
And the former called the latter 'Little Prig'.
Bun replied,
'You are doubtless very big;
But all sorts of things and weather
Must be taken in together,
To make up a year
And a sphere.' *Fable, The Mountain and the Squirrel*

19 Things are in the saddle,
 And ride mankind.
 Ode, Inscribed to W. H. Channing

20 Olympian bards who sung
 Divine ideas below,
Which always find us young,
 And always keep us so. *The Poet*

21 I like a church; I like a cowl;
I love a prophet of the soul;
And on my heart monastic aisles
Fall like sweet strains, or pensive smiles;
Yet not for all his faith can see,
Would I that cowlèd churchman be. *The Problem*

22 Not from a vain or shallow thought
His awful Jove young Phidias brought. *Ib.*

23 The hand that rounded Peter's dome,
And groined the aisles of Christian Rome,
Wrought in a sad sincerity;
Himself from God he could not free;
He builded better than he knew;—
The conscious stone to beauty grew. *Ib.*

24 Taylor, the Shakespeare of divines. *Ib.*

25 Some of your hurts you have cured,
 And the sharpest you still have survived,
But what torments of grief you endured
 From evils which never arrived!
 Quatrains. Borrowing (from the French)

26 Rhodora! if the sages ask thee why
This charm is wasted on the earth and sky,
Tell them, dear, that if eyes were made for seeing,
Then Beauty is its own excuse for being. *The Rhodora*

27 Though love repine, and reason chafe,
 There came a voice without reply,—
''Tis man's perdition to be safe,
 When for the truth he ought to die.' *Sacrifice*

28 The frolic architecture of the snow. *The Snowstorm*

29 Wilt thou seal up the avenues of ill?
Pay every debt, as if God wrote the bill. *Solution*

30 It is time to be old,
To take in sail. *Terminus*

31 House and tenant go to ground,
Lost in God, in Godhead found. *Threnody*

32 So nigh is grandeur to our dust,
 So near is God to man,
When Duty whispers low, *Thou must,*
 The youth replies, *I can.* *Voluntaries*, iii

33 There is no way to success in our art but to take off
 your coat, grind paint, and work like a digger on
 the railroad, all day and every day.
 Conduct of Life. Power

34 Art is a jealous mistress. *Ib. Wealth*

1 The louder he talked of his honour, the faster we counted our spoons. *Conduct of Life. Worship*

2 London is the epitome of our times, and the Rome of to-day. *English Traits*, xviii. *Result*

3 So . . . I feel in regard to this aged England . . . pressed upon by transitions of trade and . . . competing populations,—I see her not dispirited, not weak, but well remembering that she has seen dark days before;—indeed, with a kind of instinct that she sees a little better in a cloudy day, and that, in storm of battle and calamity, she has a secret vigour and a pulse like a cannon. *Ib. ch. 19 (Speech at Manchester, 1847)*

4 Nothing astonishes men so much as common-sense and plain dealing. *Essays*, xii. *Art*

5 Though we travel the world over to find the beautiful we must carry it with us or we find it not. *Ib.*

6 Those who listened to Lord Chatham felt that there was something finer in the man, than anything which he said. *Ib.* xv. *Character*

7 Beware when the great God lets loose a thinker on this planet. *Ib.* x. *Circles*

8 People wish to be settled: only as far as they are unsettled is there any hope for them. *Ib.*

9 Nothing great was ever achieved without enthusiasm. *Ib.*

10 Men are better than this theology. *Ib.* iii. *Compensation*

11 I knew a witty physician who found the creed in the biliary duct, and used to affirm that if there was disease in the liver, the man became a Calvinist, and if that organ was sound, he became a Unitarian. *Ib.* xiv. *Experience*

12 To fill the hour—that is happiness. *Ib.*

13 The wise through excess of wisdom is made a fool. *Ib.*

14 The years teach much which the days never know. *Ib.*

15 Yet these uneasy pleasures and fine pains are for curiosity, and not for life. *Ib.* vi. *Friendship*

16 A friend may well be reckoned the masterpiece of Nature. *Ib.*

17 Tart, cathartic virtue. *Ib.* viii. *Heroism*

18 O friend, never strike sail to a fear! Come into port greatly, or sail with God the seas. *Ib.*

19 It was a high counsel that I once heard given to a young person, 'Always do what you are afraid to do.' *Ib.*

20 Every reform was once a private opinion, and when it shall be a private opinion again it will solve the problem of the age. *Ib.* i. *History*

21 There is properly no history; only biography. *Ib.*

22 God offers to every mind its choice between truth and repose. *Ib.* xi. *Intellect*

23 He in whom the love of truth predominates . . . submits to the inconvenience of suspense and imperfect opinion; but he is a candidate for truth . . . and respects the highest law of his being. *Ib.*

24 All mankind love a lover. *Ib.* v. *Love*

25 Men are conservatives when they are least vigorous, or when they are most luxurious. They are conservatives after dinner. *Essays, New England Reformers*

26 The reward of a thing well done, is to have done it. *Ib.*

27 We are wiser than we know. *Ib.* ix. *The Over-Soul*

28 Converse with a mind that is grandly simple, and literature looks like word-catching. *Ib.*

29 Words and deeds are quite indifferent modes of the divine energy. Words are also actions, and actions are a kind of words. *Ib.* xiii. *The Poet*

30 It is not metres, but a metre-making argument, that makes a poem. *Ib.*

31 We are symbols, and inhabit symbols. *Ib.*

32 Language is fossil poetry. *Ib.*

33 The poet knows that he speaks adequately, then, only when he speaks somewhat wildly, or, 'with the flower of the mind.' *Ib.*

34 Good men must not obey the laws too well. *Ib.* xix. *Politics*

35 In skating over thin ice, our safety is in our speed. *Ib.* vii. *Prudence*

36 To believe your own thought, to believe that what is true for you in your private heart is true for all men,—that is genius. *Ib.* ii. *Self-Reliance*

37 To-morrow a stranger will say with masterly good sense precisely what we have thought and felt all the time, and we shall be forced to take with shame our own opinion from another. *Ib.*

38 Society everywhere is in conspiracy against the manhood of every one of its members. *Ib.*

39 Whoso would be a man must be a nonconformist. *Ib.*

40 A foolish consistency is the hobgoblin of little minds, adored by little statesmen and philosophers and divines. With consistency a great soul has simply nothing to do. . . . Speak what you think to-day in words as hard as cannon-balls, and to-morrow speak what to-morrow thinks in hard words again, though it contradict every thing you said to-day. *Ib.*

41 Is it so bad, then, to be misunderstood? Pythagoras was misunderstood, and Socrates, and Jesus, and Luther, and Copernicus, and Galileo, and Newton, and every pure and wise spirit that ever took flesh. To be great is to be misunderstood. *Ib.*

42 Shoves Jesus and Judas equally aside. *Ib.*

43 I like the silent church before the service begins, better than any preaching. *Ib.*

44 As men's prayers are a disease of the will so are their creeds a disease of the intellect. *Ib.*

45 Every Stoic was a Stoic; but in Christendom where is the Christian? *Ib.*

46 There are not in the world at any one time more than a dozen persons who read and understand Plato:—never enough to pay for an edition of his works; yet to every generation these come duly down, for the sake of those few persons, as if God brought them written in his hand. *Ib.* iv. *Spiritual Laws*

47 If you would not be known to do anything, never do it. *Ib.*

1 We are always getting ready to live, but never living.
Journals, 13 Apr. 1834

2 I hate quotations. *Ib. May 1849*

3 Man does not live by bread alone, but by faith, by admiration, by sympathy.
Lectures and Biographical Sketches. The Sovereignty of Ethics

4 Great men are they who see that spiritual is stronger than any material force, that thoughts rule the world.
Letters and Social Aims. Progress of Culture, Phi Beta Kappa Address, 18 July 1876

5 By necessity, by proclivity,—and by delight, we all quote. *Ib. Quotation and Originality*

6 Next to the originator of a good sentence is the first quoter of it. *Ib.*

7 I have heard with admiring submission the experience of the lady who declared that the sense of being well-dressed gives a feeling of inward tranquillity which religion is powerless to bestow. [Miss C. F. Forbes, 1817–1911.] *Ib. Social Aims*

8 When Nature has work to be done, she creates a genius to do it. *Method of Nature*

9 Every hero becomes a bore at last.
Representative Men. Uses of Great Men

10 Talent alone cannot make a writer. There must be a man behind the book. *Ib. Goethe*

11 Is not marriage an open question, when it is alleged, from the beginning of the world, that such as are in the institution wish to get out; and such as are out wish to get in. *Ib. Montaigne*

12 Belief consists in accepting the affirmations of the soul; Unbelief, in denying them. *Ib.*

13 Never read any book that is not a year old.
Society and Solitude. Books

14 Hitch your wagon to a star. *Ib. Civilization*

15 We boil at different degrees. *Ib. Eloquence*

16 One of our statesmen said, 'The curse of this country is eloquent men.' *Ib.*

17 America is a country of young men. *Ib. Old Age*

18 'Tis the good reader that makes the good book.
Ib. Success

19 Invention breeds invention. *Ib. Works and Days*

20 'Well,' said Red Jacket [to someone complaining that he had not enough time], 'I suppose you have all there is.' *Ib.*

21 Glittering generalities! They are blazing ubiquities.
Attr. remark on Rufus Choate (see 142 : 25 sneering at the ideas of the Declaration of Independence as 'glittering generalities'

22 If a man write a better book, preach a better sermon, or make a better mouse-trap than his neighbour, tho' he build his house in the woods, the world will make a beaten path to his door.
Mrs. Sarah S. B. Yule (1856–1916) credits the quotation to Emerson in her Borrowings *(1889), stating in* The Docket, *Feb. 1912, that she copied this in her handbook from a lecture delivered by Emerson. The 'mouse-trap' quotation was the occasion of a long controversy, owing to Elbert Hubbard's claim to its authorship.*

23 He who has a thousand friends has not a friend to spare,
And he who has one enemy will meet him everywhere.
Translations. From Omar Chiam

THOMAS DUNN ENGLISH
1819–1902

24 Oh! don't you remember sweet Alice, Ben Bolt,
Sweet Alice, whose hair was so brown,
Who wept with delight when you gave her a smile,
And trembled with fear at your frown? *Ben Bolt*

ENNIUS
239–169 B.C.

25 Moribus antiquis res stat Romana virisque.
The Roman state stands by ancient customs, and its manhood. *Annals*

26 Unus homo nobis cunctando restituit rem.
One man by delaying saved the state for us.
Cicero, *De Senectute*, iv. 10

HENRY ERSKINE
1746–1817

27 In the garb of old Gaul, wi' the fire of old Rome.
In the Garb of Old Gaul

THOMAS ERSKINE, BARON ERSKINE
1750–1823

28 The uncontrouled licentiousness of a brutal and insolent soldiery.
Report (1796) *of Erskine's defence of William Stone*

ROBERT DEVEREUX, EARL OF ESSEX
1566–1601

29 Reasons are not like garments, the worse for wearing.
To Lord Willoughby, 4 Jan. 1598–9. See *Notes and Queries*, Ser. X, vol. ii, p. 23

HENRI ESTIENNE
1531–1598

30 Si jeunesse savoit; si vieillesse pouvoit.
If youth knew; if age could.
Les Prémices, Épigramme cxci

SIR GEORGE ETHEREGE
1635?–1691

31 I must confess I am a fop in my heart; ill customs influence my very senses, and I have been so used to affectation that without the help of the air of the court what is natural cannot touch me.
Letter to Mr. Poley, 2/12 Jan. 1687/8

32 Few of our plays can boast of more wit than I have heard him speak at a supper. [Sir Charles Sedley.]
Letter to Mr. Will. Richards, undated

33 I walk within the purlieus of the Law.
Love in a Tub, I. iii

34 What a pretty lisp he has! *The Man of Mode*, I. i

1 Do not vow—Our love is frail as is our life, and full as little in our power; and are you sure you shall out-live this day? *The Man of Mode*, II. i

2 When love grows diseas'd, the best thing we can do is to put it to a violent death; I cannot endure the torture of a lingring and consumptive passion.
Ib. ii

3 Writing, Madam,'s a mechanic part of wit! A gentleman should never go beyond a song or a billet.
Ib. IV. i

4 None ever had so strange an art
His passion to convey
Into a listening virgin's heart,
And steal her soul away.

Fly, fly betimes, for fear you give
Occasion for your fate.
In vain, said she, in vain I strive,
Alas! 'tis now too late! *Ib.* v. i

5 What e'er you say, I know all beyond High-Park's a desart to you. *Ib.* ii

EUCLID
fl. c. 300 B.C.

6 Quod erat demonstrandum (trans. from the Greek).
Which was to be proved.

7 A line is length without breadth.

8 There is no 'royal road' to geometry.
(*Said to Ptolemy I*. Proclus, *Comment on Euclid*, Prol. G. 20.)

EURIPIDES
480–406 B.C.

9 ἡ γλῶσσ' ὀμώμοχ', ἡ δὲ φρὴν ἀνώμοτος.

'Twas but my tongue, 'twas not my soul that swore.
Hippolytus, 612. Trans. by Gilbert Murray

ABEL EVANS
1679–1737

10 When Tadlow walks the streets, the paviours cry,
'God bless you, Sir!' and lay their rammers by.
Epigram. On Dr. Tadlow

11 Under this stone, Reader, survey
Dead Sir John Vanbrugh's house of clay.
Lie heavy on him, Earth! for he
Laid many heavy loads on thee!
Epitaph on Sir John Vanbrugh, Architect of Blenheim Palace

JOHN EVELYN
1620–1706

12 This knight was indeed a valiant gentleman; but not a little given to romance, when he spake of himself. *Diary, 6 Sept. 1651*

13 Mulberry Garden, now the only place of refreshment about the town for persons of the best quality to be exceedingly cheated at. *Ib. 10 May 1654*

14 That miracle of a youth, Mr. Christopher Wren.
Ib. 11 July 1654

15 I saw Hamlet Prince of Denmark played, but now the old plays began to disgust this refined age.
Diary, 26 Nov. 1661

DAVID EVERETT
1769–1813

16 You'd scarce expect one of my age
To speak in public on the stage;
And if I chance to fall below
Demosthenes or Cicero,
Don't view me with a critic's eye,
But pass my imperfections by.
Large streams from little fountains flow,
Tall oaks from little acorns grow.
Lines Written for a School Declamation

VISCOUNT EVERSLEY
[CHARLES SHAW-LEFEVRE]
1794–1888

17 What is that fat gentleman in such a passion about?
Remark as a child on hearing Mr. Fox speak in Parliament. G. W. E. Russell, *Collections and Recollections*, ch. 11

WILLIAM NORMAN EWER
1885–

18 I gave my life for freedom—This I know:
For those who bade me fight had told me so.
Five Souls, 1917

19 How odd
Of God
To choose
The Jews. *How Odd*

FREDERICK WILLIAM FABER
1814–1863

20 Have mercy on us worms of earth.
Jesus and Mary. Have Mercy on Us, God Most High

21 My God, how wonderful Thou art!
Thy majesty how bright,
How beautiful Thy mercy-seat
In depths of burning light!
Ib. My God, How Wonderful Thou Art!

22 Thine endless wisdom, boundless power,
And awful purity! *Ib.*

23 Hark! Hark! my soul, angelic songs are swelling
O'er earth's green fields and ocean's wave-beat shore!
How sweet the truth those blessed strains are telling
Of that new life when sin shall be no more!
Oratory Hymns. The Pilgrims of the Night

24 The music of the Gospel leads us home. *Ib.*

25 Rest comes at length; though life be long and dreary,
The day must dawn, and darksome night be passed.
Ib.

26 O Paradise! O Paradise!
Who doth not crave for rest? *Ib. Paradise*

27 Faith of our fathers! holy faith!
We will be true to thee till death.
Ib. A Pledge of Faithfulness

ROBERT FABYAN
d. 1513

1 Finally he paid the debt of nature.
Chronicles, pt. ii, xli

LUCIUS CARY, VISCOUNT FALKLAND
1610?–1643

2 When it is not necessary to change, it is necessary
not to change.
A Speech concerning Episcopacy [delivered 1641].
A Discourse of Infallibility, 1660

AUGUST HEINRICH HOFFMANN VON FALLERSLEBEN
1798–1874

3 Deutschland, Deutschland über alles.
Germany, Germany over all.   *Title of Song*

GEORGE FARQUHAR
1678–1707

4 Sir, you shall taste my *Anno Domini*.
The Beaux' Stratagem, i. i

5 I have fed purely upon ale; I have eat my ale, drank
my ale, and I always sleep upon ale.   *Ib.*

6 My Lady Bountiful.   *Ib.*

7 Says little, thinks less, and does—nothing at all, faith.
Ib.

8 'Tis still my maxim, that there is no scandal like rags,
nor any crime so shameful as poverty.   *Ib.*

9 There's some diversion in a talking blockhead; and
since a woman must wear chains, I would have the
pleasure of hearing 'em rattle a little.   *Ib.* ii. ii

10 No woman can be a beauty without a fortune.   *Ib.*

11 I believe they talked of me, for they laughed consumedly.   *Ib.* iii. i

12 'Twas for the good of my country that I should be
abroad.—Anything for the good of one's country—
I'm a Roman for that.   *Ib.* ii

13 Captain is a good travelling name, and so I take it. *Ib.*

14 AIMWELL:
Then you understand Latin, Mr. Bonniface?

BONNIFACE:
Not I, Sir, as the saying is, but he talks it so very fast
that I'm sure it must be good.   *Ib.*

15 There are secrets in all families.   *Ib.* iii

16 How a little love and good company improves a
woman!   *Ib.* iv. i

17 It is a maxim that man and wife should never have it
in their power to hang one another.   *Ib.* ii

18 Spare all I have, and take my life.   *Ib.* v. ii

19 I hate all that don't love me, and slight all that do.
The Constant Couple, i. ii

20 Grant me some wild expressions, Heavens, or I shall
burst— ... Words, words or I shall burst. *Ib.* v. iii

21 Charming women can true converts make,
We love the precepts for the teacher's sake.   *Ib.*

22 Crimes, like virtues, are their own rewards.
The Inconstant, iv. ii

23 'Tis an old saying, Like master, like man; why not as
well, Like mistress, like maid?
Love and a Bottle, i. i

24 Money is the sinews of love, as of war.   *Ib.* ii. i

25 Poetry's a mere drug, Sir.   *Ib.* iii. ii

26 He answered the description the page gave to a T,
Sir.   *Ib.* iv. iii

27 And there's a pleasure in being mad,
Which none but madmen know.
The Recruiting Officer, i. iii (see also 193:33)

28 Hanging and marriage, you know, go by Destiny.
Ib. iii. ii

29 I cou'd be mighty foolish, and fancy my self mighty
witty; Reason still keeps its throne, but it nods a
little, that's all.   *Ib.*

30 A lady, if undrest at Church, looks silly,
One cannot be devout in dishabilly.
The Stage Coach, prologue

31 I'm privileg'd to be very impertinent, being an
Oxonian.   *Sir Harry Wildair*, ii. i

32 The King of Spain is dead.   *Ib.* ii

REV. FREDERICK WILLIAM FARRAR
1831–1903

33 Russell ... acted invariably from the highest principles.   *Eric, or Little by Little*, pt. i, ch. 3

34 Russell, let me always call you Edwin, and call me
Eric.   *Ib.* ch. 4

35 'What a surly devil that is,' said Eric, ...
'A surly—? Oh, Eric, that's the first time I ever
heard you swear.'   *Ib.* ch. 8

36 'By heavens, this is *too* bad!' he exclaimed, stamping
his foot with anger. 'What have I ever done to you
young blackguards, that you should treat me thus?'
Ib. pt. ii, ch. 1

37 They all drank his health with the usual honours:—
'... For he's a jolly good fe-el-low, which nobody
can deny.'   *Julian Home*, ch. 21

EMPEROR FERDINAND I
1503–1564

38 Fiat justitia, et pereat mundus.
Let justice be done, though the world perish.
Saying

JOHN FERRIAR
1761–1815

39 Now cheaply bought for thrice their weight in gold
Illustrations of Sterne. Bibliomania, l. 65

WILLIAM PITT FESSENDEN
1806–1869

40 Repudiate the repudiators.
Presidential Campaign Slogan, 1868

[203]

EUGENE FIELD
1850–1895

1 But I, when I undress me
  Each night, upon my knees
Will ask the Lord to bless me
  With apple pie and cheese. *Apple Pie and Cheese*

2 When I demanded of my friend what viands he
  preferred,
He quoth: 'A large cold bottle, and a small hot bird!'
  The Bottle and the Bird

3 A little peach in an orchard grew,—
  A little peach of emerald hue;
Warmed by the sun and wet by the dew,
  It grew. *The Little Peach*

4 Listen to my tale of woe. *Ib.*

5 Wynken, Blynken, and Nod one night
  Sailed off in a wooden shoe—
Sailed on a river of crystal light,
  Into a sea of dew. *Wynken, Blynken, and Nod*

HENRY FIELDING
1707–1754

6 '*Tace*, madam,' answered Murphy, 'is Latin for a
  candle.' *Amelia*, bk. i, ch. 10

7 It hath been often said, that it is not death, but dying,
  which is terrible. *Ib.* bk. iii, ch. 4

8 When widows exclaim loudly against second marriages, I would always lay a wager, that the man, if
  not the wedding-day, is absolutely fixed on.
  Ib. bk. vi, ch. 8

9 One fool at least in every married couple.
  Ib. bk. ix, ch. 4

10 There is not in the universe a more ridiculous, nor
  a more contemptible animal, than a proud clergyman. *Ib.* ch. 10

11 One of my illustrious predecessors.
  Covent-Garden Journal, No. 3, 11 Jan. 1752

12 I am as sober as a Judge.
  Don Quixote in England, III. xiv

13 Oh! The roast beef of England,
  And old England's roast beef.
  The Grub Street Opera, III. iii

14 He in a few minutes ravished this fair creature, or at
  least would have ravished her, if she had not, by
  a timely compliance, prevented him.
  Jonathan Wild, bk. iii, ch. 7

15 But pray, Mr. Wild, why bitch? *Ib.* ch. 8

16 To whom nothing is given, of him can nothing be
  required. *Joseph Andrews*, bk. ii, ch. 8

17 I describe not men, but manners; not an individual,
  but a species. *Ib.* bk. iii, ch. 1

18 They are the affectation of affectation. *Ib.* ch. 3

19 Public schools are the nurseries of all vice and immorality. *Ib.* ch. 5

20 Some folks rail against other folks, because other
  folks have what some folks would be glad of.
  Ib. bk. iv, ch. 6

21 Love and scandal are the best sweeteners of tea.
  Love in Several Masques, IV. xi

22 Yes, I had two strings to my bow; both golden ones,
  agad! and both cracked.
  Love in Several Masques, v. xiii

23 Map me no maps, sir, my head is a map, a map of the
  whole world. *Rape upon Rape*, I. v

24 Every physician almost hath his favourite disease.
  Tom Jones, bk. ii, ch. 9

25 Thwackum was for doing justice, and leaving mercy
  to heaven. *Ib.* bk. iii, ch. 10

26 A late facetious writer, who told the public that whenever he was dull they might be assured there was
  a design in it. *Ib.* bk. v, ch. 1

27 O! more than Gothic ignorance. *Ib.* bk. vii, ch. 3

28 'I did not mean to abuse the cloth; I only said your
  conclusion was a *non sequitur*.'—
  'You are another,' cries the sergeant, 'an you come to
  that, no more a *sequitur* than yourself.'
  Ib. bk. ix, ch. 6

29 An amiable weakness. *Ib.* bk. x, ch. 8

30 His designs were strictly honourable, as the phrase
  is; that is, to rob a lady of her fortune by way of
  marriage. *Ib.* bk. xi, ch. 4

31 Composed that monstrous animal a husband and wife.
  Ib. bk. xv, ch. 9

32 Nay, you may call me coward if you will; but if that
  little man there upon the stage is not frightened,
  I never saw any man frightened in my life.
  Ib. bk. xvi, ch. 5

33 'He the best player!' cries Partridge, with a contemp-
  tuous sneer. 'Why, I could act as well as he myself.
  I am sure, if I had seen a ghost, I should have
  looked in the very same manner, and done just as
  he did. . . . The king for my money! He speaks
  all his words distinctly, half as loud again as the
  other. Anybody may see he is an actor.' *Ib.*

34 All Nature wears one universal grin.
  Tom Thumb the Great, I. i

35 To sun my self in Huncamunca's eyes. *Ib.* iii

36 When I'm not thank'd at all, I'm thank'd enough,
  I've done my duty, and I've done no more. *Ib.*

37 The dusky night rides down the sky,
  And ushers in the morn;
The hounds all join in glorious cry,
  The huntsman winds his horn:
  And a-hunting we will go.
  A-Hunting We Will Go

L'ABBÉ EDGEWORTH DE FIRMONT
1745–1807

38 Fils de Saint Louis, montez au ciel.
  Son of Saint Louis, ascend to heaven.
  *Attr. words to Louis XVI as he mounted the
  steps of the guillotine at his execution, 1793.
  No documentary proof at all.*

JOHN ARBUTHNOT FISHER, LORD FISHER
1841–1920

39 You will always be fools! We shall never be gentlemen!
  *The Times, 26 June 1919. Quoted by him as
  'the apposite words spoken by a German naval*

[204]

officer to his English confrère. . . . On the whole I think I prefer to be the fool—even as a matter of business.'

1 Sack the lot!   *The Times, 2 Sept. 1919*

ALBERT H. FITZ

2 You are my honey, honey-suckle,
   I am the bee.   *The Honey-Suckle and the Bee*

CHARLES FITZGEFFREY
1575?–1638

3 And bold and hard adventures t' undertake,
   Leaving his country for his country's sake.
   Life and Death of Sir Francis Drake (1596), ccxiii

EDWARD FITZGERALD
1809–1883

4 Awake! for Morning in the Bowl of Night
  Has flung the Stone that puts the Stars to Flight:
      And Lo! the Hunter of the East has caught
  The Sultan's Turret in a Noose of Light.
                    Omar Khayyám, ed. 1, i

5 Wake! For the Sun, who scatter'd into flight
  The Stars before him from the Field of Night,
      Drives Night along with them from Heav'n, and strikes
  The Sultan's Turret with a Shaft of Light. *Ib.* ed. 4, i

6 Dreaming when Dawn's Left Hand was in the Sky
  I heard a Voice within the Tavern cry,
      'Awake, my Little ones, and fill the Cup
  Before Life's Liquor in its Cup be dry.' *Ib.* ed. 1, ii

7 Before the phantom of False Morning died,
  Methought a Voice within the Tavern cried,
      'When all the Temple is prepared within,
  Why nods the drowsy Worshipper outside?'
                    Ib. ed. 4, ii

8 Now the New Year reviving old Desires,
  The thoughtful Soul to Solitude retires,
      Where the White Hand of Moses on the Bough
  Puts out, and Jesus from the Ground suspires.
                    Ib. eds. 1 and 4, iv

9 Iram indeed is gone with all its Rose,
  And Jamshyd's Sev'n-ring'd Cup where no one knows;
      But still the Vine her ancient Ruby yields,
  And still a Garden by the Water blows. *Ib.* ed. 1, v

10 Iram indeed is gone with all his Rose. *Ib.* ed. 4, v

11 But still a Ruby kindles in the Vine,
   And many a Garden by the Water blows. *Ib.*

12   In divine
   High piping Pehlevi, with 'Wine! Wine! Wine!
   Red Wine!'—the Nightingale cries to the Rose
   That yellow Cheek of hers to incarnadine.
                    Ib. ed. 1, vi

13 That sallow cheek of hers to incarnadine.
                    Ib. ed. 4, vi

14 Come, fill the Cup, and in the Fire of Spring
   The Winter Garment of Repentance fling:
       The Bird of Time has but a little way
   To fly—and Lo! the Bird is on the Wing.
                    Ib. ed. 1, vii

15 Come, fill the Cup, and in the fire of Spring
   Your Winter-garment of Repentance fling:
       The Bird of Time has but a little way
   To flutter—and the Bird is on the wing.
                    Omar Khayyám, ed. 4, vii

16 The Wine of Life keeps oozing drop by drop,
   The Leaves of Life keep falling one by one.
                    Ib. ed. 4, viii. Not in ed. 1

17 And look—a thousand Blossoms with the Day
   Woke—and a thousand scatter'd into Clay.
                    Ib. ed. 1, viii

18 Each Morn a thousand Roses brings, you say;
   Yes, but where leaves the Rose of Yesterday?
       And this first Summer month that brings the Rose,
   Shall take Jamshyd and Kaikobad away.
                    Ib. ed. 4, ix

19 But come with old Khayyám, and leave the Lot
   Of Kaikobad and Kaikhosru forgot:
       Let Rustum lay about him as he will,
   Or Hatim Tai cry Supper—heed them not.
                    Ib. ed. 1, ix

20 Well, let it take them! What have we to do
   With Kaikobad the Great, or Kaikhosru?
       Let Zal and Rustum bluster as they will,
   Or Hatim call to Supper—heed not you. *Ib.* ed. 4, x

21 And pity Sultan Mahmud on his Throne.
                    Ib. ed. 1, x

22 And Peace to Mahmud on his golden Throne.
                    Ib. ed. 4, xi

23 Here with a Loaf of Bread beneath the bough,
   A Flask of Wine, a Book of Verse—and Thou
       Beside me singing in the Wilderness—
   And Wilderness is Paradise enow. *Ib.* ed. 1, xi

24 A Book of Verses underneath the Bough,
   A Jug of Wine, a Loaf of Bread—and Thou
       Beside me singing in the Wilderness—
   Oh, Wilderness were Paradise enow! *Ib.* ed. 4, xii

25 Ah, take the Cash in hand and waive the Rest;
   Oh, the brave Music of a *distant* Drum!
                    Ib. ed. 1, xii

26 Ah, take the Cash, and let the Credit go,
   Nor heed the rumble of a distant Drum!
                    Ib. ed. 4, xiii

27 The Worldly Hope men set their Hearts upon
   Turns Ashes—or it prospers; and anon,
       Like Snow upon the Desert's dusty Face
   Lighting a little Hour or two—is gone.
                    Ib. ed. 1, xiv; ed. 4, xvi

28 And those who husbanded the Golden Grain,
   And those who flung it to the Winds like Rain,
       Alike to no such aureate Earth are turn'd
   As, buried once, Men want dug up again.
                    Ib. eds. 1 and 4, xv

29 Think, in this batter'd Caravanserai
   Whose Doorways are alternate Night and Day,
       How Sultan after Sultan with his Pomp
   Abode his Hour or two, and went his way.
                    Ib. ed. 1, xv

30 Think, in this batter'd Caravanserai
   Whose Portals are alternate Night and Day,
       How Sultan after Sultan with his Pomp
   Abode his destin'd Hour, and went his way.
                    Ib. ed. 4, xvii

[205]

1 They say the Lion and the Lizard keep
The Courts where Jamshyd gloried and drank deep:
    And Bahram, that great Hunter—the Wild Ass
Stamps o'er his Head, and he lies fast asleep.
                              Omar Khayyám, ed. 1, xvii

2 Stamps o'er his Head, but cannot break his Sleep.
                              Ib. ed. 4, xviii

3 I sometimes think that never blows so red
The Rose as where some buried Caesar bled;
    That every Hyacinth the Garden wears
Dropt in her Lap from some once lovely Head.
                              Ib. ed. 1, xviii; ed. 4, xix

4 And this reviving Herb whose tender Green
Fledges the River-Lip on which we lean—
    Ah! lean upon it lightly! for who knows
From what once lovely Lip it springs unseen!
                              Ib. ed. 4, xx

5 Ah, my Belovéd, fill the Cup that clears
To-DAY of past Regrets and Future Fears:
    To-morrow!—Why, To-morrow I may be
Myself with Yesterday's Sev'n thousand Years.
                              Ib. ed. 1, xx; ed. 4, xxi

6 Lo! some we loved, the loveliest and best
That Time and Fate of all their Vintage prest,
    Have drunk their Cup a Round or two before,
And one by one crept silently to Rest. *Ib.* ed. 1, xxi

7 For some we loved, the loveliest and the best
That from his Vintage rolling Time hath prest.
                              Ib. ed. 4, xxii

8 Ah, make the most of what we yet may spend,
Before we too into the Dust descend;
    Dust into Dust, and under Dust, to lie,
Sans Wine, sans Song, sans Singer, and—sans End!
                              Ib. ed. 1, xxiii; ed. 4, xxiv

9 Oh, come with old Khayyám, and leave the Wise
To talk; one thing is certain, that Life flies;
    One thing is certain, and the Rest is Lies;
The Flower that once hath blown for ever dies.
                              Ib. ed. 1, xxvi

10 Myself when young did eagerly frequent
Doctor and Saint, and heard great argument
    About it and about: but evermore
Came out by the same Door as in I went. *Ib.* xxvii

11 Came out by the same Door wherein I went.
                              Ib. ed. 4, xxvii

12 With them the Seed of Wisdom did I sow,
And with mine own hand wrought to make it grow;
    And this was all the Harvest that I reap'd—
'I came like Water, and like Wind I go.'
                              Ib. eds. 1 and 4, xxviii

13 Into this Universe, and *Why* not knowing
Nor *Whence*, like Water willy-nilly flowing;
    And out of it, as Wind along the Waste,
I know not *Whither*, willy-nilly blowing. *Ib.* xxix

14 What, without asking, hither hurried *whence?*
And, without asking, *whither* hurried hence!
    Another and another Cup to drown
The Memory of this Impertinence! *Ib.* ed. 1, xxx

15   Oh, many a Cup of this forbidden Wine
Must drown the memory of that insolence!
                              Ib. ed. 4, xxx

16 There was a Door to which I found no Key:
There was a Veil past which I could not see:
    Some little Talk awhile of ME and THEE
There seem'd—and then no more of THEE and ME.
                              Omar Khayyám, ed. 1, xxxii

17 There was the Door to which I found no Key;
There was the Veil through which I might not see:
    Some little talk awhile of ME and THEE
There was—and then no more of THEE and ME.
                              Ib. ed. 4, xxxii

18 For in the Market-place, one Dusk of Day,
I watch'd the Potter thumping his wet clay:
    And with its all obliterated Tongue
It murmur'd—'Gently, Brother, gently, pray!'
                              Ib. ed. 1, xxxvi. Not in ed. 4

19 Ah, fill the Cup:—what boots it to repeat
How Time is slipping underneath our Feet:
    Unborn TO-MORROW, and dead YESTERDAY,
Why fret about them if TO-DAY be sweet!
                              Ib. ed. 1, xxxvii. Not in ed. 4

20 One Moment in Annihilation's Waste,
One Moment, of the Well of Life to taste—
    The Stars are setting and the Caravan
Starts for the Dawn of Nothing—Oh, make haste!
                              Ib. ed. 1, xxxviii

21 A Moment's Halt—a momentary taste
Of BEING from the Well amid the Waste—
    And lo!—the phantom Caravan has reach'd
The Nothing it set out from—Oh, make haste!
                              Ib. ed. 4, xlviii

22 Waste not your Hour, nor in the vain pursuit
Of This and That endeavour and dispute;
    Better be jocund with the fruitful Grape
Than sadden after none, or bitter, Fruit.   *Ib.* liv

23 You know, my Friends, with what a brave Carouse
I made a Second Marriage in my house;
    Divorced old barren Reason from my Bed,
And took the Daughter of the Vine to Spouse. *Ib.* lv

24 Was never deep in anything but—Wine.
                              Ib. ed. 1, xli; ed. 4, lvi

25 The Grape that can with Logic absolute
The Two-and-Seventy jarring Sects confute.
                              Ib. ed. 1, xliii; ed. 4, lix

26 Oh threats of Hell and Hopes of Paradise!
One thing at least is certain—*This* Life flies;
    One thing is certain and the rest is Lies;
The Flower that once has blown for ever dies.
                              Ib. ed. 4, lxiii

27 Strange, is it not? that of the myriads who
Before us pass'd the door of Darkness through,
    Not one returns to tell us of the Road,
Which to discover we must travel too.   *Ib.* lxiv

28 'Tis all a Chequer-board of Nights and Days
Where Destiny with Men for Pieces plays:
    Hither and thither moves, and mates, and slays,
And one by one back in the Closet lays.
                              Ib. ed. 1, xlix

29 But helpless Pieces of the Game He plays
Upon this Chequer-board of Nights and Days;
    Hither and thither moves, and checks, and slays,
And one by one back in the Closet lays.
                              Ib. ed. 4, lxix

FITZGERALD

1 The Ball no question makes of Ayes and Noes,
  But Here or There as strikes the Player goes;
    And He that toss'd you down into the Field,
He knows about it all—HE knows—HE knows!
                Omar Khayyám, ed. 4, lxx

2 The Moving Finger writes; and, having writ,
  Moves on: nor all thy Piety nor Wit
    Shall lure it back to cancel half a Line,
Nor all thy Tears wash out a Word of it. *Ib. ed. 1, li*
[Ed. 4, lxxi, reads 'your' instead of 'thy'.]

3 And that inverted Bowl we call The Sky,
  Whereunder crawling coop't we live and die,
    Lift not thy hands to *It* for help—for It
Rolls impotently on as Thou or I.   *Ib. lii*

4 And that inverted Bowl they call the Sky.
                    Ib. ed. 4, lxxii

5 As impotently moves as you or I.   *Ib.*

6 With Earth's first Clay They did the Last Man knead,
  And of the Last Harvest sow'd the Seed:
    And the first Morning of Creation wrote
What the last Dawn of Reckoning shall read.
           Ib. ed. 1, liii; ed. 4, lxxiii

7   Drink! for you know not whence you came, nor
    why:
Drink! for you know not why you go, nor where.
        Ib. ed. 4, lxxiv. Not in ed. 1

8   One glimpse of it within the Tavern caught
Better than in the Temple lost outright. *Ib. ed. 1, lvi*

9   One Flash of it within the Tavern caught.
                Ib. ed. 4, lxxvii

10 O Thou, who didst with Pitfall and with Gin
  Beset the Road I was to wander in,
    Thou wilt not with Predestination round
Enmesh me, and impute my Fall to Sin?
               Ib. ed. 1, lvii

11   Thou wilt not with Predestined Evil round
Enmesh, and then impute my Fall to Sin!
               Ib. ed. 4, lxxx

12 Oh, Thou, who Man of baser Earth didst make,
  And who with Eden didst devise the Snake;
    For all the Sin wherewith the Face of Man
Is blacken'd, Man's Forgiveness give—and take!
               Ib. ed. 1, lviii

13 And even with Paradise devise the Snake.
                Ib. ed. 4, lxxxi

14 Then said a Second—'Ne'er a peevish Boy
  Would break the Bowl from which he drank in joy;
    And He that with his hand the Vessel made
Will surely not in after Wrath destroy.'   *Ib. lxxxv*

15 After a momentary silence spake
  Some Vessel of a more ungainly Make;
    'They sneer at me for leaning all awry;
What! did the Hand then of the Potter shake?'
                  Ib. lxxxvi

16 'Who *is* the Potter, pray, and who the Pot?'
          Ib. ed. 1, lx; ed. 4, lxxxvii

17 Then said another—'Surely not in vain
  My Substance from the common Earth was ta'en,
    That He who subtly wrought me into Shape
Should stamp me back to common Earth again.'
                Ib. ed. 1, lxi

18 Another said—'Why, ne'er a peevish Boy,
  Would break the Bowl from which he drank in Joy;
    Shall He that *made* the Vessel in pure Love
And Fancy, in an after Rage destroy!'
            Omar Khayyám, ed. 1, lxii

19 Said one—'Folks of a surly Tapster tell,
  And daub his Visage with the Smoke of Hell;
    They talk of some strict Testing of us—Pish!
He's a Good Fellow, and 'twill all be well.'
           Ib. lxiv; ed. 4, lxxxviii

20 Indeed the Idols I have loved so long
  Have done my credit in this World much wrong:
    Have drown'd my Glory in a Shallow Cup
And sold my Reputation for a Song.   *Ib. ed. 4, xciii*

21 Indeed, indeed, Repentance oft before
  I swore—but was I sober when I swore?
    And then and then came Spring, and Rose-in-hand
My thread-bare Penitence apieces tore.   *Ib. xciv*

22 And much as Wine has play'd the Infidel,
  And robb'd me of my Robe of Honour—Well,
    I often wonder what the Vintners buy
One half so precious as the Goods they sell.
                Ib. ed. 1, lxxi

23 One half so precious as the stuff they sell.
                Ib. ed. 4, xcv

24 Alas, that Spring should vanish with the Rose!
  That Youth's sweet-scented Manuscript should close!
    The Nightingale that in the Branches sang,
Ah, whence, and whither flown again, who knows!
               Ib. ed. 1, lxxii

25 Yet Ah, that Spring should vanish with the Rose!
               Ib. ed. 4, xcvi

26 Ah Love! could thou and I with Fate conspire
  To grasp this sorry Scheme of Things entire,
    Would not we shatter it to bits—and then
Re-mould it nearer to the Heart's Desire!
               Ib. ed. 1, lxxiii

27 Ah Love! could you and I with Him conspire.
               Ib. ed. 4, xcix

28 Ah, Moon of my Delight who know'st no wane,
  The Moon of Heav'n is rising once again:
    How oft hereafter rising shall she look
Through this same Garden after me—in vain!
              Ib. ed. 1, lxxiv

29 Yon rising Moon that looks for us again.
  How oft hereafter will she wax and wane;
    How oft hereafter rising look for us
Through this same Garden—and for *one* in vain!
               Ib. ed. 4, c

30 And when Thyself with shining Foot shall pass
  Among the Guests Star-scattered on the Grass,
    And in thy joyous Errand reach the Spot
Where I made one—turn down an empty Glass!
              Ib. ed. 1, lxxv

31 And when like her, O Saki, you shall pass.
                Ib. ed. 4, ci

32 And in your joyous errand reach the spot.   *Ib.*

33 Mrs. Browning's death is rather a relief to me, I must
  say: no more Aurora Leighs, thank God!
      Letter, 15 July 1861 (see 91:26 for Browning's
      rejoinder)

34 Taste is the feminine of genius.
         Ib. To J. R. Lowell, Oct. 1877

1 A Mr Wilkinson, a clergyman.
  Hallam Tennyson's Tennyson, *ii. 276. An imitation of Wordsworth's worst style*

JAMES ELROY FLECKER
1884-1915

2 Voiced like a great bell swinging in a dome.
  The Bridge of Fire, iv

3 For pines are gossip pines the wide world through.
  Brumana

4 Half to forget the wandering and the pain,
  Half to remember days that have gone by,
  And dream and dream that I am home again!   *Ib.*

5 Noon strikes on England, noon on Oxford town,
  Beauty she was statue cold—there's blood upon her gown:
  Noon of my dreams, O noon!
  Proud and godly kings had built her, long ago,
  With her towers and tombs and statues all arow,
  With her fair and floral air and the love that lingers there,
  And the streets where the great men go.
  The Dying Patriot

6 Evening on the olden, the golden sea of Wales,
  When the first star shivers and the last wave pales:
  O evening dreams!   *Ib.*

7 West of these out to seas colder than the Hebrides
  I must go
  Where the fleet of stars is anchored and the young
  star-captains glow.   *Ib.*

8 The dragon-green, the luminous, the dark, the
  serpent-haunted sea.
  The Gates of Damascus. West Gate

9 We who with songs beguile your pilgrimage
  And swear that Beauty lives though lilies die,
  We Poets of the proud old lineage
  Who sing to find your hearts, we know not why,—
  What shall we tell you? Tales, marvellous tales
  Of ships and stars and isles where good men rest.
  The Golden Journey to Samarkand, Prologue

10 When the great markets by the sea shut fast
   All that calm Sunday that goes on and on:
   When even lovers find their peace at last,
   And Earth is but a star, that once had shone.   *Ib.*

11 How splendid in the morning glows the lily; with
   what grace he throws
   His supplication to the rose.   *Hassan, I. i*

12 And some to Meccah turn to pray, and I toward thy
   bed, Yasmin.   *Ib. ii*

13   For one night or the other night
   Will come the Gardener in white, and gathered
   flowers are dead, Yasmin.   *Ib.*

14 For lust of knowing what should not be known,
   We take the Golden Road to Samarkand.   *Ib. v. ii*

15 And with great lies about his wooden horse
   Set the crew laughing, and forgot his course.
   The Old Ships

16 It was so old a ship—who knows, who knows?
   And yet so beautiful, I watched in vain
   To see the mast burst open with a rose,
   And the whole deck put on its leaves again.   *Ib.*

17 And old Mæonides the blind
   Said it three thousand years ago.
   To a Poet a Thousand Years Hence

18 And walk with you, and talk with you, like any other
   boy.   *Rioupéroux*

19 A ship, an isle, a sickle moon—
   With few but with how splendid stars
   The mirrors of the sea are strewn
   Between their silver bars.
   A Ship, an Isle, and a Sickle Moon

RICHARD FLECKNOE
d. 1678?

20 Still-born Silence! thou that art
   Floodgate of the deeper heart.   *Poems, 1653*

MARJORIE FLEMING
1803-1811

21 A direful death indeed they had
   That would put any parent mad
   But she was more than usual calm
   She did not give a singel dam.   *Journal, p. 29*

22 The most devilish thing is 8 times 8 and 7 times 7
   it is what nature itselfe cant endure.   *Ib. p. 47*

23 To-day I pronounced a word which should never come
   out of a lady's lips it was that I called John a
   Impudent Bitch.   *Ib. p. 51*

24 I am going to turn over a new life and am going to be
   a very good girl and be obedient to Isa Keith, here
   there is plenty of gooseberries which makes my
   teeth watter.   *Ib. p. 76*

25 I hope I will be religious again but as for regaining
   my character I despare.   *Ib. p. 80*

26 An annibabtist is a thing I am not a member of.
   Ib. p. 99

27 Sentiment is what I am not acquainted with.   *Ib.*

28 My dear Isa,
   I now sit down on my botom to answer all your
   kind and beloved letters which you was so good as to
   write to me.   *Letters. I, To Isabella*

29 O lovely O most charming pug
   Thy graceful air and heavenly mug. . . .
   His noses cast is of the roman
   He is a very pretty weoman
   I could not get a rhyme for roman
   And was obldiged to call it weoman.   *Poems*

PAUL FLEMING
1609-1640

30 Des großen Vaters Helm ist viel zu weit dem Sohne.
   The mighty father's helm is far too big for his son.
   Sonnet (Die jetzigen Deutschen)

ANDREW FLETCHER OF SALTOUN
1655-1716

31 I knew a very wise man so much of Sir Chr—'s sentiment, that he believed if a man were permitted to
   make all the ballads, he need not care who should
   make the laws of a nation.
   Letter to the Marquis of Montrose, and Others.
   Political Works

PHINEAS FLETCHER
1582–1650

1 Poorly (poor man) he liv'd; poorly (poor man) he
di'd. *The Purple Island*, I. xix

2 His little son into his bosom creeps,
The lively picture of his father's face. *Ib.* XII. vi

3 Drop, drop, slow tears,
And bathe those beauteous feet,
Which brought from Heav'n
The news and Prince of Peace. *An Hymn*

4 In your deep floods
Drown all my faults and fears;
Not let His eye
See sin, but through my tears. *Ib.*

5 Love is like linen often chang'd, the sweeter.
Sicelides, III. v

6 The coward's weapon, poison. *Ib.* v. iii

7 Love's tongue is in the eyes.
Piscatory Eclogues, eclog. v, xiii

JOHN FLORIO
1553?–1625

8 England is the paradise of women, the purgatory of
men, and the hell of horses. *Second Frutes*

MARÉCHAL FOCH
1851–1929

9 Mon centre cède, ma droite recule, situation excellente. J'attaque!
My centre is giving way, my right is in retreat;
situation excellent. I shall attack.
Sir G. Aston, *Biography of Foch* (1929), ch. 13,
p. 122

JEAN DE LA FONTAINE
1621–1695

10 Aide-toi, le ciel t'aidera.
Help yourself, and heaven will help you.
Fables, vi. 18. *Le Chartier Embourbé*

11 Je plie et ne romps pas.
I bend and I break not.
Ib. i. 22. *Le Chêne et le Roseau*

12 C'est double plaisir de tromper le trompeur.
It is doubly pleasing to trick the trickster.
Ib. ii. 15. *Le Coq et le Renard*

13 Il connaît l'univers et ne se connaît pas.
He knows the world and does not know himself.
Ib. viii. 26. *Démocrite et les Abdéritains*

14 La raison du plus fort est toujours la meilleure.
The reason of the strongest is always the best.
Ib. i. 10. *Le Loup et l'Agneau*

15 La mort ne surprend point le sage,
Il est toujours prêt à partir.
Death never takes the wise man by surprise; he is
always ready to go.
Ib. viii. 1. *La Mort et le Mourant*

BERNARD LE BOVIER DE FONTENELLE
1657–1757

16 Si j'avais les mains pleines de vérités, je me garderais
de les ouvrir.
If my hands were filled with truths, I should be
careful not to open them.

SAMUEL FOOTE
1720–1777

17 Born in a cellar, . . . and living in a garret.
The Author, II

18 So she went into the garden to cut a cabbage-leaf, to
make an apple-pie; and at the same time a great
she-bear, coming up the street, pops its head into
the shop. 'What! no soap?' So he died, and she
very imprudently married the barber; and there
were present the Picninnies, and the Joblillies, and
the Garyalies, and the grand Panjandrum himself,
with the little round button at top, and they all fell
to playing the game of catch as catch can, till the
gun powder ran out at the heels of their boots.
In Maria Edgeworth, Harry and Lucy Concluded

19 For as the old saying is,
When house and land are gone and spent
Then learning is most excellent. *Taste*, I. i

20 He is not only dull in himself, but the cause of dullness in others. *Remark.* Boswell's *Life of Johnson*,
ed. Powell, IV, p. 178. Parody of Shakespeare,
Henry IV, Part II, I. ii. 7

HENRY FORD
1863–1947

21 History is bunk.
In the witness box during his libel suit v. *the
Chicago Tribune, July 1919*

JOHN FORD
1586–1639?

22 Hairs as gay as are Apollo's locks.
The Broken Heart, I. ii

23 Tempt not the stars, young man, thou canst not play
With the severity of fate. *Ib.* iii

24 I am . . . a mushroom
On whom the dew of heaven drops now and then.
Ib.

25 The joys of marriage are the heaven on earth,
Life's paradise, great princess, the soul's quiet,
Sinews of concord, earthly immortality,
Eternity of pleasures; no restoratives
Like to a constant woman. *Ib.* II. ii

26 I have not thoughts
Enough to think. *Ib.* IV. ii

27 He hath shook hands with time. *Ib.* v. ii

28 We can drink till all look blue.
The Lady's Trial, IV. ii

29 Tell us, pray, what devil
This melancholy is, which can transform
Men into monsters. *Ib.* III. i

1 Parthenophil is lost, and I would see him;
For he is like to something I remember,
A great while since, a long, long time ago.
The Lover's Melancholy

2 'Tis Pity She's a Whore. *Title of Play*

3 Why, I hold fate
Clasp'd in my fist, and could command the course
Of time's eternal motion, hadst thou been
One thought more steady than an ebbing sea.
'Tis Pity She's a Whore, v. iv

LENA GUILBERT FORD
d. 1916?

4 Keep the home fires burning, while your hearts are
yearning,
Though your lads are far away they dream of home;
There's a silver lining through the dark cloud shining:
Turn the dark cloud inside out, till the boys come
home. *Keep the Home Fires Burning*

THOMAS FORD
c. 1580–1648

5 There is a lady sweet and kind,
Was never face so pleased my mind;
I did but see her passing by,
And yet I love her till I die.
There is a Lady. (*Music of Sundry Kinds*,
1607, IX. i.) *But see* Corrigenda

HOWELL FORGY
1908–

6 Praise the Lord, and pass the ammunition.
*Attr. when a Naval Lt., at Pearl Harbour,
7 Dec. 1941*

E. M. FORSTER
1879–

7 Beethoven's Fifth Symphony is the most sublime
noise that has ever penetrated into the ear of man.
Howards End (1910), ch. 5

VENANTIUS FORTUNATUS
530–609

8 Vexilla regis prodeunt
Fulget crucis mysterium.

The royal banners forward go
The cross shines forth in mystic glow.
Durham Rituale. Trans. by J. M. Neale

SAM WALTER FOSS
1858–1911

9 I say the very things that make the greatest stir,
An' the most interestin' things, are things that didn't
occur.
Back Country Poems. Things That Didn't Occur

10 W'en you see a man in woe,
Walk right up and say 'hullo';
Say 'hullo' and 'how d'ye do.
How's the world a-usin' you?' *Hullo*

CHARLES FOSTER
1828–1904

11 Isn't this a billion dollar country?
*At the 51st Congress; retorting to a Democratic
gibe about a 'million dollar Congress'*

SIR GEORGE EULAS FOSTER
1847–1931

12 In these somewhat troublesome days when the great
Mother Empire stands splendidly isolated in
Europe.
*Speech, Canadian House of Commons, 16 Jan.
1896*

STEPHEN COLLINS FOSTER
1826–1864

13 I come down dah wid my hat caved in,
Doodah! doodah!
I go back home wid a pocket full of tin,
Oh! doodah day!
Gwine to run all night!
Gwine to run all day!
I'll bet my money on de bob-tail nag,
Somebody bet on de bay. *Camptown Races*

14 De blind hoss stick'n in a big mud hole,
Doodah! doodah!
Can't touch de bottom wid a ten-foot pole,
Oh! doodah day! *Ib.*

15 Weep no more, my lady,
Oh! weep no more to-day!
We will sing one song for the old Kentucky Home,
For the old Kentucky Home far away.
My Old Kentucky Home

16 'Way down upon de Swanee Ribber,
Far, far away,
Dere's where my heart is turning ebber:
Dere's where de old folks stay.
All up and down de whole creation
Sadly I roam,
Still longing for de old plantation,
And for de old folks at home.
Old Folks at Home (Swanee Ribber)

17 I'm coming, I'm coming,
For my head is bending low,
I hear their gentle voices calling
'Poor old Joe.' *Poor Old Joe*

18 He had no wool on de top of his head,
In de place where de wool ought to grow. *Uncle Ned*

19 Dere's no more hard work for poor old Ned,
He's gone whar de good niggers go. *Ib.*

CHARLES JAMES FOX
1749–1806

20 How much the greatest event it is that ever happened
in the world! and how much the best!
*On the Fall of the Bastille. Letter to Fitzpatrick,
30 July 1789. Russell's Life and Times of C. J.
Fox, vol. ii, p. 361*

21 He was uniformly of an opinion which, though not a
popular one, he was ready to aver, that the right of
governing was not property, but a trust.
*On Pitt's scheme of Parliamentary Reform.
J. L. Hammond, C. J. Fox (1903), p. 75*

1 No man could be so wise as Thurlow looked.
   Campbell's *Lives of the Lord Chancellors*, 1846, vol. v, p. 661.

2 I die happy.
   Last Words. Russell, *op. cit.*, vol. iii, ch. 69

HENRY FOX
see
FIRST BARON HOLLAND

HENRY RICHARD VASSALL FOX
see
THIRD BARON HOLLAND

ANATOLE FRANCE
1844–1924

3 Le bon critique est celui qui raconte les aventures de son âme au milieu des chefs-d'œuvre.

   The good critic is he who relates the adventures of his soul among masterpieces.
   La Vie littéraire, preface

FRANCOIS Ier
1494–1547

4 Tout est perdu fors l'honneur.

   All is lost save honour.
   Traditional words in a letter to his mother after his defeat at Pavia, 1525. The actual words were: 'De toutes choses ne m'est demeuré que l'honneur et la vie qui est saulve.' *Collection des Documents Inédits sur l'Histoire de France*, vol. i, 1847, p. 129

BENJAMIN FRANKLIN
1706–1790

5 Remember, that time is money.
   Advice to Young Tradesman, 1748. Writings, vol. ii

6 No nation was ever ruined by trade.
   Essays. Thoughts on Commercial Subjects

7 Be in general virtuous, and you will be happy.
   Ib. On Early Marriages

8 There never was a good war, or a bad peace.
   Letter to Quincy, 11 Sept. 1783

9 But in this world nothing can be said to be certain, except death and taxes.
   Letter to Jean Baptiste Le Roy, 13 Nov. 1789. Writings, vol. x

10 A little neglect may breed mischief, . . . for want of a nail, the shoe was lost; for want of a shoe the horse was lost; and for want of a horse the rider was lost.
   Maxims . . . Prefixed to Poor Richard's Almanac, (1758)

11 Some are weather-wise, some are otherwise.
   Poor Richard's Almanac, Feb. 1735

12 Necessity never made a good bargain. *Ib. Apr. 1735*

13 Three may keep a secret, if two of them are dead.
   Ib. July 1735

14 At twenty years of age, the will reigns; at thirty, the wit; and at forty, the judgement.
   Poor Richard's Almanac, June 1741

15 Dost thou love life? Then do not squander time, for that's the stuff life is made of. *Ib. June 1746*

16 Many have been ruined by buying good pennyworths.
   Ib. Sept. 1747

17 He that lives upon hope will die fasting.
   Ib. 1758, preface

18 We must indeed all hang together, or, most assuredly, we shall all hang separately.
   Remark to John Hancock, at Signing of the Declaration of Independence, 4 July 1776

19 Poor man, said I, you pay too much for your whistle.
   The Whistle, 10 Nov. 1779

20 Man is a tool-making animal.
   Boswell's Life of Johnson, 7 Apr. 1778.

21 The body of
   Benjamin Franklin, printer,
   (Like the cover of an old book,
   Its contents worn out,
   And stript of its lettering and gilding)
   Lies here, food for worms!
   Yet the work itself shall not be lost,
   For it will, as he believed, appear once more
   In a new
   And more beautiful edition,
   Corrected and amended
   By its Author!   *Epitaph for himself*

FREDERICK THE GREAT
1712–1786

22 My people and I have come to an agreement which satisfies us both. They are to say what they please, and I am to do what I please.   *Ascribed.*

23 Ihr Racker, wollt ihr ewig leben?

   Rascals, would you live for ever?
   When the Guards hesitated, at Kolin, 18 June 1757

EDWARD AUGUSTUS FREEMAN
1823–1892

24 A saying which fell from myself in one of the debates in Congregation on the Modern Language Statute has been quoted in several places . . . 'chatter about Shelley' . . . I mentioned that I had lately read a review of a book about Shelley in which the critic . . . praised or blamed the author . . . for his 'treatment of the Harriet problem'.
   Contemporary Review, Oct. 1887: 'Literature and Language'
   The two phrases are often telescoped as 'chatter about Harriet'.

JOHN HOOKHAM FRERE
1769–1846

25 The feather'd race with pinions skim the air—
   Not so the mackerel, and still less the bear!
   Progress of Man, l. 34. Poetry of the Anti-Jacobin, 1799

26 Ah! who has seen the mailed lobster rise,
   Clap her broad wings, and soaring claim the skies?
   Ib. l. 44

CHARLES FROHMAN
1860–1915

1 Why fear death? It is the most beautiful adventure in life.
His last words before going down in the Lusitania, *7 May 1915.* I. F. Marcosson and D. Frohman, *Charles Frohman, ch.* 19

ROBERT FROST
1875–1963

2 Something there is that doesn't love a wall.
North of Boston. Mending Wall

3 My apple trees will never get across
And eat the cones under his pines, I tell him.
He only says, 'Good fences make good neighbours.'
Ib.

JAMES ANTHONY FROUDE
1818–1894

4 Wild animals never kill for sport. Man is the only one to whom the torture and death of his fellow-creatures is amusing in itself. *Oceana, ch.* 5

5 Men are made by nature unequal. It is vain, therefore, to treat them as if they were equal.
Short Studies on Great Subjects. 3rd Ser. *Party Politics*

6 Experience teaches slowly, and at the cost of mistakes.
Ib.

7 Fear is the parent of cruelty. *Ib.*

THOMAS FULLER
1608–1661

8 Thus this brook hath conveyed his [Wickliff's] ashes into Avon; Avon into Severn; Severn into the narrow seas; they, into the main ocean. And thus the ashes of Wickliff are the emblem of his doctrine, which now, is dispersed all the world over.
The Church History (1655), bk. iv, sec. ii, par. 53, p. 171

9 It is a silly game where nobody wins.
Gnomologia, No. 2880

10 A proverb is much matter decocted into few words.
The History of the Worthies of England, ch. 2

11 Know most of the rooms of thy native country before thou goest over the threshold thereof.
The Holy and Profane State (1642), bk. ii, ch. 4, p. 159. *Of Travelling*

12 A little skill in antiquity inclines a man to Popery; but depth in that study brings him about again to our religion.
Ib. ch. 6, p. 69. *The True Church Antiquary*

13 Light (God's eldest daughter).
Ib. ch. 7, p. 167. *Of Building*

14 But our captain counts the Image of God nevertheless his image, cut in ebony as if done in ivory.
Ib. ch. 20. *The Good Sea-Captain*

15 Learning hath gained most by those books by which the printers have lost.
Ib. bk. iii, *ch.* 18, p. 200. *Of Books*

16 He was one of a lean body and visage, as if his eager soul, biting for anger at the clog of his body, desired to fret a passage through it.
The Holy and Profane State, bk. v, ch. 19, p. 441. *Life of the Duke of Alva*

17 Worldly wealth he cared not for, desiring only to make both ends meet. [Of Edmund Grindall.]
Worthies of England. Worthies of Cumberland

18 Many were the wit-combats betwixt him [Shakespeare] and Ben Jonson, which two I behold like a Spanish great gallion, and an English man of war: Master Jonson (like the former) was built far higher in learning; solid, but slow, in his performances. Shakespeare, with the English man of war, lesser in bulk, but lighter in sailing, could turn with all the tides, tack about, and take advantage of all winds, by the quickness of his wit and invention.
Ib. Worthies of Warwickshire

HENRY FUSELI
[JOHANN HEINRICH FUESSLI]
1741–1825

19 Blake is damned good to steal from!
Gilchrist's *Life of Blake* (1863), ch. vii

ROSE FYLEMAN
1877–1957

20 There are fairies at the bottom of our garden.
Fairies

THOMAS GAINSBOROUGH
1727–1788

21 We are all going to heaven, and Vandyke is of the company.
Attr. Last Words. Boulton, *Thomas Gainsborough,* ch. 9

REV. THOMAS GAISFORD
1779–1855

22 Nor can I do better, in conclusion, than impress upon you the study of Greek literature, which not only elevates above the vulgar herd, but leads not infrequently to positions of considerable emolument.
Christmas Day Sermon in the Cathedral, Oxford. Rev. W. Tuckwell, *Reminiscences of Oxford* (2nd ed., 1907), p. 124.

GAIUS
fl. c. 110–*c.* 180

23 Damnosa hereditas.
Ruinous inheritance. *Inst.* ii. 163

GALILEO GALILEI
1564–1642

24 E pur si muove.
But it does move.
Attr. to Galileo after his recantation in 1632. The earliest appearance of the phrase is 1761 (see E. R. Hull, *Galileo), and it is generally conceded to be apocryphal.*

RICHARD GALL
1776-1801

1 Baloo, baloo, my wee wee thing.   *Poems and Songs*

JOHN GALSWORTHY
1867-1933

2 If on a Spring night I went by
And God were standing there,
What is the prayer that I would cry
To Him? This is the prayer:
O God of Courage grave,
O Master of this night of Spring!
Make firm in me a heart too brave
To ask Thee anything.   *The Prayer*

3 He [Jolyon] was afflicted by the thought that where
Beauty was, nothing ever ran quite straight, which,
no doubt, was why so many people looked on it as
immoral.   *In Chancery*, ch. 13

4 Nobody tells me anything. [*James Forsyte.*]
   The Man of Property, pt. 1, ch. i

SIR GREGORY GANDER
[GEORGE ELLIS]
1745-1815

5 Snowy, Flowy, Blowy,
Showery, Flowery, Bowery,
Hoppy, Croppy, Droppy,
Breezy, Sneezy, Freezy.   *The Twelve Months*

AUGUSTUS P. GARDNER
1865-1918

6 Wake up, America.   *Speech, 16 Oct. 1916*

JAMES ABRAM GARFIELD
1831-1881

7 Fellow-citizens: God reigns, and the Government at
Washington lives!
   Speech on Assassination of Lincoln, 1865

DAVID GARRICK
1717-1779

8 Prologues precede the piece—in mournful verse;
As undertakers—walk before the hearse.
   Apprentice, prologue

9 Are these the choice dishes the Doctor has sent us?
Is this the great poet whose works so content us?
This Goldsmith's fine feast, who has written fine
books?
Heaven sends us good meat, but the Devil sends
cooks.
   On Doctor Goldsmith's Characteristical Cookery

10 Come, cheer up, my lads! 'tis to glory we steer,
To add something more to this wonderful year;
To honour we call you, not press you like slaves,
For who are so free as the sons of the waves?
   Heart of oak are our ships,
   Heart of oak are our men:
   We always are ready;
   Steady, boys, steady;
We'll fight and we'll conquer again and again.
   Heart of Oak

11 We ne'er see our foes but we wish 'em to stay,
They never see us but they wish us away;
If they run, why, we follow, and run 'em ashore,
For if they won't fight us, we cannot do more.
   Heart of Oak

12 Here lies Nolly Goldsmith, for shortness call'd Noll,
Who wrote like an angel, but talk'd like poor Poll.
   Impromptu Epitaph

13 I've that within—for which there are no plaisters.
   Prologue to Goldsmith's She Stoops to Conquer

14 A fellow-feeling makes one wond'rous kind.
   *An Occasional Prologue on Quitting the Theatre,
   10 June 1776*

15 Kitty, a fair, but frozen maid,
   Kindled a flame I still deplore;
The hood-wink'd boy I call'd in aid,
Much of his near approach afraid.
   So fatal to my suit before.
   A Riddle. Lady's Magazine, June 1762

16 That blessed word Mesopotamia.
   *Garrick tells of the power of George White-
   field's voice, that 'he could make men either
   laugh or cry by pronouncing the word Mesopotamia'. Related by Francis Jacox. A story
   goes (Harvey's Companion to English Literature)
   that an old woman told her pastor that she
   found great support in that comfortable word
   Mesopotamia.*
   Notes and Queries, Ser. XI, i. 458

WILLIAM LLOYD GARRISON
1805-1879

17 I am in earnest—I will not equivocate—I will not
excuse—I will not retreat a single inch—and I will
be heard!
   *Salutatory Address of The Liberator, 1 Jan.
   1831*

18 Our country is the world—our countrymen are all
mankind. *Prospectus of The Liberator, 15 Dec. 1837*

19 The compact which exists between the North and the
South is 'a covenant with death and an agreement
with hell'.
   *Resolution adopted by the Massachusetts Anti-
   Slavery Society, 27 Jan. 1843*

SIR SAMUEL GARTH
1661-1719

20 Hard was their lodging, homely was their food;
For all their luxury was doing good.
   Claremont, l. 148

21 A barren superfluity of words.
   The Dispensary, c. 2, l. 95

ELIZABETH CLEGHORN GASKELL
1810-1865

22 Get her a flannel waistcoat and flannel drawers,
ma'am, if you wish to keep her alive. But my
advice is, kill the poor creature at once. [*Capt.
Brown on Miss Betsey Barker's cow.*]
   Cranford, ch. 1

23 We were none of us musical, though Miss Jenkyns
beat time, out of time, by way of appearing to be so.
   Ib.

1 Bombazine would have shown a deeper sense of her loss. [*Miss Jenkyns.*] *Cranford*, ch. 7

JOSÉ ORTEGA Y GASSET
1883–1955

2 Orden no es una presión que desde fuera se ejerce sobre la sociedad, sino un equilibrio que se suscita en su interior.

Order is not a pressure which is imposed on society from without, but an equilibrium which is set up from within.

Mirabeau o el Político

THÉOPHILE GAUTIER
1811–1872

3 Tout passe.—L'art robuste
Seul a l'éternité,
Le buste
Survit à la cité.

See Henry Austin Dobson, *183:5. L'Art*

4 Je suis un homme pour qui le monde extérieur existe.

I am a man for whom the outside world exists.

Journal des Goncourt, 1 May 1857

GAVARNI
1801–1866

5 Les enfants terribles.

The embarrassing young. *Title of a series of prints*

JOHN GAY
1685–1732

6 I rage, I melt, I burn,
The feeble God has stabb'd me to the heart.

Acis and Galatea, ii

7 Bring me an hundred reeds of decent growth,
To make a pipe for my capacious mouth. *Ib.*

8 O ruddier than the cherry,
O sweeter than the berry. *Ib.*

9 Wou'd you gain the tender creature?
Softly, gently, kindly treat her,
Suff'ring is the lover's part.
Beauty by constraint, possessing,
You enjoy but half the blessing,
Lifeless charms, without the heart. *Ib.*

10 Love sounds the alarm, and Fear is a flying. *Ib.*

11 How, like a moth, the simple maid
Still plays about the flame!

The Beggar's Opera, Act I, sc. iv, air iv

12 Our Polly is a sad slut! nor heeds what we have taught her.
I wonder any man alive will ever rear a daughter!

Ib. viii, air vii

13 Do you think your mother and I should have liv'd comfortably so long together, if ever we had been married? *Ib.*

14 Can Love be controll'd by advice? *Ib.* air viii

15 O Polly, you might have toy'd and kist,
By keeping men off, you keep them on. *Ib.* air ix

16 Well, Polly; as far as one woman can forgive another, I forgive thee.

The Beggar's Opera, Act I, sc. viii, air ix

17 POLLY.
Then all my sorrows are at an end.
MRS. PEACHUM.
A mighty likely speech, in troth, for a wench who is just married! *Ib.*

18 Money, wife, is the true fuller's earth for reputations, there is not a spot or a stain but what it can take out.
Ib. ix

19 A fox may steal your hens, sir

If lawyer's hand is fee'd, sir
He steals your whole estate. *Ib.* air xi

20 The comfortable estate of widowhood, is the only hope that keeps up a wife's spirits. *Ib.* x

21 Oh, ponder well! be not severe;
So save a wretched wife:
For on the rope that hangs my dear
Depends poor Polly's life. *Ib.* air xii

22 Away, hussy. Hang your husband and be dutiful. *Ib.*

23 Even butchers weep! *Ib.* xii

24 Pretty Polly, say,
When I was away,
Did your fancy never stray
To some newer lover? *Ib.* xiii, air xiv

25 I sipt each flower,
I chang'd ev'ry hour,
But here ev'ry flower is united. *Ib.* air xv

26 If with me you'd fondly stray.
Over the hills and far away. *Ib.* air xvi

27 O what pain it is to part! *Ib.* air xvii

28 We retrench the superfluities of mankind. *Ib.* II. i

29 Fill ev'ry glass, for wine inspires us,
And fires us
With courage, love and joy.
Women and wine should life employ.
Is there ought else on earth desirous? *Ib.* air xix

30 If the heart of a man is deprest with cares,
The mist is dispell'd when a woman appears.
Ib. iii, air xxi

31 I must have women. There is nothing unbends the mind like them. *Ib.*

32 Youth's the season made for joys,
Love is then our duty. *Ib.* iv, air xxii

33 To cheat a man is nothing; but the woman must have fine parts indeed who cheats a woman! *Ib.*

34 Man may escape from rope and gun;
Nay, some have outliv'd the doctor's pill:
Who takes a woman must be undone,
That basilisk is sure to kill.
The fly that sips treacle is lost in the sweets,
So he that tastes woman, woman, woman,
He that tastes woman, ruin meets. *Ib.* viii, air xxvi

35 MACHEATH.
Have you no bowels, no tenderness, my dear Lucy, to see a husband in these circumstances?
LUCY.
A husband!
MACHEATH.
In ev'ry respect but the form. *Ib.* ix

1 I am ready, my dear Lucy, to give you satisfaction— if you think there is any in marriage?
The Beggar's Opera, Act II, sc. ix

2 In one respect indeed, our employment may be reckoned dishonest, because, like great Statesmen, we encourage those who betray their friends. *Ib.* x

3 I think you must ev'n do as other widows—buy yourself weeds, and be cheerful. *Ib.* xi

4 How happy could I be with either,
Were t'other dear charmer away!
But while ye thus tease me together,
To neither a word will I say. *Ib.* xiii, air xxxv

5 One wife is too much for one husband to hear,
But two at a time there's no mortal can bear.
This way, and that way, and which way I will,
What would comfort the one, t'other wife would take ill. *Ib.* III. xi, air liii

6 The charge is prepar'd; the lawyers are met;
The Judges all rang'd (a terrible show!). *Ib.* air lvii

7 That that Jemmy Twitcher should peach me, I own surprised me! *Ib.* xiv

8 She who has never lov'd, has never liv'd.
The Captives, II. i

9 If e'er your heart has felt the tender passion
You will forgive this just, this pious fraud. *Ib.* IV. x

10 She who trifles with all
Is less likely to fall
Than she who but trifles with one.
The Coquet Mother and the Coquet Daughter

11 Then nature rul'd, and love, devoid of art,
Spoke the consenting language of the heart.
Dione, prologue

12 Behold the victim of Parthenia's pride!
He saw, he sigh'd, he lov'd, was scorn'd and died.
Ib. I. i

13 He best can pity who has felt the woe. *Ib.* II. ii

14 Woman's mind
Oft' shifts her passions, like th'inconstant wind;
Sudden she rages, like the troubled main,
Now sinks the storm, and all is calm again. *Ib.* v

15 A woman's friendship ever ends in love. *Ib.* IV. vi

16 Behold the bright original appear.
Epistle to a Lady, l. 85

17 Praising all alike, is praising none. *Ib.* l. 114

18 One always zealous for his country's good. *Ib.* l. 118

19 Variety's the source of joy below.
Epistle to Bernard Lintott, l. 41

20 Life is a jest; and all things show it.
I thought so once; but now I know it.
My Own Epitaph

21 Whence is thy learning? Hath thy toil
O'er books consum'd the midnight oil?
Fables. Series I, introduction, l. 15

22 Where yet was ever found a mother,
Who'd give her booby for another?
Ib. The Mother, the Nurse, and the Fairy, iii, l. 33

23 Envy's a sharper spur than pay,
No author ever spar'd a brother,
Wits are gamecocks to one another.
Ib. The Elephant and the Bookseller, l. 74

24 An open foe may prove a curse,
But a pretended friend is worse.
Fables, xvii. *The Shepherd's Dog and the Wolf*, l. 33

25 Where there is life, there's hope, he cried,
Then why such haste? so groan'd and died.
Ib. xxvii. *The Sick Man and the Angel*, l. 49

26 Those who in quarrels interpose,
Must often wipe a bloody nose.
Ib. xxxiv. *The Mastiff*, l. 1

27 How many saucy airs we meet
From Temple-bar to Aldgate-street.
Ib. xxxv. *The Barley-Mow and Dunghill*, l. 1

28 Fools may our scorn, not envy raise,
For envy is a kind of praise.
Ib. xliv. *The Hound and the Huntsman*, l. 29

29 Friendship, like love, is but a name.
Ib. l. *The Hare and Many Friends*, l. 1

30 And when a lady's in the case,
You know, all other things give place. *Ib.* l. 41

31 Give me, kind heaven, a private station,
A mind serene for contemplation.
Ib. Series II, ii. *The Vulture, the Sparrow, and Other Birds*, l. 69

32 Studious of elegance and ease.
Ib. viii. *The Man, the Cat, the Dog, and the Fly*, l. 127

33 Whoever heard a man of fortune in England talk of the necessaries of life? . . . Whether we can afford it or no, we must have superfluities. *Polly*, I. i

34 How little are our customs known on this side of the herring-pond! *Ib.*

35 No, sir, tho' I was born and bred in England, I can dare to be poor, which is the only thing now-a-days men are asham'd of. *Ib.* xi

36 An inconstant woman, tho' she has no chance to be very happy, can never be very unhappy. *Ib.* xiv

37 Sleep, O Sleep,
With thy rod of incantation
Charm my imagination.

.   .   .   .   .

What's to sleep?
'Tis a visionary blessing;
A dream that's past expressing;
Our utmost wish possessing
So may I always keep. *Ib.* II. i

38 And one slight hair the mighty bulk commands.
Rural Sports, c. I, l. 244

39 All in the Downs the fleet was moor'd,
The streamers waving in the wind,
When black-ey'd Susan came aboard.
Sweet William's Farewell to Black-Eyed Susan

40 We only part to meet again.
Change, as ye list, ye winds; my heart shall be
The faithful compass that still points to thee. *Ib.*

41 They'll tell thee, sailors, when away,
In ev'ry port a mistress find. *Ib.*

42 If to far India's coast we sail,
Thy eyes are seen in di'monds bright,
Thy breath is Africk's spicy gale,
Thy skin is ivory, so white.
Thus ev'ry beauteous object that I view,
Wakes in my soul some charm of lovely Sue. *Ib.*

GAY—GIBBON

1 Adieu, she cries! and wav'd her lily hand.
Sweet William's Farewell to Black-Eyed Susan

2 A miss for pleasure, and a wife for breed.
The Toilette

3 Now Cynthia nam'd, fair regent of the Night.
Trivia, bk. iii, l. 4

4 Dispute the reign of some luxurious mire. *Ib.* l. 48

5 'Twas when the seas were roaring
With hollow blasts of wind;
A damsel lay deploring,
All on a rock reclin'd.
The What D'ye Call It, ii. viii

SIR ERIC GEDDES
1875-1937

6 We will get everything out of her [Germany] that you can squeeze out of a lemon and a bit more.... I will squeeze her until you can hear the pips squeak.
Speech at the Drill Hall, Cambridge, 9 Dec. 1918

DAVID LLOYD GEORGE, EARL OF DWYFOR
1863-1945

7 The stern hand of fate has scourged us to an elevation where we can see the great everlasting things that matter for a nation; the great peaks of honour we had forgotten—duty and patriotism clad in glittering white; the great pinnacle of sacrifice pointing like a rugged finger to Heaven.
Speech, Queen's Hall, London, 19 Sept. 1914

8 What is our task? To make Britain a fit country for heroes to live in.
Speech, Wolverhampton, 24 Nov. 1918

HENRY GEORGE
1839-1897

9 So long as all the increased wealth which modern progress brings goes but to build up great fortunes, to increase luxury and make sharper the contrast between the House of Have and the House of Want, progress is not real and cannot be permanent.
Progress and Poverty. Introductory, The Problem

GEORGE I OF GREAT BRITAIN
1660-1727

10 I hate all Boets and Bainters.
Campbell, *Lives of the Chief Justices*, ch. 30, *Lord Mansfield*

GEORGE II OF GREAT BRITAIN
1683-1760

11 Non, j'aurai des maîtresses.
No, I shall have mistresses.
Reply to Queen Caroline when, as she lay dying, she urged him to marry again. Her reply to this was 'Ah! mon Dieu! cela n'empêche pas'. *Hervey, Memoirs of George the Second* (1848), vol. ii

12 Oh! he is mad, is he? Then I wish he would *bite* some other of my generals.
Reply to one who complained that General Wolfe was a madman. F. Thackeray, *History of William Pitt*, vol. i, ch. 15, note

GEORGE III OF GREAT BRITAIN
1738-1820

13 Born and educated in this country I glory in the name of Briton. *Speech from the Throne, 1760*

14 'Was there ever,' cried he, 'such stuff as great part of Shakespeare? Only one must not say so! But what think you?—what?—Is there not sad stuff? what?—what?
To Fanny Burney (in her Diary, 19 Dec. 1785)

GEORGE V OF GREAT BRITAIN
1865-1936

15 Wake up, England.
Title of a reprint in 1911 of a speech made by the King when Prince of Wales in the Guildhall on 5 Dec. 1901 on his return from a tour of the Empire

I venture to allude to the impression which seemed generally to prevail among their brethren across the seas, that the old country must wake up if she intends to maintain her old position of pre-eminence in her colonial trade against foreign competitors. *Speech.*

16 How is the Empire?
Last Words. The Times, 21 Jan. 1936

EDWARD GIBBON
1737-1794

17 The successors of Charles the Fifth may disdain their brethren of England; but the romance of *Tom Jones*, that exquisite picture of human manners, will outlive the palace of the Escurial and the imperial eagle of the house of Austria.
Autobiography (World's Classics ed.), p. 4

18 My early and invincible love of reading, which I would not exchange for the treasures of India.
Ib. p. 27

19 To the University of Oxford I acknowledge no obligation; and she will as cheerfully renounce me for a son, as I am willing to disclaim her for a mother. I spent fourteen months at Magdalen College: they proved the fourteen months the most idle and unprofitable of my whole life. *Ib.* p. 36

20 The monks of Magdalen. *Ib.* p. 40

21 Decent easy men, who supinely enjoyed the gifts of the founder. *Ib.*

22 Their dull and deep potations excused the brisk intemperance of youth. *Ib.*

23 Dr. — well remembered that he had a salary to receive, and only forgot that he had a duty to perform.
Ib. p. 44

24 It was here that I suspended my religious inquiries *(aged 17).* *Ib.* p. 63

25 I saw and loved. *Ib.* p. 83

26 I sighed as a lover, I obeyed as a son. *Ib.*

27 [Of London.]
Crowds without company, and dissipation without pleasure. *Ib.* p. 90

28 The captain of the Hampshire grenadiers ... has not been useless to the historian of the Roman empire.
Ib. p. 106

1 It was at Rome, on the 15th of October, 1764, as I sat musing amidst the ruins of the Capitol, while the barefoot friars were singing vespers in the Temple of Jupiter, that the idea of writing the decline and fall of the city first started to my mind.
Autobiography, p. 160

2 The first of earthly blessings, independence.
Ib. p. 176

3 I will not dissemble the first emotions of joy on the recovery of my freedom, and, perhaps, the establishment of my fame. But my pride was soon humbled, and a sober melancholy was spread over my mind, by the idea that I had taken an ever-lasting leave of an old and agreeable companion, and that whatsoever might be the future date of my History, the life of the historian must be short and precarious.
Ib. p. 205

4 My English text is chaste, and all licentious passages are left in the decent obscurity of a learned language.
Ib. p. 212

5 The various modes of worship, which prevailed in the Roman world, were all considered by the people as equally true; by the philosopher, as equally false; and by the magistrate, as equally useful.
Decline and Fall of the Roman Empire, ch. 2

6 The principles of a free constitution are irrecoverably lost, when the legislative power is nominated by the executive.
Ib. ch. 3

7 Titus Antoninus Pius. . . . His reign is marked by the rare advantage of furnishing very few materials for history; which is, indeed, little more than the register of the crimes, follies, and misfortunes of mankind.
Ib.

8 If a man were called to fix the period in the history of the world during which the condition of the human race was most happy and prosperous, he would, without hesitation, name that which elapsed from the death of Domitian to the accession of Commodus.
Ib.

9 All taxes must, at last, fall upon agriculture. *Ib.* ch. 8

10 Corruption, the most infallible symptom of constitutional liberty.
Ib. ch. 21

11 In every deed of mischief he [Comenus] had a heart to resolve, a head to contrive, and a hand to execute.
Ib. ch. 48

12 A victorious line of march had been prolonged above a thousand miles from the rock of Gibraltar to the banks of the Loire; the repetition of an equal space would have carried the Saracens to the confines of Poland and the Highlands of Scotland; the Rhine is not more impassable than the Nile or Euphrates, and the Arabian fleet might have sailed without a naval combat into the mouth of the Thames. Perhaps the interpretation of the Koran would now be taught in the schools of Oxford, and her pulpits might demonstrate to a circumcised people the sanctity and truth of the revelation of Mahomet.
Ib. ch. 52

13 Vicissitudes of fortune, which spares neither man nor the proudest of his works, which buries empires and cities in a common grave.
Ib. ch. 71

14 All that is human must retrograde if it does not advance.
Ib.

STELLA GIBBONS
1902–

15 Something nasty in the woodshed.
Cold Comfort Farm, passim

HUMPHREY GIFFORD
1550–1600

16 Ye curious carpet knights, that spend the time in sport and play,
Abroad, and see new sights, your country's cause calls you away. *For Soldiers. Posie of Gilloflowers*

REV. RICHARD GIFFORD
1725–1807

17 Verse softens toil, however rude the sound;
She feels no biting pang the while she sings;
Nor, as she turns the giddy wheel around,
Revolves the sad vicissitude of things.
Contemplation

WILLIAM GIFFORD
1756–1826

18 In all the sad variety of woe. *The Baviad*, l. 164

19 The insatiate itch of scribbling.
Trans. of Juvenal, vii. 79

20 Virtue alone is true nobility. *Ib.* viii. 32

FRED GILBERT
1850–1903

21 At Trinity Church I met my doom. *Title of Song*

22 Woa, mare! Woa, mare!
You've earned your little bit o' corn! *Down the Road*

23 As I walk along the Bois Bou-long,
With an independent air,
You can hear the girls declare,
'He must be a millionaire';
You can hear them sigh and wish to die,
You can see them wink the other eye
At the man who broke the Bank at Monte Carlo.
The Man Who Broke the Bank at Monte Carlo

SIR HUMPHREY GILBERT
1539?–1583

24 We are as near to heaven by sea as by land!
Hakluyt's Voyages, iii (1600), p. 159

SIR WILLIAM SCHWENCK GILBERT
1836–1911

25 Among them was a Bishop, who
Had lately been appointed to
The balmy isle of Rum-ti-Foo,
And Peter was his name.
The 'Bab' Ballads, The Bishop of Rum-ti-Foo

26 It is my duty, and I will. *Ib. Captain Reece*

27 It was their duty, and they did. *Ib.*

28 A very good girl was Emily Jane,
Jimmy was good and true,
John was a very good man in the main
(And I am a good man too.)
Ib. Emily, John, James, and I

GILBERT

1 Down went the owners—greedy men whom hope of
   gain allured:
   Oh, dry the starting tear, for they were heavily
   insured.   *The 'Bab' Ballads, Etiquette*

2 He had often eaten oysters, but had never had enough.
                                                   Ib.

3 There were captains by the hundred, there were
   baronets by dozens.   *Ib. Ferdinando and Elvira*

4 Only find out who it is that writes those lovely cracker
   mottoes!   *Ib.*

5 The padre said, 'Whatever have you been and gone
   and done?'   *Ib. Gentle Alice Brown*

6 The other night, from cares exempt,
   I slept—and what d'you think I dreamt?
   I dreamt that somehow I had come
   To dwell in Topsy-Turveydom!—
   Where vice is virtue—virtue, vice:
   Where nice is nasty—nasty, nice:
   Where right is wrong and wrong is right—
   Where white is black and black is white.
                                    Ib. My Dream

7 From a highly impossible tree
   In a highly impossible scene.
                           Ib. Only a Dancing Girl

8 The mildest curate going.   *Ib. The Rival Curates*

9 Strike the concertina's melancholy string!
   Blow the spirit-stirring harp like anything!
      Let the piano's martial blast
      Rouse the Echoes of the Past,
   For of Agib, Prince of Tartary, I sing!
                           Ib. Story of Prince Agib

10 Which is pretty, but I don't know what it means. *Ib.*

11 Then they began to sing
   That extremely lovely thing,
   'Scherzando! ma non troppo ppp.'   *Ib.*

12 Roll on, thou ball, roll on!
   Through pathless realms of Space
         Roll on!
   What though I'm in a sorry case?
   What though I cannot meet my bills?
   What though I suffer toothache's ills?
   What though I swallow countless pills?
         Never *you* mind!
         Roll on! *Ib. To the Terrestrial Globe*

13 It's true I've got no shirts to wear;
   It's true my butcher's bill is due;
   It's true my prospects all look blue—
   But don't let that unsettle you!
         Never *you* mind!
         Roll on!   (*It rolls on.*)   *Ib.*

14 Oh, I am a cook and a captain bold,
      And the mate of the *Nancy* brig,
   And a bo'sun tight, and a midshipmite,
      And the crew of the captain's gig.
                     Ib. The Yarn of the 'Nancy Bell'

15 In all the woes that curse our race
   There is a lady in the case.   *Fallen Fairies*, II

16 He led his regiment from behind—
   He found it less exciting.   *The Gondoliers*, I

17 That celebrated,
   Cultivated,
   Underrated
         Nobleman,
   The Duke of Plaza Toro!   *The Gondoliers*, I

18 Of that there is no manner of doubt—
   No probable, possible shadow of doubt—
   No possible doubt whatever.   *Ib.*

19 His terrible taste for tippling.   *Ib.*

20 A taste for drink, combined with gout,
   Had doubled him up for ever.   *Ib.*

21 Oh, 'tis a glorious thing, I ween,
   To be a regular Royal Queen!
   No half-and-half affair, I mean,
   But a right-down regular Royal Queen!   *Ib.*

22 All shall equal be.
   The Earl, the Marquis, and the Dook,
   The Groom, the Butler, and the Cook,
   The Aristocrat who banks with Coutts,
   The Aristocrat who cleans the boots.   *Ib.*

23   But the privilege and pleasure
      That we treasure beyond measure
   Is to run on little errands for the Ministers of State.
                                             Ib. II

24 With the gratifying feeling that our duty has been
   done!   *Ib.*

25 Take a pair of sparkling eyes.   *Ib.*

26 Take my counsel, happy man;
   Act upon it, if you can!   *Ib.*

27 He wished all men as rich as he
   (And he was rich as rich could be),
      So to the top of every tree
      Promoted everybody.   *Ib.*

28 Dukes were three a penny.   *Ib.*

29 When every blessed thing you hold
   Is made of silver, or of gold,
         You long for simple pewter.
   When you have nothing else to wear
   But cloth of gold and satins rare,
   For cloth of gold you cease to care—
         Up goes the price of shoddy.   *Ib.*

30 When every one is somebodee,
   Then no one's anybody.   *Ib.*

31 I see no objection to stoutness, in moderation.
                                          Iolanthe, I

32 For I'm to be married to-day—to-day—
   Yes, I'm to be married to-day!   *Ib.*

33 Thou the singer; I the song!   *Ib.*

34 Bow, bow, ye lower middle classes!
   Bow, bow, ye tradesmen, bow, ye masses.   *Ib.*

35 The Law is the true embodiment
   Of everything that's excellent.
   It has no kind of fault or flaw,
   And I, my Lords, embody the Law.   *Ib.*

36 Pretty young wards in Chancery.   *Ib.*

37 A pleasant occupation for
   A rather susceptible Chancellor!   *Ib.*

38 For I'm not so old, and not so plain,
   And I'm quite prepared to marry again.   *Ib.*

1 Spurn not the nobly born With love affected,
Nor treat with virtuous scorn The well-connected.
Iolanthe, I

2 Hearts just as pure and fair
May beat in Belgrave Square
As in the lowly air
Of Seven Dials. *Ib.*

3 When I went to the Bar as a very young man,
(Said I to myself, said I). *Ib.*

4 My son in tears—and on his wedding day! *Ib.*

5 He exercises of his brains,
That is, assuming that he's got any. *Ib.* II

6 I am an intellectual chap,
And think of things that would astonish you.
I often think it's comical
How Nature always does contrive
That every boy and every gal,
That's born into the world alive,
Is either a little Liberal,
Or else a little Conservative! *Ib.*

7 The House of Peers, throughout the war,
Did nothing in particular,
And did it very well:
Yet Britain set the world ablaze
In good King George's glorious days! *Ib.*

8 Oh, Captain Shaw!
Type of true love kept under!
Could thy Brigade
With cold cascade
Quench my great love, I wonder! *Ib.*

9 When you're lying awake with a dismal headache,
and repose is taboo'd by anxiety,
I conceive you may use any language you choose
to indulge in, without impropriety. *Ib.*

10 For you dream you are crossing the Channel, and
tossing about in a steamer from Harwich—
Which is something between a large bathing machine
and a very small second class carriage. *Ib.*

11 And you're giving a treat (penny ice and cold meat)
to a party of friends and relations—
They're a ravenous horde—and they all came on
board at Sloane Square and South Kensington
Stations.
And bound on that journey you find your attorney
(who started that morning from Devon);
He's a bit undersized, and you don't feel surprised
when he tells you he's only eleven. *Ib.*

12 In your shirt and your socks (the black silk with gold
clocks), crossing Salisbury Plain on a bicycle. *Ib.*

13 From the greengrocer tree you get grapes and green
pea, cauliflower, pineapple, and cranberries,
While the pastrycook plant cherry brandy will grant,
apple puffs, and three-corners, and Banburys. *Ib.*

14 Faint heart never won fair lady!
Nothing venture, nothing win—
Blood is thick, but water's thin—
In for a penny, in for a pound—
It's Love that makes the world go round! *Ib.*

15 A wandering minstrel I—
A thing of shreds and patches,
Of ballads, songs and snatches,
And dreamy lullaby! *The Mikado*, I

16 Are you in sentimental mood?
I'll sigh with you. *Ib.*

17 But the happiest hour a sailor sees
Is when he's down
At an inland town,
With his Nancy on his knees, yo ho!
And his arm around her waist! *The Mikado*, I

18 And I am right,
And you are right,
And all is right as right can be! *Ib.*

19 I can trace my ancestry back to a protoplasmal primordial atomic globule. Consequently, my family
pride is something in-conceivable. I can't help it.
I was born sneering. *Ib.*

20 It revolts me, but I do it! *Ib.*

21 I accept refreshment at any hands, however lowly.
Ib.

22 And the brass will crash,
And the trumpets bray,
And they'll cut a dash
On their wedding day. *Ib.*

23 I am happy to think that there will be no difficulty
in finding plenty of people whose loss will be a
distinct gain to society at large. *Ib.*

24 As some day it may happen that a victim must be
found,
I've got a little list—I've got a little list
Of society offenders who might well be under ground
And who never would be missed—who never
would be missed! *Ib.*

25 The idiot who praises, with enthusiastic tone,
All centuries but this, and every country but his own.
Ib.

26 They wouldn't be sufficiently degraded in their own
estimation unless they were insulted by a very
considerable bribe. *Ib.*

27 Three little maids from school are we,
Pert as a schoolgirl well can be,
Filled to the brim with girlish glee. *Ib.*

28 Life is a joke that's just begun. *Ib.*

29 Three little maids who, all unwary,
Come from a ladies' seminary. *Ib.*

30 Modified rapture! *Ib.*

31 Awaiting the sensation of a short, sharp shock,
From a cheap and chippy chopper on a big black
block. *Ib.*

32 For he's going to marry Yum-Yum—
Yum-Yum. *Ib.*

33 There's not a trace
Upon her face
Of diffidence or shyness. *Ib.* II

34 Ah, pray make no mistake,
We are not shy;
We're very wide awake,
The moon and I! *Ib.*

35 Brightly dawns our wedding day;
Joyous hour, we give thee greeting! *Ib.*

36 Sing a merry madrigal. *Ib.*

37 Here's a how-de-doo! *Ib.*

38 Matrimonial devotion
Doesn't seem to suit her notion. *Ib.*

[219]

1 Ha! ha! Family Pride, how do you like *that*, my buck?
The Mikado, II

2 My object all sublime
I shall achieve in time—
To let the punishment fit the crime—
The punishment fit the crime. *Ib.*

3 A source of innocent merriment!
Of innocent merriment. *Ib.*

4 Sent to hear sermons
From mystical Germans
Who preach from ten till four. *Ib.*

5 The music-hall singer attends a series
Of masses and fugues and 'ops'
By Bach, interwoven
With Spohr and Beethoven,
At classical Monday Pops. *Ib.*

6 The billiard sharp whom any one catches,
His doom's extremely hard—
He's made to dwell—
In a dungeon cell
On a spot that's always barred.
And there he plays extravagant matches
In fitless finger-stalls
On a cloth untrue
With a twisted cue
And elliptical billiard balls. *Ib.*

7 The criminal cried, as he dropped him down,
In a state of wild alarm—
With a frightful, frantic, fearful frown,
I bared my big right arm. *Ib.*

8 I drew my snickersnee! *Ib.*

9 Her terrible tale
You can't assail,
With truth it quite agrees;
Her taste exact
For faultless fact
Amounts to a disease. *Ib.*

10 Though trunkless, yet
It couldn't forget
The deference due to me! *Ib.*

11 I have a left shoulder-blade that is a miracle of loveliness. People come miles to see it. My right elbow
has a fascination that few can resist. *Ib.*

12 Something lingering, with boiling oil in it, I fancy. *Ib.*

13 Merely corroborative detail, intended to give artistic
verisimilitude to an otherwise bald and unconvincing narrative. *Ib.*

14 She has a left elbow which people come miles to see!
Ib.

15 The flowers that bloom in the spring,
Tra la,
Have nothing to do with the case. *Ib.*

16 I've got to take under my wing,
Tra la,
A most unattractive old thing,
Tra la,
With a caricature of a face.
And that's what I mean when I say, or I sing,
'Oh bother the flowers that bloom in the spring.' *Ib.*

17 On a tree by a river a little tom-tit
Sang 'Willow, titwillow, titwillow!'
And I said to him, 'Dicky-bird, why do you sit
Singing 'Willow, titwillow, titwillow?' *Ib.*

18 'Is it weakness of intellect, birdie?' I cried,
'Or a rather tough worm in your little inside?'
With a shake of his poor little head he replied,
'Oh, willow, titwillow, titwillow!'
The Mikado, II

19 He sobbed and he sighed, and a gurgle he gave,
Then he plunged himself into the billowy wave,
And an echo arose from the suicide's grave—
'Oh willow, titwillow, titwillow!' *Ib.*

20 There's a fascination frantic
In a ruin that's romantic;
Do you think you are sufficiently decayed? *Ib.*

21 When your Majesty says, 'Let a thing be done,' it's
as good as done—practically, it *is* done—because
your Majesty's will is law. *Ib.*

22 Twenty love-sick maidens we,
Love-sick all against our will. *Patience*, I

23 When I first put this uniform on. *Ib.*

24 Am I alone,
And unobserved? I am! *Ib.*

25 If you're anxious for to shine in the high aesthetic line
as a man of culture rare. *Ib.*

26 You must lie upon the daisies and discourse in novel
phrases of your complicated state of mind,
The meaning doesn't matter if it's only idle chatter of
a transcendental kind.
And everyone will say,
As you walk your mystic way,
'If this young man expresses himself in terms too
deep for *me*,
Why, what a very singularly deep young man this
deep young man must be!' *Ib.*

27 For Art stopped short in the cultivated court of the
Empress Josephine. *Ib.*

28 Then a sentimental passion of a vegetable fashion
must excite your languid spleen,
An attachment à la Plato for a bashful young potato,
or a not too French French bean!
Though the Philistines may jostle, you will rank as an
apostle in the high aesthetic band,
If you walk down Piccadilly with a poppy or a lily in
your medieval hand.
And everyone will say,
As you walk your flowery way,
'If he's content with a vegetable love which would
certainly not suit *me*,
Why, what a most particularly pure young man this
pure young man must be!' *Ib.*

29 Prithee, pretty maiden—prithee, tell me true. *Ib.*

30 Nobody I care for comes a-courting me. *Ib.*

31 Prithee, pretty maiden, will you marry me?
(Hey, but I'm hopeful, willow, willow, waly!)
I may say, at once, I'm a man of propertee—
Hey willow waly O!
Money, I despise it;
Many people prize it,
Hey willow waly O! *Ib.*

32 The pain that is all but a pleasure will change
For the pleasure that's all but pain. *Ib.*

33 There will be too much of me
In the coming by and by! *Ib.* II

GILBERT

1 While this magnetic,
   Peripatetic
Lover, he lived to learn,
   By no endeavour
   Can magnet ever
Attract a Silver Churn!   *Patience*, II

2 Sing 'Hey to you—good day to you'—
Sing 'Bah to you—ha! ha! to you'—
Sing 'Booh to you—pooh, pooh to you'.   *Ib.*

3 He will have to be contented
With our heartfelt sympathy!   *Ib.*

4 'High diddle diddle'
Will rank as an idyll,
If I pronounce it chaste!   *Ib.*

5 Who's fond of his dinner
And doesn't get thinner
   On bottled beer and chops.   *Ib.*

6 Francesca di Rimini, miminy, piminy,
Je-ne-sais-quoi young man!   *Ib.*

7 A greenery-yallery, Grosvenor Gallery,
Foot-in-the-grave young man!   *Ib.*

8 A Sewell & Cross young man,
A Howell & James young man,
A pushing young particle—'What's the next article?'
Waterloo House young man!   *Ib.*

9 I'm called Little Buttercup—dear Little Buttercup,
Though I could never tell why. *H.M.S. Pinafore*, I

10 I am the Captain of the *Pinafore*;
And a right good captain too!   *Ib.*

11 And I'm never, never sick at sea!
   What, never?
   No, never!
   What, *never?*
   Hardly ever!
He's hardly ever sick at sea!
Then give three cheers, and one cheer more,
For the hardy Captain of the *Pinafore!*   *Ib.*

12 You're exceedingly polite,
And I think it only right
To return the compliment.   *Ib.*

13 I never use a big, big D.   *Ib.*

14 And so do his sisters, and his cousins and his aunts!
   His sisters and his cousins,
   Whom he reckons up by dozens,
   And his aunts!   *Ib.*

15 When I was a lad I served a term
As office boy to an Attorney's firm.
I cleaned the windows and I swept the floor,
And I polished up the handle of the big front door.
 I polished up that handle so carefullee
That now I am the Ruler of the Queen's Navee!
     Ib.

16 And I copied all the letters in a big round hand. *Ib.*

17 I always voted at my party's call,
And I never thought of thinking for myself at all. *Ib.*

18 Stick close to your desks and never go to sea,
And you all may be Rulers of the Queen's Navee! *Ib.*

19 His energetic fist should be ready to resist
A dictatorial word.   *Ib.*

20 His bosom should heave and his heart should glow,
And his fist be ever ready for a knock-down blow.
     Ib.

21 Things are seldom what they seem,
Skim milk masquerades as cream.
     H.M.S. Pinafore, II

22 The merry maiden and the tar.   *Ib.*

23 It was the cat!   *Ib.*

24 He is an Englishman!
   For he himself has said it,
   And it's greatly to his credit,
That he is an Englishman!   *Ib.*

25 For he might have been a Roosian,
A French, or Turk, or Proosian,
   Or perhaps Ital-ian!
But in spite of all temptations
To belong to other nations,
   He remains an Englishman!   *Ib.*

26 The other, upper crust,
A regular patrician.   *Ib.*

27 It is, it is a glorious thing
To be a Pirate King.   *Pirates of Penzance*, I

28 The question is, had he not been
   A thing of beauty,
Would she be swayed by quite as keen
   A sense of duty?   *Ib.*

29 Poor wandering one!
Though thou hast surely strayed,
Take heart of grace,
Thy steps retrace,
Poor wandering one!   *Ib.*

30 Take heart, fair days will shine;
Take any heart, take mine!   *Ib.*

31 I am the very model of a modern Major-General.
     Ib.

32 I'm very good at integral and differential calculus;
I know the scientific names of beings animalculous.
     Ib.

33 When the foeman bares his steel,
   Tarantara, tarantara!
We uncomfortable feel,
   Tarantara.   *Ib.* II

34 When constabulary duty's to be done,
The policeman's lot is not a happy one.   *Ib.*

35 When the enterprising burglar's not a-burgling. *Ib.*

36 When the coster's finished jumping on his mother—
He loves to lie a-basking in the sun.   *Ib.*

37 No Englishman unmoved that statement hears,
Because, with all our faults, we love our House of
   Peers.   *Ib.*

38 Politics we bar,
   They are not our bent;
On the whole we are
   Not intelligent.   *Princess Ida*, I

39 Yet everybody says I'm such a disagreeable man!
   And I can't think why!   *Ib.*

40 To everybody's prejudice I know a thing or two;
I can tell a woman's age in half a minute—and I do!
     Ib.

41 Man is Nature's sole mistake!   *Ib.* II

42 My natural instinct teaches me
   (And instinct is important, O!)
You're everything you ought to be,
   And nothing that you oughtn't, O!   *Ib.*

1 Oh, don't the days seem lank and long
When all goes right and nothing goes wrong,
And isn't your life extremely flat
With nothing whatever to grumble at!
Princess Ida, III

2 All baronets are bad. *Ruddigore*, I

3 I'll wager in their joy they kissed each other's cheek
(Which is what them furriners do). *Ib.*

4 You must stir it and stump it,
And blow your own trumpet,
Or trust me, you haven't a chance. *Ib.*

5 He combines the manners of a Marquis with the
morals of a Methodist. *Ib.*

6 When he's excited he uses language that would make
your hair curl. *Ib.*

7 For duty, duty must be done;
The rule applies to everyone. *Ib.*

8 For you are such a smart little craft—
Such a neat little, sweet little craft,
Such a bright little, tight little,
Slight little, light little,
Trim little, prim little craft! *Ib.* II

9 If a man can't forge his own will, whose will can he
forge? *Ib.*

10 Desperate deeds of derring do. *Ib.*

11 Some word that teems with hidden meaning—like
Basingstoke. *Ib.*

12 This particularly rapid, unintelligible patter
Isn't generally heard, and if it is it doesn't matter. *Ib.*

13 Time was when Love and I were well acquainted.
The Sorcerer, I

14 Forsaking even military men. *Ib.*

15 I was a pale young curate then. *Ib.*

16 Oh! My name is John Wellington Wells,
I'm a dealer in magic and spells. *Ib.*

17 If anyone anything lacks,
He'll find it all ready in stacks,
If he'll only look in
On the resident Djinn,
Number seventy, Simmery Axe! *Ib.*

18 Now for the tea of our host,
Now for the rollicking bun,
Now for the muffin and toast,
Now for the gay Sally Lunn! *Ib.*

19 So I fell in love with a rich attorney's
Elderly ugly daughter. *Trial by Jury*

20 She may very well pass for forty-three
In the dusk with a light behind her! *Ib.*

21 And many a burglar I've restored
To his friends and his relations. *Ib.*

22 For now I am a Judge,
And a good Judge too. *Ib.*

23 And a good job too! *Ib.*

24 Oh never, never, never, since I joined the human race,
Saw I so exquisitely fair a face. *Ib.*

25 Is life a boon?
If so, it must befall
That Death, whene'er he call,
Must call too soon. *The Yeomen of the Guard*, I

26 I have a song to sing O!
Sing me your song, O! *The Yeomen of the Guard*, I

27 It's a song of a merryman, moping mum,
Whose soul was sad, and whose glance was glum,
Who sipped no sup, and who craved no crumb,
As he sighed for the love of a ladye. *Ib.*

28 His pains were o'er, and he sighed no more,
For he lived in the love of a ladye! *Ib.*

29 The prisoner comes to meet his doom. *Ib.*

30 'Tis ever thus with simple folk—an accepted wit has
but to say 'Pass the mustard', and they roar their
ribs out! *Ib.* II

THOMAS GILLESPIE
1777-1844

31 An attitude, not only of defence, but defiance.
The Mountain Storm. (Wilson's *Tales of the
Borders*, No. 145.)
'Defence not defiance' *became the motto of
the Volunteer Movement in 1859.*

JAMES GILLRAY
1757-1815

32 Political Ravishment, or, The Old Lady of Threadneedle Street in Danger. *Title of Caricature, 1797*

CHARLOTTE PERKINS STETSON GILMAN
1860-1935

33 I do not want to be a fly!
I want to be a worm!
In This Our World. A Conservative

WILLIAM EWART GLADSTONE
1809-1898

34 You cannot fight against the future. Time is on our
side. *Speech on the Reform Bill, 1866*

35 [The Turks] one and all, bag and baggage, shall, I
hope, clear out from the province they have desolated and profaned.
Speech, House of Commons, 7 May 1877

36 Out of the range of practical politics.
Ib. at Dalkeith, 26 Nov. 1879

37 The resources of civilization are not yet exhausted.
Ib. Leeds, Speech at Banquet, 7 Oct. 1881

38 [The Irish Land League]. It is perfectly true that
these gentlemen wish to march through rapine to
disintegration and dismemberment of the Empire,
and, I am sorry to say, even to the placing of
different parts of the Empire in direct hostility
one with the other. *Ib. Knowsley, 27 Oct. 1881*

39 I would tell them of my own intention to keep my own
counsel . . . and I will venture to recommend them,
as an old Parliamentary hand, to do the same.
Ib. House of Commons, 21 Jan. 1886

40 All the world over, I will back the masses against the
classes. *Ib. Liverpool, 28 June 1886*

41 We are part of the community of Europe, and we must
do our duty as such. *Ib. Carnarvon, 10 Apr. 1888*

1 This is the negation of God erected into a system of Government.
First Letter to the Earl of Aberdeen on the State persecutions of the Neapolitan Government, § 8, 1851, p. 9, n.

2 The impregnable rock of Holy Scripture.
Title of Book, 1890

3 Throw his mind into the common stock.
Phrase. G. W. E. Russell, Collections and Recollections, ch. 33

HANNAH GLASSE
fl. 1747

4 Take your hare when it is cased. ....
Art of Cookery

Usually misquoted as 'First catch your hare'.

WILLIAM HENRY, DUKE OF GLOUCESTER
1743–1805

5 Another damned, thick, square book! Always scribble, scribble, scribble! Eh! Mr. Gibbon?
Best's Literary Memorials. (Boswell's Johnson, vol. ii, p. 2, n.)

JOHN A. GLOVER-KINDE d. 1918

6 I Do Like To Be Beside the Seaside.
Title of song (1909)

ALFRED DENIS GODLEY
1856–1925

7 What asks the Bard? He prays for nought
But what the truly virtuous crave:
That is, the things he plainly ought
To have ...

His taste in residence is plain:
No palaces his heart rejoice:
A cottage in a lane (Park Lane
For choice)—
Lyra Frivola, 'After Horace'

8 What is this that roareth thus?
Can it be a Motor Bus?
Yes, the smell and hideous hum
Indicat Motorem Bum

.   .   .

How shall wretches live like us
Cincti Bis Motoribus?
Domine, defende nos
Contra hos Motores Bos!
The Motor Bus. Letter to C.R.L.F., 10 Jan. 1914

HANNAH GODWIN

9 Good sense without vanity, a penetrating judgement without a disposition to satire, good nature and humility, with about as much religion as my William likes, struck me with a wish that she was my William's wife.
Letter of 29 June 1784 to her brother William, recommending Miss Gay. C. Kegan Paul, William Godwin, vol. i

WILL GODWIN
d. 1913

10 The log was burning brightly,
'Twas a night that should banish all sin,
For the bells were ringing the Old Year out,
And the New Year in. *The Miner's Dream of Home*

HERMANN GOERING
1893–1946

11 Guns will make us powerful; butter will only make us fat. *Radio Broadcast, summer of 1936*

12 When I hear anyone talk of Culture, I reach for my revolver. *But see Corrigenda.*

JOHANN WOLFGANG VON GOETHE
1749–1832

13 Lord Byron ist nur groß, wenn er dichtet; sobald er reflektiert ist er ein Kind.
Lord Byron is only great as a poet; as soon as he reflects, he is a child.
Conversations with Eckermann, 18 Jan. 1825

14 Im übrigen ist es zuletzt die größte Kunst, sich zu beschränken und zu isolieren.
For the rest of it, the last and greatest art is to limit and isolate oneself. *Ib. 20 Apr. 1825*

15 Es irrt der Mensch, so lang er strebt.
Man errs, 'till his strife is over.
Faust, pt. i. Prolog im Himmel

16 Zwei Seelen wohnen, ach! in meiner Brust.
Two souls dwell, alas! in my breast.
Ib. Vor dem Thor

17 Ich bin der Geist der stets verneint.
I am the spirit that always denies.
Ib. Studierzimmer

18 Entbehren sollst Du! sollst entbehren!
Das ist der ewige Gesang.
Deny yourself! You must deny yourself!
That is the song that never ends. *Ib.*

19 Grau, teurer Freund, ist alle Theorie
Und grün des Lebens goldner Baum.
All theory, dear friend, is grey, but the golden tree of actual life springs ever green. *Ib.*

20 Meine Ruh' ist hin,
Mein Herz ist schwer.
My peace is gone,
My heart is heavy. *Ib. Gretchen am Spinnrad*

21 Die Tat ist alles, nicht der Ruhm.
The deed is everything, its repute nothing.
Ib. pt. ii. Großer Vorhof

22 Das Ewig-Weibliche zieht uns hinan.
That which is eternal in Woman lifts us above.
Ib. last line

23 Du musst herrschen und gewinnen,
Oder dienen und verlieren,
Leiden oder triumphiren
Amboss oder Hammer sein.
You must either conquer and rule or lose and serve, suffer or triumph, and be the anvil or the hammer.
Der Gross-Cophta, Act ii

1 Ein unnütz Leben ist ein früher Tod.
A useless life is an early death. *Iphigenie*, i. 2

2 Ich singe, wie der Vogel singt,
Der in den Zweigen wohnet.

I sing but as the bird there sings,
High in the treetops nesting. *Der Sänger*

3 Der Aberglaube ist die Poesie des Lebens.

Superstition is the poetry of life.
Sprüche in Prosa (1819), iii

4 Es bildet ein Talent sich in der Stille,
Sich ein Charakter in dem Strom der Welt.

Genius develops in quiet places,
Character out in the full current of human life.
Tasso, i. 2

5 Über allen Gipfeln
Ist Ruh'.

Over all the mountain tops is peace.
Wanderers Nachtlied

6 Kennst du das Land, wo die Zitronen blühn?
Im dunkeln Laub die Gold-Orangen glühn,
Ein sanfter Wind vom blauen Himmel weht,
Die Myrte still und hoch der Lorbeer steht—
Kennst du es wohl?
Dahin! Dahin!
Möcht ich mit dir, o mein Geliebter, ziehn!

Know you the land where the lemon-trees bloom?
In the dark foliage the gold oranges glow; a soft
wind hovers from the sky, the myrtle is still and
the laurel stands tall—do you know it well?
There, there, I would go, O my beloved, with
thee! *Wilhelm Meisters Lehrjahre*, III. i

7 Mehr Licht!

More light!
Attr. dying words. (Actually: 'Macht doch den
zweiten Fensterladen auch auf, damit mehr
Licht hereinkomme': 'Open the second shutter,
so that more light can come in.')

8 Ohne Hast, aber ohne Rast.

Without haste, but without rest. *Motto*

OLIVER GOLDSMITH
1728-1774

9 For he who fights and runs away
May live to fight another day;
But he who is in battle slain
Can never rise and fight again.
Art of Poetry on a New Plan. Written by New-
bery, revised by Goldsmith

10 To the last moment of his breath
On hope the wretch relies;
And e'en the pang preceding death
Bids expectation rise.

Hope, like the gleaming taper's light,
Adorns and cheers our way;
And still, as darker grows the night,
Emits a brighter ray. *The Captivity*, II

11 A night-cap decked his brows instead of bay;
A cap by night—a stocking all the day!
Description of an Author's Bedchamber. In
Citizen of the World, letter 30. *The Author's
Club* (1760)

12 Sweet Auburn! loveliest village of the plain.
The Deserted Village, l. 1

13 The bashful virgin's side-long looks of love,
The matron's glance that would those looks reprove.
Ib. l. 29

14 Ill fares the land, to hast'ning ills a prey,
Where wealth accumulates, and men decay;
Princes and lords may flourish, or may fade;
A breath can make them, as a breath has made;
But a bold peasantry, their country's pride,
When once destroy'd, can never be supplied.
A time there was, ere England's griefs began,
When every rood of ground maintain'd its man;
For him light labour spread her wholesome store,
Just gave what life requir'd, but gave no more;
His best companions, innocence and health;
And his best riches, ignorance of wealth. *Ib.* l. 51

15 How happy he who crowns in shades like these,
A youth of labour with an age of ease. *Ib.* l. 99

16 Bends to the grave with unperceiv'd decay,
While resignation gently slopes the way;
And, all his prospects bright'ning to the last,
His heaven commences ere the world be pass'd.
Ib. l. 109

17 The watchdog's voice that bay'd the whisp'ring wind,
And the loud laugh that spoke the vacant mind.
Ib. l. 121

18 A man he was to all the country dear,
And passing rich with forty pounds a year;
Remote from towns he ran his godly race,
Nor e'er had chang'd nor wished to change his place;
Unpractis'd he to fawn, or seek for power,
By doctrines fashion'd to the varying hour;
Far other aims his heart had learned to prize,
More skill'd to raise the wretched than to rise.
Ib. l. 141

19 He chid their wand'rings, but reliev'd their pain.
Ib. l. 150

20 The broken soldier, kindly bade to stay,
Sat by his fire, and talk'd the night away;
Wept o'er his wounds, or tales of sorrow done,
Shoulder'd his crutch, and show'd how fields were
won. *Ib.* l. 155

21 Careless their merits, or their faults to scan,
His pity gave ere charity began.
Thus to relieve the wretched was his pride,
And e'en his failings lean'd to Virtue's side.
But in his duty prompt at every call,
He watch'd and wept, he pray'd and felt, for all.
And, as a bird each fond endearment tries
To tempt its new-fledg'd offspring to the skies,
He tried each art, reprov'd each dull delay,
Allur'd to brighter worlds, and led the way.
Ib. l. 161

22 At church, with meek and unaffected grace,
His looks adorn'd the venerable place;
Truth from his lips prevail'd with double sway,
And fools, who came to scoff, remain'd to pray.
Ib. l. 177

23 Even children follow'd with endearing wile,
And pluck'd his gown, to share the good man's smile.
Ib. l. 183

GOLDSMITH

1 A man severe he was, and stern to view;
I knew him well, and every truant knew;
Well had the boding tremblers learn'd to trace
The day's disasters in his morning face;
Full well they laugh'd with counterfeited glee,
At all his jokes, for many a joke had he;
Full well the busy whisper, circling round,
Convey'd the dismal tidings when he frown'd;
Yet he was kind; or if severe in aught,
The love he bore to learning was in fault.
The Deserted Village, l. 197

2 In arguing too, the parson own'd his skill,
For e'en though vanquish'd, he could argue still;
While words of learned length, and thund'ring sound
Amazed the gazing rustics rang'd around,
And still they gaz'd, and still the wonder grew,
That one small head could carry all he knew. *Ib. l. 211*

3 The white-wash'd wall, the nicely sanded floor,
The varnish'd clock that click'd behind the door;
The chest contriv'd a double debt to pay,
A bed at night, a chest of drawers by day. *Ib. l. 227*

4 The twelve good rules, the royal game of goose. *Ib. l. 232*

5 And, e'en while fashion's brightest arts decoy,
The heart distrusting asks, if this be joy. *Ib. l. 263*

6 How wide the limits stand
Between a splendid and a happy land. *Ib. l. 267*

7 Her modest looks the cottage might adorn,
Sweet as the primrose peeps beneath the thorn. *Ib. l. 329*

8 In all the silent manliness of grief. *Ib. l. 384*

9 Thou source of all my bliss, and all my woe,
That found'st me poor at first, and keep'st me so. *Ib. l. 413*

10 The fat was so white, and the lean was so ruddy. *The Haunch of Venison*, l. 4

11 Turn, gentle Hermit of the dale,
And guide my lonely way,
To where yon taper cheers the vale
With hospitable ray.
Edwin and Angelina, or The Hermit

12 No flocks that range the valleys free
To slaughter I condemn.
Taught by the Power that pities me,
I learn to pity them. *Ib.*

13 Man wants but little here below,
Nor wants that little long. *Ib.*

14 The sigh that rends thy constant heart,
Shall break thy Edwin's too. *Ib.*

15 The king himself has follow'd her,—
When she has walk'd before.
Elegy on Mrs. Mary Blaize

16 The doctor found, when she was dead,—
Her last disorder mortal. *Ib.*

17 Good people all, of every sort,
Give ear unto my song;
And if you find it wond'rous short,
It cannot hold you long.
Elegy on the Death of a Mad Dog

18 That still a godly race he ran,
Whene'er he went to pray *Ib.*

19 The naked every day he clad,
When he put on his clothes.
Elegy on the Death of a Mad Dog

20 And in that town a dog was found,
As many dogs there be,
Both mongrel, puppy, whelp, and hound,
And curs of low degree. *Ib.*

21 The dog, to gain some private ends,
Went mad and bit the man. *Ib.*

22 And swore the dog had lost his wits,
To bite so good a man. *Ib.*

23 The man recover'd of the bite,
The dog it was that died. *Ib.*

24 Brutes never meet in bloody fray,
Nor cut each other's throats, for pay.
Logicians Refuted, l. 39

25 Our Garrick's a salad; for in him we see
Oil, vinegar, sugar, and saltness agree.
Retaliation, l. 11

26 Who mix'd reason with pleasure, and wisdom with mirth:
If he had any faults, he has left us in doubt. [Dr. Barnard, Dean of Derry.] *Ib. l. 24*

27 Here lies our good Edmund, whose genius was such,
We scarcely can praise it, or blame it too much;
Who, born for the Universe, narrow'd his mind,
And to party gave up what was meant for mankind.
Though fraught with all learning, yet straining his throat
To persuade Tommy Townshend to lend him a vote;
Who, too deep for his hearers, still went on refining,
And thought of convincing, while they thought of dining;
Though equal to all things, for all things unfit,
Too nice for a statesman, too proud for a wit.
[Edmund Burke.] *Ib. l. 29*

28 Too fond of the *right* to pursue the *expedient*.
[Edmund Burke.] *Ib. l. 40*

29 His conduct still right, with his argument wrong.
[William Burke.] *Ib. l. 46*

30 Here lies David Garrick, describe me, who can,
An abridgement of all that was pleasant in man. *Ib. l. 93*

31 As a wit, if not first, in the very first line. [Garrick.] *Ib. l. 96*

32 On the stage he was natural, simple, affecting;
'Twas only that when he was off he was acting.
[Garrick.] *Ib. l. 101*

33 He cast off his friends as a huntsman his pack,
For he knew when he pleas'd he could whistle them back.
Of praise a mere glutton, he swallow'd what came,
And the puff of a dunce he mistook it for fame.
[Garrick.] *Ib. l. 107*

34 Here Reynolds is laid, and to tell you my mind,
He has not left a better or wiser behind:
His pencil was striking, resistless, and grand;
His manners were gentle, complying, and bland;
Still born to improve us in every part,
His pencil our faces, his manners our heart. *Ib. l. 137*

35 When they talk'd of their Raphaels, Correggios, and stuff,
He shifted his trumpet, and only took snuff. [Reynolds.] *Ib. l. 145*

[225]

1 Thou best-humour'd man with the worst-humour'd muse. [Whitefoord.] *Retaliation*, l. 174

2 Let schoolmasters puzzle their brain,
  With grammar, and nonsense, and learning,
Good liquor, I stoutly maintain,
  Gives genius a better discerning.
She Stoops to Conquer, 1. i, song

3 Remote, unfriended, melancholy, slow,
Or by the lazy Scheldt, or wandering Po.
The Traveller, l. 1

4 Where'er I roam, whatever realms to see,
My heart untravell'd fondly turns to thee;
Still to my brother turns with ceaseless pain,
And drags at each remove a lengthening chain.
Ib. l. 7

5 And learn the luxury of doing good. *Ib.* l. 22

6 These little things are great to little man. *Ib.* l. 42

7 Such is the patriot's boast, where'er we roam,
His first, best country ever is, at home. *Ib.* l. 73

8 Where wealth and freedom reign, contentment fails,
And honour sinks where commerce long prevails.
Ib. l. 91

9 Man seems the only growth that dwindles here.
Ib. l. 126

10 But winter ling'ring chills the lap of May. *Ib.* l. 172

11 At night returning, every labour sped,
He sits him down the monarch of a shed;
Smiles by his cheerful fire, and round surveys
His children's looks, that brighten at the blaze;
While his lov'd partner, boastful of her hoard,
Displays her cleanly platter on the board. *Ib.* l. 191

12 They please, are pleas'd; they give to get esteem,
Till, seeming bless'd, they grow to what they seem.
Ib. l. 265

13 To men of other minds my fancy flies,
Embosom'd in the deep where Holland lies.
Methinks her patient sons before me stand,
Where the broad ocean leans against the land.
Ib. l. 282

14 Pride in their port, defiance in their eye,
I see the lords of human kind pass by. *Ib.* l. 327

15 The land of scholars, and the nurse of arms.
Ib. l. 356

16 Laws grind the poor, and rich men rule the law.
Ib. l. 386

17 In every government, though terrors reign,
Though tyrant kings, or tyrant laws restrain,
How small, of all that human hearts endure,
That part which laws or kings can cause or cure!
Ib. l. 427

18 When lovely woman stoops to folly
  And finds too late that men betray,
What charm can soothe her melancholy,
  What art can wash her guilt away?
The only art her guilt to cover,
  To hide her shame from every eye,
To give repentance to her lover,
  And wring his bosom—is to die.
Song. From the *Vicar of Wakefield*, ch. 29

19 As writers become more numerous, it is natural for readers to become more indolent.
The Bee, No. 175. *Upon Unfortunate Merit*

20 The volume of nature is the book of knowledge.
Citizen of the World, letter 4

21 'The Republic of Letters' is a very common expression among the Europeans. *Ib.* letter 20

22 He writes indexes to perfection. *Ib.* letter 29

23 To a philosopher no circumstance, however trifling, is too minute. *Ib.* letter 30

24 'Did I say so?' replied he coolly; 'to be sure, if I said so, it was so.' *Ib.* letter 54

25 Had Caesar or Cromwell exchanged countries, the one might have been a sergeant, and the other an exciseman. *Essays*, i. *Introductory Paper*

26 The true use of speech is not so much to express our wants as to conceal them.
Ib. v. *The Use of Language*

27 Bacon, that great and hardy genius.
Ib. xviii. *Travel in Asia*

28 Here's to the memory of Shakespeare, Falstaff, and all the merry men of East-cheap.
Ib. xix. *At The Boar's Head Tavern*

29 I hate the French because they are all slaves, and wear wooden shoes.
Ib. xxiv. *Distresses of a Common Soldier*

30 This same philosophy is a good horse in the stable, but an arrant jade on a journey.
The Good-Natured Man, 1

31 We must touch his weaknesses with a delicate hand. There are some faults so nearly allied to excellence, that we can scarce weed out the fault without eradicating the virtue. *Ib.*

32 All his faults are such that one loves him still the better for them. *Ib.*

33 I'm now no more than a mere lodger in my own house. *Ib.*

34 Friendship is a disinterested commerce between equals; love, an abject intercourse between tyrants and slaves. *Ib.*

35 Don't let us make imaginary evils, when you know we have so many real ones to encounter. *Ib.*

36 LEONTINE:
An only son, sir, might expect more indulgence.
CROAKER:
An only father, Sir, might expect more obedience.
Ib.

37 I am told he makes a very handsome corpse, and becomes his coffin prodigiously. *Ib.*

38 Silence is become his mother tongue. *Ib.* 11

39 All men have their faults; too much modesty is his.
Ib.

40 You, that are going to be married, think things can never be done too fast; but we, that are old, and know what we are about, must elope methodically, madam. *Ib.*

41 She stoops to conquer. *Title of play*

42 In my time, the follies of the town crept slowly among us, but now they travel faster than a stage-coach. *She Stoops to Conquer*, 1

43 I love every thing that's old; old friends, old times, old manners, old books, old wines. *Ib.*

1 As for disappointing them I should not so much mind; but I can't abide to disappoint myself.
She Stoops to Conquer, 1

2 Is it one of my well-looking days, child? Am I in face to-day? *Ib.*

3 The very pink of perfection. *Ib.*

4 In a concatenation accordingly. *Ib.*

5 I'll be with you in the squeezing of a lemon. *Ib.*

6 It's a damned long, dark, boggy, dirty, dangerous way. *Ib.*

7 Your worship must not tell the story of Ould Grouse in the gun-room. I can't help laughing at that . . . We have laughed at that these twenty years. *Ib.* II

8 This is Liberty-Hall, gentlemen. *Ib.*

9 The first blow is half the battle. *Ib.*

10 We are the boys
That fears no noise
Where the thundering cannons roar. *Ib.*

11 Was there ever such a cross-grained brute? *Ib.* III

12 Women and music should never be dated. *Ib.*

13 As for murmurs, mother, we grumble a little now and then, to be sure. But there's no love lost between us. *Ib.* IV

14 A book may be amusing with numerous errors, or it may be very dull without a single absurdity.
The Vicar of Wakefield, advertisement

15 I was ever of opinion, that the honest man who married and brought up a large family, did more service than he who continued single and only talked of population. *Ib.* ch. 1

16 I chose my wife, as she did her wedding gown, not for a fine glossy surface, but such qualities as would wear well. *Ib.*

17 All our adventures were by the fire-side, and all our migrations from the blue bed to the brown. *Ib.*

18 A mutilated courtesy. *Ib.*

19 The virtue which requires to be ever guarded is scarcely worth the sentinel. *Ib.* ch. 5

20 I find you want me to furnish you with argument and intellects too. No, Sir, there I protest you are too hard for me. *Ib.* ch. 7

21 'Very well,' cried I, 'that's a good girl, I find you are perfectly qualified for making converts, and so go help your mother to make the gooseberry-pie.' *Ib.*

22 By the living jingo, she was all of a muck of sweat. *Ib.* ch. 9

23 With other fashionable topics, such as pictures, taste, Shakespeare, and the musical glasses. *Ib.*

24 Mr. Burchell . . . at the conclusion of every sentence would cry out 'Fudge!'—an expression which displeased us all. *Ib.* ch. 11

25 Conscience is a coward, and those faults it has not strength enough to prevent it seldom has justice enough to accuse. *Ib.* ch. 13

26 It seemed to me pretty plain, that they had more of love than matrimony in them. *Ib.* ch. 16

27 There is no arguing with Johnson; for when his pistol misses fire, he knocks you down with the butt end of it.
Remark. Boswell's *Life of Johnson*, 26 Oct. 1769

28 As I take my shoes from the shoemaker, and my coat from the tailor, so I take my religion from the priest.
Boswell's *Life of Johnson*, 9 Apr. 1773

29 [To Johnson who was laughing when he said that the little fishes in a proposed fable should talk like little fishes.]
Why, Dr. Johnson, this is not so easy as you seem to think; for if you were to make little fishes talk, they would talk like whales.
Ib. 27 Apr. 1773

30 [To Boswell, for talking of Johnson as entitled to the honour of unquestionable superiority.]
Sir, you are for making a monarchy of what should be a republic. *Ib.* 7 May 1773

31 [To Boswell, of Johnson.]
Is he like Burke, who winds into a subject like a serpent? *Ib.* 10 May 1773

32 He [Johnson] has nothing of the bear but his skin.
Ib. ii. 66 (Birkbeck Hill edn.)

SAMUEL GOLDWYN
1882–

33 In two words: im-possible.
Quoted in Alva Johnson: *The Great Goldwyn*

ADAM LINDSAY GORDON
1833–1870

34 Question not, but live and labour
Till yon goal be won,
Helping every feeble neighbour,
Seeking help from none;
Life is mostly froth and bubble,
Two things stand like stone,
Kindness in another's trouble,
Courage in your own.
Ye Wearie Wayfarer, Fytte 8

SIR THOMAS EDWARD GORDON
1832–1914

35 The roof of the world. *Title of a book*, 1876

EVA GORE-BOOTH
1872–1926

36 The little waves of Breffny go stumbling through my soul. *Poems. The Little Waves of Breffny*

GEORGE JOACHIM, FIRST VISCOUNT GOSCHEN
1831–1907

37 I have the courage of my opinions, but I have not the temerity to give a political blank cheque to Lord Salisbury. *Speech, House of Commons, 19 Feb. 1884*

38 If so we shall make our wills and do our duty.
Speech, 14 Apr. 1886

39 We have stood alone in that which is called isolation— our splendid isolation, as one of our colonial friends was good enough to call it. [See G. E. Foster.]
Speech at Lewes, 26 Feb. 1896

[227]

SIR EDMUND GOSSE
1849–1928

1 Papa, don't tell me that she's a Paedobaptist?
Father and Son, ch. 10

REV. EDWARD MEYRICK GOULBURN
1818–1897

2 Let the scintillations of your wit be like the coruscations of summer lightning, lambent but innocuous.
Sermon at Rugby. Rev. W. Tuckwell, *Reminiscences of Oxford* (2nd ed., 1907), p. 272

JOHN GOWER
1325?–1408

3 It hath and schal ben evermor
That love is maister wher he wile.
Confessio Amantis, prologue, l. 34

RICHARD GRAFTON
?–1572?

4 Thirty days hath November,
April, June, and September,
February hath twenty-eight alone,
And all the rest have thirty-one.
Abridgement of the Chronicles of England (1570), introductory matter, sig. 1 ¶ j. b

CHARLES GRAHAM

5 Two little girls in blue, lad,
Two little girls in blue,
They were sisters, we were brothers,
And learned to love the two.
Two Little Girls In Blue

HARRY GRAHAM
1874–1936

6 Auntie, did you feel no pain
Falling from that apple-tree?
Would you do it, please, again?
Cos my friend here didn't see.
Ruthless Rhymes for Heartless Homes. Appreciation

7 O'er the rugged mountain's brow
Clara threw the twins she nursed,
And remarked, 'I wonder now
Which will reach the bottom first?'
Ib. Calculating Clara

8 Aunt Jane observed, the second time
She tumbled off a bus,
The step is short from the Sublime
To the Ridiculous. *Ib. Equanimity*

9 'There's been an accident!' they said,
'Your servant's cut in half; he's dead!'
'Indeed!' said Mr. Jones, 'and please
Send me the half that's got my keys.' *Ib. Mr. Jones*

10 Philip, foozling with his cleek,
Drove his ball through Helen's cheek;
Sad they bore her corpse away,
Seven up and six to play. *Ib. Philip*

11 Billy, in one of his nice new sashes,
Fell in the fire and was burnt to ashes;
Now, although the room grows chilly,
I haven't the heart to poke poor Billy.
Ruthless Rhymes. Tender-Heartedness

ROBERT CUNNINGHAME-GRAHAM
1735–1797

12 If doughty deeds my lady please,
Right soon I'll mount my steed.
If Doughty Deeds My Lady Please, or *O Tell Me How To Woo Thee*

13 For you alone I ride the ring. *Ib.*

JAMES GRAHAME
1765–1811

14 Hail, Sabbath! thee I hail, the poor man's day.
The Sabbath, l. 29

KENNETH GRAHAME
1859–1932

15 'Aunt Maria flung herself on him [the curate]. "O Mr. Hodgitts!" I heard her cry, "you are brave! for my sake do not be rash!" He was not rash.'
The Golden Age, 'The Burglars'

16 Believe me, my young friend, there is *nothing*—absolutely nothing—half so much worth doing as simply messing about in boats.
The Wind in the Willows, ch. 1

17 The clever men at Oxford
Know all that there is to be knowed.
But they none of them know one half as much
As intelligent Mr. Toad. *Ib.* ch. x

JAMES GRAINGER
1721?–1766

18 What is fame? an empty bubble;
Gold? a transient, shining trouble. *Solitude*, l. 96

19 Now, Muse, let's sing of rats.
The Sugar Cane. MS. quoted in Boswell's *Life of Johnson, 21 March 1776*. The passage was not printed

SIR ROBERT GRANT
1779–1838

20 The Ancient of Days,
Pavilioned in splendour,
And girded with praise.
Bickersteth's *Church Psalmody*. *O Worship the King*

21 His chariots of wrath The deep thunder clouds form,
And dark is his path On the wings of the storm. *Ib.*

22 Frail children of dust,
And feeble as frail. *Ib.*

ULYSSES SIMPSON GRANT
1822–1885

23 I know no method to secure the repeal of bad or obnoxious laws so effective as their stringent execution. *Inaugural Address, 4 Mar. 1869*

1 I purpose to fight it out on this line, if it takes all summer.
    Dispatch to Washington, From Head-Quarters in the Field, 11 May 1864

2 Let no guilty man escape, if it can be avoided. . . . No personal considerations should stand in the way of performing a public duty.
    Indorsement of a Letter relating to the Whiskey Ring, 29 July 1875

3 Let us have peace.
    Letter of Acceptance of Nomination, 29 May 1868

4 No terms except unconditional and immediate surrender can be accepted. I propose to move immediately upon your works.
    To Simon Bolivar Buckner, whom he was besieging in Fort Donelson, 16 Feb. 1862

GEORGE GRANVILLE, BARON LANSDOWNE
1667–1735

5 I'll be this abject thing no more;
    Love, give me back my heart again.
    Adieu l'Amour

6 Who to a woman trusts his peace of mind,
    Trusts a frail bark, with a tempestuous wind.
    The British Enchanters, II. i

7 Of all the plagues with which the world is curst,
    Of every ill, a woman is the worst.   *Ib.*

8 Marriage the happiest bond of love might be,
    If hands were only joined when hearts agree. *Ib.* v. i

9 O Love! thou bane of the most generous souls!
    Thou doubtful pleasure, and thou certain pain.
    Heroic Love, II. i

10 'Tis the talk, and not the intrigue, that's the crime.
    The She Gallants, III. i

11 Cowards in scarlet pass for men of war.   *Ib.* v

12 Whimsey, not reason, is the female guide.
    The Vision, l. 81

ALFRED PERCEVAL GRAVES
1846–1931

13 Of priests we can offer a charmin' variety,
    Far renowned for larnin' and piety. *Father O'Flynn*

14 Powerfulest preacher and tinderest teacher
    And kindliest creature in ould Donegal.   *Ib.*

15 Checkin' the crazy ones, coaxin' onaisy ones,
    Liftin' the lazy ones on wid the stick.   *Ib.*

JOHN WOODCOCK GRAVES
1795–1886

16 D'ye ken John Peel with his coat so gray?
    D'ye ken John Peel at the break of the day?
    D'ye ken John Peel when he's far far away
    With his hounds and his horn in the morning?
    'Twas the sound of his horn called me from my bed,
    And the cry of his hounds has me oft-times led;
    For Peel's view-hollo would waken the dead,
    Or a fox from his lair in the morning.   *John Peel*

ROBERT GRAVES
1895–

17 Goodbye to all that.   *Title of book*

THOMAS GRAY
1716–1771

18 The social smile, the sympathetic tear.
    Alliance of Education and Government, l. 37

19 When love could teach a monarch to be wise,
    And gospel-light first dawn'd from Bullen's eyes.
    Ib. l. 108

20 Ruin seize thee, ruthless King!
    Confusion on thy banners wait,
    Tho' fann'd by Conquest's crimson wing
    They mock the air with idle state.   *The Bard*, I. i

21 To high-born Hoel's harp, or soft Llewellyn's lay.
    Ib. ii

22 Weave the warp, and weave the woof,
    The winding-sheet of Edward's race.
    Give ample room, and verge enough
    The characters of hell to trace.   *Ib.* II. i

23 Fair laughs the morn, and soft the zephyr blows,
    While proudly riding o'er the azure realm
    In gallant trim the gilded vessel goes,
    Youth on the prow, and Pleasure at the helm;
    Regardless of the sweeping whirlwind's sway,
    That, hush'd in grim repose, expects his evening prey.   *Ib.* ii

24 Ye towers of Julius, London's lasting shame,
    With many a foul and midnight murther fed. *Ib.* iii

25 Visions of glory, spare my aching sight,
    Ye unborn ages, crowd not on my soul!   *Ib.* III. i

26 And Truth severe, by fairy Fiction drest.   *Ib.* ii

27 Now my weary lips I close;
    Leave me, leave me to repose! *Descent of Odin*, l. 71

28 The curfew tolls the knell of parting day,
    The lowing herd wind slowly o'er the lea,
    The ploughman homeward plods his weary way,
    And leaves the world to darkness and to me.

    Now fades the glimmering landscape on the sight,
    And all the air a solemn stillness holds,
    Save where the beetle wheels his droning flight,
    And drowsy tinklings lull the distant folds.
    Elegy Written in a Country Churchyard, i–ii

29 Save that from yonder ivy-mantled tow'r,
    The moping owl does to the moon complain.
    Ib. iii

30 Each in his narrow cell for ever laid,
    The rude forefathers of the hamlet sleep.   *Ib.* iv

31 The breezy call of incense-breathing Morn,
    The swallow twitt'ring from the straw-built shed,
    The cock's shrill clarion, or the echoing horn,
    No more shall rouse them from their lowly bed.

    For them no more the blazing hearth shall burn,
    Or busy housewife ply her evening care:
    No children run to lisp their sire's return,
    Or climb his knees the envied kiss to share.   *Ib.* v–vi

1 Let not ambition mock their useful toil,
   Their homely joys, and destiny obscure;
Nor grandeur hear with a disdainful smile,
   The short and simple annals of the poor.

The boast of heraldry, the pomp of pow'r,
   And all that beauty, all that wealth e'er gave,
Awaits alike th' inevitable hour,
   The paths of glory lead but to the grave.
   Elegy Written in a Country Churchyard, viii–ix

2 Where thro' the long-drawn aisle and fretted vault
   The pealing anthem swells the note of praise.
   Ib. x

3 Can storied urn or animated bust
   Back to its mansion call the fleeting breath?
Can honour's voice provoke the silent dust,
   Or flatt'ry soothe the dull cold ear of death?
   Ib. xi

4 Hands, that the rod of empire might have sway'd,
   Or wak'd to ecstasy the living lyre.
   Ib. xii

5 But knowledge to their eyes her ample page
   Rich with the spoils of time did ne'er unroll;
Chill penury repress'd their noble rage,
   And froze the genial current of the soul.

Full many a gem of purest ray serene,
   The dark unfathom'd caves of ocean bear:
Full many a flower is born to blush unseen,
   And waste its sweetness on the desert air.

Some village-Hampden, that with dauntless breast
   The little tyrant of his fields withstood;
Some mute inglorious Milton here may rest,
   Some Cromwell guiltless of his country's blood.

Th' applause of list'ning senates to command,
   The threats of pain and ruin to despise,
To scatter plenty o'er a smiling land,
   And read their hist'ry in a nation's eyes.
   Ib. xiii–xvi

6 Forbad to wade through slaughter to a throne,
   And shut the gates of mercy on mankind. *Ib.* xvii

7 Far from the madding crowd's ignoble strife,
   Their sober wishes never learn'd to stray;
Along the cool sequester'd vale of life
   They kept the noiseless tenor of their way.

Yet ev'n these bones from insult to protect
   Some frail memorial still erected nigh,
With uncouth rhymes and shapeless sculpture deck'd,
   Implores the passing tribute of a sigh. *Ib.* xix–xx

8 And many a holy text around she strews,
   That teach the rustic moralist to die. *Ib.* xxi

9 For who to dumb Forgetfulness a prey,
   This pleasing anxious being e'er resign'd,
Left the warm precincts of the cheerful day,
   Nor cast one longing ling'ring look behind?

On some fond breast the parting soul relies,
   Some pious drops the closing eye requires;
Ev'n from the tomb the voice of Nature cries,
   Ev'n in our ashes live their wonted fires.
   Ib. xxii–xxiii

10 Mindful of th' unhonour'd dead. *Ib.* xxiv

11 Brushing with hasty steps the dews away
   To meet the sun upon the upland lawn. *Ib.* xxv

12 His listless length at noontide would he stretch,
   And pore upon the brook that babbles by. *Ib.* xxvi

13 Here rests his head upon the lap of Earth
   A youth to fortune and to fame unknown.
Fair Science frown'd not on his humble birth,
   And Melancholy mark'd him for her own.

Large was his bounty, and his soul sincere,
   Heav'n did a recompense as largely send:
He gave to Mis'ry all he had, a tear,
   He gain'd from Heav'n ('twas all he wish'd) a
   friend.

No farther seek his merits to disclose,
   Or draw his frailties from their dread abode,
(There they alike in trembling hope repose),
   The bosom of his Father and his God.
   Elegy written in a Country Churchyard, xxx–xxxii

14 Iron-sleet of arrowy shower
   Hurtles in the darken'd air. *The Fatal Sisters*

15 Daughter of Jove, relentless power,
   Thou tamer of the human breast,
Whose iron scourge and tort'ring hour
   The bad affright, afflict the best.
   Hymn to Adversity, l. 1

16 What sorrow was, thou bad'st her know,
   And from her own, she learn'd to melt at others' woe.
   Ib. l. 15

17 And leave us leisure to be good. *Ib.* l. 20

18 Rich windows that exclude the light,
   And passages, that lead to nothing. *A Long Story*, ii

19 Full oft within the spacious walls,
   When he had fifty winters o'er him,
My grave Lord-Keeper led the brawls;
   The Seal, and Maces, danc'd before him. *Ib.* iii

20 What female heart can gold despise?
   What cat's averse to fish?
   Ode on the Death of a Favourite Cat

21 A fav'rite has no friend! *Ib.*

22 Not all that tempts your wand'ring eyes
   And heedless hearts, is lawful prize;
Nor all, that glisters, gold. *Ib.*

23 Ye distant spires, ye antique towers,
   That crown the wat'ry glade.
   Ode on a Distant Prospect of Eton College, l. 1

24 Urge the flying ball. *Ib.* l. 30

25 Still as they run they look behind,
   They hear a voice in every wind,
   And snatch a fearful joy. *Ib.* l. 38

26 Alas, regardless of their doom,
   The little victims play!
No sense have they of ills to come,
   Nor care beyond to-day. *Ib.* l. 51

27 Ah, tell them, they are men. *Ib.* l. 60

28 Grim-visag'd comfortless Despair. *Ib.* l. 69

29 Slow-consuming Age. *Ib.* l. 90

30 To each his suff'rings: all are men,
   Condemn'd alike to groan;
The tender for another's pain,
   Th' unfeeling for his own.

Yet ah! why should they know their fate?
Since sorrow never comes too late,
   And happiness too swiftly flies.
Thought would destroy their paradise.
No more; where ignorance is bliss,
   'Tis folly to be wise. *Ib.* l. 91

1 Hence, avaunt ('tis holy ground)
Comus, and his midnight-crew.
Ode for Music, or Installation Ode, l. 1

2 Servitude that hugs her chain. *Ib.* l. 6

3 There sit the sainted sage, the bard divine,
The few, whom genius gave to shine
Thro' every unborn age, and undiscover'd clime.
Ib. l. 15

4 Their tears, their little triumphs o'er,
Their human passions now no more. *Ib.* l. 48

5 The meanest flowret of the vale,
The simplest note that swells the gale,
The common sun, the air, and skies,
To him are opening paradise.
Ode. On the Pleasure Arising from Vicissitude,
l. 49

6 The Attic warbler pours her throat,
Responsive to the cuckoo's note.
Ode on the Spring, l. 5

7 How vain the ardour of the crowd,
How low, how little are the proud,
How indigent the great! *Ib.* l. 18

8 Contemplation's sober eye. *Ib.* l. 31

9 The bloom of young desire and purple light of love.
The Progress of Poesy, i. 3

10 Nature's darling. [Shakespeare.] *Ib.* iii. 1

11 The dauntless child
Stretched forth his little arms, and smiled.
[Shakespeare.] *Ib.*

12 Or ope the sacred source of sympathetic tears. *Ib.*

13 Nor second he, that rode sublime
Upon the seraph-wings of ecstasy,
The secrets of th' abyss to spy.
He pass'd the flaming bounds of place and time:
The living throne, the sapphire-blaze,
Where angels tremble, while they gaze,
He saw; but blasted with excess of light,
Closed his eyes in endless night. [Milton.] *Ib.* iii. 2

14 Two coursers of ethereal race,
With necks in thunder clothed, and long-resounding
pace. *Ib.*

15 Bright-eyed Fancy, hovering o'er,
Scatters from her pictured urn
Thoughts, that breathe, and words, that burn. *Ib.* 3

16 Beyond the limits of a vulgar fate,
Beneath the good how far—but far above the great.
Ib.

17 Too poor for a bribe, and too proud to importune,
He had not the method of making a fortune.
Sketch of his own Character

18 To warm their little loves the birds complain.
Sonnet on the Death of Richard West

19 And weep the more because I weep in vain. *Ib.*

20 Now as the paradisaical pleasures of the Mahometans
consist in playing upon the flute and lying with
Houris, be mine to read eternal new romances of
Marivaux and Crebillon.
Letters. 103, *To West* [8] *Apr.,* [1742]

21 The language of the age is never the language of
poetry, except among the French, whose verse,
where the thought or image does not support it,
differs in nothing from prose. *Ib.*

22 It has been usual to catch a mouse or two (for form's
sake) in public once a year. [On refusing the
Laureateship.] *Letter. 259, To Mason, 19 Dec. 1757*

23 Any fool may write a most valuable book by chance,
if he will only tell us what he heard and saw
with veracity. *Ib. 475, To Walpole, 25 Feb. 1768*

24 I shall be but a shrimp of an author.
Ib. (Seventeen years after the publication of *An
Elegy Written in a Country Churchyard*)

MATTHEW GREEN
1696–1737

25 I live by pulling off the hat.
On Barclay's Apology, l. 84

26 They politics like ours profess,
The greater prey upon the less. *The Grotto,* l. 69

27 Fling but a stone, the giant dies.
Laugh and be well. *The Spleen,* l. 92

28 Or to some coffee-house I stray,
For news, the manna of a day,
And from the hipp'd discourses gather
That politics go by the weather. *Ib.* l. 168

29 Experience joined with common sense,
To mortals is a providence. *Ib.* l. 312

30 Who their ill-tasted, home-brewed prayer
To the State's mellow forms prefer. *Ib.* l. 336

31 By happy alchemy of mind
They turn to pleasure all they find. *Ib.* l. 610

ROBERT GREENE
1560?–1592

32 A noble mind disdains to hide his head,
And let his foes triumph in his overthrow.
Alphonso, King of Aragon, 1

33 Cupid abroad was lated in the night,
His wings were wet with ranging in the rain.
Sonnet: Cupid Abroad was Lated

34 Friar Bacon and Friar Bungay. *Title of play*

35 Hangs in the uncertain balance of proud time.
Friar Bacon and Friar Bungay, III. i

36 Sweet Adon, darest not glance thine eye
N'oserez vous, mon bel ami?
Upon thy Venus that must die?
Je vous en prie, pity me:
*N'oserez vous, mon bel, mon bel,
N'oserez vous, mon bel ami?* *Infida's Song*

37 Ah! were she pitiful as she is fair,
Or but as mild as she is seeming so.
Dorastus in Praise of Fawnia. Pandosto, ed. 1694

38 O glorious sun, imagine me the west!
Shine in my arms, and set thou in my breast! *Ib.*

39 Love in my bosom like a bee
Doth suck his sweet;
Now with his wings he plays with me,
Now with his feet.
Within mine eyes he makes his nest,
His bed amid my tender breast;
My kisses are his daily feast,
And yet he robs me of my rest.
Ah, wanton, will ye? *Rosalind's Madrigal*

1 Like to Diana in her summer weed,
Girt with a crimson robe of brightest dye,
　　Goes fair Samela.
Whiter than be the flocks that straggling feed,
When washed by Arethusa's fount they lie,
　　Is fair Samela. *Samela*

2 Weep not, my wanton, smile upon my knee;
When thou art old there's grief enough for thee.
　　Mother's wag, pretty boy,
　　Father's sorrow, father's joy.
　　When thy father first did see
　　Such a boy by him and me,
　　He was glad, I was woe:
　　Fortune changed made him so,
　　When he left his pretty boy,
Last his sorrow, first his joy. *Sephestia's Song*

3 The wanton smiled, father wept;
Mother cried, baby lept;
More he crowed, more we cried;
Nature could not sorrow hide.
He must go, he must kiss
Child and mother, baby bliss;
For he left his pretty boy,
Father's sorrow, father's joy. *Ib.*

4 The swain did woo, she was nice,
Following fashion nayed him twice.
The Shepherd's Ode

5 Ah! what is love! It is a pretty thing,
As sweet unto a shepherd as a king,
　　And sweeter too;
For kings have cares that wait upon a crown,
And cares can make the sweetest love to frown.
　　Ah then, ah then,
If country loves such sweet desires do gain,
What lady would not love a shepherd swain?
The Shepherd's Wife's Song

6 For there is an upstart crow, beautified with our feathers, that with his tiger's heart wrapped in a player's hide, supposes he is as well able to bumbast out a blank verse as the best of you; and being an absolute *Iohannes fac totum*, is in his own conceit the only Shake-scene in a country.
The Groatsworth of Wit Bought with a Million of Repentance

GREGORY I
540–604

7 Quasi quidam quippe est fluvius, ut ita dixerim, planus et altus, in quo et agnus ambulet et elephas natet.

This is as it were a river, if I may so use the expression, in which a lamb may walk and an elephant may swim.
Moralia in Job. Epistola Miseria, ch. 4

8 Responsum est, quod Angli vocarentur. At ille: 'Bene,' inquit; 'nam et angelicam habent faciem, et tales angelorum in caelis decet esse coheredes.'

They answered that they were called Angles. 'It is well,' he said, 'for they have the faces of angels, and such should be the co-heirs of the angels in heaven.'
Traditionally quoted: 'Non Angli sed Angeli.'
Bede, *Historia Ecclesiastica*, II. i

GREGORY VII
1020–1085

9 Dilexi iustitiam et odi iniquitatem, propterea morior in exilio.

I have loved justice and hated iniquity: therefore I die in exile. Bowden, *Life*, iii, ch. 20

STEPHEN GRELLET
1773–1855

10 I expect to pass through this world but once; any good thing therefore that I can do, or any kindness that I can show to any fellow-creature, let me do it now; let me not defer or neglect it, for I shall not pass this way again.
Attr. 'Treasure Trove', collected by John o' London, 1925. Many other claimants to authorship

FULKE GREVILLE, FIRST BARON BROOKE
1554–1628

11 More than most fair, full of that heavenly fire,
Kindled above to show the Maker's glory;
Beauty's first-born, in whom all powers conspire
To write the Graces' life, and Muses' story:
If in my heart all saints else be defaced,
Honour the shrine, where you alone are placed.
Cælica, sonnet iii

12 Fire and people do in this agree,
They both good servants, both ill masters be.
Inquisition upon Fame, lxvii

13 Do what you can: mine shall subsist by me:
I am the measure of Felicity.
Mustapha. Chorus Tertius, Eternity

14 Oh wearisome condition of humanity!
Born under one law, to another bound.
Mustapha, v. iv

15 Silence augmenteth grief, writing increaseth rage,
Stal'd are my thoughts, which loved and lost, the wonder of our age,
Yet quick'ned now with fire, though dead with frost ere now,
Enraged I write, I know not what: dead, quick, I know not how.
Elegy on the Death of Sir Philip Sidney

16 Fulke Greville, Servant to Queen Elizabeth, Councillor to King James, and Friend to Sir Philip Sidney.
Epitaph Written for Himself, on his Monument in Warwick

EDWARD, VISCOUNT GREY OF FALLODON
1862–1933

17 The British Army should be a projectile to be fired by the British Navy. *Lord Fisher, Memories*, ch. 1

18 The lamps are going out all over Europe; we shall not see them lit again in our lifetime.
3 Aug. 1914. Twenty-Five Years, vol. ii, ch. 18

GERALD GRIFFIN
1803–1840

19 I knew a gentle maid,
Flower of the hazel glade,—
Eileen Aroon. *Eileen Aroon*

1 Dear were her charms to me,
Dearer her laughter free,
Dearest her constancy,—
    Eileen Aroon!   *Eileen Aroon*

NICHOLAS GRIMALD
1519–1562

2 Of all the heavenly gifts that mortal men commend,
What trusty treasure in the world can countervail a
    friend?   *Of Friendship*

3 In working well, if travail you sustain,
Into the wind shall lightly pass the pain;
But of the deed the glory shall remain,
And cause your name with worthy wights to reign.
In working wrong, if pleasure you attain,
The pleasure soon shall fade, and void as vain;
But of the deed throughout the life the shame
Endures, defacing you with foul defame.
    Musonius the Philosopher's Saying

GEORGE GROSSMITH
1847–1912
and
WALTER WEEDON GROSSMITH
1854–1919

4 What's the good of a home if you are never in it?
    The Diary of a Nobody, ch. 1

5 I . . . recognized her as a woman who used to work
years ago for my old aunt at Clapham. It only
shows how small the world is.   *Ib.* ch. 2

6 He [Gowing] suggested we should play 'Cutlets', a
game we never heard of. He sat on a chair, and
asked Carrie to sit on his lap, an invitation which
dear Carrie rightly declined.   *Ib.* ch. 7

7 One, two, three; go! Have you an estate in Greenland?   *Ib.* ch. 10

8 That's right.   *Ib.* ch. 11

9 Without an original there can be no imitation.   *Ib.*

10 I left the room with silent dignity, but caught my
foot in the mat.   *Ib.* ch. 12

11 I am a poor man, but I would gladly give ten shillings
to find out who sent me the insulting Christmas
card I received this morning.   *Ib.* ch. 13

12 What's the matter with Gladstone? He's all right.
    Ib. ch. 17

PHILIP GUEDALLA
1889–1944

13 The little ships, the unforgotten Homeric catalogue
of *Mary Jane* and *Peggy IV*, of *Folkestone Belle,
Boy Billy,* and *Ethel Maud*, of *Lady Haig* and
Skylark . . . the little ships of England brought the
Army home.
    Mr. Churchill. [Evacuation of Dunkirk.]

14 The work of Henry James has always seemed
divisible by a simple dynastic arrangement into
three reigns: James I, James II, and the Old Pretender.
    Collected Essays, vol. iv. *Men of Letters: Mr.
    Henry James*

YVETTE GUILBERT 1867–1944

15 Linger longer Lucy,
Linger longer Lou.   *Song*

TEXAS GUINAN
1884–1933

16 Fifty million Frenchmen can't be wrong.
    Attr. New York World-Telegram, 21 Mar. 1931

DOROTHY FRANCES GURNEY
1858–1932

17 The kiss of the sun for pardon,
The song of the birds for mirth,
One is nearer God's Heart in a garden
Than anywhere else on earth.   *God's Garden*

18 O perfect Love, all human thought transcending,
Lowly we kneel in prayer before Thy throne.
    Hymn. O Perfect Love

HADRIAN
A.D. 76–138

19 Animula vagula blandula,
Hospes comesque corporis,
Quae nunc abibis in loca
Pallidula rigida nudula,
Nec ut soles dabis iocos!

Little soul, wandering, pleasant, guest and companion of the body, into what places wilt thou
now go, pale, stiff, naked, nor wilt thou play any
longer as thou art wont.
    Duff, *Minor Latin Poems* (Loeb, 1934), 445

DOUGLAS HAIG, EARL HAIG
1861–1928

20 Every position must be held to the last man: there
must be no retirement. With our backs to the wall,
and believing in the justice of our cause, each one
of us must fight on to the end.
    *Order to the British Troops, 12 Apr. 1918. The
    Times, 13 Apr.*

RICHARD BURDON HALDANE, VISCOUNT
HALDANE
1856–1928

21 I had gone to Germany too often, and had read her
literature too much, not to give ground to narrow-
minded people to say that Germany was my
'spiritual home'.   *An Autobiography,* p. 285

SIR MATTHEW HALE
1609–1676

22 Christianity is part of the Common Law of England.
    Historia Placitorum Coronae (1736). Also in
    Blackstone's *Commentaries on the Laws of
    England,* iv, 1765

SARAH JOSEPHA HALE
1788–1879

23 Mary had a little lamb,
Its fleece was white as snow,
And everywhere that Mary went
The lamb was sure to go.

'What makes the lamb love Mary so?'
    The eager children cry.
'Oh, Mary loves the lamb, you know,'
    The teacher did reply.
        Poems for Our Children. Mary's Little Lamb

THOMAS CHANDLER HALIBURTON
1796–1865

1 I want you to see Peel, Stanley, Graham, Shiel,
Russell, Macaulay, Old Joe, and so on. These men
are all upper crust here.
        Sam Slick in England, ch. 24

GEORGE SAVILE, MARQUIS OF HALIFAX
1633–1695

2 Love is a passion that hath friends in the garrison.
        Advice to a Daughter: Behaviour and Conversation

3 This innocent word 'Trimmer' signifies no more than
this, that if men are together in a boat, and one part
of the company would weigh it down on one side,
another would make it lean as much to the contrary.
        Character of a Trimmer, preface

4 He would rather die, than see a piece of English grass
trampled down by a foreign Trespasser.
        Character of a Trimmer

5 Men are not hanged for stealing horses, but that
horses may not be stolen.
        Political Thoughts and Reflections: Of Punishment

6 To the question, What shall we do to be saved in this
World? there is no other answer but this, Look to
your Moat. *A Rough Draft of a New Model at Sea*

CHARLES SPRAGUE HALL
fl. 1860

7 John Brown's body lies a mould'ring in the grave,
His soul is marching on!
        John Brown's Body. Nicholas Smith's *Stories of Great National Songs*

BISHOP JOSEPH HALL
1574–1656

8 Ah me! how seldom see we sons succeed
Their fathers' praise, in prowess and great deed.
        Satires, bk. iv, no. 3

9 I first adventure, follow me who list
And be the second English satirist.
        Virgidemiae, Prologue

10 Perfection is the child of Time.
        Works (1625), p. 670

11 All his dealings are square, and above the board.
        Virtues and Vices (1608), bk. 1, p. 15

OWEN HALL [JAMES DAVIS]
d. 1907

12 Tell me, pretty maiden, are there any more at home
like you?
        Florodora. Act II

FITZ-GREENE HALLECK
1790–1867

13 Forever, float that standard sheet!
Where breathes the foe but falls before us,
With Freedom's soil beneath our feet,
And Freedom's banner streaming o'er us?
        The American Flag
        Attr. also to Joseph Rodman Drake, 1795–1820.

14 They love their land because it is their own,
    And scorn to give aught other reason why;
Would shake hands with a king upon his throne,
    And think it kindness to his Majesty. *Connecticut*

15 Green be the turf above thee,
Friend of my better days!
None knew thee but to love thee,
Nor named thee but to praise.
        On the Death of J. R. Drake

16 Come to the bridal-chamber, Death!
    Come to the mother's, when she feels,
For the first time, her first-born's breath.
        Marco Bozzaris

FRIEDRICH HALM [FRANZ VON MÜNCH-BELLINGHAUSEN]
1806–1871

17 Mein Herz ich will dich fragen:
Was ist denn Liebe? Sag'!—
'Zwei Seelen und ein Gedanke,
Zwei Herzen und ein Schlag!'

What love is, if thou wouldst be taught,
    Thy heart must teach alone,—
Two souls with but a single thought,
    Two hearts that beat as one.
        Der Sohn der Wildniss, Act II *ad fin.*
    Trans. by Maria Lovell in *Ingomar the Barbarian*

WILLIAM FREDERICK HALSEY
1882–

18 Our ships have been salvaged and are retiring at high
speed toward the Japanese fleet.
        Radio Message, Oct. 1944 after Japanese claims that most of the American Third Fleet had been sunk or were retiring

PHILIP GILBERT HAMERTON
1834–1894

19 The art of reading is to skip judiciously.
        Intellectual Life, pt. iv, letter iv

ALEXANDER HAMILTON
1757–1804

20 A national debt, if it is not excessive, will be to us a
national blessing.
        Letter to Robert Morris, 30 Apr. 1781

GAIL HAMILTON [MARY ABIGAIL DODGE]
1838–1896

21 The total depravity of inanimate things. *Epigram*

WILLIAM HAMILTON
1704–1754

1 Busk ye, busk ye, my bonny bonny bride,
Busk ye, busk ye, my winsome marrow.
Poetical Works. The Braes of Yarrow

WILLIAM GERARD HAMILTON
1729–1796

2 Johnson is dead.—Let us go to the next best:—There
is nobody; no man can be said to put you in mind
of Johnson.
Boswell's Life of Johnson (1934), vol. iv, p. 420

SIR WILLIAM HAMILTON
1788–1856

3 Truth, like a torch, the more it's shook it shines.
Discussions on Philosophy, title-page

4 On earth there is nothing great but man; in man there
is nothing great but mind.
Lectures on Metaphysics

OSCAR HAMMERSTEIN
1895–1960

5 The last time I saw Paris, her heart was warm and
gay,
I heard the laughter of her heart in every street café.
Song. The Last Time I Saw Paris

PERCY HAMMOND
1873–1936

6 The human knee is a joint and not an entertainment.
Mark Sullivan, *Our Times*, vol. iii, ch. 10

RICHARD ROLLE DE HAMPOLE
1290?–1349

7 When Adam dalfe and Eve spane
So spire if thou may spede,
Whare was than the pride of man,
That nowe merres his mede?
Religious Pieces in Prose and Verse, vii. *Early
English Text Society, Original Series*, No. 26.
*An altered form was used by John Ball (d.
1381) as the text of his revolutionary sermon
on the outbreak of the Peasants' Revolt, 1381:*
When Adam delved and Eve span,
Who was then the gentleman?

JOHN HANCOCK
1737–1793

8 There, I guess King George will be able to read that.
*Remark on signing the Declaration of Inde-
pendence, 4 July 1776*

MINNY MAUD HANFF
fl. 1900

9 Since then they called him Sunny Jim.
*Sunny Jim. Advertisement for Force, a break-
fast food*

KATHERINE HANKEY
1834–1911

10 Tell me the old, old story,
Of unseen things above.
The Story Wanted. Tell Me the Old, Old Story

PHILIP YORKE, EARL OF HARDWICKE
1690–1764

11 His doubts are better than most people's certainties.
[Referring to the book *Dirleton's Doubts*.]
Boswell's Johnson (1934), iii, p. 205

E. J. HARDY (1849–1920)

12 How To Be Happy Though Married.
Title of book (1910)

THOMAS HARDY
1840–1928

13 'He was a man who used to notice such things.'
Afterwards

14 Some nocturnal blackness, mothy and warm,
When the hedgehog travels furtively over the lawn.
Ib.

15 As the hope-hour stroked its sum.
A Broken Appointment

16 Twin halves of one august event.
Convergence of the Twain

17 An aged thrush, frail, gaunt, and small,
In blast-beruffled plume.   *The Darkling Thrush*

18 So little cause for carolings
Of such ecstatic sound
Was written on terrestrial things
Afar or nigh around,
That I could think there trembled through
His happy good-night air
Some blessed Hope, whereof he knew
And I was unaware.   *Ib.*

19 And foreign constellations west
Each night above his mound.   *Drummer Hodge*

20 What of the Immanent Will and its designs?—
It works unconsciously as heretofore,
Eternal artistries in Circumstance.
The Dynasts, pt. i. *Fore-Scene*

21   Like a knitter drowsed,
Whose fingers play in skilled unmindfulness,
The Will has woven with an absent heed
Since life first was; and ever so will weave.   *Ib.*

22 The nether sky opens, and Europe is disclosed as a
prone and emaciated figure, the Alps shaping
like a backbone, and the branching mountain-
chains like ribs, the peninsular plateau of Spain
forming a head. Broad and lengthy lowlands stretch
from the north of France across Russia like a
grey-green garment hemmed by the Ural mountains
and the glistening Arctic Ocean.
     The point of view then sinks downwards
through space, and draws near to the surface of
the perturbed countries, where the peoples, distressed by events which they did not cause, are
seen writhing, crawling, heaving, and vibrating in
their various cities and nationalities.
Ib. Stage Direction

HARDY

1 A local cult called Christianity.   *The Dynasts*, I. vi

2 My argument is that War makes rattling good history;
but Peace is poor reading.   *Ib.* II. v

3 But O, the intolerable antilogy
Of making figments feel!   *Ib.* IV. vi

4 Each captain, petty officer, and man
Is only at his post when under fire.   *Ib.* V. i

5 The all-urging Will, raptly magnipotent.   *Ib.* VI. viii

6 But—a stirring thrills the air
Like to sounds of joyance there
   That the rages
   Of the ages
Shall be cancelled, and deliverance offered from the
   darts that were,
Consciousness the Will informing, till It fashion all
   things fair!   *Ib. pt. iii, last lines*

7 The selfsame bloody mode.   *Embarcation*

8 William Dewy, Tranter Reuben, Farmer Ledlow late
   at plough,
Robert's kin, and John's, and Ned's,
And the Squire, and Lady Susan, lie in Mellstock
   churchyard now!   *Friends Beyond*

9 Mothy curfew-tide.   *Ib.*

10 A lone cave's stillicide.   *Ib.*

11 If ye break my best blue china, children, I shan't care
   or ho.   *Ib.*

12 And shakes this fragile frame at eve
With throbbings of noontide.   *I Look Into My Glass*

13 If way to the Better there be, it exacts a full look at the
   worst.   *In Tenebris*

14 Only a man harrowing clods
   In a slow silent walk
With an old horse that stumbles and nods
   Half asleep as they stalk.

Only thin smoke without flame
   From the heaps of couch grass;
Yet this will go onward the same
   Though Dynasties pass.

Yonder a maid and her wight
   Come whispering by:
War's annals will cloud into night
   Ere their story die.
        In Time of 'The Breaking of Nations'

15 That long drip of human tears.
        On an Invitation to the United States

16 Let me enjoy the earth no less
Because the all-enacting Might
That fashioned forth its loveliness
Had other aims than my delight.
        Let Me Enjoy the Earth

17 Here's not a modest maiden elf
But dreads the final Trumpet,
Lest half of her should rise herself,
And half some sturdy strumpet!
        The Levelled Churchyard

18 What of the faith and fire within us
Men who march away
Ere the barn-cocks say
Night is growing gray?   *Men Who March Away*

19 Your face, and the God-curst sun, and a tree,
And a pond edged with grayish leaves.
        Neutral Tones

20 And both of us, scorning parochial ways,
Had lived like the wives in the patriarchs' days.
        Over the Coffin

21 Christmas Eve, and twelve of the clock.
'Now they are all on their knees,'
An elder said as we sat in a flock
By the embers in hearthside ease.   *The Oxen*

22 So fair a fancy few would weave
In these years!   *Ib.*

23 I should go with him in the gloom,
Hoping it might be so.   *Ib.*

24 Read that moderate man Voltaire.
        The Respectable Burgher

25 I have lived with Shades so long.
        Retrospect: I Have Lived with Shades

26 Love is lame at fifty years.   *The Revisitation*

27 A little ball of feather and bone.   *Shelley's Skylark*

28 Patiently adjust, amend, and heal.   *The Sleep-Worker*

29 And the spirits of those who were homing
Passed on, rushingly,
Like the Pentecost Wind.   *Souls of the Slain*

30 This is the weather the cuckoo likes,
And so do I.   *Weathers*

31 And maids come forth sprig-muslin drest.   *Ib.*

32 This is the weather the shepherd shuns,
And so do I.   *Ib.*

33 Rooks in families homeward go.   *Ib.*

34 When I set out for Lyonnesse,
A hundred miles away.
        When I Set Out for Lyonnesse

35 When I came back from Lyonnesse
With magic in my eyes.   *Ib.*

36 Goodbye is not worth while.   *Without Ceremony*

37 Life offers—to deny!   *Yellham-Wood's Story*

38 The kingly brilliance of Sirius pierced the eye with
a steely glitter, the star called Capella was yellow,
Aldebaran and Betelgueux shone with a fiery red.
To persons standing alone on a hill during a clear
midnight such as this, the roll of the world eastward is almost a palpable movement.
        Far From the Madding Crowd, ch. 2

39 A nice unparticular man.   *Ib.* ch. 8

40 We ought to feel deep cheerfulness that a happy
Providence kept it from being any worse.   *Ib.*

41 Ah! stirring times we live in—stirring times.
        Ib. ch. 1

42 Five decades hardly modified the cut of a gaiter,
the embroidery of a smock-frock, by the breadth
of a hair. Ten generations failed to alter the turn
of a single phrase. In these Wessex nooks the
busy outsider's ancient times are only old; his
old times are still new; his present is futurity.
        Ib. ch. 2

[236]

1 'And the people of Bath', continued Cain, 'never need to light their fires except as a luxury, for the water springs up out of the earth ready boiled for use.' ''Tis true as the light', testified Matthew Moon. 'I've heard other navigators say the same thing.'
Far From the Madding Crowd, ch. 33

2 Ethelberta breathed a sort of exclamation, not right out, but stealthily, like a parson's damn.
The Hand of Ethelberta

3 Done because we are too menny.
Jude the Obscure, pt. vi, ch. 2

4 Life's Little Ironies. *Title*

5 'Well, poor soul; she's helpless to hinder that or anything now,' answered Mother Cuxsom. 'And all her shining keys will be took from her, and her cupboards opened, and things a' didn't wish seen, anybody will see; and her little wishes and ways will all be as nothing.'
The Mayor of Casterbridge, ch. 18

6 Dialect words—those terrible marks of the beast to the truly genteel. *Ib.* ch. 20

7 Michael Henchard's Will.
That Elizabeth-Jane Farfrae be not told of my death, or made to grieve on account of me.
& that I be not buried in consecrated ground.
& that no sexton be asked to toll the bell.
& that nobody is wished to see my dead body.
& that no murners walk behind me at my funeral.
& that no flours be planted on my grave.
& that no man remember me.
To this I put my name. *Ib.* ch. 45

8 The heaven being spread with this pallid screen and the earth with the darkest vegetation, their meeting-line at the horizon was clearly marked. In such contrast the heath wore the appearance of an instalment of night which had taken up its place before its astronomical hour was come: darkness had to a great extent arrived hereon, while day stood distinct in the sky.
The Return of the Native, ch. 1

9 In fact, precisely at this transitional point of its nightly roll into darkness the great and particular glory of the Egdon waste began, and nobody could be said to understand the heath who had not been there at such a time. *Ib.*

10 The great inviolate place had an ancient permanence which the sea cannot claim. Who can say of a particular sea that it is old? Distilled by the sun, kneaded by the moon, it is renewed in a year, in a day, or in an hour. The sea changed, the fields changed, the rivers, the villages, and the people changed, yet Egdon remained. *Ib.*

11 A little one-eyed, blinking sort o' place.
Tess of the D'Urbervilles, ch. 1

12 Always washing, and never getting finished. *Ib.* ch. 4

13 The New Testament was less a Christiad than a Pauliad to his intelligence. *Ib.* ch. 25

14 The President of the Immortals (in Æschylean phrase) had ended his sport with Tess. *Ib.* ch. 59

15 The courses of the *Victory* were absorbed into the main, then her topsails went, and then her top-gallants. She was now no more than a dead fly's wing on a sheet of spider's web; and even this fragment diminished. Anne could hardly bear to see the end, and yet she resolved not to flinch. The admiral's flag sank behind the watery line, and in a minute the very truck of the last main-mast stole away. The *Victory* was gone.
The Trumpet Major, ch. 34

16 Good, but not religious-good.
Under the Greenwood Tree, ch. 2

17 Silent? Ah, he is silent! He can keep silence well. That man's silence is wonderful to listen to.
Ib. ch. 14

18 You was a good man, and did good things.
The Woodlanders, ch. 48

JULIUS CHARLES HARE
1795-1855
and
AUGUSTUS WILLIAM HARE
1792-1834

19 Man without religion is the creature of circumstances.
Guesses at Truth, Series 1

20 Truth, when witty, is the wittiest of all things. *Ib.*

21 The ancients dreaded death: the Christian can only fear dying. *Ib.*

22 Half the failures in life arise from pulling in one's horse as he is leaping. *Ib.*

23 Purity is the feminine, Truth the masculine, of Honour. *Ib.*

24 Every Irishman, the saying goes, has a potato in his head. *Ib.*

25 Everybody has his own theatre, in which he is manager, actor, prompter, playwright, sceneshifter, boxkeeper, doorkeeper, all in one, and audience into the bargain. *Ib.* Series 2

MAURICE EVAN HARE
1886-1967

26 There once was a man who said, 'Damn!
It is borne in upon me I am
An engine that moves
In predestinate grooves,
I'm not even a bus I'm a tram.'
Written, as above, at St. John's College, Oxford, in 1905

FRANCIS HARGRAVE
1741?-1821

27 A soil whose air is deemed too pure for slaves to breathe in. [England.]
Argument on Sommersett Habeas Corpus Case, 14 May 1772. James Sommersett was a negro slave from Jamaica, who accompanied his master to England and claimed his freedom. See Cobbett's State Trials, vol. xx

WILLIAM HARGREAVES d. 1941

28 I'm Burlington Bertie:
I rise at ten-thirty.
Burlington Bertie. First sung by Ella Shields in October 1914 at the Argyle Theatre, Birkenhead.

1 I walk down the Strand
With my gloves on my hand
And I walk down again
With them off.
Burlington Bertie

SIR JOHN HARINGTON
1561–1612

2   When I make a feast,
I would my guests should praise it, not the cooks.
Epigrams, bk. i, No. 5. *Against Writers that Carp at Other Men's Books*

3 Treason doth never prosper: what's the reason?
For if it prosper, none dare call it treason.
Ib. bk. iv, No. 5. *Of Treason*

ROBERT GOODLOE HARPER
1765–1825

4 Millions for defence but not a cent for tribute.
Toast at the dinner given by Congress at Philadelphia, 18 June 1798. Claypoole's *American Daily Advertiser*, 20 June 1798. A. J. Beveridge's *Life of John Marshall*, vol. ii.

CHARLES K. HARRIS
1865–1930

5 After the ball is over.   *After the Ball*
6 Somewhere the sun is shining.   *Somewhere*

CLIFFORD HARRIS d. 1949

7 You called me Baby Doll a year ago. *A Broken Doll*
8 You left behind a broken doll.   *Ib.*

JOEL CHANDLER HARRIS
1848–1908

9 'Law, Brer Tarrypin!' sez Brer Fox, sezee, 'you ain't see no trouble yit. Ef you wanter see sho' nuff trouble, you des oughter go 'longer me; I'm de man w'at kin show you trouble,' sezee.
Nights with Uncle Remus, ch. 17

10 W'en folks git ole en strucken wid de palsy, dey mus' speck ter be laff'd at.   *Ib.* ch. 23

11 Hit look lak sparrer-grass, hit feel like sparrer-grass, hit tas'e lak sparrer-grass, en I bless ef 'taint sparrer-grass.   *Ib.* ch. 27

12 All by my own-alone self.   *Ib.* ch. 36

13 No 'pollygy aint gwine ter make h'ar come back whar de b'iling water hit.   *Ib.* ch. 45

14 We er sorter po'ly, Sis Tempy, I'm 'blige ter you. You know w'at de jay-bird say ter der squinch-owl! 'I'm sickly but sassy.'   *Ib.* ch. 50

15 A contrapshun what he call a Tar-Baby.
Uncle Remus. Legends of the Old Plantation, ch. 2. *Tar-Baby Story*

16 How duz yo' sym'tums seem ter segashuate?   *Ib.*

17 Tar-baby ain't sayin' nuthin', en Brer Fox, he lay low.   *Ib.*

18 Bred en bawn in a brier-patch!   *Ib.* ch. 4

19 Lounjun 'roun' en suffer'n'.   *Ib.* ch. 12

20 Ole man Know-All died las' year.
Uncle Remus, ch. 34. *Plantation Proverbs*

21 Licker talks mighty loud w'en it git loose fum de jug.   *Ib.*

22 Hongry rooster don't cackle w'en he fine a wum. *Ib.*

23 Youk'n hide de fier, but w'at you gwine do wid de smoke?   *Ib.*

24 Oh, whar shill we go w'en de great day comes,
Wid de blowin' er de trumpits en de bangin' er de drums?
How many po' sinners'll be kotched out late
En find no latch ter de golden gate?
Uncle Remus. His Songs, i

FRANCIS BRETT HART
or
BRET HARTE
1839–1902

25 He read aloud the book wherein the Master
Had writ of Little Nell.
Dickens in Camp

26 And on that grave where English oak and holly
And laurel wreaths entwine
Deem it not all a too presumptuous folly,—
This spray of Western pine!   *Ib.*

27 You see this yer Dow
Hed the worst kind of luck;
He slipped up somehow
On each thing thet he struck.
Why, ef he'd a straddled that fence-rail, the derned thing 'ed get up and buck.   *Dow's Flat*

28 Thar ain't no sense
In gittin' riled!   *Jim*

29 Over the trackless past, somewhere,
Lie the lost days of our tropic youth,
Only regained by faith and prayer,
Only recalled by prayer and plaint:
Each lost day has its patron saint! *The Lost Galleon*

30 For there be women fair as she,
Whose verbs and nouns do more agree.
Mrs. Judge Jenkins

31 If, of all words of tongue and pen,
The saddest are, 'It might have been,'
More sad are these we daily see:
'It is, but hadn't ought to be!'   *Ib.*

32 Which I wish to remark,
And my language is plain,
That for ways that are dark
And for tricks that are vain,
The heathen Chinee is peculiar,
Which the same I would rise to explain.
Plain Language from Truthful James

33 But his smile it was pensive and childlike.   *Ib.*

34 But he smiled as he sat by the table,
With the smile that was childlike and bland.   *Ib.*

35 And the same with intent to deceive.   *Ib.*

36 We are ruined by Chinese cheap labour.   *Ib.*

37 And we found on his nails, which were taper,
What is frequent in tapers—that's wax.   *Ib.*

38 He wore, I think, a chasuble, the day when first we met.   *The Ritualist*

1 I reside at Table Mountain, and my name is Truthful James.   *The Society upon the Stanislaus*

2 And he smiled a kind of sickly smile, and curled up on the floor,
And the subsequent proceedings interested him no more.   *Ib.*

3 With unpronounceable awful names.
   The Tale of a Pony

MINNIE LOUISE HASKINS
1875-1957

4 And I said to the man who stood at the gate of the year: 'Give me a light that I may tread safely into the unknown'. And he replied: 'Go out into the darkness and put your hand into the hand of God. That shall be to you better than light and safer than a known way.'
God Knows. Quoted by King George VI in a Christmas Broadcast. 25 Dec. 1939

STEPHEN HAWES
fl. 1502-1521

5 When the lytle byrdes swetely dyd syng
Laudes to their maker early in the mornyng.
   Passetyme of Pleasure, cap. 33, xxxiii

6 For though the day be never so longe,
At last the belles ringeth to evensonge.   *Ib.* cap. 42

ROBERT STEPHEN HAWKER
1803-1875

7 And have they fixed the where and when?
   And shall Trelawny die?
Here's twenty thousand Cornish men
   Will know the reason why!
Song of the Western Men. The last three lines have existed since the imprisonment by James II, 1688, of the seven Bishops, including Trelawny, Bishop of Bristol

SIR ANTHONY HOPE HAWKINS
see
ANTHONY HOPE

NATHANIEL HAWTHORNE
1804-1864

8 Dr. Johnson's morality was as English an article as a beefsteak. *Our Old Home. Lichfield and Uttoxeter*

LORD CHARLES HAY
?-1760

9 Gentlemen of the French Guard, fire first! (Messieurs les gardes françaises, tirez.)
Battle of Fontenoy, 1745. E. Fournier, L'Esprit dans l'Histoire (1883), ch. 52, p. 349

WILLIAM HAZLITT
1778-1830

10 'His sayings are generally like women's letters; all the pith is in the postscript. [Charles Lamb.]
Conversations of Northcote. Boswell Redivivus

11 The only specimen of Burke is, *all that he wrote.*
English Literature, ch. ix. *Character of Mr. Burke*

12 He writes as fast as they can read, and he does not write himself down.   *Ib.* ch. xiv. *Sir Walter Scott*

13 His worst is better than any other person's best. *Ib.*

14 His works (taken together) are almost like a new edition of human nature. This is indeed to be an author!   *Ib.*

15 The round-faced man in black entered, and dissipated all doubts on the subject, by beginning to talk. He did not cease while he stayed; nor has he since, that I know of. [Coleridge.]
   Ib. ch. xvii. *My First Acquaintance with Poets*

16 'For those two hours,' he [Coleridge] afterwards was pleased to say, 'he was conversing with W. H.'s forehead!'   *Ib.*

17 He [Coleridge] lamented that Wordsworth was not prone enough to belief in the traditional superstitions of the place, and that there was a something corporeal, a *matter-of-fact-ness*, a clinging to the palpable, or often to the petty, in his poetry, in consequence.   *Ib.*

18 At Godwin's . . . they [Lamb, Holcroft, and Coleridge] were disputing fiercely which was the best—Man as he was, or man as he is to be. 'Give me,' says Lamb, 'man as he is *not* to be.' This saying was the beginning of a friendship between us, which I believe still continues.   *Ib.*

19 You will hear more good things on the outside of a stagecoach from London to Oxford than if you were to pass a twelvemonth with the undergraduates, or heads of colleges, of that famous university.   *The Ignorance of the Learned*

20 The temple of fame stands upon the grave: the flame that burns upon its altars is kindled from the ashes of great men.
   Lectures on the English Poets. Lecture viii, *On the Living Poets*

21 He [Coleridge] talked on for ever; and you wished him to talk on for ever.   *Ib.*

22 The dupe of friendship, and the fool of love; have I not reason to hate and to despise myself? Indeed I do; and chiefly for not having hated and despised the world enough.
   The Plain Speaker. On the Pleasure of Hating

23 The love of liberty is the love of others; the love of power is the love of ourselves.
   Political Essays. 'The Times' Newspaper

24 Those who make their dress a principal part of themselves, will, in general, become of no more value than their dress.   *Ib. On the Clerical Character*

25 There is nothing good to be had in the country, or, if there is, they will not let you have it.
   Ib. 1817. Observations on Mr. Wordsworth's Excursion

26 The art of pleasing consists in being pleased.
   Round Table, vol. i. *On Manner*

27 The greatest offence against virtue is to speak ill of it.
   Sketches and Essays. On Cant and Hypocrisy

28 The most fluent talkers or most plausible reasoners are not always the justest thinkers.
   Ib. On Prejudice

1 We never do anything well till we cease to think about the manner of doing it.
Sketches and Essays. On Prejudice

2 There is an unseemly exposure of the mind, as well as of the body.
Ib. On Disagreeable People

3 A nickname is the heaviest stone that the devil can throw at a man.
Ib. Nicknames

4 Rules and models destroy genius and art.
Ib. On Taste

5 But of all footmen the lowest class is *literary footmen*.
Ib. Footmen

6 His [Leigh Hunt's] light, agreeable, polished style . . . hits off the faded graces of 'an Adonis of fifty'.
The Spirit of the Age: Mr. Leigh Hunt

7 Cavanagh's blows were not undecided and ineffectual —lumbering like Mr. Wordsworth's epic poetry, nor wavering like Mr. Coleridge's lyric prose, nor short of the mark like Mr. Brougham's speeches, nor wide of it like Mr. Canning's wit, nor foul like the *Quarterly*, nor *let* balls like the *Edinburgh Review*. Cobbett and Junius together would have made a Cavanagh.
Table Talk, vii. The Indian Jugglers

8 When I am in the country I wish to vegetate like the country.
Ib. xix. On Going a Journey

9 Give me the clear blue sky over my head, and the green turf beneath my feet, a winding road before me, and a three hours' march to dinner—and then to thinking! It is hard if I cannot start some game on these lone heaths.
Ib.

10 The English (it must be owned) are rather a foul-mouthed nation.
Ib. xxii. On Criticism

11 We can scarcely hate any one that we know.
Ib.

12 Venerate art as art.
Ib. xxx

13 So have I loitered my life away, reading books, looking at pictures, going to plays, hearing, thinking, writing on what pleased me best. I have wanted only one thing to make me happy, but wanting that have wanted everything.
Winterslow. My First Acquaintance with Poets

14 Well, I've had a happy life.
Last words. W. C. Hazlitt's Memoirs of William Hazlitt, 1867

BISHOP REGINALD HEBER
1783–1826

15 Brightest and best of the sons of the morning!
Dawn on our darkness and lend us Thine aid!
Hymns, &c. Brightest and Best

16 By cool Siloam's shady rill
How sweet the lily grows!
Ib. By Cool Siloam's

17 From Greenland's icy mountains,
From India's coral strand,
Where Afric's sunny fountains
Roll down their golden sand.
Ib. From Greenland's Icy Mountains

18 What though the spicy breezes
Blow soft o'er Ceylon's isle;
Though every prospect pleases,
And only man is vile:

In vain with lavish kindness
The gifts of God are strown;
The heathen in his blindness
Bows down to wood and stone.
This is the most familiar version. Bishop Heber originally wrote 'The savage in his blindness'. He altered this, and also altered 'Ceylon's to 'Java's'.
Hymns. From Greenland's Icy Mountains

19 Holy, Holy, Holy! Lord God Almighty!
Early in the morning our song shall rise to Thee:
Holy, Holy, Holy! Merciful and Mighty!
God in Three Persons, Blessed Trinity!

Holy, Holy, Holy! all the Saints adore Thee,
Casting down their golden crowns around the glassy sea.
Ib. Holy, Holy, Holy

20 The Son of God goes forth to war,
A Kingly crown to gain;
His blood-red banner streams afar:—
Who follows in His train?
Ib. The Son of God Goes Forth

21 A noble army, men and boys,
The matron and the maid,
Around the Saviour's throne rejoice
In robes of light array'd.
Ib.

22 They climb'd the steep ascent of Heav'n
Through peril, toil and pain;
O God, to us may grace be given
To follow in their train.
Ib.

GEORG WILHELM HEGEL
1770–1831

23 What experience and history teach is this—that people and governments never have learned anything from history, or acted on principles deduced from it.
Philosophy of History. Introduction. Used by Shaw in his Revolutionist's Handbook and in the preface to Heartbreak House

HEINRICH HEINE
1797–1856

24 Ich grolle nicht, und wenn das Herz auch bricht.
I do not murmur, even if my heart break.
Buch der Lieder. Title of song

25 Ich weiss nicht, was soll es bedeuten,
Dass ich so traurig bin;
Ein Märchen aus alten Zeiten,
Das kommt mir nicht aus dem Sinn.

I know not why I am so sad; I cannot get out of my head a fairy-tale of olden times. *Die Lorelei*

26 Auf Flügeln des Gesanges.
On the wings of song. *Title of song*

27 Dieu me pardonnera. C'est son métier.
God will pardon me. It is His trade.
On his Deathbed

SIR ARTHUR HELPS
1813–1875

28 Somebody, I suppose, was excusing something on the score of temper, to which the bishop replied 'Temper is nine-tenths of Christianity.'
Friends in Council, bk. i, ch.

Reading is sometimes an ingenious device for avoiding thought. *Friends in Council*, bk. ii, ch. 1

What a blessing this smoking is! perhaps the greatest that we owe to the discovery of America.
Ib. series II, 1859, vol. i, ch. 1, *Worry*

There is one statesman of the present day, of whom I always say that he would have escaped making the blunders that he has made if he had only ridden more in omnibuses.
Ib. vol. ii, ch. 9, *On Government*

FELICIA DOROTHEA HEMANS
1793–1835

Not there, not there, my child! *The Better Land*

The boy stood on the burning deck
  Whence all but he had fled;
The flame that lit the battle's wreck
  Shone round him o'er the dead. *Casabianca*

There came a burst of thunder sound—
  The boy—oh! where was he? *Ib.*

Oh! call my brother back to me!
  I cannot play alone;
The summer comes with flower and bee—
  Where is my brother gone?
The Child's First Grief

They grew in beauty, side by side,
  They fill'd one home with glee;—
Their graves are sever'd, far and wide,
  By mount, and stream, and sea.
The Graves of a Household

One sleeps where Southern vines are drest
Above the noble slain;
He wrapt his colours round his breast
On a blood-red field of Spain. *Ib.*

She faded 'midst Italian flowers—
  The last of that bright band. *Ib.*

He Never Smiled Again! *Title*

The stately homes of England,
  How beautiful they stand!
Amidst their tall ancestral trees,
  O'er all the pleasant land. *The Homes of England*

The cottage homes of England!
  By thousands on her plains. *Ib.*

Leaves have their time to fall,
And flowers to wither at the north wind's breath,
  And stars to set—but all,
Thou hast *all* seasons for thine own, O Death!
The Hour of Death

In the busy haunts of men.
Tale of the Secret Tribunal, pt. i, l. 203

JOHN HEMING
d. 1630
and
HENRY CONDELL
d. 1627

His mind and hand went together. What he thought he uttered with that earnestness that we have scarce received from him a blot in his papers.
Preface to the First Folio Shakespeare, 1623

ERNEST HEMINGWAY
1898–1961

17 The world is a fine place and worth fighting for.
For Whom the Bell Tolls, 1940

WILLIAM ERNEST HENLEY
1849–1903

18 Out of the night that covers me,
Black as the Pit from pole to pole,
I thank whatever gods may be
For my unconquerable soul.

In the fell clutch of circumstance,
I have not winced nor cried aloud:
Under the bludgeonings of chance
My head is bloody, but unbowed.
Echoes, iv. *Invictus. In Mem. R. T. H. B.*

19 It matters not how strait the gate,
How charged with punishments the scroll,
I am the master of my fate:
I am the captain of my soul. *Ib.*

20 The friendly and comforting breast
Of the old nurse, Death. *Ib.* xxix. *To R. L. S.*

21 A late lark twitters from the quiet skies.
Ib. xxxv. *Margaritæ Sororis*

22 Night with her train of stars
And her great gift of sleep. *Ib.*

23 So be my passing!
My task accomplished and the long day done,
My wages taken, and in my heart
Some late lark singing,
Let me be gathered to the quiet west,
The sundown splendid and serene,
Death. *Ib.*

24 Or ever the Knightly years were gone
With the old world to the grave,
I was a King in Babylon
And you were a Christian Slave.
Ib. xxxvii. *To W. A.*

25 What have I done for you,
  England, my England?
What is there I would not do,
  England, my own?
For England's Sake, iii. *Pro Rege Nostro*

26 Ever the faith endures,
  England, my England:—
'Take and break us: we are yours,
  England, my own!
Life is good, and joy runs high
Between English earth and sky;
Death is death; but we shall die
  To the Song on your bugles blown, England.' *Ib.*

27   Far in the stillness a cat
Languishes loudly. *In Hospital*, vii. *Vigil*

28 Much is she worth, and even more is made of her.
Ib. viii. *Staff Nurse: Old Style*

29 Valiant in velvet, light in ragged luck,
Most vain, most generous, sternly critical,
Buffoon and poet, lover and sensualist:
A deal of Ariel, just a streak of Puck,
Much Antony, of Hamlet most of all,
And something of the Shorter-Catechist. [Stevenson.]
Ib. xxv. *Apparition*

30 Gulls in an aery morrice. *Rhymes and Rhythms*, xi

HENRI IV
1553–1610

1 Je veux qu'il n'y ait si pauvre paysan en mon royaume qu'il n'ait tous les dimanches sa poule au pot.

I want there to be no peasant in my kingdom so poor that he is unable to have a chicken in his pot every Sunday.
> Hardouin de Péréfixe, *Hist. de Henry le Grand*, 1681

2 Pends-toi, brave Crillon; nous avons combattu à Arques et tu n'y étais pas.

Hang yourself, brave Crillon; we fought at Arques and you were not there.
> *Traditional form given by Voltaire to a letter of Henri to Crillon. Lettres missives de Henri IV, Collection des documents inédits de l'histoire de France*, vol. iv, 1847, p. 848

3 Paris vaut bien une messe.

Paris is well worth a mass.
> *Attr. either to Henry IV or to his minister Sully, in conversation with Henry. Caquets de l'Accouchée*, 1622

4 The wisest fool in Christendom.
> *Of James I of England. Remark attr. to Henry IV and Sully. The French is not known*

MATTHEW HENRY
1662–1714

5 Many a dangerous temptation comes to us in gay, fine colours, that are but skin-deep.
> *Commentaries, Genesis* III. i

6 The better day, the worse deed. *Ib.* vi

7 To their own second and sober thoughts.
> *Ib. Job* VI. xxix

8 He rolls it under his tongue as a sweet morsel.
> *Ib. Ps.* XXXVI. ii

9 They that die by famine die by inches.
> *Ib. Ps.* LIX. xv

10 Men of polite learning and a liberal education.
> *Ib. Acts* x. i

11 All this and heaven too. *Life of Philip Henry*, p. 70

O. HENRY [WILLIAM SYDNEY PORTER]
1862–1910

12 Life is made up of sobs, sniffles, and smiles, with sniffles predominating. *Gifts of the Magi*

13 'Little old New York's good enough for us'—that's what they sing. *A Tempered Wind*

14 The Four Million. *Title*

15 Turn up the lights, I don't want to go home in the dark.
> *Last words, quoting popular song.* C. A. Smith's *O. Henry*, ch. 9

PATRICK HENRY
1736–1799

16 Caesar had his Brutus—Charles the First, his Cromwell—and George the Third—('Treason,' cried the Speaker) . . . *may profit by their example. If this be treason, make the most of it.*
> *Speech in the Virginia Convention, 1765.* W. Wirt's *Patrick Henry* (1818), p. 65

17 I am not a Virginian, but an American.
> *Speech in the Virginia Convention, Sept. 1774*

18 I know not what course others may take; but as for me, give me liberty, or give me death!
> *Ib. 23 Mar. 1775.* W. Wirt's *Patrick Henry* (1818), p. 123.

PHILIP HENRY
1631–1696

19 They are not amissi, but praemissi.
[Not lost, but gone before.]
> Matthew Henry, *Life of Philip Henry*, ch. 5, ed. 1825, p. 111

HENRY II OF ENGLAND
1133–1189

20 Who will free me from this turbulent priest? [Becket.]
> *History books*

21 What a parcel of fools and dastards have I nourished in my house, that not one of them will avenge me of this one upstart clerk!
> K. Norgate, in *Dict. of Nat. Biog.*

HENRY VIII OF ENGLAND
1491–1547

22 [Anne of Cleves.] The King found her so different from her picture . . . that . . . he swore they had brought him a Flanders mare.
> Smollett, *Hist. of England* (ed. 3, 1759), vi. 68

23 This man hath the right sow by the ear.
> *Of Cranmer*

HERACLEITUS
fl. 513 B.C.

24 πάντα ῥεῖ, οὐδὲν μένει.

All is flux, nothing is stationary.
> *Alluded to by Aristotle in* De Caelo, 3. 1. 18 (ed. Weise) *and elsewhere*

SIR ALAN PATRICK HERBERT
1890–

25 Don't let's go to the dogs to-night,
For mother will be there. *Don't Let's Go to the Dogs*

26 Don't tell my mother I'm living in sin,
Don't let the old folks know:
Don't tell my twin that I breakfast on gin,
He'd never survive the blow.
> *Don't Tell My Mother*

27 I'm not a jealous woman, but I *can't* see what he sees in her,
I can't see *what* he sees in her, I can't see what he *sees* in her!
> *I Can't Think What He Sees in Her*

28 It may be life, but ain't it slow? *It May Be Life*

29 I wouldn't be too ladylike in love if I were you.
> *I Wouldn't Be Too Ladylike*

30 Let's stop somebody from doing something!
> *Let's Stop Somebody*

1 Let's find out what everyone is doing,
And then stop everyone from doing it.
Let's Stop Somebody

2 As my poor father used to say
In 1863,
Once people start on all this Art
Good-bye, moralitee!
And what my father used to say
Is good enough for me. *Lines for a Worthy Person*

3 This high official, all allow,
Is grossly overpaid.
There wasn't any Board; and now
There isn't any trade.
On the President of the Board of Trade

4 Saturday night!
Saturday night!
I want to make Hammersmith hum. *Saturday Night*

5 Harriet, Hi!
Light of my eye!
Come to the pictures and have a good cry,
For it's jolly old Saturday,
Mad-as-a-hatter-day,
Nothing-much-matter-day-night! *Ib.*

6 Well, fancy giving money to the Government!
Might as well have put it down the drain.
Fancy giving money to the Government!
Nobody will see the stuff again.
Well, they've no idea what money's for—
Ten to one they'll start another war.
I've heard a lot of silly things, but, Lor'!
Fancy giving money to the Government!
Too Much!

7 Holy Deadlock.
Title of a novel satirizing the Divorce Law

8 He didn't ought to come to bed in boots.
Riverside Nights

9 The Common Law of England has been laboriously
built about a mythical figure—the figure of 'The
Reasonable Man'. *Uncommon Law* (1935), p. 1

10 People must not do things for fun. We are not here
for fun. There is no reference to fun in any Act of
Parliament. *Ib.* p. 28

11 If elderly bishops were seen leaving the Athenaeum
with jugs of stout in their hands the casual observer would form an impression of the character
of that institution which would be largely unjust.
Ib. p. 33

12 *Counsel*: But is the jury to understand, Mr. Haddock,
that in your opinion the highbrow is necessarily of
the feminine gender?
Witness: Of course. It is one of the special diseases
of women. *Ib.* p. 50

13 The critical period in matrimony is breakfast-time.
Ib. p. 98

14 The Englishman never enjoys himself except for a
noble purpose. *Ib.* p. 198

15 For any ceremonial purposes the otherwise excellent
liquid, water, is unsuitable in colour and other
respects. *Ib.* p. 272

16 An Act of God was defined as *something which no
reasonable man could have expected. Ib.* p. 316

17 A dull speaker, like a plain woman, is credited with
all the virtues, for we charitably suppose that a surface so unattractive must be compensated by
interior blessings. *Ib.* p. 412

EDWARD HERBERT, BARON HERBERT OF CHERBURY

1583–1648

18 Now that the April of your youth adorns
The garden of your face.
Poems. Ditty: Now That the April

GEORGE HERBERT

1593–1633

19 The book of books, the storehouse and magazine of
life and comfort, the holy Scriptures.
A Priest to the Temple. ch. 4

20 I read, and sigh, and wish I were a tree—
For sure then I should grow
To fruit or shade; at least some bird would trust
Her household to me, and I should be just.
The Temple. Affliction

21 Ah, my dear God, though I am clean forgot,
Let me not love Thee, if I love Thee not. *Ib.*

22 How well her name an 'Army' doth present,
In whom the 'Lord of Hosts' did pitch His tent!
Ib. Anagram, Mary

23 Like summer-friends,
Flies of estates and sunshine. *Ib. The Answer*

24 Let all the world in ev'ry corner sing
My God and King.
The heav'ns are not too high,
His praise may thither fly;
The earth is not too low,
His praises there may grow.
Let all the world in ev'ry corner sing
My God and King.
The Church with psalms must shout,
No door can keep them out:
But above all, the heart
Must bear the longest part. *Ib. Antiphon*

25 Hearken unto a Verser, who may chance
Rhyme thee to good, and make a bait of pleasure:
A verse may find him who a sermon flies,
And turn delight into a sacrifice.
Ib. The Church Porch, i

26 Drink not the third glass—which thou canst not tame
When once it is within thee. *Ib.* v

27 Dare to be true: nothing can need a lie;
A fault, which needs it most, grows two thereby.
Ib. xiii

28 Chase brave employment with a naked sword
Throughout the world. *Ib.* xv

29 O England, full of sin, but most of sloth;
Spit out thy phlegm, and fill thy breast with glory.
Ib. xvi

30 Think the king sees thee still; for his King does.
Ib. xxi

31 Never was scraper brave man. Get to live;
Then live, and use it. *Ib.* xxvi

32 Wit's an unruly engine, wildly striking
Sometimes a friend, sometimes the engineer. *Ib.* xli

33 Towards great persons use respective boldness.
Ib. xliii

34 But love is lost, the way of friendship's gone,
Though David had his Jonathan, Christ his John.
Ib. xlvi

HERBERT

1 Be calm in arguing; for fierceness makes
Error a fault and truth discourtesy.
The Temple. The Church Porch, lii

2 Calmness is great advantage; he that lets
Another chafe, may warm him at his fire. *Ib.* liii

3   Who aimeth at the sky
Shoots higher much than he that means a tree.
Ib. lvi

4 Man is God's image; but a poor man is
Christ's stamp to boot. *Ib.* lxiv

5 Kneeling ne'er spoil'd silk stocking; quit thy state;
All equal are within the Church's gate. *Ib.* lxviii

6   O, be drest;
Stay not for th' other pin! Why, thou hast lost
A joy for it worth worlds. *Ib.* lxix

7 Judge not the preacher, for he is thy Judge;
If thou mislike him, thou conceiv'st him not:
God calleth preaching folly: do not grudge
To pick out treasures from an earthen pot:
The worst speaks something good; if all want sense,
God takes a text, and preacheth patience. *Ib.* lxxii

8 Look not on pleasures as they come, but go.
Ib. lxxvii

9 I struck the board, and cried, 'No more;
      I will abroad.'
What, shall I ever sigh and pine?
My lines and life are free; free as the road,
Loose as the wind, as large as store.
      Shall I be still in suit?
Have I no harvest but a thorn
To let me blood, and not restore
What I have lost with cordial fruit?
      Sure there was wine
Before my sighs did dry it; there was corn
Before my tears did drown it;
Is the year only lost to me?
Have I no bays to crown it? *Ib. The Collar*

10   Away! take heed;
      I will abroad.
Call in thy death's-head there, tie up thy fears;
      He that forbears
To suit and serve his need
      Deserves his load.
But as I rav'd and grew more fierce and wild
      At every word,
Methought I heard one calling, 'Child';
      And I replied, 'My Lord.' *Ib.*

11 SAVIOUR:
That as I did freely part
With my glory and desert,
Left all joys to feel all smart—
MAN:
Ah, no more: Thou break'st my heart. *Ib. Dialogue*

12 Throw away Thy rod,
Throw away Thy wrath;
      O my God,
Take the gentle path. *Ib. Discipline*

13 Love is swift of foot;
Love's a man of war,
      And can shoot,
And can hit from far. *Ib.*

14 I got me flowers to strew Thy way,
I got me boughs off many a tree;
But Thou wast up by break of day,
And brought'st Thy sweets along with Thee.
Ib. Easter Song

15 Teach me, my God and King,
In all things Thee to see,
And what I do in any thing
To do it as for Thee.

A man that looks on glass,
On it may stay his eye;
Or if he pleaseth, through it pass,
And then the heaven espy.
The Temple. The Elixir

16 A servant with this clause
Makes drudgery divine;
Who sweeps a room as for Thy laws
Makes that and th' action fine. *Ib.*

17 Oh that I were an orange-tree,
      That busy plant!
Then I should ever laden be,
      And never want
Some fruit for Him that dressed me. *Ib. Employment*

18 And now in age I bud again,
After so many deaths I live and write;
I once more smell the dew and rain,
And relish versing: O, my only Light,
      It cannot be
      That I am he
On whom Thy tempests fell all night.
Ib. The Flower

19 Death is still working like a mole,
And digs my grave at each remove. *Ib. Grace*

20 I made a posy while the day ran by;
Here will I smell my remnant out, and tie
      My life within this band;
But Time did beckon to the flow'rs, and they
By noon most cunningly did steal away,
      And wither'd in my hand. *Ib. Life*

21 Love bade me welcome; yet my soul drew back,
      Guilty of dust and sin.
But quick-ey'd Love, observing me grow slack
      From my first entrance in,
Drew nearer to me, sweetly questioning
      If I lack'd any thing. *Ib. Love*

22 'You must sit down,' says Love, 'and taste My meat.'
      So I did sit and eat. *Ib.*

23   For us the winds do blow,
The earth resteth, heav'n moveth, fountains flow;
      Nothing we see but means our good,
      As our delight or as our treasure;
The whole is either our cupboard of food
      Or cabinet of pleasure. *Ib. Man*

24 Oh mighty love! Man is one world, and hath
      Another to attend him. *Ib.*

25 King of glory, King of peace,
      I will love Thee;
And, that love may never cease,
      I will move Thee. *Ib. Praise*

26 Sev'n whole days, not one in seven,
      I will praise Thee;
In my heart, though not in heaven,
      I can raise Thee. *Ib.*

27 He would adore my gifts instead of Me,
And rest in Nature, not the God of Nature:
      So both should losers be. *Ib. The Pulley*

1 Yet let him keep the rest,
But keep them with repining restlessness;
Let him be rich and weary, that at least,
If goodness lead him not, yet weariness
    May toss him to My breast.
The Temple, The Pulley

2 My God, my verse is not a crown,
No point of honour, or gay suit,
No hawk, no banquet, or renown,
Nor a good sword, nor yet a lute. *Ib. The Quiddity*

3 But Thou shalt answer, Lord, for me. *Ib. The Quip*

4 But who does hawk at eagles with a dove?
Ib. The Sacrifice, xxiii

5 Lord, with what care Thou hast begirt us round!
Parents first season us; then schoolmasters
Deliver us to laws; they send us, bound
To rules of reason, holy messengers,
Pulpits and Sundays, sorrow dogging sin,
Afflictions sorted, anguish of all sizes,
Fine nets and stratagems to catch us in,
Bibles laid open, millions of surprises. *Ib. Sin*

6 Yet all these fences and their whole array
One cunning bosom sin blows quite away. *Ib.*

7 Grasp not at much, for fear thou losest all.
Ib. The Size

8 The Sundays of man's life,
Threaded together on Time's string,
Make bracelets to adorn the wife
Of the eternal glorious King:
On Sunday heaven's gate stands ope;
Blessings are plentiful and rife,
    More plentiful than hope. *Ib. Sunday*

9 Enrich my heart, mouth, hands in me,
With faith, with hope, with charity,
That I may run, rise, rest with Thee.
Ib. Trinity Sunday

10 The God of love my Shepherd is,
And He that doth me feed,
While He is mine, and I am His,
What can I want or need? *Ib. 23rd Psalm*

11 Lord, make me coy and tender to offend:
In friendship, first I think if that agree
    Which I intend
Unto my friend's intent and end;
I would not use a friend as I use Thee.
Ib. Unkindness

12 My friend may spit upon my curious floor;
Would he have gold? I lend it instantly;
    But let the poor,
And Thou within them, starve at door:
I cannot use a friend as I use Thee. *Ib.*

13 Sweet day, so cool, so calm, so bright,
The bridal of the earth and sky,
The dew shall weep thy fall to-night;
    For thou must die.
Sweet rose, whose hue angry and brave
Bids the rash gazer wipe his eye,
Thy root is ever in its grave,
    And thou must die.
Sweet spring, full of sweet days and roses,
A box where sweets compacted lie. *Ib. Virtue*

14 Only a sweet and virtuous soul,
Like season'd timber, never gives;
But though the whole world turn to coal,
    Then chiefly lives. *Ib.*

HERODOTUS
484–424? B.C.

15 οὐ φροντὶς Ἱπποκλείδη.

Hippocleides doesn't care. *Histories, vi. 129. 4*

ROBERT HERRICK
1591–1674

16 With thousand such enchanting dreams, that meet
To make sleep not so sound, as sweet.
*Hesperides. A Country Life: to his Brother,
M. Tho. Herrick*

17 I sing of brooks, of blossoms, birds, and bowers:
Of April, May, of June, and July-flowers.
I sing of May-poles, Hock-carts, wassails, wakes,
Of bride-grooms, brides, and of their bridal-cakes.
Ib. Argument of his Book

18 A little saint best fits a little shrine,
A little prop best fits a little vine,
As my small cruse best fits my little wine.
*Ib. A Ternary of Littles, upon a Pipkin of Jelly
sent to a Lady*

19 A little stream best fits a little boat;
A little lead best fits a little float;
As my small pipe best fits my little note.

A little meat best fits a little belly,
As sweetly, Lady, give me leave to tell ye,
This little pipkin fits this little jelly. *Ib.*

20 Fair pledges of a fruitful tree,
Why do ye fall so fast?
Your date is not so past;
But you may stay yet here a while,
To blush and gently smile;
And go at last. *Ib. Blossoms*

21 Cherry ripe, ripe, ripe, I cry,
Full and fair ones; come and buy:
If so be, you ask me where
They do grow? I answer, there,
Where my Julia's lips do smile;
There's the land, or cherry-isle. *Ib. Cherry Ripe*

22 What needs complaints
When she a place
Has with the race
    Of Saints?
In endless mirth,
She thinks not on
What's said or done
    In earth.
Ib. Comfort to a Youth that had Lost his Love

23 Nor do's she mind,
Or think on't now
That ever thou
    Wast kind. *Ib.*

24 Get up, get up for shame, the blooming morn
Upon her wings presents the god unshorn.
Ib. Corinna's Going a-Maying

25 Get up, sweet Slug-a-bed, and see
The dew bespangling herb and tree. *Ib.*

26 'Tis sin,
Nay, profanation to keep in. *Ib.*

27 Come, let us go, while we are in our prime;
And take the harmless folly of the time. *Ib.*

1 So when or you or I are made
A fable, song, or fleeting shade;
All love, all liking, all delight
Lies drown'd with us in endless night.
Then while time serves, and we are but decaying;
Come, my Corinna, come, let's go a-Maying.
Hesperides. Corinna's Going a-Maying

2 Fair daffodils, we weep to see
You haste away so soon:
As yet the early-rising sun
Has not attain'd his noon.
Stay, stay,
Until the hasting day
Has run
But to the even-song;
And, having pray'd together, we
Will go with you along.　*Ib. Daffodils*

3 We have short time to stay, as you,
We have as short a Spring;
As quick a growth to meet decay,
As you or any thing.　　　　*Ib.*

4 A sweet disorder in the dress
Kindles in clothes a wantonness:
A lawn about the shoulders thrown
Into a fine distraction:
An erring lace, which here and there
Enthrals the crimson stomacher:
A cuff neglectful, and thereby
Ribbands to flow confusedly:
A winning wave (deserving note)
In the tempestuous petticoat:
A careless shoe-string, in whose tie
I see a wild civility:
Do more bewitch me, than when Art
Is too precise in every part.　*Ib. Delight in Disorder*

5 Here a solemn Fast we keep,
While all beauty lies asleep
Husht be all things; (no noise here)
But the toning of a tear:
Or a sigh of such as bring
Cowslips for her covering.　*Ib. Epitaph upon a Virgin*

6 Only a little more
I have to write,
Then I'll give o'er,
And bid the world Good-night.
Ib. His Poetry his Pillar

7 O time that cut'st down all
And scarce leav'st here
Memorial
Of any men that were.　　　*Ib.*

8 Roses at first were white,
Till thy co'd not agree,
Whether my Sappho's breast,
Or they more white sho'd be.
Ib. How Roses Came Red.

9 'Twixt kings and tyrants there's this difference known;
Kings seek their subjects' good: tyrants their own.
Ib. Kings and Tyrants

10 You say, to me-wards your affection's strong;
Pray love me little, so you love me long.
Ib. Love me Little, Love me Long

11 Love is a circle that doth restless move
In the same sweet eternity of love.
Ib. Love What It Is

12 Night makes no difference 'twixt the Priest and Clerk;
Joan as my Lady is as good i' th' dark.
Hesperides. No Difference i' th' Dark

13 I do love I know not what;
Sometimes this, and sometimes that.
Ib. No Luck in Love

14 Made us nobly wild, not mad.
Ib. Ode for Ben Jonson

15 Out-did the meat, out-did the frolic wine.　*Ib.*

16 Fain would I kiss my Julia's dainty leg,
Which is as white and hairless as an egg.
Ib. On Julia's Leg

17 Men are suspicious; prone to discontent:
Subjects still loathe the present Government.
Ib. Present Government Grievous

18 The readiness of doing, doth express
No other, but the doer's willingness.　*Ib. Readiness*

19 Attempt the end, and never stand to doubt;
Nothing's so hard, but search will find it out.
Ib. Seek and Find

20 And once more yet (ere I am laid out dead)
Knock at a star with my exalted head.
Ib. The Bad Season Makes the Poet Sad

21 It is the end that crowns us, not the fight.
Ib. The End

22 Good morrow to the day so fair;
Good morning, Sir, to you:
Good morrow to mine own torn hair
Bedabbled with the dew.　*Ib. The Mad Maid's Song*

23 Her eyes the glow-worm lend thee,
The shooting-stars attend thee;
And the elves also,
Whose little eyes glow,
Like the sparks of fire, befriend thee.

No Will-o'-th'-Wisp mislight thee;
Nor snake, or slow-worm bite thee:
But on, on thy way
Not making a stay,
Since ghost there's none to affright thee.
Ib. The Night-Piece, to Julia

24 Praise they that will times past, I joy to see
My self now live: this age best pleaseth me.
Ib. The Present Time Best Pleaseth

25 Some ask'd how pearls did grow, and where?
Then spoke I to my girl,
To part her lips, and shew'd them there
The quarelets of pearl.
Ib. The Rock of Rubies, and the Quarry of Pearls

26 Now is the time, when all the lights wax dim;
And thou (Anthea) must withdraw from him
Who was thy servant.　*Ib. To Anthea: Now is the Time*

27 For my Embalming (Sweetest) there will be
No Spices wanting, when I'm laid by thee.　*Ib.*

28 Give me a kiss, and to that kiss a score;
Then to that twenty, add a hundred more:
A thousand to that hundred: so kiss on,
To make that thousand up a million.
Treble that million, and when that is done,
Let's kiss afresh, as when we first begun.
Ib. To Anthea: Ah, My Anthea

1 Bid me to live, and I will live
Thy Protestant to be:
Or bid me love, and I will give
A loving heart to thee.

A heart as soft, a heart as kind,
A heart as sound and free,
As in the whole world thou canst find,
That heart I'll give to thee.
*Hesperides. To Anthea, Who May Command Him
Anything*

2 Bid me to weep, and I will weep,
While I have eyes to see.   *Ib.*

3 Bid me despair, and I'll despair,
Under that cypress tree:
Or bid me die, and I will dare
E'en Death, to die for thee.   *Ib.*

4 Thou art my life, my love, my heart,
The very eyes of me:
And hast command of every part,
To live and die for thee.   *Ib.*

5 No marigolds yet closed are;
No shadows great appear.
Ib. To Daisies, not to Shut so Soon

6 Sweet, be not proud of those two eyes,
Which star-like sparkle in their skies.
Ib. To Dianeme

7 That ruby which you wear
Sunk from the tip of your soft ear
Will last to be a precious stone
When all your world of beauty's gone.   *Ib.*

8 I dare not ask a kiss;
I dare not beg a smile;
Lest having that, or this,
I might grow proud the while.

No, no, the utmost share
Of my desire, shall be
Only to kiss that air,
That lately kissed thee.   *Ib. To Electra*

9 He loves his bonds, who when the first are broke,
Submits his neck unto a second yoke. *Ib. To Love*

10 Gather ye rosebuds while ye may,
Old Time is still a-flying:
And this same flower that smiles to-day,
To-morrow will be dying.

The glorious lamp of Heaven, the sun,
The higher he's a getting;
The sooner will his race be run,
And nearer he's to setting.

That age is best, which is the first,
When youth and blood are warmer;
But being spent, the worse, and worst
Times, still succeed the former.

Then be not coy, but use your time;
And while ye may, go marry:
For having lost but once your prime,
You may for ever tarry.
Ib. To Virgins, to Make Much of Time

11 Welcome maids of honour,
You do bring
In the Spring;
And wait upon her.   *Ib. To Violets*

12 Her pretty feet
Like snails did creep
A little out, and then,
As if they started at bo-peep,
Did soon draw in agen.   *Hesperides. Upon her Feet*

13 Whenas in silks my Julia goes,
Then, then (methinks) how sweetly flows
That liquefaction of her clothes.

Next, when I cast mine eyes and see
That brave vibration each way free;
O how that glittering taketh me!
Ib. Upon Julia's Clothes

14 So smooth, so sweet, so silv'ry is thy voice,
As, could they hear, the damn'd would make no noise,
But listen to thee (walking in thy chamber)
Melting melodious words, to lutes of amber.
Ib. Upon Julia's Voice

15 Here a little child I stand,
Heaving up my either hand;
Cold as paddocks though they be,
Here I lift them up to Thee,
For a benison to fall
On our meat, and on us all. Amen.
Noble Numbers. Another Grace for a Child

16 Lord, Thou hast given me a cell
Wherein to dwell,
A little house, whose humble roof
Is weather-proof;
Under the spars of which I lie
Both soft, and dry.
Ib. A Thanksgiving to God for his House

17 A little buttery, and therein
A little bin,
Which keeps my little loaf of bread
Unchipt, unflead:
Some brittle sticks of thorn or briar
Make me a fire,
Close by whose living coal I sit,
And glow like it.   *Ib.*

18 When the artless doctor sees
No one hope, but of his fees,
And his skill runs on the lees;
Sweet Spirit, comfort me!

When his potion and his pill,
Has, or none, or little skill,
Meet for nothing, but to kill;
Sweet Spirit, comfort me!
Ib. His Litany to the Holy Spirit

19 In prayer the lips ne'er act the winning part,
Without the sweet concurrence of the heart.
Ib. The Heart

20 But, for Man's fault, then was the thorn,
Without the fragrant rose-bud, born;
But ne'er the rose without the thorn. *Ib. The Rose*

21 To work a wonder, God would have her shown,
At once, a bud, and yet a rose full-blown.
Ib. The Virgin Mary

22 If any thing delight me for to print
My book, 'tis this; that Thou, my God, art in't.
Ib. To God

JAMES HERVEY
1714–1758

1 E'en crosses from his sov'reign hand
Are blessings in disguise.
Works. Reflections on a Flower-Garden

HESIOD
c. 735 B.C.

2 πλέον ἥμισυ παντός.

The half is greater than the whole.
Works and Days, 40

JOHN HEYWOOD
1497?–1580?

3 All a green willow, willow;
All a green willow is my garland. *The Green Willow*

THOMAS HEYWOOD
d. 1650?

4 Seven cities warr'd for Homer, being dead,
Who, living, had no roof to shroud his head.
Hierarchie of the Blessed Angels

5 Pack, clouds, away, and welcome day,
With night we banish sorrow;
Sweet air blow soft, mount larks aloft
To give my Love good-morrow!
Pack, Clouds, Away, st. 1

6 A Woman Killed with Kindness. *Title of play*

EMILY HENRIETTA HICKEY
1845–1924

7 Beloved, it is morn!
A redder berry on the thorn,
A deeper yellow on the corn,
For this good day new-born:
Pray, Sweet, for me
That I may be
Faithful to God and thee.
Beloved, It Is Morn

WILLIAM EDWARD HICKSON
1803–1870

8 'Tis a lesson you should heed,
Try, try again.
If at first you don't succeed,
Try, try again. *Try and Try Again*

'DR. BREWSTER HIGLEY'
nineteenth century

9 Oh give me a home where the buffalo roam,
Where the deer and the antelope play,
Where seldom is heard a discouraging word
And the skies are not cloudy all day.
Home on the Range. (1873)

AARON HILL
1685–1750

10 Tender-handed stroke a nettle,
And it stings you for your pains;
Grasp it like a man of mettle,
And it soft as silk remains.
Verses Written on Window

ROWLAND HILL
1744–1833

11 He did not see any reason why the devil should have all the good tunes.
E. W. Broome, *Rev. Rowland Hill*, vii

ARTHUR CLEMENT HILTON
1851–1877

12 The papers they had finished lay
In piles of blue and white,
They answered everything they could,
And wrote with all their might,
But though they wrote it all by rote,
They did not write it right.
The Vulture and the Husbandman. After Lewis Carroll

HIPPOCRATES
c. 460–357 B.C.

13 ὁ βίος βραχύς, ἡ δὲ τέχνη μακρή.

The life so short, the craft so long to learn.
Aphorisms, I. i. Trans. by Chaucer

ADOLF HITLER
1889–1945

14 My patience is now at an end.
Speech, 26 Sept. 1938

15 It is the last territorial claim which I have to make in Europe. *Ib.*

PRINCE HOARE
1755–1834

16 The saucy Arethusa. *Song: The Arethusa*

THOMAS HOBBES
1588–1679

17 Geometry (which is the only science that it hath pleased God hitherto to bestow on mankind).
Leviathan, pt. i, ch. 4

18 The condition of man . . . is a condition of war of everyone against everyone. *Ib.*

19 Words are wise men's counters, they do but reckon with them, but they are the money of fools. *Ib.*

20 They that approve a private opinion, call it opinion; but they that mislike it, heresy: and yet heresy signifies no more than private opinion. *Ib.* ch. 11

21 No arts; no letters; no society; and which is worst of all, continual fear and danger of violent death; and the life of man, solitary, poor, nasty, brutish, and short. *Ib.* ch. 13

22 Force, and fraud, are in war the two cardinal virtues. *Ib.*

23 The Papacy is not other than the Ghost of the deceased Roman Empire, sitting crowned upon the grave thereof. *Ib.* pt. iv, ch. 47

24 Laughter is nothing else but sudden glory arising from some sudden conception of some eminency in ourselves, by comparison with the infirmity of others, or with our own formerly.
On Human Nature, ix. (1650)

1 He was wont to say that if he had read as much as other men, he should have known no more than other men.   Aubrey, *Life of Hobbes*

2 I am about to take my last voyage, a great leap in the dark.
     Last Words. Watkins, *Anecdotes of Men of Learning*

JOHN CAM HOBHOUSE, BARON BROUGHTON
1786–1869

3 When I invented the phrase 'His Majesty's Opposition' [Canning] paid me a compliment on the fortunate hit.   *Recollections of a Long Life*, ii, ch. 12

EDWARD WALLIS HOCH
1849–1925

4 There is so much good in the worst of us,
And so much bad in the best of us,
That it hardly becomes any of us
To talk about the rest of us.
     Good and Bad. Attr. to many other authors

RALPH HODGSON
1871–

5 'Twould ring the bells of Heaven
The wildest peal for years,
If Parson lost his senses
And people came to theirs,
And he and they together
Knelt down with angry prayers
For tamed and shabby tigers
And dancing dogs and bears,
And wretched, blind, pit ponies,
And little hunted hares.   *Poems. The Bells of Heaven*

6 See an old unhappy bull,
Sick in soul and body both.   *Ib. The Bull*

7 Eve, with her basket, was
Deep in the bells and grass,
Wading in bells and grass
Up to her knees,
Plucking a dish of sweet
Berries and plums to eat,
Down in the bells and grass
Under the trees.   *Ib. Eve*

8 Picture that orchard sprite,
Eve, with her body white,
Supple and smooth to her
Slim finger tips.   *Ib.*

9 But oh, the den of wild things in
The darkness of her eyes!   *Ib. The Gipsy Girl*

10 I did not pray him to lay bare
The mystery to me;
Enough the rose was heaven to smell,
And His own face to see.   *Ib. The Mystery*

11 Reason has moons, but moons not hers,
   Lie mirror'd on her sea,
Confounding her astronomers,
   But, O! delighting me.   *Ib. Reason Has Moons*

12 God loves an idle rainbow,
No less than labouring seas.   *Ib.*

13 I climbed a hill as light fell short,
And rooks came home in scramble sort,
And filled the trees and flapped and fought
And sang themselves to sleep.
     Poems. The Song of Honour

14 Hear flocks of shiny pleiades
Among the plums and apple trees
Sing in the summer day.   *Ib.*

15 When stately ships are twirled and spun
Like whipping tops and help there's none
And mighty ships ten thousand ton
Go down like lumps of lead.   *Ib.*

16 I stood upon that silent hill
And stared into the sky until
My eyes were blind with stars and still
I stared into the sky.   *Ib.*

17 Time, you old gypsy man,
   Will you not stay,
Put up your caravan
   Just for one day?   *Ib. Time, You Old Gypsy Man*

HEINRICH HOFFMAN
1809–1874

18 Augustus was a chubby lad;
Fat ruddy cheeks Augustus had:
And everybody saw with joy
The plump and hearty, healthy boy.
He ate and drank as he was told,
And never let his soup get cold.
But one day, one cold winter's day,
He screamed out, 'Take the soup away!
O take the nasty soup away!
I won't have any soup to-day.'
     Struwwelpeter. Augustus

19 Here is cruel Frederick, see!
A horrid wicked boy was he.   *Ib. Cruel Frederick*

20 The trough was full, and faithful Tray
   Came out to drink one sultry day;
He wagged his tail, and wet his lip.   *Ib.*

21 At this, good Tray grew very red,
And growled, and bit him till he bled.   *Ib.*

22 But good dog Tray is happy now;
He has no time to say 'Bow-wow!'
He seats himself in Frederick's chair
And laughs to see the good things there:
The soup he swallows, sup by sup—
And eats the pies and puddings up.   *Ib.*

23 Let me see if Philip can
Be a little gentleman;
Let me see, if he is able
To sit still for once at table.   *Ib. Fidgety Philip*

24 But fidgety Phil,
He won't sit still;
He wriggles
And giggles,
And then, I declare,
Swings backwards and forwards,
And tilts up his chair.   *Ib.*

25 It almost makes me cry to tell
What foolish Harriet befell.
     Ib. Harriet and the Matches

1 Now tall Agrippa lived close by—
So tall, he almost touch'd the sky;
He had a mighty inkstand, too,
In which a great goose-feather grew.
Struwwelpeter. The Inky Boys

2 Look at little Johnny there,
Little Johnny Head-In-Air! *Ib. Johnny Head-In-Air*

3 Silly little Johnny, look,
You have lost your writing-book! *Ib.*

4 The door flew open, in he ran,
The great, long, red-legged scissor-man.
Ib. The Little Suck-a-Thumb

5 'Ah!' said Mamma, 'I knew he'd come
To naughty little Suck-a-Thumb.' *Ib.*

6 He finds it hard, without a pair
Of spectacles, to shoot the hare.
The hare sits snug in leaves and grass,
And laughs to see the green man pass.
Ib. The Man Who Went Out Shooting

7 And now she's trying all she can,
To shoot the sleepy, green-coat man. *Ib.*

8 Help! Fire! Help! The Hare! The Hare! *Ib.*

9 The hare's own child, the little hare. *Ib.*

10 Anything to me is sweeter
Than to see Shock-headed Peter.
Ib. Shock-Headed Peter

JAMES HOGG
1770–1835

11 And hey, then, up go we.
Jacobite Relics of Scotland, i. 15. Title

12 Wha the deil hae we goten for a King
But a wee wee German lairdie?
And when we gade to bring him hame,
He was delving in his kail-yardie.
Ib. 83. The Wee, Wee German Lairdie

13 Listen a while, and I'll tell you a tale,
Of a new device of a Protestant Flail.
Ib. 324. The Protestant Flail

14 God bless our Lord the King!
God save our lord the king!
God save the king!
Make him victorious,
Happy, and glorious,
Long to reign over us:
God save the king! *Ib. ii. 50. God Save The King.*
(But see 6:13, 125:15, and Corrigenda)

15 We'll o'er the water, we'll o'er the sea,
We'll o'er the water to Charlie;
Come weel, come wo, we'll gather and go,
And live or die wi' Charlie.
Ib. 76. O'er the Water to Charlie

16 There grows a bonny brier bush in our kail yard.
Ib. 78. An You Be He

17 'Twas on a Monday morning,
Right early in the year,
That Charlie came to our town,
The young Chevalier.
And Charlie he's my darling,
My darling, my darling,
And Charlie he's my darling,
The young Chevalier.
Ib. 93. The Young Chevalier. (See also 360:15)

18 Cock up your beaver, and cock it fu' sprush;
We'll over the Border and gi'e them a brush;
There's somebody there we'll teach better behaviour.
Hey, Johnnie lad, cock up your beaver!
Jacobite Relics, ii. 127. Cock Up Your Beaver

19 Will you no come back again?
Better lo'ed you'll never be,
And will you no come back again?
Ib. 195. Will You No Come Back Again?

20 My love she's but a lassie yet. *Title of song*

21 Bonny Kilmeny gaed up the glen.
The Queen's Wake, ii. Kilmeny. Thirteenth Bard's Song, l. 1

22 Late, late in the gloamin' Kilmeny came hame!
Ib. l. 24

23 For Kilmeny had been she knew not where,
And Kilmeny had seen what she could not declare.
Ib. l. 38

HENRY FOX, FIRST BARON HOLLAND
1705–1774

24 If Mr. Selwyn calls again, shew him up; if I am alive I shall be delighted to see him; and if I am dead he would like to see me.
Last Words. J. H. Jesse, George Selwyn and his Contemporaries, 1844, vol. iii, p. 50

HENRY RICHARD VASSALL FOX, THIRD BARON HOLLAND
1733–1840

25 Nephew of Fox, and friend of Grey,—
Enough my meed of fame
If those who deign'd to observe me say
I injur'd neither name.
Memoir of Rev. Sydney Smith (1855), i. 334

SIR RICHARD HOLLAND
c. 1450

26 O Dowglas, O Dowglas,
tendir and trewe! *Buke of the Howlat, xxxi*

JOHN HAYNES HOLMES
1879–

27 The universe is not hostile, nor yet is it friendly. It is simply indifferent.
Sensible Man's View of Religion

OLIVER WENDELL HOLMES
1809–1894

28 Lean, hungry, savage anti-everythings.
Poems. A Modest Request

29 Sweet is the scene where genial friendship plays
The pleasing game of interchanging praise.
Ib. An After-Dinner Poem

30 Uncursed by doubt, our earliest creed we take;
We love the precepts for the teacher's sake.
Ib. A Rhymed Lesson (Urania)

31 And, when you stick on conversation's burrs,
Don't strew your pathway with those dreadful *urs*. *Ib.*

1 Man wants but little drink below,
But wants that little strong.
Poems: A Song of other Days. Parody on Goldsmith

2 Day hath put on his jacket, and around
His burning bosom buttoned it with stars.
Ib. Evening

3 We greet the monarch-peasant.
Ib. For the Burns Centennial Celebration

4 Wisdom has taught us to be calm and meek,
To take one blow, and turn the other cheek;
It is not written what a man shall do
If the rude caitiff smite the other too!
Ib. Non-Resistance

5 Ay, tear her tattered ensign down!
Long has it waved on high,
And many an eye has danced to see
That banner in the sky;
Beneath it rung the battle shout,
And burst the cannon's roar;—
The meteor of the ocean air
Shall sweep the clouds no more. *Ib. Old Ironsides*

6 Have you heard of the wonderful one-hoss shay,
That was built in such a logical way
It ran a hundred years to a day?
Ib. The Deacon's Masterpiece

7 A general flavor of mild decay. *Ib.*

8 When the last reader reads no more.
Ib. The Last Reader

9 Feels the same comfort while his acrid words
Turn the sweet milk of kindness into curds.
Ib. The Moral Bully

10 And silence, like a poultice, comes
To heal the blows of sound. *Ib. The Music Grinders*

11 Call him not old, whose visionary brain
Holds o'er the past its undivided reign.
For him in vain the envious seasons roll
Who bears eternal summer in his soul.
Ib. The Old Player

12 To be seventy years young is sometimes far more
cheerful and hopeful than to be forty years old.
On the Seventieth Birthday of Julia Ward Howe

13 Man has his will,—but woman has her way.
The Autocrat of the Breakfast-Table, ch. 1

14 I think I said, I can make it plain to Benjamin
Franklin here that there are at least six person-
alities distinctly to be recognized as taking part in
that dialogue between John and Thomas.

Three Johns. { 1. The real John; known only to
his Maker.
2. John's ideal John; never the
real one, and often very unlike
him.
3. Thomas' ideal John; never the
real John, nor John's John,
but often very unlike either.

Three Thomases. { 1. The real Thomas.
2. Thomas' ideal Thomas.
3. John's ideal Thomas.
Ib. ch. 3

15 Build thee more stately mansions, O my soul,
As the swift seasons roll!
Leave thy low-vaulted past!
Let each new temple, nobler than the last,
Shut thee from heaven with a dome more vast,
Till thou at length art free,
Leaving thine outgrown shell by life's unresting sea!
The Autocrat of the Breakfast Table, ch. 4. *The
Chambered Nautilus*

16 Boston State-House is the hub of the solar system.
You couldn't pry that out of a Boston man if you
had the tire of all creation straightened out for a
crowbar. *Ib. ch. 6*

17 The axis of the earth sticks out visibly through the
centre of each and every town or city. *Ib.*

18 The world's great men have not commonly been great
scholars, nor its great scholars great men. *Ib.*

19 His humid front the cive, anheling, wipes.
And dreams of erring on ventiferous ripes.
Ib. ch. 11. Aestivation

20 Depart,—be off,—excede,—evade,—erump! *Ib.*

21 Fate tried to conceal him by naming him Smith.
[Samuel Francis Smith.] *The Boys*

22 It is the province of knowledge to speak and it is the
privilege of wisdom to listen.
The Poet at the Breakfast Table, ch. 10

23 It is the folly of the world, constantly, which confounds
its wisdom.
The Professor at the Breakfast Table, ch. 1

24 A moment's insight is sometimes worth a life's experience. *Ib. ch. 10*

JOHN HOME
1722–1808

25 In the first days
Of my distracting grief, I found myself—
As women wish to be, who love their lords.
Douglas, I. 1

26 My name is Norval; on the Grampian hills
My father feeds his flocks; a frugal swain,
Whose constant cares were to increase his store.
Ib. II. 1

27 He seldom errs
Who thinks the worst he can of womankind.
Ib. III. iii

28 Like Douglas conquer, or like Douglas die. *Ib. v*

29 Bold and erect the Caledonian stood,
Old was his mutton and his claret good;
Let him drink port, the English statesman cried—
He drank the poison and his spirit died.
Lockhart, *Life of Scott,* IV, ch. v

HOMER
c. 900 B.C.

30 μῆνιν ἄειδε, θεά, Πηληϊάδεω Ἀχιλῆος
οὐλομένην, ἣ μυρί' Ἀχαιοῖς ἄλγε' ἔθηκε.
The wrath of Peleus' son, the direful spring
Of all the Grecian woes, O Goddess, sing!
Iliad, i. 1. Trans. by Pope

31 τὸν δ' ἀπαμειβόμενος.
To him in answer spake... *Ib. 84*

32 οἵη περ φύλλων γενεή, τοίη δὲ καὶ ἀνδρῶν.
As the generation of leaves, so is that of men.
Ib. vi. 146

HOMER—HOOD

1 αἰὲν ἀριστεύειν καὶ ὑπείροχον ἔμμεναι ἄλλων.

Always to be best, and distinguished above the rest. *Iliad*, vi. 208.

2 δακρυόεν γελάσασα.

Smiling through her tears. *Ib.* 484

3 εἷς οἰωνὸς ἄριστος, ἀμύνεσθαι περὶ πάτρης.

One omen is best, to fight in defence of one's country. *Ib.* xii. 243

4 ἄνδρα μοι ἔννεπε, Μοῦσα, πολύτροπον.

Tell me, Muse, of the man of many wiles. [Odysseus.] *Odyssey*, i. 1

5 πολλῶν δ' ἀνθρώπων ἴδεν ἄστεα καὶ νόον ἔγνω.

He saw the cities of many men, and knew their mind. *Ib.* 3

6 ὡς ἀπόλοιτο καὶ ἄλλος ὅτις τοιαῦτά γε ῥέζοι.

So perish all who do the like again. *Ib.* 47

7 βουλοίμην κ' ἐπάρουρος ἐὼν θητευέμεν ἄλλῳ
ἀνδρὶ παρ' ἀκλήρῳ, ᾧ μὴ βίοτος πολὺς εἴη,
ἢ πᾶσιν νεκύεσσι καταφθιμένοισιν ἀνάσσειν.

Rather would I, in the sun's warmth divine,
Serve a poor churl who drags his days in grief,
Than the whole lordship of the dead were mine.
Ib. xi. 489

WILLIAM HONE
1780–1842

8 A good lather is half the shave.
Every-Day Book, vol. i, 1269

9 John Jones may be described as 'one of the *has* beens.'
Ib. vol. ii, 820

THOMAS HOOD
1799–1845

10 When Eve upon the first of Men
The apple press'd with specious cant,
Oh! what a thousand pities then
That Adam was not Adamant! *A Reflection*

11 It was not in the winter
Our loving lot was cast! ·
It was the time of roses,
We plucked them as we passed!
Ballad: It Was Not in the Winter

12 One more Unfortunate,
Weary of breath,
Rashly importunate,
Gone to her death!

Take her up tenderly,
Lift her with care;
Fashion'd so slenderly,
Young, and so fair!

Look at her garments
Clinging like cerements. *The Bridge of Sighs*

13 Loving, not loathing. *Ib.*

14 All that remains of her
Now is pure womanly. *Ib.*

15 Past all dishonour,
Death has left on her
Only the beautiful. *Ib.*

16 Still, for all slips of hers,
One of Eve's family. *The Bridge of Sighs*

17 Was there a dearer one
Still, and a nearer one
Yet, than all other? *Ib*

18 Alas! for the rarity
Of Christian charity
Under the sun!
Oh! it was pitiful!
Near a whole city full,
Home had she none! *Ib*

19 Even God's providence
Seeming estranged. *Ib*

20 Mad from life's history,
Glad to death's mystery,
Swift to be hurl'd—
Anywhere, anywhere,
Out of the world! *Ib*

21 Picture it—think of it,
Dissolute man!
Lave in it, drink of it,
Then, if you can! *Ib*

22 Owning her weakness,
Her evil behaviour,
And leaving, with meekness,
Her sins to her Saviour! *Ib*

23 Our very hopes belied our fears,
Our fears our hopes belied—
We thought her dying when she slept,
And sleeping when she died! *The Death Bed*

24 Much study had made him very lean,
And pale, and leaden-ey'd.
The Dream of Eugene Aram

25 But Guilt was my grim Chamberlain
That lighted me to bed. *Ib*

26 Two stern-faced men set out from Lynn,
Through the cold and heavy mist;
And Eugene Aram walked between,
With gyves upon his wrist. *Ib*

27 Where folks that ride a bit of blood,
May break a bit of bone. *The Epping Hunt*, l. 99

28 O saw ye not fair Inez? *Fair Inez*

29 Ben Battle was a soldier bold,
And used to war's alarms:
But a cannon-ball took off his legs,
So he laid down his arms! *Faithless Nelly Gray*

30 For here I leave my second leg,
And the Forty-second Foot! *Ib*

31 The love that loves a scarlet coat
Should be more uniform. *Ib*

32 His death, which happen'd in his berth,
At forty-odd befell:
They went and told the sexton, and
The sexton toll'd the bell. *Faithless Sally Brown*

33 I remember, I remember,
The house where I was born,
The little window where the sun
Came peeping in at morn;
He never came a wink too soon,
Nor brought too long a day,
But now, I often wish the night
Had borne my breath away! *I Remember*

[252]

1 I remember, I remember,
The roses, red and white,
The vi'lets, and the lily-cups,
Those flowers made of light!
The lilacs where the robin built,
And where my brother set
The laburnum on his birthday,—
The tree is living yet!   *I Remember*

2 I remember, I remember,
The fir trees dark and high;
I used to think their slender tops
Were close against the sky:
It was a childish ignorance,
But now 'tis little joy
To know I'm farther off from heav'n
Than when I was a boy.   *Ib.*

3 He never spoils the child and spares the rod,
But spoils the rod and never spares the child.
The Irish Schoolmaster, xii

4 But evil is wrought by want of thought,
As well as want of heart!   *The Lady's Dream*

5 For that old enemy the gout
Had taken him in toe!   *Lieutenant Luff*

6 Alas! my everlasting peace
Is broken into pieces.   *Mary's Ghost*

7 And then, in the fulness of joy and hope,
Seem'd washing his hands with invisible soap,
In imperceptible water.
Miss Kilmansegg. Her Christening

8 There's Bardus, a six-foot column of fop,
A lighthouse without any light atop.
Ib. Her First Step

9 For one of the pleasures of having a rout,
Is the pleasure of having it over.   *Ib. Her Dream*

10 Home-made dishes that drive one from home.
Ib. Her Misery

11 No sun—no moon!
No morn—no noon
No dawn—no dusk—no proper time of day.   *No!*

12 No warmth, no cheerfulness, no healthful ease,
No comfortable feel in any member—
No shade, no shine, no butterflies, no bees,
No fruits, no flowers, no leaves, no birds,—
November!   *Ib.*

13 I saw old Autumn in the misty morn
Stand shadowless like Silence, listening
To silence.   *Ode: Autumn*

14 Not one of those self-constituted saints,
Quacks—not physicians—in the cure of souls.
Ode to Rae Wilson, l. 13

15 Dear bells! how sweet the sound of village bells
When on the undulating air they swim!
Now loud as welcomes! faint, now, as farewells!
Ib. l. 159

16 The shrill sweet lark.
The Plea of the Midsummer Fairies, xxx

17   The bird forlorn,
That singeth with her breast against a thorn.   *Ib.*

18 We will not woo foul weather all too soon,
Or nurse November on the lap of June.   *Ib.* xcii

19 She stood breast high amid the corn,
Clasp'd by the golden light of morn,
Like the sweetheart of the sun,
Who many a glowing kiss had won.   *Ruth*

20 Thus she stood amid the stooks,
Praising God with sweetest looks.   *Ib.*

21 Sure, I said, heav'n did not mean,
Where I reap thou shouldst but glean,
Lay thy sheaf adown and come,
Share my harvest and my home.   *Ib.*

22 With fingers weary and worn,
With eyelids heavy and red,
A woman sat, in unwomanly rags,
Plying her needle and thread—
Stitch! stitch! stitch!
In poverty, hunger, and dirt.   *The Song of the Shirt*

23 O! men with sisters dear,
O! men with mothers and wives!
It is not linen you're wearing out,
But human creatures' lives!   *Ib.*

24 Sewing at once, with a double thread,
A shroud as well as a shirt.   *Ib.*

25 Oh! God! that bread should be so dear,
And flesh and blood so cheap!   *Ib.*

26 No blessed leisure for love or hope,
But only time for grief!   *Ib.*

27 My tears must stop, for every drop
Hinders needle and thread!   *Ib.*

28 There is a silence where hath been no sound,
There is a silence where no sound may be,
In the cold grave—under the deep deep sea,
Or in wide desert where no life is found.
Sonnet. Silence

29 A wife who preaches in her gown,
And lectures in her night-dress!
The Surplice Question

30 Our hands have met, but not our hearts;
Our hands will never meet again.   *To a False Friend*

31 There are three things which the public will always
clamour for, sooner or later: namely, Novelty,
novelty, novelty.
Announcement of Comic Annual for 1836

32 The sedate, sober, silent, serious, sad-coloured sect.
[Quakers.]   *The Doves and the Crows*

33 'Extremes meet', as the whiting said with its tail in
its mouth.   *Ib.*

34 Holland . . . lies so low they're only saved by being
dammed.   *Up the Rhine. To Rebecca Page*

RICHARD HOOKER
1554?–1600

35 He that goeth about to persuade a multitude, that
they are not so well governed as they ought to be,
shall never want attentive and favourable hearers.
Ecclesiastical Polity, bk. i, § 1

36 Of Law there can be no less acknowledged, than that
her seat is the bosom of God, her voice the harmony of the world: all things in heaven and earth
do her homage, the very least as feeling her care,
and the greatest as not exempted from her power.
Ib. § xvi

1 Change is not made without inconvenience, even from worse to better.
Quoted by Johnson, as from Hooker, in the Preface to the 'English Dictionary'

ELLEN STURGIS HOOPER
1816–1841

2 I slept, and dreamed that life was Beauty;
I woke, and found that life was Duty. *Life a Duty*

HERBERT CLARK HOOVER
1874–

3 The American system of rugged individualism.
Campaign speech, New York, 22 Oct. 1928

4 Our country has deliberately undertaken a great social and economic experiment, noble in motive and far-reaching in purpose. [The Eighteenth Amendment, enacting Prohibition.]
Letter to Senator W. H. Borah, 28 Feb. 1928

ANTHONY HOPE [SIR ANTHONY HOPE HAWKINS]
1863–1933

5 Economy is going without something you do want in case you should, some day, want something you probably won't want. *The Dolly Dialogues, No. 12*

6 'You oughtn't to yield to temptation.'
'Well, somebody must, or the thing becomes absurd.'
Ib. No. 14

7 'Boys will be boys——'
'And even that . . . wouldn't matter if we could only prevent girls from being girls.' *Ib. No. 16*

8 'Bourgeois,' I observed, 'is an epithet which the riff-raff apply to what is respectable, and the aristocracy to what is decent.' *Ib. No. 17*

9 He is very fond of making things which he doesn't want, and then giving them to people who have no use for them. *Ib.*

10 I wish you would read a little poetry sometimes. Your ignorance cramps my conversation.
Ib. No. 22

11 I may not understand, but I am willing to admire.
Ib.

12 Good families are generally worse than any others.
Prisoner of Zenda, ch. 1

13 His foe was folly and his weapon wit.
Inscription on the tablet to W. S. Gilbert, Victoria Embankment, London (1915)

LAURENCE HOPE [ADELA FLORENCE NICOLSON]
1865–1904

14 Pale hands I loved beside the Shalimar,
Where are you now? Who lies beneath your spell?
Indian Love Lyrics. Pale Hands I Loved

15 Pale hands, pink-tipped, like lotus-buds that float
On those cool waters where we used to dwell,
I would have rather felt you round my throat
Crushing out life than waving me farewell. *Ib.*

16 Less than the dust beneath thy chariot wheel,
Less than the weed that grows beside thy door,
Less than the rust that never stained thy sword,
Less than the need thou hast in life of me,
Even less am I.
Indian Love Lyrics. Less than the Dust

GERARD MANLEY HOPKINS
1844–1889

17 Wild air, world-mothering air,
Nestling me everywhere.
The Blessed Virgin Compared to the Air We Breathe

18 Some candle clear burns somewhere I came by.
I muse at how its being puts blissful back
With yellowy moisture mild night's blear-all black,
Or to-fro tender trambeams truckle at the eye.
The Candle Indoors

19 Not, I'll not, carrion comfort, Despair, not feast on thee;
Not untwist—slack they may be—these last strands of man
In me or, most weary, cry *I can no more.* I can;
Can something, hope, wish day come, not choose not to be. *Carrion Comfort*

20 That night, that year
Of now done darkness I wretch lay wrestling with (my God!) my God. *Ib.*

21 Towery city and branchy between towers.
Duns Scotus' Oxford

22 Cuckoo-echoing, bell-swarmèd, lark-charmèd, rook-racked, river-rounded. *Ib.*

23 Didst fettle for the great grey drayhorse his bright and battering sandal! *Felix Randal*

24 The world is charged with the grandeur of God.
God's Grandeur

25 Because the Holy Ghost over the bent
World broods with warm breast and with ah! bright wings. *Ib.*

26 Elected Silence, sing to me
And beat upon my whorlèd ear,
Pipe me to pastures still and be
The music that I care to hear.
The Habit of Perfection

27 Palate, the hutch of tasty lust,
Desire not to be rinsed with wine:
The can must be so sweet, the crust
So fresh that come in fasts divine! *Ib.*

28 And you unhouse and house the Lord. *Ib.*

29 I have desired to go
Where springs not fail,
To fields where flies no sharp and sided hail
And a few lilies blow.

And I have asked to be
Where no storms come,
Where the green swell is in the havens dumb,
And out of the swing of the sea.
Heaven-Haven

30 What would the world be, once bereft
Of wet and of wildness? Let them be left,
O let them be left, wildness and wet;
Long live the weeds and the wilderness yet.
Inversnaid

1 **All**
Life death doe s end and each day dies with sleep.
No Worst ,There Is None

2 Glory be to God for dappled things. *Pied Beauty*

3 All things counter, original, spare, strange;
Whatever is fickle, freckled (who knows how?)
With swift, slow; sweet, sour; adazzle, dim;
He fathers-forth whose beauty is past change:
Praise him. *Ib.*

4 The glassy peartree leaves and blooms, they brush
The descending blue; that blue is all in a rush.
Spring

5 Look at the stars! look, look up at the skies!
O look at all the fire-folk sitting in the air!
The bright boroughs, the circle-citadels there!
The Starlight Night

6 Ah well! it is all a purchase, all is a prize.
Buy then! bid then!—What?—Prayer, patience, alms,
vows.
Look, look: a May-mess, like on orchard boughs!
Look! March-bloom, like on mealed-with-yellow
sallows!
These are indeed the barn; withindoors house
The shocks. This piece-bright paling shuts the
spouse
Christ home, Christ and his mother and all his
hallows. *Ib.*

7 I am all at once what Christ is, since he was what I
am, and
This Jack, joke, poor potsherd, patch, matchwood,
immortal diamond,
Is immortal diamond.
That Nature is a Heraclitean Fire

8 Thou art indeed just, Lord, if I contend
With thee; but, sir, so what I plead is just.
Why do sinners' ways prosper? and why must
Disappointment all I endeavour end?
Thou Art Indeed Just, Lord

9 Birds build—but not I build; no, but strain,
Time's eunuch, and not breed one work that wakes.
Mine, O thou lord of life, send my roots rain. *Ib.*

10 To What Serves Mortal Beauty? *Title*

11 I caught this morning morning's minion, kingdom of
daylight's dauphin, dapple-dawn-drawn Falcon.
The Windhover

12 The achieve of, the mastery of the thing! *Ib.*

JOSEPH HOPKINSON
1770-1842

13 Hail, Columbia! happy land!
Hail, ye heroes! heaven-born band! *Hail, Columbia!*

HORACE
65-8 B.C.

14 **Ut turpiter atrum**
Desinat in piscem mulier formosa superne.
Make what at the top was a beautiful woman have
ugly ending in a black fish's tail.
Ars Poetica, 4. Trans. by Wickham

15 'Pictoribus atque poetis
Quidlibet audendi semper fuit aequa potestas.'
Scimus, et hanc veniam petimusque damusque
vicissim.

'Poets and painters,' you say, 'have always had
an equal licence in daring invention.' We know
it: this liberty we claim for ourselves and give
again to others. *Ars Poetica*, 9

16 Inceptis gravibus plerumque et magna professis
Purpureus, late qui splendeat, unus et alter
Adsuitur pannus.
Often on a work of grave purpose and high promises
is tacked a purple patch or two to give an effect
of colour. *Ib. 14*

17 **Amphora coepit**
Institui: currente rota cur urceus exit?
It was a wine-jar that was to be moulded: as the
wheel runs round why does it come out a pitcher?
Ib. 21

18 **Brevis essel aboro,**
Obscuru s fio.
It is when I am struggling to be brief that I be-
come unintelligible. *Ib. 25*

19 Dixeris egregie notum si callida verbum
Reddiderit iunctura novum.
You may gain the finest effects in language by the
skilful setting which makes a well-known word
new. *Ib. 47*

20 Multa renascentur quae iam cecidere, cadentque
Quae nunc sunt in honore vocabula, si volet usus,
Quem penes arbitrium est et ius et norma loquendi.
Many a term which has fallen from use shall have
a second birth, and those shall fall tha tare now
in high honour, if so Usage shall will it, in whose
hands is the arbitrament, the right and rule of
speech. *Ib. 70*

21 Grammatici certant et adhuc sub iudice lis est.
Scholars dispute, and the case is still before the
courts. *Ib. 78*

22 Proicit ampullas et sesquipedalia verba.
Throws aside his paint-pots and his words a foot
and a half long. *Ib. 97*

23 **Si vis me flere, dolendum est**
Primum ipsi tibi.
If you wish to draw tears from me, you must first
feel pain yourself. *Ib. 102*

24 **Servetur ad imum**
Qualis ab incepto processerit, et sibi constet.
Difficile est proprie communia dicere.
See that it [a fresh character in a play] is kept to
the end such as it starts at the beginning and
is self-consistent. It is a hard task to treat what is
common in a way of your own. *Ib. 126*

25 Parturient montes, nascetur ridiculus mus.
Mountains will be in labour, the birth will be a
single laughable little mouse. *Ib. 139*

26 Dic mihi, Musa, virum, captae post tempora Troiae
Qui mores hominum multorum vidit et urbis.
Of him, my Muse, who, when Troy's ramparts fell,
Saw many cities and men's manners, tell. *Ib. 141*

27 Non fumum ex fulgore, sed ex fumo dare lucem
Cogitat.
His thought is not to give flame first and then
smoke, but from smoke to let light break out.
Ib. 143

1 Semper ad eventum festinat et in medias res
Non secus ac notas auditorem rapit.

He ever hastens to the issue, and hurries his hearers
into the midst of the story as if they knew it before. *Ars Poetica*, 148. Trans. by Wickham

2 Difficilis, querulus, laudator temporis acti
Se puero, castigator, censorque minorum.
Multa ferunt anni venientes commoda secum,
Multa recedentes adimunt.

Testy, a grumbler, inclined to praise the way the
world went when he was a boy, to play the critic
and censor of the new generation. The tide of
years as it rises brings many conveniences, as it
ebbs carries many away. *Ib.* 173

3 Ne pueros coram populo Medea trucidet.

You will not let Medea slay her boys before the
audience. *Ib.* 185

4 Quodcumque ostendis mihi sic, incredulus odi.

Anything that you thus thrust upon my sight, I
discredit and revolt at. *Ib.* 188

5 Nec deus intersit, nisi dignus vindice nodus
Inciderit.

Neither should a god intervene, unless a knot be-
falls worthy of his interference. *Ib.* 191

6 Vos exemplaria Graeca
Nocturna versate manu, versate diurna.

For yourselves, do you thumb well by night and
day Greek models. *Ib.* 268

7 Fungar vice cotis, acutum
Reddere quae ferrum valet exsors ipsa secandi.

So I will play the part of a whetstone which can
make steel sharp, though it has no power itself of
cutting. *Ib.* 304

8 Grais ingenium, Grais dedit ore rotundo
Musa loqui.

It was the Greeks who had at the Muse's hand
the native gift, the Greeks who had the utterance
of finished grace. *Ib.* 323

9 Omne tulit punctum qui miscuit utile dulci,
Lectorem delectando pariterque monendo.

He has gained every vote who has mingled profit
with pleasure by delighting the reader at once
and instructing him. *Ib.* 343

10 Indignor quandoque bonus dormitat Homerus.

But if Homer, usually good, nods for a moment,
I think it shame. *Ib.* 359

11 Ut pictura poesis.

As with the painter's work, so with the poet's.
Ib. 361

12 Mediocribus esse poetis
Non homines, non di, non concessere columnae.

To poets to be second-rate is a privilege which
neither men, nor gods, nor bookstalls ever allowed. *Ib.* 372

13 Tu nihil invita dices faciesve Minerva.

You will say nothing, do nothing, unless Minerva
pleases. *Ib.* 385

14 Nonumque prematur in annum.

Let it be kept quiet till the ninth year. *Ib.* 388

15 Solve senescentem mature sanus equum, ne
Peccet ad extremum ridendus et ilia ducat.

Be wise in time, and turn your horse out to grass
when he shows signs of age, lest he end in a ludi-
crous breakdown with straining flanks.
Epistles, i. i. 8. Trans. by Wickham

16 Nullius addictus iurare in verba magistri,
Quo me cumque rapit tempestas, deferor hospes.

I am not bound over to swear allegiance to any
master: where the wind carries me, I put into
port and make myself at home. *Ib.* 14

17 Virtus est vitium fugere, et sapientia prima
Stultitia caruisse.

To flee vice is the beginning of virtue, and the beginning of wisdom is to have got rid of folly.
Ib. 41

18 Hic murus aeneus esto,
Nil conscire sibi, nulla pallescere culpa.

Be this your wall of brass, to have no guilty secrets,
no wrong-doing that makes you turn pale. *Ib.* 60

19 Si possis recte, si non, quocumque modo rem.

Money by right means if you can, if not, by any
means, money. *Ib.* 66

20 Olim quod vulpes aegroto cauta leoni
Respondit referam: 'quia me vestigia terrent,
Omnia te adversum spectantia, nulla retrorsum.'

The wary fox in the fable answered the sick lion:
'Because I am frightened at seeing that all the
footprints point towards your den and none the
other way.' *Ib.* 73

21 Qui quid sit pulchrum, quid turpe, quid utile, quid
non,
Planius ac melius Chrysippo et Crantore dicit.

Who shows us what is fair, what is foul, what is
profitable, what not, more plainly and better than
a Chrysippus or a Crantor. *Ib.* ii. 3

22 Quidquid delirant reges plectuntur Achivi.

For every folly of their princes the Greeks feel the
scourge. *Ib.* 14

23 Rursus quid virtus et quid sapientia possit
Utile proposuit nobis exemplar Ulixen.

Again, of the power of virtue and of wisdom he has
given us a profitable example in Ulysses. *Ib.* 17

24 Nos numerus sumus et fruges consumere nati.

We are the ciphers, fit for nothing but to eat our
share of earth's fruits. *Ib.* 27

25 Dimidium facti qui coepit habet: sapere aude.

He who has begun his task has half done it. Have
the courage to be wise. *Ib.* 40

26 Ira furor brevis est.

Anger is a short madness. *Ib.* 62

27 Omnem crede diem tibi diluxisse supremum.
Grata superveniet quae non sperabitur hora.
Me pinguem et nitidum bene curata cute vises
Cum ridere voles Epicuri de grege porcum.

Hold for yourself the belief that each day that
dawns is your last: the hour to which you do not
look forward will be a pleasant surprise. If you
ask of myself, you will find me, whenever you
want something to laugh at, in good case, fat and
sleek, a true hog of Epicurus' herd. *Ib.* iv. 13

HORACE

1 Nil admirari prope res est una, Numici,
Solaque quae possit facere et servare beatum.

Nought to admire is perhaps the one and only
thing, Numicius, that can make a man happy and
keep him so. *Epistles*, I. vi. 1

2 Naturam expellas furca, tamen usque recurret.

If you drive nature out with a pitchfork, she will
soon find a way back. *Ib.* x. 24

3 Tamen illic vivere vellem,
Oblitusque meorum obliviscendus et illis.

Yet I could find it in my heart to live there, forgetting my friends and forgotten by them.
Ib. xi. 8

4 Caelum non animum mutant qui trans mare currunt,
Strenua nos exercet inertia: navibus atque
Quadrigis petimus bene vivere. Quod petis hic est,
Est Ulubris, animus si te non deficit aequus.

They change their sky, not their soul, who run
across the sea. We work hard at doing nothing:
we seek happiness in yachts and four-horse
coaches. What you seek is here—is at Ulubrae—
if an even soul does not fail you. *Ib.* 27

5 Concordia discors.
Harmony in discord. *Ib.* xii. 19

6 Principibus placuisse viris non ultima laus est.
Non cuivis homini contingit adire Corinthum.

To have found favour with leaders of mankind is
not the meanest of glories. It is not every one
that can get to Corinth. *Ib.* xvii. 35

7 Et semel emissum volat irrevocabile verbum.

A word once let out of the cage cannot be whistled
back again. *Ib.* xviii. 71

8 Nam tua res agitur, paries cum proximus ardet.

It is your own interest that is at stake when your
next neighbour's wall is ablaze. *Ib.* 80

9 Tu, dum tua navis in alto est,
Hoc age, ne mutata retrorsum te ferat aura.
Oderunt hilarem tristes tristemque iocosi.

For yourself, my friend, while your bark is on the
sea, give all heed lest the breeze shift and turn
your course back again. The gloomy hate the
cheerful, the mirthful the gloomy. *Ib.* 87

10 Fallentis semita vitae.
The untrodden paths of life. *Ib.* 103

11 Sit mihi quod nunc est, etiam minus, et mihi vivam
Quod superest aevi, si quid superesse volunt di;
Sit bona librorum et provisae frugis in annum
Copia, neu fluitem dubiae spe pendulus horae.
Sed satis est orare Iovem qui ponit et aufert,
Det vitam, det opes: aequum mi animum ipse parabo.

Give me what I have, or even less; and therewith
let me live to myself for what remains of life,
if the gods will that anything remain. Let me
have a generous supply of books and of food
stored a year ahead; nor let me hang and tremble
on the hope of the uncertain hour. Nay, it is
enough to ask Jove, who gives them and takes
them away, that he grant life and subsistence; a
balanced mind I will find for myself. *Ib.* 107

12 Prisco si credis, Maecenas docte, Cratino,
Nulla placere diu nec vivere carmina possunt
Quae scribuntur aquae potoribus.

You know, Maecenas, as well as I, that, if you
trust old Cratinus, no poems can please long,
nor live, which are written by water-drinkers.
Epistles, I. xix. 1

13 O imitatores, servum pecus.
O imitators, you slavish herd. *Ib.* 19

14 Graecia capta ferum victorem cepit et artes
Intulit agresti Latio.

When Greece had been enslaved she made a slave
of her rough conqueror, and introduced the arts
into Latium, still rude. *Ib.* II. i. 156

15 Si foret in terris, rideret Democritus.

If he were on earth, Democritus would laugh at
the sight. *Ib.* 194

16 Atque inter silvas Academi quaerere verum.

And seek for truth in the garden of Academus.
Ib. ii. 45

17 Singula de nobis anni praedantur euntes.

Years as they pass plunder us of one thing after
another. *Ib.* 55

18 Multa fero, ut placem genus irritabile vatum.

I have to submit to much in order to pacify the
sensitive race of poets. *Ib.* 102

19 At qui legitimum cupiet fecisse poema,
Cum tabulis animum censoris sumet honesti.

But the man who shall desire to leave behind him
a poem true to the laws of art, when he takes
his tables to write will take also the spirit of an
honest censor. *Ib.* 109

20 Obscurata diu populo bonus eruet atque
Proferet in lucem speciosa vocabula rerum,
Quae priscis memorata Catonibus atque Cethegis
Nunc situs informis premit et deserta vetustas.

Phrases of beauty that have been lost to popular
view he will kindly disinter and bring into the
light, phrases which, though they were on the
lips of a Cato and a Cethegus of old time, now
lie uncouth because out of fashion and disused
because old. *Ib.* 115

21 Quid te exempta iuvat spinis de pluribus una?
Vivere si recte nescis, decede peritis.
Lusisti satis, edisti satis atque bibisti:
Tempus abire tibi est.

How does it relieve you to pluck one thorn out of
many? If you do not know how to live aright,
make way for those who do. You have played
enough, have eaten and drunk enough. It is time
for you to leave the scene. *Ib.* 212

22 Beatus ille, qui procul negotiis,
Ut prisca gens mortalium,
Paterna rura bubus exercet suis,
Solutus omni faenore.

Happy the man who far from schemes of business,
like the early generations of mankind, ploughs
and ploughs again his ancestral land with oxen
of his own breeding, with no yoke of usury on
his neck! *Epodes*, ii. 1. Trans. by Wickham

23 Maecenas atavis edite regibus,
O et praesidium et dulce decus meum.

Maecenas, in lineage the child of kings, but oh! to
me, my protector, pride, and joy.
Odes, I. i. 1. Trans. by Wickham

[257]

1 Indocilis pauperiem pati.

To be content without wealth he finds too hard a lesson. *Odes*, I. i. 18

2 Quodsi me lyricis vatibus inseres,
Sublimi feriam sidera vertice.

But if you give me a place among the bards of the lyre, I shall lift my head till it strikes the stars. *Ib.* 35

3 Audiet pugnas vitio parentum
Rara iuventus.

How they fought shall be told to a young generation scant in number for their parents' crimes. *Ib.* ii. 23

4 Animae dimidium meae.

The half of my own life. *Ib.* iii. 8

5 Illi robur et aes triplex
Circa pectus erat, qui fragilem truci
Commisit pelago ratem
Primus.

His heart was mailed in oak and triple brass who was the first to commit a frail bark to the rough seas. *Ib.* 9

6 Audax omnia perpeti
Gens humana ruit per vetitum nefas.

In its boldness to bear and to dare all things, the race of man rushes headlong into sin, despite of law. *Ib.* 25

7 Nil mortalibus ardui est.

No height is too arduous for mortal men. *Ib.* 37

8 Pallida Mors aequo pulsat pede pauperum tabernas
Regumque turris.

Pale Death with impartial foot knocks at the doors of poor men's hovels and of kings' palaces. *Ib.* iv. 13

9 Vitae summa brevis spem nos vetat incohare longam.

Life's short span forbids us to enter on far-reaching hopes. *Ib.* 15

10 Quis multa gracilis te puer in rosa
Perfusus liquidis urget odoribus
Grato, Pyrrha, sub antro?
Cui flavam religas comam,
Simplex munditiis?

What delicate stripling is it, Pyrrha, that now, steeped in liquid perfumes, is wooing thee on the heaped rose-leaves in some pleasant grot? For whose eyes dost thou braid those flaxen locks, so trim, so simple? *Ib.* v. 1

11 Nil desperandum Teucro duce et auspice Teucro.

No lot is desperate under Teucer's conduct and Teucer's star. *Ib.* vii. 27

12 Cras ingens iterabimus aequor.

To-morrow we set out once more upon the boundless sea. *Ib.* 32

13 Permitte divis cetera.

All else leave to the gods. *Ib.* ix. 9

14 Quid sit futurum cras fuge quaerere et
Quem Fors dierum cumque dabit lucro
Appone.

What shall be to-morrow, think not of asking. Each day that Fortune gives you, be it what it may, set down for gain. *Ib.* 13

15 Donec virenti canities abest
Morosa.

So long as youth is green and testy old age is far off. *Odes*, I. ix. 17

16 Tu ne quaesieris, scire nefas.

Pray, ask not,—such knowledge is not for us. *Ib.* xi. 1

17 Dum loquimur, fugerit invida
Aetas: carpe diem, quam minimum credula postero.

Even while we speak, Time, the churl, will have been running. Snatch the sleeve of to-day and trust as little as you may to to-morrow. *Ib.* 7

18 Velut inter ignis
Luna minores.

As shines the moon among the lesser fires. *Ib.* xii. 47

19 Felices ter et amplius
Quos irrupta tenet copula nec malis
Divulsus querimoniis
Suprema citius solvet amor die.

Thrice happy they, and more than thrice, whom an unbroken bond holds fast, and whom love, never torn asunder by foolish quarrellings, will not loose till life's last day! *Ib.* xiii. 17

20 O matre pulchra filia pulchrior.

O fairer daughter of a fair mother. *Ib.* xvi. 1

21 Mater saeva Cupidinum.

The imperious mother of Loves. *Ib.* xix. 1

22 Integer vitae scelerisque purus.

He that is unstained in life and pure from guilt. *Ib.* xxii. 1

23 Dulce ridentem Lalagen amabo,
Dulce loquentem.

Still shall I love Lalage and her sweet laughter, Lalage and her sweet prattle. *Ib.* 23

24 Quis desiderio sit pudor aut modus
Tam cari capitis?

What shame or measure should there be in grief for one so dear? *Ib.* xxiv. 1

25 Multis ille bonis flebilis occidit.

Many a good man may weep for his death. *Ib.* 9

26 Durum: sed levius fit patientia
Quidquid corrigere est nefas.

'Tis hard. But what may not be altered is made lighter by patience. *Ib.* 19

27 Parcus deorum cultor et infrequens.

A grudging and infrequent worshipper of the gods. *Ib.* xxxiv. 1

28 Nunc est bibendum, nunc pede libero
Pulsanda tellus.

Now we must drink, now beat the earth with free step. *Ib.* xxxvii. 1

29 Persicos odi, puer, apparatus.

Persian luxury, boy, I hate. *Ib.* xxxviii. 1

30 Mitte sectari, rosa quo locorum
Sera moretur.

Cease your efforts to find where the last rose lingers. *Ib.* 3

HORACE

1
> Incedis per ignis
> Suppositos cineri doloso.
>> You tread over fires hidden under a treacherous
>> crust of ashes. *Odes*, II. i. 7

2 Crescit indulgens sibi dirus hydrops.
>> The dread dropsy grows by indulging itself.
>> *Ib.* ii. 13

3 Aequam memento rebus in arduis
> Servare mentem.
>> Remember when life's path is steep to keep your
>> mind even. *Ib.* iii. 1

4 Omnes eodem cogimur.
>> We all are driven one road. *Ib.* 25

5 Ille terrarum mihi praeter omnis
> Angulus ridet.
>> That nook of earth's surface has a smile for me be-
>> fore all other places. *Ib.* vi. 13

6 Auream quisquis mediocritatem
> Diligit.
>> Whoso loves well the golden mean. *Ib.* x. 5

7 Sperat infestis, metuit secundis
> Alteram sortem bene praeparatum
> Pectus.
>> The heart that is well forearmed hopes when times
>> are adverse, and when they are favourable fears,
>> a change of fortune. *Ib.* 13

8
> Neque semper arcum
> Tendit Apollo.
>> Nor keeps Apollo his bow for ever strung. *Ib.* 19

9 Eheu fugaces, Postume, Postume,
> Labuntur anni.
>> Ah me, Postumus, Postumus, the fleeting years
>> are slipping by. *Ib.* xiv. 1

10
> Domus et placens
> Uxor.
>> House and wife of our choice. *Ib.* 21

11
> Nihil est ab omni
> Parte beatum.
>> No lot is happy on all sides. *Ib.* xvi. 27

12
> Credite posteri.
>> Believe it, after-years! *Ib.* xix. 2

13 Compesce clamorem ac sepulcri
> Mitte supervacuos honores.
>> Check all cries, and let be the meaningless honours
>> of the tomb. *Ib.* xx.-23

14 Odi profanum vulgus et arceo;
> Favete linguis; carmina non prius
> Audita Musarum sacerdos
> Virginibus puerisque canto.
>> I hate the uninitiate crowd and bid them avaunt.
>> Listen all in silence! Strains unheard before I,
>> the Muses' hierophant, now chant to maidens
>> and to boys. *Ib.* III. i. 1

15 Omne capax movet urna nomen.
>> Every name alike is shaken in her roomy urn. *Ib.* 16

16 Post equitem sedet atra Cura.
>> Black Care mounts on the horseman's pillion.
>> *Ib.* 40

17 Cur valle permutem Sabina
> Divitias operosiores?
>> Why should I exchange my Sabine valley for
>> wealth which adds to trouble? *Odes*, III. i. 47

18 Dulce et decorum est pro patria mori.
>> To die for fatherland is a sweet thing and be-
>> coming. *Ib.* ii. 13

19 Virtus repulsae nescia sordidae
> Intaminatis fulget honoribus,
> Nec sumit aut ponit securis
> Arbitrio popularis aurae.
>> Virtue, which cannot know the disgrace of rejection,
>> shines bright with honours that have no stain on
>> them, nor takes nor resigns the rods at the shift-
>> ing breath of the people's pleasure. *Ib.* 17

20 Raro antecedentem scelestum
> Deseruit pede Poena claudo.
>> Rarely has Punishment, though halt of foot, left
>> the track of the criminal in the way before her.
>> *Ib.* 31

21 Iustum et tenacem propositi virum
> Non civium ardor prava iubentium,
> Non vultus instantis tyranni
> Mente quatit solida.
>> The just man and firm of purpose not the heat of
>> fellow citizens clamouring for what is wrong,
>> nor presence of threatening tyrant can shake in
>> his rocklike soul. *Ib.* iii. 1

22 Si fractus illabatur orbis,
> Impavidum ferient ruinae.
>> If the round sky should crack and fall upon him,
>> the wreck will strike him fearless still. *Ib.* 7

23 Aurum irrepertum et sic melius situm.
>> The gold unfound, and so the better placed. *Ib.* 49

24 Non hoc iocosae conveniet lyrae:
> Quo, Musa, tendis?
>> This will not suit a mirthful lyre. Whither away,
>> my Muse? *Ib.* 69

25 Auditis an me ludit amabilis
> Insania?
>> Do you hear it? Or is it a delightful madness that
>> makes sport of me? *Ib.* iv. 5

26 Non sine dis animosus infans.
>> A brave babe, surely, and some god's special care.
>> *Ib.* 20

27 Fratresque tendentes opaco
> Pelion imposuisse Olympo.
>> The brothers who strove to leave Pelion set on the
>> top of leafy Olympus. *Ib.* 51

28 Vis consili expers mole ruit sua.
>> Force without mind falls by its own weight.
>> *Ib.* 65

29 O magna Carthago, probrosis
> Altior Italiae ruinis!
>> O mighty Carthage, lifted higher for the shameful
>> downfall of Italy! *Ib.* v. 39

30 Delicta maiorum immeritus lues.
>> For the sins of your sires albeit you had no hand
>> in them, you must suffer. *Ib.* vi. 1

1 Aetas parentum peior avis tulit
  Nos nequiores, mox daturos
    Progeniem vitiosiorem.

  Our sires' age was worse than our grandsires'.
  We their sons are more worthless than they: so
  in our turn we shall give the world a progeny
  yet more corrupt.   *Odes*, III. vi. 46

2 Docte sermones utriusque linguae.

  Learned . . . in the lore of either tongue.
                                   Ib. viii. 5

3 Donec gratus eram tibi.

  So long as I found favour in your sight.   *Ib.* ix. 1

4 Tecum vivere amem, tecum obeam libens.

  With you I should love to live, with you be ready
  to die.   *Ib.* 24

5 Splendide mendax et in omne virgo
  Nobilis aevum.

  With glorious falsehood . . ., a maid famous to
  all time.   *Ib.* xi. 35

6 Miserarum est neque amori dare ludum neque dulci
  Mala vino lavere.

  Poor maidens! who may neither let love have his
  way, nor wash away their troubles in sweet wine.
                                   Ib. xii. 1

7 O fons Bandusiae splendidior vitro.

  O spring of Bandusia, more brilliant than glass.
                                   Ib. xiii. 1

8 Non ego hoc ferrem calidus iuventa
  Consule Planco.

  I should not have borne it in my youth's hot blood
  when Plancus was consul.   *Ib.* xiv. 27

9 Magnas inter opes inops.

  A pauper in the midst of wealth.   *Ib.* xvi. 28

10 O nata mecum consule Manlio
   . . . pia testa.

  O born with me when Manlius was consul, . . .
  my gentle wine-jar.   *Ib.* xxi. 1

11   Quid leges sine moribus
   Vanae proficiunt?

  What profit laws, which without lives are empty?
                                   Ib. xxiv. 35

12 Vixi puellis nuper idoneus
   Et militavi non sine gloria;
   Nunc arma defunctumque bello
     Barbiton hic paries habebit.

  Though that life is past, I was but now still meet
  for ladies' love, and fought my battles not without
  glory. Now my armour and the lute, whose campaigns are over, will hang here on yonder wall.
                                   Ib. xxvi. 1

13 Fumum et opes strepitumque Romae.

  The smoke, and the grandeur and the noise . . .
  of Rome.   *Ib.* xxix. 12

14   Ille potens sui
   Laetusque deget, cui licet in diem
   Dixisse 'vixi: cras vel atra
     Nube polum Pater occupato
   Vel sole puro'.

  He will through life be master of himself and a
  happy man who from day to day can have said,
  'I have lived: to-morrow the Sire may fill the
  sky with black clouds or with cloudless sunshine.'
                          Odes, III. xxix. 41

15 Exegi monumentum aere perennius.

  My work is done, the memorial more enduring than
  brass.   *Ib.* xxx. 1

16 Non omnis moriar.

  I shall not all die.   *Ib.* 6

17 Non sum qualis eram bonae
   Sub regno Cinarae. Desine, dulcium
     Mater saeva Cupidinum.

  I am other than I was when poor Cinara was queen.
  Try no more, 'imperious mother of sweet loves'.
                          Ib. IV. i. 3. (*Cf. 258:21*)

18   Numerisque fertur
   Lege solutis.

  As he [Pindar] pours along in lawless rhythms.
                                   Ib. ii. 11

19 Quod spiro et placeo, si placeo, tuum est.

  Breath of song and power to please, if please I
  may, are alike of thee.   *Ib.* iii. 24

20 Fortes creantur fortibus et bonis.

  Gallant sons spring from the gallant and good.
                                   Ib. iv. 29

21 Duris ut ilex tonsa bipennibus
   Nigrae feraci frondis in Algido,
   Per damna, per caedis, ab ipso
     Ducit opes animumque ferro.

  Like the holm-oak shorn by ruthless axes on Al-
  gidus where black leaves grow thick, through
  loss, through havoc, from the very edge of the
  steel draws new strength and heart.   *Ib.* 57

22 Merses profundo: pulchrior evenit.

  Plunge it in the depth—it comes forth the fairer.
                                   Ib. 65

23   Occidit, occidit
   Spes omnis et fortuna nostri
     Nominis Hasdrubale interempto.

  Fallen, fallen is all our hope and the fortune of
  our name in the death of Hasdrubal.   *Ib.* 70

24 Diffugere nives, redeunt iam gramina campis
   Arboribusque comae.

  The snows have scattered and fled; already the
  grass comes again in the fields and the leaves on
  the trees.   *Ib.* vii. 1

25 Immortalia ne speres, monet annus et almum
   Quae rapit hora diem.

  That you hope for nothing to last for ever, is the
  lesson of the revolving year and of the flight of
  time which snatches from us the sunny days.
                                   Ib. 7

26 Damna tamen celeres reparant caelestia lunae:
     Nos ubi decidimus
   Quo pater Aeneas, quo Tullus dives et Ancus,
     Pulvis et umbra sumus.

  Yet change and loss in the heavens the swift moons
  make up again. For us, when we have descended
  where is father Aeneas, where are rich old Tullus
  and Ancus, we are but some dust and a shadow.
                                   Ib. 13

HORACE

1 Dignum laude virum Musa vetat mori.

The hero who is worthy of her praise the Muse will not let die. *Odes*, IV. viii. 28

2 Vixere fortes ante Agamemnona
Multi; sed omnes illacrimabiles
Urgentur ignotique longa
Nocte, carent quia vate sacro.

Gallant heroes lived before Agamemnon, not a few; but on all alike, unwept and unknown, eternal night lies heavy because they lack a sacred poet. *Ib.* ix. 25

3 Quotiens bonus atque fidus
Iudex honestum praetulit utili.

So often as, on a judgement-seat, generous and leal, he has set honour before expediency. *Ib.* 40

4 Non possidentem multa vocaveris
Recte beatum: rectius occupat
Nomen beati, qui deorum
Muneribus sapienter uti
Duramque callet pauperiem pati
Peiusque leto flagitium timet.

It is not the possessor of many things whom you will rightly call happy. The name of the happy man is claimed more justly by him who has learnt the art wisely to use what the gods give, and who can endure the hardships of poverty, who dreads disgrace as something worse than death. *Ib.* 45

5 Misce stultitiam consiliis brevem:
Dulce est desipere in loco.

Mix with your sage counsels some brief folly. In due place to forget one's wisdom is sweet. *Ib.* xii. 27

6 Qui fit, Maecenas, ut nemo, quam sibi sortem
Seu ratio dederit seu fors obiecerit, illa
Contentus vivat, laudet diversa sequentes?

How comes it, Maecenas, that, whether it be self-chosen or flung to him by chance, every one is discontented with his own lot and keeps his praises for those who tread some other path? *Satires*, I. i. 1. Trans. by Wickham

7 Quamquam ridentem dicere verum
Quid vetat? Ut pueris olim dant crustula blandi
Doctores, elementa velint ut discere prima.

And yet, why may one not be telling truth while one laughs, as teachers sometimes give little boys cakes to coax them into learning their letters? *Ib.* 24

8 Mutato nomine de te
Fabula narratur.

Change but the name, and it is of yourself that tale is told. *Ib.* 69

9 Est modus in rebus, sunt certi denique fines,
Quos ultra citraque nequit consistere rectum.

There is measure in everything. There are fixed limits beyond which and short of which right cannot find resting-place. *Ib.* 106

10 Hoc genus omne.

All their kith and kin. *Ib.* ii. 2

11 At ingenium ingens
Inculto latet hoc sub corpore.

But under that uncouth outside are hidden vast gifts of mind. *Satires*, I. iii. 33

12 Stans pede in uno.

Without effort. *Ib.* iv. 10

13 Faenum habet in cornu.

He carries hay on his horns. *Ib.* 34

14 Etiam disiecti membra poetae.

Even in his dismembered state, the limbs of a poet. *Ib.* 62

15 Hic niger est, hunc tu, Romane, caveto.

That man is black at heart: mark and avoid him, if you are a Roman indeed. *Ib.* 85

16 Ad unguem
Factus homo.

The pink of accomplishment. *Ib.* v. 32

17 Credat Iudaeus Apella,
Non ego.

Apella the Jew must believe it, not I. *Ib.* 100

18 Naso suspendis adunco
Ignotos.

Hang on the crook of your nose those of unknown origin. *Ib.* vi. 5

19 Sic me servavit Apollo.

So Apollo bore me from the fray. *Ib.* ix. 78

20 Satis est equitem mihi plaudere, ut audax
Contemptis aliis explosa Arbuscula dixit.

It is enough for me if the knights applaud—I care not a fig for the rest of the house.
[The actress Arbuscula, as she was being hissed from the stage.] *Ib.* x. 76

21 Solventur risu tabulae, tu missus abibis.

In a tempest of laughter the Tables will go to pieces. You will leave the court without a stain on your character. *Ib.* II. i. 86

22 Nec meus hic sermo est, sed quae praecepit Ofellus
Rusticus, abnormis sapiens crassaque Minerva.

This is no talk of my own, but the teaching of Ofellus, the countryman, a philosopher, though not from the schools, but of home-spun wit. *Ib.* ii. 2

23 Par nobile fratrum.

A noble pair of brothers. *Ib.* iii. 243

24 Hoc erat in votis: modus agri non ita magnus,
Hortus ubi et tecto vicinus iugis aquae fons
Et paulum silvae super his foret.

This used to be among my prayers—a portion of land not so very large, but which should contain a garden, and near the homestead a spring of ever-flowing water, and a bit of forest to complete it. *Ib.* vi. 1

25 O rus, quando ego te aspiciam? quandoque licebit
Nunc veterum libris, nunc somno et inertibus horis,
Ducere sollicitae iucunda oblivia vitae?

O country home, when shall I look on you again! when shall I be allowed, between my library of classics and sleep and hours of idleness, to drink the sweet draughts that make us forget the troubles of life? *Ib.* 60

26 O noctes cenaeque deum!

O nights and suppers of gods! *Ib.* 65

HORACE—HOUSMAN

1 Responsare cupidinibus, contemnere honores
Fortis, et in se ipso totus, teres, atque rotundus.

> Who has courage to say no again and again to desires, to despise the objects of ambition, who is a whole in himself, smoothed and rounded.
> *Satires*, II. vii. 85

RICHARD HENRY ['HENGIST'] HORNE
1803–1884

2 'Tis always morning somewhere in the world.
Orion, bk. iii, c. ii

3 Ye rigid Ploughmen! Bear in mind
Your labour is for future hours.
Advance! Spare not! Nor look behind!
Plough deep and straight with all your powers!
The Plough

BISHOP SAMUEL HORSLEY
1733–1806

4 The people have nothing to do with the laws but to obey them. *Speech in the House of Lords*

JOHN HOSKINS
1566–1638

5 Absence, hear thou my protestation
Against thy strength,
Distance and length:
Do what thou canst for alteration,
For hearts of truest mettle
Absence doth join, and time doth settle.
Absence: A Poetical Rhapsody. Attr.

6 By absence this good means I gain,
That I can catch her,
Where none can watch her,
In some close corner of my brain:
There I embrace and kiss her,
And so I both enjoy and miss her. *Ib.*

RICHARD MONCKTON MILNES, BARON HOUGHTON
1809–1885

7 'Lady Moon, Lady Moon, where are you roving?'
'Over the sea.'
'Lady Moon, Lady Moon, whom are you loving?'
'All that love me.' *A Child's Song: Lady Moon*

8 A fair little girl sat under a tree,
Sewing as long as her eyes could see;
Then smoothed her work, and folded it right,
And said, 'Dear work! Good Night! Good Night!'
Good Night and Good Morning

9 I wander'd by the brookside,
I wander'd by the mill,—
I could not hear the brook flow,
The noisy wheel was still;
There was no burr of grasshopper,
No chirp of any bird;
But the beating of my own heart
Was all the sound I heard. *Song: The Brookside*

ALFRED EDWARD HOUSMAN
1859–1936

10 Loveliest of trees, the cherry now
Is hung with bloom along the bough,
And stands about the woodland ride
Wearing white for Eastertide.

Now, of my threescore years and ten,
Twenty will not come again,
And take from seventy springs a score,
It only leaves me fifty more.

And since to look at things in bloom
Fifty springs are little room,
About the woodlands I will go
To see the cherry hung with snow.
A Shropshire Lad, ii

11 There sleeps in Shrewsbury jail to-night,
Or wakes, as may betide,
A better lad, if things went right,
Than most that sleep outside. *Ib. ix*

12 And naked to the hangman's noose
The morning clocks will ring
A neck God made for other use
Than strangling in a string. *Ib.*

13 In farm and field through all the shire
The eye beholds the heart's desire;
Ah, let not only mine be vain
For lovers should be loved again. *Ib. x*

14 Lovers lying two and two
Ask not whom they sleep beside,
And the bridegroom all night through
Never turns him to the bride. *Ib. xii*

15 When I was one-and-twenty
I heard a wise man say,
'Give crowns and pounds and guineas
But not your heart away.' *Ib. xiii*

16 But I was one-and-twenty,
No use to talk to me. *Ib.*

17 When I was one-and-twenty
I heard him say again,
'The heart out of the bosom
Was never given in vain;
'Tis paid with sighs a plenty
And sold for endless rue.'
And I am two-and-twenty,
And oh, 'tis true, 'tis true. *Ib.*

18 His folly has not fellow
Beneath the blue of day
That gives to man or woman
His heart and soul away. *Ib. xiv*

19 Oh, when I was in love with you,
Then I was clean and brave,
And miles around the wonder grew
How well did I behave.

And now the fancy passes by,
And nothing will remain,
And miles around they'll say that I
Am quite myself again. *Ib. xviii*

20 The garland briefer than a girl's. *Ib. xix*

21 In summertime on Bredon
The bells they sound so clear;
Round both the shires they ring them
In steeples far and near,
A happy noise to hear.

[262]

Here of a Sunday morning
　My love and I would lie,
And see the coloured counties,
　And hear the larks so high
　About us in the sky.　　　*A Shropshire Lad*, xxi

1 And I would turn and answer
　Among the springing thyme,
'Oh, peal upon our wedding,
　And we will hear the chime,
　And come to church in time.'　　　*Ib.*

2 They tolled the one bell only,
　Groom there was none to see,
The mourners followed after,
　And so to church went she,
　And would not wait for me.

The bells they sound on Bredon,
　And still the steeples hum.
'Come all to church, good people,'—
　Oh, noisy bells, be dumb;
　I hear you, I will come.　　　*Ib.*

3 The lads that will die in their glory and never be old.
　　　Ib. xxiii

4 Is my team ploughing,
　That I was used to drive?　　　*Ib.* xxvii

5 Ay, the horses trample,
　The harness jingles now;
No change though you lie under
　The land you used to plough.　　　*Ib.*

6 The goal stands up, the keeper
　Stands up to keep the goal.　　　*Ib.*

7 Yes, lad, I lie easy,
　I lie as lads would choose;
I cheer a dead man's sweetheart,
　Never ask me whose.　　　*Ib.*

8 The tree of man was never quiet:
　Then 'twas the Roman; now 'tis I.　　　*Ib.* xxxi

9 To-day the Roman and his trouble
　Are ashes under Uricon.　　　*Ib.*

10 'Oh, go where you are wanted, for you are not wanted
　here.'
And that was all the farewell when I parted from my
　dear.　　　*Ib.* xxxiv

11 And the enemies of England they shall see me and
　be sick.　　　*Ib.*

12 White in the moon the long road lies,
　The moon stands blank above;
White in the moon the long road lies
　That leads me from my love.　　　*Ib.* xxxvi

13 Oh tarnish late on Wenlock Edge,
　Gold that I never see;
Lie long, high snowdrifts in the hedge
　That will not shower on me.　　　*Ib.* xxxix

14 Into my heart an air that kills
　From yon far country blows.
What are those blue remembered hills,
　What spires, what farms are those?

That is the land of lost content,
　I see it shining plain,
The happy highways where I went
　And cannot come again.　　　*Ib.* xl

15 But play the man, stand up and end you,
　When your sickness is your soul.　　　*Ib.* xlv

16 Be still, be still, my soul; it is but for a season;
　Let us endure an hour and see injustice done.
　　　A Shropshire Lad, xlviii

17 Oh why did I awake? When shall I sleep again? *Ib.*

18 Think no more, lad; laugh, be jolly:
　Why should men make haste to die?
Empty heads and tongues a-talking
Make the rough road easy walking,
And the feather pate of folly
　Bears the falling sky.

Oh, 'tis jesting, dancing, drinking
　Spins the heavy world around.
If young hearts were not so clever,
Oh, they would be young for ever:
Think no more; 'tis only thinking
　Lays lads underground.　　　*Ib.* xlix

19 Far in a western brookland
　That bred me long ago
The poplars stand and tremble
　By pools I used to know.　　　*Ib.* lii

20 There, by the starlit fences,
　The wanderer halts and hears
My soul that lingers sighing
　About the glimmering weirs.　　　*Ib.*

21 Many a rose-lipt maiden
　And many a lightfoot lad.　　　*Ib.* liv

22 I shall have lived a little while
　Before I die for ever.　　　*Ib.* lvii

23 In all the endless road you tread
　There's nothing but the night.　　　*Ib.* lx

24 Say, for what were hop-yards meant,
　Or why was Burton built on Trent?　　　*Ib.* lxii

25 Malt does more than Milton can,
　To justify God's ways to man.　　　*Ib.*

26 Mithridates, he died old.　　　*Ib.*

27 We'll to the woods no more,
　The laurels all are cut. *Last Poems*, introductory.

28 And lads are in love with the grave.　　　*Ib.* iv

29 Peace is come and wars are over,
　Welcome you and welcome all.　　　*Ib.* viii

30 May will be fine next year as like as not:
　Oh ay, but then we shall be twenty-four.　　　*Ib.* ix

31 We for a certainty are not the first
　Have sat in taverns while the tempest hurled
Their hopeful plans to emptiness, and cursed
　Whatever brute and blackguard made the world.
　　　Ib.

32 The troubles of our proud and angry dust
　Are from eternity, and shall not fail.
Bear them we can, and if we can we must.
　Shoulder the sky, my lad, and drink your ale. *Ib.*

33 Pass me the can, lad; there's an end of May.　　*Ib.*

34 But men at whiles are sober
And think by fits and starts.
And if they think, they fasten
　Their hands upon their hearts.　　　*Ib.* x

35 I, a stranger and afraid
　In a world I never made.　　　*Ib.* xii

36 　Made of earth and sea
His overcoat for ever,
　And wears the turning globe.　　　*Ib.* xx

1 The fairies break their dances
  And leave the printed lawn,
And up from India glances
  The silver sail of dawn.

The candles burn their sockets,
  The blinds let through the day,
The young man feels his pockets
  And wonders what's to pay. *Last Poems*, xxi

2 See, in mid heaven the sun is mounted; hark,
  The belfries tingle to the noonday chime.
'Tis silent, and the subterranean dark
  Has crossed the nadir, and begins to climb.
  Ib. xxxvi

3 To air the ditty,
  And to earth I. *Ib*. xli

4 These, in the day when heaven was falling,
  The hour when earth's foundations fled,
Followed their mercenary calling
  And took their wages and are dead.

Their shoulders held the sky suspended;
  They stood, and earth's foundations stay;
What God abandoned, these defended,
  And saved the sum of things for pay.
  Ib. xxxvii. *Epitaph on an Army of Mercenaries*

5 By Sestos town, in Hero's tower
  On Hero's heart Leander lies;
The signal torch has burned his hour,
  And splutters as it dies. *More Poems*, xv

6 Experience has taught me, when I am shaving of a
  morning, to keep watch over my thoughts, because,
  if a line of poetry strays into my memory, my skin
  bristles so that the razor ceases to act.
  The Name and Nature of Poetry

RICHARD HOVEY
1864–1900

7 I do not know beneath what sky
  Nor on what seas shall be thy fate;
I only know it shall be high,
  I only know it shall be great. *Unmanifest Destiny*

BISHOP WILLIAM WALSHAM HOW
1823–1897

8 For all the Saints who from their labours rest,
Who Thee by faith before the world confess'd,
Thy name, O Jesu, be for ever blest,
  Alleluia!
  Earl Nelson's *Hymns For Saints' Days: For All
  the Saints*

9 And when the strife is fierce, the warfare long,
Steals on the ear the distant triumph-song,
And hearts are brave again, and arms are strong.
  Alleluia! *Ib*.

10 From earth's wide bounds, from ocean's farthest
  coast,
Through gates of pearl streams in the countless host,
Singing to Father, Son, and Holy Ghost,
  Alleluia! *Ib*.

11 O Lord, stretch forth thy mighty hand
And guard and bless our fatherland.
  Church Hymns, 1871. *To Thee, Our God, We Fly*

12 O Jesu, thou art standing
  Outside the fast-closed door.
  Psalms and Hymns, 1867

13 Shame on us, Christian brethren,
  His Name and sign who bear. *Ib*.

SAMUEL HOWARD
1710–1782

14 Gentle Shepherd, tell me where. *Song*

JULIA WARD HOWE
1819–1910

15 Mine eyes have seen the glory of the coming of the
  Lord:
He is trampling out the vintage where the grapes of
  wrath are stored.
  Battle Hymn of the American Republic

16 His truth is marching on. *Ib*.

17 Oh, be swift, my soul, to answer Him, be jubilant,
  my feet! *Ib*.

18 In the beauty of the lilies Christ was born, across the
  sea,
With a glory in His bosom that transfigures you and
  me:
As He died to make men holy, let us die to make men
  free. *Ib*.

JAMES HOWELL
1594?–1666

19 Some hold translations not unlike to be
The wrong side of a Turkey tapestry.
  Familiar Letters, bk. i, let. 6

20 One hair of a woman can draw more than a hundred
  pair of oxen. *Ib*. bk. ii, let. 4

21 This life at best is but an inn,
And we the passengers. *Ib*. let. 73

MARY HOWITT
1799–1888

22 Buttercups and daisies,
  Oh, the pretty flowers;
Coming ere the Springtime,
  To tell of sunny hours. *Buttercups and Daisies*

23 'Will you walk into my parlour?' said a spider to a fly:
''Tis the prettiest little parlour that ever you did spy.'
  The Spider and the Fly

EDMOND HOYLE
1672–1769

24 When in doubt, win the trick.
  *Hoyle's Games. Whist. Twenty-four Short Rules
  for Learners*

ELBERT HUBBARD
1859–1915

25 Life is just one damned thing after another.
  A Thousand and One Epigrams, p. 137

THOMAS HUGHES

1822–1896

1 He never wants anything but what's right and fair; only when you come to settle what's right and fair, it's everything that he wants and nothing that you want. And that's his idea of a compromise. Give me the Brown compromise when I'm on his side.
Tom Brown's Schooldays, pt. ii, ch. 2

2 It's more than a game. It's an institution. [Cricket.]
Ib. ch. 7

VICTOR HUGO

1802–1885

3 Souffrons, mais souffrons sur les cimes.

If we must suffer, let us suffer nobly.
Contemplations: Les Malheureux

DAVID HUME

1711–1776

4 Avarice, the spur of industry.
Essays. Of Civil Liberty

5 Beauty in things exists in the mind which contemplates them. *Ib. Of Tragedy*

6 A miracle may be accurately defined, a transgression of a law of nature by a particular volition of the Deity, or by the interposition of some invisible agent. *On Miracles*, pt. 1, note

7 No testimony is sufficient to establish a miracle, unless the testimony be of such a kind, that its falsehood would be more miraculous than the fact which it endeavours to establish: and even in that case there is a mutual destruction of arguments, and the superior only gives us an assurance suitable to that degree of force which remains after deducting the inferior. *Ib.* pt. 1

8 There is not to be found, in all history, any miracle attested by a sufficient number of men, of such unquestioned good sense, education, and learning, as to secure us against all delusion in themselves; of such undoubted integrity, as to place them beyond all suspicion of any design to deceive others; of such credit and reputation in the eyes of mankind, as to have a great deal to lose in case of their being detected in any falsehood; and at the same time attesting facts, performed in such a public manner, and in so celebrated a part of the world, as to render the detection unavoidable.
Ib. pt. 2

9 The usual propensity of mankind towards the marvellous. *Ib.*

10 The Christian religion not only was at first attended with miracles, but even at this day cannot be believed by any reasonable person without one. Mere reason is insufficient to convince us of its veracity: and whoever is moved by faith to assent to it, is conscious of a continued miracle in his own person, which subverts all the principles of his understanding, and gives him a determination to believe what is most contrary to custom and experience. *Ib.*

11 Custom, then, is the great guide of human life.
Inquiry Concerning Human Understanding, sec. 5, pt. 1

12 Never literary attempt was more unfortunate than my Treatise of Human Nature. It fell *dead-born from the press.* *My Own Life*, ch. 1

13 Opposing one species of superstition to another, set them a quarrelling; while we ourselves, during their fury and contention, happily make our escape into the calm, though obscure, regions of philosophy. *The Natural History of Religion*

MARGARET WOLFE HUNGERFORD

1855?–1897

14 Beauty is in the eye of the beholder.
Quoted in *Molly Bawn* (1878). (*See* 557:18)

G. W. HUNT

fl. 1878

15 We don't want to fight, but, by jingo if we do,
We've got the ships, we've got the men, we've got the money too.
We've fought the Bear before, and while Britons shall be true,
The Russians shall not have Constantinople.
We Don't Want to Fight. Music Hall Song, 1878

JAMES HENRY LEIGH HUNT

1784–1859

16 Abou Ben Adhem (may his tribe increase!)
Awoke one night from a deep dream of peace,
And saw, within the moonlight in his room,
Making it rich, and like a lily in bloom,
An angel writing in a book of gold:—
Exceeding peace had made Ben Adhem bold,
And to the presence in the room he said,
'What writest thou?'—The vision raised its head,
And with a look made of all sweet accord,
Answered, 'The names of those who love the Lord.'
Abou Ben Adhem and the Angel

17 'I pray thee then,
Write me as one that loves his fellow-men.' *Ib.*

18 And lo! Ben Adhem's name led all the rest. *Ib.*

19 A Venus grown fat! *Blue-stocking Revels*

20 'By God!' said Francis, 'rightly done!' and he rose from where he sat:
'No love,' quoth he, 'but vanity, sets love a task like that.' *The Glove and the Lions*

21 Green little vaulter in the sunny grass.
To the Grasshopper and the Cricket

22 It flows through old hushed Egypt and its sands,
Like some grave mighty thought threading a dream,
And times and things, as in that vision, seem
Keeping along it their eternal stands. *The Nile*

23 The laughing queen that caught the world's great hands. *Ib.*

24 If you become a nun, dear,
A friar I will be.
In any cell you run, dear,
Pray look behind for me. *The Nun*

25 Jenny kissed me when we met,
Jumping from the chair she sat in;
Time, you thief, who love to get
Sweets into your list, put that in:

Say I'm weary, say I'm sad,
Say that health and wealth have missed me,
Say I'm growing old, but add,
Jenny kissed me.   *Rondeau*

1 Stolen sweets are always sweeter,
Stolen kisses much completer,
Stolen looks are nice in chapels,
Stolen, stolen, be your apples.
                    Song of Fairies Robbing an Orchard

2 Where the light woods go seaward from the town.
                    The Story of Rimini, i, l. 18

3 But most he loved a happy human face.
                    Ib. iii, l. 110

4 The two divinest things this world has got,
A lovely woman in a rural spot!   *Ib.* l. 257

5 Places of nestling green, for poets made.   *Ib.* l. 430

6 This Adonis in loveliness was a corpulent man of fifty. [The Prince Regent.]
                    The Examiner, 22 Mar. 1812

7 A pleasure so exquisite as almost to amount to pain.
                    Letter to Alexander Ireland, 2 June 1848

ANNE HUNTER
1742–1821

8 My mother bids me bind my hair
With bands of rosy hue,
Tie up my sleeves with ribbons rare,
And lace my bodice blue.

'For why,' she cries, 'sit still and weep,
While others dance and play?'
Alas! I scarce can go or creep
While Lubin is away.
                    My Mother Bids Me Bind My Hair

JOHN HUSS
1373–1415

9 O sancta simplicitas!
O holy simplicity!
At the stake, seeing an old peasant bringing a faggot to throw on the pile. Zincgreff-Weidner, *Apophthegmata*, pub. in Amsterdam 1653, pt. iii, p. 383. Geo. Büchmann, *Geflügelte Worte* (1898), p. 509

FRANCIS HUTCHESON
1694–1746

10 Wisdom denotes the pursuing of the best ends by the best means.
Inquiry into the Original of our Ideas of Beauty and Virtue, 1725. Treatise I, sec. v, § 18

11 That action is best, which procures the greatest happiness for the greatest numbers.
Ib. Treatise II. *Concerning Moral Good and Evil*, sec. 3, § 8. (*See* 42:21)

ALDOUS LEONARD HUXLEY
1894–1963

12 But when the wearied Band
Swoons to a waltz, I take her hand,
And there we sit in peaceful calm,
Quietly sweating palm to palm.   *Frascati's*

13 Seated upon the convex mound
Of one vast kidney, Jonah prays
And sings his canticles and hymns,
Making the hollow vault resound
God's goodness and mysterious ways,
Till the great fish spouts music as he swims.   *Jonah*

14 Bewildered furrows deepen the Thunderer's scowl;
This world so vast, so variously foul—
Who can have made its ugliness? In what
Revolting fancy were the Forms begot
Of all these monsters? What strange deity—
So barbarously not a Greek was he?   *Leda*

15 Your maiden modesty would float face down,
And men would weep upon your hinder parts.   *Ib.*

16 Beauty for some provides escape,
Who gain a happiness in eyeing
The gorgeous buttocks of the ape
Or Autumn sunsets exquisitely dying.
                    The Ninth Philosopher's Song

17 Then brim the bowl with atrabilious liquor!
We'll pledge our Empire vast across the flood:
For Blood, as all men know, than water's thicker,
But water's wider, thank the Lord, than Blood.   *Ib.*

THOMAS HENRY HUXLEY
1825–1895

18 Science is nothing but trained and organized common sense, differing from the latter only as a veteran may differ from a raw recruit: and its methods differ from those of common sense only as far as the guardsman's cut and thrust differ from the manner in which a savage wields his club.
                    Collected Essays, iv. *The Method of Zadig*

19 The great tragedy of Science—the slaying of a beautiful hypothesis by an ugly fact.
                    Ib. viii. *Biogenesis and Abiogenesis*

20 The chess-board is the world; the pieces are the phenomena of the universe; the rules of the game are what we call the laws of Nature. The player on the other side is hidden from us. We know that his play is always fair, just, and patient. But also we know, to our cost, that he never overlooks a mistake, or makes the smallest allowance for ignorance.   *Lay Sermons, &c.*, iii. *A Liberal Education*

21 If some great Power would agree to make me always think what is true and do what is right, on condition of being turned into a sort of clock and wound up every morning before I got out of bed, I should instantly close with the offer.
                    On Descartes' Discourse on Method. Method & Results, iv

22 Logical consequences are the scarecrows of fools and the beacons of wise men.
                    Science and Culture, ix. *On the Hypothesis that Animals are Automata*

23 Irrationally held truths may be more harmful than reasoned errors.
                    Ib. xii. *The Coming of Age of the Origin of Species*

24 It is the customary fate of new truths to begin as heresies and to end as superstitions.   *Ib.*

25 I took thought, and invented what I conceived to be the appropriate title of 'agnostic'.
                    Science and Christian Tradition, ch. 7

EDWARD HYDE

see

EARL OF CLARENDON

HENRIK IBSEN
1828-1906

1 The minority is always right.
An Enemy of the People, Act IV

2 One should never put on one's best trousers to go out
to battle for freedom and truth. *Ib.* Act V

3 Vine-leaves in his hair. *Hedda Gabler*, Act II

4 People don't do such things. *Ib.* Act IV

5 The younger generation will come knocking at my
door. *The Master-Builder*, Act I

WILLIAM RALPH INGE
1860-1954

6 Democracy is only an experiment in government,
and it has the obvious disadvantage of merely
counting votes instead of weighing them.
Possible Recovery?

7 Literature flourishes best when it is half a trade and
half an art. *The Victorian Age* (1922), p. 49

8 A man may build himself a throne of bayonets, but
he cannot sit on it.
Marchant, *Wit and Wisdom of Dean Inge*, No.
108

9 The nations which have put mankind and posterity
most in their debt have been small states—Israel,
Athens, Florence, Elizabethan England.
Ib. No. 181

JEAN INGELOW
1820-1897

10 But two are walking apart for ever,
And wave their hands for a mute farewell.
Divided

11 When sparrows build, and the leaves break forth,
My old sorrow wakes and cries. *Supper at the Mill*

12 Play uppe 'The Brides of Enderby'.
The High Tide on the Coast of Lincolnshire, 1571

13 Come uppe, Whitefoot, come uppe Lightfoot,
Come uppe Jetty, rise and follow,
Jetty, to the milking shed. *Ib.*

14 A sweeter woman ne'er drew breath
Than my sonne's wife, Elizabeth. *Ib.*

15 And didst Thou love the race that loved not Thee?
Hymn

ROBERT GREEN INGERSOLL
1833-1899

16 An honest God is the noblest work of man.
Gods, pt. 1, p. 2. (*See also* 112:9)

17 In nature there are neither rewards nor punishments
—there are consequences.
Lectures & Essays, 3rd Series. *Some Reasons
Why*, viii

JOHN KELLS INGRAM
1823-1907

18 Who fears to speak of Ninety-Eight?
The Nation, April 1843

WASHINGTON IRVING
1783-1859

19 A tart temper never mellows with age, and a sharp
tongue is the only edged tool that grows keener
with constant use. *Rip Van Winkle*

20 They who drink beer will think beer.
The Sketch Book. Stratford

21 A woman's whole life is a history of the affections.
Ib. The Broken Heart

22 Free-livers on a small scale; who are prodigal within
the compass of a guinea. *The Stout Gentleman*

23 I am always at a loss to know how much to believe of
my own stories.
Tales of a Traveller, To the Reader

24 There is a certain relief in change, even though it be
from bad to worse; as I have found in travelling in
a stage-coach, that it is often a comfort to shift
one's position and be bruised in a new place. *Ib.*

25 The almighty dollar, that great object of universal
devotion throughout our land, seems to have no
genuine devotees in these peculiar villages.
Wolfert's Roost. The Creole Village

ANDREW JACKSON
1767-1845

26 You are uneasy; you never sailed with *me* before, I see.
J. Parton's *Life of Jackson*, vol. iii, ch. 35

27 Our Federal Union: it must be preserved.
*Toast given on the Jefferson Birthday Celebra-
tion, 13 Apr. 1830*. Benton, *Thirty Years' View*,
vol. I

RICHARD JAGO
1715-1781

28 With leaden foot time creeps along
While Delia is away. *Absence: With Leaden Foot*

JAMES I OF ENGLAND AND VI OF
SCOTLAND
1566-1625

29 A branch of the sin of drunkenness, which is the root
of all sins. *A Counterblast to Tobacco* (1604)

30 A custom loathsome to the eye, hateful to the nose,
harmful to the brain, dangerous to the lungs, and
in the black, stinking fume thereof, nearest resembling the horrible Stygian smoke of the pit that
is bottomless. *Ib.*

31 Herein is not only a great vanity, but a great contempt
of God's good gifts, that the sweetness of man's
breath, being a good gift of God, should be wilfully
corrupted by this stinking smoke. *Ib.*

32 Dr. Donne's verses are like the peace of God; they
pass all understanding.
*Saying recorded by Archdeacon Plume (1630-
1704)*

HENRY JAMES
1843–1916

1 It takes a great deal of history to produce a little literature. *Life of Nathaniel Hawthorne*

2 [Thoreau] was worse than provincial—he was parochial. *Ib.* ch. 4

3 Dramatise, dramatise! *Prefaces. Altar of the Dead, and elsewhere*

4 The note I wanted; that of the strange and sinister embroidered on the very type of the normal and easy. *Ib.*

5 The terrible *fluidity* of self-revelation. *Ib. The Ambassadors*

6 The deep well of unconscious cerebration. *Ib. The American*

7 The historian, essentially, wants more documents than he can really use; the dramatist only wants more liberties than he can really take. *Ib. The Aspern Papers, &c.*

8 I have always fondly remembered a remark that I heard fall years ago from the lips of Ivan Turgenieff in regard to his own experience of the usual origin of the fictive picture. It began for him almost always with the vision of some person or persons, who hovered before him, soliciting him, as the active or passive figure, interesting him and appealing to him just as they were and by what they were. He saw them in that fashion, as *disponibles*, saw them subject to the chances, the complications of existence, and saw them vividly, but then had to find for them the right relations, those that would bring them out. *Ib. The Portrait of a Lady*

9 The fatal futility of Fact. *Ib. The Spoils of Poynton, &c.*

10 The Real Right Ti. *Story-title*

11 The only obligation which in advance we may hold a novel, without incurring the accusation of being arbitrary, is that it be interesting. *The Art of Fiction. Partial Portraits*

12 Experience is never limited, and it is never complete; it is an immense sensibility, a kind of huge spider-web of the finest silken threads suspended in the chamber of consciousness, and catching every air-borne particle in its tissue. *Ib.*

13 What is character but the determination of incident? what is incident but the illustration of character? *Ib.*

14 We must grant the artist his subject, his idea, his *donné*: our criticism is applied only to what he makes of it. *Ib.*

15 Vereker's secret, my dear man—the general intention of his books: the string the pearls were strung on; the buried treasure, the figure in the carpet. *The Figure in the Carpet*, ch. 11

16 Cats and monkeys, monkeys and cats—all human life is there. *The Madonna of the Future*

17 Tennyson was not Tennysonian. *The Middle Years*

18 Print it as it stands—beautifully. *Terminations. The Death of the Lion*, x

THOMAS JEFFERSON
1743–1826

19 We hold these truths to be sacred and undeniable; that all men are created equal and independent, that from that equal creation they derive rights inherent and inalienable, among which are the preservation of life, and liberty, and the pursuit of happiness. Original draft for the *Declaration of Independence*. (*See* 11:11)

20 In the full tide of successful experiment. *First Inaugural Address, 4 March 1801*

21 Peace, commerce, and honest friendship with all nations—entangling alliances with none. *Ib.*

22 A little rebellion now and then is a good thing. *Letter to James Madison, 30 Jan. 1787*

23 The tree of liberty must be refreshed from time to time with the blood of patriots and tyrants. It is its natural manure. *Ib. To W. S. Smith, 13 Nov. 1787*

24 Whenever a man has cast a longing eye on them [offices], a rottenness begins in his conduct. *Ib. To Tench Coxe, 1799*

25 To seek out the best through the whole Union we must resort to other information, which, from the best of men, acting disinterestedly and with the purest motives, is sometimes incorrect. *Letter to Elias Shipman and others of New Haven, 12 July 1801*

26 If a due participation of office is a matter of right, how are vacancies to be obtained? Those by death are few; by resignation, none. *Usually quoted, 'Few die and none resign'.* *Ib.*

27 Indeed I tremble for my country when I reflect that God is just. *Notes on Virginia*, Query xviii. *Manners*

28 When a man assumes a public trust, he should consider himself as public property. *Remark to Baron von Humboldt, 1807.* Rayner's *Life of Jefferson*, p. 356

29 No duty the Executive had to perform was so trying as to put the right man in the right place. J. B. MacMaster, *History of the People of the U.S.*; vol. ii, ch. 13, p. 586

CHARLES JEFFERYS
1807–1865

30 I have heard the mavis singing
His love-song to the morn;
I have seen the dew-drop clinging
To the rose just newly born. *Mary of Argyle*

FRANCIS, LORD JEFFREY
1773–1850

31 This will never do. *On* Wordsworth's '*Excursion*'. *Edinburgh Review, Nov. 1814*, p. 1

JEROME KLAPKA JEROME
1859–1927

32 It is impossible to enjoy idling thoroughly unless one has plenty of work to do. *Idle Thoughts of an Idle Fellow. On Being Idle*

1 Love is like the measles; we all have to go through it.
Idle Thoughts of an Idle Fellow. On Being in Love

2 George goes to sleep at a bank from ten to four each day, except Saturdays, when they wake him up and put him outside at two.
Three Men in a Boat, ch. 2

3 But there, everything has its drawbacks, as the man said when his mother-in-law died, and they came down on him for the funeral expenses. *Ib.* ch. 3

4 My tooth-brush is a thing that haunts me when I'm travelling, and makes my life a misery. *Ib.* ch. 4

5 I like work: it fascinates me. I can sit and look at it for hours. I love to keep it by me: the idea of getting rid of it nearly breaks my heart. *Ib.* ch. 15

6 The Passing of the Third Floor Back. *Title of play*

DOUGLAS WILLIAM JERROLD
1803–1857

7 Honest bread is very well—it's the butter that makes the temptation. *The Catspaw*, Act III

8 Religion's in the heart, not in the knees.
The Devil's Ducat, I. ii

9 Mrs. Caudle's Curtain Lectures. *Title of Book*

10 He is one of those wise philanthropists who, in a time of famine, would vote for nothing but a supply of toothpicks.
Wit and Opinions of Douglas Jerrold (1859), p. 2. *A Philanthropist*

11 Love's like the measles—all the worse when it comes late in life. *Ib.* p. 6

12 The best thing I know between France and England is—the sea. *Ib.* p. 13. *The Anglo-French Alliance*

13 That fellow would vulgarize the day of judgment.
Ib. A Comic Author

14 The ugliest of trades have their moments of pleasure. Now, if I were a grave-digger, or even a hangman, there are some people I could work for with a great deal of enjoyment. *Ib.* p. 14. *Ugly Trades*

15 Earth is here [Australia] so kind, that just tickle her with a hoe and she laughs with a harvest.
Ib. A Land of Plenty

16 Some people are so fond of ill-luck that they run half-way to meet it.
Ib. Meeting Troubles Half-way

17 He was so good he would pour rose-water over a toad. *Ib.* p. 17. *A Charitable Man*

18 Talk to him of Jacob's ladder, and he would ask the number of the steps.
Ib. p. 29. *A Matter-of-fact Man*

19 We love peace, as we abhor pusillanimity; but not peace at any price. There is a peace more destructive of the manhood of living man than war is destructive of his material body. Chains are worse than bayonets. *Ib.* p. 155. *Peace*

20 If an earthquake were to engulf England to-morrow, the English would manage to meet and dine somewhere among the rubbish, just to celebrate the event.
Remark. Blanchard Jerrold's *Life of D. Jerrold*, ch. 14

21 The only athletic sport I ever mastered was backgammon.
W. Jerrold, *Douglas Jerrold* (1914), vol. i, ch. 1, p. 22

BISHOP JOHN JEWEL
1522–1571

22 In old time we had treen chalices and golden priests, but now we have treen priests and golden chalices.
Certain Sermons Preached Before the Queen's Majesty, 1609, p. 176

JOHN OF SALISBURY
see
SALISBURY

ANDREW JOHNSON
1808–1875

23 We are swinging round the circle.
Speech on the Presidential Reconstruction, August 1866

LIONEL PIGOT JOHNSON
1867–1902

24 There Shelley dream'd his white Platonic dreams.
Oxford

25 In her ears the chime
Of full, sad bells brings back her old springtide. *Ib.*

26 I know you: solitary griefs,
Desolate passions, aching hours.
The Precept of Silence

27 The saddest of all Kings
Crown'd, and again discrown'd.
By the Statue of King Charles I at Charing Cross

28 Stars in their stations set;
And every wandering star. *Ib.*

29 The fair and fatal King. *Ib.*

30 Speak after sentence? Yea:
And to the end of time. *Ib.*

31 King, tried in fires of woe!
Men hunger for thy grace:
And through the night I go,
Loving thy mournful face. *Ib.*

PHILANDER CHASE JOHNSON
1866–1939

32 Cheer up, the worst is yet to come.
Shooting Stars. See *Everybody's Magazine*, May 1920

SAMUEL JOHNSON
1709–1784

33 The rod produces an effect which terminates in itself. A child is afraid of being whipped, and gets his task, and there's an end on't; whereas, by exciting emulation and comparisons of superiority, you lay the foundation of lasting mischief; you make brothers and sisters hate each other.
Boswell's *Life of Johnson* (L. F. Powell's *revision of G. B. Hill's edition*), vol. i, p. 46

1 In my early years I read very hard. It is a sad reflection, but a true one, that I knew almost as much at eighteen as I do now.
Boswell's *Life of Johnson*, vol. i, p. 56. *20 July 1763*

2 *Johnson*: I had no notion that I was wrong or irreverent to my tutor.
Boswell: That, Sir, was great fortitude of mind.
Johnson: No, Sir; stark insensibility.
Ib. p. 60. *5 Nov. 1728*

3 Sir, we are a nest of singing birds. *Ib.* p. 75. *1730*

4 If you call a dog *Hervey*, I shall love him.
Ib. p. 106. *1737*

5 My old friend, Mrs. Carter, could make a pudding as well as translate Epictetus. *Ib.* p. 123 n. *1738*

6 Sleep, undisturb'd, within this peaceful shrine,
Till angels wake thee with a note like thine!
Ib. p. 149. *1741*

7 Great George's acts let tuneful Cibber sing;
For Nature form'd the Poet for the King. *Ib.*

8 Tom Birch is as brisk as a bee in conversation; but no sooner does he take a pen in his hand, than it becomes a torpedo to him, and benumbs all his faculties. *Ib.* p. 159. *1743*

9 [When asked how he felt upon the ill success of *Irene*] Like the Monument. *Ib.* p. 199. *Feb. 1749*

10 I'll come no more behind your scenes, David; for the silk stockings and white bosoms of your actresses excite my amorous propensities. *Ib.* p. 201. *1750*

11 A man may write at any time, if he will set himself doggedly to it. *Ib.* p. 203. *Mar. 1750*

12 [Of F. Lewis]
Sir, he lived in London, and hung loose upon society.
Ib. p. 226. *1750*

13 [To Beauclerk]
Thy body is all vice, and thy mind all virtue.
Ib. p. 250. *1752*

14 [On being knocked up at 3 a.m. by Beauclerk and Langton]
What, is it you, you dogs! I'll have a frisk with you.
Ib.

15 Wretched un-idea'd girls. *Ib.* p. 251. *1753*

16 I had done all I could; and no man is well pleased to have his all neglected, be it ever so little.
Ib. p. 261. *Letter to Lord Chesterfield, 7 Feb. 1755*

17 The shepherd in Virgil grew at last acquainted with Love, and found him a native of the rocks. *Ib.*

18 Is not a Patron, my Lord, one who looks with unconcern on a man struggling for life in the water, and, when he has reached ground, encumbers him with help? The notice which you have been pleased to take of my labours, had it been early, had been kind; but it has been delayed till I am indifferent, and cannot enjoy it; till I am solitary, and cannot impart it; till I am known, and do not want it. *Ib.*

19 A fly, Sir, may sting a stately horse and make him wince; but one is but an insect, and the other is a horse still. *Ib.* p. 263, n. 3

20 [Of Lord Chesterfield]
This man I thought had been a Lord among wits; but, I find, he is only a wit among Lords.
Ib. p. 266. *1754*

21 [Of Lord Chesterfield's *Letters*]
They teach the morals of a whore, and the manners of a dancing master. Boswell's *Life*, vol. i, p. 266. *1754*

22 [Of Bolingbroke and his editor, Mallet]
Sir, he was a scoundrel, and a coward: a scoundrel, for charging a blunderbuss against religion and morality; a coward, because he had not resolution to fire it off himself, but left half a crown to a beggarly Scotchman, to draw the trigger after his death! *Ib.* p. 268. *6 Mar. 1754*

23 Mr. Millar, bookseller, undertook the publication of Johnson's Dictionary. When the messenger who carried the last sheet to Millar returned, Johnson asked him, 'Well, what did he say?' 'Sir,' answered the messenger, 'he said, thank God I have done with him.'
'I am glad', replied Johnson, with a smile, 'that he thanks God for any thing.' *Ib.* p. 287. *Apr. 1755*

24 I respect Millar, Sir; he has raised the price of literature. *Ib.* p. 288. *1755*

25 There are two things which I am confident I can do very well: one is an introduction to any literary work, stating what it is to contain, and how it should be executed in the most perfect manner; the other is a conclusion, shewing from various causes why the execution has not been equal to what the author promised to himself and to the public. *Ib.* p. 292. *1755*

26 [When asked by a lady why he defined 'pastern' as the 'knee' of a horse, in his Dictionary]
Ignorance, madam, pure ignorance. *Ib.* p. 293. *1755*

27 Lexicographer: a writer of dictionaries, a harmless drudge. *Ib.* p. 296. *1755*

28 I have protracted my work till most of those whom I wished to please have sunk into the grave; and success and miscarriage are empty sounds.
Ib. p. 297. *1755*

29 A man, Sir, should keep his friendship in constant repair. *Ib.* p. 300. *1755*

30 The booksellers are generous liberal-minded men.
Ib. p. 304. *1756*

31 The worst of Warburton is, that he has a rage for saying something, when there's nothing to be said.
Ib. p. 329. *1758*

32 No man will be a sailor who has contrivance enough to get himself into a jail; for being in a ship is being in a jail, with the chance of being drowned. . . . A man in a jail has more room, better food, and commonly better company. *Ib.* p. 348. *16 Mar. 1759*

33 'Are you a botanist, Dr. Johnson?'
'No, Sir, I am not a botanist; and (alluding, no doubt, to his near sightedness) should I wish to become a botanist, I must first turn myself into a reptile.'
Ib. p. 377. *20 July 1762*

34 *Boswell*: I do indeed come from Scotland, but I cannot help it. . . .
Johnson: That, Sir, I find, is what a very great many of your countrymen cannot help.
Ib. p. 392. *16 May 1763*

35 When a butcher tells you that *his heart bleeds for his country* he has, in fact, no uneasy feeling.
Ib. p. 394. *16 May 1763*

1 [On Dr. Blair's asking whether any man of a modern age could have written *Ossian*]
Yes, Sir, many men, many women, and many children. Boswell's *Life*, vol. i, p. 396. *24 May 1763*

2 Sir, it was like leading one to talk of a book when the author is concealed behind the door. *Ib.*

3 He insisted on people praying with him; and I'd as lief pray with Kit Smart as any one else.
Ib. p. 397. *24 May 1763*

4 [Of Kit Smart]
He did not love clean linen; and I have no passion for it. *Ib.*

5 [Of literary criticism]
You may scold a carpenter who has made you a bad table, though you cannot make a table. It is not your trade to make tables. *Ib.* p. 409. *25 June 1763*

6 [Of Dr. John Campbell]
I am afraid he has not been in the inside of a church for many years; but he never passes a church without pulling off his hat. This shews that he has good principles. *Ib.* p. 418. *1 July 1763*

7 [Of Dr. John Campbell]
He is the richest author that ever grazed the common of literature. *Ib.* n.

8 Norway, too, has noble wild prospects; and Lapland is remarkable for prodigious noble wild prospects. But, Sir, let me tell you, the noblest prospect which a Scotchman ever sees, is the high road that leads him to England! *Ib.* p. 425. *6 July 1763*

9 A man ought to read just as inclination leads him; for what he reads as a task will do him little good.
Ib. p. 428. *14 July 1763*

10 But if he does really think that there is no distinction between virtue and vice, why, Sir, when he leaves our houses let us count our spoons.
Ib. p. 432. *14 July 1763*

11 Truth, Sir, is a cow, which will yield such people [sceptics] no more milk, and so they are gone to milk the bull. *Ib.* p. 444. *21 July 1763*

12 Your levellers wish to level *down* as far as themselves; but they cannot bear levelling *up* to themselves.
Ib. p. 448. *21 July 1763*

13 Sir, it is no matter what you teach them [children] first, any more than what leg you shall put into your breeches first. *Ib.* p. 452. *26 July 1763*

14 Why, Sir, Sherry [Thomas Sheridan] is dull, naturally dull; but it must have taken him a great deal of pains to become what we now see him. Such an excess of stupidity, Sir, is not in Nature.
Ib. p. 453. *28 July 1763*

15 [Of Thomas Sheridan's influence on the English language]
Sir, it is burning a farthing candle at Dover, to shew light at Calais. *Ib.* p. 454. *28 July 1763*

16 Sir, a woman's preaching is like a dog's walking on his hinder legs. It is not done well; but you are surprised to find it done at all.
Ib. p. 463. *31 July 1763*

17 I look upon it, that he who does not mind his belly will hardly mind anything else.
Ib. p. 467. *5 Aug. 1763*

18 This was a good dinner enough, to be sure; but it was not a dinner to *ask* a man to.
Boswell's *Life*, vol. i, p. 470. *5 Aug. 1763*

19 Sir, we could not have had a better dinner had there been a *Synod of Cooks*. *Ib.*

20 [Boswell happened to say it would be terrible if Johnson should not find a speedy opportunity of returning to London, from Harwich]
Don't, Sir, accustom yourself to use big words for little matters. It would *not* be *terrible*, though I *were* to be detained some time here.
Ib. p. 471. *6 Aug. 1763*

21 [Talking of Bishop Berkeley's theory of the non-existence of matter, Boswell observed that though they were satisfied it was not true, they were unable to refute it. Johnson struck his foot against a large stone, till he rebounded from it, saying]
I refute it *thus*. *Ib.*

22 [Of Sir John Hawkins]
A very unclubable man. *Ib.* p. 480 n. *1764*

23 Our tastes greatly alter. The lad does not care for the child's rattle, and the old man does not care for the young man's whore.
Ib. vol. ii, p. 14. *Spring, 1766*

24 It was not for me to bandy civilities with my Sovereign. *Ib.* p. 35. *Feb. 1767*

25 Sir, I love Robertson, and I won't talk of his book.
Ib. p. 53. *1768*

26 *Johnson*: Well, we had a good talk.
Boswell: Yes, Sir; you tossed and gored several persons. *Ib.* p. 66. *1769*

27 Let me smile with the wise, and feed with the rich.
Ib. p. 79. *6 Oct. 1769*

28 Sir, We *know* our will is free, and *there's* an end on't.
Ib. p. 82. *16 Oct. 1769*

29 Inspissated gloom. *Ib.*

30 I do not know, Sir, that the fellow is an infidel; but if he be an infidel, he is an infidel as a dog is an infidel; that is to say, he has never thought upon the subject. *Ib.* p. 95. *19 Oct. 1769*

31 Shakespeare never had six lines together without a fault. Perhaps you may find seven, but this does not refute my general assertion.
Ib. p. 96. *19 Oct. 1769*

32 I would not *coddle* the child.
Ib. p. 101. *26 Oct. 1769*

33 Let fanciful men do as they will, depend upon it, it is difficult to disturb the system of life.
Ib. p. 102. *26 Oct. 1769*

34 *Boswell*: So, Sir, you laugh at schemes of political improvement?
Johnson: Why, Sir, most schemes of political improvement are very laughable things. *Ib.*

35 It matters not how a man dies, but how he lives.
Ib. p. 106. *26 Oct. 1769*

36 Burton's *Anatomy of Melancholy*, he said, was the only book that ever took him out of bed two hours sooner than he wished to rise. *Ib.* p. 121. *1770*

1 [On Jonas Hanway, who followed his *Travels to Persia* with *An Eight Day's Journey from London to Portsmouth*]
Jonas acquired some reputation by travelling abroad, but lost it all by travelling at home.
Boswell's Life of Johnson, vol. ii, p. 122. *1770*

2 Want of tenderness is want of parts, and is no less a proof of stupidity than depravity. *Ib.*

3 That fellow seems to me to possess but one idea, and that is a wrong one. *Ib.* p. 126. *1770*

4 A gentleman who had been very unhappy in marriage, married immediately after his wife died: Johnson said, it was the triumph of hope over experience.
Ib. p. 128. *1770*

5 Every man has a lurking wish to appear considerable in his native place.
Ib. p. 141. *Letter to Sir Joshua Reynolds, 17 July 1771*

6 It is so far from being natural for a man and woman to live in a state of marriage that we find all the motives which they have for remaining in that connection, and the restraints which civilized society imposes to prevent separation, are hardly sufficient to keep them together. *Ib.* p. 165. *31 Mar. 1772*

7 Nobody can write the life of a man, but those who have eat and drunk and lived in social intercourse with him. *Ib.* p. 166. *31 Mar. 1772*

8 I would not give half a guinea to live under one form of government rather than another. It is of no moment to the happiness of an individual.
Ib. p. 170. *31 Mar. 1772*

9 [To Sir Adam Fergusson]
Sir, I perceive you are a vile Whig. *Ib.*

10 There is a remedy in human nature against tyranny, that will keep us safe under every form of government. *Ib.*

11 A man who is good enough to go to heaven, is good enough to be a clergyman. *Ib.* p. 171. *5 Apr. 1772*

12 Sir, there is more knowledge of the heart in one letter of Richardson's, than in all *Tom Jones*.
Ib. p. 174. *6 Apr. 1772*

13 Why, Sir, if you were to read Richardson for the story, your impatience would be so much fretted that you would hang yourself.
Ib. p. 175. *6 Apr. 1772*

14 [On Lord Mansfield, who was educated in England]
Much may be made of a Scotchman, if he be *caught* young. *Ib.* p. 194. *Spring 1772*

15 [On Goldsmith's apology in the *London Chronicle* for beating Evans the bookseller]
It is a foolish thing well done.
Ib. p. 210. *3 Apr. 1773*

16 *Elphinston*: What, have you not read it through? . . .
Johnson: No, Sir, do *you* read books *through*?
Ib. p. 226. *19 Apr. 1773*

17 [Quoting a college tutor]
Read over your compositions, and where ever you meet with a passage which you think is particularly fine, strike it out. *Ib.* p. 237. *30 Apr. 1773*

18 He [Goldsmith] is now writing a Natural History and will make it as entertaining as a Persian Tale. *Ib.*

19 [Of Lady Diana Beauclerk]
The woman's a whore, and there's an end on't.
Boswell's Life, vol. ii, p. 247. *7 May 1773*

20 I hope I shall never be deterred from detecting what I think a cheat, by the menaces of a ruffian.
Ib. p. 298. *Letter to James Macpherson, 20 Jan. 1775*

21 [To Dr. Barnard, Bishop of Killaloe]
The Irish are a fair people;—they never speak well of one another. *Ib.* p. 307. *1775*

22 [To William Strahan]
There are few ways in which a man can be more innocently employed than in getting money.
Ib. p. 323. *27 Mar. 1775*

23 He [Thomas Gray] was dull in a new way, and that made many people think him *great*.
Ib. p. 327. *28 Mar. 1775*

24 I never think I have hit hard, unless it rebounds.
Ib. p. 335. *2 Apr. 1775*

25 I think the full tide of human existence is at Charing-Cross. *Ib.* p. 337. *2 Apr. 1775*

26 Most vices may be committed very genteelly: a man may debauch his friend's wife genteelly: he may cheat at cards genteelly. *Ib.* p. 340. *6 Apr. 1775*

27 George the First knew nothing, and desired to know nothing; did nothing, and desired to do nothing; and the only good thing that is told of him is, that he wished to restore the crown to its hereditary successor. *Ib.* p. 342. *6 Apr. 1775*

28 A man will turn over half a library to make one book.
Ib. p. 344. *6 Apr. 1775*

29 Patriotism is the last refuge of a scoundrel.
Ib. p. 348. *7 Apr. 1775*

30 That is the happiest conversation where there is no competition, no vanity, but a calm quiet interchange of sentiments. *Ib.* p. 359. *14 Apr. 1775*

31 [On the Scotch]
Their learning is like bread in a besieged town: every man gets a little, but no man gets a full meal.
Ib. p. 363. *18 Apr. 1775*

32 Knowledge is of two kinds. We know a subject ourselves, or we know where we can find information upon it. *Ib.* p. 365. *18 Apr. 1775*

33 Politics are now nothing more than a means of rising in the world. *Ib.* p. 369. *1775*

34 Players, Sir! I look upon them as no better than creatures set upon tables and joint stools to make faces and produce laughter, like dancing dogs.
Ib. p. 404. *1775*

35 In lapidary inscriptions a man is not upon oath.
Ib. p. 407. *1775*

36 There is now less flogging in our great schools than formerly, but then less is learned there; so that what the boys get at one end they lose at the other. *Ib.*

37 When men come to like a sea-life, they are not fit to live on land. *Ib.* p. 438. *18 Mar. 1776*

38 Sir, it is a great thing to dine with the Canons of Christ-Church. *Ib.* p. 445. *20 Mar. 1776*

39 There is nothing which has yet been contrived by man, by which so much happiness is produced as by a good tavern or inn. *Ib.* p. 452. *21 Mar. 1776*

1 Marriages would in general be as happy, and often more so, if they were all made by the Lord Chancellor. Boswell's *Life*, vol. ii, p. 461. *22 Mar. 1776*

2 Questioning is not the mode of conversation among gentlemen. *Ib.* p. 472. *Mar. 1776*

3 Fine clothes are good only as they supply the want of other means of procuring respect.
Ib. p. 475. *27 Mar. 1776*

4 [Johnson had observed that a man is never happy for the present, but when he is drunk, and Boswell said: 'Will you not add,—or when driving rapidly in a post-chaise?']
No, Sir, you are driving rapidly *from* something, or *to* something. *Ib.* vol. iii, p. 5. *29 Mar. 1776*

5 If a madman were to come into this room with a stick in his hand, no doubt we should pity the state of his mind; but our primary consideration would be to take care of ourselves. We should knock him down first, and pity him afterwards.
Ib. p. 11. *3 Apr. 1776*

6 Consider, Sir, how should you like, though conscious of your innocence, to be tried before a jury for a capital crime, once a week. *Ib.*

7 We would all be idle if we could.
Ib. p. 13. *3 Apr. 1776*

8 No man but a blockhead ever wrote, except for money. *Ib.* p. 19. *5 Apr. 1776*

9 It is better that some should be unhappy than that none should be happy, which would be the case in a general state of equality. *Ib.* p. 26. *7 Apr. 1776*

10 His [Lord Shelburne's] parts, Sir, are pretty well for a Lord; but would not be distinguished in a man who had nothing else but his parts.
Ib. p. 35. *11 Apr. 1776*

11 A man who has not been in Italy, is always conscious of an inferiority. *Ib.* p. 36. *11 Apr. 1776*

12 'Does not Gray's poetry tower above the common mark?'
'Yes, Sir, but we must attend to the difference between what men in general cannot do if they would, and what every man may do if he would. Sixteenstring Jack towered above the common mark.'
Ib. p. 38. *12 Apr. 1776*

13 'Sir, what is poetry?'
'Why, Sir, it is much easier to say what it is not. We all *know* what light is; but it is not easy to *tell* what it is.' *Ib.*

14 [To Mrs. Thrale, who had interrupted him and Boswell by a lively extravagant sally on the expense of clothing children]
Nay, Madam, when you are declaiming, declaim; and when you are calculating, calculate.
Ib. p. 49. *26 Apr. 1776*

15 Every man of any education would rather be called a rascal, than accused of deficiency in *the graces.*
Ib. p. 54. *May 1776*

16 Sir, you have but two topics, yourself and me. I am sick of both. *Ib.* p. 57. *May 1776*

17 Dine with Jack Wilkes, Sir! I'd as soon dine with Jack Ketch *Ib.* p. 66. *See* Corrigenda

18 Sir, it is not so much to be lamented that Old England is lost, as that the Scotch have found it.
Ib. p. 78. *15 May 1776*

19 Olivarii Goldsmith, Poetae, Physici, Historici, Qui nullum fere scribendi genus non tetigit, Nullum quod tetigit non ornavit.
To Oliver Goldsmith, A Poet, Naturalist, and Historian, who left scarcely any style of writing untouched, and touched nothing that he did not adorn.
Boswell's *Life*, vol. iii, p. 82. *22 June 1776.*
Epitaph on Goldsmith. *See* Corrigenda

20 That distrust which intrudes so often on your mind is a mode of melancholy, which, if it be the business of a wise man to be happy, it is foolish to indulge; and if it be a duty to preserve our faculties entire for their proper use, it is criminal.
Ib. p. 135. *Letter to Boswell, 11 Sept. 1777*

21 If I had no duties, and no reference to futurity, I would spend my life in driving briskly in a postchaise with a pretty woman.
Ib. p. 162. *19 Sept. 1777*

22 Depend upon it, Sir, when a man knows he is to be hanged in a fortnight, it concentrates his mind wonderfully. *Ib.* p. 167. *19 Sept. 1777*

23 No, Sir, when a man is tired of London, he is tired of life; for there is in London all that life can afford.
Ib. p. 178. *20 Sept. 1777*

24 He was so generally civil, that nobody thanked him for it. *Ib.* p. 183. *21 Sept. 1777*

25 He who praises everybody praises nobody.
Ib. p. 225 n.

26 Round numbers are always false.
Ib. p. 226, n. 4. *30 Mar. 1778. Wks. 1787*

27 Accustom your children (said he) constantly to this; if a thing happened at one window and they, when relating it, say that it happened at another, do not let it pass, but instantly check them; you do not know where deviation from truth will end.
Ib. p. 228. *31 Mar. 1778*

28 [Of the appearance of the spirit of a person after death]
All argument is against it; but all belief is for it.
Ib. p. 230. *31 Mar. 1778*

29 John Wesley's conversation is good, but he is never at leisure. He is always obliged to go at a certain hour. This is very disagreeable to a man who loves to fold his legs and have out his talk, as I do. *Ib.*

30 Though we cannot out-vote them we will out-argue them. *Ib.* p. 234. *3 Apr. 1778*

31 [To a clergyman who asked: 'Were not Dodd's sermons addressed to the passions?']
They were nothing, Sir, be they addressed to what they may. *Ib.* p. 248. *7 Apr. 1778*

32 Seeing Scotland, Madam, is only seeing a worse England. *Ib.*

33 Goldsmith, however, was a man, who, whatever he wrote, did it better than any other man could do.
Ib. p. 253. *9 Apr. 1778*

34 Every man thinks meanly of himself for not having been a soldier, or not having been at sea.
Ib. p. 265. *10 Apr. 1778*

35 A mere antiquarian is a rugged being.
Ib. p. 278. *Letter to Boswell, 23 Apr. 1778*

1 Johnson had said that he could repeat a complete chapter of 'The Natural History of Iceland', from the Danish of Horrebow, the whole of which was exactly thus:—'CHAP. LXXII. *Concerning snakes.* 'There are no snakes to be met with throughout the whole island.'
    Boswell's Life of Johnson, vol. iii, p. 279. *13 Apr. 1778*

2 A country governed by a despot is an inverted cone.
    Ib. p. 283. 14 Apr. 1778

3 I am willing to love all mankind, *except an American.*
    Ib. p. 290. 15 Apr. 1778

4 As the Spanish proverb says, 'He, who would bring home the wealth of the Indies, must carry the wealth of the Indies with him.' So it is in travelling; a man must carry knowledge with him, if he would bring home knowledge.
    Ib. p. 302. 17 Apr. 1778

5 All censure of a man's self is oblique praise. It is in order to shew how much he can spare.
    Ib. p. 323. 25 Apr. 1778

6 [On Boswell's expressing surprise at finding a Staffordshire Whig]
    Sir, there are rascals in all countries.
    Ib. p. 326. 28 Apr. 1778

7 I have always said, the first Whig was the Devil. *Ib.*

8 It is thus that mutual cowardice keeps us in peace. Were one half of mankind brave and one half cowards, the brave would be always beating the cowards. Were all brave, they would lead a very uneasy life; all would be continually fighting; but being all cowards, we go on very well. *Ib.*

9 The King of Siam sent ambassadors to Louis XIV, but Louis XIV sent none to the King of Siam.
    Ib. p. 336. 29 Apr. 1778

10 Were it not for imagination, Sir, a man would be as happy in the arms of a chambermaid as of a Duchess. *Ib. p. 341. 9 May 1778*

11 Dr. Mead lived more in the broad sunshine of life than almost any man. *Ib. p. 355. 16 May 1778*

12 Claret is the liquor for boys; port for men; but he who aspires to be a hero must drink brandy.
    Ib. p. 381. 7 Apr. 1779

13 A man who exposes himself when he is intoxicated, has not the art of getting drunk.
    Ib. p. 389. 24 Apr. 1779

14 Remember that all tricks are either knavish or childish.
    Ib. p. 396. Letter to Boswell, 9 Sept. 1779

15 *Boswell:* Is not the Giant's-Causeway worth seeing? *Johnson:* Worth seeing? yes; but not worth going to see. *Ib. p. 410. 12 Oct. 1779*

16 If you are idle, be not solitary; if you are solitary, be not idle.
    Ib. p. 415. Letter to Boswell, 27 Oct. 1779

17 Sir, among the anfractuosities of the human mind, I know not if it may not be one, that there is a superstitious reluctance to sit for a picture.
    Ib. vol. iv, p. 4. 1780

18 [Of Kitty Clive]
    Clive, sir, is a good thing to sit by; she always understands what you say. *Ib. p. 7. 1780*

19 [On being asked why Pope had written:
    Let modest Foster, if he will, excel
    Ten metropolitans in preaching well]
    Sir, he hoped it would vex somebody.
    Boswell's Life, vol. iv, p. 9. 1780

20 A Frenchman must be always talking, whether he knows anything of the matter or not; an Englishman is content to say nothing, when he has nothing to say. *Ib. p. 15. 1780*

21 Greek, Sir, is like lace; every man gets as much of it as he can. *Ib. p. 23. 1780*

22 Are we alive after all this satire! *Ib. p. 29. 1780*

23 [Of Goldsmith]
    No man was more foolish when he had not a pen in his hand, or more wise when he had. *Ib.*

24 Depend upon it that if a man talks of his misfortunes there is something in them that is not disagreeable to him; for where there is nothing but pure misery there never is any recourse to the mention of it.
    Ib. p. 31. 1780

25 [Mr. Fowke once observed to Dr. Johnson that, in his opinion, the Doctor's literary strength lay in writing biography, in which he infinitely exceeded all his contemporaries]
    'Sir', said Johnson, 'I believe that is true. The dogs don't know how to write trifles with dignity.'
    Ib. p. 34. n. 5

26 Mrs. Montagu has dropt me. Now, Sir, there are people whom one should like very well to drop, but would not wish to be dropped by.
    Ib. p. 73. Mar. 1781

27 This merriment of parsons is mighty offensive.
    Ib. p. 76. Mar. 1781

28 [Of Lord North]
    He fills a chair. *Ib. p. 81. 1 Apr. 1781*

29 [At the sale of Thrale's brewery]
    We are not here to sell a parcel of boilers and vats, but the potentiality of growing rich, beyond the dreams of avarice. *Ib. p. 87. 6 Apr. 1781*

30 'The woman had a bottom of good sense.'
    The word '*bottom*' thus introduced, was so ludicrous, . . . that most of us could not forbear tittering . . .
    'Where's the merriment? . . . I say the *woman* was *fundamentally* sensible.' *Ib. p. 99. 20 Apr. 1781*

31 Classical quotation is the *parole* of literary men all over the world. *Ib. p. 102. 8 May 1781*

32 [To Miss Monckton, afterwards Lady Corke, who said that Sterne's writings affected her]
    Why, that is, because, dearest, you're a dunce.
    Ib. p. 109. May 1781

33 Sir, I have two very cogent reasons for not printing any list of subscribers;—one, that I have lost all the names,—the other, that I have spent all the money. *Ib. p. 111. May 1781*

34 My friend [Johnson] was of opinion, that when a man of rank appeared in that character [as an author], he deserved to have his merit handsomely allowed.
    Ib. p. 114. May 1781

35 A wise Tory and a wise Whig, I believe, will agree. Their principles are the same, though their modes of thinking are different.
    Ib. p. 117. Written statement given to Boswell, May 1781

1 Officious, innocent, sincere,
Of every friendless name the friend.

Yet still he fills affection's eye,
Obscurely wise, and coarsely kind.
Boswell's *Life*, vol. iv, p. 127. *20 Jan. 1782.*
On the death of Mr. Levett

2 In Misery's darkest caverns known,
His ready help was ever nigh. *Ib.*

3 His virtues walk'd their narrow round,
Nor made a pause, nor left a void;
And sure th' Eternal Master found
His single talent well employ'd. *Ib.*

4 Then, with no throbs of fiery pain,
No cold gradations of decay,
Death broke at once the vital chain,
And freed his soul the nearest way. *Ib.*

5 Resolve not to be poor: whatever you have, spend less. Poverty is a great enemy to human happiness; it certainly destroys liberty, and it makes some virtues impracticable and others extremely difficult.
Ib. p. 157. *7 Dec. 1782*

6 I never have sought the world; the world was not to seek me. *Ib.* p. 172. *23 Mar. 1783*

7 Thurlow is a fine fellow; he fairly puts his mind to yours. *Ib.* p. 179. *1783*

8 [Of Ossian]
Sir, a man might write such stuff for ever, if he would *abandon* his mind to it. *Ib.* p. 183. *1783*

9 [When Dr. Adam Smith was expatiating on the beauty of Glasgow, Johnson had cut him short by saying, 'Pray, Sir, have you ever seen Brentford?']
Boswell: My dear Sir, surely that was *shocking*?
Johnson: Why, then, Sir, *you* have never seen Brentford. *Ib.* p. 186. *1783*

10 [To Maurice Morgann who asked him whether he reckoned Derrick or Smart the better poet]
Sir, there is no settling the point of precedency between a louse and a flea. *Ib.* p. 192. *1783*

11 When I observed he was a fine cat, saying, 'why yes, Sir, but I have had cats whom I liked better than this'; and then as if perceiving Hodge to be out of countenance, adding, 'but he is a very fine cat, a very fine cat indeed.' *Ib.* p. 197. *1783*

12 [Johnson had said 'public affairs vex no man', and Boswell had suggested that the growing power of the Whigs vexed Johnson]
Sir, I have never slept an hour less, nor eat an ounce less meat. I would have knocked the factious dogs on the head, to be sure; but I was not *vexed*.
Ib. p. 220. *15 May 1783*

13 Clear your *mind* of cant. *Ib.* p. 221. *15 May 1783*

14 Sir, he is a cursed Whig, a *bottomless* Whig, as they all are now. *Ib.* p. 223. *26 May 1783*

15 As I know more of mankind I expect less of them, and am ready now to call a man *a good man*, upon easier terms than I was formerly.
Ib. p. 239. *Sept. 1783*

16 Boswell is a very clubable man. *Ib.* p. 254 n. *1783*

17 [Of George Psalmanazar, whom he reverenced for his piety]
I should as soon think of contradicting a Bishop.
Ib. p. 274. *15 May 1784*

18 [To Bennet Langton who brought him texts on Christian charity when he was ill]
What is your drift, Sir?
Boswell's *Life*, vol. iv, p. 281. *30 May 1784*

19 [On the roast mutton he had for dinner at an inn]
It is as bad as bad can be: it is ill-fed, ill-killed, ill-kept, and ill-drest. *Ib.* p. 284. *3 June 1784*

20 *Johnson*: As I cannot be sure that I have fulfilled the conditions on which salvation is granted, I am afraid I may be one of those who shall be damned (looking dismally).
Dr Adams: What do you mean by damned?
Johnson (passionately and loudly): Sent to Hell, Sir, and punished everlastingly. *Ib.* p. 299. *1784*

21 [To Miss Hannah More, who had expressed a wonder that the poet who had written *Paradise Lost* should write such poor Sonnets]
Milton, Madam, was a genius that could cut a Colossus from a rock; but could not carve heads upon cherry-stones. *Ib.* p. 305. *13 June 1784*

22 Don't cant in defence of savages.
Ib. p. 308. *15 June 1784*

23 [On hearing the line in Brooke's *Earl of Essex*
'Who rules o'er freemen should himself be free']
It might as well be 'Who drives fat oxen should himself be fat.' *Ib.* p. 313. *June 1784*

24 Sir, I have found you an argument; but I am not obliged to find you an understanding. *Ib.*

25 [On Sir Joshua Reynolds's observing that the real character of a man was found out by his amusements]
Yes, Sir; no man is a hypocrite in his pleasures.
Ib. p. 316. *June 1784*

26 Blown about by every wind of criticism.
Ib. p. 319. *June 1784*

27 Talking of the Comedy of 'The Rehearsal', he [Johnson] said, 'It has not wit enough to keep it sweet.' This was easy;—he therefore caught himself, and pronounced a more rounded sentence; 'It has not vitality enough to preserve it from putrefaction.' *Ib.* p. 320. *June 1784*

28 Who can run the race with Death?
Ib. p. 360. *Letter to Dr. Burney, 2 Aug. 1784*

29 Sir, I look upon every day to be lost, in which I do not make a new acquaintance. *Ib.* p. 374. *Nov. 1784*

30 I will be conquered; I will not capitulate. *Ib.*

31 Are you sick or are you sullen?
Ib. p. 380. *Letter to Boswell, 3 Nov. 1784*

32 A lawyer has no business with the justice or injustice of the cause which he undertakes, unless his client asks his opinion, and then he is bound to give it honestly. The justice or injustice of the cause is to be decided by the judge.
Boswell, *Tour to the Hebrides, 15 Aug. 1773*, p. 175

33 Let him go abroad to a distant country; let him go to some place where he is *not* known. Don't let him go to the devil where he is known!
Ib. 18 Aug., p. 194

34 I wonder, however, that so many people have written who might have let it alone. *Ib. 19 Aug.*, p. 197

1 [To Boswell who would excuse Sir Alexander Gordon's boring of them by saying it was all kindness]
True, Sir; but sensation is sensation.
Boswell, *Tour to the Hebrides*, 23 Aug., p. 219

2 I have, all my life long, been lying till noon; yet I tell all young men, and tell them with great sincerity, that nobody who does not rise early will ever do any good. *Ib. 14 Sept.*, p. 299

3 I inherited a vile melancholy from my father, which has made me mad all my life, at least not sober.
Ib. 16 Sept., p. 302

4 I am always sorry when any language is lost, because languages are the pedigree of nations.
Ib. 18 Sept., p. 310

5 [Johnson, railing against Scotland, said that the wine the Scots had before the Union would not make them drunk. Boswell assured Johnson there was much drunkenness]
No, Sir; there were people who died of dropsies, which they contracted in trying to get drunk.
Ib. 23 Sept., p. 326

6 I do not like much to see a Whig in any dress; but I hate to see a Whig in a parson's gown.
Ib. 24 Sept., p. 331

7 It was said to old Bentley upon the attacks against him, 'Why, they'll write you down.' 'No, Sir,' he replied, 'depend upon it, no man was ever written down but by himself.' *Ib. 1 Oct.*, p. 344

8 The known style of a dedication is flattery: it professes to flatter. *Ib. 4 Oct.*, p. 352

9 A cucumber should be well sliced, and dressed with pepper and vinegar, and then thrown out, as good for nothing. *Ib. 5 Oct.*, p. 354

10 [Calling for a gill of whisky]
Come, let me know what it is that makes a Scotchman happy! *Ib. 23 Oct.*, p. 393

11 Sir, are you so grossly ignorant of human nature, as not to know that a man may be very sincere in good principles, without having good practice?
Ib. 25 Oct., p. 403

12 I am sorry I have not learned to play at cards. It is very useful in life: it generates kindness and consolidates society. *Ib. 21 Nov.*, p. 433

13 This world where much is to be done and little to be known.
Johnsonian Miscellanies ed. G. B. Hill (1897), vol. i. *Prayers and Meditations. Against inquisitive and perplexing Thoughts*, p. 118

14 Wheresoe'er I turn my view,
All is strange, yet nothing new;
Endless labour all along,
Endless labour to be wrong;
Phrase that time hath flung away,
Uncouth words in disarray,
Trick'd in antique ruff and bonnet,
Ode, and elegy, and sonnet.
Ib. Anecdotes of Johnson by Mrs. Piozzi, p. 190

15 Hermit hoar, in solemn cell,
Wearing out life's evening gray;
Strike thy bosom, sage! and tell
What is bliss, and which the way?

Thus I spoke, and speaking sigh'd,
Scarce repress'd the starting tear,
When the hoary Sage reply'd,
'Come, my lad, and drink some beer.'
Johnsonian Miscellanies, vol. i, p. 193

16 If the man who turnips cries,
Cry not when his father dies,
'Tis a proof that he had rather
Have a turnip than his father
Ib. Burlesque of Lopez de Vega's lines, 'Se acquien los leones vence,' &c.

17 He [Charles James Fox] talked to me at club one day concerning Catiline's conspiracy—so I withdrew my attention, and thought about Tom Thumb.
Ib. p. 202

18 Dear Bathurst (said he to me one day) was a man to my very heart's content: he hated a fool, and he hated a rogue, and he hated a whig; he was a very good hater. *Ib.* p. 204

19 [Of a Jamaica gentleman, then lately dead]
He will not, whither he is now gone, find much difference, I believe, either in the climate or the company. *Ib.* p. 211

20 One day at Streatham . . . a young gentleman called to him suddenly, and I suppose he thought disrespectfully, in these words: 'Mr. Johnson, would you advise me to marry?' 'I would advise no man to marry, Sir,' returns for answer in a very angry tone Dr Johnson, 'who is not likely to propagate understanding.' *Ib.* p. 213

21 [To a Quaker:]
Oh, let us not be found, when our Master calls us, ripping the lace off our waistcoats, but the spirit of contention from our souls and tongues!
Ib. p. 222

22 *Goldsmith*: Here's such a stir about a fellow that has written one book [Beattie's *Essay on Truth*], and I have written many.
Johnson: Ah, Doctor, there go two-and-forty sixpences you know to one guinea. *Ib.* p. 269

23 It is very strange, and very melancholy, that the paucity of human pleasures should persuade us ever to call hunting one of them. *Ib.* p. 288

24 You could not stand five minutes with that man [Edmund Burke] beneath a shed while it rained, but you must be convinced you had been standing with the greatest man you had ever yet seen.
Ib. p. 290

25 Johnson observed that he 'did not care to speak ill of any man behind his back, but he believed the gentleman was an *attorney*'. *Ib.* p. 327, n.

26 Was there ever yet anything written by mere man that was wished longer by its readers, excepting *Don Quixote, Robinson Crusoe*, and the *Pilgrim's Progress*? *Ib.* p. 332

27 [On his Parliamentary reports]
I took care that the *Whig Dogs* should not have the best of it.
Ib. An Essay on Johnson, by Arthur Murphy, p. 379

28 Books that you may carry to the fire, and hold readily in your hand, are the most useful after all.
Ib. vol. ii. *Apophthegms from Hawkins's edition of Johnson's works*, p. 2

1 A man is in general better pleased when he has a good dinner upon his table, than when his wife talks Greek. *Johnsonian Miscellanies, vol. ii, p. 11*

2 I would rather see the portrait of a dog that I know, than all the allegorical paintings they can shew me in the world. *Ib. p. 15*

3 There is a time of life, Sir, when a man requires the repairs of a table.
Ib. Anecdotes by Joseph Cradock, p. 64

4 I have heard him assert, that a tavern chair was the throne of human felicity.
Ib. Extracts from Hawkins's Life of Johnson, p. 91.

5 I dogmatise and am contradicted, and in this conflict of opinions and sentiments I find delight. *Ib. p. 92*

6 Abstinence is as easy to me, as temperance would be difficult. *Ib. Anecdotes by Hannah More, p. 197*

7 Of music Dr. Johnson used to say that it was the only sensual pleasure without vice.
Ib. Anecdotes by William Seward, p. 301

8 [Of the performance of a celebrated violinist] Difficult do you call it, Sir? I wish it were impossible.
Ib. p. 308

9 What is written without effort is in general read without pleasure. *Ib. p. 309*

10 As with my hat upon my head
I walk'd along the Strand,
I there did meet another man
With his hat in his hand.
Ib. Anecdotes by George Steevens, p. 315

11 Where you see a Whig you see a rascal.
Ib. Anecdotes by the Rev. W. Cole, p. 393

12 Love is the wisdom of the fool and the folly of the wise.
Ib. William Cooke's Life of Samuel Foote, p. 393

13 Fly fishing may be a very pleasant amusement; but angling or float fishing I can only compare to a stick and a string, with a worm at one end and a fool at the other.
Attributed to Johnson by Hawker in Instructions to Young Sportsmen, 1859, p. 197. *Not found in his works. See* Notes and Queries, *11 Dec. 1915*

14 Madam, before you flatter a man so grossly to his face, you should consider whether or not your flattery is worth his having.
Remark to Hannah More. Mme D'Arblay's *Diary and Letters* (1891), vol. i, ch. ii, p. 55

15 I know not, madam, that you have a right, upon moral principles, to make your readers suffer so much.
To Mrs. Sheridan, after publication of her novel Memoirs of Miss Sydney Biddulph (1763)

16 Sir, your wife, under pretence of keeping a bawdy-house, is a receiver of stolen goods.
To a Thames waterman, reported by Bennet Langton to James Boswell, 1780

17 Nobody speaks in earnest, Sir; there is no serious conversation. *Attrib.*

18 A book should teach us to enjoy life, or to endure it.
Attrib. But see Corrigenda

19 No two men can be half an hour together, but one shall acquire an evident superiority over the other.
See Corrigenda

20 In all pointed sentences, some degree of accuracy must be sacrificed to conciseness.
On the Bravery of the English Common Soldier. Works (1787), vol. x, p. 286

21 I am not yet so lost in lexicography, as to forget that words are the daughters of earth, and that things are the sons of heaven.
Dictionary of the English Language. Preface

22 Every quotation contributes something to the stability or enlargement of the language. *Ib.*

23 But these were the dreams of a poet doomed at last to wake a lexicographer. *Ib.*

24 If the changes that we fear be thus irresistible, what remains but to acquiesce with silence, as in the other insurmountable distresses of humanity? It remains that we retard what we cannot repel, that we palliate what we cannot cure. *Ib.*

25 The chief glory of every people arises from its authors. *Ib.*

26 To make dictionaries is dull work. *Ib. Dull. 8*

27 *Excise.* A hateful tax levied upon commodities. *Ib.*

28 *Net.* Anything reticulated or decussated at equal distances, with interstices between the intersections. *Ib.*

29 *Oats.* A grain, which in England is generally given to horses, but in Scotland supports the people. *Ib.*

30 *Patron.* Commonly a wretch who supports with insolence, and is paid with flattery. *Ib.*

31 *Pension.* An allowance made to anyone without an equivalent. In England it is generally understood to mean pay given to a state hireling for treason to his country. *Ib.*

32 *Whig.* The name of a faction. *Ib.*

33 Every man is, or hopes to be, an idler.
The Idler, No. 1

34 When two Englishmen meet, their first talk is of the weather. *Ib. No. 11*

35 Promise, large promise, is the soul of an advertisement. *Ib. No. 41*

36 He is no wise man who will quit a certainty for an uncertainty. *Ib. No. 57*

37 A Scotchman must be a very sturdy moralist who does not love Scotland better than truth.
Journey to the Western Islands. Col.

38 At seventy-seven it is time to be in earnest. *Ib.*

39 Whatever withdraws us from the power of our senses; whatever makes the past, the distant, or the future, predominate over the present, advances us in the dignity of thinking beings.
Ib. Inch Kenneth

40 Grief is a species of idleness.
Letters of Johnson (ed. G. B. Hill, 1892), vol. i, p. 212. No. 302, to Mrs. Thrale, 17 Mar. 1773

41 There is no wisdom in useless and hopeless sorrow.
Ib. vol. ii, p. 215. No. 722, to Mrs. Thrale, 12 Apr. 1781

42 I am very ready to repay for that kindness which soothed twenty years of a life radically wretched.
Ib. p. 407. No. 972, to Mrs. Thrale, 8 July 1784

JOHNSON

1 A hardened and shameless tea-drinker, who has for twenty years diluted his meals with only the infusion of this fascinating plant; whose kettle has scarcely time to cool; who with tea amuses the evening, with tea solaces the midnight, and with tea welcomes the morning.
Review in the 'Literary Magazine', vol. ii. No. xiii. 1757

2 The true genius is a mind of large general powers, accidentally determined to some particular direction.
Lives of the English Poets, 1905, ed. G. B. Hill, vol. i, Cowley, § 3, p. 2

3 Language is the dress of thought. *Ib. § 181, p. 58*

4 An acrimonious and surly republican.
Ib. Milton, § 168, p. 156

5 The great source of pleasure is variety.
Ib. Butler, § 35, p. 212

6 The father of English criticism. [Dryden]
Ib. Dryden, § 193, p. 410

7 But what are the hopes of man! I am disappointed by that stroke of death, which has eclipsed the gaiety of nations and impoverished the public stock of harmless pleasure. [Garrick's death.]
Ib. vol. ii, Edmund Smith, § 76, p. 21

8 About things on which the public thinks long it commonly attains to think right.
Ib. Addison, § 136, p. 132

9 Whoever wishes to attain an English style, familiar but not coarse, and elegant but not ostentatious, must give his days and nights to the volumes of Addison. *Ib. § 168, p. 150*

10 By the common sense of readers uncorrupted with literary prejudices . . . must be finally decided all claim to poetical honours. *Ib. Gray, § 51, p. 441*

11 He washed himself with oriental scrupulosity.
Ib. vol. iii, Swift, § 122, p. 55

12 There are minds so impatient of inferiority that their gratitude is a species of revenge, and they return benefits, not because recompense is a pleasure, but because obligation is a pain.
The Rambler, 15 Jan. 1751

13 I have laboured to refine our language to grammatical purity, and to clear it from colloquial barbarisms, licentious idioms, and irregular combinations.
Ib. 14 Mar. 1752

14 Ye who listen with credulity to the whispers of fancy, and pursue with eagerness the phantoms of hope; who expect that age will perform the promises of youth, and that the deficiencies of the present day will be supplied by the morrow; attend to the history of Rasselas, Prince of Abyssinia.
Rasselas, ch. 1

15 The business of a poet, said Imlac, is to examine, not the individual, but the species; . . . he does not number the streaks of the tulip, or describe the different shades in the verdure of the forest. *Ib. ch. 10*

16 Human life is everywhere a state in which much is to be endured, and little to be enjoyed. *Ib. ch. 11*

17 Marriage has many pains, but celibacy has no pleasures. *Ib. ch. 26*

18 Example is always more efficacious than precept.
Ib. ch. 29

19 Integrity without knowledge is weak and useless, and knowledge without integrity is dangerous and dreadful. *Rasselas, ch. 41*

20 The endearing elegance of female friendship.
Ib. ch. 45

21 The power of punishment is to silence, not to confute.
Sermons, No. xxiii

22 Notes are often necessary, but they are necessary evils.
Shakespeare (1765), preface.

23 A quibble is to Shakespeare what luminous vapours are to the traveller: he follows it at all adventures; it is sure to lead him out of his way and sure to engulf him in the mire. *Ib.*

24 It must be at last confessed that, as we owe everything to him [Shakespeare], he owes something to us; that, if much of our praise is paid by perception and judgement, much is likewise given by custom and veneration. We fix our eyes upon his graces and turn them from his deformities, and endure in him what we should in another loathe or despise. *Ib.*

25 I have always suspected that the reading is right which requires many words to prove it wrong, and the emendation wrong that cannot without so much labour appear to be right. *Ib.*

26 How is it that we hear the loudest yelps for liberty among the drivers of negroes?
Taxation No Tyranny

27 Unmov'd tho' witlings sneer and rivals rail;
Studious to please, yet not asham'd to fail.
Irene, prologue

28 Learn that the present hour alone is man's.
Ib. III. ii. 33

29 How small, of all that human hearts endure,
That part which laws or kings can cause or cure!
Still to ourselves in every place consigned,
Our own felicity we make or find:
With secret course, which no loud storms annoy,
Glides the smooth current of domestic joy.
Lines added to Goldsmith's 'Traveller'

30 Here falling houses thunder on your head,
And here a female atheist talks you dead.
London, l. 17

31 And, bid him go to Hell, to Hell he goes. *Ib. l. 116*

32 Of all the griefs that harrass the distress'd,
Sure the most bitter is a scornful jest;
Fate never wounds more deep the gen'rous heart,
Than when a blockhead's insult points the dart.
Ib. l. 166

33 This mournful truth is ev'rywhere confess'd,
Slow rises worth by poverty depress'd. *Ib. l. 176*

34 When learning's triumph o'er her barb'rous foes
First rear'd the Stage, immortal Shakespeare rose;
Each change of many-colour'd life he drew,
Exhausted worlds, and then imagin'd new:
Existence saw him spurn her bounded reign,
And panting Time toil'd after him in vain.
Prologue at the Opening of the Theatre in Drury Lane, 1747

35 Cold approbation gave the ling'ring bays,
For those who durst not censure, scarce could praise.
Ib.

36 The wild vicissitudes of taste. *Ib.*

1 The stage but echoes back the public voice.
The drama's laws the drama's patrons give,
For we that live to please, must please to live.
Prologue at the Opening of Drury Lane

2 Let observation with extensive view,
Survey mankind, from China to Peru;
Remark each anxious toil, each eager strife,
And watch the busy scenes of crowded life.
Vanity of Human Wishes, l. 1

3 Our supple tribes repress their patriot throats,
And ask no questions but the price of votes. *Ib.* l. 95

4 Deign on the passing world to turn thine eyes,
And pause awhile from letters to be wise;
There mark what ills the scholar's life assail,
Toil, envy, want, the patron, and the jail.
See nations slowly wise, and meanly just,
To buried merit raise the tardy bust. *Ib.* l. 157

5 A frame of adamant, a soul of fire,
No dangers fright him and no labours tire. *Ib.* l. 193

6 His fall was destined to a barren strand,
A petty fortress, and a dubious hand;
He left the name, at which the world grew pale,
To point a moral, or adorn a tale. *Ib.* l. 219

7 'Enlarge my life with multitude of days!'
In health, in sickness, thus the suppliant prays:
Hides from himself its state, and shuns to know,
That life protracted is protracted woe.
Time hovers o'er, impatient to destroy,
And shuts up all the passages of joy. *Ib.* l. 225

8 An age that melts with unperceiv'd decay,
And glides in modest innocence away. *Ib.* l. 293

9 Superfluous lags the vet'ran on the stage. *Ib.* l. 308

10 In life's last scene what prodigies surprise,
Fears of the brave, and follies of the wise!
From Marlb'rough's eyes the streams of dotage flow,
And Swift expires a driv'ler and a show. *Ib.* l. 315

11 What ills from beauty spring. *Ib.* l. 321

12 Still raise for good the supplicating voice,
But leave to Heaven the measure and the choice,
Ib. l. 351

13 Secure, whate'er he gives, he gives the best. *Ib.* l. 356

14 Faith, that, panting for a happier seat,
Counts death kind Nature's signal of retreat. *Ib.* l. 363

15 With these celestial Wisdom calms the mind,
And makes the happiness she does not find. *Ib.* l. 367

JOHN BENN JOHNSTONE
1803–1891

16 I want you to assist me in forcing her on board the
lugger; once there, I'll frighten her into marriage.

(*Since quoted as:* Once aboard the lugger and the maid
is mine.) *The Gipsy Farmer*

AL JOLSON
1886–1950

17 You ain't heard nothin' yet, folks.
Remark in the first talking film, 'The Jazz Singer',
July 1927

JOHN PAUL JONES
1747–1792

18 I have not yet begun to fight.
*Remark on being hailed to know whether he had
struck his flag, as his ship was sinking, 23 Sept.
1779.* De Koven's *Life and Letters of J. P
Jones*, vol. i

SIR WILLIAM JONES
1746–1794

19 On parent knees, a naked new-born child,
Weeping thou sat'st, when all around thee smil'd;
So live, that, sinking in thy last long sleep,
Calm thou may'st smile, while all around thee weep.
Persian Asiatick Miscellany (1786), vol. ii, p.
374, *A Moral Tetrastich*

20 My opinion is, that power should always be distrusted,
in whatever hands it is placed.
Lord Teignmouth's *Life of Sir W. Jones* (1835),
vol. i. *Letter to Lord Althorpe, 5 Oct. 1782*

21 Seven hours to law, to soothing slumber seven,
Ten to the world allot, and *all* to Heaven.
Ib. vol. ii. *Lines in Substitution for Sir E. Coke's
lines*: Six hours in sleep, [&c.]. (*See 148:8*)

BEN JONSON
1573–1637

22 Fortune, that favours fools. *The Alchemist*, prologue

23 I will eat exceedingly, and prophesy.
Bartholomew Fair, I. vi

24 Neither do thou lust after that tawney weed tobacco.
Ib. II. vi

25 When I mock poorness, then heaven make me poor.
The Case is Altered, III. i

26 PEOPLE:
The Voice of Cato is the voice of Rome.
CATO:
The voice of Rome is the consent of heaven!
Catiline his Conspiracy, III. i

27 Where it concerns himself,
Who's angry at a slander makes it true. *Ib.*

28 Slow, slow, fresh fount, keep time with my salt tears:
Yet, slower, yet; O faintly, gentle springs:
List to the heavy part the music bears,
Woe weeps out her division, when she sings.
Cynthia's Revels, I. i

29 So they be ill men,
If they spake worse, 'twere better: for of such
To be dispraised, is the most perfect praise. *Ib.* III. ii

30 True happiness
Consists not in the multitude of friends,
But in the worth and choice. *Ib.*

31 Queen and huntress, chaste and fair,
Now the sun is laid to sleep,
Seated in thy silver chair,
State in wonted manner keep:
Hesperus entreats thy light,
Goddess, excellently bright. *Ib.* v. iii

32 If he were
To be made honest by an act of parliament,
I should not alter in my faith of him.
The Devil is An Ass, IV. i

1 I remember the players have often mentioned it as an honour to Shakespeare that in his writing (whatsoever he penned) he never blotted out a line. My answer hath been 'Would he had blotted a thousand'. Which they thought a malevolent speech. I had not told posterity this, but for their ignorance, who chose that circumstance to commend their friend by wherein he most faulted; and to justify mine own candour: for I loved the man, and do honour his memory, on this side idolatry, as much as any. He was (indeed) honest, and of an open and free nature; had an excellent phantasy, brave notions, and gentle expressions; wherein he flowed with that facility, that sometimes it was necessary he should be stopped: *sufflaminandus erat*, as Augustus said of Haterius. His wit was in his own power, would the rule of it had been so too. . . . But he redeemed his vices with his virtues. There was ever more in him to be praised than to be pardoned.
Discoveries. De Shakespeare Nostrati. Augustus in Haterium

2 His hearers could not cough, or look aside from him, without loss. . . . The fear of every man that heard him was, lest he should make an end. [Bacon.]
Ib. lxxviii. Dominus Verulamius

3 In his adversity I ever prayed, that God would give him strength; for greatness he could not want.
Ib. lxxx. De Augmentis Scientiarum,—Lord St. Alban

4 Yet the best pilots have needs of mariners, besides sails, anchor, and other tackle.
Ib. Illiteratus Princeps

5 Talking and eloquence are not the same: to speak, and to speak well, are two things.
Ib. Praecept. Element

6 Alas, all the castles I have, are built with air, thou know'st. *Eastward Ho, II. ii. 226*

7 Still to be neat, still to be drest,
As you were going to a feast;
Still to be powder'd, still perfum'd,
Lady, it is to be presumed,
Though art's hid causes are not found,
All is not sweet, all is not sound.

Give me a look, give me a face,
That makes simplicity a grace;
Robes loosely flowing, hair as free:
Such sweet neglect more taketh me,
Than all the adulteries of art;
They strike mine eyes, but not my heart.
Epicoene, I. i

8 HAUGHTY:
Is this the silent woman?
CENTAURE:
Nay, she has found her tongue since she was married.
Ib. III. vi

9 But that which most doth take my Muse and me,
Is a pure cup of rich Canary wine,
Which is the Mermaid's now, but shall be mine:
Of which, had Horace or Anacreon tasted,
Their lives, as do their lines, till now had lasted.
Epigrams, ci. Inviting a Friend to Supper

10 Weep with me, all you that read
This little story:
And know for whom a tear you shed
Death's self is sorry.
'Twas a child that so did thrive
In grace and feature,
As Heaven and Nature seem'd to strive
Which own'd the creature.
Years he number'd scarce thirteen
When Fates turn'd cruel,
Yet three fill'd Zodiacs had he been
The stage's jewel;
And did act, what now we moan,
Old men so duly,
As sooth the Parcae thought him one,
He play'd so truly.
So, by error, to his fate
They all consented;
But viewing him since, alas, too late!
They have repented;
And have sought (to give new birth)
In baths to steep him;
But being so much too good for earth,
Heaven vows to keep him.
Epigrams, cxx. An Epitaph on Salomon Pavy, a Child of Queen Elizabeth's Chapel

11 Underneath this stone doth lie
As much beauty as could die;
Which in life did harbour give
To more virtue than doth live.
If at all she had a fault,
Leave it buried in this vault.
One name was Elizabeth,
The other let it sleep with death:
Fitter, where it died, to tell,
Than that it lived at all! Farewell!
Ib. cxxiv. Epitaph on Elizabeth L. H.

12 Helter skelter, hang sorrow, care'll kill a cat, up-tails all, and a louse for the hangman.
Every Man in His Humour, I. iii

13 As sure as death. *Ib. II. i*

14 Ods me, I marvel what pleasure or felicity they have in taking their roguish tobacco. It is good for nothing but to choke a man, and fill him full of smoke and embers. *Ib. III. v*

15 I do honour the very flea of his dog. *Ib. IV. ii*

16 I have it here in black and white. *Ib.*

17 It must be done like lightning. *Ib. v*

18 There shall be no love lost.
Every Man out of His Humour, II. i

19 Blind Fortune still
Bestows her gifts on such as cannot use them. *Ib. ii*

20 Follow a shadow, it still flies you,
Seem to fly it, it will pursue:
So court a mistress, she denies you;
Let her alone, she will court you.
Say, are not women truly, then,
Styl'd but the shadows of us men?
The Forest, vii. Song: That Women are but Men's Shadows

21 Drink to me only with thine eyes,
And I will pledge with mine;
Or leave a kiss but in the cup,
And I'll not look for wine.

The thirst that from the soul doth rise
  Doth ask a drink divine;
But might I of Jove's nectar sup,
  I would not change for thine.

I sent thee late a rosy wreath,
  Not so much honouring thee,
As giving it a hope that there
  It could not wither'd be.
But thou thereon didst only breathe,
  And sent'st it back to me;
Since when it grows and smells, I swear,
  Not of itself, but thee.   *The Forest, ix. To Celia*

1 How near to good is what is fair!
  Which we no sooner see,
  But with the lines and outward air,
  Our senses taken be.
        Love Freed from Ignorance and Folly

2 Thou art not to learn the humours and tricks of that
  old bald cheater, Time.   *The Poetaster, I. i*

3 Ramp up my genius, be not retrograde;
  But boldly nominate a spade a spade.   *Ib. v. i*

4 Detraction is but baseness' varlet;
  And apes are apes, though clothed in scarlet.   *Ib.*

5 This is Mab, the Mistress-Fairy
  That doth nightly rob the dairy.   *The Satyr*

6 She that pinches country wenches
  If they rub not clean their benches.   *Ib.*

7 But if so they chance to feast her,
  In a shoe she drops a tester.   *Ib.*

8   Tell proud Jove,
  Between his power and thine there is no odds:
  'Twas only fear first in the world made gods.
        Sejanus, II. ii

9 This figure that thou here seest put,
  It was for gentle Shakespeare cut,
  Wherein the graver had a strife
  With Nature, to out-do the life:
  O could he but have drawn his wit
  As well in brass, as he has hit
  His face; the print would then surpass
  All that was ever writ in brass:
  But since he cannot, reader, look
  Not on his picture, but his book.
        On the Portrait of Shakespeare, To the Reader

10 While I confess thy writings to be such,
  As neither man, nor muse, can praise too much.
        *To the Memory of My Beloved, the Author, Mr.
        William Shakespeare*

11   Soul of the Age!
  The applause! delight! the wonder of our stage!
  My Shakespeare, rise; I will not lodge thee by
  Chaucer, or Spenser, or bid Beaumont lie
  A little further, to make thee a room:
  Thou art a monument, without a tomb,
  And art alive still, while thy book doth live,
  And we have wits to read, and praise to give.   *Ib.*

12 Marlowe's mighty line.   *Ib.*

13 And though thou hadst small Latin, and less Greek.   *Ib.*

14 Call forth thundering Aeschylus.   *Ib.*

15   To hear thy buskin tread,
  And shake a stage: or, when thy socks were on,
  Leave thee alone, for the comparison
  Of all, that insolent Greece, or haughty Rome
  Sent forth, or since did from their ashes come.   *Ib.*

16 He was not of an age, but for all time!   *Ib.*

17 For a good poet's made, as well as born.   *Ib.*

18 Sweet Swan of Avon! what a sight it were
  To see thee in our waters yet appear,
  And make those flights upon the banks of Thames,
  That so did take Eliza, and our James!   *Ib.*

19 THOMAS:
  They write here, one Cornelius-Son
  Hath made the Hollanders an invisible eel
  To swim the haven at Dunkirk, and sink all
  The shipping there. . . .
CYMBAL:
  It is an automa, runs under water,
  With a snug nose, and has a nimble tail
  Made like an auger, with which tail she wriggles
  Betwixt the costs of a ship, and sinks it straight.
        The Staple of News, III. i

20 Well, they talk we shall have no more Parliaments,
    God bless us!   *Ib.*

21   Hark you, John Clay, if you have
  Done any such thing, tell troth and shame the devil.
        Tale of a Tub, II. i

22 Mother, the still sow eats up all the draff.   *Ib. III. v*

23 I sing the birth was born to-night,
  The author both of life and light.
        *Underwoods. Poems of Devotion, iii. Hymn on the
        Nativity*

24 Have you seen but a bright lily grow,
  Before rude hands have touch'd it?
  Have you mark'd but the fall o' the snow
  Before the soil hath smutch'd it?

  O so white! O so soft! O so sweet is she!
        Ib. Celebration of Charis, iv. Her Triumph

25 She is Venus when she smiles;
  But she's Juno when she walks,
  And Minerva when she talks.   *Ib. v*

26 Greek was free from rhyme's infection,
  Happy Greek, by this protection,
    Was not spoiled:
  Whilst the Latin, queen of tongues,
  Is not yet free from rhyme's wrongs,
    But rests foiled.
        Ib. xlviii. A Fit of Rhyme against Rhyme

27 Vulgar languages that want
  Words, and sweetness, and be scant
    Of true measure,
  Tyrant rhyme hath so abused,
  That they long since have refused
    Other cesure.
  He that first invented thee,
  May his joints tormented be,
    Cramp'd for ever;
  Still may syllabes jar with time,
  Still may reason war with rhyme,
    Resting never!   *Ib.*

28 England's high Chancellor: the destin'd heir,
  In his soft cradle, to his father's chair.
        Ib. lxx. On Lord Bacon's [Sixtieth] Birthday

1 It is not growing like a tree
In bulk, doth make men better be;
Or standing long an oak, three hundred year,
To fall a log at last, dry, bald, and sere:
    A lily of a day,
    Is fairer far in May,
Although it fall and die that night;
It was the plant and flower of light.
In small proportions we just beauties see;
And in short measures, life may perfect be.
    Underwoods, lxxxviii. *A Pindaric Ode on the
    Death of Sir H. Morison*

2 What gentle ghost, besprent with April dew,
Hails me so solemnly to yonder yew?
    Ib. ci. *Elegy on the Lady Jane Pawlet*

3 The voice so sweet, the words so fair,
As some soft chime had stroked the air;
And though the sound were parted thence,
Still left an echo in the sense.   *Ib. Eupheme*, iv

4 Calumnies are answered best with silence.
    Volpone, II. ii

5 Come, my Celia, let us prove,
While we can, the sports of love.   *Ib.* III. v

6 Suns, that set, may rise again;
But if once we lose this light,
'Tis with us perpetual night.   *Ib.*

7 You have a gift, sir, (thank your education,)
Will never let you want, while there are men,
And malice, to breed causes. [To a lawyer.]   *Ib.* v. i

8   Mischiefs feed
Like beasts, till they be fat, and then they bleed.
    Ib. viii

9 O rare Ben Jonson.
    *Epitaph written on his tombstone in Westminster
    Abbey, by Jack Young. See* Aubrey's *Brief
    Lives, Ben Jonson*

DOROTHEA JORDAN
1762–1816

10 'Oh where, and Oh! where is your Highland laddie
    gone?'
'He's gone to fight the French, for King George
    upon the throne,
And it's Oh! in my heart, how I wish him safe at
    home!'   *The Blue Bells of Scotland*

JOSEPH JOUBERT
1754–1824

11 S'il est un homme tourmenté par la maudite ambition
de mettre tout un livre dans une page, toute une
page dans une phrase, et cette phrase dans un mot,
c'est moi.

    If there be any man cursed with the itch to com-
    press a whole book into a page, a whole page into
    a phrase, and that phrase into a word, it is I.
    Pensées

BENJAMIN JOWETT
1817–1893

12 The lie in the Soul is a true lie.
    From the Introduction to his translation of Plato's
    Republic, bk. ii

13 One man is as good as another until he has written a
book.
    Campbell and Abbott, *Life and Letters of B.
    Jowett*, i. 248

JAMES JOYCE
1882–1941

14 A portrait of the artist as a young man.   *Title of Book*

JULIAN
c. 331–363

15 Vicisti, Galilæe.
    Thou hast conquered, O Galilean.
    Dying words. Latin translation of Theodoret,
    Hist. Eccles. iii. 20

JUNIUS
fl. 1770

16 The liberty of the press is the *Palladium* of all the
civil, political, and religious rights of an Englishman.   *Letters*, dedication

17 The right of election is the very essence of the constitution.   *Ib.* Letter 11, *24 Apr. 1769*

18 Is this the wisdom of a great minister? or is it the
ominous vibration of a pendulum?
    Ib. Letter 12, *30 May 1769*

19 There is a holy mistaken zeal in politics as well as in
religion. By persuading others, we convince ourselves.   *Ib.* Letter 35, *19 Dec. 1769*

20 Whether it be the heart to conceive, the understanding to direct, or the hand to execute.
    Ib. Letter 37, *19 Mar. 1770*

21 The injustice done to an individual is sometimes of
service to the public.   *Ib.* Letter 41, *14 Nov. 1770*

EMPEROR JUSTINIAN
527–565

22 Justitia est constans et perpetua voluntas jus suum
cuique tribuens.
    Justice is the constant and perpetual wish to render
    to every one his due.   *Institutiones*, I. i. 1

JUVENAL
A.D. 60–*c.* 130

23 Probitas laudatur et alget.
    Honesty is commended, and starves.
    Satires, i. 74. Trans. by Lewis Evans

24 Si natura negat, facit indignatio versum.
    If nature denies the power, indignation would give
    birth to verses.   *Ib.* 79

25 Quidquid agunt homines, votum timor ira voluptas
Gaudia discursus nostri farrago libelli est.
    All that men are engaged in, their wishes, fears,
    anger, pleasures, joys, and varied pursuits, form
    the hotch-potch of my book.   *Ib.* 85

26 Quis tulerat Gracchos de seditione querentis?
    Who shall endure the Gracchi complaining about
    sedition?   *Ib.* ii. 24

1 Dat veniam corvis, vexat censura columbas.

Censure acquits the raven, but falls foul of the dove. *Satires*, ii. 63

2 Nemo repente fuit turpissimus.

No one ever reached the climax of vice at one step. *Ib.* 83

3 Grammaticus rhetor geometres pictor aliptes
Augur schoenobates medicus magus, omnia novit
Graeculus esuriens; in caelum miseris, ibit.
(*Alternative reading of last line*: in coelum iusseris, ibit.)

Grammarian, rhetorician, geometer, painter, trainer, soothsayer, rope-dancer, physician, wizard—he knows everything. Bid the hungry Greekling go to heaven! He'll go. *Ib.* iii. 76

4 Nil habet infelix paupertas durius in se
Quam quod ridiculos homines facit.

Poverty, bitter though it be, has no sharper pang than this, that it makes men ridiculous. *Ib.* 152

5 Haud facile emergunt quorum virtutibus opstat
Res angusta domi.

Difficult indeed is it for those to emerge from obscurity whose noble qualities are cramped by narrow means at home. *Ib.* 164

6 Omnia Romae
Cum pretio.

Everything at Rome is coupled with high price. *Ib.* 183

7 Credo Pudicitiam Saturno rege moratam
In terris visamque diu.

I believe that while Saturn still was king, Chastity lingered upon earth, and was long seen there. *Ib.* vi. 1

8 Rara avis in terris nigroque simillima cycno.

A rare bird on the earth and very like a black swan. *Ib.* 165

9 Hoc volo, sic iubeo, sit pro ratione voluntas.

I will it, I insist on it! Let my will stand instead of reason. *Ib.* 223

10 Nunc patimur longae pacis mala, saevior armis
Luxuria incubuit victumque ulciscitur orbem.

Now we are suffering all the evils of long-continued peace. Luxury, more ruthless than war, broods over Rome, and exacts vengeance for a conquered world. *Ib.* 292

11 'Pone seram, prohibe.' Sed quis custodiet ipsos
Custodes? Cauta est et ab illis incipit uxor.

'Put on a lock! keep her in confinement!' But who is to guard the guards themselves? Your wife is as cunning as you, and begins with them. *Ib.* 347

12 Tenet insanabile multos
Scribendi cacoethes et aegro in corde senescit.

An inveterate itch of writing, now incurable, clings to many, and grows old in their distempered body. *Ib.* vii. 51

13 Occidit miseros crambe repetita magistros.

It is the reproduction of the cabbage that wears out the master's life. [i.e. cabbage twice cooked.] *Ib.* 154

14 Summum crede nefas animam praeferre pudori
Et propter vitam vivendi perdere causas.

Deem it to be the summit of impiety to prefer existence to honour, and for the sake of life to sacrifice life's only end. *Satires*, viii. 83

15 Omnibus in terris, quae sunt a Gadibus usque
Auroram et Gangen, pauci dinoscere possunt
Vera bona atque illis multum diversa, remota
Erroris nebula.

In all the regions which extend from Gades even to the farthest east and Ganges, there are but few that can discriminate between real blessings and those that are widely different, all the mist of error being removed. *Ib.* x. 1

16 Nocitura toga, nocitura petuntur
Militia.

Our prayers are put up for what will injure us in peace, and injure us in war. *Ib.* 8

17 Cantabit vacuus coram latrone viator.

The traveller with empty pockets will sing even in the robber's face. *Ib.* 22

18 Verbosa et grandis epistula venit
A Capreis.

A wordy and lengthy epistle came from Capreae. *Ib.* 71

19 Duas tantum res anxius optat,
Panem et circenses.

Limits its [i.e. the Roman people's] anxious longings to two things only—bread, and the games of the circus. *Ib.* 80

20 Expende Hannibalem: quot libras in duce summo
invenies?

Put Hannibal in the scales: and how many pounds of flesh will you find in that famous general? *Ib.* 147

21 I demens et saevas curre per Alpes,
Ut pueris placeas et declamatio fias.

Go then, madman, and hurry over the rugged Alps, that you may be the delight of boys, and furnish subjects for declamations. *Ib.* 166

22 Mors sola fatetur
Quantula sint hominum corpuscula.

Death alone discloses how very small are the puny bodies of men. *Ib.* 172

23 Da spatium vitae, multos da, Iuppiter, annos.

Grant length of life, great Jove, and many years. *Ib.* 188

24 Orandum est ut sit mens sana in corpore sano.
Fortem posce animum mortis terrore carentem,
Qui spatium vitae extremum inter munera ponat
Naturae.

Your prayer must be that you may have a sound mind in a sound body. Pray for a bold spirit, free from all dread of death; that reckons the closing scene of life among Nature's kindly boons. *Ib.* 356

25 Nullum numen habes si sit prudentia, nos te,
Nos facimus, Fortuna, deam caeloque locamus.

If we have wise foresight, thou, Fortune, hast no divinity. It is we that make thee a deity, and place thy throne in heaven! *Ib.* 365

1   Prima est haec ultio quod se
Iudice nemo nocens absolvitur.

This is the punishment that first lights upon him,
that by the verdict of his own breast no guilty
man is acquitted.   *Satires*, xiii. 2

2   Quippe minuti
Semper et infirmi est animi exiguique voluptas
Ultio. Continuo sic collige, quod vindicta
Nemo magis gaudet quam femina.

Since revenge is ever the pleasure of a paltry spirit,
a weak and abject mind! Draw this conclusion
at once from the fact, that no one delights in revenge more than a woman.   *Ib.* 189

3 Maxima debetur puero reverentia, siquid
Turpe paras, nec tu pueri contempseris annos.

The greatest reverence is due to a child! If you
are contemplating a disgraceful act, despise not
your child's tender years.   *Ib.* xiv. 47

IMMANUEL KANT
1724–1804

4 Zwei Dinge erfüllen das Gemüth mit immer neuer
und zunehmender Bewunderung und Ehrfurcht,
je öfter und anhaltender sich das Nachdenken
damit beschäftigt: der bestirnte Himmel über mir,
und das moralische Gesetz in mir.

Two things fill the mind with ever-increasing wonder and awe, the more often and the more intensely the mind of thought is drawn to them:
the starry heavens above me and the moral law
within me.   *Critique of Practical Reason*, conclusion

5 There is . . . but one categorical imperative: 'Act only
on that maxim whereby thou canst at the same
time will that it should become a universal law.'
Trans. by A. D. Lindsay, *from Fundamental
Principles of . . . Morals*, p. 421

6 I ought, therefore I can.   *Attrib.*

ALPHONSE KARR
1808–1890

7 Plus ça change, plus c'est la même chose.

The more things change, the more they are the
same.   *Les Guêpes, Jan. 1849*, vi

8 Si l'on veut abolir la peine de mort en ce cas, que
MM. les assassins commencent.

If we are to abolish the death penalty, I should like
to see the first step taken by our friends the
murderers.   *Ib.*

DENIS KEARNEY
1847–1907

9 Horny-handed sons of toil.
    Speech. San Francisco, c. 1878

JOHN KEATS
1795–1821

10 Season of mists and mellow fruitfulness,
Close bosom-friend of the maturing sun;
Conspiring with him how to load and bless
With fruit the vines that round the thatch-eaves run.
    To Autumn

11   To set budding more
And still more later flowers for the bees,
Until they think warm days will never cease,
For Summer has o'erbrimmed their clammy cells.
    To Autumn

12 Who hath not seen thee oft amid thy store?
Sometimes whoever seeks abroad may find
Thee sitting careless on a granary floor,
Thy hair soft-lifted by the winnowing wind;
Or on a half-reap'd furrow sound asleep,
Drows'd with the fume of poppies, while thy hook
Spares the next swath and all its twined flowers. *Ib.*

13 Where are the songs of Spring? Ay, where are they?
    Ib.

14 Then in a wailful choir the small gnats mourn
Among the river sallows, borne aloft
Or sinking as the light wind lives or dies.   *Ib.*

15 The red-breast whistles from a garden-croft;
And gathering swallows twitter in the skies.   *Ib.*

16 Bards of Passion and of Mirth,
Ye have left your souls on earth!
Have ye souls in heaven too?
    *Written on the blank page before Beaumont
and Fletcher's Fair Maid of the Inn. Bards of
Passion and of Mirth*

17 Where the nightingale doth sing
Not a senseless, tranced thing,
But divine melodious truth.   *Ib.*

18 The imagination of a boy is healthy, and the mature
imagination of a man is healthy; but there is a space
of life between, in which the soul is in a ferment,
the character undecided, the way of life uncertain,
the ambition thick-sighted: thence proceeds mawkishness.   *Endymion*, preface

19 A thing of beauty is a joy for ever:
Its loveliness increases; it will never
Pass into nothingness; but still will keep
A bower quiet for us, and a sleep
Full of sweet dreams, and health, and quiet breathing.
    Ib. bk. i, l. 1

20   The inhuman dearth
Of noble natures.   *Ib.* l. 8

21   The grandeur of the dooms
We have imagined for the mighty dead.   *Ib.* l. 20

22 They must be always with us, or we die.   *Ib.* l. 33

23   The unimaginable lodge
For solitary thinkings; such as dodge
Conception to the very bourne of heaven,
Then leave the naked brain.   *Ib.* l. 293

24 O magic sleep! O comfortable bird,
That broodest o'er the troubled sea of the mind
Till it is hush'd and smooth!   *Ib.* l. 453

25 Wherein lies happiness? In that which becks
Our ready minds to fellowship divine,
A fellowship with essence.   *Ib.* l. 777

26   The crown of these
Is made of love and friendship, and sits high
Upon the forehead of humanity.   *Ib.* l. 800

KEATS

¹ Who, of men, can tell
That flowers would bloom, or that green fruit would
swell
To melting pulp, that fish would have bright mail,
The earth its dower of river, wood, and vale,
The meadows runnels, runnels pebble-stones,
The seed its harvest, or the lute its tones,
Tones ravishment, or ravishment its sweet
If human souls did never kiss and greet?
Endymion, bk. i, l. 835

² Never, I aver,
Since Ariadne was a vintager. *Ib*. bk. ii, l. 442

³ O Sorrow,
Why dost borrow
Heart's lightness from the merriment of May?
Ib. bk. iv, l. 164

⁴ To Sorrow,
I bade good-morrow,
And thought to leave her far away behind;
But cheerly, cheerly,
She loves me dearly;
She is so constant to me, and so kind. *Ib*. l. 173

⁵ Come hither, lady fair, and joined be
To our wild minstrelsy! *Ib*. l. 236

⁶ Great Brahma from his mystic heaven groans,
And all his priesthood moans. *Ib*. l. 265

⁷ Their smiles,
Wan as primroses gather'd at midnight
By chilly finger'd spring. *Ib*. l. 969

⁸ Sweet are the pleasures that to verse belong,
And doubly sweet a brotherhood in song.
Epistle to G. F. Mathew

⁹ Oh, never will the prize,
High reason, and the love [?lore] of good and ill,
Be my award! *Epistle to J. H. Reynolds*, l. 74

¹⁰ Lost in a sort of Purgatory blind. *Ib*. l. 80

¹¹ It is a flaw
In happiness, to see beyond our bourn,—
It forces us in summer skies to mourn,
It spoils the singing of the nightingale. *Ib*. l. 82

¹² St. Agnes' Eve—Ah, bitter chill it was!
The owl, for all his feathers, was a-cold;
The hare limp'd trembling through the frozen grass,
And silent was the flock in woolly fold.
The Eve of Saint Agnes, i

¹³ The sculptur'd dead on each side seem to freeze,
Emprison'd in black, purgatorial rails. *Ib*. ii

¹⁴ The silver, snarling trumpets 'gan to chide. *Ib*. iv

¹⁵ Upon the honey'd middle of the night. *Ib*. vi

¹⁶ The music, yearning like a God in pain. *Ib*. vii

¹⁷ A poor, weak, palsy-stricken, churchyard thing.
Ib. xviii

¹⁸ Out went the taper as she hurried in;
Its little smoke, in pallid moonshine, died. *Ib*. xxiii

¹⁹ A casement high and triple-arch'd there was,
All garlanded with carven imag'ries
Of fruits, and flowers, and bunches of knot-grass,
And diamonded with panes of quaint device,
Innumerable of stains and splendid dyes,
As are the tiger-moth's deep-damask'd wings;
And in the midst, 'mong thousand heraldries,
And twilight saints, and dim emblazonings,
A shielded scutcheon blush'd with blood of queens
and kings. *Ib*. xxiv

²⁰ Full on this casement shone the wintry moon,
And threw warm gules on Madeline's fair breast.
The Eve of Saint Agnes, xxv

²¹ By degrees
Her rich attire creeps rustling to her knees.
Ib. xxvi

²² Her soft and chilly nest. *Ib*. xxvii

²³ As though a rose should shut, and be a bud again.
Ib.

²⁴ And still she slept an azure-lidded sleep,
In blanched linen, smooth, and lavender'd. *Ib*. xxx

²⁵ And lucent syrops, tinct with cinnamon;
Manna and dates, in argosy transferr'd
From Fez; and spiced dainties, every one,
From silken Samarcand to cedar'd Lebanon. *Ib*.

²⁶ He play'd an ancient ditty, long since mute,
In Provence call'd, 'La belle dame sans mercy'.
Ib. xxxiii

²⁷ And the long carpets rose along the gusty floor.
Ib. xl

²⁸ And they are gone: aye, ages long ago
These lovers fled away into the storm. *Ib*. xlii

²⁹ The Beadsman, after thousand aves told,
For aye unsought-for slept among his ashes cold. *Ib*.

³⁰ Upon a Sabbath-day it fell;
Twice holy was the Sabbath-bell,
That call'd the folk to evening prayer.
The Eve of Saint Mark, l. 1

³¹ Dry your eyes—O dry your eyes,
For I was taught in Paradise
To ease my breast of melodies.
Fairy Song: Shed No Tear

³² Fanatics have their dreams, wherewith they weave
A paradise for a sect. *The Fall of Hyperion*, l. 1

³³ 'None can usurp this height', return'd that shade,
'But those to whom the miseries of the world
Are misery, and will not let them rest.' *Ib*. l. 147

³⁴ They are no dreamers weak,
They seek no wonder but the human face;
No music but a happy-noted voice. *Ib*. l. 162

³⁵ The poet and the dreamer are distinct,
Diverse, sheer opposite, antipodes.
The one pours out a balm upon the world,
The other vexes it. *Ib*. l. 199

³⁶ His flaming robes stream'd out beyond his heels,
And gave a roar, as if of earthly fire,
That scared away the meek ethereal hours,
And made their dove-wings tremble. On he flared.
Ib. c. ii, l. 58

³⁷ Ever let the fancy roam,
Pleasure never is at home. *Fancy*, l. 1

³⁸ O sweet Fancy! let her loose;
Summer's joys are spoilt by use. *Ib*. l. 9

³⁹ Where's the cheek that doth not fade,
Too much gaz'd at? Where's the maid
Whose lip mature is ever new? *Ib*. l. 69

⁴⁰ Where's the face
One would meet in every place? *Ib*. l. 73

1   Where—where slept thine ire,
When like a blank idiot I put on thy wreath,
     Thy laurel, thy glory,
     The light of thy story,
Or was I a worm—too low crawling, for death?
     O Delphic Apollo!   *Hymn to Apollo*

2 Far from the fiery noon, and eve's one star.
     Hyperion, bk. i, l. 3

3   No stir of air was there,
Not so much life as on a summer's day
Robs not one light seed from the feather'd grass,
But where the dead leaf fell, there did it rest. *Ib.* l. 7

4   The Naiad 'mid her reeds
Press'd her cold finger closer to her lips.   *Ib.* l. 13

5 How beautiful, if sorrow had not made
Sorrow more beautiful than Beauty's self.   *Ib.* l. 35

6 That large utterance of the early Gods.   *Ib.* l. 51

7 O aching time! O moments big as years!   *Ib.* l. 64

8 As when, upon a trancèd summer-night,
Those green-rob'd senators of mighty woods,
Tall oaks, branch-charmèd by the earnest stars,
Dream, and so dream all night without a stir.
     Ib. l. 72

9 And all those acts which Deity supreme
Doth ease its heart of love in.   *Ib.* l. 111

10 Unseen before by Gods or wondering men.
     Ib. l. 183

11 Instead of sweets, his ample palate took
Savour of poisonous brass and metal sick. *Ib.* l. 188

12 He entered, but he enter'd full of wrath. *Ib.* l. 213

13 For as in theatres of crowded men
Hubbub increases more they call out, 'Hush!'
     Ib. l. 253

14 And still they were the same bright, patient stars.
     Ib. l. 353

15 Who cost her mother Tellus keener pangs,
Though feminine, than any of her sons.
     Ib. bk. ii, l. 54

16 Now comes the pain of truth, to whom 'tis pain;
O folly! for to bear all naked truths,
And to envisage circumstance, all calm,
That is the top of sovereignty.   *Ib.* l. 202

17 A solitary sorrow best befits
Thy lips, and antheming a lonely grief.
     Ib. bk. iii, l. 5

18   Point me out the way
To any one particular beauteous star,
And I will flit into it with my lyre,
And make its silvery splendour pant with bliss.
     Ib. l. 99

19 Knowledge enormous makes a God of me. *Ib.* l. 113

20 But, for the general award of love,
The little sweet doth kill much bitterness.
     Isabella, xiii

21 Why were they proud? again we ask aloud,
Why in the name of Glory were they proud? *Ib.* xvi

22 So the two brothers and their murder'd man
Rode past fair Florence.   *Ib.* xxvii

23 And she forgot the stars, the moon, the sun,
     And she forgot the blue above the trees,
And she forgot the dells where waters run,
     And she forgot the chilly autumn breeze;
She had no knowledge when the day was done,
     And the new morn she saw not: but in peace
Hung over her sweet Basil evermore.   *Isabella*, liii

24   'For cruel 'tis,' said she,
'To steal my Basil-pot away from me.'   *Ib.* lxii

25 I stood tip-toe upon a little hill.   *Title*

26   And then there crept
A little noiseless noise among the leaves,
Born of the very sigh that silence heaves.
     I Stood Tip-toe upon a Little Hill

27 Here are sweet peas, on tiptoe for a flight.   *Ib.*

28 Oh what can ail thee, Knight at arms
     Alone and palely loitering;
The sedge is wither'd from the lake,
     And no birds sing.   *La Belle Dame Sans Merci*

29 I see a lily on thy brow,
     With anguish moist and fever dew;
And on thy cheek a fading rose
     Fast withereth too.   *Ib.*

30 I met a lady in the meads
     Full beautiful, a faery's child;
Her hair was long, her foot was light,
     And her eyes were wild.   *Ib.*

31 I set her on my pacing steed,
     And nothing else saw all day long;
For sideways would she lean, and sing
     A faery's song.   *Ib.*

32 She look'd at me as she did love,
     And made sweet moan.   *Ib.*

33 And sure in language strange she said,
     'I love thee true!'   *Ib.*

34 And there I shut her wild, wild eyes
     With kisses four.   *Ib.* (Ld. Houghton's version)

35   La belle Dame sans Merci
Hath thee in thrall!   *Ib.*

36 I saw their starv'd lips in the gloam
     With horrid warning gapèd wide,
And I awoke, and found me here
     On the cold hill side.   *Ib.*

37 She was a gordian shape of dazzling hue,
Vermilion-spotted, golden, green, and blue;
Striped like a zebra, freckled like a pard,
Eyed like a peacock, and all crimson barr'd.
     Lamia, pt. i, l. 47

38 Real are the dreams of Gods, and smoothly pass
Their pleasures in a long immortal dream. *Ib.* l. 127

39 Love in a hut, with water and a crust,
Is—Love, forgive us!—cinders, ashes, dust;
Love in a palace is perhaps at last
More grievous torment than a hermit's fast.
     Ib. pt. ii, l. 1

40 That purple-lined palace of sweet sin.   *Ib.* l. 31

41 In pale contented sort of discontent.   *Ib.* l. 135

42   Do not all charms fly
At the mere touch of cold philosophy?
There was an awful rainbow once in heaven:
We know her woof, her texture; she is given
In the dull catalogue of common things.
Philosophy will clip an Angel's wings.   *Ib.* l. 229

KEATS

1 Souls of poets dead and gone,
What Elysium have ye known,
Happy field or mossy cavern,
Choicer than the Mermaid Tavern?
Have ye tippled drink more fine
Than mine host's Canary wine?
Lines on the Mermaid Tavern

2 Pledging with contented smack
The Mermaid in the Zodiac.   *Ib.*

3 This living hand, now warm and capable
Of earnest grasping, would, if it were cold
And in the icy silence of the tomb,
So haunt thy days and chill thy dreaming nights
That thou wouldst wish thine own heart dry of blood
So in my veins red life might stream again,
And thus be conscience-calm'd—see here it is—
I hold it towards you.
Lines Supposed to have been Addressed to Fanny Brawne

4 Old Meg was brave as Margaret Queen
And tall as Amazon:
An old red blanket cloak she wore;
A chip hat had she on.   *Meg Merrilies*

5 Let none profane my Holy See of love,
Or with a rude hand break
The sacramental cake.   *Ode to Fanny*

6 Thou still unravish'd bride of quietness,
Thou foster-child of silence and slow time.
Ode on a Grecian Urn

7 What men or gods are these? What maidens loth?
What mad pursuit? What struggle to escape?
What pipes and timbrels? What wild ecstasy?   *Ib.*

8 Heard melodies are sweet, but those unheard
Are sweeter; therefore, ye soft pipes, play on;
Not to the sensual ear, but, more endear'd,
Pipe to the spirit ditties of no tone.   *Ib.*

9 For ever wilt thou love, and she be fair!   *Ib.*

10 For ever piping songs for ever new.   *Ib.*

11 All breathing human passion far above.   *Ib.*

12 Who are these coming to the sacrifice?
To what green altar, O mysterious priest,
Lead'st thou that heifer lowing at the skies,
And all her silken flanks with garlands drest?
What little town by river or sea shore,
Or mountain-built with peaceful citadel,
Is emptied of this folk, this pious morn?   *Ib.*

13 O Attic shape! Fair attitude!   *Ib.*

14 Thou, silent form, dost tease us out of thought
As doth eternity: Cold Pastoral!   *Ib.*

15 'Beauty is truth, truth beauty,'—that is all
Ye know on earth, and all ye need to know.   *Ib.*

16 For I would not be dieted with praise,
A pet-lamb in a sentimental farce! *Ode on Indolence*

17 By bards who died content on pleasant sward,
Leaving great verse unto a little clan.   *Ode to Maia*

18 Rich in the simple worship of a day.   *Ib.*

19 No, no, go not to Lethe, neither twist
Wolf's-bane, tight-rooted, for its poisonous wine.
Ode on Melancholy

20 Nor let the beetle, nor the death-moth be
Your mournful Psyche.   *Ib.*

21 She dwells with Beauty—Beauty that must die;
And Joy, whose hand is ever at his lips
Bidding adieu; and aching Pleasure nigh,
Turning to Poison while the bee-mouth sips:
Ay, in the very temple of delight
Veil'd Melancholy has her sovran shrine.
Though seen of none save him whose strenuous tongue
Can burst Joy's grape against his palate fine;
His soul shall taste the sadness of her might,
And be among her cloudy trophies hung.
Ode on Melancholy

22 My heart aches, and a drowsy numbness pains
My sense.   *Ode to a Nightingale*

23 'Tis not through envy of thy happy lot,
But being too happy in thine happiness,—
That thou, light-winged Dryad of the trees,
In some melodious plot
Of beechen green, and shadows numberless,
Singest of summer in full-throated ease.   *Ib.*

24 O, for a draught of vintage! that hath been
Cool'd a long age in the deep-delved earth,
Tasting of Flora and the country green,
Dance, and Provençal song, and sunburnt mirth!
O for a beaker full of the warm South,
Full of the true, the blushful Hippocrene,
With beaded bubbles winking at the brim,
And purple-stained mouth;
That I might drink, and leave the world unseen,
And with thee fade away into the forest dim. *Ib.*

25 Fade far away, dissolve, and quite forget
What thou among the leaves hast never known,
The weariness, the fever, and the fret,
Here, where men sit and hear each other groan. *Ib.*

26 Where youth grows pale, and spectre-thin, and dies.
Ib.

27 Where but to think is to be full of sorrow
And leaden-eyed despairs,
Where Beauty cannot keep her lustrous eyes,
Or new Love pine at them beyond to-morrow. *Ib.*

28 Away! away! for I will fly to thee,
Not charioted by Bacchus and his pards,
But on the viewless wings of Poesy,
Though the dull brain perplexes and retards. *Ib.*

29 But here there is no light,
Save what from heaven is with the breezes blown
Through verdurous glooms and winding mossy ways.
Ib.

30 I cannot see what flowers are at my feet,
Nor what soft incense hangs upon the boughs.   *Ib.*

31 Fast fading violets cover'd up in leaves;
And mid-May's eldest child,
The coming musk-rose, full of dewy wine,
The murmurous haunt of flies on summer eves. *Ib.*

32 Darkling I listen; and, for many a time
I have been half in love with easeful Death,
Call'd him soft names in many a mused rhyme,
To take into the air my quiet breath;
Now more than ever seems it rich to die,
To cease upon the midnight with no pain,
While thou art pouring forth thy soul abroad
In such an ecstasy!
Still wouldst thou sing, and I have ears in vain—
To thy high requiem become a sod.

1 Thou wast not born for death, immortal Bird!
No hungry generations tread thee down;
The voice I hear this passing night was heard
In ancient days by emperor and clown:
Perhaps the self-same song that found a path
Through the sad heart of Ruth, when sick for home,
She stood in tears amid the alien corn;
 The same that oft-times hath
Charm'd magic casements, opening on the foam
Of perilous seas, in faery lands forlorn.
Ode to a Nightingale

2 Forlorn! the very word is like a bell
To toll me back from thee to my sole self!
Adieu! the fancy cannot cheat so well
As she is fam'd to do, deceiving elf.
Adieu! adieu! thy plaintive anthem fades
Past the near meadows, over the still stream,
Up the hill-side; and now 'tis buried deep
 In the next valley-glades:
Was it a vision, or a waking dream?
Fled is that music:—Do I wake or sleep? *Ib.*

3 'Mid hush'd, cool-rooted flowers, fragrant-eyed,
Blue, silver-white, and budded Tyrian.
Ode to Psyche

4 O latest-born and loveliest vision far
Of all Olympus' faded hierarchy! *Ib.*

5 To make delicious moan
Upon the midnight hours. *Ib.*

6 Thy voice, thy lute, thy pipe, thy incense sweet
From swinged censer teeming;
Thy shrine, thy grove, thy oracle, thy heat
Of pale-mouth'd prophet dreaming. *Ib.*

7 Yes, I will be thy priest, and build a fane
In some untrodden region of my mind,
Where branched thoughts, new grown with pleasant pain,
Instead of pines shall murmur in the wind. *Ib.*

8 With buds, and bells, and stars without a name,
With all the gardener Fancy e'er could feign,
Who breeding flowers, will never breed the same. *Ib.*

9 A bright torch, and a casement ope at night,
To let the warm Love in! *Ib.*

10 Stop and consider! life is but a day;
A fragile dew-drop on its perilous way
From a tree's summit; a poor Indian's sleep
While his boat hastens to the monstrous steep
Of Montmorenci. *Sleep and Poetry*, 1. 85

11 O for ten years, that I may overwhelm
Myself in poesy; so I may do the deed
That my own soul has to itself decreed. *Ib.* 1. 96

12 They sway'd about upon a rocking horse,
And thought it Pegasus. *Ib.* 1. 186

13 The blue
Bared its eternal bosom, and the dew
Of summer nights collected still to make
The morning precious. *Ib.* 1. 189

14 A drainless shower
Of light is poesy; 'tis the supreme of power;
'Tis might half slumb'ring on its own right arm. *Ib.* 1. 235

15 The great end
Of poesy, that it should be a friend
To soothe the cares, and lift the thoughts of man. *Ib.* 1. 245

16 They shall be accounted poet kings
Who simply tell the most heart-easing things.
Sleep and Poetry, 1. 26

17 Bright star, would I were steadfast as thou art—
Not in lone splendour hung aloft the night
And watching, with eternal lids apart,
Like nature's patient, sleepless Eremite,
The moving waters at their priestlike task
Of pure ablution round earth's human shores.
Sonnet. Bright Star

18 Still, still to hear her tender-taken breath,
And so live ever—or else swoon to death. *Ib*

19 Much have I travell'd in the realms of gold,
And many goodly states and kingdoms seen;
Round many western islands have I been
Which bards in fealty to Apollo hold.
Oft of one wide expanse had I been told
That deep-brow'd Homer ruled as his demesne;
Yet did I never breathe its pure serene
Till I heard Chapman speak out loud and bold:
Then felt I like some watcher of the skies
When a new planet swims into his ken;
Or like stout Cortez when with eagle eyes
He star'd at the Pacific—and all his men
Look'd at each other with a wild surmise—
Silent, upon a peak in Darien.
Ib. On First Looking into Chapman's Homer

20 O Chatterton! how very sad thy fate!
Ib. To Chatterton

21 Mortality
Weighs heavily on me like unwilling sleep.
Ib. On Seeing the Elgin Marbles

22 The poetry of earth is never dead:
When all the birds are faint with the hot sun,
And hide in cooling trees, a voice will run
From hedge to hedge about the new-mown mead.
Ib. On the Grasshopper and Cricket

23 Happy is England! I could be content
To see no other verdure than its own;
To feel no other breezes than are blown
Through its tall woods with high romances blent.
Ib. Happy is England!

24 Happy is England, sweet her artless daughters;
Enough their simple loveliness for me. *Ib.*

25 Other spirits there are standing apart
Upon the forehead of the age to come.
Ib. To Haydon, ii. *Great Spirits Now On Earth*

26 There is a budding morrow in midnight.
Ib. To Homer

27 Four seasons fill the measure of the year.
Ib. Human Seasons

28 Glory and loveliness have pass'd away.
Ib. To Leigh Hunt

29 Son of the old moon-mountains African!
Chief of the Pyramid and Crocodile! *Ib. To the Nile*

30 It keeps eternal whisperings around
Desolate shores, and with its mighty swell
Gluts twice ten thousand Caverns. *Ib. On the Sea*

31 O soft embalmer of the still midnight. *Ib. To Sleep*

32 Turn the key deftly in the oiled wards,
And seal the hushed casket of my soul. *Ib.*

33 The sweet converse of an innocent mind.
Ib. To Solitude

1 The day is gone, and all its sweets are gone!
Sweet voice, sweet lips, soft hand, and softer breast.
Sonnet. The Day Is Gone

2 To one who has been long in city pent;
'Tis very sweet to look into the fair
And open face of heaven.
Ib. To One Who Has Been Long

3 A debonair
And gentle tale of love and languishment. *Ib.*

4 When I have fears that I may cease to be
Before my pen has glean'd my teeming brain.
Ib. When I Have Fears

5 When I behold upon the night's starr'd face,
Huge cloudy symbols of a high romance. *Ib.*

6 Then on the shore
Of the wide world I stand alone, and think
Till love and fame to nothingness do sink. *Ib.*

7 In a drear-nighted December,
Too happy, happy tree,
Thy branches ne'er remember
Their green felicity.
Stanzas. In a Drear-nighted December

8 But were there ever any
Writh'd not at passing joy?
To know the change and feel it,
When there is none to heal it,
Nor numbed sense to steel it,
Was never said in rhyme. *Ib.*

9 O fret not after knowledge—I have none,
And yet my song comes native with the warmth.
O fret not after knowledge—I have none,
And yet the Evening listens. *What the Thrush Said*

10 Woman! when I behold thee flippant, vain,
Inconstant, childish, proud, and full of fancies.
Woman! When I Behold Thee

11 Like a whale's back in the sea of prose.
Letters (ed. M. B. Forman, 1935), 14. *To Leigh Hunt, 10 May 1817*

12 What a thing to be in the mouth of fame. *Ib.*

13 I remember your saying that you had notions of a good Genius presiding over you. I have of late had the same thought—for things which [I] do half at random are afterwards confirmed by my judgment in a dozen features of propriety. Is it too daring to fancy Shakespeare this Presider?
Ib. 15. To B. R. Haydon, 10–11 May 1817

14 I am quite disgusted with literary men.
Ib. 25. To Benjamin Bailey, 8 Oct. 1817

15 A long poem is a test of invention which I take to be the Polar star of poetry, as fancy is the sails, and imagination the rudder. *Ib.*

16 A man should have the fine point of his soul taken off to become fit for this world.
Ib. 30. To J. H. Reynolds, 22 Nov. 1817

17 I am certain of nothing but the holiness of the heart's affections and the truth of imagination—what the imagination seizes as beauty must be truth—whether it existed before or not.
Ib. 31. To Benjamin Bailey, 22 Nov. 1817

18 I have never yet been able to perceive how anything can be known for truth by consecutive reasoning—and yet it must be. *Ib.*

19 O for a life of sensations rather than of thoughts! *Ib.*

20 The excellency of every art is its intensity, capable of making all disagreeables evaporate, from their being in close relationship with beauty and truth.
Letters, 32. To G. and T. Keats, 21 Dec. 1817

21 Negative Capability, that is, when a man is capable of being in uncertainties, mysteries, doubts, without any irritable reaching after fact and reason—Coleridge, for instance, would let go by a fine isolated verisimilitude caught from the Penetralium of mystery, from being incapable of remaining content with half-knowledge. *Ib.*

22 There is nothing stable in the world; uproar's your only music. *Ib. 37. To G. and T. Keats, 13 Jan. 1818*

23 So I do believe . . . that works of genius are the first things in this world. *Ib.*

24 For the sake of a few fine imaginative or domestic passages, are we to be bullied into a certain philosophy engendered in the whims of an egotist.
Ib. 44. To J. H. Reynolds, 3 Feb. 1818

25 We hate poetry that has a palpable design upon us—and if we do not agree, seems to put its hand in its breeches pocket. Poetry should be great and unobtrusive, a thing which enters into one's soul, and does not startle or amaze it with itself, but with its subject. *Ib.*

26 When man has arrived at a certain ripeness in intellect any one grand and spiritual passage serves him as a starting-post towards all 'the two-and-thirty palaces'.
Ib. 48. To J. H. Reynolds, 19 Feb. 1818

27 Poetry should surprise by a fine excess, and not by singularity; it should strike the reader as a wording of his own highest thoughts, and appear almost a remembrance. Its touches of beauty should never be half-way, thereby making the reader breathless, instead of content. The rise, the progress, the setting of imagery should, like the sun, come natural to him.
Ib. 51. To John Taylor, 27 Feb. 1818

28 If poetry comes not as naturally as leaves to a tree it had better not come at all. *Ib.*

29 I have good reason to be content, for thank God I can read and perhaps understand Shakespeare to his depths. *Ib.*

30 Scenery is fine—but human nature is finer.
Ib. 53. To Benjamin Bailey, 13 Mar. 1818

31 As if the roots of the earth were rotten, cold, and drenched. *Ib. 60. To J. H. Reynolds, 9 Apr. 1818*

32 A country which is continually under hatches.
Ib. 61. To J. H. Reynolds, 10 Apr. 1818

33 I have been hovering for some time between the exquisite sense of the luxurious and a love for philosophy—were I calculated for the former I should be glad—but as I am not I shall turn all my soul to the latter.
Ib. 62. To John Taylor, 24 Apr. 1818

34 Axioms in philosophy are not axioms until they are proved upon our pulses: we read fine things but never feel them to the full until we have gone the same steps as the author.
Ib. 64. To J. H. Reynolds, 3 May 1818

1 I am in that temper that if I were under water I would scarcely kick to come to the top.
   Letters, 66. To Benjamin Bailey, 21 May 1818

2 Were it in my choice I would reject a petrarchal coronation—on account of my dying day, and because women have cancers.
   Ib. 69. To Benjamin Bailey, 10 June 1818

3 I do think better of womankind than to suppose they care whether Mister John Keats five feet high likes them or not.
   Ib. 79. To Benjamin Bailey, 18 July 1818

4 His identity presses upon me.
   Ib. 86. To C. W. Dilke, 21 Sept. 1818

5 I never was in love—yet the voice and the shape of a woman has haunted me these two days.
   Ib. 87. To J. H. Reynolds, 22 Sept. 1818

6 There is an awful warmth about my heart like a load of immortality. *Ib.*

7 In Endymion, I leaped headlong into the sea, and thereby have become better acquainted with the soundings, the quicksands, and the rocks, than if I had stayed upon the green shore, and piped a silly pipe, and took tea and comfortable advice.
   Ib. 90. To James Hessey, 9 Oct. 1818

8 I would sooner fail than not be among the greatest.
   Ib.

9 As to the poetical character itself (I mean that sort of which, if I am anything, I am a member; that sort distinguished from the Wordsworthian or egotistical sublime; which is a thing *per se* and stands alone) it is not itself—it has no self. . . . It has as much delight in conceiving an Iago as an Imogen.
   Ib. 93. To Richard Woodhouse, 27 Oct. 1818

10 A poet is the most unpoetical of anything in existence, because he has no identity; he is continually [informing] and filling some other body. *Ib.*

11 I think I shall be among the English Poets after my death.
   Ib. 94. To George and Georgiana Keats, 14 Oct. 1818

12 The roaring of the wind is my wife and the stars through the window pane are my children. The mighty abstract idea I have of beauty in all things stifles the more divided and minute domestic happiness. . . . The opinion I have of the generality of women—who appear to me as children to whom I would rather give a sugar plum than my time, forms a barrier against matrimony which I rejoice in. *Ib.*

13 I never can feel certain of any truth but from a clear perception of its beauty.
   Ib. 98. To George and Georgiana Keats, 16 Dec. 1818–4 Jan. 1819

14 I have come to this resolution—never to write for the sake of writing or making a poem, but from running over with any little knowledge or experience which many years of reflection may perhaps give me; otherwise I shall be dumb.
   Ib. 115. To B. R. Haydon, 8 Mar. 1819

15 It is true that in the height of enthusiasm I have been cheated into some fine passages; but that is not the thing. *Ib.*

16 I should like the window to open onto the Lake of Geneva—and there I'd sit and read all day like the picture of somebody reading.
   Letters, 116. To Fanny Keats, 13 Mar. 1819

17 A man's life of any worth is a continual allegory.
   Ib. 123. To George and Georgiana Keats, 14 Feb.–3 May 1819

18 Shakespeare led a life of allegory: his works are the comments on it. *Ib.*

19 Nothing ever becomes real till it is experienced—even a proverb is no proverb to you till your life has illustrated it. *Ib.*

20 Call the world if you please 'The vale of Soul-making'. *Ib.*

21 I have met with women whom I really think would like to be married to a poem, and to be given away by a novel.
   Ib. 136. To Fanny Brawne, 8 July 1819

22 I have two luxuries to brood over in my walks, your loveliness and the hour of my death. O that I could have possession of them both in the same minute.
   Ib. 139. To Fanny Brawne, 25 July 1819

23 I am convinced more and more day by day that fine writing is next to fine doing, the top thing in the world. *Ib. 145. To J. H. Reynolds, 24 Aug. 1819*

24 Give me books, fruit, french wine and fine weather and a little music out of doors, played by somebody I do not know.
   Ib. 146. To Fanny Keats, 29 Aug. 1819

25 All clean and comfortable I sit down to write.
   Ib. 156. To George and Georgiana Keats, 17 Sept. 1819

26 I have but lately been on my guard against Milton. Life to him would be death to me. Miltonic verse cannot be written but it [for in] the vein of art—I wish to devote myself to another sensation. *Ib.*

27 The only means of strengthening one's intellect is to make up one's mind about nothing—to let the mind be a thoroughfare for all thoughts. Not a select party. *Ib.*

28 You have ravished me away by a power I cannot resist; and yet I could resist till I saw you; and even since I have seen you I have endeavoured often 'to reason against the reason of my Love'.
   Ib. 160. To Fanny Brawne, 13 Oct. 1819

29 'If I should die', said I to myself, 'I have left no immortal work behind me—nothing to make my friends proud of my memory—but I have loved the principle of beauty in all things, and if I had had time I would have made myself remembered.'
   Ib. 186. To Fanny Brawne, Feb. 1820?

30 I long to believe in immortality. . . . If I am destined to be happy with you here—how short is the longest life. I wish to believe in immortality—I wish to live with you for ever.
   Ib. 223. To Fanny Brawne, July 1820

31 I wish you could invent some means to make me at all happy without you. Every hour I am more and more concentrated in you; every thing else tastes like chaff in my mouth.
   Ib. 224. To Fanny Brawne, Aug. 1820

1 You, I am sure, will forgive me for sincerely remarking that you might curb your magnanimity, and be more of an artist, and load every rift of your subject with ore. *Letters*, 227. *To Shelley, Aug. 1820*

2 He already seemed to feel the flowers growing over him.
Words reported by Severn. W. Sharp, *Life and Letters of Severn, ch. 4*

3 Here lies one whose name was writ in water.
Epitaph. Lord Houghton, *Life of Keats, ii. 91*

JOHN KEBLE
1792–1866

4 New every morning is the love
Our wakening and uprising prove.
The Christian Year. Morning

5 If on our daily course our mind
Be set to hallow all we find,
New treasures still, of countless price,
God will provide for sacrifice. *Ib.*

6 We need not bid, for cloister'd cell,
Our neighbour and our work farewell.
Nor strive to wind ourselves too high
For sinful man beneath the sky. *Ib.*

7 The trivial round, the common task,
Would furnish all we ought to ask;
Room to deny ourselves; a road
To bring us, daily, nearer God. *Ib.*

8 And help us, this and every day,
To live more nearly as we pray. *Ib.*

9 Sun of my soul! Thou Saviour dear,
It is not night if Thou be near. *Ib. Evening*

10 Abide with me from morn till eve,
For without Thee I cannot live:
Abide with me when night is nigh,
For without Thee I dare not die. *Ib.*

11 Like infant slumbers, pure and light. *Ib.*

12 There is a book, who runs may read,
Which heavenly truth imparts,
And all the lore its scholars need,
Pure eyes and Christian hearts. *Ib. Septuagesima*

13 Bless'd are the pure in heart,
For they shall see our God. *Ib. The Purification*

14 Still to the lowly soul
He doth Himself impart,
And for His cradle and His throne
Chooseth the pure in heart. *Ib.*

15 The voice that breathed o'er Eden.
Poems. Holy Matrimony

16 The English *Virgil.* [Spenser.]
Lectures on Poetry, lect. v, 1912, vol. i, p. 82

FRANK BILLINGS KELLOGG
1856–1937

17 The high contracting parties solemnly declare in the names of their respective peoples that they condemn recourse to war for the solution of international controversies, and renounce it as an instrument of national policy in their relations with one another. The high contracting parties agree that the settlement or solution of all disputes or conflicts of whatever nature or of whatever origin they may be, which may rise among them, shall never be sought except by pacific means.
Peace Pact, signed at Paris 27 Aug. 1928

THOMAS KELLY
1769–1854

18 The Head that once was crowned with thorns
Is crowned with glory now.
Hymns on Various Passages of Scripture (1820). *The Head that Once Was Crowned*

THOMAS À KEMPIS
1380–1471

19 Opto magis sentire compunctionem quam scire eius definitionem.
I had rather feel compunction, than understand the definition thereof. *Imitatio Christi,* ch. 1, § iii. Trans. by Anthony Hoskins.

20 Nam homo proponit, sed Deus disponit.
Man proposes but God disposes. *Ib.* § xix

21 Sic transit gloria mundi.
O, how quickly doth the glory of the world pass away! *Ib.* ch. 3, § vi

22 Passione interdum movemur et zelum putamus.
We are sometimes moved with passion, and we think it to be zeal. Quoted in *ib.* ch. 5, § i

23 Multo tutius est stare in subiectione quam in praelatura.
It is much safer to obey, than to govern. *Ib.* ch. 9, § i

24 Si libenter crucem portas portabit te.
If thou bear the Cross cheerfully, it will bear thee. *Ib.* ch. 12, § v

25 Nunquam sis ex toto otiosus, sed aut legens, aut scribens, aut orans, aut meditans, aut aliquid utilitatis pro communi laborans.
Never be entirely idle: but either be reading, or writing, or praying, or meditating, or endeavouring something for the public good. *Ib.* ch. 19, § iv

26 Utinam per unam diem essemus bene conversati in hoc mundo.
O that we had spent but one day in this world thoroughly well! *Ib.* ch. 23, § ii

JOHN KEMPTHORNE
1775–1838

27 Praise the Lord! ye heavens adore Him,
Praise Him, Angels in the height;
Sun and moon, rejoice before Him,
Praise Him, all ye stars and light.
Hymns of Praise. For Foundling Apprentices (1796). *Praise the Lord! Ye Heavens Adore Him*

BISHOP THOMAS KEN
1637–1711

1 Awake my soul, and with the sun
Thy daily stage of duty run;
Shake off dull sloth, and joyful rise
To pay thy morning sacrifice.
Morning Hymn (1709). *Awake My Soul*

2 Teach me to live, that I may dread
The grave as little as my bed.
Evening Hymn. Glory to Thee My God This Night

3 Praise God, from whom all blessings flow,
Praise Him, all creatures here below,
Praise Him above, ye heavenly host,
Praise Father, Son, and Holy Ghost.
Morning and Evening Hymn

LLOYD KENYON, FIRST BARON KENYON
1732–1802

4 The Christian religion is part of the law of the land.
[England.] *Decision in William's Case. 1797*

LADY CAROLINE KEPPEL
1735–?

5 What's this dull town to me?
Robin's not near.
He whom I wished to see,
Wished for to hear;
Where's all the joy and mirth
Made life a heaven on earth?
O! they're all fled with thee,
Robin Adair.
Robin Adair

JOSEPH KESSELRING
1902–

6 Arsenic and Old Lace. *Title of Play.* (1941)

WILLIAM KETHE
d. 1608?

7 All people that on earth do dwell,
Sing to the Lord with cheerful voice;
Him serve with fear, His praise forth tell,
Come ye before Him, and rejoice.

The Lord, ye know, is God indeed;
Without our aid He did us make.
Daye's Psalter (1560). *All People That on Earth*

8 For it is seemly so to do. *Ib.*

9 For why? The Lord our God is good. *Ib.*

RALPH KETTELL
1563–1643

10 Here is Hey for Garsington! and Hey for Cuddesdon!
and Hey Hockley! but here's nobody cries, Hey
for God Almighty!
Sermon at Garsington Revel. Aubrey's *Brief Lives*,
vol. ii

FRANCIS SCOTT KEY
1779–1843

11 'Tis the star-spangled banner; O long may it wave
O'er the land of the free, and the home of the brave!
The Star-Spangled Banner

JOYCE KILMER
1888–1918

12 I think that I shall never see
A poem lovely as a tree.
Poems, Essays, and Letters, 1917, i. *Trees*

13 Poems are made by fools like me,
But only God can make a tree. *Ib.*

BENJAMIN FRANKLIN KING
1857–1894

14 Nothing to do but work,
Nothing to eat but food,
Nothing to wear but clothes
To keep one from going nude. *The Pessimist*

15 Nothing to breathe but air,
Quick as a flash 'tis gone;
Nowhere to fall but off,
Nowhere to stand but on! *Ib.*

HARRY KING

16 Young men taken in and done for. *Title of Song*

BISHOP HENRY KING
1592–1669

17 Nature's true-born child, who sums his years
(Like me) with no arithmetic but tears.
The Anniverse. Elegy

18 Accept, thou shrine of my dead Saint,
Instead of dirges this complaint;
And for sweet flowers to crown thy hearse,
Receive a strew of weeping verse
From thy griev'd friend, whom thou might'st see
Quite melted into tears for thee. *The Exequy*

19 Sleep on, my Love, in thy cold bed,
Never to be disquieted!
My last good night! Thou wilt not wake
Till I thy fate shall overtake:
Till age, or grief, or sickness must
Marry my body to that dust
It so much loves; and fill the room
My heart keeps empty in thy tomb.
Stay for me there; I will not fail
To meet thee in that hollow vale.
And think not much of my delay;
I am already on the way,
And follow thee with all the speed
Desire can make, or sorrows breed. *Ib.*

20 'Tis true, with shame and grief I yield,
Thou like the van first took'st the field,
And gotten hast the victory
In thus adventuring to die
Before me, whose more years might crave
A just precedence in the grave.
But hark! My pulse like a soft drum
Beats my approach, tells thee I come;
And slow howe'er my marches be,
I shall at last sit down by thee. *Ib.*

21 We that did nothing study but the way
To love each other, with which thoughts the day
Rose with delight to us, and with them set,
Must learn the hateful art, how to forget.
The Surrender

STODDARD KING
1889–1933

1 There's a long, long trail a-winding
Into the land of my dreams,
Where the nightingales are singing
And a white moon beams:
There's a long, long night of waiting
Until my dreams all come true;
Till the day when I'll be going down
That long long trail with you. *The Long, Long Trail*

ALEXANDER WILLIAM KINGLAKE
1809–1891

2 Soon the men of the column began to see that though
the scarlet line was slender, it was very rigid and
exact. *Invasion of the Crimea*, vol. ii, p. 455

CHARLES KINGSLEY
1819–1875

3 Airly Beacon, Airly Beacon;
Oh the pleasant sight to see
Shires and towns from Airly Beacon,
While my love climb'd up to me! *Airly Beacon*

4 Airly Beacon, Airly Beacon;
Oh the weary haunt for me,
All alone on Airly Beacon,
With his baby on my knee! *Ib.*

5 And no one but the baby cried for poor Lorraine,
Lorrèe. *Ballad: 'Lorraine, Lorraine, Lorrèe'*

6 My fairest child, I have no song to give you;
No lark could pipe in skies so dull and grey.
A Farewell. To C. E. G.

7 Be good, sweet maid, and let who can be clever;
Do lovely things, not dream them, all day long;
And so make Life, and Death, and that For Ever,
One grand sweet song. *Ib.*

8 It was Earl Haldan's daughter,
She looked across the sea.
It Was Earl Haldan's Daughter

9 The locks of six princesses
Must be my marriage fee,
'So hey bonny boat, and ho bonny boat!
Who comes a-wooing me?' *Ib.*

10 Leave to Robert Browning
Beggars, fleas, and vines;
Leave to squeamish Ruskin
Popish Apennines,
Dirty stones of Venice
And his gas-lamps seven;
We've the stones of Snowdon
And the lamps of heaven. *Letter to Thomas Hughes*

11 What we can we will be,
Honest Englishmen.
Do the work that's nearest,
Though it's dull at whiles,
Helping, when we meet them,
Lame dogs over stiles. *Ib.*

12 Welcome, wild North-easter!
Shame it is to see
Odes to every zephyr;
Ne'er a verse to thee. *Ode to the North-East Wind*

13 Jovial wind of winter
Turn us out to play! *Ode to the North-East Wind*

14 Chime, ye dappled darlings,
Down the roaring blast;
You shall see a fox die
Ere an hour be past. *Ib.*

15 'Tis the hard grey weather
Breeds hard English men. *Ib.*

16 Come; and strong within us
Stir the Vikings' blood;
Bracing brain and sinew;
Blow, thou wind of God! *Ib.*

17 I once had a sweet little doll, dears,
The prettiest doll in the world;
Her cheeks were so red and so white, dears,
And her hair was so charmingly curled.
Songs from The Water Babies. My Little Doll

18 Yet, for old sakes' sake she is still, dears,
The prettiest doll in the world. *Ib.*

19 When all the world is young, lad,
And all the trees are green;
And every goose a swan, lad,
And every lass a queen;
Then hey for boot and horse, lad,
And round the world away:
Young blood must have its course, lad,
And every dog his day.

When all the world is old, lad,
And all the trees are brown;
And all the sport is stale, lad,
And all the wheels run down;
Creep home, and take your place there,
The spent and maimed among:
God grant you find one face there,
You loved when all was young. *Ib. Young and Old*

20 The merry brown hares came leaping
Over the crest of the hill,
Where the clover and corn lay sleeping
Under the moonlight still. *The Bad Squire*

21 Oh! that we two were Maying
Down the stream of the soft Spring breeze;
Like children with violets playing,
In the shade of the whispering trees.
The Saint's Tragedy, II. ix.

22 'O Mary, go and call the cattle home,
And call the cattle home,
And call the cattle home,
Across the sands of Dee:'
The western wind was wild and dank with foam,
And all alone went she. *The Sands of Dee*

23 The western tide crept up along the sand,
And o'er and o'er the sand,
And round and round the sand,
As far as eye could see.
The rolling mist came down and hid the land:
And never home came she. *Ib.*

24 The cruel crawling foam. *Ib.*

25 Three fishers went sailing away to the west,
Away to the west as the sun went down;
Each thought on the woman who loved him the best,
And the children stood watching them out of the
town. *The Three Fishers*

26 And the night-rack came rolling up ragged and
brown. *Ib.*

[293]

1 For men must work, and women must weep,
And there's little to earn, and many to keep,
Though the harbour bar be moaning.
The Three Fishers

2 For men must work, and women must weep,
And the sooner it's over, the sooner to sleep;
And good-bye to the bar and its moaning. *Ib.*

3 To be discontented with the divine discontent, and to
be ashamed with the noble shame, is the very germ
and first upgrowth of all virtue.
Health and Education (1874), p. 20

4 Truth, for its own sake, had never been a virtue with
the Roman clergy.
Review of Froude's History of England, *in* Macmillan's *Magazine for Jan. 1864*

5 He did not know that a keeper is only a poacher
turned outside in, and a poacher a keeper turned
inside out. *The Water Babies*, ch. 1

6 As thorough an Englishman as ever coveted his
neighbour's goods. *Ib.* ch. 4

7 And still the lobster held on. *Ib.* ch. 5

8 Mrs. Bedonebyasyoudid is coming. *Ib.*

9 The loveliest fairy in the world; and her name is
Mrs. Doasyouwouldbedoneby. *Ib.*

10 All the butterflies and cockyolybirds would fly past
me. *Ib.* ch. 8

11 Till the coming of the Cocqcigrues. *Ib.*

12 Don Desperado
Walked on the Prado,
And there he met his enemy. *Westward Ho*, ch. 12

13 More ways of killing a cat than choking her with
cream. *Ib.* ch. 20

14 Eustace is a man no longer; he is become a thing, a
tool, a Jesuit. *Ib.* ch. 23

15 What, then, does Dr. Newman mean?
Title of a pamphlet, 1864

16 Some say that the age of chivalry is past, that the
spirit of romance is dead. The age of chivalry is
never past, so long as there is a wrong left unredressed on earth. *Life* (1879), vol. ii, ch. 28

RUDYARD KIPLING
1865–1936

17 When you've shouted 'Rule Britannia', when you've
sung 'God save the Queen',
When you've finished killing Kruger with your
mouth. *The Absent-Minded Beggar*

18 He's an absent-minded beggar, and his weaknesses
are great—
But we and Paul must take him as we find him—
He's out on active service, wiping something off a
slate—
And he's left a lot of little things behind him! *Ib.*

19 Duke's son—cook's son—son of a hundred Kings—
(Fifty thousand horse and foot going to Table Bay!)
Ib.

20 Pass the hat for your credit's sake, and pay—pay—
pay! *Ib.*

21 If you'd go to Mother Carey
(Walk her down to Mother Carey!),
Oh, we're bound to Mother Carey where she feeds
her chicks at sea! *Anchor Song*

22 England's on the anvil—hear the hammers ring—
Clanging from the Severn to the Tyne!
Never was a blacksmith like our Norman King—
England's being hammered, hammered, hammered
into line! *The Anvil*

23 Back to the Army again. *Title*

24 A-layin' on to the Sergeant I don't know a gun from
a bat. *Back to the Army Again*

25 I 'eard the feet on the gravel—the feet o' the men
what drill—
An' I sez to my flutterin' 'eart-strings, I sez to 'em,
'Peace, be still!' *Ib.*

26 Rolling down the Ratcliffe Road drunk and raising
Cain. *The Ballad of the 'Bolivar'*

27 Oh, East is East, and West is West, and never the
twain shall meet,
Till Earth and Sky stand presently at God's great
Judgment Seat;
But there is neither East nor West, Border, nor
Breed, nor Birth,
When two strong men stand face to face, though they
come from the ends of the earth!
The Ballad of East and West

28 With the mouth of a bell and the heart of Hell and the
head of the gallows-tree. *Ib.*

29 And the talk slid north, and the talk slid south,
With the sliding puffs from the hookah-mouth.
Four things greater than all things are,—
Women and Horses and Power and War.
Ballad of the King's Jest

30 It was not part of their blood,
It came to them very late
With long arrears to make good,
When the English began to hate. *The Beginnings*

31 There's peace in a Larañaga, there's calm in a Henry
Clay. *The Betrothed*

32 And a woman is only a woman, but a good cigar is a
Smoke. *Ib.*

33 Gentlemen unafraid.
Beyond the Path of the Outmost Sun. (*Barrack-Room Ballads: Dedication*)

34 'Oh, where are you going to, all you Big Steamers,
With England's own coal, up and down the salt seas?'
'We are going to fetch you your bread and your butter,
Your beef, pork, and mutton, eggs, apples, and
cheese.' *Big Steamers*

35 'Oh, the Channel's as bright as a ball-room already,
And pilots are thicker than pilchards at Looe.' *Ib.*

36 'For the bread that you eat and the biscuits you nibble,
The sweets that you suck and the joints that you
carve,
They are brought to you daily by all us Big Steamers—
And if any one hinders our coming you'll starve!' *Ib.*

37 We're foot—slog—slog—slog—sloggin' over Africa—
Foot—foot—foot—foot—sloggin' over Africa—
(Boots—boots—boots—boots—movin' up an' down
again!)
There's no discharge in the war! *Boots*

1 Try—try—try—try—to think o' something different—
  Oh—my—God—keep—me from goin' lunatic!
  (Boots—boots—boots—boots—movin' up an' down
  again!)   *Boots*

2 O ye who tread the Narrow Way
  By Tophet-flare to Judgement Day.
                                Buddha at Kamakura

3 I've a head like a concertina, I've a tongue like a
  button-stick,
  I've a mouth like an old potato, and I'm more than a
  little sick,
  But I've had my fun o' the Corp'ral's Guard; I've
  made the cinders fly,
  And I'm here in the Clink for a thundering drink and
  blacking the Corporal's eye.   *Cells*

4 'Drunk and resisting the Guard!'
  Mad drunk and resisting the Guard—
  'Strewth, but I socked it them hard!
  So it's pack-drill for me and a fortnight's C.B.
  For 'drunk and resisting the Guard'.   *Ib.*

5 Take of English earth as much
  As either hand may rightly clutch.
  In the taking of it breathe
  Prayer for all who lie beneath. . . .
  Lay that earth upon thy heart,
  And thy sickness shall depart!   *A Charm*

6 Land of our birth, we pledge to thee
  Our love and toil in the years to be;
  When we are grown and take our place,
  As men and women with our race.

  Father in Heaven who lovest all,
  Oh, help Thy children when they call;
  That they may build from age to age
  An undefilèd heritage.

  Teach us to bear the yoke in youth,
  With steadfastness and careful truth;
  That, in our time, Thy Grace may give
  The truth whereby the nations live.
                              The Children's Song

7 That we, with Thee, may walk uncowed
  By fear or favour of the crowd.   *Ib.*

8 That, under Thee, we may possess
  Man's strength to comfort man's distress.

  Teach us delight in simple things,
  And mirth that has no bitter springs;
  Forgiveness free of evil done,
  And love to all men 'neath the sun!

  Land of our birth, our faith, our pride,
  For whose dear sake our fathers died;
  O Motherland, we pledge to thee
  Head, heart, and hand through the years to be! *Ib.*

9 High noon behind the tamarisks—the sun is hot
  above us—
  As at Home the Christmas Day is breaking wan.
  They will drink our healths at dinner—those who
  tell us how they love us,
  And forget us till another year be gone!
                              Christmas in India

10 So Time, that is o'er-kind,
   To all that be,
   Ordains us e'en as blind,
   As bold as she:

That in our very death,
And burial sure,
Shadow to shadow, well persuaded, saith,
'See how our works endure!'
      *Cities and Thrones and Powers (Puck of Pook's
      Hill)*

11 We must go back with Policeman Day—
   Back from the City of Sleep!   *The City of Sleep*

12 The coastwise lights of England watch the ships of
   England go!   *The Coastwise Lights*

13 They know the worthy General as 'that most immoral man'.   *A Code of Morals*

14 Gold is for the mistress—silver for the maid—
   Copper for the craftsman cunning at his trade.
   'Good!' said the Baron, sitting in his hall,
   'But Iron—Cold Iron—is master of them all.'
                                          Cold Iron

15 We have learned to whittle the Eden Tree to the shape
   of a surplice-peg,
   We have learned to bottle our parents twain in the
   yolk of an addled egg,
   We know that the tail must wag the dog, for the horse
   is drawn by the cart;
   But the Devil whoops, as he whooped of old: 'It's
   clever, but is it Art?'
                          The Conundrum of the Workshops

16 Our father Adam sat under the Tree and scratched
   with a stick in the mould;
   And the first rude sketch that the world had seen was
   joy to his mighty heart.
   Till the Devil whispered behind the leaves, 'It's
   pretty, but is it Art?'   *Ib.*

17 By the favour of God we might know as much—
   as our father Adam knew!   *Ib.*

18 And that is called paying the Dane-geld;
   But we've proved it again and again,
   That if once you have paid him the Dane-geld
   You never get rid of the Dane.   *Dane-Geld*

19 'What are the bugles blowin' for?' said Files-on-
   Parade.
   'To turn you out, to turn you out,' the Colour-Ser-
   geant said.   *Danny Deever*

20 'For they're hangin' Danny Deever, you can hear the
   Dead March play,
   The Regiment's in 'ollow square—they're hangin'
   'im to-day;
   They've taken of 'is buttons off an' cut 'is stripes
   away,
   An' they're hangin' Danny Deever in the mornin'.'
                                                Ib.

21 The 'eathen in 'is blindness bows down to wood an'
   stone;
   'E don't obey no orders unless they is 'is own;
   'E keeps 'is side-arms awful: 'e leaves 'em all about,
   An' then comes up the Regiment an' pokes the 'eathen
   out.   *The 'Eathen*

22 All along o' dirtiness, all along o' mess,
   All along o' doin' things rather-more-or-less,
   All along of abby-nay*, kul†, an' hazar-ho‡,
   Mind you keep your rifle an' yourself jus' so! *Ib.*
   * not now † to-morrow ‡ wait a bit.

23 The 'eathen in 'is blindness must end where 'e began,
   But the backbone of the Army is the Non-commissioned man!   *Ib.*

KIPLING

1 The first dry rattle of new-drawn steel
Changes the world to-day! *Edgehill Fight*

2 Who are neither children nor Gods, but men in a
world of men! *England's Answer to the Cities*

3 Winds of the World, give answer! They are whimpering to and fro—
And what should they know of England who only
England know? *The English Flag*

4 I barred my gates with iron, I shuttered my doors
with flame,
Because to force my ramparts your nutshell navies
came. *Ib.*

5 Never was isle so little, never was sea so lone,
But over the scud and the palm-trees an English Flag
was flown. *Ib.*

6 I could not look on Death, which being known,
Men led me to him, blindfold and alone.
Epitaphs of the War. The Coward

7 All that pentecostal crew. *Et Dona Ferentes*

8 But it never really mattered till the English grew
polite. *Ib.*

9 Something lost behind the Ranges. *The Explorer*

10 Your 'Never-never country'. *Ib.*

11 Anybody might have found it, but—His Whisper
came to me! *Ib.*

12 For the Red Gods call us out and we must go!
The Feet of the Young Men

13 When the Himalayan peasant meets the he-bear in his
pride,
He shouts to scare the monster, who will often turn
aside.
But the she-bear thus accosted rends the peasant
tooth and nail
For the female of the species is more deadly than the
male. *The Female of the Species*

14 Man propounds negotiations, Man accepts the compromise.
Very rarely will he squarely push the logic of a fact
To its ultimate conclusion in unmitigated act. *Ib.*

15 Buy my English posies!
Kent and Surrey may—
Violets of the Undercliff
Wet with Channel spray;
Cowslips from a Devon combe—
Midland furze afire—
Buy my English posies
And I'll sell your heart's desire! *The Flowers*

16 Take the flower and turn the hour, and kiss your love
again! *Ib.*

17 So it's knock out your pipes an' follow me!
An' it's finish up your swipes an' follow me!
Oh, 'ark to the big drum callin',
Follow me—follow me 'ome! *Follow Me 'Ome*

18 For it's 'Three rounds blank' an' follow me,
An' it's 'Thirteen rank' an' follow me;
Oh, passin' the love o' women,
Follow me—follow me 'ome! *Ib.*

19 For all we have and are,
For all our children's fate,
Stand up and take the war.
The Hun is at the gate! *For All We Have and Are*

20 There is but one task for all—
One life for each to give.
What stands if Freedom fall?
Who dies if England live? *For All We Have and Are*

21 Ford, ford, ford o' Kabul river,
Ford o' Kabul river in the dark!
There's the river up an' brimmin', an' there's 'arf a
squadron swimmin'
'Cross the ford o' Kabul river in the dark.
Ford o' Kabul River

22 For to admire an' for to see,
For to be'old this world so wide
It never done no good to me,
But I can't drop it if I tried! *For to Admire*

23 So 'ere's to you, Fuzzy-Wuzzy, at your 'ome in the
Soudan;
You're a pore benighted 'eathen but a first-class
fightin' man;
An' 'ere's to you, Fuzzy-Wuzzy, with your 'ayrick
'ead of 'air—
You big black boundin' beggar—for you broke a
British square! *Fuzzy-Wuzzy*

24 'E's all 'ot sand an' ginger when alive,
An' 'e's generally shammin' when 'e's dead. *Ib.*

25 'E's the only thing that doesn't give a damn
For a Regiment o' British Infantree! *Ib.*

26 To the legion of the lost ones, to the cohort of the
damned. *Gentlemen Rankers*

27 Gentlemen-rankers out on the spree,
Damned from here to Eternity. *Ib.*

28 We have done with Hope and Honour, we are lost to
Love and Truth,
We are dropping down the ladder rung by rung;
And the measure of our torment is the measure of our
youth.
God help us, for we knew the worst too young! *Ib.*

29 The wild hawk to the wind-swept sky,
The deer to the wholesome wold,
And the heart of a man to the heart of a maid,
As it was in the days of old. *The Gipsy Trail*

30 Our England is a garden that is full of stately views,
Of borders, beds and shrubberies and lawns and
avenues,
With statues on the terraces and peacocks strutting
by;
But the Glory of the Garden lies in more than meets
the eye. *The Glory of the Garden*

31 The Glory of the Garden it abideth not in words. *Ib.*

32 Our England is a garden, and such gardens are not
made
By singing:—'Oh, how beautiful!' and sitting in the
shade,
While better men than we go out and start their
working lives
At grubbing weeds from gravel paths with broken
dinner-knives. *Ib.*

33 Then seek your job with thankfulness and work till
further orders,
If it's only netting strawberries or killing slugs on
borders;
And when your back stops aching and your hands
begin to harden,
You will find yourself a partner in the Glory of the
Garden.

Oh, Adam was a gardener, and God who made him sees
That half a proper gardener's work is done upon his knees,
So when your work is finished, you can wash your hands and pray
For the Glory of the Garden, that it may not pass away!
And the Glory of the Garden it shall never pass away! *The Glory of the Garden*

1 You may talk o' gin an' beer
When you're quartered safe out 'ere,
An' you're sent to penny-fights an' Aldershot it;
But when it comes to slaughter
You will do your work on water,
An' you'll lick the bloomin' boots of 'im that's got it.
Gunga Din

2 The uniform 'e wore
Was nothin' much before,
An' rather less than 'arf o' that be'ind. *Ib.*

3 An' for all 'is dirty 'ide
'E was white, clear white, inside
When 'e went to tend the wounded under fire! *Ib.*

4 So I'll meet 'im later on
At the place where 'e is gone—
Where it's always double drills and no canteen. *Ib.*

5 'E'll be squattin' on the coals
Givin' drink to poor damned souls,
An' I'll get a swig in Hell from Gunga Din. *Ib.*

6 Though I've belted you an' flayed you,
By the livin' Gawd that made you,
You're a better man than I am, Gunga Din! *Ib.*

7 But O, 'tis won'erful good for the Prophet!
Hal o' the Draft. (Puck of Pook's Hill)

8 Ere yet we loose the legions—
Ere yet we draw the blade,
Jehovah of the Thunders,
Lord God of Battles, aid! *Hymn Before Action*

9 There are nine and sixty ways of constructing tribal lays,
And—every—single—one—of—them—is—right!
In the Neolithic Age

10 If you can keep your head when all about you
Are losing theirs and blaming it on you,
If you can trust yourself when all men doubt you,
But make allowance for their doubting too;
If you can wait and not be tired by waiting,
Or being lied about, don't deal in lies,
Or being hated, don't give way to hating,
And yet don't look too good, nor talk too wise:

If you can dream—and not make dreams your master;
If you can think—and not make thoughts your aim;
If you can meet with Triumph and Disaster
And treat those two impostors just the same. *If—*

11 If you can make one heap of all your winnings
And risk it on one turn of pitch-and-toss,
And lose, and start again at your beginnings
And never breathe a word about your loss. *Ib.*

12 If you can talk with crowds and keep your virtue,
Or walk with Kings—nor lose the common touch,
If neither foes nor loving friends can hurt you,
If all men count with you, but none too much;

If you can fill the unforgiving minute
With sixty seconds' worth of distance run,
Yours is the Earth and everything that's in it,
And—which is more—you'll be a Man, my son!
If—

13 I have eaten your bread and salt,
I have drunk your water and wine.
I Have Eaten Your Bread. (Departmental Ditties: Prelude)

14 Dear hearts across the seas. *Ib.*

15 No doubt but ye are the People. *The Islanders*

16 Then ye returned to your trinkets; then ye contented your souls
With the flannelled fools at the wicket or the muddied oafs at the goals. *Ib.*

17 Given to strong delusion, wholly believing a lie. *Ib.*

18 He wrote that monarchs were divine,
And left a son who—proved they weren't! *James I*

19 Jane went to Paradise:
That was only fair,
Good Sir Walter met her first,
And led her up the stair.
Henry and Tobias,
And Miguel of Spain,
Stood with Shakespeare at the top
To welcome Jane. *Jane's Marriage*

20 Jane lies in Winchester, blessèd be her shade!
Praise the Lord for making her, and her for all she made.
And, while the stones of Winchester—or Milsom Street—remain,
Glory, Love, and Honour unto England's Jane! *Ib.*

21 Cold, commanded lust. *Justice*

22 Let them relearn the Law. *Ib.*

23 I've never sailed the Amazon,
I've never reached Brazil.
Just-So Stories. Beginning of the Armadilloes

24 Yes, weekly from Southampton,
Great steamers, white and gold,
Go rolling down to Rio
(Roll down—roll down to Rio!).
And I'd like to roll to Rio
Some day before I'm old! *Ib.*

25 I've never seen a Jaguar,
Nor yet an Armadill-
o dilloing in his armour,
And I s'pose I never will. *Ib.*

26 The Camel's hump is an ugly lump
Which well you may see at the Zoo;
But uglier yet is the Hump we get
From having too little to do.
Ib. How the Camel Got His Hump

27 We get the Hump—
Cameelious Hump—
The Hump that is black and blue! *Ib.*

28 The cure for this ill is not to sit still,
Or frowst with a book by the fire;
But to take a large hoe and a shovel also,
And dig till you gently perspire. *Ib.*

29 Old Man Kangaroo first, Yellow-Dog Dingo behind.
Ib. Sing-Song of Old Man Kangaroo

1 'Confound Romance!' . . . And all unseen
Romance brought up the nine-fifteen.   *The King*

2 For Allah created the English mad—the maddest of
all mankind!   *Kitchener's School*

3 I've taken my fun where I've found it,
An' now I must pay for my fun,
For the more you 'ave known o' the others
The less will you settle to one;
An' the end of it's sittin' an' thinkin',
An' dreamin' Hell-fires to see.
So be warned by my lot (which I know you will not),
An' learn about women from me!   *The Ladies*

4 An' I learned about women from 'er!   *Ib.*

5 But the things you will learn from the Yellow an'
Brown,
They'll 'elp you a lot with the White!   *Ib.*

6 For the Colonel's Lady an' Judy O'Grady
Are sisters under their skins!   *Ib.*

7 Have it jest *as* you've a mind to, but, if I was you, I'd
dreen.   *The Land*

8 'Hev it just as you've a mind to, *but*'—and here he
takes command.
For whoever pays the taxes old Mus' Hobden owns
the land.   *Ib.*

9 Thus said the Lord in the vault above the Cherubim,
Calling to the Angels and the Souls in their degree.
The Last Chantey

10 Then said the soul of the Angel of the Off-shore
Wind.   *Ib.*

11 And Ye take mine honour from me if Ye take away
the sea!   *Ib.*

12 Then cried the soul of the stout Apostle Paul to God.
Ib.

13 When they learned Thy Grace and Glory under
Malta by the sea!   *Ib.*

14 Loud sang the souls of the jolly, jolly mariners,
Plucking at their harps, and they plucked unhandily:
'Our thumbs are rough and tarred,
And the tune is something hard—
May we lift a Deepsea Chantey such as seamen use
at sea?'   *Ib.*

15 Heave or sink it, leave or drink it, we were masters
of the sea!   *Ib.*

16 Then stooped the Lord, and He called the good sea
up to Him,
And 'stablishèd its borders unto all eternity,
That such as have no pleasure
For to praise the Lord by measure,
They may enter into galleons and serve Him on the
Sea.   *Ib.*

17 And the ships shall go abroad
To the Glory of the Lord
Who heard the silly sailor-folk and gave them back
their sea!   *Ib.*

18 I ha' harpit ye up to the Throne o' God,
I ha' harpit your midmost soul in three.
I ha' harpit ye down to the Hinges o' Hell,
And—ye—would—make—a Knight o' me!
The Last Rhyme of True Thomas

19 Now this is the Law of the Jungle—as old and as true
as the sky.   *The Law of the Jungle*

20 This is the sorrowful story
Told as the twilight fails
And the monkeys walk together
Holding their neighbours' tails.
The Legends of Evil

21 Thin Noah spoke him fairly, thin talked to him
sevairely,
An' thin he cursed him squarely to the glory av the
Lord:—
'Divil take the ass that bred you, an' the greater ass
that fed you!
Divil go wid you, ye spalpeen!' an' the Donkey wint
aboard.   *Ib.*

22 Till Noah said:—'There's wan av us that hasn't paid
his fare!'   *Ib.*

23 We have had an Imperial lesson; it may make us an
Empire yet!   *The Lesson*

24 And that's how it all began, my dears,
And that's how it all began!
The Light that Failed, chapter heading

25 The Liner she's a lady, an' she never looks nor
'eeds—
The Man-o'-War's 'er 'usband, an' 'e gives 'er all
she needs;
But, oh, the little cargo-boats, that sail the wet sea
roun',
They're just the same as you an' me a-plyin' up an
down!   *The Liner She's a Lady*

26 There's a whisper down the field where the year has
shot her yield,
And the ricks stand grey to the sun,
Singing:—'Over then, come over, for the bee has quit
the clover,
And your English summer's done.'   *The Long Trail*

27 You have heard the beat of the off-shore wind,
And the thresh of the deep-sea rain;
You have heard the song—how long? how long?
Pull out on the trail again!
Ha' done with the Tents of Shem, dear lass,
We've seen the seasons through,
And it's time to turn on the old trail, our own trail,
the out trail,
Pull out, pull out, on the Long Trail—the trail that
is always new!   *Ib.*

28 It's North you may run to the rime-ringed sun,
Or South to the blind Horn's hate;
Or East all the way into Mississippi Bay,
Or West to the Golden Gate.   *Ib.*

29 The Queen was in her chamber, and she was middling
old,
Her petticoat was satin, and her stomacher was gold.
Backwards and forwards and sideways did she pass,
Making up her mind to face the cruel looking-glass.
The cruel looking-glass that will never show a lass
As comely or as kindly or as young as what she was!
The Looking Glass

30 The Queen was in her chamber, her sins were on her
head.
She looked the spirits up and down and statelily she
said:—
'Backwards and forwards and sideways though I've
been,
Yet I am Harry's daughter and I am England's
Queen!'   *Ib.*

1 There's a Legion that never was 'listed.
The Lost Legion

2 To go and find out and be damned
(Dear boys!),
To go and get shot and be damned. *Ib.*

3 Lord, Thou hast made this world below the shadow
of a dream,
An', taught by time, I tak' it so—exceptin' always
Steam.
From coupler-flange to spindle-guide I see Thy
Hand, O God—
Predestination in the stride o' yon connectin'-rod.
McAndrew's Hymn

4 Alone wi' God an' these
My engines. *Ib.*

5 Yon's strain, hard strain, o' head an' hand, for though
Thy Power brings
All skill to naught, Ye'll understand a man must
think o' things. *Ib.*

6 Ye thought? Ye are not paid to think. *Ib.*

7 Mister McAndrew, don't you think steam spoils
romance at sea? *Ib.*

8 Romance! Those first-class passengers they like it
very well,
Printed an' bound in little books; but why don't
poets tell? *Ib.*

9 While, out o' touch o' vanity, the sweatin' thrust-
block says:
'Not unto us the praise, or man—not unto us the
praise!' *Ib.*

10 By the old Moulmein Pagoda, lookin' eastward to the
sea,
There's a Burma girl a-settin', and I know she thinks
o' me;
For the wind is in the palm-trees, an' the temple-
bells they say:
'Come you back, you British soldier; come you back
to Mandalay!'
Come you back to Mandalay,
Where the old Flotilla lay:
Can't you 'ear their paddles chunkin' from Rangoon
to Mandalay?
On the road to Mandalay,
Where the flyin'-fishes play,
An' the dawn comes up like thunder outer China
'crost the Bay! *Mandalay*

11 An' I seed her first a-smokin' of a whackin' white
cheroot,
An' a-wastin' Christian kisses on an 'eathen idol's
foot. *Ib.*

12 When the mist was on the rice-fields an' the sun was
droppin' slow,
She'd git 'er little banjo an' she'd sing 'Kulla-lo-lo!'
Ib.

13 But that's all shove be'ind me—long ago an' fur away,
An' there ain' no 'buses runnin' from the Bank to
Mandalay;
An' I'm learnin' 'ere in London wot the ten-year
soldier tells:
'If you've 'eard the East a-callin', you won't never
'eed naught else.' *Ib.*

14 I am sick o' wastin' leather on these gritty pavin'-
stones,
An' the blasted English drizzle wakes the fever in my
bones;
Tho' I walks with fifty 'ousemaids outer Chelsea to
the Strand,
An' they talks a lot o' lovin', but wot do they under-
stand?
Beefy face an' grubby 'and—
Law! Wot do they understand?
I've a neater, sweeter maiden in a cleaner, greener
land! *Mandalay*

15 Ship me somewheres east of Suez, where the best is
like the worst,
Where there aren't no Ten Commandments, an' a
man can raise a thirst:
For the temple-bells are callin', an' it's there that I
would be—
By the old Moulmein Pagoda, looking lazy at the sea.
Ib.

16 Ten thousand men on the pay-roll, and forty
freighters at sea! *The 'Mary Gloster'*

17 Harrer an' Trinity College! I ought to ha' sent you
to sea. *Ib.*

18 For you muddled with books and pictures, an' china
an' etchin's an' fans,
And your rooms at college was beastly—more like a
whore's than a man's. *Ib.*

19 I've seen your carriages blocking the half o' the
Cromwell Road,
But never the doctor's brougham to help the missus
unload. *Ib.*

20 For a man he must go with a woman, which women
don't understand—
Or the sort that say they can see it, they aren't the
marrying brand. *Ib.*

21 I'm sick of the hired women. I'll kiss my girl on her
lips! *Ib.*

22 Nice while it lasted, an' now it is over—
Tear out your 'eart an' good-bye to your lover!
What's the use o' grievin', when the mother that bore
you
(Mary, pity women!) knew it all before you?
Mary, Pity Women

23 There runs a road by Merrow Down—
A grassy track to-day it is—
An hour out of Guildford town,
Above the river Wey it is. *Merrow Down*

24 But as the faithful years return
And hearts unwounded sing again,
Comes Taffy dancing through the fern
To lead the Surrey spring again. *Ib.*

25 Mines reported in the fairway,
Warn all traffic and detain.
'Sent up *Unity, Claribel, Assyrian, Stormcock,* and
Golden Gain. *Mine Sweepers*

26 Good rest to all
That keep the Jungle Law.
Morning Song in the Jungle

27 If I were hanged on the highest hill,
Mother o' mine, O mother o' mine!
I know whose love would follow me still,
Mother o' mine, O mother o' mine!
Mother O' Mine

1 If I were damned of body and soul,
I know whose prayers would make me whole,
Mother o' mine, O mother o' mine! *Mother O'Mine*

2 'Have you news of my boy Jack?'
Not this tide.
'When d'you think that he'll come back?'
Not with this wind blowing, and this tide.
My Boy Jack

3 My new-cut ashlar takes the light
Where crimson-blank the windows flare.
My New-cut Ashlar

4 The depth and dream of my desire,
The bitter paths wherein I stray—
Thou knowest Who hast made the Fire,
Thou knowest Who hast made the Clay. *Ib.*

5 One stone the more swings into place
In that dread Temple of Thy worth.
It is enough that, through Thy Grace,
I saw nought common on Thy Earth. *Ib.*

6 Now it is not good for the Christian's health to hustle
the Aryan brown,
For the Christian riles, and the Aryan smiles, and it
weareth the Christian down;
And the end of the fight is a tombstone white with
the name of the late deceased,
And the epitaph drear: 'A Fool lies here who tried to
hustle the East.' *Naulahka*, heading of ch. 5

7 The Saxon is not like us Normans. His manners are
not so polite.
But he never means anything serious till he talks
about justice and right,
When he stands like an ox in the furrow with his
sullen set eyes on your own,
And grumbles, 'This isn't fair dealing,' my son, leave
the Saxon alone. *Norman and Saxon*

8 The 'orse 'e knows above a bit, the bullock's but a
fool,
The elephant's a gentleman, the battery-mule's a
mule;
But the commissariat cam-u-el, when all is said an'
done,
'E's a devil an' a ostrich an' a orphan-child in one.
Oonts

9 Excellent herbs had our fathers of old—
Excellent herbs to ease their pain.
Our Fathers of Old

10 Anything green that grew out of the mould
Was an excellent herb to our fathers of old. *Ib.*

11 A Nation spoke to a Nation,
A Throne sent word to a Throne:
'Daughter am I in my mother's house,
But mistress in my own.
The gates are mine to open,
As the gates are mine to close,
And I abide by my Mother's House.'
Said our Lady of the Snows. *Our Lady of the Snows*

12 In the Name of the Empress, the Overland Mail!
The Overland Mail

13 The toad beneath the harrow knows
Exactly where each tooth-point goes;
The butterfly upon the road
Preaches contentment to that toad. *Pagett M.P.*

14 Pagett, M.P., was a liar, and a fluent liar therewith.
Ib.

15 After me cometh a Builder. Tell him, I too have
known. *The Palace*

16 Can't! Don't! Sha'n't! Won't!
Pass it along the line!
Somebody's pack has slid from his back,
'Wish it were only mine!
Somebody's load has tipped off in the road—
Cheer for a halt and a row!
Urrh! Yarrh! Grr! Arrh!
Somebody's catching it now!
Parade-Song of the Camp-Animals. Commissariat Camels

17 But a man in khaki kit who could handle men a bit,
With his bedding labelled Sergeant Whatsisname.
Pharaoh and the Sergeant

18 He drank strong waters and his speech was coarse;
He purchased raiment and forbore to pay;
He stuck a trusting junior with a horse,
And won gymkhanas in a doubtful way,
Then, 'twixt a vice and folly, turned aside
To do good deeds—and straight to cloak them, lied.
Plain Tales from the Hills. Chapter heading to
A Bank Fraud

19 The Three in One, the One in Three? Not so!
To my own Gods I go.
It may be they shall give me greater ease
Than your cold Christ and tangled Trinities.
Ib. Chapter heading to *Lispeth*

20 Bade farewell to Minnie Boffkin in one last, long
lingering fit. *The Post that Fitted*

21 Year by year, in pious patience, vengeful Mrs. Boffkin sits
Waiting for the Sleary babies to develop Sleary's fits.
Ib.

22 There is sorrow enough in the natural way
From men and women to fill our day;
But when we are certain of sorrow in store,
Why do we always arrange for more?
Brothers and Sisters, I bid you beware
Of giving your heart to a dog to tear.
The Power of the Dog

23 Valour and Innocence
Have latterly gone hence
To certain death by certain shame attended.
The Queen's Men

24 God of our fathers, known of old,
Lord of our far-flung battle-line,
Beneath whose awful Hand we hold
Dominion over palm and pine—
Lord God of Hosts, be with us yet,
Lest we forget—lest we forget!

The tumult and the shouting dies;
The Captains and the Kings depart:
Still stands Thine ancient sacrifice,
An humble and a contrite heart.
Lord God of Hosts, be with us yet,
Lest we forget—lest we forget! *Recessional*

25 Lo, all our pomp of yesterday
Is one with Nineveh and Tyre! *Ib.*

26 If, drunk with sight of power, we loose
Wild tongues that have not Thee in awe,
Such boastings as the Gentiles use,
Or lesser breeds without the Law. *Ib.*

1 For heathen heart that puts her trust
In reeking tube and iron shard,
All valiant dust that builds on dust,
And, guarding, calls not Thee to guard,
Thy mercy on Thy People, Lord!   *Recessional*

2 If England was what England seems,
  An' not the England of our dreams,
But only putty, brass, an' paint,
  'Ow quick we'd drop 'er! But she ain't!
                          The Return

3 There's never a law of God or man runs north of the
Fifty-Three.   *The Rhyme of the Three Sealers*

4 English they be and Japanee that hang on the Brown
Bear's flank,
And some be Scot, but the worst of the lot, and the
boldest thieves, be Yank!   *Ib.*

5 And I've lost Britain, and I've lost Gaul,
And I've lost Rome and, worst of all,
I've lost Lalage!   *Rimini*

6 I walk my beat before London Town,
Five hours up and seven down,
Up I go till I end my run
At Tide-end-town, which is Teddington.
                          The River's Tale

7 Brother, thy tail hangs down behind!
                Road Song of the Bandar-Log

8 Smokin' my pipe on the mountings, sniffin' the
mornin' cool,
I walks in my old brown gaiters along o' my old brown
mule
With seventy gunners be'ind me, an' never a beggar
forgets
It's only the pick of the Army that handles the dear
little pets—
For you all love the Screw-guns—the Screw-guns
they all love you!
So when we call round with a few guns, o' course
you'll know what to do—
Just send in your Chief an' surrender—it's worse if
you fights or you runs:
You can go where you please, you can skid up the
trees, but you don't get away from the guns!
                          Screw-guns

9 Who hath desired the Sea?—the sight of salt water
unbounded.   *The Sea and the Hills*

10 So and no otherwise—so and no otherwise—hillmen
desire their Hills!   *Ib.*

11 Cheer for the Sergeant's weddin'—
  Give 'em one cheer more!
Grey gun-'orses in the lando,
  An' a rogue is married to a whore.
                The Sergeant's Weddin'

12 Shillin' a day,
Bloomin' good pay—
Lucky to touch it, a shillin' a day!   *Shillin' a Day*

13 Give 'im a letter—
Can't do no better,
Late Troop-Sergeant-Major an'—runs with a letter!
Think what 'e's been.
Think what 'e's seen.
Think of 'is pension an'—
GAWD SAVE THE QUEEN!   *Ib.*

14 So it was 'Rounds! What Rounds?' at two of a frosty
night.
'E's 'oldin' on by the Sergeant's sash, but, sentry,
shut your eye.   *The Shut-Eye Sentry*

15 But you ought to 'ave 'eard 'em markin' time
To 'ide the things 'e said!   *Ib.*

16 There was two-an'-thirty Sergeants,
  There was Corp'rals forty-one,
There was just nine 'undred rank an' file
  To swear to a touch o' sun.   *Ib.*

17 We'll 'elp 'im for 'is mother, an' 'e'll 'elp us by-an'-
by!   *Ib.*

18 Them that asks no questions isn't told a lie.
Watch the wall, my darling, while the Gentlemen go
by!
  Five and twenty ponies
  Trotting through the dark—
  Brandy for the Parson,
  'Baccy for the Clerk;
Laces for a lady, letters for a spy,
Watch the wall, my darling, while the Gentlemen go
by!   *A Smuggler's Song*

19 Sez 'e, 'I'm a Jolly—'Er Majesty's Jolly—soldier an'
sailor too!'   *Soldier an' Sailor too!*

20 'E's a kind of a giddy harumfrodite—soldier an'
sailor too!   *Ib.*

21 I'm the Prophet of the Utterly Absurd,
Of the Patently Impossible and Vain.
                The Song of the Banjo

22 I am all that ever went with evening dress!   *Ib.*

23 There's never a wave of all her waves
But marks our English dead. *The Song of the Dead*, ii

24 If blood be the price of admiralty,
Lord God, we ha' paid in full!   *Ib.*

25 For the Lord our God Most High
He hath made the deep as dry,
He hath smote for us a pathway to the ends of all the
earth!   *A Song of the English*

26 Keep ye the Law—be swift in all obedience—
Clear the land of evil, drive the road and bridge the
ford.
Make ye sure to each his own
That he reap where he hath sown;
By the peace among our peoples let men know we
serve the Lord!   *Ib.*

27 Ere Mor the Peacock flutters, ere the Monkey People
cry,
Ere Chil the Kite swoops down a furlong sheer,
Through the Jungle very softly flits a shadow and a
sigh—
He is Fear, O Little Hunter, he is Fear!
                The Song of the Little Hunter

28 But thy throat is shut and dried, and thy heart against
thy side
Hammers: 'Fear, O Little Hunter—this is Fear!'   *Ib.*

29 Mithras, God of the Morning, our trumpets waken
the Wall!
'Rome is above the Nations, but Thou art over all!'
                A Song to Mithras

[301]

1 The Sons of Mary seldom bother, for they have inherited that good part;
   But the Sons of Martha favour their Mother of the
   careful soul and the troubled heart.
   And because she lost her temper once, and because
   she was rude to the Lord her Guest,
   Her Sons must wait upon Mary's Sons, world without
   end, reprieve, or rest.   *The Sons of Martha*

2 They do not preach that their God will rouse them a
   little before the nuts work loose.
   They do not teach that His Pity allows them to leave
   their job when they damn-well choose.   *Ib.*

3 They sit at the Feet—they hear the Word—they see
   how truly the Promise runs.
   They have cast their burden upon the Lord, and—
   the Lord He lays it on Martha's Sons!   *Ib.*

4 'Let us now praise famous men'—
   Men of little showing—
   For their work continueth,
   And their work continueth,
   Broad and deep continueth,
   Greater than their knowing!
            Stalky & Co. A School Song

5 An' it all goes into the laundry,
   But it never comes out in the wash,
   'Ow we're sugared about by the old men
   ('Eavy-sterned amateur old men!)
   That 'amper an' 'inder an' scold men
   For fear o' Stellenbosch!   *Stellenbosch*

6 You may carve it on his tombstone, you may cut it
   on his card,
   That a young man married is a young man marred.
            The Story of the Gadsbys

7 No tender-hearted garden crowns,
   No bosomed woods adorn
   Our blunt, bow-headed whale-backed Downs,
   But gnarled and writhen thorn.   *Sussex*

8 Half-wild and wholly tame,
   The wise turf cloaks the white cliff-edge
   As when the Romans came.   *Ib.*

9 The barrow and the camp abide,
   The sunlight and the sward.   *Ib.*

10 And here the sea-fogs lap and cling
   And here, each warning each,
   The sheep-bells and the ship-bells ring
   Along the hidden beach.   *Ib.*

11 Little, lost, Down churches praise
   The Lord who made the hills.   *Ib.*

12 Huge oaks and old, the which we hold
   No more than Sussex weed.   *Ib.*

13 God gives all men all earth to love,
   But, since man's heart is small,
   Ordains for each one spot shall prove
   Belovèd over all.
   Each to his choice, and I rejoice
   The lot has fallen to me
   In a fair ground—in a fair ground—
   Yea, Sussex by the sea!   *Ib.*

14 Till I 'eard a beggar squealin' out for quarter as 'e
   ran,
   An' I thought I knew the voice an'—it was me!
            That Day

15 Once on a time there was a Man.
            Things and the Man

16 And, Thomas, here's my best respects to you!
   *To Thomas Atkins. Prelude to Barrack-Room
   Ballads*

17 One man in a thousand, Solomon says,
   Will stick more close than a brother.
            The Thousandth Man

18 But the Thousandth Man will stand by your side
   To the gallows-foot—and after!   *Ib.*

19 With maids of matchless beauty and parentage unguessed,
   And a Church of England parson for the Islands of
   the Blest.   *The Three-Decker*

20 Till he heard as the roar of a rain-fed ford the roar of
   the Milky Way.   *Tomlinson*

21 Stand up, stand up now, Tomlinson, and answer
   loud and high
   The good that ye did for the sake of men or ever ye
   came to die.   *Ib.*

22 But now ye wait at Heaven's Gate and not in Berkeley Square.   *Ib.*

23 Though we called your friend from his bed this night,
   he could not speak to you,
   For the race is run by one and one and never by two
   and two.   *Ib.*

24 'Ye have read, ye have heard, ye have thought,' he
   said, 'and the tale is yet to run:
   By the worth of the body that once ye had, give
   answer—what ha' ye done?'   *Ib.*

25 Oh, this I have felt, and this I have guessed, and
   this I have heard men say,
   And this they wrote that another man wrote of a carl
   in Norroway.   *Ib.*

26 And—the faith that ye share with Berkeley Square
   uphold you, Tomlinson!   *Ib.*

27 The Wind that blows between the Worlds, it nipped
   him to the bone,
   And he yearned to the flare of Hell-gate there as the
   light of his own hearth-stone.   *Ib.*

28 For the sin ye do by two and two ye must pay for one
   by one!   *Ib.*

29 Once I ha' laughed at the power of Love and twice at
   the grip of the Grave,
   And thrice I ha' patted my God on the head that men
   might call me brave.   *Ib.*

30 Have ye sinned one sin for the pride o' the eye or the
   sinful lust of the flesh?   *Ib.*

31 Then Tomlinson he gripped the bars and yammered,
   'Let me in—
   For I mind that I borrowed my neighbour's wife to
   sin the deadly sin.'
   The Devil he grinned behind the bars, and banked
   the fires high:
   'Did ye read of that sin in a book?' said he; and
   Tomlinson said 'Ay!'   *Ib*

32 The Devil he blew upon his nails, and the little devils
   ran.   *Ib.*

33 'Ye have scarce the soul of a louse,' he said, 'but the
   roots of sin are there.'   *Ib.*

34 And—the God that you took from a printed book be
   with you, Tomlinson!   *Ib*

1 Oh, it's Tommy this, an' Tommy that, an' 'Tommy, go away';
But it's 'Thank you, Mister Atkins,' when the band begins to play. *Tommy*

2 It's Tommy this, an' Tommy that, an' 'Chuck him out, the brute!'
But it's 'Saviour of 'is country' when the guns begin to shoot. *Ib.*

3 Then it's Tommy this, an' Tommy that, an' 'Tommy, 'ow's yer soul?'
But it's 'Thin red line of 'eroes' when the drums begin to roll. *Ib.*

4 We aren't no thin red 'eroes, nor we aren't no black-guards too.
But single men in barricks, most remarkable like you;
An' if sometimes our conduck isn't all your fancy paints,
Why, single men in barricks don't grow into plaster saints. *Ib.*

5 Of all the trees that grow so fair,
Old England to adorn,
Greater are none beneath the Sun,
Than Oak, and Ash, and Thorn. *A Tree Song*

6 England shall bide till Judgement Tide,
By Oak, and Ash, and Thorn! *Ib.*

7 I tell this tale, which is strictly true,
Just by way of convincing you
How very little, since things were made,
Things have altered in the building trade.
A Truthful Song

8 Your glazing is new and your plumbing's strange,
But otherwise I perceive no change;
And in less than a month, if you do as I bid,
I'd learn you to build me a Pyramid! *Ib.*

9 The old man kindly answered them:
'It might be Japheth, it might be Shem,
Or it might be Ham (though his skin was dark),
Whereas it is Noah, commanding the Ark.'

Your wheel is new and your pumps are strange,
But otherwise I perceive no change;
And in less than a week, if she did not ground,
I'd sail this hooker the wide world round! *Ib.*

10 Much I owe to the Lands that grew—
More to the Lives that fed—
But most to Allah Who gave me two
Separate sides to my head. *The Two-Sided Man*

11 The dark eleventh hour
Draws on and sees us sold. *Ulster*

12 A fool there was and he made his prayer
(Even as you and I!)
To a rag and a bone and a hank of hair
(We called her the woman who did not care)
But the fool he called her his lady fair—
(Even as you and I!) *The Vampire*

13 But a fool must follow his natural bent
(Even as you and I!) *Ib.*

14 Oh, was there ever sailor free to choose,
That didn't settle somewhere near the sea?
The Virginity

15 They that have wrought the end unthought
Be neither saint nor sage,
But only men who did the work
For which they drew the wage. *The Wage-Slaves*

16 They shut the road through the woods
Seventy years ago. *The Way Through the Woods*

17 Steadily cantering through
The misty solitudes,
As though they perfectly knew
The old lost road through the woods—
But there is no road through the woods! *Ib.*

18 Father, Mother, and Me,
Sister and Auntie say
All the people like us are We,
And every one else is They. *We and They*

19 When Earth's last picture is painted and the tubes are twisted and dried,
When the oldest colours have faded, and the youngest critic has died,
We shall rest, and, faith, we shall need it—lie down for an æon or two,
Till the Master of All Good Workmen shall put us to work anew. *When Earth's Last Picture*

20 And those that were good shall be happy: they shall sit in a golden chair;
They shall splash at a ten-league canvas with brushes of comets' hair. *Ib.*

21 And only The Master shall praise us, and only The Master shall blame;
And no one shall work for money, and no one shall work for fame,
But each for the joy of the working, and each, in his separate star,
Shall draw the Thing as he sees It for the God of Things as They are! *Ib.*

22 When 'Omer smote 'is bloomin' lyre,
'E'd 'eard men sing by land an' sea;
An' what 'e thought 'e might require,
'E went an' took—the same as me!
When 'Omer Smote. (Barrack-Room Ballads: Introduction)

23 They knew 'e stole; 'e knew they knowed.
They didn't tell, nor make a fuss,
But winked at 'Omer down the road,
An' 'e winked back—the same as us! *Ib.*

24 Take up the White Man's burden—
Send forth the best ye breed—
Go, bind your sons to exile
To serve your captives' need;
To wait in heavy harness
On fluttered folk and wild—
Your new-caught, sullen peoples,
Half-devil and half-child.
The White Man's Burden

25 By all ye cry or whisper,
By all ye leave or do,
The silent, sullen peoples
Shall weigh your Gods and you. *Ib.*

26 Take up the White Man's burden—
And reap his old reward:
The blame of those ye better,
The hate of those ye guard. *Ib.*

27 'Ave you 'eard o' the Widow at Windsor
With a hairy gold crown on 'er 'ead?
She 'as ships on the foam—she 'as millions at 'ome,
An' she pays us poor beggars in red.
The Widow at Windsor

1 Take 'old o' the Wings o' the Mornin',
  An' flop round the earth till you're dead;
  But you won't get away from the tune that they play
  To the bloomin' old rag over 'ead.
  The Widow at Windsor

2 Down to Gehenna or up to the Throne,
  He travels the fastest who travels alone.
  The Winners

3 When the 'arf-made recruity goes out to the East
  'E acts like a babe an' 'e drinks like a beast,
  An' 'e wonders because 'e is frequent deceased
  Ere 'e's fit for to serve as a soldier.
  The Young British Soldier

4 When you're wounded and left on Afghanistan's
  plains,
  An' the women come out to cut up what remains,
  Jest roll to your rifle an' blow out your brains
  An' go to your Gawd like a soldier.   *Ib.*

5 How can I crown thee further, O Queen of the
  Sovereign South?   *The Young Queen*

6 'Ha! Ha!' said the duck, laughing.
  The Day's Work. The Brushwood Boy

7 What shall I do when I see you in the light?   *Ib.*

8 Good hunting!   *The Jungle Book. Kaa's Hunting*

9 We be of one blood, thou and I.   *Ib.*

10 'Nice,' said the small 'stute Fish. 'Nice but nubbly.'
  Just-So Stories. How the Whale Got His Throat

11 You must *not* forget the Suspenders, Best Beloved.
  Ib.

12 A man of infinite-resource-and-sagacity.   *Ib.*

13 Most 'scruciating idle.
  Ib. How the Camel Got His Hump

14 'Humph yourself!'
  And the Camel humphed himself.   *Ib.*

15 There lived a Parsee from whose hat the rays of the
  sun were reflected in more-than-oriental-splendour.   *Ib. How the Rhinoceros Got His Skin*

16 An Elephant's Child—who was full of 'satiable
  curiosity.   *Ib. The Elephant's Child*

17 The great grey-green, greasy Limpopo River, all set
  about with fever-trees.   *Ib.*

18 Led go! You are hurtig be!   *Ib.*

19 This is too butch for be!   *Ib.*

20 He was a Tidy Pachyderm.   *Ib.*

21 The Cat. He walked by himself, and all places were
  alike to him.
  Ib. The Cat That Walked By Himself

22 He went back through the Wet Wild Woods, waving
  his wild tail, and walking by his wild lone. But he
  never told anybody.   *Ib.*

23 Tho' tay is not my divarsion.
  Life's Handicap. The Courting of Dinah Shadd

24 Glory's no compensation for a belly-ache.   *Ib.*

25 What's the good of argifying?   *Ib. On Greenhow Hill*

26 I hold by the Ould Church, for she's the mother of
  them all—ay, an' the father, too. I like her bekaze
  she's most remarkable regimental in her fittings. *Ib.*

27 Asia is not going to be civilized after the methods of
  the West. There is too much Asia and she is too
  old.   *Ib. The Man Who Was*

28 Let it be clearly understood that the Russian is a de
  lightful person till he tucks in his shirt.
  Life's Handicap. The Man Who Wc

29 Man that is born of woman is small potatoes and fev
  in the hill.   *Ib. The Head of the Distri*

30 Some were married, which was bad, and some di
  other things which were worse.
  Ib. The Mark of the Bea

31 You haf too much Ego in your Cosmos.
  Ib. Bertran and Bin

32 He did not rave, as do many bridegrooms, over th
  strangeness and delight of seeing his own true lov
  sitting down to breakfast with him every mornin
  'as though it were the most natural thing in th
  world'. 'He had been there before', as the Amer
  cans say.   *Ib. Georgie Porg*

33 The Light that Failed.   *Title of Nov*

34 Every one is more or less mad on one point.
  *Plain Tales from the Hills. On the Strength c
  a Likeness*

35 Open and obvious devotion from any sort of man
  always pleasant to any sort of woman.   *I*

36 He gave way to the queer, savage feeling that som
  times takes by the throat a husband twenty year
  married, when he sees, across the table, the sam
  face of his wedded wife, and knows that, as he h
  sat facing it, so must he continue to sit until th
  day of its death or his own.
  Ib. The Bronckhurst Divorce Ca

37 'Twas like a battle field wid all the glory missin.
  Ib. The Daughter of the Regimen

38 Take my word for it, the silliest woman can mana
  a clever man; but it needs a very clever woman
  manage a fool.   *Ib. Three and—an Extr*

39 But that is another story.   *Ib.*

40 Lalun is a member of the most ancient profession i
  the world.   *Soldiers Three. On the City Wa*

41 Being kissed by a man who didn't wax his moustach
  was—like eating an egg without salt.
  Ib. The Gadsbys. Poor Dear Mamm

42 Steady the Buffs.   *I*

43 Been trotting out the Gorgonzola!   *I*

44 Almost inevitable Consequences.   *Ib. Fatim*

45 I gloat! Hear me gloat!   *Stalky and Co., ch.*

46 Your Uncle Stalky.   *I*

47 We ain't goin' to have any beastly Erickin'.
  Ib. The Moral Reforme

48 'This man,' said M'Turk, with conviction, 'is t
  Gadarene Swine.'   *Ib. The Flag of Their Countr*

49 It's boy; only boy.   *Ib. An Unsavoury Interlu*

50 'Tisn't beauty, so to speak, nor good talk neces
  sarily. It's just IT. Some women'll stay in a man
  memory if they once walked down a street.
  Traffics and Discoveries. Mrs. Bathur

51 The Waddy is an infectious disease herself.
  Wee Willie Winkie. A Second-Rate Woma

52 Once upon a time there was a Man and his Wife an
  a Tertium Quid.   *Ib. At the Pit's Mout*

53 Gawd knows, an' 'E won't split on a pal.
  Ib. Drums of the Fore and A

HORATIO HERBERT KITCHENER, EARL KITCHENER
1850–1916

1 You are ordered abroad as a soldier of the King to help our French comrades against the invasion of a common enemy. You have to perform a task which will need your courage, your energy, your patience. Remember that the honour of the British Army depends on your individual conduct. It will be your duty not only to set an example of discipline and perfect steadiness under fire but also to maintain the most friendly relations with those whom you are helping in this struggle. In this new experience you may find temptations both in wine and women. You must entirely resist both temptations, and, while treating all women with perfect courtesy, you should avoid any intimacy. Do your duty bravely. Fear God. Honour the King.
A message to the soldiers of the British Expeditionary Force, 1914, to be kept by each soldier in his Active Service Pay-Book. Sir G. Arthur's Life of Kitchener, vol. iii, p. 27.

FRIEDRICH VON KLINGER
1752–1831

2 Sturm und Drang.
    Storm and stress.   *Title of Play (1775)*

CHARLES KNIGHT

3 Here we are! here we are!! here we are again!!!
There's Pat and Mac and Tommy and Jack and Joe.
When there's trouble brewing,
When there's something doing,
Are we downhearted?
No! let 'em all come!
    Here We Are! Here We Are Again!!

MARY KNOWLES
1733–1807

4 He [Dr. Johnson] gets at the substance of a book directly; he tears out the heart of it.
    Boswell's Johnson (ed. 1934), vol. iii, p. 284. 15 Apr. 1778

JOHN KNOX
1505–1572

5 Un homme avec Dieu est toujours dans la majorité.
    A man with God is always in the majority.
    Inscription on the Reformation Monument, Geneva, Switzerland

6 The First Blast of the Trumpet Against the Monstrous Regiment of Women.   *Title of Pamphlet, 1558*

RONALD ARBUTHNOT KNOX
1888–1957

7 When suave politeness, tempering bigot zeal,
Corrected *I believe* to *One does feel.*
    Absolute and Abitofhell

8 O God, for as much as without Thee
We are not enabled to doubt Thee,
    Help us all by Thy grace
    To convince the whole race
It knows nothing whatever about Thee.
    Attr. Langford Reed, The Limerick Book

9 There was a young man of Devizes,
Whose ears were of different sizes;
    The one that was small
    Was no use at all,
But the other won several prizes.
    Attr. Langford Reed, The Limerick Book

10 There was once a man who said 'God
Must think it exceedingly odd
    If he finds that this tree
    Continues to be
When there's no one about in the Quad.'
    Ib. For the answer see 5:27

PAUL KRUGER
1825–1904

11 A bill of indemnity . . . for raid by Dr. Jameson and the British South Africa Company's troops. The amount falls under two heads—first material damage, total of claim, £577,938 3s. 3d.; second, moral or intellectual damage, total of claim, £1,000,000.
    Communicated to House of Commons by Joseph Chamberlain, 18 Feb. 1897

THOMAS KYD
1557?–1595?

12 In time the savage bull sustains the yoke,
In time all haggard hawks will stoop to lure,
In time small wedges cleave the hardest oak,
In time the flint is pierced with softest shower.
    The Spanish Tragedy, I. vi. 3

13 What outcries pluck me from my naked bed?
    Ib. II. v. I

14 Oh eyes, no eyes, but fountains fraught with tears;
Oh life, no life, but lively form of death;
Oh world, no world, but mass of public wrongs.
    Ib. III. ii. I

15 Thus must we toil in other men's extremes,
That know not how to remedy our own.   *Ib. vi. I*

16 I am never better than when I am mad. Then methinks I am a brave fellow; then I do wonders. But reason abuseth me, and there's the torment, there's the hell.   *Ib. vii a. 169 (1602 edn.)*

17 My son—and what's a son? A thing begot
Within a pair of minutes, thereabout,
A lump bred up in darkness.   *Ib. xi. Additions, l. 5*

18   Duly twice a morning
Would I be sprinkling it with fountain water.
At last it grew, and grew, and bore, and bore,
Till at the length
It grew a gallows and did bear our son,
It bore thy fruit and mine: O wicked, wicked plant.
    Ib. xii. Additions, l. 66

19 For what's a play without a woman in it?
    Ib. IV. i. 96

HENRY LABOUCHERE
1831–1912

20 He [Labouchere] did not object, he once said, to Gladstone's always having the ace of trumps up his sleeve, but only to his pretence that God had put it there.
    Dict. of Nat. Biog., 1912–1921. Cf. Thorold's Life of Labouchere, p. 375

ARTHUR J. LAMB
1870–1928

1 She's a bird in a gilded cage. *Song* (1900)

LADY CAROLINE LAMB
1785–1828

2 Mad, bad, and dangerous to know.
Of Byron, in her Journal

CHARLES LAMB
1775–1834

3 I have no ear. *Essays of Elia. A Chapter on Ears*

4 I even think that sentimentally I am disposed to harmony. But organically I am incapable of a tune.
Ib.

5 'Presents', I often say, 'endear Absents.'
Ib. A Dissertation upon Roast Pig

6 It argues an insensibility. *Ib.*

7 We are not of Alice, nor of thee, nor are we children at all. The children of Alice call Bartrum father. We are nothing; less than nothing, and dreams. We are only what might have been, and must wait upon the tedious shores of Lethe millions of ages before we have existence, and a name.
Ib. Dream Children

8 Why have we none [i.e. no grace] for books, those spiritual repasts—a grace before Milton—a grace before Shakspeare—a devotional exercise proper to be said before reading the Faerie Queene?
Ib. Grace Before Meat

9 Coleridge holds that a man cannot have a pure mind who refuses apple-dumplings. I am not certain but he is right. *Ib.*

10 I am, in plainer words, a bundle of prejudices—made up of likings and dislikings.
Ib. Imperfect Sympathies

11 I have been trying all my life to like Scotchmen, and am obliged to desist from the experiment in despair.
Ib.

12 'A clear fire, a clean hearth, and the rigour of the game.' This was the celebrated wish of old Sarah Battle (now with God), who, next to her devotions, loved a good game at whist.
Ib. Mrs. Battle's Opinions on Whist

13 All people have their blind side—their superstitions; and I have heard her declare, under the rose, that Hearts was her favourite suit. *Ib.*

14 She unbent her mind afterwards—over a book. *Ib.*

15 Methinks it is better that I should have pined away seven of my goldenest years, when I was thrall to the fair hair, and fairer eyes, of Alice W - - n, than that so passionate a love-adventure should be lost.
Ib. New Year's Eve

16 In everything that relates to science, I am a whole Encyclopaedia behind the rest of the world.
Ib. The Old and the New Schoolmaster

17 He is awkward, and out of place, in the society of his equals. . . . He cannot meet you on the square.
Ib.

18 A votary of the desk—a notched and cropt scrivener —one that sucks his substance, as certain sick people are said to do, through a quill.
Essays of Elia. Oxford in the Vacation

19 The human species, according to the best theory I can form of it, is composed of two distinct races, *the men who borrow*, and *the men who lend.*
Ib. The Two Races of Men

20 What a liberal confounding of those pedantic distinctions of *meum* and *tuum*! *Ib.*

21 I mean your *borrowers of books*—those mutilators of collections, spoilers of the symmetry of shelves and creators of odd volumes. *Ib.*

22 To lose a volume to C[oleridge] carries some sense and meaning in it. You are sure that he will make one hearty meal on your viands, if he can give no account of the platter after it. *Ib.*

23 That princely woman, the thrice noble Margaret Newcastle. *Ib.*

24 I counsel thee, shut not thy heart, nor thy library, against S. T. C[oleridge]. *Ib.*

25 I love to lose myself in other men's minds. When I am not walking, I am reading; I cannot sit and think. Books think for me.
Last Essays of Elia. Detached Thoughts on Books and Reading

26 I can read any thing which I call a book. There are things in that shape which I cannot allow for such. In this catalogue of books which are no books— biblia a-biblia—I reckon Court Calendars, Directories . . . the works of Hume, Gibbon, Robertson, Beattie, Soame Jenyns, and, generally, all those volumes which 'no gentleman's library should be without'. *Ib.*

27 Things in books' clothing. *Ib.*

28 Milton almost requires a solemn service of music to be played before you enter upon him. *Ib.*

29 A poor relation—is the most irrelevant thing in nature. *Ib. Poor Relations*

30 An Oxford scholar, meeting a porter who was carrying a hare through the streets, accosts him with this extraordinary question: 'Prithee, friend, is that thy own hare, or a wig?'
Ib. Popular Fallacies. That the Worst Puns are the Best

31 Cultivate simplicity, Coleridge.
Letter to Coleridge, 8 Nov. 1796

32 I could forgive a man for not enjoying Milton; but I would not call that man my friend who should be offended with 'the divine chit-chat of Cowper'.
Quoting Coleridge's own phrase in Letter to Coleridge, 5 Dec. 1796

33 The scene for the most part laid in a Brothel. O tempora, O mores! but as friend Coleridge said when he was talking bawdy to Miss — 'to the pure all things are pure'. *Letter to Southey, July 1798*

34 An old woman clothed in grey,
Whose daughter was charming and young,
And she was deluded away
By Roger's false flattering tongue.
Quoted in letter to Southey, 29 Oct. 1798

1 I came home . . . hungry as a hunter.
Letter to Coleridge, probably 16 or 17 Apr. 1800

2 Oh, her lamps of a night! her rich goldsmiths, print-shops, toy-shops, mercers, hardware-men, pastry-cooks, St. Paul's Churchyard, the Strand, Exeter Change, Charing Cross, with a man upon a black horse! These are thy gods, O London!
Letter to Thomas Manning, 28 Nov. 1800

3 Separate from the pleasure of your company, I don't much care if I never see another mountain in my life. *Letter to William Wordsworth, 30 Jan. 1801*

4 The man must have a rare recipe for melancholy, who can be dull in Fleet Street.
The Londoner, in letter to Thomas Manning, 15 Feb. 1802

5 Nursed amid her noise, her crowds, her beloved smoke—what have I been doing all my life, if I have not lent out my heart with usury to such scenes? *Ib.*

6 It was Lamb who, when Dr. Parr asked him how he managed to emit so much smoke, replied that he had toiled after it as other men after virtue. And Macready relates that he remarked in his presence that he wished to draw his last breath through a pipe and exhale it in a pun.
Letter to W. and D. Wordsworth, 28 Sept. 1805, note by E. V. Lucas

7 A little thin, flowery border round, neat, not gaudy.
Letter to Wordsworth, June 1806

8 To do this it will be necessary to leave off Tobacco. But I had some thoughts of doing that before, for I sometimes think it does not agree with me.
Letter to W. Wordsworth, 26 June 1806

9 I have made a little scale, supposing myself to receive the following various accessions of dignity from the king, who is the fountain of honour—As at first, 1, Mr. C. Lamb; . . . 10th, Emperor Lamb; 11th, Pope Innocent, higher than which is nothing but the Lamb of God.
Letter to Thomas Manning, 2 Jan. 1810

10 Nothing puzzles me more than time and space; and yet nothing troubles me less, as I never think about them. *Ib.*

11 I was at Hazlitt's marriage, and had like to have been turned out several times during the ceremony. Anything awful makes me laugh. I misbehaved once at a funeral. *Letter to Southey, 9 Aug. 1815*

12 This very night I am going to leave off tobacco! Surely there must be some other world in which this unconquerable purpose shall be realized. The soul hath not her generous aspirings implanted in her in vain. *Letter to Thomas Manning, 26 Dec. 1815*

13 His face when he repeats his verses hath its ancient glory, an Archangel a little damaged. [Coleridge.]
Letter to W. Wordsworth, 26 Apr. 1816

14 The rogue gives you Love Powders, and then a strong horse drench to bring 'em off your stomach that they mayn't hurt you. [Coleridge.]
Letter to Wordsworth, 23 Sept. 1816

15 Fanny Kelly's divine plain face.
Letter to Mrs. Wordsworth, 18 Feb. 1818

16 How I like to be liked, and what I do to be liked!
Letter to D. Wordsworth, 8 Jan. 1821

17 Who first invented Work—and tied the free
And holy-day rejoicing spirit down
To the ever-haunting importunity
Of business, in the green fields, and the town—
To plough—loom—anvil—spade—and, oh, most sad,
To this dry drudgery of the desk's dead wood?
Letter to Barton, Sept. 1822

18 Those fellows hate us. [Booksellers and authors.]
Letter to Barton, 9 Jan. 1823

19 Old as I am waxing, in his eyes I was still the child he [Randall Norris] first knew me. To the last he called me Charley. I have none to call me Charley now. *Letter to Robinson, 20 Jan. 1827*

20 We should be modest for a modest man—as he is for himself. *Letter to Mrs. Montagu, Summer 1827*

21 You are knee deep in clover.
Letter to C. C. Clarke, Dec. 1828

22 When my sonnet was rejected, I exclaimed, 'Damn the age; I will write for Antiquity!'
Letter to B. W. Procter, 22 Jan. 1829

23 Books of the true sort, not those things in boards that moderns mistake for books—what they club for at book clubs. *Letter to J. Gillman, 30 Nov. 1829*

24 The golden works of the dear, fine, silly old angel. [Thomas Fuller.] *Letter to J. Gillman, 1830*

25 Some cry up Haydn, some Mozart,
Just as the whim bites. For my part,
I do not care a farthing candle
For either of them, or for Handel.
Letter to Mrs. William Hazlitt, 24 May 1830

26 Did G[eorge] D[yer] send his penny tract to me to convert me to Unitarianism? Dear blundering soul! why I am as old a one-Goddite as himself.
Letter to Moxon, 24 Oct. 1831

27 Half as sober as a judge.
Letter to Mr. and Mrs. Moxon, Aug. 1833

28 The greatest pleasure I know, is to do a good action by stealth, and to have it found out by accident.
Table Talk by the late Elia. The Athenæum, 4 Jan. 1834

29 What a lass that were to go a-gipseying through the world with.
The Jovial Crew. The Examiner, July 1819

30 The uncommunicating muteness of fishes.
A Quakers' Meeting

31 For thy sake, Tobacco, I
Would do any thing but die.
A Farewell to Tobacco, l. 122

32 Gone before
To that unknown and silent shore. *Hester*

33 By myself walking,
To myself talking. *Hypochondriacus*

34 Riddle of destiny, who can show
What thy short visit meant, or know
What thy errand here below?
On an Infant Dying as soon as Born

35 Slow journeying on
To the green plains of pleasant Hertfordshire.
Sonnet: The Lord of Light Shakes Off

1 I have had playmates, I have had companions,
In my days of childhood, in my joyful school-days,—
All, all are gone, the old familiar faces.
The Old Familiar Faces

2 Free from self-seeking, envy, low design,
I have not found a whiter soul than thine.
To Martin Charles Burney

3 I like you, and your book, ingenious Hone!
To the Editor of the Every-Day Book

4 Truths, which transcend the searching School-men's vein,
And half had stagger'd that stout Stagirite.
Written at Cambridge

5 If ever I marry a wife,
I'll marry a landlord's daughter,
For then I may sit in the bar,
And drink cold brandy and water.
Written in a copy of Coelebs in Search of a Wife

6 Martin, if dirt were trumps, what hands you would hold!
Leigh Hunt's *Lord Byron and his Contemporaries* (1828), p. 299

7 I do not [know the lady]; but damn her at a venture.
E. V. Lucas, *Charles Lamb* (1905), vol. i, p. 320, note

MARY LAMB
1764–1847

8 He [Henry Crabb Robinson] says he never saw a man so happy in *three wives* as Mr. Wordsworth is.
Letter to Sarah Hutchinson, Nov. 1816

9 A child's a plaything for an hour.
Parental Recollections

10 Thou straggler into loving arms,
Young climber up of knees,
When I forget thy thousand ways,
Then life and all shall cease.
Ib.

JOHN GEORGE LAMBTON, FIRST EARL OF DURHAM
1792–1840

11 ... one of his sublimities ... too good to be lost ... he said he considered £40,000 a year a moderate income—such a one as a man *might jog on with*.
The Creevey Papers (13 Sept. 1821), ii. 32

LETITIA ELIZABETH LANDON
1802–1838

12 Few, save the poor, feel for the poor. *The Poor*

WALTER SAVAGE LANDOR
1775–1864

13 Around the child bend all the three
Sweet Graces; Faith, Hope, Charity.
Around the man bend other faces;
Pride, Envy, Malice, are his Graces.
Around the Child

14 Ah, what avails the sceptred race!
Ah, what the form divine!
What every virtue, every grace!
Rose Aylmer, all were thine.

Rose Aylmer, whom these wakeful eyes
May weep, but never see,
A night of memories and of sighs
I consecrate to thee. *Rose Aylmer*

15 There is delight in singing, tho' none hear
Beside the singer. *To Robert Browning*

16 Shakespeare is not our poet, but the world's,
Therefore on him no speech! *Ib.*

17 Browning! Since Chaucer was alive and hale,
No man hath walked along our roads with step
So active, so inquiring eye, or tongue
So varied in discourse. But warmer climes
Give brighter plumage, stronger wing: the breeze
Of Alpine heights thou playest with, borne on
Beyond Sorrento and Amalfi, where
The Siren waits thee, singing song for song. *Ib.*

18 Such stains there are—as when a Grace
Sprinkles another's laughing face
With nectar, and runs on. *On Catullus*

19 Child of a day, thou knowest not
The tears that overflow thy urn. *Child of a Day*

20 The witty and the tender Hood.
Confessions of Jealousy

21 Hail, ye indomitable heroes, hail!
Despite of all your generals ye prevail.
The Crimean Heroes

22 Stand close around, ye Stygian set,
With Dirce in one boat convey'd!
Or Charon, seeing, may forget
That he is old and she a shade. *Dirce*

23 Death stands above me, whispering low
I know not what into my ear;
Of his strange language all I know
Is, there is not a word of fear. *Epigrams, c. Death*

24 Wearers of rings and chains!
Pray do not take the pains
To set me right.
In vain my faults ye quote;
I write as others wrote
On Sunium's height. *Ib.* ci

25 I strove with none; for none was worth my strife;
Nature I loved, and, next to Nature, Art;
I warmed both hands before the fire of life;
It sinks, and I am ready to depart. *Finis*

26 I have sinuous shells, of pearly hue.
Gebir, bk. i, l. 170

27 Apply
Its polished lips to your attentive ear. *Ib.* l. 174

28 And it remembers its august abodes,
And murmurs as the ocean murmurs there. *Ib.*

29 Is this the mighty ocean? is this all?
Ib. bk. v, l. 130

30 From you, Ianthe, little troubles pass
Like little ripples down a sunny river.
Ianthe's Troubles

31 In his own image the Creator made,
His own pure sunbeam quickened thee, O man!
Thou breathing dial! since thy day began
The present hour was ever mark'd with shade!
In His own Image the Creator Made

1 I loved him not; and yet now he is gone
　　I feel I am alone.
I check'd him while he spoke; yet, could he speak,
　　Alas! I would not check. *The Maid's Lament*

2 Mother, I cannot mind my wheel. *Title*

3 No longer could I doubt him true—
　　All other men may use deceit;
He always said my eyes were blue,
　　And often swore my lips were sweet.
　　　　　　Mother, I Cannot Mind My Wheel

4 Proud word you never spoke, but you will speak
　　Four not exempt from pride some future day.
Resting on one white hand a warm wet cheek
Over my open volume you will say,
'This man loved *me*!' then rise and trip away.
　　　　　　Proud Word You Never Spoke

5 We are what suns and winds and waters make us;
The mountains are our sponsors, and the rills
Fashion and win their nursling with their smiles.
　　　　　　Regeneration

6 Well I remember how you smiled
　　To see me write your name upon
The soft sea-sand—'O! what a child!
　　You think you're writing upon stone!'

I have since written what no tide
Shall ever wash away, what men
Unborn shall read o'er ocean wide
And find Ianthe's name again.
　　　　　　Well I Remember How You Smiled

7 I know not whether I am proud,
But this I know, I hate the crowd. *With an Album*

8 Chatting on deck was Dryden too,
The Bacon of our rhyming crew.
　　*To Wordsworth: Those Who Have Laid the Harp
　　Aside*

9 Tho' never tender nor sublime,
He struggles with and conquers Time. [Dryden.]
　　　　　　Ib.

10 Thee gentle Spenser fondly led;
But me he mostly sent to bed. *Ib.*

11 George the First was always reckoned
Vile, but viler George the Second;
And what mortal ever heard
Any good of George the Third?
When from earth the Fourth descended
God be praised, the Georges ended!
　　Epigram in *The Atlas*, 28 Apr. 1855. See *Notes
　　and Queries*, 3 May 1902, pp. 318, 354

12 Laodameia died; Helen died; Leda, the beloved of
Jupiter, went before.
　　Imaginary Conversations, Æsop and Rhodope, ii

13 There are no fields of amaranth on this side of the
grave: there are no voices, O Rhodopè! that are not
soon mute, however tuneful: there is no name, with
whatever emphasis of passionate love repeated, of
which the echo is not faint at last. *Ib.*

14 He who first praises a book becomingly is next in
merit to the author. *Ib. Alfieri and Salomon*, ii

15 Prose on certain occasions can bear a great deal of
poetry: on the other hand, poetry sinks and swoons
under a moderate weight of prose.
　　Ib. Archdeacon Hare and Walter Landor

16 I hate false words, and seek with care, difficulty, and
moroseness, those that fit the thing.
　　*Imaginary Conversations. Bishop Burnet and
　　Humphrey Hardcastle*

17 Goodness does not more certainly make men happy
than happiness makes them good.
　　　　Ib. Lord Brooke and Sir Philip Sidney

18 LEONORA:
But tell him, tell Torquato . . . go again; entreat,
persuade, command him, to forget me.
PANIGAROLA:
Alas! even the command, even the command from
you and from above, might not avail perhaps.
You smile, Madonna!
LEONORA:
I die happy. *Ib. Leonora di Este and Panigarola*

19 States, like men, have their growth, their manhood,
their decrepitude, their decay. *Ib.*

20 When it was a matter of wonder how Keats, who was
ignorant of Greek, could have written his 'Hyperion', Shelley, whom envy never touched, gave
as a reason, 'Because he *was* a Greek'.
　　　　Ib. Southey and Landor, ii

21 Clear writers, like fountains, do not seem so deep as
they are; the turbid look the most profound.
　　　　Ib. Southey and Porson

22 Fleas know not whether they are upon the body of a
giant or upon one of ordinary stature. *Ib.*

ANDREW LANG

1844–1912

23 St. Andrews by the Northern Sea,
That is a haunted town to me! *Almae Matres*

24 The surge and thunder of the Odyssey.
　　　　As One that for a Weary Space has Lain

25 There's a joy without canker or cark,
　　There's a pleasure eternally new,
'Tis to gloat on the glaze and the mark
　　Of china that's ancient and blue.
　　　　　　Ballade of Blue China

26 Here's a pot with a cot in a park,
　　In a park where the peach-blossoms blew,
Where the lovers eloped in the dark,
　　Lived, died, and were changed into two
　　Bright birds that eternally flew
Through the boughs of the may, as they sang.
　　'Tis a tale was undoubtedly true
　　In the reign of the Emperor Hwang. *Ib.*

27 If the wild bowler thinks he bowls,
　　Or if the batsman thinks he's bowled,
They know not, poor misguided souls,
　　They too shall perish unconsoled.
I am the batsman and the bat,
　I am the bowler and the ball,
The umpire, the pavilion cat,
　　The roller, pitch, and stumps, and all.
　　　　Brahma (in imitation of Emerson)

28 But he shaved with a shell when he chose,—
'Twas the manner of Primitive Man.
　　　　Double Ballade of Primitive Man

FREDERICK LANGBRIDGE
1849–1923

1 Two men look out through the same bars:
One sees the mud, and one the stars.
A Cluster of Quiet Thoughts, 1896 (*Religious Tract Society Publication*)

JOHN LANGHORNE
1735–1779

2 Cold on Canadian hills, or Minden's plain,
Perhaps that parent mourn'd her soldier slain;
. . . .
The child of misery, baptiz'd in tears!
The Country Justice, pt. i. *Apology for Vagrants*

WILLIAM LANGLAND
1330?–1400?

3 In a somer seson whan soft was the sonne.
The Vision of William concerning Piers the Plowman (ed. Skeat), B Text, Prologue, l. 1.

4 A glotoun of wordes.
Ib. l. 139

5 Bakers and brewers, bouchers and cokes—
For thees men doth most harme to the mene puple.
Ib. C Text, Passus 4, l. 80

6 Grammere, that grounde is of alle.
Ib. Passus 18, l. 107

7 'After sharpest shoures,' quath Pees [Peace] 'most sheene is the sonne;
Ys no weder warmer than after watery cloudes.'
Ib. Passus 21, l. 456

8 Dowel, Dobet, and Dobest.
Ib. MS. Laud 581, Passus 8, heading

ARCHBISHOP STEPHEN LANGTON
d. 1228

9 Veni, Sancte Spiritus,
Et emitte coelitus
Lucis tuae radium.

Come, thou holy Paraclete,
And from thy celestial seat
Send thy light and brilliancy.
Trans. by J. M. Neale

SIDNEY LANIER
1842–1881

10 Into the woods my Master went,
Clean forspent, forspent.
Into the woods my Master came,
Forspent with love and shame.
Poems. A Ballad of Trees and the Master

BISHOP HUGH LATIMER
1485?–1555

11 Be of good comfort Master Ridley, and play the man. We shall this day light such a candle by God's grace in England, as (I trust) shall never be put out.
Foxe, *Actes and Monuments* (1570), p. 1937

SIR HARRY LAUDER
1870–1950

12 I love a lassie. *Title of Song*

13 Just a wee deoch-an-doris
Before we gang awa' . . .
If you can say, 'It's a braw, bricht, moonlicht nicht',
Ye're a' richt, ye ken. *Song*

14 Keep right on to the end of the road. *Song*

15 O! it's nice to get up in the mornin'
But it's nicer to lie in bed. *Song*

16 Roamin' in the gloamin'. *Title of Song*

WILLIAM L. LAURENCE
1888–

17 At first it was a giant column that soon took the shape of a supramundane mushroom.
Report in The New York Times, *26 Sept. 1945, on the first atomic explosion test held in New Mexico, U.S.A.*

ANDREW BONAR LAW
1858–1923

18 If, therefore, war should ever come between these two countries [Great Britain and Germany], which Heaven forbid! it will not, I think, be due to irresistible natural laws, it will be due to the want of human wisdom.
Speech, House of Commons, 27 Nov. 1911

19 I said [in 1911] that if ever war arose between Great Britain and Germany it would not be due to inevitable causes, for I did not believe in inevitable war. I said it would be due to human folly.
Speech, House of Commons, 6 Aug. 1914

DAVID HERBERT LAWRENCE
1885–1930

20 The terror, the agony, the nostalgia of the heathen past was a constant torture to her mediumistic soul. *The Lost Girl*, ch. 15

21 She is dear to me in the middle of my being. But the gold and flowing serpent is coiling up again, to sleep at the root of my tree.
The Man Who Died, pt. ii

22 Be a good animal, true to your animal instincts.
The White Peacock, pt. ii, ch. 2. *But see* Corrigenda

23 Along the avenue of cypresses,
All in their scarlet cloaks and surplices
Of linen, go the chanting choristers,
The priests in gold and black, the villagers.
Giorno dei Morti

24 The silence of the many villagers,
The candle-flame beside the surplices. *Ib.*

SIR AUSTEN HENRY LAYARD
1817–1894

25 I have always believed that successes would be the inevitable result if the two services, the army and navy, had fair play, and if we sent the right man to fill the right place.
Speech in Parliament, 15 Jan. 1855

STEPHEN BUTLER LEACOCK

1869–1944

1 Lord Ronald . . . flung himself upon his horse and rode madly off in all directions.
Nonsense Novels. Gertrude the Governess

EDWARD LEAR

1812–1888

2 There was an Old Man with a beard,
Who said, 'It is just as I feared!—
Two Owls and a Hen,
Four Larks and a Wren,
Have all built their nests in my beard!'
Book of Nonsense

3 There was an Old Man in a tree,
Who was horribly bored by a bee;
When they said, 'Does it buzz?'
He replied, 'Yes, it does!
It's a regular brute of a bee!' *Ib.*

4 There was an Old Man in a boat,
Who said, 'I'm afloat, I'm afloat!'
When they said, 'No, you ain't!'
He was ready to faint,
That unhappy Old Man in a boat. *Ib.*

5 There was an Old Person of Basing,
Whose presence of mind was amazing;
He purchased a steed,
Which he rode at full speed,
And escaped from the people of Basing. *Ib.*

6 There was an old Lady of Chertsey,
Who made a remarkable curtsey:
She whirled round and round,
Till she sunk underground,
Which distressed all the people of Chertsey. *Ib.*

7 There was an old man who said, 'Hush!
I perceive a young bird in this bush!'
When they said, 'Is it small?'
He replied, 'Not at all!
It is four times as big as the bush!' *Ib.*

8 Nasticreechia Krorluppia. *Nonsense Botany*

9 'How pleasant to know Mr. Lear!'
Who has written such volumes of stuff!
Some think him ill-tempered and queer,
But a few think him pleasant enough.
Nonsense Songs, preface

10 He drinks a good deal of Marsala
But never gets tipsy at all. *Ib.*

11 His body is perfectly spherical,
He weareth a runcible hat. *Ib.*

12 On the coast of Coromandel
Where the early pumpkins blow,
In the middle of the woods
Lived the Yonghy-Bonghy-Bò.
Two old chairs, and half a candle,—
One old jug without a handle,—
These were all his worldly goods.
Ib. The Courtship of the Yonghy-Bonghy-Bò

13 'Lady Jingly! Lady Jingly!
Sitting where the pumpkins blow,
Will you come and be my wife?'
Said the Yonghy-Bonghy-Bò. *Ib.*

14 One never more can go to court,
Because his legs have grown too short;
The other cannot sing a song
Because his legs have grown too long!
Nonsense Songs. The Daddy Long-Legs and the Fly

15 When awful darkness and silence reign
Over the great Gromboolian plain,
Through the long, long wintry nights.
When the angry breakers roar
As they beat on the rocky shore;—
When Storm-clouds brood on the towering heights
Of the Hills of the Chankly Bore.
Ib. The Dong with the Luminous Nose

16 Slowly it wanders,—pauses,—creeps,—
Anon it sparkles,—flashes and leaps;
And ever as onward it gleaming goes
A light on the Bong-tree stem it throws:
And those who watch at that midnight hour
From Hall or Terrace or lofty Tower,
Cry as the wild light passes along,—
'The Dong!—the Dong!
The wandering Dong through the forest goes!
The Dong!—the Dong!
The Dong with the Luminous Nose!' *Ib.*

17 A Nose as strange as a Nose could be!
Of vast proportions and painted red,
And tied with cords to the back of his head.
—In a hollow rounded space it ended
With a luminous Lamp within suspended,
All fenced about
With a bandage stout
To prevent the wind from blowing it out. *Ib.*

18 And who so happy,—O who,
As the Duck and the Kangaroo?
Ib. The Duck and the Kangaroo

19 O My agèd Uncle Arly!
Sitting on a heap of Barley
Thro' the silent hours of night,—
Close beside a leafy thicket:—
On his nose there was a Cricket,—
In his hat a Railway-Ticket;—
(But his shoes were far too tight.)
Ib. Incidents in the Life of my Aged Uncle Arly

20 Every evening found him gazing,—
Singing,—'Orb! you're quite amazing!
How I wonder what you are!' *Ib.*

21 Far and few, far and few,
Are the lands where the Jumblies live;
Their heads are green, and their hands are blue,
And they went to sea in a Sieve. *Ib. The Jumblies*

22 In spite of all their friends could say,
On a winter's morn, on a stormy day,
In a Sieve they went to sea! *Ib.*

23 Suppose we should fall down flumpetty
Just like pieces of stone!
Ib. Mr. and Mrs. Discobbolos

24 The Owl and the Pussy-Cat went to sea
In a beautiful pea-green boat.
They took some honey, and plenty of money,
Wrapped up in a five-pound note.
The Owl looked up to the Stars above
And sang to a small guitar,
'O lovely Pussy! O Pussy, my love,
What a beautiful Pussy you are.'
Ib. The Owl and the Pussy-Cat

1 Pussy said to the Owl, 'You elegant fowl!
  How charmingly sweet you sing!
O let us be married! too long we have tarried:
  But what shall we do for a ring?'
They sailed away for a year and a day,
  To the land where the Bong-tree grows,
And there in a wood a Piggy-wig stood
  With a ring at the end of his nose.
    Nonsense Songs. The Owl and the Pussy-Cat

2 'Dear Pig, are you willing to sell for one shilling
  Your ring?' Said the Piggy, 'I will'. *Ib.*

3 They dined on mince, and slices of quince,
  Which they ate with a runcible spoon;
And hand in hand, on the edge of the sand,
  They danced by the light of the moon. *Ib.*

4 We think so then, and we thought so still!
    Ib. The Pelican Chorus

5 The Pobble who has no toes
  Had once as many as we;
When they said, 'Some day you may lose them all';—
He replied,—'Fish fiddle de-dee!'
    Ib. The Pobble Who Has No Toes

6 His Aunt Jobiska made him drink
  Lavender water tinged with pink,
For she said, 'The world in general knows
  There's nothing so good for a Pobble's toes!' *Ib.*

7 For his Aunt Jobiska said, 'No harm
  Can come to his toes if his nose is warm,
And it's perfectly known that a Pobble's toes
  Are safe, provided he minds his nose.' *Ib.*

8   When boats or ships came near him
  He tinkledy-binkledy-winkled a bell. *Ib.*

9 He has gone to fish, for his Aunt Jobiska's
  Runcible Cat with crimson whiskers! *Ib.*

10   It's a fact the whole world knows,
  That Pobbles are happier without their toes. *Ib.*

11 'But the longer I live on this Crumpetty Tree
  The plainer than ever it seems to me
That very few people come this way
  And that life on the whole is far from gay!'
    Said the Quangle-Wangle Quee.
    Ib. The Quangle-Wangle's Hat

12 Two old Bachelors were living in one house;
  One caught a Muffin, the other caught a Mouse.
    Ib. The Two Old Bachelors

13 Who, or why, or which, or what,
  Is the Akond of Swat?
    Ib. 1888 edn. The Akond of Swat

14 There was an old person of Slough,
  Who danced at the end of a bough;
  But they said, 'If you sneeze,
  You might damage the trees,
You imprudent old person of Slough.'
    One Hundred Nonsense Pictures and Rhymes

15 There was an old man in a Marsh,
  Whose manners were futile and harsh. *Ib.*

16 There was an old man at a Junction,
  Whose feelings were wrung with compunction. *Ib.*

17 There was an old person of Pett,
  Who was partly consumed by regret. *Ib.*

18 There was an old person of Ware,
  Who rode on the back of a bear:
  When they asked,—'Does it trot?'—
  He said 'Certainly not!
He's a Moppsikon Floppsikon bear.'
    One Hundred Nonsense Pictures and Rhymes

19 There was an old person of Dean,
  Who dined on one pea and one bean;
  For he said, 'More than that,
  Would make me too fat,'
That cautious old person of Dean. *Ib.*

20 There was an old person of Ealing,
  Who was wholly devoid of good feeling;
  He drove a small gig,
  With three Owls and a Pig,
Which distressed all the people of Ealing. *Ib.*

21 There was an old man of Thermopylae,
  Who never did anything properly;
  But they said, 'If you choose
  To boil eggs in your shoes,
You shall never remain in Thermopylae.' *Ib.*

22 There was an old man on the Border, *Ib.*
  Who lived in the utmost disorder.

MARY ELIZABETH LEASE
1853–1933

23 Kansas had better stop raising corn and begin raising
  hell. *Attr.*

WILLIAM EDWARD HARTPOLE LECKY
1838–1903

24 The stately ship is seen no more,
  The fragile skiff attains the shore;
And while the great and wise decay,
  And all their trophies pass away,
Some sudden thought, some careless rhyme,
  Still floats above the wrecks of Time.
    On an Old Song

HENRY LEE
1756–1818

25 First in war, first in peace, first in the hearts of his
  fellow citizens.
    *Resolution in the House of Representatives on the
    death of Washington, 26 Dec. 1799*

NATHANIEL LEE
1653?–1692

26 When the sun sets, shadows, that showed at noon
  But small, appear most long and terrible.
    Œdipus, IV. i

27 Man, false man, smiling, destructive man.
    Theodosius, III. ii

28 He speaks the kindest words, and looks such things,
  Vows with so much passion, swears with so much
  grace.
  That 'tis a kind of Heaven to be deluded by him.
    The Rival Queens, Act I

29 'Tis beauty calls and glory leads the way. *Ib.*

30 Then he will talk, Good Gods,
  How he will talk. *Ib. Act III*

1 When Greeks joined Greeks, then was the tug of war!
The Rival Queens, IV. ii

2 Philip fought men, but Alexander women. *Ib.*

RICHARD LE GALLIENNE
1866–1947

3 The cry of the Little Peoples goes up to God in vain.
The Cry of the Little Peoples

4 Give back the little nation leave to live.
Christmas in War-Time

5 Loud mockers in the roaring street
Say Christ is crucified again:
Twice pierced His gospel-bearing feet,
Twice broken His great heart in vain,
The Second Crucifixion

6 The Quest of the Golden Girl. *Title of Novel*

HENRY SAMBROOKE LEIGH
1837–1883

7 In form and feature, face and limb,
I grew so like my brother
That folks got taking me for him
And each for one another.
Carols of Cockayne, The Twins

8 For one of us was born a twin
And not a soul knew which. *Ib.*

9 The rapturous, wild, and ineffable pleasure
Of drinking at somebody else's expense.
Ib. Stanzas to an Intoxicated Fly

10 I know where little girls are sent
For telling taradiddles. *Ib. Only Seven*

CHARLES GODFREY LELAND
1824–1903

11 Hans Breitmann gife a barty—
Vhere ish dat barty now? *Hans Breitmann's Party*

12 All goned afay mit de lager-beer—
Afay in de ewigkeit! *Ib.*

13 Und efery dime she gife a shoomp
She make der vinders sound. *Ib.*

14 They saw a Dream of Loveliness descending from
the train. *Brand New Ballads. The Masher*

WILLIAM LENTHALL
1591–1662

15 I have neither eye to see, nor tongue to speak here,
but as the House is pleased to direct me.
Rushworth's Historical Collections, iv. 238

LUIS DE LEÓN
c. 1528–1591

16 Dicebamus hesterna die.

We were saying yesterday.
*On resuming a lecture at Salamanca University
after five years' imprisonment.* A. F. G. Bell, *Luis
de León*, ch. 8

GOTTHOLD EPHRAIM LESSING
1729–1781

17 Ein einziger dankbarer Gedanke gen Himmel ist das
vollkommenste Gebet.

One single grateful thought raised to heaven is a
perfect prayer. *Minna von Barnhelm*, ii. 7

18 Wenn Gott in seiner Rechten alle Wahrheit und in
seiner Linken den einzigen, immer regen Trieb
nach Wahrheit, obgleich mit dem Zusatz, mich
immer und ewig zu irren, verschlossen hielte und
sprach zu mir: Wähle! ich fiele ihm mit Demut
in seine Linke und sagte: Vater, gieb! Die reine
Wahrheit ist ja doch nur für Dich allein.

If God were to hold out enclosed in His right hand
all Truth, and in His left hand just the active
search for Truth, though with the condition that
I should ever err therein, and should say to me:
Choose! I should humbly take His left hand and
say: Father! Give me this one; absolute Truth
belongs to Thee alone. *Wolfenbüttler Fragmente*

SIR ROGER L'ESTRANGE
1616–1704

19 It is with our passions as it is with fire and water, they
are good servants, but bad masters.
Æsop's Fables, no. 38, Reflection

20 Though this may be play to you, 'tis death to us.
Ib. no. 398

GEORGE LEVESON-GOWER, EARL GRANVILLE
1815–1891

21 Spheres of action.
Letter to Count Münster, 29 April 1885 (Sir
Edward Hertslet, *Map of Africa by Treaty*
(1894), vol. ii, p. 596)

GEORGE HENRY LEWES
1817–1878

22 Many a genius has been slow of growth. Oaks that
flourish for a thousand years do not spring up into
beauty like a reed. *Spanish Drama*, ch. 2

23 Murder, like talent, seems occasionally to run in
families. *The Physiology of Common Life*, ch. 12

24 We must never assume that which is incapable of
proof. *Ib.* ch. 13

SIR GEORGE CORNEWALL LEWIS
1806–1863

25 Life would be tolerable were it not for its amuse-
ments.
*According to Lord Grey of Fallodon, in his
Twenty-Five Years*

CHARLES-JOSEPH, PRINCE DE LIGNE
1735–1814

26 Le congrès ne marche pas, il danse.

The Congress makes no progress; but it dances.
*Comment on the Congress of Vienna to Comte
Auguste de La Garde-Chambonas.* La Garde-
Chambonas, *Souvenirs du Congrès de Vienne,
1814–1815*, c. 1.

GEORGE LILLO
1693–1739

1 There's sure no passion in the human soul,
But finds its food in music. *Fatal Curiosity*, I. ii

ABRAHAM LINCOLN
1809–1865

2 I think the necessity of being *ready* increases.—Look to it.
Speeches and Letters (1907). *The whole of a letter to Governor Andrew Curtin of Pennsylvania, 8 Apr. 1861*

3 I intend no modification of my oft-expressed personal wish that all men everywhere could be free.
Ib. Letter to H. Greeley, 22 Aug. 1862

4 I claim not to have controlled events, but confess plainly that events have controlled me.
Ib. Letter to A. G. Hodges, 4 Apr. 1864

5 The ballot is stronger than the bullet.
Ib. Speech, 19 May 1856

6 'A house divided against itself cannot stand.' I believe this government cannot endure permanently, half slave and half free. *Ib. Speech, 16 June 1858*

7 What is conservatism? Is it not adherence to the old and tried, against the new and untried?
Ib. Speech, 27 Feb. 1860

8 Let us have faith that right makes might; and in that faith let us to the end, dare to do our duty as we understand it. *Ib.*

9 I take the official oath to-day with no mental reservations, and with no purpose to construe the Constitution or laws by any hypercritical rules.
Ib. First Inaugural Address, 4 Mar. 1861

10 The mystic chords of memory, stretching from every battlefield and patriot grave to every living heart and hearthstone all over this broad land, will yet swell the chorus of the Union when again touched, as surely they will be, by the better angels of our nature. *Ib.*

11 In giving freedom to the slave, we assure freedom to the free,—honourable alike in what we give and what we preserve.
Ib. Annual Message to Congress, 1 Dec. 1862

12 Fourscore and seven years ago our fathers brought forth upon this continent a new nation, conceived in liberty, and dedicated to the proposition that all men are created equal. Now we are engaged in a great civil war, testing whether that nation, or any nation so conceived and so dedicated, can long endure. We are met on a great battlefield of that war. We have come to dedicate a portion of that field as a final resting-place of those who here gave their lives that that nation might live. It is altogether fitting and proper that we should do this. But in a larger sense we cannot dedicate, we cannot consecrate, we cannot hallow this ground. The brave men, living and dead, who struggled here, have consecrated it far above our power to add or detract. The world will little note, nor long remember, what we say here, but it can never forget what they did here. It is for us, the living, rather to be dedicated here to the unfinished work they have thus far so nobly advanced. It is

rather for us to be here dedicated to the great task remaining before us, that from these honoured dead we take increased devotion to that cause for which they here gave the last full measure of devotion; that we here highly resolve that the dead shall not have died in vain, that this nation, under God, shall have a new birth of freedom; and that government of the people, by the people, and for the people, shall not perish from the earth.
Speeches and Letters (1907). *Address at Dedication of National Cemetery at Gettysburg, 19 Nov. 1863*

13 With malice toward none; with charity for all; with firmness in the right, as God gives us to see the right. *Ib. Second Inaugural Address, 4 Mar. 1865*

14 You can fool all the people some of the time, and some of the people all the time, but you can not fool all the people all of the time.
Attr. words in a speech at Clinton, 8 Sept. 1858. N. W. Stephenson, *Autobiography of A. Lincoln* (1927). *Attr. also to Phineas Barnum, 1810–91*

15 It is not best to swap horses while crossing the river.
Reply to National Union League, 9 June 1864. J. E. Nicolay and J. Hay, *Abraham Lincoln*, bk. ix

16 As President, I have no eyes but constitutional eyes; I cannot see you.
Attr. reply to the South Carolina Commissioners

17 People who like this sort of thing will find this the sort of thing they like.
Judgement on a book. G. W. E. Russell, *Collections and Recollections*, ch. 30

GEORGE LINLEY
1798–1865

18 Ever of thee I'm fondly dreaming,
Thy gentle voice my spirit can cheer.
Poems. Ever of Thee

19 Among our ancient mountains,
And from our lovely vales,
Oh, let the prayer re-echo:
'God bless the Prince of Wales!'
Ib. God Bless the Prince of Wales

20 Thou art gone from my gaze like a beautiful dream,
And I seek thee in vain by the meadow and stream.
Ib. Thou Art Gone

21 Tho' lost to sight, to mem'ry dear
Thou ever wilt remain.
Song. Attr. to Linley. Notes and Queries, Ser. 5, vol. x, p. 417

SIR THOMAS LITTLETON
1422–1481

22 [From] time whereof the memory of man runneth not to the contrary. *Tenures (?1481), § 170*

LIVY
59 B.C.–A.D. 17

23 Vae victis.
Woe to the vanquished. *History*, v. xlviii. 9

MARIE LLOYD
1870–1922

1 A little of what you fancy does you good.
Title of Song

2 I'm one of the ruins that Cromwell knocked about a bit. *Ib.*

3 Oh, mister porter, what shall I do?
Ib. (*words actually by* Thomas Le Brunn)

ROBERT LLOYD
1733–1764

4 Slow and steady wins the race.
Poems. The Hare and the Tortoise

JOHN LOCKE
1632–1704

5 New opinions are always suspected, and usually opposed, without any other reason but because they are not already common.
Essay on the Human Understanding, dedicatory epistle

6 Nature never makes excellent things for mean or no uses. *Ib.* bk. ii, ch. 1, sec. 15

7 No man's knowledge here can go beyond his experience. *Ib.* sec. 19

8 It is one thing to show a man that he is in an error, and another to put him in possession of truth.
Ib. bk. iv, ch. 7, sec. 11

9 All men are liable to error; and most men are, in many points, by passion or interest, under temptation to it. *Ib.* ch. 20, sec. 17

FREDERICK LOCKER-LAMPSON
1821–1895

0 The world's as ugly, ay, as sin,
And almost as delightful. *The Jester's Plea*

1 And many are afraid of God—
And more of Mrs. Grundy. *Ib.*

2 Some men are good for righting wrongs,—
And some for writing verses. *Ib.*

3 If you lift a guinea-pig up by the tail
His eyes drop out! *A Garden Lyric*

JOHN GIBSON LOCKHART
1794–1854

4 Here lies that peerless peer Lord Peter,
Who broke the laws of God and man and metre.
Epitaph for Patrick ('Peter'), Lord Robertson.
Scott's *Journal*, vol. i, p. 259, n. 2

FRANCIS LOCKIER
1667–1740

5 In all my travels I never met with any one Scotchman but what was a man of sense. I believe everybody of that country that has any, leaves it as fast as they can. *Spence's Anecdotes* (1858), p. 55

THOMAS LODGE
1558?–1625

6 Devils are not so black as they are painted.
A Margarite of America

17 Love, in my bosom, like a bee,
Doth suck his sweet. *Love, In My Bosom*

18 Heigh ho, would she were mine!
Rosalind's Description

JOHN LOGAN
1748–1788

19 Behold congenial Autumn comes,
The sabbath of the year!
Ode on a Visit to the Country in Autumn

20 For never on thy banks shall I
Behold my love, the flower of Yarrow.
The Braes of Yarrow

21 Sweet bird! thy bow'r is ever green,
Thy sky is ever clear;
Thou hast no sorrow in thy song,
No winter in thy year!
To the Cuckoo. Attr. (See *Notes and Queries*, April 1902, p. 309; 14 June, 1902, p. 469.) *Attr. also to Michael Bruce*

FRIEDRICH VON LOGAU
1605–1655

22 Gottesmühlen mahlen langsam, mahlen aber trefflich klein;
Ob aus Langmut Er sich säumet, bringt mit Schärf' Er alles ein.

Though the mills of God grind slowly, yet they grind exceeding small;
Though with patience He stands waiting, with exactness grinds He all.
Sinngedichte, III. ii. 24 (trans. H. W. Longfellow)

JACK LONDON
[JOHN GRIFFITH LONDON]
1876–1916

23 The Call of the Wild. *Title*

HENRY WADSWORTH LONGFELLOW
1807–1882

24 I shot an arrow into the air,
It fell to earth, I knew not where.
The Arrow and the Song

25 And the song, from beginning to end,
I found again in the heart of a friend. *Ib.*

26 I know a maiden fair to see,
Take care!
She can both false and friendly be,
Beware! Beware!
Trust her not,
She is fooling thee! *Beware!* (From the German)

27 I stood on the bridge at midnight,
As the clocks were striking the hour. *The Bridge*

28 In the elder days of Art,
Builders wrought with greatest care
Each minute and unseen part;
For the Gods see everywhere. *The Builders*

29 Build me straight, O worthy Master!
Staunch and strong, a goodly vessel,
That shall laugh at all disaster,
And with wave and whirlwind wrestle!
The Building of the Ship

1 Thou, too, sail on, O Ship of State!
Sail on, O Union, strong and great!
Humanity with all its fears,
With all the hopes of future years,
Is hanging breathless on thy fate!
The Building of the Ship

2 Ye are better than all the ballads
That ever were sung or said;
For ye are living poems,
And all the rest are dead. *Children*

3 Between the dark and the daylight,
When the night is beginning to lower,
Comes a pause in the day's occupations,
That is known as the Children's Hour.
The Children's Hour

4 Singing the Hundredth Psalm, the grand old Puritan
anthem. *The Courtship of Miles Standish*, iii

5 Archly the maiden smiled, and, with eyes overrunning
with laughter,
Said, in a tremulous voice, 'Why don't you speak for
yourself, John?' *Ib.*

6 God had sifted three kingdoms to find the wheat for
this planting. *Ib.* iv

7 The day is done, and the darkness
Falls from the wings of Night,
As a feather is wafted downward
From an eagle in his flight. *The Day is Done*

8 A feeling of sadness and longing,
That is not akin to pain,
And resembles sorrow only
As the mist resembles the rain. *Ib.*

9 The bards sublime,
Whose distant footsteps echo
Through the corridors of Time. *Ib.*

10 The cares that infest the day
Shall fold their tents, like the Arabs,
And as silently steal away. *Ib.*

11 If you would hit the mark, you must aim a little above
it;
Every arrow that flies feels the attraction of earth.
Elegiac Verse

12 This is the forest primeval.
Evangeline, introduction, l. 1

13 When she had passed, it seemed like the ceasing of
exquisite music. *Ib.* pt. I. i, l. 62

14 Talk not of wasted affection, affection never was
wasted;
If it enrich not the heart of another, its waters, returning
Back to their springs, like the rain, shall fill them full
of refreshment. *Ib.* pt. II. i, l. 55

15 Sorrow and silence are strong, and patient endurance
is godlike. *Ib.* l. 60

16 And, as she looked around, she saw how Death, the
consoler,
Laying his hand upon many a heart, had healed it for
ever. *Ib.* v, l. 88

17 The shades of night were falling fast,
As through an Alpine village passed
A youth, who bore, 'mid snow and ice,
A banner with the strange device,
Excelsior! *Excelsior*

18 In happy homes he saw the light
Of household fires gleam warm and bright. *Ib.*

19 'Try not the Pass!' the old man said;
'Dark lowers the tempest overhead.' *Excelsior*

20 'O stay,' the maiden said, 'and rest
Thy weary head upon this breast!' *Ib.*

21 'Beware the pine-tree's withered branch!
Beware the awful avalanche!' *Ib.*

22 A traveller, by the faithful hound,
Half-buried in the snow was found. *Ib.*

23 Spake full well, in language quaint and olden,
One who dwelleth by the castled Rhine,
When he called the flowers, so blue and golden,
Stars, that in earth's firmament do shine. *Flowers*

24 That is best which lieth nearest;
Shape from that thy work of art. *Gaspar Becerra*

25 Giotto's tower,
The lily of Florence blossoming in stone.
Giotto's Tower

26 I like that ancient Saxon phrase, which calls
The burial-ground God's-Acre! *God's-Acre*

27 Ah, the souls of those that die
Are but sunbeams lifted higher.
The Golden Legend, pt. IV. *The Cloisters*

28 I heard the trailing garments of the Night
Sweep through her marble halls! *Hymn to the Night*

29 Hold the fleet angel fast until he bless thee. *Kavanagh*

30 Saint Augustine! well hast thou said,
That of our vices we can frame
A ladder, if we will but tread
Beneath our feet each deed of shame!
The Ladder of Saint Augustine

31 The heights by great men reached and kept
Were not attained by sudden flight,
But they, while their companions slept,
Were toiling upward in the night. *Ib.*

32 Live I, so live I,
To my Lord heartily,
To my Prince faithfully
To my Neighbour honestly,
Die I, so die I.
*Law of Life. From the Sinngedichte of Fried-
rich von Logau*

33 Know how sublime a thing it is
To suffer and be strong. *The Light of Stars*

34 Standing, with reluctant feet,
Where the brook and river meet,
Womanhood and childhood fleet! *Maidenhood*

35 You would attain to the divine perfection,
And yet not turn your back upon the world.
Michael Angelo, pt. I. v

36 Would seem angelic in the sight of God,
Yet not too saint-like in the eyes of men;
In short, would lead a holy Christian life
In such a way that even your nearest friend
Would not detect therein one circumstance
To show a change from what it was before. *Ib.*

37 The men that women marry,
And why they marry them, will always be
A marvel and a mystery to the world. *Ib.* vi

38 A boy's will is the wind's will,
And the thoughts of youth are long, long thoughts.
My Lost Youth

1 A solid man of Boston.
A comfortable man, with dividends,
And the first salmon, and the first green peas.
New England Tragedies, John Endicott, IV. i

2 *Emigravit* is the inscription on the tombstone where
he lies;
Dead he is not, but departed,—for the artist never
dies.   *Nuremberg*, xiii

3 Listen, my children, and you shall hear
Of the midnight ride of Paul Revere,
On the eighteenth of April in Seventy-five.
Paul Revere's Ride

4 Not in the clamour of the crowded street,
Not in the shouts and plaudits of the throng,
But in ourselves, are triumph and defeat. *The Poets*

5 Tell me not, in mournful numbers,
Life is but an empty dream!
For the soul is dead that slumbers,
And things are not what they seem.

Life is real! Life is earnest!
And the grave is not its goal;
Dust thou art, to dust returnest,
Was not spoken of the soul.   *A Psalm of Life*

6 Art is long, and Time is fleeting,
And our hearts, though stout and brave,
Still, like muffled drums, are beating
Funeral marches to the grave.   *Ib.*

7 Trust no Future, howe'er pleasant!
Let the dead Past bury its dead!
Act,—act in the living Present!
Heart within, and God o'erhead!   *Ib.*

8 Lives of great men all remind us
We can make our lives sublime,
And, departing, leave behind us
Footprints on the sands of time.

Footprints, that perhaps another,
Sailing o'er life's solemn main,
A forlorn and shipwrecked brother,
Seeing, shall take heart again.

Let us, then, be up and doing,
With a heart for any fate;
Still achieving, still pursuing,
Learn to labour and to wait.   *Ib.*

9 There is a Reaper, whose name is Death,
And, with his sickle keen,
He reaps the bearded grain at a breath,
And the flowers that grow between.
The Reaper and the Flowers

10 Oh, not in cruelty, not in wrath,
The Reaper came that day;
'Twas an angel visited the green earth,
And took the flowers away.   *Ib.*

11 There is no flock, however watched and tended,
But one dead lamb is there!
There is no fireside, howsoe'er defended,
But has one vacant chair!   *Resignation*

12 There is no Death! What seems so is transition;
This life of mortal breath
Is but a suburb of the life elysian,
Whose portal we call Death.   *Ib.*

13 Though the mills of God grind slowly, yet they grind
exceeding small;
Though with patience he stands waiting, with exactness grinds he all.
*Retribution. From the Sinngedichte of Friedrich
von Logau*

14 A Lady with a Lamp shall stand
In the great history of the land,
A noble type of good,
Heroic womanhood.   *Santa Filomena*

15 'Wouldst thou'—so the helmsman answered,—
'Learn the secret of the sea?
Only those who brave its dangers
Comprehend its mystery!' *The Secret of the Sea*

16 Beside the ungather'd rice he lay,
His sickle in his hand.   *The Slave's Dream*

17 He did not feel the driver's whip,
Nor the burning heat of day;
For Death had illumined the Land of Sleep,
And his lifeless body lay
A worn-out fetter, that the soul
Had broken and thrown away!   *Ib.*

18 Stay, stay at home, my heart, and rest;
Home-keeping hearts are happiest.
Song: Stay, Stay at Home

19 Should you ask me, whence these stories?
Whence these legends and traditions?
The Song of Hiawatha, introduction

20 I should answer, I should tell you,
'From the forests and the prairies,
From the great lakes of the Northland,
From the land of the Ojibways,
From the land of the Dacotahs,
From the mountains, moors, and fenlands,
Where the heron, the Shuh-shuh-gah,
Feeds among the reeds and rushes.'   *Ib.*

21 Gitche Manito, the mighty.   *Ib.* i. *The Peace-Pipe*

22 By the shore of Gitche Gumee,
By the shining Big-Sea-Water,
Stood the wigwam of Nokomis,
Daughter of the Moon, Nokomis.
Dark behind it rose the forest,
Rose the black and gloomy pine-trees,
Rose the firs with cones upon them;
Bright before it beat the water,
Beat the clear and sunny water,
Beat the shining Big-Sea-Water.
Ib. iii. *Hiawatha's Childhood*

23 Ewa-yea! my little owlet!
Who is this, that lights the wigwam?
With his great eyes lights the wigwam?   *Ib.*

24 Called them 'Hiawatha's Chickens'.   *Ib.*

25 And his heart was hot within him,
Like a living coal his heart was.
Ib. iv. *Hiawatha and Mudjekeewis*

26 From the waterfall he named her,
Minnehaha, Laughing Water.   *Ib.*

27 As unto the bow the cord is,
So unto the man is woman;
Though she bends him, she obeys him,
Though she draws him, yet she follows;
Useless each without the other!
Ib. x. *Hiawatha's Wooing*

1 Onaway! Awake, beloved!
   The Song of Hiawatha. xi. *Hiawatha's Wedding-feast*

2 He is dead, the sweet musician!
   He the sweetest of all singers!
   He has gone from us for ever,
   He has moved a little nearer
   To the Master of all music,
   To the Master of all singing!
   O my brother, Chibiabos!
   Ib. xv. *Hiawatha's Lamentation*

3 The secret anniversaries of the heart.
   Sonnets. Holidays

4 Stars of the summer night!
   Far in yon azure deeps,
   Hide, hide your golden light!
   She sleeps!
   My lady sleeps!
   Sleeps!   *The Spanish Student*, I. iii

5 Dreams of the summer night!
   Tell her, her lover keeps
   Watch! while in slumbers light
   She sleeps!   *Ib.*

6 Thinking the deed, and not the creed,
   Would help us in our utmost need.
   Tales of a Wayside Inn, pt. I, Prelude, l. 221

7 At all feasts where ale was strongest
   Sat the merry monarch longest,
   First to come and last to go.
   Ib. The Musician's Tale. The Saga of King Olaf, ii

8 He seemed the incarnate 'Well, I told you so!'
   Ib. The Poet's Tale. The Birds of Killingworth

9 Our ingress into the world
   Was naked and bare;
   Our progress through the world
   Is trouble and care;
   Our egress from the world
   Will be nobody knows where;
   But if we do well here
   We shall do well there;
   And I could tell you no more,
   Should I preach a whole year!
   Ib. pt. II. *The Student's Tale. The Cobbler of Hagenau*

10 Ships that pass in the night, and speak each other in passing;
   Only a signal shown and a distant voice in the darkness;
   So on the ocean of life we pass and speak one another,
   Only a look and a voice; then darkness again and a silence.
   Ib. pt. III. *The Theologian's Tale. Elizabeth*, iv

11 Under the spreading chestnut tree
   The village smithy stands;
   The smith, a mighty man is he,
   With large and sinewy hands;
   And the muscles of his brawny arms
   Are strong as iron bands.
   The Village Blacksmith

12 He earns whate'er he can,
   And looks the whole world in the face,
   For he owes not any man.   *Ib.*

13 Toiling,—rejoicing,—sorrowing,
   Onward through life he goes;

Each morning sees some task begin,
   Each evening sees it close;
Something attempted, something done,
   Has earned a night's repose.
   The Village Blacksmith

14 It was the schooner Hesperus,
   That sailed the wintry sea;
And the skipper had taken his little daughter,
   To bear him company.
   The Wreck of the Hesperus

15 But the father answered never a word,
   A frozen corpse was he.   *Ib.*

16 And fast through the midnight dark and drear,
   Through the whistling sleet and snow,
   Like a sheeted ghost, the vessel swept
   Towards the reef of Norman's Woe.   *Ib.*

17 There was a little girl
   Who had a little curl
   Right in the middle of her forehead,
   When she was good
   She was very, very good,
   But when she was bad she was horrid.
   B. R. T. Machetta, *Home Life of Longfellow*

18 In this world a man must be either anvil or hammer.
   Hyperion, ch. iv

ANITA LOOS
1893–

19 Gentlemen Prefer Blondes.   *Title of Novel*

LOUIS XIV
1638–1715

20 Il n'y a plus de Pyrénées.
   The Pyrenees have ceased to exist.
   At the accession of his grandson to the throne of Spain, 1700. Attr. by Voltaire *in Siècle de Louis XIV*, ch. 28

21 L'État c'est moi.
   I am the State.
   Attr. remark before the Parlement de Paris, 13 April 1655. Dulaure, *Histoire de Paris*

22 Toutes les fois que je donne une place vacante, je fais cent mécontents et un ingrat.
   Every time I make an appointment, I make one ungrateful person and a hundred with a grievance.
   Voltaire: *Siècle de Louis XIV*, ch. 26

LOUIS XVIII
1755–1824

23 L'exactitude est la politesse des rois.
   Punctuality is the politeness of kings.   *Attr.*

RICHARD LOVELACE
1618–1658

24 Am not I shot
   With the self-same artillery?
   Amyntor from Beyond the Sea to Alexis

25 Lucasta that bright northern star.   *Ib.*

26 And when she ceas'd, we sighing saw
   The floor lay pav'd with broken hearts.
   Gratiana Dancing and Singing

1 So did she move; so did she sing
Like the harmonious spheres that bring
Unto their rounds their music's aid;
Which she performed such a way,
As all th' inamour'd world will say
The Graces danced, and Apollo play'd.
Gratiana Dancing and Singing

2 Forbear, thou great good husband, little ant.
The Ant

3 Cease, large example of wise thrift a while. *Ib.*

4 When Love with unconfined wings
Hovers within my gates;
And my divine Althea brings
To whisper at the grates:
When I lie tangled in her hair,
And fettered to her eye,
The Gods, that wanton in the air,
Know no such liberty. *To Althea, From Prison*

5 When flowing cups run swiftly round
With no allaying Thames. *Ib.*

6 When thirsty grief in wine we steep,
When healths and draughts go free,
Fishes, that tipple in the deep,
Know no such liberty. *Ib.*

7 When (like committed linnets) I
With shriller throat shall sing
The sweetness, mercy, majesty,
And glories of my King;
When I shall voice aloud, how good
He is, how great should be;
Enlarged winds that curl the flood,
Know no such liberty.

Stone walls do not a prison make
Nor iron bars a cage;
Minds innocent and quiet take
That for an hermitage;
If I have freedom in my love,
And in my soul am free;
Angels alone, that soar above,
Enjoy such liberty. *Ib.*

8 If to be absent were to be
Away from thee;
Or that when I am gone,
You or I were alone;
Then my Lucasta might I crave
Pity from blust'ring wind, or swallowing wave.
To Lucasta, Going Beyond the Seas

9 And greet as angels greet. *Ib.*

10 Tell me not (Sweet) I am unkind,
That from the nunnery
Of thy chaste breast, and quiet mind,
To war and arms I fly.

True; a new mistress now I chase,
The first foe in the field;
And with a stronger faith embrace
A sword, a horse, a shield.

Yet this inconstancy is such,
As you too shall adore;
I could not love thee (Dear) so much,
Lov'd I not honour more.
To Lucasta, Going to the Wars

SAMUEL LOVER
1797–1868

11 When once the itch of literature comes over a man, nothing can cure it but the scratching of a pen.
Handy Andy, ch. 36

12 'Now women are mostly troublesome cattle to deal with mostly', said Goggins. *Ib.*

JAMES RUSSELL LOWELL
1819–1891

13 An' you've gut to git up airly
Ef you want to take in God.
The Biglow Papers, First Series, No. 1

14 God'll send the bill to you. *Ib.*

15 You've a darned long row to hoe. *Ib.*

16 This goin' ware glory waits ye haint one agreeable feetur. *Ib.* No. 2

17 But John P.
Robinson he
Sez they didn't know everythin' down in Judee.
Ib. No. 3

18 A marciful Providunce fashioned us holler,
O' purpose thet we might our principles swaller.
Ib. No. 4

19 I du believe in Freedom's cause,
Ez fur away ez Payris is;
I love to see her stick her claws
In them infarnal Phayrisees;
It's wal enough agin a king
To dror resólves an' triggers,—
But libbaty's a kind o' thing
Thet don't agree with niggers.
Ib. No. 6. *The Pious Editor's Creed*

20 An' in convartin' public trusts
To very privit uses. *Ib.*

21 I *don't* believe in princerple,
But O, I *du* in interest. *Ib.*

22 It ain't by princerples nor men
My preudunt course is steadied,—
I scent wich pays the best, an' then
Go into it baldheaded. *Ib.*

23 God makes sech nights, all white an' still
Fur'z you can look or listen,
Moonshine an' snow on field an' hill,
All silence an' all glisten.
Ib. Introduction to the Second Series. The Courtin'.

24 'Twas kin' o' kingdom-come to look
On sech a blessed cretur. *Ib.*

25 She thought no v'ice hed sech a swing
Ez hisn in the choir;
My! when he made Ole Hunderd ring,
She *knowed* the Lord was nigher. *Ib.*

26 His heart kep' goin' pity-pat,
But hern went pity Zekle. *Ib.*

27 I tell ye wut, my jedgement is you're pooty sure to fail,
Ez long 'z the head keeps turnin' back for counsel to the tail. *Ib. Second Series*, No. 3, l. 223

28 We've a war, an' a debt, an' a flag; an' ef this
Ain't to be inderpendunt, why, wut on airth is?
Ib. No. 4

1 But somehow, when the dogs hed gut asleep,
Their love o' mutton beat their love o' sheep.
The Biglow Papers. Second Series, Ib. No. 11,
l. 291

2 In life's small things be resolute and great
To keep thy muscle trained: know'st thou when Fate
Thy measure takes, or when she'll say to thee,
'I find thee worthy; do this deed for me'? *Epigram*

3 They believed—faith, I'm puzzled—I think I may
call
Their belief a believing in nothing at all,
Or something of that sort; I know they all went
For a general union of total dissent.
A Fable for Critics, l. 733

4 There comes Poe with his raven like Barnaby Rudge,
Three-fifths of him genius, and two-fifths sheer fudge.
Ib. l. 1215

5 No man is born into the world, whose work
Is not born with him; there is always work,
And tools to work withal, for those who will:
And blessèd are the horny hands of toil!
A Glance Behind the Curtain, l. 201

6 These pearls of thought in Persian gulfs were bred,
Each softly lucent as a rounded moon;
The diver Omar plucked them from their bed,
Fitzgerald strung them on an English thread.
In a Copy of Omar Khayyám

7 The birch, most shy and ladylike of trees.
An Indian-Summer Reverie

8 Before Man made us citizens, great Nature made us
men. *On the Capture of Fugitive Slaves*

9 Once to every man and nation comes the moment to
decide,
In the strife of Truth with Falsehood, for the good or
evil side. *The Present Crisis*

10 Truth forever on the scaffold, Wrong forever on the
throne. *Ib.*

11 Behind the dim unknown,
Standeth God within the shadow, keeping watch
above his own. *Ib.*

12 Then to side with Truth is noble when we share her
wretched crust,
Ere her cause bring fame and profit, and 'tis prosper-
ous to be just;
Then it is the brave man chooses, while the coward
stands aside,
Doubting in his abject spirit, till his Lord is crucified.
Ib.

13 New occasions teach new duties: Time makes ancient
good uncouth;
They must upward still, and onward, who would
keep abreast of Truth. *Ib.*

14 They are slaves who fear to speak
For the fallen and the weak. *Stanzas on Freedom*

15 They are slaves who dare not be
In the right with two or three. *Ib.*

16 May is a pious fraud of the almanac.
Under the Willows, l. 21

17 And what is so rare as a day in June?
Then, if ever, come perfect days;
Then Heaven tries earth if it be in tune,
And over it softly her warm ear lays.
Vision of Sir Launfal, pt. 1, prelude

18 Who gives himself with his alms feeds three,—
Himself, his hungering neighbour, and Me.
Vision of Sir Launfal, pt. II. viii

19 A wise scepticism is the first attribute of a good critic.
Among My Books. Shakespeare Once More

20 Let us be of good cheer, however, remembering that
the misfortunes hardest to bear are those which
never come.
Democracy and Addresses. Democracy

21 There is no good in arguing with the inevitable. The
only argument available with an east wind is to put
on your overcoat. *Ib.*

LUCAN
A.D. 39–65

22 Victrix causa deis placuit, sed victa Catoni.
The conquering cause was pleasing to the Gods,
but the conquered one to Cato.
Works, i. 128. Trans. by Ridley

23 Stat magni nominis umbra.
There stands the shadow of a glorious name.
Ib. 135

24 Nil actum credens, dum quid superesset agendum.
Thinking nothing done while anything remained to
be done. *Ib.* ii. 657

25 Clarum et venerabile nomen
Gentibus.
A name illustrious and revered by nations.
Ib. ix. 203

26 Estne Dei sedes nisi terra, et pontus, et aer,
Et coelum, et virtus? Superos quid quaerimus ultra?
Jupiter est quodcumque vides, quocumque moveris.
The abode of God, too, is, wherever is earth and
sea and air, and sky, and virtue. Why further
do we seek the Gods of heaven? Whatever
thou dost behold and whatever thou dost touch,
that is Jupiter. *Ib.* 578

LUCRETIUS
99–55 B.C.

27 Ergo vivida vis animi pervicit, et extra
Processit longe flammantia moenia mundi
Atque omne immensum peragravit, mente animoque.
And so it was that the lively force of his mind won
its way, and he passed on far beyond the fiery
walls of the world, and in mind and spirit
traversed the boundless whole.
De Rerum Natura, i. 72. Trans. by Bailey

28 Tantum religio potuit suadere malorum.
Such evil deeds could religion prompt. *Ib.* 101

29 Nil posse creari
De nilo.
Nothing can be created out of nothing. *Ib.* 155

30 Suave, mari magno turbantibus aequora ventis,
E terra magnum alterius spectare laborem;
Non quia vexari quemquamst iucunda voluptas,
Sed quibus ipse malis careas quia cernere suave est.
Suave etiam belli certamina magna tueri
Per campos instructa tua sine parte pericli.
Sed nil dulcius est, bene quam munita tenere
Edita doctrina sapientum templa serena,

[320]

Despicere unde queas alios passimque videre
Errare atque viam palantis quaerere vitae,
Certare ingenio, contendere nobilitate,
Noctes atque dies niti praestante labore
Ad summas emergere opes rerumque potiri.

Sweet it is, when on the great sea the winds are buffeting the waters, to gaze from the land on another's great struggles; not because it is pleasure or joy that any one should be distressed, but because it is sweet to perceive from what misfortune you yourself are free. Sweet is it too, to behold great contests of war in full array over the plains, when you have no part in the danger. But nothing is more gladdening than to dwell in the calm high places, firmly embattled on the heights by the teaching of the wise, whence you can look down on others, and see them wandering hither and thither, going astray as they seek the way of life, in strife matching their wits or rival claims of birth, struggling night and day by surpassing effort to rise up to the height of power and gain possession of the world.
De Rerum Natura, ii. 1

1   Sic rerum summa novatur
Semper, et inter se mortales mutua vivunt.
Augescunt aliae gentes, aliae minuuntur,
Inque brevi spatio mutantur saecla animantum
Et quasi cursores vitai lampada tradunt.

Thus the sum of things is ever being replenished, and mortals live one and all by give and take. Some races wax and others wane, and in a short space the tribes of living things are changed, and like runners hand on the torch of life. *Ib.* 75

2   Medio de fonte leporum
Surgit amari aliquid quod in ipsis floribus angat.

From the heart of this fountain of delights wells up some bitter taste to choke them even amid the flowers. *Ib.* iv. 1133

MARTIN LUTHER
1483–1546

3 Esto peccator et pecca fortiter, sed fortius fide et gaude in Christo.

Be a sinner and sin strongly, but more strongly have faith and rejoice in Christ.
Letter to Melanchthon. Epistolæ M. Lutheri (Ienae (1556), i. 345)

4 Ich kann nicht anders.

I can do no other.
Speech at the Diet of Worms, 18 Apr. 1521. On his monument at Worms

5 Wer nicht liebt Wein, Weib und Gesang,
Der bleibt ein Narr sein Leben lang.

Who loves not woman, wine, and song
Remains a fool his whole life long.
Attr. to Luther. Written in the Luther room in the Wartburg, but no proof exists of its authorship

6 Ein feste Burg ist unser Gott,
Ein gute Wehr und Waffen.

A safe stronghold our God is still,
A trusty shield and weapon.
Klug'sche Gesangbuch (1529), *Ein Feste Burg.* Trans. by Carlyle

7 Wenn ich gewisst hätte, dass so viel Teufel auf mich gezielet hätten, als Ziegel auf den Dächern waren zu Worms, wäre ich dennoch eingeritten.

If I had heard that as many devils would set on me in Worms as there are tiles on the roofs, I should none the less have ridden there.
Luthers Sämmtliche Schriften (1745), xvi. 14

JOHN LYDGATE
1370?–1451?

8 Woord is but wynd; leff woord and tak the dede.
Secrees of old Philisoffres, l. 1224

9 Sithe off oure language he [Chaucer] was the lodesterre. *The Fall of Princes*, prol. l. 252

10 Sithe he off Inglissh in makyng was the beste,
Preie onto God to yiue his soule good reste. *Ib.* l. 356

11 Comparisouns doon offte gret greuaunce.
Ib. bk. iii, l. 2188

12 Love is mor than gold or gret richesse.
The Siege of Thebes, pt. iii, l. 2716

JOHN LYLY
1554?–1606

13 CAMPASPE:
Were women never so fair, men would be false.

APELLES:
Were women never so false, men would be fond.
Campaspe, iii. iii

14 Cupid and my Campaspe play'd
At cards for kisses, Cupid paid;
He stakes his quiver, bow, and arrows,
His mother's doves, and team of sparrows;
Loses them too; then, down he throws
The coral of his lip, the rose
Growing on 's cheek (but none knows how);
With these, the crystal of his brow,
And then the dimple on his chin:
All these did my Campaspe win.
At last he set her both his eyes;
She won, and Cupid blind did rise.
O Love! has she done this to thee?
What shall, alas! become of me? *Ib.* iii. v

15 What bird so sings, yet so does wail?
O 'tis the ravish'd nightingale.
Jug, jug, jug, jug, tereu, she cries,
And still her woes at midnight rise. *Ib.* v. i

16 How at heaven's gates she claps her wings,
The morn not waking till she sings. *Ib.*

17 Be valiant, but not too venturous. Let thy attire be comely, but not costly.
Euphues, Anatomy of Wit (Arber), p. 39

18 Night hath a thousand eyes.
Maides Metamorphose, iii. i

19 If all the earth were paper white
And all the sea were ink
'Twere not enough for me to write
As my poor heart doth think.
Poems, Early Autobiographical. Lyly's Works, ed. Bond (1902), vol. iii, p. 452

HENRY FRANCIS LYTE
1793-1847

1 Abide with me; fast falls the eventide;
The darkness deepens; Lord, with me abide;
When other helpers fail, and comforts flee,
Help of the helpless, O, abide with me.

Swift to its close ebbs out life's little day;
Earth's joys grow dim, its glories pass away;
Change and decay in all around I see;
O Thou, who changest not, abide with me.
Remains. Abide with Me

2 I fear no foe with Thee at hand to bless;
Ills have no weight, and tears no bitterness;
Where is death's sting? Where, grave, thy victory?
I triumph still, if Thou abide with me.

Hold Thou Thy Cross before my closing eyes;
Shine through the gloom, and point me to the skies;
Heaven's morning breaks, and earth's vain shadows flee;
In life, in death, O Lord, abide with me. *Ib.*

GEORGE LYTTELTON, BARON LYTTELTON
1709-1773

3 What is your sex's earliest, latest care,
Your heart's supreme ambition?—To be fair.
Advice to a Lady, l. 17

4 Seek to be good, but aim not to be great;
A woman's noblest station is retreat. *Ib. l. 51*

5 Where none admire, 'tis useless to excel;
Where none are beaux, 'tis vain to be a belle.
Soliloquy of a Beauty in the Country

6 Tell me, my heart, if this be love?
Song. When Delia

EDWARD GEORGE BULWER-LYTTON, BARON LYTTON
1803-1873

7 Ah, never can fall from the days that have been
A gleam on the years that shall be! *A Lament*

8 When stars are in the quiet skies,
Then most I pine for thee;
Bend on me, then, thy tender eyes,
As stars look on the sea!
Ernest Maltravers, bk. iii, ch. i

9 Here Stanley meets,—how Stanley scorns, the glance!
The brilliant chief, irregularly great,
Frank, haughty, rash,—the Rupert of Debate.
The New Timon, pt. I. vi

10 Out-babying Wordsworth and out-glittering Keats.
[Tennyson.] *Ib.*

11 Beneath the rule of men entirely great
The pen is mightier than the sword. *Richelieu, II. ii*

12 In the lexicon of youth, which Fate reserves
For a bright manhood, there is no such word
As—*fail!* *Ib.*

13 Poverty has strange bedfellows.
The Caxtons, pt. iv, ch. 4

14 There is no man so friendless but what he can find
a friend sincere enough to tell him disagreeable
truths.
What Will He Do With It?, bk. iii, ch. 15
(heading)

EDWARD ROBERT BULWER, EARL OF LYTTON
see
OWEN MEREDITH

WARD McALLISTER
1827-1895

15 There are only about four hundred people in New
York society.
*Interview with Charles H. Crandall in the New
York Tribune, 1888*

DOUGLAS MacARTHUR
1880-

16 I shall return.
*Message on leaving Corregidor for Australia.
11 Mar. 1942*

THOMAS BABINGTON MACAULAY, BARON MACAULAY
1800-1859

17 Attend, all ye who list to hear our noble England's
praise;
I tell of the thrice famous deeds she wrought in
ancient days. *The Armada*

18 Night sank upon the dusky beach, and on the purple
sea,
Such night in England ne'er had been, nor e'er again
shall be. *Ib.*

19 The rugged miners poured to war from Mendip's
sunless caves. *Ib.*

20 The sentinel on Whitehall gate looked forth into the
night. *Ib.*

21 At once on all her stately gates arose the answering
fires;
At once the wild alarum clashed from all her reeling
spires. *Ib.*

22 And broader still became the blaze, and louder still
the din,
As fast from every village round the horse came spurring in;
And eastward straight from wild Blackheath the warlike errand went,
And roused in many an ancient hall the gallant squires
of Kent. *Ib.*

23 Till Belvoir's lordly terraces the sign to Lincoln sent,
And Lincoln sped the message on o'er the wide vale
of Trent;
Till Skiddaw saw the fire that burned on Gaunt's em-
-battled pile,
And the red glare on Skiddaw roused the burghers of
Carlisle. *Ib.*

24 Obadiah Bind - their - kings - in - chains - and - their -
nobles-with-links-of-iron. *The Battle of Naseby*

25 Oh, wherefore come ye forth in triumph from the
north,
With your hands, and your feet, and your raiment
all red?
And wherefore doth your rout send forth a joyous
shout?
And whence be the grapes of the wine-press which
ye tread? *Ib.*

1 And the Man of Blood was there, with his long
essenced hair,
And Astley, and Sir Marmaduke, and Rupert of the
Rhine. *The Battle of Naseby*

2 For God! for the Cause! for the Church! for the
laws!
For Charles King of England, and Rupert of the
Rhine! *Ib.*

3 The furious German comes, with his clarions and
his drums. *Ib.*

4 He looked upon his people, and a tear was in his eye;
He looked upon the traitors, and his glance was stern
and high. *Ivry*

5 'Press where ye see my white plume shine, amidst the
ranks of war,
And be your oriflamme to-day the helmet of Navarre.'
Ib.

6 Their ranks are breaking like thin clouds before a
Biscay gale. *Ib.*

7 To my true king I offer'd free from stain
Courage and faith; vain faith, and courage vain.
A Jacobite's Epitaph

8 And pined by Arno for my lovelier Tees. *Ib.*

9 By those white cliffs I never more must see,
By that dear language which I spake like thee,
Forget all feuds, and shed one English tear
O'er English dust. A broken heart lies here. *Ib.*

10 Lars Porsena of Clusium
By the nine gods he swore
That the great house of Tarquin
Should suffer wrong no more.
By the Nine Gods he swore it,
And named a trysting day,
And bade his messengers ride forth,
East and west and south and north,
To summon his array.
Lays of Ancient Rome. Horatius, i

11 From lordly Volaterræ,
Where scowls the far-famed hold
Piled by the hands of giants
For godlike kings of old. *Ib.* iv

12 The harvests of Arretium,
This year, old men shall reap.
This year, young boys in Umbro
Shall plunge the struggling sheep;
And in the vats of Luna,
This year, the must shall foam
Round the white feet of laughing girls
Whose sires have marched to Rome. *Ib.* viii

13 A proud man was Lars Porsena
Upon the trysting day. *Ib.* xi

14 And with a mighty following
To join the muster came
The Tusculan Mamilius,
Prince of the Latian name. *Ib.* xii

15 And plainly and more plainly
Now might the burghers know,
By port and vest, by horse and crest,
Each warlike Lucumo. *Ib.* xxiii

16 But the Consul's brow was sad,
And the Consul's speech was low,
And darkly looked he at the wall,
And darkly at the foe. *Ib.* xxvi

17 Then out spake brave Horatius,
The Captain of the Gate:
'To every man upon this earth
Death cometh soon or late.
And how can man die better
Than facing fearful odds,
For the ashes of his fathers,
And the temples of his Gods?' *Horatius,* xxvii

18 To save them from false Sextus
That wrought the deed of shame. *Ib.* xxviii

19 'Now who will stand on either hand,
And keep the bridge with me?' *Ib.* xxix

20 And straight against that great array
Forth went the dauntless Three. *Ib.* xxxi

21 Then none was for a party;
Then all were for the state;
Then the great man helped the poor,
And the poor man loved the great:
Then lands were fairly portioned;
Then spoils were fairly sold:
The Romans were like brothers
In the brave days of old. *Ib.* xxxi

22 Was none who would be foremost
To lead such dire attack;
But those behind cried 'Forward!'
And those before cried 'Back!' *Ib.* l

23 Thrice looked he at the city;
Thrice looked he at the dead;
And thrice came on in fury,
And thrice turned back in dread. *Ib.* lii

24 'Come back, come back, Horatius!'
Loud cried the Fathers all.
'Back, Lartius! back, Herminius!
Back, ere the ruin fall!' *Ib.* liii

25 But when they turned their faces,
And on the farther shore
Saw brave Horatius stand alone,
They would have crossed once more. *Ib.* liv

26 Round turned he, as not deigning
Those craven ranks to see;
Nought spake he to Lars Porsena,
To Sextus nought spake he;
But he saw on Palatinus
The white porch of his home!
And he spake to the noble river
That rolls by the towers of Rome. *Ib.* lviii

27 'Oh, Tiber! father Tiber!
To whom the Romans pray,
A Roman's life, a Roman's arms,
Take thou in charge this day!' *Ib.* lix

28 And even the ranks of Tuscany
Could scarce forbear to cheer. *Ib.* lx

29 Never, I ween, did swimmer,
In such an evil case,
Struggle through such a raging flood
Safe to the landing place. *Ib.* lxii

30 'Heaven help him!' quoth Lars Porsena,
'And bring him safe to shore;
For such a gallant feat of arms
Was never seen before.' *Ib.* lxiii

31 When the oldest cask is opened,
And the largest lamp is lit. *Ib.* lxix

[323]

1 With weeping and with laughter
  Still is the story told,
How well Horatius kept the bridge
  In the brave days of old.
                    Lays of Ancient Rome. Horatius, lxx

2 In lordly Lacedaemon,
  The city of two kings.
                    Ib. The Battle of Lake Regillus, ii

3 Those trees in whose dim shadow
  The ghastly priest doth reign,
The priest who slew the slayer,
  And shall himself be slain.   *Ib.* x

4 Herminius glared on Sextus.   *Ib.* xv

5 Ah! woe is me for the good house
  That loves the people well!   *Ib.* xvii

6 For aye Valerius loathed the wrong
  And aye upheld the right.   *Ib.* xviii

7 Away, away went Auster
  Like an arrow from the bow:
Black Auster was the fleetest steed
  From Aufidus to Po.   *Ib.* xxv

8 One of us two, Herminius,
  Shall never more go home.
I will lay on for Tusculum
  And lay thou on for Rome!   *Ib.* xxvii

9 Herminius smote Mamilius
  Through breast-plate and through breast;
And fast flowed out the purple blood
  Over the purple vest.
Mamilius smote Herminius
  Through headpiece and through head;
And side by side those chiefs of pride
  Together fell down dead.   *Ib.* xxviii

10 The pass was steep and rugged,
  The wolves they howled and whined;
But he ran like a whirlwind up the pass,
  And he left the wolves behind.   *Ib.* xxix

11 'The furies of thy brother
  With me and mine abide,
If one of your accursed house
  Upon black Auster ride!'   *Ib.* xxx

12 So spake he; and was buckling
  Tighter black Auster's band,
When he was aware of a princely pair
  That rode at his right hand.
So like they were, no mortal
  Might one from other know:
White as snow their armour was:
  Their steeds were white as snow.   *Ib.* xxxii

13 And all who saw them trembled,
  And pale grew every cheek.   *Ib.* xxxiii

14 Let no man stop to plunder,
  But slay, and slay, and slay;
The Gods who live for ever
  Are on our side to-day.   *Ib.* xxxv

15 And fliers and pursuers
  Were mingled in a mass;
And far away the battle
  Went roaring through the pass.   *Ib.* xxxvi

16 These be the great Twin Brethren
  To whom the Dorians pray.   *Ib.* xl

17   Thou, through all change,
Fix thy firm gaze on virtue and on me.
                    Lines Written in August

18 From all the angelic ranks goes forth a groan,
  'How long, O Lord, how long?'
The still small voice makes answer 'Wait and see,
  O sons of glory, what the end shall be'.
                    Marriage of Tirzah and Ahirad

19 Ye diners-out from whom we guard our spoons.
          Political Georgics. See his letter to Hannah Macaulay, 29 June 1831

20 Knowledge advances by steps, and not by leaps.
          Essays and Biographies. History

21 The business of everybody is the business of nobody.
          Historical Essays Contributed to the 'Edinburgh Review'. Hallam's Constitutional History (Sept. 1828)

22 The gallery in which the reporters sit has become a fourth estate of the realm.   *Ib.*

23 He knew that the essence of war is violence, and that moderation in war is imbecility. [John Hampden.]
          Ib. Lord Nugent's Memorials of Hampden (Dec. 1831)

24 The reluctant obedience of distant provinces generally costs more than it [the territory] is worth.
          Ib. Lord Mahon's War of the Succession (Jan. 1833)

25 The highest intellects, like the tops of mountains, are the first to catch and to reflect the dawn.
          Ib. Sir J. Mackintosh's History of the Revolution (July 1835)

26 The history of England is emphatically the history of progress.   *Ib.*

27 The rising hope of those stern and unbending Tories.
          Ib. Gladstone on Church and State (April 1839)

28 Every schoolboy knows who imprisoned Montezuma, and who strangled Atahualpa.
          Ib. Lord Clive (Jan. 1840)

29 They [the Nabobs] raised the price of everything in their neighbourhood, from fresh eggs to rotten boroughs.   *Ib.*

30 A savage old Nabob, with an immense fortune, a tawny complexion, a bad liver, and a worse heart. [Clive.]   *Ib.*

31 When some traveller from New Zealand shall, in the midst of a vast solitude, take his stand on a broken arch of London Bridge to sketch the ruins of St. Paul's.   *Ib. Von Ranke* (Oct. 1840)

32 The Chief Justice was rich, quiet, and infamous.
          Ib. Warren Hastings (Oct. 1841)

33 The great Proconsul.   *Ib.*

34 In order that he might rob a neighbour whom he had promised to defend, black men fought on the coast of Coromandel, and red men scalped each other by the Great Lakes of North America.
          Ib. Frederic the Great (Apr. 1842)

35 We hardly know any instance of the strength and weakness of human nature so striking, and so grotesque, as the character of this haughty, vigilant, resolute, sagacious blue-stocking, half Mithridates and half Trissotin, bearing up against a world in arms, with an ounce of poison in one pocket and a quire of bad verses in the other. [Frederick.]   *Ib.*

36 *Lues Boswelliana*, or disease of admiration.
          Ib. Earl of Chatham (Jan. 1834)

MACAULAY

1 The dust and silence of the upper shelf.
Literary Essays Contributed to the 'Edinburgh Review'. Milton (Aug. 1825)

2 As civilization advances, poetry almost necessarily declines. *Ib.*

3 Perhaps no person can be a poet, or can even enjoy poetry, without a certain unsoundness of mind. *Ib.*

4 Nobles by the right of an earlier creation, and priests by the imposition of a mightier hand. *Ib.*

5 That propensity which, for want of a better name, we will venture to christen Boswellism. *Ib.*

6 Out of his surname they have coined an epithet for a knave, and out of his Christian name a synonym for the Devil. *Ib. Machiavelli* (Mar. 1827)

7 Nothing is so useless as a general maxim. *Ib.*

8 We have heard it said that five per cent. is the natural interest of money. *Ib. Southey's Colloquies* (Jan. 1830)

9 His writing bears the same relation to poetry which a Turkey carpet bears to a picture. There are colours in the Turkey carpet out of which a picture might be made. There are words in Mr. Montgomery's writing which, when disposed in certain orders and combinations, have made, and will make again, good poetry. But, as they now stand, they seem to be put together on principle in such a manner as to give no image of anything 'in the heavens above, or in the earth beneath, or in the waters under the earth.'
Ib. Mr. Robert Montgomery's Poems (Apr. 1830)

10 The use of a mirror, we submit, is not to be painted upon. *Ib.*

11 But Mr. Robert Montgomery's readers must take such grammar as they can get, and be thankful. *Ib.*

12 We take this to be, on the whole, the worst similitude in the world. In the first place, no stream meanders, or can possibly meander, level with its fount. In the next place, if streams did meander level with their founts, no two motions can be less like each other than that of meandering level and that of mounting upwards. *Ib.*

13 His theory is therefore this, that God made the thunder, but that the lightning made itself. *Ib.*

14 He had a head which statuaries loved to copy, and a foot the deformity of which the beggars in the street mimicked.
Ib. Moore's Life of Lord Byron (June 1830)

15 We know no spectacle so ridiculous as the British public in one of its periodical fits of morality. *Ib.*

16 We prefer a gipsy by Reynolds to his Majesty's head on a sign-post. *Ib.*

17 The world, we believe, is pretty well agreed in thinking that the shorter a prize poem is, the better. *Ib.*

18 From the poetry of Lord Byron they drew a system of ethics, compounded of misanthropy and voluptuousness, a system in which the two great commandments were, to hate your neighbour, and to love your neighbour's wife. *Ib.*

19 Very few and very weary are those who are in at the death of the Blatant Beast.
Ib. Southey's Edition of Pilgrim's Progress (Dec. 1830)

20 What schoolboy of fourteen is ignorant of this remarkable circumstance?
Ib. Sir William Temple (Oct. 1838)

21 There is a vile phrase of which bad historians are exceedingly fond, 'the dignity of history'. *Ib.*

22 The conformation of his mind was such that whatever was little seemed to him great, and whatever was great seemed to him little.
Ib. Horace Walpole (Oct. 1833)

23 With the dead there is no rivalry. In the dead there is no change. Plato is never sullen. Cervantes is never petulant. Demosthenes never comes unseasonably. Dante never stays too long. No difference of political opinion can alienate Cicero. No heresy can excite the horror of Bossuet.
Ib. Lord Bacon (July 1837)

24 An acre in Middlesex is better than a principality in Utopia. *Ib.*

25 The checkered spectacle of so much glory and so much shame. *Ib.*

26 The Life of Johnson is assuredly a great, a very great work. Homer is not more decidedly the first of heroic poets, Shakespeare is not more decidedly the first of dramatists, Demosthenes is not more decidedly the first of orators, than Boswell is the first of biographers.
Ib. Boswell's Life of Johnson (Sept. 1831)

27 They knew luxury; they knew beggary; but they never knew comfort. *Ib.*

28 In the foreground is that strange figure which is as familiar to us as the figures of those among whom we have been brought up, the gigantic body, the huge massy face, seamed with the scars of disease, the brown coat, the black worsted stockings, the grey wig with the scorched foretop, the dirty hands, the nails bitten and pared to the quick. *Ib.*

29 Like Sir Condy Rackrent in the tale, she survived her own wake, and overheard the judgment of posterity. *Ib. Madame D'Arblay* (Jan. 1843)

30 A sort of broken Johnsonese. *Ib.*

31 He was a rake among scholars, and a scholar among rakes. [Richard Steele.]
Ib. Aikin's Life of Addison (July 1843)

32 The old philosopher is still among us in the brown coat with the metal buttons and the shirt which ought to be at wash, blinking, puffing, rolling his head, drumming with his fingers, tearing his meat like a tiger, and swallowing his tea in oceans.
Life of Johnson (ad fin.)

33 I shall cheerfully bear the reproach of having descended below the dignity of history.
History of England, vol. i, ch. 1

34 Thus our democracy was, from an early period, the most aristocratic, and our aristocracy the most democratic in the world. *Ib.*

35 Persecution produced its natural effect on them. It found them a sect; it made them a faction. *Ib.*

36 It was a crime in a child to read by the bedside of a sick parent one of those beautiful collects which had soothed the griefs of forty generations of Christians. *Ib. ch. 2*

1 The Puritan hated bear-baiting, not because it gave pain to the bear, but because it gave pleasure to the spectators.   *History of England*, vol. i, ch. 2

2 There were gentlemen and there were seamen in the navy of Charles the Second. But the seamen were not gentlemen; and the gentlemen were not seamen.   *Ib.* ch. 3

3 The English Bible, a book which, if everything else in our language should perish, would alone suffice to show the whole extent of its beauty and power.   *Edinburgh Review*, Jan. 1828. *On John Dryden*

4 His imagination resembled the wings of an ostrich. It enabled him to run, though not to soar.   *Ib.*

5 It is not easy to make a simile go on all fours.   *Ib.* Dec. 1830. *On John Bunyan*

6 The object of oratory alone is not truth, but persuasion.   *Works* (1898), vol. xi. *Essay on Athenian Orators*

7 History, abounding with kings thirty feet high, and reigns thirty thousand years long—and geography made up of seas of treacle and seas of butter.   *Minute, as Member of Supreme Council of India, 2 Feb. 1835*

8 Dark and terrible beyond any season within my remembrance of political affairs was the day of their flight. Far darker and far more terrible will be the day of their return. [The Tory Government, defeated in Nov. 1830.]   *Speech, 20 Sept. 1831*

9 A broken head in Cold Bath Fields produces a greater sensation among us than three pitched battles in India.   *Ib. 10 July 1833*

10 Thank you, madam, the agony is abated. [Reply, aged four.]   Trevelyan's *Life and Letters of Macaulay*, ch. 1

11 I shall not be satisfied unless I produce something which shall for a few days supersede the last fashionable novel on the tables of young ladies.   *Ib.* ch. 9

ANTHONY CLEMENT McAULIFFE
1898–

12 Nuts!   *Reply to German demand for surrender of 101st Airborne Division men trapped at Bastogne, Belgium, 23 Dec. 1944*

JOSEPH McCARTHY
d. 1944

13 You made me love you,
 I didn't want to do it.   *You Made Me Love You*

GEORGE McCLELLAN
1826–1885

14 All quiet along the Potomac.   *Attr. in the American Civil War*

JOHN McCRAE
1872–1918

15 We shall not sleep, though poppies grow
 In Flanders fields.
 In Flanders Fields. (*Punch*, vol. cxlix, 8 Dec. 1915)

CHARLES BAIRD MACDONALD
1885–

16 When ye come to play golf ye maun hae a heid!   *Scotland's Gift—Golf*, 1928

(A caddy at St. Andrews named Lang Willie was teaching one of the professors of the university the noble game. The professor was not a promising pupil.—Willie fairly got out of patience and said to him: 'Ye see, Professor, as long as ye are learning thae lads at the College Latin and Greek it is easy work, but when ye come to play golf ye maun hae a heid!')

GEORGE MACDONALD
1824–1905

17 Where did you come from, baby dear?
 Out of the everywhere into here.   *At the Back of the North Wind*, xxxiii, *Song*

18 Where did you get your eyes so blue?
 Out of the sky as I came through.   *Ib.*

19 Here lie I, Martin Elginbrodde:
 Hae mercy o' my soul, Lord God;
 As I wad do, were I Lord God,
 And ye were Martin Elginbrodde.   *David Elginbrod*, bk. i, ch. 13

20 Alas, how easily things go wrong!
 A sigh too much, or a kiss too long,
 And there follows a mist and a weeping rain,
 And life is never the same again.   *Phantastes: Down the Lane*

21 They all were looking for a king
 To slay their foes, and lift them high;
 Thou cam'st, a little baby thing,
 That made a woman cry.   *That Holy Thing*

CHARLES MACKAY
1814–1889

22 Cheer! Boys, cheer!   *Title of Song*

23 There's a good time coming, boys,
 A good time coming.   *The Good Time Coming*

24 Old Tubal Cain was a man of might
 In the days when earth was young.   *Tubal Cain*

HENRY MACKENZIE
1745–1831

25 The Man of Feeling.   *Title of Novel*

SIR JAMES MACKINTOSH
1765–1832

26 Men are never so good or so bad as their opinions.   *Ethical Philosophy*, § 6. *Bentham*

27 The frivolous work of polished idleness.   *Ib. Remarks on Thomas Brown*

28 The Commons, faithful to their system, remained in a wise and masterly inactivity.   *Vindiciæ Gallicæ*, § 1

MURDOCH McLENNAN
fl. 1715

1 There's some say that we wan, some say that they wan,
  Some say that nane wan at a', man;
  But one thing I'm sure, that at Sheriffmuir
  A battle there was which I saw, man:
  And we ran, and they ran, and they ran, and we ran,
  And we ran; and they ran awa', man!
    Sheriffmuir. Roxburghe Ballads (1889), vol. vi.
    In Hogg's *Jacobite Relics*, 1821, vol. ii, the last
    line is: 'But Florence ran fastest of a', man.'
    (Florence was the Marquis of Huntley's horse)

IRENE RUTHERFORD McLEOD
1891–

2 I'm a lean dog, a keen dog, a wild dog, and alone.
    Lone Dog, st. 1

NORMAN MACLEOD
1812–1872

3 Courage, brother! do not stumble,
  Though thy path is dark as night;
  There's a star to guide the humble:
  'Trust in God, and do the Right.'
    Edinburgh Christian Magazine, Jan. 1857

MAURICE DE MACMAHON
1808–1893

4 J'y suis, j'y reste.
    Here I am, and here I stay.
    Attr. remark at the taking of the Malakoff, 8 Sept.
    1855

LEONARD McNALLY
1752–1820

5 This lass so neat, with smiles so sweet,
  Has won my right good-will,
  I'd crowns resign to call thee mine,
  Sweet lass of Richmond Hill.
    The Lass of Richmond Hill. E. Duncan, *Minstrelsy
    of England* (1905), i. 254. Attr. also to W. Upton
    in *Oxford Song Book*, and to W. Hudson in
    Baring-Gould, *English Minstrelsie* (1895), iii. 54

SAMUEL MADDEN
1686–1765

6 Words are men's daughters, but God's sons are things.
    Boulter's Monument, l. 377

MAURICE DE MAETERLINCK
1862–1949

7 Il n'y a pas de morts.
  There are no dead.   *L'Oiseau bleu*, IV. ii

ARCHBISHOP WILLIAM CONNOR MAGEE
1821–1891

8 I'd rather that England should be free than that
  England should be compulsorily sober.
    See Corrigenda

MAGNA CARTA
1215

9 Nisi per legale iudicium parium suorum vel per legem
  terrae.
    Except by the legal judgement of his peers or the law
    of the land.   *Clause 39*

SIR JOHN PENTLAND MAHAFFY
1839–1919

10 [On distinguishing the Irish bull from similar freaks
  of language.] The Irish bull is always pregnant.

ALFRED THAYER MAHAN
1840–1914

11 Those far distant, storm-beaten ships, upon which
  the Grand Army never looked, stood between it
  and the dominion of the world.
    *The Influence of Sea Power upon the French
    Revolution and Empire, 1793–1812* (1892), ii.
    118

FRANCIS SYLVESTER MAHONY
see
FATHER PROUT

SIR HENRY JAMES SUMNER MAINE
1822–1888

12 Except the blind forces of Nature, nothing moves in
  this world which is not Greek in its origin.
    Rede Lecture, 1875. Village Communities

JOSEPH DE MAISTRE
1753–1821

13 Toute nation a le gouvernement qu'elle mérite.
  Every country has the government it deserves.
    Lettres et Opuscules Inédits, i, p. 215, 15 août
    1811

DAVID MALLET
1705?–1765

14 O grant me, Heaven, a middle state,
  Neither too humble nor too great;
  More than enough, for nature's ends,
  With something left to treat my friends.
    Imitation of Horace, bk. ii, sat. vi

SIR THOMAS MALORY *fl.* 1470

15 It is notoriously known through the universal world
  that there be nine worthy and the best that ever
  were. That is to wit three paynims, three Jews,
  and three Christian men. As for the paynims they
  were . . . the first Hector of Troy, . . . the second
  Alexander the Great; and the third Julius Caesar.
  . . . As for the three Jews . . . the first was Duke
  Joshua . . .; the second David, King of Jerusalem;
  and the third Judas Maccabaeus. . . . And sith the
  said Incarnation . . . was first the noble Arthur. . . .
  The second was Charlemagne or Charles the
  Great . . .; and the third and last was Godfrey of
  Bouillon.
    Le Morte D'Arthur, Caxton's Original Preface.
    See Corrigenda

1 I, according to my copy, have done set it in imprint, to the intent that noble men may see and learn the noble acts of chivalry, the gentle and virtuous deeds that some knights used in those days.
Le Morte D'Arthur. Caxton's Original Preface

2 Wherein they shall find many joyous and pleasant histories, and noble and renowned acts of humanity, gentleness, and chivalries. For herein may be seen noble chivalry, courtesy, humanity, friendliness, hardiness, love, friendship, cowardice, murder, hate, virtue, and sin. Do after the good and leave the evil, and it shall bring you to good fame and renown. *Ib.*

3 Whoso pulleth out this sword of this stone and anvil is rightwise King born of all England.
Ib. bk. i, ch. 4

4 This beast went to the well and drank, and the noise was in the beast's belly like unto the questing of thirty couple hounds, but all the while the beast drank there was no noise in the beast's belly.
Ib. ch. 19

5 Me repenteth, said Merlin; because of the death of that lady thou shalt strike a stroke most dolorous that ever man struck, except the stroke of our Lord, for thou shalt hurt the truest knight and the man of most worship that now liveth, and through that stroke three kingdoms shall be in great poverty, misery and wretchedness twelve years, and the knight shall not be whole of that wound for many years. *Ib. bk. ii, ch. 8*

6 What, nephew, said the king, is the wind in that door? *Ib. bk. vii, ch. 34*

7 Ah, my little son, thou hast murdered thy mother! And therefore I suppose thou that art a murderer so young, thou art full likely to be a manly man in thine age . . . when he is christened let call him Tristram, that is as much to say as a sorrowful birth. *Ib. bk. viii, ch. 1*

8 The questing beast. *Ib. bk. ix, ch. 12*

9 God defend me, said Dinadan, for the joy of love is too short, and the sorrow thereof, and what cometh thereof, dureth over long. *Ib. bk. x, ch. 56*

10 It is his day, said Dinadan. *Ib. ch. 70*

11 Nay, by my knighthood, said Palomides, I never espied that ever she loved me more than all the world, nor never had I pleasure with her, but the last day she gave me the greatest rebuke that ever I had, the which shall never go from my heart.
Ib. ch. 82.

12 Now I thank God, said Sir Launcelot, for His great mercy of that I have seen, for it sufficeth me. For, as I suppose, no man in this world hath lived better than I have done, to achieve that I have done.
Ib. bk. xvii, ch. 16

13 Fair lord, salute me to my lord, Sir Launcelot, my father, and as soon as ye see him, bid him remember of this unstable world. *Ib. ch. 22*

14 Thus endeth the story of the Sangreal, that was briefly drawn out of French into English, the which is a story chronicled for one of the truest and the holiest that is in this world. *Ib. ch. 23, end*

15 And thus it passed on from Candlemass until after Easter, that the month of May was come, when every lusty heart beginneth to blossom, and to bring forth fruit; for like as herbs and trees bring forth fruit and flourish in May, in likewise every lusty heart that is in any manner a lover, springeth and flourisheth in lusty deeds.
Le Morte D'Arthur, bk. xviii, ch. 25

16 Therefore all ye that be lovers call unto your remembrance the month of May, like as did Queen Guenevere, for whom I make here a little mention, that while she lived she was a true lover, and therefore she had a good end. *Ib.*

17 Through this man and me hath all this war been wrought, and the death of the most noblest knights of the world; for through our love that we have loved together is my most noble lord slain. *Ib. bk. xxi, ch. 9*

18 Therefore, Sir Launcelot, I require thee and beseech thee heartily, for all the love that ever was betwixt us, that thou never see me more in the visage. *Ib.*

19 Wherefore, madam, I pray you kiss me and never no more. Nay, said the queen, that shall I never do, but abstain you from such works: and they departed. But there was never so hard an hearted man but he would have wept to see the dolour that they made. *Ib. ch. 10*

20 And Sir Launcelot awoke, and went and took his horse, and rode all that day and all night in a forest, weeping. *Ib.*

21 Then Sir Launcelot saw her visage, but he wept not greatly, but sighed. *Ib. ch. 11*

22 Then Sir Launcelot never after ate but little meat, ne drank, till he was dead. *Ib. ch. 12*

23 I saw the angels heave up Sir Launcelot unto heaven, and the gates of heaven opened against him. *Ib.*

24 Said Sir Ector . . . Sir Launcelot . . . thou wert never matched of earthly knight's hand; and thou wert the courteoust knight that ever bare shield; and thou wert the truest friend to thy lover that ever bestrad horse; and thou wert the truest lover of a sinful man that ever loved woman; and thou wert the kindest man that ever struck with sword; and thou wert the goodliest person that ever came among press of knights; and thou wert the meekest man and the gentlest that ever ate in hall among ladies; and thou wert the sternest knight to thy mortal foe that ever put spear in the rest.
Ib. ch. 13

THOMAS ROBERT MALTHUS
1766–1834

25 Population, when unchecked, increases in a geometrical ratio. Subsistence only increases in an arithmetical ratio. *The Principle of Population, 1*

W. R. MANDALE
nineteenth century

26 Up and down the City Road,
In and out the Eagle,
That's the way the money goes—
Pop goes the weasel! *Pop Goes the Weasel*

JAMES CLARENCE MANGAN
1803–1849

1 There's wine from the royal Pope
   Upon the ocean green;
And Spanish ale shall give you hope,
   My Dark Rosaleen! *Dark Rosaleen*

2 Your holy delicate white hands
   Shall girdle me with steel. *Ib.*

3 The fair hills of Eiré, O. *Title of Poem*

4 Roll forth, my song, like the rushing river.
   The Nameless One

5 He, too, had tears for all souls in trouble
   Here, and in hell. *Ib.*

MANILIUS
A.D. 1st cent.

6 Eripuit caelo fulmen, mox sceptra tyrannis.
   He snatched the thunderbolt from heaven, soon
   the sceptres from tyrants.
   i. 104. (*Inscribed on Benjamin Franklin's Statue*)

MRS. MARY DE LA RIVIERE MANLEY
1663–1724

7 No time like the present. *The Lost Lover,* IV. i

HORACE MANN
1796–1859

8 The object of punishment is, prevention from evil; it
   never can be made impulsive to good.
   Lectures and Reports on Education, 1867, lecture
   vii

9 Lost, yesterday, somewhere between Sunrise and
   Sunset, two golden hours, each set with sixty
   diamond minutes. No reward is offered, for they
   are gone forever. *Lost, Two Golden Hours*

LORD JOHN MANNERS, DUKE OF RUTLAND
1818–1906

10 Let wealth and commerce, laws and learning die,
   But leave us still our old nobility!
   England's Trust, pt. III, l. 227

WILLIAM MURRAY, EARL OF MANSFIELD
1705–1793

11 Consider what you think justice requires, and decide
   accordingly. But never give your reasons; for your
   judgement will probably be right, but your reasons
   will certainly be wrong.
   Advice. Campbell's *Lives of the Chief Justices,*
   1874, vol. iv, p. 26

RICHARD MANT
1776–1848

12 Bright the vision that delighted
   Once the sight of Judah's seer.
   Ancient Hymns. Bright the Vision

JOHANNES MANTUANUS

13 Semel insanivimus omnes.
   We have all been mad once. *Eclogue,* i. 217

WALTER MAP or MAPES
fl. 1200

14 If die I must, let me die drinking in an inn.
   De nugis curialium

MARCUS AURELIUS ANTONINUS
A.D. 121–180

15 The poet says, Dear city of Cecrops; and wilt not
   thou say, Dear City of Zeus? *Trans. by G. Long*

WILLIAM LEARNED MARCY
1786–1857

16 To the victor belong the spoils of the enemy.
   Parton's *Life of Jackson* (1860), vol. iii, p. 378

JUAN DE MARIANA
1535–1624

17 La última camisa de que se despojan los sabios es la
   soberbia.
   The last shirt your wise man will abandon is pride.

MARIE-ANTOINETTE
1755–1793

18 Qu'ils mangent de la brioche.
   Let them eat cake.
      *On being told that her people had no bread.
      Attributed to Marie-Antoinette, but much older.
      Rousseau refers in his* Confessions, *1740, to
      a similar remark, as a well-known saying. See also*
   Corrigenda

EDWIN MARKHAM
1852–1940

19 Bowed by the weight of centuries he leans
   Upon his hoe and gazes on the ground,
   The emptiness of ages in his face,
   And on his back the burden of the world.
   The Man with the Hoe

CHRISTOPHER MARLOWE
1564–1593

20 My men, like satyrs grazing on the lawns,
   Shall with their goat feet dance an antic hay.
   Edward II, I. i. 59

21 Live and die in Aristotle's works. *Faustus,* l. 33

22 Sweet Analytics, 'tis thou hast ravished me. *Ib.* l. 34

23 I'll have them fly to India for gold,
   Ransack the ocean for orient pearl. *Ib.* l. 110

24 I'll have them wall all Germany with brass,
   And make swift Rhine circle fair Wertenberg.
   I'll have them fill the public schools with silk,
   Wherewith the students shall be bravely clad.
   Ib. l. 116

25 For when we hear one rack the name of God,
   Abjure the Scriptures, and his Saviour Christ,
   We fly, in hope to get his glorious soul. *Ib.* l. 282

MARLOWE

1 MEPHISTOPHELES:
O by aspiring pride and insolence,
For which God threw him from the face of heaven.
FAUSTUS:
And what are you that live with Lucifer?
MEPHISTOPHELES:
Unhappy spirits that fell with Lucifer,
Conspired against our God with Lucifer,
And are for ever damned with Lucifer. *Faustus*, l. 303

2 Why this is hell, nor am I out of it:
Thinkst thou that I who saw the face of God,
And tasted the eternal joys of heaven,
Am not tormented with ten thousand hells
In being deprived of everlasting bliss! *Ib.* l. 312

3   When all the world dissolves,
And every creature shall be purified,
All places shall be hell that are not heaven. *Ib.* l. 556

4 Have not I made blind Homer sing to me?
          Ib. l. 637

5 Was this the face that launch'd a thousand ships,
And burnt the topless towers of Ilium?
Sweet Helen, make me immortal with a kiss!
Her lips suck forth my soul: see, where it flies!
Come Helen, come give me my soul again.
Here will I dwell, for heaven be in these lips,
And all is dross that is not Helena. *Ib.* l. 1328

6 O thou art fairer than the evening air,
Clad in the beauty of a thousand stars,
Brighter art thou than flaming Jupiter,
When he appeared to hapless Semele,
More lovely than the monarch of the sky
In wanton Arethusa's azured arms,
And none but thou shalt be my paramour. *Ib.* l. 1341

7 Now hast thou but one bare hour to live,
And then thou must be damned perpetually;
Stand still you ever-moving spheres of heaven,
That time may cease, and midnight never come.
Fair nature's eye, rise, rise again and make
Perpetual day, or let this hour be but
A year, a month, a week, a natural day,
That Faustus may repent and save his soul.
O lente, lente currite noctis equi:
The stars move still, time runs, the clock will strike,
The devil will come, and Faustus must be damn'd.
O I'll leap up to my God: who pulls me down?
See see where Christ's blood streams in the firmament.
One drop would save my soul, half a drop, ah my
Christ. *Ib.* l. 1420

8 Mountains and hills, come, come and fall on me,
And hide me from the heavy wrath of God.
        Ib. l. 1438

9 You stars that reigned at my nativity,
Whose influence hath allotted death and hell,
Now draw up Faustus like a foggy mist,
Into the entrails of yon labouring cloud,
That when you vomit forth into the air,
My limbs may issue from your smoky mouths,
So that my soul may but ascend to heaven.
        Ib. l. 1443

10 Ah, Pythagoras' metempsychosis. *Ib.* l. 1461

11 O soul, be changed into little water drops,
And fall into the ocean, ne'er be found:
My God, my God, look not so fierce on me.
        Ib. l. 1472

12 Cut is the branch that might have grown full straight,
And burnèd is Apollo's laurel bough,
That sometime grew within this learned man.
        Faustus, l. 1478

13 It lies not in our power to love, or hate,
For will in us is over-rul'd by fate.
When two are stripped, long ere the course begin,
We wish that one should lose, the other win;
And one especially do we affect
Of two gold ingots, like in each respect.
The reason no man knows; let it suffice,
What we behold is censured by our eyes.
Where both deliberate, the love is slight;
Who ever loved that loved not at first sight?
   Hero and Leander. First Sestiad, l. 167

14 I count religion but a childish toy,
And hold there is no sin but ignorance.
      The Jew of Malta, l. 14

15 And as their wealth increases, so enclose
Infinite riches in a little room. *Ib.* l. 71

16 As for myself, I walk abroad o' nights
And kill sick people groaning under walls:
Sometimes I go about and poison wells. *Ib.* l. 939

17 Come live with me, and be my love,
And we will all the pleasures prove,
That valleys, groves, hills and fields,
Woods or steepy mountain yields.
   The Passionate Shepherd to his Love

18 By shallow rivers, to whose falls
Melodious birds sing madrigals. *Ib.*

19 And I will make thee beds of roses
And a thousand fragrant posies. *Ib.*

20 Jigging veins of rhyming mother wits.
   Conquests of Tamburlaine, prologue

21 Zenocrate, lovelier than the Love of Jove,
Brighter than is the silver Rhodope,
Fairer than whitest snow on Scythian hills.
      Ib. pt. 1, l. 283

22 Our swords shall play the orators for us. *Ib.* l. 328

23 With Nature's pride, and richest furniture,
His looks do menace heaven and dare the Gods.
      Ib. l. 351

24 His deep affections make him passionate. *Ib.* l. 359

25 These are the men that all the world admires.
      Ib. l. 418

26 Accurst be he that first invented war. *Ib.* l. 664

27 Is it not passing brave to be a King,
And ride in triumph through Persepolis? *Ib.* l. 758

28 Nature that fram'd us of four elements,
Warring within our breasts for regiment,
Doth teach us all to have aspiring minds:
Our souls, whose faculties can comprehend
The wondrous Architecture of the world:
And measure every wand'ring planet's course,
Still climbing after knowledge infinite,
And always moving as the restless Spheres,
Will us to wear ourselves and never rest,
Until we reach the ripest fruit of all,
That perfect bliss and sole felicity,
The sweet fruition of an earthly crown. *Ib.* l. 869

29 Virtue is the fount whence honour springs. *Ib.* l. 1769

[330]

1 Ah fair Zenocrate, divine Zenocrate,
Fair is too foul an epithet for thee.
Conquests of Tamburlaine, pt. I, l. 1916

2 What is beauty saith my sufferings then?
If all the pens that ever poets held,
Had fed the feeling of their masters' thoughts,
And every sweetness that inspir'd their hearts,
Their minds, and muses on admired themes:
If all the heavenly quintessence they still
From their immortal flowers of Poesy,
Wherein as in a mirror we perceive
The highest reaches of a human wit.
If these had made one poem's period
And all combin'd in beauty's worthiness,
Yet should there hover in their restless heads,
One thought, one grace, one wonder at the least,
Which into words no virtue can digest.
But how unseemly is it for my sex,
My discipline of arms and chivalry,
My nature and the terror of my name,
To harbour thoughts effeminate and faint!
Save only that in Beauty's just applause,
With whose instinct the soul of man is touched;
And every warrior that is rapt with love
Of fame, of valour, and of victory,
Must needs have beauty beat on his conceits:
I thus conceiving and subduing both,
That which hath stoopt the tempest of the Gods,
Even from the fiery-spangled veil of heaven,
To feel the lovely warmth of shepherds' flames
And march in cottages of strowed weeds,
Shall give the world to note, for all my birth,
That Virtue solely is the sum of glory,
And fashions men with true nobility. *Ib.* l. 1941

3 Now walk the angels on the walls of heaven,
As sentinels to warn th' immortal souls,
To entertain divine Zenocrate. *Ib.* pt. II, l. 2983

4 Yet let me kiss my Lord before I die,
And let me die with kissing of my Lord. *Ib.* l. 3037

5 Helen, whose beauty summoned Greece to arms,
And drew a thousand ships to Tenedos. *Ib.* l. 3055

6 More childish valourous than manly wise. *Ib.* l. 3690

7 Holla, ye pampered Jades of Asia:
What, can ye draw but twenty miles a day?
Ib. l. 3980

8 Tamburlaine, the Scourge of God, must die.
Ib. l. 4641

9 I'm arm'd with more than complete steel—
The justice of my quarrel.
Lust's Dominion, IV. iii. (*Play probably not by Marlowe. See 7:7*)

SHACKERLEY MARMION
1603–1639

10 Familiarity begets boldness. *The Antiquary*, Act I

11 Great joys, like griefs, are silent.
Holland's Leaguer, v. 1

DONALD ROBERT PERRY MARQUIS
1878–1937

12 toujours gai, archy, toujours gai.
archy's life of mehitabel, i. *the life of mehitabel the cat*

13 the great open spaces
where cats are cats.
archy's life of mehitabel, xiv. *mehitabel has an adventure*

FREDERICK MARRYAT
1792–1848

14 There's no getting blood out of a turnip.
Japhet in Search of a Father, ch. 4

15 If you please, ma'am, it was a very little one. [The nurse excusing her illegitimate baby.]
Midshipman Easy, ch. 3

16 All zeal . . . all zeal, Mr. Easy. *Ib.* ch. 9

17 As savage as a bear with a sore head.
The King's Own, ch. 26

18 I never knows the children. It's just six of one and half-a-dozen of the other. *The Pirate*, ch. 4

19 I think it much better that . . . every man paddle his own canoe. *Settlers in Canada*, ch. 8

20 I haven't the gift of the gab, my sons—because I'm bred to the sea. *The Old Navy*, st. 1

JOHN MARSTON
1575 ?–1634

21 Who winks and shuts his apprehension up.
Antonio's Revenge, prologue

MARTIAL
b. A.D. 43

22 Non est, crede mihi, sapientis dicere 'Vivam':
Sera nimis vita est crastina: vive hodie.
It sorts not, believe me, with wisdom to say 'I shall live'. Too late is to-morrow's life; live thou to-day. *Epigrammata*, I. xv. Trans. by Ker

23 Sunt bona, sunt quaedam mediocria, sunt mala plura
Quae legis hic: aliter non fit, Avite, liber.
There are good things, there are some indifferent, there are more things bad that you read here. Not otherwise, Avitus, is a book produced.
Ib. xvi

24 Non amo te, Sabidi, nec possum dicere quare:
Hoc tantum possum dicere, non amo te.
I do not love you, Sabidius, and I can't say why. This only I can say, I do not love you. *Ib.* xxxii

25 Laudant illa sed ista legunt.
Those they praise, but they read the others.
Ib. IV. xlix

26 Bonosque
Soles effugere atque abire sentit,
Qui nobis pereunt et imputantur.
And he feels the good days are flitting and passing away, our days that perish and are scored to our account. *Ib.* V. xx

27 Non est vivere, sed valere vita est.
Life is not living, but living in health. *Ib.* VI. lxx

28 Rus in urbe.
The country in town. *Ib.* XII. lvii

ANDREW MARVELL
1621–1678

1 Where the remote Bermudas ride
In th' ocean's bosom unespied. *Bermudas*

2   Orange bright,
Like golden lamps in a green night. *Ib.*

3 And makes the hollow seas, that roar,
Proclaim the ambergris on shore.
He cast (of which we rather boast)
The Gospel's pearls upon our coast. *Ib.*

4 Echo beyond the Mexique Bay. *Ib.*

5 My love is of a birth as rare
As 'tis for object strange and high:
It was begotten by despair
Upon impossibility.

Magnanimous Despair alone
Could show me so divine a thing,
Where feeble Hope could ne'er have flown
But vainly flapt its tinsel wing. *Definition of Love*

6 As lines so loves oblique may well
Themselves in every angle greet
But ours so truly parallel,
Though infinite can never meet.

Therefore the love which us doth bind,
But Fate so enviously debars,
Is the conjunction of the mind,
And opposition of the stars. *Ib.*

7 Earth cannot shew so brave a sight
As when a single soul does fence
The batteries of alluring sense,
And Heaven views it with delight.
Dialogue between the Resolved Soul and Created Pleasure

8 All this fair, and soft, and sweet,
Which scatteringly doth shine,
Shall within one Beauty meet,
And she be only thine. *Ib.*

9 And want new worlds to buy. *Ib.*

10 Not full sails hasting loaden home,
Nor the chaste lady's pregnant womb,
Nor Cynthia teeming shows so fair,
As two eyes swoln with weeping are. *Eyes and Tears*

11 Thus let your streams o'erflow your springs,
Till eyes and tears be the same things:
And each the other's difference bears;
These weeping eyes, those seeing tears. *Ib.*

12 Choosing each stone, and poising every weight,
Trying the measures of the breadth and height;
Here pulling down, and there erecting new,
Founding a firm state by proportions true.
The First Anniversary of the Government under Oliver Cromwell, l. 245

13 How vainly men themselves amaze
To win the palm, the oak, or bays;
And their uncessant labours see
Crown'd from some single herb or tree,
Whose short and narrow vergèd shade
Does prudently their toils upbraid;
While all flowers and all trees do close
To weave the garlands of repose. *The Garden*

14 Fair quiet, have I found thee here,
And Innocence thy Sister dear! *Ib.*

15 Society is all but rude,
To this delicious solitude. *The Garden*

16 The Gods, that mortal beauty chase,
Still in a tree did end their race.
Apollo hunted Daphne so,
Only that she might laurel grow.
And Pan did after Syrinx speed,
Not as a nymph, but for a reed. *Ib.*

17 What wond'rous life is this I lead!
Ripe apples drop about my head;
The luscious clusters of the vine
Upon my mouth do crush their wine;
The nectarine and curious peach,
Into my hands themselves do reach;
Stumbling on melons, as I pass,
Insnar'd with flow'rs, I fall on grass. *Ib.*

18 Meanwhile the mind, from pleasure less,
Withdraws into its happiness. *Ib.*

19 Annihilating all that's made
To a green thought in a green shade. *Ib.*

20 Here at the fountain's sliding foot,
Or at some fruit-tree's mossy root,
Casting the body's vest aside,
My soul into the boughs does glide:
There like a bird it sits, and sings,
Then whets, and combs its silver wings;
And, till prepar'd for longer flight,
Waves in its plumes the various light. *Ib.*

21 Such was that happy garden-state,
While man there walk'd without a mate. *Ib.*

22 But 'twas beyond a mortal's share
To wander solitary there:
Two Paradises 'twere in one
To live in Paradise alone. *Ib.*

23 Of a tall stature and of sable hue,
Much like the son of Kish that lofty Jew,
Twelve years complete he suffer'd in exile
And kept his father's asses all the while.
An Historical Poem

24 [*Charles I*]
He nothing common did or mean
Upon that memorable scene:
    But with his keener eye
    The axe's edge did try.
Horatian Ode upon Cromwell's Return from Ireland, l. 57

25 But bowed his comely head,
Down as upon a bed. *Ib.*

26 And now the Irish are ashamed
To see themselves in one year tamed:
    So much one man can do
    That does both act and know. *Ib. l. 75*

27 Ye living lamps, by whose dear light
The nightingale does sit so late,
And studying all the summer night,
Her matchless songs does meditate.
The Mower to the Glow-worms

28 The wanton troopers riding by
Have shot my fawn and it will die.
Nymph Complaining for the Death of her Fawn

29 Thy love was far more better than
The love of false and cruel men. *Ib.*

1 It is a wond'rous thing, how fleet
'Twas on those little silver feet.
With what a pretty skipping grace,
It oft would challenge me the race:
And when 't had left me far away,
'Twould stay, and run again, and stay.
For it was nimbler much than hinds;
And trod, as on the four winds.
Nymph Complaining for the Death of her Fawn

2 I have a garden of my own,
But so with roses overgrown,
And lilies, that you would it guess
To be a little wilderness.   *Ib.*

3 Had it liv'd long, it would have been
Lilies without, roses within.   *Ib.*

4 The Picture of little T.C. in a Prospect of Flowers.
Title of Poem

5 Who can foretell for what high cause
This darling of the Gods was born?
The Picture of Little T.C.

6 For though the whole world cannot shew such
another,
Yet we'd better by far have him than his brother.
Statue in Stocks-Market

7 He is Translation's thief that addeth more,
As much as he that taketh from the store
Of the first author.   *To Dr. Witty*

8 Had we but world enough, and time,
This coyness, Lady, were no crime.
We would sit down, and think which way
To walk, and pass our long love's day.
Thou by the Indian Ganges' side
Shouldst rubies find: I by the tide
Of Humber would complain. I would
Love you ten years before the Flood:
And you should if you please refuse
Till the conversion of the Jews.
My vegetable love should grow
Vaster than empires, and more slow.
To His Coy Mistress

9 But at my back I always hear
Time's wingèd chariot hurrying near.
And yonder all before us lie
Deserts of vast eternity.
Thy beauty shall no more be found;
Nor, in thy marble vault, shall sound
My echoing song: then worms shall try
That long preserved virginity:
And your quaint honour turn to dust;
And into ashes all my lust.
The grave's a fine and private place,
But none I think do there embrace.   *Ib.*

10 Thrice happy he who, not mistook,
Hath read in Nature's mystic book.
Upon Appleton House. To My Lord Fairfax,
lxxiii

KARL MARX
1818–1883

11 Die Proletarier haben nichts in ihr zu verlieren als
ihre Ketten. Sie haben eine Welt zu gewinnen.
Proletarier aller Lander, vereinigt euch!

The workers have nothing to lose in this [revo-
lution] but their chains. They have a world to gain.
Workers of the world, unite!
The Communist Manifesto (1848), last words

12 Jeder nach seinen Fähigkeiten, jedem nach seinen
Bedürfnissen.

From each according to his abilities, to each accord-
ing to his needs.
Criticism of the Gotha programme, 1875.
(*See* 29:14)

13 Die Religion . . . ist das Opium des Volkes.
Religion . . . is the opium of the people.
Kritik der Hegelschen Rechtsphilosophie, Intro-
duction

14 The dictatorship of the proletariat.
'*Used more than once*', *according to Mr. and Mrs.
Sidney Webb*

MARY TUDOR
1516–1558

15 When I am dead and opened, you shall find 'Calais'
lying in my heart.   Holinshed, *Chron.* iii. 1160

THEOPHILE JULIUS HENRY MARZIALS
1850–1920

16 Ahoy! and Oho, and it's who's for the ferry?
(The briar's in bud and the sun going down:)
And I'll row ye so quick and I'll row ye so steady,
And 'tis but a penny to Twickenham Town.
Twickenham Ferry

JOHN MASEFIELD
1878–1967

17 Over the grasses of the ancient way
Rutted this morning by the passing guns.
August 1914

18 Coming in solemn beauty like slow old tunes of Spain.
Beauty

19 But the loveliest things of beauty God ever has
showed to me,
Are her voice, and her hair, and eyes, and the dear red
curve of her lips.   *Ib.*

20 Quinquireme of Nineveh from distant Ophir
Rowing home to haven in sunny Palestine,
With a cargo of ivory,
And apes and peacocks,
Sandalwood, cedarwood, and sweet white wine.
Cargoes

21 Dirty British coaster with a salt-caked smoke stack,
Butting through the Channel in the mad March days,
With a cargo of Tyne coal,
Road-rail, pig-lead,
Firewood, iron-ware, and cheap tin trays.   *Ib.*

22 Oh some are fond of Spanish wine, and some are fond
of French,
And some'll swallow tay and stuff fit only for a wench.
Captain Stratton's Fancy

23 And fifteen arms went round her waist.
(And then men ask, Are Barmaids chaste?)
The Everlasting Mercy

24 To get the whole world out of bed
And washed, and dressed, and warmed, and fed,
To work, and back to bed again,
Believe me, Saul, costs worlds of pain.   *Ib.*

1 And he who gives a child a treat
Makes joy-bells ring in Heaven's street,
And he who gives a child a home
Builds palaces in Kingdom come,
And she who gives a baby birth
Brings Saviour Christ again to Earth.
The Everlasting Mercy

2 O Christ, the plough, O Christ, the laughter
Of holy white birds flying after. *Ib.*

3 The corn that makes the holy bread
By which the soul of man is fed,
The holy bread, the food unpriced,
Thy everlasting mercy, Christ. *Ib.*

4 Death opens unknown doors. It is most grand to die.
Pompey the Great. i. *The Chief Centurions*. 'Man is a sacred city'

5 He passed the spring where the rushes spread,
And there in the stones was his earth ahead.
One last short burst upon failing feet—
There life lay waiting, so sweet, so sweet,
Rest in a darkness, balm for aches.
. . . .
The earth was stopped. It was barred with stakes.
Reynard the Fox

6 Then the moon came quiet and flooded full
Light and beauty on clouds like wool,
On a feasted fox at rest from hunting,
In the beech-wood grey where the brocks were grunting.
The beech-wood grey rose dim in the night
With moonlight fallen in pools of light,
The long dead leaves on the ground were rimed;
A clock struck twelve and the church-bells chimed.
Ib.

7 The house is falling,
The beaten men come into their own.
The Rider at the Gate

8 One road leads to London,
One road runs to Wales,
My road leads me seawards
To the white dipping sails. *Roadways*

9 My road calls me, lures me
West, east, south, and north;
Most roads lead men homewards,
My road leads me forth. *Ib.*

10 I must down to the seas again, to the lonely sea and the sky,
And all I ask is a tall ship and a star to steer her by,
And the wheel's kick and the wind's song and the white sail's shaking,
And a grey mist on the sea's face and a grey dawn breaking. *Sea Fever*

11 I must down to the seas again, for the call of the running tide
Is a wild call and a clear call that may not be denied.
Ib.

12 I must down to the seas again, to the vagrant gypsy life,
To the gull's way and the whale's way where the wind's like a whetted knife;
And all I ask is a merry yarn from a laughing fellow-rover,
And quiet sleep and a sweet dream when the long trick's over.
Ib.

13 Friends and loves we have none, nor wealth nor blessed abode,
But the hope of the City of God at the other end of the road. *The Seekers*

14 It is good to be out on the road, and going one knows not where. *Tewkesbury Road*

15 It's a warm wind, the west wind, full of birds' cries;
I never hear the west wind but tears are in my eyes.
For it comes from the west lands, the old brown hills,
And April's in the west wind, and daffodils.
The West Wind

JACKSON MASON
1833–1889

16 Rise up, My love, My fair one,
Arise and come away.
For lo, 'tis past, the winter,
The winter of thy year;
The rain is past and over,
The flowers on earth appear.
And now the time of singing
Is come for every bird;
And over all the country
The turtle dove is heard.
Suppl. Hymns to Hymns A. and M., 1889.
O Voice of the Beloved

PHILIP MASSINGER
1583–1640

17 Ambition, in a private man a vice,
Is, in a prince, the virtue. *The Bashful Lover*, I. ii

18 He that would govern others, first should be
The master of himself. *The Bondman*, I. iii

19 Be wise;
Soar not too high to fall; but stoop to rise.
Duke of Milan, I. ii

20 Greatness, with private men
Esteem'd a blessing, is to me a curse;
And we, whom, for our high births, they conclude
The only freemen, are the only slaves.
Happy the golden mean! *Great Duke of Florence*, I. i

21 I am driven
Into a desperate strait and cannot steer
A middle course. *Ib.* III. i

22 A New Way to Pay Old Debts. *Title of Play*

23 The devil turned precisian!
A New Way to Pay Old Debts, I. i

24 I write *nil ultra* to my proudest hopes. *Ib.* IV. i

25 Patience, the beggar's virtue. *Ib.* V. i

26 Some undone widow sits upon my arm,
And takes away the use of 't; and my sword,
Glued to my scabbard with wrong'd orphans' tears,
Will not be drawn. *Ib.*

27 View yourselves
In the deceiving mirror of self-love.
Parliament of Love, I. v

28 What pity 'tis, one that can speak so well,
Should in his actions be so ill! *Ib.* III. iii

1   All words,
And no performance!   *Parliament of Love*, IV. ii

2 There are a thousand doors to let out life.   *Ib.*

3   Serves and fears
The fury of the many-headed monster,
The giddy multitude.
                  The Unnatural Combat, III. ii

CHARLES ROBERT MATURIN
1782–1824

4 'Tis well to be merry and wise,
'Tis well to be honest and true;
'Tis well to be off with the old love,
Before you are on with the new.   *Bertram. Motto*

SOMERSET MAUGHAM
1874–190?

5 People ask you for criticism, but they only want praise.
                  Of Human Bondage, ch. 50

FREDERICK DENISON MAURICE
1805–1872

6 I knew . . . that I was in danger of attaching myself to a party which should inscribe 'No Party' on its flag. Many had fallen into that snare.
    Life . . . chiefly told in his own Letters, ed. F. Maurice, 2nd edn. (1884), i. 239

7 Subscription no Bondage.
    Title of pamphlet (1835) against abolishing subscription to the Thirty-nine Articles.

GEORGE LOUIS PALMELLA BUSSON DU MAURIER
1834–1896

8 Life ain't all beer and skittles, and more's the pity; but what's the odds, so long as you're happy?
                  Trilby, pt. 1

9 The salad, for which, like everybody else I ever met, he had a special receipt of his own.   *Ib.*

10 A little work, a little play
To keep us going—and so, good-day!

A little warmth, a little light
Of love's bestowing—and so, good-night!

A little fun, to match the sorrow
Of each day's growing—and so, good-morrow!

A little trust that when we die
We reap our sowing! and so—good-bye!   *Ib.* (end)

TERENTIANUS MAURUS
fl. c. A.D. 200

11 Pro captu lectoris habent sua fata libelli.
    The fate of books depends on the capacity of the reader.   *De Literis, Syllabis, &c.,* l. 1286

HUGHES MEARNS
1875–?

12 As I was going up the stair
I met a man who wasn't there.
He wasn't there again to-day.
I wish, I wish he'd stay away.
                  The Psychoed (Antigonish)

WILLIAM LAMB, VISCOUNT MELBOURNE
1779–1848

13 I wish I was as cocksure of anything as Tom Macaulay is of everything.
    Earl Cowper's *Preface to Lord Melbourne's Papers*, 1889, p. xii

14 [Catholic Emancipation] What all the wise men promised has not happened, and what all the d—d fools said would happen has come to pass.
          H. Dunckley, *Lord Melbourne* (1890)

15 I like the Garter; there is no damned merit in it.
                  On the Order of the Garter

16 Things have come to a pretty pass when religion is allowed to invade the sphere of private life.
    Remark on hearing an Evangelical Sermon. G. W. E. Russell's Collections and Recollections, ch. 6

17 [At a Cabinet meeting]
Now, is it to lower the price of corn, or isn't it? It is not much matter which we say, but mind, we must all say *the same.*
    Attrib. (see Bagehot's *English Constitution,* ch. 1)

18 Damn it all, another Bishop dead,—I verily believe they die to vex me.   *Attrib.*

19 The worst of the present day [1835] is that men hate one another so damnably. For my part I love them all.   *Attrib.*

20 I don't know, Ma'am, why they make all this fuss about education; none of the Pagets can read or write, and they get on well enough. [To the Queen.]
                       Attrib.

21 While I cannot be regarded as a pillar, I must be regarded as a buttress of the church, because I support it from the outside.   *Attrib.*

THOMAS MELLOR
1880–1926

22 I wouldn't leave my little wooden hut for you!
I've got one lover and I don't want two.
    I Wouldn't Leave My Little Wooden Hut for You

GEORGE MEREDITH
1828–1909

23 With patient inattention hear him prate.
                    Bellerophon, iv

24 Sword of Common Sense!
Our surest gift.   *To the Comic Spirit*

25   And we go,
And we drop like the fruits of the tree,
          Even we,
          Even so.   *Dirge in Woods*

26 Keep the young generations in hail,
And bequeath them no tumbled house!
                    The Empty Purse

27 The Man of England circled by the sands.
           Epitaph on Gordon of Khartoum

28 Shall man into the mystery of breath
From his quick beating pulse a pathway spy?
Or learn the secret of the shrouded death,
By lifting up the lid of a white eye?
Cleave thou thy way with fathering desire
Of fire to reach to fire.   *Hymn to Colour,* ▼

1 Not forfeiting the beast with which they are crossed,
To stature of the gods they will attain.
Hymn to Colour, xiv

2 The song had ceased; my vision with the song.
Ib. xv

3   Death met I too,
And saw the dawn glow through. *Ib.*

4 Bring the army of the faithful through.
To J[ohn] M[orley]

5 I've studied men from my topsy-turvy
  Close, and, I reckon, rather true.
Some are fine fellows: some, right scurvy:
  Most, a dash between the two. *Juggling Jerry*, vii

6 I'm the bird dead-struck! *Ib.* xiii

7 Under yonder beech-tree single on the greensward,
Couched with her arms behind her golden head,
Knees and tresses folded to slip and ripple idly,
Lies my young love sleeping in the shade.
Love in the Valley, i

8 She whom I love is hard to catch and conquer,
Hard, but O the glory of the winning were she won!
Ib. ii

9 Lovely are the curves of the white owl sweeping
Wavy in the dusk lit by one large star.
Lone on the fir-branch, his rattle-note unvaried,
Brooding o'er the gloom, spins the brown eve-jar.
Darker grows the valley, more and more forgetting:
So were it with me if forgetting could be willed.
Tell the grassy hollow that holds the bubbling well-
  spring,
Tell it to forget the source that keeps it filled. *Ib.* v

10 Fain would fling the net, and fain have her free. *Ib.* vi

11 Pure from the night, and splendid for the day. *Ib.* ix

12 In arrowy rain. *Ib.* xii

13 Quaintest, richest carol of all the singing throats!
[Blackbird.] *Ib.* xvii

14 Straight rains and tiger sky. *Ib.* xix

15 Gossips count her faults; they scour a narrow
  chamber
Where there is no window, read not heaven or her.
Ib. xxii

16 Our souls were in our names. *Ib.* xxiii

17 On a starred night Prince Lucifer uprose.
Tired of his dark dominion swung the fiend . . .
He reached a middle height, and at the stars,
Which are the brain of heaven, he looked, and sank.
Around the ancient track marched, rank on rank,
The army of unalterable law. *Lucifer in Starlight*

18 Each wishing for the sword that severs all.
Modern Love, i

19 He fainted on his vengefulness, and strove
To ape the magnanimity of love, *Ib.* ii

20 Not till the fire is dying in the grate,
Look we for any kinship with the stars. *Ib.* iv

21 With hindward feather, and with forward toe
Her much-adored delightful Fairy Prince! *Ib.* x

22 And if I drink oblivion of a day,
So shorten I the stature of my soul. *Ib.* xii

23 'I play for Seasons; not Eternities!'
Says Nature. *Ib.* xiii

24 It is in truth a most contagious game:
HIDING THE SKELETON, shall be its name. *Ib.* xvii

25 They have the secret of the bull and lamb.
'Tis true that when we trace its source, 'tis beer.
Modern Love, xvii

26   We'll sit contentedly
And eat our pot of honey on the grave. *Ib.* xxi

27   That rarest gift
To Beauty, Common Sense. *Ib.* xxxi

28 O have a care of natures that are mute! *Ib.* xxx

29 God, what a dancing spectre seems the moon.
Ib. xxxi

30   In tragic life, God wot,
No villain need be! Passions spin the plot:
We are betrayed by what is false within. *Ib.* xlii

31 We saw the swallows gathering in the sky. *Ib.* xlvi

32 The pilgrims of the year waxed very loud
In multitudinous chatterings. *Ib.*

33 Their sense is with their senses all mixed in,
Destroyed by subtleties these women are! *Ib.* xlvii

34 More brain, O Lord, more brain! *Ib.*

35 Thus piteously Love closed what he begat:
The union of this ever diverse pair!
These two were rapid falcons in a snare,
Condemned to do the flitting of a bat. *Ib.*

36 Ah, what a dusty answer gets the soul
When hot for certainties in this our life! *Ib.*

37 God! of whom music
And song and blood are pure,
The day is never darkened
That had thee here obscure. *Phoebus with Admetus*

38 You with shelly horns, rams! and, promontory goats,
You whose browsing beards dip in coldest dew!
Bulls, that walk the pastures in kingly-flashing coats,
Laurel, ivy, vine, wreathed for feasts not few! *Ib.*

39 Narrows the world to my neighbour's gate.
Seed Time

40 Through the sermon's dull defile.
The Sage Enamoured,

41 Into the breast that gives the rose,
Shall I with shuddering fall?
The Spirit of Earth in Autumn

42   Broad as ten thousand beeves
At pasture! *The Spirit of Shakespeare,*

43 As the birds do, so do we,
Bill our mate, and choose our tree.
The Three Singers to Young Blood,

44   Lowly, with a broken neck,
The crocus lays her cheek to mire.
The Thrush in February

45 Full lasting is the song, though he,
The singer, passes: lasting too,
For souls not lent in usury,
The rapture of the forward view. *Ib.*

46 We spend our lives in learning pilotage,
And grow good steersmen when the vessel's crank!
The Wisdom of Eld

47 Sweet as Eden is the air,
And Eden-sweet the ray. *Woodland Peace*

48 Enter these enchanted woods,
You who dare. *The Woods of Westermain*

[336]

Love meet they who do not shove
Cravings in the van of Love. *Woods of Westermain*

2 [*On Carlyle's style*]
A style resembling either early architecture or utter dilapidation, so loose and rough it seemed; a wind-in-the-orchard style, that tumbled down here and there an appreciable fruit with uncouth bluster; sentences without commencements running to abrupt endings and smoke, like waves against a sea-wall, learned dictionary words giving a hand to street-slang, and accents falling on them haphazard, like slant rays from driving clouds; all the pages in a breeze, the whole book producing a kind of electrical agitation in the mind and the joints.
Beauchamp's Career, ch. 2

3 Thoughts of heroes were as good as warming-pans.
Ib. ch. 4

4 'Wilt thou?' said the winged minute. *Ib.* ch. 22

5 They that make of his creed a strait jacket for humanity. *Ib.* ch. 29

6 He had by nature a tarnishing eye that cast discolouration. *Diana of the Crossways*, ch. 1

7 Men may have rounded Seraglio Point: they have not yet doubled Cape Turk. *Ib.*

8 Sentimental people, in her phrase, fiddle harmonics on the strings of sensualism. *Ib.*

9 Rose pink and dirty drab will alike have passed away. *Ib.*

10 'Tis Ireland gives England her soldiers, her generals too. *Ib.* ch. 2

11 She did not seduce, she ravished. *Ib.* ch. 7

12 'Hog's my feed,' said Andrew Hedger . . . 'Ah could eat hog a solid hower!' *Ib.* ch. 8

13 She was a lady of incisive features bound in stale parchment. *Ib.* ch. 14

14 Prose can paint evening and moonlight, but poets are needed to sing the dawn. *Ib.* ch. 16

15 'But how divine is utterance!' she said. 'As we to the brutes, poets are to us.' *Ib.*

16 Brittle is foredoomed. *Ib.* ch. 28

17 Between the ascetic rocks and the sensual whirlpools. *Ib.* ch. 37

18 He had his nest of wishes piping to him all the time. *Ib.* ch. 42

19 There is nothing the body suffers the soul may not profit by. *Ib.* ch. 43

20 You see he has a leg. *The Egoist*, ch. 2

21 A Phoebus Apollo turned fasting friar. *Ib.*

22 A dainty rogue in porcelain. *Ib.* ch. 5

23 Cynicism is intellectual dandyism. *Ib.* ch. 7

24 To plod on and still keep the passion fresh. *Ib.* ch. 12

25 In . . . the book of Egoism, it is written, Possession without obligation to the object possessed approaches felicity. *Ib.* ch. 14

26 An aged and a great wine. *Ib.* ch. 20

27 I have but a girl to give! *Ib.*

28 In the middle of the night it rang a little silver bell in my ear. *The Egoist*, ch. 25

29 Are you quite well, Laetitia? *Ib.* ch. 40

30 None of your dam punctilio. *One of Our Conquerors*, ch. 1

31 I expect that Woman will be the last thing civilized by Man. *The Ordeal of Richard Feverel*, ch. 1

32 In action Wisdom goes by majorities. *Ib.*

33 Who rises from prayer a better man, his prayer is answered. *Ib.* ch. 12

34 A youth educated by a system. *Ib.* ch. 15

35 Away with Systems! Away with a corrupt world! Let us breathe the air of the Enchanted island.
Golden lie the meadows; golden run the streams; red gold is on the pine-stems. The sun is coming down to earth, and walks the fields and the waters.
The sun is coming down to earth, and the fields and the waters shout to him golden shouts. *Ib.* ch. 19

36 Kissing don't last: cookery do! *Ib.* ch. 28

37 Speech is the small change of silence. *Ib.* ch. 34

38 Italia, Italia shall be free. *Vittoria*, ch. 21

39 Much benevolence of the passive order may be traced to a disinclination to inflict pain upon oneself. *Ib.* ch. 42

OWEN MEREDITH
[EDWARD ROBERT BULWER, EARL OF LYTTON]
1831–1891

40 There's nothing certain in man's life but this:
That he must lose it. *Clytemnestra*, pt. xx

41 We may live without poetry, music and art;
We may live without conscience, and live without heart;
We may live without friends; we may live without books;
But civilized man cannot live without cooks.
Lucile, pt. 1, c. 2. xix

42 He may live without books,—what is knowledge but grieving?
He may live without hope,—what is hope but deceiving?
He may live without love,—what is passion but pining?
But where is the man that can live without dining? *Ib.* xxiv

43 Genius does what it must, and Talent does what it can.
Poems. Last Words of a Sensitive Second-Rate Poet

DIXON LANIER MERRITT
1879–

44 A wonderful bird is the pelican,
His bill will hold more than his belican.
He can take in his beak
Food enough for a week,
But I'm damned if I see how the helican. *The Pelican*

JEAN MESSELIER

eighteenth century

1 Je voudrais, et ce sera le dernier et le plus ardent de
mes souhaits, je voudrais que le dernier des rois
fût étranglé avec les boyaux du dernier prêtre.

I should like to see, and this will be the last and the
most ardent of my desires, I should like to see
the last king strangled with the guts of the last
priest. *In his Will, 1733, published by Voltaire*

PRINCE METTERNICH

1773–1859

2 Italien ist ein geographischer Begriff.

Italy is a geographical expression.
Letter, 19 Nov. 1849

ALICE MEYNELL

1847–1922

3 Flocks of the memories of the day draw near
The dovecote doors of sleep. *At Night*

4 With this ambiguous earth
His dealings have been told us. These abide:
The signal to a maid, the human birth,
The lesson, and the young Man crucified.
Christ in the Universe

5 I come from nothing; but from where
Come the undying thoughts I bear?
The Modern Poet, or A Song of Derivations

6 I must not think of thee; and, tired yet strong,
I shun the thought that lurks in all delight—
The thought of thee—and in the blue heaven's height,
And in the sweetest passage of a song.
Renouncement (ed. 1923)

7 With the first dream that comes with the first sleep
I run, I run, I am gathered to thy heart. *Ib.*

8 She walks—the lady of my delight—
A shepherdess of sheep. *The Shepherdess*

9 She holds her little thoughts in sight,
Though gay they run and leap.
She is so circumspect and right;
She has her soul to keep. *Ib.*

10 Sudden as sweet
Come the expected feet.
All joy is young, and new all art,
And He too, Whom we have by heart.
Unto us a Son is Given

HUGO MEYNELL

1727–1808

11 The chief advantage of London is, that a man is
always so near his burrow.
Boswell's Johnson (ed. 1934), vol. iii, p. 379,
1 Apr. 1779

12 For anything I see, foreigners are fools.
Ib. vol. iv, p. 15, 1780

WILLIAM JULIUS MICKLE

1735–1788

13 The dews of summer night did fall,
The moon, sweet regent of the sky,
Silver'd the walls of Cumnor Hall,
And many an oak that grew thereby.
Cumnor Hall

THOMAS MIDDLETON

1570?–1627

14 I never heard
Of any true affection, but 'twas nipt
With care. *Blurt, Master-Constable*, III. i. 39

15 By many a happy accident.
No Wit, No Help, Like a Woman's, IV. i. 66

16 Though I be poor, I'm honest. *The Witch*, III. ii

17 There's no hate lost between us. *Ib.* IV. iii. 10

18 Black spirits and white, red spirits and gray,
Mingle, mingle, mingle, you that mingle may!
Ib. V. ii. 60

ALBERT MIDLANE

1825–1909

19 There's a Friend for little children
Above the bright blue sky,
A Friend Who never changes,
Whose love will never die.
Good News for the Little Ones

JOHN STUART MILL

1806–1873

20 Ask yourself whether you are happy, and you cease
to be so. *Autobiography*, ch. 5

21 No great improvements in the lot of mankind are
possible, until a great change takes place in the
fundamental constitution of their modes of thought.
Ib. ch. 7

22 As often as a study is cultivated by narrow minds,
they will draw from it narrow conclusions.
Auguste Comte and Positivism, 1865, p. 82

23 When society requires to be rebuilt, there is no use in
attempting to rebuild it on the old plan.
*Dissertations and Discussions, Essay on Cole-
ridge*, 1859, vol. i, p. 423

24 Unearned increment. *Ib.* vol. iv, p. 299

25 The sole end for which mankind are warranted, individually or collectively, in interfering with the
liberty of action of any of their number, is self-
protection. *Liberty*, introduction

26 If all mankind minus one, were of one opinion, and
only one person were of the contrary opinion, mankind would be no more justified in silencing that
one person, than he, if he had the power, would be
justified in silencing mankind. *Ib.* ch. 2

27 We can never be sure that the opinion we are endeavouring to stifle is a false opinion; and if we
were sure, stifling it would be an evil still. *Ib.*

28 A party of order or stability, and a party of progress
or reform, are both necessary elements of a healthy
state of political life. *Ib.*

29 The liberty of the individual must be thus far limited
he must not make himself a nuisance to other
people. *Ib.* ch. 3

30 All good things which exist are the fruits of originality. *Ib.*

31 Liberty consists in doing what one desires. *Ib.* ch. 5

32 The worth of a State, in the long run, is the worth of
the individuals composing it. *Ib.*

1 A State which dwarfs its men, in order that they may be more docile instruments in its hands even for beneficial purposes—will find that with small men no great thing can really be accomplished.
Liberty, ch. 5

2 When the land is cultivated entirely by the spade and no horses are kept, a cow is kept for every three acres of land.
Political Economy. A Treatise on Flemish Husbandry

3 The great majority of those who speak of perfectibility as a dream, do so because they feel that it is one which would afford them no pleasure if it were realized. *Speech on Perfectibility, 1828*

4 If we may be excused the antithesis, we should say that eloquence is *heard*, poetry is *overheard*.
Thoughts on Poetry and its varieties (1859)

EDNA ST. VINCENT MILLAY
1892–1950

5 Euclid alone has looked on Beauty bare.
The Harp-Weaver, p. IV, sonnet xxii

6 My candle burns at both ends;
It will not last the night;
But oh, my foes, and oh, my friends—
It gives a lovely light. *Poems (1923)*

ALICE DUER MILLER
1874–1942

7 I am American bred,
I have seen much to hate here—much to forgive,
But in a world where England is finished and dead,
I do not wish to live. *The White Cliffs (1940)*

MRS. EMILY MILLER
1833–1913

8 I love to hear the story
Which angel voices tell.
The Little Corporal. I Love to Hear

WILLIAM MILLER
1810–1872

9 Wee Willie Winkie
Rins through the town,
Upstairs and downstairs
In his nicht-gown,
Tirling at the window,
Crying at the lock,
'Are the weans in their bed,
For it's now ten o'clock?' *Willie Winkie*

A. J. MILLS

10 Just like the ivy I'll cling to you. *Title of Song*

REV. HENRY HART MILMAN
1791–1868

11 When our heads are bowed with woe,
When our bitter tears o'erflow.
Hymns. When Our Heads

12 Ride on! ride on in majesty!
In lowly pomp ride on to die. *Ib. Ride On!*

ALAN ALEXANDER MILNE
1882–1956

13 There was once an old sailor my grandfather knew,
Who had so many things which he wanted to do
That, whenever he thought it was time to begin,
He couldn't, because of the state he was in.
Now We are Six, The Old Sailor

14 They're changing guard at Buckingham Palace—
Christopher Robin went down with Alice.
When We Were Very Young. Buckingham Palace

15 James James
Morrison Morrison
Weatherby George Dupree
Took great
Care of his Mother
Though he was only three. *Ib. Disobedience*

16 You must never go down to the end of the town if you don't go down with me. *Ib.*

17 The King asked
The Queen, and
The Queen asked
The Dairymaid:
'Could we have some butter for
The Royal slice of bread?' *Ib. The King's Breakfast*

18 I do like a little bit of butter to my bread! *Ib.*

19 Little Boy kneels at the foot of the bed,
Droops on the little hands, little gold head;
Hush! Hush! Whisper who dares!
Christopher Robin is saying his prayers. *Ib. Vespers*

20 Isn't it funny
How a bear likes honey?
Buzz! Buzz! Buzz!
I wonder why he does? *Winnie-the-Pooh*, ch. 1

21 I am a Bear of Very Little Brain, and long words Bother me. *Ib.* ch. 4

22 Time for a little something. *Ib.* ch. 6

23 'Pathetic', he said. 'That's what it is. Pathetic'. *Ib.*

24 On Monday, when the sun is hot,
I wonder to myself a lot:
'Now is it true, or is it not,
'That what is which and which is what?' *Ib.* ch. 7

ALFRED, LORD MILNER
1854–1925

25 [*The Peers and the Budget*] If we believe a thing to be bad, and if we have a right to prevent it, it is our duty to try to prevent it and to damn the consequences. *Speech at Glasgow, 26 Nov. 1909*

JOHN MILTON
1608–1674

26 Such sweet compulsion doth in music lie.
Arcades, l. 68

27 Before the starry threshold of Jove's Court
My mansion is. *Comus*, l. 1

28 Above the smoke and stir of this dim spot,
Which men call Earth. *Ib.* l. 5

29 Yet some there be that by due steps aspire
To lay their just hands on that golden key
That opes the palace of Eternity. *Ib.* l. 12

1 Rich and various gems inlay
The unadorned bosom of the deep.　*Comus*, l. 22

2 An old, and haughty nation proud in arms. *Ib.* l. 33

3 What never yet was heard in tale or song
From old or modern bard in hall or bower. *Ib.* l. 44

4 And the gilded car of day,
His glowing axle doth allay
In the steep Atlantic stream.　　*Ib.* l. 95

5 What hath night to do with sleep?　*Ib.* l. 122

6 Ere the blabbing eastern scout,
The nice Morn on th' Indian steep
From her cabin'd loop-hole peep.　　*Ib.* l. 138

7 Come, knit hands, and beat the ground,
In a light fantastic round.　　*Ib.* l. 143

8 　　　When the grey-hooded Even
Like a sad votarist in palmer's weed,
Rose from the hindmost wheels of Phœbus' wain.
　　　　　　Ib. l. 188

9 　　　　O thievish Night,
Why shouldst thou, but for some felonious end,
In thy dark lantern thus close up the stars,
That nature hung in heaven, and filled their lamps
With everlasting oil, to give due light
To the misled and lonely traveller?　*Ib.* l. 195

10 Calling shapes and beckoning shadows dire,
And airy tongues that syllable men's names
On sands, and shores, and desert wildernesses.
These thoughts may startle well, but not astound
The virtuous mind, that ever walks attended
By a strong siding champion, Conscience. *Ib.* l. 207

11 O welcome pure-ey'd Faith, white-handed Hope,
Thou hovering angel girt with golden wings.
　　　　　　Ib. l. 213

12 Was I deceived, or did a sable cloud
Turn forth her silver lining on the night? *Ib.* l. 221

13 Sweet Echo, sweetest nymph, that liv'st unseen
Within thy airy shell
By slow Meander's margent green,
And in the violet-embroidered vale.　*Ib.* l. 230

14 Can any mortal mixture of earth's mould
Breathe such divine enchanting ravishment?
　　　　　　Ib. l. 244

15 How sweetly did they float upon the wings
Of silence, through the empty-vaulted night,
At every fall smoothing the raven down
Of darkness till it smiled!　　*Ib.* l. 249

16 Such sober certainty of waking bliss
I never heard till now.　　*Ib.* l. 263

17 　　　Shepherd, I take thy word,
And trust thy honest offer'd courtesy,
Which oft is sooner found in lowly sheds
With smoky rafters, than in tap'stry halls
And courts of princes.　　*Ib.* l. 321

18 With thy long levell'd rule of streaming light.
　　　　　　Ib. l. 340

19 What need a man forestall his date of grief,
And run to meet what he would most avoid?
　　　　　　Ib. l. 362

20 Virtue could see to do what virtue would
By her own radiant light, though sun and moon
Were in the flat sea sunk. And Wisdom's self
Oft seeks to sweet retired solitude,
Where with her best nurse Contemplation
She plumes her feathers, and lets grow her wings
That in the various bustle of resort
Were all to ruffled, and sometimes impair'd.
He that has light within his own clear breast
May sit i' th' centre and enjoy bright day;
But he that hides a dark soul and foul thoughts
Benighted walks under the midday sun.
　　　　　　Comus, l. 373

21 　　　The unsunned heaps
Of miser's treasure.　　*Ib.* l. 398

22 'Tis Chastity, my brother, Chastity:
She that has that, is clad in complete steel. *Ib.* l. 420

23 So dear to Heaven is saintly chastity
That when a soul is found sincerely so
A thousand liveried angels lackey her,
Driving far off each thing of sin and guilt. *Ib.* l. 453

24 How charming is divine philosophy!
Not harsh, and crabbed as dull fools suppose,
But musical as is Apollo's lute,
And a perpetual feast of nectared sweets,
Where no crude surfeit reigns.　　*Ib.* l. 476

25 What the sage poets taught by th' heavenly Muse,
Storied of old in high immortal verse
Of dire chimeras and enchanted isles
And rifted rocks whose entrance leads to Hell,—
For such there be, but unbelief is blind.　*Ib.* l. 515

26 And fill'd the air with barbarous dissonance.
　　　　　　Ib. l. 550

27 A steam of rich distill'd perfumes.　*Ib.* l. 556

28 　　　I was all ear,
And took in strains that might create a soul
Under the ribs of Death.　　*Ib.* l. 560

29 　　　　That power
Which erring men call Chance.　　*Ib.* l. 587

30 Virtue may be assailed, but never hurt,
Surprised by unjust force, but not enthralled.
　　　　　　Ib. l. 589

31 　　　　If this fail,
The pillared firmament is rottenness,
And earth's base built on stubble.　*Ib.* l. 597

32 　　　The dull swain
Treads on it daily with his clouted shoon. *Ib.* l. 634

33 Hast thou betrayed my credulous innocence
With vizor'd falsehood, and base forgery? *Ib.* l. 697

34 　　　None
But such as are good men can give good things,
And that which is not good, is not delicious
To a well-govern'd and wise appetite.　*Ib.* l. 702

35 Budge doctors of the Stoic fur.　*Ib.* l. 707

36 Praising the lean and sallow abstinence.　*Ib.* l. 709

37 Beauty is Nature's coin, must not be hoarded,
But must be current, and the good thereof
Consists in mutual and partaken bliss.　*Ib.* l. 739

38 Beauty is Nature's brag, and must be shown
In courts, at feasts, and high solemnities,
Where most may wonder at the workmanship;
It is for homely features to keep home,
They had their name thence; coarse complexions
And cheeks of sorry grain will serve to ply
The sampler, and to tease the huswife's wool.
What need a vermeil-tinctur'd lip for that,
Love-darting eyes, or tresses like the morn?
　　　　　　Ib. l. 745

1 Obtruding false rules pranked in reason's garb.
Comus, l. 759

2 Through the porch and inlet of each sense
Dropt in ambrosial oils till she reviv'd. *Ib.* l. 839

3 Sabrina fair,
   Listen where thou art sitting
Under the glassy, cool, translucent wave,
   In twisted braids of lilies knitting
The loose train of thy amber-dropping hair.
Ib. l. 859

4 Thus I set my printless feet
O'er the cowslip's velvet head,
That bends not as I tread. *Ib.* l. 897

5 Love virtue, she alone is free,
She can teach ye how to climb
Higher than the sphery chime;
Or, if virtue feeble were,
Heaven itself would stoop to her. *Ib.* l. 1019

6 O fairest flower, no sooner blown but blasted,
Soft silken primrose fading timelessly.
On the Death of a Fair Infant, Dying of a Cough,
l. 1

7 Hence, vain deluding joys,
The brood of Folly without father bred.
Il Penseroso, l. 1

8 Hail divinest Melancholy. *Ib.* l. 12

9 And looks commercing with the skies,
Thy rapt soul sitting in thine eyes:
There held in holy passion still,
Forget thyself to marble. *Ib.* l. 39

10 And join with thee calm Peace, and Quiet,
Spare Fast, that oft with gods doth diet. *Ib.* l. 45

11 And add to these retired Leisure,
That in trim gardens takes his pleasure. *Ib.* l. 49

12 Him that yon soars on golden wing,
Guiding the fiery-wheeled throne,
The Cherub Contemplation. *Ib.* l. 52

13 Sweet bird, that shunn'st the noise of folly,
Most musical, most melancholy! *Ib.* l. 61

14   I walk unseen
On the dry smooth-shaven green,
To behold the wandering moon,
Riding near her highest noon,
Like one that had been led astray
Through the heav'n's wide pathless way;
And oft, as if her head she bow'd,
Stooping through a fleecy cloud. *Ib.* l. 65

15 Oft, on a plat of rising ground,
I hear the far-off curfew sound
Over some wide-watered shore,
Swinging slow with sullen roar. *Ib.* l. 73

16 Where glowing embers through the room
Teach light to counterfeit a gloom,
Far from all resort of mirth,
Save the cricket on the hearth. *Ib.* l. 79

17 Where I may oft outwatch the Bear,
With thrice great Hermes, or unsphere
The spirit of Plato. *Ib.* l. 87

18 Sometime let gorgeous Tragedy
In sceptred pall come sweeping by,
Presenting Thebes, or Pelops' line,
Or the tale of Troy divine. *Ib.* l. 97

19 Or bid the soul of Orpheus sing
Such notes as, warbled to the string,
Drew iron tears down Pluto's cheek.
Il Penseroso, l. 105

20 Or call up him that left half told
The story of Cambuscan bold. *Ib.* l. 109

21 Where more is meant than meets the ear. *Ib.* l. 120

22 While the bee with honied thigh,
That at her flowery work doth sing,
And the waters murmuring
With such consort as they keep,
Entice the dewy-feather'd sleep. *Ib.* l. 142

23 But let my due feet never fail
To walk the studious cloister's pale. *Ib.* l. 155

24 With antique pillars massy proof,
And storied windows richly dight,
Casting a dim religious light.
There let the pealing organ blow,
To the full-voiced quire below,
In service high, and anthems clear
As may, with sweetness, through mine ear,
Dissolve me into ecstasies,
And bring all Heaven before mine eyes. *Ib.* l. 158

25 Till old experience do attain
To something like prophetic strain. *Ib.* l. 173

26 Hence, loathed Melancholy,
Of Cerberus, and blackest Midnight born,
In Stygian cave forlorn,
'Mongst horrid shapes, and shrieks, and sights un-
holy. *L'Allegro*, l. 1

27 So buxom, blithe, and debonair. *Ib.* l. 24

28 Haste thee Nymph, and bring with thee
Jest and youthful jollity,
Quips and cranks, and wanton wiles,
Nods, and becks, and wreathed smiles. *Ib.* l. 25

29 Sport that wrinkled Care derides,
And Laughter holding both his sides.
Come, and trip it as ye go
On the light fantastic toe. *Ib.* l. 31

30 The mountain nymph, sweet Liberty. *Ib.* l. 36

31 Mirth, admit me of thy crew,
To live with her, and live with thee,
In unreproved pleasures free.
To hear the lark begin his flight,
And singing startle the dull night,
From his watch-tower in the skies,
Till the dappled dawn doth rise;
Then to come in spite of sorrow,
And at my window bid good-morrow. *Ib.* l. 38

32 While the cock with lively din
Scatters the rear of darkness thin,
And to the stack, or the barn door,
Stoutly struts his dames before. *Ib.* l. 49

33 Right against the eastern gate,
Where the great Sun begins his state. *Ib.* l. 59

34   The ploughman near at hand,
Whistles o'er the furrowed land,
And the milkmaid singeth blithe,
And the mower whets his scythe,
And every shepherd tells his tale
Under the hawthorn in the dale. *Ib.* l. 63

1 Meadows trim with daisies pied,
Shallow brooks and rivers wide.
Towers, and battlements it sees
Bosom'd high in tufted trees,
Where perhaps some beauty lies,
The cynosure of neighbouring eyes.   *L'Allegro*, l. 75

2 Of herbs, and other country messes,
Which the neat-handed Phyllis dresses.   *Ib.* l. 85

3 To many a youth, and many a maid,
Dancing in the chequered shade.
And young and old come forth to play
On a sunshine holiday.   *Ib.* l. 95

4 Then to the spicy nut-brown ale.   *Ib.* l. 100

5 Towered cities please us then,
And the busy hum of men.   *Ib.* l. 117

6 Store of ladies, whose bright eyes
Rain influence.   *Ib.* l. 121

7 And pomp, and feast, and revelry,
With mask, and antique pageantry,
Such sights as youthful poets dream,
On summer eves by haunted stream.
Then to the well-trod stage anon,
If Jonson's learnèd sock be on,
Or sweetest Shakespeare, Fancy's child,
Warble his native wood-notes wild,
And ever against eating cares,
Lap me in soft Lydian airs,
Married to immortal verse
Such as the meeting soul may pierce
In notes, with many a winding bout
Of linked sweetness long drawn out.   *Ib.* l. 127

8 The melting voice through mazes running;
Untwisting all the chains that tie
The hidden soul of harmony.   *Ib.* l. 142

9 Such strains as would have won the ear
Of Pluto, to have quite set free
His half regain'd Eurydice.   *Ib.* l. 148

10 Yet once more, O ye laurels, and once more
Ye myrtles brown, with ivy never sere,
I come to pluck your berries harsh and crude,
And with forc'd fingers rude,
Shatter your leaves before the mellowing year.
Bitter constraint and sad occasion dear
Compels me to disturb your season due,
For Lycidas is dead, dead ere his prime,
Young Lycidas and hath not left his peer.
Who would not sing for Lycidas? he knew
Himself to sing and build the lofty rhyme.
He must not float upon his watery bier
Unwept, and welter to the parching wind
Without the meed of some melodious tear.
    Lycidas, l. 1

11 Hence with denial vain, and coy excuse,
So may some gentle Muse
With lucky words favour my destin'd urn,
And as he passes turn,
And bid fair peace be to my sable shroud!
For we were nursed upon the self-same hill.
    Ib. l. 18

12 Under the opening eyelids of the morn.   *Ib.* l. 26

13 But, O the heavy change, now thou art gone,
Now thou art gone, and never must return!   *Ib.* l. 37

14 The gadding vine.   *Ib.* l. 40

15 As killing as the canker to the rose.   *Lycidas*, l. 45

16 Flowers that their gay wardrobe wear.   *Ib.* l. 47

17 Where were ye, Nymphs, when the remorseless deep
Closed o'er the head of your loved Lycidas?
    Ib. l. 50

18 Whom universal Nature did lament.   *Ib.* l. 60

19 Down the swift Hebrus to the Lesbian shore.
    Ib. l. 63

20 Alas! what boots it with uncessant care
To tend the homely, slighted, shepherd's trade,
And strictly meditate the thankless Muse?
Were it not better done, as others use,
To sport with Amaryllis in the shade,
Or with the tangles of Neæra's hair.
Fame is the spur that the clear spirit doth raise
(That last infirmity of noble mind)
To scorn delights, and live laborious days;
But the fair guerdon when we hope to find,
And think to burst out into sudden blaze,
Comes the blind Fury with th' abhorred shears
And slits the thin-spun life.   *Ib.* l. 64

21 Touch'd my trembling ears.   *Ib.* l. 77

22 Fame is no plant that grows on mortal soil.   *Ib.* l. 78

23 As he pronounces lastly on each deed,
Of so much fame in Heaven expect thy meed.
    Ib. l. 83

24 That strain I heard was of a higher mood.   *Ib.* l. 87

25 It was that fatal and perfidious bark
Built in th' eclipse, and rigged with curses dark,
That sunk so low that sacred head of thine.
    Ib. l. 100

26 Last came, and last did go,
The Pilot of the Galilean lake,
Two massy keys he bore of metals twain,
The golden opes, the iron shuts amain.   *Ib.* l. 108

27   Such as for their bellies' sake,
Creep and intrude, and climb into the fold.
Of other care they little reckoning make,
Than how to scramble at the shearers' feast,
And shove away the worthy bidden guest.   *Ib.* l. 114

28 Blind mouths! that scarce themselves know how to
hold
A sheep-hook, or have learn'd aught else the least
That to the faithful herdman's art belongs!
    Ib. l. 119

29   Their lean and flashy songs
Grate on their scrannel pipes of wretched straw,
The hungry sheep look up, and are not fed,
But, swoln with wind and the rank mist they draw,
Rot inwardly and foul contagion spread:
Besides what the grim wolf with privy paw
Daily devours apace, and nothing said.
But that two-handed engine at the door
Stands ready to smite once, and smite no more.
    Ib. l. 123

30   Return, Alpheus, the dread voice is past
That shrunk thy streams; return Sicilian Muse.
    Ib. l. 132

31 Throw hither all your quaint enamell'd eyes
That on the green turf suck the honied showers,
And purple all the ground with vernal flowers.
Bring the rathe primrose that forsaken dies,

The tufted crow-toe, and pale jessamine,
The white pink, and the pansy freakt with jet,
The glowing violet,
The musk-rose, and the well-attir'd woodbine,
With cowslips wan that hang the pensive head,
And every flower that sad embroidery wears.
Bid amaranthus all his beauty shed,
And daffadillies fill their cups with tears,
To strew the laureate hearse where Lycid lies.
Lycidas, l. 139

1 So to interpose a little ease,
Let our frail thoughts dally with false surmise.
Ib. l. 152

2 Whether beyond the stormy Hebrides,
Where thou perhaps under the whelming tide
Visit'st the bottom of the monstrous world;
Or whether thou, to our moist vows denied,
Sleepst by the fable of Bellerus old,
Where the great Vision of the guarded mount
Looks toward Namancos and Bayona's hold.
Look homeward, Angel, now, and melt with ruth.
Ib. l. 156

3 For Lycidas your sorrow is not dead,
Sunk though he be beneath the watery floor;
So sinks the day-star in the ocean bed,
And yet anon repairs his drooping head,
And tricks his beams, and with new spangled ore,
Flames in the forehead of the morning sky:
So Lycidas sunk low, but mounted high,
Through the dear might of Him that walked the
waves. *Ib.* l. 166

4 In solemn troops, and sweet societies. *Ib.* l. 179

5 Thus sang the uncouth swain. *Ib.* l. 186

6 He touch'd the tender stops of various quills,
With eager thought warbling his Doric lay.
Ib. l. 188

7 At last he rose, and twitch'd his mantle blue;
To-morrow to fresh woods, and pastures new.
Ib. l. 192

8 The bright morning star, day's harbinger.
On May Morning

9 This is the month, and this the happy morn,
Wherein the Son of Heaven's eternal King,
Of wedded maid, and virgin mother born,
Our great redemption from above did bring;
For so the holy sages once did sing,
That He our deadly forfeit should release,
And with His Father work us a perpetual peace.
Hymn. On the Morning of Christ's Nativity, l. 1

10 The star-led wizards haste with odours sweet!
Ib. l. 23

11   It was the winter wild
    While the Heav'n-born child
All meanly wrapt in the rude manger lies,
    Nature in awe to him
    Had doff't her gawdy trim
With her great Master so to sympathize. *Ib.* l. 29

12   Nor war, nor battle's sound
    Was heard the world around,
The idle spear and shield were high uphung.
Ib. l. 53

13 Birds of calm sit brooding on the charmèd wave.
Ib. l. 68

14 The stars with deep amaze
Stand fixt in stedfast gaze
Bending one way their precious influence
And will not take their flight
For all the morning light,
Or Lucifer that often warned them thence,
But in their glimmering orbs did glow
Until their Lord himself bespake and bid them go.
Hymn. On the Morning of Christ's Nativity, l. 69

15 Perhaps their loves, or else their sheep,
Was all that did their silly thoughts so busy keep.
Ib. l. 91

16   The helmed Cherubim
    And sworded Seraphim,
Are seen in glittering ranks with wings display'd.
Ib. l. 112

17 Ring out ye crystal spheres,
Once bless our human ears
(If ye have power to touch our senses so)
And let your silver chime
Move in melodious time;
And let the base of heav'ns deep organ blow,
And with your ninefold harmony
Make up full consort to th' angelic symphony.
Ib. l. 125

18 Time will run back, and fetch the age of gold.
Ib. l. 135

19 And speckled Vanity
Will sicken soon and die. *Ib.* l. 136

20 Swinges the scaly horror of his folded tail. *Ib.* l. 172

21   The oracles are dumb,
    No voice or hideous hum
Runs through the arched roof in words deceiving.
    Apollo from his shrine
    Can no more divine,
With hollow shriek the steep of Delphos leaving.
No nightly trance or breathèd spell,
Inspires the pale-eyed priest from the prophetic cell.
Ib. l. 173

22   From haunted spring and dale
    Edg'd with poplar pale
The parting genius is with sighing sent. *Ib.* l. 184

23 Peor and Baalim
Forsake their temples dim. *Ib.* l. 197

24   So when the sun in bed,
    Curtain'd with cloudy red,
Pillows his chin upon an orient wave. *Ib.* l. 229

25   But see the Virgin blest,
    Hath laid her Babe to rest,
Time is our tedious song should here have ending,
    Heav'n's youngest teemed star,
    Hath fixt her polisht car,
Her sleeping lord with handmaid lamp attending:
    And all about the courtly stable,
Bright-harnest Angels sit in order serviceable.
Ib. l. 237

26 Rhyme being no necessary adjunct or true ornament
of poem or good verse, in longer works especially,
but the invention of a barbarous age, to set off
wretched matter and lame metre.
The Verse. Preface to *Paradise Lost*, 1668 ed.

27 The troublesome and modern bondage of Rhyming.
Ib.

1 Of Man's first disobedience, and the fruit
Of that forbidden tree, whose mortal taste
Brought death into the world, and all our woe,
With loss of Eden.   *Paradise Lost*, bk. i, l. 1

2   Or if Sion hill
Delight thee more, and Siloa's brook that flow'd
Fast by the oracle of God.   *Ib.* l. 10

3 Things unattempted yet in prose or rhyme. *Ib.* l. 16

4   What in me is dark
Illumine, what is low raise and support;
That to the highth of this great argument
I may assert eternal Providence,
And justify the ways of God to Men.   *Ib.* l. 22

5 For one restraint, lords of the world besides.
      Ib. l. 32

6 The infernal serpent; he it was, whose guile,
Stirr'd up with envy and revenge, deceived
The mother of mankind.   *Ib.* l. 34

7   Him the Almighty Power
Hurled headlong flaming from th' ethereal sky
With hideous ruin and combustion down
To bottomless perdition, there to dwell
In adamantine chains and penal fire
Who durst defy th' Omnipotent to arms. *Ib.* l. 44

8 As far as angels' ken.   *Ib.* l. 59

9 A dungeon horrible, on all sides round
As one great furnace flam'd; yet from those flames
No light, but rather darkness visible
Serv'd only to discover sights of woe,
Regions of sorrow, doleful shades, where peace
And rest can never dwell, hope never comes
That comes to all.   *Ib.* l. 60

10 As far removed from God and light of heav'n
As from the centre thrice to th' utmost pole.
      Ib. l. 73

11   But O how fall'n! how changed
From him who, in the happy realms of light,
Clothed with transcendent brightness didst outshine
Myriads though bright.   *Ib.* l. 84

12 United thoughts and counsels, equal hope,
And hazard in the glorious enterprise.   *Ib.* l. 88

13   Yet not for those
Nor what the potent victor in his rage
Can else inflict do I repent or change,
Though changed in outward lustre; that fixed mind
And high disdain, from sense of injured merit.
      Ib. l. 94

14   What though the field be lost?
All is not lost; th' unconquerable will,
And study of revenge, immortal hate,
And courage never to submit or yield:
And what is else not to be overcome?   *Ib.* l. 105

15 Vaunting aloud, but racked with deep despair.
      Ib. l. 126

16 Fall'n Cherub, to be weak is miserable
Doing or suffering; but of this be sure,
To do ought good never will be our task,
But ever to do ill our sole delight.   *Ib.* l. 157

17 And out of good still to find means of evil. *Ib.* l. 165

18 The seat of desolation, void of light.   *Ib.* l. 181

19 What reinforcement we may gain from hope,
If not what resolution from despair.   *Ib.* l. 190

20   The will
And high permission of all-ruling Heaven
Left him at large to his own dark designs,
That with reiterated crimes he might
Heap on himself damnation.
      Paradise Lost, bk. i, l. 211

21 Is this the region, this the soil, the clime,
Said then the lost Archangel, this the seat
That we must change for Heav'n, this mournful gloom
For that celestial light?   *Ib.* l. 242

22   Farthest from him is best
Whom reason hath equalled, force hath made supreme
Above his equals. Farewell happy fields
Where joy for ever dwells: Hail horrors, hail
Infernal world, and thou profoundest Hell
Receive thy new possessor: one who brings
A mind not to be changed by place or time.
The mind is its own place, and in it self
Can make a Heav'n of Hell, a Hell of Heav'n.
      Ib. l. 247

23 Here we may reign secure, and in my choice
To reign is worth ambition though in hell:
Better to reign in hell, than serve in heav'n.
      Ib. l. 261

24 His spear, to equal which the tallest pine
Hewn on Norwegian hills, to be the mast
Of some great ammiral, were but a wand,
He walk'd with to support uneasy steps
Over the burning marle.   *Ib.* l. 292

25 Thick as autumnal leaves that strow the brooks
In Vallombrosa, where th' Etrurian shades
High over-arch'd imbower.   *Ib.* l. 302

26 Busiris and his Memphian chivalry.   *Ib.* l. 307

27 'Awake, arise, or be for ever fall'n!'
They heard, and were abashed, and up they sprung
Upon the wing, as when men wont to watch
On duty, sleeping found by whom they dread,
Rouse and bestir themselves ere well awake.
      Ib. l. 330

28 First Moloch, horrid king, besmear'd with blood
Of human sacrifice, and parents' tears.   *Ib.* l. 392

29   For spirits when they please
Can either sex assume, or both; so soft
And uncompounded is their essence pure. *Ib.* l. 423

30 Execute their aery purposes.   *Ib.* l. 430

31 Astarte, Queen of Heav'n, with crescent horns.
      Ib. l. 439

32   Thammuz came next behind,
Whose annual wound in Lebanon allur'd
The Syrian damsels to lament his fate
In amorous ditties all a summer's day,
While smooth Adonis from his native rock
Ran purple to the sea.   *Ib.* l. 446

33 A leper once he lost and gain'd a king.   *Ib.* l. 471

34 Jehovah, who in one night when he passed
From Egypt marching.   *Ib.* l. 487

35   And when night
Darkens the streets, then wander forth the sons
Of Belial, flown with insolence and wine. *Ib.* l. 500

36 Shone like a meteor streaming to the wind. *Ib.* l. 537

1 Sonorous metal blowing martial sounds:
At which the universal host upsent
A shout that tore hell's concave, and beyond
Frighted the reign of Chaos and old Night.
                              Paradise Lost, bk. i, l. 540

2   Anon they move
In perfect phalanx to the Dorian mood
Of flutes and soft recorders.   *Ib.* l. 549

3   That small infantry
Warred on by cranes.   *Ib.* l. 575

4   What resounds
In fable or romance of Uther's son
Begirt with British and Armoric knights;
And all who since, baptized or infidel
Jousted in Aspramont or Montalban,
Damasco, or Marocco, or Trebisond,
Or whom Biserta sent from Afric shore
When Charlemain with all his peerage fell
By Fontarabbia.   *Ib.* l. 579

5   He above the rest
In shape and gesture proudly eminent
Stood like a tower; his form had yet not lost
All her original brightness, nor appeared
Less than archangel ruined, and th' excess
Of glory obscur'd.   *Ib.* l. 589

6 The sun . . .
In dim eclipse disastrous twilight sheds
On half the nations, and with fear of change
Perplexes monarchs.   *Ib.* l. 594

7   His face
Deep scars of thunder had intrenched, and care
Sat on his faded cheek, but under brows
Of dauntless courage, and considerate pride
Waiting revenge.   *Ib.* l. 600

8   Who overcomes
By force, hath overcome but half his foe. *Ib.* l. 648

9   Mammon led them on,
Mammon, the least erected Spirit that fell
From heav'n, for ev'n in heav'n his looks and thoughts
Were always downward bent, admiring more
The riches of heaven's pavement, trodden gold,
Than aught divine or holy else enjoy'd
In vision beatific.   *Ib.* l. 678

10   Let none admire
That riches grow in hell; that soil may best
Deserve the precious bane.   *Ib.* l. 690

11 Anon out of the earth a fabric huge
Rose like an exhalation.   *Ib.* l. 710

12   From morn
To noon he fell, from noon to dewy eve,
A summer's day; and with the setting sun
Dropt from the zenith like a falling star. *Ib.* l. 742

13   Fairy elves,
Whose midnight revels, by a forest side
Or fountain some belated peasant sees,
Or dreams he sees, while overhead the moon
Sits arbitress.   *Ib.* l. 781

14 High on a throne of royal state, which far
Outshone the wealth of Ormus and of Ind,
Or where the gorgeous East with richest hand
Showers on her kings barbaric pearl and gold,
Satan exalted sat, by merit raised
To that bad eminence; and from despair
Thus high uplifted beyond hope. *Ib.* bk. ii, l. 1

15 The strongest and the fiercest Spirit
That fought in Heav'n; now fiercer by despair.
His trust was with th' Eternal to be deemed
Equal in strength, and rather than be less
Cared not to be at all.   *Paradise Lost*, bk. ii, l. 44

16 My sentence is for open war: of wiles
More unexpert, I boast not.   *Ib.* l. 51

17   When the scourge
Inexorably, and the torturing hour
Calls us to penance.   *Ib.* l. 90

18 Belial, in act more graceful and humane;
A fairer person lost not Heav'n; he seemed
For dignity compos'd and high exploit:
But all was false and hollow; though his tongue
Dropt manna, and could make the worse appear
The better reason.   *Ib.* l. 109

19   For who would lose,
Though full of pain, this intellectual being,
Those thoughts that wander through eternity,
To perish rather, swallowed up and lost
In the wide womb of uncreated night,
Devoid of sense and motion?   *Ib.* l. 146

20 His red right hand.   *Ib.* l. 174

21 Unrespited, unpitied, unreprieved,
Ages of hopeless end.   *Ib.* l. 185

22 Thus Belial with words clothed in reason's garb
Counselled ignoble ease, and peaceful sloth,
Not peace.   *Ib.* l. 226

23 Our torments also may in length of time
Become our elements.   *Ib.* l. 274

24   With grave
Aspect he rose, and in his rising seem'd
A pillar of state; deep on his front engraven
Deliberation sat and public care;
And princely counsel in his face yet shone,
Majestic though in ruin.   *Ib.* l. 300

25   To sit in darkness here
Hatching vain empires.   *Ib.* l. 377

26 Who shall tempt with wand'ring feet
The dark unbottom'd infinite abyss
And through the palpable obscure find out
His uncouth way.   *Ib.* l. 404

27   Long is the way
And hard, that out of hell leads up to light. *Ib.* l. 432

28 O shame to men! devil with devil damn'd
Firm concord holds, men only disagree
Of creatures rational.   *Ib.* l. 496

29   In discourse more sweet
(For eloquence the soul, song charms the sense,)
Others apart sat on a hill retir'd,
In thoughts more elevate, and reason'd high
Of providence, foreknowledge, will, and fate,
Fix'd fate, free will, foreknowledge absolute,
And found no end, in wand'ring mazes lost.
                                      Ib. l. 555

30 Vain wisdom all, and false philosophy. *Ib.* l. 565

31 A gulf profound as that Serbonian bog
Betwixt Damiata and Mount Casius old,
Where armies whole have sunk: the parching air
Burns frore, and cold performs th' effect of fire.
                                      Ib. l. 592

1
        The bitter change
Of fierce extremes, extremes by change more fierce.
        Paradise Lost, bk. ii, l. 598

2 O'er many a frozen, many a fiery Alp,
Rocks, caves, lakes, fens, bogs, dens, and shades of
   death.   *Ib.* l. 620

3   Worse
Than fables yet have feigned, or fear conceived,
Gorgons and Hydras, and Chimæras dire.   *Ib.* l. 626

4   The other shape,
If shape it might be call'd that shape had none
Distinguishable in member, joint, or limb,
Or substance might be call'd that shadow seem'd,
For each seem'd either; black it stood as night,
Fierce as ten furies, terrible as hell,
And shook a dreadful dart; what seem'd his head
The likeness of a kingly crown had on.   *Ib.* l. 666

5 Whence and what art thou, execrable shape?
                         Ib. l. 681

6 Incens'd with indignation Satan stood
Unterrifi'd, and like a comet burn'd
That fires the length of Ophiucus huge
In th' arctic sky, and from his horrid hair
Shakes pestilence and war.   *Ib.* l. 707

7   Their fatal hands
No second stroke intend.
                         Ib. l. 712

8   I fled, and cry'd out, *Death*;
Hell trembled at the hideous name, and sigh'd
From all her caves, and back resounded, *Death.*
                         Ib. l. 787

9   On a sudden open fly
With impetuous recoil and jarring sound
Th' infernal doors, and on their hinges grate
Harsh thunder.   *Ib.* l. 879

10   A dark
Illimitable ocean without bound,
Without dimension, where length, breadth, and
  highth,
And time and place are lost.   *Ib.* l. 891

11   Chaos umpire sits,
And by decision more embroils the fray
By which he reigns: next him high arbiter
Chance governs all.   *Ib.* l. 907

12   This wild abyss,
The womb of nature and perhaps her grave.
                         Ib. l. 910

13   To compare
Great things with small.   *Ib.* l. 921

14   So eagerly the fiend
O'er bog or steep, through strait, rough, dense, or
  rare.
With head, hands, wings, or feet pursues his way,
And swims or sinks, or wades, or creeps, or flies.
                         Ib. l. 947

15 Sable-vested Night, eldest of things.   *Ib.* l. 962

16 With ruin upon ruin, rout on rout,
Confusion worse confounded.   *Ib.* l. 995

17 So he with difficulty and labour hard
Moved on, with difficulty and labour he. *Ib.* l. 1021

18 Hail, holy light, offspring of Heaven first-born,
Or of th' Eternal co-eternal beam,
May I express thee unblamed? Since God is light,
And never but in unapproached light
Dwelt from eternity.   *Ib.* bk. iii, l. 1

19 So thick a drop serene hath quenched their orbs,
Or dim suffusion veiled. Yet not the more
Cease I to wander where the Muses haunt
Clear spring, or shady grove, or sunny hill.
               Paradise Lost, bk. iii, l. 25

20   Nor sometimes forget
Those other two equall'd with me in fate,
So were I equall'd with them in renown,
Blind Thamyris and blind Mæonides,
And Tiresias and Phineus, prophets old.
Then feed on thoughts, that voluntary move
Harmonious numbers; as the wakeful bird
Sings darkling, and in shadiest covert hid,
Tunes her nocturnal note. Thus with the year
Seasons return, but not to me returns
Day, or the sweet approach of ev'n or morn,
Or sight of vernal bloom, or summer's rose,
Or flocks, or herds, or human face divine;
But cloud instead, and ever-during dark
Surrounds me, from the cheerful ways of men
Cut off, and for the book of knowledge fair
Presented with a universal blank
Of Nature's works to me expung'd and raz'd,
And wisdom at one entrance quite shut out.
So much the rather thou celestial light
Shine inward.   *Ib.* l. 32

21 Freely they stood who stood, and fell who fell.
                         Ib. l. 102

22 Dark with excessive bright.   *Ib.* l. 380

23   Sericana, where Chineses drive
With sails and wind their cany waggons light.
                         Ib. l. 438

24 Embryos and idiots, eremites and friars,
White, black and grey, with all their trumpery.
                         Ib. l. 474

25 Dying put on the weeds of Dominic,
Or in Franciscan think to pass disguised. *Ib.* l. 479

26   Then might ye see
Cowls, hoods, and habits, with their wearers, tost
And fluttered into rags, then relics, beads,
Indulgences, dispenses, pardons, bulls,
The sport of winds.   *Ib.* l. 489

27 Into a Limbo large and broad, since called
The Paradise of Fools, to few unknown. *Ib.* l. 495

28 For neither man nor angel can discern
Hypocrisy, the only evil that walks
Invisible, except to God alone.   *Ib.* l. 682

29   At whose sight all the stars
Hide their diminished heads.   *Ib.* bk. iv, l. 34

30 Warring in Heav'n against Heav'n's matchless King.
                         Ib. l. 41

31 And understood not that a grateful mind
By owing owes not, but still pays, at once
Indebted and discharged.   *Ib.* l. 55

32 Me miserable! which way shall I fly
Infinite wrath, and infinite despair?
Which way I fly is Hell; myself am Hell;
And in the lowest deep a lower deep
Still threatening to devour me opens wide,
To which the Hell I suffer seems a Heaven.
                         Ib. l. 73

33 So farewell hope, and with hope farewell fear,
Farewell remorse: all good to me is lost;
Evil be thou my Good.   *Ib.* l. 108

1
      Off at sea north-east winds blow
Sabæan odours from the spicy shore
Of Araby the blest.   *Paradise Lost*, bk. iv, l. 161

2   Many a league
Cheer'd with the grateful smell old Ocean smiles.
                              Ib. l. 164

3 So clomb this first grand thief into God's fold:
So since into his church lewd hirelings climb.
Thence up he flew, and on the tree of life,
The middle tree and highest there that grew,
Sat like a cormorant.   *Ib.* l. 192

4 A heaven on earth.   *Ib.* l. 208

5 Groves whose rich trees wept odorous gums and balm,
Others whose fruit burnished with golden rind
Hung amiable, Hesperian fables true,
If true, here only.   *Ib.* l. 248

6 Flowers of all hue, and without thorn the rose.
                              Ib. l. 256

7 The mantling vine.   *Ib.* l. 258

8   Not that fair field
Of Enna, where Proserpin gathering flowers
Herself a fairer flower by gloomy Dis
Was gathered.   *Ib.* l. 268

9 Nor where Abassin kings their issue guard,
Mount Amara, though this by some supposed
True paradise.   *Ib.* l. 280

10 Two of far nobler shape erect and tall,
Godlike erect, with native honour clad
In naked majesty seemed lords of all.   *Ib.* l. 288

11 For contemplation he and valour formed;
For softness she and sweet attractive grace,
He for God only, she for God in him:
His fair large front and eye sublime declared
Absolute rule.   *Ib.* l. 297

12   Which implied
Subjection, but required with gentle sway
And by her yielded, by him best received;
Yielded with coy submission, modest pride,
And sweet reluctant amorous delay.   *Ib.* l. 307

13 Adam, the goodliest man of men since born
His sons; the fairest of her daughters Eve.   *Ib.* l. 323

14 The savoury pulp they chew, and in the rind
Still as they thirsted scooped the brimming stream.
                              Ib. l. 335

15 Sporting the lion ramped, and in his paw,
Dandled the kid; bears, tigers, ounces, pards
Gamboll'd before them, th' unwieldy elephant
To make them mirth us'd all his might, and wreathed
His lithe proboscis.   *Ib.* l. 343

16 So spake the Fiend, and with necessity,
The tyrant's plea, excus'd his devilish deeds.
                              Ib. l. 393

17   With eyes
Of conjugal attraction unreprov'd.   *Ib.* l. 492

18 Imparadised in one another's arms.   *Ib.* l. 506

19 Now came still evening on, and twilight gray
Had in her sober livery all things clad;
Silence accompanied, for beast and bird,
They to their grassy couch, these to their nests,
Were slunk, all but the wakeful nightingale;
She all night long her amorous descant sung;
Silence was pleas'd: now glow'd the firmament

With living sapphires: Hesperus that led
The starry host, rode brightest, till the moon,
Rising in clouded majesty, at length
Apparent queen unveil'd her peerless light,
And o'er the dark her silver mantle threw.
                         Paradise Lost, bk. iv, l. 598

20 God is thy law, thou mine: to know no more
Is woman's happiest knowledge and her praise.
                              Ib. l. 637

21 With thee conversing I forget all time.   *Ib.* l. 639

22 Sweet is the breath of morn, her rising sweet,
With charm of earliest birds.   *Ib.* l. 641

23   Sweet the coming on
Of grateful evening mild, then silent night
With this her solemn bird and this fair moon,
And these the gems of Heav'n, her starry train.
                              Ib. l. 646

24 Millions of spiritual creatures walk the earth
Unseen, both when we wake, and when we sleep.
                              Ib. l. 677

25   Into their inmost bower
Handed they went; and eas'd the putting off
These troublesome disguises which we wear,
Strait side by side were laid, nor turned I ween
Adam from his fair spouse, nor Eve the rites
Mysterious of connubial love refus'd:
Whatever hypocrites austerely talk
Of purity and place and innocence,
Defaming as impure what God declares
Pure, and commands to some, leaves free to all.
                              Ib. l. 738

26 Hail wedded love, mysterious law, true source
Of human offspring, sole propriety,
In Paradise of all things common else.   *Ib.* l. 750

27   Sleep on,
Blest pair; and O yet happiest if ye seek
No happier state, and know to know no more.
                              Ib. l. 773

28   Him there they found
Squat like a toad, close at the ear of Eve.   *Ib.* l. 799

29 Him thus intent Ithuriel with his spear
Touched lightly; for no falsehood can endure
Touch of celestial temper, but returns
Of force to its own likeness; up he starts
Discover'd and surpris'd.   *Ib.* l. 810

30 Not to know me argues yourselves unknown.
                              Ib. l. 830

31   Abash'd the Devil stood,
And felt how awful goodness is, and saw
Virtue in her shape how lovely.   *Ib.* l. 846

32   Of regal port,
But faded splendour wan.   *Ib.* l. 869

33 But wherefore thou alone? Wherefore with thee
Came not all hell broke loose?   *Ib.* l. 917

34 Then when I am thy captive talk of chains,
Proud limitary Cherub.   *Ib.* l. 970

35 Like Teneriff or Atlas unremov'd.   *Ib.* l. 987

36   Fled
Murmuring, and with him fled the shades of night.
                              Ib. l. 1014

37   His sleep
Was aery light, from pure digestion bred.
                              Ib. bk. v, l. 3

MILTON

1 My fairest, my espoused, my latest found,
Heaven's last best gift, my ever new delight.
Paradise Lost, bk. v, l. 18

2 Good, the more
Communicated, more abundant grows. *Ib.* l. 71

3 Best image of myself and dearer half. *Ib.* l. 95

4 These are thy glorious works, Parent of Good,
Almighty, thine this universal frame,
Thus wondrous fair; thyself how wondrous then!
Ib. l. 153

5 Him first, him last, him midst, and without end.
Ib. l. 165

6 A wilderness of sweets. *Ib.* l. 294

7 Another morn
Ris'n on mid-noon. *Ib.* l. 310

8 So saying, with despatchful looks in haste
She turns, on hospitable thoughts intent. *Ib.* l. 331

9 From many a berry, and from sweet kernels press'd
She tempers dulcet creams. *Ib.* l. 346

10 Nor jealousy
Was understood, the injured lover's hell. *Ib.* l. 449

11 Son of Heav'n and Earth,
Attend: that thou art happy, owe to God;
That thou continuest such, owe to thyself,
That is, to thy obedience; therein stand. *Ib.* l. 519

12 Freely we serve,
Because we freely love, as in our will
To love or not; in this we stand or fall. *Ib.* l. 538

13 What if earth
Be but the shadow of Heaven, and things therein
Each to other like, more than on earth is thought?
Ib. l. 574

14 Hear all ye Angels, progeny of light,
Thrones, Dominations, Princedoms, Virtues, Powers.
Ib. l. 600

15 All seemed well pleased, all seemed but were not all.
Ib. l. 617

16 And in their motions harmony divine
So smoothes her charming tones, that God's own ear
Listens delighted. *Ib.* l. 625

17 Satan, so call him now, his former name
Is heard no more in heaven. *Ib.* l. 655

18 So spake the Seraph Abdiel, faithful found
Among the faithless, faithful only he:
Among innumerable false, unmoved,
Unshaken, unseduced, unterrified
His loyalty he kept, his love, his zeal. *Ib.* l. 893

19 All night the dreadless angel unpursued
Through Heaven's wide champain held his way till morn,
Waked by the circling hours, with rosy hand
Unbarred the gates of light. *Ib.* bk. vi, l. 1

20 Servant of God, well done, well hast thou fought
The better fight, who singly hast maintained
Against revolted multitudes the cause
Of truth, in word mightier than they in arms.
Ib. l. 29

21 He onward came; far off his coming shone.
Ib. l. 768

22 Headlong themselves they threw
Down from the verge of Heaven, eternal wrath
Burnt after them to the bottomless pit. *Ib.* l. 864

23 Standing on earth, not rapt above the Pole,
More safe I sing with mortal voice, unchang'd
To hoarse or mute, though fall'n on evil days,
On evil days though fall'n, and evil tongues.
In darkness, and with dangers compass'd round,
And solitude; yet not alone, while thou
Visit'st my slumbers nightly, or when morn
Purples the east: still govern thou my song,
Urania, and fit audience find, though few:
But drive far off the barb'rous dissonance
Of Bacchus and his revellers.
Paradise Lost, bk. vii, l. 23

24 The affable Archangel. *Ib.* l. 41

25 Necessity and chance
Approach not me, and what I will is fate. *Ib.* l. 172

26 There Leviathan
Hugest of living creatures, on the deep
Stretch'd like a promontory sleeps or swims,
And seems a moving land, and at his gills
Draws in, and at his trunk spouts out a sea.
Ib. l. 412

27 Now half appear'd
The tawny lion, pawing to get free
His hinder parts. *Ib.* l. 463

28 The Planets in their stations list'ning stood,
While the bright Pomp ascended jubilant.
Open, ye everlasting gates, they sung,
Open, ye heavens, your living doors; let in
The great Creator from his work return'd
Magnificent, his six days' work, a world. *Ib.* l. 563

29 The Angel ended, and in Adam's ear
So charming left his voice that he a while
Thought him still speaking, still stood fixed to hear.
Ib. bk. viii, l. 1

30 He his fabric of the Heavens
Hath left to their disputes, perhaps to move
His laughter at their quaint opinions wide
Hereafter, when they come to model Heaven
And calculate the stars, how they will wield
The mighty frame, how build, unbuild, contrive
To save appearances, how gird the sphere
With centric and eccentric scribbled o'er,
Cycle and epicycle, orb in orb. *Ib.* l. 76

31 Heaven is for thee too high
To know what passes there; be lowly wise:
Think only what concerns thee and thy being.
Ib. l. 172

32 Liquid lapse of murmuring streams. *Ib.* l. 263

33 And feel that I am happier than I know. *Ib.* l. 282

34 In solitude
What happiness? Who can enjoy alone,
Or all enjoying, what contentment find? *Ib.* l. 364

35 I waked
To find her, or for ever to deplore
Her loss, and other pleasures all abjure. *Ib.* l. 478

36 Grace was in all her steps, heaven in her eye,
In every gesture dignity and love. *Ib.* l. 488

37 Her virtue, and the conscience of her worth,
That would be wooed, and not unsought be won.
Ib. l. 502

38 The amorous bird of night
Sung spousal, and bid haste the evening star
On his hill top, to light the bridal lamp. *Ib.* l. 518

39 The sum of earthly bliss. *Ib.* l. 522

1   So absolute she seems
And in herself complete, so well to know
Her own, that what she wills to do or say
Seems wisest, virtuousest, discreetest, best.
Paradise Lost, bk. viii, l. 547

2 To whom the Angel with contracted brow.
Accuse not Nature, she hath done her part;
Do thou but thine, and be not diffident
Of wisdom, she deserts thee not, if thou
Dismiss not her.   *Ib.* l. 560

3   Oft-times nothing profits more
Than self-esteem, grounded on just and right
Well manag'd.   *Ib.* l. 571

4   With a smile that glowed
Celestial rosy red, love's proper hue.   *Ib.* l. 618

5 My celestial Patroness, who deigns
Her nightly visitation unimplor'd,
And dictates to me slumb'ring, or inspires
Easy my unpremeditated verse:
Since first this subject for heroic song
Pleas'd me long choosing, and beginning late.
Ib. bk. ix, l. 21

6   Unless an age too late, or cold
Climate, or years damp my intended wing. *Ib.* l. 44

7 The serpent subtlest beast of all the field. *Ib.* l. 86

8   For nothing lovelier can be found
In woman, than to study household good,
And good works in her husband to promote.
Ib. l. 232

9 For solitude sometimes is best society,
And short retirement urges sweet return. *Ib.* l. 249

10 Wouldst thou approve thy constancy, approve
First thy obedience.   *Ib.* l. 367

11 As one who long in populous city pent,
Where houses thick and sewers annoy the air,
Forth issuing on a summer's morn to breathe
Among the pleasant villages and farms
Adjoin'd, from each thing met conceives delight.
Ib. l. 445

12 She fair, divinely fair, fit love for Gods. *Ib.* l. 489

13   Hope elevates, and joy
Brightens his crest.   *Ib.* l. 633

14 God so commanded, and left that command
Sole daughter of his voice; the rest, we live
Law to ourselves, our reason is our law. *Ib.* l. 652

15   Her rash hand in evil hour
Forth reaching to the fruit, she pluck'd, she eat:
Earth felt the wound, and Nature from her seat
Sighing through all her works gave signs of woe
That all was lost.   *Ib.* l. 780

16 Adam shall share with me in bliss or woe:
So dear I love him, that with him all deaths
I could endure, without him live no life. *Ib.* l. 831

17 O fairest of creation! last and best
Of all God's works! creature in whom excell'd
Whatever can to sight or thought be form'd,
Holy, divine, good, amiable, or sweet!
How art thou lost, how on a sudden lost,
Defac'd, deflower'd, and now to Death devote?
Ib. l. 896

18   For with thee
Certain my resolution is to die;
How can I live without thee, how forgo
Thy sweet converse and love so dearly joined,
To live again in these wild woods forlorn?
Should God create another Eve, and I
Another rib afford, yet loss of thee
Would never from my heart; no no, I feel
The link of nature draw me: flesh of flesh,
Bone of my bone thou art, and from thy state
Mine never shall be parted, weal or woe.
Paradise Lost, bk. ix, l. 906

19   What thou art is mine;
Our state cannot be sever'd, we are one,
One flesh; to lose thee were to lose myself.
Ib. l. 957

20   He hears
On all sides, from innumerable tongues,
A dismal universal hiss, the sound
Of public scorn.   *Ib.* bk. x, l. 506

21   Complicated monsters, head and tail,
Scorpion and asp, and Amphisbaena dire,
Cerastes horned, Hydrus, and Ellops drear.
Ib. l. 523

22 Chew'd bitter ashes, which th' offended taste
With spattering noise rejected.   *Ib.* l. 566

23   Oh! why did God,
Creator wise, that peopled highest Heaven
With Spirits masculine, create at last
This novelty on Earth, this fair defect
Of Nature?   *Ib.* l. 888

24 Demoniac frenzy, moping melancholy,
And moon-struck madness.   *Ib.* bk. xi, l. 485

25 Nor love thy life, nor hate; but what thou liv'st
Live well, how long or short permit to Heaven.
Ib. l. 553

26   The evening star,
Love's harbinger.   *Ib.* l. 588

27 The brazen throat of war had ceased to roar:
All now was turned to jollity and game,
To luxury and riot, feast and dance. *Ib.* l. 713

28   For now I see
Peace to corrupt no less than war to waste. *Ib.* l. 779

29   Then wilt thou not be loth
To leave this Paradise, but shalt possess
A Paradise within thee, happier far. *Ib.* bk. xii, l. 585

30 In me is no delay; with thee to go,
Is to stay here; without thee here to stay,
Is to go hence unwilling; thou to me
Art all things under Heaven, all places thou,
Who for my wilful crime art banished hence.
Ib. l. 615

31 They looking back, all th' eastern side beheld
Of Paradise, so late their happy seat,
Wav'd over by that flaming brand, the Gate
With dreadful faces throng'd and fiery arms.
Some natural tears they dropped, but wiped them
soon;
The world was all before them, where to choose
Their place of rest, and Providence their guide:
They hand in hand with wandering steps and slow
Through Eden took their solitary way. *Ib.* l. 641

32   Satan, bowing low
His gray dissimulation, disappeared.
Paradise Regained, bk. i, l. 497

MILTON

1 Skill'd to retire, and in retiring draw
Hearts after them tangled in amorous nets.
Paradise Regained, bk. ii, l. 161

2   Beauty stands
In the admiration only of weak minds
Led captive.   *Ib.* l. 220

3   And now the herald lark
Left his ground-nest, high tow'ring to descry
The morn's approach, and greet her with his song.
Ib. l. 279

4 Ladies of th' Hesperides, that seemed
Fairer than feign'd of old, or fabled since
Of faery damsels met in forest wide
By knights of Logres, or of Lyones,
Lancelot or Pelleas, or Pellenore.   *Ib.* l. 357

5 Of whom to be dispraised were no small praise.
Ib. bk. iii, l. 56

6 But on Occasion's forelock watchful wait.   *Ib.* l. 173

7 As he who, seeking asses, found a kingdom.
Ib. l. 242

8 Elephants endorsed with towers.   *Ib.* l. 329

9 Dusk faces with white silken turbans wreath'd.
Ib. bk. iv, l. 76

10   The childhood shows the man,
As morning shows the day. Be famous then
By wisdom; as thy empire must extend,
So let extend thy mind o'er all the world. *Ib.* l. 220

11 Athens, the eye of Greece, mother of arts
And eloquence, native to famous wits
Or hospitable, in her sweet recess,
City or suburban, studious walks and shades;
See there the olive grove of Academe,
Plato's retirement, where the Attic bird
Trills her thick-warbled notes the summer long.
Ib. l. 240

12 The first and wisest of them all professed
To know this only, that he nothing knew. *Ib.* l. 293

13 Deep versed in books and shallow in himself.
Ib. l. 327

14 In them is plainest taught, and easiest learnt,
What makes a nation happy, and keeps it so.
Ib. l. 361

15   Till morning fair
Came forth with pilgrim steps in amice grey.
Ib. l. 426

16   Without wing
Of hippogriff.   *Ib.* l. 541

17 And, as that Theban monster that proposed
Her riddle, and him who solved it not devoured;
That once found out and solved, for grief and spite
Cast herself headlong from th' Ismenian steep,
So strook with dread and anguish fell the Fiend;
And to his crew, that sat consulting, brought
Joyless triumphals of his hop't success,
Ruin, and desperation, and dismay,
Who durst so proudly tempt the Son of God.
Ib. l. 572

18   He unobserved
Home to his mother's house private returned.
Ib. l. 638

19 But headlong joy is ever on the wing.
The Passion, l. 5

20 A little onward lend thy guiding hand
To these dark steps, a little further on.
Samson Agonistes, l. 1

21 Eyeless in Gaza, at the mill with slaves. *Ib.* l. 41

22 O dark, dark, dark, amid the blaze of noon,
Irrecoverably dark, total eclipse
Without all hope of day!   *Ib.* l. 80

23 The sun to me is dark
And silent as the moon,
When she deserts the night
Hid in her vacant interlunar cave.   *Ib.* l. 86

24 To live a life half dead, a living death. *Ib.* l. 100

25 Ran on embattled armies clad in iron,
And, weaponless himself,
Made arms ridiculous.   *Ib.* l. 129

26   Wisest men
Have erred, and by bad women been deceived;
And shall again, pretend they ne'er so wise.
Ib. l. 210

27 Just are the ways of God,
And justifiable to men;
Unless there be who think not God at all. *Ib.* l. 293

28   Of such doctrine never was there school,
But the heart of the fool,
And no man therein doctor but himself. *Ib.* l. 297

29 What boots it at one gate to make defence,
And at another to let in the foe?   *Ib.* l. 560

30 My race of glory run, and race of shame,
And I shall shortly be with them that rest. *Ib.* l. 597

31 But who is this, what thing of sea or land?
Female of sex it seems,
That so bedeck'd, ornate, and gay,
Comes this way sailing
Like a stately ship
Of Tarsus, bound for th' isles
Of Javan or Gadier,
With all her bravery on, and tackle trim,
Sails fill'd, and streamers waving,
Courted by all the winds that hold them play,
An amber scent of odorous perfume
Her harbinger.   *Ib.* l. 710

32   That grounded maxim
So rife and celebrated in the mouths
Of wisest men; that to the public good
Private respects must yield.   *Ib.* l. 865

33 Yet beauty, though injurious, hath strange power,
After offence returning, to regain
Love once possess'd.   *Ib.* l. 1003

34 Love-quarrels oft in pleasing concord end.
Ib. l. 1008

35 Therefore God's universal law
Gave to the man despotic power
Over his female in due awe.   *Ib.* l. 1053

36 O how comely it is, and how reviving
To the spirits of just men long opprest,
When God into the hands of their deliverer
Puts invincible might,
To quell the mighty of the earth, th' oppressor.
Ib. l. 1268

37 He's gone, and who knows how he may report
Thy words by adding fuel to the flame? *Ib.* l. 1350

38 Lords are lordliest in their wine.   *Ib.* l. 1418

1 For evil news rides post, while good news baits.
Samson Agonistes, l. 1538

2 And as an ev'ning dragon came,
Assailant on the perched roosts
And nests in order rang'd
Of tame villatic fowl. *Ib.* l. 1692

3 Like that self-begotten bird
In the Arabian woods embost,
That no second knows nor third,
And lay erewhile a holocaust. *Ib.* l. 1699

4 And though her body die, her fame survives,
A secular bird, ages of lives. *Ib.* l. 1706

5   Samson hath quit himself
Like Samson, and heroically hath finish'd
A life heroic. *Ib.* l. 1709

6 Nothing is here for tears, nothing to wail
Or knock the breast; no weakness, no contempt,
Dispraise or blame; nothing but well and fair,
And what may quiet us in a death so noble.
Ib. l. 1721

7 All is best, though we oft doubt,
What th' unsearchable dispose
Of highest wisdom brings about,
And ever best found in the close.
Oft he seems to hide his face,
But unexpectedly returns
And to his faithful champion hath in place
Bore witness gloriously; whence Gaza mourns
And all that band them to resist
His uncontrollable intent,
His servants he with new acquist
Of true experience from this great event
With peace and consolation hath dismiss'd,
And calm of mind all passion spent. *Ib.* l. 1745

8 What needs my Shakespeare for his honour'd bones,
The labour of an age in piled stones,
Or that his hallow'd relics should be hid
Under a star-y-pointing pyramid?
Dear son of memory, great heir of fame,
What need'st thou such weak witness of thy name?
[*Epitaph*] *on Shakespeare*

9 Blest pair of Sirens, pledges of Heaven's joy,
Sphere-born harmonious sisters, Voice and Verse.
At a Solemn Music

10 Where the bright Seraphim in burning row
Their loud up-lifted Angel trumpets blow. *Ib.*

11   Till disproportion'd sin
Jarr'd against nature's chime. *Ib.*

12 O nightingale, that on yon bloomy spray
Warbl'st at eve, when all the woods are still.
Sonnet i. To the Nightingale

13 All is, if I have grace to use it so,
As ever in my great Task-Master's eye.
Ib. ii. On his having arrived at the age of twenty-three

14 Captain or Colonel, or Knight in arms.
Ib. viii. When the assault was intended to the city

15 The great Emathian conqueror bid spare
The house of Pindarus, when temple and tower
Went to the ground. *Ib.*

16   As that dishonest victory
At Chæronea, fatal to liberty,
Killed with report that old man eloquent.
Ib. x. To the Lady Margaret Ley

17 Those rugged names to our like mouths grow sleek,
That would have made Quintilian stare and gasp.
Thy age, like ours, O soul of Sir John Cheke,
Hated not learning worse than toad or asp,
When thou taught'st Cambridge, and King Edward
Greek. *Sonnet, xi. 'A book was writ of late'*

18 I did but prompt the age to quit their clogs,
By the known rules of ancient liberty,
When straight a barbarous noise environs me
Of owls and cuckoos, asses, apes, and dogs.
Ib. xii. On the Same. [*the detraction, &c.*]

19 Licence they mean when they cry Liberty;
For who loves that, must first be wise and good. *Ib.*

20 Avenge, O Lord, thy slaughtered saints, whose bones
Lie scattered on the Alpine mountains cold;
Ev'n them who kept thy truth so pure of old,
When all our fathers worshipped stocks and stones,
Forget not. In thy book record their groans
Who were thy sheep, and in their ancient fold
Slain by the bloody Piedmontese, that rolled
Mother with infant down the rocks.
Ib. xv. On the late Massacre in Piedmont

21 When I consider how my light is spent,
E're half my days, in this dark world and wide,
And that one Talent which is death to hide,
Lodg'd with me useless, though my Soul more bent
To serve therewith my Maker, and present
My true account, lest He returning chide;
'Doth God exact day-labour, light deny'd?'
I fondly ask; But Patience, to prevent
That murmur, soon replies, 'God doth not need
Either man's work or his own gifts. Who best
Bear his mild yoke, they serve him best, his State
Is Kingly. Thousands at his bidding speed
And post o'er Land and Ocean without rest:
They also serve who only stand and wait.'
Ib. xvi. On His Blindness

22 In mirth, that after no repenting draws.
Ib. xviii. To Cyriac Skinner

23 To measure life learn thou betimes, and know
Toward solid good what leads the nearest way;
For other things mild Heaven a time ordains,
And disapproves that care, though wise in show,
That with superfluous burden loads the day,
And, when God sends a cheerful hour, refrains. *Ib.*

24 Methought I saw my late espousèd Saint
Brought to me like Alcestis from the grave.
Ib. xix. On His Deceased Wife

25 Love, sweetness, goodness, in her person shined. *Ib.*

26 But O as to embrace me she inclined,
I waked, she fled, and day brought back my night. *Ib.*

27 New Presbyter is but old Priest writ large.
Ib. On the New Forcers of Conscience under the Long Parliament

28 For what can war but endless war still breed?
Ib. On the Lord General Fairfax

29   Peace hath her victories
No less renowned than war.
Ib. [*To the Lord General Cromwell, May 1652*]

30 Help us to save free conscience from the paw
Of hireling wolves, whose gospel is their maw. *Ib.*

31 Fly, envious Time, till thou run out thy race:
Call on the lazy leaden-stepping hours. *On Time,* l. 1

1 Beldam Nature.
At a Vacation Exercise in the College, l. 46

2 He who would not be frustrate of his hope to write well hereafter in laudable things ought himself to be a true poem.
Apology for Smectymnuus, introd. to § 1

3 His words . . . like so many nimble and airy servitors trip about him at command. *Ib.* § 12

4 For this is not the liberty which we can hope, that no grievance ever should arise in the Commonwealth, that let no man in this world expect; but when complaints are freely heard, deeply considered, and speedily reformed, then is the utmost bound of civil liberty attained that wise men look for.
Areopagitica

5 Books are not absolutely dead things, but do contain a potency of life in them to be as active as that soul was whose progeny they are; nay they do preserve as in a vial the purest efficacy and extraction of that living intellect that bred them. *Ib.*

6 As good almost kill a man as kill a good book: who kills a man kills a reasonable creature, God's image; but he who destroys a good book, kills reason itself, kills the image of God, as it were in the eye. *Ib.*

7 A good book is the precious life-blood of a master spirit, embalmed and treasured up on purpose to a life beyond life. *Ib.*

8 It was from out the rind of one apple tasted that the knowledge of good and evil as two twins cleaving together leaped forth into the world. *Ib.*

9 He that can apprehend and consider vice with all her baits and seeming pleasures, and yet abstain, and yet distinguish, and yet prefer that which is truly better, he is the true wayfaring Christian. I cannot praise a fugitive and cloistered virtue, unexercised and unbreathed, that never sallies out and sees her adversary, but slinks out of the race, where that immortal garland is to be run for, not without dust and heat. Assuredly we bring not innocence into the world, we bring impurity much rather: that which purifies us is trial, and trial is by what is contrary. *Ib.*

10 Our sage and serious poet Spenser. *Ib.*

11 To be still searching what we know not by what we know, still closing up truth to truth as we find it (for all her body is homogeneal and proportional), this is the golden rule in theology as well as in arithmetic, and makes up the best harmony in a church. *Ib.*

12 God is decreeing to begin some new and great period in His Church, even to the reforming of Reformation itself. What does He then but reveal Himself to His servants, and as His manner is, first to His Englishmen? *Ib.*

13 Behold now this vast city [London]; a city of refuge, the mansion-house of liberty, encompassed and surrounded with His protection. *Ib.*

14 Where there is much desire to learn, there of necessity will be much arguing, much writing, many opinions; for opinion in good men is but knowledge in the making. *Ib.*

15 Methinks I see in my mind a noble and puissant nation rousing herself like a strong man after sleep, and shaking her invincible locks. Methinks I see her as an eagle mewing her mighty youth, and kindling her undazzled eyes at the full midday beam. *Areopagitica*

16 Give me the liberty to know, to utter, and to argue freely according to conscience, above all liberties. *Ib.*

17 Though all the winds of doctrine were let loose to play upon the earth, so Truth be in the field, we do injuriously by licensing and prohibiting to misdoubt her strength. Let her and Falsehood grapple; who ever knew Truth put to the worse, in a free and open encounter. *Ib.*

18 But because about the manner and order of this government, whether it ought to be Presbyterial, or Prelatical, such endless question, or rather uproar is arisen in this land, as may be justly termed, what the fever is to the physicians, the eternal reproach of the divines.
Reason of Church Government, preface

19 This manner of writing [i.e. prose] wherein knowing myself inferior to myself . . . I have the use, as I may account it, but of my left hand.
Ib. bk. ii, introd. to ch.

20 A poet soaring in the high region of his fancies with his garland and singing robes about him. *Ib.*

21 By labour and intent study (which I take to be my portion in this life) joined with the strong propensity of nature, I might perhaps leave something so written to after-times, as they should not willingly let it die. *Ib.*

22 Inquisitorious and tyrannical duncery. *Ib.*

23 Beholding the bright countenance of truth in the quiet and still air of delightful studies. *Ib.*

24 Let not England forget her precedence of teaching nations how to live.
The Doctrine and Discipline of Divorce

25 I call therefore a complete and generous education that which fits a man to perform justly, skilfully and magnanimously all the offices both private and public of peace and war. *Of Education*

26 I will point ye out the right path of a virtuous and noble Education; laborious indeed at the first ascent, but else so smooth, so green, so full of goodly prospect, and melodious sounds on every side, that the harp of Orpheus was not more charming. *Ib.*

27 Brave men, and worthy patriots, dear to God, and famous to all ages. *Ib.*

28 Ornate rhetorick taught out of the rule of Plato, . . . To which poetry would be made subsequent, or indeed rather precedent, as being less subtle and fine, but more simple, sensuous and passionate. *Ib.*

29 In those vernal seasons of the year, when the air is calm and pleasant, it were an injury and sullenness against Nature not to go out, and see her riches, and partake in her rejoicing with Heaven and Earth. *Ib.*

30 The Wars of Kites or Crows fighting in the air.
History of Britain, ch.

1 For such kind of borrowing as this, if it be not bettered by the borrower, among good authors is accounted plagiary. *Iconoclastes, ch. 23*

2 None can love freedom heartily, but good men; the rest love not freedom, but licence.
Tenure of Kings and Magistrates

3 No man who knows aught, can be so stupid to deny that all men naturally were born free. *Ib.*

COMTE DE MIRABEAU
1749–1791

4 La guerre est l'industrie nationale de la Prusse.

War is the national industry of Prussia.
Attr. to Mirabeau by Albert Sorel, based on his Introduction to his 'Monarchie Prussienne'

MISSAL

5 O felix culpa, quae talem ac tantum meruit habere Redemptorem.

O happy fault, which has deserved to have such and so mighty a Redeemer.
'Exsultet' on Holy Saturday

MARY RUSSELL MITFORD
1787–1855

6 I have discovered that our great favourite, Miss Austen, is my country-woman. . . . with whom mamma before her marriage was acquainted. Mamma says that she was then the prettiest, silliest, most affected, husband-hunting butterfly she ever remembers.
Letter to Sir William Elford, 3 Apr. 1815. Rev. A. G. L'Estrange: *Life of Mary Russell Mitford,* vol. i, pp. 305–6

EMILIO MOLA
d. 1936

7 La quinta columna.

The fifth column.
Radio Address given when a General in the Spanish Civil War, 1936–1939

JEAN BAPTISTE POQUELIN, *called* MOLIÈRE
1622–1673

8 Vous êtes orfèvre, Monsieur Josse!

You are in the trade, Monsieur Josse!
L'Amour Médecin, I. i

9 Présentez toujours le devant au monde.

Always show your front to the world.
L'Avare, III. ii

10 Il faut manger pour vivre et non pas vivre pour manger.

One should eat to live, not live to eat. *Ib.* v

11 M. JOURDAIN: Quoi? quand je dis: 'Nicole, apportez-moi mes pantoufles, et me donnez mon bonnet de nuit', c'est de la prose?
MAÎTRE DE PHILOSOPHIE: Oui, monsieur.
M. JOURDAIN: Par ma foi! il y a plus de quarante ans que je dis de la prose sans que j'en susse rien.
M. JOURDAIN: What? when I say: 'Nicole, bring me my slippers, and give me my night-cap,' is that prose?

PROFESSOR OF PHILOSOPHY: Yes, Sir.
M. JOURDAIN: Good Heavens! For more than forty years I have been speaking prose without knowing it. *Le Bourgeois Gentilhomme,* II. iv

12 Tout ce qui n'est point prose est vers; et tout ce qui n'est point vers est prose.

All that is not prose is verse; and all that is not verse is prose. *Ib.*

13 Ah, la belle chose que de savoir quelque chose.

Knowledge is a fine thing. *Ib.* vi

14 Je voudrais bien savoir si la grande règle de toutes les règles n'est pas de plaire.

I sometimes wonder whether the greatest rule of all is not—to know how to please.
Critique de L'École des Femmes, vii

15 C'est une étrange entreprise que celle de faire rire les honnêtes gens.

It is an odd calling, to make decent folk laugh. *Ib.*

16 Je vis de bonne soupe et non de beau langage.

It's good food and not fine words that keeps me alive. *Les Femmes Savantes,* II. vii

17 Guenille, si l'on veut: ma guenille m'est chère.

Rags and tatters, maybe: but I am fond of my rags and tatters. *Ib.*

18 Un sot savant est sot plus qu'un sot ignorant.

An erudite fool is a greater fool than an ignorant fool. *Ib.* IV. iii

19 Les livres cadrent mal avec le mariage.

Reading goes ill with the married state. *Ib.* v. iii

20 Qui vit sans tabac n'est pas digne de vivre.

He who lives without tobacco is not worthy to live.
Festin de Pierre, I. i

21 Que diable allait-il faire dans cette galère?

What the devil is he doing in this galley?
Les Fourberies de Scapin, II. vii

22 Vous l'avez voulu, Georges Dandin, vous l'avez voulu.

You asked for it, George Dandin, you asked for it.
Georges Dandin, I. ix

23 L'on a le temps d'avoir les dents longues, lorsqu' on attend pour vivre le trépas de quelqu'un.

He who waits for dead men's leavings may well be sharp set before he gets a meal.
Le Médecin malgré lui, II. ii

24 Oui, cela était autrefois ainsi, mais nous avons changé tout cela.

Yes, it used to be so, but we have changed all that.
Ib. vi. *Said by the pretended doctor to justify his mistake as to the relative positions of heart and liver.*

25 Il faut, parmi le monde, une vertu traitable.

Virtue, in the great world, should be amenable.
Le Misanthrope, I. i

26 C'est une folie à nulle autre seconde,
De vouloir se mêler à corriger le monde,

Of all human follies there's none could be greater Than trying to render our fellow-men better. *Ib.*

1 On doit se regarder soi-même un fort long temps,
Avant que de songer à condamner les gens.

We should look long and carefully at ourselves
Before we pass judgement on our fellows.
Le Misanthrope, III. vii

2 Allez-vous-en la voir et me laissez enfin
Dans ce petit coin sombre avec mon noir chagrin.

Go get you gone—go, seek her out again
And leave me pent in gloom with my o'er shadow-
ing pain.
Ib. v. i

3 C'est un homme expéditif, qui aime à dépêcher ses
malades ; et quand on a à mourir, cela se fait avec lui
le plus vite du monde.

He wastes no time with patients : and if you have
to die, he will put the business through quicker
than anybody else.
Monsieur de Pourceaugnac, I. vii

4 Ils commencent ici (Paris) par faire pendre un homme
et puis ils lui font son procès.

Here, in Paris, they hang a man first, and try him
afterwards.
Ib. III. ii

5 Les gens de qualité savent tout sans avoir jamais rien
appris.

People of quality know everything without ever
having been taught.   *Les Précieuses Ridicules*, x

6 Ah, pour être dévot, je n'en suis pas moins homme.
I am not the less human for being devout.
Tartuffe, III. iii

7 Le ciel défend, de vrai, certains contentements
Mais on trouve avec lui des accommodements.

God, it is true, does some delights condemn,
But 'tis not hard to come to terms with Him.
Ib. IV. v

8 L'homme est, je vous l'avoue, un méchant animal.
Man, I can assure you, is a nasty creature. *Ib.* v. vi

9 Il m'est permis, disait Molière, de reprendre mon
bien où je le trouve.

It is permitted me, said Molière, to take good
fortune where I find it.
Grimarest, *Vie de Molière* (1704), p. 14

JAMES, DUKE OF MONMOUTH
1649-1685

10 Do not hack me as you did my Lord Russell.
Words to his executioner. Macaulay, *Hist. of
England*, vol. i, ch. 5

JOHN SAMUEL BEWLEY MONSELL
1811-1875

11 Fight the good fight with all thy might,
Christ is thy strength, and Christ thy right;
Lay hold on life, and it shall be
Thy joy and crown eternally.

Run the straight race through God's good grace,
Lift up thine eyes, and seek His Face;
Life with its way before us lies,
Christ is the path, and Christ the prize.
Hymns of Love and Praise. Fight of Faith

12 Faint not nor fear, His arms are near,
He changeth not, and thou art dear;
Only believe, and thou shalt see
That Christ is all in all to thee.
Ib.

LADY MARY WORTLEY MONTAGU
1689-1762

13 This world consists of men, women, and Herveys.
Letters, vol. i, p. 67

14 But the fruit that can fall without shaking,
Indeed is too mellow for me.
*Letters and Works. Answered, for Lord William
Hamilton*

15 And we meet, with champagne and a chicken, at last.
Ib. The Lover

16 General notions are generally wrong.
Ib. Letter to Mr. Wortley Montagu, 28 Mar. 1710

17 Civility costs nothing and buys everything.
Ib. Letter to the Countess of Bute, 30 May 1756

MICHEL EYQUEM MONTAIGNE
1533-1592

18 Le continuel ouvrage de votre vie, c'est bâtir la mort.

The ceaseless labour of a man's whole life is to build
the house of death.
Essais, I. xx

19 Il faut être toujours botté et prêt à partir.

One should be ever booted and spurred and ready
to depart.
Ib.

20 L'utilité du vivre n'est pas en l'éspace, elle est en
l'usage ; tel a vécu longtemps qui a peu vécu . . .
Il gît en votre volonté, non au nombre des ans,
que vous ayez assez vécu.

The value of life lies not in the length of days, but
in the use we make of them : a man may live long,
yet get little from life. Whether you find satisfaction in life depends not on your tale of years,
but on your will.
Ib.

21 [*Of his friend, Étienne de la Boétie*]
Si l'on me presse de dire pourquoi je l'aimais, je sens
que cela ne se peut exprimer qu'en répondant,
Parce que c'était lui ; parce que c'était moi.

If you press me to say why I loved him, I can say
no more than it was because he was he and I
was I.
Ib. xxviii

22 La gloire et le repos sont choses qui ne peuvent loger
en même gîte.

Fame and tranquillity can never be bedfellows.
Ib. xxxix

23 Il se faut réserver une arrière boutique, toute notre,
toute franche, en laquelle nous établissions notre
vraie liberté en principale retraicte et solitude.

A man must keep a little back shop where he can be
himself without reserve. In solitude alone can he
know true freedom.
Ib.

24 La plus grande chose du monde c'est de savoir être
à soi.

The greatest thing in the world is to know how to be
sufficient unto oneself.
Ib.

25 Pour juger des choses grandes et hautes, il faut une
âme de même.

Only he can judge of matters great and high whose
soul is likewise.
Ib. xlii

1 Mon métier et mon art, c'est vivre.

To know how to live is all my calling and all my art.
Essais, II. vi

2 La vertu refuse la facilité pour compagne . . . elle demande un chemin aspre et espineux.

Virtue can have naught to do with ease . . . It craves a steep and thorny path. *Ib.* xi

3 Quand je me joue à ma chatte, qui sait si elle passe son temps de moi, plus que je ne fais d'elle?

When I play with my cat, who knows whether I do not make her more sport than she makes me? *Ib.* xii

4 La vie est un songe . . . nous veillons dormants et veillants dormons.

Life is a dream . . . we waking sleep and sleeping wake. *Ib.*

5 Que sais-je?

What do I know? *Ib.*

6 Comme quelqu'un pourrait dire de moi que j'ai seulement fait ici un amas de fleurs étrangères, n'y ayant fourni du mien que le filet à les lier.

And one might therefore say of me that in this book I have only made up a bunch of other people's flowers, and that of my own I have only provided the string that ties them together.
Ib. III. xii

CHARLES DE SECONDAT, BARON DE MONTESQUIEU
1689–1755

7 Les grands seigneurs ont des plaisirs, le peuple a de la joie.

Great lords have their pleasures, but the people have happiness. *Pensées Diverses*

8 Les Anglais sont occupés; ils n'ont pas le temps d'être polis.

The English are busy folk; they have no time in which to be polite. *Ib.*

JAMES MONTGOMERY
1771–1854

9 'For ever with the Lord!'
  Amen; so let it be;
Life from the dead is in that word,
  'Tis immortality. *At Home in Heaven*

10 Here in the body pent,
  Absent from Him I roam,
Yet nightly pitch my moving tent
  A day's march nearer home. *Ib.*

11 Prayer is the soul's sincere desire,
  Uttered or unexpressed,
The motion of a hidden fire
  That trembles in the breast. *What is Prayer?*

12 A day in such serene enjoyment spent
Were worth an age of splendid discontent.
Greenland, canto ii, l. 224

ROBERT MONTGOMERY
1807–1855

13 The solitary monk who shook the world.
Luther. Man's Need and God's Supply, l. 68

14 With fearful gaze, still be it mine to see
How all is fill'd and vivified by Thee;
Upon thy mirror, earth's majestic view,
To paint Thy Presence, and to feel it too.
The Omnipresence of the Deity (ed. 1830), pt. I,
l. 105

15 And thou, vast ocean! on whose awful face
Time's iron feet can print no ruin-trace. *Ib.* l. 141

16 Ye quenchless stars! so eloquently bright,
Untroubled sentries of the shadowy night. *Ib.* l. 305

17 The soul aspiring pants its source to mount,
As streams meander level with their fount. *Ib.* l. 339

JAMES GRAHAM, MARQUIS OF MONTROSE
1612–1650

18 My dear and only love, I pray
  This noble world of thee,
Be govern'd by no other sway
  But purest Monarchy.
For if confusion have a part,
  Which virtuous souls abhor,
And hold a synod in thy heart,
  I'll never love thee more. *My Dear and Only Love*

19 He either fears his fate too much,
  Or his deserts are small,
That puts it not unto the touch,
  To win or lose it all. *Ib.*

20 But if thou wilt be constant then,
  And faithful of thy word,
I'll make thee glorious by my pen,
  And famous by my sword. *Ib.*

21 Let them bestow on every airth a limb;
Then open all my veins, that I may swim
To thee, my Maker! in that crimson lake;
Then place my parboiled head upon a stake—
Scatter my ashes—strew them in the air;—
Lord! since thou know'st where all these atoms are,
I'm hopeful thou'lt recover once my dust,
And confident thou'lt raise me with the just.
Lines Written on the Window of his Jail the Night before his Execution. Scottish Poetry of the Seventeenth Century

PERCY MONTROSE
nineteenth century

22 In a cavern, in a canyon,
  Excavating for a mine,
Dwelt a miner, Forty-niner,
  And his daughter, Clementine.
Oh, my darling, oh my darling, oh my darling Clementine!
Thou art lost and gone for ever, dreadful sorry, Clementine. *Clementine*

23 Light she was and like a fairy,
  And her shoes were number nine;
Herring boxes without topses,
  Sandals were for Clementine. *Ib.*

24 But I kissed her little sister,
  And forgot my Clementine. *Ib.*

CLEMENT C. MOORE
1779–1863

1 'Twas the night before Christmas, when all through
the house
Not a creature was stirring, not even a mouse;
The stockings were hung by the chimney with care,
In hopes that St. Nicholas soon would be there.
The Night before Christmas

EDWARD MOORE
1712–1757

2 This is adding insult to injuries. *The Foundling*, v. ii

3 I am rich beyond the dreams of avarice.
The Gamester, II. ii

GEORGE MOORE
1852–1933

4 All reformers are bachelors.
The Bending of the Bough, Act I

5 Art must be parochial in the beginning to become
cosmopolitan in the end.
Hail and Farewell! (1925), vol. i, p. 5

6 Acting is therefore the lowest of the arts, if it is an art
at all. *Mummer-Worship*

THOMAS MOORE
1779–1852

7 For you know, dear—I may, without vanity, hint—
Though an angel should write, still 'tis *devils* must
print. *The Fudges in England*, letter iii, l. 64

8 Yet, who can help loving the land that has taught us
Six hundred and eighty-five ways to dress eggs?
The Fudge Family in Paris, letter viii. l. 64

9 A Persian's Heaven is easily made;
'Tis but black eyes and lemonade.
Intercepted Letters, vi

10 And doth not a meeting like this make amends,
For all the long years I've been wand'ring away?
Irish Melodies. And Doth Not a Meeting

11 Believe me, if all those endearing young charms,
Which I gaze on so fondly to-day.
Ib. Believe Me, if All

12 And around the dear ruin each wish of my heart
Would entwine itself verdantly still. *Ib.*

13 No, the heart that has truly lov'd never forgets,
But as truly loves on to the close,
As the sun-flower turns on her god, when he sets,
The same look which she turn'd when he rose. *Ib.*

14 Eyes of most unholy blue! *Ib. By that Lake*

15 Come, rest in this bosom, my own stricken deer,
Though the herd have fled from thee, thy home is still
here. *Ib. Come, Rest In This Bosom*

16 I know not, I ask not, if guilt's in that heart,
But I know that I love thee, whatever thou art. *Ib.*

17 Erin, the tear and the smile in thine eyes,
Blend like the rainbow that hangs in thy skies!
Ib. Erin, the Tear

18 You may break, you may shatter the vase, if you will,
But the scent of the roses will hang round it still.
Ib. Farewell! But Whenever

19 Go where glory waits thee,
But, while fame elates thee,
Oh! still remember me.
Irish Melodies. Go Where Glory

20 The harp that once through Tara's halls
The soul of music shed,
Now hangs as mute on Tara's walls
As if that soul were fled.—
So sleeps the pride of former days,
So glory's thrill is o'er;
And hearts, that once beat high for praise,
Now feel that pulse no more.
Ib. The Harp that Once

21 Thus freedom now so seldom wakes,
The only throb she gives,
Is when some heart indignant breaks,
To show that still she lives. *Ib.*

22 Has sorrow thy young days shaded?
Ib. Has Sorrow Thy Young

23 And, when once the young heart of a maiden is stolen,
The maiden herself will steal after it soon.
Ib. Ill Omens

24 Lesbia hath a beaming eye,
But no one knows for whom it beameth.
Ib. Lesbia Hath

25 No, there's nothing half so sweet in life
As love's young dream. *Ib. Love's Young Dream*

26 There is not in the wide world a valley so sweet
As that vale in whose bosom the bright waters meet.
Ib. The Meeting of the Waters

27 The Minstrel Boy to the war is gone,
In the ranks of death you'll find him;
His father's sword he has girded on,
And his wild harp slung behind him.
Ib. The Minstrel Boy

28 Oh! blame not the bard. *Ib. Oh! Blame Not*

29 Oh! breathe not his name, let it sleep in the shade,
Where cold and unhonour'd his relics are laid.
Ib. Oh! Breathe not his Name

30 Rich and rare were the gems she wore,
And a bright gold ring on her wand she bore.
Ib. Rich and Rare

31 She is far from the land where her young hero sleeps,
And lovers are round her, sighing:
But coldly she turns from their gaze, and weeps,
For her heart in his grave is lying. *Ib. She is Far*

32 The light, that lies
In woman's eyes,
Has been my heart's undoing. *Ib. The Time I've Lost*

33 My only books
Were woman's looks,
And folly's all they've taught me. *Ib.*

34 This life is all chequer'd with pleasures and woes.
Ib. This Life is All Chequered

35 'Tis sweet to think, that, where'er we rove,
We are sure to find something blissful and dear,
And that, when we're far from the lips we love,
We've but to make love to the lips we are near.
Ib. 'Tis Sweet to Think

36 'Tis the last rose of summer
Left blooming alone;
All her lovely companions
Are faded and gone. *Ib. 'Tis the Last Rose*

1 Then awake! the heavens look bright, my dear;
'Tis never too late for delight, my dear;
And the best of all ways
To lengthen our days
Is to steal a few hours from the night, my dear!
Irish Melodies. The Young May Moon

2 Where I love I must not marry;
Where I marry, cannot love.
Juvenile Poems. Love and Marriage

3 'Twere more than woman to be wise;
'Twere more than man to wish thee so!
Ib. The Ring (ed. 1882)

4 To love you was pleasant enough,
And, oh! 'tis delicious to hate you!
Ib. To—When I Lov'd You

5 Oh! ever thus, from childhood's hour,
I've seen my fondest hopes decay;
I never lov'd a tree or flow'r,
But 'twas the first to fade away.
I never nurs'd a dear gazelle,
To glad me with its soft black eye,
But when it came to know me well,
And love me, it was sure to die!
Lalla Rookh. The Fire-Worshippers, i, l. 279

6 Like Dead Sea fruits, that tempt the eye,
But turn to ashes on the lips!   *Ib.* l. 484

7 One Morn a Peri at the gate
Of Eden stood, disconsolate.
Ib. Paradise and the Peri, l. 1

8 Some flow'rets of Eden ye still inherit,
But the trail of the Serpent is over them all!
Ib. l. 206

9 And, when all hope seem'd desp'rate, wildly hurl'd
Himself into the scale, and sav'd a world.
Ib. The Veiled Prophet, iii, l. 211

10 But Faith, fanatic Faith, once wedded fast
To some dear falsehood, hugs it to the last. *Ib.* l. 356

11 'Come, come', said Tom's father, 'at your time of life,
'There's no longer excuse for thus playing the
rake—
'It is time you should think, boy, of taking a wife'—
'Why, so it is, father—whose wife shall I take?'
Miscellaneous Poems. A Joke Versified

12 Disguise our bondage as we will,
'Tis woman, woman, rules us still.
Ib. Sovereign Woman

13 Oft, in the stilly night,
Ere Slumber's chain has bound me,
Fond Memory brings the light
Of other days around me;
The smiles, the tears,
Of boyhood's years,
The words of love then spoken;
The eyes that shone,
Now dimm'd and gone,
The cheerful hearts now broken!
National Airs. Oft in the Stilly Night

14 I feel like one
Who treads alone
Some banquet-hall deserted,
Whose lights are fled,
Whose garlands dead,
And all but he departed!   *Ib.*

15 Those evening bells! those evening bells!
How many a tale their music tells,
Of youth, and home, and that sweet time
When last I heard their soothing chime.
National Airs. Those Evening Bells

16 Faintly as tolls the evening chime
Our voices keep tune and our oars keep time.
Soon as the woods on shore look dim,
We'll sing at St. Ann's our parting hymn.
Row, brothers, row, the stream runs fast,
The Rapids are near and the daylight's past.
Poems Relating to America. Canadian Boat Song

17 Sound the loud timbrel o'er Egypt's dark sea!
Jehovah has triumph'd—his people are free.
*Sacred Songs. Miriam's Song. Sound the Loud
Timbrel*

18 There was a little Man, and he had a little Soul,
And he said, 'Little Soul, let us try, try, try'.
*Satirical and Humorous Poems. Little Man and
Little Soul*

19 And one wild Shakespeare, following Nature's lights,
Is worth whole planets, filled with Stagyrites.
The Sceptic

20 Your priests, whate'er their gentle shamming,
Have always had a taste for damning.
Twopenny Post-Bag, letter iv

21 Good at a fight, but better at a play,
Godlike in giving, but—the devil to pay!
*On a Cast of Sheridan's Hand. Memoirs of the Life
of R. B. Sheridan* (1825), p. 712

THOMAS OSBERT MORDAUNT
1730–1809

22 Sound, sound the clarion, fill the fife,
Throughout the sensual world proclaim,
One crowded hour of glorious life
Is worth an age without a name.
*The Bee, 12 Oct. 1791. Verses Written During
the War, 1756–1763*

HANNAH MORE
1745–1833

23 For you'll ne'er mend your fortunes, nor help the just
cause,
By breaking of windows, or breaking of laws.
Address to the Meeting in Spa Fields (1817).
H. Thompson's *Life* (1838), p. 398

24 A crown! what is it?
It is to bear the miseries of a people!
To hear their murmurs, feel their discontents,
And sink beneath a load of splendid care!
Daniel, pt. vi, l. 72

25 Small habits, well pursued betimes,
May reach the dignity of crimes.   *Florio*, l. 77

26 He lik'd those literary cooks
Who skim the cream of others' books;
And ruin half an author's graces
By plucking bon-mots from their places.   *Ib.* l. 123

27 Did not God
Sometimes withhold in mercy what we ask,
We should be ruined at our own request.
Moses in the Bulrushes, pt. i, l. 34

1 The sober comfort, all the peace which springs
From the large aggregate of little things;
On these small cares of daughter, wife, or friend,
The almost sacred joys of home depend.
Sensibility, l. 315

SIR THOMAS MORE
1478–1535

2 'In good faith, I rejoiced, son,' quoth he, 'that I had
given the devil a foul fall, and that with those Lords
I had gone so far, as without great shame I could
never go back again.'
Roper, *Life of Sir Thomas More* (1935), p. 69

3 'By god body, master More, *Indignatio principis mors
est*.'
'Is that all, my Lord?' quoth he. 'Then in good faith
is there no more difference between your grace and
me, but that I shall die to-day, and you to-morrow.'
Ib. p. 71

4 Son Roper, I thank our Lord the field is won.
Ib. p. 73

5 Is not this house [the Tower of London] as nigh
heaven as my own?
Ib. p. 83

6 I pray you, master Lieutenant, see me safe up, and
my coming down let me shift for my self. [On
mounting the scaffold.]
Ib. p. 103

7 Pluck up thy spirits, man, and be not afraid to do
thine office; my neck is very short; take heed therefore thou strike not awry, for saving of thine
honesty. [To the Executioner.]
Ib. p. 103

8 This hath not offended the king. [As he drew his
beard aside on placing his head on the block.]
Bacon, *Apophthegms*, 22

9 Yea, marry, now it is somewhat, for now it is rhyme;
before, it was neither rhyme nor reason. [Advising
an author to put his ill-written work into verse.]
A. Cayley's *Memoirs of Sir Thos. More* (1808),
vol. i, p. 247

10 They roll and rumble,
They turn and tumble,
As pigges do in a poke.
Works (1557), ¶ ii. 6. *How a Sergeant would learn
to Play the Frere*

11 This is a fair tale of a tub told us of his elects.
Ib. p. 576. *Confutation of Tyndale's Answers*

12 Your sheep, that were wont to be so meek and tame,
and so small eaters, now, as I hear say, be become
so great devourers, and so wild, that they eat up
and swallow down the very men themselves.
Utopia, bk. 1

THOMAS MORELL
1703–1784

13 See, the conquering hero comes!
Sound the trumpets, beat the drums! *Joshua*, pt. iii

AUGUSTUS DE MORGAN
1806–1871

14 Great fleas have little fleas upon their backs to bite
'em,
And little fleas have lesser fleas, and so *ad infinitum*.
A Budget of Paradoxes (1872), p. 377

ALBERT EDMUND PARKER, EARL OF MORLEY
1843–1905

15 I am always very glad when Lord Salisbury makes a
great speech, . . . It is sure to contain at least one
blazing indiscretion which it is a delight to remember. *Speech, Hull, 25 Nov. 1887*

JOHN, VISCOUNT MORLEY OF BLACKBURN
1838–1923

16 No man can climb out beyond the limitations of his
own character.
Critical Miscellanies (1886), i, *Robespierre*, p. 93

17 [Letter-writing,] that most delightful way of wasting
time. *Ib.* iii. *Life of Geo. Eliot*, p. 96

18 The whole of the golden Gospel of Silence is now
effectively compressed in thirty-five volumes.
Ib. Carlyle, p. 195

CHARLES MORRIS
1745–1838

19 If one must have a villa in summer to dwell,
Oh, give me the sweet shady side of Pall Mall!
The Contrast

20 A house is much more to my taste than a tree,
And for groves, oh! a good grove of chimneys for me.
Ib.

GEORGE POPE MORRIS
1802–1867

21 Woodman, spare that tree!
Touch not a single bough!
In youth it sheltered me,
And I'll protect it now.
Woodman, Spare That Tree

SIR LEWIS MORRIS
1833–1907

22 How far high failure overleaps the bounds of low
success. *The Epic of Hades, Marsyas*

WILLIAM MORRIS
1834–1896

23 One of these cloths is heaven, and one is hell,
Now choose one cloth for ever; which they be,
I will not tell you, you must somehow tell
Of your own strength and mightiness.
Defence of Guenevere

24 And one of these strange choosing cloths was blue,
Wavy and long, and one cut short and red;
No man could tell the better of the two.

After a shivering half-hour you said:
'God help! heaven's colour, the blue;' and he said:
'hell'.
Perhaps you then would roll upon your bed,

And cry to all good men that loved you well,
'Ah Christ! if only I had known, known, known.' *Ib.*

25 The idle singer of an empty day.
The Earthly Paradise. An Apology

1 Dreamer of dreams, born out of my due time,
　　Why should I strive to set the crooked straight?
　Let it suffice me that my murmuring rhyme
　　Beats with light wing against the ivory gate,
　Telling a tale not too importunate
　To those who in the sleepy region stay,
　Lulled by the singer of an empty day.
　　　　　　The Earthly Paradise. An Apology

2 Forget six counties overhung with smoke,
　Forget the snorting steam and piston stroke,
　Forget the spreading of the hideous town;
　Think rather of the pack-horse on the down,
　And dream of London, small and white and clean,
　The clear Thames bordered by its gardens green.
　　　　　　Ib. Prologue. The Wanderers, l. 1

3 Death have we hated, knowing not what it meant;
　Life we have loved, through green leaf and through
　　sere,
　Though still the less we knew of its intent.
　　　　　　Ib. L'Envoi, xiii

4 Had she come all the way for this,.
　To part at last without a kiss?
　Yea, had she borne the dirt and rain
　That her own eyes might see him slain
　Beside the haystack in the floods?
　　　　　　The Haystack in the Floods

5 I know a little garden close
　Set thick with lily and red rose,
　Where I would wander if I might
　From dewy dawn to dewy night,
　And have one with me wandering.
　　　　　　The Life and Death of Jason, l. 577

6 Love is enough: though the world be a-waning,
　And the woods have no voice but the voice of com-
　　plaining.
　　　　　　Love is Enough, i

7 But lo, the old inn, and the lights, and the fire,
　And the fiddler's old tune and the shuffling of feet;
　Soon for us shall be quiet and rest and desire,
　And to-morrow's uprising to deeds shall be sweet.
　　　　　　The Message of the March Winds

8 You must be very old, Sir Giles. *Old Love*

9 They hammer'd out my basnet point
　Into a round salade. *Ib.*

10 My lady seems of ivory
　Forehead, straight nose, and cheeks that be
　Hollow'd a little mournfully.
　Beata mea Domina! *Praise of my Lady*

11 Across the empty garden-beds,
　When the Sword went out to sea.
　　　　　　The Sailing of the Sword

12 There were four of us about that bed;
　The mass-priest knelt at the side. *Shameful Death*

13 He did not die in the night,
　He did not die in the day. *Ib.*

14 It is the longest night in all the year,
　Near on the day when the Lord Christ was born;
　Six hours ago I came and sat down here,
　And ponder'd sadly, wearied and forlorn.
　　　　　Sir Galahad, A Christmas Mystery, l. 1

15 O servant of the high God, Galahad! *Ib. l. 153*

16 Speak but one word to me over the corn,
　Over the tender, bow'd locks of the corn.
　　　　　　Summer Dawn

17 And ever she sung from noon to noon,
　'Two red roses across the moon.'
　　　　　　Two Red Roses Across the Moon

18 Wind, wind! thou art sad, art thou kind? *The Wind*

19 Forsooth, brothers, fellowship is heaven, and lack of
　fellowship is hell: fellowship is life, and lack of
　fellowship is death: and the deeds that ye do upon
　the earth, it is for fellowship's sake that ye do them.
　　　　　　The Dream of John Ball, ch. 4

THOMAS MORTON
1764?–1838

20 Approbation from Sir Hubert Stanley is praise indeed.
　　　　　　A Cure for the Heartache, v. ii

21 I eat well, and I drink well, and I sleep well—but
　that's all. *A Roland for an Oliver, i. ii*

22 Always ding, dinging Dame Grundy into my ears—
　what will Mrs. Grundy zay? What will Mrs.
　Grundy think? *Speed the Plough, i. i*

JOHN LOTHROP MOTLEY
1814–1877

23 As long as he lived, he was the guiding-star of a whole
　brave nation, and when he died the little children
　cried in the streets. [William of Orange.]
　　　　　　Rise of the Dutch Republic, pt. vi, ch. vii

24 Give us the luxuries of life, and we will dispense with
　its necessities.
　　Remark. O. W. Holmes, *Autocrat of the Breakfast-
　Table, ch. 6. Often mistakenly attrib. to Oscar
　Wilde.*

PETER ANTHONY MOTTEUX
1660–1718

25 The devil was sick, the devil a monk wou'd be;
　The devil was well, and the devil a monk he'd be.
　　Translation of Rabelais. *Gargantua and Panta-
　gruel, bk. iv, ch. 24*

HENRY PHIPPS, EARL OF MULGRAVE
1755–1831

26 And toast before each martial tune—
　'Howe, and the Glorious First of June!'
　　　　　　Our Line was Formed

DINAH MARIA MULOCK
see
MRS. DINAH MARIA CRAIK

ANTHONY MUNDAY
1553–1633

27 Beauty sat bathing by a spring
　　Where fairest shades did hide her;
　The winds blew calm, the birds did sing,
　　The cool streams ran beside her.
　My wanton thoughts enticed mine eye
　　To see what was forbidden:
　But better memory said, fie!
　　So vain desire was chidden.
　　　　Hey nonny, nonny.
　　　　　　England's Helicon. To Colin Clout

HECTOR HUGH MUNRO

see

SAKI

C. W. MURPHY

1 We all go the same way home. *Title of Song*

2 Has anybody here seen Kelly?
Kelly from the Isle of Man?
Has Anybody Here seen Kelly?

3 Kelly from the Em'rald Isle. *Ib.*

CHARLES MURRAY
1864–1941

4 Gin danger's there, we'll thole our share,
Gie's but the weapons, we've the will,
Ayont the main, to prove again
Auld Scotland counts for something still. *Hamewith*

FRED MURRAY

5 Carve a little bit off the top for me!
A Little Bit Off The Top

6 Our lodger's such a nice young man. *Title of Song*

ALFRED DE MUSSET
1810–1857

7 Mon verre n'est pas grand mais je bois dans mon verre.
The glass I drink from is not large, but at least it
is my own. *La Coupe et les Lèvres*

8 Le seul bien qui me reste au monde
Est d'avoir quelquefois pleuré.
The only good thing left to me
Is knowledge that I, too, have wept. *Poèmes*

9 Malgré moi l'infini me tourmente.
I can't help it, the idea of the infinite is a torment to
me. *Premières Poésies, L'Espoir en Dieu*

FREDERICK WILLIAM HENRY MYERS
1843–1901

10 Moses on the mountain
Died of the kisses of the lips of God.
Saint Paul, st. 127

11 Yea, thro' life, death, thro' sorrow and thro' sinning,
He shall suffice me, for he hath sufficed:
Christ is the end, for Christ is the beginning,
Christ the beginning for the end is Christ.
Ib. st. 150

CAROLINA, BARONESS NAIRNE
1766–1845

12 Will ye no come back again?
Better lo'ed ye canna be,
Will ye no come back again?
Life and Songs (1869), *Bonnie Charlie's now awa'*

13 Wha'll buy my caller herrin'?
They're bonnie fish and halesome farin';
Wha'll buy my caller herrin',
New drawn frae the Forth? *Ib. Caller Herrin'*

14 Oh, ye may ca' them vulgar farin',
Wives and mithers maist despairin',
Ca' them lives o' men.
Life and Songs (1869), *Caller Herrin'*

15 Charlie is my darling, my darling, my darling,
Charlie is my darling, the young Chevalier.
Ib. Charlie is My Darling

16 Gude nicht, and joy be wi' you a'. *Ib. Gude Nicht*

17 Wi' a hundred pipers an' a', an' a',
Wi' a hundred pipers an' a', an' a',
We'll up an' gie them a blaw, a blaw,
Wi' a hundred pipers an' a', an' a'.
Ib. The Hundred Pipers

18 A penniless lass wi' a lang pedigree.
Ib. The Laird of Cockpen

19 I'm wearin' awa'
To the land o' the leal. *Ib. The Land o' the Leal*

20 There's nae sorrow there, John,
There's neither cauld nor care, John,
The day is aye fair
In the land o' the leal. *Ib.*

SIR WILLIAM NAPIER
1785–1860

21 Then was seen with what a strength and majesty the
British soldier fights.
History of the War in the Peninsula, bk. xii, ch. 6,
Albuera

NAPOLEON I
1769–1821

22 L'Angleterre est une nation de boutiquiers.
England is a nation of shopkeepers.
*Attr. by B.B.E. O'Meara, Napoleon at St. Helena,
vol. ii. The original is probably 'sono mercanti',
a phrase of Paoli, quoted by Napoleon; see Gourgaud,* Journal Inédit de Ste-Hélène, *i. 69.(See
1:6, 503:11)*

23 Tout soldat français porte dans sa giberne le bâton de
maréchal de France.
Every French soldier carries in his cartridge-pouch
the baton of a marshal of France.
E. Blaze, *La Vie Militaire sous l'Empire*, I. v

24 A la guerre, les trois quarts sont des affaires morales,
la balance des forces réelles n'est que pour un
autre quart.
In war, moral considerations make up three-quar-
ters of the game: the relative balance of man-
power accounts only for the remaining quarter.
*Correspondance de Napoléon Ier, xvii, no. 14276
(Observations sur les affaires d'Espagne, Saint-
Cloud, 27 août 1808)*

25 Quant au courage moral, il avait trouvé fort rare,
disait-il, celui de deux heures après minuit; c'est-
à-dire le courage de l'improviste.
As to moral courage, I have very rarely met with
the two o'clock in the morning courage: I mean
unprepared courage.
Las Cases, *Mémorial de Ste-Hélène*, Dec. 4–5,
1815

26 La carrière ouverte aux talents.
The career open to talents.
O'Meara, *Napoleon in Exile* (1822), vol. i, p. 103

1 Soldats, songez que, du haut de ces pyramides, quarante siècles vous contemplent.

Think of it, soldiers; from the summit of these pyramids, forty centuries look down upon you.
Speech to the Army of Egypt on 21 July 1798, before the Battle of the Pyramids. Gourgaud, *Mémoires, Guerre d'Orient,* i, p. 160

2 Du sublime au ridicule il n'y a qu'un pas.

There is only one step from the sublime to the ridiculous.
To De Pradt, Polish ambassador, after the retreat from Moscow in 1812. De Pradt, *Histoire de l'Ambassade dans le grand-duché de Varsovie en 1812,* ed. 1815, p. 215.

3 Voilà le soleil d'Austerlitz.

There rises the sun of Austerlitz.
To his officers, before Moscow, 7 Sept. 1812

4 Tête d'Armée.   *Last words*

THOMAS NASHE
1567–1601

5 Brightness falls from the air;
Queens have died young and fair;
Dust hath closed Helen's eye.
I am sick, I must die.
Lord have mercy on us.   *In Time of Pestilence*

6 Spring, the sweet spring, is the year's pleasant king;
Then blooms each thing, then maids dance in a ring,
Cold doth not sting, the pretty birds do sing:
Cuckoo, jug-jug, pu-we, to-witta-woo!   *Spring*

JAMES BALL NAYLOR
1860–1945

7 King David and King Solomon
    Led merry, merry lives,
With many, many lady friends
    And many, many wives;
But when old age crept over them,
    With many, many qualms,
King Solomon wrote the Proverbs
    And King David wrote the Psalms,
                              David and Solomon

JOHN MASON NEALE
1818–1866

8 All glory, laud, and honour
    To Thee, Redeemer, King,
To whom the lips of children
    Made sweet Hosannas ring.
All Glory, Laud, and Honour, trans. from Latin *Gloria, Laus et Honor tibi sit.*

9 Around the throne of God a band
Of glorious Angels always stand.
Around the Throne of God. Hymns for Children, First Series (1842)

10 Art thou weary, art thou languid,
Art thou sore distressed?
Art Thou Weary, trans. from Greek

11 Angels, Martyrs, Prophets, Virgins,
                    Answer, Yes!   *Ib.*

12 Brief life is here our portion;
Brief sorrow, short-lived care.
Brief Life is Here, trans. from Latin, *Hic breve Vivitur*

13 Christian, dost thou see them
    On the holy ground,
How the troops of Midian
    Prowl and prowl around?

Christian, up and smite them,
    Counting gain but loss;
Smite them by the merit
    Of the holy Cross.
Christian, Dost Thou See Them, trans. from Greek

14 Laud and honour to the Father,
Laud and honour to the Son,
Laud and honour to the Spirit,
Ever Three and ever One;
Consubstantial, co-eternal,
While unending ages run.
Come ye Faithful, Raise the Anthem. The Christian Remembrancer, July 1863

15 Loosed from Pharaoh's bitter yoke
Jacob's sons and daughters;
Led them with unmoisten'd foot
Through the Red Sea waters.
Come ye Faithful, Raise the Strain, trans. from Greek

16 Endless noon-day, glorious noon-day.
Light's Abode, Celestial Salem, trans. from Latin, *Hierusalem Luminosa*

17 For thee, O dear, dear Country,
    Mine eyes their vigils keep.
For Thee, O Dear, Dear Country, trans. from Latin, *O Bona Patria*

18 Good Christian men, rejoice
With heart, and soul, and voice.
Good Christian Men, Helmore and Neale, *Carols for Christmastide*

19 Good King Wenceslas look'd out,
    On the Feast of Stephen;
When the snow lay round about,
    Deep and crisp and even.
Good King Wenceslas. Helmore and Neale, *Carols for Christmastide*

20 'Hither, page, and stand by me,
    If thou know'st it, telling,
Yonder peasant, who is he?
    Where and what his dwelling?'   *Ib.*

21 'Bring me flesh and bring me wine,
    Bring me pine-logs hither.'   *Ib.*

22 Page and monarch, forth they went,
    Forth they went together.   *Ib.*

23 'Sire, the night is darker now,
    And the wind blows stronger,
Fails my heart, I know not how;
    I can go no longer.'
'Mark my footsteps, good my page,
    Tread thou in them boldly,
Thou shalt find the winter's rage
    Freeze thy blood less coldly.'   *Ib.*

24 In his master's steps he trod,
    Where the snow lay dinted;
Heat was in the very sod
    Which the Saint had printed.
Wherefore, Christian men, be sure,
    Wealth or rank possessing,
Ye who now do bless the poor
    Shall yourselves find blessing.   *Ib.*

1 Jerusalem the golden,
　　With milk and honey blest,
　　Beneath thy contemplation
　　Sink heart and voice opprest.
　　I know not, oh, I know not,
　　What joys await us there,
　　What radiancy of glory,
　　What bliss beyond compare.
　　　　Jerusalem the Golden, trans. from Latin, *Urbs
　　　　Syon Aurea*

2 And bright with many an angel
　　And all the martyr throng.　　　　　　　*Ib.*

3 The pastures of the blessèd
　　Are deck'd in glorious sheen.　　　　　　*Ib.*

4 The shout of them that triumph,
　　The song of them that feast.　　　　　　*Ib.*

5 O sweet and blessèd country
　　That eager hearts expect!　　　　　　　*Ib.*

6 O come, O come, Emmanuel,
　　And ransom captive Israel.
　　　　O Come, O Come, Emmanuel, trans. from Latin,
　　　　Veni, Veni, Emmanuel

7 O happy band of pilgrims,
　　If onward ye will tread.
　　　　*O Happy Band of Pilgrims. Hymns of the Eastern
　　　　Church*

8 O happy band of pilgrims,
　　Look upward to the skies,
　　Where such a light affliction
　　Shall win you such a prize!　　　　　　*Ib.*

9 Oh, what the joy and the glory must be,
　　Those endless Sabbaths the blessèd ones see.
　　　　Oh, what the Joy, trans. from Latin of Abelard,
　　　　O quanta qualia sunt illa Sabbata

10 Raise the 'Trisagion' ever and aye.
　　　　*Stars of the Morning. Hymns of the Eastern
　　　　Church*

11 Safe home, safe home in port!
　　Rent cordage, shatter'd deck,
　　Torn sails, provisions short,
　　And only not a wreck.
　　　　*Safe Home, Safe Home. Hymns of the Eastern
　　　　Church*

12 The prize, the prize secure!
　　The athlete nearly fell.　　　　　　　*Ib.*

HORATIO, VISCOUNT NELSON
1758–1805

13 Palmam qui meruit, ferat.
　　Let him who merits bear the palm.　　*Motto*

14 Sent Admiral Collingwood the Nelson touch.
　　　　Private Diary, 9 Oct. 1805

15 It is my turn now; and if I come back, it is yours.
　　　　*Exercising his privilege, as second lieutenant,
　　　　to board a prize ship before the Master.* Southey's
　　　　Life of Nelson, ch. 1, *Nelson's Memoir of His
　　　　Services.*

16 You must consider every man your enemy who speaks
　　ill of your king: and . . . you must hate a French-
　　man as you hate the devil.　　*Ib.* ch. 3

17 Westminster Abbey or victory!
　　　　At the battle of Cape St. Vincent. Ib. ch. 4

18 Before this time to-morrow I shall have gained a
　　peerage, or Westminster Abbey.
　　　　Battle of the Nile. Southey's *Life of Nelson*, ch. 5

19 Victory is not a name strong enough for such a scene.
　　　　At the battle of the Nile. Ib.

20 It is warm work; and this day may be the last to
　　any of us at a moment. But mark you! I would
　　not be elsewhere for thousands.
　　　　At the battle of Copenhagen. Ib. ch. 7

21 I have only one eye,—I have a right to be blind some-
　　times: . . . I really do not see the signal!
　　　　At the battle of Copenhagen. Ib.

22 In honour I gained them, and in honour I will die with
　　them.
　　　　When asked to cover the stars on his uniform. Ib. ch. 9

23 England expects that every man will do his duty.
　　　　At the battle of Trafalgar. Ib.

24 This is too warm work, Hardy, to last long.　　*Ib.*

25 Thank God, I have done my duty.　　　　*Ib.*

26 Kiss me, Hardy.　　　　　　　　　　*Ib.*

NERO
A.D. 37–68

27 Qualis artifex pereo!
　　What an artist dies with me!
　　　　Suetonius, *Life of Nero*, xlix. 1

EDITH NESBIT
1858–1924

28 Little brown brother, oh! little brown brother,
　　Are you awake in the dark?　　*Baby Seed Song*

ALLAN NEVINS
1890–

29 The former allies had blundered in the past by offer-
　　ing Germany too little, and offering even that too
　　late, until finally Nazi Germany had become a
　　menace to all mankind.
　　　　Article in 'Current History', May 1935

SIR HENRY JOHN NEWBOLT
1862–1938

30 Effingham, Grenville, Raleigh, Drake,
　　Here's to the bold and free!
　　Benbow, Collingwood, Byron, Blake,
　　Hail to the kings of the sea!　　*Admirals All*, i

31 Admirals all, for England's sake,
　　Honour be yours, and fame!
　　And honour, as long as waves shall break,
　　To Nelson's peerless name!　　　　*Ib.*

32 He clapped the glass to his sightless eye,
　　And 'I'm damned if I see it', he said.　　*Ib.*

33 To set the Cause above renown,
　　To love the game beyond the prize,
　　To honour, while you strike him down,
　　The foe that comes with fearless eyes:
　　To count the life of battle good,
　　And dear the land that gave you birth,
　　And dearer yet the brotherhood
　　That binds the brave of all the earth.
　　　　The Island Race, Clifton Chapel

1 'Qui procul hinc', the legend's writ,—
   The frontier-grave is far away—
'Qui ante diem periit:
   Sed miles, sed pro patria.'
                    The Island Race, Clifton Chapel

2 'Take my drum to England, hang et by the shore,
   Strike et when your powder's runnin' low;
If the Dons sight Devon, I'll quit the port o' Heaven,
   An' drum them up the Channel as we drummed them
      long ago.'   *Ib. Drake's Drum*

3 Drake he's in his hammock till the great Armadas
      come.
   (Capten, art tha sleepin' there below?)
Slung atween the round shot, listenin' for the drum,
   An' dreamin' arl the time o' Plymouth Hoe.
Call him on the deep sea, call him up the Sound,
   Call him when ye sail to meet the foe;
Where the old trade's plyin' an' the old flag flyin'
   They shall find him ware an' wakin', as they found
      him long ago!   *Ib.*

4 There's a breathless hush in the Close to-night—
   Ten to make and the match to win—
A bumping pitch and a blinding light,
   An hour to play and the last man in.
And it's not for the sake of a ribboned coat,
   Or the selfish hope of a season's fame,
But his Captain's hand on his shoulder smote—
   'Play up! play up! and play the game!'
                         Ib. Vitaï Lampada

5 The voice of the schoolboy rallies the ranks:
   'Play up! play up! and play the game!'   *Ib.*

6 Now the sunset breezes shiver,
   And she's fading down the river,
But in England's song for ever
   She's the Fighting Téméraire.
                    The Fighting Téméraire

7 'Ye have robb'd', said he, 'ye have slaughter'd and
      made an end,
Take your ill-got plunder, and bury the dead.'
                    He Fell Among Thieves

8 But cared greatly to serve God and the King,
   And keep the Nelson touch.   *Minora Sidera*

MARGARET, DUCHESS OF NEWCASTLE
1624?–1673

9 Her name was Margarett Lucas, yongest sister to the
   Lord Lucas of Colchester, a noble familie; for all
   the Brothers were Valiant, and all the Sisters
   virtuous.   *Epitaph, Westminster Abbey*

JOHN HENRY, CARDINAL NEWMAN
1801–1890

10 It is very difficult to get up resentment towards
   persons whom one has never seen.
      Apologia pro Vita Sua (1864). *Mr. Kingsley's
      Method of Disputation*

11 There is such a thing as legitimate warfare: war has
   its laws; there are things which may fairly be done,
   and things which may not be done. . . . He has
   attempted (as I may call it) to *poison the wells*. *Ib.*

12 I will vanquish, not my Accuser, but my judges.
      Ib. True Mode of meeting Mr. Kingsley

13 I used to wish the Arabian Tales were true.
      Apologia pro Vita Sua (1864). *History of My
      Religious Opinions to the Year 1833*

14 Two and two only supreme and luminously self-
   evident beings, myself and my Creator.   *Ib.*

15 Growth [is] the only evidence of life.   *Ib.*

16 The motto [of *Lyra Apostolica*] shows the feeling of
   both [Hurrell] Froude and myself at the time: we
   borrowed from M. Bunsen a Homer, and Froude
   chose the words in which Achilles, on returning to
   the battle, says, 'You shall know the difference now
   that I am back again'.   *Ib.*

17 It would be a gain to the country were it vastly more
   superstitious, more bigoted, more gloomy, more
   fierce in its religion than at present it shows itself
   to be.
      *Ib. History of My Religious Opinions from
      1833 to 1839*

18 From the age of fifteen, dogma has been the fundamental principle of my religion: I know no other
   religion; I cannot enter into the idea of any other
   sort of religion; religion, as a mere sentiment, is
   to me a dream and a mockery.   *Ib.*

19 This is what the Church is said to want, not party
   men, but sensible, temperate, sober, well-judging
   persons, to guide it through the channel of no-
   meaning, between the Scylla and Charybdis of Aye
   and No.
      *Ib. History of My Religious Opinions from 1839
      to 1841*

20 I recollect an acquaintance saying to me that 'the
   Oriel Common Room stank of Logic'.
      *Ib. History of My Religious Opinions from 1841
      to 1845*

21 Cowards! If I advanced one step, you would run
   away.   *Ib.*

22 Trinity had never been unkind to me. There used
   to be much snap-dragon growing on the walls
   opposite my freshman's rooms there, and I had
   for years taken it as the emblem of my own perpetual residence even unto death in my University.
   On the morning of the 23rd I left the Observatory. I have never seen Oxford since, excepting its
   spires, as they are seen from the railway.   *Ib.*

23 Ten thousand difficulties do not make one doubt.
      Ib. Position of My Mind since 1845

24 The all-corroding, all-dissolving scepticism of the
   intellect in religious enquiries.   *Ib.*

25 It is almost a definition of a gentleman to say that he
   is one who never inflicts pain.
      *The Idea of a University. Knowledge and Religious
      Duty*

26 Take a mere beggar-woman, lazy, ragged, filthy, and
   not over-scrupulous of truth,—but if she is chaste,
   and sober, and cheerful, and goes to her religious
   duties—she will, in the eyes of the Church, have
   a prospect of heaven, quite closed and refused to
   the State's pattern-man, the just, the upright, the
   generous, the honourable, the conscientious, if he
   be all this, not from a supernatural power,—but
   from mere natural virtue.
      Lectures on Anglican Difficulties. Lecture VIII

1 She [the Catholic Church] holds that it were better for sun and moon to drop from heaven, for the earth to fail, and for all the many millions who are upon it to die of starvation in extremest agony, as far as temporal affliction goes, than that one soul, I will not say, should be lost, but should commit one single venial sin, should tell one wilful untruth, . . . or steal one poor farthing without excuse.
Lectures on Anglican Difficulties. Lecture VIII

2 Ex umbris et imaginibus in veritatem.
From shadows and types to the reality. *Motto*

3 Cor ad cor loquitur.
Heart speaks to heart.
Motto adopted for his coat-of-arms as cardinal. 1879

4 May He support us all the day long, till the shades lengthen, and the evening comes, and the busy world is hushed, and the fever of life is over, and our work is done! Then in His mercy may He give us a safe lodging, and a holy rest, and peace at the last. *Sermon, 1834. Wisdom and Innocence*

5 Firmly I believe and truly
God is Three, and God is One;
And I next acknowledge duly
Manhood taken by the Son.
The Dream of Gerontius

6 Praise to the Holiest in the height,
And in the depth be praise;
In all his words most wonderful,
Most sure in all His ways. *Ib.*

7 A secónd Adam to the fight
And to the rescue came. *Ib.*

8 O wisest love! that flesh and blood
Which did in Adam fail,
Should strive afresh against their foe,
Should strive and should prevail. *Ib.*

9 Prune thou thy words, the thoughts control
That o'er thee swell and throng;
They will condense within thy soul,
And change to purpose strong.
Flowers Without Fruit. Prune Thou Thy Words

10 Lead, kindly Light, amid the encircling gloom,
Lead thou me on;
The night is dark, and I am far from home,
Lead thou me on.
Keep Thou my feet; I do not ask to see
The distant scene; one step enough for me.
The Pillar of Cloud. Lead Kindly Light

11 I loved the garish day, and, spite of fears,
Pride ruled my will: remember not past years. *Ib.*

12 And with the morn those Angel faces smile,
Which I have loved long since, and lost awhile. *Ib.*

SIR ISAAC NEWTON
1642–1727

13 I do not know what I may appear to the world, but to myself I seem to have been only a boy playing on the sea-shore, and diverting myself in now and then finding a smoother pebble or a prettier shell than ordinary, whilst the great ocean of truth lay all undiscovered before me.
Brewster's *Memoirs of Newton*, vol. ii, ch. 27

14 O Diamond! Diamond! thou little knowest the mischief done!
Remark to a dog who knocked down a candle and so set fire to some papers and 'destroyed the almost finished labours of some years'. Thomas Maude, Wensley-Dale . . . a Poem (1780), p. 28, note

JOHN NEWTON
1725–1807

15 How sweet the name of Jesus sounds
In a believer's ear!
It soothes his sorrows, heals his wounds,
And drives away his fear.
Olney Hymns (1779), How Sweet the Name

16 Glorious things of thee are spoken,
Zion, city of our God. *Ib. Glorious Things of Thee*

NICHOLAS I OF RUSSIA
1796–1855

17 Nous avons sur les bras un homme malade—un homme gravement malade.
We have on our hands a sick man—a very sick man.
[The sick man of Europe, the Turk.]
Parliamentary Papers. Accounts and Papers, vol. lxxi, pt. 5. Eastern Papers, p. 2. Sir G. H. Seymour to Lord John Russell, 11 Jan. 1853

18 Russia has two generals in whom she can confide—Generals Janvier and Février.
Punch, 10 Mar. 1853. Speech of the late Emperor of Russia

NICIAS
c. 470–413 B.C.

19 ἄνδρες γὰρ πόλις, καὶ οὐ τείχη οὐδὲ νῆες ἀνδρῶν κεναί.
It is men who make a city, not walls or ships without crews.
Speech to his army after his defeat by the Syracusans (413 B.C.). Thucydides, vii. 77.

ADELA FLORENCE NICOLSON
see
LAURENCE HOPE

FRIEDRICH WILHELM NIETZSCHE
1844–1900

20 Jenseits von Gut und Böse.
Beyond good and evil. *Title of Book*

21 Herren-Moral und Sklaven-Moral.
Morality of masters and the morality of slaves.
Jenseits von Gut und Böse

22 Ich lehre euch den Übermenschen. Der Mensch ist Etwas, das überwunden werden soll.
I teach you the superman. Man is something to be surpassed. *Thus Spake Zarathustra. Prologue*

23 Blonde Bestie.
Blonde beast. *Zur Genealogie der Moral*

'NIMROD' [CHARLES JAMES APPERLEY]
1779-1843

1 'Who is that under his horse in the brook?'
'Only Dick Christian,' answers Lord Forester, 'and
   it's nothing new to him.'
'But he'll be drowned,' exclaims Lord Kinnaird.
'I shouldn't wonder,' observes Mr. William Coke.
'But the pace is too good to inquire.' *The Chase*

2 'Quite the cream of the thing, I suppose,' says Lord
   Gardner. *Ib.*

ALBERT JAY NOCK
1873-1945

3 It is an economic axiom as old as the hills that goods
   and services can be paid for only with goods and
   services. *Memoirs of a Superfluous Man.* iii, ch. 3

RODEN BERKELEY NOEL
1834-1894

4 After battle sleep is best,
   After noise, tranquillity. *The Old*

5 Loving, adorable,
   Softly to rest,
   Here in my crystalline,
   Here in my breast!
                        The Water-Nymph and the Boy

THOMAS NOEL
1799-1861

6 Rattle his bones over the stones;
   He's only a pauper, whom nobody owns!
                Rhymes and Roundelays, The Pauper's Drive

REV. JOHN NORRIS
1657-1711

7 Were angels to write, I fancy we should have but few
   Folios. *Collections of Miscellanies* (1678), Preface

8 How fading are the joys we doat upon!
   Like apparitions seen and gone.
   But those which soonest take their flight
   Are the most exquisite and strong,—
   Like angels' visits, short and bright;
   Mortality's too weak to bear them long.
                                      Ib. The Parting

CHRISTOPHER NORTH
[JOHN WILSON]
1785-1854

9 Minds like ours, my dear James, must always be
   above national prejudices, and in all companies it
   gives me true pleasure to declare, that, as a people,
   the English are very little indeed inferior to the
   Scotch. *Noctes Ambrosianae*, No. 28 (October 1826)

10 His Majesty's dominions, on which the sun never sets.
                        Ib. No. 20 (April 1829)

11 Laws were made to be broken.
                        Ib. No. 24 (May 1830)

12 Insultin the sun, and quarrellin wi' the equawtor.
   [*Ettrick Shepherd.*] *Ib.* (May 1830)

13 Animosities are mortal, but the Humanities live for
   ever. *Noctes Ambrosianae*, No. 35 (Aug. 1834)

14 I cannot sit still, James, and hear you abuse the
   shopocracy. *Ib.* No. 39 (Feb. 1835)

SIR STAFFORD HENRY NORTHCOTE, EARL OF IDDESLEIGH
1818-1887

15 Argue as you please, you are nowhere, that grand old
   man, the Prime Minister, insists on the other thing.
                        Speech at Liverpool, 12 Apr. 1882

CAROLINE ELIZABETH SARAH NORTON
1808-1877

16 My beautiful, my beautiful! that standest meekly by,
   With thy proudly-arched and glossy neck, and dark
      and fiery eye!
   Fret not to roam the desert now, with all thy winged
      speed:
   I may not mount on thee again!—thou'rt sold, my
      Arab steed! *The Arab's Farewell to His Steed*

17 The stranger hath thy bridle-rein, thy master hath his
      gold;—
   Fleet-limbed and beautiful, farewell; thou'rt sold, my
      steed, thou'rt sold. *Ib.*

18 And sitting down by the green well, I'll pause and
      sadly think—
   ''Twas here he bowed his glossy neck when last I saw
      him drink.' *Ib.*

19 They tempted me, my beautiful! for hunger's power
      is strong—
   They tempted me, my beautiful! but I have loved too
      long. *Ib.*

20 'Tis false! 'tis false, my Arab steed! I fling them back
      their gold! *Ib.*

21 A soldier of the Legion lay dying in Algiers—
   There was lack of woman's nursing, there was
      dearth of woman's tears. *Bingen on the Rhine*

22 I do not love thee!—no! I do not love thee!
   And yet when thou art absent I am sad.
                        I Do Not Love Thee

23 For death and life, in ceaseless strife,
   Beat wild on this world's shore,
   And all our calm is in that balm—
   Not lost but gone before. *Not Lost but Gone Before*

NOVALIS [FRIEDRICH VON HARDENBERG]
1772-1801

24 Ein Gott-betrunkener Mensch.
   A God-intoxicated man. *Remark about Spinoza*

ALFRED NOYES
1880-1958

25 Go down to Kew in lilac-time, in lilac-time, in lilac-
      time;
   Go down to Kew in lilac-time (it isn't far from
      London!)
   And you shall wander hand in hand with love in
      summer's wonderland;
   Go down to Kew in lilac-time (it isn't far from
      London!) *Barrel Organ*

1 The wind was a torrent of darkness among the gusty
    trees,
The moon was a ghostly galleon tossed upon cloudy
    seas,
The road was a ribbon of moonlight over the purple
    moor,
And the highwayman came riding—
        Riding—riding—
The highwayman came riding, up to the old inn-door.
                        The Highwayman

2   The landlord's black-eyed daughter,
    Bess, the landlord's daughter,
Plaiting a dark red love-knot into her long black hair.
                               Ib.

3   Look for me by moonlight;
    Watch for me by moonlight;
I'll come to thee by moonlight, though hell should
    bar the way!   *Ib.*

4 There's a magic in the distance, where the sea-line
    meets the sky.   *Forty Singing Seamen*, ix

5 Calling as he used to call, faint and far away,
In Sherwood, in Sherwood, about the break of day.
                              Sherwood

6 Sherwood in the red dawn, is Robin Hood asleep? *Ib.*

NURSERY RHYMES
(See Note to the Second Edition, *p. v)*

7 A was an apple-pie;
B bit it;
C cut it.
    Quoted by John Eachard, *Some Observations* (1671)

8 As I was going to St. Ives,
I met a man with seven wives,
Each wife had seven sacks,
Each sack had seven cats,
Each cat had seven kits:
Kits, cats, sacks, and wives,
How many were there going to St. Ives?
                  Harley MS., 7316 (*c.* 1730)

9 Baa, baa, black sheep,
Have you any wool?
Yes, sir, yes, sir,
Three bags full:
One for the master,
And one for the dame,
And one for the little boy
Who lives down the lane.
    Tommy Thumb's Pretty Song Book (*c.* 1744)

10 Boys and girls come out to play,
The moon doth shine as bright as day.
    In William King, *Useful Transactions in Philo-
    sophy* (1708–9)

11 Bye, baby bunting,
Daddy's gone a-hunting,
Gone to get a rabbit skin
To wrap the baby bunting in.
          Gammer Gurton's Garland (1784)

12 Cock a doodle doo!
My dame has lost her shoe;
My master's lost his fiddling-stick,
And knows not what to do.
    *Quoted in The Most Cruel And Bloody Murder
    Committed by an Innkeepers Wife* (1606)

13 Come, let's to bed, says Sleepy-head;
Tarry a while, says Slow;
Put on the pot, says Greedy-gut,
We'll sup before we go.
          Gammer Gurton's Garland (1784)

14 Cross-patch,
Draw the latch,
Sit by the fire and spin:
Take a cup,
And drink it up,
Then call your neighbours in.
        Mother Goose's Melody (*c.* 1765)

15 Cry, baby, cry,
Put your finger in your eye,
And tell your mother it wasn't I.
    Nursery Rhymes, ed. J. O. Halliwell (1853)

16 Curly locks, Curly locks,
Wilt thou be mine?
Thou shalt not wash dishes
Nor yet feed the swine.
But sit on a cushion
And sew a fine seam,
And feed upon strawberries,
Sugar and cream.
                Infant Institutes (1797)

17 Daffy-down-dilly is new come to town,
With a yellow petticoat, and a green gown.
              Songs for the Nursery (1805)

18 Ding, dong, bell,
Pussy's in the well.
Who put her in?
Little Johnny Green.
        Mother Goose's Melody (*c.* 1765)

19 Four and twenty tailors went to kill a snail,
The best man among them durst not touch her tail.
She put out her horns like a little Kyloe cow,
Run, tailors, run, or she'll kill you all e'en now.
          Gammer Gurton's Garland (1784)

20 A fox jumped up one winter's night.
        The Opera, ed. James Ballantyne (1832)

21 A frog he would a-wooing go.
'Heigh ho!' says Rowley.
        In Thomas Ravenscroft, *Melismata* (1611)

22 Georgie Porgie, pudding and pie,
Kissed the girls and made them cry;
When the boys came out to play
Georgie Porgie ran away.
    Nursery Rhymes, ed. J. O. Halliwell (1842)

23 Goosey goosey gander,
Whither shall I wander?
Upstairs and downstairs,
And in my lady's chamber;
There I met an old man
That would not say his prayers;
I took him by the left leg,
And threw him down the stairs.
        Gammer Gurton's Garland (1784)

NURSERY RHYMES

1 Hey diddle diddle,
The cat and the fiddle,
The cow jumped over the moon;
The little dog laughed
To see such sport,
And the dish ran away with the spoon.
Mother Goose's Melody (c. 1765)

2 Hickety, pickety, my black hen,
She lays eggs for gentlemen;
Gentlemen come every day
To see what my black hen doth lay.
Nursery Rhymes, ed. J. O. Halliwell (1853)

3 Hickory, dickory, dock,
The mouse ran up the clock,
The clock struck one,
The mouse ran down;
Hickory, dickory, dock.
Tommy Thumb's Pretty Song Book (c. 1744)

4 How many miles to Babylon?
Threescore miles and ten.
Can I get there by candle-light?
Yes, and back again.
If your heels are nimble and light,
You may get there by candle-light.
Songs for the Nursery (1805)

5 Humpty Dumpty sat on a wall,
Humpty Dumpty had a great fall;
All the king's horses,
And all the king's men,
Couldn't put Humpty together again.
From MS. addition to a copy of *Mother Goose's Melody* (c. 1803)

6 If I'd as much money as I could spend,
I never would cry old chairs to mend;
Cry chairs to mend, old chairs to mend;
I never would cry old chairs to mend.
Gammer Gurton's Garland (1810)

7 I had a little nut tree, nothing would it bear
But a silver nutmeg and a golden pear;
The king of Spain's daughter came to visit me,
And all for the sake of my little nut tree.
Newest Christmas Box (c. 1797)

8 I like little pussy, her coat is so warm,
And if I don't hurt her, she'll do me no harm.
So I'll not pull her tail, nor drive her away,
But pussy and I very gently will play.
Only True Mother Goose Melodies (Boston, c. 1843)

9 Jack and Jill went up the hill
To fetch a pail of water;
Jack fell down and broke his crown,
And Jill came tumbling after.
Mother Goose's Melody (c. 1765)

10 Jack Sprat could eat no fat,
His wife could eat no lean;
And so between them both, you see,
They licked the platter clean.
In John Clarke, *Paroemiologia Anglo-Latina* (1639)

11 The King of France went up the hill,
With forty thousand men;
The King of France came down the hill,
And ne'er went up again.
Quoted by James Howell in a letter to Sir James Crofts, 12 May 1620

12 Ladybird, ladybird, fly away home,
Your house is on fire, and your children all gone.
Tommy Thumb's Pretty Song Book (c. 1744)

13 The lion and the unicorn
Were fighting for the crown;
The lion beat the unicorn
All round about the town.
Some gave them white bread,
And some gave them brown;
Some gave them plum cake,
And sent them out of town.
In William King, *Useful Transactions in Philosophy* (1708–9)

14 Little Bo-Peep has lost her sheep,
And can't tell where to find them;
Leave them alone, and they'll come home,
And bring their tails behind them.
Douce MS. (c. 1805)

15 Little boy blue, come blow up your horn,
The sheep's in the meadow, the cow's in the corn;
But where is the boy that looks after the sheep?
He's under the haycock fast asleep.
Will you wake him? No, not I,
For if I do, he'll be sure to cry.
The Famous Tommy Thumb's Little Story Book (c. 1760)

16 Little Jack Horner sat in the corner,
Eating a Christmas pie:
He put in his thumb, and pulled out a plum,
And said, 'What a good boy am I!'
Quoted by Henry Carey, Namby Pamby (c. 1720)

17 Little Polly Flinders
Sat among the cinders,
Warming her pretty little toes,
Her mother came and caught her,
And whipped her little daughter
For spoiling her nice new clothes.
Original Ditties for the Nursery (c. 1805)

18 Little Tommy Tucker
Sings for his supper;
What shall we give him?
White bread and butter.

How shall he cut it
Without a knife?
How will he be married
Without a wife?
Tommy Thumb's Pretty Song Book (c. 1744)

19 London bridge is broken down,
My fair lady.
Quoted by Henry Carey, Namby Pamby (c. 1720)

20 The man in the wilderness asked me,
How many strawberries grow in the sea?
I answered him, as I thought good,
As many as red herrings grow in the wood.
MS. addition, dated 1744, to the Bath Municipal Library's copy of *The Whole Duty of Man* (1733)

21 Mary, Mary, quite contrary,
How does your garden grow?
With silver bells, and cockle shells,
And pretty maids all in a row.
Tommy Thumb's Pretty Song Book (c. 1744)

1 Monday's child is fair of face,
Tuesday's child is full of grace,
Wednesday's child is full of woe,
Thursday's child has far to go,
Friday's child is loving and giving,
Saturday's child works hard for its living,
And a child that's born on the Sabbath day
Is fair and wise and good and gay.
        Quoted by A. E. Bray, *Traditions of Devonshire*
(1838), ii. 288

2 The north wind doth blow,
And we shall have snow,
And what will poor robin do then?
        Poor thing!
He'll sit in a barn,
To keep himself warm,
And hide his head under his wing.
        Poor thing!
                Songs for the Nursery (1805)

3 Old King Cole
Was a merry old soul,
And a merry old soul was he,
He called for his pipe,
And he called for his bowl,
And he called for his fiddlers three.
Quoted by William King, *Useful Transactions in
Philosophy* (1708–9)

4 Old Mother Hubbard
Went to the cupboard,
To get her poor dog a bone;
But when she came there
The cupboard was bare,
And so the poor dog had none.
        Sarah Catherine Martin, *The Comic Adventures
of Old Mother Hubbard* (1805)

5 One a penny, two a penny, hot cross-buns;
If your daughters do not like them, give them to your
        sons.   *Christmas Box* (1797)

6 One, two,
Buckle my shoe;
Three, four,
Knock at the door;
Five, six,
Pick up sticks.
Seven, eight,
Lay them straight;
Nine, ten,
A big fat hen.   *Songs for the Nursery* (1805)

7 Oranges and lemons
Say the bells of St. Clement's.
        Tommy Thumb's Pretty Song Book (c. 1744)

8 When will you pay me?
Say the bells of Old Bailey.
When I grow rich,
Say the bells of Shoreditch.   *Ib.*

9 Here comes a candle to light you to bed,
Here comes a chopper to chop off your head.   *Ib.*

10 Pat-a-cake, pat-a-cake, baker's man,
Bake me a cake as fast as you can;
Pat it and prick it, and mark it with B,
Put it in the oven for baby and me.
        Quoted in Tom D'Urfey, *The Campaigners* (1698)

11 Pease-porridge hot, pease-porridge cold,
Pease-porridge in the pot, nine days old.
        Newest Christmas Box (c. 1797)

12 Peter Piper picked a peck of pickled pepper;
A peck of pickled pepper Peter Piper picked;
If Peter Piper picked a peck of pickled pepper,
Where's the peck of pickled pepper Peter Piper picked?
        *Peter Piper's Practical Principles of Plain and
Perfect Pronunciation* (1819)

13 Please to remember
The Fifth of November,
        Gunpowder treason and plot;
We know no reason
Why gunpowder treason
        Should ever be forgot.
        Anonymous broadsheet (1826). *See* Wm. Hone,
The Every-Day Book (1841). *See also* 9:11

14 Pussy cat, pussy cat, where have you been?
I've been up to London to look at the queen.
Pussy cat, pussy cat, what did you there?
I frightened a little mouse under the chair.
        Songs for the Nursery (1805)

15 The Queen of Hearts
She made some tarts,
        All on a summer's day;
The Knave of Hearts
He stole the tarts,
        And took them clean away.
                The European Magazine (April 1782)

16 Rain, rain, go away,
Come again another day.
                In James Howell, *Proverbs* (1659)

17 Ride a cock-horse to Banbury Cross,
To see a fine lady upon a white horse,
Rings on her fingers and bells on her toes,
And she shall have music wherever she goes.
                Gammer Gurton's Garland (1784)

18 See-saw, Margery Daw,
Jacky shall have a new master;
Jacky must have but a penny a day,
Because he can't work any faster.
                Mother Goose's Melody (c. 1765)

19 Simple Simon met a pieman
        Going to the fair:
Says Simple Simon to the pieman,
        'Let me taste your ware.'
        Simple Simon (a chapbook advertisement, 1764)

20 Sing a song of sixpence,
        A pocket full of rye,
Four and twenty blackbirds,
        Baked in a pie;
When the pie was opened,
        The birds began to sing;
Was not that a dainty dish
        To set before the king?

The king was in his counting-house
        Counting out his money;
The queen was in the parlour
        Eating bread and honey;
The maid was in the garden
        Hanging out the clothes,
There came a little blackbird,
        And snapped off her nose.
        Tommy Thumb's Pretty Song Book (c. 1744)

21 Solomon Grundy,
Born on a Monday,
Christened on Tuesday,

[368]

Married on Wednesday,
Took ill on Thursday,
Worse on Friday,
Died on Saturday,
Buried on Sunday:
This is the end
Of Solomon Grundy.
Nursery Rhymes, ed. J. O. Halliwell (1842)

1 Taffy was a Welshman, Taffy was a thief;
Taffy came to my house and stole a piece of beef:
I went to Taffy's house, Taffy was not at home;
Taffy came to my house and stole a marrow-bone.
Nancy Cock's Pretty Song Book (c. 1780)

2 Tell tale, tit!
Your tongue shall be split,
And all the dogs in the town
Shall have a little bit.
Nursery Rhymes, ed. J. O. Halliwell (1842)

3 There was a crooked man, and he walked a crooked mile,
He found a crooked sixpence against a crooked stile:
He bought a crooked cat, which caught a crooked
mouse,
And they all lived together in a little crooked house.
Ib.

4 There was an old woman who lived in a shoe,
She had so many children she didn't know what to do;
She gave them some broth without any bread,
She whipped them all soundly and put them to bed.
Gammer Gurton's Garland (1784)

5 Thirty days hath September,
April, June, and November;
All the rest have thirty-one,
Excepting February alone,
And that has twenty-eight days clear
And twenty-nine in each leap year.
Stevins MS. (c. 1555). (*See* 228:4)

6 This is the farmer sowing his corn,
That kept the cock that crowed in the morn,
That waked the priest all shaven and shorn,
That married the man all tattered and torn,
That kissed the maiden all forlorn,
That milked the cow with the crumpled horn,
That tossed the dog,
That worried the cat,
That killed the rat,
That ate the malt
That lay in the house that Jack built.
Nurse Truelove's New-Year's-Gift (1755)

7 This little pig went to market;
This little pig stayed at home;
This little pig had roast beef;
And this little pig had none;
And this little pig cried, Wee, wee, wee!
I can't find my way home.
The Famous Tommy Thumb's Little Story Book
(c. 1760)

8 Three blind mice, see how they run!
They all ran after the farmer's wife,
Who cut off their tails with a carving-knife,
Did you ever see such a thing in your life
As three blind mice?
In Thomas Ravenscroft, *Deuteromelia* (1609)

9 Three wise men of Gotham
Went to sea in a bowl:
And if the bowl had been stronger,
My song would have been longer.
Mother Goose's Melody (c. 1765)

10 Tom he was a piper's son,
He learned to play when he was young,
But all the tune that he could play,
Was 'Over the hills and far away.'
Tom, the Piper's Son (c. 1795)

11 Tom, Tom, the piper's son,
Stole a pig, and away he run;
The pig was eat, and Tom was beat,
And Tom went howling down the street. *Ib.*

12 What are little boys made of?
What are little boys made of?
Frogs and snails, and puppy-dogs' tails;
That's what little boys are made of.

What are little girls made of?
What are little girls made of?
Sugar and spice, and all that's nice;
That's what little girls are made of.
Nursery Rhymes, ed. J. O. Halliwell (1844)

13 When I was a little boy, I had but little wit,
'Tis a long time ago, and I have no more yet;
Nor ever ever shall, until that I die,
For the longer I live, the more fool am I.
Wit and Mirth, an Antidote against Melancholy
(1684)

14 Where are you going to, my pretty maid?
Quoted by William Pryce, *Archaeologia Cornu-*
Britannica (1790)

15 'My face is my fortune, sir,' she said. *Ib.*

16 'Nobody asked you, sir,' she said. *Ib.*

17 Who comes here?
A grenadier.
What do you want?
A pot of beer.
Where is your money?
I've forgot.
Get you gone,
You drunken sot!
Henry Carey, *Namby Pamby* (c. 1720)

18 'Who killed Cock Robin?'
'I,' said the Sparrow,
'With my bow and arrow,
I killed Cock Robin.'
All the birds of the air fell a-sighing and a-sobbing
When they heard of the death of poor Cock Robin.
Tommy Thumb's Pretty Song Book (c. 1744)

19 'Who saw him die?'
'I,' said the Fly,
'With my little eye,
I saw him die.' *Ib.*

FREDERICK OAKELEY

1802–1880

20 O come, all ye faithful,
Joyful and triumphant,
O come ye, O come ye to Bethlehem.
O Come, All Ye Faithful, trans. from Latin, *Adeste*
Fideles

SEAN O'CASEY
1884–

1 The whole world is in a terrible state of chassis.
Juno and the Paycock, I. i

ADOLPH S. OCHS
1858–1935

2 All the news that's fit to print.
Motto of the 'New York Times'

WILLIAM DOUGLAS O'CONNOR
1832–1889

3 The Good Gray Poet. [Whitman.] *Title of book*, 1866

JAMES OGILVY, FIRST EARL OF SEAFIELD
1664–1730

4 Now there's ane end of ane old song
*As he signed the engrossed exemplification of the
Act of Union, 1706. Lockhart Papers (1817), i. 223*

JOHN O'KEEFFE
1747–1833

5 Amo, amas, I love a lass,
As a cedar tall and slender;
Sweet cowslip's grace
Is her nom'native case,
And she's of the feminine gender.
Rorum, corum, sunt Divorum!
Harum, scarum, Divo!
Tag rag, merry derry, periwig and hatband!
Hic hoc horum Genitivo!
Agreeable Surprise, II. ii. Song: *Amo, Amas*

6 Fat, fair and forty were all the toasts of the young
men. *Irish Minnie*, ii

7 You should always except the present company.
London Hermit, I. ii

DENNIS O'KELLY
1720?–1787

8 Eclipse first, the rest nowhere.
*Epsom, 3 May 1769. Annals of Sporting, vol. ii,
p. 271*

JOHN OLDHAM
1653–1683

9 And all your fortune lies beneath your hat.
*A Satire addressed to a Friend about to leave the
University*, l. 25

10 Racks, gibbets, halters, were their arguments.
Satires Upon the Jesuits, Sat. 1, *Garnet's Ghost*,
l. 176

WILLIAM OLDYS
1696–1761

11 Busy, curious, thirsty fly.
Busy, Curious, Thirsty Fly, l. 1

JOHN OPIE
1761–1807

12 [When asked with what he mixed his colours.]
I mix them with my brains, sir.
Samuel Smiles, Self-Help, ch. 4

BARONESS ORCZY
[MRS. MONTAGUE BARSTOW]
1865–1947

13 We seek him here, we seek him there,
Those Frenchies seek him everywhere.
Is he in heaven?—Is he in hell?
That demmed, elusive Pimpernel?
The Scarlet Pimpernel, ch. 12

JOHN BOYLE O'REILLY
1844–1890

14 The organized charity, scrimped and iced,
In the name of a cautious, statistical Christ.
*Life, Poems, and Speeches (1891), In Bohemia,
l. 37*

META ORRED

15 In the gloaming, O, my darling!
When the lights are dim and low,
And the quiet shadows falling
Softly come and softly go. *In the Gloaming*

GEORGE ORWELL [ERIC BLAIR]
1903–1950

16 All animals are equal, but some animals are more
equal than others. *Animal Farm*, ch. 10

DOROTHY OSBORNE [LADY TEMPLE]
1627–1695

17 The heat of the day is spent in reading or working,
and about six or seven o'clock I walk out into a
common that lies hard by the house, where a great
many young wenches keep sheep and cows, and sit
in the shade singing of ballads. I go to them and
compare their voices and beauties to some ancient
shepherdesses I have read of, and find a vast
difference there; but, trust me, I think these are as
innocent as those could be.
Letter to Sir Wm. Temple, May 1653

18 All letters, methinks, should be as free and easy as
one's discourse, not studied as an oration, nor made
up of hard words like a charm. *Ib. Oct. 1653*

ARTHUR WILLIAM EDGAR O'SHAUGHNESSY
1844–1881

19 We are the music makers,
We are the dreamers of dreams,
Wandering by lone sea-breakers,
And sitting by desolate streams;—
World-losers and world-forsakers,
On whom the pale moon gleams:
We are the movers and shakers
Of the world for ever, it seems.
Ode: 'We are the Music Makers'

1 One man with a dream, at pleasure,
  Shall go forth and conquer a crown;
And three with a new song's measure
  Can trample a kingdom down.
          Ode: 'We are the Music Makers'

2 For each age is a dream that is dying,
  Or one that is coming to birth.   *Ib.*

SIR WILLIAM OSLER
1849–1919

3 The uselessness of men above sixty years of age,
and the incalculable benefit it would be in commercial, political, and in professional life if, as a
matter of course, men stopped work at this age.
  Address, Johns Hopkins University, Feb. 1905.
  H. Cushing's *Life of Sir W. Osler* (1925),
  vol. i, p. 667

JOHN O'SULLIVAN
1813–1895

4 Our manifest destiny to overspread the continent
allotted by Providence for the free development
of our yearly multiplying millions.
  U.S. Magazine and Democratic Review, vol. xvii,
  p. 5

5 A torchlight procession marching down your throat.
  Description of some whisky. G. W. E. Russell's
  Collections and Recollections, ch. 19

JAMES OTIS
1725–1783

6 Taxation without representation is tyranny.
  Watchword of the American Revolution. Attrib.

THOMAS OTWAY
1652–1685

7 These are rogues that pretend to be of a religion now!
Well, all I say is, honest atheism for my money.
  The Atheist, Act III, l. 31

8 Ere man's corruptions made him wretched, he
Was born most noble that was born most free:
Each of himself was lord; and unconfin'd
Obey'd the dictates of his godlike mind.
  Don Carlos, Act II, l. 3

9 Destructive, damnable, deceitful woman!
  The Orphan, Act III, l. 586

10 And for an apple damn'd mankind.   *Ib.* l. 594

11 You wags that judge by rote, and damn by rule.
  Titus and Berenice, prologue, l. 3

12 Oh woman! lovely woman! Nature made thee
To temper man: we had been brutes without you;
Angels are painted fair, to look like you;
There's in you all that we believe of heav'n,
Amazing brightness, purity, and truth,
Eternal joy, and everlasting love.
  Venice Preserved, Act I, l. 337

13 No praying, it spoils business.   *Ib.* Act II, l. 87

SIR THOMAS OVERBURY
1581–1613

14   In part to blame is she,
Which hath without consent been only tried;
He comes too near, that comes to be denied.
  Miscellaneous Works. A Wife, xxvi

15 He disdains all things above his reach, and preferreth
all countries before his own.
  Miscellaneous Works. An Affectate Traveller

16 You cannot name any example in any heathen author
but I will better it in Scripture.
  Ib. Crumms Fal'n From King James's Table, § 10

OVID
43 B.C.–A.D. 18?

17 Et nulli cessura fides, sine crimine mores,
  Nudaque simplicitas, purpureusque pudor.
  And I have good faith that will yield to none, and
  ways without reproach, and unadorned simplicity, and blushing modesty.
          Amores, I. iii. 13. Trans. by Showerman

18 Cetera quis nescit?
  The rest who does not know?   *Ib.* v. 25

19 Procul omen abesto!
  Far from us be the omen!   *Ib.* xiv. 41

20 Vilia miretur vulgus; mihi flavus Apollo
  Pocula Castalia plena ministret aqua.
  Let what is cheap excite the marvel of the crowd;
  for me may golden Apollo minister full cups
  from the Castalian fount.   *Ib.* xv. 35

21 Procul hinc, procul este, severae!
  Away from me, far away, ye austere fair!
          Ib. II. i. 3

22 Iuppiter ex alto periuria ridet amantum.
  Jupiter from on high laughs at the perjury of lovers.
          Ars Amatoria, i. 633

23 Forsitan et nostrum nomen miscebitur istis.
  Perhaps too my name will be joined to theirs.
          Ib. iii. 339

24 Nil mihi rescribas, tu tamen ipse veni!
  Yet write nothing back to me; yourself come!
          Heroides, I. i. 2. Trans. by Showerman

25 Iam seges est ubi Troia fuit.
  Now are fields of corn where Troy once was.
          Ib. 53

26 Rudis indigestaque moles.
  An unformed and confused mass.
          Metamorphoses, i. 7

27 Medio tutissimus ibis.
  You will go most safely in the middle. *Ib.* ii. 137

28 Inopem me copia fecit.
  Plenty makes me poor.   *Ib.* iii. 466

29 Ipse docet quid agam; fas est et ab hoste doceri.
  He himself teaches what I should do; it is right to
  be taught by the enemy.   *Ib.* iv. 428

30   Video meliora, proboque;
Deteriora sequor.
  I see and approve better things, but follow worse.
          Ib. vii. 20

31 Tempus edax rerum.
  Time the devourer of all things.   *Ib.* xv. 234

1 Iamque opus exegi, quod nec Iovis ira, nec ignis,
Nec poterit ferrum, nec edax abolere vetustas.

And now I have finished the work, which neither
the wrath of Jove, nor fire, nor the sword, nor
devouring age shall be able to destroy.
Metamorphoses, xv. 871

2 Principiis obsta; sero medicina paratur
Cum mala per longas convaluere moras.

Resist beginnings; too late is the medicine prepared when the disease has gained strength by
long delays.
Remedia Amoris, 91. Trans. by Showerman

3 Qui finem quaeris amoris,
Cedet amor rebus; res age, tutus eris.

You who seek an end of love, love yields to business: be busy, and you will be safe. *Ib.* 143

4 Tu quoque.
Thou also. *Tristia*, ii. 39.

5 Teque, rebellatrix, tandem, Germania, magni
Triste caput pedibus supposuisse ducis!

That thou, rebellious Germany, at length hast
lowered thy sorrowing head beneath the foot of
our leader. *Ib.* III. xii. 47

6 Virgilium vidi tantum.
I had but a glimpse of Virgil. *Ib.* IV. x. 51

7 Utque solebamus consumere longa loquendo
Tempora, sermonem deficiente die.

As we were wont to pass long hours in converse,
till daylight failed our talk. *Ib.* v. xiii. 27

8 Nescioqua natale solum dulcedine captos
Ducit et inmemores non sinit esse sui.

By what sweet charm I know not the native land
draws all men nor allows them to forget her.
Epistulae Ex Ponto, I. iii. 35. Trans. by
Wheeler

9 Adde quod ingenuas didicisse fideliter artes
Emollit mores nec sinit esse feros.

Note too that a faithful study of the liberal arts
humanizes character and permits it not to be
cruel. *Ib.* II. ix. 47

10 Gutta cavat lapidem, consumitur annulus usu.
Drops of water hollow out a stone, a ring is worn
thin by use. *Ib.* IV. x. 5

11 (Gutta cavat lapidem, non vi sed saepe cadendo.
The drop of rain maketh a hole in the stone, not
by violence, but by oft falling.
Latimer, *7th Sermon before Edw. VI*, 1549)

JOHN OWEN
1560?–1622

12 God and the doctor we alike adore
But only when in danger, not before;
The danger o'er, both are alike requited,
God is forgotten, and the Doctor slighted. *Epigrams*

13 Tempora mutantur nos et mutamur in illis
Quomodo? fit semper tempore pejor homo.

Times change, and we change with them too. How
so?
With time men only the more vicious grow. *Ib.*

EDWARD OXENFORD
1847–1929

14 I fear no foe in shining armour. *Song*

COUNT OXENSTIERNA
1583–1654

15 An nescis, mi fili, quantilla prudentia regitur orbis?

Dost thou not know, my son, with how little wisdom the world is governed?
Letter to his son, 1648

BARRY PAIN
1864–1928

16 The cosy fire is bright and gay,
The merry kettle boils away
And hums a cheerful song.
I sing the saucer and the cup;
Pray, Mary, fill the teapot up,
And do not make it strong.
The Poets at Tea. Cowper

17 Pour, varlet, pour the water,
The water steaming hot!
A spoonful for each man of us,
Another for the pot! *Ib. Macaulay*

18 As the sin that was sweet in the sinning
Is foul in the ending thereof,
As the heat of the summer's beginning
Is past in the winter of love:
O purity, painful and pleading!
O coldness, ineffably gray!
O hear us, our handmaid unheeding,
And take it away! *Ib. Swinburne*

19 I think that I am drawing to an end:
For on a sudden came a gasp for breath,
And stretching of the hands, and blinded eyes,
And a great darkness falling on my soul.
O Hallelujah! . . . Kindly pass the milk.
Ib. Tennyson

20 'Come, little cottage girl, you seem
To want my cup of tea;
And will you take a little cream?
Now tell the truth to me.'

She had a rustic, woodland grin
Her cheek was soft as silk,
And she replied, 'Sir, please put in
A little drop of milk.' *Ib. Wordsworth*

THOMAS PAINE
1737–1809

21 The sublime and the ridiculous are often so nearly
related, that it is difficult to class them separately.
One step above the sublime, makes the ridiculous;
and one step above the ridiculous, makes the
sublime again. *Age of Reason* (1795), p. ii, p. 20

22 These are the times that try men's souls.
The American Crisis, No. 1. *Writings* (1894),
vol. 1, p. 170

23 The summer soldier and the sunshine patriot will, in
this crisis, shrink from the service of their country.
Ib. In the *Pennsylvania Journal*, 19 Dec. 1785

1 Government, even in its best state, is but a necessary evil; in its worst state, an intolerable one.
Common Sense, ch. 1

2 The final event to himself [Mr. Burke] has been, that as he rose like a rocket, he fell like the stick.
Letter to the Addressers on the late Proclamation (1792), p. 4

3 [Burke] is not affected by the reality of distress touching his heart, but by the showy resemblance of it striking his imagination. He pities the plumage, but forgets the dying bird.
Rights of Man (1791), p. 26

4 My country is the world, and my religion is to do good.
Ib. pt. ii, ch. 5

5 The religion of humanity.
Attr. by Edmund Gosse

REV. WILLIAM PALEY
1743–1805

6 Who can refute a sneer?
Moral Philosophy, bk. v, ch. 9

HENRY JOHN TEMPLE, VISCOUNT PALMERSTON
1784–1865

7 Accidental and fortuitous concurrence of atoms.
Speech, House of Commons, 5 Mar. 1857

8 What is merit? The opinion one man entertains of another.
Quoted by Carlyle in *Critical and Miscellaneous Essays*, viii, 'Shooting Niagara'

9 Die, my dear Doctor, that's the last thing I shall do!
Attr. last words

EDWARD HAZEN PARKER

10 Life's race well run,
Life's work well done,
Life's victory won,
Now cometh rest.
See *Notes and Queries*, 9th Series, vol. iv, p. 167, and vol. vii, p. 406

MARTIN PARKER
d. 1656?

11 Country men of England, who live at home with ease,
And little think what dangers are incident o' th' seas:
Give ear unto the sailor who unto you will show
His case, his case: *How e'er the wind doth blow.*
Sailors for My Money (*Roxburghe Ballads*, vol. vi, p. 797)

12 You gentlemen of England
Who live at home at ease,
How little do you think
On the dangers of the seas.
The Valiant Sailors (*Early Naval Ballads* [Percy Society, 1841], p. 34)

13 But all's to no end, for the times will not mend
Till the king enjoys his own again.
Upon Defacing of Whitehall (*The Loyal Garland*, 1671). Later title: *When the King Enjoys His Own Again.* Ritson's *Ancient Songs* (1792), p. 231

14 My skill goes beyond the depths of a pond,
Or rivers, in the greatest rain:
Whereby I can tell, all things will be well,
When the King enjoys his own again.
Ib.

ROSS PARKER
1914–
and
HUGHIE CHARLES
1907–

15 There'll always be an England
While there's a country lane,
Wherever there's a cottage small
Beside a field of grain.
Song of Second World War, 1939

THEODORE PARKER
1810–1860

16 A democracy, that is, a government of all the people, by all the people, for all the people; of course, a government after the principles of eternal justice, the unchanging law of God; for shortness' sake, I will call it the idea of freedom.
The American Idea. Speech at N. E. Anti-Slavery Convention, Boston, 29 May, 1850.
Discourses of Slavery (1863), i

CHARLES STEWART PARNELL
1846–1891

17 No man has a right to fix the boundary of the march of a nation; no man has a right to say to his country —thus far shalt thou go and no further.
Speech at Cork, 21 Jan. 1885

THOMAS PARNELL
1679–1718

18 When thy beauty appears,
In its graces and airs,
All bright as an angel new dropt from the sky;
At distance I gaze, and am aw'd by my fears,
So strangely you dazzle my eye!
Poems (1894). *Song, 'When thy Beauty Appears'*

19 Still an angel appear to each lover beside,
But still be a woman to you.
Ib.

20 We call it only pretty Fanny's way.
Ib. An Elegy, to an Old Beauty, l. 34

BLAISE PASCAL
1623–1662

21 Quand on voit le style naturel, on est tout étonné et ravi, car on s'attendait de voir un auteur, et on trouve un homme.

When we encounter a natural style we are always astonished and delighted, for we expected to see an author, and found a man. *Pensées*, § i. 29

22 Le nez de Cléopâtre: s'il eût été plus court, toute la face de la terre aurait changé.

Had Cleopatra's nose been shorter, the whole history of the world would have been different.
Ib. § ii. 162

1 Le silence éternel de ces espaces infinis m'effraie.

 The eternal silence of these infinite spaces [the heavens] terrifies me.   *Pensées*, § iii. 206

2 Le dernier acte est sanglant, quelque belle que soit la comédie en tout le reste.

 The last act is bloody, however charming the rest of the play may be.   *Ib*. 210

3 On mourra seul.

 We shall die alone.   *Ib*. 211

4 Le cœur a ses raisons que la raison ne connaît point.

 The heart has its reasons which reason knows nothing of.   *Ib*. § iv. 277

5 L'homme n'est qu'un roseau, le plus faible de la nature; mais c'est un roseau pensant.

 Man is only a reed, the weakest thing in nature; but he is a thinking reed.   *Ib*. § vi. 347

6 Le moi est haïssable.

 The 'self' is hateful.   *Ib*. § vii. 434

7 Console-toi, tu ne me chercherais pas si tu ne m'avais trouvé.

 Comfort yourself, you would not seek me if you had not found me.   *Ib*. 553

8 Je n'ai fait celle-ci plus longue que parceque je n'ai pas eu le loisir de la faire plus courte.

 I have made this letter longer than usual, because I lack the time to make it short.
   Lettres Provinciales (1657), xvi

WALTER HORATIO PATER
1839–1894

9 A white bird, she told him once, looking at him gravely, a bird he must carry in his bosom across a crowded public place—his own soul was like that!
   Marius the Epicurean, pt. i, ch. 2

10 The presence that thus rose so strangely beside the waters, is expressive of what in the ways of a thousand years men had come to desire. Hers is the head upon which all 'the ends of the world are come', and the eyelids are a little weary. . . . Set it for a moment beside one of those white Greek goddesses or beautiful women of antiquity, and how would they be troubled by this beauty, into which the soul with all its maladies has passed? [Mona Lisa.]
   The Renaissance. Leonardo da Vinci

11 She is older than the rocks among which she sits; like the vampire, she has been dead many times, and learned the secrets of the grave; and has been a diver in deep seas, and keeps their fallen day about her; and trafficked for strange webs with Eastern merchants: and, as Leda, was the mother of Helen of Troy, and, as Saint Anne, the mother of Mary; and all this has been to her but as the sound of lyres and flutes, and lives only in the delicacy with which it has moulded the changing lineaments, and tinged the eyelids and the hands.
   Ib.

12 All art constantly aspires towards the condition of music.   *Ib. The School of Giorgione*

13 For art comes to you, proposing frankly to give nothing but the highest quality to your moments as they pass, and simply for those moments' sake.
   The Renaissance. Conclusion

14 To burn always with this hard, gemlike flame, to maintain this ecstasy, is success in life. *Ib*.

ANDREW PATERSON
1864–1941

15 Once a jolly swagman camped by a billabong,
 Under the shade of a coolibah tree,
And he sang as he sat and waited till his billy boiled,
 'You'll come a-waltzing, Matilda, with me.'
   Waltzing Matilda

COVENTRY PATMORE
1823–1896

16 For dear to maidens are their rivals dead.
   Amelia, l. 135

17 Grant me the power of saying things
 Too simple and too sweet for words!
  The Angel in the House (ed. 1904), bk. 1, c. 1,
  Prelude 1, *The Impossibility*, l. 7

18   Love, sole mortal thing
Of worth immortal.
   Ib. Prelude 2, *Love's Reality*, l. 9

19 The fair sum of six thousand years'
 Traditions of civility.
   Ib. The Cathedral Close, v, l. 27

20 Ah, wasteful woman, she who may
 On her sweet self set her own price,
Knowing man cannot choose but pay,
 How has she cheapen'd paradise;
How given for nought her priceless gift,
 How spoil'd the bread and spill'd the wine,
Which, spent with due, respective thrift,
 Had made brutes men, and men divine.
   Ib. c. iii, Prelude 3, *Unthrift*

21 Leave us alone! After a while,
 This pool of private charity
Shall make its continent an isle,
 And roll, a world-embracing sea.
   Ib. c. vi, Prelude 2, *Love Justified*, l. 9

22 Kind souls, you wonder why, love you,
 When you, you wonder why, love none
We love, Fool, for the good we do,
 Not that which unto us is done!
   Ib. Prelude 4, *A Riddle Solved*

23 Love wakes men, once a lifetime each;
 They lift their heavy lids, and look;
And, lo, what one sweet page can teach,
 They read with joy, then shut the book.
And some give thanks, and some blaspheme,
 And most forget; but, either way,
That and the Child's unheeded dream
 Is all the light of all their day.
   Ib. c. viii, Prelude 2, *The Revelation*, l. 5

24 I drew my bride, beneath the moon,
 Across my threshold; happy hour!
But, ah, the walk that afternoon
 We saw the water-flags in flower!
   Ib. Prelude 3, *The Spirit's Epochs*, l. 9

PATMORE

1 God's grace is the only grace,
And all grace is the grace of God.
The Angel in the House (ed. 1904), bk. I, c. x,
Prelude 1, *The Joyful Wisdom*

2 'I'll hunt for dangers North and South,
To prove my love, which sloth maligns!'
What seems to say her rosy mouth?
'I'm not convinced by proofs but signs.'
Ib. bk. II, c. iv, Prelude 3, *Valour Misdirected*

3 'I saw you take his kiss!' ''Tis true.'
'O, modesty!' ''Twas strictly kept:
He thought me asleep; at least, I knew
He thought I thought he thought I slept.
Ib. c. viii, Prelude 3, *The Kiss*

4 Why, having won her, do I woo?
Because her spirit's vestal grace
Provokes me always to pursue,
But, spirit-like, eludes embrace.
Ib. c. xii, Prelude 1, *The Married Lover*, l. 1

5 Because, though free of the outer court
I am, this Temple keeps its shrine
Sacred to Heaven; because, in short,
She's not and never can be mine. *Ib.* l. 29

6 Some dish more sharply spiced than this
Milk-soup men call domestic bliss *Olympus*, l. 15

7 Well dost thou, Love, thy solemn Feast to hold
In vestal February.
The Unknown Eros, bk. I. i. *St. Valentine's Day*,
l. 1

8 Fair as the rash oath of virginity
Which is first-love's first cry.
O 'Baby Spring,
That flutter'st sudden 'neath the breast of Earth
A month before the birth. *Ib.* l. 9

9 Thy heart with dead, wing'd innocencies fill'd,
Ev'n as a nest with birds
After the old ones by the hawk are kill'd. *Ib.* l. 51

10 But, in a while,
The immeasurable smile
Is broke by fresher airs to flashes blent
With darkling discontent.
Ib. ii. *Wind and Wave*, l. 15

11 I, singularly moved
To love the lovely that are not beloved,
Of all the Seasons, most
Love Winter. *Ib.* iii. *Winter*, l. 1

12 It *was* the azalea's breath, and she *was* dead!
Ib. vii. *The Azalea*, l. 17

13 So, till to-morrow eve, my Own, adieu!
Parting's well-paid with soon again to meet,
Soon in your arms to feel so small and sweet,
Sweet to myself that am so sweet to you! *Ib.* l. 22

14 It was not like your great and gracious ways!
Do you, that have nought other to lament,
Never, my Love, repent
Of how, that July afternoon,
You went,
With sudden, unintelligible phrase,
And frighten'd eye,
Upon your journey of so many days,
Without a single kiss, or a good-bye?
Ib. viii. *Departure*, l. 1

15 And the only loveless look the look with which you
pass'd. *Ib.* l. 31

16 My little Son, who look'd from thoughtful eyes
And moved and spoke in quiet grown-up wise,
Having my law the seventh time disobey'd,
I struck him, and dismiss'd
With hard words and unkiss'd,
His Mother, who was patient, being dead.
The Unknown Eros, bk. I. x. *The Toys*, l. 1

17 Then, fatherly, not less
Than I whom Thou hast moulded from the clay,
Thou'lt leave Thy wrath, and say,
'I will be sorry for their childishness.' *Ib.*

18 For want of me the world's course will not fail:
When all its work is done, the lie shall rot;
The truth is great, and shall prevail,
When none cares whether it prevail or not.
Ib. xii. *Magna est Veritas*, l. 7

19 In the year of the great crime,
When the false English Nobles and their Jew,
By God demented, slew
The trust they stood twice pledged to keep from
wrong,
One said, Take up thy Song,
That breathes the mild and almost mythic time
Of England's prime! *Ib.* xiii, 1867, l. 1

20 If I were dead, you'd sometimes say, Poor Child!
Ib. xiv. *'If I were dead'*, l. 1

21 With all my will, but much against my heart,
We two now part.
My Very Dear,
Our solace is, the sad road lies so clear.
It needs no art,
With faint, averted feet
And many a tear,
In our opposed paths to persevere.
Ib. xvi. *A Farewell*, l. 1

22 Haply yon wretch, so famous for his falls,
Got them beneath the Devil-defended walls
Of some high Virtue he had vow'd to win.
Ib. xx. *'Let Be'*, l. 17

23 That shaft of slander shot
Miss'd only the right blot.
I see the shame
They cannot see:
'Tis very just they blame
The thing that's not. *Ib.* l. 35

24 Through delicatest ether feathering soft their solitary
beat. *Ib.* bk. II. i. *To the Unknown Eros*, l. 8

25 What in its ruddy orbit lifts the blood,
Like a perturbed moon of Uranus,
Reaching to some great world in ungauged darkness
hid. *Ib.* l. 33

26 Who is this only happy She,
Whom, by a frantic flight of courtesy,
Born of despair
Of better lodging for his Spirit fair,
He adores as Margaret, Maude, or Cecily?
Ib. v. *Sponsa Dei*, l. 30

27 The Jebusite,
That, maugre all God's promises could do,
The chosen People never conquer'd quite;
Who therefore lived with them,
And that by formal truce and as of right,
In metropolitan Jerusalem.
Ib. vii. *To the Body*, l. 32

[375]

1 Enoch, Elijah, and the Lady, she
Who left the lilies in her body's lieu.
The Unknown Eros, bk. II. vii. *To the Body*, l. 45

2 Who has thy birth-time's consecrating dew
For death's sweet chrism retain'd,
Quick, tender, virginal, and unprofaned!
Ib. l. 51

3 There of pure Virgins none
Is fairer seen,
Save One,
Than Mary Magdalene.
Ib. l. 127

4 Shall I, the gnat which dances in thy ray,
Dare to be reverent?
Ib. xiv. *Psyche's Discontent*, l. 72

5 Maud burst in, while the Earl was there,
With 'Oh, Mama, do be a bear!'
The Victories of Love, bk. II. ii. *From Lady
Clitheroe to Mary Churchill*, l. 89

6 No magic of her voice or smile
Suddenly raised a fairy isle,
But fondness for her underwent
An unregarded increment,
Like that which lifts, through centuries,
The coral-reef within the seas,
Till, lo! the land where was the wave,
Alas! 'tis everywhere her grave.
Ib. v. *From Mrs. Graham*, l. 57

7 Faults had she, child of Adam's stem,
But only Heaven knew of them.
Ib. xii. *From Felix to Honoria*, l. 167

8 This is to say, my dear Augusta,
We've had another awful buster:
Ten thousand Frenchmen sent below!
Thank God from whom all blessings flow.
*Epigram on King William's dispatch to Queen
Augusta reported in* The Times, 8 Aug. 1870.
B. Champneys, *Coventry Patmore* (1900), i. 286.

JAMES PAYN
1830–1898

9 I had never had a piece of toast
Particularly long and wide,
But fell upon the sanded floor,
And always on the buttered side.
Chambers's Journal, 2 Feb. 1884

JOHN HOWARD PAYNE
1791–1852

10 Mid pleasures and palaces though we may roam,
Be it ever so humble, there's no place like home;
A charm from the sky seems to hallow us there,
Which, seek through the world, is ne'er met with
elsewhere.
Home, home, sweet, sweet home!
There's no place like home! there's no place like
home!
Clari, the Maid of Milan. Home, Sweet Home

THOMAS LOVE PEACOCK
1785–1866

11 Ancient sculpture is the true school of modesty. But
where the Greeks had modesty, we have cant;
where they had poetry, we have cant; where they
had patriotism, we have cant; where they had

anything that exalts, delights, or adorns humanity,
we have nothing but cant, cant, cant.
Crotchet Castle, ch. 7

12 A book that furnishes no quotations is, *me judice*, no
book—it is a plaything.
Ib. ch. 9

13 Modern literature having attained the honourable
distinction of sharing with blacking and Macassar
oil the space which used to be monopolized by
razor-strops and the lottery.
Ib. ch. 15

14 The march of mind—has marched in through my
back-parlour shutters, and out again with my
silver spoons, in the dead of the night. The
policeman, who was sent down to examine, says
my house has been broken open on the most
scientific principles.
Ib. ch. 17

15 Nothing can be more obvious than that all animals
were created solely and exclusively for the use of
man.
Headlong Hall, ch. 2

16 'Indeed, the loaves and fishes are typical of a mixed
diet; and the practice of the Church in all ages
shows—'
'That it never loses sight of the loaves and fishes.'
Ib.

17 'I distinguish the picturesque and the beautiful, and
I add to them, in the laying out of grounds, a
third and distinct character, which I call *unexpectedness.*'
'Pray, sir,' said Mr. Milestone, 'by what name do you
distinguish this character, when a person walks
round the grounds for the second time?' *Ib.* ch. 4

18 Sir, I have quarrelled with my wife; and a man who
has quarrelled with his wife is absolved from all
duty to his country.
Nightmare Abbey, ch. 11

19 He remembered too late on his thorny green bed,
Much that well may be thought cannot wisely be said.
Crotchet Castle (1831): *The Priest and the Mul-
berry Tree*, st. 5

20 Long night succeeds thy little day
Oh blighted blossom! can it be,
That this gray stone and grassy clay
Have closed our anxious care of thee?
Epitaph on his Daughter. Works of Peacock, ed.
Cole (1875), Biographical Notice by E. Nicolls

21 In his last binn Sir Peter lies,
Who knew not what it was to frown:
Death took him mellow by surprise,
And in his cellar stopped him down.
Headlong Hall, ch. 5

22 Hail to the Headlong! the Headlong Ap-Headlong!
All hail to the Headlong, the Headlong Ap-Headlong!
The Headlong Ap-Headlong
Ap-Breakneck Ap-Headlong
Ap-Cataract Ap-Pistyll Ap-Rhaiader Ap-Headlong!
Ib. ch. 13. *Chorus*

23 The mountain sheep are sweeter,
But the valley sheep are fatter;
We therefore deemed it meeter
To carry off the latter.
The Misfortunes of Elphin, ch. 11. *The War-
Song of Dinas Vawr*

24 The bowl goes trim. The moon doth shine,
And our ballast is old wine.
Nightmare Abbey, ch. 11

1 In a bowl to sea went wise men three,
   On a brilliant night in June:
They carried a net, and their hearts were set
   On fishing up the moon.
   The Wise Men of Gotham. Paper Money Lyrics

GEORGE PEELE
1558?–1597?

2 Fair and fair, and twice so fair,
   As fair as any may be;
The fairest shepherd on our green,
   A love for any lady.
   Works, ed. Bullen, vol. i. *Arraignment of Paris*,
   I. ii. 55. *Song of Oenone and Paris*

3 What thing is love for (well I wot) love is a thing.
It is a prick, it is a sting,
   It is a pretty, pretty thing;
It is a fire, it is a coal
Whose flame creeps in at every hole.
   Ib. vol. ii. *Miscellaneous Poems. The Hunting of
   Cupid*, l. 1

4 His golden locks time hath to silver turn'd;
   O time too swift, O swiftness never ceasing!
His youth 'gainst time and age hath ever spurn'd
   But spurn'd in vain; youth waneth by increasing:
Beauty, strength, youth, are flowers but fading seen;
Duty, faith, love, are roots, and ever green.

His helmet now shall make a hive for bees,
   And, lovers' sonnets turn'd to holy psalms,
A man-at-arms must now serve on his knees,
   And feed on prayers, which are age his alms:
But though from court to cottage he depart,
His saint is sure of his unspotted heart.

Goddess, allow this aged man his right,
To be your beadsman now that was your knight.
   *Ib. Polyhymnia, Sonnet ad finem. A Farewell to
   Arms*

HENRY HERBERT, EARL OF PEMBROKE
1734–1794

5 My noble friend Lord Pembroke said once to me at
Wilton, with a happy pleasantry and some truth,
that, 'Dr. Johnson's sayings would not appear so
extraordinary, were it not for his *bow-wow way*'.
   Boswell's *Life of Johnson*, 27 Mar. 1775, note

WILLIAM PENN
1644–1718

6 No Cross, No Crown.   *Title of Pamphlet*, 1669

7 It is a reproach to religion and government to suffer
so much poverty and excess.
   Reflexions and Maxims, pt. i, No. 52

8 Men are generally more careful of the breed of their
horses and dogs than of their children.   *Ib.* No. 85

9 The country life is to be preferred, for there we see
the works of God, but in cities little else but the
works of men.   *Ib.* No. 220

SAMUEL PEPYS
1633–1703

10 Strange the difference of men's talk!
   Diary, 4 *Jan.* 1659–60

11 And so to bed.   *Diary*, 20 *Apr.* 1660

12 A silk suit, which cost me much money, and I pray
God to make me able to pay for it. *Ib.* 1 *July* 1660

13 I . . . sent for Mr. Butler, who was now all full of
his high discourse in praise of Ireland, . . . but so
many lies I never heard in praise of anything as
he told of Ireland.   *Ib.* 28 *July* 1660

14 I went out to Charing Cross, to see Major-general
Harrison hanged, drawn, and quartered; which
was done there, he looking as cheerful as any man
could do in that condition.   *Ib.* 13 *Oct.* 1660

15 Very merry, and the best fritters that ever I eat in
my life.   *Ib.* 26 *Feb.* 1660–1 (*Shrove Tues.*)

16 A good honest and painful sermon.
   Ib. 17 *Mar.* 1661

17 If ever I was foxed it was now.   *Ib.* 23 *Apr.* 1661

18 But methought it lessened my esteem of a king, that
he should not be able to command the rain.
   Ib. 19 *July* 1662

19 I see it is impossible for the King to have things done
as cheap as other men.   *Ib.* 21 *July* 1662

20 But Lord! to see the absurd nature of Englishmen,
that cannot forbear laughing and jeering at everything that looks strange.   *Ib.* 27 *Nov.* 1662

21 My wife, who, poor wretch, is troubled with her
lonely life.   *Ib.* 19 *Dec.* 1662

22 Went to hear Mrs. Turner's daughter . . . play on
the harpsichon; but, Lord! it was enough to make
any man sick to hear her; yet was I forced to commend her highly.   *Ib.* 1 *May* 1663

23 Most of their discourse was about hunting, in a
dialect I understand very little.   *Ib.* 22 *Nov.* 1663

24 While we were talking came by several poor creatures
carried by, by constables, for being at a conventicle. . . . I would to God they would either conform, or be more wise, and not be catched!
   Ib. 7 *Aug.* 1664

25 Pretty witty Nell. [Nell Gwynne.]   *Ib.* 3 *Apr.* 1665

26 But Lord! what a sad time it is to see no boats upon
the River; and grass grows all up and down White
Hall Court.   *Ib.* 20 *Sept.* 1665

27 Strange to see how a good dinner and feasting reconciles everybody.   *Ib.* 9 *Nov.* 1665

28 Strange to say what delight we married people have
to see these poor fools decoyed into our condition.
   Ib. 25 *Dec.* 1665

29 And mighty proud I am (and ought to be thankful
to God Almighty) that I am able to have a spare
bed for my friends.   *Ib.* 8 *Aug.* 1666

30 I bless God I do find that I am worth more than
ever I yet was, which is £6,200, for which the
Holy Name of God be praised!   *Ib.* 31 *Oct.* 1666

31 But it is pretty to see what money will do.
   Ib. 21 *Mar.* 1667–8

CHARLES PERRAULT
1628–1703

32 'Anne, ma sœur Anne, ne vois-tu rien venir?' Et la
sœur Anne lui répondit, 'Je ne vois rien que le
soleil qui poudroye, et l'herbe qui verdoye.'

'Anne, sister Anne, do you see anybody coming?'
And her sister Anne replied, 'I see nothing but
the sun which makes a dust, and the grass looking
green.'
    Perrault, *Histoires ou Contes du Temps Passé*,
    1697. Trans. by R. Samber, 1764

PERSIUS
A.D. 34–62

1 Nec te quaesiveris extra.
    Nor ask any opinion but your own.
        Satires, i. 7. Trans. by Conington

2 At pulchrum est digito monstrari et dicier 'hic est'.
    But it is a fine thing for men to point one out and
    say 'There he goes'.   *Ib.* 28

3 Virtutem videant intabescantque relicta.
    Let them look upon virtue, and pine that they have
    lost her for ever.   *Ib.* iii. 38

4 Venienti occurrite morbo.
    Meet the disease at its first stage.   *Ib.* 64

5 De nihilo nihilum, in nihilum nil posse reverti.
    Nothing can come out of nothing, nothing can go
    back to nothing.   *Ib.* 84. Trans. by Conington

6 Tecum habita: noris quam sit tibi curta supellex.
    Live at home, and learn how slenderly furnished
    your apartments are.   *Ib.* iv. 52

MARÉCHAL PÉTAIN
1856–1951

7 Ils ne passeront pas.
    They shall not pass.   *Verdun, Feb. 1916*

PETRONIUS
d. *c.* A.D. 66

8 Cave canem.
    Beware of the dog.
        Petronii Arbitri Satyricon, 29, 1
    Found with picture of a dog on a mosaic floor in Pompeii.

9 Horatii curiosa felicitas.
    The exact felicity of Horace.   *Ib.* 118

10 Habes confitentem reum.
    You have a confessing prisoner.   *Ib.* 130

11 Abiit ad plures.
    He has joined the great majority.
        Cena Trimalchionis, xlii. 5.

EDWARD JOHN PHELPS
1822–1900

12 The man who makes no mistakes does not usually
    make anything.
        Speech at Mansion House, 24 Jan. 1899

JOHN WOODWARD PHILIP
1840–1900

13 Don't cheer, boys; those poor devils are dying.
        At the Battle of Santiago, 4 July 1898

PHILIPPIDES [PHEIDIPPIDES]
c. 490 B.C.

14 Χαίρετε, νικῶμεν.
    Joy, we win.
        *Having run to Athens with the tidings of Mara-
        thon. He died upon his message.* Lucian, *Pro Lapsu
        in Salutando*, para. iii. Trans. by Fowler

AMBROSE PHILIPS
1675?–1749

15 The flowers anew, returning seasons bring!
    But beauty faded has no second spring.
        The First Pastoral, Lobbin, l. 55

16 Timely blossom, infant fair,
    Fondling of a happy pair,
    Every morn, and every night,
    Their solicitous delight,
    Sleeping, waking, still at ease,
    Pleasing without skill to please.
    Little gossip, blithe and hale,
    Tattling many a broken tale.
        To Mistress Charlotte Pulteney, l. 1

JOHN PHILIPS
1676–1709

17 Happy the man, who, void of cares and strife,
    In silken or in leathern purse retains
    A Splendid Shilling.   *The Splendid Shilling*, l. 1

STEPHEN PHILLIPS
1864–1915

18 A man not old, but mellow, like good wine.
        Ulysses, III. ii

WENDELL PHILLIPS
1811–1884

19 One, on God's side, is a majority.
        Speeches (1880), *Lecture at Brooklyn, N.Y., 1 Nov.
        1859*

20 Every man meets his Waterloo at last.   *Ib.*

21 We live under a government of men and morning
    newspapers.   *Address: The Press*

EDEN PHILLPOTTS
1862–

22 His father's sister had bats in the belfry and was put
    away.   *Peacock House. My First Murder*

PINDAR
c. 522–442 B.C.

23 ἄριστον μὲν ὕδωρ.
    Water is best.   *Olympian Odes*, I. i

24 φωνᾶντα συνετοῖσιν. ἐς δὲ τὸ πᾶν ἑρμηνέων
    χατίζει.
    Vocal to the wise; but for the crowd they need
    interpreters.   *Ib.* ii. 85

SIR ARTHUR WING PINERO
1855–1934

1 What beautiful fruit! I love fruit when it's expensive.
The Second Mrs. Tanqueray, Act 1

WILLIAM PITT, EARL OF CHATHAM
1708–1778

2 The atrocious crime of being a young man . . . I shall neither attempt to palliate nor deny.
Speech, House of Commons, 27 Jan. 1741

3 I rejoice that America has resisted. Three millions of people, so dead to all the feelings of liberty, as voluntarily to submit to be slaves, would have been fit instruments to make slaves of the rest.
Ib. 14 Jan. 1766

4 I cannot give them my confidence; pardon me, gentlemen, confidence is a plant of slow growth in an aged bosom: youth is the season of credulity.
Ib.

5 Unlimited power is apt to corrupt the minds of those who possess it.   *Ib. House of Lords, 9 Jan. 1770*

6 There is something behind the throne greater than the King himself.   *Ib. 2 Mar. 1770*

7 We have a Calvinistic creed, a Popish liturgy, and an Arminian clergy.   *Ib. 19 May 1772*

8 If I were an American, as I am an Englishman, while a foreign troop was landed in my country, I never would lay down my arms,—never—never—never!
Ib. 18 Nov. 1777

9 You cannot conquer America.   *Ib.*

10 I invoke the genius of the Constitution!   *Ib.*

11 The poorest man may in his cottage bid defiance to all the forces of the Crown. It may be frail—its roof may shake—the wind may blow through it— the storm may enter—the rain may enter—but the King of England cannot enter—all his force dares not cross the threshold of the ruined tenement!
Ib. Date unknown. Brougham's *Statesmen in the Time of George III*, First Series

12 Our watchword is security.   *Attr.*

13 It was a saying of Lord Chatham, that the parks were the lungs of London.
William Windham, in a Speech in House of Commons, 30 June 1808

WILLIAM PITT
1759–1806

14 Necessity is the plea for every infringement of human freedom. It is the argument of tyrants; it is the creed of slaves.
Speech, House of Commons, 18 Nov. 1783

15 We must recollect . . . what it is we have at stake, what it is we have to contend for. It is for our property, it is for our liberty, it is for our independence, nay, for our existence as a nation; it is for our character, it is for our very name as Englishmen, it is for everything dear and valuable to man on this side of the grave.   *Ib. 22 July 1803*

16 England has saved herself by her exertions, and will, as I trust, save Europe by her example.
Speech. At the Guildhall, 1805

17 Roll up that map; it will not be wanted these ten years.
On a map of Europe, after hearing the news of the Battle of Austerlitz. Stanhope's *Life of the Rt. Hon. William Pitt* (1862), vol. iv, p. 369

18 Oh, my country! how I love my country.
Attr. last words. Ib. p. 382

19 Oh, my country! how I leave my country!
Attr. last words. Ib. (1879), vol. iii, p. 391

20 My country! oh, my country!
Attr. last words. G. Rose, *Diary*, 23 Jan. 1806

21 I think I could eat one of Bellamy's veal pies.
Alternative attributed last words

JAMES ROBINSON PLANCHÉ
1796–1880

22 Ching-a-ring-a-ring-ching! Feast of lanterns!
What a crop of chop-sticks, hongs and gongs!
Hundred thousand Chinese crinkum-crankums,
Hung among the bells and ding-dongs!
The Drama at Home, or An Evening With Puff

23 It would have made a cat laugh.
Extravaganzas (1879), *The Queen of the Frogs*, I. iv

PLATO
c. 429–347 B.C.

24 Σωκράτη φησὶν ἀδικεῖν τούς τε νέους διαφθείροντα καὶ θεοὺς οὓς ἡ πόλις νομίζει οὐ νομίζοντα, ἕτερα δὲ δαιμόνια καινά.
Socrates is charged with corrupting the youth of the city, and with rejecting the gods of Athens and introducing new divinities.
Apologia, 24[b] 9

25 δημοκρατία ἐσχάτη τυραννίς.
Democracy passes into despotism.
Republic, pt. iv, bk. viii. 562. Cornford's translation

PLAUTUS
B.C. 254–184

26 Miles gloriosus.
The boastful soldier.   *Title of Play*

27 GRIPUS: Tum tu mendicus es?
LABRAX: Tetigisti acu.
  GRIPUS: Then you are a beggar?
  LABRAX: You have touched the point with a needle. [You have put your finger on the spot.]
Rudens, l. 1305

PLINY
A.D. 23–79

28 Brutum fulmen.
A harmless thunderbolt.
Historia Naturalis, II. xliii

1 Ex Africa semper aliquid novi.

There is always something new from Africa. *Proverbial from Pliny*: Unde etiam vulgare Graeciae dictum 'semper aliquid novi Africam adferre'.

Whence it is commonly said among the Greeks that 'Africa always offers something new'.
Historia Naturalis, ii. viii. 42

2 In vino veritas.

Truth comes out in wine. *Proverbial from Pliny*: Vulgoque veritas iam attributa vino est.

Now truth is commonly said to be in wine.
Ib. xiv. 141

3 Sal Atticum.

Attic wit. *Ib.* xxxi. 87

4 Nulla dies sine linea.

Not a day without a line. *Proverbial from Pliny*: Apelli fuit alioqui perpetua consuetudo numquam tam occupatam diem agendi, ut non lineam ducendo exerceret artem, quod ab eo in proverbium venit.

It was moreover a regular habit of Apelles never to be so occupied in the business of the day that he could not practise his art by drawing a line, and this gave rise to the proverb.
Ib. xxxv. 36. 12

5 Ne supra crepidam sutor iudicaret.

The cobbler should not judge above his last. *Ib.* 85

JOSEPH MARY PLUNKETT
1887–1916

6 I see His blood upon the rose
And in the stars the glory of His eyes.
Poems (1916), *I See His Blood*

EDGAR ALLAN POE
1809–1849

7 This maiden she lived with no other thought
Than to love and be loved by me. *Annabel Lee*

8 I was a child and she was a child,
In this kingdom by the sea;
But we loved with a love which was more than love—
I and my Annabel Lee;
With a love that the wingèd seraphs of heaven
Coveted her and me. *Ib.*

9 The beautiful Annabel Lee. *Ib.*

10 In the sepulchre there by the sea,
In her tomb by the sounding sea. *Ib.*

11 The fever call'd 'Living'
Is conquer'd at last. *For Annie*

12 Keeping time, time, time,
In a sort of Runic rhyme,
To the tintinabulation that so musically wells
From the bells, bells, bells, bells. *The Bells*, l. 9

13 They are neither man nor woman—
They are neither brute nor human,
They are Ghouls. *Ib.* l. 86

14 Vastness! and Age! and Memories of Eld!
Silence! and Desolation! and dim Night!
The Coliseum, l. 10

15 While the angels, all pallid and **wan**,
Uprising, unveiling, affirm
That the play is the tragedy, 'Man',
And its hero the Conqueror Worm.
The Conqueror Worm, l. 39

16 All that we see or seem
Is but a dream within a dream.
A Dream within a Dream, l. 10

17 Helen, thy beauty is to me
Like those Nicean barks of yore,
That gently, o'er a perfumed sea,
The weary, wayworn wanderer bore
To his own native shore.

On desperate seas long wont to roam,
Thy hyacinth hair, thy classic face,
Thy Naiad airs have brought me home
To the glory that was Greece
And the grandeur that was Rome. *To Helen*, l. 1

18 If I could dwell where Israfel
Hath dwelt, and he where I,—
He might not sing so wildly well
A mortal melody,
While a bolder note than his might swell
From my lyre within the sky. *Israfel*

19 And, Guy de Vere, hast *thou* no tear?—weep now or nevermore! *Lenore*, l. 3

20 *Peccavimus*; but rave not thus! and let a Sabbath song
Go up to God so solemnly the dead may feel no wrong. *Ib.* l. 13

21 And all my days are trances,
And all my nightly dreams
Are where thy grey eye glances,
And where thy footstep gleams—
In what ethereal dances,
By what eternal streams. *To One in Paradise*, l. 21

22 Once upon a midnight dreary, while I pondered, weak and weary,
Over many a quaint and curious volume of forgotten lore,
While I nodded, nearly napping, suddenly there came a tapping,
As of some one gently rapping. *The Raven*, i

23 Sorrow for the lost Lenore—
For the rare and radiant maiden whom the angels name Lenore—
Nameless here for evermore. *Ib.* ii

24 Deep into that darkness peering, long I stood there wondering, fearing,
Doubting, dreaming dreams no mortal ever dared to dream before. *Ib.* v

25 Ghastly grim and ancient raven wandering from the nightly shore—
Tell me what thy lordly name is on the Night's Plutonian shore! *Ib.* viii

26 'Prophet!' said I, 'thing of evil—prophet still, if bird or devil!
By that heaven that bends above us—by that God we both adore.' *Ib.* xvi

27 Take thy beak from out my heart, and take thy form from off my door!
Quoth the Raven, 'Nevermore'. *Ib.* xvii

1 The skies they were ashen and sober;
  The leaves they were crisped and sere—
  The leaves they were withering and sere;
  It was night in the lonesome October
  Of my most immemorial year.   *Ulalume*, l. 1

2 Here once, through an alley Titanic,
  Of cypress, I roamed with my Soul—
  Of cypress, with Psyche, my Soul.   *Ib.* l. 10

JOHN POMFRET
1667–1703

3 We live and learn, but not the wiser grow.
                                   Reason, l. 112

MME DE POMPADOUR
1721–1764

4 Après nous le déluge.
    After us the deluge.
        Madame de Hausset, *Mémoires*, p. 19

JOHN POOLE
1786?–1872

5 I hope I don't intrude?   *Paul Pry*, 1. ii

ALEXANDER POPE
1688–1744

6 To wake the soul by tender strokes of art,
  To raise the genius, and to mend the heart;
  To make mankind in conscious virtue bold,
  Live o'er each scene, and be what they behold:
  For this the Tragic Muse first trod the stage.
        Prologue to Addison's *Cato*, l. 1

7 A brave man struggling in the storms of fate,
  And greatly falling, with a falling State.
  While Cato gives his little senate laws,
  What bosom beats not in his country's cause?
                                   Ib. l. 21

8 Ye gods! annihilate but space and time,
  And make two lovers happy.
        The Art of Sinking in Poetry, ch. 11

9 And thou Dalhousy, the great God of War,
  Lieutenant-Colonel to the Earl of Mar.   *Ib.*

10 A very heathen in the carnal part
   Yet still a sad, good Christian at her heart.
        Of the Character of Women

11 Poetic Justice, with her lifted scale,
   Where, in nice balance, truth with gold she weighs,
   And solid pudding against empty praise.
        The Dunciad, bk. i, l. 52

12 Now night descending, the proud scene was o'er,
   But liv'd in Settle's numbers one day more. *Ib.* l. 89

13 Pensive poets painful vigils keep,
   Sleepless themselves to give their readers sleep.
                                   Ib. l. 93

14 Or where the pictures for the page atone,
   And Quarles is sav'd by beauties not his own.
                                   Ib. l. 139

15 And gentle dullness ever loves a joke. *Ib.* bk. ii, l. 34

16 Earless on high, stood unabash'd De Foe. *Ib.* l. 147

17 Another, yet the same.   *Ib.* bk. iii, l. 40

18 Lo, where Maeotis sleeps, and hardly flows
   The freezing 'Tanais thro' a waste of snows.
        The Dunciad, bk. iii. l. 87

19 Peel'd, patch'd, and piebald, linsey-wolsey brothers,
   Grave mummers! sleeveless some, and shirtless
   others.   *Ib.* l. 115

20 All crowd, who foremost shall be damn'd to fame.
                                   Ib. l. 158

21 Some free from rhyme or reason, rule or check,
   Break Priscian's head, and Pegasus's neck. *Ib.* l. 161

22 So sweetly mawkish, and so smoothly dull. *Ib.* l. 171

23 And Alma Mater all dissolv'd in port.   *Ib.* l. 338

24 May you, my Cam and Isis, preach it long!
   The Right Divine of Kings to govern wrong.
        Ib. bk. iv, l. 187

25 Stretch'd on the rack of a too easy chair. *Ib.* l. 341

26 She comes! she comes! the sable Throne behold
   Of Night primæval, and of Chaos old!
   Before her, Fancy's gilded clouds decay,
   And all its varying rain-bows die away.   *Ib.* l. 629

27 See skulking Truth to her old cavern fled,
   Mountains of Casuistry heap'd o'er her head!
   Philosophy, that lean'd on Heav'n before,
   Shrinks to her second cause, and is no more.
   Physic of Metaphysic begs defence,
   And Metaphysic calls for aid on Sense!
   See Mystery to Mathematics fly!
   In vain! they gaze, turn giddy, rave, and die.
   Religion blushing veils her sacred fires,
   And unawares Morality expires.
   Nor public flame, nor private, dares to shine;
   Nor human spark is left, nor glimpse divine!
   Lo! thy dread empire, Chaos! is restor'd;
   Light dies before thy uncreating word;
   Thy hand, great Anarch! lets the curtain fall,
   And universal darkness buries all.   *Ib.* l. 641

28 Vital spark of heav'nly flame!
   Quit, oh quit this mortal frame:
   Trembling, hoping, ling'ring, flying,
   Oh the pain, the bliss of dying!
        The Dying Christian to his Soul

29 Tell me, my soul, can this be death?   *Ib.*

30 What beck'ning ghost, along the moon-light shade
   Invites my steps, and points to yonder glade?
        Elegy to the Memory of an Unfortunate Lady, l. 1

31 Is it, in heav'n, a crime to love too well?   *Ib.* l. 6

32 Is there no bright reversion in the sky,
   For those who greatly think, or bravely die? *Ib.* l. 9

33 Ambition first sprung from your bless'd abodes;
   The glorious fault of angels and of gods.   *Ib.* l. 13

34 By foreign hands thy dying eyes were closed,
   By foreign hands thy decent limbs composed,
   By foreign hands thy humble grave adorned,
   By strangers honoured, and by strangers mourned!
                                   Ib. l. 51

35 Yet shall thy grave with rising flow'rs be dressed,
   And the green turf lie lightly on thy breast. *Ib.* l. 63

36 So peaceful rests, without a stone, a name,
   What once had beauty, titles, wealth, and fame.
   How loved, how honoured once, avails thee not,
   To whom related, or by whom begot;
   A heap of dust alone remains of thee;
   'Tis all thou art, and all the proud shall be! *Ib.* l. 69

1 Line after line my gushing eyes o'erflow,
 Led through a sad variety of woe:
 Now warm in love, now with'ring in my bloom,
 Lost in a convent's solitary gloom!
   Eloisa to Abelard, l. 35

2 Heav'n first taught letters for some wretch's aid.
   Ib. l. 51

3 No, make me mistress to the man I love
 If there be yet another name more free
 More fond than mistress, make me that to thee!
   Ib. l. 88

4 Of all affliction taught a lover yet,
 'Tis sure the hardest science to forget.   *Ib. l. 189*

5 How happy is the blameless vestal's lot!
 The world forgetting, by the world forgot.
   Ib. l. 207

6 One thought of thee puts all the pomp to flight,
 Priests, tapers, temples, swim before my sight.
   Ib. l. 273

7 See my lips tremble, and my eye-balls roll,
 Suck my last breath, and catch my flying soul!
   Ib. l. 323

8 Teach me at once, and learn of me to die.   *Ib. l. 328*

9 You beat your pate, and fancy wit will come:
 Knock as you please, there's nobody at home.
   Epigrams. An Empty House

10 Has she no faults then (Envy says), Sir?
   Yes, she has one, I must aver;
 When all the world conspires to praise her,
   The woman's deaf, and does not hear.
   Ib. On a Certain Lady at Court

11 I am his Highness' dog at Kew;
 Pray tell me, sir, whose dog are you?
   Ib. On the Collar of a Dog which I gave to his Royal Highness

12 Here rests a woman, good without pretence.
   Epitaphs. On Mrs. Corbet

13 Heav'n, as its purest gold, by tortures tried;
 The saint sustain'd it, but the woman died.   *Ib.*

14 Whether thou choose Cervantes' serious air,
 Or laugh and shake in Rab'lais' easy chair,
 Or in the graver gown instruct mankind,
 Or, silent, let thy morals tell thy mind.
   Ib. To Swift. 22 Oct. 1727

15 In wit a man; simplicity a child.   *Ib. On Gay*

16 Form'd to delight at once and lash the age.   *Ib. l. 4*

17 Nature and Nature's laws lay hid in night:
 God said, *Let Newton be!* and all was light.
   Ib. Intended for Sir Isaac Newton

18   Prais'd, wept,
 And honour'd by the Muse he lov'd.
   Epitaph on James Craggs in Westminster Abbey

19 Ten censure wrong for one who writes amiss;
 A fool might once himself alone expose,
 Now one in verse makes many more in prose.
 'Tis with our judgments as our watches, none
 Go just alike, yet each believes his own.
   An Essay on Criticism, l. 6

20 Let such teach others who themselves excel,
 And censure freely who have written well.   *Ib. l. 15*

21 Some are bewildered in the maze of schools,
 And some made coxcombs nature meant but fools.
   An Essay on Criticism, l. 26

22 A little learning is a dang'rous thing;
 Drink deep, or taste not the Pierian spring:
 There shallow draughts intoxicate the brain,
 And drinking largely sobers us again.   *Ib. l. 215*

23 Hills peep o'er hills, and Alps on Alps arise!
   Ib. l. 232

24 'Tis not a lip, or eye, we beauty call,
 But the joint force and full result of all.   *Ib. l. 245*

25 Whoever thinks a faultless piece to see
 Thinks what ne'er was, nor is, nor e'er shall be.
   Ib. l. 253

26 Poets, like painters, thus unskilled to trace
 The naked nature, and the living grace,
 With gold and jewels cover ev'ry part,
 And hide with ornaments their want of art.
   Ib. l. 293

27 True wit is nature to advantage dressed,
 What oft was thought, but ne'er so well expressed.
   Ib. l. 297

28 Such laboured nothings, in so strange a style,
 Amaze th' unlearn'd, and make the learned smile.
   Ib. l. 326

29 Be not the first by whom the new are tried,
 Nor yet the last to lay the old aside.   *Ib. l. 335*

30   As some to church repair,
 Not for the doctrine, but the music there.
 These equal syllables alone require,
 Tho' oft the ear the open vowels tire;
 While expletives their feeble aid do join;
 And ten low words oft creep in one dull line.
   Ib. l. 342

31 Where'er you find 'the cooling western breeze',
 In the next line, it 'whispers through the trees':
 If crystal streams 'with pleasing murmurs creep',
 The reader's threatened, not in vain, with 'sleep':
 Then, at the last and only couplet fraught
 With some unmeaning thing they call a thought,
 A needless Alexandrine ends the song,
 That, like a wounded snake, drags its slow length
   along.   *Ib. l. 350*

32 True ease in writing comes from art, not chance,
 As those move easiest who have learned to dance.
 'Tis not enough no harshness gives offence,
 The sound must seem an echo to the sense.
 Soft is the strain when zephyr gently blows,
 And the smooth stream in smoother numbers flows;
 But when loud surges lash the sounding shore,
 The hoarse, rough verse should like the torrent roar:
 When Ajax strives some rock's vast weight to throw,
 The line too labours, and the words move slow:
 Not so, when swift Camilla scours the plain,
 Flies o'er th' unbending corn, and skims along the
   main.   *Ib. l. 362*

33 Yet let not each gay turn thy rapture move;
 For fools admire, but men of sense approve.
   Ib. l. 390

34 What woeful stuff this madrigal would be,
 In some starved hackney sonneteer, or me!
 But let a lord once own the happy lines,
 How the wit brightens; how the style refines.
   Ib. l. 418

POPE

1 Some praise at morning what they blame at night;
But always think the last opinion right.
An Essay on Criticism, l. 430

2 To err is human, to forgive, divine. *Ib.* l. 525

3 Men must be taught as if you taught them not,
And things unknown proposed as things forgot.
Ib. l. 574

4 The bookful blockhead, ignorantly read,
With loads of learned lumber in his head. *Ib.* l. 612

5 For fools rush in where angels fear to tread.
Ib. l. 625

6 Still pleased to teach, and yet not proud to know.
Ib. l. 632

7 Awake, my St. John! leave all meaner things
To low ambition, and the pride of kings.
Let us, since life can little more supply
Than just to look about us and to die,
Expatiate free o'er all this scene of man;
A mighty maze! but not without a plan.
An Essay on Man. Epistle i, l. 1

8 Eye Nature's walks, shoot folly as it flies,
And catch the manners living as they rise.
Laugh where we must, be candid where we can;
But vindicate the ways of God to man.
Say first, of God above or man below,
What can we reason but from what we know?
Ib. l. 13

9 Observe how system into system runs,
What other planets circle other suns. *Ib.* l. 25

10 Who sees with equal eye, as God of all,
A hero perish, or a sparrow fall,
Atoms or systems into ruin hurled,
And now a bubble burst, and now a world. *Ib.* l. 87

11 Hope springs eternal in the human breast;
Man never is, but always to be blest.
The soul, uneasy, and confined from home,
Rests and expatiates in a life to come.
Lo, the poor Indian! whose untutored mind
Sees God in clouds, or hears him in the wind;
His soul proud science never taught to stray
Far as the solar walk or milky way;
Yet simple nature to his hope has giv'n,
Behind the cloud-topped hill, an humbler heav'n.
Ib. l. 95

12 But thinks, admitted to that equal sky,
His faithful dog shall bear him company. *Ib.* l. 111

13 In pride, in reas'ning pride, our error lies;
All quit their sphere and rush into the skies!
Pride still is aiming at the bless'd abodes,
Men would be angels, angels would be gods.
Aspiring to be gods if angels fell,
Aspiring to be angels men rebel. *Ib.* l. 123

14 The first Almighty Cause
Acts not by partial, but by gen'ral laws. *Ib.* l. 145

15 Why has not man a microscopic eye?
For this plain reason, man is not a fly. *Ib.* l. 193

16 Die of a rose in aromatic pain? *Ib.* l. 200

17 The spider's touch how exquisitely fine!
Feels at each thread, and lives along the line.
Ib. l. 217

18 All are but parts of one stupendous whole,
Whose body nature is, and God the soul. *Ib.* l. 267

19 Warms in the sun, refreshes in the breeze,
Glows in the stars, and blossoms in the trees.
An Essay on Man, Ep. i, l. 271

20 As the rapt Seraph that adores and burns. *Ib.* l. 278

21 All nature is but art unknown to thee,
All chance, direction which thou canst not see;
All discord, harmony not understood;
All partial evil, universal good;
And, spite of pride, in erring reason's spite,
One truth is clear, Whatever is, is right. *Ib.* l. 284

22 Know then thyself, presume not God to scan,
The proper study of mankind is man.
Placed on this isthmus of a middle state,
A being darkly wise, and rudely great:
With too much knowledge for the sceptic side,
With too much weakness for the stoic's pride,
He hangs between; in doubt to act or rest;
In doubt to deem himself a god, or beast;
In doubt his mind or body to prefer;
Born but to die, and reas'ning but to err;
Alike in ignorance, his reason such,
Whether he thinks too little or too much;
Chaos of thought and passion, all confused;
Still by himself abused, or disabused;
Created half to rise, and half to fall;
Great lord of all things, yet a prey to all;
Sole judge of truth, in endless error hurled;
The glory, jest, and riddle of the world!
Ib. Ep. ii, l. 1

23 Go, teach eternal wisdom how to rule—
Then drop into thyself, and be a fool! *Ib.* l. 29

24 Fix'd like a plant on his peculiar spot,
To draw nutrition, propagate, and rot. *Ib.* l. 63

25 And hence one master-passion in the breast,
Like Aaron's serpent, swallows up the rest.
Ib. l. 131

26 The young disease, that must subdue at length,
Grows with his growth, and strengthens with his
strength. *Ib.* l. 135

27 Vice is a monster of so frightful mien,
As to be hated needs but to be seen;
Yet seen too oft, familiar with her face,
We first endure, then pity, then embrace.
But where th' extreme of vice, was ne'er agreed:
Ask where's the North? at York, 'tis on the Tweed;
In Scotland, at the Orcades; and there,
At Greenland, Zembla, or the Lord knows where.
Ib. l. 217

28 Till one man's weakness grows the strength of all.
Ib. l. 252

29 The learn'd is happy nature to explore,
The fool is happy that he knows no more. *Ib.* l. 263

30 Behold the child, by nature's kindly law
Pleased with a rattle, tickled with a straw:
Some livelier plaything gives his youth delight,
A little louder, but as empty quite:
Scarfs, garters, gold, amuse his riper stage,
And beads and pray'r-books are the toys of age:
Pleased with this bauble still, as that before;
Till tired he sleeps, and life's poor play is o'er.
Ib. l. 275

1 For forms of government let fools contest;
Whate'er is best administered is best:
For modes of faith let graceless zealots fight;
His can't be wrong whose life is in the right:
In faith and hope the world will disagree,
But all mankind's concern is charity.
An Essay on Man. Ep. iii, l. 303

2 O Happiness! our being's end and aim,
Good, pleasure, ease, content! whate'er thy name:
That something still which prompts th' eternal sigh,
For which we bear to live, or dare to die.
Ib. Ep. iv, l. 1

3 Order is Heav'n's first law. *Ib.* l. 49

4 Buries madmen in the heaps they raise. *Ib.* l. 76

5 Shall gravitation cease, if you go by?
Or some old temple, nodding to its fall,
For Chartres' head reserve the hanging wall?
Ib. l. 128

6 Go, like the Indian, in another life
Expect thy dog, thy bottle, and thy wife. *Ib.* l. 177

7 Worth makes the man, and want of it the fellow;
The rest is all but leather or prunella. *Ib.* l. 203

8 What can ennoble sots, or slaves, or cowards?
Alas! not all the blood of all the Howards. *Ib.* l. 215

9 A wit's a feather, and a chief a rod;
An honest man's the noblest work of God. *Ib.* l. 247

10 And more true joy Marcellus exil'd feels,
Than Caesar with a senate at his heels. *Ib.* l. 257

11 Truths would you teach, or save a sinking land?
All fear, none aid you, and few understand.
Ib. l. 265

12 If parts allure thee, think how Bacon shined,
The wisest, brightest, meanest of mankind:
Or ravished with the whistling of a name,
See Cromwell, damned to everlasting fame!
Ib. l. 281

13 Know then this truth, enough for man to know,
'Virtue alone is happiness below.' *Ib.* l. 309

14 Slave to no sect, who takes no private road,
But looks through nature up to nature's God.
Ib. l. 331

15 Formed by thy converse, happily to steer
From grave to gay, from lively to severe. *Ib.* l. 379

16 Say, shall my little bark attendant sail,
Pursue the triumph, and partake the gale? *Ib.* l. 385

17 Thou wert my guide, philosopher, and friend.
Ib. l. 390

18 That true self-love and social are the same.
Ib. l. 396

19 All our knowledge is ourselves to know. *Ib.* l. 398

20 Achilles' wrath, to Greece the direful spring
Of woes unnumbered, heavenly goddess, sing.
Iliad, i. 1

21 To observations which ourselves we make,
We grow more partial for th' observer's sake.
Moral Essays, Ep. i, *To Lord Cobham,* l. 11

22 Like following life through creatures you dissect,
You lose it in the moment you detect. *Ib.* l. 29

23 Alas! in truth the man but changed his mind,
Perhaps was sick, in love, or had not dined.
Ib. l. 127

24 'Tis from high life high characters are drawn;
A saint in crape is twice a saint in lawn.
Moral Essays, Ep. i, *To Lord Cobham,* l. 135

25 'Odious! in woollen! 'twould a saint provoke!'
(Were the last words that poor Narcissa spoke:)
Ib. l. 246

26 'One would not, sure, be frightful when one's dead:
And,—Betty,—give this cheek a little red.' *Ib.* l. 250

27 And you, brave Cobham! to the latest breath,
Shall feel your ruling passion strong in death.
Ib. l. 262

28 Most women have no characters at all.
Ib. Ep. ii. *To Mrs. M. Blount,* l. 2

29 Choose a firm cloud, before it fall, and in it
Catch, ere she change, the Cynthia of this minute.
Ib. l. 19

30 Chaste to her husband, frank to all beside,
A teeming mistress, but a barren bride. *Ib.* l. 71

31 Flavia's a wit, has too much sense to pray;
To toast our wants and wishes is her way;
Nor asks of God, but of her stars, to give
The mighty blessing, 'while we live, to live'. *Ib.* l. 87

32 Wise wretch! with pleasures too refined to please;
With too much spirit to be e'er at ease;
With too much quickness ever to be taught;
With too much thinking to have common thought.
Ib. l. 95

33 'With every pleasing, every prudent part,
Say, what can Chloe want?'—She wants a heart.
Ib. l. 159

34 Virtue she finds too painful an endeavour,
Content to dwell in decencies for ever. *Ib.* l. 163

35 In men, we various ruling passions find;
In women, two almost divide the kind;
Those, only fixed, they first or last obey,
The love of pleasure, and the love of sway. *Ib.* l. 207

36 Men, some to business, some to pleasure take;
But every woman is at heart a rake:
Men, some to quiet, some to public strife;
But every lady would be queen for life. *Ib.* l. 215

37 See how the world its veterans rewards!
A youth of frolics, an old age of cards. *Ib.* l. 243

38 She who ne'er answers till a husband cools,
Or, if she rules him, never shows she rules;
Charms by accepting, by submitting, sways,
Yet has her humour most, when she obeys. *Ib.* l. 261

39 And mistress of herself, though china fall. *Ib.* l. 268

40 Woman's at best a contradiction still. *Ib.* l. 270

41 Who shall decide, when doctors disagree,
And soundest casuists doubt, like you and me?
Ib. Ep. iii. *To Lord Bathurst,* l. 1

42 But thousands die, without or this or that,
Die, and endow a college, or a cat. *Ib.* l. 95

43 The ruling passion, be it what it will,
The ruling passion conquers reason still. *Ib.* l. 153

44 Rise, honest Muse! and sing the Man of Ross!
Ib. l. 250

1 In the worst inn's worst room, with mat half-hung,

Great Villiers lies—alas! how changed from him,

Gallant and gay, in Cliveden's proud alcove
The bower of wanton Shrewsbury and love.
Moral Essays, Ep. iii, *To Lord Bathurst*, ll. 299–308

2 Where London's column, pointing at the skies
Like a tall bully, lifts the head, and lies. *Ib.* l. 339

3 Grove nods at grove, each alley has a brother,
And half the platform just reflects the other.
Ib. Ep. iv. *To Lord Burlington*, l. 117.

4 To rest, the cushion and soft dean invite,
Who never mentions hell to ears polite. *Ib.* l. 149

5 Such were the notes, thy once-loved Poet sung,
Till Death untimely stopped his tuneful tongue.
Ib. Ep. v. *To the Earl of Oxford and Earl Mortimer*, l. 1

6 Statesman, yet friend to truth! of soul sincere,
In action faithful, and in honour clear;
Who broke no promise, served no private end,
Who gained no title, and who lost no friend.
Ib. Ep. vii. *To Mr. Addison*, l. 67

7 Where'er you walk cool gales shall fan the glade;
Trees, where you sit, shall crowd into a shade;
Where'er you tread, the blushing flow'rs shall rise,
And all things flourish where you turn your eyes.
Pastorals, Summer, l. 73

8 What dire offence from am'rous causes springs,
What mighty contests rise from trivial things!
The Rape of the Lock, c. i, l. 1

9 Here files of pins extend their shining rows,
Puffs, powders, patches, bibles, billets-doux.
Ib. l. 137

10 On her white breast a sparkling cross she wore,
Which Jews might kiss, and infidels adore.
Ib. c. ii, l. 7

11 Bright as the sun, her eyes the gazers strike,
And, like the sun, they shine on all alike. *Ib.* l. 13

12 If to her share some female errors fall,
Look on her face, and you'll forget 'em all. *Ib.* l. 17

13 Fair tresses man's imperial race insnare,
And beauty draws us with a single hair. *Ib.* l. 27

14 Here thou, great Anna! whom three realms obey,
Dost sometimes counsel take—and sometimes tea.
Ib. c. iii, l. 7

15 The hungry judges soon the sentence sign,
And wretches hang that jurymen may dine. *Ib.* l. 21

16 Let spades be trumps! she said, and trumps they were. *Ib.* l. 46

17 Not louder shrieks to pitying heav'n are cast,
When husbands, or when lap-dogs breathe their last.
Ib. l. 157

18 Sir Plume, of amber snuff-box justly vain,
And the nice conduct of a clouded cane.
Ib. c. iv, l. 123

19 Beauties in vain their pretty eyes may roll;
Charms strike the sight, but merit wins the soul.
Ib. c. v, l. 33

20 Shut, shut the door, good John! fatigued I said,
Tie up the knocker; say I'm sick, I'm dead.
Epistles and Satires of Horace Imitated. Prologue, Epistle to Dr. Arbuthnot, l. 1

21 Is there a parson, much bemused in beer,
A maudlin poetess, a rhyming peer,
A clerk, foredoomed his father's soul to cross,
Who pens a stanza, when he should engross?
Ib. Epistle to Dr. Arbuthnot, l. 15

22 Fired that the house reject him, "Sdeath I'll print it,
And shame the fools.' *Ib.* l. 61

23 You think this cruel? take it for a rule,
No creature smarts so little as a fool.
Let peals of laughter, Codrus! round thee break,
Thou unconcern'd canst hear the mighty crack:
Pit, box, and gall'ry in convulsions hurl'd,
Thou stand'st unshook amidst a bursting world.
Ib. l. 83

24 Destroy his fib or sophistry—in vain!
The creature's at his dirty work again. *Ib.* l. 91

25 As yet a child, nor yet a fool to fame,
I lisped in numbers, for the numbers came.
Ib. l. 127

26 This long disease, my life. *Ib.* l. 132

27 Pretty! in amber to observe the forms
Of hairs, or straws, or dirt, or grubs, or worms!
The things we know are neither rich nor rare,
But wonder how the devil they got there. *Ib.* l. 169

28 And he, whose fustian's so sublimely bad,
It is not poetry, but prose run mad. *Ib.* l. 187

29 Were there one whose fires
True genius kindles, and fair fame inspires;
Blest with each talent, and each art to please,
And born to write, converse, and live with ease:
Should such a man, too fond to rule alone,
Bear, like the Turk, no brother near the throne,
View him with scornful, yet with jealous eyes,
And hate for arts that caused himself to rise;
Damn with faint praise, assent with civil leer,
And, without sneering, teach the rest to sneer;
Willing to wound, and yet afraid to strike,
Just hint a fault, and hesitate dislike.
Alike reserved to blame, or to commend,
A timorous foe, and a suspicious friend;
Dreading e'en fools, by flatterers besieged,
And so obliging, that he ne'er obliged;
Like Cato, give his little senate laws,
And sit attentive to his own applause;
While wits and Templars every sentence raise,
And wonder with a foolish face of praise—
Who but must laugh, if such a man there be?
Who would not weep, if Atticus were he!
[Addison.] *Ib.* l. 193

30 Let Sporus tremble.—A. What? that thing of silk,
Sporus, that mere white curd of ass's milk?
Satire or sense, alas! can Sporus feel?
Who breaks a butterfly upon a wheel? *Ib.* l. 305

31 Yet let me flap this bug with gilded wings—
This painted child of dirt, that stinks and stings.
Ib. l. 309

32 So well-bred spaniels civilly delight
In mumbling of the game they dare not bite.
Eternal smiles his emptiness betray,
As shallow streams run dimpling all the way.
Ib. l. 313

33 A Cherub's face, a reptile all the rest. *Ib.* l. 331

34 Wit that can creep, and pride that licks the dust.
Ib. l. 333

[385]

1 That not in fancy's maze he wandered long,
But stooped to truth, and moralised his song.
Epistles and Satires of Horace Imitated. Prologue,
Epistle to Dr. Arbuthnot, l. 340

2 The dull, the proud, the wicked and the mad.
Ib. l. 347

3 A knave's a knave to me in every state.   *Ib.* l. 361

4 Unlearned, he knew no schoolman's subtle art,
No language, but the language of the heart.
By nature honest, by experience wise,
Healthy by temperance, and by exercise.   *Ib.* l. 398

5 There St. John mingles with my friendly bowl
The feast of reason and the flow of soul.
Ib. I. *Hor.* II, *Sat.* 1. *To Mr. Fortescue,* l. 127

6 For I, who hold sage Homer's rule the best,
Welcome the coming, speed the going guest.
Ib. II. *Hor.* II, *Sat.* 2. *To Mr. Bethel,* l. 159. (In
Odyssey, xv. 83 with 'parting' for 'going'.)

7 In life's cool evening satiate of applause.
Ib. III. *Hor.* I, *Ep.* 1. *To Lord Bolingbroke,* l. 9

8 Not to go back, is somewhat to advance,
And men must walk at least before they dance.
Ib. l. 53

9 Get place and wealth—if possible with grace;
If not, by any means, get wealth and place.
Ib. l. 103

10 The worst of madmen is a saint run mad.
Ib. IV. *Hor.* I, *Ep.* 6. *To Mr. Murray,* l. 27

11 Grac'd as thou art with all the Pow'r of Words,
So known, so honour'd, at the House of Lords.
Ib. l. 48

12 Shakespeare (whom you and every play-house bill
Style the divine, the matchless, what you will)
For gain, not glory, winged his roving flight,
And grew immortal in his own despite.
Ib. V. *Hor.* II, *Ep.* 1. *To Augustus,* l. 69

13 Who now reads Cowley? if he pleases yet,
His moral pleases, not his pointed wit;
Forgot his epic, nay Pindaric art,
But still I love the language of his heart.   *Ib.* l. 75

14   The people's voice is odd,
It is, and it is not, the voice of God.   *Ib.* l. 89

15 In quibbles, angel and archangel join,
And God the Father turns a school-divine.
On *Paradise Lost.*   *Ib.* l. 101

16 The mob of gentlemen who wrote with ease.
Ib. l. 108

17 Waller was smooth; but Dryden taught to join
The varying verse, the full-resounding line,
The long majestic march and energy divine.
Ib. l. 267

18 Ev'n copious Dryden wanted, or forgot,
The last and greatest art, the art to blot.   *Ib.* l. 280

19 There still remains to mortify a wit,
The many-headed monster of the pit.   *Ib.* l. 304

20 Let humble Allen, with an awkward shame,
Do good by stealth, and blush to find it fame.
Ib. Epilogue, Dial. i, l. 136

21 Argyll, the state's whole thunder born to wield,
And shake alike the senate and the field.
Ib. Dial. ii, l. 86

22 Ask you what provocation I have had?
The strong antipathy of good to bad.   *Ib.* l. 197

23 Yes, I am proud; I must be proud to see
Men not afraid of God, afraid of me.   *Ib.* l. 208

24 Vain was the chief's, the sage's pride!
They had no poet, and they died.
Imitations of Horace, Odes, IV. IX. iv

25 Bathos, the art of sinking in Poetry.
Miscellanies. Title

26 Happy the man whose wish and care
A few paternal acres bound,
Content to breathe his native air,
In his own ground.   *Ode on Solitude*

27 Thus let me live, unseen, unknown,
Thus unlamented let me die,
Steal from the world, and not a stone
Tell where I lie.   *Ib.*

28 And the touched needle trembles to the pole.
Temple of Fame, l. 431

29 Father of all! in ev'ry age,
In ev'ry clime adored,
By saint, by savage, and by sage,
Jehovah, Jove, or Lord!

Thou Great First Cause, least understood!
Who all my sense confined
To know but this, that thou art good,
And that myself am blind.   *The Universal Prayer*

30 What conscience dictates to be done,
Or warns me not to do,
This teach me more than hell to shun,
That, more than heav'n pursue.   *Ib.*

31 Teach me to feel another's woe,
To hide the fault I see;
That mercy I to others show,
That mercy show to me.   *Ib.*

32 Oft, as in airy rings they skim the heath,
The clam'rous lapwings feel the leaden death:
Oft, as the mounting larks their notes prepare,
They fall, and leave their little lives in air.
Windsor Forest, l. 131

33 Not to admire, is all the art I know
To make men happy, and to keep them so.
Trans. of Horace, Epistles, I. vi

34 This is the Jew
That Shakspeare drew.
Of Macklin's performance of Shylock, 14 Feb.
1741. Baker, Reed, & Jones, *Biographia Drama-*
tica (1812), vol. 1, pt. ii, p. 469

35 Party-spirit, which at best is but the madness of many
for the gain of a few.
Letters. To E. Blount, 27 Aug. 1714

36 'Blessed is the man who expects nothing, for he shall
never be disappointed', was the ninth beatitude
which a man of wit (who, like a man of wit, was a
long time in gaol) added to the eighth.
Ib. To Fortescue, 23 Sept. 1725

37 How often are we to die before we go quite off this
stage? In every friend we lose a part of ourselves,
and the best part.   *Ib. To Swift, 5 Dec. 1732*

38 To endeavour to work upon the vulgar with fine
sense, is like attempting to hew blocks with a razor.
Thoughts on Various Subjects

1 When men grow virtuous in their old age, they only
make a sacrifice to God of the devil's leavings.
Thoughts on Various Subjects. (*See 520:48*)

WALTER POPE
1630–1714

2 If I live to be old, for I find I go down,
Let this be my fate in a country town;
May I have a warm house with a stone at the gate,
And a cleanly young girl to rub my bald pate.
May I govern my passion with an absolute sway,
And grow wiser and better as my strength wears
away,
Without gout or stone, by a gentle decay.
The Old Man's Wish. H. Playford, *Theater of
Musick* (1685), bk. i, p. 50

RICHARD PORSON
1759–1808

3 When Dido found Æneas would not come,
She mourn'd in silence, and was Di-do-dum.
Epigram: On Latin Gerunds. J. S. Watson, *Life
of Porson* (1861), p. 418

4 The Germans in Greek
Are sadly to seek:
Not five in five score,
But ninety-five more:
All, save only Herman,
And Herman's a German.
M. L. Clarke, *Life of Porson*, ch. vii

5 Madoc will be read,—when Homer and Virgil are
forgotten. [To Southey.]
Rogers, Table Talk, p. 330

6 He sometimes draws out the thread of his verbosity
finer than the staple of his argument.
Of Gibbon's *Decline and Fall. Letters to Travis*
(1790), preface, p. xxix. (*See 455:24*)

7 I went to Frankfort, and got drunk
With that most learn'd professor, Brunck;
I went to Worts, and got more drunken
With that more learn'd professor, Ruhnken.
Facetiæ Cantabrigienses, 1825

WILLIAM SYDNEY PORTER
see
O. HENRY

BEILBY PORTEUS
1731–1808

8   In sober state,
Through the sequester'd vale of rural life,
The venerable Patriarch guileless held
The tenor of his way.   *Death*, l. 108

9   One murder made a villain,
Millions a hero.   *Ib.* l. 155

10 War its thousands slays, Peace its ten thousands.
Ib. l. 179

11   Teach him how to live,
And, oh! still harder lesson! how to die. *Ib.* l. 319

FRANCIS POTT
1832–1909

12 The strife is o'er, the battle done;
Now is the Victor's triumph won;
O let the song of praise be sung. Alleluia!
*The Strife is O'er. Hymns fitted to the Order of
Common Prayer* (1861), trans. of Latin, *Finita Iam
Sunt Praelia*

HENRY CODMAN POTTER
1835–1908

13 We have exchanged the Washingtonian dignity for the
Jeffersonian simplicity, which in due time came to
be only another name for the Jacksonian vulgarity.
Address, Washington Centennial, 30 Apr. 1889

SIR JOHN POWELL
1645–1713

14 Let us consider the reason of the case. For nothing is
law that is not reason.
Coggs v. Bernard, 2 Lord Raymond, 911

JOHN O'CONNOR POWER

15 The mules of politics: without pride of ancestry, or
hope of posterity.
*Quoted in H. H. Asquith's Memories and Reflec-
tions,* i. 123

WINTHROP MACKWORTH PRAED
1802–1839

16 I think that nought is worth a thought,
And I'm a fool for thinking.
The Chant of the Brazen Head

17 My own Araminta, say 'No!' *A Letter of Advice*

18 A happy boy, at Drury's. *School and Schoolfellows*

19 Just Eton boys grown heavy.   *Ib.*

20 Of science and logic he chatters,
As fine and as fast as he can;
Though I am no judge of such matters,
I'm sure he's a talented man. *The Talented Man*

21 Whate'er the stranger's caste or creed,
Pundit or Papist, saint or sinner,
He found a stable for his steed,
And welcome for himself, and dinner. *The Vicar*

22 If he departed as he came,
With no new light on love or liquor,—
Good sooth, the traveller was to blame,
And not the Vicarage, nor the Vicar.   *Ib.*

23 His talk was like a stream, which runs
With rapid change from rocks to roses:
It slipped from politics to puns,
It passed from Mahomet to Moses;
Beginning with the laws which keep
The planets in their radiant courses,
And ending with some precept deep
For dressing eels, or shoeing horses.   *Ib.*

24 The Baptist found him far too deep;
The Deist sighed with saving sorrow;
And the lean Levite went to sleep,
And dreamed of tasting pork to-morrow.   *Ib.*

1 For all who understood admired,
And some who did not understand them. *The Vicar*

CHARLES PRATT, EARL CAMDEN

1714–1794

2 The British Parliament has no right to tax the Americans. . . . Taxation and representation are inseparably united. God hath joined them; no British Parliament can put them asunder. To endeavour to do so is to stab our very vitals.
Speech, House of Lords, 1765

THE BOOK OF COMMON PRAYER

3 The two extremes, of too much stiffness in refusing, and of too much easiness in admitting any variation. *The Preface*

4 There was never any thing by the wit of man so well devised, or so sure established, which in continuance of time hath not been corrupted.
Ib. Concerning the Service of the Church

5 A table of the Moveable Feasts.
Section Heading in Introductory Pages, p. xxxi

6 Dearly beloved brethren, the Scripture moveth us in sundry places to acknowledge and confess our manifold sins and wickedness.
Morning Prayer. Priest's Opening Exhortation

7 We should not dissemble nor cloke them. *Ib.*

8 When we assemble and meet together. *Ib.*

9 Those things which are requisite and necessary, as well for the body as the soul. *Ib.*

10 We have erred, and strayed from thy ways like lost sheep. *Ib. General Confession*

11 We have left undone those things which we ought to have done; And we have done those things which we ought not to have done; And there is no health in us. *Ib.*

12 A godly, righteous, and sober life. *Ib.*

13 And forgive us our trespasses, As we forgive them that trespass against us. *Ib. The Lord's Prayer*

14 As it was in the beginning, is now, and ever shall be: world without end. Amen. *Ib. Gloria*

15 Lord God of Sabaoth. *Ib. Te Deum Laudamus*

16 An infinite Majesty. *Ib.*

17 The sharpness of death. *Ib.*

18 The noble army of martyrs. *Ib.*

19 O Lord, in thee have I trusted: let me never be confounded. *Ib.*

20 O all ye Works of the Lord, bless ye the Lord: praise him, and magnify him for ever. *Ib. Benedicite*

21 O all ye Green Things upon the Earth, bless ye the Lord: praise him, and magnify him for ever. *Ib.*

22 O ye Whales, and all that move in the Waters. *Ib.*

23 O Ananias, Azarias, and Misael, bless ye the Lord: praise him, and magnify him for ever. *Ib.*

24 Give peace in our time, O Lord.
Because there is none other that fighteth for us, but only thou, O God. *Ib. Versicles*

25 The author of peace and lover of concord, in knowledge of whom standeth our eternal life, whose service is perfect freedom.
Morning Prayer. Second Collect, for Peace

26 Neither run into any kind of danger.
Ib. Third Collect, for Grace

27 In Quires and Places where they sing.
Ib. Rubric after Third Collect

28 Grant her in health and wealth long to live.
Ib. A Prayer for the Queen's Majesty

29 The fountain of all goodness.
Ib. Prayer for the Royal Family

30 Almighty and everlasting God, who alone workest great marvels; Send down upon our Bishops, and Curates, and all Congregations committed to their charge, the healthful Spirit of thy grace.
Ib. Prayer for the Clergy and People

31 The continual dew of thy blessing. *Ib.*

32 With one accord to make our common supplications unto thee. *Ib. Prayer of St. Chrysostom*

33 When two or three are gathered together in thy Name thou wilt grant their requests. *Ib.*

34 From whom all holy desires, all good counsels, and all just works do proceed.
Evening Prayer. Second Collect

35 That peace which the world cannot give. *Ib.*

36 Lighten our darkness, we beseech thee, O Lord; and by thy great mercy defend us from all perils and dangers of this night. *Ib. Third Collect*

37 Whosoever will be saved: before all things it is necessary that he hold the Catholick Faith.
Which Faith except every one do keep whole and undefiled: without doubt he shall perish everlastingly. *Athanasian Creed*

38 Neither confounding the Persons: nor dividing the Substance. *Ib.*

39 As also there are not three incomprehensibles, nor three uncreated: but one uncreated, and one incomprehensible. *Ib.*

40 Not three Gods: but one God. *Ib.*

41 Of a reasonable soul and human flesh subsisting. *Ib.*

42 Not by conversion of the Godhead into flesh: but by taking of the Manhood into God. *Ib.*

43 Have mercy upon us miserable sinners. *The Litany*

44 Neither take thou vengeance of our sins. *Ib.*

45 The crafts and assaults of the devil. *Ib.*

46 Envy, hatred, and malice, and all uncharitableness. *Ib.*

47 Deceits of the world, the flesh, and the devil. *Ib.*

48 From battle and murder, and from sudden death. *Ib.*

49 Hardness of heart, and contempt of thy Word and Commandment. *Ib.*

50 Agony and bloody Sweat. *Ib.*

51 In the hour of death, and in the day of judgement. *Ib.*

52 All Bishops, Priests, and Deacons. *Ib.*

53 Unity, peace, and concord. *Ib.*

54 To bring forth the fruits of the Spirit. *Ib.*

1 To strengthen such as do stand; and to comfort and help the weak-hearted; and to raise up them that fall; and finally to beat down Satan under our feet. *The Litany*

2 All that are in danger, necessity, and tribulation. *Ib.*

3 All that travel by land or by water, all women labouring of child, all sick persons, and young children; and to shew thy pity upon all prisoners and captives. *Ib.*

4 The fatherless children, and widows. *Ib.*

5 Our enemies, persecutors, and slanderers. *Ib.*

6 The kindly fruits of the earth, so as in due time we may enjoy them. *Ib.*

7 Our sins, negligences, and ignorances. *Ib.*

8 The sighing of a contrite heart. *Ib. First Collect*

9 The craft and subtilty of the devil or man. *Ib.*

10 We have heard with our ears, and our fathers have declared unto us, the noble works that thou didst in their days, and in the old time before them. *Ib. Sentences after the First Collect*

11 Turn from us all those evils that we most righteously have deserved. *Ib. Second Collect*

12 Tied and bound with the chain of our sins. *Prayers and Thanksgivings, upon Several Occasions. 'O God, whose nature and property'*

13 Our Mediator and Advocate. *Ib.*

14 The safety, honour, and welfare of our Sovereign, and her Dominions. *Ib. Prayer for the High Court of Parliament*

15 All sorts and conditions of men. *Ib. Prayer for All Conditions of Men*

16 All who profess and call themselves Christians. *Ib.*

17 Any ways afflicted, or distressed, in mind, body, or estate. *Ib.*

18 A happy issue out of all their afflictions. *Ib.*

19 Our creation, preservation, and all the blessings of this life. *Ib. Thanksgivings. A General Thanksgiving*

20 For the means of grace, and for the hope of glory. *Ib.*

21 The former and the latter rain. *Ib. For Rain*

22 Cast away the works of darkness, and put upon us the armour of light, now in the time of this mortal life. *Collects. 1st Sunday in Advent*

23 Hear them, read, mark, learn, and inwardly digest them. *Ib. 2nd Sunday in Advent*

24 An acceptable people in thy sight. *Ib. 3rd Sunday in Advent*

25 Sore let and hindered in running the race. *Ib. 4th Sunday in Advent*

26 Children by adoption and grace. *Ib. Christmas Day*

27 The glory that shall be revealed. *Ib. St. Stephen's Day*

28 That they may both perceive and know what things they ought to do, and also may have grace and power faithfully to fulfil the same. *Ib. 1st Sunday after Epiphany*

29 Grant us thy peace all the days of our life. *Ib. 2nd Sunday after Epiphany*

30 By reason of the frailty of our nature we cannot always stand upright. *Collects. 4th Sunday after Epiphany*

31 That most excellent gift of charity. *Ib. Quinquagesima Sunday*

32 All evil thoughts which may assault and hurt the soul. *Ib. 2nd Sunday in Lent*

33 Jews, Turks, Infidels, and Hereticks. *Ib. Good Friday. Third Collect*

34 Thy special grace preventing us. *Ib. Easter Day*

35 The leaven of malice and wickedness. *Ib. 1st Sunday after Easter*

36 Those things that are contrary to their profession. *Ib. 3rd Sunday after Easter*

37 The unruly wills and affections of sinful men. *Ib. 4th Sunday after Easter*

38 Among the sundry and manifold changes of the world, our hearts may surely there be fixed where true joys are to be found. *Ib.*

39 To have a right judgement in all things. *Ib. Whitsun-day*

40 The weakness of our mortal nature. *Ib. 1st Sunday after Trinity*

41 We may so pass through things temporal, that we finally lose not the things eternal. *Ib. 4th Sunday after Trinity*

42 Such good things as pass man's understanding. *Ib. 6th Sunday after Trinity*

43 The author and giver of all good things. *Ib. 7th Sunday after Trinity*

44 Running the way of thy commandments. *Ib. 11th Sunday after Trinity*

45 Those things whereof our conscience is afraid. *Ib. 12th Sunday after Trinity*

46 Increase of faith, hope, and charity. *Ib. 14th Sunday after Trinity*

47 Because the frailty of man without thee cannot but fall. *Ib. 15th Sunday after Trinity*

48 Serve thee with a quiet mind. *Ib. 21st Sunday after Trinity*

49 Thy household the Church. *Ib. 22nd Sunday after Trinity*

50 Stir up, we beseech thee, O Lord, the wills of thy faithful people; that they, plenteously bringing forth the fruit of good works, may of thee be plenteously rewarded. *Ib. 25th Sunday after Trinity*

51 Carried away with every blast of vain doctrine. *Ib. St. Mark's Day*

52 Whom truly to know is everlasting life. *Ib. St. Philip and St. James's Day*

53 Constantly speak the truth, boldly rebuke vice, and patiently suffer for the truth's sake. *Ib. St. John Baptist's Day*

54 Ordained and constituted the services of Angels and men in a wonderful order. *Ib. St. Michael and All Angels*

55 Who hast knit together thine elect in one communion and fellowship, in the mystical body of thy Son. *Ib. All Saints' Day*

THE BOOK OF COMMON PRAYER

1 An open and notorious evil liver.
Holy Communion: Introductory Rubric

2 Truly repented and amended his former naughty life. *Ib.*

3 A fair white linen cloth. *Ib.*

4 Unto whom all hearts be open, all desires known, and from whom no secrets are hid. *Ib. Collect for Purity*

5 Thou shalt have none other gods but me. *Ib. 1st Commandment*

6 Incline our hearts to keep this law. *Ib. Response to Commandments*

7 Thou shalt not make to thyself any graven image, nor the likeness of any thing that is in heaven above, or in the earth beneath, or in the water under the earth. Thou shalt not bow down to them, nor worship them: for I the Lord thy God am a jealous God, and visit the sins of the fathers upon the children unto the third and fourth generation. *Ib. 2nd Commandment*

8 Thou shalt not take the Name of the Lord thy God in vain. *Ib. 3rd Commandment*

9 Remember that thou keep holy the Sabbath-day. Six days shalt thou labour, and do all that thou hast to do; but the seventh day is the Sabbath of the Lord thy God. *Ib. 4th Commandment*

10 The stranger that is within thy gates. *Ib.*

11 In six days the Lord made heaven and earth, the sea, and all that in them is, and rested the seventh day. *Ib.*

12 Honour thy father and thy mother; that thy days may be long in the land which the Lord thy God giveth thee. *Ib. 5th Commandment*

13 Thou shalt do no murder. *Ib. 6th Commandment*

14 Thou shalt not commit adultery. *Ib. 7th Commandment*

15 Thou shalt not steal. *Ib. 8th Commandment*

16 Thou shalt not bear false witness against thy neighbour. *Ib. 9th Commandment*

17 Thou shalt not covet thy neighbour's wife, nor his servant, nor his maid, nor his ox, nor his ass, nor any thing that is his. *Ib. 10th Commandment*

18 All things visible and invisible. *Ib. Nicene Creed*

19 Very God of very God. *Ib.*

20 The Lord and giver of life. *Ib.*

21 Who spake by the Prophets. *Ib.*

22 One Catholick and Apostolick Church. *Ib.*

23 In a decent bason to be provided by the Parish. *Ib. Rubric before the Prayer for the Church Militant*

24 The whole state of Christ's Church militant here in earth. *Ib. Prayer for the Church Militant*

25 The spirit of truth, unity, and concord. *Ib.*

26 Live in unity and godly love. *Ib.*

27 Truly and indifferently minister justice. *Ib.*

28 Thy true and lively Word. *Ib.*

29 All them, who in this transitory life are in trouble, sorrow, need, sickness, or any other adversity. *Ib.*

30 Departed this life in thy faith and fear.
Holy Communion. Prayer for the Church Militant

31 Discreet and learned Minister of God's Word. *Ib. First Exhortation*

32 Ghostly counsel and advice. *Ib.*

33 We eat and drink our own damnation. *Ib. Third Exhortation*

34 Ye that do truly and earnestly repent you of your sins, and are in love and charity with your neighbours, and intend to lead a new life. *Ib. The Invitation*

35 Meekly kneeling upon your knees. *Ib.*

36 The burden of them is intolerable. *Ib. General Confession*

37 Hear what comfortable words. *Ib. Comfortable Words*

38 It is meet and right so to do. *Ib. Versicles*

39 Therefore with Angels and Archangels, and with all the company of heaven. *Ib. Hymn of Praise*

40 Holy, holy, holy, Lord God of hosts, heaven and earth are full of thy glory: Glory be to thee, O Lord most High. *Ib.*

41 By the operation of the Holy Ghost. *Ib. Proper Preface for Christmas Day*

42 A full, perfect, and sufficient sacrifice, oblation, and satisfaction. *Ib. Prayer of Consecration*

43 Who, in the same night that he was betrayed. *Ib.*

44 This our bounden duty and service. *Ib. Prayer of Oblation, 1*

45 Not weighing our merits, but pardoning our offences *Ib.*

46 The mystical body of thy Son, which is the blessed company of all faithful people. *Ib. 2*

47 Heirs through hope of thy everlasting kingdom. *Ib.*

48 The peace of God, which passeth all understanding. *Ib. The Blessing*

49 Be amongst you and remain with you always. *Ib.*

50 All the changes and chances of this mortal life. *Ib. Collects after the Offertory, 1*

51 Prevent us, O Lord, in all our doings. *Ib. 4*

52 All our works begun, continued, and ended in thee. *Ib.*

53 Those things, which for our unworthiness we dare not, and for our blindness we cannot ask. *Ib. 5*

54 For that were Idolatry, to be abhorred of all faithful Christians. *Ib. Black Rubric*

55 In the vulgar tongue. *Publick Baptism of Infants. Introductory Rubric, 1*

56 All this I stedfastly believe. *Ib. Vow of Faith*

57 Grant that the old Adam in this Child may be so buried, that the new man may be raised up in him. *Ib. Invocation of Blessing on the Child*

58 The faith of Christ crucified. *Ib. Reception and Dedication of the Child*

59 Dead unto sin, and living unto righteousness. *Ib. Thanksgiving*

60 Crucify the old man. *Ib.*

61 Ministration of Baptism to Such as are of Riper Years. *Title*

[390]

1 Put on Christ.
   Ministration of Baptism to Such as are of Riper Years. Final Exhortation

2 What is your name?
   N. or M.
   Who gave you this name?
   My Godfathers and Godmothers in my Baptism; wherein I was made a member of Christ, the child of God, and an inheritor of the kingdom of heaven.
   What did your Godfathers and Godmothers then for you?
   They did promise and vow three things in my name. First, that I should renounce the devil and all his works, the pomps and vanity of this wicked world, and all the sinful lusts of the flesh. Secondly, that I should believe all the Articles of the Christian Faith. And thirdly, that I should keep God's holy will and commandments, and walk in the same all the days of my life.   *The Catechism*

3 Yes verily; and by God's help so I will.   *Ib.*

4 Rehearse the Articles of thy Belief.   *Ib.*

5 My duty towards God, and my duty towards my Neighbour.   *Ib.*

6 To love him as myself, and to do to all men, as I would they should do unto me.   *Ib.*

7 Governors, teachers, spiritual pastors and masters.   *Ib.*

8 To keep my hands from picking and stealing, and my tongue from evil-speaking, lying, and slandering.   *Ib.*

9 To learn and labour truly to get mine own living, and to do my duty in that state of life, unto which it shall please God to call me.   *Ib.*

10 My good child, know this.   *Ib.*

11 Amen, So be it.   *Ib.*

12 Two only, as generally necessary to salvation, that is to say, Baptism, and the Supper of the Lord.   *Ib.*

13 An outward and visible sign of an inward and spiritual grace.   *Ib.*

14 In their Mother Tongue.   *Ib. Final Rubric*

15 Confirmation, or laying on of hands.   *Title*

16 Being now come to the years of discretion.   *Confirmation*

17 Ratify and confirm the same.   *Ib.*

18 Our help is in the name of the Lord
   Who hath made heaven and earth.
   Blessed be the name of the Lord;
   Henceforth, world without end.
   Lord, hear our prayers;
   And let our cry come unto thee.   *Ib.*

19 Thy manifold gifts of grace.   *Ib.*

20 Defend, O Lord, this thy child [*or* this thy servant] with thy heavenly grace that *he* may continue thine for ever; and daily increase in thy holy Spirit more and more, until *he* come unto thy everlasting kingdom.   *Ib.*

21 If any of you know cause, or just impediment, why these two persons should not be joined together in holy Matrimony, ye are to declare it. This is the first time of asking.
   Solemnization of Matrimony. The Banns

22 Here in the sight of God, and in the face of this congregation.
   Solemnization of Matrimony. Exhortation

23 Brute beasts that have no understanding.   *Ib.*

24 First, it was ordained for the procreation of children.   *Ib.*

25 A remedy against sin.   *Ib.*

26 Such persons as have not the gift of continency.   *Ib.*

27 Let him now speak, or else hereafter for ever hold his peace.   *Ib.*

28 Wilt thou have this woman to thy wedded wife, to live together after God's ordinance in the holy estate of Matrimony?   *Ib. Betrothal*

29 Forsaking all other, keep thee only unto her, so long as ye both shall live.   *Ib.*

30 To have and to hold from this day forward, for better for worse, for richer for poorer, in sickness and in health, to love and to cherish, till death us do part, according to God's holy ordinance; and thereto I plight thee my troth.   *Ib.*

31 To love, cherish, and to obey.   *Ib.*

32 With this Ring I thee wed, with my body I thee worship, and with all my worldly goods I thee endow.   *Ib. The Wedding*

33 This Ring given and received.   *Ib. The Prayer*

34 Those whom God hath joined together let no man put asunder.   *Ib.*

35 Consented together in holy wedlock.
   Ib. Priest's Declaration

36 Peace be to this house.   *Visitation of the Sick*

37 Unto God's gracious mercy and protection we commit thee.   *Ib.*

38 The inner man.   *Ib.*

39 Against the hour of death.   *Ib.*

40 Laid violent hands upon themselves.
   Burial of the Dead. Introductory Rubric

41 Man that is born of a woman hath but a short time to live, and is full of misery.   *Ib. First Anthem*

42 In the midst of life we are in death.   *Ib.*

43 Suffer us not, at our last hour, for any pains of death, to fall from thee.   *Ib.*

44 We therefore commit *his* body to the ground; earth to earth, ashes to ashes, dust to dust; in sure and certain hope of the Resurrection to eternal life. *Ib.*

45 Sat in the seat of the scornful.   *Psalms i. 1*

46 He shall be like a tree planted by the water-side. *Ib. 3*

47 Why do the heathen so furiously rage together: and why do the people imagine a vain thing? *Ib. ii. 1*

48 Let us break their bonds asunder: and cast away their cords from us.   *Ib. 3*

49 The Lord shall have them in derision.   *Ib. 4*

50 Thou shalt bruise them with a rod of iron: and break them in pieces like a potter's vessel.   *Ib. 9*

51 Kiss the Son, lest he be angry, and so ye perish from the right way: if his wrath be kindled, (yea, but a little,) blessed are all they that put their trust in him. *Ib. 12*

52 Stand in awe, and sin not: commune with your own heart, and in your chamber, and be still. *Ib. iv. 4*

1 There be many that say: Who will shew us any good?
   Psalms iv. 6

2 Lord, lift thou up the light of thy countenance upon us. *Ib.* 7

3 The Lord will abhor both the bloodthirsty and deceitful man. *Ib.* v. 6

4 Make thy way plain before my face. *Ib.* 8

5 Their throat is an open sepulchre: they flatter with their tongue. *Ib.* 10

6 Let them perish through their own imaginations. *Ib.* 11

7 God is a righteous Judge, strong, and patient: and God is provoked every day. *Ib.* vii. 12

8 Out of the mouth of very babes and sucklings hast thou ordained strength, because of thine enemies: that thou mightest still the enemy, and the avenger. *Ib.* viii. 2

9 For I will consider thy heavens, even the works of thy fingers: the moon and the stars, which thou hast ordained. *Ib.* 3

10 What is man, that thou art mindful of him: and the son of man, that thou visitest him? *Ib.* 4

11 Thou madest him lower than the angels: to crown him with glory and worship. *Ib.* 5

12 The fowls of the air, and the fishes of the sea: and whatsoever walketh through the paths of the seas. *Ib.* 8

13 O thou enemy, destructions are come to a perpetual end. *Ib.* ix. 6

14 Their memorial is perished with them. *Ib.*

15 Up, Lord, and let not man have the upper hand. *Ib.* 19

16 That the heathen may know themselves to be but men. *Ib.* 20

17 In the Lord put I my trust: how say ye then to my soul, that she should flee as a bird unto the hill? *Ib.* xi. 1

18 That they may privily shoot at them which are true of heart. *Ib.* 2

19 For the foundations will be cast down: and what hath the righteous done? *Ib.* 3

20 They do but flatter with their lips, and dissemble in their double heart. *Ib.* xii. 2

21 The fool hath said in his heart: There is no God. *Ib.* xiv. 1

22 There is none that doeth good, no not one. *Ib.* 2

23 They are altogether become abominable. *Ib.* 4

24 Lord, who shall dwell in thy tabernacle: or who shall rest upon thy holy hill?
   Even he, that leadeth an uncorrupt life: and doeth the thing which is right, and speaketh the truth from his heart.
   He that hath used no deceit in his tongue, nor done evil to his neighbour: and hath not slandered his neighbour.
   He that setteth not by himself, but is lowly in his own eyes: and maketh much of them that fear the Lord.
   He that sweareth unto his neighbour, and disappointeth him not: though it were to his own hindrance.

He that hath not given his money upon usury: nor taken reward against the innocent.
   Whoso doeth these things shall never fall. *Psalms* xv

25 Thou shalt maintain my lot. *Ib.* xvi. 6

26 The lot is fallen unto me in a fair ground: yea, I have a goodly heritage. *Ib.* 7

27 For why? thou shalt not leave my soul in hell: neither shalt thou suffer thy Holy One to see corruption.
   Thou shalt shew me the path of life; in thy presence is the fulness of joy: and at thy right hand there is pleasure for evermore. *Ib.* 11

28 Keep me as the apple of an eye: hide me under the shadow of thy wings. *Ib.* xvii. 8

29 Thou also shalt light my candle: the Lord my God shall make my darkness to be light. *Ib.* xviii. 28

30 With the help of my God I shall leap over the wall. *Ib.* 29

31 A people whom I have not known: shall serve me. *Ib.* 44

32 The heavens declare the glory of God: and the firmament sheweth his handy-work.
   One day telleth another: and one night certifieth another.
   There is neither speech nor language: but their voices are heard among them.
   Their sound is gone out into all lands: and their words into the ends of the world.
   In them hath he set a tabernacle for the sun: which cometh forth as a bridegroom out of his chamber, and rejoiceth as a giant to run his course.
   It goeth forth from the uttermost part of the heaven, and runneth about unto the end of it again: and there is nothing hid from the heat thereof. *Ib.* xix. 1

33 More to be desired are they than gold, yea, than much fine gold: sweeter also than honey, and the honey-comb. *Ib.* 10

34 Who can tell how oft he offendeth: O cleanse thou me from my secret faults.
   Keep thy servant also from presumptuous sins, lest they get the dominion over me: so shall I be undefiled, and innocent from the great offence.
   Let the words of my mouth, and the meditation of my heart: be alway acceptable in thy sight,
   O Lord: my strength, and my redeemer. *Ib.* 12

35 The Lord hear thee in the day of trouble: the Name of the God of Jacob defend thee;
   Send thee help from the sanctuary: and strengthen thee out of Sion. *Ib.* xx. 1

36 Grant thee thy heart's desire: and fulfil all thy mind. *Ib.* 4

37 Some put their trust in chariots, and some in horses: but we will remember the name of the Lord our God.
   They are brought down, and fallen: but we are risen, and stand upright. *Ib.* 7

38 Thou hast given him his heart's desire: and hast not denied him the request of his lips. *Ib.* xxi. 2

39 He asked life of thee, and thou gavest him a long life: even for ever and ever. *Ib.* 4

40 And imagined such a device as they are not able to perform. *Ib.* 11

1 My God, my God, look upon me; why hast thou forsaken me: and art so far from my health, and from the voice of my complaint?
O my God, I cry in the day-time, but thou hearest not: and in the night-season also I take no rest.
And thou continuest holy: O thou worship of Israel. *Psalms* xxii. 1

2 But as for me, I am a worm, and no man. *Ib.* 6

3 All they that see me laugh me to scorn: they shoot out their lips, and shake their heads, saying,
He trusted in God, that he would deliver him: let him deliver him, if he will have him. *Ib.* 7

4 Many oxen are come about me: fat bulls of Basan close me in on every side. *Ib.* 12

5 For many dogs are come about me. *Ib.* 16

6 They pierced my hands and my feet; I may tell all my bones: they stand staring and looking upon me.
They part my garments among them: and cast lots upon my vesture. *Ib.* 17

7 Deliver my soul from the sword: my darling from the power of the dog.
Save me from the lion's mouth: thou hast heard me also from the horns of the unicorns. *Ib.* 20

8 For he hath not despised, nor abhorred, the low estate of the poor. *Ib.* 24

9 All they that go down into the dust shall kneel before him: and no man hath quickened his own soul. *Ib.* 30

10 The Lord is my shepherd: therefore can I lack nothing.
He shall feed me in a green pasture: and lead me forth beside the waters of comfort.
He shall convert my soul: and bring me forth in the paths of righteousness, for his Name's sake.
Yea, though I walk through the valley of the shadow of death, I will fear no evil: for thou art with me; thy rod and thy staff comfort me.
Thou shalt prepare a table before me against them that trouble me: thou hast anointed my head with oil, and my cup shall be full.
But thy loving-kindness and mercy shall follow me all the days of my life: and I will dwell in the house of the Lord for ever. *Ib.* xxiii

11 The earth is the Lord's, and all that therein is: the compass of the world, and they that dwell therein. *Ib.* xxiv. 1

12 Lift up your heads, O ye gates, and be ye lift up, ye everlasting doors: and the King of glory shall come in. *Ib.* 7

13 Who is the King of glory: even the Lord of hosts, he is the King of glory. *Ib.* 10

14 O remember not the sins and offences of my youth. *Ib.* xxv. 6

15 The sorrows of my heart are enlarged. *Ib.* 16

16 Deliver Israel, O God: out of all his troubles. *Ib.* 21

17 Examine me, O Lord, and prove me: try out my reins and my heart. *Ib.* xxvi. 2

18 I will wash my hands in innocency, O Lord: and so will I go to thine altar. *Ib.* 6

19 Lord, I have loved the habitation of thy house: and the place where thine honour dwelleth.
O shut not up my soul with the sinners: nor my life with the blood-thirsty. *Ib.* 8

20 The Lord is my light, and my salvation; whom then shall I fear: the Lord is the strength of my life; of whom then shall I be afraid? *Psalms* xxvii. 1

21 When my father and my mother forsake me: the Lord taketh me up. *Ib.* 12

22 I should utterly have fainted: but that I believe verily to see the goodness of the Lord in the land of the living. *Ib.* 15

23 The voice of the Lord maketh the hinds to bring forth young, and discovereth the thick bushes. *Ib.* xxix. 8

24 The Lord sitteth above the water-flood: and the Lord remaineth a King for ever. *Ib.* 9

25 Give thanks unto him for a remembrance of his holiness.
For his wrath endureth but the twinkling of an eye, and in his pleasure is life: heaviness may endure for a night, but joy cometh in the morning. *Ib.* xxx. 4

26 What profit is there in my blood: when I go down to the pit?
Shall the dust give thanks unto thee; or shall it declare thy truth? *Ib.* 9

27 Into thy hands I commend my spirit. *Ib.* xxxi. 6

28 But hast set my feet in a large room. *Ib.* 9

29 I am clean forgotten, as a dead man out of mind. *Ib.* 14

30 Thanks be to the Lord: for he hath shewed me marvellous great kindness in a strong city. *Ib.* 23

31 For while I held my tongue: my bones consumed away through my daily complaining. *Ib.* xxxii. 3

32 For this shall every one that is godly make his prayer unto thee, in a time when thou mayest be found: but in the great water-floods they shall not come nigh him. *Ib.* 7

33 Thou shalt compass me about with songs of deliverance. *Ib.* 8

34 Be ye not like to horse and mule, which have no understanding: whose mouths must be held with bit and bridle, lest they fall upon thee. *Ib.* 10

35 Rejoice in the Lord, O ye righteous: for it becometh well the just to be thankful.
Praise the Lord with harp: sing praises unto him with the lute, and instrument of ten strings.
Sing unto the Lord a new song: sing praises lustily unto him with a good courage. *Ib.* xxxiii. 1

36 The Lord bringeth the counsel of the heathen to nought: and maketh the devices of the people to be of none effect, and casteth out the counsels of princes. *Ib.* 10

37 There is no king that can be saved by the multitude of an host: neither is any mighty man delivered by much strength.
A horse is counted but a vain thing to save a man: neither shall he deliver any man by his great strength. *Ib.* 15

38 O taste, and see, how gracious the Lord is: blessed is the man that trusteth in him.
O fear the Lord, ye that are his saints: for they that fear him lack nothing.
The lions do lack, and suffer hunger: but they who seek the Lord shall want no manner of thing that is good. *Ib.* xxxiv. 8

1 What man is he that lusteth to live: and would fain see good days? *Psalms* xxxiv. 12

2 Eschew evil, and do good: seek peace, and ensue it. *Ib.* 14

3 Fret not thyself because of the ungodly. *Ib.* xxxvii. 1

4 He shall make thy righteousness as clear as the light: and thy just dealing as the noon-day. *Ib.* 6

5 I have been young, and now am old: and yet saw I never the righteous forsaken, nor his seed begging their bread. *Ib.* 25

6 I myself have seen the ungodly in great power: and flourishing like a green bay-tree.
I went by, and lo, he was gone: I sought him, but his place could no where be found.
Keep innocency, and take heed unto the thing that is right: for that shall bring a man peace at the last. *Ib.* 36

7 Lord, thou knowest all my desire: and my groaning is not hid from thee. *Ib.* xxxviii. 9

8 I held my tongue, and spake nothing: I kept silence, yea, even from good words; but it was pain and grief to me.
My heart was hot within me, and while I was thus musing the fire kindled: and at the last I spake with my tongue;
Lord, let me know mine end, and the number of my days: that I may be certified how long I have to live. *Ib.* xxxix. 3

9 Mine age is even as nothing in respect of thee; and verily every man living is altogether vanity.
For man walketh in a vain shadow, and disquieteth himself in vain: he heapeth up riches, and cannot tell who shall gather them. *Ib.* 6

10 Thou makest his beauty to consume away, like as it were a moth fretting a garment: every man therefore is but vanity. *Ib.* 12

11 For I am a stranger with thee: and a sojourner, as all my fathers were.
O spare me a little, that I may recover my strength: before I go hence, and be no more seen. *Ib.* 14

12 I waited patiently for the Lord: and he inclined unto me, and heard my calling.
He brought me also out of the horrible pit, out of the mire and clay: and set my feet upon the rock, and ordered my goings. *Ib.* xl. 1

13 Burnt-offerings, and sacrifice for sin, hast thou not required: then said I, Lo, I come.
In the volume of the book it is written of me, that I should fulfil thy will, O my God. *Ib.* 9

14 Thou art my helper and redeemer: make no long tarrying, O my God. *Ib.* 21

15 Yea, mine own familiar friend . . . hath lifted up his heel against me. *Ib.* xli. 9 [Bible Version]

16 Like as the hart desireth the water-brooks: so longeth my soul after thee, O God. *Ib.* xlii. 1

17 Why art thou so full of heaviness, O my soul: and why art thou so disquieted within me? *Ib.* 6

18 The little hill of Hermon. *Ib.* 8

19 One deep calleth another, because of the noise of the water-pipes: all thy waves and storms are gone over me. *Ib.* 9

20 While mine enemies that trouble me cast me in the teeth. *Psalms* xlii. 12

21 My heart is inditing of a good matter: I speak of the things which I have made unto the King.
My tongue is the pen of a ready writer. *Ib.* xlv. 1

22 Gird thee with thy sword upon thy thigh, O thou most Mighty: according to thy worship and renown.
Good luck have thou with thine honour: ride on, because of the word of truth, of meekness, and righteousness; and thy right hand shall teach thee terrible things. *Ib.* 4

23 Kings' daughters were among thy honourable women: upon thy right hand did stand the queen in a vesture of gold, wrought about with divers colours.
Hearken, O daughter, and consider, incline thine ear: forget also thine own people, and thy father's house.
So shall the King have pleasure in thy beauty. *Ib.* 10

24 And the daughter of Tyre shall be there with a gift. *Ib.* 13

25 The King's daughter is all glorious within: her clothing is of wrought gold.
She shall be brought unto the King in raiment of needle-work: the virgins that be her fellows shall bear her company, and shall be brought unto thee. *Ib.* 14

26 Instead of thy fathers thou shalt have children: whom thou mayest make princes in all lands. *Ib.* 17

27 God is our hope and strength: a very present help in trouble.
Therefore will we not fear, though the earth be moved: and though the hills be carried into the midst of the sea. *Ib.* xlvi. 1

28 God is in the midst of her, therefore shall she not be removed: God shall help her, and that right early.
The heathen make much ado, and the kingdoms are moved: but God hath shewed his voice, and the earth shall melt away. *Ib.* 5

29 He maketh wars to cease in all the world: he breaketh the bow, and knappeth the spear in sunder, and burneth the chariots in the fire.
Be still then, and know that I am God. *Ib.* 9

30 He shall subdue the people under us: and the nations under our feet. *Ib.* xlvii. 3

31 God is gone up with a merry noise: and the Lord with the sound of the trump. *Ib.* 5

32 For God is the King of all the earth: sing ye praises with understanding. *Ib.* 7

33 For lo, the kings of the earth are gathered, and gone by together.
They marvelled to see such things: they were astonished; and suddenly cast down. *Ib.* xlviii. 3

34 Thou shalt break the ships of the sea, through the east-wind. *Ib.* 6

35 Walk about Sion, and go round about her: and tell the towers thereof.
Mark well her bulwarks, set up her houses: that ye may tell them that come after.
For this God is our God for ever and ever: he shall be our guide unto death. *Ib.* 11

1 And yet they think that their houses shall continue for ever: and that their dwelling-places shall endure from one generation to another; and call the lands after their own names. *Psalms* xlix. 11

2 He shall follow the generation of his fathers: and shall never see light.

Man being in honour hath no understanding: but is compared unto the beasts that perish. *Ib.* 19

3 For all the beasts of the forest are mine: and so are the cattle upon a thousand hills. *Ib.* l. 10

4 Thinkest thou that I will eat bulls' flesh: and drink the blood of goats? *Ib.* 13

5 When thou sawest a thief, thou consentedst unto him: and hast been partaker with the adulterers. *Ib.* 18

6 O consider this, ye that forget God. *Ib.* 22

7 For I acknowledge my faults: and my sin is ever before me.

Against thee only have I sinned, and done this evil in thy sight. *Ib.* li. 3

8 Behold, I was shapen in wickedness: and in sin hath my mother conceived me.

But lo, thou requirest truth in the inward parts: and shalt make me to understand wisdom secretly.

Thou shalt purge me with hyssop, and I shall be clean: thou shalt wash me, and I shall be whiter than snow.

Thou shalt make me hear of joy and gladness: that the bones which thou hast broken may rejoice. *Ib.* 5

9 Make me a clean heart, O God: and renew a right spirit within me.

Cast me not away from thy presence: and take not thy holy Spirit from me.

O give me the comfort of thy help again: and stablish me with thy free Spirit.

Then shall I teach thy ways unto the wicked: and sinners shall be converted unto thee.

Deliver me from blood-guiltiness, O God. *Ib.* 10

10 For thou desirest no sacrifice, else would I give it thee: but thou delightest not in burnt-offerings.

The sacrifice of God is a troubled spirit: a broken and contrite heart, O God, shalt thou not despise.

O be favourable and gracious unto Sion: build thou the walls of Jerusalem. *Ib.* 16

11 Then shall they offer young bullocks upon thine altar. *Ib.* 19

12 My guide, and mine own familar friend.

We took sweet counsel together: and walked in the house of God as friends. *Ib.* lv. 14

13 His words were smoother than oil and yet be they very swords. *Ib.* 22

14 All that they imagine is to do me evil.

They hold all together, and keep themselves close. *Ib.* lvi. 5

15 Thou tellest my flittings; put my tears into thy bottle: are not these things noted in thy book? *Ib.* 8

16 For thou hast delivered my soul from death, and my feet from falling: that I may walk before God in the light of the living. *Ib.* 13

17 Under the shadow of thy wings shall be my refuge, until this tyranny be over-past. *Ib.* lvii. 1

18 God shall send forth his mercy and truth: my soul is among lions.

And I lie even among the children of men, that are set on fire: whose teeth are spears and arrows, and their tongue a sharp sword.

Set up thyself, O God, above the heavens: and thy glory above all the earth.

They have laid a net for my feet, and pressed down my soul: they have digged a pit before me, and are fallen into the midst of it themselves. *Psalms* lvii. 4

19 Awake up, my glory; awake, lute and harp: I myself will awake right early. *Ib.* 9

20 Even like the deaf adder that stoppeth her ears;

Which refuseth to hear the voice of the charmer: charm he never so wisely. *Ib.* lviii. 4

21 Let them consume away like a snail, and be like the untimely fruit of a woman: and let them not see the sun.

Or ever your pots be made hot with thorns: so let indignation vex him, even as a thing that is raw. *Ib.* 7

22 They grin like a dog, and run about through the city. *Ib.* lix. 6

23 God hath spoken in his holiness, I will rejoice, and divide Sichem: and mete out the valley of Succoth.

Gilead is mine, and Manasses is mine: Ephraim also is the strength of my head; Judah is my law-giver.

Moab is my wash-pot; over Edom will I cast out my shoe: Philistia, be thou glad of me.

Who will lead me into the strong city: who will bring me into Edom? *Ib.* lx. 6

24 As for the children of men, they are but vanity: the children of men are deceitful upon the weights, they are altogether lighter than vanity itself.

O trust not in wrong and robbery, give not yourselves unto vanity; if riches increase, set not your heart upon them.

God spake once, and twice I have also heard the same: that power belongeth unto God;

And that thou, Lord, art merciful: for thou rewardest every man according to his work. *Ib.* lxii. 9

25 My soul thirsteth for thee, my flesh also longeth after thee: in a barren and dry land where no water is. *Ib.* lxiii. 2

26 Have I not remembered thee in my bed: and thought upon thee when I was waking? *Ib.* 7

27 Thou that hearest the prayer: unto thee shall all flesh come. *Ib.* lxv. 2

28 Thou that art the hope of all the ends of the earth, and of them that remain in the broad sea.

Who in his strength setteth fast the mountains: and is girded about with power.

Who stilleth the raging of the sea: and the noise of his waves, and the madness of the people. *Ib.* 5

29 Thou that makest the outgoings of the morning and evening to praise thee. *Ib.* 8

30 Thou waterest her furrows, thou sendest rain into the little valleys thereof: thou makest it soft with the drops of rain, and blessest the increase of it.

Thou crownest the year with thy goodness: and thy clouds drop fatness.

They shall drop upon the dwellings of the wilderness: and the little hills shall rejoice on every side.

The folds shall be full of sheep: the valleys also shall stand so thick with corn, that they shall laugh and sing. *Psalms* lxv. 11

1 Who holdeth our soul in life: and suffereth not our feet to slip.
For thou, O God, hast proved us: thou also hast tried us, like as silver is tried. *Ib.* lxvi. 8

2 God be merciful unto us, and bless us: and shew us the light of his countenance, and be merciful unto us.
That thy way may be known upon earth: thy saving health among all nations. *Ib.* lxvii. 1

3 Then shall the earth bring forth her increase: and God, even our own God, shall give us his blessing. *Ib.* 6

4 Let God arise, and let his enemies be scattered: let them also that hate him flee before him.
Like as the smoke vanisheth, so shalt thou drive them away: and like as wax melteth at the fire, so let the ungodly perish at the presence of God. *Ib.* lxviii. 1

5 O sing unto God, and sing praises unto his Name: magnify him that rideth upon the heavens, as it were upon an horse; praise him in his Name JAH, and rejoice before him.
He is a Father of the fatherless, and defendeth the cause of the widows: even God in his holy habitation.
He is the God that maketh men to be of one mind in an house, and bringeth the prisoners out of captivity: but letteth the runagates continue in scarceness.
O God, when thou wentest forth before the people: when thou wentest through the wilderness,
The earth shook, and the heavens dropped at the presence of God. *Ib.* 4

6 Thou, O God, sentest a gracious rain upon thine inheritance: and refreshedst it when it was weary. *Ib.* 9

7 The Lord gave the word: great was the company of the preachers.
Kings with their armies did flee, and were discomfited: and they of the household divided the spoil.
Though ye have lien among the pots, yet shall ye be as the wings of a dove that is covered with silver wings, and her feathers like gold.
When the Almighty scattered kings for their sake: then were they as white as snow in Salmon.
As the hill of Basan, so is God's hill: even an high hill, as the hill of Basan.
Why hop ye so, ye high hills? this is God's hill, in the which it pleaseth him to dwell. *Ib.* 11

8 The chariots of God are twenty thousand, even thousands of angels. *Ib.* 17

9 Thou art gone up on high, thou hast led captivity captive, and received gifts for men. *Ib.* 18

10 God shall wound the head of his enemies: and the hairy scalp of such a one as goeth on still in his wickedness. *Ib.* 21

11 That thy foot may be dipped in the blood of thine enemies: and that the tongue of thy dogs may be red through the same. *Ib.* 23

12 The singers go before, the minstrels follow after: in the midst are the damsels playing with the timbrels. *Psalms* lxviii. 25

13 There is little Benjamin their ruler, and the princes of Judah their counsel. *Ib.* 27

14 When he hath scattered the people that delight in war. *Ib.* 30

15 Lo, he doth send out his voice, yea, and that a mighty voice. *Ib.* 33

16 I paid them the things that I never took: God, thou knowest my simpleness. *Ib.* lxix. 5

17 The zeal of thine house hath even eaten me. *Ib.* 9

18 They that sit in the gate speak against me: and the drunkards make songs upon me. *Ib.* 12

19 I looked for some to have pity on me, but there was no man, neither found I any to comfort me.
They gave me gall to eat: and when I was thirsty they gave me vinegar to drink. *Ib.* 21

20 Let them for their reward be soon brought to shame, that cry over me, There, there. *Ib.* lxx. 3

21 I am become as it were a monster unto many. *Ib.* lxxi. 6

22 Give the King thy judgements, O God: and thy righteousness unto the King's son. *Ib.* lxxii. 1

23 The mountains also shall bring peace: and the little hills righteousness unto the people. *Ib.* 3

24 He shall come down like the rain into a fleece of wool: even as the drops that water the earth. *Ib.* 6

25 His enemies shall lick the dust.
The kings of Tharsis and of the isles shall give presents: the kings of Arabia and Saba shall bring gifts.
All kings shall fall down before him: all nations shall do him service. *Ib.* 9

26 Therefore fall the people unto them: and thereout suck they no small advantage.
Tush, say they, how should God perceive it: is there knowledge in the Most High? *Ib.* lxxiii. 10

27 Then thought I to understand this: but it was too hard for me.
Until I went into the sanctuary of God: then understood I the end of these men. *Ib.* 15

28 O deliver not the soul of thy turtle-dove unto the multitude of the enemies. *Ib.* lxxiv. 20

29 The earth is weak, and all the inhabiters thereof: I bear up the pillars of it. *Ib.* lxxv. 4

30 For promotion cometh neither from the east, nor from the west: nor yet from the south. *Ib.* 7

31 For in the hand of the Lord there is a cup, and the wine is red: it is full mixed, and he poureth out of the same. *Ib.* 9

32 I have considered the days of old: and the years that are past. *Ib.* lxxvii. 5

33 A faithless and stubborn generation. *Ib.* lxxviii. 9

34 Who being harnessed, and carrying bows, turned themselves back in the day of battle. *Ib.* 10

35 So man did eat angels' food. *Ib.* 26

36 Starting aside like a broken bow. *Ib.* 58

1 So the Lord awaked as one out of sleep: and like a giant refreshed with wine.
He smote his enemies in the hinder parts: and put them to a perpetual shame. *Psalms* lxxviii. 66

2 Thou feedest them with the bread of tears. *Ib.* lxxx. 5

3 I proved thee also at the waters of strife. *Ib.* lxxxi. 8

4 They will not be learned nor understand, but walk on still in darkness: all the foundations of the earth are out of course. *Ib.* lxxxii. 5

5 O how amiable are thy dwellings: thou Lord of hosts!
My soul hath a desire and longing to enter into the courts of the Lord: my heart and my flesh rejoice in the living God.
Yea, the sparrow hath found her an house, and the swallow a nest where she may lay her young: even thy altars, O Lord of hosts, my King and my God. *Ib.* lxxxiv. 1

6 Who going through the vale of misery use it for a well: and the pools are filled with water.
They will go from strength to strength. *Ib.* 6

7 For one day in thy courts: is better than a thousand.
I had rather be a door-keeper in the house of my God: than to dwell in the tents of ungodliness. *Ib.* 10

8 Lord, thou art become gracious unto thy land: thou hast turned away the captivity of Jacob. *Ib.* lxxxv. 1

9 Mercy and truth are met together: righteousness and peace have kissed each other.
Truth shall flourish out of the earth: and righteousness hath looked down from heaven. *Ib.* 10

10 Righteousness shall go before him: and he shall direct his going in the way. *Ib.* 13

11 The congregations of naughty men have sought after my soul. *Ib.* lxxxvi. 14

12 Shew some token upon me for good, that they who hate me may see it, and be ashamed. *Ib.* 17

13 Her foundations are upon the holy hills: the Lord loveth the gates of Sion more than all the dwellings of Jacob.
Very excellent things are spoken of thee: thou city of God. *Ib.* lxxxvii. 1

14 The singers also and trumpeters shall he rehearse: All my fresh springs shall be in thee. *Ib.* 7

15 Lord, thou hast been our refuge from one generation to another.
Before the mountains were brought forth, or ever the earth and the world were made: thou art God from everlasting, and world without end.
Thou turnest man to destruction: again thou sayest, Come again, ye children of men.
For a thousand years in thy sight are but as yesterday: seeing that is past as a watch in the night.
As soon as thou scatterest them they are even as a sleep: and fade away suddenly like the grass.
In the morning it is green, and groweth up: but in the evening it is cut down, dried up, and withered. *Ib.* xc. 1

16 For when thou art angry all our days are gone: we bring our years to an end, as it were a tale that is told.
The days of our age are threescore years and ten; and though men be so strong that they come to fourscore years: yet is their strength then but labour and sorrow; so soon passeth it away, and we are gone. *Ib.* 9

17 Prosper thou the work of our hands upon us, O prosper thou our handy-work. *Psalms* xc. 17

18 For he shall deliver thee from the snare of the hunter: and from the noisome pestilence.
He shall defend thee under his wings, and thou shalt be safe under his feathers: his faithfulness and truth shall be thy shield and buckler.
Thou shalt not be afraid for any terror by night: nor for the arrow that flieth by day.
For the pestilence that walketh in darkness: nor for the sickness that destroyeth in the noon-day.
A thousand shall fall beside thee, and ten thousand at thy right hand: but it shall not come nigh thee. *Ib.* xci. 3

19 There shall no evil happen unto thee: neither shall any plague come nigh thy dwelling.
For he shall give his angels charge over thee: to keep thee in all thy ways.
They shall bear thee in their hands: that thou hurt not thy foot against a stone. *Ib.* 10

20 An unwise man doth not well consider this: and a fool doth not understand it. *Ib.* xcii. 6

21 They also shall bring forth more fruit in their age: and shall be fat and well-liking. *Ib.* 13

22 The Lord is King, and hath put on glorious apparel: the Lord hath put on his apparel, and girded himself with strength.
He hath made the round world so sure: that it cannot be moved. *Ib.* xciii. 1

23 The floods are risen, O Lord, the floods have lift up their voice: the floods lift up their waves.
The waves of the sea are mighty, and rage horribly: but yet the Lord, who dwelleth on high, is mightier. *Ib.* 4

24 He that planted the ear, shall he not hear: or he that made the eye, shall he not see? *Ib.* xciv. 9

25 Shew ourselves glad in him with psalms. *Ib.* xcv. 2

26 In his hand are all the corners of the earth: and the strength of the hills is his also.
The sea is his, and he made it: and his hands prepared the dry land. *Ib.* 4

27 O come, let us worship and fall down: and kneel before the Lord our Maker. *Ib.* 6

28 For he is the Lord our God: and we are the people of his pasture, and the sheep of his hand. *Ib.* 7

29 To-day if ye will hear his voice, harden not your hearts: as in the provocation, and as in the day of temptation in the wilderness. *Ib.* 8

30 When your fathers tempted me: proved me, and saw my works. *Ib.* 9

31 The Lord is King, the earth may be glad thereof: yea, the multitude of the isles may be glad thereof. *Ib.* xcvii. 1

32 With trumpets also, and shawms: O shew yourselves joyful before the Lord the King. *Ib.* xcviii. 7

33 The Lord is King, be the people never so impatient: he sitteth between the cherubims, be the earth never so unquiet. *Ib.* xcix. 1

34 Whoso hath also a proud look and high stomach: I will not suffer him. *Ib.* ci. 7

1 I am become like a pelican in the wilderness: and like an owl that is in the desert.

I have watched, and am even as it were a sparrow: that sitteth alone upon the house-top.

Psalms cii. 6

2 They shall perish, but thou shalt endure: they all shall wax old as doth a garment;

And as a vesture shalt thou change them, and they shall be changed: but thou art the same, and thy years shall not fail. *Ib.* 26

3 Praise the Lord, O my soul: and forget not all his benefits. *Ib.* ciii. 2

4 Who satisfieth thy mouth with good things: making thee young and lusty as an eagle. *Ib.* 5

5 He will not alway be chiding: neither keepeth he his anger for ever. *Ib.* 9

6 For look how high the heaven is in comparison of the earth: so great is his mercy also toward them that fear him.

Look how wide also the east is from the west: so far hath he set our sins from us.

Yea, like as a father pitieth his own children: even so is the Lord merciful unto them that fear him.

Ib. 11

7 The days of man are but as grass: for he flourisheth as a flower of the field.

For as soon as the wind goeth over it, it is gone: and the place thereof shall know it no more. *Ib.* 15

8 Who layeth the beams of his chambers in the waters: and maketh the clouds his chariot, and walketh upon the wings of the wind.

He maketh his angels spirits: and his ministers a flaming fire.

He laid the foundations of the earth: that it never should move at any time.

Thou coveredst it with the deep like as with a garment: the waters stand in the hills.

At thy rebuke they flee: at the voice of thy thunder they are afraid.

They go up as high as the hills, and down to the valleys beneath: even unto the place which thou hast appointed for them.

Thou hast set them their bounds which they shall not pass: neither turn again to cover the earth.

He sendeth the springs into the rivers: which run among the hills.

All beasts of the field drink thereof: and the wild asses quench their thirst.

Beside them shall the fowls of the air have their habitation: and sing among the branches.

Ib. civ. 3

9 Wine that maketh glad the heart of man: and oil to make him a cheerful countenance, and bread to strengthen man's heart.

The trees of the Lord also are full of sap: even the cedars of Libanus which he hath planted. *Ib.* 15

10 Wherein the birds make their nests: and the fir-trees are a dwelling for the stork.

The high hills are a refuge for the wild goats: and so are the stony rocks for the conies.

He appointed the moon for certain seasons: and the sun knoweth his going down.

Thou makest darkness that it may be night: wherein all the beasts of the forest do move.

The lions roaring after their prey: do seek their meat from God.

The sun ariseth, and they get them away together: and lay them down in their dens.

Man goeth forth to his work, and to his labour: until the evening. *Psalms* civ. 17

11 So is the great and wide sea also: wherein are things creeping innumerable, both small and great beasts.

There go the ships, and there is that Leviathan: whom thou hast made to take his pastime therein.

These wait all upon thee: that thou mayest give them meat in due season. *Ib.* 25

12 Whose feet they hurt in the stocks: the iron entered into his soul. *Ib.* cv. 18

13 Wonders in the land of Ham. *Ib.* 27

14 Went a whoring with their own inventions.

Ib. cvi. 38

15 Hungry and thirsty: their soul fainted in them.

So they cried unto the Lord in their trouble: and he delivered them from their distress.

He led them forth by the right way: that they might go to the city where they dwelt.

O that men would therefore praise the Lord for his goodness: and declare the wonders that he doeth for the children of men!

For he satisfieth the empty soul: and filleth the hungry soul with goodness.

Such as sit in darkness, and in the shadow of death: being fast bound in misery and iron;

Because they rebelled against the words of the Lord: and lightly regarded the counsel of the most Highest. *Ib.* cvii. 5

16 Their soul abhorred all manner of meat: and they were even hard at death's door. *Ib.* 18

17 They that go down to the sea in ships: and occupy their business in great waters;

These men see the works of the Lord: and his wonders in the deep. *Ib.* 23

18 They reel to and fro, and stagger like a drunken man: and are at their wit's end.

So when they cry unto the Lord in their trouble: he delivereth them out of their distress. *Ib.* 27

19 Then are they glad, because they are at rest: and so he bringeth them unto the haven where they would be. *Ib.* 30

20 Again, he maketh the wilderness a standing water: and water-springs of a dry ground. *Ib.* 35

21 And again, when they are minished, and brought low: through oppression, through any plague, or trouble.

Ib. 39

22 Whoso is wise will ponder these things. *Ib.* 43

23 The Lord said unto my Lord: Sit thou on my right hand, until I make thine enemies thy footstool.

Ib. cx. 1

24 The Lord sware, and will not repent: Thou art a priest for ever after the order of Melchisedech.

Ib. 4

25 The fear of the Lord is the beginning of wisdom: a good understanding have all they that do thereafter; the praise of it endureth for ever. *Ib.* cxi. 10

26 A good man is merciful, and lendeth. *Ib.* cxii. 5

27 He hath dispersed abroad, and given to the poor.

Ib. 9

1 He maketh the barren woman to keep house: and to be a joyful mother of children. *Psalms* cxiii. 8

2 The sea saw that, and fled: Jordan was driven back. *Ib.* cxiv. 3

3 The mountains skipped like rams: and the little hills like young sheep. *Ib.* 4

4 They have mouths, and speak not: eyes have they, and see not.
They have ears, and hear not: noses have they, and smell not.
They have hands, and handle not; feet have they, and walk not: neither speak they through their throat. *Ib.* cxv. 5

5 The snares of death compassed me round about: and the pains of hell gat hold upon me. *Ib.* cxvi. 3

6 And why? thou hast delivered my soul from death: mine eyes from tears, and my feet from falling. *Ib.* 8

7 I said in my haste, All men are liars. *Ib.* 10

8 The voice of joy and health is in the dwellings of the righteous: the right hand of the Lord bringeth mighty things to pass. *Ib.* cxviii. 15

9 The right hand of the Lord hath the pre-eminence. *Ib.* 16

10 I shall not die, but live: and declare the works of the Lord. *Ib.* 17

11 The same stone which the builders refused: is become the head-stone in the corner. *Ib.* 22

12 Blessed be he that cometh in the Name of the Lord: we have wished you good luck, ye that are of the house of the Lord. *Ib.* 26

13 Wherewithal shall a young man cleanse his way: even by ruling himself after thy word. *Ib.* cxix. 9

14 Make me to go in the path of thy commandments: for therein is my desire. *Ib.* 35

15 O turn away mine eyes, lest they behold vanity: and quicken thou me in thy law. *Ib.* 37

16 In the house of my pilgrimage. *Ib.* 54

17 The law of thy mouth is dearer unto me: than thousands of gold and silver. *Ib.* 72

18 For I am become like a bottle in the smoke. *Ib.* 83

19 I see that all things come to an end: but thy commandment is exceeding broad. *Ib.* 96

20 I have more understanding than my teachers: for thy testimonies are my study.
I am wiser than the aged: because I keep thy commandments. *Ib.* 99

21 Thy word is a lantern unto my feet: and a light unto my paths.
I have sworn, and am stedfastly purposed, to keep thy righteous judgements. *Ib.* 105

22 O stablish me according to thy word. *Ib.* 116

23 Princes have persecuted me without a cause. *Ib.* 161

24 What reward shall be given or done unto thee, thou false tongue: even mighty and sharp arrows, with hot burning coals.
Woe is me, that I am constrained to dwell with Mesech: and to have my habitation among the tents of Kedar. *Ib.* cxx. 3

25 I labour for peace, but when I speak unto them thereof: they make them ready to battle. *Psalms* cxx. 6

26 I will lift up mine eyes unto the hills: from whence cometh my help. *Ib.* cxxi. 1

27 He will not suffer thy foot to be moved: and he that keepeth thee will not sleep. *Ib.* 3

28 The Lord himself is thy keeper: the Lord is thy defence upon thy right hand;
So that the sun shall not burn thee by day: neither the moon by night. *Ib.* 5

29 The Lord shall preserve thy going out, and thy coming in: from this time forth for evermore. *Ib.* 8

30 I was glad when they said unto me: We will go into the house of the Lord. *Ib.* cxxii. 1

31 O pray for the peace of Jerusalem: they shall prosper that love thee.
Peace be within thy walls: and plenteousness within thy palaces.
For my brethren and companions' sakes: I will wish thee prosperity.
Yea, because of the house of the Lord our God: I will seek to do thee good. *Ib.* 6

32 Our soul is escaped even as a bird out of the snare of the fowler: the snare is broken, and we are delivered. *Ib.* cxxiv. 6

33 The hills stand about Jerusalem: even so standeth the Lord round about his people, from this time forth for evermore.
For the rod of the ungodly cometh not into the lot of the righteous: lest the righteous put their hand unto wickedness. *Ib.* cxxv. 2

34 Turn our captivity, O Lord: as the rivers in the south.
They that sow in tears: shall reap in joy.
He that now goeth on his way weeping, and beareth forth good seed: shall doubtless come again with joy, and bring his sheaves with him. *Ib.* cxxvi. 5

35 Except the Lord build the house: their labour is but lost that build it.
Except the Lord keep the city: the watchman waketh but in vain.
It is but lost labour that ye haste to rise up early, and so late take rest, and eat the bread of carefulness: for so he giveth his beloved sleep.
Lo, children and the fruit of the womb are an heritage and gift that cometh of the Lord.
Like as the arrows in the hand of the giant: even so are the young children.
Happy is the man that hath his quiver full of them: they shall not be ashamed when they speak with their enemies in the gate. *Ib.* cxxvii. 1

36 Thy wife shall be as the fruitful vine upon the walls of thine house.
Thy children like the olive-branches round about thy table. *Ib.* cxxviii. 3

37 The plowers plowed upon my back: and made long furrows. *Ib.* cxxix. 3

38 Out of the deep have I called unto thee, O Lord: Lord, hear my voice. *Ib.* cxxx. 1

39 If thou, Lord, wilt be extreme to mark what is done amiss: O Lord, who may abide it? *Ib.* 3

40 My soul fleeth unto the Lord: before the morning watch, I say, before the morning watch. *Ib.* 6

1 Lord, I am not high-minded: I have no proud looks.
I do not exercise myself in great matters: which are too high for me.
But I refrain my soul, and keep it low, like as a child that is weaned from his mother: yea, my soul is even as a weaned child. *Psalms cxxxi. 1*

2 Lord, remember David: and all his trouble.
Ib. cxxxii. 1

3 Behold, how good and joyful a thing it is, brethren, to dwell together in unity!
It is like the precious ointment upon the head that ran down unto the beard: even unto Aaron's beard, and went down to the skirts of his clothing.
Ib. cxxxiii. 1

4 His mercy endureth for ever. *Ib. cxxxvi. 1*

5 By the waters of Babylon we sat down and wept: when we remembered thee, O Sion.
As for our harps, we hanged them up: upon the trees that are therein.
For they that led us away captive required of us then a song, and melody, in our heaviness: Sing us one of the songs of Sion.
How shall we sing the Lord's song in a strange land?
If I forget thee, O Jerusalem: let my right hand forget her cunning.
If I do not remember thee, let my tongue cleave to the roof of my mouth: yea, if I prefer not Jerusalem in my mirth. *Ib. cxxxvii. 1*

6 How they said, Down with it, down with it, even to the ground.
O daughter of Babylon, wasted with misery: yea, happy shall he be that rewardeth thee, as thou hast served us.
Blessed shall he be that taketh thy children: and throweth them against the stones. *Ib. 7*

7 O Lord, thou hast searched me out, and known me: thou knowest my down-sitting, and mine up-rising; thou understandest my thoughts long before. *Ib. cxxxix. 1*

8 Such knowledge is too wonderful and excellent for me: I cannot attain unto it. *Ib. 5*

9 If I take the wings of the morning and remain in the uttermost parts of the sea;
Even there also shall thy hand lead me: and thy right hand shall hold me.
If I say, Peradventure the darkness shall cover me: then shall my night be turned to day.
Yea, the darkness is no darkness with thee, but the night is as clear as the day: the darkness and light to thee are both alike. *Ib. 8*

10 I will give thanks unto thee, for I am fearfully and wonderfully made. *Ib. 13*

11 And in thy book were all my members written.
Ib. 15

12 Thou hast covered my head in the day of battle.
Ib. cxl. 7

13 Let the lifting up of my hands be an evening sacrifice.
Set a watch, O Lord, before my mouth: and keep the door of my lips. *Ib. cxli. 2*

14 Let the righteous rather smite me friendly: and reprove me.
But let not their precious balms break my head.
Ib. 5

15 Let the ungodly fall into their own nets together: and let me ever escape them. *Psalms cxli. 11*

16 That our sons may grow up as the young plants: and that our daughters may be as the polished corners of the temple. *Ib. cxliv. 12*

17 That our oxen may be strong to labour, that there be no decay: no leading into captivity, and no complaining in our streets. *Ib. 14*

18 The Lord is gracious, and merciful: long-suffering, and of great goodness. *Ib. cxlv. 8*

19 O put not your trust in princes, nor in any child of man: for there is no help in them.
For when the breath of man goeth forth he shall turn again to his earth: and then all his thoughts perish.
Ib. cxlvi. 2

20 The Lord careth for the strangers; he defendeth the fatherless and widow: as for the way of the ungodly, he turneth it upside down. *Ib. 9*

21 Yea, a joyful and pleasant thing it is to be thankful.
The Lord doth build up Jerusalem: and gather together the out-casts of Israel.
He healeth those that are broken in heart: and giveth medicine to heal their sickness.
He telleth the number of the stars: and calleth them all by their names. *Ib. cxlvii. 1*

22 He hath no pleasure in the strength of an horse: neither delighteth he in any man's legs. *Ib. 10*

23 He giveth snow like wool: and scattereth the hoar-frost like ashes. *Ib. 16*

24 Praise the Lord upon earth: ye dragons and all deeps;
Fire and hail, snow and vapours: wind and storm, fulfilling his word. *Ib. cxlviii. 7*

25 Young men and maidens, old men and children, praise the Name of the Lord: for his Name only is excellent, and his praise above heaven and earth.
Ib. 12

26 Let the praises of God be in their mouth: and a two-edged sword in their hands. *Ib. cxlix. 6*

27 To bind their kings in chains: and their nobles with links of iron. *Ib. 8*

28 Praise him upon the well-tuned cymbals: praise him upon the loud cymbals.
Let every thing that hath breath: praise the Lord.
Ib. cl. 5

29 Such as pass on the seas upon their lawful occasions.
Forms of Prayer to be Used at Sea. 'O Eternal Lord God'

30 We therefore commit his body to the deep, to be turned into corruption, looking for the resurrection of the body (when the Sea shall give up her dead).
Ib. At the Burial of their Dead at Sea.

31 Come, Holy Ghost, our souls inspire,
And lighten with celestial fire.
Thou the anointing Spirit art,
Who dost thy seven-fold gifts impart.
Ordering of Priests. Veni, Creator Spiritus

32 Enable with perpetual light
The dulness of our blinded sight. *Ib.*

33 Anoint and cheer our soiled face
With the abundance of thy grace,
Keep far our foes, give peace at home:
Where thou art guide, no ill can come. *Ib.*

1 Cheerfully for conscience sake.
Accession Service. Almighty God, who rulest over all the kingdoms

2 We will see there shall be due Execution upon them.
Articles of Religion. His Majesty's Declaration

3 All things necessary to salvation.
Ib. vi. Of the Sufficiency of the Holy Scriptures

4 As the Pelagians do vainly talk.
Ib. Of Original Sin, ix

5 Man is very far gone from original righteousness. *Ib.*

6 Of Works of Supererogation. *Ib. Title of Article xiv*

7 Fond thing vainly invented. *Ib. xxii. Of Purgatory*

8 Understanded of the people.
Ib. xxiv. Of Speaking in the Congregation

9 The corrupt following of the Apostles.
Ib. xxv. Of the Sacraments

10 Reserved, carried about, lifted up, or worshipped.
Ib. xxviii. Of the Lord's Supper

11 Blasphemous fables, and dangerous deceits.
Ib. xxxi. Of the One Oblation

12 The Bishop of *Rome* hath no jurisdiction in this Realm of *England*.
Ib. xxxvii. Of the Civil Magistrates

13 It is lawful for Christian men, at the commandment of the Magistrate, to wear weapons, and serve in the wars. *Ib.*

14 As certain Anabaptists do falsely boast.
Ib. xxxviii. Of Christian Men's Goods

15 Table of Kindred and Affinity. *Title*

16 A Man may not marry his Grandmother.
Table of Kindred

ARCHIBALD PHILIP PRIMROSE, EARL OF ROSEBERY

see

ROSEBERY

SIR JAMES PRIOR
1790?–1869

17 Mr. Cruger . . . at the conclusion of one of Mr. Burke's eloquent harangues, finding nothing to add, or perhaps as he thought to add with effect, exclaimed earnestly, in the language of the counting-house, 'I say ditto to Mr. Burke—I say ditto to Mr. Burke.' *Life of Burke, ch. 5*

MATTHEW PRIOR
1664–1721

18 He's half absolv'd who has confess'd.
Alma, c. ii, l. 22

19 Dear Cloe, how blubber'd is that pretty face!
A Better Answer [to Cloe Jealous]

20 Odds life! must one swear to the truth of a song? *Ib.*

21 I court others in verse: but I love thee in prose:
And they have my whimsies, but thou hast my heart.
Ib.

22 Serene yet strong, majestic yet sedate,
Swift without violence, without terror great.
Carmen Seculare, l. 282

23 The song too daring, and the theme too great!
Carmen Seculare, l. 308

24 She may receive and own my flame,
For tho' the strictest prudes should know it,
She'll pass for a most virtuous Dame,
And I for an unhappy poet.
To a Child of Quality Five Years Old

25 That I shall be past making love,
When she begins to comprehend it. *Ib.*

26 Be to her virtues very kind;
Be to her faults a little blind;
Let all her ways be unconfin'd;
And clap your padlock—on her mind.
An English Padlock, l. 79

27 To John I ow'd great obligation;
But John, unhappily, thought fit
To publish it to all the nation:
Sure John and I are more than quit. *Epigram*

28 Nobles and heralds, by your leave,
Here lies what once was Matthew Prior;
The son of Adam and of Eve,
Can Bourbon or Nassau go higher? *Epitaph*

29 Without love, hatred, joy, or fear,
They led—a kind of—as it were:
Nor wish'd, nor car'd, nor laugh'd, nor cried:
And so they liv'd, and so they died.
An Epitaph, l. 59

30 All jargon of the schools.
On Exod. iii. 14. I am that I am. An Ode, l. 65

31 And oft the pangs of absence to remove
By letters, soft interpreters of love.
Henry and Emma, l. 147

32 No longer shall the bodice, aptly lac'd
From thy full bosom to thy slender waist,
That air and harmony of shape express,
Fine by degrees, and beautifully less. *Ib. l. 427*

33 From ignorance our comfort flows,
The only wretched are the wise.
To the Hon. C. Montague, l. 35

34 For the idiom of words very little she heeded,
Provided the matter she drove at succeeded,
She took and gave languages just as she needed.
Jinny the Just

35 Her religion so well with her learning did suit
That in practice sincere, and in controverse mute,
She shewed she knew better to live than dispute. *Ib.*

36 Venus, take my votive glass;
Since I am not what I was,
What from this day I shall be,
Venus, let me never see.
The Lady who Offers her Looking-Glass to Venus

37 My noble, lovely, little Peggy.
A Letter to the Honourable Lady Miss Margaret Cavendish-Holles-Harley

38 The merchant, to secure his treasure,
Conveys it in a borrowed name:
Euphelia serves to grace my measure;
But Chloe is my real flame.
An Ode, 'The Merchant to Secure his Treasure'

39 They never taste who always drink;
They always talk, who never think.
Upon this Passage in the Scaligeriana

1 He rang'd his tropes, and preach'd up patience;
Back'd his opinion with quotations.
Paulo Purganti and his Wife, l. 138

2 Entire and sure the monarch's rule must prove,
Who founds her greatness on her subjects' love.
*Prologue Spoken on Her Majesty's Birthday,
1704*, l. 17

3 Cur'd yesterday of my disease,
I died last night of my physician.
The Remedy Worse than the Disease

4 Abra was ready ere I call'd her name;
And, though I call'd another, Abra came.
Solomon, bk. ii, l. 362

5 What is a King?—a man condemn'd to bear
The public burden of the nation's care.
Ib. bk. iii, l. 275

6 Now fitted the halter, now travers'd the cart;
And often took leave: but was loth to depart.
The Thief and the Cordelier, v.

7 I never strove to rule the roast,
She ne'er refus'd to pledge my toast.
Turtle and Sparrow, l. 334

8 A Rechabite poor Will must live,
And drink of Adam's ale. *The Wandering Pilgrim*, iii

ADELAIDE ANN PROCTER
1825–1864

9 I do not ask, O Lord, that life may be
A pleasant road.
A Chaplet of Verses. Per Pacem ad Lucem

10 Joy is like restless day; but peace divine
Like quiet night:
Lead me, O Lord—till perfect Day shall shine,
Through Peace to Light. *Ib.*

11 Seated one day at the organ,
I was weary and ill at ease,
And my fingers wandered idly
Over the noisy keys.
Legends and Lyrics. A Lost Chord

12 But I struck one chord of music,
Like the sound of a great Amen. *Ib.*

13 It may be that only in Heaven
I shall hear that grand Amen. *Ib.*

14 Rise! for the day is passing,
And you lie dreaming on;
The others have buckled their armour,
And forth to the fight are gone:
A place in the ranks awaits you,
Each man has some part to play;
The Past and the Future are nothing,
In the face of the stern To-day. *Ib. Now*

BRYAN WALLER PROCTER
see
BARRY CORNWALL

PROPERTIUS
b. *c.* 51 B.C.

15 Navita de ventis, de tauris narrat arator,
Enumerat miles vulnera, pastor oves.

The seaman's story is of tempest, the ploughman's
of his team of bulls; the soldier tells his wounds
the shepherd his tale of sheep.
Elegies, ii. i. 43. Trans. by Phillimore

16 Quodsi deficiant vires, audacia certe
Laus erit: in magnis et voluisse sat est.

And if my strength fail, at least my boldness will
be a title of honour; in great enterprises the
very 'I would' is enough. *Ib.* x.

17 Cedite Romani scriptores, cedite Grai!
Nescio quid maius nascitur Iliade.

Give place, you Roman writers, give place, you
Greeks! Here comes to birth something greater
than the Iliad. *Ib.* xxxiv. 6

PROTAGORAS
c. 481–411 B.C.

18 πάντων χρημάτων ἄνθρωπον μέτρον εἶναι.

Man is the measure of all things.
Quoted by Plato in Theaetetus, 160

PIERRE-JOSEPH PROUDHON
1809–1865

19 La propriété c'est le vol.
Property is theft. *Qu'est-ce que la Propriété?* ch.

FATHER PROUT
[FRANCIS SYLVESTER MAHONY]
1804–1866

20 With deep affection,
And recollection,
I often think of
Those Shandon bells. *The Bells of Shandon*

21 'Tis the bells of Shandon,
That sound so grand on
The pleasant waters
Of the River Lee. *Ib.*

WILLIAM JEFFREY PROWSE
1836–1870

22 Though the latitude's rather uncertain,
And the longitude also is vague,
The persons I pity who know not the city,
The beautiful city of Prague. *The City of Prague*

JOHN PUDNEY
1909–

23 You shall inherit hours which are replaced,
The earth won back, the trustier human ways
From history recovered, on them based
An amplitude of noble life. *The Dead,*

24 Do not despair
For Johnny head-in-air;
He sleeps as sound
As Johnny underground. *For Johnny*, st.

25 Better by far
For Johnny-the-bright-star,
To keep your head
And see his children fed. *Ib.*

1 Live and let live.
No matter how it ended,
These lose and, under the sky,
Lie friended.   *Graves—Tobruk*, st. 1

WILLIAM PULTENEY, EARL OF BATH
1684-1764

2 Since twelve honest men have decided the cause,
And were judges of fact, tho' not judges of laws.
The Honest Jury, iii. In *The Craftsman*, 1731,
vol. 5, 337. Refers to Sir Philip Yorke's unsuccessful prosecution of *The Craftsman* (1729)

PUNCH

3 Advice to persons about to marry.—'Don't.'
Punch, vol. viii, p. 1. 1845

4 You pays your money and you takes your choice.
Ib. vol. x, p. 17. 1846. *See* Corrigenda

5 The Half-Way House to Rome, Oxford.
Ib. vol. xvi, p. 36. 1849

6 What is better than presence of mind in a railway
accident? Absence of body.
Ib. vol. xvi, p. 231. 1849

7 Never do to-day what you can put off till to-morrow.
Ib. vol. xvii, p. 241. 1849

8 No bread. Then bring me some toast!
Ib. vol. xxii, p. 18. 1852

9 Who's 'im, Bill?
A stranger!
'Eave 'arf a brick at 'im.   *Ib.* vol. xxvi, p. 82. 1854

10 What is Matter?—Never mind.
What is Mind?—No matter.
Ib. vol. xxix, p. 19. 1855

11 'Peccavi—I've Scinde' wrote Lord Ellen so proud.
More briefly Dalhousie wrote—'Vovi—I've Oude'.
Ib. vol. xxx, p. 141. 1856

12 It ain't the 'unting as 'urts 'un, it's the 'ammer,
'ammer, 'ammer along the 'ard 'igh road.
Ib. vol. xxx, p. 218. 1856

13 Oi'll tak zum o' that in a moog.
Ib. vol. xxxvii, p. 156. 1859

14 I see it's written by a lady, and I want a book that my
daughters may read. Give me something else.
Ib. vol. liii, p. 252. 1867

15 Mun, a had na' been the-erre abune two hours when
—*bang*—went saxpence!!! *Ib.* vol. liv, p. 235. 1868

16 Cats is 'dogs' and rabbits is 'dogs' and so's Parrats,
but this 'ere 'Tortis' is a insect, and there ain't no
charge for it.   *Ib.* vol. lvi, p. 96. 1869

17 Nothink for nothink 'ere, and precious little for sixpence.   *Ib.* vol. lvii, p. 152. 1869

18 Sure, the next train has gone ten minutes ago.
Ib. vol. lx, p. 206. 1871

19 It appears the Americans have taken umbrage.
The deuce they have! Whereabouts is that?
Ib. vol. lxiii, p. 189. 1872

20 Go directly—see what she's doing, and tell her she
mustn't.   *Ib.* vol. lxiii, p. 202. 1872

21 There was one poor tiger that hadn't *got* a Christian.
Ib. vol. lxviii, p. 143. 1875

22 Here was an old owl liv'd in an oak
The more he heard, the less he spoke;
The less he spoke, the more he heard
O, if men were all like that wise bird!
Punch, vol. lxviii, p. 155. 1875

23 It's worse than wicked, my dear, it's vulgar.
Ib. Almanac. 1876

24 What did you take out of the bag, Mamma? *I* only
got sixpence.   *Ib.* vol. lxx, p. 139. 1876

25 'Is Life worth living?' . . . he suspects it is, in a great
measure, a question of the Liver.
Ib. vol. lxxiii, p. 207. 1877

26 I never read books—I *write* them.
Ib. vol. lxxiv, p. 210. 1878

27 I am not hungry; but thank goodness, I am greedy.
Ib. vol. lxxv, p. 290. 1878

28 BISHOP:
Who is it that sees and hears all we do, and before
whom even I am but as a crushed worm?
PAGE:
The Missus, my Lord.   *Ib.* vol. lxxix, p. 63. 1880

29 Ah whiles hae ma doobts aboot the meenister.
Ib. p. 275. 1880

30 I used your soap two years ago; since then I have used
no other.   *Ib.* vol. lxxxvi, p. 197. 1884

31 What sort of a doctor is he?
Oh, well, I don't know very much about his ability;
but he's got a very good bedside manner!
Ib. p. 121. 1884

32 Don't look at me, Sir, with—ah—in that tone of
voice.   *Ib.* vol. lxxxvii, p. 38. 1884

33 Oh yes! I'm sure he's not so fond of me as at first.
He's away so much, neglects me dreadfully, and
he's so cross when he comes home. What *shall*
I do?
Feed the brute!   *Ib.* vol. lxxxix, p. 206. 1886

34 Hi! James—let loose the Gorgonzola!
Ib. vol. xcvi, p. 82. 1889

35 Nearly all our best men are dead! Carlyle, Tennyson,
Browning, George Eliot!—I'm not feeling very well
myself.   *Ib.* vol. civ, p. 210. 1893

36 Botticelli isn't a wine, you Juggins! Botticelli's a
cheese!   *Ib.* vol. cvi, p. 270. 1894

37 I'm afraid you've got a bad egg, Mr. Jones.
Oh no, my Lord, I assure you! Parts of it are excellent!
Ib. vol. cix, p. 222. 1895

38 Do you know, Carter, that I can actually write my
name in the dust on the table?
Faith, Mum, that's more than I can do. Sure there's
nothing like education, after all.
Ib. vol. cxxii, p. 142. 1902

39 Look here, Steward, if this is coffee, I want tea; but
if this is tea, then I wish for coffee.
Ib. vol. cxxiii, p. 44. 1902

40 We must gie it up, Alfred.
What, gie up gowff?
Nae, nae, mon. Gie up the meenistry.
Ib. vol. cxxvi, p. 117. 1904

ISRAEL PUTNAM

1718–1790

1 Men, you are all marksmen—don't one of you fire
until you see the whites of their eyes.
Bunker Hill, 1775. Frothingham, *History of the
Siege of Boston* (1873), ch. 5, note. *Also attributed
to* William Prescott (1726–95)

ERNIE PYLE

1900–1945

2 The worm's eye point of view.   *Here Is Your War*

FRANCIS QUARLES

1592–1644

3 I wish thee as much pleasure in the reading, as I had
in the writing.   *Emblems. To the Reader*

4 The heart is a small thing, but desireth great matters.
It is not sufficient for a kite's dinner, yet the whole
world is not sufficient for it.
Ib. bk. i, No. 12. *Hugo de Anima*

5 We spend our midday sweat, our midnight oil;
We tire the night in thought, the day in toil.
Ib. bk. ii, No. 2, l. 33

6 Be wisely worldly, be not worldly wise.   *Ib.* l. 46

7 Man is Heaven's masterpiece.   *Ib.* No. 6, Epig. 6

8 The road to resolution lies by doubt:
The next way home's the farthest way about.
Ib. bk. iv, No. 2, Epig. 2

9 Our God and soldiers we alike adore
Ev'n at the brink of danger; not before:
After deliverance, both alike requited,
Our God's forgotten, and our soldiers slighted.
Epigram

10 My soul, sit thou a patient looker-on;
Judge not the play before the play is done:
Her plot hath many changes; every day
Speaks a new scene; the last act crowns the play.
Epigram. Respice Finem

11 No man is born unto himself alone;
Who lives unto himself, he lives to none.
Esther, Sect. 1, Medit. 1

12 He that had no cross deserves no crown.
Ib. Sect. 9, Medit. 9

13 He teaches to deny that faintly prays.
A Feast for Worms, Sect. 7, Medit. 7, l. 2

14 Man is man's A.B.C. There is none that can
Read God aright, unless he first spell Man.
Hieroglyphics, i, l. 1

15 He that begins to live, begins to die.   *Ib.* 1, Epig. 1

16 Physicians of all men are most happy; what good
success soever they have, the world proclaimeth,
and what faults they commit, the earth covereth.
Ib. iv. *Nicocles*

17 Come then, my brethren, and be glad,
And eke rejoice with me;
Lawn sleeves and rochets shall go down,
And hey! then up go we!
The Shepherd's Oracles. Eclogue xi, *Song of
Anarchus*, i

18 We'll cry both arts and learning down,
And hey! then up go we!
The Shepherd's Oracles. Eclogue xi. *Song of
Anarchus*, iv

FRANÇOIS QUESNAY

1694–1774

19 Laissez faire, laissez passer.
No interference, and complete freedom of move-
ment.
Of Government interference. Also attributed to
Marquis d'Argenson, *Mémoires* (1736)

SIR ARTHUR QUILLER-COUCH

1863–1944

20 Know you her secret none can utter?
Hers of the Book, the tripled Crown?
Poems. Alma Mater

21 Yet if at last, not less her lover,
You in your hansom leave the High;
Down from her towers a ray shall hover—
Touch you, a passer-by!   *Ib.*

22 O pastoral heart of England! like a psalm
Of green days telling with a quiet beat.
Ib. Ode upon Eckington Bridge

23 Turns in her sleep, and murmurs of the Spring.   *Ib.*

JOSIAH QUINCY

1772–1864

24 As it will be the right of all, so it will be the duty of
some, definitely to prepare for a separation,
amicably if they can, violently if they must.
Abridgement of Debates of Congress, 14 Jan. 1811,
vol. iv, p. 327

QUINTILIAN

A.D. 40–c. 100

25 Satura quidem tota nostra est.
Satire indeed is entirely our own.
De Institutione Oratoria, x. i. 93

26 [Horatius] et insurgit aliquando et plenus est iucunditatis et gratiae et variis figuris et verbis felicissime
audax.
[Horace] soars occasionally, is full of agreeableness
and grace, and shows a most happy daring in
certain figures and expressions.   *Ib.* 96

FRANÇOIS RABELAIS

1494?–1553

27 L'appétit vient en mangeant.
The appetite grows by eating.   *Gargantua,* 1. v

28 Fay ce que vouldras
Do what thou wilt.   *Ib.* 1. lvii

29 Tirez le rideau, la farce est jouée.
Ring down the curtain, the farce is over.
Attr. to Rabelais on his death-bed

30 Je m'en vais chercher un grand peut-être.
I go to seek a great perhaps.   *Ib.*

1 Vogue la galère!
    Let her rip!
    [Literally, the words mean 'loose the galley' or
    'hoist sail'.]
                                    Works, bk. i, ch. 40

JEAN RACINE
1639-1699

2 Elle flotte, elle hésite; en un mot, elle est femme.
    She is all wavering and hesitation: in short, she is a
        woman.   *Athalie*, iii. 3

3 Ce n'est plus une ardeur dans mes veines cachée:
    C'est Vénus tout entière à sa proie attachée.
    It is no longer a passion hidden in my veins: it is
        the goddess Venus herself fastened on her prey.
                                    Phèdre, 1. iii

4 Point d'argent, point de Suisse.
    No money, no Swiss [soldiers].
                                    Les Plaideurs, 1. i.

5 Sans argent l'honneur n'est qu'une maladie.
    Honour, without money, is a mere malady.   *Ib.*

THOMAS RAINBOROWE
d. 1648

6 The poorest he that is in England hath a life to live
    as the greatest he.
    In the Army debates at Putney, 29 Oct. 1647.
    Peacock, *Life of Rainborowe.*

SIR WALTER RALEGH
1552?-1618

7 Go, Soul, the body's guest,
        Upon a thankless arrant:
    Fear not to touch the best;
        The truth shall be thy warrant:
    Go, since I needs must die,
    And give the world the lie.   *The Lie*, i

8 If all the world and love were young,
    And truth in every shepherd's tongue,
    These pretty pleasures might me move
    To live with thee, and be thy love.
        The Nymph's Reply to the [Passionate] Shepherd

9 Give me my scallop-shell of quiet,
    My staff of faith to walk upon,
    My scrip of joy, immortal diet,
    My bottle of salvation,
    My gown of glory, hope's true gage,
    And thus I'll take my pilgrimage.
                The Passionate Man's Pilgrimage

10 As you came from the holy land
        Of Walsinghame,
    Met you not with my true love
        By the way as you came?

    How shall I know your true love,
        That have met many one
    As I went to the holy land,
        That have come, that have gone?   *Walsinghame*

11 Fain would I climb, yet fear I to fall.
    Line Written on a Window-Pane. Queen Eliza-
    beth wrote under it, 'If thy heart fails thee, climb
    not at all.' Fuller, *Worthies* (1840), i. 419

12 Even such is time, which takes in trust
    Our youth, our joys, and all we have,
    And pays us but with age and dust,
    Who in the dark and silent grave,
    When we have wandered all our ways,
    Shuts up the story of our days.
    And from which earth, and grave, and dust,
    The Lord shall raise me up, I trust.
        *Written the night before his death. Found in his
        Bible in the Gate-house at Westminster*

13 O eloquent, just, and mighty Death! whom none
    could advise, thou hast persuaded; what none hath
    dared, thou hast done; and when all the world hath
    flattered, thou only hast cast out of the world and
    despised: thou hast drawn together all the far-
    stretched greatness, all the pride, cruelty, and am-
    bition of man, and covered it all over with these two
    narrow words, *Hic jacet.*
        A History of the World, bk. v, ch. vi, § 12

14 [Feeling the edge of the axe before his execution:]
    'Tis a sharp remedy, but a sure one for all ills.
        Hume, *History of Great Britain* (1754), vol. i,
        ch. iv, p. 72

15 [When asked which way he preferred to lay his head
    on the block:]
    So the heart be right, it is no matter which way the
    head lies.
        W. Stebbing, *Sir Walter Raleigh*, ch. xxx

SIR WALTER A. RALEIGH
1861-1922

16 I wish I loved the Human Race;
    I wish I loved its silly face;
    I wish I liked the way it walks;
    I wish I liked the way it talks;
    And when I'm introduced to one
    I wish I thought *What Jolly Fun!*
        Laughter from a Cloud (1923), p. 228. *Wishes of
        an Elderly Man*

JULIAN RALPH
1853-1903

17 News value.
    *Lecture to Brander Matthews's English Class,
    Columbia, 1892.* Thomas Beer's *Mauve Decade*

ALLAN RAMSAY
1686-1758

18 Farewell to Lochaber, and farewell my Jean.
        Works (1851), ii, *Lochaber No More*

JAMES RYDER RANDALL
1839-1908

19 The despot's heel is on thy shore,
        Maryland!
    His torch is at thy temple door,
        Maryland!
    Avenge the patriotic gore
    That flecked the streets of Baltimore,
    And be the battle-queen of yore,
        Maryland, my Maryland!
                Maryland! My Maryland, i

JEREMIAH EAMES RANKIN
1828–1904

1 God be with you, till we meet again,
By His counsels guide, uphold you,
With His sheep securely fold you:
God be with you, till we meet again. *Hymn*

THOMAS RAVENSCROFT
1592?–1635?

2 We be three poor mariners
Newly come from the seas.
Deuteromelia (1609). *Oxford Song Book*, vol. ii

THOMAS BUCHANAN READ
1822–1872

3 The terrible grumble, and rumble, and roar,
Telling the battle was on once more,
And Sheridan twenty miles away. *Sheridan's Ride*, i

CHARLES READE
1814–1884

4 Not a day passes over the earth, but men and women
of no note do great deeds, speak great words and
suffer noble sorrows.
The Cloister and the Hearth, ch. 1

5 Courage, mon ami, le diable est mort!
Ib. ch. 24, *and passim*

6 Sow an act, and you reap a habit. Sow a habit, and
you reap a character. Sow a character, and you reap
a destiny.
Attrib. See Notes and Queries, 9th series, vol. 12,
p. 377

ERICH MARIA REMARQUE
1898–

7 Im Westen nichts Neues.
All Quiet on the Western Front.
Title of Novel. Trans. by A. W. Wheen

EBEN REXFORD
1848–1916

8 Darling, I am growing old,
Silver threads among the gold
Shine upon my brow to-day;
Life is fading fast away.
Silver Threads among the Gold

FREDERIC REYNOLDS
1764–1841

9 How goes the enemy? [Said by Mr. Ennui, 'the time-
killer'.] *The Dramatist*, 1. i

SIR JOSHUA REYNOLDS
1723–1792

10 If you have great talents, industry will improve
them: if you have but moderate abilities, industry
will supply their deficiency.
Discourse to Students of the Royal Academy,
11 Dec. 1769

11 A mere copier of nature can never produce anything
great.
Discourse to Students of the Royal Academy,
14 Dec. 1770

12 He who resolves never to ransack any mind but his
own, will be soon reduced, from mere barrenness,
to the poorest of all imitations; he will be obliged
to imitate himself, and to repeat what he has
before often repeated. *Ib. 10 Dec. 1774*

13 I should desire that the last words which I should
pronounce in this Academy, and from this place,
might be the name of—Michael Angelo.
Ib. 10 Dec. 1790

14 He [Dr. Johnson] has no formal preparation, no
flourishing with his sword; he is through your
body in an instant.
Boswell's *Johnson* (ed. 1934), vol. ii, p. 365,
18 Apr. 1775

15 He [Johnson] qualified my mind to think justly.
Ib. vol. iii, p. 369, n. 3; *and* Northcote's, *Reynolds*,
vol. ii, p. 282.

ARCHBISHOP WALTER REYNOLDS
[De REYNEL or REGINALD]
d. 1327

16 Vox Populi, vox Dei.
The voice of the people, the voice of God.
Text of Sermon when Edward III ascended the
throne, 1 Feb. 1327. Walsingham, *Historia*
Anglicana (ed. 1863), i. 186

CECIL JOHN RHODES
1853–1902

17 So little done, so much to do.
Last words. L. Michell, *Life*, vol. ii, ch. 39

WILLIAM BARNES RHODES
1772–1826

18 'Who dares this pair of boots displace,
Must meet Bombastes face to face.'
Thus do I challenge all the human race.
Bombastes Furioso, sc. iv

19 BOMBASTES:
So have I heard on Afric's burning shore,
A hungry lion give a grievous roar;
The grievous roar echo'd along the shore.
KING:
So have I heard on Afric's burning shore
Another lion give a grievous roar,
And the first lion thought the last a bore. *Ib.*

GRANTLAND RICE
1880–

20 For when the One Great Scorer comes
To write against your name,
He marks—not that you won or lost—
But how you played the game. *Alumnus Football*

SIR STEPHEN RICE
1637–1715

21 Sir Stephen Rice . . . having been often heard to
say, before he was a judge, that he will drive a
coach and six horses through the Act of Settlement.
W. King, *State of the Protestants of Ireland*
(1672), ch. 3, § 3, par. 6

JEAN PAUL RICHTER
1763–1825

1 Providence has given to the French the empire of the land, to the English that of the sea, and to the Germans that of the air.
Quoted by Thomas Carlyle, in the Edinburgh Review, 1827

GEORGE RIDDING, BISHOP OF SOUTHWELL
1828–1904

2 I feel a feeling which I feel you all feel.
Sermon in the London Mission of 1885. G. W. E. Russell's *Collections and Recollections, ch. 29*

JAMES WHITCOMB RILEY
1852–1916

3 An' the gobble-uns 'll git you
Ef you don't watch out!
Poems. Little Orphant Annie

4 It haint no use to grumble and complane
Its jest as cheap and easy to rejoice;
When God sorts out the weather and sends rain,
W'y rain's my choice. *Ib. Wet-Weather Talk*

ROBERT LEROY RIPLEY
1893–

5 Believe it or not. *Title of newspaper feature*

ANTOINE DE RIVAROL
1753–1801

6 Ce qui n'est pas clair n'est pas français.
What is not clear is not French.
De l'Universalité de la Langue Française (1784)

SIR BOYLE ROCHE
1743–1807

7 He regretted that he was not a bird, and could not be in two places at once. *Attr.*

8 Mr. Speaker, I smell a rat; I see him forming in the air and darkening the sky; but I'll nip him in the bud. *Attr.*

DUC DE LA ROCHEFOUCAULD
1613–1680

9 Nous avons tous assez de force pour supporter les maux d'autrui.
We have all enough strength to bear the misfortunes of others. *Maximes, 19*

10 On n'est jamais si heureux ni si malheureux qu'on s'imagine.
One is never so happy or so unhappy as one thinks.
Ib. 49

11 L'hypocrisie est un hommage que le vice rend à la vertu.
Hypocrisy is homage paid by vice to virtue. *Ib. 218*

12 C'est une grande habileté que de savoir cacher son habileté.

The height of cleverness is to be able to conceal it.
Maximes, 245

13 La reconnaissance de la plupart des hommes n'est qu'une secrète envie de recevoir de plus grands bienfaits.
In most of mankind gratitude is merely a secret hope of further favours. *Ib. 298*
A saying ascribed to Sir Robert Walpole by Hazlitt in his Wit and Humour: 'The gratitude of place-expectants is a lively sense of future favours' *is obviously derived from La Rochefoucauld.*

14 Dans l'adversité de nos meilleurs amis, nous trouvons quelque chose qui ne nous déplaît pas.
In the misfortune of our best friends, we find something which is not displeasing to us.
Maximes supprimées, 583

DUC DE LA ROCHEFOUCAULD-LIANCOURT
1747–1827

15 LOUIS XVI: C'est une révolte?
LA ROCHEFOUCAULD-LIANCOURT: Non, Sire, c'est une révolution.
LOUIS XVI: Is it a revolt?
LA R.-LIANCOURT: No, Sire, it is a revolution.
When the news arrived at Versailles of the Fall of the Bastille, 1789

JOHN WILMOT, EARL OF ROCHESTER
1647–1680

16 Since 'tis Nature's law to change,
Constancy alone is strange.
Works (1926), A Dialogue between Strephon and Daphne, l. 31

17 The best good man, with the worst-natur'd muse.
To Lord Buckhurst

18 An age in her embraces past,
Would seem a winter's day. *Ib. The Mistress*

19 Nothing! thou elder brother ev'n to shade.
Ib. Upon Nothing

20 A merry monarch, scandalous and poor.
Ib. A Satire on King Charles II for which he was banished from the Court, l. 19.

21 Reason, an *ignis fatuus* of the mind.
Ib. A Satire Against Mankind, l. 11

22 Then Old Age, and Experience, hand in hand,
Lead him to Death, and make him understand,
After a search so painful, and so long,
That all his life he has been in the wrong,
Huddled in dirt the reasoning engine lies,
Who was so proud, so witty and so wise. *Ib. l. 25*

23 For all men would be cowards if they durst.
Ib. l. 158

24 Here lies a great and mighty king
Whose promise none relies on;
He never said a foolish thing,
Nor ever did a wise one.
The King's Epitaph. An alternative version of the first line is: 'Here lies our sovereign lord the King.'
For Charles II's answer see 136:4

E. W. ROGERS

1 Ev'ry member of the force
Has a watch and chain, of course;
If you want to know the time,
Ask a P'liceman!   *Ask A P'liceman*

2 Hi-tiddley-hi-ti.   *Title of Song*

JAMES EDWIN THOROLD ROGERS
1823–1890

3 Sir, to be facetious it is not necessary to be indecent.
*In imitation of Samuel Johnson. Also attributed to
Birkbeck Hill. Quo. in* John Bailey: *Dr. Johnson
and his Circle*

4 While ladling butter from alternate tubs
Stubbs butters Freeman, Freeman butters Stubbs.
Attrib. in Hutton's *Letters of Bishop Stubbs*

ROBERT CAMERON ROGERS
1862–1912

5 The hours I spent with thee, dear heart,
Are as a string of pearls to me;
I count them over, every one apart,
My rosary.   *The Rosary*

SAMUEL ROGERS
1763–1855

6 Think nothing done while aught remains to do.
Human Life, l. 49

7 But there are moments which he calls his own,
Then, never less alone than when alone,
Those whom he loved so long and sees no more,
Loved and still loves—not dead—but gone before,
He gathers round him.   *Ib. l. 755*

8 By many a temple half as old as Time.
Italy. A Farewell, ii. 5

9 Go—you may call it madness, folly;
You shall not chase my gloom away.
There's such a charm in melancholy,
I would not, if I could, be gay.   *To —, 1814*

10 Mine be a cot beside the hill;
A bee-hive's hum shall soothe my ear;
A willowy brook, that turns a mill,
With many a fall shall linger near.   *A Wish*

11 Sheridan was listened to with such attention that you
might have heard a pin drop.   *Table Talk*

12 It doesn't much signify whom one marries, for one is
sure to find next morning that it was someone else.
Ib.

13 Ward has no heart, they say; but I deny it;—
He has a heart, and gets his speeches by it.
Ib. Epigram upon Lord Dudley

14 When a new book is published, read an old one.
Attr.

MME ROLAND
1754–1793

15 O liberté! O liberté! que de crimes on commet en
ton nom!

O liberty! O liberty! what crimes are committed in
thy name!
Lamartine, *Histoire des Girondins, livre li, ch. 8*

16 The more I see of men, the better I like dogs. *Attrib.*

JAMES ROLMAZ

17 'Where did you get that hat?
Where did you get that tile?
Isn't it a nobby one, and just the proper style?
I should like to have one just the same as that!'
Wher'er I go they shout, 'Hello!
Where did you get that hat?
Where Did You Get That Hat?

PIERRE RONSARD
1529–1585

18 Quand vous serez bien vieille, au soir, à la chandelle,
Assise auprès du feu, dévidant et filant,
Direz, chantant mes vers, en vous émerveillant,
Ronsard me célébrait du temps que j'étais belle.

When you are very old, and sit in the candle-light
at evening spinning by the fire, you will say, as
you murmur my verses, a wonder in your eyes,
'Ronsard sang of me in the days when I was fair.'
Sonnets pour Hélène, ii. 43

FRANKLIN DELANO ROOSEVELT
1882–1945

19 I pledge you—I pledge myself—to a new deal for the
American people.
*Speech at Convention, Chicago, 2 July 1932.
(New York Times, 3 July, sect. 1, p. 8, col. 7.)*
E. K. Lindley, *The Roosevelt Revolution, ch. 1*

20 Let me assert my firm belief that the only thing we
have to fear is fear itself.
First Inaugural Address, 4 March 1933

21 In the field of world policy; I would dedicate this
nation to the policy of the good neighbour.   *Ib.*

22 I see one-third of a nation ill-housed, ill-clad, ill-
nourished.
Second Inaugural Address, 20 Jan. 1937

23 When peace has been broken anywhere, the peace of
all countries everywhere is in danger.
Fireside Chat, 3 Sept. 1939

24 We must be the great arsenal of democracy.
Ib. 29 Dec. 1940

25 In the future days, which we seek to make secure,
we look forward to a world founded upon four
essential freedoms.
The first is freedom of speech and expression—every-
where in the world.
The second is freedom of every person to worship
God in his own way—everywhere in the world.
The third is freedom from want. . . .
The fourth is freedom from fear.
Speech, 6 Jan. 1941

THEODORE ROOSEVELT
1858–1919

26 I wish to preach, not the doctrine of ignoble ease,
but the doctrine of the strenuous life.
Speech, Hamilton Club, Chicago, 10 Apr. 1899

27 Speak softly and carry a big stick.
Ib. Minnesota State Fair, 2 Sept. 1901

1 The first requisite of a good citizen in this Republic of ours is that he shall be able and willing to pull his weight. *Speech, New York, 11 Nov. 1902*

2 A man who is good enough to shed his blood for the country is good enough to be given a square deal afterwards. More than that no man is entitled to, and less than that no man shall have. *Ib. At the Lincoln Monument, Springfield (Illinois), 4 June 1903*

3 The men with the muck-rakes are often indispensable to the well-being of society; but only if they know when to stop raking the muck. *Ib. At the laying of the Corner-stone of the Office Building of House of Representatives, 14 Apr. 1906*

4 There can be no fifty-fifty Americanism in this country. There is room here for only 100 per cent. Americanism, only for those who are Americans and nothing else. *Ib. Republican Convention, Saratoga*

5 No man is justified in doing evil on the ground of expediency. *The Strenuous Life, Essays. Latitude and Longitude among Reformers*

6 We demand that big business give the people a square deal; in return we must insist that when any one engaged in big business honestly endeavors to do right he shall himself be given a square deal. *Autobiography (1913), p. 615*

7 Hyphenated Americans. *Metropolitan Magazine, Oct. 1915, p. 7*

ARCHIBALD PHILIP PRIMROSE, EARL OF ROSEBERY
1847–1929

8 Before Irish Home Rule is conceded by the Imperial Parliament, England as the predominant member of the three kingdoms will have to be convinced of its justice and equity. *Speech in the House of Lords, 11 March 1894*

9 It is beginning to be hinted that we are a nation of amateurs. *Rectorial Address, Glasgow, 16 Nov. 1900*

10 I must plough my furrow alone. *Speech, City of London Liberal Club, 19 July 1901*

11 What is the advice I have to offer you? The first is this—that you have to clean your slate. [To the Liberal Party.] *Speech, Chesterfield, 16 Dec. 1901*

12 The fly-blown phylacteries of the Liberal Party. *Ib.*

ALEXANDER ROSS
1699–1784

13 Marri'd an' woo'd an' a',
Marri'd an' woo'd an' a',
The dandilly toss[1] of the parish,
Is marri'd and woo'd an' a'.
The Fortunate Shepherdess (1768), p. 139

[1] = toast.

CHRISTINA GEORGINA ROSSETTI
1830–1894

14 My heart is like a singing bird
Whose nest is in a watered shoot;
My heart is like an apple-tree
Whose boughs are bent with thickset fruit;
My heart is like a rainbow shell
That paddles in a halcyon sea;
My heart is gladder than all these
Because my love is come to me. *A Birthday*

15 Because the birthday of my life
Is come, my love is come to me. *Ib.*

16 Oh where are you going with your love-locks flowing? *Amor Mundi, i*

17 We shall escape the uphill by never turning back. *Ib.*

18 This downhill path is easy, but there's no turning back. *Ib. v*

19 For there is no friend like a sister
In calm or stormy weather;
To cheer one on the tedious way,
To fetch one if one goes astray,
To lift one if one totters down,
To strengthen whilst one stands. *Goblin Market (end)*

20 In the bleak mid-winter
Frosty wind made moan,
Earth stood hard as iron,
Water like a stone;
Snow had fallen, snow on snow,
Snow on snow,
In the bleak mid-winter,
Long ago. *Mid-Winter*

21 In the bleak mid-winter
A stable-place sufficed
The Lord God almighty,
Jesus Christ. *Ib.*

22 A breastful of milk,
And a mangerful of hay. *Ib.*

23 There was no hurry in her hands,
No hurry in her feet. *The Prince's Progress, lxxxv*

24 Remember me when I am gone away,
Gone far away into the silent land. *Remember*

25 Better by far you should forget and smile
Than that you should remember and be sad. *Ib.*

26 O Earth, lie heavily upon her eyes;
Seal her sweet eyes weary of watching, Earth. *Rest*

27 Silence more musical than any song. *Ib.*

28 Oh roses for the flush of youth,
And laurel for the perfect prime;
But pluck an ivy branch for me
Grown old before my time. *Song: 'Oh Roses for the Flush'*

29 When I am dead, my dearest,
Sing no sad songs for me;
Plant thou no roses at my head,
Nor shady cypress tree:
Be the green grass above me
With showers and dewdrops wet;
And if thou wilt, remember,
And if thou wilt, forget. *Song: 'When I am Dead'*

1 And dreaming through the twilight
    That doth not rise nor set,
Haply I may remember,
    And haply may forget.   *Song: 'When I am Dead'*

2 Does the road wind up-hill all the way?
    Yes, to the very end.
Will the day's journey take the whole long day?
    From morn to night, my friend.   *Up-Hill*

3 They will not keep you standing at that door.   *Ib.*

4 Will there be beds for me and all who seek?
    Yea, beds for all who come.   *Ib.*

DANTE GABRIEL ROSSETTI
1828–1882

5 Mother of the Fair Delight,
Thou handmaid perfect in God's sight.   *Ave*, l. 1

6 Like the sweet apple which reddens upon the top-
    most bough,
    A-top on the topmost twig,—which the pluckers
        forgot, somehow,—
    Forgot it not, nay, but got it not, for none could get
    it till now.   *Beauty: A Combination from Sappho*

7 The blessed damozel leaned out
    From the gold bar of Heaven;
Her eyes were deeper than the depth
    Of waters stilled at even;
She had three lilies in her hand,
    And the stars in her hair were seven.
            The Blessed Damozel, i

8 Her hair that lay along her back
    Was yellow like ripe corn.   *Ib.* ii

9 So high, that looking downward thence,
    She scarce could see the sun.   *Ib.* v

10   As low as where this earth
Spins like a fretful midge.   *Ib.* vi

11 And the souls mounting up to God
    Went by her like thin flames.   *Ib.* vii

12 'We two,' she said, 'will seek the groves
    Where the lady Mary is,
With her five handmaidens, whose names
    Are five sweet symphonies,
Cecily, Gertrude, Magdalen,
    Margaret and Rosalys.'   *Ib.* xviii

13   Them
Who are just born, being dead.   *Ib.* xix

14 And laid her face between her hands,
    And wept. (I heard her tears.)   *Ib.* xxiv

15 Still we say as we go,—
    'Strange to think by the way,
Whatever there is to know,
    That shall we know one day.'   *Cloud Confines*

16 Heard through all spheres one song increase,—
    'Even I, even I am Beatrice.'   *Dante at Verona*, xii

17 Where the lean black craft like flies
    Seem well-nigh stagnated,
    Soon to drop off dead.   *Even So*

18 Peace in her chamber, wheresoe'er
    It be, a holy place.   *First Love Remembered*, i

19 'I saw the Sibyl at Cumæ'
    (One said) 'with mine own eye.
She hung in a cage, and read her rune
    To all the passers-by.
Said the boys, "What wouldst thou, Sibyl?"
    She answered, "I would die".'
            Fragments. The Sibyl

20 Was it a friend or foe that spread these lies?
    Nay, who but infants question in such wise?
'Twas one of my most intimate enemies.   *Fragment*

21 A sonnet is a moment's monument,—
    Memorial from the Soul's eternity
To one dead deathless hour.
            The House of Life, pt. 1. Introd.

22 Love's throne was not with these; but far above
    All passionate wind of welcome and farewell
He sat in breathless bowers they dream not of.
            Ib. i. *Love Enthroned*

23 When do I see thee most, beloved one?
            Ib. iv. *Lovesight*

24 O love, my love! if I no more should see
    Thyself, nor on the earth the shadow of thee,
Nor image of thine eyes in any spring,—
How then should sound upon life's darkening slope
The ground-whirl of the perished leaves of Hope,
The wind of Death's imperishable wing?   *Ib.*

25 Lady, I fain would tell how evermore
    Thy soul I know not from thy body, nor
Thee from myself, neither our love from God.
            Ib. v. *Heart's Hope*

26 I was a child beneath her touch,—a man
When breast to breast we clung, even I and she,—
A spirit when her spirit looked through me,—
A god when all our life-breath met to fan
Our life-blood, till love's emulous ardours ran,
Fire within fire, desire in deity.   *Ib.* vi. *The Kiss*

27 Known for my soul's birth-partner well enough!
            Ib. xv. *The Birth-Bond*

28 Beauty like hers is genius.   *Ib.* xviii. *Genius in Beauty*

29 'Tis visible silence, still as the hour-glass.
            Ib. xix. *Silent Noon*

30 Deep in the sun-searched growths the dragon-fly
Hangs like a blue thread loosened from the sky:—
So this wing'd hour is dropt to us from above.
Oh! clasp we to our hearts, for deathless dower,
This close-companioned inarticulate hour
When twofold silence was the song of love.   *Ib.*

31   Shall my sense pierce love,—the last relay
And ultimate outpost of eternity?
            Ib. xxxiv. *The Dark Glass*

32 Not in thy body is thy life at all,
But in this lady's lips and hands and eyes.
            Ib. xxxvi. *Life-in-Love*

33 The hour when you too learn that all is vain
    And that Hope sows what Love shall never reap.
            Ib. xliv. *Cloud and Wind*

34 If to grow old in Heaven is to grow young,
    (As the Seer saw and said,) then blest were he
With youth for evermore, whose heaven should be
True Woman, she whom these weak notes have sung.
            Ib. lviii. *True Woman*, sonnet iii

[410]

ROSSETTI

1 The sunrise blooms and withers on the hill
Like any hillflower; and the noblest troth
Dies here to dust. Yet shall Heaven's promise clothe
Even yet those lovers who have cherished still
This test for love:—in every kiss sealed fast
To feel the first kiss and forebode the last. *Ib.*

2 Upon the sight of lidless eyes in Hell.
Ib. pt. II. lxiii, *Inclusiveness*

3   Thenceforth their incommunicable ways
Follow the desultory feet of Death.
Ib. lxv. *Known in Vain*

4 And see the gold air and the silver fade
And the last bird fly into the last night.
Ib. lxx. *The Hill Summit*

5 Eat thou and drink; to-morrow thou shalt die.
Ib. lxxi. *The Choice,* i

6 They die not,—for their life was death,—but cease;
And round their narrow lips the mould falls close. *Ib.*

7 Think thou and act; to-morrow thou shalt die.
Ib. iii

8 Nay, come up hither. From this wave-washed mound
Unto the furthest flood-brim look with me;
Then reach on with thy thought till it be drown'd.
Miles and miles distant though the last line be,
And though thy soul sail leagues and leagues beyond,—
Still, leagues beyond those leagues, there is more sea.
Ib.

9 Give honour unto Luke Evangelist;
For he it was (the aged legends say)
Who first taught Art to fold her hands and pray.
Ib. lxxiv. *Old and New Art,* i

10 This is that Lady Beauty, in whose praise
Thy voice and hand shake still,—long known to thee
By flying hair and fluttering hem,—the beat
Following her daily of thy heart and feet,
How passionately and irretrievably,
In what fond flight, how many ways and days!
Ib. lxxvii. *Soul's Beauty*

11 Lo! as that youth's eyes burned at thine, so went
Thy spell through him, and left his straight neck bent
And round his heart one strangling golden hair.
Ib. lxxviii. *Body's Beauty*

12 And in regenerate rapture turns my face
Upon the devious coverts of dismay?
Ib. lxxix. *The Monochord*

13 The lost days of my life until to-day,
What were they, could I see them on the street
Lie as they fell? *Ib.* lxxxvi. *Lost Days*

14 I do not see them here; but after death
God knows I know the faces I shall see,
Each one a murdered self, with low last breath.
'I am thyself,—what hast thou done to me?'
'And I—and I—thyself', (lo! each one saith,)
'And thou thyself to all eternity!' *Ib.*

15   Even as, heavy-curled,
Stooping against the wind, a charioteer
Is snatched from out his chariot by the hair,
So shall Time be; and as the void car, hurled
Abroad by reinless steeds, even so the world.
Ib. xc. *'Retro me, Sathana!'*

16 Thou still, upon the broad vine-sheltered path,
Mayst wait the turning of the phials of wrath
For certain years, for certain months and days. *Ib.*

17 My name is Might-have-been;
I am also called No-more, Too-late, Farewell.
The House of Life, pt. II. xcvii. *A Superscription*

18 Sleepless with cold commemorative eyes. *Ib.*

19 When vain desire at last and vain regret
Go hand in hand to death. *Ib.* ci. *The One Hope*

20 Teach the unforgetful to forget. *Ib.*

21 The wan soul in that golden air. *Ib.*

22 Scriptured petals. *Ib.*

23   The one Hope's one name be there,—
Not less nor more, but even that word alone. *Ib.*

24 It makes a goblin of the sun. *Jenny,* l. 205

25 Between the hands, between the brows,
Between the lips of Love-Lily. *Love-Lily*

26 Whose speech Truth knows not from her thought
Nor Love her body from her soul. *Ib.*

27 This is that blessed Mary, pre-elect
God's Virgin. *Mary's Girlhood*

28 Thou fill'st from the winged chalice of the soul
Thy lamp, O Memory, fire-winged to its goal.
Mnemosyne

29 Amid the bitterness of things occult.
For Our Lady of the Rocks

30 And your own footsteps meeting you,
And all things going as they came. *The Portrait,* iii

31 Yearned loud the iron-bosomed sea. *Ib.* x

32   O Mother, Mary Mother,
Three days to-day, between Hell and Heaven!
Sister Helen

33 Unto the man of yearning thought
And aspiration, to do nought
Is in itself almost an act. *Soothsay,* x

34 I have been here before,
   But when or how I cannot tell:
I know the grass beyond the door,
   The sweet keen smell,
The sighing sound, the lights around the shore.
Sudden Light, i

35 Heavenborn Helen, Sparta's queen,
   (O Troy Town!)
Had two breasts of heavenly sheen,
The sun and moon of the heart's desire.
Troy Town, i

36 The sea hath no king but God alone.
The White Ship, l. 6

37 From perfect grief there need not be
Wisdom or even memory:
One thing then learnt remains to me,—
The woodspurge has a cup of three.
The Woodspurge

38 Conception, my boy, *fundamental brainwork,* is what
makes the difference in all art.
Letter to Hall Caine, in Caine's *Recollections of
Rossetti* (1882)

39 The Stealthy School of Criticism. *Title*

[411]

CLAUDE-JOSEPH ROUGET DE LISLE
1760–1836

1 Allons, enfants de la patrie,
Le jour de gloire est arrivé.

Come, children of our country, the day of glory has arrived.
La Marseillaise

JEAN-JACQUES ROUSSEAU
1712–1778

2 L'homme est né libre, et partout il est dans les fers.
Man was born free, and everywhere he is in chains.
Du Contrat Social, ch. 1

3 'Monseigneur, il faut que je vive,' disait un malheureux auteur satirique au ministre qui lui reprochait l'infamie de ce métier. 'Je n'en vois pas la nécessité,' lui repartit froidement l'homme en place.

'My Lord—I must live'—once said a wretched author of satire to a minister who had reproached him for following so degrading a profession. 'I fail to see why,' replied the Great Man coldly.
Émile, iii. (See *14:11*)

MARTIN JOSEPH ROUTH
1755–1854

4 You will find it a very good practice always to verify your references, sir!
Burgon, *Memoir of Dr. Routh. Quarterly Review*, July 1878, vol. cxlvi

NICHOLAS ROWE
1674–1718

5 That false Lothario! *The Fair Penitent*, II. i

6 To be good is to be happy. *Ib.* III. i

7 The evening of my age. *Ib.* IV. i

8 I feel the pangs of disappointed love. *Ib.*

9 Is this that haughty, gallant, gay Lothario? *Ib.* v. 1

10 Like Helen, in the night when Troy was sack'd,
Spectatress of the mischief which she made. *Ib.*

11 Death is the privilege of human nature,
And life without it were not worth our taking. *Ib.*

12 Had I but early known
Thy wond'rous worth, thou excellent young man,
We had been happier both. *Ib.*

13 With rough, majestic force he mov'd the heart,
With strength and nature made amends for art.
[On Shakespeare.] *Jane Shore*, prologue

14 If I boast of aught,
Be it, to have been Heaven's happy instrument,
The means of good to all my fellow-creatures;
This is a King's best praise. *Tamerlaine*, II. ii

15 Death is parting,
'Tis the last sad adieu 'twixt soul and body. *Ib.*

16 Think on the sacred dictates of thy faith,
And let that arm thy virtue, to perform
What Cato's daughter durst not,—live Aspasia,
And dare to be unhappy. *Ib.* IV. i

'RED ROWLEY'

17 Mademoiselle from Armenteers,
Hasn't been kissed in forty years,
Hinky dinky, parley-voo.
Song of the Great War, 1914–18

MATTHEW ROYDON
fl. 1580–1622

18 A sweet attractive kind of grace,
A full assurance given by looks,
Continual comfort in a face,
The lineaments of Gospel books;
I trow that countenance cannot lie,
Whose thoughts are legible in the eye.
An Elegy, or Friend's Passion, for his Astrophill (i.e. Sir Philip Sidney), xviii

19 Was never eye, did see that face,
Was never ear, did hear that tongue,
Was never mind, did mind his grace,
That ever thought the travel long—
But eyes, and ears, and ev'ry thought,
Were with his sweet perfections caught. *Ib.* xix

JOHN RUSKIN
1819–1900

20 You know there are a great many odd styles of architecture about; you don't want to do anything ridiculous; you hear of me, among others, as a respectable architectural man-milliner; and you send for me, that I may tell you the leading fashion.
The Crown of Wild Olive, § 53, lecture ii. *Traffic*

21 Thackeray settled like a meat-fly on whatever one had got for dinner, and made one sick of it.
Fors Clavigera, letter xxxi

22 [On Whistler's 'Nocturne in Black and Gold']
I have seen, and heard, much of Cockney impudence before now; but never expected to hear a coxcomb ask two hundred guineas for flinging a pot of paint in the public's face. *Ib.* letter lxxix, 18 June 1877

23 No person who is not a great sculptor or painter *can* be an architect. If he is not a sculptor or painter, he can only be a *builder*.
Lectures on Architecture and Painting, § 61, Addenda

24 There is nothing in sea-description, detailed, like Dickens' storm at the death of Ham, in 'David Copperfield'.
Modern Painters (1888), vol. i, pt. ii, p. 425, note

25 What is poetry? The suggestion, by the imagination, of noble grounds for the noble emotions.
Ib. vol. iii

26 All violent feelings . . . produce in us a falseness in all our impressions of external things, which I would generally characterize as the 'Pathetic Fallacy'. *Ib.*

27 Mountains are the beginning and the end of all natural scenery. *Ib.* vol. iv, pt. v, ch. 20, § 1

28 That mysterious forest below London Bridge.
Ib. vol. v, pt. ix, ch. 9, § 7

29 Its symmetry [be] as of thunder answering from two horizons. [A sentence of Johnson.]
Praeterita, I. xii. *Rosslyn Chapel*, § 251

1 There was a rocky valley between Buxton and Bakewell, . . . divine as the vale of Tempe; you might have seen the gods there morning and evening,—Apollo and the sweet Muses of the Light. . . . You enterprised a railroad, . . . you blasted its rocks away. . . . And now, every fool in Buxton can be at Bakewell in half-an-hour, and every fool in Bakewell at Buxton.
Praeterita, III. iv. *Joanna's Cave*, § 84, note

2 All books are divisible into two classes: the books of the hour, and the books of all time.
Sesame and Lilies, Lecture i. *Of Kings' Treasuries*, § 8

3 But whether thus submissively or not, at least be sure that you go to the author to get at *his* meaning, not to find yours. *Ib.* § 13

4 Which of us . . . is to do the hard and dirty work for the rest—and for what pay? Who is to do the pleasant and clean work, and for what pay?
Ib. § 30, note

5 What do we, as a nation, care about books? How much do you think we spend altogether on our libraries, public or private, as compared with what we spend on our horses? *Ib.* § 32

6 How long most people would look at the best book before they would give the price of a large turbot for it! *Ib.*

7 We call ourselves a rich nation, and we are filthy and foolish enough to thumb each other's books out of circulating libraries! *Ib.*

8 Will you not covet such power as this, and seek such throne as this, and be no more housewives, but queens? *Ib.* Lecture ii. *Of Queens' Gardens*, § 87

9 There is no putting by that crown; queens you must always be; queens to your lovers; queens to your husbands and your sons; queens of higher mystery to the world beyond. . . . But, alas! you are too often idle and careless queens, grasping at majesty in the least things, while you abdicate it in the greatest. *Ib.* § 90

10 I believe the right question to ask, respecting all ornament, is simply this: Was it done with enjoyment—was the carver happy while he was about it?
The Seven Lamps of Architecture, ch. 5. *The Lamp of Life*

11 Better the rudest work that tells a story or records a fact, than the richest without meaning. There should not be a single ornament put upon great civic buildings, without some intellectual intention.
Ib. ch. 6. *The Lamp of Memory*, § 7

12 When we build, let us think that we build for ever.
Ib. § 10

13 Remember that the most beautiful things in the world are the most useless; peacocks and lilies for instance. *The Stones of Venice*, vol. i, ch. 2, § 17

14 The purest and most thoughtful minds are those which love colour the most. *Ib.* vol. ii, ch. 5, § 30

15 All things are literally better, lovelier, and more beloved for the imperfections which have been divinely appointed, that the law of human life may be Effort, and the law of human judgment, Mercy. *Ib.* ch. vi, § 25

16 Fine art is that in which the hand, the head, and the heart of man go together.
The Two Paths, Lecture ii

17 Not only is there but one way of *doing* things rightly, but there is only one way of *seeing* them, and that is, seeing the whole of them. *Ib.*

18 Nobody cares much at heart about Titian; only there is a strange undercurrent of everlasting murmur about his name, which means the deep consent of all great men that he is greater than they. *Ib.*

19 No human being, however great, or powerful, was ever so free as a fish. *Ib.* Lecture v

20 Labour without joy is base. Labour without sorrow is base. Sorrow without labour is base. Joy without labour is base. *Time and Tide*, letter v

21 Your honesty is *not* to be based either on religion or policy. Both your religion and policy must be based on *it*. Your honesty must be based, as the sun is, in vacant heaven; poised, as the lights in the firmament, which have rule over the day and over the night. *Ib.* letter viii

22 To make your children *capable of honesty* is the beginning of education. *Ib.*

23 I hold it for indisputable, that the first duty of a State is to see that every child born therein shall be well housed, clothed, fed, and educated, till it attain years of discretion. But in order to the effecting this the Government must have an authority over the people of which we now do not so much as dream. *Ib.* letter xiii

24 It ought to be quite as natural and straightforward a matter for a labourer to take his pension from his parish, because he has deserved well of his parish, as for a man in higher rank to take his pension from his country, because he has deserved well of his country. *Unto this Last*, preface, § 6 (4)

25 The force of the guinea you have in your pocket depends wholly on the default of a guinea in your neighbour's pocket. If he did not want it, it would be of no use to you. *Ib.* Essay ii, § 27

26 Soldiers of the ploughshare as well as soldiers of the sword. *Ib.* Essay iii, § 54

27 Government and co-operation are in all things the laws of life; anarchy and competition the laws of death. *Ib.*

28 Whereas it has long been known and declared that the poor have no right to the property of the rich, I wish it also to be known and declared that the rich have no right to the property of the poor. *Ib.*

29 There is no wealth but life. *Ib.* Essay iv, § 77

30 There is really no such thing as bad weather, only different kinds of good weather.
Quoted by Lord Avebury

31 Trust thou thy Love: if she be proud, is she not sweet?
Trust thou thy Love: if she be mute, is she not pure?
Lay thou thy soul full in her hands, low at her feet;—
Fail, Sun and Breath!—yet, for thy peace, she shall endure. *Trust Thou Thy Love*

LORD JOHN RUSSELL
1792–1878

1 If peace cannot be maintained with honour, it is no longer peace.
   Speech. Greenock, 19 Sept. 1853. The Times, 21 Sept. 1853

2 Among the defects of the Bill, which were numerous, one provision was conspicuous by its presence and another by its absence.
   Speech to the electors of the City of London, Apr. 1859

3 A proverb is one man's wit and all men's wisdom.
   Ascribed

SIR WILLIAM HOWARD RUSSELL
1820–1907

4 [The Russians] dash on towards that thin red line tipped with steel.
   The British Expedition to the Crimea (1877), p. 156

CHARLES SACKVILLE
see
EARL OF DORSET

JOHN L. ST. JOHN

5 Archibald—certainly not!   *Title of Song*

WARHAM ST. LEGER 1850–c. 1915

6 There is a fine stuffed chavender,
   A chavender, or chub,
   That decks the rural pavender,
   The pavender, or pub,
   Wherein I eat my gravender,
   My gravender, or grub.
   The Chavender, or Chub, st. 1

CHARLES-AUGUSTIN SAINTE-BEUVE
1804–1869

7   Et Vigny plus secret,
   Comme en sa tour d'ivoire, avant midi rentrait.
        And Vigny more reserved,
   Returned ere noon, within his ivory tower.
   Quoted in Paléologue's Vigny, p. 71

'SAKI'
[HECTOR HUGH MUNRO]
1870–1916

8 'The man is a common murderer.'
   'A common murderer, possibly, but a very uncommon cook.'
   Beasts and Super-Beasts. The Blind Spot

9 When she inveighed eloquently against the evils of capitalism at drawing-room meetings and Fabian conferences she was conscious of a comfortable feeling that the system, with all its inequalities and iniquities, would probably last her time. It is one of the consolations of middle-aged reformers that the good they inculcate must live after them if it is to live at all.   *Ib. The Byzantine Omelette*

10 Waldo is one of those people who would be enormously improved by death.
   Ib. The Feast of Nemesis

11 He's simply got the instinct for being unhappy highly developed.
   Chronicles of Clovis. The Match-Maker

12 Oysters are more beautiful than any religion. . . . There's nothing in Christianity or Buddhism that quite matches the sympathetic unselfishness of an oyster.   *Ib.*

13 The cook was a good cook, as cooks go; and as cooks go she went.   *Reginald. Reginald on Besetting Sins*

14 Women and elephants never forget an injury.   *Ib.*

15 Addresses are given to us to conceal our whereabouts.
   Reginald in Russia. Cross Currents

16 The Western custom of one wife and hardly any mistresses.   *Ib. A Young Turkish Catastrophe*

17 But, good gracious, you've got to educate him first. You can't expect a boy to be vicious till he's been to a good school.   *Ib. The Baker's Dozen*

18 In baiting a mouse-trap with cheese, always leave room for the mouse.
   The Square Egg. The Infernal Parliament

19 Children with Hyacinth's temperament don't know better as they grow older; they merely know more.
   The Toys of Peace. Hyacinth

GEORGE AUGUSTUS SALA
1828–1896

20 And now, Sir, we will take a walk down Fleet Street.
   Motto of the Temple Bar *magazine. Ascribed to Dr. Johnson.*

JOHN OF SALISBURY
d. 1180

21 Siquidem uita breuis, sensus hebes, negligentiae torpor, inutilis occupatio, nos paucula, scire permittunt, et eadem iugiter excutit et auellit ab animo fraudatrix scientiae, inimica et infida semper memoriae nouerca, obliuio.

   The brevity of our life, the dullness of our senses, the torpor of our indifference, the futility of our occupation, suffer us to know but little: and that little is soon shaken and then torn from the mind by that traitor to learning, that hostile and faithless stepmother to memory, oblivion.
   Prologue to the Policraticus. (C. C. J. Webb's edition, vol. i, p. 12, ll. 13–16.) Trans. by Helen Waddell

ROBERT CECIL, LORD SALISBURY
1830–1903

22 By office boys for office boys.
   Remark about The Daily Mail. *See H. Hamilton Fyfe:* Northcliffe, an Intimate Biography, *ch. 4*

SALLUST
86–34 B.C.

23 Sed res docuit id verum esse, quod in carminibus Appius ait, fabrum esse suae quemque fortunae.

   But the case has proved that to be true which Appius says in his songs, that each man is the maker of his own fate.   *Ad Caesarem, 1. i. 2*

1 Alieni appetens, sui profusus.

    Coveting the property of others, lavish of his own.
                               Catiline, 5

2 Idem velle atque idem nolle, ea demum firma amicitia est.

    Friendship is this—to desire, and to dislike, the same thing.   *Ib.* 20

3 Pro patria, pro liberis, pro aris atque focis suis.

    On behalf of their country, their children, their altars, and their hearths.   *Ib.* 59

4 Urbem venalem et mature perituram, si emptorem invenerit.

    The venal city soon to perish, if a buyer can be found.   *Jugurtha*, 35

5 Punica fide.

    With Carthaginian faith [i.e. treachery]. *Ib.* 108, 3

IRA DAVID SANKEY (1840–1908)

See Corrigenda

6 Light in the darkness, sailor, day is at hand!
  See o'er the foaming billows fair Heaven's land.
  Drear was the voyage, sailor, now almost o'er;
  Safe within the lifeboat, sailor, pull for the shore.
  Pull for the shore, sailor, pull for the shore!
  Heed not the rolling waves, but bend to the oar.
        Sacred Songs and Solos. The Life Boat

7 Is there room for Mary there?
  Yes, there's room; yes, there's room;
  Room in the beautiful heavenly land.
                  Ib. Little Mary

8 Shall we gather at the river? . . .
  Yes, we'll gather at the river,
  The beautiful, the beautiful river,
  Gather with the saints at the river,
  That flows by the throne of God.
        Ib. No. 1000. Shall We Gather

9 In the sweet by-and-by,
  We shall meet on that beautiful shore.
               Ib. Sweet By-and-By

10 That will be glory for me.
      Ib. That Will Be Heaven For Me

EPES SARGENT

1813–1880

11 A life on the ocean wave,
  A home on the rolling deep.
          A Life on the Ocean Wave

SIEGFRIED SASSOON

1886–1967

12 If I were fierce and bald and short of breath,
  I'd live with scarlet Majors at the Base,
  And speed glum heroes up the line to death.
                Base Details

13 And when the war is done and youth stone dead
  I'd toddle safely home and die—in bed. *Ib.*

14 Everyone suddenly burst out singing.
                  Everyone Sang

15   The song was wordless;
  The singing will never be done.   *Ib.*

RICHARD SAVAGE

d. 1743

16 No tenth transmitter of a foolish face.
               The Bastard, 1. 8

17 Perhaps been poorly rich, and meanly great,
  The slave of pomp, a cipher in the state. *Ib.* 1. 39

18 May see thee now, though late, redeem thy name,
  And glorify what else is damn'd to fame.
      Character of the Rev. James Foster, 1. 45

GEORGE SAVILE, MARQUIS OF HALIFAX

see

HALIFAX

HENRY J. SAYERS

d. 1932

19 Ta-ra-ra-boom-de-ay!   *Title of Song* (1891)

FRIEDRICH VON SCHELLING

1775–1854

20 Architecture in general is frozen music.
              Philosophie der Kunst

FRIEDRICH VON SCHILLER

1759–1805

21 Freude, schöner Götterfunken,
  Tochter aus Elysium,
  Wir betreten Feuertrunken,
  Himmlische, dein Heiligtum.
  Deine Zauber binden wieder,
  Was die Mode streng geteilt,
  Alle Menschen werden Brüder
  Wo dein sanfter Flügel weilt.

    Thou radiance sprung from God Himself,
    Thou daughter of Elysium, Joy,
    Thy shrine we tread, Thou Maid Divine,
    Though light's excess our sense destroy.
    What harsh world-use has rent apart,
    Thy healing spells restore again;
    Where'er Thy gentle wings may rest,
    Brothers we find our fellow-men.   *An die Freude*

22 Die Sonne geht in meinem Staat nicht unter.
  The sun does not set in my dominions.
  [Philip II.]   *Don Carlos*, Act 1, sc. 6

23 Mit der Dummheit kämpfen Götter selbst vergebens.
  With stupidity the gods themselves struggle in vain.
           Jungfrau von Orleans, III. vi

24 Die Weltgeschichte ist das Weltgericht.
  The world's history is the world's judgement.
  1st lecture as Prof. of History, Jena. 26 May 1789

25 Ein ruheloser Marsch war unser Leben
  Und wie des Windes Sausen, heimatlos,
  Durchstürmten wir die kriegbewegte Erde.

    Our life was but a battle and a march
    And like the wind's blast, never-resting, homeless,
    We stormed across the war-convulsèd heath.
  Wallenstein's Tod, iii. 15 (Coleridge's translation)

1 Gedanken sind zollfrei.

Thoughts are free from toll.

(*Compare* William Camden, *Remains*, p. 332.)
Quoted from Luther, *Von weltlicher Oberkeit,
wie man ihr Gehorsam schuldig sei*

MAX SCHNECKENBURGER

1819–1849

2 Die Wacht am Rhein.

The watch on the Rhine.   *Title of Song*

LOUIS SCHNEIDER

3 O Tannenbaum, O Tannenbaum,
Wie grün sind deine Blätter!

O pine-tree, O pine-tree,
How green are thy leaves!
            Der Kurmärker und die Picarde

CHARLES PRESTWICH SCOTT

1846–1932

4 The newspaper is of necessity something of a monopoly, and its first duty is to shun the temptations
of monopoly. Its primary office is the gathering of
news. At the peril of its soul it must see that the
supply is not tainted. Neither in what it gives, nor
in what it does not give, nor in the mode of
presentation, must the unclouded face of truth
suffer wrong. Comment is free but facts are sacred.
            In the Manchester Guardian, 6 May 1926

ROBERT FALCON SCOTT

1868–1912

5 Great God! this is an awful place. [The South Pole.]
            Journal, 17 Jan. 1912

6 For God's sake look after our people.
            Ib. 25 March 1912

7 Had we lived, I should have had a tale to tell of the
hardihood, endurance, and courage of my companions which would have stirred the heart of every
Englishman. These rough notes and our dead
bodies must tell the tale.   *Message to the Public*

SIR WALTER SCOTT

1771–1832

8 To the Lords of Convention 'twas Claver'se who
spoke,
'Ere the King's crown shall fall there are crowns to
be broke;
So let each cavalier who loves honour and me,
Come follow the bonnet of Bonny Dundee.
   Come fill up my cup, come fill up my can,
   Come saddle your horses, and call up your men;
   Come open the West Port, and let me gang free,
   And it's room for the bonnets of Bonny Dundee!'
            Bonny Dundee. (*The Doom of Devorgoil*, Act II,
sc. ii)

9 But answer came there none.
            Bridal of Triermain, c. III. x

10 Here lies that peerless paper peer Lord Peter,
Who broke the laws of God and man and metre.
            Epitaph for Patrick ('Peter'), *Lord Robertson*

11 The stag at eve had drunk his fill,
Where danced the moon on Monan's rill,
And deep his midnight lair had made
In lone Glenartney's hazel shade.
            The Lady of the Lake, c. I.

12 A moment gazed adown the dale,
A moment snuff'd the tainted gale.   *Ib. ii*

13 Two dogs of black Saint Hubert's breed,
Unmatch'd for courage, breath, and speed.   *Ib. vii*

14 Woe worth the chase, woe worth the day,
That costs thy life, my gallant grey!   *Ib. ix*

15 In listening mood, she seem'd to stand,
The guardian Naiad of the strand.   *Ib. xvii*

16 And ne'er did Grecian chisel trace
A Nymph, a Naiad, or a Grace
Of finer form, or lovelier face!
What though the sun, with ardent frown,
Had slightly tinged her cheek with brown.   *Ib. xviii*

17 The will to do, the soul to dare.   *Ib. xxi*

18 His ready speech flow'd fair and free,
In phrase of gentlest courtesy;
Yet seem'd that tone, and gesture bland,
Less used to sue than to command.   *Ib.*

19 Soldier, rest! thy warfare o'er,
   Sleep the sleep that knows not breaking,
Dream of battled fields no more,
   Days of danger, nights of waking.   *Ib. xxxi*

20 Huntsman, rest! thy chase is done.   *Ib. xxxii*

21 Hail to the Chief who in triumph advances!
            Ib. c. II. xix

22 He is gone on the mountain,
   He is lost to the forest,
Like a summer-dried fountain,
   When our need was the sorest.   *Ib. c. III. xvi*

23 Like the dew on the mountain,
   Like the foam on the river,
Like the bubble on the fountain,
   Thou art gone, and for ever!   *Ib.*

24 Which spills the foremost foeman's life,
That party conquers in the strife!   *Ib. c. IV. vi*

25 'These are Clan Alpine's warriors true;
And, Saxon,—I am Roderick Dhu!'   *Ib. c. V. ix*

26 'Come one, come all! this rock shall fly
From its firm base as soon as I.'   *Ib. x*

27 Respect was mingled with surprise,
And the stern joy which warriors feel
In foemen worthy of their steel.   *Ib.*

28 Where, where was Roderick then?
One blast upon his bugle-horn
Were worth a thousand men!   *Ib. c. VI. xviii*

29 The way was long, the wind was cold,
The Minstrel was infirm and old;
His wither'd cheek and tresses grey,
Seem'd to have known a better day.
The harp, his sole remaining joy,
Was carried by an orphan boy.
The last of all the Bards was he,
Who sung of Border chivalry;
For, welladay! their date was fled,
His tuneful brethren all were dead;
And he, neglected and oppress'd,
Wish'd to be with them, and at rest.
            The Lay of the Last Minstrel, introd. l. 1

1 The unpremeditated lay.
The Lay of the Last Minstrel, introd. l. 18

2 Old times were changed, old manners gone;
A stranger fill'd the Stuarts' throne;
The bigots of the iron time
Had call'd his harmless art a crime. *Ib.* l. 19

3 Nine-and-twenty knights of fame
Hung their shields in Branksome Hall;
Nine-and-twenty squires of name
Brought them their steeds to bower from stall;
Nine-and-twenty yeomen tall
Waited, duteous, on them all:
They were all knights of mettle true,
Kinsmen to the bold Buccleuch. *Ib. c.* I. iii

4 They carv'd at the meal
With gloves of steel,
And they drank the red wine through the helmet
barr'd. *Ib.* iv

5 Such is the custom of Branksome Hall. *Ib.* vii

6 Vengeance, deep-brooding o'er the slain,
Had lock'd the source of softer woe;
And burning pride and high disdain
Forbade the rising tear to flow. *Ib.* ix

7 To her bidding she could bow
The viewless forms of air. *Ib.* xii

8 What shall be the maiden's fate?
Who shall be the maiden's mate? *Ib.* xvi

9 Steady of heart, and stout of hand. *Ib.* xxi

10 Sir William of Deloraine, good at need. *Ib.* xxii

11 Yet, through good heart, and Oure Ladye's grace,
At length he gain'd the landing-place. *Ib.* xxix

12 If thou would'st view fair Melrose aright,
Go visit it by the pale moonlight;
For the gay beams of lightsome day
Gild, but to flout, the ruins grey. *Ib. c.* II. i

13 Strange sounds along the chancel pass'd,
The banner wav'd without a blast. *Ib.* xvi

14 Yet somewhat was he chill'd with dread,
And his hair did bristle upon his head. *Ib.*

15 I cannot tell how the truth may be;
I say the tale as 'twas said to me. *Ib.* xxii

16 In peace, Love tunes the shepherd's reed;
In war, he mounts the warrior's steed;
In halls, in gay attire is seen;
In hamlets, dances on the green.
Love rules the court, the camp, the grove,
And men below, and saints above;
For love is heaven, and heaven is love. *Ib. c.* III. ii

17 And laugh'd, and shouted, 'Lost! lost! lost!' *Ib.* xiii

18 Why, when the volleying musket play'd
Against the bloody Highland blade,
Why was not I beside him laid!
Enough, he died the death of fame;
Enough, he died with conquering Graeme. *Ib. c.* IV. ii

19 For ne'er
Was flattery lost on poet's ear:
A simple race! they waste their toil
For the vain tribute of a smile. *Ib.* conclusion

20 Call it not vain; they do not err,
Who say, that when the Poet dies,
Mute Nature mourns her worshipper,
And celebrates his obsequies.
The Lay of the Last Minstrel, c. V. i

21 The secret sympathy,
The silver link, the silken tie,
Which heart to heart, and mind to mind,
In body and in soul can bind. *Ib.* xiii

22 Breathes there the man, with soul so dead,
Who never to himself hath said,
This is my own, my native land!
Whose heart hath ne'er within him burn'd,
As home his footsteps he hath turn'd
From wandering on a foreign strand!
If such there breathe, go, mark him well;
For him no Minstrel raptures swell;
High though his titles, proud his name,
Boundless his wealth as wish can claim;
Despite those titles, power, and pelf,
The wretch, concentred all in self,
Living, shall forfeit fair renown,
And, doubly dying, shall go down
To the vile dust, from whence he sprung,
Unwept, unhonour'd, and unsung.
O Caledonia! stern and wild,
Meet nurse for a poetic child!
Land of brown heath and shaggy wood,
Land of the mountain and the flood,
Land of my sires! what mortal hand
Can e'er untie the filial band
That knits me to thy rugged strand! *Ib. c.* VI. i–ii

23 For Love will still be lord of all. *Ib.* xi

24 The elvish page fell to the ground,
And, shuddering, mutter'd, 'Found! found! found!' *Ib.* xxiv

25 That day of wrath, that dreadful day,
When heaven and earth shall pass away. *Ib.* xxxi

26 The dew that on the violet lies
Mocks the dark lustre of thine eyes.
The Lord of the Isles, c. I. iii

27 To show the form it seem'd to hide. *Ib.* v

28 Thus, then, my noble foe I greet;
Health and high fortune till we meet,
And then—what pleases Heaven. *Ib. c.* III. vi

29 Scenes sung by him who sings no more!
His bright and brief career is o'er,
And mute his tuneful strains. *Ib. c.* IV. xi

30 O! many a shaft, at random sent,
Finds mark the archer little meant!
And many a word, at random spoken,
May soothe or wound a heart that's broken. *Ib. c.* V. xviii

31 To that dark inn, the grave! *Ib. c.* VI. xxvi

32 O hush thee, my babie, thy sire was a knight,
Thy mother a lady, both lovely and bright.
Lullaby of an Infant Chief

33 Then hush thee, my darling, take rest while you may,
For strife comes with manhood, and waking with day. *Ib.*

34 O lovers' eyes are sharp to see,
And lovers' ears in hearing. *The Maid of Neidpath*

35 Till through her wasted hand, at night,
You saw the taper burning. *Ib.*

1 November's sky is chill and drear,
November's leaf is red and sear.

Marmion, c. I, introd. i

2 To him, as to the burning levin,
Short, bright, resistless course was given. *Ib.* vi

3 Had'st thou but liv'd, though stripp'd of power,
A watchman on the lonely tower. [On Pitt.] *Ib.* viii

4 Now is the stately column broke,
The beacon-light is quench'd in smoke,
The trumpet's silver sound is still,
The warder silent on the hill! [On Pitt.] *Ib.*

5 Drop upon Fox's grave the tear,
'Twill trickle to his rival's bier;
O'er Pitt's the mournful requiem sound,
And Fox's shall the notes rebound. *Ib.* xi

6 But search the land of living men,
Where wilt thou find their like agen? *Ib.*

7 Profan'd the God-given strength, and marr'd the
lofty line. *Ib.* xvi

8 His square-turn'd joints, and strength of limb,
Show'd him no carpet knight so trim,
But in close fight a champion grim,
In camps a leader sage. *Ib.* c. I. v

9 Stout heart, and open hand! *Ib.* x

10 And come he slow, or come he fast,
It is but Death who comes at last. *Ib.* c. II. xxx

11 When Prussia hurried to the field,
And snatch'd the spear, but left the shield!

Ib. c. III, introd. l. 63

12 Where shall the lover rest,
Whom the fates sever
From his true maiden's breast,
Parted for ever?
Where, through groves deep and high,
Sounds the far billow,
Where early violets die,
Under the willow. *Ib.* c. III. x

13 In the lost battle,
Borne down by the flying,
Where mingles war's rattle
With groans of the dying. *Ib.* xi

14 Still is thy name in high account,
And still thy verse has charms,
Sir David Lindesay of the Mount,
Lord Lion King-at-arms! *Ib.* c. IV. vii

15 O, young Lochinvar is come out of the west,
Through all the wide Border his steed was the best.

Ib. c. v. xii

16 So faithful in love, and so dauntless in war,
There never was knight like the young Lochinvar.

Ib.

17 For a laggard in love, and a dastard in war,
Was to wed the fair Ellen of brave Lochinvar. *Ib.*

18 'O come ye in peace here, or come ye in war,
Or to dance at our bridal, young Lord Lochinvar?'

Ib.

19 'To lead but one measure, drink one cup of wine.'

Ib.

20 With a smile on her lips, and a tear in her eye. *Ib.*

21 'Now tread we a measure!' said young Lochinvar.

Ib.

22 'She is won! we are gone, over bank, bush, and
scaur;
They'll have fleet steeds that follow' quoth young
Lochinvar. *Marmion*, c. v. xii

23 Heap on more wood!—the wind is chill;
But let it whistle as it will,
We'll keep our Christmas merry still.

Ib. c. VI, introd. i

24 England was merry England, when
Old Christmas brought his sports again.
'Twas Christmas broach'd the mightiest ale;
'Twas Christmas told the merriest tale;
A Christmas gambol oft could cheer
The poor man's heart through half the year. *Ib.* iii

25 What skilful limner e'er would choose
To paint the rainbow's varying hues,
Unless to mortal it were given
To dip his brush in dyes of heaven? *Ib.* v

26 My castles are my King's alone,
From turret to foundation-stone—
The hand of Douglas is his own. *Ib.* xiii

27 'And dar'st thou then
To beard the lion in his den,
The Douglas in his hall?
And hop'st thou thence unscathed to go?
No, by Saint Bride of Bothwell, no!
Up drawbridge, grooms—what, warder, ho!
Let the portcullis fall.' *Ib.* xiv

28 O what a tangled web we weave,
When first we practise to deceive! *Ib.* xvii

29 Scarce could they hear, or see their foes,
Until at weapon-point they close.
They close, in clouds of smoke and dust,
With sword-sway, and with lance's thrust;
And such a yell was there,
Of sudden and portentous birth,
As if men fought upon the earth,
And fiends in upper air. *Ib.* xxv

30 Good-night to Marmion. *Ib.* xxviii

31 O Woman! in our hours of ease,
Uncertain, coy, and hard to please,
And variable as the shade
By the light quivering aspen made;
When pain and anguish wring the brow,
A ministering angel thou! *Ib.* xxx

32 'Charge, Chester, charge! On, Stanley, on!'
Were the last words of Marmion. *Ib.* xxxii

33 Where's now their victor vaward wing,
Where Huntley, and where Home?—
O, for a blast of that dread horn,
On Fontarabian echoes borne! *Ib.* xxxiii

34 The stubborn spear-men still made good
Their dark impenetrable wood,
Each stepping where his comrade stood,
The instant that he fell. *Ib.* xxxiv

35 Still from the sire the son shall hear
Of the stern strife, and carnage drear,
Of Flodden's fatal field,
Where shiver'd was fair Scotland's spear,
And broken was her shield! *Ib.*

36 To all, to each, a fair good-night,
And pleasing dreams, and slumbers light!

Ib. L'envoy

SCOTT

1 But Nora's heart is lost and won,
—She's wedded to the Earlie's son! *Nora's Vow*

2 Pibroch of Donuil Dhu,
Pibroch of Donuil,
Wake thy wild voice anew,
Summon Clan-Conuil.
Come away, come away,
Hark to the summons!
Come in your war array,
Gentles and commons. *Pibroch of Donuil Dhu*

3 Leave untended the herd,
The flock without shelter;
Leave the corpse uninterr'd,
The bride at the altar. *Ib.*

4 Come as the winds come, when
Forests are rended,
Come as the waves come, when
Navies are stranded. *Ib.*

5 Still are the thoughts to memory dear.
Rokeby, c. I. xxxiii

6 A mother's pride, a father's joy! *Ib.* c. III. xv

7 O, Brignal banks are wild and fair,
And Greta woods are green,
And you may gather garlands there
Would grace a summer queen. *Ib.* xvi

8 A weary lot is thine, fair maid,
A weary lot is thine!
To pull the thorn thy brow to braid,
And press the rue for wine! *Ib.* xxviii

9 He turn'd his charger as he spake,
Upon the river shore,
He gave his bridle-reins a shake,
Said 'Adieu for evermore,
My love!
And adieu for evermore.' *Ib.*

10 Tramp! tramp! along the land they rode,
Splash! splash! along the sea. *William and Helen*

11 You . . . whirl'd them to the back o' beyont.
The Antiquary, ch. 2

12 Praetorian here, Praetorian there, I mind the bigging
o't. *Ib.* ch. 4

13 It's no fish ye're buying—it's men's lives. *Ib.* ch. 11

14 Widow'd wife, and married maid,
Betrothed, betrayer, and betray'd!
The Betrothed, ch. 15

15 Woman's faith, and woman's trust—
Write the characters in dust. *Ib.* ch. 20

16 Look not thou on beauty's charming,—
Sit thou still when kings are arming,—
Taste not when the wine-cup glistens,—
Speak not when the people listens,—
Stop thine ear against the singer,—
From the red gold keep thy finger;—
Vacant heart and hand, and eye,—
Easy live and quiet die.
The Bride of Lammermoor, ch. 3

17 When the last Laird of Ravenswood to Ravenswood
shall ride,
And woo a dead maiden to be his bride,
He shall stable his steed in the Kelpie's flow,
And his name shall be lost for evermoe! *Ib.* ch. 18

18 I live by twa trades, sir, . . . fiddle, sir, and spade;
filling the world, and emptying of it. *Ib.* ch. 24

19 Her winding-sheet is up as high as her throat
already. *The Bride of Lammermoor*, ch. 34

20 An ower true tale. *Ib.*

21 Touch not the cat but[1] a glove.
The Fair Maid of Perth, ch. 34
[1] without.

22 But no one shall find me rowing against the stream.
I care not who knows it—I write for the general
amusement.
The Fortunes of Nigel, introductory epistle

23 It's ill taking the breeks aff a wild Highlandman.
Ib. ch. 5

24 For a con-si-de-ra-tion. *Ib.* ch. 22

25 To be plain, if your lordship does not ken when you
have a good servant, I ken when I have a kind
master. *Ib.* ch. 31

26 O Geordie, Jingling Geordie, it was grand to hear
Baby Charles laying down the guilt of dissimulation, and Steenie lecturing on the turpitude of
incontinence. *Ib.*

27 (He) was ever after designated as a 'stickit minister'.
Guy Mannering, ch. 2

28 Twist ye, twine[2] ye! even so
Mingle shades of joy and woe,
Hope and fear, and peace and strife,
In the thread of human life. *Ib.* ch. 4
[2] divide.

29 'Ride your ways,' said the gipsy, 'ride your ways,
Laird of Ellangowan—ride your ways, Godfrey
Bertram!—This day have ye quenched seven
smoking hearths—see if the fire in your ain parlour
burn the blither for that. Ye have riven the thack off
seven cottar houses—look if your ain roof-tree
stand the faster.—Ye may stable your stirks in the
shealings at Derncleugh—see that the hare does
not couch on the hearthstane at Ellangowan.'
Ib. ch. 8

30 MRS. BERTRAM:
That sounds like nonsense, my dear.
MR. BERTRAM:
May be so, my dear; but it may be very good law
for all that. *Ib.* ch. 9

31 Sophia, as you well know, followed me to India. She
was as innocent as gay; but, unfortunately for us
both, as gay as innocent. *Ib.* ch. 12

32 'Pro-di-gi-ous!' exclaimed Dominie Sampson.
Ib. ch. 14

33 Gin by pailfuls, wine in rivers,
Dash the window-glass to shivers!
For three wild lads were we, brave boys,
And three wild lads were we;
Thou on the land, and I on the sand,
And Jack on the gallows-tree! *Ib.* ch. 34

34 The ancient and now forgotten pastime of high jinks.
Ib. ch. 36

35 And Bertram's right and Bertram's might
Shall meet on Ellangowan's height. *Ib.* ch. 46

36 The hour is come, but not the man.
The Heart of Midlothian, ch. 4, heading

37 The passive resistance of the Tolbooth-gate.
Ib. ch. 6

1 Jock, when ye hae naething else to do, ye may be ay sticking in a tree; it will be growing, Jock, when ye're sleeping. *The Heart of Midlothian*, ch. 8

2 Proud Maisie is in the wood,
  Walking so early,
Sweet Robin sits in the bush,
  Singing so rarely. *Ib. ch. 40*

3 Come, trowl the brown bowl to me,
  Bully boy, bully boy,
Come, trowl the brown bowl to me:
Ho! jolly Jenkin, I spy a knave in drinking,
Come, trowl the brown bowl to me. *Ivanhoe, ch. 20*

4 'Pax vobiscum' will answer all queries. *Ib. ch. 26*

5 When Israel, of the Lord belov'd,
  Out of the land of bondage came,
Her fathers' God before her mov'd,
  An awful guide in smoke and flame. *Ib. ch. 39*

6 His morning walk was beneath the elms in the churchyard; 'for death,' he said, 'had been his next-door neighbour for so many years, that he had no apology for dropping the acquaintance.' *The Legend of Montrose*, introduction

7 But, my lord, there is a Southern proverb,—fine words butter no parsnips. *Ib. ch. 3*

8 March, march, Ettrick and Teviotdale,
Why the deil dinna ye march forward in order?
March, march, Eskdale and Liddesdale,
All the Blue Bonnets are bound for the Border. *The Monastery, ch. 25*

9 Ah! County Guy, the hour is nigh,
  The sun has left the lea,
The orange flower perfumes the bower,
  The breeze is on the sea. *Quentin Durward, ch. 4*

10 And it's ill speaking between a fou man and a fasting. *Redgauntlet*, Letter 11, *Wandering Willie's Tale*

11 Better a finger off, as ay wagging. *Ib. ch. 2*

12 The ae half of the warld thinks the tither daft. *Ib. ch. 7*

13 Over the water, and over the sea,
  And over the water to Charlie;
Come weal, come woe, we'll gather and go,
  And live or die with Charlie. *Ib. ch. 11*

14 But with the morning cool repentance came. *Rob Roy, ch. 12*

15 Come fill up my cup, come fill up my cann,
Come saddle my horses, and call up my man;
Come open your gates, and let me gae free,
I daurna stay langer in bonny Dundee. *Ib. ch. 23*

16 If your honour disna ken when ye hae a gude servant, I ken when I hae a gude master, and the deil be in my feet gin I leave ye. *Ib. ch. 24*

17 It's a far cry to Lochow. *Ib. ch. 29, note*

18 There's a gude time coming. *Ib. ch. 32*

19 Speak out, sir, and do not Maister or Campbell me— my foot is on my native heath, and my name is MacGregor! *Ib. ch. 34*

20 Fair, fat, and forty. *St. Ronan's Well, ch. 7*

21 'I doubt', said Bruce, 'that I have slain the Red Comyn.'
'Do you leave such a matter in doubt?' said Kirkpatrick. 'I will make sicker.' *Tales of a Grandfather, ch. 8*

22 The play-bill, which is said to have announced the tragedy of Hamlet, the character of the Prince of Denmark being left out. *The Talisman*, introduction. *For an earlier report of this anecdote see* T.L.S. *3 June 1939*

23 Rouse the lion from his lair. *Ib. ch. 6*

24 My heart's in the Highlands, my heart is not here,
My heart's in the Highlands a-chasing the deer;
A-chasing the wild deer, and following the roe,
My heart's in the Highlands wherever I go. *Waverley, ch. 28. But see* Corrigenda

25 Bring the bowl which you boast,
  Fill it up to the brim;
Here's to him we love most,
  And to all who love him.
Brave gallants, stand up,
  And avaunt ye, base carles!
Were there death in the cup,
  Here's a health to King Charles! *Woodstock, ch. 20*

26 But I must say to the Muse of fiction, as the Earl of Pembroke said to the ejected nun of Wilton, 'Go spin, you jade, go spin!' *Journal, 9 Feb. 1826*

27 I . . . have arrived at a *flocci-pauci-nihili-pili-fication* of money, and I thank Shenstone for inventing that long word. *Ib. 8 March 1826*

28 The Big Bow-Wow strain I can do myself like any now going; but the exquisite touch, which renders ordinary commonplace things and characters interesting, from the truth of the description and the sentiment, is denied to me. [On Jane Austen.] *Ib. 14 Mar. 1826*

29 I would like to be there, were it but to see how the cat jumps. *Ib. 7 Oct. 1826*

30 The blockheads talk of my being like Shakespeare— not fit to tie his brogues. *Ib. 11 Dec. 1826*

31 From the lone shieling of the misty island
  Mountains divide us, and the waste of seas—
Yet still the blood is strong, the heart is Highland,
  And we in dreams behold the Hebrides!
Fair these broad meads, these hoary woods are grand;
But we are exiles from our fathers' land.
Canadian Boat Song. Of disputed authorship.
See *Times Literary Supplement*, 23 Dec. 1904, G. M. Fraser's *article.*

WILLIAM SCOTT, LORD STOWELL

1745–1836

32 The elegant simplicity of the three per cents. Campbell's *Chancellors* (1857), vol. x, ch. 212, p. 218

33 A precedent embalms a principle. *An Opinion, while Advocate-General, 1788. Attrib.*

SCOTTISH METRICAL PSALMS

1650

1 The Lord's my shepherd, I'll not want.
　　He makes me down to lie
In pastures green: he leadeth me
　　the quiet waters by.
My soul he doth restore again;
　　and me to walk doth make
Within the paths of righteousness,
　　ev'n for his own name's sake.

Yea, though I walk in death's dark vale,
　　yet will I fear none ill:
For thou art with me; and thy rod
　　and staff me comfort still.
My table thou hast furnished
　　in presence of my foes;
My head thou dost with oil anoint,
　　and my cup overflows.　　　*Psalm xxiii. 1*

2 Ye gates, lift up your heads on high;
　　ye doors that last for aye,
Be lifted up, that so the King
　　of glory enter may.
But who of glory is the King?
　　The mighty Lord is this;
Ev'n that same Lord, that great in might
　　and strong in battle is.

Ye gates, lift up your heads; ye doors,
　　doors that do last for aye,
Be lifted up, that so the King
　　of glory enter may.
But who is he that is the King
　　of glory? who is this?
The Lord of hosts, and none but he,
　　The King of glory is.　　　*Ib. xxiv. 7*

3 How lovely is thy dwelling-place,
　　O Lord of hosts, to me!
The tabernacles of thy grace
　　how pleasant, Lord, they be!
My thirsty soul longs veh'mently,
　　yea faints, thy courts to see:
My very heart and flesh cry out,
　　O living God, for thee.　　　*Ib. lxxxiv. 1*

4 I to the hills will lift mine eyes,
　　from whence doth come mine aid.
My safety cometh from the Lord,
　　who heav'n and earth hath made.　　　*Ib. cxxi. 1*

5 Pray that Jerusalem may have
　　peace and felicity:
Let them that love thee and thy peace
　　have still prosperity.　　　*Ib. cxxii. 1*

6 The race that long in darkness pin'd
　　have seen a glorious light.
　　　Paraphrase 19. Isaiah ix. 2–8

SIR OWEN SEAMAN

1861–1936

7 New Art would better Nature's best,
But Nature knows a thing or two.
　　　Battle of the Bays. Ars Postera, v

8 She must know all the needs of a rational being,
Be skilled to keep counsel, to comfort, to coax;
And, above all things else, be accomplished at seeing
　　My jokes.　　　*A Plea for Trigamy*

EDMUND HAMILTON SEARS

1810–1876

9 Calm on the listening ear of night
　　Came Heaven's melodious strains,
Where wild Judea stretches far
　　Her silver-mantled plains.
　　　Boston Observer, 1834. *Christmas Hymn: Calm on the Listening Ear*

10 It came upon the midnight clear,
　　That glorious song of old,
From Angels bending near the earth
　　To touch their harps of gold;
'Peace on the earth, good will to man
　　From Heaven's all gracious King.'
The world in solemn stillness lay
　　To hear the angels sing.
　　　The Christian Register (1850). *That Glorious Song of Old*

SIR CHARLES SEDLEY

1639?–1701

11 Ah, Chloris! that I now could sit
　　As unconcerned as when
Your infant beauty could beget
　　No pleasure, nor no pain!　　　*Child and Maiden*

12 Love still has something of the sea
　　From whence his mother rose.
　　　Love still has Something

13 Phyllis is my only joy,
　　Faithless as the winds or seas;
Sometimes coming, sometimes coy,
　　Yet she never fails to please.
　　　Song. Phyllis is my Only Joy

14 　　　　She deceiving,
　　　　　I believing;
What need lovers wish for more?　　　*Ib.*

15 Phyllis, without frown or smile,
Sat and knotted all the while.
　　　Song [Phyllis Knotting]. Hears not my Phyllis

16 Not, Celia, that I juster am
　　Or better than the rest,
For I would change each hour like them,
　　Were not my heart at rest.
　　　Song [To Celia]. Not, Celia, that I juster am

17 Why then should I seek farther store,
　　And still make love anew;
When change itself can give no more,
　　'Tis easy to be true.　　　*Ib.*

ALAN SEEGER

1888–1916

18 I have a rendezvous with Death
At some disputed barricade.
　　　I Have a Rendezvous with Death

SIR JOHN ROBERT SEELEY

1834–1895

19 We [the English] seem, as it were, to have conquered and peopled half the world in a fit of absence of mind.　　　*The Expansion of England*, Lecture I

20 History is past politics, and politics present history.
　　　Growth of British Policy

JOHN SELDEN
1584–1654

1 *Scrutamini scripturas.* These two words have undone the world.
Table Talk (1892), p. 10. *Bible, Scripture*

2 Old friends are best. King James used to call for his old shoes; they were easiest for his feet.
Ib. p. 71, *Friends*

3 'Tis not the drinking that is to be blamed, but the excess. *Ib.* p. 78. *Humility*

4 Ignorance of the law excuses no man; not that all men know the law, but because 'tis an excuse every man will plead, and no man can tell how to confute him. *Ib.* p. 99. *Law*

5 Take a straw and throw it up into the air, you shall see by that which way the wind is. *Ib.* 105. *Libels*

6 Marriage is nothing but a civil contract.
Ib. p. 109. *Marriage*

7 There never was a merry world since the fairies left off dancing, and the Parson left conjuring.
Ib. p. 130. *Parson*

8 There is not anything in the world so much abused as this sentence, *Salus populi suprema lex esto.*
Ib. p. 131. *People*

9 Philosophy is nothing but discretion.
Ib. p. 132. *Philosophy*

10 Pleasure is nothing else but the intermission of pain.
Ib. Pleasure

11 Preachers say, Do as I say, not as I do.
Ib. p. 147. *Preaching*

WALTER CARRUTHERS SELLAR
1898–
and
ROBERT JULIAN YEATMAN
contemporary

12 1066 and all that. *Title of Book*

13 The Roman Conquest was, however, a *Good Thing.*
1066, And All That, ch. 1

14 James I slobbered at the mouth and had favourites; he was thus a Bad King. *Ib.* ch. 34

15 The National Debt is a very Good Thing and it would be dangerous to pay it off for fear of Political Economy. *Ib.* ch. 38

16 Napoleon's armies always used to march on their stomachs, shouting: 'Vive l'Intérieur!' *Ib.* ch. 48

17 A Bad Thing: America was thus clearly top nation, and History came to a *Ib.* ch. 62

SENECA
d. A.D. 65

18 Contra bonum morem.
Against good custom. *Dialogues*, VI. i. 2

19 Illi mors gravis incubat
Qui notus nimis omnibus
Ignotus moritur sibi.
On him does death lie heavily who, but too well known to all, dies to himself unknown.
Thyestes, ii, chorus. Trans. by Miller

ROBERT WILLIAM SERVICE
1874–

20 This is the Law of the Yukon, that only the Strong shall thrive;
That surely the Weak shall perish, and only the Fit survive.
Dissolute, damned, and despairful, crippled and palsied and slain,
This is the Will of the Yukon,—Lo! how she makes it plain!
Songs of a Sourdough. The Law of the Yukon

21 The lady that's known as Lou.
Ib. The Shooting of Dan McGrew

22 The summer—no sweeter was ever;
The sunshiny woods all athrill;
The greyling aleap in the river,
The bighorn asleep on the hill.
The strong life that never knows harness;
The wilds where the caribou call;
The freshness, the freedom, the farness—
O God! how I'm stuck on it all.
Ib. The Spell of the Yukon

WILLIAM HENRY SEWARD
1801–1872

23 The Constitution devotes the domain to union, to justice, to defence, to welfare, and to liberty. But there is a higher law than the Constitution.
Speech in U.S. Senate, 11 March 1850

24 I know, and all the world knows, that revolutions never go backward.
Ib. At Rochester on the Irrepressible Conflict, Oct. 1858

EDWARD SEXBY
d. 1658

25 Killing no Murder Briefly Discourst in Three Questions. *Title of Pamphlet*, 1657

RICHARD SHACKLOCK
c. 1575

26 Proud as peacocks. *Hatchet of Heresies* (1565), p. 26b

THOMAS SHADWELL
1642?–1692

27 Words may be false and full of art,
Sighs are the natural language of the heart.
Psyche, Act III

28 'Tis the way of all flesh. *The Sullen Lovers*, v. ii

29 And wit's the noblest frailty of the mind.
A True Widow, II. i

30 The haste of a fool is the slowest thing in the world.
Ib. III. i

31 I am, out of the ladies' company, like a fish out of the water. *Ib.*

32 Every man loves what he is good at. *Ib.* v. i

33 Instantly, in the twinkling of a bed-staff.
Virtuoso, I. i

ANTHONY ASHLEY COOPER, EARL OF SHAFTESBURY

1621–1683

1 'People differ in their discourse and profession about these matters, but men of sense are really but of one religion.' . . . 'Pray, my lord, what religion is that which men of sense agree in?' 'Madam,' says the earl immediately, 'men of sense never tell it.'
Burnet, *History of My Own Time*, vol. 1, bk. ii, ch. 1, note by Onslow

WILLIAM SHAKESPEARE

1564–1616

In the references the line number is given without brackets where the scene is all verse up to the quotation and the line number is certain. It is given in square brackets where prose makes it variable, and the references are to the Oxford Standard Authors Shakespeare in one volume.

2   It were all one
That I should love a bright particular star
And think to wed it, he is so above me.
All's Well That Ends Well, I. i. [97]

3 My friends were poor but honest. *Ib.* iii. [203]

4 They say miracles are past. *Ib.* II. iii. [1]

5 A young man married is a man that's marred.
Ib. [315]

6 I know a man that had this trick of melancholy sold a goodly manor for a song. *Ib.* III. ii. [8]

7 The web of our life is of a mingled yarn, good and ill together: our virtues would be proud if our faults whipped them not; and our crimes would despair if they were not cherished by our own virtues.
Ib. IV. iii. [83]

8 There's place and means for every man alive.
Ib. [379]

9 The flowery way that leads to the broad gate and the great fire. *Ib.* v. [58]

10   Praising what is lost
Makes the remembrance dear. *Ib.* v. iii. 19

11 The triple pillar of the world transform'd
Into a strumpet's fool. *Antony and Cleopatra*, I. i. 12

12 CLEOPATRA:
If it be love indeed, tell me how much.
ANTONY:
There's beggary in the love that can be reckoned.
CLEOPATRA:
I'll set a bourn how far to be belov'd.
ANTONY:
Then must thou needs find out new heaven, new earth. *Ib.* 14

13 The scarce-bearded Cæsar. *Ib.* 21

14 Let Rome in Tiber melt, and the wide arch
Of the rang'd empire fall! Here is my space.
Kingdoms are clay; our dungy earth alike
Feeds beast as man; the nobleness of life
Is to do thus; when such a mutual pair
And such a twain can do't. *Ib.* 33

15 Whom everything becomes, to chide, to laugh,
To weep; whose every passion fully strives
To make itself, in thee, fair and admir'd. *Ib.* 49

16 In Nature's infinite book of secrecy
A little I can read. *Ib.* ii. [11]

17 You shall be yet far fairer than you are. *Ib.* [18]

18 You shall be more beloving than belov'd.
Antony and Cleopatra, I. ii. [24]

19 O excellent! I love long life better than figs. *Ib.* [34]

20 Mine, and most of our fortunes, to-night, shall be,—drunk to bed. *Ib.* [47]

21 But a worky-day fortune. *Ib.* [57]

22   On the sudden
A Roman thought hath struck him. *Ib.* [90]

23 The nature of bad news infects the teller. *Ib.* [103]

24 These strong Egyptian fetters I must break,
Or lose myself in dotage. *Ib.* [125]

25 I have seen her die twenty times upon far poorer moment. I do think there is mettle in death which commits some loving act upon her, she hath such a celerity in dying. *Ib.* [150]

26 We cannot call her winds and waters sighs and tears; they are greater storms and tempests than almanacs can report. *Ib.* [157]

27 O sir! you had then left unseen a wonderful piece of work which not to have been blessed withal would have discredited your travel. *Ib.* [164]

28 Indeed the tears live in an onion that should water this sorrow. *Ib.* [181]

29   If you find him sad,
Say I am dancing; if in mirth, report
That I am sudden sick. *Ib.* iii. 3

30 CHARMIAN:
In each thing give him way, cross him in nothing.
CLEOPATRA:
Thou teachest like a fool; the way to lose him. *Ib.* 9

31 In time we hate that which we often fear. *Ib.* 12

32 It cannot thus be long, the sides of nature
Will not sustain it. *Ib.* 16

33 Eternity was in our lips and eyes,
Bliss in our brows bent. *Ib.* 35

34 Quietness, grown sick of rest, would purge
By any desperate change. *Ib.* 53

35 Though age from folly could not give me freedom,
It does from childishness. *Ib.* 57

36 At the last, best. *Ib.* 61

37 O! my oblivion is a very Antony,
And I am all forgotten. *Ib.* 90

38   'Tis sweating labour
To bear such idleness so near the heart
As Cleopatra this. *Ib.* 93

39   This common body,
Like to a vagabond flag upon the stream,
Goes to and back, lackeying the varying tide,
To rot itself with motion. *Ib.* iv. 44

40   On the Alps
It is reported thou didst eat strange flesh,
Which some did die to look on. *Ib.* 66

41 Give me to drink mandragora. . . .
That I might sleep out this great gap of time
My Antony is away. *Ib.* v. 4

42 The demi-Atlas of this earth, the arm
And burgonet of men. *Ib.* 23

43 Where's my serpent of old Nile? *Ib.* 25

1   Think on me,
That am with Phœbus' amorous pinches black,
And wrinkled deep in time? Broad-fronted Cæsar,
When thou wast here above the ground I was
A morsel for a monarch, and great Pompey
Would stand and make his eyes grow in my brow;
There would he anchor his aspect and die
With looking on his life.
                    Antony and Cleopatra, I. v. 27

2   My salad days,
When I was green in judgment.   *Ib.* 73

3   We, ignorant of ourselves,
Beg often our own harms, which the wise powers
Deny us for our good; so find we profit
By losing of our prayers.   *Ib.* II. i. 5

4 I do not much dislike the matter, but
The manner of his speech.   *Ib.* ii. 117

5 No worse a husband than the best of men.   *Ib.* 135

6 The barge she sat in, like a burnish'd throne,
Burn'd on the water; the poop was beaten gold,
Purple the sails, and so perfumed, that
The winds were love-sick with them, the oars were
    silver,
Which to the tune of flutes kept stroke, and made
The water which they beat to follow faster,
As amorous of their strokes. For her own person,
It beggar'd all description; she did lie
In her pavilion,—cloth-of-gold of tissue,—
O'er-picturing that Venus where we see
The fancy outwork nature; on each side her
Stood pretty-dimpled boys, like smiling Cupids,
With divers-colour'd fans, whose wind did seem
To glow the delicate cheeks which they did cool,
And what they undid did.   *Ib.* [199]

7 Her gentlewomen, like the Nereides,
So many mermaids, tended her i' the eyes,
And made their bends adornings; at the helm
A seeming mermaid steers; the silken tackle
Swell with the touches of those flower-soft hands,
That yarely frame the office. From the barge
A strange invisible perfume hits the sense
Of the adjacent wharfs. The city cast
Her people out upon her, and Antony,
Enthron'd i' the market-place, did sit alone,
Whistling to the air; which, but for vacancy,
Had gone to gaze on Cleopatra too
And made a gap in nature.   *Ib.* [214]

8   I saw her once
Hop forty paces through the public street;
And having lost her breath, she spoke, and panted
That she did make defect perfection,
And, breathless, power breathe forth.   *Ib.* [236]

9 Age cannot wither her, nor custom stale
Her infinite variety; other women cloy
The appetites they feed, but she makes hungry
Where most she satisfies; for vilest things
Become themselves in her, that the holy priests
Bless her when she is riggish.   *Ib.* [243]

10 Read not my blemishes in the world's report;
I have not kept the square, but that to come
Shall all be done by the rule.   *Ib.* iii. 5

11   Music, moody food
Of us that trade in love.   *Ib.* v. 1

12 I laugh'd him out of patience; and that night
I laugh'd him into patience: and next morn,
Ere the ninth hour, I drunk him to his bed.   *Ib.* 19

13   There is gold, and here
My bluest veins to kiss; a hand that kings
Have lipp'd, and trembled kissing.
                    Antony and Cleopatra, II. v. 28

14 Pour out the pack of matter to mine ear,
The good and bad together.   *Ib.* 54

15 Though it be honest, it is never good
To bring bad news; give to a gracious message
A host of tongues, but let ill tidings tell
Themselves when they be felt.   *Ib.* 85

16 I will praise any man that will praise me. *Ib.* vi. [88]

17 LEPIDUS:
What manner o' thing is your crocodile?
ANTONY:
It is shaped, sir, like itself, and it is as broad as it
hath breadth; it is just so high as it is, and moves
with its own organs; it lives by that which nourish-
eth it; and the elements once out of it, it trans-
migrates.
LEPIDUS:
What colour is it of?
ANTONY:
Of its own colour too.
LEPIDUS:
'Tis a strange serpent.
ANTONY:
'Tis so; and the tears of it are wet.   *Ib.* vii. [47]

18   Ah! this thou shouldst have done,
And not have spoken on't. In me 'tis villany;
In thee 't had been good service.   *Ib.* [80]

19 Come, thou monarch of the vine,
Plumpy Bacchus with pink eyne!
In thy fats our cares be drown'd,
With thy grapes our hairs be crown'd:
    Cup us, till the world go round,
    Cup us, till the world go round!   *Ib.* [119]

20   Ambition,
The soldier's virtue.   *Ib.* III. i. 22

21   The swan's down-feather,
That stands upon the swell at full of tide,
And neither way inclines.   *Ib.* ii. 48

22 The ostentation of our love, which, left unshown,
Is often left unlov'd.   *Ib.* vi. 52

23 But let determin'd things to destiny
Hold unbewail'd their way.   *Ib.* 84

24   We have kiss'd away
Kingdoms and provinces.   *Ib.* viii. 17

25   Fortune knows
We scorn her most when most she offers blows.
                            Ib. ix. 73

26 Which had superfluous kings for messengers
Not many moons gone by.   *Ib.* x. 5

27   He wears the rose
Of youth upon him.   *Ib.* xi. 20

28   Men's judgments are
A parcel of their fortunes, and things outward
Do draw the inward quality after them,
To suffer all alike.   *Ib.* 31

29 Against the blown rose may they stop their nose,
That kneel'd unto the buds.   *Ib.* 39

30   Yet he that can endure
To follow with allegiance a fall'n lord,
Does conquer him that did his master conquer,
And earns a place i' the story.   *Ib.* 43

SHAKESPEARE

Your Cæsar's father oft,
When he hath mus'd of taking kingdoms in,
Bestow'd his lips on that unworthy place,
As it rain'd kisses.

Antony and Cleopatra, III. xi. 82

2 But when we in our viciousness grow hard,—
O misery on't!—the wise gods seel our eyes;
In our own filth drop our clear judgments; make us
Adore our errors; laugh at's while we strut
To our confusion. *Ib.* 111

3 I found you as a morsel, cold upon
Dead Cæsar's trencher. *Ib.* 116

4 My playfellow, your hand; this kingly seal
And plighter of high hearts. *Ib.* 125

5 Henceforth,
The white hand of a lady fever thee,
Shake thou to look on't. *Ib.* 137

6 Let's have one other gaudy night. *Ib.* 182

7 Since my lord
Is Antony again, I will be Cleopatra. *Ib.* 185

8 Know that to-morrow the last of many battles
We mean to fight. *Ib.* IV. i. 11

9 To business that we love we rise betime,
And go to't with delight. *Ib.* iv. 20

10 O! my fortunes have
Corrupted honest men. *Ib.* v. 16

11 I am alone the villain of the earth,
And feel I am so most. *Ib.* vi. 30

12 Leap thou, attire and all,
Through proof of harness to my heart, and there
Ride on the pants triumphing. *Ib.* viii. 14

13 O infinite virtue! com'st thou smiling from
The world's great snare uncaught? *Ib.* 17

14 My nightingale,
We have beat them to their beds. *Ib.* 18

15 O sovereign mistress of true melancholy. *Ib.* ix. 12

16 Swallows have built
In Cleopatra's sails their nests; the augurers
Say they know not, they cannot tell. *Ib.* x. 16

17 The hearts
That spaniel'd me at heels, to whom I gave
Their wishes, do discandy, melt their sweets
On blossoming Cæsar. *Ib.* 33

18 The soul and body rive not more in parting
Than greatness going off. *Ib.* xi. 5

19 Sometimes we see a cloud that's dragonish;
A vapour sometime like a bear or lion,
A tower'd citadel, a pendant rock,
A forked mountain, or blue promontory
With trees upon't, that nod unto the world
And mock our eyes with air: thou hast seen these
signs;
They are black vesper's pageants. *Ib.* xii. 2

20 That which is now a horse, even with a thought
The rack dislimns, and makes it indistinct,
As water is in water. *Ib.* 9

21 Unarm, Eros; the long day's task is done,
And we must sleep. *Ib.* 35

22 I will o'ertake thee, Cleopatra, and
Weep for my pardon. So it must be, for now
All length is torture; since the torch is out,
Lie down, and stray no further. Now all labour
Mars what it does; yea, very force entangles

Itself with strength; seal then, and all is done.
Eros!—I come, my queen.—Eros!—Stay for me:
Where souls do couch on flowers, we'll hand in hand,
And with our sprightly port make the ghosts gaze;
Dido and her Æneas shall want troops,
And all the haunt be ours.

Antony and Cleopatra, IV. xii. 44

23 Since Cleopatra died,
I have liv'd in such dishonour, that the gods
Detest my baseness. *Ib.* 55

24 But I will be
A bridegroom in my death, and run into't
As to a lover's bed. *Ib.* 99

25 All strange and terrible events are welcome,
But comforts we despise. *Ib.* xiii. 3

26 ANTONY:
Not Cæsar's valour hath o'erthrown Antony
But Antony's hath triumphed on itself.
CLEOPATRA:
So it should be, that none but Antony
Should conquer Antony. *Ib.* 14

27 I am dying, Egypt, dying; only
I here importune death awhile, until
Of many thousand kisses the poor last
I lay upon thy lips. *Ib.* 18

28 The miserable change now at my end
Lament nor sorrow at; but please your thoughts
In feeding them with those my former fortunes
Wherein I liv'd, the greatest prince o' the world,
The noblest; and do now not basely die,
Not cowardly put off my helmet to
My countryman; a Roman by a Roman
Valiantly vanquished. *Ib.* 51

29 Hast thou no care of me? shall I abide
In this dull world, which in thy absence is
No better than a sty? O! see my women,
The crown o' the earth doth melt. My lord!
O! wither'd is the garland of the war,
The soldier's pole is fall'n; young boys and girls
Are level now with men; the odds is gone,
And there is nothing left remarkable
Beneath the visiting moon. *Ib.* 60

30 No more, but e'en a woman and commanded
By such poor passion as the maid that milks
And does the meanest chares. *Ib.* 73

31 What's brave, what's noble,
Let's do it after the high Roman fashion,
And make death proud to take us. *Ib.* 86

32 A rarer spirit never
Did steer humanity; but you, gods, will give us
Some faults to make us men. *Ib.* v. i. 31

33 My desolation does begin to make
A better life. 'Tis paltry to be Cæsar;
Not being Fortune, he's but Fortune's knave,
A minister of her will; and it is great
To do that thing that ends all other deeds,
Which shackles accidents, and bolts up change,
Which sleeps, and never palates more the dug,
The beggar's nurse and Cæsar's. *Ib.* ii. 1

34 Nor once be chastis'd with the sober eye
Of dull Octavia. Shall they hoist me up
And show me to the shouting varletry
Of censuring Rome? Rather a ditch in Egypt
Be gentle grave unto me! rather on Nilus' mud
Lay me stark naked, and let the water-flies
Blow me into abhorring! *Ib.* 54

[425]

1 His legs bestrid the ocean; his rear'd arm
Crested the world; his voice was propertied
As all the tuned spheres, and that to friends;
But when he meant to quail and shake the orb,
He was as rattling thunder. For his bounty,
There was no winter in't; an autumn 'twas
That grew the more by reaping; his delights
Were dolphin-like, they show'd his back above
The element they liv'd in; in his livery
Walk'd crowns and crownets, realms and islands were
As plates dropp'd from his pocket.
Antony and Cleopatra, v. ii. 82

2 He words me, girls, he words me, that I should not
Be noble to myself.   *Ib.* 190

3 Finish, good lady; the bright day is done,
And we are for the dark.   *Ib.* 192

4   Antony
Shall be brought drunken forth, and I shall see
Some squeaking Cleopatra boy my greatness
I' the posture of a whore.   *Ib.* 217

5   I am again for Cydnus,
To meet Mark Antony.   *Ib.* 227

6 His biting is immortal; those that do die of it do
seldom or never recover.   *Ib.* [246]

7 A very honest woman, but something given to lie.
Ib. [251]

8 I know that a woman is a dish for the gods, if the
devil dress her not.   *Ib.* [274]

9   I have
Immortal longings in me.   *Ib.* [282]

10   Husband, I come:
Now to that name my courage prove my title!
I am fire and air; my other elements
I give to baser life.   *Ib.* [289]

11 If thou and nature can so gently part,
The stroke of death is as a lover's pinch,
Which hurts, and is desir'd.   *Ib.* [296]

12 If thus thou vanishest, thou tell'st the world
It is not worth leave-taking.   *Ib.* [299]

13 CLEOPATRA:
If she first meet the curled Antony,
He'll make demand of her, and spend that kiss
Which is my heaven to have. Come, thou mortal
wretch,
With thy sharp teeth this knot intrinsicate
Of life at once untie; poor venomous fool,
Be angry, and dispatch. O! couldst thou speak,
That I might hear thee call great Cæsar ass
Unpolicied.
CHARMIAN:
           O eastern star! .
CLEOPATRA: Peace! peace!
Dost thou not see my baby at my breast,
That sucks the nurse asleep?   *Ib.* [303]

14 Now boast thee, death, in thy possession lies
A lass unparallel'd.   *Ib.* [317]

15 It is well done, and fitting for a princess
Descended of so many royal kings.   *Ib.* [328]

16 As she would catch another Antony
In her strong toil of grace.   *Ib.* [348]

17 She hath pursu'd conclusions infinite
Of easy ways to die.   *Ib.* [356]

18 Let us sit and mock the good housewife Fortune
from her wheel, that her gifts may henceforth be
bestowed equally.   *As You Like It*, I. ii. [35]

19 How now, wit! whither wander you?   *Ib.* [60]

20 Well said: that was laid on with a trowel. *Ib.* [113]

21 Your heart's desires be with you!   *Ib.* [214]

22 One out of suits with fortune.   *Ib.* [263]

23 My pride fell with my fortunes.   *Ib.* [269]

24 Sir, you have wrestled well, and overthrown
More than your enemies.   *Ib.* [271]

25 Hereafter, in a better world than this,
I shall desire more love and knowledge of you.
Ib. [301]

26 Thus must I from the smoke into the smother;
From tyrant duke unto a tyrant brother.   *Ib.* [304]

27 O, how full of briers is this working-day world!
Ib. iii. [12]

28 We'll have a swashing and a martial outside,
As many other mannish cowards have
That do outface it with their semblances.   *Ib.* [123]

29 Hath not old custom made this life more sweet
Than that of painted pomp? Are not these woods
More free from peril than the envious court?
Here feel we but the penalty of Adam,
The seasons' difference; as, the icy fang
And churlish chiding of the winter's wind,
Which, when it bites and blows upon my body,
Even till I shrink with cold, I smile and say,
'This is no flattery.'   *Ib.* II. i. 2

30 Sweet are the uses of adversity,
Which like the toad, ugly and venomous,
Wears yet a precious jewel in his head;
And this our life, exempt from public haunt,
Finds tongues in trees, books in the running brooks,
Sermons in stones, and good in everything. *Ib.* 12

31   The big round tears
Cours'd one another down his innocent nose,
In piteous chase.   *Ib.* 38

32 'Poor deer,' quoth he, 'thou mak'st a testament
As worldlings do, giving thy sum of more
To that which had too much.'   *Ib.* 47

33 Sweep on, you fat and greasy citizens!   *Ib.* 55

34 I love to cope him in these sullen fits,
For then he's full of matter.   *Ib.* 67

35 Unregarded age in corners thrown.   *Ib.* iii. 42

36   Though I look old, yet I am strong and lusty;
For in my youth I never did apply
Hot and rebellious liquors in my blood.   *Ib.* 47

37 Therefore my age is as a lusty winter,
Frosty, but kindly.   *Ib.* 52

38 O good old man! how well in thee appears
The constant service of the antique world,
When service sweat for duty, not for meed!
Thou art not for the fashion of these times,
Where none will sweat but for promotion,
And having that, do choke their service up
Even with the having.   *Ib.* 56

39 Ay, now am I in Arden; the more fool I. When I
was at home I was in a better place; but travellers
must be content.   *Ib.* iv. [16]

1
As true a lover
As ever sigh'd upon a midnight pillow.
As You Like It, II. iv. [26]

2 If thou remember'st not the slightest folly
That ever love did make thee run into,
Thou hast not lov'd. *Ib.* [34]

3 We that are true lovers run into strange capers.
Ib. [53]

4 Thou speakest wiser than thou art ware of. *Ib.* [57]

5 I shall ne'er be ware of mine own wit till I break my
shins against it. *Ib.* [59]

6 My master is of churlish disposition
And little recks to find the way to heaven
By doing deeds of hospitality. *Ib.* [81]

7 Under the greenwood tree
Who loves to lie with me,
And turn his merry note
Unto the sweet bird's throat,
Come hither, come hither, come hither:
    Here shall he see
    No enemy
But winter and rough weather. *Ib.* v. 1

8 I can suck melancholy out of a song as a weasel sucks
eggs. *Ib.* [12]

9 Who doth ambition shun
And loves to live i' the sun,
Seeking the food he eats,
And pleas'd with what he gets. *Ib.* [38]

10 I'll rail against all the first-born in Egypt. *Ib.* [60]

11 A fool, a fool! I met a fool i' the forest,
A motley fool. *Ib.* vii. 12

12 And rail'd on Lady Fortune in good terms,
In good set terms. *Ib.* 16

13 'Call me not fool till heaven hath sent me fortune.'
And then he drew a dial from his poke,
And, looking on it with lack-lustre eye,
Says very wisely, 'It is ten o'clock;
Thus may we see,' quoth he, 'how the world wags.'
Ib. 19

14 And so, from hour to hour, we ripe and ripe,
And then from hour to hour, we rot and rot:
And thereby hangs a tale. *Ib.* 26

15 My lungs began to crow like chanticleer,
That fools should be so deep-contemplative,
And I did laugh sans intermission
An hour by his dial. O noble fool!
A worthy fool! Motley's the only wear. *Ib.* 30

16 And says, if ladies be but young and fair,
They have the gift to know it: and in his brain,—
Which is as dry as the remainder biscuit
After a voyage,—he hath strange places cramm'd
With observation, the which he vents
In mangled forms. *Ib.* 37

17
I must have liberty
Withal, as large a charter as the wind,
To blow on whom I please. *Ib.* 47

18 The 'why' is plain as way to parish church. *Ib.* 52

19
But whate'er you are
That in this desert inaccessible,
Under the shade of melancholy boughs,
Lose and neglect the creeping hours of time;
If ever you have look'd on better days,
If ever been where bells have knoll'd to church,

If ever sat at any good man's feast,
If ever from your eyelids wip'd a tear,
And know what 'tis to pity, and be pitied,
Let gentleness my strong enforcement be.
As You Like It, II. vii. 109

20 There is an old poor man,
    .   .   .
Oppress'd with two weak evils, age and hunger.
Ib. 129

21
All the world's a stage,
And all the men and women merely players:
They have their exits and their entrances;
And one man in his time plays many parts,
His acts being seven ages. At first the infant,
Mewling and puking in the nurse's arms.
And then the whining schoolboy, with his satchel,
And shining morning face, creeping like snail
Unwillingly to school. And then the lover,
Sighing like furnace, with a woful ballad
Made to his mistress' eyebrow. Then a soldier,
Full of strange oaths, and bearded like the pard,
Jealous in honour, sudden and quick in quarrel,
Seeking the bubble reputation
Even in the cannon's mouth. And then the justice,
In fair round belly with good capon lin'd,
With eyes severe, and beard of formal cut,
Full of wise saws and modern instances;
And so he plays his part. The sixth age shifts
Into the lean and slipper'd pantaloon,
With spectacles on nose and pouch on side,
His youthful hose well sav'd a world too wide
For his shrunk shank; and his big manly voice,
Turning again towards childish treble, pipes
And whistles in his sound. Last scene of all,
That ends this strange eventful history,
Is second childishness, and mere oblivion,
Sans teeth, sans eyes, sans taste, sans everything.
Ib. 139

22 Blow, blow, thou winter wind,
Thou art not so unkind
    As man's ingratitude:
Thy tooth is not so keen,
Because thou art not seen,
    Although thy breath be rude.
Heigh-ho! sing, heigh-ho! unto the green holly:
Most friendship is feigning, most loving mere folly.
    Then heigh-ho! the holly!
    This life is most jolly.

Freeze, freeze, thou bitter sky,
That dost not bite so nigh
    As benefits forgot:
Though thou the waters warp,
Thy sting is not so sharp
    As friend remember'd not. *Ib.* 174

23 Run, run, Orlando: carve on every tree
The fair, the chaste, and unexpressive she.
Ib. III. ii. 9

24 Hast any philosophy in thee, shepherd? *Ib.* [22]

25 He that wants money, means, and content is without
three good friends. *Ib.* [25]

26 Thou art in a parlous state. *Ib.* [46]

27 I earn that I eat, get that I wear, owe no man hate,
envy no man's happiness, glad of other men's
good, content with my harm. *Ib.* [78]

28 From the east to western Ind,
No jewel is like Rosalind. *Ib.* [94]

1 This is the very false gallop of verses.
As You Like It, III. ii. [120]

2 Let us make an honourable retreat; though not with bag and baggage, yet with scrip and scrippage.
Ib. [170]

3 O wonderful, wonderful, and most wonderful wonderful! and yet again wonderful, and after that, out of all whooping! *Ib.* [202]

4 It is as easy to count atomies as to resolve the propositions of a lover. *Ib.* [246]

5 Do you not know I am a woman? when I think, I must speak. *Ib.* [265]

6 I do desire we may be better strangers. *Ib.* [276]

7 You have a nimble wit; I think 'twas made of Atalanta's heels. *Ib.* [294]

8 I will chide no breather in the world but myself, against whom I know most faults. *Ib.* [298]

9 Time travels in divers paces with divers persons. I'll tell you who Time ambles withal, who Time trots withal, who Time gallops withal, and who he stands still withal. *Ib.* [328]

10 Every one fault seeming monstrous till his fellow fault came to match it. *Ib.* [377]

11 Truly, I would the gods had made thee poetical.
Ib. iii. [16]

12 I am not a slut, though I thank the gods I am foul.
Ib. [40]

13 ROSALIND:
His hair is of a good colour.
CELIA:
An excellent colour; your chestnut was ever the only colour. *Ib.* iv. [10]

14   Down on your knees,
And thank heaven, fasting, for a good man's love.
Ib. v. 57

15 Dead shepherd, now I find thy saw of might:
'Who ever lov'd that lov'd not at first sight?' *Ib.* 81

16 It is a melancholy of mine own, compounded of many simples, extracted from many objects, and indeed the sundry contemplation of my travels, which, by often rumination, wraps me in a most humorous sadness. *Ib.* iv. i. [16]

17 Farewell, Monsieur Traveller: look you lisp and wear strange suits, disable all the benefits of your own country, be out of love with your nativity, and almost chide God for making you that countenance you are, or I will scarce think you have swam in a gondola. *Ib.* [35]

18 Break an hour's promise in love! He that will divide a minute into a thousand parts, and break but a part of the thousandth part of a minute in the affairs of love, it may be said of him that Cupid hath clapped him o' the shoulder, but I'll warrant him heart-whole. *Ib.* [46]

19 For now I am in a holiday humour. *Ib.* [70]

20 When you were gravelled for lack of matter.
Ib. [76]

21 Men have died from time to time, and worms have eaten them, but not for love. *Ib.* [110]

22 Men are April when they woo, December when they wed: maids are May when they are maids, but the sky changes when they are wives. *Ib.* [153]

23 The horn, the horn, the lusty horn
Is not a thing to laugh to scorn.
As You Like It, IV. ii. [17]

24 Chewing the food of sweet and bitter fancy.
Ib. iii. [103]

25 Cæsar's thrasonical brag of 'I came, saw, and overcame'. *Ib.* v. ii. [35]

26 No sooner met, but they looked; no sooner looked but they loved; no sooner loved but they sighed; no sooner sighed but they asked one another the reason; no sooner knew the reason but they sought the remedy. *Ib.* [37]

27 Oh! how bitter a thing it is to look into happiness through another man's eyes. *Ib.* [48]

28 PHEBE:
Good shepherd, tell this youth what 'tis to love.
SILVIUS:
It is to be all made of sighs and tears;—

It is to be all made of faith and service;—

It is to be all made of fantasy,
All made of passion, and all made of wishes;
All adoration, duty, and observance;
All humbleness, all patience, and impatience;
All purity, all trial, all obeisance. *Ib.* [90]

29 'Tis like the howling of Irish wolves against the moon. *Ib.* [120]

30 It was a lover and his lass,
With a hey, and a ho, and a hey nonino,
That o'er the green cornfield did pass,
In the spring time, the only pretty ring time,
When birds do sing, hey ding a ding, ding;
Sweet lovers love the spring. *Ib.* iii. [18]

31 Between the acres of the rye,
With a hey, and a ho, and a hey nonino,
These pretty country folks would lie,
In the spring time, &c. *Ib.* [24]

32 This carol they began that hour,
With a hey, and a ho, and a hey nonino,
How that a life was but a flower,
In the spring time, &c. *Ib.* [28]

33 And therefore take the present time,
With a hey, and a ho, and a hey nonino;
For love is crowned with the prime
In the spring time, &c. *Ib.* [32]

34 Here comes a pair of very strange beasts, which in all tongues are called fools. *Ib.* iv. [36]

35 An ill-favoured thing, sir, but mine own. *Ib.* [60]

36 Rich honesty dwells like a miser, sir, in a poor house; as your pearl in your foul oyster. *Ib.* [62]

37 The retort courteous . . . the quip modest . . . the reply churlish . . . the reproof valiant . . . the countercheck quarrelsome . . . the lie circumstantial . . . the lie direct. *Ib.* [96]

38 Your 'if' is the only peace-maker; much virtue in 'if'. *Ib.* [108]

39 He uses his folly like a stalking-horse, and under the presentation of that he shoots his wit. *Ib.* [112]

40 If it be true that 'good wine needs no bush', 'tis true that a good play needs no epilogue.
Ib. Epilogue [3]

1 They brought one Pinch, a hungry, lean-fac'd
villain,
A mere anatomy, a mountebank,
A threadbare juggler, and a fortune-teller,
A needy, hollow-ey'd, sharp-looking wretch,
A living-dead man.   *The Comedy of Errors*, v. i. 238

2 He's a very dog to the commonalty.
                                  Coriolanus, I. i. [29]

3 The kingly crowned head, the vigilant eye,
The counsellor heart, the arm our soldier,
Our steed the leg, the tongue our trumpeter.
                                  Ib. [121]

4 What's the matter, you dissentious rogues,
That, rubbing the poor itch of your opinion,
Make yourselves scabs?   *Ib.* [170]

5   They threw their caps
As they would hang them on the horns o' the moon,
Shouting their emulation.   *Ib.* [218]

6 Oh! I warrant, how he mammocked it! *Ib.* iii. [71]

7 My gracious silence, hail!   *Ib.* II. i. [194]

8 Such eyes the widows in Corioli wear,
And mothers that lack sons.   *Ib.* [197]

9   Custom calls me to 't:
What custom wills, in all things should we do't,
The dust on antique time would lie unswept,
And mountainous error be too highly heap'd
For truth to o'erpeer.   *Ib.* II. iii. [124]

10 I thank you for your voices, thank you,
Your most sweet voices.   *Ib.* [179]

11 The mutable, rank-scented many. *Ib.* III. i. 65

12 Hear you this Triton of the minnows? mark you
His absolute 'shall'?   *Ib.* 88

13 His nature is too noble for the world:
He would not flatter Neptune for his trident,
Or Jove for's power to thunder. His heart's his
mouth:
What his breast forges, that his tongue must vent.
                                  Ib. 254

14 You common cry of curs! whose breath I hate
As reek o' the rotten fens, whose loves I prize
As the dead carcases of unburied men
That do corrupt my air,—I banish you. *Ib.* iii. 118

15   The beast
With many heads butts me away.   *Ib.* IV. i. 1

16 Under the canopy . . . I' the city of kites and crows.
                                  Ib. v. [41]

17   I'll never
Be such a gosling to obey instinct, but stand
As if a man were author of himself
And knew no other kin.   *Ib.* v. iii. 34

18   Like a dull actor now,
I have forgot my part, and I am out,
Even to a full disgrace.   *Ib.* 40

19   O! a kiss
Long as my exile, sweet as my revenge!
Now, by the jealous queen of heaven, that kiss
I carried from thee, dear, and my true lip
Hath virgin'd it e'er since.   *Ib.* 44

20   Chaste as the icicle
That's curdied by the frost from purest snow,
And hangs on Dian's temple.   *Ib.* 65

21 Like a great sea-mark, standing every flaw.
                                  Coriolanus, v. iii. 74

22   Thou hast never in thy life
Show'd thy dear mother any courtesy;
When she—poor hen! fond of no second brood—
Has cluck'd thee to the wars, and safely home,
Loaden with honour.   *Ib.* 160

23 If you have writ your annals true, 'tis there,
That, like an eagle in a dove-cote, I
Flutter'd your Volscians in Corioli:
Alone I did it.   *Ib.* v. 114

24   On her left breast
A mole cinque-spotted, like the crimson drops
I' the bottom of a cowslip.   *Cymbeline*, II. ii. 37

25 Hark! hark! the lark at heaven's gate sings,
    And Phœbus 'gins arise,
His steeds to water at those springs
    On chalic'd flowers that lies;
And winking Mary-buds begin
    To ope their golden eyes:
With everything that pretty is,
    My lady sweet, arise!   *Ib.* iii. [22]

26 Is there no way for men to be, but women
Must be half-workers?   *Ib.* v. 1

27 As chaste as unsunn'd snow.   *Ib.* 13

28   There be many Cæsars
Ere such another Julius. Britain is
A world by itself, and we will nothing pay
For wearing our own noses.   *Ib.* III. i. 11

29 The natural bravery of your isle, which stands
As Neptune's park, ribbed and paled in
With rocks unscalable, and roaring waters. *Ib.* 18

30 O, for a horse with wings!   *Ib.* ii. [49]

31   What should we speak of
When we are old as you? when we shall hear
The rain and wind beat dark December, how,
In this our pinching cave, shall we discourse
The freezing hours away?   *Ib.* iii. 35

32   Some jay of Italy,
Whose mother was her painting, hath betray'd him:
Poor I am stale, a garment out of fashion.
                                  Ib. iv. [51]

33 I have not slept one wink.   *Ib.* [103]

34 Hath Britain all the sun that shines? *Ib.* [139]

35   To lapse in fulness
Is sorer than to lie for need, and falsehood
Is worse in kings than beggars.   *Ib.* vi. 12

36   Weariness
Can snore upon the flint when resty sloth
Finds the down pillow hard.   *Ib.* 33

37   Thou shalt not lack
The flower that's like thy face, pale primrose, nor
The azur'd harebell, like thy veins. *Ib.* IV. ii. 220

38 Great griefs, I see, medicine the less. *Ib.* 243

39   Though mean and mighty rotting
Together, have one dust, yet reverence—
That angel of the world—doth make distinction
Of place 'tween high and low.   *Ib.* 246

40 Thersites' body is as good as Ajax'
When neither are alive.   *Ib.* 252

[429]

1 Fear no more the heat o' the sun,
    Nor the furious winter's rages;
Thou thy worldly task hast done,
    Home art gone and ta'en thy wages:
Golden lads and girls all must,
As chimney-sweepers, come to dust.

Fear no more the frown o' the great,
    Thou art past the tyrant's stroke:
Care no more to clothe and eat;
    To thee the reed is as the oak:
The sceptre, learning, physic, must
All follow this, and come to dust.

Fear no more the lightning flash,
    Nor the all-dreaded thunder-stone;
Fear not slander, censure rash;
    Thou hast finish'd joy and moan:
All lovers young, all lovers must
Consign to thee, and come to dust.

No exorciser harm thee!
    Nor no witchcraft charm thee!
Ghost unlaid forbear thee!
    Nothing ill come near thee!
Quiet consummation have;
And renowned be thy grave!   *Cymbeline*, IV. ii. 258

2 Every good servant does not all commands.
                                                Ib. v. i. 6

3 He that sleeps feels not the toothache.   *Ib.* iv. [176]

4 He spake of her as Dian had hot dreams,
And she alone were cold.   *Ib.* v. 181

5 IMOGEN:
Why did you throw your wedded lady from you?
Think that you are upon a rock; and now
Throw me again.
POSTHUMUS:
                    Hang there like fruit, my soul,
Till the tree die!   *Ib.* 262

6 Pardon's the word to all.   *Ib.* 423

7 You come most carefully upon your hour.
                                            Hamlet, I. i. 6

8 For this relief much thanks; 'tis bitter cold,
And I am sick at heart.   *Ib.* 8

9 BERNARDO:
What! is Horatio there?
HORATIO:
                    A piece of him.   *Ib.* 19

10 What! has this thing appear'd again to-night? *Ib.* 21

11 Look, where it comes again!   *Ib.* 40

12 But in the gross and scope of my opinion,
This bodes some strange eruption to our state.
                                               Ib. 68

13   This sweaty haste
Doth make the night joint-labourer with the day.
                                               Ib. 77

14 In the most high and palmy state of Rome,
A little ere the mightiest Julius fell,
The graves stood tenantless and the sheeted dead
Did squeak and gibber in the Roman streets.
                                               Ib. 113

15   The moist star
Upon whose influence Neptune's empire stands
Was sick almost to doomsday with eclipse.   *Ib.* 118

16 I'll cross it, though it blast me.   *Ib.* 127

17 We do it wrong, being so majestical,
To offer it the show of violence;
For it is, as the air, invulnerable,
And our vain blows malicious mockery. *Hamlet*, I. i. 143

18 And then it started like a guilty thing
Upon a fearful summons.   *Ib.* 148

19 Whether in sea or fire, in earth or air,
The extravagant and erring spirit hies
To his confine.   *Ib.* 153

20 It faded on the crowing of the cock.
Some say that ever 'gainst that season comes
Wherein our Saviour's birth is celebrated,
The bird of dawning singeth all night long;
And then, they say, no spirit can walk abroad;
The nights are wholesome; then no planets strike,
No fairy takes, nor witch hath power to charm,
So hallow'd and so gracious is the time.   *Ib.* 157

21 But, look, the morn, in russet mantle clad,
Walks o'er the dew of yon high eastern hill.
                                              Ib. 166

22 The memory be green.   *Ib.* ii. 2

23 Therefore our sometime sister, now our queen. *Ib.* 8

24 With one auspicious and one dropping eye,
With mirth in funeral and with dirge in marriage,
In equal scale weighing delight and dole.   *Ib.* 11

25 The head is not more native to the heart.   *Ib.* 47

26 A little more than kin, and less than kind. *Ib.* 65

27 Not so, my lord; I am too much i' the sun. *Ib.* 67

28 Good Hamlet, cast thy nighted colour off,
And let thine eye look like a friend on Denmark.
                                              Ib. 68

29 QUEEN:
Thou know'st 'tis common; all that live must die,
Passing through nature to eternity.
HAMLET:
Ay, madam, it is common.   *Ib.* 72

30 Seems, madam! Nay, it is; I know not 'seems'.
'Tis not alone my inky cloak, good mother,
Nor customary suits of solemn black,
Nor windy suspiration of forc'd breath,
No, nor the fruitful river in the eye,
Nor the dejected 'haviour of the visage,
Together with all forms, modes, shows of grief,
That can denote me truly; these indeed seem,
For they are actions that a man might play;
But I have that within which passeth show;
These but the trappings and the suits of woe. *Ib.* 76

31   But to persever
In obstinate condolement is a course
Of impious stubbornness; 'tis unmanly grief;
It shows a will most incorrect to heaven,
A heart unfortified, a mind impatient.   *Ib.* 92

32 HAMLET:
I shall in all my best obey you, madam.
KING:
Why, 'tis a loving and a fair reply.   *Ib.* 120

33 O! that this too too solid flesh would melt,
Thaw, and resolve itself into a dew;
Or that the Everlasting had not fix'd
His canon 'gainst self-slaughter! O God! O God!
How weary, stale, flat, and unprofitable
Seem to me all the uses of this world.
Fie on't! O fie! 'tis an unweeded garden,

[430]

That grows to seed; things rank and gross in nature
Possess it merely. That it should come to this!
But two months dead: nay, not so much, not two:
So excellent a king; that was, to this,
Hyperion to a satyr: so loving to my mother,
That he might not beteem the winds of heaven
Visit her face too roughly. Heaven and earth!
Must I remember? Why, she would hang on him,
As if increase of appetite had grown
By what it fed on; and yet, within a month,
Let me not think on't: Frailty, thy name is woman!
A little month; or ere those shoes were old
With which she follow'd my poor father's body,
Like Niobe, all tears; why she, even she,——
O God! a beast, that wants discourse of reason,
Would have mourn'd longer,—married with mine uncle,
My father's brother, but no more like my father
Than I to Hercules.   *Hamlet*, I. ii. 129

1 It is not, nor it cannot come to good;
But break, my heart, for I must hold my tongue!
                                          Ib. 158

2 A truant disposition, good my lord.   *Ib.* 169

3 We'll teach you to drink deep ere you depart. *Ib.* 175

4 Thrift, thrift, Horatio! the funeral bak'd meats
Did coldly furnish forth the marriage tables.
Would I had met my dearest foe in heaven
Ere I had ever seen that day, Horatio!   *Ib.* 180

5 In my mind's eye, Horatio.   *Ib.* 185

6 He was a man, take him for all in all,
I shall not look upon his like again.   *Ib.* 187

7 Season your admiration for a while.   *Ib.* 192

8 In the dead vast and middle of the night.   *Ib.* 198

9 Armed at points exactly, cap-a-pe.   *Ib.* 200

10   Distill'd
Almost to jelly with the act of fear.   *Ib.* 204

11 These hands are not more like.   *Ib.* 212

12 But answer made it none.   *Ib.* 215

13 A countenance more in sorrow than in anger.
                                          Ib. 231

14 While one with moderate haste might tell a hundred.
                                          Ib. 237

15 HAMLET:
His beard was grizzled, no?
HORATIO:
It was, as I have seen it in his life,
A sable silver'd.   *Ib.* 239

16 Give it an understanding, but no tongue.   *Ib.* 249

17 Upon the platform, 'twixt eleven and twelve.
                                          Ib. 251

18   All is not well;
I doubt some foul play.   *Ib.* 254

19   Foul deeds will rise,
Though all the earth o'erwhelm them, to men's eyes.
                                          Ib. 256

20 A violet in the youth of primy nature,
Forward, not permanent, sweet, not lasting.
The perfume and suppliance of a minute.   *Ib.* iii. 7

21 His greatness weigh'd, his will is not his own,
For he himself is subject to his birth;
He may not, as unvalu'd persons do,
Carve for himself, for on his choice depends
The safety and the health of the whole state.
                                       Hamlet, I. iii. 17

22 And keep you in the rear of your affection. *Ib.* 34

23 Do not, as some ungracious pastors do,
Show me the steep and thorny way to heaven,
Whiles, like a puff'd and reckless libertine,
Himself the primrose path of dalliance treads,
And recks not his own rede.   *Ib.* 47

24 A double blessing is a double grace;
Occasion smiles upon a second leave.   *Ib.* 53

25 And these few precepts in thy memory
Look thou character. Give thy thoughts no tongue,
Nor any unproportion'd thought his act.
Be thou familiar, but by no means vulgar;
The friends thou hast, and their adoption tried,
Grapple them to thy soul with hoops of steel;
But do not dull thy palm with entertainment
Of each new-hatch'd, unfledg'd comrade. Beware
Of entrance to a quarrel; but, being in,
Bear't that th' opposed may beware of thee.
Give every man thine ear, but few thy voice;
Take each man's censure, but reserve thy judgment.
Costly thy habit as thy purse can buy,
But not express'd in fancy; rich, not gaudy;
For the apparel oft proclaims the man,
And they in France of the best rank and station
Are most select and generous, chief in that.
Neither a borrower, nor a lender be;
For loan oft loses both itself and friend,
And borrowing dulls the edge of husbandry,
This above all: to thine own self be true,
And it must follow, as the night the day,
Thou canst not then be false to any man.
Farewell; my blessing season this in thee!   *Ib.* 58

26   You speak like a green girl,
Unsifted in such perilous circumstance.   *Ib.* 101

27 Ay, springes to catch woodcocks. I do know,
When the blood burns, how prodigal the soul
Lends the tongue vows.   *Ib.* 115

28 Be somewhat scanter of your maiden presence.
                                          Ib. 121

29 I would not, in plain terms, from this time forth,
Have you so slander any moment's leisure.   *Ib.* 132

30 HAMLET:
The air bites shrewdly; it is very cold.
HORATIO:
It is a nipping and an eager air.   *Ib.* iv. 1

31 But to my mind,—though I am native here,
And to the manner born,—it is a custom
More honour'd in the breach than the observance.
                                          Ib. 14

32 Angels and ministers of grace defend us!
Be thou a spirit of health or goblin damn'd,
Bring with thee airs from heaven or blasts from hell,
Be thy intents wicked or charitable,
Thou com'st in such a questionable shape
That I will speak to thee: I'll call thee Hamlet,
King, father; royal Dane, O! answer me:
Let me not burst in ignorance; but tell
Why thy canoniz'd bones, hearsed in death,
Have burst their cerements; why the sepulchre,

Wherein we saw thee quietly inurn'd,
Hath op'd his ponderous and marble jaws,
To cast thee up again. What may this mean,
'That thou, dead corse, again in complete steel
Revisit'st thus the glimpses of the moon,
Making night hideous; and we fools of nature
So horridly to shake our disposition
With thoughts beyond the reaches of our souls?
Hamlet I. iv. 39

1   Look, with what courteous action
It waves you to a more removed ground.   *Ib.* 60

2 I do not set my life at a pin's fee;
And for my soul, what can it do to that,
Being a thing immortal as itself?   *Ib.* 65

3   My fate cries out,
And makes each petty artery in this body
As hardy as the Nemean lion's nerve.   *Ib.* 81

4   Unhand me, gentlemen,
By heaven! I'll make a ghost of him that lets me.
Ib. 84

5 Something is rotten in the state of Denmark. *Ib.* 90

6 Whither wilt thou lead me? speak; I'll go no further.
Ib. v. 1

7 Alas! poor ghost.   *Ib.* 4

8 I am thy father's spirit;
Doom'd for a certain term to walk the night. *Ib.* 9

9   But that I am forbid
To tell the secrets of my prison-house,
I could a tale unfold whose lightest word
Would harrow up thy soul, freeze thy young blood,
Make thy two eyes, like stars, start from their spheres,
Thy knotted and combined locks to part,
And each particular hair to stand an end,
Like quills upon the fretful porpentine:
But this eternal blazon must not be
To ears of flesh and blood. List, list, O, list! *Ib.* 13

10 Revenge his foul and most unnatural murder. *Ib.* 25

11 Murder most foul, as in the best it is;
But this most foul, strange, and unnatural. *Ib.* 27

12 And duller shouldst thou be than the fat weed
That rots itself in ease on Lethe wharf. *Ib.* 32

13   O my prophetic soul!
My uncle!   *Ib.* 40

14 That it went hand in hand even with the vow
I made to her in marriage.   *Ib.* 49

15 But, soft! methinks I scent the morning air. *Ib.* 58

16 In the porches of mine ears.   *Ib.* 63

17 Cut off even in the blossoms of my sin,
Unhousel'd, disappointed, unanel'd,
No reckoning made, but sent to my account
With all my imperfections on my head:
O, horrible! O, horrible! most horrible!
If thou hast nature in thee, bear it not. *Ib.* 76

18   Leave her to heaven,
And to those thorns that in her bosom lodge,
To prick and sting her.   *Ib.* 86

19 The glow-worm shows the matin to be near,
And 'gins to pale his uneffectual fire. *Ib.* 89

20   While memory holds a seat
In this distracted globe. Remember thee!
Yea, from the table of my memory

I'll wipe away all trivial fond records,
All saws of books, all forms, all pressures past,
That youth and observation copied there.
Hamlet, I. v. 96

21 O most pernicious woman!
O villain, villain, smiling, damned villain!
My tables,—meet it is I set it down,
That one may smile, and smile, and be a villain;
At least I'm sure it may be so in Denmark. *Ib.* 105

22 HAMLET:
There's ne'er a villain dwelling in all Denmark,
But he's an arrant knave.
HORATIO:
There needs no ghost, my lord, come from the grave,
To tell us this.   *Ib.* 123

23   And, for mine own poor part,
Look you, I'll go pray.   *Ib.* 131

24 It is an honest ghost, that let me tell you. *Ib.* 138

25   Art thou there, true-penny?
Come on,—you hear this fellow in the cellarage.
Ib. 150

26 Hic et ubique? then we'll shift our ground. *Ib.* 156

27 Well said, old mole! canst work i' the earth so fast?
Ib. 162

28 O day and night, but this is wondrous strange!
Ib. 164

29 There are more things in heaven and earth, Horatio,
Than are dreamt of in your philosophy. *Ib.* 166

30 To put an antic disposition on.   *Ib.* 172

31 Rest, rest, perturbed spirit!   *Ib.* 182

32 The time is out of joint; O cursed spite,
That ever I was born to set it right! *Ib.* 188

33 Your bait of falsehood takes this carp of truth.
Ib. II. i. 63

34 By indirections find directions out.   *Ib.* 66

35 Lord Hamlet, with his doublet all unbrac'd;
No hat upon his head; his stockings foul'd,
Ungarter'd, and down-gyved to his ankle. *Ib.* 78

36   Such thanks
As fits a king's remembrance.   *Ib.* ii. 25

37 Thou still hast been the father of good news. *Ib.* 42

38 Brevity is the soul of wit.   *Ib.* 90

39 More matter with less art.   *Ib.* 95

40 That he is mad, 'tis true; 'tis true 'tis pity;
And pity 'tis 'tis true: a foolish figure;
But farewell it, for I will use no art.   *Ib.* 97

41 That's an ill phrase, a vile phrase; 'beautified' is a
vile phrase.   *Ib.* [110]

42 Doubt thou the stars are fire;
Doubt that the sun doth move;
Doubt truth to be a liar;
But never doubt I love.   *Ib.* [115]

43 Lord Hamlet is a prince, out of thy star. *Ib.* [141]

44 If circumstances lead me, I will find
Where truth is hid, though it were hid indeed
Within the centre.   *Ib.* [157]

45 Let me be no assistant for a state,
But keep a farm, and carters.   *Ib.* [166]

1 POLONIUS:
Do you know me, my lord?
HAMLET:
Excellent well; you are a fishmonger. *Hamlet*, II. ii [173]

2 Ay, sir; to be honest, as this world goes, is to be one
man picked out of ten thousand. *Ib.* [179]

3 Still harping on my daughter. *Ib.* [190]

4 POLONIUS:
What do you read, my lord?
HAMLET:
Words, words, words. *Ib.* [195]

5 All which, sir, though I most powerfully and potently
believe, yet I hold it not honesty to have it thus set
down. *Ib.* [206]

6 Though this be madness, yet there is method in it.
Ib. [211]

7 Except my life, except my life, except my life.
Ib. [225]

8 These tedious old fools! *Ib.* [227]

9 As the indifferent children of the earth. *Ib.* [235]

10 HAMLET:
Then you live about her waist, or in the middle of
her favours?
GUILDENSTERN:
Faith, her privates we.
HAMLET:
In the secret parts of Fortune? O! most true; she is
a strumpet. What news?
ROSENCRANTZ:
None, my lord, but that the world's grown honest.
HAMLET:
Then is doomsday near. *Ib.* [240]

11 There is nothing either good or bad, but thinking
makes it so. *Ib.* [259]

12 O God! I could be bounded in a nut-shell, and
count myself a king of infinite space, were it not
that I have bad dreams. *Ib.* [263]

13 GUILDENSTERN:
The very substance of the ambitious is merely the
shadow of a dream.
HAMLET:
A dream itself is but a shadow.
ROSENCRANTZ:
Truly, and I hold ambition of so airy and light a
quality that it is but a shadow's shadow. *Ib.* [268]

14 Beggar that I am, I am poor even in thanks. *Ib.* [286]

15 It goes so heavily with my disposition that this goodly
frame, the earth, seems to me a sterile promontory;
this most excellent canopy, the air, look you, this
brave o'erhanging firmament, this majestical roof
fretted with golden fire, why, it appears no other
thing to me but a foul and pestilent congregation
of vapours. What a piece of work is a man! How
noble in reason! how infinite in faculty! in form,
in moving, how express and admirable! in action
how like an angel! in apprehension how like a god!
the beauty of the world! the paragon of animals!
And yet, to me, what is this quintessence of dust?
man delights not me; no, nor woman neither,
though, by your smiling, you seem to say so.
Ib. [316]

16 There was no such stuff in my thoughts. *Ib.* [332]

17 What lenten entertainment the players shall receive
from you. *Hamlet*, II. ii. [337]

18 Make those laugh whose lungs are tickle o' the sere.
Ib. [346]

19 There is something in this more than natural, if
philosophy could find it out. *Ib.* [392]

20 I am but mad north-north-west; when the wind is
southerly, I know a hawk from a handsaw.[1]
Ib. [405]

[1] = heron-shaw, or heron.

21 That great baby you see there is not yet out of his
swaddling-clouts. *Ib.* [410]

22 Seneca cannot be too heavy, nor Plautus too light.
Ib. [428]

23 One fair daughter and no more,
The which he loved passing well. *Ib.* [435]

24 Come, give us a taste of your quality. *Ib.* [460]

25 The play, I remember, pleased not the million; 'twas
caviare to the general. *Ib.* [465]

26 The rugged Pyrrhus, like the Hyrcanian beast.
Ib. [481]

27 Head to foot
Now is he total gules. *Ib.* [487]

28 The mobled queen. *Ib.* [533]

29 Good my lord, will you see the players well bestowed? Do you hear, let them be well used;
for they are the abstracts and brief chronicles of
the time: after your death you were better have a
bad epitaph than their ill report while you live.
Ib. [553]

30 Use every man after his desert, and who should
'scape whipping? *Ib.* [561]

31 O, what a rogue and peasant slave am I:
Is it not monstrous that this player here,
But in a fiction, in a dream of passion,
Could force his soul so to his own conceit
That from her working all his visage wann'd,
Tears in his eyes, distraction in 's aspect,
A broken voice, and his whole function suiting
With forms to his conceit? and all for nothing!
For Hecuba!
What's Hecuba to him or he to Hecuba
That he should weep for her? *Ib.* [584]

32 He would drown the stage with tears,
And cleave the general ear with horrid speech,
Make mad the guilty, and appal the free,
Confound the ignorant, and amaze, indeed,
The very faculties of eyes and ears. *Ib.* [596]

33 A dull and muddy-mettled rascal. *Ib.* [602]

34 But I am pigeon-livered, and lack gall
To make oppression bitter. *Ib.* [613]

35 I should have fatted all the region kites
With this slave's offal. *Ib.* [615]

36 I have heard,
That guilty creatures sitting at a play
Have by the very cunning of the scene
Been struck so to the soul that presently
They have proclaim'd their malefactions;
For murder, though it have no tongue, will speak
With most miraculous organ. *Ib.* [625]

37 Abuses me to damn me. *Ib.* [640]

[433]

1   The play's the thing
Wherein I'll catch the conscience of the king.
                      Hamlet, II. ii. [641]

2 Nor do we find him forward to be sounded,
But, with a crafty madness, keeps aloof,
When we would bring him on to some confession
Of his true state.   *Ib.* III. i. 7

3 'Tis too much prov'd—that with devotion's visage
And pious action, we do sugar o'er
The devil himself.   *Ib.* 47

4 To be, or not to be: that is the question:
Whether 'tis nobler in the mind to suffer
The slings and arrows of outrageous fortune,
Or to take arms against a sea of troubles,
And by opposing end them? To die: to sleep;
No more; and, by a sleep to say we end
The heart-ache and the thousand natural shocks
That flesh is heir to, 'tis a consummation
Devoutly to be wish'd. To die, to sleep;
To sleep: perchance to dream: ay, there's the rub;
For in that sleep of death what dreams may come
When we have shuffled off this mortal coil,
Must give us pause. There's the respect
That makes calamity of so long life;
For who would bear the whips and scorns of time,
The oppressor's wrong, the proud man's contumely,
The pangs of dispriz'd love, the law's delay,
The insolence of office, and the spurns
That patient merit of the unworthy takes,
When he himself might his quietus make
With a bare bodkin? Who would fardels bear,
To grunt and sweat under a weary life,
But that the dread of something after death,
The undiscover'd country from whose bourn
No traveller returns, puzzles the will,
And makes us rather bear those ills we have,
Than fly to others that we know not of?
Thus conscience doth make cowards of us all;
And thus the native hue of resolution
Is sicklied o'er with the pale cast of thought,
And enterprises of great pith and moment
With this regard their currents turn awry,
And lose the name of action.   *Ib.* 56

5   Nymph, in thy orisons
Be all my sins remember'd   *Ib.* 89

6   For, to the noble mind,
Rich gifts wax poor when givers prove unkind.
                              Ib. 100

7 Get thee to a nunnery.   *Ib.* [124]

8 I am myself indifferent honest.   *Ib.* [125]

9 I am very proud, revengeful, ambitious; with more
offences at my beck, than I have thoughts to put
them in, imagination to give them shape, or time
to act them in. What should such fellows as I do
crawling between heaven and earth? *Ib.* [128]

10 Let the doors be shut upon him, that he may play
the fool nowhere but in's own house. *Ib.* [137]

11 Be thou as chaste as ice, as pure as snow, thou shalt
not escape calumny.   *Ib.* [142]

12 I have heard of your paintings too, well enough. God
hath given you one face, and you make yourselves
another.   *Ib.* [150]

13 I say, we will have no more marriages. *Ib.* [156]

14 O! what a noble mind is here o'erthrown:
The courtier's, soldier's, scholar's, eye, tongue, sword;
The expectancy and rose of the fair state,
The glass of fashion, and the mould of form,
The observed of all observers, quite, quite, down!
And I, of ladies most deject and wretched,
That suck'd the honey of his music vows,
Now see that noble and most sovereign reason,
Like sweet bells jangled, out of tune and harsh;
That unmatch'd form and figure of blown youth,
Blasted with ecstasy: O! woe is me,
To have seen what I have seen, see what I see!
                  Hamlet, III. i. [159]

15 Speak the speech, I pray you, as I pronounced it to
you, trippingly on the tongue; but if you mouth
it, as many of your players do, I had as lief the
town-crier spoke my lines. Nor do not saw the
air too much with your hand, thus; but use all
gently: for in the very torrent, tempest, and—as
I may say—whirlwind of passion, you must
acquire and beget a temperance, that may give it
smoothness. O! it offends me to the soul to hear
a robustious periwig-pated fellow tear a passion to
tatters, to very rags, to split the ears of the groundlings, who for the most part are capable of nothing
but inexplicable dumb-shows and noise: I would
have such a fellow whipped for o'erdoing Termagant; it out-herods Herod: pray you, avoid it.
                          Ib. ii. 1

16 Be not too tame neither, but let your own discretion
be your tutor: suit the action to the word, the word
to the action; with this special observance, that
you o'erstep not the modesty of nature. *Ib.* [19]

17 The purpose of playing, whose end, both at the first
and now, was and is, to hold, as 'twere, the mirror
up to nature.   *Ib.* [24]

18 To show . . . the very age and body of the time his
form and pressure.   *Ib.* [26]

19 Neither having the accent of Christians nor the gait
of Christian, pagan, nor man.   *Ib.* [35]

20 I have thought some of nature's journeymen had
made men, and not made them well, they imitated
humanity so abominably.   *Ib.* [38]

21 FIRST PLAYER:
I hope we have reformed that indifferently with us.
HAMLET:
O, reform it altogether.   *Ib.* [41]

22 That's villanous, and shows a most pitiful ambition
in the fool that uses it.   *Ib.* [49]

23 Horatio, thou art e'en as just a man
As e'er my conversation cop'd withal. *Ib.* [59]

24   Nay, do not think I flatter:
For what advancement may I hope from thee,
That no revenue hast, but thy good spirits? *Ib.* [61]

25 Since my dear soul was mistress of her choice
And could of men distinguish, her election
Hath seal'd thee for herself.   *Ib.* [68]

26 A man that fortune's buffets and rewards
Hast ta'en with equal thanks; and bless'd are those
Whose blood and judgment are so well co-mingled
That they are not a pipe for Fortune's finger
To sound what stop she please. Give me that man
That is not passion's slave, and I will wear him
In my heart's core, ay, in my heart of heart,
As I do thee. Something too much of this. *Ib.* [72]

1 And my imaginations are as foul
As Vulcan's stithy. *Hamlet*, III. ii. [88]

2 The chameleon's dish: I eat the air, promise-crammed. *Ib.* [98]

3 Here's metal more attractive. *Ib.* [117]

4 That's a fair thought to lie between maids' legs. *Ib.* [126]

5 Die two months ago, and not forgotten yet? Then there's hope a great man's memory may outlive his life half a year; but, by'r lady, he must build churches then. *Ib.* [140]

6 For, O! for, O! the hobby-horse is forgot. *Ib.* [145]

7 Marry, this is miching mallecho. *Ib.* [148]

8 OPHELIA:
'Tis brief, my lord.
HAMLET:
As woman's love. *Ib.* [165]

9 Where love is great, the littlest doubts are fear;
When little fears grow great, great love grows there. *Ib.* [183]

10 What to ourselves in passion we propose,
The passion ending, doth the purpose lose. *Ib.* [206]

11 This world is not for aye, nor 'tis not strange
That even our love should with our fortunes change. *Ib.* [212]

12 The great man down, you mark his favourite flies;
The poor advanc'd makes friends of enemies. *Ib.* [216]

13 Our wills and fates do so contrary run
That our devices still are overthrown. *Ib.* [223]

14 Sleep rock thy brain;
And never come mischance between us twain! *Ib.* [239]

15 The lady doth protest too much, methinks. *Ib.* [242]

16 We that have free souls, it touches us not: let the galled jade wince, our withers are unwrung. *Ib.* [255]

17 The story is extant, and writ in very choice Italian. *Ib.* [277]

18 What! frighted with false fire? *Ib.* [282]

19 So runs the world away. *Ib.* [289]

20 Put your discourse into some frame, and start not so wildly from my affair. *Ib.* [325]

21 O wonderful son, that can so astonish a mother! *Ib.* [347]

22 The proverb is something musty. *Ib.* [366]

23 It will discourse most eloquent music. *Ib.* [381]

24 You would play upon me; you would seem to know my stops; you would pluck out the heart of my mystery; you would sound me from my lowest note to the top of my compass. *Ib.* [387]

25 Do you think I am easier to be played on than a pipe? Call me what instrument you will, though you can fret me, you cannot play upon me. *Ib.* [393]

26 HAMLET:
Do you see yonder cloud that's almost in shape of a camel?
POLONIUS:
By the mass, and 'tis like a camel, indeed.

HAMLET:
Methinks it is like a weasel.
POLONIUS:
It is backed like a weasel.
HAMLET:
Or like a whale?
POLONIUS:
Very like a whale. *Hamlet*, III. ii. [400]

27 They fool me to the top of my bent. *Ib.* [408]

28 By and by is easily said. *Ib.* [411]

29 'Tis now the very witching time of night. *Ib.* [413]

30 Let me be cruel, not unnatural;
I will speak daggers to her, but use none. *Ib.* [420]

31 O! my offence is rank, it smells to heaven. *Ib.* iii. 36

32 My stronger guilt defeats my strong intent;
And, like a man to double business bound,
I stand in pause where I shall first begin,
And both neglect. *Ib.* 40

33 Whereto serves mercy
But to confront the visage of offence? *Ib.* 46

34 May one be pardon'd and retain the offence? *Ib.* 56

35 'Tis not so above;
There is no shuffling, there the action lies
In his true nature, and we ourselves compell'd,
Even to the teeth and forehead of our faults
To give in evidence. *Ib.* 60

36 Now might I do it pat, now he is praying. *Ib.* 73

37 He took my father grossly, full of bread,
With all his crimes broad blown, as flush as May;
And how his audit stands who knows save heaven? *Ib.* 80

38 Tell him his pranks have been too broad to bear with. *Ib.* iv. 2

39 You go not, till I set you up a glass
Where you may see the inmost part of you. *Ib.* 19

40 How now! a rat? Dead, for a ducat, dead! *Ib.* 23

41 A bloody deed! almost as bad, good mother,
As kill a king, and marry with his brother. *Ib.* 28

42 As false as dicers' oaths. *Ib.* 45

43 A rhapsody of words. *Ib.* 48

44 Ay me! what act,
That roars so loud, and thunders in the index? *Ib.* 51

45 Look here, upon this picture, and on this. *Ib.* 53

46 Could you on this fair mountain leave to feed,
And batten on this moor? *Ib.* 66

47 You cannot call it love, for at your age
The hey-day in the blood is tame, it's humble,
And waits upon the judgment. *Ib.* 68

48 Speak no more;
Thou turn'st mine eyes into my very soul. *Ib.* 88

49 A cut-purse of the empire and the rule,
That from a shelf the precious diadem stole,
And put it in his pocket! *Ib.* 99

50 A king of shreds and patches. *Ib.* 102

51 Do you not come your tardy son to chide? *Ib.* 106

52 Conceit in weakest bodies strongest works. *Ib.* 113

1   Bring me to the test,
And I the matter will re-word, which madness
Would gambol from. Mother, for love of grace,
Lay not that flattering unction to your soul.
Hamlet, III. iv. 142

2   Confess yourself to heaven;
Repent what's past; avoid what is to come.   *Ib.* 149

3 For in the fatness of these pursy times,
Virtue itself of vice must pardon beg.   *Ib.* 153

4 QUEEN:
O Hamlet! thou hast cleft my heart in twain.
HAMLET:
O! throw away the worser part of it,
And live the purer with the other half.   *Ib.* 156

5 Assume a virtue, if you have it not.
That monster, custom, who all sense doth eat,
Of habits devil, is angel yet in this.   *Ib.* 160

6 And when you are desirous to be bless'd,
I'll blessing beg of you.   *Ib.* 171

7 I must be cruel, only to be kind.   *Ib.* 178

8 For 'tis the sport to have the enginer
Hoist with his own petar: and it shall go hard
But I will delve one yard below their mines,
And blow them at the moon.   *Ib.* 206

9 He keeps them, like an ape doth nuts, in the corner
of his jaw; first mouthed, to be last swallowed.
Ib. IV. ii. [19]

10 A knavish speech sleeps in a foolish ear.   *Ib.* [25]

11   Diseases desperate grown,
By desperate appliances are reliev'd,
Or not at all.   *Ib.* iii. 9

12 A certain convocation of politic worms are e'en at
him. Your worm is your only emperor for diet.
Ib. [21]

13 A man may fish with the worm that hath eat of a
king, and eat of the fish that hath fed of that worm.
Ib. [29]

14 We go to gain a little patch of ground,
That hath in it no profit but the name.   *Ib.* iv. 18

15 How all occasions do inform against me,
And spur my dull revenge! What is a man,
If his chief good and market of his time
Be but to sleep and feed? a beast, no more.
Sure he that made us with such large discourse,
Looking before and after, gave us not
That capability and god-like reason
To fust in us unus'd.   *Ib.* 32

16   Some craven scruple
Of thinking too precisely on the event.   *Ib.* 40

17   Rightly to be great
Is not to stir without great argument,
But greatly to find quarrel in a straw
When honour's at the stake.   *Ib.* 53

18 So full of artless jealousy is guilt,
It spills itself in fearing to be spilt.   *Ib.* v. 19

19 How should I your true love know
From another one?
By his cockle hat and staff,
And his sandal shoon.   *Ib.* [23]

20 He is dead and gone, lady,
He is dead and gone,
At his head a grass-green turf;
At his heels a stone.   *Hamlet*, IV. v. [29]

21 White his shroud as the mountain snow.   *Ib.* [36]

22 Larded with sweet flowers;
Which bewept to the grave did go
With true-love showers.   *Ib.* [38]

23 Then up he rose, and donn'd his clothes.   *Ib.* [53]

24 Come, my coach! Good-night, ladies; good-night,
sweet ladies; good night, good-night.   *Ib.* [72]

25 When sorrows come, they come not single spies,
But in battalions.   *Ib.* [78]

26   We have done but greenly
In hugger-mugger to inter him.   *Ib.* [83]

27 There's such divinity doth hedge a king,
That treason can but peep to what it would. *Ib.* [123]

28 To hell, allegiance! vows, to the blackest devil!
Conscience and grace, to the profoundest pit!
I dare damnation.   *Ib.* [130]

29 Nature is fine in love, and where 'tis fine
It sends some precious instance of itself
After the thing it loves.   *Ib.* [160]

30 They bore him barefac'd on the bier;
Hey non nonny, nonny, hey nonny;
And in his grave rain'd many a tear.   *Ib.* [163]

31 There's rosemary, that's for remembrance; pray,
love, remember: and there is pansies, that's for
thoughts.   *Ib.* [174]

32 You must wear your rue with a difference. There's
a daisy; I would give you some violets, but they
withered all when my father died.   *Ib.* [181]

33 They say he made a good end.   *Ib.* [184]

34 For bonny sweet Robin is all my joy.   *Ib.* [186]

35 No, no, he is dead;
Go to thy death-bed,
He never will come again.   *Ib.* [191]

36 He is gone, he is gone,
And we cast away moan;
God ha' mercy on his soul!   *Ib.* [196]

37 His means of death, his obscure burial,
No trophy, sword, nor hatchment o'er his bones,
No noble rite nor formal ostentation.   *Ib.* [213]

38 And where the offence is let the great axe fall.
Ib. [218]

39   You must not think
That we are made of stuff so fat and dull
That we can let our beard be shook with danger
And think it pastime.   *Ib.* vii. 30

40 It warms the very sickness in my heart,
That I shall live and tell him to his teeth,
'Thus diddest thou.'   *Ib.* 55

41 A very riband in the cap of youth.   *Ib.* 77

42   He grew into his seat,
And to such wondrous doing brought his horse,
As he had been incorps'd and demi-natur'd
With the brave beast.   *Ib.* 85

43 No place, indeed, should murder sanctuarize. *Ib.* 127

1 There is a willow grows aslant a brook,
That shows his hoar leaves in the glassy stream;
There with fantastic garlands did she come,
Of crow-flowers, nettles, daisies, and long purples,
That liberal shepherds give a grosser name,
But our cold maids do dead men's fingers call them:
There, on the pendent boughs her coronet weeds
Clambering to hang, an envious sliver broke,
When down her weedy trophies and herself
Fell in the weeping brook. Her clothes spread wide,
And, mermaid-like, awhile they bore her up;
Which time she chanted snatches of old tunes,
As one incapable of her own distress.
Hamlet, IV. vii. 167

2 Too much of water hast thou, poor Ophelia,
And therefore I forbid my tears; but yet
It is our trick, nature her custom holds,
Let shame say what it will.   *Ib.* 186

3 Is she to be buried in Christian burial that wilfully
seeks her own salvation?   *Ib.* v. i. 1

4 Ay, marry, is 't; crowner's quest law.   *Ib.* [23]

5 There is no ancient gentlemen but gardeners, ditchers
and grave-makers; they hold up Adam's profession.
          Ib. [32]

6 The gallows-maker; for that frame outlives a thousand
tenants.   *Ib.* [47]

7 Cudgel thy brains no more about it, for your dull ass
will not mend his pace with beating.   *Ib.* [61]

8 The houses that he makes last till doomsday.
          Ib. [64]

9 Has this fellow no feeling of his business?   *Ib.* [71]

10 The hand of little employment hath the daintier
sense.   *Ib.* [75]

11 The pate of a politician, . . . one that would circumvent God.   *Ib.* [84]

12 How absolute the knave is! we must speak by the
card, or equivocation will undo us.   *Ib.* [147]

13 The age is grown so picked that the toe of the peasant
comes so near the heel of the courtier, he galls his
kibe.   *Ib.* [150]

14 FIRST CLOWN:
He that is mad, and sent into England.
HAMLET:
Ay, marry; why was he sent into England?
FIRST CLOWN:
Why, because he was mad; he shall recover his wits
there; or, if he do not, 'tis no great matter there.
HAMLET:
Why?
FIRST CLOWN:
'Twill not be seen in him there; there the men are
as mad as he.   *Ib.* [160]

15 Alas! poor Yorick. I knew him, Horatio; a fellow of
infinite jest, of most excellent fancy; he hath
borne me on his back a thousand times; and now,
how abhorred in my imagination it is! my gorge
rises at it. Here hung those lips that I have kissed
I know not how oft. Where be your gibes now?
your gambols? your songs? your flashes of merriment, that were wont to set the table on a roar?
Not one now, to mock your own grinning? quite
chap-fallen? Now get you to my lady's chamber,
and tell her, let her paint an inch thick, to this
favour she must come.   *Ib.* [201]

16 To what base uses we may return, Horatio!
          Hamlet, v. i. [222]

17 'Twere to consider too curiously to consider so.
          Ib. [226]

18 Imperious Cæsar, dead, and turn'd to clay,
Might stop a hole to keep the wind away.   *Ib.* [235]

19 We should profane the service of the dead,
To sing a requiem, and such rest to her
As to peace-parted souls.   *Ib.* [258]

20   Lay her i' the earth;
And from her fair and unpolluted flesh
May violets spring! I tell thee, churlish priest,
A ministering angel shall my sister be,
When thou liest howling.   *Ib.* [260]

21 Sweets to the sweet: farewell!   *Ib.* [265]

22 I thought thy bride-bed to have deck'd, sweet maid,
And not have strewed thy grave.   *Ib.* [267]

23 For, though I am not splenetive and rash
Yet have I in me something dangerous.   *Ib.* [283]

24 I lov'd Ophelia: forty thousand brothers
Could not, with all their quantity of love,
Make up my sum.   *Ib.* [291]

25 And thus a while the fit will work on him;
Anon, as patient as the female dove,
When that her golden couplets are disclos'd,
His silence will sit drooping.   *Ib.* [307]

26 This grave shall have a living monument.   *Ib.* [319]

27 There's a divinity that shapes our ends,
Rough-hew them how we will.   *Ib.* ii. 10

28 It did me yeoman's service.   *Ib.* 36

29 HAMLET:
Dost know this water-fly?
HORATIO:
                    No, my good lord.
HAMLET:
Thy state is the more gracious; for 'tis a vice to
know him.   *Ib.* [84]

30 What imports the nomination of this gentleman?
          Ib. [134]

31 The phrase would be more german to the matter, if
we could carry cannon by our sides.   *Ib.* [165]

32 'Tis the breathing time of day with me.   *Ib.* [181]

33 But thou wouldst not think how ill all's here about
my heart.   *Ib.* [222]

34 Not a whit, we defy augury; there's a special providence in the fall of a sparrow. If it be now, 'tis
not to come; if it be not to come, it will be now;
if it be not now, yet it will come: the readiness is
all.   *Ib.* [232]

35 I have shot mine arrow o'er the house,
And hurt my brother.   *Ib.* [257]

36 Now the king drinks to Hamlet!   *Ib.* [292]

37 A hit, a very palpable hit.   *Ib.* [295]

38 Why, as a woodcock to mine own springe, Osric;
I am justly kill'd with my own treachery.   *Ib.* [320]

39 O villany! Ho! let the door be lock'd:
Treachery! seek it out.   *Ib.* [325]

40 The point envenom'd too!—
Then, venom, to thy work.   *Ib.* [335]

SHAKESPEARE

1   This fell sergeant, death,
Is strict in his arrest.   *Hamlet*, v. ii. [350]

2 Report me and my cause aright.   *Ib.* [353]

3 I am more an antique Roman than a Dane. *Ib.* [355]

4   Horatio, what a wounded name,
Things standing thus unknown, shall live behind me.
If thou didst ever hold me in thy heart,
Absent thee from felicity awhile,
And in this harsh world draw thy breath in pain,
To tell my story.   *Ib.* [358]

5 The potent poison quite o'ercrows my spirit.
     Ib. [367]

6 The rest is silence.   *Ib.* [372]

7 Now cracks a noble heart. Good-night, sweet prince,
And flights of angels sing thee to thy rest! *Ib.* [373]

8   O proud death!
What feast is toward in thine eternal cell? *Ib.* [378]

9   Purposes mistook
Fall'n on the inventors' heads.   *Ib.* [398]

10 For he was likely, had he been put on,
To have prov'd most royally.   *Ib.* [411]

11 So shaken as we are, so wan with care.
     King Henry IV, Part I, i. i. 1

12   In those holy fields
Over whose acres walk'd those blessed feet,
Which fourteen hundred years ago were nail'd
For our advantage, on the bitter cross.   *Ib.* 24

13 The blessed sun himself a fair hot wench in flame-
colour'd taffeta.   *Ib.* ii. [10]

14 I see no reason why thou shouldst be so superfluous
to demand the time of the day.   *Ib.* [11]

15 Phœbus, he 'that wandering knight so fair'. *Ib.* [16]

16 Let us be Diana's foresters, gentlemen of the shade,
minions of the moon.   *Ib.* [28]

17 FALSTAFF:
And is not my hostess of the tavern a most sweet
wench?
PRINCE:
As the honey of Hybla, my old lad of the castle.
     Ib. [44]

18 What, in thy quips and thy quiddities?   *Ib.* [50]

19 Shall there be gallows standing in England when
thou art king, and resolution thus fobbed as it is
with the rusty curb of old father antick, the law?
     Ib. [66]

20 Thou hast the most unsavoury similes.   *Ib.* [89]

21 I would to God thou and I knew where a commodity
of good names were to be bought.   *Ib.* [92]

22 O! thou hast damnable iteration, and art, indeed,
able to corrupt a saint.   *Ib.* [101]

23 Now am I, if a man should speak truly, little better
than one of the wicked.   *Ib.* [105]

24 I'll be damned for never a king's son in Christendom.
     Ib. [108]

25 Why, Hal, 'tis my vocation, Hal; 'tis no sin for a
man to labour in his vocation.   *Ib.* [116]

26 How agrees the devil and thee about thy soul, that
thou soldest him on Good Friday last for a cup
of Madeira and a cold capon's leg?   *Ib.* [126]

27 There's neither honesty, manhood, nor good fellowship in thee.   *King Henry IV, Part I*, i. ii. [154]

28 Farewell, thou latter spring! Farewell, All-hallown
summer!   *Ib.* [176]

29 If he fight longer than he sees reason, I'll forswear
arms.   *Ib.* [206]

30 I know you all, and will awhile uphold
The unyok'd humour of your idleness.   *Ib.* [217]

31 If all the year were playing holidays,
To sport would be as tedious as to work;
But when they seldom come, they wish'd for come.
     Ib. [226]

32   A certain lord, neat, and trimly dress'd,
Fresh as a bridegroom; and his chin, new-reap'd,
Show'd like a stubble-land at harvest home:
He was perfumed like a milliner,
And 'twixt his finger and his thumb he held
A pouncet-box, which ever and anon
He gave his nose and took't away again. *Ib.* iii. 33

33 And as the soldiers bore dead bodies by,
He call'd them untaught knaves, unmannerly,
To bring a slovenly, unhandsome corpse
Betwixt the wind and his nobility.
With many holiday and lady terms
He question'd me.   *Ib.* 42

34 So pester'd with a popinjay.   *Ib.* 50

35   He made me mad
To see him shine so brisk, and smell so sweet
And talk so like a waiting-gentlewoman
Of guns, and drums, and wounds,—God save the
mark!—
And telling me the sovereign'st thing on earth
Was parmaceti for an inward bruise;
And that it was great pity, so it was,
This villainous saltpetre should be digg'd
Out of the bowels of the harmless earth,
Which many a good tall fellow had destroy'd
So cowardly; and but for these vile guns,
He would himself have been a soldier.   *Ib.* 53

36 To put down Richard, that sweet lovely rose,
And plant this thorn, this canker, Bolingbroke.
     Ib. 175

37 WORCESTER:
As to o'er-walk a current roaring loud,
On the unsteadfast footing of a spear.
HOTSPUR:
If he fall in, good-night! or sink or swim:
Send danger from the east unto the west,
So honour cross it from the north to south,
And let them grapple: O! the blood more stirs
To rouse a lion than to start a hare.   *Ib.* 192

38 By heaven methinks it were an easy leap
To pluck bright honour from the pale-fac'd moon,
Or dive into the bottom of the deep,
Where fathom-line could never touch the ground,
And pluck up drowned honour by the locks;
So he that doth redeem her thence might wear
Without corrival all her dignities:
But out upon this half-fac'd fellowship! *Ib.* 201

39 Why, what a candy deal of courtesy
This fawning greyhound then did proffer me! *Ib.* 251

40 I know a trick worth two of that.   *Ib.* II. i. [40]

41 At hand, quoth pick-purse.   *Ib.* [53]

[438]

1 We have the receipt of fern-seed, we walk invisible.
King Henry IV, Part I, II. i. [95]

2 I am bewitched with the rogue's company. If the rascal have not given me medicines to make me love him, I'll be hanged. *Ib.* ii. [19]

3 Go hang thyself in thine own heir-apparent garters!
Ib. [49]

4 Farewell, and stand fast. *Ib.* [78]

5 Happy man be his dole. *Ib.* [84]

6 On, bacons, on! *Ib.* [99]

7 It would be argument for a week, laughter for a month, and a good jest for ever. *Ib.* [104]

8 Falstaff sweats to death
And lards the lean earth as he walks along. *Ib.* [119]

9 Out of this nettle, danger, we pluck this flower, safety. *Ib.* iii. [11]

10 A good plot, good friends, and full of expectation; an excellent plot, very good friends. *Ib.* [21]

11 Constant you are,
But yet a woman: and for secrecy,
No lady closer; for I well believe
Thou wilt not utter what thou dost not know.
Ib. [113]

12 Show it a fair pair of heels. *Ib.* iv. [52]

13 I am not yet of Percy's mind, the Hotspur of the North; he that kills me some six or seven dozen of Scots at a breakfast, washes his hands, and says to his wife, 'Fie upon this quiet life! I want work.'
Ib. [116]

14 Didst thou never see Titan kiss a dish of butter—pitiful-hearted Titan, that melted at the sweet tale of the sun? *Ib.* [135]

15 There live not three good men unhanged in England, and one of them is fat and grows old. *Ib.* [146]

16 Call you that backing of your friends? A plague upon such backing! give me them that will face me.
Ib. [168]

17 A plague of all cowards, still say I. *Ib.* [175]

18 I am a Jew else; an Ebrew Jew. *Ib.* [201]

19 All! I know not what ye call all. *Ib.* [208]

20 Nay that's past praying for: I have peppered two of them: two I am sure I have paid, two rogues in buckram suits. I tell thee what, Hal, if I tell thee a lie, spit in my face, call me horse. Thou knowest my old ward; here I lay, and thus I bore my point. Four rogues in buckram let drive at me—
Ib. [214]

21 O monstrous! eleven buckram men grown out of two.
Ib. [247]

22 Three misbegotten knaves in Kendal-green.
Ib. [249]

23 These lies are like the father that begets them; gross as a mountain, open, palpable. *Ib.* [253]

24 Give you a reason on compulsion! if reasons were as plentiful as blackberries I would give no man a reason upon compulsion, I. *Ib.* [267]

25 Mark now, how a plain tale shall put you down.
Ib. [285]

26 What a slave art thou, to hack thy sword as thou hast done, and then say it was in fight! *Ib.* [292]

27 Instinct is a great matter, I was a coward on instinct.
King Henry IV, Part I, II. iv. [304]

28 Ah! No more of that, Hal, an thou lovest me.
Ib. [316]

29 What doth gravity out of his bed at midnight?
Ib. [328]

30 A plague of sighing and grief! It blows a man up like a bladder. *Ib.* [370]

31 I will do it in King Cambyses' vein. *Ib.* [430]

32 QUICKLY:
O Jesu! he doth it as like one of these harlotry players as ever I see!
FALSTAFF:
Peace, good pint-pot! *Ib.* [441]

33 Shall the blessed sun of heaven prove a micher and eat blackberries? A question not to be asked.
Ib. [454]

34 There is a devil haunts thee in the likeness of a fat old man; a tun of man is thy companion.
Ib. [498]

35 That roasted Manningtree ox with the pudding in his belly, that reverend vice, that grey iniquity, that father ruffian, that vanity in years. *Ib.* [504]

36 If sack and sugar be a fault, God help the wicked!
Ib. [524]

37 No, my good lord; banish Peto, banish Bardolph, banish Poins; but for sweet Jack Falstaff, kind Jack Falstaff, true Jack Falstaff, valiant Jack Falstaff, and therefore more valiant, being, as he is, old Jack Falstaff, banish not him thy Harry's company: banish not him thy Harry's company: banish plump Jack and banish all the world.
Ib. [528]

38 Play out the play. *Ib.* [539]

39 O monstrous! but one half-pennyworth of bread to this intolerable deal of sack! *Ib.* [598]

40 GLENDOWER: At my nativity
The front of heaven was full of fiery shapes,
Of burning cressets; and at my birth
The frame and huge foundation of the earth
Shak'd like a coward.
HOTSPUR:
Why, so it would have done at the same season, if your mother's cat had but kittened. *Ib.* III. i. 13

41 And all the courses of my life do show
I am not in the roll of common men. *Ib.* [42]

42 GLENDOWER:
I can call spirits from the vasty deep.
HOTSPUR:
Why, so can I, or so can any man;
But will they come when you do call for them?
Ib. [53]

43 O! while you live, tell truth, and shame the devil!
Ib. [62]

44 See how this river comes me cranking in,
And cuts me from the best of all my land
A huge half-moon, a monstrous cantle out. *Ib.* [99]

45 I had rather be a kitten and cry mew
Than one of these same metre ballad-mongers.
Ib. [128]

46 Mincing poetry. *Ib.* [133]

SHAKESPEARE

1 And such a deal of skimble-skamble stuff
As puts me from my faith.
King Henry IV, Part I, iii. i. [153]

2   O! he's as tedious
As a tired horse, a railing wife;
Worse than a smoky house. I had rather live
With cheese and garlic in a windmill, far,
Than feed on cates and have him talk to me
In any summer-house in Christendom. *Ib*. [158]

3 I understand thy kisses, and thou mine,
And that's a feeling disputation. *Ib*. [204]

4 Makes Welsh as sweet as ditties highly penn'd,
Sung by a fair queen in a summer's bower,
With ravishing division, to her lute. *Ib*. [208]

5 Now I perceive the devil understands Welsh.
Ib. [233]

6 You swear like a comfit-maker's wife. *Ib*. [252]

7 Swear me, Kate, like a lady as thou art,
A good mouth-filling oath. *Ib*. [257]

8 The skipping king, he ambled up and down
With shallow jesters and rash bavin wits. *Ib*. ii. 60

9   Being daily swallow'd by men's eyes,
They surfeited with honey and began
To loathe the taste of sweetness, whereof a little
More than a little is by much too much.
So, when he had occasion to be seen,
He was but as the cuckoo is in June,
Heard, not regarded. *Ib*. 70

10 My near'st and dearest enemy. *Ib*. 123

11 Well, I'll repent, and that suddenly, while I am in
some liking; I shall be out of heart shortly, and
then I shall have no strength to repent. *Ib*. iii. [5]

12 Company, villanous company, hath been the spoil of
me. *Ib*. [10]

13 Come, sing me a bawdy song; make me merry.
Ib. [15]

14 Shall I not take mine ease in mine inn? *Ib*. [91]

15 I have more flesh than another man, and therefore
more frailty. *Ib*. [187]

16   That daff'd the world aside,
And bid it pass. *Ib*. iv. i. 96

17 All plum'd like estridges that wing the wind,
Baited like eagles having lately bath'd. *Ib*. 98

18 I saw young Harry, with his beaver on,
His cushes on his thighs, gallantly arm'd,
Rise from the ground like feather'd Mercury,
And vaulted with such ease into his seat,
As if an angel dropp'd down from the clouds,
To turn and wind a fiery Pegasus,
And witch the world with noble horsemanship.
Ib. 104

19 Doomsday is near; die all, die merrily. *Ib*. 134

20 I have misus'd the king's press damnably. *Ib*. ii. [13]

21 The cankers of a calm world and a long peace.
Ib. [32]

22 I am as vigilant as a cat to steal cream. *Ib*. [64]

23 Tut, tut; good enough to toss; food for powder, food
for powder; they'll fill a pit as well as better:
tush, man, mortal men, mortal men. *Ib*. [72]

24 To the latter end of a fray and the beginning of a
feast
Fits a dull fighter and a keen guest.
King Henry IV, Part I, iv. ii. [86]

25 Greatness knows itself. *Ib*. iii. 74

26 For mine own part, I could be well content
To entertain the lag-end of my life
With quiet hours. *Ib*. v. i. 23

27 Rebellion lay in his way, and he found it. *Ib*. 28

28 I do not think a braver gentleman,
More active-valiant or more valiant-young,
More daring or more bold, is now alive
To grace this latter age with noble deeds.
For my part, I may speak it to my shame,
I have a truant been to chivalry. *Ib*. 89

29 FALSTAFF:
I would it were bed-time, Hal, and all well.
PRINCE:
Why, thou owest God a death. *Ib*. [125]

30 Honour pricks me on. Yea, but how if honour prick
me off when I come on? how then? Can honour
set-to a leg? No. Or an arm? No. Or take away
the grief of a wound? No. Honour hath no skill
in surgery, then? No. What is honour? A word.
What is that word, honour? Air. A trim reckoning! Who hath it? He that died o' Wednesday.
Doth he feel it? No. Doth he hear it? No. It is
insensible then? Yea, to the dead. But will it not
live with the living? No. Why? Detraction will
not suffer it. Therefore I'll none of it: honour is
a mere scutcheon: and so ends my catechism.
Ib. [131]

31 Suspicion all our lives shall be stuck full of eyes;
For treason is but trusted like the fox,
Who, ne'er so tame, so cherish'd, and lock'd up,
Will have a wild trick of his ancestors. *Ib*. ii. 8

32 O gentlemen! the time of life is short;
To spend that shortness basely were too long,
If life did ride upon a dial's point,
Still ending at the arrival of an hour.
An if we live, we live to tread on kings;
If die, brave death, when princes die with us!
Now, for our consciences, the arms are fair,
When the intent of bearing them is just. *Ib*. 81

33 Now, *Esperance*! Percy! and set on. *Ib*. 96

34 I have led my ragamuffins where they are peppered
there's not three of my hundred and fifty left
alive, and they are for the town's end, to beg
during life. *Ib*. iii. [36]

35 I like not such grinning honour as Sir Walter hath
give me life; which if I can save, so; if not, honour
comes unlooked for, and there's an end. *Ib*. [61]

36 Two stars keep not their motion in one sphere.
Ib. iv. 65

37 But thought's the slave of life, and life time's fool;
And time, that takes survey of all the world,
Must have a stop. *Ib*. [81]

38   Fare thee well, great heart!
Ill-weav'd ambition, how much art thou shrunk!
When that this body did contain a spirit,
A kingdom for it was too small a bound;
But now two paces of the vilest earth
Is room enough: this earth, that bears thee dead,
Bears not alive so stout a gentleman. *Ib*. [87]

1 Thy ignominy sleep with thee in the grave,
But not remember'd in thy epitaph!
What! old acquaintance! could not all this flesh
Keep in a little life? Poor Jack, farewell!
I could have better spar'd a better man.
King Henry IV, Part I, v. iv. [100]

2 The better part of valour is discretion. *Ib.* [120]

3   Full bravely hast thou flesh'd
Thy maiden sword. *Ib.* [132]

4 Lord, Lord, how this world is given to lying! I grant
you I was down and out of breath; and so was he;
but we rose both at an instant, and fought a long
hour by Shrewsbury clock. *Ib.* [148]

5 For my part, if a lie may do thee grace,
I'll gild it with the happiest terms I have. *Ib.* [161]

6 I'll purge, and leave sack, and live cleanly, as a
nobleman should do. *Ib.* [168]

7 I speak of peace, while covert enmity
Under the smile of safety wounds the world.
King Henry IV, Part II, Induction, 9

8   Rumour is a pipe
Blown by surmises, jealousies, conjectures,
And of so easy and so plain a stop
That the blunt monster with uncounted heads,
The still-discordant wavering multitude,
Can play upon it. *Ib.* 15

9 Even such a man, so faint, so spiritless,
So dull, so dead in look, so woe-begone,
Drew Priam's curtain in the dead of night,
And would have told him, half his Troy was burn'd.
Ib. I. i. 70

10 Yet the first bringer of unwelcome news
Hath but a losing office, and his tongue
Sounds ever after as a sullen bell,
Remember'd knolling a departed friend. *Ib.* 100

11 The brain of this foolish-compounded clay, man, is
not able to invent anything that tends to laughter,
more than I invent or is invented on me: I am
not only witty in myself, but the cause that wit is
in other men. I do here walk before thee like a sow
that hath overwhelmed all her litter but one.
Ib. ii. [7]

12 A rascally yea-forsooth knave. *Ib.* [40]

13 Your lordship, though not clean past your youth,
hath yet some smack of age in you, some relish of
the saltness of time. *Ib.* [111]

14 This apoplexy is, as I take it, a kind of lethargy, an't
please your lordship; a kind of sleeping in the
blood, a whoreson tingling. *Ib.* [127]

15 It is the disease of not listening, the malady of not
marking, that I am troubled withal. *Ib.* [139]

16 I am as poor as Job, my lord, but not so patient.
Ib. [145]

17 Well, I am loath to gall a new-healed wound.
Ib. [169]

18 You that are old consider not the capacities of us
that are young; you measure the heat of our livers
with the bitterness of your galls; and we that are
in the vaward of our youth, I must confess, are
wags too. *Ib.* [198]

19 Have you not a moist eye, a dry hand, a yellow cheek,
a white beard, a decreasing leg, an increasing
belly? *Ib.* [206]

20 Every part about you blasted with antiquity.
King Henry IV, Part II, I. ii. [210]

21 My lord, I was born about three of the clock in the
afternoon, with a white head, and something of a
round belly. For my voice, I have lost it with
hollaing, and singing of anthems. *Ib.* [213]

22 CHIEF JUSTICE:
God send the prince a better companion!
FALSTAFF:
God send the companion a better prince! I cannot
rid my hands of him. *Ib.* [227]

23 All you that kiss our lady Peace at home. *Ib.* [236]

24 It was always yet the trick of our English nation, if
they have a good thing, to make it too common.
Ib. [244]

25 I would to God my name were not so terrible to the
enemy as it is: I were better to be eaten to death
with rust than to be scoured to nothing with perpetual motion. *Ib.* [247]

26 I can get no remedy against this consumption of the
purse: borrowing only lingers and lingers it out,
but the disease is incurable. *Ib.* [268]

27   O, thoughts of men accurst!
Past and to come seem best; things present, worst.
Ib. iii. 107

28 A poor lone woman. *Ib.* II. i. [37]

29 Away, you scullion! you rampallion! you fustilarian!
I'll tickle your catastrophe. *Ib.* [67]

30 He hath eaten me out of house and home. *Ib.* [82]

31 Thou didst swear to me upon a parcel-gilt goblet,
sitting in my Dolphin-chamber, at the round
table, by a sea-coal fire, upon Wednesday in
Wheeson week. *Ib.* [97]

32 Doth it not show vilely in me to desire small beer?
Ib. ii. [7]

33 I do now remember the poor creature, small beer.
Ib. [12]

34 Let the end try the man. *Ib.* [52]

35 Never a man's thought in the world keeps the roadway better than thine. *Ib.* [64]

36   He was indeed the glass
Wherein the noble youth did dress themselves.
Ib. iii. 21

37 Hollow pamper'd jades of Asia. *Ib.* iv [177]

38 By my troth, captain, these are very bitter words.
Ib. [183]

39 Thou whoreson little tidy Bartholomew boar-pig.
Ib. [249]

40 Patch up thine old body for heaven. *Ib.* [251]

41   O sleep! O gentle sleep!
Nature's soft nurse, how have I frighted thee,
That thou no more wilt weigh mine eyelids down
And steep my senses in forgetfulness?
Why rather, sleep, liest thou in smoky cribs,
Upon uneasy pallets stretching thee,
And hush'd with buzzing night-flies to thy slumber,
Than in the perfum'd chambers of the great,
Under the canopies of costly state,
And lull'd with sound of sweetest melody?
Ib. III. i. 5

1 Wilt thou upon the high and giddy mast
Seel up the ship-boy's eyes, and rock his brains
In cradle of the rude imperious surge,
And in the visitation of the winds,
Who take the ruffian billows by the top,
Curling their monstrous heads, and hanging them
With deaf'ning clamour in the slippery clouds,
That with the hurly death itself awakes?
King Henry IV, Part II, III. i. 18

2 With all appliances and means to boot. *Ib.* 29

3 Then, happy low, lie down!
Uneasy lies the head that wears a crown. *Ib.* 30

4 O God! that one might read the book of fate. *Ib.* 45

5 O! if this were seen,
The happiest youth, viewing his progress through,
What perils past, what crosses to ensue,
Would shut the book, and sit him down and die.
Ib. 54

6 There is a history in all men's lives,
Figuring the nature of the times deceas'd,
The which observ'd, a man may prophesy,
With a near aim, of the main chance of things
As yet not come to life, which in their seeds
And weak beginnings lie intreasured. *Ib.* 80

7 Death, as the Psalmist saith, is certain to all; all shall
die. How a good yoke of bullocks at Stamford
fair? *Ib.* ii. [41]

8 And is old Double dead? *Ib.* [58]

9 A soldier is better accommodated than with a wife.
Ib. [73]

10 Most forcible Feeble. *Ib.* [181]

11 We have heard the chimes at midnight. *Ib.* [231]

12 I care not; a man can die but once; we owe God a
death. *Ib.* [253]

13 He that dies this year is quit for the next. *Ib.* [257]

14 Lord, Lord, how subject we old men are to this vice
of lying! *Ib.* [329]

15 Like a man made after supper of a cheese-paring:
when a' was naked, he was, for all the world, like
a forked radish, with a head fantastically carved
upon it with a knife. *Ib.* [335]

16 Talks as familiarly of John a Gaunt as if he had been
sworn brother to him. *Ib.* [348]

17 Against ill chances men are ever merry,
But heaviness foreruns the good event. *Ib.* IV. ii. 81

18 A peace is of the nature of a conquest;
For then both parties nobly are subdu'd,
And neither party loser. *Ib.* 89

19 That I may justly say with the hook-nosed fellow of
Rome, 'I came, saw, and overcame.' *Ib.* iii. [44]

20 A man cannot make him laugh; but that's no marvel;
he drinks no wine. *Ib.* [95]

21 A good sherris-sack hath a two-fold operation in it.
It ascends me into the brain; dries me there all the
foolish and dull and crudy vapours which environ
it; makes it apprehensive, quick, forgetive, full of
nimble fiery and delectable shapes; which, deliver'd o'er to the voice, the tongue, which is the
birth, becomes excellent wit. The second property
of your excellent sherris is, the warming of the
blood; which, before cold and settled, left the liver

white and pale, which is the badge of pusillanimity
and cowardice: but the sherris warms it and makes
it course from the inwards to the parts extreme.
It illumineth the face, which, as a beacon, gives
warning to all the rest of this little kingdom, man,
to arm; and then the vital commoners and inland
petty spirits muster me all to their captain, the
heart, who, great and puffed up with this retinue,
doth any deed of courage; and this valour comes
of sherris. So that skill in the weapon is nothing
without sack, for that sets it a-work; and learning,
a mere hoard of gold kept by a devil till sack
commences it and sets it in act and use.
King Henry IV, Part II, IV. iii. [103]

22 If I had a thousand sons, the first human principle
I would teach them should be, to forswear thin
potations. *Ib.* [133]

23 Most subject is the fattest soil to weeds. *Ib.* iv. 54

24 Thou art a summer bird,
Which ever in the haunch of winter sings
The lifting up of day. *Ib.* [91]

25 O polish'd perturbation! golden care!
That keep'st the ports of slumber open wide
To many a watchful night! Sleep with it now!
Yet not so sound, and half so deeply sweet
As he whose brow with homely biggin bound
Snores out the watch of night. *Ib.* v. 22

26 This sleep is sound indeed; this is a sleep
That from this golden rigol hath divorc'd
So many English kings. *Ib.* 34

27 Thy wish was father, Harry, to that thought. *Ib.* 91

28 Commit
The oldest sins the newest kind of ways. *Ib.* 124

29 It hath been prophesied to me many years
I should not die but in Jerusalem,
Which vainly I suppos'd the Holy Land.
But bear me to that chamber; there I'll lie:
In that Jerusalem shall Harry die. *Ib.* 235

30 Any pretty little tiny kickshaws, tell William cook.
Ib. v. i. [29]

31 Not Amurath an Amurath succeeds,
But Harry, Harry. *Ib.* ii. 48

32 Sorrow so royally in you appears,
That I will deeply put the fashion on. *Ib.* 51

33 'Tis merry in hall when beards wag all. *Ib.* iii. [35]

34 A foutra for the world, and worldlings base!
I speak of Africa and golden joys. *Ib.* [100]

35 Under which king, Bezonian? speak, or die!
Ib. [116]

36 Let us take any man's horses; the laws of England
are at my commandment. *Ib.* [139]

37 I know thee not, old man: fall to thy prayers;
How ill white hairs become a fool and jester!
I have long dream'd of such a kind of man,
So surfeit-swell'd, so old, and so profane. *Ib.* v. [52]

38 Make less thy body hence, and more thy grace;
Leave gormandising; know the grave doth gape
For thee thrice wider than for other men. *Ib.* [57]

39 Presume not that I am the thing I was. *Ib.* [61]

40 Master Shallow, I owe you a thousand pound.
Ib. [78]

1 Where, for anything I know, Falstaff shall die of a sweat, unless already a' be killed with your hard opinions; for Oldcastle died a martyr, and this is not the man.
King Henry IV, Part II. Epilogue, [32]

2 O! for a Muse of fire, that would ascend
The brightest heaven of invention.
King Henry V, Chorus, 1

3 The flat unraised spirits. *Ib.* 9

4   Can this cockpit hold
The vasty fields of France? or may we cram
Within this wooden O the very casques
That did affright the air at Agincourt? *Ib.* 11

5 Consideration like an angel came,
And whipp'd the offending Adam out of him.
Ib. I. i. 28

6 Never came reformation in a flood,
With such a heady currance, scouring faults. *Ib.* 33

7   When he speaks,
The air, a charter'd libertine, is still. *Ib.* 47

8 O noble English! that could entertain
With half their forces the full pride of France,
And let another half stand laughing by,
All out of work, and cold for action. *Ib.* ii. 111

9 And make your chronicle as rich with praise
As is the owse and bottom of the sea
With sunken wrack and sumless treasuries. *Ib.* 163

10   For so work the honey-bees,
Creatures that by a rule in nature teach
The act of order to a peopled kingdom.
They have a king and officers of sorts;
Where some, like magistrates, correct at home,
Others, like merchants, venture trade abroad,
Others, like soldiers, armed in their stings,
Make boot upon the summer's velvet buds;
Which pillage they with merry march bring home
To the tent-royal of their emperor:
Who, busied in his majesty, surveys
The singing masons building roofs of gold,
The civil citizens kneading up the honey,
The poor mechanic porters crowding in
Their heavy burdens at his narrow gate,
The sad-ey'd justice, with his surly hum,
Delivering o'er to executors pale
The lazy yawning drone. *Ib.* 187

11 His present and your pains we thank you for:
When we have match'd our rackets to these balls,
We will in France, by God's grace, play a set
Shall strike his father's crown into the hazard.
Ib. 260

12 Now all the youth of England are on fire,
And silken dalliance in the wardrobe lies;
Now thrive the armourers, and honour's thought
Reigns solely in the breast of every man:
They sell the pasture now to buy the horse,
Following the mirror of all Christian kings,
With winged heels, as English Mercuries.
For now sits Expectation in the air
And hides a sword from hilts unto the point
With crowns imperial, crowns and coronets,
Promis'd to Harry and his followers.
Ib. II. Chorus, 1

13 O England! model to thy inward greatness,
Like little body with a mighty heart,
What might'st thou do, that honour would thee do,
Were all thy children kind and natural!
But see thy fault! *King Henry V*, II. Chorus, 16

14 I dare not fight; but I will wink and hold out mine iron. *Ib.* i. [7]

15 That's the humour of it. *Ib.* [63]

16 Base is the slave that pays. *Ib.* [100]

17 For, lambkins, we will live. *Ib.* [134]

18 Would I were with him, wheresome'er he is, either in heaven or in hell. *Ib.* iii. [7]

19 He's in Arthur's bosom, if ever man went to Arthur's bosom. A' made a finer end, and went away an it had been any christom child; a' parted even just between twelve and one, even at the turning o' the tide: for after I saw him fumble with the sheets and play with flowers and smile upon his fingers' ends, I knew there was but one way; for his nose was as sharp as a pen, and a' babbled of green fields. [Theobald's emendation of the Folio's reading: 'A table of green fields'.] *Ib.* [9]

20 So a' cried out 'God, God, God!' three or four times: now I, to comfort him, bid him a' should not think of God, I hoped there was no need to trouble himself with any such thoughts yet. *Ib.* [19]

21 As cold as any stone. *Ib.* [25]

22 BOY:
Yes, that a' did; and said they were devils incarnate.
HOSTESS:
A' never could abide carnation; 'twas a colour he never liked.
BOY:
A' said once, the devil would have him about women.
Ib. [33]

23   Trust none;
For oaths are straws, men's faiths are wafer-cakes,
And hold-fast is the only dog, my duck. *Ib.* [53]

24 Once more unto the breach, dear friends, once more;
Or close the wall up with our English dead!
In peace there's nothing so becomes a man
As modest stillness and humility:
But when the blast of war blows in our ears,
Then imitate the action of the tiger;
Stiffen the sinews, summon up the blood,
Disguise fair nature with hard-favour'd rage;
Then lend the eye a terrible aspect. *Ib.* III. i. 1

25   On, on you noblest English!
Whose blood is fet from fathers of war-proof;
Fathers that, like so many Alexanders,
Have in these parts from morn till even fought,
And sheath'd their swords for lack of argument. *Ib.* 17

26   And you, good yeomen,
Whose limbs were made in England, show us here
The mettle of your pasture. *Ib.* 25

27 I see you stand like greyhounds in the slips,
Straining upon the start. The game's afoot:
Follow your spirit; and, upon this charge
Cry 'God for Harry! England and Saint George!'
Ib. 31

28 I would give all my fame for a pot of ale, and safety.
Ib. ii. [14]

29 Men of few words are the best men. *Ib.* [40]

1 A' never broke any man's head but his own, and that was against a post when he was drunk.

King Henry V, III. ii. [43]

2 He will maintain his argument as well as any military man in the world, in the disciplines of the pristine wars of the Romans. *Ib.* [89]

3 One Bardolph, if your majesty know the man: his face is all bubukles, and whelks, and knobs, and flames o' fire. *Ib.* vi. [110]

4 I thought upon one pair of English legs
Did march three Frenchmen. *Ib.* [161]

5 Give them great meals of beef and iron and steel, they will eat like wolves and fight like devils.

Ib. vii. [166]

6 Now entertain conjecture of a time
When creeping murmur and the poring dark
Fills the wide vessel of the universe.
From camp to camp, through the foul womb of night,
The hum of either army stilly sounds,
That the fix'd sentinels almost receive
The secret whispers of each other's watch.
Fire answers fire, and through their paly flames
Each battle sees the other's umber'd face:
Steed threatens steed, in high and boastful neighs
Piercing the night's dull ear; and from the tents
The armourers, accomplishing the knights,
With busy hammers closing rivets up,
Give dreadful note of preparation. *Ib.* IV. Chorus, 1

7 The royal captain of this ruin'd band. *Ib.* 29

8 A largess universal, like the sun
His liberal eye doth give to every one,
Thawing cold fear. *Ib.* 43

9 A little touch of Harry in the night. *Ib.* 47

10 O for pity,—we shall much disgrace,
With four or five most vile and ragged foils,
Right ill dispos'd in brawl ridiculous,
The name of Agincourt. *Ib.* 49

11 Gloucester, 'tis true that we are in great danger;
The greater therefore should our courage be.

Ib. IV. i. 1

12 There is some soul of goodness in things evil,
Would men observingly distil it out. *Ib.* 4

13 Thus may we gather honey from the weed,
And make a moral of the devil himself. *Ib.* 11

14 Art thou base, common and popular? *Ib.* 37

15 Trail'st thou the puissant pike? *Ib.* 40

16 If you would take the pains but to examine the wars of Pompey the Great, you shall find, I warrant you, that there is no tiddle-taddle nor pibble-pabble in Pompey's camp. *Ib.* [69]

17 There is much care and valour in this Welshman.

Ib. [85]

18 I think the king is but a man, as I am: the violet smells to him as it doth to me. *Ib.* [106]

19 I am afeard there are few die well that die in a battle; for how can they charitably dispose of any thing when blood is their argument? *Ib.* [149]

20 Every subject's duty is the king's; but every subject's soul is his own. *Ib.* [189]

21 Upon the king! let us our lives, our souls,
Our debts, our careful wives,
Our children, and our sins lay on the king!
We must bear all. O hard condition!

King Henry V, IV. ii. [250]

22   What infinite heart's ease
Must kings neglect, that private men enjoy!
And what have kings that privates have not too,
Save ceremony, save general ceremony? *Ib.* [256]

23 'Tis not the balm, the sceptre and the ball,
The sword, the mace, the crown imperial,
The intertissued robe of gold and pearl,
The farced title running 'fore the king,
The throne he sits on, nor the tide of pomp
That beats upon the high shore of this world,
No, not all these, thrice-gorgeous ceremony,
Not all these, laid in bed majestical,
Can sleep so soundly as the wretched slave,
Who with a body fill'd and vacant mind
Gets him to rest, cramm'd with distressful bread;
Never sees horrid night, the child of hell,
But, like a lackey, from the rise to set
Sweats in the eye of Phœbus, and all night
Sleeps in Elysium; next day after dawn,
Doth rise and help Hyperion to his horse,
And follows so the ever-running year
With profitable labour to his grave:
And, but for ceremony, such a wretch,
Winding up days with toil and nights with sleep,
Hath the forehand and vantage of a king. *Ib.* [280]

24 O God of battles! steel my soldiers' hearts;
Possess them not with fear; take from them now
The sense of reckoning, if the opposed numbers
Pluck their hearts from them. *Ib.* [309]

25   O! that we now had here
But one ten thousand of those men in England
That do no work to-day. *Ib.* iii. 16

26 If we are mark'd to die, we are enow
To do our country loss; and if to live,
The fewer men, the greater share of honour. *Ib.* 20

27   I am not covetous for gold,
     .   .   .
But if it be a sin to covet honour
I am the most offending soul alive. *Ib.* 24

28 He which hath no stomach to this fight,
Let him depart; his passport shall be made,
And crowns for convoy put into his purse:
We would not die in that man's company
That fears his fellowship to die with us.
This day is called the feast of Crispian:
He that outlives this day and comes safe home,
Will stand a tip-toe when this day is nam'd,
And rouse him at the name of Crispian.
He that shall live this day, and see old age,
Will yearly on the vigil feast his neighbours,
And say, 'To-morrow is Saint Crispian:'
Then will he strip his sleeve and show his scars,
And say, 'These wounds I had on Crispin's day.'
Old men forget: yet all shall be forgot,
But he'll remember with advantages
What feats he did that day. Then shall our names,
Familiar in his mouth as household words,
Harry the King, Bedford and Exeter,
Warwick and Talbot, Salisbury and Gloucester,
Be in their flowing cups freshly remember'd.
This story shall the good man teach his son;
And Crispin Crispian shall ne'er go by,

From this day to the ending of the world,
But we in it shall be remembered;
We few, we happy few, we band of brothers;
For he to-day that sheds his blood with me
Shall be my brother; be he ne'er so vile
This day shall gentle his condition:
And gentlemen in England, now a-bed
Shall think themselves accurs'd they were not here,
And hold their manhoods cheap whiles any speaks
That fought with us upon Saint Crispin's day.
King Henry V, IV. iii. 35

1 Thou damned and luxurious mountain goat.
Ib. iv. [20]

2 I'll fer him, and firk him, and ferret him. *Ib.* [29]

3 And all my mother came into mine eyes
And gave me up to tears. *Ib.* vi. 31

4 There is a river in Macedon, and there is also moreover a river at Monmouth: ... and there is salmons in both. *Ib.* vii. [28]

5 But now behold,
In the quick forge and working-house of thought,
How London doth pour out her citizens.
Ib. v. Chorus, 22

6 Were now the general of our gracious empress,—
As in good time he may,—from Ireland coming,
Bringing rebellion broached on his sword. *Ib.* 30

7 There is occasions and causes why and wherefore in all things. *Ib.* v. i. [3]

8 Not for Cadwallader and all his goats. *Ib.* [29]

9 By this leek, I will most horribly revenge. *Ib.* [49]

10 Why that the naked, poor, and mangled Peace,
Dear nurse of arts, plenties, and joyful births.
Ib. ii. 34

11 The even mead, that erst brought sweetly forth
The freckled cowslip, burnet, and green clover,
. . . . . .
Conceives by idleness, and nothing teems
But hateful docks, rough thistles, kecksies, burs.
Ib. 48

12 If not, to say to thee that I shall die, is true; but for thy love, by the Lord, no; yet I love thee too.
Ib. [157]

13 For these fellows of infinite tongue, that can rhyme themselves into ladies' favours, they do always reason themselves out again. *Ib.* [162]

14 Shall not thou and I, between Saint Denis and Saint George, compound a boy, half-French, half-English, that shall go to Constantinople and take the Turk by the beard? *Ib.* [218]

15 It is not a fashion for the maids in France to kiss before they are married. *Ib.* [287]

16 God, the best maker of all marriages,
Combine your hearts in one. *Ib.* [387]

17 Hung be the heavens with black, yield day to night!
King Henry VI, Part I, I. i. 1

18 Expect Saint Martin's summer, halcyon days.
Ib. ii. 131

19 Unbidden guests
Are often welcomest when they are gone.
Ib. II. ii. 55

20 But in these nice sharp quillets of the law,
Good faith, I am no wiser than a daw. *Ib.* iv. 17

21 From off this brier pluck a white rose with me.
King Henry VI, Part I, II. iv. 30

22 Pluck a red rose from off this thorn with me. *Ib.* 33

23 PLANTAGENET:
Hath not thy rose a canker, Somerset?
SOMERSET:
Hath not thy rose a thorn, Plantagenet? *Ib.* 68

24 Delays have dangerous ends. *Ib.* III. ii. 33

25 I owe him little duty and less love. *Ib.* IV. iv. 34

26 So doth the swan her downy cygnets save,
Keeping them prisoners underneath her wings.
Ib. v. iii. 56

27 She's beautiful and therefore to be woo'd;
She is a woman, therefore to be won. *Ib.* 78

28 She bears a duke's revenues on her back,
And in her heart she scorns our poverty.
King Henry VI, Part II, I. iii. [83]

29 Could I come near your beauty with my nails
I'd set my ten commandments in your face. *Ib.* [144]

30 What stronger breastplate than a heart untainted!
Thrice is he arm'd that hath his quarrel just,
And he but naked, though lock'd up in steel,
Whose conscience with injustice is corrupted.
Ib. III. ii. 232

31 He dies, and makes no sign. *Ib.* iii. 29

32 Forbear to judge, for we are sinners all.
Close up his eyes, and draw the curtain close;
And let us all to meditation. *Ib.* 31

33 The gaudy, blabbing, and remorseful day
Is crept into the bosom of the sea. *Ib.* IV. i. 1

34 True nobility is exempt from fear. *Ib.* 129

35 I say it was never merry world in England since gentlemen came up. *Ib.* ii. [10]

36 There shall be in England seven halfpenny loaves sold for a penny; the three-hooped pot shall have ten hoops; and I will make it felony to drink small beer. *Ib.* [73]

37 The first thing we do, let's kill all the lawyers.
Ib. [86]

38 Is not this a lamentable thing, that of the skin of an innocent lamb should be made parchment? that parchment, being scribbled o'er, should undo a man? *Ib.* [88]

39 And Adam was a gardener. *Ib.* [146]

40 Thou hast most traitorously corrupted the youth of the realm in erecting a grammar school: and whereas, before, our forefathers had no other books but the score and the tally, thou hast caused printing to be used; and, contrary to the king, his crown and dignity, thou hast built a paper-mill. *Ib.* vii. [35]

41 Away with him! away with him! he speaks Latin.
Ib. [62]

42 Lord, who would live turmoiled in the court,
And may enjoy such quiet walks as these? *Ib.* x. [18]

43 O tiger's heart wrapp'd in a woman's hide!
King Henry VI, Part III, I. iv. 137

44 This battle fares like to the morning's war,
When dying clouds contend with growing light,
What time the shepherd, blowing of his nails,
Can neither call it perfect day nor night. *Ib.* II. v. 1

1 O God! methinks it were a happy life,
To be no better than a homely swain;
To sit upon a hill, as I do now,
To carve out dials, quaintly, point by point,
Thereby to see the minutes how they run,
How many make the hour full complete;
How many hours bring about the day;
How many days will finish up the year;
How many years a mortal man may live.
King Henry VI, Part III, II. v. 21

2 Gives not the hawthorn bush a sweeter shade
To shepherds, looking on their silly sheep,
Than doth a rich embroider'd canopy
To kings that fear their subjects' treachery? *Ib. 42*

3 See, see! what showers arise,
Blown with the windy tempest of my heart. *Ib. 85*

4 Warwick, peace;
Proud setter up and puller down of kings.
Ib. III. iii. 156

5 A little fire is quickly trodden out,
Which, being suffer'd, rivers cannot quench.
Ib. IV. viii. 7

6 Live we how we can, yet die we must. *Ib. v. ii. 28*

7 Suspicion always haunts the guilty mind;
The thief doth fear each bush an officer. *Ib. vi. 11*

8 Down, down to hell; and say I sent thee thither.
Ib. 67

9 They
Made Britain India: every man that stood
Show'd like a mine. *King Henry VIII*, I. i. 20

10 Heat not a furnace for your foe so hot
That it do singe yourself. *Ib. 140*

11 If I chance to talk a little wild, forgive me;
I had it from my father. *Ib. iv. 26*

12 The mirror of all courtesy. *Ib. II. i. 53*

13 Go with me, like good angels, to my end;
And, as the long divorce of steel falls on me,
Make of your prayers one sweet sacrifice,
And lift my soul to heaven. *Ib. 75*

14 CHAMBERLAIN:
It seems the marriage with his brother's wife
Has crept too near his conscience.
SUFFOLK:
No; his conscience
Has crept too near another lady. *Ib. ii. [17]*

15 This bold bad man. *Ib. [44]*

16 Verily,
I swear, 'tis better to be lowly born,
And range with humble livers in content,
Than to be perk'd up, in a glist'ring grief,
And wear a golden sorrow. *Ib. iii. 18*

17 I would not be a queen
For all the world. *Ib. 45*

18 Orpheus with his lute made trees,
And the mountain-tops that freeze,
Bow themselves when he did sing:
To his music plants and flowers
Ever sprung; as sun and showers
There had made a lasting spring.

Everything that heard him play,
Even the billows of the sea,
Hung their heads, and then lay by.

In sweet music is such art,
Killing care and grief of heart
Fall asleep, or hearing die. *King Henry VIII*, III. i. 3

19 Heaven is above all yet; there sits a judge,
That no king can corrupt. *Ib. 99*

20 A spleeny Lutheran. *Ib. ii. 100*

21 'Tis well said again;
And 'tis a kind of good deed to say well:
And yet words are no deeds. *Ib. 153*

22 And then to breakfast, with
What appetite you have. *Ib. 203*

23 That in all you writ to Rome, or else
To foreign princes, 'Ego et Rex meus'
Was still inscrib'd. *Ib. 314*

24 Farewell! a long farewell, to all my greatness!
This is the state of man: to-day he puts forth
The tender leaves of hope; to-morrow blossoms,
And bears his blushing honours thick upon him;
The third day comes a frost, a killing frost;
And, when he thinks, good easy man, full surely
His greatness is a-ripening, nips his root,
And then he falls, as I do. I have ventur'd,
Like little wanton boys that swim on bladders,
This many summers in a sea of glory,
But far beyond my depth: my high-blown pride
At length broke under me, and now has left me
Weary and old with service, to the mercy
Of a rude stream that must for ever hide me.
Vain pomp and glory of this world, I hate ye:
I feel my heart new open'd. O how wretched
Is that poor man that hangs on princes' favours!
There is, betwixt that smile we would aspire to,
That sweet aspect of princes, and their ruin,
More pangs and fears than wars or women have;
And when he falls, he falls like Lucifer,
Never to hope again. *Ib. 352*

25 A peace above all earthly dignities,
A still and quiet conscience. *Ib. 380*

26 A load would sink a navy. *Ib. 384*

27 There was the weight that pull'd me down. O
Cromwell!
The king has gone beyond me: all my glories
In that one woman I have lost for ever. *Ib. 408*

28 Cromwell, I did not think to shed a tear
In all my miseries; but thou hast forc'd me,
Out of thy honest truth, to play the woman. *Ib. 429*

29 Let's dry our eyes: and thus far hear me, Cromwell;
And, when I am forgotten, as I shall be,
And sleep in dull cold marble, where no mention
Of me more must be heard of, say, I taught thee,
Say, Wolsey, that once trod the ways of glory,
And sounded all the depths and shoals of honour,
Found thee a way, out of his wrack, to rise in;
A sure and safe one, though thy master miss'd it.
Ib. 432

30 Cromwell, I charge thee, fling away ambition:
By that sin fell the angels. *Ib. 441*

31 Love thyself last: cherish those hearts that hate thee;
Corruption wins not more than honesty.
Still in thy right hand carry gentle peace,
To silence envious tongues: be just, and fear not.
Let all the ends thou aim'st at be thy country's,
Thy God's, and truth's: then if thou fall'st, O Cromwell!
Thou fall'st a blessed martyr. *Ib. 444*

1 Had I but serv'd my God with half the zeal
I serv'd my king, he would not in mine age
Have left me naked to mine enemies.
King Henry VIII, III. ii. 456

2 She had all the royal makings of a queen. *Ib.* IV. i. 87

3 An old man, broken with the storms of state
Is come to lay his weary bones among ye;
Give him a little earth for charity. *Ib.* ii. 21

4 He gave his honours to the world again,
His blessed part to Heaven, and slept in peace.
Ib. 29

5 So may he rest; his faults lie gently on him! *Ib.* 31

6   He was a man
Of an unbounded stomach. *Ib.* 33

7 His promises were, as he then was, mighty;
But his performance, as he is now, nothing. *Ib.* 41

8 Men's evil manners live in brass; their virtues
We write in water. *Ib.* 45

9 He was a scholar, and a ripe and good one;
Exceeding wise, fair-spoken, and persuading:
Lofty and sour to them that lov'd him not;
But, to those men that sought him, sweet as summer.
Ib. 51

10 Those twins of learning that he rais'd in you,
Ipswich and Oxford! *Ib.* 58

11 After my death I wish no other herald,
No other speaker of my living actions,
To keep mine honour from corruption,
Than such an honest chronicler as Griffith. *Ib.* 69

12 To dance attendance on their lordships' pleasures.
Ib. v. ii. 30

13   'Tis a cruelty
To load a falling man. *Ib.* 76

14 In her days every man shall eat in safety
Under his own vine what he plants; and sing
The merry songs of peace to all his neighbours.
Ib. v. 34

15   Those about her
From her shall read the perfect ways of honour.
Ib. 37

16 Nor shall this peace sleep with her; but as when
The bird of wonder dies, the maiden phœnix,
Her ashes new-create another heir
As great in admiration as herself. *Ib.* 40

17   Some come to take their ease
And sleep an act or two. *Ib.* Epilogue, 2

18 Lord of thy presence and no land beside.
King John, I. i. 137

19 For new-made honour doth forget men's names.
Ib. 186

20 Sweet, sweet, sweet poison for the age's tooth.
Ib. 213

21 Bearing their birthrights proudly on their backs.
Ib. II. i. 70

22 For courage mounteth with occasion. *Ib.* 82

23 Saint George, that swinged the dragon, and e'er since
Sits on his horse back at mine hostess' door. *Ib.* 288

24 Mad world! Mad kings! Mad composition! *Ib.* 561

25 That smooth-fac'd gentleman, tickling Commodity,
Commodity, the bias of the world. *Ib.* 573

26 Well, whiles I am a beggar, I will rail,
And say there is no sin, but to be rich;
And, being rich, my virtue then shall be,
To say there is no vice, but beggary.
King John, II. i. 593

27   Here I and sorrows sit;
Here is my throne, bid kings come bow to it.
Ib. III. i. 73

28 Thou wear a lion's hide! doff it for shame,
And hang a calf's-skin on those recreant limbs!
Ib. 128

29   No Italian priest
Shall tithe or toll in our dominions. *Ib.* 153

30 Old Time the clock-setter, that bald sexton, Time.
Ib. 324

31 Bell, book, and candle shall not drive me back,
When gold and silver becks me to come on.
Ib. iii. 12

32 KING JOHN:
Death.
HUBERT:
    My lord?
KING JOHN:
      A grave.
HUBERT:
          He shall not live.
KING JOHN:
             Enough.
Ib. 66
I could be merry now.

33 Look, who comes here! a grave unto a soul;
Holding the eternal spirit, against her will,
In the vile prison of afflicted breath. *Ib.* iv. 17

34 Grief fills the room up of my absent child,
Lies in his bed, walks up and down with me,
Puts on his pretty looks, repeats his words,
Remembers me of all his gracious parts,
Stuffs out his vacant garments with his form. *Ib.* 93

35 Life is as tedious as a twice-told tale,
Vexing the dull ear of a drowsy man. *Ib.* 108

36 Heat me these irons hot. *Ib.* IV. i. 1

37 Methinks nobody should be sad but I:
Yet I remember, when I was in France,
Young gentlemen would be as sad as night,
Only for wantonness. *Ib.* 13

38 I knit my handkercher about your brows,—
The best I had, a princess wrought it me. *Ib.* 41

39 To gild refined gold, to paint the lily,
To throw a perfume on the violet,
To smooth the ice, or add another hue
Unto the rainbow, or with taper light
To seek the beauteous eye of heaven to garnish,
Is wasteful and ridiculous excess. *Ib.* ii. 11

40 The spirit of the time shall teach me speed. *Ib.* 176

41 Another lean unwash'd artificer. *Ib.* 201

42 It is the curse of kings to be attended
By slaves that take their humours for a warrant
To break within the bloody house of life. *Ib.* 208

43 How oft the sight of means to do ill deeds
Makes ill deeds done! *Ib.* 219

44 Whate'er you think, good words, I think, were best.
Ib. iii. 28

45 Unthread the rude eye of rebellion,
And welcome home again discarded faith. *Ib.* v. iv. 11

1 I beg cold comfort. *King John*, v. vii. 42

2 This England never did, nor never shall,
Lie at the proud foot of a conqueror,
But when it first did help to wound itself.
Now these her princes are come home again,
Come the three corners of the world in arms,
And we shall shock them: nought shall make us rue,
If England to itself do rest but true. *Ib.* 112

3 Hence! home, you idle creatures, get you home:
Is this a holiday? *Julius Cæsar*, I. i. 1

4 What trade, thou knave? thou naughty knave, what
trade? *Ib.* [15]

5 FLAVIUS:
Thou art a cobbler, art thou?
2ND COMMONER:
Truly, sir, all that I live by is with the awl: . . . I am
indeed, sir, a surgeon to old shoes. *Ib.* [22]

6 As proper men as ever trod upon neat's-leather.
Ib. [27]

7 Wherefore rejoice? What conquest brings he home?
Ib. [36]

8 You blocks, you stones, you worse than senseless
things!
O you hard hearts, you cruel men of Rome,
Knew you not Pompey? *Ib.* [39]

9 Have you not made a universal shout,
That Tiber trembled underneath her banks,
To hear the replication of your sounds
Made in her concave shores? *Ib.* [48]

10 Speak; Cæsar is turn'd to hear. *Ib.* ii. 17

11 Beware the ides of March. *Ib.* 18

12 He is a dreamer; let us leave him: pass. *Ib.* 24

13 I am not gamesome: I do lack some part
Of that quick spirit that is in Antony. *Ib.* 28

14 Brutus, I do observe you now of late:
I have not from your eyes that gentleness
And show of love as I was wont to have:
You bear too stubborn and too strange a hand
Over your friend that loves you. *Ib.* 32

15 Poor Brutus, with himself at war,
Forgets the shows of love to other men. *Ib.* 46

16 Set honour in one eye and death i' the other,
And I will look on both indifferently. *Ib.* 86

17 Well, honour is the subject of my story.
I cannot tell what you and other men
Think of this life: but, for my single self,
I had as lief not be as live to be
In awe of such a thing as I myself. *Ib.* 92

18 'Dar'st thou, Cassius, now,
Leap in with me into this angry flood,
And swim to yonder point?' Upon the word,
Accoutred as I was, I plunged in,
And bade him follow. *Ib.* 102

19 Stemming it with hearts of controversy. *Ib.* 109

20 His coward lips did from their colour fly,
And that same eye whose bend doth awe the world
Did lose his lustre. *Ib.* 122

21 Ye gods, it doth amaze me,
A man of such a feeble temper should
So get the start of the majestic world,
And bear the palm alone. *Ib.* 128

22 Why, man, he doth bestride the narrow world
Like a Colossus; and we petty men
Walk under his huge legs, and peep about
To find ourselves dishonourable graves.
Men at some time are masters of their fates:
The fault, dear Brutus, is not in our stars,
But in ourselves, that we are underlings.
Julius Cæsar, I. ii. 134

23 'Brutus' will start a spirit as soon as 'Cæsar'.
Now in the names of all the gods at once,
Upon what meat doth this our Cæsar feed,
That he is grown so great? *Ib.* 146

24 Now is it Rome indeed and room enough. *Ib.* 155

25 But, look you, Cassius,
The angry spot doth glow on Cæsar's brow. *Ib.* 181

26 Let me have men about me that are fat;
Sleek-headed men and such as sleep o' nights;
Yond' Cassius has a lean and hungry look;
He thinks too much: such men are dangerous.
Ib. 191

27 Would he were fatter! but I fear him not:
Yet if my name were liable to fear,
I do not know the man I should avoid
So soon as that spare Cassius. He reads much;
He is a great observer, and he looks
Quite through the deeds of men; he loves no plays,
As thou dost, Antony; he hears no music;
Seldom he smiles, and smiles in such a sort
As if he mock'd himself, and scorn'd his spirit,
That could be mov'd to smile at anything.
Such men as he be never at heart's ease,
Whiles they behold a greater than themselves,
And therefore are they very dangerous.
I rather tell thee what is to be fear'd
Than what I fear, for always I am Cæsar. *Ib.* 197

28 'Tis very like: he hath the falling sickness. *Ib.* [255]

29 If Cæsar had stabbed their mothers, they would have
done no less. *Ib.* [277]

30 For mine own part, it was Greek to me. *Ib.* [288]

31 Therefore 'tis meet
That noble minds keep ever with their likes;
For who so firm that cannot be seduc'd? *Ib.* [315]

32 Besides—I have not since put up my sword,—
Against the Capitol I met a lion,
Who glar'd upon me, and went surly by,
Without annoying me. *Ib.* iii. 19

33 Yesterday the bird of night did sit,
Even at noon-day, upon the market-place,
Hooting and shrieking. *Ib.* 26

34 But men may construe things after their own fashion,
Clean from the purpose of the things themselves.
Ib. 34

35 Cassius from bondage will deliver Cassius. *Ib.* 90

36 Nor stony tower, nor walls of beaten brass,
Nor airless dungeon, nor strong links of iron,
Can be retentive to the strength of spirit;
But life, being weary of these worldly bars,
Never lacks power to dismiss itself. *Ib.* 93

37 So every bondman in his own hand bears
The power to cancel his captivity. *Ib.* 101

38 I will set this foot of mine as far
As who goes furthest. *Ib.* 118

[448]

1 O! he sits high in all the people's hearts:
And that which would appear offence in us,
His countenance, like richest alchemy,
Will change to virtue and to worthiness.
Julius Cæsar, I. iii. 157

2 It is the bright day that brings forth the adder;
And that craves wary walking. *Ib.* II. i. 14

3　　　　　　　'Tis a common proof,
That lowliness is young ambition's ladder,
Whereto the climber-upward turns his face;
But when he once attains the upmost round,
He then unto the ladder turns his back,
Looks in the clouds, scorning the base degrees
By which he did ascend. *Ib.* 21

4　　　Therefore think him as a serpent's egg
Which, hatch'd, would, as his kind, grow mischievous,
And kill him in the shell. *Ib.* 32

5 Between the acting of a dreadful thing
And the first motion, all the interim is
Like a phantasma, or a hideous dream:
The genius and the mortal instruments
Are then in council; and the state of man,
Like to a little kingdom, suffers then
The nature of an insurrection. *Ib.* 63

6　　　　　　　O conspiracy!
Sham'st thou to show thy dangerous brow by night,
When evils are most free? *Ib.* 77

7 For if thou path, thy native semblance on,
Not Erebus itself were dim enough
To hide thee from prevention. *Ib.* 83

8 For he will never follow anything
That other men begin. *Ib.* 151

9 Let us be sacrificers, but not butchers, Caius.
Ib. 166

10 Let's carve him as a dish fit for the gods,
Not hew him as a carcass fit for hounds. *Ib.* 173

11 For he is superstitious grown of late,
Quite from the main opinion he held once
Of fantasy, of dreams, and ceremonies. *Ib.* 195

12 But when I tell him he hates flatterers,
He says he does, being then most flattered. *Ib.* 207

13 Enjoy the honey-heavy dew of slumber. *Ib.* 230

14　　With an angry wafture of your hand,
Gave sign for me to leave you. *Ib.* 246

15　　　　　　What! is Brutus sick,
And will he steal out of his wholesome bed
To dare the vile contagion of the night? *Ib.* 263

16　　　　　　That great vow
Which did incorporate and make us one. *Ib.* 272

17 PORTIA:
　　　　　Dwell I but in the suburbs
Of your good pleasure? If it be no more,
Portia is Brutus' harlot, not his wife.
BRUTUS:
You are my true and honourable wife,
As dear to me as are the ruddy drops
That visit my sad heart. *Ib.* 285

18 I grant I am a woman, but, withal,
A woman that Lord Brutus took to wife;
I grant I am a woman, but, withal,
A woman well-reputed, Cato's daughter.
Think you I am no stronger than my sex,
Being so fathered and so husbanded? *Ib.* 292

19 *Enter Cæsar, in his night-gown.*
Julius Cæsar, II. ii. *Stage Direction*

20 Nor heaven nor earth have been at peace to-night.
Ib. 1

21 CALPHURNIA:
　　　　These things are beyond all use,
And I do fear them.
CÆSAR:
　　　　　　What can be avoided
Whose end is purpos'd by the mighty gods? *Ib.* 25

22 CALPHURNIA:
When beggars die, there are no comets seen;
The heavens themselves blaze forth the death of
　　princes.
CÆSAR:
Cowards die many times before their deaths;
The valiant never taste of death but once.
Of all the wonders that I yet have heard,
It seems to me most strange that men should fear;
Seeing that death, a necessary end,
Will come when it will come. *Ib.* 30

23　　　　　　Danger knows full well
That Cæsar is more dangerous than he:
We are two lions litter'd in one day,
And I the elder and more terrible:
And Cæsar shall go forth. *Ib.* 44

24 The cause is in my will: I will not come. *Ib.* 71

25 See! Antony, that revels long o' nights,
Is notwithstanding up. *Ib.* 116

26 My heart laments that virtue cannot live
Out of the teeth of emulation. *Ib.* iii. [13]

27 O constancy! be strong upon my side;
Set a huge mountain 'tween my heart and tongue;
I have a man's mind, but a woman's might.
How hard it is for women to keep counsel! *Ib.* iv. 6

28 CÆSAR:
The ides of March are come.
SOOTHSAYER:
Ay, Cæsar; but not gone. *Ib.* III. i. 1

29　　　　　　Sweet words,
Low-crooked curtsies, and base spaniel fawning.
Ib. 42

30 If I could pray to move, prayers would move me;
But I am constant as the northern star,
Of whose true-fix'd and resting quality
There is no fellow in the firmament.
The skies are painted with unnumber'd sparks,
They are all fire and every one doth shine,
But there's but one in all doth hold his place:
So, in the world; 'tis furnish'd well with men,
And men are flesh and blood, and apprehensive;
Yet in the number I do know but one
That unassailable holds on his rank,
Unshak'd of motion: and that I am he,
Let me a little show it, even in this,
That I was constant Cimber should be banish'd,
And constant do remain to keep him so. *Ib.* 59

31 Et tu, Brute! *Ib.* 77

32 Ambition's debt is paid. *Ib.* 83

33 That we shall die, we know; 'tis but the time
And drawing days out, that men stand upon. *Ib.* 99

34 He that cuts off twenty years of life
Cuts off so many years of fearing death. *Ib.* 101

SHAKESPEARE

1 CASSIUS:
　　　　　　　How many ages hence
Shall this our lofty scene be acted o'er,
In states unborn, and accents yet unknown!
BRUTUS:
How many times shall Cæsar bleed in sport.
　　　　　　　Julius Cæsar, III. i. 111

2 O mighty Cæsar! dost thou lie so low?
Are all thy conquests, glories, triumphs, spoils,
Shrunk to this little measure?　　*Ib.* 148

3 　　　　Your swords, made rich
With the most noble blood of all this world. *Ib.* 155

4 　　　　　　Live a thousand years,
I shall not find myself so apt to die.　*Ib.* 159

5 The choice and master spirits of this age. *Ib.* 163

6 Let each man render me his bloody hand
First, Marcus Brutus, will I shake with you. *Ib.* 184

7 Though last, not least in love.　　*Ib.* 189

8 My credit now stands on such slippery ground,
That one of two bad ways you must conceit me,
Either a coward or a flatterer.　*Ib.* 191

9 　　　Here wast thou bay'd, brave hart;
Here didst thou fall; and here thy hunters stand,
Sign'd in thy spoil, and crimson'd in thy leth.
O world! thou wast the forest to this hart;
And this, indeed, O world! the heart of thee. *Ib.* 204

10 The enemies of Cæsar shall say this;
Then, in a friend, it is cold modesty.　*Ib.* 212

11 O! pardon me, thou bleeding piece of earth,
That I am meek and gentle with these butchers;
Thou art the ruins of the noblest man
That ever lived in the tide of times.　*Ib.* 254

12 　Cæsar's spirit, ranging for revenge,
With Ate by his side, come hot from hell,
Shall in these confines, with a monarch's voice
Cry, 'Havoc!' and let slip the dogs of war. *Ib.* 270

13 Passion, I see, is catching.　　*Ib.* 283

14 Not that I loved Cæsar less, but that I loved Rome
more.　　　　*Ib.* ii. [22]

15 As he was valiant, I honour him: but, as he was
ambitious, I slew him.　　*Ib.* [27]

16 Who is here so base that would be a bondman? If
any, speak; for him have I offended. Who is here
so rude that would not be a Roman? If any,
speak; for him have I offended. Who is here so
vile that will not love his country? If any, speak;
for him have I offended. I pause for a reply.
　　　　　　Ib. [31]

17 Friends, Romans, countrymen, lend me your ears;
I come to bury Cæsar, not to praise him.
The evil that men do lives after them,
The good is oft interred with their bones;
So let it be with Cæsar. The noble Brutus
Hath told you Cæsar was ambitious;
If it were so, it was a grievous fault;
And grievously hath Cæsar answer'd it.　*Ib.* [79]

18 For Brutus is an honourable man;
So are they all, all honourable men.　*Ib.* [88]

19 He was my friend, faithful and just to me:
But Brutus says he was ambitious;
And Brutus is an honourable man.　*Ib.* [91]

20 When that the poor have cried, Cæsar hath wept;
Ambition should be made of sterner stuff.
　　　　　Julius Cæsar, III. ii. [97]

21 You all did love him once, not without cause.
　　　　　　Ib. [108]

22 O judgment! thou art fled to brutish beasts,
And men have lost their reason.　*Ib.* [110]

23 But yesterday the word of Cæsar might
Have stood against the world; now lies he there,
And none so poor to do him reverence.　*Ib.* [124]

24 Let but the commons hear this testament—
Which, pardon me, I do not mean to read—
And they would go and kiss dead Cæsar's wounds
And dip their napkins in his sacred blood,
Yea, beg a hair of him for memory,
And, dying, mention it within their wills,
Bequeathing it as a rich legacy
Unto their issue.　　　*Ib.* [136]

25 The will, the will! we will hear Cæsar's will.
　　　　　　Ib. [145]

26 You are not wood, you are not stones, but men.
　　　　　　Ib. [148]

27 If you have tears, prepare to shed them now.
You all do know this mantle: I remember
The first time ever Cæsar put it on;
'Twas on a summer's evening, in his tent,
That day he overcame the Nervii.　*Ib.* [174]

28 See what a rent the envious Casca made. *Ib.* [180]

29 For Brutus, as you know, was Cæsar's angel.
　　　　　　Ib. [186]

30 This was the most unkindest cut of all.　*Ib.* [188]

31 Ingratitude, more strong than traitors' arms,
Quite vanquish'd him: then burst his mighty heart;
And, in his mantle muffling up his face,
Even at the base of Pompey's statua,
Which all the while ran blood, great Cæsar fell.
O! what a fall was there, my countrymen;
Then I, and you, and all of us fell down,
Whilst bloody treason flourish'd over us.
O! now you weep, and I perceive you feel
The dint of pity; these are gracious drops. *Ib.* [190]

32 Good friends, sweet friends, let me not stir you up
To such a sudden flood of mutiny.
They that have done this deed are honourable:
What private griefs they have, alas! I know not,
That made them do it; they are wise and honourable,
And will no doubt with reasons answer you.
I come not, friends, to steal away your hearts:
I am no orator, as Brutus is;
But, as you know me all, a plain, blunt man,
That love my friend.　　　*Ib.* [214]

33 For I have neither wit, nor words, nor worth,
Action, nor utterance, nor power of speech,
To stir men's blood; I only speak right on;
I tell you that which you yourselves do know.
　　　　　　Ib. [225]

34 　　　　　But were I Brutus,
And Brutus Antony, there were an Antony
Would ruffle up your spirits, and put a tongue
In every wound of Cæsar, that should move
The stones of Rome to rise and mutiny.　*Ib.* [230]

35 Here was a Cæsar! when comes such another?
　　　　　　Ib. [257]

1 Now let it work; mischief, thou art afoot,
Take thou what course thou wilt!
Julius Cæsar, III. ii. [265]

2   Fortune is merry,
And in this mood will give us anything. *Ib.* [271]

3 Tear him for his bad verses, tear him for his bad
verses.   *Ib.* iii. [34]

4 He shall not live; look, with a spot I damn him.
Ib. IV. i. 6

5 This is a slight unmeritable man,
Meet to be sent on errands.   *Ib.* 12

6 OCTAVIUS:
   He's a tried and valiant soldier.
ANTONY:
   So is my horse, Octavius; and for that
I do appoint him store of provender.   *Ib.* 28

7   We are at the stake,
And bay'd about with many enemies;
And some that smile have in their hearts, I fear,
Millions of mischiefs.   *Ib.* 48

8   Not with such familiar instances,
Nor with such free and friendly conference,
As he hath us'd of old.   *Ib.* ii. 16

9 When love begins to sicken and decay,
It useth an enforced ceremony.
There are no tricks in plain and simple faith. *Ib.* 20

10 CASSIUS:
   In such a time as this it is not meet
   That every nice offence should bear his comment.
BRUTUS:
   Let me tell you, Cassius, you yourself
   Are much condemn'd to have an itching palm.
          Ib. iii. 7

11 Remember March, the ides of March remember.
          Ib. 18

12   Shall we now
Contaminate our fingers with base bribes? *Ib.* 23

13 I had rather be a dog, and bay the moon,
Than such a Roman.   *Ib.* 27

14 Away, slight man!   *Ib.* 37

15 I'll use you for my mirth, yea, for my laughter,
When you are waspish.   *Ib.* 49

16   For mine own part,
I shall be glad to learn of noble men.   *Ib.* 53

17 You wrong me every way; you wrong me, Brutus;
I said an elder soldier, not a better:
Did I say 'better'?   *Ib.* 55

18 Do not presume too much upon my love;
I may do that I shall be sorry for.   *Ib.* 63

19 There is no terror, Cassius, in your threats;
For I am arm'd so strong in honesty
That they pass by me as the idle wind,
Which I respect not.   *Ib.* 66

20 By heaven, I had rather coin my heart,
And drop my blood for drachmas, than to wring
From the hard hands of peasants their vile trash
By any indirection.   *Ib.* 72

21 Should I have answer'd Caius Cassius so?
When Marcus Brutus grows so covetous,
To lock such rascal counters from his friends,
Be ready, gods, with all your thunderbolts;
Dash him to pieces!   *Ib.* 78

22 A friend should bear his friend's infirmities,
But Brutus makes mine greater than they are.
       Julius Cæsar, IV. iii. 85

23 A friendly eye could never see such faults. *Ib.* 89

24   All his faults observ'd,
Set in a note-book, learn'd, and conn'd by rote,
To cast into my teeth.   *Ib.* 96

25 O Cassius! you are yoked with a lamb
That carries anger as the flint bears fire;
Who, much enforced, shows a hasty spark,
And straight is cold again.   *Ib.* 109

26 O Cassius! I am sick of many griefs.   *Ib.* 143

27 I have as much of this in art as you,
But yet my nature could not bear it so. *Ib.* 193

28 Good reasons must, of force, give place to better.
          Ib. 202

29 There is a tide in the affairs of men,
Which, taken at the flood, leads on to fortune;
Omitted, all the voyage of their life
Is bound in shallows and in miseries.
On such a full sea are we now afloat,
And we must take the current when it serves,
Or lose our ventures.   *Ib.* 217

30 The deep of night is crept upon our talk,
And nature must obey necessity.   *Ib.* 225

31 This was an ill beginning of the night:
Never come such division 'tween our souls! *Ib.* 233

32 BRUTUS:
   Then I shall see thee again?
GHOST:
   Ay, at Philippi.
BRUTUS:
   Why, I will see thee at Philippi, then. *Ib.* 283

33 But for your words, they rob the Hybla bees,
And leave them honeyless.   *Ib.* v. i. 34

34 You know that I held Epicurus strong,
And his opinion; now I change my mind,
And partly credit things that do presage. *Ib.* 77

35 The gods to-day stand friendly, that we may,
Lovers in peace, lead on our days to age! *Ib.* 94

36   I know not how,
But I do find it cowardly and vile,
For fear of what might fall, so to prevent
The time of life.   *Ib.* 103

37   Think not, thou noble Roman,
That ever Brutus will go bound to Rome;
He bears too great a mind: but this same day
Must end that work the ides of March begun;
And whether we shall meet again, I know not.
Therefore our everlasting farewell take:
For ever, and for ever, farewell, Cassius!
If we do meet again, why, we shall smile!
If not, why then, this parting was well made. *Ib.* 111

38   O! that a man might know
The end of this day's business, ere it come;
But it sufficeth that the day will end,
And then the end is known.   *Ib.* 123

39 This day I breathed first: time is come round,
And where I did begin, there shall I end;
My life is run his compass.   *Ib.* iii. 23

40 O hateful error, melancholy's child!
Why dost thou show, to the apt thoughts of men,
The things that are not?   *Ib.* 67

1 O Julius Cæsar! thou art mighty yet!
Thy spirit walks abroad, and turns our swords
In our own proper entrails.   *Julius Cæsar*, v. iii. 94

2 Are yet two Romans living such as these?
The last of all the Romans, fare thee well!
It is impossible that ever Rome
Should breed thy fellow. Friends, I owe more tears
To this dead man than you shall see me pay.—
I shall find time, Cassius, I shall find time.   *Ib.* 98

3 When you do find him, or alive or dead,
He will be found like Brutus, like himself. *Ib.* iv. 24

4   I had rather have
Such men my friends than enemies.   *Ib.* 28

5 Thou seest the world, Volumnius, how it goes;
Our enemies have beat us to the pit:
It is more worthy to leap in ourselves,
Than tarry till they push us.   *Ib.* v. 22

6 Thou art a fellow of a good respect;
Thy life hath had some smatch of honour in it.
                                   Ib. 45

7   Cæsar, now be still;
I kill'd not thee with half so good a will.   *Ib.* 50

8 This was the noblest Roman of them all.   *Ib.* 68

9 He, only, in a general honest thought
And common good to all, made one of them.
His life was gentle, and the elements
So mix'd in him that Nature might stand up
And say to all the world, 'This was a man!'   *Ib.* 71

10 LEAR:
So young, and so untender?
CORDELIA:
So young, my lord, and true.   *King Lear*, i. i. [108]

11 A still-soliciting eye.   *Ib.* [234]

12   Love is not love
When it is mingled with regards that stand
Aloof from the entire point.   *Ib.* [241]

13 Fairest Cordelia, that art most rich, being poor;
Most choice, forsaken; and most lov'd, despis'd!
                                   Ib. [253]

14 Who in the lusty stealth of nature take
More composition and fierce quality
Than doth, within a dull, stale, tired bed,
Go to the creating a whole tribe of fops. *Ib.* ii. 11

15 These late eclipses in the sun and moon portend no
good to us.   *Ib.* [115]

16 We have seen the best of our time: machinations,
hollowness, treachery, and all ruinous disorders,
follow us disquietly to our graves.   *Ib.* [125]

17 This is the excellent foppery of the world. *Ib.* [132]

18 We make guilty of our disasters the sun, the moon,
and the stars; as if we were villains by necessity,
fools by heavenly compulsion.   *Ib.* [134]

19 An admirable evasion of whoremaster man, to lay
his goatish disposition to the charge of a star!
                                   Ib. [141]

20 My nativity was under Ursa Major; so that it follows
I am rough and lecherous.   *Ib.* [145]

21 Pat he comes, like the catastrophe of the old comedy;
my cue is villanous melancholy, with a sigh like
Tom o' Bedlam.   *Ib.* [150]

22 KENT:
You have that in your countenance which I would
fain call master.
LEAR:
What's that?
KENT:
Authority.   *King Lear*, i. iv. [29]

23 Not so young, sir, to love a woman for singing, nor
so old to dote on her for any thing.   *Ib.* [40]

24 Lady the brach may stand by the fire and stink.
                                   Ib. [125]

25 Have more than thou showest,
Speak less than thou knowest,
Lend less than thou owest.   *Ib.* [132]

26 LEAR:
Dost thou call me fool, boy?
FOOL:
All thy other titles thou hast given away; that thou
wast born with.   *Ib.* [163]

27 The hedge-sparrow fed the cuckoo so long,
That it had it head bit off by it young.   *Ib.* [238]

28 Ingratitude, thou marble-hearted fiend,
More hideous, when thou show'st thee in a child,
Than the sea-monster.   *Ib.* [283]

29 Into her womb convey sterility!
Dry up in her the organs of increase.   *Ib.* [302]

30 How sharper than a serpent's tooth it is
To have a thankless child!   *Ib.* [312]

31 How far your eyes may pierce I cannot tell;
Striving to better, oft we mar what's well.   *Ib.* [370]

32 A knave; a rascal; an eater of broken meats.
                                   Ib. ii. ii. [15]

33 Thou whoreson zed! thou unnecessary letter!
                                   Ib. [68]

34 I'd drive ye cackling home to Camelot.   *Ib.* [89]

35 I have seen better faces in my time
Than stands on any shoulder that I see
Before me at this instant.   *Ib.* [99]

36 Winter's not gone yet, if the wild-geese fly that way.
                                   Ib. iv. [46]

37   Down, thou climbing sorrow!
Thy element's below.   *Ib.* [57]

38 That sir which serves and seeks for gain,
And follows but for form,
Will pack when it begins to rain,
And leave thee in the storm.   *Ib.* [79]

39   O, sir! you are old;
Nature in you stands on the very verge
Of her confine.   *Ib.* [148]

40   But I'll not chide thee;
Let shame come when it will, I do not call it:
I do not bid the thunder-bearer shoot,
Nor tell tales of thee to high-judging Jove. *Ib.* [228]

41   Our basest beggars
Are in the poorest thing superfluous:
Allow not nature more than nature needs,
Man's life is cheap as beast's.   *Ib.* [267]

42 You see me here, you gods, a poor old man,
As full of grief as age; wretched in both!   *Ib.* [275]

1 I will have such revenges on you both
That all the world shall—I will do such things,—
What they are yet I know not,—but they shall be
The terrors of the earth.   *King Lear*, II. iv. [282]

2 To wilful men,
The injuries that they themselves procure
Must be their schoolmasters.   *Ib*. [305]

3 Contending with the fretful elements;
Bids the wind blow the earth into the sea,
Or swell the curled waters 'bove the main.
     Ib. III. i. 4

4 Strives in his little world of man to out-scorn
The to-and-fro conflicting wind and rain.
This night, wherein the cub-drawn bear would couch,
The lion and the belly-pinched wolf
Keep their fur dry.   *Ib*. 10

5 Blow, winds, and crack your cheeks! rage! blow!
You cataracts and hurricanoes, spout
Till you have drench'd our steeples, drown'd the
cocks!
You sulphurous and thought-executing fires,
Vaunt-couriers to oak-cleaving thunderbolts,
Singe my white head! And thou, all-shaking thunder,
Strike flat the thick rotundity o' the world!
Crack nature's moulds, all germens spill at once
That make ingrateful man!   *Ib*. ii. 1

6 I tax not you, you elements, with unkindness;
I never gave you kingdom, call'd you children,
You owe me no subscription: then, let fall
Your horrible pleasure; here I stand, your slave,
A poor, infirm, weak, and despis'd old man.
But yet I call you servile ministers,
That have with two pernicious daughters join'd
Your high-engender'd battles 'gainst a head
So old and white as this.   *Ib*. [16]

7 There was never yet fair woman but she made mouths
in a glass.   *Ib*. [35]

8 Things that love night
Love not such nights as these.   *Ib*. [42]

9 Let the great gods,
That keep this dreadful pother o'er our heads,
Find out their enemies now. Tremble, thou wretch,
That hast within thee undivulged crimes,
Unwhipp'd of justice.   *Ib*. [49]

10 Close pent-up guilts,
Rive your concealing continents, and cry
These dreadful summoners grace. I am a man
More sinned against than sinning.   *Ib*. [57]

11 The art of our necessities is strange,
That can make vile things precious.   *Ib*. [70]

12 When the mind's free,
The body's delicate.   *Ib*. iv. 11

13 O! that way madness lies; let me shun that.   *Ib*. 21

14 Poor naked wretches, wheresoe'er you are,
That bide the pelting of this pitiless storm,
How shall your houseless heads and unfed sides,
Your looped and window'd raggedness, defend you
From seasons such as these?   *Ib*. 28

15 Take physic, pomp;
Expose thyself to feel what wretches feel.   *Ib*. 33

16 Tom's a-cold.   *Ib*. [57]

17 Pillicock sat on Pillicock-hill:
Halloo, halloo, loo, loo!   *Ib*. [75]

18 Take heed o' the foul fiend!   *King Lear*, III. iv. [79]

19 A serving-man, proud in heart and mind: that curled
my hair, wore gloves in my cap, served the lust of
my mistress's heart, and did the act of darkness
with her; swore as many oaths as I spake words,
and broke them in the sweet face of heaven; one
that slept in the contriving of lust, and waked to
do it.   *Ib*. [84]

20 Keep thy foot out of brothels, thy hand out of
plackets, thy pen from lenders' books, and defy
the foul fiend.   *Ib*. [96]

21 Thou art the thing itself; unaccommodated man is
no more but such a poor, bare, forked animal as
thou art.   *Ib*. [109]

22 'Tis a naughty night to swim in.   *Ib*. [113]

23 Drinks the green mantle of the standing pool.
     Ib. [136]

24 But mice and rats and such small deer
Have been Tom's food for seven long year.   *Ib*. [142]

25 The prince of darkness is a gentleman.   *Ib*. [148]

26 I'll talk a word with this same learned Theban.
     Ib. [161]

27 Child Roland to the dark tower came,
His word was still, Fie, foh, and fum,
I smell the blood of a British man.   *Ib*. [185]

28 Nero is an angler in the lake of darkness.   *Ib*. vi. [8]

29 The little dogs and all,
Tray, Blanch, and Sweet-heart, see, they bark at me.
     Ib. [65]

30 Mastiff, greyhound, mongrel grim,
Hound or spaniel, brach or lym,
Or bobtail tike, or trundle-tail.   *Ib*. [71]

31 You, sir, I entertain for one of my hundred; only I
do not like the fashion of your garments: you will
say, they are Persian attire; but let them be
changed.   *Ib*. [83]

32 'Tis most ignobly done
To pluck me by the beard.   *Ib*. vii. [35]

33 I am tied to the stake, and I must stand the course.
     Ib. [54]

34 The sea, with such a storm as his bare head
In hell-black night endur'd, would have buoy'd up,
And quench'd the stelled fires.   *Ib*. [59]

35 Out, vile jelly!   *Ib*. [83]

36 The lowest and most dejected thing of fortune.
     Ib. IV. i. 3

37 The lamentable change is from the best;
The worst returns to laughter.   *Ib*. 5

38 I have no way, and therefore want no eyes;
I stumbled when I saw.   *Ib*. 18

39 The worst is not,
So long as we can say, 'This is the worst.'   *Ib*. 27

40 As flies to wanton boys, are we to the gods;
They kill us for their sport.   *Ib*. 36

41 You are not worth the dust which the rude wind
Blows in your face.   *Ib*. ii. 30

42 She that herself will sliver and disbranch
From her material sap, perforce must wither
And come to deadly use.   *Ib*. 34

1 Wisdom and goodness to the vile seem vile;
Filths savour but themselves. *King Lear*, IV. ii. 38

2 Crown'd with rank fumiter and furrow weeds,
With burdocks, hemlock, nettles, cuckoo-flowers,
Darnel, and all the idle weeds that grow
In our sustaining corn. *Ib.* iv. 3

3 How fearful
And dizzy 'tis to cast one's eyes so low!
The crows and choughs that wing the midway air
Show scarce so gross as beetles; half-way down
Hangs one that gathers samphire, dreadful trade!
Methinks he seems no bigger than his head.
The fishermen that walk upon the beach
Appear like mice, and yond tall anchoring bark
Diminish'd to her cock, her cock a buoy
Almost too small for sight. The murmuring surge,
That on the unnumber'd idle pebbles chafes,
Cannot be heard so high. *Ib.* vi. 12

4 The shrill-gorg'd lark so far
Cannot be seen or heard. *Ib.* 59

5 Think that the clearest gods, who make them honours
Of men's impossibilities, have preserv'd thee. *Ib.* 74

6 They told me I was every thing; 'tis a lie, I am not
ague-proof. *Ib.* [107]

7 GLOUCESTER:
Is't not the king?
LEAR:
Ay, every inch a king. *Ib.* [110]

8 The wren goes to 't, and the small gilded fly
Does lecher in my sight. *Ib.* [115]

9 Give me an ounce of civet, good apothecary, to
sweeten my imagination. *Ib.* [133]

10 A man may see how this world goes with no eyes.
Look with thine ears: see how yond justice rails
upon yond simple thief. Hark, in thine ear: change
places; and, handy-dandy, which is the justice,
which is the thief? *Ib.* [154]

11 Get thee glass eyes;
And, like a scurvy politician, seem
To see the things thou dost not. *Ib.* [175]

12 When we are born we cry that we are come
To this great stage of fools. *Ib.* [187]

13 Mine enemy's dog,
Though he had bit me, should have stood that night
Against my fire. *Ib.* vii. 36

14 Thou art a soul in bliss; but I am bound
Upon a wheel of fire, that mine own tears
Do scald like molten lead. *Ib.* 46

15 I am a very foolish, fond old man,
Fourscore and upward, not an hour more or less;
And, to deal plainly,
I fear I am not in my perfect mind. *Ib.* 60

16 For, as I am a man, I think this lady
To be my child Cordelia. *Ib.* 69

17 Pray you now, forget and forgive. *Ib.* [85]

18 Men must endure
Their going hence, even as their coming hither:
Ripeness is all. *Ib.* v. ii. 9

19 Come, let's away to prison;
We two alone will sing like birds i' the cage:
When thou dost ask me blessing, I'll kneel down,
And ask of thee forgiveness: and we'll live,

And pray, and sing, and tell old tales, and laugh
At gilded butterflies, and hear poor rogues
Talk of court news; and we'll talk with them too,
Who loses, and who wins; who's in, who's out;
And take upon 's the mystery of things,
As if we were God's spies; and we'll wear out,
In a wall'd prison, packs and sets of great ones
That ebb and flow by the moon. *King Lear*, v. iii. 8

20 Upon such sacrifices, my Cordelia,
The gods themselves throw incense. *Ib.* 20

21 The gods are just, and of our pleasant vices
Make instruments to plague us. *Ib.* [172]

22 The wheel is come full circle. *Ib.* [176]

23 His flaw'd heart,—
Alack! too weak the conflict to support;
'Twixt two extremes of passion, joy and grief,
Burst smilingly. *Ib.* [198]

24 Her voice was ever soft,
Gentle and low, an excellent thing in woman.
Ib. [274]

25 I have seen the day, with my good biting falchion
I would have made them skip. *Ib.* [278]

26 And my poor fool is hang'd! No, no, no life!
Why should a dog, a horse, a rat, have life,
And thou no breath at all? Thou'lt come no more,
Never, never, never, never, never!
Pray you, undo this button. *Ib.* [307]

27 Vex not his ghost: O! let him pass; he hates him
That would upon the rack of this tough world
Stretch him out longer. *Ib.* [314]

28 The weight of this sad time we must obey,
Speak what we feel; not what we ought to say.
The oldest hath borne most: we that are young,
Shall never see so much, nor live so long. *Ib.* [325]

29 Let fame, that all hunt after in their lives,
Live register'd upon our brazen tombs.
Love's Labour's Lost, I. i. 1

30 Spite of cormorant devouring Time. *Ib.* 4

31 Why, all delights are vain; but that most vain,
Which, with pain purchas'd, doth inherit pain.
Ib. 72

32 Study is like the heaven's glorious sun,
That will not be deep-search'd with saucy looks;
Small have continual plodders ever won,
Save base authority from others' books.
These earthly godfathers of Heaven's lights
That give a name to every fixed star,
Have no more profit of their shining nights
Than those that walk and wot not what they are.
Ib. 84

33 At Christmas I no more desire a rose
Than wish a snow in May's new-fangled mirth;
But like of each thing that in season grows. *Ib.* 105

34 So study evermore is overshot. *Ib.* [141]

35 If I break faith, this word shall speak for me,—
I am forsworn 'on mere necessity'. *Ib.* [152]

36 A child of our grandmother Eve, a female; or, for
thy more sweet understanding, a woman.
Ib. [263]

37 The world was very guilty of such a ballad some three
ages since; but, I think, now 'tis not to be found.
Ib. ii. [117]

1 Devise, wit! write, pen! for I am for whole volumes in folio! *Love's Labour's Lost*, I. ii. [194]

2 Beauty is bought by judgment of the eye,
Not utter'd by base sale of chapmen's tongues.
Ib. II. i. 15

3   A merrier man,
Within the limit of becoming mirth,
I never spent an hour's talk withal. *Ib.* 66

4 Your wit's too hot, it speeds too fast, 'twill tire.
Ib. [119]

5 Thy own wish wish I thee in every place! *Ib.* [178]

6 Warble, child; make passionate my sense of hearing.
Ib. III. i. 1

7 A very beadle to a humorous sigh. *Ib.* [185]

8 This wimpled, whining, purblind, wayward boy,
This senior-junior, giant-dwarf, Dan Cupid;
Regent of love rhymes, lord of folded arms,
The anointed sovereign of sighs and groans,
Liege of all loiterers and malcontents. *Ib.* [189]

9 With two pitch balls stuck in her face for eyes.
Ib. [207]

10 Some men must love my lady, and some Joan.
Ib. [215]

11 He hath not fed of the dainties that are bred in a book; he hath not eat paper, as it were; he hath not drunk ink. *Ib.* IV. ii. [25]

12 These are begot in the ventricle of memory, nourished in the womb of pia mater, and delivered upon the mellowing of occasion. *Ib.* [70]

13 Old Mantuan! old Mantuan! Who understandeth thee not, loves thee not. *Ib.* [102]

14 The elegancy, facility, and golden cadence of poesy.
Ib. [126]

15 By heaven, I do love, and it hath taught me to rhyme, and to be melancholy. *Ib.* iii. [13]

16 The heavenly rhetoric of thine eye. *Ib.* [60]

17 Love, whose month is ever May,
Spied a blossom passing fair,
Playing in the wanton air;
Through the velvet leaves the wind,
All unseen, 'gan passage find;
That the lover, sick to death,
Wish'd himself the heaven's breath. *Ib.* [102]

18 Thou for whom e'en Jove would swear
Juno but an Ethiop were;
And deny himself for Jove,
Turning mortal for thy love. *Ib.* [117]

19 Now step I forth to whip hypocrisy. *Ib.* [151]

20 From women's eyes this doctrine I derive:
They are the ground, the books, the academes,
From whence doth spring the true Promethean fire.
Ib. [302]

21 For where is any author in the world
Teaches such beauty as a woman's eye?
Learning is but an adjunct to ourself. *Ib.* [312]

22 But love, first learned in a lady's eyes,
Lives not alone immured in the brain,
But, with the motion of all elements,
Courses as swift as thought in every power,
And gives to every power a double power,
Above their functions and their offices.

It adds a precious seeing to the eye;
A lover's eyes will gaze an eagle blind;
A lover's ears will hear the lowest sound,
When the suspicious head of theft is stopp'd:
Love's feeling is more soft and sensible
Than are the tender horns of cockled snails:
Love's tongue proves dainty Bacchus gross in taste.
For valour, is not love a Hercules,
Still climbing trees in the Hesperides?
Subtle as Sphinx; as sweet and musical
As bright Apollo's lute, strung with his hair;
And when Love speaks, the voice of all the gods
Makes heaven drowsy with the harmony.
Never durst poet touch a pen to write
Until his ink were temper'd with Love's sighs.
Love's Labour's Lost, IV. iii. [327]

23 From women's eyes this doctrine I derive:
They sparkle still the right Promethean fire;
They are the books, the arts, the academes,
That show, contain, and nourish all the world.
Ib. [350]

24 He draweth out the thread of his verbosity finer than the staple of his argument. *Ib.* v. i. [18]

25 Priscian a little scratched; 'twill serve. *Ib.* [31]

26 MOTH:
They have been at a great feast of languages, and stolen the scraps.
COSTARD:
O! they have lived long on the alms-basket of words. I marvel thy master hath not eaten thee for a word; for thou art not so long by the head as honorificabilitudinitatibus: thou art easier swallowed than a flap-dragon. *Ib.* [39]

27 In the posteriors of this day; which the rude multitude call the afternoon. *Ib.* [96]

28   Had she been light, like you,
Of such a merry, nimble, stirring spirit,
She might ha' been a grandam ere she died;
And so may you; for a light heart lives long.
Ib. ii. 15

29 Taffeta phrases, silken terms precise,
Three-pil'd hyperboles, spruce affectation,
Figures pedantical. *Ib.* 407

30 In russet yeas and honest kersey noes. *Ib.* 414

31 When in the world I liv'd, I was the world's commander;
By east, west, north, and south, I spread my conquering might:
My scutcheon plain declares that I am Alisander.
Ib. [563]

32 Let me take you a button-hole lower. *Ib.* [705]

33 A world-without-end bargain. *Ib.* [797]

34 A jest's prosperity lies in the ear
Of him that hears it, never in the tongue
Of him that makes it. *Ib.* [869]

35 When daisies pied and violets blue
    And lady-smocks all silver-white
And cuckoo-buds of yellow hue
    Do paint the meadows with delight,
The cuckoo then, on every tree,
Mocks married men; for thus sings he,
      Cuckoo;
Cuckoo, cuckoo; O, word of fear,
Unpleasing to a married ear! *Ib.* [902]

1 When icicles hang by the wall,
    And Dick, the shepherd, blows his nail,
And Tom bears logs into the hall,
    And milk comes frozen home in pail,
When blood is nipp'd and ways be foul,
Then nightly sings the staring owl,
        Tu-who;
Tu-whit, tu-who—a merry note,
While greasy Joan doth keel the pot.

When all aloud the wind doth blow,
And coughing drowns the parson's saw;
And birds sit brooding in the snow,
And Marion's nose looks red and raw,
When roasted crabs hiss in the bowl.
        Love's Labour's Lost, v. ii. [920]

2 The words of Mercury are harsh after the songs of
    Apollo.   *Ib.* [938]

3 FIRST WITCH:
When shall we three meet again
In thunder, lightning, or in rain?
SECOND WITCH:
When the hurly-burly's done,
When the battle's lost and won.
THIRD WITCH:
That will be ere the set of sun.
FIRST WITCH:
Where the place?
SECOND WITCH:
                Upon the heath.
THIRD WITCH:
There to meet with Macbeth.
FIRST WITCH:
I come, Graymalkin!
SECOND WITCH:
                Paddock calls.
THIRD WITCH:
Anon!
ALL:
Fair is foul, and foul is fair:
Hover through the fog and filthy air.
        Macbeth, I. i. I

4 DUNCAN:
What bloody man is that? . . .
MALCOLM:
                This is the sergeant. *Ib.* ii. 1

5 Disdaining fortune, with his brandish'd steel,
Which smok'd with bloody execution,
Like valour's minion carv'd out his passage. *Ib.* 17

6 Memorize another Golgotha.   *Ib.* 41

7 So well thy words become thee as thy wounds;
They smack of honour both.   *Ib.* 44

8 Banners flout the sky.   *Ib.* 50

9 Till that Bellona's bridegroom, lapp'd in proof,
Confronted him with self-comparisons,
Point against point, rebellious arm 'gainst arm,
Curbing his lavish spirit.   *Ib.* 55

10 A sailor's wife had chestnuts in her lap,
And munch'd, and munch'd, and munch'd: 'Give
me,' quoth I:
'Aroint thee, witch!' the rump-fed ronyon cries.
Her husband's to Aleppo gone, master o' the Tiger:
But in a sieve I'll thither sail,
And, like a rat without a tail,
I'll do, I'll do, and I'll do.   *Ib.* iii. 4

11 Sleep shall neither night nor day
Hang upon his pent-house lid.
He shall live a man forbid.
Weary se'nnights nine times nine
Shall he dwindle, peak, and pine:
Though his bark cannot be lost,
Yet it shall be tempest-tost.   *Macbeth*, I. iii. 1

12 So foul and fair a day I have not seen.   *Ib.* 3

13   What are these,
So withered, and so wild in their attire,
That look not like th' inhabitants o' the earth,
And yet are on 't?   *Ib.* 3

14   You should be women,
And yet your beards forbid me to interpret
That you are so.   *Ib.* 4

15 If you can look into the seeds of time,
And say which grain will grow and which will not.
                                      Ib. 5

16 Stay, you imperfect speakers, tell me more. *Ib.* 7

17   The Thane of Cawdor lives,
A prosperous gentleman; and to be king
Stands not within the prospect of belief;
No more than to be Cawdor. Say, from whence
You owe this strange intelligence? or why
Upon this blasted heath you stop our way
With such prophetic greeting?   *Ib.* 7

18 The earth hath bubbles, as the water has,
And these are of them.   *Ib.* 7

19 Were such things here as we do speak about?
Or have we eaten on the insane root
That takes the reason prisoner?   *Ib.* 8

20 Strange images of death.   *Ib.* 9

21 What! can the devil speak true?   *Ib.* 10

22 And oftentimes, to win us to our harm,
The instruments of darkness tell us truths;
Win us with honest trifles, to betray 's
In deepest consequence.   *Ib.* 12

23   Two truths are told,
As happy prologues to the swelling act
Of the imperial theme.   *Ib.* 12

24 This supernatural soliciting
Cannot be ill, cannot be good; if ill,
Why hath it given me earnest of success,
Commencing in a truth? I am Thane of Cawdor:
If good, why do I yield to that suggestion
Whose horrid image doth unfix my hair
And make my seated heart knock at my ribs,
Against the use of nature? Present fears
Are less than horrible imaginings;
My thought, whose murder yet is but fantastical,
Shakes so my single state of man that function
Is smother'd in surmise, and nothing is
But what is not.   *Ib.* 13

25 If chance will have me king, why, chance may crown
me.   *Ib.* 14

26   Come what come may,
Time and the hour runs through the roughest day.
                                       Ib. 14

27 MALCOLM:
                Nothing in his life
Became him like the leaving it; he died
As one that had been studied in his death
To throw away the dearest thing he owed
As 'twere a careless trifle.

DUNCAN:

          There's no art
To find the mind's construction in the face;
He was a gentleman on whom I built
An absolute trust.   *Macbeth*, I. iv. 7

1 Glamis thou art, and Cawdor; and shalt be
What thou art promis'd. Yet do I fear thy nature;
It is too full o' the milk of human kindness
To catch the nearest way; thou wouldst be great,
Art not without ambition; but without
The illness should attend it; what thou wouldst
    highly,
That thou wouldst holily; wouldst not play false,
And yet wouldst wrongly win; thou'dst have, great
    Glamis,
That which cries, 'Thus thou must do, if thou have
    it';
And that which rather thou dost fear to do
Than wishest should be undone.   *Ib.* v. [16]

2   The golden round,
Which fate and metaphysical aid doth seem
To have thee crown'd withal.   *Ib.* [29]

3   The raven himself is hoarse
That croaks the fatal entrance of Duncan
Under my battlements. Come, you spirits
That tend on mortal thoughts! unsex me here,
And fill me from the crown to the toe top full
Of direst cruelty; make thick my blood,
Stop up the access and passage to remorse,
That no compunctious visitings of nature
Shake my fell purpose, nor keep peace between
The effect and it! Come to my woman's breasts,
And take my milk for gall, you murdering ministers,
Wherever in your sightless substances
You wait on nature's mischief! Come, thick night,
And pall thee in the dunnest smoke of hell,
That my keen knife see not the wound it makes,
Nor heaven peep through the blanket of the dark,
To cry 'Hold, hold!'   *Ib.* [38]

4 Greater than both, by the all-hail hereafter! *Ib.* [56]

5 Your face, my thane, is as a book where men
May read strange matters. To beguile the time,
Look like the time; bear welcome in your eye,
Your hand, your tongue: look like the innocent
    flower,
But be the serpent under't.   *Ib.* [63]

6 DUNCAN:
This castle hath a pleasant seat; the air
Nimbly and sweetly recommends itself
Unto our gentle senses.

BANQUO:
          This guest of summer,
The temple-haunting martlet, does approve
By his lov'd mansionry that the heaven's breath
Smells wooingly here: no jutty, frieze,
Buttress, nor coign of vantage, but this bird
Hath made his pendent bed and procreant cradle:
Where they most breed and haunt, I have observ'd,
The air is delicate.   *Ib.* vi. 1

7 If it were done when 'tis done, then 'twere well
It were done quickly: if the assassination
Could trammel up the consequence, and catch
With his surcease success; that but this blow
Might be the be-all and the end-all here,
But here, upon this bank and shoal of time,
We'd jump the life to come.   *Ib.* vii. 1

8 This even-handed justice.   *Macbeth*, I. vii. 10

9   Besides, this Duncan
Hath borne his faculties so meek, hath been
So clear in his great office, that his virtues
Will plead like angels trumpet-tongu'd, against
The deep damnation of his taking-off;
And pity, like a naked new-born babe,
Striding the blast, or heaven's cherubim, hors'd
Upon the sightless couriers of the air,
Shall blow the horrid deed in every eye,
That tears shall drown the wind. I have no spur
To prick the sides of my intent, but only
Vaulting ambition, which o'erleaps itself,
And falls on the other.   *Ib.* 16

10 We will proceed no further in this business:
He hath honour'd me of late; and I have bought
Golden opinions from all sorts of people. *Ib.* 31

11   Was the hope drunk,
Wherein you dress'd yourself? hath it slept since,
And wakes it now, to look so green and pale
At what it did so freely? From this time
Such I account thy love. Art thou afeard
To be the same in thine own act and valour
As thou art in desire? Wouldst thou have that
Which thou esteem'st the ornament of life,
And live a coward in thine own esteem,
Letting 'I dare not' wait upon 'I would,'
Like the poor cat i' the adage.   *Ib.* 35

12 I dare do all that may become a man;
Who dares do more is none.   *Ib.* 46

13 LADY MACBETH:
        I have given suck, and know
How tender 'tis to love the babe that milks me:
I would, while it was smiling in my face,
Have pluck'd my nipple from his boneless gums,
And dash'd the brains out, had I so sworn as you
Have done to this.

MACBETH:
        If we should fail,—

LADY MACBETH:
          We fail!
But screw your courage to the sticking-place,
And we'll not fail.   *Ib.* 54

14 That memory, the warder of the brain,
Shall be a fume.   *Ib.* 65

15   Bring forth men-children only;
For thy undaunted mettle should compose
Nothing but males.   *Ib.* 72

16 Away, and mock the time with fairest show:
False face must hide what the false heart doth know.
    Ib. 81

17   There's husbandry in heaven;
Their candles are all out.   *Ib.* II. i. 4

18   Merciful powers!
Restrain in me the cursed thoughts that nature
Gives way to in repose.   *Ib.* 7

19   Shut up
In measureless content.   *Ib.* 16

20 Is this a dagger which I see before me,
The handle toward my hand? Come, let me clutch
    thee:
I have thee not, and yet I see thee still.
Art thou not, fatal vision, sensible
To feeling as to sight? or art thou but
A dagger of the mind, a false creation,
Proceeding from the heat-oppressèd brain? *Ib.* 33

1   Now o'er the one half-world
Nature seems dead, and wicked dreams abuse
The curtain'd sleep; witchcraft celebrates
Pale Hecate's offerings; and wither'd murder,
Alarum'd by his sentinel, the wolf,
Whose howl's his watch, thus with his stealthy pace,
With Tarquin's ravishing strides, toward his design
Moves like a ghost. Thou sure and firm-set earth,
Hear not my steps, which way they walk, for fear
The very stones prate of my whereabout,
And take the present horror from the time,
Which now suits with it. Whiles I threat he lives:
Words to the heat of deeds too cold breath gives.
I go, and it is done; the bell invites me.
Hear it not, Duncan; for it is a knell
That summons thee to heaven or to hell.
              Macbeth, II. i. 49

2 That which hath made them drunk hath made me
    bold,
What hath quench'd them hath given me fire.
              Ib. ii. 1

3 It was the owl that shriek'd, the fatal bellman,
Which gives the stern'st good-night.   *Ib*. 4

4   The attempt and not the deed,
Confounds us.   *Ib*. 12

5   Had he not resembled
My father as he slept I had done 't.   *Ib*. 14

6 I have done the deed. Didst thou not hear a noise?
              Ib. 16

7 As they had seen me with these hangman's hands.
              Ib. 29

8 Consider it not so deeply.   *Ib*. 31

9 I had most need of blessing, and 'Amen'
Stuck in my throat.   *Ib*. 33

10 These deeds must not be thought
After these ways; so, it will make us mad.   *Ib*. 34

11 Methought I heard a voice cry, 'Sleep no more!
Macbeth does murder sleep,' the innocent sleep,
Sleep that knits up the ravell'd sleave of care,
The death of each day's life, sore labour's bath,
Balm of hurt minds, great nature's second course,
Chief nourisher in life's feast.   *Ib*. 36

12 Glamis hath murder'd sleep, and therefore Cawdor
Shall sleep no more, Macbeth shall sleep no more!
              Ib. 43

13 You do unbend your noble strength to think
So brainsickly of things.   *Ib*. 46

14 MACBETH:
I am afraid to think what I have done;
Look on 't again I dare not.
LADY MACBETH:
           Infirm of purpose!
Give me the daggers. The sleeping and the dead
Are but as pictures; 'tis the eye of childhood
That fears a painted devil.   *Ib*. 52

15 Will all great Neptune's ocean wash this blood
Clean from my hand? No, this my hand will rather
The multitudinous seas incarnadine,
Making the green one red.   *Ib*. 61

16 A little water clears us of this deed.   *Ib*. 68

17 Here's a farmer that hanged himself on the expectation of plenty.   *Ib*. iii. [5]

18 Faith, here's an equivocator.   *Ib*. [9]

19 The primrose way to the everlasting bonfire.
            Macbeth, II. iii. [22]

20 The labour we delight in physics pain.   *Ib*. [56]

21 The night has been unruly: where we lay
Our chimneys were blown down; and, as they say,
Lamentings heard i' the air; strange screams of
    death,
And prophesying with accents terrible
Of dire combustion and confus'd events
New-hatch'd to the woeful time. The obscure bird
Clamour'd the live-long night: some say the earth
Was feverous and did shake.   *Ib*. [60]

22 Confusion now hath made his masterpiece!
Most sacrilegious murder hath broke ope
The Lord's anointed temple, and stole thence
The life o' the building!   *Ib*. [72]

23 Shake off this downy sleep, death's counterfeit,
And look on death itself! up, up, and see
The great doom's image!   *Ib*. [83]

24 Had I but died an hour before this chance,
I had liv'd a blessed time; for, from this instant,
There's nothing serious in mortality:
All is but toys; renown and grace is dead,
The wine of life is drawn, and the mere lees
Is left this vault to brag of.   *Ib*. [98]

25 Who can be wise, amazed, temperate, and furious,
Loyal and neutral, in a moment? No man. *Ib*. [115]

26 In the great hand of God I stand, and thence
Against the undivulg'd pretence I fight
Of treasonous malice.   *Ib*. [137]

27 There's daggers in men's smiles.   *Ib*. [147]

28 A falcon, towering in her pride of place,
Was by a mousing owl hawk'd at and kill'd.
              Ib. iv. 12

29 Thriftless ambition, that wilt ravin up
Thine own life's means!   *Ib*. 28

30 Thou hast it now: King, Cawdor, Glamis, all,
As the weird women promis'd; and, I fear,
Thou play'dst most foully for 't; yet it was said
It should not stand in thy posterity,
But that myself should be the root and father
Of many kings.   *Ib*. III. i. 1

31 I must become a borrower of the night
For a dark hour or twain.   *Ib*. 27

32   To be thus is nothing;
But to be safely thus.   *Ib*. 48

33   There is none but he
Whose being I do fear; and, under him
My genius is rebuk'd: as, it is said,
Mark Antony's was by Cæsar.   *Ib*. 54

34   Mine eternal jewel
Given to the common enemy of man.   *Ib*. 68

35 FIRST MURDERER:
          We are men, my liege.
MACBETH:
Ay, in the catalogue ye go for men.   *Ib*. 91

36 SECOND MURDERER:
          I am one, my liege,
Whom the vile blows and buffets of the world
Have so incens'd, that I am reckless what
I do to spite the world.

SHAKESPEARE

FIRST MURDERER:
              I another,
So weary with disasters, tugg'd with fortune,
That I would set my life on any chance,
To mend it or be rid on 't.   *Macbeth*, III. i. 108

1 Leave no rubs nor botches in the work.   *Ib.* 134

2   Thy soul's flight,
If it find heaven, must find it out to-night. *Ib.* 141

3   Nought's had, all's spent,
Where our desire is got without content:
'Tis safer to be that which we destroy,
Than, by destruction, dwell in doubtful joy. *Ib.* ii. 4

4 LADY MACBETH:
        Things without all remedy
Should be without regard: what's done is done.
MACBETH:
We have scotch'd the snake, not killed it:
She'll close and be herself, whilst our poor malice
Remains in danger of her former tooth
But let the frame of things disjoint, both the worlds
    suffer,
Ere we will eat our meal in fear, and sleep
In the affliction of these terrible dreams
That shake us nightly. Better be with the dead,
Whom we, to gain our peace, have sent to peace,
Than on the torture of the mind to lie
In restless ecstasy. Duncan is in his grave;
After life's fitful fever he sleeps well;
Treason has done his worst: nor steel, nor poison,
Malice domestic, foreign levy, nothing,
Can touch him further.   *Ib.* 11

5 Make our faces vizards to our hearts,
Disguising what they are.   *Ib.* 34

6 But in them nature's copy's not eterne. *Ib.* 38

7 A deed of dreadful note.   *Ib.* 44

8 Be innocent of the knowledge, dearest chuck,
Till thou applaud the deed. Come, seeling night,
Scarf up the tender eye of pitiful day,
And with thy bloody and invisible hand,
Cancel and tear to pieces that great bond
Which keeps me pale! Light thickens, and the crow
Makes wing to the rooky wood;
Good things of day begin to droop and drowse,
Whiles night's black agents to their preys do rouse.
    Ib. 45

9 Things bad begun make strong themselves by ill.
    Ib. 55

10 Now spurs the lated traveller apace
To gain the timely inn.   *Ib.* iii. 6

11 Ourself will mingle with society
And play the humble host.   *Ib.* iv. 3

12 But now I am cabin'd, cribb'd, confin'd, bound in
To saucy doubts and fears.   *Ib.* 24

13 Now good digestion wait on appetite,
And health on both!   *Ib.* 38

14 Which of you have done this?   *Ib.* 49

15 Thou canst not say I did it: never shake
Thy gory locks at me.   *Ib.* 50

16 The air-drawn dagger.   *Ib.* 62

17   The times have been,
That, when the brains were out, the man would die,
And there an end; but now they rise again,
With twenty mortal murders on their crowns,
And push us from our stools: this is more strange
Than such a murder is.   *Macbeth*, III. iv. 78

18 I drink to the general joy of the whole table. *Ib.* 89

19 Thy bones are marrowless, thy blood is cold;
Thou hast no speculation in those eyes
Which thou dost glare with.   *Ib.* 94

20 What man dare, I dare;
Approach thou like the rugged Russian bear,
The arm'd rhinoceros or the Hyrcan tiger,
Take any shape but that, and my firm nerves
Shall never tremble.   *Ib.* 99

21   Hence, horrible shadow!
Unreal mockery, hence!   *Ib.* 106

22 LADY MACBETH:
You have displaced the mirth, broke the good
    meeting,
With most admir'd disorder.
MACBETH:
        Can such things be,
And overcome us like a summer's cloud,
Without our special wonder?   *Ib.* 109

23 Stand not upon the order of your going,
But go at once.   *Ib.* 119

24 MACBETH:
It will have blood, they say; blood will have blood:
Stones have been known to move and trees to speak;
Augurs and understood relations have
By maggot-pies and choughs and rooks brought forth
The secret'st man of blood. What is the night?
LADY MACBETH:
Almost at odds with morning, which is which.
    Ib. 122

25   I am in blood
Stepp'd in so far that, should I wade no more,
Returning were as tedious as go o'er. *Ib.* 136

26 You lack the season of all natures, sleep. *Ib.* 141

27 Upon the corner of the moon
There hangs a vaporous drop profound;
I'll catch it ere it come to ground.   *Ib.* v. 23

28 And you all know, security
Is mortals' chiefest enemy.   *Ib.* 32

29 Round about the cauldron go;
In the poison'd entrails throw.   *Ib.* IV. i. 4

30 Double, double toil and trouble;
Fire burn, and cauldron bubble.   *Ib.* 10

31 Eye of newt and toe of frog,
Wool of bat and tongue of dog.   *Ib.* 14

32   Slips of yew
Sliver'd in the moon's eclipse.   *Ib.* 27

33 Finger of birth-strangled babe,
Ditch-deliver'd by a drab,
Make the gruel thick and slab.   *Ib.* 30

34 *Black spirits and white,*
   Red spirits and grey,
Mingle, mingle, mingle,
   You that mingle may.
    Ib. 44. *Stage direction.* Davenant's version of
    Macbeth

[459]

1 By the pricking of my thumbs,
Something wicked this way comes.
                    Open, locks,
                    Whoever knocks.   *Macbeth*, IV. i. 44

2 How now, you secret, black, and midnight hags!
                                            Ib. 48

3 A deed without a name.   *Ib.* 49

4 Though you untie the winds and let them fight
Against the churches; though the yesty waves
Confound and swallow navigation up.   *Ib.* 52

5 Be bloody, bold, and resolute; laugh to scorn
The power of man, for none of woman born
Shall harm Macbeth.   *Ib.* 79

6 But yet I'll make assurance double sure,
And take a bond of fate.   *Ib.* 83

7 That I may tell pale-hearted fear it lies,
And sleep in spite of thunder.   *Ib.* 85

8   Wears upon his baby brow the round
And top of sovereignty.   *Ib.* 88

9   Take no care
Who chafes, who frets, or where conspirers are:
Macbeth shall never vanquish'd be until
Great Birnam wood to high Dunsinane hill
Shall come against him.   *Ib.* 90

10 Show his eyes, and grieve his heart;
Come like shadows, so depart!   *Ib.* 110

11 What! will the line stretch out to the crack of doom?
                                            Ib. 117

12 For the blood-bolter'd Banquo smiles upon me.
                                            Ib. 123

13 The weird sisters.   *Ib.* 136

14 The flighty purpose never is o'ertook,
Unless the deed go with it.   *Ib.* 145

15 The very firstlings of my heart shall be
The firstlings of my hand.   *Ib.* 147

16 His flight was madness: when our actions do not,
Our fears do make us traitors.   *Ib.* ii. 3

17 He wants the natural touch; for the poor wren,
The most diminutive of birds, will fight—
Her young ones in her nest—against the owl. *Ib.* 9

18 Angels are bright still, though the brightest fell.
                                            Ib. iii. 22

19 MACDUFF:
Stands Scotland where it did?
ROSS:
                        Alas! poor country;
Almost afraid to know itself. It cannot
Be call'd our mother, but our grave.   *Ib.* 164

20 What! man; ne'er pull your hat upon your brows;
Give sorrow words: the grief that does not speak
Whispers the o'er-fraught heart, and bids it break.
                                            Ib. 208

21   All my pretty ones?
Did you say all? O hell-kite! All?
What! all my pretty chickens and their dam,
At one fell swoop?   *Ib.* 216

22 MALCOLM:
Dispute it like a man.
MACDUFF:
                    I shall do so;
But I must also feel it as a man;

I cannot but remember such things were,
That were most precious to me. *Macbeth*, IV. iii. 219

23 DOCTOR:
You see her eyes are open.
GENTLEWOMAN:
Ay, but their sense is shut.   *Ib.* v. i. [27]

24 Out, damned spot! out, I say! One; two: why then,
'tis time to do't. Hell is murky! Fie, my lord, fie!
a soldier, and afeard? What need we fear who
knows it, when none can call our power to account?
Yet who would have thought the old man to have
had so much blood in him?   *Ib.* [38]

25 The Thane of Fife had a wife: where is she now?
What! will these hands ne'er be clean?   *Ib.* [46]

26 She has spoke what she should not, I am sure of
that: Heaven knows what she has known.   *Ib.* [52]

27 All the perfumes of Arabia will not sweeten this
little hand.   *Ib.* [56]

28 I would not have such a heart in my bosom for the
dignity of the whole body.   *Ib.* [60]

29 Foul whisperings are abroad.   *Ib.* [78]

30 More needs she the divine than the physician.
                                            Ib. [81]

31 Those he commands move only in command,
Nothing in love; now does he feel his title
Hang loose about him, like a giant's robe
Upon a dwarfish thief.   *Ib.* ii. 19

32   All that is within him does condemn
Itself for being there.   *Ib.* 24

33 Bring me no more reports; let them fly all:
Till Birnam wood remove to Dunsinane
I cannot taint with fear.   *Ib.* iii. 1

34   The spirits that know
All mortal consequences have pronounc'd me thus.
                                            Ib. 4

35 The devil damn thee black, thou cream-faced loon!
Where gott'st thou that goose look?   *Ib.* 11

36   This push
Will cheer me ever or disseat me now.
I have lived long enough: my way of life
Is fall'n into the sear, the yellow leaf;
And that which should accompany old age,
As honour, love, obedience, troops of friends,
I must not look to have; but, in their stead,
Curses, not loud but deep, mouth-honour, breath,
Which the poor heart would fain deny, and dare not.
                                            Ib. 20

37 DOCTOR:
                    Not so sick, my lord,
As she is troubled with thick-coming fancies,
That keep her from her rest.
MACBETH:
                    Cure her of that:
Canst thou not minister to a mind diseas'd,
Pluck from the memory a rooted sorrow,
Raze out the written troubles of the brain,
And with some sweet oblivious antidote
Cleanse the stuff'd bosom of that perilous stuff
Which weighs upon the heart?
DOCTOR:
                    Therein the patient
Must minister to himself.
MACBETH:
Throw physic to the dogs; I'll none of it. *Ib.* 37

SHAKESPEARE

1 If thou couldst, doctor, cast
The water of my land, find her disease,
And purge it to a sound and pristine health,
I would applaud thee to the very echo,
That should applaud again. *Macbeth*, v. iii. 50

2 Hang out our banners on the outward walls;
The cry is still, 'They come;' our castle's strength
Will laugh a siege to scorn. *Ib.* v. 1

3 I have almost forgot the taste of fears.
The time has been my senses would have cool'd
To hear a night-shriek, and my fell of hair
Would at a dismal treatise rouse and stir
As life were in't. I have supp'd full with horrors;
Direness, familiar to my slaughterous thoughts,
Cannot once start me. *Ib.* 9

4 SEYTON:
The queen, my lord, is dead.
MACBETH:
She should have died hereafter;
There would have been a time for such a word.
To-morrow, and to-morrow, and to-morrow,
Creeps in this petty pace from day to day,
To the last syllable of recorded time;
And all our yesterdays have lighted fools
The way to dusty death. Out, out, brief candle!
Life's but a walking shadow, a poor player,
That struts and frets his hour upon the stage,
And then is heard no more; it is a tale
Told by an idiot, full of sound and fury,
Signifying nothing. *Ib.* 16

5 I pull in resolution, and begin
To doubt the equivocation of the fiend
That lies like truth: 'Fear not, till Birnam wood
Do come to Dunsinane.' *Ib.* 42

6 I 'gin to be aweary of the sun,
And wish the estate o' the world were now undone. *Ib.* 49

7 Blow, wind! come, wrack!
At least we'll die with harness on our back. *Ib.* 51

8 They have tied me to a stake; I cannot fly.
But bear-like I must fight the course. *Ib.* vii. 1

9 Why should I play the Roman fool, and die
On mine own sword? *Ib.* 30

10 I bear a charmed life. *Ib.* 41

11 And let the angel whom thou still hast served
Tell thee, Macduff was from his mother's womb
Untimely ripp'd. *Ib.* 43

12 And be these juggling fiends no more believ'd,
That palter with us in a double sense;
That keep the word of promise to our ear,
And break it to our hope. *Ib.* 48

13 Live to be the show and gaze o' the time. *Ib.* 53

14 Lay on, Macduff;
And damn'd be him that first cries, 'Hold, enough!' *Ib.* 62

15 SIWARD:
Had he his hurts before?
ROSS:
Ay, on the front.
SIWARD:
Why, then, God's soldier be he!
Had I as many sons as I have hairs,
I would not wish them to a fairer death. *Ib.* 75

16 For if our virtues
Did not go forth of us, 'twere all alike
As if we had them not. Spirits are not finely touch'd
But to fine issues. *Measure for Measure*, I. i. 33

17 The sanctimonious pirate, that went to sea with the
Ten Commandments, but scraped one out of the
table. *Ib.* ii. [7]

18 And liberty plucks justice by the nose. *Ib.* iii. 29

19 I hold you as a thing ensky'd and sainted. *Ib.* iv. 34

20 A man whose blood
Is very snow-broth; one who never feels
The wanton stings and motions of the sense. *Ib.* 57

21 Our doubts are traitors,
And make us lose the good we oft might win,
By fearing to attempt. *Ib.* 77

22 We must not make a scarecrow of the law,
Setting it up to fear the birds of prey,
And let it keep one shape, till custom make it
Their perch and not their terror. *Ib.* II. i. 1

23 'Tis one thing to be tempted, Escalus,
Another thing to fall. I not deny,
The jury, passing on the prisoner's life,
May in the sworn twelve have a thief or two
Guiltier than him they try. *Ib.* 17

24 Some rise by sin, and some by virtue fall. *Ib.* 38

25 This will last out a night in Russia,
When nights are longest there. *Ib.* [144]

26 I am
At war 'twixt will and will not. *Ib.* ii. 32

27 Condemn the fault and not the actor of it? *Ib.* 37

28 No ceremony that to great ones 'longs,
Not the king's crown, nor the deputed sword,
The marshal's truncheon, nor the judge's robe,
Become them with one half so good a grace
As mercy does. *Ib.* 59

29 Why, all the souls that were were forfeit once;
And He that might the vantage best have took,
Found out the remedy. How would you be,
If He, which is the top of judgment, should
But judge you as you are? *Ib.* 73

30 O! it is excellent
To have a giant's strength, but it is tyrannous
To use it like a giant. *Ib.* 107

31 Merciful Heaven!
Thou rather with thy sharp and sulphurous bolt
Split'st the unwedgeable and gnarled oak
Than the soft myrtle; but man, proud man,
Drest in a little brief authority,
Most ignorant of what he's most assur'd,
His glassy essence, like an angry ape,
Plays such fantastic tricks before high heaven,
As make the angels weep. *Ib.* 114

32 Great men may jest with saints; 'tis wit in them,
But, in the less foul profanation. *Ib.* 127

33 That in the captain's but a choleric word,
Which in the soldier is flat blasphemy. *Ib.* 130

34 I am that way going to temptation,
Where prayers cross. *Ib.* 158

35 Having waste ground enough,
Shall we desire to raze the sanctuary
And pitch our evils there? *Ib.* 170

[461]

1 O cunning enemy, that, to catch a saint,
With saints dost bait thy hook! Most dangerous
Is that temptation that doth goad us on
To sin in loving virtue. *Measure for Measure*, II. ii. 180

2 When I would pray and think, I think and pray
To several subjects: Heaven hath my empty words.
Ib. iv. 1

3 CLAUDIO:
The miserable have no other medicine
But only hope:
I have hope to live, and am prepar'd to die.
DUKE:
Be absolute for death; either death or life
Shall thereby be the sweeter. Reason thus with life:
If I do lose thee, I do lose a thing
That none but fools would keep: a breath thou art
Servile to all the skyey influences. *Ib.* III. i. 2

4 If thou art rich, thou'rt poor;
For, like an ass whose back with ingots bows,
Thou bear'st thy heavy riches but a journey,
And death unloads thee. *Ib.* 25

5 Thou hast nor youth nor age;
But, as it were, an after-dinner's sleep,
Dreaming on both. *Ib.* 32

6 Palsied eld. *Ib.* 35

7 Dar'st thou die?
The sense of death is most in apprehension,
And the poor beetle, that we tread upon,
In corporal sufferance finds a pang as great
As when a giant dies. *Ib.* 75

8 If I must die,
I will encounter darkness as a bride,
And hug it in mine arms. *Ib.* 81

9 CLAUDIO:
Death is a fearful thing.
ISABELLA:
And shamed life a hateful.
CLAUDIO:
Ay, but to die, and go we know not where;
To lie in cold obstruction and to rot;
This sensible warm motion to become
A kneaded clod; and the delighted spirit
To bathe in fiery floods, or to reside
In thrilling region of thick-ribbèd ice;
To be imprisoned in the viewless winds,
And blown with restless violence round about
The pendant world! *Ib.* 114

10 The weariest and most loathèd worldly life
That age, ache, penury, and imprisonment
Can lay on nature, is a paradise
To what we fear of death. *Ib.* 127

11 O, fie, fie, fie!
Thy sin's not accidental, but a trade. *Ib.* 146

12 The hand that hath made you fair hath made you good.
Ib. [182]

13 Virtue is bold, and goodness never fearful. *Ib.* [214]

14 There, at the moated grange, resides this dejected
Mariana. *Ib.* [279]

15 A very superficial, ignorant, unweighing fellow.
Ib. ii. [151]

16 Take, O take those lips away,
That so sweetly were forsworn;
And those eyes, the break of day,
Lights that do mislead the morn:

But my kisses bring again, bring again;
Seals of love, but seal'd in vain, seal'd in vain.
Measure for Measure, IV. i. 1

17 Though music oft hath such a charm
To make bad good, and good provoke to harm. *Ib.* 16

18 He will discredit our mystery. *Ib.* ii. [29]

19 Every true man's apparel fits your thief. *Ib.* [46]

20 Look, here's the warrant, Claudio, for thy death:
'Tis now dead midnight, and by eight to-morrow
Thou must be made immortal. *Ib.* [66]

21 A man that apprehends death no more dreadfully
but as a drunken sleep. *Ib.* [148]

22 Look, the unfolding star calls up the shepherd.
Ib. [219]

23 I am a kind of burr; I shall stick. *Ib.* iii. [193]

24 A forted residence 'gainst the tooth of time,
And razure of oblivion. *Ib.* v. i. 12

25 Let the devil
Be sometime honour'd for his burning throne.
Ib. [289]

26 Haste still pays haste, and leisure answers leisure;
Like doth quit like, and Measure still for Measure.
Ib. [411]

27 They say best men are moulded out of faults,
And, for the most, become much more the better
For being a little bad. *Ib.* [440]

28 In sooth I know not why I am so sad:
It wearies me; you say it wearies you;
But how I caught it, found it, or came by it,
What stuff 'tis made of, whereof it is born,
I am to learn. *The Merchant of Venice*, I. i. 1

29 There, where your argosies with portly sail,—
Like signiors and rich burghers on the flood,
Or, as it were, the pageants of the sea,—
Do overpeer the petty traffickers. *Ib.* 9

30 Nature hath fram'd strange fellows in her time:
Some that will evermore peep through their eyes
And laugh like parrots at a bagpiper:
And other of such vinegar aspect
That they'll not show their teeth in way of smile,
Though Nestor swear the jest be laughable. *Ib.* 51

31 I hold the world but as the world, Gratiano;
A stage where every man must play a part,
And mine a sad one. *Ib.* 77

32 Why should a man, whose blood is warm within,
Sit like his grandsire cut in alabaster? *Ib.* 83

33 There are a sort of men whose visages
Do cream and mantle like a standing pond. *Ib.* 88

34 As who should say, 'I am Sir Oracle,
And when I ope my lips let no dog bark!'
O, my Antonio, I do know of these,
That therefore only are reputed wise,
For saying nothing. *Ib.* 93

35 Fish not, with this melancholy bait,
For this fool gudgeon, this opinion. *Ib.* 101

36 Silence is only commendable
In a neat's tongue dried and a maid not vendible.
Ib. 111

1 Gratiano speaks an infinite deal of nothing, more than any man in all Venice. His reasons are as two grains of wheat, hid in two bushels of chaff: you shall seek all day ere you find them; and, when you have them, they are not worth the search.
The Merchant of Venice, I. i. 114

2 My purse, my person, my extremest means Lie all unlock'd to your occasions. *Ib.* [139]

3 　　　　Sometimes from her eyes
I did receive fair speechless messages. *Ib.* [164]

4 By my troth, Nerissa, my little body is aweary of this great world. *Ib.* ii. 1

5 They are as sick that surfeit with too much, as they that starve with nothing. *Ib.* [5]

6 Superfluity comes sooner by white hairs, but competency lives longer. *Ib.* [9]

7 If to do were as easy as to know what were good to do, chapels had been churches, and poor men's cottages princes' palaces. *Ib.* [13]

8 It is a good divine that follows his own instructions; I can easier teach twenty what were good to be done, than be one of the twenty to follow mine own teaching. *Ib.* [15]

9 He doth nothing but talk of his horse. *Ib.* [43]

10 God made him, and therefore let him pass for a man. *Ib.* [59]

11 If I should marry him, I should marry twenty husbands. *Ib.* [66]

12 I think he bought his doublet in Italy, his round hose in France, his bonnet in Germany, and his behaviour everywhere. *Ib.* [78]

13 I will do anything, Nerissa, ere I will be married to a sponge. *Ib.* [105]

14 I dote on his very absence. *Ib.* [118]

15 Ships are but boards, sailors but men; there be land-rats and water-rats, land-thieves and water-thieves. *Ib.* iii. [22]

16 I will buy with you, sell with you, talk with you, walk with you, and so following; but I will not eat with you, drink with you, nor pray with you. What news on the Rialto? *Ib.* [36]

17 How like a fawning publican he looks!
I hate him for he is a Christian;
But more for that in low simplicity
He lends out money gratis, and brings down
The rate of usance here with us in Venice.
If I can catch him once upon the hip,
I will feed fat the ancient grudge I bear him.
He hates our sacred nation, and he rails,
Even there where merchants most do congregate,
On me, my bargains, and my well-won thrift.
Ib. [42]

18 The devil can cite Scripture for his purpose. *Ib.* [99]

19 A goodly apple rotten at the heart.
O, what a goodly outside falsehood hath! *Ib.* [102]

20 Signior Antonio, many a time and oft
In the Rialto you have rated me. *Ib.* [107]

21 For sufferance is the badge of all our tribe. *Ib.* [111]

22 'Hath a dog money? Is it possible
A cur can lend three thousand ducats?' or
Shall I bend low, and in a bondman's key,
With bated breath, and whispering humbleness,
Say this:—
'Fair sir, you spat on me on Wednesday last;
You spurn'd me such a day; another time
You call'd me dog; and for these courtesies
I'll lend you thus much moneys?'
The Merchant of Venice, I. iii. [122]

23 　　For when did friendship take
A breed for barren metal of his friend? *Ib.* [134]

24 O father Abram! what these Christians are,
Whose own hard dealing teaches them suspect
The thoughts of others! *Ib.* [161]

25 I like not fair terms and a villain's mind. *Ib.* [180]

26 Mislike me not for my complexion,
The shadow'd livery of the burnished sun.
Ib. II. i. 1

27 An honest man's son,—or rather an honest woman's son;—for, indeed, my father did something smack, something grow to, he had a kind of taste;—well, my conscience says, 'Launcelot, budge not.' 'Budge,' says the fiend. 'Budge not,' says my conscience. 'Conscience,' say I, 'you counsel well;' 'fiend,' say I, 'you counsel well.' *Ib.* ii. [16]

28 O heavens! this is my true-begotten father. *Ib.* [36]

29 An honest exceeding poor man. *Ib.* [54]

30 The very staff of my age, my very prop. *Ib.* [71]

31 It is a wise father that knows his own child. *Ib.* [83]

32 Truth will come to light; murder cannot be hid long.
Ib. [86]

33 Lord worshipped might he be! What a beard hast thou got! *Ib.* [101]

34 There is some ill a-brewing towards my rest,
For I did dream of money-bags to-night. *Ib.* v. 17

35 Then it was not for nothing that my nose fell a-bleeding on Black Monday. *Ib.* [24]

36 And the vile squealing of the wry-neck'd fife. *Ib.* [30]

37 But love is blind, and lovers cannot see
The pretty follies that themselves commit. *Ib.* vi. 36

38 What! must I hold a candle to my shames? *Ib.* 41

39 　　　　Men that hazard all
Do it in hope of fair advantages:
A golden mind stoops not to shows of dross.
Ib. vii. 18

40 Pause there, Morocco. *Ib.* 24

41 Young in limbs, in judgment old. *Ib.* 71

42 My daughter! O my ducats! O my daughter!
Fled with a Christian! O my Christian ducats!
Ib. viii. 15

43 The fool multitude, that choose by show. *Ib.* ix. 26

44 　　　　Like the martlet,
Builds in the weather on the outward wall,
Even in the force and road of casualty.
I will not choose what many men desire,
Because I will not jump with common spirits
And rank me with the barbarous multitude. *Ib.* 28

1   Let none presume
To wear an undeserved dignity.
O! that estates, degrees, and offices
Were not deriv'd corruptly, and that clear honour
Were purchased by the merit of the wearer!
The Merchant of Venice, II. ix. 39

2 The portrait of a blinking idiot.   Ib. 54

3 The fire seven times tried this:
Seven times tried that judgment is
That did never choose amiss.
Some there be that shadows kiss;
Such have but a shadow's bliss.   Ib. 63

4 Thus hath the candle sing'd the moth.
O, these deliberate fools!   Ib. 79

5 The ancient saying is no heresy:
'Hanging and wiving goes by destiny.'   Ib. 82

6 The Goodwins, I think they call the place; a very
dangerous flat, and fatal, where the carcasses of
many a tall ship lie buried, as they say, if my
gossip Report be an honest woman of her word.
Ib. III. i. [4]

7 Let him look to his bond.   Ib. [51, 52, 54]

8 Hath not a Jew eyes? hath not a Jew hands, organs,
dimensions, senses, affections, passions? fed with
the same food, hurt with the same weapons, subject
to the same diseases, healed by the same means,
warmed and cooled by the same winter and
summer, as a Christian is? If you prick us, do
we not bleed? if you tickle us, do we not laugh?
if you poison us, do we not die? and if you wrong
us, shall we not revenge?   Ib. [63]

9 The villany you teach me I will execute, and it
shall go hard but I will better the instruction.
Ib. [76]

10 Thou stick'st a dagger in me.   Ib. [118]

11 TUBAL:
One of them showed me a ring that he had of your
daughter for a monkey.
SHYLOCK:
I would not have given it for a wilderness of monkeys.
Ib. [126]

12   He makes a swan-like end
Fading in music.   Ib. ii. 44

13   Tell me where is fancy bred,
       Or in the heart or in the head?
How begot, how nourished?
       Reply, reply.

It is engender'd in the eyes,
With gazing fed; and fancy dies
In the cradle where it lies.
      Let us all ring fancy's knell:
I'll begin it,—Ding, dong, bell.
Ib. 63

14 So may the outward shows be least themselves:
The world is still deceived with ornament.
In law, what plea so tainted and corrupt
But, being season'd with a gracious voice,
Obscures the show of evil? In religion,
What damned error, but some sober brow
Will bless it and approve it with a text,
Hiding the grossness with fair ornament? Ib. 73

15   Ornament is but the guiled shore
To a most dangerous sea; the beauteous scarf
Veiling an Indian beauty; in a word,
The seeming truth which cunning times put on
To entrap the wisest.
The Merchant of Venice, III. ii. 97

16   Thou pale and common drudge
'Tween man and man.   Ib. 103

17   Rash-embrac'd despair,
And shuddering fear, and green-ey'd jealousy.
Ib. 109

18   What demi-god
Hath come so near creation?   Ib. 115

19 An unlesson'd girl, unschool'd, unpractis'd;
Happy in this, she is not yet so old
But she may learn; happier than this,
She is not bred so dull but she can learn. Ib. 160

20 I wish you all the joy that you can wish. Ib. 191

21 My eyes, my lord, can look as swift as yours:
You saw the mistress, I beheld the maid. Ib. 198

22 Here are a few of the unpleasant'st words
That ever blotted paper!   Ib. 252

23 I will have my bond.   Ib. iii. 17

24 This comes too near the praising of myself. Ib. iv. 22

25 How every fool can play upon the word! Ib. v. [48]

26 Wilt thou show the whole wealth of thy wit in an
instant? I pray thee, understand a plain man in
his plain meaning.   Ib. [62]

27   I'll not answer that:
But say it is my humour.   Ib. IV. i. 42

28 A harmless necessary cat.   Ib. 55

29 I am not bound to please thee with my answer.
Ib. 65

30 What judgment shall I dread, doing no wrong?
Ib. 89

31 I am a tainted wether of the flock,
Meetest for death: the weakest kind of fruit
Drops earliest to the ground.   Ib. 114

32 I never knew so young a body with so old a head.
Ib. [163]

33 PORTIA:
      Then must the Jew be merciful.
SHYLOCK:
On what compulsion must I? tell me that.
PORTIA:
The quality of mercy is not strain'd,
It droppeth as the gentle rain from heaven
Upon the place beneath: it is twice bless'd;
It blesseth him that gives and him that takes:
'Tis mightiest in the mightiest: it becomes
The throned monarch better than his crown;
His sceptre shows the force of temporal power,
The attribute to awe and majesty,
Wherein doth sit the dread and fear of kings;
But mercy is above this sceptred sway,
It is enthroned in the hearts of kings,
It is an attribute to God himself,
And earthly power doth then show likest God's
When mercy seasons justice. Therefore, Jew,
Though justice be thy plea, consider this,
That in the course of justice none of us
Should see salvation: we do pray for mercy,
And that same prayer doth teach us all to render
The deeds of mercy.   Ib. [182]

[464]

1 My deeds upon my head! I crave the law.
The Merchant of Venice, IV. i. [206]

2 Wrest once the law to your authority:
To do a great right, do a little wrong. *Ib.* [215]

3 'Twill be recorded for a precedent,
And many an error by the same example
Will rush into the state. *Ib.* [220]

4 A Daniel come to judgment! yea, a Daniel!
O wise young judge, how I do honour thee!
Ib. [223]

5 An oath, an oath, I have an oath in heaven:
Shall I lay perjury upon my soul?
No, not for Venice. *Ib.* [228]

6   I charge you by the law,
Whereof you are a well-deserving pillar,
Proceed to judgment. *Ib.* [238]

7 Is it so nominated in the bond? *Ib.* [260]

8 'Tis not in the bond. *Ib.* [263]

9 For herein Fortune shows herself more kind
Than is her custom: it is still her use
To let the wretched man outlive his wealth,
To view with hollow eye and wrinkled brow
An age of poverty. *Ib.* [268]

10 The court awards it, and the law doth give it.
Ib. [301]

11   Thyself shalt see the act;
For, as thou urgest justice, be assur'd
Thou shalt have justice, more than thou desir'st.
Ib. [315]

12 A second Daniel, a Daniel, Jew!
Now, infidel, I have thee on the hip. *Ib.* [334]

13 I thank thee, Jew, for teaching me that word.
Ib. [342]

14 You take my house when you do take the prop
That doth sustain my house; you take my life
When you do take the means whereby I live. *Ib.* [376]

15 He is well paid that is well satisfied. *Ib.* [416]

16 You taught me first to beg, and now methinks
You teach me how a beggar should be answer'd.
Ib. [440]

17 LORENZO:
        In such a night
Troilus methinks mounted the Troyan walls,
And sigh'd his soul toward the Grecian tents,
Where Cressid lay that night.
JESSICA:
        In such a night
Did Thisbe fearfully o'ertrip the dew,
And saw the lion's shadow ere himself,
And ran dismay'd away.
LORENZO:
        In such a night
Stood Dido with a willow in her hand
Upon the wild sea-banks, and waft her love
To come again to Carthage.
JESSICA:
        In such a night
Medea gather'd the enchanted herbs
That did renew old Æson. *Ib.* v. i. 3

18 How sweet the moonlight sleeps upon this bank!
Here will we sit, and let the sounds of music
Creep in our ears: soft stillness and the night
Become the touches of sweet harmony.
Sit, Jessica: look, how the floor of heaven

Is thick inlaid with patines of bright gold:
There's not the smallest orb which thou behold'st
But in his motion like an angel sings,
Still quiring to the young-eyed cherubins;
Such harmony is in immortal souls;
But, whilst this muddy vesture of decay
Doth grossly close it in, we cannot hear it.
The Merchant of Venice, v. i. 54

19 I am never merry when I hear sweet music. *Ib.* 69

20   Therefore the poet
Did feign that Orpheus drew trees, stones, and floods;
Since nought so stockish, hard, and full of rage,
But music for the time doth change his nature.
The man that hath no music in himself,
Nor is not mov'd with concord of sweet sounds,
Is fit for treasons, stratagems, and spoils;
The motions of his spirit are dull as night,
And his affections dark as Erebus:
Let no such man be trusted. *Ib.* 79

21 PORTIA:
How far that little candle throws his beams!
So shines a good deed in a naughty world.
NERISSA:
When the moon shone, we did not see the candle.
PORTIA:
So doth the greater glory dim the less:
A substitute shines brightly as a king
Until a king be by, and then his state
Empties itself, as doth an inland brook
Into the main of waters. *Ib.* 90

22 The crow doth sing as sweetly as the lark
When neither is attended, and I think
The nightingale, if she should sing by day,
When every goose is cackling, would be thought
No better a musician than the wren.
How many things by season season'd are
To their right praise and true perfection!
Peace, ho! the moon sleeps with Endymion,
And would not be awak'd! *Ib.* 102

23 This night methinks is but the daylight sick. *Ib.* 124

24 For a light wife doth make a heavy husband. *Ib.* 130

25 These blessed candles of the night. *Ib.* 220

26 I will make a Star-Chamber matter of it.
The Merry Wives of Windsor, I. i. 1

27 She has brown hair, and speaks small like a woman.
Ib. [48]

28 Pribbles and prabbles. *Ib.* [56]

29 Drink down all unkindness. *Ib.* [203]

30 I had rather than forty shillings I had my Book of
Songs and Sonnets here. *Ib.* [205]

31 I will make an end of my dinner; there's pippins and
seese to come. *Ib.* ii. [12]

32 'Convey,' the wise it call. 'Steal!' foh! a fico for the
phrase! *Ib.* iii. [30]

33 Here will be an old abusing of God's patience, and
the king's English. *Ib.* iv. [5]

34 We burn daylight. *Ib.* II. i. [54]

35 There's the humour of it. *Ib.* [139]

36 Faith, thou hast some crotchets in thy head now.
Ib. [158]

37 Why, then the world's mine oyster,
Which I with sword will open. *Ib.* ii. 2

1 Marry, this is the short and the long of it.
The Merry Wives of Windsor, II. ii. [62]

2 Like a fair house built upon another man's ground.
Ib. [229]

3 Ah, sweet Anne Page!
Ib. III. i. [40]

4 I cannot tell what the dickens his name is.
Ib. ii. [20]

5 He capers, he dances, he has eyes of youth, he writes verses, he speaks holiday, he smells April and May.
Ib. [71]

6 O, what a world of vile ill-favour'd faults
Looks handsome in three hundred pounds a year!
Ib. iv. [32]

7 If it be my luck, so; if not, happy man be his dole!
Ib. [67]

8 If I be served such another trick, I'll have my brains ta'en out, and buttered, and give them to a dog for a new year's gift.
Ib. v. [7]

9 I have a kind of alacrity in sinking.
Ib. [13]

10 As good luck would have it.
Ib. [86]

11 A man of my kidney.
Ib. [119]

12 Vengeance of Jenny's case!
Ib. IV. i. [65]

13 So curses all Eve's daughters, of what complexion soever.
Ib. ii. [24]

14 This is the third time; I hope good luck lies in odd numbers. . . . There is divinity in odd numbers, either in nativity, chance or death.
Ib. v. i. 2

15 Fairies, black, grey, green, and white,
You moonshine revellers, and shades of night.
Ib. v. [43]

16 To live a barren sister all your life,
Chanting faint hymns to the cold fruitless moon.
A Midsummer Night's Dream, I. i. 72

17 But earthlier happy is the rose distill'd,
Than that which withering on the virgin thorn
Grows, lives, and dies, in single blessedness.
Ib. 76

18 Ay me! for aught that ever I could read,
Could ever hear by tale or history,
The course of true love nèver did run smooth.
Ib. 132

19 O hell! to choose love by another's eye.
Ib. 140

20 If there were a sympathy in choice,
War, death, or sickness did lay siege to it,
Making it momentany as a sound,
Swift as a shadow, short as any dream,
Brief as the lightning in the collied night,
That, in a spleen, unfolds both heaven and earth,
And ere a man hath power to say, 'Behold!'
The jaws of darkness do devour it up:
So quick bright things come to confusion.
Ib. 141

21 Your tongue's sweet air
More tuneable than lark to shepherd's ear,
When wheat is green, when hawthorn buds appear.
Ib. 183

22 Love looks not with the eyes, but with the mind,
And therefore is wing'd Cupid painted blind.
Ib. 234

23 The most lamentable comedy, and most cruel death of Pyramus and Thisby.
Ib. ii. [11]

24 Masters, spread yourselves.
Ib. [16]

25 A part to tear a cat in, to make all split.
A Midsummer Night's Dream, I. ii. [32]

26 This is Ercles' vein.
Ib. [43]

27 I'll speak in a monstrous little voice.
Ib. [55]

28 I am slow of study.
Ib. [70]

29 I will roar, that I will do any man's heart good to hear me.
Ib. [73]

30 I will aggravate my voice so that I will roar you as gently as any sucking dove; I will roar you as 'twere any nightingale.
Ib. [84]

31 A proper man, as one shall see in a summer's day.
Ib. [89]

32 Hold, or cut bow-strings.
Ib. [115]

33 Over hill, over dale,
Thorough bush, thorough brier,
Over park, over pale,
Thorough flood, thorough fire.
Ib. II. i. 2

34 The cowslips tall her pensioners be;
In their gold coats spots you see;
Those be rubies, fairy favours,
In those freckles live their savours.
Ib. 10

35 I must go seek some dew-drops here,
And hang a pearl in every cowslip's ear.
Ib. 14

36 The middle summer's spring.
Ib. 82

37 Therefore the moon, the governess of floods,
Pale in her anger, washes all the air,
That rheumatic diseases do abound:
And thorough this distemperature we see
The seasons alter: hoary-headed frosts
Fall in the fresh lap of the crimson rose.
Ib. 103

38 Since once I sat upon a promontory,
And heard a mermaid on a dolphin's back
Uttering such dulcet and harmonious breath,
That the rude sea grew civil at her song,
And certain stars shot madly from their spheres,
To hear the sea-maid's music.
Ib. 149

39 But I might see young Cupid's fiery shaft
Quench'd in the chaste beams of the wat'ry moon,
And the imperial votaress passed on,
In maiden meditation, fancy-free.
Yet mark'd I where the bolt of Cupid fell:
It fell upon a little western flower,
Before milk-white, now purple with love's wound,
And maidens call it, Love-in-idleness.
Ib. 161

40 I'll put a girdle round about the earth
In forty minutes.
Ib. 175

41 I know a bank whereon the wild thyme blows,
Where oxlips and the nodding violet grows
Quite over-canopied with luscious woodbine,
With sweet musk-roses, and with eglantine:
There sleeps Titania some time of the night,
Lull'd in these flowers with dances and delight;
And there the snake throws her enamell'd skin,
Weed wide enough to wrap a fairy in.
Ib. 249

42 Some to kill cankers in the musk-rose buds,
Some war with rere-mice for their leathern wings,
To make my small elves coats.
Ib. ii. 3

43 The clamorous owl, that nightly hoots, and wonders
At our quaint spirits.
Ib. 6

44 You spotted snakes with double tongue,
Thorny hedge-hogs, be not seen;
Newts, and blind-worms, do no wrong;
Come not near our fairy queen.
Ib. 9

SHAKESPEARE

1 Weaving spiders come not here;
Hence, you long-legg'd spinners, hence!
Beetles black, approach not near;
Worm nor snail, do no offence.
A Midsummer Night's Dream, II. ii. 20

2 This green plot shall be our stage, this hawthorn-brake our tiring-house. *Ib.* III. i. [3]

3 God shield us!—a lion among ladies, is a most dreadful thing; for there is not a more fearful wild-fowl than your lion living. *Ib.* [32]

4 What hempen home-spuns have we swaggering here, So near the cradle of the fairy queen? *Ib.* [82]

5 Bless thee, Bottom! bless thee! thou art translated. *Ib.* [124]

6 The throstle with his note so true,
The wren with little quill. *Ib.* [133]

7 As wild geese that the creeping fowler eye,
Or russet-pated choughs, many in sort,
Rising and cawing at the gun's report,
Sever themselves, and madly sweep the sky.
Ib. ii. 20

8 Lord, what fools these mortals be! *Ib.* 115

9 So we grew together,
Like to a double cherry, seeming parted,
But yet an union in partition;
Two lovely berries moulded on one stem. *Ib.* 208

10 For night's swift dragons cut the clouds full fast,
And yonder shines Aurora's harbinger;
At whose approach, ghosts, wandering here and there,
Troop home to churchyards. *Ib.* 379

11 Cupid is a knavish lad,
Thus to make poor females mad. *Ib.* 440

12 Jack shall have Jill;
Nought shall go ill;
The man shall have his mare again,
And all shall be well. *Ib.* 461

13 I must to the barber's, mounsieur, for methinks I am marvellous hairy about the face. *Ib.* IV. i. [25]

14 I have a reasonable good ear in music: let us have the tongs and the bones. *Ib.* [32]

15 Methinks I have a great desire to a bottle of hay: good hay, sweet hay, hath no fellow. *Ib.* [37]

16 But, I pray you, let none of your people stir me: I have an exposition of sleep come upon me. *Ib.* [43]

17 But as the fierce vexation of a dream. *Ib.* [75]

18 My Oberon! what visions have I seen!
Methought I was enamour'd of an ass. *Ib.* [82]

19 Then, my queen, in silence sad,
Trip we after the night's shade;
We the globe can compass soon,
Swifter than the wandering moon. *Ib.* [101]

20 HIPPOLYTA:
I was with Hercules and Cadmus once,
When in a wood of Crete they bay'd the bear
With hounds of Sparta: never did I hear . . .
So musical a discord, such sweet thunder.
THESEUS:
My hounds are bred out of the Spartan kind,
So flew'd, so sanded; and their heads are hung
With ears that sweep away the morning dew;
Crook-knee'd, and dew-lapp'd like Thessalian bulls;
Slow in pursuit, but match'd in mouth like bells.
Ib. [118]

21 Saint Valentine is past:
Begin these wood-birds but to couple now?
A Midsummer Night's Dream, IV. i. [145]

22 I have had a dream, past the wit of man to say what dream it was. *Ib.* [211]

23 The eye of man hath not heard, the ear of man hath not seen, man's hand is not able to taste, his tongue to conceive, nor his heart to report, what my dream was. *Ib.* [218]

24 The lunatic, the lover, and the poet,
Are of imagination all compact:
One sees more devils than vast hell can hold,
That is, the madman; the lover, all as frantic,
Sees Helen's beauty in a brow of Egypt:
The poet's eye, in a fine frenzy rolling,
Doth glance from heaven to earth, from earth to heaven;
And, as imagination bodies forth
The forms of things unknown, the poet's pen
Turns them to shapes, and gives to airy nothing
A local habitation and a name.
Such tricks hath strong imagination,
That, if it would but apprehend some joy,
It comprehends some bringer of that joy;
Or in the night, imagining some fear,
How easy is a bush suppos'd a bear! *Ib.* v. i. 7

25 What revels are in hand? Is there no play,
To ease the anguish of a torturing hour? *Ib.* 36

26 Very tragical mirth. *Ib.* [57]

27 For never anything can be amiss,
When simpleness and duty tender it. *Ib.* [82]

28 That is the true beginning of our end.
Consider then we come but in despite.
We do not come as minding to content you,
Our true intent is. All for your delight,
We are not here. *Ib.* [111]

29 Whereat, with blade, with bloody blameful blade,
He bravely broach'd his boiling bloody breast.
Ib. [148]

30 The best in this kind are but shadows, and the worst are no worse, if imagination amend them.
Ib. [215]

31 A very gentle beast, and of a good conscience.
Ib. [233]

32 Well roared, Lion. *Ib.* [272]

33 This passion, and the death of a dear friend, would go near to make a man look sad. *Ib.* [295]

34 The iron tongue of midnight hath told twelve;
Lovers, to bed; 'tis almost fairy time. *Ib.* [372]

35 Now the hungry lion roars,
And the wolf behowls the moon;
Whilst the heavy ploughman snores,
All with weary task fordone. *Ib.* ii. 1

36 Not a mouse
Shall disturb this hallow'd house:
I am sent with broom before,
To sweep the dust behind the door. *Ib.* 17

37 A victory is twice itself when the achiever brings home full numbers.
Much Ado About Nothing, I. i. [8]

38 He hath indeed better bettered expectation than you must expect of me to tell you how. *Ib.* [15]

39 He is a very valiant trencher-man. *Ib.* [52]

[467]

SHAKESPEARE

1 I see, lady, the gentleman is not in your books.
Much Ado About Nothing, I. i. [79]

2 BEATRICE:
I wonder that you will still be talking, Signior Benedick: nobody marks you.
BENEDICK:
What! my dear Lady Disdain, are you yet living?
Ib. [121]

3 Shall I never see a bachelor of three-score again?
Ib. [209]

4 BENEDICK:
I will live a bachelor.
DON PEDRO:
I shall see thee, ere I die, look pale with love.
BENEDICK:
With anger, with sickness, or with hunger, my lord; not with love. *Ib.* [256]

5 In time the savage bull doth bear the yoke. *Ib.* [271]

6 Benedick the married man. *Ib.* [278]

7 What need the bridge much broader than the flood?
Ib. [326]

8 Would it not grieve a woman to be over-mastered with a piece of valiant dust? to make an account of her life to a clod of wayward marl? *Ib.* II. i. [64]

9 Wooing, wedding, and repenting, is as a Scotch jig, a measure, and a cinque-pace. *Ib.* [77]

10 I have a good eye, uncle: I can see a church by daylight. *Ib.* [86]

11 Speak low, if you speak love. *Ib.* [104]

12 Friendship is constant in all other things
Save in the office and affairs of love. *Ib.* [184]

13 She speaks poniards, and every word stabs: if her breath were as terrible as her terminations, there were no living near her; she would infect to the north star. *Ib.* [257]

14 Silence is the perfectest herald of joy: I were but little happy, if I could say how much. *Ib.* [319]

15 Speak, cousin, or, if you cannot, stop his mouth with a kiss. *Ib.* [322]

16 There was a star danced, and under that was I born.
Ib. [351]

17 Lie ten nights awake, carving the fashion of a new doublet. *Ib.* iii. [18]

18 Note this before my notes;
There's not a note of mine that's worth the noting.
Ib. [57]

19 Is it not strange that sheep's guts should hale souls out of men's bodies? *Ib.* [62]

20 Sigh no more, ladies, sigh no more,
Men were deceivers ever;
One foot in sea, and one on shore,
To one thing constant never.
Then sigh not so,
But let them go,
And be you blithe and bonny,
Converting all your sounds of woe
Into Hey nonny, nonny.

Sing no more ditties, sing no mo
Of dumps so dull and heavy;
The fraud of men was ever so,
Since summer first was leavy.
Ib. [65]

21 Sits the wind in that corner? *Much Ado*, II. iii. [108]

22 Doth not the appetite alter? A man loves the meat in his youth that he cannot endure in his age.
Ib. [258]

23 Paper bullets of the brain. *Ib.* [261]

24 The world must be peopled. When I said I would die a bachelor, I did not think I should live till I were married. *Ib.* [262]

25 Disdain and scorn ride sparkling in her eyes.
Ib. III. i. 51

26 One doth not know
How much an ill word may empoison liking. *Ib.* 85

27 Contempt, farewell! and maiden pride, adieu!
No glory lives behind the back of such.
And, Benedick, love on; I will requite thee,
Taming my wild heart to thy loving hand. *Ib.* 109

28 He hath a heart as sound as a bell, and his tongue is the clapper; for what his heart thinks his tongue speaks. *Ib.* ii. [12]

29 BENEDICK:
I have the toothache.
        .   .   .   .
DON PEDRO:
What! sigh for the toothache? *Ib.* [21]

30 Well, every one can master a grief but he that has it.
Ib. [28]

31 A' brushes his hat a mornings; what should that bode? *Ib.* [41]

32 The barber's man hath been seen with him; and the old ornament of his cheek hath already stuffed tennis-balls. *Ib.* [45]

33 Are you good men and true? *Ib.* iii. 1

34 To be a well-favoured man is the gift of fortune; but to write and read comes by nature. *Ib.* [14]

35 Well, for your favour, sir, why, give God thanks, and make no boast of it; and for your writing and reading, let that appear when there is no need of such vanity. You are thought here to be the most senseless and fit man for the constable of the watch.
Ib. [19]

36 You shall comprehend all vagrom men. *Ib.* [25]

37 SECOND WATCH:
How, if a' will not stand?
DOGBERRY:
Why, then, take no note of him, but let him go; and presently call the rest of the watch together, and thank God you are rid of a knave. *Ib.* [28]

38 For the watch to babble and to talk is most tolerable and not to be endured. *Ib.* [36]

39 If they make you not then the better answer, you may say they are not the men you took them for.
Ib. [49]

40 The most peaceable way for you, if you do take a thief, is, to let him show himself what he is and steal out of your company. *Ib.* [61]

41 I know that Deformed. *Ib.* [132]

42 I thank God, I am as honest as any man living, that is an old man and no honester than I. *Ib.* v. [15]

43 Comparisons are odorous. *Ib.* [18]

1 If I were as tedious as a king, I could find in my heart to bestow it all of your worship.
Much Ado About Nothing, III. v. [23]

2 A good old man, sir; he will be talking: as they say, 'when the age is in, the wit is out.' *Ib.* [36]

3 Well, God's a good man. *Ib.* [39]

4 O! what men dare do! what men may do! what men daily do, not knowing what they do! *Ib.* IV. i. [19]

5 For it so falls out
That what we have we prize not to the worth
Whiles we enjoy it, but being lack'd and lost,
Why, then we rack the value, then we find
The virtue that possession would not show us
Whiles it was ours. *Ib.* [219]

6 The idea of her life shall sweetly creep
Into his study of imagination,
And every lovely organ of her life
Shall come apparell'd in more precious habit,
More moving-delicate, and full of life
Into the eye and prospect of his soul. *Ib.* [226]

7 Write down that they hope they serve God: and write God first; for God defend but God should go before such villains! Masters, it is proved already that you are little better than false knaves, and it will go near to be thought so shortly. *Ib.* ii. [21]

8 Yea, marry, that's the eftest way. *Ib.* [39]

9 Flat burglary as ever was committed. *Ib.* [54]

10 O that he were here to write me down an ass! but, masters, remember that I am an ass; though it be not written down, yet forget not that I am an ass. *Ib.* [80]

11 A fellow that hath had losses; and one that hath two gowns, and everything handsome about him. *Ib.* [90]

12 Patch grief with proverbs. *Ib.* v. i. 17

13 For there was never yet philosopher
That could endure the toothache patiently. *Ib.* 35

14 In a false quarrel there is no true valour. *Ib.* [121]

15 What though care killed a cat, thou hast mettle enough in thee to kill care. *Ib.* [135]

16 No, I was not born under a riming planet. *Ib.* ii. [40]

17 The trumpet of his own virtues. *Ib.* [91]

18 Done to death by slanderous tongues. *Ib.* iii. 3

19 The wolves have prey'd; and look, the gentle day,
Before the wheels of Phœbus, round about
Dapples the drowsy east with spots of grey. *Ib.* 25

20 Horribly stuff'd with epithets of war.
Othello, I. i. 14

21 A fellow almost damn'd in a fair wife. *Ib.* 21

22 The bookish theoric. *Ib.* 24

23 This counter-caster. *Ib.* 31

24 'Tis the curse of the service,
Preferment goes by letter and affection,
Not by the old gradation, where each second
Stood heir to the first. *Ib.* 35

25 I follow him to serve my turn upon him;
We cannot all be masters, nor all masters
Cannot be truly follow'd. *Ib.* 42

26 Wears out his time, much like his master's ass,
For nought but provender, and when he's old,
cashier'd;
Whip me such honest knaves. *Othello*, I. i. 47

27 In following him, I follow but myself. *Ib.* 58

28 But I will wear my heart upon my sleeve
For daws to peck at: I am not what I am. *Ib.* 64

29 An old black ram
Is tupping your white ewe. *Ib.* 88

30 'Zounds! sir, you are one of those that will not serve God if the devil bid you. *Ib.* 108

31 Your daughter and the Moor are now making the beast with two backs. *Ib.* [117]

32 The gross clasps of a lascivious Moor. *Ib.* [127]

33 An extravagant and wheeling stranger
Of here and every where. *Ib.* [137]

34 I do hate him as I do hell-pains. *Ib.* [155]

35 I must show out a flag and sign of love,
Which is indeed but sign. *Ib.* [157]

36 Though in the trade of war I have slain men,
Yet do I hold it very stuff o' the conscience
To do no contriv'd murder: I lack iniquity
Sometimes to do me service. *Ib.* ii. 1

37 I fetch my life and being
From men of royal siege. *Ib.* 21

38 I would not my unhoused free condition
Put into circumscription and confine
For the sea's worth. *Ib.* 26

39 My parts, my title, and my perfect soul
Shall manifest me rightly. *Ib.* 31

40 Keep up your bright swords, for the dew will rust them. *Ib.* 59

41 The wealthy curled darlings of our nation. *Ib.* 68

42 The sooty bosom
Of such a thing as thou. *Ib.* 70

43 My particular grief
Is of so flood-gate and o'erbearing nature
That it engluts and swallows other sorrows
And it is still itself. *Ib.* iii. 55

44 The bloody book of law
You shall yourself read in the bitter letter
After your own sense. *Ib.* 67

45 Most potent, grave, and reverend signiors,
My very noble and approv'd good masters,
That I have ta'en away this old man's daughter,
It is most true; true, I have married her:
The very head and front of my offending
Hath this extent, no more. Rude am I in my speech,
And little bless'd with the soft phrase of peace;
For since these arms of mine had seven years' pith,
Till now some nine moons wasted, they have us'd
Their dearest action in the tented field;
And little of this great world can I speak,
More than pertains to feats of broil and battle;
And therefore little shall I grace my cause
In speaking for myself. Yet, by your gracious patience,
I will a round unvarnish'd tale deliver
Of my whole course of love; what drugs, what charms,
What conjuration, and what mighty magic,
For such proceeding I am charg'd withal,
I won his daughter. *Ib.* 76

1   A maiden never bold;
Of spirit so still and quiet, that her motion
Blush'd at herself.   *Othello*, I. iii. 94

2 Her father lov'd me; oft invited me;
Still question'd me the story of my life
From year to year, the battles, sieges, fortunes
That I have pass'd.
I ran it through, even from my boyish days
To the very moment that he bade me tell it;
Wherein I spake of most disastrous chances,
Of moving accidents by flood and field,
Of hair-breadth 'scapes i' the imminent deadly breach,
Of being taken by the insolent foe
And sold to slavery, of my redemption thence
And portance in my travel's history;
Wherein of antres vast and desarts idle,
Rough quarries, rocks and hills whose heads touch
   heaven,
It was my hint to speak, such was the process;
And of the Cannibals that each other eat,
The Anthropophagi, and men whose heads
Do grow beneath their shoulders. This to hear
Would Desdemona seriously incline.   *Ib.* 128

3 And often did beguile her of her tears,
When I did speak of some distressful stroke
That my youth suffer'd. My story being done,
She gave me for my pains a world of sighs:
She swore, in faith, 'twas strange, 'twas passing
   strange,
'Twas pitiful, 'twas wondrous pitiful:
She wish'd she had not heard it, yet she wish'd
That heaven had made her such a man; she thank'd
   me,
And bade me, if I had a friend that lov'd her,
I should but teach him how to tell my story,
And that would woo her. Upon this hint I spake:
She lov'd me for the dangers I had pass'd,
And I lov'd her that she did pity them.
This only is the witchcraft I have us'd. *Ib.* 156

4 I do perceive here a divided duty. *Ib.* 181

5 To mourn a mischief that is past and gone
Is the next way to draw new mischief on. *Ib.* 204

6 The robb'd that smiles steals something from the
   thief.   *Ib.* 208

7 But words are words; I never yet did hear
That the bruis'd heart was pierced through the ear.
   Ib. 218

8 The tyrant custom, most grave senators,
Hath made the flinty and steel couch of war
My thrice-driven bed of down. *Ib.* [230]

9   My heart's subdu'd
Even to the very quality of my lord. *Ib.* [252]

10 I saw Othello's visage in his mind. *Ib.* [254]

11 A moth of peace. *Ib.* [258]

12 BRABANTIO:
She has deceiv'd her father, and may thee.
OTHELLO:
My life upon her faith! *Ib.* [295]

13 I will incontinently drown myself. *Ib.* [307]

14 It is silliness to live when to live is torment; and then
have we a prescription to die when death is our
physician. *Ib.* [310]

15 Virtue! a fig! 'tis in ourselves that we are thus, or thus.
Our bodies are our gardens, to the which our wills
are gardeners.   *Othello*, I. iii. [323]

16 Put money in thy purse. *Ib.* [345]

17 The food that to him now is as luscious as locusts,
shall be to him shortly as bitter as coloquintida.
   Ib. [354]

18 There are many events in the womb of time which
will be delivered. *Ib.* [377]

19 Thus do I ever make my fool my purse. *Ib.* [389]

20   He holds me well;
The better shall my purpose work on him. *Ib.* [396]

21 Framed to make women false. *Ib.* [404]

22 The Moor is of a free and open nature,
That thinks men honest that but seem to be so.
   Ib. [405]

23 I have 't; it is engender'd; hell and night
Must bring this monstrous birth to the world's light.
   Ib. [409]

24 Our great captain's captain. *Ib.* II. i. 74

25   You are pictures out of doors,
Bells in your parlours, wild cats in your kitchens,
Saints in your injuries, devils being offended,
Players in your housewifery, and housewives in your
   beds.   *Ib.* 109

26   Do not put me to 't,
For I am nothing if not critical. *Ib.* 118

27 I am not merry, but I do beguile
The thing I am by seeming otherwise. *Ib.* 122

28 IAGO:
She never yet was foolish that was fair,
For even her folly help'd her to an heir.
DESDEMONA:
These are old fond paradoxes to make fools laugh i'
the alehouse. *Ib.* 136

29 IAGO
She that was ever fair and never proud,
Had tongue at will and yet was never loud,
Never lack'd gold and yet went never gay,
Fled from her wish and yet said 'Now I may,'
She that being anger'd, her revenge being nigh,
Bade her wrong stay and her displeasure fly,
She that in wisdom never was so frail
To change the cod's head for the salmon's tail,
She that could think and ne'er disclose her mind,
See suitors following and not look behind,
She was a wight, if ever such wight were,—
DESDEMONA:
To do what?
IAGO:
To suckle fools and chronicle small beer.
DESDEMONA:
O most lame and impotent conclusion! *Ib.* 148

30 With as little a web as this will I ensnare as great a fly
as Cassio. *Ib.* [169]

31 OTHELLO:
      If it were now to die,
'Twere now to be most happy, for I fear
My soul hath her content so absolute
That not another comfort like to this
Succeeds in unknown fate.

DESDEMONA:

The heavens forbid
But that our loves and comforts should increase
Even as our days do grow! *Othello*, II. i. [192]

1 A slipper and subtle knave, a finder-out of occasions.
Ib. [247]

2 A pestilent complete knave! and the woman hath found him already. *Ib.* [253]

3 This poor trash of Venice. *Ib.* [315]

4 Make the Moor thank me, love me, and reward me For making him egregiously an ass. *Ib.* [320]

5 Let's teach ourselves that honourable stop, Not to outsport discretion. *Ib.* iii. 2

6 She is sport for Jove. *Ib.* [17]

7 I have very poor and unhappy brains for drinking: I could well wish courtesy would invent some other custom of entertainment. *Ib.* [34]

8 My boat sails freely, both with wind and stream. *Ib.* [66]

9 And let me the canakin clink:
A soldier's a man;
A life's but a span;
Why then let a soldier drink. *Ib.* [73]

10 England, where indeed they are most potent in potting. *Ib.* [79]

11 King Stephen was a worthy peer,
His breeches cost him but a crown;
He held them sixpence all too dear,
With that he call'd the tailor lown. *Ib.* [93]

12 'Tis pride that pulls the country down. *Ib.* [99]

13 Well, God's above all; and there be souls must be saved, and there be souls must not be saved. *Ib.* [106]

14 The lieutenant is to be saved before the ancient. *Ib.* [115]

15 He is a soldier fit to stand by Cæsar And give direction. *Ib.* [128]

16 Silence that dreadful bell! it frights the isle From her propriety. *Ib.* [177]

17 But men are men; the best sometimes forget. *Ib.* [243]

18 Thy honesty and love doth mince this matter. *Ib.* [249]

19 Cassio, I love thee;
But never more be officer of mine. *Ib.* [250]

20 Reputation, reputation, reputation! O! I have lost my reputation. I have lost the immortal part of myself, and what remains is bestial. My reputation, Iago, my reputation! *Ib.* [264]

21 O thou invisible spirit of wine! if thou hast no name to be known by, let us call thee devil! *Ib.* [285]

22 O God! that men should put an enemy in their mouths to steal away their brains; that we should, with joy, pleasance, revel, and applause, transform ourselves into beasts. *Ib.* [293]

23 CASSIO:
Every inordinate cup is unblessed, and the ingredient is a devil.
IAGO:
Come, come; good wine is a good familiar creature if it be well used; exclaim no more against it. *Ib.* [312]

24 How poor are they that have not patience!
What wound did ever heal but by degrees? *Othello*, II. iii. [379]

25 O! thereby hangs a tail. *Ib.* III. i. [8]

26 Talk him out of patience. *Ib.* iii. 23

27 Excellent wretch! Perdition catch my soul But I do love thee! and when I love thee not, Chaos is come again. *Ib.* 90

28 By heaven, he echoes me,
As if there were some monster in his thought Too hideous to be shown. *Ib.* 106

29 Men should be what they seem;
Or those that be not, would they might seem none! *Ib.* 126

30 Good name in man and woman, dear my lord,
Is the immediate jewel of their souls;
Who steals my purse steals trash; 'tis something, nothing;
'Twas mine, 'tis his, and has been slave to thousands;
But he that filches from me my good name
Robs me of that which not enriches him,
And makes me poor indeed. *Ib.* 155

31 O! beware, my lord, of jealousy;
It is the green-ey'd monster which doth mock The meat it feeds on. *Ib.* 165

32 But, O! what damned minutes tells he o'er Who dotes, yet doubts; suspects, yet soundly loves! *Ib.* 169

33 Poor and content is rich, and rich enough. *Ib.* 172

34 Think'st thou I'd make a life of jealousy,
To follow still the changes of the moon
With fresh suspicions? No; to be once in doubt Is once to be resolved. *Ib.* 177

35 In Venice they do let heaven see the pranks
They dare not show their husbands; their best conscience
Is not to leave 't undone, but keep 't unknown. *Ib.* 202

36 I humbly do beseech you of your pardon For too much loving you. *Ib.* 212

37 This fellow's of exceeding honesty. *Ib.* 258

38 If I do prove her haggard,
Though that her jesses were my dear heart-strings,
I'd whistle her off and let her down the wind,
To prey at fortune. *Ib.* 260

39 For I am declin'd
Into the vale of years. *Ib.* 265

40 O curse of marriage!
That we can call these delicate creatures ours,
And not their appetites. I had rather be a toad,
And live upon the vapour of a dungeon,
Than keep a corner in the thing I love
For others' uses. *Ib.* 268

41 If she be false, O! then heaven mocks itself.
I'll not believe it. *Ib.* 278

42 Trifles light as air
Are to the jealous confirmations strong
As proofs of holy writ. *Ib.* 323

43 Not poppy, nor mandragora,
Nor all the drowsy syrups of the world,
Shall ever medicine thee to that sweet sleep
Which thou ow'dst yesterday. *Ib.* 331

1 Avaunt! be gone! thou hast set me on the rack;
I swear 'tis better to be much abus'd
Than but to know 't a little.   *Othello*, III. iii. 336

2 He that is robb'd, not wanting what is stol'n,
Let him not know 't and he's not robb'd at all.
                                                                    Ib. 343

3 I had been happy, if the general camp,
Pioners and all, had tasted her sweet body,
So I had nothing known. O! now, for ever
Farewell the tranquil mind; farewell content!
Farewell the plumed troop and the big wars
That make ambition virtue! O, farewell!
Farewell the neighing steed and the shrill trump,
The spirit-stirring drum, the ear-piercing fife,
The royal banner, and all quality,
Pride, pomp, and circumstance of glorious war!
And, O you mortal engines, whose rude throats
The immortal Jove's dread clamours counterfeit,
Farewell! Othello's occupation's gone!   *Ib.* 346

4 Be sure of it; give me the ocular proof.   *Ib.* 361

5 Never pray more; abandon all remorse;
On horror's head horrors accumulate.   *Ib.* 370

6   O wretched fool!
That liv'st to make thine honesty a vice.
O monstrous world! Take note, take note, O world!
To be direct and honest is not safe.   *Ib.* 376

7   By the world,
I think my wife be honest and think she is not;
I think that thou art just and think thou art not.
                                                                    Ib. 384

8 There are a kind of men so loose of soul
That in their sleeps will mutter their affairs.   *Ib.* 417

9 But this denoted a foregone conclusion.   *Ib.* 429

10   Swell, bosom, with thy fraught,
For 'tis of aspics' tongues!   *Ib.* 450

11 O! blood, blood, blood!   *Ib.* 452

12   Like to the Pontick sea,
Whose icy current and compulsive course
Ne'er feels retiring ebb, but keeps due on
To the Propontic and the Hellespont,
Even so my bloody thoughts, with violent pace,
Shall ne'er look back, ne'er ebb to humble love,
Till that a capable and wide revenge
Swallow them up.   *Ib.* 454

13 For here's a young and sweating devil here,
That commonly rebels.   *Ib.* iv. 43

14   The hearts of old gave hands,
But our new heraldry is hands not hearts.   *Ib.* 47

15 That handkerchief
Did an Egyptian to my mother give.   *Ib.* 56

16 'Tis true; there's magic in the web of it;
A sibyl, that had number'd in the world
The sun to course two hundred compasses,
In her prophetic fury sew'd the work;
The worms were hallow'd that did breed the silk,
And it was dy'd in mummy which the skilful
Conserv'd of maidens' hearts.   *Ib.* 70

17 But jealous souls will not be answer'd so;
They are not ever jealous for the cause,
But jealous for they are jealous.   *Ib.* 158

18 What! keep a week away? seven days and nights?
Eight score eight hours? and lovers' absent hours,
More tedious than the dial eight score times?
O, weary reckoning!   *Othello*, III. iv. 172

19 I do attend here on the general,
And think it no addition nor my wish
To have him see me woman'd.   *Ib.* 192

20   O! it comes o'er my memory,
As doth the raven o'er the infected house,
Boding to all.   *Ib.* IV. i. 20

21   Many worthy and chaste dames even thus,
All guiltless, meet reproach.   *Ib.* 47

22 To beguile many and be beguil'd by one.   *Ib.* 98

23 They laugh that win.   *Ib.* [123]

24 I would have him nine years a-killing.   *Ib.* [186]

25 My heart is turned to stone; I strike it, and it hurts
my hand.   *Ib.* [190]

26 O! the world hath not a sweeter creature; she might
lie by an emperor's side and command him tasks.
                                                                    Ib. [192]

27 O, she will sing the savageness out of a bear.
                                                                    Ib. [198]

28 But yet the pity of it, Iago! O! Iago, the pity of it,
Iago!   *Ib.* [205]

29 The justice of it pleases.   *Ib.* [221]

30 O well-painted passion!   *Ib.* [268]

31 Goats and monkeys!   *Ib.* [274]

32   Whose solid virtue
The shot of accident nor dart of chance
Could neither graze nor pierce?   *Ib.* [277]

33 Your mystery, your mystery; nay, dispatch.
                                                                    Ib. ii. 29

34   Had it pleas'd heaven
To try me with affliction, had he rain'd
All kinds of sores, and shames, on my bare head,
Steep'd me in poverty to the very lips,
Given to captivity me and my utmost hopes,
I should have found in some part of my soul
A drop of patience; but, alas! to make me
The fixed figure for the time of scorn
To point his slow and moving finger at;
Yet could I bear that too; well, very well.
But there, where I have garner'd up my heart,
Where either I must live or bear no life,
The fountain from the which my current runs
Or else dries up; to be discarded thence!
Or keep it as a cistern for foul toads
To knot and gender in! Turn thy complexion there,
Patience, thou young and rose-lipp'd cherubin;
Ay, there, look grim as hell!   *Ib.* 46

35   O thou weed!
Who art so lovely fair and smell'st so sweet
That the sense aches at thee, would thou hadst ne'er
been born!   *Ib.* 66

36 Heaven stops the nose at it and the moon winks.
                                                                    Ib. 76

37 I took you for that cunning whore of Venice
That married with Othello. You, mistress,
That have the office opposite to Saint Peter,
And keep the gate of hell!   *Ib.* 88

1 I will be hang'd, if some eternal villain,
Some busy and insinuating rogue,
Some cogging cozening slave, to get some office,
Have not devis'd this slander.   *Othello*, IV. ii. 130

2 O heaven! that such companions thou'dst unfold,
And put in every honest hand a whip
To lash the rascals naked through the world,
Even from the east to the west!   *Ib.* 141

3   Unkindness may do much;
And his unkindness may defeat my life,
But never taint my love.   *Ib.* 159

4 Why, now I see there's mettle in thee, and even from
this instant do build on thee a better opinion than
ever before.   *Ib.* [207]

5 EMILIA:
I would you had never seen him.
DESDEMONA:
So would not I; my love doth so approve him.
    Ib. iii. 18

6 The poor soul sat sighing by a sycamore tree,
Sing all a green willow;
Her hand on her bosom, her head on her knee,
Sing willow, willow, willow:
The fresh streams ran by her, and murmur'd her
    moans;
Sing willow, willow, willow:
Her salt tears fell from her, and soften'd the stones;—
Sing willow, willow, willow:
Sing all a green willow must be my garland.   *Ib.* [41]

7 DESDEMONA:
    Mine eyes do itch;
Doth that bode weeping?
EMILIA:
'Tis neither here nor there.   *Ib.* [59]

8 Who would not make her husband a cuckold to make
him a monarch?   *Ib.* [76]

9 He hath a daily beauty in his life
That makes me ugly.   *Ib.* v. i. 19

10   This is the night
That either makes me or fordoes me quite.   *Ib.* 128

11 It is the cause, it is the cause, my soul;
Let me not name it to you, you chaste stars!
It is the cause. Yet I'll not shed her blood,
Nor scar that whiter skin of hers than snow,
And smooth as monumental alabaster.
Yet she must die, else she'll betray more men.
Put out the light, and then put out the light:
If I quench thee, thou flaming minister,
I can again thy former light restore,
Should I repent me; but once put out thy light,
Thou cunning'st pattern of excelling nature,
I know not where is that Promethean heat
That can thy light relume. When I have pluck'd the
    rose,
I cannot give it vital growth again,
It needs must wither: I'll smell it on the tree.
O balmy breath, that dost almost persuade
Justice to break her sword! One more, one more.
Be thus when thou art dead, and I will kill thee,
And love thee after. One more, and this the last:
So sweet was ne'er so fatal. I must weep,
But they are cruel tears; this sorrow's heavenly,
It strikes where it doth love.   *Ib.* ii. 1

12 If you bethink yourself of any crime
Unreconcil'd as yet to heaven and grace,
Solicit for it straight.   *Othello*, v. ii. 26

13 Alas! why gnaw you so your nether lip?
Some bloody passion shakes your very frame;
These are portents, but yet, I hope, I hope
They do not point on me.   *Ib.* 43

14 For to deny each article with oath
Cannot remove nor choke the strong conception
That I do groan withal.   *Ib.* 54

15 Had all his hairs been lives, my great revenge
Had stomach for them all.   *Ib.* 74

16 It is the very error of the moon;
She comes more near the earth than she was wont,
And makes men mad.   *Ib.* 107

17 Not Cassio kill'd! then murder's out of tune,
And sweet revenge grows harsh.   *Ib.* 113

18 A guiltless death I die.   *Ib.* 120

19 Nobody; I myself; farewell.   *Ib.* 122

20 OTHELLO:
She's like a liar gone to burning hell;
'Twas I that kill'd her.
EMILIA:
    O! the more angel she,
And you the blacker devil.   *Ib.* 127

21   Nay, had she been true,
If heaven would make me such another world
Of one entire and perfect chrysolite,
I'd not have sold her for it.   *Ib.* 141

22 She was too fond of her most filthy bargain.   *Ib.* 155

23 Thou hast not half the power to do me harm
As I have to be hurt.   *Ib.* 160

24 You told a lie, an odious damned lie;
Upon my soul, a lie, a wicked lie.   *Ib.* 178

25 Curse his better angel from his side,
And fall to reprobation.   *Ib.* 206

26 With that recognizance and pledge of love.   *Ib.* 212

27   Are there no stones in heaven
But what serve for the thunder?   *Ib.* 232

28 Every puny whipster gets my sword.   *Ib.* 242

29   I will play the swan,
And die in music.   *Ib.* 245

30 Who can control his fate?   *Ib.* 264

31 Here is my journey's end, here is my butt,
And very sea-mark of my utmost sail.   *Ib.* 266

32   O ill-starr'd wench!
Pale as thy smock! when we shall meet at compt,
This look of thine will hurl my soul from heaven,
And fiends will snatch at it. Cold, cold, my girl!
Even like thy chastity.
O! cursed, cursed slave. Whip me, ye devils,
From the possession of this heavenly sight!
Blow me about in winds! roast me in sulphur!
Wash me in steep-down gulfs of liquid fire!
O Desdemona! Desdemona! dead!   *Ib.* 271

33 I look down towards his feet; but that's a fable.
If that thou be'st a devil, I cannot kill thee.   *Ib.* 285

34 An honourable murderer, if you will;
For nought did I in hate, but all in honour.   *Ib.* 293

[473]

1 OTHELLO:
Will you, I pray, demand that demi-devil
Why he hath thus ensnar'd my soul and body?
IAGO:
Demand me nothing: what you know, you know:
From this time forth I never will speak word.
Othello, v. ii. 300

2 I have done the state some service, and they know 't;
No more of that. I pray you, in your letters,
When you shall these unlucky deeds relate,
Speak of me as I am; nothing extenuate,
Nor set down aught in malice: then, must you speak
Of one that lov'd not wisely but too well;
Of one not easily jealous, but, being wrought,
Perplex'd in the extreme; of one whose hand,
Like the base Indian, threw a pearl away
Richer than all his tribe; of one whose subdu'd eyes
Albeit unused to the melting mood,
Drop tears as fast as the Arabian trees
Their med'cinable gum. Set you down this;
And say besides, that in Aleppo once,
Where a malignant and a turban'd Turk
Beat a Venetian and traduc'd the state,
I took by the throat the circumcised dog,
And smote him thus. *Ib.* 338

3 All that 's spoke is marred. *Ib.* 356

4 I kiss'd thee ere I kill'd thee. *Ib.* 357

5 See, where she comes apparell'd like the spring.
Pericles, I. i. 12

6 Few love to hear the sins they love to act. *Ib.* 92

7 O you gods!
Why do you make us love your goodly gifts,
And snatch them straight away? *Ib.* III. i. 22

8 Old John of Gaunt, time-honour'd Lancaster.
King Richard II, I. i. 1

9 Let's purge this choler without letting blood. *Ib.* 153

10 The purest treasure mortal times afford
Is spotless reputation; that away,
Men are but gilded loam or painted clay.
A jewel in a ten-times-barr'd-up chest
Is a bold spirit in a loyal breast.
Mine honour is my life; both grow in one;
Take honour from me, and my life is done. *Ib.* 177

11 We were not born to sue, but to command. *Ib.* 196

12 Stay, stay, the king hath thrown his warder down.
Ib. iii. 118

13 This must my comfort be,
That sun that warms you here shall shine on me.
Ib. 144

14 The language I have learn'd these forty years,
My native English, now I must forego;
And now my tongue's use is to me no more
Than an unstringed viol or a harp. *Ib.* 159

15 I am too old to fawn upon a nurse,
Too far in years to be a pupil now. *Ib.* 170

16 How long a time lies in one little word!
Four lagging winters and four wanton springs
End in a word; such is the breath of kings. *Ib.* 213

17 Things sweet to taste prove in digestion sour. *Ib.* 236

18 Boast of nothing else
But that I was a journeyman to grief? *Ib.* 273

19 All places that the eye of heaven visits
Are to a wise man ports and happy havens.
Teach thy necessity to reason thus;
There is no virtue like necessity.
King Richard II, I. iii. 275

20 O! who can hold a fire in his hand
By thinking on the frosty Caucasus?
Or cloy the hungry edge of appetite,
By bare imagination of a feast?
Or wallow naked in December snow
By thinking on fantastic summer's heat?
O, no! the apprehension of the good
Gives but the greater feeling to the worse. *Ib.* 294

21 Methinks I am a prophet new inspir'd,
And thus expiring do foretell of him:
His rash fierce blaze of riot cannot last,
For violent fires soon burn out themselves;
Small showers last long, but sudden storms are short;
He tires betimes that spurs too fast betimes.
Ib. II. i. 31

22 This royal throne of kings, this scepter'd isle,
This earth of majesty, this seat of Mars,
This other Eden, demi-paradise,
This fortress built by Nature for herself
Against infection and the hand of war,
This happy breed of men, this little world,
This precious stone set in the silver sea,
Which serves it in the office of a wall,
Or as a moat defensive to a house,
Against the envy of less happier lands,
This blessed plot, this earth, this realm, this England,
This nurse, this teeming womb of royal kings,
Fear'd by their breed and famous by their birth,
Renowned for their deeds as far from home,—
For Christian service and true chivalry,—
As is the sepulchre in stubborn Jewry
Of the world's ransom, blessed Mary's Son:
This land of such dear souls, this dear, dear land.
Ib. 40

23 England, bound in with the triumphant sea. *Ib.* 61

24 That England, that was wont to conquer others,
Hath made a shameful conquest of itself. *Ib.* 65

25 Can sick men play so nicely with their names?
Ib. 84

26 Lay aside life-harming heaviness,
And entertain a cheerful disposition. *Ib.* ii. 3

27 Believe me, noble lord,
I am a stranger here in Gloucestershire:
These high wild hills and rough uneven ways
Draw out our miles and make them wearisome.
Ib. iii. 2

28 I count myself in nothing else so happy
As in a soul remembering my good friends. *Ib.* 46

29 Bloody with spurring, fiery-red with haste. *Ib.* 58

30 Grace me no grace, nor uncle me no uncle. *Ib.* 87

31 The caterpillars of the commonwealth. *Ib.* 166

32 Things past redress are now with me past care.
Ib. 171

33 Eating the bitter bread of banishment. *Ib.* III. i. 21

34 I weep for joy
To stand upon my kingdom once again.
Dear earth, I do salute thee with my hand,
Though rebels wound thee with their horses' hoofs.
Ib. ii. 4

1 Not all the water in the rough rude sea
Can wash the balm from an anointed king;
The breath of worldly men cannot depose
The deputy elected by the Lord.
For every man that Bolingbroke hath press'd
To lift shrewd steel against our golden crown,
God for his Richard hath in heavenly pay
A glorious angel; then, if angels fight,
Weak men must fall, for heaven still guards the
right. *King Richard II*, III. ii. 54

2 O! call back yesterday, bid time return. *Ib.* 69

3 Is not the king's name twenty thousand names?
Arm, arm, my name! A puny subject strikes
At thy great glory. *Ib.* 85

4 The worst is death, and death will have his day.
Ib. 103

5 Sweet love, I see, changing his property,
Turns to the sourest and most deadly hate. *Ib.* 135

6   Of comfort no man speak:
Let's talk of graves, of worms, and epitaphs;
Make dust our paper, and with rainy eyes
Write sorrow on the bosom of the earth.
Let's choose executors, and talk of wills. *Ib.* 144

7 For God's sake, let us sit upon the ground
And tell sad stories of the death of kings:
How some have been depos'd, some slain in war,
Some haunted by the ghosts they have depos'd,
Some poison'd by their wives, some sleeping kill'd;
All murder'd: for within the hollow crown
That rounds the mortal temples of a king
Keeps Death his court, and there the antick sits,
Scoffing his state and grinning at his pomp;
Allowing him a breath, a little scene,
To monarchize, be fear'd, and kill with looks,
Infusing him with self and vain conceit
As if this flesh which walls about our life
Were brass impregnable; and humour'd thus
Comes at the last, and with a little pin
Bores through his castle wall, and farewell king!
Ib. 155

8 See, see, King Richard doth himself appear,
As doth the blushing discontented sun
From out the fiery portal of the east. *Ib.* iii. 62

9   O! that I were as great
As is my grief, or lesser than my name,
Or that I could forget what I have been,
Or not remember what I must be now. *Ib.* 136

10 What must the king do now? Must he submit?
The king shall do it: must he be depos'd?
The king shall be contented: must he lose
The name of king? o' God's name, let it go.
I'll give my jewels for a set of beads,
My gorgeous palace for a hermitage,
My gay apparel for an almsman's gown,
My figur'd goblets for a dish of wood,
My sceptre for a palmer's walking staff,
My subjects for a pair of carved saints,
And my large kingdom for a little grave,
A little little grave, an obscure grave;
Or I'll be buried in the king's highway,
Some way of common trade, where subjects' feet
May hourly trample on their sovereign's head;
For on my heart they tread now whilst I live;
And buried once, why not upon my head? *Ib.* 143

11 You make a leg. *Ib.* 175

12 Go, bind thou up yon dangling apricocks,
Which, like unruly children, make their sire
Stoop with oppression of their prodigal weight.
King Richard II, III. iv. 29

13 Old Adam's likeness, set to dress this garden. *Ib.* 73

14 Here did she fall a tear; here, in this place,
I'll set a bank of rue, sour herb of grace;
Rue, even for ruth, here shortly shall be seen,
In the remembrance of a weeping queen. *Ib.* 104

15 If I dare eat, or drink, or breathe, or live,
I dare meet Surrey in a wilderness,
And spit upon him, whilst I say he lies,
And lies, and lies. *Ib.* IV. i. 73

16   And there at Venice gave
His body to that pleasant country's earth,
And his pure soul unto his captain Christ,
Under whose colours he had fought so long. *Ib.* 97

17 Peace shall go sleep with Turks and infidels.
Ib. 139

18 God save the king! Will no man say, amen?
Am I both priest and clerk? Well then, amen.
Ib. 172

19 Give me the crown. Here, cousin, seize the crown;
Here cousin,
On this side my hand and on that side thine.
Now is this golden crown like a deep well
That owes two buckets filling one another;
The emptier ever dancing in the air,
The other down, unseen, and full of water:
That bucket down and full of tears am I,
Drinking my griefs, whilst you mount up on high.
Ib. 181

20 You may my glories and my state depose,
But not my griefs; still am I king of those. *Ib.* 192

21 Now mark me how I will undo myself. *Ib.* 203

22 With mine own tears I wash away my balm,
With mine own hands I give away my crown.
Ib. 207

23 God pardon all oaths that are broke to me!
God keep all vows unbroke are made to thee! *Ib.* 214

24 A mockery king of snow. *Ib.* 260

25 An if my word be sterling yet in England. *Ib.* 264

26 Julius Cæsar's ill-erected tower. *Ib.* v. i. 2

27   I am sworn brother, sweet,
To grim Necessity, and he and I
Will keep a league till death. *Ib.* 20

28 That were some love but little policy. *Ib.* 84

29 As in a theatre, the eyes of men,
After a well-grac'd actor leaves the stage,
Are idly bent on him that enters next,
Thinking his prattle to be tedious. *Ib.* ii. 23

30   Who are the violets now
That strew the green lap of the new come spring?
Ib. 46

31 Give me my boots I say. *Ib.* 77 and 87

32 He prays but faintly and would be denied. *Ib.* iii. 103

33 I have been studying how I may compare
This prison where I live unto the world. *Ib.* v. 1

34   How sour sweet music is,
When time is broke, and no proportion kept!
So is it in the music of men's lives. *Ib.* 42

1 Mount, mount, my soul! thy seat is up on high,
Whilst my gross flesh sinks downwards, here to die.
King Richard II, v. v. 112

2 Now is the winter of our discontent
Made glorious summer by this sun of York.
King Richard III, I. i. 1

3 Our stern alarums changed to merry meetings;
Our dreadful marches to delightful measures. *Ib.* 7

4 He capers nimbly in a lady's chamber
To the lascivious pleasing of a lute. *Ib.* 12

5 This weak piping time of peace. *Ib.* 24

6 And therefore, since I cannot prove a lover, ...
I am determined to prove a villain. *Ib.* 28

7 No beast so fierce but knows some touch of pity.
Ib. ii. 71

8 Was ever woman in this humour woo'd?
Was ever woman in this humour won? *Ib.* 229

9 Fram'd in the prodigality of Nature. *Ib.* 245

10 By silken, sly, insinuating Jacks. *Ib.* iii. 53

11 Since every Jack became a gentleman
There's many a gentle person made a Jack. *Ib.* 72

12 And thus I clothe my naked villany
With odd old ends stol'n forth of holy writ,
And seem a saint when most I play the devil.
Ib. 336

13 O, I have pass'd a miserable night,
So full of ugly sights, of ghastly dreams,
That, as I am a Christian faithful man,
I would not spend another such a night,
Though 'twere to buy a world of happy days,
So full of dismal terror was the time! *Ib.* iv. 2

14 Lord, Lord! methought what pain it was to drown:
What dreadful noise of water in mine ears!
What sights of ugly death within mine eyes!
Methought I saw a thousand fearful wracks;
A thousand men that fishes gnaw'd upon;
Wedges of gold, great anchors, heaps of pearl,
Inestimable stones, unvalu'd jewels,
All scatter'd in the bottom of the sea.
Some lay in dead men's skulls; and in those holes
Where eyes did once inhabit, there were crept
As 'twere in scorn of eyes, reflecting gems,
That woo'd the slimy bottom of the deep,
And mock'd the dead bones that lay scatter'd by.
Ib. 21

15 The empty, vast, and wandering air. *Ib.* 39

16 Clarence is come,—false, fleeting, perjur'd Clarence.
Ib. 55

17 As snow in harvest. *Ib.* [252]

18 Woe to the land that's govern'd by a child!
Ib. II. iii. 11

19 So wise so young, they say, do never live long.
Ib. III. i. 79

20 I moralize two meanings in one word. *Ib.* 83

21 My Lord of Ely, when I was last in Holborn,
I saw good strawberries in your garden there.
Ib. iv. 31

22 Talk'st thou to me of 'ifs'? Thou art a traitor:
Off with his head! *Ib.* 74

23 High-reaching Buckingham grows circumspect.
Ib. IV. ii. 31

24 I am not in the giving vein to-day.
King Richard III, IV. ii. 115

25 The sons of Edward sleep in Abraham's bosom.
Ib. iii. 38

26 Let not the heavens hear these tell-tale women
Rail on the Lord's anointed. *Ib.* iv. 150

27 A grievous burthen was thy birth to me;
Tetchy and wayward was thy infancy. *Ib.* 168

28 An honest tale speeds best being plainly told.
Ib. 359

29 Harp not on that string. *Ib.* 365

30 Relenting fool, and shallow, changing woman!
Ib. 432

31 Is the chair empty? is the sword unsway'd?
Is the king dead? the empire unpossess'd? *Ib.* 470

32 Thus far into the bowels of the land
Have we march'd on without impediment.
Ib. v. ii. 3

33 True hope is swift, and flies with swallow's wings;
Kings it makes gods, and meaner creatures kings.
Ib. 23

34 The king's name is a tower of strength. *Ib.* iii. 12

35 Give me another horse! bind up my wounds!
Have mercy, Jesu! Soft! I did but dream.
O coward conscience, how dost thou afflict me!
Ib. 178

36 My conscience hath a thousand several tongues,
And every tongue brings in a several tale,
And every tale condemns me for a villain. *Ib.* 194

37 I shall despair. There is no creature loves me;
And if I die, no soul will pity me:
Nay, wherefore should they, since that I myself
Find in myself no pity to myself? *Ib.* 201

38 By the apostle Paul, shadows to-night
Have struck more terror to the soul of Richard
Than can the substance of ten thousand soldiers.
Ib. 217

39 Jockey of Norfolk, be not too bold,
For Dickon thy master is bought and sold. *Ib.* 305

40 A thing devised by the enemy. *Ib.* 307

41 Conscience is but a word that cowards use,
Devis'd at first to keep the strong in awe. *Ib.* 310

42 A horse! a horse! my kingdom for a horse! *Ib.* iv. 7

43 Slave! I have set my life upon a cast,
And I will stand the hazard of the die.
I think there be six Richmonds in the field. *Ib.* 9

44 A pair of star-cross'd lovers.
Romeo and Juliet, Prologue, 6

45 The two hours' traffic of our stage. *Ib.* 12

46 ABRAHAM:
Do you bite your thumb at us, sir?
SAMPSON:
Is the law of our side if I say ay?
GREGORY:
No.
SAMPSON:
No, sir, I do not bite my thumb at you, sir; but I bite
my thumb, sir. *Ib.* I. i. [52]

47 Gregory, remember thy swashing blow. *Ib.* [68]

48 Saint-seducing gold. *Ib.* [220]

1 And 'tis not hard, I think,
For men so old as we to keep the peace.
Romeo and Juliet, I. ii. 2

2 PARIS:
Younger than she are happy mothers made.
CAPULET:
And too soon marr'd are those so early made. *Ib.* 12

3 And then my husband—God be with his soul!
A' was a merry man—took up the child:
'Yea,' quoth he, 'dost thou fall upon thy face?
Thou wilt fall backward when thou hast more wit;
Wilt thou not, Jule?' and, by my halidom,
The pretty wretch left crying, and said 'Ay.'
Ib. iii. 39

4 Pretty fool, it stinted and said 'Ay'. *Ib.* 48

5 I am proverb'd with a grandsire phrase;
I'll be a candle-holder, and look on. *Ib.* iv. 37

6 Come, we burn daylight, ho! *Ib.* 43

7 O! then, I see, Queen Mab hath been with you. . . .
She is the fairies' midwife, and she comes
In shape no bigger than an agate-stone
On the forefinger of an alderman,
Drawn with a team of little atomies
Athwart men's noses as they lie asleep:
Her waggon-spokes made of long spinners' legs;
The cover, of the wings of grasshoppers;
The traces, of the smallest spider's web;
The collars, of the moonshine's watery beams;
Her whip, of cricket's bone; the lash, of film;
Her waggoner, a small grey-coated gnat,
Not half so big as a round little worm
Prick'd from the lazy finger of a maid;
Her chariot is an empty hazel-nut,
Made by the joiner squirrel or old grub,
Time out o' mind the fairies' coach-makers.
And in this state she gallops night by night
Through lovers' brains, and then they dream of love;
O'er courtiers' knees, that dream on curtsies straight;
O'er lawyers' fingers, who straight dream on fees;
O'er ladies' lips, who straight on kisses dream;
Which oft the angry Mab with blisters plagues,
Because their breaths with sweetmeats tainted are.
Sometimes she gallops o'er a courtier's nose,
And then dreams he of smelling out a suit;
And sometimes comes she with a tithe-pig's tail,
Tickling a parson's nose as a' lies asleep,
Then dreams he of another benefice;
Sometimes she driveth o'er a soldier's neck,
And then dreams he of cutting foreign throats,
Of breaches, ambuscadoes, Spanish blades,
Of healths five fathom deep; and then anon
Drums in his ear, at which he starts and wakes;
And, being thus frighted, swears a prayer or two,
And sleeps again. This is that very Mab
That plats the manes of horses in the night;
And bakes the elf-locks in foul sluttish hairs,
Which once untangled much misfortune bodes;
This is the hag, when maids lie on their backs,
That presses them and learns them first to bear,
Making them women of good carriage. *Ib.* 53

8 For you and I are past our dancing days. *Ib.* v. [35]

9 O! she doth teach the torches to burn bright.
It seems she hangs upon the cheek of night
Like a rich jewel in an Ethiop's ear;
Beauty too rich for use, for earth too dear. *Ib.* [48]

10 We have a trifling foolish banquet towards. *Ib.* [126]

11 My only love sprung from my only hate!
Romeo and Juliet, I. v. [142]

12 Young Adam Cupid, he that shot so trim
When King Cophetua lov'd the beggar-maid.
Ib. II. i. 13

13 He jests at scars, that never felt a wound.
But, soft! what light through yonder window breaks?
It is the east, and Juliet is the sun. *Ib.* ii. 1

14 See! how she leans her cheek upon her hand:
O! that I were a glove upon that hand,
That I might touch that cheek. *Ib.* 23

15 O Romeo, Romeo! wherefore art thou Romeo?
Ib. 33

16 What's in a name? that which we call a rose
By any other name would smell as sweet. *Ib.* 43

17 For stony limits cannot hold love out. *Ib.* 67

18 Thou know'st the mask of night is on my face,
Else would a maiden blush bepaint my cheek.
Ib. 85

19 Fain would I dwell on form, fain, fain deny
What I have spoke: but farewell compliment! *Ib.* 88

20 At lovers' perjuries,
They say, Jove laughs. O gentle Romeo!
If thou dost love, pronounce it faithfully:
Or if thou think'st I am too quickly won,
I'll frown and be perverse and say thee nay,
So thou wilt woo; but else, not for the world.
In truth, fair Montague, I am too fond. *Ib.* 92

21 I'll prove more true
Than those that have more cunning to be strange.
Ib. 100

22 ROMEO:
Lady, by yonder blessed moon I swear
That tips with silver all these fruit-tree tops,—
JULIET:
O! swear not by the moon, the inconstant moon,
That monthly changes in her circled orb,
Lest that thy love prove likewise variable. *Ib.* 107

23 Do not swear at all;
Or, if thou wilt, swear by thy gracious self,
Which is the god of my idolatry. *Ib.* 112

24 It is too rash, too unadvis'd, too sudden;
Too like the lightning, which doth cease to be
Ere one can say it lightens. Sweet, good-night!
This bud of love, by summer's ripening breath,
May prove a beauteous flower when next we meet.
Ib. 118

25 Love goes toward love, as schoolboys from their
books;
But love from love, toward school with heavy looks.
Ib. 156

26 O! for a falconer's voice,
To lure this tassel-gentle back again.
Bondage is hoarse, and may not speak aloud,
Else would I tear the cave where Echo lies. *Ib.* 158

27 It is my soul that calls upon my name:
How silver-sweet sound lovers' tongues by night,
Like softest music to attending ears! *Ib.* 164

28 'Tis almost morning; I would have thee gone;
And yet no further than a wanton's bird,
Who lets it hop a little from her hand,
Like a poor prisoner in his twisted gyves,
And with a silk thread plucks it back again,
So loving-jealous of his liberty. *Ib.* 176

1 JULIET:
Yet I should kill thee with much cherishing.
Good-night, good-night! parting is such sweet sorrow
That I shall say good-night till it be morrow.
ROMEO:
Sleep dwell upon thine eyes, peace in thy breast!
Would I were sleep and peace, so sweet to rest!
Romeo and Juliet, II. ii. 183

2 Wisely and slow; they stumble that run fast.
Ib. iii. 94

3 One, two, and the third in your bosom. *Ib.* iv. [24]

4 O flesh, flesh, how art thou fishified! *Ib.* [41]

5 I am the very pink of courtesy. *Ib.* [63]

6 A gentleman, nurse, that loves to hear himself talk,
and will speak more in a minute than he will stand
to in a month. *Ib.* [156]

7 Two may keep counsel, putting one away. *Ib.* [211]

8 These violent delights have violent ends,
And in their triumph die. *Ib.* vi. 9

9 Therefore love moderately; long love doth so;
Too swift arrives as tardy as too slow. *Ib.* 14

10 O! so light a foot
Will ne'er wear out the everlasting flint. *Ib.* 16

11 Thy head is as full of quarrels as an egg is full of
meat. *Ib.* III. i. [23]

12 A word and a blow. *Ib.* [43]

13 Men's eyes were made to look, and let them gaze;
I will not budge for no man's pleasure, I. *Ib.* [59]

14 No, 'tis not so deep as a well, nor so wide as a church
door; but 'tis enough, 'twill serve: ask for me to-
morrow, and you shall find me a grave man. I am
peppered, I warrant, for this world. *Ib.* [100]

15 A plague o' both your houses!
They have made worms' meat of me. *Ib.* [112]

16 O! I am Fortune's fool. *Ib.* [142]

17 Gallop apace, you fiery-footed steeds,
Towards Phœbus' lodging. *Ib.* ii. 1

18 Come, civil night,
Thou sober-suited matron, all in black. *Ib.* 10

19 For thou wilt lie upon the wings of night,
Whiter than new snow on a raven's back. *Ib.* 18

20 Give me my Romeo: and, when he shall die,
Take him and cut him out in little stars,
And he will make the face of heaven so fine
That all the world will be in love with night,
And pay no worship to the garish sun. *Ib.* 21

21 He was not born to shame:
Upon his brow shame is ashamed to sit. *Ib.* 91

22 Romeo, come forth; come forth, thou fearful man:
Affliction is enamour'd of thy parts,
And thou art wedded to calamity. *Ib.* iii. 1

23 Thou cutt'st my head off with a golden axe. *Ib.* 22

24 Adversity's sweet milk, philosophy. *Ib.* 54

25 Hang up philosophy!
Unless philosophy can make a Juliet. *Ib.* 56

26 Wilt thou be gone? it is not yet near day:
It was the nightingale, and not the lark,
That pierc'd the fearful hollow of thine ear;
Nightly she sings on yon pomegranate tree:
Believe me, love, it was the nightingale. *Ib.* v. 1

27 Night's candles are burnt out, and jocund day
Stands tiptoe on the misty mountain tops.
Romeo and Juliet, III. v. 9

28 Villain and he be many miles asunder. *Ib.* 82

29 Thank me no thankings, nor proud me no prouds.
Ib. 153

30 Is there no pity sitting in the clouds,
That sees into the bottom of my grief? *Ib.* 198

31 Romeo's a dishclout to him. *Ib.* 221

32 'Tis an ill cook that cannot lick his own fingers.
Ib. IV. ii. [6]

33 All things that we ordained festival,
Turn from their office to black funeral;
Our instruments to melancholy bells,
Our wedding cheer to a sad burial feast,
Our solemn hymns to sullen dirges change,
Our bridal flowers serve for a buried corse,
And all things change them to the contrary. *Ib.* v. 84

34 My bosom's lord sits lightly in his throne. *Ib.* v. i. 3

35 I do remember an apothecary,
And hereabouts he dwells. *Ib.* 37

36 Being holiday, the beggar's shop is shut. *Ib.* 56

37 The world is not thy friend, nor the world's law.
Ib. 72

38 APOTHECARY:
My poverty, but not my will, consents.
ROMEO:
I pay thy poverty, and not thy will. *Ib.* 75

39 The time and my intents are savage-wild,
More fierce and more inexorable far
Than empty tigers or the roaring sea. *Ib.* iii. 37

40 Tempt not a desperate man. *Ib.* 59

41 One writ with me in sour misfortune's book. *Ib.* 82

42 How oft when men are at the point of death
Have they been merry! which their keepers call
A lightning before death. *Ib.* 88

43 Beauty's ensign yet
Is crimson in thy lips and in thy cheeks,
And death's pale flag is not advanced there. *Ib.* 94

44 Shall I believe
That unsubstantial Death is amorous,
And that the lean abhorred monster keeps
Thee here in dark to be his paramour?
For fear of that I still will stay with thee,
And never from this palace of dim night
Depart again: here, here will I remain
With worms that are thy chambermaids; O! here
Will I set up my everlasting rest,
And shake the yoke of inauspicious stars
From this world-wearied flesh. Eyes, look your last!
Arms, take your last embrace! and, lips, O you
The doors of breath, seal with a righteous kiss
A dateless bargain to engrossing death! *Ib.* 102

45 Look in the chronicles; we came in with Richard
Conqueror. *The Taming of the Shrew*, Induction i. [4]

46 As Stephen Sly, and old John Naps of Greece,
And Peter Turf, and Henry Pimpernell,
And twenty more such names and men as these,
Which never were nor no man ever saw. *Ib.* ii. [95]

47 No profit grows where is no pleasure ta'en;
In brief, sir, study what you most affect. *Ib.* I. i. 39

48 There's small choice in rotten apples. *Ib.* [137]

1 Nothing comes amiss, so money comes withal.
The Taming of the Shrew, I. ii. [82]

2 O! this learning, what a thing it is. *Ib.* [163]

3 She is your treasure, she must have a husband;
I must dance bare-foot on her wedding day,
And, for your love to her, lead apes in hell.
Ib. II. i. 32

4 Say that she rail; why then I'll tell her plain
She sings as sweetly as a nightingale:
Say that she frown; I'll say she looks as clear
As morning roses newly wash'd with dew:
Say she be mute and will not speak a word;
Then I'll commend her volubility,
And say she uttereth piercing eloquence. *Ib.* 171

5 And thereby hangs a tale. *Ib.* IV. i. [59]

6 He kills her in her own humour. *Ib.* [183]

7 She shall watch all night:
And if she chance to nod I'll rail and brawl,
And with the clamour keep her still awake.
This is the way to kill a wife with kindness. *Ib.* [208]

8 What say you to a piece of beef and mustard?
Ib. iii. [23]

9 And as the sun breaks through the darkest clouds,
So honour peereth in the meanest habit. *Ib.* [175]

10 PETRUCHIO:
It shall be what o'clock I say it is.
HORTENSIO:
Why, so this gallant will command the sun. *Ib.* [197]

11 O vile,
Intolerable, not to be endur'd! *Ib.* v. ii. 93

12 A woman mov'd is like a fountain troubled,
Muddy, ill-seeming, thick, bereft of beauty. *Ib.* 143

13 Such duty as the subject owes the prince,
Even such a woman oweth to her husband. *Ib.* 156

14 I am asham'd that women are so simple
To offer war where they should kneel for peace.
Ib. 162

15 What cares these roarers for the name of king?
The Tempest, I. i. [18]

16 He hath no drowning mark upon him; his complexion is perfect gallows. *Ib.* [33]

17 Now would I give a thousand furlongs of sea for an
acre of barren ground. *Ib.* [70]

18 The wills above be done! but I would fain die a dry
death. *Ib.* [72]

19 O! I have suffer'd
With those that I saw suffer: a brave vessel,
Who had, no doubt, some noble creatures in her,
Dash'd all to pieces. O! the cry did knock
Against my very heart. Poor souls, they perish'd.
Ib. ii. 5

20 What seest thou else
In the dark backward and abysm of time? *Ib.* 49

21 Your tale, sir, would cure deafness. *Ib.* 106

22 My library
Was dukedom large enough. *Ib.* 109

23 Knowing I lov'd my books, he furnish'd me,
From mine own library with volumes that
I prize above my dukedom. *Ib.* 166

24 From the still-vexed Bermoothes. *Ib.* 229

25 I will be correspondent to command
And do my spiriting gently. *The Tempest*, I. ii. 297

26 You taught me language; and my profit on't
Is, I know how to curse: the red plague rid you,
For learning me your language! *Ib.* 363

27 Fill all thy bones with aches. *Ib.* 370

28 Come unto these yellow sands,
And then take hands:
Curtsied when you have, and kiss'd,—
The wild waves whist,—
Foot it featly here and there;
And, sweet sprites, the burden bear.
Hark, hark!
Bow, wow,
The watch-dogs bark:
Bow, wow,
Hark, hark! I hear
The strain of strutting Chanticleer
Cock-a-diddle-dow. *Ib.* 375

29 This music crept by me upon the waters,
Allaying both their fury, and my passion,
With its sweet air. *Ib.* 389

30 Full fathom five thy father lies;
Of his bones are coral made:
Those are pearls that were his eyes:
Nothing of him that doth fade,
But doth suffer a sea-change
Into something rich and strange.
Sea-nymphs hourly ring his knell:
Ding-dong.
Hark! now I hear them,—ding-dong, bell. *Ib.* 394

31 The fringed curtains of thine eye advance,
And say what thou seest yond. *Ib.* 405

32 At the first sight
They have changed eyes. *Ib.* 437

33 There's nothing ill can dwell in such a temple:
If the ill spirit have so fair a house,
Good things will strive to dwell with 't. *Ib.* 454

34 Look, he's winding up the watch of his wit, by and by
it will strike. *Ib.* II. i. [12]

35 What's past is prologue. *Ib.* [261]

36 They'll take suggestion as a cat laps milk. *Ib.* [296]

37 Open-ey'd conspiracy
His time doth take. *Ib.* [309]

38 A very ancient and fish-like smell. *Ib.* ii. [27]

39 When they will not give a doit to relieve a lame
beggar, they will lay out ten to see a dead Indian.
Ib. [33]

40 Misery acquaints a man with strange bedfellows.
Ib. [42]

41 Well, here's my comfort. [*Drinks.*] *Ib.* [48]

42 For she had a tongue with a tang. *Ib.* [53]

43 'Ban, 'Ban, Ca-Caliban,
Has a new master—Get a new man. *Ib.* [197]

44 For several virtues
Have I lik'd several women; never any
With so full soul but some defect in her
Did quarrel with the noblest grace she ow'd,
And put it to the foil. *Ib.* III. i. 42

[479]

1 FERDINAND:
Here's my hand.
MIRANDA:
And mine, with my heart in 't. *The Tempest*, III. i. 89

2 Thou deboshed fish thou. *Ib.* ii. [30]

3 Flout 'em, and scout 'em; and scout 'em, and flout
'em;
Thought is free. *Ib.* [133]

4 He that dies pays all debts. *Ib.* [143]

5   The isle is full of noises,
Sounds and sweet airs, that give delight, and hurt
not. *Ib.* [147]

6 Spongy April. *Ib.* IV. i. 65

7 You sun-burn'd sicklemen, of August weary.
Ib. 134

8 Our revels now are ended. These our actors,
As I foretold you, were all spirits and
Are melted into air, into thin air:
And, like the baseless fabric of this vision,
The cloud-capp'd towers, the gorgeous palaces,
The solemn temples, the great globe itself,
Yea, all which it inherit, shall dissolve
And, like this insubstantial pageant faded,
Leave not a rack behind. We are such stuff
As dreams are made on, and our little life
Is rounded with a sleep. *Ib.* 148

9 I do begin to have bloody thoughts. *Ib.* [221]

10 With foreheads villanous low. *Ib.* [252]

11 Now does my project gather to a head. *Ib.* v. i. 1

12   Demi-puppets, that
By moonshine do the green sour ringlets make
Whereof the ewe not bites. *Ib.* 36

13 Deeper than did ever plummet sound,
I'll drown my book. *Ib.* 56

14 Where the bee sucks, there suck I
In a cowslip's bell I lie;
There I couch when owls do cry.
On the bat's back I do fly
After summer merrily:
Merrily, merrily shall I live now
Under the blossom that hangs on the bough. *Ib.* 88

15   O brave new world,
That has such people in 't. *Ib.* 183

16   Retire me to my Milan, where
Every third thought shall be my grave. *Ib.* [310]

17 'Tis not enough to help the feeble up,
But to support him after. *Timon of Athens*, I. i. 108

18 He that loves to be flattered is worthy o' the flatterer.
Ib. [233]

19   The strain of man's bred out
Into baboon and monkey. *Ib.* [260]

20 I wonder men dare trust themselves with men.
Ib. ii. [45]

21 Immortal gods, I crave no pelf;
I pray for no man but myself. *Ib.* [64]

22 Like madness is the glory of this life. *Ib.* [141]

23 Men shut their doors against a setting sun *Ib.* [152]

24 Nothing emboldens sin so much as mercy.
Ib. III. v. 3

25 Uncover, dogs, and lap. *Ib.* vi. [96]

26 You fools of fortune, trencher-friends time's flies.
Timon of Athens, III. vi. [107]

27 We have seen better days. *Ib.* IV. ii. 27

28 O! the fierce wretchedness that glory brings us.
Ib. 30

29 He has almost charmed me from my profession, by
persuading me to it. *Ib.* iii. [457]

30   My long sickness
Of health and living now begins to mend,
And nothing brings me all things. *Ib.* v. i. [191]

31 Life's uncertain voyage. *Ib.* [207]

32 Timon hath made his everlasting mansion
Upon the beached verge of the salt flood;
Who once a day with his embossed froth
The turbulent surge shall cover. *Ib.* [220]

33 She is a woman, therefore may be woo'd;
She is a woman, therefore may be won;
She is Lavinia, therefore must be lov'd.
What, man! more water glideth by the mill
Than wots the miller of; and easy it is
Of a cut loaf to steal a shive, we know.
Titus Andronicus, II. i. 82

34 Come, and take choice of all my library,
And so beguile thy sorrow. *Ib.* IV. i. 34

35 The eagle suffers little birds to sing,
And is not careful what they mean thereby.
Ib. iv. [82]

36 If one good deed in all my life I did,
I do repent it from my very soul. *Ib.* v. iii. [189]

37 The ravish'd Helen, Menelaus' queen,
With wanton Paris sleeps.
Troilus and Cressida, Prologue, 9

38 PANDARUS:
He that will have a cake out of the wheat must tarry
the grinding.
TROILUS:
Have I not tarried?
PANDARUS:
Ay, the grinding; but you must tarry the bolting.
TROILUS:
Have I not tarried?
PANDARUS:
Ay, the bolting; but you must tarry the leavening.
TROILUS:
Still have I tarried.
PANDARUS:
Ay, to the leavening; but here's yet in the word
'hereafter' the kneading, the making of the cake,
the heating of the oven, and the baking; nay, you
must stay the cooling too, or you may chance to
burn your lips. *Ib.* I. i. [15]

39   O! that her hand,
In whose comparison all whites are ink,
Writing their own reproach; to whose soft seizure
The cygnet's down is harsh, and spirit of sense
Hard as the palm of ploughman. *Ib.* [57]

40 I have had my labour for my travail. *Ib.* [73]

41   Women are angels, wooing:
Things won are done; joy's soul lies in the doing:
That she belov'd knows nought that knows not this:
Men prize the thing ungain'd more than it is.
Ib. ii. [310]

1   The sea being smooth
How many shallow bauble boats dare sail
Upon her patient breast.
Troilus and Cressida, I. iii. 34

2 The heavens themselves, the planets, and this centre
Observe degree, priority, and place,
Insisture, course, proportion, season, form,
Office, and custom, in all line of order.   *Ib.* 85

3   O! when degree is shak'd,
Which is the ladder to all high designs,
The enterprise is sick.   *Ib.* 101

4 Take but degree away, untune that string,
And, hark! what discord follows; each thing meets
In mere oppugnancy.   *Ib.* 109

5   The general's disdain'd
By him one step below, he by the next,
That next by him beneath; so every step,
Exampled by the first pace that is sick
Of his superior, grows to an envious fever
Of pale and bloodless emulation.   *Ib.* 129

6   Like a strutting player, whose conceit
Lies in his hamstring, and doth think it rich
To hear the wooden dialogue and sound
'Twixt his stretch'd footing and the scaffoldage.
                             Ib. 153

7   But we are soldiers;
And may that soldier a mere recreant prove,
That means not, hath not, or is not in love! *Ib.* 286

8 And in such indexes, although small pricks
To their subsequent volumes, there is seen
The baby figure of the giant mass
Of things to come at large.   *Ib.* 343

9 Mongrel beef-witted lord.   *Ib.* II. i. [14]

10 Who wears his wit in his belly, and his guts in his
head.   *Ib.* [78]

11 The wound of peace is surety,
Surety secure.   *Ib.* ii. 14

12 TROILUS:
What is aught, but as 'tis valued?
HECTOR:
But value dwells not in particular will;
It holds his estimate and dignity
As well wherein 'tis precious of itself
As in the prizer. 'Tis mad idolatry
To make the service greater than the god. *Ib.* 52

13   Young men, whom Aristotle thought
Unfit to hear moral philosophy.   *Ib.* 166

14   Thus to persist
In doing wrong extenuates not wrong,
But makes it much more heavy.   *Ib.* 186

15 I am giddy, expectation whirls me round.
The imaginary relish is so sweet
That it enchants my sense.   *Ib.* III. ii. [17]

16   To be wise, and love,
Exceeds man's might.   *Ib.* [163]

17 Time hath, my lord, a wallet at his back,
Wherein he puts alms for oblivion,
A great-siz'd monster of ingratitudes:
Those scraps are good deeds past; which are devour'd
As fast as they are made, forgot as soon
As done.   *Ib.* iii. 145

18   Perseverance, dear my lord,
Keeps honour bright: to have done, is to hang
Quite out of fashion, like a rusty mail
In monumental mockery.
Troilus and Cressida, III. iii. 150

19 For honour travels in a strait so narrow
Where one but goes abreast.   *Ib.* 154

20   Time is like a fashionable host
That slightly shakes his parting guest by the hand,
And with his arms outstretch'd, as he would fly,
Grasps in the comer: welcome ever smiles,
And farewell goes out sighing.   *Ib.* 165

21   Beauty, wit,
High birth, vigour of bone, desert in service,
Love, friendship, charity, are subjects all
To envious and calumniating time.
One touch of nature makes the whole world kin,
That all with one consent praise new-born gawds.
                           Ib. 171

22 And give to dust that is a little gilt
More laud than gilt o'er-dusted.   *Ib.* 178

23 A plague of opinion! a man may wear it on both
sides, like a leather jerkin.   *Ib.* [267]

24 How my achievements mock me!   *Ib.* IV. ii. [72]

25   Sometimes we are devils to ourselves
When we will tempt the frailty of our powers,
Presuming on their changeful potency. *Ib.* iv. [95]

26   Fie, fie upon her!
There's language in her eye, her cheek, her lip,
Nay, her foot speaks; her wanton spirits look out
At every joint and motive of her body. *Ib.* v. 54

27 What's past, and what's to come, is strew'd with
husks
And formless ruin of oblivion.   *Ib.* 165

28   The end crowns all,
And that old common arbitrator, Time,
Will one day end it.   *Ib.* 223

29 Words, words, mere words, no matter from the heart.
                    Ib. v. iii. [109]

30 If music be the food of love, play on;
Give me excess of it, that, surfeiting,
The appetite may sicken, and so die.
That strain again! it had a dying fall:
O! it came o'er my ear like the sweet sound
That breathes upon a bank of violets,
Stealing and giving odour! Enough! no more:
'Tis not so sweet now as it was before.
O spirit of love! how quick and fresh art thou,
That notwithstanding thy capacity
Receiveth as the sea, nought enters there,
Of what validity and pitch soe'er,
But falls into abatement and low price,
Even in a minute: so full of shapes is fancy,
That it alone is high fantastical. *Twelfth Night*, I. i. 1

31 O! when mine eyes did see Olivia first,
Methought she purg'd the air of pestilence.
That instant was I turn'd into a hart,
And my desires, like fell and cruel hounds,
E'er since pursue me.   *Ib.* 19

32 The element itself, till seven years' heat,
Shall not behold her face at ample view;
But, like a cloistress, she will veiled walk,
And water once a day her chamber round
With eye-offending brine.   *Ib.* 26

1 Away before me to sweet beds of flowers;
Love-thoughts lie rich when canopied with bowers.
Twelfth Night, I. i. 40

2 And what should I do in Illyria?
My brother he is in Elysium. *Ib.* ii. 2

3 O my poor brother! *Ib.* 6

4 He's as tall a man as any's in Illyria. *Ib.* iii. [21]

5 Speaks three or four languages word for word without
book. *Ib.* [28]

6 Methinks sometimes I have no more wit than a
Christian or an ordinary man has; but I am a great
eater of beef, and I believe that does harm to my
wit. *Ib.* [90]

7 SIR ANDREW:
I would I had bestowed that time in the tongues that
I have in fencing, dancing, and bear-baiting. O!
had I but followed the arts!
SIR TOBY:
Then hadst thou had an excellent head of hair.
Ib. [99]

8 Wherefore are these things hid? wherefore have
these gifts a curtain before 'em? are they like to
take dust, like Mistress Mall's picture? why dost
thou not go to church in a galliard, and come home
in a coranto? My very walk should be a jig.
Ib. [135]

9 Is it a world to hide virtues in? *Ib.* [142]

10 Diana's lip
Is not more smooth and rubious; thy small pipe
Is as the maiden's organ, shrill and sound;
And all is semblative a woman's part. *Ib.* iv. 31

11 Many a good hanging prevents a bad marriage.
Ib. v. [20]

12 What says Quinapalus? 'Better a witty fool than a
foolish wit.' *Ib.* [37]

13 Virtue that transgresses is but patched with sin; and
sin that amends is but patched with virtue.
Ib. [52]

14 Good my mouse of virtue, answer me. *Ib.* [68]

15 O! you are sick of self-love, Malvolio. *Ib.* [96]

16 A plague o' these pickle herring! *Ib.* [127]

17 Not yet old enough for a man, nor young enough for
a boy; as a squash is before 'tis a peascod, or a
codling when 'tis almost an apple: 'tis with him in
standing water, between boy and man. He is very
well-favoured, and he speaks very shrewishly: one
would think his mother's milk were scarce out of
him. *Ib.* [166]

18 I would be loath to cast away my speech, for besides
that it is excellently well penned, I have taken
great pains to con it. *Ib.* [184]

19 I can say little more than I have studied, and that
question's out of my part. *Ib.* [191]

20 OLIVIA:
'Tis in grain, sir; 'twill endure wind and weather.
VIOLA:
'Tis beauty truly blent, whose red and white
Nature's own sweet and cunning hand laid on:
Lady, you are the cruell'st she alive
If you will lead these graces to the grave
And leave the world no copy. *Ib.* [257]

21 Item, Two lips, indifferent red; Item, Two grey eyes
with lids to them; Item, One neck, one chin, and
so forth. *Twelfth Night*, I. v. [268]

22 Make me a willow cabin at your gate,
And call upon my soul within the house;
Write loyal cantons of contemned love,
And sing them loud even in the dead of night;
Halloo your name to the reverberate hills,
And make the babbling gossip of the air
Cry out, 'Olivia'. *Ib.* [289]

23 Farewell, fair cruelty. *Ib.* [309]

24 'What is your parentage?'
'Above my fortune, yet my state is well:
I am a gentleman.' *Ib.* [310]

25 She is drowned already, sir, with salt water, though
I seem to drown her remembrance again with
more. *Ib.* II. i. [31]

26 I am yet so near the manners of my mother, that upon
the least occasion more mine eyes will tell tales of
me. *Ib.* [42]

27 Not to be a-bed after midnight is to be up betimes.
.... To be up after midnight and to go to bed then,
is early; so that to go to bed after midnight is to
go to bed betimes. *Ib.* iii. [1 and 7]

28 O mistress mine! where are you roaming?
O! stay and hear; your true love's coming,
That can sing both high and low.
Trip no further, pretty sweeting;
Journeys end in lovers meeting,
Every wise man's son doth know.

What is love? 'tis not hereafter;
Present mirth hath present laughter;
What's to come is still unsure:
In delay there lies no plenty;
Then come kiss me, sweet and twenty,
Youth's a stuff will not endure. *Ib.* [42]

29 Am not I consanguineous? am I not of her blood?
Tillyvally, lady! *Ib.* [85]

30 He does it with a better grace, but I do it more
natural. *Ib.* [91]

31 Is there no respect of place, persons, nor time, in
you? *Ib.* [100]

32 SIR TOBY:
Dost thou think, because thou art virtuous, there
shall be no more cakes and ale?
CLOWN:
Yes, by Saint Anne, and ginger shall be hot i' the
mouth too. *Ib.* [124]

33 MARIA:
Marry, sir, sometimes he is a kind of puritan.
SIR ANDREW:
O, if I thought that, I'd beat him like a dog!
Ib. [153]

34 I will drop in his way some obscure epistles of love;
wherein by the colour of his beard, the shape of
his leg, the manner of his gait, the expressure of
his eye, forehead, and complexion, he shall find
himself most feelingly personated. *Ib.* [171]

35 My purpose is, indeed, a horse of that colour.
Ib. [184]

SHAKESPEARE

1 Now, good Cesario, but that piece of song,
That old and antique song we heard last night;
Methought it did relieve my passion much,
More than light airs and recollected terms
Of these most brisk and giddy-paced times:
Come, but one verse.   *Twelfth Night*, II. iv. 2

2 DUKE:
          If ever thou shalt love,
In the sweet pangs of it remember me;
For such as I am all true lovers are:
Unstaid and skittish in all motions else,
Save in the constant image of the creature
That is belov'd. How dost thou like this tune?

VIOLA:
It gives a very echo to the seat
Where love is enthron'd.   *Ib.* 15

3   Let still the woman take
An elder than herself, so wears she to him,
So sways she level in her husband's heart:
For, boy, however we do praise ourselves,
Our fancies are more giddy and unfirm,
More longing, wavering, sooner lost and worn,
Than women's are.   *Ib.* 29

4 Then let thy love be younger than thyself,
Or thy affection cannot hold the bent.   *Ib.* 36

5 Mark it, Cesario; it is old and plain.
The spinsters and the knitters in the sun
And the free maids that weave their thread with bones
Do use to chant it: it is silly sooth,
And dallies with the innocence of love,
Like the old age.   *Ib.* 43

6 Come away, come away, death,
And in sad cypress let me be laid;
Fly away, fly away, breath:
I am slain by a fair cruel maid.
My shroud of white, stuck all with yew,
O! prepare it.
My part of death no one so true
Did share it.

Not a flower, not a flower sweet,
On my black coffin let there be strown;
Not a friend, not a friend greet
My poor corse, where my bones shall be thrown.
A thousand thousand sighs to save,
Lay me, O! where
Sad true lover never find my grave,
To weep there.   *Ib.* 51

7 Now, the melancholy god protect thee, and the tailor
make thy doublet of changeable taffeta, for thy
mind is a very opal.   *Ib.* [74]

8 Get thee to yond same sovereign cruelty:
Tell her, my love, more noble than the world,
Prizes not quantity of dirty lands.   *Ib.* [82]

9   There is no woman's sides
Can bide the beating of so strong a passion
As love doth give my heart; no woman's heart
So big, to hold so much; they lack retention.
Alas! their love may be call'd appetite,
No motion of the liver, but the palate,
That suffer surfeit, cloyment, and revolt;
But mine is all as hungry as the sea,
And can digest so much.   *Ib.* [95]

10 DUKE:
And what's her history?

VIOLA:
A blank, my lord. She never told her love,
But let concealment, like a worm i' the bud,
Feed on her damask cheek: she pin'd in thought;
And with a green and yellow melancholy,
She sat like patience on a monument,
Smiling at grief. Was not this love indeed?
We men may say more, swear more; but, indeed,
Our shows are more than will; for still we prove
Much in our vows, but little in our love.
          Twelfth Night, II. iv. [111]

11 I am all the daughters of my father's house,
And all the brothers too.   *Ib.* [122]

12 How now, my metal of India!   *Ib.* v. [17]

13 Here comes the trout that must be caught with
tickling.   *Ib.* [25]

14 Contemplation makes a rare turkey-cock of him:
how he jets under his advanced plumes!   *Ib.* [35]

15 In my branched velvet gown.   *Ib.* [54]

16 Now is the woodcock near the gin.   *Ib.* [93]

17 I may command where I adore.   *Ib.* [116]

18 But be not afraid of greatness: some men are born
great, some achieve greatness, and some have greatness thrust upon them.   *Ib.* [158]

19 Let thy tongue tang arguments of state; put thyself
into the trick of singularity. She thus advises thee
that sighs for thee. Remember who commended
thy yellow stockings, and wished to see thee ever
cross-gartered.   *Ib.* [165]

20 Jove and my stars be praised! Here is yet a postscript.
          Ib. [189]

21 He will come to her in yellow stockings, and 'tis a
colour she abhors; and cross-gartered, a fashion
she detests.   *Ib.* [220]

22 Now Jove, in his next commodity of hair, send thee
a beard.   *Ib.* III. i. [51]

23 This fellow's wise enough to play the fool,
And to do that well craves a kind of wit.   *Ib.* [68]

24 Taste your legs, sir; put them to motion.   *Ib.* [88]

25 Most excellent accomplished lady, the heavens rain
odours on you!   *Ib.* [96]

26   'Twas never merry world
Since lowly feigning was called compliment.
          Ib. [110]

27 O world! how apt the poor are to be proud.
          Ib. [141]

28 O! what a deal of scorn looks beautiful
In the contempt and anger of his lip.   *Ib.* [159]

29 Love sought is good, but giv'n unsought is better.
          Ib. [170]

30 They have been grand-jurymen since before Noah
was a sailor.   *Ib.* ii. [18]

31 You should then have accosted her, and with some
excellent jests, fire-new from the mint, you should
have banged the youth into dumbness.   *Ib.* [23]

32 Where you will hang like an icicle on a Dutchman's
beard.   *Ib.* [30]

33 I had as lief be a Brownist as a politician.   *Ib.* [35]

34 Although the sheet were big enough for the bed of
Ware in England.   *Ib.* [52]

1 Let there be gall enough in thy ink, though thou write with a goose-pen, no matter.
Twelfth Night, III. ii. [54]

2 If he were opened, and you find so much blood in his liver as will clog the foot of a flea, I'll eat the rest of the anatomy. *Ib.* [68]

3 Look, where the youngest wren of nine comes. *Ib.* [73]

4 More lines than are in the new map with the augmentation of the Indies. *Ib.* [87]

5 In the south suburbs, at the Elephant. *Ib.* iii. 39

6 I think we do know the sweet Roman hand. *Ib.* iv. [31]

7 Why, this is very midsummer madness. *Ib.* [62]

8 What, man! defy the devil: consider, he's an enemy to mankind. *Ib.* [109]

9 Go, hang yourselves all! you are idle shallow things: I am not of your element. *Ib.* [138]

10 If this were played upon a stage now, I could condemn it as an improbable fiction. *Ib.* [142]

11 More matter for a May morning. *Ib.* [158]

12 Still you keep o' the windy side of the law. *Ib.* [183]

13 Fare thee well; and God have mercy upon one of our souls! He may have mercy upon mine, but my hope is better; and so look to thyself. *Ib.* [185]

14 Nay, let me alone for swearing. *Ib.* [204]

15 He is knight dubbed with unhatched rapier, and on carpet consideration. *Ib.* [260]

16 I am one that had rather go with sir priest than sir knight; I care not who knows so much of my mettle. *Ib.* [300]

17 Out of my lean and low ability I'll lend you something. *Ib.* [380]

18 I hate ingratitude more in a man Than lying, vainness, babbling drunkenness, Or any taint of vice whose strong corruption Inhabits our frail blood. *Ib.* [390]

19 In nature there's no blemish but the mind; None can be call'd deform'd but the unkind. *Ib.* [403]

20 Out, hyperbolical fiend! *Ib.* IV. ii. [29]

21 For I am one of those gentle ones that will use the devil himself with courtesy. *Ib.* [37]

22 CLOWN:
What is the opinion of Pythagoras concerning wild fowl?
MALVOLIO:
That the soul of our grandam might haply inhabit a bird.
CLOWN:
What thinkest thou of his opinion?
MALVOLIO:
I think nobly of the soul, and no way approve his opinion. *Ib.* [55]

23 Leave thy vain bibble-babble. *Ib.* [106]

24 We took him for a coward, but he's the very devil incarnate. *Ib.* v. i. [185]

25 And made the most notorious geck and gull That e'er invention play'd. *Ib.* [355]

26 And thus the whirligig of time brings in his revenges.
Twelfth Night, v. i. [388]

27 When that I was and a little tiny boy,
With hey, ho, the wind and the rain;
A foolish thing was but a toy,
For the rain it raineth every day.

But when I came to man's estate,
With hey, ho, the wind and the rain;
'Gainst knaves and thieves men shut their gates,
For the rain it raineth every day.

But when I came, alas! to wive,
With hey, ho, the wind and the rain;
By swaggering could I never thrive,
For the rain it raineth every day.

But when I came unto my beds,
With hey, ho, the wind and the rain;
With toss-pots still had drunken heads,
For the rain it raineth every day.

A great while ago the world begun,
With hey, ho, the wind and the rain;
But that's all one, our play is done,
And we'll strive to please you every day. *Ib.* [401]

28 Home-keeping youth have ever homely wits.
The Two Gentlemen of Verona, I. i. 2

29 For he was more than over shoes in love. *Ib.* 24

30 I have no other but a woman's reason:
I think him so, because I think him so. *Ib.* ii. 23

31 Fie, fie! how wayward is this foolish love
That, like a testy babe, will scratch the nurse
And presently all humbled kiss the rod! *Ib.* 55

32 Poor wounded name! my bosom, as a bed
Shall lodge thee till thy wound be throughly heal'd. *Ib.* 111

33 O! how this spring of love resembleth
The uncertain glory of an April day. *Ib.* iii. 84

34 Or as one nail by strength drives out another,
So the remembrance of my former love
Is by a newer object quite forgotten. *Ib.* II. iv. 194

35 He makes sweet music with th' enamell'd stones,
Giving a gentle kiss to every sedge
He overtaketh in his pilgrimage;
And so by many winding nooks he strays
With willing sport, to the wild ocean. *Ib.* vii. 28

36 Except I be by Silvia in the night,
There is no music in the nightingale;
Unless I look on Silvia in the day,
There is no day for me to look upon. *Ib.* III. i. 178

37 Ay,
Much is the force of heaven-bred poesy. *Ib.* ii. 71

38 A man I am cross'd with adversity. *Ib.* IV. i. 12

39 You know that love
Will creep in service where it cannot go. *Ib.* ii. 19

40 Who is Sylvia? what is she,
That all our swains commend her?
Holy, fair, and wise is she;
The heaven such grace did lend her,
That she might admired be.

Is she kind as she is fair?
For beauty lives with kindness:
Love doth to her eyes repair,
To help him of his blindness;
And, being help'd, inhabits there.

Then to Silvia let us sing,
  That Silvia is excelling;
She excels each mortal thing
  Upon the dull earth dwelling;
To her let us garlands bring.
Two Gentlemen of Verona, IV. ii. 40

1 How use doth breed a habit in a man! *Ib.* V. iv. 1

2   O heaven! were man
But constant, he were perfect. *Ib.* 110

3 Two lads that thought there was no more behind
But such a day to-morrow as to-day,
And to be boy eternal. *The Winter's Tale*, I. ii. 63

4 We were as twinn'd lambs that did frisk i' the sun,
And bleat the one at the other: what we chang'd
Was innocence for innocence; we knew not
The doctrine of ill-doing, no, nor dream'd
That any did. *Ib.* 67

5 Three crabbed months had sour'd themselves to
death,
Ere I could make thee open thy white hand
And clap thyself my love. *Ib.* 102

6 Paddling palms and pinching fingers. *Ib.* 116

7   Still virginalling
Upon his palm. *Ib.* 126

8 Affection! thy intention stabs the centre:
Thou dost make possible things not so held,
Communicat'st with dreams. *Ib.* 139

9 How like, methought, I then was to this kernel,
This squash, this gentleman. *Ib.* 160

10   A sad tale's best for winter.
I have one of sprites and goblins. *Ib.* II. i. 24

11 It is a heretic that makes the fire,
Not she which burns in 't. *Ib.* iii. 114

12   What's gone, and what's past help
Should be past grief. *Ib.* III. ii. [223]

13 *Bohemia. A desert Country near the Sea.*
Ib. iii. *Stage Direction*

14   Our ship hath touch'd upon
The desarts of Bohemia. *Ib.* 1

15 *Exit, pursued by a bear.* *Ib. Stage Direction*

16 When daffodils begin to peer,
  With heigh! the doxy, over the dale,
Why, then comes in the sweet o' the year;
  For the red blood reigns in the winter's pale.

The white sheet bleaching on the hedge,
  With heigh! the sweet birds, O, how they sing!
Doth set my pugging tooth on edge;
  For a quart of ale is a dish for a king.

The lark, that tirra-lirra chants,
  With, heigh! with, heigh! the thrush and the jay,
Are summer songs for me and my aunts,
  While we lie tumbling in the hay. *Ib.* IV. ii. 1

17 But shall I go mourn for that, my dear? *Ib.* [15]

18 A snapper-up of unconsidered trifles. *Ib.* [26]

19 For the life to come, I sleep out the thought of it.
Ib. [30]

20 Prig, for my life, prig; he haunts wakes, fairs, and
bear-baitings. *Ib.* [109]

21 Jog on, jog on the foot-path way,
  And merrily hent the stile-a:
A merry heart goes all the day,
  Your sad tires in a mile-a. *Ib.* [133]

22 For you there's rosemary and rue; these keep
Seeming and savour all the winter long.
The Winter's Tale, IV. iii. 74

23   The fairest flowers o' the season
Are our carnations and streak'd gillyvors,
Which some call nature's bastards. *Ib.* 81

24 Yet nature is made better by no mean
But nature makes that mean. *Ib.* 89

25   Here's flowers for you;
Hot lavender, mints, savory, marjoram;
The marigold, that goes to bed wi' the sun,
And with him rises weeping. *Ib.* 103

26   O Proserpina!
For the flowers now that frighted thou let'st fall
From Dis's waggon! daffodils,
That come before the swallow dares, and take
The winds of March with beauty; violets dim,
But sweeter than the lids of Juno's eyes
Or Cytherea's breath; pale prime-roses,
That die unmarried, ere they can behold
Bright Phœbus in his strength,—a malady
Most incident to maids; bold oxlips and
The crown imperial; lilies of all kinds,
The flower-de-luce being one. *Ib.* 116

27 PERDITA: Sure this robe of mine
Doth change my disposition.
FLORIZEL: What you do
Still betters what is done. When you speak, sweet,
I'd have you do it ever: when you sing,
I'd have you buy and sell so; so give alms;
Pray so; and, for the ordering your affairs,
To sing them too: when you do dance, I wish you
A wave o' the sea, that you might ever do
Nothing but that; move still, still so,
And own no other function: each your doing,
So singular in each particular,
Crowns what you are doing in the present deed,
That all your acts are queens. *Ib.* 134

28   Good sooth, she is
The queen of curds and cream. *Ib.* 160

29 Lawn as white as driven snow. *Ib.* [220]

30 I love a ballad in print, a-life, for then we are sure
they are true. *Ib.* [262]

31 The self-same sun that shines upon his court
Hides not his visage from our cottage, but
Looks on alike. *Ib.* [457]

32 Being now awake, I'll queen it no inch further,
But milk my ewes and weep. *Ib.* [462]

33 Prosperity's the very bond of love,
Whose fresh complexion and whose heart together
Affliction alters. *Ib.* [586]

34 Ha, ha! what a fool Honesty is! and Trust his sworn
brother, a very simple gentleman! *Ib.* [608]

35 Though I am not naturally honest, I am so sometimes by chance. *Ib.* [734]

36 That rare Italian master, Julio Romano.
Ib. V. ii. [108]

37 Thou art a tall fellow of thy hands. *Ib.* [185]

38 'Tis time; descend; be stone no more; approach.
Ib. iii. 99

1   O! she's warm.
If this be magic, let it be an art
Lawful as eating.   *The Winter's Tale*, v. iii. 109

2   Crabbed age and youth cannot live together:
Youth is full of pleasance, age is full of care.
                    The Passionate Pilgrim, xii

3   Age, I do abhor thee, youth, I do adore thee.   *Ib.*

4   What I have done is yours; what I have to do is
yours; being part in all I have, devoted yours.
                    The Rape of Lucrece, Preface

5   Beauty itself doth of itself persuade
The eyes of men without an orator.   *Ib.* l. 29

6   Or sells eternity to get a toy.   *Ib.* l. 214

7   Time's glory is to calm contending kings,
To unmask falsehood, and bring truth to light.
                    Ib. l. 939

8   Cloud-kissing Ilion.   *Ib.* l. 1370

9   From fairest creatures we desire increase,
That thereby beauty's rose might never die.
                    Sonnets, 1

10 When forty winters shall besiege thy brow,
And dig deep trenches in thy beauty's field.   *Ib.* 2

11 Thou art thy mother's glass, and she in thee
Calls back the lovely April of her prime.   *Ib.* 3

12 Lo! in the orient when the gracious light
Lifts up his burning head, each under eye
Doth homage to his new-appearing sight.   *Ib.* 7

13 Music to hear, why hear'st thou music sadly?
Sweets with sweets war not, joy delights in joy:
Why lov'st thou that which thou receiv'st not gladly,
Or else receiv'st with pleasure thine annoy?   *Ib.* 8

14 True concord of well-tuned sounds.   *Ib.*

15 When lofty trees I see barren of leaves,
Which erst from heat did canopy the herd,
And summer's green all girded up in sheaves,
Borne on the bier with white and bristly beard.
                    Ib. 12

16 If I could write the beauty of your eyes
And in fresh numbers number all your graces,
The age to come would say, 'This poet lies;
Such heavenly touches ne'er touch'd earthly faces.'
                    Ib. 17

17 And stretched metre of an antique song.   *Ib.*

18 Shall I compare thee to a summer's day?
Thou art more lovely and more temperate:
Rough winds do shake the darling buds of May,
And summer's lease hath all too short a date:
Sometimes too hot the eye of heaven shines,
And often is his gold complexion dimm'd;
And every fair from fair sometime declines,
By chance, or nature's changing course untrimm'd;
But thy eternal summer shall not fade,
Nor lose possession of that fair thou ow'st,
Nor shall death brag thou wander'st in his shade,
When in eternal lines to time thou grow'st;
So long as men can breathe, or eyes can see,
So long lives this, and this gives life to thee.   *Ib.* 18

19 My glass shall not persuade me I am old,
So long as youth and thou are of one date;
But when in thee time's furrows I behold,
Then look I death my days should expiate.   *Ib.* 22

20 As an unperfect actor on the stage,
Who with his fear is put besides his part.   *Sonnets*, 23

21 O! let my books be then the eloquence
And dumb presagers of my speaking breast.   *Ib.*

22 The painful warrior famoused for fight,
After a thousand victories once foil'd,
Is from the book of honour razed quite,
And all the rest forgot for which he toil'd.   *Ib.* 25

23 Weary with toil, I haste me to my bed.   *Ib.* 27

24 When in disgrace with fortune and men's eyes
I all alone beweep my outcast state,
And trouble deaf heaven with my bootless cries,
And look upon myself and curse my fate,
Wishing me like to one more rich in hope,
Featur'd like him, like him with friends possess'd,
Desiring this man's art, and that man's scope,
With what I most enjoy contented least;
Yet in these thoughts myself almost despising,
Haply I think on thee,—and then my state,
Like to the lark at break of day arising
From sullen earth, sings hymns at heaven's gate;
For thy sweet love remember'd such wealth brings
That then I scorn to change my state with kings.
                    Ib. 29

25 When to the sessions of sweet silent thought
I summon up remembrance of things past,
I sigh the lack of many a thing I sought,
And with old woes new wail my dear times' waste:
Then can I drown an eye, unus'd to flow,
For precious friends hid in death's dateless night,
And weep afresh love's long since cancell'd woe,
And moan the expense of many a vanish'd sight:
Then can I grieve at grievances foregone,
And heavily from woe to woe tell o'er
The sad account of fore-bemoaned moan,
Which I new pay as if not paid before.
But if the while I think on thee, dear friend,
All losses are restor'd and sorrows end.   *Ib.* 30

26 But since he died, and poets better prove,
Theirs for their style I'll read, his for his love.
                    Ib. 32

27 Full many a glorious morning have I seen
Flatter the mountain-tops with sovereign eye,
Kissing with golden face the meadows green,
Gilding pale streams with heavenly alchemy.   *Ib.* 33

28 But, out! alack! he was but one hour mine,
The region cloud hath mask'd him from me now.   *Ib.*

29 Suns of the world may stain when heaven's sun
staineth.   *Ib.*

30 Why didst thou promise such a beauteous day,
And make me travel forth without my cloak?   *Ib.* 34

31 Roses have thorns, and silver fountains mud;
Clouds and eclipses stain both moon and sun,
And loathsome canker lives in sweetest bud.
All men make faults.
                    Ib. 35

32 As a decrepit father takes delight
To see his active child do deeds of youth,
So I, made lame by fortune's dearest spite,
Take all my comfort of thy worth and truth.   *Ib.* 37

33 Against that time when thou shalt strangely pass,
And scarcely greet me with that sun, thine eye,
When love, converted from the thing it was,
Shall reasons find of settled gravity.   *Ib.* 49

1 Like stones of worth they thinly placed are,
Or captain jewels in the carconet. *Sonnets*, 52

2 What is your substance, whereof are you made,
That millions of strange shadows on you tend? *Ib.* 53

3 You in Grecian tires are painted new. *Ib.*

4 The spring and foison of the year. *Ib.*

5 O! how much more doth beauty beauteous seem
By that sweet ornament which truth doth give! *Ib.* 54

6 Not marble, nor the gilded monuments
Of princes, shall outlive this powerful rhyme. *Ib.* 55

7 Being your slave, what should I do but tend
Upon the hours and times of your desire?
I have no precious time at all to spend,
Nor services to do, till you require.
Nor dare I chide the world-without-end hour
Whilst I, my sovereign, watch the clock for you,
Nor think the bitterness of absence sour
When you have bid your servant once adieu;
Nor dare I question with my jealous thought
Where you may be, or your affairs suppose,
But like a sad slave, stay and think of nought
Save, where you are, how happy you make those.
So true a fool is love that in your will,
Though you do anything, he thinks no ill. *Ib.* 57

8 Like as the waves make towards the pebbled shore,
So do our minutes hasten to their end. *Ib.* 60

9 Time doth transfix the flourish set on youth
And delves the parallels in beauty's brow. *Ib.*

10 Sin of self-love possesseth all mine eye. *Ib.* 62

11 When I have seen by Time's fell hand defac'd
The rich-proud cost of outworn buried age. *Ib.* 64

12 When I have seen the hungry ocean gain
Advantage on the kingdom of the shore. *Ib.*

13 Since brass, nor stone, nor earth, nor boundless sea,
But sad mortality o'ersways their power,
How with this rage shall beauty hold a plea,
Whose action is no stronger than a flower? *Ib.* 65

14 Tir'd with all these, for restful death I cry,
As to behold desert a beggar born,
And needy nothing trimm'd in jollity,
And purest faith unhappily forsworn,
And gilded honour shamefully misplac'd,
And maiden virtue rudely strumpeted,
And right perfection wrongfully disgrac'd,
And strength by limping sway disabled,
And art made tongue-tied by authority,
And folly—doctor-like—controlling skill,
And simple truth miscall'd simplicity,
And captive good attending captain ill:
Tir'd with all these, from these I would be gone,
Save that, to die, I leave my love alone. *Ib.* 66

15 No longer mourn for me when I am dead
Than you shall hear the surly sullen bell
Give warning to the world that I am fled
From this vile world, with vilest worms to dwell. *Ib.* 71

16 That time of year thou mayst in me behold
When yellow leaves, or none, or few, do hang
Upon those boughs which shake against the cold,
Bare ruin'd choirs, where late the sweet birds sang.

In me thou see'st the twilight of such day
As after sunset fadeth in the west;
Which by and by black night doth take away,
Death's second self, that seals up all in rest. *Sonnets*, 73

17 This thou perceiv'st, which makes thy love more strong,
To love that well which thou must leave ere long. *Ib.*

18 So all my best is dressing old words new. *Ib.* 76

19 Like unletter'd clerk, still cry 'Amen'. *Ib.* 85

20 Was it the proud full sail of his great verse,
Bound for the prize of all too precious you,
That did my ripe thoughts in my brain inhearse,
Making their tomb the womb wherein they grew? *Ib.* 86

21 That affable familiar ghost
Which nightly gulls him with intelligence. *Ib.*

22 Farewell! thou art too dear for my possessing,
And like enough thou know'st thy estimate:
The charter of thy worth gives thee releasing;
My bonds in thee are all determinate.
For how do I hold thee but by thy granting?
And for that riches where is my deserving?
The cause of this fair gift in me is wanting,
And so my patent back again is swerving.
Thyself thou gav'st, thy own worth then not knowing,
Or me, to whom thou gav'st it, else mistaking;
So thy great gift, upon misprision growing,
Comes home again, on better judgment making.
Thus have I had thee, as a dream doth flatter,
In sleep a king, but, waking, no such matter. *Ib.* 87

23 Ah, do not, when my heart hath 'scap'd this sorrow,
Come in the rearward of a conquer'd woe;
Give not a windy night a rainy morrow,
To linger out a purpos'd overthrow. *Ib.* 90

24 They that have power to hurt and will do none,
That do not do the thing they most do show,
Who, moving others, are themselves as stone,
Unmoved, cold, and to temptation slow. *Ib.* 94

25 They are the lords and owners of their faces,
Others but stewards of their excellence.
The summer's flower is to the summer sweet,
Though to itself it only live and die. *Ib.*

26 Lilies that fester smell far worse than weeds. *Ib.*

27 How like a winter hath my absence been
From thee, the pleasure of the fleeting year!
What freezings have I felt, what dark days seen!
What old December's bareness every where! *Ib.* 97

28 From you have I been absent in the spring,
When proud-pied April, dress'd in all his trim,
Hath put a spirit of youth in every thing. *Ib.* 98

29 To me, fair friend, you never can be old,
For as you were when first your eye I ey'd,
Such seems your beauty still. Three winters cold
Have from the forests shook three summers' pride,
Three beauteous springs to yellow autumn turn'd
In process of the seasons have I seen,
Three April perfumes in three hot Junes burn'd,
Since first I saw you fresh, which yet are green.
Ah! yet doth beauty, like a dial-hand,
Steal from his figure, and no pace perceiv'd;
So your sweet hue, which methinks still doth stand,

Hath motion, and mine eye may be deceiv'd:
For fear of which, hear this, thou age unbred:
Ere you were born was beauty's summer dead.
Sonnets, 104

1 And beauty, making beautiful old rhyme. *Ib.* 106

2 Not mine own fears, nor the prophetic soul
Of the wide world dreaming on things to come,
Can yet the lease of my true love control,
Suppos'd as forfeit to a confin'd doom.
The mortal moon hath her eclipse endur'd,
And the sad augurs mock their own presage. *Ib.* 107

3 And thou in this shalt find thy monument,
When tyrants' crests and tombs of brass are spent. *Ib.*

4 O! never say that I was false of heart,
Though absence seem'd my flame to qualify. *Ib.* 109

5 Alas! 'tis true I have gone here and there,
And made myself a motley to the view,
Gor'd mine own thoughts, sold cheap what is most
  dear,
Made old offences of affections new;
Most true it is that I have look'd on truth
Askance and strangely; but, by all above,
These blenches gave my heart another youth,
And worse essays prov'd thee my best of love.
Ib. 110

6 　　　　　　My nature is subdu'd
To what it works in, like the dyer's hand;
Pity me, then, and wish I were renew'd. *Ib.* 111

7 Let me not to the marriage of true minds
Admit impediments. Love is not love
Which alters when it alteration finds,
Or bends with the remover to remove:
O, no! it is an ever-fixed mark,
That looks on tempests and is never shaken;
It is the star to every wandering bark,
Whose worth's unknown, although his height be
  taken.
Love's not Time's fool, though rosy lips and cheeks
Within his bending sickle's compass come;
Love alters not with his brief hours and weeks,
But bears it out even to the edge of doom.
If this be error, and upon me prov'd,
I never writ, nor no man ever lov'd. *Ib.* 116

8 What potions have I drunk of Siren tears,
Distill'd from limbecks foul as hell within. *Ib.* 119

9 O benefit of ill! now I find true
That better is by evil still made better. *Ib.*

10 'Tis better to be vile than vile esteem'd,
When not to be receives reproach of being. *Ib.* 121

11 The expense of spirit in a waste of shame
Is lust in action; and till action, lust
Is perjur'd, murderous, bloody, full of blame,
Savage, extreme, rude, cruel, not to trust. *Ib.* 129

12 Mad in pursuit, and in possession so;
Had, having, and in quest to have, extreme;
A bliss in proof,—and prov'd, a very woe;
Before, a joy propos'd; behind, a dream.
All this the world well knows; yet none knows well:
To shun the heaven that leads men to this hell. *Ib.*

13 My mistress' eyes are nothing like the sun;
Coral is far more red than her lips' red:
If snow be white, why then her breasts are dun;
If hairs be wires, black wires grow on her head.
Ib. 130

14 And yet, by heaven, I think my love as rare
As any she belied with false compare. *Sonnets*, 130

15 Whoever hath her wish, thou hast thy *Will*,
And *Will* to boot, and *Will* in over-plus. *Ib.* 135

16 When my love swears that she is made of truth,
I do believe her, though I know she lies. *Ib.* 138

17 Lo, as a careful housewife runs to catch
One of her feather'd creatures broke away. *Ib.* 143

18 Two loves I have of comfort and despair,
Which like two spirits do suggest me still:
The better angel is a man right fair,
The worser spirit a woman colour'd ill. *Ib.* 144

19 Yet this shall I ne'er know, but live in doubt,
Till my bad angel fire my good one out. *Ib.*

20 Poor soul, the centre of my sinful earth,
[Fool'd by] these rebel powers that thee array,
Why dost thou pine within and suffer dearth,
Painting thy outward walls so costly gay?
Why so large cost, having so short a lease,
Dost thou upon thy fading mansion spend? *Ib.* 146

21 So shalt thou feed on Death, that feeds on men,
And Death once dead, there's no more dying then.
Ib.

22 For I have sworn thee fair, and thought thee bright,
Who art as black as hell, as dark as night. *Ib.* 147

23 Love is too young to know what conscience is;
Yet who knows not conscience is born of love?
Ib. 151

24 The first heir of my invention.
Venus and Adonis, Preface.

25 Hunting he lov'd, but love he laugh'd to scorn.
Ib. l. 4

26 Bid me discourse, I will enchant thine ear,
Or like a fairy trip upon the green,
Or, like a nymph, with long dishevell'd hair,
Dance on the sands, and yet no footing seen:
Love is a spirit all compact of fire,
Not gross to sink, but light, and will aspire.
Ib. l. 145

27 Round-hoof'd, short-jointed, fetlocks shag and long,
Broad breast, full eye, small head and nostril wide,
High crest, short ears, straight legs and passing
  strong,
Thin mane, thick tail, broad buttock, tender hide:
Look, what a horse should have he did not lack,
Save a proud rider on so proud a back. *Ib.* l. 295

28 By this, poor Wat, far off upon a hill,
Stands on his hinder legs with listening ear,
To hearken if his foes pursue him still. *Ib.* l. 697

29 Good friend, for Jesu's sake forbear
To dig the dust enclosed here.
Blest be the man that spares these stones,
And curst be he that moves my bones.
*Shakespeare's Epitaph (chosen by himself for his
tomb at Stratford-on-Avon)*

30 Item, I give unto my wife my second best bed, with
the furniture. *Will*, 1616

DAVID TAYLOR SHAW
1813–1890

1 O Britannia, the pride of the ocean,
   The home of the brave and the free,
The shrine of the sailor's devotion,
   No land can compare unto thee!
   *The Red, White, and Blue. First line changed to
   'Columbia, the gem of the ocean', when sung by
   Shaw in America. Attrib. also to Thomas à Becket,
   1850*

GEORGE BERNARD SHAW
1856–1950

2 All great truths begin as blasphemies.
   Annajanska (1919), p. 262

3 One man that has a mind and knows it, can always
   beat ten men who havnt and dont.
   The Apple Cart (1930), Act I

4 What Englishman will give his mind to politics as
   long as he can afford to keep a motor car? *Ib.*

5 I never resist temptation, because I have found that
   things that are bad for me do not tempt me.
   Ib. Act II

6 You can always tell an old soldier by the inside of his
   holsters and cartridge boxes. The young ones carry
   pistols and cartridges: the old ones, grub.
   Arms and the Man, Act I

7 I never apologize. *Ib.* Act III

8 You're not a man, you're a machine. *Ib.*

9 When a stupid man is doing something he is ashamed
   of, he always declares that it is his duty.
   Cæsar and Cleopatra, Act III

10 He who has never hoped can never despair.
   Ib. Act IV

11 A man of great common sense and good taste,—meaning thereby a man without originality or moral
   courage. *Ib. Notes. Julius Cæsar*

12 We have no more right to consume happiness without
   producing it than to consume wealth without producing it. *Candida*, Act I

13 Do you think that the things people make fools of
   themselves about are any less real and true than
   the things they behave sensibly about? *Ib.*

14 It is easy—terribly easy—to shake a man's faith in
   himself. To take advantage of that to break a
   man's spirit is devil's work. *Ib.*

15 I'm only a beer teetotaller, not a champagne teetotaller. *Ib.* Act III

16 The worst sin towards our fellow creatures is not to
   hate them, but to be indifferent to them: that's the
   essence of inhumanity. *The Devil's Disciple*, Act II

17 I never expect a soldier to think. *Ib.* Act III

18 The British soldier can stand up to anything except
   the British War Office. *Ib.*

19 Stimulate the phagocytes.
   The Doctor's Dilemma (1906), Act I

20 All professions are conspiracies against the laity. *Ib.*

21 I believe in Michael Angelo, Velasquez, and Rem-
   brandt; in the might of design, the mystery of color,
   the redemption of all things by Beauty everlasting,
   and the message of Art that has made these hands
   blessed. *The Doctor's Dilemma* (1906), Act IV

22 With the single exception of Homer, there is no
   eminent writer, not even Sir Walter Scott, whom
   I can despise so entirely as I despise Shakespeare
   when I measure my mind against his. . . . It would
   positively be a relief to me to dig him up and
   throw stones at him.
   Dramatic Opinions and Essays (1907), vol. II,
   p. 52

23 Parentage is a very important profession; but no test
   of fitness for it is ever imposed in the interest of the
   children.
   Everybody's Political What's What, ch. ix, p. 74

24 It's all that the young can do for the old, to shock
   them and keep them up to date.
   Fanny's First Play (1911), Induction

25 You don't expect me to know what to say about a
   play when I don't know who the author is, do you?
   . . . If it's by a good author, it's a good play, naturally.
   That stands to reason. *Ib.* Epilogue

26 What God hath joined together no man shall ever
   put asunder: God will take care of that.
   Getting Married (1911), p. 216

27 When you loved me I gave you the whole sun and
   stars to play with. I gave you eternity in a single
   moment, strength of the mountains in one clasp
   of your arms, and the volume of all the seas in one
   impulse of your soul. *Ib.* p. 278

28 We possessed all the universe together; and you ask
   me to give you my scanty wages as well. I have
   given you the greatest of all things; and you ask
   me to give you little things. I gave you your own
   soul: you ask me for my body as a plaything. Was
   it not enough? Was it not enough? *Ib.*

29 I cannot bear men and women.
   Heartbreak House (1919), Act II

30 Go anywhere in England, where there are natural,
   wholesome, contented, and really nice English
   people; and what do you always find? That the
   stables are the real centre of the household.
   Ib. Act III

31 The captain is in his bunk, drinking bottled ditchwater; and the crew is gambling in the forecastle.
   She will strike and sink and split. Do you think
   the laws of God will be suspended in favour of
   England because you were born in it? *Ib.*

32 Money is indeed the most important thing in the
   world; and all sound and successful personal and
   national morality should have this fact for its basis.
   The Irrational Knot (1905), Preface, p. xiv

33 Though the Life Force supplies us with its own
   purpose, it has no other brains to work with than
   those it has painfully and imperfectly evolved in
   our heads. *Ib.* p. xxv

34 Reminiscences make one feel so deliciously aged and
   sad. *Ib.* ch. 14

35 A man who has no office to go to—I don't care who
   he is—is a trial of which you can have no conception. *Ib.* ch. 18

1 What really flatters a man is that you think him worth flattering. *John Bull's Other Island* (1907), Act IV.

2 There are only two qualities in the world: efficiency and inefficiency; and only two sorts of people: the efficien t and the inefficient. *Ib.*

3 The greatest of evils and the worst of crimes is poverty. *Major Barbara* (1907), Preface

4 Nobody can say a word against Greek: it stamps a man at once as an educated gentleman. *Ib.* Act I

5 Wot prawce Selvytion nah? *Ib.* Act II

6 I am a Millionaire. That is my religion. *Ib.*

7 I am a sort of collector of religions: and the curious thing is that I find I can believe in them all. *Ib.*

8 I cant talk religion to a man with bodily hunger in his eyes. *Ib.*

9 Nothing is ever done in this world until men are prepared to kill one another if it is not done. *Ib.* Act III

10 Our political experiment of democracy, the last refuge of cheap misgovernment.
Man and Superman (1903), Epistle Dedicatory, p. xxi.

11 He who has nothing to assert has no style and can have none: he who has something to assert will go as far in power of style as its momentousness and his conviction will carry him. *Ib.* p. xxxv

12 A lifetime of happiness: no man alive could bear it: it would be hell on earth. *Ib.* Act I

13 The more things a man is ashamed of, the more respectable he is. *Ib.*

14 Vitality in a woman is a blind fury of creation. *Ib.*

15 The true artist will let his wife starve, his children go barefoot, his mother drudge for his living at seventy, sooner than work at anything but his art. *Ib.*

16 Is the devil to have all the passions as well as all the good tunes? *Ib.*

17 Never mind her; go on talking. *Ib.*

18 You think that you are Ann's suitor; that you are the pursuer and she the pursued; that it is your part to woo, to persuade, to prevail, to overcome. Fool: it is you who are the pursued, the marked-down quarry, the destined prey. *Ib.* Act II

19 Marry Ann; and at the end of a week you'll find no more inspiration in her than in a plate of muffins. *Ib.*

20 Hell is full of musical amateurs: music is the brandy of the damned. *Ib.* Act III

21 An Englishman thinks he is moral when he is only uncomfortable. *Ib.*

22 As an old soldier I admit the cowardice: it's as universal as seasickness, and matters just as little. *Ib.*

23 When the military man approaches, the world locks up its spoons and packs off its womankind. *Ib.*

24 What is virtue but the Trade Unionism of the married? *Ib.*

25 Those who talk most about the blessings of marriage and the constancy of its vows are the very people who declare that if the chain were broken and the

prisoners left free to choose, the whole social fabric would fly asunder. You cannot have the argument both ways. If the prisoner is happy, why lock him in? If he is not, why pretend that he is? *Man and Superman* (1903), Act III

26 There are two tragedies in life. One is not to get your heart's desire. The other is to get it. *Ib.* Act IV

27 Do not do unto others as you would they should do unto you. Their tastes may not be the same. *Ib. Maxims for Revolutionists*, p. 227

28 The golden rule is that there are no golden rules. *Ib.*

29 Democracy substitutes election by the incompetent many for appointment by the corrupt few. *Ib.* p. 228

30 Liberty means responsibility. That is why most men dread it. *Ib.* p. 229

31 He who can, does. He who cannot, teaches. *Ib.* p. 230

32 Marriage is popular because it combines the maximum of temptation with the maximum of opportunity. *Ib.* p. 231

33 If you strike a child, take care that you strike it in anger, even at the risk of maiming it for life. A blow in cold blood neither can nor should be forgiven. *Ib.* p. 234

34 The reasonable man adapts himself to the world: the unreasonable one persists in trying to adapt the world to himself. Therefore all progress depends on the unreasonable man. *Ib.* p. 238

35 The man who listens to Reason is lost: Reason enslaves all whose minds are not strong enough to master her. *Ib.*

36 Home is the girl's prison and the woman's workhouse. *Ib.* p. 240

37 Every man over forty is a scoundrel. *Ib.* p. 242

38 There is nothing so bad or so good that you will not find Englishmen doing it; but you will never find an Englishman in the wrong. He does everything on principle. He fights you on patriotic principles; he robs you on business principles; he enslaves you on imperial principles. *The Man of Destiny*

39 An English army led by an Irish general: that might be a match for a French army led by an Italian general. *Ib.*

40 A great devotee of the Gospel of Getting On. *Mrs. Warren's Profession* (1893), Act IV

41 The fickleness of the women I love is only equalled by the infernal constancy of the women who love me. *The Philanderer* (1893), Act II

42 It is clear that a novel cannot be too bad to be worth publishing. . . . It certainly is possible for a novel to be too good to be worth publishing. *Plays Pleasant and Unpleasant* (1898), vol. 1, Preface, p. vi

43 There is only one religion, though there are a hundred versions of it. *Ib.* vol. 2, Preface, p. vii

44 The English have no respect for their language, and will not teach their children to speak it. . . . It is impossible for an Englishman to open his mouth, without making some other Englishman despise him. *Pygmalion* (1912), Preface

1 Not bloody likely.   *Pygmalion* (1912), Act II

2 Assassination is the extreme form of censorship.
          The Rejected Statement, Pt. 1

3 If ever I utter an oath again may my soul be blasted
   to eternal damnation!   *St. Joan* (1924), Sc. ii

4 How can what an Englishman believes be heresy?
   It is a contradiction in terms.   *Ib.* Sc. iv

5 Must then a Christ perish in torment in every age to
   save those that have no imagination? *Ib.* Epilogue

6 They tell me that So-and-So, who does not write
   prefaces, is no charlatan. Well, I am. I first caught
   the ear of the British public on a cart in Hyde Park,
   to the blaring of brass bands, and this . . . because
   . . . I am a natural-born mountebank.
          Three Plays for Puritans (1901), Preface

7 Well, sir, you never can tell. That's a principle in
   life with me, sir, if you'll excuse my having such
   a thing.   *You Never Can Tell* (1898), Act II

8 People must not be forced to adopt me as their
   favourite author, even for their own good.
          Letter to Alma Murray, 20 Oct. 1886

HENRY WHEELER SHAW
['JOSH BILLINGS']
1818–1885

9 Thrice is he armed that hath his quarrel just,
   But four times he who gets his blow in fust.
          Josh Billings, his Sayings (1865)

10 The trouble with people is not that they don't know
   but that they know so much that ain't so.
          Josh Billings' Encyclopedia of Wit and Wisdom
   (1874)

RICHARD SHEALE
sixteenth century

11 For Witherington needs must I wail,
   As one in doleful dumps;
   For when his legs were smitten off,
   He fought upon his stumps.
          Ballad of Chevy Chase, Pt. II, x

JOHN SHEFFIELD, DUKE OF BUCKINGHAM
see
BUCKINGHAM

MARY WOLLSTONECRAFT SHELLEY
1797–1851

12 Mrs. Shelley was choosing a school for her son, and
   asked the advice of this lady, who gave for advice—
   to use her own words to me—'Just the sort of
   banality, you know, one does come out with: "Oh,
   send him somewhere where they will teach him
   to think for himself!"' . . . Mrs. Shelley answered:
   'Teach him to think for himself? Oh, my God,
   teach him rather to think like other people!'
          Matthew Arnold, *Essays in Criticism, Second
   Series; Shelley*

PERCY BYSSHE SHELLEY
1792–1822

13 It might make one in love with death, to think that
   one should be buried in so sweet a place.
          Adonais. Preface

14 I weep for Adonais—he is dead!
   O, weep for Adonais! though our tears
   Thaw not the frost which binds so dear a head!
          Ib. I

15 Most musical of mourners, weep again!
   Lament anew, Urania!—He died,
   Who was the Sire of an immortal strain,
   Blind, old, and lonely, when his country's pride,
   The priest, the slave, and the liberticide,
   Trampled and mocked with many a loathed rite
   Of lust and blood; he went, unterrified,
   Into the gulf of death; but his clear Sprite
   Yet reigns o'er earth; the third among the sons of
   light.   *Ib.* IV

16 But now, thy youngest, dearest one, has perished—
   The nursling of thy widowhood.   *Ib.* VI

17 To that high Capital, where kingly Death
   Keeps his pale court in beauty and decay,
   He came.   *Ib.* VII

18 He will awake no more, oh, never more!   *Ib.* VIII

19   The quick Dreams,
   The passion-winged Ministers of thought.   *Ib.* IX

20 Lost Angel of a ruin'd Paradise!
   She knew not 'twas her own; as with no stain
   She faded, like a cloud which had outwept its rain.
          Ib. X

21   Desires and Adorations,
   Wingèd Persuasions and veiled Destinies,
   Splendours, and Glooms, and glimmering Incarna-
   tions
   Of hopes and fears, and twilight Phantasies;
   And Sorrow, with her family of Sighs,
   And Pleasure, blind with tears, led by the gleam
   Of her own dying smile instead of eyes,
   Came in slow pomp.   *Ib.* XIII

22 Ah, woe is me! Winter is come and gone,
   But grief returns with the revolving year.   *Ib.* XVIII

23 The great morning of the world when first
   God dawned on Chaos.   *Ib.* XIX

24 Alas! that all we loved of him should be,
   But for our grief, as if it had not been,
   And grief itself be mortal!   *Ib.* XXI

25 Whence are we, and why are we? Of what scene
   The actors or spectators?   *Ib.*

26 As long as skies are blue, and fields are green,
   Evening must usher night, night urge the morrow,
   Month follow month with woe, and year wake year
   to sorrow.   *Ib.*

27 Why didst thou leave the trodden paths of men
   Too soon, and with weak hands though mighty heart
   Dare the unpastured dragon in his den?
   Defenceless as thou wert, oh, where was then
   Wisdom the mirrored shield, or scorn the spear?
          Ib. XXVII

28 The herded wolves, bold only to pursue;
   The obscene ravens, clamorous o'er the dead.
          Ib. XXVIII

1 The Pilgrim of Eternity, whose fame
Over his living head like Heaven is bent,
An early but enduring monument,
Came, veiling all the lightnings of his song
In sorrow.   *Adonais*, xxx

2 A pard-like Spirit, beautiful and swift—
A Love in desolation masked;—a Power
Girt round with weakness;—it can scarce uplift
The weight of the superincumbent hour;
It is a dying lamp, a falling shower,
A breaking billow;—even whilst we speak
Is it not broken?   *Ib.* xxxii

3 A herd-abandoned deer struck by the hunter's dart.
                                                    Ib. xxxiii

4 Our Adonais has drunk poison—oh!
What deaf and viperous murderer could crown
Life's early cup with such a draught of woe?
                                                    Ib. xxxvi

5 He wakes or sleeps with the enduring dead;
Thou canst not soar where he is sitting now—
Dust to the dust! but the pure spirit shall flow
Back to the burning fountain whence it came,
A portion of the Eternal.   *Ib.* xxxviii

6 He hath awakened from the dream of life—
'Tis we, who lost in stormy visions, keep
With phantoms an unprofitable strife,
And in mad trance, strike with our spirit's knife
Invulnerable nothings   *Ib.* xxxix

7 He has out-soared the shadow of our night;
Envy and calumny and hate and pain,
And that unrest which men miscall delight,
Can touch him not and torture not again;
From the contagion of the world's slow stain
He is secure, and now can never mourn
A heart grown cold, a head grown grey in vain.
                                                    Ib. xl

8 He lives, he wakes,—'tis Death is dead, not he.
                                                    Ib. xli

9 He is made one with Nature: there is heard
His voice in all her music, from the moan
Of thunder, to the song of night's sweet bird. *Ib.* xlii

10 He is a portion of the loveliness
Which once he made more lovely.   *Ib.* xliii

11 The inheritors of unfulfilled renown
Rose from their thrones, built beyond mortal thought,
Far in the Unapparent.   *Ib.* xlv

12 Sublimely mild, a Spirit without spot. [Sidney.] *Ib.*

13 Oblivion as they rose shrank like a thing reproved.
                                                    Ib.

14 What Adonais is, why fear we to become? *Ib.* li

15 The One remains, the many change and pass;
Heaven's light forever shines, Earth's shadows fly;
Life, like a dome of many-coloured glass,
Stains the white radiance of Eternity. *Ib.* lii

16 The soul of Adonais, like a star,
Beacons from the abode where the Eternal are.
                                                    Ib. lv

17 The lone Chorasmian shore.   *Alastor*, l. 272

18   But thou art fled
Like some frail exhalation.   *Ib.* l. 686

19 Pale despair and cold tranquillity,
Nature's vast frame, the web of human things,
Birth and the grave, that are not as they were.
                                                Alastor, l. 718

20   Arethusa arose
From her couch of snows
In the Acroceraunian mountains,—
From cloud and from crag,
With many a jag,
Shepherding her bright fountains.   *Arethusa*

21 Like friends once parted
Grown single-hearted.   *Ib.*

22 'Do you not hear the Aziola cry?
Methinks she must be nigh,'
Said Mary as we sate
In dusk, ere stars were lit, or candles brought;
And I, who thought
This Aziola was some tedious woman,
Asked, 'Who is Aziola?'   *The Aziola*

23 Give yourself no unnecessary pain,
My dear Lord Cardinal. Here, Mother, tie
My girdle for me, and bind up this hair
In any simple knot; ay, that does well.
And yours I see is coming down. How often
Have we done this for one another; now
We shall not do it any more. My Lord,
We are quite ready. Well, 'tis very well.
                                    The Cenci, v. iv. 158

24 A widow bird sate mourning for her love
Upon a wintry bough;
The frozen wind crept on above,
The freezing stream below.

There was no leaf upon the forest bare,
No flower upon the ground,
And little motion in the air
Except the mill-wheel's sound.
                            Charles the First, sc. v, l. 10

25 I bring fresh showers for the thirsting flowers,
From the seas and the streams;
I bear light shade for the leaves when laid
In their noonday dreams.   *The Cloud*

26 I wield the flail of the lashing hail,
And whiten the green plains under,
And then again I dissolve it in rain,
And laugh as I pass in thunder.   *Ib.*

27 I sift the snow on the mountains below,
And their great pines groan aghast;
And all the night 'tis my pillow white,
While I sleep in the arms of the blast.
Sublime on the towers of my skiey bowers,
Lightning my pilot sits;
In a cavern under is fettered the thunder,
It struggles and howls at fits.   *Ib.*

28 And I all the while bask in Heaven's blue smile,
Whilst he is dissolving in rains.   *Ib.*

29 That orbèd maiden, with white fire laden,
Whom mortals call the Moon,
Glides glimmering o'er my fleece-like floor,
By the midnight breezes strewn;
And wherever the beat of her unseen feet,
Which only the angels hear,
May have broken the woof of my tent's thin roof,
The stars peep behind her and peer;
And I laugh to see them whirl and flee
Like a swarm of golden bees,

[492]

When I widen the rent in my wind-built tent,
  Till the calm rivers, lakes, and seas,
Like strips of the sky fallen through me on high,
  Are each paved with the moon and these.
The Cloud

1 I am the daughter of Earth and Water,
  And the nursling of the Sky;
I pass through the pores of the ocean and shores;
  I change, but I cannot die.
For after the rain when with never a stain
  The pavilion of Heaven is bare,
And the winds and sunbeams with their convex
    gleams
  Build up the blue dome of air,
I silently laugh at my own cenotaph,
  And out of the caverns of rain,
Like a child from the womb, like a ghost from the
    tomb,
  I arise and unbuild it again.   *Ib.*

2 How wonderful is Death,
  Death and his brother Sleep!
One pale as yonder wan and horned moon,
  With lips of lurid blue,
The other glowing like the vital morn,
  When throned on ocean's wave
  It breathes over the world:
Yet both so passing strange and wonderful!
The Daemon of the World, Part 1, l. 1

3 My Song, I fear that thou wilt find but few
Who fitly shall conceive thy reasoning,
Of such hard matter dost thou entertain.
Epipsychidion. Advertisement

4 My last delight! tell them that they are dull,
And bid them own that thou art beautiful. *Ib.*

5   Sweet as stops
Of planetary music heard in trance.   *Ib.* l. 85

6 The spirit of the worm beneath the sod
In love and worship, blends itself with God.
Ib. l. 128

7 The fields of Immortality.   *Ib.* l. 133

8 Are we not formed, as notes of music are,
For one another, though dissimilar.   *Ib.* l. 142

9 I never was attached to that great sect,
Whose doctrine is, that each one should select
Out of the crowd a mistress or a friend,
And all the rest, though fair and wise, commend
To cold oblivion.   *Ib.* l. 149

10 Who travel to their home among the dead
By the broad highway of the world, and so
With one chained friend, perhaps a jealous foe,
The dreariest and the longest journey go. *Ib.* l. 156

11 True Love in this differs from gold and clay,
That to divide is not to take away.   *Ib.* l. 160

12 A ship is floating in the harbour now,
A wind is hovering o'er the mountain's brow;
There is a path on the sea's azure floor,
No keel has ever ploughed that path before.
Ib. l. 408

13 An isle under Ionian skies,
Beautiful as a wreck of Paradise.   *Ib.* l. 422

14 Day and night, aloof, from the high towers
And terraces, the Earth and Ocean seem
To sleep in one another's arms, and dream
Of waves, flowers, clouds, woods, rocks, and all that we
Read in their smiles, and call reality. *Ib.* l. 508

15 I pant, I sink, I tremble, I expire!
Epipsychidion, l. 591

16 Chameleons feed on light and air:
Poets' food is love and fame. *An Exhortation*

17 And bloody Faith the foulest birth of time.
Feelings of a Republican

18   Time's printless torrent grew
A scroll of crystal, blazoning the name
Of Adonais!   *Fragment on Keats*

19 My head is wild with weeping.
Fragment: My head is wild

20 My spirit like a charmed bark doth swim
Upon the liquid waves of thy sweet singing.
Fragment: To One Singing

21 Good-night? ah! no; the hour is ill
  Which severs those it should unite;
Let us remain together still,
  Then it will be *good* night. *Good Night*

22 To hearts which near each other move
  From evening close to morning light,
The night is good; because, my love,
  They never *say* good-night.   *Ib.*

23 Life may change, but it may fly not;
Hope may vanish, but can die not;
Truth be veiled, but still it burneth;
Love repulsed,—but it returneth! *Hellas*, l. 34

24 Let there be light! said Liberty,
And like sunrise from the sea,
Athens arose!   *Ib.* l. 682

25 The world's great age begins anew,
  The golden years return,
The earth doth like a snake renew
  Her winter weeds outworn;
Heaven smiles, and faiths and empires gleam,
Like wrecks of a dissolving dream.

A brighter Hellas rears its mountains
From waves serener far;
A new Peneus rolls his fountains
Against the morning star.
Where fairer Tempes bloom, there sleep
Young Cyclads on a sunnier deep.

A loftier Argo cleaves the main,
Fraught with a later prize;
Another Orpheus sings again,
And loves, and weeps, and dies.
A new Ulysses leaves once more
Calypso for his native shore. *Ib.* l. 1060

26 Riddles of death Thebes never knew. *Ib.* l. 1083

27 Another Athens shall arise,
  And to remoter time
Bequeath, like sunset to the skies,
  The splendour of its prime;
And leave, if nought so bright may live,
All earth can take or Heaven can give.

Saturn and Love their long repose
Shall burst, more bright and good
Than all who fell, than One who rose,
Than many unsubdued:
Not gold, not blood, their altar dowers,
But votive tears and symbol flowers.

[493]

Oh cease! must hate and death return?
Cease! must men kill and die?
Cease! drain not to its dregs the urn
Of bitter prophecy.
The world is weary of the past,
Oh, might it die or rest at last!   *Hellas*, l. 1090

1 I am the eye with which the Universe
Beholds itself and knows itself divine;
All harmony of instrument or verse,
All prophecy, all medicine is mine,
All light of art or nature;—to my song
Victory and praise in its own right belong.
                                        Hymn of Apollo

2 I pursued a maiden and clasped a reed.
Gods and men, we are all deluded thus!
It breaks in our bosom and then we bleed.
                                        Hymn of Pan

3 The awful shadow of some unseen Power
   Floats though unseen among us,—visiting
   This various world with as inconstant wing
As summer winds that creep from flower to flower.
                        Hymn to Intellectual Beauty

4 Spirit of Beauty, that dost consecrate
   With thine own hues all thou dost shine upon
   Of human thought or form.   *Ib.*

5 While yet a boy I sought for ghosts, and sped
   Through many a listening chamber, cave and ruin,
   And starlight wood, with fearful steps pursuing
Hopes of high talk with the departed dead.
I called on poisonous names with which our youth
   is fed.   *Ib.*

6 The day becomes more solemn and serene
   When noon is past—there is a harmony
   In autumn, and a lustre in its sky,
Which through the summer is not heard or seen,
As if it could not be, as if it had not been!   *Ib.*

7 I arise from dreams of thee
In the first sweet sleep of night.
When the winds are breathing low,
And the stars are shining bright:
I arise from dreams of thee,
And a spirit in my feet
Hath led me—who knows how?
To thy chamber window, Sweet!

The wandering airs they faint
On the dark, the silent stream—
The Champak odours fail
Like sweet thoughts in a dream;
The nightingale's complaint,
It dies upon her heart;—
As I must on thine,
Oh, beloved as thou art!

Oh lift me from the grass!
I die! I faint! I fail!
Let thy love in kisses rain
On my lips and eyelids pale.
My cheek is cold and white, alas!
My heart beats loud and fast;—
Oh! press it to thine own again,
Where it will break at last.   *The Indian Serenade*

8 Best and brightest, come away!
Fairer far than this fair day. *To Jane: The Invitation*

9 I am gone into the fields
To take what this sweet hour yields;—
Reflection, you may come to-morrow,
Sit by the fireside with Sorrow.—
You with the unpaid bill, Despair,—
You, tiresome verse-reciter, Care,—
I will pay you in the grave,—
Death will listen to your stave.
                        To Jane: The Invitation

10 The daisy-star that never sets,
And wind-flowers, and violets,
Which yet join not scent to hue.   *Ib.*

11   Soothed by every azure breath
That under Heaven is blown.
                        To Jane: The Recollection

12 Less oft is peace in Shelley's mind,
Than calm in waters, seen.   *Ib.*

13   I love all waste
And solitary places; where we taste
The pleasure of believing what we see
Is boundless, as we wish our souls to be.
                        Julian and Maddalo, l. 14

14 Thou Paradise of exiles, Italy!   *Ib.* l. 57

15   It is our will
That thus enchains us to permitted ill—
We might be otherwise—we might be all
We dream of happy, high, majestical.   *Ib.* l. 170

16 Me—who am as a nerve o'er which do creep
The else unfelt oppressions of this earth. *Ib.* l. 449

17   Most wretched men
Are cradled into poetry by wrong:
They learn in suffering what they teach in song.
                                        Ib. l. 543

18 O world! O life! O time!
On whose last steps I climb,
Trembling at that where I had stood before;
When will return the glory of your prime?
No more—Oh, never more!   *A Lament*

19 Fresh spring, and summer, and winter hoar,
Move my faint heart with grief, but with delight
No more—Oh, never more!   *Ib.*

20 When the lamp is shattered
   The light in the dust lies dead—
When the cloud is scattered
   The rainbow's glory is shed.
When the lute is broken,
   Sweet tones are remembered not;
When the lips have spoken,
   Loved accents are soon forgot.
                        Lines: When the Lamp

21 When hearts have once mingled
   Love first leaves the well-built nest;
The weak one is singled
   To endure what it once possessed.
O Love! who bewailest
   The frailty of all things here,
Why choose you the frailest
   For your cradle, your home, and your bier?   *Ib.*

22 Many a green isle needs must be
In the deep wide sea of misery,
Or the mariner, worn and wan,
Never thus could voyage on.
        Lines written amongst the Euganean Hills, l. 1

23 Ay, many flowering islands lie
In the waters of wide Agony.   *Ib.* l. 66

SHELLEY

1 Beneath is spread like a green sea
The waveless plain of Lombardy,
Bounded by the vaporous air,
Islanded by cities fair;
Underneath Day's azure eyes
Ocean's nursling, Venice lies,
A peopled labyrinth of walls,
Amphitrite's destined halls.
Lines written amongst the Euganean Hills, l. 90

2 Sun-girt city, thou hast been
Ocean's child, and then his queen;
Now is come a darker day,
And thou soon must be his prey. *Ib.* l. 115

3   My spirit which so long
Darkened this swift stream of song. *Ib.* l. 311

4 Peopling the lone universe. *Ib.* l. 319

5 Other flowering isles must be
In the sea of Life and Agony. *Ib.* l. 335

6 What! alive, and so bold, O earth?
Lines written on hearing the News of the Death of Napoleon

7 The fountains mingle with the river,
And the rivers with the ocean;
The winds of heaven mix for ever
With a sweet emotion;
Nothing in the world is single;
All things, by a law divine,
In one another's being mingle.
Why not I with thine?—

See the mountains kiss high Heaven
And the waves clasp one another;
No sister-flower would be forgiven
If it disdained its brother;
And the sunlight clasps the earth
And the moonbeams kiss the sea:
What are all these kissings worth
If thou kiss not me? *Love's Philosophy*

8 Under the roof of blue Italian weather.
Letter to Maria Gisborne, l. 147

9   London, that great sea, whose ebb and flow
At once is deaf and loud, and on the shore
Vomits its wrecks, and still howls on for more.
Ib. l. 193

10 You will see Coleridge—he who sits obscure
In the exceeding lustre and the pure
Intense irradiation of a mind,
Which, through its own internal lightning blind,
Flags wearily through darkness and despair—
A cloud-encircled meteor of the air,
A hooded eagle among blinking owls.
You will see Hunt—one of those happy souls
Which are the salt of the earth, and without whom
This world would smell like what it is—a tomb.
Ib. l. 202

11   Have you not heard
When a man marries, dies, or turns Hindoo,
His best friends hear no more of him? *Ib.* l. 235

12   The milk-white Snowdonian antelope
Matched with this cameleopard. *Ib.* l. 239

13   His fine wit
Makes such a wound, the knife is lost in it.
[T. L. Peacock.] *Ib.* l. 240

14   Wit and sense,
Virtue and human knowledge; all that might
Make this dull world a business of delight,
Are all combined in Horace Smith.
Letter to Maria Gisborne, l. 247

15 I met Murder in the way—
He had a mask like Castlereagh.
The Mask of Anarchy, 11

16 Ye are many—they are few. *Ib.* XXXVIII

17 Its horror and its beauty are divine.
The 'Medusa' of Leonardo da Vinci

18 Some say that gleams of a remoter world
Visit the soul in sleep,—that death is slumber,
And that its shapes the busy thoughts outnumber
Of those who wake and live. *Mont Blanc,* l. 49

19   Art thou pale for weariness
Of climbing heaven, and gazing on the earth,
Wandering companionless
Among the stars that have a different birth,—
And ever changing, like a joyless eye
That finds no object worth its constancy?
To the Moon

20 Nought may endure but Mutability. *Mutability*

21 Swiftly walk over the western wave,
Spirit of Night!
Out of the misty eastern cave,
Where, all the long and lone daylight,
Thou wovest dreams of joy and fear,
Which make thee terrible and dear,—
Swift be thy flight! *To Night*

22 Wrap thy form in a mantle gray,
Star-inwrought!
Blind with thine hair the eyes of Day;
Kiss her until she be wearied out,
Then wander o'er city, and sea, and land,
Touching all with thine opiate wand—
Come, long-sought! *Ib.*

23 Thy brother Death came, and cried,
Wouldst thou me?
Thy sweet child Sleep, the filmy-eyed,
Murmured like a noontide bee,
Shall I nestle near thy side?
Wouldst thou me? *Ib.*

24 Death will come when thou art dead,
Soon, too soon—
Sleep will come when thou art fled;
Of neither would I ask the boon
I ask of thee, beloved Night—
Swift be thine approaching flight,
Come soon, soon! *Ib.*

25 A glorious people vibrated again
The lightning of the nations. *Ode to Liberty,* l. 1

26 My soul spurned the chains of its dismay,
And in the rapid plumes of song
Clothed itself, sublime and strong,
(As a young eagle soars the morning clouds among.)
Ib. l. 5

27   When o'er the Aegean main
Athens arose: a city such as vision
Builds from the purple crags and silver towers
Of battlemented cloud, as in derision
Of kingliest masonry: the ocean-floors
Pave it; the evening sky pavilions it;
Its portals are inhabited
By thunder-zoned winds. *Ib.* l. 60

[495]

1 Within the surface of Time's fleeting river
  Its wrinkled image lies, as then it lay
Immovably unquiet, and for ever
  It trembles, but it cannot pass away!
Ode to Liberty, l. 76

2 I stood within the City disinterred;
  And heard the autumnal leaves like light footfalls
Of spirits passing through the streets; and heard
The Mountain's slumbrous voice at intervals
Thrill through those roofless halls.
Ode to Naples, l. 1

3 Long lost, late won, and yet but half-regained.
Ib. l. 58

4 O wild West Wind, thou breath of Autumn's being,
Thou, from whose unseen presence the leaves dead
Are driven, like ghosts from an enchanter fleeing,

Yellow, and black, and pale, and hectic red,
Pestilence-stricken multitudes: O thou,
Who chariotest to their dark wintry bed

The winged seeds, where they lie cold and low,
Each like a corpse within its grave, until
Thine azure sister of the spring shall blow

Her clarion o'er the dreaming earth, and fill
(Driving sweet buds like flocks to feed in air)
With living hues and odours plain and hill:

Wild Spirit, which art moving everywhere;
Destroyer and preserver; hear, oh, hear!
Ode to the West Wind, l. 1

5 Shook from the tangled boughs of Heaven and Ocean,
  Angels of rain and lightning.
Ib. l. 17

6 Like the bright hair uplifted from the head
Of some fierce Maenad.
Ib. l. 20

7 Thou dirge
Of the dying year, to which this closing night
Will be the dome of a vast sepulchre.
Ib. l. 23

8 Thou who didst waken from his summer dreams
  The blue Mediterranean, where he lay,
Lulled by the coil of his crystalline streams

  Beside a pumice isle in Baiae's bay,
And saw in sleep old palaces and towers
  Quivering within the wave's intenser day,

All overgrown with azure moss and flowers
So sweet, the sense faints picturing them. *Ib.* l. 29

9 Far below
The sea-blooms and the oozy woods which wear
The sapless foliage of the ocean, know
Thy voice, and suddenly grow gray with fear,
And tremble and despoil themselves. *Ib.* l. 38

10 If I were a dead leaf thou mightest bear;
If I were a swift cloud to fly with thee;
A wave to pant beneath thy power, and share

The impulse of thy strength, only less free
Than thou, O uncontrollable! If even
I were as in my boyhood, and could be

The comrade of thy wanderings over Heaven,
As then, when to outstrip thy skiey speed
Scarce seemed a vision; I would ne'er have striven

As thus with thee in prayer in my sore need,
Oh, lift me as a wave, a leaf, a cloud!
I fall upon the thorns of life! I bleed! *Ib.* l. 43

11 Make me thy lyre, even as the forest is:
What if my leaves are falling like its own?
The tumult of thy mighty harmonies

Will take from both a deep, autumnal tone,
Sweet though in sadness. Be thou, Spirit fierce,
My spirit! Be thou me, impetuous one!

Drive my dead thoughts over the universe
Like withered leaves to quicken a new birth!
And, by the incantation of this verse,

Scatter, as from an unextinguished hearth
Ashes and sparks, my words among mankind!
Be through my lips to unawakened earth

The trumpet of a prophecy! O, Wind,
If Winter comes, can Spring be far behind?
Ode to the West Wind, 57

12 Or *anything*, as the learned Boar observed.
Oedipus Tyrannus, II. i. 105

13 I met a traveller from an antique land
Who said: Two vast and trunkless legs of stone
Stand in the desert. *Ozymandias*

14 My name is Ozymandias, king of kings:
Look on my works, ye Mighty, and despair! *Ib.*

15 Nothing beside remains. Round the decay
Of that colossal wreck, boundless and bare
The lone and level sands stretch far away. *Ib.*

16 Hell is a city much like London—
A populous and smoky city.
Peter Bell the Third, pt. 3. Hell, i

17 But from the first 'twas Peter's drift
  To be a kind of moral eunuch,
He touched the hem of Nature's shift,
  Felt faint—and never dared uplift
The closest, all-concealing tunic. *Ib.* pt. 4. Sin, xi

18 Ere Babylon was dust,
The Magus Zoroaster, my dead child,
Met his own image walking in the garden,
That apparition, sole of men, he saw.
Prometheus Unbound, I, l. 191

19 Dreams and the light imaginings of men,
And all that faith creates or love desires,
Terrible, strange, sublime and beauteous shapes.
Ib. 200

20 Cruel he looks, but calm and strong,
Like one who does, not suffers wrong. *Ib.* 238

21 It doth repent me: words are quick and vain;
Grief for awhile is blind, and so was mine.
I wish no living thing to suffer pain. *Ib.* 303

22 Kingly conclaves stern and cold
Where blood with guilt is bought and sold. *Ib.* 530

23 See a disenchanted nation
Springs like day from desolation;
To Truth its state is dedicate,
And Freedom leads it forth, her mate. *Ib.* 567

24 The good want power, but to weep barren tears.
The powerful goodness want: worse need for them.
The wise want love; and those who love want wisdom.
Ib. 625

25 Thy words are like a cloud of winged snakes;
And yet I pity those they torture not. *Ib.* 632

26 Peace is in the grave.
The grave hides all things beautiful and good:
I am a God and cannot find it there. *Ib.* 638

1 The dust of creeds outworn.
Prometheus Unbound, I. 697

2 On a poet's lips I slept
Dreaming like a love-adept
In the sound his breathing kept;
Nor seeks nor finds he mortal blisses,
But feeds on the aërial kisses
Of shapes that haunt thought's wildernesses.
He will watch from dawn to gloom
The lake-reflected sun illume
The yellow bees in the ivy-bloom,
Nor heed, nor see, what things they be;
But from these create he can
Forms more real than living man,
Nurslings of immortality! *Ib.* 737

3   That sense, which when the winds of Spring
In rarest visitation, or the voice
Of one beloved heard in youth alone,
Fills the faint eyes with falling tears which dim
The radiant looks of unbewailing flowers,
And leaves this peopled earth a solitude
When it returns no more. *Ib.* II. iv. 12

4   To be
Omnipotent but friendless is to reign. *Ib.* 47

5 He gave man speech, and speech created thought,
Which is the measure of the universe. *Ib.* 73

6 All spirits are enslaved which serve things evil.
Ib. 110

7 Fate, Time, Occasion, Chance, and Change? To
these
All things are subject but eternal Love. *Ib.* 119

8 My coursers are fed with the lightning,
They drink of the whirlwind's stream,
And when the red morning is bright'ning
They bathe in the fresh sunbeam. *Ib.* 163

9 Life of Life! thy lips enkindle
  With their love the breath between them;
And thy smiles before they dwindle
  Make the cold air fire; then screen them
In those looks, where whoso gazes
Faints, entangled in their mazes.

Child of Light! thy limbs are burning
  Through the vest which seems to hide them;
As the radiant lines of morning
  Through the clouds ere they divide them;
And this atmosphere divinest
Shrouds thee wheresoe'er thou shinest. *Ib.* v. 48

10 My soul is an enchanted boat,
  Which, like a sleeping swan, doth float
Upon the silver waves of thy sweet singing. *Ib.* 72

11 Death is the veil which those who live call life:
They sleep, and it is lifted. *Ib.* III. iii. 113

12 The loathsome mask has fallen, the man remains
Sceptreless, free, uncircumscribed, but man
Equal, unclassed, tribeless, and nationless,
Exempt from awe, worship, degree, the king
Over himself; just, gentle, wise: but man
Passionless?—no, yet free from guilt or pain,
Which were, for his will made or suffered them,
Nor yet exempt, though ruling them like slaves,
From chance, and death, and mutability,
The clogs of that which else might oversoar
The loftiest star of unascended heaven,
Pinnacled dim in the intense inane. *Ib.* 193

13 Familiar acts are beautiful through love. *Ib.* IV. 403

14 Language is a perpetual Orphic song,
Which rules with Daedal harmony a throng
Of thoughts and forms, which else senseless and
shapeless were. *Prometheus Unbound*, IV. 415

15 Elysian, windless, fortunate abodes
Beyond Heaven's constellated wilderness. *Ib.* 531

16 A traveller from the cradle to the grave
Through the dim night of this immortal day.
Ib. 551

17 To suffer woes which Hope thinks infinite;
To forgive wrongs darker than death or night;
To defy Power, which seems omnipotent;
To love, and bear; to hope till Hope creates
From its own wreck the thing it contemplates;
Neither to change, nor falter, nor repent;
This, like thy glory, Titan, is to be
Good, great and joyous, beautiful and free;
This is alone Life, Joy, Empire and Victory.
Ib. 570

18 How wonderful is Death,
Death and his brother Sleep! *Queen Mab*, c. 1, l. 1

19 That sweet bondage which is freedom's self.
Ib. c. 9, l. 76

20 I dreamed that, as I wandered by the way,
  Bare Winter suddenly was changed to Spring,
And gentle odours led my steps astray,
  Mixed with a sound of water's murmuring
Along a shelving bank of turf, which lay
  Under a copse, and hardly dared to fling
Its green arms round the bosom of the stream,
  But kissed it and then fled, as thou mightst in
  dream. *The Question*

21 There grew pied wind-flowers and violets,
  Daisies, those pearled Arcturi of the earth,
The constellated flower that never sets. *Ib.*

22 And in the warm hedge grew lush eglantine,
  Green cowbind and the moonlight-coloured may,
And cherry-blossoms, and white cups, whose wine
  Was the bright dew, yet drained not by the day;
And wild roses, and ivy serpentine,
  With its dark buds and leaves, wandering astray;
And flowers azure, black, and streaked with gold,
  Fairer than any wakened eyes behold. *Ib.*

23 And nearer to the river's trembling edge
  There grew broad flag-flowers, purple, pranked
  with white,
And starry river buds among the sedge,
  And floating water-lilies, broad and bright. *Ib.*

24 With hue like that when some great painter dips
His pencil in the gloom of earthquake and eclipse.
The Revolt of Islam, c. 5. xxiii

25 A Sensitive Plant in a garden grew.
The Sensitive Plant, pt. 1, l. 1

26 And the rose like a nymph to the bath addressed,
Which unveiled the depth of her glowing breast,
Till, fold after fold, to the fainting air
The soul of her beauty and love lay bare. *Ib.* l. 29

27 And the jessamine faint, and the sweet tuberose,
The sweetest flower for scent that blows. *Ib.* l. 37

28 It is a modest creed, and yet
Pleasant if one considers it,
To own that death itself must be
Like all the rest, a mockery. *Ib. Conclusion*

1 Hail to thee, blithe Spirit!
  Bird thou never wert,
That from Heaven, or near it,
  Pourest thy full heart
In profuse strains of unpremeditated art.
                            To a Skylark

2 And singing still dost soar, and soaring ever singest. *Ib.*

3 Like an unbodied joy whose race is just begun. *Ib.*

4 Thou art unseen, but yet I hear thy shrill delight. *Ib.*

5 Keen as are the arrows
  Of that silver sphere,
Whose intense lamp narrows
  In the white dawn clear
Until we hardly see,—we feel that it is there. *Ib.*

6 Like a Poet hidden
  In the light of thought,
Singing hymns unbidden,
  Till the world is wrought
To sympathy with hopes and fears it heeded not:

Like a high-born maiden
  In a palace-tower,
Soothing her love-laden
  Soul in secret hour
With music sweet as love, which overflows her bower.
                              Ib.

7 Chorus Hymeneal,
  Or triumphal chant,
Matched with thine would be all
  But an empty vaunt,
A thing wherein we feel there is some hidden want.
                              Ib.

8 What objects are the fountains
  Of thy happy strain?
What fields, or waves, or mountains?
  What shapes of sky or plain?
What love of thine own kind? what ignorance of
  pain? *Ib.*

9 With thy clear keen joyance
  Languor cannot be:
Shadow of annoyance
  Never came near thee:
Thou lovest—but ne'er knew love's sad satiety.

Waking or asleep,
  Thou of death must deem
Things more true and deep
  Than we mortals dream,
Or how could thy notes flow in such a crystal stream?

We look before and after;
  We pine for what is not;
Our sincerest laughter
  With some pain is fraught;
Our sweetest songs are those that tell of saddest
  thought. *Ib.*

10 Better than all measures
  Of delightful sound,
Better than all treasures
  That in books are found,
Thy skill to poet were, thou scorner of the ground!

Teach me half the gladness
  That thy brain must know,
Such harmonious madness
  From my lips would flow
The world should listen then—as I am listening now.
                              Ib.

11 Rarely, rarely, comest thou,
  Spirit of Delight! *Song: Rarely, Rarely, Comest Thou*

12 I love all that thou lovest,
  Spirit of Delight:
The fresh Earth in new leaves dressed,
  And the starry night;
Autumn evening, and the morn
  When the golden mists are born. *Ib.*

13 I love snow, and all the forms
  Of the radiant frost. *Ib.*

14   Everything almost
Which is Nature's, and may be
  Untainted by man's misery. *Ib.*

15 I love tranquil solitude,
  And such society
As is quiet, wise, and good;
  Between thee and me
What difference? but thou dost possess
  The things I seek, not love them less. *Ib.*

16 I love Love—though he has wings,
  And like light can flee,
But above all other things,
  Spirit, I love thee—
Thou art love and life! Oh, come,
  Make once more my heart thy home. *Ib.*

17 Men of England, wherefore plough
  For the lords who lay you low?
                 Song to the Men of England

18 An old, mad, blind, despised, and dying king.
                    Sonnet: England in 1819

19 Lift not the painted veil which those who live
  Call Life. *Sonnet: Lift not the Painted Veil*

20   He sought,
For his lost heart was tender, things to love,
But found them not, alas! nor was there aught
The world contains, the which he could approve.
Through the unheeding many he did move,
A splendour among shadows, a bright blot
Upon this gloomy scene, a Spirit that strove
For truth, and like the Preacher found it not. *Ib.*

21 The City's voice itself is soft like Solitude's.
       Stanzas Written in Dejection, near Naples

22 I see the waves upon the shore,
  Like light dissolved in star-showers, thrown. *Ib.*

23 How sweet! did any heart now share in my emotion.
                              Ib.

24 Alas! I have nor hope nor health,
  Nor peace within nor calm around,
Nor that content surpassing wealth
  The sage in meditation found,
  And walked with inward glory crowned. *Ib.*

25 I could lie down like a tired child,
  And weep away the life of care
Which I have borne and yet must bear,
  Till death like sleep might steal on me. *Ib.*

26 Away! the moor is dark beneath the moon,
Rapid clouds have drank the last pale beam of even:
Away! the gathering winds will call the darkness soon,
And profoundest midnight shroud the serene lights of
  heaven.
    Stanzas.—April 1814: Away! the Moor is Dark

1 Music, when soft voices die,
Vibrates in the memory—
Odours, when sweet violets sicken,
Live within the sense they quicken.

Rose leaves, when the rose is dead,
Are heaped for the beloved's bed;
And so thy thoughts, when thou art gone,
Love itself shall slumber on.
To——. Music, When Soft Voices

2 I fear thy kisses, gentle maiden,
Thou needest not fear mine;
My spirit is too deeply laden
Ever to burthen thine.

I fear thy mien, thy tones, thy motion,
Thou needest not fear mine;
Innocent is the heart's devotion
With which I worship thine.
To——. I Fear thy Kisses

3 One word is too often profaned
For me to profane it,
One feeling too falsely disdained
For thee to disdain it.
To——. One Word is too often Profaned

4 The desire of the moth for the star,
Of the night for the morrow,
The devotion to something afar
From the sphere of our sorrow. *Ib.*

5 And like a dying lady, lean and pale,
Who totters forth, wrapped in a gauzy veil.
The Waning Moon

6 A lovely lady, garmented in light
From her own beauty. *The Witch of Atlas, v*

7 For she was beautiful—her beauty made
The bright world dim, and everything beside
Seemed like the fleeting image of a shade. *Ib.* xii

8   The rapid, blind
And fleeting generations of mankind. *Ib.* lxxi

9 In honoured poverty thy voice did weave
Songs consecrate to truth and liberty,—
Deserting these, thou leavest me to grieve,
Thus having been, that thou shouldst cease to be.
To Wordsworth

10 Poets are the unacknowledged legislators of the world.
A Defence of Poetry

11 The rich have become richer, and the poor have
become poorer; and the vessel of the state is driven
between the Scylla and Charybdis of anarchy and
despotism. *Ib.*

12 Poetry is the record of the best and happiest moments
of the happiest and best minds. *Ib.*

WILLIAM SHENSTONE
1714–1763

13 Whoe'er has travell'd life's dull round,
Where'er his stages may have been,
May sigh to think he still has found
The warmest welcome, at an inn.
At an Inn at Henley

14 My banks they are furnish'd with bees,
Whose murmur invites one to sleep;
My grottoes are shaded with trees,
And my hills are white over with sheep.
A Pastoral Ballad. Pt. II, *Hope,* i

15 I have found out a gift for my fair;
I have found where the wood-pigeons breed;
But let me that plunder forbear,
She will say 'twas a barbarous deed.
A Pastoral Ballad. Pt. II, *Hope,* v

16 A little bench of heedless bishops here,
And there a chancellor in embryo,
Or bard sublime, if bard may e'er be so.
The Schoolmistress, xxviii

17 I loved him for nothing so much as his f-p-n-p-fication of money. *Letters.* xxii. *1777*

18 Laws are generally found to be nets of such a texture,
as the little creep through, the great break through,
and the middle-sized are alone entangled in.
Essays on Men and Manners. On Politics

19 A fool and his words are soon parted; a man of genius
and his money. *Ib. On Reserve*

ROBERT LOWE, VISCOUNT SHERBROOKE
1811–1892

20 I believe it will be absolutely necessary that you
should prevail on our future masters to learn their
letters.
*Speech in House of Commons (on the passing of
the Reform Bill), 15 July 1867. Popularized as
'We must educate our masters'*

PHILIP HENRY SHERIDAN
1831–1888

21 The only good Indian is a dead Indian.
Attr., at Fort Cobb, Jan. 1869

RICHARD BRINSLEY SHERIDAN
1751–1816

22 Not a translation—only *taken from the French.*
The Critic, I.

23 Steal! to be sure they may; and egad, serve your best
thoughts as gypsies do stolen children,—disfigure
them to make them pass for their own. *Ib.*

24 The newspapers! Sir, they are the most villainous—
licentious—abominable—infernal—Not that I ever
read them—no—I make it a rule never to look
into a newspaper. *Ib.*

25 If it is abuse—why one is always sure to hear of it
from one damned good-natured friend or other! *Ib.*

26 Egad, I think the interpreter is the hardest to be
understood of the two! *Ib.* ii

27 Yes, sir, puffing is of various sorts; the principal are,
the puff direct, the puff preliminary, the puff collateral, the puff collusive, and the puff oblique, or
puff by implication. *Ib.*

28 No scandal about Queen Elizabeth, I hope? *Ib.* II. i

29 I open with a clock striking, to beget an awful
attention in the audience: it also marks the time,
which is four o'clock in the morning, and saves a
description of the rising sun, and a great deal
about gilding the eastern hemisphere. *Ib.* II

30 Where they do agree on the stage, their unanimity is
wonderful! *Ib.*

31 Inconsolable to the minuet in Ariadne! *Ib.*

1 The Spanish fleet thou canst not see because—
It is not yet in sight!   *The Critic*, II. ii

2 All that can be said is, that two people happened to
hit on the same thought—and Shakespeare made
use of it first, that's all.   *Ib.* III. i

3 *Burleigh comes forward, shakes his head, and exit.*
SNEER: He is very perfect indeed. Now pray, what
did he mean by that?

. . . .

PUFF: Why, by that shake of the head, he gave you to
understand that even though they had more justice
in their cause and wisdom in their measures, yet,
if there was not a greater spirit shown on the part
of the people, the country would at last fall a sacrifice to the hostile ambition of the Spanish
monarchy.
SNEER: The devil!—did he mean all that by shaking
his head?
PUFF: Every word of it. If he shook his head as I
taught him.   *Ib.*

4 WHISKERANDOS: And Whiskerandos quits this bust-
ling scene
For all eter——
BEEFEATER: —nity—he would have added, but stern
death
Cut short his being, and the noun at once!   *Ib.*

5 I wish sir, you would practise this without me.
I can't stay dying here all night.   *Ib.*

6 O Lord, sir, when a heroine goes mad she always goes
into white satin.   *Ib.*

7 An oyster may be crossed in love.   *Ib.*

8 I ne'er could any lustre see
In eyes that would not look on me.
The Duenna, I. ii. Air

9 I loved him for himself alone.   *Ib.* iii

10 Had I a heart for falsehood framed,
I ne'er could injure you.   *Ib.* v

11 I was struck all of a heap.   *Ib.* II. ii

12 Conscience has no more to do with gallantry than it
has with politics.   *Ib.* iv

13 The throne *we* honour is the *people's choice.*
Pizarro, II. i

14 Illiterate him, I say, quite from your memory.
The Rivals, I. ii

15 'Tis safest in matrimony to begin with a little aversion.
Ib.

16 Madam, a circulating library in a town is as an ever-
green tree of diabolical knowledge! It blossoms
through the year! And depend on it, Mrs. Mala-
prop, that they who are so fond of handling the
leaves, will long for the fruit at last.   *Ib.*

17 You gentlemen's gentlemen are so hasty.   *Ib.* II. ii

18 He is the very pine-apple of politeness!   *Ib.* III. iii

19 An aspersion upon my parts of speech!   *Ib.*

20 If I reprehend any thing in this world, it is the use
of my oracular tongue, and a nice derangement of
epitaphs!   *Ib.*

21 She's as headstrong as an allegory on the banks of the
Nile.   *Ib.*

22 Too civil by half.   *Ib.* iv

23 Our ancestors are very good kind of folks; but they
are the last people I should choose to have a
visiting acquaintance with.   *The Rivals*, IV. i

24 No caparisons, miss, if you please. Caparisons don't
become a young woman.   *Ib.* ii

25 You are not like Cerberus, three gentlemen at once,
are you?   *Ib.*

26 The quarrel is a very pretty quarrel as it stands; we
should only spoil it by trying to explain it. *Ib.* iii

27 Very pretty small-sword light.   *Ib.*

28 There's nothing like being used to a thing. *Ib.* v. iii

29 My valour is certainly going!—it is sneaking off! I
feel it oozing out as it were at the palms of my
hands!   *Ib.*

30 I own the soft impeachment.   *Ib.*

31 Thro' all the drama—whether damned or not—
Love gilds the scene, and women guide the plot.
Ib. Epilogue

32 Tale-bearers are as bad as the tale-makers.
The School for Scandal, I. i

33 You shall see them on a beautiful quarto page, where
a neat rivulet of text shall meander through a
meadow of margin.   *Ib.*

34 You had no taste when you married me.   *Ib.* ii

35 MRS. CANDOUR:
I'll swear her colour is natural: I have seen it come
and go.
LADY TEAZLE:
I dare swear you have ma'am: it goes off at night,
and comes again in the morning.   *Ib.* II. ii

36 Here is the whole set! a character dead at every word.
Ib.

37 I'm called away by particular business. But I leave
my character behind me.   *Ib.*

38 Oh! plague of his sentiments!   *Ib.* iii

39 Here's to the maiden of bashful fifteen;
Here's to the widow of fifty;
Here's to the flaunting, extravagant quean;
And here's to the housewife that's thrifty.
Let the toast pass,—
Drink to the lass,
I'll warrant she'll prove an excuse for the glass.
Ib. III. iii. Song

40 Here's to the charmer whose dimples we prize;
Now to the maid who has none, sir;
Here's to the girl with a pair of blue eyes,
And here's to the nymph with but one, sir.   *Ib.*

41 Damned disinheriting countenance.   *Ib.* IV. i

42 CHARLES SURFACE:
Lady Teazle, by all that's wonderful!
SIR PETER TEAZLE:
Lady Teazle, by all that's damnable!   *Ib.* iii

43 It was an amiable weakness.   *Ib.* v. i

44 ROWLEY:
I believe there is no sentiment he has such faith in
as that 'charity begins at home'.
SIR OLIVER SURFACE:
And his, I presume, is of that domestic sort which
never stirs abroad at all.   *Ib.*

45 There is no trusting appearances.   *Ib.* ii

1 The Right Honourable gentleman is indebted to his memory for his jests, and to his imagination for his facts.
Speech in Reply to Mr. Dundas. T. Moore, *Life of Sheridan* (1825), II. 471

2 You write with ease, to show your breeding,
But easy writing's vile hard reading.
Clio's Protest. See Moore's *Life of Sheridan*, I. 55

3 Won't you come into the garden? I would like my roses to see you.
To a young lady. Attrib. in *The Perfect Hostess*

WILLIAM TECUMSEH SHERMAN
1820–1891

4 There is many a boy here to-day who looks on war as all glory, but, boys, it is all hell.
Speech, Columbus, Ohio, 11 Aug. 1880. Lewis's *Sherman, Fighting Prophet*

JAMES SHIRLEY
1596–1666

5 The glories of our blood and state
Are shadows, not substantial things;
There is no armour against fate;
Death lays his icy hand on kings:
Sceptre and crown
Must tumble down,
And in the dust be equal made
With the poor crooked scythe and spade.
The Contention of Ajax and Ulysses, I. iii

6 Only the actions of the just
Smell sweet, and blossom in their dust. *Ib.*

7 I presume you're mortal, and may err.
The Lady of Pleasure, II. ii

8 How little room
Do we take up in death, that, living know
No bounds? *The Wedding*, IV. iv

THE SHORTER CATECHISM

9 'What is the chief end of man?'
'To glorify God and to enjoy him for ever.'

JOSEPH HENRY SHORTHOUSE
1834–1903

10 'The Church of England,' I said, seeing that Mr. Inglesant paused, 'is no doubt a compromise.'
John Inglesant (1880), ch. 40

11 In all probability 'Wordsworth's standard of intoxication was miserably low'.
Remark to some Wordsworthians who were deploring W.'s confession that he got drunk at Cambridge. G. W. E. Russell's *Collections and Recollections*, ch. 8

HENRY SIDGWICK
1838–1900

12 We think so because other people all think so,
Or because—or because—after all we do think so,
Or because we were told so, and think we must think so,

Or because we once thought so, and think we still think so,
Or because having thought so, we think we *will* think so.
Memoir (1906), end of ch. II

ALGERNON SIDNEY
1622–1683

13 Liars ought to have good memories.
Discourses on Government, ch. 2, § xv

14 Men lived like fishes; the great ones devour'd the small. *Ib.* § xviii

15 'Tis not necessary to light a candle to the sun.
Ib. § xxiii

SIR PHILIP SIDNEY
1554–1586

16 High erected thoughts seated in the heart of courtesy.
The Arcadia, bk. i, ch. 2

17 Shallow brooks murmur most, deep silent slide away.
Ib. First Eclogues, Lalus and Dorus, st. ii

18 Who shoots at the mid-day sun, though he be sure he shall never hit the mark; yet as sure he is he shall shoot higher than who aims but at a bush.
Ib. bk. ii, ch. 6

19 My true love hath my heart and I have his,
By just exchange one for the other giv'n;
I hold his dear, and mine he cannot miss,
There never was a better bargain driv'n.
Ib. bk. iii, *ad fin.*

20 Doubt you to whom my Muse these notes intendeth,
Which now my breast o'ercharged to music lendeth?
To you, to you, all song of praise is due;
Only in you my song begins and endeth.
Astrophel and Stella, Song I: Doubt You to Whom

21 Have I caught my heav'nly jewel.
Ib. Song II: Have I Caught

22 Thy fair hair my heart enchained.
Ib. Certain Sonnets, To the tune of a Neapolitan Villanelle

23 'Fool!' said my Muse, to me, 'look in thy heart, and write.' *Ib. Sonnet I*

24 With how sad steps, O Moon, thou climb'st the skies!
How silently, and with how wan a face!
What! may it be that even in heavenly place
That busy archer his sharp arrows tries?
Ib. Sonnet XXXI

25 Do they call virtue there ungratefulness? *Ib.*

26 Come, Sleep! O Sleep, the certain knot of peace,
The baiting-place of wit, the balm of woe,
The poor man's wealth, the prisoner's release,
Th' indifferent judge between the high and low.
Ib. Sonnet XXXIX

27 Take thou of me smooth pillows, sweetest bed,
A chamber deaf to noise and blind to light,
A rosy garland and a weary head. *Ib.*

28 That sweet enemy, France. *Ib. Sonnet XLI*

29 They love indeed who quake to say they love.
Ib. Sonnet LIV

1 Oh heav'nly fool, thy most kiss-worthy face
Anger invests with such a lovely grace,
That Anger's self I needs must kiss again.
Astrophel and Stella, Sonnet LXXIII

2 I never drank of Aganippe well,
Nor ever did in shade of Tempe sit,
And Muses scorn with vulgar brains to dwell;
Poor layman I, for sacred rites unfit.
Ib. Sonnet LXXIV

3 Highway, since you my chief Parnassus be,
And that my Muse, to some ears not unsweet,
Tempers her words to trampling horses' feet
More oft than to a chamber melody,
Now blessed you, bear onward blessed me
To her, where I my heart, safe-left, shall meet.
Ib. Sonnet LXXXIV

4 Hundreds of years you Stella's feet may kiss. *Ib.*

5 Leave me, O Love, which reacheth but to dust;
And thou, my mind, aspire to higher things;
Grow rich in that which never taketh rust;
Whatever fades, but fading pleasure brings.
Ib. Sonnet CX: Splendidis Longum Valedico Nugis

6 Never love was so abused.
Pansies from Penshurst and Wilton. V. Love

7 O fair! O sweet! When I do look on thee,
In whom all joys so well agree,
Heart and soul do sing in me,
Just accord all music makes.
Ib. VIII. Verses, To the Tune of a Spanish Song

8 With a tale forsooth he cometh unto you, with a tale which holdeth children from play, and old men from the chimney corner.
The Defence of Poesy (1595)

9 Certainly I must confess mine own barbarousness, I never heard the old song of Percy and Douglas, that I found not my heart moved more than with a trumpet. *Ib. p. 24*

10 Philip of Macedon reckoned a horse-race won at Olympus among his three fearful felicities. *Ib.*

11 To be rhymed to death as is said to be done in Ireland. *Ib.*

12 Thy necessity is yet greater than mine.
On giving his water-bottle to a dying soldier on the battle-field of Zutphen, 1586. Sir Fulke Greville's *Life* (1907), ch. 12. *The word 'necessity' is more often quoted as 'need'*

EMMANUEL JOSEPH SIEYÈS
1748–1836

13 La mort, sans phrases.
Death, without phrases.
Attributed to Sieyès on voting in the French Convention for the death of Louis XVI, 19 Jan. 1793. Afterwards repudiated by him

SIMONIDES
556–468 B.C.

14 ὦ ξεῖν', ἀγγειλον Λακεδαιμονίοις ὅτι τῆδε
κείμεθα, τοῖς κείνων ῥήμασι πειθόμενοι.
Go, tell the Spartans, thou who passest by,
That here obedient to their laws we lie.
Select Epigrams (ed. Mackail), iii. 4

GEORGE R. SIMS (1847–1922)

15 It is Christmas Day in the workhouse.
The Dagonet Ballads

SIR OSBERT SITWELL (1892–

16 The British Bourgeoisie
Is not born,
And does not die,
But, if it is ill,
It has a frightened look in its eyes.
At the House of Mrs. Kinfoot

JOHN SKELTON
1460?–1529

17 As patient and as still
And as full of goodwill,
As the fair Isyphill,
Coliander,
Sweet pomander,
Good Cassander;
Steadfast of thought,
Well made, well wrought,
Far may be sought
Erst ye can find
So courteous, so kind,
As Merry Margaret, the midsummer flower,
Gentle as falcon or hawk of the tower.
To Mistress Margaret Hussey

18 With solace and gladness,
Much mirth and no madness,
All good and no badness;
So joyously,
So maidenly,
So womanly,
Her demeaning. *Ib.*

19 She is the violet,
The daisy delectable,
The columbine commendable,
The jelofer amiable;
For this most goodly flower,
This blossom of fresh colour,
So Jupiter me succour,
She flourisheth new and new
In beauty and virtue.
The Commendations of Mistress Jane Scrope

20 For the soul of Philip Sparrow,
That was late slain at Carrow
Among the Nunnes Black,
For that sweet soul's sake
And for all sparrows' souls
Set in our bead-rolls,
Pater noster qui
With an *Ave Mari*. *The Sparrow's Dirge*

21 The Tunning of Elynour Rumming.
Title of poem

JOHN SKINNER
1721–1807

22 Let Whig and Tory a' agree,
Whig and Tory, Whig and Tory,
Whig and Tory a' agree,
To drop their Whigmigmorum;

Let Whig and Tory a' agree
To spend the night in mirth and glee,
And cheerfu' sing alang wi' me
The reel o' Tullochgorum.

Tullochgorum, st. i. *The Songs of Scotland*, ed.
G. F. Graham. *A version of 1776 gives line 4 as*
'To drop their whipmegorum'

ADAM SKIRVING
1719–1803

1 Hey, Johnnie Cope, are ye wauking yet?
Or are your drums a-beating yet?

CHRISTOPHER SMART
1722–1771

2 He sung of God—the mighty source
Of all things—the stupendous force
    On which all strength depends;
From whose right arm, beneath whose eyes,
All period, pow'r, and enterprize
    Commences, reigns, and ends.

Song to David, st. 18

3 Tell them I am, Jehova said
To Moses; while earth heard in dread,
    And smitten to the heart,
At once above, beneath, around,
All nature, without voice or sound,
    Replied, O Lord, Thou art.   *Ib.* st. 40

4 For Adoration all the ranks
Of angels yield eternal thanks,
    And David in the midst.   *Ib.* st. 51

5 Strong is the horse upon his speed;
Strong in pursuit the rapid glede,
    Which makes at once his game:
Strong the tall ostrich on the ground;
Strong thro' the turbulent profound
    Shoots xiphias to his aim.

Strong is the lion—like a coal
His eye-ball—like a bastion's mole
    His chest against his foes:
Strong, the gier-eagle on his sail,
Strong against tide, th' enormous whale
    Emerges as he goes.

Where ask is have, where seek is find,
    Where knock is open wide.   *Ib.* st. 75–77

6 Glorious the sun in mid-career;
Glorious th' assembled fires appear;
    Glorious the comet's train:
Glorious the trumpet and alarm;
Glorious th' almighty stretch'd-out arm;
    Glorious th' enraptur'd main.

Glorious the northern lights astream;
Glorious the song, when God's the theme;
    Glorious the thunder's roar:
Glorious hosanna from the den;
Glorious the catholic amen;
    Glorious the martyr's gore.

Glorious—more glorious is the crown
Of Him that brought salvation down
    By meekness, call'd thy Son;
Thou that stupendous truth believ'd,
And now the matchless deed's achiev'd,
    Determined, dared, and done.   *Ib.* st. 84–86

FRANCIS EDWARD SMEDLEY
1818–1864

7 You are looking as fresh as paint.
Frank Fairlegh, ch. 41

SAMUEL SMILES
1812–1904

8 A place for everything, and everything in its place.
Thrift, ch. 5

9 Cecil's despatch of business was extraordinary, his maxim being, 'The shortest way to do many things is to do only one thing at once.'   *Self-Help*, ch. 9

10 His [Dr. Priestley's] appointment [to act as astronomer to Captain Cook's expedition to the southern seas] had been cancelled, as the Board of Longitude objected to his theology.
Men of Invention and Industry, ch. 3

ADAM SMITH
1723–1790

11 To found a great empire for the sole purpose of raising up a people of customers, may at first sight appear a project fit only for a nation of shopkeepers. It is, however, a project altogether unfit for a nation of shopkeepers; but extremely fit for a nation that is governed by shopkeepers.
Wealth of Nations, vol. II, bk. iv, ch. 7, pt. iii.
(*See 1:6, 360:22*)

ALEXANDER SMITH
1830–1867

12 Like a pale martyr in his shirt of fire.
A Life of Drama, ii

13 In winter, when the dismal rain
Came down in slanting lines,
And Wind, that grand old harper, smote
His thunder-harp of pines.   *Ib.*

ALFRED EMANUEL SMITH
1873–1944

14 Nothing doing. That's just boloney. Everybody knows I can't lay bricks.
Remark at the laying of the corner-stone of the New York State Office Building

ERNEST BRAMAH SMITH
1868–1942

15 It is a mark of insincerity of purpose to spend one's time in looking for the sacred Emperor in the low-class tea-shops.
The Wallet of Kai Lung. Transmutation of Ling

16 An expression of no-encouragement.
Ib. Confession of Kai Lung

17 The whole narrative is permeated with the odour of joss-sticks and honourable high-mindedness.
Ib. Kin Yen

18 However entrancing it is to wander unchecked through a garden of bright images, are we not enticing your mind from another subject of almost equal importance?
Kai Lung's Golden Hours. Story of Hien

SMITH

FREDERICK EDWIN SMITH, EARL OF BIRKENHEAD

see

BIRKENHEAD

JAMES SMITH
1775–1839

and

'HORACE' [HORATIO] SMITH
1779–1849

1 And hast thou walk'd about (how strange a story!)
In Thebes's streets three thousand years ago,
When the Memnonium was in all its glory.
Address to a Mummy

2 In Craven-street, Strand, ten attorneys find place,
And ten dark coal-barges are moor'd at its base.
Fly, Honesty, fly! seek some safer retreat;
For there's craft in the river, and craft in the street.
Craven Street, Strand

3 And when that donkey look'd me in the face,
His face was sad! and you are sad, my Public!
Playhouse Musings, l. 4

4 Hail, glorious edifice, stupendous work!
God bless the Regent and the Duke of York!
Rejected Addresses. No. 1. *Loyal Effusion*, l. 1

5 Who makes the quartern loaf and Luddites rise?
Who fills the butchers' shops with large blue flies?
Ib. l. 48

6 I saw them go: one horse was blind,
The tails of both hung down behind,
Their shoes were on their feet.
Ib. No. 2. *The Baby's Début*, vi. (Parody of Wordsworth)

7 What stately vision mocks my waking sense?
Hence, dear delusion, sweet enchantment, hence!
Ib. No. 3. *An Address Without a Phoenix*

8 I am a blessed Glendoveer:
'Tis mine to speak, and yours to hear.
Ib. No. 7. *The Rebuilding*

9 Thinking is but an idle waste of thought,
And nought is every thing, and every thing is nought.
Ib. No. 8. *Cui bono?*

10 'Why are you in such doleful dumps?
A fireman, and afraid of bumps!—
What are they fear'd on? fools! 'od rot 'em!'
Were the last words of Higginbottom.
Ib. No. 9. *Drury Lane.* (Parody of Scott)

11 In the name of the Prophet—figs!
Ib. No. 10. *Johnson's Ghost*

12 John Richard William Alexander Dwyer
Was footman to Justinian Stubbs, Esquire.
The Theatre. (Parody of Crabbe)

LANGDON SMITH
1858–1918

13 When you were a tadpole, and I was a fish,
In the Palaeozoic time,
And side by side in the ebbing tide
We sprawled through the ooze and slime.
A Toast to a Lady. (*The Scrap-Book*, April 1906)

LOGAN PEARSALL SMITH
1865–1946

14 There are two things to aim at in life: first, to get what you want; and, after that, to enjoy it. Only the wisest of mankind achieve the second.
Afterthoughts (1931), p. 4

15 There are few sorrows, however poignant, in which a good income is of no avail.
Ib. p. 12

16 People say that life is the thing, but I prefer reading.
Ib. p. 71

17 The old know what they want; the young are sad and bewildered.
All Trivia, Last Words

18 Thank heavens, the sun has gone in, and I don't have to go out and enjoy it.
Ib.

SAMUEL FRANCIS SMITH
1808–1895

19 My country, 'tis of thee,
Sweet land of liberty,
    Of thee I sing:
Land where my fathers died,
Land of the pilgrims' pride,
From every mountain-side
    Let freedom ring.
America

REV. SYDNEY SMITH
1771–1845

20 It requires a surgical operation to get a joke well into a Scotch understanding. Their only idea of wit . . . is laughing immoderately at stated intervals.
Lady Holland, *Memoir* (1st ed. 1855), vol. 1, ch. 2, p. 15.

21 I heard him [Jeffrey] speak disrespectfully of the Equator!
Ib. p. 17

22 That knuckle-end of England—that land of Calvin, oat-cakes, and sulphur.
Ib.

23 Take short views, hope for the best, and trust in God.
Ib. ch. 6, p. 48

24 Looked as if she had walked straight out of the Ark.
Ib. ch. 7, p. 157

25 No furniture so charming as books. *Ib.* ch. 9, p. 240

26 Madam, I have been looking for a person who disliked gravy all my life; let us swear eternal friendship.
Ib. p. 257

27 How can a bishop marry? How can he flirt? The most he can say is, 'I will see you in the vestry after service.'
Ib. p. 258

28 Not body enough to cover his mind decently with; his intellect is improperly exposed.
Ib.

29 I have, alas, only one illusion left, and that is the Archbishop of Canterbury.
Ib. p. 259

30 You find people ready enough to do the Samaritan, without the oil and twopence.
Ib. p. 261

31 As the French say, there are three sexes—men, women, and clergymen.
Ib. p. 262

32 Praise is the best diet for us, after all. *Ib.* p. 265

33 Daniel Webster struck me much like a steam-engine in trousers.
Ib. p. 267

1 He [Macaulay] is like a book in breeches.
  Lady Holland, *Memoir*, vol. 1, ch. 11, p. 363

2 He [Macaulay] has occasional flashes of silence, that make his conversation perfectly delightful. *Ib.*

3 Let onion atoms lurk within the bowl,
  And, scarce-suspected, animate the whole.
  Recipe for Salad, Ib. p. 373

4 Serenely full, the epicure would say,
  Fate cannot harm me, I have dined to-day. *Ib.*

5 You remember Thurlow's answer . . . you never expected justice from a company, did you? They have neither a soul to lose, nor a body to kick.
  Ib. p. 376. *See* 547: 15 *and* Corrigenda

6 Deserves to be preached to death by wild curates.
  Ib. p. 384

7 I never read a book before reviewing it; it prejudices a man so.
  H. Pearson, *The Smith of Smiths* (1934), ch. iii, p. 54

8 It is a place with only one post a day. . . . In the country I always fear that creation will expire before tea-time. *Ib.* ch. 5, p. 92

9 Minorities . . . are almost always in the right.
  Ib. ch. 9, p. 220

10 ——'s idea of heaven is, eating *pâtés de foie gras* to the sound of trumpets. *Ib.* ch. 10, p. 236

11 What a pity it is that we have no amusements in England but vice and religion! *Ib.*

12 Let the Dean and Canons lay their heads together and the thing will be done. *It being proposed to surround St. Paul's with a wooden pavement* *Ib.* p. 237

13 Death must be distinguished from dying, with which it is often confused. *Ib.* ch. 11, p. 271

14 The only way to deal with such a man as O'Connell is to hang him up and erect a statue to him under the gallows. *Ib.* p. 272

15 What two ideas are more inseparable than Beer and Britannia? *Ib.*

16 I am just going to pray for you at St. Paul's, but with no very lively hope of success.
  Ib. ch. 13, p. 308

17 Poverty is no disgrace to a man, but it is confoundedly inconvenient. *His Wit and Wisdom* (1900), p. 89

18 One of the greatest pleasures of life is conversation.
  Essays (1877). *Female Education*, p. 103

19 This great spectacle of human happiness.
  Ib. Waterton's Wanderings, p. 465

20 The moment the very name of Ireland is mentioned, the English seem to bid adieu to common feeling, common prudence, and common sense, and to act with the barbarity of tyrants, and the fatuity of idiots. *Peter Plymley's Letters* (1929), p. 9

21 A Curate—there is something which excites compassion in the very name of a Curate!!!
  Ib. p. 127. *Persecuting Bishops*

22 Dame Partington . . . was seen . . . with mop and pattens . . . vigorously pushing away the Atlantic Ocean. The Atlantic Ocean beat Mrs. Partington.
  Ib. p. 228

23 Bishop Berkeley destroyed this world in one volume octavo; and nothing remained, after his time, but mind; which experienced a similar fate from the hand of Mr. Hume in 1739.
  Sketches of Moral Philosophy. Introd.

24 We shall generally find that the triangular person has got into the square hole, the oblong into the triangular, and a square person has squeezed himself into the round hole. The officer and the office, the doer and the thing done, seldom fit so exactly that we can say they were almost made for each other. *Ib.* Lect. ix

25 I never could find any man who could think for two minutes together. *Ib.* Lect. xix

26 The motto I proposed for the [*Edinburgh*] *Review* was: *Tenui musam meditamur avena*—'We cultivate literature upon a little oatmeal.'
  Works (1859), vol. i, Preface, p. v

27 We can inform Jonathan what are the inevitable consequences of being too fond of glory;—Taxes upon every article which enters into the mouth, or covers the back, or is placed under the foot . . . taxes on everything on earth, and the waters under the earth.
  Ib. vol. i. *Review of Seybert's Statistical Annals of the United States*, p. 291

28 The schoolboy whips his taxed top—the beardless youth manages his taxed horse, with a taxed bridle, on a taxed road;—and the dying Englishman, pouring his medicine, which has paid seven per cent., into a spoon that has paid fifteen per cent.—flings himself back upon his chintz bed, which has paid twenty-two per cent.—and expires in the arms of an apothecary who has paid a licence of a hundred pounds for the privilege of putting him to death. *Ib.*

29 What bishops like best in their clergy is a dropping-down-deadness of manner.
  Ib. vol. ii, *First Letter to Archdeacon Singleton*, p. 271. *Note*

30 I like, my dear Lord, the road you are travelling, but I don't like the pace you are driving; too similar to that of the son of Nimshi. I always feel myself inclined to cry out, Gently, John, gently down hill. Put on the drag.
  Ib. vol. ii, *Letter to Lord John Russell*, p. 300

31 I look upon Switzerland as an inferior sort of Scotland.
  Letters. Lady Holland, *Memoir*, vol. ii. *To Lord Holland, 1815*

32 Tory and Whig in turns shall be my host,
  I taste no politics in boil'd and roast.
  Ib. To John Murray. Nov. 1834

33 What would life be without arithmetic, but a scene of horrors? *Ib. To Miss ——, 22 July 1835*

34 I am convinced digestion is the great secret of life.
  Ib. To Arthur Kinglake, 30 Sept. 1837

35 I have no relish for the country; it is a kind of healthy grave. *Ib. To Miss G. Harcourt, 1838*

36 I have seen nobody since I saw you, but persons in orders. My only varieties are vicars, rectors, curates, and every now and then (by way of turbot) an archdeacon. *Ib. To Miss Berry, 28 Jan. 1843*

1 One very hot evening in summer, Lady Holland and a large party of friends were suffering from the stifling atmosphere, and a general dulness had crept over the company. Then Milnes was seen to enter. 'Ah! here comes the cool of the evening,' cried Sydney Smith, and immediately everybody grew brighter. [Milnes resented this and other nicknames, and Sydney Smith wrote to him: 'The names of "Cool of the evening", "London Assurance", and "In-I-go Jones", are, I give you my word, not mine.']
T. Wemyss Reid, Life of Lord Houghton (1890), vol. i, p. 213

2 [William Whewell.] Science is his forte, and omniscience his foible.
In Isaac Todhunter, William Whewell (1876), i. 410

TOBIAS GEORGE SMOLLETT
1721–1771

3 Mourn, hapless Caledonia, mourn
Thy banish'd peace, thy laurels torn!
The Tears of Scotland

4 I think for my part one half of the nation is mad—and the other not very sound.
The Adventures of Sir Launcelot Greaves, ch. 6

5 He was formed for the ruin of our sex.
Roderick Random, ch. 22

6 That great Cham of literature, Samuel Johnson.
Letter to John Wilkes, 16 Mar. 1759. Boswell's *Johnson* (1934), vol. i, p. 348

GEORGE HUNT SMYTTAN
1822–1870
and
FRANCIS POTT
1832–1909

7 Forty days and forty nights
Thou wast fasting in the wild,
Forty days and forty nights
Tempted, and yet undefiled.
Hymn: Forty Days and Forty Nights. The Penny Post, 1856

8 Prowling beasts about Thy way;
Stones Thy pillow, earth Thy bed.
Ib.

SOCRATES
469–399 B.C.

9 ἀλλὰ γὰρ ἤδη ὥρα ἀπιέναι, ἐμοὶ μὲν ἀποθανουμένῳ, ὑμῖν δὲ βιωσομένοις. ὁπότεροι δὲ ἡμῶν ἔρχονται ἐπὶ ἄμεινον πρᾶγμα ἄδηλον παντὶ πλὴν ἢ τῷ θεῷ.
The hour of departure has arrived, and we go our ways—I to die, and you to live. Which is the better, God only knows.
Plato, Apologia, Last words

10 ὦ Κρίτων, τῷ Ἀσκληπιῷ ὀφείλομεν ἀλεκτρυόνα. ἀλλὰ ἀπόδοτε καὶ μὴ ἀμελήσητε.
Crito, we owe a cock to Aesculapius; pay it, therefore, and do not neglect it.
Last words, 399 B.C. Plato, *Phaedo,* 118a

SOLON
c. 640–c. 558 B.C.

11 γηράσκω δ' αἰεὶ πολλὰ διδασκόμενος.
I grow old ever learning many things.
Poetae Lyrici Graeci (ed. Bergk), Solon, 18

12 πρὶν δ' ἂν τελευτήσῃ, ἐπισχεῖν μηδὲ καλέειν κω ὄλβιον, ἀλλ' εὐτυχέα.
Call no man happy till he dies, he is at best but fortunate.
Herodotus, *Histories,* i. 32

WILLIAM SOMERVILLE
1675–1742

13 My hoarse-sounding horn
Invites thee to the chase, the sport of kings;
Image of war, without its guilt.
The Chase, bk. i, l. 13

14 Hail, happy Britain! highly favoured isle,
And Heaven's peculiar care!
Ib. l. 84

15 If this pale rose offend your sight,
It in your bosom wear;
'Twill blush to find itself less white,
And turn Lancastrian there.
Presenting to a Lady a White Rose and a Red on the Tenth of June

SOPHOCLES
495–406 B.C.

16 πολλὰ τὰ δεινὰ κοὐδὲν ἀνθρώπου δεινότερον πέλει.
Wonders are many, and none is more wonderful than man.
Antigone, 332. Trans. by Jebb

17 ὦ παῖ, γένοιο πατρὸς εὐτυχέστερος.
Ah, boy, may'st thou prove happier than thy sire.
Ajax, 550. Trans. by Jebb

18 μὴ φῦναι τὸν ἅπαντα νικᾷ λόγον.
Not to be born is best.
Oedipus Coloneus, 1225

CHARLES HAMILTON SORLEY
1895–1915

19 We have the evil spirits too
That shake our soul with battle-din.
But we have an eviller spirit than you,
We have a dumb spirit within:
The exceeding bitter agony
But not the exceeding bitter cry.
To Poets

20 We swing ungirded hips,
And lightened are our eyes,
The rain is on our lips,
We do not run for prize.
Song of the Ungirt Runners

21 We run because we like it
Through the broad bright land.
Ib.

JOHN BABSONE LANE SOULE
1815–1891

22 Go west, young man.
Article in the Terre Haute, Indiana, Express (1851)

REV. ROBERT SOUTH
1634–1716

1 An Aristotle was but the rubbish of an Adam, and
  Athens but the rudiments of Paradise.
  Sermons, vol. I. ii

THOMAS SOUTHERNE
1660–1746

2   And when we're worn,
  Hack'd, hewn with constant service, thrown aside
  To rust in peace, or rot in hospitals.
  Loyal Brother, Act I

ROBERT SOUTHEY
1774–1843

3 It was a summer evening,
    Old Kaspar's work was done,
  And he before his cottage door
    Was sitting in the sun,
  And by him sported on the green
  His little grandchild Wilhelmine.
  The Battle of Blenheim

4 He came to ask what he had found,
  That was so large, and smooth, and round. *Ib.*

5 Now tell us all about the war,
  And what they fought each other for. *Ib.*

6 But what they fought each other for,
  I could not well make out. *Ib.*

7 But things like that, you know, must be
  At every famous victory. *Ib.*

8 Great praise the Duke of Marlbro' won,
  And our good Prince Eugene. *Ib.*

9 'And everybody praised the Duke,
    Who this great fight did win.'
  'But what good came of it at last?'
    Quoth little Peterkin.
  'Why that I cannot tell,' said he,
  'But 'twas a famous victory.' *Ib.*

10 My name is Death: the last best friend am I.
  *Carmen Nuptiale. The Lay of the Laureate. The
  Dream*, lxxxvii

11 How does the water
  Come down at Lodore? *The Cataract of Lodore*

12 And this way the water comes down at Lodore. *Ib.*

13 Curses are like young chickens, they always come
  home to roost. *The Curse of Kehama. Motto*

14   Water shall hear me,
  And know thee and fly thee. *Ib.* II. 14

15 And Sleep shall obey me,
    And visit thee never,
  And the Curse shall be on thee
    For ever and ever. *Ib.*

16 Hark! at the Golden Palaces
  The Brahmin strikes the hour. *Ib.* V. I

17 They sin who tell us love can die.
  With life all other passions fly,
    All others are but vanity. *Ib.* X. 10

18 Thou hast been call'd, O Sleep! the friend of Woe,
  But 'tis the happy who have called thee so.
  Ib. XV. 12

19 From his brimstone bed, at break of day
    A walking the Devil is gone,
  To look at his little snug farm of the World,
    And see how his stock went on.
  The Devil's Walk, i. (*See 151:7–12*)

20 His coat was red and his breeches were blue,
  And there was a hole where his tail came through.
  Ib. iii

21 He passed a cottage with a double coach-house,
    A cottage of gentility!
  And he owned with a grin
  That his favourite sin
    Is pride that apes humility. *Ib.* viii

22 As he passed through Cold Bath fields, he looked
    At a solitary cell;
  And he was well-pleased, for it gave him a hint
    For improving the prisons of Hell. *Ib.* xv

23 And all at once to the Bishop they go.
  God's Judgment on a Wicked Bishop

24 No stir in the air, no stir in the sea,
  The ship was still as she could be. *The Inchcape Rock*

25 And then they knew the perilous rock,
  And blest the Abbot of Aberbrothok. *Ib.*

26 O Christ! It is the Inchcape Rock! *Ib.*

27 Sir Ralph the Rover tore his hair;
  He curst himself in his despair. *Ib.*

28 Day after day, day after day the same—
    A weary waste of waters!
    Madoc: Pt. I, *Madoc in Wales.* IV, *The Voyage*,
  l. 32

29 Blue, darkly, deeply, beautifully blue.
  Ib. V, *Lincoya*, l. 102

30 We wage no war with women nor with priests.
  Ib. XV, *The Excommunication*, l. 65

31 What will not woman, gentle woman dare,
  When strong affection stirs her spirit up?
    Ib. Pt. II, *Madoc in Aztlan.* II, *The Tidings*,
  l. 125

32 Yet leaving here a name, I trust,
  That will not perish in the dust.
  My Days Among the Dead

33 You are old, Father William, the young man cried,
    The few locks which are left you are grey;
  You are hale, Father William, a hearty old man,
    Now tell me the reason, I pray.
  *The Old Man's Comforts, and how he Gained
  them*

34 You are old, Father William, the young man cried
    And pleasures with youth pass away,
  And yet you lament not the days that are gone,
    Now tell me the reason, I pray. *Ib.*

35 In the days of my youth I remembered my God!
    And He hath not forgotten my age. *Ib.*

36 The Monk my son, and my daughter the Nun.
  The Old Woman of Berkeley

37 Their wintry garment of unsullied snow
  The mountains have put on.
  The Poet's Pilgrimage. Pt. I, *The Journey.* II,
  Flanders, 23

1 He ran against a shooting star,
  So fast for fear did he sail,
  And he singed the beard of the Bishop
  Against a comet's tail;
  And he passed between the horns of the moon,
  With Antidius on his back;
  And there was an eclipse that night,
  Which was not in the Almanac.
  St. Antidius, the Pope and the Devil

2 How beautiful is night!
  A dewy freshness fills the silent air;
  No mist obscures, nor cloud, nor speck, nor stain,
  Breaks the serene of heaven.
  Thalaba the Destroyer, bk. I, i

3 A vague, a dizzy, a tumultuous joy. *Ib.* bk. III. xix

4 'I had a home once—I had once a husband—
  I am a widow, poor and broken-hearted!'
  Loud blew the wind, unheard was her complaining,
  On drove the chariot. *The Widow*, v

5 Stern to inflict and stubborn to endure,
  That laughed in death.
  Poetical address to the author. In Amos Cottle,
  Icelandic Poetry (1797)

6 The arts babblative and scribblative.
  *Colloquies on the Progress and Prospects of
  Society.* Coll. x. Pt. ii

7 The march of intellect. *Ib.* Coll. xiv

8 Your true lover of literature is never fastidious.
  The Doctor, ch. 17

9 Show me a man who cares no more for one place
  than another, and I will show you in that same
  person one who loves nothing but himself. Beware
  of those who are homeless by choice. *Ib.* ch. 34

10 Live as long as you may, the first twenty years are
  the longest half of your life. *Ib.* ch. 130

11 The death of Nelson was felt in England as something
  more than a public calamity; men started at the
  intelligence, and turned pale, as if they had heard
  of the loss of a dear friend.
  The Life of Nelson, ch. 9

12 The Satanic School. *The Vision of Judgment.* Preface

13 The pander of posterity. *Ib.*

ROBERT SOUTHWELL
1561?–1595

14 As I in hoary winter's night stood shivering in the
  snow,
  Surprised I was with sudden heat which made my
  heart to glow;
  And lifting up a fearful eye to view what fire was near,
  A pretty Babe all burning bright did in the air appear.
  The Burning Babe

15 'The fuel justice layeth on, and mercy blows the
  coals;
  The metal in this furnace wrought are men's defiled
  souls:
  For which, as now on fire I am to work them to their
  good,
  So will I melt into a bath to wash them in my blood.'
  With this he vanished out of sight and swiftly shrunk
  away,
  And straight I called unto mind that it was Christmas
  Day. *Ib.*

16 Come, Raphael, this Babe must eat,
  Provide our little Toby meat.
  New Heaven, New War

17 Behold, a silly tender Babe
  In freezing winter night
  In homely manger trembling lies,
  Alas, a piteous sight! *New Prince, New Pomp*

18 With joy approach, O Christian wight,
  Do homage to thy King;
  And highly praise his humble pomp,
  Which he from heaven doth bring. *Ib.*

19 Times go by turns, and chances change by course,
  From foul to fair, from better hap to worse.
  Times go by Turns

HERBERT SPENCER
1820–1903

20 Time: That which man is always trying to kill, but
  which ends in killing him. *Definitions*

21 Science is organized knowledge. *Education*, ch. 2

22 Absolute morality is the regulation of conduct in such
  a way that pain shall not be inflicted.
  Essays (1891), vol. iii, p. 152. *Prison Ethics*

23 The ultimate result of shielding men from the effects
  of folly, is to fill the world with fools.
  Ib. p. 354. *State Tamperings with Money and
  Banks*

24 The Republican form of Government is the highest
  form of government; but because of this it requires
  the highest type of human nature—a type nowhere
  at present existing. *Ib.* p. 478. *The Americans*

25 Evolution . . . is—a change from an indefinite, incoherent homogeneity, to a definite coherent heterogeneity. *First Principles*, ch. 16, § 138

26 This survival of the fittest.
  Principles of Biology, pt. iii, ch. 12, *Indirect
  Equilibration*, § 165

27 Progress, therefore, is not an accident, but a necessity.
  . . . It is a part of nature.
  Social Statics, pt. i, ch. 2, § 4

28 Education has for its object the formation of character. *Ib.* pt. ii, ch. 17, § 4

29 Opinion is ultimately determined by the feelings, and
  not by the intellect. *Ib.* pt. iv, ch. 30, § 8

30 No one can be perfectly free till all are free; no one
  can be perfectly moral till all are moral; no one
  can be perfectly happy till all are happy. *Ib.* 16

31 It was remarked to me by the late Mr. Charles
  Roupell . . . that to play billiards well was a sign of
  an ill-spent youth.
  Remark. Duncan, *Life and Letters of Spencer*
  (1908), ch. 20, p. 298

WILLIAM ROBERT SPENCER
1769–1834

32 In fancy's ear he oft would hear
  Poor Gêlert's dying yell. *Beth-Gêlert*, xxiii

STEPHEN SPENDER

1909-

1 I think continually of those who were truly great—
The names of those who in their lives fought for life,
Who wore at their hearts the fire's centre.
I Think Continually of Those

2 Born of the sun they travelled a short while towards
the sun,
And left the vivid air signed with their honour. *Ib.*

EDMUND SPENSER

1552?-1599

3 The merry cuckoo, messenger of Spring,
His trumpet shrill hath thrice already sounded.
Amoretti. Sonnet xix

4 Most glorious Lord of life, that on this day
Didst make thy triumph over death and sin:
And, having harrow'd hell, didst bring away
Captivity thence captive, us to win. *Ib. lxviii*

5 So let us love, dear Love, like as we ought,
—Love is the lesson which the Lord us taught. *Ib.*

6 Fresh spring the herald of love's mighty king,
In whose coat armour richly are display'd
All sorts of flowers the which on earth do spring
In goodly colours gloriously array'd. *Ib. lxx*

7 One day I wrote her name upon the strand,
But came the waves and washed it away:
Again I wrote it with a second hand,
But came the tide, and made my pains his prey.
Vain man, said she, that dost in vain assay,
A mortal thing so to immortalize,
For I myself shall like to this decay,
And eke my name be wiped out likewise.
Not so, quoth I, let baser things devise
To die in dust, but you shall live by fame:
My verse your virtues rare shall eternize,
And in the heavens write your glorious name,
Where when as death shall all the world subdue,
Our love shall live, and later life renew *Ib. lxxv*

8 Triton blowing loud his wreathed horn.
Colin Clout's Come Home Again, l. 245

9 The Shepherd of the Ocean (quoth he)
Unto that Goddess' grace me first enhanc'd,
And to mine oaten pipe inclin'd her ear. *Ib.* l. 358

10 So love is Lord of all the world by right. *Ib.* l. 883

11 The woods shall to me answer and my echo ring.
Epithalamion, l. 18

12 Open the temple gates unto my love,
Open them wide that she may enter in. *Ib.* l. 204

13 Behold whiles she before the altar stands
Hearing the holy priest that to her speaks
And blesseth her with his two happy hands.
Ib. l. 223

14 Ah! when will this long weary day have end,
And lend me leave to come unto my love? *Ib.* l. 278

15 Song made in lieu of many ornaments,
With which my love should duly have been deck'd.
Ib. l. 427

16 Fierce wars and faithful loves shall moralize my song.
The Faerie Queene, bk. I, introd. i. 1

17 A gentle knight was pricking on the plain. *Ib. c.* I. i

18 But on his breast a bloody cross he bore,
The dear remembrance of his dying Lord.
The Faerie Queene, bk. I. c. I. ii

19 But of his cheer did seem too solemn sad;
Yet nothing did he dread, but ever was ydrad. *Ib.*

20 A bold bad man. *Ib.* xxxvii

21 Her angel's face
As the great eye of heaven shined bright,
And made a sunshine in the shady place;
Did never mortal eye behold such heavenly grace.
Ib. c. III. vi

22 And all the hinder parts, that few could spy,
Were ruinous and old, but painted cunningly.
Ib. c. IV. v

23 The Noble heart, that harbours virtuous thought,
And is with child of glorious great intent,
Can never rest, until it forth have brought
Th' eternal brood of glory excellent. *Ib. c.* v. i

24 A cruel crafty Crocodile,
Which in false grief hiding his harmful guile,
Doth weep full sore, and sheddeth tender tears.
Ib. xviii

25 As when that devilish iron engine, wrought
In deepest hell, and fram'd by furies' skill,
With windy nitre and quick sulphur fraught,
And ramm'd with bullet round, ordain'd to kill,
Conceiveth fire. *Ib. c.* VII. xiii

26 Still as he fled, his eye was backward cast,
As if his fear still followed him behind. *Ib. c.* IX. xxi

27 That darksome cave they enter, where they find
That cursed man, low sitting on the ground,
Musing full sadly in his sullen mind. *Ib.* xxxv

28 Sleep after toil, port after stormy seas,
Ease after war, death after life does greatly please.
Ib. xl

29 Death is the end of woes: die soon, O fairy's son.
Ib. xlvii

30 So double was his pains, so double be his praise.
Ib. bk. II, c. II. xxv

31 Upon her eyelids many Graces sate,
Under the shadow of her even brows. *Ib. c.* III. xxv

32 And all for love, and nothing for reward.
Ib. c. VIII. ii

33 So passeth, in the passing of a day,
Of mortal life the leaf, the bud, the flower,
No more doth flourish after first decay,
That erst was sought to deck both bed and bower,
Of many a Lady, and many a Paramour:
Gather therefore the Rose, whilst yet is prime,
For soon comes age, that will her pride deflower:
Gather the Rose of love, whilst yet is time,
Whilst loving thou mayst loved be with equal crime.
Ib. c. XII. lxxv

34 Let Grill be Grill, and have his hoggish mind.
Ib. lxxxvii

35 O goodly usage of those antique times,
In which the sword was servant unto right;
When not for malice and contentious crimes,
But all for praise, and proof of manly might,
The martial brood accustomed to fight:
Then honour was the meed of victory,
And yet the vanquished had no despite.
Ib. bk. III, c. I. xiii

SPENSER

1 Divine tobacco. *The Faerie Queene*, bk. III, c. v. xxxii

2 Hard is to teach an old horse amble true.
Ib. c. VIII. xxvi

3 And painful pleasure turns to pleasing pain.
Ib. c. x. lx

4 And as she look'd about, she did behold,
How over that same door was likewise writ,
Be bold, be bold, and everywhere Be bold.

. . . . .

At last she spied at that room's upper end
Another iron door, on which was writ
Be not too bold.
Ib. c. XI. liv

5 Dan Chaucer, well of English undefiled,
On Fame's eternal beadroll worthy to be filed.
Ib. bk. IV, c. II. xxxii

6 For all that nature by her mother wit
Could frame in earth.
Ib. c. x. xxi

7 O sacred hunger of ambitious minds.
Ib. bk. V, c. XII. i

8 A monster, which the Blatant beast men call,
A dreadful fiend of gods and men ydrad. *Ib.* xxxvii

9 The gentle mind by gentle deeds is known.
For a man by nothing is so well bewray'd,
As by his manners.
Ib. bk. VI, c. III. i

10 What man that sees the ever-whirling wheel
Of Change, the which all mortal things doth sway,
But that thereby doth find, and plainly feel,
How Mutability in them doth play
Her cruel sports, to many men's decay?
Ib. bk. VII, c. VI. i

11 For all that moveth doth in Change delight:
But thenceforth all shall rest eternally
With Him that is the God of Sabbaoth hight:
O that great Sabbaoth God, grant me that Sabbaoth's
sight.
Ib. c. VIII. ii

12 That beauty is not, as fond men misdeem,
An outward show of things, that only seem.
An Hymn in Honour of Beauty, l. 90

13 For of the soul the body form doth take;
For soul is form, and doth the body make. *Ib.* l. 132

14 The hearts of men, which fondly here admire
Fair seeming shows, and feed on vain delight,
Transported with celestial desire
Of those fair forms, may lift themselves up higher,
And learn to love with zealous humble duty
Th' eternal fountain of that heavenly beauty.
Hymn of Heavenly Beauty, l. 16

15 Of such deep learning little had he need,
Ne yet of Latin, ne of Greek, that breed
Doubts 'mongst Divines, and difference of texts,
From whence arise diversity of sects,
And hateful heresies.
Complaints. Mother Hubbard's Tale, l. 385

16 Full little knowest thou that hast not tried,
What hell it is, in suing long to bide:
To lose good days, that might be better spent;
To waste long nights in pensive discontent;
To speed to-day, to be put back to-morrow;
To feed on hope, to pine with fear and sorrow;
To have thy Prince's grace, yet want her Peers';
To have thy asking, yet wait many years;
To fret thy soul with crosses and with cares;
To eat thy heart through comfortless despairs;

To fawn, to crouch, to wait, to ride, to run,
To spend, to give, to want, to be undone,
Unhappy wight, born to disastrous end,
That doth his life in so long tendance spend.
Complaints. Mother Hubbard's Tale, l. 895

17 What more felicity can fall to creature,
Than to enjoy delight with liberty.
Muiopotmos, l. 209

18 I was promis'd on a time,
To have reason for my rhyme;
From that time unto this season,
I received nor rhyme nor reason.
Lines on his Pension. (*Traditional*)

19 Calm was the day, and through the trembling air,
Sweet breathing Zephyrus did softly play.
Prothalamion, l. 1

20 With that, I saw two Swans of goodly hue,
Come softly swimming down along the Lee;
Two fairer Birds I yet did never see:
The Snow which doth the top of Pindus strew,
Did never whiter show,
Nor Jove himself when he a Swan would be
For love of Leda, whiter did appear:
Yet Leda was they say as white as he,
Yet not so white as these, nor nothing near;
So purely white they were,
That even the gentle stream, the which them bare,
Seem'd foul to them, and bade his billows spare
To wet their silken feathers, lest they might
Soil their fair plumes with water not so fair
And mar their beauties bright,
That shone as Heaven's light,
Against their Bridal day, which was not long:
Sweet Thames, run softly, till I end my Song.
Ib. l. 37

21 At length they all to merry London came,
To merry London, my most kindly nurse,
That to me gave this life's first native source:
Though from another place I take my name,
An house of ancient fame.
There when they came, whereas those bricky towers,
The which on Thames' broad aged back do ride,
Where now the studious Lawyers have their bowers
There whilom wont the Templar Knights to bide,
Till they decay'd through pride.
Ib. l. 127

22 To be wise and eke to love,
Is granted scarce to God above.
The Shepherd's Calendar. March. Willy's Emblem

23 Bring hither the Pink and purple Columbine,
With Gillyflowers:
Bring Coronation, and Sops in wine,
Worn of paramours.
Strew me the ground with Daffadowndillies,
And Cowslips, and Kingcups, and loved Lilies:
The pretty Pawnce,
And the Chevisaunce,
Shall match with the fair flower Delice.
Ib. April, l. 136

24 And he that strives to touch the stars,
Oft stumbles at a straw.
Ib. July, l. 99

25 The rugged brow of careful Policy.
Dedicatory Sonnets. To Sir Christopher Hatton

26 Uncouth unkist, said the old famous Poet Chaucer.
*The Shepherd's Calendar. Letter to Gabriel
Harvey*

1 So now they have made our English tongue a gallimaufry or hodgepodge of all other speeches.
The Shepherd's Calendar. Letter to Gabriel Harvey

REV. WILLIAM ARCHIBALD SPOONER
1844–1930

2 Kinquering Congs their titles take.
*Announcing the hymn in New College Chapel,
1879. (See 135:12)*

3 You have deliberately tasted two worms and you can
leave Oxford by the town drain.
Dismissing a student. Attributed

SIR CECIL ARTHUR SPRING-RICE
1858–1918

4 I vow to thee, my country—all earthly things above—
Entire and whole and perfect, the service of my love.
Last Poem

5 I am the Dean of Christ Church, Sir:
There's my wife; look well at her.
She's the Broad and I'm the High;
We are the University.
*The Masque of Balliol, composed by and current
among members of Balliol College, Oxford, in the
late 1870s. This first couplet (identified as by
C. A. Spring-Rice) was unofficially altered to:*

6 I am the Dean, and this is Mrs. Liddell;
She is the first and I the second fiddle.
(See also 8:15, 39:5.)

CHARLES HADDON SPURGEON
1834–1892

7 The Lord gets his best soldiers out of the highlands
of affliction.
*Gleanings among the Sheaves (1864), p. 132,
Sorrow's Discipline*

SIR JOHN COLLINGS SQUIRE
1884–

8 It did not last: the Devil howling 'Ho!
Let Einstein be!' restored the status quo.
Answer to Pope's epitaph for Sir Isaac Newton

MME DE STAËL
1766–1817

9 Tout comprendre rend très indulgent.
To know all makes one tolerant.
Corinne (1807), lib. iv, ch. 3

REV. ARTHUR PENRHYN STANLEY
1815–1881

10 They claim no thrones, they only ask to share
The common liberty of earth and air. *The Gipsies*

EDWARD STANLEY, EARL OF DERBY
1799–1869

11 When I first came into Parliament, Mr. Tierney, a
great Whig authority, used always to say that
the duty of an Opposition was very simple—it
was, to oppose everything, and propose nothing.
*House of Commons, 4 June 1841. Hansard, 3rd
Ser. lviii. 1188*

12 Don't you see that we have dished the Whigs?
*With reference to the Reform Bill of 1867.
Monypenny and Buckle, Life of Disraeli, ii. 285*

SIR HENRY MORTON STANLEY
1841–1904

13 Dr. Livingstone, I presume?
How I found Livingstone, ch. 11

FRANK LEBBY STANTON
1857–1927

14 Sweetest li'l feller, everybody knows;
Dunno what to call him, but he's mighty lak' a rose;
Lookin' at his mammy wid eyes so shiny blue
Mek' you think that Heav'n is comin' clost ter you.
Mighty Lak' a Rose

JOHN STARK
1728–1822

15 We beat them to-day or Molly Stark's a widow.
*Before Battle of Bennington, 16 Aug. 1777.
Appleton's Cyclopaedia of American Biography,
vol. v*

SIR RICHARD STEELE
1672–1729

16 I have often thought that a story-teller is born, as
well as a poet. *The Guardian, No. 24*

17 Gained universal applause by explaining a passage in
the game-act. *The Spectator, No. 2*

18 I have heard Will Honeycomb say, A Woman seldom
Writes her Mind but in her Postscript. *Ib. No. 79*

19 We were in some little time fixed in our seats, and
sat with that dislike which people not too good-
natured usually conceive of each other at first sight.
Ib. No. 132

20 The noblest motive is the public good.
Ib. No. 200. Motto in Ed. 1744

21 There are so few who can grow old with a good grace.
Ib. No. 263

22 Will Honeycomb calls these over-offended ladies the
outrageously virtuous. *Ib. No. 266*

23 Fashion, the arbiter, and rule of right.
Ib. No. 478. Motto in Ed. 1744

24 It is to be noted that when any part of this paper appears dull, there is a design in it.
The Tatler, No. 38

25 Though her mien carries much more invitation than
command, to behold her is an immediate check to
loose behaviour; to love her is a liberal education.
Ib. No. 49

26 Every man is the maker of his own fortune.
Ib. No. 52

27 The insupportable labour of doing nothing.
Ib. No. 54

28 Reading is to the mind what exercise is to the body.
Ib. No. 147

29 The truth of it is, the first rudiments of education
are given very indiscreetly by most parents.
Ib. No. 173

1 Let your precept be, Be easy.   *The Tatler*, No. 196

2 The pink of courtesy.   *Ib.* No. 204. *See also* 478: 5

3 These ladies of irresistible modesty are those who make virtue unamiable.   *Ib.* No. 217

4 I fared like a distressed Prince who calls in a powerful Neighbour to his Aid; I was undone by my Auxiliary; when I had once called him in, I could not subsist without Dependance on him.
    Ib. Preface to vol. iv (*1711*). On his co-editorship, with Addison, of *The Spectator*

GEORGE STEEVENS
1736–1800

5 And when the Pye was open'd
The birds began to sing,
And was not this a dainty dish
To set before the King!
    Recorded in Lamb's Letter to Miss Sarah James, ? April, 1829. See Corrigenda

JAMES KENNETH STEPHEN
1859–1892

6 Two voices are there: one is of the deep;

And one is of an old half-witted sheep
Which bleats articulate monotony,

And Wordsworth, both are thine.
    Lapsus Calami. Sonnet

7   Good Lord! I'd rather be
Quite unacquainted with the A.B.C.
Than write such hopeless rubbish as thy worst.   *Ib.*

8 When the Rudyards cease from kipling
And the Haggards ride no more.   *Ib. To R. K.*

9 Ah! Matt.: old age has brought to me
Thy wisdom, less thy certainty:
The world's a jest, and joy's a trinket:
I knew that once: but now—I think it.
    Ib. Senex to Matt. Prior

JAMES STEPHENS
1882–1950

10 I heard a bird at dawn
Singing sweetly on a tree,
That the dew was on the lawn,
And the wind was on the lea;
But I didn't listen to him,
For he didn't sing to me.   *The Rivals*, st. 1

11 I was singing all the time,
Just as prettily as he.   *Ib.* 3

12 I heard a sudden cry of pain!
There is a rabbit in a snare.   *The Snare*

13 Little One! Oh, Little One!
I am searching everywhere!   *Ib.*

ISABELLA S. STEPHENSON
1843–1890

14 Holy Father, in Thy mercy,
Hear our anxious prayer,
Keep our loved ones, now far absent,
'Neath Thy care.
    Holy Father, in Thy Mercy. Hymns A. *and* M., **Supplement to Revised Edition**, 1889

15 When in sorrow, when in danger,
When in loneliness,
In Thy love look down and comfort
Their distress.   *Holy Father, in Thy Mercy*

LAURENCE STERNE
1713–1768

16 They order, said I, this matter better in France.
    A Sentimental Journey, l. 1

17 I had had an affair with the moon, in which there was neither sin nor shame.   *Ib. The Monk. Calais*

18 The Sentimental Traveller (meaning thereby myself) who have travell'd, and of which I am now sitting down to give an account—as much out of necessity, and the *besoin de voyager*, as any one in the class.
    Ib. Preface. In the Desobligeant

19 As an English man does not travel to see English men, I retired to my room.   *Ib.*

20 I pity the man who can travel from Dan to Beersheba, and cry, 'tis all barren.   *Ib. In the Street. Calais*

21 Having been in love with one princess or another, almost all my life, and I hope I shall go on so, till I die, being firmly persuaded, that if I ever do a mean action, it must be in some interval betwixt one passion and another.   *Ib. Montriul*

22 Vive l'amour! et vive la bagatelle!   *Ib. The letter*

23 Hail ye small sweet courtesies of life.
    Ib. The Pulse. Paris

24 There are worse occupations in this world than feeling a woman's pulse.   *Ib.*

25 'I can't get out,—I can't get out,' said the starling.
    Ib. The Passport. The Hotel at Paris

26 He gave a deep sigh—I saw the iron enter into his soul!   *Ib. The Captive. Paris*

27 I think there is a fatality in it—I seldom go to the place I set out for.   *Ib. The Address. Versailles*

28 God tempers the wind, said Maria, to the shorn lamb.
    Ib. Maria. From a French proverb, but familiar in Sterne's form of words

29 Dear sensibility! source inexhausted of all that's precious in our joys, or costly in our sorrows!
    Ib. The Bourbonnois

30 If the supper was to my taste—the grace which followed it was much more so.   *Ib. The Supper*

31 But the fille de chambre hearing there were words between us, and fearing that hostilities would ensue in due course, had crept silently out of her closet, and it being totally dark, had stolen so close to our beds, that she had got herself into the narrow passage which separated them, and had advanced so far up as to be in a line betwixt her mistress and me—
    So that when I stretched out my hand, I caught hold of the fille de chambre's.
    Ib. The Case of Delicacy

32 I live in a constant endeavour to fence against the infirmities of ill health, and other evils of life, by mirth; being firmly persuaded that every time a man smiles,—but much more so, when he laughs, that it adds something to this Fragment of Life.
    Tristram Shandy. Dedication

1 'Pray, my dear,' quoth my mother, 'have you not forgot to wind up the clock?'—'Good G——!' cried my father, making an exclamation, but taking care to moderate his voice at the same time,—'Did ever woman, since the creation of the world, interrupt a man with such a silly question?'
Tristram Shandy, bk. i, ch. 1

2 As we jog on, either laugh with me, or at me, or in short do anything,—only keep your temper.
Ib. ch. 6

3 He was within a few hours of giving his enemies the slip for ever. *Ib.* ch. 12

4 'Tis known by the name of perseverance in a good cause,—and of obstinacy in a bad one. *Ib.* ch. 17

5 Persuasion hung upon his lips. *Ib.* ch. 19

6 What is the character of a family to an hypothesis? my father would reply. *Ib.* ch. 21

7 My uncle Toby would never offer to answer this by any other kind of argument, than that of whistling half a dozen bars of Lillabullero. *Ib.*

8 Digressions, incontestably, are the sunshine;—they are the life, the soul of reading;—take them out of this book for instance,—you might as well take the book along with them. *Ib.* ch. 22

9 I should have no objection to this method, but that I think it must smell too strong of the lamp.
Ib. ch. 23

10 'I'll not hurt thee,' says my uncle Toby, rising from his chair, and going across the room, with the fly in his hand,—'I'll not hurt a hair of thy head:— Go,' says he, lifting up the sash, and opening his hand as he spoke, to let it escape;—'go, poor devil, get thee gone, why should I hurt thee?—This world surely is wide enough to hold both thee and me.' *Ib.* bk. ii, ch. 12

11 Whenever a man talks loudly against religion,— always suspect that it is not his reason, but his passions which have got the better of his creed.
Ib. ch. 17

12 'Sir,' replied Dr. Slop, 'it would astonish you to know what improvements we have made of late years in all branches of obstetrical knowledge, but particularly in that one single point of the safe and expeditious extraction of the foetus,—which has received such lights, that, for my part (holding up his hands) I declare I wonder how the world has——.'
'I wish,' quoth my uncle Toby, 'you had seen what prodigious armies we had in Flanders.' *Ib.* ch. 18

13 That's another story. *Ib.*

14 'Our armies swore terribly in Flanders,' cried my uncle Toby,—'but nothing to this.' *Ib.* bk. iii, ch. 11

15 The corregiescity of Corregio. *Ib.* ch. 12. (*See* 126:10)

16 Of all the cants which are canted in this canting world,—though the cant of hypocrites may be the worst,—the cant of criticism is the most tormenting! *Ib.*

17 Is this a fit time, said my father to himself, to talk of Pensions and Grenadiers? *Ib.* bk. iv, ch. 5

18 The nonsense of the old women (of both sexes).
Ib. ch. 16

19 There is a North-west passage to the intellectual World. *Ib.* ch. 42

20 'The poor soul will die:—'
'He shall not die, by G——', cried my uncle Toby.— The Accusing Spirit, which flew up to heaven's chancery with the oath, blush'd as he gave it in;— and the Recording Angel, as he wrote it down, dropp'd a tear upon the word, and blotted it out for ever. *Tristram Shandy*, bk. vi, ch. 8

21 An eye full of gentle salutations—and soft responses — . . . whispering soft—like the last low accents of an expiring saint. . . . It did my uncle Toby's business. *Ib.* bk. viii, ch. 25

22 'I am half distracted, Captain Shandy,' said Mrs. Wadman, . . . 'a mote—or sand—or something—I know not what, has got into this eye of mine—do look into it.' . . . In saying which, Mrs. Wadman edged herself close in beside my uncle Toby, . . . 'Do look into it'—said she. . . .
If thou lookest, uncle Toby, . . . thou art undone.
Ib.

23 That eternal separation which we are shortly to make. *Ib.* bk. ix, ch. 8

24 Said my mother, 'what is all this story about?'— 'A Cock and a Bull,' said Yorick. *Ib.* ch. 33

25 This sad vicissitude of things. *Sermon* xv

ROBERT LOUIS STEVENSON
1850–1894

26 The harmless art of knucklebones has seen the fall of the Roman empire and the rise of the United States.
Across the Plains. VII. *The Lantern-Bearers,*

27 All the while, deep down in the privacy of your fool's heart, to know you had a bull's-eye at your belt, and to exult and sing over the knowledge. *Ib.*

28 The bright face of danger. *Ib.* iv

29 Every one lives by selling something.
Ib. IX. *Beggars,* iii

30 Our frailties are invincible, our virtues barren; the battle goes sore against us to the going down of the sun. *Ib.* XI. *Pulvis et Umbra*

31 Surely we should find it both touching and inspiriting, that in a field from which success is banished, our race should not cease to labour.
Ib. ii

32 Still obscurely fighting the lost fight of virtue, still clinging, in the brothel or on the scaffold, to some rag of honour, the poor jewel of their souls! *Ib.*

33 To make our idea of morality centre on forbidden acts is to defile the imagination and to introduce into our judgments of our fellow-men a secret element of gusto. *Ib.* XII. *A Christmas Sermon,* i

34 A mortified appetite is never a wise companion. *Ib.*

35 To be honest, to be kind—to earn a little and to spend a little less, to make upon the whole a family happier for his presence, to renounce when that shall be necessary and not be embittered, to keep a few friends, but these without capitulation— above all, on the same grim condition, to keep friends with himself—here is a task for all that a man has of fortitude and delicacy. *Ib.*

36 Here lies one who meant well, tried a little, failed much:—surely that may be his epitaph, of which he need not be ashamed. *Ib.* iv

1 There goes another Faithful Failure!
Across the Plains. XII. *A Christmas Sermon,* iv

2 Lamplough was genteel, Eno was omnipresent; Lamplough was trite, Eno original and abominably vulgar. . . . Am I, then, to sink with Lamplough, or to soar with Eno?
The Dynamiter. The Superfluous Mansion

3 He who was prepared to help the escaping murderer or to embrace the impenitent thief, found, to the overthrow of all his logic, that he objected to the use of dynamite. *Ib.*

4 'Or Opulent Rotunda Strike the Sky,' said the shopman to himself, in the tone of one considering a verse. 'I suppose it would be too much to say "orotunda", and yet how noble it were! "Or Opulent Orotunda Strike the Sky." But that is the bitterness of arts; you see a good effect, and some nonsense about sense continually intervenes.'
Ib. Epilogue of the Cigar Divan

5 These are my politics: to change what we can; to better what we can; but still to bear in mind that man is but a devil weakly fettered by some generous beliefs and impositions; and for no word however sounding, and no cause however just and pious, to relax the stricture of these bonds. *Ib.*

6 Politics is perhaps the only profession for which no preparation is thought necessary.
Familiar Studies of Men and Books. 'Yoshida-Torajiro'

7 Am I no a bonny fighter? [*Alan Breck.*]
Kidnapped, ch. 10

8 I've a grand memory for forgetting, David. [*Alan Breck.*] *Ib.* ch. 18

9 I have thus played the sedulous ape to Hazlitt, to Lamb, to Wordsworth, to Sir Thomas Browne, to Defoe, to Hawthorne, to Montaigne, to Baudelaire and to Obermann.
Memories and Portraits, ch. 4

10 Each has his own tree of ancestors, but at the top of all sits Probably Arboreal. *Ib.* ch. 6, *Pastoral*

11 The devil, depend upon it, can sometimes do a very gentlemanly thing.
New Arabian Nights. The Suicide Club. Story of the Young Man with the Cream Tarts

12 Is there anything in life so disenchanting as attainment? *Ib. The Adventure of the Hansom Cab*

13 I regard you with an indifference closely bordering on aversion.
Ib. The Rajah's Diamond. Story of the Bandbox

14 For my part, I travel not to go anywhere, but to go. I travel for travel's sake. The great affair is to move.
Travels with a Donkey. Cheylard and Luc

15 I own I like definite form in what my eyes are to rest upon; and if landscapes were sold, like the sheets of characters of my boyhood, one penny plain and twopence coloured, I should go the length of twopence every day of my life. *Ib. Father Apollinaris*

16 A faddling hedonist. *Ib. The Boarders*

17 The true Babel is a divergence upon morals.
Ib. Florac

18 Fifteen men on the dead man's chest
Yo-ho-ho, and a bottle of rum!
Drink and the devil had done for the rest—
Yo-ho-ho, and a bottle of rum!
Treasure Island, ch. 1

19 Tip me the black spot. *Ib.* ch. 3

20 Pieces of eight! *Ib.* ch. 10

21 Many's the long night I've dreamed of cheese—toasted, mostly. [*Ben Gunn.*] *Ib.* ch. 15

22 In marriage, a man becomes slack and selfish, and undergoes a fatty degeneration of his moral being.
Virginibus Puerisque, I. i

23 Acidulous vestals. *Ib.*

24 They have never been in love, or in hate. *Ib.*

25 Even if we take matrimony at its lowest, even if we regard it as no more than a sort of friendship recognised by the police. *Ib.*

26 A little amateur painting in water-colour shows the innocent and quiet mind. *Ib.*

27 Lastly (and this is, perhaps, the golden rule), no woman should marry a teetotaller, or a man who does not smoke. *Ib.*

28 Marriage is a step so grave and decisive that it attracts light-headed, variable men by its very awfulness. *Ib.*

29 Marriage is like life in this—that it is a field of battle, and not a bed of roses. *Ib.*

30 Times are changed with him who marries; there are no more by-path meadows, where you may innocently linger, but the road lies long and straight and dusty to the grave. *Ib.* ii

31 To marry is to domesticate the Recording Angel. Once you are married, there is nothing left for you, not even suicide, but to be good. *Ib.*

32 Man is a creature who lives not upon bread alone, but principally by catchwords. *Ib.*

33 The cruellest lies are often told in silence.
Ib. iv. *Truth of Intercourse*

34 Old and young, we are all on our last cruise.
Ib. Crabbed Age and Youth

35 Youth is the time to go flashing from one end of the world to the other both in mind and body; to try the manners of different nations; to hear the chimes at midnight; to see sunrise in town and country; to be converted at a revival; to circumnavigate the metaphysics, write halting verses, run a mile to see a fire, and wait all day long in the theatre to applaud 'Hernani'. *Ib.*

36 The weak brother is the worst of mankind. *Ib.*

37 It is better to be a fool than to be dead. *Ib.*

38 To love playthings well as a child, to lead an adventurous and honourable youth, and to settle when the time arrives, into a green and smiling age, is to be a good artist in life and deserve well of yourself and your neighbour. *Ib.*

39 I still remember that Emphyteusis is not a disease, nor Stillicide a crime.
Ib. III. *An Apology for Idlers*

40 There is no duty we so much underrate as the duty of being happy. *Ib.*

STEVENSON

1 He sows hurry and reaps indigestion.
   Virginibus Puerisque, III. *An Apology for Idlers*

2 By the time a man gets well into the seventies his
   continued existence is a mere miracle.
   Ib. v. *Æs Triplex*

3 Into what great waters, not to be crossed by any
   swimmer, God's pale Prætorian throws us over in
   the end! *Ib.*

4 Philosophy, in its more rigid sense, has been at the
   same work for ages; and . . . has the honour of
   laying before us . . . her contribution towards the
   subject: that life is a Permanent Possibility of
   Sensation. *Ib.*

5 Even if the doctor does not give you a year, even if
   he hesitates about a month, make one brave push
   and see what can be accomplished in a week. *Ib.*

6 To travel hopefully is a better thing than to arrive,
   and the true success is to labour.
   Ib. VI. *El Dorado*

7 The great barons of the mind. *Ib.* X. *Walking Tours*

8 Though we are mighty fine fellows nowadays, we
   cannot write like Hazlitt. *Ib.*

9 You must not fancy I am sick, only over-driven and
   under the weather. *The Wrecker*, ch. 4

10 'Hebdomadary . . . well, you're a boss word', I said.
   'Before you're very much older, I'll have you in
   type as long as yourself.' *Ib.* ch. 7

11 Nothing like a little judicious levity.
   [*Michael Finsbury.*] *The Wrong Box*, ch. 7

12 'The "Athæneum", that was the name! Golly, what
   a paper!' ' "Athenæum", you mean,' said Morris.
   Ib. ch. 15

13 I believe in an ultimate decency of things.
   Letter, 23 August 1893

14 In winter I get up at night
   And dress by yellow candle-light.
   In summer, quite the other way,—
   I have to go to bed by day.

   I have to go to bed and see
   The birds still hopping on the tree,
   Or hear the grown-up people's feet
   Still going past me in the street.

   And does it not seem hard to you,
   When all the sky is clear and blue,
   And I should like so much to play,
   To have to go to bed by day?
   A Child's Garden of Verses. I. *Bed in Summer*

15 It is very nice to think
   The world is full of meat and drink,
   With little children saying grace
   In every Christian kind of place. *Ib.* II. *A Thought*

16 A child should always say what's true,
   And speak when he is spoken to,
   And behave mannerly at table:
   At least as far as he is able.
   Ib. v. *Whole Duty of Children*

17   Fairy land,
   Where all the children dine at five,
   And all the playthings come alive.
   Ib. VIII. *Foreign Lands*

18 When I am grown to man's estate
   I shall be very proud and great,
   And tell the other girls and boys
   Not to meddle with my toys.
   A Child's Garden of Verses, XII. *Looking Forward*

19 The pleasant land of counterpane.
   Ib. XVI. *The Land of Counterpane*

20 The child that is not clean and neat,
   With lots of toys and things to eat,
   He is a naughty child, I'm sure—
   Or else his dear papa is poor. *Ib.* XIX. *System*

21 The friendly cow, all red and white,
   I love with all my heart:
   She gives me cream with all her might,
   To eat with apple-tart. *Ib.* XXIII. *The Cow*

22 The world is so full of a number of things,
   I'm sure we should all be as happy as kings.
   Ib. XXIV. *Happy Thought*

23 Children, you are very little,
   And your bones are very brittle;
   If you would grow great and stately,
   You must try to walk sedately.
   Ib. XXVII. *Good and Bad Children*

24 But the unkind and the unruly,
   And the sort who eat unduly,
   They must never hope for glory—
   Theirs is quite a different story!

   Cruel children, crying babies,
   All grow up as geese and gabies,
   Hated, as their age increases,
   By their nephews and their nieces. *Ib.*

25 A birdie with a yellow bill
   Hopped upon the window-sill,
   Cocked his shining eye and said:
   'Ain't you 'shamed, you sleepy-head?'
   Ib. XXXIV. *Time to Rise*

26 Must we to bed indeed? Well then,
   Let us arise and go like men,
   And face with an undaunted tread
   The long black passage up to bed.
   Ib. XLI. *North-West Passage.* 1. *Good-Night*

27 Give to me the life I love,
   Let the lave go by me,
   Give the jolly heaven above
   And the byway nigh me.
   Bed in the bush with stars to see,
   Bread I dip in the river—
   There's the life for a man like me,
   There's the life for ever.
   Songs of Travel. 1. *The Vagabond*

28 Let the blow fall soon or late,
   Let what will be o'er me;
   Give the face of earth around
   And the road before me.
   Wealth I seek not, hope nor love,
   Nor a friend to know me;
   All I seek, the heaven above
   And the road below me. *Ib.*

29 The untented Kosmos my abode,
   I pass, a wilful stranger;
   My mistress still the open road
   And the bright eyes of danger.
   Ib. II. *Youth and Love*

[515]

1 Here, lady, lo! that servant stands
  You picked from passing men,
And should you need nor heart nor hands
  He bows and goes again.
                          Songs of Travel. VII

2 I will make you brooches and toys for your delight
Of bird-song at morning and star-shine at night.
I will make a palace fit for you and me
Of green days in forests and blue days at sea.
I will make my kitchen, and you shall keep your
  room,
Where white flows the river and bright blows the
  broom,
And you shall wash your linen and keep your body
  white
In rainfall at morning and dewfall at night.   *Ib.* XI

3 Bright is the ring of words
  When the right man rings them,
Fair the fall of songs
  When the singer sings them.
Still they are carolled and said—
  On wings they are carried—
After the singer is dead
  And the maker buried.   *Ib.* XIV

4 Low as the singer lies
  In the field of heather,
Songs of his fashion bring
  The swains together.
And when the west is red
  With the sunset embers,
The lover lingers and sings
  And the maid remembers.   *Ib.*

5 In the highlands, in the country places,
Where the old plain men have rosy faces,
And the young fair maidens
  Quiet eyes.   *Ib.* XV

6 Trusty, dusky, vivid, true,
With eyes of gold and bramble-dew,
Steel-true and blade-straight,
The great artificer
Made my mate.   *Ib.* XXV. *My Wife*

7 Sing me a song of a lad that is gone,
  Say, could that lad be I?
Merry of soul he sailed on a day
  Over the sea to Skye.   *Ib.* XLII

8 Mull was a-stern, Rum on the port,
  Eigg on the starboard bow;
Glory of youth glowed in his soul,
  Where is that glory now?   *Ib.*

9 Blows the wind to-day, and the sun and the rain are
  flying,
Blows the wind on the moors to-day and now,
Where about the graves of the martyrs the whaups
  are crying,
My heart remembers how!
                    Ib. XLV. *To S. R. Crockett*

10 Be it granted to me to behold you again in dying,
  Hills of home! and to hear again the call;
Hear about the graves of the martyrs the peewees
  crying,
  And hear no more at all.   *Ib.*

11 Of all my verse, like not a single line;
But like my title, for it is not mine.
That title from a better man I stole;
Ah, how much better, had I stol'n the whole!
                          Underwoods. Foreword

12 Go, little book, and wish to all
Flowers in the garden, meat in the hall,
A bin of wine, a spice of wit,
A house with lawns enclosing it,
A living river by the door,
A nightingale in the sycamore!
                    Underwoods, bk. I. i. *Envoy*

13 The gauger walked with willing foot,
And aye the gauger played the flute;
And what should Master Gauger play
But 'Over the hills and far away'?
                    Ib. ii. *A Song of the Road*

14 There's nothing under Heav'n so blue
That's fairly worth the travelling to.   *Ib.* iv

15 Under the wide and starry sky
Dig the grave and let me lie.
Glad did I live and gladly die,
  And I laid me down with a will.
This be the verse you grave for me:
'Here he lies where he longed to be;
Home is the sailor, home from sea,
  And the hunter home from the hill.'
                    Ib. xxi. *Requiem*

16 If I have faltered more or less
In my great task of happiness;
If I have moved among my race
And shown no glorious morning face;
If beams from happy human eyes
Have moved me not; if morning skies,
Books, and my food, and summer rain
Knocked on my sullen heart in vain:—
Lord, thy most pointed pleasure take
And stab my spirit broad awake;
Or, Lord, if too obdurate I,
Choose thou, before that spirit die,
A piercing pain, a killing sin,
And to my dead heart run them in!
                    Ib. xxii. *The Celestial Surgeon*

17 Unfrowning caryatides.
                    Ib. xxiii. *Our Lady of the Snows*

18 I am a kind of farthing dip,
  Unfriendly to the nose and eyes;
A blue-behinded ape, I skip
  Upon the trees of Paradise.   *Ib.* xxx. *A Portrait*

19   In the afternoon of time
A strenuous family dusted from its hands
The sand of granite, and beholding far
Along the sounding coast its pyramids
And tall memorials catch the dying sun,
Smiled well content, and to this childish task
Around the fire addressed its evening hours.
        Ib. xxxviii. *Say not of me that weakly I declined*

20 A mile an' a bittock, a mile or twa,
  Abüne the burn, ayont the law,
Davie an' Donal' an' Cherlie an' a',
  An' the müne was shinin' clearly!
                Ib. bk. ii. iv. *A mile an' a bittock*, 1

WILLIAM STEVENSON
1530?–1575

21 I can not eat but little meat,
  My stomach is not good:
But sure I think, that I can drink
  With him that wears a hood.
Though I go bare, take ye no care,
  I am nothing acold:

I stuff my skin, so full within,
 Of jolly good ale and old,
Back and side go bare, go bare,
 Both foot and hand go cold:
But belly God send thee good ale enough,
 Whether it be new or old.
    Gammer Gurton's Needle, Act II, *Song*

SAMUEL JOHN STONE
1839–1900

1 The Church's one foundation
 Is Jesus Christ her Lord;
She is His new creation
 By water and the Word.
    Lyra Fidelium (1866). *The Church's One Foundation*

2 Yet Saints their watch are keeping,
 Their cry goes up, 'How long?'
And soon the night of weeping
 Shall be the morn of song.   *Ib.*

3 'Mid toil and tribulation,
 And tumult of her war,
She waits the consummation
 Of peace for evermore;
Till with the vision glorious
 Her longing eyes are blest,
And the great Church victorious
 Shall be the Church at rest.   *Ib.*

4 Weary of earth and laden with my sin.
    Ib. Weary of Earth and Laden

HARRIET BEECHER STOWE
1811–1896

5 'Who was your mother?' 'Never had none!' said the child, with another grin. 'Never had any mother? What do you mean? Where were you born?' 'Never was born!' persisted Topsy.
    Uncle Tom's Cabin, ch. 20

6 'Do you know who made you?' 'Nobody, as I knows on,' said the child, with a short laugh. . . . 'I 'spect I grow'd.'   *Ib.*

7 'Cause I's wicked—I is. I's mighty wicked, any how. I can't help it.   *Ib.*

BISHOP WILLIAM STUBBS
1825–1901

8 Froude informs the Scottish youth
That parsons do not care for truth.
The Reverend Canon Kingsley cries
History is a pack of lies.
What cause for judgments so malign?
A brief reflection solves the mystery—
Froude believes Kingsley a divine,
And Kingsley goes to Froude for history.
    In Stubbs's Letter to J. R. Green, 17 Dec. 1871. Letters of Stubbs (1904), p. 162

GEOFFREY ANKETELL STUDDERT-KENNEDY
1883–1929

9 When in the darkest depths the miner striving,
Feels in his arms the vigour of the Lord,
Strikes for a Kingdom and his King's arriving,
Holding his pick more splendid than the sword.
    Songs of Faith and Doubt (1922), p. 7. *Then Will He Come: 'When Through the Whirl'*

SIR JOHN SUCKLING
1609–1642

10 Why so pale and wan, fond lover?
 Prithee, why so pale?
Will, when looking well can't move her,
 Looking ill prevail?
Prithee, why so pale?   *Aglaura*, IV. i. *Song*

11 Quit, quit, for shame, this will not move:
 This cannot take her.
If of herself she will not love,
 Nothing can make her:
 The devil take her!   *Ib.*

12 Her feet beneath her petticoat,
Like little mice, stole in and out,
 As if they fear'd the light.
    Ballad. Upon a Wedding, viii

13 For streaks of red were mingled there,
Such as are on a Catherine pear
 (The side that's next the sun).   *Ib.*

14 Her lips were red, and one was thin,
Compar'd to that was next her chin
 (Some bee had stung it newly).   *Ib.* xi

15 The Prince of Darkness is a gentleman.
    The Goblins. Act III, *A Catch.* (See 453:25)

16 I prithee send me back my heart,
 Since I cannot have thine:
For if from yours you will not part,
 Why then shouldst thou have mine?
    Song. I Prithee Send me Back

17 But love is such a mystery,
 I cannot find it out:
For when I think I'm best resolv'd,
 I then am in most doubt.   *Ib.*

18 Out upon it, I have loved
 Three whole days together;
And am like to love three more,
 If it prove fair weather.

Time shall moult away his wings,
 Ere he shall discover
In the whole wide world again
 Such a constant lover.   *A Poem with the Answer*

19 Had it any been but she,
 And that very face,
There had been at least ere this
 A dozen dozen in her place.   *Ib.*

SUETONIUS
fl. c. A.D. 120

20 Ita feri ut se mori sentiat.
 Strike him so that he can feel that he is dying.
    Caligula, xxx

21 Festina lente. [Σπεῦδε βραδέως.]
 Hasten slowly.   *Divus Augustus*, 25

22 Ave, Imperator, morituri te salutant.
 Hail, Emperor, those about to die salute thee.
    Life of Claudius, 21

MAXIMILIAN DE BETHUNE, DUC DE SULLY
1559–1641

23 Les anglais s'amusent tristement selon l'usage de leur pays.
 The English take their pleasures sadly after the fashion of their country.   *Memoirs, c.* 1630

HENRY HOWARD, EARL OF SURREY

1517?–1547

1 My friend, the things that do attain
  The happy life be these, I find:
  The riches left, not got with pain;
  The fruitful ground, the quiet mind;

The equal friend; no grudge, no strife;
  No charge of rule, nor governance;
Without disease the healthy life;
  The household of continuance.
  Martial's Quiet Life, st. i, ii

2 The faithful wife, without debate;
  Such sleeps as may beguile the night:
Content thyself with thine estate;
  Neither wish death nor fear his might. *Ib.* st. iv

3 The soote season, that bud and bloom forth brings.
  Spring

ROBERT SMITH SURTEES

1803–1864

4 More people are flattered into virtue than bullied out of vice.
  The Analysis of the Hunting Field (1846), ch. 1

5 The only infallible rule we know is, that the man who is always talking about being a gentleman never is one. *Ask Mamma* (1858), ch. 1

6 Major Yammerton was rather a peculiar man, inasmuch as he was an ass, without being a fool.
  Ib. ch. 25

7 'Unting is all that's worth living for—all time is lost wot is not spent in 'unting—it is like the hair we breathe—if we have it not we die—it's the sport of kings, the image of war without its guilt, and only five-and-twenty per cent. of its danger.
  Handley Cross (1843), ch. 7

8 'Unting fills my thoughts by day, and many a good run I have in my sleep. Many a dig in the ribs I gives Mrs. J. when I think they're running into the warmint (renewed cheers). No man is fit to be called a sportsman wot doesn't kick his wife out of bed on a haverage once in three weeks! *Ib.* ch. 11

9 Tell me a man's a fox-hunter, and I loves him at once. *Ib.*

10 Come Hup! I say, you hugly beast! *Ib.* ch. 13

11 He will bring his nightcap with him, for where the M.F.H. dines he sleeps, and where the M.F.H. sleeps he breakfasts. *Ib.* ch. 15

12 I'll fill hup the chinks wi' cheese. *Ib.*

13 Well did that great man, I think it was Sir Walter Scott, but if it warn't, 'twas little Bartley, the bootmaker, say, that there was no young man wot would not rather have a himputation on his morality than on his 'ossmanship. *Ib.* ch. 16

14 It ar'n't that I loves the fox less, but that I loves the 'ound more. *Ib.*

15 The 'oss loves the 'ound, and I loves both. *Ib.*

16 Dinner lost! 'ounds lost, self lost—all lost together!
  Ib. ch. 21

17 I can stand a wast of praise. *Ib.* ch. 24

18 From the bonded warehouse of my knowledge.
  Ib. ch. 27

19 Bishops' boots Mr. Radcliffe also condemned, and spoke highly in favour of tops cleaned with champagne and abricot jam. *Handley Cross*, ch. 27

20 Unless a man has a good many servants, he had better have them cleanin' his 'oss than cleanin' his breeches. *Ib.*

21 Full o' beans and benevolence! *Ib.*

22 Paid for catching my 'oss, 6*d*. *Ib.* ch. 29

23 Letting in the Latchfords. *Ib.* ch. 31

24 Con-found all presents wot eat! *Ib.* ch. 37

25 Hellish dark, and smells of cheese! *Ib.* ch. 50

26 I feels all over trembulation and fear, like a maid that thinks she's not a-goin' to be married. *Ib.* ch. 52

27 'Hurrah! blister my kidneys!' exclaimed he in delight, 'it is a frost!—the dahlias are dead!'
  Ib. ch. 59

28 Howsomever, never mind—the country has its charms—cheapness for one. *Hillingdon Hall* (1845), ch. 5

29 Three things I never lends—my 'oss, my wife, and my name. *Ib.* ch. 33

30 Every man shouting in proportion to the amount of his subscription.
  Jorrocks's Jaunts and Jollities (1838). No. 1. *Swell and the Surrey*

31 Jorrocks, who is not afraid of 'the pace' so long as there is no leaping. *Ib.*

32 And a nod or a wink for every pretty maid that showed at the windows; for . . . , as he says, 'there is no harm in looking'.
  Ib. No. 4. *Surrey Stag-Hounds*

33 Champagne certainly gives one werry gentlemanly ideas, but for a continuance, I don't know but I should prefer mild hale.
  Ib. No. 9. *Mr. Jorrocks in Paris*

34 No one knows how ungentlemanly he can look, until he has seen himself in a shocking bad hat.
  Mr. Facey Romford's Hounds (1865), ch. 9

35 Bob Short, who had replied to Facey's advertisement for a 'strong persevering man, to clean horses'.
  Ib. ch. 19

36 Better be killed than frightened to death. *Ib.* ch. 32

37 Thinking that life would be very pleasant if it were not for its enjoyments. *Ib.*

38 These sort of boobies think that people come to balls to do nothing but dance; whereas everyone knows that the real business of a ball is either to look out for a wife, to look after a wife, or to look after somebody else's wife. *Ib.* ch. 56

39 The young ladies entered the drawing-room in the full fervour of sisterly animosity.
  Mr. Sponge's Sporting Tour (1853), ch. 17

40 Women never look so well as when one comes in wet and dirty from hunting. *Ib.* ch. 21

41 He was a gentleman who was generally spoken of as having nothing a-year, paid quarterly. *Ib.* ch. 24

42 There is no secret so close as that between a rider and his horse. *Ib.* ch. 31

43 He had a tremendous determination of words to the mouth. *Ib.* ch. 34

1 When at length they rose to go to bed, it struck each man as he followed his neighbour upstairs that the one before him walked very crookedly.
Mr. Sponge's Sporting Tour (1853), ch. 35

CHARLES SWAIN
1801–1874

2 Time to me this truth has taught
('Tis a treasure worth revealing),
More offend from want of thought,
Than from any want of feeling.   *Want of Thought*

JONATHAN SWIFT
1667–1745

3 I conceive some scattered notions about a superior power to be of singular use for the common people, as furnishing excellent materials to keep children quiet when they grow peevish, and providing topics of amusement in a tedious winter-night.
An Argument Against Abolishing Christianity

4 Satire is a sort of glass, wherein beholders do generally discover everybody's face but their own.
The Battle of the Books, preface

5 Instead of dirt and poison we have rather chosen to fill our hives with honey and wax; thus furnishing mankind with the two noblest of things, which are sweetness and light.   *Ib.*

6 I have heard of a man who had a mind to sell his house, and therefore carried a piece of brick in his pocket, which he shewed as a pattern to encourage purchasers.
The Drapier's Letters, No. 2 (4 Aug. 1724)

7 Laws are like cobwebs, which may catch small flies, but let wasps and hornets break through.
A Tritical Essay upon the Faculties of the Mind

8 There is nothing in this world constant, but inconstancy.   *Ib.*

9 He [the emperor] is taller by almost the breadth of my nail than any of his court, which alone is enough to strike an awe into the beholders.
Gulliver's Travels. Voyage to Lilliput, ch. 2

10 The colonel and his officers were in much pain, especially when they saw me take out my penknife.   *Ib.*

11 He put this engine [a watch] to our ears, which made an incessant noise like that of a water-mill; and we conjecture it is either some unknown animal, or the god that he worships; but we are more inclined to the latter opinion.   *Ib.*

12 Flimnap, the Treasurer, is allowed to cut a caper on the straight rope, at least an inch higher than any other lord in the whole empire. I have seen him do the summerset several times together. *Ib.* ch. 3

13 It is alleged indeed, that the high heels are most agreeable to our ancient constitution: but however this be, his Majesty hath determined to make use of only low heels in the administration of the government.   *Ib.* ch. 4

14 He could not forbear taking me up in his right hand, and stroking me gently with the other, after an hearty fit of laughing, asked me whether I were a Whig or a Tory. *Ib. Voyage to Brobdingnag*, ch. 3

15 I cannot but conclude the bulk of your natives to be the most pernicious race of little odious vermin that nature ever suffered to crawl upon the surface of the earth.
Gulliver's Travels. Voyage to Brobdingnag, ch. 6

16 He was amazed how so impotent and grovelling an insect as I (these were his expressions) could entertain such inhuman ideas.   *Ib.* ch. 7

17 And he gave it for his opinion, that whoever could make two ears of corn or two blades of grass to grow upon a spot of ground where only one grew before, would deserve better of mankind, and do more essential service to his country than the whole race of politicians put together.   *Ib.*

18 He had been eight years upon a project for extracting sun-beams out of cucumbers, which were to be put into vials hermetically sealed, and let out to warm the air in raw inclement summers.
Ib. Voyage to Laputa, etc., ch. 5

19 I said the thing which was not.
Ib. A Voyage to the Houyhnhnms, ch. 3

20 I told him . . . that we ate when we were not hungry, and drank without the provocation of thirst.   *Ib.* ch. 6

21 Plaguy twelvepenny weather.
Journal to Stella, 26 Oct. 1710

22 'Tis very warm weather when one's in bed.
Ib. 8 Nov. 1710

23 With my own fair hands.   *Ib.* 4 Jan. 1711

24 We are so fond of one another, because our ailments are the same.   *Ib.* 1 Feb. 1711

25 Will she pass in a crowd? Will she make a figure in a country church?   *Ib.* 9 Feb. 1711

26 I love good creditable acquaintance; I love to be the worst of the company.   *Ib.* 17 May 1711

27 He was a fiddler, and consequently a rogue.
Ib. 25 July 1711

28 He showed me his bill of fare to tempt me to dine with him; poh, said I, I value not your bill of fare, give me your bill of company.   *Ib.* 2 Sept. 1711

29 We were to do more business after dinner; but after dinner is after dinner—an old saying and a true, 'much drinking, little thinking'. *Ib.* 26 Feb. 1712

30 Monday is parson's holiday.   *Ib.* 3 Mar. 1712

31 Not die here in a rage, like a poisoned rat in a hole.
Letter to Bolingbroke, 21 Mar. 1729

32 I have ever hated all nations, professions and communities, and all my love is towards individuals. . . . But principally I hate and detest that animal called man; although I heartily love John, Peter, Thomas, and so forth.   *Letter to Pope*, 29 Sept. 1725

33 If Heaven had looked upon riches to be a valuable thing, it would not have given them to such a scoundrel.
Letter to Miss Vanhomrigh, 12–13 Aug. 1720

34 You have but a very few years to be young and handsome in the eyes of the world; and as few months to be so in the eyes of a husband, who is not a fool.
Letter to a Young Lady on her Marriage (1723)

35 What they call 'running a man down'.   *Ib.*

SWIFT

1 Proper words in proper places, make the true definition of a style.
Letter to a Young Clergyman, 9 Jan. 1720

2 Surely man is a broomstick!
A Meditation upon a Broomstick

3 I have been assured by a very knowing American of my acquaintance in London, that a young healthy child well nursed is at a year old a most delicious, nourishing, and wholesome food, whether stewed, roasted, baked, or boiled, and I make no doubt that it will equally serve in a fricassee, or a ragout.
A Modest Proposal for Preventing the Children of Ireland from being a Burden to their Parents or Country

4 Promises and pie-crust are made to be broken.
Polite Conversation. Dialogue 1

5 Bachelor's fare; bread and cheese, and kisses. *Ib.*

6 Like an owl in an ivy-bush. *Ib.*

7 I mean, you lie—under a mistake. *Ib.*

8 Why every one as they like; as the good woman said when she kissed her cow. *Ib.*

9 Why, madam, Queen Elizabeth's dead. *Ib.*

10 The sight of you is good for sore eyes. *Ib.*

11 'Tis as cheap sitting as standing. *Ib.*

12 Prythee, Tom, sit a little farther: I believe your father was no glazier. *Ib.*

13 You were half seas over. *Ib.*

14 I won't quarrel with my bread and butter. *Ib.*

15 I swear, she's no chicken; she's on the wrong side of thirty, if she be a day. *Ib.*

16 If it had been a bear, it would have bit you. *Ib.*

17 She wears her clothes, as if they were thrown on her with a pitchfork. *Ib.*

18 Faith, that's as well said, as if I had said it myself.
Ib. Dialogue 2

19 You must take the will for the deed. *Ib.*

20 She has more goodness in her little finger, than he has in his whole body. *Ib.*

21 Lord, I wonder what fool it was that first invented kissing! *Ib.*

22 I'll give you leave to call me anything, if you don't call me spade. *Ib.*

23 The best doctors in the world are Doctor Diet, Doctor Quiet, and Doctor Merryman. *Ib.*

24 I always love to begin a journey on Sundays, because I shall have the prayers of the church, to preserve all that travel by land, or by water. *Ib.*

25 I know Sir John will go, though he was sure it would rain cats and dogs. *Ib.*

26 'Tis happy for him, that his father was before him.
Ib. Dialogue 3

27 There's none so blind as they that won't see. *Ib.*

28 She watches him, as a cat would watch a mouse. *Ib.*

29 She pays him in his own coin. *Ib.*

30 All the world and his wife. *Ib.*

31 Damn your cards, said he, they are the devil's books. *Ib.*

32 There's two words to that bargain.
Polite Conversation. Dialogue 3

33 It is a maxim, that those to whom everybody allows the second place, have an undoubted title to the first. *A Tale of a Tub.* Dedication

34 Books, like men their authors, have no more than one way of coming into the world, but there are ten thousand to go out of it, and return no more. *Ib.*

35 Satire, being levelled at all, is never resented for an offence by any. *Ib.* Preface

36 What though his head be empty, provided his commonplace book be full.
Ib. Digression in Praise of Digression

37 I never saw, heard, nor read, that the clergy were beloved in any nation where Christianity was the religion of the country. Nothing can render them popular but some degree of persecution.
Thoughts on Religion

38 We have just enough religion to make us hate, but not enough to make us love one another.
Thoughts on Various Subjects

39 What they do in heaven we are ignorant of; what they do *not* we are told expressly, that they neither marry, nor are given in marriage. *Ib.*

40 The reasons why so few marriages are happy, is, because young ladies spend their time in making nets, not in making cages. *Ib.*

41 Few are qualified to shine in company; but it is in most men's power to be agreeable. *Ib.*

42 Every man desires to live long; but no man would be old. *Ib.*

43 A nice man is a man of nasty ideas. *Ib.*

44 Old men and comets have been reverenced for the same reason; their long beards, and pretences to foretell events. *Ib.*

45 I never wonder to see men wicked, but I often wonder to see them not ashamed. *Ib.*

46 A man should never be ashamed to own he has been in the wrong, which is but saying, in other words, that he is wiser to-day than he was yesterday. *Ib.*

47 Party is the madness of many, for the gain of a few. *Ib.*

48 When men grow virtuous in their old age, they only make a sacrifice to God of the devil's leavings.
Ib. (*See* 387:1)

49 The most positive men are the most credulous. *Ib.*

50 [Of *The Tale of a Tub.*]
Good God! what a genius I had when I wrote that book.
Sir Walter Scott's *Life of Swift. Works of Swift* (1824), vol. i, p. 89

51 I shall be like that tree, I shall die at the top.
Sir Walter Scott, *Memoirs of Swift*

52 Only a woman's hair. *Ib.* ch. 5

53 How haughtily he cocks his nose,
To tell what every schoolboy knows.
The Country Life, l. 81

54 Lose no time to contradict her,
Nor endeavour to convict her. *Daphne*, l. 29

55 Only take this rule along,
Always to advise her wrong;
And reprove her when she's right;
She may then grow wise for spite. *Ib.* l. 35

1 In all distresses of our friends,
  We first consult our private ends;
  While nature, kindly bent to ease us,
  Points out some circumstance to please us.
                    On the Death of Dr. Swift, l. 7

2 Poor Pope will grieve a month, and Gay
  A week, and Arbuthnot a day.
  St. John himself will scarce forbear
  To bite his pen, and drop a tear.
  The rest will give a shrug, and cry,
  'I'm sorry—but we all must die!'   *Ib.* l. 207

3 Yet malice never was his aim;
  He lash'd the vice, but spared the name;
  No individual could resent,
  Where thousands equally were meant.   *Ib.* l. 512

4 He gave the little wealth he had
  To build a house for fools and mad;
  And show'd, by one satiric touch,
  No nation wanted it so much.   *Ib.* l. 538

5 A coming shower your shooting corns presage.
                    Description of a City Shower, l. 9

6 They never would hear,
  But turn the deaf ear,
  As a matter they had no concern in.
                    Dingley and Brent, ii

7 I often wish'd that I had clear,
  For life, six hundred pounds a-year,
  A handsome house to lodge a friend,
  A river at my garden's end,
  A terrace walk, and half a rood
  Of land, set out to plant a wood.
                    Imitation of Horace, bk. 11, sat. vi, l. 1

8 Removed from kind Arbuthnot's aid,
  Who knows his art, but not the trade.
  Preferring his regard for me
  Before his credit, or his fee.   *In Sickness*, l. 9

9 Convey a libel in a frown,
  And wink a reputation down.
                    Journal of a Modern Lady, l. 192

10 'Libertas et natale solum':
   Fine words! I wonder where you stole 'em.
   Lines written in 1724 on Chief Justice Whitshed's motto on his coach, after the trial of Drapier

11 Hail, fellow, well met,
   All dirty and wet:
   Find out, if you can,
   Who's master, who's man.
                    My Lady's Lamentation, l. 171

12 Th' artillery of words   *Ode to Sancroft*, i

13 Philosophy, the lumber of the schools.
                    Ode to Sir W. Temple, ii

14 Walls have tongues, and hedges ears.
                    Pastoral Dialogue, l. 8

15 Say, Britain, could you ever boast,—
   Three poets in an age at most?
   Our chilling climate hardly bears
   A sprig of bays in fifty years.   *On Poetry*, l. 5

16 Then, rising with Aurora's light,
   The Muse invoked, sit down to write;
   Blot out, correct, insert, refine,
   Enlarge, diminish, interline.   *Ib.* l. 85

17 As learned commentators view
   In Homer more than Homer knew.   *Ib.* l. 103

18 So geographers, in Afric-maps,
   With savage-pictures fill their gaps;
   And o'er unhabitable downs
   Place elephants for want of towns.   *On Poetry*, l. 177

19 Read all the prefaces of Dryden,
   For these our critics much confide in,
   (Tho' merely writ at first for filling
   To raise the volume's price, a shilling.)   *Ib.* l. 251

20 He gives directions to the town,
   To cry it up, or run it down.   *Ib.* l. 269

21 Hobbes clearly proves, that every creature
   Lives in a state of war by nature.   *Ib.* l. 319

22 So, naturalists observe, a flea
   Hath smaller fleas that on him prey;
   And these have smaller fleas to bite 'em,
   And so proceed *ad infinitum*.
   Thus every poet, in his kind,
   Is bit by him that comes behind.   *Ib.* l. 337

23 To guide his steps afford your kindest aid,
   And gently pity whom ye can't persuade;
   Leave to avenging Heaven his stubborn will,
   For, O, remember, he's your brother still.
                    Swan Tripe Club in Dublin, l. 489

24 Humour is odd, grotesque, and wild,
   Only by affectation spoil'd;
   'Tis never by invention got,
   Men have it when they know it not.
                    To Mr. Delany, 10 Oct. 1718, l. 25

25 Hated by fools, and fools to hate,
   Be that my motto and my fate.   *Ib.* l. 171

26 A beggarly people!
   A church and no steeple! [Of St. Ann's Church,
   Dublin]
   Attrib. to Swift by Malone. See Prior's Life of Malone (1860), p. 381

27 Ubi saeva indignatio ulterius cor lacerare nequit.
   Where fierce indignation can no longer tear his
   heart.   *Swift's Epitaph*

ALGERNON CHARLES SWINBURNE
1837–1909

28 Superflux of pain.   *Anactoria*, l. 27

29 Maiden, and mistress of the months and stars
   Now folded in the flowerless fields of heaven.
   Atalanta in Calydon. Collected Poetical Works (1924), vol. ii, p. 247, l. 1

30 When the hounds of spring are on winter's traces,
     The mother of months in meadow or plain
   Fills the shadows and windy places
     With lisp of leaves and ripple of rain;
   And the brown bright nightingale amorous
   Is half assuaged for Itylus,
   For the Thracian ships and the foreign faces,
     The tongueless vigil and all the pain.

   Come with bows bent and with emptying of quivers,
     Maiden most perfect, lady of light,
   With a noise of winds and many rivers,
     With a clamour of waters, and with might;
   Bind on thy sandals, O thou most fleet,
   Over the splendour and speed of thy feet;
   For the faint east quickens, the wan west shivers,
     Round the feet of the day and the feet of the night.

Where shall we find her, how shall we sing to her,
  Fold our hands round her knees, and cling?
O that man's heart were as fire and could spring to
    her,
  Fire, or the strength of the streams that spring!
For the stars and the winds are unto her
  As raiment, as songs of the harp-player;
For the risen stars and the fallen cling to her,
  And the southwest-wind and west-wind sing.

For winter's rains and ruins are over,
  And all the season of snows and sins;
The days dividing lover and lover,
  The light that loses, the night that wins;
And time remembered is grief forgotten,
And frosts are slain and flowers begotten,
And in green underwood and cover
  Blossom by blossom the spring begins.
        Atalanta in Calydon, Chorus, p. 249

1 And the hoofed heel of a satyr crushes
    The chestnut-husk at the chestnut-root. *Ib.* p. 250

2 And Pan by noon and Bacchus by night,
    Fleeter of foot than the fleet-foot kid,
  Follows with dancing and fills with delight
    The Maenad and the Bassarid;
  And soft as lips that laugh and hide
    The laughing leaves of the tree divide,
  And screen from seeing and leave in sight
    The god pursuing, the maiden hid.   *Ib.*

3 The ivy falls with the Bacchanal's hair
    Over her eyebrows hiding her eyes;
  The wild vine slipping down leaves bare
    Her bright breast shortening into sighs. *Ib.*

4 The wolf that follows, the fawn that flies.   *Ib.*

5 Before the beginning of years
    There came to the making of man
  Time with a gift of tears,
    Grief with a glass that ran.
  Pleasure with pain for leaven,
    Summer with flowers that fell,
  Remembrance fallen from heaven,
    And Madness risen from hell,
  Strength without hands to smite,
    Love that endures for a breath;
  Night, the shadow of light,
    And Life, the shadow of death.   *Ib.* p. 258

6 For a day and a night and a morrow,
    That his strength might endure for a span
  With travail and heavy sorrow,
    The holy spirit of man.   *Ib.* p. 259

7 Eyesight and speech they wrought
    For the veil of the soul therein,
  A time for labour and thought,
    A time to serve and to sin;
  They gave him light in his ways,
    And love, and a space for delight,
  And beauty and length of days,
    And night, and sleep in the night.
  His speech is a burning fire;
    With his lips he travaileth;
  In his heart is a blind desire,
    In his eyes foreknowledge of death;
  He weaves, and is clothed with derision;
    Sows, and he shall not reap;
  His life is a watch or a vision
    Between a sleep and a sleep.   *Ib.*

8 We have seen thee, O love, thou art fair; thou art
    goodly, O Love.
        Atalanta in Calydon, Chorus, p. 273

9 For words divide and rend;
    But silence is most noble till the end.   *Ib.* p. 299

10 Where the narrowing Symplegades whitened the
    straits of Propontis with spray.   *Ib.* p. 327

11 Shall I strew on thee rose or rue or laurel,
    Brother, on this that was the veil of thee?
  Or quiet sea-flower moulded by the sea,
  Or simplest growth of meadow-sweet or sorrel?
        Ave atque Vale, i

12 Now all strange hours and all strange loves are over,
    Dreams and desires and sombre songs and sweet,
    Hast thou found place at the great knees and feet
  Of some pale Titan-woman like a lover,
    Such as thy vision here solicited,
    Under the shadow of her fair vast head,
  The deep division of prodigious breasts,
    The solemn slope of mighty limbs asleep? *Ib.* vi

13 Sleep; and if life was bitter to thee, pardon,
    If sweet, give thanks; thou hast no more to live;
    And to give thanks is good, and to forgive.
        Ib. xvii

14 For thee, O now a silent soul, my brother,
    Take at my hands this garland and farewell.
    Thin is the leaf, and chill the wintry smell,
  And chill the solemn earth, a fatal mother,
    With sadder than the Niobean womb
  And in the hollow of her breasts a tomb.   *Ib.* xviii

15 There lies not any troublous thing before,
    Nor sight nor sound to war against thee more,
  For whom all winds are quiet as the sun,
    All waters as the shore.   *Ib.*

16 This is the end of every man's desire.
        A Ballad of Burdens

17 Poor splendid wings so frayed and soiled and torn!
  Poor kind wild eyes so dashed with light quick tears!
        Ballad of François Villon

18 Villon, our sad bad glad mad brother's name.   *Ib.*

19   Strung with subtle-coloured hair
  Of some dead lute-player.   *A Ballad of Life*

20 O slain and spent and sacrificed
  People, the grey-grown speechless Christ.
        Before a Crucifix. Poetical Works (1924), vol. i,
        p. 744

21 No soul that lived, loved, wrought and died,
  Is this their carrion crucified.   *Ib.* p. 747

22 We shift and bedeck and bedrape us,
    Thou art noble and nude and antique. *Dolores*, vii

23   Change in a trice
  The lilies and languors of virtue
    For the raptures and roses of vice.   *Ib.* ix

24 O splendid and sterile Dolores,
    Our Lady of Pain.   *Ib.*

25 Ah beautiful passionate body
  That never has ached with a heart!   *Ib.* xi

26 But sweet as the rind was the core is;
    We are fain of thee still, we are fain,
  O sanguine and subtle Dolores,
    Our Lady of Pain.   *Ib.* xiii

27 The delight that consumes the desire,
    The desire that outruns the delight.   *Ib.* xiv

1 For the crown of our life as it closes
  Is darkness, the fruit thereof dust;
No thorns go as deep as a rose's,
  And love is more cruel than lust.
Time turns the old days to derision,
  Our loves into corpses or wives;
And marriage and death and division
  Make barren our lives.   *Dolores, xx*

2 Ringed round with a flame of fair faces,
  And splendid with swords.   *Ib.* xxx

3 What ailed us, O gods, to desert you
  For creeds that refuse and restrain?
Come down and redeem us from virtue,
  Our Lady of Pain.   *Ib.* xxxv

4 On thy bosom though many a kiss be,
  There are none such as knew it of old.
Was it Alciphron once or Arisbe,
  Male ringlets or feminine gold,
That thy lips met with under the statue,
  Whence a look shot out sharp after thieves
From the eyes of the garden-god at you
  Across the fig-leaves?   *Ib.* xxxviii

5 Old poets outsing and outlove us,
  And Catullus makes mouths at our speech.   *Ib.* xliii

6 Where are they, Cotytto or Venus,
  Astarte or Ashtaroth, where?
Do their hands as we touch come between us?
  Is the breath of them hot in thy hair?
From their lips have thy lips taken fever,
  With the blood of their bodies grown red?
Hast thou left upon earth a believer
  If these men are dead?   *Ib.* lii

7 O daughter of Death and Priapus,
  Our Lady of Pain.   *Ib.* liii

8 I shall remember while the light lives yet
And in the night time I shall not forget.   *Erotion*

9 There was a poor poet named Clough,
  Whom his friends all united to puff,
    But the public, though dull,
    Had not such a skull
  As belonged to believers in Clough.
  Essays and Studies (1875), *Matthew Arnold*
  (printed as prose)

10 Bright with names that men remember, loud with
  names that men forget.   *Eton: An Ode*

11 What adders came to shed their coats?
  What coiled obscene
Small serpents with soft stretching throats
  Caressed Faustine?   *Faustine*

12 Those eyes the greenest of things blue,
  The bluest of things grey.   *Félise*

13 In a coign of the cliff between lowland and highland,
At the sea-down's edge between windward and lee,
Walled round with rocks as an inland island,
  The ghost of a garden fronts the sea.
          A Forsaken Garden

14 The fields fall southward, abrupt and broken,
  To the low last edge of the long lone land.
If a step should sound or a word be spoken,
  Would a ghost not rise at the strange guest's hand?
So long have the grey bare walls lain guestless,
Through branches and briars if a man make way,
He shall find no life but the sea-wind's, restless
  Night and day.   *Ib.*

15 Heart handfast in heart as they stood, 'Look thither,'
  Did he whisper? 'look forth from the flowers to the
    sea;
For the foam-flowers endure when the rose-blossoms
    wither
  And men that love lightly may die—but we?'
And the same wind sang and the same waves
    whitened,
And or ever the garden's last petals were shed,
In the lips that had whispered, the eyes that had
    lightened,
          Love was dead.   *A Forsaken Garden*

16 Stretched out on the spoils that his own hand spread.
As a god self-slain on his own strange altar,
          Death lies dead.   *Ib.*

17 Here, where the world is quiet;
Here, where all trouble seems
Dead winds' and spent waves' riot
In doubtful dreams of dreams.
          The Garden of Proserpine

18 I am tired of tears and laughter,
  And men that laugh and weep;
Of what may come hereafter
  For men that sow and reap:
I am weary of days and hours,
Blown buds of barren flowers,
Desires and dreams and powers
  And everything but sleep.   *Ib.*

19 Here life has death for neighbour,
  And far from eye or ear
Wan waves and wet winds labour,
  Weak ships and spirits steer.   *Ib.*

20 Pale, beyond porch and portal,
  Crowned with calm leaves, she stands
Who gathers all things mortal
  With cold immortal hands.   *Ib.*

21 Dead dreams of days forsaken,
Blind buds that snows have shaken,
Wild leaves that winds have taken,
  Red strays of ruined springs.   *Ib.*

22 We are not sure of sorrow,
  And joy was never sure.   *Ib.*

23 From too much love of living,
  From hope and fear set free,
We thank with brief thanksgiving
  Whatever gods may be
That no man lives forever,
That dead men rise up never;
That even the weariest river
  Winds somewhere safe to sea.   *Ib.*

24 Then star nor sun shall waken,
  Nor any change of light:
Nor sound of waters shaken,
  Nor any sound or sight:
Nor wintry leaves nor vernal,
Nor days nor things diurnal;
Only the sleep eternal
  In an eternal night.   *Ib.*

25 Calling a crowned man royal
That was no more than a king.   *The Halt before Rome*

26 Fiddle, we know, is diddle: and diddle, we take it,
  is dee.
          *The Heptalogia. The Higher Pantheism in a Nut-
          shell*

1
I am that which began;
Out of me the years roll;
Out of me God and man;
I am equal and whole;
God changes, and man, and the form of them bodily;
I am the soul. *Hertha*

2
But what thing dost thou now,
Looking Godward, to cry
'I am I, thou art thou,
I am low, thou art high'?
I am thou, whom thou seekest to find him; find thou
but thyself, thou art I. *Ib.*

3
A creed is a rod,
And a crown is of night;
But this thing is God.
To be man with thy might,
To grow straight in the strength of thy spirit, and live
out thy life as the light. *Ib.*

4
Green leaves of thy labour, white flowers of thy
thought, and red fruit of thy death. *Ib.*

5
Man, equal and one with me, man that is made of me,
man that is I. *Ib.*

6
Hope thou not much, and fear thou not at all.
Hope and Fear

7
In the fair days when God
By man as godlike trod,
And each alike was Greek, alike was free.
To Victor Hugo

8
And a bird overhead sang *Follow*,
And a bird to the right sang *Here*;
And the arch of the leaves was hollow,
And the meaning of May was clear. *An Interlude*

9
I remember the way we parted,
The day and the way we met;
You hoped we were both broken-hearted,
And knew we should both forget. *Ib.*

10
And the best and the worst of this is
That neither is most to blame,
If you have forgotten my kisses
And I have forgotten your name. *Ib.*

11
Swallow, my sister, O sister swallow,
How can thine heart be full of the spring?
A thousand summers are over and dead.
What hast thou found in the spring to follow?
What hast thou found in thine heart to sing?
What wilt thou do when the summer is shed?
Itylus

12
Hast thou forgotten ere I forget? *Ib.*

13
Sister, my sister, O fleet sweet swallow,
Thy way is long to the sun and the south;
But I, fulfilled of my heart's desire,
Shedding my song upon height, upon hollow,
From tawny body and sweet small mouth
Feed the heart of the night with fire.

I the nightingale all spring through,
O swallow, sister, O changing swallow,
All spring through till the spring be done,
Clothed with the light of the night on the dew,
Sing, while the hours and the wild birds follow,
Take flight and follow and find the sun. *Ib.*

14
Till life forget and death remember,
Till thou remember and I forget. *Ib.*

15
Thy lord the summer is good to follow,
And fair the feet of thy lover the spring:
But what wilt thou say to the spring thy lover?
Itylus

16
But mine goes forth among sea-gulfs hollow
To the place of the slaying of Itylus,
The feast of Daulis, the Thracian sea. *Ib.*

17
The small slain body, the flower-like face,
Can I remember if thou forget? *Ib.*

18
Thou hast forgotten, O summer swallow,
But the world shall end when I forget. *Ib.*

19
Apples of gold for the king's daughter.
The King's Daughter

20
I came as one whose thoughts half linger,
Half run before;
The youngest to the oldest singer
That England bore.
In Memory of Walter Savage Landor

21
O father of all of us, Paian, Apollo,
Destroyer and healer, hear! *The Last Oracle*

22
God by God goes out, discrowned and disanointed,
But the soul stands fast that gave them shape and
speech. *Ib.*

23
Ah, yet would God this flesh of mine might be
Where air might wash and long leaves cover me;
Where tides of grass break into foam of flowers,
Or where the wind's feet shine along the sea.
Laus Veneris

24
Until God loosen over sea and land
The thunder of the trumpets of the night. *Ib.*

25
Let us go hence, my songs; she will not hear.
Let us go hence together without fear.
A Leave-taking

26
But God, if a God there be, is the substance of men
which is man. *Hymn of Man*

27
Glory to Man in the highest! for Man is the master
of things. *Ib.*

28
If love were what the rose is,
And I were like the leaf,
Our lives would grow together
In sad or singing weather,
Blown fields or flowerful closes,
Green pleasure or grey grief. *A Match*

29
If you were thrall to sorrow,
And I were page to joy. *Ib.*

30
If you were April's lady,
And I were lord in May. *Ib.*

31
If you were queen of pleasure,
And I were king of pain. *Ib.*

32
But you would have felt my soul in a kiss,
And known that once if I loved you well;
And I would have given my soul for this
To burn for ever in burning hell. *Les Noyades*

33
Ask nothing more of me, sweet;
All I can give you I give.
Heart of my heart, were it more,
More would be laid at your feet:
Love that should help you to live,
Song that should spur you to soar. *The Oblation*

1 I turn to thee as some green afternoon
'Turns toward sunset, and is loth to die;
Ah God. ah God, that day should be so soon!
In the Orchard

2 For a day and a night Love sang to us, played with us,
Folded us round from the dark and the light;
And our hearts were fulfilled with the music he made
with us,
Made with our hands and our lips while he stayed
with us,
Stayed in mid passage his pinions from flight
For a day and a night.   *At Parting*

3 The world has no such flowers in any land,
And no such pearl in any gulf the sea,
As any babe on any mother's knee.   *Pelagius*

4 I have lived long enough, having seen one thing, that
love hath an end;
Goddess and maiden and queen, be near me now and
befriend.   *Hymn to Proserpine*

5 Yea, is not even Apollo, with hair and harpstring of
gold,
A bitter God to follow, a beautiful God to behold?
I am sick of singing: the bays burn deep and chafe:
I am fain
To rest a little from praise and grievous pleasure and
pain.   *Ib.*

6 Wilt thou yet take all, Galilean? but these thou shalt
not take,
The laurel, the palms and the paean, the breasts of
the nymphs in the brake;
Breasts more soft than a dove's, that tremble with
tenderer breath;
And all the wings of the Loves, and all the joy before
death.   *Ib.*

7 For no man under the sky lives twice, outliving his
day.   *Ib.*

8 Thou hast conquered, O pale Galilean; the world has
grown grey from Thy breath;
We have drunken of things Lethean, and fed on the
fullness of death.
Laurel is green for a season, and love is sweet for a
day;
But love grows bitter with treason, and laurel outlives
not May.   *Ib.*

9 For the old faiths loosen and fall, the new years ruin
and rend.   *Ib.*

10 O ghastly glories of saints, dead limbs of gibbeted
Gods!   *Ib.*

11 Impelled of invisible tides, and fulfilled of unspeakable things.   *Ib.*

12 All ye as a wind shall go by, as a fire shall ye pass and
be past;
Ye are Gods, and behold, ye shall die, and the waves
be upon you at last.   *Ib.*

13 Though the feet of thine high priests tread where thy
lords and our forefathers trod,
Though these that were Gods are dead, and thou
being dead art a God,
Though before thee the throned Cytherean be fallen,
and hidden her head,
Yet thy kingdom shall pass, Galilean, thy dead shall
go down to thee dead.   *Ib.*

14 As the deep dim soul of a star.   *Ib.*

15 A little soul for a little bears up this corpse which is
man.   *Hymn to Proserpine*

16 Love alone, with yearning
Heart for astrolabe,
Takes the star's height, burning
O'er the babe.   *A Rhyme*

17 Say, was not this thy Passion, to foreknow
In death's worst hour the works of Christian men?
On the Russian Persecution of the Jews

18 In the heart is the prey for gods,
Who crucify hearts, not hands.   *Satia te Sanguine*

19 Good hap to the fresh fierce weather,
The quiver and beat of the sea!
While three men hold together,
The kingdoms are less by three.
A Song in Time of Order 1852

20 They have tied the world in a tether,
They have bought over God with a fee.   *Ib.*

21 When the devil's riddle is mastered
And the galley-bench creaks with a Pope,
We shall see Buonaparte the bastard
Kick heels with his throat in a rope.   *Ib.*

22 Had you loved me once, as you have not loved;
Had the chance been with us that has not been.
The Triumph of Time

23 I have put my days and dreams out of mind,
Days that are over, dreams that are done.   *Ib.*

24 The strong sea-daisies feast on the sun.   *Ib.*

25 Who swims in sight of the great third wave
That never a swimmer shall cross or climb.   *Ib.*

26 A broken blossom, a ruined rhyme.   *Ib.*

27 I had wrung life dry for your lips to drink,
Broken it up for your daily bread.   *Ib.*

28   Content you;
The gate is strait; I shall not be there.   *Ib.*

29 I will go back to the great sweet mother,
Mother and lover of men, the sea.
I will go down to her, I and no other,
Close with her, kiss her and mix her with me.   *Ib.*

30 I shall sleep, and move with the moving ships,
Change as the winds change, veer in the tide.   *Ib.*

31 There lived a singer in France of old
By the tideless dolorous midland sea.
In a land of sand and ruin and gold
There shone one woman, and none but she.   *Ib.*

32   In heaven,
If I cry to you then, will you hear or know?   *Ib.*

33 One the last flower of Catholic love, that grows
Amid bare thorns their only thornless rose.
Two Leaders

34 Sweet red splendid kissing mouth.
*Translations from Villon. Complaint of the fair
Armouress*

35 There's no good girl's lip out of Paris.
Ib. Ballad of the Women of Paris

JOSHUA SYLVESTER
1563–1618

36 Were I as base as is the lowly plain,
And you (my Love) as high as Heaven above.
Sonnet. (Attrib.) Oxford Book of 16th Cent. Verse

JOHN ADDINGTON SYMONDS
1840–1893

1 These things shall be! A loftier race
Than e'er the world hath known shall rise,
With flame of freedom in their souls,
And light of knowledge in their eyes. *Hymn*

PUBLILIUS SYRUS
fl. 1st cent. B.C.

2 Bis dat qui cito dat.
He gives twice who gives soon.
Proverbial, attrib. to Syrus

3 Beneficium inopi bis dat, qui dat celeriter.
He doubly benefits the needy who gives quickly.
Sententiæ, 6

4 Iudex damnatur ubi nocens absolvitur.
The judge is condemned when the guilty is acquitted.
Ib. 247

5 Necessitas dat legem non ipsa accipit.
Necessity gives the law and does not itself receive
it. *Ib.* 399

6 Necessitas non habet legem.
Necessity has no law. *Proverbial, attrib. to Syrus*

JOSEPH TABRAR
1857–1931

7 In over a year and a half,
I've only sung it once,
And I don't suppose I shall sing it again
For months and months and months.
For Months and Months and Months

TACITUS
c. A.D. 55–*c.* 117

8 Atque omne ignotum pro magnifico est; sed nunc
terminus Britanniae patet.
For wonder grows where knowledge fails. But now
the very bounds of Britain are laid bare.
Agricola, 30. Trans. by Fyfe

9 Ubi solitudinem faciunt, pacem appellant.
When they make a wilderness they call it peace.
Ib.

10 Proprium humani ingenii est odisse quem laeseris.
It is human nature to hate the man whom you
have hurt. *Ib.* 42

11 Felix . . . opportunitate mortis.
Fortune favoured him . . . in the opportune moment
of his death. *Ib.* 45

12 Editis annalibus laudatoque M. Bruto C. Cassium
Romanorum ultimum dixisset.
In his history he had praised Brutus and had called
Cassius the last of the Romans. *Annals*, iv. 34

13 Elegantiae arbiter. [Petronius.]
Judge of taste. *Ib.* xvi. 18

14 Rara temporum felicitate ubi sentire quae velis et
quae sentias dicere licet.
It is the rare fortune of these days that a man may
think what he likes and say what he thinks.
Histories, I. i. Trans. by Fyfe

15 Maior privato visus dum privatus fuit, et omnium
consensu capax imperii nisi imperasset
When he was a commoner he seemed too big for
his station, and had he never been emperor, no
one would have doubted his ability to reign.
[Servius Galba] *Histories*, I. xlix

16 Etiam sapientibus cupido gloriae novissima exuitur.
For even with philosophers the passion for fame
is often their last rag of infirmity. *Ib.* IV. vi

CHARLES-MAURICE DE TALLEYRAND
1754–1838

17 Ils n'ont rien appris, ni rien oublié.
They have learnt nothing, and forgotten nothing.
*Attributed to Talleyrand by the Chevalier de Panat
in a letter to Mallet du Pan, Jan. 1796*, 'Personne
n'est corrigé, personne n'a su ni rien oublier ni rien
apprendre.' (*Mémoires et correspondance de Mallet
du Pan* (1851), II. 196.) *See also 195:1*

18 N'ayez pas de zèle.
Not too much zeal.
Sainte-Beuve, *Portraits de femmes, Madame de
Staël*, p. 131

19 Voilà le commencement de la fin.
This is the beginning of the end.
*On the announcement of Napoleon's defeat at
Borodino, 1812*

20 War is much too serious a thing to be left to military
men.
*Quoted by Briand to Lloyd George during the First
World War*

ROBERT TANNAHILL
1774–1810

21 When gloamin' treads the heels o' day,
And birds sit courin' on the spray,
Alang the flow'ry hedge I stray,
To meet mine ain dear somebody.
Songs and Poems (1911), *Mine ain dear Somebody*

NAHUM TATE
1652–1715
and
NICHOLAS BRADY
1659–1726

22 To the hills and the vales,
To the rocks and the mountains,
To the musical groves
And the cool shady fountains,
Let the triumphs of Love,
And of Beauty be shown!
Go revel, ye Cupids,
The day is your own.
Dido and Æneas, Act I (*By Nahum Tate*)

23 Take a bowsey short leave of your nymphs on the
shore,
And silence their mourning
With vows of returning,
Though never intending to visit them more.
Ib. Act III

1 As pants the hart for cooling streams
  When heated in the chase.
    New Version of the Psalms (1696). *As Pants the Hart*

2 Through all the changing scenes of life.
    Ib. Through all the Changing

3 Fear Him, ye saints, and you will then
  Have nothing else to fear.   *Ib.*

4 While shepherds watch'd their flocks by night,
  All seated on the ground,
  The Angel of the Lord came down,
  And glory shone around.

  'Fear not,' said he, for mighty dread
  Had seized their troubled mind;
  'Glad tidings of great joy I bring
  To you and all mankind.'
    Supplement to the New Version of the Psalms
    (1700). *While Shepherds Watched*

ANN TAYLOR
1782–1866
and
JANE TAYLOR
1783–1824

5 I thank the goodness and the grace
  Which on my birth have smiled,
  And made me, in these Christian days,
  A happy English child.
    Hymns for Infant Minds, 1. *A Child's Hymn of Praise*

6 O that it were my chief delight
  To do the things I ought!
  Then let me try with all my might
  To mind what I am taught.
    Ib. 18. *For a Very Little Child*

7 'Tis a *credit* to any good girl to be neat,
  But quite a *disgrace* to be fine.
    Hymns for Sunday Schools. The Folly of Finery

8 Who ran to help me when I fell,
  And would some pretty story tell,
  Or kiss the place to make it well?
  My Mother.
    Original Poems. My Mother. (By Ann Taylor)

9 How pleasant it is, at the end of the day,
  No follies to have to repent;
  But reflect on the past, and be able to say,
  That my time has been properly spent.
    Rhymes for the Nursery. The Way to be Happy.
    (By Jane Taylor)

10 Twinkle, twinkle, little star,
  How I wonder what you are!
  Up above the world so high,
  Like a diamond in the sky!
    Ib. The Star. (By Jane Taylor)

BAYARD TAYLOR
1825–1878

11 Till the sun grows cold,
  And the stars are old,
  And the leaves of the Judgment Book unfold.
    Bedouin Song. Refrain

SIR HENRY TAYLOR
1800–1886

12 Quoth tongue of neither maid nor wife
  To heart of neither wife nor maid—
  Lead we not here a jolly life
  Betwixt the shine and shade?

  Quoth heart of neither maid nor wife
  To tongue of neither wife nor maid—
  Thou wagg'st, but I am worn with strife,
  And feel like flowers that fade.
    Philip Van Artevelde, Pt. II. v. i. 1

BISHOP JEREMY TAYLOR
1613–1667

13 Too quick a sense of a constant infelicity.
    Holy Dying, ch. I, § v

14 Every school-boy knows it.
    On the Real Presence, § v, par. 1

15 The union of hands and hearts.
    Sermons. The Marriage Ring, pt. i

JOHN TAYLOR
1580–1653

16 'Tis a mad world, my masters. *Western Voyage*, l. 1

ARCHBISHOP FREDERICK TEMPLE
1821–1902

17 There is a certain class of clergyman whose mendicity
  is only equalled by their mendacity.
    Remark at a meeting of the Ecclesiastical Commissioners quoted by Sir George Leveson Gower:
    Years of Endeavour, *1942*

SIR WILLIAM TEMPLE
1628–1699

18 When all is done, human life is, at the greatest and
  the best, but like a froward child, that must be
  play'd with and humoured a little to keep it quiet
  till it falls asleep, and then the care is over.
    Essay on Poetry, ad fin.

ARCHBISHOP WILLIAM TEMPLE
1881–1944

19 'Are you not,' a Rugby master had asked him in discussing one of his [schoolboy] essays, 'a little out of
  your depth here?' 'Perhaps, Sir,' was the confident
  reply, 'but I can swim.'
    F. A. Iremonger, *William Temple*

ALFRED, LORD TENNYSON
1809–1892

20 The noblest answer unto such,
  Is kindly silence when they brawl.
    After-Thought, v

21 For nothing worthy proving can be proven,
  Nor yet disproven.   *The Ancient Sage*, l. 66

22 Cleave ever to the sunnier side of doubt.   *Ib.* l. 68

23 The rabbit fondles his own harmless face.
    Aylmer's Field, l. 851

1 Her arms across her breast she laid;
  She was more fair than words can say:
Bare-footed came the beggar maid
  Before the king Cophetua.
In robe and crown the king stept down,
  To meet and greet her on her way;
'It is no wonder,' said the lords,
  'She is more beautiful than day.'
                              The Beggar Maid

2 As shines the moon in clouded skies,
  She in her poor attire was seen:
One praised her ankles, one her eyes,
  One her dark hair and lovesome mien.
So sweet a face, such angel grace,
  In all that land had never been:
Cophetua sware a royal oath:
  'This beggar maid shall be my queen!'   *Ib.*

3 Break, break, break,
  On thy cold gray stones, O Sea!
And I would that my tongue could utter
  The thoughts that arise in me.

O well for the fisherman's boy,
  That he shouts with his sister at play!
O well for the sailor lad,
  That he sings in his boat on the bay!

And the stately ships go on
  To their haven under the hill;
But O for the touch of a vanish'd hand,
  And the sound of a voice that is still!

Break, break, break,
  At the foot of thy crags, O Sea!
But the tender grace of a day that is dead
  Will never come back to me. *Break, Break, Break*

4 A happy bridesmaid makes a happy bride.
                              The Bridesmaid, l. 4

5 I come from haunts of coot and hern,
  I make a sudden sally
And sparkle out among the fern,
  To bicker down a valley.   *The Brook*, !. 23

6 For men may come and men may go,
  But I go on for ever.   *Ib.* l. 33

7 Here and there a lusty trout,
  And here and there a grayling.   *Ib.* l. 57

8   That petitionary grace
  Of Sweet Seventeen.   *Ib.* l. 112

9 The Lord let the house of a brute to the soul of a man,
  And the man said, 'Am I your debtor?'
And the Lord—'Not yet: but make it as clean as you
    can,
  And then I will let you a better.' *By an Evolutionist*

10 He that only rules by terror
  Doeth grievous wrong.   *The Captain*, l. 1

11 Slav, Teuton, Kelt, I count them all
  My friends and brother souls,
With all the peoples, great and small,
  That wheel between the poles.
    Epilogue to The Charge of the Heavy Brigade, l. 18

12 The song that nerves a nation's heart,
  Is in itself a deed.   *Ib.* l. 81

13 Half a league, half a league,
  Half a league onward.
              The Charge of the Light Brigade

14 'Forward, the Light Brigade!'
  Was there a man dismay'd?
            The Charge of the Light Brigade *Ib*

15 Some one had blunder'd.   *Ib*

16 Their's not to make reply,
  Their's not to reason why,
  Their's but to do and die:
Into the valley of Death
  Rode the six hundred.   *Ib.*

17 Cannon to right of them
  Cannon to left of them,
  Cannon in front of them
    Volley'd and thunder'd.   *Ib.*

18 Into the jaws of Death,
  Into the mouth of Hell.   *Ib.*

19 When can their glory fade?
  O the wild charge they made!
All the world wonder'd.   *Ib.*

20   The golden guess
  Is morning-star to the full round of truth.
                          Columbus, l. 42

21 Come not, when I am dead,
  To drop thy foolish tears upon my grave,
To trample round my fallen head,
  And vex the unhappy dust thou wouldst not save.
                Come Not, When I Am Dead, i

22 Sunset and evening star,
  And one clear call for me!
And may there be no moaning of the bar,
  When I put out to sea,

But such a tide as moving seems asleep,
  Too full for sound and foam,
When that which drew from out the boundless deep
  Turns again home.

Twilight and evening bell,
  And after that the dark!
And may there be no sadness of farewell,
  When I embark;

For tho' from out our bourne of Time and Place
  The flood may bear me far,
I hope to see my Pilot face to face
  When I have crost the bar.   *Crossing the Bar*

23 O Love what hours were thine and mine,
  In lands of palm and southern pine;
  In lands of palm, of orange-blossom,
Of olive, aloe, and maize and vine.   *The Daisy*, i

24 A mount of marble, a hundred spires!   *Ib.* xv

25 Gray metropolis of the North. [Edinburgh.] *Ib.* xxvi

26 This proverb flashes thro' his head,
  'The many fail: the one succeeds.'
              The Day-dream. The Arrival, ii

27 But dallied with his golden chain,
  And, smiling, put the question by.
                      Ib. The Revival

28 And on her lover's arm she leant,
  And round her waist she felt it fold,
And far across the hills they went
  In that new world which is the old.
                      Ib. The Departure, i

29 And o'er the hills, and far away
  Beyond their utmost purple rim,
Beyond the night, across the day,
  Thro' all the world she follow'd him.   *Ib.* iv

1 And is there any moral shut
  Within the bosom of the rose?
                         The Day-dream. Moral, i

2 But any man that walks the mead,
  In bud or blade, or bloom, may find,
  According as his humours lead,
  A meaning suited to his mind.   *Ib.* ii

3 Wearing his wisdom lightly, like the fruit
  Which in our winter woodland looks a flower.
                                  A Dedication

4 And ever upon the topmost roof our banner of England blew.   *The Defence of Lucknow*

5 Out of the deep, my child, out of the deep.
                           De Profundis, i, l. 1

6 I read, before my eyelids dropt their shade,
  'The Legend of Good Women', long ago
  Sung by the morning star of song, who made
  His music heard below.
              A Dream of Fair Women, l. i

7 The spacious times of great Elizabeth.   *Ib.* l. 7

8 A daughter of the gods, divinely tall
  And most divinely fair.   *Ib.* l. 87

9 A queen, with swarthy cheeks and bold black eyes,
  Brow-bound with burning gold.   *Ib.* l. 127

10 He clasps the crag with crooked hands;
   Close to the sun in lonely lands,
   Ring'd with the azure world, he stands.
   The wrinkled sea beneath him crawls;
   He watches from his mountain walls,
   And like a thunderbolt he falls.   *The Eagle*

11 Once more the Heavenly Power
   Makes all things new,
   And domes the red-plow'd hills
   With loving blue;
   The blackbirds have their wills,
   The throstles too.   *Early Spring,* i

12 The curate; he was fatter than his cure.
                              Edwin Morris, l. 15

13 God made the woman for the man,
   And for the good and increase of the world. *Ib.* l. 50

14 Slight Sir Robert with his watery smile
   And educated whisker.   *Ib.* l. 128

15 And when they buried him the little port
   Had seldom seen a costlier funeral.   *Enoch Arden*

16 Barbarous experiment, barbarous hexameters.
   *Experiments. In quantity. On Translation of
   Homer*

17 O mighty-mouth'd inventor of harmonies,
   O skill'd to sing of Time or Eternity,
   God-gifted organ-voice of England,
   Milton, a name to resound for ages.
                          Ib. Milton. Alcaics

18 All that bowery loneliness,
   The brooks of Eden mazily murmuring.   *Ib.*

19 O you chorus of indolent reviewers.
                 Ib. Milton. Hendecasyllabics

20   A tiny poem
   All composed in a metre of Catullus,
   All in quantity, careful of my motion,
   Like the skater on ice that hardly bears him. *Ib.*

21 The mellow lin-lan-lone of evening bells.
                                  Far-Far-Away

22 O Love, O fire! once he drew
   With one long kiss my whole soul thro'
   My lips, as sunlight drinketh dew.   *Fatima,* iii

23 Read my little fable:
   He that runs may read.
   Most can raise the flowers now,
   For all have got the seed.   *The Flower,* v

24 Flower in the crannied wall,
   I pluck you out of the crannies,
   I hold you here, root and all, in my hand,
   Little flower—but *if* I could understand
   What you are, root and all, and all in all,
   I should know what God and man is.
                       Flower in the Crannied Wall

25 More black than ashbuds in the front of March.
                     The Gardener's Daughter, l. 28

26 A sight to make an old man young.   *Ib.* l. 140

27 Then she rode forth, clothed on with chastity.
                                  Godiva, l. 53

28 With twelve great shocks of sound, the shameless
   noon
   Was clash'd and hammer'd from a hundred towers.
                                      Ib. l. 74

29 Move onward, leading up the golden year.
                          The Golden Year, l. 26

30   Ah! when shall all men's good
   Be each man's rule, and universal Peace
   Lie like a shaft of light across the land? *Ib.* l. 47

31 Thro' all the circle of the golden year.   *Ib.* l. 51

32 That a lie which is all a lie may be met and fought
   with outright,
   But a lie which is part a truth is a harder matter to
   fight.   *The Grandmother,* viii

33 That man's the true Conservative
   Who lops the moulder'd branch away.
                             Hands All Round, i

34 Pray God our greatness may not fail
   Thro' craven fears of being great.   *Ib.* iii

35 Gigantic daughter of the West,
   We drink to thee across the flood . . .
   For art thou not of British blood?
      Ib. iv. In original version, published in *The
      Examiner,* 7 Feb. 1852

36   Senlac! Sanguelac,
   The lake of Blood!   *Harold,* III. i

37 Sanguelac! Sanguelac! the arrow! the arrow!   *Ib.*

38 Speak to Him thou for He hears, and Spirit with
   Spirit can meet—
   Closer is He than breathing, and nearer than hands
   and feet.   *The Higher Pantheism,* vi

39 Wearing the white flower of a blameless life,
   Before a thousand peering littlenesses,
   In that fierce light which beats upon a throne,
   And blackens every blot.
          The Idylls of the King, Dedication, l. 24

40 Man's word is God in man.
                 Ib. The Coming of Arthur, l. 132

41 A doubtful throne is ice on summer seas. *Ib.* l. 247

42 Clothed in white samite, mystic, wonderful.
       Ib. l. 284, and *The Passing of Arthur,* l. 199

1 Rain, rain, and sun! a rainbow in the sky!
A young man will be wiser by and by;
An old man's wit may wander ere he die.
The Idylls of the King, The Coming of Arthur, l. 402

2 From the great deep to the great deep he goes.
Ib. l. 410

3 Blow trumpet, for the world is white with May.
Ib. l. 481

4 Live pure, speak true, right wrong, follow the King—
Else, wherefore born? *Ib. Gareth and Lynette*, l. 117

5   The city is built
To music, therefore never built at all,
And therefore built for ever. *Ib.* l. 272

6 Lightly was her slender nose
Tip-tilted like the petal of a flower. *Ib.* l. 576

7 Lead, and I follow. *Ib.* l. 726

8 O purblind race of miserable men,
How many among us at this very hour
Do forge a lifelong trouble for ourselves,
By taking true for false, or false for true!
Ib. Geraint and Enid, l. 1

9 But o'er her meek eyes came a happy mist
Like that which kept the heart of Eden green
Before the useful trouble of the rain. *Ib.* l. 769

10 Too late, too late! ye cannot enter now.
Ib. Guinevere, l. 168

11 For manners are not idle, but the fruit
Of loyal nature, and of noble mind. *Ib.* l. 333

12 The children born of thee are sword and fire,
Red ruin, and the breaking up of laws. *Ib.* l. 422

13 To reverence the King, as if he were
Their conscience, and their conscience as their King,
To break the heathen and uphold the Christ,
To ride abroad redressing human wrongs,
To speak no slander, no, nor listen to it,
To honour his own word as if his God's. *Ib.* l. 465

14 To love one maiden only, cleave to her,
And worship her by years of noble deeds,
Until they won her; for indeed I knew
Of no more subtle master under heaven
Than is the maiden passion for a maid,
Not only to keep down the base in man,
But teach high thought, and amiable words
And courtliness, and the desire of fame,
And love of truth, and all that makes a man.
Ib. l. 472

15 Our fair father Christ. *Ib.* l. 559

16 Hereafter in that world where all are pure
We two may meet before high God, and thou
Wilt spring to me, and claim me thine, and know
I am thine husband—not a smaller soul,
Nor Lancelot, nor another. *Ib.* l. 560

17   He never mocks,
For mockery is the fume of little hearts. *Ib.* l. 627

18 I thought I could not breathe in that fine air
That pure severity of perfect light—
I yearn'd for warmth and colour which I found
In Lancelot. *Ib.* l. 640

19 It was my duty to have loved the highest:
It surely was my profit had I known:
It would have been my pleasure had I seen.
We needs must love the highest when we see it,
Not Lancelot, nor another. *Ib.* l. 652

20 To where beyond these voices there is peace.
The Idylls of the King. Guinevere, l. 69

21 For good ye are and bad, and like to coins,
Some true, some light, but every one of you
Stamp'd with the image of the King.
Ib. The Holy Grail, l. 2

22 The cup, the cup itself, from which our Lord
Drank at the last sad supper with his own. *Ib.* l. 4

23 God make thee good as thou art beautiful. *Ib.* l. 13

24 For when was Lancelot wanderingly lewd? *Ib.* l. 14

25 I, maiden, round thee, maiden, bind my belt.
Ib. l. 15

26   Ye follow wandering fires
Lost in the quagmire! *Ib.* l. 31

27 This madness has come on us for our sins. *Ib.* l. 35

28 And lifting up mine eyes, I found myself
Alone, and in a land of sand and thorns. *Ib.* l. 37

29 I saw the fiery face as of a child
That smote itself into the bread, and went. *Ib.* l. 47

30 And in the strength of this I rode,
Shattering all evil customs everywhere. *Ib.* l. 48

31 I will be deafer than the blue-eyed cat,
And thrice as blind as any noon-tide owl,
To holy virgins in their ecstasies,
Henceforward. *Ib.* l. 86

32 So spake the King: I knew not all he meant.
Ib. l. 91

33 Elaine the fair, Elaine the loveable,
Elaine, the lily maid of Astolat.
Ib. Lancelot and Elaine, l.

34   To me
He is all fault who hath no fault at all:
For who loves me must have a touch of earth.
Ib. l. 13

35   In me there dwells
No greatness, save it be some far-off touch
Of greatness to know well I am not great. *Ib.* l. 44

36 I know not if I know what true love is,
But if I know, then, if I love not him,
I know there is none other I can love. *Ib.* l. 67

37 The shackles of an old love straiten'd him,
His honour rooted in dishonour stood,
And faith unfaithful kept him falsely true. *Ib.* l. 87

38 Sweet is true love tho' given in vain, in vain;
And sweet is death who puts an end to pain.
Ib. l. 100

39   Never yet
Was noble man but made ignoble talk.
He makes no friend who never made a foe.
Ib. l. 108

40 Our bond is not the bond of man and wife.
Ib. l. 119

41 'Forgive me; mine was jealousy in love.'
He answer'd with his eyes upon the ground,
'That is love's curse; pass on, my Queen, forgiven.'
Ib. l. 134

42 Free love—free field—we love but while we may.
Ib. The Last Tournament, l. 28

43 The dirty nurse, Experience, in her kind
Hath foul'd me. *Ib.* l. 31

TENNYSON

1 The greater man, the greater courtesy.
The Idylls of the King. The Last Tournament, l. 628

2 The ptarmigan that whitens ere his hour
Woos his own end.   *Ib.* l. 692

3 Our hoard is little, but our hearts are great.
Ib. The Marriage of Geraint, l. 352

4 For man is man and master of his fate.   *Ib.* l. 355

5 Hark, by the bird's song ye may learn the nest.
Ib. l. 359

6 They take the rustic murmur of their bourg
For the great wave that echoes round the world.
Ib. l. 419

7 Mother, a maiden is a tender thing,
And best by her that bore her understood. *Ib.* l. 510

8 Brave hearts and clean! and yet—God guide them—
young.   *Ib. Merlin and Vivien,* l. 29

9 As, on a dull day in an ocean-cave,
The blind wave, feeling round his long sea-hall
In silence.   *Ib.* l. 229

10 Unfaith in aught is want of faith in all.   *Ib.* l. 387

11 It is the little rift within the lute,
That by and by will make the music mute,
And ever widening slowly silence all.   *Ib.* l. 388

12 And trust me not at all or all in all.   *Ib.* l. 396

13 Lo now, what hearts have men! they never mount
As high as woman in her selfless mood.   *Ib.* l. 440

14 Man dreams of fame while woman wakes to love.
Ib. l. 458

15 With this for motto, 'Rather use than fame'.
Ib. l. 478

16   Where blind and naked Ignorance
Delivers brawling judgments, unashamed,
On all things all day long.   *Ib.* l. 662

17 But every page having an ample marge,
And every marge enclosing in the midst
A square of text that looks a little blot.   *Ib.* l. 667

18 And none can read the text, not even I;
And none can read the comment but myself.
Ib. l. 679

19 Or some black wether of St. Satan's fold.   *Ib.* l. 748

20 O selfless man and stainless gentleman!   *Ib.* l. 790

21 Defaming and defacing, till she left
Not even Lancelot brave, nor Galahad clean.
Ib. l. 802

22 For men at most differ as Heaven and Earth,
But women, worst and best, as Heaven and Hell.
Ib. l. 812

23 Face-flatterer and backbiter are the same. *Ib.* l. 822

24   And the thicket closed
Behind her, and the forest echo'd 'fool'.   *Ib.* l. 971

25 O great and sane and simple race of brutes
That own no lust because they have no law!
Ib. Pelleas and Ettarre, l. 471

26 I found Him in the shining of the stars,
I mark'd Him in the flowering of His fields,
But in His ways with men I find Him not.
Ib. The Passing of Arthur, l. 9

27   Why is all around us here
As if some lesser god had made the world,
But had not force to shape it as he would? *Ib.* l.

28 This way and that dividing the swift mind.
The Idylls of the King. The Passing of Arthur, l. 60

29 So all day long the noise of battle roll'd
Among the mountains by the winter sea. *Ib.* l. 170

30 On one side lay the Ocean, and on one
Lay a great water, and the moon was full. *Ib.* l 179

31 Authority forgets a dying king.   *Ib.* l. 289

32 Clothed with his breath, and looking, as he walk'd,
Larger than human on the frozen hills.
He heard the deep behind him, and a cry
Before.   *Ib.* l. 350

33 When every morning brought a noble chance,
And every chance brought out a noble knight.
Ib. l. 398

34 Among new men, strange faces, other minds.
Ib. l. 406

35 And slowly answer'd Arthur from the barge:
'The old order changeth, yielding place to new,
And God fulfils himself in many ways,
Lest one good custom should corrupt the world.'
Ib. l. 407

36 If thou shouldst never see my face again,
Pray for my soul. More things are wrought by prayer
Than this world dreams of. Wherefore, let thy voice
Rise like a fountain for me night and day.
For what are men better than sheep or goats
That nourish a blind life within the brain,
If, knowing God, they lift not hands of prayer
Both for themselves and those who call them friend?
For so the whole round earth is every way
Bound by gold chains about the feet of God.
Ib. l. 414

37   I am going a long way
With these thou seest—if indeed I go
(For all my mind is clouded with a doubt)—
To the island-valley of Avilion;
Where falls not hail, or rain, or any snow,
Nor ever wind blows loudly; but it lies
Deep-meadow'd, happy, fair with orchard lawns
And bowery hollows crown'd with summer sea,
Where I will heal me of my grievous wound.
Ib. l. 424

38   Like some full-breasted swan
That, fluting a wild carol ere her death,
Ruffles her pure cold plume, and takes the flood
With swarthy webs.   *Ib.* l. 434

39 Believing where we cannot prove.
In Memoriam, prologue. (*The numbering of the Cantos follows that of the latest edition, and includes the additional Canto No. xxxix, first published in 1869*)

40 Thou madest man, he knows not why,
He thinks he was not made to die;
And thou hast made him: thou art just.   *Ib.*

41 Our little systems have their day;
They have their day and cease to be:
They are but broken lights of thee,
And thou, O Lord, art more than they.   *Ib.*

42 Let knowledge grow from more to more,
But more of reverence in us dwell;
That mind and soul, according well,
May make one music as before.   *Ib.*

TENNYSON

1 I held it truth, with him who sings
   To one clear harp in divers tones,
   That men may rise on stepping-stones
   Of their dead selves to higher things.
   In Memoriam, i

2 Who changest not in any gale,
   Nor branding summer suns avail
   To touch thy thousand years of gloom. *Ib. ii*

3 For words, like Nature, half reveal
   And half conceal the Soul within. *Ib. v*

4 But, for the unquiet heart and brain,
   A use in measured language lies;
   The sad mechanic exercise,
   Like dull narcotics, numbing pain. *Ib.*

5 And common is the commonplace,
   And vacant chaff well meant for grain. *Ib. vi*

6   Never morning wore
   To evening, but some heart did break. *Ib.*

7 His heavy-shotted hammock-shroud
   Drops in his vast and wandering grave. *Ib.*

8 Dark house, by which once more I stand
   Here in the long unlovely street,
   Doors, where my heart was used to beat
   So quickly, waiting for a hand. *Ib. vii*

9 And ghastly thro' the drizzling rain
   On the bald streets breaks the blank day. *Ib.*

10 More than my brothers are to me. *Ib. ix*

11 Or where the kneeling hamlet drains
   The chalice of the grapes of God. *Ib. x*

12 The last red leaf is whirl'd away,
   The rooks are blown about the skies. *Ib. xv*

13 Thou comest, much wept for: such a breeze
   Compell'd thy canvas. *Ib. xvii*

14 And from his ashes may be made
   The violet of his native land. *Ib. xviii*

15 There twice a day the Severn fills;
   The salt sea-water passes by,
   And hushes half the babbling Wye,
   And makes a silence in the hills. *Ib. xix*

16 I do but sing because I must,
   And pipe but as the linnets sing. *Ib. xxi*

17 The Shadow cloak'd from head to foot,
   Who keeps the keys of all the creeds. *Ib. xxiii*

18 And Thought leapt out to wed with Thought
   Ere Thought could wed itself with Speech. *Ib.*

19 I envy not in any moods
   The captive void of noble rage,
   The linnet born within the cage,
   That never knew the summer woods. *Ib. xxvii*

20 'Tis better to have loved and lost
   Than never to have loved at all. *Ib.*

21 The time draws near the birth of Christ. *Ib. xxviii*

22 'Where wert thou, brother, those four days?'
   There lives no record of reply,
   Which telling what it is to die
   Had surely added praise to praise.

   From every house the neighbours met,
   The streets were fill'd with joyful sound,
   A solemn gladness even crown'd
   The purple brows of Olivet.

Behold a man raised up by Christ!
   The rest remaineth unreveal'd;
   He told it not; or something seal'd
   The lips of that Evangelist. *In Memoriam, xxxi*

23 Her eyes are homes of silent prayer. *Ib. xxxii*

24 Leave thou thy sister when she prays,
   Her early Heaven, her happy views;
   Nor thou with shadow'd hint confuse
   A life that leads melodious days.

   Her faith thro' form is pure as thine,
   Her hands are quicker unto good:
   Oh, sacred be the flesh and blood
   To which she links a truth divine! *Ib. xxxiii*

25 And so the Word had breath, and wrought
   With human hands the creed of creeds
   In loveliness of perfect deeds,
   More strong than all poetic thought. *Ib. xxxvi*

26 Short swallow-flights of song, that dip
   Their wings in tears, and skim away. *Ib. xlviii*

27 And Time, a maniac scattering dust,
   And Life, a Fury slinging flame. *Ib. l*

28 Do we indeed desire the dead
   Should still be near us at our side?
   Is there no baseness we would hide?
   No inner vileness that we dread? *Ib. li*

29 How many a father have I seen,
   A sober man, among his boys,
   Whose youth was full of foolish noise. *Ib. liii*

30 Hold thou the good: define it well:
   For fear divine Philosophy
   Should push beyond her mark, and be
   Procuress to the Lords of Hell. *Ib.*

31 Oh yet we trust that somehow good
   Will be the final goal of ill. *Ib. liv*

32 That nothing walks with aimless feet;
   That not one life shall be destroy'd,
   Or cast as rubbish to the void,
   When God hath made the pile complete; *Ib.*

33 That not a worm is cloven in vain;
   That not a moth with vain desire
   Is shrivell'd in a fruitless fire,
   Or but subserves another's gain. *Ib.*

34   But what am I?
   An infant crying in the night:
   An infant crying for the light:
   And with no language but a cry. *Ib.*

35 So careful of the type she seems,
   So careless of the single life. *Ib. lv*

36   The great world's altar-stairs
   That slope thro' darkness up to God. *Ib.*

37 Nature, red in tooth and claw. *Ib. lvi*

38   Dragons of the prime,
   That tare each other in their slime,
   Were mellow music match'd with him. *Ib.*

39 Peace; come away: the song of woe
   Is after all an earthly song:
   Peace; come away: we do him wrong
   To sing so wildly: let us go. *Ib. lvii*

40 The passing of the sweetest soul
   That ever look'd with human eyes. *Ib.*

41 O Sorrow, wilt thou live with me
   No casual mistress, but a wife. *Ib. lix*

TENNYSON

1 As some divinely gifted man,
Whose life in low estate began
And on a simple village green;

Who breaks his birth's invidious bar,
And grasps the skirts of happy chance,
And breasts the blows of circumstance,
And grapples with his evil star. *In Memoriam*, lxiv

2 Yet feels, as in a pensive dream,
When all his active powers are still,
A distant dearness in the hill,
A secret sweetness in the stream. *Ib.*

3 So many worlds, so much to do,
So little done, such things to be. *Ib.* lxxiii

4 Death has made
His darkness beautiful with thee. *Ib.* lxxiv

5 And round thee with the breeze of song
To stir a little dust of praise. *Ib.* lxxv

6 O last regret, regret can die! *Ib.* lxxviii

7 Laburnums, dropping-wells of fire. *Ib.* lxxxiii

8 God's finger touch'd him, and he slept. *Ib.* lxxxv

9 I, the divided half of such
A friendship as had master'd Time. *Ib.*

10 Dusty purlieus of the law. *Ib.* lxxxix

11 The hard heir strides about their lands,
And will not yield them for a day. *Ib.* xc

12 When rosy plumelets tuft the larch,
And rarely pipes the mounted thrush;
Or underneath the barren bush
Flits by the sea-blue bird of March. *Ib.* xci

13 You tell me, doubt is Devil-born. *Ib.* xcvi

14 There lives more faith in honest doubt,
Believe me, than in half the creeds. *Ib.*

15 Their meetings made December June,
Their every parting was to die. *Ib.* xcvii

16 He seems so near and yet so far. *Ib.*

17 Ring out, wild bells, to the wild sky. *Ib.* cvi

18 Ring out the old, ring in the new,
Ring, happy bells, across the snow:
The year is going, let him go;
Ring out the false, ring in the true. *Ib.*

19 Ring out the feud of rich and poor. *Ib.*

20 Ring out a slowly dying cause,
And ancient forms of party strife;
Ring in the nobler modes of life,
With sweeter manners, purer laws.

Ring out the want, the care, the sin,
The faithless coldness of the times;
Ring out, ring out my mournful rhymes,
But ring the fuller minstrel in.

Ring out false pride in place and blood,
The civic slander and the spite;
Ring in the love of truth and right,
Ring in the common love of good.

Ring out old shapes of foul disease;
Ring out the narrowing lust of gold;
Ring out the thousand wars of old,
Ring in the thousand years of peace.

Ring in the valiant man and free,
The larger heart, the kindlier hand;
Ring out the darkness of the land;
Ring in the Christ that is to be. *Ib.*

21 'Tis held that sorrow makes us wise,
Whatever wisdom sleep with thee.
In Memoriam, cviii

22 Not the schoolboy hear,
The blind hysterics of the Celt. *Ib.* cix

23 And thus he bore without abuse
The grand old name of gentleman,
Defamed by every charlatan,
And soil'd with all ignoble use. *Ib.* cxi

24 Now fades the last long streak of snow
Now burgeons every maze of quick
About the flowering squares and thick
By ashen roots the violets blow. *Ib.* cxv

25 And drown'd in yonder living blue
The lark becomes a sightless song. *Ib.*

26 But trust that those we call the dead
Are breathers of an ampler day
For ever nobler ends. *Ib.* cxviii

27 There, where the long street roars, hath been
The stillness of the central sea. *Ib.* cxxiii

28 And all is well, tho' faith and form
Be sunder'd in the night of fear. *Ib.* cxxvii

29 The red fool-fury of the Seine. *Ib.*

30 Wearing all that weight
Of learning lightly like a flower. *Ib. Conclusion*, st. x

31 One God, one law, one element,
And one far-off divine event,
To which the whole creation moves. *Ib.* st. xxxvi

32 All along the valley, stream that flashest white.
In the Valley of Cauteretz

33 The voice of the dead was a living voice to me. *Ib.*

34 God gives us love. Something to love
He lends us; but, when love is grown
To ripeness, that on which it throve
Falls off, and love is left alone. *To J. S.*, iv

35 At me you smiled, but unbeguiled
I saw the snare, and I retired:
The daughter of a hundred Earls,
You are not one to be desired.
Lady Clara Vere de Vere, i

36 A simple maiden in her flower
Is worth a hundred coats-of-arms. *Ib.* ii

37 Her manners had not that repose
Which stamps the caste of Vere de Vere. *Ib.* v

38 From yon blue heavens above us bent
The gardener Adam and his wife
Smile at the claims of long descent.
Howe'er it be, it seems to me,
'Tis only noble to be good.
Kind hearts are more than coronets,
And simple faith than Norman blood. *Ib.* vi

39 Oh! teach the orphan-boy to read,
Or teach the orphan-girl to sew. *Ib.*

40 On either side the river lie
Long fields of barley and of rye.
The Lady of Shalott, pt. i

41 Willows whiten, aspens quiver,
Little breezes dusk and shiver. *Ib.*

42 But who hath seen her wave her hand?
Or at the casement seen her stand?
Or is she known in all the land,
The Lady of Shalott? *Ib.*

1 Only reapers, reaping early
In among the bearded barley,
Hear a song that echoes cheerly
From the river winding clearly
Down to tower'd Camelot.
The Lady of Shalott, pt. i

2 She hath no loyal knight and true,
The Lady of Shalott. *Ib.* pt. ii

3 Or when the moon was overhead,
Came two young lovers lately wed;
'I am half sick of shadows,' said
The Lady of Shalott. *Ib.*

4 A bow-shot from her bower-eaves,
He rode between the barley-sheaves,
The sun came dazzling thro' the leaves,
And flamed upon the brazen greaves
Of bold Sir Lancelot.
A red-cross knight for ever kneel'd
To a lady in his shield,
That sparkled on the yellow field,
Beside remote Shalott. *Ib.* pt. iii

5 All in the blue unclouded weather. *Ib.*

6 'Tirra lirra,' by the river
Sang Sir Lancelot. *Ib.*

7 She left the web, she left the loom,
She made three paces thro' the room
She saw the water-lily bloom,
She saw the helmet and the plume,
She look'd down to Camelot.
Out flew the web and floated wide;
The mirror crack'd from side to side;
'The curse is come upon me,' cried
The Lady of Shalott. *Ib.*

8 Like some bold seër in a trance,
Seeing all his own mischance—
With a glassy countenance
Did she look to Camelot. *Ib.* pt. iv

9 Heard a carol, mournful, holy,
Chanted loudly, chanted lowly,
Till her blood was frozen slowly,
And her eyes were darken'd wholly,
Turn'd to tower'd Camelot. *Ib.*

10 Who is this? and what is here?
And in the lighted palace near
Died the sound of royal cheer;
And they cross'd themselves for fear,
All the knights at Camelot:
But Lancelot mused a little space;
He said, 'She has a lovely face;
God in his mercy lend her grace,
The Lady of Shalott.' *Ib.*

11 Slander, meanest spawn of Hell. *The Letters*

12 Airy, fairy Lilian. *Lilian*

13 Comrades, leave me here a little, while as yet 'tis early morn:
Leave me here, and when you want me, sound upon the bugle-horn. *Locksley Hall*, l. i

14 The fairy tales of science, and the long result of Time.
Ib. l. 12

15 In the Spring a livelier iris changes on the burnish'd dove;
In the Spring a young man's fancy lightly turns to thoughts of love. *Ib.* l. 19

16 Love took up the glass of Time, and turn'd it in his glowing hands;
Every moment, lightly shaken, ran itself in golden sands.
Love took up the harp of Life, and smote on all the chords with might;
Smote the chord of Self, that, trembling, pass'd in music out of sight. *Locksley Hall*, l. 31

17 And our spirits rush'd together at the touching of the lips. *Ib.* l. 38

18 As the husband is, the wife is. *Ib.* l. 47

19 He will hold thee, when his passion shall have spent its novel force.
Something better than his dog, a little dearer than his horse. *Ib.* l. 49

20 The many-winter'd crow that leads the clanging rookery home. *Ib.* l. 68

21 This is truth the poet sings,
That a sorrow's crown of sorrow is remembering happier things. *Ib.* l. 75 (*See 138:35*)

22 Like a dog, he hunts in dreams. *Ib.* l. 79

23 With a little hoard of maxims preaching down a daughter's heart. *Ib.* l. 94

24 But the jingling of the guinea helps the hurt that Honour feels. *Ib.* l. 105

25 Men, my brothers, men the workers, ever reaping something new:
That which they have done but earnest of the things that they shall do:
For I dipt into the future, far as human eye could see,
Saw the Vision of the world, and all the wonder that would be. *Ib.* l. 117

26 Heard the heavens fill with shouting, and there rain'd a ghastly dew
From the nations' airy navies grappling in the central blue. *Ib.* l. 123

27 In the Parliament of man, the Federation of the world. *Ib.* l. 128

28 Science moves, but slowly slowly, creeping on from point to point. *Ib.* l. 134

29 Yet I doubt not thro' the ages one increasing purpose runs,
And the thoughts of men are widen'd with the process of the suns. *Ib.* l. 137

30 Knowledge comes, but wisdom lingers. *Ib.* l. 143

31 I am shamed thro' all my nature to have loved so slight a thing. *Ib.* l. 148

32 Woman is the lesser man, and all thy passions, match'd with mine,
Are as moonlight unto sunlight, and as water unto wine. *Ib.* l. 151

33 I will take some savage woman, she shall rear my dusky race. *Ib.* l. 168

34 Not with blinded eyesight poring over miserable books. *Ib.* l. 172

35 I the heir of all the ages, in the foremost files of time. *Ib.* l. 178

36 Forward, forward let us range,
Let the great world spin for ever down the ringing grooves of change. *Ib.* l. 181

TENNYSON

1 Better fifty years of Europe than a cycle of Cathay.
Locksley Hall, l. 184

2 He is but a landscape-painter,
And a village maiden she.
The Lord of Burleigh, l. 7

3 Let us see these handsome houses
Where the wealthy nobles dwell. *Ib.* l. 23

4 Many a gallant gay domestic
Bows before him at the door. *Ib.* l. 47

5 But he clasp'd her like a lover,
And he cheer'd her soul with love.
So she strove against her weakness,
Tho' at times her spirit sank. *Ib.* l. 67

6 And the people loved her much. *Ib.* l. 76

7 But a trouble weigh'd upon her,
And perplex'd her, night and morn,
With the burthen of an honour
Unto which she was not born. *Ib.* l. 77

8 'Oh, that he
Were once more that landscape-painter,
Which did win my heart from me!' *Ib.* l. 82

9 Three fair children first she bore him,
Then before her time she died. *Ib.* l. 87

10 Weeping, weeping late and early,
Walking up and pacing down,
Deeply mourn'd the Lord of Burleigh,
Burleigh-house by Stamford-town. *Ib.* l. 89

11 'Bring the dress and put it on her,
That she wore when she was wed.' *Ib.* l. 95

12 'Courage!' he said, and pointed toward the land.
The Lotos-Eaters

13 A land
In which it seemed always afternoon. *Ib.*

14 Music that gentlier on the spirit lies,
Than tir'd eyelids upon tir'd eyes. *Ib. Choric Song*, i

15 There is no joy but calm! *Ib.* ii

16 Ah, why
Should life all labour be? *Ib.* iv

17 Let us alone. Time driveth onward fast,
And in a little while our lips are dumb.
Let us alone. What is it that will last?
All things are taken from us, and become
Portions and parcels of the dreadful Past. *Ib.*

18 The Lotos blooms below the barren peak:
The Lotos blows by every winding creek:
All day the wind breathes low with mellower tone:
Thro' every hollow cave and alley lone,
Round and round the spicy downs the yellow Lotos-dust is blown. *Ib.* viii

19 Live and lie reclined
On the hills like Gods together, careless of mankind.
For they lie beside their nectar, and the bolts are hurl'd
Far below them in the valleys, and the clouds are lightly curl'd
Round their golden houses, girdled with the gleaming world. *Ib.*

20 Surely, surely, slumber is more sweet than toil, the shore
Than labour in the deep mid-ocean, wind and wave and oar;
Oh rest ye, brother mariners, we will not wander more. *Ib.*

21 Of love that never found his earthly close,
What sequel? Streaming eyes and breaking hearts?
Or all the same as if he had not been?
Love and Duty, l. 1

22 The long mechanic pacings to and fro,
The set gray life, and apathetic end. *Ib.* l. 17

23 Raw Haste, half-sister to Delay.
Love thou thy Land, xxiv

24 Ruining along the illimitable inane. *Lucretius*, l. 40

25 Nor at all can tell
Whether I mean this day to end myself,
Or lend an ear to Plato where he says,
That men like soldiers may not quit the post
Allotted by the Gods. *Ib.* l. 145

26 That stays the rolling Ixionian wheel,
And numbs the Fury's ringlet-snake, and plucks
The mortal soul from out immortal hell. *Ib.* l. 260

27 Passionless bride, divine Tranquillity. *Ib.* l. 265

28 Without one pleasure and without one pain.
Ib. l. 268

29 The lonely moated grange. *Mariana*

30 She only said, 'My life is dreary,
He cometh not,' she said;
She said, 'I am aweary, aweary.
I would that I were dead!' *Ib.*

31 Her tears fell with the dews at even;
Her tears fell ere the dews were dried. *Ib.*

32 She wept, 'I am aweary, aweary,
O God, that I were dead!' *Ib.*

33 I hate the dreadful hollow behind the little wood.
Maud, Pt. I. i. i

34 The smooth-faced snubnosed rogue. *Ib.* xiii

35 Faultily faultless, icily regular, splendidly null. *Ib.* II

36 A monstrous eft was of old the Lord and Master of Earth. *Ib.* IV. vi

37 The passionate heart of the poet is whirl'd into folly and vice. *Ib.* vii

38 And most of all would I flee from the cruel madness of love—
The honey of poison-flowers and all the measureless ill. *Ib.* x

39 Maud with her exquisite face,
And wild voice pealing up to the sunny sky,
And feet like sunny gems on an English green.
Ib. v. ii

40 That jewell'd mass of millinery,
That oil'd and curl'd Assyrian Bull. *Ib.* VI. vi

41 She came to the village church,
And sat by a pillar alone;
An angel watching an urn
Wept over her, carved in stone. *Ib.* VIII

42 The snowy-banded, dilettante,
Delicate-handed priest intone. *Ib.*

43 Ah God, for a man with heart, head, hand,
Like some of the simple great ones gone
For ever and ever by,
One still strong man in a blatant land,
Whatever they call him, what care I,
Aristocrat, democrat, autocrat—one
Who can rule and dare not lie.

And ah for a man to arise in me,
That the man I am may cease to be!
Maud, Pt. I. x. v–vi

1 O let the solid ground
   Not fail beneath my feet
Before my life has found
   What some have found so sweet.
Ib. XI. i

2 Birds in the high Hall-garden
When twilight was falling,
Maud, Maud, Maud, Maud,
They were crying and calling.
Ib. XII. i

3 I kiss'd her slender hand,
She took the kiss sedately;
Maud is not seventeen,
But she is tall and stately.
Ib. iv

4 I know the way she went
Home with her maiden posy,
For her feet have touch'd the meadows
And left the daisies rosy.
Ib. vi

5 Gorgonised me from head to foot
With a stony British stare.
Ib. XIII. ii

6 Go not, happy day,
From the shining fields,
Go not, happy day,
Till the maiden yields.
Rosy is the West,
Rosy is the South,
Roses are her cheeks,
And a rose her mouth.
Ib. XVII

7 Blush from West to East,
Blush from East to West,
Till the West is East,
Blush it thro' the West.
Ib.

8 A livelier emerald twinkles in the grass,
A purer sapphire melts into the sea.
Ib. XVIII. vi

9 Come into the garden, Maud,
   For the black bat, night, has flown;
Come into the garden, Maud,
   I am here at the gate alone;
And the woodbine spices are wafted abroad,
   And the musk of the rose is blown.

10 For a breeze of morning moves,
   And the planet of Love is on high,
Beginning to faint in the light that she loves
   On a bed of daffodil sky.
Ib. XXII. i–ii

11 All night have the roses heard
   The flute, violin, bassoon;
All night has the casement jessamine stirr'd
   To the dancers dancing in tune;
Till a silence fell with the waking bird,
   And a hush with the setting moon.
Ib. iii

12 Whenever a March-wind sighs
He sets the jewel-print of your feet
In violets blue as your eyes.
Ib. vii

13 The slender acacia would not shake
   One long milk-bloom on the tree;
The white lake-blossom fell into the lake
   As the pimpernel dozed on the lea;
But the rose was awake all night for your sake,
   Knowing your promise to me;
The lilies and roses were all awake,
   They sigh'd for the dawn and thee.
Ib. viii

14 Queen rose of the rosebud garden of girls.
Ib. ix

15 There has fallen a splendid tear
   From the passion-flower at the gate.
She is coming, my dove, my dear;
   She is coming, my life, my fate;
The red rose cries, 'She is near, she is near;'
   And the white rose weeps, 'She is late;'
The larkspur listens, 'I hear, I hear;
   And the lily whispers, 'I wait.'

She is coming, my own, my sweet;
   Were it ever so airy a tread,
My heart would hear her and beat,
   Were it earth in an earthy bed;
My dust would hear her and beat,
   Had I lain for a century dead;
Would start and tremble under her feet,
   And blossom in purple and red.
Maud, Pt. I. XXII. x–xi

16 The Christless code,
That must have life for a blow.
Ib. Pt. II. I. i

17 O that 'twere possible
After long grief and pain
To find the arms of my true love
Round me once again!
Ib. IV. i

18 Ah Christ, that it were possible
For one short hour to see
The souls we loved, that they might tell us
What and where they be.
Ib. iii

19 But the churchmen fain would kill their church,
As the churches have kill'd their Christ.
Ib. v. ii

20 O me, why have they not buried me deep enough?
Is it kind to have made me a grave so rough,
Me, that was never a quiet sleeper?
Ib. xi

21 Bury me, bury me
Deeper, ever so little deeper.
Ib.

22 My life has crept so long on a broken wing
Thro' cells of madness, haunts of horror and fear,
That I come to be grateful at last for a little thing.
Ib. Pt. III. VI. i

23 When the face of night is fair on the dewy downs,
And the shining daffodil dies.
Ib.

24 The blood-red blossom of war with a heart of fire.
Ib. iv

25 It is better to fight for the good, than to rail at the ill;
I have felt with my native land, I am one with my kind,
I embrace the purpose of God, and the doom assign'd.
Ib. v

26 You must wake and call me early, call me early,
   mother dear;
To-morrow 'ill be the happiest time of all the glad
   New-year;
Of all the glad New-year, mother, the maddest
   merriest day;
For I'm to be Queen o' the May, mother, I'm to be
   Queen o' the May.
The May Queen

27 It seem'd so hard at first, mother, to leave the blessed
   sun,
And now it seems as hard to stay, and yet His will be
   done!
But still I think it can't be long before I find release;
And that good man, the clergyman, has told me
   words of peace.
Ib. Conclusion

1 All in the wild March-morning I heard the angels
     call;
     It was when the moon was setting, and the dark was
     over all;
     The trees began to whisper, and the wind began to
     roll,
     And in the wild March-morning I heard them call
     my soul.   *The May Queen.* Conclusion

2 Follow the Gleam.   *Merlin and the Gleam*

3   In after-dinner talk,
     Across the walnuts and the wine.
                         The Miller's Daughter

4   What, it's you,
     The padded man—that wears the stays.
                  The New Timon and the Poets

5 What profits now to understand
     The merits of a spotless shirt—
     A dapper boot—a little hand—
     If half the little soul is dirt?   *Ib.*

6 Dosn't thou 'ear my 'erse's legs, as they canters
     awaäy?
     Proputty, proputty, proputty—that's what I 'ears 'em
     saäy.   *Northern Farmer. New Style*

7 But I knaw'd a Quaäker feller as often 'as towd me
     this:
     'Doänt thou marry for munny, but goä wheer munny
     is!'   *Ib.*

8 Taake my word for it, Sammy, the poor in a loomp
     is bad.   *Ib.*

9 An' I thowt a said whot a owt to 'a said an' I coom'd
     awaäy.   *Northern Farmer. Old Style*

10 Do godamoighty knaw what a's doing a-taäkin' o'
     meä?   *Ib.*

11 Bury the Great Duke
     With an empire's lamentation,
     Let us bury the Great Duke
     To the noise of the mourning of a mighty nation.
        Ode on the Death of the Duke of Wellington, i

12 Let the sound of those he wrought for,
     And the feet of those he fought for,
     Echo round his bones for evermore.   *Ib.* ii

13 The last great Englishman is low.   *Ib.* iii

14 Foremost captain of his time,
     Rich in saving common-sense,
     And, as the greatest only are,
     In his simplicity sublime.
     O good grey head which all men knew!   *Ib.* iv

15 O fall'n at length that tower of strength
     Which stood four-square to all the winds that blew!
                                             Ib.

16 Under the cross of gold
     That shines over city and river.   *Ib.* v

17 Mighty Seaman, this is he
     Was great by land as thou by sea.   *Ib.* vi

18 For this is England's greatest son,
     He that gain'd a hundred fights,
     Nor ever lost an English gun.   *Ib.*

19 Clash'd with his fiery few and won.   *Ib.*

20 In that world-earthquake, Waterloo!   *Ib.*

21 Thank Him who isled us here, and roughly set
     His Briton in blown seas and storming showers.
                                             Ib. vii

22 That sober freedom out of which there springs
     Our loyal passion for our temperate kings.
        Ode on the Death of the Duke of Wellington, vii

23 Who never sold the truth to serve the hour,
     Nor palter'd with Eternal God for power.   *Ib.*

24 Truth-teller was our England's Alfred named.   *Ib.*

25 Not once or twice in our rough island-story,
     The path of duty was the way to glory.   *Ib.* viii

26 He shall find the stubborn thistle bursting
     Into glossy purples, which outredden
     All voluptuous garden-roses.   *Ib.*

27   The shining table-lands
     To which our God Himself is moon and sun.   *Ib.*

28 Speak no more of his renown,
     Lay your earthly fancies down,
     And in the vast cathedral leave him,
     God accept him, Christ receive him.   *Ib.* ix

29 There lies a vale in Ida, lovelier
     Than all the valleys of Ionian hills.   *Œnone*, l. 1

30 O mother Ida, many-fountain'd Ida.   *Ib.* l. 22

31 Dear mother Ida, harken ere I die.
     It was the deep midnoon: one silvery cloud
     Had lost his way between the piney sides
     Of this long glen. Then to the bower they came,
     Naked they came to that smooth-swarded bower,
     And at their feet the crocus brake like fire,
     Violet, amaracus, and asphodel,
     Lotos and lilies.   *Ib.* l. 89

32 Self-reverence, self-knowledge, self-control,
     These three alone lead life to sovereign power.
                                             Ib. l. 142

33   Because right is right, to follow right
     Were wisdom in the scorn of consequence. *Ib.* l. 147

34 I built my soul a lordly pleasure-house,
        Wherein at ease for aye to dwell.
                         The Palace of Art, i

35 Still as, while Saturn whirls, his stedfast shade
        Sleeps on his luminous ring.   *Ib.* iv

36 A haunt of ancient Peace.   *Ib.* xxii

37 Plato the wise, and large-brow'd Verulam,
        The first of those who know.   *Ib.* xli

38 On corpses three-months-old at noon she came,
        That stood against the wall.   *Ib.* lxi

39 Act first, this Earth, a stage so gloom'd with woe
        You all but sicken at the shifting scenes.
     And yet be patient. Our Playwright may show
        In some fifth Act what this wild Drama means.
                                             The Play

40 Dower'd with the hate of hate, the scorn of scorn,
        The love of love.   *The Poet*

41 And Freedom rear'd in that august sunrise
        Her beautiful bold brow.   *Ib.*

42 Vex not thou the poet's mind
        With thy shallow wit;
     Vex not thou the poet's mind;
        For thou canst not fathom it.
     Clear and bright it should be ever,
     Flowing like a crystal river;
     Bright as light, and clear as wind.   *The Poet's Mind*

43 Dark-brow'd sophist, come not anear:
     All the place is holy ground.   *Ib.*

TENNYSON

1 And he sat him down in a lonely place,
And chanted a melody loud and sweet,
That made the wild-swan pause in her cloud,
And the lark drop down at his feet.   *The Poet's Song*

2 The swallow stopt as he hunted the fly,
The snake slipt under a spray,
The wild hawk stood with the down on his beak,
And stared, with his foot on the prey.   *Ib.*

3 For some cry 'Quick' and some cry 'Slow',
But, while the hills remain,
Up hill 'Too-slow' will need the whip,
Down hill 'Too-quick', the chain.   *Politics*

4 The cuckoo of a joyless June
Is calling out of doors.
        Prefatory Poem to my Brother's Sonnets

5 The cuckoo of a worse July
Is calling thro' the dark.   *Ib.*

6 Here, in this roaring moon of daffodil
And crocus.
    Prefatory Sonnet to the 'Nineteenth Century'

7 With prudes for proctors, dowagers for deans,
And sweet girl-graduates in their golden hair.
        The Princess, prologue, l. 141

8 A rosebud set with little wilful thorns,
And sweet as English air could make her, she.
        Ib. l. 153

9 As thro' the land at eve we went,
And pluck'd the ripen'd ears,
We fell out, my wife and I,
O we fell out I know not why,
And kiss'd again with tears.
And blessings on the falling out
That all the more endears,
When we fall out with those we love
And kiss again with tears!   *Ib.* ii. *Introd. Song*

10 O hard, when love and duty clash!   *Ib.* ii. l. 273

11 And quoted odes, and jewels five-words long,
That on the stretch'd forefinger of all Time
Sparkle for ever.   *Ib.* l. 355

12 Sweet and low, sweet and low,
Wind of the western sea,
Low, low, breathe and blow,
Wind of the western sea!
Over the rolling waters go,
Come from the dying moon, and blow,
Blow him again to me;
While my little one, while my pretty one, sleeps.
        Ib. iii. *Introd. Song*

13 A Memnon smitten with the morning Sun.
        Ib. l. 100

14 The splendour falls on castle walls
And snowy summits old in story:
The long light shakes across the lakes,
And the wild cataract leaps in glory.
Blow, bugle, blow, set the wild echoes flying,
Blow, bugle; answer, echoes, dying, dying, dying.
        Ib. iv. *Introd. Song*

15 O hark, O hear! how thin and clear,
And thinner, clearer, farther going!
O sweet and far from cliff and scar
The horns of Elfland faintly blowing!   *Ib.*

16 O love, they die in yon rich sky,
They faint on hill or field or river:
Our echoes roll from soul to soul,
And grow for ever and for ever.
        The Princess, iv. *Introd. Song*

17 Tears, idle tears, I know not what they mean,
Tears from the depth of some divine despair
Rise in the heart, and gather to the eyes,
In looking on the happy Autumn-fields,
And thinking of the days that are no more.   *Ib.* l. 21

18 So sad, so fresh, the days that are no more.   *Ib.* l. 30

19 Ah, sad and strange as in dark summer dawns
The earliest pipe of half-awaken'd birds
To dying ears, when unto dying eyes
The casement slowly grows a glimmering square;
So sad, so strange, the days that are no more.

Dear as remembered kisses after death,
And sweet as those by hopeless fancy feign'd
On lips that are for others: deep as love,
Deep as first love, and wild with all regret;
O Death in Life, the days that are no more.   *Ib.* l. 31

20 O Swallow, Swallow, flying, flying South,
Fly to her, and fall upon her gilded eaves,
And tell her, tell her, what I tell to thee.

O tell her, Swallow, thou that knowest each,
That bright and fierce and fickle is the South,
And dark and true and tender is the North.   *Ib.* l. 75

21 O tell her, Swallow, that thy brood is flown:
Say to her, I do but wanton in the South,
But in the North long since my nest is made.

O tell her, brief is life but love is long,
And brief the sun of summer in the North,
And brief the moon of beauty in the South.

O Swallow, flying from the golden woods,
Fly to her, and pipe and woo her, and make her mine,
And tell her, tell her, that I follow thee.   *Ib.* l. 90

22 Thy voice is heard thro' rolling drums,
That beat to battle where he stands;
Thy face across his fancy comes,
And gives the battle to his hands:
A moment, while the trumpets blow,
He sees his brood about thy knee;
The next, like fire he meets the foe,
And strikes him dead for thine and thee.
        Ib. l. 552

23 Man is the hunter; woman is his game.   *Ib.* v, l. 147

24 Man for the field and woman for the hearth:
Man for the sword and for the needle she:
Man with the head and woman with the heart:
Man to command and woman to obey;
All else confusion.   *Ib.* l. 427

25 Home they brought her warrior dead.
She nor swoon'd, nor utter'd cry:
All her maidens, watching, said,
'She must weep or she will die.'   *Ib.* vi. *Introd. Song*

26 Home they brought him slain with spears,
They brought him home at even-fall.
    Ib. Version reprinted in Poems (1912), p. 870

27 Rose a nurse of ninety years,
Set his child upon her knee—
Like summer tempest came her tears—
'Sweet my child, I live for thee.'   *Ib.*

28   The woman is so hard
Upon the woman.   *Ib.* l. 205

[538]

1 Ask me no more: the moon may draw the sea;
The cloud may stoop from heaven and take the shape
With fold to fold, of mountain or of cape;
But O too fond, when have I answer'd thee?
　　　　　Ask me no more.

Ask me no more: what answer should I give?
I love not hollow cheek or faded eye:
Yet, O my friend, I will not have thee die!
Ask me no more, lest I should bid thee live;
　　　　　Ask me no more.

Ask me no more: thy fate and mine are seal'd:
I strove against the stream and all in vain:
Let the great river take me to the main:
No more, dear love, for at a touch I yield;
　　　　　Ask me no more.
　　　　　The Princess, vii. *Introd. Song*

2 Now sleeps the crimson petal, now the white;
Nor waves the cypress in the palace walk;
Nor winks the gold fin in the porphyry font:
The fire-fly wakens: waken thou with me.

Now droops the milk-white peacock like a ghost,
And like a ghost she glimmers on to me.

Now lies the Earth all Danaë to the stars,
And all thy heart lies open unto me.

Now slides the silent meteor on, and leaves
A shining furrow, as thy thoughts in me.

Now folds the lily all her sweetness up,
And slips into the bosom of the lake:
So fold thyself, my dearest, thou, and slip
Into my bosom and be lost in me. *Ib.* l. 161

3 Come down, O maid, from yonder mountain height:
What pleasure lives in height? *Ib.* l. 177

4 For Love is of the valley, come thou down
And find him; by the happy threshold, he,
Or hand in hand with Plenty in the maize,
Or red with spirted purple of the vats,
Or foxlike in the vine; nor cares to walk
With Death and Morning on the silver horns.
　　　　　Ib. l. 184

5 　　　　Sweet is every sound,
Sweeter thy voice, but every sound is sweet;
Myriads of rivulets hurrying thro' the lawn,
The moan of doves in immemorial elms,
And murmuring of innumerable bees. *Ib.* l. 203

6 The woman's cause is man's: they rise or sink
Together. *Ib.* l. 243

7 Like perfect music unto noble words. *Ib.* l. 270

8 　　　　Happy he
With such a mother! faith in womankind
Beats with his blood, and trust in all things high
Comes easy to him, and tho' he trip and fall
He shall not blind his soul with clay. *Ib.* l. 308

9 No little lily-handed Baronet he,
A great broad-shoulder'd genial Englishman.
　　　　　Ib. Conclusion, l. 84

10 A pamphleteer on guano and on grain. *Ib.* l. 89

11 This laurel greener from the brows
Of him that utter'd nothing base.
　　　　To the Queen (1851), '*Revered, beloved*'

12 Her court was pure; her life serene;
　God gave her peace; her land reposed;
　A thousand claims to reverence closed
In her as Mother, Wife, and Queen;

And statesmen at her council met
　Who knew the seasons when to take
　Occasion by the hand, and make
The bounds of freedom wider yet. *To the Queen.*

13 Broad-based upon her people's will,
And compass'd by the inviolate sea. *Ib.*

14 　Our slowly-grown
And crown'd Republic's crowning common-sense.
　　　　Ib. '*O loyal to the royal in thyself*', l. 59

15 For it was in the golden prime
Of good Haroun Alraschid.
　　　Recollections of the Arabian Nights, i

16 　At Flores in the Azores Sir Richard Grenville lay,
And a pinnace, like a fluttered bird, came flying from
　far away:
'Spanish ships of war at sea! we have sighted fifty-
　three!' *The Revenge*, i

17 Then sware Lord Thomas Howard: "Fore God I am
　no coward;
But I cannot meet them here, for my ships are out of
　gear,
And the half my men are sick. I must fly, but follow
　quick.
We are six ships of the line; can we fight with fifty-
　three?' *Ib.*

18 Then spake Sir Richard Grenville: 'I know you are
　no coward;
You fly them for a moment to fight with them again.
But I've ninety men and more that are lying sick
　ashore.
I should count myself the coward if I left them, my
　Lord Howard,
To these Inquisition dogs and the devildoms of
　Spain.' *Ib.* ii

19 So Lord Howard past away with five ships of war
　that day,
Till he melted like a cloud in the silent summer
　heaven;
But Sir Richard bore in hand all his sick men from
　the land
Very carefully and slow,
Men of Bideford in Devon,
And we laid them on the ballast down below;
For we brought them all aboard,
And they blest him in their pain, that they were not
　left to Spain,
To the thumbscrew and the stake, for the glory of
　the Lord. *Ib.* iii

20 'Shall we fight or shall we fly?
Good Sir Richard, tell us now,
For to fight is but to die!
There'll be little of us left by the time this sun be set.'
And Sir Richard said again: 'We be all good English
　men.
Let us bang these dogs of Seville, the children of the
　devil,
For I never turn'd my back upon Don or devil yet.'
　　　　　Ib. iv

21 And the sun went down, and the stars came out far
　over the summer sea,
But never a moment ceased the fight of the one and
　the fifty-three.
Ship after ship, the whole night long, their high-built
　galleons came,
Ship after ship, the whole night long, with her battle-
　thunder and flame;

Ship after ship, the whole night long, drew back with her dead and her shame.
For some were sunk and many were shatter'd, and so could fight us no more—
God of battles, was ever a battle like this in the world before? *The Revenge, ix*

1 'Sink me the ship, Master Gunner—sink her, split her in twain!
Fall into the hands of God, not into the hands of Spain!' *Ib. xi*

2 And the gunner said 'Ay, ay', but the seamen made reply:
'We have children, we have wives,
And the Lord hath spared our lives.' *Ib. xii*

3 And they praised him to his face with their courtly foreign grace;
But he rose upon their decks, and he cried:
'I have fought for Queen and Faith like a valiant man and true;
I have only done my duty as a man is bound to do:
With a joyful spirit I Sir Richard Grenville die!'
And he fell upon their decks, and he died. *Ib. xiii*

4 And the little Revenge herself went down by the island crags
To be lost evermore in the main. *Ib. xiv*

5 Form, Form, Riflemen Form! *Riflemen Form!*

6 Make thou my spirit pure and clear
As are the frosty skies,
Or the first snowdrop of the year
That in my bosom lies. *St. Agnes' Eve*

7 The sabbaths of Eternity,
One sabbath deep and wide—
A light upon the shining sea—
The Bridegroom with his bride! *Ib.*

8 Battering the gates of heaven with storms of prayer.
St. Simeon Stylites, l. 7

9 What does little birdie say
In her nest at peep of day? *Sea Dreams, l. 281*

10 Birdie, rest a little longer,
Till the little wings are stronger.
So she rests a little longer, ·
Then she flies away. *Ib. l. 285*

11 My strength is as the strength of ten,
Because my heart is pure. *Sir Galahad*

12 So pass I hostel, hall, and grange;
By bridge and ford, by park and pale,
All-arm'd I ride, whate'er betide,
Until I find the holy Grail. *Ib.*

13 A man had given all other bliss,
And all his worldly worth for this,
To waste his whole heart in one kiss
Upon her perfect lips.
Sir Launcelot and Queen Guinevere

14 Alone and warming his five wits,
The white owl in the belfry sits. *Song. The Owl*

15 Thou art no sabbath-drawler of old saws,
Distill'd from some worm-canker'd homily.
Sonnet. To J. M. K.

16 Thou from a throne
Mounted in heaven wilt shoot into the dark
Arrows of lightnings. I will stand and mark. *Ib.*

17 Oh teach me yet
Somewhat before the heavy clod
Weighs on me, and the busy fret
Of that sharp-headed worm begins
In the gross blackness underneath.
Supposed Confessions of a Second-Rate Sensitive Mind

18 In tea-cup times of hood and hoop,
Or while the patch was worn.
The Talking Oak, xvi

19 And far below the Roundhead rode,
And humm'd a surly hymn. *Ib. lxxv*

20 The woods decay, the woods decay and fall,
The vapours weep their burthen to the ground,
Man comes and tills the field and lies beneath,
And after many a summer dies the swan.
Tithonus, l. 1

21 Here at the quiet limit of the world. *Ib. l. 7*

22 Why wilt thou ever scare me with thy tears,
And make me tremble lest a saying learnt,
In days far-off, on that dark earth, be true?
'The gods themselves cannot recall their gifts.'
Ib. l. 46

23 Of happy men that have the power to die,
And grassy barrows of the happier dead. *Ib. l. 70*

24 A still small voice spake unto me,
'Thou art so full of misery,
Were it not better not to be?' *The Two Voices, i*

25 This truth within thy mind rehearse,
That in a boundless universe
Is boundless better, boundless worse. *Ib. ix*

26 'Consider well,' the voice replied,
'His face, that two hours since hath died;
Wilt thou find passion, pain, or pride?' *Ib. lxxxi*

27 No life that breathes with human breath
Has ever truly long'd for death. *Ib. cxxxii*

28 For, being of that honest few,
Who give the Fiend himself his due,
Should eighty-thousand college-councils
Thunder 'Anathema', friend, at you.
To the Rev. F. D. Maurice, ii

29 A careless-order'd garden
Close to the ridge of a noble down. *Ib. iv*

30 You'll have no scandal while you dine,
But honest talk and wholesome wine. *Ib. v*

31 It little profits that an idle king,
By this still hearth, among these barren crags,
Match'd with an aged wife, I mete and dole
Unequal laws unto a savage race. *Ulysses, l. 1*

32 I will drink
Life to the lees: all times I have enjoy'd
Greatly, have suffer'd greatly, both with those
That loved me, and alone; on shore, and when
Thro' scudding drifts the rainy Hyades
Vext the dim sea: I am become a name;
For always roaming with a hungry heart
Much have I seen and known; cities of men
And manners, climates, councils, governments,
Myself not least, but honour'd of them all;
And drunk delight of battle with my peers,
Far on the ringing plains of windy Troy.
I am a part of all that I have met;
Yet all experience is an arch wherethro'

Gleams that untravell'd world, whose margin fades
For ever and for ever when I move.
How dull it is to pause, to make an end,
To rust unburnish'd, not to shine in use!
As tho' to breathe were life. Life piled on life
Were all too little, and of one to me
Little remains: but every hour is saved
From that eternal silence, something more,
A bringer of new things.   *Ulysses*, l. 6

1   This gray spirit yearning in desire
To follow knowledge like a sinking star,
Beyond the utmost bound of human thought.
                       Ib. l. 30

2 This is my son, mine own Telemachus.   *Ib.* l. 33

3 There lies the port; the vessel puffs her sail:
There gloom the dark broad seas. My mariners,
Souls that have toil'd, and wrought, and thought
   with me—
That ever with a frolic welcome took
The thunder and the sunshine, and opposed
Free hearts, free foreheads—you and I are old;
Old age hath yet his honour and his toil;
Death closes all: but something ere the end,
Some work of noble note, may yet be done,
Not unbecoming men that strove with gods.
The lights begin to twinkle from the rocks:
The long day wanes: the slow moon climbs: the deep
Moans round with many voices. Come, my friends,
'Tis not too late to seek a newer world.
Push off, and sitting well in order smite
The sounding furrows; for my purpose holds
To sail beyond the sunset, and the baths
Of all the western stars, until I die.
It may be that the gulfs will wash us down:
It may be we shall touch the Happy Isles,
And see the great Achilles, whom we knew.
Tho' much is taken, much abides; and tho'
We are not now that strength which in old days
Moved earth and heaven; that which we are, we are;
One equal temper of heroic hearts,
Made weak by time and fate, but strong in will
To strive, to seek, to find, and not to yield. *Ib.* l. 44

4 What is it all but a trouble of ants in the gleam of a
   million million of suns?   *Vastness*

5 Household happiness, gracious children, debtless
   competence, golden mean.   *Ib.*

6 An' I thowt 'twur the will o' the Lord, but Miss Annie
   she said it wur draäins.   *The Village Wife*, ii

7 All the charm of all the Muses often flowering in a
   lonely word.   *To Virgil*, iii

8 I salute thee, Mantovano,
I that loved thee since my day began,
Wielder of the stateliest measure ever moulded by
   the lips of man.   *Ib.* x

9 As 'twere a hundred-throated nightingale.
             The Vision of Sin, ii

10 God made Himself an awful rose of dawn.   *Ib.* iii

11 Bitter barmaid, waning fast!   *Ib.* iv. ii

12 Let us have a quiet hour,
Let us hob-and-nob with Death.   *Ib.* iii

13 Every moment dies a man,
Every moment one is born.   *Ib.* ix

14 Fill the can, and fill the cup:
   All the windy ways of men
Are but dust that rises up,
   And is lightly laid again.
          The Vision of Sin, iv. xviii

15 Drink to heavy Ignorance!
   Hob-and-nob with brother Death!   *Ib.* xxxiii

16 We knew the merry world was round,
   And we might sail for evermore.   *The Voyage*, i

17 Give her the wages of going on, and not to die.
                    Wages, ii

18 Sea-King's daughter from over the sea, Alexandra!
Saxon and Norman and Dane are we,
But all of us Danes in our welcome of thee, Alexandra!
           A Welcome to Alexandra

19 Oh well for him whose will is strong!
He suffers, but he will not suffer long;
He suffers, but he cannot suffer wrong.   *Will*

20 O plump head-waiter at the Cock
To which I most resort.
      Will Waterproof's Lyrical Monologue, i

21 Or that eternal want of pence,
   Which vexes public men.   *Ib.* vi

22 High over roaring Temple-bar,
   And set in Heaven's third story,
I look at all things as they are,
   But thro' a kind of glory.   *Ib.* ix

23 Right down by smoky Paul's they bore,
   Till, where the street grows straiter,
One fix'd for ever at the door,
   And one became head-waiter.   *Ib.* xviii

24 A land of settled government,
   A land of just and old renown,
   Where Freedom slowly broadens down
From precedent to precedent. '*You ask me, why*,' iii

25 While I live, the Owls!
When I die, the GHOULS!!!
   *Written by the side of an epigram on a poet's fate
   by Thomas Hood.* H. Tennyson's *Alfred, Lord
   Tennyson* (1898), ii. 96

26 A louse in the locks of literature.
   Said of Churton Collins to Edmund Gosse. Evan
   Charteris's *Life and Letters of Sir Edmund Gosse*,
   ch. xiv

TERENCE

c. 190–159 B.C.

27   Id arbitror
Adprime in vita esse utile, ut nequid nimis.
   My view is that the most important thing in life
   is never to have too much of anything.
                 Andria, 61

28 Davos sum, non Oedipus.
   I am Davos, not Oedipus.   *Ib.* 194

29 Amantium irae amoris integratio est.
   The quarrels of lovers are the renewal of love.
                    Ib. 555

30 Homo sum; humani nil a me alienum puto.
   I am a man, I count nothing human indifferent to
   me.   *Heauton Timorumenos*, I. i. 25

31 Fortis fortuna adiuvat.
   Fortune aids the brave.   *Phormio*, 203

1 Quot homines tot sententiae: suo quoique mos.
So many men, so many opinions; his own a law to
each. *Phormio*, 454

TERTULLIAN
A.D. *c.* 160–*c.* 225

2 O testimonium animae naturaliter Christianae.
O witness of the soul naturally Christian.
Apol. xvii

3 Plures efficimus quoties metimur a vobis, semen est
sanguis Christianorum.
The more ye mow us down, the more we grow, the
seed is the blood of Christians. (*Traditionally
rendered as* 'The blood of the martyrs is the seed
of the Church'.) *Ib.* l. *ad fin.*

4 Certum est quia impossibile est.
It is certain because it is impossible.
De Carne Christi, 5

EDWARD TESCHEMACHER
nineteenth century

5 There is a garden that I dream of.
The Garden of Your Heart

6 Where my caravan has rested,
Flowers I leave you on the grass.
Where My Caravan Has Rested

WILLIAM MAKEPEACE THACKERAY
1811–1863

7 He who meanly admires mean things is a Snob.
The Book of Snobs, ch. 2

8 It is impossible, in our condition of Society, not to be
sometimes a Snob. *Ib.* ch. 3

9 'Tis not the dying for a faith that's so hard, Master
Harry—every man of every nation has done that—
'tis the living up to it that is difficult.
Esmond, bk. i, ch. 6

10 'Tis strange what a man may do, and a woman yet
think him an angel. *Ib.* ch. 7

11 We love being in love, that's the truth on't.
Ib. bk. ii, ch. 15

12 Why do they always put mud into coffee on board
steamers? Why does the tea generally taste of
boiled boots? *The Kickleburys on the Rhine*

13 What woman, however old, has not the bridal-favours
and raiment stowed away, and packed in lavender,
in the inmost cupboards of her heart?
Lovel the Widower, ch. 28

14 When I say that I know women, I mean I know that
I don't know them. Every single woman I ever
knew is a puzzle to me, as, I have no doubt, she is
to herself. *Mr. Brown's Letters*

15 A military gent I see—and while his face I scan,
I think you'll all agree with me—He came from
Hindostan. *The Newcomes*, bk. i, ch. 1

16 Kind, cheerful, merry Dr. Brighton. *Ib.* ch. 9

17 What money is better bestowed than that of a schoolboy's tip? *Ib.* ch. 16

18 As the last bell struck, a peculiar sweet smile shone
over his face, and he lifted up his head a little, and
quickly said, 'Adsum!' and fell back. It was the
word we used at school, when names were called;
and lo, he, whose heart was as that of a little child,
had answered to his name, and stood in the presence of The Master.
The Newcomes, bk. i. ch. 80

19 Rake's progress.
Pendennis, title of ch. 19. *Used earlier by Hogarth*

20 Yes, I am a fatal man, Madame Fribsbi. To inspire
hopeless passion is my destiny. [*Mirobolant.*]
Ib. ch. 23

21 Remember, it is as easy to marry a rich woman as a
poor woman. *Ib.* ch. 28

22 For a slashing article, sir, there's nobody like the
Capting. *Ib.* ch. 32

23 The *Pall Mall Gazette* is written by gentlemen for
gentlemen. *Ib.*

24 Now Valoroso is a man again! [*Valoroso.*]
The Rose and the Ring, ch. 1

25 Business first; pleasure afterwards. [*Queen of
Paflagonia.*] *Ib.*

26 Runs not a river by my palace wall? Have I not sacks
to sew up wives withal? [*Valoroso.*] *Ib.* ch. 9

27 'No business before breakfast, Glum!' says the King.
'Breakfast first, business next.' [*Valoroso.*]
Ib. ch. 11

28 My bold, my beautiful, my Bulbo! [*Angelica.*] *Ib.*

29 Thorns in the Cushion. *Roundabout Papers*

30 [Quoting a newspaper:] 'Written, strange to say, on
club note-paper.' *Ib.*

31 Illuminated with the Author's own candles.
Vanity Fair. Before the Curtain

32 This I set down as a positive truth. A woman with
fair opportunities and without a positive hump,
may marry whom she likes. *Ib.* ch. 4

33 [Miss Crawley] had been in France—and loved, ever
after, French novels, French cookery, and French
wines. *Ib.* ch. 10

34 Whenever he met a great man he grovelled before
him, and my-lorded him as only a free-born Briton
can do. *Ib.* ch. 13

35 Arms and Hatchments, Resurgam.—Here is an
opportunity for moralizing! *Ib.* ch. 14

36 Them's my sentiments! [*Fred Bullock.*] *Ib.* ch. 21

37 Darkness came down on the field and city: and
Amelia was praying for George, who was lying on
his face, dead, with a bullet through his heart.
Ib. ch. 32

38 Nothing like blood, sir, in hosses, dawgs, and men.
[*James Crawley.*] *Ib.* ch. 35

39 How to live well on nothing a year.
Ib. Title of ch. 36

40 Ah! *Vanitas Vanitatum!* Which of us is happy in this
world? Which of us has his desire? or, having it,
is satisfied?—Come, children, let us shut up the
box and the puppets, for our play is played out.
Ib. ch. 67

41 There's no sweeter tobacco comes from Virginia,
and no better brand than the Three Castles.
The Virginians, ch. 1

1 Fashnable fax and polite annygoats.
The Yellowplush Papers, pt. i, title

2 My ma wrapped up my buth in a mistry.
Ib. pt. ii, *Miss Shum's Husband*, ch. 1

3 Ho, pretty page, with the dimpled chin
That never has known the barber's shear,
All your wish is woman to win,
This is the way that boys begin.
    Wait till you come to Forty Year.
The Age of Wisdom

4 Although I enter not,
Yet round about the spot
    Ofttimes I hover;
And near the sacred gate,
With longing eyes I wait,
    Expectant of her. *At the Church Gate*

5 Then sing as Martin Luther sang,
As Doctor Martin Luther sang,
'Who loves not wine, woman and song,
He is a fool his whole life long.' *A Credo*

6 The play is done; the curtain drops,
    Slow falling to the prompter's bell:
A moment yet the actor stops,
    And looks around, to say farewell.
It is an irksome word and task:
    And, when he's laughed and said his say,
He shows, as he removes the mask,
    A face that's anything but gay.
The End of the Play

7 There were three sailors of Bristol City
Who took a boat and went to sea.
But first with beef and captain's biscuits
And pickled pork they loaded she.
There was gorging Jack and guzzling Jimmy,
And the youngest he was little Billee.
Now when they got as far as the Equator
They'd nothing left but one split pea. *Little Billee*

8 Says gorging Jim to guzzling Jacky,
We have no wittles, so we must eat *we*. *Ib.*

9 There's little Bill as is young and tender,
We're old and tough—so let's eat *he*. *Ib.*

10 He scarce had said his Cathechism,
When up he jumps: 'There's land I see!
There's Jerusalem and Madagascar,
And North and South Ameri*key*.
There's the British Fleet a-riding at anchor,
With Admiral Napier, K.C.B.' *Ib.*

11 Christmas is here:
Winds whistle shrill,
Icy and chill.
Little care we;
Little we fear
Weather without,
Sheltered about
The Mahogany Tree. *The Mahogany Tree*

12 Werther had a love for Charlotte
    Such as words could never utter;
Would you know how first he met her?
    She was cutting bread and butter.

Charlotte was a married lady,
    And a moral man was Werther,
And for all the wealth of Indies,
    Would do nothing for to hurt her.

So he sighed and pined and ogled,
    And his passion boiled and bubbled,
Till he blew his silly brains out
    And no more was by it troubled.

Charlotte, having seen his body
    Borne before her on a shutter,
Like a well-conducted person,
    Went on cutting bread and butter.
Sorrows of Werther

13 Oh, Vanity of vanities!
    How wayward the decrees of Fate are;
How very weak the very wise,
    How very small the very great are!
Vanitas Vanitatum

WILLIAM MAKEPEACE THAYER

14 Log-cabin to White House.
*Title of a biography (1910) of James Garfield
(1831–1881)*

FRANCIS THOMPSON
1859–1907

15 Pontifical Death, that doth the crevasse bridge
To the steep and trifid God. *Anthem of Earth*

16   Here I shake off
The bur o' the world, man's congregation shun,
And to the antique order of the dead
I take the tongueless vows: my cell is set
Here in thy bosom; my little trouble is ended
In a little peace. *Ib.*

17 And thou—what needest with thy tribe's black tents
Who hast the red pavilion of my heart?
Arab Love Song

18 He the Anteros and Eros,
    I the body, He the Cross;
He upbeareth me, *Ischyros*,
    Agios Athanatos! *Assumpta Maria*

19 Lo! He standeth, Spouse and Brother,
    I to Him, and He to me,
Who upraised me where my mother
    Fell beneath the apple-tree. *Ib.*

20 Life is a coquetry
Of Death, which wearies me,
    Too sure
Of the amour.
To the Dead Cardinal of Westminster

21 I have no angels left
    Now, Sweet, to pray to. *A Carrier Song*

22 The hills look over on the South,
    And Southward dreams the sea;
And with the sea-breeze hand in hand,
    Came innocence and she. *Daisy*

23 Where 'mid the gorse the raspberry
    Red for the gatherer springs,
Two children did we stray and talk
    Wise, idle, childish things. *Ib.*

24 The fairest things have fleetest end,
    Their scent survives their close:
But the rose's scent is bitterness
    To him that loved the rose. *Ib.*

1 She went her unremembering way,
　　She went and left in me
　The pang of all the partings gone,
　　And partings yet to be.

　She left me marvelling why my soul
　　Was sad that she was glad;
　At all the sadness in the sweet,
　　The sweetness in the sad.　　　　*Daisy*

2 Nothing begins and nothing ends
　　That is not paid with moan;
　For we are born in other's pain,
　　And perish in our own.　　　　*Ib.*

3 Ah, for a heart less native to high Heaven,
　A hooded eye, for jesses and restraint,
　Or for a will accipitrine to pursue!
　　　　　　　　The Dread of Height

4 Go, songs, for ended is our brief sweet play;
　　Go, children of swift joy and tardy sorrow:
　And some are sung, and that was yesterday,
　　And some unsung, and that may be to-morrow
　　　　　　　　　　　　　　Envoy

5 Little Jesus, wast Thou shy
　Once, and just so small as I?
　And what did it feel to be
　Out of Heaven and just like me?　*Ex Ore Infantium*

6 　　　　Did the things
　Play 'Can you see me?' through their wings?　*Ib.*

7 Cast wide the folding doorways of the East,
　For now is light increased!
　And the wind-besomed chambers of the air,
　See they be garnished fair.
　　　From the Night of Forebeing. Ode to Easter

8 Spring is come home with her world-wandering feet.
　And all things are made young with young desires.
　　　　　　　　　　　　　　　Ib.

9 Let even the slug-abed snail upon the thorn
　Put forth a conscious horn!　　　*Ib.*

10 Look for me in the nurseries of Heaven.
　　　　　　　　　　To My Godchild

11 O nothing, in this corporal earth of man,
　That to the imminent heaven of his high soul
　Responds with colour and with shadow, can
　Lack correlated greatness.　　*The Heart*, ii

12 And all man's Babylons strive but to impart
　The grandeurs of his Babylonian heart.　*Ib.*

13 I fled Him, down the nights and down the days;
　I fled Him, down the arches of the years;
　I fled Him, down the labyrinthine ways
　　Of my own mind; and in the mist of tears
　I hid from Him, and under running laughter.
　　　　　　　　　The Hound of Heaven

14 But with unhurrying chase,
　And unperturbèd pace,
　Deliberate speed, majestic instancy,
　They beat—and a Voice beat
　More instant than the Feet—
　'All things betray thee, who betrayest Me.'　*Ib.*

15 (For, though I knew His love Who followed,
　　Yet was I sore adread
　Lest, having Him, I must have naught beside.)　*Ib.*

16 Fear wist not to evade, as Love wist to pursue.　*Ib.*

17 I said to Dawn: Be sudden—to Eve: Be soon.　*Ib.*

18 To all swift things for swiftness did I sue;
　Clung to the whistling mane of every wind.
　　　　　　　　　The Hound of Heaven

19 Came on the following Feet,
　And a Voice above their beat—
　'Naught shelters thee, who wilt not shelter Me.'　*Ib.*

20 I sought no more that after which I strayed
　　In face of man or maid;
　But still within the little children's eyes
　　Seems something, something that replies,
　They at least are for me, surely for me!
　I turned me to them very wistfully;
　But just as their young eyes grew sudden fair
　　With dawning answers there,
　Their angel plucked them from me by the hair.　*Ib.*

21 I was heavy with the even
　When she lit her glimmering tapers
　Round the day's dead sanctities.　　*Ib.*

22 My harness piece by piece Thou hast hewn from me
　And smitten me to my knee.　　　　*Ib.*

23 　Yea, faileth now even dream
　The dreamer, and the lute the lutanist;
　Even the linked fantasies, in whose blossomy twist
　I swung the earth a trinket at my wrist.　*Ib.*

24 　　　Ah! must—
　　　Designer infinite!—
　Ah! must Thou char the wood ére Thou canst limn
　　with it?　　　　　　　　*Ib.*

25 　　　Such is; what is to be?
　The pulp so bitter, how shall taste the rind?　*Ib.*

26 Yet ever and anon a trumpet sounds
　From the hid battlements of Eternity;
　Those shaken mists a space unsettle, then
　Round the half-glimpsèd turrets slowly wash again.
　　　　　　　　　　　　　　　Ib.

27 Whether man's heart or life it be which yields
　　Thee harvest, must Thy harvest-fields
　　Be dunged with rotten death?　　*Ib.*

28 　Now of that long pursuit
　　Comes on at hand the bruit;
　That Voice is round me like a bursting sea:
　　'And is thy earth so marred,
　　Shattered in shard on shard?
　Lo, all things fly thee, for thou fliest Me!'　*Ib.*

29 And human love needs human meriting:
　　How hast thou merited—
　Of all man's clotted clay the dingiest clot?
　　Alack, thou knowest not
　How little worthy of any love thou art.　*Ib.*

30 All which I took from thee I did but take,
　　Not for thy harms,
　But just that thou might'st seek it in My arms.　*Ib.*

31 　Halts by me that footfall:
　　Is my gloom, after all,
　Shade of His hand, outstretched caressingly?
　　'Ah, fondest, blindest, weakest,
　　I am He whom thou seekest!
　Thou dravest love from thee, who dravest Me.'　*Ib.*

32 There is no expeditious road
　To pack and label men for God,
　And save them by the barrel-load.
　　　　Epilogue to 'A Judgment in Heaven'

1 O world invisible, we view thee,
O world intangible, we touch thee,
O world unknowable, we know thee,
Inapprehensible, we clutch thee!

Does the fish soar to find the ocean,
The eagle plunge to find the air—
That we ask of the stars in motion
If they have rumour of thee there?

Not where the wheeling systems darken,
And our benumbed conceiving soars!—
The drift of pinions, would we hearken,
Beats at our own clay-shuttered doors.

The angels keep their ancient places;—
Turn but a stone, and start a wing!
'Tis ye, 'tis your estrangèd faces,
That miss the many-splendoured thing.

But (when so sad thou canst not sadder)
Cry;—and upon thy so sore loss
Shall shine the traffic of Jacob's ladder
Pitched betwixt Heaven and Charing Cross.

Yea, in the night, my Soul, my daughter,
Cry,—clinging Heaven by the hems;
And lo, Christ walking on the water
Not of Gennesareth, but Thames!
The Kingdom of God

2 It is little I repair to the matches of the Southron
folk,
Though my own red roses there may blow;
It is little I repair to the matches of the Southron
folk,
  Though the red roses crest the caps I know.
For the field is full of shades as I near the shadowy
    coast,
And a ghostly batsman plays to the bowling of a
    ghost,
And I look through my tears on a soundless-clapping
    host
  As the run-stealers flicker to and fro,
      To and fro:—
O my Hornby and my Barlow long ago! *At Lord's*

3 Secret was the garden,
Set i' the pathless awe. *The Mistress of Vision*

4 East, ah, east of Himalay,
Dwell the nations underground. *Ib.*

5 Where is the land of Luthany,
And where the region Elenore?
I do faint therefor.

When to the new eyes of thee
All things by immortal power,
Near or far,
Hiddenly
To each other linked are,
That thou canst not stir a flower
Without troubling of a star. *Ib.*

6 Lo, in the sanctuaried East,
Day, a dedicated priest
In all his robes pontifical exprest,
Lifteth slowly, lifteth sweetly,
From out its Orient tabernacle drawn,
Yon orbed sacrament confest
Which sprinkles benediction through the dawn.
Orient Ode

7 Ah! let the sweet birds of the Lord
With earth's waters make accord;

Teach how the crucifix may be
Carven from the laurel-tree,
Fruit of the Hesperides
Burnish take on Eden-trees,
The Muses' sacred grove be wet
With the red dew of Olivet,
And Sappho lay her burning brows
In white Cecilia's lap of snows!
To a Poet Breaking Silence

8 Summer set lip to earth's bosom bare,
And left the flushed print in a poppy there.
The Poppy

9 The sleep-flower sways in the wheat its head,
Heavy with dreams, as that with bread:
The goodly grain and the sun-flushed sleeper
The reaper reaps, and Time the reaper.

I hang 'mid men my needless head,
And my fruit is dreams, as theirs is bread:
The goodly men and the sun-hazed sleeper
Time shall reap, but after the reaper
The world shall glean of me, me the sleeper. *Ib.*

10 I had endured through watches of the dark
The abashless inquisition of each star.
Sister Songs, i

11 The innocent moon, which nothing does but shine,
Moves all the labouring surges of the world. *Ib.*

12 What heart could have thought you?—
Past our devisal
(O filigree petal!)
Fashioned so purely,
Fragilely, surely,
From what Paradisal
Imagineless metal,
Too costly for cost? *To a Snowflake*

13 His hammer of wind,
And His graver of frost. *Ib.*

14 And, while she feels the heavens lie bare,
She only talks about her hair. *The Way of a Maid*

HAROLD WILLIAM THOMPSON
1891–

15 What shall we do—or go fishing?
Body, Boots and Britches (1940), p. 504

WILLIAM HEPWORTH THOMPSON
1810–1886

16 I did not think we should miss poor Kingsley so soon.
On Seeley's inaugural lecture as Professor of History, following Charles Kingsley

17 We are none of us infallible—not even the youngest
of us.
Remark referring to G. W. Balfour, then Junior Fellow of Trinity. G. W. E. Russell's *Collections and Recollections*, ch. 18

JAMES THOMSON
1700–1748

18 When Britain first, at heaven's command,
Arose from out the azure main,
This was the charter of the land,
And guardian angels sung this strain:
  'Rule, Britannia, rule the waves;
  Britons never will be slaves.'
Alfred: a Masque (1740), Act II, Scene the last

THOMSON—THOREAU

1 The world of waters wild. *Britannia*, l. 27

2 A pleasing land of drowsyhead it was.
The Castle of Indolence, c. 1. vi

3 As when a shepherd of the Hebrid Isles,
Placed far amid the melancholy main. *Ib.* xxx

4 A bard here dwelt, more fat than bard beseems.
Ib. lxviii

5 Poured forth his unpremeditated strain. *Ib.*

6 A little, round, fat, oily man of God. *Ib.* lxix

7 For ever, Fortune, wilt thou prove
An unrelenting foe to love,
And, when we meet a mutual heart,
Come in between and bid us part? *To Fortune*

8 Come then, expressive Silence, muse His praise.
A Hymn on the Seasons, l. 118

9 How the heart listened while he pleading spoke!
While on the enlightened mind, with winning art,
His gentle reason so persuasive stole
That the charmed hearer thought it was his own.
To the Memory of the Lord Talbot, l. 103

10 Come, gentle Spring! ethereal mildness, come.
The Seasons, Spring, l. 1

11 The stately-sailing swan
Gives out his snowy plumage to the gale,
And, arching proud his neck, with oary feet
Bears forward fierce, and guards his osier-isle,
Protective of his young. *Ib.* l. 778

12 Delightful task! to rear the tender thought,
To teach the young idea how to shoot. *Ib.* l. 1152

13 An elegant sufficiency, content,
Retirement, rural quiet, friendship, books.
Ib. l. 1161

14 The sober-suited songstress. [The nightingale.]
Ib. Summer, l. 746

15 Ships, dim-discovered, dropping from the clouds.
Ib. l. 946

16 Or sighed and looked unutterable things. *Ib.* l. 1188

17 While Autumn nodding o'er the yellow plain
Comes jovial on. *Ib. Autumn*, l. 2

18 While listening senates hang upon thy tongue.
Ib. l. 15

19 For loveliness
Needs not the foreign aid of ornament,
But is when unadorned adorned the most. *Ib.* l. 204

20 Poor is the triumph o'er the timid hare! *Ib.* l. 401

21 The big round tears run down his dappled face.
Ib. l. 454

22 The Atlantic surge
Pours in among the stormy Hebrides. *Ib.* l. 864

23 Find other lands beneath another sun. *Ib.* l. 1286

24 See, Winter comes to rule the varied year,
Sullen and sad. *Ib. Winter*, l. 1

25 Welcome, kindred glooms!
Congenial horrors, hail! *Ib.* l. 5

26 The redbreast, sacred to the household gods,
Wisely regardful of the embroiling sky,
In joyless fields and thorny thickets leaves
His shivering mates, and pays to trusted man
His annual visit. Half afraid, he first

Against the window beats; then brisk alights
On the warm hearth; then hopping o'er the floor,
Eyes all the smiling family askance,
And pecks, and starts, and wonders where he is—
Till, more familiar grown, the table-crumbs
Attract his slender feet. *The Seasons, Winter*, l. 246

27 Studious let me sit,
And hold high converse with the mighty dead.
Ib. l. 431

28 Oh! Sophonisba! Sophonisba! oh! *Sophonisba*, III. ii

JAMES THOMSON
1834–1882

29 The City is of Night; perchance of Death,
But certainly of Night. *The City of Dreadful Night*

30 As we rush, as we rush in the train,
The trees and the houses go wheeling back,
But the starry heavens above that plain
Come flying on our track. *Sunday at Hampstead*, x

31 Give a man a horse he can ride,
Give a man a boat he can sail.
Sunday up the River, xv

HENRY DAVID THOREAU
1817–1862

32 The mass of men lead lives of quiet desperation.
Walden. Economy

33 It is a characteristic of wisdom not to do desperate things. *Ib.*

34 I have lived some thirty years on this planet, and I have yet to hear the first syllable of valuable or even earnest advice from my seniors. *Ib.*

35 I long ago lost a hound, a bay horse, and a turtle-dove, and am still on their trail. *Ib.*

36 It is true, I never assisted the sun materially in his rising, but, doubt not, it was of the last importance only to be present at it. *Ib.*

37 Tall arrowy white pines. *Ib.*

38 The owner of the axe, as he released his hold on it, said that it was the apple of his eye; but I returned it sharper than I received it. *Ib.*

39 For more than five years I maintained myself thus solely by the labor of my hands, and I found, that by working about six weeks in a year, I could meet all the expenses of living. *Ib.*

40 As for Doing-good, that is one of the professions which are full. Moreover, I have tried it fairly, and, strange as it may seem, am satisfied that it does not agree with my constitution. *Ib.*

41 The government of the world I live in was not framed, like that of Britain, in after-dinner conversations over the wine. *Ib. conclusion*

42 Simplify, simplify.
Ib. Where I Lived, and What I Lived For

43 The three-o'-clock in the morning courage, which Bonaparte thought was the rarest. *Ib. Sounds*

44 Wherever a man goes, men will pursue him and paw him with their dirty institutions, and, if they can, constrain him to belong to their desperate odd-fellow society. *Ib. The Village*

1 I frequently tramped eight or ten miles through the deepest snow to keep an appointment with a beech-tree, or a yellow birch, or an old acquaintance among the pines. *Walden. Winter Visitors*

2 I once had a sparrow alight upon my shoulder for a moment while I was hoeing in a village garden, and I felt that I was more distinguished by that circumstance than I should have been by any epaulet I could have worn. *Ib.*

3 It takes two to speak the truth,—one to speak, and another to hear.
A Week on the Concord and Merrimack Rivers, Wednesday

4 Some circumstantial evidence is very strong, as when you find a trout in the milk.
Unpublished MSS. in Miscellanies, Biographical Sketch (1918), vol. x, p. 30

5 Not that the story need be long, but it will take a long while to make it short.
Letter to Mr. B., 16 Nov. 1857. (See 374:8)

ROSE HARTWICK THORPE
1850–1939
6 Curfew must not ring to-night. *Title of poem*

REV. GODFREY THRING
1823–1903
7 Fierce raged the tempest o'er the deep,
Watch did thine anxious servants keep,
But thou wast wrapp'd in guileless sleep,
Calm and still.
Chope's Hymnal (1862). *Fierce Raged The Tempest*

THUCYDIDES
b. *c.* 471 B.C.
8 κτῆμα ἐς ἀεί.
A possession for ever. *Thucydides, i. 22*

9 φιλοκαλοῦμέν τε γὰρ μετ᾽ εὐτελείας καὶ φιλοσοφοῦμεν ἄνευ μαλακίας.
For we are lovers of the beautiful, yet simple in our tastes, and we cultivate the mind without loss of manliness. *Ib. ii. 40, § 1. Trans. by Jowett*

10 ἀνδρῶν γὰρ ἐπιφανῶν πᾶσα γῆ τάφος.
The whole earth is the sepulchre of famous men.
Ib. 43, § 3

11 τῆς τε γὰρ ὑπαρχούσης φύσεως μὴ χείροσι γενέσθαι ὑμῖν μεγάλη ἡ δόξα, καὶ ἧς ἂν ἐπ᾽ ἐλάχιστον ἀρετῆς πέρι ἢ ψόγου ἐν τοῖς ἄρσεσι κλέος ᾖ.
To a woman not to show more weakness than is natural to her sex is great glory, and not to be talked of for good or evil among men. *Ib. 45, § 2*

JAMES THURBER
1894–1961
12 The War Between Men and Women.
Title of series of cartoons

EDWARD, FIRST BARON THURLOW
1731–1806
13 As guardian of his Majesty's conscience.
Speech in the House of Lords, 1779. C. Butler, *Reminiscences*, vol. 1, p. 200

14 His debt of gratitude also to his Majesty was ample . . .; and which, when he forgot, might God forget him!
Speech in the House of Lords, 15 Dec. 1778. Parl. Hist. (1814), vol. xxvii, col. 680

15 Did you ever expect a corporation to have a conscience, when it has no soul to be damned, and no body to be kicked?
Attrib See 505: 5 *and* Corrigenda Appendix

EDWARD, SECOND BARON THURLOW
1781–1829
16 Nature is always wise in every part.
Select Poems. Sonnet. To a Bird, that haunted the Waters of Lacken, in the Winter

PAUL W. TIBBET
contemporary
17 A mushroom of boiling dust up to 20,000 feet.
Description of atomic bomb explosion

TIBULLUS
54?–18? B.C.
18 Te spectem, suprema mihi cum venerit hora,
Te teneam moriens deficiente manu.
Let me behold thee when my last hour is come,
thee let me hold with my dying hand. I. i. 59

19 Iuppiter pluvius.
Jupiter the rain-bringer. *Ib. vii. 26*

CHIDIOCK TICHBORNE
1558?–1586
20 My prime of youth is but a frost of cares;
My feast of joy is but a dish of pain;
My crop of corn is but a field of tares;
And all my good is but vain hope of gain.
The day is past, and yet I saw no sun;
And now I live, and now my life is done.
Verses of Praise and Joy. Elegy. (*Written in the Tower before his execution*)

THOMAS TICKELL
1686–1740
21 I hear a voice you cannot hear,
Which says I must not stay;
I see a hand you cannot see,
Which beckons me away. *Colin and Lucy, v. 4*

22 There taught us how to live; and (oh! too high The price for knowledge) taught us how to die.
Epitaph. On the Death of Mr. Addison, l. 81.
Addison's *Works* (1721), preface, p. xx

HARRY TILZER d. 1946

1 Come, Come, Come and have a drink with me
Down at the old 'Bull and Bush'.
Song sung by Florrie Ford

2 Come, Come, Come and make eyes at me. *Ib.*

MATTHEW TINDAL
1657–1733

3 Matters of fact, which as Mr. Budgell somewhere
observes, are very stubborn things.
Will of Matthew Tindal (1733), p. 23

TITUS VESPASIANUS
A.D. 40 or 41–81

4 Amici, diem perdidi.
Friends, I have lost a day.
Suetonius, *Titus*, ch. 8, i

JOHN TOBIN
1770–1804

5 The man that lays his hand upon a woman,
Save in the way of kindness, is a wretch
Whom 't were gross flattery to name a coward.
The Honeymoon, II. i

JACOPONE DA TODI
d. 1306

6 Stabat mater dolorosa
Iuxta crucem lacrimosa.

At the cross her station keeping
Stood the mournful mother weeping.
Pachen, *Jacopone da Todi. Trans. in English
Hymnal. Also ascribed to Innocent III*

LEO TOLSTOY
1828–1910

7 All happy families resemble each other, each unhappy
family is unhappy in its own way.
Anna Karenina, pt. i, ch. 1. *Trans. by Maude*

8 Pure and complete sorrow is as impossible as pure
and complete joy.
War and Peace, bk. xv, ch. 1. *Trans. by Maude*

9 Art is not a handicraft, it is the transmission of feeling
the artist has experienced.
What is Art? ch. 19. *Trans. by Maude*

10 I sit on a man's back, choking him and making him
carry me, and yet assure myself and others that
I am very sorry for him and wish to ease his lot
by all possible means—except by getting off his
back.
What Then Must We Do? ch. 16. *Trans. by
Maude*

AUGUSTUS MONTAGUE TOPLADY
1740–1778

11 Rock of ages, cleft for me,
Let me hide myself in thee.
The Gospel Magazine, Oct. 1775. *Rock of Ages*

12 Nothing in my hand I bring,
Simply to thy Cross I cling;
Naked, come to thee for dress;
Helpless, look to thee for grace;
Foul, I to the Fountain fly;
Wash me, Saviour, or I die. *Rock of Ages*

THOMAS TRAHERNE
1637?–1674

13 You never enjoy the world aright, till the sea itself
floweth in your veins, till you are clothed with the
heavens, and crowned with the stars: and perceive
yourself to be the sole heir of the whole world, and
more than so, because men are in it who are every
one sole heirs as well as you. Till you can sing and
rejoice and delight in God, as misers do in gold,
and kings in sceptres, you never enjoy the world.
Centuries of Meditations. Cent. i, § 29

14 The corn was orient and immortal wheat, which never
should be reaped, nor was ever sown. I thought it
had stood from everlasting to everlasting.
Ib. Cent. iii, § 3

15 The Men! O what venerable and reverend creatures
did the aged seem! Immortal Cherubims! And
young men glittering and sparkling Angels, and
maids strange seraphic pieces of life and beauty!
Boys and girls tumbling in the street, and playing,
were moving jewels. I knew not that they were
born or should die; but all things abided eternally
as they were in their proper places. *Ib.*

16 Contentment is a sleepy thing
If it in death alone must die;
A quiet mind is worse than poverty,
Unless it from enjoyment spring!
That's blessedness alone that makes a King!
Of Contentment

17 O yonder is the moon
Newly come after me to town,
That shin'd at Lugwardin but yesternight,
Where I enjoy'd the self-same light.
On Leaping over the Moon, viii

18 I within did flow
With seas of life, like wine. *Wonder*, iii

HENRY DUFF TRAILL
1842–1900

19 Look in my face. My name is Used-to-was;
I am also called Played-out and Done-to-death,
And It-will-wash-no-more.
*After Dilettante Concetti [i.e. Dante Gabriel
Rossetti, see 411:17]*, viii

JOSEPH TRAPP
1679–1747

20 The King, observing with judicious eyes
The state of both his universities,
To Oxford sent a troop of horse, and why?
That learned body wanted loyalty;
To Cambridge books, as very well discerning
How much that loyal body wanted learning.
*On George I's Donation of the Bishop of Ely's
Library to Cambridge University.* Nichols's
Literary Anecdotes, vol. iii, p. 330. *For the reply
see 87:26*

1 Our royal master saw, with heedful eyes,
  The wants of his two universities:
  Troops he to Oxford sent, as knowing why
  That learned body wanted loyalty:
  But books to Cambridge gave, as well discerning
  That that right loyal body wanted learning.
          Alternative version recited by Dr. Johnson.
          Johnsonian Miscellanies (1897), vol. i, p. 171

HERBERT TRENCH
1865–1923

2 But when Night is on the hills, and the great Voices
    Roll in from Sea,
  By starlight and by candlelight and dreamlight
    She comes to me.
          She Comes Not When Noon is on the Roses

3 Come, let us make love deathless, thou and I.
          To Arolilia, No. 2. '*Come, let us make love death-
          less*'

4 O dreamy, gloomy, friendly Trees.   *Title of poem*

RICHARD TRENCH, ARCHBISHOP OF DUBLIN
1807–1886

5 England, we love thee better than we know.
          Gibraltar

6 I say to thee, do thou repeat
  To the first man thou mayest meet
  In lane, highway, or open street—
  That he and we and all men move
  Under a canopy of love,
  As broad as the blue sky above. *The Kingdom of God*

7 This *is* blessing, this *is* life.   *Ib.*

GEORGE MACAULAY TREVELYAN
1876–1962

8 Disinterested intellectual curiosity is the life blood of
  real civilisation.
          English Social History (1942), preface, viii

9 Education . . . has produced a vast population able to
  read but unable to distinguish what is worth
  reading.   *Ib.* ch. 18

ANTHONY TROLLOPE
1815–1882

10 He must have known me had he seen me as he was
  wont to see me, for he was in the habit of flogging
  me constantly. Perhaps he did not recognize me
  by my face.   *Autobiography*, ch. 1

11 Take away from English authors their copyrights, and
  you would very soon take away from England her
  authors.   *Ib.* ch. 6

12 Three hours a day will produce as much as a man
  ought to write.   *Ib.* ch. 15

13 I think that Plantagenet Palliser, Duke of Omnium, is
  a perfect gentleman. If he be not, then am I unable
  to describe a gentleman.   *Ib.* ch. 20

14 She [Mrs. Stanhope] was rich in apparel, but not
  bedizened with finery . . . she well knew the great
  architectural secret of decorating her constructions,
  and never descended to construct a decoration.
          Barchester Towers, ch. 9

15 'Unhand it, sir!' said Mrs. Proudie. From what scrap
  of dramatic poetry she had extracted the word
  cannot be said; but it must have rested on her
  memory, and now seemed opportunely dignified
  for the occasion.   *Barchester Towers*, ch. 11

16 It's dogged as does it. It ain't thinking about it.
          Last Chronicle of Barset, ch. 61

17 We know that power does corrupt. [*Duke of Omnium.*]
          The Prime Minister, ch. 68

18 The tenth Muse, who now governs the periodical
  press.   *The Warden*, ch. 14

ST. VINCENT TROUBRIDGE 1895–

19 There is an iron curtain across Europe.
  Sunday Empire News, 21 Oct. 1945. *See* Corrigenda *to*
  144: 15

MARTIN FARQUHAR TUPPER
1810–1889

20 A good book is the best of friends, the same to-day
  and for ever.
          Proverbial Philosophy, Series 1. *Of Reading*

WALTER JAMES REDFERN TURNER
1889–1946

21 Chimborazo, Cotopaxi,
  They had stolen my soul away!   *Romance*, vii

THOMAS TUSSER
1524?–1580

22 Make hunger thy sauce, as a medicine for health.
          Five Hundred Points of Good Husbandry, ch.
          10. *Good Husbandry Lessons*

23 At Christmas play and make good cheer,
  For Christmas comes but once a year.
          Ib. ch. 12. *The Farmer's daily Diet*

24 Yet true it is, as cow chaws cud,
  And trees at spring do yield forth bud,
  Except wind stands as never it stood,
  It is an ill wind turns none to good.
          Ib. ch. 13. *Description of the Properties of Winds*

25 Who goeth a borrowing
  Goeth a sorrowing.
  Few lend (but fools)
  Their working tools. *Ib.* ch. 15. *September's Abstract*

26 In doing of either, let wit bear a stroke,
  For buying or selling of pig in a poke.
          Ib. September's Husbandry

27 Naught venture, naught have.
          Ib. ch. 16. *October's Abstract*

28 To dog in the manger some liken I could.
          Ib. ch. 28. *Against Fantastical Scrupleness*

29 Feb, fill the dyke
  With what thou dost like.
          Ib. ch. 34. *February's Husbandry*

30 March dust to be sold
  Worth ransom of gold.
          Ib. ch. 36. *March's Husbandry*

31 Sweet April showers
  Do spring May flowers.
          Ib. ch. 38. *April's Husbandry*

1 Cold May and windy,
Barn filleth up finely.
Five Hundred Points of Good Husbandry, ch. 40.
May's Husbandry

2 Dry August and warm
Doth harvest no harm.
Ib. ch. 46. *August's Husbandry*

3 Look ere thou leap, see ere thou go.
Ib. ch. 56. *Dialogue of Wiving and Thriving*

4 Some respite to husbands the weather may send,
But housewives' affairs have never an end.
Ib. Preface to the Book of Housewifery

5 The stone that is rolling can gather no moss,
For master and servant, oft changing is loss.
Ib. Housewifely Admonitions

6 Dry sun, dry wind;
Safe bind, safe find.   *Ib. Washing*

LAWRENCE TUTTIETT
1825–1897

7 Father, let me dedicate
All this year to thee.
Gems of Thought (1864), *Father, Let Me Dedicate*

MARK TWAIN [SAMUEL LANGHORNE CLEMENS]
1835–1910

8 There was things which he stretched, but mainly he
told the truth.
The Adventures of Huckleberry Finn, ch. 1

9 The statements was interesting, but tough.
Ib. ch. 17

10 All kings is mostly rapscallions.   *Ib.* ch. 23

11 If there was two birds sitting on a fence, he would bet
you which one would fly first.
The Celebrated Jumping Frog, p. 17

12 I don't see no p'ints about that frog that's any
better'n any other frog.   *Ib.* p. 20

13 Soap and education are not as sudden as a massacre,
but they are more deadly in the long run.
The Facts concerning the Recent Resignation.
Sketches New & Old (1900), p. 350

14 They spell it Vinci and pronounce it Vinchy;
foreigners always spell better than they pronounce.
Innocents Abroad, ch. 19

15 I do not want Michael Angelo for breakfast—for
luncheon—for dinner—for tea—for supper—for
between meals.   *Ib.* ch. 27

16 Lump the whole thing! say that the Creator made
Italy from designs by Michael Angelo!   *Ib.*

17 Guides cannot master the subtleties of the American
joke.   *Ib.*

18 If you've got a nice *fresh* corpse, fetch him out! *Ib.*

19 Are you going to hang him *anyhow*—and try him
afterward?   *Innocents at Home*, ch. 5

20 When I'm playful I use the meridians of longitude
and parallels of latitude for a seine, and drag the
Atlantic Ocean for whales! I scratch my head with
the lightning and purr myself to sleep with the
thunder!   *Life on the Mississippi*, ch. 3

21 At bottom he was probably fond of them, but he was
always able to conceal it. [On Thomas Carlyle and
Americans.]   *My First Lie*

22 An experienced, industrious, ambitious, and often
quite picturesque liar.
Private History of a Campaign that Failed

23 Adam was but human—this explains it all. He did
not want the apple for the apple's sake, he wanted
it only because it was forbidden.
Pudd'nhead Wilson, heading of ch. 2

24 Whoever has lived long enough to find out what life
is, knows how deep a debt of gratitude we owe to
Adam, the first great benefactor of our race. He
brought death into the world. *Ib.* heading of ch. 3

25 There's plenty of boys that will come hankering and
gruvvelling around when you've got an apple, and
beg the core off you; but when *they've* got one, and
you beg for the core and remind them how you
give them a core one time, they make a mouth at
you and say thank you 'most to death, but there
ain't-a-going to *be* no core.
Tom Sawyer Abroad, ch. 1

26 There ain't no way to find out why a snorer can't hear
himself snore.   *Ib.* ch. 10

27 They inwardly resolved that so long as they remained
in the business, their piracies should not again be
sullied with the crime of stealing.   *Ib.* ch. 13

28 The cross of the Legion of Honour has been con-
ferred upon me. However, few escape that distinction.   *A Tramp Abroad*, ch. 8

29 This poor little one-horse town.
The Undertaker's Chat

30 The report of my death was an exaggeration.
Cable from Europe to the Associated Press

31 There is a sumptuous variety about the New England
weather that compels the stranger's admiration—
and regret. The weather is always doing something there; always attending strictly to business;
always getting up new designs and trying them on
the people to see how they will go. But it gets
through more business in spring than in any other
season. In the spring I have counted one hundred
and thirty-six different kinds of weather inside of
four-and-twenty hours.
*The Weather. Speech at dinner of New England
Society, New York, 22 Dec. 1876. Speeches*
(1910), p. 59

HENRY TWELLS
1823–1900

32 At even ere the sun was set,
The sick, O Lord, around thee lay.
Hymns Ancient and Modern (1868), Appendix.
At Even Ere the Sun Was Set

EDWARD SMITH UFFORD
1851–1929

33 Throw out the life-line across the dark wave,
There is a brother whom someone should save,
Throw out the life-line, throw out the life-line,
Someone is sinking to-day.   *Revivalist Hymn* (1884)

[550]

UNAMUNO—VAUGHAN

MIGUEL DE UNAMUNO
1864–1937

1 Fe que no duda es fe muerta.

Faith which does not doubt is dead faith.
La Agonía del Cristianismo, p. 34

2 Cúrate de la afección de preocuparte cómo aparezcas a los demás. Cuídate sólo ... de la idea que de ti Dios tenga.

Cure yourself of the inclination to bother about how you look to other people. Be concerned only ... with the idea God has of you.
Vida de D. Quijote y Sancho, p. 27

MRS. C. UNWIN

3 The Hungry Forties. *Title of book (1905)*

RALPH R. UPTON

4 Stop; look; listen.
Slogan devised in 1912 to replace the old U.S. railway-crossing signs of 'Look out for the locomotive'

W. UPTON

5 This lass so neat, with smile so sweet,
Has won my right good will,
I'd crowns resign to call thee mine,
Sweet lass of Richmond Hill.
The Lass of Richmond Hill. Oxford Song Book.
(See 327:5)

SIR JOHN VANBRUGH
1664–1726

6 The want of a thing is perplexing enough, but the possession of it is intolerable.
The Confederacy, I. ii

7 Much of a muchness. *The Provok'd Husband, I. i*

8 BELINDA:
Ay, but you know we must return good for evil.
LADY BRUTE:
That may be a mistake in the translation.
The Provok'd Wife, I. i

9 Britons, strike home. *Ib. IV. i*

10 Thinking is to me the greatest fatigue in the world.
The Relapse, II. i

11 No man worth having is true to his wife, or can be true to his wife, or ever was, or ever will be so.
Ib. III. ii

WILLIAM HENRY VANDERBILT
1821–1885

12 The public be damned!
Reply to a question whether the public should be consulted about luxury trains. A. W. Cole's Letter, New York Times, 25 August 1918.

BARTOLOMEO VANZETTI
1888–1927

13 I found myself compelled to fight back from my eyes the tears, and quanch my heart trobling to my throat to not weep before him. But Sacco's name will live in the hearts of the people, when your name, your laws, institutions, and your false god are but a dim remomoring of a cursed past in which man was wolf to the man.
Last speech to the Massachusetts court, which was trying him and Nicolo Sacco on charges of murder and robbery. Both were self-confessed anarchists and labour agitators. Both were convicted, and were executed 23 Aug. 1927

CHARLES JOHN VAUGHAN
1816–1897

14 Must you go? Can't you stay?
Remark with which he broke up awkward breakfast parties of schoolboys who were too shy to go. Story retold with the words transposed, 'Can't you go? Must you stay?' G. W. E. Russell's Collections and Recollections, ch. 24

HENRY VAUGHAN
1622–1695

15 Man is the shuttle, to whose winding quest
And passage through these looms
God order'd motion, but ordain'd no rest.
Silex Scintillans. Man.

16 Father of lights! what sunny seed,
What glance of day hast Thou confin'd
Into this bird? To all the breed
This busy ray Thou hast assign'd;
Their magnetism works all night,
And dreams of Paradise and light.
Ib. Cock-Crowing

17 I cannot reach it; and my striving eye
Dazzles at it, as at eternity. *Ib. Childhood*

18 Through that pure virgin shrine,
That sacred veil drawn o'er Thy glorious noon,
That men might look and live, as glow-worms shine,
And face the moon;
Wise Nicodemus saw such light
As made him know his God by night.
Ib. The Night, l. 1

19 Most blest believer he!
Who in that land of darkness and blind eyes
Thy long expected healing wings could see
When Thou didst rise!
And, what can never more be done,
Did at midnight speak with the Sun!
Ib. l. 7

20 Dear Night! this world's defeat;
The stop to busy fools; care's check and curb;
The day of spirits; my soul's calm retreat
Which none disturb!
Christ's progress, and His prayer-time;
The hours to which high Heaven doth chime.
Ib. l. 25

21 There is in God—some say—
A deep, but dazzling darkness; as men here
Say it is late and dusky, because they
See not all clear.
O for that Night! where I in Him
Might live invisible and dim!
Ib. l. 49

1 My soul, there is a country
  Far beyond the stars,
Where stands a wingèd sentry
  All skilful in the wars:
There, above noise and danger,
  Sweet Peace is crown'd with smiles,
And One born in a manger
  Commands the beauteous files.
          Silex Scintillans. Peace

2 If thou canst get but thither,
    There grows the flower of Peace,
The Rose that cannot wither,
    Thy fortress, and thy ease.
Leave then thy foolish ranges;
    For none can thee secure,
But One, who never changes,
    Thy God, thy life, thy cure.   *Ib.*

3 Happy those early days, when I
Shin'd in my angel-infancy.
Before I understood this place
Appointed for my second race,
Or taught my soul to fancy aught
But a white, celestial thought;
When yet I had not walked above
A mile or two from my first love,
And looking back—at that short space—
Could see a glimpse of His bright face.
          Ib. The Retreat, l. 1

4 And in those weaker glories spy
Some shadows of eternity.   *Ib.* l. 13

5 But felt through all this fleshly dress
Bright shoots of everlastingness.   *Ib.* l. 19

6 O how I long to travel back,
And tread again that ancient track!
That I might once more reach that plain,
Where first I left my glorious train;
From whence th' enlighten'd spirit sees
The shady City of palm-trees.   *Ib.* l. 21

7 Some men a forward motion love,
But I by backward steps would move,
And when this dust falls to the urn,
In that state I came, return.   *Ib.* l. 29

8 They are all gone into the world of light,
    And I alone sit lingering here;
Their very memory is fair and bright,
    And my sad thoughts doth clear.
          Ib. They Are All Gone

9 I see them walking in an air of glory,
    Whose light doth trample on my days:
My days, which are at best but dull and hoary,
    Mere glimmering and decays.   *Ib.*

10 Dear, beauteous death! the jewel of the just,
    Shining nowhere but in the dark;
What mysteries do lie beyond thy dust,
    Could man outlook that mark!   *Ib.*

11 He that hath found some fledg'd bird's nest, may
        know
    At first sight, if the bird be flown;
But what fair well or grove he sings in now,
    That is to him unknown.   *Ib.*

12 And yet, as angels in some brighter dreams
    Call to the soul when man doth sleep,
So some strange thoughts transcend our wonted
        themes,
    And into glory peep.   *Ib.*

13 I saw Eternity the other night,
  Like a great ring of pure and endless light,
    All calm, as it was bright;
And round beneath it, Time in hours, days, years,
    Driv'n by the spheres
Like a vast shadow mov'd; in which the world
    And all her train were hurl'd.
          Silex Scintillans. The World

LUC DE CLAPIER, MARQUIS DE VAUVENARGUES
1715–1747

14 Les grandes pensées viennent du cœur.
    Great thoughts come from the heart.
          Réflexions et Maximes

THOMAS, LORD VAUX
1510–1556

15 For Age, with stealing steps,
Hath clawed me with his clutch.
    Poems (1872), p. 42. *The Aged Lover Renounceth
    Love. A Ditty . . . Representing the Image of
    Death. See* Corrigenda

VEGETIUS
4th cent. A.D.

16 Qui desiderat pacem, praeparet bellum.
    Let him who desires peace, prepare for war.
          De Re Mil. 3, prol.

PIERRE VERGNIAUD
1753–1793

17 Il a été permis de craindre que la Révolution, comme
    Saturne, dévorât successivement tous ses enfants.
    There was reason to fear that the Revolution, like
    Saturn, might devour in turn each one of her
    children.
        Lamartine, *Histoire des Girondins*, bk. xxxviii,
        ch. 20

PAUL VERLAINE
1844–1896

18 Et tout le reste est littérature.
    All the rest is mere fine writing. *Jadis et Naguère*

QUEEN VICTORIA
1819–1901

19 I will be good.
    *Letter from the Baroness Lehzen to Her Majesty,
    2 Dec. 1867.* Martin's *The Prince Consort* (1875),
    vol. i, p. 13

20 We are not amused.
    Notebooks of a Spinster Lady, 2 Jan. 1900

21 We are not interested in the possibilities of defeat.
    To A. J. Balfour, in 'Black Week', Dec. 1899

22 He [Mr. Gladstone] speaks to Me as if I was a public
    meeting.
    G. W. E. Russell's *Collections and Recollections*,
    ch. 14

ALFRED DE VIGNY

1797–1863

1 J'aime la majesté des souffrances humaines.

I love the majesty of human suffering.
La Maison du Berger

2 Seul le silence est grand; tout le reste est faiblesse . . .
Fais énergiquement ta longue et lourde tâche . . .
Puis, après, comme moi, souffre et meurs sans parler.

Silence alone is great; all else is feebleness . . .
Perform with all your heart your long and heavy task. . . .
Then as do I, say naught, but suffer and die.
La Mort du Loup

FRANÇOIS VILLON

b. 1431

3 Mais où sont les neiges d'antan?

But where are the snows of yesteryear?
Le Grand Testament, Ballade des Dames du Temps Jadis. Trans. by D. G. Rossetti

ST. VINCENT OF LERINS

d. c. A.D. 450

4 Quod semper, quod ubique, quod ab omnibus creditum est.

What is always, what is everywhere, what is by all people believed. *Commonitorium, ii*

VIRGIL

70–19 B.C.

5 Arma virumque cano, Troiae qui primus ab oris
Italiam fato profugus Lavinaque venit
Litora—multum ille et terris iactatus et alto
Vi superum, saevae memorem Iunonis ob iram.

Arms I sing, and the man, who first from the shores of Troy came, Fate-exiled, to Italy and her Lavinian strand—much buffeted he on flood and field by constraint of Heaven and fell Juno's unslumbering ire. *Aeneid, i. 1. Trans. by Jackson*

6 Quo numine laeso.

Wherein was her godhead affronted. *Ib. 8*

7 Tantaene animis caelestibus irae?

Can heavenly spirits cherish resentment so dire?
Ib. 11

8 Necdum etiam causae irarum saevique dolores
Exciderant animo; manet alta mente repostum
Iudicium Paridis spretaeque iniuria formae.

Nor yet had the causes of her wrath, nor her hot resentment, faded from her soul. Deep-written in her heart the judgement of Paris remained, and the outrage to her slighted beauty. *Ib. 25*

9 Tantae molis erat Romanam condere gentem.

So vast was the struggle to found the Roman state.
Ib. 33

10 Apparent rari nantes in gurgite vasto.

Here and there in the wastes of ocean a swimmer was seen. *Ib. 118*

11 Furor arma ministrat.

Fury ministers arms. *Ib. 150*

12 Fidus quae tela gerebat Achates.

Loyal Achates bore the weapons. *Aeneid, i. 188*

13 O passi graviora, dabit deus his quoque finem.

Friends, that have endured yet heavier blows, God will grant an ending even to this. *Ib. 199*

14 Forsan et haec olim meminisse iuvabit.

The day may dawn when this plight shall be sweet to remember. *Ib. 203*

15 Durate, et vosmet rebus servate secundis.

Then endure for a while, and live for a happier day! *Ib. 207*

16 Dux femina facti.

A woman the head of their emprize. *Ib. 364*

17 Vera incessu patuit dea.

The goddess indubitable was revealed in her step.
Ib. 405

18 'En Priamus. Sunt hic etiam sua praemia laudi;
Sunt lacrimae rerum et mentem mortalia tangunt.
Solve metus; feret haec aliquam tibi fama salutem.'
Sic ait atque animum pictura pascit inani.

'Lo, here is Priam! Even here, virtue hath her rewards, and mortality her tears: even here, the woes of man touch the heart of man! Dispel thy fears; this fame of ours is herald to some salvation.' He said, and sated his soul with the barren portraiture. *Ib. 461*

19 Impar congressus Achilli.

Fronted Achilles with unequal arm. *Ib. 475*

20 Mens sibi conscia recti.

A mind conscious of the right. *Ib. 604*

21 In freta dum fluvii current, dum montibus umbrae
Lustrabunt convexa, polus dum sidera pascet,
Semper honos nomenque tuum laudesque manebunt.

While the rivers shall run to ocean, while the shadows shall move in the mountain valleys, while the sky shall feed the stars, always shall thy honour, and thy name, and thy glory abide.
Ib. 607

22 Non ignara mali miseris succurrere disco.

Not unschooled in woe do I learn to succour unhappiness! *Ib. 630*

23 Conticuere omnes intentique ora tenebant.

Every tongue was still, every face turned rapt upon him. *Ib. ii. 1*

24 Infandum, regina, iubes renovare dolorem.

Too deep for words, O queen, lies the sorrow thou bidst me renew. *Ib. 3*

25 Quaeque ipse miserrima vidi
Et quorum pars magna fui.

All the deeds of woe mine eyes have beheld, and those whereof I was no small part. *Ib. 5*

26 Et iam nox umida caelo
Praecipitat suadentque cadentia sidera somnos.

And now dewy Night falls precipitate from heaven, and the setting stars counsel sleep! *Ib. 8*

27 Equo ne credite, Teucri.
Quidquid id est, timeo Danaos et dona ferentis.

Men of Troy, trust not the horse! Be it what it may, I fear the Danaans, though their hands proffer gifts. *Ib. 48*

VIRGIL

1   In utrumque paratus,
Seu versare dolos seu certae occumbere morti.

> Nerved to either event, whether to spin his toils, or
> to fall under death inevitable. *Aeneid*, ii. 61

2   Crimine ab uno
Disce omnes.

> From a single crime know the nation. *Ib.* 65

3 Horresco referens.

> I shudder at the word. *Ib.* 204

4 Tacitae per amica silentia lunae.

> Through the friendly silence of the mute moon.
> *Ib.* 255

5 Tempus erat quo prima quies mortalibus aegris
Incipit et dono divum gratissima serpit.

> It was the hour when the first sleep of suffering
> mortality begins, and, by the grace of Heaven,
> steals on its sweetest errand of mercy. *Ib.* 268

6   Quantum mutatus ab illo
Hectore qui redit exuvias indutus Achilli.

> How was he changed from that Hector, who
> wended homeward, clad in the spoils of Achilles.
> *Ib.* 274

7   Iam proximus ardet
Ucalegon.

> Already neighbour Ucalegon burns. *Ib.* 311

8   Fuimus Troes, fuit Ilium et ingens
Gloria Teucrorum.

> Trojans we are no more, Ilium is no more, and
> the great glory of the Teucrians is departed!
> *Ib.* 325

9 Una salus victis nullam sperare salutem.

> There is but one safety to the vanquished—to hope
> not safety! *Ib.* 354

10 Dis aliter visum.

> Heaven's thought was otherwise. *Ib.* 428

11 Non tali auxilio nec defensoribus istis
Tempus eget.

> The hour calls not for such succour, nor such
> defenders. *Ib.* 521

12 Sequiturque patrem non passibus aequis.

> Follows his father with unmatched step. *Ib.* 724

13   Quid non mortalia pectora cogis,
Auri sacra fames!

> O cursed lust of gold, to what canst thou not com-
> pel the heart of man! *Ib.* iii. 56

14 Monstrum horrendum, informe, ingens, cui lumen
ademptum.

> A monster fearful and hideous, vast and eyeless.
> *Ib.* 658

15 Agnosco veteris vestigia flammae.

> I feel again a spark of that ancient flame.
> *Ib.* iv. 23

16 Virisque adquirit eundo.

> At every step she [Fame] gathers strength. *Ib.* 175

17   Sese interea . . .
Temptaturum aditus et quae mollissima fandi
Tempora.

> Himself meanwhile . . . would assay to find access
> and watch what hour might be the smoothest
> **for his tale.** *Ib.* 291

18 Quis fallere possit amantem?

> Who shall deceive a lover's thought?
> *Aeneid*, iv. 296

19 Nec me meminisse pigebit Elissae
Dum memor ipse mei, dum spiritus hos regit artus.

> Nor ever shall the thought of Elissa be bitter to
> me, while yet I have remembrance of myself
> and the breath governs these limbs. *Ib.* 335

20   Varium et mutabile semper
Femina.

> A fickle thing and changeful is woman always!
> *Ib.* 569

21 Exoriare aliquis nostris ex ossibus ultor.

> Arise, thou avenger to come, out of my ashes.
> *Ib.* 625

22 Hos successus alit: possunt, quia posse videntur.

> To those success was good, and the semblance
> of power gave power indeed. *Ib.* v. 231

23   Facilis descensus Averni:
Noctes atque dies patet atri ianua Ditis;
Sed revocare gradum superasque evadere ad auras,
Hoc opus, hic labor est.

> Light is the descent to Avernus! Night and day
> the portals of gloomy Dis stand wide: but to
> recall thy step and issue to the upper air—there is
> the toil and there the task! *Ib.* vi. 126

24   Primo avulso non deficit alter
Aureus, et simili frondescit virga metallo.

> When the first is rent away a second, golden no
> less, succeeds, and the bough blossoms with ore
> as precious. *Ib.* 143

25 Procul, o procul este, profani.

> Hence, O hence, . . . ye that are uninitiated. *Ib.* 258

26 Nunc animis opus, Aenea, nunc pectore firmo.

> Now is the hour, Aeneas, for the dauntless spirit
> —now for the stout heart. *Ib.* 261

27 Vestibulum ante ipsum primis in faucibus Orci
Luctus et ultrices posuere cubilia Curae;
Pallentesque habitant Morbi tristisque Senectus,
Et Metus et malesuada Fames ac turpis Egestas.

> Hard before the portal, in the opening jaws of
> Hell, Grief and avenging Cares have made their
> couch; and with them dwell wan Disease and
> sorrowful Age, and Fear, and Hunger, temptress
> to Sin, and loathly Want. *Ib.* 273

28 Tendebantque manus ripae ulterioris amore.

> Their hands outstretched in yearning for the
> farther shore. *Ib.* 314

29 Inventas aut qui vitam excoluere per artis,
Quique sui memores alios fecere merendo.

> Or who ennobled life by arts discovered; with
> all whose service to their kind won them remem-
> brance among men. *Ib.* 663

30 Spiritus intus alit, totamque infusa per artus
Mens agitat molem et magno se corpore miscet.

> An indwelling spirit sustains, and a mind fused
> throughout the limbs sways the whole mass and
> mingles with the giant frame. *Ib.* 726

31 Igneus est ollis vigor et caelestis origo
Seminibus.

> To these seeds a flame-like vigour pertains and an
> origin celestial. *Ib.* 730

1 Tu regere imperio populos, Romane, memento
(Hae tibi erunt artes), pacisque imponere morem,
Parcere subiectis et debellare superbos.

Roman, be this thy care—these thine arts—to bear
dominion over the nations and to impose the law
of peace, to spare the humbled and to war down
the proud! *Aeneid*, vi. 851

2 Sunt geminae Somni portae, quarum altera fertur
Cornea, qua veris facilis datur exitus umbris,
Altera candenti perfecta nitens elephanto,
Sed falsa ad caelum mittunt insomnia manes.

There are two gates of Sleep:—of horn, fame tells,
the one, through which the spirits of truth find
an easy passage; the other, wrought smooth-
gleaming with sheen of ivory, but false the
visions that the nether powers speed therefrom
to the heaven above. *Ib.* 893

3 Geniumque loci . . .
precatur.
Implored the Genius of the place. *Ib.* vii. 136

4 Flectere si nequeo superos, Acheronta movebo.
And if Heaven be inflexible, Hell shall be un-
leashed! *Ib.* 312

5 O mihi praeteritos referat si Iuppiter annos.
O, would Jupiter restore me the years that are fled!
Ib. viii. 560

6 Quadripedante putrem sonitu quatit ungula campum.
The sound of galloping hooves shook the crumb-
ling plain. *Ib.* 596

7 Me, me, adsum qui feci, in me convertite ferrum.
On me,—here I stand who did the deed,—on me
turn your steel. *Ib.* ix. 427

8 Dum domus Aeneae Capitoli immobile saxum
Accolet imperiumque pater Romanus habebit.

So long as the house of Aeneas shall dwell by the
Capitol's unmoved rock and the Father of Rome
bear sceptre! *Ib.* 448

9 Macte nova virtute, puer, sic itur ad astra.
Good speed to thy youthful valour, child! So
shalt thou scale the stars! *Ib.* 641

10 Audentis Fortuna iuvat.
Fortune is ally to the brave. *Ib.* x. 284

11 Experto credite.
Credit one who has proved. *Ib.* xi. 283

12 Audiit et voti Phoebus succedere partem
Mente dedit, partem volucris dispersit in auras.

Phoebus heard, and in thought vouchsafed that
half his vow should prosper: half he scattered to
the fleet winds. *Ib.* 794

13 Di me terrent et Iuppiter hostis.
The gods dismay me, and Jove my foe! *Ib.* xii. 895

14 Tityre, tu patulae recubans sub tegmine fagi
Silvestrem tenui musam meditaris avena.

Tityrus, thou liest canopied beneath thy spreading
beech and wooing the silvan Muse on thy slender
oat. *Eclogue*, i. 1. *Trans. by Jackson*

15 Formosam resonare doces Amaryllida silvas.
Thou teachest the responsive woods to call
Amaryllis fair! *Ib.* 5

16 O Meliboee, deus nobis haec otia fecit.
O Meliboeus, it was a god gave us this peace.
Eclogue, i. 6

17 Non equidem invideo, miror magis.
As for me I grudge thee not—rather I marvel!
Ib. 11

18 Sic parvis componere magna solebam
Verum haec tantum alias inter caput extulit urbes
Quantum lenta solent inter viburna cupressi.

I only measured great by small but, above all other
cities, this so far exalts her head as the cypress
above the lissom osiers! *Ib.* 23

19 Et penitus toto divisos orbe Britannos.
Or where the Briton dwells utterly estranged from
all the world! *Ib.* 66

20 Formosum pastor Corydon ardebat Alexim.
Shepherd Corydon was all aflame for fair Alexis.
Ib. ii. 1

21 O formose puer, nimium ne crede colori!
Sweet boy, trust not over much to thy hue!
Ib. 17

22 Quem fugis, a, demens? Habitarunt di quoque silvas.
Ah, madman, whom dost thou flee? Even gods
have dwelt in woods. *Ib.* 60

23 Trahit sua quemque voluptas.
Each draws to his best-loved. *Ib.* 65

24 Nunc frondent silvae, nunc formosissimus annus.
Now the woods are green, and the year is loveliest. *Ib.* iii. 57

25 Ab Iove principium musae: Iovis omnia plena.
From Jove my lay begins: Jove filleth all. *Ib.* 60

26 Malo me Galatea petit, lasciva puella,
Et fugit ad salices et se cupit ante videri.

Galatea, wayward girl, pelts me with apples, then
runs behind the willows—and hopes I saw her
first! *Ib.* 64

27 Latet anguis in herba.
A snake lurks in the grass! *Ib.* 93

28 Non nostrum inter vos tantas componere lites.
Not ours to decide such high dispute! *Ib.* 108

29 Claudite iam rivos, pueri; sat prata biberunt.
Swains, close now the springs. The meadows have
drunk enough! *Ib.* 111

30 Sicelides Musae, paulo maiora canamus!
Non omnis arbusta iuvant humilisque myrica.
Si canimus silvas, silvae sint consule dignae.
Ultima Cumaei venit iam carminis aetas;
Magnus ab integro saeclorum nascitur ordo.
Iam redit et virgo, redeunt Saturnia regna
Iam nova progenies caelo demittitur alto.

Sicilian Muses, let us raise a somewhat loftier
strain. Not all do orchards and the lowly tamarisk
delight. If the woodland be our theme, let our
woods be worthy of a consul's ear! The last age,
heralded in Cumean song, is come, and the great
march of the centuries, begins anew. Now the
Virgin returns: now Saturn is king again, and a
new and better race descends from on high.
Ib. iv. 1

VIRGIL

1 Incipe, parve puer, risu cognoscere matrem.

Begin, baby boy, to know thy mother with a smile.
Eclogue, iv. 60

2 Incipe, parve puer: qui non risere parenti,
Nec deus hunc mensa, dea nec dignata cubili est.

Begin, baby boy! Him who had never a smile for a parent, no god honours with his board, no goddess with her bed!
Ib. 62

3 Arcades ambo,
Et cantare pares et respondere parati.

Both Arcadians, both ready to sing in even contest, both ready to make reply!
Ib. vii. 4

4 Saepibus in nostris parvam te roscida mala
(Dux ego vester eram) vidi cum matre legentem.
Alter ab undecimo tum me iam acceperat annus,
Iam fragilis poteram a terra contingere ramos:
Ut vidi, ut perii, ut me malus abstulit error!

Within our orchard's walls I saw thee—for I was there to point the way—a little maid gathering dewy apples with my mother! Eleven years I had numbered, and the twelfth already claimed me; from the ground already I could reach the frail boughs. Ah, how I saw! How I fell! How that fatal blindness swept me away!
Ib. viii. 37

5 Nunc scio quid sit Amor.

Now do I know what Love is!
Ib. 43

6 Non omnia possumus omnes.

All power is not to all.
Ib. 63

7 Et me fecere poetam
Pierides, sunt et mihi carmina, me quoque dicunt
Vatem pastores; sed non ego credulus illis.
Nam neque adhuc Vario videor nec dicere Cinna
Digna, sed argutos inter strepere anser olores.

Me, too, the Pierian sisters have made a singer; I, too, have songs: ay, and the shepherds dub me *poet*, but I trust them not! For as yet, methinks, my strains befit not a Varius, nor a Cinna, but, gooselike, I cackle amid quiring swans!
Ib. ix. 32

8 Omnia vincit Amor: et nos cedamus Amori.

Love is lord of all: yield we, too, to Love!
Ib. x. 69

9 Ite domum saturae, venit Hesperus, ite capellae.

Get ye home, my full-fed goats, get ye home—the Evening-star draws on!
Ib. 77

10 Ultima Thule.

Farthest Thule. *Georgics*, i. 30. *Trans. by Jackson*

11 Labor omnia vicit
Improbus et duris urgens in rebus egestas.

Never-flinching labour proved lord of all, and the stress of need in a life of struggles!
Ib. 145

12 Imponere Pelio Ossam
Scilicet, atque Ossae frondosum involvere Olympum.

In sooth . . . to pile Ossa on Pelion and roll leaf-crowned Olympus on Ossa.
Ib. 281

13 Miscueruntque herbas et non innoxia verba.

Mingled herbs and charms of bale.
Ib. ii. 129

14 Salve, magna parens frugum, Saturnia tellus,
Magna virum.

Hail, Saturn's land, great mother of the harvest, great mother of men!
Ib. 173

15 O fortunatos nimium, sua si bona norint,
Agricolas! Quibus ipsa procul discordibus armis
Fundit humo facilem victum iustissima tellus.

Ah, blest beyond all bliss the husbandmen, did they but know their happiness! On whom, far from the clash of arms, the most just Earth showers from her bosom a toilless sustenance.
Georgics, ii. 458

16 Felix qui potuit rerum cognoscere causas.

Happy he, who has availed to read the causes of things.
Ib. 490

17 Strepitumque Acherontis avari.

The roaring of the hungry stream of Death. *Ib.* 492

18 Fortunatus et ille deos qui novit agrestis.

And happy he, who has knowledge of the woodland gods.
Ib. 493

19 Temptanda via est, qua me quoque possim
Tollere humo victorque virum volitare per ora.

I must assay a path, whereby I may raise me from earth and flit conqueror through the mouths of men!
Ib. iii. 8

20 Optima quaeque dies miseris mortalibus aevi
Prima fugit: subeunt morbi tristisque senectus
Et labor, et durae rapit inclementia mortis.

It is ever the brightest day of life that is first to bid adieu to our hapless mortality: disease and gloomy eld steal upon us, and anon suffering, and the ruthless tyranny of Death, sweep us away.
Ib. 66

21 Sed fugit interea, fugit inreparabile tempus.

Meanwhile, Time is flying—flying, never to return.
Ib. 284

22 Hi motus animorum atque haec certamina tanta
Pulveris exigui iactu compressa quiescent.

Yet all this tumult of soul and all this savagery of conflict may be quelled and laid to rest by the scattering of a little dust.
Ib. iv. 86

23 Agmine facto
Ignavum fucos pecus a praesepibus arcent.

They form in array and cast out the drones and their idle bands from the homestead.
Ib. 167

24 Si parva licet componere magnis.

If it be meet to measure small by great.
Ib. 176

25 At genus immortale manet, multosque per annos
Stat fortuna domus, et avi numerantur avorum.

Yet the race abides immortal, the star of their house sets not through many years, and grandsire's grandsire is numbered in the roll.
Ib. 208

26 Victorque volentis
Per populos dat iura viamque adfectat Olympo.

Assigning in victorious march, laws to the willing nations, and assaying on earth the path to Heaven!
Ib. 561

27 Sic vos non vobis mellificatis apes.
Sic vos non vobis nidificatis aves.
Sic vos non vobis vellera fertis oves.

So you bees make your honey, not for yourselves.
So you birds make nests, not for yourselves.
So you sheep bear fleeces, not for yourselves.
Attrib. On Bathyllus' claiming the authorship of certain lines by Virgil

VOLTAIRE
1694–1778

1 Dans ce pays-ci il est bon de tuer de temps en temps un amiral pour encourager les autres.

In this country [England] it is thought well to kill an admiral from time to time to encourage the others.　　　　　　　　　　　*Candide*, ch. 23

2 Tout est pour le mieux dans le meilleur des mondes possibles.

All is for the best in the best of possible worlds.　　　　　　　　　　　　　　　　*Ib.* 30

3 Cela est bien dit, répondit Candide, mais il faut cultiver notre jardin.

'That is well said,' replied Candide, 'but we must cultivate our garden.' (We must attend to our own affairs.)　　　　　　　　　　　　　*Ib.*

4 Ils ne se servent de la pensée que pour autoriser leurs injustices, et n'emploient les paroles que pour déguiser leurs pensées.

[Men] use thought only to justify their wrongdoings, and speech only to conceal their thoughts.
　　　Dialogue xiv. Le Chapon et la Poularde

5 Le mieux est l'ennemi du bien.

The best is the enemy of the good.
　　　　Dict. Philosophique, art. *Art Dramatique*

6 Tous les genres sont bons hors le genre ennuyeux.

All styles are good save the tiresome kind.
　　　　　　　　　L'Enfant Prodigue, preface

7 Si Dieu n'existait pas, il faudrait l'inventer.

If God did not exist, it would be necessary to invent him.
　　Épîtres, xcvi. A l'Auteur du Livre des Trois Imposteurs

8 Ce corps qui s'appelait et qui s'appelle encore le saint empire romain n'était en aucune manière ni saint, ni romain, ni empire.

This agglomeration which was called and which still calls itself the Holy Roman Empire was neither holy, nor Roman, nor an empire.
　　Essai sur les Mœurs et l'Esprit des Nations, lxx

9 Quoi que vous fassiez, écrasez l'infâme, et aimez qui vous aime.

Whatever you do, trample down abuses, and love those who love you.
　　　　　Lettres. A. M. d'Alembert, 28 Nov. 1762

10 On dit que Dieu est toujours pour les gros bataillons.

It is said that God is always for the big battalions.
　　　　　Ib. A. M. Le Riche, 6 Feb. 1770

11 Le superflu, chose très nécessaire.

The superfluous is very necessary.
　　　　　　　　　　　Le Mondain, v. 22

12 La foi consiste à croire ce que la raison ne croit pas. . . . Il ne suffit pas qu'une chose soit possible pour la croire.

Faith consists in believing when it is beyond the power or reason to believe. It is not enough that a thing be possible for it to be believed.
　　　　　　　Questions sur l'Encyclopédie

13 Le secret d'ennuyer est . . . de tout dire.

The way to be a bore [for an author] is to say everything.
　　　Sept Discours en vers sur l'Homme, VI. *Sur la Nature de l'Homme*. v. 174–5

14 Habacuc était capable de tout.

Habakkuk was capable of anything.
　　　Attrib. see Notes and Queries, clxxxi. 46

15 I disapprove of what you say, but I will defend to the death your right to say it.
　　Attrib. in S. G. Tallentyre, The Friends of Voltaire (1907), p. 199

JOSEPH AUGUSTINE WADE
1796?–1845

16 Meet me by moonlight alone.　*Meet Me by Moonlight*

HENRY WALLACE
1888–

17 The century on which we are entering can be and must be the century of the common man.
　　Address: The Price of Free World Victory, 8 May 1942

LEW WALLACE
1827–1905

18 Beauty is altogether in the eye of the beholder.
　　The Prince of India (1893), III. vi. 78. (*See 265: 14*)

WILLIAM ROSS WALLACE
d. 1881

19 The hand that rocks the cradle
Is the hand that rules the world.
　　　　John o' London's Treasure Trove

GRAHAM WALLAS
1858–1932

20 The little girl had the making of a poet in her who, being told to be sure of her meaning before she spoke, said: 'How can I know what I think till I see what I say?'　　　*The Art of Thought*

EDMUND WALLER
1606–1687

21 So was the huntsman by the bear oppress'd,
Whose hide he sold—before he caught the beast!
　　　　Battle of the Summer Islands, ii, l. 111

22 Poets that lasting marble seek
Must carve in Latin or in Greek.　*Of English Verse*

23 Others may use the ocean as their road,
Only the English make it their abode.
　　　　　Of a War with Spain, l. 25

24 The seas are quiet when the winds give o'er;
So, calm are we when passions are no more!
　　　　On the Foregoing Divine Poems. l. 7

25 The soul's dark cottage, batter'd and decay'd
Lets in new light through chinks that time has made;
Stronger by weakness, wiser men become,
As they draw near to their eternal home.

Leaving the old, both worlds at once they view,
That stand upon the threshold of the new.
On the Foregoing Divine Poems, l. 18

1 That which her slender waist confin'd
Shall now my joyful temples bind;
No monarch but would give his crown
His arms might do what this has done.

It was my heaven's extremest sphere,
The pale which held that lovely deer:
My joy, my grief, my hope, my love,
Did all within this circle move.

A narrow compass! and yet there
Dwelt all that's good, and all that's fair:
Give me but what this riband bound,
Take all the rest the sun goes round. *On a Girdle*

2 Rome, though her eagle through the world had flown,
Could never make this island all her own.
Panegyric to My Lord Protector, xvii

3 Illustrious acts high raptures do infuse,
And every conqueror creates a Muse. *Ib.* xlvi

4 Go, lovely Rose!
Tell her, that wastes her time and me,
    That now she knows,
When I resemble her to thee,
How sweet and fair she seems to be.
Song: 'Go Lovely Rose!'

5 Small is the worth
Of beauty from the light retir'd;
Bid her come forth,
    Suffer'd herself to be desir'd,
And not blush so to be admir'd. *Ib.*

6 Why came I so untimely forth
Into a world which, wanting thee,
Could entertain us with no worth,
Or shadow of felicity?
To My Young Lady Lucy Sidney

7 So all we know
Of what they do above,
Is that they happy are, and that they love.
Upon the Death of My Lady Rich, l. 75

8 Under the tropic is our language spoke,
And part of Flanders hath receiv'd our yoke.
Upon the Death of the Lord Protector, l. 21

HORACE WALPOLE, FOURTH EARL OF ORFORD
1717–1797

9 Alexander at the head of the world never tasted the
true pleasure that boys of his own age have enjoyed at the head of a school.
Letters, To Montagu, 6 May 1736

10 Our supreme governors, the mob.
Ib. To Horace Mann, 7 Sept. 1743

11 [Strawberry Hill] is a little plaything-house that I got
out of Mrs. Chenevix's shop, and is the prettiest
bauble you ever saw. It is set in enamelled
meadows, with filigree hedges.
To Conway, 8 June 1747

12 But, thank God! the Thames is between me and the
Duchess of Queensberry. *Ib.*

13 Every drop of ink in my pen ran cold.
Ib. To Montagu, 3 July 1752

14 It has the true rust of the Barons' Wars.
Ib. To Bentley, Sept. 1753

15 At present, nothing is talked of, nothing admired, but
what I cannot help calling a very insipid and
tedious performance: it is a kind of novel, called
The Life and Opinions of Tristram Shandy; the
great humour of which consists in the whole narration always going backwards.
To Dalrymple, 4 Apr. 1760

16 One of the greatest geniuses that ever existed,
Shakespeare, undoubtedly wanted taste.
Ib. To Wren, 9 Aug. 1764

17 The works of Richardson . . . which are pictures of
high life as conceived by a bookseller, and romances
as they would be spiritualized by a Methodist
preacher. *Ib. To Mann, 20 Dec. 1764*

18 At Madame du Deffand's, an old blind *débauchée* of
wit. *Ib. To Conway, 6 Oct. 1765*

19 It is charming to totter into vogue.
Ib. To Selwyn, 2 Dec. 1765

20 Yes, like Queen Eleanor in the ballad, I sunk at
Charing Cross, and have risen in the Faubourg St.
Germain. *Ib. To Gray, 25 Jan. 1766*

21 The best sun we have is made of Newcastle coal.
Ib. To Montagu, 15 June 1768

22 Everybody talks of the constitution, but all sides
forget that the constitution is extremely well, and
would do very well, if they would but let it alone.
Ib. To Sir Horace Mann, 18–19 Jan. 1770

23 It was easier to conquer it [the East] than to know
what to do with it. *Ib. To Mann, 27 Mar. 1772*

24 The way to ensure summer in England is to have it
framed and glazed in a comfortable room.
Ib. To Cole, 28 May 1774

25 The next Augustan age will dawn on the other side
of the Atlantic. There will, perhaps, be a Thucydides at Boston, a Xenophon at New York, and,
in time, a Virgil at Mexico, and a Newton at
Peru. At last, some curious traveller from Lima
will visit England and give a description of the
ruins of St. Paul's, like the editions of Balbec and
Palmyra. *Ib. To Mann, 24 Nov. 1774*

26 By the waters of Babylon we sit down and weep, when
we think of thee, O America!
Ib. To Mason, 12 June 1775

27 This world is a comedy to those that think, a tragedy
to those that feel.
*Ib. To the Countess of Upper Ossory, 16 Aug.
1776*

28 Prognostics do not always prove prophecies,—at least
the wisest prophets make sure of the event first.
Ib. To Thos. Walpole, 19 Feb. 1785

29 All his [Sir Joshua Reynolds's] own geese are swans,
as the swans of others are geese.
Ib. To the Countess of Upper Ossory, 1 Dec. 1786

SIR ROBERT WALPOLE, FIRST EARL OF ORFORD
1676–1745

30 They now *ring* the bells, but they will soon *wring*
their hands.
*Remark on the declaration of war with Spain,
1739. W. Coxe, Memoirs of Sir Robert Walpole
(1798), vol. i, p. 618*

31 All those men have their price. *Ib. p. 757*

1 Madam, there are fifty thousand men slain this year in Europe, and not one Englishman.
Remark to Queen Caroline, 1734. Hervey, *Memoirs* (1848), vol. i, p. 398

2 My Lord Bath, you and I are now two as insignificant men as any in England.
To Pulteney, Earl of Bath, on their promotion to the House of Lords. W. King, *Political & Literary Anecdotes* (1819), p. 43

3 The balance of power.
Speech in the House of Commons, 13 Feb. 1741

4 Sir Robert Walpole's definition of the gratitude of place-expectants, 'That it is a lively sense of *future* favours'.
W. Hazlitt, *Lectures on the English Comic Writers, Wit and Humour*, p. 27. (See 407:13)

WILLIAM WALSH
1663–1708

5 And sadly reflecting,
That a lover forsaken
A new love may get,
But a neck when once broken
Can never be set. *The Despairing Lover, l. 17*

6 Of all the torments, all the cares,
With which our lives are curst;
Of all the plagues a lover bears,
Sure rivals are the worst!
By partners, in each other kind,
Afflictions easier grow;
In love alone we hate to find
Companions of our woe. *Song, Of All the Torments*

7 I can endure my own despair,
But not another's hope. *Ib.*

IZAAK WALTON
1593–1683

8 Angling may be said to be so like the mathematics, that it can never be fully learnt.
Compleat Angler. Epistle to the Reader

9 And for winter fly-fishing it is as useful as an almanac out of date. *Ib.*

10 As no man is born an artist, so no man is born an angler. *Ib.*

11 I shall stay him no longer than to wish him a rainy evening to read this following discourse; and that if he be an honest angler, the east wind may never blow when he goes a-fishing. *Ib.*

12 I am, Sir, a Brother of the Angle. *Ib. pt. i, ch. 1*

13 It [angling] deserves commendations; . . . it is an art, and an art worthy the knowledge and practice of a wise man. *Ib.*

14 Angling is somewhat like poetry, men are to be born so. *Ib.*

15 Sir Henry Wotton . . . was also a most dear lover, and a frequent practiser of the art of angling; of which he would say, 'it was an employment for his idle time, which was then not idly spent . . . a rest to his mind, a cheerer of his spirits, a diverter of sadness, a calmer of unquiet thoughts, a moderator of passions, a procurer of contentedness; and that it begat habits of peace and patience in those that professed and practised it.' *Ib.*

16 I remember that a wise friend of mine did usually say, 'that which is everybody's business is nobody's business.' *Compleat Angler, pt. i, ch. 2*

17 Good company and good discourse are the very sinews of virtue. *Ib.*

18 An excellent angler, and now with God. *Ib. ch. 4*

19 When I was last this way a-fishing. *Ib.*

20 I love such mirth as does not make friends ashamed to look upon one another next morning. *Ib. ch. 5*

21 A good, honest, wholesome, hungry breakfast. *Ib.*

22 No man can lose what he never had. *Ib.*

23 Thus use your frog. . . . Put your hook, I mean the arming-wire, through his mouth, and out at his gills; and then with a fine needle and silk sew the upper part of his leg, with only one stitch, to the arming-wire of your hook; or tie the frog's leg, above the upper joint, to the armed-wire; and, in so doing, use him as though you loved him. *Ib. ch. 8*

24 This dish of meat is too good for any but anglers, or very honest men. *Ib.*

25 I love any discourse of rivers, and fish and fishing. *Ib. ch. 18*

26 Look to your health; and if you have it, praise God, and value it next to a good conscience; for health is the second blessing that we mortals are capable of; a blessing that money cannot buy. *Ib. ch. 21*

27 Let the blessing of St. Peter's Master be . . . upon all that are lovers of virtue; and dare trust in His providence; and be quiet; and go a-Angling. *Ib.*

28 But God, who is able to prevail, wrestled with him, as the Angel did with Jacob, and marked him; marked him for his own. *Life of Donne*

29 The great Secretary of Nature and all learning, Sir Francis Bacon. *Life of Herbert*

30 Of this blest man, let his just praise be given,
Heaven was in him, before he was in heaven.
Written in Dr. Richard Sibbes's Returning Backslider, *now preserved in Salisbury Cathedral Library*

BISHOP WILLIAM WARBURTON
1698–1779

31 Orthodoxy is my doxy; heterodoxy is another man's doxy.
Remark to Lord Sandwich. Priestley, *Memoirs* (1807), vol. i, p. 372

ARTEMUS WARD [CHARLES FARRAR BROWNE]
1834–1867

32 I now bid you a welcome adoo.
Artemus Ward His Book. The Shakers

33 'Mister Ward, don't yur blud bile at the thawt that three million and a half of your culled brethren air a clanking their chains in the South?' Sez I, 'not a bile! Let 'em clank!' *Ib. Oberlin*

34 The College has konfired upon me the honery title of T.K., of which I'm suffishuntly prowd. *Ib.*

35 'I wish thar was winders to my Sole,' sed I, 'so that you could see some of my feelins.'
Ib. The Showman's Courtship

1 If you mean gettin hitched, I'M IN!
Artemus Ward His Book. The Showman's Courtship

2 My pollertics, like my religion, bein of a exceedin accommodatin character. *Ib. The Crisis*

3 Shall we sell our birthrite for a mess of potash? *Ib.*

4 N.B. This is rote Sarcasticul.
Ib. A Visit to Brigham Young

5 I girdid up my Lions & fled the Seen. *Ib.*

6 Did you ever hav the measels, and if so how many?
Ib. The Census

7 'Fair youth, do you know what I'd do with you if you was my sun?' 'No,' sez he. 'Wall,' sez I, 'I'd appint your funeral to-morrow arternoon & the *korps should be ready!* You're too smart to live on this yearth.' *Ib. Edwin Forrest as Othello*

8 Before he retired to his virtuous couch. *Ib.*

9 The female woman is one of the greatest institooshuns of which this land can boste. *Ib. Woman's Rights*

10 Do me eyes deceive me earsight? Is it some dreams?
Ib. Moses, the Sassy

11 By a sudden and adroit movement I placed my left eye agin the Secesher's fist.
Ib. Thrilling Scenes in Dixie

12 The ground flew up and hit me in the hed. *Ib.*

13 I presunted myself at Betty's bedside late at nite, with considerbul licker koncealed about my persun.
Ib. Betsy-Jain Re-orgunised

14 The happy marrid man dies in good stile at home, surrounded by his weeping wife and children. The old batchelor don't die at all—he sort of rots away, like a polly-wog's tail. *Ib. Draft in Baldinsville*

15 It is a pity that Chawcer, who had geneyus, was so unedicated. He's the wuss speller I know of.
Artemus Ward in London, ch. 4. At the Tomb of Shakespeare

16 Why these weeps? *Artemus Ward's Lecture*

17 One of the principal features of my Entertainment is that it contains so many things that don't have anything to do with it. *Ib.*

18 I can't sing. As a singist I am not a success. I am saddest when I sing. So are those who hear me. They are sadder even than I am. *Ib.*

19 He [Brigham Young] is dreadfully married. He's the most married man I ever saw in my life. *Ib.*

20 Why is this thus? What is the reason of this thusness? *Ib.*

21 I am happiest when I am idle. I could live for months without performing any kind of labour, and at the expiration of that time I should feel fresh and vigorous enough to go right on in the same way for numerous more months.
Pyrotechny. III. *Pettingill*

22 Why care for grammar as long as we are good?
Ib. v

23 Let us all be happy, and live within our means, even if we have to borrer the money to do it with.
Science and Natural History

MRS. HUMPHRY WARD
1851–1920

24 'Propinquity does it'—as Mrs. Thornburgh is always reminding us. *Robert Elsmere*, bk. i, ch. 2

REV. NATHANIEL WARD
1578–1652

25 The world is full of care, much like unto a bubble; Women and care, and care and women, and women and care and trouble.
Epigram. Attributed by Ward to a lady at the Court of the Queen of Bohemia. Simple Cobler's Boy (1648), p. 25

SUSAN WARNER
1819–1885

26 Jesus loves me—this I know, For the Bible tells me so. *The Love of Jesus*

HENRY STEVENSON WASHBURN
1813–1903

27 We shall meet, but we shall miss him, There will be one vacant chair: We shall linger to caress him, When we breathe our evening prayer.
The Vacant Chair, chorus

GEORGE WASHINGTON
1732–1799

28 Father, I cannot tell a lie, I did it with my little hatchet.
Attrib. remark. Mark Twain's *Mark Twain as George Washington. Another version is:* I can't tell a lie, Pa; you know I can't tell a lie. I did cut it with my hatchet.
Weems, *Washington, 1800* (Fifth edition, 1806)

29 It is our true policy to steer clear of permanent alliance with any portion of the foreign world.
His Farewell Address to the People of the United States, 17 Sept. 1796

30 Labour to keep alive in your breast that little spark of celestial fire, called conscience.
Rules of Civility and Decent Behaviour. Sparks's *Life of Washington* (1839), vol. ii, p. 109

31 We must consult Brother Jonathan.
Said to have been a frequent remark of his during the American Revolution, referring to Jonathan Trumbull, 1710–85, Governor of Connecticut. Norwich Evening Courier, 12 Nov. 1846, No. 797, p. 2. (Publications of the Colonial Society of Massachusetts (1905), vol. vii, p. 94)

32 Put none but Americans on guard to-night.
Attrib. remark, based on his circular letter to regimental commanders, 30 April 1777

ROWLAND WATKYNS
fl. 1662

33 I love him not, but shew no reason can Wherefore, but this, *I do not love* the man.
Flamma sine fumo. Antipathy

1 For every marriage then is best in tune,
When that the wife is May, the husband June.
Flamma sine fumo. To the most Courteous and Fair Gentlewoman, Mrs. Elinor Williams

WILLIAM WATSON
1559?–1603

2 Fiat justitia et ruant coeli.
Let justice be done though the heavens fall.
Quodlibets of Religion and State (1602). (*See* 203:38)

SIR WILLIAM WATSON
1858–1936

3 April, April,
Laugh thy girlish laughter;
Then, the moment after,
Weep thy girlish tears! *April*

4 O be less beautiful, or be less brief. *Autumn*

5 Slight not the songsmith. *England my Mother*

6 Plucked by his hand, the basest weed that grows
Towers to a lily, reddens to a rose. *Epigram*

7 How all her care was but to be fair,
And all her task to be sweet. *The Heart of the Rose*

8 When, upon orchard and lane, breaks the white foam
of the Spring. *Hymn to the Sea*, Pt. III, 12

9 Who never negligently yet
Fashioned an April violet,
Nor would forgive, did June disclose
Unceremoniously the rose. *Nature's Way*

10 Time and the ocean, and some fostering star,
In high cabal have made us what we are.
Ode on the Coronation of Edward VII, l. 8

11 Forget not, brother singer, that though Prose
Can never be too truthful or too wise,
Song is not Truth, not Wisdom, but the rose
Upon Truth's lips, the light in Wisdom's eyes.
Ode to J. C. Collins

12 We are children of splendour and flame,
Of shuddering, also, and tears;
Magnificent out of the dust we came,
And abject from the spheres. *Ode in May*

13 The staid, conservative, Came-over-with-the-Conqueror type of mind. *A Study in Contrasts*, i, 1. 42

14 The thirst to know and understand,
A large and liberal discontent;
These are the goods in life's rich hand,
The things that are more excellent.
Things That Are More Excellent, viii

15 And not uncrowned with honours ran
My days, and not without a boast shall end!
For I was Shakespeare's countryman;
And wert not thou my friend? *To R. H. Hutton*

16 Another bruising of the hapless head
Of a wronged people yearning to be free.
Ver Tenebrosum. 2. Hasheen

17 In this house with starry dome,
Floored with gemlike plains and seas,
Shall I never feel at home,
Never wholly be at ease? *World-Strangeness*

18 On from room to room I stray,
Yet mine Host can ne'er espy,
And I know not to this day
Whether guest or captive I. *World-Strangeness*

ISAAC WATTS
1674–1748

19 Whene'er I take my walks abroad,
How many poor I see!
What shall I render to my God
For all his gifts to me?
Divine Songs for Children, iv. *Praise for Mercies*

20 Lord, I ascribe it to Thy grace,
And not to chance, as others do,
That I was born of Christian race,
And not a Heathen, or a Jew.
Ib. vi. *Praise for the Gospel*

21 There's no repentance in the grave.
Ib. x. *Solemn Thoughts of God and Death*

22 There is a dreadful Hell,
And everlasting pains;
There sinners must with devils dwell
In darkness, fire, and chains.
Ib. xi. *Heaven and Hell*

23 But liars we can never trust,
Though they should speak the thing that's true;
And he that does one fault at first,
And lies to hide it, makes it two.
Ib. xv. *Against Lying*

24 Let dogs delight to bark and bite,
For God hath made them so;
Let bears and lions growl and fight,
For 'tis their nature too.
Ib. xvi. *Against Quarrelling*

25 But, children, you should never let
Such angry passions rise;
Your little hands were never made
To tear each other's eyes. *Ib.*

26 Whatever brawls disturb the street,
There should be peace at home.
Ib. xvii. *Love between Brothers and Sisters*

27 Birds in their little nests agree
And 'tis a shameful sight,
When children of one family
Fall out, and chide, and fight. *Ib.*

28 How doth the little busy bee
Improve each shining hour,
And gather honey all the day
From every opening flower!
Ib. xx. *Against Idleness and Mischief*

29 In works of labour, or of skill,
I would be busy too;
For Satan finds some mischief still
For idle hands to do. *Ib.*

30 One sickly sheep infects the flock,
And poisons all the rest.
Ib. xxi. *Against Evil Company*

31 Let me be dress'd fine as I will,
Flies, worms, and flowers, exceed me still.
Ib. xxii. *Against Pride in Clothes*

32 I have been there, and still would go;
'Tis like a little Heaven below.
Ib. xxviii. *Lord's Day. Evening*

1 Hush! my dear, lie still and slumber,
  Holy angels guard thy bed!
Heavenly blessings without number
  Gently falling on thy head.
          Divine Songs for Children, xxxv. *Cradle Hymn*

2 Were I so tall to reach the Pole,
  Or grasp the ocean in my span,
I must be measured by my soul;
  The mind 's the standard of the man.
                    Ib. False Greatness

3 'Tis the voice of the sluggard; I heard him complain,
'You have wak'd me too soon, I must slumber again'.
As the door on its hinges, so he on his bed,
Turns his sides and his shoulders and his heavy head.
                    Moral Songs, i. *The Sluggard*

4 Abroad in the meadows to see the young lambs
Run sporting about by the side of their dams,
With fleeces so clean and so white.
                    Ib. ii. *Innocent Play*

5 How rude are the boys that throw pebbles and mire!
                                        Ib.

6 I'll not willingly offend,
  Nor be easily offended;
What's amiss I'll strive to mend,
  And endure what can't be mended.
                    Ib. vi. *Good Resolution*

7 Lord, in the morning thou shalt hear
  My voice ascending high.   *Psalms*, v

8 Jesus shall reign where e'er the sun
  Does his successive journeys run;
His kingdom stretch from shore to shore
  Till moons shall wax and wane no more. *Ib.* lxxii

9 Our God, our help in ages past
  Our hope for years to come,
Our shelter from the stormy blast,
  And our eternal home.

Beneath the shadow of Thy Throne
  Thy saints have dwelt secure;
Sufficient is Thine Arm alone,
  And our defence is sure.

Before the hills in order stood,
  Or earth received her frame,
From everlasting Thou art God,
  To endless years the same.

A thousand ages in Thy sight
  Are like an evening gone;
Short as the watch that ends the night
  Before the rising sun.

Time, like an ever-rolling stream,
  Bears all its sons away;
They fly forgotten, as a dream
  Dies at the opening day.
          Ib. xc. *First line altered by John Wesley to
          'O God . . .'*

10 How bright these glorious spirits shine!
  Whence all their white array?
How came they to the blissful seats
  Of everlasting day?
          Hymns and Spiritual Songs, bk. i, No. 41, *How
          Bright These Glorious Spirits. First line altered
          from Watts's original:* 'These glorious minds
          how bright they shine'

11 Hark! from the tombs a doleful sound.
          Ib. bk. ii, No. 63. *Hark! from the Tombs*

12 When I can read my title clear
  To mansions in the skies,
I bid farewell to every fear,
  And wipe my weeping eyes.
          Hymns and Spiritual Songs, bk. ii, No. 65

13 There is a land of pure delight,
  Where saints immortal reign;
Infinite day excludes the night,
  And pleasures banish pain.
          Ib. No. 66. *There is a Land of Pure Delight*

14 Death, like a narrow sea, divides
  That heavenly land from ours.   *Ib.*

15 So to the Jews old Canaan stood,
  While Jordan rolled between.   *Ib.*

16 But timorous mortals start and shrink
  To cross the narrow sea,
And linger shivering on the brink,
  And fear to launch away.   *Ib.*

17 Could we but climb where Moses stood,
  And view the landscape o'er;
Not Jordan's stream, nor death's cold flood,
  Should fright us from the shore.   *Ib.*

18 When I survey the wondrous Cross,
  On which the Prince of glory died,
My richest gain I count but loss
  And pour contempt on all my pride.
          Ib. bk. iii, No. 7. *When I Survey the Wondrous
          Cross*

19 Were the whole realm of nature mine,
  That were a present far too small;
Love so amazing, so Divine,
  Demands my soul, my life, my all.   *Ib.*

FREDERIC EDWARD WEATHERLY
1848–1929

20 Where are the boys of the Old Brigade?
                              The Old Brigade

21 Not in the Abbey proudly laid
  Find they a place or part;
The gallant boys of the old brigade,
  They sleep in old England's heart.   *Ib.*

22 Why, Jack's the king of all,
  For they all love Jack!   *They All Love Jack*

SIDNEY WEBB, LORD PASSFIELD
1859–1947

23 The inevitability of gradualness.
          *Presidential address to the annual conference of the
          Labour Party, 1920*

WILLIAM WEBB
fl. 1839

24 His throat they cut from ear to ear,
  His brains they punched in,
His name was Mr. William Weare,
  Wot lived in Lyon's Inn.
          Ballad. See Lord William Lennox in *The
          Sporting Review*, July 1839, vol. ii, p. 42. Also
          attrib. to Theodore Hook (1788–1841). See C.
          Hindley's *Life and Times of James Catnach*
          (1878), p. 145

DANIEL WEBSTER
1782–1852

1 There is always room at the top.
When advised not to become a lawyer as the profession was overcrowded

2 The gentleman has not seen how to reply to this, otherwise than by supposing me to have advanced the doctrine that a national debt is a national blessing.
Second Speech in the Senate on Foot's Resolution, 26 Jan. 1830

3 The people's government, made for the people, made by the people, and answerable to the people. *Ib.*

4 He [Alexander Hamilton] smote the rock of the national resources, and abundant streams of revenue gushed forth. He touched the dead corpse of the Public Credit, and it sprung upon its feet.
Speech at a Public Dinner at New York, 10 March 1831

5 On this question of principle, while actual suffering was yet afar off, they [the Colonies] raised their flag against a power, to which, for purposes of foreign conquest and subjugation, Rome, in the height of her glory, is not to be compared; a power which has dotted over the surface of the whole globe with her possessions and military posts, whose morning drum-beat, following the sun, and keeping company with the hours, circles the earth with one continuous and unbroken strain of the martial airs of England.
Speech in the Senate on the President's Protest, 7 May 1834

6 Thank God, I—I also—am an American!
Speech on the Completion of Bunker Hill Monument, 17 June 1843

7 The Law: It has honoured us, may we honour it.
Ib.

8 I was born an American; I will live an American; I shall die an American.
Speech in the Senate on 'The Compromise Bill', 17 July 1850

9 Fearful concatenation of circumstances.
Argument on the Murder of Captain Joseph White

JOHN WEBSTER
1580?–1625?

10 She's loose i' th' hilts. *The Duchess of Malfi, II. v*

11 Rais'd by that curious engine, your white hand.
Ib. III. ii. 297

12 I am acquainted with sad misery
As the tann'd galley-slave is with his oar.
Ib. IV. ii. 25

13 I have made a soap-boiler costive. *Ib. l. 117*

14 I am Duchess of Malfi still. *Ib. l. 146*

15 Glories, like glow-worms, afar off shine bright.
But looked to near, have neither heat nor light.
Ib. l. 148

16 I know death hath ten thousand several doors
For men to take their exits. *Ib. l. 222*

17 So I were out of your whispering. *Ib. l. 226*

18 FERDINAND:
Cover her face; mine eyes dazzle: she died young.
BOSOLA:
I think not so; her infelicity
Seem'd to have years too many.
The Duchess of Malfi, IV. ii, l. 267

19 Physicians are like kings,—
They brook no contradiction. *Ib. v. ii. 72*

20 We are merely the stars' tennis-balls, struck and bandied
Which way please them. *Ib. iv. 52*

21 When I look into the fish-ponds in my garden,
Methinks I see a thing arm'd with a rake,
That seems to strike at me. *Ib. v. 5*

22 Is not old wine wholesomest, old pippins toothsomest, old wood burn brightest, old linen wash whitest? Old soldiers, sweethearts, are surest, and old lovers are soundest. *Westward Hoe, II. ii*

23 I saw him even now going the way of all flesh. *Ib.*

24 Fortune's a right whore:
If she give ought, she deals it in small parcels,
That she may take away all at one swoop.
The White Devil, I. i. 4

25 'Tis just like a summer bird-cage in a garden: the birds that are without despair to get in, and the birds that are within despair and are in a consumption for fear they shall never get out.
Ib. ii. 47

26 A mere tale of a tub, my words are idle. *Ib. II. i. 92*

27 Cowardly dogs bark loudest. *Ib. III. i. 163*

28 A rape! a rape! ... Yes, you have ravish'd justice;
Forced her to do your pleasure. *Ib. l. 271*

29 There's nothing sooner dry than women's tears.
Ib. v. iii. 192

30 Call for the robin redbreast and the wren,
Since o'er shady groves they hover,
And with leaves and flowers do cover
The friendless bodies of unburied men. *Ib. iv. 100*

31 And of all axioms this shall win the prize,—
'Tis better to be fortunate than wise. *Ib. vi. 183*

32 I am i' th' way to study a long silence. *Ib. l. 204*

33 There's nothing of so infinite vexation
As man's own thoughts. *Ib. l. 206*

34 My soul, like to a ship in a black storm,
Is driven, I know not whither. *Ib. l. 248*

35 Prosperity doth bewitch men, seeming clear;
But seas do laugh, show white, when rocks are near.
Ib. l. 250

36 I have caught
An everlasting cold; I have lost my voice
Most irrecoverably. *Ib. l. 270*

THOMAS EARLE WELBY
1881–1933

37 'Turbot, Sir,' said the waiter, placing before me two fishbones, two eyeballs, and a bit of black mackintosh. *The Dinner Knell*

ARTHUR WELLESLEY, DUKE OF WELLINGTON
1769–1852

1 Not upon a man from the colonel to the private in a regiment—both inclusive. We may pick up a marshal or two perhaps; but not worth a damn.
> *On being asked whether he calculated upon any desertion in Buonaparte's army. Creevey Papers*, ch. x, p. 228

2 It has been a damned serious business—Blücher and I have lost 30,000 men. It has been a damned nice thing—the nearest run thing you ever saw in your life.... By God! I don't think it would have done if I had not been there. *Ib.* p. 236

3 All the business of war, and indeed all the business of life, is to endeavour to find out what you don't know by what you do; that's what I called 'guessing what was at the other side of the hill'.
> *Croker Papers* (1885), vol. iii, p. 276

4 Nothing except a battle lost can be half so melancholy as a battle won.
> *Dispatch from the field of Waterloo, June 1815*

5 I never saw so many shocking bad hats in my life.
> *On seeing the first Reformed Parliament.* Sir William Fraser, *Words on Wellington* (1889), p. 12

6 The battle of Waterloo was won in the playing fields of Eton.
> Montalembert, *De l'Avenir Politique de l'Angleterre* (1855). *The attribution has been refuted by the present Duke.*

7 By God, I never saw so many whores
In all my life before.
> Hardy, *The Dynasts*, Pt. III. ii. iii

8 UXBRIDGE:
> I have lost my leg, by God!

WELLINGTON:
> By God, and have you! *Ib.* VII. viii

9 The next greatest misfortune to losing a battle is to gain such a victory as this.
> S. Rogers, *Recollections* (1859), p. 215

10 'What a glorious thing must be a victory, Sir.' 'The greatest tragedy in the world, Madam, except a defeat.' *Ib.* footnote

11 The Government was contemplating the dispatch of an expedition to Burma, with a view to taking Rangoon, and a question arose as to who would be the fittest general to be sent in command of the expedition. The Cabinet sent for the Duke of Wellington, and asked his advice. He instantly replied, 'Send Lord Combermere.'
> 'But we have always understood that your Grace thought Lord Combermere a fool.'
> 'So he is a fool, and a d—d fool; but he can take Rangoon.'
> G. W. E. Russell's *Collections and Recollections*, ch. 2

12 In refusing the dedication of a song (the Duke of Wellington) informed Mrs. Norton that he had been obliged to make a rule of refusing dedications, 'because, in his situation as Chancellor of the University of Oxford, he had been much exposed to authors.' *Ib.*

13 [*To Mrs. Arbuthnot, who asked:* 'Is it true you were surprised at Waterloo, Duke?']
Not half so surprised as I am now, Mum! *Ib.*

14 I have no small talk and Peel has no manners.
> G. W. E. Russell's *Collections and Recollections*, ch. 14

15 F.M. the Duke of Wellington presents his compliments to Mr. —— and declines to interfere in circumstances over which he has no control.
> G. A. Sala, *Echoes of the Week* in *London Illustrated News*, 23 Aug. 1884. Vol. lxxxv, p. 171, col. 1

16 Hard pounding this, gentlemen; let's see who will pound longest.
> *At Waterloo.* Sir W. Scott, *Paul's Letters* (1815)

17 I used to say of him [Napoleon] that his presence on the field made the difference of forty thousand men.
> Stanhope, *Notes of Conversations with the Duke of Wellington*, 2 Nov. 1831

18 Ours [our army] is composed of the scum of the earth—the mere scum of the earth. *Ib.* 4 Nov. 1831

19 My rule always was to do the business of the day in the day. *Ib.* 2 Nov. 1835

20 What is the best to be done for the country? How can the Government be carried on? *Ib.* 18 May 1839

('The Queen's Government must be carried on'—*and variants—was used by him on several occasions.*)

21 I don't know what effect these men will have upon the enemy, but, by God, they terrify me.
> *On a draft of troops sent to him in Spain, 1809.*
> (*Also attributed to George III*)

22 [*To a gentleman who accosted him in the street saying*, 'Mr. Jones, I believe?']
If you believe that you will believe anything. *Attrib.*

23 There is no mistake; there has been no mistake; and there shall be no mistake.
> *Wellingtoniana* (1852), p. 78

24 Up Guards and at them again!
> *Attrib. to Wellington during the Battle of Waterloo. Capt. Batty's letter, 22 June 1815, in Booth's Battle of Waterloo. J. W. Croker, in a letter to A. Greville, 14 Mar. 1852, wrote 'Perhaps I might also venture to ask his Grace whether he did say, "Up Guards and at them".' Wellington replied in an undated letter to Croker which is in Croker Correspondence and Diaries (1884), vol. iii, p. 280: 'What I must have said and possibly did say was, Stand up, Guards! and then gave the commanding officers the order to attack'*

25 I don't care a twopenny damn what becomes of the ashes of Napoleon Buonaparte.
> *Attrib.* Farmer and Henley, *Slang and its Analogues*

26 Publish and be damned. *Attrib.*

HERBERT GEORGE WELLS
1866–1946

27 'I'm a Norfan, both sides,' he would explain, with the air of one who had seen trouble.
> *Kipps*, bk. i, ch. 6, § 1

28 'I expect,' he said, 'I was thinking jest what a Rum Go everything is. I expect it was something like that.' *Ib.* bk. iii, ch. 3, § 8

29 Human history becomes more and more a race between education and catastrophe.
> *The Outline of History*, ch. 40 of the 1951 ed.

1 The Shape of Things to Come. *Title of book* (1933)

2 The Time-Machine. *Title of novel* (1895)

3 The War that will end War. *Title of book* (1914)

CHARLES WESLEY
1707–1788

4 'Christ, the Lord, is risen to-day,'
Sons of men and angels say,
Raise your joys and triumphs high,
Sing, ye heavens, and earth reply.
Hymns and Sacred Poems (1739). *Christ, the Lord, is Risen To-day*

5 Jesu, Lover of my soul,
Let me to Thy Bosom fly,
While the nearer waters roll,
While the tempest still is high;
Hide me, O my Saviour, hide,
Till the storm of life is past;
Safe into the haven guide,
O receive my soul at last.
Ib. (1740), *Jesu, Lover of My Soul*

6 Other refuge have I none;
Hangs my helpless soul on Thee. *Ib.*

7 Cover my defenceless head
With the shadow of Thy wing. *Ib.*

8 Thou of Life the Fountain art;
Freely let me take of Thee;
Spring Thou up within my heart,
Rise to all eternity. *Ib.*

9 Gentle Jesus, meek and mild,
Look upon a little child;
Pity my simplicity,
Suffer me to come to thee.
Ib. (1742), *Gentle Jesus, Meek and Mild*

10 Soldiers of Christ, arise,
And put your armour on.
Ib. (1749), *Soldiers of Christ, Arise*

11 Lift up your heart, lift up your voice;
Rejoice, again I say, rejoice.
Hymns for Our Lord's Resurrection (1746): *Rejoice, the Lord is King*

12 Hark! the herald-angels sing
Glory to the new-born King:
Peace on earth, and mercy mild,
God and sinners reconciled.
Ib. Christmas Hymn: Hark! the Herald Angels Sing. First two lines altered by George Whitefield in 1753 from Wesley's original
Hark, how all the welkin rings,
'Glory to the King of kings'.

13 Lo! He comes with clouds descending.
Hymns of Intercession for all Mankind (1758): *Lo! He Comes with Clouds. New Version of John Cennick's 'Lo! He cometh, countless trumpets', in Collection of Sacred Hymns, 1752*

14 Those who set at naught and sold Him,
Pierced and nail'd Him to the Tree,
Deeply wailing,
Shall the true Messiah see. *Ib.*

15 Let saints on earth in concert sing.
Funeral Hymns (1759): *Let saints on earth. Altered by F. H. Murray in his Hymnal for Use in the English Church* (1852), from 'Let all the saints terrestrial sing'

JOHN WESLEY
1703–1791

16 I look upon all the world as my parish.
Journal, 11 June 1739

17 Once in seven years I burn all my sermons; for it is a shame if I cannot write better sermons now than I did seven years ago. *Ib. 1 Sept. 1778*

18 Though I am always in haste, I am never in a hurry.
Select Letters (1837). *Letter to a member of the Society. 10 Dec. 1777*

19 Do all the good you can,
By all the means you can,
In all the ways you can,
In all the places you can,
At all the times you can,
To all the people you can,
As long as ever you can.
Letters (1915). *Rule of Conduct*

20 Let it be observed, that slovenliness is no part of religion; that neither this, nor any text of Scripture, condemns neatness of apparel. Certainly this is a duty, not a sin. 'Cleanliness is, indeed, next to godliness.' *Sermons*, No. xciii. *On Dress*

REV. SAMUEL WESLEY
1662–1735

21 Style is the dress of thought; a modest dress,
Neat, but not gaudy, will true critics please.
An Epistle to a Friend concerning Poetry (1700)

MAE WEST
1893–

22 Come up and see me sometime. *Diamond Lil* (1932)

EDWARD NOYES WESTCOTT
1846–1898

23 They say a reasonable amount o' fleas is good fer a dog—keeps him from broodin' over bein' a dog, mebbe. *David Harum*, ch. 32

EDITH WHARTON
1862–1937

24 Mrs. Ballinger is one of the ladies who pursue Culture in bands, as though it were dangerous to meet it alone. *Xingu*, ch. 1

RICHARD WHATELY, ARCHBISHOP OF DUBLIN
1787–1863

25 Preach not because you have to say something, but because you have something to say. *Apophthegms*

26 Happiness is no laughing matter. *Ib.* p. 218

27 It is a folly to expect men to do all that they may reasonably be expected to do. *Ib.* p. 219

28 Honesty is the best policy; but he who is governed by that maxim is not an honest man. *Ib.*

WILLIAM WHEWELL
1794–1866

1 And so no force, however great,
   Can stretch a cord, however fine,
   Into a horizontal line
That shall be absolutely straight.
   Quoted as an example of accidental metre and
   rhyme. Printed in prose in Whewell's Elementary
   Treatise on Mechanics, *1819*

JAMES ABBOTT McNEILL WHISTLER
1834–1903

2 I am not arguing with you—I am telling you.
               Gentle Art of Making Enemies

3 Art is upon the Town!   '*Ten O'Clock*'

4 Listen! There never was an artistic period. There
   never was an Art-loving nation.   *Ib.*

5 Nature is usually wrong.   *Ib.*

6 'I only know of two painters in the world,' said a
   newly introduced feminine enthusiast to Whistler,
   'yourself and Velasquez.' 'Why,' answered Whistler
   in dulcet tones, 'why drag in Velasquez?'
      D. C. Seitz, *Whistler Stories* (1913), p. 27

7 [*In answer to a lady who said that a landscape reminded*
   her of his work]
   Yes madam, Nature is creeping up.   *Ib.*, p. 9

8 [*In answer to the question* 'For two days' labour, you ask
   two hundred guineas?']
   No, I ask it for the knowledge of a lifetime. *Ib.*, p. 40

9 You shouldn't say it is not good. You should say you
   do not like it; and then, you know, you're perfectly
   safe.   *Ib.*, p. 35

10 [*Answering Oscar Wilde's* 'I wish I had said that']
   You will, Oscar, you will.
      L. C. Ingleby, *Oscar Wilde*, p. 67

HENRY KIRKE WHITE
1785–1806

11 Oft in danger, oft in woe,
   Onward, Christians, onward go.
      W. J. Hall's *Mitre Hymn Book*, 1836. *Adapted*
      by Dr. W. B. Collyer from White's original
      'Much in sorrow, oft in woe'

JOSEPH BLANCO WHITE
1775–1841

12 Mysterious Night! when our first parent knew
   Thee from report divine, and heard thy name,
   Did he not tremble for this lovely frame,
   This glorious canopy of light and blue?
                To Night, l. 1

13 Hesperus with the host of heaven came,
   And lo! Creation widened in man's view.   *Ib.* l. 8

14 If Light can thus deceive, wherefore not Life?
                Ib. l. 14

WILLIAM ALLEN WHITE
1868–1944

15 All dressed up, with nowhere to go.
   On the Progressive Party in the U.S.A. in 1916,
   after Theodore Roosevelt had retired from the
   Presidential campaign

WILLIAM LINDSAY WHITE
1900–

16 They Were Expendable.   *Title of book* (1942)

GEORGE WHITEFIELD
1714–1770

17 I had rather wear out than rust out.
          Attrib. by Robert Southey

WILLIAM WHITEHEAD
1715–1785

18 Yes, I'm in love, I feel it now,
   And Caelia has undone me;
   And yet I'll swear I can't tell how
   The pleasing plague stole on me.
        The Je ne sçay quoi, st. i. Song

19 Her voice, her touch, might give th' alarm—
   'Twas both perhaps, or neither;
   In short, 'twas that provoking charm
   Of Caelia altogether.   *Ib.*

WILLIAM WHITING
1825–1878

20 O hear us when we cry to Thee
   For those in peril on the sea.
      Hymn: Eternal Father Strong to Save

WALT WHITMAN
?1819–1892

21 Silent and amazed even when a little boy,
   I remember I heard the preacher every Sunday put
      God in his statements,
   As contending against some being or influence.
               A Child's Amaze

22 Give me the splendid silent sun with all his beams
   full-dazzling!   *Give Me the Splendid Silent Sun*

23 I dream'd in a dream I saw a city invincible to the
   attacks of the whole of the rest of the earth,
   I dream'd that was the new city of Friends.
             I Dream'd in a Dream

24 The institution of the dear love of comrades.
      I Hear it was Charged against Me

25 Joy, shipmate, joy!
   (Pleas'd to my soul at death I cry,)
   Our life is closed, our life begins,
   The long, long anchorage we leave,
   The ship is clear at last, she leaps!
   She swiftly courses from the shore,
   Joy, shipmate, joy.   *Joy, Shipmate, Joy*

26 Me imperturbe, standing at ease in Nature.
                 Me Imperturbe

27 O Captain! my Captain! our fearful trip is done,
   The ship has weather'd every rack, the prize we
      sought is won,
   The port is near, the bells I hear, the people all
   exulting.   *O Captain! My Captain!*

28 The ship is anchor'd safe and sound, its voyage closed
   and done.
   From fearful trip the victor ship comes in with object
   won;

Exult O shores, and ring O bells! But I with mournful tread
Walk the deck my Captain lies, Fallen cold and dead.
O Captain! My Captain! iii

1 Out of the cradle endlessly rocking,
Out of the mocking-bird's throat, the musical shuttle,

.   .   .

A reminiscence sing.
Out of the Cradle endlessly Rocking

2 O we can wait no longer,
We too take ship O soul,
Joyous we too launch out on trackless seas,
Fearless for unknown shores on waves of ecstasy to sail,
Amid the wafting winds (thou pressing me to thee,
I thee to me, O soul,)
Caroling free, singing our song of God,
Chanting our chant of pleasant exploration.
Passage to India, 8

3 O my brave soul!
O farther, farther, sail!
O daring joy, but safe; are they not all the seas of God?
O farther, farther, farther sail!
Ib. 9

4 Come my tan-faced children,
Follow well in order, get your weapons ready,
Have you your pistols? have you your sharp-edged axes?
Pioneers! O pioneers!
Pioneers! O Pioneers!

5 Beautiful that war and all its deeds of carnage must in time be utterly lost,
That the hands of the sisters Death and Night incessantly softly wash again, and ever again, this soil'd world;
For my enemy is dead, a man as divine as myself is dead,
I look where he lies white-faced and still in the coffin —I draw near,
Bend down and touch lightly with my lips the white face in the coffin.
Reconciliation

6 Camerado, this is no book,
Who touches this touches a man.
So Long!

7 Where the populace rise at once against the never-ending audacity of elected persons.
Song of the Broad Axe, 5, l. 12

8 Where women walk in public processions in the streets the same as the men,
Where they enter the public assembly and take places the same as the men,
Where the city of the faithfullest friends stands,
Where the city of the cleanliness of the sexes stands,
Where the city of the healthiest fathers stands,
Where the city of the best-bodied mothers stands,
There the great city stands.
Ib. l. 20

9 I celebrate myself, and sing myself.
Song of Myself, 1

10 I loafe and invite my soul.
Ib.

11 Urge and urge and urge,
Always the procreant urge of the world.
Ib. 3

12 A child said *What is the grass?* fetching it to one with full hands;

.   .   .   .

Or I guess it is the handkerchief of the Lord,
A scented gift and remembrancer designedly dropt,

Bearing the owner's name someway in the corners,
that we may see and remark, and say *Whose?*

.   .   .   .

And now it seems to me the beautiful uncut hair of graves.
Song of Myself, 6

13 Has any one supposed it lucky to be born?
I hasten to inform him or her, it is just as lucky to die, and I know it.
Ib. 7

14 The look of the bay mare shames silliness out of me.
Ib. 13

15 I also say it is good to fall, battles are lost in the same spirit in which they are won.
Ib. 18

16 I am he that walks with the tender and growing night,
I call to the earth and sea half-held by the night.
Press close bare-bosom'd night—press close magnetic nourishing night!
Night of south winds—night of the large few stars!
Still nodding night—mad naked summer night.
Ib. 21

17 Earth of the vitreous pour of the full moon just tinged with blue!
Ib.

18 Far-swooping elbow'd earth—rich apple-blossom'd earth!
Smile, for your lover comes.
Ib.

19 I believe a leaf of grass is no less than the journey-work of the stars,
And the pismire is equally perfect, and a grain of sand, and the egg of the wren,
And the tree toad is a chef-d'oeuvre for the highest,
And the running blackberry would adorn the parlors of heaven.
Ib. 31

20 I think I could turn and live with animals, they are so placid and self-contain'd,
I stand and look at them long and long.
They do not sweat and whine about their condition,
They do not lie awake in the dark and weep for their sins,
They do not make me sick discussing their duty to God,
Not one is dissatisfied, not one is demented with the mania of owning things,
Not one kneels to another, nor to his kind that lived thousands of years ago,
Not one is respectable or unhappy over the whole earth.
Ib. 32

21 Behold, I do not give lectures or a little charity,
When I give I give myself.
Ib. 39

22 My rendezvous is appointed, it is certain,
The Lord will be there and wait till I come on perfect terms,
The great Camerado, the lover true for whom I pine will be there.
Ib. 44

23 I have said that the soul is not more than the body,
And I have said that the body is not more than the soul,
And nothing, not God, is greater to one than one's self is.
Ib. 47

24 In the faces of men and women I see God, and in my own face in the glass,
I find letters from God dropt in the street, and every one is sign'd by God's name,
And I leave them where they are, for I know that wheresoe'er I go,
Others will punctually come for ever and ever.
Ib.

1 Do I contradict myself?
Very well then I contradict myself,
(I am large, I contain multitudes.)
Song of Myself, 50

2 I sound my barbaric yawp over the roofs of the world.
Ib. 51

3 Afoot and light-hearted I take to the open road,
Healthy, free, the world before me,
The long brown path before me leading wherever I
choose. *Song of the Open Road*, 1, l. 1

4 The earth, that is sufficient,
I do not want the constellations any nearer,
I know they are very well where they are,
I know they suffice for those who belong to them.
Ib. l. 8

5 I am larger, better than I thought,
I did not know I held so much goodness. *Ib.* 5, l. 1

6 I will put in my poems that with you is heroism upon
land and sea,
And I will report all heroism from an American point
of view. *Starting from Paumanok*, 6

7 This dust was once the man,
Gentle, plain, just and resolute, under whose cautious
hand,
Against the foulest crime in history known in any
land or age,
Was saved the Union of these States.
This Dust was Once the Man

8 When lilacs last in the dooryard bloom'd,
And the great star early droop'd in the western sky in
the night,
I mourn'd, and yet shall mourn with ever-returning
spring.
When Lilacs Last in the Dooryard Bloom'd, 1

9 Come lovely and soothing death,
Undulate round the world, serenely arriving, arriving,
In the day, in the night, to all, to each,
Sooner or later, delicate death.
Prais'd be the fathomless universe,
For life and joy, and for objects and knowledge
curious,
And for love, sweet love—but praise! praise! praise!
For the sure-enwinding arms of cool-enfolding death.
Ib. 14

10 These United States.
A Backward Glance O'er Travell'd Roads. 'These
States' *is passim throughout Whitman's verse*

JOHN GREENLEAF WHITTIER
1807–1892

11 Up from the meadows rich with corn,
Clear in the cool September morn,
The clustered spires of Frederick stand
Green-walled by the hills of Maryland.
Barbara Frietchie, l. 1

12 Bravest of all in Frederick town,
She took up the flag the men hauled down. *Ib.* l. 17

13 Up the street came the rebel tread,
Stonewall Jackson riding ahead. *Ib.* l. 23

14 'Shoot, if you must, this old gray head,
But spare your country's flag,' she said. *Ib.* l. 35

15 'Who touches a hair of yon gray head
Dies like a dog! March on!' he said.
Barbara Frietchie, l. 41

16 I know not where His islands lift
Their fronded palms in air;
I only know I cannot drift
Beyond His love and care. *The Eternal Goodness*, xx

17 For all sad words of tongue or pen,
The saddest are these: 'It might have been!'
Maud Muller, l. 105

18 The Indian Summer of the heart! *Memories*, ix

19 Dinna ye hear it?—Dinna ye hear it?
The pipes o' Havelock sound! *Pipes at Lucknow*, iv

20 O brother man! fold to thy heart thy brother.
Worship, l. 49

CORNELIUS WHURR
c. 1845

21 What lasting joys the man attend
Who has a polished female friend.
The Accomplished Female Friend

GEORGE JOHN WHYTE-MELVILLE
1821–1878

22 Then drink, puppy, drink, and let ev'ry puppy drink,
That is old enough to lap and to swallow;
For he'll grow into a hound, so we'll pass the bottle
round,
And merrily we'll whoop and we'll holloa.
Drink, Puppy, Drink, chorus

23 The swallows are making them ready to fly,
Wheeling out on a windy sky:
Goodbye, Summer, goodbye, goodbye.
Goodbye, Summer

24 Wrap me up in my tarpaulin jacket,
And say a poor buffer lies low,
And six stalwart lancers shall carry me,
With steps solemn, mournful, and slow.
The Tarpaulin Jacket

BISHOP SAMUEL WILBERFORCE
1805–1873

25 If I were a cassowary
On the plains of Timbuctoo,
I would eat a missionary,
Cassock, band, and hymn-book too.
Impromptu verse, Ascribed

ELLA WHEELER WILCOX
1855–1919

26 Laugh and the world laughs with you;
Weep, and you weep alone;
For the sad old earth must borrow its mirth,
But has trouble enough of its own. *Solitude*

27 So many gods, so many creeds,
So many paths that wind and wind,
While just the art of being kind
Is all the sad world needs. *The World's Need*

OSCAR WILDE
1854–1900

1 He did not wear his scarlet coat,
For blood and wine are red,
And blood and wine were on his hands
When they found him with the dead.
The Ballad of Reading Gaol (1898), pt. 1. i

2 I never saw a man who looked
With such a wistful eye
Upon that little tent of blue
Which prisoners call the sky. *Ib.* iii

3 When a voice behind me whispered low,
'That fellow's got to swing.' *Ib.* iv

4 Yet each man kills the thing he loves,
By each let this be heard,
Some do it with a bitter look,
Some with a flattering word.
The coward does it with a kiss,
The brave man with a sword! *Ib.* vii

5 It is sweet to dance to violins
When Love and Life are fair:
To dance to flutes, to dance to lutes
Is delicate and rare:
But it is not sweet with nimble feet
To dance upon the air! *Ib.* ii. ix

6 Like two doomed ships that pass in storm
We had crossed each other's way:
But we made no sign, we said no word,
We had no word to say. *Ib.* xii

7 The Governor was strong upon
The Regulations Act:
The Doctor said that Death was but
A scientific fact:
And twice a day the Chaplain called,
And left a little tract. *Ib.* iii. iii

8 And once, or twice, to throw the dice
Is a gentlemanly game,
But he does not win who plays with Sin
In the secret House of Shame. *Ib.* xxiii

9 Something was dead in each of us,
And what was dead was Hope. *Ib.* xxxi

10 And the wild regrets, and the bloody sweats,
None knew so well as I:
For he who lives more lives than one
More deaths than one must die. *Ib.* xxxvii

11 I know not whether Laws be right,
Or whether Laws be wrong;
All that we know who lie in gaol
Is that the wall is strong;
And that each day is like a year,
A year whose days are long. *Ib.* v. i

12 How else but through a broken heart
May Lord Christ enter in? *Ib.* xiv

13 Surely there was a time I might have trod
The sunlit heights, and from life's dissonance
Struck one clear chord to reach the ears of God.
Hélas! (*Lines prefixed to his Poems, Paris edition,*
1903)

14 And yet, and yet,
These Christs that die upon the barricades,
God knows it I am with them, in some ways.
Sonnet to Liberty: Not that I Love Thy Children

15 All her bright golden hair
Tarnished with rust,
She that was young and fair
Fallen to dust. *Requiescat*

16 O Singer of Persephone!
In the dim meadows desolate
Dost thou remember Sicily? *Theocritus*

17 Art never expresses anything but itself.
The Decay of Lying (1891), p. 43

18 Really, if the lower orders don't set us a good example,
what on earth is the use of them?
The Importance of Being Earnest (1895), Act 1

19 It is very vulgar to talk like a dentist when one isn't
a dentist. It produces a false impression. *Ib.*

20 The truth is rarely pure, and never simple. *Ib.*

21 In married life three is company and two none. *Ib.*

22 I have invented an invaluable permanent invalid
called Bunbury, in order that I may be able to go
down into the country whenever I choose. *Ib.*

23 To lose one parent, Mr. Worthing, may be regarded
as a misfortune; to lose both looks like carelessness.
Ib.

24 All women become like their mothers. That is their
tragedy. No man does. That's his. *Ib.*

25 The good ended happily, and the bad unhappily.
That is what Fiction means. [*Miss Prism on her novel.*]
Ib. Act 11

26 The chapter on the Fall of the Rupee you may omit.
It is somewhat too sensational. *Ib.*

27 Charity, dear Miss Prism, charity! None of us are
perfect. I myself am peculiarly susceptible to
draughts. *Ib.*

28 On an occasion of this kind it becomes more than a
moral duty to speak one's mind. It becomes a
pleasure. *Ib.*

29 Please do not shoot the pianist. He is doing his best.
Impressions of America. Leadville

30 Meredith is a prose Browning, and so is Browning.
He used poetry as a medium for writing in prose.
The Critic as Artist. Part 1. Intentions

31 A little sincerity is a dangerous thing, and a great deal
of it is absolutely fatal. *Ib.* 2

32 Ah! don't say that you agree with me. When people
agree with me I always feel that I must be wrong.
Ib.

33 As long as war is regarded as wicked, it will always
have its fascination. When it is looked upon as
vulgar, it will cease to be popular. *Ib.*

34 There is no sin except stupidity. *Ib.*

35 I couldn't help it. I can resist everything except
temptation. *Lady Windermere's Fan* (1891), Act 1

36 Many a woman has a past, but I am told that she has
at least a dozen, and that they all fit. *Ib.*

37 We are all in the gutter, but some of us are looking
at the stars. *Ib.* Act III

38 There is nothing in the whole world so unbecoming
to a woman as a Nonconformist conscience. *Ib.*

1 CECIL GRAHAM:
What is a cynic?
LORD DARLINGTON:
A man who knows the price of everything and the value of nothing. *Lady Windermere's Fan*, Act III

2 DUMBY:
Experience is the name every one gives to their mistakes.
CECIL GRAHAM:
One shouldn't commit any.
DUMBY:
Life would be very dull without them. *Ib.*

3 There is no such thing as a moral or an immoral book. Books are well written, or badly written.
Picture of Dorian Gray (1891), preface

4 The moral life of man forms part of the subject-matter of the artist, but the morality of art consists in the perfect use of an imperfect medium. *Ib.*

5 There is only one thing in the world worse than being talked about, and that is not being talked about.
Ib. ch. 1

6 A man cannot be too careful in the choice of his enemies. *Ib.*

7 The only way to get rid of a temptation is to yield to it. *Ib.* ch. 2

8 A cigarette is the perfect type of a perfect pleasure. It is exquisite, and it leaves one unsatisfied. What more can one want? *Ib.* ch. 6

9 It is better to be beautiful than to be good. But . . . it is better to be good than to be ugly. *Ib.* ch. 17

10 Anybody can be good in the country. *Ib.* ch. 19

11 As for the virtuous poor, one can pity them, of course, but one cannot possibly admire them.
Soul of Man under Socialism

12 Democracy means simply the bludgeoning of the people by the people for the people. *Ib.*

13 MRS. ALLONBY:
They say, Lady Hunstanton, that when good Americans die they go to Paris.
LADY HUNSTANTON:
Indeed? And when bad Americans die, where do they go to?
LORD ILLINGWORTH:
Oh, they go to America.
A Woman of No Importance (1893), Act I. (*See 14:1*)

14 The youth of America is their oldest tradition. It has been going on now for three hundred years. *Ib.*

15 The English country gentleman galloping after a fox—the unspeakable in full pursuit of the uneatable. *Ib.*

16 One should never trust a woman who tells one her real age. A woman who would tell one that, would tell one anything. *Ib.*

17 LORD ILLINGWORTH:
The Book of Life begins with a man and a woman in a garden.
MRS. ALLONBY:
It ends with Revelations. *Ib.*

18 Children begin by loving their parents; after a time they judge them; rarely, if ever, do they forgive them. *Ib.*

19 GERALD:
I suppose society is wonderfully delightful!
LORD ILLINGWORTH:
To be in it is merely a bore. But to be out of it simply a tragedy. *A Woman of No Importance*, Act III

20 You should study the Peerage, Gerald. . . . It is the best thing in fiction the English have ever done. *Ib.*

21 A thing is not necessarily true because a man dies for it.
Sebastian Melmoth (1904), p. 12. *Oscariana* (1910), p. 8

22 [*At the New York Custom House*]
I have nothing to declare except my genius.
F. Harris, *Oscar Wilde* (1918), p. 75

23 He [Bernard Shaw] hasn't an enemy in the world, and none of his friends like him.
Quoted in Shaw: Sixteen Self Sketches, ch. 17

24 [*A huge fee for an operation was mentioned*]
'Ah, well, then,' said Oscar, 'I suppose that I shall have to die beyond my means'.
R. H. Sherard, *Life of Oscar Wilde* (1906), p. 421

JOHN WILKES
1727–1797

25 The chapter of accidents is the longest chapter in the book.
Attributed to John Wilkes by Southey in The Doctor (1837), vol. iv, p. 166

WILLIAM WILKIE
1721–1772

26 [His] labour for his pains.
Fables. The Boy and the Rainbow, ad fin.

EMMA HART WILLARD
1787–1876

27 Rocked in the cradle of the deep. *Song*

WILLIAM III OF GREAT BRITAIN
1650–1702

28 I will die in the last ditch.
Hume, *History of Great Britain*, vol. ii (1757), p. 226. *Charles II, ch. 3*

29 Every bullet has its billet.
John Wesley, *Journal, 6 June 1765*

SIR CHARLES HANBURY WILLIAMS
1708–1759

30 Dear Betty, come, give me sweet kisses,
  For sweeter no girl ever gave:
But why in the midst of our blisses,
  Do you ask me how many I'd have?
I'm not to be stinted in pleasure,
  Then prithee, dear Betty, be kind;
For as I love thee beyond measure,
  To numbers I'll not be confin'd.
A Ballad in Imitation of Martial, Lib. 6, Ep. 34. *Works* (1822), vol. i, p. 111

WILLIAMS—WINKWORTH

HARRY WILLIAMS
and
JACK JUDGE

1 It's a long way to Tipperary, it's a long way to go;
It's a long way to Tipperary, to the sweetest girl I know!
Good-bye Piccadilly, Farewell Leicester Square;
It's a long, long way to Tipperary, but my heart's right there!

It's a Long Way to Tipperary. Chorus claimed by Alice Smythe B. Jay. Written in 1908. See New York Times, 20 Sept. 1907

2 In the shade of the old apple tree. *Title of song*

3 I'm afraid to come home in the dark. *Title of song*

ISAAC WILLIAMS
1802–1865

4 Disposer Supreme,
And Judge of the earth.
Hymns translated from the Parisian Breviary (1839), p. 271

NATHANIEL PARKER WILLIS
1806–1867

5 At present there is no distinction among the upper ten thousand of the city.
Necessity for a Promenade Drive

W. G. WILLS
nineteenth century

6 I'll sing thee songs of Araby,
And tales of wild Cashmere,
Wild tales to cheat thee of a sigh,
Or charm thee to a tear. *Lalla Rookh*

D. EARDLEY WILMOT
contemporary

7 It's a corner of heaven itself,
Though it's only a tumble-down nest,
But with love brooding there, why, no place can compare,
With my little grey home in the west.
My Little Grey Home

HARRIETTE WILSON
1789–1846

8 I shall not say why and how I became, at the age of fifteen, the mistress of the Earl of Craven.
Memoirs, First sentence

JOHN WILSON
1785–1854
see
CHRISTOPHER NORTH

JOHN WILSON
d. 1889

9 Oh for a book and a shady nook,
Either in door or out;
With the green leaves whispering overhead,
Or the street cries all about.

Where I may read all at my ease,
Both of the new and old;
For a jolly good book whereon to look,
Is better to me than gold.
Lines written as a motto to a second-hand books catalogue. Lubbock, Pleasures of Life (ed. 1887), p. 48

THOMAS WOODROW WILSON
1856–1924

10 There is such a thing as a man being too proud to fight. *Address at Philadelphia, 10 May 1915*

11 We have stood apart, studiously neutral.
Message to Congress, 7 Dec. 1915

12 Armed neutrality. *Ib. 26 Feb. 1917*

13 A little group of wilful men reflecting no opinion but their own have rendered the great Government of the United States helpless and contemptible.
Statement made on 4 March 1917 after a successful filibuster against his bill to arm American merchant ships against German submarine attacks

14 The world must be made safe for democracy.
Address to Congress, 2 Apr. 1917

15 It is indispensable that the governments associated against Germany should know beyond a peradventure with whom they are dealing.
Note to Germany, 14 Oct. 1918

16 Sometimes people call me an idealist. Well, that is the way I know I am an American. America is the only idealistic nation in the world.
Address at Sioux Falls, 8 Sept. 1919

ARTHUR WIMPERIS
1874–1953

17 Gilbert, the Filbert,
The Colonel of the Knuts. *Gilbert the Filbert*

ANNE FINCH, LADY WINCHILSEA
d. 1720

18 Nor will in fading silks compose
Faintly the inimitable rose. *The Spleen*

19 Now the Jonquille o'ercomes the feeble brain;
We faint beneath the aromatic pain. *Ib.*

WILLIAM WINDHAM
1750–1810

20 Those entrusted with arms . . . should be persons of some substance and stake in the country.
Speech in the House of Commons, 22 July 1807

CATHERINE WINKWORTH
1827–1878

21 Now thank we all our God,
With heart and hands and voices
Who wondrous things hath done
In whom His world rejoices.
Trans. of Martin Rinkart: Nun danket alle Gott

[571]

ROBERT CHARLES WINTHROP
1809–1894

1 A Star for every State, and a State for every Star.
Speech on Boston Common, 27 Aug. 1862

GEORGE WITHER
1588–1667

2 Shall I, wasting in despair,
　Die because a woman's fair?
Or make pale my cheeks with care,
　'Cause another's rosy are?
Be she fairer than the day,
Or the flow'ry meads in May;
If she think not well of me,
What care I how fair she be? *Sonnet*

3 I loved a lass, a fair one,
　As fair as e'er was seen;
She was indeed a rare one,
　Another Sheba queen. *I Loved a Lass, a Fair One*

4 But, fool as then I was,
I thought she loved me too:
But now, alas! she's left me,
Falero, lero, loo! *Ib.*

PELHAM GRENVILLE WODEHOUSE
1881–

5 He spoke with a certain what-is-it in his voice, and I could see that, if not actually disgruntled, he was far from being gruntled. *The Code of the Woosters*

6 Slice him where you like, a hellhound is always a hellhound. *Ib.*

7 Donning the soup-and-fish in preparation for the evening meal. *Jeeves and the Impending Doom*

8 Excellent browsing and sluicing.
Jeeves and the Unbidden Guest

9 There was another ring at the front door. Jeeves shimmered out and came back with a telegram.
Jeeves Takes Charge

CHARLES WOLFE
1791–1823

10 Not a drum was heard, not a funeral note,
As his corse to the rampart we hurried.
The Burial of Sir John Moore at Corunna, i

11 We buried him darkly at dead of night,
The sods with our bayonets turning. *Ib. ii*

12 But he lay like a warrior taking his rest,
With his martial cloak around him. *Ib. iii*

13 Few and short were the prayers we said,
And we spoke not a word of sorrow;
But we steadfastly gazed on the face that was dead,
And we bitterly thought of the morrow. *Ib. iv*

14 We carved not a line, and we raised not a stone—
But we left him alone with his glory. *Ib. viii*

JAMES WOLFE
1727–1759

15 The General ... repeated nearly the whole of Gray's Elegy ... adding, as he concluded, that he would prefer being the author of that poem to the glory of beating the French to-morrow.
J. Playfair, *Biogr. Acc. of J. Robinson in Transactions R. Soc. Edinb. 1814*, vii. 499

16 Now God be praised, I will die in peace.
Dying words. J. Knox, *Historical Journal of Campaigns, 1757–60.* Published 1769. Ed. 1914, vol. ii, p. 114

THOMAS, CARDINAL WOLSEY
1475?–1530

17 Father Abbot, I am come to lay my bones amongst you.
Cavendish, *Negotiations of Thomas Woolsey* (1641), p. 108

18 Had I but served God as diligently as I have served the King, he would not have given me over in my gray hairs. *Ib.* p. 113

MRS. HENRY WOOD
1814–1887

19 Dead! and ... never called me mother.
East Lynne (dramatized version by T. A. Palmer, 1874). These words do not occur in the novel

J. T. WOOD

20 Wait till the clouds roll by, Jenny,
Wait till the clouds roll by;
Jenny, my own true loved one,
Wait till the clouds roll by.
Wait Till the Clouds Roll By

REV. SAMUEL WOODFORD
1636–1700

21 To his very Worthy Friend Mr. Izaak Walton, upon his Writing and Publishing the Life of the Venerable and Judicious Mr. Richard Hooker.
Title of verses prefixed to the Life, 1670

VIRGINIA WOOLF
1882–1941

22 A Room of One's Own. *Title of book*

ELIZABETH WORDSWORTH
1840–1932

23 If all the good people were clever,
And all clever people were good,
The world would be nicer than ever
We thought that it possibly could.

But somehow, 'tis seldom or never
The two hit it off as they should;
The good are so harsh to the clever,
The clever so rude to the good!
St. Christopher and Other Poems: Good and Clever

WILLIAM WORDSWORTH
1770–1850

24 Where art thou, my beloved Son,
Where art thou, worse to me than dead?
The Affliction of Margaret

25 　　To keep
An incommunicable sleep. *Ib.*

1 My apprehensions come in crowds;
   I dread the rustling of the grass;
   The very shadows of the clouds
   Have power to shake me as they pass.
                     The Affliction of Margaret

2   Lady of the Mere,
   Sole-sitting by the shores of old romance.
   A Narrow Girdle of Rough Stones and Crags

3 And three times to the child I said,
   'Why, Edward, tell me why?'   *Anecdote for Fathers*

4 At Kilve there was no weather-cock;
   And that's the reason why.   *Ib.*

5 A Poet!—He hath put his heart to school.
   Miscellaneous Sonnets, pt. III, xxvii. *A Poet!—He Hath Put*

6 A slumber did my spirit seal;
   I had no human fears:
   She seemed a thing that could not feel
     The touch of earthly years.

   No motion has she now, no force;
   She neither hears nor sees;
   Rolled round in earth's diurnal course,
     With rocks, and stones, and trees.
                  A Slumber did My Spirit Seal

7 Action is transitory,—a step, a blow,
   The motion of a muscle, this way or that—
   'Tis done, and in the after-vacancy
   We wonder at ourselves like men betrayed:
   Suffering is permanent, obscure and dark,
   And shares the nature of infinity.
                     The Borderers, III. 1539

8 Love had he found in huts where poor men lie;
   His daily teachers had been woods and rills,
   The silence that is in the starry sky,
   The sleep that is among the lonely hills.
        Song at the Feast of Brougham Castle

9 But ne'er to a seductive lay
     Let faith be given;
   Nor deem that 'light which leads astray
   Is light from Heaven.'   *To the Sons of Burns*

10 The best of what we do and are
    Just God, forgive!
    Memorials of a Tour in Scotland, 1803. iii.
    Thoughts near Burns's Residence

11 Sweet childish days, that were as long
    As twenty days are now.
                 To a Butterfly: I've Watched You Now

12   I, with many a fear
    For my dear country, many heartfelt sighs,
    'Mongst men who do not love her, linger here.
    Poems Dedicated to National Independence. pt. I,
    i. *Near Calais, Aug. 1802: Fair Star of Evening*

13 Jones! as from Calais southward you and I
    Went pacing side by side.
    Ib. iii. *Composed near Calais, on the Road to Ardres.*

14 Isis and Cam, to patient science dear!
    Ecclesiastical Sonnets, pt. III, xlii. *Cathedrals, &c. Open your Gates, ye Everlasting Piles!*

15 To be a Prodigal's favourite,—then, worse truth,
    A Miser's Pensioner,—behold our lot!
    O Man, that from thy fair and shining youth
    Age might but take the things Youth needed not!
        The Small Celandine: There is a Flower

16 There's a flower that shall be mine,
    'Tis the little celandine.
              To the Small Celandine: Pansies, Lilies

17 Pleasures newly found are sweet
    When they lie about our feet:
    February last, my heart
    First at sight of thee was glad;
    All unheard of as thou art,
    Thou must needs, I think have had,
    Celandine! and long ago,
    Praise of which I nothing know.
          To the Same Flower: Pleasures Newly Found

18 Small service is true service while it lasts:
    Of humblest friends, bright creature! scorn not one:
    The daisy, by the shadow that it casts,
    Protects the lingering dewdrop from the sun.
             To a Child. Written in her Album

19 O blithe new-comer! I have heard,
    I hear thee and rejoice.
    O Cuckoo! Shall I call thee bird,
    Or but a wandering voice?
          To the Cuckoo: O Blithe New-comer!

20 Thrice welcome, darling of the Spring!   *Ib.*

21 'Tis the still hour of thinking, feeling, loving.
            On a High Part of the Coast of Cumberland

22 Thou unassuming common-place
    Of Nature, with that homely face,
    And yet with something of a grace
      Which love makes for thee.
    To the Same Flower [Daisy]. With Little Here To Do

23 Oft on the dappled turf at ease
    I sit, and play with similes,
    Loose types of things through all degrees.   *Ib.*

24 Degenerate Douglas! Oh, the unworthy lord!
    Memorials of a Tour in Scotland, 1803. xii.
    Sonnet: Degenerate Douglas!

25 A brotherhood of venerable trees.   *Ib.*

26 I thought of Thee, my partner and my guide,
    As being past away—Vain sympathies!
    For, backward, Duddon! as I cast my eyes,
    I see what was, and is, and will abide;
    Still glides the Stream, and shall for ever glide;
    The Form remains, the Function never dies.
              The River Duddon, xxxiv. *After-Thought*

27 Enough, if something from our hands have power
    To live, and act, and serve the future hour;
    And if, as toward the silent tomb we go,
    Through love, through hope, and faith's transcendent dower,
    We feel that we are greater than we know.   *Ib.*

28 Stern daughter of the voice of God!
    O Duty! if that name thou love
    Who art a light to guide, a rod
    To check the erring and reprove.   *Ode to Duty*

29 But thee I now will serve more strictly, if I may. *Ib.*

30 Me this uncharter'd freedom tires;
    I feel the weight of chance-desires:
    My hopes no more must change their name,
    I long for a repose that ever is the same.   *Ib.*

31 Thou dost preserve the stars from wrong;
    And the most ancient heavens, through Thee, are
    fresh and strong.   *Ib.*

1 Give unto me, made lowly wise,
The spirit of self-sacrifice;
The confidence of reason give;
And in the light of truth thy Bondman let me live!
Ode to Duty

2 Thine is the tranquil hour, purpureal Eve!
But long as god-like wish, or hope divine,
Informs my spirit, ne'er can I believe
That this magnificence is wholly thine!
—From worlds not quickened by the sun
A portion of the gift is won;
An intermingling of Heaven's pomp is spread
On ground which British shepherds tread.
Composed upon an Evening of Extraordinary Splendour

3 Not in the lucid intervals of life
That come but as a curse to party strife.
Evening Voluntaries, iv. *Not in the Lucid Intervals*

4 By grace divine,
Not otherwise, O Nature, we are thine. *Ib.*

5 On Man, on Nature, and on Human Life,
Musing in solitude. *The Excursion*, preface, l. i

6 Joy in widest commonalty spread. *Ib.* l. 18

7 The Mind of Man—
My haunt, and the main region of my song. *Ib.* l. 40

8 The discerning intellect of Man,
When wedded to this goodly universe
In love and holy passion, shall find these
A simple produce of the common day. *Ib.* l. 52

9 A metropolitan temple in the hearts
Of mighty Poets. *Ib.* l. 86

10 Oh! many are the Poets that are sown
By Nature; men endowed with highest gifts,
The vision and the faculty divine;
Yet wanting the accomplishment of verse.
Ib. bk. i, l. 77

11 What soul was his, when, from the naked top
Of some bold headland, he beheld the sun
Rise up, and bathe the world in light! *Ib.* l. 198

12 The imperfect offices of prayer and praise. *Ib.* l. 216

13 That mighty orb of song,
The divine Milton. *Ib.* l. 249

14 The good die first,
And they whose hearts are dry as summer dust
Burn to the socket. *Ib.* l. 500

15 The intellectual power, through words and things,
Went sounding on, a dim and perilous way!
Ib. bk. iii, l. 700

16 Society became my glittering bride,
And airy hopes my children. *Ib.* l. 735

17 'Tis a thing impossible, to frame
Conceptions equal to the soul's desires;
And the most difficult of tasks to *keep*
Heights which the soul is competent to gain.
Ib. bk. iv, l. 136

18 As fast as a musician scatters sounds
Out of an instrument. *Ib.* l. 524

19 We live by admiration, hope, and love;
And even as these are well and wisely fixed,
In dignity of being we ascend. *Ib.* l. 763

20 I have seen
A curious child, who dwelt upon a tract
Of inland ground, applying to his ear
The convolutions of a smooth-lipped shell;
To which, in silence hushed, his very soul
Listened intensely; and his countenance soon
Brightened with joy; for from within were heard
Murmurings, whereby the monitor expressed
Mysterious union with its native sea.
The Excursion, bk. iv, l. 1132

21 Spires whose 'silent fingers point to heaven.'
Ib. bk. vi, l. 19. Quoting Coleridge, *The Friend*, sec. i, No. 14

22 The head and mighty paramount of truths,—
Immortal life, in never-fading worlds,
For mortal creatures, conquered and secured.
Ib. l. 85

23 Amid the groves, under the shadowy hills,
The generations are prepared; the pangs,
The internal pangs, are ready; the dread strife
Of poor humanity's afflicted will
Struggling in vain with ruthless destiny. *Ib.* l. 553

24 A man of hope and forward-looking mind
Even to the last! *Ib.* bk. vii, l. 276

25 'To every Form of being is assigned',
Thus calmly spoke the venerable Sage,
'An *active* Principle.' *Ib.* bk. ix, l. 1

26 Spirit that knows no insulated spot,
No chasm, no solitude; from link to link
It circulates, the Soul of all the worlds. *Ib.* l. 13

27 And hear the mighty stream of tendency
Uttering, for elevation of our thought,
A clear sonorous voice, inaudible
To the vast multitude. *Ib.* l. 87. (*See 20:13*)

28 The primal duties shine aloft like stars;
The charities that soothe, and heal, and bless,
Are scattered at the feet of man, like flowers.
Ib. l. 238

29 Nor less I deem that there are Powers
Which of themselves our minds impress;
That we can feed this mind of ours
In a wise passiveness. *Expostulation and Reply*

30 Think you mid all this mighty sum
Of things for ever speaking,
That nothing of itself will come,
But we must still be seeking? *Ib.*

31 How nourished there through that long time
He knows who gave that love sublime. *Fidelity*

32 'What is good for a bootless bene?'
With these dark words begins my tale;
And their meaning is, whence can comfort spring
When prayer is of no avail? *The Force of Prayer*

33 My eyes are dim with childish tears,
My heart is idly stirred,
For the same sound is in my ears
Which in those days I heard. *The Fountain*

34 The wiser mind
Mourns less for what age takes away
Than what it leaves behind *Ib.*

35 And often, glad no more,
We wear a face of joy because
We have been glad of yore. *Ib.*

1 A power is passing from the earth
To breathless Nature's dark abyss;
But when the great and good depart,
What is it more than this—

That Man who is from God sent forth,
Doth yet again to God return?—
Such ebb and flow must ever be,
Then wherefore should we mourn?
Lines on the Expected Dissolution of Mr. Fox

2 Bliss was it in that dawn to be alive,
But to be young was very heaven!
French Revolution, as it Appeared to Enthusiasts,
and *The Prelude*, bk. xi, l. 108

3   Sets . . .
The budding rose above the rose full blown.
Ib. and The Prelude, bk. xi, l. 121

4 And homeless near a thousand homes I stood,
And near a thousand tables pined and wanted food.
Guilt and Sorrow, xli

5 Who is the happy Warrior? Who is he
That every man in arms should wish to be?
It is the generous spirit, who, when brought
Among the tasks of real life, hath wrought
Upon the plan that pleased his childish thought:
Whose high endeavours are an inward light
That makes the path before him always bright:
Who, with a natural instinct to discern
What knowledge can perform, is diligent to learn.
Character of the Happy Warrior

6 Who, doomed to go in company with Pain,
And Fear, and Bloodshed, miserable train!
Turns his necessity to glorious gain;
In face of these doth exercise a power
Which is our human nature's highest dower;
Controls them, and subdues, transmutes, bereaves
Of their bad influence, and their good receives. *Ib.*

7 More skilful in self-knowledge, even more pure,
As tempted more; more able to endure,
As more exposed to suffering and distress;
Thence also, more alive to tenderness. *Ib.*

8 And in himself possess his own desire. *Ib.*

9 And therefore does not stoop, nor lie in wait
For wealth, or honours, or for worldly state. *Ib.*

10 Whose powers shed round him in the common strife
Or mild concerns of ordinary life,
A constant influence, a peculiar grace;
But who if he be called upon to face
Some awful moment to which Heaven has joined
Great issues, good or bad for human kind,
Is happy as a lover; and attired
With sudden brightness, like a man inspired;
And, through the heat of conflict, keeps the law
In calmness made, and sees what he foresaw. *Ib.*

11 'Tis, finally, the Man, who, lifted high,
Conspicuous object in a Nation's eye,
Or left unthought of in obscurity,—
Who, with a toward or untoward lot,
Prosperous or adverse, to his wish or not—
Plays, in the many games of life, that one
Where what he most doth value must be won:
Whom neither shape of danger can dismay,
Nor thought of tender happiness betray. *Ib.*

12 The moving accident is not my trade;
To freeze the blood I have no ready arts:
'Tis my delight, alone in summer shade,
To pipe a simple song for thinking hearts.
Hart-leap Well, p. 2, l. 1

13 The Being that is in the clouds and air,
That is in the green leaves among the groves,
Maintains a deep and reverential care
For the unoffending creatures whom he loves.
Ib. l. 165

14 Never to blend our pleasure or our pride
With sorrow of the meanest thing that feels.
Ib. l. 179

15 High is our calling, friend! Creative Art
(Whether the instrument of words she use,
Or pencil pregnant with ethereal hues,)
Demands the service of a mind and heart,
Though sensitive, yet, in their weakest part,
Heroically fashioned.
Miscellaneous Sonnets, pt. II, iii. *To B. R. Haydon: High is our Calling, Friend!*

16 Sweet Highland Girl, a very shower
Of beauty is thy earthly dower.
Memorials of a Tour in Scotland, 1803. vi. *To a Highland Girl*

17 The rapt one, of the godlike forehead,
The heaven-eyed creature sleeps in earth:
And Lamb, the frolic and the gentle,
Has vanished from his lonely hearth.
Extempore Effusion upon the Death of James Hogg

18 How fast has brother followed brother,
From sunshine to the sunless land! *Ib.*

19 Him whom you love, your Idiot Boy. *The Idiot Boy*

20 And as her mind grew worse and worse,
Her body—it grew better. *Ib.*

21 Wisdom and Spirit of the Universe!
Thou Soul that art the Eternity of thought!
And giv'st to forms and images a breath
And everlasting motion!
Influence of Natural Objects, and *The Prelude*,
bk. i, l. 401

22 A grandeur in the beatings of the heart. *Ib.*

23   All shod with steel
We hissed along the polished ice, in games
Confederate.
Ib. and The Prelude, bk. i, l. 414

24   With the din
Smitten, the precipices rang aloud;
The leafless trees and every icy crag
Tinkled like iron; while far-distant hills
Into the tumult sent an alien sound
Of melancholy. *Ib.*

25   Leaving the tumultuous throng
To cut across the reflex of a star;
Image, that flying still before me, gleamed
Upon the glassy plain. *Ib.*

26   Yet still the solitary cliffs
Wheeled by me—even as if the earth had rolled
With visible motion her diurnal round!
Ib. and The Prelude. bk. i, l. 458

WORDSWORTH

1 There was a time when meadow, grove, and stream,
The earth, and every common sight,
  To me did seem
  Apparelled in celestial light,
The glory and the freshness of a dream.
It is not now as it hath been of yore;—
  Turn wheresoe'er I may,
  By night or day,
The things which I have seen I now can see no more.
Ode. Intimations of Immortality, i

2   The rainbow comes and goes,
      And lovely is the rose,
      The moon doth with delight
Look round her when the heavens are bare,
      Waters on a starry night
      Are beautiful and fair;
      The sunshine is a glorious birth:
      But yet I know, where'er I go,
That there hath passed away a glory from the earth.
Ib. ii

3 And while the young lambs bound
As to the tabor's sound. *Ib.* iii

4 A timely utterance gave that thought relief,
And I again am strong. *Ib.*

5 The winds come to me from the fields of sleep. *Ib.*

6 Shout round me, let me hear thy shouts, thou happy
Shepherd-boy. *Ib.*

7 And the babe leaps up on his mother's arm. *Ib.* iv

8 —But there's a tree, of many, one
A single field which I have looked upon,
Both of them speak of something that is gone:
  The pansy at my feet
  Doth the same tale repeat:
Whither is fled the visionary gleam?
Where is it now, the glory and the dream? *Ib.*

9 Our birth is but a sleep and a forgetting:
The Soul that rises with us, our life's Star,
Hath had elsewhere its setting,
  And cometh from afar:
Not in entire forgetfulness,
And not in utter nakedness,
But trailing clouds of glory do we come
  From God, who is our home:
Heaven lies about us in our infancy!
Shades of the prison-house begin to close
  Upon the growing boy,
But he beholds the light, and whence it flows,
  He sees it in his joy;
The youth, who daily farther from the east
  Must travel, still is Nature's priest,
  And by the vision splendid
  Is on his way attended;
At length the man perceives it die away,
And fade into the light of common day. *Ib.* v

10 Behold the child among his new-born blisses,
A six years' darling of a pigmy size!
See, where 'mid work of his own hand he lies,
Fretted by sallies of his mother's kisses,
With light upon him from his father's eyes! *Ib.* vii

11 As if his whole vocation
Were endless imitation. *Ib.*

12 Thou, whose exterior semblance doth belie
  Thy soul's immensity. *Ib.* viii

13   Thou Eye among the blind,
That, deaf and silent, read'st the eternal deep
Haunted for ever by the eternal mind.
Ode. Intimations of Immortality, viii

14 Thou, over whom thy immortality
Broods like the day, a master o'er a slave. *Ib.*

15   Provoke
The years to bring the inevitable yoke. *Ib.*

16 And custom lie upon thee with a weight,
Heavy as frost, and deep almost as life! *Ib.*

17   O joy! that in our embers
      Is something that doth live,
      That nature yet remembers
      What was so fugitive!
The thought of our past years in me doth breed
Perpetual benediction. *Ib.* ix

18 Not for these I raise
The song of thanks and praise;
  But for those obstinate questionings
  Of sense and outward things,
  Fallings from us, vanishings;
  Blank misgivings of a creature
Moving about in worlds not realised,
High instincts before which our mortal nature
Did tremble like a guilty thing surprised:
  But for those first affections,
  Those shadowy recollections,
Which, be they what they may,
Are yet the fountain-light of all our day,
Are yet a master-light of all our seeing. *Ib.*

19 Our noisy years seem moments in the being
Of the eternal Silence: truths that wake,
  To perish never:
Which neither listlessness, nor mad endeavour,
  Nor Man nor Boy,
Nor all that is at enmity with joy,
Can utterly abolish or destroy!

Hence in a season of calm weather
  Though inland far we be,
Our souls have sight of that immortal sea
  Which brought us hither,
  Can in a moment travel thither,
And see the children sport upon the shore,
And hear the mighty waters rolling evermore. *Ib.*

20 Though nothing can bring back the hour
Of splendour in the grass, of glory in the flower;
We will grieve not, rather find
Strength in what remains behind;
In the primal sympathy
Which having been must ever be;
In the soothing thoughts that spring
Out of human suffering;
In the faith that looks through death,
In years that bring the philosophic mind. *Ib.*

21 And O, ye fountains, meadows, hills and groves,
Forbode not any severing of our loves!
Yet in my heart of hearts I feel your might;
I only have relinquished one delight
To live beneath your more habitual sway. *Ib.* xi

22 The innocent brightness of a new-born day
  Is lovely yet;
The clouds that gather round the setting sun
Do take a sober colouring from an eye
That hath kept watch o'er man's mortality;

Another race hath been, and other palms are won.
Thanks to the human heart by which we live,
Thanks to its tenderness, its joys, and fears,
To me the meanest flower that blows can give
Thoughts that do often lie too deep for tears.
                    Ode. Intimations of Immortality, xi

1 It is a beauteous evening, calm and free,
The holy time is quiet as a nun,
Breathless with adoration; the broad sun
Is sinking down in its tranquillity;
The gentleness of heaven broods o'er the Sea;
Listen! the mighty Being is awake,
And doth with his eternal motion make
A sound like thunder—everlastingly.
Dear Child! dear Girl! that walkest with me here
If thou appear untouched by solemn thought,
Thy nature is not therefore less divine.
Thou liest in Abraham's bosom all the year;
And worshipp'st at the temple's inner shrine,
God being with thee when we know it not.
        Miscellaneous Sonnets, pt. I, xxx. *It is a Beauteous Evening*

2 It is not to be thought of that the Flood
Of British freedom, which, to the open sea
Of the world's praise, from dark antiquity
Hath flowed, 'with pomp of waters, unwithstood' . . .
Should perish.
        National Independence and Liberty. xvi. *It is not to be thought of*

3   In our halls is hung
Armoury of the invincible Knights of old:
We must be free or die, who speak the tongue
That Shakespeare spake; the faith and morals hold
Which Milton held.—In everything we are sprung
Of Earth's first blood, have titles manifold.   *Ib.*

4 I travelled among unknown men
    In lands beyond the sea;
Nor, England! did I know till then
    What love I bore to thee.
                    I Travelled among Unknown Men

5 I wandered lonely as a cloud
That floats on high o'er vales and hills,
When all at once I saw a crowd,
A host, of golden daffodils;
Beside the lake, beneath the trees,
Fluttering and dancing in the breeze.
                    I Wandered Lonely as a Cloud

6 Continuous as the stars that shine
And twinkle on the milky way.   *Ib.*

7 A poet could not but be gay,
In such a jocund company:
I gazed—and gazed—but little thought
What wealth to me the show had brought:
For oft, when on my couch I lie
In vacant or in pensive mood,
They flash upon that inward eye
Which is the bliss of solitude;
And then my heart with pleasure fills,
And dances with the daffodils.   *Ib.*

8 Vanguard of Liberty, ye men of Kent.
        National Independence and Liberty, pt. I, xxiii.
        To the Men of Kent: Vanguard of Liberty

9 Give all thou canst; high Heaven rejects the lore
Of nicely-calculated less or more.
        Ecclesiastical Sonnets, pt. III, xliii. *King's College Chapel. Tax not the Royal Saint*

10 Where light and shade repose, where music dwells
Lingering—and wandering on as loth to die;
Like thoughts whose very sweetness yieldeth proof
That they were born for immortality.   *Ib.*

11 They dreamt not of a perishable home
Who thus could build.
        Ib. xlv. *Continued. They Dreamt not of a Perishable Home*

12   The gods approve
The depth, and not the tumult, of the soul.
                    Laodamia, l. 74

13 Of all that is most beauteous—imaged there
In happier beauty; more pellucid streams,
An ampler ether, a diviner air,
And fields invested with purpureal gleams. *Ib.* l. 103

14 Milton! thou shouldst be living at this hour:
England hath need of thee; she is a fen
Of stagnant waters.
        National Independence and Liberty, pt. I, xiv.
        London. Milton! thou shouldst

15 Thy soul was like a star, and dwelt apart;
Thou hadst a voice whose sound was like the sea:
Pure as the naked heavens, majestic, free,
So didst thou travel on life's common way
In cheerful godliness; and yet thy heart
The lowliest duties on herself did lay.   *Ib.*

16 Plain living and high thinking are no more:
The homely beauty of the good old cause
Is gone; our peace, our fearful innocence,
And pure religion breathing household laws.
        Ib. xiii. *Written in London. O Friend! I Know Not*

17 I chanced to see at break of day
The solitary child.   *Lucy Gray*

18 No mate, no comrade Lucy knew;
She dwelt on a wild moor,
The sweetest thing that ever grew
Beside a human door!   *Ib.*

19 And sings a solitary song
That whistles in the wind.   *Ib.*

20   The cattle are grazing,
    Their heads never raising;
There are forty feeding like one!   *Written in March*

21 Like an army defeated
The snow hath retreated.   *Ib.*

22   Meantime Luke began
To slacken in his duty; and at length,
He in the dissolute city gave himself
To evil courses.   *Michael*, l. 442

23 Many and many a day he thither went,
And never lifted up a single stone.   *Ib.* l. 465

24 Most sweet it is with unuplifted eyes
To pace the ground, if path there be or none,
While a fair region round the traveller lies,
Which he forbears again to look upon.
                    Most Sweet It Is

25 My heart leaps up when I behold
    A rainbow in the sky:
So was it when my life began;
So is it now I am a man;
So be it when I shall grow old,
    Or let me die!
The Child is father of the Man;
And I could wish my days to be
Bound each to each by natural piety.
                    My Heart Leaps Up

1 From low to high doth dissolution climb.
   Ecclesiastical Sonnets, pt. III, xxxiv. *Mutability.*
   From Low to High

2 The unimaginable touch of time. *Ib.*

3 Soft is the music that would charm for ever;
   The flower of sweetest smell is shy and lowly.
   Miscellaneous Sonnets, pt. II, ix. *Not Love, not War*

4 Another year!—another deadly blow!
   Another mighty Empire overthrown!
   And we are left, or shall be left, alone.
   National Independence and Liberty, pt. I, xxvii.
   November. Another Year!

5 We shall exult, if they who rule the land
   Be men who hold its many blessings dear,
   Wise, upright, valiant; not a servile band,
   Who are to judge of danger which they fear,
   And honour which they do not understand. *Ib.*

6 Nuns fret not at their convent's narrow room;
   And hermits are contented with their cells.
   Miscellaneous Sonnets, pt. I, i. *Nuns Fret Not*

7 The weight of too much liberty. *Ib.*

8 There is a spirit in the woods. *Nutting*

9 But Thy most dreaded instrument
   In working out a pure intent,
   Is man,—arrayed for mutual slaughter,
   Yea, Carnage is Thy daughter.
   National Independence and Liberty, pt. II, xlv.
   Ode (1815), l. 106. *Imagination Ne'er Before Content*

10 O dearer far than light and life are dear.
   To ——: O Dearer Far than Light

11 I heard a Stock-dove sing or say
   His homely tale, this very day;
   His voice was buried among trees,
   Yet to be come-at by the breeze:
   He did not cease; but cooed—and cooed;
   And somewhat pensively he wooed;
   He sang of love, with quiet blending,
   Slow to begin, and never ending;
   Of serious faith, and inward glee;
   That was the song,—the song for me!
   O Nightingale! Thou Surely Art

12 Ye sacred Nurseries of blooming Youth!
   Miscellaneous Sonnets, pt. III, ii. *Oxford: Ye Sacred Nurseries*

13 A genial hearth, a hospitable board,
   And a refined rusticity.
   Ecclesiastical Sonnets, pt. III, xviii. *Pastoral Character. A Genial Hearth*

14 The light that never was, on sea or land,
   The consecration, and the poet's dream.
   Elegiac Stanzas Suggested by a Picture of Peele Castle in a Storm

15 A deep distress hath humanized my soul. *Ib.*

16 Farewell, farewell the heart that lives alone,
   Housed in a dream, at distance from the Kind! *Ib.*

17 But welcome fortitude, and patient cheer,
   And frequent sights of what is to be borne!
   Such sights, or worse, as are before me here.—
   Not without hope we suffer and we mourn. *Ib.*

18 I am not one who much or oft delight
   To season my fireside with personal talk.
   Personal Talk, i

19 Sweetest melodies
   Are those that are by distance made more sweet.
   Ib. ii

20 Dreams, books, are each a world; and books, we know,
   Are a substantial world, both pure and good.
   Round these, with tendrils strong as flesh and blood,
   Our pastime and our happiness will grow. *Ib.* iii

21 The gentle lady married to the Moor;
   And heavenly Una with her milk-white lamb. *Ib.*

22 Oh! might my name be numbered among theirs.
   Ib. iv

23 There's something in a flying horse,
   There's something in a huge balloon.
   Peter Bell, prologue, l. 1

24 Full twenty times was Peter feared
   For once that Peter was respected. *Ib.* pt. i, l. 204

25 A primrose by a river's brim
   A yellow primrose was to him,
   And it was nothing more. *Ib.* l. 249

26 He gave a groan, and then another,
   Of that which went before the brother,
   And then he gave a third. *Ib.* l. 443

27 Is it a party in a parlour?
   Cramm'd just as they on earth were cramm'd—
   Some sipping punch, some sipping tea,
   But, as you by their faces see,
   All silent and all damn'd! *Ib.* l. 515/6. *See* Corrigenda

28 The dew was falling fast, the stars began to blink;
   I heard a voice; it said, 'Drink, pretty creature, drink!' *The Pet Lamb*

29 Art thou a Man of purple cheer?
   A rosy Man, right plump to see? *A Poet's Epitaph*

30 A fingering slave,
   One that would peep and botanize
   Upon his mother's grave?
   A reasoning, self-sufficing thing,
   An intellectual All-in-all! *Ib.*

31 But who is He, with modest looks,
   And clad in homely russet brown?
   He murmurs near the running brooks
   A music sweeter than their own. *Ib.*

32 He is retired as noontide dew,
   Or fountain in a noon-day grove;
   And you must love him, ere to you
   He will seem worthy of your love. *Ib.*

33 Impulses of deeper birth
   Have come to him in solitude. *Ib.*

34 In common things that round us lie
   Some random truths he can impart,—
   The harvest of a quiet eye,
   That broods and sleeps on his own heart.

   But he is weak; both Man and Boy,
   Hath been an idler in the land;
   Contented if he might enjoy
   The things which others understand. *Ib*

35 Weak as is a breaking wave. *Ib.*

1
   My soul
Once more made trial of her strength, nor lacked
Aeolian visitations.   *The Prelude*, bk. i, l. 94

2 Feels immediately some hollow thought
Hang like an interdict upon her hopes. *Ib.* l. 259

3 Unprofitably travelling towards the grave. *Ib.* l. 267

4 Made one long bathing of a summer's day. *Ib.* l. 290

5 Fair seed-time had my soul, and I grew up
 Fostered alike by beauty and by fear. *Ib.* l. 301

6
   When the deed was done
I heard among the solitary hills
Low breathings coming after me, and sounds
Of undistinguishable motion, steps
Almost as silent as the turf they trod. *Ib.* l. 321

7
   Though mean
Our object and inglorious, yet the end
Was not ignoble.   *Ib.* l. 328

8 With what strange utterance did the loud dry wind
Blow through my ear! the sky seemed not a sky
Of earth—and with what motion moved the clouds!
       Ib. l. 337

9 Dust as we are, the immortal spirit grows
Like harmony in music; there is a dark
Inscrutable workmanship that reconciles
Discordant elements, makes them cling together
In one society.   *Ib.* l. 340

10
   The grim shape
Towered up between me and the stars, and still,
For so it seemed, with purpose of its own
And measured motion like a living thing,
Strode after me.   *Ib.* l. 382

11 Unknown modes of being.   *Ib.* l. 393

12
  Huge and mighty forms that do not live
Like living men, moved slowly through the mind
By day, and were a trouble to my dreams. *Ib.* l. 398

13 Not with the mean and vulgar works of man,
But with high objects, with enduring things.
       Ib. l. 408

14 Strife too humble to be named in verse. *Ib.* l. 513

15 The self-sufficing power of Solitude. *Ib.* bk. ii, l. 77

16
   A prop
To our infirmity.   *Ib.* l. 214

17 Thence did I drink the visionary power;
And deem not profitless those fleeting moods
Of shadowy exultation.   *Ib.* l. 311

18
   The soul,
Remembering how she felt, but what she felt
Remembering not, retains an obscure sense
Of possible sublimity.   *Ib.* l. 315

19
   Where the statue stood
Of Newton, with his prism and silent face,
The marble index of a mind for ever
Voyaging through strange seas of thought alone.
     Ib. bk. iii, l. 61

20 Sweet Spenser, moving through his clouded heaven
With the moon's beauty and the moon's soft pace,
I called him Brother, Englishman, and Friend!
      Ib. l. 280

21
   Here and there
Slight shocks of young love-liking interspersed.
     Ib. bk. iv. l. 316

22
  Bond unknown to me
Was given, that I should be, else sinning greatly,
A dedicated spirit. *The Prelude*, bk. iv, l. 335

23
   A day
Spent in a round of strenuous idleness. *Ib.* l. 377

24
  That uncertain heaven, received
Into the bosom of the steady lake. *Ib.* bk. v, l. 387

25
   Visionary power
Attends the motions of the viewless winds,
Embodied in the mystery of words. *Ib.* l. 595

26 Present themselves as objects recognized,
In flashes, and with glory not their own. *Ib.* l. 604

27
   Whether we be young or old,
Our destiny, our being's heart and home,
Is with infinitude, and only there;
With hope it is, hope that can never die,
Effort, and expectation, and desire,
And something evermore about to be.
     Ib. bk. vi, l. 603

28
   We were brothers all
In honour, as in one community,
Scholars and gentlemen. *Ib.* bk. ix, l. 227

29
  In the People was my trust,
And in the virtues which mine eyes had seen.
     Ib. bk. x, l. 11

30 Not in Utopia—subterranean fields,—
Or some secreted island, Heaven knows where!
But in the very world, which is the world
Of all of us,—the place where, in the end
We find our happiness, or not at all! *Ib.* l. 140

31 The dupe of folly, or the slave of crime. *Ib.* l. 320

32
   There is
One great society alone on earth:
The noble living and the noble dead. *Ib.* l. 393

33 A sensitive being, a *creative* soul. *Ib.* bk. xii, l. 207

34 Oh! mystery of man, from what a depth
Proceed thy honours. I am lost, but see
In simple childhood something of the base
On which thy greatness stands. *Ib.* l. 272

35 Animate an hour of vacant ease. *Ib.* l. 335

36 Sorrow, that is not sorrow, but delight;
And miserable love, that is not pain
To hear of, for the glory that redounds
Therefrom to human kind, and what we are.
     Ib. bk. xiii, l. 246

37
   Imagination, which, in truth,
Is but another name for absolute power
And clearest insight, amplitude of mind,
And Reason in her most exalted mood.
     Ib. bk. xiv, l. 190

38 Prophets of Nature, we to them will speak
A lasting inspiration, sanctified
By reason, blest by faith: what we have loved,
Others will love, and we will teach them how;
Instruct them how the mind of man becomes
A thousand times more beautiful than the earth
On which he dwells, above this frame of things
(Which, 'mid all revolution in the hopes
And fears of men, doth still remain unchanged)
In beauty exalted, as it is itself
Of quality and fabric more divine. *Ib.* l. 444

[579]

1 Art thou the bird whom man loves best,
The pious bird with the scarlet breast,
Our little English robin?
The Redbreast Chasing the Butterfly

2 Love him, or leave him alone! *Ib.*

3 Habit rules the unreflecting herd.
Ecclesiastical Sonnets, pt. II, xxviii. *Reflections.
Grant that by this Unsparing Hurricane*

4 There was a roaring in the wind all night.
Resolution and Independence, i

5 As high as we have mounted in delight
In our dejection do we sink as low. *Ib.* iv

6 But how can he expect that others should
Build for him, sow for him, and at his call
Love him, who for himself will take no heed at all?
Ib. vi

7 I thought of Chatterton, the marvellous boy,
The sleepless soul, that perished in his pride;
Of him who walked in glory and in joy,
Following his plough, along the mountain side:
By our own spirits are we deified:
We poets in our youth begin in gladness;
But thereof comes in the end despondency and madness. *Ib.* vii

8 The oldest man he seemed that ever wore grey hairs.
Ib. viii

9 As a huge stone is sometimes seen to lie
Couched on the bald top of an eminence. *Ib.* ix

10 Like a sea-beast crawled forth, that on a shelf
Of rock or sand reposeth, there to sun itself. *Ib.*

11 That heareth not the loud winds when they call,
And moveth all together, if it moves at all. *Ib.* xi

12 Choice words, and measured phrase, above the reach
Of ordinary men; a stately speech;
Such as grave livers do in Scotland use. *Ib.* xiv

13 And mighty poets in their misery dead. *Ib.* xvii

14 'How is it that you live, and what is it you do?' *Ib.*

15 　　　　The good old rule
Sufficeth them, the simple plan,
That they should take, who have the power,
　And they should keep who can.
Memorials of a Tour in Scotland, 1803. xi. *Rob Roy's Grave*

16 Scorn not the Sonnet; Critic, you have frowned,
Mindless of its just honours; with this key
Shakespeare unlocked his heart.
Miscellaneous Sonnets, pt. II, i. *Scorn Not the Sonnet*

17 　　　　And when a damp
Fell round the path of Milton, in his hand
The Thing became a trumpet; whence he blew
Soul-animating strains,—alas! too few. *Ib.*

18 She dwelt among the untrodden ways
　Beside the springs of Dove,
A maid whom there were none to praise
　And very few to love:

A violet by a mossy stone
　Half hidden from the eye!
Fair as a star, when only one
　Is shining in the sky.

She lived unknown, and few could know
　When Lucy ceased to be;
But she is in her grave, and, oh,
　The difference to me!
She Dwelt Among the Untrodden Ways

19 She was a phantom of delight
When first she gleamed upon my sight;
A lovely apparition, sent
To be a moment's ornament;
Her eyes as stars of twilight fair;
Like twilight's, too, her dusky hair;
But all things else about her drawn
From May-time and the cheerful dawn;
A dancing shape, an image gay,
To haunt, to startle, and waylay.
She was a Phantom of Delight

20 I saw her upon nearer view,
A spirit, yet a woman too!
Her household motions light and free,
And steps of virgin liberty;
A countenance in which did meet
Sweet records, promises as sweet;
A creature not too bright or good
For human nature's daily food;
For transient sorrows, simple wiles,
Praise, blame, love, kisses, tears, and smiles. *Ib.*

21 And now I see with eye serene,
The very pulse of the machine;·
A being breathing thoughtful breath,
A traveller betwixt life and death;
The reason firm, the temperate will,
Endurance, foresight, strength, and skill;
A perfect woman, nobly planned,
To warn, to comfort, and command;
And yet a spirit still, and bright
With something of angelic light. *Ib.*

22 For still, the more he works, the more
Do his weak ankles swell. *Simon Lee*

23 O reader! had you in your mind
Such stores as silent thought can bring,
O gentle reader! you would find
A tale in every thing. *Ib.*

24 I've heard of hearts unkind, kind deeds
With coldness still returning;
Alas! the gratitude of men
Hath oftener left me mourning. *Ib.*

25 Characters of the great Apocalypse,
The types and symbols of Eternity,
Of first, and last, and midst, and without end.
The Simplon Pass: Brook and Road, and *The Prelude*, bk. vi, l. 636

26 Ethereal minstrel! pilgrim of the sky!
Dost thou despise the earth where cares abound?
Or, while the wings aspire, are heart and eye
Both with thy nest upon the dewy ground?
Thy nest which thou canst drop into at will,
Those quivering wings composed, that music still!
To a Skylark

27 Type of the wise who soar, but never roam;
True to the kindred points of heaven and home! *Ib.*

28 Behold her, single in the field,
　Yon solitary Highland lass!
Memorials of a Tour in Scotland, 1803, ix. *The Solitary Reaper*

1 A voice so thrilling ne'er was heard
In spring-time from the Cuckoo-bird,
Breaking the silence of the seas
Among the farthest Hebrides. *The Solitary Reaper*

2 Will no one tell me what she sings?—
Perhaps the plaintive numbers flow
For old, unhappy, far-off things,
And battles long ago. *Ib.*

3 Some natural sorrow, loss, or pain
That has been, and may be again. *Ib.*

4 The music in my heart I bore,
Long after it was heard no more. *Ib.*

5 Spade! with which Wilkinson hath tilled his lands.
To the Spade of a Friend

6 She gave me eyes, she gave me ears;
And humble cares, and delicate fears;
A heart, the fountain of sweet tears;
And love, and thought, and joy.
The Sparrow's Nest

7 In that sweet mood when pleasant thoughts
Bring sad thoughts to the mind.
Lines Written in Early Spring

8 And much it grieved my heart to think
What man has made of man. *Ib.*

9 And 'tis my faith that every flower
Enjoys the air it breathes. *Ib.*

10 Have I not reason to lament
What man has made of man? *Ib.*

11 Strange fits of passion I have known.
Strange Fits of Passion

12 What fond and wayward thoughts will slide
Into a Lover's head!
'O mercy!' to myself I cried,
'If Lucy should be dead!' *Ib.*

13 Two Voices are there; one is of the sea,
One of the mountains; each a mighty Voice,
In both from age to age thou didst rejoice,
They were thy chosen music, Liberty!
National Independence and Liberty, xii. *Thought
of a Briton on the Subjugation of Switzerland: Two
Voices are There*

14 Up! up! my friend, and quit your books;
Or surely you'll grow double:
Up! up! my friend, and clear your looks;
Why all this toil and trouble? *The Tables Turned*

15 Books! 'tis a dull and endless strife:
Come, hear the woodland linnet,
How sweet his music! on my life,
There's more of wisdom in it.

And hark! how blithe the throstle sings!
He, too, is no mean preacher:
Come forth into the light of things,
Let Nature be your teacher. *Ib.*

16 Spontaneous wisdom breathed by health,
Truth breathed by cheerfulness.

One impulse from a vernal wood
May teach you more of man,
Of moral evil and of good,
Than all the sages can.

Sweet is the lore which Nature brings;
Our meddling intellect
Misshapes the beauteous forms of things:—
We murder to dissect.

Enough of science and of art;
Close up these barren leaves;
Come forth, and bring with you a heart
That watches and receives. *The Tables Turned*

17 Every gift of noble origin
Is breathed upon by Hope's perpetual breath.
National Independence and Liberty, pt. I, xx.
These Times Strike Monied Worldlings

18 The power of Armies is a visible thing,
Formal, and circumscribed in time and place.
Ib. pt. II, xxxii. *The Power of Armies*

19 A noticeable man with large grey eyes
And a pale face. [Coleridge.]
*Stanzas written in my pocket copy of Thomson's
'Castle of Indolence'*

20 I've measured it from side to side:
'Tis three feet long, and two feet wide.
The Thorn, iii [early reading]

21 Then nature said, 'A lovelier flower
On earth was never sown;
This child I to myself will take;
She shall be mine, and I will make
A lady of my own.' *Three Years She Grew*

22 The stars of midnight shall be dear
To her; and she shall lean her ear
In many a secret place
Where rivulets dance their wayward round,
And beauty born of murmuring sound
Shall pass into her face. *Ib.*

23 Sensations sweet,
Felt in the blood, and felt along the heart.
*Lines composed a few miles above Tintern Abbey,
l. 27*

24 That best portion of a good man's life,
His little, nameless, unremembered acts
Of kindness and of love. *Ib. l. 33*

25 That blessed mood,
In which the burthen of the mystery,
In which the heavy and the weary weight
Of all this unintelligible world,
Is lightened:—that serene and blessed mood,
In which the affections gently lead us on,—
Until, the breath of this corporeal frame
And even the motion of our human blood
Almost suspended, we are laid asleep
In body, and become a living soul:
While with an eye made quiet by the power
Of harmony, and the deep power of joy,
We see into the life of things. *Ib. l. 37*

26 For nature then
(The coarser pleasures of my boyish days,
And their glad animal movements all gone by)
To me was all in all.—I cannot paint
What then I was. The sounding cataract
Haunted me like a passion: the tall rock,
The mountain, and the deep and gloomy wood,
Their colours and their forms, were then to me
An appetite; a feeling and a love,
That had no need of a remoter charm,
By thought supplied, nor any interest
Unborrowed from the eye. *Ib. l. 72*

1   I have learned
To look on nature, not as in the hour
Of thoughtless youth; but hearing often-times
The still, sad music of humanity,
Nor harsh nor grating, though of ample power
To chasten and subdue. And I have felt
A presence that disturbs me with the joy
Of elevated thoughts; a sense sublime
Of something far more deeply interfused,
Whose dwelling is the light of setting suns,
And the round ocean and the living air,
And the blue sky, and in the mind of man.
        Lines composed a few miles above Tintern Abbey,
        l. 88

2   All the mighty world
Of eye, and ear,—both what they half create,
And what perceive.   *Ib.* l. 105

3   Oh! yet a little while
May I behold in thee what I was once,
My dear, dear Sister! and this prayer I make,
Knowing that Nature never did betray
The heart that loved her; 'tis her privilege,
Through all the years of this our life, to lead
From joy to joy: for she can so inform
The mind that is within us, so impress
With quietness and beauty, and so feed
With lofty thoughts, that neither evil tongues,
Rash judgments, nor the sneers of selfish men,
Nor greetings where no kindness is, nor all
The dreary intercourse of daily life,
Shall e'er prevail against us, or disturb
Our cheerful faith, that all which we behold
Is full of blessings.   *Ib.* l. 121

4   Thou hast left behind
Powers that will work for thee; air, earth, and skies;
There's not a breathing of the common wind
That will forget thee; thou hast great allies;
Thy friends are exultations, agonies,
And love, and man's unconquerable mind.
        National Independence and Liberty, pt. i, viii. *To
        Toussaint L'Ouverture: Toussaint, the Most
        Unhappy*

5 Once did she hold the gorgeous East in fee,
And was the safeguard of the West.
        Ib. vi. *On the Extinction of the Venetian Republic:
        Once Did She Hold*

6 Venice, the eldest Child of Liberty.
She was a maiden City, bright and free.   *Ib.*

7 And when she took unto herself a Mate,
She must espouse the everlasting Sea.   *Ib.*

8 Men are we, and must grieve when even the shade
Of that which once was great is passed away.   *Ib.*

9 Our tainted nature's solitary boast.
        Ecclesiastical Sonnets, pt. ii, No. xxv. *The Virgin*

10   A shy spirit in my heart,
That comes and goes—will sometimes leap
From hiding-places ten years deep.
                The Waggoner, iv, l. 210

11   A simple child, dear brother Jim
That lightly draws its breath,
And feels its life in every limb,
What should it know of death?
        We are Seven. The words 'dear brother Jim'
        were omitted in the 1815 edition of his poems.

12 I take my little porringer
And eat my supper there.   *We are Seven*

13 'But they are dead; those two are dead!
Their spirits are in Heaven!'
'Twas throwing words away; for still
The little Maid would have her will,
And said, 'Nay, we are seven!'   *Ib.*

14 Earth has not anything to show more fair:
Dull would he be of soul who could pass by
A sight so touching in its majesty:
This City now doth, like a garment, wear
The beauty of the morning; silent, bare,
Ships, towers, domes, theatres, and temples lie
Open unto the fields, and to the sky;
All bright and glittering in the smokeless air.
Never did sun more beautifully steep
In his first splendour, valley, rock, or hill;
Ne'er saw I, never felt, a calm so deep!
The river glideth at his own sweet will:
Dear God! the very houses seem asleep;
And all that mighty heart is lying still!
        Miscellaneous Sonnets, pt. ii, xxxvi. *Composed
        upon Westminster Bridge*

15 What wonder if a Poet now and then,
Among the many movements of his mind,
Felt for thee as a lover or a child! [England]
        National Independence and Liberty, pt. i, xvii.
        When I Have Borne in Memory.

16 Where lies the Land to which yon Ship must go?
        Miscellaneous Sonnets, pt. i, xxxi. *Where Lies the
        Land*

17 With Ships the sea was sprinkled far and nigh.
        Ib. xxxii. *With Ships the Sea was Sprinkled*

18 The world is too much with us; late and soon,
Getting and spending, we lay waste our powers:
Little we see in Nature that is ours;
We have given our hearts away, a sordid boon!
This Sea that bares her bosom to the moon;
The winds that will be howling at all hours,
And are up-gathered now like sleeping flowers;
For this, for everything, we are out of tune;
It moves us not; Great God! I'd rather be
A Pagan suckled in a creed outworn,
So might I, standing on this pleasant lea,
Have glimpses that would make me less forlorn;
Have sight of Proteus rising from the sea,
Or hear old Triton blow his wreathed horn.
        Ib. xxxiii. *The World is Too Much with Us*

19 Let . . .
The swan on still St. Mary's Lake
Float double, swan and shadow!
        Memorials of a Tour in Scotland, 1803. xiii.
        Yarrow Unvisited

20 But thou, that didst appear so fair
To fond imagination,
Dost rival in the light of day
Her delicate creation.
        *Memorials of a Tour in Scotland, 1814. Yarrow
        Visited*

21 Like,—but oh how different!
                Yes, it was the Mountain Echo

22   Fear and trembling Hope,
Silence and Foresight; Death the Skeleton
And Time the Shadow.   *Yew Trees*

1 Thou, while thy babes around thee cling,
Shalt show us how divine a thing
A woman may be made. *To a Young Lady*

2 But an old age, serene and bright,
And lovely as a Lapland night,
Shall lead thee to thy grave. *Ib.*

3 Poetry is the breath and finer spirit of all knowledge;
it is the impassioned expression which is in the
countenance of all science.
Lyrical Ballads, preface

4 Poetry is the spontaneous overflow of powerful feelings: it takes its origin from emotion recollected in
tranquillity. *Ib.*

5 Every great and original writer, in proportion as he
is great and original, must himself create the taste
by which he is to be relished.
Letter to Lady Beaumont

HENRY CLAY WORK
1832–1884

6 Bring the good old bugle, boys, we'll sing another
song;
Sing it with a spirit that will start the world along,
Sing it as we used to sing it—fifty thousand strong,
As we were marching through Georgia.
Marching Through Georgia

7 'Hurrah! hurrah! we bring the Jubilee!
Hurrah! hurrah! the flag that makes you free!'
So we sang the chorus from Atlanta to the sea,
As we were marching through Georgia. *Ib. Chorus*

8 Father, dear father, come home with me now,
The clock in the belfry strikes one.
Temperance song, 1864

SIR HENRY WOTTON
1568–1639

9 How happy is he born and taught
That serveth not another's will;
Whose armour is his honest thought,
And simple truth his utmost skill!
Character of a Happy Life, i

10 Who God doth late and early pray
More of his grace than gifts to lend;
And entertains the harmless day
With a religious book, or friend. *Ib.* v

11 This man is freed from servile bands,
Of hope to rise, or fear to fall:—
Lord of himself, though not of lands,
And having nothing, yet hath all. *Ib.* vi

12 He first deceas'd; she for a little tri'd
To live without him: lik'd it not, and di'd.
Death of Sir Albertus Moreton's Wife

13 You meaner beauties of the night,
That poorly satisfy our eyes,
More by your number, than your light;
You common people of the skies,
What are you when the moon shall rise?
On His Mistress, the Queen of Bohemia

14 At my departure toward Rome . . . I had won confidence enough to beg his advice [Alberto Scipioni's]
how I might carry myself securely there without
offence of others, or of mine own conscience.

'*Signor Arrigo mio*', says he, '*I pensieri stretti ed il
viso sciolto* will go safely over the whole world.'
['Sir Henry . . . the thoughts secret and the coun-
tenance open.']
Letter to Milton, 13 Apr. 1638, prefixed to
Comus

15 An ambassador is an honest man sent to lie abroad for
the good of his country.
Written in the Album of Christopher Fleckmore
(1604)

SIR CHRISTOPHER WREN
1632–1723

16 Si monumentum requiris, circumspice.
If you would see his monument look around.
*Inscription over the interior of the North Door in
St. Paul's Cathedral, London. Attributed to Wren's
son*

SIR THOMAS WYATT
1503 ?–1542

17 Blame not my lute! for he must sound
Of this and that as liketh me. *The Lute Obeys*, i

18 And wilt thou leave me thus?
Say nay, say nay, for shame! *An Appeal*

19 Forget not yet the tried intent
Of such a truth as I have meant;
My great travail so gladly spent
Forget not yet! *Steadfastness*

20 They flee from me, that sometime did me seek.
Remembrance

21 My lute, awake! perform the last
Labour that thou and I shall waste,
The end that I have now begun;
For when this song is sung and past,
My lute, be still, for I have done. *To His Lute*

WILLIAM WYCHERLEY
1640 ?–1716

22 Go to your business, I say, pleasure, whilst I go to
my pleasure, business. *Country Wife*, Act II

23 Nay, you had both felt his desperate deadly daunting
dagger:—there are your d's for you!
Gentleman Dancing-Master, Act V

24 Fy! madam, do you think me so ill bred as to love a
husband? *Love in a Wood*, III. iv

25 QUAINT:
With sharp invectives—
WIDOW:
Alias, Billingsgate. *Plain Dealer*, Act III

WYNTOUN'S CHRONICLE

26 Quhen Alysander oure kyng wes dede,
That Scotland led in luve and le,
Away wes sons of ale and brede,
Of wyne and wax, of gamyn and gle:
Oure gold wes changyd into lede,
Cryst, borne into virgynyte,
Succour Scotland, and remede,
That stad is in perplexyte.
From Andrew Wyntoun's *Cronykill*, vol. i,
p. 401, ed. 1795 (*the edition used by Scott*) *and
in the edition of 1872*, vol. ii, p. 266

XENOPHON
b. *c.* 430 B.C.

1 θάλαττα θάλαττα.

    The sea! the sea!   *Anabasis, iv. vii. 24*

WILLIAM BUTLER YEATS
1865–1939

2 A line will take us hours may be;
Yet if it does not seem a moment's thought,
Our stitching and unstitching has been naught.
     Adam's Curse

3 O heart, be at peace, because
Nor knave nor dolt can break•
What's not for their applause,
Being for a woman's sake. *Against Unworthy Praise*

4   When I was young,
I had not given a penny for a song
Did not the poet sing it with such airs
That one believed he had a sword upstairs.
     All Things Can Tempt Me

5 The phantom, Beauty, in a mist of tears.
     Anashuya and Vijaya

6 The old priest Peter Gilligan
Was weary night and day;
For half his flock were in their beds,
Or under green sods lay. *Ballad of Father Gilligan*

7 He Who is wrapped in purple robes,
With planets in His care,
Had pity on the least of things
Asleep upon a chair.   *Ib.*

8 The years like great black oxen tread the world,
And God the herdsman goads them on behind,
And I am broken by their passing feet.
     The Countess Cathleen, Act IV

9   The Light of Lights
Looks always on the motive, not the deed,
The Shadow of Shadows on the deed alone.   *Ib.*

10 God's laughing in Heaven
To see you so good.   *A Cradle Song*

11 Down by the salley gardens my love and I did meet;
She passed the salley gardens with little snow-white feet.
She bid me take love easy, as the leaves grow on the tree;
But I, being young and foolish, with her would not agree.

In a field by the river my love and I did stand,
And on my leaning shoulder she laid her snow-white hand.
She bid me take life easy, as the grass grows on the weirs;
But I was young and foolish, and now am full of tears.
     Down by the Salley Gardens

12 She was more beautiful than thy first love,
This lady by the trees.   *A Dream of Death*

13 He found the unpersuadable justice.
     Ego Dominus Tuus

14 The coarse-bred son of a livery stable keeper. [Keats.]
     Ib.

15 We who are old, old and gay
O so old!
Thousands of years, thousands of years,
If all were told.   *A Faery Song*

16 But weigh this song with the great and their pride;
I made it out of a mouthful of air,
Their children's children shall say they have lied.
     He Thinks of Those who have Spoken Evil of his Beloved

17 Had I the heavens' embroidered cloths,
Enwrought with golden and silver light,
The blue and the dim and the dark cloths
Of night and light and the half-light,
I would spread the cloths under your feet:
But I, being poor, have only my dreams;
I have spread my dreams under your feet;
Tread softly, because you tread on my dreams.
     He Wishes for the Cloths of Heaven

18 I mourn for that most lovely thing; and yet God's will be done:
I knew a phoenix in my youth, so let them have their day.   *His Phoenix*

19 Out-worn heart, in a time out-worn,
Come clear of the nets of wrong and right;
Laugh, heart, again in the grey twilight,
Sigh, heart, again in the dew of the morn.
     Into the Twilight

20 And God stands winding His lonely horn,
And time and the world are ever in flight;
And love is less kind than the grey twilight,
And hope is less dear than the dew of the morn. *Ib.*

21 Nor law, nor duty bade me fight,
Nor public men, nor cheering crowds,
A lonely impulse of delight
Drove to this tumult in the clouds;
I balanced all, brought all to mind,
The years to come seemed waste of breath,
A waste of breath the years behind
In balance with this life, this death.
     An Irish Airman Foresees His Death

22 All the wild witches, those most noble ladies,
For all their broom-sticks and their tears,
Their angry tears, are gone.
     Lines Written in Dejection

23 What were all the world's alarms
To mighty Paris when he found
Sleep upon a golden bed,
That first dawn in Helen's arms.   *Lullaby,* st. 1

24 Never give all the heart, for love
Will hardly seem worth thinking of
To passionate women if it seem
Certain, and they never dream
That it fades out from kiss to kiss.
     Never Give All the Heart

25 Why, what could she have done, being what she is?
Was there another Troy for her to burn?
     No Second Troy

26 To shake their wicked sides at youth
Restraining reckless middle-age?
    On hearing that the Students of our new University have joined the Agitation against Immoral Literature

27 Was it for this the wild geese spread
The grey wing upon every tide;
For this that all that blood was shed,
For this Edward Fitzgerald died,
And Robert Emmet and Wolfe Tone,
All that delirium of the brave?
Romantic Ireland's dead and gone,
It's with O'Leary in the grave.   *September 1913*

1 For the good are always the merry,
Save by an evil chance,
And the merry love the fiddle,
And the merry love to dance. *The Fiddler of Dooney*

2 When I play on my fiddle in Dooney
Folk dance like a wave of the sea. *Ib.*

3 One that is ever kind said yesterday
'Your well-beloved's hair has threads of grey,
And little shadows come about her eyes.'
The Folly of Being Comforted

4 Time can but make her beauty over again:
Because of that great nobleness of hers.
The fire that stirs about her, when she stirs,
Burns but more clearly. O she had not these ways
When all the wild summer was in her gaze. *Ib.*

5 O heart! O heart! if she'd but turn her head,
You'd know the folly of being comforted. *Ib.*

6 The little fox murmured,
'O what of the world's bane?'
The sun was laughing sweetly,
The moon plucked at my rein;
But the little red fox murmured,
'O do not pluck at his rein,
He is riding to the townland
That is the world's bane.' *The Happy Townland*

7 The host is riding from Knocknarea
And over the grave of Clooth-na-Bare;
Caoilte tossing his burning hair,
And Niamh calling Away, come away.
The Hosting of the Sidhe

8 Who holds the world between His bill and made us
strong or weak
Is an undying moorfowl, and He lives beyond the
sky.
The rains are from His dripping wings, the moonbeams from His eye. *The Indian upon God*

9 Who made the world and ruleth it, He hangeth on
a stalk,
For I am in His image made, and all this tinkling
tide
Is but a sliding drop of rain between His petals wide.
Ib.

10 The Stamper of the Skies,
He is a gentle roebuck; for how else, I pray, could He
Conceive a thing so sad and soft, a gentle thing like
me? *Ib.*

11 Who made the grass and made the worms and made
my feathers gay,
He is a monstrous peacock, and He waveth all the
night
His languid tail above us, lit with myriad spots of
light. *Ib.*

12 I will arise and go now, and go to Innisfree,
And a small cabin build there, of clay and wattles
made:
Nine bean-rows will I have there, a hive for the
honey-bee,
And live alone in the bee-loud glade.

And I shall have some peace there, for peace comes
dropping slow,
Dropping from the veils of the morning to where the
cricket sings;
There midnight's all a-glimmer, and noon a purple
glow,
And evening full of the linnet's wings.

I will arise and go now, for always night and day
I hear lake water lapping with low sounds by the
shore;
While I stand on the roadway, or on the pavements
gray
I hear it in the deep heart's core.
The Lake Isle of Innisfree

13 The wind blows out of the gates of the day,
The wind blows over the lonely of heart,
And the lonely of heart is withered away.
The Land of Heart's Desire

14 The land of faery,
Where nobody gets old and godly and grave,
Where nobody gets old and crafty and wise,
Where nobody gets old and bitter of tongue. *Ib.*

15 Of a land where even the old are fair,
And even the wise are merry of tongue. *Ib.*

16 Land of Heart's Desire,
Where beauty has no ebb, decay no flood,
But joy is wisdom, Time an endless song. *Ib.*

17 All things uncomely and broken, all things worn out
and old,
The cry of a child by the roadway, the creak of a
lumbering cart,
The heavy steps of the ploughman, splashing the
wintry mould,
Are wronging your image that blossoms a rose in
the deeps of my heart.
The wrong of unshapely things is a wrong too great to
be told;
I hunger to build them anew and sit on a green knoll
apart,
With the earth and the sky and the water, re-made,
like a casket of gold;
For my dreams of your image that blossoms a rose in
the deeps of my heart.
The Lover Tells of the Rose in his Heart

18 When I was a boy with never a crack in my heart.
The Meditation of the Old Fisherman

19 I heard the old, old men say,
'All that's beautiful drifts away
Like the waters.'
The Old Men Admiring Themselves in the Water

20 A pity beyond all telling
Is hid in the heart of love. *The Pity of Love*

21 Rose of all Roses, Rose of all the World!
The Rose of Battle

22 Who dreamed that beauty passes like a dream?
For these red lips, with all their mournful pride,
Mournful that no new wonder may betide,
Troy passed away in one high funeral gleam,
And Usna's children died.

We and the labouring world are passing by:
Amid men's souls, that waver and give place
Like the pale waters in their wintry race,
Under the passing stars, foam of the sky,
Lives on this lonely face.
Bow down, archangels, in your dim abode;
Before you were, or any hearts to beat,
Weary and kind one linger'd by His seat;
He made the world to be a grassy road
Before her wandering feet. *The Rose of the World*

23 Far off, most secret, and inviolate Rose,
Enfold me in my hour of hours. *The Secret Rose*

1 A woman of so shining loveliness
That men threshed corn at midnight by a tress.
The Secret Rose.

2 When shall the stars be blown about the sky,
Like the sparks blown out of a smithy, and die?
Surely thine hour has come, thy great wind blows,
Far-off, most secret, and inviolate Rose?   *Ib.*

3 It is love that I am seeking for,
But of a beautiful, unheard-of kind
That is not in the world.   *The Shadowy Waters*

4   Do you not know
How great a wrong it is to let one's thought
Wander a moment when one is in love?   *Ib.*

5 Bend lower, O king, that I may crown you with it.
O flower of the branch, O bird among the leaves,
O silver fish that my two hands have taken
Out of the running stream, O morning star,
Trembling in the blue heavens like a white fawn
Upon the misty border of the wood,
Bend lower, that I may cover you with my hair,
For we will gaze upon this world no longer.   *Ib.*

6 And pluck till time and times are done
The silver apples of the moon
The golden apples of the sun.
The Song of Wandering Ængus

7 The brawling of a sparrow in the eaves,
    The brilliant moon and all the milky sky,
And all that famous harmony of leaves,
    Had blotted out man's image and his cry.

A girl arose that had red mournful lips
And seemed the greatness of the world in tears,
Doomed like Odysseus and the labouring ships
And proud as Priam murdered with his peers;

Arose, and on the instant clamorous eaves,
    A climbing moon upon an empty sky,
And all that lamentation of the leaves,
    Could but compose man's image and his cry.
The Sorrow of Love

8 And the loud chaunting of the unquiet leaves
Are shaken with earth's old and weary cry.
The Sorrow of Love (1893 version)

9 Come away, O human child!
To the waters and the wild
With a faery, hand in hand,
For the world's more full of weeping than you can
    understand.   *The Stolen Child*

10 Nor know that what disturbs our blood
Is but its longing for the tomb.   *The Wheel*

11 I would that we were, my beloved, white birds on the
    foam of the sea!   *The White Birds*

12 But was there ever dog that praised his fleas?
*To a Poet, who would have me praise certain bad
Poets, Imitators of his and mine*

13 I know what wages beauty gives,
How hard a life her servant lives,
Yet praise the winters gone:
There is not a fool can call me friend,
And I may dine at journey's end
With Landor and with Donne.   *To a Young Beauty*

14 Know, that I would accounted be
True brother of a company
That sang, to sweeten Ireland's wrong,
Ballad and story, rann and song;

Nor be I any less of them,
Because the red-rose-bordered hem
Of her, whose history began
Before God made the angelic clan,
Trails all about the written page.
To Ireland in the Coming Times

15 For the elemental creatures go
About my table to and fro.   *Ib.*

16 Ah, faeries, dancing under the moon,
A Druid land, a Druid tune!   *Ib.*

17 Red Rose, Proud Rose, sad Rose of all my days!
To the Rose upon the Rood of Time

18 Eternal beauty wandering on her way.   *Ib.*

19 All changed, changed utterly:
A terrible beauty is born.   *Under Saturn*

20 Dwell in the house of the Fenians, be they in flames
    or at feast.   *The Wanderings of Oisin*, bk. iii

21 When you are old and gray and full of sleep,
And nodding by the fire, take down this book,
And slowly read, and dream of the soft look
Your eyes had once, and of their shadows deep;
How many loved your moments of glad grace,
And loved your beauty with love false or true,
But one man loved the pilgrim soul in you,
And loved the sorrows of your changing face.
And bending down beside the glowing bars,
Murmur, a little sadly, how Love fled
And paced upon the mountains overhead
And hid his face amid a crowd of stars.
When you are Old

ANDREW YOUNG
1807–1889

22 There is a happy land,
    Far, far away,
Where Saints in glory stand,
    Bright, bright as day.
Hymn: There is a Happy Land. C. H. Bate-
man's *Sacred Song Book*, 1843

EDWARD YOUNG
1683–1765

23   Be wise with speed;
A fool at forty is a fool indeed.
Love of Fame, Sat. ii, l. 281

24 For who does nothing with a better grace?
Ib. Sat. iv, l. 86

25 For ever most divinely in the wrong.
Ib. Sat. vi, l. 106

26 For her own breakfast she'll project a scheme,
Nor take her tea without a stratagem.   *Ib.* l. 187

27 One to destroy, is murder by the law;
And gibbets keep the lifted hand in awe;
To murder thousands, takes a specious name,
War's glorious art, and gives immortal fame.
Ib. Sat. vii, l. 55

28 How commentators each dark passage shun,
And hold their farthing candle to the sun.   *Ib.* l. 97

29 Tir'd Nature's sweet restorer, balmy sleep!
He, like the world, his ready visit pays
Where fortune smiles; the wretched he forsakes.
The Complaint: Night Thoughts, Night i, l. 1

1 Night, sable goddess! from her ebon throne
In rayless majesty, now stretches forth
Her leaden sceptre o'er a slumb'ring world.
The Complaint: Night Thoughts, Night i, l. 18

2 We take no note of Time
But from its Loss. *Ib.* l. 55

3 Be wise to-day; 'tis madness to defer. *Ib.* l. 390

4 Procrastination is the thief of time. *Ib.* l. 393

5 Of man's miraculous mistakes, this bears
The palm, 'That all men are about to live'.
Ib. l. 399

6 At thirty man suspects himself a fool;
Knows it at forty, and reforms his plan;
At fifty chides his infamous delay,
Pushes his prudent purpose to resolve;
In all the magnanimity of thought
Resolves; and re-resolves; then dies the same.
Ib. l. 417

7 All men think all men mortal, but themselves.
Ib. l. 424

8 Beautiful as sweet!
And young as beautiful! and soft as young!
And gay as soft! and innocent as gay.
Ib. Night iii, l. 81

9 Man wants but little; nor that little, long.
Ib. Night iv, l. 118

10 A God all mercy, is a God unjust. *Ib.* l. 233

11 By night an atheist half believes a God.
Ib. Night v, l. 176

12 To know the world, not love her, is thy point;
She gives but little, nor that little, long.
Ib. Night viii, l. 1276

13 Devotion! daughter of astronomy!
An undevout astronomer is mad.
The Complaint: Night Thoughts, Night ix, l. 769

14 Life is the desert, life the solitude;
Death joins us to the great majority.
The Revenge, Act IV

15 Accept a miracle, instead of wit,
See two dull lines, with Stanhope's pencil writ.
Written with Lord Chesterfield's Diamond Pencil.
Spence, *Anecdotes* (1820), p. 378

16 You are so witty, profligate, and thin,
At once we think thee Milton, Death, and Sin.
Epigram on Voltaire

ISRAEL ZANGWILL
1864–1926

17 Scratch the Christian and you find the pagan—
spoiled. *Children of the Ghetto*, bk. ii, ch. 6

18 America is God's Crucible, the great Melting-Pot
where all the races of Europe are melting and reforming! . . . God is making the American.
The Melting Pot, Act I

ÉMILE ZOLA
1840–1902

19 J'accuse.
I accuse.
*Title of an open letter to the President of the
Republic, in connexion with the Dreyfus case,
published in L'Aurore, 13 Jan. 1898*

INDEX

NOTE

THE index references show the page number followed by the numerical position of the quotation on the page (e.g. 163:15 = the fifteenth quotation on page 163).

The order of the index both in the keywords and in the entries under the keywords is strictly alphabetical.

To save space the keyword is replaced by its initial letter in the individual entries.

Foreign quotations have been included in the general alphabetical scheme and for greater clarity are printed in italic in this index. A separate Greek index follows the general one.

Irregular spellings (such as occur in Dickens, Artemus Ward, &c.), early English words, and dialect words are indexed under their normal modern equivalents except where there is no exact equivalent. Some words are given in both their original and their normal forms.

The definite and indefinite article have been dropped from the beginnings of most entries, and the alphabetical order is therefore decided by more significant words: thus—under 'Face'—'a garden in her face' and 'the garden of your face' follow each other instead of being separated by over a hundred other 'face' entries.

A

A was an apple-pie 366:7
Aaron: A.'s rod 45:42
  even unto A.'s beard 400:3
  like A.'s serpent 383:25
Abana and Pharpar 48:22
Abandon: a. all remorse 472:5
  a. his mind to it 275:8
  a. yourselves to your . . appetites 85:8
  all hope a. 168:17
Abandoned: what God a. 264:4
Abased: whosoever exalteth himself
  . . a. 62:4
  whosoever shall exalt himself . . a. 60:16
Abashed: a. the Devil stood 347:31
  heard, and were a. 344:27
  newe a. nightingale 138:34
Abashless inquisition of each star 545:10
Abassin kings their issue guard 347:9
Abate—Cardinal,—Christ 96:17
Abated: the agony is a. 326:10
Abatement: a. and low price 481:30
  earth's a. 94:1
Abba, Father 65:53
Abbey: his name on the A.-stones 92:38
  not in the A. proudly laid 562:21
Abbot: A. of Aberbrothok 507:25
  Bishop, and a., and prior 34:8
Abby-nay: all along of a. 295:22
A.B.C.: man is man's A. 404:14
  unacquainted with the A. 512:7
Abdicate it in the greatest 413:9
Abdiel: Seraph A., faithful found 348:18
Abed-nego: Meshach and A. 55:41
Abel: Cain and his brother, A. 151:10
Aberbrothok: Abbot of A. 507:25
Aberdeen: the Quaker (Lord A.) 28:25
Aberdour: half-owre to A. 32:2
Aberglaube: der A. ist die Poesie 224:3
Abhor: a. the makers 192:32
  age, I do a. thee 486:3
Abhorred: a. all manner of meat 398:16
  hath not . . a. . . the poor 393:8
  how a. in my imagination 437:15
  Idolatry, to be a. 390:54
  lean a. monster 478:44
Abhorrence: my heart's a.! 96:38
Abhorring: blow me into a. 425:34
Abide: a. in this dull world 425:29
  a. with me 322:1
  a. with me from morn till eve 291:10
  I a. by my Mother's House 300:11
  no where did a. 149:23
  there he would a. 165:10
  was, and is, and will a. 573:26
  who may a. it? 399:39

Abide (*cont.*)
  with me and mine a. 324:11
Abided: all things a. eternally 548:15
Abides: in mystery our soul a. 16:29
  much is taken, much a. 541:3
Abideth: a. not in words 296:31
  now a. faith, hope, charity 66:46(-67)
  where my Love a. 94:24
Abi-Ezer: vintage of A. 46:53
Abiit: a. ad plures 125:34, 378:11
  a., excessit, evasit, erupit 145:13
Abilities: according to his a. 333:12
  God has given you good a. 14:4
Ability: according to his several a. 60:28
  furnished with a. 57:16
  my lean and low a. 484:17
  studies serve . . for a. 27:13
  3rdly, intellectual a. 20:21
Abire: tempus a. tibi est 257:21
Abject: a. from the spheres 561:12
  doubting in his a. spirit 320:12
  I'll be this a. thing no more 229:5
  so a.—yet alive! 118:19
Abjure: a. the Scriptures 329:25
  other pleasures all a. 348:35
Ablaze: Britain set the world a. 219:7
Able: a. to do . . abundantly 67:55
  let me see if he is a. 249:23
  tempted above that ye are a. 66:38
Ablution: priest-like task of pure
  a. 288:17
Aboard: Donkey wint a. 298:21
  once a. the lugger 279:16
  we brought them all a. 539:19
Abode: a. his destin'd Hour 205:30
  a. his Hour or two 205:29
  a. where the Eternal are 492:16
  archangels, in your dim a. 585:22
  English make it their a. 557:23
  his frailties from their dread a. 230:13
  nor wealth nor blessed a. 334:13
  we live in a numble a. 174:26
Abodes: aiming at the bless'd a. 383:13
  Elysian, windless, fortunate a. 497:15
  remembers its august a. 308:28
  sprung from your bless'd a. 381:33
Abolish: utterly a. or destroy 576:19
Abominable: altogether become a. 392:23
Abomination: a. of desolation 60:24
  an a. unto the Lord, but 5:6
  incense is an a. 52:29
Abominations: the mother of
  harlots and a. 71:32
Aboon: a. the burn, ayont the law 516:20
  a heart a. them a' 108:15
Abora: singing of Mount A. 151:33(-152)
Abou Ben Adhem (may his tribe
  increase!) 265:16

Abound: grace did much more a. 65:42
  that grace may a. 65:43
  where beauties most a. 116:43
About: a., a., in reel and rout 149:6
  a. it and a. 206:10
  a. must, and a. must go 186:10
  all men are a. to live 587:5
  something evermore a. to be 579:27
  what are you a.? 87:27
Above: a. himself . . erect himself 168:5
  around, beneath, a. 81:10
  at once a., beneath, around 503:3
  every good gift . . from a. 69:29
  far a. the great 231:16
  he is so a. me 423:2
  set your affection on things a. 68:30
  some descending from a. 24:17
  square, and a. the board 234:11
  this wisdom . . not from a. 69:39
  thy glory a. all the earth 395:18
  'tis not so a. 435:35
  unseen things a. 235:10
  what they do a. 558:7
Abra was ready . . Abra came 402:4
Abraham: are they the seed of A.? 67:33
  carried . . into A.'s bosom 62:25
  God of A., . . of Isaac, . . of Jacob 45:38
  in A.'s bosom all the year 577:1
  sleep in A.'s bosom 476:25
Abreast: keep a. of Truth 320:13
  one but goes a. 481:19
Abridgement of all that was
  pleasant 225:30
Abroad: come to starve a. 192:28
  Cupid a. was lated 231:33
  for the good of my country . . a. 203:12
  I will a. 244:10
  ships shall go a. 298:17
  when he next doth ride a. 160:11
  you are ordered a. 305:1
Absalom, my son, my son 47:37
Absence: a. doth join 262:5
  a. from whom we love 160:20
  a., hear thou my protestation 262:5
  a. makes the heart grow
  fonder 5:3, 36:28
  a. of body 403:6
  a. . . of educated . . opinion 19:16
  a. of the planet Venus 177:22
  a. seemed my flame to qualify 488:4
  by a. this good means 262:6
  cannot admit a. 186:25
  conquered . . in a fit of a. of
  mind 421:19
  conspicuous . . by its a. 414:2
  how like a winter . . my a. 487:27
  I dote on his very a. 463:14
  in thy a. is . . a sty 425:29

INDEX

Absence (cont.)
pangs of a. to remove 401:31
think the bitterness of a. sour 487:7
Absence: l'a. est à l'amour 109:34
Absent: a. from Him I roam 355:10
a. in body 66:26
a. in the spring 487:28
a. one from another 45:8
a. thee from felicity 438:4
hear their a. thoughts o' ither 108:22
if to be a. were to be 319:8
loved ones, now far a. 512:14
lovers' a. hours 472:18
melancholy when thou art a. 155:27
my a. kisses 166:18
the a. are always..wrong 172:29
when thou art a. I am sad 365:22
woven with an a. heed 235:21
Absent-minded beggar 294:18
Absents: Presents..endear A. 306:5
Absents: les a. ont toujours tort 172:29
Absolute: a. power corrupts
absolutely 1:2
a. rule 347:11
a. sole Lord of life and death 166:11
bawl the A. across the hall 41:32
be a. for death 462:3
content so a. 470:31
Grape..with Logic a. 206:25
he of a. temper was so a. 189:3
how a. the knave is 437:12
so a. she seems 349:1
Absolutism moderated by assassination 6:5
Absolve him so 96:14
Absolved: half a. who has confess'd 401:18
Absolvitur: se iudice nemo nocens a. 284:1
Absorbing: my practice is never
very a. 187:20
Absorbs: daily a. a clay 121:21
Abstain: a. you from such works 328:19
and yet a., and yet distinguish 352:9
Abstinence: a. is as easy to me 277:6
A. sows sand 74:25
lean and sallow a. 340:36
made almost a sin of a. 191:40
total a. is easier 22:4
*Abstinent: facilius se a. ut non
utantur* 22:4
Abstract liberty..not to be found 100:28
Abstracts and brief chronicles 433:29
Absurd: a. nature of Englishmen 377:20
nothing so a. but.. 145:3
Prophet of the Utterly A. 301:21
proving a. all written hitherto 90:35
scientific faith's a. 91:16
so a. a view 121:10
something rather a. about the
past 39:9
Absurde: nihil tam a. dici potest 145:3
Absurdity: very dull without a
single a. 227:14
Abundance: a. of rain 48:4
a. of thy grace 400:33
he shall have a. 60:32
out of the a. of the heart 59:14
Abundant: blueness a. 97:15
good..more a. grows 348:2
Abundantly: able to do exceeding a. 67:55
Abuse: a. the shopocracy 365:14
bore without a. 533:23
if it is a...sure to hear of it 499:25
the more dangerous the a. 101:29
to a. in public 78:20
you a. snuff! 153:4
Abused: better to be much a. 472:1
by himself a. or disabused 383:22
never love was so a. 502:6
such opportunity..or a. it more 116:28
tyrant rhyme hath no a. 281:27
Abuses me to damn me 433:37
Abuseth: reason a. me 305:16
Abusing of God's patience, and the
king's English 465:33
*Abutere: quousque..a...patientia
nostra?* 145:11
Abydos: Sestos and A. of her
breasts 184:21
Abysm: dark backward and a. of
time 479:20

Abyss: breathless Nature's dark a. 575:1
dark unbottom'd infinite a. 345:26
secrets of th' a. to spy 231:13
wild a., the womb of nature 346:12
Abyssinia: Rasselas, Prince of A. 278:14
Abyssinian: an A. maid 151:33(–152)
Acacia: the slender a. would not
shake 536:13
Academe: olive grove of A. 350:11
Academes: the ground, the books,
the a. 455:20
the books, the arts, the a. 455:23
*Academi: inter silvas A. quaerere
verum* 257:16
Academy: in the groves of *their* a. 102:16
Mr. Wackford Squeers's A. 176:38
Accent: neither having the a. of
Christians 434:19
with a shrill and sad a. 145:27
Accents: a. falling on them haphazard 337:2
a. of an expiring saint 513:21
a. that are ours 168:9
a. yet unknown 450:1
caught his clear a. 93:3
follow with a. sweet 123:22
loved a. are soon forgot 494:20
prophesying with a. terrible 458:21
Accept: a., thou shrine 292:18
I a. the universe 177:32
Acceptable: alway a. in thy sight 392:34
an a. people 389:24
holy, a. unto God 65:62
the a. year of the Lord 55:3
Accepted: God in Christ a. 90:43
now is the a. time 67:29
Accepteth: God now a. thy works 51:20
Accepting: a. the affirmations of
the soul 201:12
charms by a. 384:38
Accepts: Man a. the compromise 296:14
Access and passage to remorse 457:3
Accession: to the a. of Commodus 217:8
Accident: many a happy a. 338:15
moving a. is not my trade 575:12
progress..is not an a. 508:27
shot of a. nor dart of chance 472:32
'There's been an a.!' 228:9
Accidental: a...concurrence of
atoms 373:7
thy sin's not a., but a trade 462:11
Accidents: a. will occur 174:37
a chapter of a. 139:31
chapter of a. is the longest 570:25
moving a. by flood and field 470:2
shackles a. 425:33
Acciptrine: a will a. to pursue 544:3
Accommodated: better a. than
with a wife 442:9
Accommodating: of a exceedin a.
character 560:2
*Accommodements: on trouve avec
lui des a.* 354:7
Accomplish: its highest Tribunal
will a. 101:22
Accomplished: desire a. is sweet 50:5
her warfare is a. 54:8
the a. Sofa last 162:34
Accomplishing: armourers, a. the
knights 444:6
Accomplishment: wanting the a.
of verse 574:11
Accomplishments give lustre 139:27
Accord: a look made all of sweet a. 265:16
just a. all music makes 502:7
with one a. to make our..sup-
plications 388:32
According: in peace, a. to thy word 61:20
Accordingly: in a concatenation a. 227:4
Accosted: she-bear thus a. 206:13
should then have a. her 483:31
Account: give a. thereof in the day
of judgment 59:15
give no a. of the platter 306:22
learn, nor a. the pang 95:11
make an a. of her life to a clod 468:8
present my true a. 351:21
sad a. of fore-bemoaned moan 486:25
sent to my a. 432:17
thy name in high a. 418:14
Accounted be true brother 586:14

Accounting for the moral sense 126:8
Accoutred as I was, I plunged in 448:18
Accumulate: on horror's head
horrors a. 472:5
Accumulates: wealth a., and men
decay 224:14
Accuracy..sacrificed to concise-
ness 277:20
Accursed: a. be he that first in-
vented war 330:26
a. from Christ for my brethren 65:59
think themselves a. 444:28
thoughts of men a. 441:27
what God blessed once, prove a. 89:22
Accusation: a railing a. 70:17
Accuse: a. not nature 349:2
seldom has justice enough to a. 227:25
Accused: before you be a. 135:27
Accuse: j'a. 587:19
Accuser: not my A., but my judges 363:12
Ace: Gladstone's always having
the a. of trumps 305:20
Achaians: again to the battle, A. 123:6
Achates: fidus quae tela gerebat A. 553:12
Ache: age, a., penury 462:10
make this heart rejoice, or a. 161:5
Ached: never has a. with a heart 522:25
Acheronta movebo 555:4
Acherontis: strepitumque A. avari 556:17
Aches: balm for a. 334:5
fill all thy bones with a. 479:27
my heart a. 287:22
the sense a. at thee 472:35
Achieve: I shall a. in time 220:2
some a. greatness 483:18
the a. of, the mastery of the thing 255:12
to a. that I have done 328:12
Achieved: the matchless deed's a. 503:6
Achiever: a. brings home full
numbers 467:37
Achievements: my a. mock me 481:24
such great a. cannot fail 110:40
Achieving: still a., still pursuing 317:8
Achilles: A.' wrath..sing 384:20
great A., whom we knew 541:3
I've stood upon A.' tomb 116:12
to work out A. his armour 85:17
what name A. assumed 87:12
*Achilli: exuvias indutus A.
impar congressus A.* 554:6
553:19
Aching: a. hands and bleeding
feet 17:1
a. hours 269:26
a. Pleasure 287:21
a. void 161:2
hide them from my a. sight 23:16
O a. time 286:7
spare my a. sight 229:25
terror on my a. sight 155:19
when your back stops a. 296:33
Achitophel: the false A. was first 190:13
*Achivi: quidquid delirant reges
plectuntur A.* 256:22
Acid: drank Prussic a. without any
water 34:32
Acidulous vestals 514:23
Acknowledge: a. and confess our
..sins 388:6
do you think I'd a. him 177:31
I a. my faults 395:7
I next a. duly 364:5
Acknowledgment of God in Christ 90:43
Acorned: liken his Grace to an a.
hog 92:8
Acorns: tall oaks from little a. 202:16
Acquaintance: a. I would have 158:16
an old a. among the pines 547:1
hope our a. may be a long 'un 178:41
I love good creditable a. 519:26
make a new a. 275:29
should auld a. be forgot 104:11
the last people..to have a visiting a. with 500:23
what! old a.! 441:1
Acquainted: a. with grief 54:25
a. with sad misery 563:12
at last a. with Love 270:17
better a. with the soundings 290:7
sentiment is what I am not a.
with 208:27
when Love and I were well a. 222:13

INDEX

Acquaints his soul with song 96:27
Acquent: when we were first a. 106:19
Acquiesce with silence 277:24
Acquired them with reluctance 36:5
Acquires: all perhaps which man a. 19:6
Acquist: new a. of true experience 351:7
Acre: an a. in Middlesex 325:24
for an a. of barren ground 479:17
the burial-ground God's A. 316:26
Acres: a few paternal a. 386:26
between the a. of the rye 428:31
lass that has a. o' charms 106:7
over whose a. walk'd 438:12
three a. and a cow 153:17
what mystic fruit his a. yield 199:8
Acrid: his a. words 251:9
Acrimonious and surly republican 278:4
Acroceraunian mountains 492:20
Act: a.—a. in the living Present 317:7
A. first, this Earth 537:39
a. of darkness 453:19
a. of fear 431:10
a...on that maxim 284:5
a. upon it, if you can 218:26
an A. of God was defined as.. 243:16
ancient nobility is the a. of time 26:42
any unproportion'd thought
  his a. 431:25
between the motion and the a. 197:11
commits some loving a. 423:25
did a., what now we moan 280:10
does both a. and know 332:26
drive..through the A. of Settlement 406:21
foolishest a. a wise man commits 86:34
I could a. as well as he 204:33
in a. more graceful 345:18
in doubt to a. or rest 383:22
last a. crowns the play 404:10
late a. of Parliament for securing the Church 2:16
live, and a., and serve the future
  hour 573:27
made honest by an a. of parliament 279:32
no..fun in any A. of Parliament 243:10
prologues to the swelling a. 456:23
same in thine own a. 457:11
sets it in a. and use 442:31
show in some fifth A. 537:39
sins they love to a. 474:6
sleep an a. or two 447:17
sow an a., and you reap a habit 406:6
strong upon the Regulations A. 569:7
think thou and a. 411:7
thyself shalt see the a. 465:11
time to a. them in 434:9
to do nought is..almost an a. 411:33
to see him [Kean] a. 153:5
ultimate conclusion in unmitigated a. 296:14
what a. that roars so loud 435:44
within the meaning of the A. 5:11
Acte: le dernier a. est sanglant 374:2
Acted: a. invariably from the
  highest principles 203:33
reasoned or a. consequentially 139:22
Acti: iucundi a. labores 145:4
Acting: a. of a dreadful thing 449:5
a...the lowest of the arts 356:6
danger chiefly lies in a. well 143:9
only..off he was a. 225:32
Action: a. is transitory 573:7
a. lies in his true nature 435:35
a., nor utterance 450:33
a...no stronger than a flower 487:13
an a., and not a thought 127:12
cold for a. 443:8
dearest a. in the tented field 469:45
do a good a. by stealth 307:28
do no sinful a. 3:17
every public a. which is not
  customary 157:10
imitate the a. of the tiger 443:24
in a. faithful, and in honour clear 385:6
in a. how like an angel 433:15
justice is truth in a. 180:21
liberty of a. 338:25
lose the name of a. 434:4
lust in a.; and till a., lust.. 488:11
makes that and th'a. fine 244:16

Action (cont.)
no less than a. and passion 125:31
spheres of a. 313:21
suit the a. to the word 434:16
Thought is the child of A. 182:41
with what courteous a. 432:1
youth, beauty, graceful a. 190:27
Actions: a. are a kind of words 200:29
a. in balance with my countrymen's 86:27
a. that a man might play 430:30
great a. are not always true sons 110:26
great a. speak great minds 38:3
in his a. be so ill 334:28
my a. are my ministers' 136:4
no other speaker of my living a. 447:11
one person doing interesting a. 28:29
only the a. of the just 501:6
poor centre of a man's a., himself 27:38
the best of all our a. tend 111:22
things and a. are what they are 109:37
when our a. do not, our fears do 460:16
Active: an a. Principle 574:25
more a.-valiant 440:28
out on a. service 294:18
step so a. 308:17
when all his a. powers are still 533:2
Activ'st: Love's passives are his a.
  part 165:27
Actor: after a well-grac'd a. 475:29
a moment yet the a. stops 543:6
anybody may see he is an a. 204:33
as an unperfect a. 486:20
fault and not the a. 461:27
like a dull a. now 429:18
manager, a., prompter, playwright.. 237:25
Actors: of what scene the a. 491:25
these our a...were all spirits 480:8
Actresses: white bosoms of your a. 270:10
Acts: a. his own creations 94:16
a. which Deity..doth ease its
  heart..in 286:9
all your a. are queens 485:27
familiar a. are beautiful through
  love 497:13
four first a...past 43:13
he who desires but a. not 77:10
his a. being seven ages 427:21
illustrious a. high raptures 558:3
little, nameless, unremembered
  a. 581:24
make..morality centre on forbidden a. 513:33
our a. our angels are 37:23
our own a...are mightier
  powers 15:11
with such a. fill a pen 189:8
Actum: nil a. credens 320:24
Acu: tetigisti a. 379:27
Acute: this study renders men a. 100:30
Adal sole daughter 113:21
Adage: like the poor cat i' the a. 457:11
Adair: all fled with thee, Robin A. 292:5
Adam: A. had 'em 5:4
A's ale 402:8
A. sat under the Tree 295:16
A. shall share with me 349:10
A., the first great benefactor 550:24
A., the goodliest man of men 347:13
A. was a gardener 296:33 (-297), 445:39
A. was but human 550:23
A. was not adamant 252:10
Aristotle..the rubbish of an A. 507:1
a second A. to the fight 364:7
as much as our father A. knew 295:17
brought them unto A. 44:15
child of A.'s stem 376:7
did in A. fail 364:8
grave man, nicknamed A. 146:16
hold up A.'s profession 437:5
in A. all die 67:8
old A. in this Child 390:57
old A.'s likeness 475:13
old A., the carrion crow 38:26
penalty of A. 426:29
son of A. and of Eve 401:28
the gardener A. 533:38
turned..A. from his fair spouse 347:25
when A. dalfe 235:7
when A. delved 11:18

Adam (cont.)
whilst A. slept 11:23
whipp'd the offending A. 443:5
young A. Cupid 477:12
Adamant: a frame of a. 279:5
that Adam was not a. 252:10
Adamantine chains and penal fire 344:7
Adazzle: sweet, sour; a., dim 255:3
Add: above our power to a. or
  detract 314:12
a. again years and years 184:7
a., Jenny kissed me 265:25(-266)
a. something more to this
  wonderful year 213:10
a. to golden numbers 170:21
if any..a. unto these things 72:11
Added: all..shall be a. unto you 58:14
wrote down all three dates..a.
  them up 129:28
Adder: bright day that brings
  forth the a. 449:2
stingeth like an a. 50:32
the deaf a. 395:20
Adders: what a. came 523:11
Addeth: Translation's thief that
  a. more 333:7
Adding: goes on a. one to one 91:41
Addington: Pitt is to A. 124:14
Addison: give his days and nights
  to..A. 278:9
weep if [A.] were he 385:29
what Cato did and A. approved 98:16
Addition: no a. nor my wish 472:19
Addled: yolk of an a. egg. 295:15
Address: wip'd with a little a. 162:8
Addressed: be they a. to what
  they may 273:31
Addresses..to conceal our whereabouts 414:15
Adepts in the speaking trade 143:3
Adequately: a. tall 140:8
knows that he speaks a. 200:33
Adeste, fideles 13:2
Adherence to the old and tried 314:7
Adieu: a., a., kind friends, a., a.,
  a. 10:21
a., a.! my native shore 113:6
a.! a! a! thy plaintive anthem fades 288:2
a. for evermore, My dear 106:18
a. for evermore, my love 419:9
a. my morning thoughts 156:12
a., she cries 216:1
a. 'twixt soul and body 412:15
bid you a welcome a. 559:32
bid your servant once a. 487:7
Joy..bidding a. 287:21
thou vain world, a. 124:18
Ad infinitum: lesser fleas, and so
  a. 358:14
so proceed a. 521:22
Adire: non cuivis..a. Corinthum 257:6
Adjunct: but an a. to ourself 455:21
rhyme being no necessary a. 343:26
Adjust: a., amend and heal 236:28
we never can a. it 104:8
Administered: whate'er is best a. 384:1
Administration: a criticism of a. 28:23
Admirable: how express and a. 433:15
Admiral: kill an a. from time to
  time 557:1
the a.'s flag sank 237:15
Admirals: a. all, for England's sake 362:31
a., extoll'd for standing still 162:19
Admiralty: if blood be the price of
  a. 301:24
Admirari: nil a. prope res est una 257:1
Admiration: as great in a. as herself 447:16
by a., hope, and love 574:19
by faith, by a., by sympathy 201:3
disease of a. 324:36
season your a. for a while 431:7
the a. only of weak minds 350:2
Admire: Do you a. the view? 130:18
fools a., but men of sense approve 382:33
for to a. an' for to see 296:22
I do a. of womankind but one 159:34
not to a. is all the art I know 116:19, 386:33
nought to a. 257:1

Admire (cont.)
one cannot possibly a. them 570:11
scarce begun to a. the one 194:10
Sydney, whom we yet a. 147:26
to a., we should not understand 155:15
where none a., 'tis useless to excel 322:5
willing to a. 254:11
Admired: all who understood a. 388:1
blush so to be a. 558:5
fair and a. 423:15
good things..are to be a. 25:16
needs only to be seen to be a. 159:30
that she might a. be 484:40
Admires: meanly a. mean things 542:7
men that all the world a. 330:25
Admit: a. me of thy crew 341:31
cannot a. absence 186:25
never to a. them in your sight 23:4
Admittance: no a. till the week after next 131:27
Admitting: too much easiness in a. 388:3
Admonish: fools they a. 164:34
Ado: much a. there was, God wot 80:7
the heathen make much a. 394:28
Adon: sweet A., darest not glance? 231:36
Adonais: blazoning the name of A. 493:18
I weep for A. 491:14
our A. has drunk poison 492:4
soul of A., like a star 492:16
what A. is, why fear we? 492:14
Adonis: 'an A. of fifty' 240:6
smooth A. from his native rock 344:32
this A...a corpulent man of fifty 266:6
Adopting Muses chose their sons 80:24
Adoption: children by a. and grace 389:26
Spirit of a. 65:53
their a. tried 431:25
Adorable: loving, a., softly to rest 365:5
Adoration: all a., duty, and observance 428:28
breathless with a. 577:1
for A. all the ranks 503:4
Adorations: Desires and A. 491:21
Adore: a. my gifts instead of me 244:27
a. our errors 425:2
all the Saints a. Thee 240:19
command where I a. 483:17
God and soldiers we alike a. 404:9
God and the doctor we alike a. 372:12
I positively a. Miss Dombey 175:16
I seek and a. them 81:9
in vain the saint a. 189:14
ye heavens a. Him 291:27
yet I love thee and a. 161:13
you too shall a. 486:3
Adored: a. by little statesman 319:10
in ev'ry clime a. 200:40
much-a...Fairy Prince 386:29
neglected then, a. become 336:21
Adores: a. as Margaret, Maude 164:30
Seraph that a. and burns 375:26
Adorn: a. a tale 383:20
nothing that he did not a. 279:6
old England to a. 273:19
Adorned: a. for her husband 303:5
when unadorned a. the most 71:44
Adornings: made their bends a. 546:19
Adorns and cheers our way 424:7
Adrianus: as the moles of A. 224:10
Adriatic: A. breaks in a warm bay 87:21
spouseless A. 15:14
Adsum: said, 'A.!', and fell back 114:3
me, me, a. qui feci 542:18
Adulescentiam: haec studia a. acuunt 555:7
Adullam: political Cave of A. 145:16
Adulterers: partaker with the a. 82:20
Adulteries: all the a. of art 395:5
Adulterous: evil and a. generation 280:7
Adultery: do not a. commit 59:16
men call gallantry, and gods a. 147:1
not quite a., but adulteration 115:19
thou shalt not commit a. 116:40
Advance: to a. 390:14
must retrograde if it does not a. 262:3
not to go back is somewhat to a. 217:14
see the couples a. 386:8
when we our sails a. 183:7
189:6

Advanced: if I a. one step 363:21
to have a. true friends 15:13
Advancement: what a. may I hope from thee? 434:24
Advances: a. us in the dignity of human beings 277:39
as civilization a., poetry declines 325:2
Advantage: a. rarely comes of it 147:1
calmness is great a. 244:2
for the mutual and general a. 144:2
nail'd for our a. 438:12
nature to a. dressed 382:27
private a. of the preacher 102:1
suck they no small a. 396:26
them as take a. that get a. 196:11
with equal a. content 124:6
Advantages: in hope of fair a. 463:39
remember with a. 444:28
Advent: as best such an a. becomes 117:46
Adventure: an awfully big a. 36:9
most beautiful a. in life 212:1
once more on my a. 95:18
Adventured: my ill a. youth 168:12
Adventures: a. are to the adventurous 181:34
all our a. were by the fire-side 227:17
bold and hard a. t'undertake 205:3
Adventuring: in thus a. to die 292:20
Adventurous and honourable youth 514:38
Adversary: agree with thine a. 57:46
mine a. had written a book 49:11
never..sees her a. 352:9
your a. the devil 70:6
Adversis perfugium ac solacium praebent 145:16
Adversité de nos meilleurs amis 407:14
Adversity: a. doth best discover virtue 25:21
a. is not without comforts 25:20
a. is the blessing of the New 25:18
a.'s sweet milk, philosophy 478:24
a hundred that will stand a. 126:30
bread of a. 53:41
cross'd with a. 484:38
fortunes sharp a. 138:35
good things that belong to a. 25:16
great men contending with a. 109:16
in the day of a. consider 51:13
old companions in a. 98:4
or any other a. 390:29
sweet are the uses of a. 426:30
Adversum: omnia te a. spectantia 256:20
Advertisement: promise..soul of an a. 277:35
Advice: a. is seldom welcome 139:16
can Love be controll'd by a.? 214:14
first syllable of valuable..a. 546:34
ghostly counsel and a. 390:32
in..religion and matrimony I never give any a. 139:32
to ask a. is..to tout for flattery 153:18
took tea and comfortable a. 290:7
woman seldom asks a. 2:29
Advices: lengthen'd sage a. 108:4
Advise: always to a. her wrong 520:55
whom none could a. 405:13
Adviser: than ever did th' a. 105:21
Advises: my old girl that a. 174:1
she thus a. thee 483:19
Advocate: our Mediator and A. 389:13
Aegean: among the A. isles 18:16
o'er the A. main Athens arose 495:27
Aeneae: dum domus A. Capitoli.. saxum accolet 555:8
Aeneas: decidimus quo pater A. 260:26
Dido and her A. shall want troops 425:22
when Dido found A. would not come 387:3
Aeneus: hic murus a. esto 256:18
Aeolian visitations 579:1
Aeon: lie down for an a. or two 303:19
Aequam memento..servare mentem 259:3
Aequor: cras ingens iterabimus a. 258:12
Aequum mi animum ipse parabo 257:11
Aequus: animus si te non deficit a. 257:4
Aer: estne Dei sedes nisi..a.? 320:26
Aere: exegi monumentum a. 260:15
Aery: holds an a. in its arms 93:15

Aes triplex circa pectus 258:5
Aeschylus: call forth thundering A. 281:14
sublime simplicity of A. 153:12
Aesculapius: we owe a cock to A. 506:10
Aeson: renew old A. 465:17
Aesthetic: apostle in the high a. band 220:28
shine in the high a. line 220:25
Aetas: a. parentum peior avis tulit 260:1
fugerit invida a. 258:17
ultima Cumaei venit iam carminis 555:30
Aetolian: through Europe to the A. shore 16:8
Aevi: et mihi vivam quod superest a. 257:11
Afar: a. and asunder 79:9
a. or nigh around 235:18
benefices twinkl'd from a. 192:28
cometh from a. 576:9
devotion to something a. 499:4
frightful and a. 142:11
peace to you which were a. off 67:51
Afeard: a. to be the same in thine own act 457:11
a soldier, and a.? 460:24
Affable: th' Archangel 348:24
that a. familiar ghost 487:21
Affair: an a. with the moon 512:17
Affairs: dismissed..from all further conduct of their a. 144:17
for the ordering your a., to sing them 485:27
office and a. of love 468:12
tide in the a. of men 451:29
tide in the a. of women 116:21
your a. suppose 487:7
Affect: angels a. us oft 184:4
study what you most a. 478:47
you wou'd a. a cruelty 156:4
Affectation: a. of a. 204:18
only by a. spoiled 521:24
sophistry and a. 28:13
so used to a. 201:31
spruce a. 455:29
Affected: love a. 219:1
most a., husband-hunting butterfly 353:6
Affecting: a. to seem unaffected 154:27
on the stage he was..a. 225:32
Affection: a. beaming in one eye 176:10
A.! thy intention stabs the centre 485:8
a. which grows from common names 101:10
fills a.'s eye 275:1
never heard of any true a. 338:14
preferment goes by letter and a. 469:24
rear of your a. 431:22
set your a. on things above 68:30
talk not of wasted a. 316:14
thy a. cannot hold the bent 483:4
to me-wards your a.'s strong 246:10
what unrequited a. is 175:17
when strong a. stirs her spirit up 507:31
with deep a., and recollection 402:20
Affectioned: kindly a. one to another 66:2
Affections: descend t' a. and to faculties 185:2
his a. dark as Erebus 465:20
his deep a. make him passionate 330:24
history of the a. 267:21
holiness of the heart's a. 289:17
old offences of a. new 488:5
our young a. run to waste 114:15
the a. gently lead us on 581:29
those first a. 576:18
unruly wills and a. 389:37
Affects to nod 191:1
Affinity: Table of Kindred and A. 401:15
Affirmations: accepting the a. of the soul 201:12
Afflict: a. the best 230:15
day for a man to a. his soul 54:35
what e'er a. the man 189:4
Afflicted: a., yet he opened not his mouth 54:26
any ways a., or distressed 389:17
Afflicting: most a. to a parent's mind 23:3

INDEX

Affliction: a. is enamour'd of thy
parts 478:22
a. of these terrible dreams 459:4
bread of a. 48:14
highlands of a. 511:7
in all their a. he was afflicted 55:7
in the furnace of a. 54:19
saveth in time of a. 56:30
such a light a. 362:8
try me with a. 472:34
whose fresh complexion..a. alters 485:33
a. sorted, anguish of all sizes 245:5
Afflictions: by partners..a. easier
grow 559:6
describing the a. of Job 25:19
happy issue out of all their a. 389:18
Afford: a. to it all that a soul can do 185:5
a. to keep a motor car 489:4
in London all that life can a. 273:23
where the parties could any way a. it 195:18
Affright: a. the air at Agincourt 443:4
bad a. 230:15
ghost there's none to a. thee 246:23
Affront: well-bred man will not a. me 159:15
Afghanistan: chips to..allies in A. 143:31
left on A.'s plains 304:4
Afire: midland furze a. 296:15
Afloat: 'I'm a., I'm a.' 311:4
on such a full sea..now a. 451:29
Afoot: a. and light-hearted 568:3
game's a. 443:27
mischief, thou art a. 451:1
Aforementioned: I..make the a. my last will 8:4
Afraid: a. for any terror by night 397:14
a. of being whipped 269:33
a. of that which is high 51:33
a. to come home in the dark 571:3
a. to look upon God 45:35
a. to think what I have done 458:14
almost a. to know itself 460:19
at..thy thunder they are a. 398:8
be not a., neither..dismayed 46:37
be not a. to do thine office 358:7
do what you are a. to do 200:19
I am devilishly a. 191:24
in short, I was a. 197:20
it is I; be not a. 59:36
many are a. of God 315:11
men not a. of God, a. of me 386:23
not so much a. of death 86:19
of whom..shall I be a.? 393:20
see all, nor be a. 95:13
so, I was a. 92:26
stranger and a. 263:35
they were sore a. 61:18
whereof our conscience is a. 389:45
whistling to keep..from being a. 191:25
yet a. of death 143:8
Afresh: let's kiss a. 246:28
Afric: A.'s sunny fountains 240:17
geographers, in A.-maps 521:18
heard on A.'s burning shore 406:19
sword in hand upon A.'s passes 143:3
thy breath is A.'s spicy gale 215:42
whom Biserta sent from A. shore 345:4
Africa: A. and golden joys 442:34
all A. and her prodigies in us 86:11
silent over A. 92:18
slog-slog-slog-sloggin' over A. 294:37
Africa: ex. A. semper aliquid novi 380:1
African: son of the old moon-mountains A. 288:29
After: a. dinner is a. dinner 519:29
a. many a summer 540:20
evil..lives a. them 450:17
man a. his own heart 47:13
to the gallows-foot—and a.! 302:18
After-dinner: as it were an a.'s sleep 462:5
government..framed..in a con-versations 546:41
in a. talk across the walnuts 537:3
Afternoon: in the a. of time 516:19
in which it seemed always a. 535:13
some green a. turns toward sun-set 525:1

Afternoon (cont.)
that July a. 375:14
the..multitude call the a. 455:27
After-silence on the shore 118:24
Afton: flow gently, sweet A. 105:29
Agag came unto him delicately 47:17
Again: A.! a.! and the havoc 122:5
a.—thou hearest 17:12
a. to the battle, Achaians 123:6
I do it a. and a. 128:28
I shall not pass this way a. 232:10
is it really you a.? 91:25
would you do it, please, a.? 228:6
Against: a. the wind 114:14
all argument is a. it 273:28
exclaim no more a. it 471:23
his hand..a. every man 44:49
not with me is a. me 59:11, 61:48
said he was a. it 156:24
who can be a. us? 65:57
Agam: ipse docet quid a. 371:29
Agamemnon: heroes lived before A. 261:2
sent to rouse up A. 85:21
when A. cried aloud 197:26
Agamemnona: vixere fortes ante A. 261:2
Aganippe: I never drank of A. well 502:2
Agas: quidquid a., prudenter a. 13:12
Agate: no bigger than an a.-stone 477:7
Age: a., ache, penury, and im-prisonment 462:10
a. and hunger 427:20
a. cannot wither her 424:9
a. fatal to Revolutionists 172:28
a. from folly could not give me freedom 423:35
a., I do abhor thee 486:3
a. is full of care 486:2
a. is grown so picked 437:13
a. of chivalry is gone 102:11
a. of chivalry is never past 294:16
a. of chivalry is past 182:46
A. of Machinery 125:28
a. shall not weary them 72:23
A...take the things Youth needed not 573:14
a. that melts 279:8
a., that will her pride deflower 509:33
a. too late, or cold 349:6
a. will not be defied 27:3
A., with stealing steps 552:15
an a. in her embraces past 407:18
an a. of ease 224:15
an a. of poverty 465:9
an a. of splendid discontent 355:12
arrogance of a. 103:11
as full of grief as a. 452:42
at your a. the hey-day 435:47
build from a. to a. 295:6
chooses Athens in his riper a. 193:25
common at your a. 40:21
complain of the a. we live in 101:33
crabbed a. and youth 486:2
damn the a. 307:22
days of our a. 397:16
decay of the whole a. 25:22
disgust this refined a. 202:15
do you think, at your a. 128:28
do your joys with a. diminish? 93:25
each a. is a dream 371:2
evening of my a. 412:7
fetch the a. of gold 343:18
fixed point in a changing a. 188:13
forehead of the a. to come 288:25
'gainst time and a. 377:4
grace this latter a. 440:28
green and smiling a. 514:38
hated, as their a. increases 515:24
hath not forgotten my a. 507:35
he is of a.: ask him 63:34
he is of no a. 153:14
his wealth a well-spent a. 123:25
in a. I bud again 244:18
in a good old a. 44:48, 48:34
in ev'ry a., in ev'ry clime 386:29
in mine a. have left me naked 447:1
in the flower of their a. 47:3
in the name of every a. 101:27
invention of a barbarous a. 343:26
in what stupid a. or nation 111:9
language of the a. 231:21
lash the a. 382:16

Age (cont.)
lead on our days to a. 451:35
let a. approve of youth 95:26
like the old a. 483:5
likely to be a manly man in thine a. 328:7
make the a. to come my own 158:14
mine a. is even as nothing 394:9
miracle of our a. 124:24
more fruit in their a. 397:21
my a. is as a lusty winter 426:37
never mellows with a. 267:19
not of an a. 281:16
now enjoys his a. 192:13
occupy a. with the dream of 93:1
of a 'certain a.' 116:22
Old A., and Experience 407:22
Old A. a regret 181:37
old a. has brought to me 512:9
old a. hath yet his honour 541:3
old a. of cards 384:37
old a., serene and bright 583:2
outworn buried a. 487:11
pays us but with a. and dust 405:12
prayers, which are a. his alms 377:4
prompt the a. to quit their clogs 351:18
see old a. 444:28
shame of a. 141:23
should accompany old a. 460:36
slow-consuming A. 230:29
some smack of a. 441:13
son of his old a. 45:12
soul of the A. 281:11
tell a woman's a. 221:40
that a. is best 247:10
that a. will perform the pro-mises of youth 278:14
this a. best pleaseth me 246:24
thou a. unbred 487:29(-488)
thro' every unborn a. 231:3
thy a., like ours 351:17
till a., or grief, or sickness 292:19
toys of a. 383:30
unhoped serene, that men call a. 83:19
unregarded a. in corners thrown 426:35
Vastness! and A.! 380:14
very a. and body of the time 434:18
vice and follies of the a. 134:6
virtuous in their old a. 387:1, 520:48
war, dearth, a., agues 185:14
well stricken in a. 44:50
what a. takes away 574:34
what man's a. is like to be 172:11
when a., disease, or sorrows strike him 146:32
when old a. crept over them 361:7
when the a. is in 469:2
woes that wait on a. 113:20
woman who tells one her real a. 570:16
wonder of our a. 232:15
world's great a. 493:25
worth an a. without a name 357:22
years hence..may dawn an a. 16:9
youth and a. in common—dis-content 19:7
Aged: allow this a. man his right 377:4
an a., a. man 131:22
an a. and a great wine 337:26
certainly a. 116:22
deliciously a. and sad 489:34
don't object to an a. parent 175:25
Paul the a. 69:5
slow growth in an a. bosom 379:4
what venerable..creatures did the a. seem 548:15
wiser than the a. 399:20
Agendum: dum quid superesset a. 320:24
Agent: interposition of some in-visible a. 265:6
Agents: night's black a. 459:8
Ages: a., and a. have fallen on me 172:4
a. elaps'd ere Homer's lamp ap-pear'd 162:20
a. of hopeless end 345:21
a secular bird, a. of lives 351:4
ask'd a. more 162:26
a thousand a. in Thy sight 562:9
aye, a. long ago 285:28
emptiness of a. in his fâce 329:19
heir of all the a. 534:35
his acts being seven a. 427:21

Ages (cont.)
in three distant a. born 193:9
mighty a. of eternity 127:33
my name..to..the next a. 28:15
our help in a. past 562:9
rages of the a. 236:6
rock of a. 548:11
thro' the a. one increasing purpose 534:29
to all succeeding a. curst 190:13
unborn a., crowd not on my soul 229:25
while unending a. run 361:14
Aggravate my voice 466:30
Aggravating: she was an a. child 41:14
Aggregate: large a. of little things 358:1
Aggression: secured against the menace of a. 21:6
Agib, Prince of Tartary 218:9
Agincourt: affright the air at A. 443:4
disgrace..the name of A. 444:10
Agios Athanatos 543:18
Agitation: electrical a. in the mind 337:2
A-gley: gang aft. a. 107:11
Agmine facto 556:23
Agnes: St. A.' Eve 285:12
Agnostic: invented..the appropriate title of 'a.' 266:25
Agnus: in quo et a. ambulet 232:7
Agog to dash through thick and thin 159:36
Agonies: exultations, a., and love 582:4
Agony: a. and bloody sweat 388:50
a. is abated 326:10
a...of the heathen past 310:20
exceeding bitter a. 506:19
intense the a. 83:13
my soul in a. 149:20
only a., and that has ending 84:18
sea of Life and A. 495:5
some strong swimmer in his a. 115:30
waters of wide A. 494:23
Agree: a. on the stage 499:30
a. with thine adversary 57:46
all joys so well a. 502:7
birds in their..nests a. 41:35, 561:27
care, you and I shall never a. 5:19
if that a. which I intend 245:11
let Whig and Tory a' a. 502:22
so many men a. to be of one mind 25:8
sugar and saltness a. 225:25
the more we didn't a. 125:21
this busy world and I shall ne'er a. 158:12
verbs and nouns do more a. 238:30
when people a. with me 569:32
with her would not a. 584:11
Agreeable: a. wakings 156:12
in most men's power to be a. 520:41
is the old min a.? 177:27
light, a., polished style 240:6
my idea of an a. person 182:22
Agreed: except they be a. 55:54
Agreeing: for not a. with me 86:3
Agreement: an a. with hell 213:19
with hell are we at a. 53:34
Agrees: a person who a. with me 182:22
how a. the devil and thee 438:26
with truth it quite a. 220:9
Agrestis: deos qui novit a. 556:18
Agri: modus a. non ita magnus 261:24
Agricolas: o fortunatos nimium..a.! 556:15
Agricultural: chips to the a. labourer 143:31
Agriculture: all taxes must..fall upon a. 217:9
Agrippa: I think myself happy, king A. 65:21
tall A. lived close by 250:1
Agua: a. que ahuyenta la sed 134:18
Ague-proof: I am not a. 454:6
Agues: war, dearth, age, a. 185:14
Agunt: quidquid a. homines 282:25
Ahab: ran before A. 48:6
Ahead: far, far a. 147:13
Aid: all fear, none a. you 384:11
apt Alliteration's artful a. 143:14
fate and metaphysical a. 457:2
foreign a. of ornament 546:19
from whence doth come mine a. 421:4

Aid (cont.)
God of Battles, a.! 297:8
hood-wink'd boy I call'd in a. 213:15
lend us Thine a. 240:15
saints will a. 150:23
their a. they yield to all 164:34
to fainting squadrons..a. 1:10
without our a. He did us make 292:7
Aide-toi, le ciel t'aidera 209:10
Ail: what can a. thee, Knight at arms 286:28
Ailed: what a. us, O gods, to desert you 523:3
Ailments: our a. are the same 519:24
Ailsa Craig: Meg was deaf as A. 105:14
Aim: a. a little above it 316:11
a. not to be great 322:4
great a. of culture 19:24
not make thoughts your a. 297:10
our being's end and a. 384:2
prophesy, with a near a. 442:6
shoots xiphias to his a. 503:5
Aimais: dire pourquoi je l'a. 354:21
Aimeth: who a. at the sky 244:3
Aimez: a. qui vous aime 557:9
Aiming: a. at a million 91:41
a. at the bless'd abodes 383:13
Aimless: nothing walks with a. feet 532:32
Aims: a. but at a bush 501:18
other a...had learned to prize 224:18
other a. than my delight 236:16
secret a. of nature 80:26
Ain't: as it isn't it a. 130:8
know so much that a. so 491:10
no you a. 311:4
Air: a., a charter'd libertine 443:7
a. and Angels' purity 184:5
a. bites shrewdly 431:30
a. broke into a mist 94:29
a. goes by in a wind 39:3
a. is cut away before 150:1
a. is delicate 457:6
a. nimbly..recommends itself 457:6
a. of the court 201:31
a. and harmony of shape 401:32
a. of the enchanted island 337:35
a. signed with their honour 509:2
a...too pure for slaves 237:27
all the a. a solemn stillness holds 229:28
all the a. is thy diocese 184:26
amaze the scented a. 82:4
as the a., invulnerable 430:17
babbling gossip of the a. 482:22
beateth a. 66:37
Being that is in the clouds and a. 575:13
blue regions of the a. 75:18
bounded by the vaporous a. 495:1
breathe his native a. 386:26
breathing English a. 84:21
build that dome in a. 151:33(-152)
castles..built with a. 280:6
chameleons feed on light and a. 493:16
common liberty of earth and a. 511:10
common sun, the a., the skies 231:5
dance upon the a. 569:5
diet, humour, a., anything 86:25
diviner a. 577:13
draws a moment's a. 156:11
empty, vast and wandering air 476:15
every flower enjoys the a. 581:9
fainting a. 497:26
fairer than the evening a. 330:6
fill the sea and a. 149:34
filled the a. with..dissonance 340:26
gather my skirts up in the a. 80:16
Germans that of the a. 407:1
gold a. and the silver 411:4
graceful a. and heavenly mug 208:29
growing strength in the a. 143:40
happy good-night a. 235:18
her fair and floral a. 208:5
her keel ploughs a. 135:19
his human a. 90:27
horse of a. 12:2
hurtles in the darkened a. 230:14
I eat the a., promise-crammed 435:2
if their lungs receive our a. 162:42
independent a. 217:23
in happier a. wandering 18:31(-19)

Air (cont.)
in that heavenly a. 81:18
in the smokeless a. 582:14
into my heart an a. that kills 263:14
I see him forming in the a. 407:8
I smell the Sussex a. 42:5
leave their little lives in a. 386:32
lines and outward a. 281:1
live in the a. 182:19
living a. 582:1
lowly a. of Seven Dials 219:2
make the cold a. fire 497:9
melted into a., into thin a. 480:8
mock our eyes with a. 425:19
mock the a. with idle state 229:20
moon..washes all the a. 466:37
most excellent canopy, the a. 433:15
mouthful of a. 584:16
nipping and an eager a. 431:30
no stir of a. was there 286:3
nothing to breathe but a. 292:15
now a. is hush'd 153:24
only to kiss that a. 247:8
parching a. burns frore 345:31
pibroch shake the a. 23:18
playing in the wanton a. 455:17
powers that will work for thee; a., earth 582:4
purg'd the a. of pestilence 481:31
quiet and still a. of..studies 352:23
sightless couriers of the a. 457:9
stirring thrills the a. 236:6
sweet a. blow soft 248:5
sweet as Eden is the a. 336:47
sweet as English a. could make her 538:8
take into the a. my quiet breath 287:32
through the fog and filthy a. 456:3
through the trembling a. 510:19
to a. the ditty 264:3
trifles light as a. 471:42
up to the ends of a. 80:30
viewless forms of a. 417:7
vomit forth into the a. 330:9
walking in an a. of glory 552:9
wan soul in that golden a. 411:21
waste..on the desert a. 230:5
way of an eagle in the a. 50:56
what is..honour? A. 440:30
when the a. is calm 352:29
where a. might wash me 524:23
wild a., world-mothering a. 254:17
wind-besomed chambers of the a. 544:7
Winter slumbering in the open a. 152:17
with its sweet a. 479:29
with pinions skim the a. 211:25
Air-bell: exhausted a. of the Critic 90:30
Air-borne: every a. particle 268:12
Air-drawn dagger 459:16
Airly Beacon, Airly Beacon 293:3
Airs: a. from heaven or blasts from hell 431:32
all places, all a...one country 86:28
Angels sing..their a. divine 158:4
discords make the sweetest a. 111:10
don't give yourself a. 128:29
fresher a. to flashes blent 375:10
how many saucy a. we meet 215:27
light a. and recollected terms 483:1
martial a. of England 563:5
melting a., or martial 163:48
refreshing a. of liberty 102:38
sing it with such a. 584:4
soft Lydian a. 342:7
sounds and sweet a. 480:5
thy Naiad a. 380:17
wandering a. they faint 494:7
Airt: my plaidie to the angry a. 107:24
Airth: bestow on every a. a limb 355:21
Airts: a' the a. the wind can blaw 107:17
Airy: a., fairy Lilian 534:12
a. hopes my children 574:16
a. subtleties in religion 86:7
execute their a. purposes 344:30
gives to a. nothing 407:24
gulls in an a. morrice 241:30
reveries so a. 163:11
up the a. mountain 4:18
were it ever so a. a tread 536:15

Aisle: long-drawn a. 230:2
Aisles: groined the a. of Christian Rome 199:23
  monastic a. fall like sweet strains 199:21
Aiver: a ragged cowt..mak a noble a. 105:12
Ajalon: Moon, in the valley of A. 46:42
Ajax: 'Thersites' body is as good as A.' 429:40
  when A. strives 382:32
Akond of Swat 312:13
Alabaster: an a. box 60:35
  his grandsire cut in a. 462:32
  smooth as monumental a. 473:11
Alacrity in sinking 466:9
Alarm: glorious the trumpet and a. 503:6
  her voice..might give th' a. 566:19
  in a state of wild a. 220:7
  love sounds the a. 214:10
Alarms: confused a. of struggle 15:8
  dwell in the midst of a 164:22
  used to war's a. 252:29
  what were the world's a. 584:23
Alarum: the wild a. clashed 322:21
Alarum'd by his sentinel, the wolf 458:1
Alarums: our stern a. change to merry meetings 476:3
Alas: a., a., for England 140:24
  a., and well a day 9:9
  most mournful, 'A., alack!' 170:25
Albatross: he thought he saw an A. 128:19
  I shot the A. 149:1
  the A. did follow 148:28
Albu: gallant A. fell 42:11
Alcestis: brought to me like A. 351:24
Alchemy: gilding..with heavenly a. 486:27
  happy a. of mind 231:31
  his countenance, like richest a. 449:1
Alciphron: was it A. once 523:4
Alcmena's nights 87:11
Alcoran: rather believe..the A. 25:23
Alcove: Cliveden's proud a. 385:1
Aldebaran and Betelgueux shone 236:38
Alderman: on the forefinger of an a. 477:7
Aldermanic: many an Aldermanic nose 34:2
Aldershot: penny-fights an' A. it 297:1
Aldgate-Street: from Temple-bar to A. 215:27
Aldiborontiphoscophornio! 125:12
Aldrich: *thicksides* and *hairy* A. 146:22
Ale: Adam's a. 402:8
  as tinkers do a. 109:22
  Christmas broached the mightiest a. 418:24
  drink your a. 263:32
  eat my a., drank my a. 203:5
  England talked of a. 141:25
  feasts where a. was strongest 318:7
  fed purely upon a. 203:5
  for a continuance..prefer mild ale 518:33
  God send thee good a. 516:21(-517)
  good a., the..drink of Englishmen 78:28
  jolly good a. and old 516:21(-517)
  no more cakes and a. 482:32
  ordered a glass of this a.— *would* order it 174:18
  pot of a., and safety 443:28
  quart of a. is a dish for a king 485:16
  sees bliss in a. 164:33
  sleep upon a. 203:5
  sons of a. and brede 583:26
  Spanish a. shall give you hope 329:1
  speaketh against a., that is good a. 78:28
  spicy, nut-brown a. 342:4
  take the size of pots of a. 110:10
Alea: *iacta a. est* 120:14
Alehouse: make fools laugh i' the a. 470:28
Aleppo: her husband's to A. gone 456:10
  in A. once 474:2
Alexander: A. at the head of the world 558:9
  A.'s Ragtime Band 43:16
  A. the coppersmith 69:3

Alexander (*cont.*)
  but A. women 313:2
  I am A. 455:31
  second A. the Great 327:15
  she's gane, like A. 104:25
  some talk of A. 9:24
  when A. our king was dead 583:26
  where A.'s ashes lay 33:12
Alexanders: like so many A. 443:25
Alexandra: sea-king's daughter.. A. 541:18
Alexandrine: a needless A. 382:31
Alexim: *Corydon ardebat A.* 555:20
Alfred: truth-teller..our England's A. 537:24
  when A. came to Athelney 140:12
Algebra: tell what hour..by a. 110:10
Alget: *probitas laudatur et a.* 282:23
Algido: *duris ut ilex..in A.* 260:21
Algiers: dying in A. 365:21
Alhama: woe is me, A.! 112:29
Alibi: if your governor don't prove a a. 179:8
  vy worn't there a a.! 179:17
Alice: Alice, where art thou? 98:20
  children of A. 306:7
  Christopher Robin went down with A. 339:14
  fair hair and fairer eyes of A. W..n 306:15
  remember sweet A. 201:24
Alienate: no difference..a. Cicero 325:23
Alieni appetens 415:1
Alights: brisk a. on the warm hearth 546:26
Alike: all places were a. to him 304:21
  among so many..faces..none a. 86:29
  each a. was Greek, a. was free 524:7
  like the sun, they shine on all a. 385:11
  none go just a. 382:19
Aliptes: *rhetor geometres pictor a.* 283:3
Aliquid: *tu solebas meas esse a. putare nugas* 132:10
Aliter: *dis a. visum* 554:10
Alive: a. after all this satire 274:22
  a., and so bold, O earth? 495:6
  a. for evermore 70:28
  all 'ot sand an' ginger when a. 296:24
  all the playthings come a. 515:17
  art a. still, while thy book doth live 281:11
  bliss was it in that dawn to be a. 575:2
  cockles and mussels! a., a., oh! 7:8
  he is no longer a. 42:25
  if..a. I shall be delighted to see him 250:24
  in Christ shall all be made a. 67:8
  living which are yet a. 51:4
  more a. to tenderness 575:7
  my son was dead, and is a. again 62:16
  officiously to keep a. 146:35
  she's a., she is not dead 29:24(-30)
  show that one's a. 104:2
  since Chaucer was a. and hale 308:17
  so abject—yet a. 118:19
  such a noise and tumult when a. 196:3
  who was a. and is dead 6:20
  when neither are a. 429:40
All: a., are gone 308:1
  a. along, down along 33:1
  a. are divine 15:16
  a. are needed by each one 199:9
  a., except their sun, is set 115:43
  a. for love 509:32, 173:3
  A. For Love 191:14
  a. for one, one for a. 194:33
  a. goes if courage goes 36:4
  a. I can give you I give 524:33
  a.! I know not what ye call a. 439:19
  a. is Caesar's 166:14
  a. is done that men can do 106:17
  a. is not lost 344:10
  a. is not well 431:18
  a. is well 533:28
  a. men everywhere..free 314:3
  a. my pretty ones? 460:21
  a. of Him we have in thee 165:31
  a., save..man, is divine 113:2
  a. shall be well 467:12
  a. shall die 442:7
  a. shall equal be 218:22

All (*cont.*)
  a.'s love, yet a.'s law 96:22
  a.'s to no end 373:13
  a. that a man hath 48:41
  a. that ever went with evening dress 301:22
  a. that he wrote 239:11
  a. that in them is 390:11
  a. that is, at a., lasts ever 95:22
  a. that's beautiful 585:10
  a. that they can say 147:13
  a. that thou hast done for me 106:28
  a. that we see or seem 380:16
  a. the world and his wife 520:30
  a. things bright and beautiful 3:14
  a. things through Christ 68:28
  a. things were made by him 62:59
  a. this and heaven too 242:11
  a. this for a song? 103:31
  a. to heaven 279:21
  a. was lost 349:15
  a. were for the state 323:21
  a. were his 115:45
  beareth a. things, believeth a. things 66:45
  bed-time, Hal, and a. well 440:29
  by a. the eagle in thee, a. the dove 165:23
  Christ is a. and in a. 68:31
  Christ is a. in a. 354:12
  consorts and sympathiseth with a. things 86:25
  do a. things well 143:11
  fool a. the people a. of the time 314:14
  for a. time 281:16
  for a. we have and are 296:19
  goodbye to a. that 229:17
  having nothing, yet hath a. 583:11
  his a. neglected 270:16
  I am made a. things to a. men 66:35
  if a. alas! were well at home 142:31
  if yet I have not a. thy love 185:33
  I like the jads for a. that 106:23
  in a. things Thee to see 244:15
  in London..a. that life can afford 273:23
  is this the mighty ocean? is this a.? 308:29
  I suppose you have a. there is 201:20
  judgments..on a. things a. day long 531:16
  let 'em a. come 305:3
  like Caesar's wife, a. things to a. men 8:6
  man's a man for a. that 105:31
  more than a. in heaven 115:6
  my soul, my life, my a. 562:19
  nature..to me was a. in a. 581:26
  nothing brings me a. things 480:30
  Old Uncle Tom Cobbleigh and a. 33:1
  on our meat, and on us a. 247:15
  praising a. alike 215:17
  satire, being levelled at a. 520:35
  see a., nor be afraid 95:13
  so are they a., a. honourable men 450:18
  take him for a. in a. 431:6
  that A., which always is A. 185:9
  that's how it a. began 298:24
  the Lord God made them a. 3:14
  Thou art over a. 301:29
  thou to me art a. things 349:30
  'tis a. thou art 381:36
  'twill all be well 207:19
  we must a. come to it 179:33
  where it cometh, a. things are 199:1
Allah: A. created the English mad 298:2
  A. is great, no doubt. 146:11
  A. who gave me two..sides to my head 303:10
Allay: glowing axle doth a. 340:4
Allaying: a. both their fury, and my passion 479:29
  with no a. Thames 319:5
All-corroding: the a., all-dissolving scepticism 363:24
Allegiance: religious a. 28:21
  swore to him a. 7:11
  to hell, a.! 436:28
Allegorical: all the a. paintings.. in the world 277:2

Allegory: a man's life..is a continual a.   290:17
as headstrong as an a.   500:21
Shakespeare led a life of a.   290:18
which things are an a.   67:43
Alleluia: to Father, Son, and Holy Ghost, A.!   264:10
Allemand à mon cheval   136:13
Allen: for love of Barbara A.   30:1
humble A., with an awkward shame   386:20
All-enacting Might   236:16
Alley: each a. has a brother   385:3
she lives in our a.   125:17
through an a. Titanic   381:2
thro' every hollow cave and alley lone   535:18
Alleys: vilest a. of London   187:17
Allez-vous-en la voir   354:2
All-hail: greater than both, by the a.   457:4
All-hallown: farewell, A. summer   438:28
Alliance: a Commercial A. with England   43:11
steer clear of permanent a.   560:29
Alliances: entangling a. with none   268:21
Allied: to that..which is divine they were a.   18:19
Allies: chips to the faithful a.   143:31
thou hast great a.   582:4
All-in-all: intellectual A.   578:30
Alliteration: apt A.'s artful aid   143:14
Allowance: a. for their doubting   297:10
makes the smallest a. for ignorance   266:20
Pension: An a...without an equivalent   277:31
Allowed..a part in making these days memorable   144:7
All-shattering guns   188:32
All-softening..knell   116:18
Allsopp: O Hodgson, Guinness, A., Bass!   120:23
All-terrible: God the A.   142:26
Allume: il a. le grand   109:34
Allur'd to brighter worlds   224:21
All-urging: the a. Will   236:5
Alluring: batteries of a. sense   332:7
nothing is more a. than a levée   156:9
Almack: go to Carlisle's, and to A.'s too   13:17
Alma Mater all dissolved in port   381:23
Almanac: eclipse..not in the A.   508:1
pious fraud of the a.   320:16
useful as an a. out of date   559:9
Almanacs: greater storms..than a. can report   423:26
Almighty: A.! ever-present Deity!   83:8
arrow from the A.'s bow   75:6
as thy Love is discovered a., a. be proved   96:24
God A.'s gentlemen   190:26
held the patent..from A. God   105:16
Hey for God A.!   292:10
Holy, Holy, Holy! Lord God A.!   240:19
pleased th' A.'s Orders to perform   1:11
the A. scattered kings for their sake   396:7
the A.'s form glasses itself in tempests   114:30
Almond: the a.-tree shall flourish   51:33
Almost: a. inevitable Consequences   304:44
both a., and altogether such as I am   65:27
Alms: a. for oblivion   481:17
a. of thy superfluous praise   189:19
prayer, patience, a., vows   255:6
prayers, which are age his a.   377:4
so give a.   485:27
when thou doest a.   58:2
who gives himself with his a.   320:18
Alms-basket of words   455:26
Almsman: gay apparel for an a.'s gown   475:10
Aloe: olive, a., and maize   528:23
stripes of labdanum and a.-balls   94:18
Aloft: among the river sallows, borne a.   284:14

Aloft (*cont.*)
man looks a.   194:25
now he's gone a.   173:11
Providence sits up a.   173:7
sailor-boys were all up a.   9:3
Alone: all a. went she   293:22
all we ask is to be let a.   169:26
a., a banished man   31:16
a., a., all all a.   149:20
a., and in a land of sand   530:28
a. and palely loitering   286:28
a. and warming his five wits   540:14
a. dwell for ever the kings of the sea   16:1
a. I did it   429:23
a. on a wide wide sea   149:20, 150:14
a. on earth, as I am now   113:20
a. the sun arises and a...the great streams   16:14
a. when he falleth   56:34
a. wi' God an'..my engines   299:4
a. withouten any company   137:34
am I a.?   220:24
bewilder'd, and a.   188:31
blindfold and a.   296:6
born unto himself a.   404:11
brave Horatius stand a.   323:25
Britain would fight on a.   144:9
canker, and the grief are mine a.   118:26
dangerous to meet it a.   565:24
hast been, shalt be, art, a.   16:15
heart that lives a.   578:16
I am here at the gate a.   536:9
I cannot play a.   241:7
I feel I am a.   309:1
I leave my love a.   487:14
I seem forsaken and a.   161:17
ill fortune seldom comes a.   192:7
leave them a., and they'll come home   367:14
leave us a.   374:21
left him a. with his glory   572:14
let her a., she will court you   280:22
let us a..Time driveth onward   535:17
live in Paradise a.   332:22
lives not a., nor for itself   74:3
most unfit to be a.   154:26
musing there an hour a.   115:44
never..appear the Immortals.. a.   152:16
never less a. than when a.   145:9, 408:7
not a., while thou visit'st my slumbers   348:23
nothing is fair or good a.   199:9
one who treads a.   357:14
read to thyself a.   82:11
that the man should be a.   44:14
through strange seas of thought a.   579:19
travels the fastest who travels a.   304:2
trodden the winepress a.   55:6
we are left, or shall be left, a.   578:14
we perish'd, each a.   159:3
were we long a.?   15:26
wherefore thou a.?   347:33
who can enjoy a.?   348:34
wild dog, and a.   327:2
you and I must bide a.   32:14
you and I were a.   319:8
Along: all a., down a., out a., A.   33:1
Aloof: a. from the entire point   452:12
day and night, a.   493:14
they stood a.   150:27
with a crafty madness, keeps a.   434:2
Aloud: vaunting a., but racked   344:15
Alp: many a frozen, many a fiery A.   346:2
Alpes: saevas curre per A.   283:21
Alph, the sacred river   151:32
Alpha: I am A. and Omega   70:22
Alphabet: got to the end of the a.   178:42
Alpheus: return, A., the dread voice is past   342:30
Alpine: breeze of A. heights   308:17
Clan A.'s warriors true   416:25
scattered on the A. mountains cold   351:20
streams along the A. height   114:6
through an A. village passed   316:17

Alps: A. on A. arise   382:23
A. shaping like a backbone   235:22
fading a. and archipelagoes   3:12
Johnson hewed passages through the A.   154:13
Alraschid: golden prime of good Haroun A.   539:15
Altar: a...to the unknown God   64:60
not gold, not blood, their a. dowers   493:27
one nearer to God's A.   166:13
self-slain on his own strange a.   523:16
so I will go to thine a.   393:18
thy sad floor an a.   114:34
to what green a.   287:12
whiles she before the a. stands   509:13
young bullocks upon thine a.   395:11
Altars: even thy a., O Lord of hosts   397:5
Altar-stairs: the great world's a.   532:36
Alter: not a. in my faith of him   279:32
Alteram: audi partem a.   22:2
Alteration: alters when it a. finds   488:7
do what thou canst for a.   262:5
Altered: revolving in his a. soul   191:8
things have a. in the building trade   303:7
Alternate Night and Day   205:29, 30
Alternative: an unhappy a.   22:33
Alters: a. when it alteration finds   488:7
love a. not   488:7
Althea: my divine A. brings   319:4
Altitudo: pursue my reason to an O a.!   86:8
Altogether: almost, and a. such as I am   65:27
charm of Caelia a.   566:19
Altrui: lo scendere e il salir per l'a. scale   169:1
Always: a. I am Caesar   448:27
poor a. ye have with you   63:44
remain with you a.   390:49
there'll a. be an England   373:15
Am: by the grace of God I a. what I a.   67:5
I a. not what I am   469:28
I a. that I a.   45:37
I think, therefore I a.   172:26
presume not that I a. the thing I was   442:39
since I a. not what I was   401:36
speak of me as I a.   474:2
tell them I a., Jehova said   503:3
Ama et fac quod vis   22:3
Amabam: nondum a.   21:17
Amalek: that moment A. prevailed   161:16
Amalfi: beyond Sorrento and A.   308:17
Amalgamation: Heaven and Hell A. Society   127:31
Amans amare   21:17
Amantem: quis fallere possit a.?   554:18
Amara: mount A.,..true Paradise   347:9
Amaracus: violet, a., and asphodel   537:31
Amaranth: like fields of a. lie   171:1
no fields of a. on this side of the grave   309:13
Amaranthine: only a. flower.. virtue   163:15
Amaranths grown beneath God's eye   96:31
Amaranthus: bid a. all his beauty shed   342:31(–343)
Amare: et a. amabam   21:17
Amari: de fonte..surgit a. aliquid   321:2
Amaryllida: formosam resonare doces A. silvas   555:15
Amaryllis: sport with A. in the shade   342:20
Amas de fleurs étrangères   355:6
Amateur: a little a. painting   514:26
'eavy-sterned a. old men   302:5
Amateurs: hell is full of musical a. nation of a.   490:20
409:9
Amatory poets sing their loves   116:14
Amavi: sero te a., pulchritudo   21:22
Amavit: plus quam se atque suos a. omnes   133:5
Amaze: a. the scented air   82:4
a...the very faculties of eyes and ears   433:32
how vainly men themselves a.   332:13

INDEX

Amaze (cont.)
stars with deep a.   343:14
startle or a. it with itself   289:25
ye gods, it doth a. me   448:21
Amazed: a. the gazing rustics   225:2
silent and a...a little boy   566:21
wise, a., temperate, and furious   458:25
Amazing: love so a., so Divine   562:19
orb! you're quite a.   311:20
whose presence of mind was a.   311:5
Amazon: I've never sailed the A.   297:23
tall as A.   287:4
Ambassador: A. from Britain's crown   188:30
an a. is...sent to lie abroad   583:15
Ambassadors: Parliament is not a *congress* of a.   100:14
sent a. to Louis XIV   274:9
Amber: a. scent of odorous perfume   350:31
a. torrent descended   146:17
ceiling of a.   16:1
in a. to observe the forms   385:27
lutes of a.   247:14
preserved for ever in a.   27:47
those a. locks to grey   189:10
Amber-dropping: thy a. hair   341:3
Ambergris: proclaim the a. on shore   332:3
Amberley: a good brew in A. too   42:12
Ambiguous: this a. earth   338:4
Ambition: a. can creep as well as soar   103:17
A., Distraction, Uglification and Derision   129:20
a. first sprung from your bless'd abodes   381:33
a. had..only suspended..religion   103:4
a., in a private man a vice   334:17
a.'s debt is paid   449:32
a. should be made of sterner stuff   450:20
a., the soldier's virtue   424:20
a. thick-sighted   284:18
art not without a.   457:1
fill th' a. of a private man   163:1
fling away a.   446:30
I hold a. of so airy..a quality   433:13
ill-weav'd a.   440:38
let not a. mock their useful toil   230:1
love..not with a. join'd   156:8
low a., and the pride of kings   383:7
low a. and the thirst of praise   162:27
lowliness is young a.'s ladder   449:3
most pitiful a.   434:22
pride, cruelty, and a. of man   405:13
thriftless a., that wilt ravin up   458:29
to reign is worth a.   344:23
vaulting a., which o'erleaps itself   457:9
virtue in a. is violent   26:27
wars that make a. virtue   472:3
who doth a. shun   427:9
your heart's supreme a.   322:3
Ambitions: whereby swollen a. dwindle   90:39
Ambitious: a., and..picturesque liar   550:22
as he was a., I slew him   450:15
Brutus says he was a.   450:19
proud, revengeful, a.   434:9
sacred hunger of a. minds   510:7
very substance of the a.   433:13
Amble: teach an old horse a. true   510:2
Ambled: the ambling king, he a.   440:8
Ambles: who Time a. withal   428:9
Ambo: *Arcades a.*   556:3
'Arcades a.'..blackguards both   116:11
Amboss oder *Hammer sein*   223:23
Ambree: foremost in battle was Mary A.   31:14
Ambrosial: dropt in a. oils   341:2
Ambuscadoes: breaches, a., Spanish blades   477:7
Âme: il faut une â. de même   354:25
les grands n'ont point d'â.   97:33
Amelia: A. was praying for George the author of 'A.'   542:37, 78:20
Amem: tecum vivere a.   260:4
Amemus: Vivamus, mea Lesbia, atque a.   132:15

Amen: A., so be it   391:11
A.: so let it be   355:9
'A.' stuck in my throat   458:9
glorious the catholic a.   503:6
sound of a great A.   402:12
still cry 'A.'   487:19
will no man say, a.?   475:18
Amend: adjust, a., and heal   236:28
Amended: a. his former naughty life   390:2
corrected and a. by its Author   211:21
Amends: a. for all the long years   356:10
sin that a. is but patched   482:13
America: A.! A.!   36:23
A. is a country of young men   201:17
A is God's Crucible   587:18
A. is..ourselves with the Barbarians..left out   19:23
A. is the only idealistic nation   571:16
A., thou half-brother of the world   29:10
A. was thus clearly top nation   422:17
bad Americans..go to A.   570:13
business of A. is business   156:25
huntsmen are up in A.   85:21
I rejoice that A. has resisted   379:3
my A.! my new-found-land   184:23
north and south A.   543:10
nothing less..than *whole A.*   100:27
wake up, A.   213:6
when we think of thee, O A.!   558:26
you cannot conquer A.   379:9
young man, there is A.   100:22
youth of A. is their oldest tradition   570:14
American: God is making the A.   587:18
I am A. bred   339:7
ideal A...is all wrong   142:18
if I were an A.   379:8
I was born an A.   563:8
love all mankind, *except an A.*   274:3
not a Virginian, but an A.   242:17
subtleties of the A. joke   550:17
th' A. nation in th' Sixth Ward   195:9
report all heroism from an A. point of view   568:6
thank God, I..am an A.   563:6
Americanism: fifty-fifty A.   409:4
Americans: A. and nothing else   409:4
A. have taken umbrage   403:19
[Carlyle] was probably fond of [the A.]   550:21
good A...go to Paris   14:1, 570:13
hyphenated A.   409:7
join in hand brave A. all   180:5
none but A. on guard tonight   560:32
nothing the matter with A. except their ideals   142:18
Parliament has no right to tax the A.   388:2
Amet: cras a. qui nunquam amavit   13:5
Amethyst: last an a.   87:36
the twelfth, an a.   72:1
Ami: n'oserez-vous, mon bel a.?   231:36
Amiability: gained in a. what he has lost in holiness   111:35
Amiable: a. weakness   204:29, 500:43
fruit..hung a.   347:5
jelofer a.   502:19
high thought, and a. words   530:14
holy, divine, good, a., or sweet   349:17
how a. are thy dwellings   397:5
more delighted with anything that is a.   154:37
Amiably-disposed young man   179:23
Amica: magis a. veritas   14:19
tacitae per a. silentia lunae   554:4
Amicablest: on the a. terms   179:34
Amicably: a. if they can   404:24
Amice: with pilgrim steps in a. grey   350:15
Amicus Plato, sed magis amica veritas   14:19
Amiral: tuer de temps en temps un a.   557:1
Amis: dans l'adversité de nos meilleurs a.   407:14
nos a., les ennemis   43:10
Amiss: all is a.   35:21
mark what is done a.   399:39
never anything can be a.   467:27
never choose a.   464:3

Amiss (cont.)
nothing comes a., so money comes a.   479:1
nothing shall come a.   98:15
skill not spent a.   80:18
what's a. I'll try to mend   562:6
Amissi: not a. but praemissi   242:19
Ammiral: mast of some great a.   344:24
Ammunition: praise the Lord and pass the a.   210:6
Amo: a., amas, I love a lass   370:5
non a. te, Sabidi   331:24
odi et a.   133:18
Among: a. the English Poets   290:11
a. them but not of them   113:51
a. you as he that serveth   62:44
Amongst you and remain with you   390:49
Amor: cedet a. rebus   372:3
l'a. che muove il sole   169:2
nunc scio quid sit A.   556:5
omnia vincit A.   556:8
quos..nec..suprema citius solvet a. die   258:19
Amorem: longum subito deponere a.   133:14
nec meum respectet..amorem   132:19
Amori: neque a. dare ludum   260:6
Amorites: the Hittites, and the A.   45:36
Amorous: a., and fond, and billing   111:8
a. bird of night   348:38
a. ditties all a summer's day   344:32
a. of their strokes   424:6
be a., but be chaste   117:17
excite my a. propensities   270:10
her a. descant sung   347:19
sweet reluctant a. delay   347:12
tangled in a. nets   350:1
unsubstantial Death is a.   478:44
what dire offence from a. causes springs   385:8
Amorus: to beyt thir a. of thar nychtis baill   187:4
Amos: A., what seest thou?   56:3
Amos Cottle   117:19
Amour: beginning of an A.   40:3
enforce a desperate a.   111:7
too sure of the a.   543:20
Amour: l'absence est à l'a. vive l'a.!   109:34, 512:22
Amphibious ill-born mob   170:12
Amphisbaena dire   349:21
Amphitrite's destined halls   495:1
Amphitryon: I am the true A.   191:27
Amphora coepit institui   255:17
Ample: behold her face at a. view   481:32
Ampler: a. ether, a diviner air   577:13
Amplitude: a. of noble life   402:23
clearest insight, a. of mind   579:37
Ampullas: proicit a.   255:22
Amurath: not A. an A. succeeds   442:31
Amuse you with stories of savage men   100:22
Amused: we are not a.   552:20
Amusement: cough for my own a.   22:29
I write for the general a.   419:22
topics of a. in a..winter-night   519:3
Amusements: no a. in England but vice and religion   505:11
tolerable were it not for its a.   313:25
Amusent: les anglais s'a. tristement   517:23
Amuses: with tea a. the evening   278:1
Amusing: with numerous errors   227:14
death of his fellow-creatures..   212:4
Anabaptist: an a...I am not a member of   208:26
Anabaptists: certain A.   401:14
Anacreon: of which had Horace or A. tasted   280:9
Anak: giants, the sons of A.   46:14
Analytic: profoundly skill'd in a.   110:5
Analytics: sweet A., 'tis thou hast ravished me   329:22
Ananias, Azarias, and Misael   388:23
Anapaestic: rolling a.   89:5
Anapaests: swift A.   152:5
Anarch: thy hand great A.!,   381:27
Anarchy: a. and competition the laws of death   413:27

Anarchy (cont.)
cure of a. 101:7
driven between..a. and despotism 499:11
Anathema: let him be A. Maranatha 67:20
thunder 'A.', friend, at you 540:28
Anatomy: a mere a., a mountebank 429:1
A. of Melancholy..only book 271:36
eat the rest of the a. 484:2
Ancestors: look back to their a. 102:9
our a. are very good..folks 500:23
wild trick of his a. 440:31
wisdom of our a. 101:35
Ancestral voices prophesying war 151:33(−152)
Ancestry: trace my a. back to a.. globule 219:19
without pride of a., or hope of posterity 387:15
Anchor his aspect 424:1
Anchorage: the long, long a. we leave 566:25
Anchored: a. on..immortality 83:10
where the fleet of stars is a. 208:7
Anchors: cast four a. out of the stern 65:29
great a., heaps of pearl 476:14
Ancient: a. and fishlike smell 479:38
a. forms of party strife 533:20
a. Mariner 148:18
a. nobility is the act of time 26:42
A. of days 55:43, 228:20
a. times are only old 236:42
Beauty both so a. and so fresh 21:22
china that's a. and blue 309:25
forests a. as the hills 151:32
intruders on his a. home 18:16
knowledge of the a. languages.. a luxury 82:16
lieutenant..before the a. 471:14
most a. profession 304:40
no a. gentlemen but gardeners 437:5
with the a. is wisdom 48:58
Ancients: speak..of the a. without idolatry 139:17
the a. dreaded death 237:21
wisdom of the a. 28:11
Ancona: this is A., yonder is the sea 92:3
Ancus: quo Tullus dives et A. 260:26
Anders: ich kann nicht a. 321:4
Anderson: John A., my jo 106:19
Andrea del Sarto appears 39:24
Andrew: Saint A.'s by the Northern Sea 309:23
Anecdotage: fell into his a. 182:17
Anecdotes: polite a. 543:1
Anfractuosities of the human mind 274:17
Angel: a. appear to each lover 373:19
a. dropp'd down from the clouds 440:18
A. ended 348:29
a new dropt from the sky 373:18
a. of death has been abroad 82:17
A. of Death spread his wings 118:38
A. of the Lord came down 527:4
a. of the Lord came upon them 61:18
A. of the off-shore Wind 298:10
a. of this life 95:31
A. that presided o'er my birth 75:1
A. trumpets blow 351:10
a. visited the green earth 317:10
a. watching an urn 535:41
a. whom thou still hast served 461:11
a. writing in a book of gold 265:16
ape or an a.? 180:35
beautiful and ineffectual a. 19:21
better a. is a man right fair 488:18
bright with many an a. 362:2
Brutus..was Caesar's a. 450:29
callin' a young 'ooman..a a. 179:6
consideration like an a. came 443:5
curse his better a. from his side 473:25
custom..is a. yet in this 436:5
Dante once prepared to paint an a. 93:47
dark and serious a. 80:31
dear, fine, silly old a. 307:24

Angel (cont.)
dreadless a. unpursued 348:19
drew one a. 94:12
drive an a. from your door 76:16
golden hours on a. wings 106:9
half a. and half bird 95:34
hear thy guardian a. say 198:19
heard an a. sing 5:15
her a.'s face 509:21
hold the fleet a. fast 316:29
hovering a. girt with golden wings 340:11
in action how like an a. 433:15
in heavenly pay a glorious a. 475:1
in quibbles, a. and archangel join 386:15
like an a. sings 465:18
like a.-visits, few and far between 122:40(−123)
look homeward, A. 343:2
lost A. of a ruin'd Paradise 491:20
mighty a. took up a stone 71:33
ministering a. shall my sister be 437:20
ministering a. thou 418:31
more a. she 473:20
my bad a. fire my good one out 488:19
philosophy will clip an A.'s wings 286:42
reverence—that a. of the world 429:39
she drew an a. down 191:13
shined in my a.-infancy 552:3
sigh is the sword of an A. King 75:6
story which a. voices tell 339:8
such a. grace 528:2
their a. plucked them from me 544:20
those A. faces smile 364:12
though an a. should write 356:7
white as an a. is the English child 76:13
woman yet think him an a. 542:10
wrote like an a. 213:12
Angelic: a. songs are swelling 202:23
before God made the a. clan 586:14
consort to th' a. symphony 343:17
elements, and an a. sprite 185:12
seem a. in the sight of God 316:36
something of a. light 580:21
Angelicam: nam et a. habent faciem 232:8
Angelorum: ut dicant..a. chori 13:9
Angels: a. affect us oft 184:4
a., all pallid and wan 380:15
a. all were singing out of tune 119:15
a. alone, that soar above 319:7
a. and ministers of grace defend us! 431:32
a. are bright still 460:18
a. are painted fair 371:12
A. bending near the earth 421:10
a. came and ministered 57:37
a. keep their ancient places 545:1
A., Martyrs, Prophets, Virgins 361:11
a., nor principalities, nor powers 65:58
a. of God ascending and descending 45:3
a. of rain and lightning 496:5
A. sing to thee their airs divine 158:4
a. stood round about the throne 71:4
a. tremble, while they gaze 231:13
a. wake thee with a note like thine 270:6
a. yield eternal thanks 503:4
as a. in some brighter dreams 552:12
as far as a.' ken 344:8
aspiring to be a. men rebel 383:13
band of a. comin' after me 10:2
band of glorious a. ever stand 361:9
better a. of our nature 314:10
blow your trumpets, A. 185:13
bright-harnest A. 343:25
by that sin fell the a. 446:30
calling to the A. 298:9
carried by the a. 62:25
constituted the services of A. and men 389:54
dragon fought and his a. 71:17
entertained a. unawares 69:22
even thousands of a. 396:8
flights of a. 438:7
four a. round my head 3:3

Angels (cont.)
give his a. charge over thee 397:19
glorious fault of a. and of gods 381:33
good as guardian a. are 158:13
go with me, like good a. 446:13
greet as a. greet 319:9
grew pale, as a. can 119:25
guardian a. sung this strain 545:18
hear the a. sing 421:10
holy a. guard thy bed 562:1
I am on the side of the a. 180:35
if a. fight, weak men must fall 475:1
I have no a. left 543:21
I heard the a. call 537:1
I neglect God and his A. 186:32
like a.' visits 365:8
liveried a. lackey her 340:23
lower than the a. 392:11
make the a. weep 461:31
maketh his a. spirits 398:8
man did eat a.' food 396:35
meet we no a., Pansie? 20:25
men would be a., a. would be gods 383:13
Milton wrote in fetters..of A. and God 77:7
oblivion in lost a. can infuse 16:5
o'er thee..a. mourn 82:1
only for God and a. to be lookers on 24:22
only the a. hear 492:29
our acts our a. are 37:23
plead like a. trumpet-tongu'd 457:9
praise Him, A. in the height 291:27
sad as a. for the good man's sin 122:39
saw the a. heave up Sir Launcelot 328:23
sons of men and a. say 565:4
sorrow for a. 93:6
spectacle unto the world, and to a. 66:25
they have the faces of a. 232:8
though women are a. 117:45
tongues of men and of a. 66:44
'twixt air and A.' purity 184:5
visits like those of a., short, and far between 73:13
walk the a. on the walls of heaven 331:3
walking, like two a. bright 81:17
were a. to write 365:7
where a. fear to tread 383:5
whom the a. name Lenore 380:25
with A. and Archangels 390:39
women are a., wooing 480:41
ye, like a. appear 17:20
young men glittering and sparkling A. 548:15
Anger: a. insignificantly fierce 164:2
a. invests with such a lovely grace 502:1
a. is a short madness 256:26
a. makes dull men witty 24:36
A.'s self I needs must kiss again 502:1
biting for a. at the clog of his body 212:16
carries a. as the flint bears fire 451:25
contempt and a. of his lip 483:28
do they provoke me to a.? 55:15
his a. is not turned away 53:7
keepeth he his a. for ever 398:5
moon..pale in her a. 466:37
more in sorrow than in a. 431:13
slow to a. 50:17
strike it in a. 490:33
with a., with sickness, or with hunger 468:4
Angered: she that being a. 470:29
Angiportis: nunc in quadruviis et a. 133:5
Anglais: les a. s'amusent tristement 517:23
les A. sont occupés 355:8
Angle: Brother of the A. 559:12
themselves in every a. greet 332:6
Angler: a. in the lake of darkness 453:28
excellent a., and now with God 559:18
no man is born an a. 559:10
Anglers: any but a., or very honest men 559:24
Angles: they were called A. 232:8
Angleterre: en A...une seule sauce 124:23
Angli vocarentur 232:8

INDEX

Angling: and be quiet; and go a-
A. 559:27
a...can never be fully learnt 559:8
a...I can only compare to a stick
and a string 277:13
a. is somewhat like poetry 559:14
most dear lover..of a. 559:15
Anglo-Saxon: A. Messenger..A.
attitudes 131:14
obvious and natural idol of the
A. 28:33
Angry: a. and poor and happy 142:2
a. spot doth glow on Caesar's
brow 448:25
a. with his judgment for not
agreeing with me 86:3
a. with my friend 76:5
be a., and dispatch 426:13
be ye a., and sin not 68:1
his a. soul ascended 23:24
hue a. and brave 245:13
kiss the Son, lest he be a. 391:51
proud and a. dust 263:32
speak no a. word 3:17
when he was a., one of his eyes
became so terrible 38:18
when thou art a. all our days are
gone 397:16
who's a. at a slander makes it
true 279:27
Anguis: latet a. in herba 555:27
Anguish: a. moist and fever dew 286:29
a. of a torturing hour 467:25
a. of all sizes 245:5
solitary hidden a. 196:24
Angulus: mihi praeter omnis a. ridet 259:5
Angusta: res a. domi 283:5
Anheling: the cive, a., wipes 251:19
Anima Rabelaisii habitans in sicco 153:10
Animae dimidium meae 258:4
Animal: doubt as to a. magnetism 153:8
glad a. movements all gone by 581:26
good a., true to your a. instincts 310:22
hate..that a. called man 519:32
man is a noble a. 87:20
man is..a political a. 14:14
man is..a religious a. 102:22
man is a tool-making a. 211:20
monstrous a. a husband and wife 204:31
some unknown a., or the god that
he worships 519:11
Animal: cet a. est très méchant 12:12
l'homme est..un méchant a. 354:8
Animalculous: names of beings a. 221:32
Animals: all a. were created..for
the use of man 376:15
a. are such agreeable friends 196:31
a. went in one by one 10:7
fabulous a...who used to sing
in the water 176:5
paragon of a. 433:15
some a. are more equal 370:16
turn and live with a. 567:20
wild a. never kill for sport 212:4
Animam: a. praeferre pudori
liberavi a. meam 283:14
43:17
Animate: a. an hour of vacant ease 579:35
scarce-suspected, a. the whole 505:3
Animated: storied urn or a. bust 230:3
Animis: nunc a. opus, Aenea 554:26
Animosities: a. are mortal 365:13
dissensions and a. of mankind 102:5
Animosity: sisterly a. 518:39
Animula vagula blandula 233:19
Animum: caelum non a. mutant
fortem posce a. 257:4
283:24
Anio: the A. falling 140:13
Anise: tithe of mint and a. and
cummin 60:17
Ankles: do his weak a. swell 580:22
one praised her a., one her eyes 528:2
Ankworks: 'the A. package' 176:27
Anna: great A.! whom three realms
obey 385:14
Annabel Lee: the beautiful A. 380:9
Annals: if you have writ your a.
true 429:23
short and simple a. of the poor 230:1
war's a. will cloud into night 236:14
whose a. are blank in history-
books 126:11

Anne: A. A.! Come! quick as you
can 170:25
as Saint A., the mother of Mary 374:11
John Donne, A. Donne, Un-
done 186:29
ma sœur A., ne vois-tu rien? 377:32
Queen A. was one of the smallest people 29:5
sister A., do you see anybody?
377:32(–378)
tell 'em Queen A.'s dead 154:8
we'll sing at Saint A.'s 357:16
yes, by Saint A. 482:32
Anne of Cleves: Flanders mare 242:22
Anne Page: sweet A. 466:3
Annexed: chain..by which every
creature is a. 109:24
Anni: a. labuntur, Postume, Postume! 34:1
labuntur a. 259:9
singula de nobis a. praedantur 257:17
Annie Laurie: bonnie A. 187:6
Annihilate but space and time 381:8
Annihilating all that's made 332:19
Annihilation: one Moment in A.'s
Waste 206:20
Anniversaries: secret a. of the
heart 318:3
Anno Domini: taste my A. 203:4
Annos: multos da, Iuppiter, a. 283:23
multosque per a. stat fortuna
domus 556:25
nec tu pueri contemperis a. 284:3
o mihi praeteritos referat si Juppiter a. 555:5
Annoy: he only does it to a. 129:1
receiv'st with pleasure thine a. 486:13
sewers a. the air 349:11
Annoyance: shadow of a. 498:9
Annoys: whose scent the fair a. 159:18
Annual: a. income twenty pounds 174:24
to trusted man his a. visit 546:26
Annuity: an a. is a very serious
business 23:8
Annulus: consumitur a. usu 372:10
Annus: immortalia ne speres, monet
a. 260:25
nunc formosissimus a. 555:24
Annygoats: fashnable fax and
polite a. 543:1
Anoint: a. and cheer our soiled
face 400:33
thou dost with oil a. 421:1
Anointed: a. my head with oil 393:10
I am your a. Queen 198:3
rail on the Lord's a. 476:26
touch the Lord's A. 7:9
wash the balm from an a. king 475:1
Anointing: thou the a. Spirit art 400:31
Another: 'a non sequitur'.—'You
are a.' 204:28
a. and a Cup to drown 206:14
a. to help him up 56:34
a., yet the same 381:17
as good as a. until 282:13
bind a. to its delight 76:3
can I see a.'s woe 77:3
cannot show such a. 333:6
do we look for a.? 59:5
for a. gives its ease 76:2
gaze..on a.'s..struggles 320:30 (–321)
give her booby for a. 215:22
if there's a. world he lives in
bliss 107:18
Irish..never speak well of one a. 272:21
liberal of a. man's 27:7
ne'er made a. 104:25
one a.'s best 184:29
one sure, if a. fails 96:40
quite a. thing 112:25
take..our own opinion from a. 200:37
sickens at a.'s praise 143:4
'Sir', said Mr. Pickwick, 'you're
a.' 178:33
still better than a. 6:20
that is a. story 304:39
that's a. story 513:13
when comes such a.? 450:35
Anser: arguttos inter strepere a.
olores 556:7
Anstis, Garter King at Arms 139:36

Answer: a. a fool according to his
folly 50:38
a. came there none 130:21, 416:9
a. loud and high 302:21
a. made it none 431:12
a. to 'Hi!' or to any loud cry 128:6
be swift, my soul, to a. Him 264:17
dusty a. 336:36
give a.—what ha' ye done? 302:24
give me your a., do 168:2
his a. trickled through my head 131:22
I'll not a. that 464:27
I would turn and a. 263:1
little fishes' a. was 131:10
make you not then the better a. 468:39
more than the wisest man can a. 154:21
noblest a. unto such 527:20
not bound to please thee with
my a. 464:29
not careful to a. thee 55:38
O! a. me 431:32
reduced the a. to shillings and
pence 129:28
soft a. turneth away wrath 50:10
thou shalt a., Lord, for me 245:3
waitin' for a a. 174:20
what a. should I give? 539:1
Winds of the World, give a. 296:3
woods shall to me a. 509:11
would not stay for an a. 27:29
Answerable to the people 563:3
Answered: a. the description.. to
a T 203:26
father a. never a word 318:11
grievously hath Caesar a. it 450:17
how a beggar should be a. 465:16
I a. him, as I thought good 367:20
I came, and no one a. 171:14
I have a. three questions 128:29
jealous souls will not be a. so 472:17
should I have a. Caius Cassius
so? 451:21
they a. everything they could 248:12
till it must be a. to 97:7
when have I a. thee? 539:1
Answerest thou the high priest so? 63:67
Answereth: money a. all things 51:25
Answers: dawning a. there 544:20
God a. sharp and sudden 87:29
kind are her a. 124:2
ne'er a. till a husband cools 384:38
Ant: go to the a., thou sluggard 49:45
great good husband, little a. 319:2
Antagonist: our a. is our helper 102:27
Antan: ou sont les neiges d'a.? 553:3
Antecedentem scelestum 259:20
Antecedents are rum, Romanism
and rebellion 99:42
Antediluvian: one of your a. fami-
lies 155:16
Antelope: milk-white Snowdonian
a. 495:12
where the deer and the a. play 248:9
Anteros: he the A. and Eros 543:18
Anthea: thou (A.) must withdraw 246:26
Anthem: grand old Puritan a. 316:4
pealing a. swells the note of
praise 230:2
thy plaintive a. fades 288:2
Antheming a lonely grief 286:17
Anthems: hollaing, and singing of
a. 441:21
loud your a. raise 35:2
service high, and a. clear 341:24
Anthropophagi: of the Cannibals
..the A. 470:2
Antic: dance an a. hay 329:20
old father a., the law 438:19
put an a. disposition on 432:30
there the a. sits 475:7
Anticipate: what we a. seldom
occurs 182:8
Anticipation: intelligent a. of facts 167:27
Antidius on his back 508:1
Antidote: some sweet oblivious a. 460:37
Anti-everythings: lean, hungry,
savage, a. 250:28
Antigropeloes: donn'd galligaskins, a. 121:1
Antilogy: intolerable a. of making
figments feel 236:3

INDEX

Antinoüs: hope an A. mere   146:20
Antipathies: I feel not..those
  common a.   86:27
Antipathy: no a...in diet, humour,
  air, anything   86:25
  strong a. of good to bad   386:22
Antipodes: act our A.   85:21
  diverse, sheer opposite, a.   285:35
*Antiqua: pulchritudo tam a. et tam
  nova*   21:22
Antiquarian is a rugged being   273:35
Antiquates: time, which a. antiquities   87:9
Antique: a. order of the dead   543:16
  a. pillars massy proof   341:24
  constant service of the a. world   426:38
  goodly usage of those a. times   509:35
  group that 's quite a.   115:36
  hat of a. shape   18:8
  noble and nude and a.   522:22
  stretched metre of an a. song   486:17
  traveller from an a. land   496:13
*Antiquis: moribus a. res stat
  Romana*   201:25
Antiquitas saeculi juventus mundi   25:7
Antiquities: a. are history defaced   24:15
  time, which antiquates a.   87:9
Antiquity: a little skill in a.   212:2
  blasted with a.   441:20
  I will write for A.   307:22
Antonius Pius. .His Reign   217:7
Antonio Stradivari's violins   197:1
Antony: A., enthroned i'the market-
  place   424:7
  A. shall be brought drunken
  forth   426:4
  A.'s hath triumphed on itself   425:26
  A., that revels long o' nights   449:25
  A., who lost the world for love   193:14
  A. would ruffle up your spirits   450:34
  catch another A.   426:16
  if she first meet the curled A.   426:13
  Mark A.'s was by Caesar   458:33
  much A., of Hamlet most of all   241:20
  my oblivion is a very A.   423:37
  none but A. shall conquer A.   425:26
  since my lord is A. again   425:7
  that quick spirit that is in A.   448:13
  this great gap of time my A. is
  away   423:41
  to meet Mark A.   426:5
Antres vast and desarts idle   470:2
Antro: Grato, Pyrrha, sub a.   258:10
Ants: a trouble of a.   541:4
  spiders, flies or a...in amber   27:47
Anvil: either a. or hammer   318:18
  either..the a. or the hammer   223:23
  England's on the a.   294:22
  my a. and hammer lies declined   8:13
  plough—loom—a.—spade   307:17
  this sword out of this stone and
  a.   328:3
  what the a.?   75:24(-76)
Anxiety: repose is taboo'd by a.   219:9
Anxious: if you're a. for to shine   220:25
  this pleasing a. being   230:9
Anybody: a. might have found it   296:11
  'is there a. there?'   171:13
  no one's a.   218:30
Anything: a. for a quiet life   179:28
  a. for the good of one's country   203:12
  consider a., only don't cry   131:1
  fortune..in this mood will give
  us a.   451:2
  nobody tells me a.   213:4
  or a. as the learned Boar observed   496:12
  remembering him like a.   141:30
  though you do a., he thinks no
  ill   487:7
  what is the worth of a.   121:23
  wot 's the good of A.?   142:21
  would do a. but die   307:31
Anywhere: a., a., out of the world!   252:20
  than a. else on earth   233:17
Ap: A.-Cataract A.-Pistyll A.-
  Rhaiader A.-Headlong!   376:22
Apace: gallop a.   478:13
  work a., a., a., a.,   170:21
Aparezcas: cómo a. a los demás   551:2
Apart: a., studiously neutral   571:11

Apart (cont.)
  joy a. from thee   199:13
  keep a dream or grave a.   89:3
  like a star, and dwelt a.   577:15
  of man's life a thing a.   115:25
  other spirits..standing a.   288:25
  two are walking a. for ever   267:10
Apartments: very charming a.   177:32
Apathetic end   535:22
Ape: an a. or an angel?   180:35
  a. an ancient rage   141:23
  a. the magnanimity of love   336:9
  blue-behinded a.   516:18
  gorgeous buttocks of the a.   266:16
  keeps them, like an a. doth
  nuts   436:9
  like an angry a.   461:31
  sedulous a. to Hazlitt   514:9
  take their manners from the A.   40:22
Apella: credat Iudaeus A., non ego   261:17
Apennine: wind-grieved A.   91:5
  within a folding of the A.   18:31(-19)
Apennines: on the back of the A.   127:4
  Popish A.   293:10
A per se: of townes *A.*   195:3
Apes: a. are a.,..in scarlet   281:4
  asses, a., and dogs   351:18
  ivory and a. and peacocks 47:44, 333:20
  lead a. in hell   479:3
  leave Now for dogs and a.   91:40
  made the..peple his a.   137:22
  pride that a. humility 151:11, 507:20
Apes: vos non vobis mellificatis a.   556:27
Apocalypse: characters of the
  great A.   580:25
Apollo: A...a bitter god to follow   525:5
  A. comes leading his choir   15:16
  A. from his shrine   343:21
  A. hunted Daphne so   332:16
  A., Pallas, Jove and Mars   184:2
  A.'s first, at last the true God's
  priest   124:26
  bards in fealty to A. hold   288:19
  burned is A.'s laurel bough   330:12
  father of all of us, Paian, A.   524:21
  Graces danced, and A. play'd   319:1
  hairs as gay as are A.'s locks   209:22
  harsh after the songs of A.   456:2
  mihi flavus A. pocula..ministret   371:20
  musical as bright A.'s lute   455:22
  musical as is A.'s lute   340:24
  neque semper arcum tendit A.   259:8
  not here, O A.!   15:15
  O Delphic A.!   286:1
  Phoebus A. turned fasting friar   337:21
  sic me servavit A.   261:19
  young A., golden-haired   157:8
Apollos watered   66:22
Apollyon: A. straddled quite over
  ..the way   99:12
  his name is A.   99:11
Apologize: I never a.   489:7
Apology: a. for the Devil   112:3
  never make a defence of a. before you be accused   135:27
  no a...make h'ar come back   238:13
Apoplexy: a kind of lethargy   441:14
Apostle: a. in the high aesthetic
  band   220:28
  great a. of the Philistines   19:17
  not meet to be called an a.   67:5
Apostles: all the A. would have
  done as they did   115:20
  corrupt following of the A.   401:9
  least of the a.   67:5
  men of culture..true a. of
  equality   19:26
  she, while A. shrank, could
  dangers brave   35:25
Apostolic: a. blows and knocks   110:18
  one Catholick and A. Church   390:21
  sweated through his a. skin   119:21
Apothecary: expires in the arms of
  an a.   505:28
  I do remember an a.   478:35
  ointment of the a.   51:23
Appal the free   433:32
Apparel: a. oft proclaims the man   431:25
  condemns neatness of a.   565:20
  every true man's a. fits your thief   462:19
  my gay a. for an almsman's gown   475:10

Apparel (cont.)
  ornaments of gold upon your a.   47:30
  the Lord..hath put on glorious
  a.   397:22
Apparelled: a. in celestial light   576:1
  a. like the spring   474:5
  a. in more precious habit   469:6
*Apparentibus: de non a. et de non
  existentibus*   13:6
Apparition: lovely a. sent   580:19
  that a., sole of men, he saw   496:18
Apparitions: like a. seen and gone   365:8
Appeal: a. unto Caesar   65:19
  a. from Philip drunk   5:12
  a. from tyranny to God   114:34
Appear: a...in a..more beautiful
  edition   211:21
  let that a. when..no need of
  such vanity   468:35
  never. .a. the Immortals   152:16
  Richard doth himself a.   475:8
  see thee in our waters yet a.   281:18
Appearance: a. of your Majesty,
  as of the Sun   43:25
  man looketh on the outward a.   47:18
Appearances: contrive to save a.   348:20
  keep up a.   143:12
  no trusting a.   500:45
Appeared to hapless Semele   330:6
Appeareth: vapour, that a. for a
  little time   69:41
Appetens: alieni a.   415:1
Appétit: l'a. vient en mangeant   404:27
Appetite: a. may sicken, and so die   481:30
  cloy the hungry edge of a.   474:7
  doth not the a. alter?   468:22
  good digestion wait on a.   459:13
  increase of a. had grown by what
  it fed on   430:33(-431)
  mortified a. is never a wise companion   513:34
  swich a. hath he to ete a mous   137:36
  their colours. .were then to me
  an a.   581:26
  their love may be call'd a.   483:9
  well-govern'd and wise a.   340:34
  with what a. you have   446:22
  yelps not only of a.   144:6
Appetites: abandon yourselves to
  your irregular a.   85:8
  cloy the a. they feed   424:9
  not their a.   471:40
  our a. as apt to change as theirs   191:20
  subdue your a., my dears   177:3
Applaud: a. thee to the very echo   461:1
  a. us when we run   100:15
  till thou a. the deed   459:8
  world a. the hollow ghost   16:10
Applause: a. of list'ning senates   230:5
  attentive to his own a.   385:29
  Beauty's just a.   331:2
  joy in an a. so great as thine   158:4
  joy, pleasance, revel, and a.   471:22
  satiate of a.   386:7
  the a.! delight the wonder of
  our stage   281:11
  what's not for their a.   584:3
Apple: a. puffs, and three-corners   219:13
  codling when 'tis almost an a.   482:17
  did not want the a. for the a.'s
  sake   550:23
  dusk would come in the a.
  boughs   171:21
  for a. damn'd mankind   371:10
  from out the rind of one a.
  tasted   352:8
  goodly a. rotten at the heart   463:19
  gruvvelling around when you've
  got an a.   550:25
  keep me as the a. of an eye   392:28
  like the sweet a. which reddens   410:6
  said it was the a. of his eye   546:38
  when Eve..the a. pressed   252:10
  where the a. reddens   97:25
Apple-blossomed: rich a. earth   567:18
Apple-dumplings: a pure mind
  who refuses a.   306:9
Apple-pie: a cabbage-leaf, to
  make an a.   209:18
  A was an a.   366:7
  bless me with a. and cheese   204:1

[600]

INDEX

Apples: a., cherries, hops, and
  women   178:28
a. of gold for the king's daughter   524:19
a. of gold in pictures of silver   50:34
a. on the Dead Sea's shore   113:39
cakes and a. in all the Chapels   33:21
comfort me with a.   51:45
eggs, a., and cheese   294:34
moon-washed a. of wonder   189:23
'neath no..terror's wing, a. forget to grow   140:23
porridge and a., mince, muffins   171:17
ripe a. drop about my head   332:17
silver a. of the moon   586:6
small choice in rotten a.   478:48
stolen by love   266:1
Apple-tart: cream..to eat with a.   515:21
Apple-tree: bare branch of mossy a.   151:25
falling from that a.   228:6
in the shade of an old a.   571:2
I raised the up under the a.   52:22
my heart is like an a.   409:14
the a. do lean down low in Linden Lea   35:13
where my mother fell beneath
  the a.   543:19
Apple-trees: among the plums
  and a.   249:14
my a. will never get across   212:3
Appliance: by desperate a. are
  reliev'd   436:11
Appliances: with all a. and means
  to boot   442:2
Application: lays in the a. on it   175:14
Apply: Lamb..may a. to me   153:16
you know my methods. A. them   188:21
Appointed: house a. for all living   49:10
imperfections..divinely a.   413:15
kings are by God a.   7:9
like pilgrims to th' a. place   193:17
place which thou hast a.   398:8
the blue sky..is their a. rest   149:24
wait the a. hour   193:30
Appointment: a. by the corrupt few   490:29
keep an a. with a beech-tree   547:1
Apportioning: better a. of wages
  to work   126:44
Apprehend: but a. some joy   467:24
faculties, which sense may
  reach and a.   185:2
he that can a...vice   352:9
Apprehension: in a. how like a god   433:15
shuts his a. up   331:21
the a. of the good   474:20
the sense of death is most in a.   462:7
Apprehensions: my a. come in
  clouds   573:1
Apprehensive: a., quick, forgetive   442:21
flesh and blood, and a.   449:30
Apprentice: an a. for to bind   29:23
Appris: sans avoir jamais rien a.
  rien a., ni rien oublié.   354:5
  rien oublié et..rien a.   526:17
     195:1
Approach: a. thou like the rugged
  Russian bear   459:20
a. thy grave like one..   98:3
beats my a., tells thee I come   292:20
be stone no more; a.   485:38
of his near a. afraid   213:15
snuff the a. of tyranny   100:30
sweet a. of ev'n or morn   346:20
Approaches: these drowsy a. of
  sleep   85:21
Approbation: a. from Sir Hubert
  Stanley   359:20
cold a. gave the ling'ring bays   278:35
Approve: a. it with a text   464:14
a. thy constancy, a. first thy
  obedience   349:10
aught..which he could a.   498:20
men of sense a.   382:33
my love doth so a. him   473:5
still the charmer I a.   155:37
Approved: very noble and a. good
  masters   469:45
Après nous le déluge   381:4
Apricocks: bind thou up yon
  dangling a.   475:12
Apricot: champagne and a. jam   518:19
April: A., A., laugh thy girlish
  laughter   561:3

April (cont.)
A. is the cruellest month   197:27
A., June and September   228:4
A., June and November   369:5
A.'s in the west wind   334:15
as dew in A.   7:16
besprent with A. dew   282:2
blossoming boughs of A.   80:12
eighteenth of A. in Seventy-five   317:3
if you were A.'s lady   524:30
lovely A. of her prime   486:11
March winds and A. showers   8:9
Men are A. when they woo   428:22
negligently..fashioned an A.
  violet   561:9
now that A.'s there   92:14
now that the A. of your youth   243:18
of A., May, of June,..flowers   245:17
proud-pied A., dress'd in all his
  trim   487:28
smells A. and May   466:5
so sweet love seemed that A.
  morn   82:2
spongy A.   480:6
sweet A. showers   549:31
their flag to A's breeze unfurled   199:7
three A. perfumes   487:29
uncertain glory of an A. day   484:33
whanne that A. with his shoures   136:21
April-fools: one of Love's A.   155:23
Aprons: made themselves a.   44:21
Apt: a. Alliteration's artful aid   143:14
so a. to die   450:4
Aptitude: grande a. à la patience   98:18
Aqua: in vento et rapida scribere
  oportet a.   133:11
Aquae: carmina..quae scribuntur
  a. potoribus   257:12
Arab: thou'rt sold, my A. steed   365:16
Arabia: all the perfumes of A.   460:27
far are the shades of A.   171:2
kings of A...shall bring gifts   396:25
spell of far A.   171:3
Arabian: A. fleet..into..Thames   217:12
in the A. woods embost   351:3
tears as fast as the A. trees   474:2
wish the A. Tales were true   363:13
Arabians: Cretes and A., we do
  hear them speak   64:26
Arabs: fold their tents, like the A.   316:10
Araby: A. the blest   347:1
I'll sing thee songs of A.   571:6
Aral: shine upon the A. Sea   17:28(-18)
Aram: Eugene A., though a thief   121:17
Eugene A. walked between   252:26
Araminta: my own A., say 'No!'   387:17
Araneam: quare videmus a. aut
  muscam   27:47
Arator: de tauris narrat a.   402:15
Aratro: flos..tactus a. est
  nullo contusus a.   132:19
     133:9
Arbiter: elegantiae a.   526:13
Arbiter: fashion, the a.   511:22
high a. Chance governs all   346:11
the A. of others' fate   118:20
Arbitrary: given way to an a. way   135:17
Arbitrate: who shall a.?   95:20
Arbitrator: that old common a.,
  Time   481:28
Arbitress: the moon sits a.   345:13
Arbitrium: quem penes a. est   255:20
Arboreal: probably a.   169:4, 514:10
Arbuscula dixit   261:20
Arbusta: non omnis a. iuvant   555:30
Arbuthnot: A. a day   521:2
removed from kind A.'s aid   521:8
Arcades: a. ambo   556:3
'A. ambo'..blackguards both   116:11
Arcadia: et in A. ego   13:7
Arch: all experience is an a.   540:32
A. Fear in a visible form   95:9
a. of the leaves was hollow   524:8
broken a. of London Bridge   324:31
forgot the a.—crash   178:24
o' night's black a. the key-stane   109:7
wide a. of the rang'd empire   423:14
Archangel: A. a little damaged   307:13
less than a. ruined   345:5
the affable A.   348:24
the A. bow'd, not like a modern
  beau   119:23

Archangels: bow down, a. in your
  dim abode   585:22
with Angels and A.   390:39
Archbishop: Cardinal Lord A.
  of Rheims   34:8
one illusion left..the A. of
  Canterbury   504:29
Archdeacon: (by way of turbot)
  an a.   505:36
Arched: a. and pond'rous roof   155:19
bridge that a. the flood   199:7
Archer: mark the a. little meant
  that busy a.   417:30
     501:24
Arches: among her golden a.   75:5
down the a. of the years   544:13
shot such Cyclopean a.   141:2
Arch-flatterer..a man's self   26:33
Archibald—certainly not!   414:5
Arching proud his neck   546:11
Archipelagoes: fading alps and a.   3:12
Architect: as an a., one of the
  greatest   33:23
no person..can be an a.   412:23
Architectooralooral: drawd too a.   175:26
Architectural man-milliner   412:20
Architecture: a...is frozen music   415:20
frolic a. of the snow   199:28
love's a. is his own   166:2
many odd styles of a. about   412:20
style resembling..early a.   337:2
wondrous A. of the world   330:28
Archly the maiden smiled   316:5
Arch-Mediocrity   181:31
Archways and the pavement   23:22
Archy: toujours gai, a.   331:12
Arcs: on the earth the broken a.   89:8
Arctic: Ophiucus huge in th' a. sky   346:6
the glistening A. Ocean   235:22
Arcturi: pearled A. of the earth   497:21
Arcturus: canst thou guide A.   49:25
Arcum: neque semper a. tendit
  Apollo   259:8
Arden: now am I in A.; the more
  fool I   426:39
Ardet: paries cum proximus a.   257:8
Ardeur: une a. dans mes veines
  cachée   405:3
Ardor: non civium a. prava iuben-
  tium   259:21
Ardour: daily raise our a. for more   102:38
furious a. of my zeal repress'd   143:10
radiant with a. divine   17:20
vain the a. of the crowd   231:7
Ardours: love's emulous a. ran   410:26
with a. manifold   95:2
Ardui: nil mortalibus a. est   258:7
Are: a. not as they were   492:19
because they a. not   57:26
look at all things as they a.   541:22
made us what we a.   561:10
makes us what we a.   196:21
so very undubitably a.   39:19
that which we a., we a.   541:3
Things as They a.   303:21
why then, by God, we a.   41:19
Area: on his back upon the a.
  stones   176:31
sprouting despondently at a.
  gates   197:23
Arena swims around him   114:18
Arethusa: A. arose   492:20
in wanton A.'s azured arms   330:6
saucy A.   248:16
washed by A.'s fount   232:1
Argent: point d'a., point de Suisse   405:4
sans a. l'honneur   405:5
Argentines sleep firmly   157:25
Argifying: what's the good of a.?   304:25
Argo: loftier A. cleaves the main   493:25
Argosies with portly sail   462:29
Argosy: in a. transferr'd from Fez   285:25
Argue: he could a. still   225:2
to know, to utter, and to a. freely   352:16
we will out-a. them   273:30
Argued the thing at breakfast   125:21
Argues: a. an insensibility   306:6
with women the heart a.   16:26
Argufies: what a. sniv'ling?   173:6
Arguing: be calm in a.   244:1
in a. too, the parson own'd his
  skill   225:2

[601]

Arguing (cont.)
much a., much writing, many
opinions 352:14
no a. with Johnson 227:27
no good a. with the inevitable 320:21
not a. with you..telling you 566:2
Argument: all a. is against it 273:28
a. for a week 439:7
a.'s hot to the close 93:17
finer than the staple of his a. 387:6, 455:24
furnish me with a. and intel-
lects too 227:20
'glory' doesn't mean 'a nice
knock-down a.' 131:6
heard great a. 206:10
his conduct..right with his a.
wrong 225:29
I have found you an a. 275:24
knock-down a. 191:23
maintain his a. as well as any 444:2
metre-making a. 200:30
necessity..a. of tyrants 379:14
not to stir without great a. 436:17
only a. available with an east
wind 320:21
sheath'd their swords for lack
of a. 443:25
to the highth of this great a. 344:4
Tories own no a. but force 87:26
tough customer in a. 173:17
what a. thy life..has lent 199:9
when blood is their a. 444:19
Whigs admit no force but a. 87:26
Arguments: let thy tongue tang a.
of state 483:19
mutual destruction of a. 265:7
no a. shall be wanting on my
part 23:3
racks, gibbets, halters were
their a. 370:10
Argyle: the master-fiend A.! 24:3
Argyll, the state's whole thunder 386:21
Ariadne: inconsolable to the
minuet in A. 499:31
since A. was a vintager 285:2
Arian: in three sips the A. frustrate 96:39
Ariel: a deal of A. 241:29
Aright: sought the Lord a. 104:35
Ariosto of the North 114:7
Aris: no Governor A. 119:32
Aris: *pro patria, pro liberis, pro a.* 415:3
Arisbe: Alciphron once or A. 523:4
Arise: a. and come away 334:16
a. and go now 585:12
a. and go to my father 62:14
a. and unbuild it again 493:1
a., a. 185:13
a. from their graves and aspire 76:7
a., shine; for thy light is come 54:39
awake, a., or be for ever fall'n 344:27
for a man to a. in me 535:43(–536)
I a. from dreams of thee 494:7
let God a. 396:4
let us a. and go like men 515:26
my lady sweet, a.! 429:25
Phoebus, a. 190:4
unto you..shall the Sun of righteousness 56:15
Aristocracy: A. of the Moneybag 126:20
epithet..which the a. [apply] to
what is decent 254:8
our a. the most democratic 325:34
Aristocrat: a., democrat, autocrat 535:43
A. who banks with Coutts.. A.
who cleans the boots 218:22
Aristocratic: our democracy the
most a. 325:34
Aristotle: A. and his philosophye 137:6
A...the rubbish of an Adam 507:1
A. thought unfit to hear moral
philosophy 481:13
live and die in A.'s works 329:21
Arithmetic: different branches of
A. 129:20
no a. but tears 292:17
what would life be without a. 505:33
Arithmetical: subsistence .. in-
creases in an a. ratio 328:25
Ark: a. of bulrushes 45:30

Ark (cont.)
a. of her magnificent..cause 162:45
into Noah's a. 162:2
Noah, commanding the A. 303:9
walked straight out of the A. 504:24
Arly: my aged Uncle A. 311:19
Arm: a. and burgonet of men 423:42
A.! A!..the cannon's opening
roar 113:27
a. a., my name! 475:3
a. around her waist 219:17
a. our soldier 429:3
flourish of his right a. 178:10
from whose right a. 503:2
half slumb'ring on its own right
a. 288:14
his rear'd a. crested the world 426:1
I bared my big right a. 220:7
I bit my a., I sucked the blood 149:9
let that a. thy virtue 412:16
long a. of coincidence 135:11
my a. a ladye's lilye hand 31:6
on her lover's a. she leant 528:28
rebellious a. 'gainst a. 456:9
seal upon thine a. 52:22
shewed strength with his a. 61:14
some undone widow sits upon
my a. 334:26
stretch'd-out a. 503:6
subtle wreath of hair, which
crowns my a. 185:4
sufficient is Thine A. alone 562:9
to whom is the a. of the Lord
revealed? 54:24
warning..to a. 442:21
wi' the auld moon in her a. 31:25
Arma: *a. virumque cano* 553:5
cedant a. togae 145:8
furor a. ministrat 553:11
nunc a...hic paries habebit 260:12
silent enim leges inter a. 145:19
Armadas: till the great A. come 363:3
Armadillo: nor yet an A. 297:25
Armageddon 71:30
Armaments: bloated a. 180:27
Arm-chair: loving that old a.
the Fortieth spare A. 156:21, 91:11
Armed: all-a. I ride 540:12
a. against all death's endeavour 84:19
a. at points exactly 431:9
a. in their stings 443:10
a. neutrality 571:12
a. so strong with honesty 451:19
a. with Kings to strive 118:19
a. with more than complete
steel 7:7, 331:9
gallantly a. 440:18
goeth on to meet the a. men 49:26
thrice is he a. that hath his
quarrel just 445:30, 491:9
thy want as an a. man 49:47
Armée: *Tête d'A.* 361:4
Armentiers: Mademoiselle from A. 412:17
Armes: *France, mère des..a.* 40:16
Armies: a. whole have sunk 345:31
disbanding hired a. 127:6
embattled. clad in iron 350:25
ignorant a. clash by night 15:8
kings with their a. did flee 396:7
power of A. is a visible thing 581:18
what prodigious a. we had in
Flanders 513:12
Arming: a. me from fear 83:7
when kings are a. 419:16
Arminian: an A. clergy 379:7
Armis: *procul discordibus a.* 556:15
Armoric: begirt with British and
A. knights 345:4
Armour: all his a. wherein he
trusted 61:47
a. of a righteous cause 98:1
a. of light 66:13, 389:22
a. on a. shone 189:7
dilloing in his a. 297:25
no a. against fate 501:5
no foe in shining a. 372:14
others have buckled their a. 402:14
put your a. on 565:10
there was not English a. left 140:12
white as snow their a. was 324:12
whole a. of God 68:10, 11

Armour (cont.)
whose a. is his honest thought 583:9
work out Achilles his a. 85:17
Armourers: a., accomplishing the
knights 444:6
now thrive the a. 443:12
Armours: House that a. a man 40:31
Armoury: a. of the invincible
knights 577:3
in their a. have this inscription 109:21
tower of David builded for an a. 52:5
Arms: A. and Hatchments, Resurgam! 542:35
a., and the man I sing 194:29
a. are fair 440:32
a. are strong 264:9
a. of my true love round me 536:17
a., take your last embrace 478:44
as happy in the a. of a chambermaid 274:10
come to my a., my beamish boy 129:39(–130)
dawn in Helen's a. 584:23
defy th' Omnipotent to a. 344:7
every man in a. should wish to
be 575:5
excites us to a. 191:37
expires in the a. of an apothecary 505:28
fiery a. 349:31
fifteen a. went round her waist 333:23
haughty nation proud in a. 340:2
her a. across her breast 528:1
her a. along the deep 122:3
her a. behind her golden head 336:7
His a. are near 354:12
his a. might do what this has
done 558:1
hug it in mine a. 462:8
if my love were in my a. 11:14
I'll forswear a. 438:29
imparadised in one another's a. 347:18
in the youth of a state a. 27:36
in wanton Arethusa's azured
a. 330:6
in word mightier than they in a. 348:20
in your a. to feel so small 375:13
its green a. round..the stream 497:20
laid down his a. 252:29
lord of folded a. 455:8
made a. ridiculous 350:25
more strong than traitors' a. 450:31
Moses stood with a. spread wide 161:16
muscles of his brawny a. 318:11
my a. about my dearie O 105:38
my discipline of a. and chivalry 331:2
my soul's in a. 144:28
never would lay down my a. 379:8
nurse of a. 226:15
of seeming a. 192:8
Roman's a. 323:27
seek it in My a. 544:30
shine in my a. 231:38
since these a...had seven years'
pith 469:45
so should desert in a. be
crowned 190:34
straggler into loving a. 308:10
stretched forth his little a. 231:11
sure-enwinding a. of..death 568:9
take a. against a sea of troubles 434:4
those entrusted with a. 571:20
three corners of the world in a. 448:2
to my a. restore my..love 155:35
to war and a. I fly 319:10
underneath..the everlasting a. 46:34
vigour from our a. 101:17
whose beauty summoned Greece
to a. 331:5
with his a. outstretch'd 481:20
world in a. 324:35
Army: a. marches on its stomach 12:10
a. of slaves 117:46
a. of the faithful 336:4
a. of unalterable law 336:17
Austrian a. awfully arrayed 5:7
backbone of the A. 295:23
back to the A. again 294:20
English a. led by an Irish general..French a. led by an
Italian general 490:39

Army (cont.)

her name an 'A.' doth present 243:22
honour of the British A. 305:1
hum of either a. 444:6
if..the a. and the navy had fair
  play 310:25
like an a. defeated 577:21
noble a., men and boys 240:21
noble a. of martyrs 388:18
only the pick of the A. 301:8
terrible as an a. with banners 52:15
the British A. should be a projectile 232:17
the little ships..brought the A.
  home 233:13
upon which the Grand A. never
  looked 327:11
yester-morn our a. lay 23:19
your a. would be a base rabble 101:13
your poor a. 167:12
Arno: pined by A. 323:8
Aroint thee, witch! 456:10
Aromatic: die of a rose in a. pain 383:16
  faint beneath the a. pain 571:19
Aroon: Eileen A. 232:19
Arose: a. from out the azure main 545:18
  I a. a mother in Israel 46:47
  people a. as one man 46:62
Around: a., beneath, above 81:10
  at once above, beneath, a. 503:3
  ice was all a. 148:26
Arow: tombs and statues all a. 208:5
Arques: *nous avons combattu à A.* 242:2
Arraign'st: so thou a. her 16:11
Arrange: why do we always a. for
  more? 300:22
Array: battle's magnificently stern
  a. 113:35
  rebel powers that thee a. 488:20
  straight against that great a. 323:20
  to summon his a. 323:10
  whence all their white a.? 562:10
Arrayed: a. for mutual slaughter 578:9
  a. in white robes 71:5
  Austrian army, awfully a. 5:7
  not a. like one of these 58:13
Arrears: in a minute pay glad
  life's a. 95:11
  long a. to make good 294:30
Arrest: 'A. you!' said Holmes 188:2
  strict in his a. 438:1
Arretium: harvests of A. 323:12
Arrh: Urrh! Yarrh! Grr! A.! 300:16
Arrival: silent joy at their a. 149:24
Arrive: better..than to a. 515:6
  I shall a. 94:13
  when half-gods go, the gods a. 199:14
Arrived: evils which never a. 199:25
  there a., a new admired guest 123:27
Arriving: serenely a., a. 568:9
Arrogance of age must submit 103:11
Arrow: a. from the Almighty's
  bow 75:6
  a. that flieth by day 397:18
  every a. that flies 316:11
  I shot an a. into the air 315:24
  like an a. from the bow 324:7
  Sanguelac! the a.! the a.! 529:37
  shot mine a. o'er the house 437:35
  when the last a. was fitted 140:18
Arrows: a. of lightnings 540:16
  even mighty and sharp a. 399:24
  his sharp a. tries 501:24
  keen as are the a. 498:5
  like as the a. in the hand of the
  giant 399:33
  my a. of desire 75:16
  slings and a. of outrageous fortune 434:4
  stakes his quiver, bow and a. 321:14
  whose teeth are spears and a. 395:18
Arrowy: a. rain 336:12
  iron-sleet of a. shower 230:14
  tall a. white pines 546:37
Arsenal: great a. of democracy 408:24
Arsenic and Old Lace 292:6
Art: all light of a. or nature 494:1
  all the adulteries of a. 280:7
  all this A. 243:2
  and what a. 75:24(-76)
  [angling] is an a. 559:13

Art (cont.)

A. alone enduring stays 183:5
a...aspires towards the condition of music 374:12
A...cannot exist but in..Parti-
  culars 75:7
a. for a.'s sake 157:23
a. is a jealous mistress 199:34
a. is long, and Time is fleeting 317:6
a. is not a handicraft 548:9
A. is upon the Town 566:3
a. lawful as eating 486:1
a. made tongue-tied 487:14
a. must be parochial 356:5
a. never expresses anything but
  itself 569:17
a...nothing but the highest
  quality 374:13
a. of being kind 568:27
a. of drawing sufficient conclusions 111:33
a. of getting drunk 274:13
a. of our necessities is strange 453:11
a. of reading 182:49
a. of sinking in Poetry 386:9
A. remains the one way possible 96:18
A. stopped short in the..court 220:27
a. that can immortalize 160:26
a. to make dust of all things 87:9
a. unknown to thee 383:21
as much of this in a. as you 451:27
but in the vein of a. 290:26
called his harmless a. a crime 417:2
cookery is become an a. 109:10
Creative A...demands..a mind
  and heart 575:15
desiring this man's a. 486:24
each a. to please 385:29
enough of science and of a. 581:16
entonyng every a. 187:4
excellence of every a...intensity 289:20
failed in literature and a. 182:21
fine a...the hand, the head, and
  the heart 413:16
first taught A. to fold her hands 411:9
glory and the good of A. 96:18
great a. o' letter-writin' 179:7
half a trade and half an a. 267:7
hateful a., how to forget 292:21
hide their want of a. 382:26
his pen in trust to A. 183:10
history of a...revivals 111:38
in sweet music is such a. 446:18
in the elder days of A. 315:28
it needs no a. 375:21
it's clever, but is it A.? 295:15,16
I will use no a. 432:40
knows his a., but not the trade 521:8
last and greatest a., the a. to blot 386:18
love, devoid of a. 215:11
message of A. 489:21
morality of a. 570:4
more matter with less a. 432:39
Nature..almost lost in A. 154:4
nature is the a. of God 86:12
nature's handmaid is a. 191:29
Nature that is above all a. 168:6
new all a. 338:10
new A. would better Nature's best 421:7
next to Nature, A. 308:25
no a. to find the mind's construction 456:27(-457)
none ever had so strange an a. 202:4
no schoolman's subtle a. 386:4
not to admire is all the a. I know 116:19
not without a., but yet to nature
  true 143:23
no way to success in our a. but.. 199:33
O Lord, Thou a. 503:3
only a. her guilt to cover 226:18
poetry a mere mechanic a. 162:28
poetry..in Oxford made an a. 193:24
pretend to despise A. and
  Science 75:9
rules and models destroy..a. 240:4
shape from that thy work of a. 316:24
strength and nature made
  amends for a. 412:13
tender strokes of a. 381:6
though a.'s hid causes are not
  found 280:7

Art (cont.)

true ease..comes from a. not
  chance 382:32
unpremeditated a. 498:1
venerate a. as a. 240:12
war's glorious a. 586:27
what a. can wash her guilt away? 226:18
when A. is too precise 246:4
with winning a. 546:9
work at anything but his a. 490:15
works..A. most cherishes 93:40
yield to a...supremacy 80:29

Art: *l'a. pour l'a.* 157:23
  l'a. robuste seul a l'éternité 214:3
  mon a., c'est vivre 355:1
Artery: each petty a. in this body 432:3
Artes: *a. intulit agresti Latio* 257:14
  hae tibi erunt a. 555:1
  ingenuas didicisse fideliter a. 372:9
  omnes a...commune vinclum 145:15
Artful: careless she is with a. care 154:27
  the a. Dodger 177:37
Arthur: first the noble A. 327:15
  he's in A.'s bosom 443:19
  slowly answer'd A. from the
  barge 531:35
Article: deny each a. with oath 473:14
  for a slashing a. 542:22
  snuff'd out by an a. 116:35
  'What's the next a.?' 221:8
Articles: believe all the A. of the
  Christian Faith 391:2
  the A. of thy Belief 391:4
Articulate audible voice of the
  Past 126:27
Artifex: *qualis a. pereo!* 362:27
Artificer: great a. made my mate 516:6
  lean unwash'd a. 447:41
  th' unwashed a. 162:17
Artificial: all things are a. 86:12
Artillery: a. of words 521:12
  far flashed the red a. 122:18
  Jonathan gave his a. unto his lad 47:26
  love's great a. 166:7
  shot with the self-same a. 318:24
Artis: *qui vitam excoluere per a.* 554:29
Artisan: chips to the..a. 143:31
Artist: a. never dies 317:2
  be more of an a. 291:1
  every a. writes..autobiography 198:23
  feeling the a. has experienced 548:9
  good a. in life 514:38
  grant the a. his subject 268:14
  portrait of the a. as a young man 282:14
  true a. will let his wife starve 490:15
Artistic: give a. verisimilitude 220:13
  never was an a. period 566:4
Artistries in Circumstance 235:20
Art-loving: never was an A.
  nation 566:4
Arts: a. babblative and scribblative 508:6
  a. of war and peace 115:43
  a. that caused himself to rise 385:29
  Athens..mother of a. 350:11
  books, the a., the academes 455:23
  cry both a. and learning down 404:18
  dear nurse of a. 445:10
  famed in all great a. 18:1
  had I but followed the a. 482:7
  his virtues were his a. 101:28
  learn both a. 126:33
  lowest of the a. 356:6
  'May the Devil fly away with the
  fine a.' 126:40
  mechanical a. and merchandise 27:36
  Murder..One of the Fine A. 172:22
  no a.; no letters; no society 248:21
  true begetter of all a. 42:1
Arts: France, *mère des a.* 40:16
  Aryan: hustle the A. brown 300:6
  the A. smiles 300:6
As: led—a kind of—a. it were 401:29
Ascend: a. the brightest heaven of
  invention 443:2
  base degrees by which he did a. 449:3
  in dignity of being we a. 574:19
  my soul may but a. to heaven 330:9
Ascendant: for his hour..lord of
  the a. 100:9
Ascended: bright Pomp a. jubilant 348:28

Ascendeth: smoke of their torment a. 71:26
Ascending: angels of God a. and descending 45:3
Ascends me into the brain 442:21
Ascent: laborious indeed at the first a. 352:26
steep a. of Heav'n 240:22
Ascetic rocks and sensual whirlpools 337:17
Ascribe: a. it to Thy grace 561:20
a. unto stones and stocks 56:28
Ash: Oak and A. and Thorn 303:5, 6
oak, and the a., and the bonny ivy-tree 8:22
only the A., the bonnie A. 172:7
Ashamed: ain't you a., you sleepyhead? 515:25
a. of one another ever after 156:13
a. that women are so simple 479:14
a. with the noble shame 294:3
hope maketh not a. 65:41
Irish are a. 332:26
mirth as does not make friends a. 559:20
more..a...the more respectable 490:13
nor ever once a. 14:30
not a. to fail 278:27
not be a. when they speak 399:35
not so much afraid of death, as a. 86:19
only thing..men are a. of 215:35
see it, and be a. 397:12
something he is a. of 489:9
to beg I am a. 62:18
wonder to see them not a. 520:45
Ashbourne: romantic A. 124:10
Ashbuds: more black than a. 529:25
Ashen: by a. roots the violets blow 533:24
skies they were a. and sober 381:1
Ashes: all a. to the taste 113:39
a. and sparks, my words 496:11
a. of..different varieties of.. tobacco 187:14
a. of Napoleon Buonaparte 564:25
a. of Wickliff 212:8
a. under Uricon 263:9
beauty so a. 55:4
burnt to a. 228:11
chew'd bitter a. 349:22
conveyed his a. into Avon 212:8
earth to earth, a. to a. 391:44
for the a. of his fathers 323:17
from his a...the violet 532:14
handful of grey a. 157:17
her a. new-create another heir 447:16
I am a. where once I was fire 112:37
in our a. live their wonted fires 230:9
in our a. olde 137:45
into a. all my lust 333:9
kindled from the a. of great men 239:20
love in a hut..cinders, a., dust 286:39
noble animal, splendid in a. 87:20
scatter my a. 355:21
scattereth the hoar-frost like a. 400:23
since did from their a. come 281:15
slept among his a. cold 285:29
sour grapes and a. without you 21:3
stone where Alexander's a. lay 33:12
turn to a. on the lips 357:6
turns A.—or it prospers 205:27
Ashlar: my new-cut a. 300:3
Ashore: run 'em a. 213:11
Ashtaroth: Astarte or A., where? 523:6
Asia: dwellers in Mesopotamia.. and A. 64:26
pampered Jades of A. 331:7, 441:37
seven churches which are in A. 70:21, 24
too much A. and she is too old 304:27
Aside: coward stands a. 320:12
shoves Judas and Jesus equally a. 200:42
to step a. is human 104:7
turned a. to do good deeds 300:18
Ask: above all that we a. or think 67:55
all we ought to a. 291:7
a., and it shall be given you 58:19
a. for me tomorrow 478:14
a. him; he shall speak for himself 63:34
a. if truth be there 15:18

Ask (cont.)
a. me how many I'd have 570:30
a. me no more 539:1
a. me no more where Jove bestows 125:9
a. not whom they sleep beside 262:14
a. nothing more of me, sweet 524:33
a. the Lord to bless me 204:1
a. thyself the question 175:18
a. yourself whether you are happy 338:20
came to a. what he had found 507:4
for our blindness we cannot a. 390:53
greatest fool may a. more 154:21
I only a. for information 174:30
I shall not a. Jean Jacques Rousseau 161:22
let him a. of God 69:27
never a. me whose 263:7
not a dinner to a. a man to 271:18
they a. no questions 196:31
too brave to a. Thee anything 213:2
we a. and a. 17:23
what circuit first, I a. not 94:13
where a. is have 503:5
withhold in mercy what we a. 357:27
Askance: look'd on truth a. and strangely 488:5
Asked: a. leave of Mrs. J. 121:21
a. one another the reason 428:26
I have a. to be 254:29
mercy I a. 121:25
nobody a. you, sir 369:16
Oliver Twist has a. for more 177:36
Askelon: publish it not in the streets of A. 47:29
Asketh: every one that a. receiveth 58:20
what a. men to have? 137:34
Asking: a. not wherefore nor why 171:21
first time of a. 391:21
have thy a., yet wait many years 510:16
offering too little and a. too much 124:6
what, without a. 206:14
Asks: nor a. of God, but of her stars 384:31
them that a. no questions 301:18
what a. the Bard? 223:7
Asleep: a. within the tomb 78:16
fall a., or hearing die 446:18
falls a., and then the care is over 527:18
half a. and half awake 171:21
half a. as they stalk 236:14
he lies fast a. 206:1
laid a. in body 581:25
least of things a. upon a chair 584:7
lips of those that are a. 52:20
my Mary's a. 105:29
soon will be a. 34:36
such a tide as moving seems a. 528:22
sucks the nurse a. 426:13
under the haycock fast a. 367:15
ven he vash a. in ped 1:3
very houses seem a. 582:14
when men were all a. 81:15
while all beauty lies a. 246:5
winds are all a. 15:24
Asp: as an a.'s leaf she gan to quake 138:33
scorpion and a., and Amphisbaena 349:21
play on the hole of the a. 53:19
worse than toad or a. 351:17
Asparagus: hit look lak a. 238:11
only necessary to mention A. 175:38
Aspasia: live A. 412:16
Aspect: a. anything but bland 120:27
distraction in 's a. 433:31
lend the eye a terrible a. 443:24
meet in her a. and her eyes 119:1
such vinegar a. 462:30
sweet a. of princes 446:24
there would he anchor his a. 424:1
with grave a. he rose 345:24
Aspen: light quivering a. 418:31
as an a.'s leaf she gan to quake 138:33
Aspens: willows whiten, a. quiver 533:41
Aspersion upon my parts of speech 500:19
Asphodel: violet, amaracus, and a. 537:31
Aspiciam: o rus, quando ego te a.? 261:25
Aspics: 'tis of a.' tongues 472:10

Aspiration: yearning thought and a. 411:33
Aspire: a. to higher things 502:5
a. where my Sun-flower wishes to go 76:7
bidding crouch whom the rest bade a. 93:5
by due steps a. 339:29
light, and will a. 488:26
on what wings dare he a.? 75:24
that smile we would a. to 446:24
Aspired: he that a. to know 94:15
what I a. to be, and was not 95:16
Aspireth: honour a. to it 26:2
Aspiring: a. to be gods if angels fell 383:13
by a. pride and insolence 330:1
teach us all to have a. minds 330:28
Aspirings: the soul hath not her generous a. 307:12
Aspramont: jousted in A. or Montalban 345:4
Aspre: la vertu..demande un chemin a. 355:4
Ass: an a. whose back with ingots bows 462:4
an a., without being a fool 518:6
a. [knoweth] his master's crib 52:16
call great Caesar a. unpolicied 426:13
dies of an a.'s kick 93:39
divil take the a. that bred you 298:21
egregiously an a. 471:4
enamour'd of an a. 467:18
get out, you blazing a.! 121:4
Issachar is a strong a. 45:27
law is a a. 178:1
look an a. when thou art present 155:27
much like his master's a. 469:26
nor his ox, nor his a. 390:17
Wild A. stamps o'er his Head 206:1
write me down an a. 469:10
your dull a. will not mend his pace 437:7
Assail: her terrible tale you can't a. 220:9
no more a. mine eyes 171:7
Assailant on the perched roosts 351:2
Assailed: Virtue may be a. 340:30
Assassination: absolutism moderated by a. 6:5
a. has never changed..history 180:36
a. is the extreme form of censorship 491:2
if the a. could trammel up the consequence 457:7
Assassins: que MM. les a. commencent 284:8
Assault and hurt the soul 389:32
Assaults: crafts and a. of the devil 388:45
Assay: th' a. so hard 138:22
Assemble: when we a. and meet together 388:8
Assembled: glorious th' a. fires appear 503:6
once again a. here 98:13
Assemblies: calling of a., I cannot away with 52:29
Assembling of ourselves together 69:11
Assembly: a. was confused 65:7
enter the public a. and take places 567:29
parliament is a deliberative a. 100:14
Assent: a. with civil sneer 385:29
moved by faith to a. to it 265:10
Assert: a. eternal Providence 344:4
he who has nothing to a. 490:11
Assertion: not refute my general a. 271:31
Asses: a., apes, and dogs 351:18
kept his father's a. 332:23
king Death hath a.' ears 38:27
mankind are the a. who pull 117:31
seeking a., found a kingdom 350:7
wild a. quench their thirst 398:8
Asshen: in our a. olde 137:45
Assistance: cause that lacks a. 33:8
Assistant: let me be no a. for a state 432:45
Assisted the sun materially in his rising 546:36
Associate: when bad men combine, the good must a. 101:36
Assuaged: half a. for Itylus 521:30
Assume: a. a virtue 436:5

INDEX

Assume (cont.)
never a. that which is incapable
of proof 313:24
Assumes: a. the god 191:1
Assuming: a. that he's got any 219:5
Assurance: full a. given by looks 412:18
'London A.' 506:1
make a. double sure 460:6
Assured: most ignorant of what
he's most a. 461:31
saucy look of an a. man 156:11
Assyrian: oil'd and curl'd A. Bull 535:40
the A. came down like a wolf 118:37
Unity, Claribel, A. 299:25
Assyrians: she doted upon the A. 55:32
A-stare: his every bone a. 90:21
Astarte: A. or Ashtaroth, where? 523:6
A. Queen of Heav'n 344:31
Asthmatic: a solicitor, a Free-
mason, and an a. 188:1
Astley, and Sir Marmaduke 323:1
Astolat: Elaine, the lily maid of
A. 530:33
Astonish: can so a. a mother 435:21
loore him on to skittles—and a.
him 120:3
things that would a. you 219:6
Astonished: a., and suddenly cast
down 394:33
a. at my own moderation 146:6
Astonishes: nothing a...as com-
mon-sense 200:4
Astonishment: your a.'s odd 5:27
Astound: startle well, but not a. 340:10
Astra: sic itur ad a. 555:9
Astray: if one goes a. 409:19
like sheep have gone a. 54:26
light that led a. 108:25
one that had been led a. 341:14
Astream: northern lights a. 503:6
Astrolabe: yearning heart for a. 525:16
Astronomer: an undevout a. 587:13
Astronomers: confounding her a. 249:11
Astronomy: Devotion! daughter
of a. 587:13
Asunder: cliffs which had been
rent a. 150:27
let no man put a. 391:34
let not man put a. 59:56
no British Parliament can put
them a. 388:2
taken a., seem men 86:26
when afar and a. 79:9
At: longing to be a. 'em 6:16
Atahualpa: strangled A. 324:28
Atalanta: made of A.'s heels 428:7
Ate: a. and drank as he was told 249:18
A...hot from hell 450:12
a. into itself 110:21
a. the food it ne'er had eat 148:27
a. when..not hungry 519:20
gentlest that ever a. in hall 328:24
never after a. but little 328:22
she pluck'd, she a. 349:15
Athalus, that made..ches 138:13
Athanasian Creed .. splendid
ecclesiastical lyric 182:4
Athanatos: Agios A. 543:18
Athaeneum: 'A.', that was the
name 515:12
Atheism: a little philosophy inclineth..to a. 25:25
honest a. for my money 371:7
miracle to convince a. 25:24
owlet A. 151:19
Atheist: a..laugh 105:20
by night an a. half believes 587:11
female a. talks you dead 278:30
never miracle..to convert an a. 24:18
Rebel and A. too 186:1
Turk, and the A. 140:28
village a. 142:19
Athelney: when Alfred came to A. 140:12
Athena's wisest son 113:13
Athenaeum: 'A.', you mean 515:12
leaving the A. with jugs of stout 243:11
Athenians..to hear some new
thing 64:59
Athens: another A. shall arise 493:27
A. arose 493:24
A. but the rudiments of Paradise 507:1

Athens (cont.)
A., the eye of Greece 350:11
chooses A. in his riper age 193:25
maid of A. 118:6
o'er the Aegean main A. arose 495:27
rejecting the gods of A. 379:24
small states—Israel, A. 267:9
truths as refin'd as ever A.
heard 14:26
ye men of A...too superstitious 64:60
Athirst: give unto him that is a. 71:46
let him that is a. come 72:10
Athlete nearly fell 362:12
Athletic: excel in a. sports 182:19
only a. sport.. backgammon 269:21
Athwart a cedarn cover 151:32
Atkins: thank you, Mister A. 303:1
Atlanta: from A. to the sea 583:7
Atlanteän, the load 16:11
Atlantic: drag the A. Ocean for
whales 550:20
in the steep A. stream 340:4
th' A. billows roar'd 159:1
the A. Ocean beat Mrs. Partington 505:22
the A. surge pours in 546:22
'twas in the broad A. 8:24
where the A. raves 18:16
Atlas: disencumber'd A. of the
state 161:40
like Teneriff or A. unremov'd 347:35
Atmosphere: a. of a new fal'n
year 38:30
this a. divinest 497:9
Atom: a. of meaning in it 129:34
a. that his might could render
void 83:12
Atomic: protoplasmal primordial
a. globule 219:19
Atomies: easy to count a. 428:4
team of little a. 477:7
Atoms: a. or systems into ruin
hurled 383:10
fortuitous concurrence of a. 373:7
let onion a. lurk 505:3
where all these a. are 355:21
Atrabilious liquor 266:17
Attachment: a. à la Plato 220:28
a. to their government 101:13
Attack: a. my Chesterton 41:31
I shall a. 209:9
lead such dire a. 323:22
prompt in a. 100:30
Attacks: a. of..the rest of the earth 566:23
Attain: all that I can a. 4:10
a. to the divine perfection 316:35
a. to write threescore 184:7
a. unto the resurrection of the
dead 68:22
cannot a. unto it 400:8
till old experience do a. 341:25
Attained: not a. by sudden flight 316:31
not a. his noon 246:2
Attainment: so disenchanting as
a.? 514:12
*Attaque: quand on l'a. il se défend
situation excellente. J'a.!* 209:9
Attempt: a. and not the deed 458:4
a. the end 246:19
fearing to a. 461:21
fond a. to give a deathless lot 160:37
no literary a...more unfortunate 265:12
Attempted: something a., something done 318:13
Attend: another to a. him 244:24
a., all ye who list to hear 322:17
I do a. here on the general 472:19
Son of Heav'n and Earth, a. 348:11
*Attend: lorsqu'on a...le trépas de
quelqu'un* 353:23
Attendance: dance a. on their
lordships 447:12
Attended: ever walks a. 340:10
on his way a. 576:9
the curse of kings to be a. 447:42
Attention: awful a. in the audience 499:29
I withdrew my a. 276:17
takes off my a. rather 177:11
Attentive: a. and favourable
hearers 253:35

Attentive (cont.)
a. to his own applause 385:29
minds a. to their own 163:49
Attested by a sufficient number 265:8
Attic: keep his little brain a.
stocked 187:18
mellow glory of the A. stage 16:2
O A. shape! Fair attitude! 287:13
the A. bird trills 350:11
the A. warbler 231:6
Atticum: sal A. 380:3
Atticus: if A. were he 385:29
Attire: her rich a. creeps rustling 285:21
in halls, in gay a. 417:16
in her a. doth show her wit 8:14
in her poor a. was seen 528:2
leap thou, a. and all 425:12
let thy a. be comely 321:17
so wild in their a. 456:13
walk in silk a. 77:22
Attired with sudden brightness 575:10
Attitude: O Attic shape! Fair a.! 287:13
Attitudes: Anglo-Saxon a. 131:14
Attorney: believed the gentleman
was an a. 276:25
office boy to an A.'s firm 221:15
rich a.'s elderly ugly daughter 222:19
you find your a. 219:11
Attorneys: ten a. find place 504:2
Attract: table-crumbs a. his slender feet 546:26
Attraction: conjugal a. unreprov'd 347:17
feels the a. of earth 316:11
Attractive: here's metal more a. 435:3
Oxford is..more a. than Cam-
bridge 28:20
sweet a. grace 347:11
sweet a. kind of grace 412:18
Attribute: a. to awe and majesty 464:33
a. to God himself 464:33
grandest moral a. of a Scotsman 36:17
Auburn: sweet A.! 224:12
Auctioneer: saleroom and varnish-
ing a. 126:10
Audace: de l'a., et encore de l'a. 169:3
Audacia: a. certe laus erit 402:16
Audacity of elected persons 567:7
Audax: a. omnia perpeti 258:6
verbis felicissime a. 404:26
Aude: sapere a. 256:25
*Audendi: a. semper fuit aequa
potestas* 255:15
Audentis Fortuna iuvat 555:10
Audible: a. laughter 139:7
a. voice of the past 126:27
Audi partem alteram 22:2
Audience: and a. into the bargain 237:25
fit a. find, though few 348:23
Audit: how his a. stands 435:37
Auditis an me ludit..insania? 259:25
Aufert: orare Jovem qui ponit et a. 257:11
Aufidus: from A. to Po 324:7
Auger: he bored with his a. 31:1
tail made like an a. 281:19
Augescunt aliae gentes 321:1
Aught: if a. be worth the doing 77:32
while a. remains to do 408:6
Augmentation of the Indies 484:4
Augur: they a. misgovernment 100:30
Augur: a. schoenobates medicus magus 283:3
Augurers: the a. say they know not 425:16
Augurs: a. and understood rela-
tions 459:24
sad a. mock their own presage 488:2
Augury: we defy a. 437:34
August: dry A. and warm 550:2
sicklemen, of A. weary 480:7
to recommence in A. 116:47
twin halves of one a. event 235:16
Augusta: my dear A. 376:8
Augustan: the next A. age 558:25
Augustus: A. was a chubby lad 249:18
decree from Caesar A. 61:16
unalterably, never yours, A. 176:36
Aunt: an a. in Yucatan 41:34
her A. was off to the Theatre 41:13
his A. Jobiska 312:6, 7, 9
my old a. at Clapham 233:5
Auntie A., did you feel no pain 228:6
Sister and A. say 303:18

INDEX

Aunts: his a., who are not married 142:8
his sisters and his cousins and
his a. 221:14
summer songs for me and my a. 485:16
Aura: ne mutata retrorsum te ferat
a. 257:9
Aurae: quem mulcent a. 133:9
Auras: superasque evadere ad a. 554:23
Auream quisquis mediocritatem 259:6
Aureate: to no such a. Earth 205:28
Aureus: non deficit alter a. 554:24
Auri sacra fames 554:13
Aurora: A.'s harbinger 467:10
rising with A.'s light 521:16
Aurora Leighs: no more A. 207:33
Aurum irrepertum 259:23
Auspicious: one a. and one drop-
ping eye 430:24
Austen: Miss A. is my country-
woman 353:6
Auster: away went A. 324:7
upon black A. ride 324:11
Austere: an a. man 62:38
Austerlitz: drank death like wine
at A. 141:14
voilà le soleil d'A. 361:3
Austin: use A.'s words verbatim
still 109:4
Austria: Don John of A. 141:6,8,9
outlive..the imperial eagle..of
A. 216:17
Austrian: an A. army, awfully
arrayed 5:7
Auteur: on s'attendait de voir un a. 373:21
Author: adopt me as their favourite
a. 491:8
amended by its A. 211:21
a. and finisher of our faith 69:18
a. and giver of all good things 389:43
a. both of life and light 281:23
a...concealed behind the door 271:2
a. of authors 24:12
a. of himself 429:17
a. of peace 388:25
a. who speaks about his own
books 181:5
but a shrimp of an a. 231:24
choose an a. as you choose a
friend 180:8
go to the a. to get at his meaning 413:3
if it's by a good a. 489:25
illuminated with the A.'s own
candles 542:31
man of rank appeared [as an a.] 274:34
next in merit to the a. 309:14
no a. ever spar'd a brother 215:23
pickt from the leaves of any a. 86:17
prefer being the a. of [Gray's
Elegy] 572:15
richest a. that ever grazed 271:7
ruin half an a.'s graces 357:26
sole a. of his own disgrace 160:17
this is indeed to be an a. 239:14
what the a. promised to himself 270:25
where is any a. in the world 455:15
Authority: as one having a. 58:29
a. forgets a dying king 531:31
a. over ten cities 62:36
base a. from other's books 454:32
drest in a little brief a. 461:31
every shadow of a. and credit 101:17
Government must have an a. 413:23
in a. settled and calm 26:27
man under a. 58:31
reproofs from a. 26:26
tongue-tied by a. 487:14
what's that? A. 452:22
wrest once the law to your a. 465:2
Authors: chief glory..its a. 277:25
damn those a. whom they never
read 142:29
from English a. their copyrights 549:11
invades a. like a monarch 194:13
much exposed to a. 564:12
vulgar a. in romances 110:44
'We a., Ma'am' 181:19
Autobiography: every artist writes
his own a. 198:23
Automa: an a., runs under water 281:19
Automatic: smoothes her hair
with a. hand 197:32

Autoriser leurs injustices 557:4
Autres: encourager les a. 557:1
Autrui: supporter les maux d'a. 407:9
Autumn: an a. was that grew the
more 426:1
a. evening, and the morn 498:12
A. nodding o'er the yellow plain 546:17
breath of A.'s being 496:4
congenial A. comes 315:19
descends the a. evening 17:16
happy A.-fields 538:17
harmony in a. 494:6
long dark a.-evenings 90:4
old A. in the misty morn 253:13
to yellow a. turn'd 487:29
Autumnal: a. leaves like light footfalls 496:2
deep, a. tone 496:11
one A. face 184:16
thick as a. leaves 344:25
Auxiliary: undone by my A. 512:4
Auxilio: non tali a...tempus eget 554:11
Availeth: the struggle naught a. 147:8
Avails: what a. the sceptred race 308:14
Avalanche: beware the awful a. 316:21
Avante: non vi leggemmo a. 168:23
Avarice: a., the spur of industry 265:4
beyond the dreams of a. 274:29, 356:3
take up with a. 115:27
Avatar: in Vishnu-land what A.? 97:19
Avaunt: a. ye, base carles 420:25
bidst them a. 121:18
conscience a. 144:28
hence, a. ('tis holy ground) 231:11
Ave: a. atque vale 133:20
a...morituri te salutant 13:4, 517:22
A. Maria! 'tis the hour of
prayer 116:7
A., Virgo! Gr-r-r—you swine! 96:42
with an A. Mari 502:20
Avena: tenui musam meditamur a. 505:26
tenui musam meditaris a. 555:14
Avenge: a. me of this one upstart
clerk 242:21
A., O Lord, thy slaughtered
saints 351:20
a. our blood 70:46
a. the patriotic gore 405:19
Avenger: bright a. of sly-dealing
wrong 42:1
still the enemy, and the a. 392:8
Time, the a. 114:17
Aventures: les a...au milieu des
chefs-d'œuvre 211:3
Avenue of cypresses 310:23
Avenues: seal up the a. of ill 199:29
shrubberies and lawns and a. 296:30
Averni: facilis descensus A. 554:23
Averse: what cat's a. to fish? 230:2
Aversion: begin with a little a. 500:15
business was his a. 195:21
indifference closely bordering
on a. 514:13
manner which is my a. 116:5
Aves: after thousand a. told 285:29
Aves: sic vos non vobis nidificatis a. 556:27
Avi numerantur avorum 556:25
Avilion: island-valley of A. 531:37
Avis: rara a. in terris 283:8
Avoid: a. what is to come 436:2
man I should a. 448:27
pray you, a. it 434:15
what he would most a. 340:19
Avoided: what can be a. 449:21
Avoiding: device for a. thought 241:1
superstition in a. superstition 27:21
Avon: his ashes into A.; A. into
Severn 212:8
sweet Swan of A. 281:18
Avow: an a. to God made he 30:11
Avowed: his first a. intent 99:35
the a., erect and manly foe 124:13
Await: a. no gifts from Chance 18:4
do not we..a. it too? 18:12
Awaiting: a. instructions Jellings 39:29
a. the sensation 219:31
Awaits alike th' inevitable hour 230:1
Awake: all shall a. again 85:21
are you a. in the dark? 362:28
a. and pity them that weep 123:26
a., arise, or be for ever fall'n 344:27

Awake (cont.)
a., a., the morn will never rise 169:13
a.! for Morning in the Bowl of
Night 205:4
a., my heart, to be loved 80:11
a., my Little ones 205:6
a., my St. John! 383:7
a. my soul, and with the sun 292:1
A., O north wind 52:8
a. right early 395:19
a.! the heavens look bright 357:1
a. up, my glory; a., lute and
harp 395:19
Christians a. 112:24
dream of thee, when I am a. 155:27
England! a.! a.! a.! 75:11
he will a. no more 491:18
high time to a. out of sleep 66:13
let me be a. 150:2
lie a. in the dark and weep 567:20
lie ten nights a. 468:17
lying a. with a dismal headache 219:9
my lute, a. 583:21
Onaway! A., beloved! 318:1
rose was a. all night 536:13
smiles a. you 170:23
stab my spirit broad a. 516:10
we're very wide a. 219:34
why did I a.? 263:17
with the clamour keep her still a. 479:7
Awaked: a. as one out of sleep 397:1
sleepeth, and must be a. 48:3
Awakened from the dream of life 492:6
Awaking: the great a. 35:6
Award: general a. of love 286:20
love of good and ill, be my a. 285:9
Awards: the court a. it 465:10
Aware: England bore, shaped,
made a. 84:21
a. assemblies I cannot a. with 52:29
Away: a.! a.! for I will fly to thee 287:28
a., a., went Auster 324:7
a. before me 482:1
a. from thee 319:8
a., I'm bound to go 8:21
a., slight man 451:14
a.! take heed 244:10
a.! the moor is dark 408:26
a. went Gilpin 160:1
a. went hat and wig 160:1
a. with him! he speaks Latin 445:41
a. with Systems! 337:35
a., you rolling river 8:21
boot, saddle, to horse, and a.! 90:10
come, dear children, let us a. 15:22
kiss, a sigh, and so a. 166:15
never see us but they wish us a. 213:11
Niamh calling A., come a. 585:7
think on him that's far a. 104:24
took them quite a. 129:27
when I was a. 214:24
while Lubin is a. 266:8
Awe: attribute to a. and majesty 464:33
exempt from a. 497:12
have not Thee in a. 300:26
in a. of such a thing 448:17
keep even kings in a. 169:9
nature in a. to him 343:11
over his female in due a. 350:35
pity and mournful a. 16:6
set i' the pathless a. 545:3
stand in a., and sin not 391:52
strikes an a. and terror 155:19
whose bend doth a. the world 448:20
with a. around these silent walks 164:35
Aweary: a. of the sun 461:6
I am a., a. 535:30, 32
my little body is a. 463:4
Awed by my fears 373:18
Awful: anything a. makes me
laugh 307:11
a. purity 202:22
how a. goodness is 347:31
keeps 'is side-arms a. 295:21
magnificent and a. cause 162:45
motiveless malignity—how a.! 153:1
still and a. red 149:25
this is an a. place 416:5
unpronounceable a. names 239:3
Awfulness: marriage..attracts..
by its very a. 514:28

INDEX

Awkward: an a. thing to play with
  souls 92:45
  a...in the society of his equals 306:17
  a. squad 108:40
Awl: all that I live by is with the a. 448:5
Awoke: a. one morning..famous 120:1
  a. one night 265:16
  I a., and behold..a dream 99:26
  I a., and found me here 286:36
  Sir Launcelot a. 328:20
  when I a., it rained 149:28
Awry: for leaning all a. 207:15
  not so much a. 11:5
  strike not a. 358:7
  their currents turn a. 434:4
Axe: a. is laid unto the root 57:31
  a.'s edge did try 332:24
  let the great a. fall 436:38
  Lizzie Borden took an a. 8:7
  owner of the a. 546:38
  seventy, Simmery A. 222:17
  Suffolk his a. did ply 189:8
  with a golden a. 478:23
Axes: your sharp-edged a. 567:4
Axioms in philosophy are not a.
  until.. 289:34
Axis: a. of the earth sticks out
  visibly 251:17
  soft under-belly of the A. 144:12
Axle: his glowing a. doth allay 340:4
Axletree: the fly sat upon the a. 27:35
Ay: 'A.', said Creep 171:23
  Scylla and Charybdis of A. and
  No 363:19
  stinted and said, 'A.' 477:4
  Tomlinson said, 'A.'. 302:31
Aye: in the pentameter a. falling 152:8
Ayes: no question makes of A. and
  Noes 207:1
Aylmer: Rose A., all were thine 308:14
Ayont the law 516:20
Ayr: auld A. 108:3
Azalea: it was the a.'s breath 375:12
Azarias: Ananias, A., and Misael 388:23
Aziola: did you not hear the A.? 492:22
Azores: at Flores in the A. 539:16
Azure: a., black, and streaked with
  gold 497:22
  a.-lidded sleep 285:24
  a. moss and flowers 496:8
  far in yon a. deeps 318:4
  no wrinkle on thine a. brow 114:29
  riding o'er the a. realm 229:23
  robes the mountain in its a. hue 122:31
  soothed by every a. breath 494:11
  thine a. sister 496:4
  with a., white, and red 190:4

B

B bit it 366:7
  mark it with B. 368:10
Baalim: Peor and B. forsake their
  temples dim 343:23
Babblative and scribblative 508:6
Babble: for the watch to b. 468:38
  learned b. of the saleroom 126:10
Babbled: a' b. of green fields 443:19
Babbler: what will this b. say? 64:58
Babbles: brook that b. by 230:12
Babbling gossip of the air 482:22
Babe: acts like a b. 304:3
  any b. on any mother's knee 525:3
  b. in Eternity 73:25
  b. leaps up 576:7
  B. look't up 165:36
  B. must eat 508:16
  bring the b. to rest 196:2
  burning o'er the b. 525:16
  Coleridge lull the b. at nurse 117:28
  come little b. 80:8
  finger of birth-strangled b. 459:33
  if my young b. were born 32:19(-33)
  laid her B. to rest 343:25
  let the mighty B. alone 166:2
  like a testy b. 484:31
  love the b. that milks me 457:13
  naked new-born b. 457:9
  pretty B. all burning bright 508:14
  silly tender B. 508:17

Babel: B. .. divergence upon
  morals 514:17
  stir of the great B. 163:23
Babes: as newborn b. 69:47
  old men, and b. 150:15
  out of the mouth of..b. 392:8
  revealed them unto b. 61:37
  thy b. around thee cling 583:1
Babies: as were b. all 5:16
  cruel children, crying b. 515:24
  putting milk into b. 144:14
  waiting for the Sleary b. 300:21
Bab-lock-hithe: stripling Thames
  at B. 18:9
Baboon: bred out into b. and
  monkey 480:19
Baby: b. figure of the giant mass 481:8
  little b. thing 326:21
  bye, b. bunting 366:11
  child and mother, b. bliss 232:3
  come from, b. dear? 326:17
  cry, b., cry 366:15
  down comes the b. 73:14
  his b. on my knee 293:4
  in the oven for b. and me 368:10
  mother cried, b. lept 232:3
  my b. at my breast 426:13
  no one but the b. cried 293:5
  rock-a-bye b. 73:14
  she who gives a b. birth 334:1
  that great b. 433:21
  upon his b. brow the round 460:8
  when the first b. laughed 36:7
  where a Mother laid her B. 3:20
  you called me B. Doll 238:7
Babylon: B. be thrown down 71:33
  B. in all its desolation 169:20
  B. is fallen 71:25
  by the waters of B. 400:5, 558:26
  daughter of B. 400:6
  die at thirty-five in B. 19:3
  ere B. was dust 496:18
  how many miles to B.? 367:4
  I was a King in B. 241:24
  king of B. stood at the parting 55:31
  London is a modern B. 182:37
  mystery, B. the great 71:32
Babylonian: grandeurs of his B.
  heart 544:12
  B. pulpits 102:8
Babylonish dialect 110:9
Babylons: all man's B. 544:12
Bacchanal: ivy falls with the B.'s
  hair 522:3
Bacchus: B. and his revellers 348:23
  B. by night 522:2
  B. ever fair, and ever young 191:2
  charioted by B. and his pards 287:28
  plumpy B. with pink eyne 424:19
  proves dainty B. gross 455:22
Baccy for the Clerk 301:18
Bach: fugues and 'ops' by B. 220:5
Bachelor: b., a solicitor, a Freemason 188:1
  b. of three-score 468:3
  b.'s fare 520:5
  I will live a b. 468:4
  old b. don't die 560:14
  when I said I would die a b. 468:24
Bachelors: all reformers are b. 356:4
  reasons for b. to go out 196:28
  two old B. 312:12
Back: at my b. I always hear 333:9
  b. and side go bare 516:21(-517)
  b., Lartius! b., Herminius! b.,
  ere the ruin fall! 323:24
  b. o' beyont 419:11
  b. on budding boughs 82:4
  b. the masses against the classes 222:40
  b. to Mandalay 299:10
  b. to the Army again 294:23
  be put b. tomorrow 510:16
  borne me on his b. 437:15
  die with harness on our b. 461:7
  go b. with Policeman Day 295:11
  I sit on a man's b. 548:10
  its being puts blissful b. 254:18
  laid him on his b. 176:31
  my b. unto an aik 32:18
  never come b. to me 528:3
  never turned his b. 97:4

Back (cont.)
  news..lumb'ring at his b. 163:20
  new snow on a raven's b. 478:19
  no glory lives behind the b. 468:27
  not to go b. 386:8
  not turn your b. 316:35
  now that I am b. 363:16
  on his b. the burden 329:19
  on so proud a b. 488:27
  on the bat's b. I do fly 480:14
  plowed upon my b. 399:37
  rubs its b. upon the window-
  panes 197:17
  show'd his b. above the elements 426:1
  speak ill..behind his b. 276:25
  those before cried 'B.!' 323:22
  thumps upon your b. 159:31
  turn'd my b. upon Don or devil 539:20
  turn thy b. on heaven 199:6
  what thing upon his b. had got 160:1
  when your b. stops aching 296:33
  will you no come b. again? 250:19
  with his b. to the East 148:17
  yes, and b. again 367:4
  you shall go b. for mine 160:9
Backbiter: face-flatterer and b. 531:23
Backbone: Alps shaping like a b. 235:22
  b. of the Army 295:23
Backed: it is backed like a weasel 435:26
Backgammon: only athletic sport..
  b. 269:21
Backing: a plague upon such b.! 439:16
Backs: b. to the wall 233:20
  beast with two b. 469:31
  our b. is easy ris 176:23
  their birthrights..on their b. 447:21
  when maids lie on their b. 477:7
Backward: b. and forward he
  switched his long tail 151:8
  b...as I cast my eyes 573:26
  b., turn b., O Time 4:16
  dark b. and abysm of time 479:20
  fell from off the seat b. 47:9
  his eye was b. cast 509:26
  I by b. steps would move 552:7
  never look b. to their ancestors 102:9
  revolutions never go b. 422:24
  silence surged softly b. 171:10
  so b. to comply 161:6
  thou wilt fall b. 477:3
Backwards: b...did she pass 298:29
  memory that only works b. 130:28
  swings b. and forwards 249:24
  whole narrative always going b. 558:15
Bacon: b. and..eggs..like..prim-
  roses 181:35
  B. of our rhyming crew 309:8
  B., that..hardy genius 226:27
  b. was nat fet for hem 138:6
  Friar B. and Friar Bungay 231:34
  here's to thee, B.! 121:22
  Secretary of Nature..B. 559:29
  think how B. shined 384:12
  unless you give him b. 140:25
Bacons: on, b., on! 439:6
Bad: all baronets are b. 222:2
  b. as b. can be 275:19
  B. King 422:14
  b. news infects the teller 423:23
  b.'s the best of us 37:17
  B. Thing 422:17
  bold b. man 446:15, 509:20
  brave b. man [Cromwell] 145:29
  for being a little b. 462:27
  how sad and b. and mad it was 90:38
  I have b. dreams 433:12
  I rather like b. wine 182:24
  mad, b. and dangerous to know 306:2
  make b. good 462:17
  married, which was b. 304:30
  my b. angel fire my good one
  out 488:19
  my pen in defence of a b. cause 194:14
  never good to bring b. news 424:15
  nor good compensate b. 96:14
  not really b. at heart 41:14
  obstinacy in a b. cause 86:14
  of this b. world the loveliest 41:24
  our best is b. 90:28
  our sad b. glad mad brother 522:18
  repeal of b. or obnoxious laws 228:23

[607]

Bad (cont.)
so much b. in the best 249:4
so sublimely b. 385:28
strong antipathy of good to b. 386:22
the b. affright 230:15
the b. die late 170:2
there never was..a b. peace 211:8
things b. begun 459:9
things that are b. for me 489:5
too b. to be worth publishing 490:42
when b. men combine 101:36
when she's b. 36:12
when she was b. 318:11
wiser being good than b. 89:22
Bade: those who b. me fight 202:18
Badge: b. of all our tribe 463:21
b. of pusillanimity 442:21
oars, and coat, and b. 173:14
Red B. of Courage 165:23
Badger: bar of the Black B. 175:12
Badman: Mr. B. died..like a Chrisom-child 99:2
Badness: all good and no b. 502:18
b. of her b. when she's bad 36:12
Baffled: b., get up and begin again 92:42
b. to fight better 97:4
Englishman..not easily b. 28:30
though b. oft is ever won 117:38
Baffling: beat down b. foes 15:13
Bag: B. of Parliamentary Eloquence 126:35
in the b. of one bee 97:1
though not with b. and baggage 428:2
Turks..b. and baggage 222:35
what did you take out of the b.? 403:24
Bagatelle: vive la b.! 512:22
Baggage: believe the b. loves me 155:22
Bagpiper: laugh like parrots at a b. 462:30
Bags: three b. full 366:9
Bah to you 221:2
Bahram, that great Hunter 206:1
Baiae: pumice isle in B.'s bay 496:8
Bailey: unfortunate Miss B. 154:11
Bailiff's daughter of Islington 29:24(–30)
Bait: b. in the fishes' mouth 11:21
make a b. of pleasure 243:25
with saints dost b. thy hook 462:11
with this melancholy b. 462:35
your b. of falsehood 432:33
Baited like eagles 440:17
Baiting-place of wit 501:26
Baits: b. and seeming pleasures 352:9
for subscribers b. his hook 143:6
good news b. 351:1
Bake: b. me a cake 368:10
you cannot b. or boil him whole 40:30
Baked: b. in a pie 368:20
funeral b. meats 431:4
you have b. me too brown 129:25
young healthy child..b. 520:3
Baker: a b. rhymes 96:27
pat-a-cake, b.'s man 368:10
Bakers and brewers 310:5
Baker Street irregulars 188:22
Bakewell: at B. in half-an-hour 413:1
Baking: and the b. 480:38
Hot Muffin and Crumpet B. 176:37
Balance: as the small dust of the b. 54:12
at the b. let's be mute 104:8
b. of power 559:3
in b. with this life 584:21
redress the b. of the Old 124:21
uncertain b. of proud time 231:35
weigh thy words in a b. 57:4
Balanced: I b. all 584:21
Balances: weighed in the b. 55:42
Balanza: b...que iguala al pastor con el rey 134:18
Bald: b. sexton, Time 447:30
dry, b., and sere 282:1
go up, thou b. head 48:18
his expression..b. 19:18
if I were fierce and bold 415:12
Occasion..is b. behind 158:19
otherwise b...narrative 220:13
rub my b. pate 387:2
Baldheaded: go into it b. 319:22
Baldness full of grandeur 19:18
Bales: undid his corded b. 18:16
Ball: after the b. is over 238:5

Ball (cont.)
b. into the grounded hat 164:8
B. no question makes 207:1
drove his b. through Helen's cheek 228:10
little b. of feather and bone 236:27
only wind it into a b. 75:8
real business of a b. 518:38
roll on, thou b. 218:12
urge the flying b. 230:24
Ballad: b. and story 586:14
grand old b. of Sir Patrick Spence 150:30
guilty of such a b. 454:37
I love a b. in print 485:30
I met with a b. 120:21
woful b. 427:21
Ballad-mongers: these same metre b. 439:45
Ballads: b., songs and snatches 219:15
better than all the b. 316:2
permitted to make all the b. 208:31
sit in the shade singing of b. 370:17
Ballast: our b. is old wine 376:24
we laid them on the b. 539:19
Balliol made me, Balliol fed me 40:32
Balloon: something in a huge b. 578:23
Ballot is stronger than the bullet 314:5
Ball-room: bright as a b. 294:35
Balls: elliptical billiard b. 220:6
let b. like the Edinburgh Review 240:7
two pitch b...for eyes 455:9
our rackets to these b. 443:11
Balm: all our calm is in that b. 365:23
b. for aches 334:5
b. from an anointed king 475:1
b. of hurt minds 458:11
b. of woe 501:26
b. upon the world 285:35
general b. 186:3
I wash away my b. 475:22
like b. the trickling nonsense 155:5
no b. in Gilead 55:17
odorous gums and b. 347:5
'tis not the b. 444:23
Balms break my head 400:14
Balmy: b. isle of Rum-ti-Foo 217:25
in thy b. nest 166:5
Baloo, baloo, my wee wee thing 213:1
Balsams: Pharaoh is sold for b. 87:19
Baltimore: flecked the streets of B. 405:19
Balzac: all B.'s novels occupy one shelf 89:29
Ban: spreading ruin and scattering b. 88:11
'B., 'B., Ca-Caliban 479:43
Banbury: to B. came I 79:18
to B. Cross 368:17
Banburys: three-corners, and B. 219:13
Band: Alexander's Ragtime B. 43:16
b. of glorious Angels 361:9
black Auster's b. 324:12
captain of this ruin'd b. 444:7
cassock, b., and hymn-book too 568:25
happy b. of pilgrims 362:7, 8
heaven-born b. 255:13
in the high aesthetic b. 220:28
last of that bright b. 241:10
my life within this b. 244:20
onward goes the pilgrim b. 35:4
untie the filial b. 417:22
wearied B. swoons to a waltz 266:12
we b. of brothers 444:28(–445)
we march, thy b. 92:13
when the band begins to play 303:1
Bandage: fenced about with a b. stout 311:17
Bandaged: death b. my eyes 95:10
Bandersnatch: the frumious B. 129:39
Bands: b. of love 55:48
b. of rosy hue 266:8
freed from servile b. 583:11
loose the b. of Orion 49:24
loose the b. of wickedness 54:36
pursue Culture in b. 565:24
strong as iron b. 318:11
Bandusiae: *o fons b.* 260:7
Bandy children, nor fasting 76:4
b. civilities with my Sovereign 271:24
Bane: b. of the most generous souls 229:9

Bane (cont.)
best deserve the precious b. 345:10
what of the world's b.? 585:6
Bang: b. these dogs of Seville 539:20
b. went saxpence 403:15
b.-whang-whang goes the drum 97:14
not with a b. but a whimper 197:12
Banged the youth into dumbness 483:31
Banging er de drums 238:24
Bangs me most severely 125:18
Bang-up chariot 178:16
Banish: b. plump Jack and b. all the world 439:37
I b. you 429:14
night that should b. all sin 223:10
Banished: alone, a b. man 31:16
Cimber should be b. 449:30
for my wilful crime art b. 349:30
Banishing for hours the sex 159:18
Banishment: bitter bread of b. 474:33
Banjo: she'd git 'er little b. 299:12
Bank: as I sat on a sunny b. 5:14
b. and shoal of time 457:7
breathes upon a b. of violets 481:30
broke the B. at Monte Carlo 217:23
from the B. to Mandalay 299:13
George goes to sleep at a b. 269:2
I know a b. 466:41
I'll set a b. for thee 475:14
moonlight sleeps upon this b. 465:18
pregnant b. swelled up, to rest 184:29
waly, waly, up the b. 32:18
Banked the fires high 302:31
Banker: thought he saw a B.'s Clerk 128:18
Bankrupt of life 190:14
Banks: Aristocrat who b. with Coutts 218:22
as the b. fade dimmer away 16:4
b. of the slow winding Ouse 162:7
bonnie b. o' Loch Lomon' 9:7
Brignal b. are wild 419:7
green b. of Shannon 122:10
my b...furnished with bees 499:14
never on thy b. 315:20
ye b. and braes 108:36
Banner: b. waved without a blast 417:13
b. with the strange device 316:17
Freedom's b. streaming o'er us 234:13
Freedom's lion-b. 122:30
his b. over me was love 51:44
his blood-red b. streams afar 240:20
our b. of England blew 529:4
royal b., and all quality 472:3
star-spangled b. 292:11
that b. in the sky 251:5
thy b. torn but flying 114:14
Banners: all thy b. wave 122:19
army with b. 52:15
b. flout the sky 456:8
confusion on thy b. wait 229:20
hang out our b. 461:2
royal b. forward go 210:8
Banquet: a trifling foolish b. towards 477:10
no hawk, no b., or renown 245:2
Banquet-hall: some b. deserted 357:14
Banqueting upon borrowing 56:46
Banquo: the blood-bolter'd B. 460:12
Banter: how does fortune b. us 78:2
Baphometic Fire-baptism 127:15
Baptism: B., and the Supper of the Lord 391:12
B. to Such..of Riper Years 90:61
my Godfathers..in my B. 391:2
Baptism'd: the B. found him..deep 387:24
Baptiz'd: b. in tears 310:2
b. or infidel 345:4
Bar: b. for thy mouth 57:4
b. of the Black Badger 175:12
from the gold b. of Heaven 410:7
get up and b. the door 30:22
good-bye to the b. 294:2
his birth's invidious b. 533:1
no moaning of the b. 528:22
politics we b. 221:38
sit in the b. 308:5
though the harbour be moaning 294:1
when I have crost the b. 528:22
when I went to the B. 219:3
Barabbas: B. was a publisher 123:14

Barabbas (*cont.*)
B. was a robber 63:69
how..we withstand B. 92:12
Barejar: digo, paciencia y b. 134:15
Barbara: for love of B. Allen 30:1
Barbarian, Scythian, bond nor free 68:31
Barbarians, Philistines, Populace 19:23, 29
his young b. all at play 114:19
Barbaric: b. pearl and gold 345:14
my b. yawp 568:2
Barbarism: carried on by methods of b. 123:15
Barbarisms: clear it from colloquial b. 278:13
Barbarity: act with the b. of tyrants 505:20
Barbarous: b. dissonance 340:26, 348:23
b. experiment, b. hexameters 529:16
invention of a b. age 343:26
say 'twas a b. deed 499:15
Barbarously: so b. not a Greek 266:14
Barbarousness: confess mine own b. 502:9
Barber: b.'s man..seen with him 468:32
I must to the b.'s, mounsieur 467:13
very imprudently married the b. 209:18
Barbiton: b. hic paries habebit 260:12
Bard: b. divine 231:3
b...more fat than b. beseems 546:4
b. sublime, if b. may e'er be so 499:16
blame not the b. 356:28
hail, B. triumphant 158:6
hear the voice of the B. 75:23
if the B. was weatherwise 150:30
old or modern b. 340:3
sent up to God by the..b. 89:10
what asks the B.? 223:7
wisest b. 40:4
Bardolph: banish B., banish Poins 439:37
B. of Passion and of Mirth 284:16
b., saints, heroes, if we will 15:9
b. sublime 316:9
b. who died content 287:17
last of all the B. 416:29
Lords too are b. 117:23
love that b. of old enjoy'd 75:18
Olympian b. who sung 199:20
Bardus, a six-foot column of fop 253:8
Bare: back and side go b., go b. 516:21(-517)
b. ruin'd choirs 487:16
b., sheer, penetrating power 19:19
b. the sins of many 54:28
cupboard was b. 368:4
lay b. the mystery to me 249:10
looked on Beauty b. 339:5
poor, b., forked animal 453:21
sae black and b. 107:26
silent, b., ships, towers, domes 582:14
though I go b. 516:21
Bared: b. its eternal bosom 288:13
I b. my big right arm 220:7
Barefac'd on the bier 436:30
Bare-foot: dance b. on her wedding day 479:3
him that makes shoes go b. 109:7
Bare-footed came the beggar-maid 528:1
Bare-legg'd beggarly son of a gun 121:3
Bareness: old December's b. 487:27
Bares: the foeman b. his steel 221:33
Bargain: dateless b. 478:44
necessity never made a good b. 211:12
never was a better b. 501:19
too fond of her most filthy b. 473:22
world-without-end b. 455:33
Bargains: rails..on me, my b. 463:17
Barge: answer'd Arthur from the b. 531:35
b. she sat in 424:6
Bark: b. and bite 561:24
bleat, the b., bellow, and roar 73:26
cowardly dogs b. loudest 563:27
fatal and perfidious b. 342:25
my b. is on the sea 118:14
my little b. attendant sail 384:16
my spirit like a charmed b. 493:20
off shot the spectre-b. 149:14
see, they b. at me 453:29
though his b. cannot be lost 456:11

Bark (*cont.*)
to every wandering b. 488:7
trusts a frail b. 229:6
watch-dogs b. 479:28
watch-dog's honest b. 115:22
yond tall anchoring b. 454:3
Barkis is willin' 174:17
Barks: those Nicean b. of yore 380:17
Barley: fields of b. and of rye 533:40
in among the bearded b. 534:1
sitting on a heap of B. 311:19
three measures of b. for a penny 70:44
Barleycorn: inspiring bold John B. 108:10
John B. should die 106:21
Barley-sheaves: rode among the b. 534:4
Barlow: my Hornby and my B. 545:2
Barmaid: bitter b., waning fast 541:11
Barmaids: are B. chaste? 333:23
Barmie: my b. noddle 105:26
Barn: b. filleth up finely 550:1
built the b., the forge 77:28
he'll sit in a b. 368:2
indeed the b. 255:6
to the stack, or the b. door 341:32
Barnabas..son of consolation 64:30
Barnaby Rudge: with his raven like B. 320:4
Barn-cocks: ere the b. say 236:18
Barns: nor gather into b. 58:11
Baron: 'Good!' said the B. 295:14
Baronet: no little lily-handed B. 539:9
Baronetage: never took up any book but the B. 22:25
Baronets: all b. are bad 222:2
b. by dozens 218:3
Barons: great b. of the mind 515:7
true rust of the B.' Wars 558:14
Barouche-landau: will have their b. 22:17
Barracks: single men in b. 303:4
Barred: all crimson b. 286:37
b. my gates with iron 296:4
it was b. with stakes 334:5
spot that's always b. 220:6
ten-times-b.-up chest 474:10
Barrel: handful of meal in a b. 48:1
taste the b. 107:31
Barrel-load: saved them by the b. 544:32
Barrel-organ: a kind of human b. 175:7
Barren: b. and a dry land 395:25
b. are those mountains 81:19
b. bride 384:30
b. of leaves 486:15
b. superfluity of words 213:21
b. woman to keep house 399:1
b. womb 50:55
city is b. 173:37
destined to a b. strand 279:6
I am but a b. stock 197:36
imagination cold and b. 100:23
live a b. sister 466:16
make b. our lives 523:1
most b. with best using 168:7
none so b. among them 52:5
our virtues b. 513:30
'tis all b. 512:20
Barricade: some disputed b. 421:18
Barricades: die upon the b. 569:14
Barrier against matrimony 290:12
Barring: for b. of the door 30:21
Barrow: the b. and the camp abide 302:9
Barrows: grassy b. of the happier dead 540:23
Bars: beside the glowing b. 586:21
between their silver b. 208:19
clouds..in flakes and b. 151:1
iron b. a cage 319:7
Sun was flecked with b. 149:12
through the same b. 310:1
Tomlinson he gripped the b. 302:31
weary of these worldly b. 448:36
Bartholomew: tidy B. boar-pig 441:39
Bartley: little B., the bootmaker 518:13
Bartrum: call B. father 306:7
Basan: as the hill of B. 396:7
fat bulls of B. 393:4
Base: b. as is the lowly plain 525:36
b., common, and popular 444:14
b. is the slave that pays 443:16
b. of heav'n's deep organ 343:17
b. on which thy greatness stands 579:34

Base (*cont.*)
earth's b. built on stubble 340:31
fly from its firm b. 416:26
keep down the b. in man 530:14
labour without joy is b. 413:20
like the b. Indian 474:2
rising unto place..sometimes b. 26:24
scarlet Majors at the B. 415:12
scorning the b. degrees 449:3
utter'd nothing b. 539:11
who is here so b. 450:16
Based: properly b. *Oun* 91:42
Baseless fabric of this vision 480:8
Basely: spend that shortness b. 440:32
Baseness: boldness is a child of..b. 25:32
but b.' varlet 281:4
gods detest my b. 425:23
no b. we would hide 532:28
Man of b. Earth didst make 207:12
Bashful: b. young potato 220:28
he wore a b. look 77:24
Bashfulness in everything that regards religion 2:24
Basia: da mi b. mille 132:16
Basil: hung over her sweet B. 286:23
steal my B.-pot 286:24
Basilisk: that b. is sure to kill 214:34
Basin: b. of nice smooth gruel 22:9
in a decent b. 390:23
Basing: Old Person of B. 311:5
Basingstoke: hidden meaning—like B. 222:11
Basis or substratum 120:29
Bask in the glens 15:14
Basket: Eve, with her b. 249:7
Baskets: twelve b. full 59:34
Basking: Love..does b. play 158:1
love to lie a-b. in the sun 221:36
Basnet: hammered out my b. point 359:9
is my b. a widow's curch? 31:6
Bass: Hodgson, Guinness, Allsopp, B.! 120:23
Bassarid: the Maenad and the B. 522:2
Bassoon: he heard the loud b. 148:22
flute, violin, b. 536:11
Bastard: Buonaparte the b. 525:21
Bastards: nature's b. 485:23
Bastille: ululatus of No B. 119:32
Bastion: eye-ball like a b.'s mole 503:5
Bat: b. that flits at close of eve 73:21
black b., night 536:9
don't know a gun from a b. 294:24
flitting of a b. 336:33
on the b.'s back 480:14
twinkle, twinkle, little b. 129:8
weak-ey'd b. 153:24
wool of b. 459:31
Bataillons: Dieu..pour les gros b. 557:10
Bate: sour Mr. B. 171:17
Bath: melt into a b. 508:15
nymph to the b. addressed 497:26
people of B. never..light their fires 237:1
sore against the b. 458:11
Bathe: b. in fiery floods 462:9
b. in the fresh sunbeam 497:8
b. the world in light 574:11
b. those beauteous feet 209:3
b. thy breathing tresses 153:20
Bathed: b. in joy complete 82:3
eagles having lately b. 440:17
Bathing: Beauty sat b. 359:27
caught the Whigs b. 180:16
one long b. of a summer's day 579:4
Bathing machine: something between a large b. 219:10
Bathos, the art of sinking 386:25
Bath-rabbim: by the gate of B. 52:19
Baths: b. of all the western stars 541:3
in b. to steep him 280:10
two walking b. 166:10
Bathurst..very good hater 276:18
Bâtir la mort 354:18
Bâton: le b. de maréchal 360:23
Bats: b. in the belfry 378:21
do b. eat cats? 128:21
suspicions..are like b. 27:22

Batsman: ghostly b. plays 545:2
I am the b. 309:27
if the b. thinks he's bowled 309:27
Battalion: Colour-Sergeant of the
Nonpareil b. 174:5
Battalions: God..for the big b. 557:10
inspir'd repuls'd b. to engage 1:10
sorrows come..in b. 436:25
Batten on this moor 435:46
Batter my heart, three-person'd
God 185:18
Battered: this b. Caravanserai 205:29, 30
Batteries of alluring sense 332:7
Battering: bright and b. sandal 254:23
b. the gates of heaven 540:8
Battery: by b. besieged Belgrade 5:7
Battery-mule's a mule 300:8
Battle: after b. sleep is best 365:4
again to the b., Achaians 123:6
agreed to have a b. 130:6
amidst the b.'s thunder 23:21
b. and the breeze 123:10
b. done 387:12
b. goes sore against us 513:30
b.'s magnificently stern array 113:35
b. there was which I saw 327:1
b. was on once more 406:3
b. went roaring 324:15
beat to b. where he stands 538:22
Ben B. was a soldier bold 252:29
brave that die in the b. 146:14
count the life of b. good 362:33
covered my head in the day of
b. 400:12
drunk delight of b. 540:32
each b. sees the other's..face 444:6
fallen in the midst of the b. 47:30
feats of broil and b. 469:45
few die well..in b. 444:19
first blow is half the b. 227:9
foremost in b. was Mary Ambree 31:14
Freedom's b. once begun 117:38
from b. and murder 388:48
gives the b. to his hands 538:22
he who is in b. slain 224:9
in the forefront of the hottest b. 47:32
it was not in the b. 162:11
in storm of b. and calamity 200:3
in the lost b. 418:13
lit the b.'s wreck 241:5
make them ready to b. 399:25
marriage..is a field of b. 514:29
news of b.! 23:22
next..to losing a b. 564:9
noise of b. roll'd 531:29
nor the b. to the strong 51:22
nor war, nor b.'s sound 343:12
nothing except a b. lost 564:4
now the b.-day is past 198:14
old Sarah B. 306:12
one of the most serious things..
in a b. 130:24
prepare himself to the b. 67:1
rung the b. shout 251:5
rushed the steed to b. driven 122:18
see the front o' b. lour 107:32
smelleth the b. afar off 49:27
strong in b. is 421:2
taught the doubtful b. 1:10
this b. fares like to the morning 445:44
to b. fierce came forth 122:3
turned..back in the day of b. 396:34
was ever b. like this 539:21(-540)
when the b.'s lost and won 456:3
while the b. rages loud and long 123:10
Battled: of b. fields no more 416:19
Battle-din: shake our soul with b. 506:19
Battlefield: b. wid all the glory
missin' 304:37
every b. and patriot grave 314:10
met on a great b. 314:12
Battle-line: our far-flung b. 300:24
Battlements entrance of Duncan
under my b. 457:3
hid b. of Eternity 544:26
owls came and perched on b. 39:29
towers, and b. it sees 342:1
Battle-queen: be the b. of yore 405:19
Battles: all his b. won 16:13
b. are lost in the same spirit 567:15
b. long ago 581:2

Battles (cont.)
b., sieges, fortunes that I have
pass'd 470:2
last of many b. 425:8
Lord God of B., aid! 297:8
O God of b.! 444:24
three pitched b. in India 326:9
your high-engender'd b. 453:6
Battle-thunder and flame 539:21
Bauble: delighted with my b.
coach 160:30
many shallow b. boats 481:1
pleased with this b. still 383:30
Strawberry Hill..the prettiest b. 558:11
Baubles: take away these b. 167:8
Bavin: jesters and rash b. wits 440:8
Bawdy: Coleridge..talking b. to
Miss— 306:33
sing me a b. song 440:13
Bawdy-house: pretence of keeping
a b. 277:16
Bawl: b. the Absolute across the
hall 41:32
Fitzgerald b. his creaking couplets 117:8
loud as he could b. 160:2
Bawling what it likes 19:29
Bay: Adriatic breaks in a warm b. 15:14
all the way into Mississippi B. 298:28
be a dog and b. the moon 451:13
Biscay's sleepless b. 113:8
in the B. of Biscay, O! 139:2
it split the b. 150:10
night-cap..instead of b. 224:11
outer China 'crost the B. 299:10
sings in his boat on the b. 528:3
somebody bet on de b. 210:13
thar blysfull b. entoyning every
art 187:4
Bayed: b. about with many enemies 451:7
b. the whisp'ring wind 224:17
here wast thou b. 450:9
Bayona: Namancos and B.'s hold 343:2
Bayonets: chains are worse than b. 269:19
sods with our b. turning 572:11
throne of b. 267:8
Bays: b. burn deep 525:5
have I no b. to crown it? 244:9
ling'ring b. 278:35
palm, the oak, or b. 332:13
sprig of b. in fifty years 521:15
Bay-tree: flourishing like a green b. 394:6
Be: as lief not b. as live to b. 448:17
b. off,—excede 251:20
best is yet to b. 95:13
b. what they behold 381:6
cared not to b. at all 345:15
how can these things b.? 63:8
I'd rather see than b. one 100:1
let Einstein b. 511:8
let it b. as it may 183:17
let Newton b. 382:17
ready to b. anything 87:21
something better not to b. 117:33
to b., or not to b. 434:4

Beach: all left behind on the b. 128:5
along the hidden b. 302:10
came to the b. a poor exile 122:10
dusky b. 322:18
mile of warm sea-scented b. 93:21
not the only pebble on the b. 79:16
on the b. undid his corded bales 18:16
Beached verge of the salt flood 480:32
Beaches: we shall fight on the b. 143:40
Beachy Head: Birmingham by
way of B. 141:22
Beacon: Airly B., Airly B. 293:3
as a b., gives warning 442:21
b.-light is quench'd in smoke 418:4
Beacons: b. from..where the
Eternal are 492:16
b. of hope, ye appear 17:20
b. of wise men 266:22
Beadle: b. to a humorous sigh 455:7
'cept a b. on boxin' day 179:5
Beadroll: Fame's eternal b. 510:5
Beadrolls: set in our b. 502:20
Beads: b. and pray'r-books 383:30
b., pictures, rosaries, and pixes 111:12
my jewels for a set of b. 475:10
relics, b., indulgences 346:26

Beadsman: be your b. now 377:4
the B...slept among his ashes 285:29
Beak: down on his b. 538:2
see his bones and b. 40:23
take in his b. food enough 337:44
thy b. from out my heart 380:27
Beaker full of the warm South 287:2
Beale: Miss Buss and Miss B. 8:10
Be-all: this blow might be the b. 457:7
Beam: b. that is in thine own eye 58:17
full midday b. 352:15
last pale b. of even 498:26
of th' Eternal co-eternal b. 346:18
Beameth: for whom it b. 356:24
Beaming: affection b. in one eye 176:10
Lesbia hath a b. eye 356:24
Beamish: my b. boy 129:39(-130)
oh, b. nephew 128:10
Beams: all his b. full dazzling 566:22
b. from happy human eyes 516:16
chaste b. of the wat'ry moon 466:39
layeth the b. of his chambers 398:8
my sun his b. display 158:17
some b. of wit on other souls 193:2
throws his b. 465:21
to the stars, and the cold lunar
b. 16:14
tricks his b. 343:3
Bean: a not too French French b. 220:28
dined on one pea and one b. 312:19
home of the b. and the cod 79:2
Bean-flowers' boon 91:4
Bean-rows: nine b. will I have
there 585:19
Beans: full o' b. and benevolence 518:21
you must not give him b. 140:25
Bear: all this I b. 16:25
as she [a b.] doth her young 109:5
b. it not 432:17
b. me to that chamber 442:29
B. of Very Little Brain 339:21
b. thee in their hands 397:1
b. the longest part 243:24
b. the miseries of a people 357:24
b. them we can 263:32
b. the yoke in his youth 55:25
b. those ills we have 434:4
b. with a sore head 331:17
best b. his mild yoke 351:21
bush suppos'd a b. 467:24
cub-drawn b. would couch 453:2
do be a b.! 376:5
exit, pursued by a b. 485:15
for which we b. to live 384:2
gave pain to the b. 326:1
great she-b. 209:18
hang on the Brown B.'s flank 301:4
his Name and sign who b. 264:13
how a b. likes honey 339:20
huntsman by the b. oppress'd 557:19
I b. up the pillars of it 396:29
if it had been a b. 520:16
learns them first to b. 477:7
love, and b. 497:19
meets the he-b. in his pride 296:13
Moppsikon Floppsikon b. 312:18
no dancing b. was so genteel 160:13
nothing of the b. but his skin 227:32
outwatch the B. 341:17
punishment..greater than I can
b. 44:32
rode on the back of a b. 312:18
rugged Russian b. 459:20
savageness out of a b. 472:27
she-b. thus accosted 296:13
still less the b. 211:25
their habits from the B. 40:22
they bay'd the b. 467:20
too broad to b. with 435:38
to pardon or to b. it 159:31
undying thoughts I b. 338:5
vapour..like a b. 425:19
we must b. all 444:21
we've fought the B. before 265:15
what happens, let us b. 193:17
who would b. the whips..fardels
b. 434:4
ye cannot b. them now 63:61
ye may be able to b. it 66:38
yet could I b. that too 472:34

INDEX

Bear-baiting: fencing, dancing, and b.   482:7
Puritan hated b.   326:1
Bear-baitings: wakes, fairs, and b.   485:20
Beard: b. of formal cut   427:21
  b. the lion in his den   418:27
  built their nests in my b.   311:12
  by the colour of his b.   482:34
  even unto Aaron's b.   400:3
  his b. was grizzled, no?   431:15
  icicle on a Dutchman's b.   483:32
  Jove..send thee a b.   483:22
  let our b. be shook   436:39
  long grey b. and glittering eye   148:18
  Old Man with a b.   311:12
  pluck me by the b.   453:32
  singed the b. of the Bishop   508:1
  singeing of the King of Spain's b.   188:36
  take the Turk by the b.   445:14
  this [More's b.] hath not offended   358:8
  what a b. hast thou got!   463:33
  white b., a decreasing leg   441:19
  with white and bristly b.   486:15
Bearded: b. like the pard   427:21
  scarce-b. Caesar   423:13
Beards: browsing b.   336:38
  long b., and pretences to foretell   520:44
  when b. wag all   442:33
  your b. forbid me to interpret   456:14
Beardsley: I belong to the B. period   39:8
Beareth: b. all things   66:45
  b. up things light   27:1
Bearing: b. up against a world in arms   324:35
  intent of b. them   440:32
Bearings of this observation   175:14
Bear-like I must fight the course   461:8
Bears: b. all its sons away   562:9
  b. it out..to the edge of doom   488:7
  b. not..so stout a gentleman   440:38
  b. the falling sky   263:18
  b., tigers, ounces, pards   347:15
  dancing dogs and b.   249:5
  let b. and lions growl   561:24
  so air our B.   176:24
Beast: b. and bird..were slunk   347:19
  b., but a just b.   5:2
  b., no more   436:15
  b. with many heads   429:15
  b. with two backs   469:31
  b. .. would have mourned longer   430:33(~431)
  Blatant b.   510:8
  blonde b.   364:23
  both man and bird and b.   150:16
  cocoa is a vulgar b.   142:9
  come Hup!..you hugly b.!   518:10
  confused together..one great b.   86:26
  deem himself a god, or b.   383:22
  demi-natur'd with the brave b.   436:42
  drinks like a b.   304:3
  either a b. or a god   14:15
  either a wild b., or a god   26:15
  feeds b. as man   423:14
  forth, b., out of thy stal   136:20
  frets doubt the maw-crammed b.?   95:14
  fullfed b. shall kick the empty pail   197:14
  half a b. is..Pan   88:12
  in at the death of the Blatant B.   325:19
  like a wild b. guards my way   75:19
  like the Hyrcanian b.   433:26
  man's life is cheap as b.'s   452:41
  mark..of the b.   71:21
  marks of the b. to the..genteel   237:6
  more subtil than any b. of the field   44:19
  neither good for man nor b.   11:21
  no b. so fierce   476:7
  noise in the b.'s belly   328:4
  not forfeiting the b.   336:1
  number of the b.   71:22
  questing b.   328:8
  regardeth the life of his b.   50:2
  some evil b. hath devoured him   45:15
  very gentle b.   467:31
  whan a b. is deed   137:29
  who is like unto the b.?   71:20

Beast (cont.)
  wild b. man   78:10
  worship the b.   71:26
Beastie: wee, sleekit, cow'rin, tim'rous b.   107:9
Beasties: long-leggety b.   6:9
Beastly: any b. Erickin'   304:47
  your rooms at college was b.   299:18
Beasts: all b...drink thereof   398:8
  all the b. of the forest   395:3, 398:10
  b. did leap   35:17
  b. that have no understanding   391:23
  b. that perish   395:2
  both small and great b.   308:11
  elders and the four b.   71:4
  fled to brutish b.   450:22
  fought with b. at Ephesus   67:10
  four b. full of eyes   70:37
  kin to the b. by his body   25:26
  mischiefs feed like b.   282:8
  not God's and not the b.'   91:1
  pair of very strange b.   428:34
  prowling b. about Thy way   506:8
  transform ourselves into b.   471:22
Beat: b. down Satan   389:1
  b. following her daily   411:10
  b. him when he sneezes   129:1
  b. of her unseen feet   492:29
  b. of the off-shore wind   298:27
  b. the ground   340:7
  b. the iron while it is hot   194:3
  b. them to their beds   425:14
  b. upon my whorlèd ear   254:26
  b. us to the pit   452:5
  bright before it b. the water   317:22
  feathering soft their solitary b.   375:24
  gold to aery thinness b.   186:25
  go mad, and b. their wives   121:20
  if I thought that, I'd b. him   482:33
  I walk my b. before London Town   301:6
  Miss Jenkyns b. time   213:23
  once b. high for praise   356:20
  or any hearts to b.   585:22
  sound the trumpets, b. the drums   358:13
  telling with a quiet b.   404:22
  they b.—and a Voice b.   544:14
  Tom was b.   369:11
  turban'd Turk b. a Venetian   474:2
  you b. your pate   382:9
  we b. them today or..   511:15
  when thy heart began to b.   75:24(~76)
Beata mea Domina!   359:10
Beaten: b. men come into their own   334:7
  b. till they know what wood   110:39
  b. with few stripes   61:55
  maker is him-self y-b.   138:26
Beateth: one that b. the air   66:37
Beatific: vision b.   345:9
Beating: almost hear the b. of his wings   82:17
  are your drums a-b. yet?   503:1
  b...his luminous wings in vain   19:21
  b. of my own heart   262:9
  b. of so strong a passion   483:9
  glory of b. the French   572:15
  like muffled drums, are b.   317:6
  mend his pace with b.   437:7
Beatings: grandeur in the b. of the heart   575:22
Beatitude: ninth b.   386:36
Beaton: Marie Seaton, and Marie B.   31:18
Beatrice: even I am B.   410:16
  you whisper, 'B.'   93:47
Beats: b. with light wing   359:1
  my pulse..b. my approach   292:20
Beattie: works of Hume, Gibbon, Robertson, B.   306:26
Beatum: ab omni parte b.   259:11
Beatus..qui procul negotiis   257:22
Beau: bow'd, not like a modern b.   119:23
Beaumont: B. and Willoughby   189:8
  B. lie a little nearer Spenser   36:21
  bid B. lie a little further   281:11
Beauteous: all that is most b.   577:13
  b., even where beauties most abound   116:43

Beauteous (cont.)
  b. idiot spoke   155:5
  beauty b. seem   487:5
  commands the b. files   552:1
  I love all b. things   81:9
  one particular b. star   286:18
  sublime and b. shapes   496:19
Beauties: b...their pretty eyes may roll   385:19
  b...undisgraced by..extravagancies   139:21
  compare..their b. to some ancient shepherdesses   370:17
  even where b. most abound   116:43
  forgotten crowd of common b.   125:1
  mar their b. bright   510:20
  meaner b. of the night   583:13
  our b. equal   192:10
  pale, unripened b. of the north   1:17
  sav'd by b. not his own   381:14
  we just b. see   282:1
Beautified: 'b.' is a vile phrase   432:41
  b. with our feathers   232:6
Beautiful: all heiresses are b.   192:42
  all that's b. drifts away   585:19
  all things bright and b.   3:14
  b. and ineffectual angel   19:21
  b. and swift   492:2
  b. and therefore to be woo'd   445:27
  b. Annabel Lee   380:9
  b. as a wreck of Paradise   493:13
  b. as sweet   587:8
  b. city! so venerable   19:10
  b. exceedingly   150:20
  b. face is a silent commendation   24:37
  b. God to behold   525:5
  b. must be the mountains   81:18
  b. Soup   129:26
  b. through love   497:13
  b. Tusculum   175:8
  beauty, making b. old rhyme   488:1
  be less b., or be less brief   561:4
  better to be b. than to be good   570:9
  full b., a faery's child   286:30
  good as thou art b.   530:23
  here lies a most b. lady   171:6
  hides all things b. and good   496:26
  how b. are thy feet with shoes   52:17
  how b., if sorrow   286:5
  how b. is night   508:2
  how b. they stand   241:12
  how b. Thy mercy-seat   202:21
  how b. upon the mountains   54:12
  I see, not feel, how b.   151:2
  joyous, b. and free   497:17
  made his darkness b. with thee   533:4
  more b. than any religion   414:12
  more b. than day   528:1
  more b. than the earth   579:38
  more b. than thy first love   584:12
  most b. adventure in life   212:1
  most b. things..most useless   413:13
  my b., my b.!   365:16
  my bold, my b., my Bulbo   542:28
  of a b. countenance   47:19
  of a b., unheard of kind   586:3
  'Oh, how b.!'   296:32
  one was b.   117:6
  only the b.   252:15
  own that thou art b.   493:4
  she was b.   499:7
  sorrow more b. than Beauty   286:5
  so young, so b.   115:35
  strong is the soul..and b.   15:9
  Tibur is b., too   146:13
  too b. to last   36:29
  too b. to live   177:8
  travel the world over to find the b.   200:5
  very stately palace..B.   99:9
  waters..are b. and fair   576:2
  what a deal of scorn looks b.   483:28
  yet so b.   208:16
Beautifully: as it stands—b.   268:18
  b. less   401:32
  darkly, deeply, b. blue   116:13, 507:29
Beauty: all combin'd in b.'s worthiness   331:2
  all is b.   92:2
  all that b...e'er gave   230:1
  all your world of b.'s gone   247:7

[611]

Beauty (cont.)

amaranthus all his b. shed 342:31(−343)
as much b. as could die 280:11
b. and decay 491:17
b. and length of days 522:7
b. beat on his conceits 331:2
b. beauteous seem 487:5
b. . .best of all we know 80:26
b. born of murmuring sound 581:22
b. by constraint possessing 214:9
b. calls 312:29
B. cannot keep her lustrous eyes 287:27
b. draws us 385:13
b. . .exists in the mind which contemplates 265:5
b. faded has no second spring 378:14
b. for ashes 55:4
b. for some provides escape 266:16
b. from the light retir'd 558:5
b. has no ebb 585:16
b. . .hath strange power 350:33
b. hold a plea 487:13
b. . .in the eye of the beholder 265:14, 557:18
b. is bought by judgment of the eye 455:2
B. is its own excuse 199:26
b. is Nature's brag 340:38
b. is Nature's coin 340:37
b. is not. .an outward show 510:12
b. is the lover's gift 156:5
b. is truth, truth b. 287:15
b. itself doth of itself persuade 486:5
b., like a dial-hand 487:29
b. like hers is genius 410:28
B. lives though lilies die 208:9
b. lives with kindness 484:40
b., making beautiful old rhyme 488:1
b. of a thousand stars 330:6
b. of Israel is slain 47:29
b. of the world 433:15
b. passes like a dream 585:22
b. sat bathing 359:27
b.'s ensign yet is crimson 478:43
b.'s first-born 232:11
b. she was statue cold 208:5
b.'s rose might never die 486:9
b.'s self she is 8:14
b.'s summer dead 487:29(−488)
b. stands in the admiration 350:2
b., strength, youth, are flowers 377:4
B. that must die 287:21
b., titles, wealth, and fame 381:36
b. to delight 169:17
b. took from those who loved them 171:9
b. too rich for use 477:9
b. truly bought 482:20
b. unadorn'd 40:12
b. vanishes, b. passes 171:6
b., wit, high birth 481:21
b. without a fortune 203:10
best part of b. 25:28
breast that b. cannot tame 33:3
brief the moon of b. 538:21
by b. and by fear 579:5
clear perception of its b. 290:13
come near your b. with my nails 445:29
coming in solemn b. 333:18
conscious stone to b. grew 199:23
daily b. in his life 473:9
dreamed that life was B. 7:18, 254:2
dress her b. at your eyes 169:13
dust swept from their b. 88:14
England, home and b. 79:15
eternal b. wandering 586:18
extent of its b. and power 326:3
fatal gift of b. 114:8
flow'r of youth and b.'s pride 190:34
fountain of that heavenly b. 510:14
friend of B. in distress 117:36
fruits of life and b. 74:25
garmented. .from her own b. 499:6
had he not been a thing of b. 221:28
Helen's b. in a brow of Egypt 467:24
her b. and her chivalry 113:25
her b. made the bright world dim 499:7
his b. to consume away 394:10
homely b. of the good old cause 577:16
imaged there in happier b. 577:13

Beauty (cont.)

impress with quietness and b. 582:3
in b. exalted 579:38
in B.'s just applause 331:2
in the b. of the lilies 264:18
in your b.'s orient deep 125:9
Isle of B., Fare thee well! 36:28
its horror and its b. 495:17
I wish her b. 166:18
June for b.'s heightening 18:22
King have pleasure in thy b. 394:23
laws of poetic truth and poetic b. 19:22
looked on B. bare 339:5
look not thou on b.'s charming 419:16
love built on b. soon as b. dies 184:13
loved the principle of b. 290:29
loved your b. with love false or true 586:21
loveliest things of b. 333:19
maids of matchless b. 302:19
make her b. over again 585:4
mighty abstract idea I have of b. 290:12
more beautiful than B.'s self 286:5
mortal b. chase 332:16
music even in the b. 86:32
new in b. and virtue 502:19
no b. she doth miss 8:14
no. .b. that hath not some strangeness 25:29
no b. that we should desire him 54:25
none of B.'s daughters 118:17
none the less blasphemed he b. 112:18
nor Summer b. hath such grace 184:16
of its own b. is the mind diseased 114:16
only b. purely loving 123:18
parallels in b.'s brow 487:9
phantom, b. 584:5
rarest gift to B. 336:27
power of B. I remember 192:3
redemption of all things by B. 489:21
relationship with b. and truth 289:20
Rose is B. 183:3
she dwells with B. 287:21
she walks in b. 119:1
shower of b. 575:16
simple b. and nought else 91:31
snatched away in b.'s bloom 118:23
soul of her b. and love lay bare 497:26
sounds will gather b. from their sense 80:23
Spirit of B. 494:4
spring up into b. like a reed 313:22
such b. as a woman's eye 455:21
such seems your b. still 487:29
take the winds of March with b. 485:26
terrible b. is born 586:19
that Lady B. 411:10
they grew in b. 241:8
thick, bereft of b. 479:12
thing of b. is a joy 284:19
thy b. is to me 380:17
thy b.'s birth is heavenly 123:17
thy b. shall no more be found 333:9
thy b.'s silent music 123:16
till B., Truth, and Love in thee are one 81:5
'tis not a lip. .we b. call 382:24
'tisn't b., so to speak 304:50
too late came I to love thee. .B. 21:22
touches of b. should never be half-way 289:27
To What Serves Mortal B.? 255:10
trenches in thy b.'s field 486:10
triumphs of Love and of B. 526:22
troubled by thy b. 374:10
veiling an Indian b. 464:15
wear the b. of the morning 582:14
what ills from b. spring 279:11
what is b. saith my sufferings then 331:2
what the imagination seizes as b. 289:17
what wages b. gives 586:13
when b. fires the blood 192:4
when thy b. appears 373:18
where B. was, nothing. .ran. .straight 213:3
where perhaps some b. lies 342:1
while all b. lies asleep 246:5
whose b. is past change 255:3
whose b. summoned Greece 331:5

Beauty (cont.)

with the moon's b. 579:20
within one B. meet 332:8
write the b. of your eyes 486:16
your infant b. 421:11
youth, b., graceful action seldom fail 190:27
Beaux: where none are b. 322:5
Beaver: cock up your b. 250:18
young Harry, with his b. on 440:18
Becalmed: ships, b. at eve 147:6
Because: we cannot do it, Sir, b. 131:10
Beck: more offences at my b. 434:9
Beckons me away 547:21
Becks: b. our ready minds 284:25
gold and silver b. me 447:31
nods and b. 341:28
Become: all that may b. a man 457:12
caparisons don't b. a young woman 500:24
doth so well b. her 8:14
what's b. of Waring? 97:16
what shall, alas! b. of me? 321:14
Becomes: b. his coffin prodigiously 226:37
hardly b. any of us 249:4
whom everything b. 423:15
Becometh us to fulfil all righteousness 57:32
Bed: are the weans in their b.? 339:9
as little as my b. 292:2
as to a lover's b. 425:24
at his b.'s heed twenty bokes 137:6
b. at night 225:3
B. be blest that I lie on 3:3
b. for this huge birth 166:1
b. for you and me 30:15
b. in the bush 515:27
b. of Cleopatra 85:20
b. of daffodil sky 536:10
big enough for the b. of Ware 483:34
but as a b. of flowers 186:31
by night on my b. I sought him 52:4
called me from my b. 229:16
called your friend from his b. 302:23
come to b. in boots 243:8
dark wintry b. 496:4
deck both b. and bower 509:33
die—in b. 415:13
down as upon a b. 332:25
drunk him to his b. 424:12
drunk to b. 423:20
dull, stale, tired b. 452:14
each within our narrow b. 132:3
earth Thy b. 506:8
Faith is kneeling by his b. of death 189:20
four angels to my b. 3:3
four of us about that B. 359:12
from his brimstone b. 151:7, 507:19
from the blue b. to the brown 227:17
furnish the fair Infant's b. 166:3
gentlemen in England, now a-b. 444:28(−445)
get the whole world out of b. 333:24
go to b. betimes 482:27
go to b. by day 515:14
go to b. with the lamb 80:2
goes to b. wi' the sun 485:25
gon to hys death-b. 136:17
gravity out of his b. at midnight 439:29
grief. .lies in his b. 447:34
Guilt. .lighted me to b. 252:25
heaped for the beloved's b. 499:1
his b. amid my tender breast 231:39
his pendent b. 457:6
holy angels guard thy b. 562:1
I haste me to my b. 486:23
I have to go to b. 515:14
I toward thy b., Yasmin 208:12
I in my b. again 11:14
in a manger for His b. 3:20
in going to my naked b. 196:2
in order to get to b. 196:5
kick his wife out of b. 518:8
laid in b. majestical 444:23
let's to b. 366:13
like a pillow on a b. 184:29
lovers, to b. 467:34
make my b. soon 31:10
marriage. .not a b. of roses 514:29
me mostly sent to b. 309:10

Bed (cont.)
mother, mother, make my b. 30:3
must we to b. indeed? 515:26
my b. it is fu' lowly now 30:16
my bosom, as a b. 484:32
my grave, as now my b. 87:1
nicer to lie in b. 310:15
not to be a-b. after midnight 482:27
o'erhang his wavy b. 153:24
on his thorny green b. 376:19
only book that..took him out of b. 271:36
pluck me from my naked b. 305:13
plucked them from their b. 320:6
put them to b. 369:4
remembered thee in my b. 395:26
rode their horses up to b. 171:11
rouse them from their lowly b. 229:31
second best b. 488:30
sleep on, my Love, in thy cold b. 292:19
sleep upon a golden b. 584:23
smooth pillows, sweetest b. 501:27
so he on his b. 562:3
so to b. 377:11
spare b. for my friends 377:29
steal out of his wholesome b. 449:15
sun in b. 343:24
take up thy b., and walk 63:16
thrice-driven b. of down 470:8
to more than one a b. 186:8
when he vash asleep in b. 1:3
warm weather..in b. 519:22
welcome to your gory b. 107:32
Bedabbled with the dew 246:22
Bedding labelled Sergeant Whats-isname 300:17
Bedeck and bedrape us 522:22
Bedeck'd: so b., ornate, and gay 350:31
Bedfellows:misery..strange b. 479:40
poverty has strange b. 322:13
Bedford: Harry the King, B. and Exeter 444:28
Bedonebyasyoudid: Mrs. B. is coming 294:8
Bedrape: bedeck and b. us 522:22
Beds: beat them to their b. 425:14
b. of sand and matted rushy isles 17:28(-18)
borders, b. and shrubberies 296:30
came unto my b. 484:27
half his flock were in their b. 584:6
housewifes in your b. 470:25
make thee b. of roses 330:19
stolen so close to our b. 512:31
to sweet b. of flowers 482:1
will there be b.?..yea, b. for all 410:4
Bedside: b. of a sick parent 325:36
presented myself at Betty's b. 560:13
very good b. manner 403:31
Bed-staff: in the twinkling of a b. 422:33
Bedstead: make anyone go to sleep, that b. 179:25
Bed-time: I would it were b., Hal 440:29
Bedürfnissen: jedem nach seinen B. 333:12
Bee: b. goes singing to her groom 95:2
b. has quit the clover 298:26
b.'s kiss, now! 91:35
b. with honied thigh 341:22
brisk as a b. in conversation 270:8
can you keep the b. from ranging 123:5
Hope clung feeding, like a b. 152:20
horribly bored by a b. 311:3
how doth the little busy b. 561:28
I am the b. 205:2
in the bag of one b. 97:1
love in my bosom like a b. 231:39, 315:17
murmured like a noontide b. 495:23
regular brute of a b. 311:3
some b. had stung it 517:14
where the b. sucks 480:14
Beech: shady with birch and b. 82:9
Beechen green, and shadows num-berless 287:23
spare the b. tree 122:8
Beech-tree: appointment with a b. 547:1
under yon b. 336:7
Beech-wood: in the b. grey 334:6
Beef: b. and captain's biscuits 543:7
great eater of b. 482:6
great meals of b. and iron 444:5

Beef (cont.)
roast b. of England 204:13
stole a piece of b. 369:1
this..pig had roast b. 369:7
what say you to..b. and mustard? 479:8
your b., pork, and mutton 294:34
Beef-faced boys 177:41
Beefsteak: as English..as a b. 239:8
Beef-witted: mongrel b. lord 481:9
Beefy face an' grubby 'and 299:14
Bee-hive's hum 408:10
Bee-loud: live alone in the b. glade 585:12
Bee-mouth: while the b. sips 287:21
Been: as if it had not b. 494:6
b. and gone and done 218:5
b. she knew not where 250:23
has b., and may be again 581:3
he had b. there before 304:32
I have b. here before 411:34
think what 'e's b. 301:13
thus having b. 499:9
what has b., has b. 194:21
Beer: all b. and skittles 121:7, 335:8
B. and Britannia 505:15
bottled b. and chops 221:5
chronicle small b. 470:29
desire small b. 441:32
did you ever taste b.? 177:34
drink some b. 276:15
felony to drink small b. 445:36
much bemused in b. 385:21
muddy ecstasies of b. 164:33
O B.! O Hodgson, Guinness.. 120:23
only b. teetotaller 489:15
poor creature, small b. 441:33
pot of b. 369:17
talk o' gin an' b. 297:1
they sell good b. at Haslemere 42:12
they who drink b. will think b. 267:20
very best B. I know 42:12
when we trace its source, 'tis b. 336:25
Beer-sheba: from Dan even to B. 46:61
Bees: b. are stirring 152:17
furnish'd with b. 499:14
make a hive for b. 377:4
more later flowers for the b. 284:11
murmuring of innumerable b. 539:5
no butterflies, no b. 253:12
rob the Hybla b. 451:33
swarm of b. in May 5:17
swarm of golden b. 492:29
yellow b. in the ivy-bloom 497:2
Beethoven: B.'s Fifth..most sub-lime noise 210:7
Spohr and B. 220:5
Beetle: b., nor the death-moth 287:20
b. wheels his droning flight 229:28
b. winds his..horn 153:24
poor b. that we tread upon 462:7
Beetles: b. black, approach not 467:1
scarce so gross as b. 454:3
Beeves: broad as ten thousand b. 336:42
Before: all be as b., Love 97:23
all b. us lie 333:9
b., a joy propos'd 488:12
b. I knew thy face or name 184:4
b. the morning watch 399:40
Cross of Jesus going on b. 35:1
God should go b. such villains 469:7
gone b. to that unknown..shore 307:32
had he his hurts b.? 461:11
he goes b. them 135:19
he had been there b. 304:32
I have been here b. 411:34
Leda..went b. 309:12
looking b. and after 436:15
my sin is ever b. me 395:7
not dead—but gone b. 408:7
nothin' much b. 297:2
not lost, but gone b. 242:19
not so sweet now as it was b. 481:30
righteousness shall go b. him 397:10
the Lord went b. them 45:50
those b. cried 'Back!' 323:22
those things which are b. 68:23
thou art not what thou wast b. 23:15
though it were done b. 185:24
we look b. and after 498:9
when she has walk'd b. 225:15
world was all b. them 349:31
Beforehand: so good as it seems b. 196:32

Befriend: be near me now and b. 525:4
elves also..b. thee 246:23
Beg: b. often our own harms 424:3
taught me first to b. 465:16
they b., I give 195:13
to b. during life 440:34
to b. I am ashamed 62:18
to b., or to borrow, or ask for our own 82:27
Began: all things b. in order 85:19
I am that which b. 524:1
left off before you b. 155:29
month in which the world b. 137:40
that's how it all b. 298:24
what b. best can't end worst 89:22
when Nature him b. 189:3
Begat: Love closed what he b. 336:35
Begetter: true b. of all arts that be 42:1
Begetteth: he that b. a fool 50:19
Beggar: absent-minded b. 294:18
b. by banqueting 50:46
b. may drink his fill 42:12
b.'s nurse and Caesar's 425:33
b.'s shop is shut 478:36
b. squealin' out for quarter 302:14
b. that I am 433:14
best b. in his hous 137:3
big black boundin' b. 296:23
how a b. should be answered 465:16
patience, the b.'s virtue 334:25
relieve a lame b. 479:39
to behold desert a b. born 487:14
whiles I am a b. 447:26
Beggared: b. all description 424:6
b. by fools 190:24
Beggarly: bare-legg'd b. son of a gun 121:3
b. last doit 163:44
b. people! 521:26
weak and b. elements 67:42
Beggar-maid: bare-footed came the b. 528:1
this b. shall be my queen 528:2
when King Cophetua lov'd the b. 477:12
Beggars: b., fleas, and vines 293:10
b. in the street mimicked 325:14
b. invention 162:5
our basest b...superfluous 452:41
us poor b. in red 303:27
when b. die 449:22
worse in kings than b. 429:35
Beggar-woman: take a mere b. 363:26
Beggary: b. in the love 423:12
no vice but b. 447:26
they knew b. 325:27
Begged: the living Homer b. his bread 9:15
Begging: his seed b. their bread 394:5
Begin: anything that other men b. 449:8
baffled, get up and b. again 92:42
b. at the beginning 129:30
in pause where I shall first b. 435:32
my way is to b. with the begin-ning 115:14
thought it was time to b. 339:13
warily to b. charges 26:11
where I did b., there shall I end 451:39
Beginning: as it was in the b. 388:14
before the b. of years 522:5
b. and the end of..scenery 412:27
b. and the ending 70:22
b. of an Amour 40:3
b. of the end 526:19
b. of wisdom 398:25
better is the end..than the b. 51:11
Christ is the b. 360:11
each venture is a new b. 197:9
end of the b. 144:10
ill b. of the night 451:31
in my b. is my end 197:7
in the b. God created the heaven 43:26
in the b. was the Word 62:58
long choosing, and b. late 349:5
my way is to b. with the b. 115:14
never ending, still b. 191:9
quiet homes and first b. 41:17
that was the b. of fairies 36:7
true b. of our end 467:28
Beginnings: mighty things from small b. 191:29

INDEX

Beginnings (*cont.*)
our ends by our b. know 172:11
start again at your b. 297:11
weak b. lie intreasured 442:6
Begins: he that b. to live, b. to die 404:15
in you my song b. and endeth 501:20
nothing b...not paid with moan 544:2
that's where the West b. 135:13
Begirt with British and Armoric knights 345:4
Begone, dull care..b. from me 5:19
Begot: b. in the ventricle of memory 455:12
b. within a pair of minutes 305:17
by the old fool's side that b. him 90:18
by whom b. 381:36
his mother on his father him b. 74:15
how b., how nourished? 464:13
Begotten: b. by despair 332:5
only b. of the Father 62:64
Beguile: b. her of her tears 470:3
b. many 472:22
I do b. the thing I am 470:27
so b. thy sorrow 480:34
to b. the time 457:5
Beguiled: be b. by one 472:22
serpent b. me 44:24
Beguiling: smiling of Fortune b. 147:23
your weary paths b. 87:38
Begun: as when we first b. 246:28
b., continued and ended in thee 390:52
die before I have b. to live 16:18
he who has b. his task 256:25
joke that's just b. 219:28
life's journey just b. 160:27
makes me end, where I b. 186:25
not yet b. to fight 279:18
that sin, where I b. 185:24
things bad b. 459:9
work the Ides of March b. 451:37
Behave: doth not b. itself unseemly 66:45
how well did I b. 262:19
Behaviour: her evil b. 252:22
his b...everywhere 463:12
put himself upon his good b. 116:17
we'll teach better b. 250:18
with so much sweet b. 155:36
Behead: more capital than to b. a king 111:21
Beheld: b. what never was to be 116:15
we b. his glory 62:64
Behemoth: behold now b. 49:28
Behest: darkness falls at thy b. 198:17
Behind: b., a dream 488:12
closes from b. 150:1
far, far b. 147:13
get thee b. me, Satan 59:44
in the dusk with a light b. her 222:20
led his regiment from b. 218:16
left a better or wiser b. 225:34
no more b. your scenes, David 270:10
nor look b.! 262:3
not look b. 470:29
occasion..is bald b. 158:19
one longing ling'ring look b. 230:9
pray look b. for me 265:24
rather less than 'arf o' that b. 297:2
they look b. 230:25
those b. cried 'Forward!' 323:22
those things which are b. 68:23
thought there was no more b. 485:3
true of most we leave b. 147:12
turn thee b. me 48:26
veil upon veil b. 14:28
whatever he put b. him 178:10
whole Encyclopaedia b. 306:16
Behold: all which we b. is full of blessings 582:3
b. my mother and my brethren 59:20
b. the bright original appear 215:16
b. the man! 63:70
b. thy son!..b. thy mother 63:72
b. us with Thy blessing 98:13
be what they b. 381:6
b. you again in dying 516:10
ere a man hath power to say, 'B.!' 466:20
for to b. this world so wide 296:22
he only can b. 123:24
what we b. is censured 330:13
when I b. upon the night's.. face 289:5

Beholder: in the eye of the b. 265:14, 557:18
Beholdeth: he b. himself 69:33
Beholding the bright countenance of truth 352:23
Beholds his own hereditary skies 194:25
Being: Beauty is its own excuse for b. 199:26
B., erect upon two legs 179:11
B. that is in the clouds 575:13
b. what she is 584:25
contending against some b. 566:21
dear to me in the middle of my b. 310:21
ecstasy of b. ever 87:21
for the ends of B. 88:24
his b., and the noun at once 500:4
in one another's b. 495:7
intellectual b. 345:19
its b. puts blissful back 254:18
live, and move, and have our b. 65:1
lovely b. 117:2
mighty B. is awake 577:1
momentary taste of B. 206:21
moments in the b. of..Silence 576:19
our b.'s heart and home 579:27
pleasing anxious b. 230:9
reproach of b. 488:10
respects the highest law of his b. 200:23
sounding labour-house..of b. 17:17
thou art B. and Breath 83:12
unknown modes of b. 579:11
what concerns thee and thy b. 348:31
whose b. I do fear 458:33
Beit: three hundred fought with B. 42:10
Belated: some b. peasant sees 345:13
Beldam Nature 352:1
Belfries: the b. tingle 264:2
Belfry: bats in the b. 378:21
white owl in the b. 540:14
Belgium: B.'s capital had gather'd ..her beauty 113:25
until B. receives..more than.. she has sacrificed 21:6
Belgrade: by battery besieged B. 5:7
Belgrave Square: may beat in B. 219:2
Belial: B...counselled ignoble ease 345:22
B., in act more graceful 345:18
sons of B., flown 344:35
sons of B. had a glorious time 190:25
thou son of B. 47:36
Belie: whose exterior semblance doth b. 576:12
Belief: all b. is for it 273:28
Articles of thy B. 391:4
b...accepting the affirmations of the soul 201:12
b. of truth..the enjoying of it 27:32
not within the prospect of b. 456:17
reasoning and b...are essential materials 125:31
their b. a believing in nothing 320:3
various modes of man's b. 90:31
Beliefs: fettered by some generous b. 514:5
lost causes, and forsaken b. 19:10
Believe: all this I stedfastly b. 390:56
all which, sir, though I..b. 433:5
attempted to B. Matilda 41:9
being born to b. 180:33
b. a woman or an epitaph 117:13
b. all the Articles 391:2
b. it not, O Man 147:4
b. it or not 407:5
b. only possibilities 86:22
b. the aged friend 90:42
b. what is most contrary to custom 265:10
b. your own thought 200:36
brain that won't b. 73:21
corrected I b. 305:7
don't b. there's no sich person do ye now b.? 176:33
firmly I b. and truly 63:63
how much to b. of my own stories 267:23
I b., and take it 197:35
I b. in Michael Angelo 489:21
I b. verily to see the goodness 393:22
I can b. in them all 490:7
I do b. her 488:16

Believe (*cont.*)
I *don't* b. in princerple 319:21
if you b. that you will b. anything 564:22
if you'll b. in me 131:19
I'll not b. it 471:41
I will not b. 64:9
kiss me as if you made b. 91:35
Lord, I b. 61:4
nor to b. and take for granted 27:16
only b. 354:12
so they b., because they were so bred 192:30
whom shall my soul b.? 95:20
will ne'er b., do what you please 73:28
with much toil attain to half-b. 147:9
ye b. in God, b. also in me 63:50
Believed: against hope b. in hope 65:40
b. as many as six impossible things 131:2
b. by any reasonable person 265:10
have not seen, and yet have b. 64:11
he lived while we b. 17:9
that stupendous truth b. 503:6
these juggling fiends no more b. 461:12
understood, and not be b. 77:20
who hath b. our report? 54:24
Believer: hast thou left..a b. 523:6
in a b.'s ear 364:15
most blest b. he 551:19
Believers in Clough 523:9
Believes: as one at first b. 93:8
each b. his own 382:19
half b. a God 587:11
what a man had rather were true he..b. 28:7
Believeth: b. all things 66:45
b. he that it is the sound of the trumpet 49:27
whosoever b. in him 63:9
Believing: b. in nothing at all 320:3
b. in the justice of our cause 233:20
b. their own lies 14:5
b. what we see be boundless 494:13
b. where we cannot prove 531:19
I b. 421:14
not faithless, but b. 64:10
wholly b. a lie 297:17
Belinda: only Cecilia, or Camilla, or B. 22:22
Bell: as a sullen b. 441:10
b., book, and candle shall not drive me back 447:31
b. invites me 458:17
each matin b...knells us back 150:24
enough..to have rung the b. to him 103:29
falling to the prompter's b. 543:6
for whom the b. tolls 186:28
hark the little vesper-b. 150:13
he tinkledy-binkledy-winkled a b. 312:8
heart as sound as a b. 468:28
in a cowslip's b. I lie 480:14
I shall b. the cat 5:1
little Mary B. had a Fairy in a nut 75:15
merry as a marriage b. 113:25
mouth of a b. 294:28
no sexton be asked to toll the b. 237:7
old kirk-hammer strak the b. 105:8
rang a little silver b. 337:28
sexton toll'd the b. 252:32
silence that dreadful b. 471:10
some cost a passing b. 38:28
sound of the church-going b. 164:25
surly sullen b. 487:15
they tolled the one b. only 263:2
twice holy was the Sabbath-b. 285:30
twilight and evening b. 528:22
unto the B. at Edmonton 159:33
very word is like a b. 288:2
voiced like a great b. 208:2
Bellamy: one of B.'s veal pies 379:21
Belle: vain to be a b. 322:5
Belle: du temps que j'étais b. 408:18
la b. Dame sans Merci 285:26, 286:35
Bellerus: fable of B. old 343:2
Belli: suave etiam b. certamina magna tueri 320:30

INDEX

Bellies: for their b.' sake   342:27
Bellman: B., perplexed and distressed   128:9
   fatal b.   458:3
Bellona's bridegroom   456:9
Bellow: the bleat, the bark, b., and
   roar   73:26
Bellows: my b. have quite lost
   their wind   8:13
Bell-rope: swam to the b.   39:11
Bells: air broke into a mist with b.   94:29
   all the b. on earth did ring   7:14
   at last the b. ringeth to even-
     songe   239:6
   b. I hear   566:27
   b. in your parlours   470:25
   b. of hell go ting-a-ling-a-ling   8:19
   b. on her toes   368:17
   b. they sound on Bredon   263:2
   b. they sound so clear   262:21
   b. were ringing the Old Year out   223:10
   buds, and b., and stars   288:8
   chime of full, sad b.   269:25
   church-b. chimed   334:6
   dear b.l   253:15
   deep in the b. and grass   249:7
   from the b., b., b., b.,   380:12
   hung among the b. and ding-
     dongs   379:22
   instruments to melancholy b.   478:33
   lin-lan-lone of evening b.   529:21
   match'd in mouth like b.   467:20
   Oh, noisy b., be dumb   263:2
   ring O b.   566:28(-567)
   ring out, wild b.   533:17
   say the b. of St. Clement's   368:7
   silver b., and cockle shells   367:21
   sweet b. jangled   434:14
   they now ring the b.   558:30
   those evening b.l   357:15
   those Shandon b.   402:20
   'twould ring the b. of heaven   249:5
   where b. have knoll'd to church   417:19
   with a tower and b.   164:29
Bell-swarmed: cuckoo-echoing, b.   254:22
Bellum: praeparet b.   552:16
Belly: b. God send thee good
   ale   516:21(-517)
   best fits a little b.   245:19
   filled his b. with the husks   62:14
   he who does not mind his b.   271:17
   his b. is as bright ivory   52:14
   his wit in his b.   481:10
   increasing b.   441:19
   in fair round b.   427:21
   in the b. of the fish   56:5
   I wish it was in Jonadge's b.   176:27
   more than his b. can   337:44
   my b. was bitter   71:14
   noise in the beast's b.   328:4
   pudding in his b.   439:35
   something of a round b.   441:21
   thy b. is like an heap of wheat   52:18
   whose God is their b.   68:24
Belly-ache: no compensation for a
   b.   304:24
Belly-pinched wolf   453:4
Belong: aught that wad b. thee   104:26
   secret things b. unto the Lord   46:29
Beloved: b. as thou art   494:7
   b. from pole to pole   149:27
   b., it is morn   248:7
   b. of their dams   156:19
   b. over all   302:13
   b. till life can charm no more   153:22
   Daniel, a man greatly b.   55:44
   escape me? never—b.l   92:41
   forget the Suspenders, Best B.   304:11
   giveth his b. sleep   88:25, 399:35
   heaped for the b.'s bed   499:1
   how far to be b.   423:12
   if ye find my b.   52:12
   image of the creature .. b.   483:2
   I opened to my b.   52:11
   leaning upon her b.   52:22
   Leda, the b. of Jupiter   309:12
   let us stay rather on earth, B.   88:20
   lovely that are not b.   375:11
   more beloving than b.   423:18
   my b. had withdrawn   52:11
   my b. is mine   52:3

Beloved (cont.)
   my b. is white and ruddy   52:13
   names of things b. are dear   80:23
   never be b. by men   73:22
   only b., and loving me   158:13
   that she b. knows nought   480:41
   this is my b.   52:14
   this is my b. Son   57:33
   thy power . . of being b.   96:24
   voice of my b. that knocketh   52:9
   voice of one b.   497:3
   what is thy b. more than an-
     other b.   52:12
Beloving: more b. than beloved   423:18
Below: at peace with all b.   119:2
   b. the kirk, the hill, b. the
     lighthouse-top   148:21
   down and away b.   15:22
   faithful, b., he did his duty   173:11
   fall b. Demosthenes or Cicero   202:16
   Heaven itself lies here b.   166:4
   land-lubbers lying down b.   9:3
   man wants but little drink b.   251:1
   man wants but little here b.   112:10, 225:13
   thy element's b.   452:37
Belt: my leathern b. likewise   159:39
   round thee, maiden, bind my b.   530:25
Belted you an' flayed you   297:6
Belvoir's lordly terraces   322:23
Bemused: much b. in beer   385:21
Ben: B. Adhem's name led   265:18
   B. Battle was a soldier bold   252:29
   'Next Poet'—(Manners, B.l)   93:27
   O rare B. Jonson   282:9
   Sweet Alice, B. Bolt   201:24
Benbow, Collingwood, Byron   362:30
Bench: drowsy B. protect   165:20
   little b. of heedless bishops   499:16
Benches: rub not clean their b.   281:6
Bend: b. all the three   308:13
   b. down and touch lightly   567:5
   b. lower, O king   586:5
   b. on me .. thy tender eyes   322:8
   b. to the oar   415:6
   shall I b. low   463:22
   whose b. doth awe the world   448:20
Bending: Angels b. near the earth   421:10
   b. down beside the glowing bars   586:21
   b. one way their influence   343:14
   my head is b. low   210:17
Bends: b. not as I tread   341:4
   b. the gallant mast   167:20
   b. with the remover   488:7
   blue sky b. over all   150:23
   he who b. to himself a joy   74:27
   made their b. adornings   424:7
   though she b. him   317:27
Bene: good for a bootless b.   574:32
Bene: de quoquam quicquam b. velle
   mereri   133:12
Beneath: around, b., above   81:10
   at once above, b., around   503:3
   b. the good how far   231:10
   b. the tartan plaid   23:17
   b. whose awful Hand   300:24
   prayer for all who lie b.   295:5
   some springing from b.   24:17
Benedicamus Domino   41:30
Benedick the married man   468:6
Benediction: perpetual b.   576:17
   sprinkles b. through the dawn   545:6
Benedictions: over-bowed by
   many b.   92:33
Benefacta: recordanti b. priora
   voluptas   133:13
Benefactor: Adam, the first great
   b.   550:24
Benefice: dreams he of another b.   477:7
Beneficent: zealous, b., firm   17:17
Benefices twinkl'd from afar   192:28
Benefit: o b. of ill   488:9
   without the b. o' the Clergy   155:10
Benefits: all the b. of your own
   country   428:17
   b. forgot   427:22
   forget not all his b.   398:3
Benevolence: b. of the passive
   order   337:39
   full o' beans and b.   518:21
   lazy glow of b.   90:31

Benevolence (cont.)
   whether the b. . . does most good
     or harm   29:7
Benevolent: heart b. and kind   108:35
Benight: ourselves b. our happiest
   day   184:28
Benighted: b. walks under the
   midday sun   340:20
   pore b. 'eathen   296:23
Benison: b. of hot water   83:22
   for a b. to fall   247:15
Benjamin: B.'s mess was five times
   so much   45:22
   little B. their ruler   390:13
Bent: b. head and beseeching
   hand   95:37
   fool must follow his..b.   303:13
   they are not our b.   221:38
   thy affection cannot hold the b.   483:4
   to the top of my b.   435:27
Benumbed: our b. conceiving soars   545:1
   we feel b.   118:24
Benumbs: a pen..b. all his faculties   270:8
Bequeath them no tumbled house   335:26
Bereaves of their bad influence   575:6
Bereft: b. of wet and of wildness   254:30
   of friends, of hope, of all b.   159:1
   thick, b. of beauty   479:12
Berenice's ever-burning hair   135:15
Berkeley: Bishop B. destroyed
   this world   505:23
   Bishop B. said '.. no matter'   116:30
   Coxcombs vanquish B. by a grin   85:4
Berkeley Square: faith that ye
   share with B.   302:26
   not in B.   302:22
Bermudas: from the still-vexed B.   479:24
   remote B. ride   332:1
Berries: b. and plums to eat   249:7
   two lovely b.   467:9
   your b. harsh and crude   342:10
Berry: from many a b.   348:9
   God could have made a better b.   112:21
   redder b. on the thorn   248:7
   sweeter than the b.   214:8
Berth: happen'd in his b.   252:32
Bertie: Burlington B.   237:28
Bertram's right and B.'s might   419:35
Beruffled: blast-b. plume   235:17
Beryl: eighth b.   72:1
   gold rings set with the b.   52:14
Beschränken: sich zu b.   223:14
Beseeching: bent head and b. hand   95:37
Beseems: none b. him half so well   23:24
Beset: sin which doth so easily b.
   us   69:18
   who so b. him round   99:36
Beside: b. him laid   417:18
   B. the Seaside   223:6
   Paul, thou art b. thyself   65:23
Besieged: by battery b. Belgrade   5:7
   like bread in a b. town   272:31
Besmeared: b. with blood and dust   119:16
   with blood of human sacrifice   344:28
Besoin: travell'd .. out of .. the
   b. de voyager   512:18
Besom of destruction   53:23
Besotted myriads of people   109:12
Bespake: the Lord himself b.   343:14
Bespangling: dew b. herb and tree   245:25
Bespeak her to my blisses   166:18
Besprent with April dew   282:2
Bess, the landlord's daughter   366:2
Best: about the b. thing God invents   91:31
   acts the b.   29:9
   afflict the b.   230:15
   all is b.   351:7
   all is for the b.   557:2
   all my b. is dressing old words   487:18
   all that's b. of dark and bright   119:1
   any other person's b.   239:13
   at the last, b.   423:36
   bad's the b. of us   37:17
   beauty being the b. of all we
     know   80:26
   b. and brightest, come away   494:8
   b. and happiest moments   499:12
   b. and the last   95:10
   b. and the worst of this is   524:10
   b. . . are but shadows   467:30

INDEX

Best (cont.)
b. butter 129:7
b. ends by the b. means 266:10
b. from age to age 99:31
b. good man 407:17
b. is like the worst 299:15
b. is the enemy of the good 557:5
b. is yet to be 95:13
b. men are moulded out of faults 462:27
b. of all our actions tend 111:22
b. of all possible worlds 120:6, 557:2
b. of men cannot suspend their fate 170:2
b. of men .. sometimes incorrect 268:25
b. of thieves 191:22
b. of what we do and are 573:10
b. sometimes forget 471:17
b. .. that ere wore earth 170:18
b. that is known and thought 19:12
b. that has been known or said 20:8
b. things carried to excess 143:27
b. thou canst bestow? 166:1
b. to be done for the country 564:20
b., to forget 96:20
b. which lieth nearest 316:24
b. words in the b. order 153:6
b. ye breed 303:24
both those the b. 124:26
brightest and b. 240:15
candour .. thinks the b. 143:10
ever b. found in the close 351:7
fear not to touch the b. 405:7
he does the b. he can 193:15
he gives the b. 279:13
he is doing his b. 569:29
hope for the b. 504:23
how much the b.! 210:20
it should be our very b. 90:28
kindest and the b. 107:3
lamentable change is from the b. 453:37
little do or can the b. of us 97:22
love is b. 93:12
loveliest and the b. 41:24, 206:6,7
made the b. of this 107:18
no worse a husband than the b. of men 424:5
one another's b. 184:29
our b. is bad 90:28
please her the b. you may 9:9
prov'd thee my b. of love 488:5
puppets, b. and worst, are we 94:46
said it that knew it b. 25:31
seek out the b. through the whole Union 268:25
seen the b. of our time 452:16
'tis at the very b. 11:21
we are Earth's b. 84:3
wisest, virtuousest, discreetest, b. 349:1
Best-bodied mothers 567:8
Bestial: what remains is b. 471:20
Bestie: blonde B. 304:23
Bestir: rouse and b. themselves 344:27
Bestow it all of your worship 469:1
Bestowed: divinely b. upon man 164:24
empire is on us b. 158:33
players well b. 433:29
Bestowing: a little light of love's b. 335:10
Bestows: where Jove b. ... the fading rose 125:9
Bestride the narrow world 448:22
Bet: b. my money on de bob-tail nag 210:13
b. you which one would fly first 550:11
once a pound 171:22
somebody b. on de bay 210:13
Beteem the winds of heaven 430:33(-431)
Betelgueux: Aldebaran and B. shone 236:38
Bethel: O God of B. 183:20
Bethlehem: B., thou dost all excel 132:4
but thou, B. Ephratah 56:7
come ye to B. 13:2, 369:20
O little town of B. 84:24
they sail'd in to B. 7:14
venite in B. 13:2
Betime: to business that we love we rise b. 425:9

Betimes: to be up b. ... go to bed b. 482:27
Betray: all things b. thee 544:14
b.'s in deepest consequence 456:22
else she'll b. more men 473:11
encourage those who b. their friends 215:2
finds too late that men b. 226:18
Nature never did b. 582:3
nor thought of .. happiness b. 575:11
Betrayed: b. by what is false within 336:30
b. my credulous innocence 340:33
like men b. 573:7
never .. but by ourselves b. 155:25
same night that he was b. 390:43
some jay of Italy .. hath b. him 429:32
Betrayer: betrothed, b. and betray'd 419:4
Betsey and I are out 125:20
Better: become much more the b. 462:27
begin to make a b. life 425:33
b. by far you should forget 409:25
b. day, the worse deed 242:6
b. done in Shakespeare 194:7
b. for the sun and moon to drop 364:1
b. is by evil still made b. 488:9
b. it in Scripture 371:16
b. man than I am, Gunga Din 297:6
b. men than we go out 206:32
b. one than you 83:18
b. part of valour 441:2
b. shall my purpose work 470:20
b. spar'd a b. man 441:1
b. than all measures 498:10
b. than all the ballads 316:2
b. than a play 136:3
b. the uncouther 97:11
b., the worse 25:5
b. to be much abus'd 472:1
b. to have loved and lost 112:16, 532:20
b. what we can 514:5
blame of those ye b. 303:26
boundless b., boundless worse 540:25
builded b. than he knew 199:23
can't do no b. 301:13
did I say 'b.'? 451:17
don't know b. as they grow older 414:19
even from worse to b. 254:1
far, far b. thing that I do 180:2
feed my brain with b. things 140:6
for b. for worse 391:30
from b. hap to worse 508:19
Gad! she'd b. 127:32
give place to b. men 167:9
Goldsmith .. b. than any other man 273:33
'He is no b., he is much the same' 23:14
I am .. b. than I thought 568:5
I am getting b. and b. 157:22
I didn't say there was nothing b. 131:16
if they spake worse, 'twere b. 279:29
if way to the B. there be 236:13
in a b. world than this 426:25
I will b. the instruction 464:9
I will let you a b. 528:9
left a b. or wiser behind 225:34
let us hope for b. things 23:2
little b. than one of the wicked 438:23
made b. by no mean 485:24
made to take the b. things 40:20
make men b. be 282:1
nae b. than he should be 105:9
no b. than you should be 37:18
prefer that which is truly b. 352:9
rises from prayer a b. man 337:33
shall but love thee b. after death 88:24
something b. than his dog 534:19
striving to b. 452:31
thy new wine was far more b. 332:29
title from a b. man 516:11
we have seen b. days 480:27
were it not b. not to be? 540:24
which is far b. 68:16
which is the b. God .. knows 506:9
worse appear the b. reason 345:18
Bettered: better b. expectation 467:38
nothing b., but rather .. worse 60:60
Betters: still b. what is done 485:27
Betty: B.,—give this cheek a little red 384:26

Betty (cont.)
dear B., come 570:30
hearken, Lady B., hearken 13:18
Between: b. the hands, b. the brows 411:25
b. their silver bars 208:19
dreary sea now flows b. 150:27
few and far b. 122:40(-123)
the Lord watch b. me and thee 45:8
Betwixt: all the love that ever was b. us 328:18
b. a Saturday and Monday 125:19
b. the wind and his nobility 438:33
b. us and the Sun 149:11
Bewailest: O Love! who b. 494:21
Beware: all should cry, 'B.! B.! 151:33(-152)
beamish nephew, b. of the day 128:10
b.! b.! trust her not 315:26
b. of desp'rate steps 160:40
b. the awful avalanche 316:21
b. the fury of a patient man 190:30
b. the ides of March 448:11
b. the Jabberwock 129:39
b. when .. God lets loose a thinker 200:7
Death in the cup—so b.! 105:35
I bid you b. 300:12
th'opposed may b. of thee 431:25
Beweep my outcast state 486:24
Bewept to the grave did go 436:22
Bewildered: b., and alone 188:31
b. in the maze of schools 382:21
young are sad and b. 504:17
Bewitch: do more b. me 246:4
Bewitched: b. with the rogue's company 439:2
who hath b. you? 67:41
Bewrayeth: thy speech b. thee 60:47
Beyond: all b. High-Park's a desart 202:5
b. the limits of a vulgar fate 231:16
b. the night, across the day 528:29
is there anything b.? 83:23
to the back o' b. 419:11
Bezonian: under which king, B.? 442:35
Bias of the world 447:25
Bibble-babble: leave thy vain b. 484:23
Bibendum: nunc est b. 258:28
Biberunt: sat prata b. 555:29
Bibisti: edisti satis atque b. 257:21
Bible: B. .. the religion of Protestants 142:12
B. tells me so 560:26
big ha'-B. 105:3
both read the B. day and night 74:11
English B. .. would alone suffice 326:3
'He knows', says Hebraism, 'his B.' 19:31
his studie was but litel on the b. 137:14
knows even his B. 19:31
knows .. her B. true 164:16
that book is the B. 20:4
Bibles: b., billets-doux 385:9
b. laid open 245:5
Bible-Society .. machine for converting 125:29
Biblia a-b. 306:26
Bicker down a valley 528:5
Bicycle: b. made for two 168:2
crossing Salisbury Plain on a b. 219:12
Bid: b. me to live 247:1
buy then! b. then! 255:6
do as you're b. 195:20
Bidden: worthy b. guest 342:27
Bidding: b. adieu 287:21
to her b. she could bow 417:7
Bidd'st: Thou b. me come to Thee 198:20
Bide: b. by the buff and the blue 106:6
England shall b. till Judgement Tide 303:6
coin his pouches wad na b. in 107:19
Bideford: men of B. in Devon 539:19
Bides its time and bites 90:15
Bield: thy b. should be my bosom 107:25
Bien: l'ennemi du b. 557:5
reprendre mon b. où je le trouve 354:0
Bien: no se pierde el hacer b. 120:17
Bienfaits: recevoir de plus grands b. 407:13
Bier: better b. ye cannot fashion 23:24
bore him barefac'd on the b. 436:30
borne on the b. 486:1x

Bier (*cont.*)
float upon his watery b. 342:10
your home, and your b. 494:21
Big: all you B. Steamers 294:34
  b. business give the people a square deal 409:6
  b. words for little matters 271:20
  carry a b. stick 408:27
  chopper on a b. black block 219:31
  clouds..are b. with mercy 161:18
  four times as b. as the bush 311:7
  moderate men looked b., Sir 7:12
  moments b. as years 286:7
  never use a b., b D. 221:13
  no woman's heart so b. 483:9
  plumed troop and the b. wars 472:3
  you are doubtless very b. 199:18
Bigger: a great deal b. than I am 127:24
  no b. than an agate-stone 477:7
  no b. than his head 454:3
  no b. than the Moon 149:4
Biggin: brow with homely b. bound 442:25
Bigging: I mind the b. o't 419:12
Bighorn asleep on the hill 422:22
Bigoted: more superstitious, more b. 363:17
Bigots of the iron time 417:2
Big-Sea-Water: the shining B. 317:22
Bilbo's the word 155:26
Biliary: creed in the b. duct 200:11
Bill: as if God wrote the b. 199:29
  b. our mate 336:43
  give me your b. of company 519:28
  God'll send the b. 319:14
  half-a-crown in the b. 178:26
  his b. will hold more than his belican 337:44
  holds the world between His b. 585:8
  little B. as is young and tender 543:9
  take thy b. 62:19
  this b. of my Divorce to all 185:22
  true my butcher's b. is due 218:13
  value not your b. of fare 519:28
  with the unpaid b., Despair 494:9
  you and every play-house b. 386:12
Billabong: camped by a b. 374:15
Billet: every bullet has its b. 570:29
  never go beyond a song or a b. 202:3
Billets-doux: bibles, b. 385:9
Billiard: b. sharp .. elliptical b. balls 220:6
Billiards: to play b. well 508:31
Billing: amorous and fond and b. 111:8
Billingsgate: alias, B. 583:25
Billion dollar country 210:11
Billow: breaking b. 492:2
  sounds the far b. 418:12
Billows: Atlantic b. roar'd 159:1
  b. smooth and bright 130:9
  even the b. of the sea 446:18
  take the ruffian b. 442:1
  trusted to thy b. 114:32
Billowy-bosomed: all b. 92:33
Bills: inflammation of his weekly b. 115:40
  though I cannot meet my b. 218:12
  wife and children but .. b. of charges 26:35
Billy: B. the Norman 173:16
  haven't the heart to poke poor B. 228:11
  youngest he was little B. 543:7
Billy: waited till his b. boiled 374:15
Bin: b. of wine 516:12
  in his last b. Sir Peter lies 376:21
  little b. 247:17
Bind: b. another to its delight 76:3
  b. him for thy maidens 49:30
  b. their kings in chains 400:27
  b. the wand'ring sense 155:1
  b. up my wounds 476:35
  b. up the broken-hearted 55:3
  b. your sons to exile 303:24
  in body and in soul can b. 417:21
  love which us doth b. 332:6
  mother bids me b. my hair 266:8
  Obadiah B.-their-kings 322:24
  rob me, but b. me not 185:27
  safe b., safe find 550:6
  b. the sweet influences of Pleiades 49:24
Binnorie, O Binnorie! 30:7

Bins: three black cats watch the b. 171:10
Biographers: Boswell .. the first of b. 325:26
  would have been poets, historians, b. 152:30
Biographies: history .. essence of innumerable b. 125:32
Biography: art of B. 42:23
  but the b. of great men 126:24
  no history, only b. 200:21
  read .. nothing but b. 181:44
Birch: b., most shy and ladylike 320:7
  nor fasting, nor b. 76:4
  shady with b. and beech 82:9
  that b. grew fair eneugh 33:2
  their hats were o' the b. 33:2
  Tom B. is as brisk as a bee 270:8
Bird: amorous b. of night 348:38
  as a b. each fond endearment tries 224:21
  as the b. by wandering 50:37
  as the b. wings and sings 95:17
  as when the b. of wonder dies 447:16
  Attic b. trills 350:11
  beast and b. .. were slunk 347:19
  beware the Jubjub b. 129:39
  b. among the leaves 586:5
  b. forlorn 253:17
  b. in a gilded cage 306:1
  b. in the solitude singing 119:10
  B. is on the wing 205:14, 15
  b. of dawning 430:20
  b. of night 448:33
  B. of Time has but a little way 205:14, 15
  b. overhead sang *Follow* 524:8
  b. .. shall carry the voice 51:26
  b.'s weight can break the infant tree 93:15
  b. that flutters least 164:5
  b. thou never wert 498:1
  b. whom man loves best 580:1
  both man and b. and beast 150:16
  by the b.'s song .. learn the nest 531:5
  come for every b. 334:16
  comfortable b. 284:24
  confin'd into this b. 551:16
  Dromedary is a cheerful b. 40:24
  escaped even as a b. 399:32
  flee as a b. unto the hill 392:17
  forgets the dying b. 373:3
  found some fledg'd b.'s nest 552:11
  half angel and half b. 95:34
  haply inhabit a b. 484:22
  He guides me and the b. 94:13
  her solemn b. 347:23
  household b. 184:27
  if b. or devil 380:26
  I heard a b. at dawn 512:10
  ilka b. sang of its love 108:38
  I'm the b. dead-struck 336:6
  in the sight of any b. 49:38
  I perceive a young b. 311:7
  irks care the crop-full b.? 95:14
  I would be a b. 80:30
  last b. 411:4
  like a b. it sits, and sings 332:20
  like a singing b. 409:14
  like that wise b. 403:22
  most melancholy b. 152:7
  no chirp of any b. 262:9
  no further than a wanton's b. 477:28
  not a b. .. in two places at once 407:7
  not born for death, immortal B. 288:1
  obscure b. clamour'd 458:21
  pinnace, like a fluttered b. 539:16
  pious b., with the scarlet breast 580:1
  play with him as with a b. 49:37
  poor b., as all forlorn 35:10
  rare b. on the earth 283:8
  rise up at the voice of the b. 51:33
  sea-blue b. of March 533:12
  secular b. 351:4
  self-begotten b. 351:3
  shall I call thee b. 573:19
  simple b. 169:22
  small hot b. 204:2
  some b. would trust her household to me 243:20
  song of night's sweet b. 492:9
  sweet b.'s throat 427:7

Bird (*cont.*)
  sweet b.! thy bower is ever green 97:30, 315:21
  sweet b., that shunn'st the noise of folly 341:13
  this b. hath made his pendent bed 457:6
  this is a spray the b. clung to 93:32
  thou art a summer b. 442:24
  wakeful b. sings darkling 346:20
  what b. so sings? 321:15
  with the waking b. 536:11
Bird-cage: and a b., sir 179:24
  like a summer b. 563:25
Bird-haunted: wet, b. English lawn 17:10
Birdie: b., rest a little longer 540:10
  b. with a yellow bill 515:25
  is it weakness of intellect, b.? 220:18
  what does little b. say? 540:9
Bird-song at morning 516:2
Birds: all the b. are faint 288:22
  all the b. of the air 369:18
  as b. their trackless way 94:13
  as happy as b. in the spring 76:4
  as the b. do 336:43
  back on budding boughs come b. 82:4
  b. and beasts and flowers 34:36
  b. are on the wing 152:17
  b. began to sing 368:20, 512:5
  b. build 255:9
  b. did sing 35:17, 359:27
  b. in nest would crouch to rest 171:10
  b. in the high Hall-garden 536:2
  b. in their little nests agree 41:35, 561:27
  b. .. lodge in the branches 59:29
  b. make their nests 398:10
  b. of calm sit brooding 343:13
  b. of the air have nests 58:34
  b. sit brooding in the snow 456:1
  b. sit courin' on the spray 526:21
  b. still hopping 515:14
  b. that are without 563:25
  b. went twittering by 171:21
  blossoms, b., and bowers 245:17
  charm of earliest b. 347:22
  fear the b. of prey 461:22
  frightened the b. 10:24
  full of b.' cries 334:15
  grac'd with b. that sing 87:25
  heigh! the sweet b. 485:16
  holy white b. flying after 334:2
  hours and the wild b. follow 524:13
  how can ye chant, ye little b. 108:36
  if b. confabulate or no 161:22
  little b. sang east 88:5
  melodious b. sing madrigals 330:18
  most diminutive of b. 460:17
  named all the b. without a gun 199:11
  near all the b. will sing at dawn 87:28
  nest of singing b. 270:3
  no b.,—November 253:12
  no b. sing 286:28
  no b. were flying overhead 130:11
  pipe of half-awaken'd b. 538:19
  pretty b. do sing 361:6
  she was one of the early b. 156:18
  sing like b. i' the cage 454:19
  song of b. for mirth 233:17
  suffers little b. to sing 480:35
  sweet b. of the Lord 545:7
  there were no b. to fly 130:11
  time of the singing of b. 52:1
  to warm their little loves the b. complain 231:18
  two b. sitting on a fence 550:11
  two bright b. 309:26
  two fairer B. I yet did never see 510:20
  very merciful to the b. 11:12
  when b. do sing 428:30
  when the lytle b. swetely dyd syng 239:5
  where late the sweet b. sang 487:16
  white b. on the foam of the sea 586:11
Birk: that b. grew fair eneugh 33:2
  their hats were o' the b. 33:2
Birmingham: B. by way of Beachy Head 141:22
  no great hopes from B. 22:19

Birnam wood: great B. to high
  Dunsinane hill   460:9
  till B. do come to Dunsinane   461:5
  till B. remove to Dunsinane   460:33
Birth: Angel that presided o'er my b. 75:1
  at my b. .. the earth shak'd   439:40
  bed for this huge b.   166:1
  b. and the grave   492:19
  b. of that .. word *flirtation*   139:34
  b. was born tonight   281:23
  Border, nor Breed, nor B.   294:27
  day of one's b.   51:9
  famous by their b.   474:22
  foulest b. of time   493:17
  frowned not on his humble b.   230:13
  grievous burthen was thy b.   476:27
  high b., vigour of bone   481:21
  his b.'s invidious bar   533:1
  human b.   338:4
  impulses of deeper b.   578:33
  laid us as we lay at b.   16:22
  land of our b.   295:6,8
  monstrous b.   470:23
  month before the b.   375:8
  my spiritual new-b.   127:15
  near the b. of Christ   532:21
  new b. of freedom   314:12
  nobility of b. commonly abateth
    industry   26:43
  of a b. as rare   332:5
  of H[ayley]'s b.   74:15
  one that is coming to b.   371:2
  on my b. have smiled   527:5
  our b. is but a sleep   576:9
  our Saviour's b. is celebrated   430:20
  quicken a new b.   496:11
  repeats the story of her b.   334:1
  she who gives a baby   328:7
  sorrowful b.   495:19
  stars that have a different b.   431:21
  subject to his b.   418:29
  sudden and portentous b.   576:2
  sunshine is a glorious b.   20:9
  terms like grace, new b.   442:21
  tongue, which is the b.   123:17
  thy beauty's b. is heavenly   162:26
  to give a Milton b.
  virtue, and not b. ... makes us
    noble   38:3
  where the melodious winds have
    b.   75:18
  wrapped up my b. in a mistry   543:2
Birthday: b. of my life   409:15
  laburnum on his b.   253:1
  un-b. present   131:5
Birth-partner: my soul's b.   410:27
Birth-place: of valour   107:13
Birthright: Esau selleth his b.   6:4
  he sold his b.   44:58
  sell our b. for a mess of potash   560:3
Birthrights: their b. .. on their
    backs   447:21
Births: arts, plenties, and joyful b. 445:10
  b. .. at first are ill-shapen   26:29
  innovations, which are the b. of
    time   26:29
Birth-strangled: finger of b. babe 459:33
Birth-tilme: thy b.'s consecrating
    dew   376:2
Bis dat qui cito dat   526:2
  b. dat qui dat celeriter   526:3
Biscay: before a B. gale   323:6
  in B.'s sleepless bay   113:8
  in the Bay of B., O!   139:2
Biscuit: b., or confectionary plum 160:31
  dry as the remainder b.   427:16
  here he took a captain's b.   176:9
Biscuits: beef and captain's b.   543:7
  b. you nibble   294:36
Biserta: whom B. sent from Afric
    shore   345:4
Bishop: among them was a B.   217:25
  b., and abbot, and prior were
    there   34:8
  B. of Rome hath no jurisdiction   401:12
  contradicting a B.   275:17
  damn it all, another B. dead   335:18
  desire the office of a b.   68:44
  hail, B. Valentine   184:26
  how can a b. marry?   504:27
  pardon, said the B.   31:20

Bishop (*cont.*)
  Shepherd and B. of your souls   69:52
  singed the beard of the B.   508:1
  to the B. they go   507:23
Bishoprick: his b. let another take 64:23
Bishops: all B., Priests, and
    Deacons   388:52
  b.' boots Mr. Radcliffe also
    condemned   518:19
  b. ... seen leaving the Athenae-
    um   243:11
  little bench of heedless b.   499:16
  upon our B., and Curates   388:30
  what b. like best   505:29
Bit: a b. of a chit of a boy   120:28
  a little b. off the top   360:5
  B b. it   366:7
  b. by him that comes behind   521:22
  b. him till he bled   249:21
  held with b. and bridle   393:34
  I b. my arm   149:9
  it head b. off by it young   452:27
  it would have b. you   520:16
  shall have a little b.   369:2
  though he had b. me   454:13
  went mad and b. the man   225:21
Bitch: called John a Impudent B.   208:23
  pray, Mr. Wild, why b.?   204:15
Bite: b. his pen, and drop a tear   521:2
  b. some other of my generals   216:12
  b. the hand that fed them   102:36
  dost not b. so nigh   427:22
  do you b. your thumb at us, sir? 476:46
  game they dare not b.   385:32
  man recover'd of the b.   225:23
  slow-worm b. thee   246:23
  to bark and b.   561:24
  to b. 'em   358:14, 521:22
  to b. so good a man   225:22
Bites: bides its time and b.   90:15
  b. and blows upon my body   426:29
  when a man b. a dog   168:3
Biteth like a serpent   50:32
Biting: b. all else with keen and
    angry tooth   80:27
  b. for anger at the clog of his
    body   212:16
  feels no b. pang. . while she sings 217:17
  his b. is immortal   426:6
Bits: would not we shatter it to b. 207:26
Bitten: the nails b.   325:28
Bitter: be not b. against them   68:32
  b. God to follow   525:5
  b. heart that bides its time   90:15
  b. news to hear   157:15
  bud may have a b. taste   161:19
  does truth sound b.   93:8
  her end is b. as wormwood   49:44
  if life was b. to thee   522:13
  life unto the b. in soul   48:47
  love grows b. with treason   525:8
  make oppression b.   433:34
  mirth that has no b. springs   295:8
  my belly was b.   71:14
  old and b. of tongue   585:14
  pulp so b.   544:25
  shed a b. tear   130:12
  shortly as b. as coloquintida   470:17
  sweet water and b.   69:38
  these are very b. words   441:38
  turning b. waters into sweetness 196:24
Bittern: possession for the b.   53:23
Bitterness: b. of absence   487:7
  b. of death is past   47:17
  b. of life   128:15
  b. of things occult   411:29
  b. of your galls   441:18
  curse thee in the b. of his soul 56:33
  heart knoweth his own b.   50:7
  in the b. of my soul   54:7
  in the gall of b.   64:38
  kill much b.   322:2
  no hatred or b. towards any one   134:2
  rose's scent is b.   543:24
  tears no b.   322:2
Bitters: sweets and the b. of love 117:44
Bittock: mile an' a b.   516:20
Blabbing and remorseful day   445:33
  b. eastern scout   340:6
Black: as b. as a tar-barrel   130:6
  as b. as they might be   32:13

Black (*cont.*)
  azure, b., and streaked with gold 497:22
  bar of the B. Badger   175:12
  big b. boundin' beggar   296:23
  b., as if bereav'd of light   76:13
  b. as the Pit   241:18
  B. Auster was the fleetest steed 324:7
  b. eyes and lemonade   356:9
  b. it stood as night   346:4
  b. men fought on .. Coro-
    mandel   324:34
  b.'s not so b.   124:12
  b. spirits and white   338:18, 459:34
  b., stinking fume thereof   267:30
  b. worsted stockings   325:28
  chopper on a big b. block   219:31
  fairies, b., grey, green   466:15
  fell a-bleeding on B. Monday   463:35
  devil damn thee b.   460:35
  from b. to red began to turn   110:43
  have it here in b. and white   280:16
  Hump that is b. and blue   297:27
  hung be the heavens with b.   445:17
  I am b., but comely   51:39
  I am b., but O! my soul is white 76:13
  more b. than ashbuds   529:25
  night's blear-all b.   254:18
  not so b. as they are painted   315:14
  round-faced man in b.   239:15
  secret, b., and midnight hags   460:2
  sober-suited matron, all in b.   478:18
  so b. and bare   107:26
  suits of solemn b.   430:30
  thou read'st b. where I read
    white   74:11
  though thou be as b. as night   123:20
  thy tribe's b. tents   543:17
  tip me the b. spot   514:19
  two lovely b. eyes   147:22
  wearing a b. gown   139:8
  we call it b.   89:32
  where white is b.   218:6
  whether the writer .. be a b. man 2:4
  white, b. and grey   346:24
  white shall not neutralize the b. 96:14
  who art as b. as hell   488:22
  with Phoebus' amorous pinches
    b.   424:1
  yellow, and b., and pale   496:4
Blackberries: prove a micher and
    eat b.   439:33
  reasons .. as plentiful as b.   439:24
  sit round it and pluck b.   87:35
Blackberry .. adorn the parlors of
    heaven   567:19
Blackbird: b., what a boy you are   85:11
  came a little b.   368:20
  my b. bountiful   189:22
  than to a b. 'tis to whistle   110:4
Blackbirds: b. have their wills   529:11
  four and twenty b.   368:20
  value my garden more for .. b.
    than .. cherries   2:31
Blackened: Sin wherewith the
    Face of Man is b.   207:12
Blackens: b. all the water about
    him   2:30
  b. every blot   529:39
Black-eyed: landlord's b. daughter 366:2
  when b. Susan came aboard   215:19
Blackfriars Bridge: at B. used to
    ply   173:12
Blackguard: sesquipedalian b.   146:21
  whatever .. b. made the world   263:31
Blackguards: we aren't no b. too   303:4
  b. both   116:11
  what have I ever done to you
    young b.?   203:36
Blackheath: from wild B.   322:22
Blacking: b. and Macassar oil   376:13
  b. the Corporal's eye   295:3
  Warren's b. or Rowland's oil   179:5
Blackness: gross b. underneath   540:17
  nocturnal b., mothy and warm   235:14
  reserved the b. of darkness   70:20
Blacksmith like our Norman King   294:22
Blackthorn starreth now his bough   80:10
Bladder: blows a man up like a b.   439:30
Bladders: boys that swim on b.   446:24
Blade: bloody Highland b.   417:18
  ere yet we draw the b.   297:8

INDEX

Blade (cont.)

his b. struck the water 148:1
in bud, or b., or bloom 529:2
settles back the b. 141:9
tares cling round the sickly b. 165:17
trenchant b., Toledo trusty 110:21
vorpal b. went snicker-snick 129:39(−130)
with b., with bloody blameful b. 467:29
Blades: breaches, ambuscadoes, Spanish 477:7
two b. of grass to grow 519:17
Blade-straight: steel-true and b. 516:6
Blains: breaking forth with b. 45:43
Blake: B. is damned good to steal from 212:19
Collingwood, Byron, B. 362:30
Blame: b. not my lute 583:17
b. not the bard 356:28
b. of those ye better 303:26
b. the thing that's not 375:23
bloody, full of b. 488:11
neither is most to b. 524:10
no contempt, dispraise or b. 351:6
not so much to b. 11:5
only the Master shall b. 303:21
or b. it too much 225:27
praise, b., love, kisses 580:20
reserved to b., or to commend 385:29
thine be the grief, as is the b. 23:15
what they b. at night 383:1
Blamed: ghost which b. the living man 16:10
he b. and protested 161:37
Blameful: bloody b. blade 467:29
Blameless: white flower of a b. life 529:39
Blaming it on you 297:10
Blanch: Tray, B. and Sweet-heart 453:29
when counsellors b. 25:40
Bland: aspect anything but b. 120:27
cruel, but composed and b. 17:13
gentle, complying and b. 225:34
liquid lines mellifluously b. 116:14
smile that was childlike and b. 238:34
Blandula: animula vagula b. 233:19
Blank: b., my lord 483:10
b. to Zoroaster on his terrace 94:9
moon stands b. above 263:12
no blot for us, nor b. 91:33
political b. cheque 227:37
universal b. 346:20
whose annals are b. in history-books 126:11
Blanket: b. of the dark 457:3
old red b. cloak 287:4
Blankets: rough male kiss of b. 83:21
Blaspheme: some b. 374:23
Blasphemed: none the less b. he beauty 112:18
Blasphemies: truths begin as b. 489:2
Blaspheming: brooding as b. 142:19
Blasphemous fables 401:11
Blasphemy: b. against the Holy Ghost 59:12
in a soldier is flat b. 461:33
Blast: b. of that dread horn 418:33
bleak blows the b. 124:7
down the roaring b. 293:14
East bow'd low before the b. 17:8
every b. of vain doctrine 389:51
First B. of the Trumpet 305:6
one b. upon his bugle-horn 416:28
only in the trances of the b. 151:25
owl-songs or the midnight b. 116:50
piano's martial b. 218:9
pity..striding the b. 457:9
shelter from the stormy b. 562:9
sleep in the arms of the b. 492:27
spread his wings on the b. 118:38
though it b. me 430:16
wav'd without a b. 417:13
Blast-beruffled plume 235:17
Blasted: with antiquity 441:20
b. with ecstasy 434:14
b. with excess of light 231:13
may my soul be b. 491:3
no sooner blown but b. 341:6
Blasts: hollow b. of wind 216:5
or b. from hell 431:32
Blatant: B. beast 510:8
in a b. land 535:43

Blatant (cont.)

in at the death of the B. Beast 325:19
Blätter: wie grün sind deine B. 416:3
Blaze: amid the b. of noon 350:22
brighten at the b. 226:11
broader still became the B. 322:22
burst out into sudden b. 342:20
his rash fierce b. of riot 474:21
one unclouded b. of living light 115:8
their galleys b. 115:3
western horizon was in a b. 100:9
Blazes and expires 117:29
Blazing: b. ubiquities 201:21
get out, you b. ass! 121:4
one b. indiscretion 358:15
Blazon: this eternal b. 432:9
Bleaching: white sheet b. 485:16
Bleak blows the blast 124:7
Blear-all: night's b. black 254:18
Bleat: b. the one at the other 485:4
the b., the bark, bellow, and roar 73:26
Bleating: what meaneth then this b. 47:15
Bleats articulate monotony 512:6
Bled: bit him till he b. 249:21
if it were some deed or b. 136:30
where where some buried Caesar b. 206:3
wi' Wallace b. 107:32
Bleed: Caesar b. in sport 450:1
do we not b.? 404:8
I b.! 496:10
then they b. 282:8
then we b. 494:2
Bleeding: b. from the Roman rods 158:29
my nose fell a-b. 463:35
pageant of his b. heart 16:8
thou b. piece of earth 450:11
when b., healed thy wound 161:10
with aching hands and b. feet 17:1
Bleeds: when a butcher tells you that his heart b. 270:35
Blemish: in nature there's no b. 484:19
without fear and without b. 12:13
your lamb shall be without b. 45:45
Blemishes: read not my b. 424:10
Blenches: these b. gave..another youth 488:5
Blend: b. like the rainbow 356:17
never to b. our pleasure 575:14
Blends itself with God 493:6
Blenheim: I dine at B. 8:16
Blent: beauty truly b. 482:20
Bless: be merciful unto us, and b. us 396:2
b. her when she is riggish 424:9
b. me with apple pie 204:1
b. myself with silence 94:11
b. relaxes 77:18
b. the squire 174:8
b. thee, Bottom! 667:5
b. ye the Lord 388:20
dying, b. the hand 193:35
except thou b. me 45:10
God b. all our gains 88:10
God b. our Lord the King 250:14
God b. the King 112:25
God b. thee, wheresoe'er..thou art 187:1
God b. us every one 174:10
guard and b. our fatherland 264:11
halfpenny, God b. you! 5:23
hand to b. 143:15
how to load and b. 284:10
little Lamb, God b. thee 76:10
my whole heart rises up to b. 92:31
once b. our human ears 343:17
paviours cry 'God b. you, sir!' 202:10
some sober brow will b. it 464:14
the Lord b. thee 46:10
Thee at hand to b. 322:2
tho' genius b. 153:28
until he b. thee 316:29
we stand to b. thee 198:16
wherefore b. ye, O beloved ones 121:11
who now do b. the poor 361:24
Blessed: all generations shall call me b. 61:13
all the B. Evil 89:36
always to be b. 383:11
Araby the b. 347:1

Blessed (cont.)

arise up and call her b. 50:58
b. are the horny hands of toil 320:5
b. are the poor in spirit 57:39
b. are the pure in heart 291:13
b. art thou among women 61:12
b. be her shade 297:20
b. be the art 160:26
b. be the name of the Lord 48:40, 391:18
b. by faith 579:38
b. by suns of home 84:21
b. damozel 410:7
b. is he that cometh 399:10
b. is he who has found his work 127:2
b. is the man who expects nothing 386:36
b. is the man that trusteth 393:38
b...that put their trust in him 391:51
b...that spares these stones 488:29
B. Trinity 240:19
b. were he with youth 410:34
b. were I if thou wouldst prove me 156:19
b. with each talent 385:29
b. with some new joys 191:34
b. word Mesopotamia 213:16
b. you, bear onward b. me 502:3
by all their country's wishes b. 153:29
desirous to be b. 436:6
he whom thou blessest is b. 46:17
his b. part to Heaven 447:4
I b. them unaware 149:20
it is twice b. 404:33
kings may be b. 108:6
last promotion of the b. 192:37
little b. with the soft phrase 469:45
liv'd a b. time 458:24
more b. to give 65:11
none b. before his death 56:42
not for mortals always to be b. 14:25
parson for the Islands of the B. 302:19
pastures of the b. 362:3
Sabbaths the b. ones see 362:9
seeming b. 226:12
spared and b. by time 114:22
there is a b. home 29:13
they b. him in their pain 539:19
this b. plot 474:22
thou hast altogether b. them 46:20
thy name..be for ever b. 264:8
we b. the sight 166:5
what God b. once 89:22
who win heaven, b. are they 93:43
Blessedest: vun of the B. things 179:27
Blessedness: b. alone..makes a King 548:16
in single b. 466:17
let him ask no other b. 127:2
Blesses: b. his stars, and thinks it luxury 1:15
she b. us with surprise 42:4
Blessest: b. the increase of it 395:30
he whom thou b. 46:17
Blesseth: b. her with his..hands 509:13
b. him that gives 464:33
Blessing: behold us with Thy b. 98:13
b. and cursing 46:30
b. of St. Peter's Master 559:27
boon and a b. to men 11:4
continual dew of thy b. 388:31
contrariwise b. 70:3
dismiss us with Thy b. 98:14
double b. 431:24
God shall give us his b. 396:3
hath taken away thy b. 45:2
health..a b. that money cannot buy 559:26
I had most need of b. 458:9
I'll b. beg of you 436:6
mighty b. 384:31
my b. season this 431:25
national debt.. a national b. 234:20, 563:2
no harm in b. 112:25
paid thy utmost b. 171:9
prosperity is the b. of the Old Testament 25:18
shall yourselves find b. 361:24
this *is* b. 549:7
truly it's a b. 146:31

INDEX

Blessing (cont.)
  visionary b. 215:37
  when thou dost ask me b. 454:19
  with private men esteem'd a b. 334:20
  you enjoy but half the b. 214:9
Blessings: all the b. of this life 389:19
  all which we behold is full of b. 582:3
  b. are plentiful and rife 245:8
  b. in disguise 248:1
  b. on the falling out 538:9
  break in b. on your head 161:18
  compensated by interior b. 243:17
  first of earthly b. 217:2
  from whom all b. flow 292:3, 376:8
  heavenly b. without number 562:1
  hold its many b. dear 578:5
Blew: b. a mack'rel gale 192:31
  hotched an' b. 108:13
  the Devil he b. upon his nails 302:32
Blight: ere sin could b. 151:18
Blighted: rob the b. rye 165:17
Blimber: no light nonsense about
    Miss B. 175:6
Blind: although a poor b. boy 144:22
  b. as any noon-tide owl 530:31
  b. forces of Nature 327:12
  b. guides 60:18
  b. his soul with clay 539:8
  b. Horn's hate 298:28
  b. hoss stick'n in a big mud hole 210:14
  b. leaders of the b. 59:39
  b. man..looking for a black hat 79:5
  b. mouths! 342:28
  b., old, and lonely 491:15
  b. old man of Scio's rocky isle 113:3
  b. Thamyris and b. Maeonides 346:19
  b..the eyes of Day 495:22
  b. to Galileo on his turret 94:9
  both extremely b. 119:20
  Cupid b. did rise 321:14
  Cupid painted b. 466:22
  darkness and b. eyes 551:19
  deaf man to a b. woman 152:23
  deaf to noise and b. to light 501:27
  eyes to the b. 49:9
  gaze an eagle b. 455:22
  grief for awhile is b. 496:21
  halt, and the b. 62:8
  have not I made b. Homer sing 330:4
  hour of b. old Dandolo 114:4
  if the b. lead the b. 59:39
  in a sort of Purgatory b. 285:10
  Justice, though she's painted b. 111:19
  love is b., and lovers cannot see 463:37
  my eyes were b. with stars 249:16
  myself am b. 386:29
  nourish a b. life 531:36
  old, b. débauchée of wit 558:18
  old, mad, b., despised 498:18
  old Maeonides the b. 208:17
  on the b. side of the heart 140:16
  one horse was b. 504:6
  Oppenheim, half b. with blood 42:11
  ordains us e'en as b. 295:10
  passion and party b. our eyes 152:22
  Pleasure, b. with tears 491:21
  rapid, b., and fleeting genera-
    tions 499:8
  right to be b. sometimes 362:21
  so b. as they that won't see 520:27
  thou Eye among the b. 576:13
  three b. mice 369:8
  to her faults a little b. 401:26
  through its own internal light-
    ning b. 495:10
  unbelief is b. 340:25
  whereas I was b. 63:35
Blinded: dulness of our b. sight 400:32
  no longer b. by our eyes 84:6
Blindest: fondest, b., weakest 544:31
  Nelson turned his b. eye 140:19
Blindfold and alone 296:6
Blinding: bumping pitch and a b.
    light 363:4
Blindly: lov'd sae b. 104:11
  oblivion b. scattereth her poppy 87:16
Blindness: for our b. we cannot ask 390:53
  'eathen in 'is b. 295:21
  heathen in his b. 240:18
  help him of his b. 484:40
  savage in his b. 240:18

Blinds: b. let through the day 264:1
Blind-worms: newts and b., do no
    wrong 466:44
Blinking: b. idiot 464:2
  b. in the lift sae hie 108:31
  b., puffing, rolling his head 325:32
  one-eyed, b. sort o' place 237:11
Bliss: b. in our brows bent 423:33
  b. in proof 488:12
  b. of dying! 381:28
  b. of solitude 577:7
  b. was it in that dawn 575:2
  but a shadow's b. 464:3
  child and mother, baby b. 232:3
  deprived of everlasting b. 330:2
  dream of perfect b. 36:29
  excels all other b. 195:12
  given all other b. 540:13
  he lives in b. 107:18
  hereafter b. 99:31
  hopes of earthly b. 163:35
  if souls can weep in b. 160:28
  its silvery splendour pant with
    b. 286:18
  love only b. 96:8
  milk-soup men call domestic b. 375:6
  mutual and partaken b. 340:37
  my winged hours of b. 122:40(-123)
  noting my step in b. 81:6
  one moment may with b. repay 123:2
  only b. of Paradise 163:6
  perfect b. and sole felicity 330:28
  sees b. in ale 164:33
  share with me in b. or woe 349:16
  sober certainty of waking b. 340:16
  sum of earthly b. 348:39
  thou art a soul in b. 454:14
  thou source of all my b. 225:9
  to his point of b. 96:45
  what b. beyond compare 362:1
  what is b.? 276:15
  what joy, what b. 166:9
  where ignorance is b. 230:30
Blisses: bespeake her to my b. 166:18
  finds he mortal b. 497:2
  his new-born b. 576:10
  in the midst of our b. 570:30
Blissful: b. dreams of long ago 157:1
  puts b. back 254:18
  something b. and dear 356:35
Blister my kidneys 518:27
Blisters: angry Mab with b. plagues 477:7
Blithe: be you b. and bonny 468:20
  b. new-comer 573:19
  buxom, b., and debonair 341:27
  hail to thee, b. Spirit 498:1
  milkmaid singeth b. 341:34
  no lark more b. than he 72:15
Bloated armaments 180:27
Block: chopper on a big black b. 219:31
  old b. itself 103:28
  you insensible b. 34:30
Blockade: b.'s insult 278:32
  bookful b. 383:4
  if I had not been a b. 2:17
  make a man appear..a b. 194:17
  no man but a b. ever wrote.. 273:8
  some diversion in a talking b. 203:9
Blocks: hew b. with a razor 386:38
  you b., you stones 448:8
Blonde Bestie 364:23
Blondes: Gentlemen Prefer B. 318:19
Blood: all that b. was shed 584:27
  all the b. of all the Howards 384:8
  a' the b. that's shed 32:11
  all the while ran b. 450:31
  am I not of her b.? 482:29
  besmear'd with b. and dust 119:16
  besmear'd with b. of human
    sacrifice 344:28
  b. and iron 72:33
  b. and judgment..co-mingled 434:26
  b. and wine are red 569:1
  b. and wine were on his hands 569:1
  b...fet from fathers of war-
    proof 443:25
  b. is thick, but water's thin 219:14
  b. more stirs to rouse a lion 438:37
  B. of Jesus whispers peace 72:19
  b. of patriots and tyrants 268:23
  b. of queens and kings 285:19

Blood (cont.)
  b. of the martyrs 542:3
  b., sweat, and tear-wrung mil-
    lions 112:28
  B... than water's thicker 266:17
  b. that she has spilt 158:30
  b., toil, tears and sweat 143:38
  b. upon her gown 208:5
  b. with guilt is bought and sold 496:22
  calls to heaven for human b. 73:20
  Christ's b. streams 330:7
  common names..kindred b. 101:10
  dipped in the b. of thine
    enemies 396:11
  drink the b. of goats 395:4
  drop my b. for drachmas 451:20
  drunken with the b. of the saints 71:32
  felt in the b. 581:23
  flowed out the purple b. 324:9
  fountain filled with b. 161:7
  freeze thy b. less coldly 361:23
  give me B. 174:35
  glories of our b. and state 501:5
  good enough to shed his b. 409:2
  guiltless of his country's b. 230:5
  hey-day in the b. 435:47
  his b. be on us 60:50
  His b. upon the rose 380:5
  if b. be the price of admiralty 301:24
  I'll not shed her b. 473:11
  in b. stepp'd in so far 459:25
  inhabits our frail b. 484:18
  in its ruddy orbit lifts the b. 375:25
  innocent of the b. of this just
    person 60:49
  I smell the b. 453:27
  I sucked the b. 149:9
  it will have b...b. will have b. 459:24
  judge and avenge our b. 70:46
  kind of sleeping in the b. 441:14
  lake of B. 529:36
  let me b., and not restore 244:9
  let there be b. 116:24
  make haste to shed innocent b. 54:38
  make thick my b. 457:3
  Man of B. was there 323:1
  most noble b. 450:3
  motion of our human b. 581:25
  never be purged away but with
    b. 85:6
  no getting b. out of a turnip 331:14
  nothing like b., sir 542:38
  not part of their b. 294:30
  o! b., b., b.l 472:11
  pure and eloquent b. 186:13
  red b. reigns 485:16
  ride a bit of b. 252:27
  secret'st man of b. 459:24
  sheds his b. with me 444:28(-445)
  so much b. in him 460:24
  so much b. in his liver 484:2
  song and b. are pure 336:37
  sprung of Earth's first b. 577:3
  still the b. is strong 420:31
  stir the Vikings' b. 293:16
  strong wyn, reed as b. 137:20
  summon up the b. 443:24
  their napkins in his sacred b. 450:24
  thicks man's b. with cold 149:13
  thine own heart dry of b. 287:3
  through red b. to the knee 32:11
  thy b. bought that 185:11
  thy b. is cold 459:19
  Thy b. was shed for me 198:20
  till her b. was frozen slowly 534:9
  voice of thy brother's b. 44:31
  warming of the b. 442:21
  wash them in my b. 508:15
  wash this b. clean from my hand 458:15
  water's wider..than B. 266:17
  we be of one b. 304:9
  welt'ring in his b. 191:7
  what disturbs our b. 586:10
  what profit is there in my b. 393:26
  when beauty fires the b. 192:4
  when b. is nipped 456:1
  when b. is their argument 444:19
  when the b. burns 431:27
  when the moon was b. 140:21
  when youth and b. are warmer 247:10
  white in the b. of the Lamb 71:6

Blood (cont.)

whose b. is very snow-broth 461:20
whose b. is warm within 462:32
whoso sheddeth man's b. 44:43
with the b. of their bodies
grown red 523:6
without letting b. 474:9
without shedding of b. 69:10
young b. must have its course, lad 293:19
Blood-bolter'd Banquo smiles 460:12
Blood-guiltiness: deliver me from
b. 395:9
Bloodless: all b. lay the untrodden
snow 122:17
b. categories 79:13
pale and b. emulation 481:5
Blood-red: b. blossom of war 536:24
b. field of Spain 241:9
drinking the b. wine 31:23
his b. banner streams afar 240:20
sunset ran, one glorious b. 92:17
Bloodshed: Pain, and Fear, and B. 575:6
Bloodthirsty: b. and deceitful man 392:3
b. clinging to life 19:9
nor my life with the b. 393:19
Blood-tinctured: heart within b. 88:7
Bloody: Agony and b. Sweat 388:50
begin to have b. thoughts 480:9
b. blameful blade 467:29
b., bold, and resolute 460:5
b., but unbowed 241:18
b. deed 435:41
b. Sun, at noon 149:4
b. with spurring 474:29
come out, thou b. man 47:36
each..his b. hand 450:6
even so my b. thoughts 472:12
his boiling b. breast 467:29
not b. likely 491:1
often wipe a b. nose 215:26
perjur'd, murderous, b. 488:11
selfsame b. mode 236:7
smok'd with b. execution 456:5
something wrong with our b.
ships today 37:7
thy b. and invisible hand 459:8
what b. man is that? 456:4
Bloom: all the..b. of the year 97:1
b. as they are told 84:9
b. is gone, and with the b. go I 18:25
b. of young desire 231:9
bud and b. forth brings 518:3
drives elate full on thy b. 107:8
owers that b. in the spring 220:15
flowers, which..b. the year long 81:18
flowers would b. 285:1
how can ye b. sae fresh 108:36
hung with b. along the bough 262:10
in bud, or blade, or b. 529:2
its b. is shed 108:7
sights of vernal b. 346:20
snatched away in beauty's b. 118:23
sort of b. on a woman 36:15
to look at things in b. 262:10
violets suddenly b. at her feet 42:4
with'ring in my b. 382:1
Bloomed fables 97:11
Blooming: b. good pay 301:12
left b. alone 356:36
sae bonny was their b. 147:24
Blooms: b. without a peer 107:30
Lotos b. below the barren peak 535:18
sunrise b. and withers 411:1
then b. each thing 361:6
Blossom: bade it b. there 151:18
blood-red b. of war 536:24
b. as the rose 54:1
b. by b. the spring begins 521:30(-522)
b. in purple and red 536:15
b. in their dust 501:6
broken b., a ruined rhyme 525:26
every lusty heart beginneth to b. 328:15
graces slighted b. on the tomb 164:30
oh blighted b.! 376:20
rank tongue b. into speech 90:12
spied a b. passing fair 455:17
this b. of fresh colour 502:19
timely b., infant fair 378:15
under the b. 480:14
Blossomed many an incense-bearing tree 151:32

Blossoming: b. boughs of April 80:12
b. Caesar 425:17
b. in stone 316:25
Blossoms: b. in the trees 383:19
breeze mid b. straying 152:20
even in the b. of my sin 432:17
of brooks, of b. 245:17
thousand B. with the Day woke 205:17
tomorrow b. 446:24
your image that b. a rose 585:17
Blot: art to b. 386:18
blackens every b. 529:39
b. me..out of thy book 46:4
b. out, correct, insert, refine 521:16
bright b. 498:20
I will not b. out his name 70:32
looks a little b. 531:17
only the right b. 375:23
scarce..a b. in his papers 241:16
this world's no b. for us 91:33
where is the b.? 97:15
Blotted: b. it out for ever 513:20
b. out man's image 586:7
each loved one b. from life's
page 113:20
never b. out a line 280:1
that ever b. paper 464:22
Blow: Angel trumpets b. 351:10
another deadly b. 578:4
bless the hand that gave the b. 193:35
b., b., thou winter wind 427:22
b., bugle, b. 538:14
b. him again to me 538:12
b. in cold blood 490:33
b. me about in winds 473:32
b. me into abhorring 425:34
b. on whom I please 427:17
b. out, you bugles 83:19
b. out your brains 304:4
b. the horrid deed in every eye 457:9
b. the spirit-stirring harp 218:9
b. them at the moon 436:8
b., thou wind of God 293:16
b., trumpet 530:3
b. up my garden 52:8
b., wind! come, wrack! 461:7
b., winds, and crack your cheeks 453:5
b. your own trumpet 222:4
b. your trumpets, Angels 185:13
ever ready for a knock-down b. 221:20
first b. is half the battle 227:9
gets his b. in fust 491:9
gie them a b., a b. 360:17
he'd never survive the b. 242:26
let the b. fall soon or late 515:28
liberty's in every b. 107:33
must have life for a b. 536:16
perhaps return the b. 124:13
pursued with yell and b. 148:24
step, a b. 573:7
stocks in fragrant b. 18:26
take one b., and turn the other
cheek 251:4
themselves must strike the b. 113:18
thine own genius gave the final
b. 117:25
this b. might be the be-all 457:7
when wilt thou b. 11:14
wind doth b. today 32:16
word and a b. 99:15, 191:23, 478:12
Bloweth: b. where it listeth 63:7
the spirit b. and is still 16:29
the spirit of the Lord b. upon it 54:10
Blowing: b. er de trumpets 238:24
horns of Elfland faintly b. 538:15
prevent the wind from b. it out 311:17
thoughts go b. through them 84:22
willy-nilly b. 206:13
Blown: above the rose full b. 575:3
against the b. rose 424:29
b. about by every wind of criticism 275:26
b. by surmises 441:8
b. with restless violence round 462:9
figure of b. youth 434:14
Flower that once has b. 206:26
Flower that once hath b. 206:9
his crimes broad b. 435:37
no sooner b. but blasted 341:6
rooks are b. about the skies 532:12
stars be b. about the sky 586:2

Blows: apostolic b. and knocks 110:18
bites and b. upon my body 426:29
b. a man up like a bladder 439:30
b. out his brains upon the flute 96:27
b. the wind today 516:9
Cavanagh's b. were not undecided 240:7
Dick the shepherd b. his nail 456:1
he who b. through bronze 94:5
heal the b. of sound 251:10
meanest flower that b. 576:22(-577)
never b. so red the Rose 206:3
our vain b. 430:17
sin b. quite away 245:6
unkempt about those hedges b. 84:9
vile b. and buffets of the world 458:36
when most she offers b. 424:25
wind b. it back again 75:17
wind that b. 173:8
Blowy: Snowy, Flowy, B. 213:5
Blubber'd; how b. is that pretty
face 401:19
Blücher: B. and I have lost 30,000
men 564:2
Napoleon forgot B. 143:33
Bludgeoning of the people 570:12
Bludgeonings: under the b. of
chance 241:18
Blue: all's b. 93:26
all the B. Bonnets 420:8
another b. day 125:26
as long as skies are b. 491:26
beneath the b. of day 262:18
bide by the buff and the b. 106:6
big b. cap that always fits 141:15
b. above lane and wall 90:37
b. bared its eternal bosom 288:13
b. days at sea 516:2
b. remembered hills 263:14
b. ribbon of the turf 182:11
b., silver-white, and budded
Tyrian 288:3
b., the fresh, the ever free 157:12
b. wave rolls nightly 118:37
brush the descending b. 255:4
canopy of light and b. 566:12
china that's ancient and b. 309:25
darkly, deeply, beautifully b.
116:13, 507:29
drink till all look b. 209:28
drown'd in yonder living b. 533:25
eyes of most unholy b. 356:14
eyes too expressive to be b. 15:19
forgot the b. above the trees 286:23
from the b. bed to the brown 227:17
girl with a pair of b. eyes 500:40
greenest of things b. 523:12
heaven's colour, the b. 358:24
Hump that is black and b. 297:27
in red, and b., and green 76:15
it's true my prospects all look
b. 218:13
just tinged with b. 567:17
lips of lurid b. 493:2
loving b. 529:11
noble lord in the b. riband 100:20
one of these..cloths was b. 358:24
Presbyterian true b. 110:16
said my eyes were b. 309:3
sanctuary within the holier b. 95:35
that b. is all in a rush 255:4
that little tent of b. 569:2
their hands are b. 311:21
thou deep and dark b. Ocean 114:27
twitch'd his mantle b. 343:7
two little girls in b. 228:5
violets b. as your eyes 536:12
your eyes so b. 326:18
Blue Beard's domestic chaplain 178:37
Blue-behinded: a b. ape, I skip 516:18
Blue-bottle: like a b. fly 33:18
Blue-eyed: deafer than the b. cat 530:31
Blue-fringèd lids 151:19
Blueness abundant 97:15
Bluest of things grey 523:12
Blue-stocking: this..resolute,
sagacious b. 324:35
Blunder: frae mony a b. free us 106:33
so grotesque a b. 43:4
worse than a crime..a b. 79:4
youth is a b. 181:37

Blunderbuss: charging a b. against
  religion · 270:22
Blundered: b. on some virtue una-
  awares · 143:17
  someone had b. · 528:15
Blundering: b. kind of melody · 190:32
  dear b. soul · 307:26
Blunders: b. that he has made · 241:3
  one of Nature's agreeable b. · 158:27
Blunt: b., bow-headed, whale-
  backed Downs · 302:7
  grey paper with b. type · 96:41
Blush: b. and gently smile · 245:20
  b. from West to East · 536:7
  b. to find it fame · 386:20
  b. to find itself less white · 506:15
  b. to give it in · 122:39
  born to b. unseen · 230:5
  bring a b. into the cheek of the
    young person · 178:11
  if not, with a b. retire · 175:18
  maiden b. bepaint my cheek · 477:18
  not b. so to be admir'd · 558:5
Blushed: her motion b. at herself · 470:1
  ne'er b. · 143:17
  saw its God and b. · 165:25
  shielded scutcheon b. · 285:19
Blushful Hippocrene · 287:24
Blushing: b. discontented sun · 475:8
  b. womanly discovering grace · 184:19
  his b. honours · 446:24
Bluster: let Zal and Rustum b. · 205:20
Blut und Eisen · 72:33
Blynken: Wynken, B. and Nod · 204:5
Boar: as the learned B. observed · 496:12
Board: B. of longitude · 503:10
  her cleanly platter on the b. · 226:11
  hospitable b. · 578:13
  I struck the b. · 244:9
  square, and above the b. · 234:11
  there wasn't any B. · 243:3
  wash'd headlong from on b. · 159:1
Boarded: youths are b., clothed,
  booked · 176:38
Boards: all the b. did shrink · 149:6
  ships are but b. · 463:15
  things in b. · 307:23
Boar-pig: tidy Bartholomew b. · 441:39
  and not without a b. · 561:15
Boast: Anabaptists do falsely b. · 401:14
  and not without a b. · 561:15
  b. not thyself of tomorrow · 50:43
  b. of heraldry · 230:1
  frantic and foolish word · 301:1
  if I b. of aught · 412:14
  him that girdeth on his harness b. · 48:11
  no man need b. their love · 80:9
  now b. thee, death · 426:14
  of which we rather b. · 332:3
  of wiles..I b. not · 345:16
  our..nature's solitary b. · 582:9
  such is the patriot's b. · 226:7
Boasteth: then he b. · 50:27
Boastful of her hoard · 226:11
Boastings: such b. as the Gentiles
  use · 300:26
Boasts his quiescence · 93:5
Boat: beautiful pea-green b. · 311:24
  best fits a little b. · 245:19
  enchanted b. · 497:10
  give a man a b. he can sail · 546:31
  his b. hastens to the monstrous
    steep · 288:10
  in one b. convey'd · 308:22
  my b. is on the shore · 118:14
  my b. sails freely · 471:8
  Old Man in a b. · 311:4
  once in a b. · 175:37
  sings in his b. on the bay · 528:3
  so hey bonny b. · 293:9
  took a b. and went to sea · 543:7
Boatman do not tarry · 122:23
Boats: many shallow bauble b. · 481:1
  messing about in b. · 228:16
  no b. upon the River · 377:26
  when b. or ships came near him · 312:8
Bob: bow at her and b. at her · 141:33
Bob-tail: bet my money on de b. nag · 210:13
  or b. tike · 453:30
Bode: doth that b. weeping? · 473:7
  what should that b.? · 468:31

Bodice: b., aptly lac'd · 401:32
  lace my b. blue · 266:8
Bodies: as imagination b. forth · 467:24
  conceit in weakest b. · 435:52
  friendless b. of unburied men · 563:30
  human b. are sic fools · 108:21
  our b. are our gardens · 470:15
  our b. why do we forbear? · 185:1
  their b. are buried in peace · 57:19
  these rough notes and our dead
    b. · 416:7
  those of their b. have failed · 26:46
  ye present your b. · 65:62
Boding to all · 472:20
Bodkin: with a bare b. · 434:4
Bodleian: in the name of the B. · 72:27
Body: absence of b. · 403:6
  absent in b. · 66:26
  adieu' twixt soul and b. · 412:15
  age and b. of the time · 434:18
  as well for the b. · 388:9
  beautiful passionate b. · 522:25
  b. and I pulled at one rope · 149:33
  b...capable of much curious
    pleasure · 120:5
  b. fill'd and vacant mind · 444:23
  b. gets its sop · 89:28
  b. of a weak and feeble woman · 198:11
  b. of England's · 84:21
  b. of my brother's son · 149:33
  b. of this death · 65:51
  b.'s delicate · 453:12
  b. than raiment · 58:11
  b. that once ye had · 302:24
  brief loan of his own b. · 120:5
  casting the b.'s vest aside · 332:20
  Charlotte, having seen his b. · 543:12
  clog of his b. · 212:16
  commit his b. to the deep · 400:30
  commit his b. to the ground · 391:44
  continually..filling some other
    b. · 290:10
  demd, damp, moist, unpleasant
    b. · 177:21
  disputed about the b. of Moses · 70:17
  every joint and motive of her b. · 481:26
  Eve, with her b. white · 249:8
  find thy b. by the wall · 16:20
  flavour, and b., and hue · 34:34
  follow'd my poor father's b. · 430:33(-431)
  for the dignity of the whole b. · 460:28
  fretted the pigmy b. to decay · 190:13
  gave his b. to that..country's
    earth · 475:16
  gigantic b. · 325:28
  gin a b. meet a b. · 104:31
  give my b. to be burned · 66:45
  her b...grew better · 575:20
  her b. thought · 186:13
  here in the b. pent · 355:10
  his b. is perfectly spherical · 311:11
  his lifeless b. lay · 317:17
  his mind or b. to prefer · 383:22
  I keep under my b. · 66:37
  in b. and in soul can bind · 417:21
  in his whole b. · 520:20
  in mind, b., or estate · 389:17
  I the b., He the Cross · 543:18
  its b. brevity · 151:14
  John Brown's b. lies a mould'-
    ring · 234:7
  keep your b. white · 516:2
  know not from thy b. · 410:25
  laid asleep in b. · 581:25
  language is..the b. of thought · 127:10
  lean b. and visage · 212:16
  left the lilies in her b.'s lieu · 376:1
  little b. with a mighty heart · 443:13
  make less thy b. hence · 442:38
  marry my b. to that dust · 292:19
  my b. as a plaything · 489:28
  my little b. is aweary · 463:4
  mystical b. of thy Son · 389:55, 390:46
  naught broken save this b. · 84:18
  need a b. cry? · 104:31
  no b. to be kicked · 547:15
  nobody..to see my dead b. · 237:7
  nor a b. to kick · 505:5
  nor Love her b. from her soul · 411:26
  not b. enough to cover his mind · 504:28

Body (cont.)
  not in thy b. is thy life · 410:32
  nothing the b. suffers · 337:19
  of kin to the beasts by his b. · 25:26
  of the soul the b. form doth take · 510:13
  overthrow of b. and soul · 109:22
  patch up thine old b. · 441:40
  perfect little b. · 81:22
  sick in soul and b. both · 249:6
  small slain b. · 524:17
  some b. to hew and hack · 110:21
  soul and b. part like friends · 166:15
  soul and b. rive not more · 425:18
  soul..doth the b. make · 510:13
  soul is not more than the b. · 567:23
  soul, the b.'s guest · 405:7
  so young a b. · 464:32
  still my b. drank · 149:29
  tasted her sweet b. · 472:3
  tawny b. and sweet small mouth · 524:13
  Thersites' b. is as good as Ajax' · 429:40
  this common b. · 423:39
  though her b. die · 351:4
  through your b. in an instant · 406:14
  thy b. is all vice · 270:13
  upon my buried b. lie lightly · 37:35
  what this tumultuous b. now
    denies · 84:6
  when that this b. did contain a
    spirit · 440:38
  when the b...has altogether
    vanished · 126:27
  whether in the b., I cannot tell · 67:36
  whose b. nature is · 383:18
  with my b. I thee worship · 391:32
  your b. is the temple · 66:29
Boffin: Mrs. B...is a highflyer at
    Fashion · 178:6
  when Mrs. B. does not honour
    us · 178:8
Boffkin: bade farewell to Minnie B. · 300:20
  vengeful Mrs. B. sits · 300:21
Bog: o'er b. or steep · 346:14
  that Serbonian b. · 345:31
Boggles: thing imagination b. at · 121:6
Boggy, dirty, dangerous way · 227:6
Bogs: caves, lakes, fens, b., dens · 346:2
Bohemia: B... near the Sea · 485:13
  desarts of B. · 485:14
Boil: b. breaking forth · 45:43
  the deep to b. like a pot · 49:32
  we b. at different degrees · 201:15
Boiled: his passion b. and bubbled · 543:12
  like a lobster b., the morn · 110:43
  no politics in b. and roast · 505:32
  water springs up..ready b. · 237:1
  young healthy child..b. · 520:3
Boiling his b. bloody breast · 467:29
  something lingering, with b. oil · 220:12
  whar de b. water hit · 238:13
  why the sea is b. hot · 130:15
  o'er night's brim day b. · 94:39
Bois: je b. dans mon verre · 360:7
  nous n'irons plus aux b. · 33:9
Bois Bou-long: as I walk along the
    B. · 217:23
Bold: alive, and so b., O earth? · 495:6
  as b. as she · 295:10
  be b., be b., and everywhere Be
    B. · 510:4
  be b., it will not burst thee · 56:48
  be not too b. · 166:3, 476:39, 510:4
  bloody, b. and resolute · 460:5
  b. and hard adventures t'under-
    take · 205:3
  b. bad man · 446:15, 509:20
  b. only to pursue · 491:28
  b. spirit in a loyal breast · 474:10
  here's to the b. and free · 362:30
  his servants are as b. · 190:12
  in conscious virtue b. · 381:6
  made Ben Adhem b. · 265:16
  made me b. · 458:2
  maiden never b. · 470:1
  more daring or more b. · 440:28
  my b., my beautiful, my Bulbo · 542:28
  righteous are b. as a lion · 50:49
  sagacious, b., and turbulent of
    wit · 190:13
  story of Cambuscan b. · 341:20
  virtue is b. · 462:13

Boldest · b. of hearts that ever
  braved the sun | 95:35
the b. held his breath | 122:4
Boldly: tread thou in them b. | 361:23
Boldness: b. is a child of ignorance
  and baseness | 25:32
b. is an ill keeper of promise | 25:33
familiarity begets b. | 331:10
respective b. | 243:33
what first? b. | 25:32
Bole: brushwood sheaf round the
  elm-tree b. | 92:14
Bolingbroke: every man that B.
  hath press'd | 475:1
this thorn, this canker, B. | 438:36
who now reads B.? | 102:21
Boloney: that's just b. | 503:14
Bolt: b. shot back somewhere
sweet Alice, Ben B. | 201:24
where the b. of Cupid fell | 466:39
with thy sharp and sulphurous
  b. | 461:31
Bolting: you must tarry the b. | 480:38
Bolts: b. are hurl'd far below them | 535:19
b. up change | 425:33
louder than the b. of heaven | 122:18
Olympian b. | 180:22
Bombast: b. out a blank verse | 232:6
his serious swelling into b. | 194:6
Bombastes: meet B. face to face | 406:18
Bombazine..a deeper sense of her
  loss | 214:1
Bona: pauci dinoscere possunt vera
  b. | 283:15
sua si b. norint | 556:15
sunt b., sunt..mediocria | 331:23
Bonaparte the bastard | 525:21
Bond: b. nor free | 68:31
b. unknown to me | 579:22
great b. which keeps me pale | 459:8
I will have my b. | 464:23
in the b. of iniquity | 64:38
look to his b. | 464:7
marriage the happiest b. of love | 229:8
not the b. of man and wife | 530:40
prosperity's the very b. of love | 485:33
so nominated in the b. | 465:7
sole b. which..made..the em-
  pire | 101:12
take a b. of fate | 460:6
'tis not in the b. | 465:8
Bondage: b. is hoarse | 477:26
b. of Rhyming | 343:27
Cassius from b. will deliver Cas-
  sius | 448:35
disguise our b. as we will | 357:12
out of the land of b. came | 420:5
spirit of b. | 65:53
Subscription no B. | 335:7
that sweet b. | 497:19
Bondman: every b. in his own
  hand | 448:37
in a b.'s key | 463:22
that would be a b. | 450:16
thy B. let me live | 574:1
Bonds: break their b. asunder | 391:48
except these b. | 65:27
he loves his b. | 247:9
my b. in thee | 487:22
relax the stricture of these b. | 514:5
unbound spirit into b. again | 160:34
Bondsmen: hereditary b. | 113:18
Bone: as curs mouth a b. | 143:19
b. of my b. thou art | 349:18
b. of my bones | 44:17
break a bit of b. | 252:27
bright hair about the b. | 186:9
get her poor dog a b. | 368:4
hardened into the b. of man-
  hood | 100:24
high birth, vigour of b. | 481:21
his every b. a-stare | 90:21
little ball of feather and b. | 236:27
rag and a b. and a hank of hair | 303:12
Bones: b. of a..Pomeranian
  grenadier | 72:31
b. which thou hast broken | 395:8
can these b. live? | 55:34
echo round his b. for evermore | 537:12
fill all thy b. with aches | 479:27
for his honour'd b. | 351:8

Bones (cont.)
full of dead men's b. | 60:19
grief never mended no broken
  b. | 174:7
he that moves my b. | 488:29
I may tell all my b. | 393:6
in a glas he hadde pigges b. | 137:22
interred with their b. | 450:17
Knight's b. are dust | 151:31
lay his weary b. among ye | 447:3
lay my b. amongst you | 572:17
may you see his b. and beak | 40:23
mock'd the dead b. | 476:14
my b. consumed away | 393:31
my b. would not rest in an Eng-
  lish grave | 119:33
of his b. are coral made | 479:30
rattle his b. | 365:6
rattling b. together fly | 192:40
these b. from insult to protect | 230:7
these dead b. have..quietly
  rested | 87:8
thy b. are marrowless | 459:19
thy canoniz'd b. | 431:32
tongs and the b. | 467:14
tongue breaketh the b. | 57:3
town of monks and b. | 150:28
valley..full of b. | 55:33
weave their thread with b. | 483:5
where my b. shall be thrown | 483:6
whose b. lie scattered | 351:20
your b. are very brittle | 515:23
Bonfire: the everlasting b. | 458:19
Bong-tree: a light on the B. stem | 311:16
land where the B. grows | 312:1
Bonhomie: overcame his natural b. | 43:2
Bon-mots: plucking b. from their
  places | 357:26
Bonnet: antique ruff and b. | 276:14
follow the b. of Bonny Dundee | 416:8
his b. in Germany | 463:12
in her latest new b. | 183:16
Bonnets: all the Blue B. | 420:8
b. of Bonny Dundee | 416:8
Bonnivard: worn..by B. | 114:34
Bonny: be you blithe and b. | 468:20
b. wee thing | 104:27
for b. Annie Laurie | 187:6
gin love be b. | 32:18
honest men and b. lasses | 108:3
sae b. was their blooming | 147:24
Bononcini: Signor B., compared
  to Handel | 112:22
Bono: cui b. | 145:20
Bonum: contrab. morem | 422:18
summun b. | 145:7
Booby: give her b. for another | 215:22
Booh to you | 221:2
Boojum: if your Snark by a B. | 128:10
the Snark was a B. | 128:14
Book: another damned, thick,
  square b. | 223:5
any b. that is not a year old | 201:13
anything which I call a b. | 306:26
best b...price of a large turbot | 413:6
bloody b. of law | 469:44
blot me..out of thy b. | 46:4
b. of books | 243:19
B. of Life begins with | 570:17
B. of Verses underneath the
  bough | 205:24
b.'s a b. | 117:10
b. should teach us to enjoy life | 277:18
b. wherein the Master | 238:25
b., who runs may read | 291:12
b...without pictures or con-
  versations | 128:20
dainties that are bred in a b. | 455:11
delight me for to print my b. | 247:22
do not throw this b. about | 40:19
farwel my b. and my devocion | 138:16
Flask of Wine, a Book of Verse | 205:23
for the b. of knowledge fair | 346:20
from the b. of honour razed | 486:22
frowst with a b. by the fire | 297:28
gets at the substance of a b. | 305:4
God that you took from a
  printed b. | 302:34
go, little b. | 138:41, 516:10
good b. is the best of friends | 549:20
good b. is the precious life-blood | 352:7

Book (cont.)
good b. is the purest essence of
  a human soul | 127:28
good reader..makes the good b. | 201:18
her eyes were sealed to the holy
  b. | 15:27
hers of the B. | 404:20
I like you, and your b. | 308:3
I won't talk of his b. | 271:25
I'll drown my b. | 480:13
in a b., that all may read | 76:9
in the volume of the b. it is writ-
  ten | 394:13
in thy b. record their groans | 351:20
in thy b. were all my members | 400:11
jolly good b. whereon to look | 571:9
kill a good b. | 352:6
kiss the b.'s outside | 159:29
leading one to talk of a b. | 271:2
like a b. in breeches | 505:1
like the cover of an old b. | 211:21
little volume, but large b. | 166:8
man behind the b. | 201:10
melancholy b. | 165:5
mine adversary had written a b. | 49:11
moral or an immoral b. | 570:3
my B. of Songs and Sonnets | 465:30
nature is the b. of knowledge | 226:20
Nature's infinite b. of secrecy | 423:16
Nature's mystic b. | 333:10
Nature was his b. | 77:24
never read a b. before reviewing it | 505:7
not on his picture, but his b. | 281:9
note it in a b. | 53:37
Oh for a b. | 571:9
O litel b., thou art so unconning | 138:14
one English b. and one only | 20:4
only b. that ever took him out of
  bed | 271:36
out of the b. of life | 70:32, 72:12
read of that sin in a b.? | 302:31
read the b. of fate | 442:4
religious b., or friend | 583:10
seldom peruses a b. with
  pleasure | 2:4
shut the b., and sit him down | 442:5
small old-fashioned b. | 196:24
some usefu' plan or b. could
  make | 106:3
sour misfortune's b. | 478:41
take down this b. | 586:21
take the b. along with them | 513:8
that b. is the Bible | 20:4
that they were printed in a b. | 49:5
then shut the b. | 374:23
these things noted in thy b. | 395:15
this b. I directe to thee | 138:43
this is no b. | 567:6
this square old yellow B. | 95:27
to make one b. | 272:28
unbent..over a b. | 306:14
until he has written a b. | 282:13
we present you with this B. | 157:13
what they club for at b. clubs | 307:23
what thou seest, write in a b. | 70:24
when a new b. is published | 408:14
where's the b.? | 143:6
while thy b. doth live | 281:11
who first praises a b. becomingly | 309:14
word for word without b. | 482:6
worthy to open the b. | 70:40
write a better b. | 201:22
write a most valuable b. by
  chance | 231:23
writing in a b. of gold | 265:16
written in the b. of Jasher | 46:43
written in this b. | 72:11, 12
written one b. | 276:22
your face..is as a b. | 457:5
Bookful blockhead | 383:4
Bookish theoric | 469:22
Books: a few friends and many b. | 158:13
all b. else appear so mean | 98:11
all grew out of the b. I write | 97:5
all the b. you need | 98:11
authority from other's b. | 454:32
b., and my food | 516:16
b. are not absolutely dead things | 352:5
b. are..talismans and spells | 163:51
b. are well written, or badly
  written | 570:3

Books (*cont.*)
b...a substantial world 578:20
b.l..dull and endless strife 581:15
b. by which the printers have lost 212:15
b., fruit, french wine 290:24
b. in the running brooks 426:30
b. must follow sciences 24:35
b. of the hour and..of all time 413:2
b. of the true sort 307:23
b...one way of coming into the
  world 520:34
b. that you may carry to the fire 276:28
b., the arts, the academes 455:23
b. think for me 306:25
b. to Cambridge gave 549:1
b. were opened 71:42
b. which are no b. 306:26
b. will speak plain 25:40
borrowers of b. 306:21
cards..are the devil's b. 520:31
cream of other's b. 357:20
deep versed in b. 350:13
dreams, b., are each a world 578:20
fro my b...maketh me to goon 138:16
gentleman is not in your b. 468:1
God has written all the b. 112:3
Goldsmith..who has written
  fine b. 213:9
ground, the b., the academes 455:20
his b. were read 41:23
in b...soul of the whole Past 126:27
I never read b.—I *write* them 403:26
keep my b. at the British
  Museum 111:30
knowing I lov'd my b. 479:23
lard their lean b. 109:3
learn men from b. 182:41
let my b. be then the eloquence 486:21
lineaments of Gospel b. 412:18
live without b. 337:41, 42
muddled with b. and pictures 299:18
my only b. 356:33
no furniture so charming as b. 504:25
no other b. but the score 445:40
of making many b. 51:35
old manners, old b., old wines 226:43
on b. for to rede 138:16
out of olde b. 138:23
poring over miserable b. 534:34
printed an' bound in little b. 299:8
quit your b. 581:14
rather studied b. than men 28:14
reading b., looking at pictures 240:13
read of in b. 34:8
rural quiet, friendship, b. 546:13
save their souls in new French b. 89:33
schoolboys from their b. 477:25
so many b. thou readest 17:22
some b. are to be tasted 27:17
speaks about his own b. 181:5
spectacles of b. to read Nature 194:6
things in b.' clothing 306:27
this, b. can do 164:34
three b. on the soul 90:35
thumb each other's b. 413:7
thy toil o'er b. 215:21
to Cambridge b. 87:26, 548:20
treasures that in b. are found 498:10
true University..a collection of
  b. 126:28
twenty b. clad in blak or reed 137:6
what do we..care about b.? 413:5
wise b...honoured tombs 196:36
Bookseller: high life as conceived
  by a b. 558:17
Booksellers: ask the b. of London 102:21
  b. are generous, liberal-minded
  men 270:30
Bookstall: pay sixpence at a b. 196:24
Boon: bean-flowers' b. 91:4
  b. and a blessing to men 11:4
  is life a b.? 222:25
  of neither would I ask the b. 495:24
  sordid b. 582:18
Boot: b., saddle, to horse and away 90:19
  dapper b.,—a little hand 537:5
  hey for b. and horse, lad 293:19
  make b. upon..buds 443:10
Bootmaker: little Bartley, the b. 518:13
Boots: Aristocrat who cleans the
  b. 218:22

Boots (*cont.*)
Bishops' b. Mr. Radcliffe also
  condemned 518:19
b.—b.—b.—b.— 294:37
come to bed in b. 243:8
give me my b. I say 475:31
gunpowder ran out of..their b. 209:18
lick the bloomin' b. of 'im that's
  got it 297:1
my legs when I take my b. off 175:17
spattered b., strapped waist 163:20
tea..taste of boiled b. 542:12
their heart is in their b. 141:11
then bring me my b. 34:3
this pair of b. displace 406:18
what b. it to repeat 206:19
what b. it with uncessant care 342:20
Bo-Peep: if they started at b. 247:12
Little B. has lost her sheep 367:14
Borden: Lizzie B. took an axe 8:7
Border: again in his b. see Israel
  set 92:9
as she gaed o'er the b. 104:25
B., nor Breed, nor Birth 294:27
bound for the B. 420:8
little thin, flowery b. 307:7
misty b. of the wood 586:5
old man on the B. 312:22
sung of B. chivalry 416:29
through all the wide B. 418:15
we'll over the B. 250:18
Bordered: Thames b. by its gardens 359:2
Borders: b., beds and shrubberies 296:30
enlarge the b. of their garments 60:15
killing slugs on b. 296:33
'stablished its b. unto all eternity 298:16
Bore: awhile they b. her up 437:1
b. in hand all his sick men 539:19
by her that b. her understood 531:7
every hero becomes a b. 201:9
first lion thought the last a b. 406:19
grew, and b., and b. 305:18
to be in it is..a b. 570:19
way to be a b...say everything 557:13
Bored: he b. with his augur 31:1
horribly b. by a bee 311:3
I feel a little b. 140:5
so b. with good wine 182:24
the Bores and B. 116:48
Bores: b. have succeeded to
  dragons 182:46
b. through his castle wall 475:7
the B. and Bored 116:48
Borgias: I dined last night with the
  B. 39:16
Born: all men naturally were b.
  free 353:3
as natural to die as to be b. 26:3
as soon as we were b. 56:25
being to b. to believe 180:33
birth was b. tonight 281:23
b. about three of the clock 441:21
b. and educated in this country 216:13
b. as I doubt to all our dole 80:8
b. but to die 383:22
b. 1820 5:21
b. for immortality 577:10
b. for the Universe 225:27
b. in a cellar 155:11, 209:17
b. in other's pain 544:2
b. in the garret 119:3
b. into the world alive 219:6
b. i' the rotten cheese 196:12
b. King of the Jews 57:23
b. of Christian race 561:20
b. of the sun 509:2
b. of the very sigh 286:26
b. on a Monday 368:21
b. on the Sabbath day 368:1
b. out of due time 67:5
b. out of my due time 359:1
b. so, and will please themselves 176:17
b. to be forgot 160:37
b. to improve us 225:34
b. to set it right 432:32
b. under one law 232:14
b. unto himself alone 404:11
bred en b. in a brier-patch 238:18
British Bourgeoisie is not b. 502:16
but I was free b. 65:14

Born (*cont.*)
Christ, b. into virgynyte 583:26
Christ was b., across the sea 264:18
day perish wherein I was b. 48:44
died before the god of love was b. 185:34
else, wherefore b.? 530:4
ere you were b. 487:29(-488)
ev'ry man..is b. to die 193:17
every moment one is b. 541:13
for joy Our Lord was B. 7:14
Godolphin Horne was nobly b. 40:35
he was b. in a ship 16:3
honour unto which she was not
  b. 535:7
house where I was b. 252:33
how happy is he b. and taught 583:9
I was b. in the year 1632 170:5
if he had not been b. 60:38
if my young babe were b. 32:19(-33)
in the days ere I was b. 77:34
in three distant ages b. 193:9
just b., being dead 410:13
made, as well as b. 281:17
man is b. unto trouble 48:50
man that is b. of woman
  49:1, 304:29, 391:41
men are to be b. so 559:14
'Never was b.' 517:5
no man is b. an angler 559:10
none of women b. 460:5
nor b. in any high estate 4:7
not b. to shame 478:21
not b. under a riming planet 469:16
not properly b., till flood 174:39
not to be b. is best 506:18
not to be b., or being b., to die 28:19
of..blackest Midnight b. 341:26
one and one-sixteenth is b. 6:6
One b. in a manger 552:1
one b. to love you, sweet 90:11
powerless to be b. 16:7
rose just newly b. 268:30
some men are b. great 483:18
spurn not the nobly b. 219:1
story-teller is b. 511:16
sucker b. every minute 35:24
supposed it lucky to be b. 567:13
that they were b. or should die 548:15
that thou wast b. with 452:26
then surely I was b. 140:21
thing that I was b. to do 168:8
this new Day is b. 125:27
this night shall be b. our heavenly king 5:15
thou wast not b. for death 288:1
time to be b. 51:3
to the manner b. 431:31
unto us a child is b. 53:15
we were not b. to sue 474:11
when we are b. we cry 454:12
where that thou wast b.? 29:24
whereof it is b. 462:28
who are b. of these 42:20
whose work is not b. with him 320:5
why wasn't I b. old and ugly? 173:21
world he finds himself b. into 126:26
would thou hadst ne'er been b. 472:35
Borne: b. away with every breath 118:36
b. down by the flying 418:13
b. inward into souls afar 88:25
b., like thy bubbles, onward 114:32
b. me on his back a thousand
  times 437:15
b. on beyond Sorrento 308:17
b. on the bier 486:15
b. the dirt and rain 359:4
have b. and yet must bear 498:25
he hath b. our griefs 54:25
must be b. with philosophy 174:37
oldest hath b. most 454:28
sights of what is to be b. 578:17
Borogroves: all mimsy were the b. 129:39
Boroughs: bright b. 255:5
fresh eggs to rotten b. 324:29
Borrioboola-Gha: natives of B. 173:24
Borrow: even if we have to b. the
  money 560:23
men who b. 306:19
to beg, or to b., or ask for our
  own 82:27
why dost b. 285:3

INDEX

Borrowed: b. my neighbour's wife 302:31
Borrower: b. of the night 458:31
  neither a b. nor a lender be 431:25
Borrowers: your b. of books 306:21
Borrowing: banqueting upon b. 56:46
  b. dulls the edge of husbandry 431:25
  b...lingers it out 441:26
  such kind of b. 353:1
  who goeth a b. 549:25
Böse: jenseits von Gut und B. 364:20
Bosom: bird he must carry in his b. 374:9
  around his burning b. buttoned it 251:2
  bared its eternal b. 288:13
  beneath the b. of the sea 75:18
  borne, see, on my b. 94:12
  b. of his Father 230:13
  b. of the urgent West 81:26
  breaks in our b. 494:2
  cleanse the stuff'd b. 460:37
  crept into the b. of the sea 445:33
  from thy full b. 401:32
  glory in His b. 264:18
  heart out of the b. 262:17
  her b. went in 34:20
  her hand on her b. 473:6
  her seat is the b. of God 253:36
  he's in Arthur's b. 443:19
  his b. should heave 221:20
  his little son into his b. creeps 209:2
  in the b. of her respectable family 103:35
  in th' ocean's b. unespied 332:1
  in your fragrant b. dies 125:11
  into Abraham's b. 62:25
  into the b. of the steady lake 579:24
  it in your b. wear 506:15
  leaning on Jesus' b. 63:48
  let me to Thy B. fly 505:5
  love in my b. like a bee 231:39, 315:17
  my b., as a bed 484:32
  my b.'s lord sits lightly 478:34
  my cell..here in thy b. 543:16
  one cunning b. sin 245:6
  on thy b. though many a kiss be rest in this b. 523:4 356:15
  round the b. of the stream 497:20
  Sea that bares her b. 582:18
  set lip to earth's b. 545:8
  sleep in Abraham's b. 476:25
  slip into my b. 539:2
  slips into the b. of the lake 539:2
  snowdrop..that in my b. lies 540:6
  sooty b. 469:42
  strike thy b., sage 276:15
  surmise flits across her b. young 199:13
  swell, b., with thy fraught 472:10
  take fire in his b. 49:49
  that vale in whose b. 356:26
  third in your b. 478:3
  thorns that in her b. lodge 432:18
  thy bield should be my b. 107:25
  to whose b. move 81:3
  unadorned b. of the deep 340:1
  wear thee in my b. 104:27
  what b. beats not 381:7
  wife of thy b. 46:25
  wring his b. 226:18
Bosomed: b. high in tufted trees 342:1
  no b. woods adorn 302:7
Bosom-friend: close b. of the maturing sun 284:10
Bosoms: come home, to men's business, and b. 25:15
  hang and brush their b. 97:9
  quiet to quick b. 113:42
  white b. of your actresses 270:10
  within our b. shine 132:1
Bossuet: excite the horror of B. 325:23
Boston: B. man is the east wind made flesh 13:19
  B.'s a hole 93:31
  B. State-House is the hub 251:16
  solid man of B. 317:1
  this is good old B. 79:2
Bo'sun: and a b. tight 218:14
Boswell: B. is a very clubable man 275:16
  B...first of biographers 325:26
Boswelliana: Lues B. 324:36
Boswellism: that propensity..B. 325:5

Botanist: should I wish to become a b. 270:33
Botanize: b. upon his mother's grave 578:30
  Hardy went down to b. 142:19
Botches: no rubs nor b. in the work 459:1
Both: a Norfan, b. sides 564:27
  blackguards b. 116:11
  b. perceived they had dreamed 96:43
  b. the worlds suffer 459:4
  b. those the best 124:26
  b. were faiths, and b. are gone 16:6
  b. were young 117:6
  b. worlds at once they view 557:25 (–558)
  give a specimen of b. 182:47
  good morning, gentlemen b. 198:1
  greater than b. 457:4
  to lose b. looks like carelessness 569:23
  wear it on b. sides 481:23
  Wordsworth, b. are thine 512:6
Bother: b. Mrs. Harris 176:33
  b. the flowers that bloom 220:16
  long words B. me 339:21
  sons of Mary seldom b. 302:1
Bothwell: no, by Saint Bride of B. 418:27
Botté: toujours b. et prêt à partir 354:19
Botticelli isn't a wine 403:36
Bottle: b. of rum 514:18
  b. our parents twain 295:15
  crack a b. 142:1
  farthest b. labelled 'Ether' 90:37
  first found out the leather b. 9:23
  great desire to a b. of hay 467:15
  large cold b. 204:2
  leave the b. on the chimley-piece 176:16
  like a b. in the smoke 399:18
  like magic in a pint b. 175:38
  little for the b. 173:3
  my b. of salvation 405:9
  nor a b. to give him 175:9
  put my tears into thy b. 395:15
  ten years in b. 34:34
  thy dog, thy b., and thy wife 384:6
  we'll pass the b. round 568:22
Bottled: b. wasps 161:41
  bring in the b. lightning 177:23
  drinking b. ditchwater 489:31
Bottles: new wine into old b. 58:42
Bottom: bless thee, B.! 467:5
  b. of good sense 274:30
  b. of the deep blue sea 8:24
  b. of the monstrous world 343:2
  dive into the b. of the deep 438:38
  I now sit down on my b. 208:28
  sees into the b. of my grief 478:30
  touch de b. wid a ten-foot pole 210:14
  which will reach the b. first 228:7
Bottomless: b. perdition 344:7
  b. Whig 275:14
  Key of the b. pit 71:38
  law is a bottomless pit 14:6
  pit that is b. 267:30
Bottoms: clap on Dutch b. 124:6
  wear the b. of my trousers rolled 197:21
Boue: nostalgie de la b. 21:15
Bough: Book of Verses underneath the B. 205:24
  danced at the end of a b. 312:14
  hangs on the b. 480:14
  Loaf of Bread beneath the b. 205:23
  touch not a single b. 358:21
  upon a wintry b. 492:24
  when the b. bends the cradle will fall 73:14
Boughs: back on budding b. 82:4
  blossoming b. of April 80:12
  b. which shake against the cold 487:16
  bursting b. of May 81:20
  from the b. the nightingale's high note 118:28
  got me b. off many a tree 244:14
  like on orchard b. 255:6
  lowest b. and the brushwood sheaf 92:14
  my soul into the b. does glide 332:20
  oft between the b. is seen 84:11
  shade of melancholy b. 427:19
  tangled b. of Heaven and Ocean 496:5
  through the b. of the May 309:26
  what soft incense hangs upon the b. 287:30

Boughs (cont.)
  whose b. are bent 409:14
Bought: b. over God with a fee 525:20
  b. that, the which..was thine 185:11
  Dickon..is b. and sold 476:39
  peace..b...at any price 145:28
Boulogne: an old man of B. 10:24
  at Rome she hadde been, and at B. 137:15
Bound: away, I'm b. to go 8:21
  b...about the feet of God 531:36
  b. for the prize of..you 487:20
  b. him a thousand years 71:39
  b. in misery and iron 398:15
  b. in stale parchment 337:13
  b. in to saucy doubts 459:12
  b. in with the triumphant sea 474:23
  b. to rules of reason 245:5
  b. with the chain of our sins 389:12
  ever Brutus will go b. to Rome 451:37
  I deliver'd thee when b. 161:10
  I go b. in the spirit 65:10
  my days..b. each to each 577:25
  not b. to please thee 464:29
  on, to the b. of the waste 17:21
  printed an' b. in little books 299:8
  these men were b. in their coats 55:40
  to another b. 232:14
  to them that are b. 55:3
  turn, and stop, and b. 189:16
  utmost b. of human thought 541:1
  utmost b. of the..hills 45:28
  we're b. to Mother Carey 294:21
  with a leap and a b...Anapaests 152:5
Boundary: fix the b. of..a nation 373:17
Bounded in a nut-shell 433:12
Bounden duty and service 390:44
Bounding: heart less b. at emotion new 18:30
  O b. breeze 147:7
  you big black b. beggar 296:23
Boundless: b. and bare the..sands 496:15
  b., as we wish our souls to be 494:13
  b. better, b. worse 540:25
  b. contiguity of shade 162:40
  b., endless, and sublime 114:31
  b. his wealth 417:22
  our thoughts as b. 114:42
Bounds: flaming b. of place and time 231:13
  from earth's wide b. 264:10
  living know no b. 501:8
  past the b. of freakish youth 163:5
  their b. which they shall not pass 398:8
  thin partitions do their b. divide 190:13
  wider shall thy b. be set 42:20
Bounties: thy morning b. 160:31
Bountiful: my blackbird b. 189:22
  my Lady B. 203:6
Bounty: his b., there was no winter in't 426:1
  independent on the b. of his mistress 156:11
  large was his b. 230:13
  lust of the goat..b. of God 77:16
  those his former b. fed 191:7
Bourbon: can B. or Nassau go higher? 401:28
Bourg: rustic murmur of their b. 531:6
Bourgeois..is an epithet 254:8
Bourgeoisie: the British B. is not born 502:16
Bourn: b. how far to be belov'd 423:12
  from whose b. no traveller returns 434:4
  our b. of Time and Place 528:22
  see beyond our b. 285:11
  to the very b. of heaven 284:23
Bout: many a winding b. 342:7
Boutique: reserver une arrière b. 354:23
Boutiquiers: une nation de b. 360:22
Bovril prevents that sinking feeling 5:22
Bow: arrow from the Almighty's b. 75:6
  as unto the b. the cord is 317:27
  bid kings come b. to it 447:27
  b. at her and bob at her 141:33
  b., b., ye lower middle classes 218:34
  b. down, archangels 585:22

[625]

Bow (cont.)
b. myself in the house of Rimmon 48:23
b. themselves when he did sing 446:18
b. was made in England 187:12
bring me my b. of burning gold 75:16
drew a b. at a venture 48:15
fascination in his very b. 116:41
he breaketh the b. 394:29
his quiver, b. and arrows 321:14
like a broken b. 396:36
Lord of the unerring b. 114:23
my saddle and my b. 29:24(-30)
reason doth..b. the mind 24:16
set my b. in the cloud 44:44
shalt not b. down to them 390:7
strong men shall b. themselves 51:33
to draw the b.., to ride 117:3
two strings to my b. 204:22
what of the b.? 187:12
with my b. and arrow 369:18
Bowe: scole of Stratford atte B. 136:29
Bowed: Archangel b. 119:23
as if her head she b. 341:14
at her feet he b. 46:50
b. by the weight of centuries 329:19
b. his comely head 332:25
East b. low 17:8
first it b. 32:18
nor b. to its idolatries 113:50
we b. our head 16:21
when our heads are b. with woe 339:11
Bowels: far into the b. of the land 476:32
have you no b., no tenderness? 214:35
in the b. of Christ 167:4
my b. were moved for him 52:10
out of the b. of the harmless
  earth 438:35
shutteth up his b. of compassion 70:11
Bower: b. of wanton Shrewsbury 385:1
b. quiet for us 284:19
butterfly born in a b. 36:26
deck both bed and b. 509:33
fair queen in a summer's b. 440:4
into their inmost b. 347:25
overflows her b. 408:6
this Lime-Tree B. my Prison 152:1
thy b. is ever green 97:30, 315:21
to that smooth-swarded b. 537:31
Bower-eaves: bow-shot from her b. 534:4
Bowers: blossoms, birds and b. 245:17
canopied with b. 482:1
England's green and pleasant b. 75:12
sat in breathless b. 410:22
towers of my skiey b. 492:27
Bowery: all that b. loneliness 529:18
Showery, Flowery, B. 213:5
Bow-headed: blunt, b., whale-
  backed Downs 302:7
Bowing: Satan, b. low 349:32
Bowl: B. from which he drank in
  joy 207:14
b. goes trim 376:24
brim the b. with atrabilious
  liquor 266:17
bring the b. which you boast 420:25
fill the flowing b. 5:24
golden b. be broken 51:33
he called for his b. 368:3
if the b. had been stronger 369:9
in a b. to sea 377:1
Love in a golden b. 74:2
mingles with my friendly b. 386:5
Morning in the B. of Night 205:4
onion atoms lurk within the b. 505:3
that inverted B. 207:3, 4
trowl the b., the jolly nut-
  brown b. 170:24
trowl the brown b. 420:3
went to sea in a b. 369:9
Bowler: *I* am the b. 309:27
if the wild b. thinks he bowls 309:27
Bowling: poor Tom B. 173:10
Bows: b. before him at the door 535:4
b. down to wood and stone 240:18, 295:21
come with b. bent 521:30
harnessed, and carrying b. 396:34
he b. and goes again 516:1
wood of English b. 187:12
Bowsey short leave of your
  nymphs 526:23

Bow-shot: b. from her bower-
  eaves 534:4
Bowsprit got mixed with the
  rudder 128:8
Bow-strings: hold, or cut b. 466:32
Bow-windows: expense of putting
  b. to the house 174:22
Bow-wow: Big B. strain 420:28
b., the watch-dogs bark 479:28
has not time to say 'B.!' 249:22
his *b.* way 377:5
Bow-wows: gone to the demnition b. 177:26
Box: 'B. about' 21:11
b. where sweets compacted lie 245:13
shut up the b. and the puppets 542:40
twelve good men into a b. 85:1
worth a guinea a b. 12:5
Boxes: forty-two b. 128:5
herring b. without topses 355:23
Boxing: beadle on b. day 179:5
Boxkeeper: sceneshifter, b., door-
  keeper 237:25
Boy: although a poor blind b. 144:22
and a little tiny b. 484:27
better build schoolrooms for
  'the b.' 156:22
bit of a chit of a b. 120:28
blackbird, what a b. you are 85:11
b. be virtuous still 164:13
b.—oh! where was he? 241:6
b. playing on the sea-shore 364:13
b.'s ideal of a manly career 182:26
b. stood on the burning deck 241:5
b.'s will is the wind's will 316:38
b. that looks after the sheep 367:15
b. who was bravest of all 9:1
b. with never a crack in my
  heart 585:18
bully b., bully b. 420:3
Chatterton, the marvellous b. 580:7
even when a little b. 566:21
every b. and every gal 219:6
eyes of a b. 40:31
from a b. I wanton'd with thy
  breakers 114:32
give to your b., your Caesar 191:17
glorious to be a human b. 173:34
happy b., at Drury's 387:18
hood-wink'd b. 213:15
horrid wicked b. was he 249:19
imagination of a b. is healthy 284:18
I saw a little vulgar B. 34:23
it's b.; only b. 304:49
left his pretty b. 232:2
let the b. win his spurs 195:24
like any other b. 208:18
little b. blue 367:15
Little B. kneels 339:19
Love is a b. 110:42
Minstrel B. to the war is gone 356:27
mother's wag, pretty b. 232:2
my beamish b. 129:39(-130)
my b. George quaff 90:18
ne'er a peevish B. 207:14, 18
nor Man nor B. 576:19
nor young enough for a b. 482:17
once more who would not be a
  b.? 113:14
one for the little b. 366:9
Pilot's b. 150:11
purblind, wayward b. 455:8
smiling the b. fell dead 92:24
speak roughly to your little b. 129:1
squeaking Cleopatra b. my
  greatness 426:4
such a b. by him and me 232:2
take the thanks of a b. 39:6
than when I was a b. 253:2
thou and I..compound a b. 445:14
to be a soaring human b. 173:34
to be b. eternal 485:3
upon the growing b. 576:9
well for the fisherman's b. 528:3
what a good b. am I 367:16
when I was a little b. 369:13
when the b. knows this out of
  the book 177:5
where is my..b. tonight? 9:1
your Idiot B. 575:19
Boyaux: les b. du dernier prêtre 338:1

Boyhood: as in my b. 496:10
tears of boyhood's years 357:13
Boyish: coarser pleasures of my b.
  days 581:26
even from my b. days 470:2
Boys: and be damned (Dear b.!) 299:2
as flies to wanton b. 453:40
b. and girls come out to play 366:10
b. and girls tumbling in the
  street 548:15
b. of the Old Brigade 562:20, 21
b. will be b. 254:7
by office b. for office b. 414:22
cheer, b., cheer! 326:22
Christian b. I can scarcely hope
  to make 20:22
claret..for b. 274:17
Eton b. grown heavy 387:19
give them the cold steel, b.! 14:22
go wooing in my b. 5:8
how rude are the b. 562:5
like loaded guns with b. 165:13
little wanton b...on bladders 446:24
mealy b., and beef-faced b. 177:41
men that were b. when I was a
  boy 42:7
noble army, men and b. 240:21
pretty-dimpled b. 424:6
sober man, among his b. 532:29
tallest of b. 34:4
three merry b. 37:16
till the b. come home 210:4
way that b. begin 543:3
we are the b. 227:10
what are little b. made of? 369:12
what the b. get at one end 272:36
when the b. came out to play 366:22
young b. and girls are level now 425:29
young b. in Umbro 323:12
Bozrah: dyed garments from B. 55:5
Bracelet of bright hair 186:9
Bracelets to adorn the wife 245:8
Braces: damn b., bless relaxes 77:18
Brach: b. or lym 453:19
lady the b. may..stink 452:24
Bracing brain and sinew 293:19
Bracken: do not lift him from
  the b. 23:24
hide me by the b. bush 30:6
Bradford: there goes John B. 79:12
Bradshaw: the vocabulary of 'B.' 188:27
Brae: waly, waly, doun the b. 32:18
Braes: among thy green b. 105:29
run about the b. 104:13
ye banks and b. 108:15
Brag: Beauty is Nature's b. 340:38
Caesar's thrasonical b. 428:25
left this vault to b. of 458:24
one went to b. 166:13
Brahma: great B...groans 285:6
Brahmin: B. strikes the hour 507:16
I the hymn the B. sings 199:5
Braids: twisted b. of lilies 341:3
Brain: all made out of the
  carver's b. 150:21
Bear of Very Little B. 339:21
blind life within the b. 531:36
bracing b. and sinew 293:16
b. of this foolish-compounded
  clay 441:31
b. that won't believe 73:21
b. to think again 83:13
Caesar's hand and Plato's b. 199:2
dull b. perplexes 287:28
feared it might injure the b. 128:28
feed my b. with better things 140:6
fibre from the b. does tear 73:20
flitting about..from b. unto b. 146:15
gladness that thy b. must know 408:10
glean'd my teeming b. 289:4
harmful to the b. 267:30
heat-oppressed b. 457:20
immured in the b. 455:22
in his b...strange places 427:16
in my b. I sing it 94:12
in some close corner of my b. 262:6
in what furnace was thy b. 75:24(-76)
it ascends me into the b. 442:21
Jonquille o'ercomes the feeble b. 571:19
keep his little b. attic stored 187:18
learning, that cobweb of the b. 110:35

Brain (cont.)

leave the naked b.   284:23
let my b. lie also   94:7
let schoolmasters puzzle their b.   226:2
more b. O Lord, more b.!   336:34
paper bullets of the b.   468:23
petrifactions of a plodding b.   117:20
possess a poet's b.   189:12
sleep rock thy b.   435:14
stars, which are the b. of heaven,   336:17
thought . . is . . secreted by the b.   125:30
unhinged the b. of better heads   86:7
warder of the b.   457:14
weeds and tares of mine own b.   86:17
what hand and b. went ever paired?   92:37
whose visionary b.   251:11
work like madness in the b.   150:26
written troubles of the b.   460:37
Brainless as chimpanzees   121:20
Brain-pan: weak is their b.   74:20
Brains: blew his silly b. out   543:12
  blow out your b.   304:4
  blows out his b. upon the flute   96:27
  cudgel thy b. no more   437:7
  dash'd the b. out   457:13
  exercises of his b.   219:5
  fumbles for his b.   162:25
  have not you maggots in your b.   38:15
  his b. they punched in   562:24
  make a head and b. out of a brass knob   175:36
  mix them with my b.   370:12
  my b. ta'en out, and buttered   466:8
  no other b. to work with   489:33
  rock his b.   442:1
  steal away their b.   471:22
  unhappy b. for drinking   471:7
  unhinged the b. of better heads   86:7
  when the b. were out   459:17
Brainsickly: think so b. of things   458:13
Brainwork: fundamental b.   411:38
Brake: b. that gallant ship in twain   30:19
  syne it b.   32:18
  took the Bread and b. it   197:35
  with withering b. grown o'er   165:17
Bramble-dew: eyes of gold and b.   516:6
Brambles pale with mist engarlanded   18:31
Branch: B. shall grow out   53:17
  cut is the b.   330:12
  lops the moulder'd b. away   529:33
  pine-tree's withered b.   316:21
Branch-charmèd by the earnest stars   286:8
Branched: b. thoughts   288:7
  in my b. velvet gown   483:15
Branches: birds . . lodge in the b.   59:29
  Nightingale that in the B. sang   207:24
  sing among the b.   398:8
  through b. and briars   523:14
  thy b. ne'er remember   289:7
Branchy between towers   254:21
Brand: by each gun the lighted b.   122:3
  that flaming b.   349:31
  they aren't the marrying b.   299:20
Brandy: b. for the Parson   301:18
  drink cold b. and water   308:5
  hero must drink b.   274:12
  music is the b. of the damned   490:20
  sipped b. and water gaily   154:17
  some are fou o' b.   106:13
Branksome: custom at B. Hall   417:5
  hung their shields in B. Hall   417:3
Brass: all that was ever writ in b.   281:9
  as a sounding b.   66:44
  as if this flesh . . were b. impregnable   475:7
  as well in b.   281:9
  b., nor stone, nor earth   487:13
  b. will crash   219:22
  braw b. collar   108:18
  evil manners live in b.   447:8
  head and brains out of a b. knob   175:36
  his feet like unto fine b.   70:27
  his old b. 'ill buy me a new pan   108:27
  only putty, b., an' paint   301:2
  savour of poisonous b.   286:11
  tombs of b. are spent   488:3

Brass (cont.)

wall all Germany with b.   329:24
walls of beaten b.   448:36
Brattle: wi' bickering b.   107:9
Brave: binds the b. of all the earth   362:33
  b. . . always beating the cowards   274:8
  b. as Margaret Queen   287:4
  b. days of old   323:21, 324:1
  b. hearts and clean   531:8
  b. Kempenfelt is gone   162:11
  b. man struggling in the storms of fate   381:7
  b. man with a sword   569:4
  b. men, and worthy patriots   352:27
  b. men . . who struggled here   314:12
  b. new world   480:15
  b. world, Sir   40:8
  clime of the unforgotten b.   117:37
  [Cromwell] . . a b. bad man   145:29
  delirium of the b.   584:27
  excellent phantasy, b. notions   280:1
  fair women and b. men   113:25
  fears of the b.   279:10
  heart too b.   213:2
  hearts are b. again   264:9
  home of the b.   292:11
  home of the b. and the free   489:1
  how sleep the b.   153:29
  hue angry and b.   245:13
  I'm very b. generally   130:25
  like a b. old Scottish Cavalier   24:8
  my adventure b. and new   95:18
  none but the b. deserves the fair   190:34
  not even Lancelot b.   531:21
  not too late tomorrow to be b.   14:27
  only those who b. its dangers   317:15
  on, ye b.   122:19
  O true, b. heart   187:1
  passing b. to be a King   330:27
  so b. a sight   332:7
  souls of the b.   146:14
  that men might call me b.   302:29
  then . . I am a b. fellow   305:16
  then I was clean and b.   262:19
  then it is the b. man chooses   320:12
  toll for the b.—the b.! that are no more   162:9
  unreturning b.   113:33
  what's b., what's noble   425:31
Braved: boldest . . that ever b. the sun   95:35
Bravely: b. broach'd his . . breast   467:29
  b. hast thou flesh'd thy . . sword   441:3
Braver: I have done one b. thing   186:23
  yet a b. thence doth spring   186:23
Bravery: all her b. on   350:31
  natural b. of your isle   429:29
  so, 'tis some b.   185:5
Bravest: boy who was b. of all   9:1
  b. of all in Frederick town   568:12
Brawl: if she nod I'll rail and b.   479:7
  ill disposed in b. ridiculous   444:10
  kindly silence when they b.   527:20
Brawlie: Tam kent what was what fu' b.   108:12
Brawling: b. of a sparrow   586:7
  delivers b. judgments   531:16
  with a b. woman   50:28
Brawls: my grave Lord-Keeper led the b.   230:19
  whatever b. disturb the street   561:26
Bray: and the trumpets b.   219:22
  b. a fool in a mortar   50:48
  Vicar of B.   7:9
Brazen throat of war   349:27
Brazil: I've never reached B.   297:23
Breach: i' the imminent deadly b.   470:2
  more honour'd in the b.   431:31
  not yet a b., but an expansion   186:25
  once more unto the b.   443:24
Breaches: b., ambuscadoes, Spanish blades   477:7
  through the b. . . of our prison   102:38
Bread: 'a loaf of b.' the Walrus said   130:17
  as that with b.   545:9
  away wes sons of ale and b.   583:26
  bitter b. of banishment   474:33
  b. and cheese, and kisses   520:5
  b. and flesh in the morning   47:51
  b. and . . the circus   283:19

Bread (cont.)

b. and work for all   73:12
b. eaten in secret   49:53
b. enough and to spare   62:14
b. I dip in the river   515:27
b. in a besieged town   272:31
b. of adversity   53:41
b. of affliction   48:14
b. that you eat   294:30
b. to strengthen man's heart   398:9
broken it up for your daily b.   525:27
cast thy b. upon the waters   51:27
cramm'd with distressful b.   444:23
cutting b. and butter   543:12
eating b. and honey   368:20
eat the b. of carefulness   399:35
eat thy b. with joy   51:20
having looked to government for b.   102:36
he took my father . . full of b.   435:37
his seed begging their b.   394:5
honest b. is very well   269:7
if his son ask b.   58:21
I have eaten your b. and salt   297:13
in the sweat of thy face . . eat b.   44:27
Jug of Wine, a Loaf of B.   205:24
known of them in breaking of b.   62:50
Loaf of B. beneath the bough   205:23
makes the holy b.   334:3
man does not live by b. alone   201:3
man doth not live by b. alone   46:23
man . . lives not upon b. alone   514:32
man shall not live by b. alone   57:34
money for that which is not b.   54:29
my little loaf of b.   247:17
never ate his b. in sorrow   127:30
no b. . . bring me some toast   403:8
one half-pennyworth of b.   439:39
our daily b.   58:4
quarrel with my b. and butter   520:14
Royal slice of b.   339:17
smell of b. and butter   112:36
smote itself into the b.   530:29
some gave them white b.   367:13
spoil'd the b.   374:20
that b. should be so dear   253:25
their learning is like b.   272:31
this the Wine, and this the B.   75:20
took the B. and brake it   197:35
unleavened b.   45:46
unleavened b. of sincerity   66:28
where there's no more b.   134:10
where we did eat b. to the full   45:52
white b. and butter   367:18
whole stay of b.   52:33
without any b.   369:4
with the b. of tears   397:2
wond'ring for his b.   163:22
your b. and your butter   294:34
Breadth: length, b., and highth . . are lost   346:10
  length without b.   202:7
  love thee to the depth and b. and height   88:24
  measures of the b. and height   332:12
Break: about the b. of day   366:5
  bids it b.   460:20
  b. a bit of bone   252:27
  b. a man's spirit   489:14
  b., b., b.   528:3
  b. every yoke   54:36
  b. in blessings on your head   161:18
  b. it to our hope   461:12
  b., my heart   431:1
  b. off this last lamenting kiss   184:28
  b. the eternal Sabbath of his rest   193:37
  b. them in pieces   391:50
  b. thy Edwin's too   225:14
  b. within the bloody house of life   447:42
  bruised reed shall he not b.   54:15
  cannot b. his Sleep   206:2
  counted them at b. of day   115:45
  if it be not broken, b.   161:5
  if ye b. my best blue china   236:11
  John Peel at the b. of the day   229:16
  never doubted clouds would b.   97:4
  nor knave nor dolt can b.   584:3
  take and b. us   241:26
  those eyes, the b. of day   462:16
  up by b. of day   244:14
  where it will b. at last   494:7

Break (cont.)
you may b...the vase 356:18
Breakers: I wanton'd with your b. 114:32
when the angry b. roar 311:15
Break'st: Thou b. my heart 244:11
Breaketh the bow 394:29
Breakfast: and then to b. 446:22
b., dinner, lunch, and tea are all
the human frame requires 41:3
b. first, business next 542:27
b., supper, dinner, luncheon 94:37
b. with him every morning 304:32
critical period in matrimony..
b.-time 243:13
for her own b...a scheme 586:26
hope is a good b. 24:39
I b. on gin 242:26
kills..seven dozen of Scots at a b. 439:11
Michael Angelo for b. 550:15
six impossible things before b. 131:2
we arg'd the thing at b. 125:21
where shall we our b. take? 32:13
wholesome, hungry b. 559:21
Breakfast-room: into the little b. 175:31
Breakfasts: where the M.F.H.
sleeps he b. 518:11
Breaking: boil b. forth with blains 45:43
b. of windows or b. of laws 357:23
b. Priscian's head 111:21
b. the silence of the seas 581:1
b. up of laws 530:12
b. what it likes 19:29
cheerfulness was always b. in 196:4
grey dawn b. 334:10
grey dawn is b. 166:24
known of them in b. of bread 62:56
take pleasure in b. 10:10
vainly b. 147:8
Breakneck: Ap-B. Ap-Headlong 376:22
Breaks: day b. not, it is my heart 184:10
heaven's morning b. 322:2
sooner every party b. up the
better 22:13
Breast: beats in every human b. 15:5
bold spirit in a loyal b. 474:10
bolt is shot back somewhere in
our b. 15:6
b. high amid the corn 253:19
b. that beauty cannot tame 33:3
b. that gives the rose 336:41
b. to b. we clung 410:26
broad b., full eye 488:27
broods with warm b. 254:25
comforting b. of..Death 241:20
cried still in sucking at her b. 196:2
depth of her glowing b. 497:26
dost thou not see my baby at my
b.? 426:13
ease my b. of melodies 285:31
eternal in the human b. 383:11
fill thy b. with glory 243:29
flutter'st..neath the b. of Earth 375:8
God's lamp close to my b. 94:26
God within my b. 83:8
her b. against a thorn 253:17
her b. up-till a thorn 35:17
her bright b. shortening 522:3
here in my b. 365:5
his bed amid my tender b. 231:39
his boiling bloody b. 467:29
last life-drop of his bleeding b. 117:25
light within his own clear b. 340:20
marched b. forward 97:4
my b. o'ercharged 501:20
my Sappho's b. 246:8
on her left b. a mole 429:24
on some fond b. 230:9
on the b. of the River of Time 16:3
on thy b. to be borne 114:32
peace in thy b. 478:1
peace to the soul of the man on
its b. 16:4
presagers of my speaking b. 486:21
render back from out thy b. 115:46
set thou in my b. 231:38
since that has left my b. 118:6
soft hand, and softer b. 289:1
sooth a savage b. 155:18
soul wears out the b. 119:5
tamer of the human b. 230:15
thy chaste b. 319:10

Breast (cont.)
to Chloe's b. 74:9
told but to her mutual b. 123:4
toss him to My b. 245:1
trembles in the b. 355:11
upon her patient b. 481:1
wail or knock the b. 351:6
Wedding-Guest here beat his b. 148:22
what his b. forges 429:13
with dauntless b. 230:5
with sweetness fills the b. 132:6
Breastful of milk 409:22
Breastie: what a panic's in thy b. 107:9
Breast-plate: through b. and
through breast 324:9
what stronger b. 445:30
Breasts: bore within their b. the
grief 23:25
b. more soft than a dove's 525:6
b. of the nymphs 525:6
b. the blows of circumstance 533:1
come to my woman's b. 457:3
deep division of prodigious b. 522:12
in the hollow of her b. a tomb 522:14
lie all night betwixt my b. 51:42
Sestos and Abydos of her b. 184:21
she hath no b. 52:24
sucked the b. of my mother 52:21
then her b. are dun 488:13
thy b. are like two young roes 52:5
two b. of heavenly sheen 411:35
warring within our b. 330:28
Breath: all at once their b. drew in 149:10
allowing him a b. 475:7
all the b...of the year 97:1
although thy b. be rude 427:22
bald and short of b. 415:12
boldest held his b. 122:4
borne away with every b. 118:36
borne my b. away 252:33
b. and finer spirit of all knowledge 583:3
b. between them 497:9
b. can make them, as a b. has
made 224:14
breathes with human b. 540:27
b. of Autumn's being 496:4
b. of them hot in thy hair 523:6
b. of this corporeal frame 581:25
b. of worldly men 475:1
b. thou art 462:3
but the b. of kings 105:5
call the fleeting b. 230:3
clothed with his b. 531:32
Cytherea's b. 485:26
doors of b. 478:44
draw a long b. 131:2
draw his last b. through a pipe 307:6
draw thy b. in pain 438:4
dulcet and harmonious b. 466:38
every thing that hath b. 400:28
fail, Sun and B.! 413:31
flattered its rank b. 113:50
flutter'd and fail'd for b. 17:15
fly away, b. 483:6
giv'st to forms and images a b. 575:21
having lost her b. 424:8
heaven's b. smells wooingly 457:6
her first-born's b. 234:16
her tender-taken b. 288:18
if her b. were as terrible.. 468:13
into his nostrils the b. of life 44:11
into the mystery of b. 335:28
it is by no b. 96:24
last gasp of Love's latest b. 189:20
lightly draws its b. 582:11
lost but b. 84:18
love thee with the b...of all my
life 88:24
mouth-honour, b. 460:36
now gives the hautboys b. 191:3
O balmy b. 473:11
retreating, to the b. of the night-
wind 15:7
soft as the b. of even 21:9
some of us are out of b. 130:16
soothed by every azure b. 494:11
such is the b. of kings 474:16
suck my last b. 382:7
summer's ripening b. 477:24
suspiration of forc'd b. 430:30

Breath (cont.)
sweet is the b. of morn 347:22
sweetness of man's b. 267:31
take into the air my quiet b. 287:32
thou art Being and B. 83:12
thou no b. at all 454:26
thy b. is Africk's spicy gale 215:42
too cold b. gives 458:1
to the last moment of his b. 224:10
vile prison of afflicted b. 447:33
weary of b. 252:12
what was the sound of Jesus' b.? 74:13
when the b. of man goeth forth 400:19
whose b. I hate 429:14
whose b. is in his nostrils 52:32
wish'd himself the heaven's b. 455:17
with bated b. 463:22
wither at the north wind's b. 241:14
years to come seemed waste of b. 584:21
Breathe: as though to b. were
life 540:32(-541)
b. among the pleasant villages 349:11
b. not his name 356:29
b., shine, and seek to mend 185:18
could not b. in that fine air 530:18
heart must pause to b. 119:5
if I dare..b. or live 475:15
low, low, b. and blow 538:12
may b. through silver 94:5
never b. a word about your loss 297:11
never b. its pure serene 288:19
nothing to b. but air 292:15
power b. forth 424:8
slaves cannot b. in England 162:42
so long as men can b. 486:18
thoughts, that b. 231:15
thou thereon didst only b. 280:21(-281)
too pure for slaves to b. in 237:27
Breathed: chide no b. in the world 428:8
b. upon by Hope's..breath 581:17
first true gentleman that ever b. 170:18
this day I b. first 451:39
Breather: chide no b. in the world 428:8
Breathers of an ampler day 533:26
Breathes: b. over the world 493:2
b. there the man? 417:22
b. upon a bank of violets 481:30
where the foe but falls 234:13
Breathing: all b. human passion 287:11
b. out threatenings and slaughter 64:40
b. thoughtful breath 580:21
b. time of day with me 437:32
closer is He than b. 529:38
health, and quiet b. 284:19
in fast thick pants were b. 151:32
in the sound his b. kept 497:2
not a b. of the common wind 582:4
rifle all the b. Spring 153:21
Breathings: low b. coming after me 579:6
Breathless: b., power breathe forth 424:8
b., we flung us on the windy hill 84:2
b. with adoration 577:1
hanging b. on thy fate 316:1
in b. quiet, after all their ills 15:14
making the reader b. 289:27
Breaths: in thoughts, not b. 29:9
their b. with sweetmeats tainted 477:7
Bred: ass that b. you 298:21
believe, because they so were b. 192:30
b. amongst the weeds..of mine
own brain 86:17
b. en bawn in a brier-patch 238:18
b. me long ago 263:19
I'm b. to the sea 331:20
in the kitchen b. 119:3
lump b. up in darkness 305:17
strain of man's b. out 480:19
without father b. 341:7
Brede: with b. ethereal wove 153:24
Bredon: in summertime on B. 262:21
the bells they sound on B. 263:2
Bree: a little abune her b. 32:3
Breeches: b. cost him but a crown 471:11
cleanin' his b. 518:20
his b. were blue 151:9, 507:20
like a book in b. 505:1
made themselves b. 44:21
put its hand in its b. pocket 289:25
so have your b. 124:7
what leg you shall put into your
b. first 271:13

INDEX

Breed: Border, nor B., nor Birth 294:27
b. for barren metal 463:23
careful of the b. of their horses 377:8
endless war still b. 351:28
fear'd by their b. 474:22
it might b. idolatry 185:5
my ewes b. not 35:21
not b. one work that wakes 255:9
this happy b. of men 474:22
where they most b. 457:6
wife for b. 216:2
will never b. the same 288:8
Breedest: so many schemes thou b. 17:22
Breeding: b. lilacs out of the dead land 197:27
spoil'd i' the b. 82:26
such true b. of a gentleman 115:41
write..to show your b. 501:2
Breeds: b. pestilence 77:10
invention b. invention 201:19
lesser b. without the Law 300:26
Breeks: taking the b. aff a wild Highlandman 419:23
Breeze: all the pages in a b. 337:2
battle and the b. 123:10
b. is on the sea 420:9
b. mid blossoms straying 152:20
b. of Alpine heights 308:17
b. of morning moves 536:10
cooling western b. 382:31
dancing in the b. 577:5
flag to April's b. unfurled 199:7
O bounding b. 147:7
refreshes in the b. 383:19
she forgot the chilly autumn b. 286:23
stream of the soft Spring b. 293:21
such a b. compelled thy canvas 532:13
to be come-at by the b. 578:11
tyranny in every tainted b. 100:30
volleying rain and tossing b. 18:25
with the b. of song 533:5
Breezes: b. and the sunshine 121:27
by the midnight b. strewn 492:29
feel no other b. 288:23
little b. dusk and shiver 533:41
now the sunset b. shiver 363:6
spicy b. blow soft 240:18
with the b. blown 287:29
Breezy: b. call of..Morn 229:31
B., Sneezy, Freezy 213:5
Breffny: little waves of B. 227:36
Breitmann: Hans B. gife a barty 313:11
Bremen: my father being a foreigner of B. 170:5
Brent: your bonny brow was b. 106:19
Brentford: ever seen B.? 275:9
two kings of B. 162:33
Brethren: accursed..for my b. 65:59
behold my mother and my b. 59:20
for my b. and companions' sakes 399:31
great Twin B. 324:16
shame on us, Christian b. 264:13
tuneful b. all were dead 416:29
we be b. 44:46
Brevis: in esse laboro 255:18
vita b., sensus hebes 414:21
Brevity: b. is the soul of wit 432:38
b. of our life 414:21
its body b. 151:14
Brew: good b. in Amberley too 42:12
Brewer: not a b.'s servant 73:17
wi' Bill B., Jan Stewer 33:1
Brewers: bakers and b. 310:5
Brewery: take me to a b. 7:3
Brewing: some ill a-b. 463:34
trouble b. 305:3
Briar: bonny b. bush in our kail yard 250:16
b.'s in bud 333:16
brittle sticks of thorn or b. 247:17
from off this b...a white rose 445:21
instead of the b...the myrtle 54:32
Briar-patch: bred en bawn in a b. 238:18
Briars: how full of b. is this.. world 426:27
Bribe: insulted by a very considerable b. 219:26
too poor for a b. 231:17
Bribes: contaminate our fingers with base b. 451:12
Bricht: und wenn das Herz auch b. 240:24

Brick: carried a piece of b. 519:6
found it b. and left it marble 120:8
heave 'arf a b. at 'im 403:9
Bricks: brothels with b. of Religion 77:15
I can't lay b. 503:14
Bridal: against their b. day 510:20
b. of the earth and sky 245:13
light the b. lamp 348:38
our b. flowers..for a..corse 478:33
Bridal-cakes: and of their b. 245:17
Bridal-chamber: come to the b., Death 234:16
Bridal-favours: b. and raiment stowed away 542:13
Bride: all jealousy to the b. 36:11
as a b. adorned for her husband 71:44
b. at the altar 419:3
Bridegroom with his b. 540:7
b. hath paced into the hall 148:23
busk ye, my bonny b. 235:1
dead maiden to be his b. 419:17
drew my b...across my threshold 374:24
encounter darkness as a b. 462:8
happy bridesmaid..happy b. 528:4
his b. and his darling to be 9:16
like a blooming Eastern b. 190:34
never turns him to the b. 262:14
no, by St. B. of Bothwell 418:27
passioness b.,..Tranquillity 535:27
proud b. of a ducal coronet 176:36
ready to be thy b. 29:24(-30)
society..my glittering b. 574:16
Spirit and the b. 72:10
still unravish'd b. of quietness 287:6
though a virgin, yet a b. 125:5
who will cheer my bonny b.? 122:25
Bride-bed: I thought thy b. to have deck'd 437:22
Bridechamber: children of the b. mourn 58:41
Bridegroom: as long as the b. is with them 58:41
because of the b.'s voice 63:11
Bellona's b. 456:9
b. all night through 262:14
b. in my death 425:24
B. with his bride 540:7
cometh forth as a b. 392:32
fresh as a b. 438:32
friend of the b...rejoiceth 63:11
like a b. from his room 24:6
Bridegrooms: of b., brides, and.. bridal-cakes 245:17
Brides of Enderby 267:12
Bridesmaid: happy b. 528:4
Bridge: b. much broader than the flood 468:7
b. the ford 301:26
by b. and ford 540:12
by the b. also 42:12
doth the crevasse b. 543:15
forgive you B. at dawn 140:3
golden b. 115:10
Horatius kept the b. 324:1
keep the b. with me 323:19
on the b. at midnight 315:27
on the B. of Sighs 114:1
Peschiera, when thy b. I crost 147:5
praise the b. that carried you 154:7
rude b. that arched the flood 199:7
Women, and Champagne, and B. 41:26
Bridle-rein: stranger hath thy b. 365:17
Bridle-reins: gave his b. a shake 106:18, 419:19
Bridle-ring: took him by the b. 29:24
Bridles: she heard the b. ring 32:4
Brideleth not his tongue 69:34
Brief: b. as the lightning 466:20
b. is life but love is long 538:21
b. life is here our portion, b. sorrow, short-lived care 361:12
b., my lord. As woman's love 435:8
b. the moon of beauty..b. the sun of summer 538:21
drest in a little b. authority 461:31
or be less b. 561:4
when..struggling to be b. 255:18

Briefer: garland b. than a girl's 262:20
Brig: mate of the Nancy b. 218:14
Brigade: boys of the Old B. 562:20, 21
thy B. with cold cascade 219:8
Bright: all b. and glittering 582:14
all b. as an angel new dropt 373:18
all calm, as it was b. 552:13
all things b. and beautiful 3:14
among the heather b. 131:24
angels are b. still 460:18
behold the b. original appear 215:16
best of dark and b. 119:1
bracelet of b. hair 186:9
b. and fierce and fickle 538:20
b. as light, and clear as wind 537:42
b. as the sun 385:11
b., b. as day 586:22
b. in the fruitful valleys the streams 81:18
b. day that brings forth the adder 449:2
b. eyes of danger 515:29
b. is the ring of words 516:3
b. little, tight little..craft 222:8
b. October was come 146:25
b. star, would I were stedfast 288:17
b. the lamps shone o'er fair women 113:25
b. the vision that delighted 329:12
b. things come to confusion 466:20
b. towers of silence 171:5
b. with many an angel 362:2
b. with names that men remember 523:10
brimming, and b., and large 17:28
Channel's as b. as a ball-room 294:35
dark with excessive b. 346:22
goddess, excellently b. 279:31
heavens look b., my dear 357:1
her beauty made the b. world dim 499:7
her eye was b. 148:12
he shone b. 148:21
how b. these glorious spirits 562:10
if nought so b. may live 493:27
moon be still as b. 119:4
more b. and good 493:27
myriads though b. 344:11
not..obscurely b. 115:8
not too b. or good 580:20
path before him always b. 575:5
same b., patient stars 286:14
so cool, so calm, so b. 245:13
softest clothing, woolly, b. 76:10
spirit still, and b. 580:21
thought thee b. 488:22
thy majesty how b. 202:21
thy spouse, so b. and clear 185:20
Tiger! Tiger! burning b. 75:24
westward..the land is b. 147:8
young lady named B. 98:19
Brighten at the blaze 226:11
Brightens: joy b. his crest 349:13
Brighter: allur'd to b. worlds 224:21
b...than flaming Jupiter 330:6
b. than is the silver Rhodope 330:21
look b. when we come 115:22
Brightest: b. and best 240:15
b. in dungeons 114:33
Hesperus..rode b. 347:19
though the b. fell 460:18
wisest, b., meanest of mankind 384:12
Bright-eyed: b. Fancy, hovering o'er 231:15
b. Mariner 148:20
Bright-haired sun 153:24
Brightly dawns our wedding-day 219:35
Brightness: all her original b. 345:5
amazing b., purity, and truth 371:12
attired with sudden b. 575:10
between his Darkness and his B. 119:22
b. falls from the air 361:5
b. of his glory 69:7
b. of the day 4:6
clothed with transcendent b. 344:11
innocent b. of a new-born day 576:22
sunrise brings back the b. 77:27
Brighton: merry Dr. B. 542:16
Brignal banks are wild and fair 419:7
Brig o' Dread: from B. 31:13
Brilliance: kingly b. of Sirius 236:38

[629]

INDEX

Brilliant: far less b. pen than
  mine 39:10
  the b. Frenchman never knew 164:16
Brillig: 'twas b. 129:39
Brim: bubbles winking at the b. 287:24
  filled to the b. with girlish glee 219:27
  o'er night's b. day boils 94:39
  sparkles near the b. 113:23
Brimming: b. and bright and large 17:28
  river up an' b. 296:21
Brimstone: from his b. bed 151:7, 507:19
Brine: eye-offending b. 481:32
  tunnies steeped in b. 18:16
Bring: b. another back to me 30:20
  b. down my gray hairs with sor-
    row 45:21
  b. forth the horse 118:13
  b. hither the Pink 510:23
  b. me flesh and b. me wine 361:21
  b. me my bow of burning gold 75:16
  b. with thee jest 341:28
  in sorrow..b. forth children 44:26
  those that would b. them out 268:8
  what a day may b. forth 50:43
  who will b. me into Edom? 395:23
Bringer: b. of new things 540:32(–541)
  comprehends none of that joy 467:24
  first b. of unwelcome news 441:10
Bringeth them unto the haven 107:19
Bringing: b. thy sheep in thy hand 17:19
  her b. me up by hand 175:22
Brings: one who b. a mind 344:22
Brink: dreadful outer b. 88:17
Brioche: qu'ils mangent de la b. 329:18
Brisk: as b. as a bee in conversation 270:8
  b. and giddy-paced times 483:1
  b. little somebody 89:25
  b., or grave 163:48
  easy, debonair and b. 162:21
  to see him shine so b. 438:35
Bristle: his hair did b. 417:14
Bristol: not a member of B. 100:14
  three sailors of B. city 543:7
Britain: B., could you ever boast 521:15
  B. is a world by itself 429:28
  ambassador from B.'s crown 188:30
  B. set the world ablaze 219:7
  hail, happy B.! 506:14
  hath B. all the sun? 429:34
  I've lost B. 301:5
  made B. India 446:9
  when B. first 545:18
Britannia: Beer and B. 505:15
  B. needs no bulwarks 123:11
  B. rules the waves 122:30
  B., the pride of the ocean 489:1
  rule, B. 545:18
  singing, Rule B. 8:24
  when you've shouted 'Rule B.' 294:17
Britanniae: nunc terminus B. patet 526:8
Britannos: penitus toto divisos orbe
  B. 555:19
British: art thou not of B. blood? 529:35
  blood of a B. man 453:27
  B. and Armoric knights 345:4
  B. Bourgeoisie 502:16
  B. Grenadier 9:24
  B. public..fits of morality 325:15
  B. Public, ye who like me not 95:29
  chips to the B. farmer 143:31
  come you back, you B. soldier 299:10
  fair play of the B. criminal law 187:25
  Flood of B. freedom 577:2
  ground which B. shepherds tread 567:2
  honour of the B. Army 305:1
  my grandmother's review, the
    B. 115:26
  no countries..less known by the
    B. 78:23
  normal B. sentence 144:16
  no sounder piece of B. manhood 126:3
  our ships were B. oak 20:20
  reflections on the greatness of
    the B. Nation 2:19
  Regiment o' B. Infantree 296:25
  stony B. stare 536:5
  success of the B...in political
    life 181:6
  these selfsame B. Islands 78:23
  twice tricked by the B. 38:16
  when the B. warrior queen 158:29

British (*cont.*)
  with what..majesty the B.
    soldier fights 360:21
  you broke a B. square 296:23
British Empire: B. and the United
    States..mixed up 144:2
  leave..B. to prigs 180:30
  preside over the liquidation of
    the B. 144:11
British Museum: I keep my
    books at the B. 111:30
Briton: as only a free-born B. can 542:34
  I glory in the name of B. 216:13
  set His B. in blown seas 537:21
Britons: B. never..shall be mar-
    ried 8:24
  B. never will be slaves 545:18
  B., strike home 551:9
  while B. shall be true 265:15
Brittle: b. is foredoomed 337:16
  your bones are very b. 515:23
Broach'd: bravely b. his..breast 467:29
Broad: as b. as it hath breadth 424:17
  as b. as the blue sky above 549:6
  b. and deep continueth 302:4
  b. as ten thousand beeves 336:42
  b. gate and the great fire 423:9
  b. is the way 58:23
  b. sunshine of life 274:11
  his pranks..too b. 435:38
  make b. their phylacteries 60:15
  she's the B. 511:5
  thy commandment is exceeding
    b. 399:19
  with b. and burning face 149:12
Broad-based upon her people's
    will 539:13
Broad-cloth without 160:12
Broadens: Freedom slowly b. down 541:24
Broader: b. still became the blaze 322:22
  to b. lands and better days 144:2
Broad-fronted Caesar 424:1
Broad-shoulder'd genial English-
    man 539:9
Broadsword: flashed the b. of
    Lochiell 23:20
Brocks: where b. were grunting 334:6
Brogues: not fit to tie his b. 420:30
Broil: feats of b. and battle 469:45
Broiled fowl and mushrooms—
    capital 178:27
Broke: all hell b. loose 347:33
  b. any man's head but his own 444:1
  b. no promise 385:6
  b. the Bank at Monte Carlo 217:23
  b. the good meeting 459:22
  b. them in the sweet face of
    heaven 453:19
  b. this happy dream 184:12
  fancies that b. through language 95:21
  when my grave is b. up again 186:8
  you b. a British square 296:23
Broken: among the b. men 142:10
  bones which thou hast b. 395:8
  b. and contrite heart 395:10
  b. and thrown away 317:17
  b. by their passing feet 584:8
  b. heart it kens nae second
    spring 9:8
  b. heart lies here 323:9
  b. it up for your daily bread 525:27
  b. Johnsonese 325:30
  b. open on..scientific principles 376:14
  b. with the storms of state 447:3
  but through a b. heart 569:12
  eater of b. meats 452:32
  grief never mended no b. bones 174:7
  if it be not b., break 161:5
  I live on b. wittles 174:19
  laws..to be b. 365:11
  left behind a b. doll 238:8
  London bridge is b. down 367:19
  naught b. save this body 84:18
  nor a b. thing mend 42:6
  not quickly b. 51:5
  pitcher be b. at the fountain 51:33
  promises and pie-crust..b. 520:4
  things uncomely and b. 585:17
  those that are b. in heart 400:21
  twice b. His great heart 313:5
  when the lute is b. 494:20

Broken (*cont.*)
  whilst we speak..b. 492:2
Broken-hearted: bind up the b. 55:3
  half b. 119:29
  poor and b. 508:4
  we had ne'er been b. 104:11
  you hoped we were both b. 524:9
Broker: an honest b. 72:32
Bromide: are you a b.? 99:43
Bronze: he who blows thro' b. 94:5
Brooches: I will make you b. 516:2
Brood: b. like a ghost 171:21
  b. of Folly 341:7
  eternal b. of glory 509:23
  fond of no second b. 429:22
  his b. about thy knee 538:22
  thy b. is flown 538:21
  two luxuries to b. over 290:22
Broodest o'er the troubled sea 284:24
Brooding: birds sit b. in the snow 456:1
  b. o'er the gloom 336:9
  b. on the charmed wave 343:13
  b. over bein' a dog 656:23
  Hardy..b. and blaspheming 142:19
Broods: b. with warm breast 254:25
  b. and sleeps on his own heart 578:34
  immortality b. like the day 576:14
Brook: chose a pebble from the b. 161:4
  dwelt by the b. Cherith 47:51
  Eternal B. 83:27
  fell in the weeping b. 437:1
  five smooth stones out of the b. 47:23
  he drank of the b. 47:51
  I could not hear the b. flow 262:9
  inland b. into the main 465:21
  noise like of a hidden b. 149:35
  pore upon the b. 230:12
  salad from the b. 164:1
  Siloa's b. that flow'd 344:2
  this b. hath conveyed his ashes 212:8
  where the b. and river meet 316:34
  willowy b. 408:10
Brookland: far in a western b. 263:19
Brooks: books in the running b. 426:30
  b. of Eden 529:18
  golden sands, and crystal b. 184:8
  I sing of b. 245:17
  murmurs near the running b. 578:31
  only B. of Sheffield 174:12
  shallow b. and rivers wide 342:1
  shallow b. murmur most 501:17
  strow the b. in Vallombrosa 344:25
  what sedg'd b. are Thames's 18:29
Brookside: I wandered by the b. 262:9
Broom: bright blows the b. 516:2
  on the b., green b. 169:14
  sent with b. before 467:36
Broomstick: surely man is a b. 520:2
Broomsticks: for all their b. 584:22
Broth: some b. without any bread 369:4
Brothel: scene..laid in a B. 306:33
  Still clinging, in the b. 513:32
Brothels: b. with bricks of Re-
    ligion 77:15
  thy foot out of b. 453:20
Brother: am I my b.'s keeper? 44:30
  at the hand of every man's b. 44:42
  better..him than his b. 333:6
  body of my b.'s son 149:33
  b. clasps the hand of b. 35:5
  b. of death 85:23
  B. of the Angle 559:12
  b. of the clay 122:37
  b. should not war with b. 160:41
  b., thy tail hangs down 301:7
  b. to Death 38:9, 168:12
  b. whom someone should save 550:33
  call my b. back to me 241:7
  dawn is my b. 41:20
  dear b. Jim 582:11
  Death and his b. Sleep 497:18
  elder b. ev'n to shade 407:19
  forlorn and shipwrecked b. 317:8
  furies of thy b. 324:11
  gently scan your b. man 104:7
  grew so like my b. 313:7
  had it been his b. 6:20
  hateth his b. 70:15
  he..shall be my b. 444:28(–445)
  he's your b. still 521:23
  how fast hath b. followed b. 575:18

Brother (cont.)

hurt my b.   437:35
I called him B.   579:20
if it disdained its b.   495:7
king my b.'s wreck   197:30
Land o' Cakes, and. b. Scots   107:20
little brown b.   362:28
lo'ed him like a vera b.   108:5
loveth not his b.   70:15
marry with his b.   435:41
mine uncle, my father's b.   430:33(-431)
my b. he is in Elysium   482:2
my b. John, the evil one   74:4
my b. Jonathan   47:30
my friends and b. souls   528:11
no b. near the throne   385:29
O b. man! fold to thy heart thy b.   568:20
O my poor b.   482:3
our sad bad glad mad b.   522:18
seeth his b. hath need   70:11
Sister and the B.   35:19
Spouse and B.   543:19
stick more close than a b.   302:17
sticketh closer than a b.   50:22
still to my b. turns   226:4
strong B. in God   42:2
sworn b...to grim Necessity   475:27
that thou wert as my b.   52:21
there's night and day, b.   78:24
thy b. came with subtilty   45:2
thy b. Death   495:23
true b. of a company   586:14
Trust his sworn b.   485:34
voice of thy b.'s blood   44:31
weak B. is the worst   514:36
where is my b. gone?   241:7
where my b. set the laburnum   253:1
who also am your b.   70:23
Brotherhood: b. in song   285:8
b. of venerable trees   573:25
crown thy good with b.   36:23
dearer yet the b.   362:33
love the b.   69:50
this man in b.   87:38
Brother-in-law: my b. is haberdasher   112:18
Brotherly: b. love   66:2
let b. love continue   69:22
Brothers: all the b. too   483:11
all the B. were Valiant   363:9
B. and Sisters, I bid you beware   300:22
b. be for a' that   105:33
b., lift your voices   35:2
forty thousand b. could not   437:24
make b. and sisters hate each
  other   269:33
men, my b.   534:25
more than my b.   532:10
punch, b.   83:1
Romans were like b.   323:24
two b. and their murder'd man   286:22
we band of b.   444:28(-445)
we were b.   228:5
ye are b.! ye are men   122:6
Brougham: never the doctor's b.   299:19
short of the mark like Mr. B.'s
  speeches   240:7
Brought: b. forth wind   53:32
b. reg'lar and draw'd mild   176:18
b. to you daily   294:36
b. up in this city   65:13
God..b. them unto Adam   44:15
immortal sea which b. us hither   576:19
never b. to mind   104:12
there she b. thee forth   52:12
Brought'st thy sweets along with
  Thee   244:14
Brow: Angel with contracted b.   349:2
b. of Egypt   407:24
b. with homely biggin bound   442:25
Consul's b. was sad   323:16
crystal of his b.   321:14
forty winters shall besiege thy b.   486:10
her beautiful bold b.   537:41
his eyes grow in my b.   424:1
hollow eye and wrinkled b.   465:9
king sate on the rocky b.   115:45
lily on thy b.   286:29
no wrinkle on thine azure b.   114:29
o'er that b.   119:2

Brow (cont.)

press down upon the b. of
  labor   98:2
rugged b. of careful Policy   510:25
show thy dangerous b.   449:6
sole speech in that victorious b.   17:24
some sober b. will bless it   464:14
stamps the wrinkle deeper on
  the b.   113:20
that great b.   90:7
thorn thy b. to braid   419:8
upon his baby b. the round   460:8
weariness not on your b.   17:20
whether on Ida's shady b.   75:18
your bonny b. was brent   106:19
Brow-bound with burning gold   529:9
Brown: b. coat   325:28, 32
from the blue bed to the b.   227:17
give me the B. compromise   265:1
hamlets b.   153:25
hang on the B. Bear's flank   301:4
has b. hair, and speaks small   465:27
hustle the Aryan b.   300:6
I, John B.   85:6
John Brown's body lies a
  mould'ring   234:7
learn from the Yellow an' B.   298:5
long, and lank, and b.   149:19
Long John B. had the Devil in
  his gut   75:15
rolling up ragged and b.   293:26
slightly tinged her cheek with b.   416:16
some gave them b.   367:13
whose hair was so b.   201:24
ye myrtles b.   342:10
you have baked me too b.   129:25
Browning: B...Grotesque Art   29:8
B.! since Chaucer   308:17
from B. some 'Pomegranate'   88:7
leave to Robert B.   293:10
Meredith is a prose B., and so is
  B.   569:30
Mrs. B.'s death..a relief   207:33
Robert B., you writer of plays   92:46
Brownist: as lief be a B. as a politician   483:33
Brows: between the b.   411:25
be it not seen in either of our b.   189:20
bliss in our b. bent   423:33
b. of dauntless courage   345:7
gathering her b.   108:2
my handkercher about your b.   447:38
night-cap decked his b.   224:11
purple b. of Olivet   532:22
Sappho lay her burning b.   545:7
shadow of her even b.   509:31
their b. with roses..bound   190:34
Browsing: excellent b. and sluicing   572:8
Bruce: wham B. has aften led   107:32
Brüder: alle Menschen werden B.   415:21
Bruise: b. them with a rod of iron   391:50
it shall b. thy head   44:25
parmaceti for an inward b.   438:35
thou shalt b. his heel   44:25
Bruised: b. for our iniquities   54:26
b. in a new place   267:24
Bruisers of England   78:26
Bruises: one mask of b.   177:10
Bruising of the hapless head   561:16
Bruit: comes on at hand the b.   544:28
Brunck: most learn'd professor B.   387:7
Brunswick: B.'s fated chieftain   113:28
  Hamelin Town's in B.   94:32
Brunt: bear the b.   95:11
Brush: b. the descending blue   255:4
dip his b. in dyes of heaven   418:25
gi'e them a b.   250:18
hang and b. their bosoms   97:9
never b. their hair   40:22
with so fine a b.   23:12
Brushed: their coats were b.   130:13
ne'er b. dew from lawn   119:17
Brushers: critics..b. of noble-
  men's clothes   24:41
Brushes: b. his hat a mornings   468:31
b. of comets' hair   303:20
Brushing with hasty steps the
  dews   230:11
Brushwood sheaf   92:14
Brutal and insolent soldiery   201:28
Brute: b. I might have been   95:16

Brute (cont.)

'Chuck him out, the b.!'   303:2
feed the b.   403:33
house of a b.   528:9
lord of the fowl and the b.   164:22
neither b. nor human   380:13
never saw a b. I hated so   90:22
regular b. of a bee   311:3
such a cross-grained b.   227:11
whatever b...made the world   263:31
you intoxified their soul   34:30
Brute: et tu, B.   120:12, 449:31
Brutes: as we to the b.   337:15
b. never meet in bloody fray   225:24
b. without you   371:12
made b. men   374:20
simple race of b.   531:25
Brutish: nasty, b., and short   248:21
silence is..also b. and dead   126:33
Bruto: laudatoque M. B.   526:12
Brutus: B. and Cato might discharge their souls   193:30
B. is an honourable man   450:18, 19
B. makes mine greater   451:22
B. says he was ambitious   450:19
B....was Caesar's angel   450:29
'B.' will start a spirit   448:23
Caesar had his B.   242:10
fault, dear B.   448:22
found like B., like himself   452:3
noble B.   450:17
no orator, as B. is   450:32
that ever B. will go bound   451:37
that Lord B. took to wife   449:18
were I B., and B. Antony   450:34
when Marcus B. grows so covetous   451:21
Bubble: cauldron b.   459:30
fame? an empty b.   228:18
honour but an empty b.   191:9
life is mostly froth and b.   227:34
like the b. on the fountain   416:23
much like unto a b.   560:25
now a b. burst   383:10
seeking the b. reputation   427:21
the world's a b.   28:16
Bubbled: his passion boiled and
  b.   543:12
Bubbles: beaded b. winking at the
  brim   287:24
borne, like thy b., onward   114:32
earth hath b.   456:18
Bubbling: b. and loud-hissing urn   163:21
b. cry   115:30
with b. groan   114:28
Bubukles: his face is all b., and
  whelks   444:3
Bubus: paterna rura b. exercet suis   257:22
Buccleugh: kinsmen to the bold B.   417:3
Buck: derned thing 'ed get up and
  b.   238:27
Bucket: that b. down   475:19
the nations are as a drop of a b.   54:12
Buckets: dropping b. into empty
  wells   163:11
silly b. on the deck   149:28
two b. filling one another   475:17
Buckingham: high-reaching B.   476:23
so much for B.   144:26
Buckingham Palace: changing
  guard at B.   339:14
Buckle: b. my shoe   368:6
reason doth b...the mind   24:16
Buckled: others have b. their
  armour   402:14
she takes her b. shoon   183:13
Buckler: carry the b. unto Samson   86:13
thy shield and b.   397:18
Bucklers: hang a thousand b.   52:5
Buckling tighter..Auster's band   324:12
Buckram: eleven b. men grown
  out of two   439:21
two rogues in b. suits   439:20
Bud: be a b. again   285:23
briar's in b.   333:16
b., and yet a rose   247:21
b. may have a bitter taste   161:19
canker lives in sweetest b.   486:31
I'll nip him in the b.   407:8
in age I b. again   244:18
in b., or blade, or bloom   529:2

INDEX

Bud (cont.)

leaf, the b., the flower — 509:33
like a worm i' the b. — 483:10
opening b. to Heaven convey'd — 151:18
that b. and bloom forth brings — 518:3
this b. of love — 477:24
Budded Tyrian — 288:3
Budding: b. morrow in midnight — 238:26
b. rose above the rose full blown — 575:3
to set b. more..flowers — 284:11
Budge: b. doctors of the Stoic fur — 340:35
'B.', says the fiend — 463:27
not b. for no man's pleasure — 478:13
Buds: blind b. that snows have shaken — 523:21
blown b. of barren flowers — 523:18
b., and bells, and stars — 288:8
dark b. and leaves — 497:22
darling b. of May — 486:18
driving sweet b. like flocks — 496:4
green b. they were swellin' — 30:1
hawthorn hedge puts forth its b. — 83:17
kill cankers in the musk-rose b. — 466:42
kneel'd unto the b. — 424:29
labyrinthine b. the rose — 96:32
starry river b. — 497:23
summer's velvet b. — 443:10
when hawthorn b. appear — 466:21
Buff: bide by the b. and the blue — 106:6
Buffalo: he thought he saw a B. — 128:16
where the b. roam — 248:9
Buffaloes: so air our B. — 176:24
Buffer: poor b. lies low — 568:24
Buffet: messenger of Satan to b. — 67:37
Buffeted for your faults — 69:51
Buffets: fortune's b. and rewards — 434:26
Buffoon: b. and poet — 241:29
fiddler, statesman, and b. — 190:22
Buffs: steady the B. — 304:42
Bug: flap this b. with gilded wings — 385:31
Bugaboo-baby: don't b. me — 121:4
Bughtin: b.-time is near, my jo — 106:30
Bugle: blow, b., blow — 538:14
bring the good old b., boys — 583:6
Bugle-horn: one blast upon his b. — 416:28
sound upon the b. — 534:13
Bugles: blow out, you b. — 83:19
Song on your b. blown — 241:26
what are the b. blowin' for? — 295:19
Bugloss: blue b. paints the sterile soil — 165:17
Build: birds b.—but not I b. — 255:9
b. from age to age — 295:6
b. me a pyramid — 303:8
b. me straight — 315:29
b. the lofty rhyme — 342:10
b. thee more stately mansions — 251:15
b. thou the walls of Jerusalem — 395:10
burrow awhile and b. — 89:7
except the Lord b. the house — 399:35
he's gart b. a bonny ship — 31:8
how b., unbuild, contrive — 348:30
I hunger to b. them anew — 585:17
I would b. that dome in air — 151:33(-152)
nor pair, nor b., nor sing — 152:17
that others should b. for him — 580:6
the Lord doth b. up Jerusalem — 400:21
when we b...b. for ever — 413:12
who thus could b. — 577:11
Builded better than he knew — 199:23
Builder: after me cometh a B. — 300:15
only be a b. — 412:23
Builders: b. wrought with greatest care — 315:28
our b. were with want of genius curst — 192:10
stone which the b. refused — 399:11
Building: altered in the b. trade — 303:7
ancient castle or b. not in decay — 26:41
B. up of Jerusalem — 75:10
no looking at a b. here — 103:36
stole..the life o' the b. — 458:22
tall b. with a tower — 164:29
Buildings: ornament put upon great civic b. — 413:11
Built: all we have b. — 17:1
almost lost that b. it — 87:17
b. God a church — 162:4
b. in such a logical way — 251:6
b. in th' eclipse — 342:25

Built (cont.)

b. the barn, the forge — 77:28
house that Jack b. — 369:6
love b. on beauty — 184:13
proud and godly kings had b. her — 208:5
therefore b. for ever — 530:5
which he b., lamented Jack — 152:13
Bulbo: my bold, my beautiful, my B. — 542:28
Bulk: growing like a tree in b. — 282:1
one slight hair the mighty b. — 215:38
Shakespeare..lesser in b. — 212:18
Bull: Cock and a B. — 513:24
down at the old 'B. and Bush' — 548:1
gone to milk the b. — 271:11
greatest of all is John B. — 117:31
in time the savage b. — 305:12, 468:5
Irish b. is always pregnant — 327:10
oil'd and curl'd Assyrian B. — 535:40
old unhappy b. — 249:6
secret of the b. and lamb — 336:25
Bullen: dawn'd from B.'s eyes — 229:19
Bullet: every b. has its billet — 570:29
ramm'd with b. round — 509:25
stronger than the b. — 314:5
with a b. through his heart — 542:37
Bullets: b. made of platinum — 40:27
paper b. of the brain — 468:23
Bullied: b. into a certain philosophy — 289:24
b. out of vice — 518:4
Bullock's but a fool — 300:8
Bullocks: how a good yoke of b.? — 442:7
they shall offer young b. — 395:11
whose talk is of b. — 57:12
Bulls: b., that walk the pastures — 336:38
dew-lapp'd like Thessalian b. — 467:20
dispenses, pardons, b. — 346:26
fat b. of Basan — 393:4
seated on two chairs like mad b. — 175:31
that I will eat b.' flesh — 395:4
Bull's-eye at your belt — 513:27
Bully: b. boy, b. boy — 420:3
like a tall b. — 385:2
your mentality, too, is b. — 39:28
Bulrushes: ark of b. — 45:30
Bulwark: floating b. of the island — 73:6
Bulwarks: Britannia needs no b. — 123:11
mark well her b. — 394:35
Bump: things that go b. in the night — 6:9
Bumping: b. pitch and a blinding light — 363:4
Bumps: afraid of b. — 504:10
what-hol she b.! — 131:33
Bun: B. replied — 199:18
now for the rollicking b. — 222:18
Bunbury: permanent invalid called B. — 569:22
Buncombe: speaking through reporters to B. — 126:39
Bundle: b. of contradictions — 154:23
b. of myrrh is my wellbeloved — 51:42
b. of prejudices — 306:10
the world is a b. of hay — 117:31
Bungay: Friar Bacon and Friar B. — 231:34
Bunk: history is b. — 209:21
Buns: two a penny, hot cross-b. — 368:5
Bunting: bye, baby b. — 366:11
Bunyan: Philistine of genius..B. — 20:19
Buoy: her cock a b. — 454:3
Buoy'd: the sea..would have b. up — 453:34
Burbled as it came — 129:39(-130)
Burden: b. and heat of the day — 60:7
b. and the heat — 17:1
b. of an honour — 535:7
b. of his song — 72:16
b. of my song — 8:8
b. of the desert — 53:25
b. of the incommunicable — 172:17
b. of them is intolerable — 390:36
b. of the mystery — 581:25
b. of the world — 329:19
cast their b. upon the Lord — 302:3
ever to b. thine — 499:2
fulness to such, a b. is — 99:31
grasshopper shall be a b. — 51:33
grievous b. was thy birth — 476:27
my b. is light — 59:10
public b. of a nation's care — 402:5

Burden (cont.)

sweet sprites, the b. bear — 479:28
take up the White Man's b. — 303:24
war lays a b. on the..state — 159:26
with superfluous b. loads the day — 351:23
Burdens: couching down between two b. — 45:27
crowding in their heavy b. — 443:10
undo the heavy b. — 54:36
Burdett: hallooed out at one of B.'s elections — 119:32
Burdocks, hemlock, nettles — 454:2
Burg: ein feste B. ist unser Gott — 321:6
Burgeons every maze of quick — 533:24
Burghers: b. of Carlisle — 322:23
now might the b. know — 323:15
rich b. on the flood — 462:29
Burglar: many a b. I've restored — 222:21
when the enterprising b.'s not a-burgling — 221:35
Burglary: flat b. — 469:9
Burgonet: arm and b. of men — 423:42
Burial: his obscure b. — 436:37
in one red b. blent — 113:36
in our very death, and b. sure — 295:10
to a sad b. feast — 478:33
to be buried in Christian b. — 437:3
Burial-ground God's Acre — 316:20
Buried: b. in dust — 37:13
b. in so sweet a place — 491:13
b. in the king's highway — 475:10
b. on Sunday — 368:21(-369)
b. once, Men want dug up — 205:28
leave it b. in this vault — 280:11
lie a-b. in one grave — 10:18
maker b. — 516:3
not b. in consecrated ground — 237:7
not b. me deep enough — 536:20
now 'tis b. deep — 288:2
their bodies are b. in peace — 57:19
there will I be b. — 47:1
to b. merit raise — 279:4
we b. him darkly — 572:11
where some b. Caesar bled — 206:3
Buries: b. empires and cities — 217:13
b. madmen in the heaps they raise — 384:4
Burke: B., who winds into a subject — 227:31
ditto to Mr. B. — 401:17
only specimen of B. — 239:11
Burleigh: B...shakes his head, and exit — 500:3
B.-House by Stamford-town — 535:10
mourned the Lord of B. — 535:10
Burlington Bertie — 237:28
Burma: there's a B. girl — 299:10
Burn: abune the b. — 516:20
another Troy for her to b. — 584:25
better to marry than to b. — 66:30
b. to the socket — 574:14
b. upward each — 96:45
I rage, I melt, I b. — 214:6
our heart b. within us — 62:55
shall yet terrific b. — 123:12
some trotting b.'s meander — 107:35
sun shall not b. thee — 399:28
teach the torches to b. bright — 477:9
to b. always — 374:14
to b. for ever in burning hell — 524:32
violent fires soon b. out — 474:21
we b. daylight — 465:34, 477:6
words, that b. — 231:15
you may chance to b. your lips — 480:38
Burned: as if they b. in a furnace — 70:27
bring John now to be b. alive — 92:5
b. green and blue and white — 149:6
b. is Apollo's laurel bough — 330:12
b. on the water — 424:6
b. the Temple of Diana — 87:17
b. the topless towers of Ilium — 330:5
b. to ashes — 228:11
bush b. with fire — 45:33
charmed water b. alway — 149:25
Christians have b. each other — 115:20
eternal wrath b. after them — 348:22
give my body to be b. — 66:45
half his Troy was b. — 441:9
his clothes not be b. — 49:49
ne'er within him b. — 417:22
night's candles are b. out — 478:27

INDEX

Burned (cont.)

signal torch has b. his hour 264:5
uncle George's workshops was b. 175:32
Burnet: freckled cowslip, b. and.. clover 445:11
Burneth: b. the chariots 394:29
still it b. 493:23
Burning: boy stood on the b. deck 241:5
b. and a shining light 63:18
b. for b. 45:54
b. o'er the babe 525:16
b. Sappho loved and sung 115:43
b. witches when we're only b. weeds 141:12
b. with high hope 113:34
depths of b. light 202:21
honour'd for his b. throne 462:25
keep the home fires b. 210:4
like a liar gone to b. hell 473:20
log was b. brightly 223:10
over the b. marle 344:24
plucked out of the b. 56:1
pretty Babe all b. bright 508:14
smell of b. fills the startled air 41:36
Tiger! Tiger! b. bright 75:24
time for the b. of the leaves 72:21
with broad and b. face 149:12
your lights b. 61:54
Burnish take on Eden-trees 545:7
Burnished with golden rind 347:5
Burns: b. but more clearly 585:4
b. fierce while it is green 172:7
B., Shelley, were with us 93:4
not she which b. in't 485:11
our wasted oil unprofitably b. 159:21
parching air b. frore 345:31
Seraph that adores and b. 383:20
Burn-side: waly, waly, yon b. 32:18
Burnt-offerings: b...hast thou not required 394:13
delightest not in b. 395:10
Burr: I am a kind of b. 462:23
shake off the b. o' the world 543:16
Burrow: always so near his b. 338:11
b. awhile and build 89:7
Burrs: do roses stick like b.? 97:11
rough thistles, kecksies, b. 445:11
stick on conversation's b. 250:31
Burst: be bold, it will not b. thee 56:48
b. Joy's grape 287:21
b. out singing 415:14
first that ever b. 149:3
from that..cedar what a b.! 17:11
his flaw'd heart..b. smilingly 454:23
let me not b. in ignorance 431:32
one last short b. 334:5
out of the little chapel I b. 90:24
then b. his mighty heart 450:31
think to b. out into sudden blaze 342:20
words, words, or I shall b. 203:20
Bursting: unshook amidst a b. world 385:23
Bursts: how thick the b. 17:12
Burton: why was B. built on Trent? 263:24
Bury: b. it with me 185:5
b. me, b. me deeper 536:21
b. the Great Duke 537:11
b. the lordliest lass of earth 84:5
b. under the Finite 127:18
dead b. their dead 58:35
dead Past b. its dead 317:7
disposed to b. for nothing 176:19
I b. some of you 185:5
I come to b. Caesar 450:17
I must b. sorrow 97:26
take your..plunder, and b. the dead 363:7
therewith b. in oblivion 87:22
Bus: can it be a Motor B.? 223:8
descending from the b. 223:8
Hitler has missed the b. 135:10
I'm not even a b., I'm a tram 237:26
tumbled off a b. 228:8
Busby: Dr. B., a great man 2:17
Buses: no b. runnin'..to Mandalay 299:13
Bush: aims but at a b. 501:18
bed in the b. 515:27
b. burned with fire..not consumed 45:33

Bush (cont.)

b. supposed a bear 467:24
every common b. afire with God 87:35
fear each b. an officer 446:7
flame? the b. is bare 95:7
four times as big as the b. 311:7
good wine needs no b. 428:40
hide me by the bracken b. 30:6
man in the b. with God may meet 199:16
sweet Robin sits in the b. 420:2
thorough b., thorough brier 466:33
underneath the barren b. 533:12
young bird in the b. 311:7
Bushes: discovereth the thick b. 393:23
Busied in his majesty 443:10
Busier: yet he semed b. than he was 137:8
Business: about my Father's b. 61:21
annuity is a very serious b. 23:8
big b. give the people a square deal 409:6
breakfast first, b. next 542:27
b. as usual 143:37
b. first: pleasure afterwards 542:25
b. of America is b. 156:25
b. of delight 495:14
b. of everybody 324:21
b. of the day in the day 564:19
b. was his aversion 195:21
Cecil's despatch of b. 503:9
come home to men's b. 25:15
did my uncle Toby's b. 513:21
do your own b. 68:36
end of this day's b. 451:38
everybody's is nobody's b. 559:16
for new projects than for settled b. 27:41
gets through more b. in spring 550:31
gone on b. to the Horse Guards 177:22
go to your b...pleasure 583:22
he that hath little b. 57:11
if everybody minded their own b. 128:31
if it's b. of consequence 34:7
importunity of b. 307:17
in civil b.; what first? 25:32
life's b...the terrible choice 96:14
lucrative business of mystery 103:1
my b. is to create 75:2
no feeling of his b.? 437:9
no further in this b. 457:10
no praying, it spoils b. 371:13
nothing more requisite in b. than dispatch 1:8
not slothful in b. 66:2
occupy their b. in great waters 398:17
pleasure was his b. 195:21
robs you on b. principles 490:38
servants of b. 26:22
some to b. 384:36
to be drunk, the b. of the day 192:8
to b. that we love 425:9
to double b. bound 435:32
Treasury is the spring of b. 28:22
your own foolish b. 139:36
Busiris and his Memphian chivalry 344:26
Busk: b. ye, b. ye 235:1
wherefore should I b. my heid 32:18
Buskin: hear thy b. tread 281:15
Buss: Miss B. and Miss Beale 8:10
Bust: animated b. 230:3
B. outlasts the throne 183:5
only give a b. of marriages 115:39
raise the tardy b. 279:4
Buste: le b. survit à la cité 214:3
Buster: another awful b. 376:8
Bustle: glance, and nod, and b. by 18:18
various b. of resort 340:20
Busts: picture plac'd the b. between 80:1, 139:5
Busy: b. curious, thirsty fly 370:11
b. hum of men 342:5
b. old fool, unruly Sun 186:19
b. trifler 159:27
how b. I must be this day 21:7
I would be b. too 561:29
orange-tree, that b. plant 244:17
some b. and insinuating rogue 473:1
their silly thoughts so b. keep 343:15
Busybodies: tattlers also and b. 68:49

But for the grace of God 79:12
Butcher: b...his heart bleeds 270:35
know a b. paints 96:27
shared by Miss B. 171:17
true my b.'s bill is due 218:13
Butchered to make a Roman holiday 114:19
Butchers: b. and cokes 310:5
even b. weep 214:23
fills the b.' shops 504:5
meek and gentle with these b. 450:11
sacrificers, but not b. 449:9
Butler: the Groom, the B., and the Cook 218:22
Butlers ought to know their place 41:6
Butt: here is my b. 473:31
knocks you down with the b.- end 227:27
Butter: b. and eggs and a pound of cheese 120:20
b. and honey shall he eat 53:12
b. in a lordly dish 46:49
b. will only make us fat 223:11
b.'s spread too thick 130:19
b. that makes the temptation 269:7
coffee, tea, chocolate, b. and toast 13:17
could we have some b.? 339:17
fine words b. no parsnips 420:7
it was the best b. 129:7
ladling b. from alternate tubs 408:4
little bit of b. to my bread 339:18
seas of b. 326:7
Titan kiss a dish of b. 439:14
your bread and your b. 294:34
Buttercup: I'm called Little B. 221:9
Buttercups: b. and daisies 264:22
when noontide wakes anew the b. 92:16
Buttered: always on the b. side 376:9
I sometimes dig for b. rolls 131:24
my brains ta'en out, and b. 466:8
Butterflies: b. and cockylolybirds 294:10
I look for b. 131:22
laugh at gilded b. 454:19
no b., no bees 253:12
what it concedes to the b. 173:26
white b. in the air 82:7
Butterfly: breaks a b. upon a wheel 385:30
b. upon the road 300:13
I'd be a b. born in a bower 36:26
kill not the moth nor b. 73:23
most affected, husband-hunting b. 353:6
Butters: Stubbs b. Freeman 408:4
Buttery: a little b. 247:17
Butting through the Channel 333:21
Buttock: broad b., tender hide 488:27
Buttocks: gorgeous b. of the ape 266:16
Button: I wad na gie a b. for her 108:32
little round b. at top 209:18
not a rap, not a b. 171:17
pray you, undo this b. 454:26
you press the b. 12:9
Buttoned: b. it with stars 251:2
close-b. to the chin 160:12
Button-hole: take you a b. lower 455:32
Buttons: I had a soul above b. 154:14
they've taken of 'is b. off 295:20
with the metal b. 325:32
work them into waistcoat-b. 131:24
Button-stick: tongue like a b. 295:3
Buttress: b. of the church 335:21
no jutty, frieze, b. 457:6
Butts: beast..b. me away 429:15
Buxom, blithe, and debonair 341:27
Buxton: every fool in B. can be at Bakewell 413:1
Buy: b. a world of happy days 476:13
b. my English posies 296:15
b. then! bid then! 255:6
b. yourself weeds 215:3
cherries grow, that none can b. 4:14
cherries grow, which none may b. 124:4
come and b. 245:21
come ye, b., and eat 54:29
I'd have you b. and sell so 485:27
I will b. with you 463:16
no man might b. or sell 71:21
nor peer nor prince can b. 124:5

INDEX

Buy (cont.)
want new worlds to b.   332:9
what would you b.?   38:28
Buyer: naught, saith the b.   50:27
Buying good pennyworths   211:16
Buys: costs nothing and b. everything   354:17
Buzz: B.! B.! B.!   339:20
crowd, and b., and murmurings   158:12
does it b.?   311:3
Buzzards: the B. are all gentlemen   82:26
Buzzing: hush'd with b. nightflies   441:41
what is he in my ears   90:36
By and by: b. is easily said   435:28
in the coming b.   220:33
in the sweet b.   415:9
we shall hear it b.   89:10
Byng: Kentish Sir B.   90:16
Byron: B. bore..the pageant of his bleeding heart   16:8
close thy B.   127:19
Collingwood, B., Blake   362:30
from the poetry of Lord B...a system   325:18
Goethe's sage mind and B.'s force   16:23
Lord B. is only great as a poet   223:13
Lord B. ist nur gross wenn er dichtet   223:13
when B.'s eyes were shut   16:21
Byway: and the b. nigh me   515:27
his own B. to heaven   170:15
Byword: a proverb and a b.   47:41
Byzantium: Soldan of B. is smiling   141:3

C

C: C. cut it   366:7
C Major of this life   89:12
Ça ira   12 11
Cabal: in high c.   561:10
Caballería: religión es la c.   134:12
Caballero: El C. de la Triste Figura   134:8
Cabals: kitchen-c.   164:31
Cabbage-leaf: to cut a c.   209:18
Cabbages: of c.—and kings   130:15
Cabin: make me a willow c.   482:22
small c. build there   585:12
Cabin-boy did swim   31:1
Cabin'd: c., cribb'd, confin'd   459:12
from her c. loop-hole peep   340:6
her c. ample Spirit   17:15
Cabinet: C. of Mediocrities   181:31
c. of pleasure   244:23
consequence of c. government   28:23
Cabots: the C. talk only to God   79:2
Cackle: don't c. w'en he fine a wum   238:22
Cackling: I'd drive ye c. home   452:34
when every goose is c.   465:22
Cacoethes: scribendi c.   283:12
Cad: cocoa is a c. and coward   142:9
Cadence: golden c. of poesy   455:14
harsh c. of a rugged line   193:11
to the ancient lyrical c.   146:13
Cadence: une juste c.   78:5
Cadendo: non vi sed saepe c.   372:11
Cadiz: reeking into C. Bay   92:17
Cadmus: once were C. and Harmonia   15:14
the letters C. gave   116:2
with Hercules and C. once   467:20
Cadwallader: not for C. and all his goats   445:8
Caedis: per damna, per c.   260:21
Caelum: c. non animum mutant in c. miseris, ibit   257:4   283:3
Caesar: all is C.'s   166:14
always I am C.   448:27
angry spot..on C.'s brow   448:25
as..Mark Antony's was by C.   458:33
beggar's nurse and C.'s   425:33
broad-fronted C.   424:1
Brutus..C.'s angel   450:29
but yesterday the word of C.   450:23
C. bleed in sport   450:1

Caesar (cont.)
C. had his Brutus   242:16
C. hath wept   450:20
C. is more dangerous   449:23
C. is turn'd to hear   448:10
C. shall go forth   449:23
C.'s hand, and Plato's brain   199:2
C.'s image is effac'd at last   161:29
C.'s spirit, ranging for revenge   450:12
C.'s thrasonical brag   428:25
C.'s wife..above suspicion   120:15
C.'s wife, all things to all men   8:6
C. was ambitious   450:17
C. with a senate at his heels   384:10
call great C. ass unpolicied   426:13
cold upon dead C.'s trencher   425:3
enemies of C. shall say this   450:10
enter C., in his nightgown   449:19
first time ever C. put it on   450:27
fit to stand by C.   471:15
from C.'s laurel crown   73:27
give to your boy, your C.   191:17
great C. fell   450:31
had C. or Cromwell exchanged countries   226:25
here was a C.!   450:35
I appeal unto C.   65:19
I come to bury C.   450:17
imperious C., dead   437:18
Julius C.'s ill-erected tower   475:26
melt their sweets on blossoming C.   425:17
not C.'s valour hath o'erthrown Antony   425:26
not that I loved C. less   450:14
O Julius C.! thou art mighty yet!   452:1
O mighty C.!   450:2
regions C. never knew   158:32
scarce-bearded C.   423:13
so let it be with C.   450:17
so long as C.'s self is God's   166:14
start a spirit as soon as 'C.'   448:23
that C. might be great   122:36
thou hast C. and his fortune   120:16
'tis paltry to be C.   425:33
unto C. shalt thou go   65:20
unto C. the things which are C.'s   60:12
upon what meat..C. feed?   448:23
where some buried C. bled   206:3
your C.'s father   425:1
Caesars: many C. ere such another Julius   429:28
Café: in every street c.   235:5
Cage: bird in a gilded c.   306:1
keeps a lady in a c.   141:35
nor iron bars a c.   319:7
Robin Redbreast in a C.   73:19
she hung in a c.   410:19
Cages: making nets, not..c.   520:40
Cain: C. and his brother, Abel   151:10
drunk and raising C.   294:26
first city C.   158:9
had C. been Scot   146:4
my Mont Saint Jean seems C.   116:34
old Tubal C. was a man of might   326:24
Caitiff: if the rude c. smite the other   251:4
Cake: break the sacramental c.   287:5
he that will have a c.   480:38
highly geological home-made c.   176:8
let them eat c.   329:18
making of the c.   480:38
Cakes: c. and apples in all the chapels   33:21
Land o' C., and brither Scots   107:20
no more c. and ale   482:32
Calais: 'C.' lying in my heart   333:15
fortune's malice lost her—C.   91:6
Jones! as from C.   573:13
to show light at C.   271:15
Calamity: in storm of battle and c.   200:3
makes c. of so long life   434:4
serving either c. or tyranny   56:28
thou art wedded to c.   478:22
Calamus saevior ense patet   109:13
Calcine its clods   90:20
Calculate: model Heaven and c. the stars   348:30
Calculated: nicely-c. less or more   577:9
Calculating: when you are c., calculate   273:14

Calculation shining out of the other   176:10
Calculators: sophisters, economists and c.   102:11
Calculus: integral and differential c.   221:32
Caledonia: guid to support C.'s cause   106:6
mourn, hapless C.   506:3
O C., stern and wild   417:22
Caledonian: the C. stood   251:29
Calendars: Court C., Directories   306:26
Calender: my good friend, the c.   159:34
the c., right glad to find his friend   160:6
Calf: c. and the young lion   53:18
fatted c.   62:15
golden-c. of self-love   125:25
killed a c...in a high style   21:12
Calf's-skin: hang a c. on those recreant limbs   447:28
Caliban: 'Ban, 'Ban, Ca-C.   479:43
Call: as angels..c. to the soul   552:12
c. forth thundering Aeschylus   281:14
c. him on the deep sea, c. him up the Sound   363:3
c. home the heart you gave me   189:14
c. me early, mother dear   536:26
c. me Sappho, c. me Chloris   152:5
c. my brother back to me   241:7
c. of the running tide   334:11
C. of the Wild   315:23
c. on the lazy leaden-stepping hours   351:31
c. the cattle home   293:22
c. thee mine   327:5, 551:5
c. themselves Christians   389:16
c. the rest of the watch together   468:37
c. today his own   194:20
c. upon my soul within the house   482:22
c. upon the wheels   142:14
c...while he is near   54:30
come away, children, c. no more   15:27
Death..must c. too soon   222:25
don't c. me spade   520:22
dunno what to c. him   511:14
help Thy children when they c.   295:6
I c. in..God, and his Angels   186:32
if men will c.   150:23
I know not what to c. you   198:6
let me always c. you Edwin   203:34
none to c. me Charley   307:19
obey th'important c.   163:33
one clear c. for me   528:22
only, only c. me thine   152:6
please God to c. me   391:9
prompt at every c.   224:21
Red Gods c. us out   296:12
them that c. evil good   53:6
to honour we c. you   213:10
to see what he would c. them   44:15
voted at my party's c.   221:17
whatever they c. him   535:43
what I c. God   96:12
wild c., and a clear c.   334:11
will they come when you do c.?   439:42
Callay: Callooh! C.!   129:39(-130)
Called: come when you're c.   195:20
he c. for his pipe   368:3
I c. John a Impudent Bitch   208:23
I c. not; lie down again   47:5
many are c.   60:10
provoking..to be c. an egg   131:3
science falsely so c.   68:55
she c. his name Gad   45:7
some have c. thee mighty and dreadful   185:15
the Lord c. Samuel   47:4
though I c. another, Abra came   402:4
vocation wherewith ye are c.   67:56
we are c. by his name   76:10
Calleth them all by their names   400:21
Calling: c. as he used to call   366:5
c. of assemblies   52:29
c. out of doors   538:4
c. thro' the dark   538:5
c. to the Angels   208:9
dignity of this high c.   101:15
followed their mercenary c.   264:4
high is our c., friend   575:15
if you've 'eard the East a-c.   299:13
the Lord..heard my c.   394:12

INDEX

Callooh! Callay!   129:39–(130)

Calls: c. His saints around   81:4
  if anybody c.   43:3
  Jesus c. us   3:19
  my road c. me   334:9
  till God c. you away   32:17
  'tis beauty c.   312:29
Calm: all c., as it was bright   552:13
  all is c. again   215:14
  all our c. is in that balm   365:23
  be c. in arguing   244:1
  birds of c. sit brooding   343:13
  c. and heav'nly frame   161:1
  c. and silent night   184:2
  c., c. me more   16:18
  c. in waters   494:12
  c. of mind all passion spent   351:7
  c. on the listening ear of night   421:9
  c.'s not life's crown   19:6
  c. so deep   582:14
  c. soul of all things   16:17
  c. the troubled mind   155:1
  c., though obscure, regions of
    philosophy   265:13
  c. thou may'st smile   279:19
  c. was the day   510:19
  cankers of a c. world   440:21
  cruel he looks, but c. and strong   496:20
  famous, c., and dead   91:38
  for a c. unfit   190:13
  in a season of c. weather   576:19
  in authority settled and c.   26:27
  in guileless sleep, c. and still   547:7
  more than usual c.   208:21
  nor peace within nor c. around   498:24
  peace is what I seek and public c.   16:25
  so, c. are we   557:24
  so cool, so c., so bright   245:13
  so soft, so c., yet eloquent   119:2
  stars in their c.   15:17
  taught us to be c. and meek   251:4
  there is no joy but c.   535:15
  there's c. in a Henry Clay   294:31
  there we sit in peaceful c.   266:12
  to c. contending kings   486:7
  to envisage circumstance, all c.   286:16
  tumult dwindled to a c.   119:26
  Wordsworth's sweet c.   17:5
Calmed: thus be conscience-c.   287:3
Calmer: angling..a c. of unquiet
  thoughts   559:15
Calmly in their place   26:27
Calmness: c. is great advantage   244:2
  for c. to remember   3:6
  keeps the law in c. made   575:10
Calms: celestial Wisdom c. the
  mind   279:15
  that c. each fear   21:9
Calumniating: envious and c. time   481:21
Calumnies are answered best with
  silence   282:4
Calumny: envy and c. and hate
  and pain   492:7
  thou shalt not escape c.   434:11
Calve: si quicquam..C.   133:19
Calves: Hyperion to the Piper   146:20
Calvin, oat-cakes, and sulphur   504:22
Calvinist: disease in the liver..a C.   200:11
Calvinistic: we have a C. creed   379:7
Calypso: Ulysses leaves once more
  C.   493:25
Cam: Isis and C.   573:14
  you, my C. and Isis   381:24
Cambridge: C. people rarely smile   84:13
  to C. books   87:26, 548:20
  books to C. gave   549:1
  fields of C., our dear C.   158:10
  visit C. first   28:20
  when thou taught'st C...Greek   351:17
Cambridgeshire, of all England   84:12
Cambuscan: story of C. bold   341:20
Cambyses: in King C.' vein   439:31
Came: all things going as they c.   411:30
  burbled as it c.   129:39(–130)
  c. out by the same door   206:10, 11
  c. out of great tribulation   71:6
  C.-over-with-the-Conqueror..
    mind   561:30
  for your pleasure you c. here   160:9
  found it, or c. by it   462:28
  he c. unto his own   62:63

Came (cont.)
  hinds who cut and c. again   165:7
  I c., and no one answered   171:14
  I c., I saw, I conquered   120:13
  I c. like Water   206:12
  I c., saw, and overcame   428:25, 442:19
  in prison..ye c. unto me   60:33
  last c., and last did go   342:26
  thrice c. on in fury   323:23
Cameelious Hump   297:27
Camel: almost in shape of a c.   435:26
  c...through the eye of a needle   60:3
  C.'s hump is an ugly lump   297:26
  commissariat c.   300:8
  raiment of c.'s hair   57:29
  swallow a c.   60:12
Cameleopard: matched with this
  c.   495:12
Camelot: cackling home to C.   452:34
  down to tower'd C.   534:1
Camerado: the great C., the lover
  true   567:22
Cameron: come hither, Evan C.   23:29
Camest: death, how c. thou in?   184:25
Camilla: only Cecilia, or C., or
  Belinda   22:22
  resided C.   103:15
  when swift C. scours the plain   382:32
Caminos: muchos son los c.   134:12
Camisa: la ultima c...es la soberbia   329:17
Cammin: nel mezzo del c. di..vita   168:15
Camp: barrow and the c. abide   302:9
  from c. to c.   444:6
  if the general c...had tasted her   472:3
  love rules the c.   116:37, 417:16
Campaspe: Cupid and my C.
  play'd   321:14
Campbell: do not Maister or C.
  me   420:19
Campbells: the C. are comin'   10:9
Campden Hill: strikes the stars on
  C.   141:16
  the largest lamp on C.   141:13
Camps: courts and c...learn the
  world   139:11
  in c. a leader sage   418:8
Can: act upon it, if you c.   218:26
  bear them we c., and if we c., we
    must   263:32
  c., but will not, save me   189:14
  c. must be so sweet   254:27
  c. something, hope   254:19
  come fill up my c.   416:8, 420:15
  cry I c. no more. I c.   254:19
  do what you c.   232:13
  fill the c., and fill the cup   541:14
  he who c., does   490:31
  I ought, therefore I c.   284:6
  pass me the c., lad   263:33
  talent does what it c.   337:43
  what we c. we will be   293:11
  you c. and you can't   187:7
  youth replies, I c.   199:32
Canaan: to the Jews old C. stood   562:15
Canaanites: place of the C.   45:36
Canacee: highte C.   138:4
Canadian: cold on C. hills   310:2
Canakin: let me the c. clink   471:9
  why clink the c.?   91:27
Canamus: paula maiora c.   555:30
Canary: cup of rich C. wine   280:9
  mine host's C. wine   287:1
Cancel: c. all our vows   189:20
  c...that great bond   459:8
  lure it back to c. half a line   207:2
  power to c. his captivity   448:37
Cancelled: rages of the ages shall
  be c.   236:6
Cancels: debt which c. all others   154:24
Cancers: because women have c.   290:2
Candid: be c. where we can   383:8
  one dissertates, he is c.   93:18
  save me from the c. friend   124:13
Candidate: c. of heaven   192:39
  he is a c. for truth   200:23
Candle: burning a farthing c. at
  Dover   271:15
  c.-flame beside the surplices   310:24
  c. of understanding   56:18
  c. singed the moth   464:4
  c. to light you to bed   368:9

Candle (cont.)
  Handel..scarcely fit to hold a c.   112:22
  hold a c. to my shames   463:38
  hold their farthing c. to the sun   586:28
  how far that little c.   465:21
  Latin for a c.   204:6
  light a c. to the sun   501:15
  light such a c.   310:11
  my c. burns at both ends   339:6
  not care a farthing c.   307:25
  out, out, brief c.!   461:4
  set a c. in the sun   109:25
  some c. clear burns somewhere   254:18
  thou also shalt light my c.   392:29
  two old chairs, and half a c.   311:12
  we did not see the c.   465:21
Candle-ends: called him 'C.'   128:7
Candle-holder I'll be a c., and
  look on   477:5
Candlelight: by starlight and by c.   549:2
  by sun and c.   88:24
  can I get there by c.?   367:4
  colours seen by c.   88:9
  dress by yellow c.   515:14
  fire and fleet and c.   31:12
Candles: blessed c. of the night   465:25
  c. burn their sockets   264:1
  night's c. are burnt out   478:27
  the Author's own c.   542:31
  their c. are all out   457:17
Candlestick-maker much acquaints
  his soul with song   96:27
Candlesticks: seven golden c.   70:25
Candour..still thinks this best   143:10
Candy: what a c. deal of courtesy   438:39
Cane: as a gentleman switches
  his c.   151:8
  nice conduct of a clouded c.   385:18
Canem: cave c.   378:8
Canities abest morosa   258:15
Canker: hath not thy rose a c.?   445:23
  joy without c. or cark   309:25
  killing as the c. to the rose   342:15
  loathsome c...in sweetest bud   486:31
  this thorn, this c., Bolingbroke   438:36
  worm, the c., and the grief   118:26
Cankers: c. of a calm world   440:21
  some to kill c.   466:42
Cannibals that each other eat   470:2
Cannie wee thing   104:27
Canning: like Mr. C.'s wit   240:7
Cannon: burst the c.'s roar   251:5
  c.'s opening roar   113:27
  c. to right of them   528:17
  carry c. by our sides   437:31
  even in the c.'s mouth   427:21
  pulse like a c.   200:3
  thundered the c. of France   146:12
Cannonading: Cossack commanders c. come   5:7
Cannon-ball: a c. took off his legs   252:29
Cannon-balls: words as hard as c.   200:40
Cannons: where the thundering c.
  roar   227:10
Cannot: he who c., teaches   490:31
  we c. do it, Sir, because   131:10
  what men...c. do if they would   273:12
Canoe: coffin clapt in a c.   112:33
  paddle his own c.   331:19
Canon: fixt his c. 'gainst self-
  slaughter   430:33
Canonized: many (questionless) c.
  on earth   86:16
  thy c. bones, hearsed in death   431:32
Canons: dine with the C. of
  Christ-Church   272:38
Canopied: love-thoughts..c. with
  bowers   482:1
  over-c. with luscious woodbine   466:41
Canopies: under the c. of costly
  state   441:41
Canopy: from heat did c. the herd   486:15
  glorious c. of light and blue   566:12
  than..a rich embroider'd c.   446:2
  this most excellent c., the air   433:15
  under a c. of love   549:6
  under the c.   429:16
Canossa: nach C. gehen wir nicht   72:30
Cans of poisoned meat   141:34
Canst: c. thou do likewise?   175:18
  give what thou c.   163:47

Cant: c. of criticism..most tormenting   513:16
 clear your mind of c.   275:13
 don't c. in defence of savages   275:22
 let them c. about decorum   106:25
 we have nothing but c., c., c.   376:11
 where the Greeks had modesty,
  we have c.   376:11
 with specious c.   252:10
Can't! Don't! Sha'n't! Won't!   300:16
Cantabit vacuus..viator   283:17
Cantare pares   556:3
Canteen: always double drills and
 no c.   297:4
Cantering: steadily c. through   303:17
Canticle: sweetest c. is Nunc dimittis 26:4
Canticles: sings his c. and hymns   266:13
Cantie wi' mair   104:32
Canting: sighin', c., grace-proud
 faces   106:34
Cantle: a monstrous c.   439:44
Cantons: loyal c. of contemned
 love   482:22
Cants: of all the c. which are
 canted   513:16
Canute: when C., king, rowed
 thereby   124:22
Canvas: splash at a ten-league c.   303:20
 such a breeze compell'd thy c.   532:13
 with c. drooping   147:6
Canvasses: good in c. and factions 25:41
Cany waggons light   346:23
Canyon: in a cavern, in a c.   355:22
Caoilte tossing his burning hair   585:7
Cap: big blue c. that always fits   141:15
 c. by night   224:11
 he pu'd aff his c.   32:7
 put on my considering c.   37:33
 riband in the c. of youth   436:41
Capa que cubre..pensamientos   134:18
Capability: Negative C.   289:21
 that c. and god-like reason   436:15
Capable: c. and wide revenge   472:12
 make your children c. of honesty   413:2
 now warm and c.   287:3
Capable: Habacuc était c. de tout   557:14
Capacious: pipe for my c. mouth   214:7
Capacities of us that are young   441:18
Capacity: c. for taking trouble
                                    111:40, 126:9
 notwithstanding thy c.   481:30
Cap-a-pe: armed at points ex-
 actly, c.   431:9
Caparisons don't become a young
 woman   500:24
Capax: omnium consensu c. imperii   526:15
Cape: round the C. of a sudden
 shape..of mountain or of c.   539:1
Cape of Good Hope: too old..to
 double the C.   28:3
Cape St. Vincent: nobly, nobly C.   92:17
Cape Turk: not yet doubled C.   337:7
Capella: star called C. was yellow 236:38
Capellae: ite c.   556:9
Caper: allowed to cut a c. on the
 straight rope   519:12
 first ae c., syne anither   108:13
Capers: c. nimbly in a lady's
 chamber   476:4
 he c., he dances   466:5
 true lovers run into strange c.   427:3
Capital: Belgium's c. had gather'd
 then   113:25
 Corinthian c. of polished society 102:25
 more c. than to behead a king   111:21
 that high C., where..Death
 tried..for a c. crime once a
 week   273:6
Capitis: tam cari c.   258:24
Capitol: against the C...a lion   448:32
 amidst the ruins of the C.   217:1
Capitoli: domus Aeneae C. immo-
 bile saxum   555:8
Capitulate: I will not c.   275:30
Capitulation: keep a few friends..
 without c.   513:35
Capon: belly with good c. lin'd   427:21
 Madeira and a cold c.'s leg   438:26
Cappadocia: in Judaea and C.   64:26
Capped: velvet c.   160:30
Capreis: epistula venit a C.   283:18

Caprices: public opinion, which
 has her c.   103:1c
Caps: red roses crest the c.   545:2
 they threw their c.   429:5
Captain: and a right good c. too   221:10
 C., art tha sleepin' there below? 363:3
 C. is a good travelling name   203:13
 c. is in his bunk   489:31
 c. jewels in the carconet   487:1
 C. of the Gate   323:17
 c. of the Hampshire grenadiers   216:28
 C. of the Pinafore   221:10, 11
 C. or Colonel or Knight in arms   351:14
 C.! take me in   31:1
 captive good attending c. ill   487:14
 cook and a c. bold   218:14
 crew of the C.'s gig   140:28, 218:14
 deck my C. lies   566:28(–567)
 each c., petty officer, and man   236:4
 ever hear of C. Wattle?   173:3
 foremost c. of his time   537:14
 here he took a c.'s biscuit   176:9
 his C.'s hand on his shoulder
 smote   363:4
 his pure soul unto his c. Christ   475:16
 I am the c. of my soul   241:19
 in the c...a choleric word   461:33
 nobody like the C.   542:22
 O C.! my C.!   566:27
 Oh, C. Shaw!   219:8
 our great c.'s c.   470:24
 plain russet-coated c.   167:3
 royal c. of this ruin'd band   444:7
 their c., the heart   442:21
 train-band c.   159:32
Captains: c. and rulers clothed
 most gorgeously   55:32
 C. and the Kings depart   300:24
 c. by the hundred   218:3
 c. courageous   31:14
 c. of industry   127:3
 thunder of the c.   49:27
 young star-c. glow   208:7
Captivate: while they c., inform   160:19
Captive: c. good attending captain
 ill   487:14
 c. void of noble rage   532:19
 foes they c. make   135:12
 led captivity c.   396:9
 they that led us away c.   400:5
 weak minds led c.   350:2
 when I am thy c.   347:34
 whether guest or c.   561:18
Captives: proclaim liberty to the c. 55:3
 thy pity upon all c.   389:3
 to serve your c.' need   303:24
Captivity: bring away c. thence
 captive   509:4
 bringeth the prisoners out of c.   396:5
 given to c. me and my..hopes   472:34
 led c. captive   396:9
 no leading into c.   400:17
 power to cancel his c.   448:37
 turned away the c. of Jacob   397:8
 turn our c., O Lord   399:34
Caput: haec..alias inter c. extulit
 urbes   555:18
 triste c. pedibus supposuisse ducis 372:5
Car: as the void c.   411:15
 c. rattling o'er the stony street 113:26
 fixt her polisht c.   343:25
 gilded c. of day   340:4
Caravan: join the innumerable c.   98:3
 put up your c.   249:17
 the C. starts for the Dawn of
 Nothing   206:20
 the phantom C. has reach'd the
 Nothing   206:21
 where my c. has rested   542:6
Caravanserai: in this batter'd
 C.   205:29, 30
Carcases: c. of many a tall ship   464:6
 whose loves I prize as..c.   429:14
Carcass: c. fit for hounds   449:10
 convey my c. back to your soil   119:33
 wheresoever the c. is   60:25
Carconet: captain jewels in the c. 487:1
Card: insulting Christmas c.   233:11
 we must speak by the c.   437:12
 you may cut it on his c.   302:6
Cardboard: being made entirely of c. 136:29

Cardinal: C.,—Christ,—Maria,—
 God   96:17
 C. Lord Archbishop of Rheims   34:8
 Jackdaw sat on the C.'s chair   34:8
Cards: can pack the c. and yet cannot play   25:41
 damn your c...the devil's books   520:31
 not learned to play at c.   276:12
 old age of c.   384:37
 play'd at c. for kisses   321:14
 shuffle the c.   134:15
 some were playing c.   31:1
Care: age is full of c.   486:2
 a' his weary kiaugh and c. beguile   104:33
 begone, dull c.   5:19
 beyond His love and c.   568:16
 Black C., at the horseman's back   121:18
 black C...on the..pillion   259:16
 brief sorrow, short-lived c.   361:12
 builders wrought with greatest c. 315:28
 can a woman's tender c. cease?   161:11
 c. draws on c.   189:9
 c. is heavy..sleep you   170:23
 c. less, eyes, lips, and hands to
 miss   186:26
 careless..with artful c.   154:27
 c. killed a cat   469:15
 c. 'll kill a cat   280:12
 c. no more to clothe and eat   430:1
 c. of this world   59:24
 c. sat on his faded cheek   345:7
 c.'s cheek and curb   551:20
 closed our anxious c. of thee   376:20
 dark forgetting of my c.   168:12
 death came with friendly c.   151:18
 deep and reverential c.   575:13
 deliberation..and public c.   345:24
 disapproves that c.   351:23
 for cloth of gold you cease to c. 218:22
 golden c.   442:25
 happy the man whose wish and
 c.   386:26
 hast thou no c. of me?   425:29
 have a c. of natures that are mute 336:28
 Heaven's peculiar c.   506:14
 I c. for nobody   72:16, 106:15
 I c. not very greatly   8:17
 I c. not whether a man is Good
 or Evil   75:13
 I don't care where the water
 goes   142:12
 if, full of c.   169:24
 irks at the crop-full bird?   95:14
 I shan't c. or ho   236:11
 killing c. and grief of heart   446:18
 lift her with c.   252:12
 little c. we   543:11
 load of splendid c.   357:24
 mettle enough..to kill c.   469:15
 much c. and valour in this
 Welshman   444:17
 nobody I c. for comes a-courting me   220:10
 nor c. beyond today   230:26
 nor for itself hath any c.   76:2
 not with too intense a c.   183:22
 nought but c. on ev'ry han'   105:37
 of other c. they little reckoning
 make   342:27
 past my c.   37:21
 past redress..now with me
 past c.   474:32
 primary consideration..take c.
 of ourselves   273:5
 public burden of the nation's c.   402:5
 punch with c.!   83:1
 ravell'd sleave of c.   458:11
 righteous work, the public c.   140:4
 sae weary fu' o' c.   108:36
 seek with c., difficulty   309:16
 some c. bestow on us   158:6
 Sport that wrinkled C. derides   341:29
 take c.!   315:26
 take c. of their health and their
 complexion   22:18
 take c. of the minutes   139:15
 take c. of the sense   129:17
 then the c. is over   527:18
 the very least as feeling her c.   253:63
 they sought it with c.   128:11

INDEX

Care (cont.)

things beyond our c. 193:17
tiresome verse-reciter, C. 494:9
tonight so full of c. 80:17
took great c. of his Mother 339:15
'twas nipt with c. 338:14
want, the c., the sin 533:20
we c. not which way we go 168:24
what boots it with uncessant c. 342:20
what c. I how fair she be? 572:2
whose c. is lest men see too much 95:31
with what c...begirt us round 245:5
woman who did not c. 303:12
women and c., and c. and women 560:25
world is full of c. 560:25
you are c., and c. must keep you 170:23
young ladies should take c. of themselves 22:18
your sex's earliest, latest c. 322:3
Care-charmer sleep 168:12
Care-charming Sleep 38:9
Cared: c. greatly to serve God and the King 363:8
c. not to be at all 345:15
Gallio c. for none of these things 65:3
nor wish'd, nor c. 401:29
Career: boy's ideal of a manly c. 182:26
c. of high-handed wrong 135:3
East is a c. 182:36
his bright and brief c. is o'er 417:29
nothing which might damage his c. 36:17
suspend your mad c. 162:24
Careful: c. never to set up any of their own 102:37
c. soul and the troubled heart 302:1
is not c. what they mean 480:35
so c. of the type 532:35
Carefully: most c. upon your hour 430:7
polished up that handle so c. 221:15
very c. and slow 539:19
Carefulness: eat the bread of c. 399:35
Careless: c. of mankind 535:19
c. she is with artful care 154:27
c. shoe-string 246:4
c. their merits..to scan 224:21
first fine c. rapture 92:15
sitting c. on a granary floor 284:12
so c. of the single life 532:35
Carelessness: to lose both looks like c. 569:23
Cares: against eating c. 342:7
but a frost of c. 547:20
c. can make the sweetest love to frown 232:5
c. that infest the day 316:10
friend to soothe the c. 288:15
heavier weight of c. 1:18
humble c., and delicate fears 581:6
if the heart..is deprest with c. 214:30
in thy fats our c. be drown'd 424:19
kings have c. 232:5
mean, sordid, home-bred c. 101:30
naebody c. for me 106:15
none c. whether it prevail or not 375:18
no one c. for me 72:16
poor devil has ended his c. 93:19
small c. of daughter, wife, or friend 358:1
unvex'd with anxious c. 192:13
void of c. and strife 378:16
warly men, an' warly men 105:38
what c. these roarers 479:15
worn with life's c. 165:21
Caress: we shall linger to c. him 560:27
Caressed: what .. serpents .. c. Faustine? 523:11
Carest: if thou c. not whom I love 185:21
Careth: c. not for the sheep 63:38
the Lord c. for the strangers 400:20
Carey: if you'd go to Mother C. 294:21
Cargo: c. of ivory..c. of Tyne coal 333:20
Cargo-boats: oh, the little c. 298:25
Caribou: wilds where the c. call 422:22
Caricature: with a c. of a face 220:16
Cark: joy without canker or c. 309:25
Carl: c. in Norroway 302:25
c. spak oo thing 137:27
Carles: avaunt ye, base c. 420:25
Pym and such c. 90:16

Carl-hemp: thou stalk o' c. in man 104:22
Carlisle: roused the burghers of C. 322:23
to C.'s, and to Almack's too 13:17
Carmichael: Marie C., and me 31:18
Carmina: c. non prius audita nulla placere diu..c. possunt sunt et mihi c. 259:14 257:12 556:7
Carnage: c. drear of Flodden's.. field 418:35
C...is God's daughter 116:25
C. is Thy daughter 578:9
crowning c., Waterloo 119:16
war and all its deeds of c. 567:5
where his c. and his conquests cease 113:4
Carnal: a very heathen in the c. part 381:10
contests about their c. interests 111:13
Carnally: to be c. minded is death 65:52
Carnation: a' never could abide c. 443:22
Carnations: morn of bright c. 190:6
our c. and streak'd gillyvors 485:23
soon will the musk c. break 18:26
Carol: fluting a wild c. 531:38
hear a c., mournful, holy 534:9
quaintest, richest c. 336:13
this c. they began that hour 428:32
Caroling free, caroling our song 567:2
Carolings: so little cause for c. 235:18
Carolled: still they are c. and said 516:3
Carouse: with what a brave c. 206:23
Carp: this c. of truth 432:33
Carpe diem 258:17
Carpenter: c.'s son 59:32
understood Christ was a c. 73:17
Walrus and the C. 130:12
you may scold a c. 271:5
Carpet: cliff-top has a c. 80:14
figure in the c. 268:15
knight..on carpet consideration 484:15
no c. knight so trim 418:8
Turkey c...to a picture 325:9
ye curious to c. knights 217:16
Carpet-dusting..not the imperative labour 87:27
Carpets: long c. rose 285:27
Carr: Lord Rosebery and Comyns C. 141:31
Carriage: I can't afford a c. 168:2
making them women of good c. 477:7
very small second class c. 219:10
Carriages: I've seen your c. 299:19
Carrie: dear C. rightly declined 233:6
Carried: c. about with every wind of doctrine 67:57
c. away with..vain doctrine 389:51
c. them..feet forward 87:6
Government..c. on 564:20
he hath..c. our sorrows 54:25
reserved, c. about..or worshipped 401:10
Carrière: la c. ouverte aux talents 126:2
Carrion: I'll not, c. comfort, Despair 254:19
this their c. crucified 522:21
Carrow: late slain at C. 502:20
Carry: books that you may c. to the fire 276:28
c. all he knew 225:2
c. everything before me in that House 181:26
c. thee whither thou wouldest not 64:18
c. their comfort about with them 196:25
c. them in his bosom 54:11
c. up this corpse 91:36
certain we can c. nothing out 68:51
for to c. me home 10:2
man must c. knowledge with him 274:4
to c. off the latter 376:23
to England to c. 189:8
we c. within us the wonders 86:11
we must c. it with us 200:5
Cart: creak of a lumbering c. 585:17
horse is drawn by the c. 295:15
now travers'd the c. 402:6
on a c. in Hyde Park 491:6
Carter: Mrs. C. could..translate Epictetus 270:5

Carters: keep a farm, and c. 432:45
Carthage: come again to C. 405:17
Carthago: delenda est C. 132:8
O magna C. 259:29
Cartridges: young ones carry..c. 489:6
Carve: c. a little bit off the top 360:5
c. on every tree 427:23
c. out dials, quaintly 446:1
he may not..c. for himself 431:21
let's c. him 449:10
you may c. it on his tombstone 302:6
Carved: c. biforn his fader 136:27
c. out his passage 456:5
c. with figures strange and sweet 150:21
head fantastically c. upon it 442:15
they c. at the meal 417:4
we c. not a line 572:14
Carven from the laurel-tree 545:7
Carver: all made out of the c.'s brain 150:21
was the c. happy? 413:10
Carving the fashion of a new doublet 468:17
Carving-knife: with a c. 369:8
Caryatides: unfrowning c. 516:17
Casca: what a rent the envious C. 450:28
Cascade: thy Brigade with cold c. 219:8
Case: her nom'native c. 370:5
in such an evil c. 323:29
its semblance in another's c. 159:2
lady in the c. 116:16, 218:15
lady's in the c. 215:30
my heart in a c. o' gowd 32:19
nothing to do with the c. 220:15
though I'm in sorry c. 218:12
unto you will show his c., his c. 373:11
vengeance of Jenny's c. 466:12
what appears in England's c. 159:24
Cased: your hare when it is c. 223:4
Casement: at the c. seen her stand 533:42
c. high and triple-arch'd 285:19
c. jessamine stirr'd 536:11
c. ope at night 288:9
c. slowly grows 538:19
full on this c. shone the..moon 285:20
winder, a c. 177:5
Casements: charm'd magic c. 288:1
Cash: ah, take the c. 205:25, 26
c. payment..the sole nexus 126:6,127:1
c. that goes therewith 140:2
rhyme..for needfu' c. 105:27
takes your c. 143:6
Cashier'd: when he's old, c. 469:26
Cashiering most Kings and Senates 127:6
Cashmere: tales of wild C. 571:6
Casius: betwixt Damiata and Mount C. old 345:31
Cask: when the oldest c. is opened 323:31
Casket: like a c. of gold 585:17
seal the hushed c. of my soul 288:32
Casques: very c. that did affright the air 443:4
Cassander: sweet pomander, good C. 502:17
Casse: tout passe, tout c. 12:21
Cassia: heap c., sandal-buds 94:18
Cassio: not C. kill'd! 473:17
Cassium: C. C. Romanorum ultimum 526:12
Cassius: answer'd Caius C. so 451:21
C. hath a lean and hungry look 448:26
C...will deliver C. 448:35
that spare C. 448:27
Cassock: c., band, and hymn-book too 568:25
though his c. was swarming 34:17
Cassock'd huntsman 161:25
Cassowary: if I were a c. 568:25
Cast: c. away their cords 391:48
c. away the works of darkness 389:22
c. herself..from th' Ismenian steep 350:17
c. out my shoe 395:23
c. their burden upon the Lord 302:3
c. the water of my land 461:1
c. thy bread upon the waters 51:27
c...your pearls before swine 58:18
in no wise c. out 63:22
loath to c. away my speech 482:18
pale c. of thought 434:4

INDEX

Cast (*cont.*)
sepulchre..to c. thee up
  again   431:32(-432)
set my life upon a c.   476:43
suddenly c. down   394:33
the more he c. away   99:32
thou only hast c. out   405:13
to c. into my teeth   451:24
vilely c. away   47:29
Castalia: *pocula C. plena..aqua* 371:20
Castaway: lest..I myself should
  be a c.   66:37
Castigator, censorque minorum 256:2
Castilian: old C. poor noble   119:24
Casting: c. a dim religious light 341:24
  c. down their golden crowns   240:19
Castitatem: da mihi..   21:20
Castle: ancient c...not in decay 26:41
  bores through his c. wall   475:7
  c., called Doubting-C.   99:19
  c., precipice-encurled   91:5
  coward's c.   135:20
  house of everyone is..his c.   148:9
  man's house is his c.   148:7
  my old lad of the c.   438:17
  our c.'s strength   461:2
  rich man in his c.   3:15
  splendour falls on c. walls   538:14
  this c. hath a pleasant seat   457:6
Castle Downe: look owre the C.   30:10
Castlepatrick: I come from C.   141:10
Castlereagh: intellectual eunuch
  C.   115:13
  mask like C.   495:15
Castles: all the c...built with air 280:6
  make c. than in Spayne   138:24
  my c. are my King's alone   418:26
Casual: half-believers in our c.
  creeds   18:12
Casualty: in the force and road of
  c.   463:44
Casuistry: mountains of C.   381:27
Casuists: soundest c. doubt   384:41
Cat: as a c. would watch a mouse 520:28
  but he is a very fine c.   275:11
  care killed a c.   469:15
  care'll kill a c.   280:12
  c. and the fiddle   367:1
  C...He walked by himself   304:21
  c. languishes loudly   241:27
  c. may look at a king   129:14
  Cheshire C.   129:3, 4
  deafer than the blue-eyed c. 530:31
  endow a college, or a c.   384:42
  had Tiberius been a c.   17:13
  hanging of his c. on Monday   79:18
  harmless necessary c.   464:28
  he bought a crooked c.   369:3
  his Aunt Jobiska's Runcible C. 312:9
  I don't want to swing a c.   175:1
  if your mother's c. had but-
    kittened   439:40
  I shall bell the c.   5:1
  it might have been c.   33:20
  it was the c.l   221:23
  lat take a c.   137:36
  like the poor c. i' the adage 457:11
  made a c. laugh   379:23
  more ways of killing a c.   294:13
  part to tear a c. in   466:25
  pavilion c.   309:27
  see the c. i' the dairy   196:15
  see how the c. jumps   420:29
  take suggestion as a c. laps 479:36
  touch not the c. but a glove 419:21
  turned the c. in pan again   7:11
  vigilant as a c. to steal cream 440:22
  what c.'s averse to fish?   230:20
  when I play with my c.   355:3
  worried the c.   369:6
Catalogue: dull c. of common
  things   286:42
  in the c. ye go for men   458:35
Cataract: sounding c. haunted me 581:26
  wild c. leaps in glory   538:14
Cataracts: you c. and hurricanoes 453:5
Catastrophe: I'll tickle your c. 441:29
  pat he comes, like the c.   452:21
  race between education and c. 564:29
Catch: as she would c. another
  Antony   426:16

Catch (*cont.*)
  c. a falling star   186:16
  c. him once upon the hip   463:17
  c. it ere it come to ground   459:27
  c. my flying soul   382:7
  c...the Cynthia of this minute 384:29
  c. the manners living   383:8
  first c. your hare   223:4
  first to c...the dawn   324:25
  hard to c. and conquer   336:8
  he'll c. us some more   34:16
  I can c. her   262:6
  perdition c. my soul   471:27
  perils and diseases..which c. at
    him   38:24
  toss i' the air, and c. again 95:27
Catch as catch can: fell to playing
  the game of c.   209:18
Catched: be more wise, and not be
  c.   377:24
Catching: paid for c. my 'oss, 6d. 518:22
  passion, I see, is c.   450:13
  poverty's c.   40:10
  somebody's c. it now   300:16
Catchwords: man..lives..prin-
  cipally by c.   514:32
Catechism: scarce had said his C. 543:10
  so ends my c.   440:30
Categories: unearthly ballet of
  bloodless c.   79:13
Caterpillar: c. on the leaf   73:23
  'I don't see,' said the C.   128:27
Caterpillars of the commonwealth 474:31
Cates: feed on c. and have him
  talk   440:2
Cathartic: tart, c. virtue   200:17
Cathay: cycle of C.   535:1
Cathedral: in the vast c. leave him 537:28
  sit..outside the c. at Florence 176:2
Catherine: as..on a C. pear   517:13
Catholic: and the Druse and the
  C.   140:28
  C. men that live upon wine   41:30
  glorious the c. amen   503:6
  last flower of C. love   525:33
  one C. and Apostolick Church 390:22
  that he hold the C. Faith   388:37
Catiline: [Fox] talked to me..con-
  cerning C.'s conspiracy   276:17
Cato: Brutus and C. might discharge their souls   193:30
  C. gives his little senate laws 381:7
  fate of C. and of Rome   1:13
  like C., give his little laws 385:29
  Voice of C. is the voice of Rome 279:26
  well-reputed, C.'s daughter   449:18
  what C. did   98:16
  what C.'s daughter durst not 412:16
Catoni: sed victa C.   320:22
*Catonibus: priscis memorata C. at-
  que Cethegis*   257:20
Cats: c. and monkeys   268:16
  c. is 'dogs'   403:16
  c. may have had their goose
    cooked   121:22
  do c. eat bats?   128:21
  each sack had seven c.   366:8
  his three black c.   171:10
  rain c. and dogs   520:25
  where c. are c.   331:13
  wild c. in your kitchens   470:25
Cattle: call the c. home   293:22
  c. are grazing   577:20
  c. upon a thousand hills   395:3
  lowly c. shed   3:20
  thousands of great c.   102:20
  women are mostly troublesome
    c.   319:12
Catulle: miser C.   132:17
Catullus: C. makes mouths at our
  speech   523:5
  in a metre of C.   529:20
*Catullus: gratias tibi maximas C.
  agit*   133:1
Caucasus: thinking on the frosty C. 474:20
Caudle: Mrs. C.'s Curtain Lec-
  tures   269:9
Caught: before he c. the beast   557:21
  c. his clear accents   93:3
  c. my foot in the mat   233:10
  c. my heavenly jewel   501:21

Caught (*cont.*)
  c. the world's great hands   265:23
  how I c. it, found it   462:28
  men c. out in..guilt   146:32
  ram c. in a thicket   44:56
  Scotchman..c. young   272:14
  she c. him by his garment   45:16
Cauldron: fire burn, and c. bubble 459:30
  round about the c. go   459:29
Cauliflower, pineapple and cranberries   219:13
Causa: c. finita est   22:5
  victrix c. deis placuit   320:22
Causae: necdum etiam c. irarum 553:8
Causas: rerum cognoscere c.   556:16
  vivendi perdere c.   283:14
Cause: armor of a righteous c.   98:1
  believe in Freedom's c.   319:19
  believing in the justice of our c. 233:20
  c. is in my will   449:24
  c. of dullness in others   209:20
  c. of Freedom is the c. of God 79:11
  c. of this fair gift   487:22
  c., or just impediment   391:21
  c. that lacks assistance   33:8
  c. that perishes with them   146:14
  c. that wit is in other men   441:11
  draw my pen in defence of a bad
    c.   194:14
  effect whose c. is God   163:52
  ere her c. bring fame   320:12
  events which they did not c.   235:22
  final c. of the human nose   153:4
  first Almighty C.   383:14
  for God! for the C.l   323:2
  for..no c. however just   514:5
  for what high c...born?   333:5
  her magnificent and awful c.   162:45
  homely beauty of the good old c. 577:16
  I'll try the whole c.   128:25
  it is the c., it is the c., my soul 473:11
  little shall I grace my c.   469:45
  nor help the just c.   357:23
  not..jealous for the c.   472:17
  obstinacy in a bad c.   86:14
  our c. is just   180:4
  Philosophy..shrinks to her
    second c.   381:27
  report me and my c. aright   438:2
  singly hast maintained..the c. of
    truth   348:20
  slowly dying c.   533:20
  so little c. for carolings   235:18
  Thou Great First C.   386:20
  to set the C. above renown   362:33
  which laws or kings can c. or
    cure   226:17, 278:20
  woman's c. is man's   539:6
  you all did love him..not with-
    out c.   450:21
  your country's c. calls you away 217:16
*Cause: la différence de la c. et son
  effet*   97:34
Causeless: curse c. shall not come 50:37
Causer of this   35:21
Causes: dire offence from am'rous
  c.   385:8
  former c. of her moan   87:22
  home of lost c.   19:10
  in its c. just   193:10
  malice, to breed c.   282:7
  there is occasions and c.   445:7
  these flowers, as in their c. 125:9
  though art's hid c. are not found 280:7
Cautious, statistical Christ   370:14
Cavalier: each c. who loves honour
  and me   416:8
  like a brave old Scottish C.   24:8
Cavaliero: perfect c.   112:34
Cavaliers: nation of men of
  honour, and of c.   102:11
Cavanagh's blows were not undecided   240:7
Cave: hid in her vacant interlunar c.   350:23
  his political C. of Adullam   82:20
  Idols of the C.   28:6
  in an ocean-c.   531:9
  in Stygian c. forlorn   341:26
  in this our pinching c.   429:31
  lone c.'s stillicide   236:10

Cave (cont.)
out of the misty eastern c. 495:21
tear the c. where Echo lies 477:26
thro' every hollow c. 535:18
Cave canem 378:8
Cavern: happy field or mossy c. 287:1
in a c., in a canyon 355:22
in a c. under 492:27
skulking Truth to her old c. fled 381:27
Caverns: c. measureless to man 151:32, 33
in Misery's darkest c. known 275:2
out of the c. of rain 493:1
sand-strewn c., cool and deep 15:24
twice ten thousand c. 288:30
Caves: c. of ice 151:33(−152)
dark unfathom'd c. of ocean 230:5
from Mendip's sunless c. 322:19
from the fountain and the c. 151:33(−152)
Hell..sigh'd from all her c. 346:8
ring from their marble c. 190:3
rocks, c., lakes, fens 346:2
Caveto: hunc tu, Romane, c. 261:15
Caviare to the general 433:25
Cawdor: C. shall sleep no more 458:12
Glamis thou art, and C. 457:1
I am Thane of C. 456:24
king, C., Glamis, all 458:30
no more than to be C. 456:17
Thane of C. lives 456:17
Cawing at the gun's report 467:7
C.B.: a fortnight's C. 295:4
Cease: can a woman's tender care c. 161:11
c., every joy 122:40
c., large example 319:3
c. upon the midnight with no pain 287:32
c. ye from man 52:32
ere our worship c. 198:16
fears that I may c. to be 289:4
have their day and c. to be 531:41
he did not c.; but cooed 578:11
he did not c. while he stayed 239:15
he maketh wars to c. 394:29
let the long contention c. 16:19
life and all shall c. 308:10
lightning, which doth c. to be 477:24
not the more c. I to wander 346:19
that love may never c. 244:25
that the man I am may c. to be 535:43(−536)
that thou shouldst c. to be 499:9
they die not..but c. 411:6
tongues, they shall c. 66:45
to see me c. to live 19:5
would not c., but cried still 196:2
Ceased: from ancient melody have c. 75:18
song had c. 336:2
when Lucy c. to be 580:18
Ceasing: like the c. of exquisite music 316:13
pray without c. 68:37
without c. I make mention of you 65:30
Cecidere: multa renascentur quae iam c. 255:20
Cecilia: only C., or Camilla, or Belinda 22:22
white C.'s lap of snows 545:7
Cecily: adores as Margaret, Maude, or C. 375:26
C., Gertrude, Magdalen 410:12
Cecity: term of c. 19:4
Cecrops: dear city of C. 329:15
Cedamus: *nos c. Amori* 556:8
Cedar: as a c. tall and slender 370:5
from that moonlit c. what a burst 17:11
Cedar'd: from silken Samarcand to c. Lebanon 285:25
Cedarn: athwart a c. cover 151:32
Cedars: even the c. of Libanus 398:9
excellent as the c. 52:14
Cedarwood: sandalwood, c. 333:20
Cedite Romani scriptores 402:17
Ceiling of amber 16:1
Celandine: 'tis the little c. 573:16
Célébrait: Ronsard me c. 408:18
Celebrate: dine somewhere..to c. the event 269:20
I c. myself 567:9

Celebrated: c., cultivated, under-rated nobleman 218:17
c...for his Deportment 173:29
Celeriter: qui dat c. 526:3
Celerity: such a c. in dying 423:25
Celestial: from Thy c. home 132:1
from thy c. seat 310:9
glowed c. rosy red 349:4
Peter sat by the c. gate 119:14
this mournful gloom for that c. light 344:21
thou c. light shine inward 346:20
touch of c. temper 347:29
Celestially: mud, c. fair 83:27
Celia: C. altogether 566:19
C. has undone me 566:18
come, my C. 282:5
know, C. 125:1
not, C., that I juster am 421:16
Celibacy has no pleasures 278:17
Cell: dwell in a dungeon c. 220:6
each in his narrow c. 229:30
for cloister'd c. 291:6
hermit hoar, in solemn c. 276:15
in any c. you run, dear 265:24
my c. is set here in thy bosom 543:16
priest from the prophetic c. 343:21
self-respecting lady's c. 39:26
solitary c. 151:12, 507:22
Thou hast given me a c. 247:16
what feast..in thine eternal c.? 438:8
Cellar: born in a c. 155:11, 209:17
in his c. stopped him down 376:21
Cellarage: this fellow in the c. 432:25
Cellarer: Old Simon the C. 40:15
Cells: c. and gibbets for 'the man' 156:22
o'erbrimmed their clammy c. 284:11
thro' c. of madness 536:22
Celt: blind hysterics of the C. 533:22
Slav, Teuton, C. 528:11
Cenae: noctes c.que deum 261:26
Cenotaph: laugh at my own c. 493:1
Censer: from swinged c. teeming 288:6
Censor: castigator, c.que minorum 256:2
Censoris: cum tabulis animum c. 257:19
Censorship: assassination .. extreme form of c. 491:2
Censura: vexat c. columbas 283:1
Censure: all c. of a man's self 274:5
c. freely who have written well 382:20
every trade save c. 117:11
fear not slander, c. rash 430:1
no man can justly c. 86:30
take each man's c. 431:25
ten c. wrong 382:19
those who durst not c. 278:35
Censured: what we behold is c. 330:13
Cent: not a c. for tribute 238:4
on Dutch bottoms just twenty per c. 124:6
they voted c. per c. 112:28
Centaur: that moral c., man and wife 116:20
Centipede was happy quite 166:23
Centre: at their hearts the fire's c. 509:1
c. of my sinful earth 488:20
from the c. all round to the sea 164:22
from the c. thrice to th'utmost pole 344:10
hid indeed within the c. 432:44
John A. Logan is the Head C. 83:2
of which the c. is everywhere 10:17
planets, and this c. 481:2
poor c. of a man's actions 27:38
sit i' th' c. and enjoy bright day 340:20
though it in the c. sit 186:25
thy intention stabs the c. 485:8
Centre: mon c. cède 209:9
Centric: with c. and eccentric scribbled o'er 348:30
Cents: sweet simplicity of the three per c. 182:6
Centuries: all c. but this 219:25
bowed by the weight of c. 329:19
c. ago 184:2
through what wild c. 170:26
whole c. of folly 93:11
Century: c. of the common man 557:17
in that eighteenth c. of Time 126:3
lain for a c. dead 536:15
Cerastes horned, Hydrus 349:21

Cerberus: give that C. a sop 155:7
like C., three gentlemen at once 500:25
of C. and blackest Midnight born 341:26
Cerebration: deep well of uncon-scious c. 268:6
Cerements: burst their c. 431:32
clinging like c. 252:12
Ceremonial: for any c. purposes. water 243:15
Ceremonies: of fantasy, of dreams, and c. 449:11
Ceremony: enforced c. 451:9
no c. that to great ones 'longs 461:28
save c., save general c. 444:22
thrice-gorgeous c. 444:23
Cerinthus that is lost 91:2
Certain: c. because..impossible 542:4
c. of sorrow in store 300:22
lady of a 'c. age' 116:22
love..if it seem c. 584:24
nothing..c., except death and taxes 211:9
nothing c. in man's life but this 337:40
nothing more c. than uncertain-ties 35:20
one thing is c. 206:9
thou c. pain 229:9
Certainly aged 116:22
Certainties: begin with c. 24:13
better than most people's c. 235:11
hot for c. 336:36
Certainty: quit a c. for an uncer-tainty 277:36
sober c. of waking bliss 340:16
thy wisdom, less thy c. 512:9
Certamina: haec c. tanta pulveris exigui. 556:22
Certare ingenio 320:30(−321)
Certified how long I have to live 394:8
Certifieth: one night c. another 392:32
Certum est quia impossibile est 542:4
Cervantes: C. is never petulant 325:23
C. on his galley 141:8
C.' serious air 382:14
C. smiled Spain's chivalry away 116:45
Cervicem: unam c. 120:18
Cesspool: London, that great c. 188:23
Cesure: have refused other c. 281:27
Cetera: c. quis nescit permitte divis c. 371:18, 258:13
Cethegis: prisci memorata Catoni-bus atque C. 257:20
Ceylon: soft o'er C.'s isle 240:18
Chadband style of oratory 173:33
Chaeronea: that dishonest victory at C. 351:16
Chafe: champ and c...in the spray 15:23
he that lets another c. 244:2
though..reason c. 199:27
Chafes: take no care who c. 460:9
Chaff: c. well meant for grain 532:5
everything else tastes like c. 290:31
hope..corn in c. 117:13
Chaffinch sings on the orchard bough 92:14
Chagrin: me laissez..avec mon noir c. 354:2
Chain: at each remove a lengthen-ing c. 226:4
c. of our sins 389:12
dallied with his golden c. 528:27
death broke at once the vital c. 275:4
down hill 'Too-quick', the c. 538:3
electric c. wherewith we are.. bound 114:5
ere Slumber's c. has bound me 357:13
flesh to feel the c. 83:13
Servitude that hugs her c. 231:2
subtle c. of countless rings 199:17
that Homer's golden c. 109:22
what the c.? 75:24(−76)
Chainless: eternal spirit of the c. mind 114:33
Chains: adamantine c. and penal fire 344:7
bind their kings in c. 400:27
by gold c. about the feet of God 531:36
c. and slaverie! 107:32
c. are worse than bayonets 269:19
c. of its dismay 495:26

Chains (*cont.*)
clanking their c. in the South 559:33
everywhere he is in c. 412:2
in darkness, fire, and c. 561:22
nothing to lose..but their c. 333:11
since a woman must wear c. 203:9
untwisting all the c. that tie 342:8
wearers of rings and c. 308:24
when I am thy captive talk of c. 347:34
Chair: asleep upon a c. 584:7
give Dayrolles a c. 139:37
he fills a c. 274:28
heir..to his father's c. 281:28
is the c. empty? 476:31
Jesus was sitting in Moses' c. 74:13
jumping from the c. she sat in 265:25
more wondrous still the table,
stool and c. 74:8
one vacant c. 317:11
Rab'lais' easy c. 382:14
rack of a too easy c. 381:25
seated in thy silver c. 279:31
seats himself in Frederick's c. 249:22
tavern…throne of human
felicity 277:4
there will be one vacant c. 560:27
they shall sit in a golden c. 303:20
tilts up his c. 249:24
Chairs: old c. to mend 367:6
two old c., and half a candle 311:12
Chaise: all in a c. and pair 159:33
myself and children three will
fill the c. 159:33
one-hoss c. 251:6
Chalcedony: third, a c. 72:1
third c. 87:36
Chalice: kneeling hamlet drains
the c. 532:11
winged c. of the soul 411:28
Chaliced: on c. flowers that lies 429:25
Chalices: treen c. and golden
priests 269:22
Chalky: draw the c. ring 164:8
Challenge: c. to his end 166:19
I c. all the human race 406:18
oft would c. me the race 333:1
Challenged: as any c. echo clear 123:21
Chalybeate taste 179:20
Cham: great C. of literature 506:6
Chamber: bear me to that c. 442:29
capers nimbly in a lady's c. 476:4
c. deaf to noise 501:27
commune..in your c. 391:52
each shall take his c. 98:3
get you to my lady's c. 437:15
in my lady's c. 366:23
peace in her c. 410:18
Queen was in her c. 298:30
scour a narrow c. 336:15
suspended in the c. of consciousness 268:12
than to a c. melody 502:3
through many a listening c. 494:5
throw myself down in my c. 186:32
to thy c. window, Sweet 494:7
water once a day her c. round 481:32
writ in a Roman c. 146:15
Chamberlain: Guilt was my
grim C. 252:25
Chambermaid: as happy in the
arms of a c. 274:10
Chambermaids: worms that are
thy c. 478:44
Chambers: beams of his c. in the
waters 398:8
has c. in the King's Bench Walks 144:33
perfum'd c. of the great 441:41
or in the c. of the East, the c. of
the sun 75:18
whispering c. of Imagination 176:26
wind-besomed c. of the air 544:7
Chameleon's dish 435:2
Chameleons feed on light and air 493:16
Champ and chafe..in the spray 15:23
Champagne: c…gives one werry
gentlemanly ideas 518:33
not a c. teetotaller 489:15
tops cleaned with c. and abricot
jam 518:19
we meet, with c. and a chicken 354:15
Women, and C., and Bridge 41:26

Champain: through heaven's wide
c. 348:19
Champak odours fail 494:7
Champion: in close fight a c. grim 418:8
strong siding c., Conscience 340:10
to his faithful c. 351:7
Chance: all c., direction 383:21
care o' th' main c. 111:2
C. governs all 346:11
c., or nature's changing course 486:18
despair, law, c., hath slain 185:14
either in nativity, c. or death 466:14
every c…a noble knight 531:33
every morning..a noble c. 531:33
from art, not c. 382:32
from c., and death, and mutability 497:12
grasps the skirts of happy c. 533:1
had the c. been with us 525:22
if c. will have me king..c. may
crown me 456:25
just a c. o' the prize 90:42
more weighty voice..as by c. 25:42
necessity and c. approach not 348:25
nor dart of c. 472:32
nor now to prove our c. 189:6
not naturally honest..so sometimes by c. 485:35
now and then be right, by c. 159:12
Occasion, C., and Change 497:7
power which erring men call C. 340:29
prophesy…of the main c. 442:6
set my life on any c. 458:36(-459)
that c. will bring us through 15:11
to Thy grace, and not to c. 561:20
trust me, you haven't a c. 222:4
under the bludgeonings of c. 241:18
various turns of c. below 191:8
who await no gifts from C. 18:4
with the c. of being drowned 270:32
write a most valuable book by c. 231:23
Chancel: strange sounds along the
c. 417:13
Chancellor: c. in embryo 499:16
England's high C. 281:28
rather susceptible C. 218:37
Chancery: pretty young wards in
C. 218:36
Chances: against ill c. men are..
merry 442:17
c. change by course 508:19
changes and c. of this mortal life 390:50
I spake of most disastrous c. 470:2
saw them subject to the c…of
existence 268:8
Chandelle: au soir, à la c. 408:18
Change: all..doth in C. delight 510:11
all things c. them to the contrary 478:33
as a vesture shalt thou c. them 398:2
bolts up c. 425:33
can thy soul know c.? 95:36
catch, ere she c., the Cynthia 384:29
certain relief in c. 267:24
c. and decay 322:1
c. as the winds c. 525:30
c., as ye list, ye winds 215:40
c. came o'er..my dream 117:7
c. for the worse 11:6
c. in a trice 522:23
c…in..their modes of thought 338:21
c. is inevitable..c. is constant 180:37
c. is not made without inconvenience 254:1
c. itself can give no more 421:17
c. Kate into Nan 74:22
c. of thought to find 164:35
c. places..which is the justice 454:10
each c. of many-colour'd life 278:34
Ethiopian c. his skin 55:18
ever-whirling wheel of C. 510:10
extremes by c. more fierce 346:1
fear of c. perplexes monarchs 345:6
fill my pockets with c. 177:21
full of religion, knavery, and c. 40:8
God's great *Venite* c. the song 186:11
I c., but I cannot die 493:1
in the dead there is no c. 325:23
I would not c. for thine 280:21(-281)
I would c. each hour 421:16
lamentable c. is from the best 453:37
life may c. 493:23

Change (*cont.*)
miserable c. now at my end 425:28
neither to c., nor falter 497:17
no c. though you lie under 263:5
nor any c. of light 523:24
nor wish'd to c. his place 224:18
not for those..do I repent or c. 344:13
Occasion, Chance, and C. 497:7
One remains, the many c. and
pass 492:15
O the heavy c. 342:13
otherwise I perceive no c. 303:8
our appetites are apt to c. 191:20
our love should with our fortunes c. 435:11
purge by any desperate c. 423:34
rapid c. from rocks to roses 387:23
ringing grooves of c. 534:36
seat that we must c. for Heav'n 344:21
show a c. from what it was 316:36
since 'tis Nature's law to c. 407:16
small c. of silence 337:37
state without the means of some
c. 102:6
that love could never c. 82:2
this robe..doth c. my disposition 485:27
tho' I deplore her c. 155:37
Thou dost not c. 147:14
through all c. 324:17
to c. my state with kings 486:24
to c. the name 11:6
to c. what we can 514:5
to know the c. and feel it 289:8
when it is not necessary to c. 203:2
whose beauty is past c. 255:3
Change: plus ça c. 284:7
Changé: nous avons c. tout cela 353:24
Changeable: thy doublet of c.
taffeta 483:7
Changed: all c., c. utterly 586:19
c. according to..the Sword 135:28
c. into little water drops 330:11
face of all the world is c. 88:17
how fall'n! how c. 344:11
I c. ev'ry hour 214:25
let them be c. 453:31
like linen often c. 209:5
man but c. his mind 384:23
mind not to be c. by place or
time 344:22
sea c., the fields c. 237:10
they have c. eyes 479:32
though c. in outward lustre 344:13
we have c. all that 353:24
we shall all be c. 67:16
what we c. was innocence 485:4
Changeful: presuming on their c.
potency 481:25
Changes: c. and chances of this
mortal life 390:50
c. the world today 296:1
Friend Who never c. 338:19
God c., and man 524:1
her plot hath many c. 404:10
if the c…be thus irresistible 277:24
manifold c. of the world 389:38
One, who never c. 552:2
world's a scene of c. 158:11
Changest: c. not in any gale 532:2
Thou, who c. not 322:1
Changeth: he c. not 354:12
Changing: ever c., like a joyless eye 495:19
love..c. his property 475:5
oft c. is loss 550:5
one fixed point in a c. age 188:13
through all the c. scenes of life 527:2
Chankly Bore: Hills of the C. 311:15
Channel: butting through the C. 333:21
c. of no-meaning 363:19
C.'s as bright as a ball-room 294:35
drum them up the C. 363:2
wet with C. spray 296:15
you dream you are crossing the
C. 219:10
Channels: as streams their c.
deeper wear 107:5
Chant: how can ye c., ye little
birds 108:36
or triumphal c. 498:7
our c. of pleasant exploration 567:2

INDEX

Chanted: c. loudly, c. lowly 534:9
Chantey: may we lift a Deepsea C. 298:14
Chanticleer: crow like c. 427:15
strain of strutting c. 479:28
Chanting: c faint hymns to the.. moon 466:16
c. our chant 567:2
loud c. of the unquiet leaves 586:8
Chaos: be no longer a c. 127:21
c. of thought and passion 383:22
C. umpire sits 346:11
God dawned on C. 491:23
of Night primeval, and of C. old 381:26
reign of C. and old Night 345:1
thy dread empire, C.! 381:27
when I love thee not c. is come 471:27
Chap: I am an intellectual c. 219:6
Chapel: Devil always builds a c. 170:11
devil..will have his c. 33:4
out of the little c. I burst 90:24
Chapels: cakes and apples in all the C. 33:21
c. had been churches 463:7
stolen looks are nice in c. 266:1
Chap-fallen: quite c. ? 437:15
Chaplain: Blue Beard's domestic c. 178:37
twice a day the C. called 569:7
Chapman: C. and Hall swore not at all 42:24
till I heard C. speak out 288:19
Chapmen: utter'd by base sale of c's tongues 455:2
Chaps: biography is about c. 42:23
several c. out of the City 141:29
Chapter: c. is completed from epoch to epoch 127:16
c. of accidents 139:31, 570:25
studied his last c. of St. John 89:41
Char: must Thou c. the wood 544:24
Character: as for regaining my c. I despare 208:25
as to the poetical c. itself 290:9
beyond the limitations of his own c. 358:16
c. dead at every word 500:36
c. is destiny 196:29
c...the determination of incident 268:13
c. undecided 284:18
formation of c. 508:28
for our c...as Englishmen 379:15
gave me a good c. 129:33
incident..the illustration of c. 268:13
leave my c. behind me 500:37
my wishes' cloudy c. 166:21
reap a c. 406:6
these few precepts..look thou c. 431:25
Characters: c. of hell to trace 229:22
c. of the great Apocalypse 580:25
from high life high c. 384:24
most women have no c. at all 384:28
who have c. to lose 106:25
write the c. in dust 419:15
Charakter in dem Strom der Welt 224:4
Chares: does the meanest c. 425:30
Charge: c., Chester, c.! 418:32
c. in earnest 183:8
c. is prepar'd 215:6
c. with all thy chivalry 122:19
c. you more..at a friend's 178:26
his angels c. over thee 397:19
no c. of rule, nor governance 518:1
O, the wild c. they made 528:19
take thou in c. this day 323:27
Charged: c. with the grandeur of God 254:24
rashly the troops of error 86:4
such proceeding I am c. withal 469:45
Charger: he turn'd his c. 419:9
Charges: die to save c. 109:11
goeth a warfare..at his own c. 66:34
warily to begin c. 26:11
Charing Cross: betwixt Heaven and C. 545:1
C., with a man upon a black horse 307:2
full tide of human existence..at C. 272:25
I sunk at C. 558:20
Chariot: bring me my c. of fire 75:16
c. of Israel, and the horsemen 48:16

Chariot (cont.)
dust beneath thy c. wheel 254:16
go to Hyde-Park..in a new c. 156:13
her c. is an empty hazel-nut 477:7
maketh the clouds his c. 398:8
on drove the c. 508:4
slap-up girl in a bang-up c. 178:16
snatched from out his c. 411:15
swing low, sweet c. 10:2
Time's winged c. 333:9
why is his c. so long? 46:51
Charioted: not c. by Bacchus 287:28
Charioteer: c. is snatched from out his chariot 411:15
Chariotest to their dark wintry bed 496:4
Chariots: burneth the c. in the fire 394:29
c. of God are twenty thousand 396:8
his c. of wrath 228:21
put their trust in c. 392:37
Chariot-wheel: fly sat upon the.. c. 27:35
Charitable: thy intents wicked or c. 431:32
Charitably: how can they c. dispose of any thing? 644:19
Charities: c. that soothe 574:28
cold c. of man to man 165:19
defer not c. till death 27:7
Charity: all mankind's concern is c. 384:1
and have not c. 66:44, 45
C. and Mercy. Not unholy names 176:12
c. begins at home 86:31, 500:44
c...cover the multitude of sins 70:5
c., dear Miss Prism 569:27
c. edifieth 66:33
c. envieth not 66:45
c. never faileth 66:45
c. suffereth long 66:45
c. vaunteth not itself 66:45
c. will hardly water the ground ere c. began 26:36 / 224:21
greatest of these is c. 66:46(-67)
healing voice of Christian c. 102:5
in all things, c. 36:25
increase of faith, hope and c. 389:46
in love and c. with your neighbours 390:34
lectures or a little c. 567:21
little earth for c. 447:3
living need c. more 15:1
love, friendship, c. 481:21
most excellent gift of c. 389:31
no point of c. 166:16
now abideth faith, hope, c. 66:46(-67)
organized c., scrimped and iced 370:14
pool of private c. 374:21
rarity of Christian c. 252:18
spots in your feasts of c. 70:18
with c. for all 314:13
with faith, with hope, with c. 245:9
with the c. of Paul 143:10
Charity-boy: as the c. said 178:42
Charity-meetings: in c. it stands at the door 128:13
Charlatan: defamed by every c. 533:23
no c...Well, I am 491:16
Charlemagne: second was C. 327:15
when C. with all his peerage fell 345:4
Charles: Baby C. laying down the guilt 419:26
C. Augustus Fortescue 40:33
C. the First bin Cromwell 242:16
for C. King of England 323:2
God for King C.! 90:16
here's a health to King C.! 420:25
in Hell's despite now, King C.! 90:17
keep King C...out of the Memorial 174:25
King C., and who'll do him right now? 90:17
King C.'s golden days 7:9
King C...walked and talked 8:3
my gentle-hearted C. 152:2
navy of C. the Second 326:2
some of the trouble out of King C.' head 174:27
Charlie: C. he's my darling 250:17
C. is my darling 360:15
none to call me C. 307:19

Charlie (cont.)
o'er the water to C. 250:15
over the water to C. 420:13
Charlock: o'er the young shoot the c. 165:17
Charlotte: Werther had a love for C. 543:12
Charm: all the c. of all the Muses 541:7
c. for thee, my..Charles 152:2
c. from the sky 376:10
c...loose from every..engagement 101:37
c. to stay the morning-star 151:28
made up of hard words like a c. 370:18
music oft hath such a c. 462:17
music that would c. for ever 578:3
no need of a remoter c. 581:26
or c. thee to a tear 571:6
provoking c. of Caelia altogether 566:19
sleep..c. my imagination 215:37
some c. of lovely Sue 215:42
till life can c. no more 153:22
what c. can soothe her melancholy? 226:18
why this c. is wasted 199:26
with c. of earliest birds 347:22
Charmed: almost c. me from my profession 480:29
brooding on the c. wave 343:13
c. it with smiles and soap 128:11
c. magic casements 288:1
c. water burned alway 149:25
I bear a c. life 461:10
oaks, branch-c. by the earnest stars 286:8
Charmer: here's to the c. whose dimples we prize 500:40
still the c. I approve 155:37
voice of the c. 395:20
were t'other dear c. away 215:4
Charming: c. women can true converts make 203:21
how c. is divine philosophy 340:24
in Adam's ear so c. left his voice 348:29
married, c., chaste, and twenty-three 115:17
O most c. pug 208:29
whose daughter was c. and young 306:34
Charms: all that c. or ear or sight 151:6
all those endearing young c. 356:11
c. by accepting 384:38
c. strike the sight 385:19
dear were her c. to me 233:1
do not all c. fly 286:42
freedom has a thousand c. 162:22
lass that has acres o' c. 106:7
lifeless c., without the heart 214:9
music has c. 155:18
solitude, where are the c.? 164:22
song c. the sense 345:29
what drugs, what c. 469:45
with sudden c. can bind 155:1
Charon, seeing, may forget 308:22
Charter: as large a c. as the wind 427:17
c. of thy worth 487:22
this was the c. of the land 545:18
Chartres: for C.' head reserve 384:5
Charts: busied in c. 29:6
Chase: c. brave employment 243:28
c., the sport of kings 506:13
down his nose in piteous c. 426:31
laith to rin an' c. thee 107:9
mortal beauty c. 332:16
new mistress now I c. 319:10
thy c. is done 416:20
when heated in the c. 527:1
with unhurrying c. 544:14
woe worth the c. 410:14
Chasing: a-c. the deer; c. the wild deer 107:12
Chasm: from this c...a mighty fountain 151:32
no c., no solitude 574:26
that deep romantic c. 151:32
Chassis: whole world is in a terrible state of c. 370:1
Chaste: Are Barmaids C.? 333:23
be amorous, but be c. 117:17
be thou as c. as ice 434:11
c. and fair 279:31

Chaste (cont.)
c. as the icicle 429:20
c. as unsunn'd snow 429:27
c. lady's pregnant womb 332:10
c. to her husband 384:30
ever c., except you ravish me 185:19
fair, the c., and unexpressive she 427:23
if I pronounce it c. 221:4
if she is c., and sober 363:26
justified a c. polygamy 125:5
married, charming, c., and twenty-three 115:17
my English text is c. 217:4
no natural love of the 'c. muse' 77:32
you c. stars 473:11
Chasten: of ample power to c. and subdue 582:1
Chasteneth: whom the Lord loveth he c. 69:19
Chastise: c. you with scorpions 47:47
stubborn they c. 164:34
Chastised: c. with the sober eye of dull Octavia 425:34
c. you with whips 47:47
having been a little c. 56:23
Chastisement of our peace 54:26
Chastity: clothed on with c. 529:27
even like thy c. 473:32
give me c. 21:20
so dear to Heaven is saintly c. 340:23
that c. of honour 102:13
'tis C., my brother, C. 340:22
Chasuble: he wore, I think, a c. 238:38
Chatham: C. heart-sick of his country's shame 163:2
C.'s language was his mother tongue 163:1
great C. with his sabre drawn 6:16
those who listened to Lord C. 200:6
Chatte: quand je me joue à ma c. 355:3
Chatter: c. about Harriet 211:24
hare-brained c. of irresponsible frivolity 181:13
only idle c. 220:26
Chatterings: loud in multitudinous c. 336:32
Chatters: of science and logic he c. 387:20
Chatterton: C., the marvellous boy 580:7
O C.! how very sad thy fate 288:10
Chatting on deck was Dryden 309:8
Chaucer: C...so uneducated 560:15
Dan C., mighty Shakespeare 80:24
Dan C., well of English undefiled 510:5
I will not lodge thee by C. 281:11
since C. was alive and hale 308:17
thought more nigh to learned C. 36:21
Chavender, or chub 414:6
Cheap: as c. sitting as standing 520:11
c. and chippy chopper 219:31
c. but wholesome salad 164:1
c. defence of nations 102:12
flesh and blood so c. 253:25
good counsel? 'tis c. 109:18
hold the strain 95:15
hold their manhoods c. 444:28(-445)
jest as c. and easy to rejoice 407:4
King to have things done as c. 377:19
man's life is c. as beast's 452:41
sold c. what is most dear 488:5
Cheapened: how she has c. paradise 374:20
Cheaper: c...than to keep a cow fool, but at a c. rate 112:6 161:42
Cheapest lawyer's fee 107:31
Cheaply: c. bought for thrice their weight 203:39
put him c. off 191:17
Cheapness: country has its charms —c. for one 518:28
Cheat: deterred from detecting.. a c. 272:20
fancy cannot c. so well 288:2
he may c. at cards genteelly 272:26
life, 'tis all a c. 191:34
of being cheated as to c. 111:3
so lucrative to c. 147:2
to c. a man is nothing 214:33
Cheated: c. into some fine passages 290:15

Cheated (cont.)
only place.. to be exceedingly c. at 202:13
pleasure.. of being c. 111:3
Cheater: that old bald c., Time 281:2
Cheating of our friends 143:6
Cheats: who c. a woman 214:33
Check: care's c. and curb 551:20
dreadful is the c. 83:13
free from.. rule or c. 381:21
immediate c. to loose behaviour 511:25
rod to c. the erring 573:28
Checked: I c. him while he spoke 309:1
Checking the crazy ones 229:15
Checks: moves, and c., and slays 206:29
that c. each fault 21:9
Cheek: blush into the c. of the young person 178:11
care sat on his faded c. 345:7
c. that doth not fade 285:39
concealment.. feed on her damask c. 483:10
crocus lays her c. to mire 336:44
drove his ball through Helen's c. 228:10
fragrant waters on my c. bestowed 160:32
give this c. a little red 384:26
hangs upon the c. of night 477:9
her c. was soft as silk 372:20
his c. to him that smiteth him 55:26
his wither'd c. and tresses grey 416:29
I love not hollow c. 539:1
iron tears down Pluto's c. 341:19
it fanned my c. 150:3
kissed each other's c. 222:3
language in her eye, her c., her lip 481:26
leans her c. upon her hand 477:14
loves a rosy c. 124:25
my c. is cold and white 494:7
old ornament of his c. 468:32
on that c., and o'er that brow 119:2
on thy c. a fading rose 286:29
O soul of Sir John C. 351:17
pale grew every c. 324:13
pale grew the c. 119:29
rose growing on's c. 321:14
that..C. of hers to incarnadine 205:12, 13
that I might touch that c. 477:14
turn the other c. 251:4
warm wet c. 309:4
whosoever shall smite thee on thy right c. 57:50
yellow c., a white beard 441:19
Cheeks: c. of sorry grain 340:38
c. that be hollow'd a little 359:10
crack your c. 453:5
delicate c. which they did cool 424:6
fat ruddy c. Augustus had 249:18
her.. blood spoke in her c. 186:13
her c. were so red and so white, dears 293:17
in thy lips and in thy c. 478:43
roses are her c. 536:6
rosy lips and c. 488:7
Cheer: be of good c. 59:36, 63:64
C.! Boys, c.! 326:22
c. but not inebriate 43:14, 163:21
c. for a halt and a row 300:16
c. for the Sergeant's weddin' 301:11
c. it after rain 161:21
c. me ever or disseat me now 460:36
c. my bonny bride 122:25
c. one on the tedious way 409:19
c. our soiled face 400:33
c. up, the worst is yet to come 269:32
c. us when we recover 100:15
come, c. up, my lads 213:10
died the sound of royal c. 534:10
don't c., boys 378:13
fortitude, and patient c. 578:17
for whom did he c. 90:18
give 'em one c. more 301:11
greet the unseen with a c. 97:3
I c. a dead man's sweetheart 263:7
I piped with merry c. 76:9
let thy heart c. thee 51:32
play and make good c. 549:23
scarce forbear to c. 323:28

Cheer (cont.)
thy gentle voice my spirit can c. 314:18
till a feeble c. the Dane 122:5
Cheered: c. up himself with ends of verse 110:33
c. with the grateful smell 347:2
he c. her soul with love 535:5
one of the guinea-pigs c. 129:29
ship was c., the harbour cleared 148:21
Cheerer: angling.. a c. of his spirits 559:15
Cheerful: as c. as any man could do 377:14
buy yourself weeds, and be c. 215:3
c. countenance 50:11, 398:9
c. hearts now broken 357:13
c., sing alang wi' me 502:22(-503)
entertain a c. disposition 474:2
from the c. ways of men 346:20
God loveth a c. giver 67:31
if she is chaste, and sober, and c. 363:26
when God sends a c. hour 351:32
Cheerfully: c. for conscience sake 401:1
how c. he seems to grin 128:24
Cheerfulness: c. was always breaking in 196:4
no warmth no c. 253:12
ought to feel deep c. 236:40
truth breathed by c. 581:16
Cheering: decorating and c. the elevated sphere 102:11
to our c. sent us back 122:5
Cheerly: but c., c., she loves me dearly 285:4
Cheers: adorns and c. our way 224:10
give three c., and one cheer more 221:11
Cheese: and a pound of c. 120:20
bless me with apple-pie and c. 204:1
Botticelli's a c. 403:36
bread and c. and kisses 520:5
dreamed of c.—toasted mostly 514:21
eggs, apples, and c. 294:34
fill hup the chinks wi' c. 518:12
hellish dark, and smells of c. 518:25
live with c. and garlic in a windmill 440:2
must be born i' the rotten c. 196:12
pippins and c. to come 465:31
stand a man a c. 142:1
Cheese-paring: man made.. of a c. 442:15
Chef-d'œuvre: tree toad is a c. 567:19
Chefs-d'œuvre: aventures.. au milieu des c. 211:3
Cheke: soul of Sir John C. 351:17
Chelsea: fifty 'ousemaids outer C. 299:14
Chemin: la vertu.. demande un c. aspre 355:2
Chemist, fiddler, statesman, and buffoon 190:22
Cheque: political blank c. 227:37
Chequer-board of Nights and Days 206:28, 29
Chequered: c. spectacle of.. glory and.. shame 325:25
dancing in the c. shade 342:3
this life is all c. with pleasures and woes 356:34
Chercher un grand peut-être 404:30
Chercherais: tu ne me c. pas 374:7
Cherchez la femme 194:32
Cherchons la femme 194:32
Chère: ma guenille m'est c. 353:17
Cherish: c. those hearts that hate thee 446:31
to love, c., and to obey 391:31
Cherished: crimes.. c. by our own virtues 423:7
lovers who have c. still this test 411:1
ne'er so tame, so c. 440:31
Cherishing: kill thee with much c. 478:1
Cherith: dwelt by the brook C. 47:51
Cheroot: whackin' white c. 299:11
Cherries: apples, c., hops, and women 178:22
c. fairly do enclose 124:5
more for.. blackbirds than.. c. 2:31
there c. grow 4:14, 124:4
Cherry: c. and hoary pear 82:7
c. brandy will grant 219:13
c. ripe 245:21
'C. ripe' themselves do cry 4:14, 124:4

Cherry (cont.)
like to a double c. 467:9
loveliest of trees, the c. 262:10
ruddier than the c. 214:8
see the c. hung with snow 262:10
there's the land, or c.-isle 245:21
Cherry-blossoms, and white cups 497:22
Cherry-stones: could not carve
  heads upon c. 275:21
Chertsey: old lady of C. 311:6
Cherub: C. Contemplation 341:12
C's face, a reptile all the rest 385:33
fall'n C., to be weak is miserable 344:16
proud limitary C. 347:34
Cherubim: c. does cease to sing 73:20
heaven's c., hors'd upon..the
  air 457:9
helmed C. 343:16
in the vault above the C. 298:9
Cherubims: he sitteth between
  the c. 397:33
Men!..Immortal C.! 548:15
Cherubin: fyr-reed c.'s face 137:19
thou young and rose-lipp'd c. 472:34
Cherubins: quiring to the young-
  eyed c. 465:18
Ches: to her son she c. 7:15
Cheshire Cat 129:4
Chess: life's too short for c. 120:2
made the game first of the c. 138:13
Chess-board: c. is the world 266:20
we called the c. white 89:32
Chest: c. of drawers by day 225:3
his c. against his foes 503:5
on the dead man's c. 514:18
Slingsby of the manly c. 24:9
ten-times-barr'd-up c. 474:10
Chester: charge, C., charge! 418:32
Chesterton: dared attack my C. 41:31
Chestnut: c.-husk at the c.-root 522:1
under the spreading c. tree 318:11
your c. was never the only colour 428:13
Chestnuts: c., summer through 84:8
sailor's wife had c. 456:10
to pull their c. out 38:16
Cheval: allemand à mon c. 136:13
Chevalier: young C. 250:17, 360:15
Chevalier: c. sans peur 12:13
Cheviot: hunt in the mountains of
  C. 30:11
in C. the hills so hye 30:12
Chevisaunce: and the C. 510:23
Chew: savoury pulp they c. 347:14
Chewed: some few to be c. and
  digested 27:17
Chewing: c. little bits of string 41:1
c. the food of..fancy 428:24
Chian: amber grapes, and C. wine 18:16
Chibiabos: my brother, C.! 318:2
Chicken: character called the
  Game C. 175:12
c. in his pot every Sunday 242:1
she's no c. 520:15
some c.! 144:9
we meet, with champagne and
  a c. 354:15
Chickens: all my pretty c. 460:21
as a hen gathereth her c. 60:20
count their c. 111:6
curses are like young c. 507:13
Hiawatha's C. 317:24
Chicks: where she feeds her c. at
  sea 294:21
Chid: he c. their wand'rings 224:19
never be c. 105:20
Chidden: so vain desire was c. 359:27
Chide: almost c. God 428:17
but I'll not c. thee 452:40
fall out, and c., and fight 561:27
I will c. no breather 428:8
lest He returning c. 351:21
snarling trumpets 'gan to c. 285:14
to c., to laugh 423:15
your tardy son to c. 435:51
Chiding: churlish c. of the winter's
  wind 426:29
he will not always be c. 398:5
Chief: a c. a rod 384:9
brilliant c. 322:9
c. of Scotia's food 105:2

Chief (cont.)
c. of the Pyramid and Crocodile 288:29
c. of Ulva's isle 122:24
Druid, hoary c. 158:29
hail to the C. 416:21
send in your C. an' surrender 301:8
sinners; of whom I am c. 68:43
to thy self unhappy c. 80:8
vain was the c.'s..pride 386:24
Chiefest among ten thousand 52:13
Chief Justice was rich, quiet, and
  infamous 324:32
Chiefs: those c. of pride 324:9
Chieftain: Brunswick's fated c. 113:28
c. o' the puddin'-race 106:4
c. to the Highlands bound 122:23
Chiels: Facts are c. that winna ding 105:11
Chiesa: Libera C. in libero Stato 134:3
Chil: ere C. the Kite swoops
  down 301:27
Child: aggravating c. 41:14
an it had been any christom c. 443:19
around the c. bend all the three 308:13
as a c. that is weaned 400:1
as he does with a..c. 139:23
as soon as he reflects..a c. 223:13
behold the c. 383:30
care..towards the c. she bare 161:11
c. among his new-born blisses 576:10
c. and mother, baby bliss 232:3
C.! do not throw this book about 40:19
c. I dreamed 141:16
c. imposes on the man 192:30
C. is father of the Man 577:25
c. is known by his doings 50:25
c. may rue that is unborn 30:12
c. of Adam's stem 376:7
c. of a day 308:19
C. of Light! thy limbs are burning 497:9
c. of misery 310:2
c. of our grandmother Eve 454:36
c's amang you taking notes 107:21
c.'s a plaything 308:9
c. should always say what's true 515:16
C.'s unheeded dream 374:23
c. that is not clean and neat 515:20
c. that's born on the Sabbath
  day 368:1
c. that so did thrive 280:10
come away, O human c. 586:9
cry of a c. by the roadway 585:17
Dear C.! Dear Girl! 577:1
dearer was the mother for the c. 151:22
defend, O Lord, this thy c. 391:20
died..like a Chrisom-c. 99:2
Elephant's C. 304:16
every c. born therein..housed,
  clothed 413:23
every c. may joy to hear 76:9
Experience is the c. of Thought 182:41
Fashion, though Folly's c. 164:38
fiery face of a c. 530:29
for the mother..the c. was dear 151:22
from a c...known the..scrip-
  tures 68:58
full beautiful, a faery's c. 286:30
get with c. a mandrake root 186:16
grief fills the room up of my..c. 447:34
grieved with her c. 196:2
half-devil and half-c. 303:24
happy English c. 527:5
hare's own c. 250:9
heard one calling, 'C.' 244:10
Heav'n-born c. all meanly
  wrapt 343:11
he became a little c. 76:10
here a little c. I stand 247:15
he who gives a c. a treat..a
  home 334:1
his active c. do deeds of youth 486:32
I a c. and thou a lamb 76:10
I heard a wife sing to her c. 196:2
in..simplicity a c. 382:15
is it well with the c.? 48:19
I think this lady to be my c.
  Cordelia 454:16
it was a crime in a c. 325:36
I was a c. and she was a c. 380:8
I was a c. beneath her touch 410:26
I was made..the c. of God 391:2

Child (cont.)
I would not *coddle* the c. 271:32
Jesus Christ her little C. 3:20
land that's govern'd by a c. 476:18
leave a c. alone 95:2
lie down like a tired c. 498:25
like a c. from the womb 493:1
like a froward.. 527:18
listens like a three years' c. 148:20
little c. shall lead them 53:18
look upon a little c. 565:9
love playthings well as a c. 514:38
Magus Zoroaster, my dead c. 496:18
make me a c. again 4:16
melancholy's c. 451:40
mid-May's eldest c. 287:31
Monday's c. 368:1
mother may forget the c. 106:28
my c., I live for thee 538:27
my fairest c. 293:6
my good c., know this 391:10
naked new-born c. 279:19
Nature's true-born c. 292:17
never spares the c. 253:3
nicest c. I ever knew 40:33
not a c. so small and weak 4:8
not as their friend or c. I speak 16:6
ocean's c., and then his queen 495:2
old Adam in this C. 390:57
on a cloud I saw a c. 76:9
O! what a c.! 309:6
perfection is the c. of Time 234:10
Shakespeare, Fancy's c. 342:7
simple c., dear brother Jim 582:11
singer of sweet Colonus, and its c. 16:2
sing to the c. on thy knee 82:11
solitary c. 577:17
spoil the c. 110:42
stop, c. of God 151:16
thankless c. 452:30
that gracious C., that thorn-
  crown'd Man 17:9
this c. I to myself will take 581:21
this painted c. of dirt 385:31
Thought is the c. of Action 182:41
to the lonely dreams of a c. 171:4
train up a c. 50:30
unto us a c. is born 53:15
waters wild went o'er his c. 122:29
when I was a c., I spake as a c. 66:46
where is my c.? 113:5
wise father that knows his own
  c. 463:31
with c. of glorious great intent 509:23
wretched c. expires 41:3
you'd sometimes say, Poor C. 375:20
young healthy c...in a fricassee 520:3
your trust..in any c. of man 400:19
Childe Roland to the Dark
  Tower 90:23, 453:27
Childhood: c. shows the man 350:10
ever thus from c.'s hour 121:8, 357:5
eye of c. that fears the painted
  devil 458:14
He is our c.'s pattern 4:3
in c. solac'd me 160:25
in my days of c. 308:1
in simple c. something of the
  base 579:34
with my c.'s faith 88:24
womanhood and c. fleet 316:34
Childish: all tricks are either
  knavish or c. 274:14
c., but very natural 152:11
inconstant, c., proud, and full
  of fancies 289:10
more c. valorous 331:6
pleased his c. thought 575:5
pretty, trifling, c., weak 105:9
put away c. things 66:46
sweet c. days 573:19
turning again towards c. treble 427:31
wise, idle, c. things 543:23
Wordsworth chime his c. verse 117:28
Childishly: suck'd on country
  pleasures, c. 185:6
Childishness: it does from c. 423:35
I will be sorry for their c. 375:17
second c. 427:21
Childless: c. and crownless 114:13
noblest works..from c. men 26:46

Childlike: his smile it was pensive
  and c. 238:33
Newton, c. sage! 163:13
smile that was c. and bland 238:34
Children: airy hopes my c. 574:16
all the c. dine at five 515:17
apricocks..like unruly c. 475:12
as c. fear to go in the dark 26:1
as c. with their play 160:15
as the indifferent c. of the earth 433:9
bandy c., nor fasting 76:4
become as little c. 59:48
but the young, young c. 88:2
called the c. of God 57:39
c. and the fruit of the womb 399:35
c. are to be deceived with comfits 24:31
c. born of thee are sword and fire 530:12
c. by adoption and grace 389:26
c. dear, was it yesterday? 15:25
c. follow'd with endearing wile 224:23
c. in Holland 10:10
c. in ordinary dress 40:34
c. not thine 160:30
c. of a larger growth 139:22, 191:20
c. of Alice 306:7
c. of disobedience 68:3
c. of God: and if c., then heirs 65:54
c. of men..are but vanity 395:24
c. of one family 561:27
c. of splendour and flame 561:12
c. of the bridechamber mourn 58:41
c. of the devil 539:20
c. of the future age 76:1
c. of the Lord 3:17
c. of this world..wiser than the
  c. of light 62:20
c. scream'd 160:2
c.'s teeth are set on edge 55:29
c. stood watching them 293:25
c. sweeten labours 26:45
c. walking two and two 76:15
c., you are very little 515:23
Christian c. all must be 4:2
come again, ye c. of men 397:15
come, dear c., let us away 15:22
come my tan-faced c. 567:4
cruel c., crying babies 515:24
do ye hear the c. weeping? 88:1
drinkest the tears of c. 172:18
even so are the young c. 399:35
fatherless c., and widows 389:4
for all our c.'s fate 296:19
for the procreation of c. 391:24
frail c. of dust 228:22
Friend for little c. 338:19
gathered thy c. together 60:20
go, c. of swift joy 544:4
help Thy c. when they call 295:6
her c...call her blessed 50:58
he that hath wife and c. 26:34
he..that taketh thy c. 400:6
his blood..on our c. 60:50
holdeth c. from play 502:8
household happiness, gracious
  c. 541:5
I never..call'd you c. 453:6
in sorrow..bring forth c. 44:26
instead of thy fathers..c. 394:26
known as the C.'s Hour 316:3
like c. with violets playing 293:21
little c. saying grace 515:15
little c.'s dower 92:16
more careful of the breed of
  their..dogs than of their c. 377:8
mother for her c. 72:22
mother who talks about her own
  c. 181:5
myself and c. three 159:33
neither c. nor Gods 296:2
no c. run to lisp 229:31
old men and c. 400:25
opponent of..the c. of light 19:14
our c. and our sins..on the king 444:21
provoke not your c. to wrath 68:8
Rachel weeping for her c. 57:26
round surveys his c.'s looks 226:11
secrets..must be kept from c. 193:6
see his c. fed 402:25
see the c. sport upon the shore 576:19
sick persons, and young c. 389:3
sins of the fathers upon the c. 390:7

Children (cont.)
so many c. 369:4
stars..are my c. 290:12
suffer the little c. to come 61:6
their c.'s c. shall say they have
  lied 584:16
three fair c. first she bore him 535:9
thy c. like the olive branches 399:36
till her c. came from school 109:26
to keep c. quiet 519:3
to whom the lips of c. 361:8
two c. did we stray 543:23
Usna's c. died 585:22
voices of c. are heard on the
  green 76:14
we are but little c. weak 4:7
we have c., we have wives 540:2
were all thy c. kind 443:13
when he died the little c. cried 359:23
wife and c...bills of charges 26:35
wisdom is justified of her c. 59:9
within the little c.'s eyes 544:20
women..appear to me as c. 290:12
your c. all gone 367:12
Child-wife: only my c. 175:2
Chill: ah, bitter c. it was! 285:12
c. thy dreaming nights 287:3
Chill'd: somewhat was he c. with
  dread 417:14
Chilling: our c. climate hardly
  bears 521:15
Chillon! thy prison 114:34
Chills the lap of May 226:10
Chilly: although the room grows
  c. 228:11
c. finger'd spring 285:7
her soft and c. nest 285:22
I feel c. and grown old 97:9
Chiltern: storm..on the C. Hills 140:7
you take the C. Hundreds 140:7
Chimborazo, Cotopaxi 549:21
Chime: as tolls the evening c. 357:16
c. of full, sad bells 269:25
c., ye dappled darlings 293:14
heard their soothing c. 357:15
higher than the sphery c. 341:5
jarr'd against nature's c. 351:11
some soft c. had stroked the air 282:3
we will hear the c. 263:1
your silver c. 343:17
Chimeras: dire c. and enchanted
  isles 340:25
Gorgons and Hydras, and C.
  dire 346:3
Chimes: heard the c. at midnight 442:11
hear the c. at midnight 514:35
Chimney: German who smoked
  like a c. 34:21
old men from the c. corner 502:8
Chimney-piece: Buffalo upon the
  c. 128:16
leave the bottle on the c. 176:16
Chimneys: good grove of c. for me 358:20
our c. were blown down 458:21
your c. I sweep 76:17
Chimney-sweepers: as c., come to
  dust 430:1
Chimpanzees: brainless as c. 121:20
Chin: close-button'd to the c. 160:12
her nose and c. they threaten
  ither 108:33
his c., new-reap'd 438:32
his c. upon an orient wave 343:24
item, One neck, one c. 482:21
page with the dimpled c. 543:3
China: c. an' etchin's an' fans 299:18
c. that's ancient and blue 309:25
fire a mine in C., here 111:5
if ye break my best blue c. 236:11
infusion of a C. plant 2:10
integrity of C. 43:11
mankind, from C. to Peru 279:2
outer C. 'crost the Bay 299:10
though c. fall 384:39
Chinamen: with C. but not with
  me 41:35
Chinee: heathen C. is peculiar 238:32
Chinese: C. crinkum-crankums 379:22
C. wouldn't dare to 157:25
ruined by C. cheap labour 238:36
Chineses: Sericana, where C. drive 346:23

Ching-a-ring-a-ring-ching! Feast
  of lanterns 379:22
Chink: their importunate c. 102:20
Chinks: c. that time has made 557:25
fill hup the c. wi' cheese 518:12
through the c...of our prison 102:38
Chip: c. hat had she on 287:4
not merely a c. of the old 'block' 103:28
Chipping at the countenances of
  the attendants 173:31
Chippy: from a cheap and c. chop-
  per 219:31
Chips: nothing but c...c. to the
  House of Commons 143:31
Chisel: ne'er did Grecian c. trace 416:16
Chit: bit of a c. of a boy 120:28
Chit-chat: divine c. of Cowper 306:32
Chittabob's tail was the finest 34:33
Chivalries: acts of humanity,
  gentleness, and c. 328:2
Chivalry: age of c. is gone 102:11
age of c. is never past 294:16
age of c. is past 182:46
Belgium's capital..her beauty
  and her c. 113:25
Busiris and his Memphian c. 344:26
charge with all thy c. 122:19
for Christian service and true c. 474:22
he loved c. 136:23
herein may be seen noble c. 328:2
I have a truant been to c. 440:28
learn the noble acts of c. 328:1
my discipline of arms and c. 331:2
smiled Spain's c. away 116:45
Chloe: C. is my real flame 401:38
dear C., how blubber'd 401:19
to C.'s breast young Cupid 74:9
what can C. want? 384:33
Chloris: Ah, C.! 421:11
call me Sappho, call me C. 152:6
Chocolate: coffee, tea, c., butter
  and toast 13:17
Choice: c. and master spirits of
  this age 450:5
c. between truth and repose 200:22
c. of friends 158:16
each to his c. 302:13
if there were a sympathy in c. 466:20
in the c. of his enemies 570:6
in the worth and c. 279:30
just the terrible c. 96:12
mistress of her c. 434:25
most c., forsaken 452:13
on his c. depends..the whole
  state 431:21
people's c. 500:13
rain's my c. 407:4
small c. in rotten apples 478:48
take c. of all my library 480:34
to Heaven the measure and the
  c. 279:12
you takes your c. 403:4
Choicer than the Mermaid Tavern 287:1
Choir: all the c. of heaven 43:12
full-voiced c. below 341:24
hisn in the c. 319:25
in a waiful c. 284:14
innumerable c. of day 81:20
leading his c., the Nine 15:15
may I join the c. invisible 196:34
sweet singing in the c. 10:14
with thy c. of Saints 185:25
Choirs: bare ruin'd c. 487:16
C. and Places where they sing 388:27
Choke: c. their service up 426:38
c. the strong conception 473:14
good for nothing but to c. a man 280:14
Choked: when your fountain is c.
  up 102:19
Choking her with cream 294:13
Choler: purge this c. without letting blood 474:3
Choleric: writer..mild or c. 2:4
Chommoda dicebat 133:17
Choose: c. a firm cloud 384:29
c. an author as you c. a friend 180:8
c. love by another's eye 466:19
c. one cloth for ever 358:23
c. our tree 336:43
c. the good 53:12
c. the Jews 202:19

INDEX

Choose (cont.)
c. time 26:8
c…whatever suits the line 152:6
do not c. to run for President 156:23
don't c. to have it known 139:35
he cannot c. but hear 148:20
if you c. to boil eggs in your shoes 312:21
I lie as lads would c. 263:7
leading wherever I c. 568:3
my only difficulty is to c. 194:12
never c. amiss 464:3
not c. not to be 254:19
not c. what many men desire 463:44
sailor free to c. 303:14
therefore c. life 46:30
what I c. it to mean 131:6
where to c. their place of rest 349:31
Chooses: then it is the brave man c. 320:12
Choosing: c. each stone 332:12
just c. so 90:14
long c. and beginning late 349:5
Chopper: c. to chop off your head 368:9
from a cheap and chippy c. 219:31
Chops: bottled beer and c. 221:5
c. and Tomata sauce 179:12
Chop-sticks: what a crop of c. 379:22
Chorasmian: hush'd C. waste 17:28
lone C. shore 492:17
Chord: I struck one c. 402:12
one clear c. to reach the ears of God 569:13
some c. in unison 163:48
Chords: smote on all the c. with might 534:16
there are c. in the human mind 173:35
Choristers: go the chanting c. 310:23
Chortled: he c. in his joy 129:39(-130)
Chorus: C. Hymeneal 498:7
c. of indolent reviewers 529:19
sing, boys, in joyful c. 168:14
so we sang the c. 583:7
swell the c. of the Union 314:10
Chorus-ending from Euripides 89:31
Chose: Todgers' could do it when it c. 176:11
to her son she c. 7:15
what I could say if I c. 129:18
Chosen: c. thee in the furnace 54:19
fast that I have c. 54:35, 36
few are c. 60:10
he comes on c. evenings 189:22
opponent of the c. people 19:14
where his c. lie 96:31
ye have not c. me, but I have c. you 63:58
Choughs: crows and c. that wing the midway air 454:3
maggot-pies and c. and rooks 459:24
russet-pated c. 467:7
Chrism: for death's sweet c. retain'd 376:2
Chrisom-child: an it had been any c. 443:10
died. .like a C. 99:2
Christ: abjure. .his Saviour C. 329:25
acknowledgment of God in C. 90:43
all at once what C. is 255:7
are they ministers of C.? 67:33
as the churches have killed their C. 536:19
brings Saviour C. again 334:1
but C. rises 91:18
Cardinal,—C.,—Maria,—God 96:17
cautious, statistical C. 370:14
C. and his mother and all his hallows 255:6
C., born into virgynyte 583:26
C. cannot find a chamber 12:7
C. his John 243:34
C. is all, and in all 68:31
C. is all in all to thee 354:12
C. is crucified again 313:5
C. is nigh 132:5
C. is the end. .the beginning 360:11
C. is the path, and C. the prize 354:11
C. is thy strength, and C. thy right 354:11
C. our passover 66:28
C. perish in torment in every age 491:5

Christ (cont.)
C. receive him 537:28
C. receive thy saule 31:12
C.'s lore. .he taughte 137:18
C.'s progress, and His prayer-time 551:20
C.'s stamp to boot 244:4
C. that is to be 533:20
C., the Lord, is risen 565:4
C. took the kindness 96:5
C. walking on the water. .of. . Thames 545:1
C. was born, across the sea 264:18
C. with His lamp of truth 81:4
depart, and to be with C. 68:16
do all things through C. 68:28
draws near the birth of C. 532:21
esteeming the reproach of C. 69:16
faith of C. crucified 390:58
for C.'s particular love's sake 96:2
for the testimony of Jesus C. 70:23
gain to me. .loss for C. 68:21
grey-grown speechless C. 522:20
half a drop, ah my C. 330:7
his pure soul unto his captain C. 475:16
if Jesus C. were to come today 127:25
in C. shall all be made alive 67:8
in the bowels of C. 167:4
in the kingdom and patience of Jesus C. 70:23
Jesus C. her little child 3:20
Jesus C. her Lord 517:1
Jesus C. is risen today 8:2, 13:13
joint-heirs with C. 65:54
last kind word to C. 96:5
Lord C.'s heart 199:2
Lord God almighty Jesus C. 409:21
love of C. constraineth us 67:26
love of C., which passeth knowledge 67:54
man raised up by C. 532:22
may Lord C. enter in 569:12
member of C. 391:2
now is C. risen 67:8
O C. the plough, O C. the laughter 334:2
our fair father C. 530:15
prisoner of Jesus C. 69:5
put on C. 391:1
save Jesus C., and him crucified 66:21
see the C. stand 96:25
show me, dear C., thy spouse 185:20
shuts the spouse C. home 255:6
soldiers of C., arise 565:10
to live is C. 68:15
understood C. was a carpenter 73:17
unsearchable riches of C. 67:52
uphold the C. 530:13
Vision of C. that thou dost see 74:10
was C. a man like us? 15:4
we have C.'s own promise 35:3
we withstood C. then? 92:12
when the Lord C. was born 359:14
where C. erecteth his church 33:4
where C.'s blood streams 330:7
which is in C. Jesus 65:58
whole state of C.'s Church 390:24
your cold C. 300:19
Christ-child stood at Mary's knee 140:20
Christ-Church: dine with the Canons of C. 272:38
I am the Dean of C., Sir 511:5
line of festal light in C. hall 18:11
Christendom: able to live in any place in C. 198:3
any summer-house in C. 440:2
for never a king's son in C. 438:24
in C. where is the Christian? 200:45
wisest fool in C. 242:4
Christened on Tuesday 368:21
Christiad: less a C. than a Pauliad 237:14
Christian: aisles of C. Rome 199:23
approach, O C. wight 508:18
Articles of the C. Faith 391:2
as I am a C. faithful man 476:13
as little as a C. can 188:34
C. boys I can scarcely hope to make 20:22
C. can only fear dying 237:21
C. children all must be 4:2
C., dost thou see them? 361:13

Christian (cont.)
C. religion. .at first attended with miracles 265:10
C. religion is part of the law 292:4
C. riles and the Aryan smiles 300:6
C.l seek not yet repose 198:19
C. while he sings 161:21
every C…engage. .in some mental pursuit 75:10
fled with a C.l O my C. ducats! 463:42
for C. men. .to wear weapons 401:13
for C. service and true chivalry 474:22
foreknow. .the works of C. men 525:17
gait of C., pagan, nor man 434:19
good C. men, rejoice 361:18
hadn't got a C. 403:21
healing voice of C. charity 102:5
honourable style of a C. 86:1
horror and darkness fell upon C. 99:24
how very hard it is to be a C.l 91:15
I die a C. 136:1
I hate him for he is a C. 463:17
in Christendom where is the C.? 200:45
in every C. kind of place 515:15
in these C. days 527:5
in what peace a c. can die 3:1
is she to be buried in C. burial? 437:3
it weareth the C. down 300:6
I was born of C. race 561:20
lead a holy C. life 316:36
my object. .to form C. men 20:22
no more wit than a C. 482:6
not good for the C.'s health 300:6
onward, C. soldiers 35:1
ought. .to forgive them as a c. 23:4
out of his C. name a synonym for the Devil 325:6
persuadest me to be a C. 65:26
pure eyes and C. hearts 291:12
rarity of C. charity 252:18
sad good C. at her heart 381:10
scratch the C. and you find the pagan 587:17
shame on us, C. brethren 264:13
stop, C. passer-by! 151:16
three C. men 327:15
true wayfaring C. 352:9
wherefore, C. men, be sure 361:24
you were a C. slave 241:24
Christianae: animae naturaliter C. 542:2
Christianity: all the faults. .from C. and journalism 29:21
C. .now. .discovered to be fictitious 109:35
C. part of the Common Law 233:22
for a' the gowd in C. 31:7
his C. was muscular 182:3
local cult called C. 236:1
loving C. better than Truth 152:22
temper is nine-tenths of C. 240:28
Christianorum: semen est sanguis C. 542:3
Christians: C., at your cross of hope 87:38
C., awake 112:24
C. have burnt each other 115:20
neither having the accent of C. 434:19
profess and call themselves C. 389:16
some C. have a comfortable creed 115:31
soothed the griefs of forty generations of C. 325:36
what these C. are 463:24
Christless code 536:16
Christmas: at C…desire a rose 454:33
at C. play 549:23
at Home the C. Day is breaking 295:9
C. comes but once a year 549:23
C. Day in the workhouse 502:15
C. Eve, and twelve of the clock 236:21
C. is coming 5:23
C. is here 543:11
eating a C. pie 367:16
insulting C. card 233:11
old C. brought his sports again 418:24
on C. day in the morning 5:14
that C. should fall out in the middle of Winter 2:15
that it was C. Day 508:15
'twas C. broached the mightiest ale 418:24
'twas the night before C 356:1
we'll keep our C. merry still 418:23

[645]

Christo: fortius fide et gaude in C. 321:3
Christopher Robin: C. is saying his prayers 339:19
C. went down with Alice 339:14
Christs that die upon the barricades 569:14
Christ's College: lady of C. 21:10
Christus: surrexit C. hodie 13:13
Chronic: do not repine..It is c. 176:13
Chronicle: c. of a solitary hidden anguish 196:24
c. small beer 470:29
your c. as rich with praise 443:9
Chronicler: such an honest c. as Griffith 447:11
Chronicles: brief c. of the time 433:29
look in the c. 478:45
Chrononhotonthologos: where left you C.? 125:12
Chrysippo: melius C. et Crantore 256:21
Chrysolite: one entire and perfect c. 473:21
seventh, c. 72:1
Chrysoprasus: tenth, a c. 72:1
Chub: chavender, or c. 414:6
Chubby: Augustus was a c. lad 249:18
Chuck: him out, the brute 303:2
c. it, Smith 140:2
dearest c. 459:8
Chunking: 'ear their paddles c. 299:10
Church: as some to c. repair 382:30
at c., with meek..grace 224:22
at Trinity C. I met my doom 217:21
built God a c. 162:4
buttress of the c. 335:21
c. and no steeple 521:26
C. at rest 517:3
c. for his mother 517:3
c. for peace 89:42
churchmen fain would kill their c. 536:19
c...one day's truce 102:5
C.'s one foundation 517:1
C. with psalms must shout 243:24
come all to c., good people 263:2
come to c. in time 263:1
for the C.! for the laws! 323:2
free c. in a free state 134:3
'gainst that C. prevail 35:3
go to c. in a galliard 482:8
great C. victorious 517:3
halloa! here's a c.! 175:27
I can see a c. by daylight 468:10
if undrest at C. 203:30
I like a c. 199:21
I like the silent c. 200:43
into his c. lewd hirelings 347:3
I persecuted the c. of God 67:5
make a figure in a country c. 519:25
nearer the C. the further from God 4:23
no salvation..outside the c. .22:1
not been in..a c. for many years 271:6
one Catholic and Apostolick C. 390:22
piece of mere c. furniture 164:10
plain as way to parish c. 427:18
seed of the C. 542:3
she came to the village c. 535:41
so to c. went she 263:2
stands the C. clock 84:15
thy household the C. 380:49
too close in c. and mart 89:3
upon this rock will I build my c. 59:43
what is a c.? 164:29
where Christ erecteth his c. 33:4
where bells have knoll'd to c. 427:19
who is always at c. 76:4
whole state of Christ's C. 390:24
within the C.'s gate 244:5
Church-door: housbondes at c... five 137:15
Church-going: sound of the c. bell 164:26
Church of England: C...is no doubt a compromise 501:10
C. is not a mere depositary of doctrine 180:26
C. parson for the Islands of the Blest 302:19
I die..according to..the C. 136:1
late act..for securing the C. 2:16
Church of Rome I found would suit 7:10

Churches: as the c. have kill'd their Christ 536:19
chapels had been c. 463:7
c. built to please the priest 106:24
he must build c. then 435:5
John to the seven c. 70:21
let them fight against the c. 460:4
little, lost, Down c. praise 302:11
seven c. which are in Asia 70:21, 24
Churchman: I that cowled c. be 199:21
Churchmen: c. fain would kill their church 536:19
single life doth well with c. 26:36
Churchyard: lie in Mellstock c. now 236:8
palsy-stricken, c. thing 285:17
Churchyards: troop home to c. 467:10
Churlish: my master is of c. disposition 427:6
reply c. 428:37
Churn: attract a Silver C. 221:1
Cibber: let tuneful C. sing 270:7
Cicero: fall below Demosthenes or C. 202:16
if I could have known C. 175:8
no difference..can alienate C. 325:23
Ciel: fils de St. Louis, montez au c. 204:38
Cigar: good c. is a Smoke 294:32
Smith, take a fresh c. 121:22
sweet post-prandial c. 98:7
Cigarette..perfect pleasure 570:8
Cimber: constant C. should be banished 449:30
Cimes: souffrons sur les c. 265:3
Cinarae: bonae sub regno C. 260:17
Cincinnatus of the West 118:21
Cincti Bis Motoribus 223:8
Cinder: how dry a c. this world is 185:3
Cinders: I've made the c. fly 295:3
love in a hut..c., ashes, dust 286:39
sat among the c. 367:17
Cinerem: mutam..alloquerer c. 133:20
Cineri: ignis suppositos c. doloso 259:1
Cinna: nec dicere C. digna 556:7
Cinnamon: lucent syrops, tinct with c. 285:25
nutmegs and ginger, c. and cloves 37:25
Cinque-pace: Scotch jig, a measure, and a c. 468:9
Cinque-spotted: mole c. 429:24
Cipher in the state 415:17
Ciphers: only figure among c. 25:22
Circenses: panem et c. 283:19
Circle: all the c. of the golden year 529:31
all within this c. move 558:1
c. to go into 74:24
love is a c. 246:11
mortal right-lined c. 87:13
nature of God is a c. 10:17
no happiness within this c. of flesh 86:20
small c. of a wedding-ring 144:23
thy firmness makes my c. just 186:25
we are swinging round the c. 269:23
weave a c. round him thrice 151:33(-152)
wheel come full c. 454:22
Circle-citadels there 255:5
Circled by the sands 335:27
Circles and right lines limit..all bodies 87:13
Circuit: what time, what c. first 94:13
Circuitous: foil'd c. wanderer 17:28(-18)
Circulates: from link to link it c. 574:26
Circulating library .. diabolical knowledge 500:16
Circumcised: demonstrate to a c. people 217:12
I took by the throat the c. dog 474:2
Circumcision nor uncircumcision 68:31
Circumference is nowhere 10:17
Circumlocution Office 175:29
Circumnavigate the metaphysics 514:35
Circumscribed in time and place 581:18
Circumscription: put into c. and confine 469:38
Circumspect: Buckingham grows c. 476:23
so c. and right 338:9
Circumspice: c. si monumentum requiris 33:23
si monumentum requiris, c. 583:16

Circumstance: breasts the blows of c. 533:1
c...most afflicting to a parent's mind 23:3
dance of plastic c. 95:24
detect therein one c. 316:36
eternal artistries in C. 235:20
ignorant of this remarkable c. 325:20
in the fell clutch of c. 241:18
pride, pomp, and c. of..war 472:3
some c. to please us 521:1
to a philosopher no c...too minute 226:23
to envisage c., all calm 286:16
unsifted in such perilous c. 431:26
very slave of c. 118:36
Circumstances: after many c. 110:44
c. beyond my individual control 175:3
c. over which he has no control 564:15
creature of c. 237:19
fearful concatenation of c. 563:9
if c. lead me 432:44
Circumstantial: lie c. 428:37
some c. evidence is very strong 547:4
Circumvent: one that would c. God 437:11
Circus: bread and..the c. 283:19
Cistern: c. for foul toads 472:34
wheel be broken at the c. 51:33
Citadel: mountain-built with peaceful c. 287:12
tower'd c., a pendant rock 425:19
winged sea-girt c. 113:16
Citadels: circle-c. there 255:5
Cité: le buste survit à la c. 214:3
Cities: authority over ten c. 62:36
buries empires and c. 217:13
c. of men, and manners 540:32
flower of c. all 195:5
hum of human c. torture 113:47
in c...the works of men 377:9
islanded by c. fair 495:1
silent c. of the dead 119:11
towered c. please us then 342:5
Citizen: c. of credit and renown 159:32
c. of no mean city 65:12
c. of the world 26:21
humblest c. of all the land 98:1
Citizens: before men made us c. 320:8
civil c. kneading up the honey 443:10
fat and greasy c. 426:33
first in the hearts of his fellow c. 312:25
London doth pour out her c. 445:5
Cito: qui c. dat 526:2
City: Athens..c. or suburban 350:11
back from the C. of Sleep 295:11
beautiful c.! 19:10
brought up in this c. 65:13
citizen of no mean c. 65:12
c. cast her people out 424:7
c. had no need of the sun 72:5
c. is barren 173:37
c. is built to music 530:5
C. is of Night 546:29
C. now doth..wear 582:14
c. of kites and crows 429:16
c. of the faithfullest friends 567:8
c. of the soul 114:12
c. of two kings 324:2
c. such as vision builds 495:27
C.'s voice itself is soft 498:21
c. that is set on an hill 57:41
c. which hath foundations 69:14
dear c. of Cecrops..dear c. of Zeus 329:15
except the Lord keep the c. 49:36, 399:35
falling on the c. brown 81:15
first c. Cain 158:9
he in the dissolute c. 577:22
hell is a c. much like London 496:16
here have we no continuing c. 69:24
he that taketh a c. 50:17
holy c., new Jerusalem 71:44
hope of the C. of God 334:13
in as just possession of truth as of a c. 86:5
in perils in the c. 67:35
I saw a c. invincible 566:23
I stood within the C. disinterred 496:2

INDEX

City (cont.)
kindness in a strong c. 393:30
know and not be known..in a c. 154:22
lead me into the strong c. 395:23
London; a nation, not a c. 182:15
long in c. pent 289:2
long in populous c. pent 349:11
many a noble c. 132:4
mathematics of the c. of heaven 85:19
might go to the c. 398:15
near a whole c. full 252:18
new c. of Friends 566:23
on, to the C. of God 17:21
out of the holy c. 72:12
people went up into the c. 46:40
populous and smoky c. 496:16
rose-red c. 100:3
several chaps out of the C. 141:29
shady C. of palm-trees 552:6
she was a maiden C. 582:6
street of the c. was pure gold 72:3
sun-girt c. 495:2
sweet C. with her dreaming spires 18:22
that c. which..thinks of war 109:21
that great c. 71:25, 33
there the great c. stands 567:8
this great hive, the c. 158:12
this vast c.; a c. of refuge 352:13
thou c. of God 397:13
thrice looked he at the c. 323:23
through the c.-crowds..push his way 151:27
to feel, amid the c.'s jar 16:17
towery c. and branchy 254:21
very famous c. 154:9
who know not the c...of Prague 402:22
whom the c. never called 77:28
why not their c. too? 115:3
Zion, c. of our God 364:16
City Road: up and down the C. 328:26
Cive, anheling, wipes 251:19
Civet: give me an ounce of c. 454:9
Civic independence flings the gauntlet 123:7
Civil: assent with c. leer 385:29
c. to folk he ne'er saw 13:17
in c. business..boldness 25:32
justice, whence all c. laws 24:33
marriage..a c. contract 422:6
nobility..ornament to the c. order 102:25
over violent or over c. 190:23
rude sea grew c. 466:38
shunning c. rage 192:13
so generally c. that nobody thanked him 273:24
too c. by half 500:22
utmost bound of c. liberty 110:2
what dire effects from c. discord 1:25
when c. fury first grew high 110:2
Civilian: mushroom rich c. 119:24
Civilities: bandy c. with my Sovereign 271:24
Civility: c. costs nothing 354:17
I see a wild c. 246:4
six thousand years' traditions of c. 374:19
use the c. of my knee 86:2
Civilization: as c. advances 325:2
curiosity..life blood of..c. 549:8
resources of c. 222:37
three great elements of modern c. 125:24
Civilized: Asia is not going to be c. 304:27
last thing c. by Man 337:31
Civilizers: two c. of man 181:3
Civilizes: whose presence c. ours 159:18
Civis Romanus sum 145:14
Clad: c. in complete steel 340:22
c. in the beauty of a thousand stars 330:6
lady so richly c. as she 150:20
naked every day he c. 225:19
students shall be bravely c. 320:24
Claim: all c. to poetical honours 278:10
c. me thine 530:16
I c. only a memory 92:31
last territorial c. 248:15
Claims: smile at the c. of long descent 533:38
thousand c. to reverence 539:12

Clair: ce qui n'est pas c. 407:6
Clamb: we c. the hill thegither 106:20
Clamorem: compesce c. 259:13
Clamorous: ravens, c. o'er the dead 491:28
Clamour: in the c. of the crowded street 317:4
with a c. of waters 521:30
with deaf'ning c. in the..clouds 442:1
with the c. keep her still awake 479:7
Clamoured: obscure bird c. 458:21
Clamours: immortal Jove's dread c. 472:3
Clan: against the c. M'Tavish 23:20
leaving great verse unto a little c. 287:17
Clan-Conuil: summon C. 419:2
Clang of hurrying feet 23:22
Clanging from the Severn to the Tyne 294:22
Clangour: trumpet's loud c. 191:37
Clank: let 'em c. 559:33
Clap: c. her broad wings 211:26
c. thyself my love 485:5
if you believe, c. your hands 36:10
Clapham: my old aunt at C. 233:5
Clapped: Cupid hath c. him o' the shoulder 428:18
Clapper: his tongue is the c. 468:28
Clapper-clawing: one another c. 110:45
Clapping: soundless-c. host 545:2
Clara threw the twins she nursed 228:7
Clarence: false, fleeting, perjur'd C. 476:16
Claret: c. is the liquor for boys 274:12
c...would be port if it could 43:5
his c. good 251:29
Claribel: send up *Unity, C., Assyrian* 299:25
Clarion: blow her c. o'er the dreaming earth 496:4
cock's shrill c. 229:31
sound, the c. 357:22
Clarions: with his c. and his drums 323:3
great winds thy c. 142:26
Clarum et venerabile nomen 320:25
Clash: ignorant armies c. by night 15:8
to court the country c. 105:27
Clashed: c. and thundered unthinkable wings 141:1
c. with his fiery few 537:19
noon was c. and hammer'd 529:28
Clashing: no sound..of c. wars 184:2
Clasp: c. we to our hearts for deathless dower 410:30
dare its deadly terrors c. 75:24(-76)
I shall c. thee again 95:12
very reason why I c. them 157:20
Clasped: c. by the golden light of morn 253:19
fate in my fist 210:3
he c. her like a lover 535:5
Clasps: gross c. of a lascivious Moor 469:32
Classes: bow, bow, ye lower middle c. 218:34
masses against the c. 222:40
three great c. 19:29
Classic: I seem to tread on c. ground 2:2
Classical: at c. Monday Pops 220:5
c. quotation is the *parole* of literary men 274:31
grand, old, fortifying, c. curriculum 20:1
Clause: servant with this c. 244:16
Claverhouse: 'twas C. who spoke 416:8
Clavicithern: grace of lute or c. 92:5
Claw: red in tooth and c. 532:37
Clawed me with his clutch 552:15
Claws: c. that catch 129:39
how neatly spreads his c. 128:24
pair of ragged c. 107:19
see her stick her c. 319:19
Clay: blind his soul with c. 539:8
brother of the c. 122:37
daily absorbs a c. 121:21
dead, and turn'd to c. 437:18
gilded loam or painted c. 474:10
kingdoms are c. 423:14
o'er informed the tenement of c. 190:13

Clay (cont.)
of all man's clotted c. 544:20
of c. and wattles made 585:12
or my c. mix with the earth 119:33
out of the mire and c. 394:12
potter and c. endure 95:23
power over the c. 65:60
shall the c. say.. 54:17
Sir John Vanbrugh's house of c. 202:11
there's calm in a Henry C. 294:31
this foolish-compounded c. 441:11
this gray stone and grassy c. 376:20
thousand scatter'd into C. 205:17
turf that wraps their c. 153:30
Who hast made the C. 300:4
whom Thou hast moulded from the c. 375:17
with Earth's first C. 207:6
Clayey: into a c. tenement 125:6
Clay-shuttered: our own c. doors 545:1
Clean: all c. and comfortable I sit down 290:25
child that is not c. and neat 515:20
c-l-e-a-n, c., verb active 177:5
clear fire, a c. hearth 306:12
grew more c. and white 88:22
make it as c. as you can 528:9
make me a c. heart 395:9
nor Galahad c. 531:21
purge me..and I shall be c. 395:8
strong persevering man, to c. horses 518:35
then I was c. and brave 262:19
will these hands ne'er be c.? 460:25
you have to c. your slate 409:11
Cleaned: I c. the windows 221:15
tops c. with champagne 518:19
Cleaner: in a c., greener land 299:14
Cleaning: better..c. his 'oss than c. his breeches 518:20
Cleanliness: city of the c. of the sexes 567:8
c...next to godliness 505:20
for c. finds sixpence 157:4
Cleanly: c. young girl 387:2
cold, and not too c., manger 166:1
leave sack, and live c. 441:6
so c. I myself can free 189:20
Cleanse: c. the stuff'd bosom 460:37
c. thou me 392:34
young man c. his way 399:13
Cleansed: were there not ten c.? 62:29
what God hath c. 64:47
Clear: all doctrines plain and c. 111:11
as c. as a whistle 112:23
as c. as morning roses 479:4
but c. your decks 106:23
c. and bright it should be ever 537:42
c. and gentle stream 80:13
c. as wind 537:42
c. fire, a clean hearth 306:12
c. the land of evil 301:26
c. writers, like fountains 309:21
c. your *mind* of cant 275:13
fair as the moon, c. as the sun 52:15
in honour c. 385:6
I unclothe and c. 166:21
judicious, c., succinct 159:16
night is as c. as the day 400:9
said it very loud and c. 131:12
so c. in his great office 457:9
stream..will not run c. with us 102:19
that they could get it c. 130:12
though deep, yet c. 172:10
thy righteousness as c. as the light 394:4
thy sky is ever c. 97:30, 315:21
thy spouse, so bright and c. 185:20
to friendship c. 125:4
[Turks]..shall..c. out 222:35
twilights..more c. than our mid-day 186:14
weder ginneth c. 138:28
Cleared: harbour c. 148:21
if this were only c. away 130:12
sweet, when they've c. away 121:18
Clearer: thinner, c., farther going 538:15
Clearest gods..have preserved thee 454:5
Clearing the world of its..problems 178:10

Clearing-house of the world 135:4
Clearly: fire..burns but more c. 585:4
Clears: little water c. us of this deed 458:16
Cleave: c. ever to the sunnier side 527:22
  c. the general ear 433:32
  c. the wood and there am I 9:12
  c. thou thy way 335:28
  c. to her 530:14
  c. unto his wife 44:18
  too weak to c. 147:9
Cleaving: oak-c. thunderbolts 453:5
Cleek: foozling with his c. 228:10
Cleft: c. for me 548:11
  thou hast c. my heart in twain 436:4
  who c. the Devil's foot 186:16
Clementine: oh my darling C.! 355:22
Clenches: comic wit degenerating into c. 194:6
Cleopatra: bear such idleness..as C. this 423:38
  gone to gaze on C. too 424:7
  I will be C. 425:7
  pleased with less than C. 191:17
  since C. died 425:23
  some squeaking C. boy my greatness 426:4
  swallows have built in C.'s sails 425:16
  though in the bed of C. 85:20
  your C.; Dolabella's C.; every man's C. 191:21
Cléopâtre: nez de C...plus court 373:22
Clercs: trahison des c. 42:15
Clergy: I never saw..the c...beloved 520:37
  Popish liturgy, and an Arminian c. 379:7
  truth..a virtue with the Roman c. 294:4
  without the benefit o' the C. 155:10
Clergyman: certain class of c. 527:17
  good enough to be a c. 272:11
  Mr. Wilkinson, a c. 208:1
  proud c. 204:10
  that good man, the c. 536:27
Clergymen: men, women, and c. 504:31
  with c. to do as little 188:34
Cleric before and Lay behind 110:34
Clerical: lissom, c., printless toe 84:11
Clerk: am I both priest and c.? 475:18
  'baccy for the C. 301:18
  c...his father's soul to cross 385:21
  C. Saunders and may Margaret 30:15
  C. ther was of Oxenford 137:5
  like unletter'd c. 487:19
  no difference 'twixt the Priest and C. 246:12
  scarce less illustrious..the c. 160:38
  this one upstart c. 242:21
  thought he saw a Banker's C. 128:18
  Venus c., Ovyde 138:15
Clerks: gretteste c. 138:1
Clermont: broke his heart in C. town 40:18
Clever: c. men at Oxford 228:17
  good are so harsh to the c. 572:23
  if young hearts were not so c. 263:18
  it's c., but is it Art? 295:15
  let the c. ones learn Latin 144:16
  let who can be c. 293:7
  manage a c. man 304:38
  people suppose me c. 97:29
  some parts were c. 11:7
  very c. woman to manage a fool 304:38
  you..c. to a fault 89:34
Client: but here..is our c. 188:14
Cliff: from c. and scar 538:15
  Helicon breaks down in c. 15:15
  in a coign of the c. 523:17
Cliff-edge: cloaks the white c. 302:8
Cliffs: c. I never more must see 323:9
  c. which had been rent asunder 150:27
  down cloudy c. 18:16
  solitary c. wheeled by me 575:26
Cliff-top has a carpet 80:14
Climate: c. more uncertain 154:26
  cold c...damp my intended wing 349:6
  more common where the c.'s sultry 115:19
  much difference..either in the c. or the company 276:19

Climate (cont.)
  our chilling c. hardly bears.. bays 521:15
Climates: manners, c., councils, governments 540:32
Climax of all human ills 115:40
Climb: c. not at all 198:8, 405:11
  c. out..of his own character 358:16
  could we but c. 562:17
  crossed the nadir and begins to c. 264:2
  do their best to c. 94:25
  fain would I c. 198:8, 405:11
  intrude and c. into the fold 342:27
  on whose last steps I c. 494:18
  she can teach ye how to c. 341:5
Climbed: I c. a hill 249:13
Climber: whereto the c.-upward 449:3
  young c. up of knees 308:10
Climbest: with how sad steps..c. the skies 501:24
Climbing: c., shakes his dewy wings 169:13
  still c. after knowledge infinite 330:28
  thou c. sorrow 452:37
Climbs: who c. with toil 39:4
Clime: c. of the unforgotten brave 117:37
  deeds that are done in their c. 113:1
  happy fire-side c. 104:23
  in ev'ry c. adored 386:29
  in some brighter c. 33:14
  no season knows nor c. 186:20
  that sweet golden c. 76:7
  this the soil, the c. 344:21
  thro' every..undiscover'd c. 231:3
Climes: as in northern c., obscurely bright 115:8
  cloudless c. and starry skies 119:1
  warmer c. give brighter plumage 308:17
Cling: c. with life to the maid 199:13
  I'll c. to you 339:10
  makes them c. together 579:9
  risen stars and the fallen c. to her 521:30(-522)
  sea-fogs lap and c. 302:10
Clinging: are they c. to their crosses? 140:1
  blood-thirsty c. to life 19:9
  c. Heaven by the hems 545:1
  c. like cerements 252:12
  hopeless hand was c. 87:38
Clings: as creeping ivy c. 161:30
Clink: I'm here in the C. 295:3
  let me the canakin c. 471:9
  thame quha mycht do c. it best 187:4
  why c. the cannikin? 91:27
Clip: philosophy will c. an Angel's wings 286:42
Clive: C...good thing to sit by 274:18
  what I like about C. 42:25
Cliveden: in C.'s proud alcove 385:1
Cloak: c. of grey 18:8
  his martial c. around him 572:12
  not alone my inky c. 430:30
  not dissemble nor c. them 388:7
  put thy old c. about thee 6:26
  to c. them, lied 300:18
  travel forth without my c. 486:30
  with the knyf under the c. 137:32
Cloaked: Shadow c. from head to foot 532:17
Cloaks: in their scarlet c. and surplices 310:23
Clock: c. in the belfry strikes one 583:8
  forgot to wind up the c.? 513:1
  fought a long hour by Shrewsbury c. 441:4
  I open with a c. striking 499:29
  look at the c.! 34:30
  mouse ran up the c. 367:3
  stands the Church c. 84:15
  time runs, the c. will strike 330:7
  turned into a sort of c. 266:21
  varnish'd c. that click'd 225:3
  watch the c. for you 487:7
  what hour o' th' day the c. doth strike 110:10
  what o'c. I say it is 479:10
Clocks: as the c. were striking the hour 315:27
  black silk with gold c. 219:12
  morning c. will ring 262:12

Clock-setter: old Time the c. 447:30
Clod: before the heavy c. weighs on me 540:17
  make an account of her life to a c. 468:8
  to become a kneaded c. 462:9
Clodius: to live like C. 117:22
Clods: calcine its c. 90:20
  only a man harrowing c. 236:14
Clog: biting..at the c. of his body 212:16
  c. the foot of a flea 484:2
Clogs: c. of that which else might oversoar 497:12
  to quit their c. 351:18
Cloister: walk the studious c.'s pale 341:23
Cloistered: fugitive and c. virtue 352:9
  immensity c. in thy dear womb 185:10
Cloisters: in quiet collegiate c. 146:12
Cloistress: like a c., she will veiled walk 481:32
Clomb: so c. this first grand thief 347:3
Clooth-na-Bare: grave of C. 585:7
Clootie: Satan, Nick, or C. 104:4
Close: argument's hot to the c. 93:17
  as truly loves on to the c. 356:13
  at c. of day..sweetest 121:18
  breathless hush in the C. tonight 363:4
  c. against the sky 253:2
  c., and..rather true 336:5
  c. behind him tread 150:2
  c. thy Byron 127:19
  c. up his eyes 445:32
  c. up these barren leaves 581:16
  c. with her, kiss her 525:29
  c. your eyes with holy dread 151:33(-152)
  each evening sees it c. 318:13
  ever best found in the c. 351:7
  grossly c. it in 465:14
  keep themselves c. 395:14
  never found his earthly c. 535:14
  she'll c. and be herself 459:4
  stand c. around 308:22
  stick c. to your desks 221:18
  stick more c. than a brother 302:17
  still hasten to a c. 159:16
  swift to its c. 322:1
  they c., in clouds of smoke 418:20
  walking c. at hand 130:12
Close-companioned inarticulate hour 410:30
Closed: c. his eyes in endless night 231:13
  c. up the flesh 44:16
  Love c. what he begat 336:35
Closer: c. is he than breathing 529:38
  for a c. walk with God 161:1
  sticketh c. than a brother 50:22
Closes: blown fields or flowerful c. 524:28
  c. from behind 150:1
Closet: not in a c. 139:9
  one by one back in the C. lays 206:28, 29
Closing: c. full in Man 191:35
  c. up truth to truth 352:11
  Innocence is c. up his eyes 189:20
Close-lipp'd Patience 18:13
Clot: dingiest c. 544:29
Cloth: choose one c. for ever 358:12
  c. of gold and satins rare 218:29
  coarse c. she saw 165:7
  fair white linen c. 390:3
  for c. of gold you cease to care 218:29
  her pavilion—c. of gold of tissue 424:6
  on a c. untrue 220:6
Clothe: care no more to c. and eat 430:1
  humility may c. an English dean 164:14
Clothed: apes, though c. in scarlet 281:4
  c., and in his right mind 60:58
  c. in reason's garb 345:22
  c. in purple nor in pall 5:16
  c. in white samite 529:42
  c. most gorgeously 55:32
  c. on with chastity 529:27
  c. with derision 522:7
  c. with his breath 531:32
  c. with the light of the night 524:14
  c. with transcendent brightness 344:11
  housed, c., fed, and educated 413:23

Clothed (cont.)
man c. in soft raiment? 59:6
my soul..c. itself 495:26
naked, and ye c. me 60:33
Saul, who c. you in scarlet 47:30
till you are c. with the heavens 548:13
Clothes: brushers of noblemen's c. 24:41
c...thrown on her with a pitch-fork 520:17
c. you wear—or do not wear 140:3
donn'd his c. 436:23
fine c. are good only.. 273:3
hanging out the c. 368:20
her c. spread wide 437:1
his c. not be burned 49:49
in c. a wantonness 246:4
liquefaction of her c. 247:13
nothing to wear but c. 292:14
old c. look..as weel's the new 104:34
some upo' their c. 106:11
spoiling her nice new c. 367:17
walked away with their c. 180:16
when he put on his c. 225:19
witnesses laid down their c. 64:34
Clothes-horses: mere human c. 126:37
Clothing: c. for the soul divine 73:24
c. of delight, softest c., woolly, bright 76:10
her c. is of wrought gold 394:25
in sheep's c. 58:25
things in books' c. 306:27
Cloths: dim and the dark c. 584:17
heaven's embroidered c. 584:17
one of these c. is heaven 358:23
spread the c. under your feet 584:17
Cloud: choose a firm c. 384:29
c. instead and ever-during dark 346:20
c. may stoop 539:1
c. that's dragonish 425:19
dark tremendous sea of c. 94:26
did a sable c. turn forth her.. lining? 340:12
do you see yonder c.? 435:26
entrails of yon labouring c. 330:9
fair luminous c. 151:5
fiend hid in a c. 76:8
from c. and from crag 492:20
he melted like a c. 539:19
if I were a swift c. 406:10
if you saw some western c. 92:33
joy the luminous c. 151:6
lonely as a c. 577:5
no c. was in the sky 130:11
on a c. I saw a child 76:9
one silvery c. had lost his way 537:31
overcome us like a summer's c. 459:22
pillar of a c. 45:50
region c. hath masked him 486:28
set my bow in the c. 44:44
she faded, like a c. 491:20
silver towers of battlemented c. 495:27
so fades a summer c. away 33:10
so great a c. of witnesses 69:18
stooping through a fleecy c. 341:14
there ariseth a little c. 48:5
thickest c. earth ever stretched 89:22
through the dark c. shining 210:4
turn the dark c. inside out 210:4
war's annals will c. into night 236:14
wave, a leaf, a c. 496:10
were I a c. 80:16
what a scowl of c. 97:13
when the c. is scattered 494:20
you could not see a c. 130:11
Cloud-capped towers 480:8
Cloud-continents of sunset-seas 3:12
Clouded: moon rising in c. majesty 347:19
my mind is c. with a doubt 531:37
Clouden: sounding C.'s woods amang 104:29
Cloud-encircled meteor 495:10
Cloud-kissing Ilion 486:8
Cloudless climes and starry skies 119:1
Clouds: after watery c. 310:7
Being that is in the c. and air 575:13
breaking like thin c. 323:6
certain spots and c. in the sun 109:15
c. and eclipses stain 486:31
c. are lightly curl'd 535:19
c. dispell'd 193:38
c. like wool 334:6

Clouds (cont.)
c. that gather round the setting sun 576:22
c. they are without water 70:19
c. ye so much dread 161:18
dream of waves, flowers, c. 493:14
dying c. contend with growing light 445:44
heaven is free from c. 114:6
heavily in c. brings on the day 1:13
he comes with c. descending 565:13
he cometh with c. 70:22
he that regardeth the c. 51:29
in a robe of c. 118:7
in c. of smoke and dust 418:29
looks in the c. 449:3
maketh the c. his chariot 398:8
never doubted c. would break 97:4
night's swift dragons cut the c. 467:10
no pity sitting in the c.? 478:30
nor the c. return 51:33
O c., unfold! 75:16
o'er heaven the white c. stray 82:7
or in c. hide them 158:17
pack, c., away 248:5
radiant lines of morning through the c. 497:9
rapid c. have drank the last pale beam 498:26
sees God in c. 383:11
ships..dropping from the c. 546:15
sun..through the darkest c. 479:9
sweep the c. no more 251:5
this tumult in the c. 584:21
those thin c. above 151:1
through rolling c. to soar 117:25
thy c. drop fatness 395:30
trailing c. of glory 576:9
very shadows of the c. 573:1
wait till the c. roll by 572:20
white c. build in the breezy sky 82:13
white c. on the wing 4:19
white c. scud between 80:14
with..clamour in the slippery c. 442:1
with what motion moved the c. 579:8
Cloud-topped: beyond the c. hill 383:11
Cloudy: among her c. trophies hung 287:21
c. skirts with brede ethereal wove 153:24
my wishes' c. character 166:21
sees a little better in a c. day 200:3
skies are not c. all day 248:9
Clough: poor poet named C. 523:9
Clouts: stones and c. make martyrs 87:5
Clover: bee has quit the c. 298:26
cowslip, burnet and green c. 445:11
knee deep in c. 307:21
where the c. and corn lay sleeping 293:20
Cloves: nutmegs and ginger, cinamon and c. 37:25
Clown: by emperor and c. 288:1
Cloy: c. the hungry edge of appetite 474:20
of all meats the soonest c. 158:12
other women c. the appetites 424:9
Cloyment: suffer surfeit, c., and revolt 483:9
Club: best c. in London 178:14
I call the c. to session 41:19
on c. note-paper 542:30
what they c. for at book clubs 307:23
Clubable: Boswell is a very c. man 275:16
Clubs typical of strife 163:29
Cluck'd thee to the wars 429:22
Clumsy: all is vulgar, all c. 147:18
Clung: breast to breast we c. 410:26
Clusium: Lars Porsena of C. 323:10
Clusters: luscious c. of the vine 332:17
Clutch: clawed me in his c. 552:15
come, let me c. thee 457:20
either hand may rightly c. 295:5
inapprehensible, we c. thee 545:1
in the fell c. of circumstance 241:18
to seize and c. and penetrate 197:34
Clutched: he c. a cringing Jew 141:26
Clutching: still c. the inviolable shade 18:15
Clytemnestra: moral C. of thy lord 118:25

Coach: come, my c.! 436:24
delighted with my bauble c. 160:30
drive a c...through the Act of Settlement 406:21
for the rattling of a c. 186:32
indifference and a c. and six 154:6
Coaches: in c. trouble ev'ry street 189:19
Coach-house: cottage with a double c. 151:11, 507:21
Coach-makers: fairies' c. 477:7
Coachman..on the very amicablest terms 179:34
Coal: best sun..of Newcastle c. 558:21
close by whose living c. 247:17
it is a fire, it is a c. 377:3
like a c. his eye-ball 503:5
like a living c. his heart 317:25
whole world turn to c. 245:14
with England's own c. 294:34
Coal-barges: ten dark c. 504:2
Coalitions: England does not love c. 180:23
Coals: c. of fire upon his head 50:35
'e'll be squattin' on the c. 297:5
hot burning c. 399:24
I sleep on the c. 174:19
mercy blows the c. 508:15
my c. is spent 8:13
Coarse: c. complexions and cheeks of sorry grain 340:38
familiar but not c. 278:9
his speech was c. 300:18
one of them is rather c. 7:6
Coarse-bred son of a livery stable keeper 584:14
Coarsely kind 275:1
Coarser pleasures of my boyish days 581:26
Coast: as I near the shadowy c. 545:2
from ocean's farthest c. 264:10
on the c. of Coromandel 311:12, 324:34
to far India's c. 215:42
Coaster: dirty British c. 333:21
saw the merry Grecian c. come 18:1
Coastwise lights of England 295:12
Coat: brown c. 325:28, 32
c. of many colours 45:12
he did not wear his scarlet c. 569:1
her c. is so warm 367:8
his c. was red 507:20
hold my c. and snicker 197:20
loves a scarlet c. 252:31
my c. from the tailor 227:28
oars, and c., and badge 173:14
take off your c., grind paint 199:33
with his c. so gray 229:16
Coat armour: in whose c. richly are displayed..flowers 509:6
Coats: bound in their c. 55:40
hole in a' your c. 107:21
in kingly-flashing c. 336:38
in their gold c. spots 466:34
kilted her c. o' green satin 9:16
make my small elves c. 466:42
their c. were brushed 130:13
what adders came to shed their c. 523:11
Coats-of-arms: worth a hundred c. 533:36
Coax: to keep counsel, to comfort, to c. 421:8
Coaxing onaisy ones 229:15
Cob was the strongest 34:33
Cobbett and Junius..a Cavanagh 240:7
Cobbleigh: old uncle Tom C. and all 33:1
Cobham: you, brave C.! 384:27
Cobourg: illustrative of the history of..C. 145:30
Cobweb: learning, that c. of the brain 110:35
Cobwebs: c. of the schools 163:36
laws..like c. 25:1, 519:7
Cock: before the c. crow 60:39
C. and a Bull 513:24
c.'s shrill clarion 229:31
c. that crowed in the morn 369:6
c. up your beaver 250:18
c. who thought the sun had risen 196:13

Cock (*cont.*)
c. with lively din 341:32
faded on the crowing of the c. 430:20
immediately the c. crew 60:47
more wondrous..the c. and hen 74:8
plump head-waiter at the C. 541:20
we owe a c. to Aesculapius 506:10
yond..bark diminish'd to her c. 454:3
Cock-a-doodle-doo: c.! 366:12
hark, hark! I hear..c. 479:28
Cockatrice: his hand on the c.' den 53:19
Cocking: a c. their medical eyes 180:1
Cockle: by his c. hat and staff 436:19
silver bells, and c. shells 367:21
springen c. in our clene corn 138:3
Cockled: tender horns of c. snails 455:22
Cockles: crying, C. and mussels 7:8
Cockney impudence 412:22
Cockpit: this c. hold the vasty fields 443:4
Cocks: drench'd our steeples, drown'd the c. 453:5
haughtily he c. his nose 520:53
Cocksure: as o. of anything 335:13
Cocktails: gave her c. and wine 10:25
Cockyolybirds: all the butterflies and c. 294:10
Cocoa is a cad..a vulgar beast 142:9
Cocqcigrues: till the coming of the C. 294:11
Cod: c.'s head for the salmon's tail 470:20
home of the bean and the c. 79:2
Coddle: I would not c. the child 271:32
Codlin's the friend, not Short 177:30
Codling when 'tis almost an apple 482:17
Coeli: et ruant c. 561:2
Coelitus: emitte c. lucis tuae radium 310:9
Coelum: Dei sedes..c., et virtus 320:26
Coepit: qui c. 256:25
Co-eternal: consubstantial, c. 361:14
of th' Eternal c. beam 346:18
Cœur: a c. a ses raisons 374:4
grandes pensées viennent du c. 552:14
Co-exist: two master-passions cannot c. 123:8
Coffee: always put mud into c. 542:12
for c., tea, chocolate 13:17
if this is c., I want tea 403:39
measured out my life with c. spoons 197:18
tea and c. and other slop-kettle 147:16
Coffee-house: to some c. I stray 231:28
Coffee-room: if you dined in the c. 178:26
Coffer: but litel gold in c. 137:6
Coffin: becomes his c. prodigiously 226:32
c. clapt in a canoe 112:33
not a flower..on my black c. 483:6
white-faced and still in the c. 567:5
Cogging: some c. cozening slave 473:1
Cogibundity of cogitation 125:13
Cogimur: omnes eodem c. 259:4
Cogitation: cogibundity of c. 125:13
Cogitations: interpreter of the c. 56:45
Cogitative faculties immers'd 125:13
Cogito, ergo sum 172:26
Cognatione: omnes artes..quasi c. quadam 145:15
Cognizance: such c. of men and things 92:21
Cohort: to the c. of the damned 296:26
Cohorts: his c. were gleaming 118:37
Coign: buttress, nor c. of vantage 457:6
in a c. of the cliff 523:13
Coil: c. of his crystalline streams 496:8
shuffled off this mortal c. 434:4
Coiled: what c. obscene small serpents 523:11
Coin: Beauty is Nature's c. 340:37
c. his pouches wad na bide in 107:19
c. of silvery shine 131:24
C., Tiberius 183:5
pays him in his own c. 520:29
rather c. my heart 451:20
sleep..the general c. 134:18
Coin: me laissez enfin dans ce petit c. 354:2
Coincidence: long arm of c. 135:11
'strange c.' 116:23
Coiner of sweet words 17:25
Coins: like to c...stamped with the image 530:21

Coition: this trivial and vulgar way of c. 86:34
Cold: age too late, or c. climate 349:6
arrears of pain, darkness and c. 95:11
as c. as any stone 443:21
as c. a wind as ever blew 106:26
Beauty she was statue c. 208:5
blow in c. blood 490:33
boughs which shake against the c. 487:16
c. and heat, summer and winter 44:41
c., and not too cleanly, manger 166:1
c., and to temptation slow 487:24
c. and unhonour'd his relics 356:29
c. as paddocks though they be 247:15
c. charities of man to man 105:19
c., c., my girl 473:32
c. coming we had of it 197:13
c., commanded lust 297:21
c. doth not sting 361:6
c. for action 443:8
c. in the earth 83:14
c. neutrality of an impartial judge 100:18
c. on Canadian hills 310:2
c. Pastoral! 287:14
c. performs th' effect of fire 345:31
c. queen of England 141:4
c.'s the wind 170:24
c. untroubled heart of stone 122:32
c. upon dead Caesar's trencher 425:3
dull c. ear of death 230:3
dwelleth i' the c. o' the moon 90:13
even till I shrink with c. 426:29
everlasting c. 563:36
every drop of ink..ran c. 558:13
foot and hand go c. 516:21(-517)
give them the c. steel, boys 14:22
I am nothing a-c. 516:21
I beg c. comfort 448:1
in thy c. bed 292:19
it is very c. 431:30
large c. bottle..small hot bird 204:2
neither c. nor care, John 360:20
neither c. nor hot 70:34
never mourn a heart grown c. 492:7
offspring of c. hearts 102:15
owl..was a-c. 285:12
pale grew thy cheek and c. 119:29
roots..rotten, c., and drenched 289:31
she alone were c. 430:4
sleep..the c. that moderates heat 134:18
straight is c. again 451:25
thicks man's blood with c. 149:13
this living hand..if it were c. 287:3
thy blood is c. 459:19
'tis bitter c. 430:8
Tom's a-c. 453:16
to shelter me from the c. 42:7
we called a c. a c. 42:16
wert thou in the c. blast 107:24
when 'tis auld it waxeth c. 32:18
your fleece is white but 'tis too c. 166:3
Cold Bath Fields: as he passed through C. 507:22
as he went through C. 151:12
broken head in C. 326:9
Colder: c. thy kiss 119:29
pleasanter the c. 111:24
seas c. than the Hebrides 208:7
Coldly: c. furnish forth the marriage tables 431:4
c. profane 164:40
c., sadly descends the..evening 17:16
c. she turns from their gaze 356:31
Coldness: faithless c. of the times 533:20
kind deeds with c...returning 580:24
O c., ineffably gray 372:18
Cole: old King C. 368:3
Coleridge: brother C. lull the babe 117:28
shut not thy library..against S. T. C. 306:24
to lose a volume to C. 306:22
wavering like Mr. C.'s lyric prose 240:7
you will see C. 495:10
Coliander, sweet pomander 502:17
Coliseum: while stands the C., Rome shall stand 114:21
Collar: locked, lettered, braw brass c. 108:18

Collars of the moonshine's.. beams 477:7
Collateral: puff c. 499:27
Collection: true University..a c. of books 126:28
Collections: those mutilators of c. 306:21
Collector: sort of c. of religions 490:7
Collects: c.—though it does not subscribe 128:13
one of those beautiful c. 325:30
College: eighty thousand c. councils 540:28
endow a c., or a cat 384:42
I am Master of this c. 39:5
mair than either school or c. 106:12
not of this c. or of that 148:15
your rooms at c. was beastly 299:18
Colleges: for a' their c. and schools 108:21
Collegiate: in quiet c. cloisters 146:12
Collied: lightning in the c. night 466:20
Collingwood: Benbow, C., Byron 362:30
Collins: if you do *not* marry Mr. C. 22:33
Mr. C. had only to change..to Elizabeth 22:31
Colloquial: clear it from c. barbarisms 278:13
Collusive: puff c. 499:27
Cologne: at seint Jame and at C. 137:15
wash your city of C. 150:28
Colonel: Captain or C. or knight in arms 351:14
C. of the Knuts 571:17
C.'s lady and Judy O'Grady 298:6
washed the c.'s daughter 11:8
Colonies: cease to be c. because.. independent 180:29
commerce with our c. 100:23
my hold of the c. 101:10
religion most prevalent in our northern c. 100:29
Colonnade: whispering sound of the cool c. 161:23
Colonus: singer of sweet C. 16:2
Coloquintida: shortly as bitter as c. 470:31
Colori: nimium ne crede c. 555:21
Colossus: bestride the narrow world like a C. 448:22
cut a C. from a rock 275:21
Colour: by the c. of his beard 482:34
cast thy nighted c. off 430:28
giveth his c. in the cup 50:32
good dog..cannot be of a bad c. 38:17
her c. comes and goes 183:11
his c. can't be seen 9:6
his hair is of a good c. 428:13
horse of that c. 482:35
I'll swear her c. is natural 500:35
lips did from their c. fly 448:20
mystery of c. 489:21
of its own c. too 424:17
responds with c. 544:11
sky imbrued with c. 94:8
those which love c. the most 413:14
Coloured: see the c. counties 262:21(-263)
twopence c. 514:15
Colours: all c. a suffusion from that light 151:6
all c. will agree in the dark 27:34
coat of many c. 45:12
c. seen by candle-light 88:9
goodly c. gloriously array'd 509:6
Heaven..of all c. seems to be 114:6
he turn'd all c. 119:25
his c. laid so thick 192:17
oldest c. have faded 303:19
temptation comes to us in gay, fine c. 242:5
their c...to me an appetite 581:26
under whose c. he had fought so long 475:16
wrapt his c. round his breast 241:9
wrought about with divers c. 394:23
your c. dont quite match your face 20:28
Colour-sergeant: C. of the Nonpareil battalion 174:5
C. said 295:19
Colt: I hadde alwey a c.'s tooth 138:8
oft a ragged c. 105:12
Columbas: vexat censura c. 283:1
Columbia: Hail, C.! happy land! 255:13

INDEX

Columbine: c. commendable 502:19
Pink and purple C. 510:23
Column: fifth c. 353:7
fountain's silvery c. 152:8
London's c. 385:2
now is the stately c. broke 418:4
six-foot c. of fop 253:8
urn throws up a steamy c. 163:21
Columna: quinta c. 353:7
Columnae: non concessere c. 256:12
Comae: arboribusque c. 260:24
Comam: cui flavam religas c. 258:10
Comb: wherefore should I c. my
hair 32:18
with a c. and a glass 9:3
Combat: c. deepens 122:19
to c. may be glorious 163:19
Combatants: much learned dust
involves the c. 163:10
Combattu: nous avons c. à Arques 242:2
Combe: cowslips from a Devon c. 296:15
Combinations: licentious idioms
and irregular c. 278:13
Combine: c. your hearts in one 445:16
when bad men c. 101:36
Combined: all c. in beauty's
worthiness 331:2
Combs: c. its silver wings 332:20
their gowd c. in their hair 32:2
Combustion: dire c. and confus'd
events 458:21
with hideous ruin and c. down 344:7
Come: arise and c. away 334:16
beaten men c. into their own 334:7
beds for all who c. 410:4
behold, I c. quickly 72:8
best and brightest, c. away 494:8
bid her c. forth 558:5
cannot c. again 263:14
c. again another day 368:10
c. again with joy 399:34
c. again, ye children of men 397:15
c. all to church, good people 263:2
c., all ye faithful 13:2, 369:20
c. and buy 245:21
c. and be strong 165:35
c.; and strong within us 293:16
c., and trip it as ye go 341:29
c. as the winds c. 419:4
c. away, c. away 419:2
c. away, c. away, death 483:9
c. away, O human child 586:9
c. back! c. back! 122:28
c. back, c. back, Horatius! 323:24
c., civil night 478:18
C., C., C., and make eyes at me 548:2
c., dear children, let us away 15:22
c. forth, and c. hither 55:41
c. he slow, or c. he fast 418:10
c. hither, Evan Cameron 23:29
c. hither, c. hither, c. hither 427:7
c. hither, lady fair 285:5
c. in, c. in, eternal glory..win 99:8
c. in the evening, or c. in the
morning 169:27
c. into port greatly 200:18
c. into the garden, Maud 536:9
c., let us go 245:27
c. little babe 80:8
c., long-sought 495:22
c., my Corinna 246:1
c. not near our fairy queen 466:44
c. not, when I am dead 528:21
c. one, c. all 416:26
c. out, thou bloody man 47:36
c. over into Macedonia 64:53
'C.!' said old Shellover 171:23
c. soon, soon! 495:24
c. then, my brethren 404:17
c., Thou Holy Spirit 132:1
c., thou south 52:8
c. to my arms 129:39(-130)
c. unto me 59:10
c. unto these yellow sands 479:28
c. up and see me sometime 565:22
c. uppe, Whitefoot, c. uppe,
Lightfoot 267:13
c. up.!..you hugly beast! 518:10
c. weal, c. woe 420:13
c. what c. may 456:26
c. when you're called 195:20

Come (cont.)
c. wind, c. weather 99:35
c. with old Khayyám 205:19, 206:9
c. worthy Greek, Ulysses c. 168:13
c. ye in peace here? 418:18
c., ye thankful people, c. 4:11
c. you back to Mandalay 299:10
c., you spirits 457:3
Comforter will not c. unto you 63:60
cry is still, 'They c.' 461:2
death..will c. when it will c. 449:22
dreaming on things to c. 488:2
even so, c., Lord Jesus 72:13
false, ere I c., to two or three 186:18
giant mass of things to c. 481:8
had she c. all the way for this 359:4
he never will c. again 436:35
he that should c. 59:5
husband, I c. 426:10
I c. as a thief 71:29
I c., Graymalkin! 456:3
I c., my queen 425:22
ides of March are c. 449:28
if I c. back, it is yours 362:15
if it be now, 'tis not to c. 437:34
I hear you, I will c. 263:2
I'll c. to thee by moonlight 366:3
I needed not to have c. here 135:28
let 'em all c. 305:3
let him that heareth say, C. 72:10
lo, I c. 394:13
may never c. 169:21
may not c., during our lives 179:38
my love is c. to me 409:14, 15
nay, c. up hither 411:8
nor things to c. 65:58
not..as they c., but go 244:8
nothing is there to c. 158:2
O c., O c., Emmanuel 362:6
Oh, it needn't c. to that 131:9
O Lamb of God, I c.! 198:10
one to c., and one to go 131:15
peace; away 532:39
return again, c. 171:4
rise up..and c. away 52:1
Romeo, c. forth; c. forth, thou
fearful man 478:22
shape of things to c. 565:1
softly c. and softly go 370:15
something will c. of this 173:18
Spirit and the bride say, C. 72:10
suffer me to c. to thee 565:9
tells thee I c. 292:20
that have c., that have gone 405:10
that it should c. to this! 430:33(-431)
therefore I cannot c. 62:7
they c.! they c.! 113:32
those whom never c. 320:20
Thou bidd'st me c. to Thee 198:20
thou'lt c. no more 454:26
to another, C., and he cometh 58:31
to be c.-at by the breeze 578:11
to c. in spite of sorrow 341:31
to c. unto my love 509:14
'twill c. to my father anon 21:11
until great Birnam wood..c. 460:9
very few people c. this way 312:11
was, and is, and is to c. 70:38
was, and which is to c. 70:21
we must all c. to it 179:33
what's past and what's to c. 481:27
what's to c. is still unsure 482:28
when d'you think that he'll c.
back? 300:2
when shall I c. to thee? 6:28
wherefore art thou c.? 60:45
whistle and I'll c. to you 108:28
whistle and she'll c. to you 38:13
will they c. when you do call? 439:42
will ye no c. back again? 250:19, 360:12
women c. and go 197:16
wonder what she's c. after 196:15
youth of delight, c. hither 76:6
Come-down: scandal, the incredible c. 39:25
Comedy: catastrophe of the old c. 452:21
c. to those that think 558:27
most lamentable c. 466:23
Comeliness: he hath no form nor c. 54:25
Comely: as c. or as kindly 208:29
how c. it is, and how reviving 350:36

Comely (cont.)
I am black, but c. 51:39
let thy attire be c. 321:17
spanking Jack was so c. 173:9
though all mid be c. 35:15
Comer: grasps in the c. 481:20
Comes: c. again in the morning 500:35
Demosthenes never c. un-
seasonably 325:23
hautboys breath; he c., he c. 191:3
he c. too near, that c. to be
denied 371:14
he c. with clouds descending 505:13
hope never c., that c. to all 344:9
humour'd thus, c. at the last 475:7
it all c. to the same thing 89:18
look, where it c. again 430:11
she c.! she c.! 381:26
she c. to me 549:2
who c. here? 369:17
Comes: hospes c.que corporis 233:19
Comest: rarely, rarely, c. thou 408:11
thou c., much wept for 532:13
whence c. thou, Gehazi? 48:24
when thou c. into thy kingdom 62:49
Comet: against a c.'s tail 508:1
c. of a season 114:37
glorious the c.'s train 503:6
like a c. burn'd 346:6
Cometh: blessed be he that c. 399:12
c. down from the Father of lights 69:29
c. up from the wilderness 52:22
'he c. not,' she said 535:30
he c. with clouds 70:22
him that c. to me 63:22
it c. everywhere 199:1
no man c. unto the Father 63:53
this dreamer c. 45:14
where it c. all things are 199:1
Comets: brushes of c.' hair 303:20
no c. seen 449:22
old men and c. 520:44
Comfit-maker: swear like a c.'s
wife 440:6
Comfits: children are to be deceived with c. 24:31
Comfort: all my c. of thy worth 486:32
a' the c. we're to get 108:17
any to c. me 396:19
beside the waters of c. 393:10
carry their c. about with them 196:25
c. all that mourn 55:3
c. man's distress 295:8
c. me with apples 51:45
c. of thy help 395:9
c.'s a cripple 189:2
c...the weak-hearted 389:1
c. ye, c. ye, my people 54:8
continual c. in a face 412:18
dues of fellowship and social c. 87:31
foul sluggard's c. 125:33
from ignorance our c. flows 401:33
here's my c. 479:41
I beg cold c. 448:1
I'll not, carrion c., Despair 254:19
in society c., use, and protection 24:27
look down and c. their distress 512:15
magazine of life and c. 243:19
me c. still 421:1
naught for your c. 140:13
not another c. like to this 470:31
not ecstasy but..c. 175:38
of c. no man speak 475:6
sober c. 358:1
so will I c. you 55:10
speeches that c. cruel men 141:18
sweet Spirit, c. me 247:18
they never knew c. 325:27
thy rod and thy staff c. me 393:10
tidings of c. and joy 6:12
to keep counsel, c., to coax 421:8
to warn, to c., and command 580:21
two loves..of c. and despair 488:18
what would c. the one 215:5
whence can c. spring 574:32
Comfortable: all clean and c. I sit
down 290:25
hear what c. words 390:37
no c. feel in any member 253:12
only conceive how c. they will be 23:9
some Christians have a c. creed 115:31

INDEX

Comfortably: costs a lot..to die c. 111:36
lived c. so long together 214:13
speak ye c. to Jerusalem 54:8
Comforted: folly of being c. 585:5
the Lord hath c. his people 54:23
they shall be c. 57:39
would not be c. 57:26
Comforter will not come unto you 63:60
Comforters: miserable c. are ye all 49:2
Comforteth: one whom his mother c. 55:10
Comforting: friendly and c. breast 241:20
Comfortless Despair 230:28
Comforts: adversity is not without c. and hopes 25:20
c. we despise 425:25
c. while it mocks 95:10
our loves and c. should increase 470:31(-471)
what I aspired to be..c. me 95:16
when c. are declining 161:21
when..c. flee 322:1
Comic: business of a c. poet 154:29
his c. wit degenerating into clenches 194:6
Comical: I often think it's c. 219:6
Coming: at the c. of the King of Heaven 12:7
Campbells are c. 10:9
cold c. we had of it 197:13
c. after me is preferred before me 63:2
c. down from God 71:44
c. events cast their shadows before 122:22
c. through the rye 104:31
c. to that holy room 185:25
even as their c. hither 454:18
eye will mark our c. 115:22
far off his c. shone 348:21
glory of the c. of the Lord 264:15
he is c.! he is c.! 24:6
hell..meet thee at thy c. 53:21
hold the fort, for I am c. 77:23
I'm c., I'm c. 210:17
in the c. by and by 220:33
it is on the road and c. 179:37
no more than one way of c. 520:34
she is c., my dove, my dear 536:15
sometimes c., sometimes coy 421:13
there's a good time c., boys 326:23
thy going out, and thy c. in 399:29
till the c. of the Cocqcigrues 294:11
welcome the c...guest 386:6
yours I see is c. down 492:23
Command: c. him tasks 472:26
c. my heart and me 166:17
could c. the course 210:3
even the c. from you 309:18
hast c. of every part 247:4
I may c. where I adore 483:17
I will be correspondent to c. 479:25
left that c. sole daughter of his voice 349:14
less used to sue than to c. 416:18
man to c. 538:24
more invitation than c. 511:29
move only in c. 460:31
not be able to c. the rain 377:18
not born to sue, but to c. 474:11
not in mortals to c. success 1:14
to warn, to comfort, and c. 580:21
we cannot c. nature 28:9
wide as his c. 190:8
Commanded: cold, c. lust 297:21
God so c. 349:14
woman..c. by such poor passion 425:30
Commander: I was the world's c. 455:31
whereof I am c. 12:2
Commanders: Cossack c. cannonading come 5:7
Commandment: at the c. of the Magistrate 401:13
contempt of thy Word and C. 388:49
first c. with promise 68:7
laws of England are at my c. 442:36
thy c. is exceeding broad 399:19
Commandments: fear God, and keep his c. 51:36

Commandments (cont.)
hearkened to my c. 54:20
I keep thy c. 399:20
in the path of thy c. 399:14
keep God's holy will and c. 391:2
running the way of thy c. 389:44
set my ten c. in your face 445:29
there aren't no Ten C. 299:15
went to sea with the Ten C. 461:17
Commands: c. them all 135:19
c. to some, leaves free to all 347:25
Fair c. the song 162:32
not all c. 430:2
those he c. move only in command 460:31
Commemorative: cold c. eyes 411:18
Commence: never may I c. my song 95:37
Commencement de la fin 526:19
Commencent: que MM. les assassins c. 284:8
Commences, reigns, and ends 503:2
Commend: all our swains c. her 484:40
c. to cold oblivion 493:9
forced to c. her highly 377:22
I'll c. her volubility 479:4
into thy hands I c. my spirit 62:51
to blame or to c. 385:29
virtue to c. 155:4
Commendable: columbine c. 502:19
silence is only c. 462:36
Commendation: silent c. 24:37
small matters win great c. 25:37
Commended: who c. thy yellow stockings 483:19
Commendeth: obliquely c. himself 85:14
Commends: who lavishly c. 142:28
Comment: c. is free but facts are sacred 416:4
every nice offence..his c. 451:10
none can read the c. 531:18
Commentators: as learned c. view in Homer 521:17
c. each dark passage shun 586:28
Comments: his works are the c. 290:18
Commerce: America..equal to the whole of that c. 100:22
c. with our colonies 100:23
disinterested c. between equals 226:34
in matters of c...the Dutch 124:6
let wealth and c...die 329:10
peace, c., and honest friendship 268:21
where c. long prevails 226:8
Commercial: idea of a C. Alliance with England 43:11
Commercing: looks c. with the skies 341:9
Commissariat cam-u-el 300:8
Commissary: Destiny the C. of God 186:5
Commit: c. his body to the deep 400:30
c. his body to the ground 391:44
do not adultery c. 147:1
thou shalt not c. adultery 390:14
unto God's..protection we c. thee 391:37
Committee: therefore got on a C. 141:29
Commoda: multa ferunt anni..c. 256:2
si quando c. vellet dicere 133:17
Commodities: hateful tax levied upon c. 277:27
Commodity: c. of good names 438:21
Jove, in his next c. of hair 483:22
tickling C., C., the bias of the world 447:25
Commodus: to the accession of C. 217:8
Common: adieu to c. feeling, c. prudence and c. sense 505:20
affection which grows from c. names 101:10
all things c. else 347:26
all things they have in c. 77:27
art thou base, c. and popular? 444:14
century of the c. man 557:17
c. interest always will prevail 190:27
c. love of good 533:20
c. murderer, perhaps 414:8
c. woman of c. earth 148:16
dull catalogue of c. things 286:42
earth and every c. sight 576:1
empires and cities in a c. grave 217:13
fade into the light of c. day 576:9

Common (cont.)
forgotten crowd of c. beauties 125:1
given to the c. enemy of man 458:34
good thing..make it too c. 441:24
grazed the c. of literature 271:7
I impeach the c. enemy 101:27
in c. things that round us lie 578:34
invasion of a c. enemy 305:1
I saw nought c. on Thy Earth 300:5
I walk out into a c. 370:17
nor lose the c. touch 297:12
no temptation..but such as is c. 66:38
nothing c. did or mean 332:24
not in the roll of c. men 439:41
not jump with c. spirits 463:44
of singular use for the c. people 519:3
steals a goose from off a c. 10:12
that call not thou c. 64:47
thou know'st 'tis c...Ay, madam, it is c. 430:29
throw his mind into the c. stock 223:3
touches of things c. 89:6
towered above the c. mark 273:12
to youth and age in c.—discontent 19:7
you c. people of the skies 583:13
Commonalty: joy in widest c. 574:6
very dog to the c. 429:2
Commoners: vital c. and inland petty spirits 442:21
Commonplace: common is the c. 532:5
'C.,' said Holmes 188:24
more featureless and c. a crime 187:13
provided his c. book be full 520:36
unassuming c. of Nature 573:22
Common room: Oriel C. stank of Logic 363:20
Commons: chips to the House of C. 143:31
C...in a wise..inactivity 326:28
let but the c. hear 450:24
lords and c. of this realm 103:9
Parliament, Rabble, House of C. 147:17
speak very well in the House of C. 182:47
Common sense: by the c. of readers 278:10
c...most widely shared commodity 172:27
crown'd Republic's crowning c. 539:14
experience joined with c. 231:20
man of great c. and good taste 489:11
mothers..who claim to c. 40:29
nothing astonishes..so much as c. 200:4
rarest gift to Beauty, C. 336:27
rich in saving c. 537:14
science..organised c. 266:18
sword of C. 335:24
Commonwealth: caterpillars of the c. 474:31
c. is fixed and stable 101:18
ever despaired of the C. 181:29
that no grievance..arise in the C. 352:4
Commonwealths: to raise up c. 190:11
Commune with your own heart 391:52
Communi: aliquid utilitatis pro communi 291:25
Communia: proprie c. dicere 255:24
Communicate: to do good and to c. 69:25
literature seeks to c. power.. not literature..c. knowledge 172:25
Communicated: good, the more c. 348:2
Communicatest with dreams 485:8
Communications: evil c. corrupt good manners 67:12
Communion: one c. and fellowship 389:55
Communist: what is a c.? 198:21
Community: c. of Europe 222:41
in one c., scholars and gentlemen 579:28
Compact: c...between the North and the South 213:19
of imagination all c. 467:24
Compacted: where sweets c. lie 245:13
Compagnon de la Majolaine 11:24
Compañía: el pan comido y la c. deshecha 134:10

Companion: c. in tribulation 70:23
  God send the prince a better c. 441:22
  last C.: Wine 42:2
  leave of an old and agreeable c. 217:3
  mortified appetite is never a wise c. 513:34
  only fit c...his horse 159:22
  poor, earth-born c. 107:10
  sole c. of his way 37:5
Companioned: close-c. inarticulate hour 410:30
Companionless: wandering c. 495:19
Companions: all her lovely c. 356:36
  c. for middle age 26:37
  c. of our woe 559:6
  hardihood, endurance, and courage of my c. 416:7
  his best c. innocence and health 224:14
  I have had c. 308:1
  old c. in adversity 98:4
  that such c. thou'dst unfold 473:2
  those C. true 124:17
  while their c. slept 316:31
Company: always except the present c. 370:7
  bewitched with the rogue's c. 439:2
  c. of all faithful people 390:46
  c. of the preachers 396:7
  c., villainous c...the spoil of me 440:12
  crowd is not c. 26:16
  crowds without c. 216:27
  give me your bill of c. 519:28
  good c. and good discourse 559:17
  Honest Man in much C. 158:23
  how..good c. improves a woman! 203:16
  in c. with Pain 575:6
  in jail..better c. 270:32
  in married life three is c. 569:21
  innumerable c. of the heavenly host 74:6
  in sooth a goodly c. 34:8
  in such a jocund c. 577:7
  in whose c. I delight myself 99:40
  much difference..either in the climate or the c. 276:19
  Muffin and Crumpet..C. 176:37
  never expected justice from a c. 505:5
  proper subject..in a mixed c. 139:33
  separate from the pleasure of your c. 307:3
  to bear him c. 318:14
  tone of the c. that you are in 139:13
  true brother of a c. 586:14
  Vandyke is of the c. 212:21
  very good c., and of a very ready ..wit 21:13
  we were a gallant c. 114:39
  we would not die in that man's c. 444:28
  with a goodly c. 150:15
  with all the c. of heaven 390:39
  with hounds and horsemen, a brave c. 78:1
  withouten any c. 137:34
  withouten other c. in youthe 137:15
Compare: belied with false c. 488:14
  c. thee to a summer's day 486:18
  how I may c. this prison 475:33
  I will not Reason and C. 75:2
  no land can c. unto thee 489:1
  none that can c. 9:24
  to c. great things with small 346:13
Comparison: for the c. of all 281:15
  in whose c. all whites are ink 480:39
Comparisons: c. are odorous 468:43
  c. doon offte gret grevaunce 321:11
  confronted him with self-c. 456:9
  exciting emulation and c. of superiority 269:33
  she, and c. are odious 184:15
Compass: all the c. of the notes 191:35
  c. lost 160:35
  c. of the world 393:11
  my heart..the faithful c. 215:40
  my life is run his c. 451:39
  narrow c. 558:1
  though a wide c. round be fetched 89:22
  to the top of my c. 435:24
  we the globe can c. soon 467:19

Compass (cont.)
  within his bending sickle's c. come 488:7
Compassed: c. about with..a cloud of witnesses 69:18
  c. by the inviolate sea 539:13
  with dangers c. round 348:23
Compasses: as stiff twin c. are two 186:25
  sun to course two hundred c. 472:16
Compassion: Curate..something which excites c. 505:21
  shutteth up his bowels of c. 70:11
  the Lord is full of c. 56:30
Compatriot: Wolfe's great name c. with his own 163:1
Compel: c. thee to go a mile 57:51
  c. them to come in 62:9
Compendious: portable, and c. oceans 166:10
Compensate: nor good c. bad 96:14
Compensation: no c. for a belly-ache 304:24
Competence: debtless c., golden mean 541:5
Competency lives longer 463:6
Competent: which the soul is c. to gain 574:17
Competing: pressed upon by..c. populations 200:3
Competition: all forms of c. 147:3
  anarchy and c. 413:27
  no c., no vanity 272:30
Complain: birds c. 231:18
  by the tide of Humber would c. 333:8
  farmers..flourish and c. 165:3
  I heard him c. 562:3
  never c. and never explain 181:25
  to c. of the age we live in 101:33
  to the moon c. 229:29
  when mine fail me, I'll c. 93:25
Complained: conduct c. of 187:15
Complainers: loudest c. for the public 102:2
Complaining: my daily c. 393:31
  no c. in our streets 400:17
  soft c. lute 191:38
  voice of c. 359:6
Complaint: instead of dirges this c. 292:18
  Lord, it is my chief c. 161:13
  nightingale's c. 494:7
  voice of my c. 393:1
Complaints: what needs c.? 245:22
  when c. are freely heard 352:4
Complete: again in c. steel 431:32 (-432)
  arm'd with more than c. steel 7:7, 331:9
  behold them raised, c. 88:14
  clad in c. steel 340:22
  death c. the same 95:26
  experience..is never c. 268:12
  in herself c. 349:1
  mine I saved and hold c. 93:25
  pestilent c. knave 471:2
  pure and c. sorrow..impossible 548:8
  this is not a c. education 182:19
Completeness: unities..are a c. 177:18
Complexion: his c. is perfect gallows 479:16
  his gold c. dimm'd 486:18
  mislike me not for my c. 463:26
  of what c. soever 466:13
  take care of their..c. 22:18
  tawny c., a bad liver 324:30
  that schoolgirl c. 10:4
  turn thy c. there 472:34
  whose fresh c...affliction alters 485:33
Complexions: coarse c. and cheeks of sorry grain 340:38
Compliance: by a timely c. prevented him 204:14
Complicated: c. monsters 349:21
  your c. state of mind 220:26
Complications of existence 268:8
Complies: he that c. against his will 111:18
Compliment: farewell c. 477:19
  lowly feigning..called c. 483:26
  to return the c. 221:12
Comply: so backward to c. 161:6
Complying: gentle, c., and bland 225:34
Compose: could but c. man's image 586:7

Composed: cruel, but c. and bland 17:13
Composer: contemplation of the first C. 86:33
Composition: mad kings! mad c.! 447:24
  more c. and fierce quality 452:14
Compound: c. for sins they are inclin'd to 110:20
  thou and I..c. a boy 445:14
Compounded: c. of many simples 428:16
  this foolish-c. clay 441:11
Comprehend: c. all vagrom men 468:36
  c. its mystery 317:15
  c. the wondrous Architecture 330:28
  she begins to c. it 401:25
Comprehended: darkness c. it not 62:60
Comprehending much in few words 57:7
Comprehends some bringer of that joy 467:24
Comprehensive: largest and most c. soul 194:6
Comprendre: tout c. 511:9
Compressed in thirty-five volumes 358:18
Compromise: Church of England ..a c. 501:10
  give me the Brown c. 265:1
  Man accepts the c. 296:14
Compt: when we shall meet at c. 473:32
Compulsion: fools by heavenly c. 452:18
  I will give no man a reason upon c. 439:24
  made happy by c. 152:15
  on what c. must I? 464:33
  sweet c. doth in music lie 339:26
Compunction: whose feelings were wrung with c. 312:16
Compunctionem: opto magis sentire c. 291:19
Comrade: c. of thy wanderings over heaven 496:10
  each new-hatch'd, unfledg'd c. 431:25
  no c. Lucy knew 577:18
Comrades: dear love of c. 566:24
  help our French c. 305:1
  your c. chase..the fliers 147:8
Comus, and his midnight crew 231:1
Comyn: I have slain the Red C. 420:21
Con: taken great pains to c. it 482:18
Concatenation: fearful c. of circumstances 563:9
  in a c. accordingly 227:4
Concave: in her c. shores 448:9
  shout that tore hell's c. 345:1
Conceal: addresses..to c. our whereabouts 414:15
  always able to c. it 550:21
  c. him by naming him Smith 251:21
  use of speech..to c. 226:26
  words..half c. the Soul 532:3
  yet cannot all c. 114:27
Concealed: author..c. behind the door 271:2
  considerbul licker c. about my persun 560:13
  in yon smoke c. 147:8
Concealing: hazard of c. 105:19
Concealment, like a worm i' the bud 483:10
Concedes: what it c. to the butterflies 173:26
Conceit: c. in weakest bodies 435:52
  could never forgive any c. 194:16
  force his soul so to his own c. 433:31
  infusing him with self and vain c. 475:7
  in their high c. 199:16
  from c. divinely framed 123:17
  suiting with forms to his c. 433:31
  whose c. lies in his hamstring 481:6
  wise in his own c. 50:40
  wiser in his own c. 50:42
Conceited: never any pity for c. people 196:25
Conceits: beauty beat on his c. 331:2
  be not wise in your own c. 66:5
  our best c...the greatest liars 189:5
  words..accepted for c. 24:20
Conceive: his tongue to c. 467:23
  virgin shall c. 53:12
  whether it be the heart to c. 282:20

Conceived: genuine poetry is c...in the soul 19:20
in sin hath my mother c. me 395:8
new nation, c. in liberty 314:12
there is a man child c. 48:44
worse than..fear c. 346:3
Conceivest him not 244:7
Conceiving: c. and subduing both 331:2
our benumbed c. soars 545:1
Concentrated: more and more c. in you 290:31
Concentrates his mind wonderfully 273:22
Concentred all in self 417:22
Conception: c...fundamental brainwork 411:38
c. of some eminency in ourselves 248:24
c. that I do groan withal 473:14
dodge c. to the very bourne of heaven 284:23
Conceptions equal to the soul's desires 574:17
Concern: matter they had no c. in 521:6
Concerns: mild c. of ordinary life 575:10
think only what c. thee 348:31
Concert: saints on earth in c. sing 565:15
Concertina's melancholy string 218:9
I've a head like a c. 295:3
Concessions: c. of the weak are the c. of fear 100:21
Conciseness: accuracy..sacrificed to c. 277:20
Conclave: in stately c. met 140:24
Conclaves: kingly c. stern and cold 496:22
Conclude: c. and shut up all 87:13
c. in a moist relentment 87:2
Conclusion: denoted a foregone c. 472:9
most lame and impotent c. 470:29
other is a c. 270:25
saw men hasten to a c. 26:7
to its ultimate c. 296:14
Conclusions: art of drawing sufficient c. 111:33
draw from it narrow c. 338:22
she hath pursu'd c. infinite 426:17
Concord: author of peace and lover of c. 388:25
c. of sweet sounds 465:20
devil with devil damn'd firm c. holds 345:28
love quarrels oft in..c. end 350:34
sinews of c. 209:25
true c. of well-tuned sounds 486:14
truth, unity, and c. 390:25
unity, peace, and c. 388:53
Concordia discors 257:5
Concurrence: fortuitous c. of atoms 373:7
sweet c. of the heart 247:19
Condamner: songer à c. les gens 354:1
Condemn: c. it as an improbable fiction 484:10
c. itself for being there 460:32
c. the fault and not the actor 461:27
c. you to death 128:25
neither do I c. thee 63:27
Condemned: c. alike to groan 230:30
c. to earth for ever 91:18
man c. to bear 402:5
much c. to have an itching palm 451:10
Condemns: c. a less delinquent for't 111:26
Dr. Johnson c. whatever he disapproves 103:38
Condense: they will c. within thy soul 364:9
Condescend to men of low estate 66:5
Condition: c. of man..a c. of war 248:18
c. upon which God hath given liberty 167:26
O hard c.! 444:21
poor fools decoyed into our c.
this day shall gentle his c. 444:28(-445)
wearisome c. of humanity 232:14
whine about their c. 567:20
Conditions: all sorts and c. of men 389:15
Condolement: persever in obstinate c. 430:31
Condoned we have..c. high treason 180:39

Conduct: c. complained of 187:15
c...three-fourths of life 20:10, 12
c...to the prejudice of good order 5:26
his c. still right 225:29
nice c. of a clouded cane 385:18
on your individual c. 305:1
our c. isn't all your fancy paints 303:4
2ndly, gentlemanly c. 20:21
Conductor, when you receive a fare 83:1
Cone: inverted c. 274:2
Cones: eat the c. under his pines 212:3
firs with c. upon them 317:22
Confabulate: if birds c. or no 161:22
Confectionary: biscuit, or c. plum 160:31
Confederate: in games c. 575:23
Conference: c. a ready man 27:18
such free and friendly c. 451:8
Confess: acknowledge and c. our manifold sins 388:6
c. yourself to heaven 436:2
Confessed: by faith before the world c. 264:8
half absolv'd who has c. 401:18
Confession: bring him on to some c. 434:2
Confidence: c. is a plant of slow growth 379:4
c. of reason give 574:1
in quietness and in c. 53:39
may be expected with c. 174:37
we shall fight with growing c. 143:40
Confident: assured man, c. of success 156:11
c. thou'lt raise me 355:21
Confine: hither to his c. 430:19
put into circumscription and c. 469:38
very verge of her c. 452:39
Confined: cabin'd, cribb'd, c. 459:12
to numbers I'll not be c. 570:30
uneasy, and c. from home 383:11
Confirm: c. the feeble knees 54:2
c. the wise 164:34
planets..c. the tidings 2:27
ratify and c. the same 391:17
Confirmation, or laying on of hands 391:15
Confirmations: to the jealous c. strong 471:42
Confirmeth all He did 80:29
Confiscation: we have legalized c. 180:39
Confitentem: habes c. reum 378:10
Conflict: c. of opinions 277:5
field of human c. 144:1
too weak the c. to support 454:23
Conflux of two eternities 126:14
Conform: either c., or be more wise 377:24
Confound: c. all presents wot eat 518:24
c. and swallow navigation up 460:4
c. Romance! 298:1
c. the ignorant 433:32
c. their politics 125:16
do but themselves c. 99:36
foolish..to c. the wise..the weak..to c. the..mighty 66:20
Confounded: confusion worse c. 346:16
let me never be c. 388:19
Confounding: c. her astronomers 249:11
neither c. the Persons 388:38
what a liberal c. 306:20
Confounds: attempt..c. us 458:4
folly of the world..c...wisdom 251:23
Confront the visage of offence 435:33
Confused: assembly was c. 65:7
c. jargon of their Babylonian pulpits 102:3
deal of fine c. feedin' 85:7
thought and passion, all c. 383:22
Confusedly: ribbands to flow c. 246:4
Confusion all else c. 538:24
bright things come to c. 466:20
c. now hath made his masterpiece 458:22
c. of their own faces 55:15
c. on thy banners wait 229:20
c. worse confounded 346:16
even the dream's c. 77:30
if c. have a part 355:18
in first c. 146:32
in ruin and c. hurled 3:2
levee..in some c. 156:9

Confusion (cont.)
while we strut to our c. 425:2
Confute: c., change hands, and still c. 110:5
read not to contradict and c. 27:16
to silence, not to c. 278:21
Congratulate: friends to c. their friends 193:41
Congratulatory: series of c. regrets 181:11
Congregation: in the face of this c. 391:22
latter has the largest c. 170:11
man's c. shun 543:16
pestilent c. of vapours 433:15
Congregations: all C. committed to their charge 388:30
c. of naughty men 397:11
Congregate: where merchants most do c. 463:17
Congrès: le c. ne marche pas 313:26
Congs: Kinquering C. their titles take 511:2
Conies: stony rocks for the c. 398:10
Conjecture: entertain c. of a time 444:6
not beyond all c. 87:12
Conjectures: blown by surmises, jealousies, c. 441:8
Conjugal attraction unreprov'd 347:17
Conjunction of the mind 332:6
Conjuration: what drugs, what charms, what c. 469:45
Conjuring: Parson left c. 422:7
Connaît: il c. l'univers et ne se c. pas 209:13
Connectin'-rod: yon c. 299:3
Conned: learn'd, and c. by rote 451:24
Connexion: thy c. with Mr. Spurgeon's haberdasher 112:18
Connoisseurs: as some of your c. do 34:34
Connu: peu c. dans l'histoire 43:9
Connubial: nothing wrong in a c. kiss 115:39
rites mysterious of c. love 347:25
Connubiality: wictim o' c. 178:37
Conquer: c. him that did his master c. 424:30
conquering, and to c. 70:43
determine to die here..we will c. 39:2
easier to c. it [the East] 558:23
England..wont to c. others 474:24
go forth and c. a crown 371:1
hard to catch and c. 336:8
like Douglas c. 251:26
none but Antony should c. Antony 425:26
she stoops to c. 226:41
we c. but to save 122:6
we'll c. again and again 213:10
you cannot c. America 379:9
Conquered: chosen People never c. quite 375:27
c. and peopled half the world 421:16
c. at last 380:11
I came, I saw, I c. 120:13
I will be c. 275:30
mortal creatures, c. and secured 574:24
perpetually to be c. 100:26
thou hast c., O Galilean 282:15
thou hast c., O pale Galilean 525:8
Time, not Corydon, hath c. thee 18:27
you've c. human natur 177:3
Conquering: c., and to conquer 70:43
c. kings their titles take 135:12
in c. one..enriched both 80:29
see, the c. hero comes 358:13
so sharp the c. 138:22
Conqueror: Came-over-with-the-C. type of mind 561:13
every c. creates a Muse 558:3
great Emathian c. 351:15
its hero the C. Worm 380:15
proud foot of a c. 448:2
we came in with Richard C. 478:45
we came in with the C. 82:26
Conquers: struggles with and c. Time 309:9
that party c. 416:24
Conquest: fanned by C.'s crimson wing 229:20
not lust of c. 156:27
peace..of the nature of a c. 442:18
shameful c. of itself 474:24
what c. brings he home? 448:7

Conquests: all thy c., glories,
   triumphs   450:2
drums and tramplings of three c.   87:8
only honourable c.   101:15
spread her c. farther   104:25
where his carnage and his c.
   cease   113:4
Consanguineous: am not I c.?   482:29
Conscience: argue freely according
   to c.   352:16
'Budge not,' says my c.   463:27
catch the c. of the king   434:1
celestial fire, called c.   560:30
cheerfully for c. sake   401:1
c. avaunt   144:28
c. doth make cowards of us all   434:4
c. is a coward   227:25
c. is born of love   488:23
c. is but a word   476:41
c...no more to do with gallantry 500:12
c. of her worth   348:37
c...to the profoundest pit   436:28
c. void of offence   65:18
expect a corporation to have a
   c.?   547:15
gentle beast, and of a good c.   407:31
guardian of His Majesty's c.   547:13
health..next to a good c.   559:26
help us to save free c.   351:30
his c...too near another lady   446:14
King, as if he were their c.   530:13
made some c. of what they did   167:3
my c. hath a thousand..tongues 476:36
Nonconformist c.   39:17, 569:38
O coward c...no keep   476:35
of nyce c...no fear   137:13
still and quiet c.   446:25
strong siding champion, C.   340:10
their best c...keep't unknown   471:35
thus be c.-calmed   287:3
too young to know what c. is   488:23
very stuff o' the c.   469:36
we may live without c.   337:41
what c. dictates to be done   386:30
whereof our c. is afraid   389:45
whose c. with injustice is corrupted   445:30
Consciences: for our c., the arms.. 440:32
Conscientious: honourable, the c. 363:26
Conscious: c. of none   126:25
c. stone to beauty grew   199:23
c. water..blushed   165:25
make mankind in c. virtue bold 381:6
though c. of your innocence   273:6
Consciousness: c. the Will informing   236:6
suspended in the chamber of c. 268:12
Conscire: nil c. sibi   256:18
Consecrate: c...all thou dost shine
   upon   494:4
I c. to thee   308:12
we cannot c...this ground   314:12
Consecrated: brave men..have c. it 314:12
kind of 'c. obstruction'   28:31
not buried in c. ground   237:7
we have..c. sacrilege   180:39
Consecration, and the poet's dream 578:14
Consecutive: known for truth by c.
   reasoning   289:12
Consent: c. thou not   49:37
deep c. of all great men   413:18
I will ne'er c.   115:21
voice of Rome is the c. of heaven 279:26
without c. been only tried   371:14
Consented: c. together in holy
   wedlock   391:35
to his fate they all c.   280:10
whispering, 'I will ne'er consent,' c.   115:21
Consentedest unto him   395:5
Consenting: Saul was c. unto his
   death   64:35
Consequence: betray's in deepest
   c.   456:22
if it's business of c.   34:7
it's of no c.   175:13
trammel up the c.   457:7
wisdom in the scorn of c.   537:33
Consequences: almost inevitable
   C.   304:44
c...will be what they will be   109:37

Consequences (*cont.*)
damn the c.   339:25
know all mortal c.   460:34
logical c. are the scarecrows of
   fools   266:22
neither rewards nor punishments..c.   267:17
Consequentially: reasoned or acted
   c.   139:22
Conservation: without the means
   of its c.   102:6
Conservatism: C. discards Prescription   181:32
C...the mule of politics   181:38
what is c.?   314:7
Conservative: called the C. party 166:26
C. Government .. organized
   hypocrisy   180:18
healthy stomach..nothing if
   not c.   111:37
last C. Ministry that had real
   power   29:3
or else a little C.   219:6
sound C. government   181:33
true C...lops the moulder'd
   branch   529:33
Conservatives: c. when they are
   least vigorous..c. after dinner 200:25
Conserved of maidens' hearts   472:16
Consider: c. anything, only don't
   cry   131:1
c. her ways, and be wise   49:45
c., incline thine ear   394:23
c. it not so deeply   458:8
c. the lilies   58:13
c. this, ye that forget God   395:6
c. well..his face   540:26
doth not well c. this   397:20
in the day of adversity c.   51:13
read..to weigh and c.   27:16
stop and c.!   288:10
to c. too curiously   437:17
Considerable: appear c. in his
   native place   272:5
Considerate: dauntless courage
   and c. pride   345:7
Consideration: c. like an angel came
   for a c.   419:24
Considerations: no personal c...
   in the way   229:2
Considered: I have c. the days of
   old   396:32
when complaints are..deeply c. 352:4
Considering: put on my c. cap   37:33
Consign to thee, and come to dust 430:1
Consigned: to ourselves in every
   place c.   278:29
Consili: vis c. expers   259:28
Consiliis: misce stultitiam c. brevem 261:5
Consistency: c...hobgoblin of
   little minds..with a great
   soul..nothing to do   200:40
Consolation: son of c.   64:30
that's one c.   178:39
with peace and c. hath dismissed 351:7
Console us when we fall   100:15
Consoler: Death, the c.   316:16
Consolidates society   276:12
Consort: full c. to th' angelic
   symphony   343:17
with such c. as they meet   341:22
Consorts and sympathiseth with all
   things   86:25
Conspicuous: c. by its presence 414:2
c. object in a Nation's eye   575:11
Conspiracies against the laity   489:20
Conspiracy: c. against the man-
   hood   200:38
c. of our spacious song   165:35
O c.! sham'st thou?   449:6
open-ey'd c.   479:37
Conspire: could thou and I with
   Fate c.   207:26
could you and I with Him c. 207:27
Conspired against our God   330:1
Conspirers: or where c. are   460:9
Conspiring with him how to load
   and bless   284:10
Constable: fit man for the c. of the
   watch   468:35
outrun the c. at last   110:37

Constabulary: when c. duty's to be
   done   221:34
Constancy: but c. in a good   86:14
c. alone is strange   407:16
c. lives in realms above   150:26
c. of the women who love me 490:41
c. to a bad, ugly woman   119:19
dearest her c.   233:1
grand c. of Clement Shorter 141:31
hope c. in wind   117:13
let him in c. follow   99:35
no object worth its c.   495:19
O c.! be strong   449:27
stablish dangerous c.   185:29
wouldst thou approve thy c. 349:10
Constant: as c. as the northern
   star   449:30
change is c.   180:37
c., but yet a woman   439:11
c. Cimber should be banished 449:30
c. do remain to keep him so 449:30
c. in nothing but inconstancy 35:20
friendship is c. in all other
   things   468:12
growing or full c. light   185:31
if thou wilt be c. then   355:20
no restoratives like to a c. woman 209:25
nothing..c., but inconstancy 519:8
one here will c. be   99:35
only c. mourner   117:39
sense of a c. infelicity   527:13
she is so c. to me   285:4
such a c. lover   517:18
to be c...were inconstancy 158:11
to one thing c. never   468:20
were man but c.   485:2
with c. drinking fresh and fair 158:7
Constantinople: go to C., and take
   the Turk   445:14
Patriarch of C.   152:27
Russians shall not have C. 265:15
Constellated flower that never sets 497:21
Constellations: c. any nearer   568:4
foreign c. west   235:19
Constet: et sibi c.   255:24
Constituted the services of Angels 389:54
Constitution: authority and credit
   from..our c.   101:17
c. is extremely well   558:22
C. is the game for you   141:20
higher law than the c.   422:23
I invoke the genius of the C. 379:10
of a c. so general   86:25
principles of a free c.   217:6
suit full well my c.   7:10
very essence of the c.   282:17
Constitutional: no eyes but c. eyes 314:16
symptom of c. liberty   217:10
Constitutions: talk of C.   123:1
Constrain thy..spirit into bonds 160:34
Constrained: by violence c. to do
   anything   198:3
Constraineth: love of Christ c.
   us   67:26
spirit within me c. me   49:13
Constraint: all c...is evil   163:45
beauty by c. possessing   214:9
bitter c. and sad occasion dear 342:10
Constructing tribal lays   297:9
Construction: find the mind's c. in
   the face   456:27(-457)
Constructions: decorating her c. 549:14
Construe: c. things after their own
   fashion   448:34
no purpose to c. the Constitution   314:9
Consubstantial, co-eternal   361:14
Consul's brow was sad   323:16
Consule: natam me c.   145:24
non ego hoc ferrem..c. Planco 260:8
Consult Brother Jonathan   560:31
Consults them about..serious
   matters   139:23
Consume: c. away like a snail 395:21
c. happiness without producing
   it   489:12
his beauty to c. away   394:10
Consumed: bush was not c.   45:33
my bones c. away   393:31
partly c. by regret   312:17
Consumedly: they laughed c. 203:11

Consummation: c. devoutly to be
  wished   434:4
  quiet c. have   430:1
  she waits the c.   517:3
Consumption: this c. of the purse   441:26
Consumptive: lingring and c.
  passion   202:2
Contagion: c. of the world's slow
  stain   492:7
  foul c. spread   342:29
  vile c. of the night   449:15
Contagious: most c. game   336:24
Contain: show, c., and nourish all
  the world   455:23
  stating what it is to c.   270:25
Contaminate our fingers with base
  bribes   451:12
Contemneth small things   56:47
Contemplate: let us c. existence   176:14
Contemplates: mind which c.   265:5
  thing it c.   497:17
Contemplation: beneath thy c.
  sink heart and voice   362:1
  Cherub C.   341:12
  c. makes a rare turkey-cock of
    him   483:14
  c. of the first Composer   86:33
  c.'s sober eye   231:8
  for c. he and valour   347:11
  her best nurse C.   340:20
  mind serene for c.   215:31
  my darling c.   156:12
  sundry c. of my travels   428:16
Contemplative: that fools should
  be so deep-c.   427:15
Contemporary: how it strikes a C.   92:20
Contempt: c. and anger of his lip   483:28
  c., farewell!   468:27
  c. of God's good gifts   267:31
  c. of thy Word   388:49
  for c. too high   158:15
  no weakness, no c.   351:6
  pour c. on all my pride   562:18
  speak of the moderns without c.   139:17
Contemptible: more c. animal   204:10
  rendered the..Government..c.   571:13
  those poor c. men   167:12
  unpitied sacrifice in a c. struggle   101:36
Contend: c., ye powers   166:1
  if I c. with thee   255:8
  let's c. no more   97:23
  logic and rhetoric, able to c.   27:19
Contendere nobilitate   320:30(–321)
Contending: as c. against some being   566:21
  c. with the fretful elements   453:3
  fierce c. nations   1:25
Content: as minding to c. you   467:28
  be c. with your wages   61:23
  breathless, instead of c.   289:27
  c. thyself to be obscurely good   1:21
  c. thyself with thine estate   518:2
  c. to breathe his native air   386:26
  c. to dwell in decencies   384:34
  c. with a vegetable love   220:28
  c. with my harm   427:27
  c. you..I shall not be there   525:28
  died c. on pleasant sward   287:17
  farewell C.!   472:3
  good, pleasure, ease, c.   384:2
  I am c. with what I have   99:31
  I could be well c.   440:26
  I have good reason to be c.   289:29
  land of lost c.   263:14
  make yourself c., my love   32:17
  my soul hath her c. so absolute   170:21
  O, sweet c.   170:21
  our desire is got without c.   459:3
  poor and c. is rich   471:33
  remaining c. with half-know-
    ledge   289:21
  shut up in measureless c.   457:19
  sweet C.! where doth thine
    harbour hold?   35:12
  that c. surpassing wealth   498:24
  travellers must be c.   426:39
  wants money, means, and c.   427:25
  where they went with much c.   99:18
  will no other vice c. you?   185:26
  with equal advantage c.   124:6
  with humble livers in c.   446:16

Contented: c. if he might enjoy   578:34
  c. wi' little   104:32
  he will have to be c.   221:3
  king shall be c.   475:10
  pale c. sort of discontent   286:41
  slaves, howe'er c.   162:22
  then ye c. your souls   297:16
  with what I most enjoy c. least   486:24
Contentedly: we'll sit c.   336:26
Contentedness: angling..procurer
  of c.   559:15
Contentements: le ciel défend..
  certains c.   354:7
Contention: let the long c. cease   16:19
  man of c.   55:19
  ripping..the spirit of c. from
    our tongues   276:21
Contentious: continual dropping
  ..a c. woman   50:46
Contentment: alone..what c.
  find?   348:34
  c. fails   226:8
  c. is a sleepy thing   548:16
  c. still I crave   99:31
  c. to that toad   300:13
  oh, the sweet c.   134:21
Contents: its c. worn out   211:21
Contentus: nemo..c. vivat   261:6
Contest: cease your c.   166:2
  great c. follows   163:10
Contests: saints engage in fierce c.   111:13
  what mighty c.   385:8
Conticuere omnes   553:23
Contiguity: boundless c. of shade   162:40
Continency: gift of c.   391:26
  give me..c.   21:20
Continent: C. will not suffer England   180:14
  make its c. an isle   374:21
  overspread the c. allotted by
    Providence   371:4
Continentiam: da mihi..c.
  imperas nobis c.   21:20
       21:23
Continents: over many nations and
  three..c.   188:19
  rive your concealing c.   453:10
Continuance: for a c...mild hale
  household of c.   518:33
       518:1
  patient c. in well doing   65:33
Continue: let brotherly love c.   69:2
  once begun will c.   26:11
  their houses shall c. for ever   395:1
  tree will c. to be   5:27
Continued: begun, c., and ended in
  thee   390:52
  c. miracle in his own person   265:10
  how long soever it hath c.   148:3
Continued'st: broke not, but c. it   184:12
Continues: this tree c. to be   305:10
Continuest: that thou c. such   348:11
Continueth: for their work c.   302:4
Continuing: we have no c. city   69:24
Continuous as the stars that shine   577:6
Contortions: all the c. of the Sybil   103:30
Contra hos Motores Bos   223:8
Contract: marriage..a civil c.   422:6
Contracted: Angel with c. brow   349:2
Contradict: lose no time to c. her   520:54
  read not to c. and confute   27:16
  though it c. everything you said   200:40
  very well then I c. myself   568:1
Contradicted: I dogmatize and am
  c.   277:5
Contradicting: as soon think of c.
  a Bishop   275:17
Contradiction: physicians..brook
  no c.   563:19
  woman's at best a c. still   384:40
Contradictions: bundle of c.   154:23
Contraption what he call a Tar-
  Baby   238:15
Contrarious: unfit c. moods of men   88:20
'Contrariwise,' continued Tweedledee   130:8
Contrary: all things change them
  to the c.   478:33
  c. to their profession   389:36
  everythink goes c. with me   174:13
  Mary, Mary, quite c.   367:21
  memory runneth not to the
    c.   73:7, 314:22

Contrary (cont.)
  most c. to custom and experi-
    ence   265:10
  one person..of the c. opinion   338:26
  our wills and fates do so c. run   435:13
  trial is by what is c.   352:9
Contribution: one c...to the current literature   112:1
Contrite: broken and c. heart   395:10
  humble and a c. heart   300:24
  sighing of a c. heart   389:8
Contrivance: c. enough to get himself into a jail   270:32
  Government is a c. of human
    wisdom   102:10
Contrivances: presumption in the
  wisdom of human c.   100:25
Contrive: head to c.   217:11
  head to c...mischief   145:26
  how build, unbuild, c.   348:30
  how Nature always does c.   219:6
Contrived: c. to talk about the
  Gods   116:35
  do no c. murder   469:36
Control: beyond my individual c.   175:3
  his c. stops with the shore   114:27
  leave this to c.   185:4
  man c. the wind   15:12
  over which he has no c.   564:15
  who can c. his fate?   473:30
Controlled: can Love be c. by
  advice?   214:14
  events have c. me   314:4
Controls them, and subdues   575:6
Controverse: in c. mute   401:35
Controversy: hearts of c.   448:19
Contumely: other is c.   27:20
  proud man's c.   434:4
Conturbat: timore mortis c. me   195:2
Convenience next suggested
  elbow-chairs   162:34
Conveniently low   130:15
Convent: at their c.'s narrow room   578:6
  C. of the Sacred Heart   197:26
  c.'s solitary gloom   382:1
Conventicle: for being at a c.   377:24
Convention: to the lords of C.   416:8
Conversati: per unam diem essemus
  bene c.   291:26
Conversation: as brisk as a bee
  in c.   270:8
  as e'er my c. coped withal   434:23
  by no means a proper subject of
    c.   139:33
  intrigues half-gather'd, c.-
    scraps   164:31
  John Wesley's c.   273:29
  mode of c. among gentlemen   273:2
  one of the greatest pleasures..c.   505:18
  stick on c.'s burrs   250:31
  that is the happiest c.   272:30
  there is no serious c.   277:17
  your ignorance cramps my c.   254:10
Conversations: after-dinner c.
  over the wine   546:41
  without pictures or c.   128:20
Converse: c., and live with ease   385:29
  c. with a mind..grandly simple   200:28
  c. with the mighty dead   546:27
  formed by thy c.   384:15
  how forgo thy sweet c.   349:18
  in pure c. our eternal day   84:6
  sweet c. of an innocent mind   288:33
Conversing: c. with W. H.'s forehead   239:16
  with thee c.   347:21
Conversion: c. of the Godhead
  into flesh   388:42
  till the c. of the Jews   333:8
Convert: c. and be healed   53:10
  he shall c. my soul   393:10
Converted: be c. at a revival   514:35
  except ye be c.   59:48
  love, c. from the thing it was   486:33
Converting: c. all your sounds of
  woe   468:20
  c. public trusts   319:20
  machine for c. the Heathen   125:29
Converts: charming women can
  true c. make   203:21
  qualified for making c.   227:21

INDEX

Convexa: dum..umbrae lustra-
bunt c. 553:21
'Convey' the wise it call 405:32
Conveys it in a borrowed name 401:38
Convict: nor endeavour to c. her 520:54
Convince: by persuading others,
we c. ourselves 282:19
c. the whole race 305:8
Convinced: not c. by proofs but
signs 375:2
Convinceth: which of you c. me of
sin? 63:32
Convincing: by way of c. you 303:7
oh! too c. 115:5
thought of c. 225:27
Conviviality: taper of c. 177:28
Convocation of politic worms 436:13
Convoy: crowns for c. put into his
purse 444:28
Convulsions: pit, box, and gall'ry
in c. hurl'd 385:23
Coodle would go out 174:4
Cooed: he did not cease, but c.,
and c. 578:11
Cooings: no one cares for matrimonial c. 115:39
Cook: c. and a captain bold 218:14
Duke's son—c.'s son 294:19
Groom, the Butler, and the C. 218:22
ill c...lick his own fingers 478:32
tell William c. 442:30
very uncommon c. 414:8
Cooked by tobacco-juice 121:22
Cookery: c. is become an art 109:10
kissing don't last: c. do 337:36
loved, ever after..French c. 542:33
Cooks: as c. go, she went 414:13
bouchers and c. 310:5
cannot live without c. 337:41
c. are gentlemen 109:10
Devil sends c. 213:9
had there been a Synod of C. 271:19
praise it, not the c. 238:2
those literary c. 357:26
with a legion of c. 117:46
Cool: caverns, c. and deep 15:24
c., sequester'd vale of life 230:7
delicate cheeks which they did c. 424:6
here comes the c. of the evening 506:1
in the c. of the day 44:21
kettle has scarcely time to c. 278:1
so c., so calm, so bright 245:13
when the eve is c.? 85:13
whispering sound of the c.
colonnade 161:23
Cooled: c. a long age 287:24
my senses would have c. 461:3
Cool-haired: lifting the c. creepers 18:16
Coolibah: shade of a c. tree 374:15
Cooling: you must stay the c. too 480:38
Coolness: grateful c. in the heat 132:2
Cool-rooted: hush'd, c. flowers 288:3
Cools: till a husband c. 384:38
Cooped in their winged sea-girt
citadel 113:16
Co-operation: government and c.
are ..the laws of life 413:27
Coot: haunts of c. and hern 528:5
Cope: Johnny C., are ye wauking
yet? 503:1
to c. him in these sullen fits 426:34
Coped: as e'er my conversation c.
withal 434:23
Copernicus: Pythagoras was mis-
understood..and C. 200:41
Cophetua: before the king C. 528:1
C. sware a royal oath   [maid 528:2
when king C. lov'd the beggar- 477:12
Copia: inopem me c. fecit 371:28
Copied: I c. all the letters 221:16
Copier: mere c. of nature 406:11
Copies: I find I must keep c. 156:3
Copious Dryden 386:18
Copper: but for a c. halfpenny 131:24
c. for the craftsman 295:14
in a hot and c. sky 149:4
Coppersmith: Alexander the c.
did..evil 69:3
Copula: quos irrupta tenet c. 258:19
Copy: according to my c. 328:1
head..statuaries loved to c. 325:14

Copy (cont.)
in them nature's c.'s not eterne 459:6
leave the world no c. 482:20
Copyists: shortened the labour of
c. 127:6
Copyrights: take away..their c. 549:11
Coquetry: c. of public opinion 103:10
life is a c. 543:20
Cor: c. ad c. loquitur 364:3
inquietum est c. nostrum 21:16
ulterius c. lacerare nequit 521:27
Corages: priketh hem nature in
hir c. 136:22
Coral: c. is far more red 488:13
c. lip admires 124:25
c. of his lip 321:14
from her c. lips such folly 155:5
from India's c. strand 240:17
of his bones are c. made 479:30
wand'ring in many a c. grove 75:18
Coral-reef: lifts, through centuries, the c. 376:6
Coranto: come home in a c. 482:8
Corbies: twa c. making a mane 32:15
Cord: as unto the bow the c. is 317:27
silver c. be loosed 51:33
stretch a c., however fine 566:1
threefold c. 51:5
triple c. 103:9
Cordage: rent c., shatter'd deck 362:11
Corded: undid his c. bales 18:16
Cordelia: this lady..my child C. 454:16
Cords: cast away their c. 391:48
draw iniquity with c. of vanity 53:5
scourge of small c. 63:6
tied with c. to the back of his
head 311:17
Core: ain't-a-going to be no c. 550:25
as the rind was the c. is 522:26
wear him in my heart's c. 434:26
Corinna: come, my C. 246:1
when to her lute C. sings 123:21
Corinth: thus was C. lost and won 114:40
Corinthian capital of polished
society 102:25
Corinthum: adire C. 257:6
Corioli: flutter'd your Volscians
at C. 429:23
widows in C. 429:8
Cork-heeled: wat their c. shoon 32:1
Corking-pin stuck through his tail 33:18
Corkscrew: clean tumbler and a c. 177:23
Cormorant: c. devouring Time 454:30
sat like a c. 347:3
Corn: al this newe c. 138:23
amid the alien c. 288:1
breast high amid the c. 253:19
clover and c. lay sleeping 293:20
cokkel in our clene c. 138:3
c. that makes the holy bread 334:3
c. was..immortal wheat 548:14
c. was springing fresh and green 73:11
cow's in the c. 367:15
deeper yellow on the c. 248:7
earned your little bit o' c. 217:22
flies o'er th' unbending c. 382:32
hope..in c. in chaff 117:13
idle weeds..in our sustaining c. 454:2
Kansas had better stop raising
c. 312:23
men threshed c. at midnight 586:1
my crop of c. 547:20
one word to me over the c. 359:16
raise the price of c. 112:27
reap its scanty c. 199:8
there was c. before 244:9
there was c. in Egypt 45:19
two ears of c...where only one 519:17
valleys..so thick with c. 395:30(-396)
when he treadeth out the c. 46:26
yellow like ripe c. 410:8
Cornea: Somni portae..altera fertur c. 555:2
Cornelia: these..are my jewels 109:26
Corner: c. of the street 177:32
dwell in a c. of the housetop 50:28
in ev'ry c. sing 243:24
in some close c. of my brain 262:6
it's a c. of heaven itself 571:7
Jack Horner sat in a c. 367:16
keep a c. in the thing I love 471:40

Corner (cont.)
not done in a c. 65:25
round the c. of nonsense 153:13
sits the wind in that c.? 468:21
some c. of a foreign field 84:21
upon the c. of the moon 459:27
Corners: all the c. of the earth 397:26
at the round earth's imagined c. 185:13
from the four c. of the sky 192:40
her sweet three c. in 172:7
or the green c. of the earth 75:18
polished c. of the temple 400:16
three c. of the world in arms 448:2
unregarded age in c. thrown 426:35
Cornet, flute, harp, sackbut 55:36
Cornfield: o'er the green c. did
pass 428:30
Cornish: here's twenty thousand
C. men 239:7
Corns: your shooting c. presage 521:5
Cornu: faenum habet in c. 261:13
Coromandel: on the coast of C.
311:12, 324:34
Coronation: C., and Sops in wine 510:23
reject a petrarchal c. 290:2
Coronet: her c. weeds clambering
to hang 437:1
proud bride of a ducal c. 170:36
wears a c., and prays 164:18
Coronets: more than c. 533:38
Corporal: blacking the C.'s eye 295:3
Corporals: there was C. forty-one 301:16
Corporation: expect a c. to have a
conscience? 547:15
Corporations: [C.] cannot commit
treason 148:10
Corpore: mens sana in c. sano 283:24
Corporeal: something c...in his
poetry 239:17
Corporis: hospes comesque c. 233:19
Corpse: bridal flowers serve for
a buried c. 478:33
carry up this c. 91:36
c. should be ready 560:7
dead c. of the Public Credit 563:4
each like a c. within its grave 496:4
for a little bears up this c. 525:15
frozen c. was he 318:15
good wishes to the c. 36:11
he kissed her cold c. 10:18
here's a c. in the case 34:19
his c. to the rampart we hurried 572:10
leave the c. uninterr'd 419:3
make a lovely c. 176:20
makes a very handsome c. 226:37
nice fresh c. 550:18
not a friend greet my poor c. 483:6
sad they bore her c. away 228:10
seraph-man on every c. 150:6
slovenly, unhandsome c. 438:33
thou, dead c. 431:32 (–432)
Corpses: c. three-months-old 537:38
our loves into c. or wives 523:1
Corpulent man of fifty 266:6
Corpuscula: quanta sint hominum
c. 283:22
Correct: all present and c. 5:5
blot out, c., insert, refine 521:16
easier..to be critical than..c. 180:25
like magistrates, c. at home 443:10
Corrected and amended by its
Author 211:21
Corregiescity of Correggio 513:15
Correggios: Raphaels, C., and
stuff 225:35
Correggiosity of Correggio 126:10
Correspondent to command 479:25
Corridors: through the c. of Time 316:9
Corriger: se mêler à c. le monde 353:20
Corrigere: quidquid c. est nefas 258:26
Corrival: wear without c. all her
dignities 438:23
Corroborative: merely c. detail 220:13
Corrupt: able to c. a saint 438:22
among a people generally c. 103:24
appointment by the c. few 490:29
away with a c. world 337:35
c. following of the Apostles 401:9
c. influence 101:17
c. the souls of those they rule 16:28
do c. my air 429:14

Corrupt (cont.)
evil communications c. good
manners 67:12
moth and rust doth c. 58:5
now I see peace to c. 349:28
one good custom..c. the world 531:35
power does c. 549:11
power tends to c. 1:2
that no king can c. 446:19
unlimited power is apt to c. 379:5
Corrupted: conscience with injustice is c. 445:30
c. honest men 425:10
c. the youth of the realm 445:40
which..hath not been c. 388:4
Corruptible: this c. must put on
incorruption 67:17
to obtain a c. crown 66:37
Corrupting the youth of the city 379:24
Corruption: c. of Man's Heart 91:34
c...symptom of constitutional
liberty 217:10
c. wins not more than honesty 446:31
it is sown in c. 67:14
keep mine honour from c. 447:11
suffer thy Holy One to see c. 392:27
to be turned into c. 400:30
whose strong c. inhabits our..
blood 484:18
Corruptions: ere man's c. made
him wretched 371:8
Corruptly: that estates..were not
deriv'd c. 464:1
Corryvreckan: dangerous C. 146:26
Corsair: he left a C.'s name 115:7
Cortez: like stout C. 288:19
Coruscations of summer lightning 228:2
Corvis: dat veniam c...censura 283:1
Corydon: C. would kiss her then
Phyllida and C. 80:7
Time, not C., hath conquer'd 80:7
Corydon ardebat Alexim 18:27
Cosmopolitan: become c. in the 555:20
end 356:5
c. critics 181:9
Cosmos: too much Ego in your C. 304:31
untented C. my abode 515:29
Cossack commanders cannonading
come 5:7
Cost: rich-proud c. of..age 487:11
sigh for the c. and pain 88:12
why so large c. 488:20
Coster: when the c.'s finished
jumping on his mother 221:36
Costive: make a soap-boiler c. 563:13
Costly: all that's..c. in our sorrows 512:29
c. thy habit 431:25
thy attire..comely but not c. 321:17
too c. for cost 545:12
Costs: civility c. nothing 354:17
c. a lot..to die comfortably 111:36
it c. them nothing 109:18
obedience of distant pro-
vinces..c. more than it is
worth 324:24
wriggles betwixt the c. of a ship 281:19
Cot: beside the hill 408:10
pot with a c. in a park 309:26
Cotis: fungar vice c. 256:7
Cotopaxi: Chimborazo, C. 549:21
Cottage: before his c. door 507:3
c. homes of England 241:13
c. in a lane 223:7
c. might adorn 225:7
c. with a double coach-house..
of gentility 151:11, 507:21
hides not his visage from our c. 485:31
love and a c. 154:6
soul's dark c. 557:25
though from court to c. 377:4
wherever there's a c. small 373:15
Cottages: c. of strowed reeds 331:2
poor men's c. princes' palaces 463:7
Cottage-smell: Sweet-William with
his homely c. 18:26
Cottle: oh Amos C.! 117:19
Cotton is King 142:27
Cotytto: where are they, C. or
Venus 523:6
Couch: from her c. of snows 492:20

Couch (cont.)
make his c. of silk 137:36
retired to his virtuous c. 560:8
steel c. of war 470:8
there I c. when owls do cry 480:14
they to their grassy c. 347:19
where souls do c. on flowers 425:22
wraps the drapery of his c. 98:3
Couched: c. on the bald top 580:9
c. with her arms behind her..
head 336:7
Couch grass: from the heaps of c. 236:14
Couching down between two burdens 45:27
Cough: c. for my own amusement 22:29
his hearers could not c. 280:2
keep a c. by them 143:3
Coughing drowns the parson's
saw 456:1
Coughs: no discretion in her c. 22:29
Could: as if it c. not be 494:6
Council: mortal instruments..in
c. 449:5
Councillor to King James 232:16
Councils: Her Majesty's c. his
words will grace 84:27(-85)
manners, climates, c., governments 540:32
wisdom from our c. 101:17
Counsel: by all that's..glorious
take this c. 118:35
conscience..you c. well 463:27
c. of her country's gods 158:29
c. of the heathen to nought 393:36
darkeneth c. 49:17
fitter for execution than for c. 27:41
for women to keep c. 449:27
ghostly c. and advice 390:32
if this c...be of men 64:32
keep my own c. 222:39
lightly regarded the c. of the
most Highest 398:15
princely c. in his face yet shone 345:24
princes of Judah their c. 396:13
religion, justice, c., and treasure 27:8
skilled to keep c. 421:8
sometimes c. take—and sometimes tea 385:14
spirit of c. and might 53:17
take my c., happy man 218:26
turnin' back for c. 310:27
two may keep c. 478:7
we took sweet c. together 395:12
who cannot give good c.? 109:18
Counselled ignoble ease 345:22
Counsellor: c. heart 429:3
Wonderful, C., The mighty God 53:15
Counsellors: in the multitude of c.
..safety 49:56
when c. blanch 25:40
Counsels: casteth out the c. of
princes 393:36
close designs and crooked c. 190:13
from whom..all good c. 388:34
how mony c. sweet 108:4
Count: c. five-and-twenty, Tatty-
coram 175:34
c. their chickens 111:6
he could not c. the sires and
sons 183:4
I c. them over 408:5
if all men c. with you 297:12
let me c. the ways 88:24
let us c. our spoons 271:10
makes her c. 141:35
Counted: faster we c. our spoons 200:1
he c. them at break of day 115:45
thousands c. every groan 16:8
Countenance: bright c. of truth 352:23
cheerful c. 50:11, 398:9
c. more in sorrow 431:13
damned disinheriting c. 500:41
did the C. Divine shine forth 75:16
expression..in the c. of all
science 583:3
for making you that c. you are 428:17
grim, grim grew his c. 30:18
his c. is as Lebanon 52:14
his c., like richest alchemy 449:1
his c. soon brightened with joy 574:20
his c. was as the sun 70:27

Countenance (cont.)
Knight of the Sorrowful C. 134:8
lift up his c. upon thee 46:10
light of thy c. upon us 392:2
sharpeneth the c. of his friend 50:47
shew us the light of his c. 396:2
that c. cannot lie 412:18
thoughts secret and the c. open 583:14
with a glassy c. 534:8
you have that in your c. 452:22
Countenances: chipping at the c.
of the attendants 173:31
Counter: all things c., original,
spare, strange 255:3
Counter-caster: this c. 469:23
Countercheck quarrelsome 428:37
Counterfeit: sleep, death's c. 458:23
teach light to c. a gloom 341:16
Counterpane: pleasant land of c. 515:19
Counters: lock such rascal c. 451:21
words are wise men's c. 248:19
Countervail: what..treasure.. c.
a friend 233:2
Countesses: two c. had no outlines at all 177:20
Countest the steps of the Sun 76:7
Counties: forget six c. 359:2
see the coloured c. 262:21(-263)
Counting: c. out his money 368:20
merely c. votes 267:6
Counting-house: king was in his
c. 368:20
Countries: all c. where he came 191:12
preferreth all c. before his own 371:15
there are rascals in all c. 274:6
Country: absolved from all duty
to his c. 376:18
alas, poor c. 460:19
all the benefits of your own c. 428:17
all the ends..thy c.'s 446:31
all these c. patriots 112:27
always zealous for his c.'s good 215:18
America is a c. of young men 201:17
anybody can be good in the c. 570:10
anything for the good of one's c. 203:12
beats not in his c.'s cause 381:7
billion dollar c. 210:11
blue sky..their native c. 149:24
by all their c.'s wishes blest 153:29
come from a far c. 150:8
c...continually under hatches 289:32
c. diversion, I loathe the c. 156:10
c. folks who live beneath 146:32
c. has its charms—cheapness 518:28
c. life I praise 82:5
c. life is to be preferred 377:9
c. men of England 373:11
court the c. clash 105:27
died to save their c. 41:22
every c. but his own 124:11, 219:25
every c. save their own 181:9
Father of his C. 6:7
fit c. for heroes 216:8
Flora and the c. green 287:24
for the good of my c...abroad 203:12
from yon far c. blows 263:14
genius is of no c. 143:18
God made the c. 162:38
God's own c. 6:14
great hills of the South C. 42:3
guiltless of his c.'s blood 230:5
had she been a c. maid 106:29
heart-sick of his c.'s shame 163:2
he likes the c. 162:1
his c.'s pride, the priest, the
slave 491:15
his first best c. 226:7
his virtues..undone his c. 1:20
home, home, to my ain c. 167:22
how I leave my c. 379:19
how I love my c. 379:18
if c. loves such sweet desires 232:5
I love thee still—my c.! 162:43
in a progressive c. change is
constant 180:37
in my own c. 8:22, 167:23
in the c...creation..expire 505:8
in the c. of the free 88:2
in the c. places 516:5
is this mine own c.? 150:4
I tremble for my c. 268:27

Country (cont.)
I vow to thee, my c.   511:4
I will into some far c.   29:24(-30)
I wish to vegetate like the c.   240:8
know most of..thy native c.   212:11
know thy c.   136:20
leave his c. as good   147:19
leaving his c. for his c.'s sake   205:3
left our c. for our c.'s good   36:30
lie abroad for the good of his c.   583:15
love thy c., wish it well   183:22
make unto me one c.   86:28
many a fear for my dear c.   573:12
merry c. lad   80:4
most disthressful c.   9:6
my c. is the world   373:4
my c.! oh, my c.!   379:20
my c...'tis of thee   504:19
my fate in a c. town   387:2
my soul, there is a c.   552:1
no relish for the c.   505:35
nothing good to be had in the c.   239:25
O dear, dear C.   361:17
of light and leading in the c.   182:30
Oh Rome! my c.!   114:12
O sweet and blessed c.   362:5
our c. is the world   213:18
our c., right or wrong   169:28
over all the c.   334:16
prepare the mind of the c.   180:38
pride that pulls the c. down   471:12
pride that puts this c. down   6:26
prophet..save in his own c.   59:33
saviour of 'is c.   303:2
she is my c. still   142:32
so vile..not love his c.   450:16
spare your c.'s flag   508:14
springs o' that c.   32:11
suck'd on c. pleasures   185:6
takes his pension from his c.   413:24
these pretty c. folks would lie   428:31
they touch our c.   162:42
this lady of the West C.   171:6
to a boon southern c.   18:31 (-19)
to that pleasant c.'s earth   475:16
undiscover'd c.   434:4
upon..education..the fate of this c.   181:7
who leads a c. life   192:13
whose c. he has turned into a desert   101:27
your c.'s cause calls you away   217:16
your 'Never-never c.'   296:10
Countryman: contentment the c. doth find   134:21
   put off my helmet to my c.   425:28
Countrymen: friends, Romans, c.   450:17
   our c. are all mankind   213:18
   their actions in balance with my c.'s   86:27
   what..many of your c. cannot help   270:34
Countryside: more dreadful record of sin than..the c.   187:17
Counts: Scotland c. for something still   360:4
Couple: begin..but to c. now?   467:21
   one fool..in every married c.   204:9
Coupled together for the sake of strife   143:25
Coupler-flange: from c. to spindle-guide   299:3
Couples: see the c. advance   183:7
Couplet: only c. fraught with.. a thought   382:31
Couplets: Fitzgerald bawl his creaking c.   117:8
   her golden c.   437:25
Courage: all goes if c. goes   36:4
   any deed of c.   442:21
   brows of dauntless c.   345:7
   c., brother, do not stumble   327:3
   'C.!' he said   535:12
   c. in your own   227:34
   c. is the thing   36:4
   c. mounteth with occasion   447:22
   c. never to submit or yield   344:14
   c. of my companions   416:7
   fearful saints fresh c. take   161:18
   greater therefore should our c. be   444:11

Courage (cont.)
much less than c. of heart   41:16
my c. and skill to him that can get it   99:39
my c. prove my title   426:10
O God of C. grave   213:2
or c. to forget   3:6
Red Badge of C.   165:23
screw your c. to the sticking-place   457:13
sing praises..with a good c.   393:35
strong and of a good c.   46:37
three-o'-clock in the morning c.   546:43
two o'clock in the morning c.   360:25
unmatch'd for c., breath, and speed   416:13
unprepared c.   360:25
vain faith, and c. vain   323:7
with c., love and joy   214:29
your c., your energy, your patience   305:1
Courage: c. de l'improviste   360:25
   c...le diable est mort!   406:5
Courageous: captains c.   31:14
Couriers: sightless c. of the air   457:9
   vaunt-c. to..thunderbolts   453:5
Course: bear-like I must fight the c.   461:8
   cannot steer a middle c.   334:21
   c. of true love   466:18
   forgot his c.   208:15
   foundations..out of c.   397:4
   great nature's second c.   458:11
   held in the true c. by him   126:5
   icy current and compulsive c.   472:12
   if on our daily c.   291:5
   I have finished my c.   68:60
   I must stand the c.   453:33
   in earth's diurnal c.   573:6
   insisture, c., proportion   481:2
   keen, unscrupulous c.   15:21
   long ere the c. begin   330:13
   morning-star in his steep c.   151:28
   my preudunt c. is steadied   319:22
   my whole c. of love   469:45
   short, bright, resistless c.   418:2
   what c. thou wilt   451:1
   with secret c.   278:29
   world's c. will not fail   375:18
   young blood must have its c.   293:19
Coursed: tears c. one another   426:31
Coursers: my c. are fed with.. lightning   497:8
   two c. of ethereal race   231:14
Courses: all the c. of my life   439:41
   c. as swift as thought   455:22
   gave himself to evil c.   577:22
   stars in their c.   46:48
   swiftly c. from the shore   566:25
   with which..they steer their c.   110:22
Court: at the kinges c...ech man for him-self   137:28
   birds, to c. and pair   82:4
   c. awards it   465:10
   c. for owls   53:45
   C. of King's Bench, Den of Thieves   147:17
   Death keeps his pale c.   491:17
   drink little, eat less, c. solitude   155:27
   free of the outer c.   375:5
   hear poor rogues talk of c. news   454:19
   help of the air of the c.   201:31
   her c. was pure   539:12
   I c. others in verse   401:21
   keeps Death his c.   475:7
   let her alone, she will c. you   280:20
   live turmoiled in the c.   445:42
   love rules the camp, the c.   116:37
   love rules the c.   417:16
   more free..than the envious c.   426:29
   never more can go to c.   311:14
   so c. a mistress   280:20
   starry threshold of Jove's C.   339:27
   stopped short in the cultivated c.   220:27
   sun that shines upon his c.   485:31
   though from c. to cottage   377:4
Court: le nez de Cléopâtre..plus c.   373:22
Courte: le loisir de la faire plus c.   374:8
Courted: better be c. and jilted   122:21
   c. by all the winds   350:31

Courted (cont.)
in your girls again be c.   5:8
never be c. at all   122:21
Courteous: c. he was, lowly, and servisable   136:27
   gracious and c. to strangers   26:21
   retort c.   428:37
   so c., so kind   502:17
   with what c. action it waves you   432:1
Courteoust knight that ever bare shield   328:24
Courtesies: for these c. I'll lend you..monies   463:22
   small sweet c. of life   512:23
Courtesy: by a frantic flight of c.   375:26
   by c. a man   23:13
   freedom and c.   136:23
   Grace of God is in C.   41:16
   greater man, the greater c.   531:1
   herein may be seen noble chivalry, c.   328:2
   in phrase of gentlest c.   416:18
   mirror of all c.   137:35, 440:12
   mutilated c.   227:18
   of C.—it is much less   41:16
   pink of c.   512:2
   seated in the heart of c.   501:16
   show'd thy dear mother any c.   429:22
   treating all women with perfect c.   305:1
   trust thy honest offer'd c.   340:17
   use the devil himself with c.   484:21
   very pink of c.   478:5
   what a candy deal of c.   438:39
   wish c. would invent some other custom   471:7
Courtier: c.'s, soldier's, scholar's   434:14
   gallops o'er a c.'s nose   477:7
   so near the heel of the c.   437:13
Courtiers: o'er c.' knees   477:7
Courting: he came a-c. me   35:8
   nobody I care for comes a-c. me   220:30
   when we go out a-c.   183:13
Courtliness: amiable words and c.   530:14
Courtly: all about the c. stable   343:25
Courts: Beauty..must be shown in c.   340:38
   c. and camps..learn the world   139:11
   c. for cowards were erected   106:24
   C. where Jamshyd gloried   206:1
   enter into the c. of the Lord   397:5
   in the c. of the sun   141:3
   one day in thy c.   397:7
   tap'stry halls and c. of princes   340:17
   thy c. to see   421:3
   to senates, c., and kings   123:7
Courtship to marriage   155:34
Cousin: again the C.'s whistle   89:17
   C. Swift, you will never be a poet   194:30
Cousins: his sisters and his c. and his aunts   221:14
Coutts: Aristocrat who banks with C.   218:22
Cove: as I gain the c.   93:20
Covenant with death   53:34, 213:19
Cover: athwart a cedarn c.   151:32
   c. her face   563:18
   c. my defenceless head   565:7
   like the c. of an old book   211:21
   not body enough to c. his mind   504:28
   that I may c. you with my hair   586:5
   turn again to c. the earth   398:8
Covered: thou hast c. my head   400:12
   violets c. up in leaves   287:31
Coveredest it with the deep   398:8
Covereth: faults..the earth c.   404:16
Covering: cowslips for her c.   246:5
Covers: night that c. me   241:18
Covert: c. from the tempest   53:43
   in shadiest c. hid   346:20
Coverts: devious c. of dismay   411:12
Covet: if it be a sin to c. honour   444:27
   c. thy neighbour's wife   390:17
   thou shalt not c.; but   147:3
Coveted: as ever c. his neighbour's goods   294:6
   c. her and me   380:8
Covetous: I am not c. for gold   444:27
   when..Brutus grows so c.   451:21

INDEX

Cow: cheaper..than to keep a c. 112:6
c...every three acres 339:2
c. jumped over the moon 367:1
c.'s in the corn 367:15
c. with the crumpled horn 369:6
friendly c., all red and white 515:21
kissed her c. 520:8
kiss till the c. comes home 38:5
like a little Kyloe c. 366:19
Molly smiles beneath her c. 11:20
Purple C. 100:1, 2
three acres and a c. 153:17
true..as c. chaws cud 549:24
truth, Sir, is a c. 271:11
Coward: call me c. if you will 204:32
cocoa is a cad and c., 142:9
conscience is a c. 227:25
c. does it with a kiss 569:4
c.'s castle 135:20
c.'s weapon, poison 209:6
earth shak'd like a c. 439:40
either a c. or a flatterer 450:8
'fore God I am no c. 539:17
gross flattery to name a c. 548:5
I should count myself the c. 539:18
I was a c. on instinct 439:27
live a c. in mine own esteem 457:11
no c. soul is mine 83:7
scoundrel, and a c. 270:22
while the c. stands aside 320:12
Cowardice: badge of pusillanimity and c. 442:21
hardiness, love, friendship, c. 328:2
I admit the c. 490:22
mutual c. keeps us in peace 274:8
Cowardly: c. dogs bark loudest 563:27
c. put off my helmet 425:28
find it c. and vile 451:36
many a...fellow had destroy'd so c. 438:35
Cowards: all men would be c. 407:23
being all c. 274:8
brave..always beating the c. 274:8
but a word that c. use 476:41
conscience doth make c. of us all 434:4
courts for c. were erected 106:24
c. die many times 449:22
c. in scarlet 220:11
many other mannish c. 426:28
Nonconformist Conscience makes c. 39:17
plague of all c. 439:17
what can ennoble...c.? 384:8
Cowbind: in the warm hedge.. green c. 497:22
Cowering: sleekit, c., tim'rous beastie 107:9
Cowl: I like a c. 199:21
Cowled: I that c. churchman be 199:21
Cowley: who now reads C.? 386:13
Cowls, hoods, and habits 346:26
Cowper: divine chit-chat of C. 306:32
Cows: c. are my passion 175:11
when the c. come hame 35:7
Cowslip: drops i' the bottom of a c. 429:24
freckled c. 445:11
in a c.'s bell I lie 480:14
o'er the c.'s velvet head 341:4
pearl in every c.'s ear 466:35
sweet c.'s grace 370:5
Cowslips: C. and Kingcups 510:23
c. for her covering 246:5
c. from a Devon combe 296:15
c. tall her pensioners 466:34
c. wan that hang the pensive head 342:31(-343)
Cumner c. never stirr'd 18:28
Coxcomb ask two hundred guineas 412:22
Coxcombs: C. vanquish Berkley 85:4
some made c. 382:21
Coy: denial vain, and c. excuse 342:11
make me c. and tender to offend 245:11
sometimes coming, sometimes c. 421:13
then be not c. 247:10
uncertain, c., and hard to please 418:31
Coyness: this c., Lady 333:8
Cozenage: c...upon the Providence of God 167:11
strange c. 191:34

Cozening: some cogging, c. slave 473:1
Crabbe: this fact..let C. attest 117:26
Crabbed: c. age and youth 486:2
not harsh and c. 340:24
three c. months had sour'd themselves 485:5
Crabs: roasted c. hiss in the bowl 456:1
set limed twigs for c. 131:24
Crab-tree: grievous c. cudgel 99:21
Crack: blow, winds, and c. your cheeks 453:5
c. a bottle 142:1
c. nature's moulds 453:5
hear the mighty c. 3:2, 385:23
never a c. in my heart 585:18
stretch out till the c. of doom 460:11
you'd better c. up 176:23
Cracked: it c. and growled 148:26
two strings..both c. 204:22
we must be c.-up 176:23
Cracker: those lovely c. mottoes 218:4
Crackling of thorns under a pot 51:10
Cracks: now c. a noble heart 438:7
Cradle: between the c. and the grave 195:14
but in a wooden c. 5:16
c. of the rude imperious surge 442:1
c. will rock 73:14
destin'd heir in his soft c. 281:28
for His c. and His throne 291:14
from the c. to the grave I look 165:5
grown man in the c. of an infant 103:23
hand that rocks the c. 557:19
high mountain c. in Pamere 17:28(-18)
his pendent bed and procreant c. 457:6
in the c. where it lies 464:13
near the c. of the fairy queen 467:4
out of the c. endlessly rocking 567:1
rocked in the c. of the deep 570:27
sluggard's c. 135:20
traveller from the c. to the grave 497:16
your c., your home, and your bier 494:21
Cradled: c. into poetry by wrong 494:17
day she c. me 31:19
Craft: between c. and credulity 103:20
c. and subtilty of the devil 389:9
c. in the river, and c. in the street 504:2
c. so long to learn 138:22, 248:13
lean black c. like flies 410:17
such a smart little c. 222:8
their desire is in the work of their c. 57:13
their tricks an' c. 106:23
Craftier to pley..than Athalus 138:13
Craftiness: wise in their own c. 48:51
Craftsman: copper for the c. 295:14
Crafts and assaults of the devil 388:45
Crafty: nobody gets old and c. and wise 585:14
Crag: castled c. of Drachenfels 113:43
clasps the c. with crooked hands 529:10
every icy c. tinkled 575:24
Crags: among these barren c. 540:31
at the foot of thy c., O Sea! 528:3
Crambe repetita 283:13
Crammed: c. just as they on earth were c. 578:27
c. with distressful bread 444:23
earth's c. with heaven 87:35
eat the air, promise-c. 435:2
strange places c. with observation 427:16
Cramoisie: mysel' in c. 31:4
sails o' c. 31:8
Cramped: c. for ever 281:27
long-c. scroll 92:34
Cramps: your ignorance c. my conversation 254:10
Crams with cans of poisoned meat 141:34
Cranberries: cauliflower, pineapple and c. 219:13
Cranes: warred on by c. 345:3
Crank: when the vessel's c. 336:46
Cranking: this river comes me c. in 439:44
Cranks: quips and c. and wanton wiles 341:28
Crannies: pluck you out of the c. 529:24
Crantore: melius Chrysippo et C. 256:21
Crape: saint in c. 384:24

Cras: c. amet qui nunquam amavit 13:5
c. ingens iterabimus aequor 258:12
quid sit futurum c. 258:14
vixi: c. vel atra nube.. 260:14
Crash: brass will c. 219:22
c. of worlds 1:24
Crastina: sera nimis vita est c. 331:22
Crave: c. the tuneful nightingale 189:18
I c. no pelf 480:21
I c. the law 465:1
my mind forbids to c. 195:12
who doth not c. for rest 202:26
yet still do c. 195:13
Craved: who c. no crumb 222:27
Craven-Street: in C., Strand 504:2
Craving: c. credulity 180:32
full as c. too 191:20
to feed a c. mind 164:35
Cravings: shove c. in the van of Love 337:1
Crawl: slimy things did c. with legs 149:6
suffered to c. upon..the earth 519:15
Crawling: c. between heaven and earth 434:9
cruel c. foam 293:24
whereunder c. coop't 207:3
writhing, c., heaving 235:22
Crazed with the spell of far Arabia 171:3
Crazy: checkin' the c. ones 229:15
I'm half c. 168:2
Pilot's boy..doth c. go 150:11
Creak of a lumbering cart 585:17
Creaking: constant c. of a country sign 159:11
Fitzgerald bawl his c. couplets 117:8
Cream: choking her with c. 294:13
c. and mantle like a standing pond 462:33
queen of curds and c. 485:28
quite the c. of the thing 365:2
she gives me c. 515:21
skim milk masquerades as c. 221:21
skim the c. of others' books 357:26
vigilant as a cat to steal c. 440:22
will you take a little c.? 372:20
Cream-faced: thou c. loon 460:35
Creams: she tempers dulcet c. 348:9
Creari: nil posse c. de nilo 320:29
Create: as well to c. good precedents 26:25
c. my little world 38:25
c. the taste 583:5
Father, who didst all c. 81:3
from these c. he can forms 497:2
I c. new heavens 55:9
my business is to C. 75:2
strains that might c. a soul 340:28
what they half c. 582:2
Created: all men are c. equal 314:12
for thy pleasure..c. 70:39
God c. the heaven and the earth 43:26
male and female c. he them 44:8
nothing..c. out of nothing 320:29
the Lord hath c. him 57:9
thou hast c. all things 70:39
thou hast c. us for thyself 21:16
Creating a whole tribe of fops 452:14
Creation: about the lords of the c. 108:20
blind fury of c. 490:14
come so near c. 464:18
c. widened 566:13
c. will expire before tea-time 505:8
dagger of the mind, a false c. 457:20
doubled His whole c. 80:29
first Morning of C. 207:6
man..mars c.'s plan 124:15
nobles by the right of an earlier c. 325:4
O fairest of c.! 349:17
our c., preservation 389:19
rival..her delicate c. 582:20
she is His new c. 517:1
such as c.'s dawn beheld 114:29
to which the whole c. moves 533:31
up and down de whole c. 210:16
while the mute c. downward bend 194:25
whole c. groaneth 65:5
Creations: acts his own c. 94:16
Creative: c. Art..demands.. 575:15
sensitive being, a c. soul 579:33

INDEX

Creator: creature more than the c. 65:32
depends on his C. 109:24
God, C. wise 349:23
in his own image the C. made 308:31
law of our C. 101:26
let in the great C. 348:28
myself and my C. 363:14
remember now thy C. 51:33
storehouse for the glory of the C. 24:14
voice of the great C. 128:3
Creators of odd volumes 306:21
Creature: by which every c. is annexed 109:24
constant image of the c...beloved 483:2
c. in whom excell'd.. 349:17
c. more than the creator 65:32
c. not too bright and good 580:20
c. of circumstances 237:19
c.'s at his dirty work again 385:24
every c. drink but I 158:8
every c. lives in a state of war 521:21
every c. of God is good 68:46
every c. shall be purified 330:3
God's first C...Light 28:5
I am a lone lorn c. 174:13
kill the poor c. at once 213:22
kindliest c. in ould Donegal 229:14
nor depth, nor any other c. 65:58
not a c. was stirring 356:1
poor c., small beer 441:33
she is an excellent c. 181:23
strive which own'd the c. 280:10
there is no c. loves me 476:37
to look on sech a blessed c. 319:24
wine is a good familiar c. 471:23
world hath not a sweeter c. 472:26
would you gain the tender c.? 214:9
Creatures: all c. here below 292:3
all men become good c. 93:16
call these delicate c. ours 471:40
from fairest c...increase 486:9
how many desolate c. 87:31
hugest of living c. 348:26
human c.' lives 253:23
millions of spiritual c. 347:24
one of her feather'd c. 488:17
through c. you dissect 384:22
torture and death of his fellow-c. 212:4
unoffending c. whom he loves 575:13
Crebillon: eternal new romances of Marivaux and C. 231:20
Credat Iudaeus Apella 261:16
Credence: yeve I feyth and full c. 138:16
Credit: an't much c. in that 176:6
before his c., or his fee 521:8
citizen of c. and renown 159:32
c. from..our constitution 101:17
dead corpse of the Public C. 563:4
done my c...much wrong 207:20
it's greatly to his c. 221:24
let the C. go 205:26
my c...on such slippery ground 450:8
not to thy c. 121:18
partly c. things that do presage 451:34
pass the hat for your c.'s sake 294:20
plans, c., and the Muse 199:12
some c. in being jolly 176:7
'tis a c...to be neat 527:7
world will give thee c. 143:12
Credit: id potius c. 28:7
Creditable: good c. acquaintance 519:26
Credite: c. posteri 259:12
experto c. 555:11
Creditum: quod ab omnibus c. est 553:4
Credula: quam minimum c. postero 258:17
Credulity: between craft and c. 103:20
craving c. 180:32
listen with c. to the whispers of fancy 278:14
youth is the season of c. 379:4
Credulous: most positive..the most c. 520:49
Credulus: non ego c. illis 556:7
Credunt: quod volunt c. 120:11
Creed: c. in the biliary duct 200:11
c. is a rod 524:3
c. of slaves 379:14
deed and not the c. 318:6

Creed (*cont.*)
his c. no parson ever knew 188:34
of his c. a strait-jacket 337:5
our earliest c. we take 250:30
sapping a solemn c. 113:49
some Christians have a comfortable c. 115:31
suckled in a c. outworn 582:18
thy life to thy neighbour's c. 199:9
we have a Calvinistic c. 379:7
wrought..the c. of creeds 532:25
Creeds: c. that refuse and restrain 523:3
dust of c. outworn 497:1
half-believers in our casual c. 18:12
honest doubt..than half the c. 533:14
keys of all the c. 532:17
so many c. 568:27
their c. a disease of the intellect 200:44
vain are the thousand c. 83:9
Creek: blows by every winding c. 535:18
Creeks: through c. and inlets making 147:8
Creep: ambition can c. 103:17
'Ay!' said C. 171:23
bade me c. past 95:10
c. and intrude..into the fold 342:27
c. home, and take your place 293:19
I scarce can c. or go 266:8
I wants to make your flesh c. 178:30
like snails did c. 247:12
love will c. in service 484:39
sweetly c. into his study of imagination 469:6
ten low words oft c. 382:30
with pleasing murmurs c. 382:31
wit that can c. 385:34
Creepers: lifting the cool-haired c. 18:16
Creeping: c. like snail..to school 427:21
c. on from point to point 534:28
every c. thing 44:7
Nature is c. up 566:7
things c. innumerable 398:11
Creeps: c. in this petty pace 461:4
or wades, or c., or flies 346:14
servilely c. after sense 193:43
Crepidam: ne supra c. sutor 380:5
Crept: c. by me upon the waters 479:29
follies of the town c. slowly 226:42
kings c. out again 87:39
there c. a little noiseless noise 286:26
Crescent: c. of a hair's-breadth 94:8
with c. horns 344:31
Crescit indulgens 259:2
Cressets: fiery shapes, of burning c. 439:40
Cressid: where C. lay that night 465:17
Crest: by horse and c. 323:15
high c., short ears 488:27
joy brightens his c. 349:13
over the c. of the hill 293:20
Crested: c. worm 164:4
his rear'd arm c. the world 426:1
Crete: in a wood of C. 467:20
Cretes and Arabians 64:26
Crevasse: doth the c. bridge 543:15
Crew: all that pentecostal c. 296:7
and the c. of the Captain's gig 140:28, 218:14
Bacon of our rhyming c. 309:8
Comus, and his midnight-c. 231:1
c. is gambling in the forecastle 489:31
darling of our c. 173:10
his c., that sat consulting 350:17
Mirth, admit me of thy c. 341:31
set the c. laughing 208:15
we were a ghastly c. 149:32
with all her c. complete 162:10
Crews at England's feet 122:6
Crib: ass his master's c. 52:26
Cribbed: cabin'd, c., confin'd 459:12
Cribs: liest thou in smoky c. 441:41
Cricket: her whip, of c.'s bone 477:7
on his nose there was a c. 311:19
save the c. on the hearth 341:16
to where the c. sings 585:12
Cried: c. unto the Lord 398:15
little children c. in the streets 359:23
more he crowed, more we c. 232:3
mother c., baby slept 232:3
nor laugh'd, nor c. 401:29
some therefore c. one thing 65:7
then you suddenly c. 84:4

Cried (*cont.*)
when Agamemnon c. aloud 197:26
when that the poor have c. 450:20
winced nor c. aloud 241:18
would not cease, but c. still 196:2
Crier: c. rung the bell 38:28
when the C. cried, 'O Yes!' 34:27
Cries: it sighing c., Hey ho 168:7
my old sorrow wakes and c. 267:11
night and day on me she c. 31:3
pitying the tender c. 77:2
trouble deaf heaven with my bootless c. 486:24
with the c. they make 189:7
Crieth: him that c. in the wilderness 54:9
thy brother's blood c. unto me 44:31
wisdom c. without 49:39
Crillon: pends-toi..C. 242:2
Crime: any c. so shameful as poverty 203:8
any c. unreconcil'd..to heaven 473:12
atrocious c. of being a young man 379:2
call'd his harmless art a c. 417:2
crime to love too well 381:31
for my wilful c. art banished 349:30
foulest c. in history 568:7
in the year of the great c. 375:19
it was a c. in a child 325:36
Napoleon of c. 187:26
nor Stillicide a c. 514:39
now madden to c. 113:11
punishment fit the c. 220:2
slave of c. 579:31
sullied with the c. of stealing 550:27
sweet love was thought a c. 76:1
talk..that's the c. 229:10
this coyness..were no c. 333:8
thy Godlike..was to be kind 118:30
treason was no c. 190:25
worse than a c...a blunder 79:4
Crime: pire qu'un c...une faute 79:4
Crimes: all his c. broad blown 435:37
c., like virtues, are their own rewards 203:22
c. of this guilty land 85:6
malice and contentious c. 509:35
one virtue, and a thousand c. 115:7
our c. would despair 423:7
reach the dignity of c. 357:25
register of c., follies, and misfortunes 217:7
successful c. alone are justified 193:8
what c...in thy name 408:15
with reiterated c. 344:20
within thee undivulged c. 453:9
worst of c...poverty 490:3
Crimes: que de c...en ton nom 408:15
Criminal: c. cried, as he dropped 220:7
fair play of the British c. law 187:25
melancholy which..is c. 273:20
Crimine ab uno 554:2
Crimson: all c. barr'd 286:37
beauty's ensign yet is c. 478:43
Conquest's c. wing 229:20
c.-blank the windows flare 300:3
c. of the sunset sky 4:6
fresh lap of the c. rose 466:37
girt with a c. robe 232:1
now sleeps the c. petal 539:2
Crimsoned in thy leth 450:9
Crimson-tipped: wee modest c. flow'r 107:7
Crinkum-crankums: Chinese c. 379:22
Cripple: comfort's a c. 189:2
Crippled and palsied and slain 422:20
Crisp: deep and c. and even 361:19
Crisped: leaves they were c. and sere 381:1
waters of the c. spring 170:22
Crispian: Crispin C. shall ne'er go by 444:28
this day..the feast of C. 444:28
tomorrow is Saint C. 444:28
Crispin: upon Saint C.'s Day 189:8, 444:28(-445)
Criterion: only infallible c. of wisdom 103:2
Critic: c. and whippersnapper 89:25
C., you have frowned 580:10

INDEX

Critic (*cont.*)
don't view me with a c.'s eye 202:16
exhausted air-bell of the C. 90:30
first attribute of a good c. 320:19
in logic a great c. 110:5
Jonson knew the c.'s part 154:4
youngest c. has died 303:19
Critical: c. period in matrimony 243:13
easier..to be c. than..correct 180:25
most generous, sternly c. 241:29
nothing if not c. 470:26
Criticism: bound by my own definition of c. 19:12
cant of c. is the most tormenting 513:16
c. is applied..to what he makes of it 268:14
c. of administration 28:23
c. of life 19:22
every wind of c. 275:26
father of English c. 278:6
I do not resent c. 144:4
people ask you for c. 335:5
Stealthy School of C. 411:39
wreathed the rod of c. with roses 182:48
Criticisms: they pass no c. 196:31
Criticizing: spite of all the c. elves 143:24
Critics: before you trust in c. 117:13
cosmopolitan c. 181:9
c. all are ready made 117:11
c...brushers of noblemen's clothes 24:41
therefore they turn c. 152:30
these our c. much confide in 521:19
you know who the c. are? 182:21
Critique: killed off by one c. 116:35
Croaks the fatal entrance of Duncan 457:3
Crocodile: chief of the Pyramid and C. 288:29
cruel crafty C. 509:24
how doth the little c. 128:23
to these c.'s tears 109:27
what manner o' thing is your c.? 424:17
Crocodiles: wisdom of the c. 27:40
Crocus: c. brake like fire 537:31
c. lays her cheek to mire 336:44
roaring moon of daffodil and c. 538:6
Croesus: not an intellectual C. 182:18
Croire: qu'une chose soit possible pour la c. 557:12
Cromek: O! Mr. C.—how do ye do? 74:19
Cromwell: Charles the First his C. 242:16
C., damned to everlasting fame 384:12
C...sentiments of religion 103:4
had Caesar or C. changed countries 226:25
Philistine of genius..C. 20:19
ruins that C. knocked about a bit 315:2
some C. guiltless 230:5
Cromwell Road: blockin' the half o'␣the C. 299:19
Crony: his ancient, trusty, drouthy c. 108:5
Crooked: c. man..walked a c. mile 369:3
c. shall be made straight 54:9
every rod..c. at the top 28:12
strive to set the c. straight 359:1
Crookedly: one before him walked very c. 519:1
Crook-knee'd: my hounds..c. 467:20
Crooks: develop his hooks and his c. 107:36
Crop: a-watering the last year's c. 196:7
runnable stag, a kingly c. 169:15
what a c. of chop-sticks 379:22
Crop-full: irks care the c. bird? 95:14
Crop-headed Parliament 90:16
Cropped: notched and c. scrivener 306:18
Croppy: Hoppy, C., Droppy 213:5
Cross: bloody c. he bore 509:18
by the merit of the holy C. 361:13
Christians, at your c. of hope 87:38
c. him in nothing 423:30
c. shines forth 210:8
crucify mankind upon a c. of gold 98:2
has his little c. to take 4:8
he hadde a c. of latoun 137:22
I'll c. it, though it blast me 430:16

Cross (*cont.*)
I the body, He the C. 543:18
last at His c. 35:25
nailed..on the bitter c. 438:12
No C., No Crown 377:6
no c...no crown 404:12
once upon the c. 8:2
simply to thy C. I cling 548:12
sparkling c. she wore 385:10
Thy C. before my closing eyes 322:2
to c. the narrow sea 562:16
under the c. of gold 537:16
we gave the C. 92:11
when I survey the wondrous C. 562:18
where prayers c. 461:34
with the C. of Jesus 35:1
Cross-bow: whizz of my c. 149:18
with my c. I shot the Albatross 149:1
Cross-breed: Conservatism, an unhappy c. 181:38
Crossed: man..c. with adversity 484:38
oyster may be c. in love 500:7
they c. themselves for fear 534:10
we had c. each other's way 569:6
when I have c. the bar 528:22
would have c. once more 323:25
Crosses: are they clinging to their c.? 140:1
c., relics, crucifixes 111:12
e'en c. from his sov'reign hand 248:1
fret thy soul with c. 510:16
what c. to ensue 442:5
Cross-gartered: c., a fashion she detests 483:21
wished to see thee ever c. 483:19
Cross-grained brute 227:11
Crossing: dream you are c. the Channel 219:10
Cross-patch, draw the latch 366:14
Crossways: things at home are c. 125:20
Crotchets: some c. in thy head 465:36
Crouch: make c. beneath his foot 96:13
still bidding c. 93:5
they c. in the night 171:10
to fawn, to c., to wait 510:16
Crow: c. doth sing as sweetly 465:22
c. makes wing to the rooky wood 459:8
flew down a monstrous c. 130:6
many-winter'd c. 534:20
my lungs begin to c. 427:15
old Adam, the carrion c. 38:26
risen to hear him c. 196:13
there is an upstart c. 232:6
Crowbar: straightened out for a c. 251:16
Crowd: all at once I saw a c. 577:5
all c., who foremost shall be damn'd 381:20
all the fools that c. thee so 158:22
c., and buz, and murmurings 158:12
c. is not company 26:16
c. not on my soul 229:25
far from the madding c. 230:7
fear and favour of the c. 295:7
forgotten c. of common beauties 125:1
I hate the c. 309:7
not feel the c. 163:23
not sullen from the suppliant c. 164:34
trees..shall c. into a shade 385:7
vain the ardour of the c. 231:7
we met, 'twas in a c. 37:3
will she pass in a c.? 519:25
Crowded: one c. hour of glorious life 357:22
Crowding: mechanic porters c. in 443:10
thoughts..come c. in 194:12
thy white sails c. 81:26
Crowds: apprehensions come in c. 573:1
c. without company 216:27
her noise, her c., her beloved smoke 307:5
if you can talk with c. 297:12
nor cheering c. 584:21
Crowed: more he c., more we cried 232:3
Crow-flowers, nettles, daisies 437:1
Crowing: faded on the c. of the cock 430:20
Crown: airy gold c. on 'er 'ead 303:27
ambassador from Britain's c. 188:30
better than his c. 464:33
bid defiance to all the forces of the C. 379:11

Crown (*cont.*)
both divide the c. 191:13
calm's not life's c. 19:6
cares that wait upon a c. 232:5
chance may c. me 456:25
c. him with glory and worship 392:11
c. is of night 524:3
c. of our life as it closes 523:1
c. o' the earth doth melt 425:29
c. of these..of love and friendship 284:26
c. of twelve stars 71:16
C...the 'fountain of honour' 28:22
c. the wat'ry glade 230:23
c. thy good with brotherhood 36:23
c. to her husband 50:1
c. I what is it? 357:24
ere the King's c. shall fall 416:8
fell down and broke his c. 367:9
fighting for the c. 367:13
fill me from the c. to the toe 457:3
from Caesar's laurel c. 73:27
give me the c...Here cousin, seize the c. 475:19
give thee a c. of life 70:30
go forth and conquer a c. 371:1
hairy gold c. on 'er 'ead 303:27
head that wears a c. 442:3
hers of the Book, the tripled C. 404:20
his breeches cost him but a c. 471:11
his hair was like a c. 140:20
hoary head is a c. of glory 50:16
holly bears the c. 10:14
how can I c. thee further? 304:5
I c. thee king of intimate delights 163:26
I give away my c. 475:22
kingly c. to gain 240:20
likeness of a kingly c. 346:4
might of Denmark's c. 122:3
more glorious is the c. 503:6
my verse is not a c. 245:2
no bays to c. it 244:9
No Cross, No C. 377:6
no cross..no c. 404:12
no monarch but would give his c. 558:1
no putting by that c. 413:9
not the king's c. 461:28
obtain a corruptible c. 66:37
one..never thought of hath worn the c. 56:41
power of the C...grown up anew 101:34
power of the C. has increased 20:24
receive the c. of life 69:28
sceptre and c. must tumble down 501:5
shakes from Life's fresh c. 38:28
shrewd steel against our golden c. 475:1
sorrow's c. of sorrow 534:21
strike his father's c. into the hazard 443:11
success perhaps may c. us 163:19
sweet fruition of an earthly c. 330:28
sword, the mace, the c. imperial 444:23
that I may c. you with it 586:5
this golden c. like a deep well 475:19
this I count the glory of my c. 198:12
though they possess the c. 170:17
thy joy and c. eternally 354:11
upon the brow of labor this c. of thorns 98:2
wished to restore the c. 272:27
within the hollow c...Death 475:7
Crowned: c., and again discrown'd 269:27
c. from some single herb or tree 332:13
c. with calm leaves 523:20
c. with glory now 291:18
c. with milk-white may 82:7
c. with rank fumiter 454:2
c. with the stars 548:13
love is c. with the prime 428:33
once was c. with thorns 291:18
seem to have thee c. withal 457:2
sitting c. upon the grave 248:23
so should desert in arms be c. 190:34
they c. him long ago 118:7

INDEX

Crowned (cont.)
with inward glory c. 498:24
with thy grapes our hairs be c. 424:19
Crowner: c.'s quest law 437:4
Medical C.'s..queer 34:19
Crownest the year with thy goodness 395:30
Crown imperial: bold oxlips and
the c. 485:26
Crowning mercy 167:5
Crownless: childless and c. 114:13
Crowns: casting down their golden
c. 240:19
c. are empty things 170:17
c. for convoy put into his purse 444:28
c. imperial, c. and coronets 443:12
c. o' the world 89:2
each your doing..c. what you are
doing 485:27
end c. all 481:28
end that c. us 481:28
give c. and pounds and guineas 202:15
I'd c. resign 327:5, 551:5
in his livery walk'd c. and crownets 426:1
last act c. the play 404:10
not thrones and c., but men 198:22
there are c. to be broke 416:8
twenty mortal murders on their
c. 459:17
wreath of hair which c. my arm 185:4
Crows: city of kites and c. 429:16
c...that wing the midway air 454:3
wars of Kites or C. 352:30
Crowsfeet: till c. be growe under
your yë 138:29
Crow-toe: tufted c., and pale jessamine 342:31(–343)
Croys: c. of latoun 137:22
*Crucem: juxta c. lacrimosa
si libenter c. portas* 291:24
Crucible: America is God's C. 587:18
Crucified: Christ is c. again 313:5
faith of Christ c. 390:58
Jesus Christ, and him c. 66:21
this their carrion c. 522:21
till his Lord is c. 320:12
where the dear Lord was c. 4:4
young Man c. 338:4
Crucifix: c...carven from the
laurel-tree 545:7
Crucifixes: crosses, relics, c. 111:12
Crucify: c. hearts, not hands 525:18
c. mankind upon a cross of gold 98:2
c. the old man 390:60
c...the Son of God afresh 69:9
people would not even c. him 127:25
Crucis: fulget c. mysterium 210:8
Crude: your berries harsh and c. 342:10
Cruel: c., but composed and bland 17:13
c. crawling foam 293:23
c. he looks, but calm and strong 496:20
c., not to trust 488:11
c., not unnatural 435:30
c., only to be kind 436:7
'c. 'tis', said she 286:24
here is c. Frederick 249:19
jealousy is c. as the grave 52:22
love of false and c. men 332:29
mercies of the wicked are c. 50:2
slain by a fair c. maid 483:6
speeches that comfort c. men 141:18
they are c. tears 473:11
when Fates turn'd c. 280:10
you c. men of Rome 448:8
Cruellest: April is the c. month 197:27
you are the c. she alive 482:20
Cruelly: most c. all day 141:35
Cruelty: all the pride, c., and ambition of man 405:13
C. has a human heart 77:4
c. to load a falling man 447:13
farewell, fair c. 482:23
fear is the parent of c. 212:7
hanging is too good..said Mr.
C. 99:16
not in c., not in wrath 317:10
one's c. is one's power 156:4
top full of direst c. 457:3
yond same sovereign c. 483:8
you wou'd affect a c. 156:4

Cruise: all on our last c. 514:34
Crumb: who craved no c. 222:27
Crumbs: c...from their masters'
table 59:40
c...from the rich man's table 62:24
picker-up of learning's c. 91:19
table-c. attract his slender feet 546:26
Crumpet: Muffin and C. Baking..
Company 176:37
Crumpetty Tree: longer I live on
this C. 312:11
Crumpled: cow with the c. horn 369:6
Crunch: munch on, c. on 94:37
Crusade: home from the C. 141:9
Cruse: little oil in a c. 48:1
my small c. best fits my little
wine 245:18
Crush: do c. their wine 332:17
Crushed: c. beneath the furrow's
weight 107:8
hope, once c. 18:30
people c. by law 103:12
Crushing: pale hands..c. out life 254:15
Crust: c. so fresh 254:27
other, upper c. 221:26
share her wretched c. 320:12
these men are all upper c. 234:1
with water and a c. 286:39
*Crustula: pueris olim dant c. blandi
doctores* 261:2
Crutch: shoulder'd his c. 224:20
Cry: almost makes me c. to tell 249:25
bubbling c. 115:30
but behold a c. 53:2
by all ye c. or whisper 303:25
consider anything, only don't c. 131:1
c., baby, c. 366:15
c. did knock against my..heart 479:19
c. is still, 'They come!' 461:2
c. not when his father dies 276:16
c. of a child by the roadway 585:17
c. of his hounds 229:16
c. of the Little Peoples 313:3
c. these dreadful summoners
grace 453:10
c...what shall I c.? 54:10
cuckoo's parting c. 18:25
deep behind him, and a c. before 531:32
dismal c. rose slowly 88:4
earth's old and weary c. 586:8
ere the Monkey People c. 301:27
far c. to Lochow 420:17
great c. in Egypt 45:48
harlot's c. from street to street 73:28(–74)
have a good c. 243:5
he'll be sure to c. 367:15
hounds all join in glorious c. 204:37
I c. in the daytime 393:1
if I c. to you then 525:32
kissed the girls and made them c. 366:22
let our c. come unto thee 391:18
life is our c. 84:3
made a woman c. 326:21
monstrous head and sickening c. 140:21
my very heart and flesh c. out 421:3
need a body c.? 104:31
no horse's c. was that 17:26
nor utter'd c. 538:25
not the exceeding bitter c. 506:19
or to any loud c. 128:6
Ruksh..uttered a dreadful c. 17:26
sleep..do not c. 170:23
sudden c. of pain 512:12
that we still should c. 28:19
to c. it up, or run it down 521:20
truth is the c. of all 43:15
war, war is still the c. 113:10
when they c. unto the Lord 398:18
when we are born we c. 454:12
when we c. to Thee 566:20
with no language but a c. 532:34
you common c. of curs 429:14
Crying: c. at the lock 339:9
infant c. in the night 532:34
neither sorrow, nor c. 71:45
one c. in the wilderness 57:28
pretty wretch left c. 477:3
they were c. and calling 536:2

Crystal: c. of his brow 321:14
golden sands and c. brooks 184:8
nearer the c. sea 131:32
on a river of c. light 204:5
scroll of c. 493:18
sea of glass like unto c. 70:37
whether on c. rocks ye rove 75:18
Crystalline: here in my c. 365:5
Cub-drawn bear 453:4
Cubit: add one c. unto his stature 58:12
Cuckold to make him a monarch 473:8
Cuckoo: as the c. is in June 440:9
c., c., well singes thu, c. 10:1
c., c., c.; O word of tear 455:35
c., jug-jug 361:6
c. of a joyless June 538:4
C.! shall I call thee bird? 573:19
c.'s parting cry 18:25
c. then, on every tree 455:35
hedge-sparrow fed the c. 452:27
lhude sing c. 9:26
merry c., messenger of Spring 509:3
rainbow and a c.'s song 169:21
responsive to the c.'s note 231:6
weather the c. likes 236:30
Cuckoo-bird: in spring-time from
the C. 581:1
Cuckoo-buds of yellow hue 455:35
Cuckoo-echoing, bell-swarmed 254:22
Cuckoo-flowers: hemlock, nettles,
c. 454:2
Cuckoos: owls and c. 351:18
Cucumber: c...thrown out 276:9
know'd she wouldn't have a c. 176:29
Cucumbers: lodge in a garden of c. 52:28
sunbeams out of c. 519:18
Cuddesdon: Hey for C.! 292:10
Cudgel: c. thy brains no more 437:7
grievous crab-tree c. 99:21
what wood a c.'s of 110:39
Cue: my c. is villanous melan-
choly 452:21
with a twisted c. 220:6
Cuff neglectful 246:4
Cuisses: his c. on his thighs 440:18
Cully: Man..Woman's c. 155:25
Culpa: nulla pallescere c. 256:18
O *felix c.* 353:5
qui illius c. cecidit 132:19
Cult: local c. called Christianity 236:1
Cultivate: c. literature upon a little
oatmeal 505:26
c. our garden 557:3
c. simplicity, Coleridge 306:31
Cultivated: c. by narrow minds 338:22
c., underrated nobleman 218:17
if Shakespeare's genius had been
c. 139:21
stopped short in the c. court 220:27
Cultiver notre jardin 557:3
Cultor: parcus deorum c. 258:27
Culture: as a man of c. rare 220:25
c., the acquainting ourselves
with the best 20:8
great aim of c. 19:24
men of c...true apostles of
equality 19:26
pursue C. in bands 565:29
when I hear anyone talk of C. 223:12
Cumae: I saw the Sibyl at C. 410:19
*Cumaei: ultima C. venit iam car-
minis aetas* 555:30
Cumbered: Martha was c. 61:44
Cumbereth: why..c. it the ground? 62:1
Cummin: tithe of mint and c. 60:17
Cumner cowslips never stirr'd 18:28
Cumnor Hall: walls of C. 338:13
Cunctando: unus homo..c. 201:26
Cunning: by the very c. of the
scene 433:36
craftsman c. at his trade 295:14
c. men pass for wise 25:44
c. times put on 464:15
have more c. to be strange 477:21
my right hand forget her c. 400:5
Cunningest pattern of excelling
nature 473:11
Cunningly: little world made c. 185:12
Cup: ah, fill the c. 206:19
another and another C. 206:14
awake .and fill the c. 205:6

Cup (cont.)
come, fill the C. 205:14, 15
come, fill up my c. 416:8, 420:15
crown life's early c. with..woe 492:4
c. is nearly full 135:3
c., the c. itself 330:22
c. us, till the world go round 424:19
dash down yon c. 116:3
drink one c. of wine 418:19
drown'd my glory in a shallow c. 207:20
drunk their C. a round or two before 206:6
every inordinate c. is unblessed 471:23
fill high the c. with Samian wine 116:1
fill the can, and fill the c. 541:14
fill the C. that clears TO-DAY 206:5
giveth his colour in the c. 50:32
in the hand of the Lord..a c. 396:31
Jamshyd's Sev'n-ring'd C. 205:9
leave a kiss but in the c. 280:21
let this c. pass from me 60:41
life's enchanted c. 113:23
Life's Liquor in its C. be dry 205:6
many a C. of this forbidden Wine 206:15
my c. overflows 421:1
my c. shall be full 393:10
perfect the c. as planned 95:26
pure c. of rich Canary wine 280:9
take a c. 366:14
there's Death in the c. 105:35
uses of a c. 95:25
we'll tak a c. o' kindness yet 104:15
woodspurge has a c. of three 411:37
Cupboard: c. was bare 363:4
either our c. of food 244:23
went to the c. 368:4
Cupboards: her c. opened 237:5
inmost c. of her heart 542:13
Cupid: C. abroad was lated 231:33
C. and my Campaspe played 321:14
C. hath clapped him o' the shoulder 428:18
C. is a knavish lad 467:11
C. paid 321:14
C.'s darts do not feel 8:10
giant-dwarf, Dan C. 455:8
silent note which C. strikes 86:32
to Chloe's breast young C. 74:9
where the bolt of C. fell 466:39
wing'd C. painted blind 466:22
young Adam C. 477:12
young C.'s fiery shaft 466:39
Cupidines: lugete, O Veneres C.que 132:12
Cupidinibus: responsare c. 262:1
Cupidinum: mater saeva C. 258:21, 260:17
Cupido gloriae novissima exuitur 526:16
Cupids: boys, like smiling C. 424:6
go revel, ye C. 526:22
Cupressi: inter viburna c. 555:18
Cups: c., that cheer but not ·inebriate 163:21
daffadillies fill their c. with tears 342:31(-343)
in their flowing c. freshly remembered 444:28
when flowing c. run swiftly round 319:5
white c., whose wine was the bright dew 497:22
Cur: about the ears of the old c. 110:30
already curtail'd c. 120:28
half lurcher and half c. 163:39
possible a c. can lend? 463:22
wreke him on a flye, as doth a c. 138:20
Cura: atra C. 259:16
Curae: ultrices posuere cubilia C. 554:27
Curate: c...fatter than his cure 529:12
I was a pale young c. then 222:15
mildest c. going 218:8
to sit upon the c.'s knee 141:17
very name of a C. 505:21
Curates: c., long dust 84:11
preached to death by wild c. 505:6
upon our Bishops and C. 388:30
Curb: c. a runaway young star or two 119:15
might c. your magnanimity 291:1
one c. out of the mouth of..man 78:10
rusty c. of old father antick 438:19

Curbing his lavish spirit 456:9
Curch: is my basnet a widow's c.? 31:6
Curd: mere white c. of ass's milk 385:30
Curdied: icicle..c. by the frost 429:20
Curds: queen of c. and cream 485:28
sweet milk of kindness into c. 251:9
Cure: c. for admiring the House of Lords 29:1
c. for this ill 297:28
c. her of that 460:37
c. the disease and kill the patient 26:18
death is the c. of all diseases 86:35
for c. on exercise depend 192:15
give the ill he cannot c. a name 19:5
labour against our own c...death 86:35
love's a malady without a c, 193:12
no c. for this disease 41:2
palliate what we cannot c. 277:24
quacks..in the cure of souls 253:14
thy God, thy life, thy c. 552:2
which laws or kings can cause or c. 226:17, 278:29
Cured: some of your hurts you have c. 199:25
Curfew: c. must not ring tonight 547:6
c. tolls the knell 229:28
I hear the far-off c. sound 341:15
Curfew-tide: mothy c. 236:9
Curia: quae semper celebrat superna c. 1:1
Curiosity: disinterested intellectual c. 549:8
'satiable c. 304:16
these uneasy pleasures are for c. 200:15
Curious: capable of much c. pleasure 120:5
come..the c. here 164:35
c. in unnecessary matters 56:32
spit upon my c. floor 245:12
ye c. carpet knights 217:16
Curiouser and curiouser 128:22
Curiously: to be read but not c. 27:17
to consider too c. 437:17
Curis: quid solutis est beatius c.? 132:21
Curl: had a little c. 318:17
language..make your hair c. 222:6
winds that c. the flood 319:7
Curled: clouds are lightly c. 535:19
c. minion, dancer 17:25
c. up on the floor 239:2
heavy-c...a charioteer 411:15
her hair was so charmingly c. 293:17
I saw the c. drops 166:3
serving-man..that c. my hair 453:19
wealthy c. darlings 469:41
Curling their monstrous heads 442:1
Curly locks, curly locks 366:16
Currency: debasing the moral c. 196:33
Current: Beauty..must be c. 340:37
fountain from the which my c. runs 472:34
freshening its c. 16:4
froze the genial c. of the soul 230:5
icy c. and compulsive course 472:12
o'er-walk a c. roaring loud 438:37
smooth c. of domestic joy 278:29
take the c. when it serves 451:20
Currents: split his c. 17:28(-18)
their c. turn awry 434:4
Curriculum: grand, old..classical c. 20:1
Currite: lente, lente, c. noctis equi 330:7
Curs: as c. mouth a bone 143:19
c. of low degree 225:20
you common cry of c. 429:14
Curse: all the woes that c. our race 218:15
began he to c. and to swear 60:47
c. causeless shall not come 50:37
c, God, and die 48:43
c. his better angel from his side 473:25
c. in a dead man's eye 149:22
c. is come upon me 534:7
c. my fate 486:24
c. of kings to be attended 447:42
c. of this country is eloquent men 201:16
c. on his virtues 1:20
C. shall be on thee 507:15
c. thee in the bitterness of his soul 56:33
c. thine own inconstancy 125:8

Curse (cont.)
c. to party strife 574:3
greatness..is to me a c. 334:20
I called thee to c. mine enemies 46:20
I know how to c. 479:26
man to man..the greatest c. 33:15
never was heard such a terrible c. 34:11
O c. of marriage 471:40
open foe may prove a c. 215:24
orphan's c. 149:22
O strife, O c. 88:26
that is love's c. 530:41
'tis the c. of the service 469:24
Cursed: c. be he that moves my bones 488:29
c. be the heart that thought 31:3
c. himself in his despair 507:27
c. me with his eye 149:17
c. whatever brute and blackguard 263:31
he c. him in sleeping 34:10
he is a c. Whig 275:14
O! c., c. slave 473:27
thin he c. him squarely 298:21
to all succeeding ages c. 190:13
whom thou cursest is c. 46:17
with want of genius c. 192:10
Curses: c. are like young chickens 507:13
c. from pole to pole 74:13
c., not loud, but deep 460:36
rigged with c. dark 342:25
so c. all Eve's daughters 466:13
Curset: whom thou c. is cursed 46:17
Cursing: blessing and c. 46:30
Cursores: quasi c...lampada tradunt 321:1
Curtail the already curtail'd cur 120:28
Curtain: c. drops 543:6
draw the c. close 445:32
drew Priam's c. 441:9
iron c. 144:15, 549:19
Mrs. Caudle's C. Lectures 269:9
these gifts a c. before 'em 482:8
thy hand..lets the c. fall 381:27
Curtained: abuse the c. sleep 458:1
c. with cloudy red 343:24
Curtains: as the c. of Solomon 51:39
fringed c. of thine eye 479:31
let fall the c. 163:21
through c. call on us 186:19
Curtsey: c. while you're thinking 130:1
made a remarkable c. 311:6
Curtsied when you have, and kiss'd 479:28
Curtsies: dream on c. straight 477:7
low-crooked c. 449:29
Curva: versus superiorem partem c. est 28:12
Curve: dear red c. of her lips 333:19
Curves of the white owl 336:9
Curving on a sky imbrued with colour 94:8
Curzon: my name is George Nathaniel C. 8:15
Cushes: his c. on his thighs 440:18
Cushion: c. and soft dean 385:4
he hath a cushion plump 150:8
sit on a c. 366:16
Thorns in the C. 542:29
Custodes: quis custodiet ipsos c.? 283:11
Custody: Wragg is in c. 19:11
Custom: at the receipt of c. 58:37
contrary to c. and experience 205:10
c. calls me to't 429:9
c. lie upon thee with a weight 576:16
c. loathsome to the eye 267:30
c. make it their perch 461:22
c. more honour'd in the breach 431:31
c. of Branksome Hall 417:5
c. reconciles us to everything 102:33
c. stale her infinite variety 424:9
c. that is before all law 168:6
c., that unwritten law 169:9
c...the great guide of human life 265:11
c. to whom c. 66:11
invent some other c. 471:7
lest one good c...corrupt the world 531:35
more kind than is her c. 465:9

INDEX

D

Custom (cont.)
nature her c. holds 437:2
old c. made this life more sweet 426:29
season, form, office, and c. 481:2
that monster, c. 436:5
tyrant, c. 470:8
what c. wills 429:9
Customary: every public action.. not c. 157:10
Customer: tough c. in argeyment 173:17
Customers: raising up a people of c. 503:11
Customs: how little are our c. known 215:34
ill c. influence my very senses 201:31
Cut: air is c. away before 150:1
C c. it 366:7
c. across the reflex of a star 575:25
c. down, dried up, and withered 397:15
c. each other's throats for pay 225:24
c. him out in little stars 478:20
c. is the branch 330:12
c. it down 62:1
c. off.. in the blossoms of my sin 432:17
c. off out of the land of the living 54:27
c. out of the grass 140:11
c. up what remains 304:4
from the cheerful ways of men c. off 346:70
hinds who c. and came again 165:7
hold, or c. bow-strings 466:32
if c. deep down the middle 88:7
isn't etiquette to c. anyone 131:28
laurels all are c. 33:9, 263:27
most unkindest c. of all 450:30
name, that shall not be c. off 54:33
scuttled ship or c. a throat 115:41
they'll c. a dash 219:22
Cutlets: suggested we should play 'C.' 233:6
Cut-purse of the empire 435:49
Cuts: c. me.. a huge half-moon 439:44
c. off..life, c. off..fearing death. 449:34
c. off what we possest 191:34
c. the wrong man's head off 178:39
Cut'st: O time that c. down all 246:7
thou c. my head off with a golden axe 478:23
Cutting: c. all the pictures out 40:19
c. bread and butter 543:12
c. too close..the corner of nonsense 153:13
that with most c. grows 168:7
Cutty-Sark: weel done, C.! 108:13
Cyclads: young C. on a sunnier deep 493:25
Cycle: c. and epicycle, orb in orb 348:30
c. of Cathay 535:1
Cyclopean: such C. arches 141:2
Cyeno: nigro. .simillima c. 283:8
Cydnus: I am again for C. 426:5
Cygnet's down is harsh 480:39
Cygnets: her drowsy c. save 445:26
Cymbal: sounding brass or a tinkling c. 66:44
talk but a tinkling c. 26:16
Cymbals: praise him upon the...c. 400:28
Cynara: faithful to thee, C. 187:9
I have forgot much, C. 187:10
Cynic: what is a c.? 570:1
Cynicism is intellectual dandyism 337:23
Cynosure of neighbouring eyes 342:1
Cynthia: catch..the C. of this minute 384:29
nor C. teeming 332:10
now C. nam'd, fair regent of the Night 216:3
Cypress: in sad c. let me be laid 113:1
land where the c. and myrtle 113:1
nor shady c. tree 409:29
nor waves the c. 539:2
pluck, pluck c., O pale maidens 17:2
through an alley Titanic of c. 381:2
under that c. tree 247:3
Cypresses: along the avenue of c. 310:23
rounder 'twixt the c. 94:8
Cyprian: forsake her C. groves 102:44
Cyrene: parts of Libya about C. 64:26
Cytherea: or C.'s breath 485:26
Cytherean: throned C. be fallen 525:13

D: never use a big, big D. 221:13
there are your d.'s for you 583:23
Da quod iubes 21:23
Dabis: nec ut soles d. iocos 233:19
Dacian: there was their D. mother 114:19
Dacotahs: from the land of the D. 317:20
Dad: to meet their D. 104:33
Daedal: rules with D. harmony 497:14
Daemonum: poesy vinum d. 24:25
Daffadillies fill their cups with tears 342:31(-343)
Daffadowndillies: strew me the ground with D. 510:23
Daffadowndilly: Diaphenia, like the d. 156:19
D. is new come to town 366:17
Daffed the world aside 440:16
Daffodil: bed of d. sky 536:10
moon of d. and crocus 538:6
shining d. dies 536:23
Daffodils: April..and d. 334:15
d. that come before the swallow 485:26
dances with the d. 577:7
fair d., we weep 246:2
host of golden d. 577:5
when d. begin to peer 485:16
Daft: hae put me d. 106:23
half..thinks the tither d. 420:12
Dagger: air-drawn d. 459:16
d. of the mind 457:20
deadly daunting d. 583:23
is this a d.? 457:20
thou stick'st a d. in me 464:10
Daggers: always been at d.-drawing 110:45
give me the d. 458:14
I will speak d. to her 435:30
there's d. in men's smiles 458:27
Dahin! Dahin! 224:6
Dahlias: the d. are dead 518:27
Daily: d. beauty in his life 473:9
d. labour's dull, Lethean spring 16:5
dreary intercourse of d. life 582:3
what men d. do! 469:4
Daily Mail: sandwich men of the D. 142:4
Daily Telegraph: young lions of the D. 19:8
Daintier: the d. sense 437:10
Dainties: d...bred in a book 455:11
spiced d. 285:25
Daintily dressed Walt Whitman 142:19
Dainty: every d. that is in that hous 137:36
Dairy: nightly rob the d. 281:5
see the cat i' the d. 196:15
Dairymaid: the Queen asked the D. 339:17
Daisies: buttercups and d. 264:22
crow-flowers, nettles, d. 437:1
d. pied and violets blue 455:35
d. smell-less, yet most quaint 38:8
d., those pearled Arcturi 497:21
left the d. rosie 536:4
meadows trim with d. pied 342:1
swiche as men callen d. 138:17
toes..turned up to the d. 33:19
white d. prank the ground 82:7
you must lie upon the d. 220:26
Daisy: D., D., give me your answer 168:2
d. delectable 502:19
'd.' or elles the 'ye of day' 138:19
d...protects the..dewdrop 573:18
mourn'st the D.'s fate 107:8
there's a d. 436:32
Daisy-star that never sets 494:10
Dale: from haunted spring and d. 343:22
the doxy, over the d. 485:16
through wood and d. 151:33
under the hawthorn in the d. 341:34
Dalhousy, the great God of War 381:9
Dalliance: primrose path of d. 431:23
silken d. in the wardrobe 443:12
Dallied with his golden chain 528:27
Dallies with the innocence of love 483:5
Dally with false surmise 343:1
Dam: all my.pretty chickens and their d. 460:21

Damage: first, material d... second, moral or intellectual d. 305:11
Damaged: Archangel a little d. 307:13
Damasco or Marocco or Trebisond 345:4
Damascus: looketh towards D. 52:19
rivers of D. 48:22
Damask: feed on her d. cheek 483:10
Damasked: tiger-moth's deep-d. wings 285:19
Dame: d. naturis menstralis 187:4
la belle d. sans mercy 285:26, 286:35
my d. has lost her shoe 366:12
one for the d. 366:9
pass for a most virtuous D. 401:24
our sulky sullen d. 108:2
Dames: ah, gentle d. 472:21
many worthy and chaste d. 472:21
struts his d. before 341:32
Damiata: betwixt D. and Mount Casius 345:31
Dammed: only saved by being d. 253:34
Damn: abuses me to d. me 433:37
d. braces 77:18
d. by rule 371:11
d. her at a venture 308:7
d. the age 307:22
d. the consequences 339:25
d. those authors whom they never read 142:29
d. with faint praise 385:29
d. your cards 520:31
d. your principles 181:16
he doesn't give a d. 9:14
her aged soul to d. 141:33
I don't care a twopenny d. 564:25
leave their job when they d. well choose 302:2
like a parson's d. 237:2
marshal or two..not worth a d. 564:1
only thing that doesn't give a d. 296:25
she did not give a singel d. 208:21
with a spot I d. him 451:4
young man who said, 'D.' 237:26
Damna: d. tamen..reparant caelestia lunae 260:26
per d., per caedis 260:21
Damnable: destructive, d., deceitful woman 371:1
Lady Teazle, by all that's d.! 500:42
Damnation: blasted to eternal d. 491:3
deep d. of his taking off 457:9
eat and drink..d. 390:33
eating a d. egg 177:16
gone to the d. bow-wows 177:26
heap on himself d. 344:20
hope of eternal d. 43:20
I dare d. 436:28
Damnations: twenty-nine distinct d. 96:40
Damned: all silent and all d. 578:27
almost d. in a fair wife 469:21
another d., thick, square book 223:5
brandy of the d. 490:20
cohort of the d. 296:26
Cromwell, d. to everlasting fame 384:12
d. are those who dare resist 7:9
d. be he that first cries 'Hold' 461:14
d., damp, moist, unpleasant body 177:21
d. disinheriting countenance 500:41
d. for never a king's son 438:24
d. from here to Eternity 296:27
d. long, dark..way 227:6
d. outline 177:20
d. would make no noise 247:14
devil with devil d. 345:28
dissolute, d., and despairful 422:20
drink to poor d. souls 297:5
Faustus must be d. 330:7
for an apple d. mankind 371:10
foremost shall be d. to fame 381:20
for ever d. with Lucifer 330:1
go and find out and be d. 299:2
hellish, devilish, and d. tobacco 109:22
if I were d. of body and soul 299:27(-300)
I'm d. if I see it 362:32
I will see thee d. first 124:9
no soul to be d. 547:15
one d. horrid grind 177:25
one d. thing after another 264:25
or goblin d. 431:32

[665]

Damned (cont.)
Protection is not only dead, but
d.   181:17
public be d.   551:12
publish and be d.   504:26
smiling, d. villain   432:21
then thou must be d. perpetually   330:7
what d. minutes   471:32
what do you mean by d.?   275:20
what else is d. to fame   415:18
you will be d. if you don't   187:7
Damning: always had a taste for d.   357:20
d. those they have no mind to   110:20
Damnosa hereditas   212:23
Damozel: blessed d. leaned out   410:7
Damp: demd, d., moist, unpleasant body   177:21
d. fell round..Milton   580:17
d. my intended wing   349:6
nights are very d.   128:19
Dams: as my lambs..beloved of
their d.   156:19
Damsel: d. lay deploring   216:5
d. possessed with..divination   64:55
d. with a dulcimer   151:33(–152)
to every man a d.   46:52
Damsels: allur'd the Syrian d.   344:32
d. playing with the timbrels   396:12
faery d. met in forest wide   350:4
Dan: from D...to Beer-sheba   46:61
from D. to Beersheba..all
barren   512:20
Danaë: all D. to the stars   539:2
Danaos: timeo D.   553:27
Dance: come to balls to..d.   518:38
d. an antic hay   329:20
d., and Provençal song   287:24
d. attendance   447:12
d. barefoot on her wedding day   479:3
d. is a measured pace   24:21
d. ne moe atte hallie daie   136:17
d. on the sands   488:26
d. upon the air   569:5
each d. the others would   171:22
folk d. like a wave   585:2
he fixed thee mid this d.   95:24
love's but a d.   183:7
luxury and riot, feast and d.   349:27
merry love to d.   585:1
on with the d.   113:26
or to d. at our bridal   418:18
to d. to flutes, to d. to lutes   569:5
walk at least before they d.   386:8
when you do d.   485:27
while others d. and play   266:8
who have learned to d.   382:32
will you join the d.?   129:23
you have the Pyrrhic d. as yet   116:2
Danced: d. at the end of a bough   312:14
death-fires d. at night   149:6
if he'd d. till doomsday   155:8
many an eye has d.   251:5
say the Graces d.   319:1
Seal, and Maces, d. before him   230:19
there was a star d.   468:16
they d. by the light of the moon   312:3
thro' the..heather we d. together   121:15
ye have not d.   59:8
young man that d. daintily   25:5
Dancer, coiner of sweet words   17:25
Dancers: breaks time, as d.   124:2
d. dancing in tune   536:11
Dances: d. and delight   466:41
d. with the daffodils   577:7
fairies break their d.   264:1
he capers, he d.   466:5
in hamlets, d. on the green   417:16
in what ethereal d.   380:21
when she d. in the wind   194:22
Dancing: dancers d. in tune   536:11
d. dogs and bears   249:5
d. in the chequered shade   342:3
d. to put thy..lilies out of mind   187:10
emptier ever d. in the air   475:19
faeries, d. under the moon   586:16
fencing, d., and bear-baiting   482:7
fluttering and d. in the breeze   577:5
follows with d.   522:2
manners of a d. master   270:21

Dancing (cont.)
merry, d., drinking..time   193:31
'mid these d. rocks   151:33
no d. bear was so genteel   160:13
past our d. days   477:8
say I am d.   423:29
since the fairies left off d.   422:7
Taffy d. through the fern   299:24
'tis jesting, d., drinking   263:18
Dandilly toss of the parish   409:13
Dandled: in his paw d. the kid   347:15
Dandolo: blind old D.   114:4
Dandyism: intellectual d.   337:23
Dane: king, father, royal D.   431:32
more..than a D.   438:3
never get rid of the D.   295:18
Saxon and Norman and D.   541:18
till a feeble cheer the D...sent
us   122:5
Dane-geld: once you have paid
him the D.   295:18
Danes: all of us D.   541:18
Danger: bright eyes of d.   515:29
bright face of d.   513:28
d...in acting well   143:9
d. knows..Caesar is more dangerous   449:23
d., necessity, and tribulation   389:2
d. o'er   372:12
d., the spur of all great minds   135:25
days of d.   416:19
ev'n at the brink of d.   404:9
fear and d. of violent death   248:21
gin d.'s there   360:4
in d. of her former tooth   459:4
into any kind of d.   388:26
judge of d. which they fear   578:5
let our beard be shook with d.   436:39
neither shape of d...dismay   575:11
oft in d.   566:11
Old Lady..in D.   222:32
only five-and-twenty per cent.
of its d.   518:7
only when in d.   372:12
pleased with the d.   190:13
send d. from the east   438:37
she fear'd no d.   192:20
there is no d. to a man   135:19
there's d. on the deep   36:32
this nettle, d.   439:9
till d.'s troubled night depart   123:12
true that we are in great d.   444:11
when in d.   512:15
Dangerous: all delays are d. in war   194:1
Caesar is more d.   449:23
damned, d..way   227:6
d. Corryvreckan   146:26
d. deceits   401:11
d. to know   306:2
d. to meet it alone   565:24
d. to the lungs   267:30
in me something d.   437:23
into the d. world I leapt   76:8
little learning is a d. thing   382:22
little sincerity is a d. thing   569:31
more d. the abuse   101:29
most d. is that temptation   462:1
stablish d. constancy   185:29
such men are d.   448:26
therefore are they very d.   448:27
Dangerously dear   115:5
Dangers: d...despised grow great   101:32
D. of an Honest Man   158:23
d. of the seas   373:12
hunt for d. North and South   375:2
lov'd me for the d. I had pass'd   470:3
no d. fright him   279:5
only those who brave its d.   317:15
perils and d. of this night   388:36
she..could d. brave   35:25
what d. are incident o' th' seas   373:11
what d. thou canst make us
scorn   108:10
with d. compass'd round   348:23
Daniel: D. come to judgment!   465:4
D...greatly beloved   55:44
second D., a D., Jew!   465:12
well languag'd D.   87:23
Danish: Roman-Saxon-D.-Nor-
man English   170:13
Dank: wild and d. with foam   293:22

Dankbarer: ein einziger d. Gedanke   313:17
Danket: nun d. alle Gott   167:18
Danny Deever: they're hangin'
D.   295:20
*Danse: le congrès ne marche pas..
il d.*   313:26
Dante: D. never stays too long   325:23
D. once prepared to paint an
angel   93:47
D...put leaves round his head   176:2
D. who loved well because he
hated   93:48
grete poete..that highte D.   137:39
their D. of the dread inferno   94:12
Danube: his rude hut by the D.   114:19
Daphne: Apollo hunted D. so   332:16
Dappled: for d. things   255:2
Dapple-dawn-drawn Falcon   255:11
Dapples the drowsy east   469:19
Dare: bear to live, or d. to die   384:2
d. frame thy..symmetry?   75:24(–76)
d., never grudge the throe   95:15
d. not lie   535:43
d. to be reverent   376:4
d. to be true   243:27
d. to be unhappy   412:16
d. to do our duty   314:2
enter..you who d.   336:48
for our unworthiness we d. not   390:53
gentle woman d.   507:31
I can d. to be poor   215:35
I d. damnation   436:28
I d. do all   457:12
I d. meet Surrey   475:15
I d. not ask a kiss   247:8
'I d. not' wait upon 'I would'   457:11
if I d. eat   475:15
I will d. e'en Death   247:3
menace heaven and d. the Gods   330:23
soul to d.   416:17
what man d., I d.   459:20
what men d. do!   469:4
I d. say she will do   83:18
Dared: determined, d., and done   503:6
what none hath d.   405:13
Daren't go a-hunting   4:18
Dares: before the swallow d.   485:26
who d. do more is none   457:12
wretch that d. not die   106:35
Dares: in Omer, or in D., or in
Dyte   138:5
Darest: d. not glance thine eye   231:36
d. thou die?   462:7
how d. thou put thy-self in
prees?   138:14
Darien: upon a peak in D.   288:19
Daring: d. pilot in extremity   190:13
d. to excel   143:9
more d. or more bold   440:28
song too d.   401:31
Dark: after that the d.   528:22
all colours will agree in the d.   27:34
all poor souls lost in the d.   92:7
all that's best of d. and bright   119:1
as children fear to go in the d.   26:1
as good i' th' dark   246:12
at one stride comes the d.   149:14
between the d. and the daylight   316:3
blanket of the d.   457:3
calling through the d.   538:5
Childe Roland to the D. Tower
came   90:23, 453:27
come home in the d.   571:3
damned, long, d...way   227:6
d. and true and tender   538:20
d. as winter was..Iser   122:17
d. behind it rose the forest   317:22
d., frieze-coated..Month   153:15
d. hair and d. brown eyes   171:24
d. horse   182:45
d. inscrutable workmanship   579:9
d. is his path   228:21
d. lowers the tempest overhead   316:19
d...the day of their flight   326:8
d., the serpent-haunted sea   208:8
d. tree, still sad   117:39
d. was over all   537:1
d. with dew   171:21
d. with excessive bright   346:22
each d. passage shun   586:28
ever-during d.   346:20

Dark (cont.)
folded us round from the d. 525:2
for a d. hour or twain 458:31
ford o' Kabul river in the d. 296:21
for us i' the d. to rise by 96:10
for ways that are d. 238:32
hellish d., and smells of cheese 518:25
here in d. to be his paramour 478:44
his affections d. as Erebus 465:20
hunt it in the d. 162:2
I don't want to go home in the d. 242:15
in this d. world and wide 351:21
John's soul flared into the d. 92:6
leap in the d. 249:2
leap into the d. 85:9
lovers eloped in the d. 309:26
moor is d. 498:26
my D. Rosaleen 329:1
nowhere but in the d. 552:10
O d., d., d.,..irrecoverably d. 350:22
o'er the d. her silver mantle threw 347:19
poring d. 444:6
saturnine, d., and melancholic 154:26
she has seen d. days before 200:3
subterranean d. has crossed the
  nadir 264:2
suffering..obscure and d. 573:7
sun..but the d. *simulacrum* 85:16
sun to me is d. 350:23
though his skin was d. 303:9
thy path is d. as night 327:3
trotting through the d. 301:18
void, d. and drear 150:31
we are for the d. 426:3
what d. days seen 487:27
what in me is d. 344:4
who art..as d. as night 488:22
with these d. words 574:32
Dark-browed sophist 537:43
Darkened: d. this swift stream 495:3
day is never d. 336:37
her eyes were d. wholly 534:9
those that look out..be d. 51:33
while the Sun..be not d. 51:33
Darkeneth counsel 49:17.
Darkening: forming in the air and
  d. the sky 407:8
Darkens: night d. the streets 344:35
Darker: as d. grows the night 224:10
d. grows the valley 336:9
d...the day of their return 326:8
now is come a d. day 495:2
sky grows d. yet 140:13
Dark-heaving, boundless, endless 114:31
Darkling: d. discontent 375:10
d. I listen 287:32
on a d. plain 15:8
wakeful bird sings d. 346:20
Darkly: being d. wise 383:22
d., deeply, beautifully blue
  116:13, 507:29
d. looked he at the wall 323:16
through a glass, d. 66:46(-67)
we buried him d. 572:11
Darkness: against the rulers of the
  d. 68:11
angler in the lake of d. 453:28
as light excelleth d. 51:1
awful d. and silence reign 311:15
between his D. and his Brightness 119:22
blackness of d. for ever 70:20
cast away the works of d. 389:22
cast into outer d. 58:33
cast off the works of d. 66:13
crown of our life..d. 523:1
d. and the death-hour 88:20
d. and the light..alike 400:9
d. comprehended it not 62:60
d. deepens 322:1
d. falls at thy behest 198:17
d. falls from the wings of Night 316:7
d. from light 90:44
d. had to a great extent arrived 237:8
d. is no d. with thee 400:9
d. of the land 533:20
d. quieted by hope 96:31
d. shall cover me 400:9
d. visible 344:9
d. was upon the face of the deep 44:1
d. which may be felt 45:44

Darkness (cont.)
dawn on our d. 240:15
deep but dazzling d. 551:21
deep into that d. peering 380:24
did the act of d. with her 453:19
encounter d. as a bride 462:8
go out into the d. 239:4
great d. falling on my soul 372:19
great horror and d. 99:24
horror of great d. 44:47
if the light..be d. 58:8
in d. and in storm..delight 37:6
in d., and with dangers compassed round 348:23
in d., fire and chains 561:22
in silent d. born 168:12
in spite of d...day 165:36
instruments of d. 456:22
in that land of d. 551:19
in the d. of her eyes 249:9
in ungauged d. hid 375:25
its nightly roll into d. 237:9
jaws of d. do devour it 466:20
land of d. 48:54
leaves the world to d. 229:28
lest d. come 63:46
lighten our d. 388:36
light in the d., sailor 415:6
light is as d. 48:55
light shineth in d. 62:60
long in d. pined 421:6
loved d. rather than light 63:10
lump bred up in d. 305:17
made his d. beautiful with thee 533:4
my d. to be light 392:29
pain, d. and cold 95:11
pass'd the door of D. through 206:27
people that walked in d. 53:14
pestilence that walketh in d. 397:18
Prince of D. is a gentleman
  453:25, 517:15
rear of d. thin 341:32
rose-crowned into the d. 84:3
sit in d. here 345:25
smoothing the raven down of d. 340:15
such as sit in d. 398:15
talks of d. at noon-day 161:32
terror of d.! 135:18
that the light..be not d. 61:49
that year of now done d. 254:20
them that sit in d. 61:15
then d. again and a silence 318:10
thou makest d. 398:10
through d. up to God 532:36
turn'd thy d. into light 161:10
universal d. buries all 381:27
walk on still in d. 397:4
wearily through d. and despair 495:10
where shades of d. 171:7
wind was a torrent of d. 366:1
Darks undreamed of 94:11
Darksome hours 127:30
Darling: Charlie he's my d. 250:17
Charlie is my d. 360:15
d., I am growing old 406:8
d. of our crew 173:10
d. of the Spring 573:20
even his d. popularity 101:21
Frenchman's d. 163:37
his bride and his d. to be 9:16
his d. sin 151:11
my d. Clementine 355:22
my d. from the power of the dog 393:7
Nature's d. 231:10
she is the d. of my heart 125:17
six years' d. 576:10
this d. of the Gods 333:5
Darlings: chime, ye dappled d. 293:14
wealthy curled d. 469:41
Darnel: d., and all the idle weeds 454:2
thistle and d. and dock 171:21
Dart: blockhead's insult points
  the d. 278:32
down the hill d. 39:3
his own feather on the fatal d. 117:25
launched point-blank her d. at
  ..a lie 91:34
nor d. of chance 472:32
shook a dreadful d. 346:4
struck by the hunter's d. 492:3
Time shall throw a d. at thee 87:24

Dartmouth: Shipman..of D. 137:11
Darts: Cupid's d. do not feel 8:10
deliverance..from the d. that
  were 236:6
fiery d. of the wicked 68:13
Dash: d. down yon cup 116:3
d. him to pieces 451:21
d. through thick and thin 159:36
long'd-for d. of waves 17:28(-18)
most, a d. between the two 336:5
they'll cut a d. 219:22
Dashed: d. all to pieces 479:19
d. through thick and thin 190:32
d. with light quick tears 522:17
sublime d. to pieces 153:13
Dastard in war 418:17
Dat: bis d. qui cito d. 526:2
bis d. qui d. *celeriter* 526:3
Data: theorize before one has d. 187:22
Date: forestall his d. of grief 340:19
keep them up to d. 489:24
your d. is not so past 245:20
youth and thou.. of one d. 486:19
Dated: women and music should
  never be d. 227:12
Dateless bargain 478:44
Dates: manna and d. 285:25
wrote down all three d. 129:28
Daub their natural faces unaware 87:35
Daubed it with slime 45:30
Daughter: bailiff's d. of Islington
  29:24(-30)
cares of d., wife, or friend 358:1
carnage..is God's d. 116:25
Carnage is Thy d. 578:9
Cato's d. 529:8
Cato's d. durst not 412:16
d. am I in my mother's house 300:11
d. hadde this..king..highte
  Canacee 138:4
d. of a hundred Earls 533:35
d. of astronomy 587:13
d. of Death and Priapus 523:7
d. of debate 198:5
d. of Earth and Water 493:1
d. of Jove, relentless power 230:15
d. of the gods 529:8
D. of the Moon, Nokomis 317:22
d. of the voice of God 573:28
d. of Tyre 394:24
death of your d...a blessing 23:3
Earl Haldan's d. 293:8
elderly ugly d. 222:19
ever rear a d. 214:12
farmer's d. hath soft brown
  hair 120:21
for the king's d. 524:19
gigantic d. of the West 529:35
hearken, O d., and consider 394:23
I am Harry's d. 298:30
I'll marry a landlord's d. 308:5
I won his d. 469:45
king of Spain's d. 367:7
King's d. is all glorious within 394:25
king's d. o' Noroway 31:24
landlord's black-eyed d. 366:2
Light (God's eldest d.) 212:13
like a Duke-and-a-Duchess's d. 34:32
married Noah's d. 23:27
Mrs. Porter and..her d. 197:31
my d.! oh my d.! 122:28
my d.! O my ducats! O my d.! 463:42
my d. the Nun 507:36
my little d...at the point of
  death 60:59
my Soul, my d. 545:1
O d. of Babylon 400:6
one fair d. 433:23
preaching down a d.'s heart 534:23
Sea-King's d. 541:18
skipper had taken his little d. 318:14
sole d. of his voice 349:14
sole d. of my house and heart 113:21
still harping on my d. 433:3
ta'en away this old man's d. 469:45
this Lord Ullin's d. 122:24
took the D. of the Vine 206:23
undaunted of desires 165:28
washed the colonel's d. 11:8
weep, d. of a royal line 118:3
whose d. was charming 306:34

Daughter (cont.)
your d. and the Moor — 469:31
Daughters: all the d. of musick — 51:33
book that my d. may read — 403:14
d. of Jerusalem — 51:39
d. of the Philistines rejoice..
  d. of the uncircumcised
  triumph — 47:29
fairest of her d. Eve — 347:13
horseleech hath two d. — 50:54
I am all the d. — 483:11
if your d. do not like them — 368:5
king's d...among thy..women — 394:23
none of Beauty's d. — 118:17
our d...as the polished corners — 400:16
so curses all Eve's d. — 466:13
sweet her artless d. — 288:24
with two pernicious d. join'd — 453:6
words are men's d. — 327:6
words are the d. of earth — 277:21
ye of Israel, weep — 47:30
Daulis: feast of D. — 524:16
Daunt: whom death could not d. — 31:14
Daunting: deadly d. dagger — 583:23
Dauntless: brows of d. courage — 345:7
d. the slug-horn to my lips — 90:23
d. Three — 323:20
so d. in war — 418:16
Dauphin: kingdom of daylight's d. — 255:11
Dauphiness: then the D. — 102:11
Davey: Peter D., Dan'l Whiddon — 33:1
David: D. had his Jonathan — 243:34
D., his ten thousands — 47:25
D. in the midst — 503:4
God-like D. was restored — 190:31
King D. and King Solomon — 361:7
like the tower of D. — 52:5
Lord, remember D. — 400:2
offspring of D. — 72:10
once in royal D.'s city — 3:20
second D. — 327:15
see to thine own house, D. — 47:48
teste D. cum Sibylla — 134:4
Davie an' Donal' an' Cherlie an' al' — 516:20
Davos sum, non Oedipus — 541:28
Davy Jones: as if D. were after you — 173:30
Daw: no wiser than a d. — 445:20
see saw, Margery D. — 368:18
Dawn: after d. doth rise — 444:33
awful rose of d. — 541:10
benediction through the d. — 545:6
Caravan starts for the D. of Nothing — 206:20
d. comes up like thunder — 299:10
d. is overcast — 1:13
d. on our darkness — 240:15
d. on the other — 41:20
day must d. — 202:25
dreaming when D.'s Left Hand — 205:6
first d. in Helen's arms — 584:23
first to..reflect the d. — 324:25
forgive you Bridge at d. — 140:3
from dewy d. to dewy night — 359:5
grey d. breaking — 334:10
grey d. is breaking — 166:24
innumerable choir .. welcome the d. — 81:20
in that d. to be alive — 575:2
in the white d. clear — 498:5
lasses a' lilting, before d. of day — 198:18
last D. of Reckoning — 207:6
May-time and the cheerful d. — 580:19
music of its trees at d. — 17:10
near all the birds will sing at d. — 87:28
no d.—no dusk—no proper time of day — 253:11
poets..needed to sing the d. — 337:14
roseate hues of early d. — 4:6
saw the d. glow through — 336:3
Sherwood in the red d. — 366:6
sigh'd for the d. — 536:13
silver sail of d. — 264:1
such as creation's d. beheld — 114:29
till the dappled d. doth rise — 341:31
to D.: be sudden — 544:17
watch from d. till gloom — 497:2
years hence..d. an age — 16:9
young d. of our eternal day — 166:5
Dawned: when first God d. on Chaos — 491:23

Dawning: bird of d. — 430:20
here has been d. — 125:26
Dawns: brightly d. our wedding day — 219:35
in dark summer d. — 538:19
Daws: for d. to peck at — 469:28
Day: across the d. — 528:29
all d. the same our postures — 184:31
all on a summer d. — 129:27
all on a summer's d. — 368:15
alternate Night and D. — 205:29, 30
amorous ditties all a summer's d. — 344:32
another blue d. — 125:26
arrow that flieth by d. — 397:18
as it fell upon a d. — 35:17
as morning shows the d. — 350:10
at close of d...sweetest — 121:18
a thousand Blossoms with the D. woke — 205:17
at rest for one d. — 155:7
at the end of thy d. — 17:19
back with Policeman D. — 295:11
beneath the blue of d. — 262:18
benight our happiest d. — 184:28
better d., the worse deed — 242:6
better..the d. of death — 51:9
beware of the d. — 128:10
bind..the eyes of D. — 495:22
blinds let through the d. — 264:1
breathers of an ampler d. — 533:26
bright d. is done — 426:3
bright d. that brings forth the adder — 449:2
brightness of a new-born d. — 576:22
broods like the d. — 576:14
brought too long a d. — 252:33
business of the d. in the d. — 564:19
busy larke, messenger of d. — 137:30
but..a natural d. — 330:7
by d. in a pillar of cloud — 45:50
calm was the d. — 510:19
cares that infest the d. — 316:10
child of a d. — 308:19
'daisy' or..'ye of d.' — 138:19
dark..the d. of their flight — 326:8
darkest d...will have passed away — 160:40
D., a dedicated priest — 545:6
d. after d., d. after d. — 507:28
d. and night, aloof — 493:14
d. and night shall not cease — 44:41
d. and the way we met — 524:9
d. becomes more solemn — 494:6
d. breaks not — 184:10
d. brought back my night — 351:26
d. but one — 79:5
d. by d. like us He grew — 4:3
d.! faster and more fast — 94:39
d. gone by — 171:1
d. hath put on his jacket — 251:2
d. in his hotness — 15:17
d. in such serene enjoyment — 355:12
d. in toil — 404:5
d. is at hand — 66:13
d. is aye fair — 360:20
d. is done — 316:7
d. is gone — 289:1
d. is never darkened — 336:37
d. is passing — 402:14
d. is past — 547:20
d. is past and gone — 32:14
d. is your own — 526:22
d. joins the past Eternity — 114:6
d. must dawn — 202:25
d. of my destiny's over — 119:9
d. of spirits — 551:20
d. of wrath — 134:4, 417:25
d. returns too soon — 119:6
d.'s dead sanctities — 544:21
d.'s at the morn — 94:40
d.'s march nearer home — 355:10
d. that comes betwixt — 125:19
D. that hath no pridie — 180:31
d. that is dead — 528:3
d. Thou gavest — 198:17
d...time enough to mourn — 168:12
d...to afflict his soul — 54:35
d. when first we met — 238:38
d. when heaven was falling — 264:4
d. when I'll be going down — 293:1

Day (cont.)
d. when the Lord Christ was born — 359:14
d. will be today — 82:10
death will have his d. — 475:4
despised the d. of small things — 56:11
dies at the opening d. — 562:9
dim night of this immortal d. — 497:16
dreams happy as her d. — 84:21
driven away from our immortal d. — 77:2
each d. dies with sleep — 255:1
each d. is like a year — 569:11
each lost d. has its patron saint — 238:29
end of a perfect d. — 78:17
enjoy bright d. — 340:20
entertains the harmless d. — 583:10
ere I had..seen that d. — 431:4
every d., for food or play — 148:28
every d. in every way — 157:22
every d. speaks a new scene — 404:10
every dog has his d. — 78:29
every dog his d. — 293:19
first d. — 44:3
first d. of our Jubilee is death — 86:20
for a d. and a night — 522:6, 525:2
for a year and a d. — 312:1
fountain-light of all our d. — 576:18
from this d. forward — 391:30
from this d. to the ending — 444:28(-445)
gaudy, blabbing, and remorseful d. — 445:33
gently shuts the eye of d. — 33:10
ghastly..breaks the blank d. — 532:9
gilded car of d. — 340:4
give account..in the d. of judgment — 59:15
go not, happy d. — 536:9
good morrow to the d. so fair — 246:22
good things of d. — 459:8
go to bed by d. — 515:14
greater light to rule the d. — 44:5
great, the important d. — 1:13
have their d. and cease to be — 531:41
heat of the d. — 60:7
heat of the long d. — 17:1
heaven to gaudy d. denies — 119:1
he did not die in the d. — 359:13
he fell..a summer's d. — 345:12
her performance keeps no d. — 124:2
hey to you—good d. to you — 221:2
his first, last, everlasting d. — 184:6
his rising fogs prevail upon the d. — 193:2
hope, wish d. come — 254:19
idle singer of an empty d. — 358:25
if she should sing by d. — 465:22
I have known no d...like this — 81:1
I loved the garish d. — 364:11
in a morn by break of d. — 80:7
infinite d. excludes the night — 562:13
innumerable choir of d. — 81:20
in pure converse our eternal d. — 84:6
in respect of this D. — 186:31
in spite of darkness..d. — 165:36
in the cool of the d. — 44:21
in the d., in the night — 568:19
in the d. of judgment — 388:51
in the d. that thou eatest — 44:13
in the passing of a d. — 509:33
in the Spirit on the Lord's d. — 70:23
it don't seem a d. too much — 142:12
it is his d. — 328:10
it is not yet near d. — 478:26
it was Thy d., sweet — 165:36
jam every other d. — 130:26
jocund d. — 478:27
John Peel at the break of the d. — 229:16
joy is like restless d. — 402:10
joy rul'd the d. — 193:32
joy the d. in mirth the while — 168:13
just for one d. — 249:17
knell of parting d. — 229:28
known a better d. — 416:29
large draughts of intellectual d. — 165:30
let the d. perish — 48:44
level of every d.'s most quiet need — 88:24
lifting up of d. — 442:24
lily of a d. — 282:1
live murmur of a summer's d. — 18:6

INDEX

Day (cont.)

life is but a d. 288:10
life's little d. 322:1
long d. done 241:23
long d.'s task is done 425:21
long d. wanes 541:3
look, the gentle d. 469:19
lord of lycht and lamp of d. 187:5
maddest merriest d. 536:26
make perpetual d. 330:7
Man! the pilgrim of a d. 122:37
many a canty d., John 106:20
memories of the d. 338:3
misty morwe folwen..mery
  someres d. 138:32
morning star, d.'s harbinger 343:8
neither..perfect d. nor night 445:44
news, the manna of a d. 231:28
next d., there she lay 139:2
night is as clear as the d. 400:9
night of time far surpasseth the
  d. 87:18
no d. for me to look upon 484:36
no knowledge when the d. was
  done 286:23
no proper time of d. 253:11
not look the same by d. 88:9
not to me returns d. 346:20
now's the d. 107:32
now the d. is over 34:35
O d. and night 432:28
o'er night's brim d. boils 94:39
O frabjous d. 129:39(-130)
on a stormy d., in a Sieve 311:22
once a d. with his embossed
  froth 480:32
one d. in thy courts 397:7
one d., one cold winter's d. 249:18
one d. telleth another 392:32
one d.'s truce 102:5
our triumphant holy d. 8:2, 13:13
pass our long love's d. 333:8
place to stand and love in for a d. 88:20
poor man's d. 228:14
posteriors of this d. 455:27
promise such a beauteous d. 486:30
rare as a d. in June 320:17
runs through the roughest d. 456:26
sailor, d. is at hand 415:6
sang it all d. long 81:10
seats of everlasting d. 562:10
see in a summer's d. 466:31
simple worship of a d. 287:18
since thy d. began 308:31
sing the glorious d.'s renown 122:3
sister, the whole d. long 128:2
some d. before I'm old 297:24
some future d. 147:11
sorrow enough..to fill our d. 300:22
sorrow of each d.'s growing 335:10
spent but one d...well 291:26
splendid for the d. 336:11
springs like a d. 496:23
stocking all the d. 224:11
succeeds thy little d. 376:20
such a d. tomorrow as today 485:3
sufficeth that the d. will end 451:38
sufficient unto the d. 58:15
sunbeam in a winter's d. 195:14
sure you shall outlive this d.? 202:1
sweet d., so cool 245:13
tender eye of pitiful d. 459:8
that d. should be so soon 525:1
there's night and d., brother 78:24
this and every d. 291:8
this d. shall gentle his condition 444:28(-445)
this d. we must part 166:24
this good d. new-born 248:7
this long weary d. have end 509:14
this new D. is born 125:27
this petty pace from d. to d. 461:4
this same d. must end the work 451:37
those who dwell in realms of D. 74:1
though the d. be never so longe 239:6
thou usherest in the d. 107:4
Thou wast up by break of d. 244:14
till perfect D. shall shine 402:10
tomorrow's falser than the former d. 191:34
to rest when d. is done 84:10

Day (cont.)

underneath D.'s azure eyes 495:1
until the d. break 52:3
until the hasting d. has run 246:2
unto my dying d., Sir 7:9
unto the perfect d. 49:43
upon a d. he gat him more
  moneye 137:22
vulgarize the d. of judgment 269:13
waking with d. 417:33
warm precincts of the cheerful
  d. 230:9
welcome d. 248:5
we said nothing, all the d. 184:31
what a d. may bring forth 50:43
what glance of d. 551:16
w'en de great d. comes 238:24
while d. stood..in the sky 237:8
while the d. ran by 244:20
whole long d. 410:2
wished for the d. 65:29
without all hope of d. 350:22
withstand in the evil d. 68:11
with which thoughts the d. rose 292:21
woe worth the d. 416:14
young dawn of our eternal d. 166:5
year's midnight and..the d.'s 186:2
Daybreak: some white tremendous
  d. 84:20
Day-dreams: like the d. of melancholy men 193:27
Day-labour: doth God exact d.? 351:21
Daylight: all the long and lone d. 495:21
between the dark and the d. 316:3
but the d. sick 465:23
d.'s past 357:16
kingdom of d.'s dauphin 255:11
must in death your d. finish? 93:25
see a church by d. 468:10
we burn d. 465:34, 477:6
when d. comes 147:8
Dayrolles: give D. a chair 139:37
Days: all my d. are trances 380:21
all our d. are gone 397:16
all the d. of our life 389:29
Ancient of D. 55:43, 228:20
as it was in the d. of old 296:29
as thy d., so..thy strength 46:33
because the d. are evil 68:4
born to inglorious d. 146:15
broader lands and better d. 144:2
but five d. elder than ourselves 86:9
Chequer-board of Nights and
  D. 206:28, 29
considered the d. of old 396:32
d. and moments quickly flying 132:3
d. dividing lover and lover 521:30(-532)
d. in goodness spent 119:2
d. may come, the d. may go 157:1
d. nor things diurnal 523:24
d. of danger 416:19
d. of man..as grass 398:7
d. of our age 397:16
d. of our youth..d of our glory 118:32
d. of the years of my life 45:25
d. that are no more 538:17
d. that are over 525:23
d. that have been 322:7
d. that have gone by 208:4
d. when earth was young 326:24
d. when work was scrappy 142:2
don't the d. seem lank and long 222:1
dreams of d. forsaken 523:21
even as our d. do grow 470:31(-471)
even from my boyish d. 470:2
fain see good d. 394:1
friend of my better d. 234:15
friends, kindred, d. 199:12
full of d., riches, and honour 48:34
full of sweet d. and roses 245:13
good King Charles's golden d. 7:9
good King George's glorious d. 219:7
his d. and nights to..Addison 278:9
how many d...the year 446:1
how many ways and d. 411:10
I am but two d. old 76:12
in ancient d. by emperor 288:1
in d. far-off 540:22
in the brave d. of old 323:21, 324:1
in the d. ere I was born 77:34

Days (cont.)

in the d. of my youth 507:35
lead on our d. to age 451:35
leads melodious d. 532:24
lengthen our d. 357:1
light of other d. 99:1, 357:13
live laborious d. 342:20
look'd on better d. 427:19
lose good d. 510:16
lost d. of my life 411:13
lost d. of our tropic youth 238:29
loved them in other d. 171:9
man in his hasty d. 81:9
multitude of d. 279:7
my d. and dreams out of mind 525:23
my d. are in the yellow leaf 118:26
my d. are swifter than.. 48:52
nor hours, d., months 186:20
not..of darker d. 144:7
of all the d. that's in the week 125:19
on and off, for d. and d. 128:30
scape stormy d. 185:23
seemed..but a few d. 45:6
she has seen dark d. before 200:3
shortly see better d. 40:8
shuts up the story of our d. 405:12
sweet childish d. 573:11
that thy d. may be long 390:12
then..come perfect d. 320:17
these somewhat troublesome d. 210:12
though fall'n on evil d. 348:23
time and drawing d. out 449:33
trample on my d. 552:9
weary of d. and hours 523:18
we have seen better d. 480:27
which the d. never know 200:14
winding up d. with toil 444:23
wish my d. to be bound 577:25
within a few d. dissent myself 86:3
year whose d. are long 569:11
Day-star: d. arise in your hearts 70:7
so sinks the d. 343:3
Day-time: I cry in the d. 393:1
Dazzle: I see the sights that d. 78:3
mine eyes d. 563:18
strangely you d. my eye 373:18
Dazzled: it d. their eyes 31:1
Dazzles: my striving eye d. at it 551:17
Dazzling: all his beams full-d. 566:22
De: doctrine of the enclitic D. 91:42
Dea: d. nec. dignata cubili est
  vera incessu patuit d. 556:2
553:17
Deacons: Bishops, Priests, and D. 388:52
Dead: a great deal to be said for
  being d. 42:25
all our best men are d. 403:35
all the rest are d. 316:2
antique order of the d. 543:16
as a d. man out of mind 393:29
barrows of the happier d. 540:23
be thus when thou art d. 473:11
better be with the d. 459:4
better than a d. lion 51:19
better to be a fool than..d. 514:37
blend the living with the d. 132:3
blow out..over the rich D. 83:19
books are not absolutely d.
  things 352:5
bury the d. 363:7
but they are d.; those two are d. 582:13
but two months d. 430:33(-431)
character d. at every word 500:36
come not, when I am d. 528:21
converse with the mighty d. 546:27
could not wait..he is d. 18:24
curse in a d. man's eye 149:22
cut in half: he's d. 228:9
dahlias are d. 518:27
d.! and..never called me mother 572:19
d. and turn'd to clay 437:18
d. bury their d. 58:35
d., but in the Elysian fields 181:20
d. but sceptred sovereigns 118:10
d.?..d. at last, quite, quite for
  ever d. 155:21
d. faith 551:1
d., for a ducat, d.! 435:40
d. from the waist down 91:42
d. he is not but departed 317:2
d. in trespasses 67:50
d. man win a fight 30:13

[669]

Dead (*cont.*)
d. may feel no wrong 380:20
d. men gave a groan 149:30
d. men meet on lips of living men 112:19
d. men rise up never 523:23
d. of joy 92:29
d. of winter 197:13
d. Past bury its d. 317:7
d., quick, I know not how 232:15
d. shall live, the living die 191:39
d...stand before God 71:42
d...still be near us 532:28
d., the sweet musician 318:2
d. these two years 139:35
d. unto sin 390:59
d. which are already d. 51:4
d. which die in the Lord 71:27
dear d. women with such hair 97:9
Death is d. 492:8
Death once d. 488:21
Desdemonal d.! 473:32
dew on the face of the d. 40:2
down among the d. men 195:16
drank it, and fell d. 174:18
England mourns for her d. 72:22
ere I am laid out d. 246:20
Evelyn Hope is d. 91:20
fairy somewhere..falls down d. 36:8
faith without works is d. 69:35
fame is food that d. men eat 183:9
famous, calm, and d. 91:38
flop round the earth till you're d. 304:1
found him with the d. 569:1
found, when she was d. 225:16
frightful when one's d. 384:26
gathered flowers are d., Yasmin 208:13
generally shammin' when 'e's d. 296:24
George..lying on his face, d. 542:37
hear the D. March play 295:20
he is d. and gone, lady 436:20
he left it d. 129:39(-130)
her d. and her shame 539:21(-540)
high talk with the departed d. 494:5
his Mother..being d. 375:16
Homer, being d. 248:4
Homer d. 9:15
I cheer a d. man's sweetheart 263:7
if..d. he would like to see me 250:24
if it were d. or bledde 136:30
if I were d. 375:20
if Lucy should be d. 581:12
if these men are d. 523:6
if two of them are d. 211:13
imagined for the mighty d. 284:21
immortal d. who live again 106:34
I mysel' were d. and gane 32:19(-33)
increase the number of the d. 169:12
in the d. of night 441:9, 482:22
is old Double d.? 442:8
is the king d.? 476:31
I would that I were d. 535:30
Johnson is d. 235:2
just born, being d. 410:13
King of Spain is d. 203:32
king Pandion, he is d. 35:18
lain for a century d. 536:15
lasting mansions of the d. 164:35
life from the d. is in that word 355:9
light in the dust lies d. 494:20
lilacs out of the d. land 197:27
live a life half d. 350:24
living among the d. 62:53
living-d. man 429:1
long time d. 5:20
Love was d. 523:15
Lycidas is d. 342:10
Lycidas..is not d. 343:3
man was d. 34:6
marks our English d. 301:23
mindful of th' unhonour'd d. 230:10
more tears to this d. man 452:2
mother of d. dogs 126:41
much less when he's d. 175:36
my enemy is d. 567:5
my love ys d. 136:17
my son was d. 62:16
nature seems d. 458:1
need charity more than the d. 15:1
never see..a d. postboy..a d. donkey 179:32

Dead (*cont.*)
noble d. 579:32
nobody..see my d. body 237:7
no longer mourn for me when I am d. 487:15
no, no, he is d. 436:35
not d. but gone before 408:7
not d., but sleepeth 58:43
not only d., but damned 181:17
now he is d. 17:9
once d. by fate 37:13
only constant mourner o'er the d. 117:39
only good Indian..a d. Indian 499:21
on the d. man's chest 514:18
Pan is d.! 88:4
poetry of earth is never d. 288:22
poets d. and gone 287:1
poets in their misery d. 580:13
profane the service of the d. 437:19
Queen Anne's d. 154:8
Queen Elizabeth's d. 520:9
queen, long d., was young 94:19
queen, my lord, is d. 461:4
rejoice, ye d. 81:21
remnant of our Spartan d. 115:46
resurrection of the d. 68:22
risen from the d. 67:8
romantic Ireland's d. 584:27
say I'm sick, I'm d. 385:20
sculptur'd d. on each side 285:13
sea gave up the d. 71:43
Sea..give up her d. 400:30
seen those d. men rise 149:31
sheeted d. did squeak 430:14
she has been d. many times 374:11
she's d. sir..she is not d. 29:24(-30)
she, she is d. 185:3
she *was* d. 375:12
shone round him o'er the d. 241:5
silence is..brutish and d. 126:33
silent cities of the d. 119:11
sleeping and the d. 458:14
smiling the boy fell d. 92:24
so dull, so d. in look 441:9
something was d. in each 569:9
soon to drop off d. 410:17
soul is d. that slumbers 317:5
stepping-stones of their d. selves 532:1
thanked God my wife was d. 91:26
that any man fears to be d. 27:43
their home among the d. 493:10
their rivals d. 374:11
there are no d. 327:7
they told me you were d. 157:15
those we call the d. 533:26
thou art d., as young and fair 112:30
thou being d. art a God 525:13
though d. with frost ere now 232:15
thrice looked he at the d. 323:23
thy d. shall go down to thee d. 525:13
together fell down d. 324:9
to my d. heart 516:16
took their wages and are d. 264:4
to see a d. Indian 479:39
trade both with the living and the d. 194:4
two worlds, one d. 16:7
unborn Tomorrow and d. Yesterday 206:19
voice of the d. 533:33
was alive and is d. 6:20
weep..if oon of hem were d. 136:30
what was d. was Hope 569:9
when a beast is d. 137:29
when Alysander..was d. 583:26
when I am d., I hope it may be said 41:23
when I am d., my dearest 409:29
when thou art d. 495:24
with our English d. 443:24
with soul so d. 417:22
with the d...no rivalry..no change 325:23
with the enduring d. 492:5
worse to me than d. 572:24
would waken the d. 229:16
youth stone d. 415:13
Dead-born: fell d. from the press 265:12
Deadlock: Holy D. 243:7

Dead men's fingers call them 437:1
Dead Sea: apples on the D.'s shore 113:39
like D. fruits 357:6
Dead-struck: I'm the bird d. 336:6
Deadly: come to d. use 453:42
d. daunting dagger 583:25
imminent d. breach 470:2
more d. in the long run 550:13
more d. than the male 296:13
Deaf: as d. as a door 80:6
at once..d. and loud 495:9
chamber d. to noise 501:27
d. and silent, read't 576:13
d. and viperous murderer 492:4
d. as Ailsa Craig 105:14
d. man to a blind woman 152:23
turn the d. ear 521:6
weary Titan, with d. ears 16:11
woman's d. 382:10
Deafened: loudest wit I e'er was d. with 117:5
Deafer than the blue-eyed cat 530:31
Deafness: my mother's d. is very trifling 22:12
your tale, sir, would cure d. 479:21
Deal: change of the word 'd' to 'live' 127:29
don't d. in lies 297:10
gey ill to d. wi' 127:29
intolerable d. of sack 439:39
new d. for the American people 408:19
square d. 409:2,6
Dealer in magic and spells 222:16
Dealing: know..with whom they are d. 571:15
nothing astonishes..as..plain d. 200:4
this isn't fair d. 300:7
whose own hard d. 463:24
Dealings: all his d. are square 234:11
his d. have been told us 338:4
Deam: nos facimus, Fortuna, d. 283:25
Dean: cushion and soft d. invite 385:4
humility may clothe an English d. 164:14
I am the D. 511:6
I am the D. of Christ Church 511:5
let the D. and Canons lay their heads together 505:12
no dogma, no D. 181:18
old person of D. 312:19
to your text, Mr. D. 198:2
Deans: dowagers for d. 538:7
Dear: bright eyes of the d. one 118:33
dangerously d. 115:5
d. as remembered kisses 538:19
d. dead women, with such hair 97:9
d., fine, silly old angel 307:24
d. God who loveth us 150:16
d. to God, and famous 352:27
d. to me as light and life 106:9
d. to me as..the ruddy drops 449:17
d. to me in the middle of my being 310:21
d. were her charms to me 233:1
for everything d. and valuable 379:15
hope is less d. than the dew 584:20
hug the d. deceit 157:21
I hold his d. 501:19
in thy d. womb 185:10
my dearest d. 159:34
my dove, my d. 536:15
my Very D. 375:21
names of things belov'd are d. 80:23
our d. Cambridge 158:10
Plato is d. to me 14:19
serve it right for being so d. 177:2
something blissful and d. 356:35
something d., dearer than self 113:15
such d. souls, this d., d. land 474:22
that bread should be so d. 253:25
thou art d. 354:12
to all the country d. 224:18
to kindred d. 125:4
to mem'ry d. 314:21
too d. for my possessing 487:22
when I parted from my d. 263:10
Dearer: d. far than light and life 578:10
d. her laughter free 233:1
d. than his horse 534:19
d. than self 113:15

Dearer (cont.)
d. yet the brotherhood 362:33
name d. and purer 117:32
was there a d. one? 252:17
Dearest: because, d., you're a
dunce 274:32
d. her constancy 233:1
my near'st and d. enemy 440:10
the d. girl 174:36
then, d., since 'tis so 92:31
throw away the d. thing he owed 456:27
thy youngest, d. one, has perished 491:16
Dearie: my arms about my d. O 105:38
my bonnie d. 104:29
my own kind d. O 106:30
o'er me and my d. 106:9
thinking on my d. 104:19
Dearly: she loves me d. 285:4
Dearness: distant d. in the hill 533:2
Dears: the lovely d. 106:2
Dearth: d. of noble natures 284:20
in a year of d. 77:13
pine within and suffer d. 488:20
war, d., age, agues, tyrannies 185:14
Death: absence..worse than d. 160:20
absolute sole Lord of life and d. 166:11
after d...the faces I shall see 411:14
against the hour of d. 391:39
allotted d. and hell 330:9
ancients dreaded d. 237:21
angel of d. has been abroad 82:17
Angel of D. spread his wings 118:38
any man's d. diminishes me 186:28
apprehends d. no more dreadfully 462:21
armed against all d.'s endeavour 84:19
arms of cool-enfolding d. 568:9
as sure as d. 280:13
at d. I cry 566:25
at my d., thy Sun shall shine 185:24
at the point of d. 478:42
back to a world of d. 150:24
bargain to engrossing d. 478:44
be absolute for d. 462:3
because of the d. of that lady 328:5
before you taste of d. 100:22
better..the day of d. 51:9
bitterness of d. is past 47:17
body of this d. 65:51
brave d., when princes die with
us 440:32
bridegroom in my d. 425:24
brother of d. exacteth a third part 85:23
brother to D. 38:9, 168:12
brought d. into the world 344:1, 550:24
but D. who comes at last 418:10
but one life and one d. 89:26
by man came d. 67:8
can this be d.? 381:29
certain d. by..shame attended 300:23
come away, d. 483:6
come lovely and soothing d. 568:9
come to the bridal-chamber D.! 234:16
condemn you to d. 128:25
consenting unto his d. 64:35
coquetry of D. 543:20
covenant with d. 53:34, 213:19
daughter of D. and Priapus 523:7
dear beauteous d. 552:10
d. after life does greatly please 509:28
D. and his brother Sleep 493:2, 497:18
d. and life, in ceaseless strife 365:23
d., a necessary end 449:22
D...a scientific fact 569:7
d., as the Psalmist saith 185:15
d. be not proud 185:15
d. broke..the vital chain 275:4
d. came with friendly care 151:18
d. closes all 541:3
d. comes to young men 25:4
d. cometh soon or late 323:17
d...commits some loving act 423:25
d. complete the same 95:26
d...distinguished from dying 505:13
D.! ere thou hast slain another 87:24
d. for neighbour 523:19
D. had illumined the Land of
Sleep 317:17
d. has done all d. can 89:13
d. has left on her 252:15

Death (cont.)
D. has made his darkness beautiful 533:4
d. hath no more dominion 65:45
d. hath so many doors 37:20
d. hath ten thousand..doors 563:16
d. have we hated 359:3
d...his next-door neighbour 420:6
d., in itself, is nothing 191:33
D. in the cup 105:35
d. i' the other 448:16
d. in the pot 48:20
d. is a fearful thing 462:9
d. is as a lover's pinch 426:11
d. is but a groom 186:12
D. is dead 492:8
d. is d. 241:26
d. is parting 412:15
d. is slumber 495:18
d. is the cure of all diseases 86:35
d. is the end of woes 509:29
d. is the privilege of human
nature 412:11
d. is the veil 497:11
d. itself wakes 442:1
d. itself must be..a mockery 497:28
d. I was to die 31:19
d. joins us to the great majority 587:14
d. kind Nature's signal 279:14
d. lays his icy hand on kings 501:5
D. lies dead 523:16
d., like a narrow sea 562:14
d. like sleep might steal on me 498:25
d. met I too 336:3
d. my days should expiate 486:19
d...My Lord? A grave 447:32
d., never takes..by surprise 209:15
d. of a dear friend 467:33
d. of each day's life 458:11
d. of poor Cock Robin 369:18
d. of princes 449:22
d. of the Blatant Beast 325:19
d. of the most noblest knights 328:17
d. of your daughter..a blessing 23:3
d. once dead 488:21
d...openeth the gate to good
fame 26:4
d. opens unknown doors 334:4
d.'s cold flood 562:17
d. shall all the world subdue 509:7
d. shall be no more: d., thou shalt
die 185:16
d. shall flee from them 71:12
D.'s imperishable wing 410:24
d.'s pale flag 478:43
d.'s second self 487:16
D.'s self is sorry 280:10
D.'s shadow at the door 77:27
d.'s sweet chrism 376:2
d. stands above me 308:23
d.'s untimely frost 106:10
D., the consoler 316:16
d. the journey's end 193:17
d...the least of all evils 27:42
D., the poor man's..friend 107:3
D. the Skeleton 582:22
d. took him mellow 376:21
d. unloads thee 462:32
D. untimely stopped his tuneful
tongue 385:5
D., whene'er he call 222:25
d., where is thy sting? 67:18
D., where is thy sting-a-ling-a-
ling? 8:19
D. will come when thou art dead 495:24
D. will find me 84:7
D. will listen to your stave 494:9
d., without phrases 502:13
d...working like a mole 244:19
defer not charities till d. 27:7
delicate d. 568:9
delivered my soul from d. 395:16, 399:6
dens and shades of d. 346:2
desultory feet of D. 411:3
die not, poor d. 185:15
die the d. of the righteous 46:18
direful d. 208:21
done to d. by slanderous tongues 469:18
doom'd to d., though fated not
to die 192:21
drank d. like wine 141:14

Death (cont.)
dread of something after d. 434:4
dull cold ear of d. 230:3
dunged with rotten d. 544:27
early d. 224:1
eaten to d. with rust 441:25
e'en the pang preceding d. 224:10
either d. or life..the sweeter 462:3
eloquent, just, and mighty D.! 405:13
enormously improved by d. 414:10
face to..meet d. with 93:1
fain die a dry d. 479:18
fairer d. 461:15
faithful unto d. 70:30
Faith is kneeling by his bed of d. 189:20
faith that looks through d. 576:20
fear and danger of violent d. 248:21
fear d.? 95:8
fears..only the stroke of d. 27:43
fed on the fullness of d. 525:8
feed on D., that feeds on men 488:21
field of d. survey'd 1:10
first day of our Jubilee is d. 86:20
for any pains of d. 391:47
foreknowledge of d. 522:4
for restful d. I cry 487:13
from chance, and d. 497:12
from d. to life..recover 189:20
from d. unto life 63:17
from the d. of Domitian 217:8
give me liberty or..d. 242:18
glad to d.'s mystery 252:20
go hand in hand to d. 411:19
gone to her d. 252:12
guiltless d. I die 473:18
half in love with easeful D. 287:32
hard at d.'s door 398:16
Hell..back resounded, D. 346:8
here find life in d. 151:17
hid in d.'s dateless night 486:25
his d...in his berth 252:32
his means of d. 436:37
hour of my d. 290:22
how little room..take up in d. 501:8
how wonderful is D. 493:2, 497:18
I could not look on D. 296:6
I fled, and cry'd out, D. 346:8
if ought but d. part thee and me 47:1
if thou canst D. defy 81:25
importune d. awhile 425:27
in a d. so noble 351:6
in d. alone must die 548:16
in d.'s dark vale 421:1
in d.'s worst hour 525:17
in every parting..an image of d. 196:30
in life, in d. 322:2
in nativity, chance, or d. 466:14
in our very d., and burial sure 295:10
in that sleep of d. 434:4
in the hour of d. 388:51
in their d. they were not divided 47:30
in the midst of life..in d. 391:42
in the ranks of d. 356:27
in the shadow of d. 61:15, 398:15
into the gulf of d. 491:15
into the jaws of D. 528:18
into the valley of D. 528:16
I will dare e'en D. 247:3
keep a league till d. 475:27
keeps D. his court 475:7
keys of hell and of d. 70:28
King D. hath asses' ears 38:27
kingly D. keeps his pale court 491:17
king my father's d. 197:30
kiss the image of my d. 190:5
knows what life and d. is 135:19
land of the shadow of d. 53:14
land of the..shadow of d. 48:54
lapwings feel the leaden d. 386:32
last enemy..d. 67:9
laughed in d. 508:5
laws of d. 413:27
lead him to D. 407:22
let it sleep with d. 280:11
let us hob-and-nob with D. 541:12
lieth at the point of d. 60:59
Life, and D., and that For Ever 293:7
life..but the shadow of d. 85:10
life d. does end 255:1
Life, D., Miracles 95:24
life forget and d. remember 524:18

Death (cont.)

Life is perfected by D. 89:4
life to him would be d. to me 290:26
lightning before d. 478:42
lively form of d. 305:14
living d. 350:24
look on d. itself 458:23
love is strong as d. 52:22
love. . put it to a violent d. 202:2
love thee better after d. 88:24
lover, sick to d. 455:17
make d. proud to take us 425:31
make one in love with d. 491:13
man after his d. moot wepe 137:29
marriage and d. and division 523:1
meetest for d. 464:37
men fear d. as children. . the dark 26:1
Milton, D. and Sin 587:16
must hate and d. return? 493:27(–494)
must in d. your daylight finish? 93:25
my name is D. 507:10
my part of d. 483:6
neither d., nor life 65:58
neither wish d. nor fear 518:2
never taste of d. but once 449:22
no drinking after d. 37:14
no more d. 71:45
none blessed before his d. 56:42
nor shall d. brag 486:18
not born for d. 288:1
not d., but dying 204:7
not D., but Love 88:16
nothing. . certain, except d. and taxes 211:9
not so much afraid of d. 86:19
not told of my d. 237:7
now boast thee, d. 426:14
now to D. devote 349:17
O D. in Life 538:19
old men go to d. 25:4
old nurse, D. 241:20
one of the new terrors of d. 14:8
one that had been studied in his d. 456:27
O proud d.! what feast? 438:8
our guide unto d. 394:35
outer brink of obvious d. 88:17
pain without the peace of d. 122:2
pale horse. . on him was D. 70:45
passion. . masters the fear of d. 26:2
peace instead of d. 122:6
perchance of D. 546:29
planet's tyrant, dotard D. 38:29
Pontifical D. 543:15
preached to d. by wild curates 505:6
privilege of putting him to d. 505:28
Reaper, whose name is D. 317:9
red fruit of thy d. 524:4
rendezvous with D. 421:18
report of my d. 550:30
revenge triumphs over d. 26:2
rhymed to d. 502:11
riddles of d. Thebes never knew 493:26
sad stories of the d. of kings 475:7
salvation joins issue with d. 96:24
second d. . no power 71:40
secret of the shrouded d. 335:28
sense of d. is most in apprehension 462:7
set before you life and d. 46:30
shall men seek d. 71:12
sharpness of d. 388:17
silence deep as d. 122:4
silent halls of d. 98:3
sisters D. and Night 567:5
sleep, d.'s counterfeit 458:23
sleep is a d. 87:1
sleep is. . so like d. 86:38
sleep the sleep of d. 75:11
snares of d. 399:5
some one's d., a chorus-ending 89:31
some sad lover's d. 191:19
stern d. cut short 500:4
strange images of d. 456:20
strong and long-liv'd d. 184:25
strong as d. 161:12
sudden d. 388:48
sundown splendid and serene, d. 241:23
sweet is d. 530:38
swoon to d. 288:18
sword he sung a song of d. 74:26
that d. bandaged my eyes 95:10

Death (cont.)

that one Talent which is d. to hide 351:21
their life was d. 411:6
there is no D. 317:12
there is not room for D. 83:12
this fell sergeant, d. 438:1
this is d. and the sole d. 90:44
this life, this d. 584:21
this reasonable moderator. . D. 86:18
those by d. are few 268:26
thou hast *all* seasons. . D. 241:14
thou of d. must deem 498:9
thou owest God a d. 440:29
through envy of the devil came d. 56:22
thy. . bones, hearsed in d. 431:32
thy brother D. came 495:23
till d. us do part 391:30
'tis d. to us 313:20
to be carnally minded is d. 65:52
too low crawling for d. 286:1
torture and d. of his fellow-creatures. . amusing 212:4
to what we fear of d. 462:10
triumph over d. and sin 509:4
true to thee till d. 202:27
truly long'd for d. 540:27
under the ribs of D. 340:28
unsubstantial D. is amorous 478:44
up the line to d. 415:12
valley of the shadow of d. 393:10
vasty hall of D. 17:15
wages of sin is d. 65:46
walk with D. and Morning 539:4
warrant, Claudio, for thy d. 462:20
way to dusty d. 461:4
Webster was much possessed by d. 197:33
we owe God a d. 442:12
were there d. in the cup 420:25
what's d.? you'll love me yet 94:45
what should it know of d.? 582:11
what sights of ugly d. 476:14
when Byron's eyes were shut in d. 16:21
when d. is our physician 470:14
when D. to either shall come 82:11
where is d.'s sting? 322:2
who can run the race with d.? 275:28
whom d. could not daunt 31:14
whose mortal taste brought d. 344:1
whose portal we call D. 317:12
why fear d.? 212:1
worst friend and enemy. . D. 84:18
worst is d. and d. will have his day 475:4
years of fearing d. 449:34
yet afraid of d. 143:8
your ruling passion strong in d. 384:27
Death-bed: drive me mad on my d. 119:33
gon to hys d. 136:17
go to thy d. 436:35
Jemmy Grove on his d. lay 30:1
Death-fires danced at night 149:6
Death-hour: darkness and the d. rounding it 88:20
Deathless: d. lot to names ignoble 160:37
let us make love d. 549:3
progress of a d. soul 186:4
Deathly: seal thy sense in d. slumber 171:9
Death-moth: the beetle, nor the d. 287:20
Deaths: after so many d. 244:18
by feign'd d. to die 186:15
more d. than one 569:10
with him all d. . endure 349:16
Death's-head: call in thy d. there 244:10
Debars: Fate so enviously d. 332:6
Debasing the moral currency 196:33
Debate: daughter of d. 198:5
faithful wife, without d. 518:2
Rupert of D. 322:9
Debaters: host of d. in himself 103:18
Debauch his friend's wife genteelly 272:26
Debauched with ease 190:10
Débauchée: old blind *d.* of wit 558:18
Debonair: buxom, blithe and d. 341:27
d. and gentle tale 289:3
easy, d. and brisk 162:21
Deboshed: thou d. fish, thou 480:2

Debt: ambition's d. is paid 449:32
d. which cancels all others 154:24
every d. as if God wrote the bill 199:29
in love, in d., and in drink 82:24
more than millions of d. 101:17
national d. . a national blessing 234:20, 563:2
National D. is a very Good Thing 422:15
paid the d. of nature 203:1
put mankind . . most in their d. 267:9
run in d. by disputation 110:6
war, an' a d., an' a flag 319:28
Debtor: am I your d.? 528:9
every man a d. to his profession 25:14
Debts: forgive us our d. as we forgive our debtors 58:4
he that dies pays all d. 480:4
New Way to Pay Old D. 334:22
our d., our careful wives 444:21
Decades: five d. hardly modified . . the gaiter 236:42
Decay: all human things are subject to d. 193:1
as quick a growth to meet d. 246:3
building not in d. 26:41
by a gentle d. 387:2
change and d. 322:5
cold gradations of d. 275:4
d. no flood 585:16
d. of that colossal wreck 496:15
d. of the whole age 25:22
flourish after first d. 509:33
found its d. 147:23
fretted the pigmy body to d. 190:13
general flavor of mild d. 251:7
great and wise d. 312:24
hasten its d. 161:39
in beauty and d. 491:17
melts with unperceiv'd d. 279:8
muddy vesture of d. 465:18
old Time makes these d. 124:25
only our love hath no d. 184:6
shall like to this d. 509:7
so will our hearts d. 32:17
states. . have. . their d. 309:19
that there be no d. 400:17
to many men's d. 510:10
wealth accumulates and men d. 224:14
with unperceiv'd d. 224:16
Decayed: sufficiently d.? 220:20
till they d. through pride 510:12
when I d. thy blood bought that 185:11
Decaying: we are but d. 246:1
Decays: mere glimmering and d. 552:9
Deceased: because 'e is frequent d. 304:3
Ghost of the d. Roman Empire 248:23
he first d. 583:12
nature of the times d. 442:6
working in the graves of d. languages 175:6
Deceit: all other men may use d. 309:3
men favour the d. 191:34
rumour of oppression and d. 162:40
still we hug the dear d. 157:21
used no d. in his tongue 392:24
Deceitful: bloodthirsty and d. man 392:3
d. upon the weights 395:24
destructive, damnable, d. woman 371:9
heart is d. 55:20
Deceitfulness of riches 59:24
Deceits: dangerous d. 401:11
d. of the world 388:24
prophesy d. 53:38
Deceive: d. you with vain words 68:3
if Light can thus d. 566:14
Oh, don't d. me 6:2
O Sleep, again d. me 155:35
the same with intent to d. 238:35
we d. ourselves 70:10
when first we practise to d. 418:28
Deceived: are ye also d.? 63:25
be not d. 67:47
by bad women been d. 350:26
d. the mother of mankind 344:6
disappointed. . was still d. 160:29
she has d. her father 470:12
still d. with ornament 464:14
why. . desire to be d.? 109:37
Deceiver: I'm a gay d. 154:12
welcome, thou kind d. 191:22

INDEX

Deceivers: men were d. ever 468:20
Deceiveth his own heart 69:34
Deceiving: she d. 421:14
  v hat is hope but d.? 337:42
December: D. when they wed 428:22
  in a drear-nighted D. 289:7
  made D. June 533:15
  old D.'s bareness 487:27
  rain and wind beat dark D. 429:31
  seek roses in D. 117:13
  wallow naked in D. snow 474:20
Decembers: fifteen wild D. 83:14
Decencies: dwell in d. for ever 384:34
Decency: ultimate d. of things 515:13
  want of d. is want of sense 180:9
Decent: aristocracy to what is d. 254:8
  came of d. people 42:19
  d. easy men 216:21
  d. obscurity of a learned language 217:4
Decently and in order 67:4
Decide: to d. this doubt for me 161:5
  moment to d. 320:9
  who shall d.? 384:41
Decision: by d. more embroils the
    fray 346:11
  valley of d. 55:53
Deck: d. my captain lies 566:28(-567)
  on the burning d. 241:5
  rent cordage, shatter'd d. 362:11
  they laid him on the d. 31:2
  whole d. put on its leaves 208:16
Decked: d. with jewels 12:1
  my love should duly have been d. 509:15
  thought thy bride-bed to have d. 437:22
Decks: but clear your d. 106:23
  he fell upon their d. 540:3
Declaiming: when you are d.,
    declaim 273:14
Declamatio: ut..d. fias 283:21
Declaration: make up the D. of
    Independence 142:25
Declare: d., if thou hast under-
    standing 49:19
  d. the glory of God 392:32
  d. the wonders that he doeth 398:15
  d. the works of the Lord 399:10
  him d. I unto you 64:60
  I heard him d. 129:25
  nothing to d. except my genius 570:22
  seen what she could not d. 250:23
Declares: what God d. pure 347:25
Decline: d. and fall of the city
    D.-and-Fall-Off-the-Rooshan-
    Empire 178:5
  I respectfully d. 183:14
  partakers of thy sad d. 160:23
Declined: dear Carrie rightly d. 233:6
  d. into the vale of years 471:39
  star of my fate hath d. 119:9
Declines: as civilization advances,
    poetry..d. 325:2
  d. to interfere 564:15
  professionally he d. and falls 178:3
Declining: in the d. age of a state 27:36
  when comforts are d. 161:21
  without d. West 185:8
Decocted: much matter d. into
    few words 212:10
Decomposes but to recompose 91:14
Decorate the verse herself inspires 117:26
Decorating: d. and cheering the
    elevated sphere 102:11
  d. her constructions 549:14
Decorous: dim and d. mirth 84:5
Decorum: hunt D. down 117:21
  let them cant about d. 106:25
Decorum: dulce et d. est desipere in
    loco 112:11
  dulce et d. est pro patria mori 259:18
Decoy: while fashion's brightest
    arts d. 225:5
Decoyed: poor fools d. into our
    condition 377:28
Decrease: I must d. 63:12
Decreasing leg 441:19
Decree from Caesar Augustus 61:16
Decreed: my own soul..to itself d. 288:11
Decrees: wayward the d. of Fate
    are 543:13
Decrepitude: states..have their
    ..d. 309:19

Decus: et praesidium et dulce d.
    meum 257:23
Decussated: Net. Anything..d. 277:28
Dedicate: d. your volumes to
    Prince Leopold 145:30
  let me d. all this year 550:7
  to Truth its state is d. 496:23
  we cannot d. this ground 314:12
Dedicated: d. spirit 579:22
  d. to the proposition that 314:12
  for us, the living..to be d. 314:12
Dedication: style of a d. is flattery 276:8
Deductions: fact..opposed to a
    long train of d. 188:25
Dee: across the sands of D. 293:22
  diddle, we take it, is d. 523:26
  on the river D. 72:15
Deed: attempt and not the d. 458:4
  better day, the worse d. 242:6
  bloody d. 435:41
  blow the horrid d. in every eye 457:9
  certain moment cuts the d. off 95:19
  d. of dreadful note 459:7
  d. without a name 460:3
  do this d. for me 320:2
  each d. of shame 316:30
  fit for thee d. I had to do 131:11
  if one good d...I did 480:36
  I have done the d. 458:6
  in every d. of mischief 217:11
  in itself a d. 528:12
  in prowess and great d. 234:8
  Jesu, by a nobler d. 135:12
  leff woord and tak the d. 321:8
  little water clears us of this d. 458:16
  matchless d.'s achiev'd 503:6
  motive, not the d. 584:9
  of the d. the glory shall remain
    ..of the d...the shame 233:3
  pronounces lastly on each d. 342:23
  so I may do the d. 288:11
  so shines a good d. 465:21
  take the will for the d. 520:19
  they that have done this d. 450:32
  thinking the d., and not the creed 318:6
  till in Heaven the d. appears 109:1
  till thou applaud the d. 459:8
  unless the d. go with it 460:14
  wrought the d. of shame 323:18
Deeds: d. not words shall speak me 37:29
  d. of hospitality 427:6
  d. of mercy 464:33
  d. that are done in their clime 113:1
  d. that ye do upon the earth 359:19
  d. which should not pass away 113:44
  d. will be done 93:5
  desperate d. of derring d. 222:10
  do great d., speak great words 406:4
  excus'd his devilish d. 347:16
  flourisheth in lusty d. 328:15
  foul d. will rise 431:19
  gentle and virtuous d. 328:1
  if doughty d. my lady please 228:12
  I tell of the thrice famous d. 322:17
  little d. of kindness 128:1
  looks quite through the d. of men 448:27
  loveliness of perfect d. 532:25
  my d. upon my head 465:1
  nameless in worthy d. 87:15
  our d. determine us 196:9
  our d. still travel with us 196:21
  renowned for their d. 474:22
  that doth gentil d. 138:12
  these d. must not be thought 458:10
  these unlucky d. relate 474:2
  tomorrow's uprising to d. 359:7
  turned aside to do good d. 300:18
  we live in d., not years 29:9
  words and d...indifferent
    modes 200:29
  words are no d. 446:21
  words to the heat of d. 458:1
  years of noble d. 530:14
  your better d...in water writ 38:2
Deemed: d. it meeter 376:23
  with th' Eternal to be d. equal 345:15
Deep: call spirits from the vasty d. 439:42
  commit his body to the d. 400:30
  coveredst it with the d. 398:8
  cradle of the d. 570:27
  curses not loud but d. 460:36

Deep (cont.)
  Cyclads on a sunnier d. 493:25
  danger on the d. 30:32
  d. almost as life 576:10
  d. and crisp and even 361:19
  d. and dark blue Ocean 114:27
  d. as first love 538:19
  d. in the bells and grass 249:7
  d. in the water 41:30
  d. into that darkness peering 380:24
  d. in unfathomable mines 161:18
  d. moans round 541:3
  d. of night 451:30
  d. silent slide away 501:17
  d. versed in books 350:13
  d. where Holland lies 226:13
  drew from out the boundless d. 528:22
  dull and d. potations 216:22
  fishes that tipple in the d. 319:6
  found him far too d. 387:24
  from the great d. to the great d. 530:2
  full many a fathom d. 122:7
  he heard the d. behind him 531:32
  her arms along the d. 122:3
  her home is on the d. 123:11
  his wonders in the d. 398:17
  home on the rolling d. 415:11
  horrors of the d. 123:24
  in the lowest d. a lower d. 346:32
  in your beauty's orient d. 125:9
  made the d. as dry 301:25
  maketh the d. to boil 49:32
  natural philosophy, d. 27:19
  never d. in anything but—wine 206:24
  no robin ever on the d. 171:20
  not d. the Poet sees, but wide 18:3
  not seem so d. as they are 309:21
  not so d. as a well 478:14
  one d. calleth another 394:19
  one is of the d. 512:6
  out of the d. 529:5
  out of the d...called 399:38
  read'st the eternal d. 576:13
  remorseless d. 342:17
  river Weser, d. and wide 94:32
  sweep through the d. 123:10
  terms too d. for me 220:26
  that d. romantic chasm 151:32
  though d., yet clear 172:10
  too d. for his hearers 225:27
  too d. for tears 576:22(-577)
  travail on the d. 168:13
  unadorned bosom of the d. 340:1
  upon the face of the d. 44:1
  very d. did rot 149:6
  we have not sighed d. 97:28
  what a very singularly d. young
    man 220:26
Deep-browed Homer 288:19
Deep-delved: cooled..in the d.
    earth 287:24
Deeper: d., ever so little d. 536:21
  d. sense of her loss 214:1
  d. than did ever plummet 480:13
  d. than the depths beneath 161:12
  d. waters than I had thought 188:3
  eyes..d. than the depth 410:7
  whelmed in d. gulphs than he 159:3
Deeply: consider it not so d. 458:8
  darkly, d., beautifully blue 116:13, 507:29
  sleep d. above 84:8
Deep-meadow'd: it lies d. 531:37
Deep-mouthed welcome 115:22
Deeps: dragons and all d. 400:24
  far in yon azure d. 318:4
  in what distant d. or skies 75:24
Deepsea: may we lift a D. Chantey 298:14
  thresh of the d. rain 298:27
Deep-search'd with saucy looks 454:32
Deer: a-chasing the d. 107:12, 420:24
  d. and the antelope play 248:9
  d. to the wholesome wold 206:29
  held that lovely d. 558:1
  herd-abandoned d. 492:3
  I was a stricken d. 163:8
  my own stricken d. 356:15
  'poor d.,' quoth he 426:32
  ravens..around the dying d. 24:7
  running of the d. 10:14
  such small d. 453:24

[673]

Defaced: all saints else be d. 232:11
antiquities are history d. 24:15
by Time's fell hand d. 487:11
on a sudden lost, d., deflower'd 349:17
Defacing you with foul defame 233:3
Defamed by every charlatan 533:23
Defaming: d. and defacing 531:21
d. as impure 347:25
Default of a guinea in your neighbour 413:25
Defeat: greatest tragedy..except a d. 564:10
in ourselves are triumph and d. 317:4
may d. my life 473:3
possibilities of d. 552:21
this world's d. 551:20
Defect: chief d. of Henry King 41:1
fair d. of Nature 349:23
make d. perfection 424:8
some d. in her 479:44
Defence: at one gate to make d. 350:29
cheap d. of nations 102:12
d., not defiance 5:28
d. of England 29:15
d. of philosophic doubt 29:17
don't cant in d. of savages 275:22
its greatest d. and ornament millions for d. 73:6
238:4
my pen in d. of a bad cause 194:14
never make a d...before you be accused 135:27
not only of d., but defiance 222:31
our d. is sure 562:9
ready in d., full of resources 100:30
the Lord is thy d. 399:28
Defenceless as thou wert 491:27
Defend: by thy great mercy.. us 388:36
d., O Lord, this thy child 391:20
d. thee under his wings 397:18
d...your right to say it 557:15
foremost to d. 118:22
ministers of grace d. us 431:32
Name of..God..d. thee 392:35
we shall d. our island 143:40
whom he had promised to d. 324:34
Défend: il se d. 12:12
Defende: domine, d. nos 223:8
Defended: what God abandoned, these d. 264:4
Defender: I mean the Faith's D. 112:25
Defendeth: d. the fatherless 400:20
d. the..widows 396:5
Defensive: as a moat d. 474:22
Defensoribus: non tali auxilio nec d. istis 554:11
Defer: d. not charities till death 27:7
let me not d. or neglect it 232:10
'tis madness to d. 587:3
Deference due to me 220:10
Deferor hospes 256:16
Deferred: hope d. • 50:3
Defiance: defence, not d. 5:28
d. in their eye 226:14
d. to all the forces of the Crown 379:11
not only of defence but d. 222:31
our hearts bid the tyrants d. 123:6
Deficiencies of the present day 278:14
Deficiency: accused of d. in the graces 273:15
industry will supply their d. 406:10
Defied: age will not be d. 27:3
Defile: sermon's dull d. 336:40
to d. the imagination 513:33
Defiled: he that toucheth pitch shall be d. 56:43
Defileth: that which goeth in..d. 59:38
Define it well 532:30
Definition: bound by my own d. of criticism 19:12
Definitionem: quam scire eius d. 291:19
Definitions: I hate d. 182:39
Deflowered: on a sudden lost, defac'd, d. 349:17
De Foe: earless..stood unabashed D. 381:16
Deformed: I know that D. 468:41
none..d. but the unkind 484:19
Deformities: turn them from his d. 278:24
Deformity: foot the d. of which 325:14
Defy: d. the devil 484:8

Defy (cont)
d. the foul fiend 453:20
d. th' Omnipotent to arms 344:7
every art and care d. 165:17
we d. augury 437:34
Dégagé: or half so d. 160:13
Degenerate Douglas! 573:24
Degenerating: his comic wit d. into clenches 194:6
Degeneration: fatty d. of his moral being 514:22
Degraded: reprobate, d., spiritless outcast 124:9
sufficiently d. 219:26
Degree: better suits with our d. 88:10
curs of low d. 225:20
d., priority and place 481:2
exempt from awe, worship, d. 497:12
many more of lesser d. 34:8
Souls in their d. 298:9
take but d. away 481:4
when d. is shak'd 481:3
Degrees: boil at different d. 201:15
by d. dwindle into a wife 156:14
estate, d., and offices 464:1
fine by d. 401:32
grow by slow d. brainless 121:20
heal but by d. 471:24
loose types..through all d. 573:23
Déguiser: pour d. leurs pensées 557:4
Dei: ad majorem d. gloriam 13:3
vox populi, vox d. 3:10, 406:16
Deified: by our own spirits..d. 580:7
Deigneth nat to wreke him on a flye 138:20
Deist sighed 387:24
Deity: D. supreme doth ease its heart 286:9
desire in d. 410:26
ever-present D. 83:8
for D. offended 105:20
particular volition of the D. 265:6
what strange d. 266:14
Deject: d. his cool'd imagination 86:34
of ladies most d. and wretched 434:14
Dejected: d. 'haviour of the visage 430:30
most d. thing of fortune 453:36
Dejection: in our d...sink as low 580:5
fame did not d. 587:6
Delay: chides his infamous d. 189:8
Haste, half-sister to D. 535:23
in d. there lies no plenty 482:28
in me is no d. 349:30
law's d. 434:4
no quarrels, murmurs, no d. 166:15
reprov'd each dull d. 224:21
sweet reluctant amorous d. 347:12
think not much of my d. 292:19
wanton with long d. 80:10
Delayed till I am indifferent 270:18
Delays: all d. are dangerous in war 194:1
d. have dangerous ends 445:24
Delectable:
daisy d. 502:19
D. Mountains 99:22
nimble fiery and d. shapes 442:21
Delectando pariterque monendo 256:9
Delenda est Carthago 132:8
Delia: while D. is away 267:28
Deliberate: these d. fools 464:4
where both d. 330:13
Deliberates: woman that d. is lost 1:19
Deliberation: deep on his front.. d. sat 345:24
Delicacy: all that a man has of..d. 513:35
d...which..moulded the changing lineaments 374:11
Delicate: any little d. thing to drink 175:38
body's d. 453:12
call these d. creatures ours 471:40
d. and rare 569:5
d. death 568:9
d. plain, called Ease 99:18
more moving-d. and full of life 469:6
so d. his motions be 82:2
touch his weaknesses with a d. hand 226:31
where they most breed..the air is d. 457:6
young ladies are d. plants 22:18
your holy d. white hands 329:2

Delicate-handed priest 535:42
Delicately: Agag came..d. 47:17
Delice: the fair flower D. 510:23
Delicious: d. Ah!..the gondola 146:29
make d. moan 288:5
that which is not good is not d. 340:34
this d. solitude 332:15
'tis d. to hate you 357:4
Delicta maiorum immeritus lues 259:30
Delight: all for your d. 467:28
all liking, all d. 246:1
applause! d.l..of our stage 281:11
as much d. in conceiving an Iago 290:9
as our d. or as our treasure 244:23
beauty to d. 169:17
bind another to its d. 76:3
business of d. 495:14
by d., we all quote 201:5
dances and d. 466:41
day rose with d. to us 292:21
d...and lash the age 382:16
d. in simple things 295:8
d...in the..pains of others 102:31
d. that consumes the desire 522:27
d., that they may mend 160:19
drunk d. of battle 540:32
Energy is Eternal D. 77:6
enjoy d. with liberty 510:17
feed on vain d. 510:14
fills with d. the Maenad 522:2
from each thing met conceives d. 349:11
gave thee clothing of d. 76:10
give d., and hurt not 480:5
go to't with d. 425:9
Greensleeves was my d. 6:18
Heaven views it with d. 332:7
if I e'er took d. in thy praises 118:33
if Sion hill d. thee more 344:2
in the very temple of d. 287:21
in this conflict..I find d. 277:5
labour we d. in 458:20
lady of my d. 338:8
land of pure d. 562:13
let dogs d. 561:24
lonely impulse of d. 584:21
lurks in all d. 338:6
men miscall d. 492:7
Moon of my D. 207:28
Mother of the Fair D. 410:5
mounted in d. 580:5
must d. in virtue 1:23
my d. and thy d. 81:17
my d. on a shining night 8:23
my ever new d. 348:1
my last d. 493:4
never too late for d. 357:1
not sorrow, but d. 579:36
other aims than my d. 236:16
paint the meadows with d. 455:35
people that d. in war 390:14
phantom of d. 580:19
rejoice and d. in God 548:13
relinquished one d. 576:21
space for d. 522:7
Spirit of D. 498:11
still moves d. 123:18
studies serve for d. 27:1
that it were my chief d. 527:6
their solicitous d. 378:16
there is d. in singing 308:15
thinks he takes d. in seeing thee 109:16
to d...paid thy utmost blessing 171:9
to do ill our sole d. 344:16
to rede, I me d. 138:12
to such a deep d. 151:33(–152)
turn d. into a sacrifice 243:25
weighing d. and dole 430:24
wept with d. 201:24
with d. no more 494:19
yet I hear thy shrill d. 498:4
youth of d., come hither 76:6
Delighted: d. us long enough 22:32
d. with my bauble coach 160:30
if I am alive..to see him 250:24
more d. with anything that is amiable 154:37
vision that d. 329:12
Delightest not in burnt offerings 395:10
Delighteth: neither d...in..legs 400:22
whom the king d. to honour 48:36

Delightful: almost as d. 315:10
both d. too 158:13
her..d. Fairy Prince 336:21
Delighting: but, O! d. me 249:11
d...and instructing 256:9
d. each eye 173:12
Delights: all d. are vain 454:31
all passions, all d. 152:3
his d. were dolphin-like 426:1
king of intimate d. 163:26
man d. not me 433:15
scarlet, with other d. 47:30
sovereign queen of all d. 35:22
these violent d. 478:8
to scorn d. 342:20
Delineation: happiest d. of its varieties 22:22
Delinquent: condemns a less d. for't 111:26
Delirium of the brave 584:27
Delitabill: storys to rede ar d. 33:16
Deliver: d. Israel, O God 393:16
d. me from blood-guiltiness 395:9
d. me from the body of this death 65:51
d. my soul from the sword 393:7
d. thee from the snare 397:18
d. us from evil 58:4
good Lord, d. us 6:9
I will d. him unto you 60:37
let him d. him 393:3
neither shall he d. any man 393:37
trouthe shal d. 136:20
trusted..that he would d. him 393:3
Deliverance: d. offered from the darts 236:6
songs of d. 393:33
Delivered: d. my soul from death 399:6
d. them from their distress 398:15
I d. thee when bound 161:10
many events..will be d. 470:18
Deliverer: into the hands of their d. 350:36
Delivereth them out of their distress 398:18
Delivery: Punctual D. Company 176:37
Dells: she forgot the d. 286:23
Deloraine, good at need 417:10
Delos: where D. rose 115:43
Delphos: steep of D. leaving 343:21
Deluded: heaven to be d. by him 312:28
she was d. away 306:34
we are all d. thus 494:2
Deluding: farewell dear d. Woman 105:28
Deluge: rain a d. show'r'd 139:1
Déluge: après nous le d. 381:4
Delusion: but under some d. 101:16
given to strong d. 297:17
hence, dear d. 504:7
trial by jury..will be a d. 172:12
Delusive seduction of martial music 104:1
Delve one yard below their mines 436:8
Delved: when Adam d. 11:18, 235:7
Delving: he was d. in his kailyardie 250:12
Demand: d. me nothing 474:1
d. that demi-devil 474:1
he'll make d. of her 426:13
Demanded: on the principle it was 100:5
Demas hath forsaken me 69:1
Demeaning: so womanly her d. 502:18
Demens: i d. et saevas curre per Alpes 283:21
quem fugis, a, d.? 555:22
Dementat prius 195:10
Demented: by God d. 375:19
not one is d. 567:20
Demetrius, a silversmith 65:6
Demi-Atlas of this earth 423:42
Demi-devil: demand that d. 474:1
Demi-god: what d...so near creation? 464:18
Demi-natur'd with the brave beast 436:42
Demi-paradise: other Eden, d. 474:22
Demi-puppets that .. ringlets make 480:12
Demireps that love and save their souls 89:33
Democracy: d...government of all the people 373:16
d. is only an experiment 267:6
d. is on trial 184:1

Democracy (cont.)
D. resumed her reign 41:26
d. substitutes election by the.. many 490:29
d. .. the bludgeoning of the people 570:12
great arsenal of d. 408:24
our d. the most aristocratic 325:34
perfect d...shameless 102:23
political experiment of d. 490:10
safe for d. 571:14
wine-lees and d. 89:23
Democrat: aristocrat, d., autocrat 535:43
Democratic: a whole new d. world 127:6
our aristocracy the most d. 325:34
Democritus: rideret D. 257:15
Demolished: no man is d. but by himself 43:8
Demoniac frenzy, moping melancholy 349:24
Demoniaco-seraphic 97:17
Demon-lover: woman wailing for her d. 151:32
Demonstrandum: quod erat d. 202:6
Demosthenes: D. never comes unseasonably 325:23
fall below D. or Cicero 202:16
Den: Court of King's Bench, D. of Thieves 147:17
d. of thieves 60:9
d. of wild things 249:9
glorious hosanna from the d. 503:5
his hand on the cockatrice' d. 53:19
wae to think upo' yon d. 104:5
Denial: hence, with d. vain 342:11
Denied: call that may not be d. 334:11
if it be but half d. 111:16
not d. him the request 392:38
that comes to be d. 371:14
to our moist vows d. 343:2
would be d. 475:32
Denies: she d. you 280:20
spirit that always d. 223:17
what this tumultuous body now d. 84:6
who d. of it? 176:30
Denis: between Saint D. and Saint George 445:14
Denmark: all the might of D.'s crown 122:3
it may be so in D. 432:21
look with a friend on D. 430:28
ne'er a villain dwelling in all D. 432:22
something is rotten in the state of D. 432:5
Denote: can d. me truly 430:30
Dens: lakes, fens, bogs, d. 346:2
Dense: through strait, rough, d. or rare 346:14
Dentist: vulgar to talk like a d. 569:19
Dents: avoir les d. longues 353:23
Deny: d. each article with oath 473:14
d. himself for Jove 455:18
d. them this participation of freedom 101:12
d. to Harold Skimpole 173:26
d. yourself 223:18
fain, fain d. 477:19
life offers—to d. 236:17
not d. thee 60:40
poor heart would fain d. 460:36
room to d. ourselves 291:7
teaches to d. that faintly prays 404:13
this health d. 195:16
thou shalt d. me thrice 60:39
which nobody can d. 203:37
wise powers d. us 424:3
Denying: unbelief, in d. them 201:12
Deo: ille mi par esse d. videtur 133:2
Deoch-an-doris: a wee d. 310:13
Deos: ille d. qui novit agrestis 556:18
Depart: d., be off, excede 251:20
having a desire to d. 68:16
he will not d. from it 50:30
I am ready to d. 308:25
let him d. 444:28
like shadows, so d. 460:10
loth to d. 402:6
thy servant d. in peace 61:20
when the great and good d. 575:1
when ye d. out of that house 58:48
whither d. the souls of the brave 146:14

Departed: all but he d. 357:14
dead he is not, but d. 317:2
d. never to return 108:37
d. this life 390:30
glory is d. 47:10
if he d. as he came 387:22
knolling a d. friend 441:10
souls d. but the shadows of the living 85:16
that the Lord was d. 46:59
they d...another way 57:25
Departing: at my d. 6:10
Department: fair sex is your d. 188:8
Departure: their d. is taken for misery 56:23
Dépêcher ses malades 354:3
Dependance: not subsist without D. on him 512:4
Depends: every creature..d. on his Creator 109:24
Deplore: d. her loss 348:35
flame I still d. 213:15
tho' I d. her change 155:37
though still I do d. 185:24
Deploring: damsel lay d. 216:5
Depopulating: fear of d. his dominions 38:18
Deportment: celebrated for his D. 173:29
Depose: my glories and my state d. 475:20
worldly men cannot d. 475:1
Deposed: ghosts they have d. 475:7
how some have been d. 475:7
must he be d.? 475:10
Depositary: d. of power..unpopular 181:40
mere d. of doctrine 180:26
Depravity: no less..stupidity than d. 272:2
total d. of inanimate things 234:21
Depressed: if the heart of a man is d. 214:30
Deprived of everlasting bliss 330:2
Depth: d. and dream of my desire 300:4
d. in philosophy 25:25
d. in that study 212:12
d. of some divine despair 538:17
far beyond my d. 446:24
from what a d...thy honours 579:34
gods approve thy d. 577:12
I love thee to the d. 88:24
in the d. be praise 364:6
in the search of the d. 49:22
little out of your d. 527:19
nor height nor d. 65:58
Depths: beyond the d. of a pond 373:14
d. and shoals of honour 446:29
d. of his own oceanic mind 153:14
he sinks into thy d. 114:28
his d. and his shallows 107:36
in d. of burning light 202:21
something in its d. doth glow 15:20
Deputy: d. elected by the Lord 475:1
some..read by d. 27:17
Derangement: nice d. of epitaphs 500:20
Derby dilly 124:10
Derision: clothed with d. 522:7
have them in d. 391:49
in d. of kingliest masonry 495:27
turns the old days to d. 523:1
Uglification, and D. 129:20
Derncleugh: in the shealings at D. 419:29
Derring do 222:10
Descant: her amorous d. sung 347:19
Descend: ere I d. to th' grave 158:13
pure lovers' souls d. 185:2
'tis time; d. 485:38
Descended: d. below the dignity of history 325:33
d. of so many royal kings 426:15
Descending: Dream..d. from the train 313:14
d. from the bus 128:18
some d. from above 24:17
this famous island d. incontinently 144:20
Descensus: facilis d. Averni 554:23
Descent: claims of long d. 533:38
of whatsoe'er d. their Godhead 190:12

INDEX

Describe the undescribable 114:9
Descried: d...an emerging prow 18:16
not own'd when 'tis d. 193:8
scarce long leagues apart d. 147:6
Description: answered the d...to a T 203:26
beggar'd all d. 424:6
make impertinent d. 110:44
saves a d. of the rising sun 499:29
truth of the d. 420:28
Descry the morn's approach 350:3
Desdemona: D. seriously incline 470:2
O D.! D.! dead! 473:32
Desert: all beyond High-Park's a d. 202:5
behold d. a beggar born 487:14
d. country near the sea 485:13
d. in arms be crowned 190:34
d. in service 481:21
d. of the sea 53:25
d. shall rejoice 54:1
d. were a paradise 107:26
d. were my dwelling-place 114:25
fret not to roam the d. now 365:16
in the d. a fountain 119:10
in this d. inaccessible 427:19
life is the d., life the solitude 587:14
make straight in the d. 54:9
never..d. Mr. Micawber 174:23
nothing..unrewarded but d. 190:24
owl that is in the d. 398:1
part with my glory and d. 244:11
Snow upon the D.'s dusty face 205:27
some pain'd d. lion 17:26
streams in the d. 54:3
two..legs..stand in the d. 496:13
use every man after his d. 433:30
waste its sweetness on the d. air 230:5
water but the d. 114:15
what ailed us..to d. you? 523:3
whose country he has turned into a d. 101:27
wide d. where no life is found 253:28
Deserted at his utmost need 191:7
Deserting these, thou leavest me 499:9
Deserts: antres vast and d. idle 470:2
d. of Bohemia 485:14
d. of vast eternity 333:9
or his d. are small 355:19
when she d. the night 350:23
wisdom, she d. thee not 349:2
Deserve: all who d. his love 192:13
best d. the precious bane 345:10
d. well of yourself 514:38
only d. it 144:18
we'll d. it 1:14
Deserved: d. well of his parish.. his country 413:24
most righteously have d. 389:11
Deserves: d. to carry the buckler unto Samson 86:13
none but the brave d. the fair 190:34
Deserving: d. note 246:4
where is my d.? 487:22
Deshabille: devout in d. 203:30
Desiderio: quis d...tam cari capitis? 258:24
Design: might of d. 489:21
poetry that has a palpable d. upon us 289:25
self-seeking, envy, low d. 308:2
towards his d. moves like a ghost 458:1
when..dull..a d. in it 204:26, 511:24
Designed: whom God to ruin has d. 192:33
Designer infinite 544:24
Designs: close d. and crooked counsels 190:13
from d. by Michael Angelo 50:16
his d. were strictly honourable 204:30
Immanent Will and its d. 235:20
ladder to all high d. 481:3
lofty d...like effects 92:1
to his own dark d. 344:20
treasures up his bright d. 161:18
Desine..mater saeva Cupidinum 260:17
Desipere in loco 112:11, 120:24, 261:5
Desirable young men 55:32
Desire: all their d...in..their craft 57:13
all the speed d. can make 292:19
bloom of young d. 231:9

Desire (cont.)
delight that consumes the d. 522:27
depth and dream of my d. 300:4
d. accomplished 50:5
D. gratified 74:25
d. in deity 410:26
d. not to be rinsed with wine 254:27
d. of the moth for the star 499:4
d. shall fail 51:33
end of every man's d. 522:16
expectation, and d. 579:27
eye beholds the heart's d. 262:13
few things to d. 26:9
fulfilled of my heart's d. 524:13
given him his heart's d. 392:38
grant thee thy heart's d. 392:36
great d. to a bottle of hay 467:15
having a d. to depart 68:16
I'll sell your heart's d. 296:15
in fair d...joy renew 81:5
in his heart is a blind d. 522:7
I shall d. more love..of you 426:25
kindle soft d. 191:12
Land of Heart's D. 585:16
lineaments of gratified d. 74:28
love and d. and hate 187:11
man's d. is for the woman 153:7
mixing memory and d. 197:27
my arrows of d. 75:16
my soul hath a d...to enter 397:5
naught for your d. 140:13
nearer to the Heart's D. 207:26
no beauty that we should d. him 54:25
not to get your heart's d. 490:26
our d. is got without content 459:3
our song is the voice of d. 81:19
possess his own d. 575:8
quiet and rest and d. 359:7
same..as thou art in d. 457:11
see thy heart's d. 81:25
shall d. to die 71:12
soul's sincere d. 355:11
sun and moon of the heart's d. 411:35
therein is my d. 399:14
thou knowest all my d. 394:7
times of your d. 487:7
to fill my heart's d. 41:18
transported with celestial d. 510:14
utmost share of my d. 247:8
vain d...and vain regret 411:19
vain d. was chidden 359:27
what many men d. 463:44
what..men had come to d. 374:10
whence..this fond d.? 1:22
where there is much d. to learn 352:14
which of us has his d.? 542:40
why..d. to be deceived? 109:37
with fathering d. 335:28
woman's d...for the d. of the man 153:7
wonder and a wild d. 95:34
Youth pined away with d. 76:7
Desired: d. to know nothing hurts, and is d. 272:27, 426:11
I have d. to go 254:29
more to be d...than gold 392:33
not one to be d. 533:35
suffer'd herself to be d. 558:5
who hath d. the Sea? 301:9
Desires: all d. known 390:4
D. and Adorations 491:21
d. and dreams and powers 523:18
d. but acts not 77:10
dreams and d. 522:12
equal to the soul's d. 574:17
fondly flatter our d. 189:5
from whom all holy d. 338:34
liberty..doing what one d. 338:31
my d. like..hounds 481:31
New Year reviving old D. 205:8
not what our youth d. 19:6
nurse unacted d. 77:19
submitting..shows..to the d. of the mind 24:16
such sweet d. do gain 232:5
undaunted daughter of d. 165:28
weight of chance-d. 573:30
whilst his d. were as warm 100:17
winged with vain d. 192:23
young with young d. 544:8
your heart's d. be with you 426:21

Desirest: justice, more than thou d. 465:11
thou d. no sacrifice 395:10
Desireth: heart..d. great matters 404:4
Desirous: ought else on earth d. 214:29
when you are d. to be bless'd 436:6
Desist: obliged to d. from the experiment 306:11
Desk: but a d. to write upon 110:41
drudgery of the d.'s dead wood 307:17
votary of the d. 306:18
Desks: stick close to your d. 221:18
Desolate: built d. places for themselves 48:45
d. and sick of an old passion 187:8
how many d. creatures 87:31
none are so d., but something dear 113:15
solitary griefs, d. passions 269:26
whisperings around d. shores 288:30
Desolated: province they have d. 222:35
Desolation: abomination of d. 60:24
Babylon in all its d. 169:20
like day from d. 496:23
Love in d. masked 492:2
my d...make a better life 425:33
seat of d. 344:18
Silence! and D.! 380:14
Despair: as for regaining my character I d. 208:25
begotten by d. 332:5
bid me d., and I'll d. 247:3
born of d. 375:26
can never d. 489:10
carrion comfort, D. 254:19
curst himself in his d. 507:27
depth of some divine d. 538:17
d. for Johnny head-in-air 402:24
d., law, chance 185:14
endure my own d. 559:7
eternity's d. 88:4
from d. thus high uplifted 345:14
Giant D. 99:19, 20
grim-visag'd comfortless D. 230:28
Heaven in Hell's d. 76:2
hurried question of D. 113:5
infinite wrath, and infinite d. 346:32
I shall d. 476:37
look on my works..and d. 496:14
magnanimous D. alone 332:5
now fiercer by d. 345:15
pale d. and cold tranquillity 492:19
Patience, too near neighbour to D. 18:13
racked with deep d. 344:15
rash-embrac'd d. 464:17
severer than d. 160:20
two loves..of comfort and d. 488:18
wasting in d. 572:2
wearily through darkness and d. 495:10
what resolution from d. 344:19
with the unpaid bill, D. 494:9
Despaired: neither..d. of the Commonwealth 181:29
starved, feasted, d. 97:28
Despairer: too quick d. 18:26
Despairful: dissolute, damned and d. 422:20
Despairing: wives and mithers maist d. 360:14
Despairs: leaden-eyed d. 287:27
through comfortless d. 510:16
Desperado: Don D. 294:12
Desperandum: nil d. Teucro duce 258:11
Desperate: beware of d. steps 160:40
d. deeds of derring do 222:10
diseases d. grown by d. appliances..reliev'd 436:11
his d. deadly daunting dagger 583:23
not to do d. things 546:33
tempt not a d. man 478:40
Desperation: lives of quiet d. 546:32
ruin, and d., and dismay 350:17
Despicere unde queas alios..videre errare 320:30(-321)
Despise: comforts we d. 425:25
contrite heart..not d. 395:10
dost thou d. the earth 580:26
I d. Shakespeare 489:22
I pity his ignorance and d. him 177:12
money, I d. it 220:31
pretend to d. Art and Science 75:9

INDEX

Despise (cont.)
reason to hate and d. myself 239:22
scarce begun to admire..ere you d. 194:10
some other Englishman d. him 490:44
threats of pain and ruin to d. 230:5
who know them best, d. them most 107:23
Despised: cast out of the world and d. 405:13
d. and dying king 498:18
d. and rejected of men 54:25
d. and we esteemed him not 54:25
d. the day of small things 56:11
follow only those who have d...it 112:8
he hath not d...the poor 393:8
I should not be d. 52:21
most lov'd, d. 452:13
not..hated and d. the world enough 239:22
weak and d. old man 453:6
Despises: husband frae the wife d. 108:4
thing that she d. 154:28
Despising: myself almost d. 486:24
Despite: grew immortal in his own d. 386:12
Hell in Heaven's d. 76:3
in Hell's d. now 90:17
vanquished had no d. 509:35
we come but in d. 467:28
Despoil: tremble and d. themselves 496:9
Despond: name of the slough was D. 99:5
Despondency: in the end d. and madness 580:7
Despot: country governed by a d. 274:2
d.'s heel is on thy shore 405:19
Despotic: to the man d. power 350:35
Despotism: between..anarchy and d. 499:11
d. tempered by epigrams 126:12
Destinatus obdura 132:18
Destined: d. to be happy with you here 290:30
such a d. wretch as I 159:1
Destinies: Persuasions and veiled D. 491:21
Destiny: character is d. 196:29
day of my d.'s over 119:9
D. the Commissary of God 186:5
D. with Men for Pieces plays 206:28
determin'd things to d. 424:23
hanging and marriage..go by D. 203:28
hanging and wiving goes by d. 464:5
his own funereal d. 118:31
homely joys, and d. obscure 230:1
in shady leaves of d. 166:17
manifest d. to overspread the continent 371:4
our d...is with infinitude 579:27
reap a d. 406:6
riddle of d. 307:34
struggling..with ruthless d. 574:23
Destitute of sincere friendship 25:12
Destroy: be that which we d. 459:3
doth the winged life d. 74:27
in after Wrath d. 207:14
in an after Rage d. 207:18
not..to d. the law 57:43
one sin will d. a sinner 99:28
one to d. is murder 586:27
they shall not hurt nor d. 53:19
time..impatient to d. 279:7
utterly abolish or d. 576:19
whom God would d. 195:10
Destroyed: Bishop Berkeley d. this world 505:23
d. by subtleties 336:33
many a..fellow had d. 438:35
not one life shall be d. 532:32
once d. can never be supplied 224:14
Prussia..finally d. 21:6
what's not d. by Time's..hand? 79:17
what thou art may never be d. 83:12
Destroyer: d. and healer, hear! 524:21
d. and preserver, hear 496:4
Destroyeth: sickness that d. 397:18
Destroying: fighting still, and still d. 191:9
Destroys: first d. their mind 192:33

Destruction: all other things to their d. draw 184:6
besom of d. 53:23
by d., dwell in doubtful joy 459:3
d. of the poor 49:55
d.'s devastating doom 5:7
leadeth to d. 58:23
mutual d. of arguments 265:7
pride goeth before d. 50:15
startles at d. 1:22
their going..utter d. 56:23
turnest man to d. 397:15
Destructions..a perpetual end 392:13
Destructive: d., damnable, deceitful woman 371:9
peace more destructive of..manhood 269:19
smiling, d. man 312:27
Desultory feet of Death 411:3
Detail: merely corroborative d. 220:13
occupied in trivial d. 29:6
Detain: warn all traffic and d. 299:25
Detect: not d. therein one circumstance 316:36
Detecting what I think a cheat 272:20
Detection is..an exact science 188:18
Deteriora sequor 371:30
Determinate: my bonds in thee.. 487:22
Determination: character..the d. of incident 268:13
d. of words to the mouth 518:43
Determine: our deeds d. us 196:9
Determined: accidentally d. to some..direction 278:2
d., dared, and done 503:6
d. things to destiny 424:23
Determining: I am not d. a point of law 101:5
Deterred from detecting..a cheat 272:20
Detest: d. at leisure 116:44
gods d. my baseness 425:23
Detract: above our power to add or d. 314:12
Detraction: d. is but baseness' varlet 281:4
d. will not suffer it 440:51
Detrimenti: ne quid res publica d. caperet 145:21
Deum: habere non potest D. patrem 22:1
nympha pudica D. vidit 165:25
Te D. laudamus 13:14
Deus: D. disponit 291:20
d. nobis haec otia fecit 555:16
nec d. hunc mensa..est 556:2
nec d. intersit 256:5
Deutschland über alles 203:3
Deux: courage..de d. heures après minuit 360:25
Devant: présentez toujours le d. 353:9
Develop his hooks and his crooks 107:36
Development: law of human d. 19:30
De Vere, hast thou no tear? 193:2
Deviates: never d. into sense 193:2
Device: banner with the strange d. 316:17
d...they are not able to perform 392:40
miracle of rare d. 151:33(−152)
new d. of a Protestant Flail 250:13
no work, nor d. 51:21
panes of quaint d. 285:19
Devices: d. of the people 393:36
our d. still are overthrown 435:13
Dévidant et filant 408:18
Devil: abashed the D. stood 347:31
apology for the D. 112:3
a walking the D. is gone 151:7, 507:19
can the d. speak true? 456:21
cards..the d.'s books 520:31
children of the d. 539:20
craft..of the d. or man 389:9
crafts and assaults of the d. 388:45
defy the d. 484:8
D. always builds a chapel there 170:11
d. an' a ostrich 300:8
d. be in my feet 420:16
d. can cite Scripture 463:18
d. damn thee black 460:35
D. did grin 151:11
d...do a very gentlemanly thing 514:11
D. fly away with the fine arts 126:40

Devil (cont.)
d. go wid you, ye spalpeen 298:21
d...have all the good tunes 248:11
D., having nothing else to do 41:27
D. he blew upon his nails 302:32
D. he could na scaith thee 104:26
D. he grinned 302:31
D. howling 'Ho!' 511:8
D. in his gut 75:15
d. is come down 71:18
D. knows how to row 150:11
D.'s Awa' Wi' the Exciseman 105:10
D. sends cooks 213:9
D. smiled 151:10
d.'s most devilish when respectable 87:34
d.'s walking parody 140:21
d. take her 517:11
d. take the ass that bred you 298:21
D. that prompts 'em 90:16
d. to pay 357:21
d. turned precisian 334:23
d. understands Welsh 440:5
D. was pleased 151:12
d. was sick, the d. a monk wou'd be 359:25
D. watches all opportunities 155:24
d. weakly fettered 514:5
D. whoops 295:15
d. will come 330:7
d...will have his chapel 33:4
d. with d. damn'd 345:28
d. would have him about women 443:22
dream of the d., and wake in a fright 34:10
dream'd of the d., and wak'd in a fright 13:16
drink and the d. 514:18
either..a d. frae hell 31:7
every man..was God or D. 190:23
fears a painted d. 458:14
first Whig was the D. 274:7
gifts from the D. 74:29
given the d. a foul fall 358:2
go to the d. where he is known 275:33
half-d. and half-child 303:24
heaviest stone that the d. can throw 240:3
hoard of gold kept by a d. 442:21
how agrees the d. and thee 438:26
how the d. they got there 385:27
hunting which the D. design'd 193:39
if bird or d. 380:26
if that thou be'st a d. 473:33
if the d. dress her not 426:8
ingredient is a d. 471:23
laughing d. in his sneer 115:2
let the d. be sometime honour'd 462:25
make a moral of the d. 444:13
Michael..contending with the d. 70:17
not serve God if the d. bid you 469:30
of habits d. 436:5
of the D.'s party without knowing it 77:7
old serpent, which is the D. 71:39
poor d. has ended his cares 93:19
problem must puzzle the d. 107:36
renounce the d. 391:2
resist the d. 69:40
sacrifice..of the d.'s leavings 387:1, 520:48
sugar o'er the d. himself 434:3
suspect that I worshipp'd the D. 74:29
synonym for the D. 325:6
tell truth, and shame the d. 281:21, 439:43
there is a d. haunts thee 439:34
through envy of the d. 56:22
till the D. whispered 295:16
upon Don or d. yet 539:20
use the d. himself with courtesy 484:21
very d. incardinate 484:24
vows, to the blackest d.! 436:28
wedlock's the d. 117:45
what a mischievous d. Love is 112:4
what a surly d. 203:35
what d. this melancholy is 209:29
when most I play the d. 476:12
when the d.'s riddle is mastered 525:21
who cleft the D.'s foot 186:16
wine..let us call thee d. 471:21

INDEX

Devil (*cont.*)
wi' usquebae, we'll face the d.　108:10
world, the flesh, and the d.　388:47
young and sweating d.　472:13
your adversary the d.　70:0
your father the d.　63:29
you the blacker d.　473:20
Devil-born: doubt is d.　533:13
Devil-defended: beneath the D. walls　375:22
Devildoms of Spain　539:18
Devilish: earthly, sensual, d.　69:39
excus'd his d. deeds　347:16
hellish, d., and damned tobacco　109:22
most d. thing is 8 times 8　208:22
most d. when respectable　87:34
Devils: at liberty when of D.　77:7
casteth out d. through the prince of d.　58:44
d. an' jads thegither　108:22
d. are not so black　315:16
d. being offended　470:25
d. to ourselves　481:25
fight like d.　444:5
little d. ran　302:32
one more d.'-triumph　93:6
one sees more d.　467:24
said they were d. incarnate　443:22
those poor d. are dying　378:13
'tis d. must print　356:7
whip me, ye d.　473:32
with d. dwell　561:22
Devious: drive it d.　164:8
me howling winds drive d.　160:35
Devisal: past our d.　545:12
Devise: Dant..can al d.　137:39
d., witl write, pen　455:1
Devised: d. by the enemy　470:40
never anything..so well d.　388:4
Deviseth: liberal d. liberal things　53:44
Devizes: young man of D.　305:9
Devoid: d. of sense and motion　345:19
wholly d. of good feeling　312:20
Devoir: faites votre d.　157:7
Devon: cowslips from a D. combe　296:15
if the Dons sight D.　363:2
men of Bideford in D.　539:19
started that morning from D.　219:11
Dévorât: la Révolution..d...tous ses enfants　552:17
Dévot: pour être d...pas moins homme　354:6
Devote: d. myself to another sensation　290:26
now to Death d.　349:17
Devoted yours　486:4
Devotion: d.l daughter of astronomy　587:13
d. to something afar　499:4
dollar..object of universal d.　267:25
farwel my book and my d.　138:16
innocent is the heart's d.　499:2
matrimonial d.　219:38
open..d...always pleasant　304:35
shrine of the sailor's d.　489:1
strikes me in a deep fit of d.　86:33
with d.'s visage　434:3
Devotional exercise proper to..the Faerie Queene　306:8
Devour: seeking whom he may d.　70:6
shed tears when they would d.　27:40
still threatening to d. me　346:32
worry and d. each other　160:41
Devoured: d. as fast as they are made　481:17
d. the seven good ears　45:18
d. thy living with harlots　62:17
him who solved it not d.　350:17
some evil beast hath d. him　45:15
Devourers: sheep..become so great d.　358:12
Devours: daily d. apace　342:29
Devout: d. in dishabilly　203:30
d. their peaceful temple choose　164:35
Dew: as d. in April　7:16
beards dip in coldest d.　336:38
bedabbled with the d.　246:22
besprent with April d.　282:2
bright d. is shaking　166:24
continual d. of thy blessing　388:31

Dew (*cont.*)
dark with d.　171:21
d. bespangling herb and tree　245:25
d. of summer nights collected　288:13
d. shall weep thy fall tonight　245:13
d. that on the violet lies　417:26
d. was falling fast　578:28
d. was on the lawn　512:10
d. will rust them　469:40
dreamt that they were filled with d.　149:28
fades awa' like morning d.　32:18
falls the d. on the face of the dead　40:2
fearfully o'ertrip the d.　465:17
ghastly d.　534:26
in the d. of the morn　584:19
into a sea of d.　204:5
leave the lilies in their d.　17:2
less dear than the d.　584:20
let there be no d.　47:29
like the d. on the mountain　416:23
meet the morning d.　18:30
ne'er brushed d. from lawn　119:17
newly wash'd with d.　479:4
on whom the d. of heaven drops　209:24
o'er the d. of yon high..hill　430:21
red d. of Olivet　545:7
resolve itself into a d.　430:33
retired as noontide d.　578:32
smell the d. and rain　244:18
sweep away the morning d.　467:20
thy birth-time's consecrating d.　376:2
wet by the d. it grew　204:3
who hath begotten the drops of d.?　49:23
whose wine was the bright d.　497:22
with anguish moist and fever d.　286:29
Dew-drop: fragile d. on its..way　288:10
protects the lingering d.　573:18
seen the d. clinging　268:30
woman like a d.　90:2
Dew-drops: go seek some d.　466:35
with showers and d. wet　409:29
Dewfall at night　516:2
Dew-lapp'd like Thessalian bulls　467:20
Dew-pearled: the hill-side's d.　94:40
Dews: brushing..the d. away　230:11
d. of summer night　338:13
d. of the evening..shun　139:3
with the d. at even　535:31
Dewy: from d. dawn to d. night　359:5
William D., Tranter Reuben　236:8
Dewy-feather'd sleep　341:22
Dexterity: with such skill and d.　173:12
Dexterous: acute, inquisitive, d.　100:30
Di: d. me terrent　555:13
habitarunt d. quoque silvas　555:22
non d...non..columnae　256:12
Diable: le d. est mort　406:5
Diadem: precious d. stole　435:49
with a d. of snow　118:7
Dial: as the d. to the sun　78:18
he drew a d. from his poke　427:13
laugh..an hour by his d.　427:15
life..upon a d.'s point　440:32
more tedious than the d.　472:18
not in figures on a d.　29:9
thou breathing d.　308:31
Dialect: Babylonish d.　110:9
by your d. and discourse　110:38
d. I understand very little　377:23
d. words..marks of the beast　237:6
Dial-hand: beauty, like a d.　487:29
Dialogue: hear the wooden D.　481:6
Dials: to carve out d.　446:1
Diamond: immortal d.　255:7
like a d. in the sky　527:10
more of rough than polished d.　139:24
O D.! D.!　364:14
spots quadrangular of d. form　163:29
Diamonded with panes of quaint device　285:19
Diamonds: thy eyes are seen in d. bright　215:42
Dian: as D. had hot dreams　430:4
hangs on D.'s temple　429:20
Diana: D. in her summer weed　232:1
D.'s foresters　438:16
D.'s lip is not more smooth　482:10
great is D. of the Ephesians　65:8
that burnt the Temple of D.　87:17

Diapason: d. closing full in Man　191:35
rolled its loud d.　34:2
Diaphenia, like a daffadowndilly　156:19
Diaries: let d..be brought in use　27:28
Dice: some were playing d.　31:1
to throw the d.　569:8
twain were casting d.　149:13
Dicebamus hesterna die　313:16
Dicere: et quae sentias d. licet nec possum d. quare　526:14　331:24
Dicers: false as d.' oaths　435:42
Dicho: del d. al hecho　134:16
Dichtet: Lord Byron..wem er d.　223:13
Dici: nihil tam absurde d. potest　145:3
Dick, the shepherd, blows his nail　456:1
Dickens: what the d. his name is　466:4
Dickon thy master is bought and sold　476:39
Dicky-bird, why do you sit?　220:17
Dictate: not presume to d., but　178:27
Dictates: d. of his godlike mind　371:8
d. to me slumb'ring　349:5
sacred d. of thy faith　412:16
Dictatorial: resist a d. word　221:19
Dictators ride..on tigers　144:19
Dictatorship of the proletariat　333:14
Dictionaries: to make d. is dull work　277:12
writer of d.　270:27
Dictionary: but a walking d.　135:26
learned d. words　337:2
Dictum: nihil est d. quod non est d. prius　184:3
Did: confirmeth all He d. by all He doth　80:12
d. it very well　219:7
George the First..d. nothing　272:27
it was their duty and they d.　217:27
never forget what they d. here　314:12
thou canst not say I d. it　459:15
what it d. so freely　457:11
what they undid I d.　424:19
what thou and I d. till we lov'd　185:6
Woman whom D.　4:17
Diddest: thus d. thou　436:40
Diddle: fiddle, we know, is d.　523:26
Dido: D. and her Aeneas shall want troops　425:22
D...was Di-Do-Dum　387:3
in such a night stood D.　405:17
Die: afternoon..loth to d.　525:1
all shall d.　442:7
all that live must d.　430:29
although it fall and d.　282:1
always with us, or we d.　284:22
answered, 'I would d.'　410:19
anything but d.　307:31
as loth to d.　577:10
as lucky to d.　567:13
as much beauty as could d.　280:11
as natural to d. as to be born　26:3
ay, but to d.　462:9
bear to live, or dare to d.　384:2
Beauty that must d.　287:21
because they d.　157:20
be fond to live or fear to d.　198:10
before I d. for ever　263:22
begins to d.　404:15
being born, to d.　23:19
blown about the sky..and d.　586:2
born but to d.　383:22
by feigned deaths to d.　186:15
can't d...except when the tide's ..out　174:39
costs a lot..to d. comfortably　111:36
cowards d. many times　449:22
curse God and d.　48:43
dar'st thou d.?　462:7
dead shall live, the living d.　191:39
dead which d. in the Lord　71:27
death, thou shalt d.　185:16
desire to d.　71:12
d. all, d. merrily　440:19
d. and be a riddance　174:15
d. and endow a college　384:42
d. as soon as one pleases　156:6
d. at thirty-five in Babylon　19:3
d. because a woman's fair　572:2
d., before I have begun to live　16:18
d. before they sing　151:15
d. beyond my means　570:24

INDEX

Die (*cont.*)

d. fasting	211:17
d. for thee	247:3
d.—in bed	415:13
d. in music	473:29
d. in that man's company	444:28
d. in the last ditch	103:33, 570:28
d. in the last dyke of prevarication	101:25
d. in the lost, lost fight	146:14
d. is cast	120:14
d. I, so d. I	316:32
d. not, poor death	185:15
d. of a rose	383:16
d. soon, O fairy's son	509:29
d. the death of the righteous	46:18
d...the last thing I shall do	373:9
d. to make men free	264:18
d. to save charges	109:11
d. two months ago	435:5
d. upon the barricades	569:14
d. upon the sand	17:26
d. with harness on our back	461:7
d. with kissing of my Lord	331:4
d. with looking on his life	424:1
easy ways to d.	426:17
either do or d.	37:24
ere their story d.	236:14
every man..is born to d.	193:17
fain d. a dry death	479:18
Falstaff liked..of a sweat	443:1
fears his fellowship to d. with us	444:28
few d. and none resign	268:26
few d. well that d. in a battle	444:19
gladly d.	516:15
going on, and not to d.	541:17
good d. first	574:14
greatly think, or bravely d.	381:32
Guards d.	121:24
guiltless death I d.	473:18
have the power to d.	540:23
hear them sigh and wish to d.	217:23
he did not d. in the night..in the day	359:13
hope..can d. not	493:23
how can man d. better	323:17
how often are we to d.?	386:37
I am sick, I must d.	361:5
I change, but I cannot d.	493:1
I d. a Christian	136:1
I d. as often as from thee I go	185:31
I d. happy	211:2, 309:18
I d.! I faint! I fail!	494:7
if d...when princes d. with us	440:32
if I d., no soul shall pity	476:37
if I must d.	462:8
if I should d. before I wake	8:18
if I should d...no immortal work	290:29
if I should d., think only	84:21
if it were now to d.	470:31
if these poor limbs d.	84:19
if thou d. a martir	138:37
if we are mark'd to d.	444:26
if you poison us, do we not d.?	404:8
I'll d. for him tomorrow	30:3
in Adam all d.	67:8
in that Jerusalem..d.	442:29
in what peace a Christian can d.	3:1
I shall d. at the top	520:51
I shall d. today, and you tomorrow	358:3
I Sir Richard Grenville d.	540:3
it is most grand to d.	334:4
I to d., and you to live	506:9
it was sure to d.	357:5
I will d. in peace	572:16
I will not have thee d.	539:1
lads that will d. in their glory	263:3
lay me doon and d.	187:6
learn of me to d.	382:8
leave me there to d.	7:3
let it d. with thee	56:48
let..laws and learning d.	329:10
let me d. drinking	329:14
let not God speak..lest we d.	45:53
let us determine to d. here	39:2
let us do or d.	107:33
little honey..and lo, I must d.	47:14
live and d. for thee	247:4
live or d. wi' Charlie	250:15
love her till I d.	10:20, 210:5

Die (*cont.*)

make a malefactor d. sweetly	194:19
man can d. but once	442:12
men that love lightly may d.	523:15
might it d. or rest at last	493:27(–494)
must men kill and d.?	493:27(–494)
my resolution is to d.	349:18
nor..shall, until that I d.	369:13
not d. but in Jerusalem	442:29
not d. but live	399:10
not d. here in a rage	519:31
not made to d.	531:40
not so difficult to d. in	118:11
not to live, but to d. in	86:36
not willingly let it d.	352:21
now not basely d.	425:28
now..seems it rich to d.	287:32
now that I come to d.	90:36
old batchelor don't d.	560:14
old soldiers never d.	9:2
one man..d. for the people	63:42
only art..to d.	226:18
or bid me d.	247:3
or ever ye came to d.	302:21
or hearing d.	446:18
or I d.	548:12
or let me d.	577:25
or like Douglas d.	251:28
our pattern to live and to d.	93:3
parting was to d.	533:15
perceives it d. away	576:9
play the Roman fool and d.	461:9
possess our soul before we d.	18:18
prepar'd to d.	462:3
prescription to d.	470:14
regret can d.	533:6
ride on to d.	339:12
Romeo..when he shall d.	478:20
say to thee that I shall d.	445:12
seen her d. twenty times	423:25
shall Trelawny d.?	239:7
she must weep or she will d.	538:25
sicken and so d.	481:30
sicken soon and d.	343:19
since I needs must d.	405:7
since that I must d. at last	186:15
sit him down and d.	442:5
so apt to d.	450:4
some did d. to look on	423:40
souls of those that d.	316:27
speak or d.	442:35
still harder lesson, how to d.	387:11
suffer and d.	553:2
swan-like, let me sing and d.	116:3
sweet day..thou must d.	245:13
Tamburlaine..must d.	331:8
taught us how to d.	547:22
teach the rustic moralist to d.	230:8
telling what it is to d.	532:22
that sort of king should ever d.	94:44
that we shall d., we know	449:33
then d., dear, d.	38:23
therefore I d. in exile	232:9
they d. in yon rich sky	538:16
they d. not..but cease	411:6
they d. to vex me	335:18
they seemed to d.	56:23
they that d. by famine d. by inches	242:9
those who are about to d.	13:4
those that do d. of it	426:6
though fated not to d.	192:21
though I should d. with thee	60:40
thousands d., without or this or that	384:42
thou shalt surely d.	44:13
thus adventuring to d.	292:20
thy Venus that must d.	231:36
til that myn herte d.	138:18
time to d.	51:3
to d. I leave my love alone	487:14
to d. in dust	509:7
to d. is gain	68:15
to d.: to sleep	434:4
to d. will be an awfully big adventure	36:9
to fight is but to d.	539:20
to itself, it only live and d.	487:25
to live in hearts..is not to d.	122:15
to look about us and to d.	383:7
tomorrow let us do or d.	122:14

Die (*cont.*)

tomorrow thou shalt d.	411:5, 7
tomorrow we d.	67:11
tomorrow we shall d.	53:27
trust that when we d.	335:10
try by sleeping what it is to d.	87:1
turn giddy, rave, and d.	381:27
unlamented let me d.	386:27
unto all life of mine may d.	165:31
we all must d.	521:2
were born or should d.	548:15
we shall d. to the Song	241:26
when beggars d.	449:22
when for the truth he ought to d.	199:27
when the brains were out..d.	459:17
when they d. by thousands	141:34
when they d., go to Paris	14:1
whereunder..we live and d.	207:3
whether thou live or d.	81:24
whom the gods love d. young	116:10
who saw him d.?	369:19
whose love will never d.	338:19
who would wish to d.?	78:24
why..make haste to d.?	263:18
'will d.'..'He shall not d., by God'	513:20
wisdom shall d. with you	48:57
without Thee I dare not d.	291:10
wretch that dares not d.	106:35
ye are Gods and..shall d.	525:12
yet d. we must	446:6
yet she must d.	473:11

Die: *sermonem deficiente d.* | 372:7

Died: bards who d. content | 287:17

before her time she d.	535:9
but d. an hour before	458:24
but since he d.	486:26
closed his eyes and d.	31:2
d. as firm as Sparta's king	188:33
d. as one that had been studied	456:27
d. before the god of love was born	185:34
d...but not for love	428:21
d. in a good old age	48:34
d. last night of my physician	402:3
d. of the kisses of..God	368:21(–369)
d. on Saturday	31:9
d. out of pure, pure grief	417:18
d. the death of fame	264:18
d. to make men holy	41:22
d. to save their country	31:3
d. to succour me	87:38
d. while ye were smiling	417:18
d. with conquering Graeme	225:23
dog it was that d.	540:3
fell upon their decks and..d.	440:30
he that d. o' Wednesday	65:45
in that he..he d. unto sin	19:1
I wander'd till I d.	125:5
justified a chaste polygamy and d.	309:12
Laodameia d.: Helen d.	583:12
lik'd it not, and d.	122:36
millions d. that Caesar..be great	87:25
mine only d.	99:2
Mr. Badman d...like a Chrisom-child	30:3
my love has d. for me	238:20
ole man Know-All d.	276:5
people who d. of dropsies	562:18
Prince of glory d.	361:5
queens have d. young and fair	41:34
she d. because she never knew	563:18
she d. young	461:4
she should have d. hereafter	425:23
since Cleopatra d.	81:11
since Maurice d.	215:25
so groan'd and d.	401:29
so they liv'd, and so they d.	69:15
these all d. in faith	386:24
they had no poet, and they d.	540:26
two hours since hath d.	215:12
was scorn'd and d.	209:18
'What! no soap?' So he d.	359:23
when he d. the little children cried	185:32
when I d. last	436:32
when my father d.	76:17
when my mother d.	280:11
where it d. to tell	4:4
who d. to save us all	

[679]

Died (cont.)
woman d. 382:13
woman d. also 60:13
would God I had d. for thee 47:37
would to God we had d. 45:52
youngest critic has d. 303:19
Diem: carpe d. 258:17
d. perdidi 548:4
omnem crede d...supremum 256:27
per unam d...bene conversati 291:26
Dienen und verlieren 223:23
Dies: artist never d. 317:2
because a man d. for it 570:21
d., and makes no sign 445:31
d. at the opening day 562:9
d. ere he knows it 91:41
d. in good stile at home 560:14
d. like a dog 568:15
every minute d. a man 6:6
every moment d. a man 541:13
Flower..for ever d. 206:9
giant d. 231:27
he that d. pays all debts 480:4
he that d. this year 442:13
in your fragrant bosom d. 125:11
it d. upon her heart 494:7
king never d. 73:5
light of the bright world d. 79:5
loves, and weeps, and d. 493:25
marries, d., or turns Hindoo 495:11
matters not how a man d. 271:35
more we enjoy it, more it d. 168:7
no man d. for love 193:22
no man happy till he d. 506:12
primrose that forsaken d. 342:31
soon as beauty, d. 184:13
splutters as it d. 264:5
their red it never d. 183:11
then d. the same 587:6
who d. if England live 296:20
worm that never d. 84:1
Dies: d. irae, d. illa 134:4
nulla d. sine linea 380:4
optima..d...prima fugit 556:20
Diest: where thou d., will I die 47:1
Diet: d. unparalleled 176:38
Doctor D., Doctor Quiet 520:23
immortal d. 405:9
no antipathy..in d., humour, air 86:25
oft with gods doth d. 341:10
praise is the best d. 504:32
typical of a mixed d. 376:16
Dieted with praise 287:16
Dieth: Christ..d. no more 65:45
their worm d. not 61:5
Dieu: D. me pardonnera 240:27
D...pour les gros bataillons 557:10
espagnol à D. 136:13
si D. n'existait pas 557:7
un homme avec D. 305:5
Dieux: laissez faire aux d. 157:7
Differ as Heaven and Earth 531:22
Difference: between thee and me what d.? 498:15
d. is best postponed 178:8
d. of men's talk 377:10
d. of taste in jokes 196:17
d. of texts 510:15
d. to me 580:18
each the other's d. bears 332:11
no d...alienate Cicero 325:23
only d., after all their rout 142:30
wear your rue with a d. 436:32
you shall know the d. 363:16
Different: by d. methods d. men excel 143:11
clean d. 135:28
hatched d. 196:8
how d. from us 8:10
how d., how very d. 7:2
like, but oh how d.! 582:21
other naturs thinks d. 176:17
something d. from either 197:28
think o' something d. 295:1
we boil at d. degrees 201:15
Difficile: Latin was no more d. 110:4
Difficilis, querulus 256:2
Difficult: d...?..wish it were impossible 277:8
not so d. to die 118:11
others extremely d. 275:5

Difficult (cont.)
these simple cases..so extremely d. 187:13
upon which it is d. to speak 101:24
Difficulties: pursuit of knowledge under d. 179:3
ten thousand d...one doubt 363:23
Difficulty: he wolde sowen som d. 138:3
my only d. is to choose 194:12
so he with d. and labour 346:17
Diffidence: her name was D. 99:20
not a trace..of d. or shyness 219:33
Diffident: not d. of wisdom 349:2
Dig: d. for buttered rolls 131:24
d. the grave and let me lie 516:15
d. till you gently perspire 297:28
I cannot d. 62:18
relief to me to d. him up 489:22
Digest: can d. so much 483:9
into words no virtue can d. 331:2
inwardly d. them 389:23
Digested: some few to be chewed and d. 27:17
Digestion: d. is the great secret 505:34
from pure d. bred 347:37
good d. wait on appetite 459:13
prove in d. sour 474:17
Digestions: few radicals have good d. 111:37
Digged: they have d. a pit 395:18
this..saltpetre should be d. 438:35
Digger: work like a d. 199:33
Diggeth: he that d. a pit 51:24
Dight: storied windows richly d. 341:24
Digne: pas d. de vivre 353:20
Dignify the Serpentine 183:14
Dignitate: cum d. otium 145:22
Dignities: above all earthly d. 446:25
by indignities men come to d. 26:24
speak evil of d. 70:8
without corrival all her d. 438:38
Dignity: adverting to the d. of this high calling 101:15
d. of history 78:15, 325:21, 33
for the d. of the whole body 460:28
holds his estimate and d. 481:12
I left the room with silent d. 233:10
in d. of being we ascend 574:19
in d. or honour goeth to hym nigh 195:7
in every gesture d. and love 348:36
in the d. of thinking beings 277:39
reach the d. of crimes 357:25
seemed for d. compos'd 345:18
Washingtonian d. 387:13
wear an undeserved d. 464:1
write trifles with d. 274:25
Digression: there began a lang d. 108:20
Digressions..the soul of reading 513:8
Digs my grave at each remove 244:19
Dilapidation: prevent the shameful d. 101:30
style resembling..d. 337:2
Dilemma's even 194:27
Dilettante: snowy-banded, d. 535:42
Diligence is the mother of good fortune 134:17
Diligencia: la d. es madre de la buena ventura 134:17
Diligent to learn 575:5
Dilloing in his armour 297:25
Dilly: Derby d. 124:10
Dim: adazzle, d. 255:3
d. and decorous mirth 84:5
d. and perilous way 574:15
d. emblazonings 285:19
d. religious light 341:24
d. suffusion veiled 346:19
earth's joys grow d. 322:1
live invisible and d. 551:21
made the bright world d. 499:7
nor d. nor red 149:2
not Erebus itself were d. enough 449:7
not when the sense is d. 39:6
pinnacled d. in the intense inane 497:12
when all the lights wax d. 246:26
woods on shore look d. 357:16
Dimanches: tous les d. sa poule 242:1
Dim-discovered: d. spires 153:25
ships, d. 546:15
Dimension: illimitable ocean.. without d. 346:10

Dimensions of this mercy 167:5
Dimidium: animae d. meae 258:4
d. facti qui coepit habet 256:25
Diminish: do your joys with age d. 93:25
enlarge, d., interline 521:10
Diminished: hide their d. heads ought to be d. 346:6 / 20:24
Diminishes: any man's death d. me 186:28
Diminutive: most d. of birds 460:17
Dimmed: now d. and gone 357:13
Dimness: elms fade into d. 17:16
Dimple: then the d. on his chin 321:14
Dimpled: pretty-d. boys 424:6
Dimples: whose d. we prize 500:40
Dimpling: shallow streams run d. 385:32
Din: cock with lively d. 341:23
louder still the d. 322:22
may'st hear the merry d. 148:19
raise a d. 105:27
Dinah: Villikins and his D. 10:18
Dine: more if you d. at a friend's 178:25
d. at journey's end 586:13
d. somewhere among the rubbish 269:20
d. with Jack Wilkes, Sir! 273:17
d. with the Canons of Christ-Church 272:38
gang and d. the day 32:15
going to d. with some men 43:3
go to inns to d. 141:32
I d. at Blenheim 8:16
I fear ye d. but sparely 106:32
if this should stay to d. 128:18
if wife should d. at Edmonton 160:8
no scandal while you d. 540:30
that jurymen may d. 385:15
when men asked her to d. 10:25
Dined: I d. last night with the Borgias 39:16
I have d. today 505:4
or had not d. 384:23
they d. on mince 312:3
Diner-out: philosophic d. 93:29
Diners-out: from whom we hide our spoons 324:19
Dines: where the M.F.H. d. he sleeps 518:11
Ding: always d., dinging Dame Grundy 359:22
chiels that winna d. 105:11
d. dong bell 366:18, 464:13, 479:30
Dingo: Yellow-Dog D. behind 297:29
Dining: live without d. 337:42
while they thought of d. 225:27
Dinna ye hear it? 568:19
Dinner: after d. is after d. 519:29
better..a d. of herbs 50:12
better pleased when he has a good d. 277:1
breakfast, d., lunch, and tea 41:3
Christ..they would ask him to d. 127:25
conservatives after d. 200:25
could not have had a better d. 271:19
d. lost! 'ounds lost! 518:16
d. waits—and we are tired 160:3
drink our healths at d. 295:9
fight till six, and then have d. 130:23
fond of his d. 221:5
good d...reconciles everybody 377:27
make an end of my d. 465:31
make our d. sweet 32:15
not a d. to ask a man to 271:18
not sufficient for a kite's d. 404:4
over the glass's edge when d.'s done 89:28
rolled its loud diapason after d. 34:2
settled..on whatever one had got for d. 412:21
talking politics after d. 181:6
three hours' march to d. 240:9
welcome for himself, and d. 387:21
what gat ye to your d.? 31:10
Dinner-bell: tocsin of the soul— the d. 116:18
Dinner-knives: with broken d. 296:32
Dint: you feel the d. of pity 450:31
Dinted: d. with the silver-pointed pencil 93:45
where the snow lay d. 361:24

INDEX

Diocese: all the air is thy D.   184:26
Diogenes struck the father   109:28
Dios: la idea que de ti D. tenga   551:2
Dip. kind of farthing d.   516:18
Diplomacy: Dollar D.   5:29
Dipped: I d. into the future   534:25
Dips: the sun's rim d.   149:14
Dirce: with D. in one boat   308:22
Dirck galloped   92:22
Dire: d'ennuyer..de tout d.   557:13
Direct: as the House is pleased to
   d. me   313:15
   he shall d. his going   397:10
   Homer..plain and d.   20:2
   lie d.   428:37
   puff d.   499:27
   to be d. and honest is not safe
   understanding to d.   472:6   282:20
Direction: determined to some
   particular d.   278:2
   d. which thou canst not see   383:21
   stand by Caesar and give d.   471:15
Directions: by indirections find d.
   out   432:34
   gives d. to the town   521:20
   rode madly off in all d.   311:1
Directories: Court Calendars, D.   306:26
Direful: something d. in the
   sound   22:19
Direness..cannot once start me   461:3
Dirge: by forms unseen their d. is
   sung   153:30
   d. for Saint Hugh's soul   170:24
   thou d. of the dying year   496:7
   with d. in marriage   430:24
Dirges: instead of d. this complaint   292:18
   to sullen d. change   478:33
Dirt: had she borne the d. and rain   359:4
   hairs, or straws, or d.   385:27
   half the little soul is d.   537:5
   huddled in th. reasoning engine lies   407:22
   if d. were trumps   308:6
   in poverty, hunger, and d.   253:22
   instead of d. and poison   519:5
   painted child of d.   385:31
Dirtiness: all along o' d.   295:22
Dirty: all d. and wet   521:11
   at his d. work again   385:24
   damned..d., dangerous way   227:6
   d. hands, the nails bitten   325:28
   d. nurse, Experience   530:43
   d. stones of Venice   293:10
   for all 'is d. 'ide   297:3
   life's road, so dim and d.   115:11
   rose pink and d. drab   337:9
   which..is to do the hard and d.
   work   413:4
Dis: by gloomy D. was gathered   347:8
   let'st fall from D.'s waggon   485:26
Dis: d. aliter visum   554:10
non sine d. animosus infans   259:26
Disabused: by himself abused, or
   d.   383:22
Disagree: men only d.   345:28
Disagreeable: I'm such a d. man   221:39
   sincere enough to tell him d.
   truths   322:14
Disagreeables: making all d. evaporate   289:20
Disanointed: discrowned and d.   524:22
Disappoint: can't abide to d. myself   227:1
Disappointed: d. still, was still
   deceiv'd   160:29
   never be d.   386:36
   pangs of d. love   412:8
   unhouseled, d., unaneled   432:17
Disappointeth him not   392:24
Disappointment all I endeavour
   end   255:8
Disapproves: condemns whatever
   he d.   103:38
   d. that care   351:23
Disarray: uncouth words in d.   276:14
Disaster: 'gainst all d.   99:35
   laugh at all d.   315:29
   meet with Triumph and D.   297:10
Disasters: make guilty of our d.
   the sun   452:18
   see d. fallen upon her   102:11

Disasters (*cont.*)
   so weary with d.   458:36(–459)
   trace the day's d. in his..face   225:1
Disastrous: born to d. end   510:16
Disavows: Conservatism.. d. Pro-
   gress   181:32
Disbanding hired armies   127:6
Disbelief: d. in great men   126:23
   willing suspension of d.   152:26
Disbelieve: a Napoleon and yet d.   89:35
Disbranch: that herself will sliver
   and d.   453:42
Disc: round d. of fire   74:6
Discandy, melt their sweets   425:17
Discarded: to be d. thence   472:34
Discept: two must d.—has dis-
   tinguished   93:18
Discern: all we have built do we d.   17:1
   only I d. infinite passion   97:12
   their real int'rest to d.   160:41
Discerning: gives genius a better
   d.   226:2
Discharge: might d. their souls   193:30
   no d. in that war   51:17
   no d. in the war   294:37
Discharged: at once indebted and
      346:31
Disciple: d. is not above his
   master   58:51
   d. whom Jesus loved   64:19
   in the name of a d.   59:4
Discipline: d. and perfect steadiness   305:1
   d. must be maintained   174:1
   good order and military d.   5:26
   holy spirit of d.   56:20
   my d. of arms   331:2
Disciplines of the pristine wars   444:2
Disclose: seek his merits to d.   230:13
Discobolus: gospel of the D.   112:18
Discolouration: eye that cast d.   337:6
Discomfited: kings..were d.   396:7
Discommendeth: he who d. others   85:14
Discontent: age of splendid d.   355:12
   divine d.   294:3
   in common—d.   19:7
   in pensive d.   510:16
   large and liberal d.   561:14
   more apt to d.   154:26
   pale contented sort of d.   286:41
   prone to d.   246:17
   winter of our d.   476:2
   with darkling d.   375:10
Discontented: blushing d. sun   475:8
   d. with the divine discontent   294:3
   every one that was d.   82:20
Discontents: feel their d.   357:24
Discord: all d., harmony   383:21
   dire effects from civil d.   1:25
   knows no d.   123:18
   so musical a d.   467:20
   that eke d. doth sow   198:5
   what d. follows   481:4
Discordant: reconciles d. elements   579:9
   still-d. wavering multitude   441:8
Discords make the sweetest airs   111:10
Discors: concordia d.   257:5
Discountenance every one among
   you   75:9
Discouragement: there's no d.   99:35
Discouraging: heard a d. word   248:9
Discourse: any d. of rivers   559:25
   bid me d.   488:26
   by your dialect and d.   110:38
   d. in novel phrases   220:26
   d. most eloquent music   435:23
   d. of the elders   56:37
   d. the freezing hours away   429:31
   fittest for d.   193:26
   good company and good d.   559:17
   in d. more sweet   345:29
   nor to find talk and d.   27:16
   put your d. into some frame   435:20
   rather hear thy d. than see a play   109:23
   so varied in d.   308:17
   Sydnaean showers of sweet d.   166:20
   wants of reason   430:33(–431)
   with such large d.   436:15
Discourses: from the hipp'd d.   231:28
Discourtesy: fierceness makes..
   truth d.   244:1

Discover: ere he shall d.   517:18
   happy soul she shall d.   166:9
   to d. we must travel too   206:27
Discovered: as thy love is d.
   almighty   96:24
   up he starts d.   347:29
Discoverers: ill d. that think there
   is no land   24:19
Discovereth the thick bushes   393:23
Discovering: womanly d. grace   184:19
Discredit: he will d. our mystery   462:18
Discreet and learned Minister   390:31
Discreetest: virtuousest, d., best   349:1
Discretion: better part of valour is
   d.   441:2
   fair woman..without d.   49:58
   has no d. in her coughs   22:29
   not to outsport d.   471:5
   philosophy is nothing but d.   422:9
   years of d.   391:16
   your own...your tutor   434:16
Discreto: al simple con el d.   134:18
Discrowned: crown'd and again d.   269:27
   d. and disanointed   524:22
Discussing their duty to God   567:20
Discussion: Rupert of Parliamentary d.   180:15
Disdain: d. and scorn ride sparkling   468:25
   for thee to d. it   499:3
   in patient, deep d.   17:8
   more love or more d.   125:7
   my dear Lady D.   468:2
   pride and high d.   417:6
   she did all d.   9:10
   that fixed mind and high d.   344:13
Disdained: if now I be d.   9:21
   one feeling too falsely d.   499:3
Disdains: d. all things above his
   reach   371:15
   d. to hide his head   231:32
Disease: age, d., or sorrows   146:32
   amounts to a d.   220:9
   creeds a d. of the intellect   200:44
   cur'd yesterday of my d.   402:3
   cure the d. and kill the patient   26:18
   d. is incurable   441:26
   d. of admiration   324:36
   d. of not listening   441:15
   Emphyteusis is not a d.   514:39
   every physician..his favourite d.   204:24
   find her d.   461:1
   if..d. in the liver..a Calvinist   200:11
   life is an incurable d.   158:21
   no cure for this d.   41:2
   prayers are a d. of the will   200:44
   remedy is worse than the d.   27:11
   seamed with the scars of d.   325:28
   shapes of foul d.   533:20
   strange d. of modern life   18:14
   this long d., my life   385:26
   Waddy is an infectious d.   304:51
   without d. the healthy life   518:1
   young d...grows   383:26
Diseased: d. in his feet   47:50
   minister to a mind d.   460:37
   of its own beauty is the mind d.   114:16
   when love grows d.   202:2
Diseases: death is the cure of all d.   86:35
   d. desperate grown   436:11
   one of the..d. of women   243:12
   perils and d. that he elbows   38:24
   sovereign remedy to all d.   109:22
   subject to the same d.   464:8
Disenchanted: see a d. nation   496:23
Disenchanting: so d. as attainment   514:12
Disencumbered Atlas of the state   161:40
Disentangle: cannot d.   9:21
Disertum: salaputium d.   133:4
Disfigure: gypsies..d. them   499:23
Disgrace: d. and ignominy of our
   natures   86:19
   even to a full d.   429:18
   impatient of d.   190:13
   much d...the name of Agincourt   444:10
   O the d. of it!   39:25
   poverty is no d.   505:17
   quite a d. to be fine   527:7
   sole author of his own d.   160:17
   when in d. with fortune   486:24

[681]

INDEX

Disguise: blessings in d. 248:1
  to go naked is the best d. 154:36
Disguised: in Franciscan think to
  pass d. 346:25
Disguises: these troublesome d. 347:25
Disguising: vizards..d. what they
  are 459:5
Disgust: d. and secret loathing 17:7
  in divine d. 119:16
  old plays begin to d. 202:15
Disgusted with literary men 289:14
Dish: but a d. of pain 547:20
  butter in a lordly d. 46:49
  chameleon's d. 435:2
  d. fit for the gods 449:10
  d. for a king 485:16
  d. of sweet berries 249:7
  d. ran away 367:1
  for a d. of wood 475:10
  some d. more sharply spiced 375:6
  this d...too good for any but.. 559:24
  was not that a dainty d.? 368:20
  was not this a dainty d.? 512:5
  woman is a d. for the gods 426:8
Dishclout: Romeo's a d. to him 478:31
Dishcover the riddle 131:29
Dished: we have d. the Whigs 511:12
Dishes: d. the Doctor has sent us 213:9
  d. were ill-sorted 194:16
  ever recollect half the d. 22:20
  home-made d. 253:10
  not wash d. 366:16
Dishonest: free from all d. deeds 123:23
  our employment may be
  reckoned d. 215:2
Dishonour: another unto d. 65:60
  by honour and d. 67:28
  his honour rooted in d. 530:37
  I have liv'd in such d. 425:23
  past all d. 252:15
Dishonourable: find ourselves d.
  graves 448:22
Disinclination to inflict pain 337:39
Disinheriting: damned d. countenance 500:41
Disintegration: through rapine to
  d. 222:38
Disinterested: d. endeavour to
  learn 19:12
  d. intellectual curiosity 549:10
  friendship is a d. commerce 226:34
  seldom so d. 1:6
Disinterred: within the City d. 496:2
Disjoint: let the frame of things d. 459:4
Dislike: d...at first sight 511:19
  hesitate d. 385:29
Dislikings: made up of likings and
  d. 306:10
Dislimns: the rack d. 425:20
Dismal: d. news I tell 13:18
  D. Science 126:34
  with d. stories 99:36
Dismay: chains of its d. 495:26
  devious coverts of d. 411:12
  let nothing you d. 6:11
  ruin, and desperation, and d. 350:17
  shape of danger can d. 575:11
Dismayed: neither be thou d. 46:37
  ran d. away 465:17
  was there a man d.? 528:14
Dismemberment of the Empire 222:38
Dismiss: if thou d. not her 349:2
  Lord, d. us with Thy blessing 98:14
  power to d. itself 448:36
Dismissed: d. by the British
  electorate 144:17
  d. with hard words 375:15
  may not rudely be d. 152:21
  with peace and consolation hath
  d. 351:7
Disobedience: children of d. 68:3
  excuse my d. now 158:28
  of man's first d. 344:1
Disobedient: hearts of the d. 61:11
Disobeyed: the seventh time d. 375:16
Disorder: corrupt influence..
  spring...of all d. 101:17
  her last d. mortal 225:16
  lived in the utmost d. 312:22
  most admir'd d. 459:22
  sweet d. in the dress 246:4

Disorders: all ruinous d. 452:16
Disparity: just such d. 184:5
Dispatch: be angry and d. 426:13
  Cecil's d. of business 503:9
  nothing more requisite..than d. 1:8
  your mystery, nay, d. 472:33
Dispatchful: with d. looks 348:8
Dispelled: mist is d. when a
  woman appears 214:30
Dispense: d. with..necessities 359:24
  with wine d. 164:33
Dispenses: indulgences, d., pardons 346:26
Dispersed: he hath d. abroad 398:27
  now d. all the world over 212:8
Dispirited: fainting, d. race 17:20
  not d., not weak 200:3
Displace: this pair of boots d. 406:18
Displaced: you have d. the mirth 459:22
Displayed all sorts of flowers 509:6
Displeasure: her d. fly 470:29
Disponibles: saw them..as d. 268:8
Dispose: charitably d. of anything 444:19
  unsearchable d. of highest wisdom 351:7
Disposed: sentimentally I am d.
  to harmony 306:4
  when I am so d. 176:10
Disposer Supreme 571:4
Disposes: God d. 291:20
Disposition: change my d. 485:27
  entertain a cheerful d. 474:26
  horridly to shake our d. 431:32(-432)
  lay his goatish d. to..a star 452:19
  my master is of a churlish d. 427:6
  of a mild or choleric d. 2:4
  put an antic d. on 432:30
  truant d. 431:2
Dispositions: common d. of..
  mankind 101:33
Dispraise or blame 351:6
Dispraised: of such to be d. 279:29
  of whom to be d. 350:5
Disprized: pangs of d. love 434:4
Disproportioned sin 351:11
Disproven: nor yet d. 527:21
Disputants: our d...the skuttle
  fish 2:30
Disputation: run in debt by d. 110:6
  that's a feeling d. 440:3
Disputations: doubtful d. 66:15
Dispute: better to live than d. 401:35
  d. it like a man 460:22
  d. the reign of some luxurious
  mire 216:4
  endeavour and d. 206:22
  my right there is none to d. 164:22
  on either which he would d. 110:5
  that such high d. should be 112:22
Disputed: an' downa be d. 105:11
  d. about the body of Moses 70:17
  some d. barricade 421:18
Disputes: left to their d. 348:30
Disquieted: never to be d. 292:19
  so d. within me 394:17
Disquieteth himself in vain 394:9
Disquietly: follow us d. to our
  graves 452:16
Disrespectfully of the Equator 504:21
Dissatisfied: not one is d. 567:20
Disseat: cheer me ever or d. me 460:36
Dissect: through creatures you d. 384:22
  we murder to d. 581:16
Dissemble: d. in their double heart 392:20
  d. nor cloke them 388:7
  d. sometimes your knowledge 26:6
  right to d. your love 72:14
Dissensions: one day's truce..
  to..d. 102:5
Dissent: all protestantism..a sort
  of d. 100:29
  dissidence of d. 100:29
  general union of total d. 320:3
  within a few days..d. myself 86:3
Dissenter: rigid d...eat very
  plentifully 2:16
Dissertates: one d., he is candid 93:18
Dissidence: d. of dissent 100:29
Dissimilar: though d. 493:8
Dissimulation: his gray d. 349:32
  laying down the guilt of d. 419:26
  let love be without d. 66:1
  politics in the East..d. 182:1

Dissipation without pleasure 216:27
Dissolute: d., damned, and des-
  pairful 422:20
  in the d. city 577:22
  think of it, d. man 252:21
Dissolution: from low..doth d.
  climb 578:1
  these limbs..from d. 185:4
Dissolve: all which it inherit, shall
  d. 480:8
  d. me into ecstasies 341:24
  fade far away, d. 287:25
  I d. it in rain 492:26
Dissolved: all d. in port 381:23
Dissolves: when all the world d. 330:3
Dissolving in rains 492:28
Dissonance: barbarous d. 340:26, 348:23
  from life's d. 569:13
Dissonant: no sound is d...of Life 152:2
Distance: at d. from the Kind 578:16
  at d. I gaze 373:18
  by d...more sweet 578:19
  d. lends enchantment 122:31
  for the future in the d. 33:8
  notes by d. made more sweet 154:1
  sixty second's worth of d. 297:12
  there's a magic in the d. 366:4
  thy strength, d. and length 262:5
Distance: la d. n'y fait rien 170:1
Distant: d. 205:25, 26
  d. from Heaven alike 109:20
  d...predominate over the present 277:39
  d. triumph-song 264:9
  dull prospect of a d. good 192:29
  far d., storm-beaten ships 327:11
Distasteful: found your life d.? 93:25
Distastes: prosperity is not without..d. 25:20
Distemperature: thorough this d. 466:37
Distil: observingly d. it out 444:12
Distillation: history a d. of
  rumour 126:16
Distilled: d. almost to jelly 431:10
  d. by the sun 237:10
  d. from limbecks 488:2
  rich d. perfumes 340:27
  rose d. 466:17
Distinct from harmony divine 159:11
Distinction: few escape that d. 550:28
  make d. of place 429:39
  no d. among the upper ten
  thousand 571:5
  no d. between virtue and vice 271:10
Distinctive: progress, man's d.
  mark 91:1
Distinctly: he speaks all his words d. 204:33
  so d. wrought 186:13
Distinguish: and yet abstain, and
  yet d. 352:9
  could of men d. 434:25
Distinguishable: shape had none d. 346:4
Distinguished: d. from all other
  creatures 2:32
  d. from you but by toils 1:18
  two must discept,—has d. 93:18
Distorting: I fear my speech d. 81:8
Distracted: she lay d. in the ditch 166:23
Distraction: Ambition, D. 129:20
  d. in's aspect 433:31
  into a fine d. 246:4
Distress: all pray in their d. 76:18
  called about him every one..in
  d. 82:20
  comfort man's d. 295:8
  comfort their d. 512:15
  deep d. hath humanized 578:15
  delivered them from their d. 398:15
  delivereth them out of their d. 398:18
  exposed to suffering and d. 575:7
  friend of Beauty in d. 117:36
  incapable of her own d. 437:1
  not affected by the reality of d. 373:3
  they d. them still 15:3
Distressed: afflicted, or d. 389:17
  art thou sore d.? 361:10
  d. by events which they did not
  cause 235:22
  griefs that harass the d. 278:32
  I am d. for thee 47:30
  mind d. 162:3

INDEX

Distresses: in all d. of our friends 521:1
insurmountable d. of humanity 277:24
Distressful: some d. stroke 470:3
District: of that d. I prefer 84:12
Distrust: that d...a mode of melancholy 273:20
Distrusted: power should always be d. 279:20
Disturb: difficult to d. the system of life 271:33
d. not her dream 105:29
d. our cheerful faith 582:3
d. your season due 342:10
Disturbs: presence that d. me 582:1
what d. our blood 586:10
Disused: thy needles..now rust d. 160:22
Dit: tout est à 97:32
Ditch: both shall fall into the d. 59:39
die in the last d. 103:33, 570:28
environed with a great d. 167:13
rather a d. in Egypt 425:34
Ditch-delivered by a drab 459:33
Ditchers: gardeners, d. and gravemakers 437:5
Ditches: water-land of Dutchmen and of d. 116:29
Ditchwater: drinking bottled d. 489:31
if he wasn't as dull as d. 178:19
Ditis: patet atri ianua D. 554:23
Ditties: amorous d. all a summer's day 344:32
d. of no tone 287:8
sing no more d. 468:20
Welsh as sweet as d. 440:4
Ditto to Mr. Burke 401:17
Ditty: play'd an ancient d. 285:26
sung the dolefullest d. 35:17
to air the d. 264:3
Diurna: exemplaria Graeca..versate d. 256:6
Diurnal: days nor things d. 523:24
earth's d. course 573:6
her d. round 575:26
Dive: d. into the bottom of the deep 438:38
for pearls must d. below 193:20
Heaven's great lamps do d. into the west 123:19
Diver: d. in deep seas 374:11
d. Omar 320:6
Divergence upon morals 514:17
Divers: in d. manners 69:6
time travels in d. paces 428:9
Diversa: vera bona atque illis multum d. 283:15
Diverse: d., sheer opposite 285:35
union of this ever d. pair 336:35
Diversion: d. in a talking blockhead 203:9
tay is not my d. 304:23
walking..country d. 156:10
Diversities of gifts 66:43
Diversity: whence arise d. of sects 510:15
Diverter of sadness 559:15
Divide: he could..d. a hair 110:5
he that will d. a minute 428:18
never d. my self from any man 86:3
or both d. the crown 191:13
rejoice, and d. Sichem 395:23
to d. is not to take away 493:11
when they d. the spoil 53:14
words d. and rend 522:9
Divided: d. duty 470:4
have they not d. the prey? 46:52
house..d. against itself 60:54, 314:6
in their death..not d. 47:30
more d. and minute domestic happiness 290:12
thy kingdom is d. 55:42
Dividends: comfortable..with d. 317:1
Divides that heavenly land 562:14
Dividing: by d. we fall 180:5
d. asunder of soul and spirit 69:8
d. the swift mind 531:28
in your sweet d. throat 125:10
like a d. spear 15:21
nor d. the Substance 388:38
Divination: spirit of d. 64:55
Divine: all are d. 15:16
all, save the spirit of man, is d. 113:2
Angels sing..their airs d. 158:4

Divine (cont.)
Apollo..can no more d. 343:21
as d. as myself 567:5
ask a drink d. 280:21(−281)
aught d. or holy 345:9
becks..to fellowship d. 284:25
believes Kingsley a d. 517:8
clothing for the soul d. 73:24
did the Countenance D. shine forth 75:16
distinct from harmony d. 159:11
d. discontent 294:3
d. melodious truth 284:17
d., the matchless 386:12
d. tobacco 510:1
d. Tranquillity 535:27
entertain d. Zenocrate 331:3
Fanny Kelly's d. plain face 307:15
fear of some d...powers 109:31
god-like wish, or hope d. 574:2
good d...follows his own instructions 463:8
great Mother's train d. 18:31(−19)
hand that made us is D. 2:28
heavy, but no less d. 116:4
holy, d., good, amiable 349:17
how d. a thing a woman 583:1
how d. is utterance 337:15
human face d. 346:20
inspired by d. revelation 24:17
its horror and its beauty are d. 495:17
knows itself d. 494:1
made brutes men, and men d. 374:20
majestic march and energy d. 386:17
makes drudgery d. 244:16
more needs she the d. 460:30
never could d. his real thought 115:41
nor glimpse d. 381:27
not therefore less d. 577:1
of quality and fabric more d. 579:38
radiant with ardour d. 17:20
scenery's d. 121:9
shed a ray of light D. 132:1
show me so d. a thing 332:5
silence is d. 126:33
so amazing, so D. 562:19
some d. excess 153:28
sung d. ideas below 199:20
tale of Troy d. 341:18
that in you which is d. 18:19
to forgive, d. 383:2
touch d.—and the scaled eyeball 96:33
what the form d. 308:14
wrote that monarchs were d. 297:18
Divinely: d. bestow'd upon man 164:24
d. tall and most d. fair 529:8
imperfections..d. appointed 413:15
most d. in the wrong 586:25
Divineness: poetry..some participation of d. 24:16
voice of the people hath some d. 25:8
Diviner: glad d.'s theme 190:18
Divines: D. use Austin's words verbatim still 109:4
eternal reproach of the d. 352:18
Taylor, the Shakespeare of d. 199:24
Divinest: two d. things 266:4
Divinity: as if D. had catch'd the itch 110:15
d. in odd numbers 466:14
d. that shapes our ends 437:27
d. that stirs within us 1:22
piece of d. in us 86:37
such d. doth hedge a king 436:27
tavern music..something in it of d. 86:33
what is called 'orthodox d.' 20:16
wingy mysteries in d. 86:7
Divis: permitte d. cetera 258:13
Division: deep d. of prodigious breasts 522:12
d. is as bad 8:12
equal d. of unequal earnings 198:21
marriage and death and d. 523:1
such d. 'tween our souls 451:31
with ravishing d. 440:4
woe weeps out her d. 279:28
Divisos: toto d. orbe Britannos 555:19
Divitias operosiores 259:17
Divorce: long d. of steel 446:13
my D. to all 185:22

Divorced: d. so many English kings 442:26
his aunts..demand to be d. 142:8
Divorum: rorum, corum, sunt D. 370:5
Divos: ille..superare d. 133:2
Dixerunt: ante nos nostra d. 184:3
Dizzy: how fearful and d. 'tis 454:3
Djinn: on the resident D. 222:17
Do: able to d...abundantly 67:55
by all ye leave or d. 303:25
cannot d...that ye would 67:45
d. after the good 328:2
d. all that they may..be expected to d. 565:27
d. as I say, not as I d. 422:11
d. as you're bid 195:20
d. as you would be done by 139:14
d. it with thy might 51:21
d. it yourself 34:7
d. not d. the thing they most d. show 487:24
d. not d. unto others 490:27
d. nothing and get something 182:26
d. other men, for they would d. you 176:15
d. this, and he doeth it 58:31
d. thou but thine 349:2
d. thou likewise 61:43
d. to all men as I would they should d. 391:6
d. what I will with mine own 60:8
d. what you can 232:13
d. ye even so to them 58:22
either d., or die 37:24
far, far better thing that I d. 180:2
finds out what you cannot d. 74:18
having too little to d. 297:26
I am to d. what I please 211:22
I daresay she will d. 83:18
I'd have you d. it ever 485:27
I d. nothing upon myself 186:26
if to d. were as easy 463:7
if we d. well here 318:9
I'll d., I'll d., and I'll d. 456:10
'inclined to think—'..'I should do so' 188:26
it revolts me, but I d. it 219:20
know not what they d. 62:48
know what to d. with it [the East] 558:23
let me d. it now 232:10
let us d. or die 107:33
little to d. and plenty to get 179:15
love and d. what you will 22:3
Machiavel and others..write what men d. 24:23
make me always..d. what is right 266:21
more remains to d. 115:3
not be known to d. anything, never d. it 200:47
Oh, mister porter, what shall I d.? 315:3
see thou d. it not 71:35
seemly so to d. 292:8
so little done, so much to d. 406:17
so much to d., so little done 533:3
that I would I d. not 65:49
that thou doest, d. quickly 63:49
their's but to d. and die 528:16
things that they shall d. 534:25
thing that I was born to d. 168:8
this will never d. 268:31
'tis time to d.'t 460:24
to d. thus 423:14
tomorrow let us d. or die 122:14
waked to d. it 453:19
we d. not what we ought 15:11
we shall not d. it any more 492:23
what have I to d. with thee? 63:5
what I d. in any thing to d. it as for Thee 244:15
what I d. to be liked 307:10
what I must d. then, think here 185:25
what man would d.! 96:23
what men dare d.! 469:4
what shall we d.—or go fishing? 545:15
what you d. still betters 485:27
what you say, or what you d. 8:17
which I would not, that I d. 65:49
which rather thou dost fear to d. 457:1
Wilfull will d.'t 156:16

[683]

Do (cont.)
will to d. 416:17
World..what wilt thou d.? 166:1
Doasyouwouldbedoneby: Mrs. D. 294:9
Doceri: ab hoste d. 371:29
Docet: ipse d. quid agam 371:29
Dock: d. the smaller parts-o'-speech 120:28
thistle and darnel and d. 171:21
Docks: hateful d. 445:11
Doctor: dishes the D. has sent us 213:9
D. Diet, D. Quiet, and D. Merryman 520:23
d. found, when she was dead 225:16
d. said that Death 569:7
d. slighted 372:12
D. well versed in Divinity 10:23
eagerly frequent D. and Saint 206:10
fee the d. for a nauseous draught 192:15
God and the d. we alike adore 372:12
if the d. does not give you a year 515:5
merry D. Brighton 542:16
never the d.'s brougham 299:19
no man therein d. but himself 350:28
some d. full of phrase and fame 19:5
when the artless d. sees 247:18
Doctor-like: folly, d. 487:14
Doctors: budge d. of the Stoic fur 340:35
let d. tell 105:15
medical d...cocking their medical eyes 180:1
when d. disagree 384:41
Doctrine: all the winds of d...let loose 352:17
d. of ill-doing 485:4
d. of the enclitic De 91:42
d. of the strenuous life 408:26
emblem of his d. 212:8
every blast of vain d. 389:51
every wind of d. 67:57
from women's eyes this d. 455:20, 23
lov'd the d. for the teacher's sake 170:3
not a mere depositary of d. 180:26
not for the d., but the music 382:30
of such d. never..school 350:28
Doctrines: d. fashion'd to the varying hour 224:18
makes all d. plain and clear 111:11
Documents: more d. than he can ..use 268:7
Dodd: D.'s sermons 273:31
Dodge: such as d. conception 284:23
Dodger: artful D. 177:37
Dodgers: dodgerest of the d. 178:21
Dodo never had a chance 167:25
Doeg..heroically mad 190:32
Doer: d. and the thing done 505:24
d.'s willingness 246:18
not a d. 69:33
Doers of the word 69:32
Does: d.—nothing at all 203:7
he who can, d. 490:31
not what man d. which exalts him 96:23
one who d., not suffers wrong 496:20
sees it and d. it 91:41
when the boy knows this..he ..d. it 177:5
Doest: that thou d., do quickly 63:49
Doeth: whoso d. these things 392:24
Doffed her gawdy trim 343:11
Dog: am I a d.? 47:24
as a d. is an infidel 271:30
beware of the d. 378:8
broodin' over bein' a d. 565:23
call a d. Hervey 270:4
curious incident of the d. 188:5
dies like a d. 568:15
d., a horse, a rat have life 454:26
d. had lost his wits 225:22
d. in the manger 549:28
d. it was that died 225:23
d. starved 73:20
d. that praised his fleas 586:12
d. to gain some private ends 225:21
d...to his own vomit 70:9
d...to his vomit 50:39
Dumb's a sly d. 144:24

Dog (cont.)
every d. has his day 78:29
every d. his day 293:19
from the power of the d. 393:7
get her poor d. a bone 368:4
giving your heart to a d. to tear 300:22
good d...cannot be of a bad colour 38:17
grin like a d. 395:22
hath a d. money? 463:22
his faithful d...bear him company 383:12
his Highness' d. at Kew 382:11
hold-fast is the only d. 443:23
I'd beat him like a d. 482:33
in another life expect thy d. 384:6
in that town a d. was found 225:20
is thy servant a d.? 48:25
I took by the throat the circumcised d. 474:2
lean d., a keen d. 327:2
let no d. bark 462:34
like a d., he hunts in dreams 534:22
like a d.'s walking on his hinder legs 271:16
little d. laughed 367:1
living d...better than a dead lion 51:19
mine enemy's d. 454:13
my brains..give them to a d. 466:8
my poor d. Tray 122:16
poor d., in life the firmest friend 118:22
poor d. had none 368:4
rather be a d. 451:13
rather see the portrait of a d. 277:2
something better than his d. 534:19
tail must wag the d. 295:15
tongue of d. 459:31
tossed the d. 369:6
very d. to the commonalty 429:2
very flea of his d. 280:15
when a man bites a d. 168:3
whose d. are you? 382:11
you call'd me d. 463:22
Dogged: it's d. as does it 549:16
strong, d. unenlightened opponent 19:14
Doggedly: set himself d. to it 270:11
Dog-kennel: in a empty d. 176:31
Dogma: d...the fundamental principle 363:18
no d., no Dean 181:18
Dogmatize: I d. and am contradicted 277:5
Dogs: all the d. in the town 369:2
better I like a d. 408:16
blood..in hosses, d., and men 542:38
cats is 'd.' 403:16
cowardly d. bark loudest 563:27
dancing d. and bears 249:5
d. did bark 160:2
d. eat of the crumbs 59:40
d. of..Saint Hubert's breed 416:13
don't let's go to the d. 242:25
horses and d. is some men's fancy 174:29
Inquisition d. 539:18
is it you, you d.! 270:14
knocked the factious d. on the head 275:12
lame d. over stiles 293:11
leave Now for d. and apes 91:40
let d. delight 561:24
let slip the d. of war 450:12
little d...bark at me 453:29
mad d. and Englishmen 157:25
many d. are come about me 393:5
more careful of the breed of their d. 377:8
mother of dead d. 126:41
na men but d. 108:23
players..like dancing d. 272:34
throw physic to the d. 460:37
tongue of thy d...red 396:11
uncover, d., and lap 480:25
unmiss'd but by his d. 161:24
when the d. hed gut asleep 320:1
Whig D. 276:27
Doing: d. or suffering 344:16
each your d. so singular 485:27

Doing (cont.)
Englishman..d. as he likes 19:29
find out what everyone is d. 243:1
fine writing..next to fine d. 290:23
if aught be worth the d. 77:32
joy's soul lies in the d. 480:41
one way of d. things rightly readiness of d. 413:17
246:18
see what she's d...mustn't 403:20
still be d., never done 110:19
stop somebody from d. something 242:30
such wondrous d. 436:42
when there's something d. 305:3
Doing-Good: as for D. 546:40
Doings: child is known by his d. 50:25
prevent us..in all our d. 390:51
Doit: beggarly last d. 163:44
d. to relieve a..beggar 479:39
Dolabella's Cleopatra 191:21
Dole: born..to all our d. 80:8
d. unequal laws 540:31
happy man be his d. 439:5, 466:7
weighing delight and d. 430:24
Doleful: in such d. dumps 504:10
regions of sorrow, d. shades 344:9
Dolendum est primum ipsi tibi 255:23
Doll: broken d. 238:8
prettiest d. in the world 293:17, 18
you called me Baby D. 238:7
Dollar: almighty d. 10:6, 267:25
billion d. country 210:11
D. Diplomacy 5:29
eagle..on th' back iv a d. 195:9
Dolore: accidere a nostro..d. 133:19
Dolorem: infandum..iubes renovare d. 553:24
Dolores: causae irarum saevique d. 553:8
Dolores: splendid and sterile D. 522:24
Dolorous: stroke most d. 328:5
Dolos: seu versare d. 554:1
Dolour: to see the d. that they made 328:19
Dolphin: mermaid on a d.'s back 466:38
Dolphin-chamber: sitting in my d. 441:31
Dolphin-like: his delights were d. 426:1
Domain: peace brooded o'er the hushed d. 184:2
Dome: blue d. of air 493:1
build that d. in air, that sunny d. 151:33(–152)
d. of a vast sepulchre 496:7
d. of many-coloured glass 492:15
d. of Thought 113:12
great bell swinging in a d. 208:2
hand that rounded Peter's d. 199:23
house with starry d. 561:17
shadow of the d. of pleasure 151:33(–152)
with a d. more vast 251:15
Domes: d. the red-plow'd hills 529:11
ships, towers, d., theatres 582:14
Domestic: d. happiness 163:6
gallant gay d. 535:4
imaginative or d. passages 289:24
malice d., foreign levy 459:4
more..minute d. happiness 290:12
of that d. sort 500:44
smooth current of d. joy 278:29
this milk-soup..d. bliss 375:6
Domesticate the Recording Angel 514:31
Domi: haec studia..delectant d. 145:16
res angusta d. 283:5
ridete..d. 132:21
Domina: Beata mea D. 359:10
Dominant: hark, the d.'s persistence 97:7
Domination: military d. of Prussia 21:6
Dominations: Thrones, D., Princedoms 348:14
Dominic: dying put on the weeds of D. 346:25
Dominion: between it and the d. of the world 327:11
death hath no more d. 65:45
d. over every creeping thing 44:7
d. over palm and pine 300:24
d. over the fish 44:9
lest they get the d. over me 392:34
Man's d. 107:10
tired of his dark d. 336:17

Dominions: our Sovereign, and his
  D. 389:14
tithe or toll in our d. 447:29
Domino: benedicamus D. 41:30
Dominus: d. illuminatio mea 49:35
  nisi d. frustra 49:36
Domitian: from the death of D. 217:8
Domus: d. et placens uxor 259:10
  d. sua cuique est..refugium 148:7
  dum d. Aeneae Capitoli..saxum
    accolet 555:8
  stat fortuna d. 556:25
Don: D. different from those regal
  Dons 41:32
remote and ineffectual D. 41:31
upon D. or devil yet 539:20
Dona: et d. ferentis 553:27
Done: a' is d. that men can do..
  in vain 106:17
as good as d. 220:21
been and gone and d. 218:5
better d. in Shakespeare 194:7
betters what is d. 485:27
determined, dared, and d. 503:6
do as you would be d. by 139:14
d. and not have spoken on't 424:18
d. anything that could be recalled 182:25
d. because we are too menny 237:3
d. it..least of these..d. it unto
  me 60:34
d. those things which we ought
  not to have d. 388:11
d. with Hope and Honour 296:28
game is d.! 149:13
had he not resembled my father
  ..I had d. 't 458:5
has she d. this to thee? 321:14
having d. all, to stand 68:11
having d. that, thou hast d. 185:24
how often we have d. this 492:23
I don't think it would have d. 564:2
if it were d. when 'tis d. 457:7
I go, and it is d. 458:1
I have d. the deed 458:6
I've d. it from my youth 164:32
I've d. no more 204:36
lute, be still, for I have d. 583:21
makes ill deeds d. 447:43
Mirabeau's work..is d. 125:34
much..to be d. and little..
  known 276:13
nay, I have d. 189:20
not d. in a corner 65:25
nothing is ever d...until 490:9
now my life is d. 547:20
petty d., the undone vast
  reward..to have d. at 92:36
said Francis, 'Rightly d.!' 200:26
seal then, and all is d. 265:20
servant of God, well d. 425:22
singing will never be d. 348:20
so little d. 406:17, 533:3
something attempted, something d. 318:13
still be doing, never d. 110:19
surprised to find it d. at all 271:16
taken in and d. for 292:16
thank God I have d. with him 270:23
that which is d. is that which
  shall be d. 50:61
that which they have d. but
  earnest 534:25
therefore it shall be d. 159:34
things which may fairly be d. 363:11
things won are d. 480:41
this that thou hast d. 44:23
this way or that—'tis d. 573:7
'tis d.—but yesterday a King! 118:19
to have d. 15:13, 481:18
well it were d. quickly 457:7
what hast thou d. to me? 411:14
what have I d. for you? 241:25
what have I ever d. to you? 203:36
what ha' ye d.? 302:24
what He might have d. with us 146:31
what I have d. is yours 486:4
what's d. is d. 459:4
what's d. we partly may compute 104:8
what's said or d. in earth 245:22

Done (cont.)
what *was* to be d.? 34:6
when love is d. 79:5
when thou hast d. 185:24
which of you have d. this? 459:14
wish 'twere d. 17:1
Donegal: kindliest creature in ould
  D. 229:14
Done-to-Death: also called..D. 548:19
Dong: the D.! the D.! 311:16
Donkey: D. went aboard 298:21
d. wot wouldn't go 43:23, 177:31
never see..a dead d. 179:32
once on a d. 175:37
score of d.'s years 171:21
that d...his face was sad 504:3
Donne: D., I suppose, was such
  another 197:34
D.'s verses..peace of God 267:32
D., whose muse on dromedary
  trots 151:13
John D., Anne D., Un-done 186:29
with Landor and with D. 586:13
Donné: grant the artist..his d. 268:14
Don Quixote: anything..wished
  longer..excepting *D.* 276:26
Dons: if the D. sight Devon 363:2
Don't: about to marry—'D.' 403:3
Can't! D.! Sha'n't! Won't! 300:16
you will be damned if you d. 187:7
Donuil Dhu: pibroch of D. 419:2
Doodah! doodah! 210:13
Doodle: Sir Thomas D. wouldn't
  come in 174:4
Doom: at Trinity Church I met
  my d. 217:21
crush'd..shall be thy d. 107:8
destruction's devastating d. 5:7
embrace..the d. assign'd 536:25
forfeit to a confin'd d. 488:2
great d.'s image 458:23
his d.'s extremely hard 220:6
nor strange thy d. 82:10
prisoner comes to meet his d. 222:29
reached the house of d. 24:2
regardless of their d. 230:26
stretch out to the crack of d. 460:11
to the edge of d. 488:7
to the scaffold and the d. 24:6
Doomed: d. like Odysseus 586:7
d. to death, though fated not to
  die 192:21
d...to walk the night 432:8
Dooms: grandeur of the d. 284:21
Doomsday: d. is near 440:19
houses..last till d. 437:8
if he danced till d. 155:8
sick almost to d. with eclipse 430:15
then is d. near 433:10
Doon: banks and braes o' bonny
  D. 108:36
Dooney: on my fiddle in D. 585:2
Door: as deaf as a d. 80:6
as the d. on its hinges 562:3
at my d. the Hundredth Psalm 121:13
back at mine hostess' d. 447:23
bar the d. 30:22
beside a human d. 577:18
came out by the same D. 206:10, 11
d. flew open, in he ran 250:4
d. stood open at our feast 148:17
D. to which I found no key 206:16, 17
drive an angel from your d. 76:16
either in d. or out 571:9
ev'ry d. is shut but..mercy's d. 161:17
fix'd for ever at the d. 541:23
for the whining of a d. 186:32
handle of the big front d. 221:15
his hand by the hole of the d. 52:10
I am the d. 63:36
is the wind in that d.? 328:6
it stands at the d. 128:13
keep the d. of my lips 400:13
keep you standing at that d. 410:3
knocking at Preferment's d. 18:7
knocking on the moonlit d. 171:13
let the d. be lock'd 437:39
made my sin their d. 185:24
make a beaten path to his d. 201:22
make a d...for thy mouth 57:4
my wee small d. 172:3

Door (cont.)
no d. can keep them out 243:24
nor so wide as a church 478:14
on the wrong side of the d. 140:16
open d. for all nations' trade 43:11
outside the fast-closed d. 264:12
pass'd the d. of Darkness through 206:27
posts of the d. moved 53:8
see through..a deal d. 179:16
shut stands the d. 15:27
shut the d. after you 195:20
sweep the dust behind the d. 467:36
three, four, knock at the d. 368:6
thy form from off my d. 380:27
tune the instrument here at the
  d. 185:25
when gusts shake the d. 16:1
Doorkeeper: boxkeeper, d., all in
  one 237:25
rather be a d. 397:7
Doors: be ye lift up, ye..d. 393:12
calling out of d. 538:4
death hath so many d. 37:20
death hath ten thousand..d. 563:16
death opens unknown d. 334:4
d. shall be shut 51:33
d. that do last for aye 421:2
d., where my heart 532:8
dovecote d. of sleep 338:3
he has been opening the d. 22:14
I shuttered my d. with flame 296:4
let the d. be shut upon him 434:10
lips..the d. of breath 478:44
open fly..th' infernal d. 346:9
open..your living d. 348:28
our own clay-shuttered d. 545:1
pictures out of d. 470:25
shut their d. against a setting
  sun 480:23
thousand d. to let out life 335:2
Doorways: D. are alternate Night
  and Day 205:29
folding d. of the East 544:7
Dorian: loved the D. pipe, the D.
  strain 18:28
to the D. mood 345:2
Dorians: to whom the D. pray 324:16
Doric: D. little Morgue 89:21
warbling his D. lay 343:6
Doris: call me Lalage or D. 152:6
Dormitat: bonus d. Homerus 256:10
Dotage: from Marlb'rough.
  streams of d. 279:10
or lose myself in d. 423:24
Dotages: common d. of human
  kind 109:12
Dotard: planet's tyrant, d. Death 38:29
Dote: d. on her for anything 452:23
I d. on his very absence 463:14
Doted: she d. upon the Assyrians 55:32
Dotes: who d., yet doubts 471:32
Doth: confirmeth all He did by all
  He d. 80:29
d., if the other do 186:25
Dotheboys Hall 176:38
Dots: those damned d. 143:35
Dotted over..the whole globe 563:5
Double: dissemble in their d. heart 392:20
d. blessing is a d. grace 431:24
d., d., toil and trouble 459:30
d. glass o' the inwariable 179:4
d. good 175:39
d. the vision my eyes do see 74:5
is old D. dead? 442:8
like to a d. cherry 467:9
make assurance d. sure 460:6
single thraldom or a d. strife 28:18
so d. was his pains, so d. be his
  praise 509:30
surely you'll grow d. 581:14
swan..float d. 582:19
to every power a d. power 455:22
with a d. thread 253:24
Doubled: d. him up for ever 218:20
d. his whole creation 80:29
your trouble d. 170:9
Double entendre: the horrible d. 10:24
Doublet: bought his d. in Italy 463:12
fashion of a new d. 468:17
his d. all unbrac'd 432:35
thy d. of changeable taffeta 483:7

Doubt: but live in d. 488:19
clouded with a d. 531:37
decide this d. for me 161:5
defence of philosophic d. 29:17
d. diversified by faith 89:32
doubter and the d. 199:5
d. is Devil-born 533:13
d. the equivocation of the fiend 461:5
d. thou the stars are fire 432:42
d. you to whom 501:20
enabled to d. thee 305:8
faith which does not d. 551:1
frets d. the maw-crammed beast? 95:14
'I d. it,' said the Carpenter 130:12
if the Sun and Moon should d. 73:28
in a state of philosophical d. 153:8
in d. to act or rest 383:22
knows no d. 15:21
leave such a matter in d.? 420:21
more faith in honest d. 533:14
never d. I love 432:42
never stand to d. 246:19
night of d. and sorrow 35:4
no d. but ye are the People 297:15
no longer could I d. him true 309:3
none might be in d. 81:10
no possible d. whatever 218:18
not make one d. 363:23
road to resolution lies by d. 404:8
soundest casuists d. 384:41
sunnier side of d. 527:22
then am most in d. 517:17
though we oft d. 351:7
time will d. of Rome 116:12
to be once in d. 471:34
troubled with religious d. 141:17
uncursed by d. 250:30
when all men d. you 297:10
when in d., win the trick 264:24
wherefore didst thou d. 59:37
Doubted: heard Troy d. 116:12
never d. clouds would break 97:4
Doubter and the doubt 199:5
Doubtful: d. disputations 66:15
d. throne is ice 529:41
in d. things, liberty 36:25
taught the d. battle 1:10
thou d. pleasure 229:9
Doubting: castle called D.-Castle 99:19
d., dreaming dreams 380:24
d. in his abject society 320:12
make allowance for their d. too 297:10
Doubtless God could have made a
better berry 112:21
Doubts: breed d. 'mongst Divines 510:15
d. from what he sees 73:28
end in d. 24:13
his d. are better than..certain-
ties 235:11
in uncertainties, mysteries, d. 289:21
littlest d. are fear 435:9
ma d. aboot the meenister 403:29
my d. are done 192:23
our d. are traitors 461:21
saucy d. and fears 459:12
who dotes, yet d. 471:32
Douceurs: ye d., ye sommeils du
matin 156:12
Doughtily: bare them right d. 189:8
Doughty: if d. deeds my lady please 228:12
Douglas: degenerate D. 573:24
doughty D. 30:5, 11
D., D., tender and true 165:22, 250:26
D. in his hall 418:27
hand of D. is his own 418:26
like D. conquer or like D. die 251:28
Dove: all the eagle..all the d. 165:29
as gently as any sucking d. 466:30
as the wings of a d. 396:7
beside the springs of D. 580:18
changes on the burnish'd d. 534:15
d. found no rest 44:39
hawk at eagles with a d. 245:4
my d., my dear 536:15
my d., my undefiled 52:9
patient as the female d. 437:25
Dove-cote: d. doors of sleep 338:3
eagle in a d. 429:23
Dover: burning a farthing candle
at D. 271:15
no longer think of..D. 29:15

Dover Road: milestones on the D. 175:35
Doves: as Venus yokes her d. 116:14
harmless as d. 58:49
his mother's d. 321:14
moan of d. 539:5
thou hast d.' eyes 52:5
with loves and d. 91:12
Dovetailedness: universal d. 177:18
Dove-wings: made their d.
tremble 285:36
Dow: this yer D. 238:27
Dowager's was a demd outline 177:20
Dowagers for deans 538:7
Dowel, Dobet, and Dobest 310:8
Dower: beauty is thy earthly d. 575:16
earth its d. of river 285:1
for deathless d. 410:30
human nature's highest d. 575:6
little children's d. 92:16
Dowered with the hate of hate 537:40
Down: all the stars looked d. 140:20
come d., O maid 539:3
coming d...shift for myself 358:6
cygnet's d. is harsh 480:39
does not write himself d. 239:12
d. among the dead men 195:16
d. and away below 15:22
d. at an inland town 219:17
d. by the salley gardens 584:11
d. comes the baby 73:14
d., d. to hell 446:8
d. he went like a streak 8:24
d. it merrily 170:24
D., Sir! Put it d.! 41:4
d. thou climbing sorrow 452:37
d. to the end of the town 339:16
d. to the valleys beneath 398:8
d. went the Royal George 162:10
d. with it, d. with it 400:6
drew an angel d. 191:13
float face d. 266:15
go d. like lumps of lead 249:15
he did again get d. 160:10
here's God d. on us! 87:27
he that is d. 99:31
I grant you I was d. 441:4
I rode upon the D. 78:1
let's all go d. the Strand 131:34
level d. 271:12
little, lost, D. churches 302:11
look not thou d. but up .95:25
or run it d. 521:20
other d., unseen 475:19
pack-horse on the d. 359:2
quite, quite d. 434:14
ridge of a noble d. 540:29
running a man d. 519:35
slap-dash d. in the mouth 155:30
smoothing the raven d. 340:15
so d. he came 159:38
soon came d. again 159:37
swan's d.-feather 424:21
that bucket d. 475:19
they are brought d. 392:37
thrice-driven bed of d. 470:8
when Kempenfelt went d. 162:11
when they were d., they were d. 10:19
with the d. on his beak 538:2
your d. so warm..pure 166:4
Downfall: regress..either a d. or..
an eclipse 26:24
Down-gyved to his ankle 432:35
Downhearted: are we d.? 5:13, 305:3
we are not d. 135:7
Downhill: this d. path is easy 409:18
Downs: all in the D. the fleet 215:39
fair on the dewy d. 536:23
looks on Ilsley d. 18:21
O bold majestic d. 80:19
round the spicy d. 535:18
whale-backed D. 302:7
you saw the moon from Sussex
D. 141:13
Down-sitting: thou knowest my d. 400:7
Downstairs: or I'll kick you d. 128:29
known many kicked d. 103:34
upstairs and d. 339:9, 366:23
why did you kick me d.? 72:14
Downward: his looks..always d.
bent 345:9
mute creation d. bend their sight 194:25

Downwards: could look no way
but d. 99:27
my gross flesh sinks d. 476:1
point of view..sinks d. 235:22
Doxy: heigh! the d. 485:16
orthodoxy is my d. 559:31
Orthodoxy or My-d. 126:18
Dozed: pimpernel d. on the lea 536:13
Dozen: a d. d. in her place 517:19
a d. persons who..understand
Plato 200:46
she has at least a d. 569:36
Dozens: reckons up by d. 221:14
Drab: ditch-deliver'd by a d. 459:33
rose pink and dirty d. 337:9
Drachenfels: castled crag of D. 113:43
Drachmas: drop my blood for d. 451:20
Draff: eats up all the d. 281:22
Drag: d. the Atlantic..for whales 550:20
put on the d. 505:30
why d. in Velasquez? 566:6
Draggled a' her petticoatie 104:30
Drag-net: swept like a d. 194:16
Dragon: as an ev'ning d. came 351:2
dare the unpastured d. 491:27
d. fought 71:17
fought against the d. 71:17
laid hold on the d. 71:39
swinged the d. 447:23
Dragon-fly: d. hangs like a blue
thread 410:30
with the d. on the river 88:11
Dragon-green..sea 208:8
Dragonish: cloud that's d. 425:19
Dragons: bores have succeeded to
d. 182:46
d. in their pleasant palaces 53:20
d. of the prime 532:38
habitation of d. 53:45
night's swift d. 467:10
ye d. and all deeps 400:24
Drags: d...a lengthening chain 226:4
d. its dreary length before the
court 173:22
d. its slow length along 382:31
Drain: as well..put it down the d. 243:6
d. not to its dregs 493:27(—494)
if I was you, I'd d. 298:7
leave Oxford by the town d. 511:3
Drained: d. not by the day 497:22
loungers..irresistibly d. 188:23
Drains: d. his at one gulp 96:19
she said it wur d. 541:6
Drake: D. he's in his hammock 363:3
Effingham, Grenville, Raleigh,
D. 362:30
Drama: close the d. with the day 43:13
d.'s laws the d.'s patrons give 279:1
what this wild D. means 537:39
Dramatist..wants more liberties 268:7
Dramatize, dramatize! 268:3
Drang: Sturm und D. 305:2
Drank: ate and d. as he was told 249:18
d. death like wine 141:14
d. it, and fell dead 174:18
d. without..thirst 519:20
eat my ale, d. my ale 203:5
from which our Lord d. 530:22
he d. of the brook 47:51
Jamshyd gloried and d. deep 206:1
still my body d. 149:29
Drap-de-berry: fools..such d.
things 156:7
Drapery: with the d. of his figures 153:14
wraps the d. of his couch about
him 98:3
Draught: does not think of the d. 22:14
fee the doctor for a nauseous d. 192:15
for a d. of vintage! 287:22
such a d. of woe 492:4
Draughts: d. of intellectual day 165:30
healths and d. go free 319:6
peculiarly susceptible to d. 569:27
shallow d. intoxicate 382:22
Draw: began to d. to our end 56:25
d. but twenty miles a day 331:7
d. for a thousand pounds 2:35
d. my pen in defence of a bad
cause 194:14
d. out Leviathan 49:20
d. the chalky ring 164:8

INDEX

Draw (cont.)
d. the Thing as he sees It 303:21
d. up Faustus 330:9
d. you. . with a single hair 194:28
ere yet we d. the blade 207:8
haul and d. with the mariner 189:1
in retiring d. hearts after them 350:1
let me try and d. you 95:1
rank mist they d. 342:29
soon d. in agen 247:12
to d. the bow, to ride 117:3
Drawbacks: everything has its d. 269:3
Drawbridge: up d., grooms 418:27
Drawed: brought reg'lar and d. mild 176:18
Drawers: d. of water 46:41
flannel waistcoat and flannel d. 213:22
Drawing: time is d. near 3:8
Drawler: no sabbath-d. of old saws 540:15
Drawn: d. it for a good one 194:14
d. together all the. .greatness 405:13
d. too architectooralooral 175:26
it oughtn't to be d. 174:18
new d. frae the Forth 360:13
Draws: at his gills d. in 348:26
dark eleventh hour d. on 303:11
though she d. him 317:27
Drayhorse: great grey d. 254:23
Dread: close your eyes with holy
d. 151:33(–152)
clouds ye so much d. 161:18
d. and fear of kings 464:33
d. of something after death 434:4
d. the grave as little 292:2
louder and more d. 150:10
mighty d. had seized 527:4
nothing did he d. 509:19
put thyself in prees for d. 138:14
secret d., and inward horror 1:22
somewhat was he chill'd with d. 417:14
so strook with d. and anguish 350:17
thrice turned back in d. 323:23
walk in fear and d. 150:2
what d. hand? and what d.
feet? 75:24(–76)
Dreaded: d. as thou art 163:25
once d. by our foes 162:12
Dreadful: acting of a d. thing 449:5
called thee mighty and d. 185:15
d. sorry, Clementine 355:22
each gentle and each d. scene 37:6
gathers samphire, d. trade 454:3
Dreading: d. e'en fools 385:29
Dreadless angel unpursued 348:19
Dreads: greatly his foes he d. 142:28
Dream: as a d. doth flatter 487:22
as in a pensive d. 533:2
as night is withdrawn. .d. 81:20
as youthful poets d. 342:7
beauty passes like a d. 585:22
behind, a d. 488:12
behold, it was a d. 99:26
below the shadow of a d. 299:3
body. .vanished like a d. 126:27
broke this happy d. 184:12
Child's unheeded d. 374:23
consecration, and the poet's d. 578:14
deep d. of peace 265:16
depth and d. of my desire 300:4
disturb not her d. 105:29
d. and d. that I am home again 208:4
d., and so d. all night 286:8
d. of battled fields no more 416:19
d. of joye, al but in vayne 138:24
d. of life 492:6
d. of London 359:2
D. of Loveliness descending 313:14
d. of money-bags 463:34
d. of perfect bliss 36:29
d. of spring 152:17
d. of the devil 34:10
d. of thee when I am awake 155:27
d. of the soft look 586:21
d. of waves, flowers, clouds 493:14
d. that is dying 371:2
d. that's past expressing 215:37
d., which was not all a d. 115:9
d. within a d. 380:16
empty words of a d. 81:19
even the d.'s confusion 77:30
faileth now even d. 544:23
fierce vexation of a d. 467:17

Dream (cont.)
forgotten, as a d. 562:9
freshness of a d. 576:1
garden that I d. of 542:5
glory and the d. 576:8
gone. .like a beautiful d. 314:20
housed in a d. 578:16
I dreamed, and, d. it still 141:16
I d. of the days when. . 142:2
if I d. I have you 184:17
if you can d. 297:10
in a d. of passion 433:31
in a long immortal d. 286:38
keep a d. or grave apart 89:3
life is but an empty d. 317:5
lost traveller's d. 74:22
love's young d. 356:25
my d. thou brok'st not 184:12
never saw the sun, but d. of him 94:25
not d. them all day long 293:7
occupy age with the d. of 93:1
Oh! d. of joy! 150:4
old men's d. 190:18
old men shall d. dreams 55:52
one man with a d. 371:1
perchance to d. 434:4
phantasma, or a hideous d. 449:5
quiet sleep and a sweet d. 334:12
say what d. it was 467:22
shadow of a d...A d...but a
shadow 433:13
short as any d. 466:20
sight to d. of 150:22
silently as a d. 163:40
soft! I did but d. 476:35
spirit of my d. 117:7
strange, even in a d. 149:31
then they d. of love 477:7
they d. of home 210:4
they had dreamed a d. 96:43
threading a d. 265:22
vision, or a waking d.? 288:2
we might be all we d. of 494:15
what my d. was 467:23
with the first d. 338:7
wrecks of a dissolving d. 493:25
Dreamlight: by candlelight and d. 549:2
Dreamed: child I d. 141:16
d. a dreary dream 30:13
d. not of a perishable home 577:11
d. of tasting pork 387:24
d. of the devil, and wak'd in a
fright 13:16
d. that I dwelt in marble halls 98:21
d. that life was beauty 7:18, 254:2
d. that they were filled with dew 149:28
he d...a ladder 45:3
I d...I saw a city invincible 566:23
long d. of such a kind of man 442:37
never d...wrong would triumph 97:4
nor d. that any did 485:4
they had d. a dream 96:43
willed or hoped or d. of good 89:9
Dreamer: d. of dreams 46:24, 359:1
faileth. .dream the d. 544:23
he is a d. 448:12
poet and the d. 285:35
this d. cometh 45:14
Dreamers: no d. weak 285:34
we are the d. of dreams 370:19
Dreaming: d. dreams no mortal
ever dared 380:24
d. Hell-fires to see 298:3
d. like a love-adept 497:2
d...o' Plymouth Hoe 363:3
d. on both 462:5
d. on the verge of strife 157:8
d. on things to come 488:2
d. spires 18:22
d. through the twilight 410:1
d. when Dawn's Left Hand 205:6
I'm fondly d. 314:18
you lie d. on 402:14
Dreams: all my nightly d. 380:21
as Dian had hot d. 430:4
blissful d. of long ago 157:1
communicat'st with d. 485:8
dead d. of days forsaken 523:21
desires and d. and powers 523:18
desire, that haunts our d. 81:19
doubtful d. of d. 523:17

Dreams (cont.)
dreamer of d. 46:24, 359:1
dreamers of d. 370:19
d. and desires 522:12
d. and the light imaginings 496:19
d., books, are each a world 578:20
d. happy as her day 84:21
d. no mortal ever dared 380:24
d. of Paradise and light 551:16
d. of the summer night 318:5
d. out of the ivory gate 85:22
[d.]. . serve but for winter talk 27:2
d. that are done 525:23
dreamt of in d. 34:8
embroidery of poetic d. 159:25
even in d. 120:17
fanatics have their d. 285:32
full of the foolishest d. 127:5
ghastly d. 476:13
heavy with d. 545:9
he hunts in d. 534:22
I arise from d. of thee 494:7
if there were d. to sell 38:28
I had drunken in my d. 149:29
I.. have only my d. 584:17
in d. behold the Hebrides 420:31
in some brighter d. 552:12
in their noonday d. 492:25
into the land of my d. 293:1
is it some d.? 560:10
Land of D. is better far 75:14
less than nothing, and d. 306:7
lies down to pleasant d. 98:3
my days and d. out of mind 525:23
my d. of your image 585:17
my d. under your feet 584:17
my fruit is d. 545:9
noon of my d. 208:5
not make d. your master 297:10
not the England of our d. 301:2
O evening d.! 208:6
of fantasy, of d., and ceremonies 449:11
old men shall dream d. 55:52
our d. are tales 171:1
pleasing d., and slumbers light 418:36
put man's best d. to shame 88:21
quick D. 491:19
real are the d. of Gods 286:38
rich beyond the d. of avarice
274:29, 356:3
sleep full of sweet d. 284:19
some. .peasant sees, or d. he
sees 345:13
such stuff as d. are made on 480:8
these terrible d. 459:4
these were the d. of a poet 277:23
thousand such enchanting d. 245:16
thou wovest d. 495:21
to the lonely d. of a child 171:4
trouble to my d. 579:12
until my d. all come true 293:1
waken from his summer d. 496:8
were it not that I have bad d. 433:12
what d. may come 434:4
white Platonic d. 209:24
wicked d. abuse. .sleep 458:1
you tread on my d. 584:17
Drear: d. was the voyage 415:6
void, dark and d. 150:31
Drear-nighted: in a d. December 289:7
Dreary: d. sea now flows between 150:27
my life is d. 535:30
Dregs: from the d. of life 191:34
not to its d. the urn 493:27(–494)
Drench: Love Powders. .then a
strong horse d. 307:14
Drenched: roots of the earth. .d. 289:31
till you have d. our steeples 453:5
Dress: bring the d. 535:11
children in ordinary d. 40:34
come to thee for d. 548:12
d. by yellow candle-light 515:14
d. her beauty at your eyes 169:13
if the devil d. her not 426:8
language is the d. of thought 278:3
noble youth did d. themselves 441:36
of no more value than their d. 239:24
Peace, the human d. 77:1
Secrecy the human d. 77:4
see a Whig in any d. 276:6
set to d. this garden 475:13

[687]

INDEX

Dress (cont.)
style is the d. of thought 565:21
sweet disorder in the d. 246:4
their d. a principal part 239:24
through all this fleshly d. 552:5
Dressed: all d. up and no place to go 108:42
all d. up with nowhere to go 566:15
any man..well d. 176:6
April, d. in all his trim 487:28
d. as fine as I will 561:31
d. in a little brief authority 461:31
fruit for Him that d. me 244:17
neat and trimly d. 438:32
O, be d. 244:6
still to be d. 280:7
washed and d. 333:24
wherein you d. yourself 457:11
Dresser: slept under the d. 43:1
Dresses: get the wedding d. ready 116:39
neat-handed Phyllis d. 342:2
Dressing old words new 487:18
Dressings: every season she hath
d. fit 8:14
Drew: d...everything that begins
with an M 129:12
d. from out the boundless deep 528:22
d. them..with bands of love 55:48
I d. my snickersnee 220:8
when he first d. the sword 145:25
Dried: d. up and withered 397:15
thy throat is shut and d. 301:28
tubes are twisted and d. 303:19
Dries: d...all the..vapours 442:21
or else d. up 472:34
Drift: cannot d. beyond His love 568:16
what is your d., Sir? 275:18
Drifted over Fiesole 94:8
Drifting with the tide 31:1
Drifts: dank yellow d. 17:16
through scudding d. 540:32
Drill: feet o' the men what d. 294:25
Drills: double d. and no canteen 297:4
Drink: all beasts..d. thereof 398:8
any little delicate thing to d. 175:38
ask a d. divine 280:21(-281)
Aunt Jobiska made him d. 312:6
beggar may d. his fill 42:12
canst d. the waters 170:22
come and have a d. with me 548:1
d. and no be drunk 108:16
d. and the devil 514:18
d. deep or taste not 382:22
d. down all unkindness 465:29
d. fair 176:32
d.! for you know not 207:7
d. it up 366:14
d. it with pleasure 56:40
d. life to the lees 540:32
d. no longer water 68:50
d. not the third glass 243:26
d. of Adam's ale 402:8
d., pretty creature, d. 578:28
d., puppy, d. 568:22
d. that quenches thirst 134:18
d. the blood of goats 395:4
d. the visionary power 579:17
d. till all look blue 209:28
d. to heavy Ignorance 541:15
d. to me only 280:21
d. to thee across the flood 529:35
d...with a merry heart 51:20
d. ye to her that each loves best 123:4
d. your ale 263:32
eat and d...damnation 390:33
eat and d.; for tomorrow 53:27
eat, d., and be merry 61:52
eat thou and d. 411:5
every creature d. but I 158:8
five reasons we should d. 3:11
follow strong d. 53:4
gapes for d. again 158:7
give to d. unto one of these 59:4
givin' d. to poor damned souls 297:5
I d. to the general joy 459:18
I eat well and I d. well 359:21
if I dare eat, or d. 475:15
in love, in debt, and in d. 82:24
in the Clink for a thundering d. 295:3
I think that I had.. 516:21
it snewed..of mete and d. 137:10
I will not..d. with you 463:16

Drink (cont.)
lave in it, d. of it 252:21
leave or d. it 298:15
leeze me on d. 106:12
let a soldier d. 471:9
never taste who always d. 401:39
nor any drop to d. 149:6
Parson might preach, and d. 76:4
sigh much, d. little 155:27
sit and d. with me 42:7
strong d. is raging 50:23
taste any d. once 120:4
taste for d., combined with gout 218:20
teach you to d. deep 431:3
that I might d. 287:24
they who d. beer will think beer 267:20
they will d. our healths 295:9
tippled d. more fine 287:1
Tray came out to d. 249:20
wants but little d. below 251:1
when last I saw him d. 365:18
wittles and d. to me 174:29
Drinking: as they were d. all 149:10
d. at somebody else's expense 313:9
d. is the soldier's pleasure 191:4
d. largely sobers us 382:22
d. my griefs 475:19
d. the blude-red wine 31:23
d. watered orange-pulp 96:39
I spy a knave in d. 420:3
let me die d. 329:14
much d., little thinking 519:29
next to d. and sabbath-breaking 172:23
no d. after death 37:14
not the d...but the excess 422:3
spoiled ta Flood by d. 23:27
then to deep d. 10:23
'tis jesting, dancing, d. 263:18
unhappy brains for d. 471:7
very merry dancing, d...time 193:31
with constant d. fresh and fair 158:7
Drinks: d. and gapes for drink
again 158:7
d. the green mantle 453:23
'e d. like a beast 304:3
he d. no wine 442:20
king to Hamlet 437:36
long time between d. 7:21
Drip: long d. of human tears 236:15
Drive: but difficult to d. 85:3
d. a coach.. through the Act 406:21
d. far off the barb'rous dissonance 348:23
d. it devious 164:8
d. ye cackling home 452:34
nor d. her away 367:8
one heat..doth d. out another 135:22
shall not d. me back 447:31
so shall thou d. them away 396:4
that I used to d. 263:4
tomorrow shall not d. it out 186:31
Driveller: Swift expires a d. 279:10
Driven: d. away from our immortal day 77:2
d. by the spheres 552:13
d., I know not whither 563:34
d. into a desperate strait 334:21
Jordan was d. back 399:2
Driver: did not feel the d.'s whip 317:17
Drivers: among the d. of negroes 278:26
Drives: by strength d. out another 484:34
who d. fat oxen 275:23
Driveth: d. o'er a soldier's neck 477:7
Jehu..d. furiously 48:27
Time d. onward fast 535:17
Driving: d. briskly in a post-
chaise 273:21
d. far off each thing of sin 340:23
d...like the d. of Jehu 48:27
d. rapidly in a post-chaise 273:4
Drizzle: blasted English d. 299:14
Droite: ma d. recule 209:9
Drollery: fatal d...representative
government 182:33
Dromedary: D. is a cheerful bird 40:24
whose muse on d. trots 151:13
Drone: lazy yawning d. 443:10
Droop: begin to d. and drowse 459:8
honest folk d. 90:16
Drooping: his silence will sit d. 437:25
so soon the d. spirits..raise 158:18

Drop: apples d. about my head 332:17
as a d. of a bucket 54:12
can't d. it if I tried 296:22
d., d., slow tears 209:3
d. into poetry 178:4
d. into thyself..a fool 383:23
d. the brynie teare wythe mee 136:17
d. thy pipe, thy happy pipe 76:9
d. upon the dwellings of the
wilderness 395:30
every d. hinders needle and
thread 253:27
every d. of ink 558:13
every d. of the Thames 104:3
his eyes d. out 315:13
how quick we'd d. 'er 301:2
merrily did we d. 148:21
nor any d. to drink 149:6
one d. would save my soul, half a d. 330:7
oozing d. by d. 205:16
people..one should..like to d. 274:26
soon to d. off dead 410:17
so thick a d. serene 346:19
vaporous d. profound 459:27
we'd. like the fruits 335:25
Dropped: angel d. down 440:18
angel new d. from the sky 373:18
as he d. him down 220:7
d. from the ruin'd sides of Kings 37:13
d. from the zenith 345:12
d. in ambrosial oils 341:2
every Hyacinth..d. in her Lap 206:3
glory d. from their youth 96:43
Mrs. Montagu has d. me 274:26
not wish to be d. by
remembrancer designedly d. 567:12
Droppeth as the gentle rain 464:33
Dropping: continual d. 50:46
d. from the clouds 546:15
one d. eye 430:24
peace comes d. slow 585:12
we are d. down the ladder 296:28
Dropping-down-deadness of manner 505:29
Droppings: his d. of warm tears 89:6
Dropping-wells: laburnums, d. of
fire 533:7
Droppy: Hoppy, Croppy, D. 213:5
just a d. in our ee 108:30
Drops: as a friend he d. into
poetry 178:3
crimson d. i' the..cowslip 429:24
dear to me as..the ruddy d. 449:17
d. earliest to the ground 464:31
d. that water the earth 396:24
few small d. of rain 32:16
into little water d. 330:11
I saw the curl'd d. 166:3
little d. of water 127:33
nations..like kindred d. 162:41
some pious d. 230:7
these are gracious d. 450:31
who hath begotten the d. of dew 49:23
Dropsies..trying to get drunk 276:5
Dross: all is d. that is not Helena 330:5
stoops not to shows of d. 463:39
Drought of Marche 136:21
Drove: d. his ball through Helen's
cheek 228:10
d. suddenly betwixt us and the
Sun 149:11
d. them all out of the temple 63:6
Drown: d. all my faults and fears 209:4
d. myself in the Thames 177:21
d. the memory of that insolence 206:15
d. the Memory of this Impertinence 206:14
d. the stage with tears 433:32
I'll d. my book 480:13
incontinently d. myself 470:13
neither can the floods d. it 52:23
seem to d. her remembrance 482:25
then can I d. an eye 486:25
what pain it was to d. 476:14
Drowned: but he'll be d. 365:1
d. already..with salt water 482:25
d. in the depth of the sea 59:49
d. in yonder living blue 533:25
d. the cocks 453:5
d. with us in endless night 246:1
with the chance of being d. 270:32

Drowning: no d. mark upon him 479:16
Drowns: fame..d. things weighty 27:1
Drowse: begin to droop and d. 459:8
Drowsed with the fume of poppies 284:12
Drowsy: all the d. syrups 471:43
 d. Bench protect 165:20
 d. frowzy poem 116:5
 d. numbness pains my sense 287:22
 d. unimpassioned grief 150:31
 dull ear of a d. man 447:35
 makes heaven d. 455:22
 who can be d. at that hour 85:21
Drowsyhead: pleasing land of d. 546:2
Drudge: lexicographer..a harmless d. 270:27
 pale and common d. 464:16
Drudgery: dry d. of the desk 307:17
 makes d. divine 244:16
Drug: literature is a d. 78:27
 poetry's a mere d., Sir 203:25
Drugs: what d., what charms 469:45
Druid: a D. land, a D. tune 586:16
 the D., hoary chief 158:29
Drum: as an unbrac'd d. 134:7
 bang-whang-whang goes the d. 97:14
 distant D. 205:25, 26
 d. now to d. did groan 189:7
 d. them up the Channel 363:3
 dumb as a d. vith a hole 178:40
 hark to the big d. callin' 296:17
 my pulse like a soft d. 292:20
 not a d. was heard 572:10
 pulpit, d. ecclesiastick 110:3
 spirit-stirring d. 472:3
 take my d. to England 363:2
Drum-beat: morning d., following
  the sun 563:5
Drumming with his fingers 325:32
Drums: anon d. in his ear 477:7
 are your d. a-beating yet? 503:1
 bangin' er de d. 238:24
 d. and tramplings of three conquests 87:8
 heard thro' rolling d. 538:22
 like muffled d., are beating 317:6
 of guns, and d., and wounds 438:35
 sound the trumpets, beat the d.
  191:3
 when the d. begin to roll 303:3
 with his clarions and his d. 323:3
Drunk: against a post when he
  was d. 444:1
 all learned, and all d. 163:32
 art of getting d. 274:13
 contracted in trying to get d. 276:5
 drink and no be d. 108:16
 d. and raising Cain 294:26
 d. and resisting the Guard 295:4
 d. deep of the Pierian spring 189:13
 d. their Cup a Round or two before 206:6
 d. the milk of Paradise 151:33(-152)
 d. to bed 423:20
 d. with sight of power 300:26
 gloriously d. 163:33
 hasten to be d. 192:8
 I d. him to his bed 424:12
 I have d. your water and wine 297:13
 man..must get d. 115:34
 never happy..but when he
  is d. 273:4
 partly she was d. 106:22
 Philip d. to Philip sober 5:12
 that which hath made them d. 458:2
 th' hydroptic earth hath d. 186:3
 this meeting is d. 179:10
 though he never was d. 154:17
 was the hope d.? 457:11
 went to Frankfort and got d. 387:7
 who have eat and d...with him 272:7
Drunkard: reel in a d. 143:13
 rolling English d. 141:21
Drunkards make songs 396:18
Drunken: Antony..brought d.
  forth 426:4
 do with the d. sailor 11:16
 d. and overbold 95:2
 d., but not with wine 53:35
 d. of things Lethean 525:8
 d. with the blood of the saints 71:32
 got more d. 387:7

Drunken (*cont.*)
 stagger like a d. man 398:18
 sure I had d. in my dreams 149:29
 toss-pots still had d. heads 484:27
Drunkenness: babbling d. 484:18
 branch of the sin of d. 267:29
Drury's: happy boy, at D. 387:18
Druse: the Thug and the D. 140:28
Dry: all the week to d. 11:5
 as d. as the remainder biscuit 427:16
 before Life's Liquor..be d. 205:6
 dark tarn d. 172:1
 d. August and warm 550:2
 d., bald, and sere 282:1
 d. sun, d. wind 550:6
 d. up..the organs of increase 452:29
 d. your eyes 285:31
 fain die a d. death 479:18
 good wine..or being d. 3:11
 hearts..d. as summer dust 574:14
 how d. a cinder this world is 185:3
 I am so d. 7:3
 I lie both soft and d. 247:16
 keep your powder d. 73:2
 let's d. our eyes 446:29
 made the deep as d. 301:25,
 moist eye, a d. hand 441:19
 nothing sooner d. 563:29
 passed over on d. ground 46:39
 prepared the d. land 397:26
 rivers of water in a d. place 53:43
 she was d. and sandy 175:6
 soul of Rabelais..in a d. place 153:10
 thine own heart d. of blood 287:3
 what shall be done in the d.? 62:47
Dryad: light-winged, D. of the
  trees 287:23
Dryden: all the prefaces of D. 521:19
 chatting on deck was D. 309:8
 D. fails to render him 20:3
 D. taught to join 386:17
 ev'n copious D. wanted 386:18
 genuine poetry..the poetry of D. 19:20
Dubious: d. hand 279:6
 naming a d. name 92:10
Dublin: built a church in D. town 42:19
 in D.'s fair city 7:8
Ducal: proud bride of a d. coronet 176:36
Ducat: dead, for a d., dead! 435:40
Ducats: lend three thousand d. 463:22
 my d.!..my Christian d.! 463:42
Duce: *quot libras in d.* 283:20
Duchess: I am D. of Malfi still 563:14
 my last D. 93:34
 of a chambermaid as of a D. 274:10
 the D. in a hoarse growl 128:31
 the D.! The D.! 128:26
Duck: D. and the Kangaroo 311:18
 said the d., laughing 304:6
Ducks: four d. on a pond 4:19
 go about..stealing d. 4:4
Duct: creed in the biliary d. 200:11
Duda: *fe que no d.* 551:1
Duddon: backward, D.! as I cast 573:26
Du Deffand: Madame d. 587:26
Due: as d. by many titles I resign 185:11
 commence my song, my d. 95:37
 deference d. to me 220:10
 give the Fiend..his d. 540:28
 keeps d. on to the Propontic 472:12
 not travel d. West 128:9
Dues: simple d. of fellowship 87:31
 to all their d. 66:11
Dug: Men want d. up again 205:28
 Miss Blimber d. them up 175:6
 never palates more the d. 425:33
Duke: bears a d.'s revenues 445:28
 bury the Great D. 537:11
 died like a D.-and-a-Duchess's
  daughter 34:32
 D. of Plaza Toro 218:17
 D.'s son—cook's son 294:19
 Earl, the Marquis, and the D. 218:22
 everybody praised the D. 507:9
 from tyrant d. 426:20
 marquis, d., and a' that 105:32
 naked D. of Windlestraw 127:9
 parson..who knows a d. 164:9
Dukedom: my library was d. large
  enough 479:22
 prize above my d. 479:23

Dukes were three a penny 218:28
Dulce: d. est desipere in loco 120:24, 261:5
 d. et decorum est desipere in loco 112:11
 d. et decorum est pro patria mori 259:18
 d. ridentem Lalagen amabo 258:23
Dulcet: such d. and harmonious
  breath 466:38
Dulci: qui miscuit utile d. 256:9
Dulcimer: damsel with a d...
  on her d. she played 151:33(-152)
 sackbut, psaltery, d. 55:36
Dull: all d., all torpid inanity 147:18
 anger makes d. men witty 24:36
 be d. in Fleet Street 307:4
 but d. and hoary 552:9
 d. and deep potations 216:22
 d. and muddy-mettled 433:33
 d. cold ear of death 230:3
 d. prospect of a distant good 192:29
 d. speaker..all the virtues 243:17
 d. sublunary lovers' love 186:25
 d., the proud, the wicked 386:2
 d. thy palm with entertainment 431:25
 d. would he be of soul 582:14
 [Gray] was d. in a new way 272:23
 her name was D. 99:29
 how d. it is to pause 540:32(-541)
 if he wasn't as d. as ditchwater 178:19
 in one d. line 382:30
 life..very d. without them 570:2
 lock was d. 119:14
 motions of his spirit are d. 465:20
 not only d. in himself 209:20
 on a d. day in an ocean-cave 531:9
 public, though d. 523:9
 Sherry is d., naturally d. 271:14
 so d. but she can learn 464:19
 so d., so dead in look 441:9
 so smoothly d. 381:22
 tell them that they are d. 493:4
 though gentle, yet not d. 172:10
 though it's d. at whiles 293:11
 to make dictionaries is d. work 277:26
 two d. lines 587:15
 venerably d. 143:22
 very d. without a single absurdity 227:14
 what's this d. town to me? 292:5
 when..d...a design in it 511:24
 whenever he was d...a design in it 204:26
 witty prologue to a very d. Play 155:34
Duller..than the fat weed 432:12
Dullness: cause of d. in others 209:20
 d. ever loves a joke 381:15
 d. of our blinded sight 400:32
Dumb: as a sheep..is d. 54:26
 d. as a drum vith a noise 178:40
 d., inscrutable and grand 17:13
 D.'s a sly dog 144:24
 d. to Homer, d. to Keats 94:9
 in a little while our lips are d. 535:17
 in the havens d. 254:29
 Oh, noisy bells, be d. 263:2
 oracles are d. 343:21
 otherwise I shall be d. 290:14
 tongue of the d. sing 54:3
 we have a d. spirit within 506:19
 wise of the world have made d. 171:4
Dumbness: banged the youth into
  d. 483:31
Dumb-shows: inexplicable d. and
  noise 434:15
*Dummheit: mit der D. kämpfen
  Götter* 415:23
Dumps: in such doleful d. 504:10
 of d. so dull and heavy 468:20
 one in doleful d. 491:11
Dumpy: I hate a d. woman 115:18
Dun: then her breasts are d. 488:13
Duncan: D. is in his grave 459:4
 D. sighed baith out and in 105:14
 fatal entrance of D. 457:3
 gart poor D. stand abeigh 105:13
 hear it not, D. 458:1
 this D...hath been so clear 457:9
Duncan Gray came here to woo 105:13
Dunce: because, dearest, you're a
  d. 274:32
 d. that has been sent to roam 161:31
 nobody calls you a d. 97:29
 puff of a d. 225:33
 Satan, thou art but a d. 74:22

Duncery: tyrannical d. 352:22
Dundee: bonnet of Bonny D. 416:8
   stay longer in bonny D. 420:15
Dunfermline: in D. town 31:23
Dunged with rotten death 544:27
Dungeon: d. horrible 344:9
   live upon the vapour of a d. 471:40
   nor airless d. 448:36
   quarry-slave..scourged to his d. 98:3
   this D., that I'm rotting in 124:17
Dungeon-grate: as if through a d.
      he peered 149:12
Dungeons: brightest in d. 114:33
Dunghill: hard by his own stable 151:10
Dunkirk: swim the haven at D. 281:19
Dunmow: in Essex at D. 138:6
Dunsinane: come to D. 461:5
   remove to D. 460:33
   to high D. hill 460:9
Duodecimos: humbler band of d. 164:36
Dupe: d. of folly 579:31
   d. of friendship 239:22
Dupes: if hopes were d. 147:8
Dupree: Weatherby George D. 339:15
Durate et vosmet rebus servate
   secundis 553:15
Durchstürmten wir die..Erde 415:25
Dureth: the sorrow..d. over long 328:9
Dusk: breezes d. and shiver 533:41
   d. faces 350:9
   d. mis-featured messenger 95:31
   d. the hall with yew 17:2
   d. would come 171:21
   in d., ere stars were lit 492:22
   in the d. with a light behind her 222:20
   no dawn—no d.—no proper
      time of day 253:11
   wavy in the d. 336:9
Dusky: d. night rides down the
      sky 204:37
   late and d. 551:21
   rear my d. race 534:33
   trusty, d., vivid, true 516:6
Dust: all valiant d. that builds on
      d. 301:1
   blossom in their d. 501:6
   buried in d. 37:13
   but writes in d. 28:17
   by Time..written in the d. 33:12
   come to d. 430:1
   curates, long d. 84:11
   dig the d. enclosed here 488:29
   dry as summer d. 574:14
   d. as we are 579:9
   d. hath closed Helen's eye 361:5
   d. of creeds outworn 497:1
   d...of the upper shelf 325:1
   d. on antique time 429:9
   d. swept from their beauty 88:14
   d. that is a little gilt 481:22
   d. that rises up 541:14
   d. thou art, to d. returnest 317:5
   d. thou art..unto d...return 44:28
   d. to d. 391:44
   d. to the d. 492:5
   d. whom England bore 84:21
   earth and grave and d. 405:12
   fallen to d. 569:15
   fear in a handful of d. 197:28
   formed man of the d. 44:11
   frail children of d. 228:22
   go down into the d. 393:9
   go down to the vile d. 417:22
   guilty of d. and sin 244:21
   heap of d. alone remains 381:36
   his enemies shall lick the d. 396:25
   in the d. be equal made 501:5
   into the D. descend, D. into D.,
      and under D. 206:8
   Knight's bones are d. 151:31
   less than the d. 254:16
   lie beyond thy d. 552:10
   light in the d. lies dead 494:20
   like to take d.? 482:8
   little d. of praise 533:5
   Love in a hut..cinders, ashes,
      d. 286:39
   magnificent out of the d. 561:12
   make d. of all things 87:9
   make d. our paper 475:6
   maniac scattering d. 532:27

Dust (*cont.*)
   March d. to be **sold** 549:30
   much learned d. 163:10
   mushroom of boiling d. 547:17
   my d. would hear her 536:15
   noblest troth dies here to d. 411:1
   not perish in the d. 507:32
   not without d. and heat 352:9
   not worth the d. 453:41
   one English tear o'er English d. 323:9
   pays us but with age and d. 405:12
   piece of valiant d. 468:8
   pride that licks the d. 385:34
   proud and angry d. 263:32
   provoke the silent d. 230:3
   reacheth but to d. 502:5
   richer d. concealed 84:21
   shake off the d. 58:48
   shall the d. give thanks? 393:26
   small d. of the balance 54:12
   so nigh is grandeur to our d. 199:32
   sweep the d. behind the door 467:36
   that d. it so much loves 292:19
   then shall the d. return 51:33
   this d. was once the man 568:7
   this quintessence of d. 433:15
   thou'lt recover once my d. 355:21
   to die in d. 509:7
   tread..on an Empire's d. 113:24
   vex the unhappy d. 528:21
   what a d. do I raise 27:35
   what of vile d.? 141:19
   when this d. falls 552:7
   write my name in the d. 403:38
   write the characters in d. 419:15
   your quaint honour turn to d. 333:9
Dusted from its hands..sand 516:19
Dust-heap: great d. called 'his-
      tory' 72:26
Dustman: Golden D. 178:22
Dusty: d. purlieus of the law 533:10
   what a d. answer 336:36
Dutch: behold with prejudice the
      French..or D. 86:27
   fault of the D. 124:6
   on D. bottoms just twenty per
      cent. 124:6
   'swop' for my dear old D. 142:22
Dutchman: icicle on a D.'s beard 483:32
Dutchmen: water-land of D. and
      of ditches 116:29
Duteous: 'tis a d. thing 12:7
Duties: goes to her religious d. 363:26
   lowliest d. 577:15
   new occasions teach new d. 320:13
   primal d. 574:28
   property has its d. 189:24
Dutiful: hang your husband and
      be d. 214:22
Duty: absolved from all d. to his
      country 376:18
   adoration, d., and observance 428:28
   began to slacken in his d. 577:22
   below, he did his d. 173:11
   dare to do our d. 314:8
   declares that it is his d. 489:9
   discussing their d. to God 567:20
   divided d. 470:4
   do my d. in that state of life 391:9
   done my d. and..no more 204:36
   do your d., and leave the issue 157:7
   do your d. bravely 305:1
   d...clad in glittering white 216:7
   d., d. must be done 222:7
   d., faith, love, are **roots** 377:4
   d. of an Opposition 143:34
   d. of being happy 514:40
   d. which lies nearest 127:20
   England expects..do his duty 362:23
   every subject's d. is the king's 444:20
   forgot that he had a d. 254:21
   found that life was D. 7:18, 254:2
   I have only done my d. 540:3
   in his d. prompt 224:21
   in the way of..a public d. 229:2
   I owe a d., where I cannot love 40:7
   it is my d., and I will 217:26
   little d. and less love 445:25
   love is then our d. 214:32
   love with zealous humble d. 510:14
   make our wills and do our d. 227:38

Duty (*cont.*)
   more than a moral d...a
      pleasure 569:28
   my d. to have loved the highest 530:19
   my d. towards God..towards
      my Neighbour 391:5
   nor law, nor d. bade me fight 584:21
   O D.! 573:28
   our bounden d. and service 390:44
   owes not all his d. to gaudy tire 166:18
   path of d. 537:25
   picket's off d. forever 40:2
   quite as keen a sense of d.? 221:28
   such d. as the subject owes 479:13
   thank God, I have done my d. 362:25
   that our d. has been done 218:24
   that which was our d. 62:28
   thy daily stage of d. run 292:1
   thy second d...already..clearer 127:20
   when constabulary d.'s to be
      done 221:34
   when D. whispers low, *Thou
      must* 199:32
   when love and d. clash 538:10
   when service sweat for d. 426:38
   when simpleness and d. tender
      it 467:22
   whole d. of man 51:36
Dux: d. ego vester eram 556:4
   d. femina facti 553:16
Dwarf sees farther than the giant 152:29
Dwarfish: d. whole 151:14
   giant's robe upon a d. thief 460:31
Dwarfs: State which d. its men 339:1
Dwell: cell wherein to d. 247:16
   constrained to d. with Mesech 399:24
   d. a weeping hermit there 153:30
   d. in adamantine chains 344:7
   d.—in a dungeon cell 220:6
   d. in realms of Day 74:1
   d. in such a temple 479:33
   d. in the house of the Fenians 586:20
   d. in the midst of alarms 164:22
   d. in the tents of ungodliness 397:7
   d. together in unity 400:3
   d. where Israfel hath dwelt 380:18
   d. with sothfastnesse 136:20
   here will I d. 330:5
   it pleaseth him to d. 396:7
   I will d. in the house of the Lord 393:10
   strive to d. with't 479:33
   such as d. in tents 44:34
   that on earth do d. 292:7
   they that d. therein 393:11
   who shall d. in thy tabernacle? 392:24
Dwellers in Mesopotamia 64:20
Dwelleth: d. by the castled Rhine 316:23
   d. i' the cold o' the moon 90:13
   sin that d. in me 65:48
Dwelling: any plague come nigh
      thy d. 397:10
   d. for the stork 398:10
   d. in tents 44:57
   where and what his d.? 361:20
   whose d. is the light 582:1
Dwelling-place: how lovely is thy
      d. 421:3
   that the desert were my d. 114:25
Dwelling-places: their d. shall
      endure 395:1
Dwellings: d. of the wilderness 395:30
   how amiable are thy d. 397:5
   in the d. of the righteous 399:8
   more than all the d. of Jacob 397:13
Dwells: she d. with Beauty 287:21
   where joy forever d. 344:22
Dwelt: d. from eternity 346:15
   d. in the land of Nod 44:33
   I d. in marble halls 98:21
   the Word..d. among us 62:64
   where Israfel hath d. 380:18
   where once we d. 160:30
Dwindle: by degrees d. into a wife 156:14
   d., peak, and pine 456:11
   smiles before they d. 497:9
Dwindles: only growth that d.
      here 226:9
Dwyer: John Richard..D. 504:12
Dyed: d. garments from Bozrah 55:5
   it was d. in mummy 472:16
Dyer: like the d.'s hand 488:6

Dyes: in d. of heaven 418:25
stains and splendid d. 285:19
Dying: as a d. man to d. men 36:24
behold you again in d. 516:10
Christian can only fear d. 237:21
death must be distinguished from d. 505:13
despised and d. king 498:18
doubly d. 417:22
dream that is d. 371:2
d., bless the hand 193:35
d. Englishman 505:28
d., has made us rarer gifts 83:19
d. put on the weeds of Dominic 346:25
d., we live 96:20
echoes, d., d., d. 538:14
groans of the d. 418:13
I am d., Egypt, d. 425:27
it had a d. fall 481:30
lay d. in Algiers 365:21
living indisposeth us for d. 87:10
not death, but d...is terrible 204:7
not the d. for a faith 542:9
not till the fire is d. 336:20
on account of my d. day 290:2
pain, the bliss of d. 381:28
stay d. here all night 500:5
such a celerity in d. 423:25
sunsets exquisitely d. 266:16
there's no more d. then 488:21
those poor devils are d. 378:13
thought her d. when she slept 252:23
to d. ears 538:19
to-morrow will be d. 247:10
Truth..upon the lips of d. men 17:27
unconscionable time d. 136:11
unmoved see thee d. 178:32
unto d. eyes the casement 538:19
young man, I think you're d. 30:2
Dyke: Feb, fill the d. 549:29
last d. of prevarication 101:25
yon auld fail d. 32:15
Dynamite: objected to the use of d. 514:1
Dynasties: though D. pass 236:14
Dyte: in Omer, or in Dares, or in D. 138:25

E

E please 175:39
Each: all are needed by e. one 199:9
e. for one another 313:7
e. man for him-self 137:28
e. one..fight on to the end 233:20
e. seem'd either 346:4
e. shall take his chamber 98:3
e. to his great Father 150:15
e. warning 302:10
e. within our narrow bed 132:3
from e...to e. 29:14, 333:12
make ye sure to e. his own 301:26
one life for e. to give 296:20
think e. in e. 84:6
two hearts beating e. to e. 93:22
useless e. without the other 317:27
Eadem: semper e. 198:9
Eager: all e. for the treat 130:13
e. air 431:30
e. for the fray 144:28
his e. soul 212:16
his hopes as e. as ours 100:17
Eagle: as a young e. soars 495:26
by all the e. in thee 165:29
does the E. know? 74:2
e. in a dove-cote 429:23
e. mewing her mighty youth 352:15
e. on th' back iv a dollar 195:9
e. plunge to find the air 545:1
e. suffers little birds 480:35
gaze an e. blind 455:22
her e. through the world 558:2
hooded e. 495:10
in and out the E. 328:26
lusty as an e. 398:4
outlive..the imperial e. 216:17
so the struck e. 117:25
upon my e.'s wings 191:16
way of an e. 50:56
Eagle-feather: moulted feather, an e. 93:24
Eagles: baited like e. 440:17
e. be gathered together 60:25

Eagles (cont.)
hawk at e. with a dove 245:4
mount up..as e. 54:14
swifter than e. 47:30
where his e. never flew 158:32
Ealing: old person of E. 312:20
Ear: beat upon my whorlèd e. 254:26
by the hearing of the e. 49:33
came o'er my e. 481:30
caught the e. of the..public 491:6
charms or e. or sight 151:6
cleave the general e. 433:32
close at the e. of Eve 347:28
dull cold e. of death 230:3
dull e. of a drowsy man 447:35
e. begins to hear 83:13
e. filled with hearing 50:61
e...hath not seen 467:23
e. is pleased 163:48
e. of jealousy heareth all 56:21
e. the open vowels tire 382:30
fearful hollow of thine e. 478:26
flea in his e. 14:21
flea in's e. 37:32
from e. to e. 562:24
give e. unto my song 225:17
give e. unto the sailor 373:11
give every man thine e. 431:25
give no sound unto the e. 86:32
God's own e. listens 348:16
hearing e. 50:26
her warm e. lays 320:17
he that planted the e. 397:24
hope..to soothe thine e. 153:23
I have no e. 306:3
incline thine e. 394:23
into the Queen's e. 73:16
I was all e. 340:28
jest's prosperity lies in the e. 455:34
keep the..promise to our e. 461:12
lend an e. to Plato 535:25
listening e. of night 421:9
mighty world of eye, and e. 582:2
more..than meets the e. 341:21
more than the e. discovers 86:33
not to the sensual e. 287:8
one e. it herde 138:36
one the e. the..triumph-song 264:9
pierced through the e. 470:7
reasonable good e. in music 467:14
right sow by the e. 242:23
she shall lean her e. 581:22
shouted in his e. 131:12
sleeps in a foolish e. 436:10
so nice his e. 162:28
stillness..invades the e. 191:31
stop thine e. against the singer 419:16
tip of your soft e. 247:7
to your attentive e. 308:27
turn the deaf e. 521:6
unpleasing to a married e. 455:35
was never e. 412:19
whom he whispers in the e. 89:11
with sweetness through mine e. 341:24
won the e. of Pluto 342:9
Earl: e. by right 23:13
E., the Marquis, and the Dook 218:22
while the E. was there 376:5
Earless on high..De Foe 381:16
Earlie: wedded to the E.'s son 419:1
Earlier: by the right of an e. creation 325:4
Earliest: at his grave 35:25
e., latest care 322:3
leaves, the e. of the year 118:23
Earls: daughter of a hundred E. 533:35
Early: and that right e. 394:28
awake right e. 395:19
call me e., mother dear 536:26
e. in the morning 11:16, 240:19
e. one morning 6:2
good die e. 170:2
had it been e., had been kind 270:18
happy those e. days 552:3
if Emma comes away e. 22:13
one of the e. birds 156:18
play-place of our e. days 164:7
right e. in the year 250:17
those so e. made 477:2
up in the morning e. 108:24
utterance of the e. Gods 286:6
you've gut to git up e. 319:13

Early-rising sun 246:2
Earn: e. a little and..spend..less 513:35
I e. that I eat 427:27
there's little to e. 294:1
Earned: e. a night's repose 318:13
e. your little bit o' corn 217:22
Earnest: charge in e. 183:8
e. of success 456:24
e. of the things..they shall do 534:25
I am in e. 213:17
intermingle..jest with e 26:5
life is e.! 317:5
nobody speaks in e., Sir 277:17
time to be in e. 277:38
Earnings: unequal e. 198:21
Earns whate'er he can 318:12
Ear-piercing fife 472:3
Ears: adder that stoppeth her e. 395:20
Death hath asses' e. 38:27
do thyne e. glowe 138:30
eyes and e. and every thought 412:19
e., and hear not 399:4
e. like errant wings 140:21
e...of different sizes 305:9
e. of every one that heareth 47:7
e. that sweep away the..dew 467:20
fly 'bout the e. of the old cur 110:30
harvest waves its wither'd e. 165:17
hath e. to hear 60:55
hedges e. 521:14
high crest, short e. 488:27
I have e. in vain 287:32
in e. and eyes match me 95:20
'Jug Jug' to dirty e. 197:29
leathern e. of stock-jobbers 162:20
lend me your e. 450:17
lest they..hear with their e. 53:10
look with thine e. 454:10
lover's e...hear the lowest sound 455:22
lovers' e. in hearing 417:34
make their e. heavy 53:10
make two e. of corn..grow 519:17
mentions hell to e. polite 385:4
once bless our human e. 343:17
plucked the ripen'd e. 538:9
porches of mine e. 432:16
reach the e. of God 569:13
she gave me e. 581:6
shout about my e. 140:22
split the e. of the groundlings 434:15
stopped his e. in a..dog-kennel 176:31
thin e. devoured the seven good e. 45:18
to dying e. 538:19
to e. of flesh and blood 432:9
to some e. not unsweet 502:3
touch'd my trembling e. 342:21
weary Titan! with deaf e. 16:11
we have heard with our e. 389:10
Earsight: deceive me e.? 560:10
Earth: Act first, this E. 537:39
air, e., and skies 582:4
alive, and so bold, O e.? 495:6
all e. can take 493:27
all e. to love 302:13
all the corners of the e. 397:26
all the e. were paper 321:19
anywhere else on e. 233:17
arising from sullen e. 486:24
attraction of e. 316:11
axis of the e. sticks out 251:17
between English e. and sky 241:26
blow the e. into the sea 453:3
bowels of the harmless e. 438:35
bridal of the e. and sky 245:13
centre of my sinful e. 488:20
chill the solemn e. 522:14
come back, as a king, to e. 83:20
comes more near the e. 473:16
common liberty of e. and air 511:10
common woman of common e. 148:16
condemned to e. for ever 91:18
cool flowery lap of e. 16:22
created the heaven and the e. 43:26
crown o' the e. 425:29
daughter of E. and Water 493:1
dear e., I do salute thee 474:34
differ as Heaven and E. 531:22
dim spot which men call E. 339:28
dost thou despise the e.? 580:26
E. all Danaë to the stars 539:2

Earth (cont.)

e., and every common sight 576:1
E. and Ocean..in one another's arms 493:14
e. bring forth her increase 396:15
e...but the shadow of Heaven 348:13
e. changes 95:22
e. felt the wound 349:15
e...fill'd with the glory of God 3:8
e...full of dreary noises 88:26
e...full of the knowledge of the Lord 53:19
e. has many a noble city 132:4
e. has not anything..more fair 582:14
e. hath bubbles 456:18
e. hath no good but yours 82:1
e. hath no sin but thine 82:1
e. heard in dread 503:3
e. his sober inn 123:25
e. in an earthy bed 536:15
e. is all the home I have 24:10
E. is but a star 208:10
e. is here so kind 269:15
e. is not too low 243:24
e. is the Lord's 66:40, 393:11
e. is weak 396:29
e. its dower 285:1
E., lie heavily 409:26
e...like a snake 493:25
e. may be glad thereof 397:31
e. never so unquiet 397:33
e...not filled with water 50:55
e. of the vitreous pour 567:17
e. received her frame 562:9
E.I render back 115:46
e. resteth 244:23
e...rolled with visible motion 575:26
e.'s base built on stubble 340:31
e.'s crammed with heaven 87:35
e.'s diurnal course 573:6
e. shak'd like a coward 439:40
e. shall melt away 394:28
e. shook..at the presence of God 396:5
e.'s joys grow dim 322:1
e.'s old and weary cry 586:8
e.'s returns 93:11
E.'s shadows fly 492:15
e. stood hard as iron 409:20
e.'s vain shadows flee 322:2
e., that is sufficient 568:4
e. Thy bed 506:8
e., tideless and inert 29:19
e. to e. 391:44
e. was feverous 458:21
e. was nigher heaven 94:43
e. was stopped 334:5
e. was without form 44:1
E. will live by hers 17:14
e., with her thousand voices 151:30
e. with the darkest vegetation 237:8
e. won back 402:23
e'er wore e. about him 170:18
elbow'd e. 567:18
enjoy the e. no less 236:16
enveloping the E. 151:5
face of e. around 515:28
faults..the e. covereth 404:16
first heaven and the first e. 71:44
flop round the e. 304:11
for e. too dear 477:9
found E. not grey 93:26
fresh E. in new leaves 498:12
from e.'s wide bounds 264:10
from which e., and grave 405:12
furniture of e. 43:12
give him a little e. 447:3
glance from heaven to e. 467:24
heaven and e. are full of thy glory 390:40
heaven on e. 347:4
Heaven tries e. 320:17
her all on e. 115:6
his snug little farm the e. 151:7
hydroptic e. 186:3
I call to the e. and sea 567:16
in e. as it is in heaven 58:4
inherit the e. 57:39
in that rich e. 84:21
in the shadow of the e. 85:23
I swung the e. 544:23
it fell to e. 315:24
Judge of the e. 571:4

Earth (cont.)

King of all the e. 394:32
laid the foundations of the e. 49:19, 398:8
lards the lean e. 439:8
lay her i' the e. 437:20
leaves this peopled e. a solitude 497:3
left your souls on e. 284:16
let us stay rather on e. 88:20
lie heavy on him, E. 202:11
lie lightly, gentle e. 37:35
lived on e. our Saviour 4:1
Lord and Master of E. 535:36
made of e. and sea his overcoat 263:36
man marks the e. with ruin 114:27
Man of baser E. 207:12
many..canonized on e. 86:16
militant here in e. 390:24
must have a touch of e. 530:34
my Substance from the common E. 207:17
new heaven and a new e. 71:44
new heaven, new e. 423:12
new heavens and a new e. 55:9
nightly to the listening E. 2:26
nor stone, nor e. 487:13
not a sky of e. 579:8
not perish from the e. 314:12
nought common on Thy E. 300:5
o'er e.'s green fields 202:23
of the e., earthy 67:15
on e. was never sown 581:21
on that dark e. 540:22
on the bare e. expos'd 191:7
on the e. the broken arcs 89:8
on the e. the shadow of thee 410:24
or ever the e...were made 397:15
or in the e. beneath 325:9, 390:7
our dungy e. alike 423:14
plants suck in the e. 158:7
power which..circles the e. 563:5
rich apple-blossomed e. 567:18
round e.'s imagined corners 185:13
sacred names of e. and Heaven 158:3
sad old e. 568:26
salt of the e. 57:40
Saviour Christ again to E. 334:1
scum of the e. 564:18
Sea of Faith..round e.'s shore 15:7
sing..and e. reply 565:4
smile o' the brown old e. 92:28
so much too good for e. 280:10
sprung of E.'s first blood 577:3
stamp me back to common E. 207:17
standing on e. 348:23
sure and firm-set e. 458:1
swear not..by the e. 57:48
take of English e. 295:5
takes e.'s abatement 94:1
that on e. do dwell 292:7
the Lord made heaven and e. 390:11
them that dwell on the e. 70:46
there in the stones was his e. 334:5
there is our e. here 97:6
things learned on e. 93:40
thirsty e. soaks up the rain 158:7
this ambiguous e. 338:4
this corporal e. of man 544:11
this e. in fast thick pants 151:32
this e. of majesty 474:22
this e., that bears thee dead 440:38
this e., this realm, this England 474:22
this goodly frame, the e. 433:15
thou bleeding piece of e. 450:11
thou upon e. 51:6
though all the e. o'erwhelm 431:19
though e. and man were gone 83:11
though the e. be moved 394:27
thy e. so marred 544:28
till E. and Sky stand 294:27
to e. I 264:3
to e.'s bosom bare 545:8
to no such aureate E. 205:28
to that pleasant country's e. 475:16
to unawakened e. 496:11
turn again to his e. 400:19
two paces of the vilest e. 440:38
upon the dull e. dwelling 484:40(–485)
upon the lap of E. 230:13
us worms of e. 202:20

Earth (cont.)

very e. did shake 189:7
visited the green e. 317:10
wasted on the e. and sky 199:26
way of all the e. 46:44
we are E.'s best 84:3
weary of e. 517:4
what's said or done in e. 245:22
when e. was young 326:24
where this e. spins 410:10
while the e. remaineth 44:41
whole e. is full of his glory 53:8
whole round e. is..bound 531:36
with the e. and the sky 585:17
words are the daughters of e. 277:21
ye powers of heaven and e. 166:1
yet on e. your fame 81:21
yours is the E. 297:12
Earth-born: thine e. joy renew 81:5
Earthern: flaws..in the e. vessel 90:33
treasure in e. vessels 67:23
treasures from an e. pot 244:7
Earthlier happy 466:17
Earthly: all e. things above 511:4
e., sensual, devilish 69:39
e. song 532:39
fruition of an e. crown 330:28
nothing e. could surpass her 115:15
to their e. mother tend 194:25
Earthquake: after the wind an e. 48:8
e...engulf England 269:20
e.'s spoil 113:24
gloom of e. 497:24
very good against an e. 2:34
Earthy: of the earth, e. 67:15
Ease: age of e. 224:15
another's loss of e. 76:3
at e. for aye to dwell 537:34
at e. in Zion 56:2
come to take their e. 447:17
counselled ignoble e. 345:22
debauched with e. 190:10
delicate plain, called E. 99:18
doctrine of ignoble e. 408:26
done with so much e. 190:9
e. after war 509:28
e. its heart of love 286:9
e. my weary limb 29:24
e. the anguish of a torturing hour 467:25
equal e. unto my pain 125:7
for another gives its e. 76:2
full-throated e. 287:23
good, pleasure, e., content 384:2
greater e. than your cold Christ 300:19
hour of vacant e. 579:35
in hearthside e. 236:21
in our hours of e. 418:31
interpose a little e. 343:1
kindly bent to e. us 521:1
never at heart's e. 448:27
never wholly be at e.? 561:17
no healthful e. 253:12
press your point with..e 159:13
prodigal of e. 190:14
put to hazard his e. 101:21
rots itself in e. 432:12
standing at e. in nature 566:26
still at e. 378:16
studious of elegance and e. 215:32
studious of laborious e. 163:17
take mine e. in mine inn 440:14
take thine e., eat, drink 61:52
thy fortress, and thy e. 552:2
to be e'er at e. 384:32
to e. my breast of melodies 285:31
true e. in writing 382:32
wrote with e. 386:16
you write with e. 501:2
Eased the putting off 347:25
Easer of all woes 38:9
Easier: call a man..good..on e. terms 275:15
Easily: how e. things go wrong 326:20
one not e. jealous 474:2
Easiness: too much e. in admitting 388:3
East: argument..with an e. wind 320:21
Boston man..the e. wind made flesh 13:19
by e., west, north, and south 455:31
daily farther from the e. 576:9
dapples the drowsy e. 469:19

East (cont.)
easier to conquer. . [the E.]   558:23
e., ah, e. of Himalay   545:14
E. all the way   298:28
e. and west and south and
    north   323:10
E. bow'd low   17:8
E. is a career   182:36
E. is E.   294:27
e. wind. . never blow   559:11
even from the e. to the west   473:2
faint e. quickens   521:30
fiery portal of the e.   475:8
folding doorways of the E.   544:7
from the e. to western Ind   427:28
goes out to the E.   304:3
gorgeous E. with richest hand   345:14
hold the gorgeous E. in fee   582:5
how wide. .the e.. is from the
    west   398:6
Hunter of the E.   205:4
if e. or west the Phoenix builds   125:11
if you've 'eard the E.   299:13
in the chambers of the E.   75:18
in the sanctuaried E.   545:6
it is the e.   477:13
little birds sang e.   88:5
man with his back to the E.   148:17
morn purples the e.   348:23
neither E. nor West   294:27
not from the E.   165:36
politics in the E.   182:1
promotion. . neither from the e.   396:30
send danger from the e.   438:37
somewheres e. of Suez   299:15
South, E., and on   92:13
thine eyes break from their E.   166:5
this window for the e.   169:13
tried to hustle the E.   300:6
through the e.-wind   394:34
when the wind blew due E.   128:9
when the wind is in the e.   11:21
when the wind is.. in the e.   173:25
wise men from the e.   57:23
East-Cheap: merry men of E.   226:28
Easter-Day breaks   91:18
Eastern: all th'e. side.. of Paradise 349:31
blabbing e. scout   340:6
like a blooming E. bride   190:34
not by e. windows only   147:8
O e. star!   426:13
o'er the hill the e. star   106:30
right against the e. gate   341:33
yon high e. hill   430:21
Eastertide: white for E.   262:10
Eastward: e.. . from wild Black-
    heath   322:22
garden e. in Eden   44:11
lookin' e. to the sea   299:10
roll of the world e.   236:38
some e.. . and all wrong   160:16
Easy: all zeal, Mr. E.   331:16
as e. to marry a rich woman   542:21
be e.   512:1
decent e. men   216:21
e., debonair, and brisk   162:21
e. live and quiet die   419:16
e. ways to die   420:17
e. writing   501:2
embroidered on.. the normal
    and e.   268:4
from all the e. speeches   141:18
good e. man   446:24
I lie e.   263:7
inspires e. my.. verse   349:5
my yoke is e.   59:10
of so e.. . a stop   441:8
Rab'lais' e. chair   382:14
rack of a too e. chair   381:25
she bid me take love e.   584:11
'tis e. to be true   421:17
Eat: all presents wot e.   518:24
all sense doth e.   436:5
come ye, buy and e.   54:29
drink little, e. less   155:27
e.. . and be merry   51:18, 61:52
e. and drink our own damna-
    tion   390:33
e. but little meat   516:21
e. his pleasant fruits   52:8
e. like wolves   444:5

Eat (cont.)
e. not of it raw   45:46
e. one of Bellamy's veal pies   379:21
e. our meal in fear   459:4
e. the cones under his pines   212:3
e. the fat of the land   45:23
e. the rest of the anatomy   484:2
e. thou and drink   411:5
e. to live   353:10
e. up the.. fat kine   45:17
e. up.. the very men   358:12
every man shall e. in safety   447:14
I did e.   44:22, 24
I did sit and e.   244:22
I earn that I e.   427:27
I e. the air   435:2
I e. well, and I drink well   359:21
if I dare e., or drink   475:15
I have e. my ale   203:5
I'll e. my head   177:40
I see what I e.   129:6
I will e. exceedingly   279:23
I will not e. with you   463:16
let us e. and drink   53:27, 67:11
neither should he e.   68:39
nor e. an ounce less   275:12
nothing to e. but food   292:14
pig was e.   369:11
sat down to e. and to drink   46:3
she pluck'd, she e.   349:15
some hae meat and canna e.   107:34
that hath e. of a king   436:13
that I will e. bulls' flesh   395:4
those who have e. and drunk..
    with him   272:7
thou shalt not e. of it   44:13
to e. thy heart through.. de-
    spairs   510:16
to e. with apple-tart   515:21
toys and things to e.   515:20
whether therefore ye e.   66:41
who e. unduly   515:24
ye shall e. it in haste   45:47
Eaten: e. me out of house and home   441:30
e. on the insane root   456:19
e. thee for a word   455:26
e. to death with rust   441:25
he was e. of worms   64:50
I have e. your bread and salt   297:13
see God made and e.   89:44
they'd e. every one   130:21
zeal of thine house.. e. me   396:17
Eater: e. of broken meats   452:32
great e. of beef   482:6
out of the e.. . meat   46:55
Eaters: your sheep.. so small e.   358:12
Eatest: day that thou e. thereof   44:13
Eateth: e. grass as an ox   49:28
e.. . with publicans   58:38
Eating: against e. cares   342:7
e. and drinking, marrying   60:26
e. an egg without salt   304:41
lawful as e.   486:1
Eats: e. the pies and puddings up   249:22
whatever Miss T. e.   171:17
Eau: 'L'e.'.. 'Lo, eh?'   177:15
Eave-drops: whether the e. fall   151:25
Eaves: clamorous e.   586:7
upon her gilded e.   538:20
Ebb: beauty has no e.   585:16
e. and flow by the moon   454:19
London.. whose e. and flow   495:9
ne'er e. to humble love   472:12
ne'er feels retiring e.   472:12
such e. and flow   575:1
Ebbs out life's little day   322:1
Ebony: his image, cut in e.   212:14
Ebrew: an E. Jew   439:18
Ecce homo   63:70
Eccentric: centric and e. scribbled
    o'er   348:30
Dante.. an e. man   176:2
Eccentricities of genius   179:1
Ecclesiam: qui e. non habet matrem   22:1
salus extra e. non est   22:1
Ecclesiastic: e. tyranny   170:16
pulpit, drum e.   110:3
Ecclesiastical: splendid e. lyric   182:4
Echo: applaud thee to the very e.   461:1
as any challeng'd e. clear   123:21
cave where E. lies   477:26

Echo (cont.)
distant footsteps e.   316:9
e. answers—'Where?'   113:5
e. arose from the suicide's grave   220:19
e. beyond the Mexique Bay   332:4
e.. . faint at last   309:13
e. round his bones   537:12
e. to the sense   382:32
gives a very e.   483:2
left an e. in the sense   282:3
my e. ring   509:11
sweet E., sweetest nymph   340:13
Echoed: the grievous roar e.   406:19
Echoes: answer, e., dying   538:14
by heaven, he e. me   471:28
e. of that voice   151:6
e. roll from soul to soul   538:16
e. round the world   531:6
e. which he made relent   190:3
Fontarabian e.   418:33
rouse the E. of the Past   218:9
set the wild e. flying   538:14
Eckstein: where E. stood   42:11
Éclat: despising all manner of é.   29:6
Eclipse: at least an e.   26:24
built in th' e.   342:25
dark, total e.   350:22
E. first   370:8
e.. . not in the Almanac   508:1
gloom of earthquake and e.   497:24
mortal moon.. her e.   488:2
sick almost to doomsday with e.   430:15
sliver'd in the moon's e.   459:32
sun in dim e.   345:6
Eclipsed the gaiety of nations   278:7
Eclipses: these late e.   452:15
Economic: social and e. experi-
    ment   254:4
Economists: sophisters, e., and cal-
    culators   102:11
Economy: e. is going without   254:5
for fear of Political E.   422:15
no e. where.. no efficiency   181:28
wrote, 'Principles of Political E.' 43:2
Écrasez l'infâme   557:9
Écris: si j'é. quatre mots   78:7
Écrivain: l'e. original   136:18
Ecstasies: dissolve me into e.   341:24
holy virgins in their e.   530:31
muddy e. of beer   164:33
with e. so sweet   82:6
Ecstasy: blasted with e.   434:14
e. of being ever   87:21
in such an e.   287:32
lie in restless e.   459:4
not e. but.. comfort   175:38
on waves of e. to sail   567:2
seraph-wings of e.   231:13
think thereof without an e.   86:9
to maintain this e.   374:14
wak'd to e. the.. lyre   230:4
what wild e.?   287:7
Ecstatic: such e. sound   235:18
Edax: tempus e. rerum   371:31
Eden: at the gate of E. stood   357:7
breathed o'er E.   291:15
brooks of E.   529:18
garden eastward in E.   44:11
kept the heart of E. green   530:9
make this earth an E.   128:1
some flow'rets of E.   357:8
sweet as E. is t.e air   336:47
this other E.   474:22
through E. took their.. way   349:31
told in dim E.   171:1
whittle the E. Tree   295:15
with E... the snake   207:12
with loss of E.   344:1
Edens: lest we lose our E.   97:25
Eden-sweet the ray   336:47
Eden-trees: burnish take on E.   545:7
Edge: dulls the e. of husbandry   431:25
hungry e. of appetite   474:20
low last e. of the.. land   523:14
on the e. of the sand   312:3
teeth.. set on e.   55:29
to the e. of doom   488:7
with the e. of the sword   46:16
Edged: only e. tool that grows
    keener   267:19
secrets are e. tools   193:6

Edges: down the vast e. drear 15:7
Edifice: hail, glorious e. 504:4
Edifieth: charity e. 66:33
Edinburgh Review: *let balls like the E.* 240:7
motto for the E. 505:26
Edisti satis atque bibisti 257:21
Edition: never enough to pay for an e. 200:46
new and more beautiful e. 211:21
new e. fifty volumes long 89:29
new e. of human nature 239:14
Edmonton: if wife should dine at E. 160:8
unto the Bell at E. 159:33
Edmund: here lies our good E. 225:27
Edom: bring me into E. 395:23
cometh from E. 55:5
over E...cast out my shoe 395:23
Educate: e. our masters 499:20
e. our party 180:38
Educated: absence..of any..e. opinion 19:16
as an e. gentleman 490:4
born and e. in this country 216:13
e. by a system 337:34
e. man 96:15
e. whisker 529:14
every child..clothed, fed, and e. 413:23
Educating the natives of Borrioboola-Gha 173:24
Education: all this fuss about e. 335:20
beginning of e. 413:22
by e. most have been misled 192:30
complete and generous e. 352:25
e...formation of character 508:28
e. makes a people easy to lead 85:3
first rudiments of e. 511:29
liberal e. 242:10
not a complete e...highest e. since the Greek 182:19
nothing like e. 403:38
path of a virtuous and noble E. 352:26
race between e. and catastrophe 564:29
soap and e...more deadly 550:13
thank your e. 282:7
to love her is a liberal e. 511:25
travel..a part of e. 27:27
upon the e. of the people 181:7
Edward: E. the Confessor slept 43:1
proud E.'s power 107:32
taught...King E. Greek 351:17
the sons of E. sleep 476:25
why, E.? 573:3
winding sheet of E.'s race 229:22
Edwin: break thy E.'s too 225:14
let me always call you E. 203:34
Eel: I have seen but an e. 173:37
invisible e. 281:19
Eels: e. boil'd in broo' 31:10
precept..for dressing e. 387:23
Eface: may note those marks e. 114:34
Effaced: Caesar's image is e. 161:29
Effacerai: j'en e. trois 78:7
Effect: between the e. and it 457:3
greet e. men wryte in place lyte 138:40
name for an e. whose cause is God 163:52
persecution produced its natural e. 325:35
to be of none e. 393:36
what e...upon the enemy 564:21
you see a good e. 514:4
Effects: close in like e. 92:1
Effeminate: thoughts e. and faint 331:2
Efficacious: example.. more e. than precept 278:18
Efficacy: preserve..the purest e. 352:5
Efficiency: e. and inefficiency 490:2
no economy where..no e. 181:28
Efficient and the inefficient 490:2
Effingham, Grenville 362:30
Effort: e., and expectation 579:27
good without e. 114:24
if that e. be too great 8:11
law of human life..E. 413:15
what is written without e. 277:9
Effugies: non e. meos iambos 134:1
Eft: a monstrous e. 535:36
Eftest: that's the way 469:8
Égalité: Liberté! E.! Fraternité 12:16
Egdon: E. remained 237:10
glory of the E. waste 237:9

Egestas: duris urgens in rebus e. 556:11
Fames ac turpis E. 554:27
Egg: as an e. is full of meat 478:11
e. boiled very soft..not unwholesome 22:7
e. does not match any waistcoat 177:16
e. of the wren 567:19
I'm afraid you've got a bad e. 403:37
like eating an e. without salt 304:41
radish and an e. 163:27
remorse, the fatal e. 161:27
serpent's e. 449:4
to be called an e. 131:3
white and hairless as an e. 246:16
yolk of an addled e. 295:15
Eggs: as a weasel sucks e. 427:8
as the partridge sitteth on e. 55:21
boil e. in your shoes 312:21
but to roast their e. 27:39
e., apples, and cheese 294:34
e...like..primroses 181:35
fresh e. to rotten boroughs 324:29
lays e. for gentlemen 367:2
ways to dress e. 356:8
Eglantine: lush e. 497:22
with e. 466:41
Ego: too much E. in your Cosmos 304:31
Ego: E. et Rex meus 446:23
et in Arcadia e. 13:7
Egoism: in..the book of E. 337:25
Egotist: whims of an e. 289:24
Egotistical: Wordsworthian or e. sublime 290:9
Egregiously: making him e. an ass 471:4
Egress: our e. from the world 318:9
Egypt: against all the first-born in E. 427:10
corn in E. 45:19
dying, E., dying 425:27
from E. marching 344:34
great cry in E. 45:48
in a brow of E. 467:24
in..Pamphylia, in E. 64:26
new king over E. 45:19
o'er E.'s dark sea 357:17
rather a ditch in E. 425:34
this bruised reed..E. 48:33
through old hushed E. 265:22
through the land of E. 45:47
treasures in E. 69:16
wonders in the land of E. 45:41
Egyptian: an E. to my mother give 472:15
chips to the E. fellah 143:31
these strong E. fetters 423:24
Egyptians: they spoiled the E. 45:49
Eheu fugaces 34:1, 259:9
Ehrlicher Makler 72:32
Eigg on the starboard bow 516:8
Eight: by e. tomorrow..immortal 462:20
e.-foot-high..serving-man 184:14
e. score e. hours? 472:18
pieces of e. 514:20
take a fellow e. years old 91:32
the most devilish thing is e. times 208:22
Eight hundred: he and his e. 162:13
Eighteen: knew almost as much at e. 270:1
Eighteenth: in that e. century of Time 126:3
on the e. of April 317:3
Eighty: e. mile o' females 179:34
Eighty thousand: takes up about e. lines 121:6
the impending e. lines 120:29
Eildon Tree: by the E. 32:6
Eileen Aroon 232:19
Eingeritten: wäre ich dennoch e. 321:7
Einstein: let E. be 511:8
Eire: fair hills of E. 329:3
Eisen: Blut und E. 72:33
Either: each seem'd e. 346:4
how happy..with e. 215:4
Ekenhead: Leander, Mr. E., and I did 115:32
Elaine the fair 530:33
Elamites: Medes, and E. 64:26
Elate: Ruin's ploughshare drives e. 107:8
Elates: while fame e. thee 356:19
Elbow: left e...come miles to see 220:14
my right e. 220:11
Elbow-chairs: suggested e. 162:34

Elbowed: far-swooping e. earth 567:18
Elbows: diseases that he e. 38:24
Eld: Memories of E. 380:14
palsied e. 462:6
Elder: e. man not at all 26:38
e. than herself 483:3
e. unto the elect lady 70:16
I said an e. soldier 451:17
I the e. and more terrible 449:23
Oak, E., Elm and Thorn 172:6
travel..in the e...experience 27:27
Elderly: e. single woman 222:19
Mr. Salteena..an e. man of 42 20:26
Elders: e. and the four beasts 71:4
miss not the discourse of the e. 56:37
Elder-tree: the wood and the pool and the e. 172:4
Eldest: Earl of Fitzdotterel's e. son 84:27(-85)
e. Child of Liberty 582:6
God's e. daughter 212:13
Night, e. of things 346:15
Elect: elder unto the e. lady 70:16
knit together thine e. 389:55
Elected: audacity of e. persons 567:7
deputy e. by the Lord 475:1
e. Silence 254:26
Election: at the moment of the e. 100:17
e. by the incompetent many 490:29
her e. hath seal'd thee 434:25
Particular E. 187:7
right of e. 282:17
Elections: hallooed out at one of Burdett's e. 119:32
Electorate: dismissed by the British e. 144:17
Electric: e. light i' the West 82:8
e. message came 23:14
striking the e. chain 114:5
Electrical agitation in the mind 337:2
Electrician is no longer there 41:36
Electro: quare videmus araneam.. in e. 27:47
Elegance: endearing e. of female friendship 278:20
studious of e. and ease 215:32
Elegancy, facility, and golden cadence 455:14
Elegant: e. but not ostentatious 278:9
e. simplicity of the three per cents 420:32
e. sufficiency 546:13
Gibbon's e. 154:13
you e. fowl 312:1
Elegantem: neque e...neque urbanum 132:22
Elegantiae arbiter 526:13
Elegy: ode, and e., and sonnet 276:14
prefer being the author of [Gray's E.] 572:15
Element: e. itself, till seven years 481:32
his back above the e. 426:1
not of your e. 484:9
one God, one law, one e. 533:31
thy e.'s below 452:37
Elementa velint ut discere prima 261:7
Elemental creatures go 586:15
'Elementary,' said he 187:24
Elemented: those things which e. it 186:25
Elements: amidst the wars of e. 1:24
e. once out of it 424:17
e. so mixed in him 452:9
framed out of four e. 330:28
fretful e. 453:3
I tax not you, you e. 453:6
made cunningly of e. 185:12
my other e. 426:10
our torments..become our e. 345:23
reconciles discordant e. 579:9
so mix'd the e. 189:3
something that was before the e. 86:37
three..e. of..civilization 125:24
weak and beggarly e. 67:42
with the motion of all e. 455:22
Elenore: the region E. 545:5
Elephant: at the E. 484:5
E.'s Child 304:16
e.'s a gentleman 300:8
he thought he saw an E. 128:15
unwieldy e. 347:15
Elephanto: candenti perfecta nitens e. 555:2

Elephants: e. endorsed with towers 350:8
e. for want of towns 521:18
women and e. never forget 414:14
Elephas: in quo..e. natet 232:7
Elevate: in thoughts more e. 345:29
Elevated: joy of e. thoughts 582:1
Elevates: e. above the vulgar herd 212:22
hope e. 349:13
Elevation: for e. of our thought 574:27
scourged us to an e. 216:7
Eleven: e. buckram men 439:21
he's only e. 219:11
second e. sort of chap 36:2
'twixt e. and twelve 431:17
Eleventh: dark e. hour 303:11
Elf: deceiving e. 288:2
negligent e. 34:7
not a modest maiden e. 236:17
Elfland: horns of E. 538:15
Road to fair E. 32:10
Elf-locks: bakes the e. 477:7
Elgin: stands in E.'s place 188:30
Elginbrodde: here lie I, Martin E. 326:19
Eli, Eli, lama sabachthani? 60:52
Elias: unto none..was E. sent 61:26
Elijah: E. passed by him 48:10
Enoch, E., and the Lady 376:1
spirit of E. 48:17
Eliminated: when you have e. the impossible 188:20
Elisha: when..shall E. slay 48:9
rest upon E. 48:17
Elissae: nec me meminisse pigebit E. 554:19
Eliza: so did take E. 281:18
Elizabeth: bright Occidental Star, Queen E. 43:24
Mr. Collins..only to change..to E. 22:31
my sonne's wife, E. 267:14
no scandal about Queen E.? 499:28
one name was E. 280:11
Queen E.'s dead 520:9
Servant to Queen E. 232:16
times of great E. 529:7
Elizabeth-Jane Farfrae..not told of my death 237:7
Ellangowan: hearthstane at E. 419:29
on E.'s height 419:35
ride your ways..E. 419:29
Ellen: to wed the fair E. 418:17
Elliot of Kellynch-Hall 22:25
Elliptical billiard balls 220:6
Ellops drear 349:21
Elm: Oak, Elder, E. and Thorn 172:6
signal-e...looks on Ilsley downs 18:21
Elms: e. fade into dimness 17:16
in immemorial e. 539:5
Elm-tree: round the e. bole 92:14
Elope methodically 226:40
Elopement: worked..an e. into.. Euclid 188:18
Eloquence: Bag of Parliamentary E. 126:35
e. is heard 339:4
e. the soul 345:29
intoxicated with my own e. 181:43
mother of arts and e. 350:11
my books..the e. 486:21
say she uttereth..e. 479:4
talking and e...not the same 280:5
Eloquent: curse of this country ..e. men 201:16
discourse most e. music 435:23
e. just, and mighty Death 405:13
her pure and e. blood 186:13
so calm, yet e. 110:2
that old man e. 351:16
Eloquently: so e. bright 355:16
Else: anywhere e. on earth 233:17
never read much..something e. to do 22:24
Elsewhere: not be e. for thousands 362:20
Elsinore: thy wild and stormy steep, E.! 122:7
Elucescebat quoth our friend? 90:1
Elusive: demmed, e. Pimpernel 370:13
Elves: all the criticizing e. 143:24
e. also, whose little eyes glow 246:23
fairy e...some..peasant sees 345:13
make my small e. coats 466:42

Ely: merrily sang the monks in Ely 124:22
Elysian: dead, but in the E. fields 181:20
E., windless, fortunate abodes 497:15
suburb of the life e. 317:12
Elysium: all night sleeps in E. 444:23
my brother he is in E. 482:2
Tochter aus E. 415:21
what E. have ye known? 287:1
Emaciated: prone and e. figure 235:22
Emanation: my E. far within 75:19
Emathian: great E. conqueror 351:15
Embalmed and treasured up 352:7
Embalmer: soft e. of the still midnight 288:31
Embalming: for my E. (Sweetest) 246:27
Embalms: a precedent e. 180:20, 420:33
Embark: when I e. 528:22
Embarking: your friends are all e. 13:18
Embarras: l'e. des richesses 4:15
Embarrassed: Jack was e. 118:1
transient and e. phantom 182:2
Embattled farmers 199:7
Embers: by the e. in hearthside ease 236:21
full of smoke and e. 280:14
glowing e. through the room 341:16
in our e. 576:17
sunset e. 516:4
Emblazonings: dim e. 285:19
Emblem: e. of his doctrine 212:8
e. o' my dear 107:30
e. of untimely graves 163:29
Emblems of deeds 113:1
Embodied: e. in the mystery of words 579:25
man is an e. paradox 154:23
Embodiment: the Law is the true e. 218:35
Embody: I..e. the Law 218:35
Emboldens: nothing e. sin..as mercy 480:24
Embosomed in the deep 226:13
Embost: in the Arabian woods e. 351:3
Embower: high over-arch'd e. 344:25
Embrace: as to e. me 351:26
eludes e. 375:4
e. the purpose of God 536:25
his right hand doth e. me 51:45
honour, love, and e. them 86:27
none I think do there e. 333:9
take your last e. 478:44
then pity, then e. 383:27
there I e. and kiss her 262:6
with a stronger faith e. 319:10
Embraced: rash-embraced despair 464:17
Embraces: an age in her e. past 407:18
Embracing the knight e. Jane 123:2
Embroidered: the strange and sinister e. 268:4
Embroidery: e. of a smock-frock 236:42
e. of poetic dreams 159:25
sad e. wears 342:31(-343)
Embroils: more e. the fray 346:11
Embryo: Chancellor in e. 499:16
Embryos and idiots 346:24
Emendation wrong that cannot 278:25
Emerald: as green as e. 148:25
fourth, an e. 72:1
Kelly from the E. Isle 360:3
like unto an e. 70:36
livelier e. twinkles 536:8
men of the E. Isle 189:21
peach of e. hue 204:3
Emerge: I shall e. one day 94:26
new-bath'd stars e. 17:28(-18)
Emerges: enormous whale e. 503:5
Emerging: descried..an e. prow 18:16
Emergunt: haud facile e. 283:5
Emigravit: is the inscription 317:2
Emily: up roos E. 137:33
Emily Jane: a very good girl was E. 217:28
Eminence: bald top of an e. 580:9
that bad e. 345:14
Eminency: some e. in ourselves 248:24
Eminent: proudly e. 345:5
Emit: managed to e. so much smoke 307:6
Emmanuel: come, E. 362:6
Emmet: Robert E. and Wolfe Tone 584:27
Emollit: artes e. mores 372:9

Emolument: derived any..e. from it 103:3
positions of considerable e. 212:22
Emori: quid moraris e.? 133:3
Emotion: e. recollected in tranquillity 583:4
heart less bounding at e. new 18:30
morality touched by e. 20:11
share in my e. 498:23
with a sweet e. 495:7
Emotions: grounds for the noble e. 412:25
Empêche: cela n'e. pas 216:11
Emperor: by e. and clown 288:1
E. Lamb 307:9
lie by an e.'s side 472:26
looking for the sacred E. 503:15
tent-royal of their e. 443:10
your only e. for diet 436:13
Emphasis: for the sake of e. 144:4
whatever e. of passionate love 309:13
Emphyteusis is not a disease 514:39
Empire: another mighty E. overthrown 578:4
arch of the rang'd e. fall 423:14
as thy e. must extend 350:10
cut-purse of the e. 435:49
deceased Roman E. 248:23
different parts of the E. in., hostility 222:38
dilapidation into which a great e. must fall 101:30
dismemberment of the E. 222:38
e. is on us bestow'd 158:33
e...power in trust 100:19
every rod..of e. 28:12
Fall-Off-The-Rooshan-E. 178:5
great e. and little minds 101:14
great Mother E...isolated 210:12
historian of the Roman E. 216:28
how is the E.? 216:16
is the ..e. unpossess'd? 476:31
Joy, E. and Victory 497:17
love of order..basis of E. 156:27
make us an E. yet 298:23
Neptune's e. 430:15
nor Roman, nor an e. 557:8
on an E.'s dust 113:24
pledge our E. 266:17
preserve the unity of the e. 101:12
rod of e. might have sway'd 230:4
savage wilderness into a glorious e. 101:15
seem to stay a falling e. 161:39
westward the course of e. 43:13
Empire Day: meaning of E. 142:15
Empire: ni romain, ni e. 557:8
Empires: buries e. and cities 217:13
day of E. has come 135:6
faiths and e. gleam 493:25
hatching vain e. 345:25
vaster than e. and more slow 333:8
Employ: fit to e. all the heart 96:21
in some unknown Power's e. 17:6
Employment: chase brave e. 243:28
e. for his idle time 559:15
hand of little e. 437:10
pleasantness of an e...its propriety 23:10
Empoison: an ill word may e. liking 468:26
Empress: court of the E. Josephine 220:27
e...of floures alle. 138:19
general of our gracious e. 445:6
in the Name of the E. 300:12
Emptied of this folk 287:12
Emptier ever dancing in the air 475:19
Empties: his state e. itself 465:21
Emptiness: e. of ages in his face 320:19
hurled their..plans to e. 263:31
little e. of love 84:17
smiles his e. betray 385:32
Emptorem: si e. invenerit 415:4
Empty: as e. quite 383:30
crowns are e. things 170:17
e. heads and tongues a-talking 263:18
e., swept, and garnished 59:18
e., vast, and wandering air 476:15
e. words of a dream 81:9
heaven hath my e. words 462:2
idle singer of an e. day 358:25
satisfieth the e. soul 398:15

INDEX

Empty (*cont.*)
sent e. away	61:14
success and miscarriage are e. sounds	270:28
tall men..e. heads	24:38
turn down an e. Glass	207:30
Emptying: and e. of it	419:18
Emulation: by exciting e.	269:33
pale and bloodless e.	481:5
out of the teeth of e.	449:26
shouting their e.	429:5
Enable with perpetual light	400:32
Enamelled: set in e. meadows	558:11
your quaint e. eyes	342:31
Enamour: those which most e. us	112:35
Enamoured: affliction is e. of thy parts	478:22
e. of an ass	467:18
Enchained: my heart e.	501:22
Enchains us to permitted ill	494:15
Enchant: I will e. thine ear	488:26
Enchanted: as holy and e.	151:32
E. island	337:35
enter these e. woods	336:48
Enchanter: from an e. fleeing	496:4
Enchanting: divine e. ravishment	340:14
Enchantment: distance lends e.	122:31
sweet e., hence!	504:7
Enchantments: last e. of the Middle Age	19:10
Enchants: it e. my sense	481:15
Enclitic: doctrine of the e. *De*	91:42
Enclosed: a garden e. is my sister	52:7
Encompassed..with his protection	352:13
Encourage those who betray their friends	215:2
Encouragement: an expression of no-e.	503:16
Encourager: pour e. les autres	557:1
Encumbers him with help	270:18
Encyclopaedia: whole E. behind	306:16
End: ages of hopeless e.	345:21
all's to no e.	373:13
all things come to an e.	399:19
apathetic e.	535:22
attempt the e.	246:19
began to draw to our e.	56:25
beginning of the e.	526:19
better is the e.	51:11
born to disastrous e.	510:16
bring our years to an e.	397:16
by opposing e. them	434:4
can't e. worst	89:22
challenge to his e.	166:19
Christ is the e.	360:11
come to a perpetual e.	392:13
death, a necessary e.	449:22
death the journey's e.	193:17
dull..to make an e.	540:32(–541)
e. crowns all	481:28
e. in sight was a vice	96:46
e. is not yet	60:22
e. of a golden string	75:8
e. of all things is at hand	70:4
e. of ane old song	370:4
e. of a perfect day	78:17
e. of every man's desire	522:16
e. of man is an action	127:12
e. of Solomon Grundy	368:21(–369)
e. of the beginning	144:10
e. of things created	6:17
e. of this day's business	451:38
e. that crowns us	246:19
e. that I have now begun	583:21
e. the heartache	434:4
e. to these bloated armaments	180:27
e. try the man	441:34
e. was not ignoble	579:7
e. where 'e began	295:23
fight on to the e.	233:20
found no e.	345:29
God be at my e.	6:10
go on till you come to the e.	129:30
go with me..to my e.	446:13
great e. of poesy	288:15
hardly bear to see the e.	237:15
here is my journey's e.	473:31
her e. is bitter	49:44
I am drawing to an e.	372:19
in my beginning is my e.	197:7
journeys e. in lovers meeting	482:28

End (*cont.*)
lest he should make an e.	280:2
let me know mine e.	394:8
let there be an e.	94:22
life death does e.	255:1
likewise is the e. of all things	176:22
love hath an e.	525:4
made a finer e.	443:19
made a good e.	436:33
make an e. the sooner	26:7
makes me e., where I begun	186:25
my last e...like his	46:18
of making..books..no e.	51:35
our being's e. and aim	384:2
quiet-coloured e. of evening	93:10
reserved for some e.	146:7
right true e. of love	184:20
same thing at the e.	89:18
sans E.	206:8
served no private e.	385:6
she had a good e.	328:16
sleep itself must e.	85:21
so shall they e.	85:19
stand up and e. you	263:15
swan-like e.	464:12
then the e. is known	451:38
there's an e.	440:35
there's an e...of kissing	84:23
there's an e. of May	263:33
there shall I e.	451:39
they are for the town's e.	440:34
this is not the e.	144:10
this same day..e. that work	451:37
till I e. my run	301:6
till I e. my song	510:20
to e. myself	535:25
to the e. of the road	310:14
to the e. of the town	339:16
to the very e.	410:2
true beginning of our e.	467:28
what is the chief e. of man?	501:9
what the boys get at one e.	272:36
what the e. shall be	324:18
what will ye do in the e.?	55:13
whose e. is purpos'd	449:21
wish it all at an e.	103:37
world without e., reprieve, or rest	302:1
wrought the e. unthought	303:15
End-all: be-all and the e. here	457:7
Endear: Presents e. Absents	306:5
old loves e. thee	148:14
Endeared: more e., pipe to the spirit	287:8
Endearing: e. elegance of female friendship	278:20
those e. young charms	356:11
Endearment: each fond e. tries	224:21
Endears: all the more e.	538:9
Endeavour: all death's e.	84:19
by no e.	221:1
disappointment all I e. end	255:8
disinterested e. to learn..the best	19:12
e. and dispute	206:22
nor mad e.	576:19
too painful an e.	384:34
Endeavours: whose high e.	575:5
Ended: day Thou gavest..is e.	198:17
e. in thee	390:52
Georges e.	309:11
no matter how it e.	403:1
summer is e.	55:16
Enderby: The Brides of E.	267:12
Ending: agony, and that has e.	84:18
beginning and the e.	70:22
never e., still beginning	191:9
our tedious song..have e.	343:25
slow to begin and never e.	578:11
still e. at..an hour	440:32
to the e. of the world	444:28(–445)
Endings: sentences..running to abrupt e.	337:2
Endless: all the e. road you tread	263:23
boundless, e., and sublime	114:31
e. extinction of unhappy hates	16:25
e. noon-day	361:16
Endorsed: elephants e. with towers	350:8
Endow: e. a college, or a cat	384:42
I thee e.	391:32
Ends: all the e. thou aim'st at	446:31
best e. by the best means	266:10
commences, reigns, and e.	503:2

Ends (*cont.*)
delays have dangerous e.	445:24
e. all other deeds	425:33
e. all our month-long love?	81:12
e. of Being	88:24
e. of the world	374:10
enough for nature's e.	327:14
ever nobler e.	533:26
from the e. of the earth	294:27
hope of all the e. of the earth	395:28
make both e. meet	212:17
nothing begins and nothing e.	544:2
odd old e. stol'n forth of holy writ	476:12
our e. by our beginnings know	172:11
shapes our e.	437:27
to gain some private e.	225:21
to serve our private e.	143:6
to the e. of all the earth	301:25
to the undiscovered e.	41:17
Endued: thank God..e. with such qualities	198:3
Endurance: e. and courage of my companions	416:7
e., foresight, strength	580:21
patient e. is godlike	316:15
Endure: all deaths I could e.	349:16
all pains the..spirit must e.	17:24
all that human hearts e.	278:29
but thou shalt e.	398:2
can e. the stings	158:12
e. in him	278:24
e. my own despair	559:7
e. not yet a breach	186:25
e. their going hence	454:18
e. what can't be mended	562:16
e. what it once possessed	494:21
e. you a little longer	156:14
let us e. an hour	263:16
more able to e.	575:7
nought..e. but Mutability	495:20
potter and clay e.	95:23
see how our works e.	295:10
she shall e.	413:31
stubborn to e.	508:5
stuff will not e.	482:28
their dwelling-places shall e.	395:1
this government cannot e.	314:6
to enjoy life, or to e. it	277:18
we first e.	383:27
what nature itselfe cant e.	208:22
Endured: e. through watches of the dark	545:10
intolerable, not to be e.	479:11
most tolerable and not to be e.	468:38
much is to be e.	278:16
what torments..you e.	199:25
Endures: Love that e. for a breath	522:5
shame e.	233:3
since to be loved e.	82:11
Endureth: e. all things	66:45
he that e. to the end	58:50
his mercy e. for ever	400:4
praise..e. for ever	398:25
Enduring: art alone e. stays	183:5
e. power, not ourselves	20:14
with e. things	579:13
Endymion: in E., I leaped headlong	290:7
the moon sleeps with E.	465:22
Enemies: all our e. having surrendered	144:17
bay'd about with many e.	451:7
choice of his e.	570:6
curse mine e.	46:20
dipped in the blood of thine e.	396:11
e. of Caesar shall say this	450:10
e. of England	263:11
find out their e. now	453:9
giving his e. the slip	513:3
his e. shall lick the dust	396:25
his e., 'Toasted-cheese'	128:7
if laws are their e.	103:12
let his e. be scattered	396:4
makes friends of e.	435:12
mine e...cast me in the teeth	394:20
mountains..make e. of nations	162:41
multitude of the e.	396:28
my most intimate e.	410:20
naked to mine e.	447:1
our e...and slanderers	389:5
our e. have beat us to the pit	452:5

INDEX

Enemies (cont.)

overthrown more than your e.	426:24
smote his e. in the hinder parts	397:1
speak with their e. in the gate	399:35
thine e. thy footstool	398:23
to forgive e. H— does pretend	74:16
trophies unto the e. of truth	86:4
we ought to forgive our e.	25:3
wound the head of his e.	396:10

Enemy: common e. of man

common e. of man	458:34
consider every man your e. who	362:16
devised by the e.	476:40
do be my e.	74:17
e. faints not	147:8
e. hath done this	59:26
e. in their mouths	471:22
e. of the good	557:5
e. to mankind	484:8
for a flying e.	115:10
found me, O mine e.?	48:12
great e. of reason, virtue	86:26
hasn't an e. in the world	570:23
here comes the e.	154:25
here shall he see no e.	427:7
he who has one e.	201:23
his e...sowed tares	59:25
how goes the e.?	406:9
I impeach the common e.	101:27
invasion of a common e.	305:1
last e...death	67:9
mine e.'s dog	454:13
mortal's chiefest e.	459:28
my e. is dead	567:5
my name..terrible to the e.	441:25
my vision's greatest e.	74:10
near'st and dearest e.	440:10
O cunning e.	462:1
O thou e.	392:13
our friends, the e.	43:10
poverty..great e. to..happiness	275:5
spoils of the e.	329:16
still the e.	392:8
sweet e., France	501:28
that old e. the gout	253:5
there he met his e.	294:12
weak invention of the e.	144:27
what effect..upon the e.	564:21
worst friend and e...Death	84:18

Energetic: his e. fist 221:19

Energies: the e. of our system will decay 29:19

Energy: E. is Eternal Delight 77:6

majestic march and e. divine	386:17
modes of the divine e.	200:29
your courage, your e., your patience	305:1

Enfants: dévorât..tous ses e. 552:17

e. de la patrie	412:1
les e. terribles	214:5

Enfold: inviolate Rose e. me 585:23

Enfolding sunny spots 151:32

Enforce a desperate amour 111:7

Enforced: e. ceremony 451:9

much e., shows a hasty spark 451:25

Enforcement: gentleness my strong e. 427:19

Enforcing thame 187:4

Engagement: loose from every honourable e. 101:37

Engarlanded: brambles pale with mist e. 18:31

Engendered: e. in the eyes 464:13

it is e. 470:23

Engenders: mule that e. nothing 181:38

Engine: e. that moves 237:26

put this e. to our ears	519:11
reasoning e. lies	407:22
that curious e., your white hand	563:11
that devilish iron e.	509:25
two-handed e. at the door	342:29
wit's an unruly e.	243:32

Engineer: e. hoist with his own petar 436:8

sometimes the e. 243:32

Engines: e. to play a little on our own 102:4

these, my e.	299:4
you mortal e.	472:3

England: alas, alas, for E. 140:24

be E. what she will	142:32
between France and E...the sea	269:12

England (cont.)

body of E.'s	84:21
bow was made in E.	187:12
Cambridgeshire of all E.	84:12
children in E...breaking	10:10
cold queen of E.	141:4
cottage homes of E.	241:13
country men of E.	373:11
crews at E.'s feet	122:6
defence of E.	29:15
dust whom E. bore	84:21
enemies of E.	263:11
E.—a happy land	143:1
E. as the predominant member	409:8
E.! awake!	75:11
E., bound in	474:23
E. breed again	189:8
E. does not love coalitions	180:23
E. expects	362:23
E., full of sin	243:29
E. has saved herself	379:16
E. hath need of thee	577:14
E., home and beauty	79:15
E. is a paradise for women	109:29
E.! model to thy inward greatness	443:13
E...most potent in potting	471:10
E. mourns for her dead	72:22
E., my E.	241:25, 26
E...rest but true	448:2
E. shall bide	303:6
E.'s on the anvil	294:22
E.'s the one land	84:12
E. talked of ale	141:25
E...the workshop of the world	180:14
E. was merry E.	418:24
E., we love thee better	549:5
E. will have her neck wrung	144:9
E., with all thy faults	162:43
E...wont to conquer others	474:24
E.'s greatest son	537:18
E.'s green and pleasant land	75:16
E's green and pleasant bowers	75:12
E.'s Jane	297:20
E.'s Milton equals both	160:24
ere E.'s griefs began	224:14
for E.'s sake	362:31
for ever E.	84:21
France..influenced manners in E.	102:19
further off from E.	129:24
get me to E. once again	84:12
Greece, Italy and E. did adorn	193:9
green fields of E.	147:10
happy is E.	288:23, 24
Harry! E. and Saint George	443:27
heralds of E.'s Marshal	142:4
here did E. help me	92:18
high road that leads him to E.	271:8
I am E.'s Queen	298:30
I am in E. everywhere	86:28
if E. was what E. seems	301:2
in E...given to horses	277:29
in E.—now!	92:14
in E. to take a prey	30:5
in E.'s song for ever	363:6
in this Realm of E.	401:12
Ireland gives E. her soldiers	337:10
knew what E. means	140:25
let not E. forget her precedence	352:24
lights of E. watch the ships of E.	295:12
lost the last of E.	42:14
mad, and sent into E.	437:14
Man of E. circled by the sands	335:27
martial airs of E.	563:5
men of E.	102:24
men of E., wherefore plough?	498:17
men that worked for E.	140:24
meteor flag of E.	123:12
noon strikes on E.	208:5
nor, E.! did I know	577:4
not..that Old E. is lost	273:18
of a king of E. too	198:11
of all the trees in E.	172:6, 7
Oh, to be in E.	92:14
old E. to adorn	303:5
old E.'s winding sheet	73:28(—74)
oldest singer..E. bore	524:20
on E.'s pleasant pastures seen	75:16
organ-voice of E.	529:17
our banner of E. blew	529:4
our E. is a garden	296:30

England (cont.)

our E.'s Alfred	537:24
our E. to his Italy	96:19
our noble E.'s praise	322:17
pastoral heart of E.	404:22
poison E. at her roots	79:3
rather..E. should be free than ..sober	327:8
rightwise King born of all E.	328:3
roast beef of E.	204:13
since he stood for E.	140:25
slaves cannot breathe in E.	162:42
sleep in old E.'s heart	562:21
small states..Elizabethan E.	267:9
stately homes of E.	241:12
such night in E. ne'er had been	322:18
suspended in favour of E.	489:31
take my drum to E.	363:2
that knuckle-end of E.	504:22
that shire..the heart of E.	189:17
there'll always be an E.	373:15
they that rule in E.	140:24
this aged E.	200:3
this E.	474:22
this E. never did	448:2
thoughts by E. given	84:21
to E. to carry	189:8
unless proud E. keep	188:32
upon E.'s mountains green	75:16
wake up, E.	216:15
we are the people of E.	141:28
we have in E. a..bashfulness	2:24
what appears in E.'s case	159:24
where an immortal E. sits	141:14
who dies if E. live?	296:20
whoever wakes in E.	92:14
who only E. know	296:3
whose limbs were made in E.	443:26
with E.'s own coal	294:34
world where E. is finished	339:7
worse E.	273:32
ye Mariners of E.	123:10
you gentlemen of E.	373:12

English: abusing..the king's E. 465:33

among the E. Poets	290:11
attain an E. style	278:9
boy, half-French, half-E.	445:14
breathing E. air	84:21
buy my E. posies	296:15
created the E. mad	298:2
Dr. Johnson's morality..as English	239:8
E. army..Irish general	490:39
E. Flag was flown	296:5
E...foul-mouthed	240:10
E. grew polite	296:8
E...least..philosophers	28:32
E. lord should lightly me	31:6
E. make it their abode	557:23
E...meet and dine somewhere	269:20
E. Mercuries	443:12
E. subject's sole prerogative	193:42
E. take their pleasures sadly	517:23
E. that of the sea	125:23, 407:1
E. they be and Japanee	301:4
E. unofficial rose	84:9
E...very little..inferior to the Scotch	365:9
E. Virgil	291:16
E. winter	116:47
father of E. criticism	278:6
fine old E. gentleman	8:5
good E. hospitality	77:5
grave where E. oak	238:26
happy E. child	527:5
humility..clothe an E. dean	164:14
if he went among the E.	36:16
in favour of boys learning E.	144:16
made our E. tongue a galli-maufry	511:1
make his E. swete	137:4
marks our E. dead	301:23
my E. text is chaste	217:4
my native E.	474:14
not E. armour left, nor any E. thing	140:12
not rest in an E. grave	119:33
off E. in makyng was the beste	321:10
one E. book..only..the Bible	20:4
one E. tear o'er E. dust	323:9
one pair of E. legs	444:4

English (cont.)
O noble E.! 443:8
on, you noblest E.! 443:25
our E. dead 443:24
out of French into E. 328:14
piece of E. grass trampled 234:4
rolling E. drunkard 141:21
Roman-Saxon-Danish-Norman E. 170:13
strung them on an E. thread 320:6
take of E. earth 295:5
talent of our E. nation 193:23
these E. fields, this upland 18:31
to be an E. king 140:12
trick of our E. nation 441:24
well of E. undefiled 510:5
wet bird-haunted E. lawn 17:10
when the E. began to hate 294:30
when shall E. men 189:8
when you can't think of the E. 130:2
white..the E. child 76:13
with E. instinct fraught 188:31
wood of E. bows 187:12
Englishman: as I am an E. 379:8
as thorough an E. 294:6
broad-shoulder'd genial E. 539:9
Brother, E., and Friend 579:20
dying E. 505:28
either for E. or Jew 74:14
E...content to say nothing 274:20
E. does not travel to see Englishmen 512:19
E...flatter'd, is a lamb 135:14
E. never enjoys himself except 243:14
E...not easily baffled 28:30
E.'s..privilege of doing as he likes 19:29
for an E. to open his mouth 490:44
he is an E.! 221:24
ill-natur'd thing, an E. 170:12
last great E. 537:13
never find an E. in the wrong 490:38
no E. unmoved 221:37
not deserving of the name of E. 78:28
not one E. 559:1
one E. could beat three Frenchmen 2:19
prejudices which..cleave to..a true E. 2:19
religious rights of an E. 282:16
unintelligent..young E. of our upper class 19:27
what an E. believes..heresy 491:4
woo'd an E. 12:1
Englishmen: absurd nature of E. 377:20
breeds hard E. 293:15
find E. doing it 490:38
first to His E. 352:12
for our very name as E. 379:15
honest E. 293:11
mad dogs and E. 157:25
proper drink of E. 78:28
we all be good E. 539:20
when two E. meet 277:34
Engluts..other sorrows 469:43
Engross: when he should e. 385:21
Engrossing: bargain to e. death 478:44
Enjoy: after that, to e. 504:14
book should teach us to e. life 277:18
both e. and miss her 262:6
can neither, when we will, e. 17:6
don't have to go out and e. it 504:18
e. but half the blessing 214:9
e. her while she's kind 194:22
e. him for ever 501:9
e. such liberty 319:7
e. the earth no less 236:16
e. the things..others understand 578:34
he can thoroughly e. the pepper 129:2
hope I shall e. myself with you 20:27
indifferent, and cannot e. it 270:18
more we e. it 168:7
never e. the world aright 548:13
prize not..whiles we e. it 469:5
we may e. them 389:6
what I most e. 486:24
which I can ne'er e. 144:21
who can e. alone? 348:34
Enjoyed: all times I have e. 540:32
e. his youth 192:13
e. the gifts of the founder 216:21

Enjoyed (cont.)
e. the self-same light 548:17
if not e. 168:7
little to be e. 278:16
that bards of old e. in you 75:18
what peaceful hours I once e. 161:2
Enjoying: all e., what contentment? 348:34
forgive a man for not e. Milton 306:32
think it worth e. 191:9
which is the e. of it 27:32
Enjoyment: such serene e. 355:12
unless it from e. spring 548:16
was it done with e.? 413:10
Enjoyments: fireside e. 163:25
if it were not for its e. 518:37
Enjoys: e. himself..for a noble purpose 243:14
every flower e. the air 581:9
now e. his age 192:13
Enlarge: e., diminish, interline 521:16
e. my life 279:7
to e. or illustrate this 109:25
enlargement of the language 277:22
Enlightened: on the e. mind 546:9
Enmesh: with Predestination round e. me 207:10
with Predestined Evil round e. 207:11
Enmity: at e. with joy 576:19
covert e. 441:7
Enna: that fair field of E. 347:8
Ennemi: l'e. du bien 557:5
voilà l'e.! 154:25
Ennemies: les oreilles e. vous écoutent 12:19
Ennemis: nos amis, les e. 43:10
Ennui: Mr. E., 'the time-killer' 406:9
Ennuyer: le secret d'e. 557:13
Ennuyeux: hors le genre e. 557:6
End: E. was omnipresent 514:2
soar with E. 514:2
Enoch: E., Elijah, and the Lady 376:1
E. walked with God 44:35
Enormous through the Sacred Town 41:32
Enough: e. for modesty 98:6
e. for nature's ends 327:14
e., if something 573:27
e. of science and of art 581:16
e. that he heard it once 89:10
first cries, 'Hold, e.!' 461:14
it is e. 50:55
Lord Lilac had had quite e. 141:31
love is e. 359:6
oysters..never had e. 218:2
patriotism is not e. 134:2
quite e. to get 179:15
three questions, and that is e. 128:29
'tis e., 'twill serve 478:14
was it not e.? 489:28
Enraged I write 232:15
Enraptured main 503:6
Enrich: e. my heart, mouth, hands 245:9
e. not the heart of another 316:14
e. unknowing nations 168:9
Enriched: so e. both 80:29
Enriches: not e. him 471:30
Enrichment of our native language 194:4
Ensample: this noble e. to his sheep 137:17
Ensanguined hearts 163:29
Ense: quam sit calamus sævior e. 109:13
Ensham: above by E. 18:29
Ensign: beauty's e. yet is crimson 478:43
tear her tattered e. down 251:5
Enskied: thing e. and sainted 461:19
Enslave: impossible to e. 85:3
Enslaved: all..e. which serve things evil 497:6
be e. by another man's 75:2
still e. 116:27
Enslaves: e. you on imperial principles 490:38
Reason e. 490:35
Ensnared: e. with flowers 332:17
thus e. my soul and body 474:1
Ensue: seek peace, and e. it 394:2
slaughter will e. 155:26
Entangled: e. in the cobwebs 163:36
e. in their mazes 497:9
middle-sized are alone e. 499:18
Entangles: very force e. itself 425:22
Entangling alliances with none 268:21

Entbehren sollst Du! 223:18
Enter: although I e. not 543:4
before you e. upon him 306:28
e. Caesar 449:19
e. into the courts of the Lord 397:5
e...into the joy of thy lord 60:30
e. these enchanted woods 336:48
hardly..e. into the kingdom 62:35
King of England cannot e. 379:11
King of glory e. may 421:2
rich man..e. into the kingdom 60:3
that she may e. in 509:12
ye cannot e. now 530:10
ye who e. here 168:17
Entered: e. into their labours 63:15
e. into the springs of the sea 49:22
he e. full of wrath 286:12
ne'er to be e. more 119:21
Entergraft: to e. our hands 184:30
Enterprise: all period, pow'r and e. 503:2
e. is sick 481:3
hazard in the glorious e. 344:12
nurse of..heroic e. 102:12
Enterprised: you e. a railroad 413:1
Enterprises: e. of great pith and moment 434:4
impediments to great e. 26:34
Enterprising burglar 221:35
Enters: e. into one's soul 289:25
him that e. next 475:29
Entertain: e. divine Zenocrate 331:3
e. Him..like a stranger 12:7
e...the full pride of France 443:8
e. this starry stranger 166:1
e. us with no worth 558:6
some second guest to e. 186:8
you, sir, I e. 453:31
Entertained angels unawares 69:22
Entertaining: as e. as a Persian Tale 272:18
very e. to myself 155:27
Entertainment: dull thy palm with e. 431:25
joint and not an e. 235:6
my E. 560:17
some other custom of e. 471:7
what lenten e. 433:17
Entertains the harmless day 583:10
Enthrall: except you e. me 185:19
Enthralled: surprised..but not e. 340:30
what her eyes e. 155:5
Enthralls the crimson stomacher 246:4
Enthroned: e. in the hearts of kings 464:33
e. i' the market-place 424:7
Enthusiasm: e. moves the world 29:20
in the height of e. 290:15
nothing..achieved without e. 29:20
Enthusiastic: praises with e. tone 219:25
Enthusiasts: few e...speak the truth 29:20
Entice: the dewy-feather'd sleep 341:22
if sinners e. thee 49:37
Enticed: my..thoughts e. mine eye 359:27
Entire: e. and whole and perfect 511:4
e. of itself 186:27
one e. and perfect chrysolite 473:21
this sorry Scheme of Things e. 207:26
Entomb: sage to e. it 34:34
Entrails: e. of yon labouring cloud 330:9
in our own proper e. 452:1
poison'd e. 459:29
Entrance: beware of e. to a quarrel 431:25
fatal e. of Duncan 457:3
from my first e. in 244:21
whose e. leads to Hell 340:25
wisdom at one e. 346:20
Entrances: their exits and their e. 427:21
Entrap: to e. the wisest 464:15
Entrate: voi ch'e. 168:17
Entreat: e...him to forget me 309:18
e. me not to leave thee 47:1
not missed by any that e. 87:37
Entreats: Hesperus e. thy light 279:31
Entuned in her nose full semely 136:29
Entwine itself verdantly still 356:12
Enveloping the Earth 151:5
Envenomed: the point e. too 437:40
Envie de recevoir de plus grands bienfaits 407:13

Envieth: charity e. not 66:45
Envious: e. and calumniating time 481:21
e. fever 481:5
Environ: what perils do e. 110:29
Environed with a great ditch 167:13
Envisage circumstance, all calm 286:16
Envy: attracts the e. of the world 100:22
by whim, e., or resentment 142:29
death..extinguisheth e. 26:4
e. and calumny 492:7
e. and wrath shorten the life 57:5
e., hatred, and malice 388:46
e. is a kind of praise 215:28
e. never makes holiday 25:9
e. no man's happiness 427:27
e.'s a sharper spur 215:23
e...the dull unletter'd small 164:17
I e. not..the captive 532:19
our scorn, not e. raise 215:28
Pride, E., Malice 308:13
self-seeking, e., low design 308:1
Shelley, whom e. never touched 309:20
stirr'd up with e. and revenge 344:6
through e. of the devil 56:22
toil, e., want 279:4
too low for it 158:15
Enwrought with golden..light 584:17
Epaulet: any e. I could have worn 547:2
Ephesians: great is Diana of the E. 65:8
Ephesus: fought with beasts at E. 67:10
Ephod: girded with a linen e. 47:2
Ephraim: E...the strength of my head 395:23
grapes of E. 46:53
Epic: forgot his e...art 386:13
legend of an e. hour 141:16
Mr. Wordsworth's e. poetry 240:7
Epictetus: as well as translate E. 270:5
Epicure: the e. would say 505:4
Epicuri de grege porcum 256:27
Epicurus: he was E. owne sone 137:9
I held E. strong 451:34
Epicycle: cycle and e. 348:30
Epigram: what is an E.? 151:14
Epigrams: despotism tempered by e. 126:12
Epilogue: needs no e. 428:40
Epistles: obscure e. of love 482:34
Epistula: verbosa et grandis e. 283:18
Epitaph: believe a woman or an e. 117:13
better have a bad e. 433:29
not remembered in thy e. 441:1
that may be his e. 513:36
Epitaphs: nice derangement of e. 500:20
of worms and e. 475:6
Epithet: too foul an e. for thee 331:1
Epithets: sensitive to e. like these 40:26
stuff'd with e. of war 469:20
Epitome: all mankind's e. 190:22
London is the e. of our times 200:2
Epoch: chapter..completed from e. to e. 127:16
Equal: admitted to that e. sky 383:12
all men are created e. 11:11, 268:19, 314:12
all shall e. be 218:22
as if they were e. 212:5
e. and one with me 524:5
e. division of unequal earnings 198:21
e. friend 518:1
e. society with them 158:4
e. to the whole of that commerce 100:22
e. to what the author promised 270:25
e...within the Church's gate 244:5
I am e. and whole 524:1
in the dust be made 501:5
man e., unclassed 497:12
Nature, with e. mind 15:12
sees with e. eye 383:10
some animals..more e. than others 370:16
though e. to all things 225:27
with e. mind 193:17
with th' Eternal..e. in strength 345:15
Equality: men of culture..true apostles of e. 19:26
never be in the servants' hall 36:1
Equalled: e. with them in renown 346:20
whom reason hath e. 344:22
Equally: her gifts..bestowed e. 426:18

Equals: awkward..in the society of his e. 306:17
disinterested commerce between e. 226:34
little friendship..between e. 26:13
supreme above his e. 344:22
Equator: as far as the E. 543:7
quarrellin wi' the e. 365:12
speak disrespectfully of the E.! 504:21
Equi: lente currite noctis e. 330:7
Equilibrio: Orden..es..un e. 214:2
Equilibrium: order is..an e. 214:2
Equinox: who knows when was the e.? 87:18
Equipment: shabby e. always deteriorating 197:9
Equitem: post e....Cura 259:16
satis est e. mihi plaudere 261:20
Equity: convinced of its justice and e. 409:8
law of humanity, justice, e. 101:26
Equivalent: allowance..without an e. 277:31
Equivocate: I will not e. 213:17
Equivocation: e. of the fiend 461:5
e. will undo us 437:12
Equivocator: here's an e. 458:18
Equo ne credite 553:27
Equum: solve senescentem..e. 256:15
Eradicating: without e. the virtue 226:31
Erastian: Essene, E. Whig 140:12
Ercles: this is E.' vein 466:26
Erebus: dark as E. 465:20
not E. itself 449:7
Erect: above himself..e. himself 168:5
e. and tall, godlike e. 347:10
e. upon two legs 179:11
grows e., as that comes home 186:25
our two souls..e. and strong 88:19
raise and e. the mind 24:16
Erected: e. into a system of Government 223:1
for cowards were e. 106:24
high e. thoughts 501:16
least e. spirit 345:9
with e. eyes 194:25
with e. look 193:41
Erecting: there e. new 332:12
Eremite: nature's..sleepless E. 288:17
Eremites and friars 346:24
Eric: call me E. 203:34
Erickin': an beastly E. 304:47
Erin: E. go bragh! 122:11
E., the tear and the smile 356:17
poor Exile of E. 122:10
Eros: Anteros and E. 543:18
unarm, E. 425:21
Err: better to e. with Pope 117:14
mortal, and may e. 501:7
most may e. as grossly 190:28
reas'ning but to e. 383:22
shall not e. therein 54:4
to e. is human 383:2
unbelief is sure to e. 161:20
Errand: joyous E. 207:30,32
upon a thankless e. 405:7
warlike e. went 322:22
what thy e.? 307:34
Errands: e. for the Ministers of State 218:23
meet to be sent on e. 451:5
Errant: ears like e. wings 140:21
Errare: e....malo cum Platone 145:23
unde..passimque videre e. 320:30(-321)
Erred: we have e. 388:10
wisest men have e. 350:26
Erring: e. lace 246:4
e. on ventiferous ripes 251:19
e. sister's shame 117:40
extravagant and e. spirit 430:19
to check the e. 573:28
which e. men call Chance 340:29
Erroneous: profane, e., and vain 110:35
Error: all men are liable to e. 315:9
by e. to his fate..consented 280:10
charged the troops of e. 86:4
e. is immense 78:11
e. of the moon 473:16
he was guilty of no e. 85:1
if this be e. 488:7
in endless e. hurled 383:22

Error (cont.)
makes e. a fault 244:1
many an e...rush into the State 465:3
most gratuitous form of e. 196:20
mountainous e. 429:9
O hateful e. 451:40
show..that he is in e. 315:8
stalking horse to e. 78:12
stronger than all the hosts of e. 98:1
what damned e., but 464:14
Error: me malus abstulit e. 556:4
Erroris: remota e. nebula 283:15
Errors: adore our e. 425:2
amusing with numerous e. 227:14
e., like straws 193:20
e. of a wise man 73:15
more harmful than reasoned e. 266:23
some female e. 385:12
Errs: man e., till his strife is over 223:15
Ers: those dreadful e. 250:31
Erubuit: Deum vidit, et e. 165:25
Eruet: obscurata diu..e...vocabula 257:20
Erump: excede,—evade,—e. 251:20
Erupit: excessit, evasit, e. 145:13
Eruption: some strange e. to our state 430:12
Esau: E...is a hairy man 44:59
E. selleth his birthright 6:4
E. was a cunning hunter 44:57
hands of E. 45:1
Escalier: l'esprit de l'e. 180:6
Escape: beauty..provides e. 266:16
e. from rope and gun 214:34
e. into..philosophy 265:13
e. me? Never 92:41
e. the uphill 409:17
few e. that distinction 550:28
let me ever e. them 400:15
let no guilty man e. 229:2
make a way to e. 66:38
what struggle to e.? 287:7
Escaped: e. even as a bird 399:32
e. from the people of Basing 311:5
e. with the skin of my teeth 49:4
fancies that e. 95:21
Escapes: painful e. of fitful life 80:17
Escapeth: him that e. the sword 48:9
Eschew evil 394:2
Escorial: Tom Jones..outlive.. the E. 216:17
Eskdale and Liddesdale 420:8
Espace: l'utilité..n'est pas en l'e. 354:20
Espaces: le silence éternel de ces é. 374:1
Espagnol: je parle e. à Dieu 136:13
Esperance! Percy 440:33
Espineux: un chemin aspre et e. 355:2
Espouse the everlasting Sea 582:7
Espoused: my fairest, my e. 348:1
my late e. Saint 351:24
Esprit: l'e. de l'escalier 180:6
le peuple n'a guère d'e. 97:33
Esquire: an e.'s son 29:22
Essay: make a short e. 192:8
Essays: my e...come home to men 25:15
worse e. 488:5
Essence: e. of innumerable biographies 125:32
e. of war is violence 324:23
fellowship with e. 284:25
his glassy e. 461:31
purest e. of a human soul 127:28
so..uncompounded is their e. 344:29
Essenced: his long e. hair 323:1
Essene, Erastian Whig 140:28
Establish: revere, e. and defend 42:1
Established: every word..e. 67:39
in mercy..e. 53:24
or so sure e. 388:4
Estate: comfortable e. of widowhood 214:20
content thyself with thine e. 518:2
e., good fame 199:12
fallen from his high e. 191:7
Fourth E. 126:29
fourth e. of the realm 324:22
had a great e. 5:10
have you an e. in Greenland? 233:7
man of mean e. 188:33
mind, body, or e. 389:17
nor born in any high e. 4:7
order'd their e. 3:15

Estate (cont.)
relief of man's e.   24:14
steals your whole e.   214:19
they had his e.   190:24
wish the e. o' the world..un-
done   461:6
Estates: e., degrees and offices
flies of e.   464:1
Esteem: lessened my e. of a king   243:23
they give to get e.   377:18
Esteemed: vile e.   226:12
we e. him not   488:10
Estimable: Mr. F...an e. man   54:25
Estimate holds his e. and dignity   175:38
thou know'st thy e.   481:12
Estimation: degraded in their own
e.   219:26
Estranged: seeming e.   252:19
Estranging: unplumb'd, salt, e. sea   16:16
Estribo: el pie en el e.   134:20
Estridges: plumed like e.   440:17
Esurienti: mihi..   21:18
Et tu, Brute   120:12, 449:31
Étais: tu n'y é. pas   242:2
État: l'É. c'est moi   318:21
Etchings: china an' e. an' fans   299:18
Étient: l'absence..é. le petit   109:34
Eternal: condition..is e. vigilance   167:26
Energy is E. Delight   77:6
e. artistries in Circumstance   235:20
e. glory thou shalt win   99:8
e. in the heavens   67:24
e. not ourselves   20:17
e. Now   158:2
E. Passion! E. Pain!   17:12
e. Sabbath of his rest   193:37
e. spirit of the chainless mind   114:33
e. summer gilds them yet   115:43
e. summer in his soul   251:11
e. triangle   10:11
haunted..by the e. mind   576:13
heav'n's e. year is thine   192:38
hope springs..   383:11
in e. lines to trine   486:18
in themselves e.   123:18
let us swear an e. friendship   124:16
let us swear e. friendship   504:26
lose not the things e.   389:41
mine e. jewel   458:34
mounts..to e. life   16:13
of th' E. co-e. beam   346:18
our e. home   562:9
our e. life   388:25
portion of the E.   492:5
sleep e. in an e. night   523:24
their 'E.' and 'God'   20:14
thy e. summer shall not fade   486:18
to be boy e.   485:3
where the E. are   492:16
with e. lids apart   288:17
with th' E. to be deemed equal   345:15
Eternally: thy joy and crown e.   354:11
we wake e.   185:16
Eterne: nature's copy's not e.   459:6
Éternité: seul à l'é.   214:3
Eternities: conflux of two e.   126:14
for Seasons; not E.   336:23
Eternity: as doth e.   287:14
babe in E.   73:25
damned from here to E.   296:27
day joins the past E.   114:6
dazzles at it, as at e.   551:17
deserts of vast e.   333:9
dwelt from e.   346:18
E. in an hour   73:18
e. is in love with..time   77:12
E. of thought   575:21
E.'s too short   2:23
e. shut in a span   166:6
E.! thou pleasing, dreadful
thought!   1:22
e. was in our lips   423:33
e. was in that moment   155:28
from e., and shall not fail   263:32
from the Soul's e.   410:21
hid battlements of E.   544:26
I gave you e.   489:27
image of e.   114:31
in E.'s sunrise   74:27
intimates e. to man   1:22

Eternity (cont.)
into E.   125:27
I saw E. the other night   552:13
I to thee E. shall give   189:19
latest flakes of E.   38:30
lovers' hours be full e.   185:32
mighty ages of e.   127:33
opes the palace of E.   339:29
out of E.   125:27
outpost of e.   410:31
Pilgrim of E.   492:1
sabbaths of E.   540:7
sells e. to get a toy   486:6
shadows of e.   552:4
silence is deep as E.   126:1
Silence is of E.   127:22
sing of Time or E.   529:17
speak of e. without a solecism   86:9
sweet e. of love   246:11
symbols of E.   580:25
thoughts that wander through e.   345:19
thou thyself to all e.   411:14
through all E. to thee   2:23
through nature to e.   430:29
throughout all E.   75:20
white radiance of E.   492:15
Eter-nity: for all e. he would have
added   500:4
Eternize: your virtues rare..e.   509:7
Ether: ampler e.   577:13
bottle labelled 'E'   90:37
through delicatest e.   375:24
Ethereal: all the blue e. sky   2:25
flaming from th'e. sky   344:7
in what e. dances   380:21
meek e. hours   285:36
with brede e. wove   153:24
Etherized: patient e. upon a table   197:15
Ethics: Byron..drew a system of
e.   325:18
Ethiop: jewel in an E.'s ear   477:9
Juno but an E.   455:18
Ethiopian change his skin   55:18
Etiquette: it isn't e. to cut anyone   131:12
Eton: E. boys grown heavy   387:19
playing fields of E.   564:6
Étranglé: le dernier des rois..é.   338:1
Etrurian shades   344:25
Ettrick and Teviotdale   420:8
Euclid: E...looked on Beauty bare   339:5
worked a love-story..into..E.   188:18
Eugene: our good Prince E.   507:8
Eugenia: listen, E.   17:12
Eundo: virisque adquirit e.   554:16
Eunuch: a kind of moral e.   496:17
intellectual e. Castlereagh   115:13
strain, Time's e.   255:9
Euphelia serves   401:38
Eureka!   14:9
Euripides: chorus-ending from E.   89:31
E., the human   89:6
passionate outpourings of E.   153:12
Europe: better fifty years of E.   535:1
community of E.   222:41
E...a prone..figure   235:22
E. by her example   379:16
E. made his woe her own   16:8
E.'s latter hour   16:23
'E.'s Liberator'   116:27
glory of E. is extinguished   102:11
going out all over E.   232:18
rights of smaller nationalities of
E.   21:6
sheep-worry of E.   82:14
splendidly isolated in E.   210:12
through E. to the Aetolian shore   16:8
Eurydice: his half regain'd E.   342:9
Eustace is a man no longer   294:14
Evade: excede, —e., —erump!   251:20
Fear wist not to e.   544:16
Evaded: revolutions..not to be e.   181:39
Evangelist: honour unto Luke E.   411:9
lips of that E.   532:22
Evaporate: all disagreeables e.   289:20
Evasion of whoremaster man   452:19
Evasit: excessit, e., erupit   145:13

Eve (cont.)
E. from his side arose   11:23
E. upon the first of Men   252:10
E., with her basket   249:7
E., with her body white   249:8
e.'s one star   286:2
every e. I say   81:6
fairest of her daughters E.   347:13
fallen sons of E.   142:5
from noon to dewy e.   345:12
meekest E.   153:26
nor E. the rites..refused   347:25
not sure, this e.   91:35
one of E.'s family   252:16
on St. Gallowglass's E.   141:10
O pensive E.   153:23
purpureal E.   574:2
ships, becalmed at e.   147:6
so curses all E.'s daughters   466:13
summer's e.—or spring   114:5
through the land at e.   538:9
to E.: Be soon   544:17
warblest at e.   351:12
when..E. span   11:18, 235:7
when the e. is cool   85:13
Eve-jar: spins the brown e.   336:9
Evelyn Hope is dead   91:20
Even: at e. ere the sun was set   550:32
deep and crisp and e.   361:19
dilemma's e.   194:27
e. so, come, Lord Jesus   72:13
grey-hooden E.   340:8
heavy with the e.   544:21
how can you..write so e.?   22:30
soft as the breath of e.   21:9
sweet approach of e.   346:20
with the dews at e.   535:31
would God it were e.   46:28
Even-fall: brought him home at e.   538:26
Even-handed justice   457:7
Evening: addressed its e. hours   516:19
all that ever went with e. dress   301:22
as an e. dragon came   351:2
autumn e.   498:12
bid haste the e. star   348:38
came still e. on   347:19
come in the e.   169:27
cool of the e.   506:1
dews of the e...shun   139:3
each e. sees it close   318:13
e. and the morning..the first
day   44:3
e. full of the linnet's wings   585:12
e. is spread out against the sky   197:15
e. must usher night   491:26
e. of my age   412:7
e. on the olden   208:6
e. sacrifice   400:13
e. star, Love's harbinger   349:26
expects his e. prey   229:23
fairer than the e. air   330:6
from e. close to morning   493:22
grateful e. mild   347:23
in the e. it is cut down   397:15
in the e. withhold not   51:30
it is a beauteous e.   577:1
it was a summer's e.   507:3
life's cool e.   386:7
like an e. gone   562:9
never morning wore to e.   532:6
O e. dreams   208:6
on a summer's e., in his tent   450:27
ply her e. care   229:31
prose can paint e.   337:14
quiet-coloured end of e.   93:10
sadly descends the autumn e.   17:16
shadows of the e.   34:35
soon as the e. shades prevail   2:26
Soup of the e.   129:26
till the..e. comes   364:4
twilight and e. bell   528:22
until the e.   398:10
wearing out life's e.   276:15
welcome peaceful e. in   163:21
when e. shuts   95:19
wish him a rainy e.   559:11
with tea amuses the e.   278:1
yet the E. listens   289:9
your shadow at e.   197:28
Evenings: he comes on chosen e.   180:22
long dark autumn-e.   90:4

Evening-star: e., Love's harbinger 349:26
  moon's and e.'s at once 92:33
  sunset and e.' 528:22
Evensong: at last the belles ringeth
    to e. 239:6
  but to the e. 246:2
Event: experience from this great
    e. 351:7
  how much the greatest e. 210:20
  make sure of the e. first 558:28
  one august e. 235:16
  one e. happeneth to..all 51:2
  one far-off divine e. 533:31
  too precisely on the e. 436:16
Eventful: this strange e. history 427:21
Eventide: fast falls the e. 322:1
Events: confus'd e. new-hatch'd 458:21
  coming e. cast their shadows 122:22
  e. have controlled me 314:4
  e. in the womb of time 470:18
  e. which they did not cause 235:22
  strange and terrible e. 425:25
Eventum: ad e. festinat 256:1
Ever: at once and e. 151:33
  be loved by, for e. 96:25
  cramp'd for e. 281:27
  ecstasy of being e. 87:21
  e. do nothing but that 48:27
  e. shall be 388:14
  fades for e. and for e. 540:32(–541)
  for e. and for e. farewell, Cas-
    sius 451:37
  for e. dead 155:21
  for e. in joy 96:21
  for e. wilt thou love 287:9
  for e. with the Lord 355:9
  gone, and for e. 410:23
  gone for e. and e. by 535:43
  if for e., still for e. 117:34
  it may be for e. 166:24
  lost it for e. 97:29
  punctually come for e. and e. 567:24
  talked on for e. 239:21
  that e. this should be 149:6
  that For E. 293:7
  they are gone for e. 329:9
  think that we build for e. 413:12
  yesterday, and today, and for e. 69:23
Ever-burning: Berenice's e. hair 135:15
Ever-during: e. dark 346:20
  one e. night 123:19
Ever-fixed mark 488:7
Ever-haunting importunity 307:17
Everlasting: e. arms 46:34
  e. cold 563:36
  e. farewells! 172:21
  E...fix'd his canon 430:33
  e. light 84:25
  e. mercy, Christ 334:3
  e. name 54:33
  e. night 185:23
  e. No 127:13
  e. things that matter for a
    nation 216:7
  e. Yea 127:17
  first, last, e. day 184:6
  from e. Thou art God 562:9
  God from e. 397:15
  hill of e. youth 81:4
  set up my e. rest 478:44
  stood from e. to e. 548:14
  Timon..his e. mansion 480:32
Everlastingness: shoots of e. 552:5
Evermore: e. came out by the same
    door 206:10
  from this time forth for e. 399:29
  there is pleasure for e. 392:27
  with thy..Saints for e. 185:25
Ever-present Deity 83:8
Ever-weeping Paddington 75:3
Every: e. man..do if he would 273:12
  e. man..God or Devil 190:23
  e. man's Cleopatra 191:21
  God bless us e. one 174:10
  his hand..against e. man 44:49
  strive to please you e. day 484:27
Everybody: always suspect e. 177:35
  business of e. 324:21
  e.'s business 559:16
  he who praises e. 273:25
  if e. minded their own business 128:31

Everyone: e. against e. 248:18
  e...comes round by Rome 96:4
  e. else is 'They' 303:18
  rule applies to e. 222:7
  stop e. from doing it 243:1
  when e. is somebodee 218:30
Everything: as..Macaulay is of e. 335:13
  carry e. before me in that House 181:26
  e. by starts 190:22
  e...good for something 193:36
  e...hath two handles 109:17
  e. that he wants 265:1
  e. that lives, lives not alone 74:3
  e. that's in it 297:12
  e. you ought to be 221:42
  I'll tell thee e. I can 131:22
  know a little of e. 7:4
  knows the price of e. 570:1
  nought is e. 504:9
  place for e. 503:8
  sans e. 427:21
  smattering of e. 174:6
  they told me I was e. 454:6
  way to be a bore..say e. 557:13
Everywhere: always is All e. 185:9
  centre is e. 10:17
  e. that Mary went 233:23
  Gods see e. 315:28
  his behaviour e. 463:12
  I am in England e. 86:28
  it cometh e. 199:1
  one enemy..e. 201:23
  out of the e. 326:17
  that all men e. could be free 314:3
  water, water, e. 149:6
Eves: dream on summer e. 342:7
Evidence: compelled..to give in e. 435:35
  evidence of things not seen 69:13
  it's not e. 179:15
  only e. of life 363:15
  some circumstantial e. is very
    strong 547:4
Evil: Alexander..did me much e. 69:3
  all constraint..is e. 163:45
  all e. shed away 84:21
  all e. thoughts 389:32
  all...is to do me e. 395:14
  all partial e. 383:21
  all punishment..e. 42:22
  be not overcome of e. 66:7
  by e. still made better 488:9
  call e. good 53:6
  charity..thinketh no e. 66:45
  clear the land of e. 301:26
  days are e. 68:4
  deliver us from e. 58:4
  do e., that good may come 65:37
  done this e. in thy sight 395:7
  enslaved which serve things e. 497:6
  eschew e. 394:2
  e. and adulterous generation 59:16
  E. be thou my Good 346:33
  e...by want of thought 253:4
  e. communications corrupt 67:12
  e. is present with me 65:50
  e. manners live in brass 447:8
  e. news rides post 351:1
  e. that men do 450:17
  e. which I would not 65:49
  fall'n on e. days..e. tongues 348:23
  fat ox with e. will 50:13
  few and e... the years 45:25
  for the good or e. side 320:9
  gave himself to e. courses 577:22
  goodness in things e. 444:12
  government..a necessary e. 373:1
  his good and his e. 107:36
  his sun to rise on the e. 57:52
  imagination of man's heart is e. 44:40
  in e. hour 349:15
  I will fear no e. 393:10
  John, the e. one 74:4
  justified in doing e. 409:5
  knowing good and e. 44:20
  knowledge of good and e. 44:13
  know to refuse the e. 53:12
  leave the e. 328:2
  my tongue from e. speaking 391:8
  no e. happen unto thee 397:19
  nor done e. to his neighbour 392:24
  not a terror to good works, but..e. 66:10

Evil (cont.)
  notorious e. liver 390:1
  not rendering e. for e. 70:3
  obscures the show of e. 464:14
  of moral e. and of good 581:16
  only e. that walks invisible 346:28
  out of good..find means of e. 344:17
  overcome e. with good 66:7
  prevention from e. 329:8
  resist not e. 57:50
  resist the e. 3:18
  root of all e. 68:52
  shall there be e. in a city 55:55
  shattering all e. customs 530:30
  some e. beast hath devoured him 45:15
  speak e. of dignities 70:8
  stifling it would be an e. 338:27
  sufficient unto the day is the e. 58:15
  their deeds were e. 63:10
  thing of e. 380:26
  unruly e. 69:37
  vice..lost half its e. 102:14
  we have the e. spirits too 506:19
  what all the blessed E.'s for 89:36
  while the e. days come not 51:33
  wisdom lays on e. men 163:45
  with Predestined E. 207:11
  withstand in the e. day 68:11
Eviller spirit than you 506:19
Evils: death..the least of all e. 27:42
  don't..make imaginary e. 226:35
  e. which never arrived 199:25
  greatest of e...poverty 490:3
  must expect new e. 26:30
  notes..necessary e. 278:22
  pitch our e. there 461:35
  turn from us all those e. 389:11
  two weak e. 427:20
  when e. are most free 449:6
Evolution: e...homogeneity to..
    heterogeneity 508:25
  some call it e. 131:30
Ewe: at the e. milking 198:18
  one little e. lamb 47:33
  tupping your white e. 469:29
  whereof the e. not bites 480:12
Ewer: as safe in a golden e. 90:33
Ewes: milk my e. and weep 485:32
  my e. breed not 35:21
Ewigkeit: afay in de e. 313:12
Ewig-Weibliche: das E. 223:22
Exact: busied in charts, e. in sums 29:6
  detection is..an e. science 188:18
  greatness not..e. 100:6
  her taste e. for..fact 220:9
  very rigid and e. 293:2
  writing an e. man 27:18
Exactitude..la politesse des rois 318:23
Exactness: with e. grinds he all 315:22, 317:13
Exaggeration: chargeable with no
    e. 85:1
  report of my death..an e. 550:30
Exalt: whosoever shall e. himself 60:16
Exalted: every valley..e. 54:9
  e. them of low degree 61:14
  he..shall be e. 60:16, 62:4
  in beauty e. 579:38
  proud to be e. so 7:13
  Reason in her most e. 579:37
  Satan e. sat 345:14
Exalteth: righteousness e. a nation 50:9
  whosoever e. himself 62:4
Exalts: e., delights, or adorns
    humanity 376:11
  not what man does which e. him 96:23
Examinations are formidable 154:21
Examine me, O Lord 393:17
Example: both by precept and e. 117:16
  by the same e. 465:3
  cease, large e. 319:3
  Europe by her e. 379:16
  e. is the school of mankind 103:15
  e...more efficacious than pre-
    cept 278:18
  lower orders..set us a good e. 569:18
  profit by their e. 242:16
  thy stream my great e. 172:10
Examples: Philosophy teaching
    by e. 78:13, 180:12
Excavating for a mine 355:22

Excede, —evade, —erump! 251:20
Exceedingly: beautiful e. 150:20
Excel: Bethlehem, thou dost all e. 132:4
  daring to e. 143:9
  different men e. 143:11
  thou shalt not e. 45:26
  useless to e. 322:5
  who themselves e. 382:20
Excelled: in whom e. 349:17
Excellence: but stewards of their e. 487:25
  faults so nearly allied to e. 226:31
  in new e. divine 81:1
  ne'er will reach an e. 193:43
Excellent: everything that's e. 218:35
  e. as the cedars 52:14
  'E.!' I cried 187:24
  e. gift of charity 389:31
  e. thing in woman 454:24
  e. things are spoken of thee 397:13
  e. things for mean..uses 315:6
  e. well; you are a fishmonger 433:1
  e. wretch! 471:27
  his Name only is e. 400:25
  learning is most e. 209:19
  parts of it are e. 403:37
  so e. a king 430:33(–431)
  things that are more e. 561:14
  thou e. young man 412:12
  too wonderful and e. for me 400:8
Excellently: goddess, e. bright 279:31
Excelleth: wisdom e. folly..as light
  e. darkness 51:1
Excelling: e. in his kind 154:38
  Silvia is e. 484:40(–485)
Excels: e. all other bliss 195:12
  she e. each mortal thing 484:40(–485)
Excelsior! 316:17
Except: always e. the present company 370:7
  e. my life 433:7
Excess: best things carried to e. 143:27
  blasted with e. of light 231:13
  e. of glory obscur'd 345:5
  e. of wisdom 200:13
  give me e. of it 481:30
  moderation even in e. 182:42
  nothing in e. 12:22
  not the drinking..but the e. 422:3
  road of e. 77:8
  some divine e. 153:28
  such an e. of stupidity 271:14
  suffer so much poverty and e. 377:7
  surprise by a fine e. 289:27
  wasteful and ridiculous e. 447:39
Excessit, evasit, erupit 145:13
Excessive: dark with e. bright 346:22
  great right of an e. wrong 96:3
Exchange: by just e. 501:19
  e. thy sullen skies 162:44
  love to frequent..the Royal E. 2:9
  not e. for the treasures of India 216:18
Excise. A hateful tax 277:27
Exciseman: awa' wi' the E. 105:10
  the other an e. 226:25
Excite my amorous propensities 270:10
Excites us to arms 191:37
Exciting: found it less e. 218:16
Exclaim no more against it 471:23
Exclamation: breathed a sort of e. 237:2
Excommunicate: nor be outlawed,
  nor e. 148:10
  poor e. 125:8
Excrucior: fieri sentio et e. 133:18
Excruciating: most e. idle 304:13
Excursion: drowsy frowzy poem..
  the 'E.' 116:5
Excursions in my own mind 153:2
Excuse: all..began to make e. 62:5
  Beauty is its own e. 199:26
  denial vain, and coy e. 342:11
  e. for the glass 500:39
  e. my disobedience now 158:28
  e. my having such a thing 491:7
  I will not e. 213:17
  steal one..farthing without e. 364:1
Excused: I pray thee have me e. 62:6
Execrable shape 346:5
Execute: e. their aery purposes 344:30
  hand to e. 145:26, 217:11, 282:20
Executing: thought-e. fires 453:5
Execution: due E. upon them 401:2

Execution (*cont.*)
  fitter for e. than counsel 27:41
  smoked with bloody e. 456:5
  their stringent e. 228:23
  why the e. has not been equal 270:25
Executioner: mine own E. 186:26
Executions: marriages and public
  e. 182:23
Executive: legislative .. nominated by the e. 217:6
Executors: let's choose e. 475:6
  to e. pale 443:10
Exempt: e. from awe 497:12
  e. from public haunt 426:30
  nor yet e... from chance 497:12
Exempted: the greatest..not e. 253:36
Exercise: by temperance and e. 386:4
  devotional e. proper to..the
    Faerie Queene 306:8
  e. all functions of a man 163:12
  e. myself in great matters 400:1
  on e. depend 192:15
  sad mechanic e. 532:4
  what e. is to the body 511:28
  when I do e. 159:39
Exercises: he e. his brains 219:5
Exertions: herself by her e. 379:16
Exeter: Bedford and E. 444:28
Exeter Change 307:2
Exhalation: like some frail e. 492:18
  rose like an e. 345:11
Exhale it in a pun 307:6
Exhales her odours 117:29
Exhausted: e. air-bell of the Critic 90:30
  e. worlds 278:34
  range of e. volcanoes 181:2
Exhilarate: rural sounds e. the
  spirit 162:36
Exile: bind your sons to e. 303:24
  he suffer'd in e. 332:23
  long as my e. 429:19
  poor E. of Erin 122:10
  therefore I die in e. 232:9
Exiled: Marcellus e. 384:10
Exiles: e. from our father's land 420:31
  Paradise of e. 494:14
  woe which none save e. feel 23:25
Exilio: propterea morior in e. 232:9
Exist: for the people..all must e. 182:43
  if God did not e. 557:7
Existait: si Dieu n'e. pas 557:7
Existe: pour qui le monde extérieur e. 214:4
Existed: whether it e. before or not 289:17
Existence: before we have e., and a
  name 306:7
  called the New World into e. 124:21
  every e. would exist in Thee 83:11
  e. saw him spurn her 278:34
  for our e. as a nation 379:15
  full tide of human e. 272:25
  let us contemplate e. 176:14
  put out of e. 178:10
  struggle for e. 169:7
  subject to..the complications of
    e. 268:8
  'tis woman's whole e. 115:25
  when e. or when hope is gone 22:27
Existentibus: de non e...ratio 13:6
Existing: a type nowhere at present e. 508:24
Exists: beauty..e. in the mind 265:5
  e. with and for it 96:24
Exit: e., pursued by a bear 485:15
  shakes his head and e. 500:3
Exits: doors for men to take their e. 563:16
  their e. and their entrances 427:21
Exorciser: no e. harm thee 430:1
Exorna: hanc e. 145:2
Expanse: grey e. where he floats 16:4
  one wide e. 288:19
Expansion: not..a breach, but an
  e. 186:25
Expatiate free 383:7
Expatiates in a life to come 383:11
Expect: e. men to do 565:27
  e. thy dog 384:6
  I e. less of them 275:15
  mus' e. ter be laff'd at 238:10
  scarce e. one of my age 202:16
  what else did you e.? 91:25
  what we least e. 182:8

Expect'(*cont.*)
  what you may e. to see 183:12
Expectancy and rose 434:14
Expectant of her 543:4
Expectation: better bettered e. 467:38
  bids e. rise 224:10
  effort, and e., and desire 579:27
  e. whirls me round 481:15
  full of e. 439:10
  now sits E. in the air 443:12
  on the e. of plenty 458:17
  songs of e. 35:4
Expected: come the e. feet 338:10
  lords that are certainly e. 149:24
  may be e. with confidence 174:37
  no reasonable men could have e. 243:16
  reasonably be e. to do 565:27
Expects: England e. 362:23
  man who e. nothing 386:36
Expediency: doing evil on the
  ground of e. 409:5
Expedient: all things are not e. 66:39
  e...that I go away 63:60
  e...that one man should die 63:42
  not a principle, but an e. 180:17
  to pursue the e. 225:28
Expéditif: c'est un homme e. 354:3
Expeditious: no e. road 544:32
Expel: one passion doth e. another 135:22
Expendable: they were e. 566:16
Expende Hannibalem 283:20
Expenditure: annual e. nineteen
  nineteen six 174:24
Expense: at the e. of two? 146:34
  drinking at somebody else's e. 313:9
  e. of many a vanish'd sight 486:25
  e. of spirit 488:11
Expenses: meet all the e. of living 546:39
Expensive: fruit when it's e. 379:1
Experience: all e. is an arch 540:32
  as its e. widens 20:15
  beyond his e. 315:7
  by e. wise 386:4
  by long e., and in learned schools 4:10
  contrary to custom and e. 265:10
  dirty nurse, E. 530:43
  e...a lantern in the stern 152:24
  e. is never limited 268:12
  E. is the child of Thought 182:41
  e. joined with common-sense 231:29
  e. of women which extends 188:13
  e. teaches slowly 212:6
  e...their mistakes 570:2
  expert beyond e. 197:34
  I have had good e. of this world 198:10
  in the elder, a part of e. 27:27
  knowledge...recorded e. 125:31
  new acquist of true e. 351:7
  Old Age and E. 407:22
  old e. do attain 341:25
  perfected by e. 27:15
  running over with..e. 290:14
  triumph of hope over e. 272:4
  worth a life's e. 251:24
Experienced: e. industrious..liar 550:22
  nothing..real till..e. 290:19
Experientia does it 174:21
Experiment: barbarous e. 529:16
  democracy is only an e. 267:6
  desist from the e. in despair 306:11
  full tide of successful e. 268:20
  social and economic e. 254:4
Expert beyond experience 197:34
Experto credite 555:11
Expiate: death my days should e. 486:19
Expire: creation will e. before tea-
  time 505:8
  I tremble, I e. 493:15
Expires: blazes, and e. 117:29
  e. in the arms of an apothecary 505:28
  unawares Morality e. 381:27
  wretched child e. 41:3
Expiring frog 178:32
Explain: by trying to e. it 500:26
  e. his explanation 115:12
  I can e. all the poems 131:8
  I can't e. *myself* 128:27
  never e. 181:25
  rise to e. 238:32
Explaining a passage in the game-
  act 511:17

Explanation: explain his e. 115:12
Explanations: I do loathe e. 36:6
Expletives their feeble aid 382:30
Exploit: for dignity..and high e. 345:18
Exploration: our chant of pleasant e. 567:2
Expolitum: libellum..pumico e. 132:9
Expose: e. thyself to feel 453:15
himself alone e. 382:19
Exposed: his intellect is improperly e. 504:28
more e. to suffering 575:7
much e. to authors 564:12
on the bare earth e. 191:7
Exposes himself when..intoxicated 274:13
Exposition: I have an e. of sleep 467:16
Exposure: unseemly e. of the mind 240:12
Express: how e. and admirable may I e. thee unblamed? 433:15 / 346:18
not so much to e. our wants 226:26
picture cannot e. 25:28
to e. my nerves this night 176:35
what I can ne'er e. 114:26
Expressed: ne'er so well e. 382:27
not e. in fancy 431:25
Expresses: art never e. anything but itself 569:17
Expressing: dream that's past e. 215:37
Expression: e...in the countenance of all science 583:3
e. of no-encouragement 503:16
his e. may..be called bald 19:18
such a vulgar e. 154:31
Expressions: brave notions and gentle e. 280:1
grant me some wild e. 203:20
Expressive: eyes too e. to be blue 15:19
Expressure of his eye 482:34
Expunged: to me e. and raz'd 346:20
Exquisite: e...leaves one unsatisfied 570:8
most e. and strong 365:8
pleasure so e. 266:7
Exquisitely: so e. fair a face 222:24
Extant: the story is e. 435:17
Extend: e. from here to Mesopotamy 121:6
so let e. thy mind 350:10
Extensive and peculiar 178:35
Extent: this e., no more 469:45
whole e. of its beauty 326:3
Extenuate: nothing e. 474:2
Extenuates not wrong 481:14
Extérieur: pour qui le monde e. existe 214:4
Extinct: purpose of becoming e. 167:25
Extinction: endless e. of unhappy hates 16:25
nature is..seldom e. 26:39
Extirpate: to e. the vipers 23:26
Extol: how shall we e. thee 42:20
Extolled for standing still 162:19
Extracted from many objects 428:16
Extraction: e. of that living intellect 352:5
safe..e. of the foetus 513:12
Extracts made..by others 27:17
Extras: no e., no vacations 176:38
Extravagancies: Shakespeare..undisgraced by e. 139:21
Extravagant: e. and erring spirit 430:19
e. and wheeling stranger 469:33
plays e. matches 220:1
Extreme: e. to mark what is done amiss 399:39
had, having..e. 488:12
perplexed in the e. 474:2
savage, e., rude 488:11
where th' e. of vice 383:27
Extremes: e. by change more fierce 346:1
e. meet 253:33
toil in other men's e. 305:15
two e...like man and wife 143:25
two e. of passion 454:23
Extremity: daring pilot in e. 190:13
Extremum: spatium vitae e. 283:24
Exuberance of his own verbosity 181:12
Exult O Shores 566:28(-567)

Exultation: shadowy e. 579:17
Exultations, agonies 582:4
Exuvias indutus Achilli 554:6
Eye: affection beaming in one e. 176:10
as it were in the e. 352:6
as the apple of an e. 392:28
as the great e. of heaven 509:21
Athens, the e. of Greece 350:11
beauteous e. of heaven to garnish 447:39
blacking the Corporal's e. 295:3
broad breast, full e. 488:27
but the twinkling of an e. 393:25
by judgment of the e. 455:2
cast a longing e. on [offices] 268:24
changing, like a joyless e. 495:19
choose love by another's e. 466:19
closing e. requires 230:9
Contemplation's sober e. 231:8
cursed me with his e. 149:17
curse in a dead man's e. 149:22
darest not glance thine e. 231:36
dark and fiery e. 365:16
dayesye..the e. of day 138:19
defiance in their e. 226:14
delighting each e. 173:12
drappie in our e. 108:30
dull e. of scorn 82:1
dust hath closed Helen's e. 361:5
each under e. doth homage 486:12
enter into life with one e. 59:51
enticed mine e. 359:27
every e. shall see him 70:22
every tear from every e. 73:25
expressure of his e. 482:34
e. and prospect of his soul 469:6
e. begins to see 83:13
e. beholds the heart's desire 262:13
e. for e. 45:54
e. full of gentle salutations 513:21
e. is not satisfied 50:61
e. of heaven visits 474:19
e. of man hath not heard 467:23
e. of newt 459:31
e. that hath kept watch 576:22
e., tongue, sword 434:14
e. to see, nor tongue to speak 313:15
e. whose bend doth awe the world 448:20
e. will mark our coming 115:22
fair large front and e. sublime 347:11
fair nature's e. 330:7
far as human e. could see 534:25
fettered to her e. 319:4
fills affection's e. 275:1
flatter..with sovereign e. 486:27
fringed curtains of thine e. 479:31
fruitful river in the e. 430:30
gently shuts the e. of day 33:10
glad me with its soft black e. 177:33, 357:5
glazed each e...each weary e. 149:8
got into this e. of mine 513:22
grown beneath God's e. 96:31
guard me with a watchful E. 2:21
had but one e. 177:1
harvest of a quiet e. 578:34
have you not a moist e. 441:19
heaven in her e. 348:36
he that made the e. 397:24
his liberal e. 444:8
his mild and magnificent e. 93:3
hollow cheek or faded e. 539:1
hooded e. 544:3
I am the e. 494:1
if thine e. offend thee 59:51
I have a good e. 468:10
I have only one e. 362:21
in my mind's e. 431:5
in the e. of the beholder 265:14, 557:18
in woman's e. the..tear 115:5
lack-lustre e. 427:13
language in her e. 481:26
lend the e. a terrible aspect 443:24
Lesbia hath a beaming e. 356:24
let thine e. look like a friend 430:28
lid of a white e. 335:28
lifting up a fearful e. 508:14
light of my e. 243:5
loathsome to the e. 267:30
lock'd up from mortal e. 166:17

Eye (cont.)
long grey beard and glittering e. 148:18
many an e. has danced 251:5
microscopic e. 383:15
mighty world of e. and ear 582:2
mine e. may be deceived 487:29(-488)
moonbeams from His e. 585:8
more than meets the e. 296:30
most seeming-virtuous e. 118:9
my great Task-Master's e. 351:13
my left e. agin the Secesher's fist 560:11
my striving e. dazzles 551:17
my tiny watching e. 172:8
neither a wit in his own e. 155:17
no breath, turn of e. 96:24
nor let His e. see sin 209:4
now mine e. seeth thee 49:33
one auspicious and one dropping e. 430:24
one sin for the pride o' the e. 302:30
poet's e. 467:24
Pope..with his e. on his style 20:3
precious seeing to the e. 455:22
reverent e. must see 83:24
rhetoric of thine e. 455:10
rude e. of rebellion 447:45
see e. to e. 54:23
seeing e. 50:26
self-love possesseth all mine e. 487:10
sentry, shut your e. 301:14
set honour in one e. 448:16
sniv'ling and piping your e. 173:6
sober e. of dull Octavia 425:34
so inquiring e. 308:17
still-soliciting e. 452:11
such beauty as a woman's e. 455:21
tarnishing e. 337:6
tear was in his e. 323:4
tender e. of pitiful day 459:8
that sun, thine e. 486:33
then I saw her e. was bright 148:12
thine e. shall see thy..desire 81:25
through the e. of a needle 60:3
thou E. among the blind 576:13
to his sightless e. 362:32
too hot the e. of heaven 486:18
truckle at the e. 254:18
turned his blindest e. 140:19
unborrowed from the e. 581:26
unintelligible phrase and frightened e. 375:14
vigilant e. 429:3
Virgil..with his e. on the object 20:3
was never e... 412:19
whales..with unshut e. 15:24
what immortal hand or e. 75:24
what the e. brings means of seeing 126:13
when first your e. I ey'd 487:29
where thy grey e. glances 380:21
with a critic's e. 202:16
with an e. made quiet 581:25
with a poet's e. 122:35
with his e. on the object 20:3
with his glittering e. 148:20
with his keener e. 332:24
with hollow e. and wrinkled brow 465:9
with my inward e. 74:5
with my little e. 369:19
with, not thro', the e. 74:12
worm's e. point of view 404:2
your finger in your e. 366:15
Eye-ball: like a coal his e. 503:5
scaled e. 96:33
Eye-balls: my e. roll 382:7
two fishbones, two e. 563:37
Eyebrow: to his mistress' e. 427:21
Eyebrows: over her e. 522:3
Eyed: e. like a peacock 286:37
when first your eye I e. 487:29
Eyeing the gorgeous buttocks of the ape 266:16
Eyeless in Gaza 350:21
Eyelids: before my e. dropt 529:6
e. are a little weary 374:10
e. heavy and red 253:22
from your e...a tear 427:19
my lips and e. pale 494:7
opening e. of the morn 342:12

INDEX

Eyelids (*cont.*)

take thee with her e. 49:48
tinged the e. and the hands 374:11
tired e. 535:14
upon her e. many Graces 509:31
weigh mine e. down 441:41
Eye-offending brine 481:32
Eyes: all Heaven before mine e. 341:24
as long as her e. could see 262:8
as that youth's e. burned 411:11
before her closing e. 322:2
bein' only e. 179:16
beneath whose e. 503:2
black e. and lemonade 356:9
bold black e. 529:9
brave, joyful e. 82:1
bright e. of danger 515:29
bright e. of the dear one discover 118:33
bright e. rain influence 342:6
brightness in their failing 77:27
brings tears into his e. 127:4
cannot keep her lustrous e. 287:27
cast one's e. so low 454:3
censured by our e. 330:13
closed his e. and died 31:2
closed his e. in endless night 231:13
close up his e. 445:32
close your e. with holy dread
                         151:33(–152)
cocking their medical e. 180:1
cold commemorative e. 411:18
come and make e. at me 548:2
crowes-feet..under your e. 138:29
cynosure of neighbouring e. 342:1
dark brown e. 171:24
dark lustre of thine e. 417:26
darkness of her e. 249:9
dawned from Bullen's e. 229:19
Day's azure e. 495:1
death bandaged my e. 95:10
do me e. deceive me earsight? 560:10
dress her beauty at your e. 169:13
engendered in the e. 464:13
ever look'd with human e. 532:40
e. all the smiling family 546:26
e., and ears, and ev'ry thought 412:19
e...and see not 399:4
e. and tears be the same 332:11
e...kindled in the upper skies 199:10
e., lips, and hands to miss 186:25
e., look your last 478:44
e. of a boy 40:31
e. of conjugal attraction 347:17
e. of gold and bramble-dew 516:6
e. of most unholy blue 356:14
e. of the garden-god 523:4
e. overrunning with laughter 316:5
e. so shiny blue 511:14
e. that had lightened 523:15
e. that shone 357:13
e. that would not look on me 500:8
e. to behold the sun 51:31
e. too expressive to be blue 15:19
fair hair, and fairer e. 306:15
faith in their happy e. 42:4
fills the faint e. 497:3
fire of thine e. 75:24
five e. 171:10
foreign hands thy dying e...
    closed 381:34
four beasts full of e. 79:37
from happy human e. 516:16
from her e...messages 463:3
from his father's e. 576:10
from Marlb'rough's e. 279:10
from star-like e. 124:25
from thine e. 165:36
from women's e. 455:20, 23
full of e. within 70:38
gasp for breath..and blinded e. 372:19
gather to the e. 538:17
get thee glass e. 454:11
glory of His e. 380:6
God be in my e. 6:10
golden slumbers kiss your e. 170:23
good for sore e. 520:10
grat his e. 105:14
happiness through another
    man's e. 428:27
hath not a Jew e.? 464:8
having two e...cast into hell 59:51

Eyes (*cont.*)

heavily upon her e. 409:26
he has e. of youth 466:5
her aspect and her e. 119:1
her e. are homes of silent prayer 532:23
her e. are open 460:23
her e. as stars of twilight 580:19
her e. the gazers strike 385:11
her e. the glow-worm lend thee 246:23
her e. were darken'd wholly 534:9
her e. were deeper than the
    depth 410:7
her e. were seal'd to the holy book 15:27
her e. were wild 286:30
her hair, and e. 333:19
her longing e. are blest 517:3
her own dying smile instead of e. 491:21
her own e...see him slain 359:4
his bonny blue e. 32:15
his e...as a flame of fire 70:27
his e. drop out 315:13
his e. grow in my brow 424:1
his e. went to and fro 150:11
his e. were with his heart 114:19
his flashing e. 151:33(–152)
his sullen set e. on your own 300:7
how far your e. may pierce 452:31
if e. were made for seeing 199:26
I gave her e. my own e. to take 92:44
I have a pair of e. 179:16
I hunt for haddock's e. 131:24
in a nation's e. 230:5
in a theatre, the e. of men 475:29
in ears and e. match me 95:20
in his e. foreknowledge of death 522:7
in Huncamunca's e. 204:35
Innocence is closing up his e. 189:20
in our lips and e. 423:33
in scorn of e. 470:14
in the e. of a husband 519:34
in the optics of these e. 86:20
it dazzled their e. 31:1
item, two grey e. 482:21
I was e. to the blind 49:9
I..will lift mine e. 421:4
I will lift up mine e. 399:26
kindling her undazzled e. 352:15
knowledge to their e. 230:5
labour-dimmed e. 16:11
learned in a lady's e. 455:22
lest they see with their e. 53:10
let waking e. suffice 168:12
lidless e. in Hell 411:2
lids of Juno's e. 485:26
lift up thine e. 354:11
light in Wisdom's e. 561:11
light that lies in woman's e. 356:32
lion's ruddy e. 77:2
look'd from thoughtful e. 375:16
love-darting e. 340:38
love in her sunny e. 158:1
love looks not with the e. 466:22
lover's e. 455:22
lovers' e. are sharp 417:34
love's tongue is in the e. 209:7
maidens quiet e. 516:5
men's e. were made to look 478:13
mine e., but not my heart 280:7
mine e. dazzle 563:18
mine e. do itch 473:7
mine e. from tears 399:6
mine e. have seen the glory 264:15
mine e. their vigils keep 361:17
mine e. will tell tales 482:26
moistens my e. 191:19
my e. are dim 574:33
my e. are tired of weeping 83:3
my e...can look as swift 464:21
my e. make pictures 150:29
my e. were blind with stars 249:16
my gushing e. o'erflow 382:1
my hand before my e. 41:18
my mistress' e. 488:13
my mother came into mine e. 445:3
night has a thousand e. 79:5
Night hath a thousand e. 321:18
no e. but constitutional e. 314:16
no longer blinded by our e. 84:6
no more assail mine e. 171:7
nor image of thine e. 410:24
no speculation in those e. 459:19

Eyes (*cont.*)

not a friend to close his e. 191:7
noticeable man with large grey e. 581:19
o'er her meek e. 530:9
o'erwhelm them, to men's e. 431:19
Oh e., no e., but fountains 305:14
Oh e. sublime 89:2
one her e. 528:2
one of his e. became so terrible 38:18
one whose subdu'd e. 474:2
on his grave, with shining e. 17:9
only with thine e. 280:21
ope their golden e. 429:25
painted to the e. 183:11
pair of sparkling e. 218:25
pearls that were his e. 479:30
persuade the e. of men 486:5
pictures in our e. to get 184:30
pitch balls..for e. 455:9
poor kind wild e. 522:17
proud of those two e. 247:6
pure e. and Christian hearts 291:12
said my e. were blue 309:3
sans e. 427:21
seal her sweet e. 409:26
seel up the ship-boy's e. 442:1
see the whites of their e. 404:1
see..with no e. 454:10
set her both his e. 321:14
seven horns and seven e. 70:41
she gave me e. 581:6
show his e. 460:10
shut her wild, wild e. 286:34
shut their e. 53:10
sleep dwell upon thine e. 478:1
slepen all the night with open e. 136:22
smile in thine e. 356:17
soft e. look'd love to e. 113:25
soft look your e. had once 586:21
Sorrow..in those fair e. 7:13
soul sitting in thine e. 341:9
sparkling in her e. 468:25
streaming e. and breaking hearts 535:21
stuck full of e. 440:31
such e. the widows..wear 429:8
tear each other's e. 561:25
tempts your wand'ring e. 230:22
their pretty e. may roll 385:19
their young e. 544:20
therefore want no e. 453:38
these wakeful e. 308:14
these weeping e. 332:11
they have changed e. 479:32
thine e. break from their East 166:5
thine e. like the fishpools 52:19
this lady's lips and hands and e. 410:32
those e., the break of day 462:16
those e. the greenest 523:12
thou hast doves' e. 52:5
thou turn'st mine e. 435:48
thy e. are seen in di'monds 215:42
thy tender e. 322:8
thy two e., like stars 432:9
to dry one's e. 92:42
to her e. repair 484:40
to keep our e. open longer 85:21
to provoke e. and whispers 156:13
to the new e. of thee 545:5
turn away mine e. 399:15
two e. swoln with weeping 332:10
two lovely black e. 147:22
unfriendly to the nose and e. 516:18
unto dying e. 538:19
upon tired e. 535:14
very e. of me 247:4
very faculties of e. and ears 433:32
vision my e. do see 74:5
wanton e. 52:35
what her e. enthral'd 155:5
where e. did once inhabit 476:14
where you turn your e. 385:7
while I have e. to see 247:2
whose little e. glow 246:23
wipe my weeping e. 562:12
wise gods seel our e. 425:2
with a pair of blue e. 500:40
with erected e. 194:25
with e. as wise 83:18
with e. of flame 129:39(–130)
with e. severe 427:21
with e. uprais'd 154:1

INDEX

Eyes (cont.)
with his great e. lights the wigwam 317:23
within mine e...his nest 231:39
within the little children's e. 544:20
with longing e. I wait 543:4
with magic in my e. 236:35
with pink e. 424:19
with rainy e. 475:6
with their own e. should see 83:16
with the West in her e. 148:17
with unaffrighted e. 123:24
Wordsworth's e. avert their ken 17:3
write the beauty of your e. 486:16
your e. so blue 326:18
your quaint enamell'd e. 342:31
Eyeservice: not with e. 68:9
Eyesight: e. and speech they
 wrought 522:7
not with blinded e. 534:34

F

F: I revere the memory of Mr. F. 175:38
Fable: but that's a f. 473:33
 f., song, or fleeting shade 246:1
 life's sweet f. 166:15
 read my little f. 529:23
 sleepst by the f. of Bellerus 343:2
 that thai be nocht bot f. 33:16
 what resounds in f. or romance 345:4
Fables: blasphemous f. 401:11
 f. and endless genealogies 68:41
 Hesperian f. true 347:5
 Luther bloomed f. 97:11
 old wives' f. 68:47
 rather believe all the f. 25:23
 worse than f. yet have feigned 346:3
Fabric: baseless f. of this vision 480:8
 f. huge rose 345:11
 his f. of the Heavens 348:30
 quality and f. more divine 579:38
 silently..the f. rose 163:40
Fabrum esse suae quemque fortunae 414:23
Fabula: mutato nomine de te f. narratur 261:8
Fabulous animals..who used to
 sing 176:5
Fac: ama et f. quod vis 22:3
Face: am I in f. to-day? 227:2
 as he has hit his f. 281:9
 beautiful f. is a..commendation 24:37
 beauty..shall pass into her f. 581:22
 beefy an' grubby 'and 299:14
 behold her f. at ample view 481:32
 beholding his natural f. in a
 glass 69:33
 blubber'd..that pretty f. 401:19
 bright f. of danger 513:28
 called..to f. some awful moment 575:10
 carnations..o'erspread her f. 190:6
 cheer our soiled f. 400:33
 Cherub's f. 385:33
 continual comfort in a f. 412:18
 cover her f. 563:18
 Desert's dusty F. 205:27
 divine plain f. 307:15
 dont quite match your f. 20:28
 dost thou fall upon thy f.? 477:3
 down his dappled f. 546:21
 each turned his f. 149:17
 emptiness of ages in his f. 329:19
 everybody's f. but their own 519:4
 F. like my f. 96:25
 f. of all the world is changed 88:17
 f. of earth around 515:28
 F. of Man..blacken'd 207:12
 f. of night is fair 536:23
 f. that launch'd a thousand ships 330:5
 f. that's anything but gay 543:6
 f. the index 165:15
 f. to lose youth for 93:1
 false f. must hide..false heart 457:16
 fiery f. as of a child 530:29
 find one f. there 293:19
 finer form, or lovelier f. 416:16
 flower-like f. 524:17
 fondles his own harmless f. 527:23
 foolish f. of praise 385:29

Face (cont.)
 garden in her f. 124:4
 garden of your f. 243:18
 gazed on the f. that was dead 572:13
 give me a f. 280:7
 glimpse of His bright f. 552:3
 God hath given you one f. 434:12
 good f. is a letter 2:14
 grey mist on the sea's f. 334:10
 her f. between her hands 410:14
 her f. was full of woe 7:13
 he shows his honest f. 191:3
 hides a smiling f. 161:18
 hid his f. amid a crowd of stars 586:21
 his colours..hid the f. 192:17
 his f., that..hath died 540:26
 his f...thunder had intrenched 345:7
 his f. when he repeats his verses 307:13
 His own f. to see 249:10
 honest labour bears a lovely f. 170:21
 huge massy f. 325:28
 human f. divine 346:20
 in..f. and limb 313:7
 in f. of man or maid 544:20
 in his morning f. 225:1
 in my own f. in the glass 567:24
 in one Autumnal f. 184:16
 in the f. of this congregation 391:22
 in the sweat of thy f. 44:27
 in the sweet f. of heaven 453:19
 it illumineth the f. 442:21
 I who saw the f. of God 330:2
 Jealousy a human f. 77:4
 kindred soul out to his f. 95:35
 kissing with golden f. 486:27
 knew thy f. or name 184:4
 Lake Leman..with its crystal f. 113:45
 languid patience of thy f. 152:19
 lives on this lonely f. 585:22
 looked up and shew'd his f. 165:36
 look in my f. 548:19
 look into thy bonnie f. 104:26
 look on her f. 385:12
 looks the whole world in the f. 318:12
 loved a happy human f. 266:3
 loved its silly f. 405:16
 loving thy mournful f. 269:31
 make his f. shine upon thee 46:10
 make the f. of heaven so fine 478:20
 many a f...groweth to fair 80:23
 mask of night is on my f. 477:18
 Maud with her exquisite f. 535:39
 mind's construction in
 the f. 456:27(-457)
 mist in my f. 95:8
 Monday's child is fair of f. 368:1
 Moses hid his f. 45:35
 most kiss-worthy f. 502:1
 moved upon the f. of the waters 44:1
 my f. is my fortune 369:15
 my f. is pink 8:16
 my f., your flower 91:35
 my Pilot f. to f. 528:22
 neither by hir wordes ne hir f. 137:24
 never f. so pleased 10:20, 210:5
 no glorious morning f. 516:16
 noo mwore do zee your f. 35:16
 nor turn my f. 97:27
 not a trace upon her f. 219:33
 not recognize me by my f. 549:10
 no wonder but the human f. 285:34
 on his smiling f. a dream 152:17
 on the f. of the tiger 11:2
 on whose awful f. 355:15
 other's umber'd f. 444:6
 Pity a human f. 77:1
 praised him to his f. 540:3
 sages have seen in thy f. 164:22
 same f. of his wedded wife 304:36
 seek His F. 354:11
 seems to hide his f. 351:7
 seen God f. to f. 45:11
 set upon it a good f. 29:16
 she has a lovely f. 534:10
 she look'd in my f. 35:9
 shining morning f. 427:21
 since first I saw your f. 9:21
 singing f. 38:11
 so exquisitely fair a f. 222:24
 some features of my father's f. 118:29
 so sweet a f. 528:2

Face (cont.)
 spirituality about the f. 188:9
 sprinkles another's laughing f. 308:18
 spy in thy f. 184:19
 stand f. to f. 294:27
 still we find her f. 94:8
 that donkey..his f. was sad 504:3
 that homely f. 573:22
 that lovely f. who view 15:18
 that moment that his f. I see 150:12
 that one F...grows 91:14
 that very f. 517:19
 them that will f. me 439:16
 then f. to f. 66:46(-67)
 thy classic f. 380:17
 thy f. across his fancy comes 538:22
 thy way plain before my f. 392:4
 to draw a full f. 194:17
 transmitter of a foolish f. 415:16
 truth has such a f. 192:22
 two souls..f. to f. 88:19
 unclouded f. of truth 416:4
 visit her f. too roughly 430:33(-431)
 watered the..f. of the ground 44:10
 we wear a f. of joy 574:35
 where's the f. ? 285:40
 white f. in the coffin 567:5
 with a caricature of a f. 220:10
 with a sad swell'd f. 34:19
 with broad and burning f. 149:12
 with his prism and silent f. 579:19
 with twain he covered his f. 53:8
 wi' usquebae, we'll f. the devill 108:10
 your f., and the God-curst sun 236:19
 your f...is as a book 457:5
 your f. my quarry was 78:2
 your honest sonsie f. 106:4
Face-flatterer and backbiter 531:23
Faces: bend other f. 308:13
 brake them to our f. 88:14
 confusion of their own f. 55:15
 daub their natural f. 87:35
 dusk f. 350:9
 f. are but a gallery 26:16
 flame of fair f. 523:2
 Gate with dreadful f. throng'd 349:31
 grace-proud f. 106:34
 grind the f. of the poor 52:34
 his pencil our f. 225:34
 I know the f. I shall see 411:14
 in the f. of men and women..
 God 567:24
 make our f. vizards 459:5
 mild monastic f. 146:12
 millions of f...none alike 86:29
 ne'er touched earthly f. 486:16
 new men, strange f. 531:34
 nice clean f. 34:9
 old familiar f. 308:1
 owners of their f. 487:25
 seen better f. in my time 452:35
 set upon tables..to make f. 272:34
 set your f. like a flint 99:13
 [Shakespeare]..wears..two f. 194:10
 slope of f. 163:28
 their f. washed 130:13
 their innocent f. clean 76:15
 Thracian ships and the foreign f. 521:30
 'tis your estrangèd f. 545:1
 when they turned their f. 323:25
Facetious..not necessary to be
 indecent 408:3
Facilis descensus Averni 554:23
Facilité: la vertu refuse la f. 355:2
Facility: elegance, f...of poesy 455:14
 f. of the octo-syllabic verse 114:41
 flowed with that f. 280:1
Facing: as he has sat f. it 304:36
 f. fearful odds 323:17
Fact: Death was but a scientific f. 569:7
 f...opposed to..deductions 188:25
 fatal futility of F. 268:9
 for faultless f. 220:9
 irritable reaching after f. 289:21
 judges of f. 403:2
 man's religion is the chief f. 126:21
 matters of f...very stubborn 548:3
 more miraculous than the f. 265:7
 omitted to mention the f. 128:5
 push the logic of a f. 296:14
 rudest work that..records a f. 413:11

[705]

Fact (cont.)
slaying..by an ugly f. 266:19
Faction: it made them a f. 325:35
Whig..a f. 277:32
Factions: good in canvasses and f. 25:41
old religious f. are volcanoes 101:31
Fac totum: absolute *Iohannes* f. 232:6
Facts: at the same time attesting f. 265:8
F. alone are wanted in life 175:28
f. are f. and flinch not 96:1
f. are sacred 416:4
f. were never pleasing to him 36:5
F...winna ding 105:11
fashionable f. and polite anygoats 543:1
intelligent anticipation of f. 107:27
to his imagination for f. 501:1
Faculties: borne his f. so meek 457:9
duty to preserve our f. 273:20
f. which sense may reach 185:2
from each according to his f. 29:14
his cogitative f. immers'd 125:13
very f. of eyes and ears 433:32
whose f. can comprehend 330:28
Faculty: f. divine 574:10
how infinite in f. 433:15
Faddling hedonist 514:16
Fade: banks f. dimmer away 16:4
cheek that doth not f. 285:39
elms f. into dimness 17:16
f. away suddenly like the grass 397:15
f. far away, dissolve 287:25
f. into the light of common day 576:9
feel like flowers that f. 527:12
first to f. away 121:8, 357:5
how fast they f. away 4:6
may flourish, or may f. 224:14
nothing of him that doth f. 479:30
pleasure soon shall f. 233:3
see the gold air..f. 411:4
sorrow f. 151:18
they only f. away 9:2
we all do f. as a leaf 55:8
with thee f. away 287:24
Faded: f. and gone 356:36
f. 'midst Italian flowers 241:10
f. on the crowing of the cock 430:20
f. splendour wan 347:32
hits off the f. graces 240:6
light of other days is f. 99:1
oldest colours have f. 303:19
she f., like a cloud 491:20
Fades: f. awa' like morning dew 32:18
f. out from kiss to kiss 584:24
memory f. 171:8
my native shore f. 113:6
now f. the glimmering landscape 229:28
now f. the last long streak 533:24
until she f. away 141:35
whatever f.,..fading pleasure 502:5
Fadeth: after sunset f. in the west 487:16
grass withereth, the flower f. 54:10
Fading: f. down the river 363:6
flowers but f. seen 377:4
how f. are the joys 305:8
in f. silks compose 571:18
life is f. fast away 406:8
primrose f. timelessly 341:6
Fadler: like my Lady F. 156:13
Faece: in *Romuli* f. 145:1
Faenore: *solutis omni* f. 257:22
Faenum habet in cornu 261:13
Faerie Queene: before reading the
F. 306:8
Faery: in f. lands forlorn 288:1
land of f. 585:14
Fagi: *recubans sub tegmine* f. 555:14
Fähigkeiten: *jeder nach seinen* F. 333:12
Fail: desire shall f. 51:33
f...in the House of Lords 182:47
f., Sun and Breath 413:31
heart and voice would f. me 35:11
I die! I faint! I f.! 494:7
if we should f. 457:13
in that it seems to f. 95:16
I will not f. thee 46:36
I will not f. to meet thee 292:19
I would sooner f. 290:8
let no man's heart f. 47:21
many f.; the one succeeds 528:26
my due feet never f. 341:23
no such word as—f. 322:12

Fail (cont.)
not ashamed to f. 278:27
not f. beneath my feet 536:1
not o word wol he f. 137:39
O then it did not f. 77:5
prophecies, they shall f. 66:45
some night you'll f. us 95:1
that cannot f. 35:3
thy years shall not f. 398:2
troubles..shall not f. 263:32
we'll not f. 457:13
we shall not flag or f. 143:40
you're pooty sure to f. 319:27
Failed: f. in literature and art 182:21
f.; therefore..turn critics 152:30
fluttered and f. for breath 17:15
Light that F. 304:33
tried a little, f. much 513:36
Faileth: charity never f. 66:45
f. now even dream 544:23
faints not, nor f. 147:8
whose goodness f. never 29:12
Failing: every f. but their own 117:40
his pulse f., Passion 189:20
principal f...in the sailing 128:9
she had one f. 106:31
Failings: his f. lean'd to Virtue 224:21
Fails: f. my heart 361:23
if thy heart f. thee 198:8, 405:11
one sure, if another f. 96:40
Failure: another Faithful F. 514:1
high f. overleaps the bounds 358:22
pays the f. of years 89:20
Failures: half the f. in life 237:22
Fain: f. die a dry death 479:18
f...fling the net 336:10
f. would I climb 198:8, 405:11
home f. wad I be 167:22
we are f. of thee still, we are f. 522:26
Faint: beginning to f. in the light 536:10
damn with f. praise 385:29
eating hay when you're f. 131:16
f. and far away 366:5
f. and partial 142:4
f. beneath the aromatic pain 571:19
f. heart ne'er wan 104:22
f. heart never won fair lady 219:14
f. not nor fear 354:12
f., now, as farewells 253:15
f. on hill or field or river 538:16
f., yet pursuing 46:54
he was ready to f. 311:4
I die! I f.! I fail! 494:7
I do f. therefor 545:5
if we f. not 67:48
my love is weak and f. 161:13
of which the echo..f. at last 309:13
so f., so spiritless 441:9
to pray, and not to f. 62:32
touched the hem..felt f. 496:17
walk, and not f. 54:14
whole heart f. 52:27
with study f. 143:13
Fainted: f. on his vengefulness 336:19
I should utterly have f. 393:22
their soul f. in them 398:15
Faintest: why f. thou? 19:1
Fainting: f., dispirited race 17:20
to f. Squadrons 1:10
Faintly, gentle springs 279:28
Faints: enemy f. not 147:8
f. the cold work 153:28
sense f. picturing them 496:8
where whoso gazes f. 497:9
Fair: all so excellently f. 151:2
all that's good, and all that's f. 558:1
all this f., and soft 332:8
almost damn'd in a f. wife 469:21
angels are painted f. 371:12
anything but what's right and f. 265:1
as f. as e'er was seen 572:3
as young and f. as aught 112:30
Bacchus f. 191:2
black man or a f. man 2:4
bloom sae fresh and f. 108:36
chaste and f. 279:31
deserves the f. 190:34
die because a woman's f. 572:2
drink f. 176:32
Elaine the f. 530:33
ever f. and never proud 470:29

Fair (cont.)
every f. from f...declines 486:18
f. and f., and twice so f. 377:2
f. and fatal King 269:29
f. and flagrant things 165:26
f. and learn'd and good as she 87:24
f. and yet not fond 173:1
f. and wise and good and gay 368:1
f. as is the rose in May 138:21
f. as the lily 156:19
f. as the moon 52:15
f. as the rash oath 375:8
f. be their wives 195:6
F. commands the song 162:32
f. days will shine 221:30
f. fa' your..face 106:4
f., fat, and forty 420:20
f. hair, and fairer eyes 306:15
f. is foul and foul is f. 456:3
f. is too foul an epithet 331:1
f. sex is your department 188:8
f. stood the wind for France 189:6
f. terms and a villain's mind 463:25
f., the chaste 427:23
f. the fall of songs 516:3
f. these broad meads 420:31
f. with orchard lawns 531:37
f. woman..without discretion 49:58
f. women and brave men 113:25
fashion all things f. 236:6
fat, f., and forty..all the toasts 370:6
for ever..she be f. 287:9
full and f. ones 245:21
gift for my f. 499:15
going to the f. 368:19
hand that hath made you f. 462:12
her care was but to be f. 561:7
her f. and floral air 208:5
holy, f., and wise is she 484:40
how sweet and f. she seems 558:4
if the two services..had f. play 310:25
I have sworn thee f. 488:22
I loved a lass, a f. one 572:3
in a f. ground 302:13, 392:26
in Heaven ye wander f. 75:18
in thee f. and admir'd 423:15
Irish are a f. people 272:21
is she kind as she is f.? 484:40
just as pure and f. 219:2
Lady Jane was f. 34:13
loving and a f. reply 430:32
magnificent f. play of the British
criminal law 187:25
maiden f. to see 315:26
man right f. 488:18
many a face..groweth to f. 80:23
Mistress moderately f. 158:13
Monday's child is f. of face 368:1
more f. than words can say 528:1
more than most f. 232:11
more wondrous..the charming F. 74:8
most divinely f. 529:8
mud, celestially f. 83:27
near to good..what is f. 281:1
never..foolish that was f. 470:28
never won f. lady 219:14
nor Cynthia teeming shows so f. 332:10
not anything to show more f. 582:1
not f. to outward view 148:12
nothing but well and f. 351:6
nothing is f...alone 199:9
O f.! O sweet! 502:7
O love, thou art f. 522:8
outward be f. 143:12
pitiful as she is f. 231:37
rise up, my love, my f. one 52:1
Sabrina f. 341:3
say that thou wast f. 15:18
she f., divinely f. 349:12
so exquisitely f. a face 222:24
so foul and f. a day 456:12
so young, so f. 114:24
that f. mot she falle 138:19
that f. thou ow'st 486:18
that was only f. 297:19
this f. defect of Nature 349:23
this isn't f. dealing 300:7
thou art all f., my love 52:6
thou art f., my love 52:5
thou, that didst appear so f. 582:20
to be f. 322:3

INDEX

Fair (cont.)

to Widdicombe F.   33:1
true and f.   186:17
universal frame, thus wondrous f.   348:4
were women never so f.   321:13
what care I how f. she be   572:2
where even the old are f.   585:15
who art so lovely f.   472:35
whose scent the f. annoys   159:18
wind was f.   192:31
with constant drinking fresh and f.   158:7
with my own f. hands   519:23
women f. as she   238:30
ye say it will be f. weather   59:41
young, and so f.   252:12
Faire: laissez f., laissez passer   404:19
Fairer: be she f. than the day   572:2
can't say no f. than that   175:4
f. far in May   282:1
f. far than this fair day   494:8
f. person lost not heaven   345:18
f. than feign'd of old   350:4
f. than the evening air   330:6
f. than..wakened eyes behold   497:22
f. than whitest snow   330:21
f. way is not much about   24:32
none is f. seen   376:3
yet far f. than you are   423:17
Fairest: f. among women   51:41
f. of her daughters Eve   347:13
f. things have fleetest end   543:24
leader is f.   15:16
my f., my espoused   348:1
O f. of creation   349:17
water f. meadows   164:5
with flowers of the f.   147:24
Fairies: beginning of f.   36:7
do you believe in f.?   36:10
f. at the bottom of our garden   212:20
f. black, grey, green   466:15
f. break their dances   264:1
f.' coach-makers   477:7
f., dancing under the moon   586:16
farewell rewards and f.   157:3
I don't believe in f.   36:8
she is the f.' midwife   477:7
since the f. left off dancing   422:7
Fairing: thou'll get thy f.   108:14
Fairly: which may f. be done   363:11
Fairs: wakes, and bear-baitings   485:20
Fair-spoken: wise, f., and per-
    suading   447:9
Fairway: mines reported in the f.   299:25
Fairy: almost f. time   467:34
by f. Fiction drest   229:26
by f. hands   153:30
calls up the realms of f.   110:15
come not near our f. queen   466:44
cradle of the f. queen   467:4
delightful F. Prince   336:21
die soon, O f.'s son   509:29
F. in a nut   75:15
f. kind of writing   192:41
f. land..dine at five   515:17
f. Queen Proserpina   123:26
f. tales of science   534:14
'f. way of writing'   2:20
full beautiful, a f.'s child   286:30
light she was and like a f.   355:23
like a f. trip   488:26
loveliest in the world   294:9
Mab, the Mistress-F.   281:5
no f. takes   430:20
quoth the F., nidding, nodding   171:18
raised a f. isle   376:6
rubies, f. favours   466:34
sing a f.'s song   286:31
to wrap a f. in   466:41
with a f., hand in hand   586:9
Fais ce que vouldras   404:28
Fait: un lieu..un seul f.   78:6
Faith: all made of. and service   428:28
all that f. creates   496:19
Articles of the Christian F.   391:2
author and finisher of our f.   69:18
blest by f.   579:38
bloody F. the foulest birth   493:17
by f., by admiration   201:3
constitutes poetic f.   152:26
disturb our cheerful f.   582:3

Faith (cont.)

doubt diversified by f.   89:32
duty, f., love, are roots   377:4
ever the f. endures   241:26
f. and fire within us   236:18
f. and morals..which Milton
    held   577:3
f. as a grain of mustard seed   59:47
F., fanatic F.   357:10
f., hope and charity   66:46(-67), 389:46
f. in a nation of sectaries   181:41
f. in their happy eyes   42:4
f. in womankind   539:8
F. is kneeling by his bed   189:20
f. is..things hoped for   69:13
f. of Christ crucified   390:58
f. of our fathers   202:27
f. of the poor   142:4
f...panting for a happier seat   279:14
f. shines equal   83:7
f. that launched point-blank   91:34
f. that looks through death   576:20
f. that ye share   302:26
f. unfaithful   530:37
f. which does not doubt is dead f.   551:1
f. without works is dead   69:35
f.'s daughter   35:21
f.'s transcendent dower   573:27
fight the good fight of f.   68:53
for modes of f.   384:1
fought for Queen and F.   540:3
gather his f. together   81:23
gentleness, goodness, f.   67:46
guid f. he mauna fa' that   105:32
her f. thro' form   532:24
his f...might be wrong   158:5
if I break f.   454:35
if thy F. is entire   81:25
I have kept the f.   68:60
I mean the F.'s Defender   112:25
impossibilities enough..for an
    active f.   86:6
in f. and hope..disagree   384:1
in thy f. and fear   390:30
just shall live by f.   65:31
land of..our f., our pride   295:8
more f. in honest doubt   533:14
moved by f. to assent   265:10
my life upon her f.   470:12
my staff of f.   405:9
my strong f. shall purchase   125:8
not alter in my f. of him   279:32
not f. but mere Philosophy   86:22
not for all his f.   199:21
not found so great f.   58:32
no tricks in plain and simple f.   451:9
now abideth f., hope, charity   66:46(-67)
purest f. unhappily forsworn   487:14
puts me from my f.   440:1
regained by f.   238:29
sacred dictates of thy f.   412:16
scientific f.'s absurd   91:11
Sea of F.   15:7
serious f., and inward glee   578:11
shake a man's f. in himself   489:14
shield of f.   68:13
simple f. than Norman blood   533:38
Thee by f...confess'd   264:8
their f. upon..pike and gun   110:17
them that do not have the f.   142:7
these all died in f.   69:15
tho' f. and form be sunder'd   533:28
though I have all f.   66:45
thou of little f.   59:37
three sweet Graces; F., Hope,
    Charity   308:13
'tis a point of f.   166:16
'tis not dying for a f.   542:9
to a seductive lay..f.   573:9
to hem yeve I f.   138:16
vain f., and courage vain   323:7
want of f. in all   531:10
we have kept the f.   84:3
welcome..discarded f.   447:45
welcome pure-ey'd F.   340:11
we walk by f.   67:25
what more could fright my f.?   192:23
which F. except every one do
    keep   388:37
with a stronger f. embrace   319:10
with f., with hope, with charity   245:9

Faith (cont.)

with my childhood's f.   88:24
woman's f., and woman's trust   419:15
Faithful: among the faithless, f.
    only he   348:18
another F. Failure   514:1
army of the f.   336:4
as the f. years return   299:24
be thou f. unto death   70:30
come, all ye f.   13:2, 369:20
company of all f. people   390:46
f. and just to me   450:19
f. are the wounds of a friend   50:45
f., below   173:11
f. in that which is least   62:22
f. of thy word   355:20
f. to God and thee   248:7
f. to thee, Cynara   187:9
God is f.   66:38
he..was called F. and True   71:36
in action f.   385:6
love..free and f.   161:12
O f. shepherd!   17:19
so f. in love   418:16
these words are true and f.   71:45
Faithfully: pronounce it f.   477:20
to my Prince f.   316:32
Faithfulness: his f. and truth   397:18
Faithless: faithful found among
    the f.   348:18
f. and stubborn generation   396:33
f. as the winds or seas   421:13
f. was she   16:1
not f., but believing   64:10
Faiths: both were f.   16:6
f. and empires gleam   493:25
men's f. are wafer-cakes   443:23
old f. loosen and fall   525:9
Falchion: my good biting f.   454:25
Falcon: dapple-dawn-drawn F.   255:11
f...hawk'd at and kill'd   458:28
gentle as f.   502:17
Falconer: for a f.'s voice   477:26
Falernian: real F. winged the pen   120:24
Falero, lero, loo!   572:4
Faliero my Leipsic   116:34
Falkland: like F. fall   117:22
Fall: all kings shall f. down before
    him   396:25
although it f. and die   282:1
another thing to f.   461:23
beheld Satan as lightning f.   61:36
both shall f. into the ditch   59:39
by dividing we f.   180:5
chapter on the F. of the Rupee   569:26
console us when we f.   100:15
diggeth a pit shall f. into it   51:24
dost thou f. upon thy face?   477:3
fair the f. of songs   516:3
f...an unpitied sacrifice   101:36
f. at her flying feet   123:22
f. behind and graze him   38:24
f. below Demosthenes   202:16
f. by little and little   56:47
f. down flumpetty   311:23
f. into the hands of God   540:1
f. into the hands of..God   69:12
f. into the hands of the Lord   56:31
f. into the ocean   330:11
f. not out by the way   45:24
f. on us, and hide us   71:2
f. out, and chide, and fight   561:27
f. out with those we love   538:9
f. without shaking   354:14
fear I to f.   405:11
frighted thou let'st f.   485:26
given the devil a foul f.   358:2
great was the f. of it   58:28
had a great f.   367:5
half to f.   383:22
haughty spirit before a f.   50:15
here didst thou f.   450:9
his f. was destined   279:6
hope to rise, or fear to f.   583:11
if he f. in, good-night   438:37
if I slip, Thou dost not f.   147:14
impute my F. to Sin   207:10, 11
in the f. of a sparrow   437:34
in this we stand or f.   348:12
it had a dying f.   481:30
it is good to f.   567:15

INDEX

Fall (cont.)
laugh at a f.   92:42
less likely to f.   215:10
lest I should fear and f.   87:37
lest they f. upon thee   393:34
let f. your horrible pleasure   453:6
let us worship and f. down   397:27
like Falkland f.   117:22
mountains..come and f. on me   330:8
needs fear no f.   99:31
nodding to its f.   384:5
not too high to f.   334:19
nowhere to f. but off   292:15
one of them shall not f.   58:52
raise up them that f.   389:1
safe where men f.   84:19
some by virtue f.   461:24
sparrow f.   383:10
survived the f.   163:6
suffer us not..to f. from thee   391:43
take heed lest he f.   66:38
take warning by the f.   30:4
therefore f. the people unto
  them   396:26
tho' he trip and f.   539:8
thousand shall f. beside thee   397:18
thou wilt f. backward   477:3
we f. to rise   97:4
what a f. was there   450:31
what stands if Freedom f.?   296:20
whoso doeth these things shall
  never f.   392:24
why do ye f. so fast?   245:20
wither long before it f.   113:38
with many a f.   408:10
without thee cannot but f.   389:47
with shuddering f.   336:41
Fallacy: the 'Pathetic F.'   412:26
Fallen: Babylon is f., is f.   71:25
brought down, and f.   392:37
f. at length that tower of strength 537:15
f. by the tongue   57:3
f. cold and dead   566:28(-567)
f. from his high estate   191:7
f. on evil days   348:23
f. to dust   569:15
follow..a f. lord   424:30
for the f. and the weak   320:14
how are the mighty f.   47:29, 30
how art thou f. from heaven   53:22
how f., how changed   344:11
or be for ever f.   344:27
risen stars and the f. cling to
  her   521:30(-522)
though f., great   113:17
ye are f. from grace   67:44
Fallere: quis f. possit amantem?   554:18
Fallest: if thou f...thou f. a
  blessed martyr   446:31
Falleth: alone when he f.   56:34
flower thereof f. away   69:46
that f. on the grass   7:16
where the tree f.   51:28
Falling: Anio, f., f. yet   146:13
bears the f. sky   263:18
catch a f. star   186:16
f. from that apple-tree?   228:6
f. one by one   205:16
f. out of faithful friends   196:2
f. stars are shooting   118:8
gently f. on thy head   562:1
greatly f., with a f. State   381:7
he hath the f. sickness   448:28
Lady, the stars are f.   140:26
like a f. star   345:12
load a f. man   447:12
my feet from f.   395:16, 399:6
shades of night were f. fast   316:17
when heaven was f.   264:4
Fallings from us, vanishings   576:18
Falls: brightness f. from the air   361:5
darkness f. from..Night   316:7
famous for his f.   375:22
fast f. the eventide   322:1
o'erleaps..and f. on the other   457:9
professionally he declines and f.   178:3
sing of her with f.   88:13
then he f., as I do   446:24
when he f. he f. like Lucifer   446:24
when Rome f.   114:21
where breathes the foe but f.   234:13

Falsa..mittunt insomnia manes   555:2
False: all was f. and hollow   345:18
among innumerable f.   348:18
any other thing that's f.   117:13
beware of f. prophets   58:25
both f. and friendly   315:26
by the philosopher, as equally f.   217:5
f. Achitophel   190:13
f. as dicers' oaths   435:42
f., ere I come, to two or three   186:18
f. face must hide..f. heart   457:16
f., fleeting, perjur'd Clarence   476:16
f. philosophy   345:30
f. though she be   155:37
for f. quantities..whipt   194:26
framed to make women f.   470:21
if she be f.   471:41
I hate f. words   309:16
in a f. quarrel..no true valour   469:14
in perils among f. brethren   67:35
love of f. and cruel men   332:29
man, f. man   312:27
men would be f.   321:13
my f. lover stole my rose   108:39
none was f. to you   80:7
not bear f. witness   390:16
not f. to others   27:37
opinion..a f. opinion   338:27
prove f. again   111:11
ring out the f.   533:18
round numbers are always f.   273:26
some f. impossible shore   18:20
taking true for f., or f. for true   530:8
that I was f. of heart   488:4
thou canst not then be f.   431:25
thou f. tongue   399:24
'tis f., my Arab steed   365:20
'tis hard if all is f.   159:12
to bring the f. to light   81:13
what is f. within   336:30
what the f. heart doth know   457:16
words may be f.   422:27
wouldst not play f.   457:1
Falsehood: f. has a perennial
  spring   100:7
f. is worse in kings   429:35
heart for f. framed   500:10
its f. would be more miraculous   265:7
let her and F. grapple   352:17
no f. can endure   347:29
some dear f.   357:10
strife of Truth with F.   320:9
their being detected in any f.   265:8
time..to unmask f.   486:7
vizor'd f.   340:33
what a goodly outside f. hath   463:19
your bait of f.   432:33
Falsely: kept him f. true   530:37
  prophets prophesy f.   55:13
Falseness in all our impressions   412:26
Falser: tomorrow's f.   191:34
Falstaff: F., and all the merry men
  of East-cheap   226:28
F. shall die of a sweat   443:1
F. sweats to death   439:8
sweet Jack F.   439:37
Falter: change, nor f., nor repent   497:17
f., are lost in the storm   17:18
f. life away   18:12
Faltered: if I have f. more or less   516:16
Fama: feret haec aliquam..f. salu-
  tem   553:18
Fame: blush to find it f.   386:20
bring you to good f.   328:2
damned to everlasting f.   384:12
damned to f.   381:20, 415:18
desire of f.   530:14
enough my meed of f.   250:25
ere her cause bring f.   320:12
establishment of my f.   217:3
estate, good f.   199:12
fair f. inspires   385:29
f...an empty name   143:2
f. can never heal   23:25
f...dead men eat   183:9
f. is like a river   27:1
f. is no plant..mortal soil   342:22
f. is the spur   342:20
F. sounds the heroic syllables   116:26
f., that all hunt after   454:29
F.'s eternal beadroll   510:5

Fame (cont.)
for his f. the ocean sea   35:23
full of phrase and f.   19:5
great heir of f.   351:8
he died the death of f.   417:18
he mistook it for f.   225:33
her f. survives   351:4
his f. soon spread around   160:2
honour be yours, and f.   362:31
hope of a season's f.   363:4
house of ancient f.   510:21
imped the wings of f.   125:1
in the mouth of f.   280:12
love and f. to nothingness   289:6
man dreams of f.   531:14
my f. for a pot of ale   443:28
no one shall work for f.   303:21
oh F.!—if I e'er took delight   118:33
of so much f. in Heaven   342:23
openeth the gate to good f.   26:4
passion for f.   100:11
poet's food is love and f.   493:19
rapt with love of f.   331:2
rather use than f.   531:15
servants of f.   26:22
speaking trump of future f.   117:19
temple of f...upon the grave   239:20
titles, wealth, and f.   381:36
to fortune and to f. unknown   230:13
to grow great in f.   173:4
what is f.?   228:12
which f. did not delay   189:8
while f. elates thee   356:19
whose f. over his living head   492:1
yet..your f. is bright   81:21
you shall live by f.   509:7
Famed in all great arts   18:1
Fames: malesuada F.   554:27
Familiar: don't let us be f. or fond   156:13
f. acts are beautiful through
  love   497:13
f., but by no means vulgar   431:25
f. but not coarse   278:9
more f. grown   546:26
old f. faces   308:1
our names f. in his mouth   444:28
that once f. word   36:31
wine..a good f. creature   471:23
with such f. instances   451:8
Familiarity begets boldness   331:10
Familiarly: as f. of John a Gaunt   442:17
Families: all happy f. resemble
  each other   548:7
good f...worse than any others   254:12
great f. of yesterday   170:14
in the best-regulated f.   174:37
mothers of large f.   40:29
murder..seems..to run in f.   313:23
old f. last not three oaks   87:14
rooks in f. homeward   236:33
secrets in all f.   203:15
your antediluvian f.   155:19
Family: character of a f. to an
  hypothesis   513:6
each unhappy f...in its own way   548:7
eyes all the smiling f.   546:26
Ha! ha! F. Pride   220:1
his f. was not unworthy of him   182:12
honest man..brought up a large
  f.   227:15
in the bosom of her respectable
  f.   103:35
my f. pride is..inconceivable   219:17
one of Eve's f.   252:16
strenuous f.   516:19
Famine: they that die by f.   242:9
Famous: be f. then by wisdom   350:10
f. by my sword   355:20
f. by their birth   474:22
f., calm, and dead   91:38
f. for his falls   375:22
f. to all ages   352:27
found myself f.   120:1
now praise f. men   57:14, 302:4
Fan: f. the sinking flame of hilarity   177:29
this was the Pompadour's F.   183:18
with her f. spread and streamers
  out   156:1
Fanatics have their dreams   285:32
Fancies: f. flee away   99:37
f. fugitive   96:26

INDEX

Fancies (cont.)

f. that broke through language 95:21
full of f. as to a love-lady 29:6
heart of furious f. 12:2
high region of his f. 352:20
lay your earthly f. down 537:28
our f. are more giddy 483:3
my f., fly before ye 166:22
proud and full of f. 289:10
set your f. free 97:2
thick-coming f. 460:37

Fancy: bright-eyed F. 231:15
by hopeless f. feign'd 538:19
did your f. never stray 214:24
ever let the f. roam 285:37
f. cannot cheat so well 288:2
f. dies in the cradle 464:13
f. from a flower-bell 89:31
f. giving money to the Government 243:6
f. is the sails 289:15
f. never taught to steer 164:33
f. outwork nature 424:6
F.'s gilded clouds 381:26
f.'s meteor ray 108:25
food of sweet and bitter f. 428:24
gardener F. 288:8
horses and dorgs is some men's f. 174:29
in f.'s maze 386:1
in what revolting f. 266:14
isn't all your f. paints 303:4
listen..to the whispers of f. 278:14
little of what you f. 315:1
makes f. lame 162:5
not express'd in f. 431:25
now the f. passes by 262:19
of most excellent f. 437:15
ring f.'s knell 464:13
Shakespeare, F.'s child 342:7
so fair a f. 236:22
so full of shapes is f. 481:30
sweet F.! let her loose 285:38
taste and f. of the speller 179:13
thy face across his f. comes 538:22
to..other minds my f. flies 226:13
where is f. bred? 464:13
young man's f. 534:15

Fancy-free: free be she, f. 199:13
in maiden meditation, f. 466:39

Fanda: omnia f. nefanda. .permixta 133:10
Fandi: quae mollissima f. tempora 554:17

Fane: build a f. in..my mind 288:7
Fang: icy f. .. of the winter's wind 426:29
Fanged with murderous stones 150:28
Fanhope: Ferrers and F. 189:8
Fanned: by Conquest's..wing 229:20
it f. my cheek 150:3
Fanny: pretty F.'s way 373:20
Fanny Kelly's divine plain face 307:15
Fans: china an' etchin's an' f. 299:18
with divers-colour'd f. 424:6
wi² their f. into their hand 32:2
Fantasies: even the linked f. 544:23
twilight F. 491:21
Fantastic: f. summer's heat 474:20
in a light f. round 340:7
light f. toe 341:29
Fantastical: it alone is high f. 481:30
our joys are but f. 184:17
whose murder yet is but f. 450:24
Fantasy: all made of f. 428:28
had an excellent f. 280:1
opinion he held once of f. 449:11
too strong for f. 184:12
Far: alas, so long, so f. 185:1
as f. as eye could see 293:24
as f. as who goes furthest 448:38
beneath the good how f. 231:16
faint and f. away 366:5
f. and few, f. and few 311:21
f. are the shades of Arabia 171:2
f. be it from God 49:15
f., f. ahead 147:13
f., f. away 210:16, 586:22
f., f. better thing that I do 180:2
f., f. from here 15:14
f. from eye or ear 523:19
f. from sorrow, f. from sin 183:2
f. from the fiery noon 286:2
f. from the lips we love 356:35
f. from the madding crowd 230:7

Far (cont.)

f. in a western brookland 263:19
f. in the Unapparent 492:11
f. may be sought 502:17
f. off, most secret..Rose 585:23
f. or forgot 199:4
few and f. between 122:40(-123)
good news from a f. country 50:36
how f. your eyes may pierce 452:31
I am f. from home 364:10
isle in the f. seas 94:42
isn't f. from London 365:25
it doesn't go f. enough 177:13
keep f. our foes 400:33
man is very f. gone 401:5
nor f. away deem 82:10
one near one is too f. 90:10
O sweet and f. 538:15
over the hills and f. away
214:26, 369:10, 516:13
o'er the hills, and f. away 528:29
peace to him that is f. off 54:34
placed f. amid the..main 546:3
she is f. from the land 356:31
so near and yet so f. 533:16
their graves..f. and wide 241:8
think on him that's f. away 104:24
though your lads are f. away 210:4
Thursday's child..f. to go 368:1
thus f. shalt thou go 373:17
when he's f. f. away 229:16
when the other f. doth roam 186:25
Farce: Fate act the same grey f. 141:2
pet-lamb in a sentimental f. 287:16
Farce: la f. est jouée 404:29
Fardels: who would f. bear 434:4
Fare: bachelor's f. 520:5
f. thee well, for I must leave thee 10:21
f. thee well, great heart 440:38
f. you weel, auld Nickie-ben! 104:5
for ever, f. thee well 117:34
hasn't paid his f. 298:22
Isle of Beauty, F. thee well 36:28
last of all the Romans, f. thee well 452:2
value not your bill of f. 519:28
when you receive a f. 83:1
Fared sumptuously every day 62:23
Farewell: bade the world f. 122:33
bid f. to every fear 562:12
bid..our work f. 291:6
but f. compliment 477:19
but f. it 432:40
contempt, f. 468:27
f.! a long f., to..greatness 446:24
f. al the snowe of ferne yere 138:39
f., and stand fast 439:4
f. content 472:3
f. dear..woman 105:28
f., fair cruelty 482:23
f. goes out sighing 481:20
f. happy fields 344:22
f. hope..f. fear..f. remorse 346:33
f., Horace 114:11
f. house, and f. home 166:12
f. king 475:7
f. Leicester Square 571:1
f. my book 138:16
f., my trim-built wherry 173:14
f. rewards and fairies 157:3
f. the heart that lives alone 578:16
f. the neighing steed 472:3
f. the plumed troop 472:3
f. the tranquil mind 472:3
f.! thou art too dear 487:22
f. to Lochaber, and f. my Jean 405:18
f. to Minnie Boffkin 300:20
f. to the Highlands 107:13
f. to the shade 161:23
f...ye virgins all 30:4
for ever and for ever f. 451:37
looks around, to say f. 543:6
mute f. 267:10
No-more, Too-late, F. 411:17
no sadness of f. 528:22
oars and coat and badge, f. 173:14
only feel—F.! —F.! 117:35
our everlasting f. take 451:37
pale hands..waving me f. 254:15
poor Jack, f. 441:1
sweets to the sweet: f. 437:21

Farewell (cont.)

that it lived at all. F.! 280:11
that was all the f. 263:10
thou sayest f. 81:14
wind of welcome and f. 410:22
Farewells: everlasting f. 172:21
faint, now, as f. 253:15
Far-heard: with f. whisper 149:14
Faring: halesome f. 360:13
Farm: his snug little f. of the World 507:19
his snug little f. the earth 151:7
in f. and field 262:13
keep a f., and carters 432:45
Farmer: better f. ne'er 119:17
chips to the British f. 143:31
F. Ledlow late at plough 236:8
f.'s daughter 120:21
f. sowing his corn 369:6
f. that hanged himself 458:17
ran after the f.'s wife 369:8
Farmers: embattled f. 199:7
our f... flourish and complain 165:3
three jolly F. 171:22
Farms: what f. are those? 263:14
wi' the weel-stockit f. 106:7
Farness: the freedom, the f. 422:22
Far-off: isle in f. seas 94:42
old, unhappy, f. things 581:2
Farrago: nostri f. libelli 282:25
Far-reaching in purpose 254:4
Far-set: to one f. goal 19:4
Far-stretched: all the f. greatness 405:13
Far-swooping elbow'd earth 567:18
Farther: f., f., sail! 567:3
f. off from heav'n 253:2
nature could no f. go 193:9
on the f. shore 323:15
thinner, clearer, f. going 538:15
Farthest: as far as who goes f. 448:38
f. from him is best 344:22
f. way about 404:8
next unto the f. 199:17
Farthing: for a f. less 1:28
kind of f. dip 516:18
never pay a f. for it 167:7
paid the uttermost f. 57:47
steal one poor f. without excuse 364:1
Fascinating: tea..this f. plant 278:1
Fascination: f. few can resist 220:11
f. frantic 220:20
f. in his very bow 116:41
Fashion: deeply put the f. on 442:32
faithful..in my f. 187:9
f. all things fair 236:6
f.!—a word 143:20
f. of a new doublet 468:17
f. of this world passeth 66:32
f., the arbiter 511:20
F., though Folly's child 164:38
f.'s brightest arts decoy 225:5
following f. nayed him 232:4
for the f. of these times 426:38
garment out of f. 429:32
glass of f. 434:14
highflyer at F. 178:6
high Roman f. 425:31
marriage ever out of f.? 111:9
not like the f. of your garments 453:31
out of the world as out of the f. 144:25
rills f.. their nurslings 309:5
songs of his f. 516:4
tell you the leading f. 412:20
to hang quite out of f. 481:18
worn-out poetical f. 197:8
Fashionable: with other f. topics 227:23
Fashioned: f. forth its loveliness 236:16
f. so purely 545:12
f. so slenderly 252:12
f. to the varying hour 224:18
heroically f. 575:15
Fashions men with true nobility 331:2
Fast: all rowed f. but none so f. 148:1
as f. as you can 368:10
as fine and as f. as he can 387:20
at least twice as f. 130:4
by the sea shut f. 208:10
f. by the oracle of God 344:2
f. from every village 322:22
grew f. and furious 108:11
hold f...sound words 68:57
hold f. that which is good 68:38

Fast (cont.)
is it such a f.? 54:35
join with thee..spare F. 341:10
more grievous..than a hermit's f. 286:39
no, no, no, my heart is f. 9:21
so f. for fear did he sail 508:1
solemn F. we keep 246:5
talks it so very f. 203:14
they stumble that run f. 478:2
thick and f. they came at last 130:14
things can never be done too f. 226:40
thoughts..come..so f. 194:12
too f. we live 17:5
what need you flow so f.? 11:10
will not f. in peace 164:41
work i' the earth so f. 432:27
writes as f. as they can read 239:12
Fast-closed: the f. door 264:12
Fasten: f. him as a nail 53:28
f. their hands upon their hearts 263:34
Faster: f. and more fast 94:39
f.I f.I 130:3
f. than a stage-coach 226:42
f. we counted our spoons 200:1
he can't work any f. 368:18
nobody walks much f. 131:17
walk a little f. 129:22
world..go round..f. 128:31
Fastest: he travels the f. 304:2
Fastidious: true lover of literature..never f. 508:8
Fasting: Apollo turned f. friar 337:21
die f. 211:17
f. in the wild 506:7
fou man and a f. 420:10
nor f., nor birch 76:4
thank heaven, f. 428:14
Fasts divine 254:27
Fat: all of us are f. 130:16
could eat no f. 367:10
fair, f. and forty 420:20
f. and greasy citizens 426:33
f.. fair and forty 370:6
f. of others' works 109:3
f. of the land 45:23
f., oily man of God 546:6
f. was so white 225:10
feast of f. things 53:37
feed f. the ancient grudge 463:17
first seven f. kine 45:11
grow f. and look young till forty 193:4
heart of this people f. 53:10
incredibly f. or incredibly thin 36:14
in the likeness of a f. old man 439:34
Jeshurun waxed f., and kicked 46:32
men about me that are f. 448:26
mischiefs feed..till they be f. 282:8
more f. than bard beseems 546:4
more..would make me too f. 312:19
O f. white woman 157:9
of stuff so f. and dull 436:39
one of them is f. and grows old' 439:15
out of the f...'Alas!' 170:25
shall be f. and well-liking 397:21
she help'd him to f. 33:20
should himself be f. 275:23
that f. gentleman 202:17
to hearken than the f. of rams 47:16
Venus grown f. 265:19
who's your f. friend? 97:31
Fatal: f. and perfidious bark 342:25
f. facility of..octo-syllabic
verse 114:41
f. gift of beauty 114:8
f. to liberty 351:16
f. to my suit before 213:15
so sweet was ne'er so f. 473:11
strange and f. interview 184:18
yes, I am a f. man 542:20
Fatality: there is a f. in it 512:27
Fate: Arbiter of others' f. 118:20
at length my f. I know 92:31
big with the f. of Cato 1:13
build that nation's f. 73:28(-74)
cannot suspend their f. 170:2
equall'd with me in f. 346:20
F. act the same grey farce 141:2
f. and metaphysical aid 457:2
f. cannot harm me 505:4
f. has scourged us 216:7

Fate (cont.)
f. never wounds more deep 278:32
F. reserves for a bright manhood 322:12
F. so enviously debars 332:6
F., Time, Occasion Chance 497:7
F. tried to conceal him 251:21
f. wrote her a..tremendous
tragedy 39:18
fears his f. too much 355:19
fixed f., free will 345:29
for all our children's f. 296:19
forced by f. 194:29
foreknowledge, will, and f. 345:29
full reward and glorious f. 125:8
give occasion for your f. 202:4
half of human f. 17:3
hanging breathless on thy f. 316:1
heart for any f. 317:8
heart for every f. 118:15
he fits for f. 192:33
he that knows not f. 141:7
his was an untoward f. 116:35
hold f. clasp'd in my fist 210:2
how very sad thy f.I 288:20
I thy f. shall overtake 292:19
limits of a vulgar f. 231:16
maiden's f. 417:8
master of his f. 531:4
master of my f. 241:19
mind..experienced a similar f. 505:23
my f. cries out 432:3
my f. in a country town 387:2
my life, my f. 536:15
my motto and my f. 521:25
no armour against f. 501:5
not fear nor wish my f. 158:17
once dead by f. 37:13
on what seas..thy f. 264:7
play with the severity of f. 209:23
read the book of f. 442:4
star of my f. hath declined 119:9
struggling in the storms of f 381:7
take a bond of f. 460:6
that f. is thine 107:8
they..have conquer'd F. 18:4
thou and I with F. conspire 207:26
thy f. and mine are seal'd 539:1
Time and F. of all their Vintage
prest 206:6
to his F. they all consented 280:10
too vast orb of her f. 16:11
triumph'd over f. 117:24
wayward the decrees of F. are 543:13
what I will is f. 348:25
when f. summons 193:1
when F. thy measure takes 320:2
who can control his f.? 473:30
why should they know their f? 230:30
will..over-rul'd by f. 330:13
Fated not to die 192:21
Fates: F. turn'd cruel 280:10
masters of their f. 448:22
whom the f. sever 418:12
Father: about my F.'s business 61:21
arise and go to my f. 62:14
as a f. pitieth his own children 398:6
because I go to the F. 63:62
between his f.'s knees 164:11
cometh down from the F. of
lights 69:29
cry not when his f. dies 276:16
decrepit f. takes delight 486:32
Diogenes struck the f. 109:28
each to his great F. bends 150:15
eternal F., who didst all create 81:3
everlasting F. 53:15
f. and mither and a'..gae mad 108:28
f. answered never a word 318:15
f., dear f., come home 583:8
F., in Thy gracious keeping 198:15
f. is rather vulgar 176:1
F., Mother, and Me 303:18
f. of all 386:29
f. of all of us 524:21
f., O f.I what do we here? 75:14
f. of English criticism 278:6
f. of good news 432:37
f. of his country 6:7
f. of such as dwell in tents 44:34
F. of the fatherless 396:5
f. of the Man 577:25

Father (cont.)
f. wept 232:3
F...who lovest all 295:6
f.'s joy 419:6
f.'s sorrow, f.'s joy 232:2, 3
followed my poor f.'s body 430:33(-431)
forget also..thy f.'s house 394:23
full fathom five thy f. lies 479:30
gave her f. forty-one 8:7
had he not resembled my f. 458:5
had it been his f. 6:20
happy..that his f. was before
him 520:26
hath the rain a f.? 49:23
have God for his F. 22:1
have we not all one f.? 56:14
her f. lov'd me 470:2
he took my f. grossly 435:37
his F. and his God 230:13
his f.'s soul to cross 385:21
his mother on his f. him begot 74:15
honour thy f. and thy mother 390:12
I am thy f.'s spirit 432:8
I had it from my f. 446:11
in my F.'s house 63:51
king, f.; royal Dane 431:32
king my f.'s death 197:30
laud and honour to the F. 361:14
lead us, Heavenly F. 195:23
leave his f. and his mother 44:18
liar, and the f. of it 63:31
light upon him from his f.'s eyes 576:10
many a f. have I seen 532:29
my f. argued sair 35:9
my f. did something smack 463:27
my f...eminent button-maker 154:14
my f. feeds his flocks 521:26
my f. hath chastised you with
whips 47:47
my f. sold me 76:17
my f. wept 76:8
my true-begotten f. 463:28
nearer my F.'s house 131:32
no man cometh unto the F. 63:53
no more like my f. 430:33(-431)
not an angry f. 122:26
of your f. the devil 63:29
old f. antick, the law 438:19
only f., Sir 226:36
our fair f. Christ 530:15
picture of his f.'s face 209:2
praise F., Son, and Holy Ghost 292:3
rather..a turnip than his f. 276:16
root and f. of many kings 458:30
she has deceiv'd her f. 470:12
show us the F. 63:54
singing to F., Son 264:10
Sir Launcelot, my f. 328:13
some features of my f.'s face 118:22
that f. ruffian 439:35
these lies are like the f. 439:23
thicker than my f.'s loins 47:46
Thou F. of the poor 132:1
thy f...durst not have used that
word 198:13
thy wish was f...to that thought 442:27
Tiber, f. Tiber! 323:27
'twill come to my f. anon 21:11
what my f. used to say 243:2
when my f. and my mother forsake me 393:21
when my f. died 436:32
when thy f. first did see 232:2
whereby we cry, Abba, F. 65:53
wise f. that knows his own child 463:31
wise son maketh a glad f. 49:54
with hir f...dwelleth this flour 137:24
with His F. work..peace 343:9
without f. bred 341:7
would not strike his f. 21:11
you are old, F. William
128:28, 507:33, 34
your Caesar's f. 425:1
your f. was no glazier 520:12
Fathered: so f. and so husbanded 449:18
Fathering: with f. desire 335:23
Fatherland: guard and bless our f. 264:11
Fatherless: defendeth the f. and
widow 400:20
f. children, and widows 389:4

INDEX

Fatherless (*cont.*)
Father of the f.   396:5
visit the f. and widows   69:34
Fatherly, not less than I   375:17
Fathers: ashes of his f.   323:17
as my f. were   77:34
city of the healthiest f.   567:8
cried the F. all   323:24
excellent herbs had our f.   300:9
faith of our f.   202:27
f. have eaten sour grapes   55:29
f...like so many Alexanders   443:25
f. of war-proof   443:25
f., provoke not your children   68:8
follow the generation of his f.   395:2
God of our f.   183:20, 300:24
hast all our f. led   183:20
he f.-forth   255:3
instead of thy f...children   394:26
land where my f. died   504:19
our f. died   295:8
our f. have declared unto us   389:10
our f. that begat us   57:14
our f. worshipped stocks and stones   351:20
sins of the f. upon the children   390:7
slept with his f.   47:49
sons succeed their f.' praise   234:8
the Lord God of your f.   45:38
to our f. of old   300:10
when your f. tempted me   397:30
your f., where are they?   56:10
Fathom: canst not f. it   537:42
full f. five   479:30
full many a f. deep   122:7
nine f. deep..followed us   149:7
Fathom-line: where f. could never touch   438:38
Fathoms: 'tis fifty f. deep   32:2
Fatigue: thinking..the greatest f.   551:10
Fatling: young lion and the f. together   53:18
Fatness: f. of these pursy times   436:3
thy clouds drop f.   395:30
Fats: in thy f. our cares be drown'd   424:19
Fatted all the region kites   433:35
Fatter: f. than his cure   529:12
would he were f.   448:27
Fatty degeneration of his moral being   514:22
Fatuity of idiots   505:20
Faubourg: risen in the F. St. Germain   558:20
Faucibus: primis in f. Orci   554:27
Fault: checks each f.   21:9
every one f. seeming monstrous   428:10
f. and not the actor   461:27
f., dear Brutus   448:22
f...grows two thereby   243:27
faultless to a f.   96:11
f. was Nature's f.   119:31
fierceness makes error a f.   244:1
for Man's f.   247:20
glorious f. of angels   381:33
he is all f. who hath no f.   530:34
he that does one f.   561:23
hide the f. I see   386:31
if at all she had a f.   280:11
if sack and sugar be a f.   439:36
it was a grievous f.   450:17
just hint a f.   385:29
Nature's f. alone   143:26
never had six lines..without a f.   271:31
no kind of f. or flaw   218:35
only f.'s with time   93:16
scarce weed out the f.   226:31
see thy f.   443:13
shun the f. I fell in   30:4
without f. before..God   71:24
without f. or stain   81:22
Faultless: faultily f.   535:35
f. piece to see   382:25
f. to a fault   96:11
for f. fact   220:9
Faults: against whom I know most f.   428:8
all his f. observ'd   451:24
all his f...one love him..better   226:32
all men have their f.   226:39
all men make f.   486:31

Faults (*cont.*)
buffeted for your f.   69:51
drown all my f. and fears   209:4
England..with all her f.   142:32
England, with all thy f.   162:43
f. had she   376:7
f...not strength..to prevent   227:25
f. so nearly allied to excellence   226:31
forehead of her f.   435:35
from my secret f.   392:34
gossips count her f.   336:15
greatest of f...conscious of none   126:25
has she no f. then?   382:10
his f. lie gently on him   447:5
I acknowledge my f.   395:7
if he had any f.   225:26
if our f. whipped them not   423:7
in vain my f. ye quote   308:24
moulded out of f.   462:27
never see such f.   451:23
not for thy f., but **mine**   114:11
old f. and follies   147:11
scouring f.   443:6
some f. to make us **men**   425:32
their f. to scan   224:21
to her f. a little blind   401:26
what f...the earth covereth   404:16
with all our f.   221:37
with all thy f. I love thee still   112:12
world of vile ill-favour'd f.   466:6
Faustine: what .. serpents .. caressed F.   523:11
Faustus must be damn'd   330:7
Faute: pire qu'un crime..une f.   79:4
Favete linguis   259:14
Favilla: solvet saeclum in f.   134:4
Favour: f. my destin'd urn   342:11
fear or f. of the crowd   295:7
flop in f. of your husband   179:36
for your f...give God thanks   468:35
her refusal..almost like a f.   155:36
in f. with God and man   61:22
men f. the deceit   191:34
to this f. she must come   437:15
Favourable: be f. and gracious unto Sion   395:10
never want..f. hearers   253:35
Favoured: thou that art highly f.   61:12
Favourite: f. has no friend   230:21
his f. flies   435:12
to be a Prodigal's f.   573:15
Favourites: James I..had f...a Bad King   422:14
Favours: felt all its f.   147:23
fortune, that f. fools   279:22
hangs on princes' f.   446:24
lively sense of *future* f.   407:13, 559:4
rubies, fairy f.   466:34
Fawn: f. that flies   522:4
shot my f.   332:28
to f., to crouch   510:16
to old to f. upon a nurse   474:15
trembling..like a white f.   586:5
unpractis'd he to f.   224:18
Fawning: base spaniel f.   449:29
Fe: f. que no duda es f. muerta   551:1
Fear: act of f.   431:10
all f., none aid you   384:11
all it yields of..hope and f.   90:42
angels f. to tread   383:5
Arch F. in a visible form   95:9
arming me from f.   83:7
as if his f. still followed   509:26
be just and f. not   446:31
bid farewell to every f.   562:12
by beauty and by f.   579:5
concessions of f.   100:21
continual f. and danger   248:21
danger which they f.   578:5
doth Job f. God for naught?   48:39
drives away his f.   364:15
eat our meal in f.   459:4
faint not nor f.   354:12
F. and trembling Hope   582:22
f. death?   95:8
f. first..made gods   281:8
f. God, and keep his commandments   51:36
f. God, and take your own part   78:30
f. God. Honour the King   69:50, 305:1

Fear (*cont.*)
f. Him, ye saints   527:3
f. in a handful of dust   197:28
F. is a flying   214:10
f. is the parent of cruelty   212:7
f. I to fall   405:11
f...lest he should make an end   280:2
f. no more the heat o' the sun   430:1
f. not, but trust in Providence   36:33
'f. not,' said he   527:4
f. not, till Birnam wood   461:5
f. not to touch the best   405:7
f. of some divine..powers   109:31
f. of the Lord..beginning of wisdom   398:25
f. or favour of the crowd   295:7
f., the last of ills   193:38
f. the Lord, ye..saints   393:38
f. thou not at all   524:6
f. to launch away   562:16
f. to whom f.   66:11
F. wist not to evade   544:16
fond to live or f. to die   198:10
for f. o' Stellenbosch   302:5
for f. of what might fall   451:36
for f. the very stones prate   458:1
freedom from f.   408:25
from hope and f. set free   523:23
hate that which we often f.   423:31
haunts of horror and f.   536:22
he is F., O Little Hunter   301:27
hence together without f.   524:25
him serve with f.   292:7
hope to rise, or f. to fall   583:11
I cannot taint with f.   460:33
I f. no foe in shining armour   372:14
I f. no foe with thee at hand   322:2
I f. thee, ancient Mariner   149:19
I f., thy kisses, gentle maiden   499:2
I f. thy mien   499:2
I f. thy skinny hand   149:19
if my name were liable to f.   448:27
I have a sin of f.   185:24
I'll f. not what men say   99:37
imagining some f.   467:24
in company with Pain, and F.   575:6
in thy faith and f.   390:30
I will f. no evil   393:10
knight without f.   12:13
knowledge and of the f. of the Lord   53:17
lest I should f. and fall   87:37
little we f.   543:11
love, hatred, joy, or f.   401:29
many a f. for my dear country   573:12
many things to f.   26:9
masters the f. of death   26:2
men f. death   26:1
merciful unto them that f. him   398:6
needs f. no fall   99:31
never strike sail to a f.   200:18
no f. in love   70:14
not a word of f.   308:23
not f. nor wish my **fate**   158:17
nothing else to f.   527:3
not..the spirit of f.   68:56
only thing..to f. is f. itself   408:20
O word of f.   455:35
perfect love casteth out f.   70:14
pine with f. and sorrow   510:16
possess them not with f.   444:24
quietly and without f.   99:2
severity breedeth f.   26:26
shuddering f.   464:17
slaves who f. to speak   320:14
so fast for f. did he sail   508:1
so..robs the mind..as f.   102:32
spirit of bondage again to f.   65:53
strange that men should f.   449:22
such..as had the f. of God   167:3
sunder'd in the night of f.   533:28
tell pale-hearted f. it lies   460:7
that calms each f.   21:9
thawing cold f.   444:8
their one f.   77:27
them that f. the Lord   392:24
therefore will we not f.   394:27
they that f. him lack nothing   393:38
trembled with f. at your frown   201:24
true nobility is exempt from f.   445:34
walk in f. and dread   150:2

Fear (cont.)

watch not one another out of f. 185:7
we f. to be we know not what 191:33
what need we f. who knows it 460:24
what we f. of death 462:10
which feels no f. 15:21
which rather thou dost f. to do 457:1
whom then shall I f. 393:20
who never had a f. 164:15
whose being I do f. 458:33
why f. death? 212:1
why f. we to become? 492:14
wise f...forbids..robbing 143:6
wish death nor f. his might 518:2
with f. and trembling 68:19
with his f...beside his part 486:20
with hope farewell f. 346:33
worse than..f. conceived 346:3
yet do I f. thy nature 457:1
yet will I f. none ill 421:11
Feared: f. by their breed 474:22
it is just as I f. 311:2
monarchize, be f. 475:7
she f. no danger 192:20
tell thee what is to be f. 448:27
twenty times was Peter f. 578:24
what are they f. on? 504:10
Fearest nor sea rising 81:26
Fearful: come forth, thou f. man 478:22
f...to fall into the hands of..God 69:12
frame thy f. symmetry 75:24
frightful frantic f. frown 220:7
goodness never f. 462:13
lovely and a f. thing 115:37
snatch a f. joy 230:25
three f. felicities 502:10
ye f. saints 161:18
Fearfully and wonderfully **made** 400:10
Fearing: f. to attempt 461:21
years of f. death 449:34
Fearless: f. for unknown shores 567:2
stepping f. through the night 35:5
Fears: craven f. of being great 529:34
drown all my faults and f. 209:4
f. his fate too much 355:19
f. may be liars 147:8
f. of the brave 279:10
f. shall be in the way 51:33
f. that I may cease to be 289:4
f. to speak of Ninety-Eight 267:18
fifty hopes and f. 89:31
forgot the taste of f. 461:3
from sudden f. 114:35
hopes and f. it heeded not 498:6
hopes and f. of all the years 84:25
hopes belied our f. 252:23
humanity with all its f. 316:1
humble cares, and delicate f. 581:6
I had no human f. 573:6
Incarnations of hopes and f. 491:21
its tenderness, its joys, and f.
576:22(−577)
not mine own f. 488:2
our f. do make us traitors 460:16
past Regrets and Future F. 206:5
present f. are less 456:24
prosperity is not without..f. 25:20
Religion..f. her friends 164:39
saucy doubts and f. 459:12
serves and f...the giddy multitude 335:3
so are their griefs and f. 26:44
spite of f. 364:11
that any man f. to be dead 27:43
thro' its joys and f. 93:22
tie up thy f. 244:10
when f. attack 121:18
when little f. grow great 435:9
within were f. 67:30
Feast: as you were going to a f. 280:7
at a great f. of languages 455:26
at any good man's f. 427:19
bare imagination of a f. 474:20
beginning of a f. 440:24
chief nourisher in life's f. 458:11
door stood open at our f. 148:17
f. is set 148:19
f. of Crispian 444:28
f. of Daulis 524:16
f. of fat things 53:31
f. of lanterns 379:22
f. of reason 386:5

Feast (cont.)

f. of wines on the lees 53:31
Goldsmith's fine f. 213:9
if so they chance to f. her 281:7
in flames or at f. 586:20
let us keep the f. 66:28
liberty's a glorious f. 106:24
Love, thy solemn F. 375:7
luxury and riot, f. and dance 349:27
my f. of joy 547:20
my kisses are his daily f. 231:39
not f. on thee 254:19
on the vigil f. his neighbours 444:28
perpetual f. of nectared sweets 340:24
pomp, and f., and revelry 342:7
scramble at the shearers' f. 342:27
song of them that f. 362:4
what f. is toward? 438:8
when I make a f. 238:2
Feasted: starved, f., despaired 97:28
Feasting: f. reconciles everybody 377:27
go to the house of f. 51:9
Feasts: beauty..must be shown..
at f. 340:38
f. where ale was strongest 318:7
spots in your f. of charity 70:18
table of the Moveable F. 388:5
wreathed for f. not few 336:38
Feat: empty f. 147:2
f. on which ourselves we prided 115:32
such a gallant f. of arms 323:30
Feather: as a f. is wafted downward 316:7
ball of f. and bone 236:27
f. pate of folly 263:18
friendship never moults a f. 177:28
his own f. on the..dart 117:25
moulted f., an eagle-f. 93:24
stuck a f. in his cap 33:7
swan's down-f. 424:21
with hindward f. 336:21
wit's a f. 384:9
Feathered: catch one of her f.
creatures 488:17
f. race with pinions 211:25
he f. his oars 173:12
Feathering soft their..beat 375:24
Feathers: beautified with our f. 232:6
her f. like gold 396:7
made my f. gay 585:11
owl, for all his f. 285:12
safe under his f. 397:18
she plumes her f. 340:20
two-legged animals without f. 127:5
wet their silken f. 510:20
Featly: foot if f. here and there 479:28
Feats: f. of broil and battle 469:45
one of my f. 118:2
what f. he did that day 444:28
Feature: every f. works 22:10
in form and f. 313:7
thrive in grace and f. 280:10
Featured like him 486:24
Featureless: the more f...a crime 187:13
Features: for homely f. to keep
home 340:38
lady of incisive f. 337:13
some f. of my father's face 118:20
Feb, fill the dyke 549:29
February: excepting F. alone 369:5
F. hath twenty-eight alone 228:4
F. last, my heart 573:17
vestal F. 375:7
Fecisti nos ad te 21:16
Fed: bite the hand that f. them 102:36
clothed, f., and educated 413:23
dressed and warmed, and f. 333:24
f. on the fullness of death 525:8
f. purely upon ale 203:5
f. with the same food 464:8
greater ass that f. you 298:21
grown by what it f. on 430:33(−431)
ill-f., ill-killed 275:19
it is f. and watered 121:27
look up and are not f. 342:29
on honey-dew hath f. 151:33(−152)
thy people still are f. 183:20
Federal: our F. Union 267:27
Federation of the world 534:27
Fee: before his credit, or his f. 521:8
bought over God with a f. 525:20
cheapest lawyer's f. 107:31

Fee (cont.)

f. the doctor for a nauseous
draught 192:15
gorgeous East in f. 582:5
my life at a pin's f. 432:2
my marriage f. 293:9
Feeble: confirm the f. knees 54:2
f. and restless youths 146:15
f. as frail 228:22
f. God has stabb'd me 214:6
help the f. up 480:17
if virtue f. were 341:5
man of such a f. temper 448:21
most forcible F. 442:10
religion of f. minds 102:26
Feed: bid thee f. 76:10
but to sleep and f. 436:15
f. fat the ancient grudge 463:17
f. his flock like a shepherd 54:11
f. his sacred flame 152:3
f. me in a green pasture 393:10
f. my brain with better things 140:6
f. my lambs 64:15
f. my sheep 64:16
f. on vain delight 510:14
f. the brute 403:33
f. the titled knave 108:17
f. with the rich 271:27
He that doth me f. 245:10
hog's my f. 337:12
keep us, f. us 195:23
mischiefs f. like beasts 282:8
on this fair mountain leave to f. 435:46
sea-beasts..f. in the ooze 15:24
so f. with lofty thoughts 582:3
so shalt thou f. on Death 488:21
than f. on cates 440:2
then f. on thoughts 346:20
we can begin to f. 130:17
we can f. this mind of ours 574:29
which f. among the lilies 52:5
Fee'd: if lawyer's hand is f. 214:19
Feeder: Mr. F., B.A. 175:7
Feedest: f. them with the bread of
tears 397:2
so many wishes f. 17:22
tell me..where thou f. 51:40
Feedeth among the lilies 52:3
Feeding: deal of fine confused f. 85:7
forty f. like one 577:20
Feeds: Death, that f. on men 488:21
f. on the aërial kisses 497:2
ruin that it f. upon 161:30
where she f. her chicks 294:21
Feel: also f. it as a man 460:22
f. another's woe 386:31
f...happier than I know 348:33
f. I am so most 425:11
f. it more than other people 174:14
f. the first kiss 411:1
f. what I can ne'er express 114:26
f., who have laid our..hands
away 84:6
few..f. for the poor 308:12
I f. a feeling which I f. you all f. 407:2
I see, not f. 151:2
know the change and f. it 289:8
make us f., must f. themselves 143:24
making figments f. 236:3
never f. them to the full 289:34
no comfortable f. 253:12
not f. the crowd 163:23
one does f. 305:7
speak what we f. 454:28
thing that could not f...years 573:6
to f. it too 355:14
tragedy to those that f. 558:27
we f. that it is there 498:5
we f. that we are greater 573:27
we uncomfortable f. 221:33
Feeleth: He f. for our sadness 4:3
Feeling: appeals to diffused f. 28:29
appetite; a f. and a love 581:26
art is..the transmission of f. 548:9
as old as he's f. 153:19
f. disputation 440:3
f. of sadness and longing 316:8
f. of their masters' thoughts 331:2
gratifying f. that our duty 218:24
greater f. to the worse 474:20
he has, in fact, no uneasy f. 270:35

Feeling (cont.)
high mountains are a f. 113:47
hour of thinking, f., loving 573:21
I feel a f. 407:2
index of a f. mind 165:15
lost pulse of f. 15:6
love's f. is more soft 455:22
Man of F. 326:25
no f. of his business 437:9
one f. too falsely disdained 499:3
petrifies the f. 105:19
sensible to f. as to sight 457:20
than from any want of f. 519:2
that Kruschen f. 10:3
wholly devoid of good f. 312:20
Feelings: f. by which the heroic
  kings governed 28:27
f...wrung with compunction 312:16
[Furies'] f. are strong 182:10
in f., not in figures 29:9
opinion..determined by the f. 508:29
reasoned out of the f. of humanity 73:4
see some of my f. 559:35
spontaneous overflow of powerful f. 583:4
what we call our f. 176:25
Feels: f. at each thread 383:17
f. the noblest 29:9
finding how it f. 142:14
universe that f. and knows 91:14
Fees: hope, but of his f. 247:18
straight dream on f. 477:7
Feet: about the f. of God 531:36
aching hands and bleeding f. 17:1
at her f. he bowed 46:50
at the f. of Gamaliel 65:13
bathe those beauteous f. 209:3
beat down Satan under our f. 389:1
beat of her unseen f. 492:29
beat..of thy heart and f. 411:10
beautiful upon the mountains
  are the f. 54:22
before her wandering f. 585:22
be jubilant, my f. 264:17
beneath our f...shame 316:30
broken by their passing f. 584:8
came on the following F. 544:19
clang of hurrying f. 23:22
come the expected f. 338:10
crews at England's f. 122:6
desultory f. of Death 411:3
devil be in my f. 420:16
diseased in his f. 47:50
dost thou wash my f.? 63:47
faint, averted f. 375:21
fair the f. of thy lover 524:15
fall at her flying f. 123:22
f. have they, and walk not 399:4
f. like sunny gems 535:39
f. of joy in idleness 82:6
f. of the day and the f. of the
  night 521:30
f. of the men what drill 294:25
f. of thine high priests 525:13
f. of those he fought for 537:12
f. was I to the lame 49:9
glowing Hours with flying f. 113:26
guide our f. into..peace 61:15
hear the grown-up people's f. 515:14
her f. beneath her petticoat 517:12
her f. have touch'd the meadows 536:4
her pretty f. like snails 247:12
his f. like unto fine brass 70:27
how beautiful are thy f. with
  shoes 52:17
I look down towards his f. 473:33
jewel print of your f. 536:12
keep Thou my f. 364:10
lantern unto my f. 399:21
last short burst upon failing f. 334:5
little snow-white f. 584:11
low at her f. 413:31
making a tinkling with their f. 52:35
more instant than the F. 544:14
my dreams under your f. 584:17
my due f. never fail 341:23
my f. from falling 395:16, 399:6
nations under our f. 394:30
no hurry in her f. 409:23
no room at my f. 30:16
not sweet with nimble f. 569:5

Feet (cont.)
now with his f. 231:39
palms before my f. 140:22
pierced His gospel-bearing f. 313:5
pierced my hands and my f. 393:6
sea beneath my f. 80:15
set my f. in a large room 393:28
set my f. upon the rock 394:12
set my printless f. 341:4
skull, and the f. 48:32
slipping underneath our F. 206:19
splendour and speed of thy f. 521:30
Stella's f. may kiss 502:4
subjects' f. may hourly trample 475:10
suddenly bloom at her f. 42:4
suffereth not our f. to slip 396:1
table-crumbs attract his slender
  f. 546:26
tempt with wand'ring f. 345:26
they hadn't any f. 130:13
they sit at the F. 302:3
those f. in ancient time 75:16
those little silver f. 333:1
thy shoes from off thy f. 45:34
time's iron f. 355:15
walk'd those blessed f. 438:12
wash their f. in soda water 197:31
what dread f.? 75:24(-76)
what flowers are at my f. 287:30
white f. of laughing girls 323:12
whose f. they hurt in the stocks 398:12
with head, hands, wings, or f. 346:14
with lifted f., hands still 39:3
with oary f. 540:11
with reluctant f. 316:34
with their f. forward 87:6
with twain he covered his f. 53:8
with your hands, and your f...
  red 322:25
world-wandering f. 544:8
your f. are always in the water 4:21
your f. shod with..the gospel 68:12
your shoes on your f. 45:47
Feign: telle his tale untrewe or f.
  thing 137:23
Feigned: by f. deaths to die 186:15
f. necessities 167:11
story, f. for pleasure 191:19
worse than fables yet have f. 346:3
Feigning: lowly f...called compliment 483:26
most friendship is f. 427:22
Felice: ricordarsi del tempo f. nella
  miseria 168:22
Felicem: infelicissimum..fuisse f. 78:4
Felices ter et amplius 258:19
Felicitas: Horatii curiosa f. 378:9
Felicities: f. of this 87:7
more..than the f. of Solomon 25:19
three fearful f. 502:10
Felicity: absent thee from f. awhile 438:4
boast sincere f. 193:17
Jerusalem..peace and f. 421:5
measure of F. 232:13
our own f. we make 278:29
perfect bliss and sole f. 330:28
shadow of f. 558:6
their green f. 289:7
throne of human f. 277:4
to behold f. 86:20
what more f. can fall 510:17
Felix: f...opportunitate mortis 526:11
f. qui potuit..cognoscere causas 556:16
O f. culpa 353:5
Fell: all of us f. down 450:31
all who f...One who rose 493:27
athlete nearly f. 362:12
enough, that when it f. 183:22
f. among thieves 61:39
f. before the throne 71:4
f. beneath the apple-tree 543:19
f. by the wayside 59:21
f. from off the seat backward 47:9
f. out they knew not why 110:2
f. upon the sanded floor 376:9
foremost fighting, f. 113:29
freely they..f. who f. 346:21
from morn to noon he f. 345:12
great Caesar f. 450:31
he bowed, he f., he lay down 46:50
he f. like the stick 373:2

Fell (cont.)
he f. upon their decks 540:3
I do not love you, Dr. F. 85:10
I f. at his feet as dead 70:27
I f. at his feet to worship 71:35
instant that he f. 418:34
it f. to earth 315:24
Jack f. down 367:9
least erected Spirit that f. from
  heaven 345:9
lying where he f. 23:24
one f. swoop 460:21
other f. into good ground 59:23
ran to help me when I f. 527:8
so strook..f. the Fiend 350:17
spirits that f. with Lucifer 330:1
together f. down dead 324:9
wall f. down flat 46:40
we f. out, my wife and I 538:9
Fellah: chips to the Egyptian f. 143:31
Felled: the poplars are f. 161:23
Fellow: among his f. roughs 188:29
ever Rome should breed thy f. 452:2
f. of a good respect 452:6
f. of infinite jest 437:15
for he's a jolly good f. 203:37
hail, f., well met 521:11
have such a f. whipped 434:15
He's a Good F. 207:19
he was a good f. 137:12
his folly has not f. 262:18
Magna Charta is such a f. 148:2
no f. in the firmament 449:30
old F. of Trinity 10:23
on the unjust f. 79:7
sweetest li'l f. 511:14
take a f. eight years old 91:32
that f.'s got to swing 569:3
this f. in the cellarage 432:25
till his f. fault came 428:10
till she met a city f. 9:18
touchy, testy, pleasant f. 2:8
want of it the f. 384:7
you're a f...you're another 178:33
Fellow-citizens: F.: God reigns 213:7
first in the hearts of his f. 312:25
Fellow-creature: kindness .. to
  any f. 232:10
Fellow-creatures: torture and
  death of his f. 212:4
Fellow-feeling makes one..kind 213:14
Fellow-men: one that loves his f. 265:17
Fellow-rover: laughing f. 334:12
Fellows: nature hath fram'd
  strange f. 462:30
those f. hate us 307:18
Fellow-servant: I am thy f. 71:35
Fellowship: fears his f. to die with
  us 444:28
f. divine, a f. with essence 284:25
f. is heaven..f. is life 359:19
for f.'s sake 359:19
neither honesty, manhood, nor
  good f. 438:27
one communion and f. 389:55
right hands of f. 67:40
simple dues of f. 87:31
this half-fac'd f. 438:38
your f. a trouble 169:18
Felonious: for some f. end 340:9
Felony to drink small beer 445:36
Felt: darkness which may be f. 45:44
f. for thee as a lover 582:15
f. in the blood, and f. along the
  heart 581:23
f. with my native land 536:25
I f. it was glory 118:34
our soul had f. him 16:21
pray'd and f. for all 224:21
remembering how she f. but
  what she f. remembering not 579:18
say..what we have thought and
  f. 200:37
this I have f. 302:25
Female: child of our grandmother Eve, a f. 454:36
despotic power over his f. 350:35
endearing elegance of f. friendship 278:20
f. of sex it seems 350:31
f. of the species..more deadly 296:13

INDEX

Female (cont.)
f. woman 560:9
for one fair f. 193:39
male and f. created he them 44:8
polished f. friend 568:21
some f. errors 385:12
what f...gold despise? 230:20
whimsey..is the f. guide 229:12
Females: eighty mile o' f. 179:34
make poor f. mad 467:11
Femina: dux f. facti 553:16
varium et mutabile semper f. 554:20
vindicta nemo magis gaudet quam f. 284:2
Feminine: highbrow..of the f. gender? 243:12
keener pangs, though f. 286:15
male ringlets or f. gold 523:4
of the f. gender 370:5
Purity is the f. 237:23
Femme: cherchez la f. 194:32
cherchons la f. 194:32
en un mot, elle est f. 405:2
Femmes: je parle..italien aux f. 136:13
Fen of stagnant waters 577:14
Fence: f. against the infirmities 512:32
when a single soul does f. 332:7
Fenced about with a bandage 311:17
Fence-rail: straddled that f. 238:27
Fences: all these f. 245:6
by the starlit f. 263:20
good f. make good neighbours 212:3
Fencing, dancing, and bear-baiting 482:7
Fenians: dwell in the house of the F. 586:20
Fenlands: mountains, moors and f. 317:20
Fens: reek o' the rotten f. 429:14
rocks, caves, lakes, f. 346:2
Fer: I'll f. him, and firk him 445:2
Fercula: illa erant f. 21:18
Feri: ut f. ut se mori sentiat 517:20
Ferly: f. he spied wi' his e'e 32:6
ye crowlin' 106:32
Ferment: the soul is in a f. 284:18
Ferments: love..f. and frets 111:24
Fern: grasshoppers under a f. 102:20
sparkle out among the f. 528:5
Taffy dancing through the f. 299:24
Fern-seed: the receipt of f. 439:1
Fero: multa f. ut placem genus..vatum 257:18
Feros: nec sinit esse f. 372:9
Ferrers and Fanhope 189:8
Ferret: firk him, and f. him 445:2
Ferro: ab ipso ducit opes animumque f. 260:21
Ferrum: in me convertite f. 555:7
nec poterit f...abolere 372:1
Ferry: to row us o'er the f. 122:23
who's for the f.? 333:16
Fers: partout il est dans les f. 412:2
Fertile: twice five miles of f. ground 151:32
Fervent in spirit; serving the Lord 66:2
Festal: line of f. light 18:11
Fester: lilies that f. 487:26
Festina lente 517:21
Festival: things that we ordained f. 478:33
Fetch: f. my life..from men of royal siege 469:37
f. one if one goes astray 409:19
Fetlocks shag and long 488:27
Fetter: a worn-out f. 317:17
Fettered: devil weakly f. 514:5
f. to her eye 319:4
nor f. Love from dying 123:5
so f. fast we are 89:14
Fetters: in love with his f. 27:44
Milton wrote in f...of Angels 77:7
strong Egyptian f. 423:24
Fettle for the great grey drayhorse 254:23
Feu: assise auprès du f. 408:18
ce qu'est au f. le vent 109:34
Feud: f. of rich and poor 533:19
old f. 'twixt things and me 80:22
'Pherson swore a f. 23:26
Feuds: forget all f. 323:9
their ineffectual f. 15:3
Feuertrunken: wir betreten F. 415:21
Fever: after life's fitful f. 459:4
f. and the fret 287:25

Fever (cont.)
f. call'd 'Living' 380:11
f. of life is over 364:4
grows to an envious f. 481:5
thy lips taken f. 523:6
wakes the f. in my bones 299:14
what the f. is to the physicians 352:18
white hand of a lady f. thee 425:5
with anguish moist and f. dew 286:29
Feverous: earth was f. and did shake 458:21
Fever-trees: set about with f. 304:17
Février: Generals Janvier and F. 364:18
Few: appointment by the corrupt f. 490:29
clashed with his fiery f. 537:19
comprehending much in f. words 57:7
far and f., far and f. 311:21
f. and evil..the days 45:25
f. and far between 122:40(-123)
f. are chosen 60:10
f. die and none resign 268:26
f., f. shall part 122:20
f. honest men 167:2
f. in the hill 304:29
f., save the poor 308:12
f. there be that find it 58:24
f. whom genius gave 231:3
fit audience find, though f. 348:23
for the gain of a f. 386:35, 520:47
God has f. of us 89:11
grinders cease because they are f. 51:33
how f. know their own good 194:23
let thy words be f. 51:6
most may err..as the f. 190:28
of f. days 49:1
so much owed..to so f. 144:1
thou wilt find but f. 493:3
very f. and very weary 325:19
we f., we happy f. 444:28(-445)
with f. but with how splendid stars 208:19
ye are many—they are f. 495:16
Fewer: f. men, the greater.. honour 444:26
Fez: transferred from F. 285:25
Fezziwig: in came Mrs. F. 174:9
Fiat: bit of f. in my soul 38:25
f. lux 44:2
Fib: destroy his f. or sophistry 385:24
Fibre from the brain 73:20
Fickle: bright and fierce and f. 538:20
made thee f. 119:31
whatever is f., freckled 255:3
Fickleness of the women I love 490:41
Fico: a f. for the phrase 465:32
Fiction: best thing in f. the English have..done 570:20
by fairy F. drest 229:26
condemn it as an improbable f. 484:10
f. lags after truth 100:23
in a f., in a dream of passion 433:31
say to the Muse of f. 420:26
stranger than f. 117:1
what F. means 569:25
Fictions: be ye my f. 166:22
Fictitious: Christianity .. discovered to be f. 109:35
Fictive: origin of the f. picture 268:8
Fiddle: cat and the f. 367:1
f...and spade 419:18
f. harmonics on..sensualism 337:8
f., we know, is diddle 523:26
good tune..on an old f. 112:15
his lass, his f., and his frisk 162:21
I the second f. 511:6
merry love the f. 585:1
play on my f. in Dooney 585:2
robes riche, or f. 137:6
Time plays the f. 183:7
Fiddlepin's end! 121:4
Fiddler: chemist, f., statesman 190:22
f., and..a rogue 519:27
f.'s old tune 359:7
f.'s standing by 5:25
in came a f. 174:9
kissed the f.'s wife 107:15
Fiddlers: called for his f. three 368:3
Fiddlestick: imperial f.! 129:38
Fiddle-strings: which f. is weakness 176:35

Fiddling priest 161:25
Fiddling-stick: lost his f. 366:12
Fide: fortius f. et gaude Punica f. 321:3, 415:5
Fidele: F.'s grassy tomb 153:20
Fides: et nulli cessura f. 371:17
Fidgety Phil 249:24
Fie: better memory said, f. 359:27
f., f., f., now would she cry 35:17
f., f. upon her 481:26
f., foh, and fum 453:27
f., my lord, f. 460:24
f. on't! O f.! 430:33
f. upon this quiet life 439:13
Field: beside a f. of grain 373:15
blood-red f. of Spain 241:9
but for you, possess the f. 147:8
F...and the elms 17:16
f. from which success is banished 513:31
f. is full of shades 545:2
f. of death survey'd 1:10
flying from f. and tree 80:12
free love—free f. 530:42
from the F. of Night 205:5
from the wet f. 18:25
goodliness..as the flower of the f. 54:10
happy f. or mossy cavern 287:1
in a f. by the river 584:11
in the f. of human conflict 144:1
in the tented f. 469:45
I thank our Lord the f. is won 358:4
man for the f. 538:24
man of the f. 44:57
marriage..a f. of battle 514:29
rush'd into the f. 113:29
senate and the f. 386:21
sickle in the fruitful f. 74:26
single f. which I have looked upon 576:8
single in the f. 580:28
sparkled on the yellow f. 534:4
some corner of a foreign f. 84:21
that fair f. of Enna 347:8
that lay f. to f. 53:3
thou..first took'st the f. 292:20
tills this lonely f. 199:8
till the f. ring again 79:10
what though the f. be lost 344:14
whisper down the f. 298:20
Fields: alone through f. and woods 151:27
as long as..f. are green 491:26
babbled of green f. 443:19
better to hunt in f. 192:15
blown f. or flowerful closes 524:28
farewell happy f. 344:22
f. fall southward 523:14
f. from Islington to Marybone 75:4
F. his study 77:24
f. invested with purpureal gleams 577:13
f. of Immortality 493:7
f. where flies no .. hail 254:29
f. without a flower 162:44
flowerless f. of heaven 521:29
from the f. of sleep 576:5
from the shining f. 536:6
green f. of England 147:10
gone into the f. 494:9
in the green f., and the town 307:17
in those holy f. 438:12
joyless f. and thorny thickets 546:26
like f. of amaranth lie 171:1
lilied f. of France 122:12
little tyrant of his f. 230:5
long f. of barley and of rye 533:40
no f. of amaranth 309:13
nor f. of offerings 47:29
o'er earth's green f. 202:23
of battled f. no more 416:19
open unto the f. 582:14
out of olde f. 138:23
poetic f. encompass me 2:2
show'd how f. were won 224:20
subterranean f. 579:30
table of green f. 443:19
these English f. 18:31
valleys, groves, hills and f. 330:17
vasty f. of France 443:4
walk through the f. in gloves 157:9
we plough the f. 121:27

Fields (*cont.*)
what f., or waves 498:8
ye f. of Cambridge 158:10
Fiend: 'Budge,' says the f. 463:27
defy the foul f 453:20
equivocation of the f. 461:5
f. a pride na pride had he 108:19
f. hid in a cloud 76:8
f. of gods and men ydrad 510:8
foul F. coming over the field 99:11
frightful f...close behind him 150:2
give the F. himself his due 540:28
marble-hearted f. 452:28
out, hyperbolical f. 484:20
so eagerly the f. o'er bog 346:14
so strook..fell the F. 350:17
take heed o' the foul f. 453:18
tired..swung the F. 336:17
Fiends: f. in upper air 418:29
f. that plague thee 149:1
f. will snatch at it 473:32
these juggling f. 461:12
Fierce: bears forward f. 546:11
bright and f. and fickle 538:20
extremes by change more f. 346:1
f. as ten furies 346:4
f. wretchedness that glory brings 480:28
grew more f. and wild 244:10
his rash f. blaze of riot 474:21
if I were f. and bald 415:12
insignificantly f. 164:2
look not so f. on me 330:11
more f. and more inexorable 478:39
more f. in its religion 363:17
safer being meek than f. 89:22
when the strife is f. 264:9
Fierceness: f. makes error a fault 244:1
swalloweth the ground with f. 49:27
Fiercer: now f. by despair 345:15
Fiercest: strongest and the f. Spirit 345:15
Fiere: a hand, my trusty f. 104:16
Fiery: clashed with his f. few 537:19
far from the f. noon 286:2
f. four-in-hand 153:13
f. soul 190:13
heaven..full of f. shapes 439:40
many a f. Alp 346:2
nimble, f. and delectable shapes 442:21
that very f. particle 116:35
Fiery-footed: you f. steeds 478:17
Fiery-red with haste 474:29
Fiery-spangled veil of heaven 331:2
Fiery-wheeled throne 341:12
Fiesole: drifted over F. 94:8
Fife: ear-piercing f. 472:3
fill the f. 357:22
practised on a f. 128:15
sound the f. 23:18
Thane of F. had a wife 460:25
tootle-te-tootle the f. 97:14
wry-neck'd f. 463:36
Fifes: treble of her f. 77:31
Fifteen: f. men on the dead man's chest 514:18
f. wild Decembers 83:14
maiden of bashful f. 500:39
Fifth: Beethoven's F. Symphony 210:7
f. column 353:7
F. of November 9:11, 368:13
in some f. Act 537:39
under the f. rib 47:31
Fifty: Adonis of f. 240:6
at f. chides his infamous delay 587:6
better f. years of Europe 535:1
corpulent man of f. 266:6
f. hopes and fears 89:31
f. springs are little room 262:10
f. winters o'er him 230:19
gallows f. cubits high 48:37
leaves me f. more 262:10
love is lame at f. years 236:26
my f. men and women 93:44
new edition f. volumes long 89:29
sit down quickly, and write f. 62:19
sprig of bays in f. years 521:15
'tis f. fathoms deep 32:2
were it f. times as fair 73:12
widow of f. 500:39
Fifty million Frenchmen 233:16

Fifty thousand: f. horse and foot 294:19
f. men slain this year in Europe 559:1
f. strong 583:6
Fifty-fifty Americanism 409:4
Fifty-score strong 90:16
Fifty-three: can we fight with f.? 539:17
north of the F. 301:3
one and the f. 539:21
Fig: a f. for those..protected 106:24
pig, or f.? 129:3
Virtue! a f.! 470:15
Fight: baffled to f. better 97:4
better to f. for the good 536:25
Britain would f. on alone 144:9
come ye here to f.? 31:5
eat like wolves and f. like devils 444:5
end that crowns us, not the f. 246:21
end of the f. 300:6
even to f. against God 64:32
fall out, and chide, and f. 561:27
f. against the churches 460:4
f. and no be slain 108:16
f. begins within himself 89:38
f. it out on this line 229:1
f. longer than he sees reason 438:29
f. on to the end 233:20
f. the good f. 354:11
f. the good f. of faith 68:53
f., to be found fighting 82:10
forth to the f. are gone 402:14
gone to f. the French 282:10
good at a f. 357:21
he that flies mought f. again 24:43
I dare not f. 443:14
if they won't f. us 213:11
I give the f. up 94:22
I have fought a good f. 68:60
I must f. the course 461:8
in the lost, lost f. 146:14
I will not cease from Mental F. 75:16
let's f. till six 130:23
live to f. another day 6:25, 224:9
lost f. of virtue 513:32
martial brood accustomed to f. 509:35
never a moment ceased the f. 539:21
never rise and f. again 224:9
no peril in the f. 157:6
nor law, nor duty bade me f. 584:21
not yet begun to f. 279:18
one f. more 95:10
saw a dead man win a f. 30:13
second Adam to the f. 364:7
shall we f. or shall we fly? 539:20
so could f. us no more 539:21(-540)
they now to f. are gone 189:7
those that fly may f. again 111:17
those who bade me f. 202:18
to f. is but to die 539:20
to f. with them again 539:18
too proud to f. 571:10
Ulster will f. 143:29
warrior famoused for f. 486:22
we don't want to f. 11:9, 265:15
we'll f. and we'll conquer 213:10
we shall f. in France 143:40
who's ripe for f. now? 90:17
you cannot f. against the future 222:34
Fighter: am I no a bonny f.? 514:7
fits a dull f. 440:24
I was ever a f. 95:10
Fighteth: none other that f. for us 388:24
Fighting: f. as low as.. 192:19
f. for the crown 367:13
f. still, and still destroying 191:9
F. Téméraire 363:6
first-class f. man 296:23
foremost f., fell 113:29
for want of f...rusty 110:21
single pilgrim f. unarmed 38:24
world is..worth f. for 241:17
Fightings: without were f. 67:30
Fights: captain that knows what he f. for 167:3
f. you on patriotic principles 490:38
gain'd a hundred f. 537:18
he that f. and runs away 6:25
he who f. and runs away 224:9
it's worse if you f. 301:8
sent to penny-f. 297:1
with what a strength..the British soldier f. 360:21

Fig-leaves: across the f. 523:4
sewed f. together 44:21
Figments: making f. feel 236:3
Figs: f. grew upon thorn 140:21
gather..f. of thistles? 58:26
green bursting f. 18:16
in the name of the Prophet—f.! 504:11
long life better than f. 423:19
Fig-tree: as a f. casteth her..figs. 71:1
every man..under his f. 56:6
train up a f. 175:10
Figura: el Caballero de la Triste F. 134:8
Figurative: his f. naval manner 173:30
Figure: baby f. of the giant mass 481:8
beauty..steal from his f. 487:29
Europe..a prone..f. 235:22
f. in the carpet 268:15
f. of blown youth 434:14
fixed for the time of scorn 472:34
foolish f. 432:40
make a f. in a country church 519:25
only f. among ciphers 25:22
strangest f. 94:36
that strange f. 325:28
this f. that thou here seest 281:9
what a f...in the republic of letters 1:7
Figures: carved with f. strange 150:21
f. pedantical 455:29
in feelings, not in f. 29:9
prove anything by f. 126:4
Figuring..the times deceas'd 442:6
Filbert: Gilbert, the F. 571:17
Filches from me my good name 471:30
File: Dante..in the nature of an Old F. 176:2
Files: commands the beauteous f. 552:1
gaps in our f. 17:21
in the foremost f. of time 534:35
Files-on-Parade: said F. 295:19
Filet: que le f. à les lier 355:6
Filia: matre pulchra filia pulchrior 258:20
Filigree hedges 558:11
Fill: ah, f. the Cup 206:19
awake..and f. the Cup 205:6
come, f. the Cup 205:14, 15
Feb, f. the dyke 549:29
f. all the glasses there 158:8
f. ev'ry glass 214:29
f. high the cup 116:1
f. it up to the brim 420:25
f. the can, and f. the cup 541:14
f. them full of refreshment 316:14
f. the unforgiving minute 297:12
take our f. of love 49:50
to f. the hour 200:12
Filled: f. and vivified by Thee 355:14
f. to the brim with girlish glee 219:27
for they shall be f. 57:39
rooks..f. the trees 249:13
source that keeps it f. 336:9
Fille de chambre: I caught hold of the f.'s 512:31
Filleth: barn f. up finely 550:1
Filling: continually .. f. some other body 290:10
f. the world 419:18
writ at first for f. 521:19
Fills: he f. a chair 274:28
he f. affection's eye 275:1
Film: that f., which fluttered 151:24
the lash, of f. 477:7
Filmy-eyed: Sleep, the f. 495:23
Fils de Saint Louis, montez 204:38
Filth: in our own f. 425:2
Filths savour but themselves 454:1
Filthy: her most f. bargain 473:22
he which is f...be f. still 72:8
Fin: nor winks the gold f. 539:2
that Almighty F. 83:26
Fin: le commencement de la f. 526:19
Final cause of the human nose 153:4
Finality is not the language of politics 180:24
Finching: Mr. F. proposed seven times 175:37
Find: by searching f. out God 48:56
can't tell where to f. them 307:14
ever f. joy's language 81:2
f. him ware an' wakin' 363:3
f. it after many days 51:27

Find (*cont.*)
f. me, and turn thy back 199:6
f. out, if you can 521:11
f. out their enemies now 453:9
f. out what everyone is doing 243:1
f. out what you don't know 564:3
go and f. out and be damned 299:2
God and cannot f. it there 496:26
hallow all we f. 291:5
happiness she does not f. 279:15
he that loseth..shall f. it 59:3
I cannot f. it out 517:17
if it f. heaven..f. it out tonight 459:2
if ye f. my beloved 52:12
I waked to f. her 348:35
lost thing could I never f. 42:6
make his opportunity, as oft as
  f. it 24:28
safe bind, safe f. 550:6
seek, and ye shall f. 58:19
seeking shall f. Him 91:41
take him as we f. him 294:18
to strive, to seek, to f. 541:3
travel the world..to f. the beautiful 200:5
until I f. the holy Grail 540:12
where seek is f. 503:5
where shall we f. her? 521:30(-522)
where we can f. information 272:32
with men I f. Him not 531:26
your sin will f. you out 46:21
Finder-out of occasions 471:1
Findeth: he that f. his life 59:3
he that seeketh f. 58:20
whatsoever thy hand f. to do 51:21
Finding how it feels 142:14
Finds: more opportunities than he f. 25:39
who f. himself 18:17
Fine: as f. and as fast as he can 387:20
bring in f. things 98:9
cheated into some f. passages 290:15
dear, f., silly old angel 307:24
face of heaven so f. 478:20
f. by degrees 401:32
f. things to be seen 141:24
f. words!..where you stole 'em 521:10
f. writing..next to f. doing 290:23
finely touch'd but to f. issues 461:16
frets until 'tis f. 111:24
how exquisitely f. 383:17
less subtle and f. 352:28
May will be f. next year 263:30
mighty f. fellows nowadays 515:8
not to put too f. a point 173:27
night is f. 130:18
passage which you think..f. 272:17
quite a *disgrace* to be f. 527:7
scenery is f. 289:30
some are f. fellows 336:5
that f. madness 189:12
world is a f. place 241:17
Fine art is that in which.. 413:16
Fine arts: Devil fly away with the
  f. 126:40
Murder..one of the F. 172:22
Finely: spirits are not f. touch'd 461:16
Finem: dabit deus his quoque f. 553:13
qui f. quaeris amoris 372:3
respice f. 13:12
Finer: than the staple of his
  argument 387:6, 455:24
something f. in the man 200:6
Fines: sunt certi denique f. 261:9
Finesse: his musical f. was such 162:28
Finest: this was their f. hour 143:41
Finger: better a f. off 420:11
f. idly some..knot 147:9
f. of birth-strangled babe 459:33
God's f. touch'd him 533:8
his slow and moving f. 472:34
lazy f. of a maid 477:7
more goodness in her little f. 520:20
Moving F. writes 207:2
my f. into the print of the nails 64:9
my little f. shall be thicker 47:46
not a pipe for Fortune's f. 434:26
Old Harry's got a f. in it 190:23
pointing like a rugged f. 216:7
press'd her cold f...to her lips 286:4
put your f. in your eye 366:15
Time's slow f. 33:12

Fingered: chilly f. spring 285:7
Fingering slave 578:30
Fingers: cannot lick his own f. 478:32
contaminate our f. with..bribes 451:12
dead men's f. 437:1
even the works of thy f. 392:9
f. play in..unmindfulness 235:21
f. weary and worn 253:22
my f. wandered idly 402:11
o'er lawyers' f. 477:7
only kissed the f. 88:22
pinching f. 485:6
silent f. point to heaven 574:21
smile upon his f.' ends 443:19
with forc'd f. rude 342:10
Finger-stalls: in fitless f. 220:6
Fingertips: her slim f. 249:8
Finical: polish of the latter..f. 154:13
Finish: f., good lady 426:3
f. up your swipes 296:17
we will f. the job 144:5
Finished: f. gentleman 116:42
heroically hath f. 351:5
I have f. my course 68:60
it is f. 64:2
washing and never..f. 237:12
when your work is f. 296:33(-297)
world where England is f. 339:7
Finisher: author and f. of our faith 69:18
Finita: causa f. est 22:5
Finite: cannot quite bury under
  the F. 127:18
f. hearts that yearn 97:12
Fir-branch: lone on the f. 336:9
Fire: adamantine chains and penal
  f. 344:7
after the earthquake a f. 48:8
after the f. a still small voice 48:8
Aha,..I have seen the f. 54:16
all compact of f. 488:26
all the youth of England are on
  f. 443:12
around the f...its evening hours 516:19
as a f. shall ye pass 525:12
as now on f. I am 508:15
as the flint bears f. 451:25
at his post when under f. 236:4
at their hearts the f.'s centre 509:1
awkward squad f. over me 108:40
bad angel f. my good one out 488:19
before the f. of life 308:25
beside my lonely f. 3:6
Billy..fell in the f. 228:11
books that you may carry to the f. 276:28
broad gate and the great f. 423:9
bush burned with f. 45:33
by night in a pillar of f. 45:50
children born of thee are sword
  and f. 530:12
children of men..set on f. 395:18
clear f., a clean hearth 306:12
coals of f. upon his head 50:35
cold performs th' effect of f. 345:31
cosy f. is bright and gay 372:16
dare seize the f. 75:24
desire of f. to reach to f. 335:28
don't one of you f. until 404:1
dropping-wells of f. 533:7
every time she shouted, 'F.!' 41:12
f. a mine in China 111:5
f. and fleet and candle-lighte 31:12
f. and hail, snow and vapours 400:24
f. and people..agree 232:12
f. answers f. 444:6
f. burn and cauldron bubble 459:30
F.! Help! The Hare! 250:8
f. in your ain parlour 419:29
f. is not quenched 61:5
f. of old Rome 201:27
f. of soul is kindled 177:28
f. of thine eyes 75:24
f. seven times tried 464:3
f. shall never make thee shrink 31:13
f. that saith not, It is enough 50:55
f. that stirs about her 585:4
f. that warms cold 134:18
f. when you are ready 173:2
f. which in the heart resides 16:29
f. within f. 410:26
fretted with golden f. 433:15
frighted with false f. 435:18

Fire (*cont.*)
full of that heavenly f. 232:11
gentlemen of the French Guard,
  f. first 239:9
given me f. 458:2
Great F...not the f. in which 175:32
gulfs of liquid f. 473:32
heart of the night with f. 524:13
heretic that makes the f. 485:11
his ministers a flaming f. 398:8
his speech is a burning f. 522:7
hold a f. in his hand 474:20
I am f. and air 426:10
in darkness, f. and chains 561:22
in his shirt of f. 503:12
in our asshen olde is f. 137:45
in the F. of Spring 205:14, 15
it is a f., it is a coal 377:3
I will sit beside the fire 41:18
Last Judgment's f. 90:20
lighten with celestial f. 400:31
lights, and the f. 359:7
like f. he meets the foe 538:22
like the sparks of f. 246:23
little f. kindleth 69:36
little f. is quickly trodden out 446:5
little spark of celestial f. 560:30
make me a f. 247:17
man take f. in his bosom 49:49
motion of a hidden f. 355:11
my chariot of f. 75:16
my f.'s extinct 8:13
not the resolution to f. it 270:22
not till the f. is dying 336:20
now stir the f. 163:21
O! for a Muse of f. 443:2
O Love, O f.! 529:22
ordain'd to kill, conceiveth f. 509:25
our little torches at his f. 147:26
our neighbour's house..on f. 102:4
our passions as..f. and water 313:19
pale his uneffectual f. 432:19
perfect steadiness under f. 305:1
quick'ned now with f. 232:15
right Promethean f. 455:23
roar, as if of earthly f. 285:36
roast with f. 45:46
rosy fleece of f. 166:4
run a mile to see a f. 514:35
sea of glass mingled with f. 71:38
set a house on f. 27:39
shrivell'd in a fruitless f. 532:33
Skiddaw saw the f. 322:23
smiles by his cheerful f. 226:11
soldier..sat by his f. 224:20
soul of f. 279:5
spark o' Nature's f. 105:24
stand by the f. and stink 452:24
stood that night against my f. 454:13
that man's heart were as f. 521:30(-522)
they are all f. 449:30
tongues like as of f. 64:25
to Purgatory f. thou com'st 31:13
to view what f. was near 508:14
true Promethean f. 455:20
two irons in the f. 37:22
warm him at his f. 244:2
what of the faith and f.? 236:18
when his pistol misses f. 227:27
where once I was f. 112:37
while I was..musing the f.
  kindled 394:8
while Mrs. Bennet was stirring
  the f. 22:31
Who hast made the F. 300:4
with a book by the f. 297:28
with a heart of f. 536:24
with white f. laden 492:29
years steal f. from the mind 113:23
youk'n hide de f. 238:23
Fire Brigade: summoned..Lon-
  don's Noble F. 41:10
Fireballs: hail, or blinding f. 94:13
Fire-baptism: Baphometic F. 127:15
Firebrand plucked out of the burning 56:1
Fired: f. another Troy 191:11
projectile..f. by the British
  Navy 232:17
Fire-drake: as far as the f. swings 141:1
Fire-flames noondays kindle 90:39

Fire-fly wakens 539:2
Fire-folk sitting in the air 255:5
Fireman, and afraid of bumps 504:10
Fire-new from the mint 483:31
Fire-red cherubinnes face 137:19
Fires: arose the answering f. 322:21
 banked the f. high 302:31
 fuel to maintain his f. 124:25
 glorious th' assembled f. 503:6
 keep the home f. burning 210:4
 light of household f. 316:18
 light their f...a luxury 237:1
 live their wonted f. 230:9
 misled by wandering f. 192:23
 phoenix 'midst her f. 117:29
 quench'd the stelled f. 453:34
 thought-executing f. 453:5
 tried in f. of woe 269:31
 Truth..lend her noblest f. 117:26
 violent f. soon burn out 474:21
 whose f. true genius kindles 385:29
 wine inspires us, and f. us 214:30
 ye follow wandering f. 530:26
Fire-side: all our adventures were
  by the f. 227:17
 by the f. with Sorrow 494:9
 f. enjoyments 163:26
 happy f. clime 104:23
 season my f. with personal talk 578:18
 there is no f. 317:11
 winter talk by the f. 27:2
Fire-winged to its goal 411:28
Firewood, ironware 333:21
Firk: I'll fer him, and f. him 445:2
Firm: as f. as Sparta's king 188:33
 f. I can meet..the blow 124:13
 make f. in me a heart 213:2
 so f. that cannot be seduc'd 448:31
 zealous, beneficent, f. 17:17
Firmament: f. showeth his handy-
  work 392:32
 in earth's f...shine 316:23
 no fellow in the f. 449:30
 now glow'd the f. 347:19
 pillared f. is rottenness 340:31
 spacious f. on high 2:25
 streams in the f. 330:7
 this brave o'erhanging f. 433:15
Firmness: little objects with like f. 113:40
 thy f. makes my circle just 186:25
 with f. in the right 314:13
Firm-set: sure and f. earth 458:1
Firs: f. with cones upon them 317:22
 sight of bleak Scotch f. 127:4
First: after Last, returns the F. 89:22
 be not the f. 382:29
 came f. to the sepulchre 64:5
 dislike..at f. sight 511:19
 each second..heir to the f. 469:24
 else made f. in vain 96:10
 ever since afore her F. 176:31
 Eve upon the f. of Men 252:10
 f. and wisest 350:12
 f. day 44:3
 f. heaven and the f. earth 71:44
 f. in war, f. in peace 312:25
 f.-love's f. cry 375:8
 f. man is of the earth 67:15
 f. man thou mayest meet 549:6
 f. of biographers 325:26
 f. of those who know 537:37
 f. shall be last 60:5
 f. that ever burst 149:3
 f. to come and last to go 318:7
 f. to fade away 121:8
 f. to his Englishmen 352:12
 f. to me 82:11
 f. true gentleman 170:31
 f. Whig was the Devil 274:7
 for which the f. was made 95:13
 Glorious F. of June 147:15, 359:26
 Great F. Cause 386:29
 he'd have been here f. 131:17
 him f., him last 348:5
 his f. avow'd intent 99:35
 his f., best country 226:7
 his f., last, everlasting day 184:6
 if at f. you don't succeed 248:8
 if not f., in the very f. line 225:31
 in her f. passion 115:38
 last his sorrow, f. his joy 232:2

First (cont.)
 like Tom the F. 192:11
 never remember which came f. 181:23
 no last nor f. 94:46
 no matter what you teach them f. 271:13
 nothing should ever be done for
  the f. time 157:10
 not th.. f. have sat in taverns 263:31
 of f., and last, and midst 580:25
 rather be f. in a village 24:29
 reach the bottom f. 228:7
 that lov'd not at f. sight 330:13, 428:15
 that the f. poets had 189:11
 undoubted title to the f. 520:33
 when f. we kissed 82:2
 when f. we met 82:12
 worse than the f. 59:19
First-born: against all the f. in
  Egypt 427:10
 Beauty's f. 232:11
 feels..her f.'s breath 234:16
 offspring of Heaven f. 346:18
 smite all the f. in...Egypt 45:47
First-class: those f. passengers 299:8
Firstfruits of them that slept 67:8
Firstlings: f. of my heart..f. of my
  hand 460:15
Fir-tree: instead of the thorn..the
  f. 54:32
Fir-trees: f...for the stork 398:10
 the f. dark and high 253:2
Fish: discourse of..f. and fishing 559:25
 does the f. soar? 545:1
 dominion over the f. of the sea 44:9
 f. diddle-de-dee 312:5
 f...have bright mail 285:1
 f. not with this melancholy bait 462:35
 f. say 83:23, 27
 f. that talks 170:25
 f. with the worm that hath eat of
  a king 436:13
 great f. spouts music 266:13
 harmless f. monastic silence
  keep 184:24
 impaling worms to torture f. 154:16
 it's no f. ye're buying 419:13
 I was a f. 504:13
 Jonah..in the belly of the f. 56:5
 like a f. out of the water 422:31
 littlest f. may enter in 83:26
 no more land, say f. 84:1
 O silver f. 586:5
 piece of a broiled f. 62:57
 small 'stute F. 304:10
 so free as a f. 413:19
 they're bonnie f. 360:13
 thou deboshed f. thou 480:2
 to f. for his Aunt Jobiska's .. cat 312:9
 un-dish-cover the f. 131:29
 what cat's averse to f.? 230:20
Fishbones: two f., two eyeballs 563:37
Fished: who f. the murex up? 95:3
Fisher: skilful f. goes not forth 11:21
Fisherman: well for the f.'s boy 528:3
Fishermen..appear like mice 454:3
Fishers: f. of men 57:38
 three f. went sailing 293:25
Fishes: bait in the f.' mouth 11:21
 f. first to shipping 191:29
 f. of the sea 392:12
 f. that tipple 319:6
 little f.' answer 131:10
 little f. of the sea 131:10
 loses sight of the loaves and f. 376:16
 make hors-d'œuvres for f. 183:14
 make little f. talk 227:29
 men lived like f. 501:14
 men that f. gnaw'd upon 476:14
 uncommunicating muteness of f. 307:30
 waiting..so are the f. 144:3
 welcomes little f. in 128:24
 when f. flew 140:21
Fishified: flesh, how art thou f.! 478:4
Fishing: discourse of..fish and f. 559:25
 f. up the moon 377:1
 fly f...angling or float f. 277:13
 I go a f. 64:12
 or go f.? 545:15
 when I was last this way a-f. 559:19
Fish-like: very ancient and f.
  smell 479:38

Fishmonger: you are a f. 433:1
Fishpond: that great f. 170:19
Fish-ponds in my garden 563:19
Fishpools: eyes like the f. in
  Heshbon 52:19
Fish-sauce: crack a bottle of f. 142:1
Fishy: of f. form and mind 83:26
Fist: beat with f. 110:3
 his energetic f. 221:19
 his f. be ever ready 221:20
 my left eye agin the Seceesher's
  f. 560:11
Fit: all the news that's f. to print 370:2
 doer and the thing done seldom
  f. 505:24
 fell down in a f. 150:11
 f. audience find 348:23
 f. for the deed 131:11
 f. for to serve as a soldier 304:3
 f. will work on him 437:25
 most senseless and f. man 468:35
 not f. to tie his brogues 420:30
 one last long lingering f. 300:20
 only the F. survive 422:20
 punishment f. the crime 220:2
 soldier f. to stand by Caesar 471:15
 therefore needs must f. 160:7
 they all f. 569:36
 those that f. the thing 309:16
Fitless finger-stalls 220:6
Fitly: word f. spoken 50:34
Fitness: parentage..no test of f.
  for it 489:23
Fits: bein' took with f. 176:31
 big blue cap that always f. 141:15
 develop Sleary's f. 300:21
 periodical f. of morality 325:15
 strange f. of passion 581:11
 their f. and freaks 183:12
 think by f. and starts 263:34
Fitted: the last arrow was f. 140:18
Fitter: f. being sane than mad 89:22
 f. Love for me 186:15
 f., where it died, to tell 280:11
Fittest: Survival of the F. 169:8, 508:26
Fitting for a princess 426:15
Fittings: remarkable regimental
  in her f. 304:26
Fitzdotterel: Earl of F.'s eldest
  son 84:27(–85)
Fitzgerald: F. strung them 320:6
 F...'thanked God my wife was
  dead' 91:26
 for this Edward F. died 584:27
 hoarse F. 117:8
Five: Benjamin's mess was f. times 45:22
 but f. days elder 86:9
 children dine at f. 515:17
 f. hours up and seven down 301:6
 f. miles meandering 151:33
 f. minutes too late all my lifetime 158:25
 f. ports of knowledge 85:18
 f. steep flights 171:24
 full fathom f. 479:30
 healths f. fathom deep 477:7
 housbondes..she hadde f. 137:15
 jewels f.-words long 538:11
 life's f. windows 74:12
 Mister John Keats f. feet high 290:3
 must rise at f. 145:31
 not f. in f. score 387:4
 of f. things have a care 7:5
 received the use of the f. operations 56:45
 their f. eyes smouldering 171:10
 twice f. miles 151:32
Five-and-thirty pipers 23:26
Five-and-twenty: count f., Tatty-
  coram 175:34
 f. ponies 301:18
 only f. per cent. of its danger 518:7
 reputation of f. 193:4
Five hundred a year 23:9
Five per cent..the natural interest 325:8
Five-pound: as the gen'l'm'n
  said to the f. note 178:41
 wrapped up in a f. note 311:24
Fix thy firm gaze 324:17
Fixed: commonwealth is f. 101:18
 f. fate, free will 345:29

Fixed (cont.)
f. figure for the time of scorn 472:34
f. for ever at the door 541:23
f. in stedfast gaze 343:14
f. like a plant 383:24
f. thee mid this dance 95:24
f. the where and when 239:7
great gulf f. 62:26
man..absolutely f. on 204:8
our hearts..there be f. 389:38
still stood f. to hear 348:29
that f. mind and high disdain 344:13
Watson..the one f. point 188:13
well and wisely f. 574:19
Flag: admiral's f. sank 237:15
death's pale f. 478:43
English F. was flown 296:5
f. and sign of love 469:35
f. that makes you free 583:7
meteor f. of England 123:12
old f. flyin' 363:3
raised their f. against a power 563:5
she took up the f. 568:12
spare your country's f. 568:14
their f. to April's breeze 199:7
vagabond f. 423:39
war, an' a debt, an' a f. 319:28
we shall not f. or fail 143:40
whose f. has braved 123:10
Flag-flowers: there grew broad f. 497:23
Flagitium: peiusque leto f. timet 261:4
Flagons: stay me with f. 51:45
Flagrant: fair and f. things 165:26
Flags wearily through darkness 495:10
Flail: f. of the lashing hail 492:26
Protestant F. 250:13
Flakes: clouds..in f. and bars 151:1
large white f. 81:15
latest f. of Eternity 38:30
Flame: adding fuel to the f. 350:37
but f.? 95:7
candle-f. beside the surplices 310:24
children of splendour and f. 561:12
Chloe is my real f. 401:38
fed with Shakespeare's f. 141:30
feed his sacred f. 152:3
f. I still deplore 213:15
f. of fair faces 523:2
f. that lit the battle's wreck 241:5
f...upon its altars 239:20
full of subtil f. 37:12
Fury slinging f. 532:27
hard, gemlike f. 374:14
his eyes were as a f. of fire 70:27
if you nurse a f. 123:4
my f. to qualify 488:4
she may receive..my f. 401:24
shuttered my doors with f. 296:4
sinking f. of hilarity 177:29
softer f. 104:20
so in a shapeless f. 184:4
spark of heav'nly f. 381:28
steel and scorching f. 23:21
still plays about the f. 214:11
thin smoke without f. 236:14
whose f. creeps in 377:3
with eyes of f. 129:39(–130)
with her battle-thunder and f. 539:21
Flame-coloured: in f. taffeta 438:13
Flamed: as one great furnace f. 344:9
f. upon the brazen greaves 534:4
Flamens: here lies two f. 124:26
Flames: f. in the forehead of the
..sky 343:3
his f. must waste away 124:25
in f. or at feast 586:20
like thin f. 410:11
rich f., and hired tears 87:3
thou king of f. 135:18
whelks and knobs and f. o' fire 444:3
Flaming: f. from th' ethereal sky 344:7
thou f. minister 473:11
wav'd over by the f. brand 349:31
Flammae: agnosco veteris vestigia f. 554:15
Flammantia moenia mundi 320:27
Flanders: F. mare 242:22
in F. fields 326:15
part of F. hath receiv'd our yoke 558:8
prodigious armies we had in F. 513:12
Flank: on the Brown Bear's f. 301:4
Flanks: all her silken f. 287:12

Flannel: f. waistcoat and f. drawers 213:22
infant negroes..f. waistcoats 178:43
Flannelled fools at the wicket 297:16
Flap; let me f. this bug 385:31
Flap-dragon: easier swallowed
than a f. 455:26
Flapped: rooks..f. and fought 249:13
vainly f. its tinsel wing 332:5
Flare: to the f. of Hell-gate 302:27
Flared: forth John's soul f. 92:6
full she f. it 94:8
on he f. 285:36
Flash: f. upon that inward eye 577:7
one F. of it within the Tavern 207:9
quick as a f. 'tis gone 292:15
Flashes: f. blent with..discontent 375:10
f. struck from midnights 90:39
objects recognized in f. 579:26
occasional f. of silence 505:2
your f. of merriment 437:15
Flashest: stream that f. white 533:32
Flashing: f. from one end of the
world to the other 514:35
his f. eyes 151:33(–152)
Flashy: lean and f. songs 342:29
Flask of Wine, a book of Verse 205:23
Flat: f. and flexible truths 85:17
f. burglary 469:9
half so f. as Walter Scott 9:5
life extremely f. 222:1
many times f., insipid 194:6
stale, f. and unprofitable 430:33
strike f. the thick rotundity 453:5
therefore it's f. and plain 9:10
wall fell down f. 46:40
Flat-irons: flavour o' warm f. 179:20
Flats: fifty different sharps and f. 94:33
Flatten: sure to f. 'em 40:27
Flatter: before you f. a man 277:14
but f. with their lips 392:20
dedication..professes to f. 276:8
do not think I f. 434:24
f. ourselves that I may be the
survivor 23:2
fondly f. our desires 189:5
not f. me at all 167:7
they f. with their tongue 392:5
would not f. Neptune 429:13
Flattered: being then most f. 449:12
Englishman, being f. 135:14
f. into virtue 518:4
he that loves to be f. 480:18
not f. its rank breath 113:50
whom all the world hath f. 405:13
Flatterer: arch-f...a man's self 26:33
either a coward or a f. 450:8
f. of happy minds 154:39
plea of the..f. 75:7
worthy o' the f. 480:18
Flatterers: by f. besieged 385:29
tell him he hates f. 449:12
Flattering: some with a f. word 569:4
that f. unction 436:1
think him worth f. 490:1
Flatters: humours and f. them 139:23
lie that f. 162:16
what really f. a man 490:1
Flattery: ask advice..tout for f. 153:18
everyone likes f. 181:22
f. lost on poet's ear 417:19
f. soothe the ..ear of death 230:3
gained by every sort of f. 139:30
gross f. to name a coward 548:5
known style of a dedication..f. 276:8
patron..paid with f. 277:30
this is no f. 426:29
whether your f. is worth..having 277:14
with feyned and japes 137:22
Flaunting, extravagant quean 500:39
Flavia's a wit 384:31
Flavour: f. o' warm flat-irons 179:20
general f. of mild decay 251:7
gives it all its f. 163:4
till it's losing its f. 34:34
vich wanity do you like the f. on? 179:30
Flaw: f. in happiness 285:11
no kind of fault or f. 218:35
standing every f. 429:21
Flawed: his f. heart 454:23
Flaws: wished the f. were fewer 90:33
Flax: smoking f. shall he not quench 54:15

Flayed: belted you an' f. you 297:6
Flea: clog the foot of a f. 484:2
f. hath smaller fleas 521:22
f. in his ear 14:21
f. in's ear 37:32
not take the life of a f. 34:17
precedency between a louse and
a f. 275:10
very f. of his dog 280:15
Fleas: beggars, f., and vines 293:10
dog that praised his f. 586:12
f. know not whether..upon..a
giant 309:22
f. that tease 42:9
great f. have little f. 358:14
reasonable amount of f. 565:23
smaller f. 521:22
Flebilis: multis ille bonis f. occidit 258:25
Flecked: f. the streets of Baltimore 405:19
Sun was f. with bars 149:12
Flectere si nequeo superos 555:4
Fled: all but he had f. 241:9
f., and cry'd out, *Death* 346:8
f. from her wish 470:20
f. is that music 288:2
f. like some frail exhalation 492:18
f. the Seen 560:5
f. with a Christian 463:42
I f. Him 544:13
I waked, she f. 351:26
sea saw..and f. 399:2
still as he f. 509:26
they're all f. with thee 292:5
to a boon..country he is f. 18:31(–19)
when earth's foundations f. 264:4
with him f. the shades of night 347:36
Fledges: Green f. the River-Lip 206:4
Flee: at thy rebuke they f. 398:8
death shall f. from them 71:12
fancies f. away! 99:37
f. as a bird 392:17
f. fro the press 136:20
f. from the wrath to come 57:30
f. when no man pursueth 50:49
he can speak and f. 30:20
he will f. from you 69:40
kings with their armies did f. 396:7
sorrow and sighing shall f. 54:5
them also that hate him f. 396:4
they f. from me, that..did me
seek 583:20
thousand shall f. at the rebuke of
one 53:40
Fleece: its f. was white as snow 233:23
like the rain into a f. of wool 396:24
rosy f. of fire 166:4
your f. is white 166:5
Fleeces so clean and so white 562:4
Fleet: all in the Downs the f. 215:39
fire and f. and candle-lighte 31:12
f. of stars 208:7
O thou most f. 521:30
retiring..towards the Japanese
f. 234:18
Spanish f. thou canst not see 500:1
there's the British F. 543:10
took care of our f. 2:19
wondrous thing, how f. 333:1
yield..thy f. 122:6
Fleeter of foot than the..kid 522:2
Fleetest: fairest things have f. end 543:24
Fleeth: hireling f. 63:38
my soul f. unto the Lord 399:40
Fleeting: false, f., perjur'd Clarence 476:16
rapid, blind, and f. generations 499:8
Time is f. 317:9
Fleet-limbed and beautiful 365:17
Fleets: mightiest f. of iron 188:13
ten thousand f. sweep over thee 114:27
Fleet Street: dull in F. 307:4
take a walk down F. 414:20
Flere: si vis me f. 255:23
Flesh: all f. is as grass 69:46
all f. is grass 54:10
all f. shall see it 54:9
all this f. keep in..life 441:1
bring me f. 361:21
closed up the f. instead 44:16
conversion of the Godhead into
f. 388:42

Flesh (*cont.*)
east wind made f. 13:19
every..spirit that ever took f. 200:41
fedde with rosted f. 136:30
f. and blood, and apprehensive 449:30
f. and blood..in Adam fail 364:8
f. and blood so cheap 253:25
f. f., how art thou fishified! 478:4
f. is weak 60:43
f. lusteth against the Spirit 67:45
f. of f., bone of my bone 349:18
f. of my f. 44:17
f. to feel the chain 83:13
f. which walls about our life 475:7
her fair and unpolluted f. 437:20
in my f. shall I see God 49:6
make not provision for the f. 66:14
milk and tendre f. 137:36
more f. than another man 440:15
much study is a weariness of the f. 51:35
my f. also longeth after thee 395:25
my gross f. sinks downwards 476:1
my..heart and f. cry out 421:3
my heart and my f. rejoice 397:5
my kinsmen according to the f. 65:59
not against f. and blood 68:11
one f...two fools 154:32
pour out my spirit upon all f. 55:52
present joys are more to f. and blood 192:29
prisons of f. 186:7
reasonable soul and human f. 388:41
sacred be the f. and blood 532:24
set..our f. upright 184:22
shocks that f. is heir to 434:4
since f. must live 96:26
sinful lust of the f. 302:30
sinful lusts of the f. 391:2
soul helps f. 95:17
soul to feel the f. 83:13
spite of this f. today 95:17
ta'en out thy heart o' f. 32:5
that I will eat bull's f. 395:4
thorn in the f. 67:37
they shall be one f. 44:18
they that are after the f. 65:52
this f. of mine might be 524:23
this too too solid f. 430:33
this world-wearied f. 478:44
thou didst eat strange f. 423:40
unto thee shall all f. come 395:27
wants to make your f. creep 178:30
way of all f. 155:39, 422:28, 563:23
we are one, one f. 349:19
weyveth milk and f. and al 137:36
within this circle of f. 86:20
Word was made f. 62:64
world, the f., and the devil 388:47
Fleshed: full bravely..f. thy maiden sword 441:3
Flesh-garment: language is the f. 127:10
Fleshly: abstain from f. lusts 69:49
F. School of Poetry 98:5
through all this f. dress 552:5
Flesh pots: we sat by the f. 45:52
Fleshy tables of the heart 67:21
Fletu: fraterno multum manantia f. 133:20
Fleurs: amas de f. étrangères 355:6
Flew: birds that eternally f. 309:26
round and round it f. 148:27
thence up he f. 347:3
Flewed: so f., so sanded 467:20
Flexible: flat and f. truths 85:17
Flichterin' noise an' glee 104:33
Flicker: run-stealers f. to and fro 545:2
Fliers: chase e'en now the f. 147:8
f. and pursuers 324:15
Flies: as f. to wanton boys 453:40
dead f...stinking savour 51:23
f. o'er th'unbending corn 382:32
f. of estates 243:23
f., or ants..in amber 27:47
f., worms and flowers, exceed me 561:31
happiness too swiftly f. 230:30
he that f. mought fight again 24:43
immortal f. 84:1
Joy as it f. 74:27
large blue f. 504:5
lean black craft like f. 410:17
may catch small f. 519:7
Flies (*cont.*)
murmurous haunt of f. 287:31
see, where it f. 330:5
shadow, it still f. you 280:20
small f...caught 25:1
then she f. away 540:10
This Life f. 206:26
time's f. 480:26
unto you at last she f. 125:11
wades, or creeps, or f. 346:14
Flieth: grief f. to it 26:2
Flight: attained by sudden f. 316:31
confused alarms of struggle and f. 15:8
dark..the day of their f. 326:8
eagle in his f. 316:7
frantic f. of courtesy 375:26
hear the lark begin his f. 341:31
his f. was madness 460:16
in what fond f. 411:10
on tiptoe for a f. 286:27
puts the Stars to F. 205:4
scattered into f. the Stars 205:5
soonest take their f. 365:8
swift be thy f. 495:21
take f. and follow 524:13
thy soul's f. 459:2
till prepar'd for longer f. 332:20
Time, in your f. 4:16
wheels his droning f. 229:28
will not take their f. 343:14
Flights: five steep f. 171:24
f. upon the banks of Thames 281:18
Flighty purpose never is o'ertook 460:14
Flim-flam: pretty f. 37:26
Flimnap..allowed to cut a caper 519:12
Flinch: facts..f. not 96:1
Flinders: little Polly F. 367:17
Fling: f. but a stone 231:27
f. them back their gold 365:20
I'll have a f. 38:4
Winter Garment..f. 205:14, 15
Flint: as the f. bears fire 451:25
in time the f. is pierced 305:12
set your faces like a f. 99:13
snore upon the f. 429:36
wear out the everlasting f. 478:10
Flippant: woman..f., vain 289:10
Flirt: how can he f.? 504:27
Flirtation: merely innocent f. 116:40
most significant word, *f.* 139:34
Flit: I will f. into it 286:18
Flits: he f. across the stage 182:2
surmise f. across her bosom 199:13
Flitting: I am f. about many years 146:15
Flittings: thou tellest my f. 395:15
Float: angling or f. fishing 277:13
f. face down 266:15
f. that standard sheet 234:13
f. upon his watery bier 342:10
f. upon the wings of silence 340:15
little lead best fits a little f. 245:19
Floated: f. midway on the waves 151:33(-152)
out flew the web and f. wide 534:7
Floating: f. bulwark of the island 73:6
his f. hair 151:33(-152)
his f. home for ever left 159:1
Floats: cloud that f. on high 577:5
f. above the wrecks of Time 312:24
grey expanse where he f. 16:4
Flocci-pauci-nihili-pili-fication of money 420:27, 499:17
Flock: as we sat in a f. 236:21
feed his f. like a shepherd 54:11
f. without shelter 419:3
half his f...in their beds 584:6
silent was the f. 285:12
there is no f. 317:11
thou makest thy f. to rest 51:40
thy hair is as a f. of goats 52:5
thy teeth are like a f. of sheep 52:5
Flocks: fleecy f. of light 82:7
f. of shiny pleiades 249:14
f. of the memories 338:3
f., or herds, or human face 346:20
f. that straggling feed 232:1
like f. to feed in air 496:4
my father feeds his f. 251:26
my f. feed not 35:21
no f. that range the valleys 225:12
Flodden's fatal field 418:35
Flogging: habit of f. me constantly 549:10
less f...than formerly 272:36
Flood: accidents by f. and field 470:2
beached verge of the salt f. 480:32
beauty has no ebb, decay no f. 585:16
bridge that arched the f. 199:7
drink to thee across the f. 529:35
f. could not wash away 155:16
f. may bear me far 528:22
F. of British freedom 577:2
giant race before the f. 192:9
into this angry f. 448:18
land of the mountain and the f. 417:22
much broader than the f. 468:7
nearly spoiled ta F. 23:27
nobler tenants of the f. 161:34
not properly born, till f. 174:39
passage o'er a restless f. 160:14
reformation in a f. 443:6
rich burghers on the f. 462:29
sudden f. of mutiny 450:32
taken at the f. 116:21, 451:29
takes the f. with swarthy webs 531:38
ten years before the F. 333:8
thorough f., thorough fire 466:33
through such a raging f. 323:29
vast across the f. 266:17
winds that curl the f. 319:7
Flood-brim: unto the furthest f. 411:8
Flooded full light and beauty 334:6
Flood-gate: f. of the deeper heart 208:20
of so f...nature 469:43
Flooding in, the main 147:8
Floods: bathe in fiery f. 462:9
f. are risen..the f. have lift up their voice: f. lift up their waves 397:23
governess of f. 466:37
haystack in the f. 359:4
in your deep f. 209:4
neither can the f. drown it 52:23
to his f. decline 82:9
Floor: along the gusty f. 285:27
beneath the watery f. 343:3
careless on a granary f. 284:12
faces from the f. to th' roof 163:28
fell upon the sanded f. 376:9
f. of heaven is thick inlaid 465:18
f...pav'd with broken hearts 318:26
from whose f. the new-bathed stars 17:28(-18)
hopping o'er the f. 546:26
I could f. them all 181:26
I swept the f. 221:15
my fleece-like f. 492:29
nicely sanded f. 225:3
spit upon my curious f. 245:12
thy sad f. an altar 114:34
trod my nursery f. 160:30
Floored with gemlike plains 561:17
Floors: across the f. of silent seas 197:19
Flop: f. in favour of your husband 179:36
f. round the earth 304:1
Flora: nor F.'s pride 87:25
tasting of F. 287:24
Floral: her fair and f. air 208:5
Florence: F. ran fastest of all 327:1
lily of F. 316:25
Lord of Parys, Venyce, or F. 195:7
past fair F. 286:22
sit..outside the cathedral at F. 176:2
small states—Israel, Athens, F. 267:9
yonder late in F. 94:8
Florentine: what the F. 81:1
Flores: at F. in the Azores 539:16
Floribus: quod in ipsis f. angat 321:2
Flos: cecidit velut prati ultimi f. 132:19
ut f. in saeptis secretus..hortis 133:9
Flourish: all things f. 385:7
almond tree shall f. 51:33
f. at home in my own country 8:22
f. in immortal youth 1:24
f. in May 328:15
f. set on youth 487:9
in the youth..arms do f. 27:36
no more doth f. after first decay 509:33
our farmers..f. and complain 165:3
peculiar f. of his right arm 178:10
princes and lords may f. 224:14
truth shall f. out of the earth 397:9
Flourished: treason f. over us 450:31

INDEX

Flourisheth: f. as a flower of the field 398:7
f. in lusty deeds 328:15
she f. new and new 502:19
Flourishing: f. like a green bay-tree 394:6
no f. with his sword 406:14
Flotilla: where the old F. lay 299:10
Flotte: elle f., elle hésite 405:2
Flout: banners f. the sky 456:8
f. 'em and scout 'em 480:3
gild but to f. 417:12
Flouts: master of gibes and f. and jeers 181:8
Phillida f. me 9:9, 10
Flow: aware of his life's f. 15:6
could I f. like thee 172:10
ebb and f. by the moon 454:19
eye, unus'd to f. 486:25
f. gently, sweet Afton 105:29
f. of Iser, rolling rapidly 122:17
f. of soul 386:5
f. with seas of life 548:18
ribbands to f. confusedly 246:4
that the spices..may f. out 52:8
what need you f. so fast? 11:10
Flowed with that facility 280:1
Flower: action..no stronger than a f. 487:13
as the f. of the grass 69:46
constellated f. that never sets 497:21
creep from f. to f. 494:3
crimson-tippèd f. 107:7
every f. enjoys the air 581:9
fairest f., no sooner blown 341:6
fields without a f. 162:44
finest f. that e'er was seen 32:17
flourisheth as a f. of the field 398:7
f. in the crannied wall 529:24
f. of cities all 195:5
f. of floures alle 138:19
f. of Peace 552:2
f. of sweetest smell 578:3
f. of the hazel glade 232:19
f. of their age 47:3
f. of Yarrow 315:20
F. that once hath blown 206:9
f. that shall be mine 573:16
f. that's like thy face 429:37
f. that smiles today 247:10
f. thereof falleth away 69:46
f.—the wind—the Ocean 114:5
from every opening f. 561:28
fruit which..looks a f. 529:3
glory in the f. 576:20
goodliness..as the f. of the field 54:10
grass withereth, the f. fadeth 54:10
Heaven in a Wild F. 73:18
he paints the wayside f. 122:1
here ev'ry f. is united 214:25
herself a fairer f. 347:8
in f. of youth 190:34
I sipt each f. 214:25
last f. of Catholic love 525:33
leaf, the bud, the f. 509:33
life was but a f. 428:32
lightly like a f. 533:30
little western f. 466:39
look like the innocent f. 457:5
many a f. is born to blush unseen 230:5
meanest f. that blows 576:22 (-577)
midsummer f. 502:17
my face, your f. 91:35
nature said, 'A lovelier f.' 581:21
nipt my f. sae early 106:10
no f. upon the ground 492:24
no sister-f. would be forgiven 495:7
not a f., not a f., sweet 483:6
of all the king's knights 'tis the f. 11:24
O f. of the branch 586:5
only amaranthine f. on earth 163:15
plant and f. of light 282:1
prove a beauteous f. 477:24
simple maiden in her f. 533:36
speaks..'with the f. of the mind' 200:33
summer's f. is to the summer sweet 487:25
sweet will be the f. 161:19
Flower (*cont.*)
take the f. 296:16
this f. of wyfly pacience 137:24
this f., safety 439:9
this most goodly f. 502:19
thou canst not stir a f. 545:5
white f. of a blameless life 529:39
with f. and bee 241:7
you seize the f. 108:7
Flower-bell: fancy from a f. 89:31
Flower-de-luce being one 485:26
Floweret: meanest f. of the vale 231:5
Flowerets of Eden 357:8
Flowering: f. in a lonely word 541:7
in the f. of His fields 531:26
Flowerless fields of Heaven 521:29
Flower-pots: water your damned f., do! 96:38
Flowers: all f. and all trees do close 332:13
all its twined f. 284:12
all sorts of f. 509:6
all that loven f. 138:19
all the f. looked up at Him 140:20
birds and beasts and f. 34:36
blown buds of barren f. 523:18
blushing f. shall rise 385:7
break into foam of f. 524:23
breeding f...never breed the same 288:8
bridal f...for a buried corse 478:33
bringeth vo'th May f. 8:9
but as a bed of f. 186:31
called the f...stars 316:23
cool-rooted f. 288:3
crown old Winter..with f. 166:20
do spring May f. 549:31
ensnar'd with f. 332:17
faded 'midst Italian f. 241:10
fairest f. o' the season 485:23
feel like f. that fade 527:12
flies, worms, and f., exceed me 561:31
flour of f. alle 138:19
f. and fruits of love 118:26
f. appear on the earth 52:1
f. azure, black 497:22
f. begotten 521:30(-522)
f. but fading seen 377:4
f. ginnen for to springe 138:16
f. growing over him 291:2
f. I leave you on the grass 542:6
f. in the garden 516:12
f. made of light 253:1
f. of all hue 347:6
f. of the forest 147:25, 198:18
f. on earth appear 334:16
f. on furze 97:11
f... returning seasons bring 378:15
f. that bloom in the spring 220:15, 16
f. that grow between 317:9
f. that their gay wardrobe wear 342:16
f. to crown thy hearse 292:18
f. to strew Thy way 244:14
f. to wither 241:14
from the f. to the sea 523:15
gathered f. are dead 208:13
here's f. for you 485:25
her f. to love 84:21
I have loved f. that fade 81:7
immortal f. of Poesy 331:2
in a Prospect of F. 333:4
in thee all f...spring 87:25
larded with sweet f. 436:22
later f. for the bees 284:11
lulled in these f. 466:41
most can raise the f. now 529:23
no f., by request 3:7
no f...on my grave 237:7
no fruits, no f. 253:12
no such f. in any land 525:3
of alle the f. in the mede 138:17
of June and July-f. 245:17
oh, the pretty f. 264:22
on chalic'd f. that lies 429:25
other people's f. 355:6
play with f. 443:19
Proserpina! for the f. now 485:26
Proserpin gathering f. 347:8
purple..with vernal f. 342:31
scattered at the feet of man, like f. 574:28
showers for the thirsting f. 492:25
Flowers (*cont.*)
smelt for f. 121:15
summer with f. that fell 522:5
that f. would bloom 285:1
these f., as in their causes 125:9
these f. whyte and rede 138:17
thy grave with rising f. 381:35
Time did beckon to the f. 244:20
took the f. away 317:10
to sweet beds of f. 482:1
unbewailing f. 497:3
up-gathered..like sleeping f. 582:18
votive tears and symbol f. 493:27
wander there among the f. 81:18
waves, f., clouds 493:14
what f. are at my feet 287:30
where souls do couch on f. 425:22
white f. of thy thought 524:4
with f. of the fairest 147:24
Flower-soft: those f. hands 424:7
Flowery: as you walk your f. way 220:28
at her f. work doth sing 341:22
cool f. lap of earth 16:22
f. way 423:9
Showery, F., Bowery 213:5
Floweth: sea itself f. in your veins 548:13
Flowing: f. like a crystal river 537:42
f. sea 167:20
f. with milk and honey 45:36
springs renewed by f. 123:18
your love-locks f. 409:16
Flown: English Flag was f. 296:5
f. with insolence and wine 344:35
Hope could ne'er have f. 332:5
if the bird be f. 552:11
was fitted and was f. 140:18
whither f. again 207:24
Flows: f. by the throne of God 415:18
hardly f. the freezing Tanais 381:18
how sweetly f. 247:13
light, and whence it f. 576:9
thence f. all that charms 151:6
Flowy: Snowy, F., Blowy 213:5
Flügel: wo dein sanfter F. weilt 415:21
Flügeln: auf F. des Gesanges 240:26
Fluidity of self-revelation 268:5
Flummoxed: reg'larly f. 179:8
Flumpetty: fall down f. 311:23
Flung: f. himself upon his horse 311:1
f. it to the winds like Rain 205:28
f. up..the sacred river 151:33
Flunkey: most f. world 126:46
Flush: as f. as May 435:37
roses for the f. of youth 409:28
Flush'd with a purple grace 191:3
Flute: blows out his brains upon the f. 96:27
cornet, f., harp, sackbut 55:36
f., violin, bassoon 536:11
gauger played the f. 516:13
playing upon the f...Houris 231:20
soft complaining f. 191:38
Flutes: f. and soft recorders 345:2
Gibbon moved to f. 154:13
sound of lyres and f. 374:11
to dance to f. 569:5
to the tune of f. kept stroke 424:6
Fluting a wild carol 531:38
Fluttered: f. and fail'd for breath 17:15
f. folk and wild 303:24
f. into rags 346:26
f. your Volscians 429:23
Flutterest: Spring that f. sudden 375:8
Fluttering: f. and dancing in the breeze 577:5
freshening and f. in the wind 92:34
my f. 'eart-strings 294:25
Flutters: bird that f. least 164:5
ere Mor the Peacock f. 301:27
that film..still f. there 151:24
Fluvii: in freta dum f. current 553:21
Fluvius..in quo et agnus..et elephas 232:7
Flux of mortal things 19:4
Fly: above the world you f. 129:8
all things f. thee 544:28
arms outstretch'd, as he would f. 481:20
as great a f. as Cassio 470:30
as he hunted the f. 538:2
as pigs have to f. 129:19
as the sparks f. upward 48:50
awey the f. smyteth 138:20

INDEX

Fly (*cont.*)

bees in July..not worth a f. 5:17
curious, thirsty, f. 370:11
ever f. by twilight 27:22
f. away, f. away, breath 483:6
f. away home 367:12
f., envious Time 351:31
f. fishing..very pleasant 277:13
f., f. betimes 202:4
f., Honesty, f. 504:2
f. I well know whither 80:16
f...may sting a stately horse 270:29
f. not..from the suppliant crowd 164:34
f. sat upon the axle-tree 27:35
f. that sips treacle 214:34
f. to her 538:21
f. to others that we know not of 434:4
for the noise of a f. 186:32
her full Glory..f. before ye 166:22
his praise may thither f. 243:24
I cannot f. But..must fight 401:8
I do not want to be a f. 222:33
I must f., but follow quick 539:17
in my 'solitary f.' 121:11
'I', said the F. 369:19
it may f. not 493:23
I will f. to thee 287:28
know thee and f. thee 507:14
let them f. all 460:33
life so fast doth f. 169:10
man is not a f. 383:15
never f. conceals a hook 83:27
no birds to f. 130:11
no more than a dead f.'s wing 237:15
on the bat's back I do f. 480:14
rattling bones together f. 192:40
said a spider to a f. 264:23
seem to f. it 280:20
shall we fight or shall we f.? 539:20
small gilded f. does lecher 454:8
Swallow, Swallow..f. to her 538:20
they f. forgotten 562:9
those that f., may fight again 111:17
to f. from, need not be to hate 113:46
to f. is safe 163:19
we f...to get his glorious soul 329:25
when a f. offendeth 138:20
which way I f. is Hell 346:32
which way shall I f.? 346:32
with the f. in his hand 513:10
with twain he did f. 53:8
wreke him on a f. 138:20
you f. them for a moment 539:18
Fly-blown phylacteries 409:12
Fly-fishing: for winter f. 559:9
Flying: as the swallow by f. 50:37
borne down by the f. 418:13
come f. on our track 546:30
Fear is a f. 214:10
f., f. South 538:20
f. from the golden woods 538:21
f. still before me, gleamed 575:25
for a f. enemy 115:10
hoping, ling'ring, f. 381:28
moments quickly f. 132:3
old Time is still a-f. 247:10
pinnace..came f. from far away 539:16
white birds f. after 334:2
Flying-fishes: where the f. play 299:10
Foal: poor little F. 152:19
Foaled: since he was f. 171:21
Foam: cruel crawling f. 293:23
f. of the sky 585:22
like the f. on the river 416:23
opening on the f. 288:1
ships on the f. 303:27
spotted with f. 16:4
this year, the must shall f. 323:12
through sheets of f. 18:16
to Noroway o'er the f. 31:24
white birds on the f. of the sea 586:41
white f. of the Spring 561:8
wild and dank with f. 293:22
Foam-flowers endure 523:15
Foaming out their own shame 70:20
Fobbed: resolution thus f. as it is 438:19
Focis: pro aris atque f. suis 415:3
Foe: angry with my f. 76:5
at another to let in the f. 350:29
avowed, erect, and manly f. 124:13

Foe (*cont.*)

darkly at the f. 323:16
first f. in the field 319:10
f. of tyrants 122:38
f. that comes with fearless eyes 362:33
f.! they come! 113:32
furnace for your f. 446:10
great without a f. 114:24
his f. was folly 254:13
I fear no f. 322:2
like fire he meets the f. 538:22
manxome f. 129:39(–130)
met my dearest f. in heaven 431:4
my noble f. I greet 417:28
neither seeks nor shuns his f. 191:28
no f. in shining armour 372:14
open f. may prove a curse 215:24
overcome but half his f. 345:8
perhaps a jealous f. 493:10
rider and horse,—friend, f. 113:36
robbing a f. 143:6
sternest knight to thy mortal f. 328:24
strive afresh against their f. 364:8
taken by the insolent f. 470:2
thou arraign'st her, her f. 16:11
timorous f. 385:29
to match another f. 123:10
treads the shadow of his f. 148:24
unrelenting f. to love 546:7
was it a friend or f.? 410:20
where breathes the f. but falls 234:13
who never made a f. 530:39
willing f. and sea room 5:18
wish my deadly f. no worse 80:3
yield, proud f., thy fleet 122:6
Foeman: beneath the f.'s frown 188:30
spills the foremost f.'s life 416:24
when the f. bares his steel 221:33
Foemen worthy of their steel 416:27
Foes: against her f. Religion 164:39
beat down baffling f. 15:13
f. they captive make 135:12
greatly his f. he dreads 142:28
hearken if his f. pursue 488:28
in presence of my f. 421:1
in the midst of f. 198:19
keep far our f. 400:33
king to slay their f. 326:21
let his f. triumph 231:32
long inveterate f. saluted 193:41
man's f...of his own household 59:2
neither f. nor loving friends 297:12
oh, my f., and oh, my friends 339:6
once dreaded by our f. 162:12
scarce could they hear..their f. 418:29
thrice he routed all his f. 191:6
we ne'er see our f. 213:11
Foetus: expeditious extraction of the f. 513:12
Fog: feel the f. in my throat 95:8
f. of the good man's mind 90:26
hover through the f. 456:3
London particular..a f. 173:23
yellow f. that rubs its back 197:17
Fogs: his rising f. prevail 193:2
Foible: omniscience his f. 506:2
Foie gras: eating *pâtés de f.* to the sound of trumpets 505:10
Foil: put it to the f. 479:44
Foiled: f. circuitous wanderer 17:28(–18)
Latin..rests f. 281:26
though f. he does the best he can 193:15
Foils: most vile and ragged f. 444:10
Foison: spring and f. of the year 487:4
Fold: climb into the f. 342:27
flock in woolly f. 285:12
f. after, to the fainting air 497:26
f. our hands round her knees 521:30(–522)
f. to thy heart thy brother 568:20
in their ancient f. 351:20
like a wolf on the f. 118:37
loves to f. his legs 273:29
not of this f. 63:39
so f. thyself 539:2
taught Art to f. her hands 411:9
thief into God's f. 347:3
walking round the f. 77:2
when the sheep are in the f. 35:7
Folded: f. in the flowerless fields 521:29
f. it right 262:8

Folded (*cont.*)

f. us round 525:2
its sweetest leaves yet f. 117:2
lord of f. arms 455:8
Folding: a-f. let us gang 104:29
f. of the Apennine 18:31(–19)
little f. of the hands 49:46
Folds: f. shall be full of sheep 395:30(–396)
like the f. of a bright girdle 15:7
lull the distant f. 229:28
Foliage: sapless f. of the ocean 496:9
Folio: whole volumes in f. 455:1
Folios: but few F. 365:7
mighty f. first 164:36
Folk: emptied of this f. 287:12
fluttered f. and wild 303:24
Sabbath-bell that call'd the f. 285:30
Folks: hand f. over to God's mercy 196:14
kind to those dear little f. 33:19
old f. at home 210:16
other f. have..some f...glad of 204:20
O yonge fresshe f. 138:42
pretty country f. would lie 428:31
where de old f. stay 210:16
Follies: f. laid him low 104:20
f. of the town crept 226:42
f. of the wise 279:10
f. that themselves commit 403:37
lash the..f. of the age 134:6
no f. to have to repent 527:9
old faults and f. 147:11
paint..vices and f. 154:29
register of the crimes, f. and misfortunes 217:7
where f. naturally grow 143:1
Follow: as well create..precedents as to f. 26:25
bird overhead sang F. 524:8
f...a fall'n lord 424:30
f. a shadow 280:20
f., as the night the day 431:25
f. in their train 240:22
f. me—f. me 'ome 296:17
f. mine own teaching 463:8
f. still the changes of the moon 471:34
f. thee with all the speed 292:19
f. the Gleam 537:2
f. this, and come to dust 430:1
f. thy fair sun 123:20
f. up! f. up! 79:10
f. us disquietly to our graves 452:16
f. well in order 567:4
f. your Saint 123:22
f. your spirit 443:27
he will never f. anything 449:8
I f. but myself 469:27
I f. him to serve my turn 469:25
if they run..we f. 213:11
in constancy f. the Master 99:35
lead, and I f. 530:7
shun what I f. 95:20
take flight and f. 524:13
tell her, that I f. thee 538:21
their works do f. them 71:27
they'll have fleet steeds that f. 418:22
water..to f. faster 424:6
what you may expect..when I f. you 188:12
whose love would f. me still 299:27
ye f. wandering fires 530:26
Followed: first he f. it him-selve 137:18
f. him, honoured him 93:3
f. my poor father's body 430:33(–431)
king himself has f. her 225:15
nine fathom deep he had f. us 149:7
nor all masters..truly f. 469:25
she f. him 110:28, 528:29
Following: corrupt f. of the Apostles 401:9
f. after thee 47:1
f. the roe 107:12
f. him 469:27
in f. him 323:14
with a mighty f. 452:38
Follows: f. but for form 452:38
who f. in His train? 240:20
wind that f. fast 167:20
yet she f. 317:27
Folly: age from f...give me freedom 423:35
all my joys to this are f. 109:2

Folly (cont.)
answer a fool according to his f. 50:38
brood of F. 341:7
call it madness, f. 408:9
due to human f. 310:19
dupe of f. 579:31
Fashion..F.'s child 164:38
feather pate of f. 263:18
f., doctor-like 487:14
f. of being comforted 585:5
f. of the world..confounds its wisdom 251:23
f.'s all they've taught me 356:33
F.'s at full length 80:1, 139:5
f. to be wise 230:30
fool returneth to his f. 50:39
from her coral lips such f. 155:5
God calleth preaching f. 244:7
harmless f. of the time 245:27
her f. help'd her to an heir 470:28
his foe was f. 254:13
his f. has not fellow 262:18
knavery and f. to excuse 143:20
love is..the f. of the wise 277:12
most loving mere f. 427:22
odd and unworthy piece of f. 86:34
O f.! 286:16
persist in his f. 77:14
public schools..public f. 164:6
remember's not the slightest f. 427:2
shielding men from the effects of f. 508:23
shoot f. as it flies 383:8
shunn'st the noise of f. 341:13
stretch the f. of our youth 141:23
too presumptuous f. 238:26
'twixt a vice and f. 300:18
uses..f. like a stalking horse 428:39
when lovely woman stoops to f. 197:32, 226:18
when the forts of f. fall 16:20
whirl'd into f. and vice 535:37
whole centuries of f. 93:11
wisdom excelleth f. 51:1
Fond: don't let us be familiar or f. 156:13
fair and yet not f. 173:1
f. of each gentle..scene 37:6
f. of no second brood 429:22
f. of them..able to conceal it 550:2
f. thing vainly invented. 401:7
f. to live or fear to die 198:10
his f. and foolish mind 29:23
I am too f. 477:20
men would be f. 321:13
more f. than mistress 382:3
so f. of one another..our ailments 519:24
too f. of glory 505:27
too f. of her most filthy bargain 473:22
too f. to rule alone 385:29
very foolish, f. old man 454:15
Fonder: makes the heart grow f. 5:3, 36:28
Fondest, blindest, weakest 544:31
Fondling of a happy pair 378:16
Fondly: f. sae did I 108:38
Fondness for her 376:6
Fons: O f. Bandusiae 260:7
tecto vicinus iugis aquae f. 261:24
Fontarabbia: fell by F. 345:4
Fontarabian: on F. echoes 418:33
Fonte: medio de f. leporum 321:2
Food: books, and my f. 516:16
chief of Scotia's f. 105:2
either our cupboard of f. 244:23
fed with the same f. 464:8
f. enough for a week 337:44
f. for powder 440:23
f. it ne'er had eat 148:27
f. of sweet and bitter fancy 428:24
f. that appeases hunger 134:18
f. that dead men eat 183:9
f. unpriced 334:3
for f. or play 148:28
for human nature's daily f. 580:20
homely was their f. 213:20
if music be the f. of love 481:30
in a jail..better f. 270:32
its f. in music 314:1
lies here, f. for worms 211:21
man did eat angels' f. 396:35

Food (cont.)
music, moody f. 424:11
nothing to eat but f. 292:14
poet's f. is love and fame 493:16
seeking the f. he eats 427:9
Tom's f. 453:24
Fool: answer a f. according to his folly 50:38
any f...write a most valuable book 231:23
ass, without being a f. 518:6
become the golden f. 74:7
better a witty f. 482:12
better to be a f. than..dead 514:37
bray a f. in a mortar 50:48
busy old f. 186:19
by the old f.'s side 90:18
call me not f. 427:13
dost thou call me f., boy? 452:26
drop into thyself, and be a f. 383:23
every f. can play upon the word 464:25
every f. in Buxton 413:1
every f. will be meddling 50:24
f. all the people all of the time 314:14
f., and a d—d f...take Rangoon 564:11
f. and his words..soon parted 499:19
f. as then I was 572:4
f. at forty is a f. indeed 586:23
f. doth not understand it 397:20
f. hath said..no God 392:21
f. he called her his lady 303:12
f. his whole life long 543:5
f. is happy 383:29
F. lies here 300:6
f. me to the top of my bent 435:27
f. might once himself alone expose 382:19
f. multitude 463:43
f. must follow his natural bent 303:13
f. must now and then be right 159:12
f., not to know 193:13
f. of love 239:22
f. returneth to his folly 50:39
'F.!' said my Muse 501:23
f. sees not the same tree 77:11
f. that I was 191:16
f. there was 303:12
f. uttereth all his mind 50:51
forest echo'd 'f.' 531:24
greatest f. may ask more 154:21
hard to make a man appear a f. 194:17
haste of a f. 422:30
heart of the f. 350:28
he hated a f. 276:18
he that begetteth a f. 50:19
how ill white hairs become a f. 442:37
I am Fortune's f. 478:16
if the f. would persist 77:14
I hate a f. 175:33
I have played the f. 47:28
I'm a f. for thinking 387:16
in Arden: the more f. I 426:39
in the privacy of your f.'s heart 513:27
I speak as a f. 67:33
life time's f. 440:37
love is the wisdom of the f. 277:12
Love's not Time's f. 488:7
make my f. my purse 470:19
manage a f. 304:38
man suspects himself a f. 587:6
met a f. i' the forest, a motley f. 427:11
more f. am I 369:13
more hope of a f. than of him 50:40
more of the f. than of the wise 25:30
my poor f. is hang'd 454:20
never was patriot yet but was a f. 190:29
nor a f. in the eye of the world 155:17
nor yet a f. to fame 385:25
not a f. can call me friend 586:13
oh heav'nly f. 502:1
one f...in every married couple 204:9
only f. in the world 93:31
O noble f.! a worthy f. 427:15
O wretched f. 472:6
perfections of a f. 73:15
play the f...at a cheaper rate 161:42
play the f...in 's own house 434:10
play the Roman f. and die 461:9
poor venomous f. 426:13
pretty f., it stinted 477:4
relenting f. 476:30

Fool (cont.)
resolved to live a f. 37:12
smarts so little as a f. 385:23
so is the laughter of a f. 51:10
so true a f. is love 487:7
strumpet's f. 423:11
swear, f., or starve 194:27
wise..made a f. 200:13
Wise man or a F. 75:13
what f...first invented kissing 520:21
whosoever shall say, Thou f. 57:45
wise enough to play the f. 483:23
wisest f. in Christendom 242:4
worm..and a f. 277:13
Fooled: f. by these rebel powers 488:20
f. with hope 191:34
Fool-fury: red f. of the Seine 533:29
Fooling: she is f. thee 315:26
Foolish: better a witty fool than a f. wit 482:12
f., as if in pain 141:26
f. face of praise 385:29
f. figure 432:40
f. son..heaviness of his mother 49:54
f. thing to make a long prologue 57:20
f. thing well done 272:15
f. thing was but a toy 484:27
f...to confound the wise 66:20
f. when he had not a pen 274:23
frantic boast and f. word 301:1
his fond and f. mind 29:23
I being young and f. 584:11
I cou'd be mighty f. 203:29
know your own f. business 139:36
never..f. that was fair 470:28
never said a f. thing 407:24
O f. Galatians 67:41
paltry, f., painted things 189:40
sleeps in a f. ear 436:10
trifling f. banquet 477:10
very f. fond old man 454:15
what f. Harriet befell 249:25
women are f. 196:16
Foolish-compounded clay, man 441:11
Foolishest act a wise man commits 86:34
Foolishness: f. of preaching 66:19
yet will not his f. depart 50:48
Fools: as dull f. suppose 340:24
beggar'd by f. 190:24
build a house for f. 521:4
dreading e'en f. 385:29
Fashion..guide of f. 164:38
few lend (but f.) 549:25
flannelled f. at the wicket 297:16
f. admire 382:33
f. and knaves 98:8
f. are my theme 117:9
f. by heavenly compulsion 452:18
f. decoyed into our condition 377:28
F.! for I also had my hour 140:22
f. may our scorn..raise 215:28
f. never wear out 156:7
f.! 'od rot 'em! 504:10
f. rush in 383:5
f...so deep-contemplative 427:15
f. that crowd thee so 158:22
f. they admonish 164:34
f. who came to scoff 224:22
foreigners are f. 338:12
fortune, that favours f. 279:22
hated by f. and f. to hate 521:25
human bodies are sic f. 108:21
I am two f. 186:21
if..Nature made you f. 105:23
in all tongues..called f. 428:34
knaves and f. may use 143:20
lighted f. the way to dusty death 461:44
little wise, the best f. 186:22
made by f. like me 292:13
make f. laugh i' the alehouse 470:28
nature meant but f. 382:21
none but f. would keep 462:3
one flesh..two f. 154:32
Paradise of F. 346:27
scarecrows of f. 266:22
secrets..kept..from f. 193:6
see how f. are vexed 170:21
shoal of f. for tenders 156:1
silence is the virtue of f. 25:11
stop to busy f. 551:20
suffer f. gladly 67:32

Fools (*cont.*)
Sussex men are noted **f.** 74:20
their f...known by this..livery 155:27
these deliberate f. 464:4
these tedious old f. 433:8
this great stage of f. 454:12
think them wise..greatest f. 4:10
things people make f. of themselves about 489:13
to fill the world with f. 508:23
to suckle f. 470:29
twenty-seven millions mostly f. 126:39
wayfaring men, though f. 54:4
we f. of nature 431:32(-432)
what all the d—d f. said 335:14
what..f. call Nature 96:12
what f. these mortals be 467:8
wit of f. 135:20
words..are the money of f. 248:19
you f. of fortune 480:26
you will always be f. 204:39
Foolscap: of f. subjects..king 116:33
Foot: at the f. of thy crags, O Sea! 528:3
caught my f. in the mat 233:10
clog the f. of a flea 484:2
fifty thousand horse and f. 294:19
f. and hand go cold 516:21(-517)
f. for f. 45:54
f. it featly here and there 479:28
f. less prompt 18:30
f.-slog..sloggin' over Africa 294:37
f. the deformity of which 325:14
Forty-second F. 252:30
fountain's sliding f. 332:20
gorgonised me from head to f. 536:5
Hercules is not only known by
his f. 87:4
her f. speaks 481:20
her f. the..cowslips never stirr'd 18:28
her f. was light 286:30
his f. upon the stirrup 171:16
like th'other f. 186:25
love is swift of f. 244:13
make crouch beneath his f. 96:13
my f. is on my native heath 420:19
no man's f. can pass 79:3
no rest for the sole of her f. 44:39
on an 'eathen idol's f. 299:11
one f. in sea 468:20
print of a man's naked f. 170:7
proud f. of a conqueror 448:2
rights..trodden under f. 101:27
sets f. upon a worm 164:3
set this f. of mine as far 448:38
so light a f. 478:10
squeeze a right-hand f. 131:25
suffer thy f. to be moved 399:27
thy f. against a stone 397:19
thy f...dipped in the blood of
thine enemies 396:11
thy f. out of brothels 453:20
thy soul the fixt f. 186:25
with his f. on the prey 538:2
with leaden f. time creeps 267:28
with shining F. shall pass 207:30
who cleft the Devil's f. 186:16
with unmoisten'd f. 361:15
Footfall: halts by me that f. 544:31
Footfalls: autumnal leaves like
light f. 496:2
no f. seen 481:6
unsteadfast f. of a spear 488:26
Footing: his stretch'd f. 438:37
Foot-in-the-grave young man 221:7
Footman: eternal F. 197:20
f. to Justinian Stubbs 504:12
Footmen: literary f. 240:5
Foot-path: jog on the f. way 485:21
narrow f. of a street 104:28
Footprint: Zuleika..looking for
a man's f. 39:27
Footprints: f. of a gigantic hound 188:17
f. on the sands of time 317:8
Footstep: where thy f. gleams 380:21
Footsteps: distant f. echo 316:9
f. of thy soul 88:17
his f. in the sea 161:18
mark my f. 361:23
your own f. meeting you 411:30
Footstool: earth; for it is his f. 57:48
thine enemies thy f. 398:23

Foozling with his cleek 228:10
Fop: I am a f. in my heart 201:31
six-foot column of f. 253:8
Foppery: excellent f. of the world 452:17
Fops: whole tribe of f. 452:14
For: all belief is f. it 273:28
if God be f. us 65:57
Forbear: f., said I 166:3
f., thou great good husband 319:2
f. to dig the dust 488:29
our bodies why do we f.? 185:1
Forbearance ceases to be a virtue 101:38
Forbears: f. again to look upon 577:24
he that f. to suit 244:10
Forbid: f. them not 61:6
live a man f. 456:11
they said, God f. 62:41
Forbidden: because it was f. 550:23
morality centre on f. acts 513:33
see what was f. 359:27
this f. Wine 206:15
Forbore: bandaged my eyes, and f. 95:10
f. to pay 300:18
Force: Byron's f. 16:23
ev'ry member of the f. 408:1
f. and fraud 248:22
f. hath made supreme 344:22
f. is not a remedy 82:22
f. of heaven-bred poesy 484:37
f. of the guinea 413:25
had not f. to shape it 531:27
his f. dares not cross the threshold 379:11
his pomp, without his f. 103:30
in the f. and road of casualty 463:44
joint f. and full result 382:24
Life F. 489:33
long'd for trenchant f. 15:21
no argument but f. 87:26
no f., however great 566:1
no motion has she now, no f. 573:6
of no f. in law 148:3
patience..achieve more than
our f. 102:28
stupendous f. 503:2
surprised by unjust f. 340:30
their little f. resign 160:23
this player .. could f. his soul 433:31
to f. my ramparts 296:4
use of f...temporary 100:26
very f. entangles itself 425:22
violent take it by f. 59:7
who overcomes by f. 345:8
with rough, majestic f. 412:13
Forced: f. by fate 194:29
momently was f. 151:32
with f. fingers rude 342:10
Forces: except the blind f. of
nature 327:12
Forces: la balance des f. réelles 360:24
Forcible: most f. Feeble 442:10
Forcibly if we must 146:3
Ford: bridge the f. 301:12
by bridge and f. 540:12
f., f., f. o' Kabul river 296:21
rain-fed f. 302:20
Fording through the rising flood 42:11
Fordoes: makes me or f. me quite 473:10
Forebode: f. not any severing 576:21
f. the last 411:1
Foredoomed: brittle is f. 337:16
Forefathers: our rude f. deemed it
two 121:10
rude f. of the hamlet 229:30
think of your f.! 1:5
thy lords and our f. trod 525:13
Forefinger: on the f. of an alderman 477:7
stretched f. of all Time 538:11
Forefront: set ye Uriah in the f. 47:32
Foregone: f. conclusion 472:9
Forehand and vantage of a king 444:23
Forehead: conversing with W. H.'s
f. 239:16
f. straight nose 359:10
in the f. of the morning sky 343:3
in the middle of her f. 318:17
of the godlike f. 575:17
on whose f. climb the crowns 89:2
upon the f. of humanity 284:26
upon the f. of the age to come 288:25
Foreheads: f. villanous low 480:10

Foreheads (*cont.*)
free hearts, free f. 541:3
seal of God in their f. 71:11
Foreign: by f. hands 381:34
cutting f. throats 477:7
f. constellations west 235:19
leave it to..f. nations 28:15
malice domestic, f. levy 459:4
some corner of a f. field 84:21
Foreigners: f. are fools 338:12
f...spell better 550:14
what them f. do 222:3
Foreknowledge: f. absolute 345:29
providence, f., will and fate 345:29
Forelock: on Occasion's f...wait 350:6
Fore-mast: strack..the f. wi' his
knee 30:19
Foremost: adorn'd the f. 147:24
f...damn'd to fame 381:20
f. in battle was Mary Ambree 31:14
none who would be f. 323:22
Foresaw: sees what he f. 575:10
Foresee his own funereal destiny 118:31
Foresight: endurance, f., strength,
and skill 580:21
Silence and F. 582:22
Forest: all that day and all night in
a f. 328:20
beasts of the f. are mine 395:3
by a f. side 345:13
damsels met in f. wide 350:4
dark..rose the f. 317:22
different shades in the .. f. 278:15
Dong through the f. goes 311:16
flowers of the f. 147:25, 198:18
fool i' the f. 427:11
f. adorn'd the foremost 147:24
f. below London Bridge 412:28
f. echo'd 'fool' 531:24
f. primeval 316:12
f. to this hart 450:9
he is lost to the f. 416:22
into the f. dim 287:24
thy lyre, even as the f. is 496:11
Forestall his date of grief 340:19
Forest-brook: lag my f. along 150:9
Foresters: Diana's f. 438:16
Forests: f. ancient as the hills 151:32
from the f. and the prairies 317:20
from the f. shook 487:29
green days in f. 516:2
in the f. of the night 75:24
when f. are rended 419:4
when..f. walked 140:21
Foretell: expiring do f. of him 474:21
pretences to f. events 520:44
Foretop: scorched f. 325:28
Forever: F.! 'tis a single word 121:10
man has f. 91:40
Forfeit: all the souls..were f. once 461:29
f. to a confin'd doom 488:2
He our deadly f. should release 343:9
Forfeiting: not f. the beast 336:1
Forgave: Christ.. f. the theft 96:5
f. th'offence 192:6
never in his life f. a friend 74:16
Forge: built the barn, the f. 77:28
can't f. his own will 222:9
f. a lifelong trouble 530:8
in the quick f...of thought 445:5
my f. decay'd 8:13
Forgery: falsehood and base f. 340:33
Forges: what his breast f. 429:13
Forget: apples f. to grow 140:23
best sometimes f. 471:17
best, to f. 96:20
Charon, seeing, may f. 308:22
command him to f. me 309:18
courage to f. 3:6
dissolve, and quite f. 287:25
do not quite f. 141:28
even them..f. not 351:20
f. all feuds 323:9
f. also thine own people 394:23
f. and forgive 454:17
f. me..Augustus 176:36
f. not all his benefits 398:3
f. not yet 583:10
f. six counties 359:2
f. the human race 114:25
f. those other two 346:20

INDEX

Forget (cont.)

f. thyself to marble	341:9
f. thy thousand ways	308:10
f. us till another year be gone	295:9
f. what I have been	475:9
half to f. the wandering	208:4
haply may f.	410:1
hardest science to f.	382:4
hateful art, how to f.	292:21
if I f. thee, do not thou f. me	21:7
if I f. thee, O Jerusalem	400:5
I f. all time	347:21
I f. the rest	93:24
in the night time I shall not f.	523:8
I shall never, *never* f.!	129:37
knew we should both f.	524:9
learn so little and f. so much	168:16
lest we f.	300:24
most f.	374:23
names that men f.	523:10
never f. what they did here	314:12
nor worms f.	176:34
not a breathing..will f. thee	582:4
not f. the Suspenders	304:11
old men f.	444:28
soon f. the..beauties of the north	1:17
teach the unforgetful to f.	411:20
tell it to f. the source	336:9
thou remember and I f.	524:14
till life f.	524:14
trunkless, yet it couldn't f.	220:10
we f. because we must	15:2
when he forgot, might God f. him	547:14
women and elephants never f.	414:14
world shall end when I f.	524:18
ye that f. God	395:6
you'll f. 'em all	385:12
you should f. and smile	409:25

Forgetful: not f. to entertain

strangers	69:22
she may f. be	161:11

Forgetfulness: not in entire f. | 576:9

steep my senses in f.	441:41
to dumb F. a prey	230:9

Forgetive: apprehensive, quick, f. | 442:21

Forgets: f. the dying bird | 373:3

truly lov'd never f.	356:13
while she laughs..f.	154:28

Forgetteth what manner of man | 69:33

Forgetting: but a sleep and a f. | 576:9

dark f. of my care	168:12
f. the bright speed	17:28(-18)
f. those good stars	140:26
f. those things which are behind	68:23
grand memory for f.	514:8
if f. could be willed	336:9
more and more f.	336:9
world f.	382:5

Forgive: as far as one woman can

f..I f.	214:16
as we f. our debtors	58:4
as we f. them	388:13
but they never can f.	9:10
father, f. them	62:48
forget and f.	454:17
f...for not enjoying Milton	306:32
f. me; mine was jealousy	530:41
f. this just..fraud	215:9
f. us our debts	58:4
f. us our trespasses	388:13
God may f. you	198:7
good, to f.	96:20
I f. you, you f. me	75:20
I have seen .. much to f.	339:7
just God, f.	573:10
lambs could not f.	176:34
mercy to f.	192:24
not..f. our friends	25:3
ought to f. them as a christian	23:4
parents..rarely..do they f. them	570:18
to f., divine	383:2
to f. wrongs	497:17
to give thanks..and to f.	522:13
wilt thou f. that sin?	185:24

Forgiven: blasphemy..shall not be f. | 59:12

it shall not be f. you	140:4
pass on, my Queen, f.	530:41

Forgiveness: ask of thee f. | 454:19

f. free of evil done	295:8
f. to the injured	191:42

Forgiveness (cont.)

Man's F. give—and take	207:12
Mutual F.	74:21

Forgiveth: the Lord..f. sins | 56:30

Forgo: how f. thy sweet converse | 349:18

Forgot: all shall be f., but he'll

remember	444:28
all the rest f.	486:22
born to be f.	160:37
by the world f.	382:5
ever be f.	368:13
far or f.	199:4
f. as soon as done	481:17
f. his course	208:15
f. his epic...art	386:13
f. it not, nay	410:6
f. that he had a duty	216:23
f. the taste of fears	461:3
giver is f.	154:40
I have f. much, Cynara	187:10
I have f. my part	429:18
in new excellence..old f.?	81:1
I've f.	369:17
lest they f., lest they f.	141:31
loved accents are soon f.	494:20
Napoleon f. Blücher, I f. Goschen	143:33
old acquaintance be f.	104:12
old faults and follies..f.	147:11
she f. the stars	286:23
things unknown proposed as things f.	383:3
though I am clean f.	243:21
when he f., might God forget	547:14

Forgotten: all words f. | 172:1

always a f. thing	140:16
by a newer object quite f.	484:34
f. crowd of common beauties	125:1
f. how soon we must sever	166:24
f. nothing and learnt nothing	195:1
God is f.	372:12
God's f.	404:9
hast thou f. ere I forget?	524:12
hath not f. my age	507:35
how many..things..f.	189:19
I am all f.	423:37
I am clean f.	393:29
I have f. your name	524:10
injury..sooner f.	139:10
I want to be f. even by God	94:22
learnt nothing and f. nothing	526:17
not f. yet?	435:5
not one of them is f.	61:51
Shakespeare..quite f.	141:29
they fly f.	562:9
thou hast f..swallow	524:18
when I am f.	446:29
you have f. my kisses	524:10

Fori: Idola F. | 28:6

Foris: haec studia..non impediunt f. | 145:16

Forked: poor, bare, f. animal | 453:21

Forks: pursued it with f. and hope | 128:11

Forlorn: f. and shipwrecked brother | 317:8

f.! the very word	288:2
glimpses..make me less f.	582:18
in faery lands f.	288:1
in Stygian cave f.	341:26
in these wild woods f.	349:18
is of sense f.	150:17
poor bird, as all f.	35:17
them that lie f.	172:6
wearied and f.	359:14

Form: all the spires of f. | 199:17

Almighty's f. glasses itself	114:30
fain would I dwell on f.	477:19
finer f. or lovelier face	416:16
follows but for f.	452:38
F., F., Riflemen, F.!	540:5
f. of sound words	68:57
f. of them bodily	524:1
F. remains	573:26
her faith thro' f.	532:24
Human F. display	74:1
human thought or f.	494:4
I like definite f.	514:15
in ev'ry respect but the f.	214:35
in f. and feature	313:7
in f., in moving, how express	433:15
lick it into f.	109:5
lively f. of death	305:14
Love, the human f. divine	77:1

Form (cont.)

mould of f.	434:14
no f. nor comeliness	54:25
of fishy f. and mind	83:26
of the soul the body f. doth take	510:13
proportion, season, f.	481:2
show the f. it seem'd to hide	417:27
show..the time..his f. and pressure	434:18
soul is f.	510:13
stuffs out..with his f.	447:34
take thy f. from off my door	380:27
Terror the human f. divine	77:4
that unmatch'd f.	434:14
thou, silent f.	287:14
to every F...an *active* Principle	574:25
what the f. divine	308:14
without f., and void	44:1

Formal: beard of f. cut | 427:21

f., and circumscribed	581:18

Formation of character | 508:28

Formed: f. by thy converse | 384:15

scarcely f. or moulded	117:2

Former: f. and the latter rain | 389:21

f. days were better	51:12
f. things are passed away	71:45
his f. name is heard no more	348:17
know that in a f. time	76:1
remembrance of my f. love	484:34

Formicam: videmus..f. in electro | 27:47

Forming: see him f. in the air | 407:8

Formosissimus: nunc..f. annus | 555:24

Forms: all f., all pressures past | 432:20

all f., modes, shows of grief	430:30
by f. unseen	153:30
f. more real than living man	497:2
f. of things unknown	467:24
f. that do not live	579:12
from outward f. to win	151:3
giv'st to f. and images	575:21
in what revolting fancy..the F.	266:14
lovely f. do flow	123:17
misshapes the beauteous f. of things	581:16
State's mellow f.	231:30
their colours and their f.	581:26
throng of thoughts and f.	497:14
vents in mangled f.	427:16

Fors: quem F. dierum cumque dabit | 258:14

seu f. obiecerit | 261:6

Forsake: f. not an old friend | 56:40

not fail thee, nor f. thee	46:36
when my father and my mother f. me	393:21

Forsaken: Demas hath f. me | 69:1

home of..f. beliefs	19:10
I seem f. and alone	161:17
lover f.	559:15
most choice, f.	452:13
primrose that f. dies	342:31
saw I never the righteous f.	394:5
why hast thou f. me?	60:52, 393:1

Forsaking: f. all other | 391:29

f. even military men	222:14

Forspent: clean f., f. | 310:10

Forswear: f. thin potations | 442:12

I'll f. arms	438:29

Forsworn: faith unhappily f. | 487:14

f. 'on mere necessity'	454:35
so sweetly were f.	462:16

Fort: hold the f. | 77:14

Truth's sacred F.	85:4

Fort: la raison du plus f. | 209:14

Forte: science is his f. | 506:2

Fortem posce animum | 283:24

Fortes: f. creantur fortibus et bonis | 260:20

vixere f. ante Agamemnona | 261:2

Fortescue: Charles Augustus F. | 40:33

Forth: Caesar shall go f. | 449:23

f. John's soul flared	92:6
f., pilgrim, f.! f., beste	136:20
f. they went together	361:22
if our virtues did not go f.	461:16
my road leads me f.	334:9
new drawn frae the F.	360:13

Forties: Hungry F. | 551:3

Fortieth spare Arm-chair | 91:11

Fortifies: it f. my soul to know | 147:14

Fortis fortuna adiuvat | 541:31

Fortitude: all..a man has of f. and delicacy | 513:35

INDEX

Fortitude (cont.)

great f. of mind 270:2
welcome f. 578:17
Fortnight's C.B. 295:4
Fortress: his castle and f. 148:9
petty f. 279:6
this f. built by Nature 474:22
thy f. and thy ease 552:2
Forts: when the f. of folly fall 16:20
Fortuitous concurrence of atoms 373:7
Fortuna: audentis F. iuvat 555:10
fortis f. adiuvat 541:31
f. mihi tete abstulit ipsum 133:20
nos facimus, F., deam 283:25
*Fortunae: fabrum esse suae quemque
f.* 414:23
16:9
Fortunate: age more f.
better to be f. than wise 563:31
Elysian, windless, f. abodes 497:15
Fortunatos: O f. nimium 556:15
Fortunatus . . deos qui novit agrestis 556:18
Fortune: above my f. 482:24
arrows of outrageous f. 434:4
beauty without a f. 203:10
blind f. still bestows 280:19
but a worky-day f. 423:21
Caesar and his f. with thee 120:16
disdaining f. 456:5
do F. what she can 189:4
ere f. made him so 192:2
for ever, F. 546:7
f. changed made him so 232:2
f. is full of fresh variety 35:20
f. is merry 451:2
f. knows we scorn her most 424:25
F.'s a right whore 563:24
f.'s buffets and rewards 434:26
F. shows herself more kind 465:9
f.'s malice lost her Calais 91:6
f., that favours fools 279:22
good housewife F. 426:18
health and high f. 417:28
his . . visit pays where f. smiles 586:29
hostages to f. ·26:34
how does f. banter us 78:9
I am F.'s fool 478:16
ill f. seldom comes alone 192:7
in disgrace with f. 486:24
in possession of a good f. 22:28
in the secret parts of F. 433:10
maker of his own f. 511:26
man of f. in England 215:33
man's f. . . in his own hands 26:14
method of making a f. 231:17
most dejected thing of f. 453:36
my face is my f. 369:15
Nabob, with an immense f. 324:30
not a pipe for F.'s finger 434:26
not being F. . . but F.'s knave 425:33
of f.'s sharp adversitee 138:35
out of suits with f. 426:22
rail'd on Lady F. 427:12
rob a lady of her f. 204:30
ruined Mr. Hampden's f. 100:5
smiling of F. beguiling 147:23
taken at the flood, leads on to f. 451:29
till heaven hath sent me f. 427:13
to prey at f. 471:38
to f. and to fame unknown 230:13
tugg'd with f. 458:36(-459)
vicissitudes of f. 217:13
well-favoured . . the gift of f. 468:34
who lets slip F. 158:19
you fools of f. 480:26
your f. . . beneath your hat 370:9
Fortunes: battles, sieges, f. 470:2
but to build up great f. 216:9
f. and lives he will vote away
84:27(-85)
f. . . come tumbling 24:30
men's judgements are a parcel
of their f. 424:28
my f. have corrupted honest
men 425:10
my pride fell with my f. 426:23
ne'er mend your f. 357:23
our love . . with our f. change 435:11
those my former f. 416:22
Fortune-teller: one Pinch . . a f. 429:1
Forty: at f., the judgement 211:14
every man over f. 490:37

Forty (cont.)

fair, fat, and f. 420:20
fat, fair and f. 370:6
fool at f. 586:22
f. days and f. nights 506:7
f. feeding like one 577:20
f. freighters at sea 299:16
f. pounds a year 224:18
f. stripes save one 67:34
f. years old 251:12
f. years on 79:9
griefs of f. generations of Christians 325:36
his death . . at f.-odd befell 252:32
knows it at f., and reforms 587:6
look young till f. 193:4
round about the earth in f.
minutes 466:40
together now for f. years 142:22
wait till you come to F. Year 543:3
when f. winters 486:10
Forty-niner: miner, F. 355:22
Forty-one: gave her father f. 8:7
Forty thousand: difference of f.
men 564:17
Forty-three: very well pass for f. 222:20
Forty-two boxes 128:5
Forward: f. bends his head 148:24
f., f. let us range 534:36
f., not permanent 431:20
F., the Light Brigade 528:14
f. to be sounded 434:2
look f. to posterity 102:9
rapture of the f. view 336:45
some men a f. motion love 552:7
those behind cried 'F!' 323:22
with f. toe 336:21
with their feet f. 87:6
Forward-looking mind 574:24
Forwards: swings backwards and
f. 249:24
Fossil: language is f. poetry 200:32
Foster him wel with milk 137:36
Foster-child of silence 287:6
Fostered alike by beauty and by fear 579:5
Fou: f. for weeks thegither 108:5
I wasna f. 105:7
some are f. o' love divine and
some are f. o' brandy 106:13
we are na f. 108:30
when we were f. 105:13
Fought: as if men f. upon the
earth 418:32
fiercest Spirit that f. in Heav'n 345:15
f. a long hour by Shrewsbury
clock 441:4
f. and lost 147:5
f. was this noble fray 189:8
f. with beasts at Ephesus 67:10
from morn till even f. 443:25
if that he f. 137:13
I have f. a good fight 68:60
I have f. for Queen and Faith 540:3
never to have f. at all 147:5
rooks . . flapped and f. 249:13
stars . . f. against Sisera 46:48
those he f. for 537:12
those who . . f. for life 509:1
under whose colours he had f. 475:16
well hast thou f. 348:20
what they f. each other for 507:5, 6
whiles any speaks that f. with us
444:28(-445)
Foul: defy the f. fiend 453:20
fair is f. and f. is fair 456:3
fair is too f. an epithet 331:1
f. and midnight murther 229:24
f. as Vulcan's stithy 435:1
f., I to the Fountain fly 548:12
f. like the *Quarterly* 240:7
from f. to fair 508:19
however f. within 143:12
I doubt some f. play 431:18
murder most f. 432:11
not woo f. weather 253:18
sin . . f. in the ending thereof 372:18
so f. and fair a day 456:12
so variously f. 266:14
take heed o' the f. fiend 453:18
thank the gods I am f. 428:12
ways be f. 456:1

Fouled: Experience . . hath f. me 530:40
Foulest: shortest way . . the f. 24:32
Foully: play'dst most f. for it 458:30
Foul-mouthed: English . . a f.
nation 240:10
Found: anybody might have f. it 296:11
as good as he had f. it 147:19
as 'ow I've always f. 135:1
f. . . a drop of patience 472:34
f.! f.! f.! f.! 417:24
f. my sheep which was lost 62:11
f. no more at all 71:33
hast thou f. me? 48:12
have it f. out by accident 307:28
he was lost, and is f. 62:16
he will be f. like Brutus 452:3
his place could no where be f. 394:6
how I caught it, f. it 462:28
I awoke and f. me 286:36
in Godhead f. 199:31
it f. them a sect 325:35
less often sought than f. 118:27
looked inwards and f. her there 194:6
mercy f. 121:25
my espoused, my latest f. 348:1
not f. out my riddle 46:56
O soul . . ne'er be f. 330:11
Scotch have f. it 273:18
seek . . while he may be f. 54:30
song . . I f. again 315:25
thy beauty shall no more be f. 333:9
victim must be f. 219:24
watchmen . . f. me 52:12
woman hath . . f. him already 471:2
when f., make a note of 175:9
when thou mayest be f. 393:32
Foundation: Church's one f. 517:1
first f. was jasper 72:1
huge f. of the earth 439:40
wine, the f. 42:1
Foundations: city which hath f. 69:14
earth's f. stay 264:4
f. of the earth . . out of course 397:4
f. will be cast down 392:19
hell's f. quiver 35:2
her f. are upon the holy hills 397:13
laid the f. of the earth 49:19, 398:8
when earth's f. fled 264:4
Foundation-stone: from turret to
f. 418:26
Founder: enjoyed the gifts of the
f. 216:21
Fount: count . . to Jesse's f. 183:4
f. of fiery life 16:21
f. whence honour springs 330:29
meander level with their f. 355:17
meanders . . level with its f. 325:12
slow, slow, fresh f. 279:28
washed by Arethusa's f. 232:1
Fountain: back to the burning f. 492:5
f. and the caves 151:33(-152)
f. fill'd with blood 161:7
f. from the which my current 472:34
f. heads, and pathless groves 37:37
f. in a noon-day grove 578:32
f. of all goodness 388:29
f. of honour 27:45, 28:22
f. of sweet tears 581:6
f. of that heavenly beauty 510:14
f. of the water of life 71:46
f. sealed 52:7
f. send forth . . sweet water and
bitter 69:38
f.'s silvery column 152:8
f.'s sliding foot 332:20
in the desert a f. 119:10
I to the F. fly 548:12
let thy voice rise like a f. 531:36
like a f. troubled 479:12
like the bubble on the f. 416:23
mighty f. momently was forced 151:32
perpetual f. of good sense 194:15
pitcher . . broken at the f. 51:33
sprinkling it with f. water 305:18
summer-dried f. 416:22
Thou of Life the F. art 565:8
your f. . . choked up 102:19
Fountain-light of all our day 576:18
Fountains: Afric's sunny f. 240:17
certain f. of justice 24:33
cool shady f. 526:22

INDEX

Fountains (*cont.*)

for us..f. flow 244:23
f. mingle with the river 495:7
from little f. 202:16
new Peneus rolls his f. 493:25
no eyes, but f. 305:14
O, ye f. 576:21
shepherding her bright f. 492:20
silver f. mud 486:31
weep you no more, sad f. 11:10
what objects are the f. 498:8
whose f. are within 151:3
Founts: white f. falling 141:3
Four: f. angels to my bed 3:3
f. corners of the sky 192:40
f. great walls 89:16
f. lagging winters 474:16
f. o'clock in the morning 499:29
f. of us about that bed 359:12
f. pillars of government 27:8
f. rogues in buckram 439:20
f. seasons fill the measure 288:27
f. spend in prayer 148:8
f. things greater 294:29
f. things say not, It is enough 50:55
f. times as big as the bush 311:7
f. times he who gets his blow in
    fust 491:9
fram'd us of f. elements 330:28
just f. feet ten 34:4
kisses f. 286:34
letters f. do form his name 151:20
preach from ten till f. 220:4
Four-and-twenty: f. leaders of
    revolt 96:37
with f. men 23:26
Fourfold: your threefold, f. tomb 36:21
Four-footed: parody of all f.
    things 140:21
Four hundred people in New
    York Society 322:15
Four-in-hand: fiery f. 153:13
Four Million: the F. 242:14
Fours: make a simile go on all f. 326:5
Fourscore: come to f. years 397:16
f. and upward 454:15
Four-square: stood f. to all the
    winds 537:15
Fourteen hundred years ago..
    nail'd 438:12
Fourth: f. estate of the realm 324:22
from earth the F. descended 309:11
there sat a F. Estate 126:29
unto the third and f. generation 390:7
Fous: le monde est plein de f. 12:15
Fouth o' auld nick-nackets 107:22
Foutra: a f. for the world 442:34
Fowl: broiled f. and mushrooms 178:27
lord of the f. and the brute 164:22
over the f. of the air 44:9
Pythagoras concerning wild f. 484:22
tame villatic f. 351:2
you elegant f. 312:1
Fowler: creeping f. eye 467:7
out of the snare of the f. 399:32
Fowls: all small f. singis 187:5
behold the f. of the air 58:11
beside them..the f. of the air 398:8
f. of the air, and the fishes 392:12
small f. maken melodye 136:22
that I here the f. singe 138:16
Fox: better than that of the f. 77:33
Brer F., he lay low 238:17
Daun Russel the f. 137:41
feasted f. at rest 334:6
f. jumped up 366:20
f. may steal your hens 214:19
F.'s..notes rebound 418:5
little red f. murmured 585:6
nephew of F. 250:25
or a f. from his lair 229:16
see a f. die 293:14
that I loves the f. less 518:14
trusted like the f. 440:31
upon F.'s grave 418:5
Foxed: if ever I was f. 377:17
Foxes: f. have holes 58:34
little f., that spoil the vines 52:2
Foxey—our revered father 177:35
Fox-hunter: tell me a man's a f. 518:9
Foxlike in the vine 539:4

Frabjous: O f. day 129:39(–130)
Fraction: infinitesimal f. of a pro-
    duct 127:21
thou wretched f. 126:7
Fragilely, surely 545:12
Fragment: adds something to this
    F. of Life 512:32
Fragments: gather up the f. 63:21
they took up of the f. 59:34
Fragrant: f. weed 163:37
in your f. bosom 125:11
Fragrant-eyed: flowers, f. 288:3
Frail: feeble as f. 228:22
f. as is our life 202:1
f. children of dust 228:22
f., gaunt, and small 235:17
in wisdom never was so f. 470:29
it may be f. 379:11
some f. memorial 230:7
trusts a f. bark 229:6
Frailes: no todos podemos ser f. 134:12
Frailest: why choose you the f.? 494:21
Frailties: his f. from their dread
    abode 230:13
our f. are invincible 513:30
Frailty: f. of all things here 494:21
f. of a man 25:17
f. of man 389:47
f. of our nature 389:30
f., thy name is woman 430:33(–431)
love's but a f. of the mind 156:8
more flesh..more f. 440:15
noblest f. of the mind 192:34, 422:29
tempt the f. of our powers 481:25
Frame: above this f. of things 579:38
all that nature..could f. 510:6
all the human f. requires 41:3
breath of this corporeal f. 581:25
calm and heav'nly f. 161:1
earth received her f. 562:9
f. and huge foundation of the
    earth 439:40
f. of adamant 279:5
f. of things disjoint 459:4
f. thy fearful symmetry 75:24
mighty f. of the world 43:12
quit this mortal f. 381:28
rapture-smitten f. 122:34
shakes this fragile f. 236:12
shakes your very f. 473:13
stirs this mortal f. 152:3
that f. outlives a thousand 437:6
thine this universal f. 348:4
this goodly f., the earth 433:15
this universal f. began 191:35
this universal f...without a mind 25:23
tremble for this lovely f. 566:12
whole f. of nature..break 3:2
wield the mighty f. 348:30
your discourse into some f. 435:20
Framed: conceit divinely f. 123:17
f. by furies' skill 509:25
f. in the prodigality of Nature 476:9
f. to make women false 470:21
Nature that f. us 330:28
summer..f. and glazed 558:24
*Français: je parle..f. aux hommes
    pas clair..pas f.* 136:13
    407:6
Françaises: les gardes f., tirez 239:9
France: best thing between F. and
    England 269:12
better in F. 512:16
entertain..the full pride of F. 443:8
fair stood the wind for F. 189:6
F., fam'd in all great arts 18:1
F...influenced..England 102:19
his round hose in F. 463:12
King of F. went up the hill 367:11
lilied fields of F. 122:12
maids in F. to kiss 445:15
nearer is to F. 129:24
since I saw the Queen of F. 102:11
singer in F. of old 525:31
sweet enemy, F. 501:28
they in F. of the best rank 431:25
thundered the cannon of F. 146:15
until F. is adequately secured 21:6
vasty fields of F. 443:4
warmer F. with all her vines 162:44
when I was in F. 447:37
France, mère des arts 40:16

Francesca di Rimini, niminy, piminy 221:6
Franciscan: in F...pass disguised 346:25
Frank: f., haughty, rash 322:9
f. to all beside 384:30
Frankfort: I went to F. 387:7
Frankie and Johnny 6:8
Frankincense: gold, and f., and
    myrrh 57:24
Franklin: body of Benjamin F. 211:21
Frantic: animated by f. sentiment 29:6
fascination f. 220:20
f. boast and foolish word 301:1
frightful f. fearful frown 220:7
lover, all as f. 467:24
*Frater: heu miser indigne f. ad-
    empte mihi* 133:20
Fraternité: Liberté! Égalité! F.! 12:16
Fratresque tendentes 259:27
Fratrum: par nobile f. 261:23
Fraud: force and f. 248:22
f. of men was ever so 468:20
pious f. 215:9
pious f. of the almanac 320:16
Fraudatrix scientiae 414:21
Frauds: pious f. 102:1
Fraught: f. with a later prize 493:25
swell, bosom, with thy f. 472:10
though f. with all learning 225:27
Fray: by decision more embroils
    the f. 346:11
eager for the f. 144:28
fought was this noble f. 189:8
never meet in bloody f. 225:24
to the latter end of a f. 440:24
Frayed: poor splendid wings so f. 522:17
Freaked: pansy f. with jet 342:31(–343)
Freakish youth 163:5
Freaks: their fits and f. 183:12
Freckled like a pard 286:37
whatever is fickle, f. 255:3
Freckles: in those f...their
    savours 466:34
Fred: here lies F. 6:20
Frederick: bravest of all in F.
    town 568:12
clustered spires of F. 568:11
here is cruel F. 249:19
Free: alike was Greek, alike was f. 524:7
all letters..as f. and easy 370:18
all men..born f. 353:3
all men everywhere..f. 314:3
another name more f. 382:3
appal the f. 433:32
as f. as nature first made man 191:41
assure freedom to the f. 314:11
at length art f. 251:15
beautiful and f. 497:17
bond nor f. 68:31
born most f. 371:8
comment is f. 416:4
country of the f. 88:2
fain have her f. will 336:10
fixed fate, f. will 345:29
flag that makes you f. 583:7
f. and faithful, strong as death 161:12
f. and holy-day..spirit 307:17
f. as the road 244:9
f. be she, fancy-f. 199:13
f. church in a f. state 134:3
f. from all meaning 190:32
f. from rhyme or reason 381:21
f. from self-seeking 308:2
f. from this restraint 155:38
f. love, f. field 530:42
f. the world of a poisonous thing 188:7
fresh, the ever f. 157:12
from hope and fear set f. 523:23
hair as f. 280:7
half slave and half f. 314:6
healths and draughts go f. 319:6
heart as sound and f. 247:1
here we may be f. 168:13
himself..he could not f. 199:23
his people are f. 357:17
home of the brave and the f. 489:1
I..never shall be f. 185:19
I only ask to be f. 173:26
Italia shall be f. 337:38
I was f. born 65:14
land of the f. 123:6, 292:11
leaves f. to all 347:25

[726]

INDEX

Free (cont.)

leaves soul f. a little   89:28
let me gae f.   420:15
let me gang f.   416:8
let the oppressed go f.   54:36
let us die to make men f.   264:18
man was born t.   412:2
mind is f.   189:4
Mother of the F.   42:20
my unhoused f. condition   469:38
no one..perfectly f. till all are f.   508:30
not sighed deep, laughed f.   97:28
of a f. and open nature   470:22
of an open and f. nature   280:1
offer'd f. from stain   323:7
only less f. than thou   496:10
our souls as f.   114:42
principles of f. constitution   217:6
rather..England should be f. than..sober   327:8
sceptreless, f., uncircumscribed   497:12
set f...Eurydice   342:9
set your fancies f.   97:2
she alone is f.   341:5
should himself be f.   83:16, 275:23
so cleanly I myself can f.   189:20
so f. as a fish   413:19
so f. as the sons of the waves   213:10
so f. we seem   89:14
such f. and friendly conference   451:8
that Greece might still be f.   115:44
that moment they are f.   162:42
thou art f.   17:23
thought is f.   480:3
till..thou f. my soul   185:21
truth shall make you f.   63:28
vibration each way f.   247:13
we *know* our will is f.   271:28
we must be f. or die   577:3
we that have f. souls   435:10
what a f. government is   103:21
when evils are most f.   449:6
when the mind's f.   453:12
wholly slaves or wholly f.   192:26
whom the truth makes f.   163:46
who would be f.   113:18
will is f.   15:9
wine, privilege of the completely f.   42:1
wronged people yearning to be f.   561:16

Freed: f. from servile bands   583:11
f. his soul the nearest way   275:4
f. us from everlasting sleep   85:21
thousands He hath f.   135:12

Freedom: bondage which is f.'s self   497:19
bounds of f. wider yet   539:12
but what is F.?   148:11
cause of F.   79:11
deny them..f.   101:12
every infringement of..f.   379:14
fair F.'s classic line   123:1
few men talked of f.   141:25
flame of f. in their souls   526:1
Flood of British f.   577:2
f. and curteisye   136:23
F. and Whisky gang thegither   104:18
F. hallows with her tread   119:11
F. has a thousand charms   162:22
f. in my love   319:7
f. is a noble thing   33:17
F. leads it forth   496:23
f. mays man to haiff liking   33:17
f. now so seldom wakes   356:21
f. of speech..worship..from want..fear   408:25
F. rear'd..her..brow   537:41
F.'s banner streaming   234:13
F.'s battle once begun   117:38
F. shall awhile repair   153:30
F. shrieked   122:33
F.'s lion-banner   122:30
F. slowly broadens down   541:24
f...sole prerogative   193:42
F.'s soil beneath our feet   101:7
f... the cure of anarchy   101:7
f. to the slave..f. to the free   314:11
f. which in no other land   193:42
freshness, the f.   422:22
govern..on the principles of f.   101:4

Freedom (cont.)

idea of f.   373:16
I du believe in F.'s cause   319:19
I gave my life for f.   202:18
let f. ring   504:19
lost is our f.   124:3
me this unchartered f. tires   573:30
new birth of f.   314:12
none..love f...but good men   353:2
not f., but licence   353:2
recovery of my f.   217:3
regain'd my f. with a sigh   114:36
that sober f.   537:22
what stands if F. fall?   296:20
where wealth and f. reign   226:8
whose service is perfect f.   388:25
with a great sum obtained..f.   65:14
yet, F.! yet thy banner   114:14
Freedoms: four essential f.   408:25
Free-livers on a small scale   267:22
Freely: f. they stood who stood   346:21
f. we serve   348:12
f. ye have received, f. give   58:47
I love thee f.   88:24
what it did so f.   457:11
Freeman: f. whom the truth makes free   163:46
Stubbs butters F.   408:4
Freemason: obvious..that you are a F.   188:1
Freemen: only f...the only slaves to rule o'er f.   334:20, 83:16
who rules o'er f.   275:23
Freeport: Sir Andrew F...monied interest   2:13
Free-thinking: he took to f.   10:23
Freeze: f., f., thou bitter sky   427:22
f. thy blood less coldly   361:23
f. thy young blood   432:9
on each side seem to f.   285:13
to f. the blood   575:12
Freezings: what f. have I felt   487:27
Freezy: Breezy, Sneezy, F.   213:5
Freighted with amber grapes   18:16
Freighters: forty f. at sea   299:16
French: beating the F. to-morrow   572:15
books, fruit, f. wine   290:24
boy, half-F., half-English   445:14
drawn out of F. into English   328:14
F. are wiser than they seem   27:12
F. are with equal advantage content   124:6
F. army led by an Italian general   490:39
F. Guard, fire first!   239:9
F. novels, F. cookery, and F. wines   542:33
F. of Paris was to hir unknowe   136:29
F. or Turk or Proosian   221:25
F. she spak ful faire   136:29
help our F. comrades   305:1
I hate the F.   226:29
love..in new F. books   89:33
my scrofulous F. novel   96:41
nor..behold with prejudice.. F., Italian   86:27
not too F. F. bean   220:28
only taken from the F.   499:22
reading F. novels   182:32
some are fond of F.   333:22
speak in the F.   130:2
to fight the F.   282:10
to men F.   136:13
to the F...the land   125:23, 407:1
we F. stormed Ratisbon   92:23
your new F. proselytes   192:28
Frenchies: those F. seek him   370:13
Frenchman: F...always talking   274:20
F., easy, debonair   162:21
F.'s darling   163:37
hate a F. as..the devil   362:16
I praise the F.   162:6
truth the brilliant F. never knew   164:16
Frenchmen: did march three F.   444:4
fifty million F.   233:16
one Englishman could beat three F.   2:19
ten thousand F. sent below   376:8
Frenzy: demoniac f.   349:24
in a fine f. rolling   467:24
Frequent: eagerly f. Doctor and Saint   206:10

Frequented: in more f. rows   164:36
Frequently done before   120:20
Fresh: bloom sae f. and fair   108:36
blossom of f. colour   502:19
blue, the f., the ever free   157:12
crust so f.   254:27
first I saw you f.   487:29
f. as a bridegroom   438:32
f. as is the month of May   136:25
f. as paint   503:7
f. eggs to rotten boroughs   324:29
f. from Natur's mould   176:24
how quick and f. art thou   481:30
keep the passion f.   337:24
most ancient heavens..f. and strong   573:31
O yonge f. folkes   138:42
so ancient and so f.   21:22
so sad, so f.   538:18
with constant drinking f. and fair   158:7
Freshening: f. and fluttering in the wind   92:34
f. its current   16:4
Freshness: dewy f.   508:2
f. of a dream   576:1
f., the freedom   422:22
Fret: fever and the f.   287:25
f. a passage through it   212:16
f. not after knowledge   289:9
f. not thyself because of the ungodly   394:3
f. not to roam the desert   365:16
f. of that sharp-headed worm   540:17
f. thy soul with crosses   510:16
living, we f.   96:20
though you can f. me   435:25
why f. about them   206:19
Frets: f. until 'tis fine   111:24
I think it f. the saints   87:31
no care who chafes, who f.   460:9
Fretted: f. by sallies of..kisses   576:10
f. the pigmy body   190:13
f. with golden fire   433:15
long-drawn aisle and f. vault   230:2
Freude, schöner Götterfunken   415:21
Friar: Apollo turned fasting f.   337:21
F. Bacon and F. Bungay   231:34
f. I will be   265:24
f. ther was   137:1
many a f.   34:8
Friars: barefoot f. were singing vespers   217:1
eremites and f.   346:24
we cannot all be f.   134:12
Fricassee: equally serve in a f.   520:3
Friday: F. morn when we set sail   9:3
F.'s child   368:1
on a F. fil al this   137:42
takes my man F. with me   170:8
worse on F.   368:21
Friend: angry with my f.   76:5
as a f. he drops into poetry   178:3
believe the aged f.   90:42
Brother, Englishman, and F.   579:20
called your f. from his bed   302:23
candid f.   124:13
choose an author as.. a f.   180:8
Codlin's the f.   177:30
countervail a f.   233:2
crack a bottle with a f.   142:1
daughter, wife or f.   358:1
death of a dear f.   407:33
debauch his f.'s wife genteelly   272:24
equal f.   518:1
every f...part of ourselves   386:37
faithful are the wounds of a f.   50:45
faithful f. is the medicine of life   56:36
favourite has no f.   230:21
forsake not an old f.   56:40
F. for little children   338:19
f., go up higher   62:3
f. in my retreat   162:6
f. of Beauty in distress   117:36
f. of every country but his own   124:11
f. of Grey   250:25
f. of man   122:38
f. of my better days   234:15
f. of the bridegroom   63:11
f. remember'd not   427:22
f. should bear his f.'s infirmities   451:22
f...tell him disagreeable truths   322:14

INDEX

Friend (cont.)

f. that sticketh closer than a brother — 50:22
f...the masterpiece of Nature — 200:16
F. to Sir Philip Sidney — 232:16
f. to soothe the cares — 288:15
f. to truth — 385:6
F. Who never changes — 338:19
from thy griev'd f. — 292:18
gain'd from Heav'n..a f. — 230:13
good wine, a f. — 3:11
guide, philosopher, and f. — 384:17
handsome house to lodge a f. — 521:7
he was my f. — 450:19
his f. in merry pin — 160:6
I could not see my little f. — 34:26
if I had a f. that lov'd her — 470:3
in a f...cold modesty — 450:10
in every mess I finds a f. — 173:5
in life the firmest f. — 118:22
in the heart of a f. — 315:25
I think on thee, dear f. — 486:25
I've a F., over the sea — 97:5
Jack lov'd his f. — 173:9
knolling a departed f. — 441:10
known Cicero, and been his f. — 175:8
last best f. am I — 507:10
look like a f. on Denmark — 430:28
makes no f. who never made a foe — 530:39
mankind's mysterious f. — 42:1
marry your old f.'s love — 96:36
mine own familiar f. — 394:15, 395:12
mistress or a f. — 493:9
more if you dine at a f.'s — 178:26
my f. here didn't see — 228:6
need be very much his f. — 159:31
never..forgave a f. — 74:16
never want a f. in need — 175:9
new f. is as new wine — 56:40
no f. like a sister — 409:19
nor a f. to know me — 515:28
not a fool can call me f. — 586:13
not a f., not a f. greet — 483:6
not a f. to close his eyes — 191:7
not a f. to spare — 201:23
not as their f. or child — 16:6
of every friendless name the f. — 275:1
one damned good-natured f. or other — 499:25
Patience for our only f. — 18:13
polished female f. — 568:21
poor man's dearest f. — 107:3
pretended f. is worse — 215:24
rider and horse,—f., foe — 113:36
Satan met his ancient f. — 119:24
say, 'Welcome F.'— — 166:19
sharpeneth the countenance of his f. — 50:47
Sleep, the f. of Woe — 507:18
soul of a f. we've made — 78:17
suspicious f. — 385:29
that love my f. — 450:32
this f. happen to be—God? — 91:23
this is my f., O daughters of Jerusalem — 52:14
those who call them f. — 531:36
thou art not my f. — 199:15
truest f. to thy lover — 328:24
use a f. as I use Thee — 245:11, 12
was it a f. or foe — 410:20
wert not thou my f.? — 561:15
who lost no f. — 385:6
who's your fat f.? — 97:31
wildly striking sometimes a f. — 243:32
with a religious book, or f. — 583:10
with one chained f. — 493:10
world is not thy f. — 478:37
worst f. and enemy — 84:18
you're my f. — 91:28
your f. that loves you — 448:14
your nearest f...not detect — 316:36
Friended: under the sky lie f. — 403:1
Friendless: every f. name — 275:1
no man so f. — 322:14
omnipotent but f. — 497:4
Friendliness, hardiness, love — 328:2
Friendly: both false and f. — 315:26
death..with f. care — 151:18
f. and comforting breast — 241:20
f. eye could never see — 451:23

Friendly (cont.)

f. swarry — 179:19
f. to peace, but not to me — 162:14
gods today stand f. — 451:35
maintain the most f. relations — 305:1
righteous rather smite me f. — 400:14
social, f., honest man — 105:25
Friends: all their f. could say — 311:22
all thy f. are lapp'd in lead — 35:18
animals are such agreeable f. — 196:31
babes and loving f. — 150:15
backing of your f. — 439:16
best of f. must part — 10:21
cast off his f. as a huntsman — 225:33
cheating of our f. — 143:6
choice of f. — 158:16
city of the faithfullest f. — 567:8
excellent plot, very good f. — 439:10
falling out of faithful f. — 196:2
few f., and many books — 158:13
f. and loves we have none — 334:13
f., kindred, days — 199:12
f. of every country save their own — 181:9
f. of the mammon of unrighteousness — 62:21
f., Romans, countrymen — 450:17
f. thou hast — 431:25
f. to congratulate their f. — 193:41
f. who set forth at our side — 17:18
good book is the best of f. — 549:20
good thoughts his only f. — 123:25
had been f. in youth — 150:25
hard to part when f. are dear — 33:14
he who has a thousand f. — 201:23
his best f. hear no more of him — 495:11
his intimate f. — 128:7
humblest f...scorn not — 573:18
in all distresses of our f. — 521:1
keep a few f. — 513:35
keep f. with himself — 513:35
laughter and the love of f. — 41:17
laughter, learnt of f. — 84:21
lay down his life for his f. — 63:57
like f. once parted — 492:21
like him with f. possess'd — 486:24
like summer-f. — 243:23
live without f. — 337:41
love..hath f. in the garrison — 234:2
makes f. of enemies — 435:12
more his f. — 142:28
my f. and brother souls — 528:11
my f. proud of my memory — 290:29
my list of f. — 164:3
neither foes nor loving f. — 297:12
new city of F. — 566:23
none of his f. like him — 570:23
not..forgive our f. — 25:3
not in the multitude of f. — 279:30
of f., of hope, of all bereft — 159:1
oh, my foes, and oh, my f. — 339:6
old f., old times — 226:43
our f., the enemy — 43:10
party of f. and relations — 219:11
precious f. hid in death's..night — 486:25
rather have such men my f. — 452:4
Religion..fears her f. — 104:39
remembering my good f. — 474:28
separateth very f. — 50:18
something left to treat my f. — 327:14
soul and body part like f. — 166:15
that to f. — 426:1
those who betray their f. — 215:2
to have advanced true f. — 15:13
to his f. and his relations — 222:21
to meet one's f. — 104:2
trencher-f. — 480:26
troops of f. — 460:36
walked in the house of God as f. — 395:12
want of f. — 80:3
when his f. did understand — 29:23
without three good f. — 427:25
wounded in the house of my f. — 56:13
wretched have no f. — 191:18
Friendship: crown..made of love and f. — 284:26
destitute of sincere f. — 25:12
dupe of f. — 239:22
endearing elegance of female f. — 278:20
f...but a name — 215:29
f. is a disinterested commerce — 226:34
f. is constant in all..save..love — 468:12

Friendship (cont.)

F. is Love without his wings — 117:43
f. recognized by the police — 514:25
[f.] redoubleth joys — 26:17
f. take a breed of barren metal — 463:23
f. with all nations — 268:21
his f. in constant repair — 270:29
in f., first I think — 245:11
let us swear an eternal f. — 124:16
let us swear eternal f. — 504:26
little f. in the world — 26:13
love, f., charity — 481:21
love, f, cowardice — 328:2
most f. is feigning — 427:22
my enemy—for f.'s sake — 74:17
part in f. — 119:8
rural quiet, f., books — 546:13
society, f., and love — 164:24
such a f. as had master'd Time — 533:9
thy f...made my heart to ache — 74:17
to f. clear — 125:4
way of f.'s gone — 243:34
what a thing f. is — 91:28
where genial f. plays — 250:20
wing of f. — 177:28, 29
woman's f. — 215:15
Friendships begin with liking — 196:19
Frieze: no jutty, f., buttress — 457:6
Frieze-coated: dark, f...Month — 153:15
Fright: f. us from the shore — 562:17
Nature stood recover'd of her f. — 193:38
no dangers f. him — 279:5
wake in a f. — 34:10
wak'd in a f. — 13:16
Frighted: being thus f. — 477:7
f. the reign of Chaos — 345:1
f. thou let'st fall — 485:26
f. with false fire — 435:18
Frightened: better be killed than f. to death — 518:36
f. both the heroes so — 130:6
f. look in its eyes — 502:16
if that little man..is not f. — 204:32
words which f. the birds — 10:24
Frightful: f. and afar — 142:11
f. frantic fearful frown — 220:7
f. when one's dead — 384:26
monster of so f. mien — 383:27
'twas f. there to see — 150:20
Frights: it f. the isle — 471:16
Fringed: f. curtains of thine eye — 479:13
his blue-f. lids — 151:19
Fringes of a southward-facing brow — 18:16
Frío que templa el ardor — 134:18
Frisk: his lass, his fiddle, and his f. — 162:21
I'll have a f. with you — 270:14
lambs that did f. i' the sun — 485:4
Fritillaries: what purple f. — 18:29
Fritter-my-wig! — 128:6
Fritters: best f. that ever I eat — 377:15
Friuli: blue F.'s mountains — 114:6
Frivolity: chatter of irresponsible f. — 181:13
gay without f. — 16:9
Frivolous work of polished idleness — 326:27
Frog: better'n any other f. — 550:12
expiring f. — 178:32
f. he would a-wooing go — 366:21
F. is justly sensitive — 40:26
thus use your f. — 559:23
toe of f. — 459:31
Frolic: f. architecture of the snow — 199:39
Lamb, the f. and the gentle — 575:17
Frolics: youth of f. — 384:37
From: driving rapidly f. something — 273:4
Frondent: nunc f. silvae — 555:24
Frondescit: simili f. virga metallo — 554:24
Frondis: nigrae feraci f. in Algido — 260:21
Front: head and f. of my offending — 460:45
his fair large f. — 347:11
see the f. o' battle lour — 107:32
won't go to the f. ourselves — 11:9
Frontier: the f.-grave — 363:1
Frore: parching air burns f. — 345:31
Frost: but a f. of cares — 547:10
comes a f., a killing f. — 446:24
curdied by the f. — 429:20
dead with f. ere now — 232:15
death's untimely f. — 106:10

Frost (cont.)
  forms of the radiant f.   498:13
  f. performs its secret ministry   151:23
  heavy as f.   576:16
  His graver of f.   545:13
  it is a f.l   518:27
  our tears thaw not the f.   491:14
  secret ministry of f.   151:25
Frosts: f. are slain   521:30(-522)
  hoary-headed f.   466:37
Frosty: as are the f. skies   540:6
  f., but kindly   426:37
  thinking on the f. Caucasus   474:20
Froth: his embossed f.   480:32
  idlest f. amid the..main   83:9
  mostly f. and bubble   227:34
Froude: F. believes Kingsley a divine   517:8
  F. informs the Scottish youth   517:8
Froward: human life..like a f. child   527:18
Frown: beneath the foeman's f.   188:30
  convey a libel in a f.   521:9
  fear at your f.   201:24
  frightful frantic fearful f.   220:7
  f. o' the great   430:1
  I'll f. and be perverse   477:20
  knew not what it was to f.   376:21
  say that she f.   479:4
  sweetest love to f.   232:5
  they f. on you for weeks   183:12
  without f. or smile   421:15
Frowned: fair Science f. not   230:13
  not true to say I f.   140:5
  when he f.   225:1
Frowning: behind a f. providence   161:18
Frowns: f. o'er the..Rhine   113:43
  her very f.   148:13
Frowst with a book by the fire   297:28
Frowzy: drowsy, f. poem   116:5
Froze the genial current   230:5
Frozen: architecture..is f. music   415:20
  fair, but f. maid   213:15
  f. up within   16:10
  her blood was f. slowly   534:9
  milk comes f. home   456:1
  o'er many a f...Alp   346:2
  or the f. zone   125:7
  strapp'd waist, and f. locks   163:20
Frugal: she had a f. mind   159:35
Fruges consumere nati   256:24
Frugis: provisae f. in annum copia   257:11
Frugum: salve, magna parens f.   556:14
Fruit: after none, or bitter, F.   206:22
  bent with thickest f.   409:14
  bless with f. the vines   284:10
  books, f., french wine   290:24
  bore thy f. and mine   305:18
  bring forth f...in May   328:15
  bring forth more f. in their age   397:21
  brought forth f.   59:23
  every lusty heart..bring forth f.   328:15
  f. burnished with golden rind   347:5
  f. of good works   389:50
  f. of loyal nature   530:11
  f. of that forbidden tree   344:1
  f. of the Hesperides   545:7
  f. of the Spirit   67:46
  f. that can fall without shaking   354:14
  f. thereof dust   523:1
  f. which..looks a flower   529:3
  give them f. for their songs   2:31
  grow to f. or shade   243:20
  hang there like f., my soul   430:5
  I love f. when it's expensive   379:1
  known by his f.   59:13
  last season's f. is eaten   197:14
  like the untimely f. of a woman   395:21
  long for the f. at last   500:16
  my f. is dreams   545:9
  never want some f.   244:17
  planteth..eateth not of the f.   66:34
  reach the ripest f. of all   330:28
  red f. of thy death   524:4
  restore..with cordial f.   244:9
  that green f. would swell   285:1
  weakest..f. drops earliest   464:31
  what mystic f.   199:8
Fruitful: be f., and multiply   44:9
  f. ground   518:1
  vineyard in a..f. hill   52:37

Fruitfulness: mists and mellow f.   284:10
Fruition: sweet f. of an earthly crown   330:28
Fruits: by their f...know them   58:27
  eat his pleasant f.   52:8
  flowers and f. of love   118:26
  f. of originality   338:30
  f. of the Spirit   388:54
  imag'ries of f. and flowers   285:19
  kindly f. of the earth   389:6
  like Dead Sea f.   357:6
  like the f. of the tree   335:25
  no f., no flowers   253:12
  plants f. of life and beauty   74:25
  wherein all pleasant f.   124:4
Fruit-tree: all these f. tops   477:22
  some f.'s mossy root   332:20
Frumious: the f. Bandersnatch   129:39
Frustra: nisi dominus f.   49:36
Frustrate: Arian f.   96:39
  each f. ghost   96:46
  f. hope severer   160:20
  f. their knavish tricks   125:16
Frying-pan: fish that talks in the f.   170:25
Fry me!   128:6
Fucos: ignavum f. pecus..arcent   556:23
Fudge: cry out 'F.!'   227:24
  two-fifths sheer f.   320:4
Fuego que calienta el frío   134:18
Fuel: adding f. to the flame   350:37
  f. justice layeth on   508:15
  f. to maintain his fires   124:25
Fuere: sed haec prius f.   132:14
Fugaces: eheu f.   34:1
  eheu f., Postume, Postume   259:9
Fugis: quem f., a, demens?   555:22
Fugit interea, f. inreparabile tempus   556:21
Fugitive: fancies f.   96:26
  f. and cloistered virtue   352:9
  what was so f.   576:17
Fugues: masses and f. and 'ops'   220:5
Fuimus Troes   554:8
Fulfil: faithfully to f. the same   389:28
  f. all righteousness   57:32
  f. all thy mind   392:36
  f. the law of their being   20:13
  not to destroy but to f.   57:43
  that I should f. thy will   394:13
Fulfilled: f. of my heart's desire   524:13
  f. of unspeakable things   525:11
  he that loveth..hath f. the law   66:11
  our hearts were f. with the music   525:2
  through hours of gloom f.   16:29
Fulfilling: love is the f. of the law   66:12
  wind and storm f. his word   400:24
Fulfils: God f. himself in many ways   531:35
Fulget: virtus..intaminatis f. honoribus   259:19
Fulgore: non fumum ex f.   255:27
Full: between a f. man and a fasting   420:10
  f. and fair ones   245:21
  f. as craving..f. as vain   191:20
  f. fathom five   479:30
  if the moon shine at f.   111:4
  never any with so f. soul   479:44
  reading maketh a f. man   27:18
  Sea of Faith..at the f.   15:7
  serenely f., the epicure   505:4
  too f. for sound and foam   528:22
  without o'erflowing f.   172:10
  yet the sea is not f.   50:60
Full-blown: yet a rose f.   247:21
Full-breasted: some f. swan   531:38
Fuller: silly old angel [Thomas F.]   307:24
Fuller's earth: true f. for reputations   214:18
Fullfed beast shall kick   197:14
Full-resounding line   386:17
Full-stop: History came to a f.   422:17
Full-throated ease   287:23
Full-voiced: to the f. quire   341:24
Fulmen: brutum f.   379:28
  eripuit caelo f.   329:6
Fulness: and the f. thereof   66:40
  f. to such, a burden is   99:31
  in the f. of joy and hope   253:7
  in thy presence is the f. of joy   392:27
  to lapse in f.   429:35
Fumble: saw him f. with the sheets   443:19

Fumbles for his brains   162:25
Fume: black, stinking, f.   267:30
  f. of little hearts   530:17
  f. of poppies   284:12
  memory..shall be a f.   457:14
Fumiter: crown'd with rank f.   454:2
Fumum: f. et opes strepitumque Romae   260:13
  non f. ex fulgore   255:27
Fun: I rhyme for f.   105:27
  little f.   335:10
  mirth and f. grew   108:11
  my f. o' the Corp'ral's Guard   295:3
  no..f. in any Act of Parliament   243:10
  taken my f. where I've found it   298:3
  to come and spoil the f.   130:10
  what he had to say..make f. of it   127:25
  What Jolly F.   405:16
  will not have the f.   142:7
Function: f. is smother'd in surmise   456:24
  F. never dies   573:26
  his whole f. suiting with forms   433:31
  own no other f.   485:27
  proper f. of women   196:28
Functions: above their f.   455:22
  all f. of a man   163:12
Fundamental brainwork   411:38
Fundamentally: woman was f. sensible   274:30
Fundit: f. humo facilem victum   556:15
Funeral: costlier f.   529:15
  fancy to see my own f.   195:19
  f. bak'd meats   431:4
  f. marches to the grave   317:6
  her f. sermon   41:15
  I'd appint your f. to-morrow afternoon   560:7
  misbehaved once at a f.   307:11
  no murners..at my f.   237:7
  not a f. note   572:10
  one high f. gleam   585:22
  prepare vault for f. Monday   39:30
  to black f.   478:33
  with mirth in f.   430:24
Funereal: his own f. destiny   118:31
Funny how a bear likes honey   339:20
Fur: doctors of the Stoic f.   340:35
  f. fly 'bout the ears   110:30
  keep their f. dry   453:4
  oh my f. and whiskers   128:26
Furca: naturam expellas f.   257:2
Furies: fierce as ten f.   346:4
  fram'd by f.' skill   509:25
  [F.] mean well   182:10
  f. of thy brother   324:11
Furious: grew fast and f.   108:11
  temperate and f.   458:25
Furiously: he driveth f.   48:27
Furlong: swoops down a f. sheer   301:27
Furloughs for another world   193:30
Furnace: as one great f. flam'd   344:9
  burning fiery f.   55:37, 40
  f. for your foe   440:10
  heat the f... seven times more   55:39
  in the f. of affliction   54:19
  in what f.   75:24(-76)
  sighing like f.   427:21
Furnish: coldly f. forth the marriage tables   431:4
  f. all we ought to ask   291:7
  f. you with argument and intellects   227:20
Furnished: f. well with men   449:30
  my table thou hast f.   421:1
Furniture: all the f. he is likely to use   187:18
  all the..f. of earth   43:12
  mere church f.   164:10
  Nature's pride and richest f.   330:23
  no f. so charming as books   504:25
Furor: f. arma ministrat   553:11
  ira f. brevis est   256:26
Furrow: beneath the f.'s weight   107:8
  leaves a shining f.   539:2
  like an ox in the f.   300:7
  on a half-reap'd f.   284:12
  plough my f. alone   409:10
  rank fumiter and f. weeds   454:2
Furrows: bewildered f.   266:14
  in thee time's f...behold   486:19
  made long f.   399:37

Furrows (cont.)
smite the sounding f. 541:3
thou waterest her f. 395:30
Further: Beaumont lie a little f. 281:11
f. from God 4:23
f. off from England 129:24
hitherto..but no f. 49:21
little f. on 350:20
Furthest: as far as who goes f. 448:38
Furtively: hedgehog travels f. 235:14
Fury: allaying both their f. 479:29
blind f. of creation 490:14
comes the blind F. 342:20
cunning old F. 128:25
full of sound and f. 461:4
f. of a patient man 190:30
f. of the many-headed monster 335:3
F. slinging flame 532:27
in her prophetic f. 472:16
nor Hell a f. 155:20
numbs the F.'s ringlet-snake 535:26
thrice came on in f. 323:23
when civil f. first grew high 110:2
Furze: flowers on f. 97:11
midland f. afire 296:15
Fusees: they who use f. 121:20
Fuss: didn't tell, nor make a f. 303:23
Fust in us unus'd 436:15
Fustian..so sublimely bad 385:28
Fustilarian: you f. 441:29
Futile: whose manners were f. and harsh 312:15
Futility: fatal f. of Fact 268:9
Future: both..present in time f. 197:4
cannot fight against the f. 222:34
children of the f. age 76:1
extravagant hopes of the f. 101:33
for the f. in the distance 33:8
f. predominate over the present 277:39
hopes of f. years 316:1
I dipt into the f. 534:25
leave the f. to..Providence 24:24
lively sense of f. favours 559:4
no preparation for the f. 181:32
Past and the F. are nothing 402:14
plan the f. by the past 103:6
present, past, and f. sees 75:23
serve the f. hour 573:27
some f. day 147:11
trust no F. 317:7
your labour is for f. hours 262:3
Futurity: his present is f. 236:42
Futurum: quid sit f. cras 258:14
Fuzzy-Wuzzy: so 'ere's to you, F. 296:23
Fyle the Logan-water 108:34

G

Gab: haven't the gift of the g. 331:20
Gabble o' the goose 121:4
Gabies: grow up as geese and g. 515:24
Gad: liberty to g. abroad 57:2
she called his name G. 45:7
Gadarene: *the* G. Swine 304:48
Gadding vine 342:14
Gadier: Javan or G. 350:31
Gaels: great G. of Ireland 140:15
spoke the speech of the G. 140:14
Gage: hope's true g. 405:9
Gai: toujours g., archy 331:12
Gaiety: eclipsed the g. of nations 278:7
take me back to the G. hotel 21:4
Gaily the Troubadour 37:2
Gain: counting g. but loss 361:13
distinct g. to society at large 219:23
for g., not glory 385:1
for the g. of a few 386:35, 520:47
if he shall g. the whole world 59:45, 61:3
loss comes..from his g. 90:44
my good is but vain hope of g. 547:20
necessity to glorious g. 575:6
pleased with constant g. 165:3
richest g. I count but loss 562:18
serves and seeks for g. 452:38
subserves another's g. 532:33
this g. of our best glory 168:9
to die is g. 68:15
to g. our peace 459:4

Gain (cont.)
weather that bringeth no g. 170:24
what things were g. to me 68:21
which the soul is competent to g. 574:17
whom hope of g. allured 218:1
would you g. the tender creature 214:9
Gained: all we have g...by...unbelief 89:32
g. a hundred fights 537:18
g. a king 344:33
g. ground upon the whole 95:17
g. no title..lost no friend 385:6
in honour I g. them 362:22
learning hath g. most 212:15
Gains: God bless all our g. 88:10
light g. make heavy purses 25:36
Gait: manner of his g. 482:34
nor the g. of Christian 434:19
Gaiter: hardly modified the cut of a g. 236:42
Gaiters: all is gas and g. 177:24
in my old brown g. 301:8
Galahad: nor G. clean 531:21
servant of the high God, G. 359:15
Galatea: malo me G. petit 555:26
Galatians: great text in G. 96:40
O foolish G. 67:41
Gale: Africk's spicy g. 215:42
before a Biscay g. 323:6
blew a mack'rel g. 192:31
changest not in any g. 532:2
his snowy plumage to the g. 546:11
note that swells the g. 231:5
partake the g. 384:16
snuff'd the tainted g. 416:12
so sinks the g. 33:10
Galeotto fu il libro e chi lo scrisse 168:23
Galère: dans cette g. 353:21
vogue la g.! 405:1
Gales: cool g. shall fan the glade 385:7
'mid the equinoctial g. 8:24
Galice: in G. at Seint Jame 137:15
Galilæ: vicisti, G. 282:15
Galilean: conquered, O G. 282:15
conquered, O pale G. 525:8
pilot of the G. lake 342:26
thy kingdom shall pass, G. 525:13
yet take all, G.? 525:6
Galilee: rolls nightly on deep G. 118:37
Galileo: blind, to G. 94:9
Pythagoras was misunderstood ..and G. 200:41
Gall: g. a new-healed wound 441:17
g. enough in thy ink 484:1
in the g. of bitterness 64:38
lack g. to make oppression bitter 433:34
take my milk for g. 457:3
they gave me g. to eat 396:19
wormwood and the g. 55:24
Gallant: g. and gay 385:1
he was a braw g. 30:9
in a nation of g. men 102:11
that haughty, g., gay Lothario 412:9
this g. will command the sun 479:10
very g. gentleman 21:8
Gallantry: conscience..no more to do with g. 500:12
what men call g. 115:19
Gallants: brave g., stand up 420:25
Galleon: like a Spanish great g. 212:18
moon was a ghostly g. 366:1
Galleons: may enter into g. 298:16
their high-built g. came 539:21
where are the g. of Spain? 183:6
Gallery: faces are but a g. of pictures 26:16
g. in which the reporters sit 324:22
Grosvenor G...young man 221:7
in the Reporters' G. yonder 126:29
Galley: Cervantes on his g. 141:8
taken by a Spanish G. 30:23
Galley-bench creaks with a Pope 525:21
Galleys: over the sea our g. went 94:20
their g. blaze 115:3
Galley-slave: as the tanned g. 563:12
Gallia..in partes tres 120:10
Galliard: go to church in a g. 482:8
Galligaskins: donn'd g. 121:1
Gallimaufry or hodge-podge 511:1
Gallio cared for none of these things 65:3

Gallop: false g. of verses 428:1
g. apace, you..steeds 478:17
to g. and to trot 189:16
Galloped: I g., Dirck g. 92:22
Gallops: g. o'er a courtier's nose 477:7
she g. night by night 477:7
who Time g. withal 428:9
Gallowglass: on·St. G.'s Eve 141:10
Gallows: erect a statue..under the g. 505:14
g. fifty cubits high 48:37
g. in my garden 140:8
g. standing in England 438:19
his complexion is perfect g. 479:16
it grew a g. 305:18
nothing but the g. 102:16
Gallows-foot: to the g.—and after 302:18
Gallows-maker 437:6
Gallows-tree: head of the g. 294:28
Jack on the g. 419:33
under the g. 37:16
Galls: bitterness of your g. 441:18
he g. his kibe 437:13
Galumphing: he went g. back 129:39(-130)
Gamaliel: at the feet of G. 65:13
Gambler: whore and g. 73:28(-74)
Gambol: Christmas g. 418:24
which madness would g. from 436:1
Gambolled: bears..g. before them 347:15
Gambols: your g.? your songs? 437:15
Game: g. for you 141:20
g. is done! 149:13
g...never lost till won 165:14
g. of interchanging praise 250:29
g. of the few 43:15
g.'s afoot 443:27
g. they dare not bite 385:32
gentlemanly g. 569:8
hard if I cannot start some g. 240:9
helpless Pieces of the G. 206:29
how you played the g. 406:20
love the g. beyond the prize 362:33
made the g. first of the chess 138:13
more than a g...an institution 265:2
most contagious g. 336:24
not a g. at which two can play 39:31
play the g.! 363:4, 5
rigour of the g. 306:12
royal g. of goose 225:4
silly g. where nobody wins 212:9
ther is g. noon 138:16
turned to jollity and g. 349:27
war's a g. 163:42
win this g. and..thrash the Spaniards 188:35
woman is his g. 538:23
Game-act: explaining a passage in the g. 511:17
Game Chicken 175:12
Gamecocks: wits are g. 215:23
Game-preservers: idlers, g. 126:37
Games: he's up to these grand g. 120:3
in g. confederate 575:23
in the many g. of life 575:11
playing our g. 164:8
Gamesome: I am not g. 448:13
Gamesters: see more than g. 26:12
Gammon: world of g. and spinnage 174:32
Gamyn: of g. and gle 583:26
Gang: g. a kennin wrang 104:7
old g. 143:30
will ye g. wi' me 9:17
Ganges: by the Indian G.' side 333:9
Gaol: long time in g. 386:36
we..who lie in g. 569:11
Gap: made a g. in nature 424:7
this great g. of time 423:41
Gape: grave doth g...wider 442:18
Gapèd with horrid warning g. 286:36
Gapes for drink again 158:7
Gaps: g. in our files 17:21
with savage-pictures fill their g. 521:18
Garb: clothed in reason's g. 345:22
in the g. of old Gaul 201:27
Garde: la G. meurt 121:24
Garden: blow upon my g. 52:8
careless-order'd g. 540:29
come into the g., Maud 536:9
cultivate our g. 557:3

Garden (cont.)

down in yonder g. green	32:17
every Hyacinth the G. wears	206:3
fairies at the bottom of our g.	212:20
first g. of Liberty's tree	123:6
gallows in my g.	140:8
G. by the Water blows	205:9, 11
g. inclosed is my sister	52:7
g. in her face	124:4
g. is a lovesome thing	85:12
g. of bright images	503:18
g. of my own	333:2
g. of your face	243:18
g.'s last petals	523:15
g. that I dream of	570:17
ghost of a g.	523:13
Glory of the G.	296:30
God Almighty first planted a g.	26:19
God the first g. made	158:9
God walking in the g.	44:21
how does your g. grow?	367:21
I know a little g. close	359:5
into the g. to cut a cabbage-leaf	209:18
lodge in a g. of cucumbers	52:28
look through this same G.	207:28, 29
man and a woman in a g.	570:17
my beloved come into his g.	52:8
nearer God's Heart in a g.	233:17
nidding, nodding in the g.	171:18
no tender-hearted g.	302:7
our England is a g.	296:30
owre yon g. green	30:15
rosebud g. of girls	536:14
secret was the g.	545:3
set to dress this g.	475:13
small house and large garden	158:13
that happy g.-state	332:21
the Lord God planted a g.	44:11
through his g. walketh God	96:33
unweeded g.	430:33
who loves a g.	163:18
Garden-beds: across the empty g.	359:11
Garden-croft: whistles from a g.	284:15
Gardener: Adam was a g.	296:33(–297), 445:39
g. Fancy	288:8
g. Robin	160:30
G., Time	183:3
half a proper g.'s work	296:33(–297)
supposing him to be the g.	64:6
will come the G. in white	208:13
Gardeners: no ancient gentlemen but g.	437:5
our wills are g.	470:15
Garden-god: eyes of the g.	523:4
Garden-roses: voluptuous g.	537:26
Gardens: bordered by its g. green	359:2
down by the salley g.	584:11
g. bright with sinuous rills	151:32
in the g. of the night	81:17
Leisure. .in trim g.	341:11
levelled walks through .. g.	154:13
not God! in g.!	85:13
our bodies are our g.	470:15
such g. are not made	296:32
sweetest delight of g.	85:20
Garden-trees: through the vext g.	18:25
Gardes: messieurs les g. françaises	239:9
Garish: I loved the g. day	364:11
Garland: all a green willow is my g.	248:3
g. briefer than a girl's	262:20
green willow must be my g.	473:6
his g. and singing robes	352:20
take at my hands this g.	522:14
that immortal g.	352:9
wither'd is the g.	425:29
Garlanded with carven imag'ries	285:19
Garlands: her silken flanks with g. drest	287:12
to her. .g. bring	484:40(–485)
weave the g. of repose	332:13
whose g. dead	357:14
with fantastic g.	437:1
you may gather g. there	419:7
Garlic: wel loved he g.	137:20
with cheese and g. in a windmill	440:2
Garment: g. down to the foot	70:26
g. of praise	55:4
g. out of fashion	429:32
know the g. from the man	74:22
language. .the g. of thought	127:10

Garment (cont.)

like a g. wear. .the morning	582:14
like as with a g.	398:8
lowlands. .like a grey-green g.	235:22
moth fretting a g.	394:10
she caught him by his g.	45:16
wax old as doth a g.	398:2
Winter G. of Repentance	205:14, 15
wintry g. of unsullied snow	507:37
Garmented in light	499:6
Garments: enlarge the borders of their g.	60:15
g. gay and rich	12:1
look at her g.	252:12
not like the fashion of your g.	453:31
reasons are not like g.	201:29
stuffs out his vacant g.	447:34
they part my g.	393:6
trailing g. of the Night	316:28
with dyed g. from Bozrah	55:5
Garnered up my heart	472:34
Garnish: beauteous eye of heaven to g.	447:39
Garnished: see they be g. fair	544:7
swept and g.	59:18
Garret: born in the g.	119:3
her precious jewels into a g.	24:38
living in a g.	209:17
Garrick: here lies David G.	225:30
our G.'s a salad	225:25
Garrison: hath friends in the g.	234:2
Garsington: hey for G.!	292:10
Garter: take away that star and g.	23:16
the G.. .no damned merit	335:15
Garters: scarfs, g., gold	383:30
thine own heir-apparent g.	439:3
Garyalies: Joblillies, and the G.	209:18
Gas: all is g. and gaiters	177:24
Gash: in a g. of the. .Apennine	91:5
Gas-lamps: his g. seven	293:10
Gasp: at the last g.	57:21
Dreadful Lies, it made one G.	41:9
last g. of Love's latest breath	189:20
on a sudden came a g. for breath	372:19
Gate: after we pass the g.	187:11
against the ivory g.	359:1
a-sitting on a g.	131:22
at his narrow g.	443:10
at one g. to make defence	350:29
broad g. and the great fire	423:9
by the g. of Bath-rabbim	52:19
Captain of the G.	323:17
dreams out of the ivory g.	85:22
g. is strait	525:28
G. with dreadful faces throng'd	349:31
Godfrey in the g.	141:7
heaven's g. stands ope	245:8
he gazed upon the g.	119:21
here at the g. alone	536:9
how strait the g.	241:19
Hun is at the g.	296:19
keep the g. of hell	472:37
lead you in at Heaven's g.	75:8
Mede is at his g.	119:13
near the sacred g.	543:4
no latch ter de golden g.	238:24
openeth the g. to good fame	26:4
poor man at his g.	3:15
sat by the celestial g.	119:14
sound at heaven's high g.	81:3
stood at the g. of the year	239:4
strait is the g.	58:24
they that sit in the g.	396:18
this is the g. of heaven	45:5
to my neighbour's g.	336:39
unlock the g. of Heav'n	4:5
watchful at His G.	183:21
West to the Golden G.	298:28
wide is the g.	58:23
ye wait at Heaven's G.	302:22
Gates: at heaven's g. she claps her wings	321:16
at the g. o' Paradise	33:2
battering the g. of heaven	540:8
despondently at area g.	197:23
even from the g. of heaven	99:25
g. are mine to open	300:11
g. of heaven opened against him	328:23
g. of hell can never. .prevail	35:3
g. of hell. .not prevail	59:43
g. of new life	96:25

Gates (cont.)

Gaul is at her g.	158:31
hovers within my g.	319:4
I barred my g. with iron	296:4
lift up your heads. .g.	393:12
men shut their g.	484:27
on all her stately g.	322:21
open the temple g.	509:12
open, ye everlasting g.	348:28
out of the g. of the day	585:13
shut the g. of mercy	230:6
stranger. .within my g.	390:10
such are the G. of Paradise	74:21
the Lord loveth the g. of Sion	397:13
through g. of pearl	264:10
twelve g. were twelve pearls	72:2
two g. of Sleep	555:2
unbarred the g. of light	348:19
ye g. lift up your heads	421:2
Gath: tell it not in G.	47:29
Gather: g. at the river	415:8
g. therefore the Rose	509:33
g. together the outcasts	400:21
g. up the fragments	63:21
g. ye rosebuds	247:10
God. .shall g. them	24:5
he shall g. the lambs	54:11
nor g. into barns	58:11
we'll g. and go	250:15, 420:13
who shall g. them	394:9
Gathered: all is safely in g.	4:11
by gloomy Dis was g.	347:8
cannot be g. up again	47:35
flowers, some g. at six	186:31
g. flowers are dead	208:13
g. them together into. .Armageddon	71:30
g. thy children together	60:20
g. to the quiet west	241:23
I am g. to thy heart	338:7
kings of the earth are g.	394:33
safely, safely g. in	183:2
when two or three are g.	388:33
where two or three are g.	59:52
Gatherer: red for the g.	543:23
Gathering: g. her brows like g. storm	108:2
g. where thou hast not strawed	60:31
swallows g. in the sky	336:31
Gathers: g. all things mortal	523:20
those. .he g. round him	408:7
Gat-toothed I was	138:8
Gaude: fide et g. in Christo	321:3
Gaudeamus igitur	13:8
Gaudete vosque O Lydiae lacus undae	132:21
Gaudy: g., blabbing. .day	445:33
neat but not g.	565:21
neat, not g.	307:7
one other g. night	425:6
owes not all. .to g. tire	166:18
rich, not g.	431:25
this g. melon-flower	92:16
to g. day denies	119:1
Gauger: g. played the flute	516:13
what should Master G. play?	516:13
Gaul: G. is at her gates	158:31
G.. .three parts	120:10
in the garb of old G.	201:27
I've lost G.	301:5
to G., to Greece	162:2
Gaunt: as familiarly of John a G.	442:16
frail, g., and small	235:17
old John of G.	474:8
on G.'s embattled pile	322:23
siege of the city of G.	31:14
Gauntlet: flings the g. down to senates	123:7
g. with a gift in't	87:29
Gauze: owre g. and lace	106:32
Gave: g. up the ghost	64:50
g. what life requir'd	224:14
no man g. unto him	62:14
return unto God who g. it	51:33
she g. me of the tree	44:22
that we g., we have	10:5
the Lord g.	48:40
what were g., we have	11:17
Gavest: the day Thou g.	108:17
Gawds: praise new-born g.	481:21
Gay: all will be g.	92:16

Gay (cont.)
always g.!	11:24
bedeck'd, ornate, and g.	350:31
each g. turn	382:33
face that's anything but g.	543:6
from grave to g.	384:15
g. as soft!	587:8
G. a week	521:2
g. gilded scenes	2:2
g. in the mazy	146:23
g. Robin is seen no more	80:20
g., the g. and festive scene	178:12
g. without frivolity	16:9
gild and make them g.	189:10
I'm a g. deceiver	154:12
impiously g.	164:40
innocent as g.	419:31, 587:8
life on the whole is far from g.	312:11
though g. they run	338:9
thy outward walls so costly g.	488:20
went never g.	470:29
wise and good and g.	368:1
would not, if I could, be g.	408:9

Gaza: eyeless in G. 350:21
whence G. mourns	351:7

Gaze: coldly she turns from their g. 356:31
fix thy firm g. on virtue	324:17
fixt in stedfast g.	343:14
g. an eagle blind	455:22
g. on so fondly to-day	350:11
g. upon this world no longer	586:5
gone to g. on Cleopatra too	424:7
let them g.	478:13
show and g. o' the time	461:13
they g., turn giddy	381:27
thou art gone from my g.	314:20
wild summer..in her g.	585:4
with fearful g.	355:14

Gazed: g. adown the dale 416:12
g. on the face that was dead	572:13
I g.—and g.	577:7
too much g. at	285:39

Gazelle: never nursed a dear G. 177:33, 357:5
Gazer: rash g. wipe his eye 245:13
Gazes: g. on the ground 329:19
whoso g. faints	497:9

Gazing: every evening found him g. 311:20
g. on the earth	495:19
why stand ye g. up?	64:22
with g. fed	464:13

Gear: tho' poor in g. 108:1
Gebet: das vollkommenste G. 313:17
Geck: notorious g. and gull 484:25
Gedanke: ein einziger dankbarer G. 313:17
ein G.	234:17

Gedanken sind zollfrei 416:1
Geese: all his own g. are swans 558:29
g. are getting fat	5:23
g. are swans	16:19
grow up as g. and gabies	515:24
wild g. spread the grey wing	584:27
wild g...the creeping fowler eye	467:7

Gehazi: whence comest thou, G.? 48:24
Gehenna: down to G. 304:2
Geist: der G. der stets verneint 223:17
Gêlert's dying yell 508:32
Gem: consider'd a perfect g. 120:22
g. of all joy	195:5
many a g. of purest ray	230:5

Gems: brilliant..with thousand g. 82:9
feet like sunny g.	535:39
g. she wore	356:30
in scorn of eyes, reflecting g.	476:14
rich and various g.	340:1
these the g. of Heav'n	347:23

Gender: for foul toads to knot and g. in 472:34
of the feminine g.	370:5

Genealogies: fables and endless g. 68:41
General: attend here on the g. 472:19
by g. laws	383:14
caviare to the g.	433:25
English army led by an Irish g...French army led by an Italian g.	490:39
g.'s disdain'd	481:5
G. Good is the plea of the scoundrel	75:7

General (cont.)
g. notions are generally wrong	354:16
g. of our gracious empress	445:6
mind of large g. powers	278:2
not local prejudices..but the g. good	100:14
so useless as a g. maxim	325:7
worthy G...'immoral man'	295:13

Generalities: glittering and sounding g. 142:25
glittering g.!..blazing ubiquities	201:21

Generally: so g. civil 273:24
Generals: bite some other of my g. 216:12
despite of all your g. ye prevail	308:21
G. Janvier and Février	364:18
Ireland gives England her..g.	337:10

Generate: spirituality..typewriter does not g. 188:9
Generation: evil and adulterous g. 59:16
faithless and stubborn g.	396:33
follow the g. of his fathers	395:2
had it been the whole g.	6:20
O g. of vipers	57:30
one g. passeth..another g. cometh	50:59
to every g. these come..down	200:46
unto the third and fourth g.	390:7
ye are a chosen g.	69:48

Generations: all g...call me blessed 61:13
fleeting g. of mankind	499:8
g. are prepared	574:23
no hungry g.	288:1
soothed the griefs of forty g.	325:36
ten g. failed to alter	236:42
young g. in hail	335:26

Generous: bane of the most g. souls 229:9
booksellers are g...men	270:30
g. aspirings..in vain	307:12
g. nature..her own way	100:25
it is the g. spirit	575:5
just, the upright, the g.	363:26
like g. wine	111:24
most select and g.	431:25
most vain, most g.	241:29

Genesis: square with G. again 89:37
Geneva: grim G. ministers 24:7
open onto the Lake of G.	290:16

Genevieve: G., sweet G. 157:1
Genial: froze the g. current 230:5
great..g. Englishman	539:9

Génie: le g...aptitude à la patience vous vous croyez un grand g. 37:11
Genitivo: hic hoc horum G. 370:5
Geniumque loci...precatur 555:3
Genius: beauty like hers is g. 410:28
creates a g. to do it	201:8
eccentricities of g.	179:1
Edmund, whose g. was such	225:27
g. and the mortal instruments	449:5
g...aptitude for patience	98:18
'g'...capacity of taking trouble	111:40, 126:9
G. does what it must	337:43
g. found respectable	87:33
g...getting its possessors into trouble	111:40
g. is of no country	143:18
g...ninety-nine per cent. perspiration	195:22
g. of the Constitution	379:10
gives g. a better discerning	226:2
good G. presiding	289:13
great and hardy g.	226:27
if Shakespeare's g. had been cultivated	139:21
man of g. and his money	499:19
many a g...slow of growth	313:22
most singular g.	78:20
nothing to declare except my g.	570:22
parting g.	343:22
Philistine of g.	20:19
ramp up my g.	281:3
right sphere for Shelley's g.	19:13
rules and models destroy g.	240:4
talent instantly recognizes g.	188:28
taste is the feminine of g.	207:34
thine own g. gave the..blow	117:25
tho' g. bless	153:28
three fifths of him g.	320:4

Genius (cont.)
to believe your own thought..g.	200:36
to raise the g.	381:6
under him my g. is rebuk'd	458:33
what a g. I had	520:50
whom g. gave to shine	231:3
whose fires true g. kindles	385:29
with want of g. curst	192:10
works of g...the first things	289:23

Gennesareth: not of G., but Thames 545:1
Genteel: Lamplough was g. 514:2
no dancing bear was so g.	160:13
to the truly g.	237:6

Genteelly: debauch his friend's wife g. 272:26
Genterye: of his g. him deyneth nat 138:20
Gentes: augescunt aliae g. 321:1
multas per g.	133:20

Gentile: might of the G. 118:39
Gentiles: boastings as the G. use 300:26
Gentility: cottage of g. 151:11, 507:21
Gentle: brave notions and g. expressions 280:1
each g. and each dreadful scene	37:6
g. and virtuous deeds	328:1
g. as falcon	502:17
g. Jesus, meek and mild	565:9
g. kind of the lioun	138:20
g. lady married to the Moor	578:21
g. mind by g. deeds is known	510:9
g., plain, just	568:7
g. shepherd, tell me where	264:14
g. thing like me	585:10
he is g. that doth g. dedis	138:12
her voice..g. and low	454:24
his life was g.	452:9
his manners were g.	225:34
I knew a g. maid	232:19
just, g., wise	497:12
many a g. person..a Jack	476:11
one of those g. ones	484:21
pitee..in g. herte	137:31
Sleep! it is a g. thing	149:27
some g. Muse	342:11
this day..g. his condition	444:28(-445)
though g., yet not dull	172:10
very g. beast	467:31
very parfit g. knight	136:24

Gentle-hearted: my g. Charles 152:2
Gentleman: as a g. switches his cane 151:8
be a little g.	249:23
cannot make a g.	103:27
fat g. in such a passion	202:17
fine old English g.	8:5
fine puss-g.	159:19
finish'd g.	116:42
first true g.	170:18
g. and scholar	108:18
g...never go beyond a song	202:3
g...never inflicts pain	363:25
g. on whom..absolute trust	456:27(-457)
g. said to the fi' pun' note	178:41
g., though spoiled i' the breeding	82:26
g. to haul..with the mariner	189:1
G. who held the patent for his honours	105:16
grand old name of g.	533:23
'I am a g.'	482:24
'no g.'s library..without'	306:26
not..a braver g.	440:28
not quite a g.	20:27
old worshipful g.	5:10
once a g., and always a g.	176:3
Prince of Darkness is a g.	453:25, 517:15
prosperous g.	456:17
since every Jack..a g.	476:11
so stout a g.	440:38
stainless g.	531:20
stamps a man..as an educated g.	490:4
St. Patrick was a g.	42:19
talking about being a g.	518:5
tea..is a g.	142:9
this knight..a valiant g.	202:12
true breeding of a g.	115:41
unable to describe a g.	549:13
very gallant g.	21:8

INDEX

Gentleman (*cont.*)
very simple g. 485:34
who was then a g.? 11:18
who was then the g.? 235:7
worthy g...snatched from us 100:17
Gentlemanly: champagne..werry
  g. ideas 518:33
devil..do a very g. thing 514:11
2ndly, g. conduct 20:21
Gentleman-rankers out on the
  spree 296:27
Gentlemen: Buzzards are all g.
cooks are g. 109:10
g. in England 444:28(–445)
g. of the French Guard, fire first 239:9
g. of the shade 438:16
G. Prefer Blondes 318:19
g.'s g. 500:17
g. unafraid 294:33
g. who wrote with ease 386:16
God Almighty's g. 190:26
good-morning, g. both 198:1
great-hearted g. 90:16
no ancient g. but gardeners 437:5
not a religion for g. 136:6
scholars and g. 579:28
seamen were not g. 326:2
she lays eggs for g. 367:2
since g. came up 445:35
three g. at once 500:25
three jolly g. 171:11
two single g. roll'd into one 154:18
we shall never be g. 204:39
while the G. go by 301:18
written by g. for g. 542:23
you g. of England 373:12
young g. would be as sad 447:37
Gentleness: from your eyes that g. 448:14
g., goodness, faith 67:46
g., in hearts at peace 84:21
g. my strong enforcement 427:19
g. of heaven 577:1
humanity, g., and chivalries 328:2
Gentlest: meekest man and the g. 328:24
Gentlewomen: her g., like the
  Nereides 424:7
Gentlier on the spirit lies 535:14
Gently: as g. lay my head 87:1
flow g., sweet Afton 105:29
g. as any sucking dove 466:30
g., Brother, g., pray! 206:18
g., John, g. down hill 505:30
g., kindly treat her 214:9
g. prest, press g. mine 160:23
his faults lie g. 447:5
use all g. 434:15
Genus: g. immortale manet 556:25
hoc g. omne 261:10
nullum..scribendi g. non tetigit 273:19
Geographers, in Afric-maps 521:18
Geographical expression 338:2
Geographischer: ein g. Begriff 338:2
Geography: different from G. 42:23
g... seas of treacle 326:7
Geological: highly g...cake 176:8
Geometres pictor aliptes 283:3
Geometric: by g. scale 110:10
Geometrical: population..in a g.
  ratio 328:25
Geometry: g...it hath pleased
  God to bestow 248:17
no 'royal road' to g. 202:8
Geordie: Jingling G. 419:26
George: Amelia was praying for
  G. 542:37
between Saint Denis and Saint
  G. 445:14
for King G. upon the throne 282:10
G. in pudding time 7:12
G. the First knew nothing 272:27
G. the First was always reck-
  oned vile 309:11
G. III..'consecrated obstruc-
  tion' 28:31
G. the Third..never to have
  occurred 43:4
G. the Third..profit by their
  example 242:16
God save great G. 6:13
great G.'s acts 270:7
Harry! England and Saint G. 443:27

George (*cont.*)
in which your Uncle G.'s work-
  shops was burned 175:32
King G...able to read that 235:8
King G.'s glorious days 219:7
Saint G., that swinged the
  dragon 447:23
streets leading from St. G.'s,
  Hanover Square 112:13
when your Uncle G. was living 175:36
Georges: the G. ended 309:11
Georgia: marching through G. 583:7
Georgie Porgie, pudding and pie 366:22
Geranium: your own g.'s red 91:21
Germ: very g...of all virtue 294:3
German: by the side of the G.
  tiger 144:6
furious G. comes 323:3
G., who smoked 34:21
Herman's a G. 387:4
more g. to the matter 437:31
to my horse—G. 136:13
wee G. lairdie 250:12
Germania: rebellatrix..G. 372:5
Germans: G. in Greek 387:4
sermons from mystical G. 220:4
to the G...the air 125:23, 407:1
Germany: G...my 'spiritual
  home' 233:21
governments associated against
  G. 571:15
his bonnet in G. 463:12
offering G. too little 362:29
wall all G. with brass 329:24
Germens: all g. spill at once 453:5
Germinal: trumpet of G. 140:10
Gertrude: Cecily, G., Magdalen 410:12
Gesang: das ist der ewige G. 223:18
Wein, Weib und G. 321:5
Gesanges: auf Flügeln des G. 240:26
Gesetz: das moralische G. in mir 284:4
Gestes: Troyane g. 138:25
Gesture: g. bland 416:18
in every g. dignity 348:36
in shape and g. proudly eminent 345:5
Get: do nothing and g. something 182:26
first, to g. what you want 504:14
g. but thither 552:2
g. that I wear 427:27
g. thee to a nunnery 434:7
g. them away together 398:10
g. to live 243:31
g. up, g. up for shame 245:24
if you want to g. somewhere
  else 130:4
my practice could g. along 187:29
nice to g. up in the mornin' 310:15
Pagets..g. on well enough 335:20
pictures in our eyes to g. 184:30
plenty to g...quite enough to g. 179:15
to him that can g. it 99:39
wish you may g. it 34:18
you g. no more of me 189:20
Gets: every man g. as much..as he
  can 274:21
Getting: g. and spending 582:18
g. ready to live 201:1
Gospel of G. On 490:40
King Charles..constantly g. into it 174:25
with all thy g. get understanding 49:42
Gettysburg: [address at G.] 314:12
Gewinnen: herrschen und g. 223:23
Gewgaw: this g. world 191:17
Gey ill to deal wi' 127:29
Ghastly: g. through the drizzling
  rain 532:9
we were a g. crew 149:32
Ghost: affable familiar g. 487:21
alas! poor g. 432:7
applaud the hollow g. 16:10
brood like a g. 171:21
each frustrate g. 96:46
gave up the g. 64:50
g. of a garden 523:13
G. of the deceased Roman Empire 248:23
there's none to affright thee 246:23
g. unlaid forbear thee 430:1
if I had seen a g. 204:33
I saw my Jamie's g. 35:10

Ghost (*cont.*)
it is an honest g. 432:24
lat thy g. thee lede 136:20
like a g. from the tomb 493:1
like a g. she glimmers on 539:2
like an ill-us'd g. 73:13
like a sheeted g. 318:16
make a g. of him that lets me 432:4
moves like a g. 458:1
murmur of the mourning g. 183:1
raise up the g. of a rose 85:20
some old lover's g. 185:34
there needs no g. 432:22
to a woman but a kind of g. 184:9
turn thou g. that way 184:28
vex not his g. 454:27
what beck'ning g. 381:30
what gentle g. 282:2
would a g. not rise 523:14
your g. will walk 91:3
Ghosties: from ghoulies and g. 6:9
Ghostly: g. counsel and advice 390:32
Ghosts: they have depos'd 475:7
g...troop home 467:10
I sought for g. 494:5
like g. from an enchanter 490:4
make the g. gaze 425:22
Ghoulies: from g. and ghosties 6:9
Ghoul: Miss Blimber dug them
  up like a G. 175:6
Ghouls: they are G. 380:13
when I die, the G.!!! 541:25
Giant: arrows in the hand of the g. 399:35
as when a g. dies 462:7
baby figure of the g. mass 481:8
excellent to have a g.'s strength 461:30
fleas..upon the body of a g. 309:22
G. Despair 99:19
g. dies 231:27
g. race before the flood 192:9
g. rat of Sumatra 188:16
like a g. refreshed 397:1
like a g.'s robe 460:31
rejoiceth as a g. 392:32
sees farther than the g. 152:29
use it like a g. 461:30
Giant-dwarf, Dan Cupid 455:8
Giant's-Causeway worth seeing 274:15
Giants: g., the sons of Anak 46:14
piled by the hands of g. 323:11
sleeps with the primeval g. 125:34
there were g. in the earth 44:37
Gibber: squeak and g. in the..
  streets 430:14
Gibbets: g. for 'the man' 156:22
g. keep..in awe 586:27
racks, g., halters 370:10
Gibbon: G. moved to flutes..
  levelled walks 154:13
G.'s [style] elegant 154:13
scribble, scribble, scribble! Eh!
  Mr. G.? 223:5
works of Hume, G., Robertson 306:29
Gibeon: stand thou still upon G. 46:42
Gibes: great master of g. 181:8
where be your g. now? 437:15
Gibraltar: a thousand miles from
  the rock of G. 217:12
Giddy: I am g. 481:15
our fancies are more g. 483:3
turn g., rave, and die 381:27
Giddy-paced: brisk and g. times 483:1
Gier-eagle: strong, the g. 503:5
Gift: beauty is the lover's g. 156:5
breath..a good g. of God 267:31
cause of this fair g. 487:22
daughter of Tyre..with a g. 394:24
every g. of noble origin 581:17
every good g. and every perfect g. 69:29
every other g. but..love 16:12
excellent g. of charity 389:31
fatal g. of beauty 114:8
for a new year's g. 466:8
for g. or grace, surpassing 88:25
gauntlet with a g. in't 87:29
g. for my fair 499:15
g. of martyrdom 192:25
g. to know it 427:16
g...will never let you want 282:7
have not the g. of continency 391:26
haven't the g. of the gab 331:20

[733]

Gift (cont.)
heaven's g. takes earth's abatement 94:1
Heaven's last best g. 348:1
her great g. of sleep 241:22
her priceless g. 374:20
our surest g. 335:24
portion of her g. 574:2
rarest g. to Beauty 336:27
scented g. and remembrancer 567:12
taught song by g. of thee 95:37
thy great g. 487:22
Gifted: noble nature poetically g. 20:5
some divinely g. man 533:1
Gift-horse: look a g. in the mouth 110:24
Giftie: some Pow'r the g. gie us 106:33
Gifts: all good g. around us 121:27
all his g. to me 561:19
all the g. from all the heights 94:4
cannot recall their g. 540:22
contempt of God's good g. 267:31
diversities of g. 66:43
endowed with highest g. 574:10
enjoyed the g. of the founder 216:21
g. from the Devil 74:29
g. of God are strown 240:18
God's g. . .man's best dreams 88:21
her g. . .henceforth. .bestowed
  equally 426:18
her g. on such as cannot use them 280:19
kings. .shall bring g. 396:25
make us love your goodly g. 474:7
manifold g. of grace 391:19
man's work or his own g. 351:21
more of his grace than g. 583:10
my g. instead of me 244:27
of all the heavenly g. 233:2
pretending to. .g. of the Holy
  Ghost 109:38
rarer g. than gold 83:19
received g. for men 396:9
rich g. wax poor 434:6
these g. a curtain before 'em 482:8
they presented onto him g. 57:24
thy seven-fold g. impart 400:31
Gig: crew of the Captain's g. 140:28, 218:14
he drove a small g. 312:20
Gigadibs the literary man 89:39
Gigantic body 325:28
Giggles: he wriggles and g. 249:24
Gilbert, the Filbert 571:17
Gilboa: ye mountains of G. 47:29
Gild: g. but to flout 417:12
g. it with the happiest terms 441:5
g. refined gold 447:39
my verse again shall g. 189:10
silly to 'g. refined gold' 115:42
Gilded: men are but g. loam 474:10
small g. fly 454:8
Gilding: g. pale streams 486:29
g. the eastern hemisphere 499:29
stript of its lettering and g. 211:21
Gilds: eternal summer g. them yet 115:43
love g. the scene 500:31
Gilead: G. is mine 395:23
goats, that appear from mount G. 52:5
no balm in G.? 55:17
Giles: very old, Sir G. 359:8
Gill: look out of your window,
  Mrs. G.? 171:18
Gilliflower amiable 502:19
Gilliflowers: Columbine, with G. 510:23
streak'd g. 485:23
Gilligan: old priest Peter G. 584:6
Gills: at his g. draws in 348:26
Gilpin: away went G. 160:1
G. long live he 160:11
John G. was a citizen 159:32
Gilt: dust that is a little g. . .g.
  o'er-dusted 481:22
Gimble: gyre and g. 129:39
Gin: g. by pailfuls 419:33
talk o' g. an' beer 297:1
that I breakfast on g. 242:26
with Pitfall and with G. 207:10
woodcock near the g. 483:16
Ginger: all 'ot sand an' g. 296:24
g. shall be hot i' the mouth 482:32
nutmegs and g. 37:25
Giotto's tower, the lily of Florence 316:25
Gipfeln: über allen G. ist Ruh' 224:5

Gipseying: go a-g. through the
  world with 307:29
Gipsies: as g. do stolen children 499:23
the same the G. wore 18:8
Gipsy: prefer a g. by Reynolds 325:16
Time, you old g. man 249:17
to the vagrant g. life 334:12
Gird: another shall g. thee 64:18
g. on thy sword, O man 81:5
g. thee with thy sword 394:22
g. up now thy loins 49:18
how g. the sphere 348:30
Girded: g. himself with strength 397:22
g. with a linen ephod 47:2
g. with praise 228:20
he g. up his loins 48:6
his father's sword he has g. on 356:27
I g. up my Lions 560:5
let your loins be g. 61:54
with your loins g. 45:47
Girdedst: thou g. thyself 64:18
Girdle: folds of a bright g. furl'd 15:7
g. me with steel 329:2
g. round about the earth 466:40
girt. .with a golden g. 70:26
leathern g. 57:29
tie my g. for me 492:23
truth is the golden g. 159:4
Girdled: g. with the gleaming world 535:19
with walls and towers. .g. round 151:32
Girl: Burma g. a-settin' 299:10
but a g. to give 337:27
cleanly young g. 387:2
cold, cold, my g.! 473:32
come, little cottage g. 372:20
dear Child! dear G.! 577:1
every boy and every g. 219:6
fair little g. 262:8
find some g. perhaps 83:18
garland briefer than a g.'s 262:20
g. arose 586:7
g. I left behind me 10:13
g. with a pair of blue eyes 500:40
going to be a very good g. 208:24
Golden G. 313:6
home is the g.'s prison 490:36
I'll kiss my g. 299:21
like a green g. 431:26
my old g. that advises 174:1
she's the dearest g. 174:36
slap-up g. in a. .chariot 178:16
sweeter no g. ever gave 570:30
sweetest g. I know 571:1
sweet Highland G. 575:16
then spoke I to my g. 246:25
there was a little g. 318:17
unlesson'd g. 464:19
we all love a pretty g. 72:17
Girl-graduates: sweet g. 538:7
Girlish: filled. .with g. glee 219:27
laugh thy g. laughter 561:3
Girls: boys and g. come out 366:10
hear the g. declare 217:23
in your g. again be courted 5:8
kissed with the g. and made them cry 366:22
of all the g. 125:17
prevent g. from being g. 254:7
rosebud garden of g. 530:14
secrets with g. 165:13
swear never to kiss the g. 91:32
two little g. in blue 228:5
un-idea'd g. 270:15
what are little g. made of? 369:12
where little g. are sent 313:10
white feet of laughing g. 323:12
young boys and g. are level 425:29
Girt: g. about the paps with a. .
  girdle 70:26
g. with a crimson robe 232:1
Gitche Gumee: by the shores of G. 317:22
Gitche Manito, the mighty 317:21
Give: all I can g. you I g. 524:33
blush to g. it in 122:39
freely g. 58:47
g. all thou canst 577:9
g. all to love 199:12
g., and it shall be given 61:31
g. me my Romeo 478:20
g. me my soul again 330:5
'G. me,' quoth I 456:10
g. me the lass 106:7

Give (cont.)
g., oh g. me back my heart 118:6
g. to me the life I love 515:27
g. unto this last 60:8
g. what thou canst 163:47
g., you gods, g. to your boy 191:17
if she g. ought. .in small parcels 563:24
in each thing g. him way 423:30
I will g. a loving heart 247:1
law doth g. it 465:10
more blessed to g. 65:11
not a joy the world can g. 118:18
one life for each to g. 296:20
or Heaven can g. 493:27
receive but what we g. 151:4
such as I have g. I thee 64:27
that heart I'll g. to thee 247:1
then I'll g. o'er 246:6
they beg, I g. 195:13
they g. to get esteem 226:12
to lend, and to g. in 82:27
to spend, to g., to want 510:16
two daughters crying, G., g. 50:54
what we g. and what we preserve 314:11
what will ye g. me? 60:37
when I g. I g. myself 567:21
Given: ask, and it shall be g. you 58:19
give, and it shall be g. 61:31
g. all other bliss 540:13
g. away by a novel 290:21
g. me over in my gray hairs 572:18
g. to hospitality 66:3
g. to strong delusion 297:10
g. unsought is better 483:29
not g. for thee alone 109:1
other titles thou has g. away 452:26
something g. that way 37:28
to whom nothing is g. 204:16
unto every one that hath. .g. 60:32
when all have g. him over 189:20
Giver: cheerful g. 67:31
g. is forgot 154:40
g. of all good things 389:43
Lord and g. of life 390:20
Givers: when g. prove unkind 434:6
Gives: g. to man or woman 262:18
it blesseth him that g. 464:33
like season'd timber, never g. 245:14
she g. but little 587:12
whate'er he g., he g. the best 279:13
whoever g., takes liberty 185:21
who g. himself with his alms 320:18
Giveth: God, that g. to all men 69:27
He g. His beloved, sleep 88:25
Giving: godlike in g. 357:21
loving and g. 368:1
not in the g. vein 476:24
Gizzards: into their g. 121:20
Glad: come then. .and be g. 404:17
earth may be g. thereof 397:31
g. because. .at rest 398:19
g. did I live 516:15
g. me with its soft black eye 177:33, 357:5
g. no more. .g. of yore 574:35
g. of other men's good 427:27
g. to death's mystery 252:20
g. to learn of noble men 451:16
g. when they said 399:30
g., yea g. with all my heart 189:20
God must be g. 94:41
hark, the sound! 183:19
he was g., I was woe 232:2
Janet was as g. 32:4
live in heart so g. 80:4
our sad bad g. mad brother 522:18
Philistia, be thou g. of me 395:23
shew ourselves g. in him 397:25
what some folks would be g. of 204:20
wine that maketh g. 398:9
wise son maketh a g. father 49:54
Gladder: my heart is g. than all
  these 409:14
Glade: bee-loud g. 585:12
cool gales shall fan the g. 385:7
crown the wat'ry g. 230:23
points to yonder g. 381:30
Gladly: g. wolde he lerne and g.
  teche 137:7
suffer fools g. 67:32
travail so g. spent 583:19

Gladness: g. of her g. 36:12
in our youth begin in g. 580:7
make me hear of joy and g. 395:8
shareth in our g. 4:3
solemn g. 532:22
teach me half the g. 498:10
whose music is the g. of the world 196:35
with solace and g. 502:18
Gladsome light of jurisprudence 148:5
Gladstone: G.'s always having the ace 305:20
what's the matter with G.? 233:12
Glamis: G. hath murder'd sleep 458:12
G. thou art 457:1
King, Cawdor, G., all 458:30
thou'dst have, great G. 457:1
Glance: darest not g. thine eye 231:36
g., and nod, and bustle by 18:18
g. from heaven to earth 467:24
his g. was stern and high 323:4
how Stanley scorns the g.l 322:9
in the g. of the Lord 118:39
matron's g. 224:13
mutual g. of great politeness 119:22
whisper, a g. 183:7
whose g. was glum 222:27
Glances: up from India g. 264:1
Glare: eyes which thou dost g. with 459:19
red g. on Skiddaw 322:23
Glared: lion, who g. upon me 448:32
Glasgow: expatiating on the beauty of G. 275:9
through G. town 31:4
Glass: beholding his natural face in a g. 69:33
comb and a g. 9:3
dome of many-coloured g. 492:15
double o' the invariable 179:4
excuse for the g. 500:39
fill ev'ry g. 214:29
get the g. eyes 454:11
g. of fashion 434:14
g. to his sightless eye 362:32
grief with a g. that ran 522:5
he was indeed the g. 441:36
in a g...pigges bones 137:22
looking in the g. 141:4
Love took up the g. of Time 534:16
made mouths in a g. 453:7
man that looks on g. 244:15
my g. shall not persuade me 486:19
ordered a g. of this ale 174:18
out of the fat, as clear as g. 170:25
peeps over the g.'s edge 89:28
pure gold, like unto clear g. 71:47
satire is a sort of g. 519:4
sea of g. like unto crystal 70:37
sea of g. mingled with fire 71:28
take my votive g. 401:36
thou art thy mother's g. 486:11
through a g., darkly 66:46(-67)
till I set you up a g. 435:39
turn down an empty G. 207:30
Glasses: fill all the g. there 158:8
Shakespeare, and the musical g. 227:23
the Almighty's form.. itself 114:30
Glassy: around the g. sea 240:19
g. peartree leaves 255:4
his g. essence 461:31
Glaze: to gloat on the g. and the mark 309:25
Glazed: how g. each weary eye 149:8
summer..framed and g. 558:24
Glazier: your father was no g. 520:12
Glazing: your g. is new 303:8
Gleam: follow the G. 537:2
g. of her own dying smile 491:21
g. on the years that shall be 322:7
in the g. of a million..suns 541:4
one high funeral g. 585:22
spent lights quiver and g. 15:24
visionary g. 576:8
Gleamed: g. upon my sight 580:19
g. upon the glassy plain 575:25
Gleams: convex g. 493:1
g. of a remoter world 495:18
g. that untravell'd world 540:32(-541)
invested with purpureal g. 577:13
Glean: thou shouldst but g. 253:21
world shall g. of me 545:9

Gleaned my teeming brain 289:4
Gleaning of the grapes of Ephraim 46:53
Glede: rapid g. 503:5
Glee: fill'd one home with g. 241:8
filled..with girlish g. 219:27
inward g. 578:11
laugh'd with counterfeited g. 225:1
of gamyn and g. 583:26
Glen: down the rushy g. 4:18
Kilmeny gaed up the g. 250:21
this long g. 537:31
Glenartney: lone G.'s hazel shade 416:11
Glencairn: remember thee, G. 106:28
Glendoveer: blessed G. 504:8
Glenlivet: only half G. 23:28
Glens: bask in the g. 15:14
Glide: into the boughs does g. 332:20
shall for ever g. 573:26
Glides: still g. the Stream 573:26
Glideth: thus the living g. 94:24
Glimmering: about the g. weirs 263:20
g. o'er my fleece-like floor 492:29
mere g. and decays 552:9
their g. tapers to the sun 165:2
Glimmerings: see such g. of light 102:38
Glimmers: like a ghost she g. on 539:2
Glimpse: g. of His bright face 552:3
nor g. divine 381:27
one g. of it within the Tavern 207:8
Glimpses: g...make me less forlorn 582:18
g. of the moon 431:32(-432)
Glisten: all silence an' all g. 319:23
Glistering shoe-tie 166:18
Glisters: nor all that g., gold 230:22
Glitter: Sirius..with a steely g. 236:38
Glittering: all bright and g. 582:14
continues to offer g. prizes 72:25
g. and sounding generalities 142:25
g. generalities!..blazing ubiquities 201:21
g. like the morning star 102:11
how that g. taketh me 247:13
long grey beard and g. eye 148:18
Gloam: starv'd lips in the g. 286:36
Gloaming: in the g., O, my darling 370:15
late, late in the g. 250:22
Roamin' in the G. 310:16
when g. treads the heels o' day 526:21
Gloat: I g.l hear me g.l 304:45
to g. on the glaze and the mark 309:25
Globe: dotted over..the whole g. 563:5
golden girdle of the g. 159:4
great g. itself 480:8
rattle of a g. 191:17
this distracted g. 432:20
wears the turning g. 263:36
we the g. can compass 467:19
Globule: protoplasmal primordial atomic g. 219:19
Gloire: la g. et le repos..ne peuvent loger 354:22
le jour de g. 412:1
on triomphe sans g. 157:6
Gloom: amid the encircling g. 364:10
brooding o'er the g. 336:9
counterfeit a g. 341:16
end of toil and g. 35:6
g. of earthquake 497:24
g. the dark broad seas 541:3
go with him in the g. 236:23
in silence and in g. 24:2
inspissated g. 271:29
its splendour..pierce the g. 94:26
Lethe's g. 122:2
my g...shade of His hand 544:31
not chase my g. away 408:9
shine through the g. 322:2
this mournful g. 344:21
through hours of g. fulfill'd 16:29
thy thousand years of g. 532:2
tunnel of green g. 84:8
watch from dawn to g. 497:2
Glooms: Splendours, and G. 491:21
through verdurous g. 287:29
welcome, kindred g. 546:25
Gloomy: bright blot upon this g. scene 498:20
more bigoted, more g. 363:17
Gloria: ingens g. Teucrorum 554:8
sic transit g. mundi 291:21

Gloriae: etiam sapientibus cupido g. 526:16
Gloriam: ad majorem Dei g. 13:3
Gloried: Jamshyd g. and drank deep 206:1
Glories: all my g. in that one woman 446:27
all thy conquests, g. 450:2
ghastly g. of saints 525:10
g., like glow-worms 563:15
g. of my King 319:7
g. of our blood and state 501:5
in those weaker g. 552:4
I see heaven's g. shine 83:7
its g. pass away 322:1
my g. and my state depose 475:20
Glorified, new Memnons 88:14
Glorify: g. what else is damn'd 415:18
to g. God and to enjoy him 501:9
Gloriosus: miles g. 379:26
Glorious: all g. within 394:25
by all that's good and g. 118:35
g. by my pen 355:20
G. First of June 147:15, 359:26
g. the northern lights 503:6
g. thing, I ween 218:21
g. things of thee are spoken 364:16
g. thing to be a Pirate King 221:27
g. to be a human boy 173:34
had a g. time 190:25
happy and g. 250:14
hooting at the g. sun 151:19
more g. is the crown 503:6
Tam was g. 108:6
thou g. mirror 114:30
to combat may be g. 163:19
Gloriously drunk 163:33
Glory: all g., laud, and honour 361:8
all the g. missin' 304:37
all the g. of man as..grass 69:46
all their g. past 99:1
awake up, my g. 395:19
be Thine the g. 192:23
brightness of his g. 69:7
calls the g. from the grey 95:19
chief g...its authors 277:25
come short of the g. of God 65:38
crowned with g. now 291:18
crown him with g. and worship 392:11
cursed..to the g. av the Lord 298:21
days of our g. 118:32
differeth from another star in g. 67:13
do all to the g. of God 66:41
drown'd my G. in a Shallow Cup 207:20
eternal brood of g. excellent 509:23
eternal g. thou shalt win 99:8
excess of g. obscur'd 345:5
fill'd with the g. of God 3:8
fill thy breast with g. 243:29
for gain, not g. 386:12
for the hope of g. 389:20
g. and loveliness have pass'd away 288:28
g. and good of Art 96:18
g. and the freshness of a dream 576:1
g. and the dream 576:8
g. and the nothing of a name 114:38
g. be to God for dappled things 255:2
g. be to thee, O Lord most High 390:40
'g.' doesn't mean 'a nice knockdown argument' 131:6
g. dropped from their youth 96:43
g. in the flower 576:20
g. is departed 47:10
g., jest and riddle 383:22
g. leads the way 312:29
g., like the phoenix 117:29
G., Love, and Honour 297:20
g. of Europe is extinguished 102:11
g. of God did lighten it 72:5
g. of my crown 198:12
g. of the Egdon waste 237:9
G. of the Garden 296:30
g. of the Lord is risen 54:39
g. of the Lord..revealed 54:9
g. of the Lord shone round 61:18
g. of the winning 336:8
g. of the world pass away 291:21
g. of your prime 494:18
g. of youth 516:8
g. shall remain 233:3
g. shone around 527:4

Glory (cont.)

g.'s no compensation 304:24
g.'s thrill is o'er 356:20
g. that redounds 579:36
g. that shall be revealed 389:27
g. that was Greece 380:17
g. to God in the highest 61:19
g. to Man 524:27
g. to the king of kings 565:12
g. to the new-born king 565:12
gout and g. 91:11
go where g. waits 356:19
greater g. dim the less 465:21
heaven and earth are full of thy g. 390:40
heavens declare the g. of God 392:32
her full G...fly before ye 166:22
him who walked in g. 580:7
his work of g. done 162:11
hoary head is a crown of g. 50:16
I felt it was g. 118:34
I g. in the name of Briton 216:13
in a blaze with his descending. 100:9
in a sea of g. 446:24
into g. peep 552:12
King of g. enter may 421:2
King of g., King of peace 244:25
King of g. shall come in 393:12
lads that will die in their g. 263:3
laughter is...sudden g. 248:24
learned Thy Grace and G. under Malta 298:13
left him alone with his g. 572:14
light, a g. 151:5
like madness..the g. of this life 480:22
long hair..a g. to her 66:42
looks on war as all glory 501:4
mellow g. of the Attic stage 16:2
Memnonium..in all its g. 504:1
mine eyes have seen the g. 264:15
my gown of g. 405:9
my race of g. run 350:30
never hope for g. 515:24
no g. lives behind..such 468:27
once trod the ways of g. 446:29
on which the Prince of g. died 562:18
part with my g. and desert 244:11
paths of g. 230:1
power and the g. 58:4
pride of the peacock is the g. of God 77:16
sea of g. streams along 114:6
ships..to the G. of the Lord 298:17
show the Maker's g. 232:11
soil'd g. 16:5
so much g. and so much shame 325:25
storehouse for the g. of the Creator 24:14
strikes at thy great g. 475:3
that will be g. for me 415:10
there has passed away a g. 576:2
there's g. for you 131:6
this gain of our best g. 168:9
this goin' ware g. waits ye 319:16
thro' a kind of g. 541:22
thy g. above all the earth 395:18
thy laurel, thy g. 286:1
'tis to g. we steer 213:10
too fond of g. 505:27
to the greater g. of God 13:3
trailing clouds of g. 576:9
uncertain g. of an April day 484:33
Virtue solely is the sum of g. 331:2
visions of g. 229:25
wait and see, O sons of g. 324:18
walking in an air of g. 552:9
way to g. 537:25
we behold his g...g. as of the only begotten 62:64
What Price G. 4:22
what their joy and their g. 1:1
what the joy and the g. 362:9
when can their g. fade? 528:19
where is that g. now? 516:8
where Saints in g. stand 586:22
who is the King of g. 393:13
whole earth is full of his g. 53:8
who of g. is the king? 421:2
who rush to g. 122:19
who to your g. came 14:20
whose g. is in their shame 68:24

Glory (cont.)

why in the name of G. 286:21
with a g. in His bosom 264:18
with g. not their own 579:26
with inward g. crowned 498:24
wretchedness that g. brings us 480:28
write for g. or reward 157:5
Gloss: read every text and g. over 110:11
Gloucester: Salisbury and G. 444:28
Gloucestershire: stranger here in G. 474:27
Glove: g. upon that hand 477:14
he play'd at the g. 30:10
touch not the cat but a g. 419:21
world and they..hand and g. 162:18
Gloves: my g. on my hand 238:1
walk through the fields in g. 157:9
wore g. in my cap 453:19
Glow: felt the friendly g. 104:20
his heart should g. 221:20
lazy g. of benevolence 90:31
noon a purple g. 585:12
saw the dawn g. through 336:3
see to g. the delicate cheeks 424:6
sit and g. like it 247:17
to do thyne eres g. 138:30
Glowed: now g. the firmament 347:19
smile that g. celestial 349:4
Glowing: g. like the vital morn 493:2
unbutton'd, g. hot 164:8
Glows in the stars 383:19
Glow-worm: g. in the grass 118:8
g. shows the matin..near 432:19
green of the g. shine 171:21
her eyes the g. lend thee 246:23
Glow-worms: as g. shine 551:18
glories, like g. 503:15
Glubit magnanimis Remi nepotes 133:5
Glued: my sword g. to my scabbard 334:26
Glum: whose glance was g. 222:27
Glutinous: turtle, green and g. 94:34
Gluts twice ten thousand Caverns 288:30
Glutton: g. of wordes 310:4
of praise a mere g. 225:33
Gnarled and writhen thorn 302:7
Gnashing: weeping and g. of teeth 376:4
Gnat: I, the g. 477:7
small grey-coated g. 60:18
strain at a g. 284:14
Gnats: small g. mourn 473:13
Gnaw: g...your nether lip
Time may g. Tantallan 107:27
Go: against Nature not to g. out 352:29
all cowards, we g. on very well 274:8
all dressed up, with nowhere to g. 566:15
and g. at last 245:20
and we g. 335:25
as cooks g. she went 414:13
as often as from thee I g. 185:31
before I g. hence 394:11
bind me not, and let me g. 185:27
can't you g.? 551:14
come, let us g. 245:27
creep..where it cannot g. 484:39
donkey wot wouldn't g. 43:23, 177:31
expedient..that I g. away 63:60
friend, g. up higher 62:3
get the men to g. away 41:11
g., and catch a falling star 186:16
g., and do thou likewise 61:43
g. and find out and be damned 299:2
g., and he goeth 58:31
g., and sin no more 63:27
g., and the Lord be with thee 47:22
g. at once 459:23
g. away at any rate 8:11
g., for they call you 18:5
g. into it yourself 74:24
g., litel book 138:41
g., little book 516:12
g., lovely Rose 558:4
g., my Love 89:17
g. not, happy day 536:6
g. on till you come to the end 129:30
g., poor devil, get thee gone 513:10
g. thy way, eat thy bread 51:20
g. to your Gawd like a soldier 304:4
g. up, thou bald head 48:18
g. we know not where 462:0
g. wheer munny is 537:7

Go (cont.)

g. where glory waits 356:19
g. where you are wanted 263:10
g. with him twain 57:51
g. ye into all the world 61:9
he must g., he must kiss 232:3
how you do g. it 85:11
I can g. no longer 361:23
I can't remember how they g. 120:25
I could never g. back again 358:2
if I g. not away 63:60
I find I g. down 387:2
I g., and it is done 458:1
I g. from you to Him 24:5
I g. on for ever 528:6
I g. to the Father 63:62
I know, where'er I g. 576:2
I'll g. no further 432:6
I scarce can g. or creep 266:8
it doesn't g. far enough 177:13
I will arise and g. now 585:12
I will not let thee g. 81:13
last did g. 342:26
let them g. 468:20
let us g. hence, my songs 524:25
like Wind I g. 206:12
must you g.? 551:14
neither g. nor hang 72:20
neither will I let Israel g. 45:40
never g. from my heart 328:11
not sit nor stand but g. 95:15
not..pleasures as they come, but g. 244:8
not to g. anywhere, but to g. 514:14
obliged to g. at a certain hour 273:29
o' God's name, let it g. 475:10
one to come and one to g. 131:15
reasons for bachelors to g. out 196:28
still would g. 561:32
sweetest love, I do not go 186:15
ten thousand to g. out of it 520:34
their Lord..bid them g. 343:14
those who g. about doing good 166:25
though I must g. 186:25
Thursday's child has far to g. 368:1
thus far shalt thou g. 373:17
Time stays, we g. 183:15
to g. hence unwilling 349:30
unto Caesar shalt thou g. 65:20
we'll g. no more a-roving 119:4
we must g. 296:12
west of these..I must g. 208:7
we will g. into the house of the Lord 399:30
we will g. with you along 246:2
we will not g. again 141:23
what a Rum G. everything is 564:28
where'er I g. they shout 'Hello!' 408:17
who will g. for us? 53:9
with thee to g. 349:30
Goad us on to sin 462:1
Goads: God..g. them on 584:8
words of the wise are as g. 51:34
Goal: final g. of ill 532:31
fire-winged to its g. 411:28
g. stands up 263:6
grave is not its g. 317:5
one far-set g. 19:4
staggering on to her g. 16:11
stands up to keep the g. 263:6
till yon g. be won 227:34
Goals: muddied oafs at the g. 297:16
Goat: Llama..sort of fleecy hairy g. 41:33
lust of the g. 77:16
luxurious mountain g. 445:1
with hoofs of g. 88:11
with their g. feet dance 329:20
Goatish: his g. disposition 452:19
Goats: better than sheep or g. 531:36
Cadwallader and all his g. 445:8
drink the blood of g. 395:4
g. and monkeys! 472:31
promontory g. 336:38
refuge for the wild g. 398:10
thy hair is as a flock of g. 52:5
Gobble-uns'll git you 407:3
Goblet: thy navel is like a round g. 52:18
upon a parcel-gilt g. 441:31
Goblets: my figur'd g. 475:10
Goblin: makes a g. of the sun 411:24
spirit of health or g. damn'd 431:32

INDEX

Goblins: g.'ll git you 407:3
one of sprites and g. 485:10
God: about the feet of G. 531:36
abusing of G.'s patience 465:33
acknowledgement of G. in Christ 90:43
Act of G...defined 243:16
again to G. return 575:1
ah, my dear G. 243:21
all love is lost but upon G. 195:8
all the sons of G. shouted 49:20
almost chide G. 428:17
appeal from tyranny to G. 114:34
as a g. self-slain 523:16
as far removed from G. 344:10
as G. gives us to see the right 314:13
as if G. brought them written in his hand 200:46
as if G. wrote the bill 199:29
as if we were G.'s spies 454:19
assumes the g. 191:1
as the sunflower turns on her g. 356:13
at G.'s great Judgment Seat 294:27
attribute to G. himself 464:33
avow to G. made he 30:11
before G. made the angelic clan 586:14
before the g. of love was born 185:34
best thing G. invents 91:31
better..no opinion of G. 27:20
bitter G. to follow, a beautiful G. to behold 525:5
blends itself with G. 493:6
blow, thou wind of G.! 293:16
built G. a church 162:4
but for the grace of G. 79:12
by G.'s Almighty Hand 121:27
by searching find out G. 48:56
by the grace of G. I am what I am 67:5
by the livin' G. that made you 297:6
Cabots talk only to G. 79:2
Caesar's self is G.'s 166:14
called the children of G. 57:39
call in and invite G. 186:32
Cardinal,—Christ,—Maria,—G. 96:17
cared greatly to serve G. 363:8
Carnage..is G.'s daughter 116:25
charged with the grandeur of G. 254:24
chariots of G. 396:8
child of G. 391:2
closer walk with G. 161:1
conspired against our G. 330:1
cried out 'G., G., G.!' 443:20
cry out, O living G., for thee 421:3
curse G., and die 48:43
daily, nearer G. 291:7
daughter of the voice of G. 573:28
dear G. who loveth us 150:16
deem himself a g., or beast 383:22
Destiny the Commissary of G. 186:5
Donne's verses..like the peace of G. 267:32
door-keeper in the house of my G. 397:7
earth..praises G. 151:30
effect whose cause is G. 163:52
either a beast or a g. 14:15
either a wild beast, or a g. 26:15
eternal G. is thy refuge 46:34
even G.'s providence 252:19
even to fight against G. 64:32
every..bush afire with G. 87:35
every man..G. or Devil 190:23
every word..out of the mouth of G. 57:34
excellent angler..now with G. 559:18
faithful to G. and thee 248:7
fall into the hands of G. 540:1
fall into the hands of the living G. 69:12
far be it from G. 49:15
fast by the oracle of G. 344:2
fat, oily man of G. 546:6
fear G., and keep his commandments 51:36
fear G., and take your own part 78:30
fear G... Honour the King 69:50, 305:1
feeble G. has stabb'd me 214:6
fellow-citizens: G. reigns 213:7
first G. dawned on Chaos 491:23
forgotten even by G. 94:22

God (cont.)
for G.! for the Cause! 323:2
for G.'s sake hold your tongue 184:11
Freedom is the cause of G.! 79:11
from everlasting Thou art G. 562:9
from G. sent forth 575:1
from G., who is our home 576:9
further from G. 4:23
gifts of G. are strown 240:18
glory of G. did lighten it 72:5
glory to G. in the highest 61:19
G. accept him 537:28
G. all mercy..a G. unjust 587:10
G. Almighty's gentlemen 190:26
G. and sinners reconciled 565:12
G. and soldiers we alike adore 404:9
G. and the doctor 372:12
G. answers sharp and sudden 87:29
G. appears, and G. is Light 74:1
G. become her lover 166:9
G. being with thee 577:1
G. be in my head 6:10
G. be thanked who has matched us 84:16
G. be with you, Balliol men 40:32
G. be with you till we meet 406:1
G. bless our Lord the king 250:14
G. bless the Regent 504:4
G. by G. goes out 524:22
G. cannot change the past 3:5
G. changes, and man 524:1
G. could have made a better berry 112:21
G. created the heaven 43:26
G. disposes 291:20
G., even our own G...blessing 396:3
G. first planted a garden 26:19
G. for Harry! 443:27
G. for his Richard 475:1
G. for King Charles 90:16
G. fulfils himself 531:35
G. gave the increase 66:22
G. gives skill 197:1
G. grant you find one face 293:19
G. ha' mercy on his soul 436:36
G. has a few of us 89:11
G. has not said a word 95:6
G. has written all the books 112:3
G. hath given you one face 434:12
G. hath joined them 388:2
G. hath made them so 561:24
G. hath made the pile complete 532:32
G. hath no better praise 81:9
G. help the wicked 439:36
G. Himself is moon and sun 537:27
G. himself scarce seemed 150:14
G., if a G. there be 524:26
G., if there be a G. 8:20
G. in his holy habitation 396:5
G. in Three Persons 240:19
G. into the hands of their deliverer 350:36
G. is always for the big battalions 557:10
G. is a Spirit 63:13
G. is faithful 66:38
G. is forgotten 372:12
G. is his own interpreter 161:20
G. is in heaven 51:6
G. is in the midst of her 394:28
G. is love 70:12
G. is Love, I dare say 112:4
G. is making the American 587:18
G. is not a man 46:19
G. is not mocked 67:47
G. is our hope and strength 394:27
G. is..stream of tendency 20:13
G. is the perfect poet 94:16
G. is, they are 91:1
G. is Three, and G. is One 364:5
G. is thy law, thou mine 347:20
G. is working His purpose out 3:8
G. knoweth 67:36
G. knows, an' 'E won't split 304:53
G. 'll send the bill to you 319:14
G. loves an idle rainbow 249:12
G. Lyæus ever young 38:10
G...made 'em to match the men 196:16
G. made him..pass for a man 463:10
G. made Himself an awful rose 541:10

God (cont.)
G. made the country 162:38
G. made them, high or lowly 3:15
G. made the thunder 325:13
G. made the wicked Grocer 141:32
G...make a man miserable 136:5
G...marked him for his own 559:28
G. may forgive you 198:7
G. moves in a mysterious way 161:18
G. must be glad 94:41
G. must think it exceedingly odd 305:10
G. never made his work for man to mend 192:15
G. now accepteth thy works 51:20
G. o'erhead 317:7
G. of life, and poesy 114:23
G. of Love my Shepherd is 245:10
g. of my idolatry 477:23
G. of our fathers, be the G. 183:20
G. of our fathers, known of old 300:24
g. of our idolatry, the press 161:33
G. of Things as they are 303:21
g. pursuing 522:2
G. rest you merry 6:11
G.'s a good man 469:3
G. save great George 6:13
G. save our gracious king 125:15
G. save the king 47:12, 125:15, 250:14
G. save the king! Will no man say amen? 475:18
G. save the Queen 301:13
G. saw that it was good 44:4
G.'s eldest daughter 212:13
G.'s first Creature 28:5
G.'s forgotten 404:9
G.'s gifts..man's best dreams 88:21
G.'s grace is the only grace 375:1
G.'s greatness flowed around 88:5
G.'s great Venite 186:11
G. shall help her 394:28
G.'s hill 396:7
G. should go before such villains 469:7
G.'s in his heaven 94:40
G.'s laughing in Heaven 584:10
G.'s own country 6:14
G.'s own ear listens 348:16
G.'s soldier he 401:15
G.'s sons are things 327:6
G. stands winding His..horn 584:20
G. stooping shows sufficient 96:10
G. strikes a silence 88:26
G. tempers the wind 512:28
g. that he worships 519:11
G. that hidest thyself 54:18
G. that you took from a printed book 302:34
G. the All-terrible 142:26
G. the Father turns a school-divine 386:15
G. the first garden made 158:9
G. the herdsman 584:8
G. the soul 383:18
G. the word that spake it 197:35
G. threw him from..heaven 330:1
G. took him 44:35
G. unmakes but to remake 96:16
G. walks in mine 85:13
G. was very merciful to the birds 11:12
g. when all our life-breath met 410:26
G. who best taught song 95:37
G. who made him sees 296:33(-297)
G. who made shall gather them 24:5
G. who made thee mighty 42:20
G., whose puppets..are we 94:46
G. will provide..a lamb 44:55
G. within my breast 83:8
G. wot! 85:12
good G. pardon all good men 87:32
go to your G. like a soldier 304:4
grace is given of G. 146:24
Grace of G. is in Courtesy 41:16
grace of G...with me 67:6
granted scarce to G. 510:22
great G. of War 381:9
great g. of Loves name 138:15
great, just, good G. 96:6
grown beneath G.'s eye 96:31
had I but served G. as diligently 572:18

God (cont.)

had I but serv'd my G. 447:1
hand folks over to G.'s mercy 196:14
happen to be—G.? 91:23
have G. for his Father 22:1
have G. to be his guide 99:31
he for G. only 347:11
heirs of G. 65:54
he is the Lord our G. 397:28
he liveth unto G. 65:45
here in the sight of G. 391:22
here is G., and there is G. 147:4
here is G.'s plenty 194:13
here's G. down on us 87:27
her fathers' G. 420:5
her last republic cried to G. 142:3
her seat is the bosom of G. 253:36
he sung of G. 503:2
he trusted in G. 393:3
hey for G. Almighty! 292:10
higher than G.'s 96:15
himself from G...not free 199:23
his Father and his G. 230:13
Holy, Holy, Holy! Lord G.
    Almighty! 240:19
holy Lamb of G. 75:16
honest G. 112:9, 267:16
hope for the best, and trust in G. 504:23
hope of the City of G. 334:13
how can he love G...not seen? 70:15
how odd of G. 202:19
I am a G. and cannot find it 496:26
idea G. has of you 551:2
I embrace the purpose of G. 536:25
if G. be for us 65:57
if G. choose..love thee better 88:24
if G. did not exist 557:7
if..G. were standing there 213:2
I find letters from G. 567:24
if it be of G. 64:32
if you want to take in G. 319:13
I'll leap up to my G. 330:7
in apprehension how like a g.! 433:15
inclines to think there is a G. 146:32
in my flesh shall I see G. 49:6
in the faces..I see G. 567:24
in the great hand of G. 458:26
invisible, except to G. 346:28
I remembered my G. 507:35
is, and..is not, the voice of G. 386:14
it is the voice of a g. 64:49
I who saw the face of G. 330:2
just are the ways of G. 350:27
just G., forgive 573:10
justify G.'s ways to man 263:25
justify the ways of G. 344:4
kills the image of G. 352:5
kingdom of G. is within 62:30
kin to G. by his spirit 25:26
know his G. by night 551:18
knowledge..makes a G. of me 286:19
know that I am G. 394:29
know what G. and man is 529:24
laws of G. and man and metre
    315:14, 416:10
laws of G...suspended 489:31
leads—G. knows where 116:21
leave the word of G. 64:33
led him to confess a G. 24:18
let G. arise 396:4
let G. be true 65:36
let not G. speak with us 45:53
light but the shadow of G. 85:16
like a G. in pain 285:16
like G.'s own head 149:2
Lord G. of Battles 297:8
Lord G. of hosts 300:24, 390:40
Lord G. of Sabaoth 388:15
lost in G., in Godhead found 199:31
lost my leg, by G.! By G., and
    have you! 564:8
lovesome thing, G. wot! 85:12
make..the will of G. prevail 19:25
man in the bush with G...meet 199:16
man is G.'s image 244:4
man sent from G. 62:61
man's word is G. in man 529:40
man with G...in the majority 305:5
many are afraid of G. 315:11
melancholy g. protect thee 483:7
men that G. made mad 140:15

God (cont.)

mills of G. 15:22, 317:13
Mithras, G. of the Morning 301:29
more just than G. 48:49
most resembles G. 108:35
Mother of G.! no lady 148:16
much ado...G. wot 80:7
music sent up to G. 89:10
my duty towards G. 391:5
my G. and King 243:24
my G., how wonderful 202:21
my G., I love thee 132:7
my G., look not so fierce 330:11
my G., my G., look upon me 393:1
my G., my verse is not 245:2
my G., why..forsaken me? 60:52
my King and my G. 397:5
myself a g. 78:2
mysteries of G. 66:24
Name of the G. of Jacob 392:35
names G. in oaths 184:14
nature is the art of G. 86:12
nature of G. is a circle 10:17
nearer G.'s Heart in a garden 233:17
neck G. made for other use 262:12
ne'er said, 'G. be praised' 88:3
negation of G. erected into a
    system 223:1
neglect G. and his Angels 186:32
neither our love from G. 410:25
neither should a g. intervene 256:5
new treasures..G. will provide 291:5
noblest work of G. 105:5, 384:9
no G. could please 190:10
no—G. knows what 119:32
'no G.,' the wicked saith 146:31
no king but G. alone 411:36
no man hath seen G. 63:1, 70:13
none other but the house of G. 45:5
none that can read G. aright 404:14
nor asks of G., but of her stars 384:31
not afraid of G., afraid of me 386:23
not G.! in gardens! 85:13
not G.'s and not the beasts' 91:1
not the G. of Nature 244:27
not three Gods: but one G. 388:40
now thank we all our G. 571:21
obey G. rather than men 64:31
of all the thoughts of G. 88:25
of G. above or man below 383:8
of such is the kingdom of G. 61:6
O G. of battles 444:24
O G. of Bethel 183:20
O, G. of Mercy, when? 198:22
O G.! oh Montreal! 112:17
O G., our help 562:9
O Lamb of G., I come 198:20
O—my—G.—keep—me 295:1
one G. created us 56:14
one G., one law 533:31
one G. only 146:34
one more insult to G. 93:6
one, on G.'s side 378:19
one that would circumvent G. 437:11
only..G. and angels..lookers on 24:22
only G. can make a tree 292:13
O that great Sabbaoth G. 510:11
others call it G. 131:30
our G., our help 562:9
out of me G. and man 524:1
owe G. a death 442:12
owest G. a death 440:29
paltered with Eternal G. 537:23
patent for his honours..from..
    G. 105:16
patted my G. on the head 302:29
peace of G. 68:26, 267:32, 390:48
praise G. from whom all bless-
    ings 292:3
'Praise G.!' sang Theocrite 90:3
praising G. with sweetest looks 253:20
presents the g. unshorn 245:24
press G.'s lamp close 94:26
presume not G. to scan 383:22
pretence that G. had put it there 305:20
pride of the peacock is the glory
    of G. 77:16
put G. in his statements 566:21
put your trust in G., my boys 73:2
rack the name of G. 329:25
ranks the same with G. 94:46

God (cont.)

reader of the works of G. 163:13
rebellion..obedience to G. 79:14
rejoice and delight in G. 548:13
rejoice in the living G. 397:5
resound G.'s goodness 266:13
rest for the people of G. 93:41
sacrifice of G. 395:10
sacrifice to G. of the devil's
    leavings 387:1, 520:48
sail with G. the seas 200:18
saw its G., and blushed 165:25
say, 'G. be pitiful' 88:3
seas of G. 567:3
security of a G. 25:17
see G. made and eaten 89:44
seek ye first the kingdom of G. 58:14
seen G. face to face 45:11
sees G. in clouds 383:11
separate us from the love of G. 65:58
serve G. and mammon 58:10
service greater than the g. 481:12
she for G. in him 347:11
should not think of G. 443:20
sign'd by G.'s name 567:24
since G. is light 346:18
some lesser g...made the world 531:27
so near is G. to man 199:32
Son of G. goes forth 240:20
spirit shall return unto G. 51:33
stamps G.'s own name 162:23
standeth G. within the shadow 320:11
steep and trifid G. 543:15
stop, child of G. 151:16
such a lady G.'s mother 7:17
take the Name of..G. in vain 390:8
taking of the Manhood into G. 388:42
Tamburlaine, the Scourge of G. 331:8
teach me, my G. and King 244:15
thank'd my G. for worldly things 74:29
thank G. of all! 136:20
that G. we both adore 380:26
that I should keep G.'s holy will 391:2
that thou art happy, owe to G. 348:11
their 'Eternal' and 'G.' 20:14
the Lord G. almighty 409:21
the Lord G. made them all 3:14
the Lord G. of your fathers, the
    G. of Abraham, the G. of
    Isaac, and the G. of Jacob 45:38
the Lord..is G. indeed 292:7
the Lord our G. Most High 301:25
The mighty G. 53:15
then show likest G.'s 464:33
there is no G. 392:21
there we see the works of G. 377:9
they heard the voice of..G. 44:21
they hope they serve G. 469:7
they said, G. forbid 62:41
they shall see G. 57:39
they shall see our G. 291:13
they that deny a G. 25:26
think not G. at all 350:27
this G. is our G. for ever 394:35
this thing is G. 524:3
thou art G. from everlasting 397:15
thou being dead art a G. 525:13
though G. hath raised me high 198:12
Thou, my G., art in't 247:22
three person'd G. 185:18
through darkness up to G. 532:36
through his garden walketh G. 96:33
through nature up to nature's G. 384:14
throws himself on G. 91:41
thy country's, thy G.'s, and
    truth's 446:31
thy G. my G. 47:1
thy G., thy life, thy cure 552:2
thy soul and G. stand sure 95:22
to glorify G. and to enjoy him 501:9
to G. I speak Spanish 136:13
to see G. only 185:23
to the Altar's G. 166:13
to the City of G. 17:21
to the greater glory of G. 13:3
to the judgement-seat of G. 23:24
To The Unknown G. 64:60
true G.'s priest 124:26
trust G.: see all 95:13
trust in G., and do the Right 327:3
unchanging law of G. 373:10

INDEX

God (cont.)

unless G. send his hail   94:13
very G. of very G.   390:19
vindicate the ways of G.   383:8
voice of the people is the voice of G.   3:10, 406:16
walked in the house of G.   395:12
we are the children of G.   65:54
well, G.'s above all   471:13
were I Lord G.   326:19
what G. abandoned   264:4
what G. declares pure   347:25
what G. hath cleansed   64:47
what G. hath joined..G. will take care of that   489:26
what...G. hath joined   59:56
what I call G.   96:12
when G. by man..trod   524:7
when g. first maked man   137:40
when..G. lets loose a thinker   200:7
when G.'s will be done   503:6
when G.'s the theme   77:7
when he wrote of Angels and G.   77:7
when I reflect that G. is just   268:27
when you've sung 'G. save the Queen'   294:17
wheresoe'er in G.'s great universe   187:1
wherever G. erects a house   170:11
whom G. hath joined..put asunder   391:34
whom G. to ruin has designed   192:33
whose G. is their belly   68:24
with G. all things are possible   60:4
with G. be the rest   95:12
wonderful works of G.   64:26
word was with G...was G.   62:58
worketh not the righteousness of G.   69:30
world, as G. has made it   92:2
wrestling with (my G.!) my G.   254:20
write G. first   469:7
ye believe in G.   63:50
yet G.'s will be done   584:18
ye that forget G.   395:6
your false g...but a dim remomoring   551:13
yours faithfully, G.   5:27
zeal of G.   65:61
God-curst sun   236:19
Goddess: g., allow this aged man   377:14
g. and maiden and queen   525:4
g., excellently bright   279:31
unto that G.' grace   509:9
Goddesses: set it..beside one of those...g.   374:10
Godfathers: earthly g. of Heaven's lights   454:32
my G. and Godmothers   391:2
Godfrey: in the gate   141:7
last was G. of Bouillon   327:15
God-gifted organ-voice   529:17
Godhead: conversion of the G. into flesh   388:42
lost in God, in G. found   199:31
of whatso'er descent their G. be   190:12
God-intoxicated man   365:24
God-light: singing in the great G.   88:14
Godlike: for g. kings of old   323:11
God by man as g.   524:7
G. David was restored   190:31
g. erect   347:10
g. hero sate   190:34
g. in giving   357:21
g. reason to rust in us unus'd   436:15
patient endurance is g.   316:15
seeds of g. power   15:9
thy G. crime   118:30
Godliness: in cheerful g.   577:15
Godly: every one that is g.   393:32
g. race he ran   225:18
g., righteous, and sober   388:12
nobody gets old and g.   585:14
proud and g. kings   208:5
Godolphin Horne was nobly born   40:35
Gods: angels would be g.   383:13
as flies..are we to the g.   453:40
be ready, g.   451:21
by the nine g. he swore   323:10
clearest g.   454:5
contrived to talk about the G.   116:35

Gods (cont.)

counsel of her country's g.   158:29
dare the G.   330:23
dish fit for the g.   449:10
dish for the g.   426:8
fault of angels and of g.   381:33
fear first in the world made g.   281:8
fit love for G.   349:12
give, you g., give to your boy   191:17
g. approve the depth   577:12
g. are come down   64:51
g. are just   454:21
g. are we   15:9
g...cannot recall their gifts   540:22
g. detest my baseness   425:23
G. see everywhere   315:28
g. that made the g.   140:11
G., that mortal beauty chase   332:16
G., that wanton in the air   319:4
g. themselves throw incense   454:20
g. today stand friendly   451:35
G. who live for ever   324:14
great g...find out their enemies   453:9
in the names of all the g.   448:23
kings it makes g.   476:33
large utterance of the early G.   286:6
leave the issue to the G.   157:7
limbs of gibbeted G.   525:10
men that strove with g.   541:3
neither children nor G.   296:2
none other g. but me   390:5
not three G.   388:40
on the hills like G.   535:19
post allotted by the G.   535:25
purpos'd by the mighty g.   449:21
real are the dreams of G.   286:38
Red G. call us out   296:12
rejecting the g. of Athens   379:24
so many g.   568:27
stooped the tempest of the G.   331:2
take the good the g. provide   191:9
temples of his G.   323:17
these are thy g., O London   307:2
these that were G. are dead   525:13
thinking of his own G.   16:6
this darling of the G.   333:5
to my own G. I go   300:19
to stature of the g.   336:1
true g. sigh   88:12
unseen before by G.   286:10
voice of all the g.   455:22
weigh your G. and you   303:25
whatever g. may be   241:18, 523:23
what men or g. are these?   287:7
when half-gods go the g. arrive   199:14
whom the g. love   116:10
wise g. seel our eyes   425:2
with g. doth diet   341:10
with stupidity the g...struggle   415:23
woman is a dish for the g.   426:8
wondrous the g.   74:8
ye are G. and..shall die   525:12
ye shall be as g.   44:20
you might have seen the g. there   413:1
you see me here, you g.   452:42
God's-acre: the burial-ground G.   316:26
Godward: looking G.   524:2
Goes: he bows and g. again   516:1
her colour..g. off at night   500:33
mostly they g. up and down   135:1
onward it gleaming g.   311:16
regard not how it g.   106:25
sea where it g.   15:6
ship that g.   173:8
Sunday that g. on and on   208:10
Time g., you say?   183:15
wren g. to't   454:8
Goest: grave, whither thou g.   51:21
whithersoever thou g.   46:37
whither thou g. I will go   47:1
Goeth: g. on still in his wickedness   396:10
g. to his long home   51:33
it g. forth from..heaven   392:32
man g. forth to his work   398:10
wine..that g. down sweetly   52:20
Goethe: G.'s sage mind   16:23
G.'s wide and luminous view   17:5
open thy G.   127:19
Going: all things g. as they came   411:30
endure their g. hence   454:18
g. down that long long trail   293:1

Going (cont.)

g. on before   35:1
g. one knows not where   334:14
g. out with the tide   174:39
g. to and fro in the earth   48:38
g. to run all night   210:13
he shall direct his g.   397:10
not worth g. to see   274:15
Oh where are you g.?   409:16
perceive how the world is really g.   19:27
preserve thy g. out   399:29
safe shall be my g.   84:19
softly she was g. up   149:23
their g. from us..utter destruction   56:23
to keep us g.   335:10
upon the order of your g.   459:23
wages of g. on   541:17
worth while g. through so much   178:42
Goings: ordered my g.   394:12
Gold: apples of g.   50:34, 524:19
as its purest g.   382:13
as misers do in g.   548:13
barbaric pearl and g.   345:14
better to me than g.   571:9
beyond all their panaceas, potable g.   109:22
born of beaten g.   190:12
brow-bound with..g.   529:9
builded over with pillars of g.   75:4
building roofs of g.   443:10
but litel g. in cofre   137:6
cheaply..for thrice their weight in g.   203:39
city was pure g.   71:47
dearer..than thousands of g.   399:17
fetch the age of g.   343:18
flowers..streaked with g.   497:22
flow with tears of g.   77:2
fly to India for g.   329:23
for a' the g. in Christentie   31:7
for cloth of g. you cease to care   218:29
from the red g. keep thy finger   419:16
gild refined g.   115:42, 447:39
gleaming in purple and g.   118:37
g. air and the silver fade   411:4
g. and bramble-dew   516:6
g., and frankincense   57:24
g.? a transient..trouble   228:18
g...at the root of wisdom   111:39
g. is for the mistress   295:14
g. that I never see   263:13
g. to airy thinness beat   186:25
hair and harpstring of g.   525:5
her clothing is of wrought g.   394:25
her feathers like g.   396:7
her locks were yellow as g.   149:13
her stomacher was g.   298:29
his fetters, though of g.   27:44
his g. complexion dimm'd   486:18
his hands are as g. rings   52:14
I do not sell for g.   131:24
I fling them back their g.   365:20
in their g. coats spots   466:34
is she not pure g.?   96:28
jewel of g. in a swine's snout   49:58
learning a mere hoard of g.   442:21
lilac, g. and green   80:14
Love..differs from g. and clay   493:11
love is mor than g.   321:12
made of silver, or of g.   218:29
male ringlets or feminine g.   523:4
man's the g.   105:30
mast was o' the beaten g.   31:8
more than g. was in a ring   140:26
more to be desired..than g.   392:33
my bow of burning g.   75:16
my heart in a case o' g.   32:19
my heart of g.   6:18
narrowing lust of g.   533:20
never lack'd g.   470:29
no g., no Holy Ghost   111:39
nor all that glisters, g.   230:22
nor winks the g. fin   539:2
not covetous for g.   444:27
not g., not blood   493:27
O delvèd g.   88:26
of two g. ingots   330:13
ornaments of g.   47:30
oure g. wes changyd into lede   583:26
patines of bright g.j   465:18

INDEX

Gold (*cont.*)

poop was beaten g.   424:6
queen in a vesture of g.   394:23
rare g. ring of verse   96:19
rarer gifts than g.   83:19
red g. is on the pine-stems   337:35
ring..is yet of g.   165:21
rottenness of eighty years in g.   119:18
saint-seducing g.   476:48
scarfs, garters, g.   383:30
set upon sockets of fine g.   52:14
silver and g. have I none   64:27
silver threads among the g.   406:8
straight was a path of g.   94:27
streets are paved with g.   154:9
street..was pure g.   72:3
sumpshous spot all done up in g.   20:31
there is g. and here my bluest veins   424:13
thy master hath his g.   365:17
travell'd in the realms of g.   288:19
trodden g.   345:9
truth with g. she weighs   381:11
upon a cross of g.   98:2
wedges of g.   476:14
what female..g. despise?   230:20
what's become of all the g.?   97:9
when g. and silver becks me   447:31
wisdom cannot be gotten for g.   111:39
with g. and jewels cover   382:26
worth ransom of g.   549:30
would he have g.?   245:12
writing in a book of g.   265:16
Gold-dusted snapdragon   18:26
Golden: add to g. numbers   170:21
become the g. fool   74:7
both g...and both cracked   204:22
burnished with g. rind   347:5
debtless competence, g. mean   541:5
fretted with g. fire   433:19
from the g. woods   538:21
g. and silver light   584:17
g. bowl be broken   51:33
g. bridge   115:10
g.-calf of self-love   125:25
g. care   442:25
G. Dustman   178:22
G. Girl   313:6
g. hours on angel wings   106:9
g. lads and girls   430:1
g. lamps in a green night   332:2
g. lie the meadows   337:35
g. mind stoops not   463:39
g. opes, the iron shuts   342:26
g. opinions from all sorts   457:10
G. Road to Samarkand   208:14
g. rule..no g. rules   490:28
g. sands and crystal brooks   184:8
g. sea of Wales   208:6
g. slumbers kiss your eyes   170:23
G. Vanity   30:23
g. works of the .. angel   307:24
g. years return   493:25
happy the g. mean   334:20
hast thou g. slumbers?   170:21
husbanded the G. grain   205:28
Jerusalem the g.   362:1
Love in a g. bowl   74:2
Mahmud on his g. Throne   205:22
no latch ter de g. gate   238:24
observ'd the g. rule   74:7
shrewd steel against our g. crown   475:1
Silence is g.   127:22
Stormcock, and G. Gain   299:25
that Homer's g. chain   109:24
treen chalices and g. priests   269:22
truth is the g. girdle   159:4
wear a g. sorrow   446:16
West to the G. Gate   298:28
with a g. axe   478:23
Golden: Schweigen ist g.   127:22
Goldenest: seven of my g. years   306:15
Goldsmith: G.'s fine feast   213:9
G...whatever he wrote   273:33
here lies Nolly G.   213:12
Olivarii G., Poetae   273:19
Goldsmiths: her rich g.   307:2
Golf: to play g. ye maun hae a heid   326:16
what, gie up g.?   403:40

Golgotha: memorize another G.   456:6
Goltman, silent on his horse   42:11
Gondola: g. of London   182:16
scarce..swam in a g.   428:17
what else is like the g.?   146:29
Gone: all, all are g.   308:1
ay, Caesar; but not g.   449:28
been and g. and done   218:5
both are g.   16:6
days that have g. by   208:4
from these I would be g.   487:14
gathered, and g. by together   394:33
g. from us for ever   318:2
g. into the world of light   552:8
g. over to the majority   125:34
g. the way of all flesh   155:39
g. to her death   252:12
g. to-morrow   40:6
g. to the demnition bow-wows   177:26
g. up with a merry noise   394:31
g. whar de good niggers go   210:19
g. with the wind   187:10
he is g., he is g.   436:36
I have g. here and there   488:5
Iram indeed is g.   205:9, 10
I would have thee g.   477:28
like Snow upon the Desert..is g.   205:27
lo, he was g.   394:6
lost and g. for ever   355:22
make what haste I can to be g.   167:14
not dead—but g. before   408:7
not lost but g. before   242:19, 365:23
now thou art g.   342:13
odds is g.   425:29
passeth it away and we are g.   397:16
place where 'e is g.   297:4
she is won! we are g.   418:22
she's g., like Alexander   104:25
soon as she was g. from me   75:22
speke of thee..whan thou art g.   138:30
that have come, that have g.   405:10
that when I am g.   319:8
their sound is g. out   392:32
they are g.: aye, ages long ago   285:28
they are g. forever   329:9
thou art g., and for ever   416:23
thou art g. up   396:9
virtue had g. out of him   61:1
welcomest when they are g.   445:19
what's g...past grief   485:12
when house and land are g.   209:19
when I am g. away   409:24
wilt thou be g.?   478:26
with those Lords..g. so far   358:2
yet now he is g.   309:1
Gongs: strong g. groaning   141:5
Good: ale, that is g. ale   78:28
all g. and no badness   502:18
all g. gifts around us   121:27
all g. things are ours   95:17
all g. to me is lost   346:33
all his hopes of g.   19:2
all meaning, whether g. or bad   190:32
all men's g...each man's rule   529:30
all my g. is but vain hope   547:20
all things beautiful and g.   496:26
all things work together for g.   65:56
all times when old are g.   112:26
all we have..hoped or dreamed of g.   89:9
and a g. job too   222:23
and a g. Judge too   222:22
and the g. to do   3:18
answered him as I thought g.   367:20
antipathy of g. to bad   386:22
anybody can be g. in the country   570:10
any g...came of telling truth   191:26
any g. of George the Third   309:11
any g. thing..out of Nazareth   63:3
any g. thing..that I can do   232:10
anything for the g. of one's country   203:12
apprehension of the g.   474:20
are you g. men and true?   468:33
as full of g. will   502:17
as g. people's wery scarce   174:7
as long as we are g.   560:22
at any g. man's feast   427:19
be g., sweet maid   293:7
beneath the g. how far   231:16

Good (*cont.*)

better .. beautiful than .. g. . .
better .. g. than .. ugly   570:9
better to fight for the g.   536:25
bite so g. a man   225:22
bored with g. wine   182:24
by all that's g. and glorious   118:35
call a man á g. man upon easier terms   275:15
cannot be ill..be g.   456:24
captive g.   487:14
choose the g.   53:12
common g. to all   452:9
common love of g.   533:20
deny us for our g.   424:3
do after the g.   328:2
do all the g. you can   565:19
do any man's heart g.   466:29
do evil that g. may come   65:37
do g. by stealth   386:20
don't look too g.   297:10
drawn it for a g. one   194:14
dull prospect of a distant g.   192:29
enemy of the g.   557:5
English..if they have a g. thing   441:24
E please. Double g.l   175:39
eschew evil, and do g.   394:2
everything..g. for something   193:29
Evil be thou my G.   346:33
fair and learn'd, and g. as she   87:24
few know their own g.   194:23
fire my g. one out   488:19
first be wise and g.   351:19
for g. the supplicating voice   279:12
for the g. and increase   529:13
for the g. of my country..abroad   203:12
for the g. or evil side   320:9
for the g. we do   374:22
foundation of all g. things   102:29
fruit of g. works   389:50
full of g. works   64:44
General G...plea of the scoundrel   75:7
giver of all g. things   389:43
glad of other men's g.   427:27
glory and g. of Art   96:19
God's a g. man   469:3
God saw that it was g.   44:4
going to be a very g. girl   208:24
g. Americans..go to Paris   14:1, 570:13
g. and bad together   424:14
g. are always merry   585:1
g. are so harsh to the clever   572:29
g. as another until he has written   282:13
g. as guardian angels   158:13
g. as thou art beautiful   530:23
g. at need   417:10
g., but not religious-g.   237:16
g. deed in a naughty world   465:21
g. die early   170:2
g. die first   574:14
g. ended happily   569:25
g. enough for me   243:2
g. enough to be a clergyman   272:11
g. enough to shed his blood   409:2
g. families..worse than any others   254:12
g. fences make g. neighbours   212:3
g. for sore eyes   520:10
g. for us to be here   59:16
g. God pardon all g. men   87:32
G. Gray Poet   370:3
g. he scorn'd stalk'd off   73:13
g. hunting!   304:8
g. in everything   426:30
g...in mutual..bliss   340:37
g. is oft interred   450:17
g. life be now my task   192:23
g. man, and a just   62:52
g. man, and did g. things   237:18
g. man is merciful   398:26
g. man's love   428:12
g. man's sin   122:39
g. man teach his son   444:28
g. men..not obey the laws too well   200:34
g. men starve   193:21
g. must associate   101:36
g...must live after them   414:9
g. nature and humility   223:9
g. news baits   351:1

INDEX

Good (cont.)

g. of subjects   170:17
g. people all   225:17
g. pleasure, ease, content   384:2
g. provoke to harm   462:17
g. reader..makes the g. book   201:18
g. receiv'd   154:40
'G.!' said the Baron   295:14
g. shall come of water   83:24
g. that I can do   33:8
g. that I would I do not   65:49
g. that ye did   302:21
g., the more communicated   348:2
g. things of day   459:8
g. things..strive to dwell with't   479:33
g. time coming   326:23
g. to be merry and wise   7:22, 106:6
g., to forgive   96:20
g. to the poor   125:4
g. want power   496:24
g. will to man   421:10
g. will toward men   61:19
g. without effort   114:24
g. without pretence   382:12
g. words..were best   447:44
g. ye are and bad   530:21
greatest g. that mortals know   1:26
great, just, g. God   96:6
hand..hath made you g.   462:12
hanging is too g. for him   99:16
happiness makes them g.   309:17
heaviness foreruns the g. event   442:17
he was wery g. to me   173:28
he who would do g.   75:7
his chief g. and market   436:15
his g. and his evil   107:36
hold fast that which is g.   68:38
hold thou the g.   532:30
holy, divine, g., amiable   349:17
how g. and joyful a thing   400:3
how g. he is   319:7
how g. is man's life   96:21
how near to g. is what is fair   281:1
I am a g. man too   217:28
if g., why do I yield?   456:24
if one g. deed..I did   480:36
ill wind turns none to g.   542:24
in a g. old age   44:48, 48:34
it cannot come to g.   431:1
I will be g.   552:19
I will seek to do thee g.   399:31
Jimmy was g. and true   217:28
John was a very g. man   217:28
kind of g. deed to say well   446:21
kings seek their subjects' g.   246:9
knowing g. and evil   44:20
knowledge of g. and evil   44:13
knowledge of g. and evil as two twins   352:8
know what were g. to do   463:7
leave his country as g.   147:19
left our country for our country's g.   36:20
leisure to be g.   230:17
licence to be g.   148:11
likes that little g.   112:10
love of g. and ill   285:9
loves what he is g. at   422:32
luxury..doing g.   165:12, 213:20, 226:5
means intensely, and means g.   91:33
means of g. to all   412:14
meek lover of the g.   199:6
mild, obedient, g. as He   4:2
much too g. for earth   280:10
my religion is to do g.   373:4
National Debt is a..G. Thing   422:15
neither g. for man nor beast   11:21
never done no g. to me   296:22
never g. to bring bad news   424:15
never..impulsive to g.   329:8
night is g.   493:22
noblest motive is the public g.   511:20
no g. but yours   82:1
none but..g. men..give g. things   340:34
none..love freedom..but g. men   353:2
none that doeth g.   392:22
nor g. compensate bad   96:14
not a terror to g. works   66:10

Good (cont.)

not g. that the man should be alone   44:14
nothing..but means our g.   244:23
nothing either g. or bad   433:11
nothing g...in the country   239:25
nothing is fair or g. alone   199:9
nothing left..but to be g.   514:31
nothing so g. for a Pobble's toes   312:6
not local prejudices..but the general g.   100:14
obscurely g.   1:21
of moral evil and of g.   581:16
O g. old man!   426:38
only noble to be g.   533:38
only truly great who are truly g.   135:23
other fell into g. ground   59:23
our acts..or g. or ill   37:23
our doubts..make us lose the g.   461:21
out of g...find..evil   344:17
overcome evil with g.   66:7
Parent of G.   348:4
partial evil, universal g.   383:21
pelting each other for the public g.   159:8
policy of the g. neighbour   408:21
quiet, wise, and g.   498:15
rhyme thee to g.   243:25
rich in g. works   68:54
rise on the evil and on the g.   57:52
Roman Conquest..a G. Thing   422:13
seek to be g.   322:4
seemed g...to write to thee   61:10
seven g. ears   45:18
shouldn't say it is not g.   566:9
so g. or so bad as their opinions   326:26
so it seemed g. in thy sight   61:37
somehow g...final goal of ill   532:31
something g. and bad of every land   29:10
so much g. in the worst of us   249:4
sovereign g. of human nature   27:32
such g. things as pass..understanding   389:42
take the g. the gods provide   191:9
that thou art g.   386:29
that which is not g.   340:34
their g. receives   575:6
the Lord our God is g.   292:9
them that call evil g.   53:6
there dwelt all that's g.   558:1
there never was a g. war   211:8
there's a g. time coming   420:18
these late eclipses..portend no g.   452:15
these scraps are g. deeds past   481:17
they bid for g. and all   80:7
they love the G.   84:14
they say he made a g. end   436:33
those that were g. shall be happy   303:20
those who go about doing g.   166:25
to be g., great and joyous   497:17
to be g. is to be happy   412:6
to do g...forget not   69:25
to do ought g.   344:16
to make bad g.   462:17
too g. to be worth publishing   490:42
to see you so g.   584:10
toward solid g. what leads   351:23
very g. girl was Emily Jane   217:28
victuals and the wine rather g.   121:9
want no manner of thing that is g.   393:38
we must return g. for evil   551:8
what a g. boy am I   367:16
what g. came of it?   507:9
what is g. for them   167:6
what's the g. of a home?   233:4
what's the g. of Hanyfink?   142:21
what were g. to be done   463:8
when I would do g.   65:50
when she was g.   318:17
when the great and g. depart   575:1
whether a man is G. or Evil   75:13
which you was so g. as to write   208:28
whoso hath this world's g.   70:11
who will shew us any g.?   392:1
wise and g. and gay   368:1
wiser being g. than bad   89:22
woe is me for the g. house   324:5
won'erful g. for the Prophet   297:7
won my right g. will   327:5

Good (cont.)

worst speaks something g.   244:7
you will hear more g. things   239:19
zealous for his country's g.   215:18
Good-bye: and so—g.   335:10
g. is not worth while   236:36
g., moralitee   243:2
g. Piccadilly   571:1
g., proud world   199:15
g., Summer, g., g.   568:23
g. to all that   229:17
g. to the bar   294:2
g. to your lover   299:22
nod g. to Rochefoucauld   197:3
without..a g.   375:14
Good-day: and so g.   335:10
Goodliest: g. man of men   347:13
thou wert the g. person   328:24
Goodliness: all the g. thereof   54:10
Goodly: g. grain..the g. men   545:9
g. outside falsehood hath   463:19
g. to look to   47:19
thou art g., O Love   522:8
Goodman: g. is not at home   49:50
when our g.'s awa'   10:22
Good-morning: bid me G.   33:14
g., gentlemen both   198:1
G.!..Pears' Soap?   6:15
g. Sir to you   246:22
my brother, g.   41:20
Good-morrow: and so, g.   335:10
at my window bid g.   341:31
give my Love g.   248:5
g. to our waking souls   185:7
g. to the day so fair   246:22
to sorrow I bade g.   285:4
Good-natured: one damned g. friend or other   499:25
Goodness: crownest the year with thy g.   395:30
days in g. spent   119:2
filleth the hungry soul with g.   398:15
fountain of all g.   388:29
gentleness, g., faith   67:46
g. and the grace   527:5
g. never fearful   462:13
g...not make men happy   309:17
g. only knowses   142:6
how awful g. is   347:31
if g. lead him not   245:1
I held so much g.   508:5
inclination to g.   26:20
love, sweetness, g.   351:25
more g. in her little finger   520:20
of great g.   400:18
powerful g. want   496:24
praise the Lord for his g.   398:15
resound God's g.   266:13
see the g. of the Lord   393:22
some soul of g. in things evil   444:12
whose g. faileth never   29:12
wisdom and g. to the vile   454:1
Good-night: and so g.   335:10
bid the world G.   246:6
Dear work! G.! G.!   262:8
g.! ah! no   493:21
g., and joy be wi' you   360:16
g., sweet ladies: g.   436:24
g., sweet prince   438:7
g. to Marmion   418:30
his happy g. air   235:18
if he fall in, g.   438:37
my last g.   292:19
my native land—G.   113:7
my sister, g.   41:20
part in friendship—and bid g.   119:8
say g. till it be morrow   478:1
say not G.   33:14
smiled and said 'G.'   41:24
stern'st g.   458:3
sweet, g.!   477:24
they never say g.   493:22
to each, a fair g.   418:36
Goods: all his worldly g.   311:12
all my worldly g.   391:32
as ever coveted his neighbour's g.   294:6
g. and services..paid for only with g. and services   365:3
g. in life's rich hand   561:14
his g. are in peace   61:46

INDEX

Goods (*cont.*)

much g. laid up for many years   61:52
so precious as the G. they sell   207:22
their *Life* and their G...most their own   135:28
Good-sense: for solid, reasoning, g.   139:22
Goodwins: the G...they call the place   464:6
Goose: every g. a swan, lad   293:19
gabble o' the g.   121:4
royal game of g.   225:4
steals a g.   10:12
their g. cooked by tobacco-juice   121:22
when every g. is cackling   465:22
where gott'st thou that g. look?   460:35
Gooseberries which makes my teeth watter   208:24
Gooseberry-pie: make the g.   227:21
Goose-feather: in which a great g. grew   250:1
Goose-pen: though thou write with a g.   484:1
Goosey: g. g. gander   366:23
Gordian: she was a g. shape   286:37
some old G. knot   147:9
Gore: avenge the patriotic g.   405:19
glorious the martyr's g   503:6
hope it mayn't be human g.   173:18
Gored: g. mine own thoughts   488:5
tossed and g. several persons   271:26
Gorge: my g. rises at it   437:15
Gorgeous: g. East   345:14, 582:5
g. Tragedy   341:18
thrice-g. ceremony   444:23
Gorging Jack   543:7
Gorgonised me   536:5
Gorgons and Hydras   346:3
Gorgonzola: let loose the G. trotting out the G.   403:34 304:43
Gormandising: leave g.   442:38
Gormed: I'm G.   175:4
Gorse: 'mid the g. the raspberry   543:23
Gory: welcome to your g. bed   107:32
Goschen: I forgot G.   143:33
Gosling: such a g. to obey instinct   429:17
Gospel: golden G. of Silence   358:18
g. according to Jean Jacques   126:17
G. of Getting On   490:40
g. of Montreal..the g. of Hellas   112:18
G.'s pearls   332:3
g. to every creature   61:9
lineaments of G. books   412:18
music of the G.   202:24
shod with..the g. of peace   68:12
whose g. is their maw   351:30
Gospel-bearing: His g. feet   313:5
Gospel-light first dawn'd   229:19
Goss-hawk: my gay g.   30:20
Gossip: babbling g. of the air   482:22
little g., blithe and hale   378:16
pines are g. pines   208:3
Gossips count her faults   336:15
Got: assuming that he's g. any   219:5
boots of 'im that's g. it   297:1
g. it not   410:6
how the devil they g. there up he g.   385:27 159:37
Gotham: three wise men of G.   369:9
Gothic: more than G. ignorance   204:27
sunset..through a G. skylight   119:25
Gott: ein feste Burg ist unser G.   321:6
Gott-betrunkener Mensch   365:24
Gotten: wha..hae we g. for a King   250:12
Götter: wha mit der Dummheit kämpfen G.   415:23
Götterfunken: Freude, schöner G.   415:21
Gottesmühlen mahlen langsam   315:22
Gottingen: University of G.   124:17
Gout: combined with g.   218:20
g. and glory   91:11
that old enemy the g.   253:5
without g. or stone   387:2
Goût: entre le bon sens et le bon g.   97:34
Gouvernement: le g. qu'elle mérite   327:13
Govern: all did g.   189:3
easy to g.   85:3
go out and g. New South Wales   41:8
g. two millions..on the principles of freedom   101:4
he that would g. others   334:18
may I g. my passion   387:2

Govern (*cont.*)

Right Divine..to g. wrong   381:24
still g. thou my song   348:23
such should g.   38:3
Governance: by pryncely g.   195:7
no charge of rule, nor g.   518:1
Governed: g. by no other sway   355:18
g. by shopkeepers   503:11
not so well g. as they ought to be   253:35
not g.   100:26
with how little wisdom the world is g.   372:15
Governess of floods   466:37
Governing: right of g...a trust   210:21
Government: consequence of cabinet g.   28:23
Conservative G. .. organized hypocrisy   180:18
fatal drollery..representative g.   182:33
for forms of g. let fools contest   384:1
four pillars of g.   27:8
Freedom..in having the G. of those Laws   135:28
giving money to the G.   243:6
g. and co-operation   413:27
g...a necessary evil   373:1
G. at Washington lives   213:7
g. is a contrivance of human wisdom   102:10
G. must have an authority   413:23
g. of..by..for all the people   373:16
g. of..morning newspapers   378:21
g. of the people   314:29
g. shall be upon his shoulder   53:15
g. without a king   33:5
great g. of the United States helpless   571:13
how can the G. be carried on?   564:20
intelligible g.   28:26
land of settled g.   541:24
loathe the present G.   246:17
looked to g. for bread   102:36
negation..a system of G.   223:1
no G...secure without..opposition   181:30
not for having share in G.   135:28
of the increase of his g.   53:15
one..g. rather than another   272:8
paper g.   100:19
Queen's g. must be carried on   564:20
reproach to religion and g.   377:7
safe under every form of g.   272:10
sound Conservative g.   181:33
their attachment to their g.   101:13
there has been no G.   174:4
this g. cannot endure   314:6
this g...Presbyterial or Prelatical   352:18
what a free g. is   103:21
without party Parliamentary g...impossible   181:21
your sister is given to g.   175:21
Governments: climates, councils, g.   540:32
g. associated against Germany   571:15
Governor: no G. Aris   119:32
the G. was strong   569:7
t'other g.   178:20
Governors: g., teachers   391:7
our supreme g., the mob   558:10
Gowans: pu'd the g. fine   104:13
Gower: O moral G.   138:43
Gown: and a green g.   366:17
as she did her wedding g.   227:16
blood upon her g.   208:5
for an almsman's g.   475:10
for wearing a black g.   139:8
in amply billowing g.   41:32
in the graver g.   382:14
my branched velvet g.   483:15
my g. of glory   405:9
pluck'd his g.   224:23
preaches in her g.   253:29
Whig in a parson's g.   276:6
Gowns: one that hath two g.   469:11
Gracchos: quis tulerat G...querentis?   282:29
Grace: abundance of thy g.   400:33
all g. is the g. of God   375:1
also may have g. and power   389:28
ascribe it to Thy g.   561:20

Grace (*cont.*)

Being and ideal G.   88:24
bride to every G.   125:5
but for the g. of God   79:12
by g. divine..we are thine   574:4
by the g. of God I am what I am   67:5
children by adoption and g.   389:26
defend..with thy heavenly g.   391:20
does it with a better g.   482:30
double g.   431:24
every virtue, every g.   308:14
extent and stretch of g.   190:10
flush'd with a purple g.   191:3
for gift or g., surpassing   88:25
for g. to love thee more   161:13
for the means of g.   389:20
full of g. and truth   62:64
God..lend her g.   534:10
God's g. is the only g.   375:1
g. as lang's my arm   100:43
g. before Milton   306:8
g. be unto you, and peace   70:21
g. did much more abound   65:42
g. is given of God   146:24
g. me no g.   474:30
G. of God is in Courtesy   41:16
g. of God..with me   67:6
g. this latter age   440:28
g. was in all her steps   348:36
g. which followed it   512:30
grow old with a good g.   511:21
healthful Spirit of thy g.   388:30
Heaven's Mother send us g.!   149:12
help us all by Thy g.   305:8
her gracious, graceful, graceless G.   117:4
her spirit's vestal g.   375:4
if I have g. to use it so   351:13
if possible with g.   386:9
in her strong toil of g.   426:16
inward and spiritual g.   391:13
learned Thy G. and Glory under Malta   298:13
less thy body..more thy g.   442:38
liken his G. to a..hog   92:8
little children saying g.   515:15
little shall I g. my cause   469:45
living g.   382:26
look to thee for g.   548:12
makes simplicity a g.   280:7
manifold gifts of g.   391:19
meek and unaffected g.   224:22
men hunger for thy g.   269:31
mind his g.   412:19
ministers of g. defend us   431:32
moments of glad g.   586:21
more of his g. than gifts   583:10
noblest g. she ow'd   479:44
no Spring..beauty hath such g.   184:16
one thought, one g.   331:2
peculiar g.   575:10
power of g.   122:34
renown and g. is dead   458:24
serves to g. my measure   401:38
shed His g. on thee   36:23
sour herb of g.   475:14
such a lovely g.   502:1
such g. did lend her   484:40
such heavenly g.   509:21
swears with so much g.   312:28
sweet attractive g.   347:11
sweet attractive kind of g.   412:18
tabernacles of thy g.   421:3
take heart of g.   221:29
tender g. of a day   528:3
terms like g., new birth   20:9
that g. may abound   65:43
their courtly foreign g.   540:3
this in him was the peculiar g.   91:39
thrive in g. and feature   280:10
through God's good g.   354:11
thy G. may give the Truth   295:6
thy special g. preventing us   389:34
to have thy Prince's g.   510:16
to us may g. be given   240:22
trust him for his g.   161:18
Tuesday's child is full of g.   368:1
unbought g. of life   102:12
wanteth there g. of lute   92:5
what a pretty skipping g.   333:1
when a G. sprinkles another   308:18
who does nothing with a better g.?   586:24

Grace (cont.)
with something of a g. 573:22
with what g. he throws 208:11
womanly discovering g. 184:19
ye are fallen from g. 67:44
your speech be alway with g. 68:33
Graced: never g. with birds that
sing 87:25
Graceful: her gracious, g., graceless Grace 117:4
in act more g. 345:18
youth, beauty, g. action 190:27
Graceless: her gracious, graceful,
g. Grace 117:4
Grace-proud faces 106:34
Graces: accused of deficiency in
the g. 273:15
all the three sweet G. 308:13
faded g. of 'an Adonis of fifty' 240:6
fix our eyes upon his g. 278:24
G. danced 319:1
G...not..natives of Great
Britain 139:24
g. slighted blossom 164:30
half-mile g. 106:34
in its g. and airs 373:18
lead these g. to the grave 482:20
number all your g. 486:16
Pride, Envy, Malice..his G. 308:13
sacrifice to the G. 139:19
upon her eyelids many G. sate 509:31
write the G.' life 232:11
Gracing: either other sweetly g. 123:16
Gracious: all his g. parts 447:34
become g. unto thy land 397:8
be..g. unto Sion 395:10
be g. unto thee 46:10
g. and courteous to strangers 26:21
her g., graceful, graceless Grace 117:4
how g. the Lord is 393:38
in g. twilights 96:31
so g. is the time 430:20
the Lord is g., and merciful 400:18
thy state is the more g. 437:29
your great and g. ways 375:14
Graciousness: thy g. a warmer zest 80:27
Gradation: not by the old g. 469:24
Gradations: cold g. of decay 275:4
Gradualness: inevitability of g. 562:23
Graeca: exemplaria G. 26:6
Graecas: ad G. Kalendas 120:9
Graecia capta ferum victorem cepit 257:14
Graeculus: omnia novit G. esuriens 283:3
Graeme: died with conquering G. 417:18
spirit of the G. 23:21
Grai: cedite, G. 402:17
Grail: until I find the holy G. 540:12
Grain: chaff well meant for g. 532:5
cheeks of sorry g. 340:38
goodly g. 545:9
g. of mustard seed 59:28, 47
he reaps the bearded g. 317:9
husbanded the Golden g. 205:28
on guano and on g. 539:10
'tis in g., sir 482:20
warmth to swell the g. 121:27
which g. will grow 456:15
without one g. of sense 193:21
Grains: little g. of sand 127:33
two g. of wheat 463:1
Grais: G. ingenium, G...ore rotundo..loqui 256:8
Gramercy! they for joy did grin 149:10
Gramina: redeunt iam g. campis 260:24
Grammar: g., and nonsense, and
learning 226:2
g., that grounde is of alle
heedless of g. 310:6
take such g. as they can get 34:12
why care for g.? 325:11
Grammars: what sairs your g.? 560:22
Grammar school: in erecting a g. 105:23
Grammatical: refine our language 445:40
to g. purity 278:13
Grammatici certant 255:21
Gramophone: puts a record on the
g. 197:32
Grampian: on the G. hills 251:26
Granary: careless on a g. floor 284:12
Grand: dumb, inscrutable and g. 17:13
g. rough old Martin Luther 97:11

Grand (cont.)
g. style 20:5
it is most g. to die 334:4
it would be g. 130:12
Johnson's style was g. 154:13
sound so g. on 402:21
striking, resistless, and g. 225:34
that g. old man 365:15
upon which the G. Army never
looked 327:11
Grand: il allume le g. 109:34
Grandam: g. ere she died 455:28
soul of our g. 484:22
Grandchild: his little g. Wilhelmine 507:3
Grandes: pour juger des choses g. 354:25
Grandeur: baldness full of g. 19:18
charged with the g. of God 254:24
g. hear with a disdainful smile 230:1
g. in the beatings of the heart 575:22
g. of the dooms 284:21
g. that was Rome 380:17
old Scotia's g. 105:5
so nigh is g. to our dust 199:32
Grandeurs of his Babylonian
heart 544:12
Grandfather: whipped my g. 2:17
Grandis: verbosa et g. epistula 283:18
Grand-jurymen since before Noah 483:30
Grandly: mind that is g. simple 200:28
Grandmother: my g.'s review 115:26
not marry his G. 401:16
Grands: les g. n'ont point d'âme 97:33
Grandsire: g. phrase 477:5
sit like his g. 462:32
Grange: at the moated g. 462:14
lonely moated g. 535:29
Granite: from its hands the sand of
g. 516:19
over a ledge of g., into a g. bason 146:17
Grant: God g. you find one face 293:19
g. me some wild expressions 203:20
g. the artist his subject 268:14
g. thee thy heart's desire 392:36
thou wilt g. their requests 388:33
Grantchester: lovely hamlet G. 84:12
Granted: never take anything for
g. 180:31
Granting: by thy g. 487:22
Grape: burst Joy's g. 287:21
G. that can..Sects confute 206:25
jocund with the fruitful G. 206:22
Grapes: fathers have eaten sour g. 55:29
freighted with amber g. 18:16
gather g. of thorns 58:26
gleaning of the g. of Ephraim 46:53
g. of God 532:11
it brought forth wild g. 53:1
looked that it should bring forth
g. 53:1
my life will be sour g. 21:3
whence be the g. 322:25
where the g. of wrath are stored 264:15
with thy g...crown'd 424:19
you get g. and green pea 219:13
Grapeshot: whiff of g. 126:15
Graphic: penman's latest piece of
g. 97:17
Grapple: g. them to thy soul 431:25
let her and Falsehood g. 352:17
let them g. 438:37
Grapples with his evil star 533:1
Grasp: exceed his g. 89:15
g. it like a man of mettle 248:10
g. not at much 245:7
g. this sorry Scheme 207:26
what dread g.? 75:24(–76)
Grasping: capable of earnest g. 287:3
Grasps in the corner 481:20
Grass: all flesh is as g. 69:46
all flesh is g. 54:10
as the flower of g. 69:46
as the g. grows on the weirs 584:11
cut out of the g. 140:11
days of man..as g. 398:7
deep in the bells and g. 249:7
destroy a blade of g. 79:3
dread the rustling of the g. 573:1
eateth g. as an ox 49:28
fade away suddenly like the g. 397:15
flowers I leave you on the g. 542:6

Grass (cont.)
from the feather'd g. 286:3
glow-worm in the g. 118:8
go to g. 37:27
g. beyond the door 411:34
g. grows all up and down White
Hall 377:26
g. withereth 54:10, 69:46
green g. above me 409:29
green g. growing over me 32:19(–33)
Guests Star-scattered on the G. 207:30
I fall on g. 332:17
kissed the lovely g. 84:2
lift me from the g. 494:7
piece of English g. trampled 234:4
sits snug in leaves and g. 250:6
splendour in the g. 576:20
surely the people is g. 54:10
that falleth on the g. 7:16
through the frozen g. 285:12
tides of g. 524:23
vaulter in the sunny g. 265:21
what is the g.? 507:12
who made the g. 585:11
Grass-bank beyond 4:19
Grasses: over the g. 333:17
Grasshopper: g. shall be a burden 51:33
no burr of g. 262:9
Grasshoppers: half a dozen g.
under a fern 102:20
of the wings of g. 477:7
Grassy: Fidele's g. tomb 153:20
g. track to-day it is 299:23
search the g. knolls 131:24
they to their g. couch 347:19
Grata superveniet..hora 256:27
Grate: fluttered on the g. 151:24
g. on their scrannel pipes 342:29
on their hinges a 346:9
Grateful: g...for a little thing 530:22
g. mind..owes not 346:31
Grates: to whisper at the g. 319:4
Grati—: most g.—most interesting 188:2
Gratiâ: there's Vespers! Plena g. 96:42
Gratiano speaks..nothing 463:1
Gratified: lineaments of g. desire 74:28
Gratifying feeling that our duty has
been done 218:24
Grating: nor harsh nor g. 582:1
Gratis: he lends out money g. 463:17
Gratitude: begin with liking or g. 196:19
g. of men 580:24
their g. is a species of revenge 278:12
Gratuitous: most g. form of error 196:20
Gratulations: our g. flow 125:14
Gratus: donec g. eram tibi 260:3
Grau, teurer Freund, ist alle Theorie 223:19
Grave: approach thy g. like one 98:3
bends to the g. 224:16
between the cradle and the g. 195:14
bewept to the g. did go 436:22
brisk, or g. 163:48
buried in one g. 10:18
Death. My lord? A g. 447:32
digs my g. at each remove 244:19
dig the g. 516:15
ditch in Egypt be gentle g. 425:34
dread the g. as little 292:2
Duncan is in his g. 459:4
each like a corpse within its g. 496:4
earliest at His g. 35:25
eat our pot of honey on the g. 336:26
empires and cities in a common
g. 217:13
ere I descend to th' g. 158:13
every battlefield and patriot g. 314:10
every third thought..my g. 480:16
everywhere her g. 376:6
find me a g. man 478:14
from g. to gay 384:15
from the cradle to the g. I look 165:5
from the suicide's g. 220:19
from which earth, and g. 405:12
frontier-g. is far away 363:1
funeral marches to the g. 317:6
gently steer from g. to light 193:19
gone with the old world to the g. 241:24
g., and not taunting 26:26
g.; and the barren womb 50:55
g. doth gape..wider 442:38
g. hides all things 496:26

INDEX

Grave (cont.)
g. is not its goal 317:5
g. man . . Adam 146:16
g.'s a fine and private place 333:9
g.'s one violet 94:45
g. so rough 536:20
g. unto a soul 447:33
g. where English oak 238:26
g., where is thy victory? 67:18
her heart in his g. 356:31
in cold g. she was lain 32:16
in his g. rain'd many a tear 436:30
in his vast and wandering g. 532:7
in love with the g. 263:28
in the cold g. 253:28
in the dark and silent g. 405:12
jealousy is cruel as the g. 52:22
keep a dream or g. apart 89:3
kind of healthy g. 505:35
lead but to the g. 230:1
lead thee to thy g. 583:2
lead these graces to the g. 482:20
learned the secrets of the g. 374:11
lies a mould'ring in the g. 234:7
little little g., an obscure g. 475:10
marriage is a step so g. 514:28
meteor on the g. 118:8
mild o'er her g. 18:19
moral, g. 27:19
most . . have sunk into the g. 270:28
mourn all at her g. 32:16
my g., as now my bed 87:1
never find my g. 483:6
no repentance in the g. 561:21
not have strewed thy g. 437:22
not rest in an English g. 119:33
now in his colde g. 137:34
no work . . in the g. 51:21
O G., thy victoree? 8:19
old and godly and g. 585:14
on his g. . . the Syrian stars 17:9
our mother, but our g. 460:19
over the g. of Clooth-na-Bare 585:7
pay you in the g. 494:9
peace is in the g. 496:26
perhaps her g. 346:12
pompous in the g. 87:20
potent, g., and reverend signiors 469:45
precedence in the g. 292:20
renowned be thy g. 430:1
she is in her g. 580:18
sitting crowned upon the g. 248:23
soldier . . a quiet, g. man 29:6
soldier's g. 118:27
straight and dusty to the g. 514:30
temple of fame . . upon the g. 239:20
that ayont the g. 108:17
that dark inn, the g. 417:31
there lies a lonely g. 3:16
this g. . . a living monument 437:26
thy g. with rising flow'rs 381:35
thy humble g. adorned 381:34
thy root is ever in its g. 245:13
to glory, or the g. 122:19
tongue . . silent in the g. 161:8
travelling towards the g. 579:3
twice at the grip of the G. 302:29
untimely g. 125:3
upon his mother's g. 578:30
when my g. is broke up 186:8
where, G., thy victory? 322:2
without a g. 114:28
with profitable labour to his g. 444:23
with sorrow to the g. 45:21
Grave-digger: if I were a g. 269:14
Gravel: grubbing weeds from g. paths 296:32
I 'eard the feet on the g. 294:25
Gravelled for lack of matter 428:20
Grave-makers: gardeners, ditchers, and g. 437:5
Graven: not make . . any g. image 390:7
Gravender: my g., or grub 414:6
Graver: g. had a strife 281:9
His g. of frost 545:13
Graves: about the g. of the martyrs 516:9
arise from their g. and aspire 76:7
emblem of untimely g. 163:29
find ourselves dishonourable g. 448:22
follow us disquietly to our g. 452:16
g. have learnt 186:8

Graves (cont.)
g. of deceased languages 175:6
g. stood tenantless 430:14
have no g. as yet 140:24
have their g. at home 140:24
let's talk of g. 475:6
their g. are sever'd 241:8
they watch from their g. 93:4
uncut hair of g. 567:12
Gravitation: shall g. cease? 384:5
Gravity: g. out of his bed 439:29
reasons find of settled g. 486:33
Gravy: person who disliked g. 504:26
Gray: Auld Robin G . . . came a-courting 35:8
G.'s poetry . . above the common mark 273:12
Grayling: g. aleap in the river 422:22
here and there a g. 528:7
Graymalkin: I come, G. 456:3
Graze: g. him as he passes 38:24
neither g. nor pierce 472:32
Grazed: g the common of literature 271:7
Grazing: satyrs g. on the lawns 329:20
Greasy: fat and g. citizens 426:33
g. Joan 456:1
grey-green, g. Limpopo River 304:17
Great: aim not to be g. 322:4
all creatures g. and small 3:14
all g. men make mistakes 143:33
applause so g. as thine 158:4
as g. as is my grief 475:9
because his soul was g. 188:33
between the small and g. 164:12
biography of g. men 126:24
both g. and small 150:16
compare g. things with small 346:13
consent of all g. men 413:18
darkly wise, and rudely g. 383:22
disbelief in g. men 126:23
do this g. thing 48:25
Dr. Busby, a g. man 2:17
dull . . made many people think him g. 272:23
even g. men have . . poor relations 174:2
everything that is g. . . done by youth 181:36
far above the g. 231:16
fears of being g. 529:34
from the ashes of g. men 239:20
frown o' the g. 430:1
good, g. and joyous 497:17
g. and hardy genius 226:27
g. as a king 173:9
g. break through 499:18
g. by land 537:17
g. empire and little minds 101:14
g., ere fortune made him so 192:2
g. grey-green, greasy 304:17
g. is Diana of the Ephesians 65:8
g. is Truth 56:17
g., just, good God 96:6
g. man down 435:12
g. man helped the poor 323:21
g. man's memory . . outlive his life 435:5
g. Marlbro's mighty soul 1:9
g. men are not always wise 49:12
g. men are the guide-posts 100:10
g. men contending with adversity 109:16
g. men . . inspired texts 127:16
g. men may jest with saints 461:32
g. men . . not . . g. scholars 251:18
g. men . . see . . that thoughts rule 201:4
g. no heart 97:33
g. ones devour'd the small 501:14
g. right of an excessive wrong 96:3
g. to do that thing that ends 425:33
g. to little man 226:6
g. was the fall of it 58:28
g. without a foe 114:24
he bears too g. a mind 451:37
heights by g. men reached 316:31
he is always g. 194:6
how g. should be 319:7
how indigent the g. 231:7
how very small the very g. 543:13
if you would grow g. 515:23
in man . . nothing g. but mind 235:4

Great (cont.)
instinct of all g. souls 100:11
I shall be very proud and g. 515:18
just as he really promised something g. 116:35
know well I am not g. 530:35
Life of Johnson . . a very g. work 325:26
lives of g. men 317:8
men in g. place 26:22
nearer the g. white throne 131:32
no g. and no small 199:1
no g. man lives in vain 126:24
not exercise myself in g. matters 400:1
nothing . . without enthusiasm 200:9
not ignorant . . in a g. matter 56:35
on earth . . nothing g. but man 235:4
only know it shall be g. 264:7
only truly g. . . from the passions 181:42
only truly g. who are truly good 135:23
packs and sets of g. ones 454:19
poetry . . g. and unobtrusive 289:25
poorly rich, and meanly g. 415:17
rightly to be g. 436:10
rising to g. place 26:28
rule of men entirely g. 322:11
seekest thou g. things for thyself? 55:22
silence alone is g. 553:2
simple g. ones 535:43
smallest . . ever set in a g. place 29:5
some men are born g. 483:18
streets where the g. men go 208:5
that Caesar might be g. 122:36
that he is grown so g. 448:23
that which once was g. 582:7
these are g. days 144:7
those who were truly g. 509:1
though fallen, g. 113:17
thou wouldst be g. 457:1
to be g. is to be misunderstood 200:41
to do a g. right 465:2
to g. ones 'longs 461:28
to grow g. in fame 173:4
too humble nor too g. 327:14
weigh this song with the g. 584:16
what did you do in the G. War? 11:15
whatever was little seemed . . g. 325:22
whenever he met a g. man 542:34
when the g. and good depart 575:1
while the g. and wise decay 312:24
with a g. thing to pursue 91:41
with consistency a g. soul 200:40
without terror g. 401:22
with small men no g. thing 339:1
worship of the g. of old 118:30
your g. and gracious ways 375:14
Great-coat: shaggy white g. 175:12
Greater: Brutus makes mine g. 451:22
consent . . that he is g. than they 413:18
four things g. than all things 294:29
g. are none 303:5
g. glory dim the less 465:21
g. man, the g. courtesy 531:1
g. prey upon the less 231:26
g. than both 457:4
g. than Solomon 59:17
g. than their knowing 302:4
g. than the King 379:6
g. than themselves 448:27
g. than we know 573:27
there's something g. 128:3
thy necessity . . g. than mine 502:12
Greatest: as the g. he 405:14
given you the g. of all things 489:28
g. as not exempted 253:36
g. happiness for the g. numbers 266:11
g., nor the worst of men 113:40
g. of these is charity 66:46(-67)
how much the g. event 210:20
not be among the g. 290:8
one of the g. . . poems 194:11
standing with the g. man 276:24
Great-heart: one G. 99:30
Great-hearted gentlemen 90:15
Greatly: come into port g. 200:18
Greatness: all g. . . not . . exact 100:5
all the far-stretched g. 405:13
base on which thy g. stands 579:34
be not afraid of g. 483:18
boy my g. 426:4
farewell to all my g. 446:24

Greatness (cont.)
God's g. flowed around — 88:5
g. going off — 425:18
g. he could not want — 280:3
g. . . is to me a curse — 334:20
g. knows itself — 440:25
g. of the world in tears — 586:7
g. thrust upon them — 483:18
her g. on her subjects' love — 402:2
his g. weigh'd — 431:21
if honour gives g. — 173:9
in me there dwells no g. — 530:35
lack correlated g. — 544:11
man's unhappiness . . comes of his g. — 127:18
model to thy inward g. — 443:13
our g. may not fail — 529:34
reflections on the g. of the British — 2:19
some achieve g. — 483:18
some far-off touch of g. — 530:35
thinks . . his g. is a-ripening — 446:24
Greaves: flamed upon the brazen g. — 534:4
Grecian: merry G. coaster — 18:16
ne'er did G. chisel — 416:16
sigh'd his soul toward the G. tents — 465:17
you in G. tires — 487:3
Greece: Athens, the eye of G. — 350:11
fair G.! sad relic — 113:17
feelings by which . . later G. ruled — 28:27
glory that was G. — 380:17
G., Italy, and England did adorn — 193:9
G., sound thy Homer's . . name — 160:24
insolent G. or haughty Rome — 281:15
isles of G. — 115:43
light wave lisps 'G.' — 90:34
old John Naps of G. — 478:46
that G. might still be free — 115:44
to G., and into Noah's ark — 162:2
to G. the direful spring — 384:20
whose beauty summoned G. — 331:5
Greedy: not g. of filthy lucre — 68:45
owners—g. men — 218:1
thank goodness, I am g. — 403:27
Greedy-gut: says G. — 366:13
Greek: at the G. Kalends — 120:9
because he *was* a G. — 309:20
come worthy G. — 168:13
each alike was G. — 524:7
Germans in G. — 387:4
G. in pity and mournful awe — 16:6
G., Sir, is like lace — 274:21
G. was free from rhyme — 281:26
happy G. . . was not spoiled — 281:26
he could speak G. as naturally — '110:4
highest education since the G. — 182:19
it was G. to me — 448:30
Keats, who was ignorant of G. — 309:20
learn . . G. as a treat — 144:16
loving, natural, and G. — 115:36
neither G. nor Jew — 68:31
ne yet of Latin, ne of G. — 510:15
nothing . . not G. in its origin — 327:12
poets . . must carve in Latin or in G. — 557:22
questioned him in G. — 128:17
say a word against G. — 490:4
small Latin, and less G. — 281:13
so barbarously not a G. — 266:14
study of G. literature — 212:22
taught'st Cambridge and King Edward G. — 351:17
what the G. did — 81:1
when his wife talks G. — 277:1
whisky's name in G. — 104:17
without G. . . talk about the Gods — 116:35
Greeks: when G. joined G. — 313:1
where the G. had modesty — 376:11
which came first, the G. or the Romans — 181:23
Green: all the trees are g. — 293:19
all ye G. Things — 388:21
anything g. that grew — 300:10
as g. as emerald — 148:25
as long as . . fields are g. — 491:26
babbled of g. fields — 443:19
burns fierce while it is g. — 172:7
burnt g. and blue and white — 149:6

Green (cont.)
do these things in a g. tree — 62:47
dry smooth-shaven g. — 341:14
feed me in a g. pasture — 393:10
first g. peas — 317:1
Flora and the country g. — 287:24
golden lamps in a g. night — 332:2
g. and happy in first love — 146:32
g. and smiling age — 514:38
g. and yellow melancholy — 483:10
g. be the turf above thee — 234:15
g. days in forests — 516:2
g. fields of England — 147:10
g. grow the rashes O — 105:37
g. hill far away — 4:4
g. Illyrian hills — 15:14
g. in judgment — 424:2
g. little vaulter — 265:21
g. plant groweth — 140:16
g. pleasure or grey grief — 524:28
g. thought in a g. shade — 332:19
heard on the g. — 76:14
in red and blue and g. — 76:15
in the morning it is g. — 397:15
keeps his own wounds g. — 27:6
laid him on the g. — 30:8
laughs to see the g. man pass — 250:6
like a g. girl — 431:26
lilac, gold and g. — 80:14
little Johnny g. — 366:18
look so g. and pale — 457:11
making the g. one red — 458:15
many a g. isle — 494:22
memory be g. — 430:22
misbegotten knaves in Kendal-g. — 439:22
on an English g. — 535:39
on a simple village g. — 533:1
places of nestling g. — 266:5
psalm of g. days — 404:22
remember their g. felicity — 289:7
roots, and ever g. — 377:4
so smooth, so g. — 352:26
sported on the g. — 507:3
summer's g. all girded up — 486:15
table of g. fields — 443:19
their heads are g. — 311:21
this . . Herb whose tender G. — 206:4
thy bower is ever g. — 97:30, 315:21
turtle, g. and glutinous — 94:34
upon England's mountains g. — 75:16
upon the ocean g. — 329:1
wearin' o' the G. — 9:6
where evermore no g. life shoots — 79:3
which yet are g. — 487:29
Green-coat: sleepy g. man — 250:7
Greener: in a cleaner, g. land — 299:14
laurel g. from the brows — 539:11
Greenery: sunny spots of g. — 151:32
Greenery-yallery . . young man — 221:7
Greenest of things blue — 523:12
Green-eyed: g. jealousy — 464:17
g. monster — 471:31
Greengrocer: from the g. tree — 219:13
Greenhouse: loves a g. — 163:18
Greenland: G. . . or the Lord knows where — 383:27
G.'s icy mountains — 240:17
have you an estate in G.? — 233:7
Greenly: we have done but g. — 436:26
Greenness: clothe the general earth with g. — 151:25
Green-robed senators — 286:8
Greensleeves was all my joy — 6:18
Greensward: single on the g. — 336:7
Green-walled by the hills of Maryland — 568:11
Greenwood: to the g. go — 31:16
under the g. tree — 427:7
Greet: gentle dames! it gars me g. — 108:14
g. as angels g. — 319:9
g. her with his song — 350:3
g. the unseen with a cheer — 97:3
how should I g. thee? — 119:30
never kiss and g. — 285:1
scarcely g. me with that sun — 486:33
we g. the monarch-peasant — 251:3
Greeting: cease frae their g. — 9:8
joyous hour . . g. — 219:35
such prophetic g. — 456:17
Greetings where no kindness is — 582:3

Gremio: matris e g. suae — 133:9
Grenadier: British G. — 9:24
who comes here? a g. — 369:17
Grenadiers: captain of the Hampshire g. — 216:28
talk of Pensions and G. — 513:17
Grenville: at Flores . . Sir Richard G. lay — 539:16
Effingham, G., Raleigh — 302:30
I Sir Richard G. die — 540:3
Greta woods are green — 419:7
Greville: Fulke G., Servant to Queen Elizabeth — 232:16
Grew: at last it g., and g. — 305:18
g. up fostered . . by beauty — 579:5
he g. into his seat — 436:42
like us He g. — 4:3
neither g. in dike nor ditch — 33:2
sometime g. within this . . man — 330:12
so we g. together — 467:9
stone to beauty g. — 199:23
they g. in beauty — 241:8
wet by the dew it g. — 204:3
Grey: bluest of things g. — 523:12
bring down my g. hairs — 45:21
calls the glory from the g. — 95:19
cloak of g. — 18:8
dapples . . with spots of g. — 469:19
earth not g. but rosy — 93:26
friend of G. — 250:25
given me over in my g. hairs — 572:18
Good G. Poet — 370:3
green pleasure or g. grief — 524:28
g. expanse where he floats — 16:4
grown g. from Thy breath — 525:8
head grown g. in vain — 492:7
his coat so g. — 229:16
his g. dissimulation — 349:32
in amice g. — 350:15
little g. home — 571:7
my gallant g. — 114:35
my hair is g. — 236:18
night is growing g. — 372:18
O coldness, ineffably g. — 537:14
O good g. head — 306:34
old woman clothed in g. — 96:41
on g. paper — 153:30
pilgrim g. — 338:18, 459:34
red spirits and g. — 298:26
ricks stand g. to the sun — 535:22
set g. life — 496:9
suddenly grow g. with fear — 439:35
that g. iniquity — 189:10
those amber locks to g. — 585:3
threads of g. — 15:19
too lovely to be g. — 346:24
white, black and g. — 148:20
Grey-beard loon — 304:17
Grey-green, greasy Limpopo River — 522:20
Grey-grown speechless Christ — 453:30
Greyhound: mastiff, g., mongrel — 438:39
this fawning g. — 443:27
Greyhounds: like g. in the slips — 173:2
Gridley: fire when you are ready, G. — 54:25
Grief: acquainted with g. — 536:17
after long g. and pain — 292:19
age, or g., or sickness — 286:17
antheming a lonely g. — 452:42
as full of g. as age — 475:9
as great as is my g. — 478:30
bottom of my g. — 491:24
but for our g. — 77:3
can I see another's g. — 118:26
canker and the g. — 446:18
care and g. of heart — 31:9
died out of pure, pure g. — 468:30
every one can master a g. — 340:19
forestall his date of g. — 350:17
for g. and spite cast herself — 411:37
from perfect g. — 446:16
glist'ring g. — 524:28
green pleasure or grey g. — 447:34
g. fills the room up — 26:2
g. flieth to it — 499:21
g. for awhile is blind — 521:30(~522)
g. forgotten — 277:40
g. is a species of idleness — 159:5
g. is itself a med'cine — 491:24
g. itself be mortal — 174:7
g. never mended no broken bones

INDEX

Grief (cont.)
g. returns with the..year 491:22
g. that does not speak 460:20
g. that fame can never heal 23:25
g...upon the heels of pleasure 155:32
g. with a glass that ran 522:5
g. without a pang 150:31
hopeless g. is passionless 88:15
in false g. 509:24
it was pain and g. to me 394:8
journeyman to g. 474:18
move my faint heart with g. 494:19
my distracting 251:25
my joy, my g. 558:1
my particular g. 469:43
one g. brings forth twain 189:9
only time for g. 253:26
patch g. with proverbs 469:12
plague of sighing and g. 439:30
should be past g. 485:12
shows of g. 430:30
silence augmenteth g. 232:15
silent manliness of g. 225:8
smiling at g. 483:10
stifled, drowsy, unimpassioned g. 150:31
take away the g. of a wound 440:30
there's g. enough 232:2
thine be the g. 23:15
thirsty g. in wine we steep 319:6
thy mother's g. 73:23, 80:8
'tis unmanly g. 430:31
two extremes..joy and g. 454:23
what torments of g. you endured 190:25
when others' g. is fled 117:39
with shame and g. I yield 292:20

Griefs: all g. that bow 17:24
but not my g. 475:20
cutteth g. in halves 26:17
drinking my g. 475:19
ere England's g. began 224:14
great g...medicine the less 429:38
great joys, like g., are silent 331:11
g. that harass the distress'd 278:32
he hath borne our g. 54:25
I am sick of many g. 451:26
passion..in my old g. 88:24
so are their g. and fears 26:44
solitary g. 269:26
soothed the g. of forty generations 325:36
what private g. they have 450:32
Grievance: no g...arise in the Commonwealth 352:4
Grievances: grieve at g. foregone 486:25
Grieve: g. his heart 460:10
made to g. on account of me 237:7
men are we and must g. 582:8
nor joy nor g. too much 193:17
Pope will g. a month 521:2
than a nation g. 190:20
thou leavest me to g. 499:9
we will g. not 576:20
Grieved: although it g. him sore 159:38
g. and obscure waters 96:31
g. with her child 196:2
here come the g. 164:35
they soothe the g. 164:34
Grieves: if aught inanimate e'er g. 113:33
Grieving: g...over the unreturning brave 113:33
what is knowledge but g.? 337:42
what's the use o' g.? 299:22
Grievous: it was a g. fault 450:17
Grievously hath Caesar answer'd it 450:17
Griffin: I John G. 8:4
Griffith: honest chronicler as G. 447:11
Grill: let G. be G. 509:34
Grim: g., g. grew his countenance 30:18
heaven not g. 93:26
there look g. as hell 472:34
Grim-visag'd comfortless Despair 230:28
Grin: Devil did g. 151:11
ending with the g. 129:4
how cheerfully he seems to g. 128:24
one universal g. 204:34
rustic, woodland g. 372:20
they for joy did g. 149:10
they g. like a dog 395:22
universal g. 163:28
vanquish Berkley by a g. 85:4

Grind: g. in the prison house 46:60
g. the faces of the poor 52:34
laws g. the poor 226:16
mills of God g. slowly 315:22, 317:13
one demd horrid g. 177:25
Grinder, who serenely grindest 121:13
Grinders cease 51:33
Grindest: grinder, who serenely g. 121:13
Grinding: sound of the g. is low 51:33
tarry the g. 480:38
Grinds: with exactness g. he all 315:22, 317:13
Grinned: Devil he g. 302:31
Grinning: g. at his pomp 475:7
mock your own g. 437:15
such g. honour 440:35
Grip: twice at the g. of the Grave 302:29
Gripped: he g. the bars 302:31
Gristle: people..still..in the g. 100:24
Grizzled: his beard was g., no? 431:15
Groan: bitter g. of the martyr's woe 75:6
conception that I do g. withal 473:14
condemn'd alike to g. 230:30
counted every g. 16:8
dead men gave a g. 149:30
he gave a g. 578:26
sit and hear each other g. 287:25
with bubbling g. 114:28
Groaned inly while he taught 87:38
Groaneth: whole creation g. 65:55
Groaning: my g. is not hid 394:7
sick people g. under walls 330:16
strong gongs g. 141:5
Groans: g. of the dying 418:13
in thy book record their g. 351:20
Grocer: G. treat housemaids 142:1
wicked G. 141:32
Groined the aisles of Christian Rome 199:23
Grolle: ich g. nicht 240:24
Gromboolian: great G. plain 311:15
Groom: by his dogs and by his g. 161:24
death is but a g. 186:12
goes singing to her g. 95:2
G., the Butler, and the Cook 218:22
g. there was none to see 263:2
Grooves: predestinate g. 237:26
ringing of change 534:36
Groping: laid our g. hands away 84:6
Gross: dainty Bacchus g. in taste 455:22
g. and scope of my opinion 430:12
lies..as a mountain 439:23
not g. to sink 488:26
things rank and g. 430:33(-431)
Grosser: shepherds give a g. name 437:1
Grossly: err as g. as the few 190:28
he took my father g. 435:37
Grossness: by losing all its g. 102:14
hiding the g. 464:14
spare the g. of the names 194:17
Grosvenor Gallery..young man 221:7
Grotesque: from the g. to the horrible 188:15
Pure, Ornate, and G. 29:8
Grottoes: my g. are shaded 499:14
Ground: acre of barren g. 479:17
another man's g. 466:2
beat the g. 340:7
betwixt the stirrup and the g. 121:25
choose thy g. 118:27
daisies prank the g. 82:7
dance the others..off the g. 171:22
fruitful g. 518:1
gained g. upon the whole 95:17
gazes on the g. 329:19
Grammere, that g. is of alle 310:6
g. flew up and hit me 560:12
g. which British shepherds tread 574:2
guide into poetic g. 162:29
haunted, holy g. 113:19
he swalloweth the g. 49:27
his body to the g. 391:44
house and tenant go to g. 199:31
if she did not g. 303:9
in a fair g. 302:13, 392:26
in his own g. 386:26
Jesus from the G. suspires 205:8
let us sit upon the g. 475:7
man of the dust of the g. 44:11
might well be under g. 219:24
old hope goes to g. 92:43

Ground (cont.)
on a plat of rising g. 341:15
on such slippery g. 450:8
on the holy g. 361:13
outside our happy g. 18:24
passion that left the g. 89:10
place..is holy g. 45:34
purple all the g. 342:31
scarce..stand on any g. 189:16
solid g. not fail 536:1
they are the g., the books 455:20
thou scorner of the g. 498:10
thy brother's blood crieth.. from the g. 44:31
'tis holy g. 231:1
to a more removed g. 432:1
tread on classic g. 2:2
twice five miles of fertile g. 151:32
up-on the g. I see thee stare 138:5
watered the whole face of the g. 44:10
why cumbereth it the g.? 62:1
Grounded on just and right 349:2
Groundlings: split the ears of the g. 434:15
Ground-nest: lark left his g. 350:3
Grounds: noble g. for the noble emotions 412:25
Ground-whirl of the perished leaves 410:24
Group: g. that's quite antique 115:36
little g. of wilful men 571:13
Grouse: Ould G. in the gun-room 227:7
Grove: camp, the court, the g. 116:37
clear spring, or shady g. 346:19
good g. of chimneys 358:20
g. nods at g. 385:3
g. of myrtles 35:17
meadow, g., and stream 576:1
Muses' sacred g. be wet 545:7
olive g. of Academe 350:11
thy shrine, thy g. 288:6
young Jemmy G. 30:1
Grovel: souls that g. 121:12
Grovelled: he g. before him 542:34
Grovelling: so impotent and g. an insect 519:16
Groves: amid the g. 574:23
for g. 358:20
forsake her Cyprian g. 192:44
g. whose rich trees 347:5
in the g. of their academy 102:16
meadows, hills and g. 576:21
o'er shady g. they hover 563:30
pathless g. 37:37
through g. deep and high 418:12
to the musical g. 526:22
valleys, g., hills and fields 330:17
we two..will seek the g. 410:12
Grow: as our days do g. 470:31(-471)
g. for ever and for ever 538:16
g. to what they seem 226:12
he'll g. into a hound 568:22
his eyes g. in my brow 424:1
his praises there may g. 243:24
I g. old..I g. old 197:21
I should g. to fruit or shade 243:20
let both g. together 59:27
my wrath did g. 76:5
something smack, something g. to 463:22
where de wool ought to g. 210:18
where follies naturally g. 143:1
where they do g.? 245:21
which grain will g. 456:15
Growed: I 'spect I g. 517:6
Growing: green grass g. over me 32:19(-33)
g. or full constant light 185:31
g...when ye're sleeping 420:1
is young and is g. 32:14
not g. like a tree 282:1
sorrow of each day's g. 335:10
Growl: Duchess in a hoarse g. 128:31
Growled: g. and bit him 249:12
it cracked and g. 148:26
Grown: both full g. 10:14
g. beneath God's eye 96:31
g. man in the cradle 103:23
might have g. full straight 330:12
new g. with pleasant pain 288:7
when we are g. 295:6

Grown-up: hear the g. people's feet 515:14
in quiet g. wise 375:16
Grows: all other bliss that..g.
by kind 195:12
far from vanish, rather g. 91:14
g., lives, and dies..single 466:17
g. on mortal soil 342:22
g. with his growth 383:26
since when it g. 280:21(–281)
Growth: as quick a g. to meet decay 246:3
children of a larger g. 139:22, 191:20
genius..slow of g. 313:22
give it vital g. again 473:11
g. the only evidence of life 363:15
only g. that dwindles 226:9
reeds of decent g. 214:7
states..their g., their manhood 309:19
Growths: in the sun-searched g. 410:30
Grr: Urrh! Yarrh! G.! Arrh! 300:16
Gr-r-r: g. there go..abhorrence 96:38
g.—you swine! 96:42
Grub: joiner squirrel or old g. 477:7
my gravender, or g. 414:6
old ones, g. 489:6
Grubbing: weeds from gravel
paths 296:32
Grubby: beefy face an' g. 'and 299:14
John G., who was short 141:17
Grubs: dirt, or g., or worms 385:27
Grudge: feed fat the ancient g. 463:17
never g. the throe 95:15
no g., no strife 518:1
Gruel: basin of nice smooth g. 22:9
g. thick and slab 459:33
Grumble: g. a little now and then 227:13
it haint no use to g. 407:4
nothing whatever to g. at 222:1
terrible g. 406:3
Grün: g. des Lebens goldner Baum 223:19
wie g. sind deine Blätter 416:3
Grundy: end of Solomon G. 368:21(–369)
more of Mrs. G. 315:11
what will Mrs. G. zay? 359:22
Grunt and sweat under a weary life 434:4
Gruntled: far from being g. 572:5
Guano: pamphleteer on g. 539:10
Guanoed her mind 182:32
Guarantee: no one can g. success
in war 144:18
Guard: calls not Thee to g. 301:1
changing g. at Buckingham
Palace 339:14
drunk and resisting the G. 295:4
from whom we g. our spoons 324:19
gentlemen of the French G. 239:9
g. and bless our fatherland 264:11
g. me with a watchful Eye 2:21
g. our native seas 123:10
g. the sailors 34:37
g. us, guide us, keep us 195:23
hate of those ye g. 303:26
my fun o' the Corp'ral's G. 295:3
none but Americans on g. 560:32
on my g. against Milton 290:26
Guarda: ma g., e passa 168:18
Guarded: virtue which requires to
be ever g. 227:19
Vision of the g. mount 343:2
Guardian: good as g. angels 158:13
g. of his Majesty's conscience 547:13
hear thy g. angel say 108:19
Guarding, calls not Thee to guard 301:1
Guards: G. die..not surrender 121:24
g. his osier-isle 546:11
up G. and at them 564:24
Gudgeon: this fool g. 462:35
Gudgeons: swallow g. ere th'are
catched 111:6
Guenevere..a true lover 328:16
Guenille: ma g. m'est chère 353:17
Guerdon: fair g. 342:20
Guerre: ce n'est pas la g. 79:1
la g. est l'industrie..de la Prusse 353:4
Guess: golden g. 528:20
g. now who holds thee? 88:16
g. where he may be 94:25
Guessed: this I have g. 302:25
Guessing: g. what was at the other
side 564:3
it's better only g. 146:31

Guest: at the strange g.'s hand 523:14
be your g. tomorrow night 12:6
body's g. 405:7
dull fighter and a keen g. 440:24
g. that tarrieth but a day 56:26
made me a closer g. 80:27
poor nigh-related g. 152:21
shakes his parting g. by the
hand 481:20
some second g. to entertain 186:8
speed the going g. 386:6
this g. of summer 457:6
was rude to the Lord her G. 302:1
whether g. or captive 561:18
worthy bidden g. 342:27
Guests: g. are met 148:19
G. star-scattered 207:30
hosts and g. 39:15
my g. should praise it 238:2
unbidden g. 445:19
Guide: awful g. 420:5
canst thou g. Arcturus? 49:25
except some man should g. me 64:39
Fashion..g. of fools 164:38
guard us, g. us 195:23
g. my lonely way 225:11
g., philosopher, and friend 384:17
have God to be his g. 99:31
light to g. 573:28
my g. and..familiar friend 395:12
my partner and my g. 573:26
our g. unto death 394:35
probability is the..g. of life 109:36
Providence their g. 349:31
skilful g. into poetic ground 162:29
to g. his steps 521:23
where thou art g. 400:33
whimsey..is the female g. 229:12
women g. the plot 500:31
Guide-posts: great men are the g. 100:10
Guides: blind g. 60:18
he g. me and the bird 94:13
Guiding: g.-star of a whole..
nation 359:23
g. the fiery-wheeled throne 341:12
Guildford: an hour out of G. town 299:23
Guildford Hill: under G. 42:12
Guile: he it was, whose g. 344:6
hiding his harmful g. 509:24
in their mouth..no g. 71:24
Israelite..in whom is no g. 63:4
packed with g. 84:13
Guileless held..his way 387:8
Guilt: blood with g. is bought and
sold 496:22
each thing of sin and g. 340:23
free from g. or pain 497:12
g. of dissimulation 419:26
G. was my grim Chamberlain 252:25
her g. to cover 226:18
if g.'s in that heart 356:16
image of war, without its g.
506:13, 518:1
my stronger g. 435:32
other pens dwell on g. 22:21
so full of..jealousy is g. 436:18
wash her g. away 226:18
what the world calls g. 146:32
Guiltier than him they try 461:23
Guiltless: all g., meet reproach 472:21
g. death I die 473:18
g. of his country's blood 230:5
Guilts: close pent-up g. 453:10
Guilty: better that ten g...escape 73:9
crimes of this g. land 85:6
g. creatures..at a play 433:36
g. of dust and sin 244:21
g. of such a ballad 454:37
g. splendour 163:7
haunts the g. mind 446:7
let no g. man escape 229:2
make g. of our disasters the sun 452:18
make mad the g. 433:32
started like a g. thing 430:18
strength of g. kings 16:28
tremble like a g. thing 576:18
Guinea: but the g.'s stamp 105:30
default of a g. 413:25
force of the' g. 413:25
jingling of the g. 534:24
sixpences..to one g. 276:22

Guinea (cont.)
somewhat like a g. 74:6
within the compass of a g. 267:22
worth a g. a box 12:5
Guinea-pig: if you lift a g. up 315:13
Guinea-pigs: one of the g. cheered 129:29
Guineas: crowns and pounds and
g. 262:15
nice yellow g. for me 106:8
Guinness, Allsopp, Bass 120:23
Guitar: sang to a small g. 311:24
Troubadour touch'd his g. 37:2
Gules: now is he total g. 433:27
warm g. on Madeline's fair breast 285:20
Gulf: great g. fixed 62:26
g. profound 345:31
into the g. of death 491:15
Gulfs: g. of liquid fire 473:32
g. will wash us down 541:3
in Persian g. were bred 320:6
whelm'd in deeper g. than he 159:3
Gull: g.'s way 334:12
notorious geck and g. 484:25
Gulls: g. in an aery morrice 241:30
nightly g. him 487:21
Gulp: drains his at one g. 96:39
Gum: med'cinable g. 474:2
Gums: my nipple from his boneless g. 457:13
odorous g. and balm 347:5
Gun: all the birds without a g. 199:11
beggarly son of a g. 121:3
by each g. the lighted brand 122:3
cawing at the g.'s report 467:7
don't know a g. from a bat 294:24
escape from rope and g. 214:34
nor ever lost an English g. 537:18
pointing a g. at the horny 146:23
summons of the rock g.'s roar 77:31
text of pike and g. 110:17
Gunga Din: better man than I am,
G. 297:6
Gun-horses: grey g. in the lando 301:11
Gunner: sink me the ship, Master
G. 540:1
Gunners: with seventy g. behind me 301:8
Gunpowder: g. and sealing-wax 131:21
G., Printing 125:24
G. Treason and Plot 9:11, 368:13
sympathetic g. 111:5
till the g. ran out 209:18
Gun-room: Ould Grouse in the g. 227:7
Guns: as the g. boom far 141:5
but for these vile g. 438:35
don't get away from the G. 301:8
g. will make us powerful: butter
..make us fat 223:11
loaded g. with boys 165:13
of g., and drums, and wounds 437:35
rutted..by the passing g. 333:17
those all-shattering g. 188:32
though winds blew great g. 173:9
when the g. begin to shoot 303:2
Gurgite: in g. vasto 553:10
Gurgle he gave 220:19
Gurly grew the sea 220:19
Gurney: Peter G., Peter Davey 33:1
Gushed: love g. from my heart 149:26
Gusto: secret element of g. 513:33
Gusts: when g. shake the door 16:1
Gut: Devil in his g. 75:15
Gut; jenseits von G. und Böse 364:20
Guts: g. of the last priest 338:1
his g. in his head 481:10
sheep's g...hale souls 468:19
Gutta cavat lapidem 372:10, 11
Gutter: we are all in the g. 569:37
Guy: ah! County G. 420:9
G. de Vere, has thou no tear? 380:10
Guzzling Jimmy 543:7
Gymkhanas: won g. in a doubtful
way 300:18
Gyre and gimble 129:39
Gyves: with g. upon his wrist 252:26

H

Ha: h.-h.-h., you and me 6:19
'h.! h.!' quoth he 150:11
'H.! H.!' said the duck 304:6

Ha (*cont.*)
h., h., the wooing o't — 105:13
h.! h.! to you — 221:2
saith among the trumpets, H., h. — 49:27
Habacuc était capable de tout — 557:14
Haberdasher to Mr. Spurgeon — 112:18
Habileté .. de savoir cacher son h. — 407:12
Habit: apparell'd in more precious h. — 469:6
costly thy h. as thy purse — 431:25
h. rules the unreflecting herd — 580:3
h. with him..the test of truth — 164:32
honour.. in the meanest h. — 479:9
how use doth breed a h. — 485:1
in the h. of flogging me — 549:10
long h. of living — 87:10
reap a h. — 406:6
Habitable: look round the h. world — 194:23
Habitation: beside them..the fowls..their h. — 398:8
God in his holy h. — 396:5
h. of dragons — 53:45
I have loved the h. of thy house — 393:19
local h. and a name — 467:24
my h. among the tents of Kedar — 399:24
Habitations: living peaceably in their h. — 57:16
Habits: begat h. of peace and patience — 559:15
cowls, hoods, and h. — 346:26
of h. devil — 436:5
small h., well pursued — 357:25
their h. from the Bear — 40:22
Habitual: your more h. sway — 576:21
Hack: do not h. me — 354:10
some body to hew and h. — 110:21
to h. thy sword — 439:12
Hacked, hewn with constant service — 507:2
Hackney: see to H. Marshes — 36:22
some starved h. sonneteer — 382:34
Hackney-coach: once in a h. — 175:37
Had: h., having, and in quest to have — 488:12
I have h. my hour — 194:21
more he h. — 99:32
that we spent we h. — 10:5
thus have I h. thee — 487:22
what wee spent, wee h. — 11:17
Haddocks: I hunt for h.' eyes — 131:24
Hadn't ought to be — 238:31
Hag: this is the h. — 477:7
Haggard: all h. hawks will stoop — 305:12
if I do prove her h. — 471:38
with h. eyes I view — 124:17
Haggards ride no more — 512:8
Hags: black and midnight h. — 460:2
rags, and h. — 150:28
Hail: congenial horrors, h. — 546:25
fire and h., snow and vapours — 400:24
flail of the lashing h. — 492:26
h., Bard triumphant — 158:6
h., Columbia! — 255:13
h. divinest Melancholy — 341:8
h., fellow, well met — 521:11
h., glorious edifice — 504:4
h., happy Britain! — 506:14
h., holy light — 346:18
h., horrors, h. infernal world — 344:22
h., master; and kissed him — 60:44
h., Sabbath! thee I h. — 228:14
h. to the Chief — 416:21
h. to thee, blithe Spirit — 498:1
h. to the Headlong — 376:22
h. to the kings of the sea — 362:30
h. wedded love — 347:26
h., ye heroes — 255:13
h., ye indomitable heroes, h. — 308:21
h. ye small sweet courtesies — 512:23
no sharp and sided h. — 254:29
unless God send his h. — 94:13
where falls not h. — 531:37
young generations in h. — 335:26
Hailed: he h. them o'er the wave — 122:6
Hails: h. you Tom or Jack — 159:31
what gentle ghost..h. me? — 282:2
Hair: ae lock o' his gowden h. — 32:15
all her bright golden h. — 569:15
beauty draws us with a single h. — 385:13
beg a h. of him — 450:24
Berenice's ever-burning h. — 135:15
bids me bind my h. — 266:8

Hair (*cont.*)
bind up this h. — 492:23
blind with thine h. — 495:22
bone and a hank of h. — 303:12
bracelet of bright h. — 186:9
braided her yellow h. — 32:3
bright h. uplifted — 496:6
brushes of comets' h. — 303:20
Caoilte tossing his burning h. — 585:7
cover you with my h. — 586:5
divide a h. — 110:5
drew me backward by the h. — 88:16
each particular h. — 432:9
Ethel patted her h. — 21:2
excellent head of h. — 482:7
fair h., and fairer eyes — 306:15
from his horrid h...pestilence — 346:6
h. and harpstring of gold — 525:5
h. as free — 280:7
h. of my flesh stood up — 48:48
h. was so charmingly curled — 293:17
her dusky h. — 580:19
her h. in one long yellow string — 95:5
her h. that lay along her back — 410:8
her h. was long — 286:30
her voice, and her h. — 333:19
his flashing eyes, his floating h. — 151:33(-152)
his h. did bristle — 417:14
his h. is of a good colour — 428:13
his h. was like a crown — 140:20
his long essenced h. — 323:1
horrid image..unfix my h. — 456:24
I must sugar my h. — 129:25
into her long black h. — 366:2
it raised my h. — 150:3
Jove, in his next commodity of h. — 483:22
known to thee by flying h. — 411:10
long dishevell'd h. — 488:26
long h...a glory to her — 66:42
make your h. curl — 222:6
my fell of h. .. rouse and stir — 461:3
my h. is grey — 114:35
my h. is sleek — 8:16
never brush their h. — 40:22
never pin up my h. with prose — 156:3
no 'pollygy aint gwine ter make h. come back — 238:13
one h. of a woman — 264:20
one her dark h. — 528:2
one lock o' his gowden h. — 32:15
one slight h. — 215:38
one strangling golden h. — 411:11
only a woman's h. — 520:52
only talks about her h. — 545:14
pin up your h. with all your letters — 156:3
pleasant mazes of her h. — 158:1
ruddy limbs and flaming h. — 74:25
serve one to pin up one's h. — 156:2
she has brown h. — 465:27
smoothes her h. with automatic hand — 197:32
snatched..by the h. — 411:15
soft brown h. — 120:21
strung with his h. — 455:22
subtle-coloured h. — 522:19
tangled in her h. — 319:4
that subtle wreath of h. — 185:4
thy amber-dropping h. — 341:3
thy fair h. my heart enchained — 501:22
thy h. is as a flock of goats — 52:5
thy h. soft-lifted — 284:12
thy hyacinth h. — 380:17
to mine own torn h. — 246:22
uncut h. of graves — 567:12
vine-leaves in his h. — 267:3
wherefore should I kame my h.? — 32:18
whose h. was so brown — 201:24
who touches a h. of yon..head — 568:15
with a single h. — 194:28
with his h. on end — 163:22
with such h., too — 97:9
with the tangles of Neaera's h. — 342:20
your h. has become very white — 128:28
your well-beloved's h. — 585:3
Hair-breadth 'scapes — 470:2
Hairless: white and h. as an egg. — 246:16
Hairs: as many sons as I have h. — 461:15
bring down my grey h. with sorrow — 45:21

Hairs (*cont.*)
foul sluttish h. — 477:7
had all his h. been lives — 473:15
h. as gay as are Apollo's locks — 209:22
his head and his h. were white — 70:27
if h. be wires — 488:13
observe the forms of h., or straws — 385:27
our h. be crown'd — 424:19
those set our h...upright — 184:22
very h. of your head..numbered — 58:53
Hair's-breadth: crescent of a h. — 94:8
Hairy: Esau my brother is a h. man — 44:59
marvellous h. about the face — 467:13
thicksides and h. Aldrich — 146:22
Haïssable: le moi est h. — 374:6
Halcyon: paddles in a h. sea — 409:14
Saint Martin's summer, h. days — 445:18
Haldan: Earl H.'s daughter — 293:8
Hale: sheep's guts should h. souls — 468:19
you are h., Father William — 507:33
Half: another h. stand..by — 443:8
but h. denied..h. as good as justified — 111:16
dearer h. — 348:3
entertain with h. their forces — 443:8
h. a drop — 330:7
h. a league, h. a league — 528:13
h. as old as Time — 100:3, 408:8
h. as sober as a judge — 307:27
h. a time — 71:19
h. a trade and h. an art — 267:7
h. is greater than the whole — 248:2
h. Mithridates and h. Trissotin — 324:35
h. of her should rise herself — 236:17
h. of human fate — 17:3
h. of one order, h. another — 110:34
h. of such a friendship — 533:9
h. our days..in the shadow — 85:23
h. seas over — 520:13
h. slave and h. free — 314:6
h. some sturdy strumpet — 236:17
h. that's got my keys — 228:9
h. to forget the wandering — 208:4
h. to remember days — 208:4
h. was not told me — 47:43
how they will spend h. of it — 23:9
left h. told the story — 341:20
longest h. of your life — 508:10
lost him h. the kind — 193:39
not h. the power to do me harm — 473:23
one h. of the nation is mad — 506:4
one h. of the warld thinks the tither daft — 420:12
one h. of the world cannot understand — 22:8
one h. so precious — 207:22, 23
only h. way up — 10:19
overcome but h. his foe — 345:8
payment of h. twenty shillings — 100:5
purer with the other h. — 436:4
swept it for h. a year — 130:12
your servant's cut in h. — 228:9
youth shows but h. — 95:13
Half-a-crown: h. in the bill — 178:26
left h. to a..Scotchman — 270:22
Half-a-dozen of the other — 331:18
Half-and-half: no h. affair — 218:21
Half-an-hour: always did it for h. a day — 131:2
be at Bakewell in h. — 413:1
h. after his head was cut off — 8:3
silence..about the space of h. — 71:9
Half-believe: attain to h. — 147:9
Half-believers: light h. — 18:12
Half-brother of the world — 29:10
Half-buried in the snow — 316:22
Half-cities: walls, palaces, h. — 114:20
Half-devil and half-child — 303:24
Half-faced: this h. fellowship — 438:38
Half-French, half-English — 445:14
Half-gathered: intrigues h. — 164:31
Half-gods: when h. go — 199:14
Half-held by the night — 507:16
Half-kisses: poor h. — 189:15
Half-knowledge: remaining content with h. — 289:21
Half-light: night and light and the h. — 584:17
Half-men and their dirty songs — 84:17
Half-mile graces — 106:34

Half-moon: a huge h. 439:44
Half-owre: h., h. to Aberdour 32:2
Halfnence: change for a sove-
reign in h. 177:21
Halfpenny: for a copper h. 131:24
if you haven't got a h. 5:23
Half-pennyworth: one h. of bread 439:39
Half-regained: h. Eurydice 342:9
yet but h. 496:3
Half-sister to Delay 535:23
Half-way: H. House to Rome 403:5
its touches of beauty..h. 289:27
Half-wild and wholly tame 302:8
Half-workers: women must be h. 429:26
Half-world: o'er the one h. 458:1
Hall: Absolute across the h. 41:32
Chapman and H. swore not 42:24
Douglas in his h. 418:27
equality in the servants' h. 36:1
from H. or Terrace 311:16
gentlest that ever ate in h. 328:24
he slept in the h. 43:1
hung in the castle h. 36:30
in many an ancient h. 322:22
sparrow..fly..into the h. 38:31(-39)
vasty H. of Death 17:15
Hallelujah!..kindly pass the milk 372:19
Hallelujahs: from out the h. 87:37
Hall-gardens: birds in the high H. 536:2
Hallo: they shout, 'H.!' 408:17
walk right up and say 'h.' 210:10
Halloo: h. your name 482:22
h., h., loo, loo! 453:17
Hallooed out at one of Burdett's
elections 119:32
Hallow: bright names will h. song 113:37
h. thus the Sabbath-day 151:27
seems to us there 376:10
set to h. all we find 291:5
we cannot h. this ground 314:12
Hallowed: h. be thy name 58:4
place of justice..h. 26:31
so h. and so gracious 430:20
worms were h. 472:16
Hallows: all his h. 255:6
Halls: Amphitrite's destined h. 495:1
dwelt in marble h. 98:21
h., the h. of dazzling light 178:12
in h., in gay attire 417:16
in tap'stry h. 340:17
silent h. of death 98:3
sweep through her marble h. 316:28
those roofless h. 496:2
through Tara's h. 356:20
your dreary marble h. 121:12
Halt: cheer for a h. 300:16
h., and the blind 62:8
h...between two opinions 48:2
Moment's H. 206:21
Halter: now fitted the h. 402:6
Halters: racks, gibbets, h. 370:10
Halts by me that footfall 544:31
Halves: cutteth griefs in h. 26:17
h. of one august event 235:16
Ham: it might be H. 303:9
Shem, H., and Japheth 44:36
storm at the death of H. 412:24
when there's h. 178:7
with h. and sherry 84:5
wonders in the land of H. 398:13
Hambre: la mejor salsa..el h. 134:9
Hamelin Town's in Brunswick 94:32
Hamilton: Marie H.'s to the kirk
gane 31:17
Hamlet: H. most of all 241:29
H...the Prince..left out 420:22
I'll call thee H., king 431:32
I saw H...played 202:15
king drinks to H. 437:36
kneeling 532:11
Lord H...all unbrac'd 432:35
Lord H. is a prince 432:43
lovely h. Grantchester 84:12
rude forefathers of the h. 229:30
Hamlets: h. brown 153:25
in h., dances 417:16
Hammer: beat out by every h. 85:17
either anvil or h. 318:18
either..the anvil or the h. 223:23
h., h., h. along the 'ard 'igh
road 403:12

Hammer (cont.)
His h. of wind 545:13
his little h. under the pillow 173:31
my anvil and h. lies declined 8:13
no sound of h. or of saw 163:40
took an h. in her hand 46:46
what the h. 75:24(-76)
Hammer: Amboss oder H. sein 223:23
Hammered: England's being h.,
h., h. into line 294:22
h. out my basnet point 359:9
Hammers: busy h. closing rivets
up 444:6
hear the h. ring 294:22
Hammersmith: want to make H.
hum 243:4
Hammock: Drake he's in his h. 363:3
Hammock-shroud: heavy-shotted
h. 532:7
Hampden: ruined Mr. H.'s fortune 100:5
some village-H. 230:5
Hamper an' 'inder an' scold men 302:5
Hampshire: captain of the H.
grenadiers 216:28
Hamstring: whose conceit lies in
his h. 481:6
Ha'nacker Hill: gone from H. 41:29
Hand: as an old Parliamentary h. 222:39
as arrows in the h. of the giant 399:35
at h., quoth pick-purse 438:41
at the h. of every man's brother 44:42
beefy face an' grubby h. 299:14
beneath whose awful h. 300:24
bent head and beseeching h. 95:37
bite the h. that fed them 102:36
bless the h. that gave the blow 193:35
books..hold readily in your h. 276:28
bringing me up by h. 175:22
but of my left h. 352:19
by God's Almighty H. 121:27
Caesar's h. and Plato's brain 199:2
clasps the h. of brother 35:5
crosses from his sov'reign h. 248:1
curious engine, your white h. 563:11
Dawn's Left H. 205:6
did the H...of the Potter shake? 207:15
dubious h. 279:6
each..his bloody h. 450:6
each waved his h. 150:6
either h. may rightly clutch 295:5
end of all things is at h. 70:4
every bondman in his own h. 448:37
for a man with heart, head, h. 535:43
gie's a h. o' thine 104:16
glove upon that h. 477:14
God brought them written in
his h. 200:46
God of Bethel, by whose h. 183:20
go h. in h. to death 411:19
h. folks over to God's mercy 196:14
h. in h. even with the vow 432:14
h. in h. on the edge of the sand 312:3
h. in h...through Eden 349:31
h. in h. we'll go 106:20
handle toward my h. 457:20
H. like this h. 96:25
h. of Douglas is his own 418:26
h. of little employment 437:10
h. that fired the shot 31:3
h. that kings have lipp'd 424:13
H. that made us 2:28
h. that made you fair 462:12
h. that rocks the cradle 557:19
h. that rounded Peter's dome 199:23
h. that waited for the heart 196:24
h., the head, and the heart 413:16
h. to bless 143:15
h. to execute 145:26, 217:11, 282:20
h. you cannot see 547:21
head, heart, and h. 295:8
heaving up my either h. 247:15
her cheek upon her h. 477:14
here's my h. 480:1
her h. on her bosom 473:6
her rash h. in evil hour 349:15
his Captain's h. on his shoulder 363:4
his h. dropt he 148:20
his h. is stretched out still 53:7
his h. on the cockatrice' den 53:19
his h. upon many a heart 316:16

Hand (cont.)
his h. will be against every man 44:49
his hat in his h. 277:10
his icy h. on kings 501:5
his mind and h. went together 241:16
his red right h. 345:20
hold a fire in his h. 474:20
hold your h. but as long 93:9
hop a little from her h. 477:28
I fear thy skinny h. 149:19
if lawyer's h. is fee'd 214:19
if that he..hadde the hyer h. 137:13
if you want to win her h. 79:16
I kiss'd her slender h. 536:3
imposition of a mightier h. 325:4
in a big round h. 221:16
in a bold determined h. 122:3
in every honest h. a whip 473:2
in his h. are all the corners of the
earth 397:26
in the great h. of God 458:26
in the h. of God 56:23
in the h. of the Lord..a cup 396:31
in your mediaeval h. 220:28
I see Thy H., O God 299:3
I take her h. 266:12
it hurts my h. 472:25
it will go into his h. 48:33
join in h. brave Americans 180:5
kindlier h. 533:20
kingdom of heaven is at h. 57:27
kissed the fingers of this h. 88:22
lays his h. upon a woman 548:5
lay their h. upon the ark 162:45
lend thy guiding h. 350:20
lifted h. in awe 586:27
little cloud..like a man's h. 48:5
man's h. is not able to taste 467:23
moist eye, a dry h. 441:19
my arm a ladye's lilye h. 31:6
my beloved put in his h. 52:10
my h. before my eyes 41:18
my h. sought hers 92:44
my knee, my hat and h. 86:2
my playfellow, your h. 425:4
my right h. forget her cunning 400:5
my times be in Thy h. 95:20
my wild heart to thy loving h. 468:27
nature's own..cunning h. 482:20
nothing in my h. I bring 548:12
one lovely h. she stretched 122:27
one whose h...threw a pearl
away 474:2
on this side my h. 475:19
open thy white h. 485:5
O! that her h. 480:39
other h. held a weapon 485:3
our times are in His h. 95:13
potent quack..whose murderous h. 165:20
put its h. in its breeches pocket 289:25
refuse to set his h. to a rope 189:1
resting on one white h. 309:4
righteous put their h. unto
wickedness 399:33
salute thee with my h. 474:34
sandwich in her h. 178:24
shade of His h. 544:31
sheep of his h. 397:28
she laid her snow-white h. 584:11
smoothes her hair with automatic h. 197:32
spirit-small h. 90:7
spoils that his own h. spread 523:16
stand on either h. 323:19
stout heart and open h. 418:9
stout of h. 417:9
strack the top-mast wi' his h. 30:19
stretch forth thy mighty h. 264:11
subject made to your h. 92:46
sweeten this little h. 460:27
sweet lips, soft h. 289:1
sweet Roman h. 484:6
take the Cash in h. 205:25
there also shall thy h. lead me 400:9
there's a h., my trusty fiere 104:16
this blood clean from my h. 458:15
this h. hath offended 165:24
this living h. 287:3
this my h. will rather 458:15
through her wasted h. 417:35

INDEX

Hand (*cont.*)

thrust my h. into his side 64:9
thy bloody and invisible h. 459:8
thy defence upon thy right h. 399:28
thy h. out of plackets 453:20
thy right h. shall hold me 400:9
thy sheep in thy h. 17:19
thy voice and h. shake still 411:10
too strange a h. 448:14
tooth for tooth, h. for h. 45:54
touch of a vanish'd h. 528:3
turn of eye, wave of h. 96:24
under whose cautious h. 568:7
waiting for a h. 532:8
walking close at h. 130:12
wav'd her lily h. 216:1
we'll h. in h. 425:22
what dread h.? 75:24(—76)
what h. and brain..paired? 92:37
what immortal h. or eye 75:24
whatsoever thy h. findeth to do 51:21
what the h. dare seize 75:24
when I stretched out my h. 512:31
when people walk h. in h. 154:34
white h. of a lady fever thee 425:5
White H. of Moses 205:8
whose h. is ever at his lips 287:21
with a rude h. break 287:5
with his skinny h. 148:20
withhold not thine h. 51:30
world and they..h. and glove 162:18
written unto you with mine own h. 67:49
your h. into the h. of God 239:4
your staff in your h. 45:47
you shall wander h. in h. 365:25
Handclasp's a little stronger 135:13
Handed they went 347:25
Handel: Bononcini compar'd to H. 112:22
  or for H. 307:25
Handfast: heart h. in heart 523:15
Handful: fear in a h. of dust 197:28
  for a h. of silver 93:2
  h. of grey ashes 157:17
  h. of meal in a barrel 48:1
Handicraft: art is not a h. 548:9
Handkercher: knit my h. about
  your brows 447:38
Handkerchief: h. of the Lord 567:12
  he had no little h. 34:24
  holding his pocket-h. 130:20
  snuffle and sniff and h. 84:5
  that h...an Egyptian to my
  mother 472:15
Handkerchiefs: moral pocket h. 178:43
Handle: could h. men a bit 300:17
  h. nòt 68:29
  h. toward my hand 457:20
  hands, and h. not 399:4
  him that can h. them 126:2
  I polished up that h. 221:15
  one old jug without a h. 311:12
Handled: never in that sort had h.
  been 160:1
Handles: everything..hath two h. 109:17
Handmaid: h. to religion 24:26
  nature's h. art 191:29
  our h. unheeding 372:18
  riches are a good h. 25:6
  thou h. perfect in God's sight 410:5
  with h. lamp attending 343:25
Handmaiden: low estate of his h. 61:13
Handmaidens: her five h. 410:12
Hands: accept refreshment at any
  h. 219:21
  aching h. and bleeding feet 17:1
  at my h. this garland 522:14
  bear thee in their h. 397:19
  before rude h. have touch'd it 281:24
  between the h. 411:25
  by foreign h. 381:34
  cannot rid my h. of him 441:22
  caught the world's great h. 265:23
  cold immortal h. 523:20
  come, knit h. 340:7
  command all h. to work 12:6
  confute, change h. 110:5
  crucify hearts, not h. 525:18
  dirty h., the nails bitten 325:28
  do their h...come between us? 523:6
  enrich my heart, mouth, h. 245:9
  eyes, lips, and h. to miss 186:25

Hands (*cont.*)

fall into the h. of God 540:1
fall into the h. of the living God 69:12
fall into the h. of the Lord 56:31
fasten their h. upon their hearts 263:34
from the hard h. of peasants 451:20
h., and handle not 399:4
h. are the h. of Esau 45:1
h. not hearts 472:14
h., that the rod of empire 230:4
hearts of old gave h. 472:14
he hath shook h. with time 200:27
her h. are quicker 532:24
his h. are as gold rings 52:14
his h. prepared the dry land 397:26
his two happy h. 509:13
horny h. of toil 320:5
house not made with h. 67:24
if h. were only joined 229:8
I have thee by the h. 81:14
in judicious h. 121:6
in this lady's lips and h. 410:32
into my h. themselves do reach 332:17
into other's h. these relics 185:5
into the h. of their deliverer 350:36
into the h. of the spoilers 46:45
into thy h. I commend my
  spirit 62:51, 393:27
I warmed both h. 308:25
laid our groping h. away 84:6
laid violent h. upon themselves 391:40
large and sinewy h. 318:11
laying on of h. 391:15
lay their just h. on that..key 339:29
lifted feet, h. still 39:3
lifting up of my h. 400:13
lift not thy h. to *It* 207:3
little folding of the h. 49:46
made these h. blessed 489:21
man's fortune is in his own h. 26:14
my h. from picking and stealing 391:8
nearer than h. and feet 529:38
never took his h. away 176:31
no hurry in her h. 409:23
not into the h. of men 56:31
not into the h. of Spain 540:1
not without men's h. 197:1
on the little h. little gold head 339:19
our h. have met..will never
  meet again 253:30
pale h. 254:14, 15
prosper thou the work of our h. 397:17
right h. of fellowship 67:40
shake h. for ever 189:20
shake h. with a king 234:14
should you need nor heart nor h. 516:1
solely by the labor of my h. 546:39
something from our h. 573:27
soon *wring* their h. 558:30
so to 'entergraft our h. 184:30
strengthen ye the weak h. 54:2
Strength without h. 522:5
stretching of the h. 372:19
tall fellow of thy h. 485:37
their fatal h. 346:7
their h. are blue 311:21
then take h. 479:28
these h. are not more like 431:11
these hangman's h. 458:7
they pierced my h. 393:6
those flower-soft h. 424:7
thou shalt stretch forth thy h. 64:18
thy h. their little force resign 160:23
thy soul full in her h. 413:31
turn'd it in his glowing h. 534:16
union of h. and hearts 527:15
wash your h. and pray 296:33(—297)
wave their h. for a mute farewell 267:10
weak h. though mighty heart 491:27
will these h. ne'er be clean? 460:25
with crooked h. 529:10
with head, h., wings 346:14
with mine own h. 475:22
with my own fair h. 519:23
with one of his h. wrought 48:35
with your h., and your feet 322:25
your h. begin to harden 296:33
your holy delicate white h. 329:2
your little h. were made to take 40:20
your little h. were never made 561:25
Handsaw: I know a hawk from a h. 433:20

Handsome: everything h. about
  him 469:11
  h. man, but..a gay deceiver 154:12
  h., well-shaped man 21:13
  she is a h. wee thing 107:16
  very few years to be young and
  h. 519:34
  very h. corpse 226:37
  what a world of..faults looks h. 466:6
Handy: with the girls be h. 33:6
Handy-dandy, which is the justice? 454:10
Handy-work: firmament sheweth
  his h. 392:32
  prosper thou our h. 397:17
Hang: all h. together, or..h.
  separately 211:18
  clambering to h. 437:1
  cowslips wan that hang the..
  head 342:31(—343)
  go, h. yourselves all 484:9
  h. a man first and try him afterwards 354:4
  h. and brush their bosoms 97:9
  h. a pearl in every cowslip 466:35
  h. him *anyhow* 550:19
  h. him..erect a statue to him 505:14
  h. it by the shore 363:2
  h. the man over again 34:6
  h. them on the horns o' the
  moon 429:5
  h. them up in silent icicles 151:25
  h. there like fruit 430:5
  h. thyself in thine own heir-
  apparent garters 439:3
  h. up philosophy! 478:25
  h. your husband and be dutiful 214:20
  helter skelter, h. sorrow 280:12
  icicles h. by the wall 456:1
  I'll h. my harp 10:21
  in their power to h. one another 203:17
  neither go nor h. 72:20
  not h. myself to-day 140:9
  or none, or few, do h. 487:16
  read Richardson for the story..
  h. yourself 272:13
  senates h. upon thy tongue 546:18
  she would h. on him 430:33(—431)
  some hollow thought h. like an
  interdict 579:2
  to h. quite out of fashion 481:18
  wretches h. that jurymen may
  dine 385:15
Hanged: farmer that h. himself 458:17
  Harrison h., drawn, and quartered 377:14
  if I were h. 299:27
  knows he is to be h. 273:22
  millstone..h. about his neck 62:27
  my poor fool is h. 454:26
  not h. for stealing horses 234:5
  our harps, we h. them up 400:5
Hangeth: He h. on a stalk 585:9
Hanging: bare h. 194:19
  good h. prevents a bad marriage 482:11
  h. and marriage..go by Destiny 203:28
  h. and wiving goes by destiny 464:5
  h. is too good for him 99:16
  h.-look to me 155:10
  h. of his cat on Monday 79:18
  h. out the clothes 368:20
  h. them..in the slippery clouds 442:1
  they're h. Danny Deever 295:20
  they're h. men and women now 9:6
Hangman: h.'s hands 458:7
  if I were a..h. 269:14
  louse for the h. 280:12
  naked to the h.'s noose 262:12
Hangs: blossom that h. on the
  bough 480:14
  h. in the uncertain balance 231:35
  h. my helpless soul on Thee 565:6
  h. on princes' favours 446:24
  h. upon the cheek of night 477:9
  he h. between 383:22
  now h. as mute 356:20
  thereby h. a tail 471:25
  thereby h. a tale 427:14, 479:5
  thy tail h. down behind 301:7
Hank: bone and a h. of hair 303:12
Hannibalem: expende H. 283:20
Hanover: by famous H. city 94:32

Hans: in H.' old Mill 171:10
Hansom: in your h. leave the High 404:21
Hansom-cabs: for wheels of h. 131:24
Haply I may remember 410:1
Happen: what then did h...? 72:28
Happened: could but have h. once 97:29
  what all the wise men promised
  has not h. 335:14
Happeneth: one event h. to them
  all 51:2
Happens: what h., let us bear 193:17
  what we least expect..h. 182:8
Happier: feel that I am h. than I
  know 348:33
h. for his presence 513:35
h. without their toes 312:10
Paradise within thee, h. far 349:29
remembering h. things 534:21
seek no h. state 347:27
we had been h. both 412:12
Happiest: benight our h. day 184:28
best and h. moments 499:12
h. if ye seek no happier 347:27
h. when I am idle 560:21
h. women, like the h. nations 196:26
to-morrow 'ill be the h. time 536:26
Happily: the good end h. 569:25
Happiness: all the h. mankind can
  gain 192:36
by no greatest h. principle 126:8
consume h. without producing 489:12
domestic h. 163:6
envy no man's h. 427:27
for the h. 'twill bring 121:23
gain a h. in eyeing 266:16
greatest h. for the greatest numbers 266:11
greatest h. of the greatest number 42:21
great spectacle of human h. 505:19
h. is no laughing matter 565:26
h. makes them good 309:17
h. of the human race 101:15
h. of the next world 87:7
H.! our being's end 384:2
h. through another man's eyes 428:27
h. too swiftly flies 230:30
home-born h. 163:26
in solitude what h.? 348:34
it is a flaw in h. 285:11
lifetime of h. 490:12
love match..only thing for h. 195:18
makes the h. she does not find 279:15
more divided..domestic h. 290:12
my great task of h. 516:16
no h. within this circle of flesh 86:20
of no moment to the h. of an individual 272:8
our pastime and our h. 578:20
poverty is a great enemy to..h. 275:5
pursuit of h. 11:11, 268:19
result h. 174:24
thought of tender h. betray 575:11
to fill the hour—that is h. 200:12
too happy in thine h. 287:23
to recall a time of h. 168:22
travelling is the ruin of all h. 103:36
virtue alone is h. 384:13
wherein lies h.? 284:25
where in the end we find our h. 579:30
withdraws into its h. 332:18
Happy: accounted yourselves h. 167:13
ah! h. years! 113:14
all h. families resemble each
  other 548:7
always h., reign whoever may 162:21
angry and poor and h. 142:2
ask yourself whether you are h. 338:20
be h. as ever at home 82:11
be h. while y'er leevin 5:20
between a splendid and a h. land 225:6
business of a wise man to be h. 273:20
but a little h. if I could say 468:14
call no man h. till he dies 506:12
deep-meadow'd, h. 531:37
despaired—been h. 97:28
duty of being h. 507:18
earthlier h. is the rose 466:17
farewell h. fields 344:22
flatterer of h. minds 154:39
good dog Tray is h. now 249:22
goodness..make men h. 309:17

Happy (cont.)
h. and glorious 250:14
h. as a lover 575:10
h. as birds in the spring 76:4
h. as kings 515:22
h. as we once 164:8
h., h., h. pair 190:34
h...he..that rewardeth thee 400:6
h. he with such a mother 539:8
h., high, majestical 494:15
h. human face 266:3
h. in the arms of a chambermaid 274:10
h. in this..not yet so old 464:19
h. is England! 288:23
h. issue 389:18
h. land we know 143:1
h. man be his dole 439:5, 466:7
h. men that have the power to
  die 540:23
h. noise to hear 262:21
h...that his father was before
  him 520:26
h. the man, and h. he alone 194:20
h. the man whose wish and care 386:26
h. the man, who, void of cares 378:17
h. those early days 552:3
H. though Married 235:12
h. who have called thee so 507:18
h. who in his verse 193:19
help to make earth h. 128:1
how h. is he born and taught 583:9
how h...with either 215:4
how h. you make those 487:7
human race..most h. 217:8
I die h. 211:2, 309:18
if I am destined to be h. with
  you 290:30
if the prisoner is h. 490:25
I had been h. 472:3
I h. am 76:12
I should be h...but I have a
  partner 174:34
I've had a h. life 240:14
let us all be h. 560:23
lucid intervals and h. pauses 27:46
made h. by compulsion 152:15
make me at all h. without you 290:31
make men h., and to keep them
  so 386:33
makes a Scotchman h. 276:10
make two lovers h. 381:8
marriages..as h...made by the
  Lord Chancellor 273:1
methinks it were a h. life 446:1
more h., if less wise 117:47
never h. for the present 273:4
no chance to be very h. 215:36
no one..perfectly h. till all are
  h. 508:30
not a h. one 221:34
now to be most h. 470:31
O h. band of pilgrims 362:7
one of those h. souls 495:10
Queen Elizabeth of most h.
  memory 43:24
so h. in three wives 308:8
take my counsel, h. man 218:26
than that none should be h. 273:9
that h. garden-state 332:21
that thou art h., owe to God 348:11
there is a h. land 586:22
they h. are 558:7
things that do attain the h. life 518:1
think myself h., king Agrippa 65:21
this h. breed of men 474:22
those that were good shall be h. 303:20
to be good is to be h. 412:6
to have been h. 78:4
too h., h. tree 289:7
too h. in thine happiness 287:23
virtuous, and you will be h. 211:7
wanted only one thing to make
  me h. 240:13
was the carver h.? 413:10
what makes a nation h. 350:14
what's the odds, so long as
  you're h.? 335:8
which of us is h.? 542:40
who is the h. Warrior? 575:5
who so h., O who? 311:18
won't be h. till he gets it 6:27

Happy Isles: touch the H. 541:3
Happy-noted voice 285:34
Harassed: too h. 17:5
Harbinger: amber scent..her h. 350:31
  Aurora's h. 467:10
  day's h. 343:8
  evening star, love's h. 349:26
  Spring-time's H. 38:8
Harbour: H. cleared 148:21
in life did h. give 280:11
ship is floating in the h. 493:12
though the h. bar be moaning 294:1
where doth thine h. hold? 35:12
Hard: bold and h. adventures 205:3
dismiss'd with h. words 375:16
does it not seem h. to you? 515:14
for earth too h. 89:10
'H.'..'As nails' 177:38
h. as..the nether millstone 49:31
h. as the palm of ploughman 480:39
h. at death's door 398:16
h. Englishmen 293:15
h. grey weather 293:15
h., the selfish, and the proud 164:34
h. to catch and conquer 336:8
h...to kick against the pricks 64:42
h. was their lodging 213:20
h., when love and duty clash 538:10
in h. words again 200:40
in our viciousness grow h. 425:2
it seem'd so h. at first 536:27
it seems as h. to stay 536:27
it was too h. for me 396:27
long is the way and h. 345:27
made up of h. words like a
  charm 370:18
never think I have hit h. 272:24
nothing's so h., but search 246:19
of such h. matter 493:3
stockish, h. and full of rage 465:20
thou art an h. man 60:31
though h. be the task 131:31
though 'tis h. for you 3:18
very h... to be a Christian 91:15
words as h. as cannon-balls 200:40
you are too h. for me 227:20
Harden: h. not your hearts 397:29
your hands begin to h. 296:33
Hardened: h. into the bone of
  manhood 100:24
he h. Pharaoh's heart 45:42
Hardens: it h. a' within 105:19
Hardest time of all 187:3
Hardihood, endurance, and courage 416:7
Hardiness: friendliness, h., love 328:2
Hardly: h. ever 221:11
  mounts, and that h. 16:13
Hardness: h. of heart, and contempt 388:49
  without h...sage 16:9
Hardware-men: mercers, h.,
  pastrycooks 307:2
Hardy: great and h. genius 226:27
h. and high the slimy mallow 165:17
h. Captain of the Pinafore 221:11
H...a sort of village atheist 142:19
h. as the Nemean lion 432:3
H. went down to botanize 142:19
kiss me, H. 362:26
Hare: as thou woldest finde an h. 138:5
first catch your h. 223:4
hard..to shoot the h. 250:6
h. limp'd trembling 285:12
h. sits snug 250:6
h.'s own child, the little h. 250:9
H.! the H.! 250:8
I like the hunting of the h. 77:33
it look'd like h. 33:20
outcry of the hunted h. 73:20
see that the h. does not couch 419:29
take your h. when it is cased 223:4
than to start a h. 438:37
thy own h., or a wig? 306:30
triumph o'er the timid h. 546:20
Harebell: azur'd h. 429:37
Harebells: among the heath and h. 83:15
Hare-brained chatter 181:13
Hares: little hunted h. 249:5
  merry brown h. 293:20
Hark: H.! a thrilling voice 132:5
  H., H.! Bow, wow 479:28

Hark (cont.)
H.! H.! my soul 202:23
h.! h.! the lark 429:25
h., my soul! 161:9
h.! now I hear them 479:30
h., the glad sound! 183:19
h.! the herald-angels 565:12
h. to the big drum callin' 296:17
O h., O hear! 538:15
Harlot: every h. was a virgin once 74:22
h.'s cry 73:28(–74)
Portia is Brutus' h. 449:17
Harlotry: like one of these h. players 439:32
Harlots: devoured thy living with h. 62:17
mother of h. 71:32
Harm: beef..does h. to my wit 482:6
content with my h. 427:27
do not h. nor question much 185:4
doth harvest no h. 550:2
doth most h. to the mene puple 310:5
good provoke to h. 462:17
I fear we'll come to h. 31:25
no h. can come to his toes 312:7
no h. in looking 518:32
none of woman born..h. Macbeth 460:5
no people do so much h. 166:25
not half the power to do me h. 473:23
thinks no creature h. 80:8
to win us to our h. 456:22
Harmful: h. to the brain 267:30
more h. than reasoned errors 266:23
Harmless: h. as doves 58:49
h. drudge 270:27
h. fish 184:24
h. necessary cat 464:28
his own h. face 527:23
Harmonia: once were Cadmus and H. 15:14
Harmonics: fiddle h. on..sensualism 337:8
Harmonies: inventor of h. 529:17
tumult of thy mighty h. 496:11
Harmonious: dulcet and h. breath 466:38
sphere-born h. sisters 351:9
such h. madness 498:10
Harmony: air and h. of shape 401:32
all h. of instrument 494:1
best h. in a church 352:11
distinct from h. divine 159:11
famous h. of leaves 586:7
from h., from heavenly h. 191:35
h. not understood 383:21
heaven drowsy with the h. 455:22
her voice the h. of the world 253:36
hidden soul of h. 342:8
in their motions h. divine 348:16
like h. in music 579:9
made quiet by the power of h. 581:25
music wherever there is a h. 86:32
note most full of h. 86:32
other h. of prose 194:12
rules with Daedal h. 497:14
sentimentally I am disposed to h. 306:4
such h. is in immortal souls 405:18
there is a h. in autumn 494:6
touches of sweet h. 405:18
with your ninefold h. 343:17
Harms: beg often our own h. 424:3
not for thy h. 544:30
Harness: between the joints of the h. 48:15
die with h. on our back 461:7
h. and not the horses 124:20
h. jingles now 263:5
him that girdeth on his h. boast 48:11
life that never knows h. 422:22
my h. piece by piece 544:22
through proof of h. 425:12
to wait in heavy h. 303:24
Harnessed, and carrying bows 396:34
Haroun Alraschid: good H. 539:15
Harp: blow the spirit-stirring h. 218:9
cornet, flute, h., sackbut 55:36
h., his sole remaining joy 416:29
h. not on that string 476:29
h. of Orpheus was not more charming 352:26
h. that once 356:20

Harp (cont.)
h. the monarch minstrel swept 117:41
high-born Hoel's h. 229:21
his h., the sole companion 37:5
his wild h. slung behind him 356:27
I'll hang my h. 10:21
Love took up the h. of Life 534:16
no h. like my own 122:16
praise the Lord with h. 393:35
sings to one clear h. 532:1
unstringed viol or a h. 474:14
Harped ye up to the Throne o' God 298:18
Harper: Wind, that grand old h. 503:13
Harping: still h. on my daughter 433:3
Harp-player: as songs of the h. 521:30(–522)
Harps: our h., we hanged them up 400:5
plucking at their h. 298:14
touch their h. of gold 421:10
Harpsichon: Mrs. Turner's daughter..on the h. 377:22
Harpstring: hair and h. of gold 525:5
Harriet: chatter about H. 211:24
H., Hi! 243:5
what foolish H. befell 249:25
Harris: bother Mrs. H. 176:33
Mr. H. who was dreadful timid 176:31
words she spoke of Mrs. H. 176:34
Harrison: see Major-general H. hanged 377:14
Harrow: H. an' Trinity College! 299:17
h. up thy soul 432:9
toad beneath the h. 300:13
Harrowing: only a man h. clods 236:14
Harry: banish not him thy H.'s company 439:37
crowns..promis'd to H. 443:12
God for H.! 443:27
H. the King, Bedford 444:28
I am H.'s daughter 298:30
in that Jerusalem shall H. die 442:29
little touch of H. 444:9
not Amurath an Amurath..but H. H. 442:31
Old H...a finger in it 196:32
such a King H. 189:8
young H., with his beaver on 440:18
Harsh: cygnet's down is h. 480:39
good are so h. to the clever 572:23
h. cadence of a rugged line 193:11
not h., and crabbed 340:24
not h. nor grating 582:1
out of tune and h. 434:14
sweet revenge grows h. 473:17
whose manners were futile and h. 312:15
words of Mercury are h. 456:2
your berries h. and crude 342:10
Harshness: no h. gives offence 382:32
Hart: as pants the h. 527:1
as the h. desireth the water-brooks 394:16
forest to this h. 450:9
here wast thou bay'd, brave h. 450:9
lame man leap up as an h. 54:3
like to a..young h. 52:25
was I turn'd into a h. 481:31
Harum, scarum, Divo 370:5
Harumfrodite: kind of a giddy h. 301:20
Harvest: according to the joy in h. 53:14
all the H. that I reap'd 206:12
as snow in h. 476:17
beneath the h. moon 183:13
doth h. no harm 550:2
grassy h. of the river-fields 18:29
grow together until the h. 59:27
h. is past 55:16
h. of a quiet eye 578:34
h. truly is plenteous 58:45
like a stubble-land at h. home 438:32
no h. but a thorn 244:9
seed its h. 285:1
seedtime and h. 44:41
share my h. 253:21
she laughs with a h. 269:15
there of the last H. 207:6
thin h. 165:17
white already to h. 63:14
yields Thee h. 544:27
Harvest-fields: Thy h. be dunged with..death 544:27

Harvest-home: song of H. 4:11
Harvests of Arretium 323:12
Harwich: in a steamer from H. 219:10
Has beens: one of the h. 252:9
Hasdrubale: nominis H. interempto 260:23
Haslemere: good beer at H. 42:12
Hast: thou h. it now 458:30
Hast: ohne H., aber ohne Rast 224:8
Haste: always in h...never in a hurry 565:18
bid h. the evening star 348:38
fiery-red with h. 474:29
h. of a fool 422:30
h. to rise up early 399:35
h. still pays h. 462:26
h. thee Nymph 341:28
h. you, sad notes 123:22
he that maketh h. to be rich 50:50
I h. me to my bed 486:23
I said in my h. 399:7
make h., my beloved 52:25
make h. to die 263:18
make h. to shed innocent blood 54:38
marry'd in h. 155:32
men love in h. 116:44
mounting in hot h. 113:30
oh, make h.! 206:20, 21
raw H., half-sister to Delay 535:23
repent in h. 155:32
this sweaty h. 430:13
we weep to see you h. away 246:2
what h. I can to be gone 167:14
whither doth h. the nightingale 125:10
why such h.? 215:25
with despatchful looks in h. 348:8
with like h. 172:9
ye shall eat it in h. 45:47
Hasten: h. slowly 517:21
h. to be drunk 192:8
minutes h. to their end 487:24
still h. to a close 159:16
Hasting: full sails h. loaden home 332:10
Hasty: man in his h. days 81:9
Hat: away went h. and wig 160:1
ball into the grounded h. 164:8
beneath your h. 370:9
blind man..looking for a black h. 79:8
brushes his h. a mornings 468:31
chip h. had she on 287:4
h. of antique shape 18:8
his h. in his hand 277:10
in a shocking bad h. 518:32
live by pulling off the h. 231:25
my h. and wig will soon be here 160:5
my knee, my h., and hand 86:2
ne'er pull your h. upon your brows 460:20
no h. upon his head 432:35
Parsee from whose h. 304:20
pass the h. for your credit's sake 294:20
runcible h. 311:11
where did you get that h.? 408:17
with my h. caved in 210:13
with my h. upon my head 277:10
without pulling off his h. 271:6
your h. has got a hole in't 124:7
Hatched: chickens ere th' are h. 111:6
h. different 196:8
h., would..grow mischievous 449:4
Hatches: continually under h. 289:32
Hatchet: I did it with my little h. 560:28
Hatcheth them not 55:21
Hatching vain empires 345:25
Hatchment: no trophy, sword, nor h. 436:37
Hatchments: Arms and H., Resurgam 542:35
Hate: calumny and h. and pain 492:7
cherish those hearts that h. thee 446:31
delicious to h. you 357:4
dower'd with the h. of h. 537:40
English began to h. 294:30
enough religion to make us h. 520:38
fools to h. 521:25
glance of supernatural h. 119:21
h. a Frenchman as you h. the devil 362:16
h. all that don't love me 203:19

INDEX

Hate (cont.)
h. for arts 385:29
h. him as I do hell-pains 469:34
h. of those ye guard 303:26
h. that which we often fear 423:31
h. the traitor 168:4
h. your neighbour 325:18
haughty Juno's unrelenting h. 194:29
I h. a fool 175:33
I h. all Boets and Bainters 216:10
I h. him for he is a Christian 463:17
I h. the crowd 309:7
I h. the French 226:29
I have seen much to h. here 339:7
immortal h. 344:14
in love, or in h. 514:24
let them also that h. him flee 396:4
love and desire and h. 187:11
love what I h. 95:20
make brothers and sisters h. each other 269:33
men h. one another so damnably 335:19
murder, h., virtue, and sin 328:2
must h. and death return? 493:27(-494)
need not to be h. 113:46
no h. lost between us 338:17
nor love thy life, nor h. 349:25
not in our power to love or h. 330:13
nought did I in h. 473:34
owe no man h. 427:27
principally I h...that animal called Man 519:32
reason to h. and to despise myself 239:22
roughness breedeth h. 26:26
scarcely h. anyone...we know 240:11
smile to those who h. 118:15
sourest and most deadly h. 475:5
sprung from my only h. 477:11
they who h. me may see it 397:12
those fellows h. us 307:18
to the blind Horn's h. 298:28
traitor h. 170:20
vain pomp..I h. ye 446:24
ye profane; I h. ye all 158:24
Hated: brute I h. so 90:22
death have we h. 359:3
h., as their age increases 515:24
h. by fools 521:25
h. not learning worse 351:17
he h. a fool and he h. a rogue 276:18
Horace, whom I h. so 114:11
I have ever h. all nations 519:32
loved well because he h. 93:48
not having h...the world enough 239:22
or being h. 297:10
she might have h. 92:35
to be h. needs but to be seen 383:27
Hateful: h. to the nose 267:30
shamed life a h. 462:9
Hater: very good h. 276:18
Hates: extinction of unhappy h. 16:25
feeble h., shadows of h. 15:3
yet others h. 154:28
Hateth: I love God, and h. his brother 70:15
spareth his rod h. his son 50:6
Hath: even that which he h. 60:32
from him that h. not 60:32
h. not, or is not in love 481:7
thing that h. been 50:61
unto every one that h. 60:32
Hatim: H. call to Supper 205:20
H. Tai cry Supper 205:19
Hating: don't give way to h. 297:10
h. no one, loved but only her 114:25
loving not, h. not 90:14
Hatred: envy, h., and malice 388:46
h...the longest pleasure 116:44
healthy h. of scoundrels 126:36
I must have no h. or bitterness 134:2
love to h. turn'd 155:20
stalled ox and h. 50:12
without love, h., joy, or fear 401:29
Hats: so many shocking bad h. 564:5
their h. were o' the birk 33:2
they wat their h. aboon 32:1
Hatta: the other Messenger's called H. 131:15
Hatter: 'can't take *less*', said the H. 129:9
mad-as-a-h.-day 243:5

Haughtiness: rank pride, and h. of soul 1:16
Haughty: Byron bore with h. scorn 16:8
frank, h., rash 322:9
h. Juno's unrelenting hate 194:29
h. spirit before a fall 50:15
h., vigilant, resolute,..blue-stocking 324:35
insolent Greece or h. Rome 281:15
that h., gallant, gay Lothario 412:9
Haul: gentleman to h...with the mariner 189:1
Haunch: in the h. of winter 442:24
Haunt: all the h. be ours 425:22
exempt from public h. 426:30
h. of ancient Peace 537:36
Mind of Man—my h. 574:7
murmurous h. of flies 287:31
Oh the weary h. for me 293:4
so h. thy days 287:3
to h. thy sleep 171:20
to h., to startle 580:19
Haunted: beneath a waning moon was h. 151:32
h. by the ghosts they have de-pos'd 475:7
h. for ever by the eternal mind 576:13
h., holy ground 113:19
h. town to me 309:23
shape of a woman has h. me 290:5
sounding cataract h. me 581:26
Haunts: desire, that h. our dreams 81:19
h. meet for thee 15:15
h. of coot and hern 528:5
h. of horror and fear 536:22
in the busy h. of men 241:15
Hause-bane: ye'll sit on his white h. 32:15
Hautboys: Gibbon moved to flutes and h. 154:13
now gives the h. breath 191:3
Hauteur: Satan..with more h. 119:24
Have: for all we h. and are 296:19
h. it when they know it not 521:24
h. more than thou showest 452:25
House of H. 216:9
I am content with what I h. 99:31
if I dream I h. you, I h. you 184:17
if you h. it [charm] 36:15
I h. thee not 457:20
I h. 't: it is engender'd 470:23
in quest to h. 488:12
such as I h. give I thee 64:27
that we gave we h. 10:5
thou'dst h., great Glamis 457:1
thus thou must do, if thou h. it 457:1
to h. and to hold 391:30
whatever you h., spend less 275:5
what wee gave wee h. 11:17
what we h. been..what we are 196:21
what we h. we prize not 469:5
where ask is h. 503:5
Have-his-carcase 179:27
Havelock: pipes o' H. sound 568:19
Haven: h. where they would be rowing home to h. 333:20
safe into the h. guide 565:5
swim the h. at Dunkirk 281:19
their h. under the hill 528:3
Have-nots: the Haves and the H. 134:14
Havens: in the h. dumb 254:29
ports and happy h. 474:19
Haves: the H. and the Have-nots 134:14
Having: choke their service.. with the h. 426:38
had, h. and in quest to have 488:12
h. been must ever be 576:20
lest, h. Him 544:15
your flattery is worth his h. 277:14
Havoc: cry, 'H.!' 450:12
h. did not slack 122:5
Hawk: after the old ones by the h. are kill'd 375:9
Dan'l Whiddon, Harry H. 33:1
falcon or h. of the tower 502:17
h. at eagles with a dove 245:4
his h., his hound, and his lady 32:15
his h. to fetch the wild-fowl 32:15
I know a h. from a handsaw 433:20
no h., no banquet 245:2
wild h. stood 538:2
wild h. to the..sky 296:29

Hawked: by a mousing owl h. at 458:28
Hawks: all haggard h. will stoop 305:12
Hawthorn: h. bush a sweeter shade 446:2
h. hedge puts forth 83:17
under the h. in the dale 341:34
when h. buds appear 466:21
Hawthorn-brake: this h. our tiring-house 467:2
Hay: dance an antic h. 329:20
good h., sweet h., hath no fellow 467:15
great desire to a bottle of h. 467:15
lie tumbling in the h. 485:16
mangerful of h. 409:22
nothing like eating h. 131:16
when husbands win their h. 30:5
with my love in the scented h. 82:13
world is a bundle of h. 117:31
worth a load of h. 5:17
Haycock: under the h. fast asleep 367:15
Haydn: some cry up H. 307:25
Hayley: H. does pretend 74:16
when H. finds out 74:18
Hayrick: your h. 'ead of 'air 296:23
Haystack: beside the h. in the floods 359:4
Hazael: him that escapeth the sword of H. 48:9
Hazard: h. in the glorious enterprise 344:12
h. of concealing 105:19
he has put to h. his ease 101:21
his father's crown into the h. 443:11
men that h. all 463:39
stand the h. of the die 476:43
Hazar-ho: kul, an' h. 295:22
Hazel: flower of the h. glade 232:19
Hazel-nut: her chariot is an empty h. 477:7
Hazlitt: I was at H.'s marriage 307:11
we cannot write like H. 515:8
He: cannot be that I am h. 244:18
every h. has got him a she 5:25
h. for God only 347:11
h. that is down..h. that is low 99:31
H. whom thou seekest 544:31
h. who would valiant be 99:35
let's eat h. 543:9
poorest h...as the greatest h. 405:6
that I am h. 449:30
yonge fresshe folkes, h. or she 138:42
Head: after his h. was cut off 8:3
Alexander at the h. of the world 558:9
apples drop about my h. 332:17
as gently lay my h. 87:1
as if her h. she bowed 341:14
at his h. a grass-green turf 436:20
at the h. of a school 558:9
bear with a sore h. 331:17
behind her golden h. 336:7
binds so dear a h. 491:14
blessings on your h. 161:18
bowed his comely h. 332:25
breaking Priscian's h. 111:21
break Priscian's h. 381:21
broke any man's h. but his own 444:1
broken h. in Cold Bath Fields 326:9
bruising of the hapless h. 561:16
closed o'er the h. of..Lycidas 342:17
cod's h. for the salmon's tail 470:29
complicated monsters, h. and tail 349:21
covered my h. in the day of battle 400:12
cover my defenceless h. 565:7
cowslip's velvet h. 341:4
crown old Winter's h. 166:20
cuts the wrong man's h. off 178:39
cutt'st my h. off with a golden axe 478:23
disdains to hide his h. 231:32
excellent h. of hair 482:7
except with bent h. 95:37
fame over his living h. 492:11
fit to snore his h. off 130:22
for a man with heart, h., hand 535:43
for Chartres' h. reserve the..wall 384:5
forward bends his h. 148:24
gently falling on thy h. 562:1
get one's h. cut off 130:24
God be in my h. 6:10
God shall wound the h. of his enemies 396:10

[753]

Head (*cont.*)
good grey h. 537:14
gorgonised me from h. to foot 536:5
ground..hit me in the h. 560:12
hair uplifted from the h. 413:16
hand, the h. and the heart 496:6
hang the pensive h. 342:31(-343)
h. and front of my offending 469:45
h. fantastically carved 442:15
h. grown grey in vain 492:7
h., heart and hand 295:8
h. is not more native 430:25
h. keeps turnin' back 319:27
h. like a concertina 295:3
h. of a family off 178:24
h. of the gallows-tree 294:28
h. of the literary profession 181:24
h...of truths 574:22
h. so old and white as this 453:6
H. that once 291:18
h. to contrive 145:26, 217:11
h. which statuaries loved to copy 325:14
her fair vast h. 522:12
her h. on her knee 473:6
hers is the h. 374:10
hide her drowsy h. 169:12
his bare h...endur'd 453:34
his guts in his h. 481:10
his h. and his hairs were white 70:27
his h. not yet..completely silver'd 163:5
his h. under his wing 368:2
his h. upon the lap of Earth 230:13
his h. with his legs 45:46
his heart runs away with his h. 154:15
his left hand is under my h. 51:45
his Majesty's h. on a sign-post 325:16
his shoulders and his heavy h. 562:3
hovering o'er the place's h. 166:3
ideas of its 'h.' 29:3
if she'd but turn her h. 585:5
if you can keep your h. 297:10
I'll eat my h. 177:40
I'll give you my h. 13:17
in the heart or in the h.? 464:13
I strove, made h. 95:17
it had it h. bit off 452:27
it shall bruise thy h. 44:25
John A. Logan is the H. Centre 83:2
kingly crowned h. 429:3
knock at a star with my exalted h. 246:20
knocked Mr. Toots about the h. 175:12
lifts up his burning h. 486:12
like God's own h. 149:2
little gold h. 339:19
make a h...out of a brass knob 175:36
make you shorter by the h. 198:4
man with the h. 538:24
mother's h. off 178:24
my deeds upon my h. 465:1
my hat upon my h. 277:10
my h. is a map 204:23
my h. is bending low 210:17
my h. is bloody 241:18
my h. is twice as big 160:7
my h. is wild with weeping 493:19
my h. thou dost with oil anoint 421:1
my needless h. 545:9
my parboiled h. upon a stake 355:21
my project gather to a h. 480:11
nail my h. on yonder tower 24:5
no bigger than his h. 454:3
no room at my h. 30:16
not of the h., but heart 118:5
not where to lay his h. 58:34
no wool on de top of his h. 210:18
off with his h.! 129:13, 144:26, 476:22
one small h. 225:2
out of King Charles's h. into my h. 174:27
patted my God on the h. 302:29
potato in his h. 237:24
put leaves round his h. 176:2
repairs his drooping h. 343:3
rosy garland and a weary h. 501:27
shake of his poor little h. 220:18
she has the h. 174:1
singe my white h. 453:5
small h. and nostril wide 488:27
some crotchets in thy h. 465:36

Head (*cont.*)
some once lovely H. 206:3
Spain forming a h. 235:22
stamps o'er his H. 206:1, 2
stand 'On my h.' 181:27
sunk so low that sacred h. 342:25
suspicious h. of theft 455:22
take lodgings in a h. 110:14
their h. the prow 191:29
this old gray h. 568:14
through headpiece and through h. 324:9
thumped him on the h. 131:23
thy h. is as full of quarrels 478:11
thy poor h. almost turns 17:22
thy weary h. upon this breast 316:20
to deck her mistress' h. 119:3
to keep your h. 402:25
to play golf ye maun hae a h. 326:16
trample on their sovereign's h. 475:10
trickled through my h. 131:22
turn his h. as if he said 171:21
two separate sides to my h. 303:10
uneasy lies the h. 442:3
violet's reclining h. 184:29
we bow'd our h. 16:21
what seem'd his h. 346:4
wherefore should I busk my h.? 32:18
which way the h. lies 405:15
whole h. is sick 52:27
whose h. proud fancy never taught 164:33
why not upon my h.? 475:10
with a white h. 441:21
with h., hands, wings 346:14
with its h. 129:39(-130)
with monstrous h. 140:21
with so old a h. 464:32
you incessantly stand on your h. 128:28
your royal h. may fall 140:10
Headache: awake with a dismal h. 219:9
today I happen to have a h. 130:25
Head-in-air: Johnny H. 250:2, 402:24
Headland: naked top of some bold h. 574:11
Headlong: cast herself h. 350:17
hail to the H.! 376:22
h. from on board 159:1
h. joy is ever on the wing 350:19
h. themselves they threw down 348:22
hurled h. flaming 344:7
Headpiece: through h. and through head 324:9
Heads: beast with many h. 429:15
billows..hung their h. 446:18
carve h. upon cherry-stones 275:21
curling their monstrous h. 442:1
Dean and Canons lay their h. together 505:12
empty h. and tongues a-talking 263:18
facts..stood them on their h. 36:5
h. do grow beneath their shoulders 470:2
h., h.! 178:24
h. I win 167:1
h. replete with thoughts of other men 163:49
hills whose h. touch heaven 470:2
in their restless h. 331:2
lift up your h., O ye gates 393:12
monster with uncounted h. 441:8
our h. are bowed with woe 339:11
pigging together, h. and points 100:8
pillars rear their marble h. 155:19
stars hide their diminished h. 346:29
tall men..empty h. 24:38
their h. all in nightcaps 127:5
their h. are green 311:21
their h. are hung with ears 467:20
their h. never raising 577:20
this dreadful pother o'er our h. 453:9
your houseless h. 453:14
Head-stone: become the h. in the corner 399:11
Headstrong: as h. as an allegory 500:21
h., moody, murmuring race 190:10
Head-waiter: one became h. 541:23
plump h. at the Cock 541:20
Heady: such a h. currance 443:6
Heal: adjust, amend, and h. 236:28
fame can never h. 23:25
h. it, if it be 161:5

Heal (*cont.*)
h. me of my grievous wound 531:37
none to h. it 289:8
physician, h. thyself 61:25
Healed: convert, and be h. 53:10
had h. it for ever 316:16
h. by the same means 464:8
when wounded, h. thy wound 161:10
with his stripes we are h. 54:26
Healeth: he h. those that are broken 400:21
Healing: h. in his wings 56:15, 161:21
h. of the nations 72:7
of the most High cometh h. 57:10
Wordsworth's h. power 16:23
Health: art so far from my h. 393:1
be thou a spirit of h. 431:32
by His h., sickness 77:2
double h. to thee 118:14
fence against the infirmities of ill h. 512:32
for h. unbought 192:15
h. and high fortune 417:28
h. is the second blessing 559:26
h. of the whole state 431:21
h. on both 459:13
h. to all those that we love 6:21
h. to King Charles 420:25
hunger..a medicine for h. 549:22
I have nor hope nor h. 498:24
in h. and wealth long to live 388:28
in h., in sickness 279:7
innocence and h. 224:14
long sickness of h. and living 480:30
look to your h. 559:26
not good for the Christian's h. 300:6
sound and pristine h. 461:1
sweet dreams and h. 284:19
take care of their h. 22:18
that h. and wealth have missed me 265:25(-266)
there is no h. in us 388:11
thine h. shall spring forth 54:37
this h. deny 195:16
thy saving h. among all nations 396:2
voice of joy and h. 399:8
wisdom breathed by h. 581:16
Healthful: h. Spirit of thy grace 388:30
no h. ease 253:12
Healthiest: city of the h. fathers 567:8
Healths: drink our h. at dinner 295:9
h. and draughts go free 319:6
h. five fathom deep 477:7
Healthy: h. by temperance 386:4
h., free, the world before me 568:3
h. hatred of scoundrels 126:36
imagination of a boy is h. 284:18
kind of h. grave 505:35
plump and hearty, h. boy 249:18
without disease the h. life 518:1
Heap: h. on himself damnation 344:20
h. on more wood 418:23
one h. of all your winnings 297:11
struck all of a h. 500:11
thy belly is like an h. of wheat 52:18
wailers h. 88:26
Heaped: error be too highly h. 429:9
Heaps: h. of couch-grass 236:14
in h. they run 194:24
in the h. they raise 384:4
unsunned h. 340:21
Hear: abuse..always sure to h. of it 499:25
all that h. me this day 65:27
another to h. 547:3
at my back I always h. 333:9
be swift to h. 69:30
but to h. a story 191:19
Caesar is turn'd to h. 448:10
cannot choose but h. 148:20
come on and h. 43:16
deaf, and does not h. 382:10
destroyer and healer, h. 524:21
destroyer and preserver, h., oh, h.! 496:4
did ye not h. it? 113:26
dinna ye h. it 568:19
do any man's heart good to h. me 466:29
do you not h. the Aziola? 492:22
ears, and h. not 399:4

INDEX

Hear (*cont.*)

few love to h. the sins 474:6
good news yet to h. 141:24
h. each other groan 287:25
h. her tender-taken breath 288:18
h. his word 161:9
h. it not, Duncan 458:1
h., know, and say 84:6
h. no more at all 516:10
h. not my steps 458:1
h. our noble England's praise 322:17
h. Sordello's story told 96:29
h. the hammers ring 294:22
h. the larks so high 262:21(-263)
h. them, read, mark, learn 389:23
h. the voice of the Bard 75:23
h. the voice of the charmer 395:20
h. thy guardian angel 198:19
h. us, our handmaid unheeding 372:18
h. what comfortable words 390:37
h. what he had to say 127:25
he that hath ears to h., let him
  h. 60:55
I h. a smile 167:16
I h. a voice you cannot h. 547:21
I h., I h. 536:15
I h. it in the deep heart's core 585:12
I h. thee and rejoice 573:19
I h. you, I will come 263:2
I long to h. you 8:21
lest they..h. with their ears 53:10
Lord, h. my voice 399:38
Lord, h. our prayers 391:18
loves to h. himself talk 478:6
make me h. of joy and gladness 395:8
man that must h. me 150:12
music that I care to h. 254:26
none h. beside the singer 308:15
now I h. them 479:30
O hark, O h.! 538:15
risen to h. him crow 196:13
scarce could they h. 418:29
shall he not h.? 397:24
she will not h. 524:25
snorer can't h. himself snore 550:26
so are those who h. me 560:18
still must I h.? 117:8
still stood fixed to h. 348:29
tempting sounds I h. 78:3
that I h. the foules singe 138:16
the Lord h. thee in the day of
  trouble 392:35
they h. the Word 302:3
they never would h. 521:6
to h. again the call 516:10
to h. some new thing 64:59
to h. the angels sing 421:10
to h. those things which ye h. 61:38
to h., was wonder 189:7
unfit to h. moral philosophy 481:13
water shall h. me 507:14
we do h. them speak in our
  tongues 64:26
we cannot h. it 465:18
we shall h. it by and by 89:10
what do I see and h.? 6:17
when you will h. me 180:13
will you h. or know? 525:32
wished for to h. 292:5
ye must not h. him 3:18
yet I h. thy shrill delight 498:4
yours to h. 504:8
Heard: all who h. 151:33(-152)
cannot be h. so high 454:3
eloquence is h. 339:4
enough that he h. it once 89:10
have ye not h.? 54:13
h. for their much speaking 58:3
h., not regarded 440:9
h. of Philip Slingsby 24:9
h. Sordello's story told 96:35
h. through all spheres 410:16
he h. it, but he heeded not 114:19
his former name is h. no more 348:17
his prayer shall be h. 56:33
if you've the East a-callin' 299:13
I have h., I hear thee 573:19
I have h. of thee 49:33
I h. her tears 410:14
I never h. till now 340:16
isn't generally h. 222:12

Heard (*cont.*)

I've h. them lilting 198:18
I will be h. 213:17
knowing none would be h...so
  oft 80:24
long after it was h. no more 581:4
more he h. the less he spoke 403:22
not so much as h...any Holy
  Ghost 65:5
one ere it h. 138:36
only h. one side of the case 112:3
only tell us what he h. 231:23
our name is h. no more 160:30
shot h. round the world 199:7
since I h. thee last 160:25
then is h. no more 461:4
they h. and were abashed 344:27
they h. the voice of the Lord God 44:21
this I have h. men say 302:25
trumpet shall be h. on high 191:39
twice I have also h. the same 395:24
voice of the turtle is h. 52:1
we have h. with our ears 389:10
what never yet was h. 340:3
when complaints are freely h. 352:4
when she is sung and h. 157:5
while earth h. in dread 503:3
who hath ever h.? 81:2
wish'd she had not h. it 470:3
ye have read, ye have h. 302:24
you ain't h. nothin' yet 279:17
Hearer: charmed h. 546:9
h. of the word 69:33
Hearers: never want..favour-
  able h. 253:35
not h. only 69:32
too deep for his h. 225:27
Hearest: thou h. not 393:1
thou h. the sound thereof 63:7
thou h. the prayer 395:27
Heareth: ear of jealousy h. all 56:21
ears of every one that h. it 47:7
him that h. say, Come 72:10
thy servant h. 47:6
Hearing: by the h. of the ear 49:33
h. die 446:18
h. ear 50:26
h., thinking, writing 240:13
lover's ears in h. 417:34
make passionate my sense of h. 455:6
nor the ear filled with h. 50:61
their names..in your h. 23:4
Hearken: h. ere I die 537:31
h., Lady Betty, h. 13:18
h., O daughter 394:23
h. unto a Verser 243:25
to h. than the fat of rams 47:16
Hearkened: O that thou hadst h. 54:20
Hearkens after it 186:25
Hears: ear of him that h. it 455:34
for He h. 529:38
she neither h. nor sees 573:6
Hearsay: I have formerly lived by h. 99:40
Hearse: laureate h. where Lycid
  lies 342:31(-343)
to crown thy h. 292:18
underneath this sable h. 87:24
walk before the h. 213:8
Hearsed in death 431:32
Heart: absence makes the h. grow
  fonder 5:3, 36:28
all that mighty h...still 582:14
all the h. and the soul 96:21
all thy h. lies open 539:2
any h. now share in my emotion 498:23
apple rotten at the h. 463:19
as a seal upon thine h. 52:22
as if you entered gay my h. 91:35
as my poor h. doth think 321:19
as well as want of h. 253:4
awake, my h., to be loved 80:11
bad liver, and a worse h. 324:30
batter my h. 185:18
beating of my own h. 262:9
beat..of thy h. 411:10
because my h. is pure 540:11
betray the h. that loved her 582:3
bitter h. that bides its time 90:15
borrow h.'s lightness 285:3
bread to strengthen man's h. 398:9
bring with you a h. 581:16

Heart (*cont.*)

broke his h. in Clermont 40:18
broken and contrite h. 395:10
broken h. lies here 323:9
broken h...nae second spring 9:8
bruised h...pierced through the
  ear 470:7
butcher..that his h. bleeds 270:35
call home the h. 189:14
careful soul and the troubled h. 302:1
Christian at her h. 381:10
cleft my h. in twain 436:4
cold untroubled h. of stone 122:32
command my h. and me 166:17
commune with your own h. 391:52
consenting language of the h. 215:11
corruption of Man's H. 91:34
counsellor h. 429:3
Cruelty has a human h. 77:4
cure thine h. of love 38:23
curst be the h. 31:3
darling of my h. 125:17
day breaks not..my h. 184:10
deceiveth his own h. 69:34
did not our h. burn within us? 62:55
dissemble in their double h. 392:20
do any man's h. good to hear me 466:29
drops that visit my sad h. 449:17
ease its h. of love in 286:9
ease thine h. of love 38:22
Englishman whose h. is in a
  matter 28:30
enrich my h., mouth, hands 245:9
enrich not the h. of another 316:14
every living h. and hearthstone 314:10
every lusty h. beginneth to
  blossom 328:15
every warbler has his tune by h. 162:28
faint h. ne'er wan a lady 104:22
faint h. never won fair lady 219:14
fare thee well, great h. 440:38
feed the h. of the night 524:13
felt along the h. 581:23
find 'Calais' lying in my h. 333:15
fire which in the h. resides 16:29
firstlings of my h...of my
  hand 460:15
fleshy tables of the h. 67:21
floodgate of the deeper h. 208:20
for a man with h., head, hand 535:43
for pitee renneth sone in gentil
  h. 137:31
for the unquiet h. 532:4
for Witherington my h. was woe 30:14
found in thine h. to sing 524:11
from the h. of joy 39:6
gathered to thy h. 338:7
gave my h. another youth 488:5
give a loving h. to thee 247:1
give me back my h. 118:6, 229:5
given him his h.'s desire 392:38
gives..his h. and soul away 262:18
giving your h. to a dog 300:22
glad with all my h. 189:20
God be in my h. 6:10
grandeur in the beatings of the
  h. 575:22
grandeurs of his Babylonian h. 544:12
grant thee thy h.'s desire 392:36
great no h. 97:33
great sick h. of a Sir Walter Scott 127:4
grieve his h. 460:10
hand, the head, and the h. 413:16
hardness of h. 388:49
haven't the h. to poke 228:11
head, h., and hand 295:8
healeth those that are broken
  in h. 400:21
h. aboon them a' 108:15
h. and eye both with thy nest 580:26
h. and soul do sing 502:7
h. and stomach of a king 198:11
h. and voice would fail me 35:11
h. as soft..kind..sound and
  free 247:1
h. as sound as a bell 468:28
h. aye's the part aye 105:22
h. benevolent and kind 108:35
h. be still as loving 119:4
h. but one 79:5
h. distrusting 225:5

Heart (cont.)

h. doth need a language 152:10
h. for any fate 317:8
h. for every fate 118:15
h. for falsehood framed 500:10
h...gets his speeches by it 408:13
h. grown cold 492:7
h. handfast in h. 523:15
h. hath ne'er..burn'd 417:22
h. is a small thing 404:4
h. is deceitful 55:20
h. is Highland 420:31
h. knoweth his own bitterness 50:7
h. less bounding 18:30
h. must bear the longest part 243:24
h. must pause to breathe 119:5
h. of a man to the h. of a maid 296:29
h. of a ranger 40:31
h. of England 189:17
h. of Hell 294:28
h. of kings is unsearchable 50:33
h. of my h., were it more 524:33
h. of neither wife nor maid 527:12
h. of oak 213:10
h. of the fool 350:28
h. on h. 89:3
h. out of the bosom 262:17
h. ran o'er 118:10
h. replies 163:48
h.'s denying 35:21
h. that has truly loved 356:13
h. that lives alone 578:16
h. that's broken 417:30
h., the fountain of sweet tears 581:6
h. the Queen leant on 93:33
h. to conceive 282:20
h. to h. 417:21
h. too brave to ask 213:2
h. to pity 143:15
h. to resolve 217:11
h. unfort_ 430:31
h. untainted 445:30
h. whose love is innocent 119:2
h. with English instinct fraught 188:31
h. within and God o'erhead 317:7
heathen h. that puts her trust 301:1
he hardened Pharaoh's h. 45:42
her h. in his grave is lying 356:31
her h. was warm and gay 235:5
hid in the h. of love 585:20
his eyes were with his h. 114:19
his flaw'd h. 454:23
his hand upon many a h. 316:16
his h. kep' goin' pity-pat 319:26
his h. runs away with his head 154:15
his h. should glow 221:20
his h. was hot within him 317:25
his h. *was* true 103:32
his h...wax to receive 112:35
his lost h. was tender 498:20
his manners our h. 225:34
his tiger's h. 232:6
holiness of the h.'s affections 289:17
how ill all 's here about my h. 437:33
how the h. listened 546:9
humble and a contrite h. 300:24
I feel my h.—I can't tell how 11:20
I feel my h. new open'd 446:24
if e'er your h. has felt 215:9
if guilt's in that h. 356:16
if the h. of a man is deprest 214:30
if thy h. fails thee 198:8, 405:11
if your h. be only true 103:32
I hear it in the deep h.'s core 585:12
I'll sell your h.'s desire 296:15
imagination of man's h. is evil 44:40
I my h., safe-left, shall meet 502:3
Indian Summer of the h. 568:18
in her h. she scorns 445:28
in his h. is a blind desire 522:7
in my h. all saints else 232:11
in my h., how I wish him safe 282:10
in my h. of h. 434:26
in my h. of hearts 576:21
in my h. some late lark 241:23
in my h., though not in heaven 244:26
in myn h. have hem in reverence 138:16
in the h. is the prey for gods 525:18
in the h. of a friend 315:25
in the h. or in the head? 464:13
into my h. an air 263:14

Heart (cont.)

I said to H. 41:25
I shall be out of h. shortly 440:11
it dies upon her h. 494:7
I would not have such a h. 460:28
joy in his mighty h. 295:16
knock against my very h. 479:19
knocked on my sullen h. 516:16
knowledge of the h. in..
Richardson 272:12
land of H.'s Desire 585:16
language of his h. 386:13
language of the h. 386:4
languor is not in your h. 17:20
larger h. 533:20
laugh, h., again 584:19
laughing h.'s long peace 84:18
laughter of her h. 235:5
lent out my h...to such scenes 307:5
let no man's h. fail 47:21
let not your h. be troubled 63:50
let thy h. cheer thee 51:32
level in her husband's h. 483:3
lifeless charms, without the h. 214:9
lift up your h. 565:11
light of step and h. 171:6
like a living coal his h. was 317:25
like music on my h. 150:7
little body with a mighty h. 443:13
live without h. 337:41
lock'd my h. in a case o' gowd 32:19
lonely of h. 585:13
look in thy h., and write 501:23
loos'd our h. in tears 16:22
Lord Christ's h. 199:2
loss of thee would never from
my h. 349:18
love gushed from my h. 149:26
majestic force..mov'd the h. 412:13
make me a clean h. 395:9
make the h. of this people fat 53:10
maketh glad the h. 398:9
maketh the h. sick 50:3
man after his own h. 47:13
meditation of my h. 392:34
Mercy has a human h. 77:1
merry h...cheerful countenance 50:11
merry h. doeth good 50:20
merry h. goes all the day 485:20
mine eyes, but not my h. 280:7
mine, with my h. in't 480:1
mountain 'tween my h. and
tongue 449:27
move my faint h. with grief 494:19
much against my h. 375:21
my h. aches 287:22
my h. and my flesh rejoice 397:5
my h. beats loud and fast 494:7
my h. is fast 9:21
my h. is idly stirred 574:33
my h. is like a singing bird 409:14
my h. is not here 107:12
my h. is on me sleeve 141:10
my h. is sair 105:34
my h. is sick of woe 83:3
my h. is turned to stone 472:25
my h. leaps up 577:25
my h. moved more than with a
trumpet 502:9
my h. of gold 6:18
my h. puts forth its pain 83:17
my h. remembers how 516:9
my h.'s abhorrence 96:38
my h.'s in the Highlands
107:12, 420:24
my h.'s right there 571:1
my h.'s subdu'd..to..my lord 470:9
my h.'s undoing 356:32
my h...the faithful compass 215:40
my h. thy home 498:16
my h. trobling to my throat 551:13
my h. untravelled 226:4
my h. upon my sleeve 469:28
my h. waketh 52:9
my h. was hot within me 394:8
my h. with pleasure fills 577:7
my h. would hear her 536:15
my life, my love, my h. 247:4
my seated h. knock at my ribs 456:24
my true love hath my h. 501:19
my very h. and flesh cry out 421:3

Heart (cont.)

my whole h. rises up 92:31
naked thinking h. 184:9
natural language of the h. 422:27
nearer God's H. in a garden 233:17
nearer to the H.'s Desire 207:26
nerves a nation's h. 528:12
never at h.'s ease 448:27
never give all the h. 584:24
never go from my h. 328:11
never has ached with a h. 522:25
Noble h...can never rest 509:23
no longer tear his h. 521:27
no matter from the h. 481:29
nor his h. to report 467:23
not more native to the h. 430:25
not of the head, but h. 118:5
not your h. away 262:15
now cracks a noble h. 438:7
nowhere beats the h. so kindly 23:17
no woman's h. so big 483:9
obey thy h. 199:12
O h., be at peace 584:3
O h.! O h.! 585:5
O make this h. rejoice 161:5
once the young h. of a maiden
is stolen 356:23
on Hero's h. Leander lies 264:5
on my h. they tread 475:10
on the blind side of the h. 140:16
open my h. 91:6
open not thine h. to every man 56:38
O that man's h. were as fire
521:30(-522)
O true, brave h. 187:1
our being's h. and home 579:27
our h. cannot be quieted 21:16
out of the abundance of the h. 59:14
out-worn h. 584:19
O world! the h. of thee 450:9
pageant of his bleeding h. 16:8
passionate h. of the poet 535:37
pastoral h. of England 404:22
pluck out the h. of my mystery 435:24
poor h. would fain deny 460:36
possess thy h., my own 82:11
pourest thy full h. 498:1
pure in h. 57:39, 291:13, 14
put his h. to school 573:5
red pavilion of my h. 543:17
red-ripe of the h. 95:35
religion's in the h. 269:8
revolting and a rebellious h. 55:12
roaming with a hungry h. 540:32
room my h. keeps empty 202:19
rose in the deeps of my h. 585:17
round his h. one..hair 411:11
sad h. of Ruth 288:1
same h. beats 15:5
seated in the h. of courtesy 501:16
secret anniversaries of the h. 318:3
seeing, shall take h. again 317:8
see thy h.'s desire 81:25
send me back my h. 517:16
service of a mind and h. 575:15
set not your h. upon them 395:24
shaft that quiver'd in his h. 117:25
Shakespeare unlocked his h.
92:19, 580:16
she wants a h. 384:33
should you need nor h. nor
hands 516:1
shut not thy h., nor thy library 306:24
sighing of a contrite h. 389:8
sigh that rends thy constant h. 225:14
since man's h. is small 302:13
sinews of thy h. 75:24(-76)
sink h. and voice opprest 362:1
sleep in old England's h. 562:21
sleeps on his own h. 578:34
smitten to the h. 503:3
sole daughter of my house and
h. 113:21
so long as the human h. is strong 28:29
some h. did break 532:6
some h. indignant breaks 356:21
sorrows of my h. 393:15
so the h. be right 405:15
speaks to the h. alone 128:3
stabb'd me to the h. 214:12
stay at home, my h. 317:18

INDEX

Heart (*cont.*)

steady of h. 417:9
stirred the h. of every Englishman 416:7
stout h., and open hand 418:9
strong h. of her sons 188:32
such idleness so near the h. 423:38
sure of his unspotted h. 377:4
sweet concurrence of the h. 247:19
ta'en out thy h. o' flesh 32:5
take any h., take mine 221:30
take h. of grace 221:29
taming my wild h. 468:27
tear out your h. 299:22
tears out the h. of it 305:4
tell me, my h. 322:6
thanks to the human h. 576:22(–577)
that earth upon thy h. 295:5
that h. I'll give to thee 247:1
their captain, the h. 442:21
their h. is in their boots 141:11
the Lord looketh on the h. 47:18
then burst his mighty h. 450:31
there are strings..in the human h. 173:20
there will your h. be 58:7
thine h. be full of the spring 524:11
think, this h. 84:21
this h...to be long lov'd 15:20
thou break'st my h. 244:11
thou hast my h. 401:21
thou voice of my h. 166:24
throe of the h. 81:19
through a broken h. 569:12
through good h. 417:11
through..harness to my h. 425:12
thy beak from out my h. 380:27
thy fair hair my h. enchained 501:22
thy h. against thy side 301:28
thy h. the lowliest duties 577:15
thy h. with..innocencies fill'd 375:9
tiger's h. wrapp'd in a woman's hide 445:43
till my h. was like to break 35:9
till that myn h. dye 138:18
to eat thy h. 510:16
to mend the h. 381:6
to my dead h. 516:16
true for you in your private h. 200:36
try out my reins and my h. 393:17
twice broken His great h. 313:5
understand with their h. 53:10
vacant h. and hand 419:16
waited for the h.'s prompting 196:24
Ward has no h. 408:13
warm h. within 160:12
waste his whole h. in one kiss 540:13
watched my foolish h. expand 90:31
weak hands though mighty h. 491:27
wear him in my h.'s core 434:26
weighs upon the h. 460:37
were not my h. at rest 421:16
what can a tired h. say? 171:4
what female h. can gold despise? 230:20
what h. could have thought you? 545:12
what..h.'s ease must kings neglect 444:22
what his h. thinks 468:28
what the false h. doth know 457:16
when my h. hath 'scap'd 487:23
when thy h. began to beat 75:24(–76)
where I have garner'd up my h. 472:34
where my h. is turning ebber 210:16
where my h. lies 94:7
where my h. was used to beat 532:8
whether man's h. or life 544:27
whispers the o'er-fraught h. 460:20
whole h. faint 52:27
Whom we have by h. 338:10
whose fresh complexion and whose h. 485:33
whose guiltless h. is free 123:23
windy tempest of my h. 446:3
win my h. from me 535:8
winning each h. 173:12
wish my h. had never known ye 9:21
wish thine own h. dry 287:3
with a h. of fire 536:24
with a h. of furious fancies 12:2
with h. and hand and voices 571:21
with h. and soul and voice 361:18
with women the h. argues 16:26

Heart (*cont.*)

woman with the h. 538:24
wounded is the wounding h. 165:27
yearning h. for astrolabe 525:16
your h.'s desires be with you 426:21
Heart-ache: say we end the h. 434:4
Heart-easing: most h. things 288:16
Heartfelt: contented with our h. sympathy 221:3
Hearth: alights on the warm h. 546:26
by this still h. 540:31
clear fire, a clean h. 306:12
cricket on the h. 341:16
from an unextinguished h. 496:11
genial h. 578:13
no more the blazing h. 229:31
vanished from his lonely h. 575:17
woman for the h. 538:24
Hearths: quenched seven smoking h. 419:29
Hearth-stone: every living heart and h. 314:10
h. at Ellangowan 419:29
his clean h. 104:33
light of his own h. 302:27
Heartily: h. know 199:14
to my Lord h. 316:32
Hearts: all that human h. endure 278:29
any h. to beat 585:22
at their h. the fire's centre 509:1
boldest of h. 95:35
brave h. and clean 531:8
but our h. are great 531:3
cheerful h. now broken 357:13
clasp we to our h. 410:30
conserv'd of maidens' h. 472:15
creeds that move men's h. 83:9
crucify h., not hands 525:18
dear h. across the seas 297:14
Dons with h. of gold 41:32
ensanguin'd h. 163:29
enthroned in the h. of kings 464:33
equal temper of heroic h. 541:3
finite h. that yearn 97:12
hands not h. 472:14
harden not your h. 397:29
h. are brave again 264:9
h. at peace 84:21
h. just as pure and fair 219:2
h. of controversy 448:19
h. of men..may lift themselves 510:14
h. of oak 20:20
h. of old gave hands 472:14
h. of truest mettle 262:5
h. that once beat high 356:20
h. that spaniel'd me 425:17
h. unwounded sing again 299:24
H. was her favourite suit 306:13
h. which near each other move 493:22
home-keeping h. are happiest 317:18
if young h. were not so clever 263:18
in all the people's h. 449:1
incline our h. to keep this law 390:6
in retiring draw h. after them 350:1
in the h. of his fellow-citizens 312:25
in the h. of mighty Poets 574:9
in the imagination of their h. 61:14
I've heard of h. unkind 580:24
jining of h. and housekeepings 177:42
kind h. are more than coronets 533:38
Knave of H. 129:27, 368:15
live in h. we leave 122:15
men with splendid h. 84:12
neither have the h. to stay 111:15
nor helps good h. 170:24
numbers pluck their h. from them 444:24
offspring of cold h. 102:15
only joined when h. agree 229:8
opposed free h., free foreheads 541:3
other lips and other h. 98:22
our hands..not our h. 253:30
our h. bid the tyrants defiance 123:6
our h. may surely there be fixed 389:38
our h., though stout and brave 317:6
our h. were fulfilled 525:2
O valiant h. 14:20
O you hard h. 448:8
pav'd with broken h. 318:26
plighter of high h. 425:4
prizes to those who have stout h. 72:25

Hearts (*cont.*)

pure eyes and Christian h. 291:12
Queen of H. 129:27, 368:15
simple song for thinking h. 575:12
sing to find your h. 208:9
steal away your h. 450:32
streaming eyes and breaking h.? 535:21
such a woe..as wins more h. 7:13
that eager h. expect 362:5
their hands upon their h. 263:34
their h. are in the right place 182:10
their h. were set on..the moon 377:1
those whose h. are dry 574:14
thousand h. beat happily 113:25
turn the h. of the disobedient 61:11
two fond h...joined 33:11
two h. beating each to each 93:22
union of hands and h. 527:15
unto whom all h. be open 390:4
vizards in their h. 459:5
wand'ring eyes and heedless h. 230:22
we have given our h. away 582:18
what h. have men! 531:13
when h. have once mingled 494:21
while your h. are yearning 210:4
Worldly Hope men set their H. upon 205:27
your image at our h. 147:10
you will wring no more h. 188:7
Heart-sick: Chatham h. 163:2
Heart-strings: her jesses..my dear h. 471:38
I sez to my fluttering' h. 294:25
Heart-throbs: count time by h. 29:9
Heart-whole· I'll warrant him h. 428:18
Hearty: plump and h., healthy boy 249:18
Heat: bear the burden and the h. 17:1
blazing h. of the day 171:21
borne the burden and h. of the day 60:7
burning h. of day 317:17
coolness in the h. 132:2
fantastic summer's h. 474:20
from h... canopy the herd 486:15
h. me these irons hot 447:36
h. of the summer's beginning 372:18
h. o' the sun 430:1
h. the furnace one seven times more 55:39
h. was in the very sod 361:24
measure the h. of our livers 441:18
neither h. nor light 563:15
nor any h. 71:7
nothing hid from the h. thereof 392:32
not without dust and h. 352:9
one h...drive out another 135:22
surprised I was with sudden h. 508:14
through the h. of conflict 575:10
thy h. of pale-mouth'd prophet 288:6
till seven years' h. 481:32
where is that Promethean h. 473:11
Heated: when h. in the chase 527:1
Heath: h...an instalment of night 237:8
h., with..brake o'ergrown 165:17
land of brown h. 417:22
my foot is on my native h. 420:19
nobody..understand the h. 237:9
on the barren h. 74:26
they skim the h. 380:32
upon the h. 456:3
upon this blasted h. 456:17
wind on the h. 78:24
Heathen: counsel of the h. to nought 393:36
h. heart that puts her trust 301:1
h. in his blindness 240:18
h. in 'is blindness 295:21
h. in the carnal part 381:10
h...know themselves..men 392:16
h. make much ado 394:28
machine for converting the H. 125:29
nostalgia of the h. past 310:20
not a H., or a Jew 561:20
on an h. idol's foot 299:11
pokes the h. out 295:21
to break the h. 530:13
why do the h...rage 391:47
you're a pore benighted h. 296:23
Heather: among the h. bright 131:24
bare and broken h. 23:24
in the field of h. 516:4
through the rare red h. 121:15

[757]

Heaths: start some game on these lone h. 240:9
Heat-oppressed brain 457:20
Heave: angels h. up Sir Launcelot 328:23
h. or sink it 298:15
his bosom should h. 221:20
Heaven: above my head the h. 80:15
all H. before mine eyes 341:24
all I seek, the h. above 515:28
all of h. we have below 1:26
all places..hell that are not h. 330:3
all that we believe of h. 371:12
all the choir of h. 43:12
all this and h. too 242:11
all to H. 279:21
all we know of h. 180:3
angels on the walls of h. 331:3
any thing that is in h. above 390:7
as high as H. above 525:36
as it is in h. 58:4
as near to h. by sea 217:24
Astarte, Queen of H. 344:31
at h.'s command 545:18
at h.'s gates she claps her wings 321:16
at h.'s high gate 81:3
azure breath that under H. is blown 494:11
battering the gates of h. 540:8
bask in H.'s blue smile 492:28
beat on H.'s shore 73:26
beauteous eye of h. to garnish 447:39
between Hell and H. 411:32
betwixt H. and Charing Cross 545:1
Brahma from his mystic h. 285:6
brightest h. of invention 443:2
bring up the rear in h. 86:24
bring with thee airs from h. 431:32
brought from H. the news 209:3
calls to H. for human blood 73:20
candidate of h. 192:39
confess yourself to h. 436:2
consent of h. 279:26
corner of h. itself 571:7
crawling between h. and earth 434:9
distant from H. alike 109:20
down from the verge of H. 348:22
earth happy, like the h. above 128:1
earth resteth, h. moveth 244:23
earth's crammed with h. 87:35
even from the gates of h. 99:25
fair H.'s land 415:6
farther off from h. 253:2
Father in H. who lovest all 295:6
fellowship is h. 359:19
fiery-spangled veil of h. 331:2
find out new h., new earth 423:12
find the way to h. 427:6
floor of h. is thick inlaid 465:18
flowerless fields of h. 521:29
from H., or near it 498:1
from h...with the breezes blown 287:29
gain'd from H...a friend 230:13
gazing up into h. 64:22
gentleness of h. 577:1
gentle sleep from H. 149:27
glance from h. to earth 467:24
God created the h. and the earth 431:26
God is in h. 51:6
God's in his h. 94:40
gold bar of H. 410:7
golden chain..from H. to earth 109:24
good enough to go to h. 272:11
heart less native to high H. 544:3
h. and earth are full of thy glory 390:40
h. and earth! must I remember? 430:33(-431)
H. and Hell Amalgamation Society 127:31
H. and Nature..strive 280:10
h. awards the vengeance 158:33
h. be in these lips 330:5
H...comin' clost ter you 511:14
H. did a recompense..send 230:13
h. did not mean 253:21
h. drowsy with the harmony 455:22
h. first taught letters 382:2
h...full of fiery shapes 439:40
h. had made her such a man 470:3
H. had wanted one..song 190:17
H. has no rage 155:20
Heaven (*cont.*)
h. hath my empty words 462:2
H. help him! 323:30
H. in a Wild Flower 73:18
H. in Hell's despair 76:2
h. in her eye 348:36
h. is above all yet 446:19
H. is everywhere at home 141:15
H. is for thee too high 348:31
H. is free from clouds 114:6
h. is music 123:17
H. itself lies here below 166:4
h. itself..points out an hereafter 1:22
h. itself would stoop 341:5
h. knows what she has known 460:26
h. lies about us in our infancy 576:9
h. make me poor 279:25
h...make me such another world 473:21
h. not grim 93:26
H. of all their wish 84:1
H. of Hell, a Hell of H. 344:22
h. on earth 347:4
h. peep through the blanket 457:3
h.'s colour, the blue 358:24
H.'s constellated wilderness 497:15
H. sends us good meat 213:9
h.'s eternal year 192:38
H.'s gift takes earth's abatement 94:1
H.'s great lamps do dive 123:19
h. shall forgive you Bridge 140:3
H.'s happy instrument 412:14
H.'s last best gift 348:1
H.'s light forever shines 492:15
H.'s melodious strains 421:9
h. smiles 493:25
H.'s morning breaks 322:2
H.'s Mother send us grace 149:12
h. soon sets right 90:33
H.'s peculiar care 506:14
h...spread with this pallid screen 237:8
h. still guards the right 475:1
h. stops the nose at it 472:36
h. such grace did lend her 484:40
h.'s wide pathless way 341:14
H.'s youngest teemed star 343:25
H., that but once was prodigal 192:12
H. to be deluded by him 312:28
h. to gaudy day denies 119:1
h. upon earth 27:33
H. views it with delight 332:7
H. vows to keep him 280:10
h. was in him before he was in h. 559:30
heave up Sir Launcelot unto h. 328:23
Hell in H.'s despite 76:3
Hell I suffer seems a H. 346:32
herald of H.'s King 190:2
her early H. 532:24
his h. commences 224:16
his looks do menace h. 330:23
his own By-way to h. 170:15
his praise above h. and earth 400:25
how art thou fallen from h. 53:22
how long or short permit to H. 349:25
humbler h. 383:11
hurl my soul from h. 473:32
I call h. and earth to witness 46:22
if earth be but the shadow of H. 348:13
if it find h. 459:2
if thou deye a martir, go to h. 138:37
imminent h. of his..soul 544:11
in h., a crime to love 381:31
in h., if I cry to you 525:32
in H.'s third story 541:22
in H. the deed appears 109:1
inheritor of the kingdom of h. 391:2
in mid h. the sun is mounted 264:2
in my heart, though not in h. 244:26
in six days..h. and earth 390:11
in the blue h.'s height 338:6
in the h., a perfect round 89:8
in the nurseries of H. 544:10
I saw h. opened 71:36
I see H.'s glories shine 83:7
is he in h.? 370:13
it smells to h. 435:31
its shrine sacred to H. 375:5
jolly h. above 515:27
joy-bells ring in H.'s street 334:1
joy..in h. over one sinner 62:12
Heaven (*cont.*)
kindred points of h. and home 580:27
kingdom of h. is at hand 57:27
kingdom of h. is like to a grain 59:28
lamps of h. 293:10
lead you in at H.'s gate 75:8
leave to H. the measure 279:12
leaving mercy to h. 204:25
let h. see the pranks 471:35
light from H. 108:25, 573:9
like a little H. below 561:32
look how high the h. is 398:6
louder than the bolts of h. 122:18
love is h. and h. is love 116:37, 417:16
make life a h. on earth 292:5
make the face of h. so fine 478:20
man is H.'s masterpiece 404:7
mathematics of the city of h. 85:19
men..differ as H. and Earth 531:22
met my dearest foe in h. 431:4
mild H. a time ordains 351:23
model H. and calculate the stars 348:30
Moon of H. is rising 207:28
more than all in h. 115:6
more than h. pursue 386:30
more things in h. and earth 432:29
most sacred names of earth and H. 158:3
moving through his clouded h. 579:20
my h.'s extremest sphere 558:1
my h. to have 426:13
never be saints in H. 86:16
new h. and a new earth 71:44
niche in H. 88:14
Night along with them from H. 205:5
nor h. nor earth..at peace 449:20
not because I hope for h. 132:7
not H. itself upon the past 194:21
nothing under H. so blue 516:14
not scorn'd in h. 160:33
o'er h. the white clouds 82:7
offspring of H. first-born 346:18
of so much fame in H. 342:23
one from h. 171:24
one h., one hell 89:26
one of these cloths is h. 358:23
only H. knew of them 376:7
only in H. 402:13
on Sunday h.'s gate 245:8
open face of h. 289:2
opening bud to H. convey'd 151:18
order is H.'s first law 384:3
or H. can give 493:27
or what's a h. for? 89:15
our Father which art in h. 58:4
out of H. and just like me 544:5
patch up thine old body for h. 441:40
pavement of her H. 168:1
pavilion of H. is bare 493:1
permission of all-ruling H. 344:20
Persian's H. 356:9
Philosophy, that lean'd on H. 381:27
places that the eye of h. visits 474:19
pledges of H.'s joy 351:9
pointing like a rugged finger to H. 216:7
quit the port o' H. 363:2
read not h. or her 336:15
ring the bells of H. 249:5
rose was h. to smell 249:10
sent from H. above 121:27
she will..have a prospect of h. 363:26
shun the h. that leads 488:12
shut from h. 91:18
shut thee from h. 251:15
some call it the Road to H. 32:9
Son of H.'s eternal King 343:9
souls in h. too 284:16
spark from H. 18:10
speaks of h. 21:9
star of unascended h. 497:12
stars, that nature hung in h. 340:9
steep and thorny way to h. 431:23
steep ascent of H. 240:22
summons thee to h. or to hell 458:1
swear not..by h. 57:48
tangled boughs of H. and Ocean 496:5
tasted the eternal joys of h. 330:2
that h. that bends above us 380:26
that my soul may but ascend to h. 330:9

INDEX

Heaven (cont.)
that uncertain h. 579:24
than serve in h. 344:23
their's is the kingdom of h. 57:39
then h. mocks itself 471:41
then H. tries earth 320:17
then the h. espy 244:15
these the gems of H. 347:23
there may be h. 97:6
there's h. above 92:30
there's husbandry in h. 457:17
things are the sons of h. 277:21
this house as nigh h. 358:5
this is the gate of h. 45:5
those who win h. 93:43
threw him from the face of h. 330:1
throne mounted in h. 540:16
through H.'s wide champain 348:19
thy wanderings over H. 496:10
till h. hath sent me fortune 427:13
to be young was very h. 575:2
to grow old in H. 410:34
to h. being gone 185:4
too hot the eye of h. 486:18
top of it reached to h. 45:3
to the very bourne of h. 284:23
to which high H. doth chime 551:20
tradesman..hope to go to h. 194:27
treasures in h. 58:6
tricks before high h. 461:31
trouble dark in h. 486:24
turn thy back on h. 199:6
under an English h. 84:21
unextinguishable laugh in h. 85:15
unfolds both h. and earth 466:20
unlock the gate of H. 4:5
unreconcil'd as yet to h. 473:12
warring in H. against H.'s..
  King 346:30
water'd h. with their tears 75:24(-76)
way to h...as ready by water 198:24
we are all going to h. 212:21
weariness of climbing h. 495:19
we must change for H. 344:21
we shall practise in h. 93:40
what pleases h. 417:28
what they do in h. 520:39
when earth was nigher h. 94:43
when h. and earth shall pass
  away 417:25
when h. was falling 264:4
whether in H. ye wander 75:18
who hath made h. and earth 391:18
who h. and earth hath made 421:4
whose h. should be true
  Woman 410:34
will most incorrect to h. 430:31
with all the company of h. 390:39
with him..in h. or in hell 443:18
without a thought of H. or Hell 86:21
women..as H. and Hell 531:22
ye powers of h. and earth 166:1
ye wait at H.'s Gate 302:22
yon are the hills o' H. 30:18
your honesty..based..in vacant
  h. 413:21

Heaven-born: Englishman's h.
  privilege 19:29
h. band 255:13
H. child 343:11
Heaven-bred: force of h. poesy 484:37
Heaven-eyed creature 575:17
Heavenly: calm and h. frame 161:1
even in h. place 501:24
from h. harmony 191:35
in h. truths attir'd 159:30
it was a h. sight 150:6
knows ye not, ye h. Powers 127:30
lead us, H. Father 195:23
Music, h. maid 153:31
observant of His h. word 183:21
possession of this h. sight 473:32
this sorrow's h. 473:11
thy beauty's birth is h. 123:17
Heavens: all the H. thou hast in
  Him 165:31
ancient H. 74:13
by h., this is too bad 203:36
distorts the H. 74:12
from yon blue h. 533:38
h. are not too high 243:24

Heavens (cont.)
h. declare the glory of God 392:32
h. dropped at the presence of God 396:5
h.' embroidered cloths 584:17
h. fill with shouting 534:26
h. free from strife 157:18
h. look bright, my dear 357:1
h. my..roof-tree 24:10
h. rain odours on you 483:25
h. themselves blaze forth 449:22
h. themselves..observe degree 481:2
him that rideth upon the h. 396:5
his fabric of the H. 348:30
house..eternal in the h. 67:24
how many h. at once 166:9
I create new h. 55:9
in the h. write your..name 509:7
I will consider thy h. 392:9
most ancient h. 573:31
no image of anything 'in the h.
  above' 325:9
on the opposite quarter of the h. 100:9
pure as the naked h. 577:15
set up thyself..above the h. 395:18
she feels the h. lie bare 545:14
sing, ye h. 505:4
starry h. above that plain 546:30
till you are clothed with the h. 548:13
trembling in the blue h. 586:5
when the h. are bare 576:2
ye h. adore Him 291:27
Heavily: h. in clouds brings on
  the day 1:13
lie h. upon her eyes 409:26
Heaviness: for the spirit of h. 55:4
h. foreruns the good event 442:17
h. may endure for a night 393:25
h. of his mother 49:54
life-harming h. 474:17
why art thou so full of h. 394:17
Heaving: crawling, h. and vibrating 235:22
h. up my either hand 247:15
Heavy: Eton boys grown h. 387:19
h. and the weary weight 581:25
h. as frost 576:16
h., but no less divine 116:4
h. husband 465:24
h. purses 25:36
h. with the even 544:21
lie h. on him, Earth 202:11
list to the h. part 279:28
makes it much more h. 481:14
make their ears h. 53:10
Seneca cannot be too h. 433:22
Heavy-curled..a charioteer 411:15
Heavy-shotted hammock-shroud 532:7
Heavy-sterned amateur old men 302:5
Hebdomadary..you're a boss
  word 515:10
He-bear: meets the h. in his pride 296:13
Heber: Jael, H.'s wife 46:46
Hebes: sensus h. 414:21
Hebraism and Hellenism 19:30
Hebrew: an H. of the Hebrews 68:20
Hebrews: are they H.? so am I 67:33
Hebrid: each cold H. isle 153:27
shepherd of the H. Isles 546:3
Hebrides: among the farthest H. 581:1
among the stormy H. 546:22
beyond the stormy H. 343:2
colder than the H. 208:7
we in dreams behold the H. 420:31
Hebrus: down the swift H. 342:19
Hecate: pale H.'s offerings 458:1
Hecho: del dicho al h. 134:16
Hector: first H. of Troy 327:15
of H. and Lysander 9:24
Hectore: quantum mutatus ab illo H. 554:6
Hecuba: for H.! what's H. to him 433:31
Hedge: along the flow'ry h. I stray 526:21
hawthorn h. puts forth 83:17
high snowdrifts in the h. 263:13
run from h. to h. 288:22
sheet bleaching on the h. 485:16
Hedgehog travels furtively 235:14
Hedgehogs: thorny h. 466:44
Hedges: filigree h. 558:11
go out into the highways and h. 62:9
h. ears 521:14
unkempt about those h. 84:9
Hedge-sparrow fed the cuckoo 452:27

Hedonist: faddling h. 514:16
Heed: away! take h. 244:10
for himself will take no h. 580:6
h. not the rolling waves 415:6
h. them not 205:20
h. not you 205:19
nor h...a distant Drum 205:26
nor h., nor see 497:2
take h. o' the foul fiend 453:18
take h. unto the thing that is
  right 394:6
Heeded: heard it but he h. not 114:19
Heedful: dart, with h. mind 39:3
Heedless: borne in h. hum 153:24
Heeds what we have taught her 214:12
Heel: despot's h. 405:19
h. of the courtier 437:13
lifted up his h. against me 394:15
thou shalt bruise his h. 44:25
Heels: at his h. a stone 436:20
fair pair of h. 439:12
high h...agreeable to our ancient
  constitution 519:13
if your h. are nimble and light 367:4
made of Atalanta's h. 428:7
only low h. in the administration 519:13
out at the h. of their boots 209:18
see Buonaparte..kick h. 525:21
stream'd out beyond his h. 285:36
upon the h. of pleasure 155:32
with a senate at his h. 384:10
with winged h. 443:12
Heifer: plowed with my h. 46:56
that h. lowing at the skies 287:12
Height: although his h. be taken 488:7
Angels in the h. 291:27
h. of this great argument 344:4
he reached a middle h. 336:17
know the sacred h. 42:10
length, breadth, and h...lost 346:10
measures of the breadth and h. 332:12
measure your mind's h. 94:17
none can usurp this h. 285:33
nor h., nor depth 65:58
on Ellangowan's h. 419:35
on Sunium's h. 308:24
think up to the h. of his..style 142:12
to the depth and breadth and h. 88:24
what pleasure lives in h.? 539:3
Heightening: for beauty's h. 18:22
Heights: all the gifts from all the h. 94:4
breeze of Alpine h. 308:17
brood on the towering h. 311:15
from Janiculan h. 146:15
h. by great men reached 316:31
higher than the h. 161:12
on the h. of Killiecrankie 23:19
other h. in other lives 94:4
to keep h. 574:17
trod the sunlit h. 569:13
Heiligtum: wir betreten..dein H. 415:21
Heimatlos: wie des Windes Sausen,
  h. 415:25
Heine for songs 91:10
Heir: ashes new-create another h. 447:16
destin'd h. 281:28
each second stood h. to the first 469:24
first h. of my invention 488:24
flesh is h. to 434:4
folly help'd her to an h. 470:28
great h. of fame 351:8
hard h. strides about 533:11
h. of all the ages 534:35
sole h. of the whole world 548:13
Heir-apparent: thine own h.
  garters 439:3
Heiresses: all h. are beautiful 192:42
Heirs: every one sole h. as well as
  you 548:13
h. of God, and joint-h. with
  Christ 65:54
h. through hope 390:47
if children, then h. 65:54
Held: h. to the last man 233:20
still the lobster h. on 294:7
Helen: dawn in H.'s arms 584:23
dust hath closed H.'s eye 361:5
heavenborn H. 411:35
H.'s beauty in a brow of Egypt 467:24
H...spectatress of the mischief 412:10
H., thy beauty is to me 380:17

Helen (cont.)

H., whose' beauty summoned
Greece 331:5
his ball through H.'s cheek 228:10
in my arms burd H. dropt 31:3
Laodameia died, H. died 309:12
like another H. 191:11
mother of H. of Troy 374:11
ravish'd H. 480:37
sweet H., make me immortal 330:5
where H. lies 31:3
white Iope, blithe H. 123:27
Helena: all is dross that is not H. 330:5
Helicon: watered our horses in H. 135:21
where H. breaks down 15:15
Hell: agreement with H. 213:19
airs from heaven or blasts from h. 431:32
all h. broke loose 347:33
allotted death and h. 330:9
all places . . h. that are not heaven 330:3
all we need of h. 180:3
begin raising h. 312:23
bells of H. 8:19
better to reign in h. 344:23
between H. and Heaven 411:32
bid him go to H., to H. he goes 278:31
boys, it is all h. 501:4
burn for ever in burning h. 524:32
cast into h. fire 59:51
characters of h. to trace 229:22
come hot from h. 450:12
damned if I see how the h. he
can 337:44
down, down to h. 446:8
down to the Hinges o' H. 298:18
drag to h. a spirit 149:22
dunnest smoke of hell 457:3
engine, wrought in deepest h. 509:25
England . . h. for horses 109:29
England . . h. of horses 209:8
for the fiery gulf of hell 13:18
from out immortal h. 535:26
gates of h. can never 35:3
gates of h. shall not prevail 59:43
go to h. like lambs 141:11
having harrow'd h. 509:4
heart of H. 294:28
Heaven and H. Amalgamation
Society 127:31
Heaven in H.'s despair 76:2
Heav'n of H., a H. of Heav'n 344:22
heaven that leads men to this h. 488:14
h. and night . . this monstrous
birth 470:23
h. from beneath is moved 53:21
H. in Heaven's despite 76:3
H. is a city much like London 496:16
h. is full of musical amateurs 490:20
h. is murky 460:24
H. I suffer seems a Heaven 346:32
h.'s foundations quiver 35:2
H. trembled at the hideous name 346:8
here, and in h. 329:5
he said: 'h.' 358:24
horrid night, the child of h. 444:23
improving his prisons in H. 151:12
improving the prisons of H. 507:22
in H.'s despite now 90:17
in h. they'll roast thee 108:14
injured lover's h. 348:10
into the mouth of H. 528:18
is he in h.? 370:13
Italy . . h. for women 109:29
keep the gate of h. 472:37
keys of h. and of death 70:28
lead apes in h. 479:3
let H. afford the pavement 168:1
lidless eyes in h. 411:2
like a liar gone to burning h. 473:20
limbecks foul as h. within 488:8
Lord George H. 39:14
made human life a h. 17:7
make a h. of this world 38:19
meanest spawn of H. 534:11
Milton wrote . . at liberty when
of . . H. 77:7
mockery of h. 119:18
more devils than vast h. can hold 467:24
never married, and that's his h. 109:14
never mentions h. 385:4
nor H. a fury, like a woman 155:20

Hell (cont.)

not leave my soul in h. 392:27
one heaven, one h. 89:26
one of these cloths is . . h. 358:23
out of h. leads up to light 345:27
pains of h. 399:5
procuress to the Lords of H. 532:30
quiet to quick bosoms is a h. 113:42
sent to H., Sir 275:20
shout that tore h.'s concave 345:1
swig in H. from Gunga Din 297:5
teach me more than h. to shun 386:30
terrible as h. 346:4
that riches grow in h. 345:10
there is a dreadful H. 561:22
there look grim as h. 472:34
there must be h. 97:6
there's the torment, there's the
h. 305:16
this is h., nor am I out of it 330:2
thou fool . . danger of h. fire 57:45
though h. should bar the way 366:3
thou profoundest H. 344:22
threats of H. and Hopes of
Paradise 206:20
to h., allegiance! 436:28
way to h., even from . . heaven 99:25
what h. it is, in suing 510:16
which way I fly is H., myself am
H. 346:32
who art as black as h. 488:22
whose entrance leads to H. 340:25
whose music h. can move 123:27
with h. . . at an agreement 53:34
with him . . in heaven or in h. 443:18
without a thought of Heaven or
H. 86:21
women . . as Heaven and H. 531:22
Hellas: brighter H. 493:25
gospel of H. 112:18
Hellenism: Hebraism and H. 19:30
Hellespont: H. between . . her
breasts 184:21
pass'd the H. 115:32
to the Propontic and the H. 472:12
Hell-fires: dreamin' H. to see 298:3
Hell-gate: to the flare of H. there 302:27
Hellhound is always a hellhound 572:6
Hellish: h. dark, and smells of
cheese 518:25
h., devilish . . tobacco 109:22
Hell-kite: O h.! 460:21
Hell-pains: hate him as I hate h. 469:34
Hells: tormented with ten thou-
sand h. 330:2
Helm: at the h. a seeming mermaid 424:7
Pleasure at the h. 229:23
Helm: des grossen Vaters H. 208:30
Helmet: h. of Navarre 323:5
his h. now shall make a hive 377:4
not cowardly put off my h. 425:28
red wine through the h. 417:4
she saw the h. 534:7
Helmsman steered us through 148:27
Help: by God's h. so I will 391:3
come . . into Macedonia, and h. us 64:53
comfort of thy h. again 395:9
encumbers him with h. 270:18
from whence cometh my h. 399:26
God h. us 296:28
God shall h. her 394:28
hath not another to h. him up 56:34
h. 'im for 'is mother . . 'e'll h.
us by-an'-by 301:17
h. him of his blindness 484:40
h. of the helpless 322:1
h. there's none 249:15
h. thou mine unbelief 61:4
h. Thy children when they call 295:6
h. us in our utmost need 318:6
h. us this and every day 291:8
h. you a lot with the White 298:5
h. yourself, and heaven will h.
you 209:10
his ready h. was ever nigh 275:2
how can I h. England? 92:18
I will make him an h. meet for him 44:14
love that should h. you to live 524:33
love without the h. of anything 75:1
many of your countrymen cannot h. 270:34

Help (cont.)

no h. but Thee 195:23
our h. in ages past 502:9
our h. is in the name of the Lord 391:18
seeking h. from none 227:34
send these h. from the sanctuary 392:35
since there's no h. 189:20
there is no h. in them 400:19
very present h. 5:6, 394:27
what is past my h. 37:21
what's past h. 485:12
with the h. of my God 392:30
Helped: being h., inhabits there 484:40
over, and can't be h. 178:39
she h. him to lean 33:20
we shall have h. it 179:38
Helper: our antagonist is our h. 102:27
thou art my h. and redeemer 394:14
Helpers: when other h. fail 322:1
Helping: h. every feeble neighbour 227:34
h., when we meet them 293:11
Helpless: great Government of the
United States h. 571:13
h., look to thee for grace 548:12
h., naked, piping loud 76:8
help of the h. 322:1
little, weak, and h. 4:3
so lonely, loving, h. 115:35
Helpmeet for him 44:14
Helps: nor h. good hearts 170:24
used h., undergirding the ship 65:28
what h. it now 16:8
Helter skelter, hang sorrow 280:12
Hem: flying hair and fluttering
h. 411:10
h. his watery march 17:28(–18)
red-rose-bordered h. 586:14
touched the h. of Nature's shift 496:17
Hemisphere: gilding the eastern h. 499:29
Hemlock: burdocks, h., nettles 454:2
Hempen: h. home-spuns 467:4
sing in a h. string 37:16
Hems: clinging Heaven by the h. 545:1
Hen: as a h. gathereth her chickens 60:20
good fat h. 368:6
he yaf not . . a pulled h. 136:31
more wondrous . . the cock and h. 74:8
my black h. 367:2
she—poor h.! 429:22
two Owls and a H. 311:2
Hence: h., avaunt 231:1
h., dear delusion 504:7
h., horrible shadow! Unreal
mockery h.! 459:21
h., loathed Melancholy 341:26
h., vain deluding joys 341:7
h., ye profane 158:24
h., you long-legg'd spinners, h. 467:1
hundred years h. 177:6
latterly gone h. 300:23
to go h. unwilling 349:30
whither hurried h. 206:14
Henchard: Michael H.'s Will 237:7
Hen-pecked: have they not h. you
all 115:16
Henry and Tobias and Miguel 297:19
Henry Clay: calm in a H. 294:31
Henry King: chief defect of H. 41:1
Henry Pimpernell 478:46
Hens: fox may steal your h. 214:19
Hent: merrily h. the stile-a 485:21
Her: *h.* lips were red, *h.* looks were
free 149:13
read not heaven or h. 336:15
told me you had been to h. 129:33
Heraclitus: they told me, H. 157:15
Herald: hark! the h.-angels 505:12
h. of a noisy world 163:20
h. of love's mighty king 509:6
last and greatest h. 190:2
no other h. 447:11
perfectest h. of joy 468:14
Heraldries: 'mong thousand h. 285:19
Heraldry: boast of h. 230:1
our new h. is hands 472:14
Heralds: chosen h. of England's
Marshal 142:4
Herb: excellent h. to our fathers 300:10
some single h. or tree 332:13
sour h. of grace 475:14
this . . H. whose tender Green 206:4

INDEX

Herba: latet anguis in h. 555:27
Herbas: miscueruntque h. 556:13
Herbe: l'h. qui verdoye 377:32
Herbs: dinner of h. 50:12
  excellent h. had our fathers 300:9
  h. and other country messes 342:2
  h. and trees..in May 328:15
  Medea gather'd the enchanted h. 465:17
  with bitter h. shall they eat it 45:46
Hercules: H. is not only known by
  his foot 87:4
  is not love a H.? 455:22
  I to H. 430:33(−431)
  I was with H. and Cadmus 467:20
  some of H. 9:24
Herd: canopy the h. 480:15
  elevates above the vulgar h. 212:22
  habit rules the unreflecting h. 580:3
  leave untended the h. 419:3
  lowing h. 229:28
  stricken deer, that left the h. 163:8
  though the h. have fled from
  thee 356:15
Herdman: faithful h.'s art 342:28
Herds: flocks, or h., or human
  face 346:20
Herdsman: God the h. 584:8
Here: bird to the right sang H. 524:8
  but h...is our client 188:14
  good for us to be h. 59:46
  h. a little, and there a little 53:33
  h. am I; for thou calledst me 47:5
  h. am I; send me 53:9
  h. and h. did England help me 92:18
  h., and in hell 329:5
  h., h. will I remain 478:44
  h. is God's plenty 194:13
  h. kind mate to thee 170:24
  h. little, and hereafter bliss 99:31
  h. may we sit 168:13
  h...my everlasting rest 478:44
  H. or There as strikes the Player 207:1
  h.'s the sex 106:23
  h.'s to thee, Bacon 121:22
  h. today and gone tomorrow 40:6
  h., upon this bank and shoal 457:7
  h. we are! 305:3
  lo, h. is God 147:4
  my heart is not h. 107:12, 420:24
  neither h. nor there 473:7
  not h., O Apollo 15:15
  stranger of h. and every where 469:33
  that we now had h. 444:25
  we're h. because we're h. 11:13
  who comes h.? 369:17
Hereafter: heaven..points out an
  h. 1:22
  h. bliss 99:31
  she should have died h. 461:4
  what is love? 'tis not h. 482:28
  what may come h. 523:18
Hereditary: every h. monarch..
  insane 29:4
  h. bondsmen 113:18
  his own h. skies 194:25
  restore the crown to its h. successor 272:27
Hereditas: damnosa h. 212:23
Heresies: diversity of sects and
  hateful h. 510:15
  new truths..begin as h. 266:24
Heresy: h...no more than private
  opinion 248:20
  no h...excite the horror of Bossuet 325:23
  they that mislike it, h. 248:20
  what an Englishman believes..
  h. 491:4
Heretic that makes the fire 485:11
Heretics: poor h. in love 185:29
  Turks, Infidels, and H. 389:33
Heretofore: shines now, and h. 185:24
Heritage: children..are an h. 309:35
  come into our h. 83:20
  I have a goodly h. 392:26
  our h. the sea 167:21
  that h. of woe 118:4
  undefiled h. 295:6
Herman's a German 387:4
Hermaphrodite: kind of a giddy h. 301:20
Hermes: with thrice great H. 341:17

Herminius: back, H.! 323:24
  H. glared on Sextus 324:4
  H. smote Mamilius 324:9
  one of us two, H. 324:8
Hermit: dwell a weeping h. there 153:30
  gentle H. of the dale 225:11
  h. hoar in solemn cell 276:15
  holy H. raised his eyes 150:11
  more..torment than a h.'s fast 286:39
  this H. good 150:8
Hermitage: my..palace for a h. 475:10
  take that for an h. 319:7
Hermits are contented 578:6
Hermon: little hill of H. 394:18
Hernani: wait..to applaud 'H.' 514:35
Hero: conquering h. comes 358:13
  embarrassed—never h. more 118:1
  every h. becomes a bore 201:9
  god-like h. sate 190:34
  h. can be Poet, Prophet, King 126:26
  h. from his prison 24:6
  h. must drink brandy 274:12
  h. perish or a sparrow fall 383:10
  h. to his valet 157:11
  in H.'s tower on H.'s heart 264:5
  its h. the Conqueror Worm 380:15
  millions a h. 387:9
  one non-flunkey..one h. 126:46
  to his very valet..a h. 112:34
  where her young h. sleeps 356:31
Hero gaude 132:21
Herod: it out-h.s H. 434:15
Heroes: country for h. to live in 216:8
  frightened both the h. so 130:6
  hail, ye h. 255:13
  hail, ye indomitable h. 308:21
  my peers, the h. of old 95:11
  of all the world's brave h. 9:24
  saints, h., if we will 15:9
  speed glum h. 415:12
  thin red line of h. 303:3
  thoughts of h...warning-pans 337:3
  two h. to begin with 126:46
  we aren't no thin red h. 303:4
Heroic: finished a life h. 351:5
  good, h. womanhood 317:14
  h. for earth too hard 89:10
  h. poem of its sort 125:35
  h. syllables both ways 116:26
  manly sentiment and h. enterprise 102:12
  subject for h. song 349:5
Heroically: h. fashioned 575:15
  h. hath finished a life heroic 351:5
  h. mad 190:32
Heroine: when a h. goes mad 500:6
Heroism: I will report all h. 568:6
  with you is h. 568:6
Heron, the Shuh-shuh-gah 317:20
Héros: point de h. pour son valet 157:11
Herostratus lives 87:17
Herren-Moral and Sklaven-Moral 364:21
Herring: buy my caller h. 360:13
  h. boxes without topses 355:23
  plague o' these pickle h. 482:16
  roast thee like a h. 108:14
Herring-pond: h. is wide 93:31
  Neighbours o'er the H. 195:11
  this side of the H. 215:34
Herrings: as many as red h. 367:20
Herrschen und gewinnen 223:23
Herself: gave me h. indeed 92:44
  half of her should rise h. 236:17
Hertfordshire: plains of pleasant
  H. 307:35
Hervey: if you call a dog H. 270:4
Herveys: men, women, and H. 354:13
Herz: mein H. ich will dich fragen 234:17
  mein H. ist schwer 223:20
  und wenn das H. auch bricht 240:24
Herzen: zwei H. und ein Schlag 234:17
Heshbon: fishpools in H. 52:19
Hesitate: h. and falter life away 18:12
  h. dislike 385:29
Hésite: elle flotte, elle h. 405:2
Hesper: slippered H. 84:10
Hesperian fables true 347:5
Hesperides: climbing trees in the
  H. 455:22
  fruit of the H. 545:7
  ladies of th' H. 350:4

Hesperus: H. entreats thy light 279:31
  H. that led the starry host 347:19
  H. with the host of heaven 566:13
  schooner H. 318:14
Hesperus: venit H...ite capellae 556:9
Hesterna: dicebamus h. die 313:16
Het: ye' se a' be h. ere I come back 106:26
Heterodoxy is another man's doxy 559:31
Heterogeneity: definite coherent
  h. 508:25
Heureux: h. qui comme Ulysse 40:17
  jamais si h...qu'on s'imagine 407:10
Hew: h. him as a carcass 449:10
  some body to h. and hack 110:21
Hewed: Johnson h. passages 154:13
Hewers of wood 46:41
Hewn: hacked, h. with constant
  service 507:2
  my harness..thou hast h. from
  me 544:22
Hexameter: in the h. rises 152:8
Hexameters: barbarous h. 529:16
Hey: h. diddle diddle 221:4, 367:1
  h. ding a ding, ding 428:30
  h. for boot and horse 293:19
  h. for Garsington!..h. for God
  Almighty! 292:10
  h. ho, how I do love thee 156:19
  h. ho! says Rowley 366:21
  h.-ho! sing h.-ho! 427:22
  h., ho, the wind and the rain 484:27
  h. non nonny, nonny, h. nonny 436:30
  h. nonny nonny 170:21, 359:37, 468:20
  h.! the doxy 485:16
  h., then up go we 250:11, 404:17
  h.! the sweet birds 485:16
  h. to you—good day to you 221:2
  sighing cries, H. ho 168:7
  so h. bonny boat 293:9
  with a h. and a ho 428:32
Hey-day in the blood is tame 435:47
Hi: answer to 'H.!' 128:6
  Harriet, H.! 243:5
  h. diddle diddle 221:4
Hiawatha's Chickens 317:24
Hic: h. est 378:2
  h. et ubique? 432:26
  h. hoc horum Genitivo 370:5
  two narrow words, *H. jacet* 405:13
Hickety, pickety, my black hen 367:2
Hickory, Dickory, Dock 367:3
Hid: Achilles..when he h. himself 87:12
  city..on an hill cannot be h. 57:41
  find where truth is h. 432:44
  h. these things from the wise 61:37
  in shadiest covert h. 346:20
  in the mist of tears I h. from
  Him 544:13
  Moses h. his face 45:35
  murder cannot be h. long 463:32
  my groaning is not h. 394:7
  nothing h. from the heat thereof 392:32
  to keep that h. 186:23
  we h. as it were our faces 54:25
  wherefore are these things h.? 482:8
Hidden: half h. from the eye 580:18
  nature is often h. 26:39
  solitary h. anguish 196:24
  teems with h. meaning 222:11
Hiddenly: near or far, h. 545:5
Hide: broad buttock, tender h. 488:27
  death to h. 351:21
  disdains to h. his head 231:32
  for all 'is dirty h. 297:3
  form it seem'd to h. 417:27
  h., h. your golden light 318:4
  h. in cooling trees 288:22
  h. me by the bracken bush 30:6
  h. me from the..wrath of God 330:8
  h. me, O my Saviour, h. 565:5
  h. the fault I see 386:31
  h. us from the face of him 71:2
  let me h. myself in thee 548:11
  seems to h. them 497:9
  stars h. their diminished heads 346:29
  thou wear a lion's h.! 447:28
  to h. the things 'e said 301:15
  whose h. he sold 557:21
  world to h. virtues in? 482:9
  wrapped in a player's h. 232:6
  wrapped in a woman's h. 445:43

Hideous: hags and h. wenches 150:28
horrid, h. notes of woe 116:50
making night h. 431:32(~432)
more h...than the sea-monster 452:28
too h. to be shown 471:28
Hides: he that h. a dark soul 340:20
h. from himself its state 279:7
h. not his visage from our cottage 485:31
h. the ruin that it feeds upon 161:30
Hidest: God that h. thyself 54:18
Hiding the Skeleton 336:24
Hiding-place: dark and lonely h. 151:19
h. from the wind 53:43
now issuing from its h. 19:29
Hiding-places ten years deep 582:10
Hiemis tempestate non tangitur 38:31
Hierarchy: all Olympus' faded h. 288:4
Hierusalem, my happy home 6:28
Higden: O Mrs. H., Mrs. H. 178:18
Higginbottom: last words of H. 504:10
High: afraid of that which is h. 51:33
as h. as Heaven above 525:36
as h. as metaphysic wit 110:13
bosom'd h. in tufted trees 342:1
dignity of this h. calling 101:15
divine h. piping Pehlevi 205:12
even an h. hill 396:7
every man who is h. up 36:19
fixed mind and h. disdain 344:13
for contempt too h. 158:15
for object strange and h. 332:5
from h. life h. characters 384:24
God made them, h. or lowly 3:15
happy, h., majestical 494:15
hardy and h...the slimy mallow 165:17
Heaven is for thee too h. 348:31
heav'ns are not too h. 243:24
he sits h. 449:1
h. and triple-arch'd 285:19
h. as we have mounted in delight 580:5
h. erected thoughts 501:16
h. is our calling, friend 575:15
h. life as conceived by a bookseller 558:17
h. Midsummer pomps 18:26
h. on a throne of royal state 345:14
h. over roaring Temple-bar 541:22
h. that proved too h. 89:10
his glance was stern and h. 323:4
hold the h. wey 136:20
I am low, thou art h. 524:2
I'm the H. 511:5
in your hansom leave the H. 404:21
I only know it shall be h. 264:7
it alone is h. fantastical 481:30
just so h. as it is 424:17
knowledge in the Most H. 396:26
look how h. the heaven is 398:6
matters which are too h. for me 400:1
mind not h. things 66:5
of the most H. cometh healing 57:10
O Lord most H. 390:40
pitch this one h. 15:4
place 'tween h. and low 429:39
plain living and h. thinking 577:16
sing both h. and low 482:28
six feet h. and look'd..higher 165:6
slain in thine h. places 47:30
slain upon thy h. places 47:29
soar not too h. to fall 334:19
so h. that looking downward 410:9
spirit from on h. 149:22
teach h. thought 530:14
they go up as h. as the hills 398:8
this h. man 91:41
though G. hath raised me h. 198:12
to wind ourselves too h. 291:6
trumpet shall be heard on h. 191:39
trust in all things h. 539:8
upon a throne, h. and lifted up 53:8
upon the h. horse 85:5
wickedness in h. places 68:11
with h. objects 579:13
ye'll tak the h. road 9:7
High-blown: my h. pride 446:24
High-born Hoel's harp 229:21
Highbrow..feminine 243:12
High-Churchman: furious H.
was I 7:9
High-cultured as her soil 123:7

High diddle diddle 221:4
High-engender'd: your h. battles 453:6
Higher: aspire to h. things 502:5
Bourbon or Nassau go h.? 401:28
built far h. in learning 212:18
but sunbeams lifted h. 316:27
friend, go up h. 62:3
he shall shoot h. 501:18
h. he's a getting 247:10
h. law than the Constitution 422:23
h. than the heights 161:12
h. than the sphery chime 341:5
look'd six inches h. 165:6
mediocrity knows nothing h. 188:28
new tribunal..h. than God's 96:15
of a h. mood 342:24
rise..to h. things 532:1
sea rises h. 140:13
steps were h. 193:41
who aimeth at the sky shoots h. 244:3
Highest: acted..from the h. principles 203:33
hanged on the h. hill 299:27
h. education since the Greek 182:19
h. type of human nature 508:24
trouthe is the h. thing 137:26
we needs must love the h. 530:19
Highflyer at fashion 178:6
High-handed: career of h. wrong 135:3
High jinks: pastime of h. 419:34
Highland: bloody H. blade 417:18
forgive your H. chief 122:28
heart is H. 420:31
my sweet H. Mary 106:9
sweet H. Girl 575:16
where is your H. laddie gone? 282:10
yon solitary H. lass 580:28
Highlandman: breeks aff a wild
H. 419:23
Highlands: farewell to the H. 107:13
in the h. 516:5
my heart's in the H. 107:12, 420:24
out of the h. of affliction 511:7
to the H. bound 122:23
will ye gang to the H. 9:17
ye H. and ye Lawlands 30:8
Highly: h. impossible tree 218:7
Mr. Reilly, they speak of so h. 7:19
what thou wouldst h. 457:1
High-minded: Lord, I am not h. 400:1
High-mindedness: honourable h. 503:17
Highness: his H.' dog at Kew 382:11
High Park: all beyond H.'s a desert 202:5
High Priest: answerest thou the h.
so 63:67
revilest thou God's h.? 65:16
High-reaching Buckingham 476:23
High-sounding: thy h. phrases 118:33
Highway: broad h. of the world 493:10
buried in the king's h. 475:10
h. for our God 54:9
h...my chief Parnassus 502:3
lane, h. or open street 549:6
Highwayman came riding 366:1
Highways: go out into the h. and
hedges 62:9
happy h. where I went 263:14
Hilarem: oderunt h. tristes 257:9
Hilarity: sinking flame of h. 177:29
Hill: as the h. of Basan, so is God's
h.: even an high h. 396:7
at the other side of the h. 564:3
behind the cloud-topped h. 383:11
below the kirk, below the h. 148:21
blooms and withers on the h. 411:1
city that is set on an h. 57:41
cot beside the h. 408:10
distant dearness in the h. 533:2
down the green h. 151:32
down the h. dart 39:3
down thy h., romantic Ashbourne 124:10
every..h. shall be made low 54:9
few in the h. 304:29
green h. far away 4:4
hanged on the highest h. 299:27
heard on the h. 76:14, 166:24
h. beside the silver Thames 82:9
h. of everlasting youth 81:4
hunter home from the h. 516:15
I climbed a h. 249:13

Hill (cont.)
if Sion h. delight thee more 344:2
in a very fruitful h. 52:37
in the shadow of the h. 118:8
is this the h.? 150:4
Jack and Jill went up the h. 367:9
King of France went up the h. 367:11
little h. of Hermon 394:18
longest h...end in a vale 39:4
Mahomet will go to the h. 25:34
on a huge h...Truth stands 186:10
on the windy h. 84:2
others apart sat on a h. 345:29
our Tree yet crowns the h. 19:1
over h., over dale 466:33
over the crest of the h. 293:20
Pillicock set on Pillicock-h. 453:17
red coats marching from the h. 77:31
rest upon thy holy h. 392:24
shady grove, or sunny h. 346:19
stood upon that silent h. 249:16
sweet lass of Richmond H.
327:5, 551:5
this is God's h. 396:7
tip-toe upon a little h. 286:25
to persons standing alone on a h. 236:38
to sit upon a h. 446:1
traveller's dream under the h. 74:22
upon the self-same h. 342:11
up to the top of the h. 10:19
valley, rock, or h. 582:14
we clamb the h. thegither 106:20
yon high eastern h. 430:21
Hill flower: sunrise..like any h. 411:1
Hillmen desire their Hills 301:10
Hills: among the lonely h. 573:8
among the solitary h. 579:6
before the h. in order stood 562:9
cold on Canadian h. 310:2
domes the red-plow'd h. 529:11
fair h. of Eiré 329:3
far across the h. they went 528:28
far-distant h...sent an alien
sound 575:24
forests ancient as the h. 151:32
from those brown h. 83:14
great h. of the South Country 42:3
green Illyrian h. 15:14
her foundations are upon the
holy h. 397:13
high h. are a refuge 398:10
hillmen desire their H. 301:10
h. look over on the South 543:22
h. of home! 516:10
H. of the Chankly Bore 311:15
h. peep o'er h. 382:23
h. stand about Jerusalem 399:33
h. where his life rose 15:6
h. whose heads touch heaven 470:2
h. with thunder riven 122:18
I to the h. 421:4
lift up mine eyes unto the h. 399:26
little h. like young sheep 399:3
little h. righteousness 306:23
little h. shall rejoice 395:30
meadows, h. and groves 576:21
my h. are white over 499:14
o'er the h., and far away 528:29
old brown h. 334:15
over the h. and far away
214:26, 369:10, 516:13
pine hewn on Norwegian h. 344:24
reclined on the h. like Gods 535:19
silence in the h. 532:15
storm..on the Chiltern H. 140:7
strength of the h. is his 397:26
the Lord who made the h. 302:11
these high wild h. 474:27
they go up as high as the h. 398:8
those blue remembered h. 263:14
though the h. be carried into..
the sea 394:27
to the h. and the vales 526:22
under the shadowy h. 574:23
upon our clouded h. 75:16
utmost bound of the everlasting
h. 45:28
valleys, groves, h. and fields 330:17
what h. are yon, yon pleasant h. 30:18
while the h. remain 538:3
whitest snow on Scythian h. 330:21

INDEX

Hills (cont.)

why hop ye so, ye high h.? 396:7
yon are the h. o' Heaven 30:18
your name to the reverberate h. 482:22
Hill-side: h.'s dew-pearled 94:40
loved h. 19:1
on the cold h. 286:36
up the h. 288:2
Hill top: evening star on his h. 348:38
Hilts: she's loose i' th' h. 563:10
Him: all cried, 'That's h.!' 34:12
all the flowers looked up at H. 140:20
be with H. in whose company 99:40
h. first, h. last, h. midst 348:5
h. that's far awa' 104:24
H. that walked the waves 343:3
I go from you to H. 24:5
I found H. in the..stars 531:26
I to H. and He to me 543:19
I would remember H. 39:6
mentioned me to h. 129:33
what's Hecuba to h.? 433:31
Himalay: east of H. 545:4
Himalayan peasant meets the he-bear 296:13
Himmel: der bestirnte H. über mir 284:4
Himself: Brutus, with h. at war 448:15
by h. he learned to wander 107:35
calls H. a Lamb 76:10
can h. know 137:38
Cat..walked by h. 304:21
demolished but by h. 43:8
ech man for h. 137:28
end by loving h. better than all 152:22
fight begins within h. 89:38
first he folwed it h. 137:18
He doth H. impart 291:14
he h. with his human air 90:27
h. from God he could not free 199:23
h. he cannot save 60:51
h., his..neighbour, and Me 320:18
in h. possess his own desire 575:8
like Brutus, like h. 452:3
lord of h. 118:4
loved him for h. alone 500:9
loving h. better than me 27:5
master of h. 334:18
poor centre of a man's actions, h. 27:38
Richard's h. again 144:28
think for h.? 491:12
when he spake of h. 202:12
who finds h. 18:17
who lives unto h. 404:11
written down but by h. 276:7
Hinder: all the h. parts..painted 509:22
'amper an' h. an' scold men 302:5
helpless to h. that or anything 237:5
poor Wat..on his h. legs 488:28
smote his enemies in the h. parts 397:1
to get free his h. parts 348:27
weep upon your h. parts 266:15
Hindered: sore let and h. 389:25
Hinders: h. needle and thread 253:27
if any one h. our coming 294:36
Hindrance: pointing at h. 80:17
though it were to his own h. 392:24
Hindrances: what various h. we meet 161:14
Hinds: h. to bring forth young 393:23
nimbler much than h. 333:1
soil'd by rude h. 165:7
Hindu: marries, dies, or turns H. 495:11
we'll send the mild H. 11:9
Hindus and Argentines sleep firmly 157:25
Hindustan: he came from H. 542:15
Hindward: with h. feather 336:21
Hinges: as the door on its h. 562:3
down to the H. o' Hell 298:18
on their h. grate 346:9
Hinky dinky, parley-voo 412:17
Hint: gave him a h. for..Hell 151:12, 507:22
h. at any little delicate thing 175:38
just h. a fault 385:29
upon this h. I spake 470:3
with shadow'd h. confuse 532:24
Hip: catch him once upon the h. 463:17
he smote them h. and thigh 46:57
infidel, I have thee on the h. 465:12
Hipped: from the h. discourses 231:28
Hippocrene: blushful H. 287:24

Hippogriff: without wing of h. 350:16
Hippopotamus: big h. stuck 10:8
found it was a H. 128:18
I shoot the H. 40:27
Hips: we swing ungirded h. 506:20
Hire: worthy of his h. 61:35
Hired: I'm sick of the h. women 299:21
they h. the money, didn't they? 156:26
Hireling: h. fleeth because he is an h. 63:38
pay given to a state h. 277:31
Hirelings: into his church lewd h. 347:3
His: H. that gentle voice 21:9
my beloved is mine, and I am h. 52:3
sealed thee h. 165:31
'twas mine, 'tis h. 471:30
Hiss: dismal universal h. 349:20
roasted cares h. 456:1
Hissed: we h. along the polished ice 575:23
Historian: h. of the Roman empire 216:28
h...wants more documents 268:7
life of the h...short 217:3
Historians: God cannot alter the past, h. can 111:28
these gentle h. 103:8
would have been poets, h. 152:30
Histories: h. make men wise 27:19
many joyous and pleasant h. 328:2
History: antiquities are h. defaced 24:15
assassination..never changed.. history 180:36
attend to the h. of Rasselas 278:14
become a h. little known 160:30
by some named H. 127:16
dignity of h. 78:15, 325:21, 33
dust-heap called 'h.' 72:26
exceeds an infamous h. 87:15
from h. recovered 402:23
great deal of h...little literature 268:1
great h. of the land 317:14
happiest..no h. 196:26
her, whose h. began 586:14
h. a distillation of rumour 126:16
h...biography of great men 126:24
H. came to a 422:17
h...essence of innumerable biographies 125:32
h. in all men's lives 442:6
h. is a pack of lies 517:8
h. is bunk 209:21
h. is past politics 421:20
H. is Philosophy teaching by examples 78:13, 180:12
h...kings thirty feet high 326:7
h. of art is the h. of revivals 111:38
h. of progress 324:26
h. of the affections 267:21
h. of the human spirit 20:8
if men could learn from h. 152:24
Kingsley goes to Froude for h. 517:8
knowledge..product of h. 125:31
liquid h. 104:3
mad from life's h. 252:20
never...learned anything from h. 240:23
no h., only biography 200:21
poetry..of graver import than h. 14:17
portance in my travel's h. 470:2
read no h. 181:44
read their h. in a nation's eyes 230:5
some remnants of h. 24:15
strange eventful h. 427:21
very few materials for h. 217:7
War makes rattling good h. 236:2
what's her h.? 483:10
whatsoever..the future date of my H. 217:3
History-books: whose annals are blank in h. 126:11
Hit: can h. from far 244:13
h., a very palpable h. 437:37
if you would h. the mark 316:11
never think I have h. hard 272:24
two h. it off 572:23
two people..h. on the same thought 500:2
Hitch your waggon to a star 201:14
Hitched: h. his trousers up 34:28
if you mean gettin h. 560:1
Hither: come h., come h., come h. 427:7
h. and thither moves 206:28

Hither (cont.)

h. hurried whence 206:14
h., page, and stand by me 361:20
let him come h. 99:35
Hitherto shalt thou come 49:21
Hi-tiddley-hi-ti 408:2
Hitler has missed the bus 135:10
Hits off the faded graces 240:6
Hittites: Canaanites, and the H. 45:36
Hive: his helmet now shall make a h. 377:4
h. for the honey-bee 585:12
this great h., the city 158:12
Hives: fill our h. with honey and wax 519:5
Hivites, and the Jebusites 45:36
Ho: I shan't care or h. 236:11
Hoard: boastful of her h. 226:11
learning a mere h. of gold 442:21
little h. of maxims 534:23
our h. is little 531:3
Hoarded: Beauty..must not be h. 340:37
Hoar-frost: scattereth the h. like ashes 400:23
Hoarse: bondage is h. 477:26
h. Fitzgerald 117:8
h., teeth-chattering Month 153:15
h. with having little else to do 119:15
raven himself is h. 457:3
unchang'd to h. or mute 348:23
Hoary: but dull and h. 552:9
Druid, h. chief 158:29
h. head is a crown of glory 50:16
in h. winter's night 508:14
Hob-and-nob: let us h. with Death 541:12
Hobbes clearly proves 521:21
Hobby-horse is forgot 435:6
Hobden: old Mus' Hobden owns the land 298:8
Hobgoblin: consistency..h. of little minds 200:40
Hock-carts: of May-poles, H. 245:17
Hockley: Hey H.! 292:10
Hodge: perceiving H...out of countenance 275:11
Hodgepodge: gallimaufry or h. 511:1
Hodgson, Guinness, Allsopp 120:23
Hodie: vive h. 331:22
Hoe: darned long row to h. 319:15
just tickle her with a h. 269:15
leans upon his h. 329:19
take a large h. 297:28
Hoel: high-born H.'s harp 229:21
Hog: acorned h. 92:8
h.'s my feed..eat h. a solid hower 337:12
Hoggish: have his h. mind 509:34
Hoi polloi..no matter what they think 194:9
Hoist: h. with his own petar 436:8
shall they h. me up 425:34
Holborn: when I was last in H. 476:21
Hold: books..h. readily in your hand 276:28
cry, 'H., h.!' 457:3
ever h. me in thy heart 438:4
first cries, 'H., enough!' 461:14
for ever h. his peace 391:27
for God sake h. your tongue 184:11
h. fast that which is good 68:38
h. fast the form of sound words 68:57
h. off! unhand me! 148:20
h., or cut bow-strings 466:32
h. the fleet angel fast 316:29
h. the fort 77:23
h. the hye wey 136:20
h. Thou Thy Cross 322:2
h. your hand but as long 93:9
how do I h. thee 487:22
how to h. a sheep-hook 342:28
I h. it towards you 287:3
I h. you here, root and all 529:24
I must h. my tongue 431:1
lay h. on eternal life 68:53
Namancos and Bayona's h. 343:2
no woman's heart..to h. so much 483:9
scowls the far-famed h. 323:11
they h. all together 395:14
to have and to h. 391:30
Holdeth: who h. our soul in life 396:1

INDEX

Hold-fast is the only dog 443:23
Holding: h. both his sides 341:29
  h. on by the Sergeant's sash 301:14
  h. their neighbours' tails 298:20
Holds: he h. me well 470:20
  h. him with his glittering eye 148:20
  h. him with his skinny hand 148:20
Hole: Caesar..stop a h. 437:18
  creeps in at every h. 377:3
  drum vith a h. 178:40
  his hand by the h. of the door 52:10
  h. in a' your coats 107:21
  h. where his tail came through 507:20
  h. where the tail came through 151:9
  if you knows of a better h. 29:11
  old Sallie Worm from her h. 171:23
  play on the h. of the asp 53:19
  poisoned rat in a h. 519:31
  stick'n in a big mud h. 210:14
  your hat has got a h. in't 124:7
Holes: foxes have h. 58:34
  h. where eyes did..inhabit 476:14
Holiday: butcher'd to make a Roman h. 114:19
  but seldom, on the h. 138:16
  daunce ne moe atte h. 136:17
  envy never makes h. 25:9
  free and h. rejoicing spirit 307:17
  he speaks h. 466:5
  in a h. humour 428:19
  is this a h.? 448:3
  many h. and lady terms 438:33
  Monday is parson's h. 519:30
  on a sunshine h. 342:3
  regular h. to them 179:20
  we no h. have seen 159:32
Holidays: if all the year were..h. 438:31
Holier: within the h. blue 95:35
Holiest: h. thing alive 152:14
  one of the truest and the h. 328:14
  praise to the H. 364:6
Holily: that wouldst thou h. 457:1
Holiness: courage of heart or h. 41:16
  h. of the heart's affections 289:17
  put off H. 75:13
  remembrance of his h. 393:25
  what he has lost in h. 111:35
Hollaing: lost it with h. 441:21
Holland: children in H. 10:10
  deep where H. lies 226:13
  H...saved by being dammed 253:34
  Lowlands o' H. 31:11
Hollo: came to the mariner's h. 148:28
Holloa: we'll whoop and we'll h. 568:22
Hollow: all was false and h. 345:18
  applaud the h. ghost 16:10
  fearful h. of thine ear 478:26
  h. pamper'd jades 441:37
  h. seas that roar 332:3
  I hate the dreadful h. 535:33
  in the h. of her breasts a tomb 522:14
  Providence fashioned us h. 319:18
  tell the grassy h. 336:9
  touched the h. of his thigh 45:9
  we are the h. men 197:10
  within the h. crown 475:7
Hollowed a little mournfully 359:10
Hollow-ey'd, sharp-looking wretch 429:1
Hollowness: machinations, h., treachery 452:16
Hollows: bowery h. 531:37
Holly: English oak and h. 238:26
  h. and the ivy 10:14
  h. bears the crown 10:14
  h. branch shone 36:30
  unto the green h. 427:22
Holocaust: lay erewhile a h. 351:3
Holy: as h. and enchanted 151:32
  as you came from the h. land 405:10
  come thou H. Spirit 132:1
  coming to that h. room 185:25
  died to make men h. 264:18
  haunted, h. ground 113:19
  her foundations are upon the h. hills 397:13
  he that is h...h. still 72:8
  h., acceptable unto God 65:62
  H. Deadlock 243:7
  h., divine, good, amiable 349:17
  h., fair, and wise is she 484:40
  H., H., H. is the Lord God 74:6

Holy (cont.)
  h., h., h. is the Lord of hosts 53:8
  H., H., H.! Lord God Almighty! 70:38, 240:19
  h., h., h., Lord God of hosts 390:40
  h. text of pike and gun 110:17
  h. time is quiet 577:1
  keep h. the Sabbath-day 390:9
  neither h., nor Roman 557:8
  O Lord, h. and true 70:46
  place is h. ground 537:43
  place whereon thou standest is h. ground 45:34
  seal'd to the h. book 15:27
  seems half h. 88:13
  suffer thy H. One to see corruption 392:27
  that hunters been nat h. men 136:31
  thou continuest h. 393:1
  'tis h. ground 231:1
  'twas on a H. Thursday 76:15
  twice h. was the Sabbath-bell 285:30
  wheresoe'er it be, a h. place 410:18
Holy Ghost: blasphemy against the H. 59:12
  come H., our souls inspire 400:31
  H. over the bent world 254:25
  no gold, no H. 111:39
  operation of the H. 390:41
  pencil of the H. 25:19
  praise Father, Son, and H. 292:3
  pretending to..gifts of the H. 109:38
  whether there be any H. 65:5
  your body is the temple of the H. 66:29
Holy Land: vainly I suppos'd the H. 442:29
Holy Writ: ends stol'n forth of h. 476:12
  proofs of h. 471:42
Homage: all things..do her h. 253:36
  claims the h. of a tear 113:15
  do h. to thy king 508:18
  each under eye doth h. 486:12
  owes no h. unto the sun 86:37
Home: afraid to come h. in the dark 571:3
  all go the same way h. 360:1
  all the h. I have 24:10
  almost sacred joys of h. 358:1
  any more at h. like you? 234:12
  at H. the Christmas Day 295:9
  at your h. in the Soudan 296:23
  because they starv'd at h. 192:28
  before Irish H. Rule is concluded 409:8
  blest by suns of h. 84:21
  by water he sente hem h. 137:13
  call h. the heart 189:14
  charity begins at h. 86:31, 500:44
  cluck'd thee..safely h. 429:22
  come h...to marry thee 35:10
  come h...with a flood of tears 174:22
  comin' for to carry me h. 10:2
  confined him h. 146:4
  creep h., and take your place there 293:19
  day's march nearer h. 355:10
  dream that I am h. again 208:4
  dunce that has been kept at h. 161:31
  eaten me out of house and h. 441:30
  England, h. and beauty 79:15
  ere I left my h. 160:31
  farewell h. 166:12
  father, come h. with me 583:8
  fill'd one h. with glee 241:8
  first, best country..at h. 226:7
  follow me—follow me h. 296:17
  for homely features to keep h. 340:38
  for husbands to stay at h. 196:28
  from thy celestial h. 132:1
  full sails hasting loaden h. 332:10
  Germany was my 'spiritual h.' 233:21
  go back h. wid a pocket full 210:13
  God, who is our h. 576:9
  goodman is not at h. 49:50
  grows erect as that comes h. 186:25
  happy as ever at h. 82:11
  Heaven is everywhere at h. 141:15
  hence! h., you idle creatures 448:3
  her h. is on the deep 123:11
  her princes are come h. again 448:2
  he that..comes safe h. 444:28
  he who gives a child a h. 334:1

Home (cont.)
  his floating h. for ever left 159:1
  h. art gone 430:1
  h. had she none 252:18
  h. his footsteps..turn'd 417:22
  h., h., h. to my ain countree 167:22
  h., h., sweet, sweet h.! 376:10
  h. I'd trudge to mine 171:17
  h. is h...never so homely 14:7, 146:1
  h. is the girl's prison 490:36
  h. is the sailor, h. from sea 516:15
  h. life of our own dear Queen 7:2
  h. of lost causes 19:10
  h. of the brave 292:11, 489:1
  h. on the rolling deep 415:11
  h., Rose, and h. 146:33
  h.'s h., be it never so hamely 14:7, 146:1
  h. they brought her warrior 538:25
  h. to his mother's house 350:18
  h. to shades of under ground 123:27
  h. where the buffalo roam 248:9
  h. with her maiden posy 536:4
  hunter h. from the hill 516:15
  I am far from h. 364:10
  I can't find my way h. 369:7
  I don't want to go h. in the dark 242:15
  if all..were well at h. 142:31
  I had a h. once 508:4
  I'm going h. 199:15
  intruders on his ancient h. 18:16
  it never is at h. 159:20
  it's h. and it's h., h. fain would I be 167:22
  keep the h. fires burning 210:4
  kindred points of heaven and h. 580:27
  lark shall sing me h. 167:23
  late..Kilmeny came h. 250:22
  little grey h. in the west 571:7
  live at h. with ease 373:11, 12
  lost it all by travelling at h. 272:1
  man goeth to his long h. 51:33
  music of the Gospel leads us h. 202:24
  my happy h. 6:28
  my heart thy h. 498:16
  near to their eternal h. 557:25
  never h. came she 293:24
  never more go h. 324:8
  next way h. 404:8
  no place like h. 376:10
  not of a perishable h. 577:11
  of youth, and h. 357:15
  old folks at h. 210:16
  old Kentucky H. 210:15
  our being's heart and h. 579:27
  our eternal h. 562:9
  pleasure never is at h. 285:37
  Ruth..sick for h. 288:1
  safe h., safe h. in port 362:11
  shall I never feel at h.? 561:17
  share my harvest and my h. 253:21
  shuts the spouse Christ h. 255:6
  start it at h. 162:2
  stay, stay at h., my heart 317:18
  Taffy was not at h. 369:1
  that drive one from h. 253:10
  their h. among the dead 493:10
  there is a blessed h. 29:13
  there's nobody at h. 382:9
  they dream of h. 210:4
  they have their graves at h. 140:24
  they'll come h. 367:14
  things at h. are crossways 125:20
  this little pig stayed at h. 369:7
  thou must bring her h. 31:24
  thy h. is still here 356:15
  thy Naiad airs..brought me h. 380:17
  till the boys come h. 210:4
  turns again h. 528:22
  welcome as we draw near h. 115:22
  what's the good of a h. 233:4
  when I was at h. 426:39
  When Johnny Comes Marching H. 11:19
  when we gade to bring him h. 250:12
  where Huntley, and where H.? 418:33
  white porch of his h. 323:26
  wish him safe at h. 282:10
  won't go h. till morning 98:15
  you'd best be getting h. 128:19
  your cradle, your h. 494:21

[764]

INDEX

Home-born happiness 163:26
Home-bred: mean, sordid, h. cares 101:30
Home-brewed: ill-tasted, h. prayer 231:30
Home-keeping: h. hearts are happiest 317:18
h. youth 484:28
Homeless: h. near a thousand homes 575:4
those who are h. by choice 508:9
Homely: be it never so h. 14:7
home-keeping youth..h. wits 484:28
h. was their food 213:20
though it be never so h. 146:1
with that h. face 573:22
Home-made: geological h. cake 176:8
h. dishes 253:10
Homer: deep-brow'd H. 288:19
dumb to H. 94:9
ere H.'s lamp appear'd 162:26
for H., being dead 248:4
for H. dead 9:15
Greece, sound thy H.'s..name 160:24
H...his eye on the object 20:3
H.'s golden chain 109:24
H. sometimes sleeps 116:6
H. will be all..you need 98:11
if H...nods 256:10
in H. more than H. knew 521:17
in H. or in Dares 138:25
made blind H. sing to me 330:4
our poets steal from H. 109:4
read H. once 98:11
sage H.'s rule the best 386:6
though Somnus in H. be sent 85:21
translator of H. 20:2
when H. smote 'is bloomin' lyre 303:22
you must not call it H. 43:6
Homerus: bonus dormitat H. 256:10
Homes: cottage h. of England 241:13
from quiet h. 41:17
homeless near a thousand h. 575:4
h. of silent prayer 532:23
in happy h. he saw the light 316:18
stately h. of England 241:12
their own natural h. 149:24
Home-spuns: hempen h. 467:4
Homeward: Don John of Austria rides h. 141:8
look h., Angel 343:2
ploughman h. plods 229:28
rooks in families h. go 236:33
Homewards: most roads lead men h. 334:9
Homily: some worm-canker'd h. 540:15
Homines: non h., non di 256:12
quidquid agunt h. 282:25
quot h. tot sententiae 542:1
Homing: those who were h. 236:29
Hominum: qui mores h. multorum vidit 255:26
Hominy: presented..by a H. 176:25
Hommage que le vice rend à la vertu 407:11
Homme: le style est l'h. même 98:17
on trouve un h. 373:21
pour être dévot..pas moins h. 354:6
un h. avec Dieu 305:5
Hommes: français aux h. 136:13
Homo: ecce h. 63:70
fit semper tempore pejor h. 372:13
h. proponit 291:20
h. sum 541:30
Homocea touches the spot 7:1
Homogeneal: all her body is h. 352:11
Homogeneity: indefinite, incoherent h. 508:25
Hone: ingenious H. 308:3
Honest: ambassador is an h. man 583:15
anglers, or very h. men 559:24
as h. as any man living 468:42
but she was h. 9:18
by nature h. 386:4
Dangers of an H. Man 158:23
few h. men 167:2
good h. and painful sermon 777:16
good to be h. and true 7:22, 106:6
h., and of an open..nature 280:1
h. atheism for my money 371:7
h. broker 72:32
h. Englishmen 293:11

Honest (cont.)
h. exceeding poor man 463:29
h. folk droop 90:16
h. God 112:9, 267:16
h. labour bears a lovely face 170:21
h. man, close-button'd 160:12
h. man's aboon his might 105:32
h. man's the noblest work 105:5, 384:9
h. men and bonnie lasses 108:3
h. without a thought of Heaven 86:21
I am myself indifferent h. 434:8
in a general h. thought 452:9
in every h. hand a whip 473:2
I think my wife be h. 472:7
it is an h. ghost 432:24
made h. by an act of parliament 279:32
makes an h. man a knave 170:10
my fortunes have corrupted h. men 425:10
not an h. man 565:28
poor but h. 423:3
rather, an h. woman's son 463:27
shows his h. face 191:3
social, friendly, h. man 105:25
that h. few 540:28
thinks man h. 470:22
though I be poor, I'm h. 338:16
though it be h. 424:15
though..not naturally h. 485:35
to be direct and h. is not safe 472:6
to be h., as this world goes 433:2
to be h., to be kind 513:35
very h...something given to lie 426:7
well to be h. and true 335:4
whatsoever things are h. 68:27
world's grown h. 433:10
Honester: no h. than I 468:42
Honestly: to my Neighbour h. 316:32
Honestum: iudex h. praetulit utili 261:3
Honesty: arm'd so strong in h. 451:19
corruption..not more than h. 446:31
fly, H., fly! 504:2
h. is the best policy 565:28
h., manhood, nor good fellowship 438:27
make thine h. a vice 472:6
make your children capable of h. 413:22
not h. to have it thus set down 433:5
rich h. dwells like a miser 428:36
this fellow's of exceeding h. 471:37
thy h...doth mince this matter 471:18
what a fool H. is! 485:34
your h...based .. in vacant heaven 413:21
Honey: as the h. of Hybla 438:17
butter and h. shall he eat 53:12
citizens kneading up the h. 443:10
eating bread and h. 368:20
eat our pot of h. on the grave 336:26
fill our hives with h. and wax 519:5
flowing with milk and h. 45:36
gather h. all the day 561:28
gather h. from the weed 444:13
h. of all earthly joy 158:12
h. of his music vows 434:14
h. of poison-flowers 535:38
how a bear likes h. 339:20
I did but taste a little h. 47:14
in my mouth sweet as h. 71:14
is there h. still for tea? 84:15
locusts and wild h. 57:29
nor h. make 152:17
some h., and plenty of money 311:24
sweeter also than h. 392:33
they surfeited with h. 440:9
with milk and h. blest 362:1
you are my h., h.-suckle 205:2
Honey-bee: hive for the h. 585:12
Honey-bees: so work the h. 443:10
Honey-comb: drop as an h. 49:44
of an h. 62:57
Honey-dew: he on h. hath fed 151:33(-152)
Honeyed: bee with h. thigh 341:22
h. middle of the night 285:15
Honey-heavy dew of slumber 449:13
Honeyless: leave them h. 451:33
Honey-suckle: you are my honey, h. 205:2
Hongs: chop sticks, h. and gongs 379:22

Honnêtes: faire rire les h. gens 353:15
Honneur: sans argent l'h. 405:5
tout est perdu fors l'h. 211:4
Honores: contemnere h. 262:1
sepulcri mitte supervacuos h. 259:13
Honorificabilitudinitatibus 455:26
Honos: semper h. nomenque..manebunt 553:21
Honour: as he was valiant I h. him 450:15
brothers all in h. 579:28
by h. and dishonour 67:28
can h. set-to a leg? 440:30
can h.'s voice provoke 230:3
chivalrye, trouthe and h. 136:23
clear h...purchased by the merit 464:1
clinging..to some rag of h. 513:32
depths and shoals of h. 446:29
done with Hope and H. 296:28
each cavalier who loves h. and me 416:8
Fear God. H. the King 69:50, 305:1
fountain of h. 27:45, 28:22
fount whence h. springs 330:29
from the book of h. razed 486:22
full of days, riches, and h. 48:34
gilded h...misplac'd 487:14
giving h. unto the wife 70:2
Glory, Love, and H. unto..Jane 297:20
good luck..with thine h. 394:22
greater share of h. 444:26
great peaks of h. 216:7
his h. rooted in dishonour 530:37
h. all men 69:50
h. a physician 57:9
h. aspireth to it 26:2
h. be yours and fame 362:31
h. but an empty bubble 191:9
h. comes unlooked for 440:35
h. has come back 83:20
h. hath no skill in surgery 440:30
h. is a mere scutcheon 440:30
h. is the subject 448:17
h., love, obedience 460:36
h. of the British Army 305:1
h. peereth in the meanest habit 479:9
h. pricks me on 440:30
h. sinks 226:8
h.'s thought reigns solely 443:12
h...them in the same degree 86:27
h. the shrine 232:11
h. the very flea of his dog 280:15
h. thou hast got 110:32
h. thy father and thy mother 390:10
h...to Nelson's peerless name 362:31
h. to whom h. 66:11
h. travels in a strait 481:19
h. unto Luke Evangelist 411:9
h. unto which she was not born 535:7
h. was the meed of victory 509:35
h. which they do not understand 578:5
h., while you strike him down 362:33
how I do h. thee 465:4
hurt that H. feels 534:24
idiot race to h. lost 107:23
I do h. his memory 280:1
if h. gives greatness 173:9
if it be a sin to covet h. 444:27
if peace cannot be maintained with h. 414:1
I like not such grinning h. 440:35
in h. clear 385:6
in..h. goeth to hym nigh 195:7
in h. I gained them 362:22
in h. preferring one another 66:2
jealous in h. 427:21
laud and h. to the Father 361:14
loaden with h. 429:22
louder he talked of his h. 200:1
loved I not h. more 319:10
make one vessel unto h. 65:60
man being in h. 395:2
mine h. from corruption 447:11
mine h. is my life 474:10
nation of men of h. 102:11
new-made h. doth forget 447:19
no point of h. 245:2
nought..in hate, but all in h. 473:34
old age hath yet his h. 541:3
on her left hand riches and h. 49:40
peace I hope with h. 181:10
peace with h. 135:9
pension list..a roll of h. 146:5

INDEX

Honour (*cont.*)

perfect ways of h.	447:15
perseverance..keeps h. bright	481:18
pluck bright h. from the..moon	438:38
pluck up drowned h.	438:38
post of h. is a private station	1:21
prophet is not without h.	59:33
resolved to h. and renown ye	9:21
robb'd me of my Robe of H.	207:22
safety, h., and welfare of our Sovereign	389:14
set h. in one eye	448:16
so h. cross it	438:37
some smatch of h.	452:6
stain in thine h.	57:8
take h. from me	474:10
that chastity of h.	102:13
that h. could not move	84:17
that h. would thee do	443:13
there H. comes	153:30
they smack of h. both	456:7
throne *we* h.	500:13
to h. his own word	530:13
to h. we call you	213:10
Truth the masculine of H.	237:23
two men I h.	127:23
vivid air signed with their h.	509:2
welcome maids of h.	247:11
what is h.? A word	440:30
when h.'s at the stake	436:17
where thine h. dwelleth	393:19
whom the king delighteth to h.	48:36
with native h. clad	347:10
Ye take mine h. from me	298:11
your quaint h.	333:9

Honourable: adventurous and h. youth 514:38
Brutus is an h. man..all h. men	450:18
his designs were strictly h.	204:30
h. alike in what we give	314:11
h. high-mindedness	503:17
h. murderer	473:34
h. style of Christian	86:1
loose from every h. engagement	101:37
make an h. retreat	428:2
teach ourselves that h. stop	471:5
they that have done this deed are h.	450:32
upright, the generous, the h.	363:26

Honoured: by strangers h. 381:34
devil be sometime h.	462:25
ever h., ever sung	38:10
followed him, h. him	93:3
he hath h. me of late	457:10
h. of them all	540:32
how loved, how h. once	381:36
Law. It has h. us	563:7
man..h. for them	81:9
more h. in the breach	431:31
praised, wept, and h.	382:18
so known, so h.	386:11

Honouring: not so much h. thee 280:21(−281)

Honours: all claim to poetical h. 278:10
bears his blushing h.	446:24
from what a depth proceed thy h.	579:34
held the patent for his h.	105:16
his h. to the world	447:4
lie in wait for wealth, or h.	575:9
make them h. of..impossibilities	454:5
mindless of its just h.	580:10
not uncrowned with h.	561:15
piled-up h. perish	90:39

Hood: here lies bold Robin H. 31:22
him that wears a h.	516:21
is Robin H. asleep?	366:6
tea-cup times of h. and hoop	540:18
witty and the tender H.	308:20

Hoods: cowls, h., and habits 346:26

Hood-winked boy 213:15

Hoofs: plunging h. were gone 171:10
wound thee with their horses' h.	474:34

Hook: draw out leviathan with an h. 49:29
for subscribers baits his h.	143:6
never fly conceals a h.	83:27
thine has a great h. nose	74:10
thy h. spares the next swath	284:12
with saints dost bait thy h.	402:1

Hookah-mouth: puffs from the h. 294:29

Hooker: Life of..Mr. Richard H. 572:21
sail this h. the wide world round	303:9

Hook-nosed fellow of Rome 442:19

Hooks: develop his h. and his crooks 107:36
silken lines, and silver h.	184:8

Hoop: tea-cup times of hood and h. 540:18

Hoops: grapple them..with h. of steel 431:25

Hooter: because the h. hoots 141:11

Hooting: h. and shrieking 448:33
h. at the glorious sun	151:19
remained there through night h.	39:29

Hoots: because the hooter h. 141:11
owl, that nightly h.	466:43

Hop: I saw her once h. forty paces 424:8
lets it h. a little	477:28
why h. ye so, ye high hills	396:7

Hope: against h. believed in h. 65:40
all h. abandon	168:17
all it yields of..h. and fear	90:42
beacons of h.	17:20
because I do not h. to turn	197:2
break it to our h.	461:12
burning with high h.	113:34
by admiration, h. and love	574:19
can something,	254:19
Christians, at your cross of h.	87:38
darkness quieted by h.	96:31
done with H. and Honour	296:28
equal h., and hazard	344:12
farewell h., and with h. farewell fear	346:33
Fear and trembling H.	582:22
feeble H. could ne'er have flown	332:5
fool'd with h.	191:34
forks and h.	128:11
for the h. of glory	389:20
from h. and fear set free	523:23
frustrate h. severer than despair	160:20
giving it a h. that there	280:21(−281)
God is our h. and strength	394:27
god-like wish, or h. divine	574:2
heirs through h.	390:47
he may live without h.	337:42
he that lives upon h.	211:17
high uplifted beyond h.	345:14
H. an Antinoüs mere	146:20
h. and fear, and peace and strife	419:28
h...bade the world farewell	122:33
h. deferred	50:3
h. elevates	349:13
h. is a good breakfast	24:39
h. is less dear	584:20
h., like the gleaming taper	224:10
h. maketh not ashamed	65:41
h. may vanish	493:23
h. never comes	344:9
h. nor love	515:28
h. of all the ends of the earth	395:28
h. of the City of God	334:13
h., once crushed	18:30
H. sows	410:33
H.'s perpetual breath	581:17
h. springs eternal	383:11
h.'s true gage	405:9
h. thou not much	524:6
h. till H. creates	497:17
h. to rise or fear to fall	583:11
h. without an object	152:18
I have h. to live	462:3
I have nor h. nor health	498:24
I h., I h. they do not point at me	473:13
increase of faith, h. and charity	389:46
in faith and h...disagree	384:1
in h. of fair advantages	463:39
in h. the world can show	186:15
in the fulness of joy and h.	253:7
in trembling h. repose	230:13
Land of H. and Glory	42:20
leave the light of H. behind	122:40
leisure for love or h.	253:26
let us h. for better things	23:2
man of h.	574:24
mock the h. of toil	165:17
more h. of a fool	50:40
more plentiful than h.	245:8
much to h. and nothing to lose	103:12
my grief, my h., my love	558:1
my h. is better	484:13

Hope (*cont.*)
my own h. is	89:12
Nature, H., and Poesy	152:20
never h. to see one	100:1
never to h. again	446:24
no h. who never had a fear	104:15
no other medicine but only h.	462:3
not another's h.	559:7
not because I h. for heaven	132:7
not without h. we suffer	578:17
no very lively h. of success	505:16
now abideth faith, h., charity	66:46(−67)
of friends, of h., of all bereft	159:1
old h. goes to ground	92:43
one H.'s one name	411:23
one more rich in h.	486:24
on h. the wretch relies	224:10
our h. for years to come	562:9
only h. that keeps up a wife's spirits	214:20
only..unsettled is there any h.	200:8
perished leaves of H.	410:24
pursue..the phantoms of h.	278:10
rising h. of those..Tories	324:27
simple nature to his h.	383:11
some blessed H.	235:18
Spanish ale shall give you h.	329:1
take back the h.	92:31
take short views, h. for the best	504:23
tender leaves of h.	446:24
their h. full of immortality	56:23
their h. of eternal damnation	43:20
they h. they serve God	469:7
this pleasing h., this fond desire	1:22
through love, through h.	573:27
to feed on h.	510:16
tradesman..h. to go to heaven	194:27
triumph of h. over experience	272:4
true h. is swift	476:33
unconquerable h.	18:15
was the h. drunk	457:11
what advancement may I h.	434:24
what I faintly h.	193:17
what is h. but deceiving?	337:42
what reinforcement..from h.	344:17
what was dead was H.	569:9
when all h. seem'd desp'rate	357:9
when h. is gone	22:27
where H. clung feeding	152:30
where there is life, there's h.	215:25
white-handed H.	340:11
with faith, with h., with charity	245:9
with h. it is, h. that can never die	579:27
without all h. of day	350:22
woes which H. thinks infinite	497:17
work without h.	152:18
Worldly H.	205:27
ye prisoners of h.	56:12
youth whose h. is high	81:24

Hoped: all we have willed or h. 89:9
he who has never h.	489:10
h. it would vex somebody	274:17
h. we were both broken-hearted	524:9
substance of things h. for	69:13

Hopeful: hey, but I'm h. 220:31
h. thou'lt recover once my dust	355:21

Hope-hour: as the h. stroked 235:15

Hopeless: ages of h. end 345:21
h. grief is passionless	88:15
h. horn blown	140:18
h. lance..in rest	140:18
perennially h.	173:22
useless and h. sorrow	277:41

Hopes: airy h. my children 574:16
all his h. of good	19:2
all revolution in the h. and fears of men	579:38
all the h. of future years	316:1
dashing at forlorn h.	29:6
extravagant h. of the future	101:33
fifty h. and fears	89:31
had h. to win her	155:38
his h. as eager as ours	100:17
h. and fears it heeded not	498:24
h. and fears of all the years	84:25
h. of earthly bliss	163:35
h. of high talk	494:5
if h. were dupes	147:8
Incarnations of h. and fears	491:21

INDEX

Hopes (cont.)
like an interdict upon her h. 579:2
me and my utmost h. 472:34
my fondest h. decay 357:5
my fondest h. would not decay 121:8
my h. no more must change 573:30
nil ultra to my proudest h. 334:24
no great h. from Birmingham 22:19
not without comforts and h. 25:20
our very h. belied 252:23
threats of Hell and H. of Paradise 206:26
wholly h. to be 91:1
Hopeth all things 66:45
Hoping: h. it might be so 236:23
trembling, h., ling'ring 381:28
Hopkins, hail! 162:30
Hopped with his song 171:20
Hopping: h. o'er the floor 546:26
meagre, h...insects of the hour 102:20
Hoppy, Croppy, Droppy 213:5
Hops: apples, cherries, h., and women 178:28
Hop-yards: for what were h. meant? 263:24
Hora: almum quae rapit h. diem 260:25
quae non sperabitur h. 256:27
quid..felici optatius h. 133:8
suprema mihi cum venerit h. 547:18
Horace: farewell, H. 114:11
had H. or Anacreon tasted 280:9
Horatii curiosa felicitas 378:9
Horatio: H... as just a man is H. there? 434:23, 430:9
Horatius: brave H. stand alone 323:25
come back, H.! 323:24
how well H. kept the bridge 324:1
out spake brave H. 323:17
Horatius: [H.] et insurgit aliquando 404:26
Horde: society..one polish'd h. 116:48
they're a ravenous h. 219:11
Horizon: I saw her just above the h. 102:11
their meeting-line at the h. 237:8
western h...in a blaze 100:9
Horizons: thunder answering from two h. 412:29
Horizontal: lie around us in h. positions 127:5
Horn: blast of that dread h. 418:33
blow up your h. 367:15
cow with the crumpled h. 369:6
echoing h. 229:31
his small but sullen h. 153:24
hopeless h. blown 140:18
h. of the hunter 166:24
h., the h., the lusty h. 428:23
huntsman winds his h. 204:37
my hoarse-sounding h. 506:13
put forth a conscious h. 544:9
Saint John sate in the h. 7:14
sound of his h. 229:16
sound upon the bugle h. 534:13
south to the blind H.'s hate 298:28
thro' the mellow h. 154:1
Triton blow his wreathed h. 582:18
Triton blowing..his wreathed h. 509:8
winding His lonely h. 584:20
with his hounds and his h. 229:16
you have a h. 40:28
Hornby: O my H. and my Barlow 545:2
Horne: Godolphin H. was nobly born 40:35
Horned Moon 149:16
Horner: little Jack H. 367:16
Hornets: let wasps and h. break through 519:7
Hornie: Auld H., Satan 104:4
Horns: also from the h. of unicorns 393:7
between the h. of the moon 508:1
hang them on the h. o' the moon 429:5
h. of Elfland 538:15
Latin names for h. and stools 105:23
on the silver h. 539:4
Queen of Heaven, with crescent h. 344:31
seven h. and seven eyes 70:41
she put out her h. 366:19
tender h. of cockled snails 455:22
you with shelly h., rams! 336:38

Horny: pointing a gun at the h. 146:23
Horny-handed sons of toil 284:9
Horrendous: ingens-h. 97:17
Horrendum: monstrum h. 554:14
Horresco referens 554:3
Horrible: dungeon h. 344:9
from the grotesque to the h. 188:15
more h. than that 149:22
O h.! O h.! most h.! 432:17
reign in this h. place 164:22
Horrid: are they all h.? 22:23
h., hideous notes of woe 116:50
h. stillness 191:31
h. thing, a very h. thing 109:38
h. wicked boy 249:19
Moloch, h. king 344:28
O h. provisos 156:15
one demd h. grind 177:25
when she was bad she was h. 318:17
Horridly to shake our disposition 431:32(-432)
Horror: excite the h. of Bossuet 325:23
great h. and darkness 99:24
haunts of h. and fear 536:22
h. heavy sat 193:38
h. of great darkness 44:47
h. of that moment 129:37
its h. and its beauty 495:17
on h.'s head horrors 472:5
scaly h. of his folded tail 343:20
secret dread and inward h. 1:22
take the present h. from the time 458:1
Horrors: congenial h., hail 546:25
hail, h., hail 344:22
h. of the deep 123:24
on horror's head h. accumulate 472:5
supp'd full with h. 461:3
without arithmetic..a scene of h. 505:33
Hors-d'œuvres: make h. for fishes 183:14
Horse: behold a pale h. 70:45
behold a white h. 71:36
better have them cleanin' his h. 518:20
blind h. stick'n 210:14
bring forth the h.! 118:13
by h. and crest 323:15
calender will lend his h. 159:34
call me h. 439:20
dark h. 182:45
dog, a h., a rat have life 454:26
e'er since sits on his h. 447:23
fifty thousand h. and foot 294:19
flung himself upon his h. 311:1
for catching my h., 6d. 518:22
for want of a h. 211:10
give a man a h. he can ride 546:31
give me another h.! 476:35
good h. in the stable 226:30
help Hyperion to his h. 444:23
hey for boot and h., lad 293:19
his h...wonder more and more 160:1
h.! a h.! my kingdom for a h.! 476:42
h. came spurring in 322:22
h. 'e knows above a bit 300:8
h. is counted but a vain thing 393:37
h. is drawn by the cart 295:15
h. loves the 'ound 518:15
h. of air 12:2
h. of that colour 482:35
h. misus'd upon the road 73:20
h. was lost 211:10
I long ago lost a hound, a bay h. 546:35
lady upon the h. 368:17
lies about his wooden h. 208:15
little dearer than his h. 534:19
man upon a black h. 307:2
my h. a thing of wings 78:2
my h., my wife, and my name 518:29
no h.'s cry was that 17:26
no pleasure in the strength of an h. 400:22
nothing but talk of his h. 463:9
not like to h. and mule 393:34
O, for a h. with wings 429:30
old h. that stumbles 236:14
one h. was blind 504:6
one stiff blind h. 90:21
only fit companion..his h. 159:22
other is a h. still 270:19
pulling in one's h...leaping 237:22

Horse (cont.)
ride a cock-h. 368:17
rider and h. 113:36
Ruksh, the h. 17:26
secret..between a rider and his h. 518:42
silent on his h. 42:11
so is my h., Octavius 451:6
something in a flying h. 578:23
strong is the h. 503:5
sword, a h., a shield 319:10
teach an old h. amble true 510:2
tedious as a tired h. 440:2
that which is now a h. 425:20
to buy the h. 443:12
to h., and away 90:19
to h., away 144:28
to my h.—German 136:13
to Oxford sent a troop of h. 87:26, 548:20
to such..doing brought his h. 436:42
truest friend..that ever bestrad h. 328:24
trusting junior with a h. 300:18
two things about the h. 7:6
upon the heavens as it were..an h. 396:5
upon the high h. 85:5
what a h. should have 488:27
White H. of the White H. Vale 140:11
Horseback: ride on h. after we 159:33
Horse drench: Love Powders, and then a..h. 307:14
Horsed upon the sightless couriers 457:9
Horse Guards: gone on business to the H. 177:22
Horseleach hath two daughters 50:54
Horseman: at the h.'s back 121:18
Horsemanship: himputation..on his h. 518:13
with noble h. 440:18
Horsemen: chariot of Israel, and the h. 48:16
h. riding upon horses 55:32
with hounds and h. 78:1
Horse-race won at Olympus 502:10
Horses: all the king's h. 367:5
as fed h. in the morning 55:11
ay, the h. trample 263:5
careful of the breed of their h. 377:8
come saddle my h. 420:15
come saddle your h. 416:8
dressing eels, or shoeing h. 387:23
harness and not the h. 124:20
hell for h. 109:29
hell of h. 209:8
h. and dorgs is some men's fancy 174:29
h. of instruction 77:17
in England..given to h. 277:29
Italy a paradise for h. 109:29
let us take any man's h. 442:36
no h. are kept 339:2
not hanged for stealing h. 234:5
nothing like blood..in h., dawgs and men 542:38
plats the manes of h. 477:7
rode their h. up to bed 171:11
some put their trust in..h. 392:37
swap h. while crossing the river 314:15
to clean h. 518:35
to trampling h.' feet 502:3
watered our h. in Helicon 135:21
what we spend on our h. 413:5
wild white h. play 15:23
Women and H. and Power and War 294:29
wound thee with their h.'s hoofs 474:34
Hortus: modus agri non ita magnus, h. 261:24
Hosanna: glorious h. from the den 503:6
Hosannas: made sweet H. ring 361:8
Hose: his round h. in France 463:12
youthful h. well sav'd 427:21
Hospes: deferor h. 256:16
h. comesque corporis 233:19
Hospitable: native to famous wits, or h. 350:11
on h. thoughts intent 348:8
Hospital: learnt..fellowship..in a h. 87:31
not an inn, but an h. 86:36

[767]

Hospitality: doing deeds of h. 427:6
given to h. 66:3
good English h. 77:5
Hospitals: rot in h. 507:2
Host: Hesperus that led the starry
h. 347:19
Hesperus with the h. of heaven 566:13
h. is riding from Knocknarea 585:7
h. of debaters in himself 103:18
h. of golden daffodils 577:5
if you find such a h. 13:17
innumerable company of the
heavenly h. 74:6
mine H. can ne'er espy 561:18
now for the tea of our h. 222:18
play the humble h. 459:11
saved by the multitude of an h. 393:37
streams in the countless h. 264:10
Time is like a fashionable h. 481:20
Tory and Whig in turns..my h. 505:32
ye heavenly h. 292:3
Hostages to fortune 26:34
Hoste: fas est et ab h. doceri 371:29
Hostel: so pass I h., hall, and
grange 540:12
Hostess: back at mine h.' door 447:23
my h...a most sweet wench 438:17
Hostile: universe is not h. 250:27
Hostility: parts of the Empire in
direct h. 222:38
Hostis: Iuppiter h. 555:13
Hosts: even the Lord of h. 393:13
holy, holy, holy is the Lord of h. 53:8
holy, holy, holy, Lord God of h. 390:40
h. and guests 39:15
Lord God of H. 300:24
stronger than all the h. of error 98:1
who is this? the Lord of H. 421:2
Hot: argument's h. to the close 93:17
as Dian had h. dreams 430:4
come h. from hell 450:12
ginger shall be h. i' the mouth 482:32
his heart was h. within him 317:25
honour..piping h. 110:32
h. for certainties 336:36
in a h. and copper sky 149:4
iron while it is h. 194:3
lull in the h. race 15:6
my heart was h. within me 394:8
small h. bird 204:2
too h. the eye of heaven 486:18
unbutton'd, glowing h. 164:8
when you make pitch h. 173:30
why the sea is boiling h. 130:15
your pots be made h. with
thorns 395:21
Hotched an' blew 108:13
Hotel: Mr. Reilly that owns the h. 7:19
take me back to the Gaierty h. 21:4
Hoti: he settled H.'s business 91:42
Hotness: day in his h. 15:17
Hotspur of the North 439:13
Hottentot: respectable H. 139:28
Hound: by the faithful h. 316:22
footprints of a gigantic h. 188:17
he'll grow into a h. 568:22
his hawk, his h., and his lady 32:15
his h. is to the hunting gane 32:15
horse loves the h. 518:15
h. or spaniel 453:30
I long ago lost a h., a bay horse 546:35
I loves the h. more 518:14
puppy, whelp and h. 225:20
sleping h. to wake 138:31
take that, you h. 188:7
Hounds: carcass fit for h. 449:10
cry of his h. 229:16
desires, like..cruel h. 481:31
dinner lost! h. lost, self lost 518:16
h...in glorious cry 204:37
h. of spring 521:30
my h...of the Spartan kind 467:20
of smale h. had she 136:30
questing of thirty couple h. 328:4
with his h. and his horn 229:16
with h. and horsemen 78:1
with h. of Sparta 467:20
Houndsditch: housebreaker, of H. 120:26
Hour: abode his destin'd H. 205:30
abode his H. or two 205:29
against the h. of death 391:39

Hour (cont.)
anguish of a torturing h. 467:25
at our last h. 391:43
awaits alike th'inevitable h. 230:1
books of the h. 413:2
break an h.'s promise in love 428:18
but an h. ago 185:31
but one h. mine 486:28
canny h. at e'en 105:38
carefully upon your h. 430:7
carol they began that h. 428:32
clocks were striking the h. 315:27
close-companioned inarticulate
h. 410:30
dark eleventh h. 303:11
dark h. or twain 458:31
dead h. of the night 32:4
died an h. before this chance 458:24
ending at the arrival of an h. 440:32
enfold me in my h. of hours 585:23
ere an h. be past 293:14
every h. is saved 540:32(−541)
every h. that passes O 105:37
fashioned to the varying h. 224:18
for his h...lord of the ascendant 100:9
fought a long h. 441:4
from h. to h. 427:14
happiest h. a sailor sees 219:17
happy h.! 374:24
her rash hand in evil h. 349:15
h. is come, but not the man 419:36
h. of blind old Dandolo 114:4
h. of vacant ease 579:35
h. out of Guildford town 299:23
h. to play 363:4
h. when earth's foundations fled 264:4
h. when from the boughs 118:28
h. when lovers' vows 118:28
h. when you too learn 410:33
how many make the h. 446:1
I also had my h. 140:22
I chang'd every h. 214:25
I have had my h. 194:21
improve each shining h. 561:28
in secret h. 498:6
insects of the h. 102:20
in such h. of need 17:20
iron scourge and tort'ring h. 230:15
joyous h...greeting 219:35
known as the Children's H. 316:3
legend of an epic h. 141:16
let this h. be but a year 330:7
let us have a quiet h. 541:12
lighting a little H. or two 205:27
look thy last..every h. 171:9
matched us with His h. 84:16
mine h. is not yet come 63:5
musing there an h. alone 115:44
nothing can bring back the h. 576:20
now's the h. 107:32
one bare h. to live 330:7
one crowded h. of glorious life 357:22
one dead deathless h. 410:21
one far fierce h. 140:22
present h. alone is man's 278:28
present h...mark'd with shade 308:31
some wee short h. 105:8
still h. of thinking 573:21
struts and frets his h. 461:4
superincumbent h. 492:2
surely thine h. has come 586:2
that h...the key-stane 108:9
that h. which freed us 85:21
their finest h. 143:41
this wing'd h. is dropt 410:30
time and the h. runs through 456:26
'tis the h. of prayer..of love 116:7
to fill the h. 200:12
torturing h. 230:15, 345:17, 467:25
turn the h. 206:16
wait the 'pointed h. 193:30
what h...by algebra 110:10
what this sweet h. yields 494:9
wonder of an h. 113:11
world-without-end h. 487:7
your loveliness and the h. of my
death 290:22
Hour-glass: still as the h. 410:29
Houris: lying with H. 231:20
Hours: banishing for h. the sex 159:18
chase the glowing H. 113:26

Hours (cont.)
desolate passions, aching h. 269:26
discourse the freezing h. away 429:31
for future h. 262:3
golden h. on angel wings 106:9
his brief h. and weeks 488:7
h. and the wild birds follow 524:13
h. and times of your desire 487:7
h. I spent with thee 408:5
h. to which high Heaven doth
chime 551:20
h. will take care or themselves 139:15
how many h. 446:1
inherit h. which are replaced 402:23
leaden-stepping h. 351:31
line will take us h. 584:2
lost..two golden h. 329:9
lovers' absent h. 472:18
lover's h. be full eternity 185:32
meek ethereal h. 285:36
my wingèd h. of bliss 122:40(−123)
neglect the creeping h. 427:19
nor h., days, months 186:20
six h. in sleep 148:8
spent the darksome h. weeping 127:30
steal a few h. from the night 357:1
sweetest h. that e'er I spend 105:37
to tell of sunny h. 264:22
waked by the circling h. 348:19
weary of days and h. 523:18
well content..with quiet h. 440:26
what h. were thine and mine 528:23
what peaceful h. I once enjoy'd 161:2
white and sable h. 38:30
with one voice about the space
of two h. 65:8
House: all the substance of his h.
for love 52:23
as the H. is pleased to direct me 313:15
barren woman to keep h. 399:1
because of the h. of the Lord 399:31
bequeath them no tumbled h. 335:26
better to go to the h. of mourning 51:9
bloody h. of life 447:42
bow myself in the h. of Rimmon 48:23
bring thee into my mother's h. 52:21
build a h. for fools and mad 521:4
dark h. 532:8
disturb this hallow'd h. 467:36
doorkeeper in the h. of my God 397:7
dwell in the h. of the Fenians 586:20
dwell in the h. of the Lord for
ever 393:10
eaten me out of h. and home 441:30
except the Lord build the h. 399:35
fair h...upon another man's
ground 466:2
farewell h. 166:12
forget..thy father's h. 394:23
from every h. the neighbours 532:22
go into the h., and die 174:15
great h. of Tarquin 323:10
had a mind to sell his h. 519:6
handsome h. to lodge a friend 521:7
home to his mother's h. 350:18
h. and tenant go to ground 199:31
h. appointed for all living 49:10
h. divided against itself 314:6
h. is falling 334:37
h. is much more to my taste 358:20
h. not made with hands 67:24
h. o'ertopping all 90:37
h. of ancient fame 510:21
h. of everyone..his castle 148:9
h. of feasting 51:9
H. of Have..H. of Want 216:9
H. that armours a man 40:31
h. that Jack built 369:6
h. was filled with smoke 53:8
h. where I was born 252:33
h. with lawns 516:12
if a h. be divided 00:54
I have loved the habitation of
thy h. 393:19
in a little crooked h. 369:3
in my Father's h. are many mansions 63:51
in the h. of my pilgrimage 399:16
I went to Taffy's h. 369:1
I will build a h. 42:7
little h. 247:16

INDEX

House (cont.)

lodger in my own h.   226:33
lost sheep of the h. of Israel   58:46
man's h. his castle   148:7
may I have a warm h.   387:2
my h...called the h. of prayer   60:9
my h. in the high wood   42:7
my mother's h.   300:11
nearer my Father's h.   131:32
none other but the h. of God   45:5
nowhere but in's own h.   434:10
one of your accursed h.   324:11
our neighbour's h...on fire   102:4
peace be to this h.   61:34, 391:36
prop that doth sustain my h.   465:14
raven o'er the infected h.   472:20
reached the h. of doom   24:2
return no more to his h.   48:53
secret H. of Shame   569:8
see to thine own h., David   47:48
set a h. on fire..to roast..eggs   27:39
set thine h. in order   54:6
small h. and large garden   158:13
so fair a h.   479:33
sole daughter of my h.   113:21
spare the h. of Pindarus   351:15
sparrow hath found her an h.   397:5
that h. cannot stand   60:54
the Lord let the h. of a brute   528:9
them that join h. to h.   53:3
this h. as nigh heaven   358:5
this h. with starry dome   561:17
this reft h.   152:13
tho' he build his h. in the woods   201:22
unless you leave this h.   128:16
Vanbrugh's h. of clay   202:11
walked in the h. of God   395:12
we will go into the h. of the Lord   399:30
when h. and land are gone   209:19
wherever God erects a h.   170:11
withindoors h. the shocks   255:6
woe is me for the good h.   324:5
worse than a smoky h.   440:2
wounded in the h. of my friends   56:13
ye that are of the h. of the Lord   399:12
your h. is on fire   367:12
zeal of thine h...eaten me   396:17
Housebreaker, of Houndsditch   120:26
Housed: h., clothed, fed, and educated   413:23
h. in a dream   578:16
Household: as h. words   444:28
her h. motions   580:20
h. bird   184:27
h. happiness, gracious children   541:5
h. of continuance   518:1
religion breathing h. laws   577:16
sacred to the h. gods   546:26
some bird would trust her h. to me   243:20
they of his own h.   59:2
they of the h. divided the spoil   396:7
thy h. the Church   389:49
to study h. good   349:8
Householder, which bringeth forth   59:31
Housekeepings: jining of hearts and h.   177:42
Houseless: your h. heads   453:14
Housemaids: damp souls of h.   197:23
I walks with fifty h.   299:14
treat h. to his teas   142:1
Houses: here falling h. thunder   278:30
h. are built to live in   25:35
h. in between   36:22
h. that he makes   437:8
h. thick and sewers   349:11
laws, like h., lean on one another   102:34
let us see these handsome h.   535:3
plague o' both your h.   478:15
round their golden h.   535:19
set up her h.   394:35
their h. shall continue for ever   395:1
trees and h. go wheeling   546:30
very h. seem asleep   582:14
House-top: dwell in a corner of the h.   50:28
sparrow..upon the h.   398:1
Housewife: as a careful h. runs   488:17
h. ply her evening care   229:31

Housewife (cont.)

h. that's thrifty   500:39
mock the good h. Fortune   426:18
tease the h.'s wool   340:38
Housewifery: players in your h.   470:25
Housewives: h.' affairs have never an end   550:4
h. in your beds   470:25
no more h., but queens   413:8
Hovel: prefer in fact a h.   121:12
Hover: h. in their restless heads   331:2
h. through the fog   456:3
ofttimes I h.   543:4
Hovered: person or persons who h. before him   268:8
Hovering o'er the place's head   166:3
Hovers within my gates   319:4
How: and h. and when and where   7:5
dead, quick, I know not h.   232:15
h. do I love thee?   88:24
h. is it that you live?   580:14
h. is it you live?   131:22
h. long, O lord, h. long?   324:18
h. not to do it   175:29
h. now, you..hags!   460:2
if I could say h. much   468:14
know not h. nor why   82:23
say 'Hullo' and 'H. d'ye do?'   210:10
when or h. I cannot tell   411:34
without knowing h. or why   190:32
Howard: sware Lord Thomas H.   539:17
Howards: all the blood of all the H.   384:8
How-de-doo: here's a h.   219:37
Howe, and the Glorious First   359:26
Howell and James young man   221:8
Howl: h., ye ships of Tarshish   53:30
wolf knows h.'s his watch   458:1
Howled: roared and h.   148:26
Howling: hear the winds h.   16:1
h. of Irish wolves   428:29
Tom went h. down the street   369:11
waste h. wilderness   46:31
when thou liest h.   437:20
winds that will be h.   582:18
Howls: his h. was organs   176:31
h. the sublime   176:26
still h. on for more   495:9
struggles and h. at fits   492:27
Hub: h. of the solar system   251:16
H., the King Pin   83:2
Hubbard: old Mother H.   368:4
Hubbub increases   286:13
Hubert: approbation from Sir H.   359:20
of black Saint Hubert's breed   416:13
Huddled in dirt   407:22
Hue: add another h. unto the rainbow   447:39
bands of rosy h.   266:8
flavour and body and h.   34:34
flowers of all h.   347:6
gordian shape of dazzling h.   286:37
h. angry and brave   245:13
join not scent to h.   494:10
native h. of resolution   434:4
not grim but fair of h.   93:26
your sweet h.   487:29
Hues: consecrate with thine own h.   494:4
living h. and odours   496:4
rich h. have marriage made   81:7
Hug: h. it in mine arms   462:8
h. the dear deceit   157:21
Hugest of living creatures   348:26
Hugged: she h. th'offender   192:6
Hugger-mugger: in h. to inter him   436:26
Hugh: dirge for Saint H.'s soul   170:24
Saint H. be our good speed   170:24
Hugs: h. it to the last   357:10
servitude that h. her chain   231:2
Hulk: naked h. alongside came   149:13
sheer h.   173:10
Hull: settled first at H.   170:5
Hum: bee-hive's h.   408:10
borne in heedless h.   153:24
busy h. of men   342:5
h. of either army   444:6
h. of human cities torture   113:47
justice, with his surly h.   443:10
no voice or hideous h.   343:21
out of the mist and h.   17:28

Hum (cont.)

smell and hideous h.   223:8
want to make Hammersmith h.   243:4
Human: all h. things..decay   193:1
all that is h. must retrograde   217:14
blood of h. sacrifice   344:28
breathing h. passion far above   287:11
chords in the h. mind   173:35
conquered h. natur   177:3
Cruelty has a h. **heart**   77:4
due to h. folly   310:19
Euripides, the h.   89:6
flocks, or herds, or h. face   346:20
for h. nature's daily food   580:20
glorious to be h.   173:34
glory that redounds..to h. kind   579:36
happiness of the h. race   101:15
happy h. face   266:3
he himself with his h. air   90:27
held the h. race in scorn   40:35
highest reaches of a h. wit   331:2
history of the h. spirit   20:8
hope it mayn't be h. gore   173:18
h. at the red-ripe   95:35
h. bodies are sic fools   108:21
h. creatures' lives   253:23
H. Form display   74:1
h. kind cannot bear very much reality   197:5
h. love needs h. meriting   544:29
h. mind in ruins   169:20
h. nature is finer   289:30
h. thought or form   494:4
in the name of h. nature itself   101:27
I wish I loved the H. Race   405:16
larger than h.   531:32
lord of h. kind   193:34
lords of h. kind   226:14
march of the h. mind   101:6
Mercy has a h. **heart**   77:1
my Treatise of H. Nature.. dead-born   265:12
new edition of h. nature   239:14
no h. spark is left   381:27
nothing but the milk of h. kindness   103:8
observer of h. nature, sir   178:25
of reasonable soul and h. flesh   388:41
on Nature and on H. Life   574:5
our h. nature's highest dower   575:6
porcelain of h. kind   193:29
purest essence of a h. soul   127:28
purest of h. pleasures   26:19
round earth's h. shores   288:17
soaring h. boy   173:34
so long as the h. heart is strong   28:29
speech is h.   126:33
strength and weakness of h. nature   324:35
sublime of h. life   104:23
sum of h. wretchedness   118:30
sweet milk of h. kindness   143:10
tamer of the h. breast   230:15
thanks to the h. heart   576:22(–577)
throne of h. felicity   277:4
to err is h.   383:2
to step aside is h.   104:7
want of h. wisdom   310:18
web of h. things   492:19
when first the h. race began   105:25
wisdom of h. contrivances   100:25
wrought with h. hands   532:25
Humane: in act more graceful and h.   345:18
Humani nil a me alienum puto   541:30
Humanities: fair h. of old religion   152:9
H. live for ever   365:13
Humanity: acts of h., gentleness, and chivalries   328:2
anything that exalts..h.   376:11
chivalry, courtesy, h.   328:2
h. with all its fears   316:1
imitated h. so abominably   434:20
law of h., justice, equity   101:26
rarer..never did steer h.   425:32
reasoned out of the feelings of h.   73:4
religion of h.   373:5
still, sad music of h.   582:1
strait jacket for h.   337:5
such popular h. is treason   1:20

Humanity (cont.)
upon the forehead of h.   284:26
veined h.   88:7
wearisome condition of h.   232:14
what h..and justice tell me I ought   101:3
Humanized: deep distress hath h.   578:15
Humano pro solamine   13:13
Humber: I by the tide of H.   333:8
Humble: be it ever so h.   376:10
he that is h.   99:31
he that shall h. himself   60:16
hey-day..is tame, it's h.   435:47
h. and a contrite heart   300:24
h., tranquil spirit   170:18
minutes, though they be   127:33
play the h. host   459:11
range with h. livers   446:16
star to guide the h.   327:3
strife too h. to be named   579:14
too h. nor too great   327:14
very h. person   174:26
we are so very h.   174:28
wisdom is h.   163:50
Humbleness: all h., all patience   428:28
whispering h.   463:22
Humbler band of duodecimos   164:36
Humblest: h. citizen of all the land   98:1
h. person going   174:26
of h. friends   573:18
Humbleth: he that h. himself   62:4
Humbly: walk h. with thy God   56:8
Humbug in a Pickwickian..view   178:23
Humdrum: spliced in the h. way   83:6
Hume: similar fate from the hand of Mr. H.   505:23
works of H., Gibbon, Robertson   306:26
Humiliation: valley of H.   99:10
Humility: as 'twas h.   185:5
good nature and h.   223:9
h. may clothe an English dean   164:14
modest stillness and h.   443:24
pride that apes h.   151:11, 507:21
Hummed a surly hymn   540:19
Humo: qua me quoque possim tollere h.   556:19
Humorous: most h. sadness   428:16
Humour: has her h. most   384:38
h. is odd, grotesque   521:24
in a holiday h.   428:19
in this h. woo'd..won?   476:8
kills her in her own h.   479:6
liveliest effusions of wit and h.   22:12
most perfect h...unconscious   111:31
no antipathy..in diet, h., air   86:25
phrase 'unconscious h.'   112:1
say it is my h.   464:27
that's the h. of it   443:15
there's the h. of it   465:35
unyok'd h. of your idleness   438:30
Humoured: best-h. man..worst-h. muse   226:1
froward child that must be..h.   527:18
h. thus, comes at the last   475:7
Humours: h. and flatters them   139:23
in all thy h.   2:8
learn the h. and tricks of..Time   281:2
take their h. for a warrant   447:42
Hump: Camel's h. is an ugly lump   297:26
uglier yet is the H. we get   297:26
we get the H.—Cameelious H., the H. that is black and blue   297:27
without a positive h.   542:32
Humph yourself!   304:14
Humpty Dumpty: H. sat on a wall   367:5
'very provoking,' H. said   131:3
Humus: nos habebit h.   13:8
Hun is at the gate   296:19
Huncamunca: in H.'s eyes   204:35
Hunchback: little h. of the snow   169:23
Hundred: add a h. more   246:28
all the same a h. years hence   177:6
captains by the h.   218:3
for one of my h.   453:31
his h.'s soon hit   91:41
h. miles away   236:34
h. per cent. Americanism   409:4
h. versions of it   490:43
made Ole H. ring   319:25
more than a h. pair of oxen   264:20

Hundred (cont.)
ran a h. years to a day   251:6
son of a h. Kings   294:19
throned on her h. isles   114:2
while one..might tell a h.   431:14
Hundred and fifty: not three of my h. left   440:34
Hundred and forty and four thousand   71:23
Hundredfold: some an h.   59:23
Hundreds: h. of years..Stella's feet   502:4
Methusalem, with all his h. of years   186:31
Hundredth: at my door the H. Psalm   121:13
practising the h. psalm   119:26
singing the H. Psalm   316:4
Hundred-throated nightingale   541:9
Hung: cherry now is h. with bloom   262:10
fruit..h. amiable   347:5
h. aloft the night   288:17
h. among the bells   379:22
h. be the heavens with black   445:17
h. loose upon society   270:12
Hunger: best sauce..h.   134:9
bodily h. in his eyes   490:8
h. and thirst after righteousness   57:39
h.'s power is strong   365:19
h. thy sauce   549:22
I h. to build them anew   585:17
in poverty, h. and dirt   253:22
I perish with h.   62:14
lions do..suffer h.   393:38
men h. for thy grace   269:31
sacred h. of ambitious minds   510:7
they shall h. no more   71:7
two weak evils, age and h.   427:20
with h...not with love   468:4
Hungry: as h. as the sea   483:9
ate when we were not h.   519:20
filled the h. with good things   61:14
filleth the h. soul with goodness   398:15
h. and thirsty: their soul fainted   398:15
h. as a hunter   307:1
H. Forties   551:3
h., savage anti-everythings   250:28
h. sheep look up   342:29
lean and h. look   448:26
makes h. where most she satisfies   424:9
not h...greedy   403:27
roaming with a h. heart   540:32
tigers are getting h.   144:19
Hunt: better to h. in fields   192:15
fame, that all h. after   454:29
h. a poetaster down   117:30
h. Decorum down   117:21
h. down a tired metaphor   116:46
h. it in the dark   162:2
I h. for haddocks' eyes   131:24
I'll h. for dangers   375:2
that he would h. in the mountains   30:11
to h., and vote   112:27
you will see H.   495:10
Hunter: Bahram, that great H.   206:1
Esau was a cunning h.   44:57
Fear, O Little H.   301:27, 28
from the snare of the h.   397:18
horn of the h.   166:24
hungry as a h.   307:1
h. home from the hill   516:15
H. of the East   205:4
man is the h.   538:23
Nimrod the mighty h.   44:45
trailed the h.'s javelin   17:26
Hunters: here thy h. stand   450:9
that h. been nat holy men   136:31
Hunting: a-h. we will go   204:37
Daddy's gone a-h.   366:11
for at rest from h.   334:6
good h.   304:8
his hound is to the h. gane   32:15
h. fills my thoughts by day   518:8
h. he lov'd   488:25
h. is all that's worth living for   518:7
h. which the Devil design'd   193:39
I like the h. of the hare   77:33
I'm weary wi' h.   31:10
it ain't the h. as 'urts 'un   403:12

Hunting (cont.)
most of their discourse was about h.   377:23
passion for h. something   177:39
pleasures..call h. one of them   276:23
we daren't go a-h.   4:18
wet and dirty from h.   518:40
Huntley: where H., and where Home?   418:33
Huntlie: lay on H. bank   32:6
Huntress: Queen and h.   279:31
Hunts: he h. in dreams   534:22
Huntsman: as a h. his pack   225:33
cassock'd h.   161:25
h. by the bear oppress'd   557:21
h., rest!   416:20
h. winds his horn   204:37
Huntsmen are up in America   85:21
Hurl my soul from heaven   473:32
Hurled: h. himself into the scale   357:9
swift to be h.   252:20
systems into ruin h.   383:10
Hurly: with the h. death..awakes   442:1
Hurly-burly: when the h.'s done   456:3
Hurrah: h.! h.! we bring the Jubilee   583:7
Hurray and up she rises   11:16
Hurricane of steel   23:20
Hurricanoes: you cataracts and h.   453:5
Hurried: four young Oysters h. up   130:13
Hurry: always in haste..never in a h.   565:18
no h. in her hands   409:23
old man in a h.   143:32
sows h. and reaps indigestion   515:1
Hurrying: clang of h. feet   23:22
Time's winged chariot h.   333:9
Hurt: assailed, but never h.   340:30
do nothing for to h. her   543:11
give delight and h. not   480:5
h. my brother   437:31
h. that Honour feels   534:24
h. with the same weapons   464:8
if I don't h. her   367:8
I'll not h. thee   513:10
lie..that doth the h.   27:31
may assault and h. the soul   389:32
most power to h. us that we love   37:36
nor loving friends can h. you   297:12
power..as I have to be h.   473:23
that thou h. not thy foot   397:19
they shall not h. nor destroy   53:19
they that have power to h.   487:24
thou shalt h. the truest knight   328:5
whose feet they h. in the stocks   398:12
Hurting: led go! You are h. be!   304:18
Hurtles in the darken'd air   230:14
Hurts: had he his h. before?   461:15
he h. me most   142:28
h., and is desir'd   426:11
it h. my hand   472:25
some of your h...cured   199:25
Husband: as the h. is the wife is   534:18
being a h...whole-time job   42:17
bride adorned for her h.   71:44
chaste to her h.   384:30
crown to her h.   50:1
flop in favour of your h.   179:36
good works in her h.   349:8
hang your h. and be dutiful   214:19
heavy h.   465:24
here comes my h.   91:13
her h.'s to Aleppo gone   456:10
his sister's h.'s niece   128:16
h. frae the wife despises   108:4
h., I come   426:10
h.! In ev'ry respect but the form   214:35
h. in these circumstances   214:35
h. June   561:1
h. twenty years married   304:36
I am thine h.   530:10
I had once a h.   508:4
in the eyes of a h., who is not a fool   519:34
level in her h.'s heart   483:3
make her h. a cuckold..a monarch   473:8
Man-o'-War's 'er h.   298:25
monstrous animal a h. and wife   204:31
most indulgent h.   175:38
no worse a h. than the best   424:5

Husband (cont.)
she must have a h. 479:3
so ill bred as to love a h. 583:24
thou great good h. 319:2
till a h. cools 384:38
too much for one h. to hear 215:5
unbelieving h. 66:31
woman oweth to her h. 479:13
Husbanded: h. the golden grain 205:28
so fathered and so h. 449:18
Husband-hunting: affected, h. butterfly 353:6
Husbandry: dulls the edge of h. 431:25
there's h. in heaven 457:17
Husbands: as wel over hir h. as hir love 138:11
for h. to stay at home 196:28
h. at chirche-dore..fyve 137:15
h., love your wives 68:32
I should marry twenty h. 463:11
let them ask their h. 67:3
pranks they dare not show their h. 471:35
queens to your h. 413:9
some respite to h. 550:4
submit yourselves unto your own h. 68:6
when h. or..lap-dogs 385:17
when h. win their hay 30:5
Hush: breathless h. in the Close 363:4
h. and bless myself 94:11
H.! H.! Whisper who dares 339:19
h.! my dear, lie still 562:11
h. of the grey expanse 16:4
h. thee, my babie 417:32
h. with the setting moon 536:11
more they call out, 'H.!' 286:13
old man who said, 'H!' 311:7
Hushed: h. be all things 246:5
h. casket of my soul 288:32
h. Chorasmian waste 17:28
h., cool-rooted flowers 288:3
h. in grim repose 229:23
o'er the h. domain 184:2
till it is h. and smooth 284:24
Hushes half the babbling Wye 532:15
Husks: h. that the swine did eat 62:14
strew'd with h. 481:27
Hustle: h. the Aryan brown 300:6
tried to in the East 300:6
Hut: his rude h. by the Danube 114:19
leave my little wooden h. 335:22
love in a h. 286:39
Hutch of tasty lust 254:27
Huts: love had he found in h. 573:8
Hwang: in the reign of the Emperor H. 309:26
Hyacinth: every H. the Garden wears 206:3
thy h. hair 380:17
Hyades: rainy H. 540:32
Hybla: as the honey of H. 438:17
rob the H. bees 451:33
Hyde Park: all beyond H.'s a desart 202:5
go to H. together 156:13
on a cart in H. 491:6
Hydras: Gorgons and H. 346:3
Hydrops: crescit indulgens sibi..h. 259:2
Hydroptic earth 186:3
Hydrus, and Ellops drear 349:21
Hymeneal: chorus H. 498:7
Hymn: at St. Ann's our parting h. 357:16
humm'd a surly h. 540:19
I the h. the Brahmin sings 199:5
Hymn-book: cassock, band, and h. too 568:25
Hymns: chanting faint h. 466:16
h. and spiritual songs 68:5
singing h. unbidden 498:6
sings his canticles and h. 266:13
sings h. at heaven's gate 486:24
solemn h. to sullen dirges 478:33
Hyperbole: speaking in a perpetual h. 26:32
Hyperboles: three-pil'd h. 455:29
Hyperbolical: out, h. fiend 484:20
Hypercritical: construe the Constitution..by any h. rules 314:9
Hyperion: help H. to his horse 444:23
H. of calves the Piper 146:20
H. to a satyr 430:33(–431)

Hyphenated Americans 409:7
Hypocrisie: l'h. est un hommage..à la vertu 407:11
Hypocrisy: organized h. 29:3, 180:18
h., the only evil..invisible 346:28
to whip h. 455:19
Hypocrite: no man is a h. in his pleasures 275:25
scoundrel, h. and flatterer 75:7
Hypocrites: cant of h...the worst 513:16
whatever h. austerely talk 347:25
Hypothesis: character of a family to an h. 513:6
slaying of a beautiful h. 266:19
Hyrcanian: like the H. beast 433:26
Hyssop: thou shalt purge me with h. 395:8
Hysterics: blind h. of the Celt 533:22

I

I: are they Hebrews? so am I 67:33
Eve and I 97:25
even as you and I 303:12
fly..as soon as I 416:26
I a child and thou a lamb 76:10
I am I, thou art thou 524:2
I am the batsman 309:27
I and no other 525:29
I, and you, and all of us 450:31
'I,' said the Sparrow 369:18
I the song 218:33
I think that man was I 30:13
it is I; be not afraid 59:36
I to Him and He to me 543:19
I too..have not been idle 7:20
Leander..and I did 115:32
lived on; and so did I 149:21
man that is I 524:5
moon and I 219:34
nobody; I myself 573:19
no more I that do it 65:48
not I, but the grace of God 67:6
now 'tis I 263:8
reverend sir, not I 90:36
so do I 236:30
soon will you and I be lying 132:3
that I am he 449:30
thou, Lord, and I 172:1
'twas I that kill'd her 473:20
why not I with thine? 495:7
with the bloom go I 18:25
I demens et..curre per Alpes 283:21
Iacet: two narrow words, Hic i. 405:13
Iactatus: multum ille et terris i. et alto 553:5
Iago: as much delight in conceiving an I. 290:9
pity of it, I. 472:28
Iambics march 152:5
Iambos: non effugies meos i. 134:11
Ianthe: find I.'s name again 309:6
from you, I...troubles pass 308:30
Ianua: patet atri i. Ditis 554:23
Iberians: dark I. come 18:16
Ice: be thou as chaste as i. 434:11
bore 'mid snow and i. 316:17
caves of i. 151:33(–152)
good to break the i. 25:42
i. did split 148:27
i. in June 117:13
i. mast-high 148:25
i. on summer seas 529:41
i. that hardly bears him 529:20
i. was here, the i. was there 148:26
in skating over thin i. 200:35
penny i. and cold meat 219:11
region of thick-ribbèd i. 462:9
to smooth the i. 447:39
we hissed along the polished i. 575:23
Iced: charity, scrimped and i. 370:14
I-chabod..the glory is departed 47:10
Ichor: his perspiration was but i. 119:21
Icicle: chaste as the i. 429:20
i. on a Dutchman's beard 483:32
Icicles: silent i. 151:25
when i. hang 456:1
Icily regular 535:35
Ida: dear mother I. 537:31

Ida (cont.)
mother I., many-fountained I. 537:30
on I.'s shady brow 75:18
vale in I. 537:29
Idea: between the i. and the reality 197:11
i. God has of you 551:2
I. of a Patriot King 78:8
i. of freedom 373:16
i. of her life 469:6
mighty abstract i. I have of beauty 290:12
no i. what money's for 243:6
one i., and that..wrong 182:28, 272:3
teach the young i. 540:12
Idea: la i. que de ti Dios tenga 551:2
Ideal: boy's i. of a manly career 182:26
i. American..all wrong 142:18
John's i. John 251:14
sleeps the calm I. 176:26
Idealistic: America is the only i. nation 571:16
Ideas: entertain such inhuman i. 519:16
man of nasty i. 520:43
sung divine i. below 199:20
Idem: i. velle atque i. nolle 415:2
Identity: his i. presses upon me 290:4
poet..has no i. 290:10
Ides of March: beware the I. 448:11
i. are come 449:30
i. remember 451:11
that work the i. begun 451:37
Idiom of words..little she heeded 401:34
Idioms: clear it from..licentious i. 278:13
Idiosyncrasy: I have no antipathy or..i. 86:25
Idiot: beauteous i. 155:5
blaspheming over the village i. 142:19
blinking i. 464:2
i. race 107:23
i. who praises 219:25
law is a ass—a i. 178:1
like a blank i. 286:1
tale told by an i. 461:4
your I. Boy 575:19
Idiots: embryos and i. 346:24
fatuity of i. 505:20
Idle: all be i. if we could 273:7
angling..'employment for his i. time 559:15
as i. as a painted ship 149:5
be not solitary, be not i. 109:33
fourteen months the most i 216:19
happiest when I am i. 560:21
if you are i. be not solitary 274:16
I too..have not been i. 7:20
manners are not i. 530:11
mischief..for i. hands 561:29
most 'scruciating i. 304:13
oh! i. thought! 152:7
why stand ye here..i.? 60:6
wise, i., childish things 543:23
you are i. shallow things 484:9
Idleness: conceives by i. 445:11
grief is a species of i. 277:40
i...never brought a man 134:17
i...the refuge of weak minds 139:25
joy in i. 82:6
strenuous i. 579:23
such i. so near the heart 423:38
unyok'd humour of your i. 438:30
work of polished i. 326:27
Idler: every man..an i. 277:33
i. in the land 578:34
Idlers, game-preservers 126:37
Idling: enjoy i. thoroughly 268:32
Idly bent on him that enters next 475:29
Idol: dearest i. I have known 161:3
natural i. of the Anglo-Saxon 28:33
on an 'eathen i.'s foot 299:11
Idola Tribus .. Specus .. Fori .. Theatri 28:6
Idolatries: bow'd to its i. 113:50
Idolatry: god of my i. 477:23
god of our i., the press 161:33
it might breed i. 185:5
of the ancients without i. 139:17
that were I. 390:54
this side i. 280:1
'tis mad i. 481:12
Idolorum: quatuor sunt genera I. 28:6

INDEX

Idols: four classes of I...I. of the
  Tribe..Cave..Market-place
  ..Theatre 28:6
I. I have loved so long 207:20
  to hold our i. 88:14
Idyll: rank as an i. 221:4
If: go and wake them, i. 131:12
  'i.' is the only peace-maker 428:38
  i. you can keep your head 297:10
  much virtue in 'i.' 428:38
Ifs: talk'st thou to me of 'i.' 476:22
Ignara: non i. mali 553:22
Ignes: nec Iovis ira, nec i. 372:1
Ignis: per i. suppositos cineri doloso 259:1
Ignis fatuus: reason, an i. 407:21
Ignoble: counselled i. ease 345:22
  deathless lot to names i. 160:37
  end was not i. 579:7
  madding crowd's i. strife 230:7
  soiled with all i. use 533:23
Ignominy: disgrace and i. of our
  natures 86:19
  thy i. sleep with thee 441:1
Ignoramus: quid autem sequatur..i. 38:31
Ignorance: alike in i. 383:22
  blind and naked I. 531:16
  boldness is a child of i. 25:32
  drink to heavy I. 541:15
  from i. our comfort 401:33
  from knowledge i. 90:44
  his best riches i. of wealth 224:14
  i. is not innocence 92:25
  i., madam, pure i. 270:26
  i. of the law excuses no man 422:4
  I pity his i. and despise him 177:12
  it was a childish i. 253:2
  let me not burst in i. 431:32
  more than Gothic i. 204:27
  no sin but i. 330:14
  putting us to i. again 90:35
  smallest allowance for i. 266:20
  through i. ye did it 64:28
  understand a writer's i. 152:25
  what i. of pain? 498:8
  where i. is bliss 230:30
  your i. cramps my conversation 254:10
Ignorances: sins, negligences, and i. 389:7
Ignorant: be not i. of anything 56:35
  confound the i. 433:32
  i...guided by the wiser 126:5
  i. of his understanding 152:25
  i. of ourselves 424:3
  i., unweighing fellow 402:15
  most i...most assur'd 461:31
  of what follows..we are..i. 38:31(–39)
  what schoolboy..i. of this 325:20
  where i. armies clash 15:8
Ignorantly: I did it i. in unbelief 68:42
  whom..ye i. worship 64:60
Ignore: qu'un homme comme vous i.
  quelque chose 37:10
Ignotos: naso suspendis adunco i. 261:18
Ignotum pro magnifico est 526:8
Ignotus moritur sibi 422:19
Iguala al pastor con el rey 134:18
Ilex: duris ut i. tonsa bipennibus 260:21
Ilia ducat 256:15
Iliad: I. of woes 172:20
  in the I...perfect plainness 20:4
Iliade: nescio quid maius nascitur I. 402:17
Ilion: cloud-kissing I. 486:8
Ilium: topless towers of I. 330:5
Ilium: fuimus Troes, fuit I. 554:8
Ill: against i. chances men are..
  merry 442:17
  all the measureless i. 535:38
  cannot be i., cannot be good 456:24
  captive good attending captain i. 487:14
  cure for this i. 297:28
  enchains us to permitted i. 494:15
  final goal of i. 532:31
  gey i. to deal wi' 127:29
  give the i. he cannot cure a name 19:5
  he thinks no i. 487:7
  how i. all's here about my heart 437:33
  if it is i...a frightened look 502:16
  i. customs influence my..senses 201:31
  i. fares the land 224:14
  i. fortune seldom comes alone 192:7
  i. is the weather..no gain 170:24
  i. news hath wings 189:2

Ill (cont.)
  i. spirit..so fair a house 479:33
  i. wind turns none to good 549:24
  i. word may empoison liking 468:26
  in his actions be so i. 334:28
  let i. tidings tell themselves 424:15
  love of good and i. 285:9
  make strong themselves by i. 459:9
  means to do i. deeds makes i.
    deeds done 447:43
  no i. can come 400:33
  not care to speak i. of any man 276:25
  nothing i. come near thee 430:1
  nothing i...in such a temple 479:33
  nought shall go i. 467:12
  O benefit of i.! 488:9
  of every i., a woman is the worst 229:7
  our angels..or good or i. 37:23
  seal up the avenues of i. 199:29
  some i. a-brewing 463:34
  so they be i. men 279:29
  their i. report while you live 433:29
  to do i. our sole delight 344:16
  took i. on Thursday 368:21
  to rail at the i. 536:25
  virtue..speak i. of it 239:27
  will I fear none i. 421:1
  will..looking i. prevail? 517:10
Illacrimabiles: omnes i. urgentur..
  nocte 261:2
Ill-born: this amphibious i. mob 170:12
Ill-bred: nothing so..i., as audible
  laughter 139:7
  so i. as to love a husband 583:24
Ill-clad: ill-housed, i., ill-nourished 408:22
Ill-doing: knew not the doctrine of i. 485:4
Ill-erected: Caesar's i. tower 475:26
Ill-favoured: i. kine 45:17
  i. thing..but mine own 428:35
  vile, i. faults 466:6
Ill-fed, ill-killed, ill-kept and ill-
  drest 275:19
Ill-housed: one-third of a nation i. 408:22
Illiberal: nothing so i...as audible
  laughter 139:7
Illimitable: dark i. ocean 346:10
  i. inane 535:24
Illiterate him..from your memory 500:14
Ill-luck: so fond of i. 269:16
Ill-natured: vain i. thing, an Englishman 170:12
Illness: without the i. should attend it 457:1
Ill-nourished: ill-housed, ill-
  clad, i. 408:22
Ills: after all their i. 15:14
  bear those i. we have 434:4
  climax of all human i. 115:40
  fear, the last of i. 193:38
  i. have no weight 322:2
  long versed in human i. 165:20
  no sense..of i. to come 230:26
  o'er a' the i. o' life victorious 108:6
  sure one for all i. 405:14
  to hastening i. a prey 224:14
  what i. from beauty spring 279:11
  what i. the scholar's life assail 279:4
  when nae real i. perplex them 108:21
Ill-seeming: muddy, i., thick 479:12
Ill-shapen: births..at first are i. 26:29
Ill-sorted: dishes were i. 194:16
Ill-spent: billiards..an i. youth 508:31
Ill-starred: O i. wench! 473:32
Ill-tasted, home-brewed prayer 231:30
Ill-tempered: some think him i. 311:9
Illuminated with the Author's own
  candles 542:11
Illuminatio: dominus i. mea 49:35
Illumine: what in me is dark i. 344:4
Illumineth: it i. the face 442:21
Ill-used: like an i. ghost 73:13
Illusion: Great I. 4:24
  one i...Archbishop of Canter-
  bury 504:29
  thankful for i. 146:32
Illustrated: till your life has i. it 290:19
Illustration: incident..the i. of
  character 268:13
Illustrious: i. acts high raptures 558:3
  one of my i. predecessors 204:11

Illustrious (cont.)
  parson, oh! i. spark 160:38
  scarce less i...the clerk 160:38
Ill-weav'd ambition 440:38
Illyria: as tall..as any's in I. 482:4
  what should I do in I.? 482:2
Illyrian: among the green I. hills 15:14
Ilsley: looks on I. downs 18:21
Image: beast and his i. 71:26
  best i. of myself 348:3
  Caesar's i. is effac'd at last 161:29
  constant i. of the creature 483:2
  every parting..an i. of death 196:30
  express i. of his person 69:7
  fleeting i. of a shade 499:7
  great doom's i. 458:23
  horrid i. doth unfix my hair 456:24
  I am in His i. made 585:9
  i...flying still before me 575:25
  i. gay 580:19
  i. of eternity 114:31
  I. of God nevertheless his i. 212:14
  i. of the King 530:21
  i. of truth new-born 76:7
  i. of war without its guilt 506:13, 518:7
  i. that Nebuchadnezzar..set up 55:35
  in his own i. the Creator made 308:31
  its wrinkled i. 496:1
  kills the i. of God 352:6
  kiss the i. of my death 190:5
  make man in our i. 44:6
  man is God's i. 244:4
  man's i. and his cry 586:7
  met his own i. 496:18
  nor i. of thine eyes 410:24
  not make..any graven i. 390:7
  scatter'd his Maker's i. 190:8
  to give no i. of anything 325:9
  whose is this i.? 60:11
  wronging your i. that blossoms 585:17
  your i. at our hearts 147:10
Imaged there in happier beauty 577:13
Imageries: garlanded with carven i. 285:19
Imagery: rise, the progress..of i. 289:27
Images: express the i. of their
  minds 26:46
  garden of bright i. 503:18
  strange i. of death 456:20
  to forms and i. a breath 575:21
Imaginary: don't let us make i. evils 226:35
  i. necessities 167:11
  i. relish 481:15
Imagination: as i. bodies forth 467:24
  bare i. of a feast 474:20
  charm my i. 215:37
  deject his cool'd i. 86:34
  depends only upon..i. 192:41
  his i...the wings of an ostrich 326:4
  how abhorred in my i. 437:15
  if i. amend them 467:30
  i. boggles 121:6
  i...but another name for 579:37
  i. cold and barren 100:23
  i. droops her pinion 116:8
  i. of a boy is healthy 284:18
  i. of man's heart is evil 44:40
  i. the rudder 289:15
  i. to give them shape 434:9
  in ages of i. 77:21
  in the i. of their hearts 61:14
  into his study of i. 469:6
  of i. all compact 467:24
  refined play of the i. 102:30
  save those that have no i. 491:5
  showy resemblance..striking
  his i. 373:3
  so fair to fond i. 582:20
  such tricks hath strong i. 467:24
  suggestion, by the i., of noble
  grounds 412:25
  sweeten my i. 454:9
  to defile the i. 513:33
  to his i. for his facts 501:11
  truth of i. 289:17
  were it not for i. 274:10
  what the i. seizes as beauty 289:17
  whispering chambers of I. 176:26
Imaginations: my i. are as foul 435:1
  perish through their own i. 392:6
Imaginative: few fine i...passages 289:24
Imagine: all that they i. is..evil 395:14

Imagine (*cont.*)
i. me the west 231:38
people i. a vain thing 391:47
Imagined: dooms..i. for the mighty dead 284:21
i. such a device 392:40
round earth's i. corners 185:13
then i. new 278:34
Imagineless metal 545:12
Imaginibus: ex umbris et i. in veritatem 364:2
Imaginings: less than horrible i. 456:24
light i. of men 496:19
Imbecility: moderation in war is i. 324:23
Imber: educat i. 133:9
Imbibing the rosy 146:23
Imitan: los buenos pintores i. la naturaleza 134:19
Imitate: i. the action of the tiger 443:24
obliged to i. himself 406:12
Imitated humanity so abominably 434:20
Imitation: endless i. 576:11
not a good i. of Johnson 103:30
without an original..no i. 233:9
Imitations: reduced .. to the poorest of i. 406:12
Imitatores, servum pecus 257:13
Imiter: celui que personne ne peut i. 136:18
Immanent: what of the I. Will 235:20
Immanuel: call his name I. 53:12
Immediate: unconditional and i. surrender 229:4
Immediately the cock crew 60:47
Immemorial: doves in i. elms 539:5
my most i. year 381:1
Immense, of fishy form 83:26
Immensity: belie thy soul's i. 576:12
i. cloistered in thy dear womb 185:10
vortex of i. 176:26
Imminent deadly breach 470:2
Immoderately: laughing i. at.. intervals 504:20
Immodest words..no defence 180:9
Immoral: no such thing as..an i. book 570:3
that most i. man 295:13
Immorality: nurseries of all..i. 204:19
Immortal: flourish in i. youth 1:24
his biting is i. 426:6
I have left no i. work 290:29
I have i. longings 426:9
I. Cherubims! 548:15
i. diamond 255:7
i. flowers of Poesy 331:2
i. hate 344:14
i. in his own despite 386:12
i. life..conquered 574:22
i., though no more 113:17
lost the i. part of myself 471:20
make me i. with a kiss 330:5
married to i. verse 342:7
minute makes i. 94:2
sole mortal thing of worth i. 374:18
thing i. as itself 432:2
those i. dead 196:34
thou must be made i. 462:20
wanted one i. song 190:17
where an i. England sits 141:14
Immortalia ne speres 260:25
Immortality: born for i. 577:10
earthly i. 209:25
fields of I. 493:7
I long to believe in i. 290:30
load of i. 290:6
nurslings of i. 497:2
over whom thy i. broods 576:14
slumber out their i. 164:37
steadfast rock of i. 83:10
their hope full of i. 56:23
their sons they gave, their i. 83:19
this longing after i. 1:22
this mortal must put on i. 67:17
'tis i. 355:9
Immortalize: art that can i. 160:26
mortal thing so to i. 509:7
Immortalizes whom it sings 164:21
Immortals: never..appear the I. 152:16
President of the I. 237:14
Immoveable: by its own weight..i. 155:19
Immured: not alone i. in the brain 455:22
Imogen: an Iago as an I. 290:9
Impaired: sometimes i. 340:20
Impairs: all weakness which i. 17:24
Impaling worms to torture fish 154:16
Impar congressus Achilli 553:19
Imparadised in one another's arms 347:18
Impart: He doth Himself i. 291:14
solitary, and cannot i. it 270:18
Impartial: neutrality of an i. judge 100:18
Impassable: Rhine..not more i. than the Nile 217:12
Impatience: all patience, and i. 428:28
your i...so much fretted 272:13
Impatient: i. of disgrace 190:13
i. of servitude 101:4
i. to destroy 279:7
mind i. 430:31
minds so i. of inferiority 278:12
people never so i. 397:33
Impavidum ferient ruinae 259:22
Impeach the common enemy 101:27
Impeachment: I own the soft i. 500:30
Imped the wings of fame 125:1
Impediment: cause or just i. 391:21
march'd on without i. 476:32
Impediments: i. to great enterprises 26:34
let me not..admit i. 488:7
Impelled of invisible tides 525:11
Impending eighty thousand lines 120:29
Impetuous: be thou me, i. one! 496:11
Imperatur: naturae enim non i. 28:9
Imperceptible: in i. water 253:7
Imperfect: perfect use of an i. medium 570:4
suspense and i. opinion 200:23
Imperfections: i...divinely appointed 413:15
my i. on my head 432:17
pass my i. by 202:16
Imperial: enslaves you on i. principles 490:38
i. theme 456:23
i. votaress 466:39
my i. kitten! I. fiddlestick! 129:38
on his i. throne 190:34
we have had an I. lesson 298:23
Imperially: learn to think I. 135:5
Imperii: omnium consensu capax i. 526:15
Imperium et Libertas 181:14
Impertinence: Memory of this I. 206:14
Impertinent: privileg'd to be..i. 203:31
Imperturbe: me i. 566:26
Impious men bear sway 1:21
Impiously gay 164:40
Implication: puff by i. 499:27
Implore: to i. your light 169:13
we thee i. to go away 8:11
Implores the passing tribute 230:7
Importance: of the last i...to be present 546:36
subject of almost equal i. 503:18
Important: i.—unimportant 129:31
little things..most i. 187:16
most i. peers..most i. 28:34
Imports: what i. the nomination 437:30
Importunate: rashly i. 252:12
tale not too i. 359:1
their i. chink 102:20
Importune: I here i. death awhile 425:27
too proud to i. 231:17
Importunity: ever-haunting i. of business 307:17
Imposes: child i. on the man 192:30
Imposition of a mightier hand 325:4
Impositions: some generous beliefs and i. 514:5
Impossibile: certum est quia i. est 542:4
Impossibilities: make..honours of men's i. 454:5
no i. enough in Religion 86:6
Impossibility: by despair upon i. 332:5
likely i. 14:18
Impossible: because it is i. 542:4
difficult..wish it were i. 277:8
highly i. tree 218:7
i. loyalties 19:10
i. to be silent 101:24
in two words: i. 227:33
Impossible (*cont.*)
more than i. 156:12
our peace..in i. things 141:1
Patently I. and Vain 301:21
six i. things before breakfast 131:2
some false i. shore 18:20
that not i. she 166:17
think on things i. 193:27
when you have eliminated the i. 188:20
with men this is i. 60:4
Impostors: those two i. just the same 297:10
Impotent: lame and i. conclusion 470:29
so i. and grovelling an insect 519:16
Impotently: as i. moves 207:5
rolls i. on 207:3
Impoverished the public stock of ..pleasure 278:7
Impracticable: makes some virtues i. 275:5
Imprecision: mess of i. of feeling 197:9
Impregnable: i. rock of Holy Scripture 223:2
this flesh..brass i. 475:7
Impress: of themselves our minds i. 574:29
so i. with quietness and beauty 582:3
Impression: i. deeper makes 107:5
i. of pleasure in itself 24:11
Impressions: falseness in all our i. 412:26
Impressive: few more i. sights 36:18
Impressiveness on what we call our feelings 176:25
Imprint: set it in i. 328:1
Imprison: take me to you, i. me 185:19
Imprisoned: i. in the viewless winds 462:9
who i. Montezuma 324:28
Imprisonment: ache, penury, and i. 462:10
Improbable: condemn it as an i. fiction 484:10
whatever remains, *however i.* 188:20
Impropriety: any language..without i. 219:9
Improve: i. each shining hour 561:28
i. his shining tail 128:23
still born to i. us 225:34
Improved: enormously i. by death 414:10
I. Hot Muffin..Company 176:37
Improvement: schemes of political i. 271:34
Improvements: no great i... possible 338:21
Improving: i. his prisons in Hell 151:12
i. the prisons of Hell 507:22
Improviste: le courage de l'i. 360:25
Imprudent: nobody could be so i. 22:15
Imprudently: very i. married the barber 209:18
Impudence: much of Cockney i. 412:22
starve for want of i. 193:21
your i. protects you sairly 106:32
Impudent: called John a I. Bitch 208:23
not so i. a thing..as..an assured man 156:11
Impulse: lonely i. of delight 584:21
one i. from a vernal wood 581:16
share the i. of thy strength 496:10
slave of circumstance and i. 118:36
this or that poor i. 90:39
to its own i...stirs 17:14
Impulses of deeper birth 578:33
Impulsive: never..made i. to good 329:8
Impune: nemo me i. lacessit 13:10
Impunity: ravage with i. a rose 96:34
Impure what God declares pure 347:25
Impurer: from th' i. matter free 111:24
Impurity: we bring i. much rather 352:9
Imputantur: soles..qui nobis pereunt et i. 331:26
Imputation on his..'ossmanship 518:13
Impute: i. my Fall to Sin 207:10, 11
i. to each frustrate ghost 96:46
Imum: ad i. qualis ab incepto 255:24
In: being i. 431:25
born, unless it's pretty nigh i. 174:39
despair to get i. 563:25
i. and out the Eagle 328:26
i. did come the strangest 94:36
never *i.* the way 136:7
one is i. 142:30

In (cont.)
profanation to keep i. 245:26
Sir Thomas Doodle wouldn't
come i. 174:4
such as are i. the institution 201:11
they were i. the well. .well i. 129:11
Thou, my God, art i.'t 247:22
to be i. it is merely a bore 570:19
who's in, who's out 454:19
Inaccuracy: I hate i. 112:7
Inactivity: masterly i. 326:28
Inalienable: [i.] rights 11:11
rights inherent and i. 268:19
Inane: illimitable i. 535:24
in the intense i. 497:12
Inanimate: depravity of i. things 234:21
if aught i. e'er grieves 113:33
Inanity: all torpid i. 147:18
Inapprehensible, we clutch thee! 545:1
Inarticulate: close-companioned i.
hour 410:30
raid on the i. 197:9
Inattention: with patient i. 335:23
Inaudible to the vast multitude 574:27
Inauspicious: yoke of i. stars 478:44
Incantation: by the i. of this verse 496:11
thy rod of i. 215:37
Incapable: i. of her own distress 437:1
that which is i. of proof 313:24
Incapacity: old maid courted by I. 77:9
Incardinate: very devil i. 484:24
Incarnadine: multitudinous seas i. 458:15
that. .Cheek. .to i. 205:12, 13
Incarnate: said they were devils i. 443:22
Incarnations: glimmering I. 491:21
Incense: gods themselves throw i. 454:20
i. is an abomination 52:29
thy i. sweet 288:6
what soft i. hangs 287:30
Incense-bearing: many an i. tree 151:32
Incense-breathing Morn 229:31
Incensed: i. with indignation 346:6
vile blows. .have so i. 458:36
Incense-smoke: stupefying i. 89:45
Incepto: ad imum qualis ab i. 255:24
Incertainties: nothing more cer-
tain than i. 35:20
Incertum: eius, quod nobis i. est,
temporis 38:31
Incessantly stand on your head 128:28
Incessu: vera i. patuit dea 553:17
Inch: every i. a king 454:7
no painful i. to gain 147:8
Inchcape: it is the I. Rock 507:26
Inches: die by famine. .by i. 242:9
looked six i. higher 165:6
Incident: curious i. of the dog 188:5
determination of i. 268:13
i. . . .illustration of character 268:13
malady most i. to maids 485:26
Incidents well link'd 159:16
Incipe, parve puer 556:1, 2
Incisive: lady of i. features 337:13
Incivility: to i. and procrastination 172:23
Inclination: i. to goodness 26:20
read. .as i. leads him 271:9
Incline: consider, i. thine ear 394:23
Desdemona seriously i. 470:2
i. . .our hearts to keep this law 390:6
Inclined: he i. unto me 394:12
Inclines: neither way i. 424:21
Income: annual i. twenty pounds 174:24
£40,000 pounds a year a mode-
rate i. 308:11
good i. of no avail 504:15
live beyond its i. 111:34
Incommunicable: burden of the i. 172:17
i. name 56:28
i. sleep 572:25
their i. ways 411:3
Incomparable: thine 'i. oil',
Macassar 115:15
Incompetent: election by the i.
many 490:29
Incompleteness: flowed around
our i. 88:5
Incomprehensibles: not three i. 388:39
Inconsolable to the minuet in
Ariadne 499:31
Inconstancy: constant in nothing
but i. 35:20

Inconstancy (cont.)
curse thine own i. 125:8
nothing. .constant, but i. 519:8
this i. is such 319:10
to be constant. .were i. 158:11
Inconstant: i., childish, proud 289:10
i. woman. .never very unhappy 215:36
like th' i. wind 215:14
swear not by. .the i. moon 477:22
Incontinence: Steenie. .on the
turpitude of i. 419:26
Incontinently drown myself 470:13
Inconvenience: change is not made
without i. 254:1
submits to the i. of suspense 200:23
Inconvenient: i. to be poor 159:6
poverty. .confoundedly i. 505:17
Incorporate and make us one 449:16
Incorpsed and demi-natur'd 436:42
Incorrect: from the best of men. .
sometimes i. 268:25
will most i. to heaven 430:31
Incorruptible: seagreen I. 126:19
we an i. 66:37
Incorruption: raised in i. 67:14
this corruptible must put on i. 67:17
Increase: blessest the i. of it 395:30
daily i. in the holy spirit 391:20
dry up. .the organs of i. 452:29
earth bring forth her i. 396:3
from fairest. .desire i. 486:9
God gave the i. 66:22
good and i. of the world 529:13
he must i. 63:12
if riches i. 395:24
i. of appetite 430:33(-431)
i. of faith, hope, and charity 389:46
of the i. of his government 53:15
our loves and comforts. .i.
470:31(-471)
Increased: has i., is increasing, and
ought to be diminished 20:24
i. means and i. leisure 181:3
Jesus i. in wisdom 61:22
knowledge shall be i. 55:45
not i. the joy 53:14
Increases: as their wealth i. 330:15
its loveliness i. 284:19
what judgment I had i. 194:12
Increaseth: he that i. knowledge i.
sorrow 50:63
Increasing: i. belly 441:19
youth waneth by i. 377:4
Incredible: round an i. star 141:1
Incredulity! the wit of fools 135:20
Incredulus odi 256:4
Increment: unearned i. 338:24
unregarded i. 376:6
Inculto. .hoc sub corpore 261:11
Incurable: disease is i. 441:26
life is an i. disease 158:21
Ind: east to western I. 427:28
wealth of Ormus and of I. 345:14
Indebted: at once i. and discharged 346:31
i. to his memory for his jests 501:1
Indecent: not necessary to be i. 408:3
Indelible stamp of his lowly origin 169:5
Independence: civic i. flings the
gauntlet down 123:7
first of. .blessings, i. 217:2
generalities. .Declaration of I. 142:25
it is for our i. 379:15
Independent: all men are created
equal and i. 268:19
cease to be colonies because. .i. 180:29
if this ain't to be i. 319:28
i. on the bounty of his mistress 156:11
with an i. air 217:23
Indestructible: i. Union composed
of i. States 136:15
Index: i. of a feeling mind 165:15
marble i. of a mind 579:19
thunders in the i. 435:44
Indexes: in such i. 481:8
writes i. to perfection 226:22
India: fly to I. for gold 329:23
if to far I.'s coast 215:42
impeach him in the name of. .I. 101:27
I.'s coral strand 240:17
I.'s spicy shores 159:7

India (cont.)
key of I. is in London 181:15
my metal of I. 483:12
not exchange for the treasures
of I. 216:18
they made Britain I. 446:9
three pitched battles in I. 326:9
up from I. glances 264:1
Indian: I., in another life 384:6
I. Summer of the heart 568:18
like the base I. 474:2
lo, the poor I. 383:11
nice Morn on th' I. steep 340:6
only good I. is a dead I. 499:21
poor I.'s sleep 288:10
sweetened with. .an I. cane 2:10
ten to see a dead I. 479:39
Indicat Motorem Bum 223:8
Indictment against an whole people 101:2
Indies: bring home the wealth of
the I. 274:4
with the augmentation of the I. 484:4
Indifference: i. and a coach and six 154:6
i. . .bordering on aversion 514:13
so fatal to religion as i. 103:25
Indifferent: I am myself i. honest 434:8
i., and cannot enjoy it 270:18
i. children of the earth 433:9
to be i. to them 489:16
universe. .is simply i. 250:27
words and deeds. .i. modes 200:29
Indifferently: i. minister justice 390:27
look on both i. 448:16
Indigent: how i. the great 231:7
Indigestion: reaps i. 515:1
Indignant: reading this i. page 76:1
Indignantly: held on i. 18:16
Indignatio: facit i. versum 282:24
i. principis mors est 358:3
saeva i. . .cor lacerare 521:27
Indignation: fierce i. . . . tear the
heart 521:27
incens'd with i. 346:6
let i. vex him 395:21
Indignities: by i. . .come to dig-
nities 26:24
Indigo: deep i. transparent skies 127:4
Indirection: by any i. 451:20
Indirections: by i. find directions
out 432:34
Indiscreetly: education given very
i. 511:20
Indiscretion: at least one blazing i. 358:15
Indisposeth: habit. .is up for dying 87:10
Indisputablest: this right. .the i. 126:5
Indite: songes make and wel i. 136:26
we men, at sea, i. 187:2
Inditing: my heart is i. of a good
matter 394:21
Individual: beyond my i. control 175:3
coachman's a privileged i. 179:34
injustice done to an I. 282:21
liberty of the i. . .limited 338:29
no i. could resent 521:3
no moment to. .an i. 272:8
not an i., but a species 204:17
not the i., but the species 278:15
your i. conduct 305:1
your i. whiskers 110:38
Individualism: rugged i. 254:3
Individuals: all my love is towards i. 519:32
i. pass like shadows 101:18
worth of the i. composing it 338:32
Indolent: agreeable wakings, i.
slumbers 156:19
chorus of i. reviewers 529:19
i. vacuity of thought 163:30
readers. .become more i. 226:19
with an i. expression 41:33
Indubitably: they so very i. are 39:19
Indulge: i. the loud unseemly jape 40:22
melancholy. .foolish to i. 273:20
Indulgence: only son. .expect more
i. 226:36
Indulgences: relics, beads, i. 346:26
Indulgens: crescit i. sibi. .hydrops 259:2
Indulgent: most i. husband 175:38
Indulgent: tout comprendre rend très
i. 511:9
Industrie: l'i. nationale de la
Prusse 353:4

Industrious, ambitious..liar 550:22
Industry: avarice, the spur of i. 265:4
captains of i. 127:3
i. will supply their deficiency 406:10
national i. of Prussia 353:4
nobility of birth..abateth i. 26:43
Inebriate: cheer but not i. 43:14, 163:21
Inebriated with..his own ver-
bosity 181:12
Ineffectual: beautiful and i. angel 19:21
remote and i. Don 41:31
their i. feuds 15:3
Ineptire: desinas i. 132:17
Inequity of oblivion 87:16
Inert: earth, tideless and i. 29:19
Inertia: strenua nos exercet i. 257:4
Inertibus: nunc somno et i. horis 261:25
Inevitability of gradualness 562:23
Inevitable: almost i. Consequences 304:44
arguing with the i. 320:21
change is i. 180:37
I did not believe in i. war 310:19
i. hour 230:1
Inexactitude: terminological i. 143:36
Inexorable: more fierce and more i. 478:39
Inexplicable dumb-shows and noise 434:15
Inez: saw ye not fair I. 252:28
Infallible: none of us i. 545:17
Infâme: quoi que vous fassiez, écra-
sez l'i. 557:9
Infamous: exceeds an i. history 87:15
rich, quiet, and i. 324:32
Infancy: heaven lies about us in
our i. 576:9
my angel-i. 552:3
nations, like men, have their i. 78:14
tetchy and wayward was thy i. 476:27
Infandum..iubes renovare dolorem 553:24
Infans: non sine dis animosus i. 259:26
Infant: i. crying in the night 532:34
break the i. tree 93:15
describe the i. phenomenon 177:17
furnish the fair I.'s bed 166:3
grown man in the cradle of an i. 103:23
i., mewling and puking 427:21
like i. slumbers 291:11
lisping i. prattling 104:33
on every i.'s tongue 120:23
providing the i. negroes..with
flannel waistcoats 178:43
sooner murder an i. 77:19
timely blossom, i. fair 378:16
to a little i...as painful 26:3
to the ragged i. threaten 165:17
where the noble I. lay 165:36
your i. beauty could beget 421:11
Infantry: Regiment of British I. 296:25
that small i. 345:3
Infants: who but i. question 410:20
Infatuated and besotted myriads 109:12
Infect: she would i. to the north
star 468:13
Infected: raven o'er the i. house 472:20
Infection: against i. and the hand
of war 474:22
free from rhyme's i. 281:26
Infectious: Waddy is an i. disease 304:51
Infects: one sickly sheep i. 561:30
Infelicissimum..fuisse felicem 78:14
Infelicity: constant i. 527:13
her i...years too many 563:18
Inferias: advenio has miseras..ad i.
tristi munere ad i. 133:20
133:20
Inferior: after deducting the i. 265:7
English..little..i. to the Scotch 365:9
knowing myself i. to myself 352:19
pleasing i. people 146:9
Inferiority: minds so impatient of i. 278:12
not been in Italy..an i. 273:11
Infernal: hail i. world 344:22
Inferno: Dante of the dread I. 94:12
Infidel: baptized or i. 345:4
i. as a dog is an i. 271:30
now, i., I have thee 465:12
Wine has played the I. 207:32
worse than an i. 68:48
Infidelity: indifference..half i. 103:25
Infidels: i. adore 385:10
Jews, Turks, I. 389:33
sleep with Turks and i. 475:17
Infini: l'i. me tourmente 360:9

Infinite: fellow of i. jest 437:15
her i. variety 424:9
how i. in faculty 433:15
i. majesty 388:16
i. mercy..as i. a justice 92:4
i. passion and the pain 97:12
i.-resource-and-sagacity 304:12
i. riches in a little room 330:15
i. wrath and i. despair 346:32
king of i. space 433:12
mercy every way is i. 91:18
there is an I. in him 127:18
though i. can never meet 332:6
unbottom'd i. abyss 345:26
woes which Hope thinks i. 497:17
Infinitely: I would love i. 94:15
Infinitude: our destiny..is with i. 579:27
Infinity: I. in the palm of your
hand 73:18
shares the nature of i. 573:7
Infirm: i. of purpose 458:14
i., weak, and despis'd old man 453:6
Infirmities: bear his friend's i. 451:22
bear the i. of the weak 66:17
fence against the i. of ill health 512:32
thine often i. 68:50
Infirmity: last i. of noble mind 342:20
prop to our i. 579:17
Inflammation of his weekly bills 115:40
Inflict: stern to i. 508:5
Inflicts: one who never i. pain 363:25
Influence: bereaves of their bad i. 575:6
between these two points of i. 19:30
constant i. 575:10
corrupt i. 101:17
i. of Woman 174:37
moist star upon whose i. 430:15
spheres of i. 9:25
their precious i. 343:14
under the name of I. 101:34
whose bright eyes rain i. 342:6
whose i. hath allotted death 330:9
Influenced: France has always..i.
..England 102:19
Influences: all the skyey i. 462:3
sweet i. of Pleiades 49:24
Influenza: no i. in my young days 42:16
Inform: all occasions do i. 436:15
i.'-ingens-horrend-ous 97:17
she can so i. the mind 582:3
while they captivate, i. 160:19
Information: I only ask for i. 174:30
i. upon..practical politics 182:40
resort to other i. 268:25
where we can find i. 272:32
Informe: monstrum horrendum, i. 554:14
Informed: o'er i. the tenement 190:13
Infortune: worst kinde of i. 138:35
Infrequens: parcus deorum cultor
et i. 258:27
Infringement: every i. of human
freedom 379:14
Infusa per artus mens 554:30
Infuse: oblivion in lost angels..i. 16:5
Infusion of a China plant 2:10
Ingeminate the word Peace, Peace 145:27
Ingenio: certare i. 320:30(−321)
Ingenious Hone! 308:3
Ingenium: Grais i. 256:8
i. ingens latet hoc sub corpore 261:11
Ingens: i.-horrend-ous 97:17
monstrum horrendum, informe, i. 554:14
Ingle: his wee bit i. 104:33
Inglorious: born to i. days 146:15
some mute i. Milton 230:5
Ingots: ass whose back with i.
bows 462:4
one..of two gold i. 330:13
Ingrat: cent mécontents et un i. 313:22
Ingrateful: all germens..that make
i. man 453:5
Ingratitude I hate i. 484:18
i., more strong 450:31
i., thou marble-hearted fiend 452:28
unkind as man's i. 427:22
Ingratitudes: monster of i. 481:17
Ingredient is a devil 471:23
Ingres's the modern man 91:9
Ingress: out i. into the world 318:9
Inhabit: we..i. symbols 200:31
Inhabitant: poor i. below 104:20

Inhabitants: not like th' i. o' the
earth 456:13
Inhabiters: all the i. thereof 396:29
Inhabits: being helped, i. there 484:40
Inhearse: ripe thoughts in my
brain i. 487:20
Inherent: rights i. and inalienable 268:19
Inherit: all which it i. 480:8
they shall i. the earth 57:39
tonight it doth i. 17:15
Inheritance: ruinous i. 212:23
Inherited: they have i. that good
part 302:1
Inheritor of the kingdom of heaven 391:2
Inheritors of unfulfilled renown 492:11
Inhuman: entertain such i. ideas 519:16
i. dearth of noble natures 284:20
Inhumanity: man's i. to man 107:2
In-I-go Jones 506:1
Inimitable rose 571:18
Iniquitatem: dilexi iustitiam et odi i. 232:9
Iniquities: bruised for our i. 54:26
Iniquity: bond of i. 64:38
draw i. with cords of vanity 53:5
I lack i. sometimes 469:36
loved justice and hated i. 232:9
on him the i. of us all 54:26
rejoiceth not in i. 66:45
that grey i. 439:35
ye have reaped i. 55:47
Iniuria: spretaeque i. formae 553:8
Injure: I ne'er could i. you 500:10
Injured: forgiveness to the i. 191:42
I i. neither name 250:25
i. lover's hell 348:10
sense of i. merit 344:13
Injuries: adding insult to i. 356:2
i...themselves procure 453:2
saints in your i. 470:25
Injurious: beauty, though i. 350:33
Injury: i...against Nature not to
go out 352:29
i. is much sooner forgotten 139:10
Injustice: conscience with i...cor-
rupted 445:30
i. done to an Individual 282:21
see i. done 263:16
Injustices: la pensée..autoriser
leurs i. 557:4
Ink: all the sea were i. 321:19
every drop of i...ran cold 558:13
gall enough in thy i. 484:1
he hath not drunk i. 455:11
his i...temper'd with Love's
sighs 455:22
in whose comparison all whites
are i. 480:39
Inkstand: he had a mighty i. 250:1
Inky: not alone my i. cloak 430:30
Inlaid: floor of heaven is thick i. 405:18
Inland: though i. far we be 576:19
Inlet: porch and i. of each sense 341:2
Inlets: through creeks and i.
making 147:8
Inly: moving i. to one far-set goal 19:4
Inmemores non sinit esse sui 372:8
Inmost: see the i. part of you 435:39
Inn: cannot find a chamber in the
i. 12:7
do you remember an I.? 42:8
earth his sober i. 123:25
gain the timely i. 459:10
lo, the old i. 359:7
no room for them in the i. 61:17
so much happiness..as by a good
..i. 272:39
take mine ease in mine i. 440:14
that dark i., the grave 417:31
this life at best is but an i. 264:21
unto mine i. must I 121:11
warmest welcome at an i. 409:13
world..not an i. 86:36
world's an i. 193:17
worst i.'s worst room 385:1
Innate: untaught i. philosophy 113:41
Inn-door: up to the old i. 366:1
Inner man 67:53, 301:38
Innisfree: go to I. 585:12
Innkeepers: righteous minds of i. 142:1
Innocence: best companions i. and
health 224:14

Innocence (cont.)
betrayed my credulous i.   340:33
came i. and she   543:22
dallies with the i. of love   483:5
glides in modest i. away   279:8
ignorance is not i.   92:25
i. for i.   485:4
I. is closing up his eyes   189:20
I. thy Sister dear   332:14
not to know we sinned is i.   169:10
our fearful i.   577:16
purity and place and i.   347:25
though conscious of your i.   273:6
Valour and I...gone hence   300:23
we bring not i. into the world   352:9
Innocencies: dead, wing'd i.   375:9
Innocency: keep i.   394:6
wash my hands in i.   393:18
Innocent: be i. of the knowledge   459:8
converse of an i. mind   288:33
heart whose love is i.   119:2
i. as gay   419:31, 587:8
i. brightness of a new-born day   576:22
i. from the great offence   392:34
i. is the heart's devotion   499:2
i. of the blood of this just person   60:40
make haste to shed i. blood   54:38
maketh haste to be rich..not i.   50:50
minds i. and quiet   319:7
officious, i., sincere   275:1
source of i. merriment   220:3
taken reward against the i.   392:24
than one i. suffer   73:9
these are as i. as those could be   370:17
water-colour shows the i...mind   514:26
Innocently employed .. getting money   272:22
Innocuous: lambent but i.   228:2
Innovate: to i. is not to reform   103:7
Innovations..the births of time   26:29
Innovator: time is the greatest i.   26:30
Innoxia: herbas et non i. verba   556:13
Inns: all I. have been driven   42:14
go to i. to dine   141:32
when you have lost your I.   42:14
Innumerable: among i. false   348:18
i. bees   539:5
i. of stains   285:19
join the i. caravan   98:3
Inopem me copia fecit   371:28
Inops: magnas inter opes i.   260:9
Inordinate: every i. cup   471:23
Inquest: greatest i. of the nation   101:22
Inquietum est cor nostrum   21:16
Inquire: pace is too good to i.   365:1
thou dost not i. wisely   51:12
Inquiries: here..suspended my religious i.   216:24
scepticism .. in religious i.   363:24
Inquiring: step so active, so i. eye   308:17
Inquiry of truth   27:32
Inquisition: abashless i. of each star   545:10
these i. dogs   539:18
Inquisitive: acute, i., dexterous   100:30
Inquisitorious and tyrannical duncery   352:22
Insane: eaten on the i. root   456:19
every hereditary monarch..i.   29:4
Insania: an me ludit amabilis i.?   259:25
Insanivimus: semel i. omnes   329:13
Insatiable: full of i. curtiosity   304:16
Insatiate itch of scribbling   217:19
Inscriptions: in lapidary i...not upon oath   272:35
Inscrutable: dark i. workmanship   579:9
dumb, i. and grand   17:13
Insect: so impotent and grovelling an i.   519:16
this 'ere 'Tortis' is a i.   403:16
Insects: troublesome i. of the hour   102:20
Insensibility: it argues an i.   306:6
stark i.   270:2
Inseparable: i...Beer and Britannia   505:15
i. propriety of time   24:34
Insert: correct, i., refine   521:16
Inside: lady i.   11:2
not been in the i. of a church   271:6
tough worm in your little i.   220:18

Insides: carrying Three I.   124:10
Insight: clearest i.   579:37
in hours of i. will'd   16:29
moment's i.   251:24
Insignificant: two as i. men as any   559:2
Insignificantly: anger i. fierce   164:2
Insincerity: mark of i. of purpose   503:15
Insinuating: busy and i. rogue   473:1
sly, i. Jacks   476:10
Insipid: he is many times flat, i.   194:6
Insists: Prime Minister i. on the other thing   365:15
Insisture, course, proportion   481:2
Insolence: by aspiring pride and i.   330:1
flown with i. and wine   344:35
i. of office   434:4
memory of that i.   206:15
wretch who supports with i.   277:30
Insolent: i. Greece or haughty Rome   281:15
taken by the i. foe   470:2
Insomnia: falsa..mittunt i. manes   555:2
Inspiration: contortions..without the i.   103:30
lasting i.   579:38
marry Ann..no more i. in her one per cent. i.   490:19 / 195:22
Inspire: our souls i.   400:31
till thou i. the whole   153:28
to i. hopeless passion   542:20
Inspired: as one i. pale Melancholy   154:1
great men are the i. texts   127:16
i. repuls'd battalions to engage   1:10
like a man i.   575:10
prophet new i.   474:21
sweetness that i. their hearts   331:2
Inspires easy my..verse   349:5
Inspiring bold John Barleycorn   108:10
Inspissated gloom   271:29
Instalment: heath..an i. of night   237:8
Instance: some precious i. of itself   436:29
Instances: wise saws and modern i.   427:21
with such familiar i.   451:8
Instancy: majestic i.   544:14
Instant: i. in season, out of season   68:59
more i. than the Feet   544:14
Instead: good abilities, i. of which   14:4
Instinct: all healthy i. for it   112:5
England..with a kind of i.   200:3
i. for being unhappy   414:11
i. is a great matter, I was a coward on i.   439:27
i. is important, O!   221:42
i. of all great souls   100:11
my natural i. teaches me   221:42
natural i. to discern   575:5
old i.   152:10
such a gosling to obey i.   429:17
with English i. fraught   188:31
with whose i...touched   331:2
Instincts: high i.   576:18
true to your animal i.   310:22
Institution: deep stake .. in such a glorious i.   101:13
more than a game..an i.   265:2
such as are in the i.   201:11
Institutions: female woman is one of the greatest i.   560:9
their dirty i.   546:44
your laws, i., and your false god   551:13
Instruct: in the graver gown i.   382:14
Instructed in all languages   176:38
Instructing: delighting..and i.   256:9
Instruction: horses of i.   77:17
I will better the i.   464:9
Instructions: awaiting i. Jellings   39:29
follows his own i.   463:8
Instructor: grand I., Time   103:13
Instrument: call me what i. you will   435:25
harmony of i. or verse   494:1
Heaven's happy i.   412:14
i. of ten strings   393:35
i. to know if the moon shine   111:4
I tune the i.   185:25
scatters sounds out of an i.   574:18
sweeter than the sound of an i.   86:32
Thy most dreaded i.   578:9
Instruments: fit i. to make slaves of the rest   379:3
genius and the mortal i.   449:5
i. of darkness   456:22

Instruments (cont.)
i. to plague us   454:21
our i. to melancholy bells   478:33
Insubstantial: like this i. pageant   480:8
Insufferable: Oxford that has made me i.   39:13
Insufficient: i. premises   111:33
mere reason is i.   265:10
Insulated: knows no i. spot   574:26
Insult: adding i. to injuries   356:2
blockhead's i.   278:32
injury..sooner forgotten than an i.   139:10
one more i. to God   93:6
these bones from i. to protect   230:7
threatened her with i.   102:11
Insulted by a very considerable bribe   219:26
Insulting: i. Christmas card   233:11
i. the sun   365:12
Insults: first i. the victim   165:20
Insured: they were heavily i.   218:1
Insurgit: [Horatius] et i. aliquando   404:26
Insurrection: nature of an i.   449:5
Intangible: O world i.   545:1
Integer vitae   258:22
Integratio: irae amoris i. est   541:29
Integrity: based on the i. of China   43:11
i. without knowledge is weak   278:19
Intellect: certain ripeness in i.   289:26
creeds a disease of the i.   200:44
discerning i. of Man   574:8
his i. is improperly exposed   504:28
is it weakness of i.?   220:18
march of i.   508:7
opinion..determined..not by the i.   508:29
our meddling i.   581:16
put on I.   75:13
scepticism of the i.   363:24
strengthening one's i.   290:27
that living i. that bred them   352:5
Intellects: argument and i. too   227:20
highest i., like the tops of mountains   324:25
Intellectual: disinterested i. curiosity   549:8
draughts of i. day   165:30
I am an i. chap   219:6
i. All-in-all   578:30
i. eunuch Castlereagh   115:13
i. power   574:15
lords of ladies i.   115:16
moral or i. damage   305:11
not an i. Croesus   182:18
passage to the i. World   513:19
tear is an i. thing   75:6
thirdly, i. ability   20:21
this i. being   345:19
unravaged by the fierce i. life   19:10
without some i. intention   413:11
yet, being i.   121:17
Intelligence: gulls him with i.   487:21
people have little i.   97:33
whence..this strange i.?   456:17
Intelligencies: we are the i.   185:1
Intelligent: i. anticipation of facts   167:27
we are not i.   221:38
Intelligible: Monarchy..an i. government   28:26
Shakespeare was not..more i.   153:14
something great, if not i.   116:35
Intemperance: brisk i. of youth   216:22
Intend: if that agree which I i.   245:11
i. to lead a new life   390:14
Intended: damp my i. wing   349:6
I i. an Ode   183:14
Intending: never i. to visit them more   526:29
Intense: i. inane   497:12
not with too i. a care   133:22
Intensely: means i. and means good   91:33
Intensity: excellency of every art ..i.   289:20
Intent: agree..unto my friend's i.   245:11
defeats my strong i.   435:32
forget not yet the tried i.   583:19
glorious great i.   509:23
his first avow'd i.   99:35
i. is al   138:40
on hospitable thoughts i.   348:8

Intent (cont.)
our true i. is | 467:28
prick the sides of my i. | 457:9
resist his uncontrollable i. | 351:7
still the less we knew of its i. | 359:3
truth..told with bad i. | 73:24
when the i...is just | 440:32
with i. to deceive | 238:35
working out a pure i. | 578:9
Intentique ora tenebant | 553:23
Intention: general i. of his books | 268:15
thy i. stabs | 485:8
without some intellectual i. | 413:11
Intents: my i. are savage-wild | 478:39
thy i. wicked or charitable | 431:32
Inter: in hugger-mugger to i. him | 436:26
Inter-assured of the mind | 186:25
Intercession: made i. for the transgressors | 54:28
Interchange: quiet i. of sentiments | 272:30
Interchanging praise | 250:29
Intercourse: dreary i. of daily life | 582:3
lived in social i. with him | 272:7
love, an abject i. | 226:34
Interdict: hang like an i. | 579:2
Interest: common i. always will prevail | 190:27
false estimation of our i. | 101:30
fresh i. to a twice-told tale | 117:42
his ease, his security, his i. | 101:21
I du in i. | 319:21
i. unborrowed from the eye | 581:26
it's i. that keeps peace | 167:10
natural i. of money | 325:8
their real i. to discern | 160:41
to damn the public i. | 111:14
Interested: i. him no more | 239:2
not i. in the possibilities of defeat | 552:21
Interesting: i., but tough | 550:9
most grati—most i. | 188:2
most i. things..didn't occur | 210:9
one person doing i. actions | 28:29
some person..i. him | 268:8
that I. Play | 41:13
that it be i. | 268:11
Interests: about their carnal i. | 111:13
ambassadors from..hostile i. | 100:14
Interfere: declines to i. | 564:15
Interfering with the liberty of action | 338:25
Interfused: something far more deeply i. | 582:1
Intérieur: vive l'I.! | 422:16
Interim: all the i. is like a phantasma | 449:5
Interior: compensated by i. blessings | 243:17
touch'd with an i. ray | 165:33
Interior: un equilibrio que se suscita en su i. | 214:2
Interire: nil vere i. | 25:13
Interline: enlarge, diminish, i. | 521:10
Interlunar: her vacant i. cave | 350:23
Intermeddle with his joy | 50:7
Intermingling of Heaven's pomp | 574:2
Intermission: but the i. of pain | 422:10
laugh sans i. | 427:15
Interpose: to i. a little ease | 343:1
who in quarrels i. | 215:26
Interposition of some invisible agent | 265:6
Interpret: your beards forbid me to i...so | 456:14
Interpretation: capable of..some other i. | 188:25
Interpreter: God is his own i. | 161:20
i. is the hardest to be understood | 499:26
i. of the cogitations thereof | 56:45
Interpreters: soft i. of love | 401:31
Interred: good is oft i. | 450:17
Interstices between the intersections | 277:28
Intertissued robe | 444:23
Interval: i. betwixt one passion and another | 512:21
make a lucid i. | 193:2
Intervalos: lúcidos i. | 134:13
Intervals: full of lucid i. | 134:13
laughing..at stated i. | 504:20
lucid i. and happy pauses | 27:46
not in the lucid i. | 574:3
Interview: strange and fatal i. | 184:18

Interviews: these our i. | 114:26
Interwoven: Bach, i. with Spohr | 220:5
Intestines: product of the smaller i. | 125:30
Intimacy: avoid any i. | 305:1
Intimate: king of i. delights | 163:26
one of my most i. enemies | 410:20
Into: constantly getting i. it | 174:25
Intolerable: burden of them is i. | 390:36
i., not to be endur'd | 479:11
this i. deal of sack | 439:39
Intoxicate: shallow draughts i. | 382:22
Intoxicated: exposes himself when ..i. | 274:13
i. with my own eloquence | 181:43
once i. with power | 103:3
Intoxication: best of life..i. | 115:34
Wordsworth's standard of i. | 501:11
Intoxified: you i. brute | 34:30
Intreasured: in their seeds..lie i. | 442:6
Intrenched: deep scars of thunder had i. | 345:7
Intricated: poor i. soul | 186:30
Intrigue: talk and not the i. | 229:10
Intrigues half-gather'd | 164:31
Intrinsicate: this knot i. of life | 426:13
Introduced: cut anyone you've been i. to | 131:28
when I'm i. to one | 405:16
Introduction: one is an i. | 270:25
Intrude: I hope I don't i.? | 381:5
Intruders on his ancient home | 18:16
Intrudes: society, where none i. | 114:26
Intus: ecce i. eras | 21:22
Inurned: saw thee quietly i. | 431:32(–432)
Inutilis occupatio | 414:21
Invade: dare to i...my realm | 198:11
Invades: he i. authors like a monarch | 194:8
stillness first i. the ear | 191:31
Invalid: permanent i. called Bunbury | 569:22
Invariable: double glass o' the i. | 179:4
Invasion: i. of a common enemy | 305:1
waiting for the long-promised i. | 144:3
Invectives: sharp i.—Alias, Billingsgate | 583:25
Invent: fitter to i. than to judge | 27:41
necessary to i. him | 557:7
not able to i...more than I i. | 441:11
Invented: all the poems that ever were i. | 131:8
fond thing vainly i. | 401:7
good many that haven't been i. | 131:8
he that first i. thee | 281:27
he that first i. war | 330:26
more than..is i. on me | 441:11
not a regular rule: you i. it | 129:32
Inventer: il faudrait l'i. | 557:7
Invention: beggars i. and makes fancy lame | 162:5
brightest heaven of i. | 443:2
first heir of my i. | 488:24
happy i. | 13:1
i. breeds i. | 201:19
i. is unfruitful | 100:23
i. of a barbarous age | 343:26
it's my own i. | 131:20
long poem is a test of i. | 289:15
never by i. got | 521:24
quickness of his wit and i. | 212:18
weak i. of the enemy | 144:27
Inventions: a whoring with their own i. | 398:14
sought out many i. | 51:16
Inventor of harmonies | 529:17
Inventors: on the i.' heads | 438:9
Inverted: i. cone | 274:2
ruler of th' i. year | 163:24
that i. Bowl | 207:3, 4
Investment..putting milk into babies | 144:14
Inveterate: long i. foes saluted | 193:41
Invideo: non equidem i. | 555:17
Invincible: none i. as they | 158:32
our frailties are i. | 513:30
shaking her i. locks | 352:15
Inviolable: clutching the i. shade | 18:15
Inviolate: compass'd by the i. sea | 539:13
great i. place | 237:10
most secret and i. Rose | 585:23

Invisible: fern-seed, we walk i. | 439:1
i. eel | 281:19
i. spirit of wine | 471:21
join the choir i. | 196:34, 35
live i. and dim | 551:21
only evil that walks i. | 346:28
O world i. | 545:1
some i. agent | 265:6
things visible and i. | 390:18
with i. soap | 253:7
Invisibly: silently, i. | 75:21, 22
Invitation: i...rightly declined | 233:6
more i. than command | 511:25
Invite: friendly himself i. | 12:6
I loafe and i. my soul | 567:10
i. God and his Angels | 186:32
Invited: her father..oft i. me | 470:2
Invites: what beck'ning ghost..i. my steps | 381:30
Invoke the genius of the Constitution | 379:10
Involved: I am i. in Mankind | 186:28
night i. the sky | 159:1
Invulnerable: as the air, i. | 430:17
i. nothings | 492:6
Inward: borne i. unto souls afar | 88:25
draw the i. quality after them | 424:28
endeavours..an i. light | 575:5
i. and spiritual grace | 391:13
that i. eye | 577:7
thou celestial light shine i. | 346:20
truth in the i. parts | 395:8
well-dressed..a feeling of i. tranquillity | 201:7
with i. glory crowned | 498:24
with my i. eye | 74:5
Inwardly..ravening wolves | 58:25
Inwards: from the i. to the parts extreme | 442:21
he looked i. and found her | 194:6
Iocos: nec ut soles dabis i. | 233:19
Iohannes fac totum | 232:6
Ionian: isle under I. skies | 493:13
valleys of I. hills | 537:29
Iope: white I., blithe Helen | 123:27
Iove: ab I. principium musae | 555:25
Iovem: satis est orare I. | 257:11
Iovis: I. omnia plena | 555:25
nec I. ira..poterit..abolere | 372:1
Ipse: 'I. dixit'. 'I.' autem erat Pythagoras | 145:6
Ipswich and Oxford | 447:10
Ira: ça i. | 12:11
Ira: i. furor brevis est | 256:26
nec Iovis i...poterit..abolere | 372:1
Irae: amantium i. amoris integratio est | 541:29
dies i., dies illa | 134:4
tantaene animis caelestibus i.? | 553:7
Iram indeed is gone | 205:9, 10
Ire: where slept thine i.? | 286:1
Ireland: discourse in praise of I. | 377:13
general..from I. coming | 445:6
great Gaels of I. | 140:15
how's poor ould I.? | 9:6
I'll not forget old I. | 73:12
I. gives England her soldiers | 337:10
moment..I. is mentioned | 505:20
romantic I.'s dead and gone | 584:27
to sweeten I.'s wrong | 586:14
Iris: in the Spring a livelier i. | 534:15
one vast I. of the West | 114:6
Irish: before I. Home Rule is conceded | 409:8
forbid to grow on I. ground | 9:6
howling of I. wolves | 428:29
I. are a fair people | 272:21
I. bull is always pregnant | 327:10
led by an I. general | 490:39
never hae trodden on I. ground | 30:17
no blithe I. lad | 122:16
now the I. are ashamed | 332:26
upon the I. shore | 106:18
Irishman: every I...a potato in his head | 237:24
Irked: it. him to be here | 18:24
Iron: beat the i. while it is hot | 194:3
bigots of the i. time | 417:2
blood and i. | 72:33
bound in misery and i. | 398:15
bruise them with a rod of i. | 391:50
earth stood hard as i. | 409:20

Iron (cont.)
  embattled armies clad in i.   350:25
  every..crag tinkled like i.   575:24
  great meals of beef and i.   444:5
  I barred my gates with i.   296:4
  i. bars a cage   319:7
  I.—Cold I.—is master   295:14
  i. curtain   144:15, 549:19
  i. entered into his soul   398:12
  i. enter into his soul   512:26
  i. sharpeneth i.   50:47
  i. shuts amain   342:26
  i. tongue of midnight   467:34
  meddles with cold i.   110:29
  mightiest fleets of i.   188:32
  my i. gone   8:13
  nor strong links of i.   448:36
  painted to look like i.   73:1
  reeking tube and iron shard   301:1
  sound of i. on stone   171:16
  strong as i. bands   318:11
  strong as links of i.   101:10
  their nobles with links of i.   400:27
  whose i. scourge   230:15
  wink and hold out mine i.   443:14
Iron-bosomed sea   411:31
Iron-bound serving-man   184:14
Ironies: Life's Little I.   237:4
Irons: heat me these i. hot   447:36
  two i. in the fire   37:22
Iron-sleet of arrowy shower   230:14
Iron-ware: firewood, i.   333:21
Irony: most perfect..i...unconscious   111:31
Irradiation: intense i. of a mind   495:10
Irrationally held truths   266:23
Irrecoverably: i. dark   350:22
  lost my voice most i.   563:36
Irregular: licentious idioms and i. combinations   278:13
  your i. appetites   85:8
Irregularly great   322:9
Irregulars: Baker Street i.   188:22
Irrelevant: poor relation..most i. thing   306:29
Irresistible: if the changes..be thus i.   277:24
  ladies of i. modesty   512:3
  theatre is i.   20:6
  war..due to i. natural laws   310:18
Irresponsible: chatter of i. frivolity   181:13
Irretrievably: passionately and i.   411:10
Irreverent to my tutor   270:2
Irrevocabile: volat i. verbum   257:7
Irritabile: genus i. vatum   257:18
Irrt: es i. der Mensch   223:15
Is: all that i., at all   95:22
  him which i. and which was   70:21
  I see what was, and i.   573:26
  it i., but hadn't ought to be   238:31
  nay, it i.; I know not 'seems'   430:30
  was, and i., and i. to come   70:38
  whatever i., i...just   193:10
  whatever i., i. right   383:21
Isaac: God of I.   45:38
  I., whom thou lovest   44:54
Iscariot: Judas..not I.   63:56
Ischyros: He upbeareth me, I.   543:18
Iser: flow of I., rolling rapidly   122:17
Isis: I. and Cam to..science dear   573:14
  my Cam and I.   381:24
Island: as an inland i.   523:13
  Enchanted I.   337:35
  floating bulwark of the i.   73:6
  make this i. all her own   558:2
  misty i.   420:31
  no man is an i.   186:27
  no snakes..throughout the..i.   274:1
  some secreted i.   579:30
  watched this famous i. descending   144:20
  we shall defend our i.   143:40
  what a snug little I.   173:15
  Zuleika, on a desert i.   39:27
Islanded by cities fair   495:1
Islands: many flowering i.   494:23
  parson for the I. of the Blest   302:19
  round many western i.   288:19
  these selfsame British I.   78:23
  where His i. lift   568:16
Island-story: our rough i.   537:25
Island-valley of Avilion   531:37

Isle: balmy i. of Rum-ti-Foo   217:25
  beyond the I. of Sky   30:13
  blow soft o'er Ceylon's i.   240:18
  Britain, highly favoured i.   506:14
  each cold Hebrid i.   153:27
  fairest I., all isles excelling   192:44
  i. is full of noises   480:5
  I. of Beauty   36:28
  i. that is called Patmos   70:23
  i. under Ionian skies   493:13
  it frights the i.   471:16
  Kelly from the Em'rald I.   360:3
  make its continent an i.   374:21
  many a green i.   494:22
  men of the Emerald I.   189:21
  natural bravery of your i.   429:29
  never was i. so little   296:5
  Scio's rocky i.   113:3
  ship, an i.   208:19
  some unsuspected i.   94:42
  suddenly raised a fairy i.   376:6
  this scepter'd i.   474:22
Isled: Him who i. us here   537:21
Isle of Man: Kelly from the I.   360:2
Isles: among the Aegean i.   18:16
  bound for th' i. of Javan or Gadier   350:31
  chimeras and enchanted i.   340:25
  he taketh up the i.   54:12
  i. of Greece   115:43
  i. where good men rest   208:9
  kings of Tharsis and of the i.   396:25
  matted rushy i.   17:28(-18)
  multitude of the i...glad   397:31
  on her hundred i.   114:2
  other flowering i. must be   495:5
  sprinkled i.   90:34
  touch the Happy I.   541:3
Islington: at I., kind sir   29:24
  bailiff's daughter..in I.   29:22
  fields from I.   75:4
  village less than I.   158:22
Ismenian: headlong from th' I. steep   350:17
Isn't: as it i., it ain't   130:8
  'There i. any,' said the March Hare   129:5
Isolate: i. pure spirits   88:20
  to limit and i. oneself   223:14
Isolated: fine i. verisimilitude   289:21
  splendidly i. in Europe   210:12
Isolation: our splendid i.   227:39
Isolieren: zu beschränken und zu i.   223:14
Israel: beauty of I. is slain   47:29
  better than all the waters of I.   48:22
  chariot of I.   48:16
  deliver I., O God   393:16
  gather together the out-casts of I.   400:21
  in his border see I. set   92:9
  I. loved Joseph   45:12
  I., of the Lord belov'd   420:5
  I. scattered upon the hills   48:13
  lost sheep of the house of I.   58:46
  mother in I.   46:47
  neither will I let I. go.   45:40
  O thou worship of I.   393:1
  prophet in I.   48:21
  ransom captive I.   362:6
  small states—I., Athens   267:9
  so great faith, no, not in I.   58:32
  success..on I.'s side   161:16
  sweet psalmist of I.   47:38
  to your tents, O I.   47:48
  ye daughters of I., weep   47:30
Israelite..in whom there is no guile   63:4
Israelites: are they I.? so am I   67:33
  I. passed over   46:39
Israfel: where I. hath dwelt   380:18
Issachar is a strong ass   45:27
Issue: Abassin kings their i. guard   347:9
  happy i.   389:18
  joins i. with death   96:24
  rich legacy unto their i.   450:24
Issues: Heaven has joined great i.   575:10
  to fine i.   461:16
Issuing: forth i. on a summer's morn   349:11
Isthmus: this i. of a middle state   383:22
Isyphill: fair I.   502:17
It: I. rolls impotently on   207:3
  'tisn't beauty..just i.   304:50
Italia: I., I, shall be free   337:38
  I.! oh I.!   114:8
Italiae: probrosis altior I. ruinis   259:29

Italiam fato profugus..venit   553:5
Italian: led by an I. general   490:39
  like I. twilight   119:25
  'midst I. flowers   241:10
  no I. priest shall tithe   447:29
  nor..behold with prejudice the French, I.   86:27
  or perhaps I.   221:25
  roof of blue I. weather   495:8
  that rare I. master   485:36
  to women I.   136:13
  writ in very choice I.   435:17
Italians: what the I. call..flummoxed   179:8
Italien aux femmes   136:13
Italien ist ein geographischer Begriff   338:2
Italy: bought his doublet in I.   463:12
  graved inside of it, 'I.'   91:6
  great poete of I.   137:39
  Greece, I., and England   193:9
  I. a paradise for horses   109:29
  I. a vassal state   144:6
  I. is a geographical expression   338:2
  I., my I.   91:6
  made I. from designs by Michael Angelo   550:16
  man who has not been in I.   273:11
  no extract from Moore's I.   119:32
  no looking at a building here after..I.   103:36
  our England to his I.   96:19
  Paradise of exiles, I.   494:14
  some jay of I.   429:32
  transparent skies of I.   127:4
Itch: Divinity had catch'd the i.   110:15
  insatiate i. of scribbling   217:19, 283:12
  i. of literature   319:11
  mine eyes do i.   473:7
  poor i. of your opinion   429:4
Itching palm   451:10
Ite: i. domum saturae..i. capellae   556:9
Item, two lips   482:21
Iter: per i. tenebricosum   132:13
Iteration: any i. of nuptials   156:17
  thou hast damnable i.   438:12
Ithuriel: him..I. with his spear touched   347:29
Itself: art never expresses anything but i.   569:17
  in i., but not in fine weather   146:18
  it is not i.—it has no self   290:9
  it is still i.   469:43
  nor for i. hath any care   76:2
  not alone, nor for i.   74:3
  not of i., but thee   280:21(-281)
  nought but i. to teach it   81:2
  seeketh not i. to please   76:2
  shaped, sir, like i.   424:17
  thou art the thing i.   453:21
Itur: sic i. ad astra   555:9
It-will-wash-no-more   548:19
Itylus: half assuaged for I.   521:30
  slaying of I.   524:16
Iubeo: hoc volo, sic i.   283:9
Iubes: da quod i. et iube quod vis   21:23
Iucunditatis: plenus est i. et gratiae   404:26
Iudex: i. damnatur ubi nocens absolvitur   526:4
  i. honestum praetulit utili   261:3
Iudicat: securus i. orbis terrarum   21:24
Iudice: adhuc sub i. lis est   255:21
  se i. nemo nocens absolvitur   284:1
Iudicium: manet alta mente repostum i. Paridis   553:8
  per legale i. parium suorum   327:9
Iunctura: callida verbum reddiderit i. novum   255:19
Iunonis: saevae memorem I. ob iram   553:5
Iuppiter: I. est quodcumque vides   320:20
  I. hostis   555:13
  I...periuria ridet amantum   371:22
  I. pluvius   547:19
  quem I. vult perdere   195:10
Iura: per populos dat i.   556:25
Iurare: nullius addictus i...magistri   256:10
Ius: i. et norma loquendi   255:20
  voluntas i. suum cuique tribuens   282:22
Iustitia: fiat i., et pereat mundus   203:38
  fiat i. et ruant coeli   561:2
  i. est..voluntas ius suum cuique   282:22

Iustitiam: dilexi i. et odi iniquitatem 232:9
Iustum et tenacem propositi 259:21
Iuvabit: forsan et haec olim meminisse i. 553:14
Iuvenes dum sumus 13:8
Iuventa: non ego hoc ferrem calidus i. 260:8
Iuventus: antiquitas saeculi i. mundi vitio parentum rara i. 25:6, 258:3
Iuventutem: post iucundam i. 13:8
Ivoire: Vigny..en sa tour d'i. 414:7
Ivory: against the i. gate 359:1
  dreams out of the i. gate 85:22
  his belly is as bright i. 52:14
  in ebony..as in i. 212:14
  i. and apes and peacocks 47:44, 333:20
  little bit..of i. 23:12
  my lady seems of i. 359:10
  other..of i. 555:2
  thy neck is as a tower of i. 52:19
  thy skin is i. 215:42
Ivy: as creeping i. clings 161:30
  holly and the i. 10:14
  i. falls 522:3
  i. never sere 342:10
  i. of sweet two-and-twenty 118:32
  laurel, i., vine 336:38
  like the i. I'll cling to you 339:10
  pluck an i. branch 409:28
  wild roses and i. serpentine 497:22
Ivy-bloom: bees in the i. 497:2
Ivy-bush: owl in an i. 520:6
Ivy-mantled: yonder i. tow'r 229:29
Ivy-tod is heavy with snow 150:9
Ivy-tree: bonny i. 8:22
Ivywood: between the trees in I. 140:26
Ixionian: rolling I. wheel 535:26

J

Jabberwock: beware the J. 129:39
  hast thou slain the J. 129:39(-130)
  J. with eyes of flame 129:39(-130)
Jacinth: eleventh, a j. 72:1
Jack: banish plump J. 439:37
  every J...a gentleman 476:11
  for the life of poor J. 173:7
  gorging J. and guzzling Jimmy 543:7
  hails you Tom or J. 159:31
  house that J. built 369:6
  J. and Jill 367:9
  J. lov'd his friend 173:9
  j. shall have Jill 467:12
  J.'s the king of all 562:22
  J. was embarrassed 118:1
  lamented J. 152:13
  news of my boy J. 300:2
  poor J., farewell 441:1
  Sixteen-string J. 273:12
  spanking J. was so comely 173:9
  they all love J. 562:22
  this J., joke, poor potsherd 255:7
  Tommy and J. and Joe 305:3
Jackal: this whipped j. 144:6
Jackdaw sat on the Cardinal's chair 34:8
Jacket: day hath put on his j. 251:2
  his j. was red 151:9
  I could thresh his old j. 164:26
Jack Falstaff: sweet J. 439:37
Jack Horner: little J. 367:16
Jack Ketch: as soon dine with J. 273:17
Jack Redskin: I'll read 'J.' 140:6
Jacks: sly, insinuating J. 476:10
Jackson: J. standing like a stone wall 39:2
  Stonewall J. riding ahead 568:13
Jacksonian vulgarity 387:13
Jack Sprat could eat no fat 367:10
Jack Wilkes: dine with J., Sir! 273:17
Jacky shall have a new master 368:18
Jacob: God of J. 45:38
  J. served seven years 45:6
  J.'s sons and daughters 361:15
  J. was a plain man 44:57
  mercy on J. yet 92:9
  more than all the dwellings of J. 397:13
  Name of the God of J. 392:35
  sold his birthright unto J. 44:58
  talk to him of J.'s ladder 269:18
  traffic of J.'s ladder 545:1

Jacob (cont.)
  turned away the captivity of J. 397:8
  voice is J.'s voice 45:1
Jade: arrant j. on a journey 220:30
  go spin, you j. 420:26
  let the galled j. wince 435:16
Jades: I like the j. for a' that 106:23
  pampered J. of Asia 331:7, 441:37
  run deils an' j. thegither 108:22
Jael Heber's wife 46:46
Jag: with many a j. 492:20
Jaguar: I've never seen a J. 297:25
Jah: praise him in his name J. 396:5
Jail: being in a ship is being in a j. 270:32
  in j...better company 270:32
  in Shrewsbury j. tonight 262:11
  nothing was now left but a j. 174:22
  patron and the j. 279:4
Jam: j. every other day 130:26
  j., junket, jumbles 171:17
  never j. to-day 130:26
James: Councillor to King J. 232:16
  J. J. Morrison Morrison 339:15
  J. I, J. II, and the Old Pretender 233:14
  K. I. slobbered 422:14
  King J...call for his old shoes 422:2
  my name is Truthful J. 239:1
  take Eliza, and our J. 281:18
James Lee: dead of joy, J. 92:29
Jamie: I saw my J.'s ghaist 35:10
  my J. was at sea 35:8
Jamshyd: Courts where J. gloried 206:1
  J.'s Sev'n-ring'd Cup 205:9
  take J. and Kaikobad away 205:18
Jane: change from J. to Elizabeth 22:31
  England's J. 297:20
  J. lies in Winchester 297:20
  J. went to Paradise 297:19
  knight embracing J. 123:2
  Lady J. was fair 34:13
  to welcome J. 297:19
  Willie shall dance with J. 5:25
Janet was as glad at that 32:4
Jangled: like sweet bells j. 434:14
Janiculan: from J. heights 146:15
Janus: very J. of poets 194:10
Janvier: Generals J. and Février 364:18
Japanee: English they be and J. 301:4
Japanese: J. don't care to 157:25
  retiring..towards the J. fleet 234:18
Jape: indulge the loud unseemly j. 40:22
Japes: with feyned flaterye and j. 137:22
Japheth: it might be J. 303:9
  Shem, Ham, and J. 44:36
Jar: amid the city's j. 16:17
  may syllabes j. with time 281:27
Jardin: *cultiver notre j.* 557:3
Jargon: j. of their Babylonian pulpits 102:8
  j. of the schools 401:30
  j. o' your schools 105:23
Jargoning: their sweet j. 149:34
Jarley: Mrs. J.'s waxwork show 177:31
Jarndyce: J. and J...perennially hopeless 173:22
Jarr'd against nature's chime 351:11
Jarring: j. sectaries may learn 160:41
  recoil and j. sound 346:9
Jasher: written in the book of J. 46:43
Jasper: first foundation was j. 72:1
  'J. first,' I said 87:36
  j. of jocunditie 195:5
  to look upon like a j. 70:36
Java: blow soft o'er J.'s isle 240:18
Javan: isles of J. or Gadier 350:31
Javelin: trailed the hunter's j. 17:26
Jaws: into the j. of Death 528:18
  j. of darkness do devour it 466:20
  j. that bite 129:39
  ponderous and marble j. 431:32(-432)
  with gently smiling j. 128:24
Jay: poor Jim J. 171:12
  some j. of Italy 429:32
  thrush and the j. 485:16
Jay-bird: you know w'at de j. say 238:14
Jealous: art is a j. mistress 199:34
  as thou art j., Lord, so I am j. 185:21
  I'm not a j. woman 242:27
  j. for they are j. 472:17
  J. God 390:7
  j. in honour 427:21
  j. souls will not be answer'd 472:17

Jealous (cont.)
  loving-j. of his liberty 477:28
  not ever j. for the cause 473:17
  one not easily j. 474:12
  question with my j. thought 487:7
  to the j. confirmations 471:42
  with scornful, yet with j. eyes 385:29
  wit with j. eye surveys 143:4
Jealousies: surmises, j., conjectures 441:8
Jealousy: all j. to the bride 30:11
  beware, my lord, of j. 471:31
  green-ey'd j. 464:17
  j. a human face 77:4
  j. heareth all things 56:21
  j. is cruel as the grave 52:22
  j...the injured lover's hell 348:10
  life of j. 471:34
  mine was j. in love 530:41
  so full of artless j. is guilt 436:18
  tyrant, tyrant J. 192:46
Jean: farewell my J. 405:18
Jean Jacques: gospel according to J. 126:17
Jebusite..maugre all God's promises 375:27
Jebusites: Hivites, and the J. 45:36
Jeder nach seinem Fähigkeiten 333:12
Jeering at everything that looks strange 377:20
Jeers: master of gibes and flouts and j. 181:8
Jeeves shimmered out 572:9
Jeffersonian simplicity 387:13
Jehovah: I am, I said 503:3
  J. has triumph'd 357:17
  J., Jove, or Lord! 386:29
  J. of the thunders 207:8
  J...when he passed from Egypt 344:34
  names divine of Jesus and J. 74:22
Jehu: him..shall J. slay 48:9
  J...driveth furiously 48:27
Jekkel and Jessup 171:10
Jellings: awaiting instructions J. 39:29
Jelly: distill'd almost to j. 431:10
  fits this little j. 245:19
  meaty j. too..is mellering 178:7
  out, vile j. 453:35
Jelofer amiable 502:19
Jemmy Grove: young J. 30:1
Jemmy Twitcher..peach me 215:7
Je-ne-sais-quoi young man 221:6
Jenkin: hol jolly J. 420:3
Jenny: J. kissed me 265:25
  J., my own true loved one 572:20
  vengeance of J.'s case 406:12
Jenyns: Robertson, Beattie, Soame J. 306:26
Jeopardy: in j. of their lives 47:39
Jerkin: on both sides, like a leather j. 481:23
Jerks: bring me up by j. 175:22
Jerusalem: build thou the walls of J. 395:10
  built in J.'s wall 75:8
  daughters of J. 52:12, 14
  for the Building up of J. 75:10
  four squeal walls in the New J. 89:16
  he hath redeemed J. 54:23
  hills stand about J. 399:33
  holy city, new J. 71:44
  if I forget thee, O J. 400:5
  if I prefer not J. 400:5
  I go bound in the spirit unto J. 65:10
  in that J. shall Harry die 442:29
  J. the golden 362:1
  J. thy sister calls 75:11
  metropolitan J. 375:27
  not die but in J. 442:29
  O J., J., thou that killest the prophets 60:20
  pray for the peace of J. 399:31
  pray that J. may have 421:5
  speak ye comfortably to J. 54:8
  the Lord doth build up J. 400:21
  there J.'s pillars stood 75:4
  there's J. and Madagascar 543:10
  thryes hadde she been at J. 137:15
  till we have built J. 75:16
  was J. builded here? 75:16
Jeshurun waxed fat and kicked 46:32
Jessamine: casement j. stirr'd 536:11
  crow-toe, and pale j. 342:31(-343)
  j. faint 497:27

Jesse: count..to J.'s fount 183:4
rod out of the stem of J. 53:17
Jesses: eye for j. and restraint 544:3
her j...my dear heart-strings 471:38
Jessup: Jekkel and J. 171:10
Jest: fellow of infinite j. 437:15
glory, j., and riddle 383:22
good j. for ever 439:7
great men may j. with saints 461:32
he had his j. 190:24
his whole wit in a j. 37:12
intermingle..j. with earnest 26:5
j. and youthful jollity 341:28
j.'s prosperity 455:34
life is a j. 215:20
rueful j. 161:25
scornful j. 278:32
swear the j. be laughable 462:30
tells the j. without the smile 152:21
to use my self in j. 186:15
world's a j. 512:9
Jested: he j., quaff'd, and swore 188:29
Jester: how ill white hairs become a..j. 442:37
Jesters: ambled up and down with shallow j. 440:8
Jesting: j. Pilate 27:29
nor foolish talking, nor j. 68:2
'tis j., dancing, drinking 263:18
Jestings: our common j. 88:13
Jests: he j. at scars 477:13
some excellent j., fire-new 483:31
to his memory for his j. 501:1
Jesu: J., by a nobler deed 135:12
J., Lover of my soul 565:5
J., Mary, and Joseph they bare 7:14
J., the very thought 132:6
O J., thou art standing 264:12
thy Name, O J. 264:8
Jesuit: thing, a tool, a J. 294:14
Jesus: at the name of J. 68:18
Blood of J. whispers peace 72:19
disciple whom J. loved 64:19
do for J.' sake 4:8
even so, come, Lord J. 72:13
gentle J., meek and mild 565:9
how sweet the name of J. 364:15
J. calls us 3:19
J. from the Ground suspires 205:8
J. increased in wisdom 61:22
J. loves me 560:26
J. shall reign 562:8
J. speaks..to thee 161:9
J. was sitting in Moses' chair 74:13
J. wept 63:41
J.! with all thy faults 112:12
little J., wast Thou shy? 544:5
looking unto J. the author 69:18
names divine of J. and Jehovah 74:22
one of his disciples, whom J. loved 63:48
Pythagoras was misunderstood ..and J. 200:41
shoves J. and Judas equally aside 200:42
sound of J.' breath 74:13
stand up for J. 194:31
sweet reasonableness of J. 20:18
they had been with J. 64:29
this J. will not do 74:14
we would see J. 63:45
with the Cross of J. 35:1
ye belong to J. 3:17
Jésus: bon Sansculotte J. 172:28
Jesus Christ: if J. were to come to-day 127:25
in the kingdom and patience of J. 70:23
J. and him crucified 66:21
J. her little child 3:20
J. her Lord 517:1
J. is risen to-day 8:2, 13:13
prisoner of J. 69:5
Jet: pansy freakt with j. 342:31(-343)
Jets: how he j. 483:14
Jetty: come uppe J. 267:13
Jeunesse: si j. savoit 201:30
Jew: Daniel, J. 465:12
either for Englishman or J. 74:14
false English Nobles and their J. 375:19
hath not a J. eyes? 464:8

Jew (cont.)
he clutched a cringing J. 141:26
I am a J. else, an Ebrew J. 439:18
I thank thee, J. 405:13
J. that Shakspeare drew 386:34
Kish that lofty J. 332:23
neither Greek nor J. 68:31
not a Heathen, or a J. 561:20
then must the J. be merciful 464:33
Jewel: caught my heav'nly j. 501:21
immediate j. of their souls 471:30
j. in an Ethiop's ear 477:9
j...in a swine's snout 49:58
j. in a ten-times-barr'd-up chest 474:10
j. of the just 552:10
lest my j. it should tine 104:27
mine eternal j. 458:34
no j. is like Rosalind 427:28
poor j. of their souls 513:32
precious j. in his head 426:30
stage's j. 280:10
Jewelled mass of millinery 535:40
Jewel-print of your feet 536:12
Jewels: boys and girls..moving j. 548:15
captain j. in the carconet 487:1
decked with j. 12:1
her precious j. into a garret 24:38
j. five-words long 538:11
many j. make women either..fat 36:14
my j. for a set of beads 475:10
these, said she, are my j. 109:26
unvalu'd j. 476:14
Jewry: sepulchre in stubborn J. 474:22
Jews: born King of the J. 57:23
cross..which Jews might kiss 385:10
ears of stock-jobbers and J. 162:20
J., a headstrong..race 190:10
J. and proselytes 64:26
J., Turks, Infidels, and Heretics 389:33
three Paynims, three J. 327:15
till the conversion of the J. 333:8
to choose the J. 202:19
to the J. old Canaan stood 562:15
Jig: my very walk should be a j. 482:8
wooing..a Scotch j. 468:9
Jigging veins 330:20
Jill: Jack and J. 367:9
Jack shall have J. 467:12
one-eyed J. 171:10
Jilted: better be courted and j. 122:21
Jim: dear brother J. 582:11
they called him Sunny J. 235:9
Jim Jay: poor J. 171:12
Jimmy: gorging Jack and guzzling J. 543:7
J. was good and true 217:28
Jingle: made his pension j. 164:26
Jingles: harness j. now 263:5
Jingling of the guinea 534:24
Jingly: Lady J.! Lady J.! 311:13
Jingo: by j., if we do 11:9, 265:15
by the living j. 227:22
Jo: John Anderson my j. 106:19, 20
Joan: greasy J. doth keel 456:1
J...as good i' th' dark 246:12
Johnny has got his J. 5:25
some..my lady, and some J. 455:10
Job: and a good j. too 222:23
blessed the latter end of J. 49:34
describing the afflictions of J. 25:19
doth J. fear God for naught? 48:39
leave their j. when they..choose 302:2
patience of J. 69:42
poor as J...not so patient 441:16
seek your j. with thankfulness 296:33
we will finish the j. 144:5
Jobiska: his Aunt J. 312:6, 7
his Aunt J.'s Runcible Cat 312:9
Joblillies and the Garyalies 209:18
Jockey of Norfolk 476:39
Jocund: better be j. 206:22
such a j. company 577:7
Jocunditie: jasper of j. 195:5
Joe: poor old J. 210:17
Tommy and Jack and J. 305:3
Jog: income..a man might j. on with 308:11
j. on, j. on 485:21
John: Christ his J. 243:34
Don J. of Austria 141:6

John (cont.)
forth J.'s soul flared 92:6
gently, J., gently down hill 505:30
his last chapter of St. J. 89:41
I heartily love J., Peter, Thomas 519:32
I J., who also am your brother 70:23
J. and I are more than quit 401:27
J. he cried in vain 159:40
J. to the seven churches 70:21
J. was a very good man 217:28
Matthew, Mark, Luke, and J. 3:3
my brother J., the evil one 74:4
O No J.! 9:4
Robert's kin, and J.'s 236:8
Saint J. sate in the horn 7:14
shut the door, good J.! 385:20
Thomas' ideal J. 251:10
to J. I ow'd great obligation 401:27
we bring J. now to be burned 92:5
whose name was J. 62:61
John Anderson my jo 106:19, 20
John Barleycorn: bold J. 108:10
John Brown: J.'s body 234:7
Long J. 75:15
John Bull: greatest of all is J. 117:31
John Donne, Anne Donne, Undone 186:29
John Grubby, who was short and stout 141:17
John Naps of Greece 478:46
Johnny: Frankie and J. were lovers 6:8
J. has got his Joan 5:25
J. underground 402:24
silly little J., look 250:3
When J. Comes Marching Home 11:19
Johnny Cope are ye wauking yet? 503:1
Johnny Green: little J. 366:18
Johnny Head-in-air 250:2, 402:24
Johnny-the-bright-star 402:25
John of Gaunt: as familiarly of J. 442:61
old J. 474:8
John Peel: d'ye ken J.? 229:16
Johns: three J. 251:14
Johnson: Dr. J.'s morality 239:8
freedom with which Dr. J. condemns 103:38
J. is dead..no man can..put you in mind of J. 235:2
J.'s style..and Gibbon's 154:13
Life of J...a very great work 325:26
no arguing with J. 227:27
not a good imitation of J. 103:30
that great Cham..J. 506:6
Johnsonese: broken J. 325:30
John Wellington Wells 222:16
Joie: le peuple a de la j. 355:7
Join: j. in hand brave Americans 180:5
j. the choir invisible 196:34
j. the innumerable caravan 98:3
j. with thee calm Peace, and Quiet 341:10
will you j. the dance? 129:23
Joined: if hands were only j. 229:8
j. be to our wild minstrelsy 285:5
love so dearly j. 349:18
she j. the former two 193:9
taxation and representation.. God hath j. 388:2
what..God hath j. 59:56
what God hath j...God will take care of 489:26
whom God hath j. 391:34
why these two persons should not be j. 391:21
Joiner squirrel 477:7
Joining of hearts and housekeepings 177:42
Joins: salvation j. issue with death 96:24
Joint: at every j. and motive 481:26
in member, j., or limb 346:4
Jacob's thigh was out of j. 45:9
j. and not an entertainment 235:6
remove the j. 131:28
time is out of joint 432:32
Joint-heirs with Christ 65:54
Joint-labourer: night j. with the day 430:13
Joints: agitation in the mind and the j. 337:2

Joints (cont.)
between the j. of his harness 48:15
his square-turn'd j. 418:8
j. that you carve 294:36
may his j. tormented be 281:27
Joint stools: creatures set upon..j. 272:34
Joke: American j. 550:17
dullness ever loves a j. 381:15
it's our only j. 36:19
j.'s a very serious thing 143:7
j. well into a Scotch understand-ing 504:20
life is a j. that's just begun 219:28
this Jack, j., poor potsherd 255:7
truth or j.? 97:20
Jokes: accomplished at seeing my j. 421:8
difference of taste in j. 196:17
Round-heads..are standing j. 1:27
they laughed..at all his j. 225:1
Jollity: jest and youthful j. 341:28
nothing trimmed in j. 487:14
turned to j. and game 349:27
Jolly: I'm a J.—'Er Majesty's J. 301:19
j. young waterman 173:12
laugh, be j. 263:18
lead we not here a j. life 527:12
nose, nose, j. red nose 37:25
so comely, so pleasant, so j. 173:9
some credit in being j. 176:7
this life is most j. 427:22
three j. Farmers 171:22
three j. gentlemen 171:11
What J. Fun! 405:16
Jonah: J. prays and sings 266:13
J. was in..the fish 56:5
lot fell upon J. 56:4
wish it was in J.'s belly 176:27
Jonas: grave J. Kindred 165:6
Jonathan: consult Brother J. 560:31
David had his J. 243:34
J. gave his artillery unto his lad 47:26
O J., thou wast slain..my bro-ther J. 47:30
Saul and J. were lovely 47:30
Jones: J.! as from Calais 573:13
J...daily absorbs a clay 121:21
J., the tobacco-jar 121:22
Tom J...picture of human manners 216:17
Jonquille o'ercomes the feeble brain 571:19
Jonson: J.'s learnèd sock 342:7
learn'd J. 189:13
O rare Ben J. 282:9
too nicely J. knew the critic's part 154:4
wit-combats betwixt him and Ben J. 212:18
Jordan: I looked over J. 10:2
J. was driven back 399:2
not J.'s stream 562:17
this side J.'s wave 3:16
while J. rolled between 562:15
Joris, and he 92:22
Jorkins: I have a partner. Mr. J. 174:34
Joseph: as J. was a-walking 5:15
Israel loved J. more 45:12
Jesus, Mary, and J. they bare 7:14
J. did whistle 7:14
new king..which knew not J. 45:29
Josephine: court of the Empress J. 220:27
Joshua: first was Duke J. 327:15
J. the son of Nun 46:6
Joss-sticks: permeated with the odour of J. 503:17
Jostle: Philistines may j. 220:28
Jostling: not done by j. in the street 74:23
Jot: one j. of former love 189:20
Jour: le j. de gloire est arrivé 412:1
qu'en un lieu..un j. 78:6
Journalism: Christianity .. but why j.? 29:21
Journalists say a thing they know isn't true 42:18
Journey: arrant jade on a j. 226:30
bear'st thy..riches but a j. 462:4
begin a j. on Sundays 520:24
day's j. take the..day 410:2

Journey (cont.)
death the j.'s end 193:17
dine at j.'s end 586:13
dreariest and the longest j. 493:10
for a j., and such a long j. 197:13
he is gone a long j. 49:50
here is my j.'s end 473:31
life's j. just begun 160:27
on that j...your attorney 219:11
or he is in a j. 48:3
where the traveller's j. is done 76:7
your j. of so many days 375:14
Journeying: slowly j. on 307:35
Journeyman to grief 474:18
Journeymen: nature's j. had made men 434:20
Journeys: his successive j. run 562:8
j. end in lovers meeting 482:28
Journey-work of the stars 567:19
Jours: tous les j., à tous points de vue 157:22
Jousted in Aspramont 345:4
Jove: Apollo, Pallas, J. and Mars 184:2
at lovers' perjuries..J. laughs 477:20
daughter of J. 230:15
deny himself for J. 455:18
his awful J. 199:22
immortal J.'s dread clamours 472:3
Jehovah, J., or Lord 386:29
J. and my stars be praised 483:20
J. but laughs at lovers' perjury 193:13
J. for's power to thunder 429:13
J...send thee a beard 483:22
J. would swear Juno but an Ethiop 455:18
lovelier than the Love of J. 330:21
might I of J.'s nectar sup 280:21(-281)
nor J. himself..whiter 510:20
she is sport for J. 471:6
tell proud J. 281:8
tell tales..to high-judging J. 452:40
threshold of J.'s Court 339:27
where J. bestows..the fading rose 125:9
while J.'s planet rises 92:18
Jovial: Autumn..comes j. on 546:17
j. wind of winter 293:13
Jowett: my name is J. 39:5
Joy: ah heavenly j.! 82:12
all it yields of j. and woe 90:42
all j. is young 338:10
all the j. before death 525:6
all the j. that you can wish 464:20
all the passages of j. 279:7
asks if this be j. 225:5
at enmity with j. 576:19
bathed in j. complete 82:3
before, a j. propos'd 488:12
bends to himself a J. 74:27
break forth into j. 54:23
burst J.'s grape 287:21
but apprehend some j. 467:24
cease, every j. 122:40
come again with j. 399:34
countenance..brightened with j. 574:20
deep power of j. 581:25
dizzy, a tumultuous j. 508:3
dreme of j., al but in vayne 138:24
dwell in doubtful j. 459:3
each for the j. of the working 303:21
enter thou into the j. of thy Lord 60:30
eternal j., and everlasting love 371:12
everybody saw with j. 249:18
every child may j. to hear 76:9
father's j. 232:2, 419:6
fields where j. for ever dwells 344:22
finish'd j., and moan 430:1
for ever in j. 96:21
form'd of j. and mirth 75:1
from the heart of j. 39:6
from which he drank in j. 207:14
full of life, and splendour, and j. 102:11
fulness of j. 392:27
general j. of the..table 459:18
glad tidings of great j. 527:4
Greensleeves was all my j. 6:18
harp, his sole remaining j. 416:29
headlong j. is ever on the wing 350:19

Joy (cont.)
he chortled in his j. 129:39(-130)
he sees it in his j. 576:9
honey of all earthly j. 158:12
I j. to see my self now live 246:24
intermeddle with his j. 50:7
in the fulness of j. and hope 253:7
I should be dead of j. 92:29
I weep for j. 474:34
j. apart from thee 199:13
j. before thee according to the j. in harvest 53:14
j. be wi' you a' 360:16
j. brightens his crest 349:13
j. cometh in the morning 393:25
j. delights in j. 486:13
j. for ever 284:19
j. in an applause so great 158:4
j. in idleness 82:6
j. in the making 81:9
j. in widest commonalty 574:6
j. is like restless day 402:10
j. is my name 76:12
j. is the sweet voice, j. the lumin-ous cloud 151:6
j. is wisdom 585:16
j. of elevated thoughts 582:1
j. of love is too short 328:9
J. rul'd the day 193:32
j. runs high 241:26
j.'s a trinket 512:9
j. shall be in heaven 62:12
j., shipmate, j.! 566:25
j.'s soul lies in the doing 480:41
j. the day in mirth 168:13
j. to his mighty heart 295:16
j. was never sure 523:22
j. where'er he dwell 9:23
J., whose hand is ever at his lips 287:21
j. without canker or cark 309:25
kisses the J. as it flies 74:27
labour without j. is base 413:20
lead from j. to j. 582:3
Life, J., Empire 497:17
London..gemme of all j. 195:5
lost a j. for it worth worlds 244:6
love, and thought, and j. 581:6
love, j., peace, long-suffering 67:46
make me hear of j. and gladness 395:8
man was made for J. and Woe 73:24
more true j. Marcellus 384:10
my feast of j. 547:20
my j., my grief, my hope 558:1
my j., of youthful sports 114:32
my scrip of j. 405:9
no j. but calm 535:15
nor j. nor grieve too much 193:17
not a j. the world can give 118:18
not increased the j. 53:14
now 'tis little j. 253:2
O daring j., but safe 567:3
oh! dream of j.! 150:4
oil of j. for mourning 55:4
O j.! that in our embers 576:17
page to j. 524:29
perfectest herald of j. 468:14
Phyllis is my only j. 421:13
pledges of Heaven's j. 351:9
pure and complete j. 548:8
reap in j. 399:34
riding's a j. 92:39
Robin is all my j. 436:34
silent j. at their arrival 149:24
smooth current of domestic j. 278:29
snatch a fearful j. 230:25
some bringer of that j. 467:24
sons of God shouted for j. 49:20
stern j. which warriors feel 416:27
stream of sparkling j. 173:34
sweet j. befall thee 76:12
they for j. did grin 149:10
thine earth-born j. renew 81:5
thy j. and crown eternally 354:11
tidings of comfort and j. 6:12
'twixt two extremes..j. and grief 454:23
unbodied j. 498:3
variety's the source of j. below 215:19
voice of j. and health 309:8
walked in glory and in j. 580:7
we wear a face of j. 574:35

Joy (cont.)
what j., what bliss 166:9
what their j. and their glory 1:1
what the j. and the glory 362:9
where's all the j. and mirth 292:5
who hath seen j.? 81:2
who shall ever find j.'s language 81:2
with courage, love, and j. 214:29
with j. approach 508:18
with j., pleasance, revel 471:22
without love, hatred, j. or fear 401:29
Woman, the j. of joys 105:28
writh'd not at passing j. 289:8
years to be of work and j. 83:19
Joyance: like to sounds of j. 236:6
thy clear keen j. 498:9
Joy-bells ring in Heaven's street 334:1
Joyful: how good and j. a thing 400:3
in. . prosperity be j. 51:13
j. and pleasant. .to be thankful 400:21
j. and triumphant 13:2, 369:20
j. rise 292:1
shew yourselves j. 397:32
with a j. spirit I. .die 540:3
Joyless: like a j. eye 495:19
j. triumphals 350:17
Joyous: good, great and j. 497:17
j. errand 207:30, 32
many j. and pleasant histories 328:2
Joyously: so j., so maidenly 502:18
Joys: Africa and golden j. 442:34
all my j. to this are folly 109:2
all our j. are but fantastical 184:17
all that's precious in our j. 512:29
almost sacred j. of home 358:1
blest with some new j. 191:34
do your j. with age diminish 93:25
excommunicate from all the j. of love 125:8
[friendship] redoubleth j. 26:17
great j., like griefs, are silent 331:11
hence, vain deluding j. 341:7
how fading are the j. 365:8
in whom all j. . .agree 502:7
its tenderness, its j., and fears 576:22(–577)
j. and sorrows sailors find 113:16
j. in another's loss of ease 76:3
j. of parents are secret 26:44
left all j. to feel all smart 244:11
less loud, through its j. and fears 93:22
minds me o' departed j. 108:37
our j. three-parts pain 95:15
present j. are more 192:29
profanation of our j. 186:24
raise your j. and triumphs 565:4
season made for j. 214:32
she knows, in j. and woes 150:23
society's chief j. 159:18
such present j. therein I find 195:12
summer's j. are spoilt by use 285:38
takes in trust our youth, our j. 405:12
tasted the eternal j. of heaven 330:2
their homely j. 230:1
thy j. when shall I see? 6:28
thy visionary j. remove 155:35
Time. .rob us of our j. 5:8
what j. await us there 362:1
where true j. are to be found 389:38
Juan was my Moscow 116:34
Jubilant: be j., my feet 264:17
Jubilee: first day of our J. is death 86:20
we bring the J. 583:7
Jubjub: beware the J. bird 129:39
Judah: among the thousands of J. 56:7
J. is my law-giver 395:23
princes of J. their counsel 396:13
sight of J.'s seer 329:12
Judas: shoves Jesus and J. equally aside 200:42
Judas Maccabaeus: the third J. 327:15
Judea: in Mesopotamia, and in J. 64:26
where wild J. stretches 421:9
Judee: know everythin' down in J. 319:17
Judge: after a time they j. them 570:18
as sober as a J. 204:12
fitter to invent than to j. 27:41
forbear to j. 445:32
for . . monarchs justly to j. 83:16
God is a righteous J. 392:7

Judge (cont.)
half as sober as a j. 307:27
how long. .dost thou not j. 70:46
if He. .j. you as you are 461:29
I'll be j., I'll be jury 128:25
indifferent j. 501:26
J., and a good J. too 222:22
j. none blessed before his death 56:42
j. not 58:16, 61:30
j. not me 121:25
j. not the Lord 161:18
j. not the play 169:19, 404:10
j. not the preacher, for he is thy J. 244:7
j. of danger which they fear 578:5
J. of the earth 571:4
j.'s robe become them. .as mercy 461:28
j., that no king can corrupt 446:19
neutrality of an impartial j. 100:18
out of thine own mouth. .j. thee 62:37
O wise young j. 465:4
shall not the J. . .do right? 44:52
sole j. of truth 383:22
though I am no j. 387:20
thou seest I j. not thee 121:25
wags that j. by rote 371:11
who made thee a prince and a j.? 45:31
Judgement: at forty, the j. 211:14
blood and j. . .co-mingled 434:26
bring every work into j. 51:36
by j. of the eye 455:2
Daniel come to j. 465:4
green in j. 424:2
he looked for j. 53:2
He, which is the top of j. 461:29
in j. old 463:41
in the day of j. 59:15, 388:51
j. of the great whore 71:31
Last J. draweth nigh 73:23
Last J.'s fire must cure 90:20
O j.! thou art fled 450:22
on better j. making 487:22
overheard j. of posterity 325:29
penetrating j. without. .satire 223:9
people's j. always true 190:28
proceed to j. 465:6
reserve thy j. 431:25
right j. in all things 389:39
seven times tried that j. 464:3
their j. is a mere lottery 194:9
vulgarize the day of j. 269:13
waits upon the j. 435:47
what j. I had increases 194:12
what j. shall I dread? 464:30
your j. . .probably. .right 329:11
Judgement Book: leaves of the J. unfold 527:11
Judgement Day: by Tophet-flare to J. 295:2
Judgement Seat: at God's great J. 294:27
to the j. of God 23:24
Judgement Tide: England shall bide till J. 303:6
Judgements: criterion of wisdom to vulgar j. 103:2
differing j. 160:18
drop our clear j. 425:2
evil tongues, rash j. 582:3
give the King thy j. 396:22
Ignorance delivers brawling j. 531:16
j. so malign 517:8
men's j. are a parcel of their fortunes 424:28
to keep thy righteous j. 399:21
with our j. as our watches 382:19
Judges: hungry j. 385:15
J. all rang'd 215:6
j. of fact, tho' not j. of laws 403:2
not my Accuser, but my J. 363:12
Judicious: in j. hands 121:6
little j. levity 515:11
tale should be j. 159:16
Judiciously: to skip j. 234:19
Judy O'Grady: Colonel's Lady an' J. 298:6
Jug: cuckoo, j.-j. 361:6
j., j., j., j., tereu 321:15
'J. J.' to dirty ears 197:29
J. of Wine 205:24
little brown J. 6:19
one old j. without a handle 311:12
w'en it git loose fum de j. 238:21

Juger: pour . des choses grandes 354:25
Juggler: least perceive a j.'s sleight 111:3
threadbare j. 429:1
Julia: kiss my J.'s dainty leg 246:16
whenas in silks my J. goes 247:13
where my J.'s lips do smile 245:21
Juliet: J. is the sun 477:13
philosophy. .make a J. 478:25
Julius: ere the mightiest J. fell 430:14
such another J. 429:28
ye towers of J. 229:24
Julius Caesar: J.'s ill-erected tower 475:20
O J., thou art mighty yet 452:1
third J. 327:15
July: cuckoo of a worse J. 538:5
English winter—ending in J. 116:47
of June, and J.-flowers 245:17
swarm of bees in J. 5:17
Jumbles: jam, junket, j. 171:17
Jumblies: lands where the J. live 311:21
Jump: efery dime she gife a j. 313:13
j., as Mr. Levi did 34:25
j. the life to come 457:7
not j. with common spirits 463:44
with old rules j. right 110:30
Jumping: finished j. on his mother 221:36
j. from the chair she sat in 265:25
Jumps: see how the cat j. 420:29
Junction: old man at a J. 312:16
June: all J. I bound the rose 93:42
April, J., and November 369:5
April, J., and September 228:4
as the cuckoo is in J. 440:9
cuckoo of a joyless J. 538:4
for the old J. weather 90:37
Glorious First of J. 147:15, 359:26
husband J. 561:7
ice in J. 117:13
in the leafy month of J. 149:35
J. disclose unceremoniously the rose 561:9
J.'s twice J. since 91:30
made December J. 533:15
newly sprung in J. 107:14
November on the lap of J. 253:18
of J., and July-flowers 245:17
she needs not J. 18:22
so rare as a day in J. 320:17
swarm of bees in J. 5:17
when J. is come 82:13
when J. is past 125:9
Junes: in three hot J. burn'd 487:29
Jungle: all that keep the J. Law 299:26
Law of the J. 298:19
through the J. very softly 301:27
Junior: stuck a. .j. with a horse 300:18
Juniper: sat down under a j. 48:7
Junius: Cobbett and J. together 240:7
Junket: jam, j., jumbles 171:17
Juno: haughty J.'s unrelenting hate 194:29
J. but an Ethiop 455:18
lids of J.'s eyes 485:26
she's J. when she walks 281:25
Jupiter: brighter. .than flaming J. 330:6
Leda, the beloved of J. 309:12
so J. me succour 502:19
vespers in the Temple of J. 217:1
Jurisdiction: Bishop of Rome hath no j. 401:12
Jurisprudence: gladsome light of J. 148:5
Jury: I'll be judge, I'll be j. 128:25
j. all wrote down 129:34
j. . .have a thief or two 461:23
j. . .wrote down all three dates 129:28
trial by j. . .will be a delusion 172:12
Jurymen: that j. may dine 385:15
Just: becometh well the j. to be thankful 393:13
be j., and fear not 446:31
blood of this j. person 60:49
faithful and j. to me 450:19
gentle, plain, j. and resolute 568:7
gods are j. 454:21
good man, and a j. 62:52
great, j., good God! 96:6
grounded on j. and right 349:3
hath his quarrel j. 445:30, 491:9
in its causes j. 193:10
I should be j. 243:20
I think that thou art j. 472:7

INDEX

Just (cont.)
jewel of the j. 552:10
j. are the ways of God 350:27
j. as I am 198:20
j. beast 5:2
j., gentle, wise 497:12
j. men made perfect 69:21
j. shall live by faith 65:31
j., subtle, and mighty opium 172:19
j., the upright, the generous 363:26
Lord, make us j. 14:29
meanly j. 279:4
more j. than God 48:49
ninety and nine j. persons 62:12
nothing to do with that j. man 60:48
only the actions of the j. 501:6
our cause is j. 180:4
path of the j. 49:43
prosperous to be j. 320:12
pursue things which are j. in present 24:24
rain it raineth on the j. 79:7
rain on the j. and..unjust 57:52
spirits of j. men long opprest 350:36
this j., this pious fraud 215:9
thou art e'en as j. a man 434:23
thou art indeed j., Lord 255:8
thou art j. 531:40
thou'lt raise me with the j. 355:21
thy j. dealing as the noon-day 394:4
'tis very j. they blame 375:23
to the wisdom of the j. 61:11
we j. beauties see 282:1
whatsoever things are j. 68:27
when I reflect that God is j. 268:27
when the intent..is j. 440:32
your rifle an' yourself j. so 295:22
Juster: not, Celia, that I j. am 421:16
Justice: as infinite a j. too 92:4
as thou urgest j...shalt have j. 465:11
believing in the j. of our cause 233:20
certain fountains of j. 24:33
crimes unwhipp'd of j. 453:9
England..convinced of its j. 409:8
equal piece of j., Death 86:18
even-handed j. 457:8
expected j. from a company? 505:5
fuel j. layeth on. 508:15
indifferently minister j. 390:27
in..j. none..see salvation 464:33
j. enough to accuse 227:25
j., in fair round belly 427:21
j. is truth in action 180:21
j. of it pleases 7:7, 331:9
J....to the weaker side inclin'd 111:19
law of humanity, j., equity 101:26
let j. be done 203:38, 561:2
loved j. and hated iniquity 232:9
no business with the j...of the cause 275:32
persuade j. to break her sword 473:11
place of j...hallowed 26:31
plucks j. by the nose 461:18
poetic J., with her lifted scale 381:11
principles of eternal j. 373:16
religion, j., counsel, and treasure 27:8
revenge is a kind of wild j. 27:4
sad-ey'd j. 443:10
see how yond j. rails 454:10
sword of j. first lay down 170:17
though j. be thy plea 464:33
Thwackum was for doing j. 204:25
till he talks about j. and right 300:7
unpersuadable j. 584:13
what humanity..and j. tell me I ought 101:3
what you think j. requires 329:11
when mercy seasons J. 464:33
where mystery begins, j. ends 102:39
which is the j. 454:10
with sword of j. thee ruleth 195:7
you have ravish'd j. 563:28
Justifiable to men 350:27
Justification: terms like grace, new birth, j. 20:9
Justified: half as good as j. 111:16
j. a chaste polygamy 125:5
little j. with thee 14:29
successful crimes alone are j. 193:8
wisdom is j. of her children 59:9

Justify: j. God's ways to man 263:25
j. the ways of God 344:4
Justly: j., skilfully, and magnanimously 352:25
to do j. and to love mercy 56:8
to think j. 406:15
Jutty: no j., frieze, buttress 457:6
Juxtaposition: J. his prophet 146:11
j., in short; and what is j.? 146:10

K

Kabul: ford o' K. river 296:21
Kaikhosru: Kaikobad the Great or K. 205:20
lot of Kaikobad and K. 205:19
Kaikobad: K. the Great or Kai-Khosru 205:20
leave the lot of K. 205:19
take Jamshyd and K. away 205:18
Kailyard: brier bush in our k. 250:16
Kail-yardie: delving in his k. 250:12
Kalendas: ad Graecas k. soluturos 120:9
Kalends: pay at the Greek K. 120:9
Kangaroo: Duck and the K. 311:18
Old Man K. first 297:29
Kansas had better stop raising corn 312:23
Karshish, the picker-up 91:19
Kaspar: old K.'s work was done 507:3
Kate: change K. into Nan 74:22
swear me, K. 440:7
Kathleen Mavourneen! 166:24
Katterfelto..hair on end 163:22
Keats: dumb to K.—him, even John K., who was kill'd off 116:35
K...was a Greek 309:20
Mister John K. five feet high 290:3
out-glittering K. 322:10
what porridge had John K.? 95:3
who killed John K.? 118:2
Kecksies: rough thistles, k., burs 445:11
Kedar: among the tents of K. 399:24
as the tents of K. 51:39
Keel: her k. ploughs air 135:19
no k. has ever ploughed 493:12
Keen: k. as are the arrows 498:5
k., unscrupulous course 15:21
k. were his pangs 117:25
quite as k. a sense of duty 221:28
thy tooth is not so k. 427:22
Keener: grows k. with constant use 267:19
Keep: always k. us so 199:20
bless thee, and k. thee 46:10
care must k. you 170:23
guard us, guide us, k. us 195:23
k. an incommunicable sleep 572:25
k. it now, and take the rest 118:6
k. King Charles..out of the Memorial 174:25
k. thee in all thy ways 397:19
k. thee unto him 391:29
k. the home fires burning 210:4
k. the Jungle Law 299:26
k. Thou my feet 364:10
k. thy righteous judgements 399:21
k. up appearances 143:12
k. up your bright swords 469:40
k. ye the Law 301:26
k. yourself to yourself 179:2
let him k. the rest 245:1
many to k. 294:1
profanation to k. in 245:26
so may I always k. 215:37
still k. something to yoursel 105:18
subtle ways I k. 199:3
they should k. who can 580:15
to k. heights 574:17
with such consort as they k. 341:22
Yankee Doodle, k. it up 33:6
you k. them on 214:15
Keeper: boldness is an ill k. of promise 25:33
k. is only a poacher 294:5
k. stands up 263:6
my brother's k. 44:30
son of a livery stable k. 584:14
the Lord himself is thy k. 399:28

Keepers: k. of the house..tremble 51:33
k. of the walls 52:12
their k. call a lightning 478:42
Keepest: found'st me poor..k. me so 225:9
Keepeth: he that k. thee 399:27
neither k. he his anger 398:5
Keeping: by k. men off 214:15
if k. it does it much good 34:34
in Thy gracious k. 198:15
k. along it their eternal stands 265:22
k. time, time, time 380:12
opening the doors..and k. them open 22:14
Keeps: makes a nation happy, and k. it so 350:14
Keith of Ravelston 183:1
Kelly: anybody here seen K.? K. from the Isle of Man 360:2
Fanny K.'s divine plain face 307:15
K. from the Em'rald Isle 360:3
Kellynch-Hall: Elliot of K. 22:25
Kelpie: in the K.'s flow 419:17
Kelt: blind hysterics of the K. 533:22
Slav, Teuton, K. 528:11
Kempenfelt: brave K. is gone 162:11
when K. went down 162:11
Ken: as far as angels' k. 344:8
what I k. this night 32:5
Wordsworth's eyes avert their k. 17:3
Kendal: misbegotten knaves in K.-green 439:22
Kenned: mair they talk I'm k. the better 107:28
they hae been k., in holy rapture 105:6
Kenning: they may gang a k. wrang 104:7
Kennst du das Land 224:6
Kensal Green: Paradise by way of K. 141:24
Kent: gallant squires of K. 322:22
K. and Surrey may 296:15
K., sir—everybody knows K. 178:28
ye men of K. 577:8
young lady of K. 10:25
Kentish Sir Byng 90:10
Kentish Town: Pancras and K. repose 75:5
Kentucky: old K. Home 210:15
Kept: secrets..must be k. from children 193:6
that I k. my word 171:14
what wee k., wee lost 11:17
Kernel: this k., this squash 485:9
Kernels: from sweet k. press'd 348:9
Kersey: honest k. noes 455:30
Ketch: as soon dine with Jack K. 273:17
Ketten: nichts..als ihre K. 333:11
Kettle: how agree the k. and the..pot? 56:44
I took a k. 131:11
merry k. boils 372:16
Polly put the k. on 173:19
whose k. has scarcely time to cool 278:1
Kettle-drums: Johnson marched to k. 154:13
Kew: go down to K. in lilac-time 365:25
his Highness' dog at K. 382:11
Key: Door to which I found no K. 206:16, 17
k. of India is in London 181:15
k. of the bottomless pit 71:38
k. of the street 179:31
taken away the k. of knowledge 61:50
that golden k. 339:29
turn the k. deftly 288:32
with an easy k...open life 191:22
with this k. Shakespeare 580:16
with this same k. Shakespeare 92:19
Keys: all her shining k...took 237:5
half that's got my k. 228:9
his k. were rusty 119:14
k. of all the creeds 532:17
k. of hell and death 70:28
over the noisy k. 402:11
pattered with his k. 119:21
thou hast the k. of Paradise 172:19
two massy k. he bore 342:26
Key-stone: of night..the k. 108:9

Khaki: man in k. kit 300:17
Khayyam: come with old K.
    205:19, 206:9
Kiaugh: his weary k. and care beguile 104:33
Kibe: he galls his k. 437:13
Kick: dies of an ass's k. 93:39
  k. against the pricks 64:42
  k. his wife out of bed 518:8
  nor a body to k. 505:5
  or I'll k. you downstairs 128:29
  scarcely k. to come to the top 290:1
  wheel's k. 334:10
  why did you k. me downstairs? 72:14
Kicked: k., until they can feel
  whether 110:39
  never knew any k. upstairs 103:34
  no body to be k. 547:15
  waxed fat, and k. 46:32
Kicking you seems the common lot 91:26
Kickshaws: any pretty little tiny
  k. 442:30
Kid: fleet-foot k. 522:2
  in his paw dandled the k. 347:15
  leopard. .lie down with the k. 53:18
  thou shalt not seethe a k. 46:1
Kidney: man of my k. 466:11
  one vast k. 266:13
Kidneys: blister my k. 518:27
Kill: as k. a king 435:41
  for nothing, but to k. 247:18
  if. .a devil, I cannot k. thee 473:33
  I'll k. you if you quote it 100:2
  k. a man as k. a good book 352:6
  k. an admiral from time to time 557:1
  k. a wife with kindness 479:7
  k. him in the shell 449:4
  k. not the moth 73:23
  k. thee and love thee after 473:11
  k. thee with much cherishing 478:1
  k. the patient 26:18
  k. the poor creature at once 213:22
  k. with looks 475:7
  let's k. all the lawyers 445:37
  mettle enough. .to k. care 469:15
  must men k. and die? 493:27(–494)
  prepared to k. . .if it is not done 490:9
  that basilisk is sure to k. 214:34
  these poor half-kisses k. me 189:15
  they k. us for their sport 453:40
  thou shalt not k.; but. . 146:35
  which man is always trying to k. 508:20
  wild animals never k. for sport 212:4
Killed: better be k. than frightened 518:36
  effort very nearly k. her 41:9
  I kiss'd thee ere I k. thee 474:4
  I'm k., Sire! 92:24
  justly k. with my own treachery 437:38
  k. hisself on principle 179:29
  k. not thee with half so good a
    will 452:7
  k. off by one critique 116:35
  k. with report that old man 351:16
  k. with your hard opinions 443:1
  not Cassio k. 473:17
  some sleeping k. 475:7
  'twas I that k. her 473:20
  when he k. a calf 21:12
  who k. Cock Robin? 369:18
  who k. John Keats? 118:2
  Woman K. with Kindness 248:6
Killest: thou that k. the prophets 60:20
Killeth: letter k. 67:22
Killibeate: you disliked the k.
  taste? 179:20
Killiecrankie: on the heights of
  K. 23:19
Killing: as k. as the canker 342:15
  ends in k. him 508:20
  K. no Murder 422:25
  k. of a mouse on Sunday 79:18
  more ways of k. a cat 294:13
  nine years a-k. 472:24
  when you've finished k. Kruger 294:17
Kills: air that k. 263:14
  k. her in her own humour 479:6
  k. me some six. .dozen of Scots 439:13
  k. reason itself, k. the image of
    God 352:6
  k. the thing he loves 569:4
  victim whom he k. 165:20

Kilmeny: bonny K. gaed up the
  glen 250:21
  K. came home 250:22
  K. had been 250:23
Kilted: k. her coats o' green satin 9:16
  k. her green kirtle 32:3
Kilve: at K. . .no weather-cock 573:4
Kin: if. .not of k. to God by his
  spirit 25:26
  knew no other k. 429:17
  little less than 'k.' 34:31
  little more than k. 430:26
  of k. to the beasts by his body 25:26
  Robert's k., and John's 236:8
  whole world k. 481:21
Kind: all other bliss that. .grows
  by k. 195:12
  at distance from the K. 578:16
  charity. .is k. 66:45
  coarsely k. 275:1
  cruel, only to be k. 436:7
  dear Betty, be k. 570:30
  enjoy her while she's k. 194:22
  Fortune shows herself more k. 465:9
  gentil k. of the lioun 138:20
  had it been early, had been k. 270:18
  heart as k. 247:1
  heart benevolent and k. 108:35
  his k. that lived thousands of
    years ago 567:20
  k. are her answers 124:2
  k. as she is fair 484:40
  k. deeds with coldness. .return-
    ing 580:24
  k. hearts are more than coronets 533:38
  k. Jack Falstaff 439:37
  k. of—as it were 401:29
  k. souls. .love you 374:22
  lady sweet and k. 10:20, 210:5
  last k. word to Christ 96:5
  less than k. 430:26
  lost him half the k. 193:39
  love is less k. 584:20
  makes one wondrous k. 213:14
  not k. sir. .quite usual 20:30
  one with my k. 536:25
  rather more than 'k.' 34:31
  so constant to me and so k. 285:4
  so courteous, so k. 502:17
  that ever thou wast k. 245:23
  thou art sad, art thou k.? 359:18
  thy Godlike crime was to be k. 118:30
  to be honest, to be k. 513:35
  to her virtues very k. 401:26
  to servants k. 125:4
  weary and k. one linger'd 585:22
  were all thy children k. 443:13
  what he has done in any one. .k. 154:38
  what k. of people do they think
    we are? 144:8
  yet he was k. 225:1
Kind: *sobald er reflektiert. .ein K.* 223:13
Kindest: k. and the best 107:3
  speaks the k. words 312:28
  thou wert the k. man 328:24
Kind-hearted: loving, kissing, k.
  gentleman 164:28
Kindle: or k. soft desire 191:12
  we cannot k. when we will 16:29
Kindled: if his wrath be k. 391:51
  k. in the upper skies 199:10
  that fire, k. above 232:11
Kindles in clothes a wantonness 246:4
Kindlier: k. hand 533:20
  eyes as wise, but k. 83:18
Kindliest creature in ould Donegal 229:14
Kindliness: cool k. of sheets 83:21
Kindling her undazzled eyes 352:15
Kindly: as comely or as k. 298:29
  beats the heart so k. 23:17
  be k. affectioned 66:2
  frosty, but k. 426:37
  gently, k. treat her 214:9
  k. mood of melancholy 195:15
  never lov'd sae k. 104:11
  Sally is gone that was so k. 41:29
Kindness: acts of k. and of love 581:24
  any k. that I can show 232:10
  beauty lives with k. 484:40
  Christ took the k. 96:5
  cup o' k. 104:15

Kindness (*cont.*)
  greetings where no k. is 582:3
  have you had a k. shown? 109:1
  in vain with lavish k. 240:18
  kill a wife with k. 479:7
  k. in another's trouble 227:34
  little deeds of k. 128:1
  milk of human k. 143:10, 457:1
  nothing but the milk of human k. 103:8
  save in the way of k. 548:5
  shewed me marvellous great k. 393:30
  sweet milk of k. 251:9
  that k. which soothed twenty
    years 277:42
  think it k. to his Majesty 234:14
  to play at cards. .generates k. 276:12
  Woman Killed with K. 248:6
Kindred: friends, k., days 199:12
  from k. blood 101:10
  Jonas K., Sybil K.'s sire 165:6
  like k. drops. .mingled 162:41
  sang a k. soul out 95:35
  table of K. and Affinity 401:15
  to k. dear 125:4
Kindreds: all k. of the earth shall
  wail 70:22
  all nations, and k. 71:3
Kine: ill-favoured k. 45:17
  keeps the shadowy k. 183:1
King: abusing of. .the k.'s English 465:33
  against Heav'n's matchless K. 346:30
  all honour to an earthly k. 12:7
  all the k.'s horses 367:5
  all were looking for a k. 326:21
  apples of gold for the k.'s
    daughter 524:19
  as a soldier of the K. 305:1
  as firm as Sparta's k. 188:33
  as I have served the K. 572:18
  as kill a k. 435:41
  as tedious as a k. 469:1
  as to the K. 135:28
  at the k.'s court. .ech man for
    him-self 137:28
  authority forgets a dying k. 531:31
  Bad K. 422:14
  balm from an anointed k. 475:1
  bend lower, O k. 586:5
  blacksmith like our Norman K. 294:22
  blessedness alone. .makes a K. 548:16
  born K. of the Jews 57:23
  born our heavenly k. 5:15
  brightly as a k. until a k. be by 465:21
  brought unto the K. in raiment 394:25
  buried in the k.'s highway 475:10
  but yesterday a K. 118:19
  catch the conscience of the k. 434:1
  cat may look at a k. 129:14
  chief defect of Henry K. 41:1
  come back, as a k., to earth 83:20
  coming of the K. of Heaven 12:7
  contrary to the k., his crown 445:40
  Cotton is K. 142:27
  damned for never a k.'s son 438:24
  despised and dying k. 498:18
  dish for a k. 485:16
  do homage to thy K. 508:18
  equals the shepherd with the k. 134:18
  eternal glorious K. 245:8
  every inch a k. 454:7
  every subject's duty is the k.'s 444:20
  fair and fatal K. 269:29
  farewell k. 475:7
  fear God. Honour the K. 69:50, 305:1
  fits a k.'s remembrance 432:36
  follow the K. 530:4
  forehand and vantage of a k. 444:23
  form'd the Poet for the K. 270:7
  gain'd a k. 344:33
  give the K. thy judgements 396:20
  glad the K. should have bought
    it 145:28
  glories of my K. 319:7
  glory to the K. of kings 565:12
  glory to the new-born K. 565:12
  God bless our Lord the K. 250:14
  God bless the K. 112:25
  God is the K. of all the earth 394:32
  God save our gracious k. 125:15
  God save the K. 47:12, 125:15, 250:14
  God save the k. . .amen 475:18

King (cont.)

government without a k.	33:5
greater than the K. himself	379:6
greatest herald of Heaven's K.	190:2
great George our K.	6:13
Heaven's all-gracious K.	421:10
he might hae been a k.	30:9
here lies a great..k.	407:24
here lies a K.	124:26
Hero can be Poet, Prophet, K.	126:26
his K.'s arriving	517:9
Idea of a Patriot K.	78:8
idle k.	540:31
if chance will have me k.	456:25
image of the K.	530:21
impossible..to discharge my duties as K.	196:1
in sleep a k.	487:22
is a k. indeed	135:17
I speak..unto the K.	394:21
is the k. dead?	476:31
it was a' for our rightfu' K.	106:16
I was a K. in Babylon	241:24
I were k. of pain	524:31
Jack's the k. of all	562:22
judge..no k. can corrupt	446:19
k. and his faithful subjects	103:9
K. asked the Queen	339:17
k. can do no wrong	73:8
K., Cawdor, Glamis, all	458:30
k. drinks to Hamlet	437:36
K. dropp'd a tear	73:16
k., father; royal Dane	431:32
k. for my money	204:33
k. has gone beyond me	446:27
K. have pleasure in thy beauty	394:23
K...have things done as cheap	377:19
k. himself has followed	225:15
k. is but a man	444:18
k. is the strongest	56:16
K. looked up	140:18
k. may make a nobleman	103:27
k. my brother's wreck	197:30
k. my father's death	197:30
k. never dies	73:5
k...not able to command the rain	377:18
k. of all kings	7:15
k. of Babylon..at the parting	55:31
K. of England cannot enter	379:11
K. of France went up	367:11
K. of glory enter may	421:2
K. of Glory, K. of Peace	244:25
K. of glory shall come in	393:12
k. of infinite space	433:12
k. of intimate delights	163:26
K. of Kings, and Lord of Lords	71:37
K. of Love my Shepherd	29:12
k. of shreds and patches	435:50
K. of Siam sent ambassadors	274:9
K. of Spain is dead	203:32
K. of Spain's daughter	367:7
k. of terrors	49:3
k. over himself	497:12
K. over the Water	10:15
K.'s a K.	189:4
k. sate on the rocky brow	115:45
K.'s best praise	412:14
K.'s daughter is all glorious	394:25
k. shall be contented	475:10
k. shall do it	475:10
K. sits in Dunfermline	31:23
k.'s name is a tower	476:34
k.'s name twenty thousand names	475:3
k. stept down	528:1
K. thought mair o' Marie Hamilton	31:17
K. to Oxford sent a troop	87:26
k., tried in fires of woe	269:31
k. was in his counting-house	368:20
K., Who ordainest	142:26
misus'd the k.'s press	440:20
mockery k. of snow	475:24
Moloch, horrid k.	344:28
more capital than to behead a k.	111:21
must he lose the name of k.?	475:10
my castles are my K.'s	418:26
my God and K.	243:24
my K. and my God	397:5
neither k. nor prince..tempt me	23:16

King (cont.)

new k. over Egypt	45:29
no k. could govern	190:10
no k...saved by..an host	393:37
no more than a k.	523:25
not the k.'s crown	461:28
of all the k.'s knights	11:24
of foolscap subjects..k.	116:33
our k. has written a braid letter	31:24
our sins lay on the k.	444:21
Ozymandias, k. of kings	496:14
passing brave to be a K.	330:27
rightwise K. born	328:3
ruthless K.	229:20
sea hath no k. but God	411:36
see the last k. strangled	338:1
shake hands with a k.	234:14
singeing of the K. of Spain's Beard	188:36
sing, long live the K.	160:11
Sir Byng stood for his K.	90:16
skipping k.	440:8
so excellent a k.	430:33(–431)
Son of Heaven's eternal K.	343:9
so spake the K.	530:32
speaks ill of your k.	362:16
still am I k. of those	475:20
stomach of a k., and of a k. of England	198:11
submission meet to our K.	122:6
such divinity doth hedge a k.	436:27
sweet unto a shepherd as a k.	232:5
sword of an Angel k.	75:6
take away my life to make you K.	136:10
teach me, my God and K.	244:15
that sort of k...ever die	94:44
the Lord is K.	397:22, 31, 33
the Lord remaineth a K.	393:24
they have a k. and officers	443:10
think the k. sees thee..his K. does	243:30
this hath not offended the k.	358:8
thou k. of flames	135:18
till the k. enjoys his own	373:13
to be an English k.	140:12
to be a Pirate K.	221:27
to be k.	456:17
to my true k. I offered	323:7
to reverence the K.	530:13
to serve God and the K.	363:8
to set before the K.	368:20, 512:5
to Thee, Redeemer, K.	361:8
under which k., Bezonian?	442:35
upon the k.!	444:21
was great as a k.	173:9
well enough agin a k.	319:19
what cares these roarers for..k.?	479:15
what is a K.?	402:5
what must the k. do now?	475:10
whatsoever k. shall reign	7:9
when Cnut, K., rowed thereby	124:22
whilst thus I sing, I am a K.	144:22
who is the K. of glory?	393:13
whom the k. delighteth to honour	48:36
who of glory is the k.?	421:2
who Pretender..who is K.	112:25
who the deil hae we goten for a K.	250:12
with half the zeal I serv'd my K.	447:1
worm that hath eat of a k.	436:13
worse k. never	119:17
year's pleasant k.	361:6

King-at-Arms: Lord Lion K. | 418:14
Kingcups: Cowslips, and K. | 510:23
Kingdom: best walls of this k. | 157:24

come unto thy everlasting K.	391:20
full k. of that final kiss	165:31
God hath numbered thy k.	55:42
heirs..of thy everlasting k.	390:47
his k. stretch	562:8
his mind his k.	164:19
I never gave you k.	453:6
inheritor of the k. of heaven	391:2
in the k. and patience of Jesus Christ	70:23
k. against k.	60:23
k. for it was too small	440:38
k. of daylight's dauphin	255:11
K. of God is within you	62:30
k. of heaven..grain of mustard	59:28

Kingdom (cont.)

k. of heaven is at hand	57:27
k...suffereth violence	59:7
like to a little k.	449:5
my k. for a horse	476:42
my large k. for a little grave	475:10
my mind to me a k. is	195:12
not enter into the k.	59:48
of such is the k. of God	61:6
order to a peopled k.	443:10
rich man to enter into the k.	60:3
seeking asses, found a k.	350:7
seek ye first the k.	58:14
stand upon my k. once again	474:34
strikes for a K.	517:9
their's is the k. of heaven	57:39
they that have riches enter into the k.	62:35
thine is the k.	58:4
this k. by the sea	380:8
this little k., man	442:21
thy k. come	58:4
thy k. is divided	55:42
thy k. shall pass, Galilean	525:13
trample a k. down	371:1
when thou comest into thy k.	62:49

Kingdom-come: kin' o' k. | 319:24
| palaces in K. | 334:1 |

Kingdoms: God had sifted three k. | 316:6

k. are clay	423:14
k. are less by three	525:19
k. are moved	394:28
k. of this world..the k. of our Lord	71:15
kiss'd away k.	424:24
many goodly..k. seen	288:19
mused of taking k. in	425:1
showed unto him all the k. of the world	61:24
showeth him all the k. of the world	57:36
three k...in great poverty	328:5

King-like rolls the Rhine | 121:9
Kingly: k. crop | 169:15
| K. crown to gain | 240:20 |
| his State is K. | 351:21 |

Kingly-flashing: bulls..in k. coats | 336:38
King Pin, the Main Spring | 83:2
Kings: accounted poet k. | 288:16

all k. is mostly rapscallions	550:10
all k. shall fall down	396:25
all the powerful K. and Queens	186:31
arm'd with K. to strive	118:19
at rest, with k. and counsellors	48:45
bid k. come bow	447:27
bind their k. in chains	400:27
blood of queens and k.	285:19
but the breath of k.	105:5
cabbages—and k.	130:15
calm contending k.	486:7
Captains and the K. depart	300:24
cashiering most K. and Senates	127:6
change my state with k.	486:24
city of two k.	324:2
conquering k. their titles take	135:12
curse of K. to be attended	447:42
death lays his icy hand on k.	501:5
delight..as..k. in sceptres	548:13
descended of so many royal k.	426:15
divorc'd so many English k.	442:26
dread and fear of k.	464:33
enthroned in the hearts of k.	464:33
feelings by which the heroic k. governed	28:27
from the Devil and earthly k.	74:29
game..k. would not play at	163:42
gart k. ken they had a lith	21:14
godlike k. of old	323:11
good of subjects is the end of k.	170:17
hand that k. have lipp'd	424:13
heart of k. is unsearchable	50:33
keep even k. in awe	169:9
k. are by God appointed	7:9
k. crept out again	87:39
k.' daughters were among thy..women	394:23
k...gods..meaner creatures k.	476:33
k. have cares	232:5
k. may be blest	108:6
k. may love treason	170:20
k. of Arabia and Saba..gifts	396:25

Kings (*cont.*)

k. of Tharsis..**give presents** 396:25
k. of the earth are gathered 394:33
k. of the sea 16:1, 362:30
k. seek their subjects' good 246:9
k. thirty feet high 326:7
k. will be tyrants from policy 102:17
k. with their armies did flee 396:7
laws or k...cause or cure 226:17, 278:29
mad world! mad k.! 447:24
many k. have sat down 56:41
many prophets and k. have desired 61:38
mirror of all Christian k. 443:12
necessary things to..ruin k. 190:11
Obadiah Bind-their-k. 322:24
our temperate k. 537:29
physicians are like k. 563:19
politeness are k. 318:23
pride of k. 383:7
proud and godly k. 208:5
puller down of k. 446:4
rich embroider'd canopy to k. 446:2
Right Divine of K. to govern
wrong 381:24
root and father of many k. 458:30
ruin'd sides of K. 37:13
saddest of all k. 269:27
sad stories of the death of k. 475:7
showers on her k. barbaric pearl 345:14
son of a hundred K. 294:19
sport of k. 169:12, 506:13, 518:7
such is the breath of k. 474:16
superfluous k. for messengers 424:26
teeming womb of royal k. 474:22
they are no k. 170:17
this royal throne of k. 474:22
three k. into the east 106:21
to senates, courts, and k. 123:7
true strength of guilty k. 16:28
'twixt k. and tyrants 246:9
two k. of Brentford 162:33
walk with K. 297:12
war is the trade of k. 192:43
we live to tread on k. 440:32
what have k. that privates have
not 444:22
what..heart's ease must k. neglect 444:22
what they show to k. 164:34
when k...justice first lay down 170:17
when the Almighty scattered k. 396:7
where Abassin k. their issue
guard 347:9
worse in k. than beggars 429:35
King's Bench: Court of K., Den
of Thieves 147:17
King's Bench Walks: chambers in
the K. 144:33
Kingsley: believes K. a divine 517:8
miss poor K. so soon 545:16
Reverend Canon K. 517:8
Kinquering Congs their titles take 511:2
Kinship with the stars 336:20
Kinsmen: k. to the bold Buccleugh 417:3
my k. according to the flesh 65:19
Kipling: Rudyards cease from k. 512:8
Kirk: below the k. 148:21
caulder k. 106:26
is this the k.? 150:4
Marie Hamilton's to the k. gane 31:17
walk together to the k. 150:15
Kirkconnell: on fair K. leal 31:3
Kirk-hammer: auld k. strak 105:8
Kirtle: kilted her green k. 32:3
Kish that lofty Jew 332:23
Kismet: he that saith not 'K.' 141:7
Kiss: ae fond k. 104:9
all humbled k. the rod 484:31
Anger's self I needs must k. 502:1
bee's k., now 91:35
close with her, k. her 525:29
colder thy k. 119:29
come let us k. and part 189:20
Coridon would k. her then 80:7
coward does it with a k. 569:4
envied k. to share 229:31
fades out from k. to k. 584:24
felt my soul in a k. 524:32
gav'st me, though unseen, a k. 160:28
gentle k. to every sedge 484:35

Kiss (*cont.*)

gin a body k. a body 104:31
golden slumbers k. your eyes 170:23
he must k. child and mother 232:3
holy k. 66:18
I dare not ask a k. 247:8
if human souls did **never** k. 285:1
if thou k. not me 495:7
I'll k. my girl 299:21
in every k. sealed fast 411:1
I saw you take his k. 375:3
I would k. thee 52:21
kingdom of that final k. 165:31
k. again with tears 538:9
k., and to that k. a score 246:28
k., a sigh, and so away 166:15
k. before they are married 445:15
k. dead Cæsar's wounds 450:24
k. her until she be wearied 495:22
k. long as my exile 429:19
k. me and never no more 328:19
k. me as if 91:35
k. me, Hardy 362:20
k. me times a thousand 132:16
k. me with the kisses of his mouth 51:37
k. my Julia's dainty leg 246:16
k. of the sun 233:17
k. our lady Peace 441:23
k. the book's outside 159:29
k. the image of my death 190:5
k. the place to make it well 527:8
k. the Son 391:51
k. till the cow comes home 38:5
k. too long 326:20
k. your love again 296:16
leave a k. but in the cup 280:21
let's k. afresh 246:28
maids must k. no men 80:7
make me immortal with a k.! 330:5
man may k. a bonnie lass 108:16
many a glowing k. 253:19
moth's k., first 91:35
mountains k. high Heaven 495:7
my bluest veins to k. 424:13
nor k. before folks 156:13
nothing wrong in a connubial k. 115:39
one fond k. 104:9
only to k. that air 247:8
on thy bosom..many a k. 523:4
part at last without a k.? 359:4
quit in a single k. 81:12
rough male k. of blankets 83:21
seal with a righteous k. 478:44
shadows k. 464:3
she took the k. sedately 536:3
so k. on 246:28
Stella's feet may k. 502:4
stop his mouth with a k. 468:15
swear never to k. the girls 91:32
that k. I carried from thee 429:19
that k. which is my heaven to have 426:13
then come k. me 482:28
there I embrace and k. her 262:6
this last lamenting k. 184:28
to feel the first k. 411:1
waste his whole heart in one k. 540:13
went..without a single k. 375:14
which Jews might k. 385:10
will she k. me to-morrow? 183:17
with one long k. my whole soul 529:22
you must not k. and tell 155:13

Kissed: curtsied when you have,
and k. 479:28
first time he k. me 88:22
had I wist, before I k. 32:19
hail, master: and k. him 60:44
hasn't been k. in forty years 412:17
he k. her cold corpus 10:18
he k. likewise the maid 164:28
I k. her little sister 355:24
I k. her slender hand 536:3
I k. thee ere I kill'd thee 474:4
Jenny k. me 265:25
k. away kingdoms 424:24
k. by a man who didn't wax his
moustache 304:41
k. her cow 520:8
k. it and then fled 497:20
k. the girls 366:22
k. the lovely grass 84:2
only k. the fingers of this hand 88:22

Kissed (*cont.*)

righteousness and peace have k. 397:9
Rose k. me to-day 183:17
that lately k. thee 247:8
they k. each other's cheek 222:3
those lips that I have k. 437:15
when first we k. 82:2
you might have toy'd and k. 214:15
Kisses: as it rain'd k. 425:1
a-wastin' Christian k. 299:11
bread and cheese, and k. 520:5
come, give me sweet k. 570:30
died of the k. of..God 360:10
feeds on the aërial k. 497:2
for k., how? 91:10
I fear thy k. 499:2
I understand thy k. 440:3
k. four 286:34
k., tears, and smiles 580:20
k. the Joy as it flies 74:27
my absent k. 166:18
my k. are his daily feast 231:39
my k. bring again 462:16
of many thousand k. the poor
last 425:27
our close k...impair their white 88:14
play'd at cards for k. 321:14
reaps a thousand k. there 158:1
remembered k. after death 538:19
sallies of his mother's k. 576:10
stolen k. much completer 266:1
straight on k. dream 477:7
these poor half-k. kill me 189:15
thy love in k. rain 494:7
with the k. of his mouth 51:37
you have forgotten my k. 524:10
Kissing: die with k. of my Lord 331:4
end, I think, of k. 84:23
k. don't last 337:36
k. with golden face 486:27
loving, k., kind-hearted gentleman 164:28
splendid k. mouth 525:34
trembled k. 424:13
what fool..invented k. 520:21
when the k. had to stop 97:8
Kissings: all these k. worth 495:7
Kiss-worthy: thy most k. face 502:1
Kit: man in khaki k. 300:17
Kit-bag: your troubles in your old
k. 20:23
Kitchen: in the k. bred 119:3
I will make my k. 516:2
k.-cabals 164:31
Kitchens: wild cats in your k. 470:25
Kite: Chil the K. 301:27
not sufficient for a k.'s dinner 404:4
Kites: city of k. and crows 429:16
fatted all the region k. 433:35
wars of K. or Crows 352:30
Kits: every cat had seven k. 366:8
Kitten: my imperial k. 129:38
rather be a k. 439:45
Kittened: your mother's cat..but
k. 439:40
Kitty: if any young men come for
..K. 23:7
K., a fair but frozen maid 213:15
K. has no discretion in her coughs 22:29
Knappeth the spear in sunder 394:29
Knave: but he's an arrant k. 432:22
coined an epithet for a k. 325:6
he's but Fortune's k. 425:33
k., a rascal 452:32
K. of Hearts 129:27, 368:15
k.'s a k. to me 386:3
make a man appear a..k. 194:17
necessity makes an honest man
a k. 170:10
nor k. nor dolt can break 584:3
pestilent complete k. 471:2
petty sneaking k. 74:19
rascally yea-forsooth k. 441:12
slipper and subtle k. 471:1
spy a k. in drinking 420:3
thank God you are rid of a k. 468:37
to feed a titled k., man 108:17
what trade, thou k.? thou
naughty k. 448:4
Knavery: religion, k., and change 40:8
their k. and folly to excuse 143:20

Knaves: bold k. thrive 193:21
call'd them untaught k. 438:33
fools and k. 98:8
'gainst k. and thieves 484:27
little better than false k. 469:7
three misbegotten k. 439:22
whip me such honest k. 469:26
word which k. and fools may use 143:20
Knavish: all tricks..k. or childish 274:14
frustrate their k. tricks 125:16
k. speech 436:10
Knead two virtuous souls 116:20
Kneaded by the moon 237:10
Kneading: k., the making 480:38
k. up the honey 443:10
Knee: at Mary's k. 140:20
civility of my k. 86:2
every k. should bow 68:18
fore-mast wi' his k. 30:19
fought on his k. 30:14
her head on her k. 473:6
human k. is a joint 235:6
kilted them up to the k. 9:16
k. deep in clover 307:21
little abune her k. 32:3
louted low down on his k. 32:7
play the tambourine on her other k. 177:19
prattling on his k. 104:33
set upon the nurse's k. 32:19(-33)
sing to the child on thy k. 82:11
sit upon the curate's k. 141:17
smiles sae sweetly on her k. 106:28
smitten me to my k. 544:22
stood by me, k. to k. 140:33
to its idolatries a patient k. 113:50
Kneel: I'll k. down and ask of thee 454:19
k. and draw the chalky ring 164:8
k. before the Lord 397:27
lowly we k. in prayer 233:18
they that go down..shall k. 393:9
when they should k. for peace 479:14
Kneeled: k. and fought on his knee 30:14
k. unto the buds 424:29
Kneeling: Faith is k. by his bed 189:20
k. ne'er spoiled silk stocking 244:5
lowly k., wait Thy word 198:10
meekly k. upon your knees 390:35
Kneels: he k. at morn, and noon 150:8
little Boy k. 339:19
not one k. to another 567:20
Knees: all on their k. 236:21
between his father's k. 164:11
climber up of k. 308:10
climb his k. 229:31
confirm the feeble k. 54:2
done upon his k. 296:33(-297)
down on your k. 428:14
each night, upon my k. 204:1
fold our hands round her k. 521:30(-522)
his Nancy on his k. 219:17
k. and tresses folded 336:7
meekly kneeling upon your k. 390:35
now serve on his k. 377:4
o'er courtiers' k. 477:7
on her apron'd k. 120:20
on parent k. 279:19
petticoats up to the k. 146:19
place at the great k. 522:12
religion..not in the k. 269:8
rest on his k. 175:37
rustling to her k. 285:21
saint upon his k. 161:15
up to her k. 249:7
Knell: by fairy hands their k. 153:30
hourly ring his k. 479:30
k. of parting day 229:28
k. that summons thee 458:1
like a rising k. 113:25
ring fancy's k. 464:13
sigh'd at the sound of a k. 164:25
that..overpowering k. 116:18
Knells us back to a world of death 150:24
Knelt down with angry prayers 249:5
Knew: as much as our father Adam k. 295:17
as though they perfectly k. 303:17
before I k. thy face 184:4
builded better than he k. 199:23
died because she never k. 41:34

Knew (cont.)
George the First k. nothing 272:27
he k. himself to sing 342:10
he k. not what to say 118:1
he k. they knowed 303:23
he said it that k. it best 25:31
I k. him well, and every truant k. 225:1
I k. it was love 118:34
I k. not all he meant 530:32
I k. that once 512:9
I k. you once 97:27
in this place; and I k. it not 45:4
I thought I k. my Watson 188:11
I thought I k. the voice 302:14
king..which k. not Joseph 45:29
k. almost as much at eighteen 270:1
k. it all before you 299:22
k. not, and did commit things 61:55
k. not what to think 160:39
k. not wherefore..come together 65:7
k. only..that he k. nothing 40:4
k. we should both forget 524:9
k. what England means 140:25
k. you, and named a star 95:1
k. you not Pompey? 448:8
none k. thee but to love thee 234:15
none such as k. it of old 523:4
she k. no sin 192:20
she k. not where 250:23
she k. what it meant 10:25
some..Hope, whereof he k. 235:18
this only, that he nothing k. 350:12
we k. the worst too young 296:28
Knewest: thou k. that I was an austere man 62:38
Knife: k. is lost in it 495:13
my keen k. see not the wound 457:3
smyler with the k. 137:32
strike with our spirit's k. 492:6
war even to the k. 113:10
wind's like a whetted k. 334:12
without a k. 367:18
Knife-grinder: needy K. 124:7
Knight: brought out a noble k. 531:33
Colonel or K. in arms 351:14
courteous k. 328:24
gentle k. was pricking 509:17
k. dubbed with unhatched rapier 484:15
k. embracing Jane 123:2
K. of the Sorrowful Countenance 134:8
K.'s bones are dust 151:31
k. shall not be whole 328:5
k. to be their wooer 30:7
k. without fear 12:13
make a K. o' me! 298:18
many a k., and many a squire 34:8
never matched of earthly k.'s hand 328:24
new-slain k. 32:15
no carpet k. so trim 418:8
no loyal k. and true 534:2
prince can mak a belted k. 105:32
rather..sir priest than sir k. 484:16
red-cross k. for ever kneel'd 534:4
that wandering k. so fair 438:15
that was your k. 377:4
there never was k. like 418:16
this k...given to romance 202:12
thou shalt hurt the truest k. 328:5
thou were the sternest k. 328:24
thy sire was a k. 417:32
verray parfit gentil k. 136:24
what can ail thee, K. at arms? 286:28
Knighterrantry: Religion is k. 134:12
Knightly: or ever the K. years were gone 241:24
Knights: accomplishing the k. 444:6
among them k. 328:24
British and Armoric k. 345:4
death of the most noblest k. 328:17
invincible K. of old 577:3
k. of Logres or of Lyones 350:4
k. of mettle true 417:3
nine-and-twenty k. of fame 417:3
of all the king's k. 11:24
row, my k. 124:22
virtuous deeds that some k. used 328:1
ye curious carpet k. 217:16
Knit: come, k. hands 340:7
k. together thine elect 389:55

Knits me to thy rugged strand 417:22
Knitter: like a k. drowsed 235:21
Knitters in the sun 483:5
Knitting: in twisted braids of lilies k. 341:3
Knives: razors and carving k. 121:20
Knob: head..out of a brass k. 175:36
Knobs: whelks, and k., and flames 444:3
Knochen eines..pommerschen Musketiers 72:31
Knock: k. against my very heart 479:10
k. and it shall be opened 58:19
k. as you please 382:9
k. at a star 246:20
k. him down first 273:5
k. out your pipes an' follow me 296:17
stand at the door, and k. 70:35
wail or k. the breast 351:6
when you k. 159:20
where k. is open wide 503:5
you as yet but k., breathe 185:18
Knock-down: k. argument 191:23
nice k. argument 111:6
ready for a k. blow 221:20
Knocked: k. 'em in the Old Kent Road 142:23
k. Mr. Toots about the head 175:12
k. on my sullen heart 516:16
k. the factious dogs on the head 275:12
that Cromwell k. about a bit 315:2
Knocker: tie up the k. 385:20
Knocketh: my beloved that k. 52:9
Knocking: k. at Preferment's door 18:7
k. on the moonlit door 171:13
someone came k. 172:3
younger generation will come k. 267:5
Knocknarea: riding from K. 585:7
Knocks: apostolic blows and k. 110:18
k. you down with the butt end 227:27
whoever k. 460:1
Knoll: sit on a green k. apart 585:17
Knolled: where bells have k. to church 427:19
Knolling a departed friend 441:10
Knolls: search the grassy k. 131:24
Knot: any simple k. 492:23
certain k. of peace 501:26
k. there's no untying 123:5
some old Gordian k. 147:9
this k. intrinsicate of life 426:13
toads to k. and gender in 472:34
Knot-grass: bunches of k. 285:19
Knots: pokers into true-love k. 151:13
Knotted: sat and k. all the while 421:15
thy k. and combined locks 432:9
Know: all that we k. is 113:13
all we k. of heaven 180:3
all ye k...all ye need to k. 287:15
almost afraid to k. itself 460:19
as I k. more of mankind 275:15
augurers say they k. not 425:16
but to k.'t a little 472:1
by their fruits..k. them 58:27
confined to k. but this 386:29
dangerous to k. 306:2
determined not to k. anything 66:21
didn't k. everythin' down in Judee 319:17
does both act and k. 332:26
don't k. a gun from a bat 294:24
don't..k. anything about music ..k. what I like 40:1
dost thou k. who made thee? 76:10
do you k. me, my lord? 433:1
even k. your own foolish business 139:36
feel..happier than I k. 348:33
first of those who k. 537:37
greater than we k. 573:27
hate anyone that we k. 240:11
hear, k., and say 84:6
heartily k. 199:14
he that aspired to k. 94:15
he that can him-selven k. 137:38
how can I k. what I think? 557:20
how few k. their own good 194:23
I k. nothing..about you 188:1
I k. not, oh, I k. not 362:1
I k. not the Lord 45:40
I k. not the man 60:47
I k. not what they mean 538:17

Know (*cont.*)

I k. not what ye call all   439:19
I k. not why I am so sad   462:28
I k. thee not, old man   442:37
I k. there is none other   530:36
I k., where'er I go   576:2
I k. women..k. that I don't k.
    them   542:14
I k. you all   438:30
I k. you: solitary griefs   269:26
I k. you will not   298:3
impossible precept, 'K. thyself'   127:14
I only k. it shall be high   264:7
I want to k. a butcher paints   96:27
I write, I k. not what   232:15
k. all..there is to be knowed   228:17
k., and not be known   154:22
k. as much as..Adam   295:17
k. even as also I am known   66:46(-67)
k. most of..thy native country   212:11
k. my stops   435:24
k. no such liberty   319:4
k. not what's resisted   104:8
k. our proper stations   174:8
k. so much that ain't so   491:10
k...that he nothing knew   350:12
k. that I am God   394:29
k. thee and fly thee   507:14
k. the end of this day's business   451:38
k. themselves..but men   392:16
k. then thyself   383:22
k. thy contree   136:20
k. thyself   12:23
k. to k. no more   347:27
k. what God and man is   529:24
k. what I mean to do   90:4
k. what things they ought to do   389:28
k. what thou canst work at   127:14
k...with whom they are dealing   571:15
let him not k.'t   472:2
let me k. mine end   394:8
let men k. we serve the Lord   301:26
liberty to k., to utter, and to
    argue   352:16
little do we k. wot lays afore   176:28
living, k. no bounds   501:8
love I k. not what   246:13
my good child, k. this   391:10
my Lord, we k. them well   42:11
nor, England! did I k.   577:4
not proud to k.   383:6
not to k. me   347:30
not to k. we sinned   169:10
now I k. in part   66:46(-67)
now I k. it   215:20
old, and k. what we are about   226:40
old k. what they want   504:17
others that we k. not of   434:4
other women k. so much   89:19
ourselves k. not what it is   186:25
ourselves to k.   384:19
perfection not to k. them   155:2
place..k. it no more   398:7
reason but from what we k.   383:8
saying you want to k., you k.   175:30
sir, we *k.* our will is free   271:28
somebody I do not k.   290:24
so well to k. her own   349:1
suffer us to k. but little   414:21
suspect much..k. little   27:23
that which you yourselves do k.   450:33
that you are thought to k.   26:6
they k. not, poor..souls   309:27
they k. not what they do   62:48
they leave you, and you k. them   94:21
thirst to k.   561:14
this I k. full well   85:10
this shall I ne'er k.   488:10
thought..to k. that you k. not   26:6
'tis a vice to k. him   437:29
to be we k. not what   191:33
to do..as easy as to k.   463:7
to k. all makes one tolerant   511:9
to k. the change and feel it   289:8
to k. the world   587:12
true poet..I k. you   95:1
utter what thou dost not k.   439:11
we all *k.* what light is   273:13
we k. a subject..or..where we
    can find information   272:32
we k. in part   66:45

Know (*cont.*)

whatever there is to k...shall
    we k.   410:15
what I don't k.   39:5
what we k. not by what we k.   352:11
what you don't k. by what you do   564:3
what you k., you k.   474:1
when it came to k. me well
    177:33, 357:5
where no man doth me k.   29:24(-30)
whispering low I k. not what   308:23
who k. them best, despise them   107:23
whom truly to k.   389:52
who only England k.   296:3
wiser than we k.   200:27
wise to k.   104:20
with thee when we k. it not   577:1
world unknowable, we k. thee   545:1
you k. my methods   187:23, 28
you k. not whence   207:7
Know-all: ole man K.   238:20
Knowed: all..there is to be k.   228:17
    she k. the Lord was nigher   319:25
Knowest: full little k. thou   510:16
    k. thou what argument   199:9
    Lord, thou k. all things   64:17
    speak less than thou k.   452:25
    thou k. my simpleness   396:16
    thou k. not how little worthy   544:29
    thou k. not the tears   308:19
    thou k. that I love thee   64:17
    thou k. thy estimate   487:22
    Thou k. Who hast made   300:4
    thou that k. each   538:20
    when thou k. this   185:3
Knoweth: God k.   67:36
    heart k. his own bitterness   50:7
    he that loveth not k. not God   70:12
    name..which no man k.   70:31
    no man k. of his sepulchre   46:35
    sun k. his going down   398:10
Knowing: greater than their k.   302:4
    k. God, they lift not hands   531:36
    k. good and evil   44:20
    k. it, pursue   194:23
    k. what should not be known   208:14
    k. your promise to me   536:13
    not k. what they do   469:4
    Why not k.   206:13
    without k. how or why   190:32
Knowledge: all k. and wonder..
    pleasure   24:11
    all k...my province   28:1
    be innocent of the k.   459:8
    bonded warehouse of my k.   518:18
    climbing after k. infinite   330:28
    dissemble sometimes your k.   26:6
    exult and sing over the k.   513:27
    finer spirit of all k.   583:3
    five ports of k.   85:18
    follow k. like a sinking star   541:1
    for objects and k. curious   568:9
    for the book of k. fair   346:20
    for the k. of a lifetime   566:8
    fret not after k.   289:9
    full of the k. of the Lord   53:19
    increaseth k. increaseth sorrow   50:63
    in k. of whom..life   388:25
    integrity without k. is weak   278:19
    k. advances by steps   324:20
    k...but recorded experience   125:31
    k. by suffering entereth   89:4
    k. comes, but wisdom lingers   534:30
    k. dwells in heads replete   163:49
    k. enormous makes a God of me   286:19
    k. in the Most High   396:26
    k. is bought in the market   146:24
    k. is of two kinds   272:32
    k. is proud   163:50
    k. itself is power   28:10
    k. may give weight   139:27
    k. of good and evil   44:13
    k. of good and evil as two twins   352:8
    k. of man is as the waters   24:17
    k. of nothing   174:6
    k. of the heart in..Richardson   272:12
    k. of the world   139:9
    k. of truth   27:32
    k. puffeth up   66:33
    k. shall be increased   55:45
    k. to their eyes   230:5

Knowledge (*cont.*)

know my k. is but vain   4:10
Lamb, if he wants any *k.*   153:16
let k. grow   531:42
light of k. in their eyes   526:1
literature of *k.*   172:24
love..which passeth k.   67:54
more love and k. of you   426:25
Mr. Weller's k. of London   178:35
must carry k. with him   274:4
nature..the book of k.   226:20
no k. but I know it   39:5
no k. when the day was done   286:23
no man's k...beyond his experi-
    ence   315:7
nor device, nor k.   51:21
not according to k.   65:61
not any law exceeds his k.   135:19
from k. ignorance   90:44
opinion..k. in the making   352:14
out-topping k.   17:23
province of k. to speak   251:22
pursuit of k. under difficulties   179:3
running over with..k.   290:14
science is organized k.   508:21
spirit of k.   53:17
such k. is too wonderful   400:8
taken away the key of k.   61:50
to communicate k.   172:25
too high the price for k.   547:22
too much k. for the sceptic side   383:22
tree of diabolical k.   500:16
tree of the k. of good and evil   44:13
true antithesis to k...power   172:25
what I don't know isn't k.   39:5
what is k. but grieving?   337:42
what k. can perform   575:5
whether there be k.   66:45
woman's happiest k.   347:20
wonder..the seed of k.   24:11
words without k.   49:16, 17
Known: all desires k.   390:4
    among the leaves..never k.   287:25
    become a history little k.   160:30
    be k. and not know   154:22
    best that has been k. and said   20:8
    best that is k. and thought   19:12
    better..than I have ever k.   180:2
    but early k. thy..worth   412:12
    dead..don't choose to have it k.   139:35
    God of our fathers, k. of old   300:24
    go to the devil where he is k.   275:33
    hast thou not k. me, Philip?   63:55
    have ye not k.?   54:13
    heaven knows what she has k.   460:26
    if I had k. it had been you   31:20
    if only I had k., k., k.   358:24
    if you would not be k. to do any-
       thing   200:47
    is she k. in all the land?   533:42
    it's perfectly k.   312:7
    knowing what should not be k.   208:14
    k. and loved so long   80:13
    k. for my soul's birth-partner   410:27
    k. of them in breaking of bread   62:56
    k. only to his Maker   251:14
    lady that's k. as Lou   422:21
    little to be k.   276:13
    Lord, thou hast..k. me   400:7
    more than they have k.   84:22
    more you 'ave k. o' the others   298:3
    needs only to be k.   192:13
    no countries..less k. by the
       British   78:23
    nothing can be k.   113:13
    not k. sin, but by the law   65:47
    people whom I have not k.   392:31
    read as much..k. no more   249:1
    safer than a k. way   239:4
    so I had nothing k.   472:3
    so k., so honour'd   386:11
    some place where he is *not* k.   275:33
    tell him, I too have k.   300:15
    that thy way may be k.   396:2
    then the end is k.   451:38
    till I am k., and do not want it   270:18
    to be for ever k.   158:14
    tree is k. by his fruit   59:13
Knows: all this the world well k.   488:12
    as a lawyer k. how   161:38
    dies ere he k. it   91:41

INDEX

Knows (cont.)
every school-boy k. it   527:14
fact the whole world k.   312:10
Gawd k., an' 'E won't split   304:53
greatness. itself   440:25
happy that he k. no more   383:29
heaven k. what she has known   460:26
He k. about it all—He k.—He k.   207:1
he k., a frightful fiend   150:2
he k. ye not   127:30
humble that he k. no more   163:50
k., and k. no more, her Bible true   164:16
k. nothing whatever about thee   305:8
k. not what to do   366:12
k. nought that k. not this   480:41
k. what he fights for and loves what he k.   167:3
k. what life and death is   135:19
my universe that feels and k.   91:14
Nature k. a thing or two   421:7
no man k.   170:26
no man truly k. another   86:30
none k. well to shun   488:12
one man that has a mind and k. it   489:3
parson k. enough who k. a duke   164:9
she k. her man   194:28
she k. wot's wot   179:21
so old a ship—who k., who k.?   208:16
then he thinks he k.   15:6
this she k.   150:23
what ev'ry body k.   159:16
what every schoolboy k.   520:53
what need we fear who k. it   460:24
who k. nothing else, k...his Bible   19:31
Knowes: goodness only k.   142:6
Knuckle down at taw   164:8
Knucklebones: harmless art of k.   513:26
Knuckle-end of England   504:22
Knuts: Colonel of the K.   571:17
Köhln, a town of monks   150:28
Koran..taught in..Oxford   217:12
Kosciusko: as K. fell   122:33
Kosmos: untented K.   515:29
Kriegbewegte Erde   415:25
Krorluppia: Nasticreechia K.   311:8
Kruger: when you've finished killing K.   294:17
Kruschen: that K. feeling   10:3
Kubla: 'mid this tumult K. heard   151:33(-152)
Kubla Khan: in Xanadu did K.   151:32
Kul: abby-nay, k., an' hazar-ho   295:22
Kulla-lo-lo: she'd sing, 'K.'   299:12
Kurd: same about the K.   40:24
Kyloe: little k. cow   366:19

L

Labdanum: stripes of l.   94:18
Label men for God   544:32
Labelled Sergeant Whatsisname   300:17
Labor: *hoc opus, hic l. est*   554:23
l. omnia vicit   556:11
subeunt morbi tristisque senectus et l.   556:20
Laborare: *orare est l.*   13:11
Laborem: *alterius spectare l.*   320:30
Labores: *iucundi acti l.*   145:4
Laboribus: *pro l. tantis*   132:21
Laborious: l. indeed at the first ascent   352:26
live l. days   342:20
studious of l. ease   163:17
Labour: all l. mars what it does   425:22
all things are full of l.   50:61
all ye that   59:10
but l. and sorrow   397:16
by l. and intent study   352:21
by the l. of my hands   546:39
Chinese cheap l.   238:36
daily l.'s..spring   16:5
endless l. all along..to be wrong   276:14
every l. sped   226:11
forget his l. an' his toil   104:33
green leaves of thy l.   524:4
[his] l. for his pains   570:26

Labour (cont.)
honest l...a lovely face   170:21
I l. for peace   399:25
I'll l. night and day   99:37
in all l...profit   50:8
in our l. rest most sweet   132:2
in works of l.   561:29
it is but lost l.   399:35
l. against our own cure   86:35
l. and the wounds are vain   147:8
l. in his vocation   438:25
l. in the deep mid-ocean   535:20
l. of an age   351:8
l. of doing nothing   511:27
l. of love   68:35
l. we delight in   458:20
l. without joy is base   413:20
learn to l. and to wait   317:8
light l. spread her..store   224:14
live and l.   227:34
many still must l.   115:1
my l. for my travail   480:40
not the imperative l.   87:27
our race should not cease to l.   513:31
perform the last l.   583:21
pleasure is l. too   161:36
six days shalt thou l.   390:9
sore l.'s bath   458:11
sweating l. to bear such idleness   423:38
think no l. lost   12:7
time for l. and thought   522:7
to learn and l. truly   391:9
true success is to l.   515:6
upon the brow of l. this crown   98:2
we l. soon, we l. late   108:17
what profit..of all his l.   50:59
why should life all l. be?   535:16
with difficulty and l. hard   346:17
without..any kind of l.   560:21
with profitable l.   444:23
your l. for that which satisfieth not   54:29
your l. is for future hours   262:3
youth of l.   224:15
Labour-dimmed eyes   16:11
Laboured: I l. more abundantly   67:6
other men l.   63:15
Labourer: chips to the agricultural l.   143:31
l. is worthy of his hire   61:35
l.'s task is o'er   198:14
l. to take his pension   413:24
Labourers are few   58:45
Labour-house: sounding l. vast   17:17
Labouring: all women l.   389:3
no less than l. seas   249:12
sleep is sweet to the l. man   99:23
sleep of a l. man   51:8
we and the l. world   585:22
Labours: children sweeten l.   26:45
clay after his l.   121:21
entered into their l.   63:15
l. of a servile state   117:24
line too l.   382:32
no l. tire   279:5
notice..of my l.   270:18
their uncessant l. see   332:13
who from their l. rest   264:8
Laburnum: my brother set the l.   253:1
Laburnums, dropping-wells of fire   533:7
Labyrinth: peopled l. of walls   495:1
Labyrinthical: perplexed, l. soul!   186:30
Labyrinthine: down the l. ways   544:13
still more l...the rose   96:32
Lace: Arsenic and Old L.   292:6
erring l.   246:4
Greek, Sir, is like l.   274:21
l. my bodice blue   266:8
owre gauze al.   106:32
ripping the l. off our waistcoats   276:21
Laced: bodice, aptly l.   401:32
Lacedaemon: in lordly L.   324:2
Laces for a lady   301:18
Lacessit: *nemo me impune l.*   13:10
Lack: can I l. nothing   393:10
good l.! quoth he   159:39
gravelled for l. of matter   428:20
I sigh the l. of many   486:25
l. of love from love   90:44
lions do l.   393:38
needs spirit l. all life behind   96:26

Lack (cont.)
they l., I have   195:13
they that fear him l. nothing   393:38
Lacked: being l. and lost   469:5
if I l. anything   244:21
learn all we l. before   84:6
Lackey: like a l.   444:23
thousand..angels l. her   340:23
Lackeying the varying tide   423:39
Lack-lustre: with l. eye   427:13
Lacks: if anyone anything l.   222:17
Lacrimae: *sunt l. rerum*   553:18
Lacrimarum: *ut filius istarum l. pereat*   21:19
Lad: better l., if things went right   262:11
could that l. be I?   516:7
Cupid is a knavish l.   467:11
his artillery unto his l.   47:26
I'll come to you, my l.   108:28
l. does not care for the child's rattle   271:23
many a lightfoot l.   263:21
my old l. of the castle   438:17
no blithe Irish l.   122:16
song of a l. that is gone   516:7
when I was a l.   221:15
whilst my pretty l. is young   32:14
Ladder: behold a l.   45:3
dropping down the l.   296:28
Jacob's l...ask the number of the steps   269:18
l. to all high designs   481:3
of our vices..a l.   316:30
traffic of Jacob's l.   545:1
unto the l. turns his back   449:3
wiv a l. and some glasses   36:22
young ambition's l.   449:3
Laddie: your Highland l. gone   282:10
Laden: I should ever l. be   244:17
labour and are heavy l.   59:10
l. with my sin   517:4
Ladies: all you l. now at land   187:2
ate in hall among l.   328:24
for l.' love unfit   192:3
from a l.' seminary   219:29
good-night, sweet l.   436:24
I am parshial to l.   20:27
if l. be but young and fair   427:16
l. of St. James's   183:12
l. of th' Hesperides   350:4
l. that do sleep   123:26
lion among l.   407:3
long, may the l. sit   32:2
lords of l. intellectual   115:16
misogyn a l.' man!   39:21
o'er l.' lips   477:7
of l. most deject   434:14
on the tables of young l.   326:11
out of the l.' company   422:31
rhyme themselves into l.' favours   445:13
store of l., whose bright eyes   342:6
these over-offended l.   511:22
when he has l. to please   22:10
witches, those most noble l.   584:22
young l. are delicate plants   22:18
Lads: cheer up, my l.!   213:10
golden l. and girls   430:1
I lie as l. would choose   263:7
l. are in love with the grave   263:28
l. that will die in their glory   263:3
thinking lays l. underground   263:18
though your l. are far away   210:4
three wild l. were we   419:33
two l.   485:3
Lady: as sweetly, L.   245:19
because of the death of that l.   328:5
capers nimbly in a l.'s chamber   476:4
Colonel's L. an' Judy O'Grady   298:6
come hither, l. fair   285:5
courting his l. in the spring   81:8
elect l.   70:16
Enoch, Elijah, and the L.   376:1
every l. would be queen   384:36
faint heart ne'er wan a l. fair   104:22
faint heart never won fair l.   219:14
fine l. upon a white horse   368:17
for the love of a l.   222:27
gentle l. married to the Moor   578:21
get you to my l.'s chamber   437:15
good heart, and Oure L.'s grace   417:11

Lady (cont.)
he called her his l. fair 303:12
he keeps a l. in a cage 141:35
here lies a most beautiful l. 171:6
his hound, and his l. fair 32:15
his l.'s ta'en anither mate 32:15
holiday and l. terms 438:33
if doughty deeds my l. please 228:12
if you were April's l. 524:30
I met a l. in the meads 286:30
in this l.'s lips and hands 410:32
I see it's written by a l. 403:14
Joan as my L. is as good 246:12
laces for a l. 301:18
l. doth protest too much 435:15
l., if undrest at Church 203:30
l. in the case 116:16, 218:15
l. inside 11:2
l. is a musician 188:9
L. Jane was fair 34:13
L. Moon, L. Moon 262:7
l. of a 'certain age' 116:22
l. of Christ's College 21:10
l. of incisive features 337:13
l. of light 521:30
l. of my delight 338:8
L. of Shalott 533:42
L. of the Mere 573:2
l. so richly clad as she 150:20
l. stole it from me 141:10
l. sweet and kind 10:20, 210:5
L. Teazle, by all that's wonder-ful! 500:42
l. that's known as Lou 422:21
l. the brach may stand 452:24
L.! we receive but 151:4
L. with a Lamp 317:14
learned in a l.'s eyes 455:22
like a dying l. 499:5
Liner she's a l. 298:25
long will his L. look owre 30:10
love for any l. 377:2
lovely l., garmented in light 499:6
make a l. of my own 581:21
many a L., and many a Para-mour 509:33
many, many l. friends 361:7
my arm a l.'s lilye hand 31:6
my dear L. Disdain 468:2
my fair l. 367:19
my L. Bountiful 203:6
my l. seems of ivory 359:10
my l. sleeps! 318:4
my l. sweet. arise! 429:25
never come out of a l.'s lips 208:23
no l. closer 439:11
no l. thou 148:16
Old L. of Threadneedle Street 222:32
our L. of Pain 523:7
our L. of the Snows 300:11
rob a l. of her fortune 204:30
self-respecting l.'s cell 39:26
some lost l. of old years 97:18
some men must love my l. 455:10
such a l. God's mother be 7:17
swear me, Kate, like a l. 440:7
talk . with the same single l. 116:39
there ain't a l. livin' 142:22
there he saw a l. bright 32:6
think this l. to be my child 454:16
this l. by the trees 584:12
this l. of the West Country 171:6
thy mother a l. 417:32
to a l. in his shield 534:4
too near another l. 446:14
weep no more, my l. 210:15
what l. would not love 232:5
when a l.'s in the case 215:30
white hand of a l. fever thee 425:5
who but L. Greensleeves? 6:18
will you hear a Spanish l. 12:1
Ladybird: l., l., fly away home 367:12
Ladylike: most . l. of trees 320:7
too l. in love 242:29
Lady-smocks all silver-white 455:35
Laeseris: odisse quem l. 526:10
Laeti triumphantes 13:2
Laetitia: quite well, L.? 337:29
Lag-end: entertain the l. of my life 440:26
Lager-beer: goned afay mit de l. 313:12
Laggard in love 418:17
Lags: superfluous l. the vet'ran 279:9

Laid: best l. schemes 107:11
ere I am l. out dead 246:20
I l. me down with a will 516:15
in his narrow cell for ever l. 229:30
in sad cypress let me be l. 483:6
l. him on the deck 31:2
l. him on the green 30:8
l. many heavy loads on thee 202:11
l. on him the iniquity of us all 54:26
l. on with a trowel 426:20
lightly l. again 541:14
not in the Abbey..l. 562:21
we l. them on the ballast 539:19
when I'm l. by thee 246:27
Lain: l. for a century dead 536:15
should I have l. still 48:45
Lair: deep his midnight l. 416:11
fox from his l. 229:16
lion from his l. 420:23
slugs leave their l. 152:17
Laird: last L. of Ravenswood 419:17
Lairdie: wee wee German l. 250:12
Laissez: l. faire aux dieux 157:7
l. faire, l. passer 404:19
me l. enfin dans ce petit coin 354:2
Laity: conspiracies against the l. 489:20
tell the l. our love 186:24
Lake: angler in the l. of darkness 453:28
beside the l. 577:5
bosom of the steady l. 579:24
I hear l. water lapping 585:12
in that crimson l. 355:21
into the bosom of the l. 539:2
l.-blossom fell into the l. 536:13
l. of Blood 529:36
on still St. Mary's L. 582:19
open onto the L. of Geneva 290:16
Pilot of the Galilean l. 342:26
sedge is wither'd from the l. 286:28
Lake-blossom: white l. 536:13
Lake-reflected sun 497:2
Lakes: from the great l. 317:20
rocks, caves, l., fens 346:2
scalped each other by the Great L. 324:34
shakes across the l. 538:14
Lalage: call me L. or Doris 152:6
I've lost L. 301:5
Lalagen: dulce ridentem L. amabo 258:23
Lama sabachthani? 60:52
Lamb: as a l. to the slaughter 54:26
being flatter'd is a l. 135:14
blood of the L. 71:6
did he who made the L. make thee? 75:24(-76)
God will provide himself a l. 44:55
go to bed with the l. 80:2
He calls Himself a L. 76:10
I a child, and thou a l. 76:10
L. as it had been slain 70:41
L., if he wants any *knowledge* 153:16
L. is the light thereof 72:5
L. of God, I come! 198:20
L., the frolic and the gentle 575:17
l. was sure to go 233:23
l...without blemish 45:45
leads me to the L. 161:1
little L., who made thee? 76:10
London's towers receive the L. 75:12
marriage supper of the L. 71:34
Mary had a little l. 233:23
Mary loves the l. 233:23(-234)
nothing but the L. of God 307:9
one dead l. is there 317:11
one little ewe l. 47:33
pet-l. in a sentimental farce 287:16
secret of the bull and l. 336:25
skin of an innocent l...parch-ment 445:38
song about a L. 76:9
10th, Emperor L. 307:9
to the shorn l. 512:28
Una with her milk-white l. 578:21
was the holy L. of God..seen 75:16
wolf..dwell with the L. 53:18
wrath of the L. 71:2
yoked with a l. 451:25
Lambent but innocuous 228:2
Lambkins, we will live 443:17
Lambs: as my l. are beloved 156:19
feed my l. 64:15
gather the l. with his arm 54:11

Lambs (cont.)
go to hell like l. 141:11
l. could not forgive 176:34
to see the young l. 562:4
we were as twinn'd l. 485:4
while the young l. bound 576:3
Lame: feet was l to the l. 49:9
l. and impotent conclusion 470:29
l. dogs over stiles 293:11
l. man leap as an hart 54:3
l. of a leg and old 171:21
love is l. at fifty years 236:26
made l. by fortune 486:32
wretched matter and l. metre 343:26
Lament: have I not reason to l. 581:10
l. anew, Uranial 491:15
miserable change..l. nor sor-row at 425:28
nought other to l. 375:14
to l. the past 101:33
universal Nature did l. 342:18
yet you l. not the days 507:34
Lamentation: empire's l. 537:11
that l. of the leaves 586:7
Lamented: L. Jack 152:13
ye have not l. 59:8
Lamenting: break off this last l. kiss 184:28
he was left l. 122:29
Lamentings heard i' the air 458:21
Lammas: about the L. tide 30:5
Lamp: Christ with His l. of truth 81:4
dying l. 492:2
ere Homer's l. appear'd 162:26
fluttered round the l. 128:19
glorious l. of Heaven, the sun 247:10
God's l. close to my breast 94:26
Lady with a L. 317:14
largest l. is lit 323:31
largest l. on Campden Hill 141:13
light the bridal l. 348:38
lord of lycht and l. of day 187:5
luminous L. within suspended 311:17
Slaves of the L. 14:30
smell too strong of the l. 513:9
thy l., O Memory 411:28
unlit l. 96:46
when the l. is shattered 494:20
whose intense l. narrows 498:5
with handmaid l. attending 343:25
Lampada: vitai l. tradunt 321:1
Lamping Samminiato 94:8
Lamp-lit: o'er his l. desk 80:28
Lamplough was genteel 514:2
Lamps: bright the l. shone 113:25
filled their l. with everlasting oil 340:9
golden l. in a green night 332:2
Heav'n's great l. do dive 123:19
hidden l. in old sepulchral urns 159:21
l. are going out 232:18
l. of heaven 293:10
new l. for old 14:2
oh, her l. of a night! 307:2
ye living l. 332:27
Yew alone burns l. of peace 172:6
Lancaster: time-honour'd L. 474:8
Lancastrian: turn L. there 506:15
Lance: hopeless l...in rest 140:18
lay his l. in rest 183:8
my l. a wand? 31:6
with l.'s thrust 418:29
Lancelot: angels heave up Sir L. 328:23
bold Sir L. 534:18
found in L. 530:18
L., budge not 463:12
L. mused a little space 534:10
L. or Pelleas, or Pellenore 350:4
L. wanderingly lewd 530:24
left not even L. brave 531:11
my lord, Sir L., my father 328:13
not L.. nor another 530:19
Sir L. awoke 328:20
Lancers: six stalwart l. 568:24
Land: all you ladies now at l. 187:2
along the l. they rode 419:10
and the pleasant l. 127:33
as signals to the l. 150:6
beyond this l. of woe 29:13
by sea as by l. 217:24
by water as by l. 198:24
came from the holy l. 405:10
cast the water of my l. 461:1

INDEX

Land (cont.)

clear the l. of evil 301:26
Columbial happy l.1 255:13
divides that..l. from ours 562:14
dry l. where no water is 395:25
England—a happy l. we know 143:1
England's green & pleasant L. 75:16
exiles from our fathers' l. 420:31
fat of the l. 45:23
freedom..in no other l. 193:42
from the best of all my l. 439:44
gaze from the l. on another's ..struggles 320:30(-321)
good and bad of every l. 29:10
goodness..in the l. of the living 393:22
good seed on the l. 121:27
great by l. as thou by sea 537:17
great rock in a weary l. 53:43
her l. reposed 539:12
his Maker's image through the l. 190:8
ill fares the l. 224:14
illumined the L. of Sleep 317:17
in a cleaner, greener l. 299:14
in the beautiful heavenly l. 415:7
in the l. which..God giveth 390:12
into the silent l. 409:24
I pass..from l. to l. 150:12
l. flowing with milk and honey 45:36
l. is scattered with light 80:12
l. of brown heath 417:22
L. o' Cakes 107:20
l. of darkness 48:54
L. of Dreams is better far 75:14
l. of faery 585:14
l. of Heart's Desire 585:16
L. of Hope and Glory 42:20
l. of lost content 263:14
l. of mist and snow 149:7
l. of my dreams 293:1
l. of my sires 417:22
l. of Nod 44:33
l. of our birth 295:6, 8
l. of pure delight 562:13
l. of sand and thorns 530:28
l. of scholars 226:15
l. of settled government 541:24
l. of the free 123:6, 292:11
l. o' the leal 360:19, 20
l. of the Ojibways 317:20
l. of the shadow of death 53:14
l.-rats and water-rats, l.-thieves 463:15
l. that gave you birth 362:33
l. to which the ship 147:13
l. to which yon Ship 582:16
l. where her young hero sleeps 356:31
l. where my fathers died 504:19
l. where the Bong-tree grows 312:1
l. where the cypress 113:1
l...where the light is as darkness 48:55
l. where was the wave 376:6
l. you used to plough 263:5
last l. 84:7
lilacs out of the dead l. 197:27
look, the l. is bright 147:8
marched into their l. 23:26
my America! my new-found-l. 184:23
my native l.—Good Night! 113:7
my own, my native l. 417:22
nakedness of the l. 45:20
no l. beside 447:18
no l. can compare unto thee 489:1
no more l., say fish 84:1
not fit to live on l. 272:37
ocean leans against the l. 226:13
o'er all the pleasant l. 241:12
o'er the furrowed l. 341:34
old Mus' Hobden owns the l. 298:8
on to the Pleasant L. 92:13
our l., the first garden 123:6
our ship not far from l. 9:3
out of the l. of the living 54:27
pleasant l. of counterpane 515:19
Prince of all the l. 122:3
Queen of l. and sea 184:2
room in the..heavenly l. 415:7
row, my knights, near the l. 124:22
save a sinking l. 384:11
scatter plenty o'er a smiling l. 230:5
seems a moving l. 348:26
spy out the l. 46:13
sweet l. of liberty 504:19

Land (cont.)

there's l. I seel 543:10
there's the l., or cherry-isle 245:21
they love their l...their own 234:14
think there is no l. 24:19
this l. of such dear souls, this dear, dear l. 474:22
thou on the l. 419:33
through the broad bright l. 506:21
to the French..the l. 125:23, 407:1
to the Promised L. 35:4
what thing of sea or l.? 350:31
when house and l. are gone 209:19
where is the l. of Luthany? 545:5
where lies the l.? 147:13
where the l. she travels from? 147:13
who can help loving the l. 356:8
wonders in the l. of Egypt 45:41
wonders in the l. of Ham 398:13
Land: kennst du das L.? 224:6
Landau: gun-'orses in the l. 301:11
Land-breeze shook the shrouds 162:10
Landed: Sir Roger..inclined to the l...interest 2:13
Landing-place: he gain'd the l. 417:11
safe to the l. 323:29
Landlord: come, l., fill 5:24
l.'s black-eyed daughter 366:2
Land-lubbers lying down below 9:3
Landmark: removeth his neigh-bour's l. 46:27
Landmarks: great men..l. in the state 100:10
Landor: with L. and with Donne 586:13
Land-rats and water-rats 463:15
Lands: broader l. and better days 144:2
call the l. after their own names 395:1
hundred little l. within one 41:21
in faery l. forlorn 288:1
it comes from the west l. 334:15
l. beyond the sea 577:4
l. I was to travel in 31:19
l. were fairly portioned 323:21
l. where the Jumblies live 311:21
much I owe to the L. that grew 303:10
other l. beneath another sun 546:23
quantity of dirty l. 483:8
though not of l. 583:11
Landscape: fades the glimmering l. 229:28
view the l. o'er 562:17
Landscape-painter: he is but a l. once more that l. 535:2, 535:8
Landscapes: if l. were sold 514:15
Land-travel: in l. or sea-faring? 97:20
Lane: blue above l. and wall 90:37
cottage in a l. (Park L.) 223:7
in an English l. 91:3
l., highway, or open street 549:6
little boy who lives down the l. 366:9
while there's a country l. 373:15
Langage: de bonne soupe et non de beau l. 353:16
Langmut: ob aus L. Er sich säumet 315:22
Language: Chatham's l. was his mother-tongue 163:1
consenting l. of the heart 215:11
decent obscurity of a learned l. 217:4
don't think anything of that l. 177:15
English..no respect for their l. 490:44
enrichment of our native l. 194:4
fancies that broke through l. 95:21
finality is not the l. of politics 180:24
for learning me your l. 479:26
heart doth need a l. 152:10
if everything else in our l. should perish 326:3
I love the l. of his heart 386:13
in l. quaint and olden 316:23
in the best chosen l. 22:22
l. all nations understand 40:11
l. I have learn'd these forty years 474:14
l. is a perpetual Orphic song 497:14
l. is fossil poetry 200:32
l. is the dress of thought 278:3
l. is the flesh-garment, the body, of thought 127:10
l. of the age is never the l. of poetry 231:21
l. plain 159:16
l. that would make your hair curl 222:6

Language (cont.)

l. was not powerful enough 177:17
learned his great l. 93:3
my l. fails! 41:8
my l. is plain 238:32
natural l. of the heart 422:27
neither speech nor l. 392:32
no l. but a cry 532:34
no l., but the l. of the heart 386:4
of his strange l. all I know 308:23
of oure l...the lodesterre 321:9
only speak one l. 182:19
persuasive l. of a tear 143:28
quotation..enlargement of the l. 277:22
some entrance into the l. 27:27
sure in l. strange 286:33
that dear l. which I spake like thee 323:9
that those lips had l.1 160:25
there's l. in her eye 481:26
under the tropic is our l. spoke 558:8
use any l. you choose 219:9
use in measured l. 532:4
who shall ever find joy's l.? 81:2
you taught me l. 479:26
Languages: great feast of l. 455:26
instructed in all l. living and dead 176:38
in the graves of deceased l. 175:6
knowledge of the ancient l. 82:16
l. are the pedigree of nations 276:4
none of your live l. 175:6
silent in seven l. 29:6
speaks three or four l. 482:5
took and gave l. 401:34
vulgar l. that want words 281:27
wit in all l. 194:5
Languid: art thou l.? 361:10
l. patience of thy face 152:19
restore the tone of l. Nature 162:36
Languish: relieve my l. 168:12
Languishes: cat l. loudly 241:27
Languishment: tale of love and l. 289:3
Languor: l. cannot be 498:9
l. is not in your heart 17:20
Languors: lilies and l. of virtue 522:23
Lank: days seem l. and long 222:1
thou art long, and l. 149:19
Lantern: experience..a l. on the stern 152:24
in thy dark l. 340:9
l. unto my feet 399:21
Lanterns: feast of l. 379:22
Laodameia died 309:12
Lap: asked Carrie to sit on his l. 233:6
chills the l. of May 226:10
cool flowery l. of earth 16:22
dropt in her L. 206:3
fresh l. of the crimson rose 466:37
l. me in soft Lydian airs 342:7
l. of the new come spring 475:30
old enough to l. 568:22
on the l. of June 253:18
sea-fogs l. and cling 302:10
sing lullaby and l. it warm 80:8
sun..in the l. of Thetis 110:43
uncover, dogs, and l. 480:25
upon the l. of Earth 230:13
La Palie: Provence and L. 146:33
Lap-dogs: when l. breathe their last 385:17
Lapidary: in l. inscriptions..not upon oath 272:35
Lapidem: gutta cavat l. 372:10, 11
Lapland: lovely as a L. night 583:2
Lapped: all thy friends are l. in lead 35:18
l. in proof 456:9
Lapping: I hear lake water l. 585:12
Laps: tumbling into some men's l. 24:30
Lapse: liquid l. of murmuring streams 348:32
to l. in fulness 429:35
Lapwings feel the leaden death 386:32
Larañaga: there's peace in a L. 294:31
Larch: plumelets tuft the L. 533:12
Lard their lean books 109:3
Larded with sweet flowers 436:22
Lards the lean earth 439:8
Larem: venimus l. ad nostrum 132:21
Large: as l. as store 244:9

Large (cont.)

brimming, and bright, and l. 17:28
how l. a letter I have written 67:49
I am l., I contain multitudes 568:11
l. as life and twice as natural 131:18
l. cold bottle 204:2
l. draughts of intellectual day 165:30
l. utterance of the early Gods 286:6
left him at l. 344:20
little volume, but l. book 166:8
old Priest writ l. 351:27
set my feet in a l. room 393:28
so l., and smooth, and round 507:4
speke he never so rudeliche and l. 137:23
things to come at l. 481:8
Large-brained woman 88:6
Large-hearted man 88:6
Largely: drinking l. sobers us 382:22
Larger: I am l., better 568:5
l. heart 533:20
l. than human 531:32
Largess universal 444:8
Largest: l. and most comprehensive soul 194:6
shout with the l. 178:31
those of the l. size 130:20
Lark: as sweetly as the l. 465:22
bisy l., messenger of day 137:30
hark! hark! the l. 429:25
herald l. 350:3
l. becomes a sightless song 533:25
l. begin his flight 341:31
l.-charmèd, rook-racked 254:22
l. drop down at his feet 538:1
l. from her light wing 166:24
l. now leaves his wat'ry nest 169:13
l. sang loud and high 73:11
l. shall sing me hame 167:23
l. soars 87:30
l.'s on the wing 94:40
l., that tirra-lirra chants 485:16
late l. twitters 241:21
more tuneable than l. 466:21
music soars within the little l. 87:30
my state, like to the l. 486:24
nightingale, and not the l. 478:26
no l. could pipe 293:6
no l. more blithe 72:15
shrill-gorg'd l. 454:4
shrill sweet l. 253:16
some late l. singing 241:23
swallow for the holy l. 87:28
we rise with the l. 80:2
Larks: four L. and a Wren 311:2
hear the l. so high 262:21(-263)
mounting l. 386:32
mount l. aloft 248:5
Larkspur listens 536:15
Lars Porsena of Clusium 323:10
Lartius: back, L.! 323:24
Lasciate ogni speranza 168:17
Lasciva: Galatea..l. puella 555:26
Lascivious: clasps of a l. Moor 469:32
Lash: delight at once and l. the age 382:16
l., of film 477:7
l. the vice and follies 134:6
neebor's name to l. 105:27
Lashed: he l. the vice 521:3
Lashes: ordered him three hundred and fifty l. 179:15
Lass: amo, amas, I love a l. 370:5
drink to the l. 500:39
every l. a queen 293:19
for a l. wi' a tocher 106:8
give him his l., his fiddle 162:21
I loved a l., a fair one 572:3
kiss a bonnie l. 108:16
l. that has acres o' charms 106:7
l. that loves a sailor 173:8
l...to go a-gipseying..with 307:29
l. unparallel'd 426:14
lordliest l. of earth 84:5
lover and his l. 428:30
never show a l. as comely 298:29
penniless l. wi' a lang pedigree 360:18
solitary Highland l. 580:28
sweet l. of Richmond Hill 327:5, 551:5
Tents of Shem, dear l. 298:27
this l. so neat 327:5, 551:5
Lasse: tout casse, tout l. 12:21

Lasses: come l. and lads 5:25
honest men and bonny l. 108:3
l. a' lilting 198:18
spent amang the l. O! 105:37
Lassie: I love a l. 310:12
my love she's but a l. yet 250:20
young l...wi' an auld man 108:26
Last: after L., returns the First 89:22
all on our l. cruise 514:34
at l., at l., unite them there! 147:7
at our l. hour..fall from thee 391:43
at the l., best 423:36
beggarly l. doit 163:44
best and the l. 95:10
die in the l. ditch 103:33
Earl can l. but a few years 84:27
eternal Now does always l. 158:2
even to the l.! 574:24
eyes, look your l.! 478:44
fear, the l. of ills 193:38
first, l., everlasting day 184:6
first to come and l. to go 318:7
forebode the l. 411:11
happy. .to be but the l. man 86:24
held to the l. man 233:20
her l. disorder mortal 225:16
he that comes l. is commonly best 109:4
in both the l. 193:9
in life's l. scene 279:10
it will l. my time 125:33
I will give unto this l. 60:8
l. and best of all God's works 349:17
l. and greatest herald 190:2
l. arrow 140:18
l. at His cross 35:25
l. enemy 67:9
l. great Englishman is low 537:13
l. his sorrow, first his joy 232:2
l. kind word to Christ 96:5
l. man in 363:4
l. of all he was seen of me also 67:5
l. of all the Romans 452:2
l. of a race in ruin 140:14
l. of life 95:13
l. of that bright band 241:10
L. of the Mohicans 157:2
l. out a night in Russia 461:25
l. reader reads no more 251:8
l. sad squires ride slowly 141:27
l. state..worse than the first 59:19
l. thing I shall do! 373:9
l. this way a-fishing 559:19
l., till you write your letter 186:18
l. time I saw Paris 235:5
l. to lay the old aside 382:29
l. words..Michael Angelo 406:13
l. words..Narcissa spoke 384:25
l. year's words 197:14
look thy l. on all things lovely 171:9
many that are first shall be l. 60:5
my l. Duchess 93:34
no l. nor first 94:46
of many..kisses the poor l. 425:27
one more, and this the l. 473:11
sex to the l. 192:6
system..l. her time 414:9
think the l. opinion right 383:1
this day may be the l. 362:20
though l., not least in love 450:7
too warm work..to l. long 362:24
to the l. moment of his breath 224:10
what is it that will l.? 535:17
when I saw Waring 97:20
world's l. night 185:17
would that this might be the l. 160:21
Last Judgement: L. draweth nigh 73:23
L.'s fire must cure 90:20
Lasted: nice while it l. 299:22
their lives..till now had l. 280:9
Lasting: full l. is the song 336:45
l. too, for souls not lent 336:45
sweet, not l. 431:20
what l. joys the man attend 568:21
Lastly: as he pronounces l. 342:23
Lasts: all that is. .l. ever 95:22
Latch: draw the l. 366:14
no l. ter de golden gate 238:24
Latchet: whose shoe's l. I am not worthy 63:2
Latchfords: letting in the L. 518:23
Late: age too l. 349:6
alas! 'tis now too l.! 202:4

Late (cont.)

bad die l. 170:2
beginning l. 349:5
finds too l. that men betray 226:18
five minutes too l. all my life 158:25
it came to them very l. 294:30
l. and early pray 583:10
l. and soon 582:18
l. at plough 236:8
l., l. in the gloamin' 250:22
never too l. for delight 357:1
nightingale does sit so l. 332:27
not too l. to-morrow 14:27
say it is l. and dusky 551:21
she is l. 536:15
sorrow never comes too l. 230:30
tarnish l. on Wenlock Edge 263:13
too l. and I to love thee 21:22
too l., too l.! 530:10
too l. to seek a newer world 541:3
viewing him since, alas, too l.! 280:10
when others cry, 'Too l.' 88:23
whom still he found too l. 190:24
who of l. for cleanliness 157:4
worse when it comes l. in life 269:11
Lated: Cupid abroad was l. 231:33
Later: I'll meet 'im l. on 297:4
Latericiam: quam l. accepisset 120:8
Latest: l.-born and loveliest vision 288:4
Love's l. breath 189:20
Lath of good wood painted. . like iron 73:1
Lather: l. good l. is half the shave 252:8
Latian: prince of the L. name 323:14
Latin: he speaks L. 445:41
L. for a candle 204:6
L. names for horns and stools 105:23
L., queen of tongues 281:26
L. was no more difficile 110:4
learn L. as an honour 144:16
must carve in L. or in Greek 557:22
ne yet of L., ne of Greek 510:15
small L., and less Greek 281:13
you understand L.? 203:14
Latio: artes intulit agresti L. 257:14
Latitude: l.'s rather uncertain 402:22
longtitude and..l. for a seine 550:20
Latoun: he hadde a croys of l. 137:22
Latrone: cantabit..coram l. 283:17
Latter: blessed the l. end of Job 49:34
carry off the l. 376:23
Europe's l. hour 16:23
farewell, thou l. spring! 438:28
former and the l. rain 389:21
stand at the l. day 49:6
Laud: l. and honour to the Father 361:14
to dust. .a little gilt more l. 481:22
Laudable: write well..in l. things 352:2
Laudamus: Te Deum l. 13:14
Laudant illa sed ista legunt 331:25
Laudator temporis acti se puero 256:2
Laudatur: probitas l. et alget 282:23
Laude: dignum l. virum Musa vetat mori 261:1
Laudes: semper..nomen..l.que manebunt 553:21
Laudi: concedant laurea l. 145:8
Lauds: lytle byrdes..syng l. 239:5
Laugh: anything awful makes me l. 307:11
atheist-l. 105:20
cannot make him l. 442:20
for whom did he. .l. else 90:18
if I l. at any mortal thing 116:9
l. and be well 231:27
l. and the world laughs 568:26
l. as he sits by the river 88:12
l. a siege to scorn 461:2
l. as I pass in thunder 492:26
l. at a fall 92:42
l. at all disaster 315:29
l. at all you trembled at 161:35
l. at gilded butterflies 454:19
l. at my own cenotaph 493:1
l. at's while we strut 425:2
l. at them in our turn 23:5
l., be jolly 263:18
l., heart, again 584:19
l. like parrots at a bagpiper 462:30
l. or mourn with me 161:25
l. sans intermission 427:15
l. their pride 90:34
l. to scorn the power of man 460:5
l. to see how fools are vexed 170:21

Laugh (*cont.*)
l. to see them whirl 492:29
l. uproariously in youth 84:14
l. where we must 383:8
l. with me, or at me 513:2
loud l... the vacant mind 224:17
made a cat l. 379:23
make fools l. i' the alehouse 470:28
men that l. and weep 523:18
nobody has ever heard me l. 139:20
not a thing to l. to scorn 428:23
they..l. me to scorn 393:3
they l. that win 472:23
those l. whose lungs are tickle 433:18
tickle us, do we not l.? 464:8
to chide, to l., to weep 423:15
truth..th' exploded l. shall win 85:4
unbecoming a man of quality..
  to l. 154:31
unextinguishable l. in heaven 85:15
valleys..l. and sing 395:30(-396)
wherefore did Sarah l.? 44:51
who but must l. 385:29

Laughable: schemes of political
  improvement..l. 271:34
swear the jest be l. 462:30

Laughed: folks..mus' speck ter
  be l. at 238:10
I l. him out of patience 424:12
l. and moaned about 89:24
l. at that these twenty years 227:7
l. at the power of Love 302:29
l. his word to scorn 162:4
l. in death 508:5
l. in the sun 84:2
l. loud and long 150:11
l. with counterfeited glee 225:1
nor l., nor cried 401:29
sighed deep, l. free 97:28
so loud, loud l. he 31:24
they l. consumedly 203:11
when he's l. and said his say 543:6
when the first baby l. 36:7

Laughing: another half stand l. by 443:8
cannot forbear l. and jeering 377:20
God's l. in Heaven 584:10
happiness is no l. matter 565:26
he l. said to me 76:9
l. devil in his sneer 115:2
l. heart's long peace 84:18
l. immoderately at stated intervals 504:20
l. is heard on the hill 76:14
l., quaffing..time 193:31
l. queen 265:23
L. Water 317:26
set the crew l. 208:15
sun was l. sweetly 585:6

Laughs: at lovers' perjuries..
  Jove l. 477:20
fair l. the morn 229:23
he l. like anything 141:34
Jove but l. at lovers' perjury 193:13
l. the sense of misery away 162:21
l. to see the good things 249:22
l. to see the green man pass 250:6
more so, when he l. 512:32
she l. with a harvest 269:15
while she l. at them 154:28

Laughter: boughs of April in l. shake 80:12
dearer her l. free 233:1
eyes overrunning with l. 316:5
his l. at their quaint opinions 348:30
in her lovely l. shows 124:5
invent anything that tends to l. 441:11
l. and the love of friends 41:17
l. for a month 439:7
L. holding both his sides 34:29
l. is..sudden glory 248:24
l., learnt of friends 84:21
l. of a fool 51:10
l. of her heart 235:5
laugh thy girlish l. 561:3
man is distinguished..by..l. 2:32
'mid l. free 10:21
O Christ, the l. 334:2
our sincerest l. 498:9
peals of l...round thee break 385:23
present l. 482:28
so ill-bred as audible l. 139:7
to make faces and produce l. 272:34
under running l. 544:13

Laughter (*cont.*)
weeping and the l. 187:11
wine and women, mirth and l. 115:33
with weeping and with l. 324:1
worst returns to l. 453:37
yea, for my l. 451:15

Laughters: tears and l. for all time 89:2
Launch: fear to l. away 562:16
joyous we too l. out 567:2
your glorious standard l. again 123:10
Launched a thousand ships 330:5
Laundry: it all goes into the l. 302:5
Laura: if L. had been Petrarch's
  wife 115:39
rose-cheeked L., come 123:16
Laurea: concedant l. laudi 145:8
Laureate: strew the l. hearse 342:31(-343)
Laurel: Apollo's l. bough 330:12
l. for the perfect prime 409:28
l. is green for a season 525:8
l., ivy, vine 336:38
l. outlives not May 525:8
l., the palms, and the paean 525:6
l. wreaths entwine 238:26
that she might l. grow 332:16
this l. greener from the brows 539:11
thy l., thy glory 286:1
Laurels: l. all are cut 33:9, 263:27
once more, O ye l. 342:10
thy l. torn 506:3
worth all your l. 118:32
Laurel-tree: carven from the l. 545:7
Lauriers: les l. sont coupés 33:9
Laus: non ultima l. est 257:6
Lave: l. in it, drink of it 252:21
let the l. go by me 515:27
whistle owre the l. o't 108:29
Lavender: hot l., mints 485:25
l. water tinged with pink 312:6
Lavender'd: linen, smooth, and l. 285:24
Lavinia: she is L. 480:33
Lavishly: who l. commends 142:28
Law: against reason..of no force
  in l. 148:3
all's love, yet all's l. 96:22
all that keep the Jungle L. 299:26
army of unalterable l. 336:17
as touching the l., a Pharisee 68:20
ayont the l. 516:20
become a universal l. 284:5
bloody book of l. 469:44
born under one l. 232:14
Common L. of England..
  laboriously built 243:9
crowner's quest l. 437:4
Custom that is before all l. 168:6
custom, that unwritten l. 169:9
despair, l., chance 185:14
fair play of the..criminal l. 187:25
first is l., the last prerogative 192:24
fulfilling of the l. 66:12
fulfil the l. of their being 20:13
God is thy l., thou mine 347:20
having my l...disobey'd 375:16
he that loveth..fulfilled the l. 66:11
higher l. than the Constitution 422:23
highest l. of his being 200:23
his will his l. 164:19
I am not determining a point of l. 101:5
I crave the l. 465:1
I find them a l. 65:50
if he only knew a little of l. 7:4
if the l. supposes that 178:1
ignorance of the l. 422:4
I, my Lords, embody the L. 218:35
incline our hearts to keep this l. 390:6
in l.'s grave study six 148:8
is the l. of our side if I say ay? 476:46
is the l. sin? 65:47
keeps the l. in calmness made 575:10
keep ye the L. 301:26
laid His hand on Moses' l. 74:13
l. agin the wearin' o' the Green 9:6
l. can take a purse 111:26
l. doth give it 465:10
L....her seat is the bosom of God 253:36
l. is a ass 178:1
L. is a bottomless pit 14:6
L. is the true embodiment 218:35
L.: It has honoured us 563:7
l. of thy mouth is dearer 399:17

Law (*cont.*)
l...perfection of reason 148:4
l.'s delay 434:4
l. so general a study 100:30
l...take care o' raskills 196:22
l. unto themselves 65:35
l. which governs all l. 101:20
lesser breeds without the L. 300:26
let them relearn the L. 297:22
make a scarecrow of the l. 461:22
more ought l. to weed it out 27:4
nature's great l., and l. of all
  men's minds 17:14
nature's l., that man was made to
  mourn 107:1
necessity hath no l. 167:11
never a l. of God or man 301:3
no l...no transgression 65:39
no lust because..no l. 531:25
nor l., nor duty bade me fight 584:21
nor the world's l. 478:37
not any l. exceeds his knowledge 135:19
not..come to destroy the l. 57:43
nothing is l. that is not reason 387:14
not known sin, but by the l. 65:47
offends no l. 135:19
old father antick, the l. 438:11
one God, one l. 533:37
one l. for all 101:26
our reason is our l. 349:14
part of the Common L. of England 233:22
part of the law of the land 292:4
people crushed by l. 103:12
prisons are built with stones of
  L. 77:15
progress is the l. of life 94:23
purlieus of the l. 201:33, 533:10
quicken thou me in thy l. 399:15
quillets of the l. 445:20
reason is the life of the l. 148:4
Reign of L. 14:12
rich men rule the l. 226:16
seven hours to l. 279:21
shamrock is by l. forbid 9:6
stoop to any other l. 135:19
this is l., I will maintain 7:9
this is the l. and the prophets 58:22
this is the L. of the Jungle 208:19
this is the L. of the Yukon 422:20
this is the royal L. 157:13
those by l. protected 106:24
to himself is a l. rational 135:19
transgression of a l. of nature 265:6
unchanging l. of God 373:16
very good l. for all that 419:30
wedded love, mysterious l. 347:26
we live l. to ourselves 349:14
who to himself is l., no l. doth
  need 135:17
windward of the l. 143:5
windy side of the l. 484:12
wrest once the l. 465:2
your Majesty's will is l. 220:21
Lawful: all things are l. for me 66:39
art l. as eating 486:1
l. that he should stoop 135:19
l...to do what I will with mine
  own 60:8
l...to wear weapons 401:13
nations knew their l. lord 190:31
neither quite l. nor quite right 111:35
that which is l. and right 55:30
their l. occasions 400:29
Law-giver: Judah is my l. 395:23
Lawless linsy-woolsy brother 110:34
Lawn: bird-haunted English l. 17:10
brushed dew from l. 119:17
furtively over the l. 235:14
l. about the shoulders thrown 246:4
l. as white as..snow 485:29
leave the printed l. 264:1
rivulets hurrying thro' the l. 539:5
twice a saint in l. 384:24
upon the upland l. 230:11
Lawns: house with l. enclosing it 516:12
l. and avenues 296:30
like satyrs grazing on the l. 329:20
Laws: as for 'Thy l. 244:16
bad l. are the worst sort of
  tyranny 100:16
base l. of servitude 191:41

Laws (cont.)
beginning with the l. 387:23
breaking of l. 357:23
breaking up of l. 530:12
breathing household l. 577:16
drama's l. 279:1
for the l.l 323:2
fountains..whence all civil l. 24:33
give his little senate l. 385:29
gives his little senate l. 381:7
had l. not been 169:10
if l. are their enemies 103:12
L., by which their Life and their
Goods 135:28
l. grind the poor 226:16
l...lean on one another 102:34
l...like cobwebs 25:1, 519:7
l...nets 499:18
l. of England are at my commandment 442:36
l. of God and man and metre 315:14, 416:10
l. of life..l. of death 413:27
l. of poetic truth and..beauty 19:22
L. of the Land will..instruct
you 135:28
l. or kings can cause or cure 226:17, 278:29
l. were made to be broken 365:11
let..l. and learning die 329:10
Nature's l. lay hid in night 382:17
not care who should make the l. 208:31
not..due to irresistible..l. 310:18
nothing to do with the l. but to
obey 262:4
not obey the l. too well 200:34
repeal of bad..l. 228:23
rules of the game..l of Nature 266:20
schoolmasters deliver us to l. 245:5
sweeter manners, purer l. 533:20
their l. approve 192:32
think the l. of God will be suspended 489:31
tho' not judges of l. 403:2
to have all L. chang'd 135:28
unequal l. unto a savage race 540:31
war has its l. 363:11
whether L. be right 569:11
your l., institutions, and your
false god 551:13
Lawyer: as a l. knows how 161:38
cheapest l.'s fee 107:31
for her the l. pleads 35:22
he leaned on a staggering l. 141:26
if l.'s hand is fee'd 214:19
L. killing a viper 151:10
l...no business with the justice
or injustice 275:32
what a l. tells me I may do 101:3
Lawyers: l. are met 215:6
let's kill all the l. 445:37
o'er l.' fingers 477:7
studious L. have their bowers 510:21
woe unto you, l.l 61:50
Lay: beside the ungather'd rice he l. 317:16
Brer Fox, he l. low 238:17
Cleric before, and L. behind 110:34
he fell, he l. down 46:50
help you with her l. 189:18
here I l. 439:20
hung their heads, and then l. by 446:18
I can't l. bricks 503:14
I'd l. me doun and dee 187:6
I never would l. down my arms 379:8
I will l. on for Tusculum 324:8
laid us as we l. at birth 16:22
l. aside every weight 69:18
l. hold on life 354:11
l. it on with a trowel 181:22
l. me, O! where 483:6
l. on, Macduff 461:14
l. that earth upon thy heart 295:5
l. them down in their dens 398:10
l. them straight 368:6
l. thou on for Rome 324:8
l. thy sheaf adown and come 253:21
let Rustum l. about him 205:19
like sepulchral statues l. 184:31
next day, there she l. 139:2
not where to l. his head 58:34
now I l. me down to sleep 8:18
rebellion l. in his way 440:27

Lay (cont.)
soft Llewellyn's l. 229:21
to a seductive l. 573:9
unpremeditated l. 417:1
warbling his Doric l. 343:6
where Cressid l. that night 465:17
yester-morn our army l. 23:19
your sweet responsive l. 168:14
Laying on of hands 391:15
Layman: poor l. I 502:2
Lays: constructing tribal l. 297:9
know wot l. afore us 176:28
she l. it on with a trowel 154:33
thinking l. lads underground 263:18
Lazy: l. finger of a maid 477:7
liftin' the l. ones on 229:15
looking l. at the sea 299:15
Lea: on fair Kirconnell l. 31:3
on yonder l., on yonder lea 107:24
slowly o'er the l. 229:28
standing on this pleasant l. 582:18
sun has left the l. 420:9
Lead: affections gently l. us on 581:25
all thy friends are lapp'd in l. 35:18
changyd into l. 583:26
down like l. 150:10
down like lumps of l. 249:15
if the blind l. the blind 59:39
I would l. thee 52:21
l., and I follow 530:7
l., kindly Light 364:10
l. me forth beside the waters 393:10
l. me, O Lord 402:10
l. on our days to age 451:35
l. the Surrey spring again 299:24
l. those that are with young 54:11
l. us, Heavenly Father, l. us 195:23
l. us not into temptation 58:4
let thy gost thee l. 136:20
little child shall l. them 53:18
little l. best fits a little float 245:19
people easy to l. 85:3
scald like molten l. 454:14
sure to l. him out of his way 278:23
to l. but one measure 418:19
to l. from joy to joy 582:3
to l. such dire attack 323:22
when we think we l. 119:12
whither wilt thou l. me? 432:6
who will l. me into the strong
city? 395:23
Leaden: if I use l. ones 40:27
lapwings feel the l. death 386:32
with l. foot time creeps 267:28
Leaden-eyed: l. despairs 287:27
pale, and l. 252:24
Leaden-stepping: lazy l. hours 351:31
Leader: in camps a l. sage 418:8
l. is fairest 15:16
Leaders: *Four-and-twenty* l. of
revolts 96:37
Leadeth: he l. me the quiet waters
by 421:1
Leading: Apollo comes l. his choir 15:16
l. up the golden year 529:29
l. wherever I choose 568:3
of light and l. in England 102:24
of light and l. in the country 182:30
Leads: l.—God knows where 116:21
l. me from my love 263:12
l. me to the Lamb 161:1
Leaf: fade as a l. 55:8
her silky l. 165:17
I believe a l. of grass 567:19
if I were a dead l. 496:10
in tiny l. 92:14
I were like the l. 524:28
last red l. 532:12
l., the bud, the flower 509:33
my days are in the yellow l. 118:26
no l. upon the forest bare 492:24
November's l. is red 418:1
right as an aspes l...quake 138:33
sear, the yellow l. 460:36
thin is the l. 522:14
through green l. and through
sere 359:3
wave, a l., a cloud 496:10
where the dead l. fell 286:3
with the l. still in October 37:15
Leafy: in the l. month of June 149:35
since summer first was l. 468:20

League: for many a l. the..Oxus 17:28(-18)
half a l., half a l. 528:13
keep a l. till death 475:27
l. but barely three 30:18
many a l...Ocean smiles 347:2
she hadna sail'd a l., a l., 30:18
Leagues: l. beyond those l. 411:8
long l. apart descried 147:6
Leah: this Rachel-and-L. is marriage 146:27
Leak: one l. will sink a ship 99:28
she sprang no fatal l. 102:11
Leal: land o' the l. 360:19, 20
Lean: his wife could eat no l. 367:10
lard their l. books 109:3
laws..l. on one another 102:34
l. abhorred monster 478:44
l. and flashy songs 342:29
l. and hungry look 448:26
l. and slipper'd pantaloon 427:21
l. and the ill favoured kine 45:17
l.,..anti-everythings 250:28
l. as much to the contrary 234:3
l. body and visage 212:16
l. down low in Linden Lea 35:13
l. unwash'd artificer 447:41
l. upon it lightly! 206:12
l. upon the thought 15:11
l. was so ruddy 225:10
my l. and low ability 484:17
on which if a man l. 48:33
she help'd him to l. 33:20
study had made him very l. 252:24
Leander: L., Mr. Ekenhead, and I 115:32
on Hero's heart L. lies 264:5
Leaned: he l. on a staggering
lawyer 141:26
l. her breast up-till a thorn 35:18
Leaning: l. across..the West 81:26
l. on Jesus' bosom 63:48
l. together 197:10
l. upon her beloved 52:22
Leans: he l. upon his hoe 329:19
how she l. her cheek 477:14
l., and hearkens after it 186:25
Leap: great l. in the dark 249:2
I'll l. up to my God 330:7
I shall l. over the wall 392:30
it were an easy l. 438:38
lame man l. up 54:3
l. in ourselves 452:5
l. thou, attire and all 425:12
look before you ere you l. 111:2
look ere thou l. 550:3
made a l. into the dark 85:9
sometimes l. from hiding-
places 582:10
though gay they run and l. 338:9
with a l. and a bound 152:5
Leaped: baby l. 232:3
I l. headlong into the sea 290:7
into the dangerous world I l. 76:8
knowledge of good and evil..l.
forth 352:8
Leaping: pulling in one's horse as
he is l. 237:22
so long as there is no l. 518:31
spak o' l. o'er a linn 105:14
Leaps: babe l. up 576:7
knowledge..not by l. 324:20
my heart l. up 577:25
wild cataract l. 538:14
Leap-year: twenty-nine in each l. 369:5
Lear: how pleasant to know Mr. L. 311:9
Lea-rig: meet thee on the l. 106:30
Learn: cannot l. men from books 182:41
craft so long to l. 138:22
diligent to l. 575:5
gladly wolde he l. 137:7
glad to l. of noble men 451:16
he'd l. how to live 91:39
he lived to l. 221:1
how I caught it..I am to l. 462:28
if men could l. from history 152:24
if they will l. any thing 67:3
I l. to pity tears 225:12
l. about women from me 298:3
l. all we lacked before 84:6
l. and propagate the best 19:12
l. from the Yellow an' Brown 298:5
l., nor account the pang 95:15

INDEX

Learn (cont.)
l. of me   59:10
l. of me to die   382:8
l. the hateful art..to forget   292:21
l. to labour and to wait   317:8
l. to write well, or not to write   193:28
neither..l. war any more   52:31
quick to l. and wise to know   104:20
read, mark, l.   389:23
see and l. the noble acts   328:1
so dull but she can l.   464:19
so old but she may l.   464:19
so much to l. so little   178:42
to l. and labour truly   391:9
we l. so little   169:16
we live and l.   381:3
wherefrom ye l. your song   81:18
where there is most desire to l.   352:14
Learned: all l., and all drunk   163:32
decent obscurity of a l. language   217:4
fair and l., and good   87:24
grew within this l. man   330:12
he was naturally l.   194:6
l., and conn'd by rote   451:24
l. aught else the least   342:28
l. his great language   93:3
l. in a lady's eyes   455:22
l. is happy nature to explore   383:29
l. Thy Grace and Glory   208:13
l. to love the two   228:5
l. without sense   143:22
less is l. there   272:36
loads of l. lumber   383:4
make the l. smile   382:28
much l. dust   163:10
never.. l. anything from history   240:23
of the opinion with the l.   155:3
proud that he has l. so much   163:50
that l. body wanted loyalty   548:20, 549:1
they will not be l.   397:4
things l. on earth   93:40
words of l. length   225:2
Learning: all that weight of l.   533:30
a' the l. I desire   105:24
cry both arts and l. down   404:18
enough of l. to misquote   117:12
fraught with all l.   225:27
grammar, and nonsense, and l.   226:2
hated not l. worse than toad   351:17
her religion so well with her l.   401:35
I'm l. 'ere in London   299:13
in l. rules   164:38
in the middle age of a state, l.   27:36
Jonson..higher in l.   212:18
knew all that ever l. writ   40:4
l., a mere hoard of gold   442:21
l. hath gained most by those books   212:15
l. is but an adjunct to ourself   455:21
l.'s triumph   278:34
l. that cobweb of the brain   110:35
l. will be cast into the mire   102:18
let..laws and l. die   329:10
little l.   382:22
love he bore to l.   225:1
men of polite l.   242:10
much l. doth make thee mad   65:23
of light, of liberty, and of l.   181:4
of such deep l.   510:15
picker-up of l.'s crumbs   91:19
renowned for l. and piety   229:13
sceptre, l., physic   430:1
Secretary of Nature and all l.   559:20
that loyal body wanted l.   548:20, 549:1
their l. is like bread in a besieged town   272:31
then l. is most excellent   209:19
this l., what a thing it is   479:2
those twins of l.   447:10
wear your l...in a private pocket   139:18
whence is thy l.?   215:21
Learnt: angling..can never be fully l.   559:8
forgotten nothing and l. nothing   195:1
l. nothing and forgotten nothing   526:17
plainest taught, and easiest l.   350:14
Lease: having so short a l.   488:20
l. of my true love   488:2
summer's l...all too short   486:18
Least: death..the l. of all evils   27:42
faithful in that which is l.   62:22

Least (cont.)
I am the l. of the apostles   67:5
not l. in love   450:7
unto one of the l. of these   60:34
very l. as feeling her care   253:36
what we l. expect   182:8
Leather: as ever trod upon neat's-l.   448:6
I'm sick o' wastin' l.   299:14
l. bottel   9:23
l. or prunella   384:7
on both sides, like a l. jerkin   481:23
Spanish or neats-l.   110:39
Leathern: flits by on l. wing   153:24
l. ears of stock-jobbers   162:20
l. girdle   57:29
my l. belt likewise   159:39
Leave: all to l. what..he won   190:15
bowsey short l. of your nymphs   526:23
by all ye l. or do   303:25
comrades, l. me here a little   534:13
deil be in my feet gin I l. ye   420:16
everlasting l. of an old..companion   217:3
for I must l. thee   10:21
gave sign for me to l. you   449:14
get l. of your dads   5:25
how I l. my country!   379:19
I l. my character behind me   500:37
I l. them where they are   567:24
intreat me not to l. thee   47:1
I pray thee l.   189:14
l. a child alone   96:2
l...all earth can take   493:27
l. her to heaven   432:18
l. him lying where he fell   23:24
l. his country as good   147:19
l. it buried in this vault   280:11
l. it to men's charitable speeches   28:15
l. me, l. me to repose   229:27
l. me, O Love   502:5
l. my little wooden hut for you   335:22
l. nothing of myself in me   165:31
l. off first   57:6
l. off Tobacco   307:8, 12
l., oh! l. the light of Hope   122:40
l. or drink it   298:15
l. the bottle on the chimley-piece   176:16
l. the evil   328:2
l. their job when they..choose   302:2
l. their little lives in air   386:32
l. the Lot of Kaikobad   205:19
l. the naked brain   284:23
l. then thy foolish ranges   552:2
l. the Saxon alone   300:7
l. the sick hearts   84:17
l. the Wise to talk   206:9
l. the word of God   64:33
l. this barren spot to me   122:8
l. to Heaven the measure   279:12
l. to Robert Browning   293:10
l. we now Thy servant   198:15
little nation l. to live   313:4
live in hearts we l.   122:15
love him, or l. him alone!   580:2
man l. his father   44:18
not l. my soul in hell   392:27
not..loth to l. this Paradise   349:29
often took l.   402:6
oh, never l. me!   6:2
sleep, why dost thou l. me?   155:35
smiles upon a second l.   431:24
they lack, I l.   195:13
they l. you, and you know them   94:21
to l. her far away behind   285:4
which thou must l. ere long   487:17
wilt thou l. me thus?   583:18
Leaven: l. of malice and wickedness   66:28, 389:35
little l. leaveneth the whole lump   66:27
not with the old l.   66:28
Leavening: you must tarry the l.   480:38
Leaves: as l. to a tree   289:28
as the l. grow on the tree   584:11
autumnal l. like light footfalls   496:2
brown skeletons of l.   150:9
burning of the l.   72:21
chaunting of the unquiet l.   586:8
close up these barren l.   581:16
crowding through the l.   17:12
crowned with calm l.   523:20
dazzling thro' the l.   534:4
Earth in new l. dressed   498:12

Leaves (cont.)
edged with grayish l.   236:19
famous harmony of l.   586:7
fond of handling the l.   500:16
green l. of thy labour   524:4
green l. whispering   571:9
in the green l.   575:13
its sweetest l. yet folded   117:2
laughing l.   522:2
l. break forth   267:11
l. dead are driven   496:4
l. have their time to fall   241:14
l. it as fast as they can   315:15
L. of Life keep falling   205:16
l. of the Judgment Book   527:11
l. of the tree were for..healing   72:7
l. them all about   295:21
l. the world to darkness   229:28
l. they are so green   32:14
l. they were crisped and ser   381:1
light shade for the l.   492:25
lisp of l.   521:30
lofty trees..barren of l.   486:15
long dead l.   334:6
long l. cover me   524:23
my dead thoughts..like withered l.   496:11
noiseless noise among the l.   286:26
no l., no birds   253:12
perished l. of Hope   410:24
pickt from the l. of any author   86:17
put l. round his head   176:2
roses rear their l.   118:23
shady l. of destiny   166:17
shatter your l.   342:10
shows his hoar l.   437:1
silent l. are still   118:8
snug in l. and grass   250:6
tender l. of hope   440:24
that lamentation of the l.   586:7
thick as autumnal l.   344:25
thou among the l.   287:25
through the velvet l. the wind   455:17
violets cover'd up in l.   287:31
what if my l. are falling?   496:11
what it l. behind   574:34
where l. the Rose of Yesterday?   205:18
whole deck put on its l.   208:16
wild l. that winds have taken   523:21
wintry l. nor vernal   523:24
with l. and flowers do cover   563:30
yellow l., or none, or few   487:16
Leavest: scarce l. here memorial   246:7
Leave-taking: world..not worth l.   426:12
Leaving: became him like the l. it   456:27
l...for his country's sake   205:3
l...her sins to her Saviour   252:22
l. mercy to heaven   204:25
Leavings: devil's l.   387:1, 520:48
Lebanon: annual wound in L.   344:32
his countenance is as L.   52:14
thy nose..as the tower of L.   52:19
to cedar'd L.   285:25
Leben: ein ruheloser Marsch war unser L.   415:25
ein unnütz L. ist ein früher Tod   224:1
wollt ihr ewig l.?   211:23
Lebens: grün des L. goldner Baum   223:19
Lecher in my sight   454:8
Lecherous: I am rough and l.   452:20
Lecto: acquiescimus l.   132:21
Lectoris: pro captu l...fata libelli   335:11
Lecture: read to thee a l., Love   185:30
Lectures: I do not give l.   567:21
l. in her night-dress   253:29
Mrs. Caudle's Curtain L.   269:9
Led: Ben Adhem's name l.   265:18
he l. them forth   398:15
l. her up the stair   297:19
l. me to him, blindfold   296:6
l. my ragamuffins   440:34
l. the way   224:21
most l.   119:12
Prince..l. them on   122:3
that Scotland l. in luve and le   583:26
thee gentle Spenser fondly l.   309:10
they l.—a kind of   401:29
Leda: as L., was the mother of Helen of Troy   374:11
for love of L.   510:20
L., the beloved of Jupiter   309:12
L. was..as white as he   510:20

Ledge: over a l. of granite 146:17
Ledlow: Farmer L. late at plough 236:8
Lee: beautiful Annabel L. 380:9
  dead of joy, James L. 92:29
  swimming down along the L. 510:20
  waters of the River L. 402:21
  when 'tis settled on the l. 111:24
Leek: by this l. 445:9
Leeks: garleek, oynons, and eek l. 137:20
Leer: assent with civil l. 385:29
Lees: drink life to the l. 540:32
  his skill runs on the l. 247:18
  mere l. is left this vault 458:24
  wines on the l. 53:31
Leeze me on drink! 106:12
Left: all l. behind on the beach 128:5
  better to be l. 155:40
  girl I l. behind me 10:13
  his l. hand is under my head 51:45
  in her l. hand riches 49:40
  l. a lot of little things 294:18
  l. his pretty boy 232:3
  l. not even Lancelot brave 531:21
  l. our country for our country's good 36:20
  l. the room with silent dignity 233:10
  l. thy first love 70:29
  let not thy l. hand know 58:2
  let them be l. 254:30
  moon on my l. 41:20
  not l. to Spain 539:19
  now, alas! she's l. me 572:4
  one..taken, and the other l. 60:27
  riches l. 518:1
  Sun came up upon the l. 148:21
  that we l., we lost 10:5
  thou hast l. behind powers 582:4
  use..but of my l. hand 352:19
  we are l., or shall be l., alone 578:4
  we, we only, are l. 17:18
  when't had l. me far away 333:1
  where l. you Chrononhoton-thologos? 125:12
  you l. off before you began 155:29
Left-hand: into a l. shoe 131:25
Leg: can honour set-to a l.? 440:30
  could stand upon one l. 177:19
  decreasing l. 441:19
  he has a l. 337:20
  here I leave my second l. 252:30
  l. of mutton with the usual trimmings 179:19
  literary man—with a wooden l. 178:2
  lost my l., by God! 564:8
  my Julia's dainty l. 246:16
  our steed the l. 429:3
  shape of his l. 482:34
  what l...into your breeches first 271:13
  which l. goes after which? 166:23
  you make a l. 475:11
Legacy: as a rich l. 450:24
Legalized: we have l. confiscation 180:39
Lege: numerisque..l. solutus tolle l. 260:18
   21:21
Legem: iudicium parium..vel per l. terrae 327:9
  necessitas dat l. 526:5
  necessitas non habet l. 526:6
Legend: l. of an epic hour 141:16
  L. of Good Women 529:6
Legends: whence these l. and traditions? 317:19
Legens: aut l., aut scribens 291:25
Leges: l. sine moribus vanae 260:11
  silent enim l. inter arma 145:19
Leggemmo: non vi l. avante 168:23
Legible: whose thoughts are l. 412:18
Legion: l. of the lost ones 296:26
  L. that never was 'listed 299:1
  my name is L. 60:57
  with a l. of cooks 117:46
Legion of Honour: cross of the L. ..few escape 550:28
Legiones: Vare, l. redde 120:7
Legions: ere yet we loose the l. 297:8
  give me back my l. 120:7
  she let the l. thunder past 17:8
Legislation: would give them.. much l. 143:31
Legislative power..nominated by the executive 217:6
Legislator: people is the rue l. 102:35

Legislators: unacknowledged l. 499:10
Legislature: sentiments..no l. can manufacture 28:21
Legitimate warfare 363:11
Legs: all l. and wings 34:15
  brought me to my last l. 192:19
  cannon-ball took off his l. 252:29
  delighteth..in any man's l. 400:22
  ever recuvver the use of his l. 177:9
  fold his l. and have out his talk 273:29
  his head with his l. 45:46
  his l. are as pillars of marble 52:14
  his l. bestrid the ocean 426:1
  his l. have grown too long 311:14
  his l. have grown too short 311:14
  his l...hewn in two 30:14
  if you could see my l. 175:17
  l. without the man 163:38
  lie between maids' l. 435:4
  my 'erse's l., as they canters 537:6
  never have stood upon his l. 174:11
  poor Wat..on his hinder l. 488:28
  short ears, straight l. 488:27
  slimy things did crawl with l. 149:6
  taste your l. 483:24
  trunkless l. of stone 496:13
  upon one pair of English l. 444:4
  walk under his huge l. 448:22
  when his l. were smitten off 491:11
Legunt: laudant illa sed ista l. 331:25
Leicester Square: farewell L. 571:1
Leiden oder triumphiren 223:23
Leipsic: Faliero my L. 116:34
  type they get up well at L. 89:30
Leisure: add to these retired L. 341:11
  at l. marry'd 155:32
  detest at l. 116:44
  increased means and increased l. 181:3
  John Wesley..never at l. 273:29
  l. answers l. 462:26
  l. to be good 230:17
  no blessed l. for love 253:26
  polish it at l. 194:3
  repent at l. 155:32
  slander any moment's l. 431:29
  what l. to grow wise? 17:4
  wisdom..by opportunity of l. 57:11
Leman: Lake L. woos me 113:45
Lemon: in the squeezing of a l. 227:5
  take a suck at the l. 33:22
  that you can squeeze out of a l. 216:6
Lemonade: black eyes and l. 356:9
  essayed to drink l. 11:1
Lend: few l. (but fools) 549:25
  l. l. it instantly 245:12
  I'll l. you something 484:17
  l. less than thou owest 452:25
  l. me your ears 450:17
  l. us Thine aid! 240:15
  men who l. 306:19
  to spend, and to l. 82:27
Lender: neither a borrower, nor a l. 431:25
Lenders: thy pen from l.' books 453:20
Lendeth: good man..l. 398:26
Lends: he l. out money gratis 463:17
  something to love he l. us 533:34
  three things I never l. 518:29
Length: all l. is torture 425:22
  at full l. people's wooings 115:39
  at l. I realize 128:15
  beauty and l. of days 522:7
  distance and l. 262:5
  drags its dreary l. 173:22
  fires the l. of Ophiucus 346:6
  folly's at full l. 80:1, 139:5
  his listless l. 230:12
  in l. of days understanding 48:58
  l. and breadth enough 31:22
  l., breadth and highth..are lost 346:10
  l. of burning sand 165:17
  l. of days is in her right hand 49:40
  l. without breadth 202:7
Lengthen: to l. our days 357:1
Lengths: carry nature l. unknown before 162:30
Lenore: sorrow for the lost L. 380:23
Lent out my heart with usury 307:5
Lente: festina l. 517:21
  l., l., currite noctis equi 330:7
Lenten entertainment 433:17

Leoni: vulpes aegroto cauta l. 256:20
Leopard: l. his spots 55:18
  l. shall lie down with the kid 53:18
Leopold: dedicate your volumes to Prince L. 145:30
Leper once he lost 344:33
Leporum: medio de fonte l. 321:2
Leprosy: her skin was white as l. 149:13
Lesbia: L. hath a beaming eye 356:24
  L. nostra, L. illa, illa L. 133:5
  sweetest L. let us live 123:19
Lesbian: down..to the L. shore 342:19
Lesley: saw ye bonnie L.? 104:25
Less: beautifully l. 401:32
  care l., eyes..to miss 186:25
  condemns a l. delinquent 111:26
  for nothing l. than thee 184:12
  greater glory dim the l. 465:21
  greater prey upon the l. 231:26
  infinitely l. 165:34
  in the l. foul profanation 461:32
  l. is learned there 272:36
  l. Sav'narola he 39:22
  l. than 'kin' 34:31
  l. than kind 430:26
  l. than that no man shall have 409:2
  l. than the dust..even l. am I 254:16
  little l. 90:9
  make l. thy body hence 442:38
  much l. when he's dead 175:36
  nicely-calculated l. or more 577:9
  nor be I any l. of them 586:14
  not l. nor more 411:23
  pleased with l. than Cleopatra 191:17
  rather than be l. 345:15
  small Latin, and l. Greek 281:13
  you mean you can't take l. 129:9
Lessen: because they l. from day to day 129:21
Lesser: or l. than my name 475:9
  some l. god..made the world 531:27
  woman is the l. man 534:32
Lesson: human birth, the l. 338:4
  Imperial l. 298:23
  l. you should heed 248:8
  love is the l. 509:5
  own..the l. just 33:12
  that learnt her l. here 84:3
Lessons: called l...because they lessen 129:21
  of two such l., why forget 116:2
Lest: l. they forgot 141:31
  l. we forget 300:24
  l. we should be by and by 3:11
Let: bind me not, and l. me go 185:27
  head..to be l. unfurnished 110:14
  here's a church!..l.'s go in! 175:27
  I will not l. thee go 45:10
  l. balls like the Edinburgh Review 240:7
  l. go, Sir! Down, Sir! 41:4
  l. go! you are hurtig be! 304:18
  l. him go 533:18
  l. in the great Creator 348:28
  l. it be as it may 183:17
  l. it take them 205:20
  l.'s all go down the Strand 131:34
  l. there be light 44:2
  l. us pass on! 100:15
  neither will I l. Israel go 45:40
  sore l. and hindered 389:25
  they will not l. you have it 239:25
  written who might have l. it alone 275:34
  yammered, 'L. me in' 302:31
Leth: crimson'd in thy l. 450:9
Lethargy: kind of l. 441:14
Lethe: go not to L. 287:19
  rots itself..on L. wharf 432:12
  tedious shores of L. 306:7
  'tis L.'s gloom 122:2
Lethean: drunken of things L. 525:8
  labour's dull, L. spring 16:5
Lets: him that l. me 432:4
Letter: better..by speech than by l. 26:40
  carry a l. to my love 30:20
  give 'im a l. 301:13
  good face a l. 2:14
  how large a l. I have written 67:49
  l. from his wife 128:15
  l. killeth 67:22

Letter (cont.)
name, and not the l. — 11:6
not of the l. — 67:22
one l. of Richardson's — 272:12
preferment goes by l. — 469:24
runs with a l. — 301:13
thou unnecessary l.! — 452:33
till you write your l. — 186:18
written a braid l. — 31:24
yourself read in the bitter l. — 469:44
Lettered: lockèd, l., braw brass collar — 108:18
Lettering: stript of its l. and gilding — 211:21
Letters: all your kind and beloved l. — 208:28
Heav'n first taught l. — 382:2
I copied all the l. — 221:16
I pray you, in your l. — 474:2
l. Cadmus gave — 116:2
l. for a spy — 301:18
l. four do form his name — 151:20
l...free and easy as one's discourse — 370:18
l. from God — 567:24
l.—I had l.—I am persecuted with l. — 156:2
l., soft interpreters of love — 401:31
like women's l.; all..in the postscript — 239:10
no arts; no l.; no society — 248:21
no Manual, no l. — 119:32
nought the l.' space — 138:40
our future masters to learn their l. — 499:20
pause awhile from l. — 279:4
pin up your hair with all your l. — 156:3
Republic of L. — 226:21
Letter-writing: great art o' l. — 179:7
Lettest thou thy servant depart — 61:20
Letting in the Latchfords — 518:23
Levee from a couch in..confusion — 156:9
Level: l. now with men — 425:29
l. of every day's..need — 88:24
meander l. with its fount — 325:12
meander l. with their fount — 355:17
so sways she l. — 483:3
Levelled: thy long l. rule — 340:18
Levellers: your l. wish to level down — 271:12
Leven: lies across the lily l. — 32:9
Levi: jump, as Mr. L. did — 34:25
Leviathan: draw out l. with an hook — 49:29
L., hugest of living creatures that L. — 348:26 / 398:11
Levin: as to the burning l. — 418:2
Levite: lean L. went to sleep — 387:24
Levity: little judicious l. — 515:11
Levy: malice domestic, foreign l. — 459:4
Lewd: certain l. fellows — 64:56
Lancelot wanderingly l.? — 530:24
Lex: salus populi suprema l. — 422:8
Lexicographer: l...a harmless drudge — 270:27
wake a l. — 277:23
Lexicography: not yet so lost in l. — 277:21
Lexicon: in the l. of youth — 322:12
two men wrote a l. — 11:7
Liar: doubt truth to be a l. — 432:42
every man a l. — 65:36
l., and a fluent l. therewith — 300:14
l., and the father of it — 63:31
like a l. gone to burning hell — 473:20
only answered, 'Little l.!' — 41:12
picturesque l. — 550:22
though a thief, a l., and a murderer — 121:17
thou l. of the first magnitude — 155:9
Liars: all men are l. — 399:7
fears may be l. — 147:8
l. ought to have good memories — 501:13
l. we can never trust — 561:23
our best conceits..greatest l. — 189:5
Libanus: cedars of l. — 398:9
Libel in a frown — 521:9
Libelli: pro captu lectoris..fata l. — 335:11
quidquid agunt homines..farrago l. — 282:25
Libellum: cui dono..novum l. — 132:9
Libens: tecum obeam l. — 260:4

Liber: aliter non fit..l. — 331:23
Libera Chiesa in libero Stato — 134:3
Liberal: either a little L. — 219:6
fly-blown phylacteries of the L. Party — 409:12
l. deviseth l. things — 53:44
l. education — 242:10
l. of another man's — 27:7
panted for a l. profession — 154:14
that l. obedience — 101:13
to love her is a l. education — 511:25
watchword of the great L. party — 82:18
Liberally: giveth to all men l. — 69:27
Liberal-minded: booksellers..l. men — 270:30
Liberator: 'Europe's L.' — 116:27
Liberavi animam meam — 43:17
Liberis: pro patria, pro l. — 415:3
Libertas: Imperium et L. — 181:14
l. et natale solum — 521:10
Liberté: établissions notre vraie l. — 354:23
L.! Égalité! Fraternité! — 12:16
l.! que de crimes..en ton nom! — 408:15
Liberticide: slave, and the l. — 491:15
Liberties: give up their l...under some delusion — 101:16
more l. than he can really take — 268:7
Libertine: charter'd l. — 443:7
puffed and reckless l. — 431:23
Liberty: abstract l...not to be found — 100:28
among a people..corrupt, l. cannot..exist — 103:24
brightest in dungeons, L.! — 114:33
common l. of earth and air — 511:10
condition upon which God hath given l. — 167:26
dead to all the feelings of l. — 379:3
delight with l. — 510:17
eldest Child of L. — 582:6
first garden of L.'s tree — 123:6
give me l., or give me death! — 242:18
he that commands the sea is at great l. — 27:26
I must have l. withal — 427:17
in doubtful things, l. — 36:25
interfering with the l. of action — 338:25
it is for our l. — 379:15
let there be light! said L. — 493:24
l. connected with order — 100:13
l...doing what one desires — 338:31
l...don't agree with niggers — 319:19
l. means responsibility — 490:30
l...must be limited — 103:22
l. of the individual..limited — 338:29
l. of the press — 282:16
l. plucks justice by the nose — 461:18
l.'s a glorious feast — 106:24
l.'s in every blow — 107:33
l. still more — 93:31
l. to know, to utter, and to argue — 352:16
l.! what crimes..in thy name — 408:15
life, and l., and the pursuit of happiness — 268:19
life, l., and the pursuit of happiness — 11:11
loudest yelps for l. — 278:26
love of l. is the love of others — 239:23
loving-jealous of his l. — 477:28
manly, moral, regulated l. — 102:3
mansion-house of l. — 352:13
Milton wrote..at l. when of Devils — 77:7
mountain nymph, sweet L. — 341:30
my dear l., shall I leave thee? — 156:12
new nation, conceived in l. — 314:12
no such l. — 319:4
of light, of l., and of learning — 181:4
on Naples and on l. — 140:19
pardon something to the spirit of l. — 100:25
poverty..certainly destroys l. — 275:5
proclaim l. to the captives — 55:3
rules of ancient l. — 351:18
spirit of divinest L. — 151:21
steps of virgin l. — 580:20
such refreshing airs of l. — 102:38
sweet land of l. — 504:10
symptom of constitutional l. — 217:10
that little is achieved through L. — 97:22

Liberty (cont.)
their L...consists in..the Government of those Laws — 135:28
too much l. — 578:7
to seek power and to lose l. — 26:23
thy chosen music, L. — 581:10
Transatlantic l. — 122:13
tree of l...refreshed..with..blood — 268:23
truly I desire their L. — 135:30
utmost bound of civil l. — 352:4
vanguard of L. — 577:8
victory..fatal to l. — 351:16
when they cry L. — 351:19
whoever gives, takes l. — 185:21
wicked woman l. to gad — 57:2
Liberty Hall: this is L. — 227:8
Libraries: books out of circulating l. — 413:7
how much..on our l. — 413:5
Library: circulating l...tree of diabolical knowledge — 500:16
furnish'd me from mine own l. — 479:23
my l. was dukedom large enough — 479:22
no gentleman's l...without — 306:26
shut not thy..l. against S.T.C. — 306:24
take choice of all my l. — 480:34
turn over half a l. — 272:28
Libras: quot l. in duce summo invenies? — 283:20
Libre: né l., et partout il est dans les fers — 412:2
Libris: nunc veterum l., nunc somno — 261:25
Libro: il l. e chi lo scrisse — 168:23
Librorum: sit bona l. — 257:11
Libya: parts of L. about Cyrene — 64:26
Licence: apothecary who has paid a l. — 505:28
L. they mean — 351:19
rest love not freedom, but l. — 353:2
universal l. to be good — 148:11
Licensed: by the state l. — 73:28(-74)
Licensing: by l...to misdoubt her — 352:17
Licentious: all l. passages..decent obscurity — 217:4
l. idioms, and irregular combinations — 278:13
rapacious and l. soldiery — 101:20
Licentiousness: uncontrouled l. of a brutal..soldiery — 201:28
Licht: mehr L.! — 224:7
Lick: cannot l. his own fingers — 478:32
his enemies shall l. the dust — 396:15
l. it into form — 109:5
l. the bloomin' boots — 297:1
Licks: pride that l. the dust — 385:34
Lid: lifting up the l. of a white eye — 335:28
upon his pent-house l. — 450:11
Liddell: L. and Scott — 11:7
this is Mrs. L. — 511:6
Liddesdale: Eskdale and L. — 420:8
Lidless eyes in Hell — 411:12
Lids: drops his blue-fringèd l. — 151:19
eyes, with l. to them — 482:21
l. of Juno's eyes — 485:26
they lift their heavy l. — 374:13
with eternal l. apart — 288:17
Lie: after all, what is a l.? — 116:32
country folks would l. — 428:31
dare not l. — 535:43
dost thou l. so low? — 450:2
fain wald l. down — 31:10
give the world the l. — 405:7
God's own name upon a l. — 162:23
happy low, l. down! — 442:3
he loves to l. a-basking — 221:36
he makes me down to l. — 421:11
here let her l.! — 192:18
here l. I, Martin Elginbrodde — 326:19
how still we see thee l. — 84:24
I cannot tell a l. — 560:28
if a l. may do thee grace — 441:5
if I tell thee a l. — 439:20
I l...among the children of men — 395:18
I l. easy, I l. as lads would choose — 263:7
in a cowslip's bell I l. — 480:14
in the street l. as they fell — 411:13
isn't told a l. — 301:18
launched..at the head of a l. — 91:34
leads you to believe a l. — 74:12
leopard shall l. down with the kid — 53:18

Lie (cont.)

let me l. 516:15
l. all night betwixt my breasts 51:42
l. between maids' legs 435:4
l. by an emperor's side 472:26
l. circumstantial..l. direct 428:37
l. down again 47:5
l. down, and stray no further 425:22
l. down for an aeon or two 303:19
l. down like a tired child 498:25
l. in the Soul is a true l. 282:12
l. in wait for wealth 575:9
l. long, high snowdrifts 263:13
l. reclined on the hills 535:19
l. shall rot 375:18
l. still and slumber 562:1
l. till seven 145:31
l. that flatters 162:16
l. upon the wings of night 478:19
l. which is all a l. may be met 529:32
loveth and maketh a l. 72:9
mixture of a l...add pleasure 27:30
my love and I would l. 262:21(-263)
nature admits no l. 126:38
nicer to l. in bed 310:15
no change though you l. under 263:5
not a man, that he should l. 46:19
not a stone tell where I l. 386:27
nothing can need a l. 243:27
not the l. that passeth through 27:31
saying, L. with me 45:16
sent to l. abroad 583:15
something given to l. 426:7
sorer than to l. for need 429:35
Spenser, l. a thought more nigh 36:21
that countenance cannot l. 412:18
they l. beside their nectar 535:19
though it be a foul great l. 29:16
to l. in cold obstruction 462:9
twilights where his chosen l. 96:31
under Dust to l. 206:8
when I l. where shades 171:7
when they l. about our feet 573:17
where'er she l. 166:17
wholly believing a l. 297:17
who loves to l. with me 427:7
you l.—under a mistake 520:7
you must l. upon the daisies 220:26
you told a l., an odious damned l. 473:24
Liebe: was ist denn L.? 234:17
Lied: being l. about 297:10
but it l. 41:25
say they have l. 584:16
to cloak them, l. 300:18
Liege of all loiterers 455:8
Lien among the pots 396:7
Lies: all the l. you can invent 73:24
believing their own l. 14:5
cruellest l...told in silence 514:33
don't deal in l. 297:10
expos'd he l. 191:7
far hence he l. 17:9
fiend that l. like truth 461:5
great l. about his wooden horse 208:15
great Prince in prison l. 185:2
he l. in his rights of a man 89:13
he l. now in the little valley 89:24
here he l. where he longed 516:15
here l. bold Robin Hood 31:22
history is a pack of l. 517:8
I say he l., and l., and l. 475:15
l. down to pleasant dreams 98:3
l. to hide it, makes it two 561:23
l. worse 191:34
life with its way before us l. 354:11
lifts the head, and l. 385:2
lone and alone she l. 171:24
Matilda told such Dreadful L. 41:9
naebody kens that he l. there 32:15
now l. he there 450:23
open truth to cover l. 154:36
Passion speechless l. 189:20
Rest is L. 206:9
so many l. I never heard 377:13
spread these l. 410:20
tell pale-hearted fear it l. 460:7
there l. gude Sir Patrick Spens 32:2
these l. are like the father 439:23
this poet l. 486:16
though I know she l. 488:16
tills the field and l. beneath 540:20

Lies (cont.)

uneasy l. the head 442:3
where Helen l. 31:3
which way the head l. 405:15
who l. beneath your spell? 254:14
Lieu: qu'en un l...un seul fait 78:6
Lieutenant..saved before the ancient 471:14
Lieutenant-Colonel to the Earl of Mar 381:9
Life: adds..to this Fragment of L. 512:32
after l.'s fitful fever 459:4
all human l. is there 268:16
all is lost, except a little l. 118:24
all l. death does end 255:1
all my l. seemed meant for 92:31
all that a man hath..for his l. 48:41
all the blessings of this l. 389:19
all the courses of my l. 439:41
angel of this l. 95:31
anythin' for a quiet l. 179:28
asked l...thou gavest..long l. 392:39
author both of l. and light 281:23
awakened from the dream of l. 492:6
aware of his l.'s flow 15:6
bankrupt of l. 190:14
before L.'s Liquor..be dry 205:6
before my l. has found 536:1
before the fire of l. 308:25
bitterness of l. 128:15
bloodthirsty clinging to l. 19:9
bloody house of l. 447:42
books..contain a potency of l. 352:5
book..teach us to enjoy l., or to endure it 277:18
breath, smiles, tears of all my l. 88:24
brevity of our l. 414:21
brief is l. but love is long 538:21
brief l. is here our portion 361:12
busy scenes of crowded l. 279:2
but one l. and one death 89:26
by l.'s unresting sea 251:15
by which their L. and..Goods ..most their own 135:28
calamity of so long l. 434:4
calm's not l.'s crown 19:6
certain, that L. flies 206:9
chances of this mortal l. 390:50
cling with l. to the maid 199:13
C Major of this l. 89:12
concerns of ordinary l. 575:10
conduct..three-fourths of l. 20:10, 22
criticism of l. 19:22
crushing out l. 254:15
days of the years of my l. 45:25
dearer far than light and l. 578:10
death of each day's l. 458:11
deep almost as l. 576:16
defeat my l. 473:3
departed this l. in thy faith 390:30
depends poor Polly's l. 214:21
desert where no l. is found 253:28
disease of member l. 18:14
doors to let out l. 37:20, 335:2
dost thou love l.? 211:15
dreamed that l. was Beauty 7:18, 254:2
drink l. to the lees 540:32
ebbs out l.'s little day 322:1
either death or l...the sweeter 462:3
either live or bear no l. 472:34
envy and wrath shorten the l. 57:5
except my l. 433:7
expatiates in a l. to come 383:11
facts alone are wanted in l. 175:28
feels its l. in every limb 582:11
fellowship is l. 359:19
following l. through creatures you dissect 384:22
for curiosity and not for l. 200:15
for l. and joy 568:9
for the l. to come, I sleep 485:19
found that l. was Duty 7:18, 254:2
found your l. distasteful? 93:25
fount of fiery l. 16:21
from death to l...yet recover 189:20
from death unto l. 63:17
from L.'s fresh crown 38:28
from the dregs of l. 191:34
gates of new l. 96:25
gave the l., and bid thee feed 76:10
gave what l. requir'd 224:14

Life (cont.)

giveth his l. for the sheep 63:37
give me l. 440:35
give new views to l. 164:34
give thee a crown of l. 70:30
give to me the l. I love 515:27
glory of this l. 480:22
God of l., and poesy 114 23
growth is the only evidence of l. 363:15
hath man no second l.? 15:4
here find l. in death 151:17
her l. serene 539:12
he studied from the l. 14:24
he that findeth his l. 59:3
hills where his l. rose 15:6
his former naughty l. 390:2
his l. in so long tendance 510:16
his l. is a watch 522:7
his l. was gentle 452:9
his l...was in the right 158:5
his unkindness may defeat my l. 473:3
holdeth our soul in l. 396:1
how good is man's l. 96:21
how short is the longest l. 290:30
I bear a charmed l. 461:10
idea of her l. 469:6
I fetch my l. and being 469:37
if l. did ride upon a dial 440:32
if l. was bitter to thee, pardon 522:13
I gave my l. for freedom 202:18
in balance with this l. 584:21
in l. did harbour give 280:11
in l., in death, O Lord 322:2
in London all that l. can afford 273:23
in newness of l. 65:44
in our l. alone..Nature 151:4
intend to lead a new l. 390:34
in their lives fought for l. 509:1
in the midst of l. 391:42
in the time of this mortal l. 389:22
is l. a boon? 222:25
is L. worth living? 403:17
is not the l. more than meat? 58:11
isn't your life extremely flat 222:1
it may be l., but ain't it slow? 242:28
jump the l. to come 457:7
keep in a little l. 441:1
known no day in all my l. 81:6
knows what l. and death is 135:19
large as l., and twice as natural 131:18
last of l. 95:13
later l. renew 509:7
laws of l. 413:21
lay down his l. for his friends 63:57
lay hold on eternal l. 68:53
lay hold on l. 354:11
lead a holy Christian l. 316:36
Leaves of L. keep falling 205:16
let me so read thy l. 165:31
L., a Fury slinging flame 532:27
l. and all shall cease 308:10
L., and Death, and that For Ever 293:7
l. and light be thine for ever! 94:30
l., and splendour, and joy 102:11
l., being weary 448:36
l. can little more supply 383:7
L., Death, Miracles 95:28
l. for a blow 536:16
l. for l. 45:54
l. from the dead 355:9
l. has death for neighbour 523:19
l. has pass'd with me but roughly 160:25
l. heroic 351:5
l. is a coquetry of Death 543:20
l. is a jest 215:20
l. is a joke that's just begun 219:28
l. is all a variorum 106:25
l. is an incurable disease 158:21
l. is as tedious 447:35
l. is but a day 288:10
l. is but an empty dream 317:5
l...is but the shadow of death 85:16
l. is fading fast away 406:8
l. is good 241:26
l. is made up of sobs 242:12
l. is mostly froth and bubble 227:34
l. is never the same again 326:20
l. is one long..getting tired 111:32
l. is our cry 84:3

INDEX

Life (*cont.*)

L. is perfected by Death   89:4
l. is real! l. is earnest!   317:5
l. is the desert, l. the solitude   587:14
l. is thorny   150:26
l. is very sweet, brother   78:24
l. just a stuff   89:27
l. lay waiting, so sweet   334:5
l., liberty, and the pursuit of happiness   11:11
l...liberty, and the pursuit of happiness   268:19
l., like a dome of..glass   492:15
l. may change   493:23
l. of doubt diversified   89:32
l. offers—to denyl   236:37
L. of Johnson..very great work   325:26
L. of L.!   497:9
l. of man..a heroic poem   125:35
l. of man less than a span   28:16
l. of man, solitary, poor   248:21
l. of poor Jack   173:7
l. of the historian must be short   217:3
l. on the ocean wave   415:11
l. on the whole is far from gay   312:11
l. piled on l.   540:32(–541)
l. protracted is protracted woe   279:7
l. radically wretched   277:42
L.'s a single pilgrim   38:24
l.'s business..the..choice   96:14
l.'s but a span   471:9
l.'s but a walking shadow   461:4
l.'s common way   577:15
l.'s enchanted cup   113:23
l.'s journey just begun   160:27
L.'s Little Ironies   237:4
l. so fast doth fly   169:16
l. so short, the craft so long   138:22, 248:13
l.'s race well run   373:10
l.'s too short for chess   120:12
l. succeed in that it seems to fail   95:16
l.'s uncertain voyage   480:31
l.'s wild restless sea   3:19
l., that dares send   166:19
l.—that in me has rest   83:8
l. that leads melodious days   532:24
l. that never knows harness   422:22
L., the shadow of death   522:5
l. time's fool   440:37
l. to him would be death to me   290:26
l. treads on l.   89:3
l. unto the bitter in soul   48:47
l. was but a flower   428:32
l. we have loved   359:3
l. went-a-maying   152:20
l.! we've been long together   33:14
l., with all it yields   90:42
l. with its way   354:11
l. without it..not worth our taking   412:11
l. without theory   181:44
l. would be very dull without them   570:2
light of a whole l. dies   79:5
live a l. half dead   350:24
live thou thy l.   81:5
long l. better than figs   423:19
looking on his l.   424:1
Lord and giver of l.   390:20
loseth his l. for my sake   59:3
made l. a heaven on earth   292:5
mad from l.'s history   252:20
magazine of l. and comfort   243:19
make a l. of jealousy   471:34
man of l. upright   123:23
man's l...allegory   290:17
man's l. is cheap as beast's   452:41
many-colour'd l.   278:34
married to a single l.   165:32
men deal with l. as children   160:15
mine honour is my l.   474:10
most beautiful adventure in l.   212:1
most glorious Lord of l.   509:4
most loathèd worldly l.   462:10
mounts..hardly, to eternal l.   16:13
my l. did..smack sweet   93:25
my l. is one demd...grind   177:25
my l. is preserved   45:11
my l. is run his compass   451:39
my l., my fate   536:15

Life (*cont.*)

my l. upon her faith!   470:12
my l. with the blood-thirsty   393:19
my lines and l. are free   244:9
my soul, my l., my all   562:19
my way of l. is fall'n into the sear   460:36
neither death, nor l., nor angels   65:58
nobody can write the l. of a man, but those who   272:7
no l. but the sea-wind's   523:14
no l. that breathes   540:27
no, no, no l.!   454:26
no sound..which tells of L.   152:2
nothing in his l. became him   456:27
not in thy body is thy l.   410:32
not one l. shall be destroy'd   532:32
not perish, but have everlasting l.   63:9
not so much l.   286:3
O Death in L.   538:19
of man's l. a thing apart   115:25
of mortal l. the leaf, the bud   509:33
O l., no l.   305:14
O lover of my l.   96:9
one crowded hour of glorious l.   357:22
one l. for each to give   296:20
on the tree of l...sat   347:3
on this l.'s rough sea   135:19
our l., exempt from public haunt   426:30
our l. is closed, our l. begins   566:25
our little l. is rounded with a sleep   480:8
our love is frail as is our l.   202:1
out of the book of l.   70:32, 72:12
O world! O life! O time!   494:18
painful escapes of fitful l.   80:17
passing on the prisoner's l.   461:23
passion and the l.   151:3
pay glad l.'s arrears   95:11
people say that l. is the thing   504:16
plants fruits of l. and beauty   74:25
poorest l...hath a l. to live   405:6
present l. of men   38:31
progress is the law of l.   94:23
railing at l.   143:8
ravin up thine own l.'s means   458:29
reason is the l. of the law   148:4
reason thus with l.   462:3
receive the crown of l.   69:28
reck'd not of the l. he lost   114:19
red l. might stream again   287:3
regardeth the l. of his beast   50:2
require the l. of man   44:42
rest of his dull l.   37:12
resurrection, and the l.   63:40
righteous, and sober l.   388:12
Roman's l.   323:27
saw l. steadily   16:2
sea of L. and Agony   495:5
seas of l., like wine   548:18
see into the l. of things   581:25
sequester'd vale of l.   230:7
sequester'd vale of rural l.   387:8
set before you l. and death   46:30
set my l. at a pin's fee   432:2
set my l. on any chance   458:36(–459)
set my l. upon a cast   476:43
Shakespeare led a l. of allegory   290:18
shamed l. a hateful   462:9
shew me the path of l.   392:27
simple l. that Nature yields   165:18
since l. first was   235:21
slits the thin-spun l.   342:20
so careless of the single l.   532:35
sole Lord of l. and death   166:11
so was it when my l. began   577:25
spare all I have, and take my l.   203:18
spend my l. in driving briskly   273:21
spirit giveth l.   67:22
spirit lack all l. behind   96:26
stir as l. were in't   461:3
stole thence the l. o' the building   458:22
struggling for l. in the water   270:18
stuff l. is made of   211:15
sublime of human l.   104:23
suburb of the l. elysian   317:12
such is L.   175:23, 176:22
Sundays of man's l.   245:8
sunset of l.   122:22
sweat under a weary l.   434:4

Life (*cont.*)

take away my l. to make you King   136:10
take honour..my l. is done   474:10
that l. may be a pleasant road   402:9
that new l.   202:23
their l. was death   411:6
therefore choose l.   46:30
there's the l. for a man like me.. for ever   515:27
this gives l. to thee   486:18
this is alone L., Joy   497:17
this *is* l.   549:7
this knot intrinsicate of l.   426:13
this l. at best is but an inn   264:21
this L. flies   206:26
this l. is all chequer'd   356:34
this l. is most jolly   427:22
this l.'s first native source   510:21
this l.'s five windows   74:12
this long disease, my l.   385:26
those who live call L.   497:11, 498:19
thou art my l., my love, my heart   247:4
though l. be long and dreary   202:25
thought's the slave of l.   440:37
throughout the l. the shame   233:3
thy God, thy l., thy cure   552:2
thy l. hath had some..honour   452:6
tie my l. within this band   244:20
till l. can charm no more   153:22
till l. forget   524:14
till your l. has illustrated it   290:19
time of l. is short   440:32
tired of London...of l.   273:23
to a l. beyond l.   352:7
to measure l. learn thou   351:23
took a man's l. along with him   126:3
to out-do the l.   281:9
to write the Graces' l.   232:11
travell'd l.'s dull round   499:13
tree of l.   44:12
true l. is only love   96:8
turn over a new l.   208:24
unbought grace of l.   102:12
undying L.   83:8
unto all l. of mine..die   165:31
variety's the very spice of l.   163:4
villain to bereave my l.   74:10
walks the waters like a thing of l.   114:43
walls about our l.   475:7
water of l.   71:46, 72:6
way, the truth, and the l.   63:53
way, which leadeth unto l.   58:24
weep away the l. of care   498:25
Well of L. to taste   206:20
well-written L....rare   125:22
we will not live if l. be all   140:26
what argument thy l...has lent   199:9
what is this l., if   169:24
what is your l.?   69:41
what signifies the l. o' man   105:37
what wond'rous l. is this   332:17
when I consider l.   191:34
when Love and L. are fair   569:5
when l.'s sweet fable ends   166:15
where evermore no green l. shoots   79:3
wherefore not L.?   566:14
where there is l., there's hope   215:25
who leads a country l.   192:13
whom truly to know is..l.   389:52
whose l. is in the right   384:1
why should a dog..have l.?   454:26
why should l. all labour be?   535:16
Wine of L. keeps oozing   205:16
winged l. destroy   74:27
with an easy key dost open l.   191:22
with l. all other passions fly   507:17
worth a l.'s experience   251:24
yea, thro' l., death   360:11
you take my l.   465:14
Life-blood: l. of a master spirit   352:7
to fan our l.   410:26
Lifeboat: safe within the l.   415:6
Life-breath: all our l. met   410:26
Life-drop: drank the last l.   117:25
Life Force   489:33
Life-harming heaviness   474:26
Life-in-Death: Night-mare L.   149:13
Lifeless: l. charms, without the heart   214:9
l. ocean   151:33

Life-line: throw out the l. 550:33
Lifetime: five minutes too late all
   my l. 158:25
knowledge of a l. 566:8
l. of happiness 490:12
not..lit again in our l. 232:18
sole work of a l. 90:39
Lift: king to..l. them high 326:21
blinkin' in the l. sae hie 108:31
brothers, l. your voices 35:2
do not l. him 23:24
I l. them up to Thee 247:15
I will l. up mine eyes 399:26
l. a Deepsea Chantey 298:14
l. her with care 252:12
l. me as a wave 496:10
l. me from the grass! 494:7
l. my soul to heaven 446:13
l. not the painted veil 498:19
l. not thy hands to It 207:3
l. one if one totters down 409:19
l. themselves up higher 510:14
l. thou up..thy countenance 392:2
l. up thine eyes 354:11
l. up your heads, O ye gates 393:12
l. up your heart..voice 565:11
the Lord l. up his countenance 46:10
they l. their heavy lids 374:23
veil after veil will l. 14:28
ye gates, l. up your heads 421:2
Lifted: high and l. up 53:8
l. up, or worshipped 401:10
Man, who, l. high 575:11
never l. up a single stone 577:23
they sleep, and it is l. 497:11
thy hair soft-l. 284:12
Lifteth: l. slowly, l. sweetly 545:6
Lifting: l. the lazy ones on 229:15
l. up a fearful eye 508:14
l. up mine eyes 530:28
l. up of day 442:24
l. up of my hands 400:13
Lifts the head, and lies 385:2
Light: above the l. of the morning star 75:14
after l.'s term..cecity 19:4
all l. of art or nature 494:1
all the l. of all their day 374:23
all ye stars and l. 291:27
apparelled in celestial l. 66:13, 389:22
armour of l. 76:13
as if bereav'd of l. 517:12
as if they fear'd the l. 51:1
as l. excelleth darkness 249:13
as l. fell short 311:16
as the wild l. passes along 281:23
author both of life and l. 574:11
bathe the world in l. 558:5
beauty from the l. retir'd 239:4
better than l. 231:13
blasted with excess of l. 363:4
blinding l. 501:27
blind to l. 537:42
bright as l. 63:18
burning and a shining l. 340:20
by her own radiant l. 119:6
by the l. of the moon 166:5
by thine own sweet l. 493:16
chameleons feed on l. 497:9
child of L.! 524:13
clothed with the l. of the night 147:8
comes in the l. 351:21
consider how my l. is spent 445:44
contend with growing l. 312:3
danced by the l. of the moon 400:9
darkness and l...alike 90:44
darkness from l. 63:10
darkness rather than l. 578:10
dearer far than l. and life 202:21
depths of burning l. 344:18
desolation, void of l. 341:24
dim religious l. 288:14
drainless shower of l. is poesy 150:6
each one a lovely l. 400:32
enable with perpetual l. 351:21
exact day-labour, l. deny'd? 27:1
fame..beareth up things l. 334:6
flooded full l. and beauty 343:14
for all the morning l. 344:21
for that celestial l. 193:10
from grave to l. 344:9
from those flames no l.

Light (cont.)
garmented in l. 499:6
gave him l. in his ways 522:7
give due l. to the..traveller 340:9
give me a l. 239:4
gladsome l. of Jurisprudence 148:5
God is L. 74:1
God of life, and poesy, and l. 114:23
God's first Creature..L. 28:5
golden l. of morn 253:19
gone into the world of l. 552:8
greater l. to rule the day 44:5
growing or full constant l. 185:32
had she been l., like you 455:28
hail, holy l. 346:18
halls of dazzling l. 178:12
happy realms of l. 344:11
he beholds the l. 576:9
here there is no l. 287:29
Hesperus entreats thy l. 279:31
hide your golden l. 318:4
his sleep was aery l. 347:37
if L. can thus deceive 566:14
if once we lose this l. 282:6
infant slumbers, pure and l. 291:11
in fleecy flocks of l. 82:7
in happy homes he saw the l. 316:18
in its plumes the various l. 332:20
in robes of l. array'd 240:21
in the l. of the living 395:16
in the l. of thought 498:6
in the orient when the gracious l. 486:12
into the l. of things 581:15
inward l. 575:5
it gives a lovely l. 339:6
Lamb is the l. thereof 72:5
lamps, by whose dear l. 332:27
land is scattered with l. 80:12
lead, kindly L. 364:10
lesser l. to rule the night 44:5
Let Newton be! and all was l. 382:17
lets in new l. through chinks 557:25
let there be l.: and there was l. 44:1
'Let there be l.,' said God 116:24
let there be l.! said Liberty 493:24
let your l. so shine 57:42
levell'd rule of streaming l. 340:18
lie like a shaft of l. 529:30
life and l. be thine for ever! 94:30
l., a glory, a fair..cloud 151:5
l., agreeable .. style [Leigh
   Hunt's] 240:6
L. and Mrs. Humphry Ward 140:5
l., and will aspire 488:26
l. but the shadow of God 85:16
l. dies before thy..word 381:27
l. dissolved in star-showers 498:22
l. fantastic toe 341:29
l. gains make heavy purses 25:36
L. (God's eldest daughter) 212:13
l. heart lives long 455:28
lighthouse without any l. 253:8
l. in ragged luck 241:29
l. in the darkness, sailor 415:6
l. in the dust lies dead 494:20
l. in Wisdom's eyes 561:11
l. is sweet 51:31
l. of common day 576:9
l. of his countenance 396:2
l. of his own hearth-stone 302:27
L. of Lights 584:9
l. of my eye 243:5
l. of other days is faded 99:1
l. of setting suns 582:11
l. of step and heart was she 171:6
l. of Terewth 173:36
l. of the bright world dies 79:5
l. of thy countenance 392:2
l. of truth 173:36
l. on the Bong-tree stem 311:16
l. she was 355:23
l. shineth in darkness 62:60
l. such a candle 310:11
L. that Failed 304:33
l. that led astray 108:25
l., that lies in woman's eyes 356:32
l. that loses 521:30(-522)
l. that never was 578:14
l. that she loves 536:10
l. the bridal lamp 348:38
l. thickens 459:8

Light (cont.)
l. to guide 573:28
l...to him that is in misery 48:47
l. to shine upon the road 161:1
l. to them that sit in darkness 61:15
l. unto my paths 399:21
l. up my own mind 93:30
l. upon him from his father's eyes 576:10
l. upon the shining sea 540:7
l. we sought 19:1
l. which beats upon the throne 529:39
l. which is in thee be not darkness 61:49
l. wife..heavy husband 465:24
l. within his own clear breast 340:20
like l. can flee 498:16
line of festal l. 18:11
little warmth, a little l. 335:10
lived l. in the spring 15:13
live out thy life as the l. 524:3
long l. shakes 538:14
make my darkness to be l. 392:29
man all l., a seraph-man 150:6
mellow'd to that tender l. 119:1
more by your number than..l. 583:13
more l.! 224:7
more than l. airs 483:1
my burden is l. 59:10
my only L. 244:18
never but in unapproached l. 346:18
no new l. on love or liquor 387:22
Noose of L. 205:4
nothing goes for sense, or l. 110:36
now is l. increased 544:7
of l. and leading in England 102:24
of l. and leading in the country 182:30
of l., of liberty, and of learning 181:4
of night and l. and the half-l. 584:17
once put out thy l. 473:11
opponent of the..children of l. 19:14
out of hell leads up to l. 345:27
plant and flower of l. 282:1
Plautus too l. 433:22
progeny of l. 348:14
purple l. of love 231:9
put out the l., and then 473:11
ray of l. Divine 132:1
remember while the l. lives 523:8
restore the l. 168:12
ring of pure and endless l. 552:13
river of crystal l. 204:5
seen a glorious l. 421:6
seen a great l. 53:14
Servants of L. 14:30
severity of perfect l. 530:18
shall never see l. 395:2
Shaft of L. 205:5
she made all of l. 123:20
shineth the everlasting l. 84:25
shining l., that shineth more
   and more 49:43
since God is l. 346:18
sky resum'd her l. 193:38
slight little, l. little 222:8
so l. a foot 478:10
sometimes a l. surprises 161:21
some true, some l. 530:21
soon as once set is our little l. 123:19
speed..far faster than l. 98:19
spring of l. 148:12
such a l. affliction 362:8
sufficient of His l. 96:10
suffusion from that l. 151:6
sun, or the l...not darkened 51:33
Sweet Muses of the L. 413:1
sweetness and l. 19:25, 519:5
take his l. away 89:35
teach l. to counterfeit a gloom 341:16
that 'l. which leads astray is l.
   from Heaven' 573:9
that shone as Heaven's l. 510:20
the Lord is my l. 49:35, 393:20
third among the sons of l. 491:15
those flowers made of l. 253:1
thou celestial l. shine inward 346:20
through Peace to L. 402:10
thy former l. restore 473:11
thy l. break forth 54:37
thy l. is come 54:39
thy l. relume 473:11
thy righteousness as clear as the l. 394:4

Light (*cont.*)
ties..though l. as air 101:10
till the hours of l. return 17:1
to bring the false to l. 81:13
to implore your l. 169:13
trifles l. as air 471:42
true L. 62:62
truth will come to l. 463:32
turn'd thy darkness into l. 161:10
unbarred the gates of l. 348:19
unclouded blaze of living l. 115:8
unveil'd her peerless l. 347:19
upon them hath the l. shined 53:14
very pretty small-sword l. 500:27
walk while ye have the l. 63:46
we all *know* what l. is 273:13
welcum the lord of l. 187:5
we see such glimmerings of l. 102:38
what is that thing called L. 144:21
what l. through yonder window 477:13
when I see you in the l. 304:7
where l. and shade repose 577:10
where the l. is as darkness 48:55
whose l. doth trample 552:9
windows that exclude the l. 230:18
with a l. behind her 222:20
with golden and silver l. 584:17
ye are the l. of the world 57:41
Light Brigade: forward, the L.! 528:14
Lighted: that l. me to bed 252:25
torch that l. mine 199:10
Lighten: glory of God did l. it 72:5
l. our darkness 388:36
l. with celestial fire 400:31
Lightened are our eyes 506:20
Lightens: ere one can say it l. 477:24
Lighter: English man of war..l. in
  sailing 212:18
l. of a fair son 197:36
l. than vanity itself 395:24
town..l. than vanity 99:14
Lighteth: light, which l. every man 62:62
many a l. lad 263:21
Light-headed: marriage..attracts
  l...men 514:28
Light-hearted: afoot and l. 568:3
l. Masters of the waves 18:16
Lighthouse: below the l. top 148:21
is this indeed the l. top 150:4
l. without any light 253:8
took the sitivation at the l. 179:28
Lighting: l. a little Hour or two 205:27
l. our little torches at his fire 147:26
Lightly: English lord..l. me 31:6
green turf lie l. 381:35
lean upon it l.! 206:4
lie l., gentle earth 37:35
l. as it comth..spende 137:43
men that love l. may die 523:15
my bosom's lord sits l. 478:34
Lightness: borrow heart's l. 285:3
Lightning: angels of rain and l. 496:5
beneath the l. and the Moon 149:30
brief as the l. 466:20
bring in the bottled l. 177:23
coruscations of summer l. 228:2
distant l. on the horizon 119:25
done like l. 280:17
fear no more the l. flash 430:1
fed with the l. 497:8
in thunder, l., or in rain 456:3
l. before death 478:42
l. made itself 325:13
l. my pilot sits 492:27
l. of the nations 495:25
Satan as l. fall 61:36
scratch my head with the l. 550:20
Shakespeare by flashes of l. 153:5
through its own internal l. blind 495:10
too like the l. 477:24
Lightnings: all the l. of his song 492:1
arrows of l. 540:16
l. Thy sword 142:26
Lights: become of all these l. of the
  world 102:21
but broken l. of thee 531:41
coastwise l. of England 295:12
cometh down from the Father
  of l. 69:29
earthly godfathers of Heaven's l. 454:32

Lights (*cont.*)
father of l.! 551:16
followed false l. 192:23
following Nature's l. 357:19
glorious the northern l. 503:6
he l. the evening star 122:1
l. around the shore 411:34
l. begin to twinkle 541:3
l. that do mislead 462:16
old inn, and the l. 359:7
poised, as the l. in the firmament 413:21
serene l. of heaven 498:26
silent silver l. 94:11
spent l. quiver and gleam 15:24
this that l. the wigwam 317:23
turn up the l. 242:15
two great l. 44:5
when all the l. wax dim 246:26
when the l. are dim and low 370:15
whose l. are fled 357:14
your l. burning 61:54
Light-winged Dryad of the trees 287:23
Lignum...versus superiorem partem
  curva est 28:12
Like: each to other l. 348:13
every one as they l. 520:8
find their l. agen 418:6
how do you l. that, my buck? 220:1
how I l. to be liked 307:16
I'd l. to roll to Rio 297:24
I know what I l. 40:1
I l. him, but he loves me 97:5
I l. you, and your book 308:3
ingots, l. in each respect 330:13
I said there was nothing l. it 131:16
l.,—but oh how different! 582:21
l. doth quit l. 462:26
less we l. you 41:28
l. master, l. man 203:23
l. mistress, l. maid 203:23
l. not a single line 516:11
look upon his l. again 431:6
people who l. this sort of thing 314:17
say you do not l. it 566:9
so l. they were 324:12
something very l. Him 146:32
sort of thing they l. 314:17
these hands are not more l. 431:11
trying..to l. Scotchmen 306:11
we run because we l. it 506:21
what thou dost l. 549:29
who want it the most..l. it the
  least 139:16
women..more l. each other than
  men 139:26
ye who l. me not 95:29
Liked: he l. the 'Sermon on the
  Mount' 183:4
how I like to be l. 307:16
I that loved and you that l. 9:21
l. it not, and died 583:12
wish I l. the way it walks 405:16
Likely: l. impossibility 14:18
l...to have prov'd most royally 438:10
mighty l. speech 214:17
not bloody l. 491:1
Likeness: after our l. 44:6
gods..in the l. of men 64:51
in l. of my love 81:10
in the l. of a fat old man 439:34
l. of a kingly crown 346:4
not make..the l. of any thing 390:7
old Adam's l. 475:13
returns..to its own l. 347:29
Likes: but l. that little good 112:10
doing as he l. 19:29
she l. her self 154:28
whether Mister John Keats..l.
  them or not 290:3
Liketh: of this and that as l. me 290:3
Likewise: canst thou do l.? 175:18
do thou l. 61:43
Liking: all love, all l., all delight 246:1
fredome mayse man to haiff l. 33:17
friendships begin with l. 196:19
I have a l. old for them 121:18
ill word may empoison l. 468:26
Likings: made up of l. and dislikings 306:10
Lilac: l., gold and green 80:14
Lord L. was of slighter stuff 141:31

Lilacs: l. out of the dead land 197:27
l. where the robin built 253:1
when l. last..bloom'd 568:8
Lilac-time: go down to Kew in l. 365:25
Lilian: airy, fairy L. 534:12
Lilied: gay l. fields of France 122:12
Lilies: Beauty lives though l. die 208:9
breaking the golden l. afloat 88:11
consider the l. of the field 58:13
feed among the l. 52:5
feedeth among the l. 52:3
few l. blow 254:29
in the beauty of the l. 264:18
Kingcups, and loved L. 510:23
leave the l. in their dew 17:2
l. and languors of virtue 522:23
l. and roses were all awake 536:13
l. in her body's lieu 376:1
l. of all kinds 485:26
l. that fester 487:26
l. without, roses within 333:3
lotos and l. 537:31
peacocks and l. for instance 413:13
roses and l. meet 36:26
roses and white l. grow 124:4
three l. in her hand 410:7
thy pale, lost l. out of mind 187:10
twisted braids of l. knitting 341:3
wheat set about with l. 52:18
with roses overgrown, and l. 333:2
Lillabullero: whistling..L. 513:7
Lilting: I've heard them l. 198:18
Lily: fair as the l. 156:19
folds the l. all her sweetness 539:2
how splendid..glows 208:11
how sweet the l. grows! 240:16
it trembles to a l. 183:11
lies across the l. leven 32:9
like a l. in bloom 265:16
l. maid of Astolat 530:33
l. of a day 282:1
l. of Florence 316:25
l. of the valleys 51:43
l. on l. 90:34
l. on thy brow 286:29
l. whispers, 'I wait.' 536:15
my precious L.! 129:38
seen but a bright l. grow? 281:24
set thick with l. and red rose 359:5
to paint the l. 447:39
towers to a l. 561:6
wav'd her l. hand 216:1
with a poppy or a l. 220:28
Lily-cups: vi'lets, and the l. 253:1
Lily-handed: no little l. Baronet 539:9
Lily-lea: on yonder l. 30:6
Limb: as vigour from the l. 113:23
ease my weary l. 29:24
give every town a l. 24:5
in..face and l. 313:7
in member, joint, or l. 346:4
joints, and strength of l. 418:8
on every airth a l. 355:21
perils both of wind and l. 110:28
Limbecks foul as hell 488:8
Limbo large and broad 346:27
Limbs: great smooth marbly l. 89:43
if these poor l. die 84:19
l. of gibbeted Gods 525:10
my l...issue from your smoky
  mouths 330:9
ruddy l. and flaming hair 74:25
solemn slope of mighty l. 522:12
these l., her Province 185:4
those recreant l. 447:28
thy decent l. composed 381:34
thy l. are burning 497:9
tired pilgrim's l. 124:1
whose l. were made in England 443:26
young in l., in judgement old 403:41
Limed: set l. twigs for crabs 131:24
Lime-Tree: this L. Bower 152:1
Limit: greatest art is to l. and
  isolate oneself 223:14
l. at which forbearance ceases to
  be a virtue 101:38
l. of becoming mirth 455:3
quiet l. of the world 540:21
Limitary: proud l. Cherub 347:34
Limitations of his own character 358:16
Limited: experience is never l. 268:12

Limited (*cont.*)
liberty..l...to be possessed   103:22
my wision's l.   179:16
vocabulary of 'Bradshaw'..l.   188:27
Limits: l. of a vulgar fate   231:16
stony l. cannot hold love out   477:17
Limner: what skilful l.   418:25
Limns the water   28:17
Limpets: stuck like l. to the spot   141:31
Limping: strength by l. sway disabled   487:14
Limpopo: greasy L. River   304:17
Linages: *dos l. sólos..el tenir y el no tenir*   134:14
Lincoln: Belvoir..the sign to L. sent   322:23
Linden: on L., when the sun was low   122:17
Linden Lea: lean down low in L.   35:13
Lindesay: Sir David L. of the Mount   418:14
Lindsay: gang wi' me, Lizzy L.   9:17
Line: fight it out on this l.   229:1
Freedom's classic l.   123:1
full-resounding l.   386:17
hammered into l.   294:22
harsh cadence of a rugged l.   193:11
in all l. of order   481:2
in the very first l.   225:31
into a horizontal l.   566:1
like not a single l.   516:11
l. after l. my gushing eyes   382:1
l. is length without breadth   202:7
l. of festal light   18:11
l. too labours   382:32
l. upon l., l. upon l.   53:33
l. will take us hours   584:2
lives along the l.   383:17
Marlowe's mighty l.   281:12
marr'd the lofty l.   418:7
move on a rigorous l.   17:6
one dull l.   382:30
pass it along the l.l   300:16
poet does not work by square or l.   159:23
sorrows of thy l.   183:1
strengthen the wavering l.   17:21
Thebes, or Pelops' l.   341:18
thin red l. tipped with steel   414:4
this l. of scarlet thread   46:38
though the scarlet l. was slender   293:1
to cancel half a L.   207:2
up the l. to death   415:12
victorious l. of march..prolonged   217:12
whatever suits the l.   152:6
will the l. stretch out   460:11
Linea: nulla dies sine l.   380:4
Lineage: Poets of the proud old l.   208:9
Lineaments: in my l. they trace   118:29
l. of Gospel books   412:18
l. of gratified desire   74:28
moulded the changing l.   374:11
Linen: all in fair l.   5:16
blanched l., smooth, and lavender'd   285:24
clothed in purple and fine l.   62:23
did not love clean l.   271:4
fair white l. cloth   390:3
girded with a l. ephod   47:2
love is like l.   209:5
not l. you're wearing out   253:23
old l. wash whitest   563:22
surplices of l.   310:23
you shall wash your l.   516:2
Linen-draper bold   159:34
Liner she's a lady   298:25
Lines: about eighty thousand l.   121:6
as l, so loves oblique   332:6
circles and right l. limit..all bodies   87:13
impending eighty thousand l.   120:29
l. and outward air   281:1
liquid l. mellifluously bland   116:14
my l. and life are free   244:9
radiant l. of morning   497:9
rain..in slanting l.   503:13
silken l., and silver hooks   184:8
their lives, as do their l...lasted   280:9
wholly consisted of l. like these   120:21
Linger: I...l. here   573:12

Linger (*cont.*)
l. longer Lucy   233:15
l. out a purpos'd overthrow   487:23
l. shivering on the brink   562:16
l. to caress him   560:27
whose thoughts half l.   524:20
willowy brook..l. near   408:10
Lingered: I l. round them   83:15
l. by His seat   585:22
Lingering: hoping, l., flying   381:28
I alone sit l. here   552:8
l. and consumptive passion   202:2
one longing, l. look   230:9
something l. with boiling oil   220:12
where music dwells l.   577:10
Lingers: l. and l. it out   441:26
love that l. there   208:5
my soul that l. sighing   263:20
Linguae: docte sermones utriusque l.   260:2
Lining: silver l.   210:4
turn forth her silver l.   340:12
Link: from l. to l. it circulates   574:26
I feel the l. of nature   349:18
silver l.   417:21
Linked: incidents well l.   159:16
l. with one virtue   115:7
to each other l.   545:5
Linking our England to his Italy   96:19
Links: nor strong l. of iron   448:36
their nobles with l. of iron   400:27
Lin-lan-lone of evening bells   529:21
Linnet: full of the l.'s wings   585:12
hear the woodland l.   581:15
I heard a l. courting   81:8
l. born within the cage   532:19
Linnets: but as the l. sing   532:16
like committed l.   319:7
Linsey-woolsey: l. brother   110:34
l. brothers   381:19
Lion: beard the l. in his den   418:27
better than a dead l.   51:19
devil, as a roaring l.   70:6
first l.   406:19
gentil kind of the l.   138:20
half appear'd the tawny l.   348:27
hardy as the Nemean l.   432:3
hungry l. give a..roar   406:19
hungry l. roars   467:35
I hear the l. roar   161:17
I met a l.   448:32
l. among ladies   467:3
l. and the belly-pinched wolf   453:4
L. and the Lizard   206:1
l. beat the unicorn   367:13
l. in the way: a l. is in the streets   50:41
l. shall eat straw like the ox   53:19
l.'s ruddy eyes   77:2
l. who dies of an ass's kick   93:39
Lord L. King-at-Arms   418:14
more fearful wild-fowl than your l.   467:3
righteous are bold as a l.   50:49
rouse the l. from his lair   420:23
save me from the l.'s mouth   393:7
saw the l.'s shadow   465:17
some pain'd desert l.   17:26
sporting the l. ramped   347:15
strong is the l.   503:5
thou wear a l.'s hide!   447:28
threaten'd, a l.   135:14
to rouse a l.   438:37
well roared, L.   467:32
wrath of the l.   77:16
young l. and the fatling   53:18
Lion-banner: Freedom's l.   122:30
Lions: I girdid up my L.   560:5
let bears and l. growl   561:24
l. do lack   393:38
l. roaring after their prey   398:10
my soul is among l.   395:18
they were stronger than l.   47:30
we are two l.   449:23
young l. of the *Daily Telegraph*   19:8
Lip: anger of his l.   483:28
coral l. admires   124:25
coral of his l.   321:14
Diana's l. is not more smooth   482:10
from what once lovely L.   206:4
her eye, her cheek, her l.?   481:26
my true l. hath virgin'd it   429:19
no good girl's l. out of Paris   525:35

Lip (*cont.*)
set l. to earth's bosom bare   545:8
stiff upper l.   131:31
'tis not a l., or eye   382:24
vermeil-tinctur'd l.   340:38
wagged his tail, and wet his l.   249:20
whose l. mature is ever new   285:39
why gnaw you so your nether l.?   473:13
Lipp'd: hand that kings have l.   424:13
Lips: at the touching of the l.   534:17
best befits thy l.   286:17
between the l. of Love-Lily   411:25
but flatter with their l.   392:20
causing the l...to speak   52:20
chance to burn your l.   480:38
crimson in thy l.   478:43
dear red curve of her l.   333:19
eternity was in our l.   423:33
eyes, l., and hands to miss   186:25
far from the l. we love   356:35
for these red l.   585:22
for your l. to drink   525:27
from her coral l. such folly   155:5
from their l...thy l. taken fever   523:6
harmonious madness from my l.   498:10
heaven be in these l.   330:5
here hung those l.   437:15
her l. suck forth my soul   330:5
her l. were red   517:14
her l. were red   149:13
his coward l.   448:20
his l. on that unworthy place   425:1
I'll kiss my girl on her l.   299:21
I moved my l.   150:11
in prayer the l.   247:19
in this lady's l. and hands   410:32
item, Two l. indifferent red   482:21
its polished l. to your..ear   308:27
keep the door of my l.   400:13
kisses of the l. of God   360:10
let me put my l. to it   176:16
l. as soft, but true   183:18
l. cannot fail of taking their plie   100:4
l. of a strange woman   49:44
l. of dying men   17:27
l. of lurid blue   493:2
l. of that Evangelist   532:22
l. of those who love you well   81:21
l., O you the doors of breath   478:44
l. say, 'God be pitiful'   88:3
l. that are for others   538:19
l. that had whispered   523:15
more red than her l.' red   488:13
moulded by the l. of man   541:8
my l. are now forbid   36:31
my weary l. I close   229:27
my whole soul thro' my l.   529:22
never come out of a lady's l.   208:23
o'er ladies' l.   477:7
of unclean l.   53:8
on a poet's l. I slept   497:2
on both her l. for ever stray   158:1
on l. of living men   112:19
other l., and other hearts   98:22
our l. are dumb   535:17
persuasion hung upon his l.   513:5
poor last I lay upon thy l.   425:27
pretty form to the l.   176:1
rain is on our l.   506:20
rain on my l. and eyelids   494:7
red mournful l.   586:7
request of his l.   392:38
rose upon Truth's l.   561:11
round their narrow l.   411:16
see my l. tremble   382:7
slug-horn to my l. I set   90:23
soft as l. that laugh and hide   522:2
spitting from l. once sanctified   91:26
sweet voice, sweet l.   289:1
swore my l. were sweet   309:3
take those l. away   462:16
that those l. had languagel   160:25
that thy l. met with   523:4
their starv'd l. in the gloam   286:36
they shoot out their l.   393:3
those l. are thine   160:25
though rosy l. and cheeks   488:7
through my l...the trumpet   496:11
thy l. are like a thread of scarlet   52:5
thy l. enkindle   497:9
to part her l.   246:25

Lips (*cont.*)
touch lightly with my l.	567:5
to whom the l. of children	361:8
upon her perfect l.	540:13
when the l. have spoken	494:20
where my Julia's l. do smile	245:21
whispering, with white l.	113:32
whose hand is ever at his l.	287:21
with his l. he travaileth	522:7
your l. would keep from slips	7:5

Liquefaction of her clothes   247:13
Liquid: l. lapse of murmuring
streams	348:32
l. lines mellifluously bland	116:14
Thames is l. 'istory	104:3

Liquidation of the British Empire   144:11
Liquidity: purpose in l.   83:24
Liquor: atrabilious l.   266:17
before Life's L…be dry	205:6
considerbul l. koncealed	560:13
good l., I stoutly maintain	226:2
l. talks mighty loud	238:21
no new light on love or l.	387:22
or some such other spiritual l.	119:21
wanteth not l.	52:18
when the l.'s out	91:27

Liquors: hot and rebellious l.
in my blood   426:36
Lisp: l. and wear strange suits   428:17
| l. their sire's return | 229:31 |
| what a pretty l. he has! | 201:34 |

Lisped: I l. in numbers   385:25
| somewhat he l. | 137:4 |

Lisping: poor l. stammering
tongue   161:8
Lissom, clerical, printless toe   84:11
List: get sweets into your l.   265:25
I've got a little l.	219:24
l., l., O, l.!	432:9
l. to the heavy part	279:28
my l. of friends	164:3

'Listed: for a soldier I 'l.   173:4
| Legion that never was 'l. | 299:1 |

Listen: damn'd…l. to thee   247:14
darkling I l.	287:32
fur'z you can look or l.	319:23
I didn't l. to him	512:10
l. all day to such stuff	128:29
l., Eugenia	17:12
l. to my tale of woe	204:4
l. where thou art sitting	341:3
l. with credulity to..fancy	278:14
privilege of wisdom to l.	251:22
silence..wonderful to l. to	237:17
stop; look; l.	551:4
world should l. then	498:10

Listened: his very soul l.   574:27
| those who l. to Lord Chatham | 200:6 |
| we l. and looked sideways up | 149:15 |

Listeners: the l.   171:15
Listening: disease of not l.
in l. mood   441:15
   416:15
l. for the drum	363:3
l. to silence	253:13
Planets..l. stood	348:28
poor Wat..with l. ear	488:28

Listens: God's own ear l. delighted   348:16
| l. like a three years' child | 148:20 |

Listeth: bloweth where it l.   63:7
Listlessness, nor mad endeavour   576:19
Lit: not..l. again in our lifetime   232:18
Literary: any force of educated l.
..opinion   19:16
disgusted with l. men	289:14
Gigadibs the l. man	89:39
head of the l. profession	181:24
immense l. misapprehension	20:16
l. footmen	240:5
l. man—*with* a wooden leg	178:2
never l. attempt was more un-	
fortunate	265:12
parole of l. men	274:31
unsuccessful l. man	41:33
with St. Paul..l. terms	20:9

Literature: cultivate l. upon a little
oatmeal   505:26
every other branch of classical l.	176:38
grazed the common of l.	271:7
great Cham of l.	506:6
itch of l.	319:11

Literature (*cont.*)
l…communicate power	172:25
l..half a trade and half an art	267:7
l. is a drug	78:27
l. looks like word-catching	200:28
l. of *knowledge*	172:24
l. of *power*	172:24
louse in the locks of l.	541:26
men who have failed in l.	182:21
modern l…sharing with black-	
ing and Macassar oil	376:13
not l…communicate knowledge	172:25
Philistine of genius in l.	20:19
produce a little l.	268:1
raised the price of l.	270:24
true lover of l.	508:8

Lites: *non nostrum..componere l.*   555:28
Lith in their neck   21:14
Lithe: wreathed his l. proboscis   347:15
Litter: all her l. but one   441:11
Littérature: *tout le reste est l.*   552:18
Litter'd: lions l. in one day   449:23
Little: all the rest were l. ones   24:40
any l. delicate thing to drink	175:38
as a very l. thing	54:12
ask me to give you l. things	489:28
as l. as a Christian can	188:34
as l. in our power	202:1
awake, my L. ones	205:6
big words for l. matters	271:20
but likes that l. good	112:10
but l. drink below	251:1
but wants that l. strong	251:1
contented wi' l.	104:32
cry of the L. Peoples	313:3
do a l. wrong	465:2
eagle suffers l. birds to sing	480:35
every man gets a l.	272:31
for fear of l. men	4:18
fume of l. hearts	530:17
gives but l., nor that l., long	587:12
go, l. book, go l. myn tragedie	138:41
grateful at last for a l. thing	536:22
great empire and l. minds	101:14
having l. else to do	119:15
here a l., and there a l.	53:33
here l., and hereafter bliss	99:31
he taught us l.	16:21
his all neglected, be it ever so l.	270:16
hobgoblin of l. minds	200:40
how l. are the proud	231:7
I am a l. world	185:12
I l. have	195:13
it was a very l. one	331:15
I were but l. happy	468:14
large aggregate of l. things	358:1
left a lot of l. things	294:18
life piled on life..too l. 540:32(−541)	
l. among the thousands of Judah	56:7
l. be it, or much	99:31
l. creature, form'd of joy and	
mirth	75:1
l. creep through	499:18
l. devils ran	302:32
l. do or can the best of us	97:22
l. do we know what lays afore	176:28
l. drops of water	127:33
l. for the bottle	173:3
l. Lamb, who made thee?	76:10
l. less than 'kin'	34:31
l. l. grave	475:10
l. man, l. man!	108:13
l. more than a l.	440:9
l. more than kin	430:26
l., nameless..acts	581:24
l. nation leave to live	313:4
l. of this great world	469:45
l. of what you fancy	315:1
l. old New York	242:13
L. One! Oh, L. One!	512:13
l. one shall become a thousand	55:1
l. ones moan	15:26
l. ones, unbutton'd	164:8
l. rule, a l. sway	195:14
l. saint best fits a l. shrine	245:18
l. ships of England	233:13
l. things affect l. minds	182:27
l. things are great to l. man	226:6
l. things..most important	187:16
l. to be enjoyed	278:16
l. to be known	276:13

Little (*cont.*)
l. to do and plenty to get	179:15
l. to earn	294:1
l. town of Bethlehem	84:24
l. volume, but large book	166:8
l., weak, and helpless	4:3
l. we see in Nature	582:18
l. while	63:62
l. work, a l. play	335:10
love me l.	8:8, 246:10
make l. fishes talk	227:29
monstrous l. voice	466:27
much drinking, l. thinking	519:29
my l. finger..thicker	47:46
nor that l. long	587:9
nor wants that l. long	225:13
offend one of these l. ones	59:49
offering Germany too l.	362:29
offering too l.	124:6
of one to me l. remains 540:32(−541)	
O l. book	138:14
on l. objects..fixt	113:40
only a l. more I have to write	246:6
precious l. for six-pence	403:17
smart l. craft	222:8
snug l. Island	173:15
so l. done, so much to do	406:17
so the l. minutes	127:33
stay a l., that we may make an	
end the sooner	26:7
suspect much..know l.	27:23
that l. is achieved through	
Liberty	97:22
that l. man..upon the stage	204:32
that low man seeks a l. thing	91:41
there'll be l. of us left	539:20
too l. to do	297:26
unto one of these l. ones	59:4
wants but l. here below 112:10, 225:13	
wants but l., nor that l. long	587:9
what a l. thing to remember	4:19
whatever was l. seemed to him	
great	325:22
while my l. one..sleeps	538:12
who think too l.	190:21
you are very l.	515:23

Little Buttercup: I'm called L.   221:9
Little Cowfold: at L. as I've been
told   42:12
Littleness: l…disbelief in great
men   126:23
| long l. of life | 157:8 |

Littlenesses: thousand peering l.   529:39
Littlest fish may enter   83:26
Liturgy: Popish l.   379:7
Live: able to l. in any place   198:3
about to l.	587:5
after so many deaths I l.	244:18
age and youth cannot l. together	486:2
all that l. must die	430:29
always getting ready to l.	201:1
before I have begun to l.	16:18
bid me to l., and I will l.	247:1
both thou and thy seed..l.	46:30
can these bones l.?	55:34
come l. with me	184:8, 330:17
come, tell me how you l.!	131:23
converse, and l. with ease	385:29
dead shall l.	191:39
dying, we l.	96:20
eat to l., not l. to eat	353:10
either..l. or bear no life	472:34
every man desires to l. long	520:42
fond to l. or fear to die	198:10
forms that do not l.	579:12
for which we bear to l.	384:2
get to l.; then l., and use it	243:31
gey ill to l. wi'	127:29
Gilpin long l. he	160:11
glad did I l.	516:15
Gods who l. for ever	324:14
he'd learn how to l.	91:39
help you to l.	524:33
he may l. without books	337:42
he shall not l.	447:32, 451:4
he that begins to l.	404:15
he that lusteth to l.	394:1
hope without an object cannot	
l.	152:18
houses are built to l. in	25:35
how can I l. without thee?	349:18

INDEX

Live (cont.)

how is it that you l.? 580:14
how is it you l.? 131:22
how long I have to l. 394:8
human heart by which we l. 576:22(–577)
Humanities l. for ever 365:13
if I dare..breathe or l. 475:15
if we l., we l. to tread on kings 440:32
I have hope to l. 462:3
I l. not in myself 113:47
I must l. 14:11, 412:3
in him we l., and move 65:1
in our life alone..Nature l. 151:4
in whom we l. 81:3
I shall not die, but l. 399:10
I to die and you to l. 506:9
I wish to l. with you for ever 290:30
I would gladly l. for ever 78:25
joy to see my self now l. 246:24
just shall l. by faith 65:31
knew better to l. than dispute 401:35
lambkins, we will l. 443:17
Lesbia let us l. and love 123:19, 132:15
lest I should bid thee l. 539:1
let us love nobly, and l. 184:7
little nation leave to l. 313:4
l. after them if it is to l. at all 414:9
l. a man forbid 456:11
l. and die in Aristotle's works 329:21
l. and labour 227:34
l. and let l. 403:1
l. and tell him to his teeth 436:40
l. Aspasia 412:16
l. at home with ease 373:11
l. a thousand years 450:4
l. beyond its income 111:34
l. by pulling off the hat 231:25
l. by thy light 17:14
l. cleanly, as a nobleman should 441:6
l. in hearts we leave 122:15
l. in unity 390:26
l. invisible and dim 551:21
l. I, so l. I 316:32
l. o'er each scene 381:6
l. or die wi' Charlie 250:15
l. or die with Charlie 420:13
l. out thy life as the light 524:3
l. pure, speak true 530:4
l., that I may dread 292:2
l. thou thy life 81:5
l. till I were married 468:24
l. till to-morrow 160:40
l. to fight another day 6:25, 224:9
l. together after God's ordinance 391:28
l. to study, and not study to l. 28:4
l. upon our daily rations 174:8
l. we how we can, yet die we must 446:8
l. well on nothing a year 542:39
l. with her, and l. with thee 341:31
l. within our means 560:23
l. without dining 337:42
longer I l. the more fool 369:13
long l. our noble king 125:15
long l. the king 160:11
long to l. 388:28
loves to l. i' the sun 427:9
man cannot l. without cooks 337:41
martyrdom to l. 87:7
merrily shall I l. now 480:14
more virtue than doth l. 280:11
my child, I l. for thee 538:22
never l. long 476:19
none of your l. languages 175:6
none would l. past years again 191:34
nor l. so long 454:28
not fit to l. on land 272:37
not l. by bread alone 57:34, 201:3
not l. by bread only 46:23
not l. with the living? 440:30
not suffer a witch to l. 45:55
not to l., but to die in 86:36
now I l., and now my life is done 547:20
one bare hour to l. 330:7
our love shall l. 509:7
our pattern to l. and to die 93:3
prophets..l. for ever? 56:10
Queens..glad to l. 189:19
rather l. with cheese and garlic 440:2

Live (cont.)

Sacco's name will l. 551:13
see me, and l. 46:7
silliness to l. when to l. is torment 470:14
since flesh must l. 96:26
so l. ever 288:18
so l., that..thou may'st smile 279:19
so l., that when thy summons 98:3
so long as ye both shall l. 391:29
something that doth l. 576:17
Sorrow, wilt thou l. with me 532:41
taught us how to l. 547:22
teach him how to l. 387:11
teaching nations how to l. 352:24
teach us how to l. 164:34
tell me whom you l. with 139:12
they do l. in the air 182:19
they l. as long as one pleases 156:6
they pine, I l. 195:13
those immortal dead who l. again 196:34
those who l. call life 497:11, 498:19
those who wake and l. 495:18
thou hast no more to l. 522:13
thus let me l., unseen, unknown 386:27
to itself it only l. and die 487:25
to l. and act 573:27
to l. and die for thee 247:4
to l. is Christ 68:15
to l. is like love 112:5
to l. like Clodius 117:22
to l. more nearly as we pray 291:8
to l. with thee, and be thy love 405:8
too beautiful to l. 177:8
too smart to l. 560:7
to see me cease to l. 19:5
tri'd to l. without him 583:12
turn and l. with animals 567:20
we l. and learn 381:3
we l. law to ourselves 349:14
we'll l., and pray, and sing 454:19
we may l. without poetry 337:41
we that l. to please, must please to l. 279:1
we will not l. if life be all 140:26
what thou liv'st l. well 349:25
where England is finished..not wish to l. 339:7
where I shall l. by sight 99:40
whereunder..we l. and die 207:3
whether thou l. or die 81:24
while we l., to l. 384:31
who dies if England l.? 296:20
without him l. no life 349:16
without Thee I cannot l. 291:10
wouldn't l. under Niagara 127:27
would you l. for ever? 211:23
wounded name..l. behind me 438:4
write too much, and l. too long 168:10
your names..l. on the lips 81:21
you shall l. by fame 509:7

Lived: had'st thou but l...a watchman 418:3
he l. to learn 221:1
he l. while we believed 17:9
I had l. a blessed time 458:24
I have formerly l. by hearsay 99:40
I have l. in such dishonour 425:23
I have l. long enough 460:36, 525:4
I have l. today 158:17, 194:20
I l. a Pharisee 65:22
I shall have l. a little while 263:22
l. in his..eye 93:3
l. in London and hung loose 270:12
l. in social intercourse with him 272:7
l. in the love of a ladye 222:28
l. with Shades so long 236:25
my former fortunes wherein I l. 425:28
never loved,..never l. 215:8
no man..hath l. better than I 328:12
poorly (poor man) he l. 209:1
so they l., and so they died 401:29
that it l. at all 280:11
therefore l. with them 375:27
they all l. together 369:3
thousand slimy things l. on 149:21
while she l...a true lover 328:16

Liveliest effusions of wit and humour 22:22
Lively: from l. to severe 384:15

Lively (cont.)

l. form of death 305:14
true and l. Word 390:28
Liver: bad l., and a worse heart 324:30
if..disease in the l...a Calvinist 200:11
l. white and pale 442:21
no motion of the l. 483:9
notorious evil l. 390:1
question of the L. 403:25
so much blood in his l. 484:2
Liverpool: folk that live in L. 141:11
Livers: grave l...in Scotland 580:12
measure the heat of our l. 441:18
Livery: in her sober l. 347:19
in his l. walk'd crowns 426:1
known by this party-coloured l. 155:27
l. of the burnished sun 463:26
son of a l. stable keeper 584:14
Lives: after shocking l. 121:20
ca' them l. o' men 360:14
everything that l., l. not alone 74:3
evil..l. after them 450:17
Government at Washington l. 213:7
had all his hairs been l. 473:15
he l., he wakes 492:8
he most l. who thinks most 29:9
he that l. upon hope 211:17
he who l. more l. than one 569:10
human creatures' l. 253:23
if you join two l. 90:10
in jeopardy of their l. 47:39
it's no fish..men's l. 419:13
leave their little l. in air 386:32
light heart l. long 455:28
l. along the line 383:17
l. by that which nourisheth it 424:17
l. in Eternity's sunrise 74:27
l. of great men 317:8
l. of quiet desperation 546:32
make our l. sublime 317:8
more to the L. that fed 303:10
no man l. forever 523:23
no man..l. twice 525:7
not how a man dies, but..l. 271:35
one really l. no where 103:37
other heights in other l. 94:4
our l., our souls 444:21
our l. would grow together 524:28
pleasant in their l. 47:30
ruin no more l. 188:7
secular bird, ages of l. 351:4
so long l. this 486:18
spend our l. in learning pilotage 336:46
start their working l. 296:32
their l., as do their lines..lasted 280:9
the Lord hath spared our l. 540:2
then chiefly l. 245:14
to show that still she l. 356:21
whiles I threat, he l. 458:1
who l. unto himself..l. to none 404:11
Livest: what thou l. live well 349:25
Liveth: I am he that l. 70:28
in that he l., he l. unto God 65:45
my redeemer l. 49:6
their name l. 57:19
Living: become a l. soul 581:25
be happy while y'er l. 5:20
blamed the l. man 16:10
blend the l. with the dead 132:3
by the l. jingo 227:22
catch the manners l. 383:8
devoured thy l. with harlots 62:17
every man l. is..vanity 394:9
fever call'd 'L.' 380:11
for us, the l. 314:12
get mine own l. 391:9
goodness..in the land of the l. 393:22
house appointed for all l. 49:10
I'm l. in sin 242:26
in the light of the l. 395:16
into the hands of the l. God 69:12
like a l. thing strode 579:10
l. by taking in one another's washing 6:3
l.-dead man 429:1
l. death 350:24
l. die 191:39
l. dog 51:19
l...forfeit fair renown 417:25
l. in a garret 209:17
l. know no bounds 501:8

INDEX

Living (cont.)
l. need charity more — 15:1
l. unto righteousness — 390:59
l. up to it that is difficult — 542:9
l. voice to me — 533:33
l., we fret — 96:20
l. which are yet alive — 51:4
long habit of l. — 87:10
long sickness of health and l. — 480:30
man became a l. soul — 44:11
man's life, the mere l. — 96:21
mother of all l. — 44:29
noble l. and the noble dead — 579:32
no l. thing to suffer pain — 496:21
no l. with thee, nor without thee — 2:8
not live like l. men — 579:12
not live with the l. — 440:30
on lips of l. men — 112:19
out of the land of the l. — 54:27
over every l. thing — 44:9
plain l. and high thinking — 577:16
rejoice in the l. God — 397:5
riotous l. — 62:13
shadows of the l. — 85:16
Snake l. yet — 41:34
thou shouldst be l. — 577:14
thou wert l. the same poet — 158:4
too much love of l. — 523:23
trade..with the l. and the dead — 194:4
unclouded blaze of l. light — 115:8
wak'd to ecstasy the l. lyre — 230:4
when your Uncle George was l. — 175:36
who, l., had no roof — 248:4
why seek ye the l. among the dead? — 62:53
ye are l. poems — 316:2
Livingstone: Dr. L., I presume? — 511:13
Livre: tout un l. dans une page — 282:11
Livres: les l. cadrent mal avec le mariage — 353:19
Lizard: Lion and the L. — 206:1
Lizards: meagre as l. — 121:20
Lizzy Lindsay: gang wi' me, L. — 9:17
Llama is a..sort of fleecy hairy goat — 41:33
Llewellyn: soft L.'s lay — 229:21
Lo, eh? — 177:15
Load: bearing..Atlantèan, the l. — 16:11
deserves this l. — 244:10
how to l. and bless — 284:10
like a l. of immortality — 290:6
l. every rift..with ore — 291:1
l. of splendid care — 357:24
l. would sink a navy — 446:26
somebody's l. has tipped off — 300:16
to l. a falling man — 447:13
Loaded: always ready to be l. — 180:28
like l. guns with boys — 165:13
Loaden: hasting l. home — 332:10
l. with honour — 429:22
Loads: laid many heavy l. on thee — 202:11
with superfluous burden l. the day — 351:23
Loaf: L. of Bread — 205:23, 24
of a cut l. to steal a shive — 480:33
quartern l. and Luddites — 504:5
Loafe: I l. and invite my soul — 567:10
Loam: gilded l. or painted clay — 474:10
Loan: brief l. of his own body — 120:5
l. oft loses both itself and friend — 431:25
Loaning: on ilka green l. — 198:18
Loathe: in another l. or despise — 278:24
l. the present Government — 246:17
l. the taste of sweetness — 440:9
we l. our manna — 193:7
Loathed: hence, l. Melancholy — 341:26
Valerius l. the wrong — 324:6
Loathing: disgust and secret l. — 17:7
loving, not l. — 252:13
Loathsome to the eye — 267:30
Loaves: laid sight of the l. and fishes — 376:16
seven halfpenny l...a penny — 445:36
Lobster: like a l. boil'd, the morn — 110:43
l. held on — 294:7
mailed l. rise — 211:26
voice of the l. — 129:25
Loca: quae nunc abiis in l. — 233:19
Local: l. habitation — 467:24
not l. purposes..but the general good — 100:14

Localism: spirit of l. — 78:22
Lochaber: farewell to L. — 405:18
Lochiel: broadsword of L. — 23:20
Lochinvar: young L. is come — 418:15
Lochow: a far cry to L. — 420:17
Loci: geniumque l...precatur — 555:3
Lock: crying at the l. — 339:9
l. such rascal counters — 451:21
l. was dull — 119:14
why l. him in? — 490:25
Locked: l., lettered, braw brass collar — 108:18
l. my heart in a case o' gowd — 32:19
l. the source of softer woe — 417:6
l. up from mortal eye — 166:17
so cherished, and l. up — 440:31
Locks: Curly l., Curly l. — 366:16
doves' eyes within thy l. — 52:5
few l. which are left you — 507:33
gay as are Apollo's l. — 209:22
her l. were yellow as gold — 149:13
his golden l. — 377:4
l. of six princesses — 293:9
l. of the corn — 359:16
louse in the l. of literature — 541:26
never shake thy gory l. — 459:15
open, l. — 460:1
pluck up drowned honour by the l. — 438:38
shaking her invincible l. — 352:15
strapp'd waist, and frozen l. — 163:20
thy knotted and combined l. — 432:9
turn those amber l. to grey — 189:10
your l. were like the raven — 106:19
Loco: dulce est desipere in l. — 120:24, 261:5
dulce et decorum est desipere in l. — 112:11
Locust: that..hath the l. eaten — 55:50
years that the l. hath eaten — 55:51
Locusts: as luscious as l. — 470:17
l. and wild honey — 57:29
Locuta: Roma l. est — 22:5
Lodestar: off oure language..the l. — 321:9
Lodge: birds..l. in the branches — 59:29
l. in a garden of cucumbers — 52:28
l. in some vast wilderness — 162:40
l. thee till thy wound be..heal'd — 484:32
not l. thee by Chaucer — 281:11
unimaginable l. for solitary thinkings — 284:23
Lodged with me useless — 351:21
Lodger: l. in my own house — 226:33
our l.'s such a nice young man — 360:6
Lodgers: Queer Street is full of l. — 178:17
Lodgest: where thou l., I will lodge — 47:1
Lodging: despair of better l. — 375:26
give us a safe l. — 364:4
hard was their l. — 213:20
towards Phoebus' l. — 478:17
Lodgings: take l. in a head — 110:14
Lodore: come down at L. — 507:11, 12
Loftiness: first in l. of thought — 193:9
Lofty: l. and sour — 447:9
l. designs..like effects — 92:1
Log: l. was burning brightly — 223:10
on a l., expiring frog — 178:32
to fall a l. at last — 282:1
Logan: John A. L. is the Head Centre — 83:2
Logan-water: fyle the L. — 108:34
Log-cabin to White House — 543:14
Logic: good, too, L., of course — 146:18
in l. a great critic — 110:5
l. and rhetoric, able to contend — 27:19
of science and l. he chatters — 387:20
push the l. of a fact — 296:14
stank of L. — 363:20
that's l. — 130:8
with L. absolute — 206:25
Logical: built in such a l. way — 251:6
l. consequences — 266:22
Logres: knights of L., or of Lyones — 350:4
l. — 456:1
Logs: Tom bears l. — 96:46
Loin: ungirt l. — 48:6
gird up now thy l. — 49:18
I gird up my L. — 560:5
let your l. be girded about — 61:54
thicker than my father's l. — 47:46
your l. girded — 45:47
Loire: from..Gibraltar to..the L. — 217:12

Loisir: pas eu le l. de la faire plus courte — 374:8
Loitered my life away — 240:13
Loiterers: leige of all l. — 455:8
Loitering: alone and palely l. — 286:28
Loix: mère des..l. — 40:16
Lombardy: waveless plain of L. — 495:1
Lomond: banks o' Loch L. — 9:7
London: as L. is to Paddington — 124:14
dream of L., small and white — 359:2
famous L. town — 159:32
Fire of L...not the fire — 175:32
gondola of L. — 182:16
Hell is a city much like L — 496:16
I'm learnin' 'ere in L. — 299:13
in L. all that life can afford — 273:23
in L. only is a trade — 193:24
it isn't far from L. — 365:25
I've been up to L. — 368:14
key of India is in L. — 181:15
L.; a nation, not a city — 182:15
'L. Assurance' — 506:1
L. doth pour out her citizens — 445:5
L. is a fine town — 154:9
L. is the epitome of our times — 200:2
L. is a modern Babylon — 182:37
L., my most kindly nurse — 510:21
L...of townes A per se — 195:3
L. particular — 173:23
L.'s column — 385:2
L.'s lasting shame — 229:24
L...so near his burrow — 338:11
L.'s towers receive the Lamb — 75:12
L., that great sea — 495:9
L...the clearing-house of the world — 135:4
L., thou art the flower — 195:5
lungs of L. — 379:13
midst fallen L. — 33:12
Mr. Weller's knowledge of L. — 178:35
moon's self. Here in L. — 94:8
my beat before L. Town — 301:6
one road leads to L. — 334:8
sent him up to fair L. — 29:23
these are thy gods, O L.! — 307:2
to merry L. came — 510:21
vilest alleys of L. — 187:17
when a man is tired of L. — 273:23
London Bridge: broken arch of L. — 324:31
forest below L. — 412:28
L...greater..than any of the seven Wonders — 2:19
L. is broken down — 367:19
Lone: I'm a l. lorn creetur — 174:13
l. and alone she lies — 171:24
l. on the fir-branch — 336:9
poor l. woman — 441:28
walking by his wild l. — 304:22
Loneliness: all that bowery l. — 529:18
shade and l. and mire — 84:7
when in l. — 512:15
Lonely: antheming a l. grief — 286:17
blind, old, and l. — 491:15
from my l. room this night — 23:16
guide my l. way — 225:11
in l. lands — 529:10
l. as a cloud — 577:5
l. dreams of a child — 171:4
l. of heart — 585:13
none of these so l. — 83:19
sat him down in a l. place — 538:1
smooth, fair, and l. — 80:19
so l., loving, helpless — 115:35
so l. 'twas — 150:14
still it's l. lies — 171:24
troubled with her l. life — 377:21
Lonesome: on a l. road — 150:2
Long: alas, so l., so far — 185:1
appear most l. and terrible — 312:26
art is l. — 317:6
as l. as ever you can — 565:19
as l. as twenty days are now — 573:11
as l.'s my arm — 106:4
because his legs have grown tool. — 311:14
blissful dreams of l. ago — 157:1
calamity of so l. life — 434:4
craft so l. to learn — 248:13
craft so l. to lerne — 138:22
damned l., dark, boggy..way — 227:6
delighted us l. enough — 22:32
don't the days seem lank and l. — 222:1

[805]

Long (*cont.*)

every man desires to live l. 520:42
everything by starts, and nothing l. 190:22
Gilpin l. live he 160:11
goeth to his l. home 51:33
how l.? 53:11, 517:2
how l. a time lies 474:16
how l.? how l.? 298:27
how l. I have to live 394:8
how l., O Lord 70:46
how l., O lord, how l.? 324:18
how l. or short permit to Heaven 349:25
I am going a l. way 531:37
I l. to talk 185:34
in the bleak mid-winter, l. ago 409:20
it cannot hold you l. 225:17
I think it can't be l. 536:27
it's a l. way to Tipperary 571:1
it sha'n't be l. 139:4
lie l., high snowdrifts 263:13
light heart lives l. 455:28
l. ago an' fur away 299:13
l. as my exile 429:19
l. hair. .a glory to her 66:42
l. has it waved on high 251:5
l. is the way and hard 345:27
L. John Brown 75:15
l. live the king 160:11
l. live the weeds 254:30
l., l. may the ladies sit 32:2
l., l. may the maidens sit 32:2
l., l. thoughts 316:38
l., l. time ago 210:1
l. may it wave 292:11
l. poem is a test of invention 289:15
l. prayers 15:26
l. shot, Watson 188:4
l. time on the road 179:37
l. to reign over us 250:14
l. while to make it short 547:5
look at them l. and l. 567:20
Lord, how l.? 53:11
love is l. 538:21
love me l. 8:8, 246:10
march from short to l. 152:5
nor that little l. 587:9, 12
nor wants that little l. 225:13
not that the story need be l. 547:5
not too l. in coming 112:10
now we sha'n't be l. 121:26
on which the public thinks l. 278:8
our acquaintance. .a l. 'un 178:41
pull out, on the L. Trail 208:27
Saviour promised l. 183:19
seas are too l. 28:3
short and the l. of it 466:1
so l. as ye both shall live 391:29
so l. lives this 486:18
sorrow. .dureth over l. 328:9
so you love me l. 246:10
sweetness l. drawn out 342:7
that thy days may be l. 590:12
they are not l. 187:11
thou art l., and lank 149:19
though life be l. and dreary 202:25
though the day be never so l. 239:6
to be l. loved 15:20
too l. a day 252:33
trips from l. to short 152:4
warfare l. 264:9
we l. for quails 193:7
Long-cramped scroll 92:34
Long-drawn aisle 230:2
Longed: truly l. for death 540:27
where he l. to be 516:15
Longed-for dash of waves 17:28(–18)
Longer: linger l. Lucy 233:15
my song. .l. 369:9
nor now. .l. will tarry 189:6
so very little l. 93:9
stretch him out l. 454:27
wished l. by its readers 276:26
Longest: how short is the l. life 290:30
l. half of your life 508:10
l. night in all the year 359:14
loving l. 22:27
see who will pound l. 564:16
Longeth: my flesh also l. after thee 395:25
Longing: feeling of sadness and l. 316:8
its l. for the tomb 586:10
l. for de old plantation 210:16

Longing (*cont.*)

l. to be at 'em 6:16
more l., wavering 483:3
my soul hath a. .l. 397:5
one l. ling'ring look 230:9
this l. after immortality 1:22
Longings: I have immortal l. 426:9
Longitude: Board of L. 503:10
l. also is vague 402:22
l. and. .latitude for a seine 550:20
Long-leggety beasties 6:9
Long-lived: strong and l. death 184:25
Long Melford: tip them L. 78:31
Long-resounding pace 231:14
Long-sought: come, l.l 495:22
Long-suffering: l., and of great goodness 400:18
l., and very pitiful 56:30
love, joy, peace, l. 67:46
Longue: je n'ai fait celle-ci plus l. que 374:8
Looe: pilchards at L. 294:35
Look: afraid to l. upon God 45:35
be a candle-holder, and l. on 477:5
cat may l. at a king 129:14
do I l. like it? 129:36
don't l. too good 297:10
do we l. for another? 59:5
eyes that would not l. on me 500:8
far'z you can look or listen 319:23
forbears again to l. upon 577:24
full l. at the worst 236:13
give me a l. 280:7
goodly to l. to 47:19
hereafter rising l. for us 507:29
her wanton spirits l. out 481:26
his hearers could not. .l. aside 280:2
how you l. to other people 551:2
hungry sheep l. up 342:29
I could not l. on Death 296:6
if he'll only l. in 222:17
if you l. at the waiter 178:26
I l. at all things as they are 541:22
I l. right through its. .roof 92:30
I must not l. to have 460:36
I stand and l. at them 567:20
lean and hungry l. 448:26
let him l. to his bond 464:7
l. after our people 416:6
l. around and choose thy ground 118:27
l. at least on love's remains 94:45
l. at me. .in that tone of voice 403:32
l. at the stars! 255:5
l. before you ere you leap 111:2
l. behind for me 265:24
l. ere thou leap 550:3
l. for me by moonlight 366:3
l. for me in the nurseries 544:10
l. here, upon this picture 435:45
l. homeward, Angel 343:2
l. in my face 548:19
l. in thy heart, and write 501:23
l. into the seeds of time 456:15
l. into thy bonnie face 104:26
l. like the time 457:5
l. not back nor tire 81:24
l. not on his picture 281:9
l. not on pleasures as they come 244:8
l. not thou down but up 95:25
l. not thou on beauty's charming 419:16
l. not thou upon the wine 50:32
l. on both indifferently 448:16
l. on her face 385:12
l. on my works, ye Mighty 496:14
l. on't again I dare not 458:14
l. out for a wife, to l. after a wife 518:38
l. out of your window, Mrs. Gill? 171:18
l. round, l. up 87:27
l. round the habitable world 194:23
l. thither 523:15
l. through this same Garden 207:28, 29
l. thy last on all things lovely 171:9
l. to your health 559:26
l. to your Moat 234:12
l. upon a little child 565:9
l. upon myself 486:24
l. up, thank God of all! 136:20
l. with thine ears 454:10
men's eyes were made to l. 478:13
met. .with erected l. 193:41
my God, l. upon me 393:1

Look (*cont.*)

my wife; l. well at her 511:5
ne'er l. back 472:12
never to l. into a newspaper 499:24
no day for me to l. upon 484:36
not l. upon his like again 431:6
O l. at the trees! 81:16
one longing ling'ring l. 230:9
only a l. and a voice 318:10
only loveless l. 375:15
row one way and l. another 109:6
same l. . .when he rose 356:13
see his monument l. around 583:16
shake thou to l. on't 425:5
she gave me never a l. 15:27
silly little Johnny, l. 250:3
spare not! Nor l. behind! 262:3
stop; l.; listen 551:4
that men might l. and live 551:18
that we may l. upon thee 52:16
this eye. .do l. into it 513:22
this l. of thine 473:32
to live in and not to l. on 25:35
to l. about us and to die 383:7
Twelve-pound L. 36:13
two men l. out 310:1
unless I l. on Silvia in the day 484:36
unto the. .flood-brim l. with me 411:8
we l. before and after 498:9
westward, l., the land is bright 147:8
whence a l. shot out 523:4
when I do l. on thee 502:7
with a bitter l. 569:4
with delight l. round her 576:2
your l.? 94:45
Looked: all his men l. at each other 288:19
as she l. around 316:16
Babe l. up 165:36
but l. to near 563:15
come when you're l. for 169:27
ever l. with human eyes 532:40
he l. again, and found 128:15
he l. inwards, and found her 194:6
he l. upon his people 323:4
his wife l. back 44:53
I l. over Jordan 10:2
I should have l. . .the very same 204:33
King l. up 140:18
l. asklent and unco skeigh 105:13
l. forth into the night 322:20
l. on better days 427:19
l. on truth askance 488:5
l. out at a window 48:28
l. that it should bring forth grapes 53:1
mother of Sisera l. out 46:51
no sooner met, but they l. 428:26
righteousness hath l. down 397:9
she l. across the sea 293:8
she l. at me as she did love 286:32
she l. in my face 35:9
she l. the spirits up and down 298:30
sigh'd and l., and sigh'd again 191:10
the Lord. .l. upon Peter 62:46
thrice l. he at the city 323:23
when her spirit l. through me 410:20
wise as Thurlow l. 211:1
Looker-on: patient l. 404:10
Lookers-on: l. feel most delight 111:3
l. . .see more 26:12
only for God and angels to be l. 24:22
Lookest: if thou l., uncle Toby 513:22
why l. thou so? 149:1
Looketh: l. forth as the morning 52:15
the Lord l. on the heart 47:18
which l. toward Damascus 52:19
Looking: all were l. for a king 326:21
in my l. 6:10
l. back. .see a glimpse 552:3
l. before and after 436:15
l. down the throat of Old Time 175:19
l. one way, and rowing another 99:17
l. on his life 424:1
l. tranquillity 114:22
l. unto Jesus 69:18
no harm in l. 518:32
no l. at a building here 103:36
they l. back 349:31
when l. well can't move her 517:10
Looking-glass: cruel l. 298:29
Looking-glasses: plenty of l. 20:31

INDEX

Looks: actor stops, and l. around 543:6
assurance given by 412:18
clear your l. 581:14
deep-search'd with saucy l. 454:32
her l. were free 149:13
her modest l. 225:7
his l. adorn'd the venerable place 224:22
his l. do menace heaven 330:23
his wit invites you by his l. 159:20
kill with l. 475:7
Liner..never l. nor 'eeds 298:25
l. commercing with the skies 341:9
l. in the clouds 449:3
l. quite through the deeds of men 448:27
l. such things 312:28
l. through nature 384:14
l. toward Namancos 343:2
l. with unconcern on a man struggling 270:18
man l. aloft 194:25
Moon that l. for us again 207:29
praising God with sweetest l. 253:20
puts on his pretty l. 447:34
radiant l. of..flowers 497:3
screen them in those l. 497:9
she l. another way 9:9
side-long l. of love 224:13
stolen l. are nice in chapels 266:1
woman as old as she l. 153:19
woman's l. 356:33
Loom: plough—l.—anvil 307:17
she left the l. 534:7
Looms: passage through these l. 551:15
Loon: thou cream-faced.l! 460:35
unhand me, grey-beard l.l! 148:20
with that he call'd the tailor l. 471:11
Looped and window'd raggedness 453:14
Loop-hole: from her cabin'd l. 340:6
Loopholes of retreat 103:23
Loose: all hell broke l. 347:33
before the nuts work l. 302:2
check to l. behaviour 511:25
ere yet we l. the legions 297:8
Fancy! let her l. 285:38
God lets l. a thinker 200:7
his title hang l. about him 460:31
hung l. upon society 270:12
let l. the Gorgonzola! 403:34
l. as the wind 244:9
l., plain, rude writer 109:9
l. the bands of Orion 49:24
l. the bands of wickedness 54:36
l. the seals thereof 70:40
men so l. of soul 472:8
she's l. i' th' hilts 563:10
wear those things so l. 34:28
w'en it git l. fum de jug 238:21
young Scotsman..let l. 36:16
Loosed from Pharaoh's bitter yoke 361:15
Loosely: robes l. flowing 280:7
Loosen: until God l...the trumpets 524:24
Lops the moulder'd branch 529:33
Loquendi: ius et norma l. 255:20
Loquendo: consumere longa l. tempora 372:7
Loquentem: Lalagen..dulce l. 258:23
Loquimur: dum l., fugerit..aetas 258:17
Lor: non ragionem di l. 168:18
Lorbeer: und hoch der L. steht 224:6
Lord: absolute sole l. 166:11
acceptable year of the L. 55:3
Adriatic mourns her l. 114:3
angel of the L. came upon them 61:18
arm of the L. revealed 54:24
cast their burden upon the L. 302:3
certain l., neat 438:32
coming of the L. 264:15
dear L. was crucified 4:4
deputy elected by the L. 475:1
die with kissing of my L. 331:4
dwell in the house of the L. 393:10
each of himself was l. 371:8
earth is the L.'s 66:40
English l...lightly me 31:6
even so standeth the L. 399:33
even that same L. 421:2
even the L. of hosts 393:13

Lord (*cont.*)
evil..and the L. hath not done it? 55:55
except the L. build the house 399:35
except the L. keep the city 49:36, 399:35
fall into the hands of the L. 56:31
fear of the L. 53:17, 398:25
fie, my l., fie! 460:24
for ever with the L.! 355:9
for he is the L. our God 397:28
for joy Our L. was born 7:14
for the L. hath created him 57:9
from which our L. drank 530:22
glory of the L. is risen 54:39
glory of the L...revealed 54:9
God bless our L. the King! 250:14
great l. of all things 383:22
hark, my soul! it is the L. 161:9
her sleeping l. 343:25
holy, holy, holy is the L. of hosts 53:8
if his majesty our sovereign l. 12:6
I know not the L. 45:40
in the glance of the L. 118:39
in the L. put I my trust 392:17
in whom the L...did pitch 243:22
I replied, 'My L.' 244:10
it is the L. who rises 161:21
I were l. in May 524:30
Jehovah, Jove, or L. 386:29
judge not the L. 161:18
kneel before the L. our Maker 397:27
knowledge of the L. 53:19
lesson which the L. us taught 509:5
let men know we serve the L. 301:20
L. among wits 270:20
L., behold us 98:13
L. God of Sabaoth 388:15
l. how it talk't 38:7
L., how long? 53:11
l. of folded arms 455:8
l. of himself 118:4, 583:11
l. of humankind 193:34
L. of lords 71:37
L. of our far-flung battle-line 300:24
l. of the ascendant 100:9
l. of the fowl and the brute 164:22
L. of the unerring bow 114:23
l. of thy presence and no land 447:18
l. of yourself 192:14
l. once own the..lines 382:34
love is L. of all the world 509:10
Love will still be l. of all 417:23
mongrel beef-witted l. 481:9
monstrous eft was..the L. 535:36
moral Clytemnestra of thy l. 118:25
most glorious L. of life 509:4
mourn'd the L. of Burleigh 535:10
mouth of the L. hath spoken 54:9
my bosom's l. sits lightly 478:34
my gude l. in the black velvet 31:4
my L. in the Peers will take his place 84:27(-85)
my most noble l. slain 328:17
nations knew their lawful l. 190:31
noble l. in the blue riband 100:20
no L. of Parys..or Floraunce 195:7
nor the servant above his l. 58:51
O L. most High 390:40
O L., stretch forth 264:11
O, the unworthy l.! 573:24
our help is in the name of the L. 391:18
parents..the L. knows who 170:14
praise the L.! 291:27
prepare ye the way of the L. 54:9, 57:28
pretty well for a L. 273:10
rejoice in the L. 393:35
remembrance of his dying L. 509:18
salute me to my l., Sir Launcelot 328:13
sapient sutlers of the L. 197:24
seek ye the L. while he may be found 54:30
since my l. is Antony again 425:7
sing the L.'s song 400:5
sought the L. aright 104:35
speak, L. 47:6
spirit of the L. bloweth upon it 54:10
Spirit of the L. God is upon me 55:2
spirit of the L...upon him 53:17
thank the L., O thank the L. 121:27

Lord (*cont.*)
their L. himself bespake 343:14
the L. and giver of life 390:20
the L. be thankit 107:34
the L. be with thee 47:22
the L. He lays it on Martha's Sons 302:3
the L. himself is thy keeper 399:28
the L. is a man of war 45:51
the L. is in this place 45:4
the L. is King 397:22, 31, 33
the L...is mightier 397:23
the L. is my light 49:35, 393:20
the L. is my shepherd 393:10
the L. is thy defence 399:28
the L. is with thee 61:12
the L. knows where 383:27
the L. No Zoo 176:4
the L. of Hosts, and none but he 421:2
the L. our God is good 292:9
the L. our God Most High 301:25
the L. remaineth a King 393:24
the L. said unto my L. 398:23
the L. shall raise me up 405:12
the L.'s my shepherd 421:1
the L.'s passover 45:47
the L. taketh me up 393:21
the L. thy God is with thee 46:37
the L. was not in the wind 48:8
the L. went before them 45:50
the L. who made the hills 302:11
the L. will be there 567:22
the L. will have mercy on Jacob 92:9
the L., ye know, is God 292:7
they cried unto the L. 398:15
they that wait upon the L. 54:14
they who seek the L. 393:38
those who view the L. 265:16
Thou, L., and I 172:1
thus said the L. in the vault 208:9
thy l. the summer 524:15
till his L. is crucified 320:12
to my L. heartily 316:32
to the very quality of my l. 470:9
unhouse and house the L. 254:28
voice of the L. 393:23
welcum the l. of lycht 187:5
whom the L. loveth 69:19
ye servants of the L. 183:21
zeal of the L. of hosts 53:16
Lord Chancellor: marriages.. made by the L. 273:1
Lord-Keeper: my grave L. 230:19
Lordliest: l. lass of earth 84:5
lords are l. in their wine 350:38
Lordly: butter in a l. dish 46:49
l., lovely Rhine 122:9
Lords: about the l. of the creation 108:20
addressing a naked House of L. 127:9
cure for admiring the House of L. 29:1
fail..in the House of L. 182:47
l. and commons of this realm 103:9
l. and owners of their faces 487:25
l. are lordliest in their wine 350:38
l. of human kind 226:14
l. of ladies intellectual 115:16
l. of the world besides 344:5
l. that are certainly expected 149:24
l. too are bards 117:23
l. who lay you low 498:17
l. whose parents were.. 170:14
our gude Scots l. 32:1
princes and l...but the breath 105:5
princes and l. may flourish 224:14
procuress to the L. of Hell 532:30
Scots l. at his feet 32:2
seemed l. of all 347:10
so honour'd, at the House of L. 386:11
with those L. I had gone so far 358:2
women..who love their l. 251:25
Lordships: attendance on their l.' pleasures 447:12
Lore: all the l. its scholars need 291:12
Cristes l...he taught 137:18
gives me mystical l. 122:22
l. which Nature brings 581:16
volume of forgotten l. 380:22
Lorn: I'm a lone l. creetur 174:13
Lorraine Lorrèe: poor L. 293:5
Lose: gain the whole world, and l. his own soul 59:45, 61:3

INDEX

Lose (cont.)

get at one end. .l. at the other 272:36
he must l. it 337:40
he that findeth his life shall l. it 59:3
if I do l. thee I do l. a thing 462:3
if once we l. this light 282:6
lest we l. our Edens 97:25
l. and neglect the creeping hours 427:19
l., and start again 297:11
l. it in the moment you detect 384:22
l. myself in a mystery 86:8
l. myself in dotage 423:24
l. myself in other men's minds 306:25
l. not the things eternal 389:41
l. the good we oft might win 461:21
l. the name of action 434:4
l. the name of king 475:10
l. . .this intellectual being 345:19
l. to-morrow the ground won 18:12
l. what he never had 559:22
l. who may 93:43
love I seemed to l. 88:24
more lust again to l. 140:17
much to hope and nothing to l. 103:12
neither a soul to l. 505:5
nothing to l. . .but their chains 333:11
some day you may l. them all 312:5
tails you l. 167:1
these l., and under the sky, lie friended 403:1
to l. a volume to C. 306:22
to l. good days 510:16
to l. one parent. .to l. both 569:23
to l. thee were to l. myself 349:19
to seek power and to l. liberty 26:23
to win or l. it all 355:19
way to l. him 423:30
we may l. the way 142:13
wish that one should l. 330:13
Loser: neither party l. 442:18
Losers: both should l. be 244:27
in war. .all are l. 135:8
l. must have leave to speak 144:30
Loses: l. both itself and friend 431:25
l. his misery 18:17
l. them too 321:14
who l. and who wins 454:19
Losest: for fear thou l. all 245:7
Loseth his life for my sake 59:3
Losing: all about you are l. theirs 297:10
but a l. office 441:10
next. .to l. a battle 564:9
profit by l. of our prayers 424:3
Loss: counting gain but l. 361:13
deeper sense of her l. 214:1
enow to do our country l. 444:26
for ever to deplore her l. 348:35
for the l. of the sun 139:3
l. for Christ 68:21
l. of thee. .never from my heart 349:18
man's l. . .from his gain 90:44
natural sorrow, l., or pain 581:3
never breathe. .about your l. 297:11
no note of Time but from its L. 587:2
richest gain I count but l. 562:18
upon thy so sore l. 545:1
whose l. . .a distinct gain 219:23
with l. of Eden 344:1
Losses: all l. are restor'd 486:25
fellow that hath had l. 469:11
God bless all our l. 88:10
Lost: all good to me is l. 346:33
all is l., except a little life 118:24
all is not l. 344:14
all love is l. but upon God 195:8
battle l. . .melancholy as a battle won 564:4
better to have fought and l. 147:5
112:16, 532:20
books by which the printers have l. 212:15
Cerinthus that is l. 91:2
compass l. 160:35
Corinth l. and won 114:40
die in the l., l. fight 146:14
dinner l.l 'ounds l., self l. 518:16
ever l. an English gun 537:18
fairer person l. not Heav'n 345:18
falter, are l. in the storm 17:18
he was l., and is found 62:16

Lost (cont.)

his bark cannot be l. 456:11
home of l. causes 19:10
how art thou l. . .on a sudden l. 349:17
I am l., but see 579:34
I have l. all the names 274:33
in the Temple l. outright 207:8
I've l. Britain. .I've l. Lalage 301:5
land of l. content 263:14
legion of the l. ones 296:26
leper once he l. 344:33
like the l. Pleiad seen no more 112:32
long l., late won 496:3
lose with my l. saints 88:24
l. a joy. .worth worlds 244:6
l. days of my life 411:13
l. evermore in the main 540:4
l. her honest name 9:18
l. him half the kind 193:39
l. in a sort of Purgatory blind 285:10
l. in God, in Godhead found 199:31
l. in the same spirit 567:15
l. is our freedom 124:3
l. no friend 385:6
l. sheep of the house of Israel 58:46
l. the world for love 193:14
l. thing could I never find 42:6
l. to Love and Truth 105:1, 296:28
l. to me, l. to me 34:1
l. . .two golden hours 329:9
l. upon the roundabouts 135:2
loved long since, and l. awhile 364:12
missed it, l. it forever 97:29
my sheep which was l. 62:11
my thoughts, which loved and l. 232:15
never l. till won 165:14
never star was l. here 97:21
never to have l. at all 112:16
no hate l. between us 338:1
no love l. 280:18
no love l. between us 227:13
not l. but gone before 242:19, 365:23
not so much. .that Old England is l. 273:18
not that you won or l. 406:20
not yet so l. in lexicography 277:21
one silvery cloud had l. his way 537:31
Parthenophil is l. 210:1
poor souls l. in the dark 92:7
praising what is l. 423:10
shoe was l. 211:10
shouted, 'L.! l.! l.!' 417:17
some l. lady of old years 97:18
something l. behind the Ranges 296:9
sooner l. and worn 483:3
that nothing be l. 63:21
that we left, we l. 10:5
thou art l. and gone for ever 355:22
though l. to sight 314:21
unknowe, unkist, and l. that is unsought 138:27
war. .in time be utterly l. 567:5
what though the field be l.? 344:14
what wee kept, wee l. 11:17
when the battle's l. and won 456:3
woe that all was l. 349:15
woman that deliberates is l. 1:19
work itself shall not be l. 211:21
World Well L. 191:14
you have l. your writing-book 250:3
Lot: attempt to give a deathless l. 160:37
be warned by my l. 298:3
into the l. of the righteous 399:33
leave the L. of Kaikobad 205:19
l. fell upon Jonah 56:4
l. has fallen to me 302:13
l. is fallen unto me 392:26
neither part nor l. in this 64:37
no great improvements in the l. of mankind 338:21
our loving l. 252:11
policeman's l. 221:34
remember L.'s wife 62:31
sack the l.l 205:1
Shepherd's sweet l. 76:11
thou shalt maintain my l. 392:25
weary l. is thine, fair maid 419:8
Loth: not. .l. to leave this Paradise 349:29
was l. to depart 402:6
what maidens l.? 287:7

Lothario: gallant, gay L. 412:9
that false L.! 412:5
Lotos: l. and lilies 537:31
L. blooms 535:18
Lotos-buds: like l. that float 254:15
Lotos-dust: yellow L. is blown 535:18
Lots: cast l. upon my vesture 393:6
Lottery: razor strops and the l. 370:13
their judgement is a mere l. 194:9
Lou: lady that's known as L. 422:21
linger longer L. 233:15
Loud: at once. .deaf and l. 495:9
curses, not l., but deep 460:36
half as l. again as the other 204:33
I said it very l. and clear 131:12
l. and troublesome *insects* 102:20
l. in multitudinous *chatterings* 336:32
l. prays the priest 15:27
l. sang the souls 298:14
l. with names 523:10
melody l. and sweet 538:1
now l. as welcomes 253:15
voice less l. 93:22
with music l. and long 151:33(–152)
yet was never l. 470:29
you needn't shout so l. 131:12
Louder: little l., but as empty 383:30
l. he talked of his honour 200:1
l. still the din 322:22
still l. and more dread 150:10
Loudest: l. complainers for the public 102:2
l. will I. 117:5
Loud-hissing: bubbling and l. urn 163:21
Loudly: cat languishes l. 241:27
l. his sweet voice he rears 150:8
Louis: fils de Saint L., montez 204:38
Louis XIV: ambassadors to L. 274:9
Lounge: treated as a l. 39:26
Loungers: all the l. of the Empire 188:23
Lounging 'roun' en suffer'n' 238:15
Louse: l. for the hangman 280:12
l. in the locks of literature 541:26
precedency between a l. and a flea 275:10
scarce the soul of a l. 302:33
Louted low down on his knee 32:7
Love: absence from whom we l. 160:20
acts of kindness and of l. 581:24
against the reason of my L. 290:28
ah! what is l.! 232:5
alas! the l. of women! 115:37
all earth to l. 302:13
all for l. 173:3, 509:32
All For L. 191:14
all for the l. of you 168:2
all l., all liking, all delight 246:1
all l. at first. .'terments 111:24
all l. is lost but upon God 195:8
all mankind l. a lover 200:24
all my l. is towards individuals 519:32
all she loves is l. 115:38
all's l., yet all's law 96:22
all. .subject but eternal L. 497:7
all that l. me 262:7
all the l. that ever was betwixt us 328:18
all the substance of his house for l. 52:32
all the world and l. were young 405:8
all who deserve his l. 192:13
ape the magnanimity of l. 336:19
arms of my true l. 536:17
as great in l. as in religion 158:20
as L. wist to pursue 544:16
as she did l. 286:32
as thy L. is discovered almighty 96:24
as woman's l. 435:8
at his call l. him 580:6
at last acquainted with L. 270:17
beautiful through l. 497:13
Beauty, Truth, and L. . .one 81:5
because my l. is come 409:14
because we freely l. 348:12
before the god of l. was born 185:34
Benedick, l. on 468:27
better than secret l. 50:44
beyond His l. and care 568:16
bid me l. 247:1
bid me take l. easy 584:11
boast their l. possessing 80:9

INDEX

Love (cont.)
bower of wanton Shrewsbury
  and l.   385:1
break an hour's promise in l.l   428:18
brotherly l. continue   69:22
but ministers of L.   152:3
by a l. so much refined   186:25
call a dog *Hervey*. .l. him   270:4
cantons of contemned l.   482:22
carry a letter to my l.   30:20
Cassio, I l. thee   471:19
caught up into l.   88:17
cheer'd her soul with l.   535:5
choose l. by another's eye   466:19
Christ's particular l.'s sake   96:2
clap thyself my l.   485:5
comely in nothing but in l.   26:32
common l. of good   533:20
conscience is born of l.   488:23
content with a vegetable l.   220:28
could L. for ever run   119:7
courage, l. and joy   214:29
course of true l.   466:18
crime to l. too well   381:31
crown. .made of l. and friendship 284:26
cruel madness of l.   535:38
cure thine heart of l.   38:23
dallies with the innocence of l.   483:5
dear l. of comrades   566:24
dearly l. but one day   125:19
deep and heavy was the l.   30:15
deep as first l.   538:19
didst Thou l. the race   267:15
dinner of herbs where l. is   50:12
distorting his tender l.   81:8
doesn't l. a wall   212:2
don't I l. thee   6:19
dost thou l. life?   211:15
dropped from their youth and l.   96:43
dull sublunary lovers' l.   186:25
duty, faith, l., are roots   377:4
duty, where I cannot l.   40:7
ease its heart of l. in   286:9
ease thine heart of l.   38:22
emphasis of passionate l. repeated   309:13
England does not l. coalitions   180:23
England, we l. thee better   549:5
enkindle with their l. the breath 497:9
enough to make us l. one another 520:38
eternal joy, and everlasting l.   371:12
every other gift, but wanted l.   16:12
every warrior that is rapt with l. 331:2
excommunicate from. .l.   125:8
exultations, agonies, and l.   582:4
faith creates or l. desires   496:19
fall out with those we l.   538:9
feeling and a l.   581:26
fettered L. from dying   123:5
few l. to hear the sins they l. to act 474:6
first-l.'s first cry   375:8
fit l. for Gods   349:12
flowers and fruits of l.   118:26
folly that. .l. did make thee run
  into   427:2
fool of l.   239:22
for a good man's l.   428:14
for all His l.   121:27
for ever wilt thou l.   287:9
for ladies' l. unfit   192:3
for l. of Barbara Allen   30:1
for l.'s sake only   88:18
for l., sweet l.   568:9
forspent with l. and shame   310:10
for the general award of l.   286:20
for the l. he had to her   45:6
for the l. of a ladye   222:27
for thy l.. .no; yet I l. thee   445:12
for your l. to her, lead apes   479:3
freedom in my l.   319:7
free l.—free field   530:42
friendship ever ends in l.   215:15
friendship, like l., is but a name 215:29
from my first l.   552:3
fruit of the Spirit is l.   67:46
gather the Rose of l.   509:33
gin l. be bonnie   32:18
give all to l.   199:12
give my L. good-morrow!   248:5
Glory, L. and Honour unto. .
  Jane   297:20

Love (cont.)
God gives us l.   533:34
God is l.   70:12
God is L., I dare say   112:4
God l. you!   95:29
God of L. my Shepherd is   245:10
grace to l. thee more   161:13
grace which l. makes for thee   573:22
greater l. hath no man   63:57
great god of L.'s name   138:15
great l. grows there   435:9
green and happy in first l.   146:32
hail, wedded l.   347:26
half in l. with easeful Death   287:32
happiest bond of l.   229:8
hate all that don't l. me   203:19
hath not, or is not in l.   481:7
having not seen, ye l.   69:45
health to all those that we l.   6:21
heart whose l. is innocent   119:2
he'll never l. me mair   32:18
help. .of the woman I l.   196:1
he may live without l.   337:42
herald of l.'s mighty king   509:6
her subjects'l.   402:2
he sang of l.   578:11
he was the Queen's l.   30:10
he would l., and she would not   80:7
hid in the heart of l.   585:20
his banner over me was l.   51:44
his for his l.   486:26
his l., his zeal   348:18
his song of l.   81:8
hold your tongue and let me l.   184:11
honour, l., obedience   460:36
hope nor l.   515:28
how can he l. God   70:15
how do I l. thee?   88:24
how I do l. thee!   156:19
how I l. my country   379:18
how little worthy of any l.   544:29
how l. exalts the mind   192:4
how many times do I l. thee   38:30
how shall I know your true l. ?   405:10
how should I your true l. know?   436:19
how wayward is this. .l.   484:31
human l. needs human meriting   544:29
I am sick of l.   51:45, 52:12
I could not l. thee (Dear)   319:10
I do know l.   82:23
I do l. I know not what   246:13
I do l.. .taught me to rhyme   455:15
I do l. thee! and when I l. thee
  not   471:27
I do l. thee as my lambs   156:19
I do l. thee, meek *Simplicity!*   152:12
I do not l. thee!   365:22
I do not l. the man   560:33
I do not l. you, Dr. Fell   85:10
if a man say, I l. God   70:15
if ever thou shalt l.   483:2
if I know what true l. is   530:36
if I l. not him   530:36
if it be l. indeed   423:12
if l. were what the rose is   524:28
if music be the food of l.   481:30
if my l. were in my arms   11:14
if of herself she will not l.   517:11
if this be not l., it is madness   155:27
if thou car'st not whom I l.   185:21
if thou dost l., pronounce it   477:20
if thou must l. me   88:18
if yet I have not all thy l.   185:33
I heartily l. John, Peter, Thomas 519:32
I honour, l. and embrace them   86:27
I knew it was l.   118:34
ilka bird sang of its l.   108:38
I'll never l. thee more   355:18
I l. a lass   370:5
I l. a lassie   310:12
I l. all beauteous things   81:9
I l. all that thou lovest   498:12
I l. but you alone   31:15
I l. her so sincerely   560:33
I l. her till I die   10:20, 210:5
I l. him not   560:33
I l. it, I l. it   156:21
I l. L.   498:16
I l. my L. and my L. loves me   150:18
I l. not hollow cheek   539:1

Love (cont.)
I l. Robertson, and I won't
  talk of his book   271:25
I l. thee, all unlovely   163:25
I l. thee beyond measure   570:30
I l. thee in prose   401:21
I l. thee still   112:12, 162:43
I l. thee to the depth   88:24
I l. thee true   286:33
I l. thee, whatever thou art   356:16
I l. thee with a l. I seemed to
  lose   88:24
I l. the languid patience   152:19
I l. them all   335:19
I l. to give pain   156:4
I l. to hear the story   339:8
I l. with all my heart   515:21
in all her outward parts L.   158:1
I never had but one true l.   32:16
I never was in l.   290:5
in every gesture dignity and l.   348:36
in likeness of l.   81:10
in l. alone we hate. .companions 559:6
in l. and charity with your
  neighbours   390:34
in l. and holy passion   574:8
in l., and in debt, and in drink   82:24
in l. and worship blends itself   493:6
in l., or had not dined   384:23
in l. with his fetters   27:44
in l. with night   478:20
in l. with one princess or another 512:21
in l. with the grave   263:28
in l. with the productions of
  time   77:12
in our will to l. or not   348:12
in Thy l. look down   512:15
invincible l. of reading   216:18
I shall be past making l.   401:25
is not l. a Hercules?   455:22
I think my l. as rare   488:14
it is the l. of the people   101:13
it strikes where it doth l.   473:11
I will l. Thee   244:25
I would l. infinitely   94:15
joy of l. is too short   328:9
keep a corner in the thing I l.   471:40
kill thee, and l. thee after   473:11
kind souls. . l. you   374:22
King of L. my Shepherd is   29:12
kiss your l. again   296:16
know me well, and l. me   177:35, 357:5
know the world, not l. her   587:12
labour of l.   68:35
lack of l. from l. made manifest   90:44
laggard in l.   418:17
last flower of Catholic l.   525:33
laughed at the power of L.   302:29
leads me from my l.   263:12
learned to l. the two   228:5
learn to l.   510:14
lease of my true l. control   488:2
leave me, O L.   502:5
leave to come unto my l.   509:14
lecture, L., in l.'s philosophy   185:30
left the ancient l.   75:18
leisure for l. or hope   253:26
Lesbia let us live and l.   123:19
let one's thought wander . .in l. 586:4
let's contend no more, L.   97:23
let the warm L. in   288:9
let thy l. be younger   483:4
let thy l. in kisses rain   494:7
let us l., deare L., like as we
  ought   509:5
let us l. nobly, and live   184:7
let us l. our occupations   174:8
lies my young l.   336:7
life I l.   515:27
light of l.'s bestowing   335:10
like to l. three more   517:18
lips of those who l. you   81:21
little duty and less l.   445:25
little emptiness of l.   84:17
little in our l.   483:10
little l. and good company   203:16
little words of l.   128:1
live with me and be my l. 184:8, 330:17
live with thee, and be thy l.   405:8
long l. doth so   478:9
lost the world for l.   193:14

Love (cont.)
lost to L. and Truth   105:1, 296:28
l. a bright particular star   423:2
l., all alike, no season knows   186:20
l. all..except an American   274:3
l. alone, with yearning heart   525:16
l. alters not   488:7
l., an abject intercourse   226:34
l. and a cottage   154:6
l., and a space for delight   522:7
l. and desire and hate   187:11
l. and do what you will   22:3
l. and fame to nothingness   289:6
L. and I were well acquainted   222:13
l. and murder will out   154:35
l. and save their souls   89:33
l. and scandal   204:21
l., and thought, and joy   581:6
l. a woman for singing   452:23
l. bade me welcome   244:21
L. be controll'd by advice   214:14
l. betwixt us two   158:10
l. built on beauty   184:13
l. but her, and l. for ever   104:10
l. but her for ever   104:25
l. but only her   114:25
l. ceases to be a pleasure   40:5
L. closed what he begat   336:35
l., converted   486:33
l. could teach a monarch   229:19
l., devoid of art   215:11
L.. .differs from gold and clay   493:11
l. does on both her lips   158:1
l. doth to her eyes repair   484:40
l. endures no tie   193:13
l. false or true   586:21
l., first learned in a lady's eyes   455:22
L. first leaves the..nest   494:21
l. for any lady   377:2
l. for philosophy   289:33
l., friendship, charity   481:21
l., friendship, cowardice   328:2
l. from l.   477:25
l. gilds the scene   500:31
l. goes toward l.   477:25
l. grows bitter with treason   525:8
l. had he found in huts   573:8
L.l has she done this to thee?   321:14
l...hath friends in the garrison   234:2
l. he bore to learning   225:1
l. he laugh'd to scorn   488:25
L. her body from her soul   411:26
l. him as myself   391:6
l. him, or leave him alone   580:2
L. in a golden bowl   74:2
l. in a hut   286:39
l. in a palace   286:39
l. indeed who quake to say they l.   501:29
L. in desolation masked   492:2
L. in her sunny eyes   158:1
l. in my bosom   231:39, 315:17
l. is a boy   110:42
l. is a circle   246:11
l. is a growing or full constant light   185:31
l. is a sickness full of woes   168:7
l. is a spirit all compact   488:26
l. is best   93:12
l. is blind   463:37
l. is crowned with the prime   428:33
l. is dying   35:21
l. is enough   359:6
l. is heaven, and heaven is l.   116:37, 417:16
l. is lame at fifty years   236:26
l. is left alone   533:34
l. is less kind   584:20
l. is like linen often chang'd   209:5
l. is like the measles   269:1, 11
l. is long   538:21
l. is Lord of all the world   509:10
l. is lost   243:34
l. is maister wher he wile   228:3
l. is more cruel than lust   523:1
l. is mor than gold   321:12
l. is not l. when it is mingled   452:12
l. is not l. which alters   488:7
l. is not secure   140:16
L. is of the valley   539:4
l. is slight   330:13

Love (cont.)
l. is strong as death   52:22
l. is such a mystery   517:17
l. is sweet for a day   525:8
L. is swift of foot   244:13
l. is the fulfilling of the law   66:12
l. is the lesson   509:5
l. is then our duty   214:32
l. is the wisdom of the fool   277:12
l. is too young to know   488:23
l. itself have rest   119:5
l. itself shall slumber on   499:1
lovelier than the L. of Jove   330:21
l. looks not with the eyes   466:22
l. match..only thing for happiness   195:18
l. meet they who do not shove   337:1
l. me little, l. me long   8:8
l. me little, so you l. me long   246:10
l. me no more   189:14
l. moderately   478:9
L. ne'er will from me flee   158:13
l. now who never lov'd   13:5
l. of Christ constraineth us   67:26
l. of Christ. .passeth knowledge   67:54
l. of false and cruel men   332:29
l. of good and ill   285:9
l. of liberty is the l. of others   239:23
l. of l.   537:40
l. of money   68:52
l. of news   165:1
l. of order..basis of Empire   156:27
l. of pleasure, and the l. of sway   384:35
l. of power is the l. of ourselves   239:23
l. of the turtle   113:1
l. of truth predominates   200:23
l. repulsed..returneth   493:23
l. rules the camp   116:37
l. rules the court   417:16
l.'s a malady without a cure   193:12
L.'s a man of war   244:13
L. sang to us   525:2
L.'s architecture is his own   166:2
L.'s but a dance   183:7
L.'s but a frailty of the mind   156:8
l. seeketh not itself to please   76:2
l.'s great artillery   166:7
l.'s harbinger   349:26
l. should have no wrong   80:7
L.'s latest breath   189:20
l. slights it   26:2
l.'s like the measles   269:1, 11
l.'s long since cancell'd woe   486:25
L.'s not Time's fool   488:7
l. so amazing, so Divine   562:19
l. so dearly joined   349:18
L...so hard a master   82:12
l...so ill to win   32:19
l., sole mortal thing   374:18
l. sought is good   483:29
l. sounds the alarm   214:10
l. so young..so sweet   82:3
l.'s passives   165:27
l.'s proper hue   349:4
l.'s remains   94:45
l.'s sad satiety   498:9
L.'s sweetest part, Variety   185:28
l.'s the noblest frailty   192:34
l.'s throne was not with these   410:22
L. still has something of the sea   421:12
l.'s tongue is in the eyes   209:7
l., sweet l., was thought a crime   76:1
l., sweetness, goodness   351:25
l.'s young dream   356:25
l. that can be reckoned   423:12
l. that endures for a breath   522:5
l. that he hath never woo'd   80:28
l. that I am seeking for   586:3
l. that lingers there   208:5
l. that loves a scarlet coat   252:31
L. that makes the world go round   7:23, 129:15, 219:14
l. that never found his..close   535:21
l. that never told can be   75:21
l. that should help you   524:33
l. that the..seraphs..coveted   380:8
l. that well which thou must leave   487:17
l. the brotherhood   69:50
L., the human form divine   77:1
L. the night   193:32

Love (cont.)
l., thou art absolute   166:11
L.l thou bane   229:9
l. thy country, wish it well   183:22
l. thy neighbour as thyself   46:9, 59:57
l. thyself last   446:31
l. to all men   295:8
l. to hatred turn'd   155:20
l. took up the glass of Time   534:16
L. tunes the shepherd's reed   417:16
l. virtue, she alone is free   341:5
l. wakes men   374:23
L. walks the pleasant mazes   158:1
l. warps the mind a little   165:16
l. was dead   523:15
l. was not a little thing   140:26
L. watching Madness   114:10
l. what I hate   95:20
l...when it ceases to be a secret   40:5
l. which us doth bind   332:6
l. which was more than l.   380:8
l., whose month is ever May   455:17
l. will change   82:2
l. will creep in service   484:39
l. will hardly seem worth   584:24
L. will still be lord of all   417:29
L. will venture in   107:29
l...without dissimulation   66:1
L. without his wings   117:43
l. without the help of anything   75:1
L. with unconfined wings   319:4
l. yet was l.   165:21
l. your neighbour's wife   325:18
l. your wives   68:32
l. you ten years before the Flood   333:8
made the Vessel in pure L.   207:18
make l. anew   421:17
make l. deathless   549:3
make l. to the lips we are near   350:35
make one in l. with death   491:13
makes thy l. more strong   487:17
make the Moor..l. me   471:4
make us l. your..gifts   474:7
man's l...a thing apart   115:25
many waters cannot quench l.   52:23
marry your old friend's l.   96:36
me and my true l.   9:7
medicines to make me l. him   439:2
men have died..not for l.   428:21
men l. in haste   116:44
men that l. lightly may die   523:19
men who do not l. her   573:12
mess of pottage with l.   50:13
met you not with my true l.   405:10
mine is an unchanging l.   161:12
mine was jealousy in l.   530:41
miserable l.   579:36
money is the sinews of l.   203:24
more beautiful than thy first l.   584:12
more l. and knowledge of you   426:29
more l. or more disdain   125:7
more of l. than matrimony   227:25
most power to hurt us that we l.   37:36
music sweet as l.   498:6
my dear and only l.   355:18
my dear l. sits him down   10:21
my God, I l. Thee   132:7
my Holy See of l.   287:5
my hope, my l.   558:7
my l. and I did meet   584:11
my l. and I did stand   584:11
my l. and I would lie   262:21(-263)
my l. doth so approve him   473:5
my l. has died for me to-day   30:3
my L. in her attire   8:14
my l. is dedde   136:17
my l. is of a birth as rare   332:5
my l. is weak and faint   161:13
my l. is the maïd ov all maïdens   35:15
my l., more noble than the world   483:8
my l.'s a noble madness   191:15
my l. she's but a lassie yet   191:15
my l. should..have been deck'd   509:15
my L.'s like a red red rose   107:14
my l., the flower of Yarrow   315:20
my only l...my only hate   477:11
my people l. to have it so   55:13
my sister, my l., my dove   52:9
my true L. did lichtlie me   32:18
my true L. has me forsook   32:18

INDEX

Love (cont.)

my true l. hath my heart	501:19
my vegetable l. should grow	333:8
my whole course of l.	469:45
nature is fine in l.	436:29
ne'er ebb to humble l.	472:12
neither our l. from God	410:25
never been in l., or in hate	514:24
never doubt I l.	432:42
never knew l. was so abused	502:6
never seek to tell thy l.	75:21
never taint my l.	473:3
new every morning is the l.	291:4
new l. may get	559:5
new L. pine at them	287:27
no fear in l.	70:14
no l. lost	280:18
no l. lost between us	227:13
no l...sets l. a task like that	265:20
no man dies for l.	193:22
none knew thee but to l. thee	234:15
none other I can l.	530:36
no new light on l. or liquor	387:22
nor l. thy life, nor hate	349:25
not Death, but L.	88:16
nothing all my l. avails	92:31
nothing in l.	460:31
not in our power to l., or hate	330:13
not least in l.	450:7
not l. thee (Dear) so much	319:10
not l. Thee if I l. Thee not	243:21
not l. them less	498:15
not unworthy to l. her	118:33
not with l.	468:4
now warm in l.	382:1
now with his l.	137:34
obscure epistles of l.	482:34
office and affairs of l.	468:12
off with the old l.	7:22, 335:4
of power, and of l.	68:56
O l. my Williel	121:15
O L., O firel	529:22
O l., thou art fair	522:8
O l., they die	538:16
O L. what hours	528:23
O L.! who bewailest	494:21
O lyric L., half angel	95:34
O mighty l.!	244:24
one born to l. you, sweet!	90:11
one jot of former l. retain	189:20
one of l.'s April-fools	155:23
open the temple gates unto my l.	509:12
O perfect l.	233:18
O spirit of l.!	481:30
ostentation of our l.	424:22
our l. and toil	295:6
our l. hath no decay	184:6
our l. is frail as is our life	202:1
our l. shall live	509:7
our l...with our fortunes change	435:11
out of l. with your nativity	428:17
over hir housbond as hir l.	138:11
over shoes in l.	484:29
O wisest l.!	364:8
oyster may be crossed in l.	500:7
pains of l. be sweeter far	194:2
pale with l.	468:4
pangs of disappointed l.	412:8
pangs of dispriz'd l.	434:4
partly wi' l. o'ercome	106:22
passing the l. of women	47:30
passin' the l. o' women	296:19
pass our long l.'s day	333:8
perfect l. casteth out fear	70:14
planet of L. is on high	536:10
pledge of l.	473:26
poets' food is l. and fame	493:16
poor heretics in l.	185:29
possible to l. such a man?	139:28
praise, blame, l., kisses	580:20
prize of learning l.	90:42
prosperity's the very bond of l.	485:33
prov'd thee my best of l.	488:5
prove..the sports of l.	282:5
purple light of l.	231:9
purple with l.'s wound	466:39
quench my great l.	219:8
quick-ey'd L.	244:21
regent of l. rhymes	455:8
remembrance of my former l.	484:34
renewing is of l.	196:2

Love (cont.)

restore my wand'ring L.	155:35
right true end of l.	184:20
rise up, my l.	52:1, 334:16
rites..of connubial l.	347:25
rogue gives you L. Powders	307:14
same sweet eternity of l.	246:11
Saturn and L. their long repose	493:27
seals of l.	462:16
seem worthy of your l.	578:32
separate us from the l. of God	65:58
service of my l.	511:4
shackles of an old l.	530:37
shall my sense pierce l.?	410:31
she never told her l.	483:10
shepherd—of his l.	33:13
she whom I l.	336:8
shove cravings in the van of L.	337:1
show a fitter L. for me	186:15
show out a flag and sign of l.	469:35
shows of l. to other men	448:15
side-long looks of l.	224:13
sigh to those who l. me	118:15
since I am L.'s martyr	185:5
sit with my l. in the..hay	82:13
sleep on, my L.	292:19
society, friendship, and l.	164:24
so dear I l. him	349:16
so faithful in l.	418:16
soft eyes look'd l.	113:25
soft interpreters of l.	401:31
soft philosopher of l.	192:45
so I fell in l.	222:19
so ill bred as to l. a husband	583:24
some are fou o' l. divine	106:13
some l. but little policy	475:28
something..moves me to l.	82:23
something to l. he lends us	533:34
so strong a passion as l. doth give	483:9
so sweet l. seemed	82:2
so true a fool is l.	487:7
sought..things to l.	498:20
soul of her beauty and l.	497:26
speak low, if you speak l.	468:11
spirit, I l. thee	498:16
spring of l. gushed	149:26
stand and l. in for a day	88:20
stony limits cannot hold l. out	477:17
stories of thy finish! l.	123:27
such ever was l.'s way	90:41
such I account thy l.	457:11
sweetest l., I do not go	186:15
sweetest l. to frown	232:5
sweet is true l.	530:38
sweet l...changing his property	475:5
sweets and the bitters of l.	117:44
sworn servant unto l.	168:11
take our fill of l.	49:50
tale of l. and languishment	289:3
tell me..if this be l.?	322:6
tell the laity our l.	186:24
tell this youth what 'tis to l.	428:28
tell us l. can die	507:17
temper'd with L.'s sighs	455:22
that gentleness and show of l.	448:14
that is l.'s curse	530:41
that l. could never change	82:2
that l. hath an end	525:4
that l. may never cease	244:25
that l. my friend	450:32
that they l.	558:7
their l. may be call'd appetite	483:9
their tales of l. shall tell	98:22
them that l.	65:56
them that l. thee and thy peace	421:5
then must the l. be great	35:19
then they dream of l.	477:7
therefore I l. it	93:35
they all l. Jack	562:22
things that l. night l. not such nights as these	453:8
this bud of l.	477:24
this spring of l.	484:33
this test for l.	411:1
those who l. the Lord	265:16
those who l. want wisdom	496:24
thou art goodly, O L.	522:8
thou art l. and lifel	498:16
thou art my life, my l., my heart	247:4
thou dravest l. from thee	544:31
thou hast left thy first l.	70:29

Love (cont.)

though I knew His l.	544:15
though l. repine	199:27
though they l. the treason	168:4
thou knowest that I l. thee	64:17
thou shalt l. and be loved by	96:25
thro' l.'s long residence	80:23
through l., through hope	573:27
through our l. that we have loved	328:17
thy honesty and l.	471:18
thy l. is better than wine	51:37
thy l. prove likewise variable	477:22
thy l. to me was wonderful	47:30
thy l. was far more better	332:29
Thy name..which is L.	81:3
thy sweet l. remember'd	486:24
'tis the hour of l.l	116:7
to be wise and eke to l.	510:22
to be wise, and l.	481:16
to be wroth with one we l.	150:26
to business that we l.	425:9
to die, I leave my l. alone	487:14
to dissemble your l.	72:14
to him we l. most	420:25
to live is like l.	112:5
to l., and bear	497:17
to l. and be loved by me	380:7
to l. and to be wise	100:12
to l. and to cherish	391:30
to l., cherish, and to obey	391:31
to l. her is a liberal education	511:25
to l. is wise	82:1
to l. one another	66:11
to l. one maiden only	530:14
to l. you was pleasant enough	357:4
to Mercy, Pity, Peace, and L.	76:18
too ladylike in l.	242:29
too late came I to l. thee	21:22
too much l. of living	523:23
to prove my l.	375:2
to regain l. once possess'd	350:33
to see her is to l. her	104:25
to see her was to l. her	104:10
to thoughts of l.	534:15
triumphs of L.	526:22
true life is only l., l. only bliss	96:8
trust thou thy L.	413:31
turning mortal for thy l.	455:18
twin'd my l. and me	31:11
'twixt women's l., and men's	184:5
twofold silence was the song of l.	410:30
two fond hearts in equal l.	33:11
two passions, vanity and l.	139:26
type of true l. kept under	219:8
under a canopy of l.	549:6
unity and godly l.	390:26
unrelenting foe to l.	546:7
us that trade in l.	424:11
very few to l.	580:18
virgins l. thee	51:38
waft her l...to Carthage	465:17
was not this l. indeed?	483:10
way to l. each other	292:21
we live by..hope, and l.	574:19
well dost thou, L.	375:7
well of l.	148:12
we l. being in l.	542:11
we l. but while we may	530:42
we l., Fool, for the good we do	374:22
we l. our House of Peers	221:37
we needs must l. the highest	530:19
we're rich in l.	108:1
what a mischievous devil L. is	112:4
what is l.?	482:28
what l. I bore to thee	577:4
what l. of thine own kind?	498:8
what L. shall never reap	410:33
what thing is l.	377:3
when I was in l. with you	262:19
when l. and duty clash	538:10
when L. and Life are fair	569:5
when l. begins to sicken	451:9
when l. grows diseas'd	202:2
when l. is done	79:5
when l. is grown to ripeness	533:34
when L. speaks	455:22
when my l. swears	488:16
where I and my L. wont	32:18
where I l. I must not marry	357:2

INDEX

Love (*cont.*)

where l. is enthron'd 483:2
where l. is great 435:9
where my L. abideth 94:24
where there is no l. 26:16
while my l. climb'd up to me 293:3
who gave that l. sublime 574:31
whom the gods l. die young 116:10
whose l. will never die 338:19
whose l. would follow me 299:27
wise want l. 496:24
with all their quantity of l. 437:24
with all thy faults I l. thee still 112:12, 162:43
with bands of l. 55:48
with l. affected 219:1
with l. brooding there 571:7
without l., hatred 401:29
woman wakes to l. 531:14
women I l…women who l. me 490:41
women..who l. their lords 251:25
Wonder, L., and Praise 2:22
words of l. then spoken 357:13
worst that l. could do 186:1
yes, I'm in l. 566:18
yet I l. thee and adore 161:13
you all did l. him once 450:21
you cannot call it l. 435:47
you'll l. me yet! 94:45
you..l. none 374:22
you made me l. you 326:13
you must l. him 578:32
your true l.'s coming 482:28
youth means l. 95:33
you, who do not l. her 96:28
Loveable: Elaine the l. 530:33
Love-adept: dreaming like a l. 497:2
Love-adventure: so passionate a l...lost 306:15
Loved: all we l. of him 491:24
awake, my heart, to be l. 80:11
betray the heart that l. her 582:3
better l. ye canna be 360:12
better l. you'll never be 250:19
better to have l. and lost 112:16, 532:20
Cophetua l. the beggar-maid 477:12
disciple whom Jesus l. 64:19
each l. one blotted from life 113:20
from those who l. them 171:9
God so l. the world 63:9
had we never l. sae kindly 104:11
had you l. me..as you have not l. 525:22
having l. this present world 69:1
heart that has truly l. 356:13
he had l. her long 80:7
her father l. me 470:2
how l., how honoured once 381:36
hunting he l. 488:25
if I had a friend that l. her 470:3
if I l. you well 524:32
I have l. thee, Ocean! 114:32
I have l. the principle of beauty 290:29
I have l. three whole days 517:18
I have l. too long 365:19
I have not l. the world 113:50
I l. a lass 572:1
I l. her that she did pity them 470:3
I l. him for himself alone 500:9
I l. him not 309:1
I l. Ophelia 437:24
I l. Rome more 450:14
I l. thee once 23:15
I l. the man 280:1
I saw and l. 216:25
I that l. 9:21
I wish I l. the Human Race 405:16
keep our l. ones 512:14
known all l. so long 80:13
life we have l. 359:3
l. a happy human face 266:3
l. and still loves 408:7
l. him like a vera brither 108:5
l. not honour more 319:10
l. so slight a thing 534:31
l. that l. not at first sight 330:13, 428:15
l. the bailiff's daughter 29:22
l. the doctrine for the teacher 170:3
l. thee since my day began 541:8
l., was scorn'd and died 215:12
l. well because he hated 93:48
l. your beauty 586:21

Loved (*cont.*)

lovers should be l. again 262:13
makes her l. at home 105:5
many l. your moments 586:21
might she have l. me? 92:35
most l., despis'd 452:13
my own true l. one 572:20
my thoughts, which l. and lost 232:15
Nature I l. 308:25
never espied that ever she l. me 328:11
never l. a tree or flower 357:5
never to have been l. 155:40
never to have l. at all 532:20
nor no man ever l. 488:7
no sooner looked but they l. 428:26
not that I l. Caesar less 450:14
one face there you l. 293:19
one that l. not wisely 474:2
one..whom Jesus l. 63:48
our love that we have l. together 328:17
pale hands I l. 254:14
people l. her much 535:6
she l. me for the dangers 470:3
she who has never l. 215:8
since to be l. endures 82:1
Solomon l. many strange women 47:45
some we l. 206:6, 7
them that l. him not 447:9
therefore must be l. 480:33
this man l. *me* 309:4
those whom he l. so long 408:7
thought she l. me too 572:4
thou hast not l. 427:2
thou shalt love and be l. by 96:25
time..place and the l. one 93:38
to be long l. 15:20
to be l. himself 192:13
to be l. needs only to be seen 192:22
to have l., to have thought 15:13
to love and be l. by me 380:7
truest..that ever l. woman 328:24
twice or thrice had I l. thee 184:4
use him as though you l. him 559:23
we l. in vain 117:35
we l. with a love 380:8
we that had l. him so 93:3
what thou, and I did, till we l. 185:6
what we have l., others will love 579:38
when you l. me 489:27
where burning Sappho l. 115:43
which he l. passing well 433:23
which I have l. long since 364:12
with those that l. me 540:32
woman who l. him the best 293:25
Love-darting eyes 340:38
Love-in-idleness 466:39
Love-knot: dark red l. 366:2
Lovel: Lord L. he died out of sorrow 31:9
Love-laden: her l. soul 498:6
Loveless: only l. look 375:15
Lovelier: l. than the Love of Jove 330:21
l. things have mercy shown 117:40
nothing l…in woman 349:8
Loveliest: l. and best 206:6
l. and the best 206:7
l. of trees 262:10
of this bad world the l. 41:24
Love-light in your eye 73:11
Love-liking: shocks of young l. 579:21
Love-Lily: between the lips of L. 411:25
Loveliness: Dream of L. 313:14
enough their simple l. 288:24
fashioned forth its l. 236:16
glory and l. have pass'd away 288:28
her l. I never knew 148:12
its l. increases 284:19
l. needs not..ornament 546:19
l. of perfect deeds 532:25
of so shining l. 586:1
portion of the l. 492:10
shoulder-blade..miracle of l. 220:11
this Adonis in l. 266:6
your l. and..my death 290:22
Love-locks: with your l. flowing 409:16
Lovely: do l. things 293:7
each one a l. light 150:6
he'd make a l. corpse 176:20
he is altogether l. 52:14
labour bears a l. face 170:21
look thy last on all things l. 171:9

Lovely (*cont.*)

lordly, l. Rhine 122:9
l. and a fearful thing 115:37
l. and pleasant in their lives 47:30
l. Thais by his side 190:34
l. Thais sits beside thee 191:9
l. that are not beloved 375:11
l. wee thing 104:27
l. woman in a rural spot 266:4
more l. and more temperate 486:18
more l. ere his race be run 115:8
more l. than the monarch of the sky 330:6
mourn for that most l. thing 584:18
O l. O most charming pug 208:29
once he made more l. 492:10
one l. hand she stretched 122:27
that extremely l. thing 218:11
too l. to be grey 15:19
virtue in her shape how l. 347:31
whatsoever things are l. 68:27
when l. woman stoops 197:32, 226:18
Love-making, or wooing of it 27:32
Love-quarrels oft in pleasing concord end 350:34
Lover: all mankind love a l. 200:24
all the plagues a l. bears 559:6
as to a l.'s bed 425:24
as true a l. 427:1
beauty is the l.'s gift 156:5
by the l. and the bard 89:10
clasp'd her like a l. 535:5
dividing l. and l. 521:30(-522)
felt for thee as a l. 582:15
God become her l. 166:7
goodbye to your l. 299:22
happy as a l. 575:10
her l. keeps watch 318:5
in any manner a l. 328:15
injured l.'s hell 348:10
I sighed as a l. 216:21
it was a l. and his lass 428:30
I've got one l. 335:22
like a true l. brave 10:18
l., all as frantic 467:24
l. and sensualist 241:29
l. forsaken a new love, get 559:5
l. lingers and sings 516:4
l. never find my grave 483:6
l. of concord 388:25
L. of my soul 565:5
l.'s eyes 455:22
l., sick to death 455:17
l., sighing like a furnace 427:21
l. that can dare to think 156:11
l. true for whom I pine 507:22
lunatic, the l., and the poet 467:24
magnetic, peripatetic l. 221:1
meek l. of the good 199:6
my fause l. stole my rose 108:39
not less her l. 404:21
O l. of my life 96:9
one was round her l. 122:27
on her l.'s arm 528:28
repentance to her l. 226:18
resolve the propositions of a l. 428:4
she was a true l. 328:16
since I cannot prove a l. 476:1
slide into a L.'s head 581:12
some newer l. 214:24
some sad l.'s death 191:19
spring thy l. 524:15
such a constant l. 517:18
suffering is the l.'s part 214:9
talk with some old l.'s ghost 185:34
thou l. of souls 56:27
thy l. the spring 524:15
to each l. beside 373:19
true l. of literature 508:8
truest friend to thy l. 328:24
truest l. of a sinful man 328:24
what is a l., that it can give? 156:6
when they have slain her l. 122:25
where shall the l. rest 418:12
why so pale and wan, fond l.? 517:10
woman loves her l. 115:38
your l. comes 567:18
Lovers: ages long ago these l. fled 285:28
all l. young, all l. must 430:1
all that are l. of virtue 559:27
all ye that be l. 328:16

INDEX

Lovers (cont.)
almighty l. in the spring | 140:16
at l.' perjuries..Jove laughs | 477:20
dull sublunary l.' love | 186:25
end in l. meeting | 482:28
even l. find their peace | 208:10
Frankie and Johnny were l. | 6:8
Heaven's promise clothe..those
  l. | 411:1
laughs at l.' perjury | 193:13
l.' absent hours | 472:18
l. are round her | 356:31
l. cannot see | 463:37
l.' eyes are sharp to see | 417:34
l.' hours be full eternity | 185:31
l. in peace | 451:35
l. lying two and two | 262:14
l. run into strange capers | 427:3
l. should be loved again | 262:13
l., to bed | 467:34
l.' tongues by night | 477:27
makes l. as fast as one pleases | 156:6
make two l. happy | 381:8
nectareous poppy l. use | 16:5
old l. are soundest | 563:22
pair of star-cross'd l. | 476:44
pure l.' souls descend | 185:2
queens to your l. | 413:9
such as I am all true l. are | 483:2
sweet l. love the spring | 428:30
through l.' brains | 477:7
to thy motions l.' seasons run | 186:19
two young l. lately wed | 534:3
what need l. wish for more? | 421:14
when l.' vows seem sweet | 118:28
where the l. eloped | 309:26

Loves: all l. except what trade can
  give | 96:26
all she l. is love | 115:38
all strange l. are over | 522:12
all the wings of the L. | 525:6
all ye L. and Cupids..mourn | 132:12
amatory poets sing their l. | 116:14
any severing of our l. | 576:21
as lines so l. oblique | 332:6
a-waiting for their..l. | 32:2
bird whom man l. best | 580:1
captain that..l. what he knows | 167:3
fierce wars and faithful l. | 509:16
first..woman l. her lover | 115:38
fox-hunter..I l. him | 518:9
friends and l. we have none | 334:13
glad one l. His world | 94:41
he l. to lie a-basking | 221:36
her that each l. best | 123:4
he that l. a rosy cheek | 124:25
his faults..one l. him still the
  better | 226:32
I believe the baggage l. me | 155:22
if country l. | 232:5
if our l. remain | 91:3
I have reigned with your l. | 198:12
I like him, but he l. me | 97:5
I l. the 'round more | 518:14
Jesus l. me | 560:26
kills the thing he l. | 569:4
lass that l. a sailor | 173:8
l., and weeps, and dies | 493:25
l. nothing but himself | 508:9
l. to hear himself talk | 478:6
l. what he is good at | 422:32
Mary l. the lamb | 233:23(−234)
my Love l. me | 150:18
no creature l. me | 476:37
old l. endear thee | 148:14
one that l. his fellow-men | 265:17
our l. and comforts..increase | 470:31(−471)
our l. into corpses or wives | 523:1
sends..after the thing it l. | 436:29
she l. me dearly | 285:4
show..when he l. her | 94:10
solace ourselves with l. | 49:50
suspects, yet soundly l. | 471:32
that dust it so much l. | 292:19
that I l. the fox less | 518:14
that l. the people well | 324:5
their l., or else their sheep | 343:15
to warm their little l. | 231:18
truly l. on to the close | 356:13
two l. I have | 488:18

Loves (cont.)
understandeth thee not, l. thee
  not | 455:13
whoever l. if..not propose | 184:20
who l. me..a touch of earth | 530:34
who l. not wine | 543:5
who l. that..wise and good | 351:19
whose l. I prize as..carcases | 429:14
with l. and doves | 91:12
woman whom nobody l. | 157:9
Love-sick: l. all against our will | 220:22
Savonarola l.l | 39:21
twenty l. maidens we | 220:22
winds were l. | 424:6
Lovesome: garden is a l. thing | 85:12
l. wee thing | 107:16
l., white and small | 195:6
Love-song: mavis singing his l. | 268:30
Lovest: alas, thou l. not me | 185:21
Father in Heaven who l. all | 295:6
Isaac, whom thou l. | 44:54
l. thou me more than these? | 64:14
l. to greet the early morn | 107:4
poor sinner, l. thou me? | 161:9
thou l.—but ne'er..satiety | 498:9
thou l. not, till..thou free | 185:21
thou l. the one | 35:19
why l. thou that | 486:13
Love-story: worked a l...into..
  Euclid | 188:18
Loveth: dear God who l. us | 150:16
he made and l. all | 150:16
he that l. another | 66:11
he that l. not his brother | 70:15
he that l. not knoweth not God | 70:12
l. and maketh a lie | 72:9
prayeth best, who l. best | 150:16
prayeth well, who l. well | 51:40, 52:4
whom my soul l. | 69:19
whom the Lord l. | 482:1
Love-thoughts lie rich | 482:1
Loving: babes, and l. friends | 150:15
begin by l. their parents | 570:18
for l., and for saying so | 186:21
for l. that old arm-chair | 156:21
from l. more..free my soul | 185:21
l., adorable | 365:5
l. and a fair reply | 430:32
l. and giving | 368:1
l. heart to thee | 247:1
l. himself better than all | 152:22
l. himself better than me | 27:5
l.-jealous of his liberty | 477:28
l., kissing, kind-hearted gentle-
  man | 164:28
l. longest | 22:27
l., natural, and Greek | 115:36
l. not, hating not | 90:14
l., not loathing | 252:13
most l. mere folly | 427:22
most l. of you all | 89:1
night was made for l. | 119:6
only beauty purely l. | 123:18
only belov'd, and l. me | 158:13
perfectly sore with l. her | 175:16
so lonely, l., helpless | 115:35
so l. to my mother | 430:33(−431)
they talks a lot o' l. | 299:14
thinking, feeling, l. | 573:21
though the heart be still as l. | 119:4
too much l. you | 471:36
whilst l. thou mayst loved be | 509:33
whom are you l.? | 262:7
wickedness that hinders l. | 93:48
Loving-kindness: thy l. and
  mercy | 393:10
Low: as l. as..Squire Widdrington | 192:19
cast one's eyes so l. | 454:3
conveniently l. | 130:15
daughters of musick..brought l. | 51:33
dost thou lie so l.? | 450:2
earth is not too l. | 243:24
envy, l. design | 308:2
every mountain..made l. | 54:9
exalted them of l. degree | 61:14
follies laid him l. | 104:20
foreheads villanous l. | 480:10
from l. to high..dissolution | 578:1
happy l., lie down | 442:3
her voice..gentle and l. | 454:24
he that is l. no pride | 99:31

Low (cont.)
how l...the proud | 231:7
I am l., thou art high | 524:2
I'll tak' the l. road | 9:7
in l. estate began | 533:1
in our defection..sink as l. | 580:5
it is not that I deem them l. | 120:25
lords who lay you l. | 498:17
l. as the singer lies | 516:4
l. as where this earth spins | 410:10
l. estate of his handmaiden | 61:13
l. estate of the poor | 393:8
l., l., breathe and blow | 538:12
men of l. estate | 66:5
my head is bending l. | 210:17
narrow, and l. | 165:34
poor buffer lies l. | 568:24
quincunx of heaven runs l. | 85:18
refrain my soul, and keep it l. | 400:1
sing both high and l. | 482:28
speak l., if you speak love | 468:11
speak l. to me, my Saviour | 87:37
sweet and l. | 538:12
ten l. words | 382:30
that l. man seeks a little thing | 91:41
thou's but of l. degree | 6:26
too l. for envy | 158:15
weep when I am l. | 112:31
what is l. raise and support | 344:4
winds are breathing l. | 494:7
Low-born: rude, l., untaught | 188:31
Low-class: in the l. tea-shops | 503:15
Low-crooked curtsies | 449:29
Lowells talk to the Cabots | 79:2
Lower: button-hole l. | 455:32
in the lowest deep a l. deep | 346:32
l. orders..set us a good example | 569:18
l. than the angels | 392:11
night is beginning to l. | 316:3
ye l. middle classes | 218:34
Lowers: dark l. the tempest
  morning l. | 316:19 / 1:13
Lowest: in the l. deep | 346:32
l. and most dejected thing | 453:36
take the l. room | 62:2
Lowing: l. of the oxen | 47:15
that heifer l. at the skies | 287:12
Lowland: between l. and highland | 523:13
Lowlands: l...like a grey-green
  garment | 235:22
L. o' Holland | 31:11
sails by the L. low | 30:23
ye Highlands and ye L. | 30:8
Lowliness is young ambition's
  ladder | 449:3
Lowly: any happs, however l. | 219:21
better to be l. born | 446:16
God made them, high or l. | 3:15
l. air of Seven Dials | 219:2
l., and servisable | 136:27
l. in his own eyes | 392:24
l. wise | 348:31, 574:1
l., with a broken neck | 336:44
meek and l. in heart | 59:10
poor, and mean, and l. | 4:1
stamp of his l. origin | 169:5
still to the l. soul | 291:14
Lowpin: spak o' l. o'er a linn | 105:14
Low-vaulted: l. past | 251:15
Loy: but by sëynt L. | 136:28
Loyal: bold spirit in a l. breast | 474:10
fruit of l. nature | 530:11
l. and neutral | 458:25
that l. body wanted learning | 548:20, 549:1
Loyalties: impossible l. | 19:10
Loyalty: his l. he kept | 348:18
that learned body wanted l. | 548:20, 549:1
when l. no harm meant | 7:9
Lubin: while L. is away | 266:8
Lucasta: L. that bright northern
  star | 318:25
then my L. might I crave | 319:8
Lucem: ex fumo dare l. | 255:27
Lucent: each softly l. | 320:6
l. syrops | 285:25
Lucid: full of l. intervals | 134:13
l. intervals and happy pauses | 27:46
make a l. interval | 193:2
not in the l. intervals | 574:3

[813]

Lúcidos intervalos 134:13
Lucifer: he falls like L. 446:24
  L., son of the morning 53:22
  L. that often warned them thence 343:14
  Prince L. uprose 336:17
  spirits that fell with L. 330:1
Luck: as good l. would have it 466:10
  good l. have thou 394:22
  good l...in odd numbers 466:14
  if it be my l., so 466:7
  light in ragged l. 241:29
  nae l. about the house 10:22
  we have wished you good l. 399:12
  worst kind of l. 238:27
Lucky: l. to be born?..as l. to die 567:13
  l. to touch it 301:12
Lucrative: l. business of mystery 103:1
  so l. to cheat 147:2
Lucre: greedy of filthy l. 68:45
Lucro: quem Fors..dabit l. appone 258:14
Lucumo: each warlike L. 323:15
Lucy: if L. should be dead! 581:12
  linger longer L. 233:15
  no comrade L. knew 577:18
  when L. ceased to be 580:18
Luddites: quartern loaf and L. 504:5
Lues: delicta maiorum immeritus l. 259:30
  l. Bostwelliana 324:36
Lugete, O Veneres Cupidinesque 132:12
Lugger: forcing her on board the l. 279:16
Lugwardin: shin'd at L. 548:17
Lui: parce que c'était l. 354:21
Luke: honour unto L. Evangelist 411:9
  L. began to slacken 577:22
  L., the beloved physician 68:34
  Matthew, Mark, L. and John 3:3
  only L. is with me 69:2
Lukewarm: because thou art l. 70:34
Lukewarmness I account a sin 158:20
Lull: l. in the hot race 15:6
  l. the distant folds 229:28
Lullaby: I will sing a l. 170:23
  sing l. and lap it warm 80:8
  snatches, and dreamy l. 219:15
Lulled: l. by the coil 496:8
  l. in these flowers 466:41
  l. with..sweetest melody 441:41
Lumber: loads of learned l. 383:4
  l. of the schools 521:13
Lumbering: l. like Mr. Words-worth's epic 240:7
  news..l. at his back 163:20
Lumen: cui l. ademptum 554:14
Lumina: Vesper Olympo..l. tollit 133:7
Luminary: arose another l. 10:0
Luminous: Dong with the L. Nose 311:16
  dragon-green, the l. 208:8
  fair l. cloud 151:5
  Goethe's wide and l. view 17:5
  his l. home of waters 17:28(–18)
  his l. wings 19:21
Lump: leaveneth the whole l. 66:27
  l. bred up in darkness 305:17
  l. the whole thing 550:16
  poor in a l. is bad 537:8
  spewed up a good l. 194:18
Luna: in the vats of L. 323:12
Luna: inferebatur sol et l. 21:18
  velut inter ignis l. minores 258:18
Lunae: damna..reparant caelestia! 260:26
  per amica silentia l. 554:12
Lunar: cold l. beams 16:14
  on the l. world securely pry 191:30
Lunatic: keep me from goin' l. 295:1
  l., the lover, and the poet 467:24
Lunch: breakfast, dinner, l. and tea 41:3
  when they've cleared away l. 121:18
Luncheon: supper, dinner, l. 94:37
Lundy: Lord L. from his earliest years 41:5
Lungs: dangerous to the l. 267:30
  if then l. receive our air 162:42
  l. of bronze 41:32
  l. of London 379:13
  my l. begin to crow 427:15
  whose l. are tickle o' the sere 433:18
Lurch: modest Dame L. 76:4
Lurcher: half l. and half cur 163:39
Lure: haggard hawks will stoop to l. 305:12

Lure (cont.)
  l. him on to skittles 120:3
  l. it back to cancel 207:2
  l. this tassel-gentle back 477:26
Lures: calls me, l. me 334:9
Lurks: thought that l. in all delight 338:6
Luscious: as l. as locusts 470:17
Lusisti satis 257:21
Lust: cold, commanded l. 297:21
  for l. of knowing 208:14
  hutch of tasty l. 254:27
  into ashes all my l. 333:9
  l. in action 488:11
  l. of the goat 77:16
  more cruel than l. 523:1
  more l. again to lose 140:17
  narrowing l. of gold 533:20
  neither..l. after ..tobacco 279:24
  no l. because..no law 531:25
  not l. of conquest 156:27
  not serving shame or l. 183:10
  served the l. of my mistress 453:19
  sinful l. of the flesh 302:30
  slept in the contriving of l. 453:19
  till action, l. is perjur'd 488:11
  weariness and sated l. 17:7
Lusteth: flesh l. against the Spirit 67:45
  he that l. to live 394:1
Lustre: accomplishments give l. 139:27
  changed in outward l. 344:13
  dark l. of thine eyes 417:26
  l...in eyes that would not look 500:8
  l. in its sky 494:6
  obscure in the exceeding l. 495:10
  that same eye..lose his l. 448:20
Lustres: my six l. almost now out-wore 186:6
Lusts: abstain from fleshly l. 69:49
  fulfil the l. thereof 66:14
  sinful l. of the flesh 391:2
Lusty: every l. heart beginneth to blossom 328:15
  flourisheth in l. deeds 328:15
  l. as an eagle 398:4
  thou l. Troynovaunt 195:4
  yet I am strong and l. 426:36
Lute: awake, l. and harp 395:19
  blame not my l. 583:17
  bright Apollo's l. 455:22
  faileth..the l. the lutanist 544:23
  lascivious pleasing of a l. 476:4
  little rift within the l. 531:11
  l. its tones 285:1
  musical as is Apollo's l. 340:24
  my l., awake..be still 583:21
  nor yet a l. 245:2
  Orpheus with his l. 446:18
  sing praises..with the l. 393:35
  sung..to her l. 440:4
  thy voice, thy l., thy pipe 288:6
  to her l. Corinna 123:21
  wanteth there grace of l. 92:5
  when the l. is broken 494:20
Lute-player: some dead l. 522:19
Lutes: to dance to l. 569:5
  to l. of amber 247:14
Luthany: land of L. 545:5
Luther: as Martin L. sang 543:5
  L., and Mahomet..prisons of flesh 186:7
  Philistine of genius..L. 20:19
  Pythagoras was misunderstood .. and L. 200:41
  rough old Martin L. 97:11
Lutheran: spleeny L. 446:20
Lux: cum semel occidit brevis l. 132:15
  fiat l. 44:2
Luxuria: saevior armis l. 283:10
Luxuries: give us the l. 359:24
  two l. to brood over 290:22
Luxurious: conservatives..when they are most l. 200:25
  exquisite sense of the l. 289:33
  l. mountain goat 445:1
  some l. mire 216:4
Luxury: all their l. was doing good 213:20
  ancient languages..a l. 82:16
  blesses his stars, and thinks it l. 1:15
  fortunes, to increase l. 216:9
  l. of doing good 165:12, 226:5
  l. the accomplish'd Sofa last 162:34

Luxury (cont.)
  they knew l. 325:27
  to l. and riot 349:27
Lyaeus: god L. ever young 38:10
Lycid: hearse where L. lies 342:31(–343)
Lycidas: for L. is dead 342:10
  L. your sorrow is not dead 343:3
  so L. sunk low 343:3
  your loved L. 342:17
Lydia, a seller of purple 64:54
Lydiae lacus undae 132:21
Lydian: in L. measures 191:9
  lap me in soft L. airs 342:7
Lying: all my life long..l. till noon 276:2
  George..l. on his face 542:37
  how this world is given to l. 441:4
  I do not mind l. 112:7
  l., and slandering 391:8
  l., vainness..drunkenness 484:18
  l. with Houris 231:20
  settling and loosely l. 81:15
  soon will you and I be l. 132:3
  this vice of l. 442:14
Lym: brach or l. 453:30
Lynn: set out from L. 252:26
  young lady of L. 11:1
Lyones: knights of Logres or of L. 350:4
Lyonnesse: when I set out for L. 236:34
Lyon's Inn: lived in L. 562:24
Lyra Apostolica: motto [of L.] 363:16
Lyrae: non hoc iocosae conveniet l. 259:24
Lyre: flit into it with my l. 286:18
  l. with other strings 164:20
  make me thy l. 496:11
  my l. within the sky 380:18
  not from his l. 93:5
  wak'd to ecstasy the living l. 230:4
  when 'Omer smote 'is bloomin' l. 303:22
Lyres: but as the sound of l. 374:11
Lyric: Mr. Coleridge's l. prose 240:7
  O l. Love 95:34
  splendid ecclesiastical l. 182:4
Lysander: of Hector and L. 9:24

M

M: begins with an M.—' 'Why with an M?' 129:12
  N. or M. 391:2
Ma says it's sinful 177:14
Ma'am: call his mother 'M.' 141:33
Mab: angry M. 477:7
  M., the Mistress-Fairy 281:5
  Queen M. hath been with you 477:7
  that very M. 477:7
Mac: Pat and M. and Tommy 305:3
Macaroni: called it M. 33:7
Macassar: sharing with blacking and M. oil 376:13
  thine 'incomparable oil', M. 115:15
Macaulay: apostle of the Philis-tines..M. 19:17
  as cocksure..as Tom M. 335:13
  M. is well for a while 127:27
Macbeth: M. does murder sleep 458:11
  M. shall never vanquish'd be 460:9
  M. shall sleep no more 458:12
  none of woman born..harm M. 460:5
  to meet with M. 456:3
Macdonald: aff wi' Lord Ronald M. 9:16
  slogan of M. 23:20
Macduff: M...from his mother's womb 461:11
  lay on, M. 461:14
Mace: sword, the m., the crown 444:23
Macedon: great war from M. 19:3
  river in M. 445:4
Macedonia: come over into M. 64:53
Maces: Seal, and M., danc'd 230:19
MacGregor: my name is M. 420:19
Machiavel: much beholden to M. 24:23
Machinations, hollowness, treach-ery 452:16
Machine: m. for converting the Heathen 125:29
  pulse of the m. 580:12
  you're not a man.. a m. 489:8

INDEX

Machinery: Age of M. 125:28
  whole m. of the State 85:1
Mackail: I'm M.,—and who are you? 8:17
Mackerel: blew a m. gale 192:31
  not so the m. 211:25
Mackintosh: bit of black m. 563:37
M'Tavish: against the clan M. 23:26
Macte nova virtute, puer 555:9
Mad: Allah created the English m. 298:2
  all poets are m. 109:8
  as m. as he 437:14
  because he was m. 437:14
  drive me m. on my deathbed 119:33
  everyone is more or less m. 304:34
  fitter being sane than m. 89:22
  go m., and beat their wives 121:20
  He first sends m. 195:10
  heroically m. 190:32
  m. all my life 276:3
  m., and sent into England 437:14
  m., bad, and dangerous 306:2
  m. from life's history 252:20
  m. in pursuit 488:12
  m., is he? 216:12
  m. March days 333:21
  m. naked summer night 567:16
  m. north-north-west 433:20
  M. World 80:5, 527:16
  m. world! m. kings! m. composition 447:24
  make m. the guilty 433:32
  make poor females m. 467:11
  makes men m. 473:16
  makes the wise man m. 93:14
  man's m., friend 89:35
  men that God made m. 140:15
  much learning doth make thee m. 65:23
  never better than when I am m. 305:16
  nobly wild, not m. 246:14
  old, m., blind, despised 498:18
  one half of the nation is m. 506:4
  one man merry, another m. 86:33
  our sad bad glad m. brother 522:18
  pleasure..in being m. 193:33, 203:27
  Practice drives me m. 8:12
  prose run m. 385:28
  put any parent m. 208:21
  sad and bad and m. it was 90:38
  Saint run m. 386:10
  so, it will make us m. 458:10
  some did count him m. 99:32
  suspend your m. career 162:24
  that he is m., 'tis true 432:40
  tho'..a' should gae m. 108:28
  undevout astronomer is m. 587:13
  went m. and bit the man 225:21
  when a heroine goes m. 500:6
  wicked and the m. 386:2
Madagascar: Jerusalem and M. 543:10
Madam I may not call you 198:6
Mad-as-a-hatter-day 243:5
Madden: now m. to crime 113:1
Maddest: m. merriest day 536:26
  m. of all mankind 298:2
Madding crowd 230:7
Made: all things were m. by him 62:59
  annihilating all that's m. 332:19
  as a breath has m. 224:14
  even more is m. of her 241:28
  fearfully and wonderfully m. 400:10
  first I was m. by thee 185:11
  for all she m. 297:20
  good poet's m. 281:17
  it m. them a faction 325:35
  little Lamb, who m. thee? 76:10
  m. and loveth all 150:10
  m. for each other 505:24
  m. for the people 563:3
  m. the world and ruleth it 585:9
  m. with our hands and our lips 525:2
  marriages..m. by the Lord Chancellor 273:1
  not anything m. that was m. 62:59
  such gardens are not m. 296:32
  'thinketh He m. it 90:13
  thou hast m. him 531:40
  well m., well wrought 502:17
  world I never m. 263:35
  you m. me love you 326:13
Madeira: sold him..for a cup of M. 438:26

Mademoiselle from Armentiers 412:17
Madest: thou m. man 531:40
Madly squeeze a right-hand foot 131:25
Madman: if a m. were to come in 273:5
Madmen: buries m. in the heaps 384:4
  none but m. know 193:33, 203:27
  worst of m. 386:10
Madness: cruel m. of love 535:38
  despondency and m. 580:7
  his flight was m. 460:16
  his m. was not of the head 118:5
  if..not love, it is m. 155:27
  like m. in the brain 150:26
  like m. is the glory 480:22
  Love watching M. 114:10
  m...method in it 433:6
  m. of many 386:35, 520:47
  m. of the people 395:28
  M. risen from hell 522:5
  m. to defer 587:3
  m. would gambol from 436:1
  moon-struck m. 349:24
  much mirth and no m. 502:18
  noble m. 191:15
  such harmonious m. 498:10
  that fine m. 189:12
  that way m. lies 453:13
  this m...for our sins 530:27
  thro' cells of m. 536:22
  to m. near allied 190:13
  very midsummer m. 484:7
  with a crafty m. 434:2
  you may call it m. 408:9
Madoc will be read 387:5
Madonnas: only used to draw M. 93:45
  Rafael of the dear M. 94:12
Madrigal: sing a merry m. 219:36
  woeful stuff this m. 382:34
Madrigals: in lovely m. 88:13
  melodious birds sing m. 330:18
Maecenas atavis edite regibus 257:23
Maenad: M. and the Bassarid 522:2
  some fierce M. 496:6
Mænides: blind M. 346:20
  old M. the blind 208:17
Mæotis: where M. sleeps 381:18
Maestro: il M. di color che sanno 168:21
Magazine of life and comfort 243:19
Magdalen: Cecily, Gertrude, M. 410:12
  fourteen months at M. 216:19
  monks of M. 216:20
Magdalene: fairer..than Mary M. 376:3
Maggie coost her head 105:13
Maggot must be born 190:12
Maggot-pies and choughs 459:24
Maggots in your brains 38:15
Magic: came like m. in a pint bottle 175:38
  dealer in m. and spells 222:11
  if this be m. 486:1
  m. casements 288:1
  m. in my eyes 236:35
  m. in the distance 366:4
  m. like thee 118:17
  m. of a name 122:34
  no m. of her voice 376:6
  once it was a m. sound 116:15
  secret m. of numbers 86:10
  there's m. in the web 472:16
  what mighty m. 469:45
Magistrate: at the commandment of the M. 401:13
  by the m., as equally useful 217:5
Magistrates: some, like m. 443:10
Magna: m. est veritas 56:19, 84:26
  parvis componere m. 555:18
Magna Charta is such a fellow 148:2
Magnanimity: curb your m. 291:11
  m. in politics 101:14
  m. of love 336:19
  m. of thought 587:6
Magnanimous Despair 332:5
Magnanimously: justly, skilfully and m. 352:25
Magnet ever attract a Silver Churn 221:1
Magnetic, peripatetic lover 221:1
Magnetism: doubt as to animal m. 153:8
  their m. works all night 551:16
Magnificence: this m...wholly thine 574:2

Magnificent: from his work return'd m. 348:28
  her m. and awful cause 162:45
  m., but..not war 79:1
  m. out of the dust 561:12
  mild and m. eye 93:3
  mute and m. 193:40
Magnifico: ignotum pro m. est 526:8
Magnifique: c'est m...pas la guerre 79:1
Magnify: m. him for ever 388:20
  m. him that rideth 396:5
  my soul doth m. the Lord 61:13
Magnipotent: raptly m. 236:5
Magnis: parva..componere m. 556:24
Magnitude: liar of the first m. 155:9
Magus Zoroaster 496:18
Magus: schoenobates medicus m. 283:3
Mahlen aber trefflich klein 315:22
Mahmud: Peace to M. 205:22
  pity Sultan M. 205:21
Mahogany Tree 543:11
Mahomet: from M. to Moses 387:23
  her pulpits..the revelation of M. 217:12
  Luther and M...prisons of flesh 186:7
  M. will go to the hill 25:34
Mahometans: pleasures of the M. 231:20
Maid: Abyssinian m. 151:33(-152)
  be good, sweet m. 293:7
  cling with life to the m. 199:13
  Elaine, the lily m. 530:33
  espy a fair pretty m. 9:3
  fair, but frozen m. 213:15
  fair m. dwellin' 30:1
  had she been a country m. 106:29
  I beheld the m. 464:21
  I heard a m. sing 6:2
  I knew a gentle m. 232:19
  kissed likewise the m. 164:28
  lazy finger of a m. 477:7
  like a moth, the simple m. 214:11
  like mistress, like m. 203:23
  little M. would have her will 582:13
  maiden passion for a m. 530:14
  m. not vendible 462:36
  m. of Athens 118:6
  m. ov all maidens 35:15
  m. remembers 516:4
  m. that milks 425:30
  m. was in the garden 368:20
  m. who has none, sir 500:40
  many a m. 342:3
  married m. 419:14
  matron and the m. 240:21
  Music, heav'nly m. 153:31
  my pretty m. 369:14
  neither m. nor wife 527:12
  nor his m., nor his ox 390:17
  O fair and stately m. 199:10
  of her scorn the m. repented 33:13
  signal to a m. 338:4
  silver for the m. 295:14
  slain by a fair cruel m. 483:6
  sphere-descended m. 154:3
  to the heart of a m. 296:29
  way of a man with a m. 50:56
  wedded m., and virgin mother 343:9
  where's the m. 285:39
  yonder a m. and her wight 236:14
Maiden: archly the m. smiled 316:5
  as the m.'s organ 482:10
  flesh'd thy m. sword 441:3
  heart of a m...stolen 350:23
  his true m.'s breast 418:12
  I, m., round thee m. 530:25
  in m. meditation 466:39
  I pursued a m. 494:2
  I sing of a m. 7:15
  kissed the m. all forlorn 369:6
  let the m. understand 79:16
  like a high-born m. 498:6
  m., and mistress 521:29
  m. fair to see 315:26
  m. herself..steal after it 350:23
  m. hid 522:2
  m. is a tender thing 531:7
  m. most perfect 521:30
  m. never bold 470:1
  m. of bashful fifteen 500:39
  m. passion for a maid 530:14
  m. pride, adieu! 468:27

INDEX

Maiden (*cont.*)

many a rose-lipt m.   263:21
merry m. and the tar   221:22
mother and m.   7:17
neater, sweeter m.   299:14
not a modest m. elf   236:17
prithee, pretty m.   220:31
rare and radiant m.   380:23
scanter of your m. presence   431:28
she was a m. City   582:6
simple m. in her flower   533:36
'Stay,' the m. said   316:20
that orbèd m.   492:29
this m...no other thought   380:7
till the m. yields   536:6
to love one m. only   530:14
use a poor m. so   6:2
village m. she   535:2
what shall be the m.'s fate?   417:8
woo a dead m.   419:17
your m. modesty would float   266:15
Maidenly: so m.   502:18
Maidens: all the m. pretty   154:9
bind him for thy m.   49:30
conserv'd of m.' hearts   472:16
dear to m. are their rivals dead   374:16
lang may the m. sit   32:2
sing, ye gentle m.   168:14
smiles of other m.   148:13
twenty love-sick m. we   220:22
what m. loth?   287:7
young fair m. quiet eyes   516:5
young men and m.   400:25
youths and m. gay   150:15
Maids: for the m. in France to kiss   445:15
free m. that weave   483:5
lie between m.' legs   435:4
m. come forth   236:31
m. dance in a ring   361:6
m. must kiss no men   80:7
m. of matchless beauty   302:19
m. strange seraph.c pieces   548:15
malady most incident to m.   485:26
May when they are m.   428:22
our cold m.   437:1
pretty m. all in a row   307:21
seven m. with seven mops   130:12
three little m. from school   219:27
welcome m. of honour   247:11
when m. lie on their backs   477:7
Maid-servants..instructed in the 'ologies   126:32
Mail: fish would have bright m.   285:1
like a rusty m.   481:18
Overland M.   300:12
Mailed lobster   211:26
Maimed: poor, and the m.   62:8
spent and m. among   293:19
Main: amid the melancholy m.   546:3
ayont the m., to prove again   360:4
care o' th' m. chance   111:2
curled waters 'bove the m.·   453:3
enraptur'd m.   503:6
flooding in, the m.   147:8
froth amid the boundless m.   83:9
into the m. of waters   465:21
lost evermore in the m.   540:4
M. Spring, Mogul   83:2
o'er life's solemn m.   317:8
rages, like the troubled m.   215:14
skims along the m.   382:32
very good man in the m.   217:28
Maine: remember the M.   9:13
Mains: les m. pleines de vérités   209:16
Maintain: m. the state of the world   57:13
thou shalt m. my lot   392:25
to m. this ecstasy   374:14
Maintained: discipline must be m.   174:1
every rood..m. its man   224:14
I m. myself thus   546:39
singly hast m. against..multitudes   348:20
Maior privato visus   526:15
Maisie: proud M.   420:2
Maîtresses: j'aurai des m.   216:11
Maize: aloe, and m. and vine   528:23
with Plenty in the m.   539:4
Majesté: la m. des souffrances   553:1
Majestic: m. River floated on   17:28
m. though in ruin   345:24
m. yet sedate   401:22

Majestical: being so m.   430:17
happy, high, m.   494:15
laid in bed m.   444:23
Majesty: appearance of Your M.   43:25
as his m. is   56:31
busied in his m.   443:10
grasping at m. in the least   413:9
her M.'s councils..grace   84:27(–85)
Her M.'s Jolly   301:19
Her M.'s Opposition   28:23
his M.'s head on a sign-post   325:16
if his m. our sovereign lord   12:6
infinite M.   388:16
in naked m.   347:10
in rayless m.   587:1
m. of human suffering   553:1
next in m.   193:9
ride on in m.   339:12
rising in clouded m.   347:19
sweetness, mercy, m.   319:7
think it kindness to his M.   234:14
this earth of m.   474:22
Thy m. how bright   202:21
touching in its m.   582:14
with what a strength and m.   360:21
Majolaine: Compagnon de la M.   11:24
Major: C M. of this life   89:12
Major-General: model of a modern M.   221:31
Majorité: avec Dieu..dans la M.   305:5
Majorities: Wisdom goes by m.   337:32
Majority: gone over to the m.   125:34
joins us to the great m.   587:14
m...best repartee   182:34
one, on God's side, is a m.   378:19
with God..in the m.   305:5
Majors: live with scarlet M.   415:12
Make: breath can m. them   224:14
could not well m. out   507:6
did not m., and cannot mar   16:17
I too will something m.   81:9
m. him once relent   99:35
m. more opportunities   25:39
m. the most of what we yet may spend   206:8
m. the most on 'em   174:7
m. up one's mind about nothing   290:27
not usually m. anything   378:12
Scotsman on the m.   36:18
treason, m. the most of it   242:16
what m. ye   81:1
what suns and winds..m. us   309:5
what the word did m. it   197:35
without our aid..us m.   292:7
Maked: whan god first m. man   137:40
Makeless: maiden that is m.   7:15
Maker: best m. of all marriages   445:16
known only to his M.   251:14
m. buried   516:3
m. is him-self y-beten   138:26
m. of his own fortune   511:26
more pure than his m.   48:49
scatter'd his M.'s image   190:8
syng laudes to their m.   239:7
to show the M.'s glory   232:11
Makers: t'abhor the m.   192:32
Makes: m. me or fordoes me   473:10
m. the happiness she does not find   279:15
m. us what we are   196:21
Makest: what m. thou?   54:17
Maketh: m. much of them   392:24
Soul that m. all   199:1
Making: joy in the m.   81:9
m. things which he doesn't want   254:9
praise the Lord for m. her   297:20
take pleasure in m.   10:10
to the m. of man   522:5
Makings: royal m. of a queen   447:2
Makler: ehrlicher M.   72:32
Mala: m. per longas convaluere moras   372:2
parvam te roscida m...legentem sunt m. plura   556:4 / 331:23
Malade: un homme gravement m.   364:17
Malades: dépêcher ses m.   354:3
Maladie: sans argent l'honneur.. une m.   405:5
Maladies: m. of Society   126:45
soul with all its m.   374:10
Malady: m. most incident to maids   485:26

Malady (*cont.*)

m. of not marking   441:15
m. without a cure   193:12
medicine worse than the m.   37:31
Malcontents: loiterers and m.   455:8
Male: m. and female created he them   44:8
m. ringlets   523:4
more deadly than the m.   296:13
Malefactions: proclaim'd their m.   433:36
Males: nothing but m.   457:15
Malfi: Duchess of M. still   563:14
Malherbe: enfin M. vint   78:5
Malice: envy, hatred, and m.   388:46
fortune's m. lost her Calais   91:6
leaven of m.   66:28, 389:35
m. domestic, foreign levy   459:4
m. toward none   314:13
much m...a little wit   192:27
not for m.   509:35
our poor m.   459:4
pretence..of treasonous m.   458:26
Pride, Envy, M.   308:13
set down aught in m.   474:2
where there are men, and m.   282:7
Malign: judgments so m.   517:8
Malignant..Turk   474:2
Malignity: motiveless m.   153:1
Malis: quibus ipse m. careas..cernere   320:30
Mall: like Mistress M.'s picture   482:8
Mallecho: this is miching m.   435:7
Mallow: slimy m.   165:17
Malmsey and Malvoisie   40:15
Malo me Galatea petit   555:26
Malone: sweet Molly M.   7:8
Malt: m. does more than Milton   263:25
that ate the m.   369:6
Malta: under M. by the sea   208:13
Malvoisie: Malmsey and M.   40:15
Mama: Oh, M., do be a bear!   376:5
when your M. came   175:31
Mamilius: Herminius smote M.   324:9
Tusculan M.   323:14
Mammocked: how he m. it   429:6
Mammon: m. of unrighteousness   62:21
M., the least erected   345:9
serve God and m.   58:10
Man: aged, aged m.   131:22
all functions of a m.   163:12
all perhaps which m. acquires   19:6
all, save the spirit of m.   113:2
all that makes a m.   530:14
all that may become a m.   457:12
all, that might be in a m.   189:3
all this scene of m.   383:7
also feel it as a m.   460:22
animals..for the use of m.   376:15
appear like m. and wife   143:25
arms, and the m.   194:29, 553:5
arose as one m.   46:62
around the m. bend other faces   308:13
as nature first made m.   191:41
be a m.   15:10
before M. made us citizens   320:7
behold the m.   63:70
believe it not, O M.   147:4
bestow'd upon m.   164:24
blamed the living m.   16:10
bold bad m.   509:20
but the last m.   86:24
by courtesy a m.   23:13
by m. came death, by m...re-surrection   67:8
came to m.'s estate   484:27
cease ye from m.   52:32
century of the common m.   557:17
charities of m. to m.   165:19
childhood shows the m.   350:10
child imposes on the m.   192:30
Christian, pagan, nor m.   434:19
closing full in M.   191:35
confirm'd misogyn a ladies' m.   39:21
corruption of M.'s Heart   91:34
deaf m. to a blind woman   152:23
delighteth..in any m.'s legs   400:22
desire of the m.   153:7
discerning intellect of M.   574:8
dissolute m.   252:21
each m. has some part   402:14
each..petty officer, and m.   236:4
end try the m.   441:34

Man (cont.)

enslav'd by another M.'s 75:2
estimable m. and..husband 175:38
Eustace is a m. no longer 294:14
every m. a liar 65:36
every m.'s Cleopatra 191:21
every rood..maintained its m. 224:14
father of the M. 577:25
first m. is of the earth 67:15
first spell M. 404:14
for a m. with heart 535:43
frailty of a m. 25:17
friend of m. 122:38
from any sort of m. 304:35
fury of a patient m. 190:30
get a new m. 479:43
gibbets for 'the m.' 156:22
Gigadibs the literary m. 89:39
gives to m. or woman 262:18
glory to M. 524:27
God above or m. below 383:8
God formed m. of the dust 44:11
God is not a m. 46:19
God never made..for m. to mend 192:15
good for m. nor beast 11:21
goodliest m. of men 347:13
Good Lord, what is m.! 107:36
good m., and did good things 237:18
grown m. in the cradle 103:23
grown to m.'s estate 515:18
handsome, well-shaped m. 21:13
happy the m...alone 194:20
happy the m. whose wish 386:26
hath m. no second life? 15:4
heart of a m. 296:29
her prentice han' she tried on m. 106:2
he was a m. 431:6
he was her m. 6:8
honest exceeding poor m. 463:29
honest m.'s aboon his might 105:32
honest m.'s the noblest work 105:5, 384:9
hour..but not the m. 419:36
how good is m.'s life 96:21
I have a m.'s mind 449:27
I'm sure he's a talented m. 387:20
in his little world of m. 453:4
in his rights of a m. 89:13
in the mind of m. 582:1
in wit a m. 382:15
is m. an ape or an angel? 180:35
justify God's ways to m. 263:25
king is but a m. 444:18
know the garment from the m. 74:22
large-hearted man 88:6
Last M. knead 207:6
last strands of m. 254:19
last thing civilized by M. 337:31
laws of..m. and metre 315:14, 416:10
legs without the m. 163:38
let him pass for a m. 463:10
life for a m. like me 515:27
life of a m...a heroic poem 125:35
life of m., solitary, poor 248:21
like a m. of mettle 248:10
likely to be a manly m. 328:7
like master, like m. 203:23
literary m.—with a wooden leg 178:2
love not the m. the less 114:26
love's a m. of war 244:13
made her such a m. 470:3
make m. in our image 44:6
makes m. and wife one flesh 154:32
making a poet out of a m. 88:12
M. accepts the compromise 296:14
m. after his death moot wepe 137:29
m. after his own heart 47:13
m. and a woman in a garden 570:17
m. and bird and beast 150:16
M. and Boy..an idler 578:34
M. and his Wife and a Tertium Quid 304:52
m. and wife..hang one another 203:17
m. as he is *not* to be 239:18
m. before thy mother 37:30
m. before your mother 159:10
m. behind the book 201:10
m. being in honour 395:2
m., being reasonable, must get drunk 115:34

Man (cont.)

m. be more pure than his maker 48:49
m. can have but one life 89:26
m. cannot utter it 50:61
m. child conceived 48:44
m. clothed in soft raiment 59:6
m. comes and tills the field 540:20
m. control the wind 15:12
m. delights not me 433:15
m. did eat angels' food 396:35
m. does not live by bread alone 201:3
m. doth not live by bread alone 46:23
m. dreams of fame 531:14
m., equal and one with me, m. that is made of me, m. that is I 524:5
m. equal, unclassed 497:12
m., false m. 312:27
m. for the field 538:24
m. for the sword 538:24
m. goeth forth to his work 398:10
m. has Forever 91:40
m. has his will 251:13
m. has shop to mind 96:26
m. hath all which Nature hath 19:2
m. have the upper hand 392:15
m. he must go with a woman 299:20
m. I am..cease 535:43(−536)
m., if not the wedding-day.. fixed 204:8
m. in his hasty days 81:9
m. in portions can foresee 118:31
m. in the bush with God 199:16
m. is an embodied paradox 154:23
m. is a noble animal 87:20
m. is..a political animal 14:14
m. is..a religious animal 102:22
m. is as old as he's feeling 153:19
m. is a tool-making animal 211:20
m...is..born to believe 180:33
m. is born unto trouble 48:50
m. is God's image 244:4
m. is Heaven's masterpiece 404:7
m. is m. 531:14
m. is m.'s A.B.C. 404:14
m. is Nature's sole mistake 221:41
m. is not a fly 383:15
m. is not m. as yet 94:23
m. is one world 244:24
m. is the hunter 538:23
M. is the master of things 524:27
m. is the measure 402:18
m. leave his father 44:18
M. like to me 96:25
m. looks aloft 194:25
m. made the town 162:38
m. marks the earth with ruin 114:27
m. may drink 108:16
m. may escape from rope 214:34
manner of Primitive M. 309:28
m. never is..blest 383:11
M. of baser Earth didst make 207:12
M. of Blood was there 323:1
M. of England 335:27
M. of Feeling 326:25
m. of mean estate 188:33
M. of purple cheer 578:29
m. of sorrows 54:25
m. of strife 55:19
m. of the field 44:57
m. of unclean lips 53:8
m. of wit..long..in gaol 386:36
m. of yearning thought 411:33
m. only..starts from his rank 124:15
m. partly is 91:1
m. passionless? 497:12
m. perceives it die away 576:9
m. proposes 291:20
M. propounds negotiations 296:14
m., proud m. 461:31
m. put off the prophet 94:3
m. recover'd of the bite 225:23
m. remains, sceptreless 497:12
m. right fair 488:18
m.'s a m. for a' that 105:31
m.'s best dreams 88:21
m.'s congregation shun 543:16
m.'s desire is for the woman 153:7
m.'s distinctive mark 91:1
M.'s dominion has broken 107:10
m. seems the only growth that dwindles 226:9

Man (cont.)

M.'s first disobedience 344:1
M.'s Forgiveness 207:12
m. shall have his mare 467:12
m. sharpeneth the countenance 50:47
m.'s house is his castle 148:7
m.'s inhumanity to m. 107:2
m.'s life is cheap as beast's 452:41
m.'s love..a thing apart 115:25
m.'s strength to comfort m.'s distress 295:8
m.'s the gowd 105:30
m. struggling for life 270:18
m.'s unconquerable mind 582:4
m.'s waitin' for a answer 174:20
m.'s word is God in m. 529:40
m.'s worth something 89:38
m. that hath no music 465:20
m. that is born of woman 49:1, 391:41
m. that must hear me 150:12
M.! the pilgrim of a day 122:37
m. there walked without a mate 332:21
m. there was 99:32
m. to arise in me 535:43(−536)
m...to be surpassed 364:22
m. to command 538:24
m. to m...greatest curse 33:15
m. to m. the warld o'er 105:33
m. under authority 58:31
m. upon a black horse 307:2
m. wants but little 225:13
m. was formed for society 73:3
m. was made for Joy and Woe 73:24
m. was made to mourn 107:1
m. was wolf to the m. 551:13
m. w'at kin show you trouble 238:9
m. when breast to breast 410:26
m. who broke the Bank 217:23
m. who does not smoke 514:27
M. who is from God sent forth 575:1
M., who, lifted high 575:11
m. who used to notice 235:13
m. who wasn't there 335:12
M. will go down into the pit 29:19
m. with God..majority 305:5
m. with his back to the East 148:17
m. with the head 538:24
M...Woman's cully 155:25
measureless to m. 151:32, 33
Mind of M.—my haunt 574:7
moral centaur, m. and wife 116:20
more like a whore's than a m.'s 299:18
more than m. to wish thee so 357:3
more than the wisest m. can answer 154:21
my m. Friday 170:8
my only study, is m. 78:21
my single state of m. 456:24
mystery of m. 579:34
neither m., nor muse 281:10
neither m. nor woman 380:13
never m. spake like this m. 63:24
never m. was true 80:7
new tribunal..the educated m.'s 96:15
noblest work of m. 112:9, 267:16
no m. does. That's his 569:24
no m. put asunder 391:34
nor M. nor Boy 576:19
Noselessness of M. 142:6
nothing great but m. 235:4
not the bond of m. and wife 530:40
not what m. does 96:23
not yet old enough for a m. 482:17
now I am a m. 577:25
number of a m. 71:22
oft proclaims the m. 431:25
O M., that from thy..youth 573:15
O men, this m. in brotherhood 87:38
once on a time there was a M. 302:15
once to every m. and nation 320:9
one m. in his time 427:21
one m. with a dream 371:1
one wrong more to m. 93:6
only a m. harrowing 236:14
only m. is vile 240:18
on M., on Nature 574:5
outward semblance of a m. 179:11
Parliament of m. 534:27
peace..m. did not make 16:17
play the m. 263:15
poor m.'s day 228:14

Man (cont.)

print of a m.'s naked foot — 170:7
proper study of mankind is m. — 383:22
reading maketh a full m. — 27:18
refined, presumptuous m. — 124:15
relief of m.'s estate — 24:14
right m. in the right place — 268:29
right m. to fill the right place — 310:25
rough and ready m. — 89:34
round, fat, oily m. of God — 546:6
Sabbath was made for m. — 60:53
sadder and a wiser m. — 150:17
scan your brother m. — 104:7
sensible, and well-bred m. — 159:15
she knows her m. — 194:28
sing the M. of Ross — 384:44
social, friendly, honest m. — 105:25
soldier's a m. — 471:9
sole nexus of m. to m. — 126:6
sole nexus of m. with m. — 127:1
so near is God to m. — 199:32
soul of the m. on its breast — 16:4
so unto the m. is woman — 317:27
spake on that ancient m. — 148:20
spares neither m. nor..his works — 217:13
stand a m. a cheese — 142:1
standard of the m. — 562:2
stand five minutes with that m. — 276:24
strain of m.'s bred out — 480:19
striving to be m. — 199:17
substance of men which is m. — 524:26
subtilty of the devil or m. — 389:9
such a m., so faint — 441:9
take hold of one m. — 52:36
temptation but for m. to meet — 96:13
that animal called m. — 519:32
that thorn-crown'd M. — 17:9
that wild beast m. — 78:10
their murdered m. — 286:22
the Lord is a m. of war — 45:51
there was a crooked m. — 369:3
there was a little M. — 357:18
this is not the m. — 443:1
this is the state of m. — 446:24
this little kingdom, m. — 442:21
this m. loved me — 309:4
this was a m.! — 452:9
thou art the m. — 47:34
though earth and m. were gone — 83:11
Thousandth M. — 302:18
thou turnest m. to destruction — 397:15
thou were the kindest m. — 328:24
through this m. and me — 328:17
time whereof the memory of m. — 314:22
to be m. with thy might — 524:3
to bite so good a m. — 225:22
to every m...death cometh — 323:17
to m. despotic power — 350:35
took a m.'s life along with him — 126:3
to the last m. — 233:30
touches a m. — 567:6
tragedy, 'M.' — 380:15
truest lover of a sinful m. — 328:24
unsuccessful literary m. — 41:33
Valoroso is a m. again — 542:24
vindicate the ways of God to m. — 383:8
voice of a god..not of a m. — 64:49
wanderer is m. — 16:3
was Christ a m. like us? — 15:4
way of a m. with a maid — 50:56
were m. but constant — 485:2
what a m. may do — 542:10
what a piece of work is a m.! — 433:15
what is m., that thou art mindful — 392:10
what m. has made of m. — 581:8, 10
what m. would do — 96:23
when a m. bites a dog — 168:3
when god first maked m. — 137:40
when I became a m. — 66:46
when M. is the Turk — 140:28
where is the m. who has the power — 11:22
wherewith the Face of M. is blacken'd — 207:12
who's master, who's m., — 521:11
whoso sheddeth m.'s blood — 44:43
whoso would be a m. — 200:39
why, m. of morals — 158:8
woman's cause is m.'s — 539:6

Man (cont.)

worm, and no m. — 393:2
worth makes the m. — 384:7
wrath of m. — 69:30
you'll be a M. — 297:12
young M. crucified — 338:4
you're not a m...a machine — 489:8
Manage: m. clever man..m. a fool — 304:38
Managed: just and right well m. — 349:3
Manager, actor, prompter — 237:25
Manasses is mine — 395:23
Man-at-arms..on his knees — 377:4
Mandalay: back to M. — 299:10
Mandate: thus the royal m. — 105:25
Mandragon: Mr. M., the Millionaire — 140:27
Mandragora: give me to drink m. — 423:41
not poppy, nor m. — 471:43
Mandrake: get with child a m. — 186:16
Mane: grasp'd the m. — 159:41
laid my hand upon thy m. — 114:32
seiz'd fast the flowing m. — 159:37
thin m., thick tail — 488:27
whistling m. of every wind — 544:18
Manes: plats the m. of horses — 477:7
Mangeant: l'appétit vient en m. — 404:27
Manger: dog in the m. — 549:28
in homely m. — 508:17
in the rude m. lies — 343:11
lodge Him in the m. — 12:7
m. for His bed — 3:20
not too cleanly, m. — 166:1
One born in a m. — 552:1
Manger pour vivre — 353:10
Mangerful of hay — 409:22
Mangle: immense pecuniary M. — 179:35
Mangled: vents in m. forms — 427:16
Mangler in a million — 178:18
Manhood: bone of m. — 100:24
conspiracy against..m. — 200:38
honesty, m., nor good fellowship — 438:27
in the glory of his m. — 23:21
M. a struggle — 181:37
m. taken by the Son — 364:5
no sounder piece of British m. — 126:3
peace more destructive of..m. — 269:19
promise of strength and m. — 81:22
reserves for a bright m. — 322:12
robs me of my m. — 191:19
states..their growth, their m. — 309:19
strife comes with m. — 417:33
taking of the M. into God — 388:42
Manhoods: hold their m. cheap — 444:28(-445)
Mania of owning things — 567:20
Maniac: from a m.'s tongue — 87:38
m. scattering dust — 532:27
Manifest: every man's work..m. — 66:23
from love made m. — 90:44
m. me rightly — 469:39
Manifesto: awful, though monotonous, m. — 180:22
Manifold: m. stories..are told — 121:19
sundry and m. changes — 389:38
with ardours m. — 95:2
Manjar que quita la hambre — 134:18
Mankind: all m.'s epitome — 190:22
amongst the noblest of m. — 121:17
careless of m. — 535:19
example is the school of m. — 103:15
he's an enemy to m. — 484:8
I am involved in M. — 186:28
improvements in the lot of m. — 338:21
in th' original perus'd m. — 14:24
let observation..survey m. — 279:2
maddest of all m. — 298:2
m...not deny to Harold Skimpole — 173:26
need not be to hate, m. — 113:46
our countrymen are all m. — 213:18
proper study of m. — 383:22
shut the gates of mercy on m. — 230:6
superfluities of m. — 214:28
teach it to m. — 81:2
that they may mend m. — 160:19
things..ride m. — 199:19
what was meant for m. — 225:27
you shall not crucify m. — 98:2
Manlier one — 116:2
Manliness: silent m. of grief — 225:8

Manlio: nata mecum consule M. — 260:10
sit suo similis patri M. — 133:6
Manly: boy's idea of a m. career — 182:26
his big m. voice — 427:21
likely to be a m. man — 328:7
m., moral..liberty — 102:3
m. wise — 331:6
nurse of m. sentiment — 102:12
proof of m. might — 509:35
Man-milliner: architectural m. — 412:20
Manna: his tongue dropt m. — 345:18
m. and dates — 285:25
m. of a day — 231:28
we loathe our m. — 193:7
Manned: get you m. by Manning — 95:30
Manner: cease to think about the m. — 240:1
dislike..the m. of his speech — 424:4
in wonted m. keep — 279:31
m. of Primitive Man — 309:28
m. rude and wild — 40:21
m. which is my aversion — 116:5
no m. of doubt — 218:18
they..shall want no m. of thing — 393:38
to the m. born — 431:31
Mannerly: behave m. at table — 515:16
Manners: as by his m. — 510:9
catch the m. living — 383:8
corrupt good m. — 67:12
describe not men, but m. — 204:17
exquisite picture of human m. — 216:17
for m.' sake — 57:6
her m. had not that repose — 533:37
his m. are not so polite — 300:7
his m. our heart — 225:34
his m. were gentle — 225:34
in divers m. — 69:6
m. are not idle — 530:11
m., Ben! — 93:27
m., climates, councils — 540:32
m. of a dancing master — 270:21
m. of a Marquis — 222:5
m. of different nations — 514:35
m. of my mother — 482:26
not good m. to mention — 85:8
old m. gone — 417:2
old m., old books — 226:43
Peel has no m. — 564:14
polish'd m. and fine sense — 164:3
savage men, and uncouth m. — 100:22
sweeter m., purer laws — 533:20
take their m. from the Ape — 40:22
their tricks and their m. — 178:13
whose m. were futile and harsh — 312:15
Manning: get you manned by M. — 95:30
Manningtree: roasted M. ox — 439:35
Mannish cowards — 426:28
Man-of-war: English m. — 212:18
M.'s 'er 'usband — 298:25
Manor: goodly m. for a song — 423:6
Mansion: back to its m...breath — 230:3
before the starry threshold..my m. — 339:27
his everlasting m. — 480:32
m.-house of liberty — 352:13
thy fading m. — 488:20
Mansionry: his lov'd m. — 457:6
Mansions: lasting m. of the dead — 164:35
m. in the skies — 562:12
many m. — 63:51, 131:32
more stately m. — 251:15
Mantle: cast his m. upon him — 48:10
drinks the green m. — 453:23
in his m. muffling — 450:31
in scarlet m. warm — 160:30
morn, in russet m. — 430:22
o'er the dark her silver m. — 347:19
twich'd his m. blue — 343:7
whose visages do cream and m. — 462:33
wrap thy form in a m. gray — 495:22
you all do know this m. — 450:27
Mantling vine — 347:7
Mantovano: I salute thee, M. — 541:8
Mantuan: M. swan — 162:26
old M.! old M.! — 455:13
pretty i' the M. — 121:5
Manu: te teneam..deficiente m. — 547:18
Manual: no M., no letters — 119:32
Manufacturer: chips to the m. — 143:31
Manure: its natural m. — 268:23
Manus: porrigens teneras m. — 133:6
tendebantque m. ripae ulterioris — 554:28

Manuscript: Youth's sweet-
  scented M.   207:24
Manxome foe   129:39(-130)
Many: among so m.   63:20
  because we are too m.   237:3
  election by the incompetent m.   490:29
  madness of m.   386:35, 520:47
  m. are called   60:10
  m. a time and oft   463:20
  m. change and pass   492:15
  m...doing uninteresting actions   28:29
  m. fail; the one succeeds   528:26
  m. people prize it   220:31
  m. still must labour   115:1
  m. there be that go in   58:23
  m. to keep   294:1
  m. to save with thyself   17:19
  rank-scented m.   429:11
  so much owed by so m.   144:1
  we are m.   60:57
  what...m...cannot help   270:34
  ye are m.—they are few   495:16
Many-coloured life   278:34
Many-fountain'd Ida   537:30
Many-headed: fury of the m.
  monster   335:3
  m. monster of the pit   386:19
Many-memoried name   72:24
Many-splendoured thing   545:1
Map: m. me no maps..my head is
  a m.   204:23
  new m. with the..Indies   484:4
  roll up that m.   379:17
Maple Grove: like M.   22:16
Maps: Geography is about m.   42:23
Mar: did not make, and cannot m.   16:17
  Lieutenant-Colonel to the Earl
    of M.   381:9
  m. what,'s well   452:31
Maran-atha: Anathema M.   67:20
Marathon looks on the sea   115:44
Marble: as pillars of m.   52:14
  dwelt in m. halls   98:21
  forget thyself to m.   341:9
  left it m.   120:8
  m., nor the gilded monuments   487:6
  m. to retain   112:35
  mount of m.   528:24
  pillars rear their m. heads   155:19
  poets that lasting m. seek   557:22
  ponderous and m. jaws   431:32(-432)
  sleep in dull cold m.   446:29
  this in m.   38:2
  your dreary m. halls   121:12
Marbled: Sunium's m. steep   116:3
Marble-hearted fiend   452:28
Marbly: great smooth m. limbs   89:43
Marcellus: more true joy M.
  exil'd feels   384:10
March: ashbuds in the front of M. 529:25
  beware the Ides of M.   448:11
  continue our m.   17:21
  droghte of M.   136:21
  hear the Dead M. play   295:20
  hem his watery m.   17:28(-18)
  her m. is o'er the..waves   123:11
  iambics m.   152:5
  ides of M. are come   449:28
  ides of M. remember   451:11
  long majestic m.   386:17
  mad M. days   333:17
  M. dust to be sold   549:30
  m. forward in order   420:8
  m., m., Ettrick   420:8
  m. of a nation   373:17
  m. of intellect   508:7
  m. of mind   376:14
  m. of the human mind   101:6
  'M. on!' he said   568:15
  m. on their stomachs   422:16
  M. sun feels like May   93:13
  m. through rapine   222:38
  m. to the siege of..Gaunt   31:14
  M., whan god first maked man   137:40
  M. winds and April showers   8:9
  men who m. away   236:18
  sea-blue bird of M.   533:12
  take the winds of M.   485:26
  three hours' m. to dinner   240:9
  we m., thy band   92:13
  we shall m. prospering   93:5

March (cont.)
  with merry m. bring home   443:10
  work the ides of M. begun   451:37
March-bloom: look! M.   255:6
March Hare: '..some wine,' the
  M. said   129:5
Marche: le congrès ne m. pas   313:20
Marched: Johnson m. to kettle-
  drums   154:13
  m. breast forward   97:4
  m. in through my..shutters   376:14
  m. into their land   23:26
  m. on without impediment   476:32
  m., rank on rank   336:17
  m. them along, fifty-score   90:16
  m. them up to the top   10:19
  whose sires have m. to Rome   323:12
Märchen: ein M. aus alten Zeiten 240:25
Marches: dreadful to delightful
  measures   476:3
  funeral m. to the grave   317:6
  slow howe'er my m. be   292:20
Marching: his soul is m. on   234:7
  his truth is m. on   264:16
  Johnny Comes M. Home   11:19
  m. as to war   35:1
  m. through Georgia   583:6, 7
  m. to the Promised Land   35:4
  m. where it likes   19:29
March-morning: all in the wild M. 537:1
March-wind: whenever a M. sighs   536:12
Mare: Flanders m.   242:22
  have his m. again   467:12
  lend me your grey m.   33:1
  look of the bay m.   567:14
  woa, m.!   217:22
Mare: qui trans m. currunt   257:4
Maréchal: la bâton de m. de France 360:23
Marengo: this is our M.   188:6
Margaret: adores as M.   375:26
  brave as M. Queen   287:4
  Clerk Saunders and may M.   30:15
  Magdalen, M. and Rosalys   410:12
  Merry M.   502:17
Margaret Newcastle: thrice noble
  M.   306:23
Margate: in M. last July   34:23
Marge: ample m... every m. en-
  closing   531:17
  m. of each cold..isle   153:27
Margent: slow Meander's m. green 340:13
Margery Daw: see-saw, M.   368:18
Margin: meadow of m.   500:33
  some picture on the m.   190:1
  whose m. fades for ever   540:32(-541)
Mari magno turbantibus aequora
  ventis   320:30
Maria: Ave M.! 'tis the hour of
  prayer   116:7
  Cardinal,—Christ,—M.,—God   96:17
Mariana: this dejected M.   462:14
Maries: Queen had four M.   31:18
Marigold..to bed wi' the sun   485:25
Marigolds: no m. yet closed   247:5
Mariner: ancient M.   148:18
  bright-eyed M.   148:20
  gentlemen..draw with the m.   189:1
  M. hath his will   148:20
  m., worn and wan   494:22
  to the m.'s hollo   148:28
Mariners: best pilots have needs
  of m.   280:4
  jolly, jolly m.   298:14
  my m.   541:3
  rest ye, brother m.   535:20
  three poor m.   406:2
  to talk with m.   150:8
  ye M. of England   123:10
Marino Falieri: no extract..con-
  cerning M.   119:32
Marion's nose looks red   456:1
Maris: serenitas m...prosequetur   39:1
Marivaux: eternal new romances
  of M.   231:20
Mark: could man outlook that m.   552:10
  ever-fixed m.   488:7
  glaze and the m.   309:25
  if you would hit the m.   316:11
  I will stand and m.   540:16
  man's distinctive m.   91:1
  m. him well   417:22

Mark (cont.)
  m. it with B   368:10
  m. me..undo myself   475:21
  m. my footsteps   361:23
  m... of the beast   71:21
  m. of the beast   142:2
  m. the archer little meant   417:30
  m. well her bulwarks   394:35
  m. what is done amiss   399:39
  Matthew, M., Luke and John   3:3
  press toward the m.   68:23
  push beyond her m.   532:30
  read, m., learn   389:23
  to the self-same m.   92:43
Mark Antony: as..M.'s was by
  Caesar   458:33
  to meet M.   426:5
Marked: ever m. with shade   308:31
  m. him for his own   559:28
Market: knowledge is bought in
  the m.   146:24
  m. of his time   436:15
  this little pig went to m.   369:7
Market-gardener: marry a m.   177:33
Market-place: bird of night..up-
  on the m.   448:33
  enthron'd i' the m.   424:7
  Idols of the M.   28:6
  in the M., one Dusk   206:18
Markets: great m. by the sea   208:10
Marking: 'eard 'em m. time   301:15
  malady of not m.   441:15
Marks: m.—not that you won   406:20
  m. our English dead   301:23
  may none those m. efface!   114:34
  nobody m. you   468:2
  terrible m. of the beast   237:6
Marksmen: you are all m.   404:1
Marjoram: mints, savory, m.   485:25
Marl: clod of wayward m.   468:8
  over the burning m.   344:24
Marlborough: from M.'s eyes   279:10
  Great M.'s mighty soul was
    proved   1:9
  great praise..M. won   507:8
Marlowe's mighty line   281:12
Marmaduke: Astley and Sir M.   323:1
Marmion: good-night to M.   418:30
  last words of M.   418:32
Marmoream..relinquere   120:8
Marocco: Damasco or M.   345:4
Marquis: manners of a M.   222:5
  m., duke, and a' that   105:32
  M. gazed a moment   24:4
Marred: all that's spoke is m.   474:3
  man that's m.   423:5
  m. the lofty line   418:7
  too soon m.   477:2
  young man married is..m.   302:6
Marriage: coldly furnish..the m.
  tables   431:4
  courtship to m.   155:34
  every m...best in tune   561:1
  frighten her into m.   279:16
  giving in m.   60:26
  hanging and m...by Destiny   203:28
  if you think there is any in m. 215:1
  I made a Second M.   206:23
  in m...slack and selfish   514:22
  I was at Hazlitt's m.   307:11
  joys of m.   209:25
  m. and death and division   523:1
  m. ever out of fashion?   111:9
  m. has many pains   278:17
  m. is..a civil contract   422:6
  m. is..a field of battle   514:29
  m. is a step so grave   514:28
  m. is popular because..   490:32
  m. of true minds   488:7
  m. supper of the Lamb   71:34
  m. the happiest bond   229:8
  m. with his brother's wife   446:14
  merry as a m. bell   113:25
  more for a m. than a ministry   28:28
  most happy m. I can picture   152:23
  my m. fee   293:9
  natural..to live in a state of m. 272:6
  nor are given in m.   60:14, 520:39
  O curse of m.!   471:40
  prevents a bad m.   482:11
  rich hues have m. made   81:7

[819]

INDEX

Marriage (cont.)
rob a lady..by way of m. 204:30
talk most about the blessings of m. 490:25
this Rachel-and-Leah is m. 146:27
tho' m. makes..one flesh 154:32
vow I made to her in m. 432:14
with dirge in m. 430:24
won't be a stylish m. 168:2

Marriage-feast: sweeter than the m. 150:15
Marriages: best maker of all m. 445:16
exclaim..against second m. 204:8
m. would..be as happy 273:1
no more m. 434:13
only..a bust of m. 115:39
so few m...happy 520:40
taste for m. 182:23
Married: at leisure m. 155:32
Benedick the m. man 468:6
Charlotte was a m. lady 543:12
dreadfully m...most m. man 560:19
found her tongue since she was m. 280:8
happy m. man dies in good stile 560:14
Happy Though M. 235:12
his aunts, who are not m. 142:8
how will he be m. 367:18
I have m. a wife 62:7
I'm to be m. today 218:32
intended to be m. in this way 83:6
kiss before they are m. 445:15
let us be m. 312:1
liv'd comfortably so long..m. 214:13
live till I were m. 468:24
m. a great while 156:13
m. and brought up a..family 227:15
m. and gone to New Zealand 146:28
m. an' woo'd an' a' 409:13
m., charming, chaste 115:17
m. in haste 155:32
m. on Wednesday 368:21
m. past redemption 193:5
m. the barber 209:18
m. to a mer-ma-id 8:24
m. to a poem 290:21
m. to a single life 165:32
m. to a sponge 463:13
m. to a whore 301:11
m. to immortal verse 342:7
m. to the Moor 578:21
m., which was bad 304:30
m. within these three days 193:5
m. with mine uncle 430:33(-431)
mocks m. men 455:35
mostly m. people 146:32
never m., and that's his hell 109:14
no taste when you m. me 500:34
not m. at all 156:13
now we're m. 108:29
once you are m. 514:31
one fool..in every m. couple 204:9
Reader, I m. him 83:5
that m. with Othello 472:37
thinks she's not a-goin' to be m. 518:26
till anes we m. be 30:15
Trade Unionism of the m. 490:24
true, I have m. her 469:45
unpleasing to a m. ear 455:35
we m. people 377:28
wench who is just m. 214:17
wen you're a m. man, Samivel 178:42
woo'd and m. and a' 12:3
writer..m. or a bachelor 2:4
young man m. 302:6, 423:5
you, that are going to be m. 226:40
Marries: m., dies, or turns Hindoo 495:11
signify whom one m. 408:12
times are changed with him who m. 514:30
Marrow: my winsome m. 235:1
Marrow-bone: stole a m. 369:1
Marrowless: thy bones are m. 459:19
Marry: as easy to m. a rich woman 542:21
better to m. than to burn 66:30
doänt thou m. for munny 537:12
every woman should m. 182:20
he's going to m. Yum-Yum 219:32
home, my love, to m. thee 35:10
how can a bishop m.? 504:27
if ever I m. a wife 308:5

Marry (cont.)
if you do *not* m. Mr. Collins 22:33
I'll m. a landlord's daughter 308:5
m. a market-gardener 177:33
m. Ann 490:19
m. any vun among them 179:34
m...domesticate the Recording Angel 514:31
m. my body to that dust 292:19
m. these..to be rid of thee 155:33
m. twenty husbands 463:11
m. whom she likes 542:32
m. with his brother 435:41
m. your old friend's love 96:36
men that women m. 316:37
neither m., nor are given 60:14, 520:39
not m. his Grandmother 401:16
no woman should m. a teeto-taller 514:27
persons about to m. 403:3
prepared to m. again 218:38
when a man should m. 26:38
where I love I must not m. 357:2
while ye may, go m. 247:10
will you m. me? 220:31
Marrying: m. and giving in marriage 60:26
they aren't the m. brand 299:20
Mars: all labour m. what it does 425:22
nowe m. his mede 235:7
Pallas, Jove, and M. 184:2
this seat of M. 474:22
Marsala: good deal of M. 311:10
Marsch: ein ruheloser M. 415:25
Marsh: old man in a M. 312:15
Marshal: heralds of England's M. 142:4
m.'s truncheon 461:28
pick up a m. or two 564:1
Mart: in church and m. 89:3
Martha: lays it on M.'s Sons 302:3
M. was cumbered about 61:44
Sons of M. 302:1
Martial: blowing m. sounds 345:1
m. airs of England 563:5
m. brood 509:35
m. outside 426:28
melting airs, or m. 163:48
overlaid with taxes..m. 27:25
seduction of m. music 104:1
Martin: M., if dirt were trumps 308:6
Saint M.'s summer 445:18
Martin Elginbrodde: here lie I, M. 326:19
Martinmass: fell about the M. 33:2
Martlet: like the m. 463:44
temple-haunting m. 457:6
Martyr: all the m. throng 362:2
glorious the m.'s gore 503:6
groan of the m.'s woe 75:6
if thou deye a m. 138:37
like a pale m. 503:12
M. of the People 135:28
Oldcastle died a m. 443:1
since I am love's m. 185:5
thou fall'st a blessed m. 446:31
Martyrdom: for the Moors, and m. 166:12
gift of m. 192:25
m. to live 87:7
Martyrs: about the graves of the m. 516:10
Angels, M., Prophets 361:11
blood of the m. 542:3
noble army of m. 388:18
stones and clouts make m. 87:5
Marvel and a mystery 316:37
Marvelled to see such things 394:33
Marvelling: she left me m. 544:1
Marvellous: m. boy 580:7
propensity..towards the m. 265:9
Marvels: alone workest great m. 388:30
Mary: at M.'s knee 140:20
blessed M.'s Son 474:22
everywhere that M. went 233:23
if any young men come for M. 23:7
is there room for M. there? 415:7
Jesu, M. and Joseph they bare 7:14
M. did sing 7:14
M. had a little lamb 233:23
M. hath chosen that good part 61:45
M.! I want a lyre 164:20
M. loves the lamb 233:23(-234)
M., pity women 299:22
M., quite contrary 367:21

Mary (cont.)
M. Seaton, and M. Beaton 31:18
M. was that Mother mild 3:20
Mother, M. Mother 411:32
my M.! 160:21
my M. from my soul 107:4
my M.'s asleep 105:29
my sweet Highland M. 106:9
name of 'M'. 116:15
Philip and M. on a shilling 111:8
Queen M.'s saying serves 91:6
Saint Anne, the mother of M. 374:11
sitting on the stile, M. 73:10
Sons of M. seldom bother 302:1
that blessed M., pre-elect 411:27
to M. Queen the praise 149:27
where the lady M. is 410:12
Mary Ambree: foremost..was M. 31:14
Mary Bell: little M. had a Fairy 75:15
Marybone: from Islington to M. 75:4
Mary-buds: winking M. 429:25
Maryland: by the hills of M. 568:11
M., my M.! 405:19
Mary Magdalene: cometh M. early 64:4
fairer..than M. 376:3
Mary Morison: ye are na M. 107:6
Masculine: peopled..Heaven with Spirits m. 349:23
Truth the m., of Honour 237:23
Masefield: to M. something more 39:12
Mask: as he removes the m. 543:6
loathsome m. has fallen 497:12
m., and antique pageantry 342:7
m. like Castlereagh 495:15
m. of night 477:18
no m. like open truth 154:36
one m. of brooses 177:10
Masonry: kingliest m. 495:27
Masons: singing m. 443:10
Masquerade: truth in m. 116:32
Masquerades: skim milk m. 221:21
Mass: baby figure of the giant m. 481:8
from its m. walls, palaces 114:20
m. of mankind—understand it 28:26
m. of public wrongs 305:14
mingled in a m. 324:15
one m. of brooses 177:10
yawning at the M. 141:4
Massacre: not as sudden as a m. 550:13
Masses: bow, ye m. 218:34
m. against the classes 222:40
m. and fugues and 'ops' 220:5
Mass-priest knelt 359:12
Massy: pillars m. proof 341:24
Mast: bends the gallant m. 167:20
m. of some great ammiral 344:24
m...o' the beaten gold 31:8
right up above the m. 149:4
see the m. burst open 208:16
upon the high and giddy m. 442:1
Master: ass his M.'s crib 52:26
blessing of St. Peter's M. 559:27
choice and m. spirits 450:5
Cold Iron—is m. 295:14
disciple is not above his m. 58:51
do not M. or Campbell me 420:19
fain call m. 452:22
follow the M. 99:35
for m. and servant 550:5
has a new m. 479:43
him that did his m. conquer 424:30
in his m.'s steps 361:24
into the woods my M. 310:10
Jacky shall have a new m. 368:18
ken when I hae a gude m. 420:16
ken when I have a kind m. 419:25
lets your m. in 168:11
life-blood of a m. spirit 352:7
like m., like man 203:23
love is m. wher he wile 228:3
Love would prove so hard a m. 82:12
Man is the m. of things 524:27
m. and make crouch 96:13
m. o'er a slave 576:14
M. of All Good Workmen 303:19
M. of all music 318:2
m. of gibes 181:8
m. of himself 334:18
m. of his fate 531:4
m. of my fate 241:19
m. of the Tiger 456:10

Master (cont.)
M. of this college 39:5
M. of this night of Spring 213:2
m. of unmeaning rhyme 117:27
m...the American joke 550:17
monstrous eft..the Lord and M. 535:36
my m. comes like any Turk 125:18
my m. is..churlish 427:6
my m.'s lost his fiddling-stick 366:12
no more subtle m. 530:14
not make dreams your m. 297:10
one for the m. 366:9
only The M. shall praise 303:21
slew his m. 48:29
soul of an ancient M. 93:39
straight, O worthy M. 315:29
sure th' Eternal M. found 275:3
that rare Italian m. 485:36
this is our m. 91:38
though thy m. miss'd it 446:29
thy m. hath his gold 365:17
we've got a private m. 177:14
wherein the M. had writ 238:25
which is to be m. 131:7
who's m., who's man 521:11
with her great M...sympathise 343:11
M.F.H.: where the M. dines he sleeps 518:11
Master-light of all our seeing 576:18
Masterly inactivity 326:28
Masterpiece: confusion..his m. 458:22
friend..the m. 200:16
man is Heaven's m. 404:7
Master-passion: m. is the love of news 165:1
one m. in the breast 383:25
Master-passions: two m. cannot co-exist 123:8
Masters: all m. cannot be truly follow'd 469:25
approv'd good m. 469:45
both ill m. be 232:12
educate our m. 499:20
Mad World, My M. 80:5
m. of their fates 448:22
m. of the sea 298:15
m. the fear of death 26:2
morality of m. 364:21
our..m...learn their letters 499:20
our passions..bad m. 313:19
people are the m. 101:19
serve two m. 58:9
spiritual pastors and m. 391:7
we cannot all be m. 469:25
young..M. of the waves 18:16
Master-fiend Argyle 24:3
Master-spring: one m. controll'd them 163:28
Mastery: m. of the thing 255:12
voice said in m. 88:16
Mast-high: ice, m. 148:25
Mastiff, greyhound, mongrel 453:30
Masts: his m. crack 135:19
Mat: caught my foot in the m. 233:10
with m. half-hung 385:1
Match: in ears and eyes m. me 95:20
love m...the only thing 195:18
made 'em to m. the men 196:3
m. to win 363:4
m. with the fair flower 510:23
spurt of a lighted m. 93:22
your colors dont quite m. your face 20:28
Matched: m. in mouth like bulls 467:20
m. our rackets to these balls 443:11
m. us with His hour 84:16
m. with thine 498:7
thou wert never m. 328:24
Matches: m. of the Southron folk 545:2
plays extravagant m. 220:6
Matchless: against Heav'n's m. King 346:30
divine, the m., what you will 386:12
maiden that is in. 7:15
Matchwood: potsherd, patch, m. 255:7
Mate: bill our m. 336:43
great artificer made my m. 516:6
here kind m. to thee 170:24
m. of the *Nancy* brig 218:14
no m., no comrade 577:18

Mate (cont.)
ta'en anither m. 32:15
took unto herself a M. 582:7
walk'd without a m. 332:21
who shall be the maiden's m.? 417:8
Mater: m. saeva Cupidinum 258:21, 260:17
scientiarum m. 28:8
stabat m. dolorosa 548:6
Materiae: summam m...manere 25:13
Material: first m. damage 305:11
m sublime 153:3
m. substance of it..vanished 126:27
stronger than any m. force 201:4
Materials: reasoning and belief.. essential m. 125:31
very few m. for history 217:7
Mates: his m. were idly sporting 81:8
leaves his shivering m. 546:26
moves, and m. and slays 206:28
Mathematics: m...never be fully learnt 559:8
m., subtile 27:19
Mystery to M. fly 381:27
mystical m. 85:19
Matilda: attempted to believe M. 41:9
waltzing M. 374:15
Matin: each m. bell..knells us back 150:24
m. to be near 432:19
Matin: ye sommeils du m. 156:12
Matre pulchra filia pulchrior 258:20
Matrem: qui ecclesiam non habet m. 22:1
risu cognoscere m. 556:1
Matrimonial: m. cooings 115:39
m. devotion 219:38
Matrimony: barrier against m. 290:12
holy estate of M. 391:28
in m...a little aversion 500:15
in..m. I never give..advice 139:32
joined together in holy M. 391:21
more of love than m. 227:26
take m. at its lowest 514:25
Matris: pudicitiam..m. indicet 133:6
Matron: m. and the maid 240:21
m.'s glance 224:13
sober-suited m. 478:18
Matter: Berkeley said '..no m.' 116:30
gravelled for lack of m. 428:20
he that repeateth a m. 50:18
I am full of m. 49:13
if it is it doesn't m. 222:12
I the m. will re-word 436:1
little m. mend all 80:18
m. enough to save one's own 92:45
m. for a May morning 484:11
m. she drove at 401:34
m. they had no concern in 521:6
meaning, however, is no great m. 121:14
mind and m...glide swift 176:20
more m. with less art 432:39
much m. decocted into few words 212:10
no m. from the heart 481:29
no m. what he said 116:30
no m. what you do 103:32
nothing-much-m.-day 243:5
not much dislike the m. 424:4
order..this m. better in France 512:16
pour out the pack of m. 424:14
prevent seditions..take away the m. 27:9
root of the m. 49:7
then he's full of m. 426:34
there the m. ended it 40:18
things that m. for a nation 216:7
waking, no such m. 487:22
what is M.? 403:10
what's the m. with Gladstone? 233:12
wrecks of m. 1:24
wretched m. and lame metre 343:26
Mattered: it never really m. 296:8
Matter-of-fact-ness: a m. 239:17
Matters: big words for little m. 271:20
m. not how a man dies 271:35
no judge of such m. 387:20
sets right all other m. 90:33
small m. win great commendation 25:37
trusts them with, serious m. 139:23
Matthew, Mark, Luke, and John 3:3

Mature: lip m. is ever new 285:39
Maud: into the garden, M. 536:9
M. burst in 376:5
M. is not seventeen 536:3
M., M., M., M. 536:2
M. with her exquisite face 535:39
Maude: adores as Margaret, M. 375:26
Maudlin poetess 385:21
Maugre: in the m. of..Douglas 30:11
m. all God's promises 375:27
Maurice: since M. died 81:11
Maux: supporter les m. d'autrui 407:9
Mavis: heard the m. singing 268:30
m.' evening sang 104:29
merl, the m. 187:4
Mavourneen: Kathleen M. 166:24
Maw: whose gospel is their m. 351:30
Maw-crammed beast 95:14
Mawkish: so sweetly m. 381:22
Mawkishness: thence proceeds m. 284:18
Maxim: m. he had often tried 165:10
that m...become a universal law 284:5
useless..a general m. 325:7
Maxims: little hoard of m. 534:23
Maximum: m. of temptation...m. of opportunity 490:32
May: as flush as M. 435:37
bursting boughs of M. 81:20
bush, in the corner, of m. 171:21
call unto your remembrance.. M. 328:16
chief music of our M. 189:18
chills the lap of M. 226:10
cold M. and windy 550:1
crowned with milk-white m. 82:7
darling buds of M. 486:18
fairer far in M. 282:1
flourish in M. 328:15
fresh as is the month of M. 136:25
from the merriment of M. 285:3
I'm to be Queen o' the M. 536:26
in M.'s new-fangled mirth 454:33
I were lord in M. 524:30
Kent and Surrey m. 296:15
laurel outlives not M. 525:8
let it be as it m. 183:17
love, whose month is ever M. 455:17
March sun feels like M. 93:13
matter for a M. morning 484:11
M.l be thou never grac'd 87:25
M. flowers 8:9, 549:31
M. is a pious fraud 320:16
M. when they are maids 428:22
M. will be fine next year 263:30
meaning of M. 524:8
merry month of M. 30:1, 31:21, 35:17, 80:7
month of M. was come 328:15
moonlight-coloured m. 497:22
nuts in M. 6:23
of April, M. 245:17
on the eve of M. 80:10
rose in M. 138:21
steal from all I m. be 114:26
swarm of bees in M. 5:17
there m. be heaven 97:6
there's an end of M. 263:33
through the boughs of the m. 309:26
what a lawyer tells me I m. do 101:3
what men m. do 469:4
whenas M. was in his pride 80:7
when M. is past 125:10
when that..M. is comen 138:16
wife is M. 561:1
world is white with M. 530:3
Maying: let's go a-M. 246:1
life went a-m. 152:20
that we two were M. 293:21
May-mess: look: a M. 255:6
Mayne: thus the M. glideth 94:24
Mayor: thy famous M. 195:7
Maypole: away to the M. hie 5:5
where's the M. in the Strand? 79:17
Maypoles: I sing of M. 245:17
May-time: from M. and the.. dawn 580:19
Maze: burgeons every m. of quick 533:24
m. of schools 382:21
mighty m. 383:7
not in fancy's m. 386:1
wander in that golden m. 193:27

Mazes: entangled in their m. 497:9
in wand'ring m. lost 345:29
pleasant m. of her hair 158:1
through m. running 342:8
Mazy: gay in the m. 146:23
with a m. motion 151:33
Me: believe they talked of m. 203:11
but not for m. 8:19
command my heart and m. 166:17
Father, Mother, and M. 303:18
feud 'twixt things and m. 80:22
first to m. 82:11
grow old along with m. 95:13
his hungering neighbour, and M. 320:18
it was m.! 302:14
just like m. 544:5
Man like to m. 96:25
m. miserable! 346:32
m., my bargains 463:17
m., to whom thou gav'st it 487:22
minister of thee to m. 80:21
miserable m.! 96:6
no more of THEE and M. 206:16, 17
not afraid of God, afraid of m. 386:23
on virtue and on m. 324:17
out of m. the years roll 524:1
same as m. 303:22
Talk awhile of M. and THEE 206:16, 17
they at least are for m. 544:20
this man loved *m.*! 309:4
to darkness and to m. 229:28
to peace, but not to m. 162:14
Me: m., m., adsum qui feci 555:7
Mead: bloweth m. 9:26
Dr. M…in the broad sunshine 274:11
even m., that erst 445:11
o'er the m. 76:10
of alle the floures in the m. 138:17
walks the m. 529:2
Meadow: deep-m., happy 531:37
Meadowed-gale of spring 150:3
Meadows: golden lie the m. 337:35
her feet have touch'd the m. 536:4
in the dim m. desolate 569:16
m. runnels 285:1
m. trim with daisies pied 342:1
no more by-path m. 514:30
paint the m. with delight 455:35
past the near m. 288:2
set in enamelled m. 558:11
up from the m. 568:11
water fairest m. 164:5
with golden face the m. 486:27
ye fountains, m., hills 576:21
Meadow-sweet or sorrel 522:11
Meads: fair these broad m. 420:31
flow'ry m. in May 572:2
lady in the m. 286:30
these sweet-springing m. 81:20
Meagre: m. as lizards 121:20
m., hopping…*insects* 102:20
Meal: handful of m. 48:1
make one hearty m. 306:22
no man gets a full m. 272:31
Roman m. 163:27
winding up every m. 187:15
Mealed-with-yellow sallows 255:6
Meals of beef and iron 444:5
Mealy boys 177:41
Mean: debtless competence, golden m. 541:5
excellent things for m…uses 315:6
[Furies] m. well 182:10
happy the golden m. 334:20
heav'n did not m. 253:21
if I ever do a m. action 512:21
I m. what I say 129:6
man of m. estate 188:33
m. and mighty rotting together 429:39
m. and vulgar works of man 579:13
meanly admires m. things 542:7
m. reparations upon mighty ruins 101:30
m., sordid, home-bred cares 101:30
nature makes that m. 485:24
not careful what they m. 480:35

Mean (cont.)
nothing common did or m. 332:24
poor, and m., and lowly 4:1
say what you m. 129:6
though m. our object 579:7
what..Dr. Newman m.? 294:15
what I choose it to m. 131:6
what I m. when I say 220:16
Meander: m. level 325:12, 355:17
m. through a meadow of margin 500:33
slow M.'s margent 340:13
some trotting burn's m. 107:35
Meandering: five miles m. 151:33
Meaner: leave all m. things 383:7
motives m. than your own 36:3
you m. beauties 583:13
Meanest: m. flower that blows 576:22(-577)
m. flowret 231:5
m. of his creatures 94:10
m. of mankind 384:12
sorrow of the m. thing 575:14
Meaneth: what m. then this bleating 47:15
Meaning: as to the m. 120:22
atom of m. in it 129:34
free from all m. 190:32
inexhaustible m. 126:13
its m. is my meat and drink 91:33
m. doesn't matter 220:26
m…no great matter 121:14
m. of Empire Day 142:15
m. of May 524:8
m. suited to his mind 529:2
richest without m. 413:11
some faint m. 193:2
teems with hidden m. 222:11
to get at *his* m. 413:3
within the m. of the Act 5:11
Meanings: m. that he never had 163:9
two m…one word 131:13, 476:20
Meanly: all m. wrapt 343:11
m. admires mean things 542:7
m. just 279:4
thinks m. of himself 273:34
Means: all appliances and m. to boot 442:2
all the m. to make us one 184:30
best m. 266:10
by all the m. you can 565:19
die beyond my m. 570:24
for the m. of grace 389:20
increased m. and increased leisure 181:3
knew what England m. 140:25
live within our m. 560:23
m. just what I choose 131:6
m. not, hath not 481:7
m. whereby I live 465:14
my extremest m. 463:2
my m. may lie 158:15
place and m. for every man 423:8
politics..a m. of rising 272:33
pretty, but I don't know what it m. 218:10
ravin up thine own life's m. 458:29
sight of m. to do ill 447:43
this good m. I gain 262:6
wants money, m., and content 427:25
what the eye brings m. of seeing 126:13
Meant: all, my life seemed m. for 92:31
I knew not all he m. 530:32
m. well 513:36
more is m. 341:21
she knew what it m. 10:25
what ere she m. by it 185:5
Measles: ever hav the m.? 560:6
love..like the m. 269:1, 11
Measure: does it hold good m.? 90:33
fill the m. of the year 288:27
good m., pressed down 61:31
lead but one m. 418:19
leave to Heaven the m. 279:12
man is the m. 402:18
m. every..planet's course 330:28
m. my mind against his 489:22
m. of Felicity 232:13
m. of our torment 296:28
m. of the universe 497:5
M. still for M. 462:26
mingled m. 151:33(-152)

Measure (cont.)
now tread we a m. 418:21
number, weight, and m. in a year of dearth 77:13
praise the Lord by m. 298:16
scant of true m. 281:27
Scotch jig, a m. 468:9
shrunk to this little m. 450:2
to grace my m. 401:38
to m. life learn 351:23
treasure beyond m. 218:23
when Fate thy m. **takes** 320:2
wielder of the stateliest m. 541:8
with what m. ye mete 60:56
Measured: dance is a m. pace 24:21
it shall be m. to you 60:56
m. by my soul 562:2
m. it from side to side 581:20
m. out my life with coffee spoons 197:18
use in m. language 532:4
Measureless to man 151:32, 33
Measures: better than all m. 498:10
in Lydian m. 191:9
in short m. 282:1
m. comparatively nothing 124:20
m. not men 124:20
not men, but m. 101:37
to delightful m. 476:3
Tory men and Whig m. 181:33
trying the m. 332:12
Meat: abhorred all manner of m. 398:16
as an egg is full of m. 478:11
as it buys its m. 112:6
cans of poisoned m. 141:34
eat an ounce less m. 275:12
eat but little m. 516:21
ever..gavest m. or drink 31:13
full of m. and drink 515:15
have ye any m.? 64:13
heaven sends us good m. 213:9
his m. was locusts 57:29
its meaning is my m. and drinke 91:33
it snewed..of m. and drinke 137:10
life more than m. 58:11
little m. 245:19
little m. for men 194:16
loves the m. in his youth 468:22
made worms' m. of me 478:15
m. in due season 398:11
m. in the hall 516:12
mock the m. it feeds on 471:31
no stomach for such m. 183:9
on our m., and on us all 247:15
out-did the m. 246:15
out of the eater..m. 46:55
penny ice and cold m. 210:11
provide our little Toby m. 508:16
seek their m. from God 398:10
some hae m. 107:34
taste My m. 244:22
tearing his m. like a tiger 325:32
upon what m…Caesar feed 448:23
Meat-fly: Thackeray settled like a m. 412:21
Meats: eater of broken m. 452:32
funeral baked m. 431:4
of all m. the soonest cloy 158:12
Meaty jelly, too 178:7
Meccah: some to M. turn 208:12
Mechanic: m. part of wit 202:3
mere m. operation 111:12
poetry a mere m. art 162:28
Mechanical arts and merchandise 27:36
Méchant: cet animal est très m. 12:12
l'homme..un m. animal 354:8
Mécontents: cent m. et un ingrat 318:22
Meddle: not to m. with my toys 515:18
Meddling: every fool will be m. 50:24
Mede is at his gate 119:13
Medea: M. gather'd the..herbs 465:17
pueros coram populo M. trucidet 256:3
Medes: given to the M. and Persians 55:42
Parthians, and M. 64:26
Medias: in m. res 256:1
Mediator: our M. and Advocate 389:13
Medical: M. Crowner 34:12
m. doctors..cocking their m. eyes 180:1
Medicina: sero m. paratur 372:2
Medicinable: their m. gum 74:2

Medicine: all m. is mine 494:1
doeth good like a m. 50:20
great griefs. .m. the less 429:38
grief itself is a m. 159:5
hunger..m. for health 549:22
m. of life 56:36
m. thee to that sweet sleep 471:43
m. to heal their sickness 400:21
m., which has paid seven per
cent. 505:28
m. worse than the malady 37:31
no other m. but only hope 462:3
Medicines to make me love him 439:2
Medicus: schoenobates m. magus 283:3
Medieval: your m. hand 220:28
Medio tutissimus ibis 371:27
Mediocria: sunt quaedam m. 331:23
Mediocribus esse poetis 256:12
Mediocritatem: auream. .m. diligit 259:6
Mediocrity: Arch-M... Cabinet of
Mediocrities 181:31
m. knows nothing higher 188:28
Meditamur: tenui musam m. avena 505:26
Meditans: aut orans, aut m. 291:25
Meditaris: tenui musam m. avena 555:14
Meditate: her matchless songs..
m. 332:27
m. the thankless Muse 342:20
Meditation: in maiden m. 466:39
let us all to m. 445:32
m. of my heart 392:34
Mediterranean: waken. .the blue
M. 496:8
Medium: m. for writing in prose 569:30
perfect use of an imperfect m. 570:4
Mediumistic: her m. soul 310:20
Meed: for duty, not for m. 426:38
in Heaven expect thy m. 342:23
m. of some melodious tear 342:10
m. of victory 509:35
nowe merres his m. 235:7
Meek: blessed are the m. 57:39
borne his faculties so m. 457:9
He is m., and He is mild 76:10
m. and lowly in heart 59:10
m. and quiet spirit 70:1
m. and unaffected grace 224:22
Moses was very m. 46:12
safer being m. than fierce 89:22
soft, m., patient 170:18
taught us to be calm and m. 251:4
that I am m. and gentle 450:11
Meekest: thou wert the m. man 328:24
Meekly kneeling upon your knees 390:35
Meekness: brought salvation down
by m. 503:1
faith, m., temperance 67:46
leaving, with m., her sins 252:22
word of truth, of m. 394:22
wrath, by His m. 77:2
Meet: assemble and m. together 388:8
cannot m. you on the square 306:17
extremes m. 253:33
firm I can m. 124:13
I cannot m. them here 539:17
if I should m. thee 119:30
if we do m. again 451:37
I'll m. 'im later on 297:4
I'll m. thee on the lea-rig 106:30
in Paradise, if we m. 97:27
I there did m. another man 277:10
I will not fail to m. thee 292:19
make both ends m. 213:17
m., and either do, or die 37:24
m. and greet her 528:1
m. and right so to do 390:38
m. at any time again 189:20
m. him everywhere 201:23
m. it is I set it down 432:21
m. me by moonlight alone 557:16
m. on that beautiful shore 415:9
m. we shall. .where dead men
m. 112:19
m. you her my wishes 166:18
merely. . to m. one's friends 104:2
never m. again 9:7
never the twain shall m. 294:27
one would m. in every place 285:40
our hands will never m. again 253:30
run half-way to m. it 269:16
run to m...most avoid 340:19

Meet (cont.)
soon again to m. 375:13
temptation but for man to m. 96:13
though infinite can never m. 332:6
till we m. again 406:1
to m. the armed men 49:26
to m. thee at thy coming 53:21
we m., with champagne 354:15
we only part to m. again 215:40
we shall m., but. .miss him 560:27
we three m. again 456:3
when we shall m. at compt 473:32
where many m. 122:20
your shadow. .rising to m. you 197:28
Meeter: deemed it m. 376:23
Meeting: as if I was a public m. 552:22
broke the good m. 459:22
lovers m. 482:28
m. like this make amends 356:10
m. where it likes 19:29
neither over-taking nor m. 154:34
this m. is drunk, sir! 179:10
Meetings: changed to merry m. 476:3
their m. made December June 533:15
Meets: here Stanley m. 322:9
m. in mere oppugnancy 481:4
more. .than the ear 341:21
more than m. the eye 296:30
Méfiez-vous 12:19
Meg: M. grew sick 105:15
M. was deaf 105:14
old M. was brave 287:4
Meilleur: le m. des mondes possibles 557:2
Melancholic: saturnine, dark, and
m. 154:26
Melancholy: alien sound of m. 575:24
day-dreams of m. men 193:27
error, m.'s child 451:40
full of spirit's m. 88:4
green and yellow m. 483:10
hail divinest M. 341:8
hence, loathed M. 341:26
I can suck m. 427:8
inherited a vile m. 276:3
in Nature. .nothing m. 152:7
kindly mood of m. 195:15
lovely m. 38:1
m. as an unbrac'd drum 134:7
m...foolish to indulge 273:20
m. god protect thee 483:7
m., long. .roar 15:7
M. mark'd him for her own 230:13
m. of mine own 428:16
m. when thou art absent 155:27
mine I conceive a m. book 165:5
mistress of true m. 425:15
moping m. 349:24
most musical, most m. 152:7, 341:13
my cue is villainous m. 452:21
naught so sweet as M. 109:2
pale M. sate retir'd 154:1
rare recipe for m. 307:4
soothe her m. 226:18
such a charm in m. 408:9
this trick of m. 423:6
to rhyme, and to be m. 455:15
unfriended, m., slow 226:3
veil'd M. has her. .shrine 287:21
what devil this m. is 209:29
Melchisedech: after the order of M. 398:24
Meliora: video m., proboque 371:30
Mellow: death took him m. 376:21
m. glory of the Attic stage 16:2
not old, but m. 378:18
thro' the m. horn 154:1
too m. for me 354:14
Mellowed to that tender light 119:1
Mellowing: before the m. year 342:10
m. to the grape 178:7
upon the m. of occasion 455:12
Mellows: tart temper never m. 267:19
Mellstock: in M. churchyard 236:8
Melodies: all m. the echoes 151:6
ease my breast of m. 285:31
heard m. are sweet 287:8
sweetest m. 578:19
Melodious: goodly prospect and
m. sounds 352:26
melting m. words 247:14
some m. plot 287:23
some m. tear 342:10

Melody: blund'ring kind of m. 190:32
chanted a m. loud 538:1
falling in m. back 152:8
from ancient m. have ceas'd 75:18
lull'd with. .sweetest m. 441:41
m., in our heaviness 400:5
mortal m. 380:18
my Luve's like the m. 107:14
smale fowles maken m. 136:22
Melon-flower: this gaudy m. 92:16
Melons: stumbling on m. 332:17
Melrose: view fair M. aright 417:12
Melt: crown o' the earth doth m. 425:29
earth shall m. away 394:28
I rage, I m., I burn 214:6
m. at others' woe 230:16
m. their sweets on. .Caesar 425:17
m. with ruth 343:2
now m. into sorrow 113:1
so let us m. 186:24
so will I m. into a bath 508:15
this too too solid flesh. .m. 430:33
Melted: m. at the sweet tale of the
sun 439:14
m. into air 480:8
m. like a cloud 539:19
m. like snow 118:39
m. to one vast Iris 114:6
quite m. into tears 292:18
Melting: all the races of Europe
are m. 587:18
m. airs, or martial 163:48
m. melodious words 247:14
unused to the m. mood 474:2
Melting-pot: great M. 587:18
Melts: m. with unperceiv'd decay 279:8
purer sapphire m. 536:8
then m. for ever 108:7
Member: comfortable feel in any
m. 253:12
ev'ry m. of the force 408:1
m. of Christ 391:2
not m. of Bristol. .a m. of parliament 100:14
shape. .distinguishable in m. 346:4
thing I am not a m. of 208:26
Members: all my m. written 400:11
m. one of another 67:58
Membra: etiam disiecti m. poetae 261:14
Même: plus c'est la m. chose 284:7
Meminisse: nec me m. pigebit Elissae 554:19
Memnon smitten 538:13
Memnonium. .in all its glory 504:1
Memnons: new M. singing 88:14
Memoirs: prosperous people..
write their m. 112:2
Memor: dum m. ipse mei 554:19
Memorable: making these days m. 144:7
Memorandum: if you don't make
a m. 129:37
Memores: sui m. alios fecere merendo 554:29
Memorial: have no m. 57:18
keep King Charles. .out of the
M. 174:25
m. from the Soul's eternity 410:21
scarce leav'st here m. 246:7
singest with vois m. 136:19
some frail m. 230:7
their m. is perished with them 392:14
Memorials catch the dying sun 516:19
Memories: liars ought to have
good m. 501:13
M. of Eld! 380:14
m. of the day 338:3
night of m. and of sighs 308:14
Memorize another Golgotha 456:6
Memory: begot in the ventricle of
m. 455:12
better m. said, fie! 359:27
deals with the m. of men 87:16
dear son of m. 351:8
do honour his m. 280:1
Elizabeth of most happy m. 43:24
fond M. brings the light 357:13
for my name and m. 28:15
from the m. a rooted sorrow 460:37
from the table of my m. 432:20
grand m. for forgetting 514:8
great man's m. 435:5
hands of m. weave 157:1
how sweet their m. still! 161:2

Memory (cont.)
I claim only a m. — 92:31
illiterate him..from your m. — 500:14
I revere the m. of Mr. F. — 175:38
it comes o'er my m. — 472:20
m. be green — 430:22
m. fades — 171:8
m. of that insolence — 206:15
M. of this Impertinence — 206:14
m., the warder of the brain — 457:14
mixing m. and desire — 197:27
my friends proud of my m. — 290:29
mystic chords of m. — 314:10
poor sort of m. — 130:28
stay in a man's m. — 304:50
their very m. is fair — 552:8
thy lamp, O M. — 411:28
thy tablets, M.! — 16:24
time whereof the m. of man — 73:7, 314:22
to his m. for his jests — 501:1
to m. dear — 314:21, 419:5
to the m. of Shakespeare — 226:28
vibrates in the m. — 499:1
while m. holds a seat — 432:20
wisdom or even m. — 411:37
Memphian: his M. chivalry — 344:26

Men: all are m. — 230:30
all m. all earth to love — 302:13
all m. become good creatures — 93:16
all m. everywhere..free — 314:3
all m. mortal but themselves — 587:7
all sorts and conditions of m. — 389:15
all the m. and women..players — 427:21
any m. that were — 246:7
be such m. as he — 15:4
blood..in hosses, dawgs and m. — 542:38
brave m., living and dead — 314:12
brutes m. and m. divine — 374:20
busy hum of m. — 342:5
cannot learn m. from books — 182:41
England..the purgatory of m. — 209:8
fair women and brave m. — 113:25
faults to make us m. — 425:32
few honest m. — 167:2
gods..in the likeness of m. — 64:51
Gods or wondering m. — 286:10
good will toward m. — 61:19
heart of oak are our m. — 213:10
hearts of oak our m. — 20:20
her m. robust for toil — 123:7
honest m. and bonnie lasses — 108:3
honour all m. — 69:50
I cannot bear m. and women — 489:29
I describe not m. but manners — 204:17
if this counsel..of m. — 64:32
I'll fear not what m. say — 99:37
in cities..the works of m. — 377:9
in the catalogue ye go for m. — 458:35
I see m. as trees, walking — 61:2
justifiable to m. — 350:27
justify the ways of God to M. — 344:4
know themselves to be but m. — 392:16
level now with m. — 425:29
made in the likeness of m. — 68:17
made m., and not made them well — 434:20
maids must kiss no m. — 80:7
makes m. mad — 473:16
maketh m. to be of one mind — 396:5
measures not m. — 124:20
m. and morning newspapers — 378:21
m. are April when they woo — 428:22
m. are better than this theology — 200:10
m. are but children — 191:20
m. are everything — 124:20
m. are made by nature unequal — 212:5
m. are we — 471:17
m. are we and must grieve — 582:8
m. at most differ as Heaven and Earth — 531:22
m. below, and saints above — 417:16
m. dare trust themselves with m. — 480:20
m. in a world of m. — 296:2
m. like soldiers may not quit — 535:25
m. may come and m. may go — 528:6
m. must work — 294:1
m., my brothers, m. the workers — 534:25
m. of England..of light and leading — 102:24
m. of like passions with you — 64:52

Men (cont.)
m. of little showing — 302:4
m. of renown — 44:38
m. of sense never tell it — 423:1
m. only disagree — 345:28
M.!O what venerable..creatures — 548:15
m.'s m.: gentle or simple — 196:18
m. that God made mad — 140:15
m. that strove with gods — 541:3
m. that were boys — 42:5
m. that women marry — 316:37
m. that worked for England — 140:24
m. were deceivers ever — 468:20
m. who did the work — 303:15
m. who march away — 236:18
m. with sisters..mothers and wives — 253:23
m. with splendid hearts — 84:12
m., with wailing in your voices — 88:26
m., women, and clergymen — 504:31
m., women, and Herveys — 354:13
m. would be angels — 383:13
m. would be false — 321:13
merry m. of East-cheap — 226:28
more I see of m. — 408:16
more wondrous are the m. — 74:8
mortal m., mortal m. — 440:23
most wretched m. — 494:17
my fifty m. and women — 93:44
my m., like satyrs — 329:20
Nature made us m. — 320:8
need of a world of m. — 94:27
noble army, m. and boys — 240:21
not into the hands of m. — 56:31
not m. but dogs — 108:23
not m., but measures — 101:37
not stones, but m. — 450:26
not the m. you took them for — 468:39
not thrones and crowns, but m. — 198:22
no way for m. to be — 429:26
obey God rather than m. — 64:31
O m., this man in brotherhood — 87:38
pass for m. of war — 229:11
Philip fought m. — 313:2
practise if you please with m. — 96:2
praise famous m. — 57:14
praises from the m., whom all m. praise — 158:18
priests are only m. — 95:33
quit you like m., be strong — 67:19
quit yourselves like m. — 47:8
rather..books than m. — 28:14
sailors but m. — 463:15
schemes o' mice an' m. — 107:11
sensible m. never tell — 182:5
shadows of us m. — 280:20
shame to m.! — 345:28
shortest of m. — 34:4
states, like m., have their growth — 309:19
such cognizance of m. and things — 92:21
swallow down the very m. — 358:12
taken asunder, seem m. — 86:26
take our place as m. and women — 295:6
tell them, they are m. — 230:27
that m. betray — 226:18
to form Christian m. — 20:22
to match the m. — 196:16
to m. French — 136:13
to m. of other minds — 226:13
too saint-like in the eyes of m. — 316:36
Tory m. and Whig measures — 181:33
transform m. into monsters — 200:29
twelve good m. into a box — 85:1
twice four hundred m. — 162:11
War between M. and Women — 547:12
weak m. must fall — 475:1
wealth accumulates, and m. decay — 224:14
we m., at sea, indite — 187:2
we m. may say more — 483:10
we've got the m. — 265:15
what are m. better — 531:36
what is it m. in women do require? — 226:13
what m. or gods are these? — 74:28
when m. and mountains meet — 74:23
while there are m., and malice — 282:7
why don't the m. propose? — 37:4
with M. for Pieces plays — 206:28
with m. he can be rational — 22:10

Men (cont.)
with m. this is impossible — 60:4
with small m. no great thing — 339:1
with the tongues of m. — 66:44
women's love and m.'s — 184:5
women walk..the same as the m. — 567:8
words are m.'s daughters — 327:6
ye are m.! — 122:6
yes, Sir, many m. — 271:1
Menace: his looks do m. heaven — 330:23
Nazi Germany had become a m. — 362:29
Menaces: deterred..by the m. of a ruffian — 272:20
Menacing almighty lovers — 140:16
Men-children only — 457:15
Mend: broken thing m. — 42:6
delight, that they may m. — 160:19
God never made..for man to m. — 192:15
m. it or be rid on't — 458:36(-459)
my long sickness..begins to m. — 480:30
shine, and seek to m. — 185:18
strive to m. — 562:6
tak a thought an' m. — 104:5
times will not m. — 373:13
to m. the heart — 381:6
Mendacity: mendacity..equalled by their m. — 527:17
Mendax: splendide m. — 260:5
Mended: at Pontigibaud they m. it — 40:18
endure what can't be m. — 562:6
nothing else but to be m. — 110:19
Mendez Pinto: Ferdinand M. was but a type of thee — 155:9
Mendicity..equalled by their mendacity — 527:17
Mendicus: tum tu m. es? — 379:27
Mendip: from M.'s sunless caves — 322:19
Mene: m., m., tekel, upharsin — 55:42
Menelaus: Helen, M.' queen — 480:37
Menpleasers: as m. — 68:9
Mens: m. agitat molem — 554:30
m. cuiusque is est quisque — 145:10
m. sana in corpore sano — 283:24
m. sibi conscia recti — 553:20
Mensch: der M...überwunden — 364:22
Menschen: alle M. werden Brüder — 415:21
Mental: engage..in some m. pursuit — 75:10
not cease from M. Fight — 75:16
Mentality: your m., too, is bully — 39:28
Mente: non vultus..tyranni m. qualit solida — 259:21
peragravit, m. animoque — 320:27
Menten: iustificam nobis m. avertere deorum — 133:10
Mention: make m. of you always — 65:30
m. it within their wills — 450:24
no m. of me more — 446:29
omitted to m. the fact — 128:5
only necessary to m. Asparagus — 175:38
recourse to the m. of it — 274:24
we never m. her — 36:31
Mentioned: m. me to him — 129:33
or allow their names to be m. — 23:4
Mercenary: followed their m. calling — 264:4
Mercers: toy-shops, m., hardware-men — 307:2
Merchandise: mechanical arts and m. — 27:36
mummy is become m. — 87:19
Merchant, to secure his treasure — 401:38
Merchantman: monarchy is a m. — 4:21
Merchants: others, like m. — 443:10
trafficked..with Eastern m. — 374:11
where m. most do congregate — 463:19
whose m. are princes — 53:29
Merci: la belle Dame sans M. — 285:26, 286:35
Mercies: all thy M., O my God — 2:22
tender m. of the wicked — 50:2
thanks for m. past receive — 98:14
Merciful: blessed are the m. — 57:39
God be m. to me a sinner — 62:34
God be m. unto us — 396:2
m., and lendeth — 398:26
M. and Mighty! — 240:19

INDEX

Merciful (cont.)
m. unto them that fear him 398:6
the Lord is gracious, and m. 400:18
then must the Jew be m. 464:33
thou, Lord, art m. 395:24
very m. to the birds 11:12
Mercuries: English M. 443:12
Mercury: like feather'd M. 440:18
words of M. are harsh 456:2
Mercy: as his majesty..his m. 56:31
become them..as m. 461:28
big with m. 161:18
by thy great m. defend us 388:36
Charity and M...Not unholy names 176:12
crowning m. 167:5
dimensions of this m. 167:5
full of compassion and m. 56:30
God all m. 587:10
God ha' m. on his soul! 436:36
hand folks over to God's m. 196:14
have m. o' my soul 326:19
have m. on Jacob yet 92:9
have m. on us worms 202:20
have m. upon us..sinners 388:43
his m. endureth for ever 400:4
infinite m. 92:4
in m. shall the throne be established 53:24
law of human judgment, M. 413:15
leaving m. to heaven 204:25
Lord have m. on us 361:5
lovelier things have m. shown 117:40
m. and truth are met 397:9
m. blows the coals 508:15
m. every way is infinite 91:18
M. has a human heart 77:1
m. I asked, m. I found 121:25
m. is above this..sway 464:33
m. to forgive 192:24
m. upon one of our souls 484:13
most tender m. is neglect 165:20
nothing emboldens sin..as m. 480:24
O, God of M.! when? 198:22
'O m.!' to myself I cried 581:12
peace on earth, and m. mild 565:12
quality of m. 464:33
send forth his m. and truth 395:18
shut the gates of m. 230:6
so great is his m. 398:6
sometimes withhold in m. 357:27
sweetness, m., majesty 319:7
teach us all to render..m. 464:33
that is m.'s door 161:17
that m. I to others show 386:31
they shall obtain m. 57:39
thy everlasting m., Christ 334:3
thy loving-kindness and m. 393:10
Thy m. on Thy People 301:1
to do justly and to love m. 56:8
to M., Pity, Peace and Love 76:18
to the m. of a rude stream 446:24
unto God's gracious m. 391:37
we do pray for m. 464:33
when m. seasons justice 464:33
whereto serves m. 435:33
Mercy-seat: coming to a m. 161:14
how beautiful Thy m. 202:21
Mere: Lady of the M. 573:2
Mère: France, m. des arts 40:16
Meredith: M...a sort of..Walt Whitman 142:19
M. climbed towards the sun 142:19
M. is a prose Browning 569:30
Mereri: bene velle m. 133:12
Meridian: in England..under any m. 86:28
Merit: by m. raised to that bad eminence 345:14
by the m. of the holy Cross 361:13
his m. handsomely allowed 274:34
how he esteems your m. 159:31
m. of perpetuity 87:16
m. of the wearer 464:1
m.'s all his own 143:26
m. that which he obtains 151:26
m. wins the soul 385:19
no damned m. in it 335:15
patient m. of the unworthy takes 434:4
preacher's m. or demerit 90:33

Merit (cont.)
sense of injured m. 344:13
to buried m. raise a..bust 279:4
what is m.? 373:8
Mérite: le gouvernement qu'elle m. 327:13
Merited: how hast thou m.? 544:29
Meriting: human m. 544:29
Merits: careless their m...to scan 224:21
his m. to disclose 230:13
m. of a spotless shirt 537:5
not weighing our m. 390:45
obtain that which he m. 151:26
Merle, the mavys 187:4
Mermaid: at the M. 37:12
choicer than the M. Tavern 287:1
mar-ri-ed to a m. 8:24
M. in the Zodiack 287:2
m. on a dolphin's back 466:38
M.'s now 280:9
seeming m. steers 424:7
until he came to a m. 8:24
Mermaid-like..bore her up 437:1
Mermaids: I have heard the m. 197:22
so many m. 424:7
Merrier man..never 455:3
Merriest: maddest, m. day 536:26
Merrily: after summer m. 480:14
die all, die m. 440:19
down it m. 170:24
m. did we drop 148:21
m., m. shall I live now 480:14
m. sang the monks 124:22
we went m.! 114:39
Merriment: from the m. of May 285:3
innocent m. 220:3
this m. of parsons 274:27
your flashes of m. 437:15
Merrow Down: road by M. 299:23
Merry: against ill chances..m. 442:17
all their wars are m. 140:15
at the point of death..m. 478:42
eat, and to drink, and to be m. 51:18
eat, drink, and be m. 61:52
England was m. England 418:24
folwen..a m. someres day 138:32
Fortune is m. 451:2
God rest you m., gentlemen 6:11
gone up with a m. noise 394:31
good are always the m. 585:1
good to be m. and wise 7:22
guid to be m. and wise 106:6
hear the m. din 148:19
he was a m. man 477:3
I am not m. 470:27
I could be m. now 447:32
let us be m. 176:9
makes one man m. 86:33
m. and sad to tell 38:28
m. as a marriage bell 113:25
m., dancing, drinking..time 193:31
m. Grecian coaster 18:16
m. heart..a cheerful countenance 50:11
m. heart doeth good 50:20
m. love the fiddle 585:1
m. maiden and the tar 221:22
m. men of East-cheap 226:28
m., m. lives 361:7
m. monarch 407:20
m. month of May 30:1, 31:21, 35:17, 80:7
m. of soul 516:7
m. old soul 368:3
never m. when I hear..music 465:19
never m. world in England 445:35
never m. world since 483:26
of such a m. nimble..spirit 455:28
sing a m. madrigal 219:36
tag rag, m. derry 370:5
three m. boys 37:16
tonight we'll m. be 5:24
very m., and the best fritters 377:15
wantown and a m. 137:1
well to be m. and wise 335:4
we were m. 148:17
wine maketh m. 51:25
wise are m. of tongue 585:15
Merryman: Doctor M. 520:23
song of a m. 222:27
Merses profundo 260:22
Meruit: palmam qui m., ferat 362:13

Mesech: constrained to dwell with M. 399:24
Meshach: Shadrach, M., and Abed-Nego 55:41
Mesopotamia: blessed word M. 213:16
dwellers in M. 64:26
Mesopotamy: from here to M. 121:6
Mess: all along o' m. 295:22
Benjamin's m. 45:22
for a m. of potage 6:4
for a m. of potash 560:3
in every m. I finds a friend 173:5
m. of imprecision of feeling 197:9
m. of pottage with love 50:13
Message: electric m. came 23:14
give to a gracious m. 424:15
Lincoln sped the m. on 322:23
m. of Art 489:21
Messages: fair speechless m. 463:3
Messe: Paris vaut bien une m. 242:3
Messenger: Anglo-Saxon M. 131:14
bisy larke, m. of day 137:30
m. of Satan to buffet me 67:37
m. of Spring 509:3
mis-featured m. 95:31
other M.'s called Hatta 131:15
Messengers: bade his m. ride forth 323:10
holy m. 245:5
superfluous kings for m. 424:26
Messes: other country m. 342:2
Messiah: found the new M. 192:28
true M. see 565:14
Messieurs les gardes françaises 239:9
Messing about in boats 228:16
Met: all a lie may be m. 529:32
day and the way we m. 524:9
day when first we m. 238:38
hail fellow, well m. 521:11
have m. many one 405:10
mercy and truth are m. 397:9
m. in thee tonight 84:25
m. my dearest foe in heaven 431:4
m...with erected look 193:41
m. you not with my true love? 405:10
ne'er m. with elsewhere 376:10
never be m. with again 128:10
never m.—or never parted 104:11
night that first we m. 37:1
no sooner m. but..looked 428:26
true when you m. her 186:18
we m., 'twas in a crowd 37:3
Metal: breed for barren m. 463:23
brown coat with the m. buttons 325:32
imagineless m. 545:12
m. in this furnace wrought 508:15
m. more attractive 435:3
m. sick 286:11
my m. of India 483:12
sonorous m. blowing 345:1
Metallo: simili frondescit virga m. 554:24
Metals: keys..of m, twain 342:26
Metaphor: all slang is m. and all m. is poetry 142:16
betrayed..into no m. 85:1
hunt down a tired m. 116:46
Metaphysic: as high as m. wit 110:13
M. calls for aid on Sense 381:27
of M. begs defence 381:27
Metaphysical: fate and m. aid 457:2
Metaphysics: circumnavigate the m. 514:35
Mete: m. and dole unequal laws 540:31
m. out the valley of Succoth 395:23
with what measure ye m. 60:56
Metempsychosis: Pythagoras' m. 330:10
Meteor: cloud-encircled m. 495:10
fancy's m. ray 108:25
m. flag of England 123:12
m. of the ocean air 251:5
m. on the grave 118:8
now slides the silent m. on 539:2
shone like a m. 344:36
Method: madness..m. in it 433:6
m. and secret..of Jesus 20:18
m. of making a fortune 231:17
Methodically: elope m. 226:40
Methodist: morals of a M. 222:5
spiritualized by a M. 558:17
Methods: by different m. different men 143:11
you know my m. 187:23, 28

Methusalem..but a mushroom 186:31
Métier: c'est son m. 240:27
  mon m. et mon art, c'est vivre 355:1
Metre: laws of..man and
  m. 315:14, 416:10
  m. of Catullus 529:20
  stretched m. of an antique song 486:17
  understanding what m. is 153:11
  wretched matter and lame m. 343:26
Metre-making argument 200:30
Metropolis: gray m. of the North 528:25
  m. of the empire 147:20
Metropolitan: M. Improved Hot
  Muffin 176:37
  m. temple in the hearts 574:9
Mettle: I see there's m. in thee 473:4
  knights of m. true 417:3
  like a man of m. 248:10
  m. enough..to kill care 469:15
  m. of your pasture 443:26
  so full of m. 189:16
  there is m. in death 423:25
  thy undaunted m. 457:15
Metuant: oderint, dum m. 145:17
Metuit secundis alteram sortem 259:7
Metus: et M. et malesuada Fames 554:27
  solve m. 553:18
Meum: distinctions of *m.* and *tuum* 306:20
Meurs sans parler 553:2
Meurt: la Garde m. 121:24
Mew: kitten and cry m. 439:45
Mewing: eagle m. her mighty
  youth 352:15
Mewling and puking 427:21
Me-wards: to m. your affection 246:10
Mexique: echo beyond the M. Bay 332:4
Mezzo: nel m. del cammin 168:15
Micawber: I never will desert Mr.
  M. 174:23
Mice: feet..like little m. 517:12
  fishermen..appear like m. 454:3
  m. and rats..Tom's food 453:24
  schemes o' m. an' men 107:11
  three blind m. 369:8
Michael: M. and his angels fought 71:17
  M...when contending 70:17
  Saint M. was the steresman 7:14
  when M. saw this host 119:25
Michael Angelo: enter M. 39:24
  from designs by M. 550:16
  I believe in M. 489:21
  last words..M. 406:13
  M. for breakfast 550:15
  talking of M. 197:16
Micher: blessed sun..prove a m. 439:33
Miching: this is m. mallecho 435:7
Mickle: many a pickle makes a m. 134:11
Microcosm of a public school 182:38
Microscopes: magnifyin' gas m. 179:16
Microscopic eye 383:15
Mid: i' the m. o' the day 120:28
Mid-career: sun in m. 503:6
Midday: at the full m. beam 352:15
  go out in the m. sun 157:25
  more clear, than our m. 186:14
  spend our m. sweat 404:5
  under the m. sun 340:20
Middle: because it was the m. of
  the night 130:9
  cannot steer a m. course 334:21
  dead vast and m. of the night 431:8
  honey'd m. of the night 285:15
  in the m. of her favours 433:10
  in the m. of her forehead 318:17
  in the m. of my being 310:21
  in the m. of the woods 311:12
  isthmus of a m. state 383:22
  m. of my song 160:4
  M. of Next Week 128:17
  m. state 164:12, 327:14, 383:22
  m. Summer's spring 466:36
  no m. ways 82:5
  tenants of life's m. state 164:12
  twirl down the m. 183:7
  ye lower m. classes 218:34
Middle age: companions for m. 26:37
  in the m. of a state 36:36
  last enchantments of the M. 19:10
  reckless m. 584:26
Middle Class was quite prepared 41:8
Middlesex: acre in M. 325:24

Middle sized are alone entangled 499:18
Midge: like a fretful m. 410:10
Midian: troops of M. 361:13
Midland: dolorous m. sea 525:31
  m. furze afire 296:15
  o'er the blue M. waters 18:16
Midlands: living in the M. 42:3
Mid-May's eldest child 287:31
Midnight: at m. and at morn 199:8
  at m. speak with the Sun 551:19
  at the m. in the silence 97:2
  black and m. hags 460:2
  budding morrow in m. 288:26
  cease upon the m. 287:32
  elves, whose m. revels 345:13
  embalmer of the still m. 288:31
  fast through the m. 318:16
  foul and m. murther 229:24
  gravity out of his bed at m. 439:29
  heard the chimes at m. 442:11
  hear the chimes at m. 514:35
  his m. crew 231:1
  in the solemn m. 184:2
  iron tongue of m. 467:34
  m. never come 330:7
  m. oil 215:21, 404:5
  m.'s all a-glimmer 585:12
  not to be a-bed after m. 482:27
  of..blackest M. born 341:26
  on the bridge at m. 315:27
  primroses gather'd at m. 285:7
  profoundest m. 498:26
  sadder than..the m. blast 116:50
  still her woes at m. rise 321:15
  threshed corn at m. 586:1
  'tis now dead m. 462:20
  tis the year's m. 186:2
  to be up after m. 482:27
  upon a m. dreary 380:22
  upon the m. clear 421:10
  upon the m. hours 288:5
  visions before m. 85:22
  with tea solaces the m. 278:1
Midnights: flashes struck from m. 90:39
Mid-noon: another morn ris'n on
  m. 348:7
  it was the deep m. 537:31
Mid-ocean: labour in the deep m. 535:20
Midshipmite: and a m. 218:14
Midst: fallen into the m. of it 395:18
  God is in the m. of her 394:28
  him m. and without end 348:5
  in the m. of foes 198:19
  in the m. of life 391:42
  there am I in the m. 59:52
Midsummer: high M. pomps 18:26
  m. flower 502:17
  very m. madness 484:7
Mid-watch: at m. came 92:10
Midway: floated m. on the
  waves 151:33(–152)
  wing the m. air 454:3
Midwife: fairies' m. 477:7
Mid-winter: in the bleak m. 409:20
Mien: I fear thy m. 499:2
  lovesome m. 528:2
  such a face and such a m. 192:22
  with an indignant m. 158:29
  with unalterable m. 114:10
Mieux: je vais de m. en m. 157:22
  le m. est l'ennemi du bien 557:5
  tout est pour le m. 557:2
Might: all-enacting M. 236:16
  Bertram's m. 419:35
  dissolv'd by m. 190:28
  do it with thy m. 51:21
  eke with all his m. 159:41
  great in m. 421:2
  I feel your m. 576:21
  if it was so, it m. be 130:8
  I spread my conquering m. 455:31
  it m. have been 238:31, 568:17
  m. half slumb'ring 288:14
  m. of Denmark's crown 122:3
  m. of design 489:21
  m. of the Gentile 118:39
  m. she have loved me? 92:35
  puts invincible m. 350:36
  right makes m. 314:8
  Rome been growing up to m. 184:2
  sadness of her m. 287:21

Might (cont.)
  shining with all his m. 130:9
  spirit of counsel and m. 53:17
  through the dear m. 343:3
  to be man with thy m. 524:3
  to be strengthened with m. 67:53
  Tubal Cain was a man of m. 326:24
  we are only what m. have been 306:7
  woman's m. 449:27
Might-have-been: my name is M. 411:17
Mightier: imposition of a m. hand 325:4
  our own acts..m. powers 15:11
  the Lord..is m. 397:23
Mightiest: m. fleets of iron 188:32
  m. in the m. 464:33
  one moment of the m. 113:40
Mighty: all the proud and m. have 195:14
  any m. man delivered 393:37
  better than the m. 50:17
  bringeth m. things to pass 399:8
  confound the things which are m. 66:20
  Gitche Manito, the m. 317:21
  God who made the m. 42:20
  he hath put down the m. 61:14
  his promises were..m. 447:7
  how are the m. fallen 47:29, 30
  let the m. Babe alone 166:2
  look on my works, ye M. 496:14
  Marlowe's m. line 281:12
  mean and m. rotting together 429:39
  mean reparations upon m. ruins 101:30
  Merciful and M.! 240:10
  m. above all things 56:17
  m. dead 284:21
  m. in the scriptures 65:4
  m. man is he 318:11
  m. master of unmeaning rhyme 117:27
  m. men which were of old 44:38
  m. opium 172:19
  m. poets in their misery dead 580:13
  m. things from small beginnings 191:29
  shield of the m...cast away 47:29
  some have called them m. 185:15
  thou art m. yet! 452:1
  to quell the m. of the earth 350:36
Migrations from the blue bed 227:17
Miguel of Spain 297:19
Mihi vivam quod superest aevi 257:11
Milan: retire me to my M. 480:16
Mild: brought reg'lar and draw'd
  m. 176:18
  He is meek, and He is m. 76:10
  m. and magnificent eye 93:3
  m. as she is seeming so 231:37
  m., obedient, good as He 4:2
  m. or choleric disposition 2:4
  sublimely m. 492:12
Mildest: m. curate going 218:8
  m. manner'd man 115:41
Mildness: m. ethereal m., come 546:10
Mile: compel thee to go a m. 57:51
  eighty m. o' females 179:34
  m. an' a bittock, a m. or twa 516:20
  m. of warm..beach 93:21
  m. or two from my first love 552:3
  run a m. to see a fire 514:35
  walked a crooked m. 369:3
  walked on a m. or so 130:15
Miles: draw out our m. 474:27
  five m. meandering 151:33
  how many m. to Babylon? 367:4
  m. and m. distant 411:8
  m. around the wonder grew 262:19
  m. around they'll say 262:19
  people come m. to see it 220:11
  twice five m. 151:32
  villain and he..m. asunder 478:28
Miles: enumerat m. vulnera 402:15
  m. gloriosus 379:26
  sed m., sed pro patria 363:1
Milestones on the Dover Road 175:35
Militant: Christ's Church m. 390:24
  Poets M. 158:6
Military: as well as any m. man 444:2
  forsaking even m. men 222:14
  m. domination of Prussia 21:6
  m. gent I see 542:15
  War..left to m. men 526:20
  when the m. man approaches 490:23
Militavi non sine gloria 260:12
Militia: nocitura..petuntur m. 283:16

Milk: adversity's sweet m. 478:24
  as it..takes in its m. 112:6
  breastful of m. 409:22
  buy wine and m. without money 54:29
  drunk the m. of Paradise 151:33(-152)
  flowing with m. and honey 45:36
  fostre him wel with m. 137:36
  gone to m. the bull 271:11
  he weyveth m. 137:36
  his mother's m...scarce out of
    him 482:17
  kindly pass the m. 372:19
  little drop of m. 372:20
  m. and wastel-breed 136:30
  m. comes frozen home 456:1
  m. my ewes and weep 485:32
  nothing but the m. of human
    kindness 103:8
  putting m. into babies 144:14
  seethe a kid in his mother's m. 46:1
  sincere m. of the word 69:47
  sweet m. of human kindness 143:10
  sweet m. of kindness 251:9
  take my m. for gall 457:3
  too full o' the m. of human kind-
    ness 457:1
  trout in the m. 547:4
  white curd of ass's m. 385:30
  with m. and honey blest 362:1
  yield such people no more m. 271:11
Milk-bloom: one long m. 536:13
Milking: at the ewe m. 198:18
  to the m. shed 267:13
Milkmaid singeth blithe 341:34
Milks: love the babe that m. me 457:13
  maid that m. 425:30
Milk-soup..domestic bliss 375:6
Milk-white: before m., now
    purple 466:39
  crowned with m. may 82:7
Milky Way: roar of the M. 302:20
  solar walk or m. 383:11
  twinkle on the m. 577:6
Mill: all..that goes by his m. 109:30
  at the m. with slaves 350:21
  barn, the forge, the m. 77:28
  brook, that turns a m. 408:10
  in Hans' old M. 171:10
  I wander'd by the m. 262:9
  John Stuart M. 43:2
  more water glideth by the m. 480:33
  were it but a m. 183:8
Millar: I respect M., Sir 270:24
Milldams: bonny m. o' Binnorie 30:7
Miller: jolly m. 72:15
  m. sees not all the water 109:30
  more..than wots the m. 480:33
Milliner: perfumed like a m. 438:32
Millinery: jewell'd mass of m. 535:40
Million: aiming at a m. 91:41
  Four M. 242:14
  make that thousand..m. 246:28
  m. m. of suns 541:4
  pleased not the m. 433:25
Millionaire: he must be a m. 217:23
  M...my religion 490:6
  Mr. Mandragon, the M. 140:27
Millions: m. a hero 387:9
  m. for defence 238:4
  m. of mischiefs 451:7
  m. of spiritual creatures 347:24
  m. of strange shadows 487:2
  m. of surprises 245:5
  our yearly multiplying m. 371:4
  she 'as m. at 'ome 303:27
  tear-wrung m. 112:28
  thy m. boast 158:22
  twenty-seven m. mostly fools 126:39
  what m. died 122:36
Mills: m. of God 315:22, 317:13
  these dark Satanic m. 75:16
Millstone: m...hanged about his
    neck 59:49, 62:17
  nether m. 49:31
  stone like a great m. 71:33
Mill-wheel's sound 492:24
Milsom Street: Winchester—or
    M. 297:20
Milton: Classic M. 80:24
  divine M. 574:13
  England's M. equals both 160:24

Milton (cont.)
  faith and morals..M. held 577:3
  grace before M. 306:8
  malt does more than M. can 263:25
  M., a name to resound 529:17
  M...could cut a Colossus 275:27
  M., Death, and Sin 587:16
  M...requires a solemn service 306:28
  M.'s the prince of poets 116:4
  M.! thou shouldst be living 577:14
  M. was for us 93:4
  M. wrote in fetters..of Angels 77:7
  not enjoying M. 306:32
  on my guard against M. 290:26
  round the path of M. 580:17
  some mute inglorious M. 230:5
  to give a M. birth 162:26
Miltonic verse..in the vein of art 290:26
Mimicked: foot..which the beg-
    gars..m. 325:14
Miminy, piminy 221:6
Mimsy: all m. were the borogoves 129:39
Min: is the old m. agreeable? 177:27
Mince: m., muffins and mutton 171:17
  m. this matter 471:18
  they dined on m. 312:3
Mincing: m. as they go 52:35
  m. poetry 439:46
Mind: all my m. is clouded 531:37
  amplitude of m. 579:37
  any subsistence without a m. 43:12
  as a dead man out of m. 393:29
  as her m. grew worse 575:29
  as the m. is pitch'd 163:48
  because a man has shop to m. 96:26
  better than presence of m. 403:6
  body fill'd and vacant m. 444:23
  brought all to m. 584:21
  but a frailty of the m. 156:8
  calm of m. all passion spent 351:7
  calm the troubled m. 155:1
  cannot have a pure m. 306:9
  certain unsoundness of the m. 325:3
  chainless m. 114:33
  chords in the human m. 173:35
  clear your m. of cant 275:13
  come back into my m. 42:3
  conjunction of the m. 332:6
  cover his m. decently 504:28
  dictates of his godlike m. 371:8
  dividing the swift m. 531:28
  electrical agitation in the m. 337:2
  excursions in my own m. 153:2
  fair terms and a villain's m. 463:25
  farewell the tranquil m. 472:3
  feed a craving m. 164:35
  feed this m. of ours 574:29
  first destroys their m. 192:33
  flower of the m. 200:33
  fog of the good man's m. 90:26
  fool uttereth all his m. 50:51
  fulfil all thy m. 392:36
  golden m. stoops not 463:39
  grateful m...owes not 346:31
  great barons of the m. 515:7
  great fortitude of m. 270:2
  happy alchemy of m. 231:31
  haunted.. by the eternal m. 576:13
  he who does not m. his belly 271:17
  his m. and hand went together 241:16
  his m. his kingdom 164:19
  his m. into the common stock 223:3
  his m. or body to prefer 383:22
  his own oceanic m. 153:14
  horror heavy sat on ev'ry m. 193:38
  how love exalts the m. 192:4
  human m. in ruins 169:20
  I cannot m. my wheel 309:2
  I have a man's m. 449:27
  index of a feeling m. 165:15
  inform the m. 160:19
  inform the m. that is within us 582:3
  in his right m. 60:58
  in m., body, or estate 389:17
  in my m., of all mankind 31:15
  in my m.'s eye, Horatio 431:5
  inter-assured of the m. 186:25
  in the m. of man 582:1
  in the m. which contemplates 265:5
  irradiation of the m. 495:10
  jest as you've a m. to 298:7, 8

Mind (cont.)
  last infirmity of noble m. 342:20
  let the m. be a thoroughfare 290:27
  let the world m. him! 91:41
  light up my own m. 93:30
  love warps the m. 165:16
  maketh men to be of one m. 396:5
  make up one's m. about nothing 290:27
  man's m...turn upon..truth 27:33
  man's unconquerable m. 582:4
  marble index of a m. 579:19
  march of m. 376:14
  march of the human m. 101:6
  Matter?—never m. 403:10
  measure your m.'s height 94:17
  m. and matter..glide swift 176:26
  m. and soul..make one music 531:42
  m. at peace with all below 119:2
  m...experienced a similar fate 505:23
  m., from pleasure less 332:18
  m. has a thousand eyes 79:5
  m. impatient 430:31
  m. is free 189:4
  m. is its own place 344:22
  m. not to be changed 344:22
  m. of man..more beautiful 579:38
  M. of Man—my haunt 574:7
  m. quite vacant is a m. distress'd 162:3
  m.'s construction in the face 456:27(-457)
  m. serene for contemplation 215:31
  m.'s the standard of the man 562:2
  m. that is grandly simple 200:28
  m., that very fiery particle 116:35
  m. the music and the step 33:6
  m. to m. 417:21
  m. what I am taught 527:6
  minister to a m. diseas'd 460:37
  my m., aspire to higher things 502:5
  my m. forbids to crave 195:12
  my m. to me a kingdom is 195:12
  narrow'd his m. 225:27
  nature, with equal m. 15:12
  ne'er disclose her m. 470:29
  never brought to m. 104:12
  never m., did m. his grace 412:19
  philosophic m. 82:5, 576:20
  quiet m. 518:1
  never you m.! 218:12
  noble m. disdains 231:32
  no blemish but the m. 484:19
  nobler in the m. to suffer 434:4
  noblest frailty of the m. 192:34
  nor do's she m. 245:23
  not astound the virtuous m. 340:10
  nothing great but m. 235:4
  nothing unbends the m. like
    them 214:31
  not in my perfect m. 454:15
  not with the eyes..the m. 466:22
  of its own beauty is the m.
    diseased 114:16
  of love, and of a sound m. 68:56
  one man that has a m. 489:3
  on the torture of the m. 459:4
  Othello's visage in his m. 470:10
  out of sight is out of m. 147:12
  persuaded in his own m. 66:16
  pleased to call his m. 43:21
  prepare the m. of the country 180:38
  pulse in the eternal m. 84:21
  puts his m. to yours 275:7
  put you in m. of Johnson 235:2
  raise and erect the m. 24:16
  ransack any m. but his own 406:12
  reason doth..bow the m. 24:16
  rest to his m. 559:15
  robs the m. of all its powers 102:32
  serve thee with a quiet m. 389:48
  service of a m. and heart 575:15
  she had a frugal m. 159:35
  so let extend thy m. 350:10
  so pleased my m. 10:20, 210:5
  spoke the vacant m. 224:17
  steal fire from the m. 113:23
  that fixed m. 344:13
  this universal frame..without a
    m. 25:23
  those they have no m. to 110:20
  thy chaste breast and quiet m. 319:10
  thy..lilies out of m. 187:10

Mind (cont.)
 thy m. all virtue 270:13
 thy m. is a very opal 483:7
 thy morals tell thy m. 382:14
 too great a m. 451:37
 to the desires of the m. 24:16
 tyrant of the m. 192:46
 unbent her m...over a book 306:14
 unseemly exposure of the m. 240:2
 what a noble m...o'erthrown 434:14
 when the m.'s free 453:12
 Wisdom calms the m. 279:15
 with equal m. 193:17
 with heedful m. 39:3
 with woman the heart..not the
  m. 16:26
 woman's m. oft' shifts 215:14
 your complicated state of m. 220:26
 your padlock—on her m. 401:26
Minded: to be carnally m. is death 65:52
Minden: on M.'s plain 310:2
Mindful: m. how..we withstand
 Barabbas 92:12
 m. of th' unhonour'd dead 230:10
 man, that thou art m. of him 392:10
Minding: as m. to content 467:28
Minds: affect little m. 182:27
 aspiring m. 330:28
 balm of hurt m. 458:11
 by chance our m. do muse 190:1
 express the images of their m. 26:46
 flatterer of happy m. 154:39
 great actions speak great m. 38:3
 great empire and little m. 101:14
 happiest and best m. 499:12
 hobgoblin of little m. 200:40
 inspir'd their hearts, their m. 331:2
 lose myself in other men's m. 306:25
 marriage of true m. 488:7
 m. attentive to their own 163:49
 m. innocent and quiet 319:7
 m. made better 196:34
 m. me o' departed joys 108:37
 refuge of weak m. 139:25
 religion of feeble m. 102:26
 righteous m. of innkeepers 142:1
 spur of all great m. 135:25
 strange faces, other m. 531:34
 to men of other m. 226:13
 virtue of weak m. 192:35
 wars begin in the m. of men 9:22
Mine: any heart, take m. 221:30
 call thee m. 327:5, 551:5
 every man..show'd like a m. 446:9
 excavating for a m. 355:22
 fire a m. in China 111:5
 I am m. and yours 94:6
 m. has a snub nose 74:10
 m. has been a fine one 78:29
 m. is all as hungry as the sea 483:9
 m. only died 87:25
 m. own Executioner 186:26
 m. shall subsist by me 232:13
 m. to speak 504:8
 never can be m. 375:5
 not for thy faults, but m. 114:11
 she shall be m. 581:21
 to mouths like m. 96:18
 'twas m., 'tis his 471:30
 what thou art is m. 349:19
 while He is m. 245:10
 why..thou have m.? 517:16
 wilt thou be m.? 366:16
 would she were m. 315:18
Miner: in the..depths the m. 517:9
 m., Forty-niner 355:22
Miners: rugged m. poured to war 322:19
Minerva when she talks 281:25
Minerva: abnormis sapiens crassaque M. 261:22
 nihil invita dices..M. 256:13
Mines: in unfathomable m. 161:18
 like plants in m. 94:25
 m. reported in the fairway 299:25
 one yard below their m. 436:8
Mingle: in one another's being m. 495:7
 m., m., m., you that m. may
  338:18, 459:34
 m. with society 459:11
 m. with the Universe 114:26
Mingled: like kindred drops..m. 162:41

Mingled (cont.)
 m. in a mass 324:15
 m. measure 151:33(–152)
 m. with a little wit 192:27
 m. with regards 452:12
 when hearts have once m. 494:21
Minion: curl'd m., dancer 17:25
 like valour's m. 456:5
 morning's m. 255:11
Minions of the moon 438:16
Minished, and brought low 398:21
Minister: discreet and learned M. 390:31
 doobts aboot the m. 403:29
 indifferently m. justice 390:27
 m. kiss'd the fiddler's wife 107:15
 m. of her will 425:33
 m. of thee to me 80:21
 m. to a mind diseas'd 460:37
 not become the King's First M. 144:11
 one fair spirit for my m. 114:25
 patient must m. to himself 460:37
 stickit m. 419:27
 thou flaming m. 473:11
 wisdom of a great m. 282:18
Ministered: angels..m. unto him 57:37
Ministers: angels and m. of grace 431:32
 are they m. of Christ? 67:33
 but m. of Love 152:3
 errands for the M. of State 218:23
 grim Geneva m. 24:7
 his m. a flaming fire 398:8
 I call you servile m. 453:6
 m...exhausted volcanoes 181:2
 m...hae been kenn'd 105:6
 my actions are my m.' 136:4
 passion-winged M. of thought 491:19
 you murdering m. 457:3
Ministration of Baptism 390:61
Ministries: the Times has made
 many m. 28:24
Ministry: gie up the m. 403:40
 last Conservative M...real power 29:3
 m. of all the talents 10:16
 more for a marriage than a m. 28:28
 secret m. 151:23, 25
Minnehaha, Laughing Water 317:26
Minnie Boffkin: farewell to M. 300:20
Minnows: this Triton of the m. 429:12
Minor: spared these m. monuments 87:9
Minorities..in the right 505:9
Minority is always right 267:1
Minstrel: ethereal m.l 580:26
 for him no M. raptures 417:22
 fuller m. 533:20
 M. Boy 356:27
 M. was infirm 416:29
 monarch m. 117:41
 wandering m. I 219:15
Minstrels: dame naturis m. 187:4
 m. follow after 396:12
Minstrelsy: our wild m. 285:5
Mint: fire-new from the m. 483:31
 rare..the mark of the m. 142:2
 ye pay tithe of m. 60:17
Mints, savory, marjoram 485:25
Minuet: inconsolable to the m. 499:31
Minute: divided and m. domestic
 happiness 290:12
 each m... part 315:28
 every m. dies a man 6:6
 his first m., after noon 185:31
 in a m. pay glad 95:11
 in M. Particulars 75:7
 m. into a thousand parts 428:18
 m. makes immortal 94:2
 m.'s success 89:20
 mortal in the m. 94:2
 no circumstance..too m. 226:23
 sucker born every m. 35:24
 suppliance of a m. 431:20
 thousandth part of a m. 428:18
 unforgiving m. 297:12
 winged m. 337:4
Minutes: begot within a pair of m. 305:17
 five m. too late all my life 158:23
 our m. hasten to their end 487:8
 see the m. how they run 446:1
 sixty diamond m. 329:9
 so the little m. 127:33
 take care of the m. 139:15
 what damned m. 471:32

Minx: a M., or a Sphinx 178:15
Mirabeau's work..is done 125:34
Miracle: accept a m. 587:15
 continued existence..a mere m. 515:2
 continued m. in his own person 265:10
 establish a m. 265:7
 m. may be..defined 265:6
 m. of our age 124:24
 m. of rare device 151:33(–152)
 never m...to convert an atheist 24:18
 never..m. to convince atheism 25:24
 not to be found..any m. 265:8
 that m. of a youth 202:14
Miracles: at first attended with m. 265:10
 book..works m. 196:24
 Life, Death, M. 95:28
 m. do not happen 20:7
 sapping the proof from m. 20:15
 they say m. are past 423:4
Miraculous: its falsehood..more m. 265:7
 most m. organ 433:36
Miranda: remember an Inn, M.? 42:9
Mire: engulf him in the m. 278:23
 her cheek to m. 336:44
 learning..cast into the m. 102:18
 out of the m. and clay 394:12
 shade and loneliness and m. 84:7
 some luxurious m. 216:4
 throw pebbles and m. 562:5
Mirk: sun through the m. 167:24
Miroir: casser son m. 12:15
Miroir: non..invideo, m. magis 555:17
Mirror: deceiving m. of self-love 334:27
 hold..the m. up to nature 434:17
 m. cracked 534:7
 m...not to be painted upon 325:10
 m. of all Christian kings 443:12
 m. of all courtesy 446:12
 m. of alle curteisye 137:35
 thou glorious m. 114:30
 upon thy m...paint Thy Presence 355:17
 wherein as in a m. 331:2
Mirror'd on her sea 249:11
Mirrors of the sea 208:19
Mirth: all resort of m. 341:16
 all the joy and m. 292:5
 Bards of Passion and of M. 284:16
 borrow its m. 568:26
 dim and decorous m. 84:5
 displaced the m. 459:22
 elephant to make them m. 347:15
 fence against..evils of life, by m. 512:32
 form'd of joy and m. 75:1
 if you find him..in m. 423:29
 I'll use you for my m. 451:15
 in endless m. 245:22
 joy the day in m. 168:13
 limit of becoming m. 455:3
 May's new-fangled m. 454:33
 M., admit me 341:31
 m. and fun grew fast 108:11
 m. and laughter 115:33
 m...no bitter springs 295:8
 m., that after no repenting draws 351:22
 much m. and no madness 502:18
 prefer not Jerusalem in my m. 400:5
 present m. 482:28
 public mischief in your m. 162:39
 so much wit, and m. 2:8
 song of the birds for m. 233:17
 spend the night in m. 502:22(–503)
 such m. as does not make..
  ashamed 559:20
 sunburnt m. 287:24
 very tragical m. 467:26
 wins more hearts, than M. 7:13
 wisdom with m. 225:26
 with m. in funeral 430:24
Misael: Azarias, and M. 388:23
Misanthropy and voluptuousness 325:18
Misapprehension: immense literary m. 20:16
Misbegotten: three m. knaves 439:22
Misbehaved: I m. once at a funeral 307:11
Miscarriage: success and m...
 empty sounds 270:28
Miscet: mens..magno se corpore m. 554:30
Mischance: never come m. 435:14
 on a Friday..this m. 137:42
 seeing all his own m. 534:8

Mischief: all punishment is m. 42:22
draw new m. on 470:5
foundation of lasting m. 269:33
in every deed of m. 217:11
hand to execute any m. 145:26
little knowest the m. 364:14
m., thou art afoot 451:1
mourn a m...past 470:5
public m. in your mirth 162:39
Satan finds some m. 561:29
spectatress of the m. 412:10
tobacco..a plague, a m. 109:22
wait on nature's m. 457:3
Mischiefs: millions of m. 451:7
m. feed like beasts 282:8
record the m. he has done 162:37
Mischievous: what a m. devil
Love is 112:4
Misdoubt: by licensing..m. her
strength 352:17
Miser: heaps of m.'s treasure 340:21
honesty dwells like a m. 428:36
M.'s Pensioner 573:15
Miserable: God would make a man
m. 136:5
me m.! 346:32
m. comforters are ye all 49:2
m. have no other medicine 462:3
m. me! 96:6
of all men most m. 67:7
to be weak is m. 344:16
Miserarum est 260:6
Miseria: ricordarsi del tempo felice
nella m. 168:22
Miseries: m. of a people 357:24
m. of the world are misery 285:33
Miseris succurrere disco 553:22
Miserrima: ipse m. vidi 553:25
Misers: rejoice..as m. do in gold 548:13
Misery: acquainted with sad m. 563:12
child of m. 310:2
fast bound in m. 398:15
finds himself, loses his m. 18:17
full of m. 391:41
gave to M. all he had 230:13
him that is in m. 48:47
laughs the sense of m. far away 162:21
let other pens dwell on..m. 22:21
miseries of the world are m. 285:33
m. makes Alcmena's nights 87:11
M.'s darkest caverns 275:2
m. still delights to trace 159:2
m...strange bedfellows 479:40
poets in their m. dead 580:13
poverty, m. and wretchedness 328:5
pure m. there never is any..
mention of it 274:24
result m. 174:24
so full of m. 540:24
their departure is taken for m. 56:23
through the vale of m. 397:6
untainted by man's m. 498:14
wasted with m. 400:6
wide sea of m. 494:22
Mis-featured messenger 95:31
Misfortune: alleviate so severe a m. 23:3
m. of our best friends 407:14
much m. bodes 477:7
sour m.'s book 478:41
to lose one parent..a m. 569:23
Misfortunes: children..make m.
more bitter 26:45
if a man talks of his m. 274:24
m. great and sma' 108:15
m. hardest to bear 320:20
real m... of others 102:31
register of the crimes, follies,
and m. 217:7
Misgivings: blank m. of a creature 576:18
Misgovernment: refuge of cheap
m. 490:10
they augur m. 100:30
Misguiding: gi'en to great m. 107:19
Mishaps: nursery-m. 164:31
Misled: by education most..m. 192:30
m. by fancy's meteor ray 108:25
m. by wandering fires 192:23
Misletoe hung 36:30
Mislight: Will-o'-th'-Wisp m. thee 246:23
Mislike: if thou m. him 244:7
m. me not for my complexion 463:26

Misogyn: confirm'd m. 39:21
Mis-placed: those words m. 155:32
Misprision: upon m. growing 487:22
Misquote: enough of learning to m. 117:12
Miss: both enjoy and m. her 262:6
calls her 'M.' 141:35
eyes, lips, and hands to m. 186:25
mine he cannot m. 501:19
m. for pleasure 216:2
m. poor Kingsley 545:16
m. the many-splendoured 545:1
we shall m. him 560:27
whatever M. T. eats 171:17
Missed: health and wealth have m.
me 265:25(−266)
m. by any that entreat 87:37
no one would have m. her 6:20
we m. it, lost it for ever 97:29
who never would be m. 219:24
Misses: m. an unit 91:41
when his pistol m. fire 227:27
Misshapes the beauteous forms 581:16
Missing so much 157:9
Mission: never have a m. 174:3
Missionary: eat a m. 568:25
Mississippi: into M. Bay 298:28
Missouri: wide M. 8:21
Missus: help the m. unload 299:19
the M., my Lord 403:28
Missus: tu m. abibis 261:21
Mist: air broke into a m. 94:29
as the m. resembles the rain 316:8
cold and heavy m. 252:26
Faustus like a foggy m. 330:9
grey m. on the sea's face 334:10
happy m. 530:9
land of m. and snow 149:7
m. in my face 95:8
m. is dispell'd 214:30
m. was on the rice-fields 299:12
no m. obscures 508:2
out of the m. and hum 17:28
rank m. they draw 342:29
rolling m. came down 293:24
there follows a m. 326:20
there went up a m. 44:10
with m. engarlanded 18:31
Mistake: is no m...has been no m. 564:23
m. in the translation 551:8
Nature's sole m. 221:41
never overlooks a m. 266:20
pray make no m. 219:34
you lie—under a m. 520:7
Mistaken: here, unless I am m. 188:14
holy m. zeal in politics 282:19
m. and over-zealous piety 101:23
possible you may be m. 167:4
Mistakes: at the cost of m. 212:6
I hope will excuse m. 177:11
man's miraculous m. 587:5
man who makes no m. 378:12
name..to their m. 570:2
Mistaking: else m. 487:22
Mistook: he who, not m. 333:10
Mistress: art is a jealous m. 199:34
ballad..to his m.' eyebrow 427:21
gold is for the m. 295:14
how I became..m. of the Earl 571:8
independent on the bounty of
his m. 156:11
in ev'ry port a m. 215:41
like m., like maid 203:23
Mab, the M.-Fairy 281:5
maiden, and m. 521:29
m. I am ashamed to call you 198:6
m. in my own 300:11
M. moderately fair 158:13
m. of her choice 434:25
m. of herself 384:39
m. or a friend 493:9
m. to the man I love 382:3
more fond than m. 382:3
my m.' eyes 488:13
my m...the open road 515:29
new m. now I chase 319:10
O m. mine 482:28
pure gold, my m. 96:28
riches..the worst m. 25:6
so court a m. 280:20
Sorrow..no casual m. 532:41
sovereign m. of true melancholy 425:15

Mistress (cont.)
teeming m. 384:30
to deck her m.' head 119:3
you saw the m. 464:21
Mistresses: hardly any m. 414:16
m. with great..limbs 89:43
young men's m. 26:37
Mists: season of m. 284:10
those shaken m...unsettle 544:26
when the golden m. are born 498:12
Misty: ful m. morwe 138:32
Misty-bright October 146:25
Misunderstood: to be great is to
be m. 200:41
Misuse: first m...their toys 160:15
Mites: threw in two m. 61:8
Mithras, God of the Morning 301:29
Mithridates: half M. and half
Trissotin 324:35
M., he died old 263:26
Mix: m. her with me 525:29
m. them with my brains 370:12
my clay m. with the earth 119:33
Mixed: antithetically m. 113:40
elements so m. in him 452:9
in whom so m. the elements 189:3
it is full m. 396:31
proper subject..in a m. company 139:33
somewhat m. up together 144:2
typical of a m. diet 376:16
Mixing memory and desire 197:27
Mixture: any mortal m. 340:14
had the m. peen 23:28
m. of a lie 27:30
Mizpah..the Lord watch 45:8
Mizraim cures wounds 87:19
Moab: in the land of M. 3:16
M. is my wash-pot 395:23
Moan: everything did banish m. 35:17
fore-bemoaned m. 486:25
former causes of her m. 87:22
little ones m. 15:26
made sweet m. 286:32
make delicious m. 288:5
m. of doves 539:5
m. of thunder 492:9
not paid with m. 544:2
we cast away m. 436:36
Moaned: laughed and m. about 89:24
Moaning: harbour bar be m. 294:1
no m. of the bar 528:22
now they are m. 198:18
Moans: deep m. round 541:3
murmur'd her m. 473:6
Moat: as a m. defensive 474:22
look to your M. 234:6
Mob: amphibious ill-born m. 170:12
do what the m. do 178:31
m. of gentlemen 386:16
M., Parliament, Rabble 147:17
M. was the wrongest 34:33
our..governors, the m. 558:10
Mobled queen 433:28
Mobs: suppose there are two m.? 178:31
Mock: m. on, m. on, Voltaire 75:17
m. our eyes with air 425:19
m. the air with idle state 229:20
m. the good housewife Fortune 426:18
m. the hope of toil 165:17
m. their useful toil 230:1
m. the meat it feeds on 471:31
m. the time 457:16
m. your own grinning 437:15
my achievements m. me 481:24
when I m. poorness 279:25
Mocked: as if he m. himself 448:27
God is not m. 67:47
m. the dead bones 476:14
m. with many a loathed rite 491:15
scorn which m. the smart 16:8
Mocker: wine is a m. 50:23
Mockers: loud m. in the..street 313:5
Mockery: death itself..a m. 497:28
delusion, a m. 172:12
m. is the fume of little hearts 530:17
m. king of snow 475:24
m. of hell 119:18
monumental m. 481:18
our vain blows malicious m. 430:17
unreal m., hence! 459:21

Mocking-bird: out of the m.'s throat 567:1
Mocks: comforts while it m. 95:16
m. married men 455:35
m. my waking sense 504:7
then heaven m. itself 471:41
Mode: selfsame bloody m. 236:7
Mode: it began à la m. 183:16
Mode: was die M. streng geteilt 415:21
Model: come to m. Heaven 348:30
m. of a man 176:20
m. of a modern Major-General 221:31
m. to thy inward greatness 443:13
Models: rules and m. destroy genius 240:4
Moderate: m. men looked big 7:12
that m. man Voltaire 236:24
Moderately: love m. 478:9
Mistress m. fair 158:13
Moderation: abstinence is easier than..m. 22:4
astonished at my own m. 146:6
m...a sort of treason 103:19
m. even in excess 182:42
m. in war is imbecility 324:23
no terms of m...with the vulgar 25:10
stoutness, in m. 218:31
Moderator: m. of passions 559:15
this reasonable m...Death 86:18
Modern: disease of m. life 18:14
elements of m. civilization 125:24
m. Babylon 182:37
m. Major-General 221:31
m. man who paints 91:9
saws and m. instances 427:21
Moderns: of the m. without contempt 139:17
Modes: indifferent m. of the divine energy 200:29
nobler m. of life 533:20
their m. of thinking are different 274:35
unknown m. of being 579:11
various m. of man's belief 90:31
Modest: be m. for a m. man 307:20
He, with m. looks 176:21
I was a m., good-humoured boy 39:13
m. dress 565:21
quip m. 428:37
wee m...flow'r 107:7
Modester: people ought to be m. 127:24
Modesty: enough for m. 98:6
in a friend..cold m. 450:10
ladies of irresistible m. 512:3
m. of nature 434:16
too much m. 226:39
true school of m. 376:11
where the Greeks had m. 376:11
with m. and ease 159:13
your maiden m. would float 266:15
Modified rapture! 219:30
Modo: sed noli m. 21:20
Modus: est m. in rebus 261:9
Moenia: flammantia m. mundi 320:27
Mogul: Main Spring, M., and Mugwump 83:2
Mohicans: Last of the M. 157:2
Moi: le m. est haïssable 374:6
l'État c'est m. 318:21
parce que c'était m. 354:21
Moist: demd, damp, m...body 177:21
m. eye, a dry hand 441:19
m. relentment 87:2
our m. vows 343:2
with anguish m. and fever dew 286:29
Moistens my eyes 191:19
Moisture: yellowy m. 254:18
Mole: death..working like a m. 244:19
go ask the M. 74:2
like a bastion's m. 503:5
m. cinque-spotted 429:24
well said, old m. 432:27
Molem: mens agitat m. 554:30
Moles: m. of Adrianus 87:21
rudis indigestaque m. 371:26
Molis: tantae m. erat 553:9
Mollissima: quae m. fandi 554:17
Molly: true to his M. 173:9
when M. smiles 11:20
Molly Malone: sweet M. 7:8
Moloch, horrid king 344:28
Moltke: like Count M. 29:6

Mome raths outgrabe 129:39
Moment: all be changed, in a m. 67:16
certain m. cuts the deed off 95:19
eternity was in that m. 155:28
every m. dies a man 541:13
every m., lightly shaken 534:16
in some unreasonable m. 127:29
m. gazed adown the dale 416:12
M.'s Halt 206:21
m.'s insight 251:24
m.'s monument 410:21
m.'s ornament 580:19
m. when the moon was blood 140:21
not seem a m.'s thought 584:2
of great pith and m. 434:4
of no m. to the .. individual 272:8
one M. in Annihilation's Waste 206:20
one m...with bliss repay 123:2
some awful m. 575:10
to the last m. 224:10
Momentary: m. as a sound 466:20
m. taste 206:21
Momently: flung up m. 151:33
m. was forced 151:32
Moments: best and happiest m. 499:12
days and m. quickly flying 132:3
highest quality to your m. 374:13
m. big as years 286:7
m. which he calls his own 408:7
our noisy years seem m. 576:19
your m. of glad grace 586:21
Monan: moon on M.'s rill 416:11
Monarch: becomes the throned m. better 464:33
entire and sure the m.'s rule 402:2
every hereditary m...insane 29:4
invades authors like a m. 194:8
merry m. 318:7, 407:20
m. minstrel 117:41
m. of all I survey 164:22
m. of a shed 226:11
m. of mountains 118:7
m. of the sky 330:6
m. of the vine 424:19
morsel for a m. 424:1
no m. but would give his crown 558:1
page and m. 361:22
teach a m. to be wise 229:19
to make him a m. 473:8
with a m.'s voice 450:12
Monarchies: four M... as a bed of flowers 186:31
Monarchize: little scene, to m. 475:7
Monarch-peasant 251:3
Monarchs: fear of change perplexes m. 345:6
m. must obey 193:1
righteous men, justly to judge 83:16
wrote that m. were divine 297:18
Monarchy: characteristic of the English M. 28:27
essential to a true m. 28:21
m. is a merchantman 4:21
m...should be a republic 227:30
purest M. 355:18
universal m. of wit 124:26
why M. is a strong government 28:26
Monastic: fish m. silence keep 184:24
mild m. faces 146:12
on my heart m. aisles 199:21
Monday: a-bleeding on Black M. 463:35
began on a M. at morn 30:12
betwixt a Saturday and M. 125:19
born on a M. 368:21
classical M. Pops 220:5
hanging of his cat on M. 79:18
M. is parson's holiday 519:30
M.'s child is fair of face 368:1
on a M. morning 250:17
on M., when the sun is hot 339:24
wash on M. 11:5
Monde: pour qui le m. extérieur existe 214:4
Mondes: le meilleur des m. possibles 557:2
Moneda: el sueño..m. general 134:18
Monendo: delectando pariterque m. 256:9
Money: as much m. as I could spend 367:6
blessing that m. cannot buy 559:26
buy wine and milk without m. 54:29
counting out his m. 368:20
doänt thou marry for m., but goä wheer m. is 537:7

Money (cont.)
flocci-pauci-nihili-pili-fication of m. 420:27
f-p-n-p-fication of m. 499:17
giving m. to the Government 243:6
hath a dog m.? 463:22
he that hath no m. 54:29
how pleasant..to have m. 146:30
I give thee my m. 155:27
I have spent all the m. 274:33
king for my m. 204:33
lot of m. to die comfortably 111:36
love of m...root of all evil 68:52
man of genius and his m. 499:19
m. answereth all things 51:25
m. for that which is not bread 54:29
m. has a power above 111:20
m., I despise it 220:31
m. in the Three per Cents 91:12
m. is like muck 27:10
m. is the sinews of love 203:24
m...language all nations understand 40:11
m...most important thing 489:32
m. of fools 248:19
m. the sinews of war 27:24
m...true fuller's earth 214:18
more innocently..than in getting m. 272:22
my m. on de bob-tail nag 210:13
no idea what m.'s for 243:6
no one shall work for m. 303:21
not given his m. upon usury 392:24
put m. in thy purse 470:10
some honey, and plenty of m. 311:24
so m. comes withal 479:1
so much M. as 'twill bring 110:23
they hired the m. 156:26
thy m. perish with thee 64:36
time is m. 211:5
up-on a day..more m. 137:22
wants m., means, and content 427:25
way the m. goes 328:20
we've got the m. too 265:15
what m. will do 377:31
where is your m.? 369:17
wrote, except for m. 273:8
you pays your m. 403:4
Moneybag: Aristocracy of the M. 126:20
Money-bags: I did dream of m. 463:34
Moneys: as m. are for values 24:20
lend you thus much m. 463:22
Mongrel: greyhound, m. grim 453:30
m. beef-witted lord 481:9
m., puppy, whelp, and hound 225:20
Monied: inclined to the..m. interest 2:13
Monitor expressed..union 574:20
Monk: borrowed from a Greek m. 152:27
devil a m. wou'd be 359:25
many a m. 34:8
M. my son 507:36
m. who shook the world 355:13
Monkey: bred out into baboon and m. 480:19
look long upon a m. 155:6
ring..for a m. 464:11
Monkey People: ere the M. cry 301:27
Monkeys: cats and m. 268:16
goats and m.! 472:31
m. walk together 298:20
wilderness of m. 464:11
Monks: hear we these m.'s song 124:22
merrily sang the m. 124:22
m. of Magdalen 216:20
town of m. and bones 150:28
Monmouth: river at M. 445:4
Monograph on the ashes of..tobacco 187:14
Monopoly: newspaper..a m. 416:4
Monotony: bleats articulate m. 512:6
Monster: as that Theban m. 350:17
become as it were a m. 396:21
blunt m. with uncounted heads 441:8
chief m. 162:15
faultless m. 98:12
green-ey'd m. 471:31
lean abhorred m. 478:44
man, and not of a m. 179:11
many-headed m. 335:3
m. of ingratitudes 481:17

INDEX

Monster (cont.)
m. ot so frightful mien 383:27
m. of the pit 386:19
m…the metropolis 147:20
shouts to scare the m. 296:13
some m. in his thought 471:28
that m., custom 436:5
Monsters: complicated m. 349:21
Forms…of all these m. 266:14
transform men into m. 209:29
Monstr'—inform'—ingens 97:17
Monstrosity: m. more prodigious
than Hydra 86:26
numerous piece of m. 86:26
Monstrous: bottom of the m.
world 343:2
every one fault seeming m. 428:10
m. animal a husband and wife 204:31
m. head and sickening cry 140:21
m. little voice 466:27
M. Regiment of Women 305:6
O m. world! 472:6
this m. birth 470:23
Monstrum horrendum 554:14
Mont Blanc is the monarch 118:7
Mont Saint Jean: my M. seems
Cain 116:34
Montagu: Mrs. M. has dropt me 274:26
Montague: in truth, fair M. 477:20
Montalban: in Aspramont or M. 345:4
Monte Carlo: broke the Bank at
M. 217:23
Monte Testaceo: like its own M. 146:8
Montes: parturient m. 255:25
Montez au ciel 204:38
Montezuma: who imprisoned M. 324:28
Montgomery: Mr. M.'s writing 325:9
Month: April is the cruellest m. 197:27
fresh as is the m. of May 136:25
in less than a m. 303:8
laughter for a m. 439:7
leafy m. of June 149:35
little m. 430:33(-431)
merriest m. in all the year 31:21
merry m. of May 30:1, 31:21, 35:17,
80:7
m. before the birth 375:8
m. follow m. with woe 491:26
m. in which the world began 137:40
m. of May…comen 138:16
m. of May was come 328:15
Pope will grieve a m. 521:2
teeth-chattering M. 153:15
this first Summer m. 205:18
this is the m. 343:9
whose m. is ever May 455:17
within a m. 430:33(-431)
year, a m., a week 330:7
Month-long: our m. love 81:12
Monthly changes in her…orb 477:22
Months: as few m…in the eyes of
a husband 519:34
for m. and m. and m. 526:7
hours, days, m. 186:20
mistress of the m. and stars 521:29
mother of m. 521:30
Montmorenci: monstrous steep of
M. 288:10
Montreal: gospel of M. 112:18
Oh God! Oh M.! 112:17
Monument: early but enduring m. 492:1
from off the M. 34:25
his m. look around 583:16
in this…thy m. 488:3
like the M. 270:9
living m. 437:26
moment's m. 410:21
patience on a m. 483:10
thou art a m. 281:11
Monumental: earn a m. pile 162:37
m. mockery 481:18
Monumento plus quam regio 27:47
Monuments: gilded m. of princes 487:6
spared these minor m. 87:9
*Monumentum: m. aere perennius
si M. requiris* 33:26, 583:16
Mood: in listening m. 416:15
in this m…give us anything 451:2
kindly m. of melancholy 195:15
of a higher m. 342:24
that blessed m. 581:25

Mood (cont.)
that sweet m. 581:7
to the Dorian m. 345:2
unused to the melting m. 474:2
Moods: contrarious m. of men 88:20
not profitless those fleeting m. 579:17
Moody: headstrong, m., murmuring race 190:10
Moon: affair with the m. 512:17
appointed the m. for certain
seasons 398:10
as shines the m. 528:2
bares her bosom to the m. 582:18
behold the wandering m. 341:14
beneath a waning m. 151:32
beneath the harvest m. 183:13
beneath the lightning and the
M. 149:30
beneath the visiting m. 425:29
benedictions—sun's and m.'s 92:33
between the horns of the m. 508:1
blow them at the m. 436:8
brief the m. of beauty 538:21
brilliant m. 586:7
by the light of the m. 119:6
by yonder blessed m. 477:22
carry the m. in my pocket 93:19
chaste beams of the wat'ry m. 466:39
climbing m. 586:7
cold fruitless m. 466:16
come from the dying m. 538:12
cow jumped over the m. 367:1
danced by the light of the m. 312:3
danced the m. on Monan's rill 416:11
Daughter of the M. 317:22
drew my bride, beneath the m. 374:24
dwelleth i' the cold o' the m. 90:13
ebb and flow by the m. 454:19
face the m. 551:18
fair as the m. 52:15
fishing up the m. 377:1
follow…the changes of the m. 471:34
forgot the stars, the m. 286:23
glimpses of the m. 431:32(-432)
God himself…m. and sun 537:27
hornèd M. 149:16
hush with the setting m. 536:11
if the m. shine at full 111:4
if the Sun and M. should doubt 73:28
innocent m. 545:11
in…one revolving m. 190:22
Irish wolves against the m. 428:29
I saw the new m. 31:15
it is the m., I ken her horn 108:31
kneaded by the m. 237:10
Lady M. 262:7
lo, the m.'s self 94:8
lucent as a rounded m. 320:6
minions of the m. 438:16
m. and I 219:34
m. and the stars 392:9
m. be still as bright 119:4
m. came quiet 334:6
m. doth shine 366:10, 376:24
m. doth with delight 576:2
m. is up 114:6
m. may draw the sea 539:1
m. of moons 173:36
M. of my Delight 207:28
m. on the one hand 41:20
m. plucked at my rein 585:6
m., rising in clouded majesty 347:19
m.'s beauty and the m.'s soft
pace 579:20
m. shone bright on Mrs. Porter 197:31
m. sits arbitress 345:13
m. sleeps with Endymion 465:22
m. stands blank above 263:12
m., sweet regent 338:13
m. takes up the wondrous tale 2:26
m. that was the town's 141:13
m., the governess of floods 466:37
m. under her feet 71:16
m. was a ghostly galleon 366:1
m. was full 531:30
m. was shinin' clearly 516:20
m. winks 472:36
mortal m…her eclipse 488:2
mortals call the m. 492:29
moving M. went up the sky 149:23
neither the m. by night 399:28

Moon (cont.)
no bigger than the M. 149:4
no need of the sun…of the m. 72:5
no sun, no m. 253:11
not by the m., the inconstant
m. 477:22
on the horns o' the m. 429:5
on whom the pale m. gleams 370:19
or the m…be not darkened 51:33
pale-fac'd m. 438:38
perturbed m. of Uranus 375:25
red roses across the m. 359:17
shining to the quiet m. 151:25
shone the wintry m. 285:20
sickle m. 208:19
silent as the m. 350:23
silently, now the m. 172:2
sliver'd in the m.'s eclipse 459:32
slow m. climbs 541:3
stain both m. and sun 486:31
sun and m. of the heart's desire 411:35
sun and m., rejoice 291:27
sun, m., and stars, brother 78:24
sun, m., and thou vain world 124:18
Sussex m. 141:13
swifter than the wandering m. 467:19
this fair m. 347:23
this roaring m. of daffodil 538:6
thou, M., in the valley of Ajalon 46:42
to the m. complain 229:29
under the solitary m. 17:28
upon the corner of the m. 459:27
very error of the m. 473:16
vitreous pour of the full m. 567:17
wan and hornèd m. 493:2
what a dancing spectre…the m. 336:29
when the m. is on the wave 118:8
when the m. shall rise 583:13
when the m. shone 465:21
when the m. was blood 140:21
when the m. was overhead 534:3
when the m. was setting 537:1
white in the m. 263:12
white m. beams 293:1
with how sad steps, O M. 501:24
wolf behowls the m. 467:35
yonder is the m. 548:17
yon rising M. 207:29
you saw the m. 141:13
Moonbeams: m. from His eye 585:8
m. kiss the sea 495:7
Moonlight: along the m. shade 381:30
as m. unto sunlight 534:32
how sweet the m. sleeps 465:18
in the m., dark with dew 171:21
look for me by m. 366:3
meet me by m. alone 557:16
m. fallen in pools 334:6
m. in his room 265:16
prose can paint…m. 337:14
ribbon of m. 366:1
under the m. still 293:20
visit it by the pale m. 417:12
Moonlight-coloured may 497:22
Moonlit: from that m. cedar 17:11
on the m. door 171:13
Moon-mountains African 288:29
Moons: m…wax and wane no
more 562:8
new m. and sabbaths 52:29
reason has m., but m. not hers 249:11
Moonshine: by m…sour ringlets
make 480:12
in pallid m., died 285:18
m. an' snow 319:23
m.'s watery beams 477:7
transcendental m. 126:43
you m. revellers 466:15
Moon-struck madness 349:24
Moon-washed apples 189:23
Moor: batten on this m. 435:46
lascivious M. 409:32
make the M. thank me 471:4
married to the M. 578:21
m. is dark 498:26
M. is of a free…nature 470:22
over the purple m. 366:1
she dwelt on a wild m. 577:18
your daughter and the M. 469:31
Moore: before I go, Tom M. 118:14
no *extract* from M.'s *Italy* 119:32

Moorfowl: undying m. 585:8
Moors: from the mountains, m. 317:20
  she's for the M 166:12
  wind on the m. 516:9
Moping: merryman, m. mum 222:27
  m. owl 229:29
Moppsikon Floppsikon bear 312:18
Mops: seven maids with seven m. 130:12
Mor the Peacock 301:27
Moral: accounting for the m. sense 126:8
  debasing the m. currency 196:33
  everything's got a m. 129:16
  fatty degeneration of his m. being 514:22
  1st, religious and m. principles 20:21
  his m. pleases 386:13
  let us be m. 176:14
  make a m. of the devil 444:13
  manly, m...liberty 102:3
  m. Clytemnestra of thy lord 118:25
  m. Gower 138:43
  m., grave 27:19
  m. life..part of the subject-matter 570:4
  m. man was Werther 543:12
  m. of that is 129:15
  m. or an immoral book 570:3
  m. or intellectual damage 305:11
  m. pocket handkerchiefs 178:43
  m., sensible..man 159:15
  m. shut within..the rose 529:1
  no one..m. till all are m. 508:30
  of m. evil and of good 581:16
  that m. centaur 116:20
  thinks he is m...only uncomfortable 490:21
  to point a m. 279:6
Moral: Herren-M. und Sklaven-M. 364:21
Moral Philosophy: m...handmaid to religion 24:26
  unfit to hear m. 481:13
Morales: trois quarts sont des affaires m. 360:24
Moralische: das m. Gesetz in mir 284:4
Moralist: rustic m. 230:8
  very sturdy m. 277:37
  your 'poor m.' 121:11
Morality: absolute m. 508:22
  blunderbuss against..m. 270:22
  Dr. Johnson's m. 239:8
  good-bye, m. 243:2
  m. of art 570:4
  m. of masters..m. of slaves 364:21
  m. touched by emotion 20:11
  national m...this fact for its basis 489:32
  periodical fits of m. 325:15
  rather have a himputation on his m. 518:13
  some people talk of m. 195:17
  unawares M. expires 381:27
Moralize: m. my song 509:16
  m. two meanings 476:20
Moralized his song 386:1
Moralizing: opportunity for m. 542:35
Morals: divergence upon m. 514:17
  m. of a Methodist 222:5
  m. of a whore 270:21
  thy m. tell thy mind 382:14
  why, man of m. 158:8
Moraris: quid m. emori? 133:3
Moras: mala per longas convaluere m. 372:2
Morass: wisp on the m. 118:8
Morbi: pallentesque habitant M. 554:27
  subeunt m. tristisque senectus 556:20
Morbo: venienti occurrite m. 378:4
Morbum: hunc habet m. 132:22
More: and m., and m., and m. 130:14
  any m. at home like you 234:12
  bravel that are no m. 162:9
  cantie wi' m. 104:32
  could not give him m. 192:12
  days that are no m. 538:17
  doin' things rather-m.-or-less 295:22
  easy to take m. than nothing 129:9
  enough for modesty—no m. 98:6
  he m. had pleased us 2:1
  his strength the m. is 99:36
  I am m. 67:33
  I can't take m. 129:9

More (cont.)
  I feel it m. 174:14
  if one pleases one makes m. 156:6
  I have m. 185:24
  in that m...all his hopes 19:2
  kiss me and never no m. 328:19
  little m. 90:9
  m. he cast away, the m. he had 99:32
  m. is meant 341:21
  m...laid at your feet 524:33
  m...no man is entitled to 409:2
  m. than most fair 232:11
  m. than that..too fat 312:19
  m. than thou desir'st 465:11
  m. than usual calm 208:21
  m. they talk I'm kent the better 107:28
  m. things are wrought by prayer 531:36
  neither m. nor less 131:6
  no m., dear love 539:1
  no m. do zee your feàce 35:16
  no m. of that 474:2
  no m. of that, Hal 439:28
  no m.—Oh, never m. 494:18
  Oliver Twist has asked for m. 177:36
  seek no m. 195:13
  she'll vish there wos m. 179:7
  they merely know m. 414:19
  thou, O Lord, art m. 531:41
  to Masefield something m. 39:12
  two hundred m. 111:11
  whyles do m. 104:22
  you get no m. of me 189:20
Morea: along M.'s hills 115:8
Morem: contra bonum m. 422:18
Mores: artes emollit m. 372:9
  m. hominum multorum vidit 255:26
  o tempora, o m.! 145:12
  sine crimine m. 371:17
More-than-oriental-splendour 304:15
Morgue: Doric little M. 89:21
Mori: ita feri ut se m. sentiat 517:20
  Musa vetat m. 261:1
  pro patria m. 259:18
Moriar: non omnis m. 260:16
Moribus: leges sine m. 260:11
  m. antiquis res stat Romana 201:25
Moriens: te teneam m... manu 547:18
Morior: propterea m. in exilio 232:9
Morison: ye are na Mary M. 107:6
Morituri te salutant 13:4, 517:22
Morn: another m. ris'n. 348:7
  at midnight and at m. 199:8
  autumn evening, and the m. 498:12
  Autumn in the misty m. 253:13
  beloved, it is m. 248:7
  blooming m. 245:24
  day's at the m. 94:40
  descry the m.'s approach 350:3
  each M. a thousand Roses brings 205:18
  every m., and every night 378:16
  fair laughs the m. 229:23
  forth..on a summer's m. 349:11
  from m. till eve 291:10
  from m. till even fought 443:25
  from m. to night, my friend 410:2
  from m. to noon he fell 345:12
  glowing like the vital m. 493:2
  golden light of m. 253:19
  greet the early m. 107:4
  held his way till m. 348:19
  his love-song to the m. 268:30
  in a m. by break of day 80:7
  incense-breathing M. 229:31
  like a lobster boil'd, the m. 110:43
  mislead the m. 462:16
  m., in russet mantle 430:21
  m. not waking 321:16
  m. of bright carnations 190:6
  m. of song 517:2
  m. will never rise 169:13
  morrow m. 150:17
  new m. she saw not 286:23
  nice M. 340:6
  no m.—no noon 253:11
  on a winter's m. 311:22
  on Christ's Sunday at m. 7:14
  opening eyelids of the m. 342:12
  peeping in at m. 252:33
  salute the happy m. 112:24

Morn (cont.) sang from m. till night 72:15
  see the opening m. 76:6
  Son of M. in..Night's decline 74:22
  sweet approach of ev'n or m. 346:20
  sweet is the breath of m. 347:22
  that April m. 82:2
  this pious m. 287:12
  this the happy m. 343:9
  tresses like the m. 340:38
  ushers in the m. 204:37
  when m. purples the east 348:23
  when the m. is grey 121:18
  while as yet 'tis early m. 534:13
  with the m. those Angel faces 364:12
Morning: almost at odds with m. 459:24
  always m. somewhere 262:2
  as fed horses in the m. 55:11
  ashamed..next m. 559:20
  as m. shows the day 350:10
  beauty of the m. 582:14
  before the m. watch 399:40
  breeze of m. moves 536:10
  caught this m. m.'s minion 255:11
  clear as m. roses 479:4
  cold and frosty m. 6:23
  disasters in his m. face 225:1
  each m. sees some task 318:13
  early in the m. 11:16, 240:19
  early one m. 6:2
  evening and the m. 44:3
  evening close to m. light 493:22
  every m...a noble chance 531:33
  first M. of Creation 207:6
  forehead of the m. sky 343:3
  from his lair in the m. 229:16
  from the veils of the m. 585:12
  full many a glorious m. 486:27
  gathered..all in one m. 186:31
  go home till m. 98:15
  great m. of the world 491:23
  Heaven's m. breaks 322:2
  here of a Sunday m. 262:21(−263)
  he's for the m. 91:37
  his horn in the m. 229:16
  in the m. it is green 397:15
  in the m. of the world 94:43
  in the m...remember them 72:23
  in the m. sow 51:30
  in the m. thou shalt hear 562:7
  in the m. thou shalt say 46:28
  I scent the m. air 432:15
  joy cometh in the m. 393:25
  laudes..early in the m. 239:5
  like to the m.'s war 445:44
  looketh forth as the m. 52:15
  Lucifer, son of the m. 53:22
  make the m. precious 288:13
  matter for a May m. 484:11
  men and m. newspapers 378:21
  Mithras, God of the M. 301:29
  m. cometh 53:26
  m., evening, noon and night 90:3
  m. fair came forth 350:15
  M. in the Bowl of Night 205:4
  m. lowers 1:13
  m.'s at seven 94:40
  m. stars sang together 49:20
  my m. thoughts 156:12
  never glad confident m. again 93:7
  never m. wore to evening 532:6
  new every m. 291:4
  next m...someone else 408:12
  'No,' this m. 88:9
  or come in the m. 169:27
  outgoings of the m. and evening 395:29
  phantom of False M. 205:7
  radiant lines of m. 497:9
  red m...bright'ning 497:8
  shining m. face 427:21
  sniffin' the m. cool 301:8
  some m., unaware 92:14
  sons of the m. 240:15
  take our fill of love until the m. 49:50
  thy light break forth as the m. 54:37
  thy m. bounties 160:31
  thy m. sacrifice 292:1
  'tis almost m. 477:28
  up in the m. early 108:24
  walk with Death and M. 539:4
  wings of the m. 400:9
  Wings o' the M. 304:1

Morning (cont.)
with tea welcomes the m. 278:1
with the m. cool repentance
came 420:14
your shadow at m. 197:28
Mornings: brushes his hat a m. 468:31
Morning star: above the light of
the m. 75:14
against the m. 493:25
bright and m. 72:10
bright m., day's harbinger 343:8
glittering like the m. 102:11
m. of song 529:6
m. to..truth 528:20
stay the m. 151:28
Morocco: Damasco, or M. 345:4
pause there, M. 463:40
Moron: see the happy m...I wish
I were a m. 9:14
Morosa: canities abest m. 258:15
Moroseness: care, difficulty, and
m. 309:16
Morrice: gulls in an aery m. 241:30
Morrison: James James M. M. 339:15
no M.'s Pill for..Society 126:45
Morrow: bitterly thought of the m. 572:13
budding m. in midnight 288:26
m. morn 150:17
night for the m. 499:4
night urge the m. 491:26
no thought for the m. 58:15
of a ful misty m. 138:32
say good-night till it be m. 478:1
supplied by the m. 278:14
watching for the m. 127:30
windy night a rainy m. 487:23
Mors: illi m. gravis incubat 422:19
indignatio principis m. est 358:3
m. sola fatetur..corpuscula 283:22
pallida M. aequo..pede 258:8
Morsel: found you as a m., cold 425:3
m. for a monarch 424:1
sweet m . 242:8
Mort: bâtir la m. 354:18
la m. ne surprend point le sage 209:15
la m., sans phrases 502:13
Mortal: all men m., but themselves 587:7
animosities are m. 365:13
beyond a m.'s share 332:22
beyond m. thought 492:11
chances of this m. life 390:50
companion an' fellow-m. 107:10
dreams no m. ever dared 380:24
excels each m. thing 484:40(-485)
fair as aught of m. birth 112:30
flux of m. things 19:4
gathers all things m. 523:20
genius and the m. instruments 449:5
grief itself be m. 491:24
here came a m. 16:1
her last disorder m. 225:16
in the time of this m. life 389:22
I presume you're m. 501:7
lock'd up from m. eye 166:17
m. in the minute 94:2
m. man be more just than God? 48:49
m. men, m. men 440:23
m. right-lined circle 87:13
m. thing so to immortalize 509:7
my m. part..nigh this stone 8:13
never-fading worlds, for m.
creatures 574:22
nor seeks..m. blisses 497:2
of m. life the leaf 509:33
our m. nature did tremble 576:18
plant that grows on m. soil 342:22
purest treasure m. times afford 474:10
rais'd a m. to the skies 191:13
shuffled off this m. coil 434:4
sing with m. voice 348:23
sole m. thing of worth immortal 374:18
tend on m. thoughts 457:3
this m... put on immortality 67:17
turning m. for thy love 455:18
weakness of our m. nature 389:40
Mortales: inter se m. mutua vivunt 321:1
Mortalia: mentem m. tangunt 553:18
Mortalibus: nil m. ardui 258:7
Mortality: m.'s too weak 365:8
m. weighs heavily on me 288:21

Mortality (cont.)
nothing serious in m. 458:24
sad m. o'ersways 487:13
to frail m...trust 28:17
watch o'er man's m. 576:22
Mortals: greatest good that m.
know 1:26
m.' chiefest enemy 459:28
not for m. always to be blest 14:25
not in m. to command success 1:14
timorous m. start and shrink 562:16
to m...a providence 231:29
what fools these m. be 467:8
Mortar: bray a fool in a m. 50:48
Morti: seu certae occumbere m. 554:1
Mortify a wit 386:19
Mortifying: monkey..m. reflections 155:6
Mortis: animum m. terrore carentem 283:24
felix..opportunitate m. 526:11
postremo..munere m. 133:20
rapit inclementia m. 556:20
timor m. conturbat me 195:2
Morts: il n'y a pas de m. 327:7
Mos: suo quoique m. 542:1
Moscow: Juan was my M. 116:34
Moses: as I was with M. 46:36
climb where M. stood 562:17
disputed about the body of M. 70:17
from Mahomet to M. 387:23
His hand on M.' law 74:13
Jesus..in M.' chair 74:13
M. hid his face 45:35
M. on the mountain 360:10
M. was very meek 46:12
while M. stood 161:16
White Hand of M. 205:8
Moss: azure m. and flowers 496:8
cushion plump..the m. 150:8
gather no m. 550:5
Mossy: winding m. ways 287:29
Most: make the m. of what we yet
may spend 206:8
make the m. on 'em 174:7
m. may err 190:28
m. musical, m. melancholy 152:7
treason, make the m. of it 242:16
Mot: cette phrase dans un m. 282:11
Mote..in thy brother's eye 58:17
Motes: thikke as m. in the sonne-
beem 138:10
Moth: candle sing'd the m. 464:4
desire of the m. 499:4
kill not the m. 73:23
like..a m. fretting a garment 394:10
like a m., the simple maid 214:11
m. and rust..corrupt 58:5
m. of peace 470:11
m.'s kiss 91:35
not a m. with vain desire 532:33
Mother: as is the m. 55:28
as M., Wife, and Queen 539:12
behold my m. 59:20
behold thy m. 63:72
botanize upon his m.'s grave 578:30
call his m. 'Ma'am' 141:33
call me early, m. dear 536:26
cannot be call'd our m. 460:19
child and m. 232:3
Christ and his m. 255:6
church for his m. 22:1
come to the m.'s 234:16
daughter..in my m.'s house 300:11
dearer..than his own m. University 193:25
dearer was the m. 151:22
deceived the m. of mankind 344:6
does your m. know 34:29
don't tell my m. 242:26
earth, a fatal m. 522:14
Father, M., and Me 303:18
favour their M. 302:1
finished jumping on his m. 221:36
for the m.'s sake 151:22
gave her m. forty whacks 8:7
great care of his M. 339:15
great M. Empire 210:12
great M.'s train divine 18:31(-19)
great sweet m. 525:29
happy he with such a m. 539:8
Heaven's M. send us grace 149:12

Mother (cont.)
heaviness of his m. 49:54
her m. came and caught her 367:17
his m. a witch maun be 31:7
his M...being dead 375:16
his m. on his father him begot 74:15
his m.'s doves 321:14
home to his m.'s house 350:18
honour thy father and thy m. 390:12
I arose a m. in Israel 46:47
in sin hath my m. conceived me 395:8
into my m.'s house 52:21
joyful m. of children 399:1
little did my m. ken 31:19
man before thy m. 37:30
man before your m. 159:10
Mary was that M. mild 3:20
m. and lover of men 525:29
m. and maiden 7:17
m. cried 232:3
m. for her children 72:22
m. Ida 537:30
m. is a m. still 152:14
M. laid her Baby 3:20
m., make my bed soon 31:10
M., Mary M. 411:32
m. may forgot the child 106:28
m., m., make my bed 30:3
m. of all living 44:29
m. of arts 350:11
m. of dead dogs 126:41
m. of God! no lady 148:16
m. of harlots 71:32
m. of months 521:30
m. of Parliaments 82:19
m. of Sisera looked out 46:51
M. of the Fair Delight 410:5
M. of the Free 42:20
m. of the sciences 28:8
m. o' mine 299:27
m.'s allocution to me 127:29
m.'s head off 178:24
m.'s pride 419:6
m.'s wag 232:2
m. that bore you 299:22
m., who'd give her booby 215:22
m. who talks about her own
children 181:5
m. will be there 242:25
m., wi' her needle 104:34
my M. 527:8
my m. bids me 266:8
my m. bore me in the..wild 76:13
my m. didna speak 35:9
my m. groan'd 76:8
my m...into mine eyes 445:3
my m. she fell sick 35:8
nature by her m. wit 510:6
near the manners of my m. 482:26
never called me m. 572:19
on any m.'s knee 525:3
one whom his m. comforteth 55:10
only son of his m. 61:32
Pembroke's m. 87:24
rhyming m. wits 330:20
rolled m. with infant 351:20
seethe a kid in his m.'s milk 46:1
show'd thy..m...courtesy 429:22
so astonish a m. 435:21
so loving to my m. 430:33(-431)
such a lady God's m. 7:17
sucked the breasts of my m. 52:21
tell your m. it wasn't I 366:15
their Dacian m. 114:19
there thy m. brought thee forth 52:22
thou art thy m.'s glass 486:11
thou hast murdered thy m. 328:7
thy m. a lady 417:32
thy m.'s grief 73:23
to their earthly m. tend 194:25
wedded maid, and virgin m. 343:9
we'll 'elp 'im for 'is m. 301:17
whence his m. rose 421:12
when my father and my m. forsake me 393:21
when my m. died 76:17
where His m. was 7:16
where my m. fell 543:19
whose m. was her painting 429:32
who was your m.? 517:5
woman and a m. 178:18

INDEX

Mother (cont.)

your m. and I..liv'd comfortably 214:13
your m...never see you again 22:33
Mother Carey: to M. 294:21
Mothering: world-m. air 254:17
Mother-in-law: when his m. died 269:3
Motherland, we pledge to thee 295:8
Mothers: all women..like their m. 569:24
city of the best-bodied m. 507:8
if Caesar had stabbed their m. 448:29
men with m. and wives 253:23
m. of large families 40:29
m. that lack sons 429:8
younger than she..m. 477:2
Mother tongue: his m. 163:1
in their M. 391:14
silence..his m. 226:38
Moths: m. fluttering among the heath 83:15
unfading m. 84:1
Mothy: m. and warm 235:14
m. curfew-tide 236:9
Motion: between the acting..and the first m. 449:5
between the m. and the act 197:11
breath and everlasting m. 575:21
careful of my m. 529:20
devoid of sense and m. 345:19
give away their m. to the stars 151:1
God order'd m., but..no rest 551:15
her m. blush'd at herself 470:1
in his m. like an angel 465:18
little m. in the air 492:24
meandering with a mazy m. 151:33
measured m. like a living thing 579:10
m. of a hidden fire 355:11
m. of all elements 455:22
m. of a muscle 573:7
m. of our human blood 581:25
next to the perpetual m. 179:27
no m. has she now 573:6
no m. of the liver 483:9
rolled with visible m. 575:26
rot itself with m. 423:39
scoured..with a perpetual m. 441:25
short uneasy m. 149:36
their m. in one sphere 440:36
this sensible warm m. 462:9
undistinguishable m. 579:6
unshak'd of m. 449:30
with his eternal m. 577:1
with what m. moved the clouds 570:8
your sweet hue..hath m. 487:29(–488)
Motions: her household m. 580:20
m. of his spirit are dull 465:20
m. of the viewless winds 579:25
no two m. can be less like 325:12
skittish in all m. else 483:2
so delicate his m. 82:2
stings and m. of the sense 461:20
those well ordered m. 86:32
to thy m. lovers' seasons 186:19
two weeping m. 166:10
Motive: every joint and m. 481:26
experiment, noble in m. 254:4
m., not the deed 584:9
noblest m...public good 511:20
Motive-hunting 153:1
Motiveless malignity 153:1
Motives meaner than your own 36:3
Motley: made myself a m. 488:5
m. fool 427:11
m.'s the only wear 427:15
Motor Bus: can it be a M.? 223:8
Motor car: afford to keep a m. 489:4
Motto: m. [of *Lyra Apostolica*] 363:16
my m. and my fate 521:25
Mottoes: those lovely cracker m. 218:4
Motus: hi m. animorum 556:22
Mould: fresh from Natur's m. 176:24
grew out of the m. 300:10
mixture of earth's m. 340:14
m. of a man's fortune 26:14
m. of form 434:14
round their narrow lips the m. 411:6
scratched..in the m. 295:16
so soft a m. 191:19
Moulded: m. out of faults 462:27
scarcely form'd or m. 117:2
stateliest measure ever m. 541:8

Moulder cold and low 113:34
Mouldering: a-m. in the grave 234:7
Moulds: crack nature's m. 453:5
Moulmein: old M. Pagoda 299:10, 15
Moult: time shall m. away 517:18
Moults: never m. a feather 177:28
Mound: each night above his m. 235:19
from this wave-washed m. 411:8
upon the convex m. 266:13
Mount: by m., and stream, and sea 241:8
guarded m. 343:2
liked the 'Sermon on the M.' 183:4
m., m., my soul 476:1
m. of marble 528:24
m. up with wings as eagles 54:14
never m. as high as women 531:31
not m. on thee again 365:16
whilst you m. up 475:19
Mount Abora: singing of M. 151:33(–152)
Mountain: every m...made low 54:9
exceeding high m. 57:36
forked m. 425:19
from his m. walls 529:10
from yonder m. height 539:3
gross as a m. 439:23
he is gone on the m. 416:22
his high m. cradle 17:28(–18)
hovering o'er the m.'s brow 493:12
if I never see another m. 307:3
in all my holy m. 53:19
land of the m. 417:22
like the dew on the m. 416:23
looked over the m.'s rim 94:27
m. and the squirrel 199:18
m. nymph..Liberty 341:30
m. sheep are sweeter 376:23
M.'s slumbrous voice 496:2
m. 'tween my heart and tongue 449:27
Nebo's lonely m. 3:16
o'er the m.'s brow 228:7
of m. or of cape 539:1
on this fair m. leave 435:46
robes the m. 122:31
say unto this m., Remove 59:47
tall rock, the m. 581:26
upon the m. of spices 52:25
up the airy m. 4:18
white..as the m. snow 436:21
woods or steepy m. 330:17
Mountain-built with peaceful citadel 287:12
Mountain-chains like ribs 235:22
Mountains: Acroceraunian m. 492:20
among our ancient m. 314:19
among the m. by the..sea 531:29
barren are those m. 81:19
beautiful must be the m. 81:18
before the m. were brought forth 397:15
blue Friuli's m. 114:6
Delectable M. 99:22
from the m., moors, and fenlands 317:20
Greenland's icy m. 240:17
high m. are a feeling 113:47
how beautiful upon the m. 54:22
hunt in the m. of Cheviot 30:11
monarch of m. 118:7
m. and hills..fall on me 330:8
m. are our sponsors 309:5
m. are the beginning and the end 412:27
m...bring peace 396:23
m. divide us 420:31
m. interpos'd make enemies 162:41
m. kiss high Heaven 495:7
m. look on Marathon 115:44
m. of Casuistry 381:27
M. of Necessity 18:2
m. skipped 399:3
m. will be in labour 255:25
o'er her grave, ye m. 18:19
one of the m. 581:13
paced upon the m. 586:21
rears its m. 493:25
scattered on the Alpine m. 351:20
setteth fast the m. 395:28
so that I could remove m. 66:45
to the m...Fall on us 71:2
upon England's m. green 75:16
waves, or m. 498:8
when men and m. meet 74:23

Mountains (cont.)

wintry garment..the m. have put on 507:37
ye m. of Gilboa 47:29
Mountain-side: from every m. 504:19
Mountain-tops: as..m. are bald 19:18
flatter the m. 486:27
m. that freeze 446:18
tiptoe on the misty m. 478:27
Mount Amara..true paradise 347:9
Mountebank: mere anatomy, a m. 429:1
m. who sold pills..against an earthquake 2:34
natural-born m. 491:6
Mounted: m. on her milk-white steed 32:8
sunk low, but m. high 343:3
Mounteth: courage m. with occasion 447:22
Mounting: meandering level and ..m. upwards 325:12
m. in hot haste 113:30
Mounts: m., and that hardly 16:13
now he m. above me 191:17
worm m. 199:17
Mourir: quand on a à mourir 354:3
Mourn: angels m. 82:1
blessed are they that m. 57:39
children of the bridechamber m. 58:41
comfort all that m. 55:3
countless thousands m. 107:2
I m. for that most lovely thing 584:18
in summer skies to m. 285:11
man was made to m. 107:1
m. all at her grave 32:16
m. a mischief that is past 470:5
m., hapless Caledonia 506:3
m. with ever-returning spring 568:8
no longer m. for me 487:15
not without hope..m. 578:17
now can never m. 492:7
shall I go m. for that? 485:17
time enough to m. 168:12
wherefore should we m.? 575:1
Mourned: beast..m. longer 430:33(–431)
by strangers m. 381:34
I m., and yet shall mourn 568:8
m. the Lord of Burleigh 535:10
m., till Pity's self be dead 153:22
she m. in silence 387:3
we have m. unto you 59:8
Mourner: only constant m. 117:39
Mourners: most musical of m. 491:15
m. followed after 263:2
m. go about 51:33
no m. walk behind me 237:7
Mournful: each sundown makes them m. 77:27
in pity and m. awe 16:6
loving thy m. face 269:31
m. ever-weeping Paddington 75:3
m. that no new wonder 585:22
oh, most m. 170:25
this m. gloom 344:21
Mournfully: hollow'd a little m. 359:10
Mourning: house of m. 51:9
M. Bride 193:18
m. of a mighty nation 537:11
murmur of the m. ghost 183:1
oftener left me m. 580:24
oil of joy for m. 55:4
she doth of m. speak 123:21
silence their m. 526:23
Mourns: wiser mind m. less 574:34
Mourra: on m. seul 374:3
Mouse: appetyt..to ete a m. 137:36
as a cat would watch a m. 520:28
birth will be a..m. 255:25
catch a m. or two..in public 231:22
caught a crooked m. 369:3
frightened a little m. 368:14
good my m. of virtue 482:14
killing of a m. on Sunday 79:18
leave room for the m. 414:18
let him seen a m. 137:36
m. caught in a trappe 136:30
m. ran up the clock 367:3
not a m. shall disturb 467:36
not even a m. 356:1
other caught a M. 312:12
so quiet as a m. 1:3

Mouse-trap: make a better m. 201:22
Moustache: didn't wax his m. 304:41
Mouth: as curs m. a bone 143:19
bar for thy m. 57:4
could not ope his m., but 110:7
determination of words to the m. 518:43
down in the m. 155:30
enrich my heart, m., hands 245:9
every article which enters.. the m. 505:27
for an Englishman to open his m. 490:44
God be in my m. 6:10
great strawberries at the m. 24:40
he opened not his m. 54:26
he put up his m. 170:25
her m. is smoother than oil 49:44
her rosy m. 375:2
his heart's his m. 429:13
his m. is most sweet 52:14
if you m. it 434:15
in the cannon's m. 427:21
in their m...no guile 71:24
in the m. of fame 289:12
in the m. of two or three witnesses 67:39
into the m. of Hell 528:18
kisses of his m. 51:37
law of thy m. 399:17
look a gift-horse in the m. 110:24
made his m. to water 110:31
match'd in m. like bulls 467:20
most beautiful m. in the world 139:34
m...Freedom's classic line 123:1
m. like an old potato 295:3
m. of a bell 294:28
m. of the Lord hath spoken 54:9
m. of your own geranium's red 91:21
my capacious m. 214:7
no m. to put it in 178:24
our mouths are one with M. 84:23
out of his m. went a..sword 70:27
out of..the heart the m. speaketh 59:14
out of the m. of..babes 392:8
out of the m. of God 57:34
out of the m. of the Lord 46:23
out of thine own m. 62:37
praises of God..in their m. 400:26
purple-stained m. 287:24
rose her m. 536:6
satisfieth thy m. 398:4
splendid kissing m. 525:34
spue thee out of my m. 70:34
stop his m. with a kiss 468:15
sweet small m. 524:13
upon my m...their wine 332:17
watch..before my m. 400:13
which goeth into the m. 59:38
words of my m. 392:34
Mouthed: first m...last swallowed 436:9
Mouth-filling: good m. oath 440:7
Mouthful: out of a m. of air 584:16
Mouth-honour 460:36
Mouths: blind m.! 342:18
Catullus makes m. 523:5
enemy in their m. 471:22
issue from your smoky m. 330:9
made m. in a glass 453:7
m. and speak not 399:4
m. a sentence 143:19
our m. are one with Mouth 84:23
to m. like mine 96:18
to our like m. grow sleek 351:17
whose m. must be held 393:34
Moutons: revenons à ces m. 12:18
Movable: M. Feasts 388:5
M. Types 127:6
Move: all m. one place 129:10
great affair is to m. 514:14
in him we live, and m. 65:1
I will m. Thee 244:25
makes no show to m. 186:25
m. immediately upon your works 229:4
m. still, still so 485:27
m. the stones of Rome 450:34
never should m. at any time 398:8
prayers would m. me 449:30
so did she m. 319:1
stones have been known to m. 459:24

Move (cont.)
that honour could not m. 84:17
they m. in perfect phalanx 345:2
things m. violently to their place 26:27
this will not m. 517:11
those m. easiest 382:32
voluntary m. harmonious numbers 346:20
we and all men m. 549:6
Movebo: Acheronta m. 555:4
Moved: Gibbon m. to flutes 154:13
hell from beneath is m. 53:21
kingdoms are m. 394:28
m. a little nearer 318:2
m. among my race 516:16
m. earth and heaven 541:3
m...in quiet grown-up wise 375:16
m. me not 516:16
m. on, with difficulty 346:17
m. slowly through the mind 579:12
m. upon the face of the waters 44:1
my bowels were m. 52:10
my heart m. more 502:9
not suffer thy foot to be m. 399:27
round world..cannot be m. 397:22
though the earth be m. 394:27
woman m...fountain troubled 479:12
Movement: almost a palpable m. 236:38
sudden and adroit m. 560:11
Movements: many m. of his mind 582:15
Moveris: Jupiter..quocumque m. 320:26
Movers: we are the m. and shakers 370:19
Moves: as impotently m. 207:5
God m. in a mysterious way 161:18
having writ m. on 207:2
it m. us not 582:18
m. in predestinate grooves 237:26
m. like a ghost 458:1
m. with its own organs 424:17
nothing m...which is not Greek 327:12
Moveth: all that m. 510:11
every living thing that m. 44:9
m. all together 580:11
Moving: always m. as the..Spheres 330:28
gay in the mazy m. 146:23
his slow and m. finger 472:34
in form, in m., how express 433:15
m. about in worlds not realized 576:18
M. Finger writes 207:2
m. inly to one..goal 19:4
m. others, are..as stone 487:24
m. through his clouded heaven 579:20
m. up an' down again 294:37
seems a m. land 348:26
which art m. everywhere 496:4
Moving-delicate: more m. 469:6
Mower whets his scythe 341:34
Mozart: some cry up..M. 307:25
Much: asking too m. 124:6
by m. too m. 440:9
how m. it is 90:9
missing so m. and so m. 157:9
m. drinking, little thinking 519:29
m. is she worth 241:28
m. is to be done 276:13
m. is to be endured 278:10
m. might be said on both sides 2:12
m. of a muchness 196:18, 551:7
none too m. 297:2
poor though m. they have 195:13
some have too m. 195:13
something too m. of this 434:26
so m. owed by so many 144:1
so m. they talk'd 143:21
so m. to do 406:17, 533:3
talk too m. 190:21
tell me how m. 423:12
this is too m. for bel 304:19
tho' m. is taken, m. abides 541:3
though m. I want 195:12
too m. Asia 304:27
too m. of me 220:33
won't be m. for us 128:18
Muchness: much of a m. 196:18, 551:7
Mucho: muchos pocos hacen un m. 134:11
Muck: all of a m. of sweat 227:22
money is like m. 27:10
when to stop raking the m. 409:3
Muckrake in his hand 99:27
Muck-rakes: men with the m. 409:3

Mud: me name is M. 172:13
m., celestially fair 83:27
of water and of m. 83:24
one sees the m. 310:1
on Nilus' m. lay me 425:34
put m. into coffee 542:12
stick'n in a big m. hole 210:14
Muddied oafs at the goals 297:16
Muddle through 82:15
Muddled with books and pictures 299:18
Muddy: m. ecstasies of beer 164:33
m., ill-seeming 479:12
m. understandings 102:15
m. vesture of decay 465:18
tickled best in m. water 111:27
Muddy-mettled rascal 433:33
Mudie's: keep my books at..M. 111:30
Muerta: fe m. 551:1
Muffin: Improved Hot M... Company 176:37
now for the m. 222:18
one caught a M. 312:12
Muffins: mince, m. and mutton 171:17
no more inspiration in her than..m. 490:19
Muffling up his face 450:31
Mug: graceful air and heavenly m. 208:29
zum o' that in a m. 403:13
Mugwump: Main Spring, Mogul, and M. 83:2
Mulberry Garden 202:13
Mule: along o' my old brown m. 301:8
battery-mule's a m. 300:8
m. of politics 181:38
not like to horse and m. 393:34
Mules of politics 387:15
Mulier: desinat in piscem m. formosa 255:14
m...quod dicit amanti 133:11
Mull was a-stern 516:8
Multiplication is vexation 8:12
Multiplied: I have m. visions 55:49
m. the nation 53:14
Multiplieth: he m. words 49:16
Multiply: be fruitful, and m. 44:9
Multitude: cover the m. of sins 70:5, 463:43
fool m. 335:3
giddy m. 335:3
great enemy of reason..the m. 86:26
inaudible to the vast m. 574:27
in the m. of counsellors 49:56
m...in the wrong 180:10
m...no matter what they think 194:9
m. of days 279:7
m. of the isles..glad 397:31
m., which no man could number 71:3
not in the m. of friends 279:30
nouns of number, or m. 147:17
rank me with the barbarous m. 463:44
saved by the m. of an host 393:37
still-discordant wavering m. 441:8
swinish m. 102:18
Multitudes: against revolted m. 348:20
I contain m. 568:1
m. in the valley of decision 55:53
pestilence-striken m. 496:4
Multitudinous: m. chatterings 336:32
m. seas incarnadine 458:15
Mum: merryman, moping m. 222:27
m.'s the word 154:5
Mumbling of the game 385:32
Mummers: grave m. 381:19
Mummy: it was dy'd in m. 472:16
m. is become merchandise 87:19
Munch on, crunch on 94:37
Munched: m., and m., and m. 456:10
Mundane: more than m. weeds 83:27
Mundi: iuventus m. 25:7
Mundus: et pereat m. 203:38
Munera: vitae extremum inter m... Naturae 283:24
Munere: tristi m. ad inferias 133:20
Muneribus: deorum m. sapienter uti 261:14
Munich: wave, M.! all thy banners 122:19
Munita: nil dulcius..quam m. tenere 320:30
Muove: e pur si m. 212:24
Murder: foul and midnight m. 229:24
from battle and m. 388:48
I met M. 495:15
killing no M. 422:25

INDEX

Murder (cont.)
love and m. will out 154:35
Macbeth does m. sleep 458:11
more strange than such a m. 459:17
most unnatural m. 432:10
m. cannot be hid 463:32
m., hate, virtue, and sin 328:2
m. hath broke ope the. .temple 458:22
m. most foul 463:32
M.. .One of the Fine Arts 172:22
m.. .run in families 313:23
m. sanctuarize 436:43
m.'s out of tune 473:17
m., though it have no tongue 433:36
no contriv'd m. 469:36
once. .indulges himself in m. 172:23
one m. made a villain 387:9
one to destroy, is m. 586:27
sooner m. an infant 77:19
thou shalt do no m. 390:13
to m. and to rafish 23:26
to m. thousands 586:27
vanity, like m., will out 158:26
we m. to dissect 581:16
whose m.. .but fantastical 456:24
will you let them m. me? 96:17
wither'd m. 458:1
Murdered: all m. 475:7
Priam m. with his peers 586:7
their m. man 286:22
thou hast m. thy mother 328:7
Murderer: common m., possibly 414:8
deaf and viperous m. 492:4
first m.'s son 163:43
help the escaping m. 514:3
honourable m. 473:34
m. so young 328:7
thief, a liar, and a m. 121:17
Murderous: fang'd with m. stones 150:28
perjur'd, m., bloody 488:11
whose m. hand 165:20
Murders: twenty mortal m. 459:17
Murex: who fished the m. up? 95:3
Murky: hell is m. 460:24
Murmur: creeping m. 444:6
everlasting m. about his name 413:18
live m. of a summer's day 18:6
m. at. .possessors of power 101:33
m.. .how Love fled 586:21
m. in the wind 288:7
m. of the mourning ghost 183:1
rustic m. of their bourg 531:6
whose m. invites one 499:14
why m. I 186:1
with reason m. at his case 160:17
Murmured: m. her moans 473:6
m. like a noontide bee 495:23
Murmuring: fled m. 347:36
lapse of m. streams 348:32
mazily m. 529:18
moody, m. race 190:10
m. of innumerable bees 539:5
m. poor 164:41
waters m. 341:22
Murmurings: buz, and m. 158:12
from within were heard m. 574:20
Murmurous haunt of flies 287:31
Murmurs: as for m. 227:13
in hollow m. died away 154:2
m. and scents of the. .Sea 16:4
m. as the ocean m. 308:28
m. near the running brooks 578:31
m. of the Spring 404:23
no quarrels, m., no delay 166:15
our mutual m. sweep 116:3
to hear their m. 357:24
Murray: my M. 118:16
slain the Earl of M. 30:8
Murus: hic m. aeneus esto 256:18
Mus: nascetur ridiculus m. 255:25
Musa: M. vetat mori 261:1
quo, M., tendis? 259:24
Musae: ab Iove principium m. 555:25
Sicelides M. 555:30
Musam: tenui m. meditamur avena 505:26
tenui m. meditaris avena 555:14
Muscam: aut m. aut formicam 27:47
Muscle: keep thy m. trained 320:2
Muscles of his brawny arms 318:11
Muscular: his Christianity was m. 182:3
Muse: by chance our minds do m. 190:1

Muse (cont.)
every conqueror creates a M. 558:3
'Fooll' said my M. 501:23
I m. at how its being 254:18
love of the 'chaste m.' 77:32
meditate the thankless M. 342:20
meets his favouring m. 164:35
move the m. to tears 159:24
M. he lov'd 382:18
M. invoked 521:16
M., let's sing of rats 228:19
M., nae poet ever fand 107:35
m. on Nature 122:35
my M., to some ears not unsweet 502:3
neither man, nor m. 281:10
O! for a M. of fire 443:2
plans, credit, and the M. 199:12
return Sicilian M. 342:30
Silence, m. His praise 546:8
so may some gentle M. 342:11
take my M. and me 280:9
talked about like a tenth m. 6:24
taught by th' heavenly M. 340:25
tenth M. 549:18
to the M. of Fiction. .'Go spin' 420:26
to whom my M. 501:20
whose m. on dromedary trots 151:13
worst-humour'd m. 226:1
worst-natur'd m. 407:17
Mused: Lancelot m. a little 534:10
m. of taking kingdoms in 425:1
Muses: adopting m. 80:24
charm of all the M. 541:7
m. on admired themes 3 1:2
M.' sacred grove 545:7
M. scorn. .vulgar brains 502:2
sitteth in the M.' bower 80:28
where the M. haunt 346:19
write the. .M.' story 232:11
Museum: all in the M. 40:23
Mushroom: I am. .a m. 209:24
Methusalem. .but a m. 186:31
m. of boiling dust 547:17
m. rich civilian 119:24
supramundane m. 310:17
Mushrooms: broiled fowl and m. 178:27
Music: all kinds of m. 55:36
all the daughters of m. 51:33
along the Psalmist's m. deep 88:25
architecture. .frozen m. 415:20
ceasing of exquisite m. 316:13
chief m. of our May 189:18
city is built to m. 530:5
die in m. 473:29
discourse most eloquent m. 435:23
don't. .know anything about m. 40:1
eating ortolans to. .soft music 182:44
fading in m. 464:12
finds its food in m. 314:1
fled is that m. 288:2
formed, as notes of m. 493:8
from their own M.. .stray 124:2
great fish spouts m. 266:13
have m. wherever she goes 368:17
heaven is m. 123:17
heavy part the m. bears 279:28
he hears no m. 448:27
his voice in all her m. 492:9
honey of his m. vows 434:14
how sour sweet m. is 475:34
how sweet his m. 581:15
if M. and. .Poetry agree 35:19
if m. be the food of love 481:30
in sweet m. is such art 446:18
just accord all m. makes 502:7
let the sounds of m. creep 465:18
like harmony in m. 579:9
like m. on my heart 150:7
made his m. heard below 529:6
made thy M. 185:25
maintain the m. of the spheres 86:32
make one m. as before 531:42
make the m. mute 531:11
man that hath no m. 465:20
Master of all m. 318:2
mellow m. match'd with him 532:38
mind the m. and the step 33:6
m. alone. .can bind 155:1
m.. .change his nature 465:20
m. even in. .the silent note 86:32
m. has charms 155:18

Music (cont.)
M., heav'nly maid 153:31
m. he made with us 525:2
m. in its roar 114:26
m. in my heart I bore 581:4
m. is the brandy of the damned 490:20
m., moody food 424:11
M. of a distant Drum 205:25
m. of its trees 17:10
m. of men's lives 475:34
m. oft hath such a charm 462:17
m. of the Gospel 202:24
m.. .only sensual pleasure 277:7
m. out of doors 290:24
m. sent up to God 89:10
M. shall untune the sky 191:39
m. soars within. .lark 87:30
M., sphere-descended 154:3
m. sweet as love 498:6
m. sweeter than their own 578:31
m. that gentlier. . lies 535:14
m. that I care to hear 254:26
M., the greatest good 1:26
m. to hear, why hear'st thou m.
sadly? 486:13
m., when soft voices die 499:1
m. wherever there is a harmony 86:32
m., yearning like a god 285:16
no m. but a happy-noted voice 285:34
no m. in the nightingale 484:36
not for the doctrine, but the m. 382:30
of m., not of poetry 19:13
of whom m. and song. .are pure 336:37
pass'd in m. out of sight 534:16
perfect m. unto noble words 539:7
reasonable good ear in m. 467:14
sea-maid's m. 466:38
seduction of martial m. 104:1
Shelley with liquid m. 80:24
softest m. to attending ears 477:27
soft is the m. 578:3
solemn service of m. 306:28
some strain of m. 80:18
soul of m. shed 356:20
still, sad m. of humanity 582:1
stops of planetary m. 493:5
sweet compulsion. .in m. 339:26
sweet m. of speech 164:23
sweet m. with th' enamelled
stones 484:35
that m. still 580:26
that vulgar and tavern m. 86:33
their m.'s aid 319:1
this m. crept by me 479:29
thy beauty's silent m. 123:16
thy chosen m., Liberty 581:13
to his m. plants and flowers 446:18
to m. lendeth 501:20
tone of m.. .shall wound 114:5
towards the condition of m. 374:12
uproar's your only m. 289:22
we are the m. makers 370:19
what passion cannot M. raise 191:36
when I hear sweet m. 465:19
when m. arose 113:25
where m. dwells lingering 577:10
whose m. hell can move 123:27
whose m. is the gladness 196:35
with m. loud and long 151:33(–152)
women and m.. .dated 227:12
your voice is m. 40:1
Musical: as sweet and m. 455:22
most m., most melancholy
152:7, 341:13
most m. of mourners 491:15
m. as is Apollo's lute 340:24
Shakespeare, and the m. glasses 227:23
silence more m. 409:27
we were none of us m. 213:23
Music-hall singer 220:5
Musician: as a m. scatters sounds 574:18
dead, the sweet m. 318:2
lady is a m. 188:9
no better a m. than the wren 465:22
Musicians: we m. know 89:11
Music-maker: Schumann's our m.
now 91:8
Musing: m. full sadly 509:27
m. in solitude 574:5
m. there an hour alone 115:44
m. upon the king my brother 197:30

Musk: m. carnations break 18:26
  m. of the rose is blown 536:9
Musket: volleying m. 417:18
Musketiers: eines einzigen pommer-
  schen M. 72:31
Musk-rose: cankers in the m. buds 466:42
  coming m. 287:31
  m., and..woodbine 342:31(–343)
Musk-roses: sweet m. 466:41
Mussels: Cockles and m. 7:8
Must: forget because we m. 15:2
  Genius does what it m. 337:43
  if we can we m. 263:32
  in vain; which m. not be 96:16
  is *m.* a word..to princes? 198:13
  m. shall foam 323:12
  there m. be hell 97:6
  whispers low, *Thou m.* 199:32
Mustard: but to say, 'Pass the m.' 222:30
  grain of m. seed 59:28, 47
  what say you to..beef and m.? 479:8
Muster: inland petty spirits m. 442:21
  to join the m. came 323:14
Mustered: they m. their soldiers 31:14
Mustn't: tell her she m. 403:20
Musty: proverb is something m. 435:22
Mutable, rank-scented many 429:11
Mutability: M...her cruel sports 510:10
  m. of human affairs 178:25
  nor yet exempt..from..m. 497:12
  nought may endure but M. 495:20
Mutamur: nos et m. in illis 372:13
  nos m. in illis 13:15
Mutantur: tempora m. 13:15, 372:13
Mutari: omnia m. 25:13
Mutatus: quantum m. ab illo Hectore 554:6
Mute: ditty, long since m. 285:26
  haply m. 96:27
  if she be m. 413:31
  let's be m. 104:8
  m. and magnificent 193:40
  m. creation downward bend 194:25
  m. inglorious Milton 230:5
  natures that are m. 336:28
  now hangs as m. 356:20
  say she be m. 479:4
  soon m., however tuneful 309:13
Muteness: uncommunicating m.
  of fishes 307:30
Mutilated courtesy 227:18
Mutilators of collections 306:21
Mutiny: stones of Rome to ..m. 450:34
  sudden flood of m. 450:32
Mutter: in their sleeps..m. their
  affairs 472:8
Mutton: boiled leg of m. 179:19
  mince, muffins and m. 171:17
  old was his m. 251:29
  their love o' m. 320:1
  your beef, pork, and m. 294:34
Mutton-pies: make them into m. 131:22
Mutua: inter se mortales m. vivunt 321:1
Mutual: but to her m. breast 123:4
  m. and partaken bliss 340:37
  m. cowardice keeps us in peace 274:8
  m. destruction of arguments 205:7
  m. glance of great politeness 119:22
  such a m. pair 423:14
  when we meet a m. heart 546:7
Muzzle: not m. the ox 46:26
My: Orthodoxy or M.-doxy 126:18
My-lorded him 542:34
Mynheer Vandunck 154:17
Myra: at M.'s pocket-hole 74:9
Myriad-minded: our *m.* Shakespeare 152:27
Myriads: besotted m. of people 109:12
  of the m. who before us 206:27
  outshine the m. though bright 344:11
Myrica: arbusta..humilisque m. 555:30
Myrrh: bundle of m. is my well-
  beloved 51:42
  frankincense, and m. 57:24
Myrte: die M. still 224:6
Myrtle: cypress and m. 113:1
  instead of the brier..the m. 54:32
  m. and ivy 118:32
  soft m. 461:31
Myrtles: grove of m. 35:17
  with roses and with m. 190:34
  ye m. brown 342:10

Myself: best image of m. 348:3
  by m. walking 307:33
  celebrate m., and sing m. 567:9
  disappoint m. 227:1
  I can't explain *m.* 128:27
  I contradict m. 568:1
  I'm not m., you see 128:27
  know not..thee from m. 410:25
  m. am Hell 346:32
  m. and my Creator 363:14
  m. not least 540:32
  nothing of m. in me 165:31
  pray for no man but m. 480:21
  quite m. again 262:19
  resign m. to thee, O God 185:11
  thinking for m. 221:17
  when I give I give m. 567:21
Mysteries: stewards of the m. of
  God 66:24
  uncertainties, m., doubts 289:21
  what m... beyond thy dust 552:10
  wingy m. in divinity 86:7
Mysterious: moves in a m. way 161:18
  m. virtue of wax and parchment 101:1
  rites m. of connubial love 347:25
  that m. realm 98:3
  wedded love, m. law 347:26
Mystery: burthen of the m. 581:25
  comprehend its m. 317:15
  discredit our m. 462:18
  glad to death's m. 252:20
  in m. our soul abides 16:29
  into the m. of breath 335:28
  lay bare the m. to me 249:10
  lose myself in a m. 86:8
  love is such a m. 517:17
  lucrative business of m. 103:1
  marvel and a m. 316:37
  m. and a sign 141:32
  m., Babylon the Great 71:32
  m. of colour 489:21
  m. of man 579:34
  m. of words 579:25
  M. to Mathematics fly 381:27
  m...you must not touch 185:4
  Penetralium of m. 289:21
  pluck out the heart of my m. 435:24
  queens of higher m. 413:9
  reflection solves the m. 517:8
  take upon 's the m. of things 454:19
  where m. begins religion ends..
  justice ends 102:39
  wrapped up my buth in a m. 543:2
  your m., your m. 472:33
Mystic: m., wonderful 529:42
  owns the m. rod 96:33
  walk your m. way 220:26
  what m. fruit 199:8
Mystical: m. body of thy Son
  389:55, 390:46
  m. Germans 220:4
  m. lore 122:22
  m. mathematics 85:19
  m. way of Pythagoras 86:10
Mythic: almost m. time 375:19

N

N. or M. 391:2
Nabob: savage old N. 324:30
Nactus: Spartam n. es 145:2
Nadir: crossed the n. 264:2
Nag: de bob-tail n. 210:13
Naiad: guardian N. 416:15
  N. 'mid her reeds 286:4
  thy N. airs 380:17
Nail: Dick..blows his n. 456:1
  fasten him as a n. 53:28
  for want of a n. 211:10
  n. my head on yonder tower 24:5
  n.'t wi' Scripture 105:6
  one n...drives out another 484:34
  smote the n. into his temples 46:46
  taller by..the breadth of my n. 519:9
Nailed: n. for our advantage 438:12
  pierced and n. Him 565:14
Nails: blowing of his n. 445:44
  come near..with my n. 445:29
  Devil he blew upon his n. 302:32

Nails (cont.)
  'Hard'..'As n.' 177:38
  his n., which were taper 238:37
  my n. are drove 8:13
  n. bitten 325:28
  print of the n. 64:9
  system of Prince's n. 174:33
Naître: vous vous êtes donné la peine
  de n. 37:11
Naked: half n., loving, natural 115:36
  he but n., though..in steel 445:30
  helpless, n., piping loud 76:8
  in n. majesty 347:10
  lash the rascals n. 473:2
  leave the n. brain 284:23
  n., and ye clothed me 60:33
  n., come to thee 548:12
  n. Duke of Windlestraw 127:9
  n. every day he clad 225:19
  n. hulk alongside came 149:13
  n...like a forked radish 442:15
  n. new-born babe 457:9
  n. new-born child 279:19
  n. shingles of the world 15:7
  n. summer night 567:16
  n...the best disguise 154:36
  n. they came 537:31
  n. thinking heart 184:9
  n. to mine enemies 447:1
  n. to the hangman's noose 202:12
  on Nilus' mud..stark n. 425:34
  our ingress..n. and bare 318:9
  poor n. wretches 453:14
  wallow n. in December snow 474:20
Nakedness: n. of the land 45:20
  n. of woman 77:16
  not in utter n. 576:9
Namancos: looks toward N. 343:2
Name: age without a n. 357:22
  arm, arm, my n.! 475:3
  bearing the owner's n. 507:12
  before we have..a n. 306:7
  Ben Adhem's n. led 265:18
  blazoning the n. of Adonais 493:18
  bless your n. 92:31
  breathe not his n. 356:29
  but a n. for an effect 163:32
  calls upon my n. 477:27
  change the n. 11:6
  deed without a n. 460:3
  everlasting n. 54:33
  filches from me my good n. 471:30
  for his own n.'s sake 421:1
  form his n. 151:20
  frailty, thy n. is woman 430:33(–431)
  friendship..is but a n. 215:29
  from another place..my n. 510:21
  gathered together in my n. 59:52
  gathered together in thy N. 388:33
  give the ill..a n. 19:5
  God's own n. upon a lie 162:23
  good n. 50:29, 51:9, 471:30
  good travelling n. 203:13
  halloo your n. 482:22
  hallowed be thy n. 58:4
  he is callèd by thy n. 76:10
  he left a Corsair's n. 115:7
  her n. is never heard 36:31
  her n. upon the strand 509:7
  his former n. is heard no more 348:17
  his N. and sign who bear 264:13
  his N. only is excellent 400:25
  his n. on the Abbey-stones 92:38
  his n. painted..on each 128:5
  his n. shall be called Wonderful 53:15
  his n. shall be lost for evermoe 419:17
  how sweet the n. of Jesus 364:15
  I am become a n. 540:32
  if my n. were liable to fear 448:27
  if that n. thou love 573:28
  if thou hast no n. 471:21
  I have forgotten your n. 524:10
  I have no n. 76:12
  in a borrowed n. 401:38
  injur'd neither n. 250:25
  in the N. of the Empress 300:12
  in the N. of the Lord 391:18, 399:12
  in the n. of the Prophet 504:11
  in the stone a new n. 70:31
  I sing the N. 165:33
  king's n. is a tower 476:34

Name (*cont.*)

king's n. twenty thousand names 475:3
knew thy face or n. 184:4
leaving here a n. 507:32
left a n. behind them 57:17
lesser than my n. 475:9
let me not n. it to you 473:11
local habitation and a n. 467:24
lose the n. of action 434:4
lose the n. of king 475:10
lost her honest n. 9:18
magic of a n. 122:34
many-memoried n. 72:24
my n. and memory, I leave 28:15
my n. be wiped out 509:7
my n. is Legion 60:57
my n. is Mud 172:13
my n. is Used-to-was 548:19
my n...not so terrible 441:25
my n...numbered among theirs 578:22
my 'oss, my wife, and my n. 518:29
my verse extoll'd thy n. 125:1
n., at which the world grew pale 279:6
n. dearer or purer 117:32
n. great in story 118:32
n. of...God..defend thee 392:35
n. of the beast 71:21
n. of the one was Obstinate 99:5
n. to all..ages curst 190:13
n. to every fixed star 454:32
n. which is above every n. 68:18
naming a dubious n. 92:10
Nelson's peerless n. 362:31
no more must change their n. 573:30
no n...not faint at last 309:13
no profit but the n. 436:14
not blot out his n. 70:32
nothing but an empty n. 143:2
nothing of a n. 114:38
of every friendless n. 275:1
o' Hope's one n., let it go 475:10
one Hope's one n. be there 411:23
one n. was Elizabeth 280:11
our n. is heard no more 160:30
our very n. as Englishmen 379:15
poor wounded n. 484:32
praise the N. of the Lord 400:25
proud his n. 417:22
rack the n. of God 329:25
remember the N. of the Lord 392:37
rose by any other n. 477:16
Sacco's n. will live 551:13
set down my n., Sir 99:7
signed by God's n. 567:24
spared the n. 521:3
stain'd his n. 104:20
still the n. do bide the seäme 35:14
takes a specious n. 586:27
take the N. of..God in vain 390:8
terror of my n. 331:2
that slow sweet n. 91:29
that was the n.! 515:12
their n. liveth 57:19
thy n. in high account 418:14
thy n. is an ointment 51:38
thy N., O Jesu 264:8
to all men be Thy n. known 81:3
to that n...prove my title 426:10
trembled at the hideous n 346:8
we are callèd by His n. 76:10
we will not ask her n. 123:4
what a wounded n. 438:4
what crimes..in thy n. 408:15
what is your n.? 391:2
what n. Achilles assumed 87:12
what's in a n.? 477:16
what the dickens his n. is 466:4
what thy lordly n. is 380:25
whistling of n. 384:12
whose n. was writ in water 291:3
with a n. like yours..any shape 131:4
without a stone, a n. 381:36
Wolfe's great n. compatriot 163:1
write upon him my new n. 70:33
write your glorious n. 509:7
your n. with worthy wights to reign 233:3
your n., your laws..a cursed past 551:13

Named: n. all the birds without a gun 199:11
nor n. thee but to praise 234:15

Nameless: n. here for evermore 380:23
n. in worthy deeds 87:15
n., unremembered acts 581:24
now thou art a n. thing 118:19
Names: all by their n. 400:21
allow their n. to be mentioned 23:4
all the other n. there are 141:31
bright n. will hallow song 113:37
bring back the old n. 152:10
call'd him soft n. 287:32
called on poisonous n. 494:5
called them by wrong n. 89:40
commodity of good n. 438:21
deathless lot to n. ignoble 160:37
five handmaidens, whose n. 410:12
forget men's n. 447:19
from common n. 101:10
home of..unpopular n. 19:10
I have lost all the n. 274:33
I know the scientific n. 221:32
in the n. of all the gods 448:23
lands after their own n. 395:1
n. of those who love the Lord 265:16
n...on every infant's tongue 120:23
n. that men remember 523:10
n. that must not wither 113:44
not unholy n. 176:12
our n., familiar in his mouth 444:28
our souls were in our n. 336:16
play so nicely with their n. 474:25
seeing our n. in print 142:2
such great n. as these 9:24
syllable men's n. 340:10
those rugged n. 351:17
twenty more such n. 478:46
two most sacred n. 158:3
unpronounceable awful n. 239:3
very n. of things beloved 80:23
worshipp'd by the n. divine 74:22
your n., remembered 81:21
Nan: change Kate into N. 74:22
Nancy: his N. on his knees 219:17
Lady N. she died 31:9
mate of the N. brig 218:14
Nantes: apparent rari n. 553:10
Nap: the sun.. his n. 110:43
Napier: Admiral N., K.C.B. 543:10
Napkins: their n. in his sacred blood 450:24
Naples: his blindest eye on N. 410:19
Napoleon: ashes of N. Buonaparte 564:25
be a N. and yet disbelieve 89:35
N. forgot Blücher 143:33
N. of crime 187:26
N. of the realms of rhyme 116:33
such opportunity, except N. 116:28
Napping: I nodded, nearly n. 380:22
Naps: old John N. of Greece 478:46
Narcissa: poor N. 384:25
Narr: der bleibt ein N. 321:5
Narration: whole n. always going backwards 558:15
Narrative: bald and unconvincing n. 220:13
Narrow: cultivated by n. minds 338:22
make it saft and n. 30:3
n., and low 165:34
n. is the way 58:24
n. vergèd shade 332:13
that plain was but n. 99:18
these two n. words 405:13
tread the N. Way 295:2
wand'rer from the n. way 161:26
Narrow'd his mind 225:27
Narrows the world 336:39
Naso suspendis adunco ignotos 261:18
Nassau go higher? 401:28
Nasticreechia 311:8
Nasty: man of n. ideas 520:43
n., brutish, and short 248:21
something n. in the woodshed 217:15
where nice is n. 218:6
Nasum: totum ut te faciant..n. 132:20
Nata mecum consule Manlio 260:10
Natale: libertas at n. solum 521:10
n. solum..ducit 372:8
Nation: American n. in th' Sixth Ward 195:9
better for the n. 6:20
better..than a n. grieve 190:20

Nation (*cont.*)

burden of the n.'s care 402:5
clearly top n. 422:17
curled darlings of our n. 469:41
disenchanted n. 496:23
greatest inquest of the n. 101:22
guiding-star of a..n. 359:23
he hates our sacred n. 403:17
holy n. 69:48
in a N.'s eye 575:11
little n. leave to live 313:4
march of a n. 373:17
mourning of a mighty n. 537:11
n., not a city 182:15
n. of amateurs 409:9
n. of gallant men 102:11
n. of pure philosophers 28:32
n. of sectaries 181:41
n. of shopkeepers 1:6, 360:22, 503:11
n...perpetually to be conquered 100:26
n. shall not lift up sword against n. 52:31
n. shall rise against n. 60:23
N. spoke to a N. 300:1
nerves a n.'s heart 528:12
new n., conceived in liberty 314:19
noble and puissant n. 352:15
no n...ruined by trade 211:6
no n. wanted it so much 521:4
old, and haughty n. 340:2
publish it to all the n. 401:27
rather a foul-mouthed n. 240:10
righteousness exalteth a n. 50:9
talent of our English n. 193:23
things that matter for a n. 216:7
this n., under God 314:12
thou hast multiplied the n. 53:14
what makes a n. happy 350:14
with us, or..with any n. 102:19
Youth of a N...trustees 182:31
Nation: une n. de boutiquiers 360:22
National Debt: N. is a very Good Thing 422:15
n...national blessing 234:20, 563:2
Nationalities: rights of the smaller n. 21:6
Nationless: tribeless, and n. 497:12
Nations: all n., and kindreds 71:3
all n. shall do him service 396:25
among all n. 396:2
belong to other n. 221:25
cheap defence of n. 102:12
day of small n. 135:6
eclipsed the gaiety of n. 278:7
eclipse..on half the n. 345:6
enrich unknowing n. 168:9
extends over many n. 188:19
fierce contending n. 1:25
friendship with all n. 268:21
healing of the n. 72:7
language all n. understand 40:11
law of nature, and of n. 101:26
lightning of the n. 495:25
like the happiest n...no history 196:26
make enemies of n. 162:41
manners of different n. 514:35
men in n.;—all were his 115:45
n.' airy navies 534:22
n. are as a drop 54:12
n., like men..infancy 78:14
n. slowly wise 279:4
n. touch at their summits 29:2
n. underground 545:4
n. under our feet 394:30
news from all n. 163:20
Niobe of n. 114:13
pedigree of n. 276:2
plagued the n. 162:15
Privileged and..People.. Two N. 182:29
Rome is above the N. 301:29
Saviour of the N. 116:22
teaching n. how to live 352:24
to foreign n. 28:15
truth whereby the n. live 295:6
willing n. knew their..lord 190:31
Native: blue sky..their n. country 149:24
breathe his n. air 386:26
considerable in his n. place 272:5
fast by their n. shore 162:9

Native (cont.)
guard our n. seas	123:10
less n. to high Heaven	544:3
my n. land—Good Night	113:7
my n. shore fades	113:6
my song comes n.	289:9
n. of the rocks	270:17
n. to famous wits	350:11
not more n. to the heart	430:25
this is..my n. land	417:22
though I am n. here	431:31
trusting n. races	143:31
with n. honour clad	347:10
Natives: Graces..not..n.	139:24
n. of Borrioboola-Gha	173:24
Nativity: at my n...fiery shapes	439:40
my n. was under Ursa Major	452:20
n., chance or death	466:14
out of love with your n.	428:17
stars that reigned at my n.	330:9
Natura: si n. negat	282:24
Naturae..non imperatur, nisi parendo	28:9
Natural: all thy children..n.	443:13
as n. to die	26:3
childish, but very n.	152:11
follow his n. bent	303:13
from mere n. virtue	363:26
generalities of n. right	142:25
he wants the n. touch	460:17
I do it more n.	482:30
imagery should..come n. to him	289:27
irresistible n. laws	310:18
loving, n., and Greek	115:36
more than n.	433:19
n. interest of money	325:8
n. to please	190:9
on the stage he was n.	225:32
ruined on the side of their n. propensities	103:14
so far from being n...marriage	272:6
twice as n.	131:18
what is n. cannot touch me	201:31
Natural History: [Goldsmith] writing a N.	272:18
Natural Philosophy: mother of the sciences [n.]	28:8
n., deep	27:19
Natural Selection	169:6
Naturaleza: los buenos pintores imitan la n.	134:19
Naturally: he was n. learn'd	194:6
if poetry comes not as n.	289:28
Naturam expellas furca	257:2
Nature: accuse not N.	349:2
action lies in his true n.	435:35
against the use of n.	450:24
all n. cries aloud	1:23
all n. is but art unknown	383:21
all N. seems at work	152:17
all N. was degraded	73:16
all n., without voice	503:3
allow not n. more than n. needs	452:41
all that n...could frame	510:6
at ease in N.	566:26
beauty is N.'s brag	340:38
beauty is N.'s coin	340:37
Beldam N.	352:1
better N.'s best	421:7
bow the mind unto the n. of things	24:16
breathless N.'s dark abyss	575:1
built by N. for herself	474:22
by n. honest	386:4
by viewing n., n.'s handmaid art	191:29
can't be N...not sense	142:33
carry n. lengths unknown	162:26
command n. except by obeying	28:9
common-place of N.	573:22
Dame n.'s menstralis	187:4
disguise fair n.	443:24
drive n. out with a pitchfork	257:2
enough, for n.'s ends	327:14
everything..which is N.'s	498:14
except the blind forces of N.	327:12
eye N.'s walks	383:8
fair defect of N.	349:23
fancy outwork n.	424:6
fault was N.'s fault	119:31
following N.'s lights	357:19

Nature (cont.)
fools call N.	96:12
frailty of our n.	389:30
free as n. first made man	191:41
fresh from N.'s mould	176:24
from the tomb the voice of N.	230:9
fulfils great N.'s plan	105:25
graver had a strife with N.	281:9
great Secretary of N.	559:29
happy n. to explore	383:29
Heaven and N...strive	280:10
hem of N.'s shift	496:17
hold..the mirror up to n.	434:17
I do fear thy n.	457:1
I feel the link of n.	349:18
if honest N. made you fools	105:23
if thou hast n. in thee	432:17
in a state of war by n.	521:21
in N...nothing melancholy	152:7
in N.'s mystic book	333:10
in n...there are consequences	267:17
in N. were inconstancy	158:11
in our life alone..N. live	151:4
I suppose it is my n.	20:27
jarr'd against n.'s chime	351:11
law of n., and of nations	101:26
learned to look on n.	582:1
let N. be your teacher	581:15
light of n...led him to..God	24:18
little we see in N.	582:18
lore which N. brings	581:16
made one with N.	492:9
man hath all which N. hath	19:2
masterpiece of N.	200:16
mere copier of n.	406:11
muse on N.	122:35
music..change his n.	465:20
mute N. mourns	417:20
my n. and the terror	331:2
my n. could not bear it so	451:27
my n. is subdu'd	488:6
naked n., and the living grace	382:26
n. admits no lie	126:38
N...almost lost in Art	154:4
N. always does contrive	219:6
N. and N.'s laws lay hid	382:17
n...better by no mean but n. makes	485:24
n. could no farther go	193:9
n. could not sorrow hide	232:3
N. from her seat sighing	349:15
n. has cast me in so soft a mould	191:19
n. hath fram'd strange fellows	462:30
n. her custom holds	437:2
N., Hope, and Poesy	152:20
N. I loved	308:25
n. in awe to him	343:11
n. in you..on the very verge	452:39
N. is always wise	547:16
n. is but a name	163:52
N. is creeping up	566:7
n. is fine in love	436:29
n. is loth to yield to art	80:29
n. is often hidden	26:39
n. is the art of God	86:12
n. is usually wrong	566:5
n., kindly bent	521:1
N. knows a thing or two	421:7
N. made her what she is	104:25
n. made thee to temper man	371:12
N. made us men	320:8
n. must obey necessity	451:30
N. never did betray	582:3
N., not the God of N.	244:27
n. of the times deceas'd	442:6
N., red in tooth and claw	532:37
N. say one thing	103:16
n.'s changing course	486:18
n.'s copy's not eterne	459:6
N.'s darling	231:10
n. seems dead	458:1
N.'s fault alone	143:26
n.'s great law	17:14
N.'s infinite book of secrecy	423:16
n.'s journeyman	434:20
N.'s law..made to mourn	107:1
N.'s law to change	407:16
n.'s own sweet..hand	482:20
n.'s patient..Eremite	288:17
N.'s pride, and richest furniture	330:23
N.'s priest	576:9

Nature (cont.)
n.'s second course	458:11
N.'s signal of retreat	279:14
N.'s social union	107:10
n.'s soft nurse	441:41
N.'s sole mistake	221:41
n.'s sternest painter	117:26
N.'s sweet restorer	586:29
N. stood recover'd	193:38
n.'s true-born child	292:17
n.'s vast frame	492:19
N...take the pen	19:19
n. that fram'd us	330:28
N. that is above all art	168:6
n. then..to me was all in all	581:26
n. to advantage dressed	382:27
N. was his book	77:24
N. wears one..grin	204:34
n., with equal mind	15:12
n. yet remembers	576:17
not man the less but N. more	114:26
not otherwise, O N.	574:4
o'erbearing n.	469:43
o'erstep not the modesty of n.	434:16
of a free and open n.	470:22
of an open and free n.	280:1
old n. swears	106:2
one informed by the light of n.	24:17
one of N.'s agreeable blunders	158:27
one spark o' N.'s fire	105:24
one touch of n.	481:21
on Man, on N...musing	574:5
paid the debt of n.	203:1
pattern of excelling n.	473:11
Poets that are sown by N.	574:10
prodigality of N.	476:9
prophets of N.	579:38
rest on N. fix	148:8
restore the tone of languid N.	162:36
secret aims of n.	80:26
shares the n. of infinity	573:7
simple life that N. yields	165:18
simple n. to his hope	383:11
so priketh hem n.	136:22
stars, that n. hung in heaven	340:9
strong propensity of n.	352:21
such by n. still I am	192:23
such..stupidity..not in N.	271:14
sullenness against N. not to go out	352:29
that age..can lay on n.	452:9
that N. might stand up	452:9
then n. rul'd	215:11
they perfect n.	27:15
thorough knowledge of human n.	22:22
thou and n...so gently part	426:11
thoughts that n. gives way to	457:18
through n. to eternity	430:29
through n. up to n.'s God	384:14
thy n. is not..less divine	577:1
'tis their n. too	561:24
to n. true	143:23
to read N.; he looked inwards	194:6
to write..comes by n.	468:34
transgression of a law of n.	265:6
universal blank of N.'s works	346:20
universal N. did lament	342:18
visitings of n.	457:3
volume of n...book of knowledge	226:20
vows can't change n.	95:33
wait on n.'s mischief	457:3
weakness of our mortal n.	389:40
we fools of n.	431:32(-432)
what n. itselfe cant endure	208:22
what we call the laws of N.	266:20
when N. has work to be done	201:8
when N. him began	189:3
whole frame of n...break	3:2
whole realm of n.	562:19
whose body n. is	383:18
with strength and n. make amends for art	412:13
womb of n.	346:12
youth of primy n.	431:20
Naturel: le style n.	373:21
Natures: dearth of noble n.	284:20
ignominy of our n.	86:19
n. that are mute	336:28
other n. thinks different	176:17
season of all n., sleep	459:26

Naughtiness: n. of thine heart 47:20
  superfluity of n. 69:31
Naughty: congregations of n. men 397:11
  good deed in a n. world 465:21
  he is a n. child 515:20
  his former n. life 390:2
  n. night to swim in 453:22
Nauseate: I n. walking 156:10
Nauseous draught 192:15
Naval: his figurative n. manner 173:30
Navarre: helmet of N. 323:5
Navel: thy n. is like a round goblet 52:18
Navem: ubi n. ascenderitis 39:1
Navibus atque quadrigis 257:4
Navies: nations' airy n. 534:26
  when n. are stranded 419:4
  your nutshell n. came 296:4
Navigation: swallow n. up 460:4
Navigators: heard other n. say the same 237:1
Navis: dum tua n. in alto est 257:9
Navita de ventis 402:15
Navy: fired by the British N. 232:17
  if..the..n., had fair play 310:25
  load would sink a n. 446:26
  n. of Charles the Second 326:2
  royal n. of England 73:6
  Ruler of the Queen's N. 221:15
  upon the n...safety..attend 136:2
  your n...rotten timber 101:13
Nay: Mr. Hall's n. was n. 42:24
  say n., say n., for shame 583:18
  say thee n. 477:20
  Yea, yea; N., n. 57:49
  your n., n. 69:43
Nayed him twice 232:4
Nazareth: any good thing..out of N. 63:3
Né: l'homme est n. libre 412:2
Neæra: tangles of N.'s hair 342:20
Near: be n. me now 525:4
  come not n. our fairy queen 466:44
  dead..still be n. us 532:28
  far or forgot..is n. 199:4
  he comes too n...to be denied 371:14
  n. and far, ray on ray 97:13
  n. each other move 493:22
  n. or far, hiddenly 545:5
  one n. one is too far 90:10
  she is n., she is n. 536:15
  so n. and yet so far 533:16
  so n. is God to man 199:32
  to him that is n. 54:34
  while he is n. 54:30
Nearer: daily, n. God 291:7
  Love..drew n. to me 244:21
  moved a little n. 318:2
  n. and n. draws the time 3:8
  n. is to France 129:24
  n. my Father's house 131:32
  n. one yet, than all others 252:21
  n. than hands and feet 529:38
  n. the Church 4:23
  one n. to God's Altar 166:13
  our salvation n. 66:13
  saw her upon n. view 580:20
Nearest: best which lieth n. 316:24
  catch the n. way 457:1
  duty which lies n. 127:20
  freed his soul the n. way 275:4
  n. and dearest enemy 440:10
  n. run thing you ever saw 564:2
Nearly: live more n. as we pray 291:8
Neat: credit..to be n. 527:7
  n., and trimly dress'd 438:32
  n. as can be..Miss T. 171:17
  n., but not gaudy 565:21
  n. little, sweet little craft 222:8
  n., not gaudy 307:7
  n.'s tongue dried 462:36
  new and n. and..tall 140:8
  not clean and n. 515:20
  still to be n. 280:7
  this lass so n. 327:5, 551:5
Neater, sweeter, maiden 299:14
Neat-handed Phyllis 342:2
Neatness of apparel 565:20
Neat's-leather: ever trod upon n. 448:6
  Spanish or n. 110:39
Nebo's lonely mountain 3:16

Nebuchadnezzar the king 55:35
Nebula: remota erroris n. 283:15
Necessaries: talk of the n. of life 215:33
Necessary: death, a n. end 449:22
  government..a n. evil 373:1
  harmless n. cat 464:28
  in n. things, unity 36:25
  n. to salvation 391:12, 401:3
  notes..n. evils 278:22
  only n. to mention Asparagus 175:38
  plots..n. things 190:11
  requisite and n. 388:9
  when it is not n. to change 203:2
Necessitas: n. dat legem 526:5
  n. non habet legem 526:6
Nécessité: je n'en vois pas la n.
              14:11, 412:3
Necessities: art of our n. 453:11
  dispense with its n. 359:24
  feigned n., imaginary n. 167:11
Necessity: by n...all quote 201:5
  danger, n., and tribulation 389:2
  forsworn 'on mere n.' 454:35
  his n. to glorious gain 575:6
  I do not see the n. 14:11, 412:3
  Mountains of N. 18:2
  nature must obey n. 451:30
  n. and chance approach not me 348:25
  n. hath no law 167:11
  n. invented stools 162:34
  n. is the plea 379:14
  n. makes..a knave 170:10
  n. never made a good bargain 211:12
  n. of subduing again 100:26
  n., the tyrant's plea 347:10
  no virtue like n. 474:19
  progress..a n. 508:27
  sworn brother..to grim N. 475:27
  teach thy n. to reason 474:19
  thy n. is yet greater 502:12
  travelled..out of n. 512:18
  villains by n. 452:18
Neck: bowed his glossy n. 365:18
  his n. brake 47:9
  his n. unto a second yoke 247:9
  Item, One n. 482:21
  left his straight n. bent 411:11
  lith in their n. 21:14
  my n. is very short 358:7
  n. God made for other use 262:12
  n. or nought 160:1
  n. when once broken 559:5
  o'er a soldier's n. 477:7
  Pegasus's n. 381:21
  proudly-arched and glossy n. 365:16
  ringdove's n. from changing 123:5
  Roman people..but one n. 120:18
  some chicken! some n.! 144:9
  thy n. is as a tower 52:19
  thy n. is like the tower 52:5
  with a broken n., the crocus 336:44
Necks: n. in thunder clothed 231:14
  stretched forth n. 52:35
Nectar: draws n. in a sieve 152:18
  of Jove's n. sup 280:21(-281)
  sprinkles..with n. 308:18
  they lie beside their n. 535:19
Nectared: feast of n. sweets 340:24
Nectarine and curious peach 332:17
Nectarous: not the n. poppy 16:5
Ned: John's, and N.'s 236:8
  poor old N. 210:19
Need: all we n. of hell 180:3
  all ye n. to know 287:15
  as in earnest n. 92:44
  deserted at his utmost n. 191:7
  England hath n. of thee 577:14
  faith, we shall n. it 303:19
  God doth not n...man's work 351:10
  good at n. 417:10
  helps good hearts in n. 170:24
  help us in our utmost n. 318:6
  in such hour of n. 17:20
  most quiet n. 88:24
  n. a body cry? 104:31
  n. nor heart nor hands 516:1
  n. of a world of men 94:27
  n. thou hast..of me 254:16
  never want a friend in n. 175:9
  no n. of such vanity 468:35
  nothing can n. a lie 243:27

Need (cont.)
  sorrow, n., sickness 390:29
  suit and serve his n. 244:10
  thy n. is yet greater than mine 502:12
  wash in n. 11:5
  what can I want or n.? 245:10
  what we chiefly n. 130:17
  when our n. was the sorest 416:22
  why do we n. them? 124:3
Needed: all are n. by each 199:9
  he n. not the spectacles of books 194:6
  I n. not to have come 135:28
  showing them they were not n. 41:11
  things Youth n. not 573:15
Needest: what n. thou such weak witness? 351:8
Needful: one thing is n. 61:45
Needle: for the n. she 538:24
  hinders n. and thread 253:27
  plying her n. and thread 253:22
  through the eye of a n. 60:3
  touched n. trembles 386:28
  true as the n. 78:18
  wi' her n. an' her sheers 104:34
Needles: thy n...now rust 160:22
Needle-work: in raiment of n. 394:25
Needn't: it n. come to that 131:9
  you n. shout so loud 131:12
Needs: according to his n. 29:14, 333:12
  more than nature n. 452:41
  n. of a rational being 421:8
  n. spirit lack all life behind? 96:26
  what n. my Shakespeare 351:8
Needy Knife-grinder 124:7
Nefanda: omnia fanda n...permixta 133:10
Nefas: ruit per vetitum n. 258:6
Negation of God erected into a system 223:1
Negative Capability 289:21
Neglect: both n. 435:32
  I n. God and his Angels 186:32
  most tender mercy..n. 165:20
  not defer or n. it 232:10
  such sweet n. 280:7
  wise and salutary n. 100:25
Neglected: have his all n. 270:16
  he, n. and oppress'd 416:29
  virtues n. then 164:30
Neglectful: cuff n. 246:4
Negligences: sins, n., and ignorances 389:7
Negligent: too often a n. elf 34:7
Negligentiae torpor 414:21
Negligently: never n. yet 561:9
Negotiate: whilst our souls n. 184:31
Negotiations: Man propounds n. 296:14
Negro: respecting his n. friend 38:17
Negroes: among the drivers of n. 278:20
  providing the infant n. 178:43
Neiges: les n. d'antan 553:3
Neighbour: accommodating n. 187:27
  better mouse-trap than his n. 201:22
  borrowed my n.'s wife 302:31
  calls in a powerful N. 512:4
  coveted his n.'s goods 294:6
  death..his next-door n. 420:6
  done evil to his n. 392:24
  hate your n...love your n.'s wife 325:18
  helping every feeble n. 227:34
  his hungering n. 320:18
  life has death for n. 523:19
  love thy n. as thyself 46:9, 59:57
  my duty towards my N. 391:5
  n.'s name to lash 105:27
  n. to Despair 18:13
  neighed after his n.'s wife 55:11
  our n. and our work 291:6
  our n.'s house..on fire 102:4
  policy of the good n. 408:21
  removeth his n.'s landmark 46:27
  that he might rob a n. 324:34
  to my N. honestly 316:32
  to my n's gate 336:39
  to thy n.'s creed 199:9
Neighbouring: cynosure of n. eyes 342:1
Neighbours: call your n. in 366:14
  from every house..n. met 532:22
  good fences make good n. 212:3

Neighbours (cont.)
good n. I have had 198:10
holding their n.' tails 298:20
in love and charity with your n. 390:34
make sport for our n. 23:5
n. o'er the Herring Pond 195:11
what is happening to our n. 135:7
Neighed after his neighbour's wife 55:11
Neighs: high and boastful n. 444:6
Neither: 'tis n. here nor there 473:7
n. way inclines 424:21
to n. a word will I say 215:4
Nell: pretty witty N. 377:25
writ of Little N. 238:25
Nelly: let not poor N. starve 136:8
Nelson: death of N. 508:11
end by N.'s urn 141:14
keep the N. touch 363:8
N.'s peerless name 362:31
N. turned his blindest eye 140:19
of N. and the North 122:3
of N. only a touch 93:36
sent..the N. touch 362:14
Nemean: hardy as the N. lion 432:3
Nephew: beamish n. 128:10
n. of Fox 250:25
Nephews: their n. and their nieces 515:24
Neptune: all great N.'s ocean 458:15
flatter N. for his trident 429:13
N.'s park 429:29
upon whose influence N.'s empire 430:15
Nequiores: nos n. 260:1
Nereides: her gentlewomen, like the N. 424:7
Nero is an angler 453:28
Nerve: who am as a n. 494:16
Nerves: my firm n...never tremble 459:20
my poor n. 23:1
strengthens our n. 102:27
to expredge my n. 176:35
Nervii: day he overcame the N. 450:27
Nervous: vocabulary of 'Bradshaw' is n. 188:27
Nest: as a n. with birds 375:9
builds the phoenix' n. 166:2
heart and eye both with thy n. 580:26
her soft and chilly n. 285:22
her young ones in her n. 460:17
his n. of wishes 337:18
in her n. at peep of day 540:9
in the North..my n. 538:21
in thy balmy n. 166:5
learn the n. 531:5
leaves his wat'ry n. 169:13
leaves the well-built n. 494:21
n. of singing birds 270:3
n. which thou canst drop into 580:26
only a tumble-down n. 571:7
Phoenix..her spicy n. 125:11
plumage that had warm'd his n. 117:25
swallow a n...lay her young 397:5
we'll theek our n. 32:15
whose n. is in a watered shoot 409:14
within mine eyes..his n. 231:39
Nestle: shall I n. near thy side? 495:23
Nestling me everywhere 254:17
Nestor swear..laughable 462:30
Nests: birds..have n. 58:34
birds in their little n. 41:35, 561:27
built their n. in my beard 311:2
in Cleopatra's sails their n. 425:16
n. in order rang'd 351:2
these to their n...slunk 347:19
wherein the birds make their n. 398:10
Net: at thy word..let down the n. 61:27
fain would fling the n. 336:10
in vain the n. is spread 49:38
laid a n. for my feet 395:18
N. Anything reticulated 277:28
they carried a n. 377:1
Nether: gnaw..your n. lip 473:13
piece of the n. millstone 49:31
within the n. tip 149:16
Nets: fall into their own n. 400:15
fine n. and stratagems 245:5
laws are..n. 499:18
making n., not..cages 520:40
n. of wrong and right 584:19
tangled in amorous n. 350:1

Netting: only n. strawberries 296:33
Nettle: stroke a n. 248:10
this n., danger 439:9
Nettles: burdocks, hemlock, n. 454:2
crow-flowers, n., daisies 437:1
Neues: im Western nichts N 406:7
Neutral: loyal and n. 458:25
studiously n. 571:11
Neutrality: armed n. 571:12
cold n. of an impartial judge 100:18
for a word—'n.' 43:22
Neutralize: white shall not n. the black 96:14
Never: beheld what n. was to be 116:15
escape me? N. 92:41
he n. will come again 436:35
kiss me and n. no more 328:19
n. alone 152:16
n. be met with again 128:10
n. doubted clouds would break 97:4
n. ending, still beginning 191:9
n. glad confident morning 93:7
n., I aver, since Ariadne 285:2
n. jam to-day 130:27
n...lay down my arms 379:8
n. lov'd sae kindly 104:11
n. may I commence my song 95:37
n. met—or n. parted 104:11
n. more, Sailor 171:19
n., n., n., n., n. 454:26
n., n., since I joined 222:24
n. pry—lest we lose 97:25
N. Smiled Again 241:11
n. the time and the place 93:38
n. the twain shall meet 294:27
n. to be disquieted 292:19
n. *you* mind 218:12
no more—Oh, n. more 494:18
such names and men..which n. were 478:46
this will n. do 268:31
unalterably, n. yours 176:36
what, n.? No, n.! 221:11
what n. yet was heard 340:3
whose goodness faileth n. 29:12
Nevermore: grows n. again 88:12
quoth the Raven, 'N.' 380:27
weep now or n. 380:19
Never-never: your 'N. country' 296:10
New: adversity is the blessing of the N. 25:18
against the n. and untried 314:7
always old and always n. 95:39
among n. men, strange faces 531:34
as n. what ev'ry body knows 159:16
avoid the wild and n. 141:20
both of the n. and old 571:9
brave n. world 480:15
bringer of n. things 540:32 (-541)
by whom the n. are tried 382:29
dull in a n. way 272:23
finde wordes n. 137:23
fitter for n. projects 27:41
hear some n. thing 64:59
his old times are still n. 236:42
how strange it seems, and n. 93:23
I make all things n. 71:45
intend to lead a n. life 390:34
look amaist as weel's the n. 104:34
makes all things n. 529:11
my adventure brave and n. 95:18
n. all art 338:10
n. and neat and..tall 140:8
n. deal 408:19
n. every morning 291:4
n. friend is as n. wine 56:40
n. heaven and a n. earth 71:44
n. heavens and a n. earth 55:9
n. is not comparable 56:40
n. man..raised up 390:57
n. nation, conceived in liberty 314:12
n. nobility..act of power 26:42
n. one, straight to the self-same 92:43
n. people takes the land 141:27
n. truths..begin as heresies 266:24
N. Way to Pay Old Debts 334:22
n. wine into old bottles 58:42
no n. thing under the sun 50:61
on with the n. 7:22, 335:4
out of his treasure things n. and old 59:31

New (cont.)
pleasure eternally n. 309:25
ring in the n. 533:18
she flourisheth n. and n. 502:19
songs for ever n. 287:10
that n. world which is the old 528:28
trail that is always n. 298:27
when a n. book is published 408:14
whether it be n. or old 516:21(-517)
whose lip mature is ever n. 285:39
yet nothing n. 276:14
New-bath'd stars emerge 17:28(-18)
New-birth: my spiritual n. 127:15
New-born: n. King 565:12
naked n. babe 457:9
naked n. child 279:19
praise n. gawds 481:21
Newcastle: best sun..N. coal 558:21
New-caught, sullen peoples 303:24
New-comer: O blithe n. 573:19
New-cut: my n. ashlar 300:3
New England weather 550:31
Newer: by a n. object..forgotten 484:34
New-fledged: tempt its n. offspring 224:21
New-found-land: my n. 184:23
New-hatched: confus'd events n. 458:21
each n...comrade 431:25
New Jerusalem: holy city, N. 71:44
walls in the N. 89:16
Newly: n. come from the seas 406:2
n. sprung in June 107:14
New-made honour 447:19
Newman: new-manned by N. 95:30
what..does Dr. N. mean? 294:15
New-mown: about the n. mead 288:22
Newness of life 65:44
New-reaped: his chin, n. 438:32
News: all the n. that's fit to print 370:2
any n. in the paper 23:11
bad n. infects the teller 423:23
bitter n. to hear 157:15
bringer of unwelcome n. 441:10
dismal n. I tell 13:18
evil n. rides post 351:1
father of good n. 432:37
from Heaven the n. 209:3
gathering of n. 416:4
good n. from a far country 50:36
good n. yet to hear 141:24
ill n. hath wings 189:2
love of n. 165:1
man bites a dog..n. 168:3
never good to bring bad n. 424:15
n. from all nations 163:20
n. of battle! 23:22
n. of my boy Jack 300:2
n. that's goin' round 9:6
n., the manna of a day 231:28
n. value 405:17
others..may tell the n. 77:32
what n. on the Rialto? 463:16
New South Wales: govern N. 41:8
Newspaper: never to look into a n. 499:24
n. is..a monopoly 416:4
Newspapers: men and morning n. 378:21
Newt: eye of n. 459:31
New Testament..a Pauliad 237:13
Newton: *Let N. be!* 382:17
N., childlike sage 163:13
Pythagoras was misunderstood ..and N. 200:41
statue..of N. 579:19
Newts, and blind-worms 466:44
New World: called the N. into existence 124:21
New Year: of all the glad N. 536:26
N. reviving old Desires 205:8
ringing..the N. in 223:10
New York: four hundred people in N. society 322:15
little old N. 242:13
New Zealand: married and gone to N. 146:28
some traveller from N. 324:31
Next: happiness of the n. world 87:7
n. train has gone 403:18
n. unto the farthest 199:17
n. year's words 197:14
quit for the n. 442:13
should he need the n. 91:41
week after n. 131:27

Nexus: sole n. of man   126:6, 127:1
Nex: le n. de Cléopâtre   373:22
Niagara: wouldn't *live* under N.   127:27
Niamh calling Away   585:7
Nice: all that's n.   369:12
   damned n. thing   564:2
   more n. than wise   160:36
   n. but nubbly   304:10
   n. man..nasty ideas   520:43
   n. to get up   310:15
   n. unparticular man   236:39
   n. while it lasted   299:22
   she was n...nayed him twice   232:4
   such a n. young man   360:6
   too n. for a statesman   225:27
   where n. is nasty   218:6
Nicean: those N. barks   380:17
Nicely: play so n. with their names   474:25
Nicely-calculated less or more   577:9
Nicer: world would be n.   572:23
Nicest child   40:33
Niche: God keeps a n.   88:14
   within a window'd n.   113:28
Nicholas: St. N. soon would be
   there   356:1
Nicholas Nye   171:21
Nick: Satan, N., or Clootie   104:4
Nickie-ben: auld N.   104:5
Nick-nackets: auld n.   107:22
Nickname is the heaviest stone   240:3
Nicknamed Adam   146:16
Nicodemus saw such light   551:18
Nidding, nodding in the garden   171:18
Niece: his sister's husband's n.   128:16
Nieces: their nephews and their n.   515:24
Nieve: his n. a nit   106:5
Niger: on the left bank of the N.   173:24
Niger: *hic n. est*   261:15
Niggers: don't agree with n.   319:19
   whar de good n. go   210:19
Nigh: Christ is n.   132:5
   drawing n. and nigher   88:19
   goeth to hym n.   195:7
   lie a thought more n.   36:21
   not come n. him   393:32
   not come n. thee   397:18
   she must be n.   492:22
   slowly she came n. him   30:2
   so n. in grandeur   199:32
   them that were n.   67:51
   this house as n. heaven   358:5
   when night is n.   291:10
Nigher: *knowed* the Lord was n.   319:25
Nigh-related: some poor n. guest   152:21
Night: about the dead hour of the
   n.   32:4
   afraid for any terror by n.   397:18
   after the n.'s shade   467:19
   all n. betwixt my breasts   51:42
   all n. have the roses heard   536:11
   all n. long we have not stirred   95:6
   alternate N. and Day   205:29, 30
   always n. and day   585:12
   amorous bird of n.   348:38
   another such a n.   476:13
   as dark as n.   488:22
   as darker grows the n.   224:10
   as n. is withdrawn   81:20
   at n. returning   226:11
   bare-bosom'd n.   567:16
   beloved N.—come soon   495:24
   beyond the night, across the day   528:29
   black bat, n.   536:9
   black it stood as n.   346:4
   black n. doth take away   487:16
   blessed candles of the n.   465:25
   boldly say each n.   158:17
   borrower of the n.   458:31
   braw brecht moonlecht n.   310:13
   brilliant n. in June   377:1
   by n. an atheist   587:11
   by n. in a pillar of fire   45:50
   by n. on my bed   52:4
   by n. or day   576:1
   by Silvia in the n.   484:36
   calm and silent n.   184:2
   cap by n.   224:11
   Chaos and old N.   345:1
   choose an everlasting n.   185:23
   City is of N.   546:29
   closed his eyes in endless n.   231:13

Night (*cont.*)
   cloths of n. and light   584:17
   cloud into n.   236:14
   come, civil n.   478:18
   comes at n. to die   17:26
   come, seeling n.   459:8
   come, thick n.   457:3
   crown is of n.   524:3
   dangers of this n.   388:36
   danger's troubled n.   123:12
   darksome n. be passed   202:25
   day brought back my n.   351:26
   day excludes the n.   562:13
   dear N.!   551:20
   death-fires danced at n.   149:6
   Desolation! and dim N.!   380:14
   dim n. of this immortal day   497:16
   doom'd..to walk the n.   432:8
   drives N. along with them   205:5
   drown'd with us in endless n.   246:1
   dusky n. rides down the sky   204:37
   each n. above his mound   235:19
   each n. upon my knees   204:1
   earned a n.'s repose   318:13
   evening must usher n.   491:26
   every n. and alle   31:12
   fair regent of the N.   216:3
   fearless through the n.   35:5
   feed the heart of the n.   524:13
   first minute. .n.   185:31
   first sweet sleep of n.   494:7
   fled the shades of n.   347:36
   fly into the last n.   411:4
   follow, as the n. the day   431:25
   from morn to n., my friend   410:2
   from my lonely room this n.   23:16
   from the Field of N.   205:5
   from the wings of N.   316:7
   from this palace of dim n.   478:44
   get up at n.   515:14
   gloomy n. embrac'd the place   165:36
   going to run all n.   210:13
   golden lamps in a green n.   332:2
   heaviness may endure for a n.   393:25
   he did not die in the n.   359:13
   her silver lining on the n.   340:12
   honey'd middle of the n.   285:15
   how beautiful is n.   508:2
   I answered you last n.   88:9
   ignorant armies clash by n.   15:8
   I'll labour n. and day   99:37
   in an eternal n.   523:24
   in beauty, like the n.   119:1
   in freezing winter n.   508:17
   in hell-black n. endur'd   453:34
   in hoary winter's n.   508:14
   in love with n.   478:20
   in one n. when he pass'd   344:34
   instalment of n.   237:8
   in such a n.   465:17
   in the day, in the n.   568:9
   in the dead of n.   441:9
   in the forests of the n.   75:24
   in the gardens of the n.   81:17
   in the n., my Soul   545:1
   in the n. of fear   533:28
   in the n. time I shall not forget   523:8
   in the silent n.   131:24
   into Eternity at n.   125:27
   in weary N.'s decline   74:22
   I pass, like n.   150:12
   it is cold winter's n.   32:14
   know his God by n.   551:18
   last n...he jested   188:29
   last out a n. in Russia   461:25
   lated in the n.   231:33
   lay hid in n.   382:17
   let no n. seal thy sense   171:9
   let's have one other gaudy n.   425:6
   lightning in the collied n.   466:20
   light of the n.   524:13
   like quiet n.   402:10
   like the quarry-slave at n.   98:3
   longest n. in all the year   359:14
   long, long n. of waiting   293:1
   long n. succeeds   376:20
   looked forth into the n.   322:20
   lovely as a Lapland n.   583:2
   lovers' tongues by n.   477:27
   Love by n.   193:32
   makest darkness that it may be n.   398:10

Night (*cont.*)
   making n. hideous   431:32(–432)
   mask of n.   477:18
   middle of the n.   130:9
   mirk, mirk n.   32:11
   miserable n.   476:13
   moon walks the n.   172:2
   morning cometh, aad also the n.   53:26
   Morning in the Bowl of N.   205:4
   mushroom of a n.'s growth   186:31
   my n. be turned to day   400:9
   mysterious N.!   566:12
   naked summer n.   567:16
   naughty n. to swim in   453:22
   never sees horrid n.   444:23
   n. and day on me she cries   31:3
   n., and sleep in the n.   522:7
   n. by n. I look   92:30
   n. cometh   63:33
   n. for the morrow   499:4
   n. had borne my breath away   252:33
   n. has a thousand eyes   79:5
   n. has been unruly   458:12
   n. hath a thousand eyes   321:18
   n. in her silence   15:17
   n. in the lonesome October   381:1
   n. is as clear as the day   400:9
   n. is beginning to lower   316:3
   n. is dark   364:10
   n. is darker now   361:23
   n. is drawing nigh   34:35
   n. is far spent   66:13
   n. is fine   130:18
   n. is good   493:22
   n. is growing gray   236:18
   n. joint-labourer with the day   430:13
   n. makes no difference   246:12
   n. of memories   308:14
   n. of south winds   567:16
   n. of the large few stars   567:16
   n. of time far surpasseth the day   87:18
   n. of weeping   517:2
   N., sable goddess!   587:1
   n. sank upon the dusky beach   322:18
   n.'s black agents   459:8
   n.'s black arch   108:9
   n.'s blear-all black   254:18
   n.'s candles are burnt out   478:27
   n.'s sweet bird   492:9
   n.'s swift dragons   467:10
   n. that either makes me   473:10
   n. that first we met   37:1
   n. that should banish all sin   223:10
   n. that wins   521:30(–522)
   n., the shadow of light   522:5
   n. urge the morrow   491:26
   n. was made for loving   119:6
   n. we went to Birmingham   141:22
   n. when Troy was sack'd   412:10
   N. with her train of stars   241:22
   nothing but the n.   263:23
   not n. if Thou be near   291:9
   now n. descending   381:12
   obscurest n. involv'd the sky   159:1
   o'er n.'s brim, day boils   94:39
   O for that N.!   551:21
   of thar n.'s baill   187:4
   oft in the stilly n.   357:13
   on a shining n.   8:23
   one ever-during n.   123:19
   one n. certifieth another   392:32
   one n. or the other n.   208:13
   one winter's n.   366:20
   on the N.'s Plutonian shore   380:25
   O thievish N.   340:9
   out of the n. that covers me   241:18
   piercing the n.'s dull ear   444:6
   poor souls who dwell in N.   74:1
   pure from the n.   336:11
   returned home the previous n.   98:19
   revelry by n.   113:25
   sable-vested N., eldest of things   346:15
   same n. that he was betrayed   390:43
   sentries of the shadowy n.   355:16
   shades of n. were falling   316:17
   shadow of our n.   492:7
   Shadwell's genuine n.   193:2
   she all n. long   347:19
   she gallops n. by n.   477:7
   ships that pass in the n.   318:10
   show thy dangerous brow by n.   449:6

Night (cont.)
silent hours of n. 311:19
singeth all n. long 430:20
sisters Death and N. 567:5
sleep..neither n. nor day 456:11
sleeps as may beguile the n. 518:2
soft stillness and the n. 465:18
so late into the n. 119:4
some n. you'll fail us 95:1
son of the sable N. 168:12
spend the n. in mirth 502:22(–503)
spend the n. in sleep 168:13
spirit of N. 495:21
starry n. 498:12
stars of the summer n.! 318:4
startle the dull n. 341:31
steal a few hours from the n. 357:1
still nodding n. 567:16
such n. in England ne'er 322:18
tender and growing n. 567:16
that n., that year 254:20
there's n. and day, brother 78:24
things that love n. 453:8
this ae n. 31:12
this closing n. 496:7
this n...is but the daylight sick 405:23
this n. of Spring 213:2
this n. thy soul..required 61:53
thou and I this n. maun gae 32:10
though thou be black as n. 123:20
throne..of N. primæval 381:26
through the empty-vaulted n. 340:15
through the foul womb of n. 444:6
through the n. I go 209:31
through the n. of doubt 35:4
thy path is dark as n. 327:3
Thy tempests fell all n. 244:18
tire the n. in thought 404:5
'tis a fearful n. 36:32
toiling upward in the n. 316:31
torment of the n.'s untruth 168:12
to rule the n. 44:5
to the sleeping woods all n. 149:35
touch of Harry in the n. 444:9
trailing garments of the N. 316:28
trancéd summer-n. 286:8
upon the cheek of n. 477:9
upon the n.'s starr'd face 289:5
upon the wings of n. 478:19
vile contagion of the n. 449:15
voice I hear this passing n. 288:1
waters on a starry n. 576:2
what hath n. to do with sleep? 340:5
what is the n.? 459:24
what of the n.? 53:26
when n. darkens the streets 344:35
when n. is nigh 291:10
when N. is on the hills 549:2
when she deserts the n. 350:23
where Cressid lay that n. 465:17
white in a single n. 114:35
will not last the n. 339:6
windy n. a rainy morrow 487:23
witching time of n. 435:29
with n. we banish sorrow 248:5
with us perpetual n. 282:6
womb of uncreated n. 345:19
world's last n. 185:17
yet it is not n. 114:6
Night-air: burst into the fresh n. 90:24
Night-cap: bring his n. with him 518:11
n. decked his brows 224:11
Nightcaps: their heads all in n. 127:5
Night-dress: lectures in her n. 253:29
Nighted: cast thy n. colour off 430:28
Night-flies: buzzing n. 441:41
Night-gown: Caesar, in his n. 449:19
downstairs in his n. 339:9
Nightingale: all but the wakeful n. 347:19
brown bright n. 521:30
crave the tuneful n. 189:18
hark! ah, the N.! 17:11
hundred-throated n. 541:9
I the n. all spring through 524'13
it was the n. 478:26
merl, the mavys, and the n. 187:4
my n. 425:14
newe abaysshed n. 138:34
N. cries to the Rose 205:12
n. does sit so late 332:27

Nightingale (cont.)
n., if she should sing by day 465:22
n. in the sycamore 516:12
n.'s complaint 494:7
n.'s high note is heard 118:28
N. that in the Branches sang 207:24
n., that on yon bloomy spray 351:12
no music in the n. 484:36
ravish'd n. 321:15
roar you as 'twere any n. 466:30
save the n. alone 35:17
singing of the n. 285:11
sweetly as a n. 479:4
where the n. doth sing 284:17
whither doth haste the n. 125:10
Nightingales: Eve's n. 171:1
n. are singing 197:26, 293:1
till the n. applauded 94:8
Nightly: blue wave rolls n. 118:37
n. she sings 478:26
n. sings the staring owl 456:1
n. to the listening Earth 2:26
shake us n. 459:4
visit'st my slumbers n. 348:23
Night-mare Life-in-Death 149:13
Night-rack came rolling up 293:26
Nights: Alcmena's n. 87:11
Chequer-board of N. and Days 206:28
chill thy dreaming n. 287:3
dew of summer n. 288:13
fled Him, down the n. 544:13
God makes sech n. 319:23
long, long wintry n. 311:15
love not such n. 453:8
n. are very damp 128:19
n. are wholesome 430:20
n. of waking 416:19
profit of their shining n. 454:32
stand in starless n. 193:30
to waste long n. 510:16
when n. are lang and mirk 33:2
when n. are longest there 461:25
winding up..n. with sleep 444:23
Night-season: in the n...no rest 393:1
Night-shriek: to hear a n. 461:3
Night-wind: breath of the n. 15:7
n. brings up the stream 16:4
Nigrae feraci frondis in Algido 260:21
Nihil: tu n. invita dices faciesve Minerva 256:13
Nihilo: de n. nihilum 378:5
Nil: n. admirari 257:1
n. desperandum Teucro 258:11
n. posse creari de nilo 320:29
n. ultra to my proudest hopes 334:24
Nile: allegory on the banks of the N. 500:21
my serpent of old N. 423:43
pour the waters of the N. 128:23
Nilus: rather on N.' mud 425:34
Nimble: has a n. tail 281:19
if your heels are n. and light 367:4
merry, n., stirring spirit 455:28
n. fiery..shapes 442:21
words that have been so n. 37:12
Nimbler much than hinds 333:1
Nimini-pimini 100:4
Nimis: nequid n. 541:27
Nimrod the mighty hunter 44:45
Nimshi: Jehu, the son of N. 48:27
that of the son of N. 505:30
Nine: by the n. gods 323:10
fair N., forsaking Poetryl 75:18
his choir, the N. 15:16
n. days old 368:11
n. fathom deep 149:7
n. worthy 327:15
n. years a-killing 472:24
now some n. moons wasted 469:45
se'nnights n. times n. 456:11
that will purchase n. 131:24
where are the n.? 62:29
Nine-and-sixty ways 297:9
Nine-and-twenty knights of fame 417:3
Nine-fifteen: Romance brought up the n. 298:1
Ninefold harmony 343:17
Nine hundred rank and file 301:16
Ninepence: but n. in ready money 2:35
Nineteen: expenditure n. n. six 174:24
Nine-tenths of Christianity 240:28

Ninety: n. men and more 539:18
nurse of n. years 538:27
Ninety and nine: leave the n. 62:10
n. just persons 62:12
Ninety-eight: fears to speak of N.? 267:18
Ninety-nine per cent. perspiration 195:22
Nineveh: one with N. and Tyre 300:25
Quinquireme of N. 333:20
Ninny: to Handel's a mere n. 112:22
Ninth: n. part..of a tailor 126:7
till the n. year 256:14
Niobe: like N., all tears 430:33(–431)
N. of nations! 114:13
Niobean: sadder than the N. womb 522:14
Nip: I'll n. him in the bud 407:8
Nipped: n. him to the bone 302:27
n. with care 338:14
when blood is n. 456:1
Nipping and an eager air 431:30
Nipple: pluck'd my n. from his.. gums 457:13
Nit: his nieve a n. 106:5
Niti: noctes atque dies n. 320:30(–321)
Nitidum: pinquem et n. 256:27
Nitre: with windy n. 509:25
Nives: diffugere n. 260:24
No: Araminta, say 'N.!' 387:17
cried 'N. more' 244:9
everlasting N. 127:13
Lord N. Zoo 176:4
N. Bastille! N. Governor Aris! 119:32
n. John! 9:4
n. Manual, n. letters 119:32
n. more of Tom 116:31
n. more—Oh, never more! 494:18
n., n., go not to Lethe 287:19
n., not in Israel 58:32
'N. Party' 335:6
'N.,' this morning 88:9
people cried, 'O N.!' 34:27
Scylla and Charybdis of Aye and N. 363:19
Noah: before N. was a sailor 483:30
into N.'s ark 162:2
married N.'s daughter 23:27
N. begat Shem, Ham, and Japheth 44:36
N. he often said 142:12
N. spoke him fairly 298:21
whereas it is N. 303:9
Nobby: isn't it a n. one 408:17
Nobilitate: contendere n. 320:30(–321)
Nobility: all were noble, save N. 113:9
ancient n. 26:42
betwixt the wind and his n. 438:33
deny a God destroy man's n. 25:26
fashions men with true n. 331:2
leave us..our old n. 329:10
new n. 26:42
n. is a graceful ornament 102:25
n. is of great use 28:33
n. of birth..abateth industry 26:43
true n. is exempt from fear 445:34
virtue alone is true n. 217:20
Noble: all were n., save Nobility 113:9
amplitude of n. life 402:23
ashamed with the n. shame 294:3
born most n. 371:8
dearth of n. natures 284:20
Earth has many a n. city 132:4
except for a n. purpose 243:14
experiment, in n. motive 254:4
fruit..of n. mind 530:11
glad to learn of n. men 451:16
greatest, most n...poems 194:11
he was a n. steed 118:13
Homer..eminently n. 20:2
how n. in reason! 433:15
in a death so n. 351:6
man with all his n. qualities 169:5
more n. than the world 483:8
my n., lovely, little Peggy 401:37
n. and approv'd good masters 469:45
n. and nude and antique 522:22
n. and puissant nation 352:15
n. grounds for the n. emotions 412:25
N. heart, that harbours 500:23
n. living and the n. dead 579:32
n. lord in the blue riband 100:20
n. man..ignoble talk 530:39

INDEX

Noble (cont.)
n. mind disdains to hide 231:32
n. minds..with their likes 448:31
n. nature, poetically gifted 20:5
n. savage 191:41
n., the grand style 20:5
not be n. to myself 426:2
old Castilian poor n. 119:24
only n. to be good 533:38
our n. society 178:43
silence is most n. 522:9
some n. creatures in her 479:19
some work of n. note 541:3
that n. men may see 328:1
that n..reason 434:14
too n. for the world 429:13
virtue..makes us n. 38:3
what a n. mind 434:14
what's brave, what's n. 425:31
where the n. Infant lay 165:36
years of n. deeds 530:14
Nobleman: cultivated, underrated n. 218:17
king may make a n. 103:27
live cleanly, as a n. should 441:6
what may a N. find to do? 34:5
Nobleness: greatest n. principle 126:8
n. of life is to do thus 423:14
N. walks in our ways 83:20
perfect plainness..perfect n. 20:4
that great n. of hers 585:4
Nobler: n. and the manlier one 116:2
n. in the mind to suffer 434:4
n. modes of life 533:20
n. tenants of the flood 161:34
Nobles: false English N. 375:19
n. and heralds 401:28
n. by..an earlier creation 325:4
their n. with links of iron 400:27
their-n.-with-links-of-iron 322:24
where the wealthy n. dwell 535:3
Noblest: greatest prince..the n. 425:28
her n. work she classes O 106:2
love's the n. frailty 192:34
n. motive 511:20
n. of mankind 121:17
n. production of human nature 2:7
n. Roman of them all 452:8
n. work of God 105:5, 384:9
n. work of man 112:9, 267:16
not a thought, though..the n. 127:12
ruins of the n. man 450:11
thinks most, feels the n. 29:9
Nobly: I think n. of the soul 484:22
let us love n., and live 184:7
n., n. Cape St. Vincent 92:17
n. wild, not mad 246:14
spurn not the n. born 219:1
Nobody: business of n. 324:21
I care for n. 72:16, 106:15
n. calls you a dunce 97:29
n. cares for me 106:15
n. gets old and godly 585:14
n. I care for comes a-courting 220:30
n.; I myself; farewell 473:19
n. is on my side 23:1
n. knows where 318:9
n. walks much faster 131:17
there's n. at home 382:9
Nocens: nemo n. absolvitur 284:1
ubi n. absolvitur 283:16
Nocitura: n. toga, n...militia 283:16
Nocte: omnes..urgentur..longa n. 261:2
Noctes: n. atque dies niti 320:30(-321)
n. atque dies patet..ianua 554:23
n. cenaeque deum! 261:26
Noctis: lente currite n. equi 330:7
Nocturna versate manu 256:6
Nocturnal: some n. blackness 235:14
tunes her n. note 346:20
Nod: affects to n. 191:1
if she chance to n. 479:7
in the land of N. 44:33
n., and bustle by 18:18
n. good-bye to Rochefoucauld 197:3
n. unto the world 425:19
Wynken, Blynken, and N. 204:5
Nodded: while I n. 380:22
Nodding: if he sees anybody else n. 2:11
n. by the fire 586:21
n. o'er the yellow plain 546:17

Nodding (cont.)
n. to its fall 384:5
still n. night 567:16
Noddle: my barmie n. 105:26
Nodosities of the oak 103:30
Nods: horse that stumbles and n. 236:14
if Homer..n. 256:10
n., and becks 341:28
Reason..n. a little 203:29
why n. the drowsy Worshipper? 205:7
Nodus: nisi dignus vindice n. 256:5
Noes: honest kersey n. 455:30
Nohow! 130:7
Noise: above n. and danger 552:1
after n., tranquillity 365:4
barbarous n. environs me 351:18
body..holds its n. 89:28
chamber deaf to n. 501:27
damn'd would make no n. 247:14
didst thou not hear a n.? 458:6
dumb-shows and n. 434:15
fears no n. 227:10
folly, n. and sin 93:11
for the n. of a fly 186:32
full of foolish n. 532:29
gone up with a merry n. 394:31
happy n. to hear 262:21
her n., her crowds 307:5
little noiseless n. 286:26
melt, and make no n. 186:24
most sublime n. 210:7
n. like of a hidden brook 149:35
n. of battle roll'd 531:29
n. of his waves 395:28
n. of the water-pipes 394:19
n. was in the beast's belly 328:4
no n. here 246:5
pleasant n. till noon 149:35
shunn'st the n. of folly 341:13
such a n. and tumult when alive 196:3
those who make the most n. 102:20
valued till they make a n. 165:13
wi' flichterin n. an' glee 104:33
Noiseless: little n. noise 286:26
n. tenor of their way 230:7
Noises: isle is full of n. 480:5
like n. in a swound 148:26
so full of dreary n. 88:26
Noisome: from the n. pestilence 397:18
Noisy: n. bells, be dumb 263:2
n. man..in the right 159:14
Nokomis: wigwam of N. 317:22
Noll: for shortness call'd N. 213:12
N.'s damned troopers 90:18
Nolle: idem velle atque idem n. 415:2
Nom: que de crimes..en ton n.! 408:15
Noman: dear Mr. N. 41:28
No-meaning: channel of n. 363:19
Nomen: clarum et venerabile n. 320:25
nostrum n. miscebitur istis 371:23
omne capax movet urna n. 259:15
semper honos n.que..manebunt 553:21
Nominated: so n. in the bond? 465:7
Nomination of this gentleman? 437:30
Nominative: her n. case 370:5
Nomine: mutato n. de te fabula 261:8
Nominis: stat magni n. umbra 320:23
No-more: also called N. 411:17
Non sequitur—'You are another' 204:28
Non-commissioned man 295:23
Nonconformist: man must be a n. 200:39
N. conscience 569:38
N. Conscience 39:17
None: cared for n. of those things 65:3
flew away n. knows whither 39:29
if there is n. 107:18
I strove with n. 308:25
never had n.! 517:5
never n. but she 7:17
n. but the brave 190:34
b. but thou..my paramour 330:6
n. can call our power to account 460:24
n. other gods but me 390:5
n. resign 268:26
n. such as knew it of old 523:4
n. to call me Charley now 307:19
n. to one could sovereignty impute 189:3
n. was for a party 323:21
perfectly sure I have n. 128:28
save n. of me 185:5

Non-flunkey: *one n.*, one hero 126:46
Nonpareil battalion 174:5
Nonsense: good lump of clotted n. 194:18
grammar, and n. 226:2
his n. suits their n. 136:12
no light n. about Miss Blimber 175:6
n. of the old women 513:18
round the corner of n. 153:13
some n. about sense 514:4
sounds like n... very good law 419:30
those extravagancies, and that n. 139:21
through sense and n. 190:32
time and n. scorning 98:15
trickling n. 155:5
Nonumque prematur in annum 256:14
Nook: book and a shady n. 571:9
obscure n. for me 94:22
Nooks: by many winding n. 484:15
in these Wessex n. 236:42
Noon: amid the blaze of n. 350:22
athwart the n. 151:19
bloody Sun, at n. 149:4
by n...steal away 244:20
far from the fiery n. 286:2
from morn to n. he fell, from n. to dewy eve 345:12
high n. behind the tamarisks 295:9
his first minute, after n. 185:31
lying till n. 276:2
no morn—no n.! 253:11
n. a purple glow 585:12
n. strikes on England..n. of my dreams, O n. 208:5
not attain'd his n. 246:2
o'er Thy glorious n. 551:18
pleasant noise till n. 149:35
Princes ride at n. 171:2
riding near her highest n. 341:14
shameless n. 529:28
showed at n. but small 312:26
when n. is past 494:6
Noonday: destroyeth in the n. 397:18
endless n., glorious n. 361:16
my heart at some n. 91:35
talks of darkness at n. 161:32
thy just dealing as the n. 394:4
tingle to the n. chime 264:2
Noondays: fire-flames n. kindle 90:39
No one's anybody 218:30
Noontide: his listless length at n. 230:12
throbbings of n. 236:12
when n. wakes anew 92:16
Noose: naked to the hangman's n. 262:12
N. of Light 205:4
Nora's heart is lost and won 419:1
Norfan: a N., both sides 564:27
Norma: ius et n. loquendi 255:20
Normal: very type of the n. 268:4
Norman: Billy the N. 173:16
blacksmith like our N. King 294:22
Danish-N.-English 170:13
Saxon and N. and Dane 541:18
simple faith than N. blood 533:38
Norman's Woe: reef of N. 318:16
Normans: not like us N. 300:7
Noroway: carl in N. 302:25
to N., to N. 31:24
North: Ariosto of the N. 114:7
awake, O n. wind 52:8
between the N. and the South 213:19
cross it from the n. to the south 438:37
farewell to the N. 107:13
infect to the n. star 468:13
in the N...my nest is made 538:21
in triumph from the n. 322:25
metropolis of the N. 528:25
n. of the Fifty-Three 301:3
n. wind doth blow 368:2
N. you may run 298:28
of Nelson and the N. 122:3
ship..in the N. Country 30:23
sun of summer in the N. 538:21
talk slid in. 294:29
tender is the N. 538:20
unripened beauties of the n. 1:17
west, east, south and n. 334:9
when the wind is in the n. 11:21
where's the N.? 383:27
wither at the n. wind's breath 241:14
without sharp N. 185:8

North America: by the Great
Lakes of N. 324:34
Northeast: off at sea n. winds 347:1
North-easter: wild N. 293:12
Northern: as in n. climes 115:8
constant as the n. star 449:30
glorious the n. lights 503:6
on some far n. strand 16:6
religion. .in our n. colonies 100:29
St. Andrews, by the N. Sea 309:23
Northland: great akes of the N. 317:20
North-north-west: but mad n. 433:20
North-west: N. passage to the intellectual World 513:19
to the N. died away 92:17
Norval: my name is N. 251:26
Norwegian: tallest pine hewn on
N. hills 344:24
Nos: n. et mutamur in illis 372:13
n. mutamur in illis 13:15
Nose: against the blown rose. .stop
their n. 424:29
any n. may ravage 96:34
down his innocent n. 426:31
entuned in hir n. 136:29
ever and anon he gave his n. 438:32
final cause of the human n. 153:4
forehead, straight n. 359:10
heaven stops the n. at it 472:36
he cocks his n. 520:53
her n. and chin 108:33
her slender n. tip-tilted 530:6
his n.'s cast is of the roman 208:29
his n. was as sharp as a pen 443:19
if his n. is warm 312:7
many an Aldermanic n. 34:2
Marion's n. looks red 456:1
my n. fell a-bleeding 463:35
n., n., jolly red n. 37:25
o'er a courtier's n. 477:7
on his n. there was a Cricket 311:19
plucks justice by the n. 461:18
provided he minds his n. 312:7
snapped off her n. 368:20
spectacles on n. 427:21
strange as a N. could be 311:17
thine has a great hook n. 74:10
thy n. is as the tower 52:19
unfriendly to the n. 516:18
wipe a bloody n. 215:26
wipe his little n. 34:24
with a snug n. 281:19
with the Luminous N. 311:16
Noselessness of Man 142:6
Noses: athwart men's n. 477:7
haven't got no n. 142:5
n. have they, and smell not 399:4
wearing our own n. 429:28
Nostalgia of the heathen past 310:20
Nostalgie de la boue 21:15
Nostril wide 488:27
Nostrils: into his n. the breath of
life 44:11
whose breath is in his n. 52:32
Nostrum: non n...componere 555:28
Not: Archibald—certainly n.! 414:5
easier to say what it is n. 273:13
he said, 'Certainly n.!' 312:18
how n. to do it 175:29
man as he is n. to be 239:18
nay, n. so much, not two 430:33(-431)
n. choose n. to be 254:19
n. men, but measures 101:37
thing that's n. 375:23
thing which was n. 519:19
when what is now is n. 147:11
Notas: non secus ac n. 256:11
Notched and cropt scrivener 306:18
Note: bolder n. than his 380:18
deed of dreadful n. 459:7
deserving n. 246:4
dreadful n. of preparation 444:6
fits my little n. 245:19
from my lowest n. 435:24
give the world to n. 331:2
men and women of no n. 406:4
merry n. 456:1
nightingale's high n. is heard 118:28
n. it in a book 53:37
n. I wanted 268:4
n. most full of harmony 86:32

Note (cont.)
n. this. .not a n. of mine 468:18
responsive to the cuckoo's n. 231:6
silent n. which Cupid strikes 86:32
simplest n. that swells 231:5
swells the n. of praise 230:2
take n., take n., O world! 472:6
throstle with his n. so true 467:6
tunes her nocturnal n. 346:20
turn his merry n. 427:7
we take no n. of Time 587:2
when found, make a n. of 175:9
with a n. like thine 270:6
world will little n. 314:12
Note-book: set in a n. 451:24
Noted in thy book 395:15
Note-paper: on club n. 542:30
Notes: all the compass of the n. 191:35
both in highest n. appear 123:21
chield. .taking n. 107:21
formed, as n. of music are 493:8
Fox's shall the n. rebound 418:5
haste you, sad n. 123:22
hideous n. of woe 116:50
how could thy n. flow 498:9
larks their n. prepare 386:32
meeting soul may pierce in n. 342:7
n. are few! 75:18
n. by distance. .sweet 154:1
n...necessary evils 278:22
note this before my n. 468:18
such n. as, warbled 341:10
such were the n. 385:5
these n. intendeth 501:20
these rough n. and our dead
bodies 416:7
these weak n. have sung 410:34
thinks two n. a song 160:22
with mery n. myrthfully 187:4
Nothing: although there's n. in't 117:10
as n., Charles 36:12
believing in n. at all 320:3
bettre than a good wowman? N. 137:37
brought n. into this world 68:51
bury for n. 176:19
death, in itself, is n. 191:33
did n. and desired to do n. 272:27
did n. in particular 219:7
doing n. with. .skill 162:19
do n. and get something 182:26
drawing n. up 163:11
ever do n. but that 485:27
for n. less than thee 184:12
George the First knew n. 272:27
having n., and yet possessing all 67:29
having n., yet hath all 583:11
his performance. .n. 447:7
I come from n. 338:5
infinite deal of n. 463:1
is it n. to you? 55:23
it was n. more 578:25
I've had n. yet 129:9
knowledge of n. 174:6
knows n. whatever about Thee 305:8
labour of doing n. 511:27
make up one's mind about n. 290:27
needy n. trimmed in jollity 487:14
no n. 119:32
n. a year 542:39
n. a-year, paid quarterly 518:41
n. beside remains 496:15
n. brings me all things 480:30
n. but the night 263:23
n. but what hath been said 109:4
n. can be created out of n. 320:29
n. can be known 113:13
n. can bring back the hour 576:20
n. can come out of n. 378:5
n. can need a lie 243:27
n., can touch him further 459:4
n. comes amiss 479:1
n. did he say 24:4
n. doing 503:14
n. done while aught remains 408:6
n. else saw all day long 286:31
n. extenuate 474:2
n. for n. 'ere 403:17
n. for reward 509:32
n. if not critical 470:26
n. in love 460:31
n. in my hand I bring 548:12

Nothing (cont.)
n. is but what is not 456:24
n. is fair or good alone 199:9
n. is here for tears 351:6
n. is so good as it seems 196:32
n. is there to come, and n. past 158:2
N. it set out from 206:21
n. left remarkable 425:29
n. less. .than whole America 100:27
n. like it 131:16
n. long 190:22
n. more certain than incertainties 35:20
n. much before 297:2
n.-much-matter-day night 243:5
n. of a name 114:38
n. of itself will come 574:30
n. of myself in me 165:31
n. refuse 199:12
n. shall come amiss 98:15
n. that you oughtn't, O! 221:42
n. that you want 265:1
n.! thou elder brother 407:19
n. to do but work 292:14
n. to do to-day 187:20
n. to do with that just man 60:48
n. to do with the case 220:15
n. to say, say n. 154:20
n. to what I could say 129:18
n. was now left but a jail 174:22
n. went unrewarded but desert 190:24
n. we see but means our good 244:23
n. whatever to grumble at 222:1
n. will remain 262:19
n. would it bear 367:7
passages, that lead to n. 230:18
reputed wise for saying n. 462:34
saying something. .n. to be said 270:31
say n., when he has n. to say 274:20
signifying n. 461:4
so I had n. known 472:3
starts for the Dawn of N. 206:20
that he knew n. yet 40:4
that he n. knew 350:12
that n. be lost 63:21
they that starve with n. 463:5
they were n., Sir 273:31
thinking of n. at all 173:13
'tis something, n. 471:30
to airy n. a local habitation 467:24
touched n. that he did not adorn 273:19
to whom n. is given. .n...re-
quired 204:16
value of n. 570:1
we are n.; less than n. 306:7
we said n., all the day 184:31
'wot's the good. .?'. .'N.!' 142:21
who does n. with a better grace? 586:24
Nothing-much-matter-day-night 243:5
Nothingness: love and fame to n. 289:6
never pass into n. 284:19
Nothings: invulnerable n. 492:6
such laboured n. 382:28
Notice: n. . .you have been pleased
to take 270:18
used to n. such things 235:13
you would hardly n. it 20:27
Noticeable man with large grey
eyes 581:19
Noticed: little n. here 160:33
Noting my step in bliss 81:6
Notion: blunder. .and foolish n. 106:33
Notions: excellent phantasy, brave
n. 280:1
general n. are generally wrong 354:16
Notorious evil liver 390:1
Notus nimis omnibus 422:19
Notwithstanding up 449:25
Nought: counsel of the heathen to
n. 393:36
count for n. what the Greek did 81:1
falling into n. 1:22
for n. except for love's sake 88:18
have n. beside 544:15
it is n., it is n. 50:27
n. broken save this body 84:18
n. could be done 34:6
n. did I in hate 473:34
n. for your comfort 140:13
n. is everything 504:9
n. is worth a thought 387:16
n.'s had, all's spent 459:3

Nought (*cont.*)
n. shall go ill 467:12
struggle n. availeth 147:8
those who set at n. 565:14
to do n...almost an act 411:33
Noun: his being and the n. at once 500:4
Nouns: n. of number 147:17
verbs and n. do more agree 238:30
Nourish: n. a blind life 531:36
n. all the world 455:23
Nourished: how begot, how n.? 464:13
how n. there 574:31
Nourisher: chief n. in life's feast 458:11
Nourisheth: lives by that which n. it 424:17
Nova: pulchritudo..tam n. 21:22
Novatur: rerum summa n. semper 321:1
Novel: given away by a n. 290:21
I've read in many a n. 121:12
my scrofulous French n. 96:41
n. cannot be too bad 490:42
obligation to which..hold a n. 268:11
only a n. 22:22
supersede the last fashionable n. 326:11
when I want to read a n. 181:21
Novels: Balzac's n...one shelf 89:29
French n., French cookery 542:33
reading French n. 182:32
Novelty: create at last this n. 349:23
n., n., n. 253:31
November: April, June, and N. 369:5
Fifth of N. 9:11, 368:13
no birds—N.! 253:12
N.'s sky is chill and drear 418:1
nurse N. on..June 253:18
thirty days hath N. 228:4
Noverca: inimica et infida semper memoriae n. 414:21
Novi: ex Africa semper aliquid n. 380:1
Novum: iunctura n. 255:19
Now: eternal N. 158:2
if it be n. 437:34
in England—n.! 92:14
leave N. for dogs and apes! 91:40
let me do it n. 232:10
not n. as it hath been 576:1
n., and ever shall be 388:14
n. I may 470:29
'N.! N.!' cried the Queen 130:3
n.'s the day 107:32
n. the day is over 34:35
n. we sha'n't be long 121:26
when what is n. is not 147:11
Now-a-days: settled n. 116:23
Nowhere: circumference is n. 10:17
n. did abide 149:23
n. to fall but off 292:15
n. to go 566:15
rest n. 370:8
swear n. 186:17
Nox: iam n. umida caelo praecipitat 553:26
n. est perpetua una dormienda 132:15
Nubly: nice but n. 304:10
Nube: vel atra n...vel sole puro 260:14
Nude: keep one from going n. 292:14
noble and n. and antique 522:22
Nudula: pallidula rigida n. 233:19
Nugas: meas esse aliquid putare n. 132:10
Nuisance: not make himself a n. 338:29
Null: splendidly n. 535:35
Nullum quod tetigit non ornavit 273:19
Numbed sense to steel it 289:8
Number: happiness of the greatest n. 42:21
it ought to be N. One 129:32
more by your n., than your light 583:13
no man could n. 71:3
not on the n., but the choice 158:16
nouns of n. 147:17
n. of a man 71:22
n. of his name 71:21
n. of the beast 71:22
n. the streaks of the tulip 278:15
n., weight, and measure 77:13
telleth the n. of the stars 400:21
wealth, the n., the happiness 101:15
Numbered: God hath n. thy kingdom 55:42
n. with the transgressors 54:28
very hairs..n. 58:53
Numbers: better than n. 167:2

Numbers (*cont.*)
brings home full n. 467:37
golden n. 170:21
greatest happiness for the greatest n. 266:11
in fresh n. 486:16
in mournful n. 317:5
lisped in n., for the n. came 385:25
liv'd in Settle's n. 381:12
move harmonious n. 346:20
opposed n. 444:24
plaintive n. flow 581:2
round n. are always false 273:26
secret magic of n. 86:10
to n. I'll not be confin'd 570:30
Numbness: drowsy n. pains 287:22
Numen: nullum n. habes 283:25
Numerisque fertur lege solutis 260:18
Numerous: as writers become more n. 226:19
n. piece of monstrosity 86:20
Numerus: nos n. sumus 256:24
Numine: quo n. laeso 553:6
Nun: if you become a n., dear 265:24
my daughter the N. 507:36
quiet as a n. 577:1
son of N. 46:6
Nunc: sit mihi quod n. est 257:11
Nunc Dimittis: sweetest canticle is N. 26:4
Nuncheon: take your n. 94:37
Nunnery: get thee to a n. 434:7
n. of thy chaste breast 319:10
Nuns: among the N. Black 502:20
n. fret not 578:6
Nuptials: iteration of n. 156:17
Nurse: beggar's n. and Caesar's 425:33
continues what the n. began 192:30
dear n. of arts 445:10
dirty n., Experience 530:43
her best n. Contemplation 340:20
if you n. a flame 123:4
London, my most kindly n. 510:21
nature's soft n. 441:41
n. for a poetic child 417:22
n. November on..June 253:18
n. of arms 226:15
n. of manly sentiment 102:12
n. of ninety years 538:27
n. sleeps sweetly 162:35
n. unacted desires 77:19
old n., Death 241:20
puking in the n.'s arms 427:21
scratch the n. 484:31
sucks the n. asleep 426:13
this n., this teeming womb 474:22
too old to fawn upon a n. 474:15
Nursed: never n. a dear gazelle 177:33, 357:5
n. amid her noise 307:5
n. upon the self-same hill 342:11
Nurseries: n. of all vice 204:19
N. of blooming Youth 578:12
n. of heaven 544:10
Nursery: n.-mishaps 164:31
n. of future revolutions 102:7
trod my n. floor 160:30
Nurses: old men's n. 26:37
Nursing: lack of woman's n. 365:21
n. her wrath 108:2
n. the unconquerable hope 18:15
Nursling: n. of the Sky 493:1
n. of thy widowhood 491:16
Ocean's n., Venice lies 495:1
Nurslings: n. of immortality 497:2
win their n. with their smiles 309:5
Nut: Fairy in a n. 75:15
Nut-brown: jolly n. bowl 170:24
spicy n. ale 342:4
Nutmeg: but a silver n. 367:7
Nutmegs and ginger 37:25
Nutrition: draw n.,..and rot 383:24
Nuts: before the n. work loose 302:2
like an ape doth n. 436:9
n.! 326:12
n. in May 6:23
Nut-shell: bounded in a n. 433:12
your n. navies came 296:4
Nut-tree: I had a little n. 367:7
Nye: Nicholas N. 171:21
Nymph: haste thee N. 341:28

Nymph (*cont.*)
mountain n., sweet Liberty 341:30
not as a n., but for a reed 332:16
N., a Naiad, or a Grace 416:16
n., in thy orisons 434:5
n. to the bath addressed 497:26
n., with long dishevell'd hair 488:26
sweet Echo, sweetest n. 340:13
to the n. with but one 500:40
Nympha pudica Deum vidit 165:25
Nymphs: breasts of the n. 525:6
N. that reign o'er sewers 150:28
short leave of your n. 526:23
Thames, attended by two n. 167:17
where were ye, N.? 342:17

O

O: O! Sophonisba! Sophonisba! O! 546:28
this wooden O 443:4
Oafs: muddied o. 297:16
Oak: beneath a spreading o. 158:29
cleave the hardest o. 305:12
English o. and holly 238:26
heart of o. are our ships 213:10
hearts of o. our men 20:20
hollow o. our palace is 167:21
many an o. 338:13
my back unto an o. 32:18
nodosities of the o. 103:30
O., and Ash, and Thorn 303:5, 6
o. and the ash 8:22
O., Elder, Elm and Thorn 172:6
our ships were British o. 20:20
palm, the o., or bays 332:13
reed is as the o. 430:1
shadow of the British o. 102:20
standing long an o. 282:1
unwedgeable and gnarled o. 461:31
Oak-cleaving thunderbolts 453:5
Oaks: huge o. and old 302:12
o...do not spring up 313:22
old families last not three o. 87:14
tall o., branch-charmèd 286:8
tall o. from little acorns grow 202:16
Oak-stump: rotted old o. 150:8
O altitudo: to an O.! 86:8
Oar: bend to the o. 415:6
galley-slave..with his o. 563:12
wind and wave and o. 535:20
Oars: feather'd his o. with such skill 173:12
I took the o. 150:11
o., and coat, and badge 173:14
o. were silver 424:6
our o. keep time 357:16
Oat-cakes: Calvin, o., and sulphur 504:22
Oaten: o. stop or pastoral song 153:23
to mine o. pipe 509:9
Oath: deny each article with o. 473:14
good mouth-filling o. 440:7
hir grettestè o. 136:28
if ever I utter an o. again 491:3
I take the official o. to-day 314:9
not upon o. 272:35
o., an o., I have an o. in heaven 465:5
rash o. of virginity 375:8
sworn a solemn o. 106:21
to heaven's chancery with the o. 513:20
Oaths: all o...broke to me 475:23
as many o. as I spake words 453:19
false as dicers' o. 435:42
full of strange o. 427:21
men with o. 24:31
names God in o. 184:14
o. are but words 110:46
o. are straw 443:23
Oatmeal: upon a little o. 505:26
Oats..given to horses 277:29
Obadiah Bind-their-kings 322:24
Obdurate: if too o. I 516:10
Obeam: tecum o. libens 260:4
Obedience: approve first thy o. 349:10
expect more o. 226:36
fear..keeps men in o. 109:31
honour, love, o. 460:36
into both that liberal o. 101:11
my o. then 158:28

INDEX

Obedience (cont.)
o. to God 79:14
owe to thyself..to thy o. 348:11
reluctant o. of distant provinces 324:24
swift in all o. 301:26
Obedient: mild, o., good as He 4:2
o. to Isa Keith 208:24
Obeisance: all trial, all o. 428:28
o. to my sheaf 45:13
Obey: all did o. 189:3
don't o. no orders 295:21
in all my best o. you, madam 430:32
monarchs must o. 193:1
nothing..with the laws but to o. 262:4
o. God rather than men 64:31
o. th' important call 163:33
o. thy heart 199:12
to love, cherish, and to o. 391:31
to o. is better than sacrifice 47:16
woman to o. 538:24
Obeyed as a son 216:26
Obeying: except by o. her 28:9
Obeys: most when she o. 384:38
she o. him 317:27
Object: by a newer o...forgotten 484:34
conspicuous o. in a Nation's eye 575:11
ev'ry beauteous o. 215:42
for o. strange and high 332:5
his eye on the o. 20:3
hope without an o. 152:18
my o. all sublime 220:2
no o. worth its constancy 495:19
o. of universal devotion 267:25
though mean our o. 579:7
with o. won 566:28
Objected to the use of dynamite 514:3
Objection: no o. to stoutness 218:31
Objects: extracted from many o. 428:16
for o. and knowledge 568:9
o. recognized in flashes 579:26
what o. are the fountains 498:8
Oblation and satisfaction 390:42
Oblations: no more vain o. 52:29
Obligation: because o. is a pain 278:12
I ow'd great o. 401:27
Possession without o. 337:25
Obliged: always o. to go 273:29
ne'er o. 385:29
o. to call it weoman 208:29
o. to stand in starless nights 193:30
Obliging: so o., that he ne'er obliged 385:29
Oblique: o. praise 274:5
puff o. 499:27
so loves o. 332:6
Obliquely: o. commendeth himself 85:14
o. run 186:25
Obliterated: its all o. Tongue 206:18
Oblitusque meorum 257:3
Oblivio: memoriae noverca, o. 414:21
Oblivion: alms for o. 481:17
bury in o. 87:22
commend to cold o. 493:9
formless ruin of o. 481:27
if I drink o. of a day 336:22
iniquity of o. 87:16
mere o. 427:21
my o. is a very Antony 423:37
o. as they rose shrank 492:13
o. in lost angels 16:5
razure of o. 462:24
stepmother to memory, o. 414:21
Oblivious: sweet o. aɪitidote 460:37
Oblong into the triangular 505:24
Obnoxious: repeal of..o. laws 228:23
Obscene: coiled o...serpents 523:11
on o. wings 151:19
Obscurata diu 257:20
Obscure: calm, though o., regions 265:13
destiny o. 230:1
grievèd and o. waters slope 96:31
had thee here o. 336:37
he who sits o. 495:10
o. bird clamour'd 458:21
o. grave 475:10
o. nook for me 94:22
o. sequestered state 96:16
suffering is permanent, o. 573:7
through the palpable o. 345:26
Obscured: excess of glory o. 345:5

Obscurely (cont.)
o. good 1:21
o. wise, and coarsely kind 275:1
Obscurest night involv'd the sky 159:1
Obscurity: decent o. of a learned language 217:4
unthought of in o. 575:11
Obscurus: brevis esse laboro, o. fio 255:18
Obsequies: celebrates his o. 417:20
solemnised their o. 87:3
Obsequious Seraphims 166:4
Observance: breach than the o. 431:31
duty, and o. 428:28
Observant of His heav'nly Word 183:21
Observation: bearings of this o. 175:14
cramm'd with o. 427:16
his o. and reading..the drapery 153:14
o., with extensive view 279:2
youth and o. copied there 432:20
Observations which ourselves we make 384:21
Observatory: I left the O. 363:22
Observed: o. by Yours faithfully 5:27
o. of all observers 434:14
Observer: he is a great o. 448:27
o. of human n., sir 178:25
partial for th' o.'s sake 384:21
Observeth: he that o. the wind 51:29
Obstinacy: o. in a bad cause 86:14
o. in a bad one 513:4
Obstinate: o. questionings 576:18
one was o. 99:4
Obstruction: consecrated o. 28:31
to lie in cold o. 462:9
Obtain that which he merits 151:26
Obtruding false rules 341:1
Occasion: courage mounteth with o. 447:22
Fate, Time, O. 497:7
give o. for your fate 202:4
giveth another o. of satiety 25:38
had o. to be seen 440:9
mellowing of o. 455:12
O. once pass'd by 158:19
o. smiles upon a second leave 431:24
on O.'s forelock..wait 350:6
postponed to some other o. 178:8
sad o. dear 342:10
some o. is presented 194:6
such an o. as this 98:15
take o. by the hand 539:12
Occasions: all o. do inform 436:15
finder-out of o. 471:1
new o. teach new duties 320:13
o. and causes why 445:7
upon their lawful o. 400:29
Occident: yet unformed O. 168:9
Occidental: bright O. Star 43:24
Occidit: o., o. spes omnis 260:23
Occult: bitterness of things o 411:29
Occupatio: inutilis o. 414:21
Occupation: absence of o. 162:3
Othello's o. 's gone! 472:3
pleasant o. for 218:37
Occupations: let us love our o. 174:8
pause in the day's o. 316:3
Occupés: les Anglais sont o. 355:8
Occupy age with the dream of 93:1
Occur: accidents will o. 174:37
facts..before they o. 167:27
things that didn't o. 210:9
Occurred: ought never to have o. 43:1
Occurs: what we anticipate seldom o. 182:8
Ocean: all great Neptune's o. 458:15
as it draws to the O. 16:4
as the o. murmurs there 308:28
dark illimitable o. 346:10
day-star in the o. bed 343:3
deep and dark blue O. 114:27
Earth and O. seem to sleep 493:14
fall into the o. 330:11
flower—the wind—the o. 114:5
for his fame the o. sea 35:23
from o.'s farthest coast 264:10
glistening Arctic O. 235:22
grasp the o. in my span 562:2
great o. of truth 364:13
his legs bestrid the o. 426:1
hungry o. gain 487:12
I have loved thee, O.! 114:32

Ocean (cont.)
in th' o.'s bosom unespied 332:1
into the main o. 212:8
is this the mighty o.? 308:29
life on the o. wave 415:11
make the mighty o. 127:33
meteor of the o. air 251:5
o.-floors pave it 495:27
O.'s child 495:2
O.'s nursling, Venice 495:1
o.'s wave-beat shore 202:23
old O. smiles 347:2
on one side lay the O. 531:30
on the o. of life we pass 318:10
pride of the o. 489:1
ransack the o. for..pearl 329:23
read o'er o. wide 309:6
rivers with the o. 495:7
round o. and the living air 582:1
sapless foliage of the o. 496:9
Shepherd of the O. 509:9
sky bounds the o. 80:14
thou, vast o.! 355:15
throned on o.'s wave 493:2
time, and the o. 561:10
to a lifeless o. 151:33
to the wild o. 484:35
unfathom'd caves of o. 230:5
upon a painted o. 149:5
upon the o. green 329:1
use the o. as their road 557:23
where the broad o. leans 226:13
Ocean-cave: dull day in an o. 531:9
Oceanic mind 153:14
Oceans: compendious o. 166:10
swallowing his tea in o. 325:32
Octavia: sober eye of dull O 425:34
Octavos: light o. 164:30
October: bright O...misty-bright O. 146:25
in the lonesome O. 381:1
leaf still in O. 37:15
Octo-syllabic verse 114:41
Ocular: give me the o. proof 472:4
Odd: creators of o. volumes 306:21
divinity in o. numbers 466:14
good luck..in o. numbers 466:14
how o. of God 202:19
think it exceedingly o. 305:10
this was o. 130:9, 13
this was scarcely o. 130:21
very o. thing—as o. as can be 171:17
Odd-fellow: desperate o. society 540:44
Odds: almost at o. with morning 459:24
Caesar's; and what o.? 166:14
facing fearful o. 323:17
his power and thine..no o. 281:8
o. is gone 425:29
what is the o. 177:28
what's the o. 335:8
Odds-bobs, sir! 121:6
Ode: I intended an O. 183:16
o., and elegy, and sonnet 276:14
Oderint, dum metuant 145:17
Odes: o. to every zephyr 293:12
quoted o. 538:11
Odi: incredulus o. 256:4
o. et amo 133:18
Odious: o.! in woollen! 384:25
she, and comparisons are o. 184:15
Odisse quem laeseris 526:10
Odium: more strength and far less o. 101:34
Odoribus: perfusus liquidis..o. 258:10
Odorous: comparisons are o. 468:43
wept o. gums and balm 347:5
Odour: o. of joss-sticks 503:17
stealing and giving o. 481:30
Odours: Champak o. fail 494:7
exhales her o. 117:29
gentle o. led my steps astray 497:20
haste with o. sweet 343:10
heavens rain o. on you! 483:25
living hues and o. 496:4
o., when sweet violets sicken 499:1
Sabæan o. 347:1
shakes hands with delectable o. 85:20
vials full of o. 70:42
Odysseus: doomed like O. 586:7
Odyssey: thunder of the O. 309:24
Odysseys: last of all our O. 41:18

INDEX

Oedipus: Davos sum, non O. 541:28
O'er: o. and o. the sand 293:23
O'erbrimmed their clammy cells 284:11
O'ercome: partly wi' love o. 106:22
O'ercrows my spirit 438:5
O'erdoing Termagant 434:15
O'erdusted: gilt o. 481:22
O'erflow: let your streams o. 332:11
O'erflowing: without o. full 172:10
O'erhang his wavy bed 153:24
O'erhanging: brave o. firmament 433:15
O'er informed the tenement 190:13
O'erjoyed was he to find 159:35
O'erkind: Time, that is o. 295:10
O'erlace the sea 90:34
O'erleaps: ambition..o. itself 457:9
O'erstep not the modesty of nature 434:16
O'ertake: I will o. thee, Cleopatra 425:22
O'ertook: flighty purpose never is o. 460:14
O'ertopping: house o. all 90:37
O'ertrip: fearfully o. the dew 465:17
O'erwhelm: all the earth o. them 431:19
Of: among them, but not o. them 113:51
Ofellus: quae praecepit O. 261:22
Off: if honour prick me o. 440:30
  nowhere to fall but o. 292:15
  o. with his head 129:13, 144:26, 476:22
  o. with the old love 7:22, 335:4
  walk down again with them o. 238:1
Offal: this slave's o. 433:35
Offence: after o. returning 350:33
  appear o. in us 449:1
  by whom the o. cometh 59:50
  confront the visage of o. 435:33
  conscience void of o. 65:18
  do no o. 467:1
  every nice o...comment 451:10
  forgave th' o. 192:6
  greatest o. against virtue 239:27
  innocent from the great o. 392:34
  my o. is rank 435:31
  retain the o. 435:34
  rock of o. 53:13
  satire..never resented for an o. 520:35
  that hir was doon o. 137:24
  what dire o. 385:8
  where the o. is 436:38
Offences: more o. at my beck 434:9
  needs be that o. come 59:50
  old o. of affections new 488:5
  pardoning our o. 390:45
  remember not the..o. of my youth 393:14
Offend: if thine eye o. thee 59:51
  if this pale rose o. 506:15
  I'll not willingly o. 519:2
  o. from want of thought 519:2
  o. one of these little ones 59:49
  tender to o. 245:11
Offended: Deity o. 105:20
  devils being o. 470:25
  him have I o. 450:16
  nor be easily o. 562:6
  not o. the king 358:8
  o. with 'the divine chit-chat' 306:32
  this hand hath o. 165:24
Offender: hugg'd th' o. 192:6
Offenders: society o. 219:24
Offendeth: tell how oft he o. 392:34
Offending: front of my o. 469:45
  most o. soul alive 444:27
  o. Adam 443:5
Offends: o. me to the soul 434:15
  o. no law 135:17
Offensive: mighty o. 274:27
Offer: nothing to o. but blood 143:38
  o. young bullocks 395:11
Offering: o. Germany too little 362:29
  o. too little 124:6
Offerings: nor fields of o. 47:29
  pale Hecate's o. 458:1
Offers: life o.—to deny! 236:37
Office: but a losing o. 441:10
  during his o. treason 190:25
  each in his o. wait 183:21
  form, o., and custom 481:2
  from their o. to black funeral 478:33
  insolence of o. 434:4
  in the o. of a wall 474:22

Office (cont.)
  no o. to go to 489:35
  not afraid to do thine o. 358:7
  o. and affairs of love 468:12
  officer and the o. 505:24
  o. he'll hold 84:27(-85)
  o. of perpetual president 127:31
  o. opposite to Saint Peter 472:37
  single o...between them 100:8
  so clear in his great o. 457:9
  to get some o. 473:1
  yarely frame the o. 424:7
Office boy to an Attorney's firm 221:15
Office boys: by o. for o. 414:22
Officer: each bush an o. 446:7
  each captain, petty o. 236:4
  never more be o. of mine 471:19
  o. and the office 505:24
Officers: king and o. of sorts 443:10
Offices: cast a longing eye on [o.] 268:24
  o. both private and public 352:25
  o...not derived corruptly 464:1
  o. of prayer and praise 574:12
  their functions and their o. 455:22
Official: this high o. 243:3
Officious, innocent, sincere 275:1
Officiously: strive o. to keep alive 146:35
Off-shore: Angel of the O. Wind 298:10
  beat of the o. wind 298:27
Offspring: o. of cold hearts 102:15
  o. of David 72:10
  o. of Heaven first-born 346:18
  source of human o. 347:26
  tempt its new-fledg'd o. 224:21
  time's noblest o. is the last 43:13
Oft: o. in danger, o. in woe 566:11
Often: how o. have we done this 492:23
Oft-times: me o. led 229:16
Ogled: sighed and pined and o. 543:12
O'Grady: the Colonel's Lady an' Judy O. 298:6
Oil: anointed my head with o. 393:10
  everlasting o. 340:9
  her mouth..smoother than o. 49:44
  his words..smoother than o. 395:13
  hurt not the o. and the wine 70:44
  'incomparable o.', Macassar! 115:15
  little o. in a cruse 48:1
  midnight o. 215:21, 404:5
  o...a cheerful countenance 398:9
  o. of joy for mourning 55:4
  o., vineyard, sugar 225:25
  our wasted o. 159:21
  this o. that I give you 39:1
  Warren's blackin' or Rowland's o. 179:5
  with boiling o. in it 220:12
  with o. anoint 421:1
  without the o. and twopence 504:30
Oiled: in the o. wards 288:32
Oils: dropt in ambrosial o. 341:2
  like a witch's o. 149:6
Oily: fat, o. man of God 546:6
Ointment: better than precious o. 51:9
  like the precious o. 400:3
  o. of the apothecary 51:23
  thy name is an o. 51:38
  very precious o. 60:35
  why was not this o. sold? 63:43
Ojibways: land of the O. 317:20
Old: act...o. men so duly 280:10
  all..the young can do for the o. 480:24
  all times when o. are good 112:26
  ancient times are only o. 236:42
  Asia..is too o. 304:27
  as o. and as true as the sky 298:19
  as o. as he's feeling 153:19
  as o. as she looks 153:19
  before I'm o. 297:19
  blind, o., and lonely 491:15
  born o. and ugly 173:21
  brave days of o. 323:21, 324:1
  busy o. fool, unruly Sun 186:19
  call him not o. 251:11
  considered the days of o. 396:32
  crucify the o. man 390:60
  darling, I am growing o. 406:8
  don't let the o. folks know 242:26
  even the o. are fair 585:15
  foolish, fond o. man 454:15
  for o. lang syne 104:14

Old (cont.)
  forget that he is o. 308:32
  forty years o. 251:10
  grand o. man 365:15
  growing o. in drawing nothing 163:11
  grow o. along with me! 95:13
  grow o. with a good grace 511:21
  half as o. as Time 100:3, 408:8
  head so o. and white as this 453:6
  heard the o., o. men say 585:19
  his o. brass 108:27
  how subject we o. men 442:14
  humanities of o. religion 152:9
  I am but two days o. 76:12
  I am too o. 28:3
  I am too o. to fawn 474:15
  I feel chilly and grown o. 97:9
  if ever I grow to be o. 42:6
  if I live to be o. 387:2
  I grow o. 197:21
  I have a liking o. for thee 121:19
  I know thee not, o. man 442:37
  I'm not so o. 218:38
  in judgment o. 463:41
  in the days of o. 296:29
  in the o. time before them 389:10
  is the o. min agreeable? 177:27
  it is o. and plain 483:5
  last to lay the o. aside 382:29
  leaving the o. 557:25
  likeness of a fat o. man 439:34
  lost lady of o. years 97:18
  love everything that's o. 226:43
  love will change in growing o. 82:2
  make an o. man young 529:26
  marry your o. friend's love 96:36
  mighty men which were of o. 44:38
  Mithridates, he died o. 263:26
  never be o. 263:3
  new world which is the o. 528:38
  nobody gets o. and godly 585:14
  no man would be o. 520:42
  not o., but mellow 378:18
  not persuade me I am o. 486:19
  not yet o. enough for a man 482:17
  now am o. 394:5
  off with the o. love 7:22, 335:4
  o. and haughty nation 340:2
  o. and tried 314:7
  o. and well stricken in age 44:50
  o. as I am, for ladies' love unfit 192:3
  o. before my time 409:28
  o. block itself 103:28
  o. bottles 58:42
  o. chairs to mend 367:6
  o. claes look amaist as weel 104:34
  o. companions in adversity 98:4
  o. enough to lap 568:22
  o. familiar faces 308:1
  o. folks at home 210:16
  o. friends are best 422:2
  o. friends, o. times 226:43
  o. gang 143:30
  O. Hornie, Satan, Nick 104:4
  o. instinct bring back the o. names 152:10
  o. is better 61:28
  O. Jack Falstaff 439:37
  o. know what they want 504:17
  O. Lady..in Danger 222:32
  o. lovers are soundest 563:22
  o. loves endear thee 148:14
  o., mad, blind, despised 498:18
  o. man and no honester than I 468:42
  o. man, broken 447:3
  o. man does not care for 271:23
  O. Man grey 74:5
  o. man in a hurry 143:32
  o. man Know-All 238:20
  o. man..so much blood 460:24
  o. man's wit may wander 530:1
  o. man.! 'tis not so difficult 118:11
  O. Man with a beard 311:2
  o. man with an o. soul 119:20
  o. men, and babes 150:15
  o. men and children 400:25
  o. men and comets 520:44
  o. men forget 444:28
  o. men from the chimney 502:8
  o. men go to death 25:4
  o. men's dream 190:18

INDEX

Old (cont.)

o. men shall dream dreams 55:52
o. men shall reap 323:12
o. men's nurses 26:37
o., o, and gay, O so o.! 584:15
o. o. story 235:10
o. ones by the hawk..kill'd 375:9
o. order changeth 531:35
o. plain men have rosy faces 516:5
o. plays begin to disgust 202:15
o. religious factions 101:31
O. Robin Grey 35:8
o. times are still new 236:42
o. times unqueen thee 148:14
o. times were changed 417:2
o., unhappy, far-off things 581:2
o. wine wholesomest 563:22
o. women (of both sexes) 513:18
one of them is fat and grows o. 439:15
one's o. and ugly 156:4
O, sir! you are o. 452:39
out of o. feldes..o. bokes 138:23
poor o. Joe 210:17
poor o. man 452:42
rebuild it on the o. plan 338:23
redress the balance of the O. 124:21
ring out the o. 533:18
say I'm growing o. 265:25(-266)
say of a particular sea..o. 237:10
say the o. 158:4
she was middling o. 298:29
should o. acquaintance be forgot 104:12
some o. lover's ghost 185:34
so o. a ship 208:16
so o. but she may learn 464:19
so o. to dote on her 452:23
so o...to keep the peace 477:1
story always o. and always new 95:39
sugared about by the o. men 302:5
summits o. in story 538:14
that o. man eloquent 351:16
there I met an o. man 366:23
there is an o. poor man 427:20
they all shall wax o. 398:3
they shall grow not o. 72:23
thinking of the o. 'un 174:16
though I look o. 426:36
time to be o. 199:30
to grow o. in Heaven 410:34
too o. for him 174:18
too o. to go again to my travels 136:9
unattractive o. thing 220:16
very o. are we men 171:1
weak, and despis'd o. man 453:6
we that are o. 226:40
when folks git o. 238:10
when he is o...not depart 50:30
when he's o., cashier'd 469:26
when I shall grow o. 577:25
when it is o...drink it 56:40
when they get to feeling o. 84:14
when thou art o. 232:2
when thou shalt be o. 64:18
when 'tis o. it waxeth cauld 32:18
when we are o. as you 429:31
when you are o. and gray 586:21
when you are o. sit under the shade 175:10
where de o. folks stay 210:16
whether it be new or o. 516:21(-517)
with so o. a head 464:32
worship of the great of o. 118:10
you and I are o. 541:3
you are o., Father William 128:28, 507:33
you must be very o., Sir Giles 359:8
you never can be o. 487:29
young lassie do wi' an o. man 108:26
you that are o. consider not 441:18
Old Bailey: bells of O. 368:8
Old Brigade: boys of the O.? 562:20
Oldcastle died a martyr 443:1
Olden: all of the o. time 8:5, 24:8
evening on the o. 208:6
Older: know better as they grow o. 414:19
o. than the rocks 374:11
richer still the o. 111:24
Oldest: o. hath borne most 454:28
o. man he seemed 580:8

Oldest (cont.)

o. rule in the book 129:32
o. sins the newest..ways 442:28
Old-fashioned: small o. book 196:24
Old-gentlemanly vice 115:27
Old Hundred: made O. ring 319:25
Old Kent Road: in the O. 142:23
Old maid: rich, ugly o. 77:9
Old Pretender: James II, and the O. 233:14
Old Testament: blessing of the O. 25:18
Old Year: ringing the O. out 223:10
O'Leary: with O. in the grave 584:27
Oleum: hoc o...mittas in mare 39:1
Olive: o., aloe, and maize 528:23
o. grove of Academe 350:11
Olive-branches: children like the o. 399:36
Oliver Twist has asked for more! 177:36
Olivet: purple brows of O. 532:22
red dew of O. 545:7
Olivia: cry out, 'O.' 482:22
see O. first 481:31
Ologies: instructed in the 'o.' 126:32
Olores: instrepere anser o. 556:7
Olympian: O. bards who sung 199:20
o. bolts 180:22
Olympo: Pelion imposuisse O. 259:27
viamque adfectat O. 556:26
Olympum: Ossae..involvere O. 556:12
Olympus: all O.' faded heirarchy 288:4
Omar: the diver O. 320:6
Ombrifuge (Lord love you!) 121:2
Omega: I am Alpha and O. 70:22
Omen: procul o. abesto! 371:19
quod di o. avertant 145:18
Ominous vibration of a pendulum 282:18
Omitted: o., all the voyage 451:29
o. to mention the fact 128:5
Omnes eodem cogimur 259:4
Omnia: labor o. vicit 556:11
non o. possumus omnes 556:6
o. mutari 25:13
o. vincit Amor 556:8
Omnibus: ab o. creditum est 553:4
Omnibuses: ridden more in o. 241:3
Omnipotent: defy th' O. to arms 344:7
o. but friendless 497:4
Power, which seems o. 497:17
squamous, o., and kind 83:26
Omnipresent: Eno was o. 514:2
Omnis: non o. moriar 260:16
Omniscience: his specialism is o. 188:10
o. his foible 506:2
Omnium: Plantagenet Palliser, Duke of O...gentleman 549:13
On: let us pass on! 100:15
nowhere to stand but o.! 292:15
o., bacons, o.! 439:6
o., o. thy way 246:23
o., o., you noblest English! 443:25
o., Stanley, o.! 418:32
o. with the dance! 113:26
o. with the new 7:22, 335:4
sit here..o. and off 128:30
Sunday that goes o. and o. 208:10
their utmost up and o. 95:38
Onaway! Awake, beloved! 318:1
Once: at o. and ever 151:33
but o. a year 549:23
could but have happened o. 97:29
man can die but o. 442:12
o. a gentleman 176:3
o. more unto the breach 443:24
o. more, O ye laurels 342:10
o. more upon the waters! 113:22
o. more who would not be a boy? 113:14
o. to every man and nation 320:9
taste any drink o. 120:4
that o. had shone 208:10
through this world but o. 232:10
to be o. in doubt 471:34
One: adding o. to o. 91:41
all the means to make us o. 184:30
as o. man 46:62
but o...doth hold his place 449:30
clock struck o. 367:3
day but o. 79:5
ever Three and ever O. 361:14
flee at the rebuke of o. 53:40

One (cont.)

formed..for o. another 493:8
for o. in vain 207:29
God is O. 364:5
have o. with me wandering 359:5
he had but o. eye 177:1
his qualifications?—O.! 84:27(-85)
I dearly love but o. day 125:19
I do know but o. 449:30
incorporate and make us o. 449:16
in thee are o. 81:5
labour for the o. 115:1
looking o. way 99:17
made o. of them 452:9
members o. of another 67:58
more than o. a bed 186:8
none is fairer seen, save O. 376:3
none to o...sovereignty 189:3
not three Gods: but o. 388:40
nymph with but o. 500:40
of o. to me little remains 540:32(-541)
o. among a thousand 49:14
o. and o.-sixteenth is born 6:6
o. and the fifty-three 539:21
o. another's best 184:29
o. a penny, two a penny 368:5
o. born to love you, sweet! 90:11
o. by o. back in the Closet 206:28, 29
o. by o. crept silently to Rest 206:6
o. damned thing after another 264:25
o. dissertates, he is candid 93:18
o. does feel 305:7
o. especially do we affect 330:13
o. far-off divine event 533:31
o. flesh..two fools 154:32
o. from other know 324:12
o. God, o. law, o. element 533:31
o. God only 146:34
o. here will constant be 99:35
o. idea..wrong 182:28, 272:3
o. leak will sink a ship 99:28
o. life for each to give 296:20
o. man among a thousand 51:15
o. man..die for the people 63:42
o. man in a thousand 302:17
o. man..out of ten thousand 433:2
o. more, and this the last 473:11
o. more, o. more 473:11
o. more Unfortunate 252:12
O., most loving of you all 89:1
o. near o. is too far 90:10
o. of Eve's family 252:16
o. of two bad ways 450:8
o. of us that hasn't paid 298:22
o. of us two, Herminius 324:8
o. of us was born a twin 313:8
o., on God's side 378:19
o. per cent. inspiration 195:22
o. person doing interesting actions 28:29
O. remains 492:15
o. shall be taken 60:27
o. sin..destroy a sinner 99:28
o. succeeds 528:26
o. sure, if another fails 96:40
o. task for all 296:20
o. that lov'd not wisely 474:2
o. to come, and o. to go 131:15
o. to destroy is murder 586:27
o. to face the world with 94:10
o. to show a woman 94:10
o., two, and the third 478:3
o., two, buckle my shoe 368:6
o., two! o., two! 129:39(-130)
o., two, three; go! 233:7
o.; two; thy then, 'tis time 460:24
o. was beautiful 117:6
o. way possible 96:18
o. who never turned his back 97:4
o. with my kind 536:25
only o...of the contrary opinion 338:26
only o. thing at once 503:9
ought to be Number O. 129:32
our two souls..which are o. 186:25
poor wandering o.! 221:29
putting o. away 478:7
run by o. and o. 302:23
so much o. man can do 332:26
stoppeth o. of three 148:18
than O. who rose 493:27
that's all o. 484:27

One (cont.)
they are o. and o. 90:10
they'd eaten every o. 130:21
thinking of the old o. 174:16
thou lov'st the o. 35:19
to o. thing constant never 468:20
watch with me o. hour 60:42
we are o., o. flesh 349:19
we be of o. blood, thou and I 304:9
went in o. by o. 10:7
when only o. is shining 580:18
One-and-twenty: when I was o. 262:17
One-eyed..sort o' place 237:11
One-goddite: as old a o. 307:26
One-horse: o. town 550:29
wonderful o. shay 251:6
Onion: let o. atoms lurk 505:3
tears live in an o. 423:28
Onions: wel loved he garleek, o. 137:20
Only: o., o. call me thine 152:6
o. sleep! 97:23
o. son..o. father 226:36
o. thou, O God 388:24
worship o. thee 161:3
Onus: cum mens o. reponit 132:21
Onward: he o. came 348:21
if o. ye will tread 362:7
little o. lend thy..hand 350:20
o., Christian soldiers 35:1
o., Christians, go 566:11
o. goes the pilgrim band 35:4
o., leading up the golden year 529:29
o. through life he goes 318:13
upward still, and o. 320:13
Onwards: o.—always o. 24:2
Ooze: o. and bottom of the sea 443:9
o. of their pasture-ground 15:24
sprawled through the o. 504:13
Oozing: I feel it o. out 500:29
Wine of Life keeps o. 205:16
Oozy woods 496:9
Opal: thy mind is a very o. 483:7
Ope: could not o. his mouth 110:7
when I o. my lips 462:34
Oped his ponderous..jaws 431:32(-432)
Open: all hearts be o. 390:4
come o. your gates 420:15
gates are mine to o. 300:11
great o. spaces 331:13
gross as a mountain, o. 439:23
her eyes are o. 460:23
I take to the o. road 568:3
my sentence is for o. war 345:16
of a free and o. nature 470:22
of an o. and free nature 280:1
o. and notorious evil liver 390:1
o. door for all nations' trade 43:11
o. face of heaven 289:2
o. foe may prove a curse 215:24
o., locks 460:1
o. my heart 91:6
o. not thine heart to every man 56:38
o. quickly! 23:23
o. rebuke is better 50:44
o. Sesame! 14:3
o. the temple gates 509:12
o. thy Goethe 127:19
o. thy white hand 485:5
o. to me, my sister 52:9
o. unto the fields 582:14
o., ye everlasting gates 348:28
o…your living doors 348:28
slumbering in the o. air 152:17
throw o. the gates of new life 96:25
where knock is o. wide 503:5
Opened: gates of heaven o. 328:23
I o. to my beloved 52:11
knock, and it shall be o. 58:19
my heart new o. 446:24
o. not his mouth 54:26
Open-ey'd conspiracy 479:37
Opening: he has been o. the doors 22:14
o. of the prison 55:3
o. on the foam 288:1
o. paradise 231:5
o. the windows at Randalls 231:5
Operation: mere mechanic o. 111:12
o. of the Holy Ghost 390:41
requires a surgical o. 504:20
Operations: five o. of the Lord 56:45
Opes: ab ipso ducit o…ferro 260:21

Opes (cont.)
ad summas emergere o. 320:30(-321)
det vitam, det o. 257:11
fumum et o. strepitumque Romae 260:13
inter o. inops 260:9
Ophelia: I lov'd O. 437:24
Ophir: from distant O. 333:20
Ophiucus: fires the length of O. 346:6
Opinion: back'd his o. with quotations 402:1
better to have no o. of God 27:20
build on these a better o. 473:4
coquetry of public o. 103:10
educated literary and scientific o. 19:16
great organ of public o. 180:22
gross and scope of my o. 430:12
heresy..private o. 248:20
imperfect o. 200:23
justifies th'ill o. 107:10
last o. right 383:1
of his own o. still 111:18
of the o. with the learned 155:3
once a private o. 200:20
one..of the contrary o. 338:26
o…determined by the feelings 508:29
o…knowledge in the making 352:14
o. one man entertains of another 373:8
o. we are endeavouring to stifle 338:27
our own o. from another 200:37
party is organized o. 180:34
plague of o.! 481:23
poor itch of your o. 429:4
quite from the main o. 449:11
this fool gudgeon, this o. 462:35
upon the difference of an o. 86:3
Opinions: golden o. 457:10
halt ye between two o.? 48:2
killed with your hard o. 443:1
laughter at their quaint o. 348:30
much writing, many o. 352:14
new o. are always suspected 315:5
public buys its o. 112:6
so bad as their o. 326:26
so many men, so many o. 542:1
stiff in o. 190:22
this conflict of o. 277:5
Opium: o. of the people 333:13
subtle and mighty o.! 172:19
Opium: das O. des Volkes 333:13
Oppenheim, half blind 42:11
Opponent: o. of the chosen people 19:14
to an o. motives meaner 36:3
Opportunitae: felix..o. mortis 526:11
Opportunities: make more o. 25:39
watches all o. 155:24
woman with fair o. 542:32
Opportunity: make his o. 24:28
maximum of o. 490:32
mortal man such o. 116:28
o. for moralizing 542:35
o. makes a thief 28:2
seducer, o. 192:1
what a o. 177:42
wisdom..by o. of leisure 57:11
Oppose: o. every system 102:37
Opposition..to o. 143:34
to o. everything 511:11
Opposed: new opinions..usually o. 315:5
o. may beware of thee 431:25
Opposing: by o. end them 434:4
o. one..superstition to another 265:13
Opposite: diverse, sheer o. 285:35
on the o. quarter 100:9
Opposition: duty of an O. 143:34, 511:11
Her Majesty's O. 28:23
'His Majesty's O.' 249:3
not in o. to 'em 179:36
o. of the stars 332:6
without a formidable O. 181:30
Oppressed: Foal of an o. race! 152:19
heart and voice o. 362:1
he was o. 54:26
just men long o. 350:36
let the o. go free 54:36
o. with two weak evils 427:20
Oppression: but behold o. 53:2
make o. bitter 433:34
o. makes the wise man mad 93:14
rumour of o. and deceit 162:40

Oppression (cont.)
stoop with o. 475:12
through o…any plague 398:21
Oppressions: else unfelt o. 494:16
Oppressor: common enemy and o. 101:27
mighty of the earth, th' o. 350:36
o.'s wrong 434:4
Opprobrious: without using..o. terms 194:17
Oppugnancy: meets in mere o. 481:4
Ops: fugues and 'o.' 220:5
Optics: in the o. of these eyes 86:20
Optimist proclaims 120:6
Opulent Rotunda 514:4
Opus: hoc o., hic labor est 554:23
iamque o. exegi 372:1
nunc animis o., Aenea 554:23
Oracle: fast by the o. of God 344:12
I am Sir O. 462:34
thy o., thy heat 288:6
Oracles: lively O. of God 157:13
o. are dumb 343:21
Oracular: my o. tongue 500:20
Orange: o. bright like golden lamps 332:2
o. flower perfumes 420:9
Orange-blossom: of palm, of o. 528:23
Orangen: die Gold-O. glühn 224:6
Orange-pulp: watered o. 96:39
Oranges and lemons 368:7
Orange-tree: that I were an o. 244:17
Orans: aut scribens, aut o. 291:25
Orare est laborare 13:1
Oration: not studied as an o. 370:18
Orator: I am no o., as Brutus 459:32
persuade..without an o. 486:5
Orators: our swords shall play the o. 330:22
Oratory: Chadband style of o. 173:33
object of o. 326:6
Orb: changes in her circled o. 477:22
mighty o. of song 574:19
never lighted on this o. 102:11
not the smallest o. 465:18
o. in o. 348:30
O.! you're quite amazing! 311:20
quail and shake the o. 426:1
this splendid o…set 100:9
too vast o. of her fate 16:11
Orbis: securus iudicat o. terrarum 21:24
si fractus illabatur o. 259:22
Orbit: in its ruddy o. 375:25
Orbs: in their glimmering o. 343:14
quenched their o. 346:19
Orcades: in Scotland, at the O. 383:21
Orchard: fair with o. lawns 531:37
like on o. boughs 255:6
o. slopes and the Anio 146:13
picture that o. sprite 249:8
pleasant o. closes 88:10
sings on the o. bough 92:14
Orci: in faucibus O. 554:23
Ordained: o. and constituted.. Angels 389:54
o. for the procreation of children 391:24
powers that be are o. of God 66:9
stars, which thou hast o. 392:9
Ordainer of order 85:19
Ordainest: King, Who o. 142:26
Ordains: o. for each one spot 302:13
o. us e'en as blind 295:10
Orden no es una presión 214:2
Order: all things began in o. 85:19
before the hills in o. stood 562:9
decently, and in o. 67:4
good o. is the foundation 102:29
half of one o., half another 110:34
harmony, o. or proportion 86:32
in a wonderful o. 389:54
in all line of o. 481:2
liberty connected with o. 100:13
old o. changeth 531:35
ordainer of o. 85:19
o…basis of Empire 156:27
o. is Heav'n's first law 384:3
o. is not a pressure 214:2
o. of your going 459:23
o…this matter better in France 512:16
ornament to the civil o. 102:25
party of o. 338:28
set thine house in o. 54:6

Order (cont.)
teach the act of o. 443:10
to the prejudice of good o. 5:26
words in the best o. 153:6
Ordered my goings 394:12
Ordering: for the o. your affairs 485:27
Orders: Almighty's o. to perform 1:11
don't obey no o. 295:21
work till further o. 296:33
Ordinance: God's holy o. 391:30
God's o. 391:28
Ordinary: above the reach of o. men 580:12
o. young Englishman 19:27
Ordo: saeclorum nascitur o. 555:30
Ordre: l'o. règne à Varsovie 12:17
Ore: load every rift..with o. 291:1
with new spangled o. 343:3
Ore rotundo 256:8
Oreilles: les o. ennemies 12:19
Orfèvre: vous êtes o. 353:8
Organ: as the maiden's o. 482:10
every lovely o. 469:6
heav'n's deep o. 343:17
mellering to the o. 178:7
most miraculous o. 433:36
o. of public opinion 180:22
pealing o. blow 341:24
playing of the merry o. 10:14
seated one day at the o. 402:11
Organically..incapable of a tune 306:4
Organism: desire on the part of every o. 111:34
Organize the theatre! 20:6
Organized: minutely o. Particulars 75:7
Organized: o. hypocrisy 29:3, 180:18
party is o. 180:34
science is o. knowledge 508:21
Organs: dry up..the o. of increase 452:29
his owls was o. 176:31
moves with its own o. 424:17
Organ-voice: God-gifted o. 529:17
Orgunjè: past O. 17:28
Oriel Common-Room stank 363:20
Orient: his chin upon an o. wave 343:24
in the o. when the..light 486:12
of o. pearl a double row 124:5
your beauty's o. deep 125:9
Oriental: more-than-o.-splendour 304:15
tea, although an O. 142:9
with o. scrupulosity 278:11
Orientals make hither 82:8
Oriflamme: be your o. today 323:5
Origin: gift of noble o. 581:17
nothing..not Greek in its o. 327:12
o. of the fictive picture 268:8
stamp of his lowly o. 169:5
Original: all things counter, o. 255:3
behold the bright o. 215:16
Eno o. 514:2
from o. righteousness 401:5
in th'o. perus'd mankind 14:24
nothing o...excepting O. Sin 123:13
o. something 123:13
taught O. Sin 91:34
without an o. 233:9
Original: l'écrivain o. 136:18
Originality: fruits of o. 338:30
without o. or moral courage 489:11
Originator: next to the o...the first quoter 201:6
Origo: caelestis o. 554:31
Orion: loose the bands of O. 49:24
Orisons: nymph, in thy o. 434:5
Orlando: run, run, O. 427:23
Ormus: wealth of O. 345:14
Ornament: deceived with o. 464:14
for delight, for o. 27:13
foreign aid of o. 546:19
graceful o. to the civil order 102:25
greatest defence and o. 73:6
hiding..with fair o. 464:14
moment's..with o. 580:19
not a single o. 413:11
old o. of his cheek 468:32
o. of a meek..spirit 70:1
o. of life 457:11
o...the guiled shore 404:15
o. to her profession 99:33
rhyme being no..true o. 343:20
that sweet o...truth 487:5

Ornaments: hide with o. their want of art 382:26
in lieu of many o. 509:15
put on o. of gold 47:30
Ornate: bedeck'd, o., and gay 350:31
o. rhetorick 352:28
Pure, O., and Grotesque 29:8
Ornavit: nullum quod tetigit non o. 273:19
Orotunda: Opulent O. 514:4
Orphan: an o., both sides 564:27
o.'s curse 149:22
Orphan-boy: carried by an o. 416:29
o. to read 533:39
Orphan-child: ostrich an' a o. 300:8
Orphan-girl to sew 533:39
Orphans: sighs of o. 172:18
wrong'd o.' tears 334:26
Orpheus: another O. sings again 493:25
feign that O. drew trees 465:20
harp of O. 352:26
O. with his lute made trees 446:18
soul of O. sing 341:19
Orphic: perpetual O. song 497:14
Orthodox: called 'o. divinity' 20:16
prove their doctrine o. 110:18
Orthodoxy: o. is my doxy 559:31
O. or My-doxy 126:18
Ortolans: die eating o. 182:44
Oscar: you will, O. 566:10
Oserez: n'o. vous 231:36
Osier-isle: guards his o. 546:11
Ossam: imponere Pelio O. 556:12
Ossian: could have written O. 271:1
Ossibus: ex o. ultor 554:21
Ostendis: quodcumque o. mihi 256:4
Ostentation: o. of our love 424:22
rite nor formal o. 436:37
Ostentatious: elegant but not o. 278:7
Ostrich: devil an' a o. 300:8
resembled the wings of an o. 326:4
strong the tall o. 503:5
Othello: married with O. 472:37
O.'s occupation's gone! 472:3
O.'s visage in his mind 470:10
Other: all o. things give place 215:30
all o. things, to their destruction 184:6
at the o. out it wente 138:36
feel it more than o. people 174:14
find o. lands 546:23
in o. men's minds 306:25
I the o. 35:19
not so as men are 62:33
nuisance to o. people 338:29
o. folks have 204:20
o. lips, and o. hearts 98:22
o. things..all very well 174:35
o. to the Altar's God 166:13
smite the o. too 251:4
some did o. things 304:30
sounded..on the o. side 99:41
think like o. people 491:12
t'o. dear charmer away 215:4
t'o. governor 178:20
Others: as o. see us 106:33
love of o. 239:23
misfortunes and pains of o. 102:31
not false to o. 27:37
o. abide our question 17:23
o...tell the news 77:32
that o. should build for him 580:6
Otherwise: so, and no o. 301:10
some are o. 211:11
stars came o. 90:13
we might be o. 494:15
Otia: deus nobis haec o. fecit 555:16
Otiosum: numquam se minus o. esse 145:9
Otiosus: numquam sis ex toto o. 291:25
Otium: cum dignitate 145:22
Otto: in your pipe, my Lord O. 34:22
Oublié: rien appris, ni rien o. 526:17
rien o. et..rien appris 195:1
Oude: vovi—I've O. 403:11
Ought: do the things I o. 527:6
everything you o. to be 221:42
hadn't o. to be 238:31
I. o., therefore I can 284:6
love..lyke as we o. 509:5
not what they o. to do 24:23
not what we o. to say 454:28
things he plainly o. to have 223:7
we do not what we o. 15:11

Ought (cont.)
what..I o. to do 101:3
what things they o. to do 389:28
Oughtn't: nothing that you o. 221:42
Oun: properly based O. 91:42
Ounce of poison in one pocket 324:35
Ounces: tigers, o., pards 347:15
Our Father 58:4
Ours: little we see..that is o. 582:18
they're o. 185:1
Ourselves: America is just o. 19:23
by o. betrayed 155:25
enduring power, not o. 20:14
eternal not o. 20:17
in o. are triumph and defeat 317:4
in o. that we are thus 470:15
love of o. 239:23
not in our stars, but in o. 448:22
o. know not 186:25
o. to know 384:19
phantom of o. 16:10
steal us from o. 191:22
to o...consigned 278:29
truth is within o. 94:14
unsafe..with o. 154:26
Ouse: slow winding O. 162:7
Ousel and the throstlecock 189:18
Out: bachelors to go o. 196:28
beat time, o. of time 213:23
Betsey and I are o. 125:20
came o. by the same door 206:10, 11
creep a little o., and then 247:12
get o., you blazing ass! 121:4
going o. with the tide 174:39
I can't get o. 512:25
immediately go o. 73:28
in the way, nor o. of the way 136:7
know that you are o. 34:29
Lord Coodle would go o. 174:4
love and murder will o. 154:35
never o. nor in 190:32
nor am I o. of it 330:2
not to go o. 352:29
other o. 142:30
o., damned spot! 460:24
o., even to a full disgrace 429:18
o. of it, as Wind 206:13
o. of it..a tragedy 570:29
o. of sight is o. of mind 147:12
o. of the world! 252:20
o., o., brief candle! 461:4
o., vile jelly! 453:35
o. with it, then 127:21
shall not be put o. 56:18
vanity, like murder, will o. 158:26
went o...with the Stuarts 182:7
when the tide's pretty nigh o. 174:39
who's in, who's o. 454:19
wish to get o. 201:11
Out-argue: we will o. them 273:30
Out-babying Wordsworth 322:10
Outcast: beweep my o. state 486:24
spiritless o.! 124:9
Outcasts: gather together the o. 400:21
Outcries: what o. plague me? 305:13
Outcry of the hunted hare 73:20
Out-did the meat 246:15
Outface it with their semblances 426:28
Out-glittering Keats 322:10
Outgoings of the morning 395:29
Outgrabe: mome raths o. 129:39
Outgrown: thine o. shell 251:15
Outlawed: [corporations] cannot..be o. 148:10
Outlet: finds no natural o. 150:31
Outline: demd o. 177:20
Outlines: no o. at all 177:20
Outlive: o. this powerful rhyme 487:6
sure you shall o. this day? 202:1
Outlived the doctor's pill 214:34
Outlives: he that o. this day 444:28
Outlook that mark 552:10
Outlove: outsing and o. us 523:5
Outpost: ultimate o. of eternity 410:31
Outpourings: passionate o. of Euripides 153:12
Outrageous fortune 434:4
Outrageously virtuous 511:22
Outredden all..garden-roses 537:26
Outrun: thou hast o. the constable 110:37
Out-scorn the..wind and rain 453:4

INDEX

Outshine myriads, though bright 344:11
Outshone: far o. the wealth 345:14
Outside: I support it from the o. 335:21
  kiss the book's o. 159:29
  martial o. 426:28
  o. the fast-closed door 264:12
Outsider: busy o. 236:42
Outsing: o. and outlove us 523:5
Out-soared the shadow of our night 492:7
Outsport discretion 471:5
Outstayed his welcome 152:21
Outstretched: with his arms o. 481:20
Outstrip thy skiey speed 496:10
Out-topping knowledge 17:23
Out-vote: though we cannot o. 273:30
Outward: from o. forms to win 151:3
  in all her o. parts 158:1
  my o. soul 185:4
  not fair to o. view 148:12
  o. and visible sign 391:13
  o. appearance 47:18
  o. be fair 143:12
  o. show of things 510:12
  sense and to o. things 576:18
  taper to the o. room 186:12
  things o. do draw the inward quality 424:28
  with my o. a Thistle 74:5
Outwatch the Bear 341:17
Outwore: six lustres almost..o. 186:6
Outworn: o. buried age 487:11
  o. heart, in a time o. 584:19
Ouverte aux talents 126:2
Oven: heating of the o. 480:38
  in the o. for baby and me 368:10
Over: after the ball is o. 238:5
  all's o., then 93:8
  all thy waves..gone o. me 394:19
  half seas o. 520:13
  now it is o. 299:22
  o. and can't be helped 178:39
  o. hill, o. dale 466:33
  o. the hills and far away 214:26, 369:10, 516:13
  o. then, come o. 298:26
  o. the sea 250:15, 262:7, 420:13
  o. the water 10:15, 250:15, 420:13
  pleasure of having it o. 253:9
  so he passed o. 99:41
  sooner it's o. 294:2
  Thou art o. all! 301:29
  view of—of o. the way 177:32
  when all have given him o. 189:20
Over-arched: shades high o. 344:25
Overboard: yellow fellow fell o. 8:24
Overbold: drunken and o. 95:2
Over-bowed by many benedictions 92:33
Overcame: came, saw, and o. 428:25, 442:19
  day he o. the Nervii 450:27
Over-canopied with..woodbine 466:41
Overcast: dawn is o. 1:13
  our sky was o. 160:21
Overcoat: his o. for ever 263:36
  only argument..put on your o. 320:21
Overcome: I have o. the world 63:64
  nature..sometimes o. 26:39
  not o. of evil, but o. evil 66:7
  o. us like a summer's cloud 459:22
  what is else not to be o. 344:14
Overcomes: who o. by force 345:8
Over-driven: only o. 515:9
Overflow: o. of powerful feelings 583:4
  o. thy urn 308:19
Overflows her bower 498:6
Overgrown with azure moss 496:8
Overheard: poetry is o. 339:4
  o. the judgment of posterity 325:29
Overland Mail 300:12
Over-mastered: woman to be o. 468:8
Overpaid: grossly o. 243:3
Over-past: until this tyranny be o. 395:17
Over-plus: Will in o. 488:15
Overpowering knell 116:18
Over-ruled: will in us is o. 330:13
Overset: she was o. 162:10
Overshot: study evermore is o. 454:34
Oversoar the loftiest star 497:12
Overspread the continent 371:4
Overtake: I thy fate shall o. 292:19

Overtaking: neither o. nor meeting 154:34
Overthrow: of God, ye cannot o. it 64:32
  o. of body and soul 109:22
  purpos'd o. 487:23
  think'st thou dost o. 185:15
  triumph in his o. 231:32
Overthrown: our devices still are o. 435:13
  o. more than your enemies 426:24
Overtook: so soon as the man o. me 99:15
Overwhelm myself in poesy 288:11
Overwhelmed all her litter 441:11
Over-zealous piety 101:23
Oves: enumerat..pastor o. 402:15
  non vobis vellera fertis o. 556:27
Ovid: O., the soft philosopher 192:45
  Venus clerk, O. 138:15
Owe: continuest such, o. to thy-self 348:11
  happy, o. to God 348:11
  I o. you a thousand pound 442:40
  much I o. to the Lands 303:10
  o. no man anything 66:11
  o. no man hate 427:27
  we o. God a death 442:12
  you o. me no subscription 453:6
Owed: never..was so much o. 144:1
Owedst: sleep which thou o. yesterday 471:43
Owes: by owing o. not 346:31
  he o. not any man 318:12
  he o. something to us 278:24
Owest: lend less than thou o. 452:25
  pay me that thou o. 59:55
  thou o. God a death 440:29
Owing: by o. owes not 346:31
Owl: as any noon-tide o. 530:31
  by a mousing o. hawk'd at 458:28
  clamorous o. 466:43
  fight..against the o. 460:17
  it was the o. that shriek'd 458:3
  moping o. 229:29
  old o. liv'd in an oak 403:22
  O. and the Pussy-Cat 311:24
  o., for all his feathers 285:12
  o. in an ivy-bush 520:6
  O. looked up to the Stars 311:24
  o. that is in the desert 398:1
  Pickwick, the O. 11:4
  sings the staring o. 456:1
  white o. in the belfry sits 540:14
  white o. sweeping 336:9
Owlet: my little o.! 317:23
  o. Atheism 151:19
  o. whoops to the wolf 150:9
Owls: answer'd o. are hooting 118:8
  court for o. 53:45
  eagle among blinking o. 495:10
  o. and cuckoos 351:18
  three O. and a Pig 312:20
  two black o. came 39:29
  two O. and a Hen 311:2
  when o. do cry 480:14
  while I live, the O.! 541:25
Owl-songs: sadder than o. 116:50
Own: all countries..his o. 191:32
  ask for our o. 82:27
  beaten men come into their o. 334:7
  because it is their o. 234:14
  but mine o. 428:35
  came unto his o...received him not 62:63
  do what I will with mine o. 60:8
  I o. the soft impeachment 500:30
  keeping watch above his o. 320:11
  liberal..of his o. 27:7
  makes his o. 192:13
  make the age to come my o. 158:14
  make ye sure to each his o. 301:26
  Melancholy mark'd him for her o. 230:13
  moments which he calls his o. 408:7
  most their o. 135:28
  my o., my sweet 536:15
  o. that thou art beautiful 493:4
  Room of One's O. 572:22
  till the King enjoys his o. 373:13
  wiser than his o. 84:22
  yet can call his o. 188:31
Own-alone: by my o. self 238:12

Owned: treason is not o. 193:8
Owner: I am the o. of the sphere 199:2
  ox knoweth his o. 52:26
Owners: down went the o. 218:1
Owning: mania of o. things 567:20
  o. her weakness 252:22
Owns: whom nobody o. 365:6
Ox: eateth grass as an o. 49:28
  eat straw like the o. 53:19
  fat o. with evil will 50:13
  nor his o., nor his ass 390:17
  not muzzle the o. 46:26
  o. knoweth his owner 52:26
  o...to the slaughter 49:51
  o. to wrath has mov'd 73:22
  roasted Manningtree o. 439:35
  stalled o. and hatred 50:12
  stands like an o. in the furrow 300:7
Oxen: lowing of the o. 47:15
  many o. are come about me 393:4
  more than a hundred pair of o. 264:20
  that our o. may be strong 400:17
  who drives fat o. 275:23
  years like great black o. 584:8
Oxenford: Clerk..of O. 137:5
Oxford: Half-Way House to Rome, O. 403:5
  in O. made an art 193:24
  Ipswich and O.! 447:10
  Koran..taught in..O. 217:12
  never seen O. since 363:22
  noon on O. town 208:5
  O...made me insufferable 39:13
  O...more attractive 28:20
  O. to him..dearer 193:25
  stage coach from London to O. 239:19
  to..O..no obligation 216:19
  to O. sent a troop 87:26, 548:20
  troops he to O. sent 549:1
  what a whole O. is! 148:15
Oxford Street, stony-hearted step-mother 712:18
Oxlips: bold o. 485:26
  o. and the nodding violet 466:41
Oxonian: privileg'd..being an O. 203:31
Oxus: O., forgetting 17:28(–18)
  shorn and parcell'd O. 17:28(–18)
Oyster: o...crossed in love 500:7
  pearl in your foul o. 428:36
  unselfishness of an o. 414:12
  world's mine o. 465:37
Oysters: all the little O. stood 130:15
  by no means unlike o. 176:5
  four young O. hurried up 130:13
  often eaten o. 218:2
  o...more beautiful than..religion 414:12
  poverty and o. 178:38
Ozymandias, king of kings 496:14

P

Pace: creeps in this petty p. 461:4
  dance is a measured p. 24:21
  exampled by the first p. 481:5
  I don't like the p. 505:30
  long-resounding p. 231:14
  mend his p. with beating 437:7
  moon's soft p. 579:20
  no p. perceiv'd 487:29
  not afraid of 'the p.' 518:31
  p. is too good to inquire 365:1
  to p. the ground 577:24
  unperturbed p. 544:14
  with his stealthy p. 458:1
  with violent p. 472:12
Pace: e'n la sua volontade è nostra p. 168:26
Paced: bride hath p. 148:23
  p. upon the mountains 586:21
Pacem: qui desiderat p., praeparet bellum 552:16
  solitudinem..p. appellant 526:9
Paces: p. about her room again 197:32
  regular p. 86:32
Pachyderm: Tidy P. 304:20
Paciencia y barajar 134:15
Pacific: except by p. means 291:17
  star'd at the P 288:19

INDEX

Pacing side by side 573:13
Pacings: mechanic p. to and fro 535:22
Pacis: longae p. mala 283:10
  p.que imponere morem 555:1
Pack: God! I will p. 84:12
  huntsman his p. 225:33
  p. and label men for God 544:32
  p. when it begins to rain 452:38
  pour out the p. of matter 424:14
  somebody's p. has slid 300:16
  that can p. the cards 25:41
Package: Ankworks p. 176:27
Pack-drill for me 295:4
Packed: all carefully p. 128:5
Pack-horse: p. on the down 359:2
  posterity..a p. 180:28
Packs and sets of great ones 454:19
Padded man 537:4
Paddington: as London is to P. 124:14
  ever-weeping P. 75:3
Paddle his own canoe 331:19
Paddles: 'ear their p. chunkin' 299:10
  p. in a halcyon sea 409:14
Paddling: p. palms 485:6
  splashing and p. 88:11
Paddock calls 456:3
Paddocks: cold as p. 247:15
Paddy: O P. dear 9:6
Padlock: your p. on her mind 401:26
Paedobaptist: a P.? 228:1
Pagan: Christian, p., nor man 434:19
  find the p.—spoiled 587:17
  hard P. world 17:7
  I'd rather be a P. 582:18
Page: all about the written p. 586:14
  blotted from life's p. 113:20
  description the p. gave 203:26
  elvish p. fell to the ground 417:24
  every p. having an ample marge 531:17
  hither, p. 361:20
  ho, pretty p. 543:3
  knowledge..her ample p. 230:5
  one sweet p. 374:23
  p. and monarch 361:22
  p. to joy 524:29
  p. was so besmear'd 119:16
  pictures for the p. atone 381:14
  sweet Anne P.! 466:3
  this indignant p. 76:1
Page: un livre dans une p. 282:11
Pageant: dreary p. laboured 24:2
  insubstantial p. 480:8
  p. of his bleeding heart 16:8
Pageantry: antique p. 342:7
Pageants: black vesper's p. 425:19
  p. of the sea 462:29
Pages: all the p. in a breeze 337:2
  untouch'd the p. lie 164:37
Pagets: none of the P. can read 335:20
Pagett, M.P., was a liar 300:14
Pagoda: old Moulmein P. 299:10, 15
Paian, Apollo 524:21
Paid: Cupid p. 321:14
  hasn't p. his fare 298:22
  nothing-a-year, p. quarterly 518:41
  not p. to think 299:6
  not p. with moan 544:2
  p. him the Dane-geld 295:18
  p. them...things..I never took 396:16
  p. the uttermost farthing 57:47
  p. thy utmost blessing 171:9
  p. with flattery 277:30
  p. with sighs a plenty 262:17
  we ha' p. in full! 301:24
  well p. that is well satisfied 465:15
Pail: fetch a p. of water 367:9
  frozen home in p. 456:1
  kick the empty p. 197:14
Pain: after long grief and p. 536:17
  all the p. 521:30
  any more p. 71:45
  aromatic p., darkness 383:16, 571:19
  arrears of p., darkness 95:11
  beest..hath no p. 137:29
  blest him in their p. 539:19
  born in other's p. 544:2
  but a dish of p. 547:20
  calumny and hate and p. 492:7
  costs worlds of p. 333:24
  did you feel no p.? 228:6
  draw thy breath in p. 438:4

Pain (cont.)
  equal ease unto my p. 125:7
  eternal P.! 17:12
  foolish, as if in p. 141:26
  for another's p. 230:30
  forget the wandering and the p. 208:4
  free from guilt or p. 497:12
  gave p. to the bear 326:1
  hark—what p.! 17:11
  herbs to ease their p. 300:9
  I love to give p. 156:4
  in company with P. 575:6
  inflict p. upon oneself 337:39
  in rest from p. 192:36
  intermission of p. 422:10
  king of p. 524:31
  labour we delight in physics p. 458:20
  lightly pass the p. 233:3
  love that is not p. to hear of 579:36
  my heart puts forth its p. 83:17
  narcotics, numbing p. 532:4
  never inflicts p. 363:25
  new grown with pleasant p. 288:7
  no living thing to suffer p. 496:21
  no p. dear mother now 7:3
  no pleasure, nor no p. 421:11
  not akin to p. 316:8
  not got with p. 518:1
  no throbs of fiery p. 275:4
  no unnecessary p. 492:23
  obligation is a p. 278:12
  our Lady of P. 522:24, 26, 523:3, 7
  owes its pleasures to another's
    p. 163:16
  p. and grief to me 394:8
  p. for leaven 522:5
  p. of finite hearts 97:12
  p. of truth, to whom 'tis p. 286:16
  p. shall not be inflicted 508:22
  p. that is all but a pleasure 220:32
  p., the bliss of dying! 381:28
  p. without the peace of death 122:2
  passion, p., or pride 540:26
  peril, toil, and p. 240:22
  piercing p. 516:16
  pleasure..almost to amount to
    p. 266:7
  pleasures banish p. 562:13
  reliev'd their p. 224:19
  she felt no p. 95:5
  sigh for the cost and p. 88:12
  sorrow, loss, or p. 581:3
  sudden cry of p. 512:12
  superflux of p. 521:28
  sweet is pleasure after p. 191:5
  thou asked p. 229:9
  though full of p. 345:19
  threats of p. and ruin 230:5
  three-parts p. 95:15
  travaileth in p. together 65:55
  turns to pleasing p. 510:3
  turns with ceaseless p. 226:4
  unnumbered hours of p. 123:2
  upon the midnight with no p. 287:32
  what p. it is to part! 214:27
  what p. it was to drown 476:14
  when p. and anguish wring 418:31
  wicked to deserve such p. 90:22
  without one p. 535:28
  with p. purchas'd..inherit p. 454:31
  with some p. is fraught 408:9
  yearning like a God in p. 285:16
Painful: honest and p. sermon 377:16
  no p. inch to gain 147:8
  one is as p. as the other 26:3
  p. passage 160:14
  p. pleasure turns 510:3
  p. pre-eminence! 1:18
  virtue she finds too p. 384:34
Pains: all p. the immortal spirit
    must endure 17:24
  by p. men come to greater p. 26:24
  do not take the p. 308:24
  double was his p. 509:30
  everlasting p. 561:22
  for any p. of death 391:43
  for my p. a world of sighs 470:3
  great p. to con it 482:18
  [his] labour for his p. 570:26
  his p. were o'er 222:28
  his present and your p. 443:11

Pains (cont.)
  marriage has many p. 278:17
  misfortunes and p. of others 102:31
  my p. his prey 509:7
  no p. with its sums 128:12
  p. of hell gat hold upon me 399:5
  p. of love be sweeter far 194:2
  pays a thousand p. 94:45
  pleasure in poetic p. 163:3
  stings you for your p. 248:10
  uneasy pleasures and fine p. 200:15
Paint: does he p.? 93:49
  flinging a pot of p. 412:22
  fresh as p. 503:7
  grind p., and work 199:33
  I cannot p. what I then was 581:26
  let her p. an inch thick 437:15
  only showed the p. 192:17
  p. my picture truly 167:7
  p. the lily 115:42, 447:39
  p. the meadows with delight 455:35
  p. 'em truest 1:12
  p. the sable skies 190:4
  p. Thy Presence 355:14
  putty, brass, an' p. 301:2
Painted: Earth's last picture..p. 303:19
  fears a p. devil 458:14
  gilded loam or p. clay 474:10
  his name p. clearly 128:5
  in Grecian tires..p. new 487:3
  mirror..not to be p. upon 325:10
  old, but p. cunningly 509:22
  p. child of dirt 385:31
  p. meadow 2:3
  p. on the wall 93:34
  p. ship, upon a p. ocean 149:5
  p. to the eyes 183:11
  paltry, foolish, p. things 189:19
  she p. her face 48:28
  so black as they are p. 315:16
  so young as they are p. 39:7
  wood p. to look like iron 73:1
Painter: H—the p...a Sussex man? 74:20
  I, too, am a p. 157:14
  nature's sternest p. 117:26
  not a great sculptor or p. 412:23
  some great p. dips his pencil 497:24
Painters: I hate all Boets and P. 216:10
  only..two p. 566:6
  poets, like p., thus unskilled 382:26
Painting: amateur p. in water-
    colour 514:26
  p. thy outward walls 488:20
  two styles of portrait p. 177:7
  whose mother was her p. 429:32
Paintings: heard of your p. too 434:12
Paints: he p. the wayside flower 122:1
  I want to know a butcher p. 96:27
  modern man who p. 91:9
Pair: aware of a princely p. 324:12
  blest p. of Sirens 351:9
  court and p. 82:4
  ever diverse p. 336:35
  fair p. of heels 439:12
  fondling of a happy p. 378:16
  happy, happy, happy p.! 190:34
  nor honey make, nor p. 152:17
  p. of ragged claws 197:19
  p. of sparkling eyes 218:25
  p. of very strange beasts 428:34
  p. their rhymes 116:14
  sleep on, blest p. 347:27
  such a mutual p. 423:14
Paired: hand and brain..p. 92:37
Pal: 'E won't split on a p. 304:53
Palace: cypress in the p. walk 539:2
  hollow oak our p. 167:21
  in at the p. door one day 178:25
  in the lighted p. near 534:19
  I will make a p. 516:2
  love in a p. 286:39
  my gorgeous p. for a hermitage 475:19
  opes the p. of Eternity 339:29
  p. and a prison 114:1
  p. of dim night 478:44
  p. of the Soul 113:12
  p. of wisdom 77:8
  purple-lined p. of sweet sin 286:40
  strong man armed keepeth his
    p. 61:46
  very stately p. 99:9

Palaces: at the Golden P. 507:16
builds p. in Kingdom come 334:1
cottages princes' p. 463:7
dragons in their pleasant p. 53:20
fair, frail p. 3:12
gorgeous p. 480:8
no p. his heart rejoice 223:7
old p. and towers 496:8
sunshot p. high 82:13
two-and-thirty p. 289:26
walls, p., half-cities 114:20
Palace-tower: hidden in a p. 498:6
Paladin: starry p. 96:30
Palaeozoic: in the P. time 504:13
Palate: his ample p. took savour 286:11
Joy's grape against his p. 287:21
no motion of the liver, but the p. 483:9
p., the hutch of tasty lust 254:27
Palates: never p. more the dug 425:33
Palatinus: he saw on P. 323:26
Pale: at which the world grew p. 279:6
behold a p. horse 70:45
edg'd with poplar p. 343:22
God's p. prætoriat 515:3
grew p., as angels can 119:25
keeps me p. 459:8
large grey eyes and a p. face 581:19
make p. my cheeks with care 572:2
men started..and turned p. 508:11
p. and bloodless emulation 481:5
p. and common drudge 464:16
p., and hectic red 496:4
p., and leaden-ey'd 252:24
p. as thy smock! 473:32
p. as yonder..moon 493:2
p., beyond porch and portal 523:20
p. contented..discontent 286:41
p. for weariness 495:19
p. grew every cheek 324:13
p. grew thy cheek and cold 119:29
p. hands I loved 254:14
p. his uneffectual fire 432:19
p. in her anger 466:37
p. prime-roses 485:26
p., unripened beauties 1:1
p. which held that lovely deer 558:1
p. young curate 222:15
pink pills for p. people 6:1
reigns in the winter's p. 485:16
see thee..p. with love 468:4
so thin, so p., is yet of gold 165:21
thy p., lost lilies 187:10
turn not p., beloved snail 129:24
where youth grows p. 287:26
why so p. and wan? 517:10
Paled: ribbed and p. in 429:29
Pale-eyed priest 343:21
Pale-faced moon 438:38
Pale-hearted: tell p. fear it lies 460:7
Pale-mouthed prophet dreaming 288:6
Pales: last wave p. 208:6
Palestine: in sunny P. 333:20
Paling: piece-bright p. 255:6
Pall: p. thee in the dunnest smoke 457:3
Tragedy in sceptred p. 341:18
when that began to p. 43:1
Palladium of all..rights 282:16
Pallas: Apollo, P., Jove and Mars 184:2
Pallescere: nulla p. culpa 256:18
Pallets: upon uneasy p. 441:41
Palliate what we cannot cure 277:24
Pallid: angels, all p. and wan 380:15
Pallidula rigida nudula 233:19
Pall Mall: shady side of P. 358:19
Pall Mall Gazette..written by gentlemen 542:23
Palls: everything p. 12:21
Palm: bear the p. alone 448:21
dominion over p. and pine 300:24
dull thy p. with entertainment 431:25
hard as the p. of ploughman 480:39
itching p. 451:10
p. and southern pine 528:23
strife with the p. 15:17
sweating p. to p. 266:12
to win the p., the oak 332:13
virginalling upon his p. 485:7
Palmam qui meruit, ferat 362:13
Palmer: p.'s walking staff 475:10
votarist in p.'s weed 340:8
Palmerston: the pugilist (Lord P.) 28:25

Palmerworm: which the p. hath left 55:50
Palms: lift their fronded p. 508:16
other p. are won 576:22(–577)
paddling p. 485:6
p. before my feet 140:22
p. of her hands 48:32
Palm-trees: City of p. 552:6
over the scud and the p. 296:5
wind is in the p. 299:10
Palmy state of Rome 430:14
Palpable: almost a p. movement 236:38
clinging to the p. 239:17
gross as a mountain, open, p. 439:23
through the p. obscure 345:26
very p. hit 437:37
Palsied: crippled and p. and slain 422:20
p. eld 462:6
Palsy: ole an strucken wid de p. 238:10
Palsy-stricken, churchyard thing 285:17
Palter with in a double sense 461:12
Paltry: p., foolish, painted things 189:19
p. to be Caesar 425:33
Pamere: mountain cradle in P. 17:28(–18)
Pampered: God's p. people 190:10
p. Jades of Asia 331:7, 441:37
Pamphleteer on guano 539:10
Pamphylia: Phrygia and P. 64:26
Pan: buy me a new p. 108:27
great god P. 88:11, 12
P. by noon 522:2
P. did after Syrinx speed 332:16
P. is dead! 88:4
Pan: el p. comido 134:10
Panaceas: beyond all their p. 109:32
Pancras and Kentish Town 75:5
Pander of posterity 508:13
Pandion: King P., he is dead 35:18
Pane: tap at the p. 93:22
Pane: lo p. altrui 169:1
Panem et circenses 283:19
Panes of quaint device 285:19
Pang: ghastly p. 149:17
grief without a p. 150:31
learn, nor account the p. 95:15
p. as great 462:7
p. of all the partings gone 544:1
p. preceding death 224:10
she feels no biting p. 217:17
Pangs: cost..Tellus keener p. 286:15
in the sweet p. of it 483:2
keen were his p. 117:25
more p. and fears 446:24
p. of absence to remove 401:31
p. of disappointed love 412:8
p. of dispriz'd love 434:4
p., the internal p., are ready 574:23
Panic: what a p. 107:9
Panjandrum: grand P. himself 209:18
Pannus: purpureus..p. 255:16
Pansie: no angels, P.? 20:25
Pansies, that's for thoughts 436:31
Pansy: p. at my feet 576:8
p. freakt with jet 342:31(–343)
pretty P. 510:23
Pant: I p., I sink, I tremble 493:15
p. with bliss 286:18
Pantaloon: lean and slipper'd p. 427:21
Panted: p. for a liberal profession 154:14
she spoke, and p. 424:8
Panting: chase a p. syllable 162:2
p. for a happier seat 279:14
Pants: as p. the hart 527:1
in fast thick p. 151:32
ride on the p. triumphing 425:12
soul aspiring p. 355:17
Papa: as p. used to say 174:21
his dear p. is poor 515:20
made a scene of it with my P. 175:31
P., potatoes, poultry 176:1
word P. 176:1
Papacy: P...Ghost of the deceased Roman Empire 248:23
Paper: any news in the p. 23:11
ever blotted p. 464:22
Golly, what a p.! 515:12
he hath not eat p. 455:11
if all the earth were p. 321:19
just for a scrap of p. 43:22
make dust our p. 475:6

Paper (cont.)
on grey p. with blunt type 96:41
p. bullets of the brain 468:23
p. government 100:19
peerless p. peer 416:10
Paper-mill: built a p. 445:40
Papers they had finished 248:12
Papist: Pundit or P. 387:21
Paraclete: holy P. 310:9
Paradisaical pleasure of the Mahometans 231:20
Paradisal imagineless metal 545:12
Paradise: all P. opens! 182:44
all th'eastern side beheld of P. 349:31
Angel of a ruin'd P. 491:20
before us go to P. by way of Kensal Green 141:24
by some supposed true p. 347:9
cheapen'd p. 374:20
desert were a p. 107:26
destroy their p. 230:30
dreams of P. and light 551:16
drunk the milk of P. 151:33(–152)
England is a p. for women 109:29
England is the p. of women 209:8
enjoy p. in the next 38:19
Gates of P. 74:21
gates o' P. 33:2
heav'nly p. is that place 124:4
Hopes of P. 206:26
in P., if we meet 97:27
Italy a p. for horses 109:29
I was taught in P. 285:31
Jane went to P. 297:19
leave this P. 349:29
life's p., great princess 209:25
live in P. alone 332:22
only bliss of P...surviv'd 163:6
O P.! O P.! 202:26
opening p. 231:5
p. for a sect 285:32
P. of exiles, Italy! 494:14
P. of Fools 346:27
p. to what we fear of death 462:10
P. within thee, happier far 349:29
rudiments of P. 507:1
sole propriety, in P. 347:26
thou hast the keys of P. 172:19
trees of P. 516:18
Wilderness..P. enow 205:23, 24
with me in p. 62:50
with P...the Snake 207:13
wreck of P. 493:13
Paradises: two P. 'twere in one 332:22
Paradox: embodied p. 154:23
p. which comforts 95:16
Paradoxes: old fond p. 470:28
Paragon of animals! 433:15
Parallel: ours so truly p. 332:6
Parallelograms: princess of P. 119:34
Parallels in beauty's brow 487:9
Paramount: mighty p. of truths 574:22
Paramour: many a P. 509:33
none but thou..my p. 330:6
to be his p. 478:44
Paramours: worn of p. 510:23
Parasol: your Mama's p. between them 175:31
Paratus: in utrumque p. 554:1
Parboiled: my p. head 355:21
Parcae thought him one 280:10
Parcel of their fortunes 424:28
Parcel-gilt: upon a p. goblet 441:31
Parcelled Oxus 17:28(–18)
Parcels: deals it in small p. 563:24
p. of the dreadful Past 535:17
Parcere subiectis 555:1
Parched: each throat was p. 149:21
Parchment: bound in stale p. 337:13
innocent lamb..made p. 445:38
p...undo a man 445:38
virtue of wax and p. 101:1
Parcus deorum cultor 258:27
Pard: bearded like the p. 427:21
freckled like a p. 286:37
Pard-like Spirit 492:2
Pardon: bret-ful of p. 137:21
God might p. her 198:7
God p. all good men! 87:32
God p. all oaths 475:23
if life was bitter to thee, p. 522:13

INDEX

Pardon (*cont.*)
kiss of the sun for p. 233:17
of vice..p. beg 436:3
p. me, thou bleeding piece 450:11
'p.', said the Bishop 31:20
p. something to the spirit of liberty 100:25
p.'s the word to all 430:6
they ne'er p. 191:42
to p. or to bear it 159:31
weep for my p. 425:22
your p. for too much loving 471:36
Pardonable: madness and..p. 155:27
Pardoned: more..than to be p. 280:1
p. and retain the offence? 435:34
Pardoning our offences 390:45
Pardonnera: *Dieu me p.* 240:27
Pardons: dispenses, p., bulls 346:26
Pards: Bacchus and his p. 287:28
tigers, ounces, p. 347:15
Parendo: *nisi p.* 28:9
Parens: *magna p. frugum* 556:14
Parent: afflicting to a p.'s mind 23:3
aged p. 175:25
bedside of a sick p. 325:36
fear is the p. of cruelty 212:7
on p. knees 279:19
P. of Good 348:4
p. of settlement 102:7
perhaps that p. mourn'd 310:2
put any p. mad 208:21
to lose one p. 569:23
Parentage: p. is a very important profession 489:23
p. unguessed 302:19
what is your p.? 482:24
Parents: begin by loving their p. 570:18
bottle our p. twain 295:15
her p. was the same 9:18
joys of p. are secret 26:44
p. first season us 245:5
p.' tears 344:28
p...the Lord knows who 170:14
stranger to one of your p. 22:33
Paridis: *iudicium p.* 553:8
Paries cum proximus ardet 257:8
Paris: far away ez P. 319:19
Frensh of P. was to hir unknowe 136:29
good Americans..go to P. 14:1, 570:13
good girl's lip out of P. 525:35
last time I saw P. 235:5
no Lord of P., Venyce 195:7
P. vaut bien une messe 242:3
P. when he found sleep 584:23
with wanton P. sleeps 480:37
Parish: all the world as my p. 565:16
dandilly toss of the p. 409:13
his pension from his p. 413:24
plain as way to p. church 427:18
provided by the P. 390:23
Parium: *per legale iudicium p.* 327:9
Park: by p. and pale 540:12
cot in a p. 309:26
Neptune's p. 429:29
over p., over pale 466:33
Park Lane for choice 223:7
Parks: levelled walks through p. 154:13
p...the lungs of London 379:13
Parler: *meurs sans p.* 553:2
Parles: treasonous p. 90:16
Parley-voo: hinky dinky, p. 412:17
Parliament: crop-headed P. 90:16
made honest by an act of p. 279:32
Mob, P., Rabble 147:17
no British P. can put them asunder 388:2
not member of Bristol, but.. of p. 100:14
P. of man 534:27
P. speaking through reporters 126:39
Three Estates in P. 126:49
Parliamentary: Bag of P. Eloquence 126:35
P. government..impossible 181:1
Rupert of P. discussion 180:15
Parliaments: mother of P. 82:19
no more P. 281:20
Parlour: party in a p. 578:27
prettiest little p. 264:23
prison'd in a p. 161:41
queen was in the p. 368:20

Parlour (*cont.*)
walk into my p. 264:23
Parlours: adorn the p. of heaven 567:19
bells in your p. 470:25
Parlous: in a p. state 427:26
Parma or Spain..dare to invade 198:11
Parmeceti for an inward bruise 438:35
Parnassus: my chief P. 502:3
Parochial: art must be p. 356:5
scorning p. ways 236:20
worse than provincial..p. 268:2
Parody: devil's walking p. 140:21
Parole of literary men 274:31
Paroles: *les p...déguiser leurs pensées* 557:4
Paronomasia: you catch the p. 120:28
Parrots: laugh like p. 462:30
Pars: *quorum p. magna fui* 553:25
Parsee from whose hat 304:15
Parsnips: butter no p. 420:7
Parson: brandy for the P. 301:18
drowns the p.'s saw 456:1
his creed no p. ever knew 188:34
like a p.'s damn 237:2
Monday is p.'s holiday 519:30
p. and the p.'s wife 146:32
p. and the people his apes 137:22
p. for the Islands of the Blest 302:19
p. knows enough 164:9
P. left conjuring 422:7
P. lost his senses 249:5
P. might preach 76:4
p., much bemused in beer 385:21
povre P. 137:16, 22
there goes the p. 160:38
tickling a p.'s nose 477:7
Whig in a p.'s gown 276:6
Parsons: p. are very like other men 139:8
p. do not care for truth 517:8
merriment of p. 274:27
Part: bear the longest p. 243:24
best of friends must p. 10:21
better p. of valour 441:2
bid us p. 546:7
command of every p. 247:4
each man has some p. to play 402:14
ere we p. 118:6
every man must play a p. 462:31
every pleasing, every prudent p. 384:33
few shall p. 122:20
freely p. with my glory 244:11
hard to p. when friends are dear 33:14
heart aye's the p. aye 105:22
I have forgot my p. 429:18
in every friend..p. of ourselves 386:37
know in p., but then 66:46(-67)
know in p...prophesy in p. 66:45
let us kiss and p. 189:20
Love's sweetest p., Variety 185:28
Mary hath chosen that good p. 61:45
minute and unseen p. 315:28
my p. of death 483:6
neither p. nor lot in this matter 64:37
not p. of their blood 294:30
only p. to meet again 215:40
ought but death p. thee and me 47:1
p., and meet again 112:19
p. at last without a kiss 359:4
p. in all I have 486:4
p. in friendship 119:8
p. in making these days memorable 144:7
p. of all that I have met 540:32
p. of the thousandth p. 428:18
p. of wisdom 163:31
p. to tear a cat in 466:25
put beside his p. 486:20
she hath done her p. 349:2
take your own p. 78:30
this day we must p. 166:24
thou and nature..so gently p. 426:11
till death us do p. 391:30
too precise in every p. 246:4
we two now p. 375:21
what pain it is to p.! 214:27
Partagee: *la chose..la mieux p.* 172:27
Partake: p. in her rejoicing 352:29
p. the gale 384:16
Partaken: mutual and p. bliss 340:37
Partaker with the adulterers 395:5
Partakers of thy sad decline 160:23

Parted: fool and his words are soon p. 499:19
from thy state mine never..p. 349:18
or never p. 104:11
p. are those who are singing 79:9
p...between twelve and one 443:19
p. for ever 418:12
way we p. 524:9
when I p. from my dear 263:16
when one has p. with that 156:4
when we two p. 119:29
Partem: *audi p. alteram* 22:2
succedere p... p... dispersit 555:12
Parthenia: victim of P.'s pride 215:12
Parthenophil is lost 210:1
Parthians and Medes 64:26
Partial: faint and p. 142:4
I am p. to ladies 20:27
not by p...laws 383:14
p. evil universal good 383:21
p. for th' observer's sake 384:21
Participation of freedom 101:12
Particle: every air-borne p. 268:12
pushing young p. 221:8
that very fiery p. 116:35
Particular: Christ's p. love's sake 96:2
London p. 173:23
love a bright p. star 423:2
not in p. will 481:12
one p. beauteous star 286:18
P. Election 187:7
so singular in each p. 485:27
your p. wanity 179:30
Particularly long and wide 376:9
Particulars: Minute P. 75:7
Parties: both p. join'd to do their best 111:14
both p. nobly are subdu'd 442:18
p. must ever exist 101:9
Parting: Death is p. 412:15
do not let this p. grieve thee 10:21
in every p...an image of death 196:30
p. hour 16:24
p. is all we know of heaven 180:3
p. is such sweet sorrow 478:1
p. of the way 55:31
p.'s well-paid 375:13
rive not more in p. 425:13
their every p. was to die 533:15
this p. was well made 451:37
Partings: p. gone and p. yet to be 544:1
Partington: Atlantic..beat Mrs. P. 505:22
Partir: *botté et prêt à p.* 354:19
toujours prêt à p. 209:15
Partition: union in p. 467:9
Partitions: thin p. 190:13
Partly: man p. is 91:1
p. she was drunk 106:22
Partner: find yourself a p. 296:33
his lov'd p. 226:11
I have a p. 174:34
my p. and my guide 573:26
Partners, in each other kind 559:6
Partridge: as the p. sitteth 55:21
Parts: all his gracious p. 447:34
different p. of the Empire in.. hostility 222:38
dock the smaller p.-o'-speech 120:28
if p. allure thee 384:12
my p., my title 469:39
my p. of speech 500:19
nothing else but his p. 273:10
p. for the time with reality 144:4
p. of it are excellent! 403:37
p. of one stupendous whole 383:18
p...pretty well for a Lord 273:10
plays many p. 427:21
read only in p. 27:17
want of p. 272:2
Parturient montes 255:25
Party: Breitmann gife a p. 313:11
called the Conservative, p. 166:26
educate our p. 180:38
forms of p. strife 533:20
none was for a p. 323:21
'No P.' on its flag 335:6
not a select p. 290:27
of the Devil's p. 77:7
p. in a parlour 578:27
p. is organised opinion 180:34
p. is the madness of many 520:47

Party (cont.)
  p. of order or stability   338:28
  p. of two   82:21
  p.-spirit..madness of many   386:35
  p. whose antecedents are   99:42
  passion and p. blind our eyes   152:24
  sooner every p. breaks up   22:13
  stick to your p.   181:16
  that p. conquers in the strife   416:24
  to p. gave up   225:27
  voted at my p.'s call   221:17
  where ish dat p. now?   313:11
  without p. Parliamentary
    government..impossible   181:1
Party-coloured livery   155:27
Parva..componere magnis   556:24
Parvam..vidi cum matre legentem   556:4
Parvis componere magna   555:18
Pas: le premier p. qui coûte   170:1
Pass: after we p. the gate   187:11
  all ye that p. by   55:23
  bid it p.   440:16
  bounds which they shall not p.   398:8
  cannot p. away   496:1
  deeds which should not p. away   113:44
  heaven and earth shall p. away   417:25
  if he pleaseth, through it p.   244:15
  I p., like night   150:12
  I shall not p. this way again   232:10
  its glories p. away   322:1
  I will p. nor turn my face   97:27
  I will p. through..Egypt   45:47
  let him p. for a man   463:10
  let us p. on!   100:15
  lightly p. the pain   233:3
  like her, O Saki, you shall p.   207:31
  lords of human kind p. by   226:14
  make them p. for their own   499:23
  never p. into nothingness   284:19
  O! let him p.   454:27
  p. and speak one another   318:10
  p. by me as the idle wind   451:19
  p. for forty-three   222:20
  p. into her face   581:22
  p. it along the line!   300:16
  p. it on!   109:1
  p. man's understanding   389:42
  p. me the can, lad   263:33
  p. no criticisms   106:31
  p. on, my Queen, forgiven   530:41
  p. our long love's day   333:8
  p. the hat for your credit   294:20
  'P. the mustard'   222:30
  p. the rosy wine   177:29
  p. through this world but once   232:10
  p. was steep and rugged   324:10
  pay us, p. us   141:28
  roaring through the p.   324:15
  ships that p. in the night   318:10
  sideways did she p.   298:29
  so p. I hostel   540:12
  so p. through things temporal   389:41
  such as p. on the seas   400:29
  that it may not p. away   296:33(-297)
  they p. all understanding   267:32
  they shall not p.   378:7
  though Dynasties p.   236:14
  try not the P.!   316:19
  ways I keep, and p.   199:3
  when thou shalt strangely p.   486:33
  will she p. in a crowd?   519:25
Passa: guarda, e p.   168:18
Passage: black p. up to bed   515:26
  explaining a p. in the game-act   511:17
  fret a p. through it   212:16
  North-West p. to the intellectual   513:19
  painful p.   160:14
  p. through these looms   551:15
  p. to remorse   457:3
  sweetest p. of a song   338:6
  unseen, 'gan p. find   455:17
Passages: all the p. of joy   279:7
  cheated into some fine p.   290:15
  Johnson hewed p.   154:13
  p. that lead to nothing   230:18
Passe: si elle p. son temps de moi   355:3
  tout p...L'art..survit   214:3
  tout p., tout casse, tout lasse   12:21
Passed: alike have p. away   337:9
  darksome night be p.   202:25
  Elijah p. by him   48:10

Passed (cont.)
  first heaven..p. away   71:44
  foes saluted as they p.   193:41
  glory and loveliness..p. away   288:28
  Israelites p. over   46:39
  life has p. with me but roughly   160:25
  look with which you p.   375:15
  Lord Howard p. away   539:19
  p. as a watch in the night   397:15
  p. by on the other side   61:40
  p. on, rushingly   236:29
  plucked them as we p.   252:11
  so he p. over   99:41
  spirit p. before my face   48:48
  Thee..p. away   573:26
  when he p. from Egypt   344:34
  when it p. is   138:35
  when she had p.   316:13
  will have p. away   160:40
Passenger: in the presence of the p.   83:1
Passengers: those first-class p.   299:8
  we the p.   264:21
Passer: laissez p.   404:19
Passer mortuus est   132:12
Passer-by: stop, Christian p.!   151:16
  you, a p.   404:21
Passeront: ils ne p. pas   378:7
Passerum: adveniens unus p.   38:31
Passes: beauty p.   171:6
  everything p.   12:21
  graze him as he p.   38:24
  he, the singer, p.   336:45
  never p. a church   271:6
  who p. by this road so late?   11:24
Passeth: fashion of this world p.   66:32
  lie that p. through   27:31
  one generation p. away   50:59
  p. all understanding   68:26, 390:48
  p. away as..a guest   56:26
  p. knowledge   67:54
  so p. in the passing of a day   509:33
  so soon p. it away   397:16
Passi graviora   553:13
Passibus: sequiturque patrem non p.
    aequis   554:12
Passing: but see her p. by   10:20, 210:5
  he could not wait their p.   18:24
  on the p. world to turn thine
    eyes   279:4
  p. of the sweetest soul   532:40
  P. of the Third Floor Back   269:6
  p. the love of women   47:30
  p. the love o' women   296:18
  p. through nature to eternity   430:29
  power is p. from the earth   575:1
  so be my p.!   241:23
  some cost a p. bell   38:28
  speak each other in p.   318:10
  we and the..world are p. by   585:22
Passion: all made of p.   428:28
  all p. spent   351:7
  bards of P. and of Mirth   284:16
  beating of so strong a p.   483:9
  breathing human p.   287:11
  by p. driven   108:25
  chaos of thought and p.   383:22
  cows are my p.   175:11
  e'er..felt the tender p.   215:9
  eternal P.!   17:12
  fat gentleman in such a p.   202:17
  govern my p.   387:2
  haunted me like a p.   581:26
  held in holy p. still   341:9
  his p. boiled and bubbled   543:12
  his p. shall have spent   534:19
  his p. to convey   202:4
  if a p. is in you   73:28
  I have no p. for it   271:4
  in a dream of p.   433:31
  infinite p.   97:12
  in her first p.   115:38
  in love and holy p.   574:8
  interval betwixt one p. and an-
    other   512:21
  keep the p. fresh   337:24
  lingring and consumptive p.   202:2
  maiden p. for a maid   530:14
  no less than action and p.   125:31
  no p...but..masters the fear of
    death   26:2
  no p. in the human soul   314:1

Passion (cont.)
  no p. so..robs the mind   102:32
  not p.'s slave   434:26
  one p. doth expel another   135:22
  p. and party blind our eyes   152:24
  p. ending   435:10
  p. for fame   100:11
  p. for hunting something   177:39
  p. for our temperate kings   537:22
  p. for the name of 'Mary'   116:15
  p., I see, is catching   450:13
  p., pain, or pride   540:26
  p. put to use   88:24
  P. speechless lies   189:20
  p. such it was to prove   165:21
  p. that left the ground   89:10
  places which pale p. loves   37:37
  Queen was in a furious p.   129:13
  relieve my p. much   483:1
  ruling p.!   173:31
  ruling p. conquers reason   384:43
  ruling p. strong in death   384:27
  sentimental p.   220:28
  sick of an old p.   187:8
  some bloody p.   473:13
  strange fits of p.   581:11
  such poor p.   425:30
  tear a p. to tatters   434:15
  their fury and my p.   479:29
  this p...make a man look sad   467:33
  to be in a p. you good may do   73:28
  to inspire hopeless p.   542:20
  to ourselves in p...propose   435:10
  two extremes of p.   454:23
  vows with so much p.   312:28
  vulgar expression of the p.   154:31
  was not this thy P.   525:17
  well-painted p.!   472:30
  what is p. but pining?   337:42
  what p. cannot Music raise   191:36
  whirlwind of p.   434:15
  whose every p. fully strives   423:15
  win the p. and the life   151:3
Passionate: deep affections make
    him p.   330:24
  make p. my sense of hearing   455:6
  simple, sensuous and p.'   352:28
  so p. a love-adventure   306:15
  to p. women   584:24
Passionately and irretrievably   411:10
Passione interdum movemur   291:22
Passion-flower at the gate   536:15
Passionless: hopeless grief is p.   88:15
  man p.?   497:12
  p. bride, divine Tranquillity   535:27
Passions: all other p. fly   507:17
  all thoughts, all p.   152:3
  desolate p.   269:26
  devil to have all the p.   490:16
  great when he acts from the p.   181:42
  his p...the better of his creed   513:11
  let such angry p. rise   561:25
  men of like p. with you   64:52
  moderator of p.   559:15
  our p...good servants   313:19
  p. spin the plot   330:30
  shifts her p.   215:14
  their human p. now no more   231:4
  thy p., match'd with mine   534:32
  various ruling p.   384:25
  when p. are no more   557:24
Passion-winged Ministers of
    thought   491:19
Passive: benevolence of the p.
    order   337:39
  p. resistance of the Tolbooth
    gate   419:37
Passiveness: wise p.   574:29
Passives: Love's p.   165:29
Passover: Christ our p.   66:28
  the Lord's p.   45:47
Passport: his p. shall be made   444:28
Past: absurd about the p.   39:9
  all their glory p.   99:1
  day is p. and gone, sweet-heart   32:14
  dead P. bury its dead   317:7
  dim remembering of a cursed p.   551:13
  God cannot alter the p.   111:28
  God cannot change the p.   3:5
  harvest is p.   55:16
  history is p. politics   421:20

Past (*cont.*)
lament the p. 101:33
leave thy low-vaulted p.! 251:15
live p. years again 191:34
lo, the winter is p. 52:1
lo, 'tis p., the winter 334:16
many a woman has a p. 569:36
mischief that is p. and gone 470:5
nothing p. 158:2
o'er the p. its undivided reign 251:11
over the trackless p. 238:29
parcels of the dreadful P. 535:17
p. all dishonour 252:15
P. and the Future are nothing 402:14
p. and to come seem best 441:27
p. help..p. grief 485:12
p. my help..p. my care 37:21
p., the distant, or the future 277:39
plan the future by the p. 103:6
praise they that will times p. 246:24
present, p. and future sees 75:23
remember not p. years 364:11
remembrance of things p. 486:25
repent what's p. 436:2
rouse the Echoes of the P. 218:9
soul of the whole P. Time 126:27
thought of our p. years 576:17
time present and time p. 197:4
upon the p. has pow'r 194:21
voice of the P. 126:27
weary of the p. 493:27(–494)
what's p. and what's to come 481:27
what's p. is prologue 479:35
when May is p. 125:10
where all p. years are 186:16
years that are p. 396:32
Pastern..the knee of a horse 270:26
Pastime: our p. and our happiness 578:20
take his p. therein 398:11
think it p. 436:39
Pastor: iguala al p. con el rey 134:18
Pastor: enumerat..p. oves 402:15
Pastoral: cold P.! 287:14
oaten stop or p. song 153:23
p. heart of England! 404:22
Pastores: me quoque dicunt vatem p. 556:7
Pastors: some ungracious p. 431:23
spiritual p. and masters 391:7
Pastrycook plant 219:13
Pastrycooks: hardware-men, p. 307:2
Pasture: feed me in a green p. 393:10
mettle of your p. 443:26
people of his p. 397:28
ten thousand beeves at p. 336:42
the Lord my P. shall prepare 2:21
they sell the p. 443:12
Pasture-ground: ooze of their p. 15:24
Pastures: bulls, that walk the p. 336:38
in p. green 421:1
on England's pleasant p. 75:16
p. new 343:7
p. of the blessèd 362:3
pipe me to p. still 254:26
Pat: now might I do it p. 435:36
p. he comes 452:21
p. it and prick it 368:10
there's P. and Mac 305:3
with a dext'rous p. 164:8
Pat-a-cake: p., p., baker's man 368:10
Patch: gain a little p. of ground 436:14
p. grief with proverbs 469:12
p. up thine old body 441:40
potsherd, p., matchwood 255:7
while the p. was worn 540:18
Patched: but p. with sin 482:13
peel'd, p., and piebald 381:19
Patches: king of shreds and p. 435:50
puffs, powders, p. 385:9
thing of shreds and p. 219:15
Pate: aged old p. 5:10
feather p. of folly 263:18
p. of a politician 437:11
rub my bald p. 387:2
you beat your p. 382:9
Patent: my p. back again is swerving 487:22
p. for his honours 105:16
Patently Impossible and Vain 301:21
Pater: imperiumque p. Romanus habebit 555:8
P. noster qui 502:20
Paterna rura bubus exercet suis 257:22
Pâtés de foie gras to..trumpets 505:10
Path: beaten p. to his door 201:22
Christ is the p. 354:11
dark is his p. 228:21
if thou p. 449:7
long brown p. before me 568:3
'midst the twilight p. 153:24
p. before him always bright 575:5
p. of a..noble Education 352:26
p. of gold for him 94:27
p. of the just 49:43
p. of thy commandments 399:14
p. on the sea's..floor 493:12
p. through the sad heart of Ruth 288:1
primrose p. of dalliance 431:23
shew me the p. of life 392:27
take the gentle p. 244:12
though thy p. is dark 327:3
vine-sheltered p. 411:16
Pathetic: P. Fallacy 412:26
that's what it is. P. 339:23
Pathless: heav'ns wide p. way 341:14
pleasure in the p. woods 114:26
Pathos: true p. and sublime 104:23
Paths: all her p. are peace 49:41
bitter p. wherein I stray 300:4
grubbing weeds from gravel p. 296:32
light unto my p. 399:21
make his p. straight 57:28
our opposed p. 375:21
p. of glory 230:1
p. of righteousness 393:10
so many p. 568:27
through the p. of the seas 392:12
trodden p. of men 491:27
Pathway: p. spy 335:28
smote for us a p. 301:25
strew your p. with..*urs* 250:31
Patience: abusing of God's p. 465:33
all humbleness, all p. 428:28
by your gracious p. 469:45
close-lipp'd P. 18:13
drop of p. 472:34
flour of wyfly p. 137:24
God..preacheth p. 244:7
habits of peace and p. 559:15
I laugh'd him out of p. 424:12
in pious p. 300:21
in your p. possess ye your souls 62:42
kingdom and p. of Jesus Christ 70:23
languid p. of thy face 152:19
Lord, have p. with me 59:54
my p. is now at an end 248:14
p., and shuffle the cards 134:15
p. have her perfect work 69:26
p. of Job 69:42
p. on a monument 483:10
p., the beggar's virtue 334:25
P., thou young..cherubin 472:34
P., to prevent that murmur 351:21
p. will achieve more 102:28
prayer, p., alms 255:6
preach'd up p. 402:1
run with p. the race 69:18
they that have not p. 471:24
with p. He stands waiting 315:22,317:13
your energy, your p. 305:1
Patience: grande aptitude à la p. 98:18
Patient: as p. and as still 502:17
fury of a p. man 190:30
her p. sons 226:13
his Mother, who was p. 375:16
kill the p. 26:18
like a p. etherized 197:15
not so p. 441:16
O soul, be p. 80:18
p. as the female dove 437:25
p...minister to himself 460:37
righteous Judge, strong and p. 392:7
same bright, p. stars 286:14
soft, meek, p. 170:18
with p. inattention 335:23
yet be p. 537:39
Patientia: abutere..p. nostra 145:11
levius fit p. 258:26
Patiently: take it p. 69:51
Patines of bright gold 465:18
Patmos: isle that is called P. 70:23
Patrem: habere non potest Deum p. sequiturque p. 22:1
554:12
Patri: sit suo similis p. 133:6
Patria: pro p. mori 259:18
pro p., pro liberis 415:3
sed pro p. 363:1
Patriarch: applies it to a P. 152:27
venerable P. 387:8
Patriarchs: wives in the p.' days 236:20
Patrician: regular p. 221:26
Patrick: no more St. P.'s Day 9:6
St. P. was a gentleman 42:19
Patrick Spens: ballad of Sir P. 150:30
to Sir P. 31:24
Patrie: enfants de la p. 412:1
Patriot: Idea of a P. King 78:8
never was p. yet, but was a fool 190:29
p. of the world alone 124:11
repress their p. throats 279:3
such is the p.'s boast 226:7
sunshine p. 372:23
Patriotic: fights you on p. principles 490:38
Patriotism: duty and p. 216:7
p. is not enough 134:2
p. is the last refuge 272:29
where they had p. 376:11
Patriots: all these country p. 112:27
blood of p. and tyrants 268:23
brave men and worthy p. 352:27
true p. we 36:20
Patron: p. and the jail 279:4
P. Commonly a wretch 277:30
P., one who 270:18
Patronage sway 84:27(–85)
Patroness: my celestial P. 349:5
Patrons: drama's p. 279:1
Patronum: optimus omnium's p. 133:1
Patted: Ethel p. her hair 21:2
p. my God on the head 302:29
Patter: unintelligible p. 222:12
Pattern: made him our p. 93:3
our childhood's p. 4:3
p. to encourage purchasers 519:6
State's p.-man 363:26
thou cunning'st p. 473:11
Pattle: wi' murd'ring p. 107:9
Paucity of human pleasures 276:23
Paucula: nos p. scire 414:21
Paul: by the apostle P. 476:38
P. the aged 69:5
stout Apostle P. 298:12
with St. P...literary terms 20:9
with the charity of P. 143:10
Paul Revere: ride of P. 317:3
Pauliad: less a Christiad than a P. 237:13
Paul's: down by smoky P. 541:23
Paunch, tripe, or thairm 106:4
Pauper: only a p. 365:6
Pauperiem: duram..p. pati 261:4
indocilis p. pati 258:1
Pauperum tabernas regumque turris 258:8
Paupertas: nil habet..p. durius 283:4
Pause: how dull it is to p. 540:32(–541)
I p. for a reply 450:16
I stand in p. 435:32
must give us p. 434:4
nor made a p. 275:3
p. and ask thyself 175:18
p. and puff..p. again 159:17
p. awhile from letters 279:4
p. in the day's occupations 316:3
p. there, Morocco 463:40
Pauses: happy p. 27:46
Paved: p. with broken hearts 318:26
p. with gold 154:9
p. with the moon 492:29(–493)
Pavement: archways and the p. 23:22
p. of her Heaven 168:1
p. of pearl 16:1
riches of heaven's p. 345:9
surround St. Paul's with a wooden p. 505:12
thy cold p...a sod 114:34
Pavements: p. fang'd 150:28
p. gray 585:12
Pavender, or pub 414:6
Pavilion: p. of Heaven is bare 493:1
red p. of my heart 543:17
she did lie in her p. 424:6
umpire, the p. cat 309:27
Pavilioned in splendour 228:20
Pavilions: evening sky p. it 495:27

Paving-stones: these gritty p. 299:14
Paviours cry 202:10
Paw: in his p. dandled the kid 347:15
p. him with..institutions 546:44
p. of hireling wolves 351:30
wolf with privy p. 342:29
Paweth in the valley 49:26
Pawing to get free 348:27
Pawnce: pretty P. 510:23
Paws: massive p. of elder persons 40:20
oh my dear p.l 128:26
'Pax vobiscum' will answer all 420:4
Pay: bloomin' good p. 301:12
cut each other's throats for p. 225:24
devil to p.l 357:21
enough to p. for an edition 200:46
even then she had to p. 41:11
forbore to p. 300:18
for what p.? 413:4
God..hath in heavenly p. 475:1
I was to p. the piper 155:8
I will p. thee all 59:54
make me able to p. for it 377:12
man cannot choose but p. 374:20
now I must p. for my fun 298:3
p. as if not paid before 486:25
p. at the Greek Kalends 120:9
p. every debt as if God wrote 199:29
p. for by one and one 302:28
p. given to a state hireling 277:31
p. glad life's arrears 95:11
p. me that thou owest 59:55
P. Old Debts 334:22
p.—p.—p.l 294:20
p. too much for your whistle 211:19
p. you in the grave 494:9
saved the sum of things for p. 264:4
sharper spur than p. 215:23
smile at us, p. us, pass us 141:28
vow and not p. 51:7
waxworks, you ought to p. 130:7
we will nothing p. 429:28
when will you p. me? 368:8
wonders what's to p. 264:1
Payment of half twenty shillings 100:5
Paynim: called each P. voice 123:9
Paynims: three p., three Jews 327:15
Pay-roll: ten thousand men on the p. 299:16
Pays: he that dies p. all debts 480:4
I scent wich p. the best 319:22
owes not, but still p. 346:31
p. a thousand pains 94:45
p. him in his own coin 520:29
p. us but with age and dust 405:12
p. us poor beggars in red 303:27
slave that p. 443:16
whoever p. the taxes 298:8
you p. your money 403:4
Pea: grapes and green p. 219:13
one p. and one bean 312:19
one split p. 543:7
Peace: all her paths are p. 49:41
all the p. which springs 358:1
arts of war and p. 115:43
author of p. 388:25
been at p. tonight 449:20
begat habits of p. and patience 559:15
belong unto thy p. 62:40
beyond these voices..p. 530:20
bring a man of p. at the last 394:6
burns lamps of p. 172:6
calls it—p. 113:4, 319:22
calm world and a long p. 440:21
certain knot of p. 501:26
chastisement of our p. 54:26
church for p. 89:42
come ye in p.? 418:18
deep dream of p. 265:16
ended in a little p. 543:16
even lovers find their p. 208:10
exceeding p. 265:16
fair p. be to my sable shroud 342:11
first in p. 312:25
flower of P. 552:2
for ever hold his p. 391:27
for thy p. 413:31
friendly to p., but not to mel 162:14
give p. at home 400:33
give thee p. 46:10
God gave her p. 539:12

Peace (cont.)
grace be unto you, and p. 70:21
grant us thy p. 389:29
had Zimri p.? 48:29
haunt of ancient P. 537:36
hearts at p. 84:21
his goods are in p. 61:46
I came not to send p. 59:1
if p. cannot be..with honour 414:1
if these should hold their p. 62:39
if thou return at all in p. 48:14
I labour for p. 399:25
increase of his government and p. 53:13
inginate the word P., P. 145:27
in p., Love 417:16
in p. there's nothing so becomes 443:24
in thy right hand carry p. 446:31
in time of p. thinks of war 109:21
into the way of p. 61:15
I sez to 'em, 'P., be still.' 294:25
I shall have some p. there 585:12
is it p.?..what hast thou to do with p.? 48:26
I speak of p. 441:7
I will die in p. 572:16
join with thee calm P., and Quiet 341:10
King of p. 244:25
kiss our lady P. 441:23
laughing heart's long p. 84:18
let us have p. 229:3
like the p. of God 267:32
love, joy, p., long-suffering 67:46
lovers in p. 451:35
love thee and thy p. 421:5
Mercy, Pity, P. and Love 76:18
merry songs of p. 447:14
mind at p. 119:2
moth of p. 470:11
mourn thy banish'd p. 506:3
mutual cowardice keeps us in p. 274:8
my..p. is broken into pieces 253:6
never..a bad p. 211:8
news and Prince of P. 209:3
no p...unto the wicked 54:21
now I see p. to corrupt 349:28
offices..of p. and war 352:25
O heart, be at p. 584:3
on earth p., good will 61:19
our p...in impossible things 141:1
our p., our fearful innocence 577:16
pain without the p. of death 122:2
p. above all earthly dignities 446:25
p. among our peoples 301:26
p. and felicity 421:5
p. and rest can never dwell 344:9
p. and strife 419:28
p. at the last 364:4
p. be to this house 61:34, 391:36
p. between the effect and it 457:3
p. be within thy walls 399:31
p. brooded 184:2
p.; come away 532:39
p. comes dropping slow 585:12
p., commerce, and honest friendship 268:21
p. divine like quiet night 402:10
p. does nothing to relieve 159:26
p. for evermore 517:3
p. for our time..p. with honour 135:9
peaceful sloth, not p. 345:22
p., good pint-pot! 439:32
p. hath her victories 351:29
p., hol the moon sleeps 465:22
p. in a Larañaga 294:31
p. in her chamber 410:18
p. in our time 388:24
p. in Shelley's mind 494:12
p. in thy breast 478:1
p. instead of death 122:6
p. is come and wars are over 263:29
P. is crown'd with smiles 552:1
p. is in the grave 496:26
p. is of the nature of a conquest 442:18
P. is poor reading 236:2
p. is what I seek 16:25
P. its ten thousands 387:10
p. more destructive 269:19
p. of God 68:26, 390:48
p. of Jerusalem 399:31

Peace (cont.)
p. on earth, and mercy mild 565:12
p. on the earth 421:10
p., perfect p. 72:19
p., retrenchment, and reform 82:18
p. shall go sleep with Turks 475:17
P., the human dress 77:1
p. to him that is far off 54:34
P. to Mahmud 205:22
p. to you which were afar off 67:51
p. which the world cannot give 388:35
p...with honour 181:10
p. within nor calm around 498:24
poor, and mangled P. 445:10
preparation of the gospel of p. 68:12
Prince of P. 53:15
prosperity, and universal p. 143:31
publisheth p. 54:22
righteousness and p. 397:9
rust in p. 507:2
saying, p., p.; when there is no p. 55:14
seek p., and ensue it 394:2
should be p. at home 561:26
should kneel for p. 479:14
slept in p. 447:4
so enamoured on p. 145:28
soft phrase of p. 469:45
so old..keep the p. 477:1
star of p. return 123:12
strike p. to the soul of the man 16:4
studying p. 192:13
their bodies are buried in p. 57:19
then had thy p. been as a river 54:20
there abides a p. of thine 16:17
they are in p. 56:23
this p. sleep with her 447:16
though p. be made..interest that keeps p. 167:10
thousand years of p. 533:20
through P. to Light 402:10
thy mountains also shall bring p. 396:23
to a woman trusts his p. 229:3
to gain our p., have sent to p. 459:4
told me words of p. 536:27
two nymphs..P. and Plenty 167:17
unity, p., and concord 388:53
universal P. 529:30
until I come in p. 48:14
wait Thy word of p. 108:16
weak piping time of p. 476:5
we love p...not p. at any price 269:19
what is p.? Is it war? 173:32
when p...broken anywhere 408:23
where lazy P. 169:12
while he taught you p. 87:38
whispers p. within 72:19
who desires p., prepare for war 552:11
will not fast in p. 164:41
with p. and consolation 351:7
work us a perpetual p. 343:9
would I were sleep and p. 478:1
wound of p. is surety 481:11
Peaceably: p. if we can 146:3
p. in their habitations 57:16
Peaceful: in p. thought 1:10
p. sloth, not peace 345:22
so p. rests 381:36
their p. temple 164:35
Peace-maker: 'if' is the only p. 428:38
Peacemakers: blessed are the p. 57:39
Peace-parted: as to p. souls 437:16
Peach: Jemmy Twitcher..p. me 215:7
little p. in an orchard 204:3
nectarine and curious p. 332:17
Peach-blossoms: where the p. blew 309:16
Peacock: as a p.'s tail 119:25
droops the milk-white p. 539:2
ere Mor the P. flutters 301:27
eyed like a p. 286:37
he is a monstrous p. 585:11
pride of the p. 77:16
Peacocks: apes, and p. 47:44, 333:20
p. strutting by 296:30
proud as p. 422:26
useless; p. and lilies 413:13
Pea-green: beautiful p. boat 311:24
Peak: dwindle, p. and pine 456:11
upon a p. in Darien 288:19
Peaks: great p. of honour 216:7
solemn p. 16:14

Peal: deep thunder p. on p. 113:31
p. upon our wedding 263:1
wildest p. for years 249:5
Pealing: p. anthem 230:2
p. up to the sunny sky 535:39
Pear: cherry and hoary p. 82:7
golden p. 367:7
on a Catherine p. 517:13
Pearl: barbaric p. and gold 345:14
heaps of p. 476:14
no such p. in any gulf 525:3
p. in every cowslip's ear 466:35
of orient p. a double row 124:5
one p. of great price 59:30
pavement of p. 16:1
quarelets of p. 246:25
ransack the ocean for orient p. 329:23
threw a p. away 474:2
through gates of p. 264:10
your p. in your foul oyster 428:36
Pearled Arcturi of the earth 497:21
Pearls: as a string of p. to me 408:5
Gospel's p. 332:3
he who would search for p. 193:20
how p. did grow 246:25
p. before swine 58:18
p. that were his eyes 479:30
string the p. were strung on 268:15
these p. of thought 320:6
twelve gates were twelve p. 72:2
Pearly: shells of p. hue 308:26
used P.' Soap? 6:15
Pearse: Tom P., Tom P. 33:1
Peartree: glassy p. leaves 255:4
Peas: first green p. 317:1
Peasant: Hymalayan p. 296:13
rogue and p. slave 433:31
some belated p. 345:13
toe of the p. 437:13
yonder p., who is he? 361:20
Peasantry: bold p. 224:14
Peasants: from the hard hands of
p. 451:20
Peascod: before 'tis a p. 482:17
Pease-porridge hot 368:11
Pebble: not the only p. 79:16
p. from the brook 161:4
Pebbles: throw p. and mire 562:5
unnumber'd idle p. 454:3
Pebble-stone: you see this p.? 120:28
Pebble-stones: runnels p. 285:1
Peccator: esto p. et pecca fortiter 321:3
Peccavi—I've Scinde 403:11
Peccavimus'; but rave not thus! 380:20
Peck: for daws to p. at 469:28
p. of pickled pepper 368:12
Pecks, and starts 546:26
Pecori: ignotus p. 133:9
Pectora: quid non mortalia p. cogis 554:13
Pectore: nunc p. firmo 554:26
Pectus: bene praeparatum p. 259:7
Peculiar: extensive and p. 178:35
p. people 69:48
Pecunia: [P.] is the sovereign queen 35:22
Pecuniary: immense p. Mangle 179:23
Pecus: imitatores, servum p. 257:13
Pedantic: former was sometimes p. 154:13
Pedantical: figures p. 455:29
Pedants: learned p. much affect 110:9
prigs and p. 180:30
Pede: p. libero pulsanda tellus 258:28
stans p. in uno 261:12
Pedestalled in triumph 96:13
Pedibus: caput p. supposuisse ducis 372:5
Pedigree: languages..p. of nations 276:4
lass wi' a lang p. 360:18
or other homely p. 190:12
Peel: d'ye ken John P. 229:16
P. has no manners 564:14
P. knows what he is about 127:31
Sir Robert P.'s Ministry 29:3
Peeled, patch'd, and piebald 381:19
Peep: at p. of day 540:9
from her cabin'd loop-hole p. 340:6
into glory p. 552:12
p. about to find..graves 448:22
p. and botanize 578:30
p. at such a world 163:23
p. through their eyes 462:30
treason can but p. 436:27

Peeping in at morn 252:33
Peer: blooms without a p. 107:30
daffodils begin to p. 485:16
hath not left his p. 342:10
nor p. nor prince can buy 124:5
peerless paper p. 416:10
peerless p. Lord Peter 315:14
rhyming p. 385:21
worthy p. 471:11
Peerage: Charlemain with all his p. 345:4
p. or Westminster Abbey 362:18
study the P., Gerald 570:20
Peers: fare like my p. 95:11
his valiant p. 190:34
House of P. throughout the war 219:7
in p. to write at all 117:23
in the P...take his place 84:27(-85)
most important p. 28:34
Priam murdered with his p. 586:7
want her P.' 510:16
we love our House of P. 221:37
Peewees crying 516:10
Pegasus: break..P.'s neck 381:21
thought it P. 288:12
wind a fiery P. 440:18
Peggy: lovely, little P. 401:37
Pehlevi: high piping P. 205:12
Pejor: fit semper tempore p. homo 372:13
Pelagians do vainly talk 401:4
Pelago: fragilem truci commisit p.
ratem 258:5
Pelf: I crave no p. 480:21
titles, power, and p. 417:22
Pelican: have me turn p. 155:12
p. in the wilderness 398:1
wonderful bird is the p. 337:44
Pelio: imponere P. Ossam 556:12
Pelion imposuisse Olympo 259:27
Pelleas: Lancelot or P. 350:4
Pellenore: Pelleas or P. 350:4
Pelops: Thebes, or P.' line 341:18
Pelting: bide the p. of this..storm 453:14
p. each other 159:8
Pembroke's mother 87:24
Pen: all sad words of tongue or p. 568:17
all words of tongue and p. 238:31
before my p. has glean'd 289:4
bite his p. 521:2
draw my p. in defence 194:14
far less brilliant p. than mine 39:10
glorious by my p. 355:20
held his p. in trust to Art 183:10
his fingers held the p. 162:11
I made a rural p. 76:9
more foolish when he had not a
p. 274:23
my tongue is the p. 394:21
never durst poet touch a p. 455:22
no sooner..take a p. 270:8
p. is mightier 322:11
p. is worse 109:13
poet's p. 467:24
prevents his holding a p. 177:9
real Falernian winged the p. 120:24
scratching of a p. 319:11
sharp as a p. 443:19
take the p. out of his hand 19:19
thy p. from lenders' books 453:20
Waverley p. 11:4
with such acts fill a p. 189:8
write, p.l 455:1
Penal fire 344:7
Penalty of Adam 426:29
Penance: calls us to p. 345:17
p. done..p. more will do 149:37
Pence: eternal want of p. 541:21
loss of p. 159:38
took out two p. 61:41
Pencil: dips his p. in the gloom 497:24
his p. our faces 225:34
his p. was striking 225:34
p. of the Holy Ghost 25:19
p. pregnant with ethereal lines 575:15
silver-pointed p. 93:45
Stanhope's p. 587:15
Pendre: ils commencent ici par faire
p. 354:4
Pends-toi, brave Crillon 242:2
Pendulum: ominous vibration of
a p. 282:18
Penetralium of mystery 289:21

Penetrate: seize and clutch and p. 197:34
Penetrating: p. judgement without
..satire 223:9
sheer, p. power 19:19
Peneus: new P. 493:25
Penitence: my thread-bare P. 207:21
Penknife: saw me take out my p. 519:10
Penman: demoniaco-seraphic p.'s
latest 97:17
Penned: ditties highly p. 440:4
excellently well p. 482:18
Penny: but a p. a day 368:18
but a p. to Twickenham 333:16
dukes were three a p. 218:28
give me one p. 29:24
if you haven't got a p. 5:23
in for a p. 219:14
measure of wheat for a p. 70:44
one a p., two a p. 368:5
one p. plain 514:15
one p. the worse 34:11
p. for a song 584:4
put a p. in the old man's hat 5:23
sent to p.-fights 297:1
turn a p. 162:23
Penny-postage-stamp 128:19
Pennyworths: good p. 211:16
Pens: dip their p. in nothing but 103:8
if all the p. 331:2
other p. dwell on guilt 22:21
p. a stanza 385:21
threw their p. down 119:16
Pensamientos: cubre todos los humanos p. 134:18
Pensant: roseau p. 374:5
Pensée: la p... autoriser leurs injustices 557:4
Pensées: déguiser leurs p. 557:4
les grandes p. viennent du cœur 552:14
Pensent: qu'il y a des hommes et qui
.p. 97:32
Pensieri: i p. stretti 583:14
Pension: made his p. jingle 164:26
P... An allowance 277:31
p. list..a roll of honour 146:5
take his p. 413:24
think of 'is p. 301:13
Pensioner: Miser's p. 573:15
Pensioners: cowslips tall her p. 466:34
Pensions and Grenadiers 513:17
Pensive: her p. soul 154:1
his smile it was p. 238:33
in vacant or in p. mood 577:7
p. Eve 153:23
Pent: in populous city p. 349:11
long in city p. 289:2
Pentameter: in the p. aye falling 152:8
Pentecost: like the P. Wind 236:29
Pentecostal crew 296:7
Pent-house: upon his p. lid 456:11
Pentridge by the river 35:14
Penury: age, ache, p. 462:10
chill p. 230:5
People: acceptable p. 389:24
all p. that on earth 292:7
all the p. like us are We 303:18
all the p. you can 565:19
answerable to the p. 563:3
bear the miseries of a p. 357:24
beggarly p.l 521:26
bludgeoning of the p., by the p. 570:12
broad-based upon her p.'s will 539:13
by the p. as equally true 217:5
by the p...understand the multitude 194:9
came of decent p. 42:19
chosen P. never conquer'd 375:27
city cast her p. out 424:7
devices of the p. 393:36
education of the p. 181:7
escaped from the p. of Basing 311:5
fall the p. unto them 396:26
fire and p...agree 232:12
fool all the p. all of the time 314:14
forget also thine own p. 394:23
for the P...their Liberty 135:28
from the p. and for the p. 182:43
glorious p. vibrated again 495:25
God's pampered p. 190:10
good p. all 225:17
good p.'s wery scarce 174:7

People (cont.)
has such p. in 't 480:15
heart of this p. fat 53:10
he looked upon his p. 323:4
he shall subdue the p. 394:30
indictment against an whole p. 101:2
in Scotland supports the p. 277:29
in the name of the p. of India 101:27
in the P. was my trust 579:29
Irish are a fair p. 272:21
kill sick p. 330:16
kindreds, and p., and tongues 71:3
live in the hearts of the p. 551:13
look after our p. 416:6
love of the p. 101:13
loves the p. well 324:5
made..the p. his apes 137:22
madness of the p. 395:28
Martyr of the P. 135:28
most harme to the mene p. 310:5
mostly married p. 146:32
my p. love to have it so 55:13
new p. takes the land 141:27
no doubt but ye are the P. 48:57, 297:15
no vision, the p. perish 50:52
of all the p., by all the p. 373:16
of the p., by the p., and for the p. 314:12
one man..die for the p. 63:42
opium of the p. 333:13
O stormy p.! 137:25
peculiar p. 69:48
p. all exulting 566:27
p. are the masters 101:19
p. arose as one man 46:62
p. came to theirs 249:5
p. don't do such things 267:4
p. generally corrupt 103:24
p. have little intelligence 97:33
p. imagine a vain thing 391:47
p. is grass 54:10
p. is the true legislator 102:35
p. keep even kings in awe 169:9
p., Lord, the p. 198:22
p. loved her much 535:6
p. never give up their liberties 101:16
p. never so impatient 397:33
p. of customers 503:11
p. of his pasture 397:28
p. overlaid with taxes 27:25
p.'s choice 500:13
p.'s judgement 190:28
p.'s prayer 190:18
p. suppose me clever 97:29
p.'s voice is odd 386:14
p.'s wrongs his own 190:27
p. that delight in war 396:14
p. that walked in darkness 53:14
p. went up into the city 46:40
p. who are still..in the gristle 100:24
p. who like this sort of thing 314:17
p. whom he has never seen 101:21
p. whom I have not known 392:31
Priveleged and the P. 182:29
round about his p. 399:33
save the p. 198:22
stiff-necked p. 46:5
this p. hath a revolting..heart 55:12
thy p. shall be my p. 47:1
thy p. still are fed 183:20
understanded of the p. 401:8
very few p. come this way 312:11
voice of the p. 3:10, 25:8, 406:16
we are the p. of England 141:28
wentest forth before the p. 396:5
what kind of p. do they think we are? 144:8
what the p. think so 103:21
when the p. listens 419:16
wronged p. 561:16
Peopled: p...Heaven with Spirits masculine 349:23
world must be p. 468:24
Peoples: all the p. 528:11
cry of the Little P. 313:3
new-caught, sullen p. 303:24
peace among our p. 301:26
p...are seen writhing 235:22
souls of Christian p. 140:2
Peopling the lone universe 495:4
Peor and Baalim 343:23
Pepper: peck of pickled p. 368:12

Pepper (cont.)
p. and vinegar besides 130:17
thoroughly enjoy the p. 129:2
Peppered: I am p. 478:14
p. two of them 439:20
where they are p. 440:34
Peragravit: omne immensum p. 320:27
Perceive: both p. and know 389:28
half create and what p. 582:2
how should God p. it 396:26
I p. no change 303:8
p. a juggler's sleight 111:3
Perception: clear p. of its beauty 290:13
Perch: their p. and not their terror 461:22
Perchance to dream 434:4
Percy: Esperance! P.! 440:33
old song of P. and Douglas 502:9
P. out of Northumberland 30:11
Perdere: quem Juppiter vult 195:10
Perdition: bottomless p. 344:7
man's p. to be safe 199:27
p. catch my soul 471:27
son of p. 63:65
Perdrix: toujours p.! 12:20
Perdu: tout est p. fors l'honneur 211:4
Pereat: fiat justitia, et p. mundus 203:38
Peregrinantur, rusticantur 145:16
Perennial: falsehood has a p. spring 100:7
p. spring of all prodigality 101:17
Perennially hopeless 173:22
Perennius: monumentum aere p. 260:15
Pereo: qualis artifex p.! 362:27
Peres: Thy kingdom is divided 55:42
Pereunt: qui nobis p. et imputantur 331:26
Pereza: la p... jamás llegó al término 134:17
Perfect: be ye therefore p. 58:1
but constant, he were p. 485:2
end of a p. day 78:17
entire and p. chrysolite 473:21
ever p. 123:18
handmaid p. in God's sight 410:5
if thou wilt be p. 60:1
in short measures life..p. 282:1
just men made p. 69:21
made p. in weakness 67:38
my p. soul 469:39
none of us are p. 569:27
not in my p. mind 454:15
our union is p. 180:4
patience have her p. work 69:26
p. day nor night 445:44
p. democracy..most shameless 102:23
p. the cup as p'anned! 95:26
p. till the nightingales 94:8
p. type of a p. pleasure 570:8
p. use of an imperfect medium 570:4
they p. nature 27:15
unto the p. day 49:43
verray p. gentil knight 136:24
Perfected by experience 27:15
Perfectibility as a dream 339:3
Perfection: ascertain what p. is 19:24
attain to the divine p. 316:35
her own way to p. 100:25
he writes indexes to p. 226:22
make defect p. 424:8
p. is the child of Time 234:10
p. not to know them 155:2
p. of reason 148:4
p. wrongfully disgrac'd 487:14
pursuit of p. 19:25
right praise and true p. 465:22
very pink of p. 227:3
what's come to p. perishes 93:40
Perfections: eyes where all p. keep 7:13
know everything..but your p. 155:2
p. of a fool 73:15
with his sweet p. caught 412:19
Perfidious: fatal and p. bark 342:25
Perform: duty to p. 216:23
his wonders to p. 161:18
not able to p. 392:40
p. the last labour 583:21
zeal of the Lord..p. this 53:16
Performance: all words, and no p. 335:1
her p. keeps no day 124:2
his p...nothing 447:7
Performed: which she p. 319:1
Perfume: p. and suppliance of a minute 431:20

Perfume (cont.)
puss-gentleman that's all p. 159:19
scent of odorous p. 350:31
strange invisible p. 424:7
throw a p. on the violet 447:39
Perfumed: p. chambers of the great 441:41
p. like a milliner 438:32
purple the sails, and so p. 424:6
still p. 280:7
Perfumes: all the p. of Arabia 460:27
rich distill'd p. 340:27
three April p. 487:29
Perfuming: their scent the air p. 147:24
Perhaps: grand P. 89:31
p. I am! 9:14
p. turn out a sermon 105:17
Peri at the gate 357:7
Perii: ut vidi, ut 556:4
Periit: qui ante diem p. 363:1
Peril: p., toil, and pain 240:22
these woods more free from p. 426:19
those in p. on the sea 566:20
Péril: à vaincre sans p. 157:6
Perilous: dim and p. way 574:15
p. in steep places 80:19
p. seas 288:1
that p. stuff 460:37
Perils: defend us from all p. 388:36
if man could see the p. 38:24
in p. in the city 67:35
p. both of wind and limb 110:28
what p. do environ 110:10
what p. past 442:5
when our p. are past 124:19
Period: I belong to the Beardsley p. 39:8
made one poem's p. 331:2
new and great p. in His Church 352:12
p...most happy 217:8
p., pow'r, and enterprize 503:2
Periodical: governs the p. press 549:18
Peripatetic: magnetic, p. lover 221:1
Periphrastic study 197:8
Perish: all his thoughts p. 400:19
all his thoughts will p. 29:19
beasts that p. 395:2
better to p. 127:26
day p. wherein I was born 48:44
everything else in our language ..p. 326:3
hero p., or a sparrow fall 383:10
he shall p. everlastingly 388:37
I p. with hunger! 62:11
let the ungodly p. 396:4
not p., but have..life 63:9
not p. from the earth 314:12
not p. in the dust 507:32
no vision, the people p. 50:52
p. from the right way 391:51
p. in our own 544:2
p. on the shore 185:24
p. the thought! 144:29
p. through their own imaginations 392:6
p. unconsoled 309:27
p. with the sword 60:46
Rome shall p. 158:30
they shall p. 398:2
thy money p. with thee 64:36
to p. rather 345:12
wake, to p. never 576:19
Perishable: not of a p. home 577:11
Perished: p. in his pride 580:7
p. in the waters 58:36
poor souls, they p. 479:19
their memorial is p. with them 392:14
we p., each alone 159:3
Perishes: cause that p. with them everything p. 146:14
what's come to perfection p. 12:21 / 93:40
Perishing: must the remembered p. be? 171:8
Periuria: Iuppiter..p. ridet amantum 371:22
Periwig and hatband! 370:5
Periwig-pated: robustious p. fellow 434:15
Perizzites and the Hivites 45:36
Perjured: fleeting, p. Clarence 476:16
p., murderous, bloody 488:11
Perjuries: at lovers' p...Jove laughs 477:20

Perjury: Jove..laughs at lovers' p. 193:13
shall I lay p. upon my soul? 465:5
Perked up, in a glist'ring grief 446:16
Permanence which the sea cannot claim 237:10
Permanent: forward, not p. 431:20
nought's p. 116:36
P. Possibility of Sensation 515:4
suffering is p. 573:7
Permission of all-ruling Heaven 344:20
Permit: how long or short p. to Heaven 349:25
Permitted: not p. unto them to speak 67:2
Pernicious: most p. woman! 432:21
p. weed! 159:18
two p. daughters 453:6
Pernoctant nobiscum 145:16
Perpeti: audax omnia p. 258:6
Perpetual: next to the p. motion 179:27
p. fountain of good sense 194:15
p. president 127:31
p. quarrel 101:8
p. shame 397:1
with us p. night 282:6
Perpetually: p. settling 81:15
p. to be conquered 100:26
thou must be damned p. 330:7
Perpetuity: merit of p. 87:16
Perplex: when nae real ills p. 108:21
Perplexed: p. her, night and morn 535:7
p. in the extreme 474:2
p., labyrinthical soul! 186:30
yet is thy mind p.? 170:21
Perplexes: dull brain p. and retards 287:28
p. monarchs 345:6
Perplexity: stad is in p. 583:26
Persecuted: I p. the church of God 67:5
p. with letters 156:2
princes have p. me 399:23
Persecutest: why p. thou me? 64:41
Persecution: p...made them a faction 325:35
p...way to plant religion 86:15
religious p. may shield itself 101:23
some degree of p. 520:37
Persecutors: enemies, p., and slanderers 389:5
Persephone: singer of P.! 569:16
Persepolis: in triumph through P. 330:27
Perseverance: p. in a good cause 513:4
p...keeps honour bright 481:18
Persevere: in our opposed paths to p. 375:21
p. in obstinate condolement 430:31
Persevering: strong p. man 518:35
Persia: past their first sleep in P. 85:21
Persian: entertaining as a P. Tale 272:18
in P. gulfs..bred 320:6
P. on his throne! 119:13
P.'s heaven is easily made 356:9
say they are P. attire 453:31
Persians: antique P. taught 117:3
given to the Medes and P. 55:42
Persicos odi, puer, apparatus 258:29
Persist in doing wrong 481:14
Persistence: dominant's p. 97:7
Person: cheek of the young P. 178:11
express image of his p. 69:7
fairer p. lost not Heav'n 345:18
I am a most superior p. 8:15
my purse, my p. 463:2
no sich a p. 176:33
p. who agrees with me 182:22
thou wert the goodliest p. 328:24
vision of some p. or persons 268:8
well-conducted p. 543:12
Personal: no p. considerations 229:2
p. talk 578:18
Personated: most feelingly p. 482:34
Persons: neither confounding the P 388:38
no respecter of p. 64:48
no respect of p. 65:34
no respect of place, p. 482:31
paws of elder p. 40:20
p. I pity 402:22
p. whom one has never seen 363:10
towards great p. 243:32
Perspiration: his p. was but ichor 119:21
ninety-nine per cent. p. 195:22

Perspire: till you gently p. 297:28
Persuade: almost p. Justice 473:11
of itself p. the eyes of men 486:5
p. Tommy Townshend 225:27
pity whom ye can't p. 521:23
tongue to p. 145:26
wit to p. 169:17
Persuaded: fully p. in his own mind 66:16
shadow, well p. 295:10
thou hast p. 405:13
Persuadest: almost thou p. me 65:26
Persuading: by p. me to it 480:29
by p. others 282:19
fair-spoken and p. 447:9
Persuasion: not capable of a firm p. 77:21
not truth but p. 326:6
p. hung upon his lips 513:5
p. that a thing is so 77:21
p. tips his tongue 144:33
Persuasions: wingèd P. 491:21
Persuasive: p. language of a tear 143:28
reason so p. stole 546:9
Pert as a schoolgirl 219:27
Pertaining: nothing p. to 'em 135:28
Perturbation: polish'd p.! 442:25
Perturbed: rest, p. spirit! 432:31
Peru: from China to P. 279:2
Perused: in th' original p. mankind 14:24
Pervading: that p. influence 174:37
Perverse: all women born are so p. 80:9
I'll frown and be p. 477:20
widows..the most p. creatures 2:18
Perverts the Prophets 117:18
Peschiera, when thy bridge I crost 147:5
Pessimist fears this is true 120:6
Pessimus omnium poeta 133:1
Pester'd with a popinjay 438:34
Pestilence: breeds p. 77:10
from his horrid hair shakes p. 346:6
from the noisome p. 397:18
p. that walketh in darkness 397:18
purg'd the air of p. 481:31
Pestilence-stricken multitudes 496:4
Pestilent complete knave! 471:2
Pestle: bray a fool..with a p. 50:48
Pests of society 78:10
Pet: kept it for a p. 41:34
Petal: filigree p.! 545:12
like the p. of a flower 530:6
now sleeps the crimson p. 539:2
Petals: garden's last p. 523:15
pursed its p. up 91:35
rain between His p. wide 585:9
scriptured p. 411:22
Petar: hoist with his own p. 436:8
Peter: blessing of St. P.'s Master 559:27
in his last binn Sir P. 376:21
looked upon P. 62:46
once that P. was respected 578:24
opposite to Saint P. 472:37
paper peer Lord P. 416:10
peerless peer Lord P. 315:14
P.'s drift 496:17
P. was his name 217:25
raree-show of P.'s successor 90:32
rounded P.'s dome 199:23
Saint P. sat by the celestial gate 119:14
Saint P. wish himself within 119:21
Shock-headed P. 250:10
thou art P. 59:43
twenty times was P. feared 578:24
Peter Gilligan: old priest P. 584:6
Peterkin: little P. 507:9
Peter Piper picked a peck 368:12
Peter Turf 478:46
Petis: quod p. hic est 257:4
Petit: il éteint le p. 109:34
Petitionary grace 528:8
Pet-lamb in a sentimental farce 287:16
Peto: banish P. 439:37
Petrarch: if Laura had been P.'s wife 115:39
Petrarchal: reject a p. coronation 290:2
Petrifactions of a plodding brain 117:20
Petrifies the feeling 105:19
Pets: handles the dear little p. 301:8
Pett: old person of P. 312:17
Petticoat: her feet beneath her p. 517:12
her p. was satin 298:29
I for one venerate a p. 116:49

Petticoat (cont.)
out of the Realm in my p. 198:3
tempestuous p. 246:4
with a yellow p. 366:17
Petticoatie: draiglet a' her p. 104:30
Petticoats up to the knees 146:19
Petty: clinging to the..p. 239:17
overpeer the p. traffickers 462:29
p. done, the undone vast 92:36
p. fortress 279:6
we p. men 448:22
Petulant: Cervantes is never p. 325:23
Peuple: je veux être p. 97:33
le p. a de la joie 355:7
le p. n'a guére d'esprit 97:33
Peur: sans p. et sans reproche 12:13
Peut-être: un grand p. 404:30
Pew: once in a p. 175:37
Pews: talk about the p. 140:2
Pewter: you long for simple p. 218:29
Phagocytes: stimulate the p. 489:19
Phalanx: in perfect p. 345:2
where is the Pyrrhic p.? 116:2
Phantasma: interim is like a p. 449:5
Phantom: p., Beauty 584:5
p. Caravan 206:21
p. of delight 580:19
p. of False Morning 205:7
p. of ourselves 16:10
transient and embarrassed p. 182:2
Phantoms: pursue..p. of hope 278:14
with p...strife 492:6
Pharaoh: from P.'s bitter yoke 361:15
hardened P.'s heart 45:42
P. is sold for balsams 87:19
Pharisee: I lived a P. 65:22
P., the son of a P. 65:17
touching the law, a P. 68:20
Pharisees: righteousness of the scribes and P. 57:44
them infarnal P. 319:19
Pharphar: Abana and P. 48:22
Phenomena: pieces are the p. 266:20
Phenomenon: infant p. 177:17
Pherson: P. had a son 23:27
P. swore a feud 23:26
Phials of wrath 411:16
Phidias: his awful Jove young P. 199:22
Phil: fidgety P. 249:24
Philanthropists: one of those wise p. 269:10
Philip: not known me, P.? 63:55
P. and Mary on a shilling 111:8
P. drunk to P. sober 5:12
P., foozling with his cleek 228:10
P. fought men 313:2
P...reckoned a horse-race won 502:10
P. Slingsby 24:9
P. Sparrow 502:20
P.'s peerless son 19:3
see if P. can 249:23
Philippi: I will see thee at P. 451:32
Philistia, be thou glad 395:23
Philistine: P. of genius 20:19
P...originally meant 19:14
Philistines: Barbarians, P...Populace 19:23, 29
daughters of the P. rejoice 47:29
designation of P. 19:28
great apostle of the P. 19:17
P. be upon thee, Samson 46:58
P. may jostle 220:28
Philistinism! 19:15
Phillida: P. and Coridon 80:7
P. flouts me 9:9, 10
P., my P.! 183:11
Philologists who chase 162:2
Philosopher: al be that he was a p. 137:6
ancient sage p. 110:27
by the p. as equally false 217:5
great poet..profound p. 152:28
guide, p., and friend 384:17
he was a shrewd p. 110:11
old p. is still among us 325:32
p...endure the toothache 469:13
p., sir? 178:25
p.'s stones 109:22
soft p. of love 192:45
some p. has said it 145:3
to a p. no circumstance..too minute 226:23

INDEX

Philosophers: nation of pure p. 28:32
sayings of p. 110:33
Philosophic: bring the p. mind 576:20
defence of p. doubt 29:17
p. diner-out 93:29
p. mind..no middle ways 82:5
poetry..more p...than history 14:17
Philosophical: state of p. doubt 153:8
Philosophorum: dicatur ab aliquo p. 145:3
Philosophy: adversity's sweet milk, p. 478:24
Aristotle and his p. 137:6
axioms in p. 289:34
bullied into a certain p. 289:24
calm..regions of p. 265:13
dreamt of in your p. 432:29
false p. 345:30
hang up p.l unless p...make a Juliet 478:25
hast any p. in thee? 427:24
how charming is divine p.l 340:24
if p. could find it out 433:19
little p...depth in p. 25:25
love for p. 289:33
love's p. 185:30
must be borne with p. 174:37
not faith, but mere P. 86:22
p. is a good horse in the stable 226:30
p. is nothing but discretion 422:9
P. teaching by examples 78:13, 180:12
P., that lean'd on Heav'n 381:27
p., the lumber of the schools 521:13
p. will clip an Angel's wings 286:42
some fear divine P. 532:30
touch of cold p. 286:42
unfit to hear moral p. 481:13
untaught innate p. 113:41
Phineus: Tiresias and P. 346:20
Phlegm: spit out thy p. 243:29
Phoebus: before the wheels of P. 469:19
bright P. in his strength 485:26
Delos rose and P. sprung 115:43
P.' amorous pinches 424:1
P. Apollo turned fasting friar 337:21
P., arise 190:4
P. 'gins arise 420:25
P., he 'that wandering knight' 438:15
P.l what a name 117:19
sweats in the eye of P. 444:23
towards P.' lodging 478:17
voti P. succedere partem mente dedit 555:12
wheels of P.' wain 340:8
Phoenix: if east or west the P. builds 125:11
I knew a p. in my youth 584:18
maiden p. 447:16
p. builds the p.' nest 166:2
p. 'midst her fires 117:29
Phrase: a fico for the p.l 465:32
alter..a single p. 236:42
full of p. and fame 19:5
grandsire p. 477:5
ill p., a vile p. 432:41
measured p. 580:12
p. of gentlest courtesy 416:18
p. that time hath flung away 276:14
p. would be more german 437:31
soft p. of peace 469:45
that portentous p. 116:50
unintelligible p. 375:11
well turned p. 4:13
Phrase: une page dans une p. 282:11
Phrases: death, without p. 502:13
discourse in novel p. 220:26
high-sounding p. 118:33
taffeta p. 455:29
Phrases: la mort, sans p. 502:13
Phrygia, and Pamphylia 64:26
Phylacteries: make broad their p. 60:15
p. of the Liberal Party 409:12
Phyllis: neat-handed P. 342:2
P. is my only joy 421:13
P., without frown or smile 421:15
Physic: P. of Metaphys c begs 381:27
sceptre, learning, p. 430:1
take p., pomp 453:15
throw p. to the dogs 460:37
Physician: died..of my p. 402:3
every p...favourite disease 204:24
honour a p. 57:9

Physician (cont.)
Luke, the beloved p. 68:34
more needs she the divine than the p. 460:30
p., heal thyself 61:25
time is the great p. 182:9
when death is our p. 470:14
whole need not a p. 58:39
Physicians: many things of many p. 60:60
p. are like kings 563:19
p. of all men are most happy 404:16
p. of the utmost fame 41:2
quacks—not p. 253:14
what the fever is to the p. 352:18
Physics: labour we delight in p. pain 458:20
Pia mater: never stretched the p. 86:7
nourished in the womb of p. 455:12
Pianist: do not shoot the p. 569:29
Piano's martial blast 218:9
Piano-forte is a fine resource 89:29
Pibble-pabble: no tiddle-taddle nor p. in Pompey's camp 444:16
Pibroch: of Donuil Dhu 419:2
p. shake the air 23:18
Piccadilly: down P. with a poppy 220:28
goodbye p. 571:1
Pick: his p. more splendid 517:9
not scruple to p. a pocket 172:14
only the p. of the Army 301:8
Picked: age is grown so p. 437:13
not p. from the leaves 86:17
p. from passing men 516:1
Picker-up of learning's crumbs 91:19
Picket's off duty for ever 40:2
Picking: my hands from p. and stealing 391:8
Pickle: a plague o' these p. herring 482:16
many a p. makes a mickle 134:11
Pick-lock to a place 159:28
Pick-purse: at hand, quoth p. 438:41
Pickwick: old unbroken P. 142:10
P., the Owl 11:4
yours, P. 179:12
Pickwickian sense..point of view 178:23
Picninnies, and the Joblillies 209:18
Pictor: geometres p. aliptes 283:3
Pictoribus atque poetis..audendi 255:15
Pictura: animum p. pascit inani ut p. poesis 553:18
256:11
Picture: Earth's last p. 303:19
exquisite p. of human manners 216:17
fain would paint a p. 93:49
like Mistress Mall's p. 482:8
like the p. of sombody reading 290:16
look here, upon this p. 435:45
look not on his p. 281:9
origin of the fict've p. 268:8
paint my p. truly like me 167:7
p. cannot express 25:28
p. it—think of it 252:21
p. of his father's face 209:2
P. of little T.C. 333:4
p. plac'd the busts between 80:1, 139:5
p. that orchard sprite 249:8
reluctance to sit for a p. 274:17
some p. on the margin wrought 190:1
Turkey carpet..to a p. 325:9
Pictured: from her p. urn 231:15
Pictures: all his p. faded 73:16
beads, p., rosaries, and pixes 111:12
but a gallery of p. 26:16
but as p. 458:14
come to the p. 243:5
cutting all the p. out 40:19
looking at p. 240:13
muddled with books and p. 299:18
my eyes make p. 150:29
p. for the page atone 381:14
p. in our eyes to get 184:30
p. of silver 50:34
p. out of doors 470:25
p., taste, Shakespeare 227:23
without p. or conversations 128:20
with savage-p. fill their gaps 521:18
Picturesque liar 550:22
Picturing: sense faints p. them 496:8
Pie: baked in a p. 368:20
eating a Christmas p. 367:16
when the p. was opened 368:20, 512:5

Pie: el p. in el estribo 134:20
Piebald: peel'd, patch'd, and p. 381:19
Piece: equal p. of justice 86:18
faultless p. to see 382:25
numerous p. of monstrosity 86:26
p. of divinity in us 86:37
p. of him 430:9
p. of the nether millstone 49:31
prologues precede the p. 213:8
that p. of song 483:1
what a p. of work is a man! 433:15
Piece-bright paling 255:6
Pieces: dash him to p.l 451:21
helpless P. of the Game 206:29
Men for P. 206:28
my everlasting peace..into p. 253:6
p. are the phenomena 266:22
p. of eight! 514:20
seraphic p. of life and beauty 548:15
sublime dashed to p. 153:13
thirty p. of silver 60:37
Pie-crust: promises and p. 520:4
Pied: daisies p. and violets blue 455:35
Piedmontese: slain by the bloody P. 351:20
Pieman: Simple Simon met a p. 368:19
Pier: from this here p. 34:25
I walk'd upon the p. 34:33
Pierce: into his hand, and p. it 48:33
meeting soul may p. 342:7
neither graze nor p. 472:32
sun will p. 89:22
Pierced: p. and nail'd Him 565:14
p. through the ear 470:7
they also which p. him 70:22
they p. my hands 393:6
twice p. His..feet 313:5
Piercing even to the dividing 69:8
Pierian: deep of the P. spring 189:13
taste not the P. spring 382:20
Pierides: me fecere poetam P. 556:7
Pies: eats the p. and puddings 249:22
one of Bellamy's veal p. 379:21
Pietate: reddite mi hoc pro p. mea 133:16
Piety: all thy P. nor Wit 207:2
mistaken and over-zealous p. 101:23
natural p. 577:25
renowned for larnin' and p. 229:13
to p. more prone 4:9
Piffle before the wind 21:1
Pig: dear P., are you willing? 312:2
p. in a poke 549:26
p., or fig? 129:3
p.'s bones 137:22
stole a p...the p. was eat 369:11
this little p. went to market 369:7
three Owls and a P. 312:20
Pigeon-livered: I am p. 433:34
Pigging together 100:8
Piggy-wig: in a wood a P. stood 312:1
Pig-lead: road-rail, p. 333:21
Pigmy: darling of a p. size 576:10
fretted the p. body to decay 190:13
Pigs: as p. do in a poke 358:50
as p. have to fly 129:19
naturally as p. squeak 110:4
whether p. have wings 130:15
Pike: puissant p. 444:15
text of p. and gun 110:17
Pilate: jesting P. 27:29
Pilchards: thicker than p. 294:35
Pile: earn a monumental p. 162:37
face of this tall p. 155:19
Gaunt's embattled p. 322:23
God hath made the p. complete 532:32
Piled by the hands of giants 323:11
Pilgrim: against the p. borne 153:24
forth, p., forth! 136:20
Honour comes, a p. grey 153:30
Life's a single p. 38:24
onward goes the p. band 35:4
p. of a day 122:37
P. of Eternity 492:1
p. of the sky! 580:26
p. soul in you 586:21
p. steps of spring 80:25
tired p.'s limbs 124:1
to be a p. 99:35, 37
with p. steps 350:12
Pilgrimage: house of my p. 399:16
I'll take my p. 405:9

Pilgrimage (cont.)
in return outlandish p. 82:8
overtaketh in his p. 484:35
quiet p. 123:25
succeed me in my p. 99:39
that go on p. 99:31
through this weary p. 183:20
with songs beguile your p. 208:9
Pilgrimages: to goon on p. 136:22
Pilgrims: happy band of p. 362:7, 8
land of the p.' pride 504:19
like p. to th' appointed place 193:17
p. of the year 336:32
Pilgrim's Progress: wished longer..
excepting..the P. 276:26
Pill: his potion and his p. 247:18
no Morrison's P. for..Society 126:45
outliv'd the doctor's p. 214:34
Pillage: which p. they..bring home 443:10
Pillar: I cannot be regarded as a p. 335:21
p. of cloud 45:50
p. of fire 45:50
p. of salt 44:53
sat by a p. alone 535:41
seem'd a p. of state 345:24
triple p. of the world 423:11
well-deserving p. 465:6
Pillared firmament 340:31
Pillars: among her golden p. 75:5
ancient p. rear their..heads 155:19
antique p. massy proof 341:24
four p. of government 27:8
his legs are as p. of marble 52:14
I bear up the p. of it 396:29
with p. of gold 75:4
Pillicock: P. sat on P.-hill 453:17
Pillow: like a p. on a bed 184:29
little hammer under the p. 173:31
my p. white 492:27
sighed upon a midnight p. 427:1
sloth finds the down p. hard 429:36
stones Thy p. 506:8
Pillows: smooth p., sweetest bed 501:27
sun..p. his chin 343:24
Pills: p...against an earthquake 2:34
pink p. for pale people 6:1
swallow countless p. 218:12
Pilot: daring p. in extremity 190:13
lightning my p. sits 492:27
oh, P.! 36:32
P. of the Galilean lake 342:26
P.'s boy..crazy 150:11
P. shrieked 150:11
p. that weathered the storm 124:19
see my P. face to face 528:22
Pilotage: learning p. 336:46
Pilots: best p. have needs 280:4
p. are thicker than pilchards 294:35
Pimpernel: elusive P. 370:13
p. dozed on the lea 536:13
Pimpernell: Henry P. 478:46
Pimples: roughnesses, p., warts 167:7
Pin: at a p.'s fee 432:2
heard a p. drop 408:11
in merry p. 160:6
pinn'd it wi' a siller p. 32:19
serve..to up one's hair 156:2
stay not for th' other p.! 244:6
with a little p. 475:7
Pinafore: Captain of the P. 221:10, 11
Pinch: death is as a lover's p. 426:11
they brought one P. 429:1
Pinches: Phoebus' amorous p. 424:1
p. country wenches 281:6
Pinching fingers 485:6
Pindaric: forgot his..P. art 386:13
Pindarus: spare the house of P. 351:15
Pindus: top of P. strow 510:20
Pine: beech and odorous p. 82:9
dwindle, peak, and p. 456:11
over palm and p. 300:24
palm and southern p. 528:23
p. for what is not 498:9
p. with fear and sorrow 510:16
shall I ever sigh and p.? 244:9
spray of Western p. 238:26
sun doth p. 82:1
tallest p. 344:24
then most I p. for thee 322:8
they p., I live 195:13
why dost thou p. within 488:20

Pineapple: p., and cranberries 219:13
p. of politeness 500:18
Pined: near a thousand tables p. 575:4
p. away seven..years 306:15
p. by Arno for..Tees 323:8
she p. in thought 483:10
sighed and p. and ogled 543:12
Pine-logs: bring me p. hither 361:21
Pines: arrowy white p. 546:37
eat the cones under his p. 212:3
I never get between the p. 42:5
old acquaintance among the p. 547:1
p. are gossip p. 208:3
their great p. groan aghast 492:27
thoughts..instead of p. 288:7
thunder-harp of p. 503:13
Pine-stems: red gold is on the p. 337:35
Pine-tree's withered branch 316:21
Pine-trees: black and gloomy p. 317:22
Pinguem: me p. et nitidum 256:27
Pining: what is passion but p.? 337:42
Pinion: he nursed the p. 117:25
imagination droops her p. 116:8
Pinions: drift of p. 545:1
stayed..his p. from flight 525:2
with p. skim the air 211:25
Pink: bring hither the P. 510:23
I will pu' the p. 107:30
my face is p. 8:16
p. of courtesy 478:5, 512:2
p. of perfection 227:3
p. o' womankind 107:30
rose p. and dirty drab 337:9
tinged with p. 312:6
white p. and the pansy 342:31(-343)
Pink-tipped: pale hands, p. 254:15
Pinnace, like a fluttered bird 539:16
Pinnacle of sacrifice 216:7
Pinnacled dim in the..inane 497:12
Pinned it wi' a siller pin 32:19
Pins: here files of p. 385:9
have magic in a p. bottle 175:38
p. o' wine 105:36
Pintores: los buenos p. imitan 134:19
Pint-pot: peace, good p.! 439:32
Pioneers: p. and all 472:3
p.! O p.! 567:4
Pious: devotion's visage and p.
action 434:3
he was rarther p. 20:29
in p. times 190:7
stored with p. frauds 102:1
Pipe: called for his p. 368:3
easier to be played on than a p. 435:25
his last breath through a p. 307:6
my small p. 245:19
p. and woo her 538:21
p. a simple song 575:12
p. a song about a Lamb 76:9
p. but as the linnets sing 532:16
p. for Fortune's finger 434:26
p. for my capacious mouth 214:7
p. me to pastures still 254:26
p. of half-awaken'd birds 538:19
p. to the spirit 287:8
p., with solemn..puff 159:17
put that in your p. 34:22
rumour is a p. 441:8
she loved the Dorian p. 18:28
smokin' my p. on the mountings 301:8
three-p. problem 187:19
thy tube, thy p. 288:6
thy small p. 482:10
Piped: p. a silly pipe 290:7
p. with merry cheer 76:9
we have p. unto you 59:8
Piper: Hyperion of calves the P. 146:20
I was to pay the P. 155:8
Peter P. picked a peck 368:12
p., pipe that song again 76:9
p.'s son 369:10, 11
Pipers: especially p. 94:38
five-and-thirty p. 23:26
wi' a hundred p. 360:17
Pipes: knock out your p. 296:17
p. and whistles in his sound 427:21
p. o' Havelock 568:19
scrannel p. 342:29
soft p., play on 287:8
what p. and timbrels? 287:7
Piping: for ever p. 287:10

Piping (cont.)
high p. Pehlevi 205:12
his p. took a troubled sound 18:24
naked, p. loud 76:8
p. down the valleys wild 76:9
p. hot 110:32
p. your eye 173:6
weak p. time of peace 476:5
wishes p. to him 337:18
Pipkin: this little p. 245:19
Pippa passes 39:24, 94:39
Pippin: right as a Ribstone P.! 41:25
Pippins: old p. toothsomest 563:22
p. and seese to come 465:31
Pips: hear the p. squeak 216:6
Piracies..sullied with..stealing 550:27
Pirate: sanctimonious p. 461:17
to be a P. King 221:27
Piscem: desinat in p. mulier 255:14
Pismire is equally perfect 567:19
Pistol: when his p. misses fire 227:27
Pistols: have you your p.? 567:4
young ones carry p. 489:6
Piston: steam and p. stroke 359:2
Pit: beat us to the p. 452:5
black as the P. 241:18
blind p. ponies 249:5
he that diggeth a p. 51:24
key of the bottomless p. 71:38
law is a bottomless p. 14:6
man..go down into the p. 29:19
monster of the p. 386:19
out of the horrible p. 394:12
p., box, and gall'ry 385:23
p. that is bottomless 267:30
they have digged a p. 395:18
they'll fill a p. 440:23
to the bottomless p. 348:22
to the profoundest p. 436:28
what is in the p. 74:2
when I go down to the p. 393:26
Pit-a-pat: my heart go p. 94:35
Pitch: bumping p. 363:4
he that toucheth p. 56:43
of what validity and p. 481:30
p. His tent 243:22
p. my moving tent 355:10
p. this one high! 15:4
roller, p., and stumps, and all 309:27
two p. balls..for eyes 455:9
when you make p. hot 173:30
Pitch-and-toss: one turn of p. 297:11
Pitched: as the mind is p. 163:48
p. betwixt Heaven and.. 545:1
Pitcher be broken at the fountain 51:33
Pitchfork: drive nature out with a
p. 257:2
thrown on her with a p. 520:17
Piteous sight 508:17
Piteously Love closed 336:35
Pitfall: with P. and with Gin 207:10
Pith: enterprises of great p. 434:4
men of p. and thew 77:28
p...in the postscript 239:10
p. of an Indian cane 2:10
Pitied: p. the man 161:37
what 'tis to pity, and be p. 427:19
Pities: he p. the plumage 373:3
Power that p. me 225:12
what a thousand p. then 252:10
Pitieth: as a father p. 398:6
Pitiful: God be p. 88:3
it was p.! 252:18
long-suffering, and very p. 56:30
p. as she is fair 231:37
'twas p., 'twas wondrous p. 470:3
Pitiful-hearted Titan 439:14
Pitiless: ruffians, p. as proud 158:33
Pitt: o'er P.'s the mournful requiem sound 418:5
P. is to Addington 124:14
Pittore: anch' io sono p.! 157:14
Pity: any p. for conceited people 196:25
feel the dint of p. 450:31
first endure, then p. 383:27
for some to have p. on me 396:15
heart to p. 143:15
he best can p. who has felt 215:13
his p. gave ere charity began 224:21
I learn to p. them 225:12
in p. and mournful awe 16:6

INDEX

Pity (cont.)

I p. his ignorance 177:12
it was the more p. 30:12
je vous en prie, p. me 231:36
know what 'tis to p. 427:19
never a saint took p. 149:20
no p. sitting in the clouds 478:30
no p. to myself 476:37
no soul will p. me 476:37
persons I p. 402:22
P. a human face 77:1
p. beyond all telling 585:20
p. from blust'ring wind 319:8
p. him afterwards 273:5
p. is sworn servant unto love 168:11
p., like a naked new-born babe 457:9
p. me, then 488:6
p. my simplicity 565:9
p. never ceases to be shown 190:27
p. of it, Iago! 472:28
p. on the least of things 584:7
p. renneth sone 137:31
P. She's a Whore 210:2
p. Sultan Mahmud 205:21
p. them that weep 123:26
p. those they torture not 496:25
p. 'tis 'tis true 432:40
p. whom ye can't persuade 521:23
some touch of p. 476:7
that His P. allows them 302:2
that she did p. them 470:3
then cherish p. 76:16
they (methinks) deserve my p. 158:12
thy p. upon all prisoners 389:3
till P.'s self be dead 153:22
to hear it was great p. 35:17
to Mercy, P., Peace, and Love 76:18
virtuous poor, one can p. 570:11
Pitying the tender cries 77:2
Pity-pat: his heart. .p. 319:26
Pity-zekle: hern went p. 319:26
Pium: aliquem fieri posse putare p. 133:12
Pius: Titus Antoninus P...His reign 217:7
Pixes: rosaries and p. 111:12
Place: adorn'd the venerable p. 224:22
all move one p. 129:10
all other things give p. 215:30
all the p. is holy ground 537:43
bourne of Time and P. 528:22
calmly in their p. 26:27
cares no more for one p. 508:9
changed by p. or time 344:22
choose their p. of rest 349:31
cure this p. 90:20
degree, priority, and p. 481:2
dovetailedness with regard to p. 177:18
earns a p. i' the story 424:30
even in heavenly p. 501:24
find they a p. or part 562:21
fine and private p. 333:9
flaming bounds of p. and time 231:13
from another p. . .my name 510:21
get p. and wealth 386:9
give p. to better men 167:9
good reasons. .give p. to better 451:28
great effect. .in p. lyte 138:40
great inviolate p. 237:10
grown and take our p. 295:6
his p. could nowhere be found 394:6
his p. know him any more 48:53
I go to prepare a p. for you 63:52
keep in the same p. 130:4
live in any p. in Christome 198:3
meet in every p. 285:40
men in great p. 26:22
mind is its own p. 344:22
never the time and the p. 93:38
night embrac'd the p. 165:16
no p. to go 108:42
no respect of p., persons 482:31
not getting into p. 116:36
one in all doth hold his p. 449:30
one of the smallest. .in a great p. 29:5
on sic a p. 106:32
p. and means for every man 423:8
p. for everything 503:8
p. in the ranks awaits you 402:14
I set out for 512:27
p. of justice is a hallowed p. 26:31
p. of the Canaanites 45:36

Place (cont.)

p. thereof shall know it no more 398:7
p. to stand and love in 88:20
p. where 'e is gone 297:4
p. where men can pray 142:13
p. whereon thou standest 45:34
p. where the tree falleth 51:28
p. where thine honour dwelleth 393:19
p. where. .we find our happiness 579:30
p. which thou hast appointed 398:8
purity and p. and innocence 347:25
reign in this horrible p. 164:22
right man in the right p. 268:29
right man to fill the right p. 310:25
rising to great p. 26:28
rising unto p. is laborious 26:24
savage p.! 151:32
she a p. has 245:22
shop to mind in time and p. 96:26
so thick on every p. 192:17
take your p. there 293:19
their hearts. . in the right p. 182:10
the Lord is in this p. 45:4
this is an awful p. 416:5
thy prison is a holy p. 114:34
till there be no p. 53:3
time and p. are lost 346:10
to th' appointed p. 193:17
towering in her pride of p. 458:28
unfixed in principles and p. 190:13
upon the p. beneath 464:33
where the p.? 456:3
your reward in a certain p. 85:8
Place: toutes les fois que je donne une p. 318:22
Placeas: ut pueris p. 283:21
Placed: where you alone are p. 232:11
Placeo: spiro et p., si p., tuum est 260:19
Places: all p., all airs 86:28
all p. that the eye of heaven 474:19
all p. thou 349:30
all p. were alike to him 304:21
all the p. you can 565:19
bon-mots from their p. 357:26
built desolate p. for themselves 48:45
in their proper p. 548:15
in two p. at once 407:7
keep their ancient p. 545:1
moveth us in sundry p. 388:6
p. of nestling green 266:5
P. where they sing 388:27
p. which pale passion loves 37:37
proper words in proper p. 520:1
strange p. cramm'd 427:16
Placid: so p. and self-contained 567:20
Plackets: thy hand out of p. 453:20
Plagiary: accounted p. 353:1
Plague: any p. come nigh 397:19
a p., a mischief 109:22
a p. o' both your houses! 478:15
a p. of all cowards 439:17
a p. of opinion! 481:23
a p. of sighing and grief! 439:30
a p. o' these pickle herring! 482:16
a p. upon such backing! 439:16
fiends that p. thee thus 149:1
instruments to p. us 454:21
p. of his sentiments! 500:38
pleasing p. stole on me 566:18
red p. rid you 479:26
that's his p. 109:14
through any p., or trouble 398:21
Plagued the nations 162:15
Plagues: add unto him the p. 72:11
all the p. a lover bears 559:6
Mab with blisters p. 477:7
of all p. 170:16
two main p. . .of human kind 109:12
Plaguy twelvepenny weather 519:21
Plaid: beneath the tartan p. 23:17
Plaidie: my p. to the angry airt 107:24
Plain: after his deeth. .p. 137:29
all doctrines and clear 111:11
astonishes. .p. dealing 200:4
base as is the lowly p. 525:36
best p. set 25:27
divine p. face 307:15
dull speaker, like a p. woman 243:17
eminently p. and direct 20:2
fair instead of p. and sere 80:23
gentle, p., just and resolute 568:7

Plain (cont.)

glassy p. 575:25
great Gromboolian p. 311:15
heavens above that p. 546:30
he will make it p. 161:20
I'll tell her p. 479:4
I see it shining p. 263:14
it is old and p. 483:5
Jacob was a p. man 44:57
language p. 159:16
lo, how she makes it p.! 422:20
loose, p., rude, writer 109:9
loveliest village of the p. 224:12
make it p. upon tables 56:9
make thy way p. 392:4
my language is p. 238:32
not so p. 218:38
on a darkling p. 15:8
once more reach that p. 552:6
one penny p. 514:15
or Minden's p. 310:2
p. as way to parish church 427:18
p., blunt man 450:32
p. living and high thinking 577:16
p. man in his p. meaning 464:26
p. tale shall put you down 439:25
rough places p. 54:9
see Shelley p. 93:23
shapes of sky or p. 498:8
stretched upon the p. 117:25
that p. was but narrow 99:18
they came at a delicate p. 99:18
Waterloo's ensanguin'd p. 9:5
waveless p. of Lombardy 495:1
way is all so very p. 142:13
Plainly: p. and more p. 323:15
p. told 476:28
Plainness: perfect p. of speech 20:4
Plains: by thousands on her p. 241:13
gemlike p. and seas 561:17
her silver-mantled p. 421:9
left on Afghanistan's p. 304:4
p. of pleasant Hertfordshire 307:35
p. of windy Troy 540:32
sunny p. and. .transparent skies 127:4
Plain-speaking: apology for p. 173:27
Plaint: recalled by prayer and p. 238:29
tease her with our p. 18:28
Plaintive treble of the Treasury Bench 180:22
Plaire: la grande règle. .de p. 353:14
Plaisirs: les grands seigneurs ont des p. 355:7
Plaits the manes of horses 477:7
Plan: form'd a p. that flatter'd me 163:35
fulfils great Nature's p. 105:25
his 'simple p.' 188:34
joined in the p. 161:37
not without a p. 383:7
p. that pleased his childish thought 575:5
p. the future by the past 103:6
Prince-Elective on the modern p. 140:7
rebuild it on the old p. 338:23
some usefu' p. or beuk 106:3
Planco: consule P. 260:8
Planet: absence of the p. Venus 177:22
born under a riming p. 469:16
every wand'ring p.'s course 330:28
Jove's p. rises yonder 92:18
new p. swims into his ken 288:19
p. of Love is on high 536:10
p.'s tyrant, dotard Death 38:29
Planetary: stops of p. music 493:5
Planets: laws which keep the p. 387:23
no p. strike 430:20
p., and this centre 481:2
p., filled with Stagyrites 357:19
P. in their stations list'ning 348:28
p. in their turn 2:27
with p. in His care 584:7
what other p. 383:9
Plank: only have to swab a p. 173:30
Planned: perfect the cup as p.! 95:26
perfect woman, nobly p. 580:21
whole I p. 95:13
Plans: p. credit, and the Muse 199:12
their hopeful p. to emptiness 263:31
Plant: confidence is a p. of slow growth 370:4

[864]

Plant (cont.)
fix'd like a p. 383:24
green p. groweth 140:16
indirect way to p. religion 86:15
no p...on mortal soil 342:22
p. and flower of light 282:1
p. that with most cutting grows 168:7
Sensitive P. 497:25
this fascinating p. 278:1
wicked, wicked p. 305:18
Plantation: longing for de old p. 210:16
Planted: God..first p. a garden 26:19
I have p., Apollos watered 66:22
Planting: wheat for this p. 316:6
Plants: grow up as the young p. 400:16
like p. in mines 94:25
p. did spring 35:17
p. his footsteps 161:18
p. suck in the earth 158:7
to his music p. and flowers 446:18
young ladies are delicate p. 22:18
Plaster: don't grow into p. saints 303:4
Plasters: for which..no p. 213:13
Plastic circumstance 95:24
Plat of rising ground 341:15
Plate: moment they're out of her p. 171:17
Plateau: peninsular p. of Spain 235:22
Plates dropp'd from his pocket 426:1
Platform: half the p. just reflects 385:3
upon the p. 431:17
Platinum: bullets made of p. 40:27
Plato: attachment à la P. 220:28
lend an ear to P. 535:25
out of the rule of P. 352:28
P. is dear to me 14:19
P. is never sullen 325:23
P.'s brain 199:2
P.'s retirement 350:11
P. the wise 537:37
P., thou reason'st well! 1:22
rather be wrong with P. 145:23
read and understand P. 200:46
unsphere the spirit of P. 341:17
Plato: amicus P. 14:19
Platone: errare..malo cum P. 145:23
Platonic: white P. dreams 269:24
Platter: displays her cleanly p. 226:11
give no account of the p. 306:22
licked the p. clean 367:10
Plaudere: satis est equitem mihi p. 261:20
Plautus too light 433:22
Play: actions that a man might p. 430:30
all her sons at p. 15:12
all the tune that he could p. 359:10
as children with their p. 160:15
at Christmas 549:23
better at a p. 357:21
better than a p. 136:3
come forth to p. 342:3
come out to p. 366:10
come to the p. without knowing 104:2
come ye here to p.? 31:5
craftier to p. she was 138:13
fair p. of the British criminal law 187:25
for food or p. 148:28
game..kings would not p. at 163:42
globe to p. withal 191:17
good author..good p. 489:25
good p. needs no epilogue 428:40
guilty creatures sitting at a p. 433:36
heard him p. 446:18
his p. is always fair 266:20
holdeth children from p. 502:8
I cannot p. alone 241:7
I doubt some foul p. 431:18
if the two services..had fair p. 310:25
I p. for Seasons 336:23
is there no p.? 467:25
I will p. the swan 473:29
judge not the p. 169:19, 404:10
last act crowns the p. 404:10
learned to p. when he was young 369:10
life's poor p. is o'er 383:30
like so much to p. 515:14
little p. 335:10
little victims p. 230:26
not let my p. run 172:15
or a' the p. was play'd 32:1
our brief sweet p. 544:4
our p. is done 484:27

Play (cont.)
our p. is played out 542:40
p. is done 543:6
p. is the tragedy, 'Man' 380:15
p. on; give me excess of it 481:30
p. on the hole of the asp 53:19
p. out the p. 439:38
p. 'po' words 120:28
p.'s the thing 434:1
p. the fool..cheaper 161:42
p. the fool..in's own house 434:10
p. the man..and end you 263:15
p. the Roman fool 461:9
p. to you..death to us 313:20
p. up! p. up! and p. the game! 363:4, 5
p. up 'The Brides of Enderby' 267:12
p. with flowers and smile 443:19
p. with him as with a bird 49:30
pussy and I very gently will p. 367:8
rather..than see a p. 109:23
refined p. of the imagination 102:30
rose up to p. 46:3
sick men p. so nicely 474:25
six to p. 228:10
soft pipes, p. on 287:8
spend the time in sport and p. 217:16
that Interesting P. 41:13
turn us out to p. 293:13
very dull P. 155:34
when I p. on my fiddle 585:2
when the band begins to p. 303:1
wouldst not p. false 457:1
you cannot p. upon me 435:25
you would p. upon me 435:24
Play-bills: no time to read p. 104:2
Played: Apollo p. 319:1
child, that must be p. with 527:18
easier to be p. on 435:25
he p. so truly 280:10
how you p. the game 406:20
if this were p. upon a stage now 484:10
I have p. the fool 47:28
Love sang to us, p. with us 525:2
p. before you enter upon him 306:28
sweetly p. in tune 107:14
Played-out: also called P. 548:19
Playedst most foully for it 458:30
Player: as strikes the P. 207:1
like a strutting p. 481:6
p. on the other side is hidden 266:20
poor p. 461:4
this p. here 433:31
wrapped in a p.'s hide 232:6
Players: lenten entertainment the p. shall receive 433:17
merely p. 427:21
one of these harlotry p. 439:32
p...creatures set upon tables 272:34
p. in your housewifery 470:25
see the p. well bestowed 433:29
Playfellow: my p., your hand 425:4
Playing: amid our p. 128:2
p. in the wanton air 455:17
p. of the merry organ 10:14
p. on the sea-shore 364:13
p. our games 164:8
p. upon the flute 231:20
Playing fields of Eton 564:6
Playmates: I have had p. 308:1
Play-place of our early days 164:7
Plays: few of our p...more wit 201:32
going to p. 240:13
he loves no p. 448:27
old p. begin to disgust 202:15
p. about the flame 214:11
p., in the many games of life 575:11
p. many parts 427:21
p. with them, humours..them 139:23
with his wings he p. with me 231:39
you writer of p. 92:46
Plaything: child's a p. for an hour 308:9
little p.-house 558:11
some livelier p. 383:30
Playthings: great princes have great p. 163:41
love p. well as a child 514:38
p. come alive 515:17
Playtime: in the p. of the others 88:2
Playwright: actor, prompter, p. 237:25
our P. may show 537:39
Plaza Toro: Duke of P. 218:17

Plea: necessity the tyrant's p. 347:16
though justice be thy p. 404:33
what p. so tainted 464:14
without one p. 198:20
Plead: p. like angels 457:9
so what I p. is just 255:8
Pleading: while he p. spoke 546:9
Pleasance: joy, p., revel 471:22
youth is full of p. 486:2
Pleasant: abridgement of all that was p. 225:30
bread eaten in secret is p. 49:53
few think him p. enough 311:9
from p. to severe 193:19
how p. it is 146:30, 527:9
how p. to know Mr. Lear! 311:9
joyful and p. thing 400:21
joyous and p. histories 328:2
lovely and p. in their lives 47:30
most p. and gay 147:24
on to the P. Land 92:13
p. noise till noon 149:35
p. road 402:9
p. smooth wit 21:13
p...to behold the sun 51:31
so comely, so p., so jolly 173:9
that p. country's earth 475:16
'tis p., sure 117:10
to love you was p. enough 357:4
very p. hast thou been 47:30
Pleasanter the colder 111:24
Pleasantness: p. of an employment 23:10
ways of p. 49:41
Please: cities p. us then 342:5
coy, and hard to p. 418:31
E p..Double good! 175:39
if you mean to p. 159:13
Love seeketh not itself to p. 76:2
natural to p. 190:9
never fails to p. 421:13
not bound to p. thee 464:29
not difficult to p. 121:7
not to p. ourselves 66:17
p. her the best you may 9:9
p. your thoughts 425:28
studious to p. 278:27
they p., are pleas'd 226:12
those whom I wished to p. 270:28
to tax and to p. 100:12
we'll strive to p. you 484:27
we that live to p. 279:1
will p. themselves 176:17
you can go where you p. 301:8
Pleased: all seemed well p. 348:15
better p. when he has a good dinner 277:1
Devil was p. 151:12
ear is p. 163:48
face so p. my mind 10:20, 210:5
I'll not be p. with less 191:17
in whom I am well p. 57:33
p. his childish thought 575:5
p. th' Almighty's orders to perform 1:11
p. to call his mind 43:21
p. to have his all neglected 270:16
p. to my soul at death I cry 566:25
p. us, had he p. us less 2:1
p. with a rattle 383:30
p. with constant gain 165:3
p. with the danger 190:13
p. with this bauble still 383:30
p. with what he gets 427:9
pleasing consists in being p. 239:26
silence was p. 347:19
so he be p. 12:7
still p. to teach 383:6
what p. me best 240:13
Pleases: as long as one p. 156:6
every prospect p. 240:18
justice of it p. 472:29
Pleaseth: p. him to dwell 396:7
this age best p. me 246:24
Pleasing: art of p. 239:26
every p., every prudent part 384:33
lascivious p. of a lute 476:4
p. anxious being 230:9
p., dreadful thought! 1:22
p. inferior people 146:9
p. without skill to please 378:16
true vanity in..p. 156:4
turns to p. pain 510:3

Pleasure: aching P. nigh 287:21
all hope p. 191:34
at p., shall go forth 371:1
bait of p. 243:25
blend our p. or our pride 575:14
budge for no man's p. 478:13
cabinet of p. 244:23
capable of much curious p. 120:5
dissipation without p. 216:27
dome of p. 151:33(–152)
drinking is the soldier's p. 191:4
egg by p. laid 161:27
fading p. brings 502:5
feigned for p. 191:19
for thy p...created 70:39
for your p. you came here 160:9
from p. less 332:18
gave p. to the spectators 326:1
good, p., ease, content! 384:2
go to your business..p. 583:22
great source of p. is variety 278:5
green p. or grey grief 524:28
grievous p. and pain 525:5
hatred..the longest p. 116:44
if p. you attain 233:3
I have no p. in them 51:33
impression of p. in itself 24:11
in his p. is life 393:25
in trim gardens..his p. 341:11
King have p. in thy beauty 394:23
let fall your horrible p. 453:6
love of p. 384:35
man's chief p. is society 169:18
mingled profit with p. 256:9
miss for p. 216:2
mix'd reason with p. 225:26
mixture of a lie..add p. 27:30
more than a..duty..a p. 569:28
my heart with p. fills 577:7
never had I p. with her 328:11
no p. if it were realized 339:3
no p. in..an horse 400:22
no p., nor no pain 421:11
no profit grows where is no p. 478:47
not in p., but in rest from pain 192:36
not p., but power 172:25
only for taking a little p. 136:5
only sensual p. without vice 277:7
on p. she was bent 159:35
painful p. turns 510:3
pain that is all but a p. 220:32
perfect type of a perfect p. 570:8
p. afterwards 542:25
P. at the helm 229:23
P., blind with tears 491:21
p. eternally new 309:25
p. for evermore 392:27
p. gives way 183:17
p...in being mad 193:33, 203:27
p. in poetic pains 163:3
p. in the pathless woods 114:26
p. is as great 111:3
p. is..intermission of pain 422:10
p. is labour too, and tries 161:36
p. never is at home 285:37
p. of having it over 3:259
p. of pleasing inferior people 146:9
p. of the fleeting year 487:27
p.'s a sin 115:24
p. so exquisite 266:7
p. soon shall fade 233:3
p. was his business 195:21
p. with pain for leaven 522:5
privilege and p. 218:23
public stock of harmless p. 278:7
queen of p. 524:31
read without p. 277:9
recompense is a p. 278:12
separate from the p. of your company 307:3
some to p. take 384:36
suburbs of your good p. 449:17
such as have no p. 298:16
sweet is p. after pain 191:5
take p. in making 10:10
thou doubtful p. 229:9
thy most pointed p. take 516:16
turn to p. all they find 231:31
unholy p. 40:19
upon the heels of p. 155:32
variety is the soul of p. 40:9

Pleasure (cont.)
what p. lives in height? 539:3
when Youth and P. meet 113:26
wild and ineffable p. 313:9
without one p. 535:28
would have been my p. had I seen 530:19
your youth of p. 93:25
Pleasure-dome: stately p. 151:32
sunny p. 151:33(–152)
Pleasure-house: lordly p. 537:34
Pleasures: all the p. prove 330:17
baits and seeming p. 352:9
celibacy has no p. 278:17
chequer'd with p. and woes 356:34
English take their p. sadly 517:23
eternity of p. 209:25
hypocrite in his p. 275:25
its p. to another's pain 163:16
look not on p. as they come 244:8
mid p. and palaces 376:10
new p. prove 184:8
other p. all abjure 348:35
paucity of human p. 276:23
p. are like poppies spread 108:7
p. banish pain 562:13
p. newly found are sweet 573:17
p. of the Mahometans 231:20
p. that to verse belong 285:8
p. too refined to please 384:32
p. with youth pass away 507:34
purest of human p. 26:19
seat of p. 192:44
smoothly pass their p. 286:38
sooth'd his soul to p. 191:9
suck'd on country p. 185:6
sweeter far than all other p. are 194:2
these pretty p. might me move 405:8
understand the p. of the other 22:8
uneasy p. and fine pains 200:15
unreproved p. free 341:31
Pledge: I will p. with mine 280:21
ne'er refused to p. my toast 402:7
p. of love 473:26
we p. to thee 295:6, 8
Pledged: twice p. 375:19
Pledges: p. of a fruitful tree 245:20
p. of Heaven's joy 351:9
Pledging with contented smack 287:2
Pleiad: like the lost P. 112:32
Pleiades: flocks of shiny p. 249:14
sweet influences of P. 49:24
Plena gratia 96:42
Plenteous: harvest truly is p. 58:45
Plenteously: p. bringing forth..p. rewarded 389:50
Plenteousness within thy palaces 399:31
Plenties: nurse of arts, p. 445:10
Plentiful: blessings are p. 245:8
more p. than hope 245:8
p. as blackberries 439:24
Plenty: hand in hand with P. 539:4
here is God's p. 104:13
in delay there lies no p. 482:28
just had p. 105:7
on the expectation of p. 458:17
p. enough, but the dishes were ill-sorted 194:16
p. to get 179:15
scatter p. 230:5
two nymphs..Peace and P. 167:17
Pleuré: d'avoir quelquefois p. 360:8
Pleurer: peur d'être obligé d'en p. 37:9
Pliable: the other P. 99:4
Plie: the lips..taking their p. 100:4
Plie: je p. et ne romps pas 209:11
Plight: I p. thee my troth 391:30
Plighter of high hearts 425:4
Plod on a d still keep the passion fresh 337:24
Plodders: continual p. 454:32
Plodding: petrifactions of a p. brain 117:20
Plods: ploughman homeward p. 229:28
Plot: good p., good friends 439:10
Gunpowder Treason and P. 9:11, 368:13
her p. hath many changes 404:10
passions spin the p. 336:30
p. thickens 98:10
some melodious p. 287:23

Plot (cont.)
this blessed p., this earth 474:22
this green p. shall be our stage 467:2
what..does the p. signify 98:9
women guide the p. 500:31
Plots, true or false 190:11
Plotting some new reformation 193:23
Plough: following his p. 580:7
land you used to p. 263:5
late at p. 236:8
O Christ, the p. 334:2
p. deep and straight 262:3
p. my furrow alone 409:10
p. the wave no more 162:13
speed his p. 135:16
tested his first p. 89:41
to p.—loom—anvil 307:17
we p. the fields 121:27
wherefore p. 498:17
Ploughed: p. with my heifer 46:56
ye have p. wickedness 55:47
Ploughers plowed upon my back 399:37
Ploughing: is my team p.? 263:4
Ploughman: hard as the palm of p. 480:39
heavy p. snores 467:35
heavy steps of the p. 585:17
p. homeward plods 229:28
p. near at hand 341:34
Ploughmen: ye rigid P.! 262:3
Ploughshare: soldiers of the p. 413:26
stern Ruin's p. drives 107:8
Ploughshares: swords into p. 52:31
Pluck: do not p. at his rein 585:6
I come to p. your berries 342:10
I p. you out of the crannies 529:24
p. bright honour 438:17
p. from the memory 460:37
p. me by the beard 453:32
p. out the heart of my mystery 435:24
p. till time and times are done 586:6
p. up drowned honour 438:38
thine eye..p. it out 59:51
Plucked: p. by his hand 561:6
p. his gown 224:23
p. out of the burning 56:1
p. them as we passed 252:11
p. the ripen'd ears 538:9
she p., she eat 349:15
when I have p. the rose 473:11
Plucker of amaranths 96:31
Pluckers: which the p. forgot 410:6
Plucking: p. a dish 249:7
p. at their harps 298:14
Plum: confectionary p. 160:31
pulled out a p. 367:16
some gave them p. cake 367:13
Plumage: brighter p. 308:17
gives out his snowy p. 546:11
he pities the p. 373:3
same p. that had warm'd 117:25
Plumbing: your p.'s strange 303:8
Plumbline in his hand 56:3
Plume: blast-beruffled p. 235:17
helmet and the p. 534:7
ruffles her pure cold p. 531:38
Sir P. 385:18
where ye see my white P. 323:5
Plumed: farewell the p. troop 472:3
p. like estridges 440:17
Plumelets: rosy p. 533:12
Plumes: in its p. the various light 332:20
jets under his advanced p. 483:14
rapid p. of song 495:26
soil their fair p. 510:20
Plummet: deeper than..p. 480:13
Plump: banish p. Jack 439:37
cushion p. 150:8
p. and hearty, healthy boy 249:18
right p. to see 578:29
Plum-porridge: eat very plentifully of his p. 2:16
Plums: among the p. 249:14
berries and p. to eat 249:7
Plunder: he shar'd in the p. 161:37
no man stop to p. 324:14
take your ill-got p. 363:7
that p. forbear 499:15
what a place to p.! 177:20
Plündern: was für P.! 77:26

Plunge: p...razors and carving knives 121:20
p. the struggling sheep 323:12
Plunged: accoutred as I was, I p. in 448:18
p. himself into the..wave 220:19
p. in thought again 17:8
Plunging hoofs were gone 171:16
Plures: abiit ad p. 125:34, 378:11
Plus quam se atque suos amavit 133:5
Pluto: tears down P.'s cheek 341:19
won the ear of P. 342:9
Pluvius: Iuppiter p. 547:19
Ply the sampler 340:38
Plying: a-p. up an' down 298:25
p. her needle and thread 253:22
where the old trade's p. 363:3
Plymouth Hoe: dreamin'..o' P. 363:3
Po: from Aufidus to P. 324:7
lazy Scheldt, or wandering P. 226:3
Poacher turned outside in 294:5
Pobble: P.'s toes 312:6, 7
P. who has no toes 312:10
Pobbles are happier 312:10
Pocket: moon in my p. 93:19
not scruple to pick a p. 172:14
plates dropp'd from his p. 426:1
p. full of rye 368:20
p. full of tin 210:13
put it in his p. 435:49
put its hand in its breeches p. 289:25
your learning..in a private p. 139:18
Pocket handkerchiefs: moral p. 178:43
Pocket-hole: at Myra's p. 74:9
Pocket-money: furnished with p. 176:38
Pockets: feels his p. 264:1
p...full of sixpences 182:18
rare in our p. 142:2
Pocos: muchos p. hacen un mucho 134:11
Pocula: mihi flavus Apollo p...ministret 371:20
Pods went pop in the broom 169:14
Poe: there comes P. 320:4
Poem: drowsy frowzy p. 116:5
fain would write a p. 93:49
for the sake of..making a p. 290:14
heroic p. of its sort 125:35
himself to be a true p. 352:2
long p. is a test of invention 289:15
made one p.'s period 331:2
married to a p. 290:21
not metres..makes a p. 200:30
p. lovely as a tree 292:12
p., whose subject is not truth 135:24
pretty p., Mr. Pope 43:6
shorter a prize p. 325:17
tiny p. 529:20
Poema: legitimum cupiet fecisse p. 257:19
Poems: all the p...ever..invented 131:8
I will put in my p. 568:6
one of the greatest..p. 194:11
p. are made by fools like me 292:13
ye are living p. 316:2
Poena: raro antecedentem scelestum deseruit pede P. claudo 259:20
Poesie: der Aberglaube ist die P. 224:3
Poesis: ut pictura p. 256:11
Poesy: drainless shower of light is p. 288:14
God of life, and p. 114:23
golden cadence of p. 455:14
great end of p. 288:15
heaven-bred p. 484:37
immortal flowers of P. 331:2
Nature, Hope, and P. 152:20
overwhelm myself in p. 288:11
p...some participation of divineness 24:16
p. vinum daemonum 24:25
Sense and wit with p. allied 117:15
viewless wings of P. 287:28
Poet: accounted p. kings 288:16
be a p...a certain unsoundness 325:3
buffoon and p. 241:29
Byron is only great as a p. 223:13
business of a comic p. 154:29
business of a p. 278:15
durst p. touch a pen to write 455:22
every p., in his kind 521:22
flattery lost on p.'s ear 417:19
God is the perfect p. 94:16

Poet (cont.)
Good Gray P. 370:3
good p.'s made 281:17
great p. of Itaille 137:39
great p...profound philosopher 152:28
Hero can be P. 126:26
if any p. knew her 88:13
if a P. now and then 582:15
I for an unhappy p. 401:24
is this the great p. 213:9
like a P. hidden 498:6
lover and the p. 467:24
making a p. out of a man 88:12
many a would-be p. 80:28
nae p. ever fand her 107:35
next P. 93:27
not..called a p. 77:32
not deep the P. sees 18:3
on a p.'s lips I slept 497:2
passionate heart of the p. 535:37
P. and Saint! 158:3
p. and the dreamer 285:35
p. could not but be gay 577:7
p. does not work by square 159:23
P. for the King 270:7
p. is the most unpoetical 290:10
p. meets his favouring muse 164:35
p. praised 96:19
P...put his heart to school 573:5
p.'s dream 578:14
p.'s eye 122:35, 467:24
p. sing it with such airs 584:4
p. soaring in the high region 352:20
p...speaks adequately 200:33
p.'s pen 467:24
p...spewed up a good lump 194:18
p...wake a lexicographer 277:23
possess a p.'s brain 189:12
sage and serious p. Spenser 352:10
Shakespeare is not our p. 308:16
spare the p. for his subject 159:9
they had no p. 386:24
this p. lies 486:16
thou wert living the same p. 158:4
thy skill to p. 498:10
true P...of the Devil's party 77:7
true p. that you are 95:1
truth the p. sings 534:21
vex not thou the p.'s mind 537:42
when the P. dies 417:20
whom no p. sings 189:19
you will never be a p. 194:30
Poeta: onorate l'altissimo p. 168:20
Poeta: pessimus omnium p. 133:1
Poetae: membra p. 261:14
Poetam: me fecere p. Pierides 556:7
Poetaster: hunt a p. down 117:30
Poetess: maudlin p. 385:21
Poetic: all p. thought 532:25
constitutes p. faith 152:26
embroid'ry of p. dreams 159:25
guide into p. ground 162:29
laws of p. truth and p. beauty 19:22
nurse for a p. child 417:22
pleasure in p. pains 163:3
p. fields encompass me around 2:2
P. Justice 381:11
warbler of p. prose 163:34
Poetical: all claim to p. honours 278:10
gods...made thee p. 428:11
p. character 290:9
Poetically: noble nature, p. gifted 20:5
Poetis: mediocribus esse p. 256:12
pictoribus atque p...audendi 255:15
Poet-race: what p. 141:2
Poetry: all metaphor is p. 142:16
angling is somewhat like p. 559:14
as a friend he drops into p. 178:3
bear a great deal of p. 309:15
civilization advances, p...declines 325:2
cradled into p. by wrong 494:17
drop into p. 178:4
Fleshly School of P. 98:5
fossil p. 200:32
from the p. of Lord Byron 325:18
genuine p. 19:20
grand style arises in p. 20:5
Grotesque..in English P. 29:8
his writing..relation to p. 325:9
I can repeat p. 131:9

Poetry (cont.)
if Music and sweet P. agree 35:19
if p. comes not as naturally 289:28
line of p. strays 264:6
made and will make..good p. 325:9
mincing p. 439:46
Mr. Wordsworth's epic p. 240:7
never the language of p. 231:21
Nine, forsaking P. 75:18
no man ever talked p. 179:5
not p., but prose run mad 385:28
of music, not of p. 19:13
p. a mere mechanic art 162:28
p...criticism of life 19:22
p.=the best words 153:6
p...finer spirit of all knowledge 583:2
p...great and unobtrusive 289:25
p...in Oxford made an art 193:24
p. is overheard 339:4
p. is the record of the best 499:12
p. is the spontaneous overflow 583:4
p...more philosophic 14:17
p...must be good sense 153:9
p...noble grounds 412:25
p. of earth is never dead 288:22
P...product of the..intestines 125:30
p.'s a mere drug 203:25
p. should surprise 289:27
p. sinks..under..prose 309:15
p.'s unnatural 179:5
p. that has a palpable design 289:25
p. would be made subsequent 352:28
read a little p. sometimes 254:10
sinking in P. 386:25
Sir, what is p.? 273:13
that with p. is won 110:41
used p...for writing in prose 569:30
we may live without p. 337:41
where they had p. 376:11
whining P. 186:21
Poets: all p. are mad 109:8
all P. believe that it does 77:21
all the pens that ever p. held 331:2
among the English P. 290:11
as youthful p. dream 342:7
certain also of your own p. 65:2
first p. 189:11
for p. made 266:5
hearts of mighty P. 574:9
I hate all P. and Painters 216:10
Janus of p. 194:10
Love is a boy, by p. styl'd 110:42
mighty p. in their misery dead 580:13
Milton's the prince of p. 116:4
old p. outsing and outlove us 523:5
only p. know 163:3
O p., from a maniac's tongue 87:38
our p. steal from Homer 109:4
p. are needed to sing the dawn 337:14
p. are to us 337:15
p. better prove 486:26
p. food is love and fame 493:16
p., like painters, thus unskilled 382:26
P. Militant below 158:6
P. of the proud old lineage 208:9
p. painful vigils keep 381:13
P. that are sown by Nature 574:10
p...the best writers 24:42
p...unacknowledged legislators 499:10
p., witty 27:19
reviewers..would have been p. 152:30
sage p. taught by the..Muse 340:25
souls of p. 287:1
theft in other p. 194:8
three p. in an age at most 521:15
three p. in three distant ages 193:9
we p. in our youth 580:7
when amatory p. sing 116:14
why don't p. tell? 299:8
wise p. that wrapt Truth 125:2
Pogram: presented to a P. 176:25
Poins: banish P. 439:37
Point: al devyse fro p. to p. 137:39
aloof from the entire p. 452:12
creeping on from p. to p. 534:28
each to his p. of bliss 96:45
fine p. of his soul taken off 289:16
I hope they do not p. on me 473:13
no p. of charity 166:16
no p. of honour 245:2
not determining a p. of law 101:4

Point (*cont.*)
one fixed p. 188:13
Pickwickian p. of view 178:23
p. against p. 456:9
p. envenom'd too! 437:40
p. me out the way 286:18
p. me to the skies 322:2
p. of faith 166:16
p. of view then sinks 235:22
press your p. with modesty 159:13
put too fine a p. upon it 173:27
quaintly, p. by p. 446:1
ride upon a dial's p. 440:32
silent fingers p. to heaven 574:21
still p. of the turning world 197:6
swim to yonder p. 448:18
thus I bore my p. 439:20
to p. a moral 279:6
Point-blank: launched p. her dart 91:34
Pointed toward the land 535:12
Points: armed at p. exactly 431:9
pigging together, heads and p. 100:8
p. her to the skies 195:15
p. of practical politics 182:40
p. to yonder glade 381:30
still p. to thee 215:40
Poised: I am p. 39:3
p., as the lights 413:21
Poising every weight 332:12
Poison: Adonais has drunk p. 492:4
attempted . . to *p. the wells* 363:11
coward's weapon, p. 209:6
go about and p. wells 330:16
he drank the p. 251:29
he swallowed the p. 10:18
if you p. us 464:8
instead of dirt and p. 519:5
nor steel, nor p. 459:4
ounce of p. in one pocket 324:35
Pleasure . . turning to P. 287:21
potent p. quite o'ercrows 438:5
strongest p. ever known 73:27
sweet, sweet, sweet p. 447:20
Poisoned: cans of p. meat 141:34
some p. by their wives 475:7
Poison-flowers: the honey of p 535:38
Poisonous: I called on p. names 494:5
p. thing 188:7
p. wine 287:19
Poisons all the rest 561:30
Poke: as pigges do in a p. 358:10
pig in a p. 549:26
p. poor Billy 228:11
Pokers: wreathe iron p. 151:13
Pokes the 'eathen out 295:21
Poland: Saracens to . . P. 217:12
Polar Star: P. of poetry 289:15
right for the P. 17:28
Pole: all sights from p. to p. 18:18
as the needle to the p. 78:18
beloved from p. to p. 149:27
distorts . . from p. to p. 74:12
not rapt above the P. 348:23
soldier's p. is fall'n 425:29
so tall to reach the P. 562:2
spread the truth from p. to p. 2:27
thrice to th' utmost p. 344:10
trembles to the p. 386:28
wid a ten-foot p. 210:14
writ with curses from p. to p. 74:13
Poles: p. of truth 27:33
wheel between the p. 528:11
Police: friendship recognised by the p. 514:25
I'll send for the P. 128:16
Policeman: ask a P. 408:1
back with P. Day 295:11
p.'s lot is not a happy one 221:34
Policy: brow of careful P. 510:25
honesty is *not* to be based . . on . . p. 413:21
honesty is the best p.; but . . 565:28
some love but little p. 475:28
tyrants from p. 102:17
Polis: le temps d'être p. 355:8
Polish: p. it at leisure 194:3
p. of the latter 154:13
Polished: her p. car 343:25
I p. up that handle 221:15
light, agreeable, p. style 240:6
more of rough than p. diamond 139:24

Polished (*cont.*)
p. corners of the temple 400:16
p. female friend 568:21
p. perturbation! golden care! 442:25
work of p. idleness 326:27
Polite: his manners are not so p. 300:7
men of p. learning 242:10
never mentions hell to ears p. 385:4
till the English grew p. 296:8
you're exceedingly p. 221:12
Politeness: glance of great p. 119:22
pine-apple of p. 500:18
p. of kings 318:23
Politesse: la p. des rois 318:23
Political: man . . p. animal 14:14
p. blank cheque 227:37
P. Ravishment 222:32
schemes of p. improvement 271:34
success of the British . . in p. life 181:6
Political Economy: Dismal Science [P.] 126:34
for fear of P. 422:15
wrote 'Principles of P.' 43:2
Politician: lief be a Brownist as a p. 483:33
like a scurvy p. 454:11
pate of a p. 437:11
Politicians: more . . than the whole race of p. 519:17
Politics: confound their p. 125:16
from p. to puns 387:23
history is past p. 421:20
magnanimity in p. 101:14
mistaken zeal in p. 282:19
mule of p. 181:38
mules of p. 337:15
my p. . . exceedin accommodatin 560:2
no more to do with gallantry than . . p. 500:12
no p. in boil'd and roast 505:32
not the language of p. 180:24
Philistine of genius in p. 20:19
p. . . a means of rising 272:33
p. and the pulpit 102:5
p. go by the weather 231:28
p. in the East 182:1
p. like ours profess 231:26
p. . . no preparation . . necessary 514:6
p. . . not an exact science 72:29
p. we bar 221:38
practical p. 182:40, 222:36
shoved him into p. 41:7
talking p. after dinner 181:6
what Englishman will give his mind to p. 489:4
Politik: die P. ist keine exakte 72:29
Poll: talk'd like poor P. 213:12
true to P. 103:32
Polloi: multitude, the hoi p. 194:9
Polluted: your fountain . . p. 102:19
Polly: P. is a sad slut 214:12
P. put the kettle on 173:19
poor P.'s life 214:21
pretty P., say 214:24
Polly Flinders: little P. 367:17
Polly-wog: like a p.'s tail 560:14
Polonies: with fine p. 33:21
Poltagrue: tempt my Lady P. 41:27
Polygamy: before p. was made a sin 190:7
chaste p. 125:5
Pomander: sweet p. 502:17
Pomegranate: from Browning some 'P.' 88:7
like a piece of a p. 52:5
sings on yon p. tree 478:26
Pommerschen: einzigen p. Muske-tiers 72:31
Pomp: all his p., without his force 103:30
all our p. of yesterday 300:25
bright P. ascended jubilant 348:28
came in slow p. 491:21
flowed 'with p. of waters' 577:2
grinning at his p. 475:7
in lowly p. ride on to die 339:12
intermingling of Heaven's p. 574:2
nor the tide of p. 444:23
p., and feast, and revelry 342:7
p. of power 230:1
praise his humble p. 508:18
pride, p. and circumstance 472:3

Pomp (*cont.*)
puts all the p. to flight 382:6
slave of p. 415:17
Sultan after Sultan with his P. 205:29, 30
take physic, p. 453:15
that of painted p. 426:29
vain p. and glory 446:24
world of p. and state 37:13
Pompadour's Fan 183:18
Pompey: at the base of P.'s statua 450:31
great P. would stand 424:1
in P.'s camp 444:16
knew you not P.? 448:8
Pompilia, will you let them 96:17
Pompous in the grave 87:20
Pomps: high Midsummer p. 18:26
p. and vanities of this . . world 391:2
Pond: beyond the depths of a p. 373:14
four ducks on a p. 4:19
have their stream and p. 83:23
mantle like a standing p. 462:33
neighbours o'er the Herring P. 195:11
pop Sir Thomas again in the p. 34:16
tree, and a p. edged with grayish leaves 236:19
Ponder: p. well 214:21
whoso is wise will p. 398:22
Pondered: p., weak and weary 380:22
p. sadly, wearied and forlorn 359:14
Ponderous: arch'd and p. roof 155:19
p. and marble jaws 431:32(-432)
Poniards: she speaks p. 468:13
Ponies: blind pit p. 249:5
five-and-twenty p. 301:18
Ponit: Iovem qui p. et aufert 257:11
Pontgibaud: at P. they mended it 40:18
Pontick: like to the P. sea 472:12
'Pontol' he cried 41:4
Pontus: in P., and Asia 64:26
Pontus: estne Dei sedes nisi . . p. 320:26
Pony: riding on a p. 33:7
Pooh: p., p., to you 221:2
Pool: first fill a p. 26:36
green mantle of the standing p. 453:23
on the wood and the p. 172:4
p. of private charity 374:21
Pools: moonlight fallen in p. 334:6
p. are filled with water 397:6
p. I used to know 263:19
p. of water 53:23
Poop was beaten gold 424:6
Poor: anger . . keeps them p. 24:36
angry and p. and happy 142:2
art thou p. 170:21
as p. as Job 441:16
being so p. 77:27
blessed are the p. in spirit 57:39
cheer the p. man's heart 418:24
dare to be p. 215:35
destruction of the p. 49:55
die not, p. death 185:15
even great men . . p. relations 174:2
faith of the p. is faint 142:4
Father of the p. 132:1
few, save the p., feel for the p. 308:12
found'st me p. at first 225:9
given to the p. 398:27
give to the p. 60:1
good to the p. 125:4
great man helped the p. 323:21
grind the faces of the p. 52:34
heaven make me p. 279:25
his dear papa is p. 515:20
honest exceeding p. man 463:29
how apt the p. are to be proud 483:27
how many p. I see 561:19
how p. are they . . not patience 471:24
how p. a thing is man 168:5
huts where p. men lie 573:8
I, being p., have only my dreams 584:17
if thou art rich, thou'rt p. 462:4
inconvenient to be p. 159:6
laws grind the p. 226:16
let the p. and Thou starve 245:12
lonely and p. of old 83:19
low estate of the p. 393:8
makes me p. indeed 471:30
most rich, being p. 452:13
murmuring p. 164:41
my goods to feed the p. 66:45
none so p. to do him reverence 450:23

Poor (*cont.*)
no right to the property of the p. 413:28
old Castilian p. noble 119:24
old p. man 427:20
p. advanc'd makes friends 435:12
p. always ye have 63:44
p. and content is rich 471:33
p., and the maimed 62:8
p. but honest 423:3
p. but she was honest 9:18
P. Child! 375:20
p. even in thanks 433:14
p. have become poorer 499:11
p. in a loomp is bad 537:8
p., infirm, weak, and despis'd 453:6
poorly (p. man) he liv'd 209:1
p. man at his gate 3:15
p. man had nothing 47:33
p. man is Christ's stamp 244:4
p. man's day 228:14
p. man's dearest friend 107:3
p. man's wealth 501:26
p. Miss 7 171:24
p...no right to the property 413:28
p. old Joe 210:17
p. old man 452:42
p. person 137:22
p. Persoun 137:16
p., reckless, rude 188:31
p. relation..irrelevant 306:29
p. Robin Crusoe 170:6
p. robin do then? p. thing! 368:2
p. sort of memory 130:28
p., wandering one! 221:29
p. what gets the blame 9:20
p. World (said I) 166:1
resolve not to be p. 275:5
rich gifts wax p. 434:6
scandalous and p. 407:20
simple annals of the p. 230:1
sold..and given to the p. 63:43
solitary p., nasty 248:21
they are but p. 195:13
they p., I rich 195:13
tho' p. in gear 108:1
though I be p., I'm honest 338:16
too p. for a bribe 231:17
virtuous p. 570:11
warms the neighbouring p. 165:17
when that the p. have cried 450:20
who now do bless the p. 361:24
without thee we are p. 163:47
with the p., and mean 4:1
your p. army 167:12
Poorest: in the p. thing superfluous 452:41
p. he..in England 405:6
p...in his cottage 379:11
Poorly: p. (poor man) he liv'd 209:1
sorter p., Sis Tempy 238:14
Poorness: when I mock p. 279:25
Pop: p. goes the weasell 328:26
when the pods went p. 169:14
Pope: better to err with P. 117:14
creaks with a P. 525:21
poetry of Dryden, P. 19:20
poor P. will grieve a month 521:2
P...eye on his style 20:3
wine from the royal P. 329:1
Popery: inclines a man to P. 212:12
never be in danger of P. 2:19
Popinjay: pester'd with a p. 438:34
Popish: Calvinistic creed, a P.
liturgy 379:7
P. Apennines 293:10
Poplar: edg'd with p. pale 343:22
Poplars: p. are felled 161:23
p. stand and tremble 263:19
Poppies: fume of p. 284:12
pleasures are like p. spread 108:7
p., nodding, mock 165:17
p. was nothing to it 179:25
though p. grow 326:15
Poppy: blindly scattereth her p. 87:16
left the flushed print in a p. 545:8
nectarous p. lovers use 16:5
not p., nor mandragora 471:43
with a p. or a lily 220:28
Pops: Classical Monday P. 220:5
Populace: Barbarians, Philistines,
P. 19:23, 29

Populace (*cont.*)
name of P. 19:29
p. rise at once 567:7
Popular: base, common and p. 444:14
p. prejudice runs 177:1
such p. humanity is treason 1:20
Popularis: arbitrio p. aurae 259:19
Popularity: even his darling p. 101:21
Population: only talked of p. 227:15
p...in a geometrical ratio 328:25
Populations: competing p. 200:3
Populi: salus p. suprema est lex 145:5
salus p. suprema lex esto 422:8
vox P., vox Dei 3:10, 406:16
Populous: in p. city pent 349:11
Populus Romanus unam cervicem 120:18
Porcelain: dainty rogue in p. 337:22
p. of humankind 193:19
Porch: beyond p. and portal 523:20
p. and inlet of each sense 341:2
white p. of his home 323:26
Porches of mine ears 432:16
Porcum: Epicuri de grege p. 256:27
Porcupine: fretful p. 432:9
Pore: p. by the hour 34:14
p. upon the brook 230:12
Pores of the ocean and shores 493:1
Poring dark 444:6
Pork: captain's biscuits and
pickled p. 543:7
dreamed of tasting p. 387:24
your beef, p. and mutton 294:34
Porpentine: fretful p. 432:9
Porphyry: in the p. font 539:2
Porpoise close behind us 129:22
Porridge: p. and apples 171:17
what p. had John Keats? 95:3
wholesome p. 105:2
Porringer: I take my little p. 582:12
Porsena: Lars P. of Clusium 323:10
Port: all dissolv'd in p. 381:23
bent to make some p. 18:20
by p. and vest 323:1
come into p. greatly 200:18
in ev'ry p. a mistress find 215:41
in every p. a wife 173:5
in every p. he finds a wife 72:18
let him drink p. 251:29
little p. had seldom seen 529:15
of regal p. 347:32
p. after stormy seas 509:28
p. for men 274:12
p. is near, the bells I hear 566:27
p. should have age 34:34
p. wine that she sends 'em 9:19
pride in their p. 226:14
there lies the p. 541:3
with our sprightly p. 425:22
would be p. if it could 43:5
Portabit te 291:24
Portable: p. and compendious
oceans 166:10
p. property 175:24
Portae: geminae Somni p. 555:2
Portal: fiery p. of the east 475:8
whose p. we call Death 317:12
Portals: its p. are inhabited 495:27
P...alternate Night and Day 205:30
Portance in my travel's history 470:2
Portcullis: let the p. fall 418:27
Portend no good to us 452:15
Portentous: p. sight 151:19
that p. phrase 116:50
Portents: these are p. 473:13
Porter: all p. and skittles 179:26
bright on Mrs. P. 197:31
Oh, mister p. 315:3
Porters: poor mechanic p. 443:10
Portia is Brutus' harlot 449:17
Portion: become p. of that around 113:47
brief life is here our p. 361:12
he wales a p. 105:4
my p. in this life 352:21
no p. in us after 187:11
p. of the Eternal 492:5
p. of the gift is won 574:2
p. of the loveliness 492:10
Portioned: lands were fairly p. 323:21
Portions: man in p. can forsee 118:31
p...of the dreadful Past 535:17

Portmanteau: like a p. 131:13
Portrait: p. of a dog that I know 277:2
p. of the artist 282:14
two styles of p. painting 177:7
Ports: five p. of knowledge 85:18
p. of slumber open 442:25
to the wise man p. 474:19
Posies: buy my English p. 296:15
thousand fragrant p. 330:19
Position: every p. must be held 233:20
Positive: most p...most credulous 520:49
Possess: but for you, p. the field 147:8
in himself p. his own desire 575:8
in your patience p. ye your souls 62:42
never once p. our soul 18:18
p. a poet's brain 189:12
p. man's strength to comfort 295:8
p. these shores with me 168:13
p. thy heart, my own 82:11
things rank..p. it merely 430:33(−431)
thou dost p. the things I seek 408:15
though they p. the crown 170:17
Possessed: cuts off what we p. 191:34
endure what it once p. 494:21
limited in order to be p. 103:22
much p. by death 197:33
regain love once p. 350:33
Possesses: man p. nothing 120:5
p. or possess'd a thought 113:15
Possessing: beauty by constraint, p. 214:9
our utmost wish p. 215:37
too dear for my p. 487:22
yet p. all things 67:29
Possession: death, in thy p. lies 426:14
in as just p. of truth 86:5
in p. so 488:12
lose p. of that fair thou ow'st 486:18
p. for the bittern 53:23
p. of it is intolerable 551:6
p. of them both 290:22
p. of this heavenly sight 473:32
P. without obligation 337:25
that p. would not show 469:5
Possessions: her p. and military
posts 563:5
sorrowful: for he had great p. 60:2
Possessor: Hell receive thy new p. 344:22
Possible: best of all p. worlds 120:6, 557:2
if it be p., let this cup pass 60:41
make p. things not so held 485:8
no..p. shadow of doubt 218:18
one way p. of speaking truths 96:18
p. you may be mistaken 167:4
with God all things are p. 60:4
*Possible: il ne suffit pas qu'une chose
soit p. pour la croire* 557:12
Possibilities: believe only p. 86:22
not interested in the p. of defeat 552:21
Possibility: Permanent P. of
Sensation 515:4
unconvincing p. 14:18
Possibly sweetest 121:18
Possidentem: non p. multa 261:4
Possumus: non omnia p. omnes 556:6
Possunt, quia posse videntur 554:22
Post: against a p...drunk 444:1
at his p. when under fire 236:4
evil news rides p. 351:1
not quit the p. allotted 535:25
one p. a day 505:8
p. o'er Land and Ocean 351:21
p. of honour..private 1:21
still as a p. 171:21
Postage: penny-p.-stamp 128:19
Postboy: dead p. 179:32
Post-chaise: driving briskly in a p. 273:21
driving rapidly in a p. 273:4
Posteri: credite p. 259:12
Posteriors of this day 455:27
Posterity: not look forward to p. 102:9
not stand in thy p. 458:30
overheard the judgment of p. 325:29
pander of p. 508:13
p...a pack-horse 180:28
P. do something for us 2:33
think of your p.! 1:5
thy p. shall sway 158:32
trustees of P. 182:31
without..hope of p. 387:15

INDEX

Postero: quam minimum credula p. 258:17
Postponed to some other occasion 178:8
Post-prandial cigar 98:7
Postridie: no pridie, nor p. 186:31
Posts: her possessions and military
  p. 563:5
  p. of the door moved 53:8
Postscript: here is yet a p. 483:20
  most material in the p. 25:43
  pith. . in the p. 239:10
  Writes her Mind. . in her P. 511:18
Postume: eheu fugaces, P., P. 259:9
  P., P.! 34:1
Posture of a whore 426:4
Postures: all day, the same our p.
  were 184:31
Posy: home with her maiden p. 536:4
  I made a p. 244:20
  I pluck a p. 93:26
Pot: another for the p. 372:17
  at the mouth of their p. 24:40
  chicken in his p. every Sunday 242:1
  death in the p. 48:20
  deep to boil like a p. 49:32
  eat our p. of honey 336:26
  flinging a p. of paint 412:22
  greasy Joan doth keel the p. 456:1
  kettle and the. .p. 56:44
  p. of beer 369:17
  p. with a cot in a park 309:26
  put on the p. 366:13
  thorns under a p. 51:10
  three-hooped p. 445:36
  treasures from an earthern p. 244:7
  who the P.? 207:16
Pot: sa poule au p. 242:1
Potable gold 109:22
Potage: mess of p. 6:4
Potash: mess of p. 560:3
Potations: dull and deep p. 216:22
  forswear thin p. 442:22
Potato: bashful young p. 220:28
  mouth like an old p. 295:3
  p. in his head 237:24
Potatoes: Papa, p., poultry 176:1
  small p. and few in the hill 304:29
Potatori: Deus. .propitius isti p. 13:9
Potency: contain a p. of life 352:5
  their changeful p. 481:25
Potent: most p. in potting 471:10
  p., grave, and reverend 469:45
  p. quack 165:20
Potentiality of growing rich 274:29
Potestas: scientia p. est 28:10
Pother: keep this dreadful p. 453:9
Potion: his p. and his pill 247:18
Potions: what p. have I drunk 488:8
Potomac: all quiet along the P.
  40:2, 326:14
Pots: lien among the p. 396:7
  your p. be made hot with thorns 395:21
Potsherd: poor p. 255:7
  p. to scrape himself withal 48:42
Pottage: mess of p. with love 50:13
Potter: I watch'd the P. 206:18
  like a p.'s vessel 391:50
  p. and clay endure 95:23
  p. power over the clay 65:60
  who *is* the P., pray? 207:16
Potting: most potent in p. 471:10
Pouch on side 427:21
Pouches: coin his p. wad na bide in 107:19
Poule: tous les dimanches sa p. 242:1
Poultice: silence like a p. 251:10
Poultry: Papa, potatoes, p. 176:1
Pouncet-box: he held a p. 438:32
Pound: for a thousand p. 160:2
  I'll give thee a silver p. 122:23
  in for a p. 219:14
  once bet a p. 171:22
  Twelve-P. Look 36:13
Pounding: hard p. this. .who will
  pound longest 564:16
Pounds: draw for a thousand p. 2:35
  give crowns and p. 262:15
  income twenty p. 174:24
  two hundred p. a year 111:11
Pour: p. out my spirit upon all 55:52
  p. out the pack of matter 424:14
  p., varlet, p. the water 372:17
  vitreous p. of the full moon 567:17

Poured thro' the mellow horn 154:1
Poureth out of the same 396:31
Pourvu: chacun pense en être bien p. 172:27
Pouvait: si vieillesse p. 201:30
Poverty: age of p. 465:9
  destruction. .their p. 49:55
  honoured p. 499:9
  I pay thy p. 478:38
  neither p. nor riches 50:53
  p. and oysters 178:38
  p. has strange bedfellows 322:13
  p., hunger, and dirt 253:22
  p. is a great enemy to. .happi-
  ness 275:5
  p. is no disgrace to a man 505:17
  p.'s catching 40:10
  she scorns our p. 445:28
  so much p. and excess 377:7
  so shall thy p. come 49:47
  so shameful as p. 203:8
  steep'd me in p. 472:34
  three kingdoms. .in great p. 328:5
  worse than p. 548:16
  worst of crimes is p. 490:3
  worth by p. depress'd 278:33
Powder: food for p. 440:23
  keep your p. dry 73:2
  when your p.'s runnin' low 363:2
Powdered: still to be p. 280:7
Powders: gives you Love P. 307:14
  puffs, p., patches 385:9
Power: above our p. to add 314:12
  accursed p. which stands on
  Privilege 41:26
  acquired the chief p. in the State 144:17
  act of p. 26:42
  all p. is a trust 182:43
  all the pride of p. sink 100:25
  ample p. to chasten 582:1
  as little in our p. 202:1
  balance of p. 559:3
  beauty. .hath strange p. 350:33
  between his p. and thine 281:8
  boundless p. 202:22
  breathless, p. breathe forth 424:8
  by immortal p.. .linked 545:5
  call our p. to account 460:24
  courses. .in every p. 455:22
  covet such p. as this 413:8
  deep p. of joy 581:25
  depositary of p.. .unpopular 181:40
  drunk with sight of p. 300:26
  earthly p.. .likest God's 464:33
  empire. .p. in trust 190:19
  enduring p., not ourselves 20:14
  extent of its beauty and p. 326:3
  fawn, or seek for p. 224:18
  force of temporal p. 464:33
  from the p. of our senses 277:39
  girded about with p. 395:28
  good want p. 496:24
  greater the p. 101:29
  half the p. to do me harm 473:23
  have p. to hurt 487:24
  Heavenly P. makes. .new 529:11
  him the Almighty P. hurled 344:7
  his wit was in his own p. 280:1
  if there's a p. above us 1:23
  in face of these doth exercise a p. 575:6
  in p. unpleas'd 190:13
  knowledge itself is p. 28:10
  laugh to scorn the p. of man 460:5
  legislative p.. .nominated by
  the executive 217:6
  literature of p. 172:24
  love of p.. .of ourselves 239:23
  man who has the p. and skill 11:22
  may have grace and p. 389:28
  name for absolute p. 579:37
  no hopes but from p. 103:12
  not exempted from her p. 253:36
  not in our p. to love, or hate 330:13
  notions about a superior p. 519:3
  not *pleasure*, but *p.* 172:25
  of p., and of love 68:56
  once intoxicated with p. 103:3
  one's cruelty is one's p. 156:4
  palter'd with Eternal God for p. 537:23
  period, p., and enterprize 503:2
  pomp of p. 230:1
  p., and the glory 58:4

Power (*cont.*)
  p. belongeth unto God 395:24
  p. does corrupt 549:17
  P. girt round with weakness 492:2
  p. I cannot resist 290:28
  p. is passing from the earth 575:1
  p. of beauty I remember yet 192:3
  p.. .of being beloved 96:24
  p. of grace 122:34
  p. of harmony 581:25
  p. of punishment is to silence 278:21
  p. of saying things 374:17
  p. of the crown. .has grown 101:34
  p. of the Crown has increased 20:24
  p. should always be distrusted 279:20
  p. tends to corrupt 1:2
  P. that pities me 225:12
  p. to cancel his captivity 448:37
  p. to dismiss itself 448:36
  p. to touch our senses so 343:17
  present possessors of p. 101:33
  put to hazard. .his p. 101:21
  relentless p. 230:15
  second death hath no p. 71:40
  seeds of godlike p. are in us 15:9
  self-sufficing p. of Solitude 579:15
  shadow of some unseen P. 494:3
  sheer, penetrating p. 19:19
  some P. the giftie gie us 106:33
  something from our hands have
  p. 573:27
  strange p. of speech 150:12
  supreme p. of p. 288:14
  that p.. .men call Chance 340:29
  though stripp'd of p. 418:3
  Thy P. brings all skill to naught 299:5
  titles, p. and pelf 417:22
  to communicate p. 172:25
  to defy P. 497:17
  to every p. a double p. 455:22
  to seek p. and to lose liberty 26:23
  to the man despotic p. 350:35
  true vanity. .p. of pleasing 156:4
  unknown P.'s employ 17:6
  unlimited p. is apt to corrupt 379:5
  upon the past has p. 194:21
  visionary p. 579:17, 25
  want of p. to sin 193:16
  Women and Horses and P. 294:29
  Wordsworth's healing p. 16:23
Powerful: p. goodness want 496:16
  word. .quick and p. 69:8
Powerfulest preacher 229:14
Powerless: religion. .p. to bestow 201:7
Powers: against principalities,
  against p. 68:11
  contend, ye p. 166:1
  desires and dreams and p. 523:18
  fear of some divine. .p. 109:31
  frailty of our p. 481:25
  in whom all p. conspire 232:11
  knows ye not, ye heavenly P. 127:30
  mind of large general p. 278:2
  nor principalities, nor p. 65:58
  our own acts. .mightier p. 15:11
  p. that be are ordained of God 66:9
  p. that will work for thee 582:4
  P. which. .our minds impress 574:29
  Princedoms, Virtues, P. 348:14
  robs the mind of all its p. 102:32
  subject unto the higher p. 66:8
  we lay waste our p. 582:18
  whose p. shed round him 575:10
  wise p. deny us 424:3
Poyser: Mrs. P. 'has her say out' 196:10
PPP: non troppo p. 218:11
Practical politics 182:40, 222:36
Practice: good principles without
  . .p. 276:11
  haven't had much p. 131:12
  in p. sincere 401:35
  my p. could get along 187:29
  my p. is never very absorbing 187:20
  not wear them out in p. 37:8
  P. drives me mad 8:12
  p. is quiet 187:27
  p. of politics in the East 182:1
Practise: go p.. .with men and
  women 96:2
Practised: p. that strength 17:17
  p. what he preach'd 14:26

Practising the hundredth psalm 119:26
Prado: walked on the P. 294:12
Praecesserit: quidve p. 38:31
Praedantur: singula de nobis anni p. 257:17
Praelatura: tutius..in subiectione quam in p. 291:23
Praemia: sua p. laudi 553:18
Praemissi: not amissi but p. 242:19
Praesidium: et p. et dulce decus meum 257:23
Praetorian: God's pale P. 515:3
P. here, P. there 419:12
Praevalebit: magna est veritas et p. 84:26
Praevalet: magna est veritas et p. 56:19
Prague: beautiful city of P. 402:22
Prairies: forests and the p. 317:20
Praise: added p. to p. 532:22
all for p. 509:35
all things thou wouldst p. 171:9
as rich with p. 443:9
as they turn from P. 88:24
at the shout of p. 35:2
conspires to p. her 382:10
damn with faint p. 385:29
dieted with p. 287:16
dispraised..no small p. 350:5
dispraised..perfect p. 279:29
envy is a kind of p. 215:28
everything that hath breath p. 400:28
foolish face of p. 385:29
garment of p. 55:4
girded with p. 228:20
God hath no better p. 81:9
happiest knowledge and her p. 347:20
his p. above heaven and earth 400:25
His p. forth tell 292:7
his p. may thither fly 243:24
however we do p. ourselves 483:3
if there be any p. 68:27
interchanging p. 250:29
I will p. Thee 244:26
king's best p. 412:14
let the song of p. be sung 387:12
let us now p. famous men 57:14, 302:4
little dust of p. 533:5
men, whom all men p. 158:18
morning and evening to p. thee 395:29
muse His p. 546:8
named thee but to p. 234:15
noble England's p. 322:17
none to p. him 580:18
not to p. him 450:17
not unto us the p. 299:9
oblique p. 274:5
once beat high for p. 356:20
only the Master shall p. us 303:21
open sea of the world's p. 577:2
paint 'em truest p. 'em most 1:12
p. any man that will p. me 424:16
p. at morning 383:1
p., blame, love, kisses 580:20
p. enough 163:1
p. God from whom all blessings 292:3
'P. God!' sang Theocrite 90:3
p. him 359:20
p. him and magnify him 388:20, 21, 23
p. him in his Name JAH 396:5
p. him upon the..cymbals 400:28
p. his humble pomp 508:18
p. indeed 359:20
p. is the best diet for us 504:32
p. new-born gawds 481:21
p. of it endureth for ever 398:25
p. of which I nothing know 573:17
p.! p.! p.! 568:9
p. the bridge that carried you 154:7
p. the honest worker 4:13
p. the Lord! 291:27
p. the Lord, and pass the ammunition 210:6
p. the Lord by measure 298:16
p. the Lord for his goodness 398:15
p. the Lord for making her 297:20
p. the Lord, O my soul 398:3
p. the Lord upon earth 400:24
p. the Lord with harp 393:35
p. the Name of the Lord 400:25
p. they that will times past 246:24
p. to give 281:11
p. too much 281:10
p. to the Holiest in the height 364:6

Praise (cont.)
pudding against empty p. 381:11
rest a little from p. 525:5
scarce could p. 278:35
sickens at another's p. 143:4
so double be his p. 509:30
some p. in peers to write at all 117:23
some p. for skill 80:18
song in thy p. 105:29
song of thanks and p. 576:18
stand a wast of p. 518:17
succeed their fathers' p. 234:8
swells the note of p. 230:2
they only want p. 335:5
thirst of p. 162:27
thy superfluous p. 189:19
to Mary Queen the p. 149:27
to p. and pray 92:18
to p., revere, establish 42:1
to their right p. 465:22
utter all thy p. 2:23
we p. thee, O God 13:14
we scarcely can p. it 225:27
Wonder, Love, and P. 2:22
your hymn of p. 168:14
Praised: everybody p. the Duke 507:9
I p. the dead 51:4
more in him to be p. 280:1
ne'er said, 'God be p.' 88:3
poet p. 96:19
p. be the fathomless universe 568:9
p. him to his face 540:3
p., wept and honour'd 382:18
Praises: delight in thy p. 118:33
earth..p. God 151:30
he who first p. a book 309:14
his p. there may grow 243:24
idiot who p. 219:25
its loud p. sound 81:3
p. everybody p. nobody 273:25
p. from the men 158:18
p. of God be in their mouth 400:26
sing p. lustily unto him 393:35
sing p. unto him 393:35
sing p. unto his Name 396:5
sing ye p. with understanding 394:32
Praising: doing one's p. for oneself 112:14
p. all alike, is p. none 215:17
p. God with sweetest looks 253:20
p...sallow abstinence 340:36
p. what is lost 423:10
too near the p. of myself 464:24
Pranked in reason's garb 341:1
Pranks: his p. have been too broad 435:38
let heaven see the p. 471:15
Prata: sat p. biberunt 555:29
Prate: hear him p. 335:23
very stones p. 458:1
Prattle: his p...tedious 475:29
Prattling on his knee 104:33
Prava: civium ardor p. iubentium 259:21
Praxed: Saint P.'s 89:42
Pray: all p. in their distress 76:18
all together p. 150:15
as lief p. with Kit Smart 271:3
fold her hands and p. 411:9
I'll go p. 432:23
I p. for no man but myself 480:21
I p. the Lord my soul to keep 8:18
just going to p. for you 505:16
late and early p. 583:10
more nearly as we p. 291:8
never p. more 472:5
no angels left..to p. to 543:21
nor p. with you 463:16
not p. him to lay bare 249:10
one to p. 3:3
other to p. 166:13
place where men can p. 142:13
p. for my soul 531:36
p. for the peace of Jerusalem 399:31
p. for wisdom yet 3:6
p. God..able to pay 377:12
p. make no mistake 219:34
p., Mr. Wild, why bitch? 204:15
p. so 485:27
p., Sweet, for me 248:7
p. that Jerusalem may have 421:5
p...to give his soule good reste 321:10
p. without ceasing 68:37
remained to p. 224:22

Pray (cont.)
some to Meccah turn to p. 208:12
too much sense to p. 384:31
to praise and p. 92:18
to p., and not to faint 62:32
to whom the Romans p. 323:27
two went to p.? 166:13
wash your hands and p. 296:33(-297)
watch and p. 198:19
we do p. for mercy 464:33
we'll live, and p., and sing 454:19
whene'er he went to p. 225:18
when I would p. and think 462:2
Prayed: caught at God's skirts, and p. 92:26
having p. together 246:2
p. and felt for all 224:21
p. where he did sit 150:11
thing we have p. for 87:29
without sucess, have p. 143:14
Prayer: biddeth me to p. 150:13
call'd the folk to evening p. 285:30
called the house of p. 60:9
each Paynim voice to p. 123:9
effectual fervent p. 69:44
four spend in p. 148:8
hear our anxious p. 512:14
he made his p. 303:12
his p. shall be heard 56:33
home-brewed p. 231:30
homes of silent p. 532:23
in p. the lips 247:19
let the p. re-echo 314:19
lift not hands of p. 531:36
make his p. unto thee 393:32
more things are wrought by p. 531:36
offices of p. and praise 574:12
our evening p. 560:27
people's p. 190:18
p. for all who lie beneath 295:5
p. is the soul's sincere desire 355:11
p., patience, aims, vows 255:6
p. that I would cry to Him 213:2
recalled by p. and plaint 238:29
regained by faith and p. 238:29
storms of p. 540:8
striven as thus with thee in p. 496:10
swears a p. or two 477:7
that same p. doth teach us 464:33
thou that hearest the p. 395:27
'tis the hour of p.! 116:7
when p. is of no avail 574:32
wherever..a house of p. 170:11
who rises from p. a better man 337:33
Prayer-books: beads and p. 383:30
Prayers: angry p. 249:5
by losing of our p. 424:3
fall to thy p. 442:37
feed on p. 377:4
few p. in the hall 20:29
for a pretence make long p. 61:7
long p...in the world they say 15:26
Lord, hear our p. 391:18
mention of you always in my p. 65:30
of your p. one sweet sacrifice 446:13
our vows, our p. 183:20
p...disease of the will 200:44
p. of saints 70:42
p. would move me 449:30
saying his p. 339:19
short were the p. we said 572:13
sudden on some p. 87:29
three-mile p. 106:34
trust it without my p. 86:38
where p. cross 461:34
whose p...make me whole 299:27(-300)
would not say his p. 366:23
Prayer-time: His p. 551:20
Prayeth: he p. well..he p. best 150:16
Praying: Amelia was p. for George 542:37
insisted on people p. with him 271:3
no p., it spoils business 371:13
now he is p. 435:36
past p. for 439:20
Prays: he p. but faintly 475:32
that faintly p. 404:13
wears a coronet and p. 164:18
when she p. 532:24
Preach: could na p. for thinkin' 107:15
I p. for ever..in vain 165:4
Parson might p. 76:4

INDEX

Preach (cont.)
p. a better sermon 201:22
p. a whole year 318:9
p. from ten till four 220:4
p. not..to say something 565:25
p. the gospel to every creature 61:9
Preached: I daily p. 7:9
I p. as never sure 36:24
practis'd what he p. 14:26
p. to death by wild curates 505:6
p. up patience 402:1
when I have p. to others 66:37
Preacher: caulder p. never spak 106:26
heard the p. every Sunday 566:21
judge not the p. 244:7
like the P. found it not 498:20
no mean p. 581:15
powerfulest p. 229:14
p.'s merit or demerit 90:33
private advantage of the p. 102:1
saith the P. 50:59
Preachers: company of the p. 396:7
Preaches in her gown 253:29
Preacheth: God..p. patience 244:7
Preaching: better than any p. 200:43
foolishness of p. 66:19
God calleth p. folly 244:7
p. down a daughter's heart 534:23
p. man's immense stupidity 90:25
woman's p. 271:16
Preamble: long p. of a tale 138:9
Precarious: earned a p. living 6:3
Precedence: her p. of teaching nations 352:24
just p. in the grave 292:20
Precedency between a louse and a flea 275:10
Precedent: dangerous p. 157:10
from p. to p. 541:24
poetry..indeed rather p. 352:28
p. embalms a principle 180:20, 420:33
recorded for a p. 465:3
Precedents: as well to create good p. 26:25
Precept: by p. and example 117:16
ending with some p. deep 387:23
more efficacious than p. 278:18
p. upon p. 53:33
Precepts: live up to the p. of the Gospel 85:8
render with thy p. less 118:30
these few p. in thy memory 431:25
we love the p. 203:21, 250:30
Precincts of the cheerful day 230:9
Precious: all that's p. in our joys 512:29
all too p. you 487:20
make the morning p. 288:13
make vile things p. 453:11
my p. Lily! 129:38
one half so p. 207:22, 23
p. bane 345:10
this p. stone 474:22
were most p. to me 460:22
wherein 'tis p. of itself 481:12
Precipice-encurled: castle, p. 91:5
Precipices rang aloud 575:24
Precise: too p. in every part 246:4
Precisely: thinking too p. 436:16
Precisian: devil turned p. 334:23
Predecessors: my illustrious p. 204:11
Predestinate grooves 237:26
Predestination: p. in the stride 299:3
with P. round enmesh me 207:10
Predestined: with P. Evil round 207:11
Predicate: bully, as we all p. 39:28
Predictions: dreams and p. 27:2
Predilection to mean..cares 101:30
Predominant: England as the p. member 409:8
Predominates: love of truth p. 200:23
Predominating: sniffles p. 242:12
Pre-elect God's Virgin 411:27
Pre-eminence: painful p.! 1:18
right hand..the p. 399:9
Prefaces: all the p. of Dryden 521:19
nothing but his P. 154:38
Prefer: folks p. in fact a hovel 121:12
Gentlemen P. Blondes 318:19
if I p. not Jerusalem 400:5
State's..forms p. 231:30
yet p. that which is truly better 352:9

Preferment: knocking at P.'s door 18:7
p. goes by letter and affection 469:24
so I gain'd p. 7:9
Preferred before me 63:2
Preferrest thou the gospel of Montreal? 112:18
Preferreth all countries before his own 371:15
Preferring: in honour p. one another 66:2
Pregnant: chaste lady's p. womb 332:10
Irish bull is always p. 327:10
p. bank swelled up 184:29
Prejudice: nor..behold with p. the French 86:27
popular p. runs in favour 177:1
to everybody's p. 221:40
to the p. of good order 5:26
Prejudices: bundle of p. 306:10
honest p. 2:19
p. a man so 505:7
uncorrupted with literary p. 278:10
Prelate: religion without a p. 33:5
Prelatical: Presbyterial, or P. 352:18
Preliminary: puff p. 499:27
Prematur: nonumque p. in annum 256:14
Premises: insufficient p. 111:33
Prentice: her p. han' she tried 106:2
Preparation: dreadful note of p. 444:6
no formal p. 406:14
no p. for the future 181:32
politics..no p...necessary 514:6
p. of the gospel of peace 68:12
Prepare: I go to p. a place 63:52
O! p. it 483:6
p. a table before me 393:10
p. the mind of the country 180:38
p. to shed them now 450:27
p. ye the way 54:9, 57:28
who shall p. himself to the battle? 67:1
Prepared: charge is p. 215:6
p. as a bride adorned 71:44
p. to marry again 218:38
when all the Temple is p. 205:7
world is not yet p. 188:16
Preposterous sight! 163:38
Preposterousest end 111:22
Prerogative: dead and rotten as P. 101:34
English subject's sole P. 193:42
last p. 192:24
Presage: augurs mock their own p. 488:2
credit things that do p. 451:34
Presagers of my speaking breast 486:21
Presbyter: new P...old Priest 351:27
Presbyterial, or Prelatical 352:18
Presbyterian true blue 110:16
Prescription: Conservatism discards P. 181:32
p. to die 470:14
Presence: at the p. of God 396:4
better by their p. 196:34
better than p. of mind 403:6
from whose unseen p. 496:4
his p. on the field 564:17
his P. shall my wants supply 2:21
in thy p. is the fulness of joy 392:27
lord of thy p. and no land 447:18
not away from thy p. 395:9
not thro' his p. 93:5
paint Thy P. 355:14
p. that disturbs me 582:1
p. that thus rose so strangely 374:10
punch in the p. 83:1
scanter of your maiden p. 431:28
to the p. in the room 265:16
truth..the p. of it 27:32
whose p. civilizes ours 159:18
whose p. of mind was amazing 311:5
your p. I..accept 38:20
Present: act in the living P.! 317:7
all p. and correct 5:5
crowns..the p. deed 485:27
deficiencies of the p. day 278:14
except the p. company 370:7
his p. and your pains 443:11
his p. is futurity 236:42
like an ass when thou art p. 155:27
no redress for the p. 181:32
nor things p. 65:58
no time like the p. 329:7

Present (cont.)
only to be p. at it 546:36
predominate over the p. 277:39
p. far too small 562:19
p. horror from the time 458:1
p. hour alone is man's 278:28
p. in spirit 66:26
p. joys are more 192:29
p. life of men on earth 38:31
p. mirth hath p. laughter 482:28
p. my true account 351:21
p., past, and future sees 75:23
p. your bodies a living sacrifice 65:62
pursue things which are just in p. 24:24
sons of God came to p. themselves 48:38
take the p. time 428:33
things p., worst 441:27
this p...the world's last night 185:17
time p. and time past 197:4
un-birthday p. 131:5
very p. help 5:6, 394:27
Presented: p. myself at Betty's bedside 560:13
p. to a Pogram 176:25
p. with a universal blank 346:20
Presenting Thebes 341:18
Presents: all p. wot eat 518:24
by these p. 8:4
kings..shall give p. 396:25
P...endear Absents 306:5
Preservation: our creation, p. 389:19
Preserve: p. as in a vial..living intellect 352:5
p. our faculties entire 273:22
p. the stars from wrong 573:31
p. thy going out 399:29
what we give and what we p. 314:11
Preserved: each slight variation.. p. 169:6
gods..have p. thee 454:5
long p. virginity 333:9
must be p. 267:27
seen God..and my life is p. 45:11
Preserver: destroyer and p. 496:4
Preside over the liquidation 144:17
President: not choose to run for P. 156:23
perpetual p. 127:31
P. of the Immortals 237:14
rather be right than be P. 146:2
Presider: Shakespeare this P.? 289:13
Presión: orden no es una p. 214:2
Press: among p. of knights 328:24
darst..put thy-self in p. 138:14
dead-born from the p. 265:12
flee fro the p. 136:20
gently pressed, p. gently 160:23
god of our idolatry, the p. 161:33
governs the periodical p. 549:18
I p. toward the mark 68:23
liberty of the p. 282:16
misus'd the king's p. 440:20
not p. you like slaves 213:10
p. close bare-bosom'd night 567:16
p. it to thine own again 494:7
p. no ponderous tomb 118:23
p. onward 81:25
P. was squared 41:8
p. where ye see my white plume 323:5
we p. too close 89:3
Pressed: gently p., press gently 160:23
good measure, p. down 61:31
p. down my soul 395:18
p. upon by transitions 200:3
Presses: hag..that p. them 477:7
his identity p. upon me 290:4
Pressing: thou p. me to thee 567:2
Press-men: so we named P. 14:30
Pressure: his form and p. 434:17
order is not p. 214:2
Pressures: all p. past 432:20
Presume: Dr. Livingstone, I p.? 511:13
do not p. too much 451:18
not p. to dictate 178:27
p. not God to scan 383:22
p. not that I am 442:39
Presumed: it is to be p. 280:7
Presumption: all p...die away 100:25
Presumptuous: from p. sins 392:34
refined, p. man 124:15
too p. folly 238:26

INDEX

Prêt. botté et p. à partir 354:19
toujours *p. à partir* 209:15
Pretence: for a p. make long
   prayers 61:7
   good without p. 382:12
p. of keeping a bawdy-house 277:16
to some faint meaning make p. 193:2
undivulg'd p. 458:26
Pretences to break known rules 107:11
Pretend they ne'er so wise 350:26
Pretended friend 215:24
Pretender: James II, and the Old
   P. 233:14
who P. is 112:25
Pretending to extraordinary revelations 109:38
Pretexts: tyrants seldom want p. 103:5
Pretio: omnia Romae cum p. 283:6
Prêtre: les boyaux du dernier p. 338:1
Prettiest, silliest, most affected 353:6
Prettily: just as p. as he 512:11
Pretty: all my p. ones? 460:21
   all the maidens p. 154:9
   driving briskly..with a p.
   woman 273:21
   everything that p. is 429:25
   it is a p., p. thing 377:3
   it is a p. thing 232:5
   p., but I don't know what it
   means 218:10
   p., but is it Art? 295:16
   p. i' the Mantuan! 121:5
   p. to see what money will do 377:31
   p. witty Nell 377:25
   p. young wards in Chancery 218:36
   prithee, p. maiden 220:31
   puts on his p. looks 447:34
   uncommon p. young woman 196:6
   where girls are so p. 7:8
   while my p. one sleeps 538:12
   wife was p., trifling 165:9
Prevail: common interest..will p. 190:27
   despite of all your generals ye p. 308:21
   e'er p. against us 582:3
   'gainst that Church 35:3
   great is truth and shall p. 84:26
   looking ill p.? 517:10
   p. upon the day 193:2
   soon as the evening shades p. 2:26
   strive and should p. 364:8
   whether it p. or not 375:18
Prevailed: Amalek p. 161:16
Prevails: great is truth and it p. 56:19
Prevaricate: thou dost p. 110:25
Prevarication: last dyke of p. 101:25
Prevent: not strength enough to
   p. 227:25
   p. it and to damn the consequences 339:25
   p. the time of life 451:36
   p. us, O Lord 390:51
Prevention: hide thee from p. 449:7
   p. from evil 329:8
Preventing: thy..grace p. us 389:34
Prevents his holding a pen 177:9
Previous: returned home the p.
   night 98:19
Prey: destined p. 490:18
   divided the p. 46:52
   expects his evening p. 229:23
   his foot on the p. 538:2
   in England to take a p. 30:5
   p. for gods 525:18
   p. to all 383:22
   p. upon the less 231:26
   soon must be his p. 495:2
   to dumb Forgetfulness a p. 230:9
   to p. at fortune 471:38
Preys: to their p. do rouse 459:8
Priam: drew P.'s curtain 441:9
   proud as P. 586:7
Priamus: en P. 553:18
Priapus: Death and P. 523:7
Pribbles and prabbles 465:28
Price: abatement and low p. 481:30
   at any price 145:28, 269:19
   her price is far above rubies 50:57
   knows the p. of everything 570:1
   no question but the p. of votes 279:3
   of countless p. 291:5
   p. of admiralty 301:24

Price (cont.)
   p. of shoddy 218:29
   p. of wisdom is above rubies 49:8
   raised the p. of everything 324:29
   raised the p. of literature 270:24
   set her own p. 374:20
   those men have their p. 558:31
   too high the p. for knowledge 547:22
   What P. Glory 4:22
   wot p. Selvytion nah? 490:5
   without money and without p. 54:29
Prick: if you p. us 464:8
   it is a p., it is a sting 377:3
   pat it and p. it 368:10
   p. and sting her 432:18
   p. the sides of my intent 457:9
Pricked from the lazy finger 477:7
Pricketh: so p. hem nature 136:22
Pricking: p. of my thumbs 460:1
   p. on the plain 509:17
Prickly: stretch their p. arms 165:17
Pricks: honour p. me on 440:30
   kick against the p. 64:42
   small p. to their subsequent
   volumes 481:8
Pride: age..her p. deflower 509:33
   all their mournful p. 585:22
   all the p. of power sink 100:25
   ambition, and the p. of kings 383:7
   burning p. and high disdain 417:6
   by aspiring p. and insolence 330:1
   considerate p. 345:7
   contempt on all my p. 562:18
   decay'd through p. 510:21
   Family P. 220:1
   fient a p. na p. had he 108:19
   for the p. o' the eye 302:30
   four not exempt from p. 309:4
   full p. of France 443:8
   he that is low no p. 99:31
   I know thy p. 47:20
   in p. and thankfulness 92:31
   in p., in reas'ning p. 383:13
   land of the pilgrims' p. 504:19
   laugh their p. 90:34
   maiden p., adieu! 468:27
   May was in his p. 80:7
   modest p. 347:12
   mother's p., a father's joy! 419:6
   my family p...in-conceivable 219:19
   my high-blown p. 446:24
   my p. fell with my fortunes 426:23
   my p. struck out new sparkles 192:23
   nor Flora's p. 87:25
   our faith, our p. 295:8
   our pleasure or our p. 575:14
   own with humbled p. 33:12
   passion, pain, or p. 540:26
   perished in his p. 580:7
   p., cruelty and ambition of man 405:13
   P., Envy, Malice 308:13
   p. goeth before destruction 50:15
   p. in their port 226:14
   p. of former days 356:20
   p. of the ocean 489:1
   p. of the peacock 77:16
   p. of the rich is all for sale 142:4
   p., pomp, and circumstance 472:3
   p. ruled my will 364:11
   p. still is aiming 383:13
   p. that apes humility 151:11, 507:21
   p. that licks the dust 385:34
   p. that pulls the country down 471:12
   p. that puts this country down 6:26
   ring out false p. 533:20
   soldier's p. 92:24
   spite of p. 383:21
   their country's p. 224:14
   then the p. of man? 235:7
   'tis p., rank p. 1:16
   towering in her p. of place 458:28
   vain was the chief's..p. 386:24
   victim of Parthenia's p. 215:12
   with Nature's p. 330:23
   youth and beauty's p. 190:34
Prided: feat on which ourselves
   we p. 115:32
Pridie: no p., nor postridie 186:31
Prie: je vous en p., pity me 231:36
Priest: as a p...church furniture 164:10
   both p. and clerk? 475:18

Priest (cont.)
   churches built to please the p. 106:24
   day, a dedicated p. 545:6
   delicate-handed p. 535:42
   fiddling p. 161:25
   ghastly p. doth reign 324:3
   guts of the last p. 338:1
   hearing the holy p. 509:13
   I will be thy p. 288:7
   loud prays the p. 15:27
   mair o' Marie Hamilton than..
   the p. 31:17
   my religion from the p. 227:28
   Nature's p. 576:9
   no Italian p. shall tithe 447:29
   old p. Peter Gilligan 584:6
   old P. writ large 351:27
   O mysterious p. 287:12
   pale-eyed p. 343:21
   Poet, Prophet, King, P. 125:26
   p. all shaven and shorn 369:6
   p. continues 192:30
   p., the slave 491:15
   p. who slew the slayer 324:3
   rather go with sir p. 484:16
   this turbulent p. 242:20
   thou art a p. for ever 398:24
   true God's p. 124:26
   'twixt the P. and Clerk 246:12
Priestcraft: ere p. did begin 190:7
Priesthood: all his p. moans 285:6
   royal p. 69:48
Priestlike task 288:17
Priests: Bishops, P., and Deacons 388:52
   feet of thine high p. tread 525:13
   holy p. bless her 424:9
   no war with..p. 507:30
   of p...charmin' variety 229:13
   p. are only men 95:33
   p. bear rule by their means 55:13
   p. by..a mightier hand 325:4
   p. in gold and black 310:23
   p. of all religions are the same 190:12
   p., tapers, temples 382:6
   treen chalices and golden p. 269:22
   your p., whate'er their..sham-
   ming 357:20
Prig: Little P. 199:18
   p., for my life, p. 485:20
Prigs and pedants 180:30
Prim little craft 222:8
Primate: served the Lord P. 34:8
Prime: crowned with the p. 428:33
   dead ere his p. 342:10
   glory of your p. 494:18
   laurel for the perfect p. 409:28
   lost but once your p. 247:10
   lovely April of her p. 486:11
   my barmie noddle's working p. 105:26
   my p. of youth 547:20
   splendour of its p. 493:27
   time of England's p. 375:19
   whilst yet is p. 509:33
   while we are in our p. 245:27
Prime Minister: next P. but three 41:8
Primeval: forest p. 316:12
   sleeps with the p. giants 125:34
Primitive: manner of P. Man 309:28
Primo avulso 554:24
Primordial atomic globule 219:19
Primrose: like thy face, pale p. 429:37
   p. by a river's brim 578:25
   p. first born child of Ver 38:8
   p. path of dalliance 431:23
   p. way 458:19
   rathe p. 342:31
   soft silken p. 341:6
   sweet as the p. 225:7
Primrose Hill: to P. 75:4
Primroses: brought you some p. 182:13
   like tufts of p. 181:35
   pale p. 485:26
   p. make a capital salad 182:13
   wan as p. 285:7
Prince: any p. of Europe 198:11
   as the subject owes the p. 479:13
   delightful Fairy P. 336:21
   God send the p. a better companion 441:22
   good-night, sweet p. 438:7
   greatest p. o' the world 42<:28

Prince (*cont.*)
great P. in prison lies   185:2
have thy P.'s grace   510:16
in a p., the virtue   334:17
Lord Hamlet is a p.   432:43
Milton's the p. of poets   116:4
neither king nor p.   23:16
news and P. of Peace   209:3
nor peer nor p. can buy   124:5
on which the P. of Glory died   562:18
p. can mak a..knight   105:32
P., I can hear the trumpet   140:10
P. of all the land   122:3
p. of darkness is a gentleman   453:25, 517:15
P. of Denmark..left out   420:22
P. of Peace   53:15
p. of the Latian name   323:14
P., P.-Elective   140:7
P. who calls in a..Neighbour   512:4
Rasselas, P. of Abyssinia   278:14
system of P.'s nails   174:33
through the p. of the devils   58:44
to my P. faithfully   316:32
who made thee a p.?   45:31
Princedoms, Virtues, Powers   348:14
Princely: by p. governaunce   195:7
p. counsel in his face   345:24
that p. woman   306:23
Prince of Wales: God bless the P.   314:19
Princes: counsels of p.   393:36
courts of p.   340:17
death of p.   449:22
great p. have great playthings   163:41
hangs on p.' favours   446:24
her p. are come home again   448:2
make p. in all lands   394:26
p. and lords may flourish   224:14
p...but the breath of kings   105:5
p. have persecuted me   399:23
p. in this case   168:4
p. of Judah their counsel   396:13
P. ride at noon   171:2
sweet aspect of p.   446:24
when p. die with us   440:32
whose merchants are p.   53:29
your trust in p.   400:19
Princess: fitting for a p.   426:15
in love with one p. or another   512:21
P. of Parallelograms   119:34
p. wrought it me   447:38
Princesses: locks of six p.   293:9
Principal: wisdom is the p. thing   49:42
Principalities: against p., against
    power   68:11
nor p., nor powers   65:58
Principality: better than a p. in
    Utopia   325:24
Principibus placuisse viris   257:6
Principiis obsta   372:2
Principle: active P.   574:25
any p. whatever   126:8
does everything on p.   490:38
I *don't* believe in p.   319:21
killed hisself on p.   179:22
loved the p. of beauty   290:29
on the p. it was demanded   100:5
precedent embalms a p.   180:20, 420:33
p. in life with me   491:7
protection is not a p.   180:17
rebels from p.   102:17
refinement on the p. of resistance   100:29
sensibility of p.   102:13
shrinks from P.   181:32
Principles: broken open on..
    scientific p.   376:14
damn your p.   181:16
fights you on patriotic p.   490:38
1st, religious and moral p.   20:21
from the highest p.   203:33
he has good p.   271:6
it ain't by p. nor men   319:22
on the p. of freedom   101:4
our p. swaller   319:18
p. of eternal justice   373:16
p. of his understanding   265:10
sincere in good p.   276:11
their p. are the same   274:35
unfixed in p. and place   190:13
wrote 'P. of Political Economy'   43:2
Print: delight me for to p.   247:22

Print (*cont.*)
devils must p.   356:7
faith, he'll p. it   107:21
fit to p.   370:2
I'll p. it   385:22
I love a ballad in p.   485:30
p. it as it stands—beautifully   268:18
p. of a man's naked foot   170:7
p. of the nails   64:9
p. to him   176:21
p. would then surpass   281:9
seeing our names in p.   142:2
see one's name in p.   117:10
so many Scarers in P.   178:9
Printed: from a p. book   302:34
leave the p. lawn   264:1
p. an' bound in little books   299:8
that they were p. in a book!   49:5
what p. thing soever   127:11
Printers: books by which the p.
    have lost   212:15
Printing: caused p. to be used   445:40
Gunpowder, P., and..   125:24
invented the art of p.   127:6
Printless: clerical, p. toe   84:11
my p. feet   341:4
Print-shops: her rich goldsmiths,
    p.   307:2
Prior: abbot and p. were there   34:8
what once was Matthew P.   401:28
Priority: degree, p., and place   481:2
Prithee, pretty maiden   220:29, 31
Prisca: ut p. gens   257:22
Priscian: breaking P.'s head   111:21
break P.'s head   381:21
P. a little scratched   455:25
Prism: Newton, with his p.   579:19
prunes and p.   176:1
Prison: breaches of our p.   102:38
compare this p.   475:33
great Prince in p. lies   185:2
hero from his p.   24:6
home is the girl's p.   490:36
in p., and ye came unto me   60:33
let's away to p.   454:19
Lime-tree Bower my P.   152:1
not a p. make   319:7
opening of the p.   55:3
palace and a p.   114:1
pretty sort of p.   39:26
p. in a p.   179:24
ship..a p.   109:19
thy p. is a holy place   114:34
vile p. of afflicted breath   447:33
wear out in a wall'd p.   454:19
Prisoned: his p. time   80:27
p. in a parlour   161:41
Prisoner: if the p. is happy   490:25
p. comes to meet his doom   222:29
p. in his twisted gyves   477:28
p. of Jesus Christ   69:5
p.'s release   501:20
takes the reason p.   456:19
Prisoners: bringeth the p. out   396:5
p. call the sky   569:2
p. of hope   56:12
p. underneath her wings   445:26
set my p. free   90:20
thy pity upon all p.   389:3
Prison-house: grind in the p.   46:60
secrets of my p.   432:9
shades of the p.   576:9
Prisons: improving his p. in Hell   151:12
improving the p. of Hell   507:22
p. are built with stones of Law   77:15
p. of flesh   186:7
Privacy: a p., an obscure nook   94:22
Private: ambition of a p. man   163:1
consult our p. ends   521:1
fine and p. place   333:9
gain some p. ends   225:21
heresy..p. opinion   248:20
in a p. man a vice   334:17
once a p. opinion   200:20
pool of p. charity   374:21
p. respects must yield   350:32
p. station   1:21, 215:31
public flame, nor p.   381:27
religion..invade..p. life   335:16
secure of p. right   190:28
served *no* p. end   385:6

Private (*cont.*)
serve our p. ends   143:6
takes no p. road   384:14
that p. men enjoy   444:22
to his mother's house p. re-
    turned   350:18
true..in your p. heart   200:36
very p. uses   319:20
we've got a p. master   177:14
what p. griefs they have   450:32
with p. men esteem'd a blessing   334:20
Privates: her p. we   433:10
that p. have not too   444:22
Privato: maior p. visus   526:15
Privilege: death is the p.   412:11
Englishman's heaven-born p.   19:29
power which stands on P.   41:26
p. and pleasure   218:23
p. of putting him to death   505:28
p. o' sitting down   196:27
p. of wisdom to listen   251:22
wine, p. of the completely free   42:1
Privileged: P. and the People   182:29
p. individual   179:34
p. to be very impertinent   203:31
Privileges: from similar p.   101:10
Prize: all is a p.   255:6
Christ the p.   354:11
fraught with a later p.   493:25
game beyond the p.   302:33
many people p. it   220:31
not all..lawful p.   230:22
one receiveth the p.   66:36
other aims..learned to p.   224:18
p. above my dukedom   479:23
p. of all too precious you   487:20
p. of learning love   90:42
p., the p. secure!   362:12
p. the thing ungain'd   480:41
p. we sought is won   566:27
shorter a p. poem..better   325:17
Timotheus yield the p.   191:13
we do not run for p.   506:20
what we have we p. not   469:5
win you such a p.   362:8
Prizer: as well..as in the p.   481:24
Prizes: in herself she p.   154:28
offer glittering p.   72:25
other won several p.   305:9
Probability is the very guide of life   109:36
Probable: no p., possible shadow   218:18
Probably Arboreal   169:4, 514:10
Probationer: yet a young p.   192:39
Probitas laudatur et alget   282:23
Problem: all in all, he's a p.   107:36
solve the p. of the age   200:20
three-pipe p.   187:19
Problems: clearing the world of its
    most difficult p.   178:10
Proboscis: wreathed his lithe p.   347:15
Proceed: we will p. no further   457:10
Proceedeth: p. from the wicked   47:27
p. out of the mouth of God   57:34
Proceeding I am charg'd withal   469:45
Proceedings: subsequent p.   239:2
Procès: puis ils lui font son p.   354:4
Process: long p. of getting tired   111:32
Procession: torchlight p...down
    your throat   371:5
years in long p. ran   190:31
Processions: women walk in pub-
    lic p.   567:8
Proclaim the acceptable year   55:3
Proclaimed their malefactions   433:36
Proclaimeth: what good success..
    the world p.   404:16
Proclivity: by p...all quote   201:5
Proconsul: great P.   324:33
Procrastination: p. is the thief of
    time   587:4
to incivility and p.   172:23
Procreant: always the p. urge   567:11
Procreate: that we might p. like
    trees   86:34
Procreation: for the p. of children   391:24
Proctors: prudes for p.   538:7
Procul: p. hinc, p. este, severael   371:21
p., o p. este, profani   554:25
qui p. hinc   363:1
Procure: injuries..they them-
    selves p.   453:2

Procurer of contentedness 559:15
Procuress to the Lords of Hell 532:30
Prodigal: how p. the soul 431:27
  once was p. before 192:12
  p. of ease 190:14
  P.'s favourite 573:15
  p. within..a guinea 267:22
Prodigality: p. of Nature 476:9
  spring of all p. 101:17
Prodigies: all Africa and her p. 86:11
  what p. surprise 279:10
'Prodigious!' 419:32
Produce: p. of the common day 574:8
  p.! p.!..p. it in God's name! 127:21
Producing: consume..without p. 489:12
Product: fraction of a p. 127:21
  knowledge..p. of history 125:31
  p. of the smaller intestines 125:30
Production: noblest p. of human nature 2:7
Profanation: in the less foul p. 461:32
  p. of our joys 186:24
  p. to keep in 245:26
Profane: coldly p. 164:40
  for me to p. it 499:3
  hence, ye p. 158:24
  none p.! my Holy See of love 287:5
  O p. one! 79:18
  p., erroneous, and vain 110:35
  p. the service of the dead 437:19
  so old, and so p. 442:37
  so surpassingly p. 120:26
Profaned: p. the God-given strength 418:7
  province they have..p. 222:35
  too often p. 499:3
Profani: procul este, p. 554:25
Profess: politics like ours p. 231:26
  p. and call themselves 389:16
Professes to flatter 276:8
Profession: Adam's p. 437:5
  charmed me from my p. 480:29
  contrary to their p. 389:36
  debtor to his p. 25:14
  head of the literary p. 181:24
  most ancient p. 304:40
  ornament to her p. 99:33
  panted for a liberal p. 154:14
  parentage is a very important p. 489:23
Professionally he declines and falls 178:3
Professions: all p. are conspiracies 489:20
  p. which are full 546:40
Professor: most learn'd p., Brunk 387:7
Professors of the Dismal Science 126:34
Profit: body suffers the soul..p. by 337:19
  ere her cause bring..p. 320:12
  in all labour there is p. 50:8
  mingled p. with pleasure 256:9
  my p. had I known 530:19
  my p. on't is.. 479:26
  no p. but the name 436:14
  no p...where is no pleasure 478:47
  p. by their example 242:16
  p. of their shining nights 454:32
  so find we p. 424:3
  what p. is there in my blood 393:26
  what p...of all his labour 50:59
Profiteth me nothing 66:45
Profitless: not p. those fleeting moods 579:17
Profits: it little p. 540:31
  nothing p. more than self-esteem 349:3
Profligate: so witty, p., and thin 587:16
Profound: thro' the turbulent p. 503:5
  turbid look the most p. 309:21
Profoundest: thou p. Hell 344:22
Profusus: sui p. 415:1
Progeniem vitiosiorem 260:1
Progenies: iam nova p. 555:30
Progeny: p. of light 348:14
  whose p. they are 352:5
Prognostics..not always..prophecies 558:28
Programme for a British Ministry 181:14
Progress: all p. is based upon 111:34
  Christ's p. 551:20
  disavows P. 181:32
  history of p. 324:26
  our p. through the world 318:9

Progress (cont.)
  party of p. 338:28
  p. depends on the unreasonable 490:34
  p...is not an accident 508:27
  p. is not real 216:9
  p. is the law of life 94:23
  p., man's distinctive mark 91:1
  p. of a deathless soul 186:4
  p. of human society consists 126:44
  p. spiring round 140:5
  rake's p. 542:19
  rise, the p...of imagery 289:27
  viewing his p. through 442:5
Progression: nothing in p. can rest 103:23
Progressive: in a p. country 180:37
Prohibiting: by licensing and p. 352:17
Project: my p. gather to a head 480:11
Projectile: British Army..a p. 232:17
Projects: fitter for new p. 27:41
Proletariat: dictatorship of the p. 333:14
Proletarier: die P. haben nichts.. als ihre Ketten..P...vereinigt euch! 333:11
Prologue: make a long p. 57:20
  very witty p. 155:34
  what's past is p. 479:35
Prologues: happy p. 456:23
  nothing but his..P. 154:38
  p. precede the piece 213:8
Promethean: right P. fire 455:23
  true P. fire 455:20
  where is that P. heat 473:11
Promise: break an hour's p. in love! 428:18
  broke no p. 385:6
  Christ's own p. 35:3
  first commandment with p. 68:7
  Heaven's p. clothe 411:1
  how truly the P. runs 302:3
  ill keeper of p. 25:33
  keep the word of p. to our ear 461:12
  knowing your p. to me 536:13
  p., large p. 277:35
  p. such a beauteous day 486:30
  they did p...three things 391:2
  whose p. none relies on 407:24
  with p. of strength and manhood 81:22
  you p. heavens 157:18
Promise-crammed: air, p. 435:2
Promised: as the weird women p. 458:30
  marching to the P. Land 35:4
  really p. something great 110:35
  Saviour p. long 183:19
  what the author p. 270:25
  what thou art p. 457:1
  whom he had p. to defend 324:34
Promises: his p. were..mighty 447:7
  maugre all God's p. 375:27
  perform the p. of youth 278:14
  p. and pie-crust 520:4
  p. as sweet 580:20
Promontory: blue p. with trees 425:19
  p. goats 336:38
  sat upon a p. 466:38
  sterile p. 433:15
  stretch'd like a p. 348:26
Promoted: p. everybody 218:27
  p. thence to deck 119:3
Promotion: last p. of the blest 192:37
  p. cometh neither from the east 396:30
  sweat but for p. 426:38
Prompt: foot less p. 18:30
  p. at every call 224:21
  p. in attack 100:30
Prompter: falling to the p.'s bell 543:6
  manager, actor, p. 237:25
Prompting: heart's p. 106:24
Prone: p. and emaciated figure 235:22
  p. to any iteration of nuptials 156:17
  to piety more p. 4:9
Pronounce: p. it faithfully 477:20
  spell better than they p. 550:14
Pronounced me thus 460:34
Pronounces: as he p. lastly 342:23
Proof: bliss in p. 488:12
  dost thou ask p.? 19:1
  give me the ocular p. 472:4
  incapable of p. 313:24
  lapp'd in p. 456:9

Proof (cont.)
  p. of manly might 509:35
  through p. of harness 425:12
Proofs: not convinced by p. 375:2
  p. of holy writ 471:42
Prop: little p. 245:18
  my very p. 463:30
  p. to our infirmity 579:16
  when you do take the p. 465:14
Propagate: learn and p. the best 19:12
  not likely to p. understanding 276:20
  p. and rot 383:24
Propagation: all our p. 184:30
Propensities: my amorous p. 270:10
  ruined on the side of their..p. 103:14
Propensity: p...towards the marvellous 265:9
  strong p. of nature 352:21
  that p...Boswellism 325:5
Proper: in their p. places 548:15
  no p. time of day 253:11
  p. man as one shall see 466:31
  p. men as ever trod 448:6
  p. words in p. places 520:1
Properly: never did anything p. 312:21
  not p. born 174:39
  p. spent 527:9
Propertied: his voice was p. as.. spheres 426:1
Property: changing his p. 475:5
  consider himself as public p. 268:28
  give me a little snug p. 195:17
  I'm a man of p. 220:31
  it is for our p. 379:15
  no right to the p. of the rich 413:28
  not p., but a trust 210:21
  portable p. 175:24
  p. has its duties 189:24
  p. is theft 402:19
  P., p., p. 537:6
Prophecies: prognostics .. not always..p. 558:28
  whether there be p. 66:45
Prophecy: all p., all medicine 494:1
  p...most gratuitous form of error 196:20
  trumpet of a p. 496:11
  urn of bitter p. 493:27(-494)
Prophesy: eat exceedingly and p. 279:23
  man may p. 442:6
  p. deceits 53:38
  prophets p. falsely 55:13
  we p. in part 66:45
  your sons and your daughters shall p. 55:52
Prophesying: p. war 151:33(-152)
  p. with accents terrible 458:21
Prophet: confound the p. with the whale 176:27
  good for the P. 297:7
  in the name of the P.—figs! 504:11
  Juxtaposition his p. 146:11
  man put off the p. 94:3
  pale-mouth'd p. 288:6
  Poet, P., King, Priest 126:26
  p. in Israel 48:21
  p. is not without honour 59:33
  p. new inspired 474:21
  p. of the soul 199:21
  P. of the Utterly Absurd 301:21
  'P.!' said I 380:26
  p.? Yea..more than a p. 59:6
  What-you-may-call-it is his p. 175:15
Prophetess: more than a p. 196:6
Prophetic: from the p. cell 343:21
  in her p. fury 472:16
  like p. strain 341:25
  my p. soul! 432:13
  p. soul of the wide world 488:2
  such p. greeting 456:17
Prophets: all the Lord's people..p. 46:11
  beware of false p. 58:25
  many p. and kings have desired 61:38
  Martyrs, P., Virgins 361:11
  perverts the P. 117:18
  p...live for ever? 56:10
  p. of Nature 579:38
  p. old 346:20
  p. prophesy falsely 55:13
  Saul also among the p.? 47:11
  spake by the P. 390:21

Prophets (*cont.*)
this is the law and the p.   58:22
thou that killest the p.   60:20
wisest p. make sure   558:28
Propinquity does it   560:24
Propitius: Deus. .p. isti potatori   13:9
Propontic: due on to the P.   472:12
Propontis: whitened the straits of P.   522:10
Proportion: harmony, order or p.   86:32
insisture, course, p.   481:2
no p. kept   475:34
some strangeness in the p.   25:29
Proportional: her body is homogeneal and p.   352:11
Proportions: by p. true   332:12
in small p.   282:1
of vast p. and painted red   311:17
Propose: if he do not p.   184:20
why don't the men p.?   37:4
Proposed: before, a joy p.   488:12
he p. seven times   175:37
Proposes: man p.   291:20
Proposition: dedicated to the p.   314:12
fifth p. of Euclid   188:18
Propositions: resolve the p. of a lover   428:4
Propping: spirit-small hand p. it   90:7
Proprie communia dicere   255:24
Propriété: la p. c'est le vol   402:19
Propriety: frights the isle from her p.   471:16
inseparable p. of time   24:34
not always evince its p.   23:10
sole p. in Paradise   347:26
study first p.   121:16
with more p. be called. . Conservative   166:26
Prose: differs in nothing from p.   231:21
I love thee in p.   401:21
in a sea of p.   289:11
many more in p.   382:19
medium for writing in p.   569:30
Mr. Coleridge's lyric p.   240:7
nearest p.   193:26
never pin up my hair with p.   156:3
next to those that write p.   24:42
only p.   90:5
other harmony of p.   194:12
p. . .bear a great deal of poetry   309:15
p. Browning   569:30
P. can never be too truthful   561:11
p. can paint evening   337:14
p. = words in their best order   153:6
p. run mad   385:28
[p.] wherein knowing myself inferior   352:19
shows that p. is verse   117:16
unattempted yet in p. or rhyme   344:3
under a moderate weight of p.   309:15
warbler of poetic p.   163:34
Prose: quarante ans que je dis de la p.   353:11
tout ce qui n'est point p. est vers   353:12
Proselytes: Jews and p.   64:26
new French p.   192:28
p. of one another's trade   111:23
Proserpin gathering flowers   347:8
Proserpina: fairy Queen P.   123:26
P.! for the flowers now   485:26
Prospect: every p. pleases   240:18
eye and p. of his soul   469:6
in a P. of Flowers   333:4
noblest p. . .a Scotchman. .sees   271:8
p. of a distant good   192:29
p. of heaven   363:26
so full of goodly p.   352:26
what a p. this opens!   177:42
within the p. of belief   456:17
Prospects: my p. all look blue   218:13
p. bright'ning to the last   224:16
shining p. rise   2:2
Prosper: p. that love thee   399:31
p. thou our handy-work   397:17
treason doth never p.   238:3
why do sinners' ways p.?   255:8
Prospering: we shall march p.   93:5
Prosperity: good things which belong to p.   25:16
have still p.   421:5
in the day of p. be joyful   51:13

Prosperity (*cont.*)
jest's p. lies in the ear   455:34
much legislation, great p.   143:31
one man who can stand p.   126:30
p. doth best discover vice   25:21
p. doth bewitch men   563:35
p. is not without many fears   25:20
p. is the blessing of the Old Testament   25:18
p.'s the very bond of love   485:33
to have been in p.   138:35
wish thee p.   399:31
Prosperous: most happy and p.   217:8
p. or adverse   575:11
p. people. .write their memoirs   112:2
p. to be just   320:12
Prospers: turns Ashes—or it p.   205:27
Prostitute: I puff the p. away   194:22
Protect: I'll p. it now   358:21
Protected: those by law p.   106:24
Protection: comfort, use and p.   24:27
God's gracious mercy and p.   391:37
Greek, by this p.   281:26
p. is not a principle   180:17
p. is not only dead   181:17
similar privileges and equal p.   101:10
surrounded with His p.   352:13
Protective of his young   546:11
Protest: lady doth p. too much   435:15
Protestant: Printing, and the P. Religion   125:24
P. Flail   250:13
P. . .can only go to his solicitor   182:14
protestantism of the P. religion   100:29
thy P. to be   247:1
Protestantism: all p. . .dissent   100:29
p. of the Protestant religion   100:29
Protestants: religion of P.   142:24
Protestation: hear thou my p.   262:5
Protested: he blam'd and p.   161:37
Proteus rising from the sea   582:18
Protoplasmal primordial atomic globule   219:19
Protracted: life p. is p. woe   279:7
p. my work till. .   270:28
Proud: all the p. and mighty have   195:14
all the p. shall be   381:36
balance of p. time   231:35
death be not p.   185:15
death p. to take us   425:31
dull, the p., the wicked   386:2
ever fair and never p.   470:29
friends p. of my memory   200:29
hath also a p. look   397:34
how apt the poor are to be p.   483:27
how little are the p.   231:7
I am p.; I must be p. to see   386:23
if she be p., is she not sweet?   413:31
I have no p. looks   400:1
I know not whether I am p.   309:7
I might grow p.   247:8
knowledge is p.   163:50
man, p. man   461:31
mighty I am   377:29
of which I'm suffishuntly p.   559:34
our virtues would be p.   423:7
pitiless as p.   158:33
p. and angry dust   263:32
p. and godly kings   208:5
p. as peacocks   422:26
p. as Priam   586:7
p. clergyman   204:10
p. in arms   340:2
p. in heart and mind   453:19
p. limitary Cherub   347:34
p. man's contumely   434:4
p. man was Lars Porsena   323:13
p. me no prouds   478:29
p. of one another the first week   156:13
p. of seeing our names in print   142:2
p., revengeful, ambitious   434:9
p. rider on so p. a back   488:27
p., the cold untroubled heart   122:32
p. word you never spoke   309:4
p. world, said I   166:2
scattered the p.   61:14
selfish, and the p.   164:34
since thou art so p.   125:1
sweet, be not p.   247:6
too p. for a wit   225:27
too p. to fight   571:10

Proud (*cont.*)
too p. to importune   231:17
unless p. England keep   188:32
very p. and great   515:18
very stiff and p.   131:12
we ain't p.   177:14
who was so p., so witty   407:22
why were they p.?   286:21
yet not p. to know   383:6
Prouder. .than. .Archbishop   34:8
Proudest: nor the p. of his works   217:13
Prove: believing where we cannot p.   531:39
Celia, let us go   282:5
examine me. .and p. me   393:17
if thou wouldst p. me   156:19
I'll p. more true   477:21
p. all things   68:38
p., and make thine own   16:15
p. anything by figures   126:4
p. false again   111:11
p. it—as clear as a whistle   112:23
p. much in our vows   483:10
wakening and uprising p.   291:4
Proved: almighty be p. thy power   96:24
God p. them   56:23
I p. thee also   397:3
Marlbro's mighty soul was p.   1:9
p. already. .false knaves   469:7
p., a very woe   488:12
p. it again and again   295:18
p. it—'twas no matter   116:30
p. me, and saw my works   397:30
p. most royally   438:10
p. they weren't   297:18
p. upon our pulses   289:34
thou, O God, hast p. us   396:1
upon me p.   488:7
Proven, nor yet disproven   527:21
Provençal: dance, and P. song   287:24
Provence: in P. call'd   285:26
P. and La Palie   146:33
Provender: appoint him store of p.   451:6
nought but p.   469:26
Proverb: p. and a byword   47:41
p. is much matter   212:10
p. is no p. . .till. .illustrated   290:19
p. is one man's wit   414:3
p. is something musty   435:22
Proverb'd with a grandsire phrase   477:5
Proverbs: King Solomon wrote the P.   361:7
patch grief with p.   469:12
Provide: God will p. for sacrifice   291:5
God will p. himself a lamb   44:55
good the gods p.   191:9
Provided: p. by the Parish   390:23
p. for   174:38
Providence: assert eternal P.   344:4
behind a frowning p.   161:18
dare trust in His p.   559:27
even God's p.   252:19
leave the future to. .P.   24:24
P. fashioned us holler   319:18
p., foreknowledge   345:29
P. in it all   179:33
p. in the fall of a sparrow   437:34
P. kept it from being. .worse   236:40
P. sits up aloft   173:7
P. their guide   349:31
to mortals is a p.   231:29
trust in P.   36:33
Province: all knowledge. .my p.   28:1
p. they have desolated   222:35
these limbs, her P.   185:4
Provinces: kiss'd away kingdoms and p.   424:24
obedience of distant p.   324:24
Provincial: worse than p. . . parochial   268:2
Proving: nothing worthy p.   527:21
Provision: make not p. for the flesh   66:14
Provisions short   362:11
Provisos: horrid p.   156:15
Provocation: as in the p.   397:29
what p. I have had   386:22
Provoke: do they p. me to anger?   55:15
p. eyes and whispers   156:13
p. not your children   68:8
p. themselves to the confusion   55:15
p. the silent dust   230:3
p. the years to bring   576:15

INDEX

Provoked: God is p. every day 392:7
  not easily p. 66:45
Provoking..to be called an egg 131:3
Prow: emerging p. 18:16
  their head the p. 191:29
  with pushing p. 93:20
  Youth on the p. 229:23
Prowess: in p. and great deed 234:8
Prowl: p. and p. around 361:13
Prowling beasts 506:8
Prudence is a rich..old maid 77:9
Prudent: every pleasing, every p.
  part 384:33
  my p. course 319:22
Prudenter agas 13:12
Prudentia: quantilla p. regitur 372:15
  si sit p. 283:25
Prudently: thee ruleth p. 195:7
Prudes: p. for proctors 538:7
  strictest p...know it 401:24
Prune thou thy words 364:9
Prunella: leather or p. 384:7
Prunes and prism 176:1
Pruninghooks: spears into p. 52:31
Prusse: industrie nationale de la P. 353:4
Prussia: military domination of P. 21:6
  national industry of P. 353:4
  when P. hurried 418:11
Prussian: French, or Turk, or P. 221:25
Prussians: others may be P. 176:17
Prussic acid: she drank P. 34:32
Pry: never p. 97:25
  p. that out of a Boston man 251:16
  securely p. 191:30
Psalm: grindest..the Hundredth
  P. 121:13
  practising the hundredth p. 119:26
  p. of green days 404:22
  singing the Hundredth P. 316:4
Psalmist: along the P.'s music 88:25
  sweet p. of Israel 47:38
Psalms: Church with p. must shout 243:24
  glad in him with p. 397:25
  King David wrote the P. 361:7
  p. and hymns 68:5
  purloins the P. 117:18
  sonnets turn'd to holy p. 377:4
Psaltery: gay p. 137:6
  sackbut, p., dulcimer 55:36
Psyche: with P., my Soul 381:2
  your mournful P. 287:20
Ptarmigan that whitens 531:2
Pub: pavender, or p. 414:6
  take me to a p. 140:5
Public: abuse in p. 78:20
  across a crowded p. place 374:9
  along the p. way 160:30
  as if I was a p. meeting 552:22
  assumes a p. trust..p. property 268:28
  bear the p. burden 402:5
  British p...fits of morality 325:15
  catch a mouse..in p. 231:22
  convartin' p. trusts 319:20
  coquetry of p. opinion 103:10
  dead corpse of the P. Credit 563:4
  deliberation..and p. care 345:24
  echoes back the p. voice 279:1
  exempt from p. haunt 426:30
  first caught the ear of the British
    p. 491:6
  for the p. good 159:8
  great organ of p. opinion 180:22
  injustice..of service to the p. 282:21
  in the way of..a p. duty 229:2
  loudest complainers for the p. 102:2
  mass of p. wrongs 305:14
  noblest motive is the p. good 511:20
  nor p. flame..dares to shine 381:27
  nor p. men, nor cheering crowds 584:21
  on which the p. thinks long 278:8
  peace..and p. calm 16:25
  pot of paint in the p.'s face 412:22
  p. affairs vex no man 275:12
  p. be damned 551:12
  p. care..not forgiven 140:4
  p. folly breeds 164:6
  p. man of light and leading 182:30
  p. mischief in my mirth 162:39
  p. stock of harmless pleasure 278:7
  p., though dull 523:9
  some to p. strife 384:36

Public (cont.)
  sound of p. scorn 349:20
  speak in p. on the stage 202:16
  taste for..p. executions 182:23
  to the p. good..yield 350:32
  vexes p. men 541:21
  well, British P. 95:29
  you are sad, my P. 504:3
Publican: like a fawning p. 463:17
Publicans: eateth..with p. and
  sinners 58:38
  even the p. the same 57:53
Public school: microcosm of a p. 182:38
Public schools: fill the p. with silk 329:24
  p...nurseries of all vice 204:19
  p...public folly 164:6
Publish: I'll p., right or wrong 117:9
  p. and be damned 564:26
  p. it not in the streets 47:29
  p. it to all the nation 401:27
Publisher: Barabbas was a p. 123:14
Publishing: to good too be worth p. 490:42
Puck: streak of P. 241:20
Pudding: chieftain o' the p.-race 106:4
  George in p. time 7:12
  make a p...translate Epictetus 270:5
  p. against empty praise 381:11
  p. and pie 366:22
  p. in his belly 439:35
Puddings: eats the pies and p. 249:22
Pudicitiam: P. Saturno rege mora-
  tam in terris 283:7
  p. suo matris indicet ore 133:6
Pudor: purpureusque p. 371:17
Pudori: animam praeferre p. 283:14
Puellae: multae optavere p. 133:9
Puellis: vixi p. nuper idoneus 260:12
Puer: formose p. 555:21
  incipe, parve p. 556:1, 2
  quis..p. in rosa perfusus 258:10
Pueri: multi illum p. 133:9
Puero: laudator temporis acti se p. 256:2
  maxime debetur p. reverentia 284:3
Pueros: ne p. coram populo..trucidet 256:3
Puff: his friends all united to p. 523:9
  pause, and p. 159:17
  p. direct..p. preliminary 499:27
  p. of a dunce 225:33
  p. the prostitute away 194:22
  solemn interposing p. 159:17
Puffed: not p. up 66:45
  p. and reckless libertine 431:23
  p. up with this retinue 442:21
Puffeth: knowledge p. up 66:33
Puffing: blinking, p., rolling his
  head 325:32
  p. is of various sorts 499:27
Puffs: p., powders, patches 385:9
  sliding p. 294:29
Pug: most charming p. 208:29
Pugging: my p. tooth 485:16
Pugilist: put in the p. 28:25
Pugnas vitio parentum 258:3
Puissant: noble and p. nation 352:15
  p. pike 444:15
Puking: mewling and p. 427:21
Pulchrior evenit 260:22
Pulchritudo tam antiqua 21:22
Pulchrum: qui quid sit p. 256:21
Pull: I will p. the pink 107:30
  ne'er p. your hat 460:20
  p. for the shore 415:6
  p. his weight 409:1
  p. it out and strike it 139:18
  p. out on the trail 298:27
  rather a sudden p. up 179:7
Pulled: can be p. up 196:19
  p. the gowans fine 104:13
Puller down of kings 446:4
Pulling: here p. down 332:12
  live by p. off the hat 231:25
  p. in one's horse 237:22
Pulls: p. up on the swings 135:2
  who p. me down? 330:7
Pulp: p. so bitter 544:25
  savoury p. they chew 347:14
  swell to melting p. 285:1
Pulpit: politics and the p. 102:5
  p., drum ecclesiastic 110:3
Pulpits: Babylonian p. 102:8
  p. and Sundays 245:5

Pulsanda: pede libero p. tellus 258:28
Pulse: feeling a woman's p. 512:24
  feel that p. no more 356:20
  his p. failing 189:20
  his quick beating p. 335:28
  lost p. of feeling 15:6
  my p. like a soft drum 292:20
  p. begins to throb 83:13
  p. in the eternal mind 84:21
  p. like a cannon 200:3
  very p. of the machine 580:21
Pulses: proved upon our p. 289:34
Pulveris exigui iactu 556:22
Pulvis et umbra sumus 260:26
Pumice: beside a p. isle 496:8
Pumpkins: where the early p. blow 311:12
Pumps: your p. are strange 303:9
Pun: exhale it in a p. 307:6
  make so vile a p. 172:14
Punch: p. in the presence 83:1
  some sipping p. 578:27
Punched: his Brains they p. in 562:24
Punctilio: your dam p. 337:30
Punctual Delivery Company 176:37
Punctuality is the politeness of
  kings 318:23
Punctually: others will p. come 567:24
Pundit or Papist 387:21
Punica fide 415:5
Punished: p. in the sight of men 56:23
  sent to Hell, Sir, and p. 275:20
Punishment: all p. is mischief 42:22
  object of p. 329:8
  oh, p.! 170:21, 22
  power of p. is to silence 278:21
  p. fit the crime 220:2
  p...greater than I can bear 44:32
Punishments: charged with p. 241:19
  neither rewards nor p. 267:17
Puns: from politics to p. 387:23
Punt: as the slow p. swings 18:9
Puny subject strikes 475:3
Pupil: too far in years to be a p. 474:15
Puppets: p., best and worst 94:46
  shut up the box and the p. 542:40
Puppy: drink, p., drink 568:22
  mongrel, p., whelp 225:20
Puppy-dogs' tails 369:12
Purblind: p. race 530:8
  p., wayward boy 455:8
Purchase: it is all a p. 255:6
Pure: because my heart is p. 540:11
  be thou..as p. as snow 434:11
  be warm, but p. 117:17
  bless'd are the p. in heart 291:13
  blessed are the p. in heart 57:39
  chooseth the p. in heart 291:14
  every p. and wise spirit 200:41
  hearts just as p. and fair 219:2
  is she not p.? 413:31
  kept thy truth so p. 351:20
  live p., speak true 530:4
  more p., as tempted more 575:7
  more p. than his maker 48:49
  my spirit p. and clear 540:6
  nation of p. philosophers 28:32
  not quite—so p. as you 112:20
  particularly p. young man 220:28
  p. and complete sorrow 548:8
  p. and eloquent blood 186:13
  p. as the naked heavens 577:15
  p. from the night 336:11
  p. lovers' souls 185:2
  p. mind..refuses apple-dump-
    lings 306:9
  P., Ornate, and Grotesque 29:8
  real Simon P. 134:5
  slumbers, p. and light 291:11
  song and blood are p. 336:37
  to the p. all things are p. 306:33
  truth is rarely p. 569:20
  unto the p. all things are p. 69:4
  what God declares p. 347:25
  whatsoever things are p. 68:27
  world where all are p. 530:16
  your down..p. 166:4
Purely: I love thee p. 88:24
Purer: name dearer and p. 117:32
  p. than the purest 90:2
  p. with the other half 436:4
Purest: gem of p. ray serene 230:5

Purest (cont.)
purer than the p. 90:2
p. and most thoughtful minds 413:14
p. of human pleasures 26:19
p. soul..clayey tenament 125:6
Purgatorial: black, p. rails 285:13
Purgatory: in a sort of P. blind 285:10
no other p. but a woman 38:6
p. of men 209:8
to P. fire thou com'st 31:13
Purge: I'll p., and leave sack 441:6
p. it to..health 461:1
p. me with hyssop 395:8
p. this choler 474:9
quietness..would p. 423:34
Purged: p. away but with blood 85:6
p. the air of pestilence 481:31
Purger: violent p. of goods 109:22
Purified: every creature shall be p. 330:3
Purifies: that which p. us is trial 352:9
Puritan: grand old P. anthem 316:4
I saw a P.-one 79:18
kind of p. 482:33
P. hated bear-baiting 326:1
Puriter: si vitam p. egi 133:15
Purity: air and Angels' p. 184:5
all p., all trial 428:28
awful p. 202:22
brightness, p., and truth 371:12
grammatical p. 278:13
p. and place and innocence 347:25
p. is the feminine 237:23
p., painful and pleading 372:18
Purlieus: dusty p. of the law 533:10
within the p. of the Law 201:33
Purling stream 2:3
Purloins the Psalms 117:18
Puro e disposto a salire 168:25
Purple: blossom in p. and red 536:15
flush'd with a p. grace 191:3
gleaming in p. and gold 118:37
in p. nor in pall 5:16
Man of p. cheer 578:29
on the p. sea 322:18
over the p. vest 324:9
p. all the ground 342:31
p. and fine linen 62:23
P. Cow 100:1, 2
p. light of love 231:9
p. the sails 424:6
p. with love's wound 466:39
ran p. to the sea 344:32
seller of p. 64:54
spirted p. of the vats 539:4
what p. fritillaries 18:29
wrapped in p. robes 584:7
Purple-lined palace 286:40
Purples: daisies, and long p. 437:1
morn p. the east 348:23
Purple-stained mouth 287:24
Purpose: better shall my p. work 470:20
carry p. up 80:30
change to p. strong 364:9
clean from the p. 448:34
embrace the p. of God 536:25
enjoys himself except for a noble p. 243:14
far-reaching in p. 254:4
for some unaccountable p. 176:2
infirm of p. 458:14
mark of insincerity of p. 503:15
my p. holds 541:3
one increasing p. 534:29
p. in liquidity 83:24
p. lose 435:10
pushes his prudent p. 587:6
shake my fell p. 457:3
their flighty p. 460:14
this unconquerable p...realized 307:12
time to every p. 51:3
to what p. is this waste? 60:36
with p. of its own 579:10
working His p. out 3:8
Purposed: p. by the mighty gods 449:21
sworn, and..stedfastly p. 399:21
Purposes: execute their aery p. 344:30
p. mistook 438:9
Purpureal: invested with p. gleams 577:13
Purpureus..pannus 255:10
Purr myself to sleep 550:20
Purse: consumption of the p. 441:26

Purse (cont.)
costly..as thy p. can buy 431:25
empty p. 80:3
in silken or in leathern p. 378:17
my fool my p. 470:19
my p., my person 463:2
take a p. in open court 111:26
who steals my p. 471:30
Purses: light gains..heavy p. 25:36
Pursue: accipitrine to p. 544:3
as Love wist to p. 544:16
bold only to p. 491:28
great thing to p. 91:41
I'll ne'er p. revenge 155:37
it will p. 280:20
knowing it, p. 194:23
my desires..e'er since p. me 481:31
provokes me always to p. 375:4
p. him and paw him 546:44
p. my reason to an O altitudo! 86:8
p...the phantoms of hope 278:14
p. the triumph 384:16
p. things which are just 24:24
what shadows we p. 100:17
Pursued: p. by a bear 485:15
p. it with forks and hope 128:11
p. with yell and blow 148:24
you who are the p. 490:18
Pursuers: fliers and p. 324:15
Pursueth: flee when no man p. 50:49
Pursuing: faint, yet p. 46:54
or he is p. 48:3
p. of the best ends 266:10
still p., learn to labour 317:8
Pursuit: mad in p. 488:12
p. of happiness 11:11, 268:19
p. of knowledge under difficulties 179:3
rhymes for his p. 96:27
slow in p. 467:20
strong in p. 503:5
that long p. 544:28
vain p. of This and That 206:22
what mad p.? 287:7
Pursy: these p. times 436:3
Purtenance: with the p. thereof 45:46
Purus: integer vitae scelerisque p. 258:22
Push: Philosophy..p. beyond her mark 532:30
p. off..well in order 541:3
p. us from our stools 459:17
squarely p. the logic 296:14
tarry till they p. us 452:5
through city crowds..p. 151:27
Pushes his prudent purpose 587:6
Pushing young particle 221:8
Pusillanimity: badge of p. 442:21
Puss-gentleman..all perfume 159:19
Pussy: I like little P. 367:8
O lovely P.! O P., my love 311:24
p. and I very gently will play 367:8
p.'s in the well 366:18
what a beautiful P. 311:24
Pussy-cat: Owl and the P. 311:24
p., where have you been? 368:14
Put: God had p. it there 305:20
never be p. out 310:11
p. away childish things 66:46
p. down Richard 438:36
p. it down a we 179:14
p. off Holiness 75:13
p. off thy shoes 45:34
p. on Christ 391:1
p. out the light 473:11
when I p. out to sea 528:22
who p. her in? 366:18
Putrefaction: preserve it from p. 275:27
Puts: p. his mind to yours 275:7
today he p. forth 446:24
Putting: eas'd the p. off..disguises 347:25
Putty, brass, an' paint 301:2
Puzzle: every single woman..a p. 542:14
p. the devil 107:36
schoolmasters p. their brain 226:2
Puzzles: nothing p. me more than time and space 307:10
p. the will 434:4
Puzzling world 196:23
Pye: when the P. was open'd 512:5
shine with P. 117:14
Pym and such carles 90:16

Pyramid: build me a P. 303:8
chief of the P. 288:29
star-y-pointing p. 351:8
Pyramides: du haut de ces p. 361:1
Pyramids: its p. and tall memorials 516:19
p. of sweetmeats 194:16
Pyramus: death of P. and Thisby 466:23
Pyrenees: tease in the high P. 42:9
Pyrénées: il n'y a plus de P. 318:20
Pyrrha: quis..puer..P.? 258:10
Pyrrhic: P. dance as yet 116:2
where is the P. phalanx 116:2
Pyrrhus: rugged P. 433:26
Pythagoras: ah, P.' metempsychosis 330:10
'Ipse' autem erat P. 145:6
mystical way of P. 86:10
opinion of P. 484:22
P. was misunderstood 200:41
Python: bought a P. from a man 41:34

Q

Quack: potent q. 165:20
Quacks—not physicians 253:14
Quad: about in the Q. 5:27, 305:10
Quadrangular: with spots q. 163:29
Quadrigis petimus bene vivere 257:4
Quadripedante..sonitu quatit ungula 555:6
Quadruped: hairy q...probably arboreal 169:4
Quadruviis: in q. et angiportis 133:5
Quaerebam: ibi te q. 21:22
q. quid amarem 21:17
Quaerimus: superos quid q. ultra 320:26
Quaesieris: tu ne q., scire nefas 258:16
Quaesiveris: nec te q. extra 378:1
Quaff: my boy George q. else 90:18
Quaffed: jested, q., and swore 188:29
Quaffing: laughing, q., and unthinking 193:31
Quagmire: lost in the q. 530:26
Quail: when he meant to q. 426:1
Quails: we long for q. 193:7
Quaint: what q. honour 333:9
Quake: as an aspes leef she gan to q. 138:33
q. to say they love 501:29
Quaker: we turned out the Q. 28:25
Qualifications: what are his q.? 84:27(-85)
Qualified my mind to think justly 406:15
Qualis: non sum q. eram 260:17
Qualité: les gens de q. savent tout 354:5
Qualities: endued with such q. 198:3
his q. are reigning still 119:19
Quality: all q., pride, pomp 472:3
composition and fierce q. 452:14
give..highest q. to your moments 374:13
persons of the best q..cheated 202:13
q. and fabric more divine 579:38
q. of mercy 464:33
q. of my lord 470:9
taste of your q. 433:24
unbecoming a man of q. 154:31
Qualms: with many, many q. 361:7
Quangle-Wangle Quee 312:11
Quanta qualia sunt..sabbata 1:1
Quantities: for false q., was whipt 194:26
Quantity: all in q. 529:20
q. of dirty lands 483:8
Quantum o' the sin 105:19
Quarelets of pearl 246:25
Quarles is saved 381:14
Quarrel: entrance to a q. 431:25
find q. in a straw 436:17
hath his q. just 445:30, 491:9
in a false q...no true valour 460:14
justice of my q. 7:7, 331:9
mountain and the squirrel..had a q. 199:18
q...very pretty q. 500:26
q. with my bread and butter 520:14
q. with the noblest grace 479:44
quick in q. 427:21
quite forgot their q. 130:6
standing revenue..perpetual q. 101:8

INDEX

Quarrelled with his wife 376:18
Quarrelling: one species of super-
  stit'on . . a q. 265:13
  q. wi' the equawtor 365:12
Quarrels: no q., murmurs 166:15
  thy head is as full of q. 478:11
  who in q. interpose 215:26
Quarrelsome: countercheck q. 428:37
Quarries: rough q. rocks 470:2
Quarry: marked-down q. 490:18
  your face my q. was 78:2
Quarry-slave: like the q. at night 98:3
Quarter: beggar squealin' out for q. 302:14
  opposite q. of the heavens 100:9
Quartered safe out 'ere 297:1
Quarterly: foul like the Q. 240:7
  'I,' says the Q. 118:2
  nothing a-year, paid q. 518:41
Quartern loaf and Luddites rise 504:5
Quartos: then q. . . well-order'd 164:36
Quatit: mente q. solida 259:21
Quatuor sunt genera Idolorum 28:6
Quean: flaunting, extravagant q. 500:39
Queen: another Sheba 572:3
  Astarte, Q. of Heaven 344:31
  at length apparent q. 347:19
  British warrior q. 158:29
  cold q. of England 141:4
  come not near our fairy q. 466:44
  cradle of the fairy q. 467:4
  every lady would be q. 384:36
  every lass a q. 293:19
  fought for Q. and Faith 540:3
  Gawd save the Q. 301:13
  grace a summer q. 419:7
  heart the Q. leant on 93:33
  Helen, Sparta's q. 411:35
  he was the Q.'s luve 30:10
  home life of our . . Q. 7:2
  I am England's Q. 208:30
  I come, my q. 425:22
  if you were q. of pleasure 524:31
  I'm to be Q. o' the May 536:26
  I saw the Q. of France 102:11
  I would not be a q. 446:17
  jealous q. of heaven 429:19
  King asked the Q. 339:17
  laughing q. 265:23
  Menelaus' q. 480:37
  mobled q. 433:28
  Mother, Wife, and Q. 539:12
  now our q. 430:23
  old Soldier of the Q.'s 5:9
  q. and huntress 279:31
  Q. had four Maries 31:18
  q. in a vesture of gold 394:23
  q. it no inch further 485:32
  q., long dead 94:19
  Q. Mab hath been with you 477:7
  q., my lord, is dead 461:4
  q. of curds and cream 485:28
  Q. of Hearts 129:27, 368:15
  Q. of land and sea 184:2
  q. of Scots . . a fair son 197:36
  Q. of Sheba 47:42
  Q. of the Sovereign South 304:5
  q. of tongues 281:26
  q. rose 536:14
  Q.'s government . . carried on 564:20
  Q. was in her chamber 208:29
  q. was in the parlour 368:20
  Q., we thee implore 8:11
  q., with swarthy cheeks 529:9
  regular royal Q. 218:21
  remembrance of a weeping q. 475:14
  royal makings of a q. 447:2
  Ruler of the Q.'s Navee 221:15
  sovereign q., of all delights 35:22
  sung by a fair q. 440:4
  sung 'God save the Q.' 294:17
  tear into the Q.'s ear 73:16
  then his q. 495:2
  this beggar maid . . be my q. 528:2
  to look at the q. 368:14
  to Mary Q. the praise 149:27
  your anointed Q. 198:3
Queens: all the powerful Kings
  and Q. 186:31
  all your acts are q. 485:27
  blood of q. and kings 285:19
  idle and careless q. 413:9

Queens (cont.)
  no more housewives, but q. 413:8
  q. have died 361:5
  Q. hereafter shall be glad 189:19
  q. to your lovers 413:9
  q. you must always be 413:9
Queensberry: between me and the
  Duchess of Q. 558:12
Queer: ill-tempered q. 311:9
Queer Street: is full of lodgers 178:17
Quell: Music raise and q. 191:36
  q. the mighty 350:36
Quench: if I q. thee 473:11
  q. its speed 93:20
  q. my great love 219:8
  smoking flax . . not q. 54:15
  waters cannot q. love 52:23
Quenched: q. in the chaste beams 466:39
  q. their orbs 346:19
  q. the stelled fires 453:34
  what hath q. them 458:2
Querentis: Gracchos de seditione q. 282:26
Querimoniis: nec malis divulsus q. 258:19
Querulus: difficilis, q. 256:2
Quest: crowner's q. law 437:4
  Jack Redskin on the Q. 140:6
  Q. of the Golden Girl 313:6
  to whose winding q. 551:15
  what thy q.? 81:26
Questing: q. beast 328:8
  q. of thirty couple hounds 328:4
Question: harm nor q. much 185:4
  immediately struck out of the q. 126:42
  in danger to be called in q. 65:9
  more we arg'ed the q. 125:21
  others abide our q. 17:23
  put the q. by 528:27
  'q. is,' said Humpty Dumpty 131:7
  q. not, but . . labour 227:34
  q. not to be asked 439:33
  q. with my jealous thought 487:7
  such a silly q. 513:1
  that is the q. 434:4
  that q.'s out of my part 482:19
  who but infants q. 410:20
Questionable: such a q. shape 431:32
Questioned: still q. me 470:2
Questioning: q. is not the mode
  of conversation 273:2
  sweetly 244:21
Questionings: obstinate q. 576:18
Questions: answered three q. 128:29
  ask no q. but the price 279:3
  solves for thee all q. 90:43
  them that asks no q. 301:18
  they ask no q. 196:31
Quibble is to Shakespeare 278:23
Quibbles: in q., angel and archangel join 386:15
Quick: apprehensive, q., forgetive 442:21
  as q. a growth 246:3
  dead, q., I know not how 232:15
  how q. and fresh art thou 481:30
  less q. to spring again 18:30
  q. as a flash 'tis gone 292:15
  q. as you can 170:25
  q. in quarrel 427:21
  quiet to q. bosoms 113:42
  some cry 'Q.' 538:3
  word of God is q. 69:8
Quicken thou me in thy law 399:15
Quickened: pure sunbeam q. thee 308:31
  q. his own soul 393:9
  q. now with fire 232:15
  you hath he q. 67:50
Quickeneth: spirit that q. 63:23
Quicker unto good 532:24
Quick-ey'd Love 244:21
Quickly: I am too q. won 477:20
  I come q. 72:8
  sit down q. 62:19
  well it were done q. 457:7
  went q. over it 99:18
Quickness: q. of his wit and invention 212:18
  too much q. ever to be taught 384:32
Quicksands: better acquainted
  with . . the q. 290:7
Quid: his Wife and a Tertium Q. 304:52
Quiddities: in thy quips and thy
  q.? 438:18

Quies: prima q. mortalibus 554:5
Quiescence: boasts his q. 93:5
Quiescent: pulveris exigui . . q. 556:22
Quiet: all q. along the Potomac 40:2, 326:14
  All Q. on the Western Front 406:7
  anythin' for a q. life 179:28
  be q.; and go a-Angling 559:27
  breathless q., after . . ills 15:14
  Doctor Q. 520:23
  easy live and q. die 419:16
  entertain . . with q. hours 440:26
  eye made q. 581:25
  fair q. . . and Innocence 332:14
  fie upon this q. life! 439:13
  lain still and been q. 48:45
  Lethe's gloom but not its q. 122:2
  lives of q. desperation 546:32
  materials to keep children q. 519:3
  meek and q. spirit 70:1
  men, come to q. 384:36
  my scallop-shell of q. 405:9
  q. and rest and desire 359:7
  q. as a nun 577:1
  q. did q. remain 172:5
  q. mind 518:1
  q. mind is worse 548:16
  q. sleep and a sweet dream 334:12
  q. to quick bosoms 113:42
  q. us in a death so noble 351:6
  retirement, rural q. 546:13
  rich, q., and infamous 324:32
  seas are q. 557:24
  shining to the q. moon 151:25
  soldier . . a q., grave, man 29:6
  soul's q. 209:25
  spirit so still and q. 470:1
  study to be q. 68:36
  such society as is q., wise 498:15
  tree of man was never q. 263:8
  where the world is q. 523:17
  with a q. mind 389:48
Quiet-coloured end of evening 93:10
Quieted by hope 96:31
Quietly: q. and without fear 99:2
  q. inurn'd 431:32(-432)
  q. shining to the quiet moon 151:25
  when dead, lie as q. 196:3
Quietness: bride of q. 287:6
  impress with q. and beauty 582:3
  in q. and in confidence 53:39
  q., grown sick of rest 423:34
Quietus: his q. make 434:4
Quill: his substance . . through a q. 306:18
  read or hold a q. 77:28
  wren with little q. 467:6
Quillets: sharp q. of the law 445:20
Quills: q. upon the fretful por-
  pentine 432:9
  stops of various q. 343:6
Quinapalus: what says Q.? 482:12
Quince: slices of q. 312:3
Quincunx of heaven runs low 85:18
Quinquereme of Nineveh 333:20
Quinta: la q. columna 353:7
Quintessence: all the heavenly q. 331:2
  this q. of dust 433:15
Quintilian: made Q. stare 351:17
Quip modest 428:37
Quips: q. and cranks 341:28
  thy q. and thy quiddities? 438:18
Quire: full-voiced q. below 341:24
  q. of bad verses 324:35
Quires and Places where they sing 388:27
Quiring to the young-eyed cherubins 465:18
Quit: all q. their sphere 383:13
  John and I are more than q. 401:27
  may not q. the post 535:25
  q. for the next 442:13
  q. himself like Samson 351:5
  q. in a single kiss 81:12
  q., oh q. this mortal frame 381:28
  q., q., for shame 517:11
  q. thy state 244:5
  q. you like men 67:19
  q. yourselves like men 47:8
Quite: q. another thing 112:25
  q., q. for ever dead 155:21
  that young man is not q. the thing 22:14

R

Quiver: he stakes his q. 321:14
his q. full of them 399:35
q. and beat of the sea 525:19
spent lights q. and gleam 15:24
Quivering within the wave's..day 496:8
Quivers: emptying of q. 521:30
Quo: q., *Musa, tendis?* 259:24
q. *vadis?* 63:59
Quocumque modo rem 256:19
Quotation: classical q...the *parole* 274:31
every q. contributes 277:22
Quotations: back'd..with q. 402:1
furn shes no q. 376:12
I hate q. 201:2
Quote: kill you if you q. it 100:2
my faults ye q. 308:24
we all q. 201:5
Quoter: first q. 201:6

Rabbit: gone to get a r. skin 366:11
r. fondles his..face 527:23
r. in a snare 512:12
Rabble: *Mob*, Parliament, R. 147:17
your army..a base r. 101:13
Rabboni: saith unto him, R. 64:7
Rabelais: *Mob*,' easy chair 382:14
soul of R...in a dry place 153:10
Rabelaisii: anima R. *habitans in sicco* 153:10
Race: all is r. 182:35
another r. hath been 576:22(−577)
challenge me the r. 333:1
coursers of ethereal r. 231:14
didst Thou love the r.? 267:15
fainting, dispirited r. 17:20
feather'd r. with pinions 211:25
Foal of an oppressed r. 152:19
giant r. before the flood 192:9
godly r. 224:18, 225:18
held the human r. in scorn 40:35
he rides a r.! 160:2
hindered in running the r. 389:25
human r., to which so many
of my readers belong 142:17
idiot r. to honour lost 107:23
in a tree did end their r. 332:16
I wish I loved the Human R. 405:16
last of a r. in ruin 140:14
life's r. well run 373:10
loftier r...shall rise 526:1
lull in the hot r. 15:6
moody, murmuring r. 190:10
most pernicious r. of..vermin 519:15
moved among my r. 516:16
my r. of glory run, and r. of
shame 350:30
no longer tolerate the r. 29:19
our r. should not cease to labour 513:31
purblind r. of miserable men 530:8
r. between education and catastrophe 564:29
r. is not to the swift 51:22
r. that is set before us 69:18
r. that long in darkness 421:6
run out thy r. 351:31
run the r. with Death 275:28
run the straight r. 354:11
since I joined the human r. 222:24
slinks out of the r. 352:9
slow and steady wins the r. 315:4
sooner will his r. be run 247:10
their succeeding r. 183:20
type of all her r. 188:30
waters in their wintry r. 585:22
what avails the sceptred r.! 308:14
when first the human r. 105:25
whose r. is just begun 498:3
winding-sheet of Edward's r. 229:22
with the r. of Saints 245:22
woes that curse our r. 218:15
Races: chips to the trusting native
r. 143:31
r. of Europe are melting 587:18
soft in the level r. 80:19
Rachel: R. weeping for her children 57:26
seven years for R. 45:6

Rachel-and-Leah: this R. is mar-
riage 146:27
Rack: leave not a r. behind 480:8
r. dislimns 425:20
r. of a too easy chair 381:25
r. of this tough world 454:27
r. the name of God 329:25
set me on the r. 472:1
then we r. the value 469:5
Racked with deep despair 344:15
Racker: ihr R., *wollt ihr ewig leben?* 211:23
Rackets: our r. to these balls 443:11
Rackrent: like Sir Condy R. 325:29
Racks, gibbets, halters 370:10
Radiance: white r. of Eternity 492:15
Radiancy: what r. of glory 362:1
Radiant: r. frost 498:13
r. with ardour divine 17:20
rare and r. maiden 380:23
Radicals: few r. have good diges-
tions 111:37
Radish: like a forked r. 442:15
r. and an egg 163:27
Radium: lucis tuae r. 310:9
Raft: republic is a r. 4:21
Rafters: sheds with smoky r. 340:17
Rag: bloomin' old r. over 'ead 304:1
to a r. and a bone 303:12
Ragamuffins: led my r. 440:34
Rage: all Heaven in a R. 73:19
ape an ancient r. 141:23
doubtful battle where to r. 1:10
hard, and full of r. 465:20
hard-favour'd r. 443:24
heathen so furiously r. 391:47
Heav'n has no r. 155:20
in an after R. destroy 207:18
I r., I melt, I burn 214:6
not die here in a r. 519:31
potent victor in his r. 344:13
r. for saying something 270:31
r. of the vulture 113:1
r. to set things right 89:25
repress'd their noble r. 230:5
shunning civil r. 192:13
strong without r. 172:10
swell the soul to r. 191:12
void of noble r. 532:19
waves..r. horribly 397:23
with this r. shall beauty hold a
plea? 487:13
writing increaseth r. 232:15
Rages: furious winter's r. 430:1
r. of the ages 236:6
sudden she r. 215:14
Ragged: pair of r. claws 197:19
r. cowt's been known 105:12
rolling up r. and brown 293:26
to the r. infant 165:17
Raggedness: looped and window'd
r. 453:14
Raging: r. of the sea 395:28
r. of the skies 122:26
strong drink is r. 50:23
Ragioniam: non r. di lor 168:18
Ragout: child..in a..r. 520:3
Rags: fluttered into r. 346:26
no scandal like r. 203:8
our righteousnesses..filthy r. 55:8
r., and hags 150:28
r. of time 186:20
tear a passion..to very r. 434:15
unwomanly r. 253:22
Ragtime: Alexander's R. Band 43:16
Raid on the inarticulate 197:9
Rail: her six young on the r. 92:27
I'll r. and brawl 479:7
r. against all the first-born 427:10
r. at the ill 536:25
r. on the Lord's anointed 476:26
rivals r. 278:27
say that she r. 479:4
suffers anybody else to r. at me 155:22
whiles I am a beggar, I will r. 447:26
Rail'd on Lady Fortune 427:12
Railing: r. at life 143:8
r. for r. 70:3
tedious as a..r. wife 440:2
Railroad: work like a digger on the
r. 199:33
you enterprised a r. 413:1

Rails: he r...on me, my bargains 463:17
purgatorial r. 285:13
Railway: its spires..seen from the
r. 363:22
Railway-share: threatened..with
a r. 128:11
Railway-Ticket: in his hat a R. 311:19
Raiment: body than r. 58:11
clothed in soft r. 59:6
he purchased r. 300:18
in r. of needle-work 394:25
in sparkling r. bright 4:12
r. of camel's hair 57:29
winds..unto her as r. 521:30(−522)
your r. all red 322:25
Rain: abundance of r. 48:4
after the r. 493:1
angels of r. and lightning 496:5
arrowy r. 336:12
borne the dirt and r. 359:4
case o' r. 121:2
caverns of r. 493:1
cheer it after r. 161:21
cloud..outwept its r. 491:20
come down like the r. 396:24
deep-sea r. 298:27
dismal r. 503:13
droppeth as the gentle r. 464:33
flung it to the Winds like R. 205:28
former and the latter r. 389:21
hath the r. a father? 49:23
heavens r. odours 483:25
in thunder, lightning, or in r. 456:1
like the r...full of refreshment 316:14
mist resembles the r. 316:8
neither let there be r. 47:29
not be able to command the r. 377:18
not hail, or r. 531:37
pack when it begins to r. 452:38
r. and wind beat dark December 429:31
r. cats and dogs 520:25
r. into the little valleys 395:30
r. is on our lips 506:20
r. is over and gone 52:1
r. is past and over 334:16
r. it raineth every day 484:29
r. it raineth on the just 79:7
r. may enter 379:11
r. on the just and..unjust 57:52
r., r., and sun! 530:1
r., r., go away 368:32
r. set early in 95:4
r.'s my choice 407:4
ripple of r. 521:30
rivers, in the greatest r. 373:14
send my roots r. 255:9
sentest a gracious r. 396:6
sliding drop of r. 585:9
small drops of r. 32:16
small r. down can r. 11:11
smell the dew and r. 244:18
soaks up the r. 158:7
soft refreshing r. 121:27
soft with the drops of r. 395:30
stirring dull roots with spring r. 197:27
summer r. 516:16
r. a deluge show'rd 139:1
thro' the drizzling r. 532:9
under snow or r. 142:13
useful trouble of the r. 530:9
volleying r. 18:25
weeping r. 326:20
wet's the r. 170:20
wet with ranging in the r. 231:33
when God..sends r. 407:4
Rainbow: another hue unto the
r. 447:39
awful r. once in heaven 286:42
blend like the r. 356:17
God loves an idle r. 249:12
like a r. shell 409:14
or a fresh r. 119:21
paint the r.'s..hues 418:25
r. and a cuckoo's song 169:21
r. comes and goes 576:2
r. in the sky 530:1, 577:25
r. round about the throne 70:36
r.'s glory is shed 494:20
when I behold a r. 577:25
Rainbows: its varying r. die away 381:26
Rained: as it r. kisses 425:12

Rained (cont.)
beneath a shed while it r.   276:24
r. all kind of sores   472:34
when I awoke, it r.   149:28
Rainfall at morning   516:2
Rain-fed: roar of a r. ford   302:20
Rains: dissolving in r.   492:28
r. are from His dripping wings   585:8
straight r. and tiger sky   336:14
winter's r. and ruins   521:30(–522)
Rainy: dropping in a very r. day   50:46
windy night a r. morrow   487:23
wish him a r. evening   559:11
with r. eyes write sorrow   475:6
Raise: I can r. Thee   244:26
loud your anthems r.   35:2
not for these I r. the song   576:18
r. and erect the mind   24:16
r. me with the just   355:21
r. the genius   381:6
r. the wretched   224:18
r. up commonwealths   190:11
r. up them that fall   389:1
r. your joys   565:4
the Lord shall r. me up   405:12
what is low r. and support   344:4
what passion cannot Music r.?   191:36
Raised: Christ being r.   65:45
he r. a mortal to the skies   191:13
it r. my hair   150:3
r. in incorruption   67:14
r. thee up under the apple tree   52:22
r. the price of everything   324:29
r. the price of literature   270:24
r. up by Christ   532:22
that the new man may be r. up   390:57
though God hath r. me high   198:12
we shall behold them r.   88:14
Raising: by only r. my voice   22:12
drunk and r. Cain   294:26
stop r. corn. . begin r. hell   312:23
Raison: la r. *du plus fort*   209:14
tout le monde a r.   138:44
Raisons: le cœur a ses r.   374:4
Rake: every woman. . a r.   384:36
r. among scholars   325:31
r.'s progress   542:19
thing arm'd with a r.   563:21
Raking: stop r. the muck   409:3
Raleigh: Grenville, R., Drake   362:30
Rallies the ranks   363:5
Rally behind the Virginians   39:2
Ralph: Sir R. the Rover   507:27
Ralpho, thou dost prevaricate   110:25
Ram: old black r.   460:29
r. caught in a thicket   44:56
Rammers: lay their r. by   202:10
Ramos: a terra contingere r.   556:4
Ramp up my genius   281:3
Rampage: on the R.   175:23
Rampallion: you r.   441:29
Rampart: his corse to the r.   572:10
Ramparts: to force my r.   296:4
Rams: mountains skipped like r.   399:3
my r. speed not   35:21
to hearken than the fat of r.   47:16
with shelly horns, r.!   336:38
Ran: in r. . . scissor-man   250:4
I r. it through   470:2
little devils r.   302:32
r. about the room and roared   140:5
r. a hundred years   251:6
r. before Ahab   48:6
r. dismay'd away   465:17
r. down unto the beard   400:3
r. on embattled armies   350:25
they r. both together   64:5
we r., and they r.   327:1
Randal: Lord R., my Son   31:10
Randalls: opening the windows at R.   22:15
Random: to a r. rhyme   183:3
Range: forward let us r.   534:36
r. of practical politics   222:36
Ranged: sea-beasts r. all round   15:24
Ranger: heart of a r.   40:31
Ranges: leave then thy foolish r.   552:2
lost behind the R.   296:9
Ranging: r. for revenge   450:12
wet with r. in the rain   231:33
Rangoon: from R. tó Mandalay   299:10
he can take R.   564:11

Rank: holds on his r.   449:30
in France of the best r.   431:25
in the name of every r.   101:27
man of r. . .[as an author]   274:34
man starts from his r.   124:15
marched, r. on r.   336:17
my offence is r.   435:31
nine 'undred r. an' file   301:16
r. is but the guinea's stamp   105:30
r. me with the. .multitude   463:44
r. tongue blossom into speech   90:12
things r. and gross   430:33(–431)
Ranks: all the r. of angels   503:4
amidst the r. of war   323:5
even the r. of Tuscany   323:28
forming in the r. of war   113:31
in the r. of death   356:27
place in the r.   402:14
quartos, their well-order'd r.   164:36
rallies the r.   363:5
seen in glittering r.   343:16
their r. are breaking   323:6
those craven r.   323:26
Rank-scented many   429:11
Rann and song   586:14
Ransack r. any mind but his own   406:12
r. the ocean   329:23
Ransom: r. captive Israel   362:6
r. of gold   549:30
world's r.   474:22
Rant: when you r. and swear   194:28
Rap: not a r., not a button   171:17
Rapacious and licentious soldiery   101:20
Rape: a r.! a r.!   563:28
Raphael: come, R., this Babe must eat   508:16
R. made a century of sonnets   93:45
R. of the dear Madonnas   94:12
Raphaels: talk'd of their R.   225:35
Rapid: Homer. .eminently r.   20:2
r., blind and fleeting generations   499:8
r., unintelligible patter   222:12
Rapidly: driving r. in a post-chaise   273:4
works done least r.   93:40
Rapids are near   357:16
Rapier: dubbed with unhatched r.   484:15
Rapine: march through r.   222:38
Rapping: some one gently r.   380:22
Rapscallions: kings is mostly r.   550:10
Rapt: not r. above the Pole   348:23
r. one. . godlike forehead   575:17
r., twirling in thy hand   18:10
Rapture: fine careless r.   92:15
in holy r.   105:6
in regenerate r.   411:12
modified r.!   219:30
r. of the forward view   336:45
r. on the lonely shore   114:26
thy r. move   382:33
Raptures: high r. do infuse   558:3
r. and roses of vice   522:23
Rapture-smitten frame   122:34
Rapturous, wild, and ineffable   313:9
Rara: r. avis   283:8
vitio parentum r. *iuventus*   258:3
Rare: delicate and r.   569:5
however r.—r. it be   171:6
indeed a r. one   572:3
miracle of r. device   151:33(–152)
neither rich nor r.   385:27
of a birth as r.   332:5
r. as a day in June   320:17
r. Ben Jonson   282:9
r. gold ring of verse   96:19
r. in our pockets   142:2
rich and r. were the gems   356:30
rough, dense, or r.   346:14
think why love as r.   488:14
Raree-show of Peter's successor   90:32
Rarely: r., r., comest thou   498:11
Rarity of Christian charity   252:18
Rascal: knave, a r.   452:32
lock such r. counters   451:21
muddy-mettled r.   433:33
r. . given me medicines   439:2
rather be called a r.   273:15
Whig. .a r.   277:11
Rascally yea-forsooth knave   441:12
Rascals: lash the r. naked   473:2
law. .take care o' r.   196:22

Rascals (cont.)
r. in all countries   274:6
r., would you live for ever?   211:23
Rash: be not r.   115:10
'do not be r.!' He was not r.   228:15
frank, haughty, r.   322:9
her r. hand in evil hour   349:15
not splenetive and r.   437:23
r. fierce blaze of riot   474:21
r., refined, presumptuous man   124:15
too r., too unadvis'd   477:24
you look rather r.   20:28
Rash-embrac'd despair   464:17
Rashes: green grow the r. O   105:37
Rashly importunate   252:12
Raspberry: 'mid the gorse the r.   543:23
Rasselas: attend to the history of R.   278:14
Rast: ohne Hast, aber ohne R.   224:8
Rat: giant r. of Sumatra   188:16
horse, a r., have life   454:26
how now! a r.?   435:40
I smell a r.   110:25, 407:8
killed the r.   369:6
like a poisoned r. in a hole   519:31
like a r. without a tail   456:10
sound of a r.   94:35
Ratcliffe Road : rolling down the R.   294:26
Rate: play the fool. .at a cheaper r.   161:42
Rated: in the Rialto. .r. me   463:20
rocked it, and r. it   196:2
Ratem: fragilem truci commisit pelago r.   258:5
Rathe primrose   342:31
Rather: I'd r. be a Pagan   582:18
I had much r.   6:20
what a man had r. were true   28:7
Raths: mome r. outgrabe   129:39
Ratify and confirm   391:17
Ratio: seu r. *dederit*   261:6
Ratiocination: pay with r.   110:6
Rational: needs of a r. being   421:8
to himself is a law r.   135:19
with men he can be r.   22:10
Ratione: pro r. *voluntas*   283:9
Rations: live upon our daily r.   174:8
Ratisbon: we French stormed R.   92:23
Rat-riddled stairs   93:19
Rats: for the thieving r.   171:10
land-r. and water-r.   463:15
let's sing of r.   228:19
mice and r. . . Tom's food   453:24
Rattle: hearing 'em r. a little   203:9
not care for the child's r.   271:23
pleased with a r.   383:30
r. his bones   365:6
r. of a globe   191:17
r. of new-drawn steel   296:1
spoiled his nice new r.   130:6
war's r. . .groans of the dying   418:13
Rattle-note: his r. unvaried   336:9
Rattlesnake: thought he saw a R.   128:17
Rattling: for the r. of a coach   186:32
r. bones together fly   192:40
r. o'er the stony street   113:26
Ravage with impunity   96:34
Rave: r. not thus   380:20
turn giddy, r., and die   381:27
Raved and grew more fierce   244:10
Ravell'd sleave of care   458:11
Ravelston: Keith of R.   183:1
Raven: grim and ancient r.   380:25
Poe with his r.   320:4
quoth the R., 'Nevermore'   380:27
r. himself is hoarse   457:3
r. o'er the infected house   472:20
smoothing the r. down   340:15
snow on a r.'s back   478:19
your locks were like the r.   106:19
Ravening: inwardly. .r. wolves   58:25
Ravens: obscene r.   491:28
r. brought him bread   47:51
seen the r. flock   24:7
three r. sat on a tree   32:13
Ravenswood: last Laird of R. to R. . .ride   419:17
Raves: where the Atlantic r.   18:16
Ravin up thine own life's means   458:29
Ravish: chaste, except you r. me   185:19
to murder and to r.   23:26

Ravished: Analytics..hast r. me 329:22
r. with the whistling 384:12
she did not seduce, she r. 337:11
turn my r. eyes 2:2
would have r. her 204:14
you have r. justice 563:28
you have r. me away 290:28
Ravishing: Tarquin's r. strides 458:1
Ravishment: divine enchanting r. 340:14
Political R. 222:32
tones r., or r. its sweet 285:1
Raw: as a thing that is r. 395:21
eat not of it r. 45:46
nose looks red and r. 456:1
Ray: Eden-sweet the r. 336:47
emits a brighter r. 224:10
fancy's meteor r. 108:25
from her towers a r. 404:21
gem of purest r. serene 230:5
hospitable r. 225:11
r. of light Divine 132:1
r. of rays 173:36
r. on r. split the shroud 97:13
Shadwell's..night admits no r. 193:2
this busy r. 551:16
touch'd with an interior r. 165:33
with lessening r. 107:4
Raymond: it is Richard, it is R. 141:7
Rays: from whose hat the r. of the
sun 304:15
Raze: r. out the written troubles 460:37
r. the sanctuary 461:35
Razed: expung'd and r. 346:20
Razor: hew blocks with a r. 386:38
Razors and carving knives 121:20
Razor-strops and the lottery 376:13
Razure of oblivion 462:24
Reach: all things above his r. 371:15
I cannot r. it 551:17
man's r. should exceed 89:15
never r. me more 162:40
r. on with thy thought 411:8
r. the bottom first 228:7
themselves do r. 332:17
which sense may r. 185:2
Reaches: beyond the r. of our
souls 431:32(-432)
highest r. of a human wit 331:2
Reacheth but to dust 502:5
Reaching: r. after fact and reason 289:21
r. forth unto those things 68:23
r. to some great world 375:25
Read: all you that r. 280:10
authors whom they never r. 142:26
did you r. of that sin in a book? 302:31
do you r. books through? 272:16
he that runs may r. 529:23
his books were r. 41:23
I cannot r. it 142:7
I do not mean to r. 450:24
ignorantly r. 383:4
I never r. books 403:26
I never r. much 22:24
I r., and sigh 243:20
I r. very hard 270:1
I will r. to thee a lecture, Love 185:30
King George..able to r. that 235:8
let me so r. thy life 165:31
little I can r. 423:16
men may r. strange matters 457:5
more, he r. it 183:4
much had he r. 14:24
never r. any book..not a year
old 201:13
none of the Pagets can r. 335:20
not that I ever r. them 499:24
on bokes for to r. 138:16
population able to r. 549:9
r. a book before reviewing it 505:7
r. all at my ease 571:9
r. and perhaps understand
Shakespeare 289:29
r. an old one 408:14
r. any thing which I call a book 306:26
r. as much as other men 249:1
r. eternal new romances 231:20
r. God aright 404:14
r. hem as they wryte 138:25
r. Homer once 98:11
r. in Nature's mystic book 333:10
r. in secret 78:20

Read (cont.)
r. in the bitter letter 469:44
r. just as inclination leads 271:9
r., mark, learn 389:23
r. no history 181:44
r. not heaven or her 336:15
r. not my blemishes 424:10
r. not to contradict 27:16
r. somewhat seldomer 89:34
r. that moderate man Voltaire 236:24
r. the book of fate 442:4
r. their hist'ry in a nation's eyes 230:5
r. the perfect ways of honour 447:15
r. to thyself alone 82:11
r. without pleasure 277:9
scarce could r. or hold a quill 77:28
sit and r. all day 290:16
slowly r. and dream 586:21
some few to be r. wholly 27:17
teach the orphan-boy to r. 533:39
that all may r. 76:9
that day..we r. no more 168:23
they never r. 182:19
they r. with joy 374:23
to write and r. comes by nature 468:34
we have wits to r. 281:11
we r. fine things 289:34
what do you r., my lord? 433:4
what..I could meet with I r. 127:11
what the last Dawn..shall r. 207:6
when I want to r. a novel 181:21
who runs may r. 291:12
writes as fast as they can r. 239:12
ye have r., ye have heard 302:24
Reader: good r...the good book 201:18
last r. reads no more 251:8
R., I married him 83:5
r., look not on his picture 281:9
r. of the works of God 163:13
r. seldom peruses..with pleasure 2:4
r.'s threatened..with 'sleep' 382:31
Readers: give their r. sleep 381:13
r. to become more indolent 226:19
so many of my r. belong 142:17
your r. suffer so much 277:15
Readest: r. the eternal deep 576:13
so many books thou r. 17:22
thou r. black 74:11
understandest..what thou r.? 64:39
Readeth: run that r. 56:9
Readiness: r. is all 437:34
r. of doing 246:18
Reading: art of r...as well.. 182:49
art of r. is to skip 234:19
as much pleasure in the r. 404:3
before r. the Faerie Queene 306:8
digressions..the soul of r. 513:8
distinguish what is worth r. 549:9
invincible love of r. 216:18
I prefer r. 504:16
not walking..r. 306:25
observation and r...the drapery 153:14
Peace is poor r. 236:2
r...avoiding thought 241:1
r. is right 278:25
r. is to the mind 511:28
r. maketh a full man 27:18
r. Shakespeare by flashes of
lightning 153:5
vile hard r. 501:2
Reads: he r. much 448:27
last reader r. no more 251:8
what he r. as a task 271:9
who often r...wish to write 165:8
Ready: Abra was r. 402:4
always getting r. to live 201:1
always r. to go 209:15
as r. by water 198:24
but ninepence in r. money 2:35
conference a r. man 27:18
critics all are r. made 117:11
fire when you are r., Gridley 173:2
his fist be ever r. 221:20
I am r. to depart 308:25
if you're r., Oysters 130:17
necessity of being r. 314:2
pen of a r. writer 394:21
r. and pleasant smooth wit 21:13
r. enough to do the Samaritan 504:30
r. in defence 100:30
r. to be any thing 87:21

Ready (cont.)
rough and r. man 89:34
we always are r. 213:10
we are quite r. 492:23
Real: any less r. and true 489:13
forms more r. than living man 497:2
life is r.! life is earnest! 317:5
r. are the dreams of Gods 286:38
r. John..the r. Thomas 251:17
r. misfortunes..of others 102:31
R. Right Thing 268:10
r. Simon Pure 134:5
r. till it is experienced 290:19
so many r. ones to encounter 226:35
tasks of r. life 575:5
Reality: bear very much r. 197:5
between the idea and the r. 197:11
call r. 493:17
parts for the time with r. 144:4
Realize: at length I r. 128:15
Realized: no pleasure if it were r. 339:3
this unconquerable purpose..r. 307:12
worlds not r. 576:18
Really you again? 91:15
Realm: fourth estate of the r. 324:22
into the Soudan's r. 19:3
invade the borders of my r. 198:11
lords and commons of this r. 103:9
never left a r. undone 119:17
no jurisdiction in this R. 401:12
out of the R. in my petticoat 198:3
riding o'er the azure r. 229:23
this r., this England 474:22
to that mysterious r. 98:3
whole r. of nature mine 562:19
Realms: calls up the r. of fairy 116:15
constancy lives in r. above 150:26
in the r. of gold 288:19
pathless r. of Space 218:12
r. and islands were as plates 426:1
whatever r. to see 226:4
whom three r. obey 385:14
Reap: he shall not r. 522:7
in due season we shall r. 67:48
neither do they r. 58:11
old men shall r. 323:12
r. a habit 406:6
r. his old reward 303:26
r. in joy 399:34
r. its scanty corn 199:8
r. the whirlwind 55:46
r. where he hath sown 301:26
regardeth the clouds..not r. 51:29
that shall he also r. 67:47
Time shall r. 545:9
what Love shall never r. 410:33
where I r. thou shouldst..glean 253:21
you are like to r. 111:2
Reaped: never should be r. 548:14
r. iniquity 55:47
Reaper: after the r...the sleeper 545:9
R. came that day 317:10
r. reaps, and Time the r. 545:9
R. whose name is Death 317:9
Reapers: only r., reaping early 534:1
Reaping: ever r. something new 534:25
grew the more by r. 426:1
reapers, r. early 534:1
r. where thou hast not sown 60:31
Reaps: r. indigestion 515:1
r. the bearded grain 317:9
Rear: bring up the r. in heaven 86:24
ever r. a daughter 214:12
in the r. of your affection 431:22
r. my dusky race 534:33
scatters the r. of darkness 341:32
Rearward of a conquer'd woe 487:23
Reason: all r. is against it 112:5
any other r. why 3:11
aught other r. why 234:14
by r. of the frailty 389:30
clothed in r.'s garb 345:22
confidence of r. 574:1
divorced old barren R. 206:23
feast of r. 386:5
fight longer than he sees r. 438:29
free from rhyme or r. 381:21
general r. of the whole 100:14
God in Christ accepted by thy
r. 90:43
god-like reason 436:15

INDEX

Reason (cont.)

high r.	285:9
his gentle r. so persuasive	546:9
his r. such	383:22
how noble in r.	433:15
humanity, r., and justice	101:3
human r. weak	28:29
if it be against r.	148:3
I'll tell the r.	104:17
in erring r.'s spite	383:21
in R.'s ear they all rejoice	2:28
it was a theme for r.	184:12
I will not R. and Compare	75:2
kills r. itself	352:6
know the r. why	239:7
law that is not r.	387:14
lost their r. in..religion	87:5
love repine, and r. chafe	199:27
men have lost their r.	450:22
mere r. is insufficient	265:10
mix'd r. with pleasure	225:26
most sovereign r.	434:14
no man a r. upon compulsion	439:24
no other but a woman's r.	484:30
no r. why gunpowder treason	368:13
no sooner knew the r.	428:26
not his r., but his passions	513:11
not to r. why	528:16
our r. is our law	349:14
pursue my r. to an *O altitudo*	86:8
reaching after fact and r.	289:21
r. abuseth me	305:16
r. against the r. of my Love	290:28
r., and the will of God	19:25
r., an *ignis fatuus*	407:21
r. but from what we know	383:8
r. doth.. bow the mind	24:16
R. enslaves all..not strong enough	490:35
r. firm..temperate will	580:21
r. for my rhyme	510:18
r. has moons	249:11
R. in her most exalted	579:37
r. is the life of the law	148:4
R. still keeps its throne	203:29
r. themselves out again	445:13
r. thus with life	462:3
r. to rule	192:24
r. war with rhyme	281:27
render a r.	50:42
rest may r.	89:11
rhyme nor r.	358:9, 510:18
right deed for the wrong r.	197:25
rules of r.	245:5
rules pranked in r.'s garb	341:1
ruling passion conquers r.	384:43
sanctified by r.	579:38
shew no r. can	560:33
takes the r. prisoner	456:19
'Tam tint his r.	108:13
teach thy necessity to r. thus	474:19
tell me the r., I pray	507:33
that's the r. why	573:4
very r. why	157:20
voice of r. is stifled	103:20
wants discourse of r.	430:33(–431)
what r. I should be the same?	23:15
what's the r.?	238:3
whimsey, not r.	229:12
whom r. hath equalled	344:22
with r. murmur at his case	160:17
woman's r.	108:41

Reasonable: believed by any r.

person	265:10
man, being r.	115:34
no r. man could have expected	243:16
of a r. soul	388:41
R. Man	243:9
this r. moderator	86:18

Reasonableness: sweet r. of Jesus 20:18

Reasoned: r. errors 266:23

r. high of providence	345:29
r. or acted consequentially	139:22
r. out of..humanity	73:4

Reasoners: most plausible r. 239:28

Reasonest: Plato, thou r. well! 1:22

Reasoning: fitly shall conceive thy r. 493:3

r. and belief..essential materials	125:31
r. but to err	383:22
r., self-sufficing thing	578:30

Reasoning (cont.)

solid, r. good-sense	139:22
truth by consecutive r.	289:18

Reasons: five r. we should drink 3:11

good r...give place to better	451:28
his r. are as two grains	463:1
never give your r.	329:11
r. are not like garments	201:29
r. for bachelors to go out	196:28
r. made his mouth to water	110:31
r...plentiful as blackberries	439:2
when love..shall r. find	486:33
with r. answer you	450:32
your r...certainly be wrong	329:11

Rebel: r. and Atheist too 186:1

r. powers that thee array	488:20
r. tread	568:13
to be angels men r.	383:13

Rebellatrix: teque, r...Germania 372:5

Rebelled against the words of the Lord 398:15

Rebellion: little r. now and then 268:22

r. broached on his sword	445:6
r. is as the sin of witchcraft	47:16
r. lay in his way	440:27
r. to tyrants	79:14
rude eye of r.	447:45
rum, Romanism, and r.	99:42

Rebellious: revolting and a r. heart 55:12

Rebels: all that they leave of r. 142:11

devil here that commonly r.	472:13
hear now, ye r.	46:15
though r. wound thee	474:34
when subjects are r.	102:17

Rebounds: hit hard, unless it r. 272:24

Rebuff: welcome each r. 95:15

Rebuild it on the old plan 338:23

Rebuke: at the r. of one 53:40

at thy r. they flee	398:8
boldly r. vice	389:53
open r. is better	50:44
she gave me the greatest r.	328:11

Rebuked: my genius is r. 458:33

Recall: cannot r. their gifts 540:22

lasts ever, past r.	95:22
r. a time of happiness	168:22

Recalled: anything that could be r. 182:25

once spoke. .never be r.	180:7
r. by prayer and plaint	238:29

Recapture: never could r. 92:15

Recedentes: multa r. adimunt 256:2

Receipt: at the r. of custom 58:37

salad..of his own	335:9
we have the r. of fern-seed	439:1

Receive: *Christe r. thy saule* 31:12

from the dregs..think to r.	191:34
had a salary to r.	216:23
r. but what we give	151:4
r. him as..such an advent becomes	117:46
r. my soul at last	565:5
r. thy new possessor	344:22
slight what I r.	95:20
to give than to r.	65:11
wax to r.	112:35

Received: by him best r. 347:12

freely ye have r.	58:47
good r., the giver is forgot	154:40
his own r. him not	62:63
r. with thanksgiving	68:46
sharper than I r. it	546:38

Receiver: r. as bad 139:6

r. of stolen goods	277:16

Receives: like my face that r. thee 96:25

watches and r.	581:16

Receivest: r. not gladly 486:13

r. with pleasure thine annoy	486:13

Receiveth: every one that asketh r. 58:20

he that r. it	70:31
r. as the sea	481:30

Recess: in her sweet r. 350:11

Rechabite poor Will must live 402:8

Recipe: rare r. for melancholy 307:4

Reck: better r. the rede 105:21

Recked not of the life 114:19

Reckless: poor, r., rude 188:31

puff'd and r. libertine	431:23
r. what I do	458:36
restraining r. middle-age	584:26

Reckon: but r. with them 248:19

Reckoned: love that can be r. 423:12

Reckoning: last Dawn of R. 207:6

no r. made	432:17
O, weary r.!	472:18
take..the sense of r.	444:24
they little r. make	342:27
trim r.	440:30

Reckons up by dozens 221:14

Recks: little r. to find the way 427:6

r. not his own rede	431:23

Reclined: on a rock r. 216:5

Reclining: violet's r. head 184:29

Recognizance and pledge of love 473:26

Recognize: not r. me by my face 549:10

Recognized: objects r., in flashes 579:26

Recoil: moods of men r. away 88:20

with impetuous r.	346:9

Recollect half the dishes 22:20

Recollected: emotion r. in tranquillity 583:4

r. terms	483:1

Recollecting with tears 128:12

Recollection: affection, and r. 402:20

Recollections: shadowy r. 576:18

Recommendation: good face.. letter of r. 2:14

Recommends: the air..r. itself 457:6

Recompense: Heav'n did a r... send 230:13

not because r. is a pleasure	278:12

Recompose: decomposes but to r. 91:14

Reconciled: God and sinners r. 565:17

Reconciles: custom r. us to everything 102:33

feasting r. everybody	377:27
r. discordant elements	579:9

Reconnaissance: la r...une secrète envie 407:13

Record: no r. of reply 532:12

~ puts a r. on the gramophone	197:32
r. of the best and happiest moments	499:12
r. the mischiefs he has done	162:37
weep to r.	122:39

Recordanti: siqua r. benefacta 133:13

Recorded: knowledge..r. experience 125:31

life of a man, faithfully r.	125:35
r. for a precedent	465:3

Recorders: flutes and soft r. 345:2

Recording Angel: domesticate the R. 514:31

R...dropp'd a tear	513:20

Records: sweet r. 580:20

trivial fond r.	432:20

Recover: cheer us when we r. 100:15

r. his wits there	437:14
r. my strength	394:11
r. once my dust	355:21
r. the use of his legs	177:9
seldom or never r.	426:6
thou might'st him yet r.	189:20

Recovered: man r. of the bite 225:23

Nature stood r. of her fright	193:38
tyme y-lost..not r.	138:38

Recreant: soldier a mere r. prove 481:7

those r. limbs	447:28

Recruity: 'arf-made r. 304:3

Recte: si possis r. 256:19

Recti: mens sibi conscia r. 553:20

Rectum: nequit consistere r. 261:9

Recubans sub tegmine fagi 555:14

Red: azure, white, and r. 190:4

bird, with the r. stomacher	184:27
blood and wine are r.	569:1
blossom in purple and r.	536:15
celestial rosy r.	349:4
coral..more r. than her lips' r.	488:13
curtain'd with cloudy r.	343:24
floures whyte and r.	138:17
from black to r. began to turn	110:43
give this cheek a little r.	384:26
her r. coats marching	77:31
his r. right hand	345:20
in coats of r.	171:11
in my veins r. life	287:3
in r. and blue and green	76:15
like a r. r. rose	107:14
lips, indifferent r.	482:21
making the green one r.	458:15
Marion's nose looks r. and raw	456:1
never blows so r.	206:3

Red (*cont.*)
nor dim nor r. 149:2
one cut short and r. 358:24
pale, and hectic r. 496:4
pluck a r. rose 445:22
r. as any rose 29:24
r. as a r. is she 148:23
r. for the gatherer 543:23
R. Gods call us 296:12
r. in tooth and claw 532:37
r. men scalped each other 324:34
r. pavilion of my heart 543:17
r. plague rid you 479:26
r. rose cries 536:15
r. Rose, Proud Rose 586:17
r. slayer think he slays 199:3
r. spirits and gray 338:18, 459:34
r. sweet wine of youth 83:19
r. was on your lip 73:11
r. with spirted purple 539:4
sky is r. 59:41
so r. and so white 293:17
still and awful r. 149:25
streaks of r...mingled there 517:13
strong wyn, r. as blood 137:20
their r. it never dies 183:11
thin r. line 414:4
tongue of thy dogs may be r. 396:11
Tray grew very r. 249:21
us poor beggars in r. 303:27
vast..and painted r. 311:17
vindictive scribble of r. 91:17
whose r. and white Nature..laid on 482:20
wine is r. 396:31
Wine! r. Wine! 205:12
wine when it is r. 50:32
your own geranium's r. 91:21
your raiment all r. 322:25
Redbreast: r., sacred 546:26
r. sit and sing 151:25
r. whistles 284:15
Red-cross knight 534:4
Reddens: apple which r. 410:6
r. to a rose 561:6
where the apple r. 97:25
Reddite mi hoc pro pietate mea 133:16
Rede: better reck the r. 105:21
recks not his own r. 431:23
Redeem: he that doth r. her 438:38
r. thy name 415:18
r. us from virtue 523:3
suffer to r. our loss 8:2
Redeemed: he hath r. Jerusalem 54:23
r. from the earth 71:23
r. his vices with his virtues 280:1
Redeemer: as our dear R. said 75:20
my helper and r. 394:14
my r. liveth 49:6
my strength, and my r. 392:34
R., King 361:8
Redeeming the time 68:4
Redemption: married past r. 193:5
my r. thence 470:2
our great r. 343:9
r. of all things by Beauty 489:21
Redemptorem: tantum meruit habere R. 353:5
Redire: unde negant r. quenquam 132:13
Red-legged scissor-man 250:4
Red-plow'd hills 529:11
Redress: no r. for the present 181:32
r. the balance of the Old 124:21
things past r. 474:32
Redressing human wrongs 530:13
Red-ripe of the heart 95:35
Red-rose-bordered hem 586:14
Red Sea: through the R. waters 361:15
Redskin: Jack R. on the Quest 140:6
Redtape Talking-machine 126:35
Redundant: summer r. 97:15
Reed: bruised r...not break 54:15
clasped a r. 494:2
not as a nymph, but..r. 332:16
pluck'd a hollow r. 76:9
r. is as the oak 430:1
r. shaken with the wind 59:6
r. which grows never more 88:12
r. with the reeds 88:12
spring up into beauty like a r. 313:22
this bruised r. 48:33
Reeds: among the r. and rushes 317:20
bring me an hundred r. 214:7
cottages of strowed r. 331:2
down in the r. 88:11
my worn r. broken 172:1
Naiad 'mid her r. 286:4
Reef: swept towards the r. 318:16
Reek o' the rotten fens 429:14
Reeking: her trust in r. tube 301:1
r. into Cadiz Bay 92:17
Reel: in r. and rout 149:6
r. in a drunkard 143:13
r. o' Tullochgorum 502:22(-503)
r. to and fro 398:18
References: verify your r. 412:4
Referens: horresco r. 554:3
Refine: correct, insert, r. 521:16
laboured to r. our language 278:13
Refined: by a love so much r. 186:25
disgust this r. age 202:15
in more r. ages 28:27
pleasures too r. to please 384:32
r., presumptuous man 124:15
r. with th' accents that are ours 168:9
truths as r. 14:26
Refinement on the principle of resistance 100:29
Refines: how the style r. 382:34
Refining: still went on r. 225:27
Reflect on the past 527:9
Reflecting: sadly r. ..a lover forsaken 559:5
Reflection: brief r. solves 517:8
many years of r. 290:14
R...come to-morrow 494:9
Reflections: monkey..very mortifying r. 155:6
Reflects: as soon as he r...a child 223:13
half the platform just r. 385:3
Reflektiert: sobalder. r...ein Kind 223:13
Reflex of a star 575:25
Reform: every r...once a private opinion 200:20
party of progress or r. 338:28
peace, retrenchment and r. 82:18
r. it altogether 434:21
to innovate is not to r. 103:7
Reformation: never came r. in a flood 443:6
plotting some new r. 193:23
reforming of R. 352:12
what then did happen at the R.? 72:28
Reformed: considered, and speedily r. 352:4
r. that indifferently 434:21
Reformers: all r. are bachelors 356:4
consolations of middle-aged r. 414:9
Reforms his plan 587:6
Refrain: I r. my soul 400:1
r. from the unholy pleasure 40:19
Refrains: cheerful hour, r. 351:23
Refreshedst it when it was weary 396:6
Refreshes in the breeze 383:19
Refreshment: accept r. at any hands 219:21
full of r. 316:14
only place of r. 202:13
Reft: this r. house 152:13
Refuge: city of r. 352:13
eternal God is thy r. 46:34
last r. of a scoundrel 272:29
last r. of cheap misgovernment 490:10
other r. have I none 565:6
r. for the wild goats 398:10
r. of weak minds 139:25
thou hast been our r. 397:15
under..thy wings shall be my r. 395:17
Refugium: tutissimum r. 148:7
Refusal: great r. 168:19
her r., through her skill 155:36
Refuse: how to r. the evil 53:12
if you please r. 333:8
nothing r. 199:12
Refused: nothing to be r. 68:46
r. about the age of three 141:17
r. other cesure 281:27
Refuses: whom she r...like a favour 155:36
Refusing: stiffness in r. 388:3
Refute: I r. it *thus* 271:21
not r. my general assertion 271:31
who can r. a sneer? 373:6
Regain love once possessed 350:33
Regained: half r. Eurydice 342:9
r. by faith and prayer 238:29
r. my freedom with a sigh 114:36
yet but half-r. 496:3
Regaining: as for r. my character 208:25
Regal: of r. port 347:32
Regard: preferring his r. for me 521:8
r. not how it goes 106:25
should be without r. 459:4
Regarded: heard, not r. 440:9
lightly r. the counsel 398:15
r. the low estate 61:13
Regarder: se r. soi-même 354:1
Regardeth: he that r. the clouds 51:29
Regardful of the embroiling sky 546:26
Regardless: r. of their doom 230:26
r. of the sweeping whirlwind 229:23
Regards: mingled with r. 452:12
Regent: fair r. of the Night 216:3
God bless the R. 504:4
r. of love rhymes 455:8
revelled with the R. 39:14
sweet r. of the sky 338:13
Reges: quidquid delirant r. 256:22
Regibus: Maecenas atavis edite r. 257:23
Regiment: House of Commons, R. 147:17
led his r. from behind 218:16
Monstrous R. of Women 305:6
R. o' British Infantree 296:25
R.'s in 'ollow square 295:20
then comes up the R. 295:21
within our breasts for r. 330:28
Regimental in her fittings 304:26
Regiments: review of thirty r. 119:25
Region: fair r. round 577:24
high r. of his fancies 352:20
in the sleepy r. stay 359:1
is this the r.? 344:21
main r. of my song 574:7
r. of thick-ribbèd ice 462:9
untrodden r. of my mind 288:7
where the r. Elenore? 545:5
Regions: blue r. of the air 75:18
obscure, r. of philosophy 265:13
r. Caesar never knew 158:32
r. of sorrow 344:9
r. of the West 24:9
Register of the crimes, follies 217:7
Register'd upon our brazen tombs 454:29
Regitur: quantilla prudentia r. orbis 372:15
Regress .. a downfall, or .. an eclipse 26:24
Regret: deeply r. inform your grace 39:29
last r., r. can die 533:6
Old Age a r. 181:37
partly consumed by r. 312:17
vain desire..and vain r. 411:19
wild with all r. 538:19
Regrets: clears TO-DAY of past R. 206:5
series of congratulatory r. 181:11
wild r. 569:10
Regretted that he was not a bird 407:7
Regular: brought r. and draw'd mild 176:18
icily r. 535:35
not a r. rule 129:32
r. Royal Queen 218:21
Regulated: best-r. families 174:37
moral, r. liberty 102:3
Regulation of conduct 508:22
Regulations Act 569:7
Regum: pauperum tabernas r. que turris 258:8
Rehearse: he moot r...everich a word 137:23
r. the Articles 391:4
trumpeters shall he r. 397:14
Rehearsal: talking of..'The R.' 275:27
Reign: better to r. in hell 344:23
dispute the r. of some..mire 216:4
frighted the r. of Chaos 345:1
here we may r. secure 344:23
his r...few materials for history 217:7
Jesus shall r. 562:8
long to r. over us 250:14
o'er the past its undivided r. 251:11
omnipotent but friendless..to r. 497:4
r. in this horrible place 164:22
R. of Law 14:12

Reign (*cont.*)
r. whoever may 162:21
second of our r. 184:7
to r. is worth ambition 344:23
undisturbed their ancient r. 184:2
weeds..r. o'er the land 165:17
Reigned: I have r. with your loves 198:12
Reigneth: Thy God r. 54:22
Reigns: commences, r., and ends 503:2
fray by which he r. 346:11
his clear Sprite yet r. 491:15
Reilly: is that Mr. Reilly? 7:19
Reinforcement..gain from hope 344:19
Reins: try out my r. 393:17
Reiterated: with r. crimes 344:20
Reject: difficulty..to choose or r. 194:12
Rejected: despised and r. of men 54:25
Rejecting the gods of Athens 379:24
Rejoice: again I say, R. 68:25
all the vales r. 76:10
as cheap and easy to r. 407:4
as men r. when they divide 53:14
bones which thou has broken
..r. 395:8
Christian men, r. 361:18
come ye before Him, and r. 292:7
daughters of the Philistines r. 47:29
desert shall r. 54:1
I hear thee and r. 573:19
in both..thou didst r. 581:13
in Reason's ear they all r. 2:28
I r. the lot has fallen 302:13
I will r., and divide Sichem 395:23
little hills shall r. 395:30
make this heart r. 161:5
my heart and my flesh r. 397:5
r., again I say, r. 565:11
r. and delight in God 548:13
r. before Him 291:27, 396:5
r. in the Lord alway 68:25
r. in the Lord, O ye righteous 393:35
r., O young man 51:32
r. that yet on earth 81:21
r. with me 62:11, 404:17
r. with them that do r. 66:4
r. ye dead 81:21
we in ourselves r. 151:6
wherefore r.? 448:7
Rejoiced: my spirit hath r. 61:13
r. they were na men 108:23
Rejoices: in whom His world r. 571:21
Rejoiceth: friend of the bridegroom..r. 63:11
r. as a giant 392:32
r. in his strength 49:26
r. not in iniquity, but r. in the
truth 66:45
Rejoicing: partake in her r. 352:29
there mov'd, r. 17:28
toiling,—r.,—sorrowing 318:13
Relate: little to r. 131:22
Related: to whom r. 381:36
Relation: poor r...irrelevant 306:29
Relations: augurs and understood
r. 459:24
find for them the right r. 268:8
great men have their poor r. 174:2
maintain the most friendly r. 305:1
party of friends and r. 219:11
squire and his r. 174:8
to his friends and his r. 222:21
Relationship with beauty and
truth 289:20
Relative: in a r. way 98:19
Relaxed into a universal grin 163:28
Relaxes: bless r. 77:18
Relearn: let them r. the Law 297:22
Release: before I find r. 536:27
our deadly forfeit should r. 343:9
prisoner's r. 501:26
Releasing: gives thee r. 487:22
Relent: echoes which he made r. 190:3
make him once r. 99:35
Relenting fool 476:30
Relentless power 230:15
Relentment: conclude in a moist r. 87:2
Relents: my rigour r. 100:25
Relic of departed worth 113:17
Relics: crosses, r., crucifixes 111:12
his hallow'd r...hid 351:8
into other's hands these r. 185:5

Relics (*cont.*)
r., beads, indulgences 346:26
unhonour'd his r. are laid 356:29
with thise r. 137:22
Relief: certain r. in change 267:24
for this r. much thanks 430:8
gave that thought r. 576:4
no..outlet, no r. 150:31
not seek for kind r. 77:3
r. of man's estate 24:14
Relieve: r. my passion much 483:1
r. the wretched 224:21
Relieved: r...it was only Brooks 174:12
r. their pain 224:19
*Religio: tantum r. potuit suadere
malorum* 320:28
Religion: about as much r. 223:9
against her foes R. well defends 164:39
all of the same r. 182:5
as great in love as in r. 158:20
as if R. were intended 110:19
based either on r. or policy 413:21
bashfulness in..r. 2:14
Bible..r. of Protestants 142:24
blunderbuss against r. 270:22
bringeth..about to r. 25:25
brings him..again to our r. 212:12
brothels with bricks of R. 77:15
enough r. to make us hate 520:38
good man was ther of r. 137:16
handmaid to r. 24:26
her r. so well with her learning 401:35
humanities of old r. 152:9
indirect way to plant r. 86:15
in nothing so much as their r. 87:5
in politics as well as in r. 282:19
in..r. and matrimony..advice 139:32
in r., what damned error 464:14
in their r...so uneven 170:15
man's r...the chief fact 126:21
man without r. 237:19
men of sense..of one r. 423:1
Millionaire..my r. 490:6
more beautiful than any r. 414:12
more fierce in its r. 363:17
my r. from the priest 227:28
my r. is to do good 373:4
no amusements..but vice and r. 505:11
not a r. for gentlemen 136:6
not impossibilities enough in R. 86:6
one r. is as true as another 109:32
only one r...hundred versions 490:43
Philistine of genius in r. 20:19
protestantism of the Protestant
r. 100:29
pure r. and undefiled 69:34
pure r. breathing 577:16
r., as a mere sentiment 363:18
R. blushing veils 381:27
r. but a childish toy 330:14
r. has so seldom found 162:29
r., if in..truths attir'd 159:30
r...invade..private life 335:16
r. *is* knight-errantry 134:12
r...is the opium 333:13
r., justice, counsel, and treasure 27:8
r., knavery, and change 40:8
r...morality touched with emotion 20:11
r. most prevalent 100:29
r. of feeble minds 102:26
r. of humanity 373:5
r...powerless to bestow 201:7
R...product of the..intestines 125:30
r...remedy for superstition 101:7
r.'s in the heart 269:8
r...subject of conversation 139:33
r. without a prelate 33:5
reproach to r. and government 377:7
rum and true r. 115:28
so fatal to r. as indifference 103:25
some people talk of..r. 195:17
subtleties in r. 86:7
suspended the sentiments of r. 103:4
talk r...with bodily hunger 490:8
talks loudly against r. 513:11
this man's r. is vain 69:34
where mystery begins, r. ends 102:39
writers against r. 102:37
Religion: die R...das Opium 333:13
Religión es la caballería 134:12

Religions: collector of r. 490:7
sixty..r...only one sauce 124:23
Religious: dim r. light 341:24
1st, r. and moral principles 20:21
hope I will be r. again 208:25
man..a r. animal 102:22
not r.-good 237:16
old r. factions 101:31
O ye R. 75:9
r. persecution..shield itself 101:23
seem to be r. 69:34
suspended my r. inquiries 216:24
troubled with r. doubt 141:17
Relinquished one delight 576:21
Relish: imaginary r. is so sweet 481:15
some r. of the saltness of time 441:13
Reluctance: acquired them with r. 36:5
r. to sit for a picture 274:17
Reluctant: r. amorous delay 347:12
stalk'd off r. 73:13
with r. feet 316:34
Relume: thy light r. 473:11
Rem: quocumque modo r. 256:19
Remain: as things have been,
things r. 147:8
constant do r. 449:30
fragments that r. 63:24
glory shall r. 233:3
here will I r. 478:44
r. in the broad sea 395:28
r. with you always 390:49
still would r. my wit to try 172:1
thou ever wilt r. 314:21
Remainder: dry as the r. biscuit 427:16
Remained: Egdon r. 237:10
r. to pray 224:22
Remaineth: when nothing else r. 189:19
Remains: all that r. of her 252:14
cut up what r. 304:4
love's r. 94:45
strength in what r. 576:20
the One r. 492:15
what r. is bestial 471:20
what then r., but ..to die 28:19
while aught r. to do 408:6
Remake: unmakes but to r. the
soul 96:16
Remark: r. all these roughnesses 167:7
which I wish to r. 238:32
Remarkable: most r. like you 303:4
nothing left r. 425:29
Remedies: all r. refusing 168:7
will not apply new r. 26:30
Remedy: force is not a r. 82:22
He..found out the r. 461:29
how to r. our own 305:15
no r. against this consumption 441:26
r. against sin 391:25
r...against tyranny 272:10
r. is worse than the disease 27:11
sharp r...sure..for all ills 405:14
sought the r. 428:20
sovereign r. to all diseases 109:22
succour Scotland, and r. 583:26
things without all r. 459:4
Remember: calmness to r. 3:6
can't you r. how they go 120:25
death r. 524:14
don't you r. sweet Alice 201:24
half to r. days that have gone by 208:4
haply I may r. 410:1
ides of March r. 451:11
if I do not r. thee 400:5
I'll r. thee, Glencairn 106:28
in the sweet pangs..r. me 483:2
I r. how you smiled 309:6
I r., I r. 253:1
I shall r. while the light 523:8
I would r. Him 39:6
like to something I r. 210:1
little note, nor long r. 314:12
Lord, r. David 400:2
Lord, r. me 62:49
must I r.? 430:33(-431)
names that men r. 523:10
no man r. me 237:7
not r. what I must be now 475:9
please to r. the Fifth 9:11, 368:13
power of beauty I r. 192:3
r. and be sad 409:25
r. Lot's wife 62:31

Remember (cont.)
r. me when I am gone 409:24
r. not past years 364:11
r. not the sins 393:14
r. now thy Creator 51:33
r. of this unstable world 328:13
r. one man saw you 95:1
r. such things were 460:22
r. thee! 432:20
r. the Maine 9:13
r. the name of the Lord 392:37
r. the poor creature 441:33
r. thy swashing blow 476:47
r. who commended 483:19
r. with advantages 444:28
still r. me 356:19
thou r. and I forget 524:14
thy branches ne'er r. 289:7
to have been in prosperitee, and
  it r. 138:35
to r. for years 4:19
we will r. them 72:23
who will r. this **lady** 171:6
yet will I r. thee 161:11
you will wake, and r. 91:22
Remembered: blue r. hills 263:14
friend r. not 427:22
in their flowing cups..r. 444:28
I r. my God 507:35
made myself r. 290:29
must the r. perishing be? 171:8
not r. in thy epitaph 441:1
r. on waking 81:9
r. that he had a salary 216:23
r. that he once was young 14:23
r. thee in my bed 395:26
said anything that was r. 182:25
sweet tones are r. not 494:20
we in it shall be r. 444:28(–445)
wept when we r. thee 400:5
your names, r. day and night 81:21
Remember'st not the slightest
  folly 427:2
Remembering: r. happier things 534:21
r. him like anything 141:30
r. how she felt 579:18
r. my good friends 474:28
r. that she has seen dark days 200:3
Remembers: my heart r. how! 516:9
nature rest r. 576:17
r. its august abodes 308:28
r. me of all his gracious parts 447:34
Remembrance: appear almost a r. 289:27
drown her r. again 482:25
every r. of you 68:14
fits a king's r. 432:36
makes the r. dear 423:10
r. fallen from heaven 522:5
r. of a guest 56:26
r. of a weeping queen 475:14
r. of his dying Lord 509:18
r. of his holiness 393:25
r. of my former love 484:34
r. of things past 486:25
rosemary, that's for r. 436:31
Remembrancer designedly dropt 567:12
Remi: glubit magnanimis R. nepotes 133:5
Reminiscence sing 567:1
Reminiscences make one feel.. 489:34
Remission: without..blood is no r. 69:10
Remnant: r. of our Spartan dead 115:46
smell my r. out 244:20
Remnants: some r. of history 24:15
Remorse: abandon all r. 472:5
farewell r. 346:33
passage to r. 457:3
r., the fatal egg 161:27
Remorseful day 445:33
Remote: r. and ineffectual Don 41:31
r. Bermudas 332:1
r. from towns 224:18
r., unfriended, melancholy 226:3
Remoter: gleams of a r. world 495:18
no need of a r. charm 581:26
Re-mould it nearer 207:26
Remove: digs my grave at each r. 244:19
r. the joint 131:28
r...the strong conception 473:14
r. those things which elemented
  it 186:25
unto this mountain, R. hence 59:47

Removed: as far r. from God 344:10
I shape me—ever r.! 92:43
shall she not be r. 394:28
to a more r. ground 432:1
Remover: with the r. to remove 488:7
Removeth his neighbour's landmark 46:27
Renascentur: multa r. 255:20
Rend: ne se r. *pas* 121:24
Render: Dryden fails to r. him 20:3
earth! r. back 115:46
r. me his bloody hand 450:6
r. the deeds of mercy 464:33
r. therefore unto Caesar 60:12
r...to all their dues 66:11
r. with thy precepts less 118:30
that can r. a reason 50:42
what shall I r. to my God? 561:19
Rendezvous: my r. is appointed 567:22
r. with Death 421:18
Rending of the tomb 35:6
Rends thy constant heart 225:14
Renew: r. a right spirit 395:9
r. their strength 54:14
Renewed: r. in a year 237:10
springs r. by flowing 123:18
wish I were r. 488:6
Renewing is of love 196:2
Renidet: quodcumque agit, r. 132:22
Renounce: r. me for a son 216:19
r. the devil 391:2
r. when that shall be necessary 513:35
Renown: Cause above r. 362:33
credit and r. 159:32
equall'd with them in r. 346:20
forfeit fair r. 417:22
gave thee thy r. 125:1
glorious day's r. 122:3
just and old r. 541:24
men of r. 44:38
no banquet, or r. 245:2
no more of his r. 537:28
r., and grace is dead 458:24
to good fame and r. 328:2
unfulfilled r. 492:11
wight of high r. 6:26
Renowned: far r. for larnin' 229:13
no less r. than war 351:29
r. for their deeds 474:22
Rent: blood, sweat..for r. 112:28
r. for Mrs. Rip Van Winkle 97:35
r. in my wind-built tent 492:29(–493)
what a r. the envious Casca 450:28
Repair: Freedom shall awhile r. 153:30
friendship in constant r. 270:29
r. unto the Bell 159:33
Repairs: r. his drooping head 343:3
r. of a table 277:3
Reparations: mean r. upon mighty
  ruins 101:30
Repartee: majority..the best r. 182:34
Repasts: spiritual r. 306:8
Repay: I will r. 66:6
I will r. thee 61:42
think to-morrow will r. 191:34
Repeal of bad or obnoxious laws 228:23
Repeat: do thou r. 549:6
r. poetry as well as other folk 306:13
r. what he has..repeated 406:12
what boots it to r. 206:19
Repeated: emphasis of passionate
  love r. 309:13
Repeateth: he that r. a matter 50:18
Repeats: r. his words 447:34
when he r. his verses 307:13
Repel: retard what we cannot r. 277:24
Repent: do I r. or change 344:13
from their marble caves, r., r. 190:3
I'll r., and that suddenly 440:11
it doth r. me 496:21
never, my Love, r. 375:14
no follies to have to r. 527:9
nor falter, nor r. 497:17
no strength to r. 440:11
r. at leisure 155:32
r. in haste 155:32
r. it from my very soul 480:36
r. what's past 436:2
r. ye..kingdom of heaven.. 57:27
r. you of your sins 390:34
should I r. me 473:11

Repent (cont.)
sware, and will not r. 398:24
that Faustus may r. 330:7
weak alone r. 115:4
Repentance: give r. to her lover 226:18
just persons..need no r. 62:12
no place of r. 69:20
no r. in the grave 561:21
R. oft before I swore 207:21
r...virtue of weak minds 192:35
r...want of power to sin 193:16
sinners to r. 58:40
Winter-garment of R. 205:14, 15
with the morning cool r. 420:14
Repented: maid r. 33:13
strove, and much r. 115:21
they have r. 280:10
truly r. and amended 390:2
Repenteth: one sinner that r. 62:12
Repenting: after no r. draws 351:22
wooing, wedding, and r. 468:9
Repetita: crambe r. 283:13
Repetitions: vain r. 58:3
Repine: do not r., my friends 176:13
though love r. 199:27
Replenish the earth 44:9
Replete: heads r. with thoughts 163:49
Replication of your sounds 448:9
Replied: all nature..r. 503:3
I r., 'My Lord' 244:10
Replies: heart r. 163:48
Reply: I pause for a r. 450:16
loving and a fair r. 430:32
no record of r. 532:22
r. churlish 428:37
r., r. 464:13
teacher did r. 233:23(–234)
their's not to make r. 528:16
voice without r. 199:27
Report: believed our r.? 54:24
evil r. and good r. 67:28
how he may r. thy words 350:37
killed with r. 351:16
knew thee from r. divine 566:12
my gossip R. 464:6
of good r. 68:27
r. all heroism 568:6
r. me and my cause aright 438:2
r. of my death 550:30
their ill r. while you live 433:29
Reporters: gallery in which the r.
  sit 324:22
Parliament speaking through r. 126:39
R.' Gallery 126:29
Reports: bring me no more r. 460:33
Repos: la gloire et le r. 354:22
Repose: choice between truth and
  r. 200:22
earned a night's r. 318:13
find r. in thee 21:16
garlands of r. 332:13
her manners had not that r. 533:37
his last r. 11:23
hush'd in grim r. 229:23
I long for a r. 573:30
leave me to r. 229:27
nature gives way to in r. 457:18
r. is taboo'd by anxiety 219:9
seek not yet r. 198:12
their long r. shall burst 493:27
Reposes: in quiet she r. 17:15
Reprehend: if I r. any thing 500:20
Representation: taxation and r. 388:2
taxation without r. 371:16
Representative: drollery .. r.
  government 182:33
Repressed: ardour of my zeal r. 143:10
scarce r. the..tear 276:15
Reprieve: world without end, r. 302:1
Reproach: eternal r. of the divines 352:12
guiltless, meet r. 472:21
receives r. of being 488:10
r. of Christ 69:16
r. to religion and government 377:7
writing their own r. 480:39
Reprobate, degraded 124:9
Reprobation: fall to r. 473:25
Reproche: sans peur et sans r. 12:13
Reproof valiant 428:37
Reproofs from authority 26:16
Reprove: check the erring and r. 573:24

INDEX

Reprove (cont.)
r. her when she's right 520:55
sager sort our deeds r. 123:19
would those looks r. 224:13
Reproved: r. each dull delay 224:21
shrank like a thing r. 492:13
Reptile: r. all the rest 385:33
turn myself into a r. 270:33
Republic: crown'd R. 539:14
her last r. 142:3
pension list of the r. 146:5
r. is a raft 4:21
R. of Letters 1:7, 226:21
what should be a r. 227:30
Republican: R. form of Government 508:24
surly r. 278:4
Republicans: we are R. 99:42
Republics..appeal to the understanding 28:29
Repudiate the repudiators 203:40
Repugnances: national r. do not touch me 86:27
Repulsae: virtus r. nescia sordidae 259:19
Repulsed: inspir'd r. battalions 1:10
love r. 493:23
Reputation: acquired some r. by travelling 272:1
bubble r. 427:21
made himself of no r. 68:17
my R. for a Song 207:20
r. of five-and-twenty 193:4
r., r., r.!..my r., Iago 471:20
spotless r. 474:10
wink a r. down 521:9
written out of r. 43:7
Reputations: fuller's earth for r. 214:18
Request: no flowers, by r. 3:7
r. of his lips 392:38
ruined at our own r. 357:27
Requests: grant their r. 388:33
Requiem: o'er Pitt's the mournful r. sound 418:5
to sing a r. 437:19
to thy high r. 287:32
Requiescat: donec r. in te 21:16
Require: r. the life of man 44:42
services to do, till you r. 487:7
the Lord r. of thee 56:8
thought 'e might r. 303:22
Required: burnt-offerings..not r. 394:13
nothing be r. 204:16
thy soul shall be r. 61:53
Requires: what you think justice r. 329:11
Requisite: things..r. and necessary 388:9
Requite: I should ill r. thee 160:34
I will r. thee 468:27
Requited: both alike r. 404:9
both are alike r. 372:12
Rere-mice: war with r. 466:42
Res age, tutus eris 372:3
Rescribas: nil mihi r. 371:24
Rescue: to the r. came 364:7
Resemblance: showy r. 373:3
Resemble: when I r. her to thee 558:4
Resembled my father 458:5
Resembles: most r. God 108:35
r. sorrow only 316:8
Resented: never r. for an offence 520:35
Resentment: r. towards persons.. never seen 363:10
whim, envy, or r. 142:29
Reservations: no mental r. 314:9
Reserved: r., carried about 401:10
r. for some end 146:7
Reside: r. at Table Mountain 239:1
r. in thrilling region 462:9
Residence: emblem of my..r. 363:22
his taste in r. is plain 223:7
love's long r. 80:23
r. 'gainst the tooth of time 462:24
Residuum: vast r...Populace 19:29
Resign: none r. 268:26
nor, when we will, r. 17:6
r. my self to thee 185:11
Resignation: by r., none 268:26
while r. gently slopes 224:16
Resigned: anxious being e'er r. 230:9
Resist: cannot r...could r. till I saw you 290:28

Resist (cont.)
ready to r. 221:19
r. everything except temptation 569:35
r. his uncontrollable intent 351:7
r. not evil 57:50
r. the devil 69:40
r. the evil 3:18
Resistance: passive r. of the Tolbooth-gate 419:37
refinement on the principle of r. 100:29
wrong that needs r. 33:8
Resisted: know not what's r. 104:8
rejoice that America has r. 379:3
Resisting the Guard 295:4
Resistless: bright, r. course 418:2
striking, r., and grand 225:34
Resolute: bloody, bold, and r. 460:5
haughty, vigilant, r. 324:35
in..small things be r. 320:2
just and r. 568:7
Resolution: I pull in r. 461:5
my r. is to die 349:18
native hue of r. 434:4
not r. to fire it off himself 270:22
r. thus fobbed 438:19
road to r. 404:8
what r. from despair 344:9
Resolutions: great and mighty r. 110:26
Resolve: come, Firm R. 104:22
heart to r...head to contrive 217:11
his prudent purpose to r. 587:6
r. itself into a dew 430:33
r. the propositions of a lover 428:4
r. to be thyself 18:17
Resolved: once to be r. 471:34
r. to ruin or to rule 190:16
think I'm best r. 517:17
Resolves: dror r. an' triggers 319:19
r.; and re-r. 587:6
Resort: all r. of mirth 341:16
various bustle of r. 340:20
Resound: name to r. for ages 529:17
Resounded: back r., *Death* 346:8
Resounding: full-r. line 386:17
Resounds: what r. in fable 345:4
Resource: infinite-r.-and-sagacity 304:12
piano-forte is a fine r. 89:29
Resources: full of r. 100:30
r. of civilization 222:37
rock of the national r. 563:4
Respect: fellow of a good r. 452:6
in ev'ry r. but the form 214:35
I r. Millar, Sir 270:24
no r. for their language 490:44
no r. of persons 65:34
no r. of place, persons 482:31
other means of procuring r. 273:3
r. was mingled with surprise 416:27
there's the r...makes calamity 434:4
wind, which I r. not 451:19
Respectable: bosom of her r. family 103:35
genius found r. 87:33
more..ashamed of, the more r. 490:13
most devilish when r. 87:34
not one is r. or unhappy 567:20
r. Hottentot 139:28
r. Professors of the Dismal Science 126:34
riff-raff apply to what is r. 254:8
Respected: once that Peter was r. 578:24
Respecter of persons 64:48
Respectfully: I r. decline 183:14
Respects: my best r. to you 302:16
r. the highest law of his being 200:23
Respice finem 13:12
Respite: some r. to husbands 550:4
Respondere parati 556:3
Responds with colour 544:11
Responses: soft r. 513:21
Responsibility: liberty means r. 490:30
Responsive: r. to the cuckoo's note 231:6
sweet r. lay 168:14
Rest: absence of occupation is not r. 162:3
all shall r. eternally 510:11
all the r...to cold oblivion 493:9
angels sing thee to thy r. 438:7
at r. for one day 155:7
away the r. have trifled 90:39
Church at r. 517:3

Rest (cont.)
crept silently to R. 206:6
die or r. at last 493:27(−494)
done for the r. 514:18
dove found no r. 44:39
eternal Sabbath of his r. 193:37
ever put spear in the r. 328:24
far, far better r. 180:2
find r. unto your souls 59:10
give his soule good r. 321:10
glad, because they are at r. 398:19
God order'd motion, but..no r. 551:15
God r. you merry 6:11
good r. to all 299:26
grown sick of r. 423:34
he could not r. 18:24
holy r. 364:4
I forget the r. 93:24
in doubt to act or r. 383:22
in our labour r. 132:2
in r. from pain 192:36
in the night-season..no r. 393:1
isles where good men r. 208:9
I will give you r. 59:10
lay his lance in r. 183:8
long long ago at r. 157:17
love itself have r. 119:5
makest thy flock to r. 51:40
my everlasting r. 478:44
my heart at r. 421:16
not r. in an English grave 119:33
now cometh r. 373:10
now she's at r. 192:18
o'er Land and Ocean without r. 351:21
our r. is as far 141:1
our restlessness, His r. 88:5
quiet and r. and desire 359:7
r. a little from praise 525:5
r. a little longer 540:10
r. comes at length 202:30
r. for the people of God 93:41
r. from their labours 71:27
r. in a darkness 334:5
r. in this bosom 356:15
r. I well know where 80:16
r. on its original plan 103:23
r., r., perturbed spirit! 432:31
r. thy weary head 316:20
r. to his mind 559:15
r. upon thy holy hill 392:24
r. ye, brother mariners 535:20
run, rise, r. with Thee 245:9
said 'Good-Night,' and gone to r. 41:24
softly to r. 365:5
so late take r. 399:35
soldier, r.! 416:19
so may he r. 447:5
so sweet to r. 478:1
spirit of the Lord..r. upon him 53:17
such r. to her 437:19
take r. while you may 417:33
take the r. 118:6
take thy r. 118:27
talk about the r. of us 249:4
that in me has r. 83:8
their appointed r. 149:24
then, had I been at r. 48:45
the r. be all men's 94:6
the R. is Lies 206:9
the r. is mere fine writing 552:18
the r. is silence 438:6
the r. may reason and welcome 89:11
the r. nowhere 370:8
the r. on his knees 175:37
the r. on Nature fix 148:8
the r. remaineth unreveal'd 532:22
they have no r. 71:26
they r. not day and night 70:38
to r. the violet's reclining head 184:29
waive the R. 205:25
we are taking r., master 142:14
wear ourselves and never r. 330:28
weary be at r. 48:46
weary world to quiet r. 35:7
we'll do the r. 12:9
we shall r., and..need it 303:19
who doth not crave for r.? 202:26
who sink to r. 153:29
will not let them r. 285:33
without end, reprieve, or r. 302:1
with them, and at r. 416:29

INDEX

Rest (cont.)
 with them that r. 350:30
 with those that r. 78:16
Reste: j'y suis, j'y r. 327:4
 le r. est littérature 552:18
Rested: quietly r. under..three
  conquests 87:8
 r. he by the Tumtum tree 129:39(−130)
 r. the seventh day 390:11
 they r. on a rock 130:15
Resting never! 281:27
Restless: circle that doth r. move 246:11
 for my sake r. 160:22
 hover in their r. heads 331:2
 joy is like r. day 402:10
 o'er a r. flood 160:14
 r. ecstasy 459:4
 r. night and day 523:14
 r., unfixed in principle 190:13
 too strange, too r. 15:20
 wind-ridden r. sea 171:19
Restlessness: round our r. 88:5
 with repining r. 245:1
Restoratives like to a constant
  woman 209:25
Restore: each lonely scene shall
  thee r. 153:22
 he wished to r. the crown 272:27
 my soul he doth r. 421:1
 not r. what I have lost 244:9
 r. the light 168:12
 r. the tone of languid Nature 162:36
 thy former light r. 473:11
 Time may r. us 16:23
Restored: God-like David was r. 190:31
 r. to his friends 222:21
Restorer: tired Nature's sweet r. 586:29
Restoring: I am r. tranquillity 101:5
Restrain in me the cursed thoughts 457:18
Restraining reckless middle-age 584:26
Restraint: for one r. 344:5
 free from this r. 155:38
Rests: r. and expatiates 383:11
 r. foiled 281:26
 she r. a little longer 540:10
Result: full r. of all 382:24
 long r. of Time 534:14
 r. happiness 174:24
Resume: way to resumption is to r. 136:10
Resurgam: Arms and Hatchments,
 R. 542:35
Resurrection: attain unto the r. 68:22
 by man came also the r. 67:8
 certain hope of the R. 391:44
 I am the r. 63:40
 looking for the r. 400:30
Retain: marble to r. 112:35
 r. the offence 435:34
Retainer: play the Old R. 41:6
Retard what we cannot repel 277:24
Retards: perplexes and r. 287:28
Retention: they lack r. 483:9
Retentive to the strength of spirit 448:36
Reticulated: Net. Anything r. 277:28
Retinue: puffed up with this r. 442:21
Retire: r. me to my Milan 480:16
 sign for him to r. 182:17
 skill'd to r. 350:1
 with a blush r. 175:18
Retired: I r. to my room 512:19
 I saw the snare, and I r. 533:35
 Melancholy sate r. 154:1
 r. as noontide dew 578:32
 r. to his virtuous couch 560:8
 r. to their tea and scandal 154:30
Retirement: in his r. at Tusculum 175:8
 no r...our backs to the wall 233:20
 Plato's r. 350:11
 r., rural quiet 546:13
 short r. urges sweet return 349:9
Retiring..toward the Japanese
  fleet 234:18
Retort courteous 428:37
Retrace: thy steps r. 221:29
Retreat: friend in my r. 162:6
 honourable r. 428:2
 loopholes of r. 163:23
 my soul's calm r. 551:20
 Nature's signal of r. 279:14
 noblest station is r. 322:4

Retreat (cont.)
 not r. a single inch 213:17
 seek some safer r. 504:2
Retreated: snow hath r. 577:21
Retreating, to the breath.. 15:7
Retreats: never r., and never stops 179:37
Retrench the superfluities of mankind 214:28
Retrenchment: peace, r., and reform 82:18
Retrograde: be not r. 281:3
 r. if it does not advance 217:14
Retrorsum: nulla r. 256:20
Return: bid time r. 475:2
 day of their r. 326:8
 departed never to r. 108:37
 dust r. to the earth 51:33
 if thou r. at all in peace 48:14
 ill-us'd ghost, not to r. 73:13
 in that state I came, r. 552:7
 I shall r. 322:16
 never must r. 342:13
 perhaps r. the blow 124:13
 retirement urges sweet r. 349:9
 r. again, come! 171:4
 r., Alpheus..r. Sicilian Muse 342:30
 r. from following after thee 47:1
 r. no more 520:34
 r. no more to his house 48:53
 r., r., O Shulamite 52:16
 seasons r. 346:20
 spirit shall r. unto God 51:33
 unto dust shalt thou r. 44:28
 we must r. good for evil 551:8
Returned: I r. it sharper 546:38
 r. to your trinkets 297:16
Returnest: to dust r. 317:5
Returneth: repulsed,—but it r. 493:23
Returning: lest He r. chide 351:21
 r. seasons bring 378:15
 r. were as tedious 459:25
 vows of r. 526:23
Returns: earth's r. 93:11
 not one r. to tell us 206:27
 not to me r. day 346:20
 unexpectedly r. 351:7
 when it r. no more 497:3
Reuben: Tranter R. 236:8
Reveal: r. Himself to His servants 352:12
 words, like Nature, half r. 532:3
Revealed: arm of the Lord r. 54:24
 glory of the Lord..r. 54:9
 glory that shall be r. 389:27
 r. them unto babes 61:37
Revel: go r., ye Cupids 526:22
 pleasance, r., and applause 471:22
Revelation: other inspired by
  divine r. 24:17
 Oxford..r. of Mahomet 217:12
Revelations: divine Book of R. 127:16
 ends with R. 570:17
 pretending to extraordinary r. 109:38
Revelled: all who r. with the Regent 39:14
Revellers: you moonshine r. 466:15
Revelry: feast, and r. 342:7
 sound of r. by night 113:25
Revels: midnight r. 345:13
 our r. now are ended 480:8
 r. long o' nights 449:25
 what r. are in hand? 467:25
Revenge: capable and wide r. 472:12
 her r. being high 470:29
 I'll ne'er pursue r. 155:37
 I will most horribly r. 445:9
 little R...went down 540:4
 man that studieth r. 27:6
 my great r. had stomach 473:15
 ranging for r. 450:12
 r. his foul..murder 432:10
 r. is a kind of wild justice 27:4
 r. triumphs over death 26:2
 shall we not r.? 464:8
 spur my dull r. 436:15
 study of r. 344:14
 sweet as my r. 429:19
 sweet is r. 115:23
 sweet r. grows harsh 473:17
 their gratitude is a species of r. 278:12
 waiting r. 345:7
Revengeful: proud, r., ambitious 434:9

Revenges: such r. on you both 453:1
 time brings in his r. 484:26
Revenons à ces moutons 12:18
Revenue: instead of a standing r. 101:8
 no r. hast, but..good spirits 434:24
 streams of r. 563:4
Revenues: she bears a duke's r. 445:28
Reverberate hills 482:22
Reverberated: again r...farewells 172:21
Revere: praise, r., establish 42:1
 ride of Paul R. 317:3
Revered abroad 105:5
Reverence: in myn herte have hem
  in r. 138:16
 more of r. in us dwell 531:42
 mystic r. 28:21
 none so poor to do him r. 450:23
 r.—that angel of the world 429:39
 thousand claims to r. 539:12
 to r. the King 530:17
Reverend: ah, r. sir, not I 90:36
 grave and r. signiors 469:45
 how r...this tall pile 155:19
 that r. vice 439:35
Reverent: dare to be r. 376:4
Reverentia: maxima debetur puero r. 284:3
Reveries: from r. so airy 163:11
Reversion: no bright r. in the sky 381:32
Review: my grandmother's r. 115:26
 or a grand r. 119:25
Reviewers: chorus of indolent r. 529:19
 r...would have been poets, his-
  torians 152:30
Reviewing: read a book before r. it 505:7
Revilest thou God's high priest? 65:16
Revisit'st thus the glimpses 431:32(−432)
Revival: be converted at a r. 514:35
Revivals: history of r. 111:38
Revive: could I r. within me
  151:33(−152)
 straight again r. 123:19
Reviving: how r. to the spirits 350:13
 r. old Desires 205:8
Revocare gradum 554:23
Revolt: cloyment, and r. 483:9
Révolte: c'est une r.? 407:15
Revolted: against r. multitudes 348:20
Revolting and a rebellious heart 55:12
Revolts: leaders of r. 96:37
 r. me, but I do it 219:20
Revolution: 'mid all r. in the hopes 579:38
 R. a parent of settlement 102:7
Révolution: la R...dévorât..ses
  enfants 552:17
 non, Sire, c'est une r. 407:15
Revolutions: nursery of future r. 102:7
 r. are not to be evaded 181:39
 r. never go backward 422:12
Revolver: I reach for my r. 223:12
Revolves the sad vicissitude 217:17
Revolving in his alter'd soul 191:28
Reward: for their r...brought to
  shame 396:20
 full r. and glorious fate 125:8
 in no wise lose his r. 59:4
 love me, and r. me 471:4
 no r. is offered 329:9
 nothing for r. 509:32
 reap his old r. 303:26
 r. of a thing well done 200:26
 taken r. against the innocent 392:24
 the Lord r. him 69:3
 what r. shall be given 399:24
 write for glory or r. 157:5
 your r. in a certain place 85:8
Rewarded: plenteously r. 389:50
 they shall be greatly r. 56:23
Rewardest: thou r. every man 395:24
Rewardeth: he that r. thee 400:6
Rewards: crimes..their own r. 203:12
 farewell r. and fairies 157:3
 fortune's buffets and r. 434:26
 its veterans r. 384:37
 neither r. nor punishments 267:17
Re-word: I the matter will r. 436:1
Rex: Ego et R. meus 446:23
Rey: iguala al pastor con el r. 134:18
Reynolds: here R. is laid 225:34
 prefer a gipsy by R. 325:22
 when Sir Joshua R. died 73:16
Rhapsody of words 435:43

Rheims: Archbishop of R. 34:8
Rhein: die Wacht am R. 416:2
Rhetor geometres pictor 283:3
Rhetoric: for r. he could not ope 110:7
  heavenly r. of thine eye 455:16
  ornate r. 332:28
  r., able to contend 27:19
Rhetorician: r.'s rules 110:8
  sophistical r. 181:12
Rheumatic diseases do abound 466:37
Rhine: by the castled R. 316:23
  king-like rolls the R. 121:9
  lordly, lovely, R. 122:9
  R. circle fair Wertenberg 329:24
  R. is not more impassable 217:12
  R...our frontier 29:15
  Rupert of the R. 323:1, 2
  wash the river R. 150:28
  watch on the R. 416:2
  wide and winding R. 113:43
Rhinoceros: arm'd r. 459:20
  R., you are an ugly beast 40:28
Rhodopè: no voices, O R.! 309:13
Rhodora! if the sages ask 199:26
Rhyme: build the lofty r. 342:10
  free from r. or reason 381:21
  free from r.'s infection 281:26
  free from r.'s wrongs 281:26
  I r. for fun 105:27
  it hath taught me to r. 455:15
  making beautiful old r. 488:1
  many a mused r. 287:32
  master of unmeaning r. 117:27
  my murmuring r. 359:1
  Napoleon of the realms of r. 116:33
  neither r. nor reason 358:9
  nevre said in r.! 289:8
  nor r. nor reason 510:18
  now it is r. 358:9
  outlive this powerful r. 487:6
  reason for my r. 510:18
  reason war with r. 281:27
  r. being no necessary adjunct 343:26
  r. for roman 208:29
  r. is the rock 190:33
  r. thee to good 243:25
  r. themselves into ladies' favours 445:13
  r. the rudder is of verses 110:22
  ruined r. 525:26
  some careless r. 312:24
  some r...for needfu' cash 105:27
  sort of Runic r. 380:12
  to a random r. 183:3
  tyrant r. 281:27
  unattempted yet in prose or r. 344:3
Rhymed to death 502:11
Rhymes: know a baker r. 96:27
  my mournful r. 533:20
  pair their r. 116:14
  regent of love r. 455:8
  r. are so scarce 121:15
  r. of a love 80:28
  uncouth r. 230:7
Rhyming: Bacon of our r. crew 309:8
  modern bondage of R. 343:27
  r. mother wits 330:20
  r. peer 385:21
  under a r. planet 469:16
Rhythm: the whole of a new r. 88:17
Rialto: oft in the R. 463:20
  what news on the R.? 463:16
Rib: another r. afford 349:18
  r...made he a woman 44:16
  under the fifth r. 47:31
Ribbed: r. and paled in 429:29
  r. sea-sand 149:19
Ribbon: blue r. of the turf 182:11
  just for a r. 93:2
  lord in the blue r. 100:20
  r. in the cap of youth 436:41
  r. of moonlight 366:1
  what this r. bound 558:1
Ribboned coat 363:4
Ribbons: my sleeves with r. rare 266:8
  r. on her breast 31:17
  r. to flow confusedly 246:4
Ribs: mountain-chains like r. 235:22
  roar their r. out 222:30
  took one of his r. 44:16
  under the r. of Death 340:28
Ribstone Pippin: right as a R. 41:25

Rice: beside the ungather'd r. 317:16
Rice-fields: mist was on the r. 299:12
Rich: all men as r. as he 218:27
  art thou r. 170:21
  as easy to marry a r. woman 542:21
  beauty too r. for use 477:9
  being r., my virtue then 447:26
  certain r. man 62:23
  feed with the r. 271:27
  feud of r. and poor 533:19
  from the r. man's table 62:24
  grow r. in that 502:5
  he was r. as r. could be 218:27
  if I ever become a r. man 42:7
  if thou art r., thou'rt poor 462:4
  let him be r. and weary 245:1
  maketh haste to be r. 50:50
  making it r. 265:16
  most r., being poor 452:13
  mushroom r. civilian 119:24
  neither r. nor rare 385:27
  no sin, but to be r. 447:26
  one more r. in hope 486:24
  poor and content is r., and r.
    enough 471:33
  poorly r., and meanly great 415:17
  pride of the r. 142:4
  r. and rare were the gems 356:30
  r. and various gems 340:1
  r. beyond the dreams of avarice
    274:29, 356:3
  r. gifts wax poor 434:6
  r. have become richer 499:11
  r. have no right 413:28
  r. he hath sent empty away 61:14
  r. in good works 68:54
  r. in saving common-sense 537:14
  r. in the simple worship 287:18
  r. man in his castle 3:15
  r. man to enter..the kingdom 60:3
  r. men furnished with ability 57:16
  r. men rule the law 226:16
  r., not gaudy 431:25
  r., quiet, and infamous 324:32
  r. the treasure 191:5
  r. to hear the wooden dialogue 481:6
  r. what gets the pleasure 9:20
  r. with forty pounds a year 224:18
  r. with little store 195:13
  r. with the most noble blood 450:3
  r. with the spoils of time 230:5
  seems it r. to die 287:32
  something r. and strange 479:30
  they poor, I r. 195:13
  to the property of the r. 413:28
  virtue is like a r. stone 25:27
  we're r. in love 108:1
  when I grow r. 368:8
  with thee r. 163:47
Richard: came in with R. Con-
    queror 478:45
  God for his R. 475:1
  it is R., it is Raymond 141:7
  King R. doth himself appear 475:8
  R.'s himself again 144:28
  R., that sweet lovely rose 438:36
  terror to the soul of R. 476:38
Richardson: one letter of R.'s
    read R. for the story 272:12
    272:13
  works of R. 558:17
Richer: for r. for poorer 391:30
  r. still the older 111:24
  r. than all his tribe 474:2
  rich have become r. 499:11
Riches: all the r. of this world 74:29
  bear'st thy heavy r. 462:4
  deceitful of r. 59:24
  for that r. where is my deserv-
    ing? 487:22
  full of days, r., and honour 48:34
  good name..rather..than great
    r. 50:29
  go out, and see her r. 352:29
  hardly shall they that have r.
    enter 62:35
  he heapeth up r. 394:9
  his heart, ignorance of wealth 224:14
  if r. increase 395:24
  infinite r. in a little room 330:15
  in her left hand r. 49:40
  mor than gold or gret r. 321:12

Riches (*cont.*)
  neither poverty nor r. 50:53
  reproach of Christ greater r. 69:16
  r. are a good handmaid 25:6
  r. are for spending 26:10
  r. have wings 163:14
  r. left, not got with pain 518:1
  r...make themselves wings 50:31
  r. of heaven's pavement 345:9
  r. to be a valuable thing 519:33
  that r. grow in hell 345:10
  unsearchable r. of Christ 67:52
Richesses: embarras des r. 4:15
Richest: r. author 271:7
  r. without meaning 413:11
Richly: windows r. dight 341:24
Richmond Hill: lass of R. 327:5, 551:5
Richmonds: six R. in the field 476:43
Richness: here's r. 177:4
Rich-proud cost of..age 487:11
Ricks stand grey 298:26
Ricordarsi: che r. del tempo felice 168:22
Rid: cannot r. my hands of him 441:22
  he r. at the ring 30:9
  marry thee..to be r. of thee 155:33
  mend it or be r. on't 458:36(-459)
  thank God you are r. of a knave 468:37
Riddance: die and be a r. 174:15
Riddle: devil's r. is mastered 525:21
  dishcover the r. 131:29
  found out my r. 46:56
  glory, jest, and r. 383:22
  proposed her r. 350:17
  r. of destiny 307:34
Riddles of death 493:26
Riddling, perplexed..soul 186:30
Ride: about the woodland r. 262:10
  all-arm'd I r. 540:12
  as I r., as I r. 97:10
  for me, I r. 92:39
  for you alone I r. the ring 228:13
  his messengers r. forth 323:10
  in haste to r. 159:37
  returned from the r. 11:2
  r. a bit of blood 252:27
  r. a cock-horse 368:17
  r. in triumph through Persepolis 330:27
  r. mankind 199:19
  r. of Paul Revere 317:3
  r. on because..of meekness 394:22
  r. on! r. on in majesty 339:12
  r. on the pants triumphing 425:12
  r., r. together, forever r. 92:40
  r. your ways..Ellangowan 419:29
  to draw the bow, to r. 117:3
  to r., to run 510:16
  upon black Auster r. 324:11
  when he next doth r. 160:11
  where the Princes r. 171:2
  you must r. on horseback 159:33
Rideat: dulce r. ad patrem 133:6
Rideau: tirez le r. 404:29
Ridentem: dulce r. Lalagen 258:23
  r. dicere verum 261:7
  spectat et audit dulce r. 133:2
Rider: between a r. and his horse 518:42
  for want of a horse the r. was lost 211:10
  proud r. on so proud a back 488:27
  r. and horse 113:36
  steed that knows his r. 113:22
Rideret Democritus 257:15
Rides upon the storm 161:18
*Ridet: Iuppiter..periuria r. aman-
    tum* 371:22
  mihi..angulus r. 259:5
*Ridete quidquid est domi cachin-
    norum* 132:21
Rideth upon the heavens 396:5
Ridge of a noble down 540:29
Ridges: like a tempest down the r. 23:20
Ridicule is the best test of truth 139:29
Ridicule: du sublime au r. 361:2
*Ridiculos: paupertas..r. homines
    facit* 283:4
Ridiculous: don't want to do any-
    thing r. 412:20
  in brawl r. 444:10
  made arms r. 350:25
  more r...than a proud clergy-
    man 204:10
  sublime and the r. 372:21

Ridiculous (*cont.*)
 sublime to the r.   228:8, 361:2
 wasteful and r. excess   447:39
Riding: highwayman came r.   366:1
 my r. is better   92:38
 r. down by the Eildon Tree   32:6
 r. near her highest noon   341:14
 r. o'er land   114:39
 r. o'er the azure realm   229:23
 r.'s a joy   92:39
 r. to the townland   585:6
Rife: blessings are plentiful and r. 245:8
Riff-raff..to what is respectable 254:8
Rifiuto: il gran r.   168:19
Rifle: r. all the breathing Spring 153:21
 roll to your r.   304:4
 your r. an' yourself jus' so   295:22
Riflemen Form!   540:5
Rift: little r. within the lute 531:11
 load every r..with ore   291:1
Riga: young lady of R.   11:2
Rigdum-Funnidos: gentle R.   125:14
Rigged with 'curses dark   342:25
Riggish: bless her when she is r. 424:9
Right: all is r. as r. can be 219:18
 all's r. with the world   94:40
 always in the r.   159:14
 and I am r., and you are r.   219:18
 as God gives us to see the r.   314:13
 as men strive for R.   88:24
 as much r...as pigs have to fly 129:19
 attains to think r.   278:8
 at thy r. hand..pleasure   392:27
 aye upheld the r.   324:6
 because not all was r.   165:11
 because r. is r., to follow r. 537:33
 Bertram's r.   419:35
 born to set it r.   432:32
 by the r. way   398:15
 Christ thy r.   354:11
 circles and r. lines   87:13
 dare not be in the r. with two
   or three   320:15
 dawn on my r.   41:20
 did not write it r.   248:12
 do the R.   327:3
 do what is r.   266:21
 earl by r.   23:13
 every single one..is r.   297:9
 firmness in the r.   314:13
 generalities of natural r.   142:29
 great r. of an excessive wrong 96:3
 heaven still guards the r.   475:1
 he's all r.   233:12
 his conduct still r.   225:29
 his life..was in the r.   158:5
 his r. hand doth embrace me   51:45
 in his r. mind   60:58
 in thy r. hand..peace   446:31
 it must be r.   104:32
 Judge of all the earth do r.   44:52
 length of days is in her r. hand 49:40
 little from the r.   105:16
 makes us r. or wrang   105:22
 meet and r. so to do   390:38
 minorities..always in the r.   505:9
 my r. good-will   327:5
 my r. hand forget her cunning   400:5
 my r. there is none to dispute 164:22
 of r. and wrong he taught   14:26
 on the r. went down   148:21
 our country, r. or wrong   169:28
 publish, r. or wrong   117:9
 quite lawful nor quite r.   111:35
 rage to set things r.   89:25
 rather be r. than be President 146:2
 reading is r.   278:25
 Real R. Thing   268:10
 renew a r. spirit   395:9
 reprove her when she's r.   520:55
 r. against the eastern gate   341:33
 r. and round about   106:18
 r. as a Ribstone Pippin   41:28
 r., by chance   159:12
 r. deed for the wrong reason   197:25
 R. Divine..to govern wrong   381:24
 r. good captain too   221:10
 r. hand of the Lord   399:8, 9
 r. hands of fellowship   67:40
 r. it should be so   73:24
 r. little, tight little Island 173:15

Right (*cont.*)
 r. makes might   314:8
 r. man in the r. place   268:29
 r. man to fill the r. place   310:25
 r. of an earlier creation   325:4
 r. of election   282:17
 r. of governing   210:21
 r. of the ignorant   126:5
 r. part wrote Liddell   11:7
 r. was r.   165:10
 secure of private r.   190:28
 servant unto r.   509:35
 serve it r. for being so dear   177:2
 set thee r.   161:10
 sit thou on my r. hand   398:23
 smite thee on thy r. cheek   57:50
 sometimes in the r.   194:9
 speak true, r. wrong   530:4
 talks about justice and r.   300:7
 ten thousand at thy r. hand   397:18
 that which is lawful and r.   55:30
 thing that is r.   394:6
 thing which is r.   392:24
 think, at your age, it is r.?   128:28
 think it only r.   221:12
 though r. were worsted   97:4
 thy r. hand shall hold me   400:9
 thy r. hand shall teach thee   394:22
 to do a great r.   465:2
 too fond of the r.   225:28
 to set me r.   308:24
 Ulster will be r.   143:29
 upon thy r. hand..the queen   394:23
 whatever is, is r.   383:21
 what's r. and fair   265:1
 what thy r. hand doeth   58:2
 when all goes r.   222:1
 when the r. man rings them   516:3
 where r. is wrong   218:6
 who'll do him r. now?   90:17
 whose life is in the r.   384:1
 without so much labour appear
   to be r.   278:25
 your judgement..probably .. r. 329:11
 your r. to say it   557:15
Right-doing: relinquish r., even in
   dreams   120:17
Right-down regular Royal Queen 218:21
Righteous: armor of a r. cause 98:1
 be not r. over much   51:14
 death of the r.   46:18
 dwellings of the r.   399:8
 fervent prayer of a r. man   69:44
 God is a r. Judge   392:7
 godly, r. and sober   388:12
 let the r. rather smite me   400:14
 not come to call the r.   58:40
 O ye r.   393:35
 r. are bold as a lion   50:49
 r., let him be r. still   72:8
 r. man regardeth..his beast   50:2
 r. minds of inn-keepers   142:1
 r. put their hand unto wickedness 399:33
 r. work..not be forgiven   140:4
 saw I never the r. forsaken   394:5
 souls of the r.   56:23
 what hath the r. done?   392:19
 when the r. man turneth away   111:35
Righteousness: from original r. 401:5
 fulfil all r.   57:32
 he looked for..r   53:2
 little hills to r.   396:23
 living unto r.   390:59
 makes for r.   20:14, 17
 paths of r.   393:10, 421:1
 r. and peace have kissed   397:9
 r. exalteth a nation   50:9
 r. hath looked down   397:9
 r. shall go before him   397:10
 Sun of r. arise   56:15
 thirst after r.   57:39
 thy r. as clear   394:4
 thy r. as the waves   54:20
 thy r. unto the King's son   396:22
 what r. really is   20:18
 word of..r.   394:22
 worketh not the r. of God   69:30
 your r...exceed the r. of the
   scribes   57:44
Righteousnesses: our r...as filthy
   rags   55:8

Rightful: for our r. King   106:16
Right-hand foot   131:25
Righting: good for r. wrongs   315:12
Right-lined: mortal r. circle 87:13
Rightly done!   265:20
Rights: its duties as well as its r. 189:24
 lies in his r. of a man   89:13
 r. inherent and inalienable   268:17
 r. of an Englishman   282:16
 unalienable r.   11:11
 whose r. he has trodden   101:27
Rigid: very r. and exact   293:2
Rigida: pallidula r. nudula   233:19
Rigol: this golden r.   442:26
Rigour: my r. relents   100:25
Riled: no sense in gittin' r. 238:28
Riles: Christian r.   300:5
Rill: Siloam's shady r.   240:16
Rills: bright with sinuous r. 151:32
 r. fashion..their nursling   309:5
Rim: over the mountain's r.   94:27
 Sun's r. dips   149:14
 utmost purple r.   528:29
Rime-ringed: to the r. sun   298:28
Rimini: Francesca di R.   221:6
Rimmon: in the house of R.   48:23
Rind: burnished with golden r. 347:5
 from out the r. of one apple   352:8
 how shall taste the r.?   544:25
 in the r...scooped   347:14
 sweet as the r. was   522:20
Ring: bright gold r.   356:30
 curfew must not r. to-night   547:5
 draw the chalky r.   164:8
 for one shilling your r.   312:2
 for you alone I ride the r.   228:13
 he rid at the r.   30:9
 maids dance in a r.   361:6
 more than gold was in a r.   140:26
 only pretty r. time   428:30
 rare gold r. of verse   96:19
 r. at the end of his nose   312:1
 r. from their marble caves   190:3
 r. O bells   566:28(-567)
 r. of pure and endless light   552:13
 r. of words   516:3
 r. out..r. in   533:18, 19, 20
 r. out, wild bells   533:17
 r. out ye crystal spheres   343:17
 r. so worn   165:21
 r. that he had of your daughter 464:11
 r. the bells of Heaven   249:5
 round both the shires they r.   262:21
 sleeps on his luminous r.   537:35
 they now r. the bells   558:30
 this R. given and received   391:33
 unconquered in a r.   141:30
 what shall we do for a r.?   312:1
 with this R. I thee wed   391:32
Ringdove's neck   123:5
Ringed: r. round with a flame 523:2
 r. with the azure world   529:10
Ringing down the street   23:22
Ringlets: green sour r.   480:12
 male r.   523:4
Ringlet-snake: Fury's r.   535:26
Rings: as in airy r.   386:32
 chain of countless r.   199:17
 his hands are as gold r.   52:14
 right man r. them   516:3
 r. on her fingers   368:17
 wearers of r. and chains   308:24
Rinsed with wine   254:27
Rio: rolling down to R.   297:24
Riot: luxury and r.   349:27
 rash fierce blaze of r.   474:21
Riotous living   62:13
Ripae ulterioris amore   554:28
Ripe: cherry r.   4:14, 124:5, 245:21
 r. and good one   447:9
 we r. and r.   427:14
 what shelter to grow r.   17:4
Ripeness: certain r. in intellect 289:26
 r. is all   454:18
 when love is grown to r.   533:34
Ripening: his greatness is a-r. 446:24
Riper: of R. Years   390:61
Ripes: ventiferous r.   251:19
Ripped: from his mother's womb
   untimely r.   461:11
Ripple: slip and r. idly   336:7

INDEX

Ripples : little r. down a sunny river 308:30
Rip Van Winkle: when R. went
  away 97:35
Rire: faire r. les honnêtes gens 353:15
  je me presse de r. 37:9
Ris : our backs is easy r. 176:23
Rise : arts that caused himself to r. 385:29
  awake you when you r. 170:23
  beheld the sun r. up 574:11
  created half to r. 383:22
  haste to r. up early 399:35
  held we fall to r. 97:4
  his sun to r. on the evil 57:52
  hope to r., or fear to fall 583:11
  I r. at ten-thirty 237:28
  i' the dark to r. by. And I r. 96:10
  Jetty, r. and follow 267:13
  mailed lobster r. 211:26
  morn will never r. 169:13
  my Shakespeare, r. 281:11
  nation shall r. against nation 60:23
  nature's eye, r., r. again 330:7
  never r. and fight again 224:9
  not r. nor set 410:1
  now they r. again 459:17
  quartern loaf and Luddites r. 504:5
  r. at five 145:31
  r.! for the day is passing 402:14
  r. from the ground like..
    Mercury 440:18
  r. not from the East 165:36
  r. on stepping-stones 532:1
  r., take up thy bed 63:16
  r., the progress..of imagery 289:27
  r. to all eternity 565:8
  r. up at the voice of the bird 51:33
  r. up, My love 52:1, 334:16
  r. with the lark 80:2
  run, r., rest with Thee 245:9
  seen those dead men r. 149:31
  sets to r. again 93:25
  some r. by sin 461:24
  stoop to r. 334:19
  suns..may r. again 282:6
  tears..r. in the heart 538:17
  they r. or sink together 539:6
  thy voice r. like a fountain 531:36
  to r., it stoops 90:41
  when afar you r. 95:1
  who does not r. early 276:1
  woe unto them that r. up 53:4
Risen : Christ, the Lord, is r. 565:4
  glory of the Lord is r. 54:39
  now is Christ r. 67:8
  r. in the Faubourg St. Germain 558:20
  r. to hear him crow 196:13
  we are r., and stand upright 392:37
Risere: qui non r. parenti 556:2
Rises : or they r., and we snarls 176:23
  the Lord who r. 161:21
  up she r. 11:16
  with him r. weeping 485:25
Rising : all r. to great place 26:28
  assisted the sun..in his r. 546:36
  at evening r. to meet you 197:28
  her r. sweet 347:22
  his r. fogs prevail 193:2
  how oft hereafter r. 207:28, 29
  my r. Soul surveys 2:22
  politics..a means of r. 272:33
  r. hope of those..Tories 324:27
  r. in clouded majesty 347:19
  r. of the sun 10:14
  r. unto place is laborious 26:24
  r. with Aurora's light 521:16
  yon r. Moon 207:29
Risk it on one turn 297:11
Risu: r. cognoscere matrem 556:1
  r. inepto 132:23
  solventur r. tabulae 261:21
Rite : many a loathed r. 491:15
  no noble r. 436:37
Rites : r. mysterious of connubial
    love 347:25
  when r. unholy called' 123:9
Rival : r. in the light of day 582:20
  trickle to his r.'s bier 418:5
Rivalry : with the dead .. no r. 325:23
Rivals : r. are the worst 559:6
  r. rail 278:27
  their r. dead 374:16

Rive not more in parting 425:18
Riveder le stelle 168:24
River : Alph, the sacred r. 151:32
  beautiful r. 415:8
  beside the r. make for you 84:8
  bread I dip in the r. 515:27
  brook and r. meet 316:34
  by a r.'s brim 578:25
  by r. or sea shore 287:12
  craft in the r. 504:2
  dower of r., wood, and vale 285:1
  dragon-fly on the r. 88:11
  even the weariest r. 523:23
  fading down the r. 363:6
  fame is like a r. 27:1
  flung up..the sacred r. 151:33
  ford o' Kabul r. 296:21
  for ever run like a r. 119:7
  fountains mingle with the r. 495:7
  fruitful r. in the eye 430:30
  greasy Limpopo R. 304:17
  in a field by the r. 584:11
  let the great r. take me 539:1
  like a crystal r. 537:42
  like a reynynge r. bee 136:17
  like the foam on the r. 416:23
  like the rushing r. 329:4
  living r. by the door 516:12
  majestic R. floated on 17:28
  on a tree by a r. 220:17
  on either side the r. 533:40
  one more r. to cross 10:7
  Pentridge by the r. 35:14
  pure r. of water of life 72:6
  reeds by the r. 88:11
  ripples down a sunny r. 308:30
  r. at my garden's end 521:7
  r. glideth at his own.. will 582:14
  r. in Macedon..at Monmouth 445:4
  r. of crystal light 204:5
  r. of Time 16:3
  r.'s trembling edge 497:23
  r. up an' brimmin' 296:21
  r. winding clearly 534:1
  runs not a r. by my palace wall? 542:26
  rush of the r. 40:2
  sacred r. ran 151:33
  shall we gather at the r.? 415:8
  snow falls in the r. 108:7
  spake to the noble r. 323:26
  swap horses while crossing the
    r. 314:15
  this r. comes me cranking in 439:44
  thy peace been as a r. 54:20
  Time's fleeting r. 496:1
  'Tirra lirra,' by the r. 534:6
  upon the r. shore 419:9
  upon the Swanee R. 210:16
  where white flows the r. 516:2
  you rolling r. 8:21
River-fields : harvest of the r. 18:29
River-Lip : fledges the R. 206:4
River-rounded 254:22
Rivers : all the r. run into the sea 50:60
  any discourse of r., and fish 559:25
  as r. of water in a dry place 53:43
  as the r. in the south 399:34
  by shallow r., to whose falls 330:18
  noise of winds and many r. 521:30
  r. cannot quench 446:5
  r., in the greatest rain 373:14
  r. of Damascus 48:22
  r. with the ocean 495:7
  shallow brooks and r. wide 342:1
  springs into the r. 398:8
  washed by the r. 84:21
Rivets : closing r. up 444:6
Rivos: claudite iam r., pueri 555:29
Rivulet : neat r. of text 500:33
Rivulets : myriads of r. 539:5
  where r. dance 581:22
Road : because the r. is rough 83:4
  butterfly upon the r. 300:13
  drive the r. 301:26
  force and r. of casualty 463:44
  free as the r. 244:9
  Golden R. to Samarkand 208:14
  good to be out on the r. 334:14
  hammer along the 'ard 'igh r. 403:12
  high r...leads him to England 271:8
  I like..the r. you are travelling 505:30

Road (*cont.*)
  in all the endless r. you tread 263:23
  I take to the open r. 568:3
  life..a pleasant r. 402:9
  life's r., so dim and dirty 115:11
  long r. lies 263:12
  my mistress still the open r. 515:29
  my r. calls me, lures me 334:9
  no expeditious r. 544:32
  no r. or ready way to virtue 86:23
  no 'royal r.' to geometry 202:8
  on a lonesome r. 150:2
  one r. leads to London 334:8
  on the r. and coming 179:37
  other end of the r. 334:13
  r. before me..below me 515:28
  R. I was to wander in 207:10
  r. lies long and straight 514:30
  r. of excess 77:8
  r. through the woods 303:16, 17
  R. to fair Elfland 32:10
  r. to resolution lies by doubt 404:8
  r. was a ribbon of moonlight 366:1
  r. went up, the r. went down 40:18
  r. wind up-hill all the way? 410:2
  rolling English r. 141:21
  rough r. easy walking 263:18
  sad r. lies so clear 375:21
  sustain to-morrow's r. 77:30
  there runs a r. by Merrow Down 299:23
  they are upon the r. 160:5
  to shine upon the r. 161:1
  to tell us of the R. 206:27
  to the end of the r. 310:14
  who passes by this r. so late? 11:24
  winding r. before me 240:9
  world to be a grassy r. 585:22
  yon braid, braid r. 32:9
Road-rail, pig-lead 333:21
Roads : most r. lead men 334:9
  walked along our r. 308:17
Roadway : keeps the r. better 441:35
  while I stand on the r. 585:12
Roam : absent from Him I r. 355:10
  dunce that has been sent to r. 161:31
  her ways to r. 84:21
  long wont to r. 380:17
  other far doth r. 186:25
  r. on! 19:1
  sadly I r. 210:16
  soar, but never r. 580:27
  though we may r. 376:10
  where'er I r. 226:4
  where'er we r. 226:7
Roamed with my Soul 381:2
Roaming : R. in the Gloamin' 310:16
  r. with a hungry heart 540:32
  where are you r.? 482:28
Roar : bark, bellow, and r. 73:26
  burst the cannon's r. 251:5
  cannon's opening r. 113:27
  glorious the thunder's r. 503:6
  grievous r. echo'd 406:19
  grumble, and rumble, and r. 406:3
  hear the waves r. 16:1
  I will r. 466:29, 30
  like the torrent r. 382:32
  long, withdrawing r. 15:7
  r., as if of earthly fire 285:36
  r. of a rain-fed ford 302:20
  r. of some..desert lion 17:26
  r. of the Milky Way 302:20
  r. their ribs out 222:30
  rock gun's r. 77:31
  set the table on a r. 437:15
  thundering cannons r. 227:10
  with sullen r. 341:15
Roared : Atlantic billows r. 159:1
  growled, and r. and howled 148:26
  loud r. the dreadful thunder 139:1
  ran about the room and r. 140:5
  well r., Lion 467:32
Roarers : what cares these r.? 479:15
Roareth : this that r. thus? 223:8
Roaring : mockers in the r. street 313:5
  r. in the wind all night 580:4
  r. of the young lions 19:8
  r. through the pass 324:15
  when the seas were r. 216:5
Roars : act, that r. so loud 435:44
Roast : but to r. their eggs 27:39

Roast (*cont.*)
no politics in boil'd and r. 505:32
r. beef of England 204:13
r. me in sulphur! 473:32
r. with fire 45:46
strove to rule the r. 402:7
Roasted: she fedde with r. flesh 136:30
young healthy child. .r. 520:3
Rob: nightly r. the dairy 281:5
r. a lady of her fortune 204:30
r. me, but bind me not 185:27
r. us of our joys 5:8
that he might r. a neighbour 324:34
Robbed: he that is r., not wanting 472:2
not r. at all 472:2
r. me of my Robe of Honour 207:22
r. that smiles steals something 470:6
ye have r. 363:7
Robber: Barabbas was a r. 63:69
Robbery: in scandal, as in r. 139:6
trust not in wrong and r. 395:24
Robbing: comes to think little of r. 172:23
r. of a foe 143:6
Robe: girt with a crimson r. 232:1
in a r. of clouds 118:7
intertissued r. of gold 444:23
like a giant's r. 460:31
nor the judge's r. 461:28
robb'd me of my R. of Honour 207:22
this r. of mine 485:27
Robert: R.'s kin, and John's 236:8
slight Sir R. 529:14
Robertson: Sir, I love R. 271:25
works of Hume, Gibbon, R. 306:26
Robes: arrayed in white r. 71:5
his flaming r. stream'd out 285:36
in all his r. pontifical exprest 545:6
in r. of light array'd 240:21
r. loosely flowing 280:7
r. riche, or fithele 137:6
r. the mountain 122:31
singing r. about him 352:20
washed their r. 71:6
when all her r. are on 8:14
Robin: bonny sweet R. 436:34
call for the r. redbreast 563:30
gard'ner R. 160:30
gay R. is seen no more 80:20
lilacs where the r. built 253:1
no r. ever on the deep 171:20
our little English r. 580:1
R. Redbreast in a cage 73:19
R., R., R. Crusoe 170:6
R.'s not near 292:5
sweet R. sits in the bush 420:2
what will poor r. do then? 368:2
who killed Cock R.? 369:18
Robin Adair 292:5
Robin Hood: here lies bold R. 31:22
is R. asleep? 366:6
Robinson: John P. Robinson he 319:17
Robinson Crusoe: wished longer
. .R. 276:26
Robs: r. me of my rest 231:39
r. me of my manhood 191:19
r. me of that which not enriches 471:30
r. not one light seed 286:3
r. you on business principles 490:38
Robur: illi r. et aes triplex 258:5
Robust: men r. for toil 123:7
Robustious periwig-pated fellow 434:15
Rochefoucauld: nod good-bye to
R. 197:3
Rochets: lawn sleeves and r. 404:17
Rock: Adonis from his native r. 344:32
Colussus from a r. 275:21
for a r. of offence 53:13
it is the Inchcape R.! 507:26
monarchy. .strike on a r. 4:21
on a r. reclin'd 216:5
pendant r. 425:19
rhyme is the r. 190:33
r. his brains 442:1
r. of ages, cleft for me 548:11
r. of Holy Scripture 223:2
r. of immortality 83:10
r. them, r. them, lullaby 170:23
serpent upon a r. 50:56
shadow of a great r. 53:43
she ran upon no r. 162:11
sleep r. thy brain 435:14

Rock (*cont.*)
smote the r. of the national resources 563:4
some r.'s vast weight to throw 382:32
summons of the r. gun's roar 77:31
tall r., the mountain 581:26
they knew the perilous r. 507:25
they rested on a r. 130:15
think that you are upon a r. 430:5
this r. shall fly 416:26
upon this r. . .my church 59:43
valley, r., or hill 582:14
water out of this r. 46:15
Rock-a-bye-baby 73:14
Rocked: he neither shall be r. 5:16
r. in the cradle of the deep 570:27
she r. it, and rated it 196:2
Rocket: he rose like a r. 373:2
Rocking: cradle endlessly r. 567:1
r. a grown man 103:23
Rocking horse: upon a r. 288:12
Rocks: ascetic r. 337:17
flowers, clouds, woods, r. 493:14
from r. to roses 387:23
hand that r. the cradle 557:19
'mid these dancing r. 151:33
mother with infant down the r. 351:20
on a throne of r. 118:7
quicksands, and the r. 290:7
rifted r. whose entrance leads 340:25
r. among which she sits 374:11
r., and stones, and trees 573:6
r., caves, lakes, fens 346:2
r. on the mould 5:16
r. unscalable 429:29
stony r. for the conies 398:10
these valleys and r. 164:25
to the r. and the mountains 526:22
walled round with r. 523:13
whether on crystal r. ye rove 75:18
Rod: Aaron's r. 45:42
bruise them with a r. of iron 391:50
chief a r. 384:9
creed is a r. 524:3
every r. or staff of empire 28:12
eyeball owns the mystic r. 96:33
he that spareth his r. 50:6
humbled kiss the r. 484:31
r. of empire might have sway'd 230:4
r. of incantation 215:37
r. of the ungodly 399:33
r. produces an effect 269:33
r. to check the erring 573:28
spare the r. 110:42
spoils the r. 253:3
there shall come forth a r. 244:12
throw away Thy r. 244:12
thy r. and staff me comfort 421:1
thy r. and thy staff comfort me 393:10
Wisdom be put in a silver r. 74:2
with the end of the r. 47:14
wreathed the r. of criticism 182:48
Rode: for it I r. 78:2
he r. at the ring 30:9
Hesperus. .r. brightest 347:19
in the strength of this I r. 530:30
I r. upon the Down 78:1
r. all that day. .in a forest 328:20
r. at full speed 311:5
r. at his right hand 324:12
r. between the barley-sheaves 534:4
r. madly off in all directions 311:1
r. past fair Florence 286:22
Roderick: where was R. then? 416:28
Roderick Dhu: I am R.! 416:25
Rods: bleeding from the Roman r. 158:29
Roe: be thou like to a r. 52:25
following the r. 107:12, 420:24
Roebuck: he is a gentle r. 585:10
Roes: thy breasts are like two
young r. that are twins 52:5
Roger's false flattering tongue 306:34
Rogue: bewitched with the r.'s
company 439:2
dainty r. in porcelain 337:22
fiddler. .consequently a r. 519:27
has he not a r.'s face? 155:10
hated a r. 276:18
how easy it is to call r. 194:17
insinuating r. 473:1
r. and peasant slave 433:31

Rogue (*cont.*)
r. gives you Love Powders 307:14
r. is married to a whore 301:11
snubnosed r. 535:34
Rogues: hear poor r. talk 454:19
see the r. flourish 90:16
two r. in buckram suits 439:20
you dissentious r. 429:4
Roi: plus royaliste que le r. 12:14
un r. d'Yvetot 43:9
Rois: la politesse des r. 318:23
le dernier des r. . .étranglé 338:1
Roland: Childe R. to the Dark
Tower came 90:23, 453:27
Roll: all away began to r. 74:13
felt him like the thunder's r. 16:21
few more years shall r. 78:16
let it r. on full flood 144:2
not in the r. of common men 439:41
our echoes r. 538:16
pension list. .a r. of honour 146:5
r. down—r. down to Rio 297:24
r. down their golden sand 240:17
r. forth, my song 329:4
r. of the world eastward 236:38
r. on, thou ball 218:12
r. on, thou. .Ocean 114:27
r. to your rifle 304:4
r. upon your bed 358:24
r. up that map 379:17
they r. and rumble 358:10
when the drums begin to r. 303:3
Rolled: as if the earth had r. 575:26
bottoms of my trousers r. 197:21
r. mother with infant 351:20
r. round in earth's diurnal course 573:6
Roller, pitch, and stumps, and all 309:27
Rollest: thou r. now 114:29
Rollicking bun 222:18
Rolling: in a fine frenzy r. 467:24
Iser, r. rapidly 122:17
night-rack came r. up 293:29
r. down the Ratcliffe Road 294:26
r. down to Rio 297:24
r. English drunkard 141:21
r. his head 325:32
stone that is r. 550:5
you r. river 8:21
Rolls: dig for buttered r. 131:24
r. by the towers of Rome 323:20
r. impotently on as Thou or I 207:3
r. it under his tongue 242:8
Roma locuta est 22:5
Romae: omnia R. cum pretio 283:6
opes strepitumque R. 260:13
si fueris R. 4:20
Romain: ni saint, ni r., ni empire 557:8
*Romam: fortunatam natam me con-
sule R.* 145:24
Roman: before the R. came to Rye 141:21
bleeding from the R. rods 158:29
Ghost of the deceased R. Empire 248:23
high R. fashion 425:31
his noses cast is of the r. 208:29
historian of the R. empire 216:28
I'm a R. for that 203:12
make a R. holiday 114:19
more an antique R. 438:3
neither holy, nor R. 557:8
noblest R. of them all 452:8
No, sir. R. R. 178:8
play the R. fool, and die 461:9
rather be a dog. .than such a R. 451:13
rhyme for r. 208:29
R. and his trouble 263:9
R. by a R. valiantly vanquished 425:28
R. Conquest. .a *Good Thing* 422:13
R. meal 163:27
R.-Saxon-Danish-Norman 170:13
R.'s life, a R.'s arms 323:27
R. thought hath struck him 423:22
sweet R. hand 484:6
then 'twas the R. 263:8
truth. .with the R. clergy 294:4
would not be a R. 450:16
writ in a R. chamber 146:15
*Romana: moribus antiquis res stat
R. virusque* 201:25
Romanam condere gentem 553:9
Romance: any historical r. 145:30

Romance (cont.)
confound R. 298:1
not a little given to r. 202:12
R. brought up the nine-fifteen 298:1
R.! those first-class passengers 299:8
shores of old r. 573:2
spirit of r. is dead 294:16
steam spoils r. at sea 299:7
symbols of a high r. 289:5
Romances : read eternal new r. 231:20
r. paint at full length 115:39
r. . .spiritualized 558:17
vulgar authors in r. 110:44
woods with high r. blent 288:23
Romane: tu regere, . .R., memento 555:1
Romani: cedite R. scriptores 402:17
Romanism: rum, R., and rebellion 99:42
Romano: Italian master, Julio R. 485:36
Romanorum ultimum 526:12
Romans : as when the R. came 302:8
first, the Greeks, or the R. 181:23
friends, R., countrymen 450:17
last of all the R. 452:2
pristine wars of the R. 444:2
R. call it stoicism 1:16
R. were like brothers 323:21
to whom the R. pray 323:27
yet two R. living 452:2
Romantic: deep r. chasm 151:32
not a r. animal 29:6
ruin that's r. 220:20
Romantics: detection. .tinge it
with r. 188:18
Romanus: civis R. sum 145:14
populus R. unam cervicem 120:18
Rome: aisles of Christian R. 199:23
all you writ to R. 446:23
at R. she hadde been 137:15
Bishop of R. . .no jurisdiction 401:12
Church of R. I found 7:10
comes round by R. 96:4
ever R. should breed thy fellow 452:2
fate, of Cato and of R. 1:13
fire of old R. 201:27
go bound to R. 451:37
grandeur that was R. 380:17
Half-Way House to R. 403:5
if you are at R. 4:20
I loved R. more 450:14
insolent Greece or haughty R. 281:15
it was at R. 217:1
I've lost R. 301:5
lay thou on for R.! 324:8
let R. in Tiber melt 423:14
marched to R. 323:12
move the stones of R. to rise 450:34
palmy state of R. 430:14
pardoun come from R. al hoot 137:21
rolls by the towers of R. 323:26
R. been growing up to might 184:2
R. indeed and room enough 448:24
R. is above the Nations 301:29
R. . .like its own Monte Testaco 114:12
R.! my country! 114:12
R. . .not to be compared 563:5
R. of to-day 200:2
R. shall perish 158:30
R. shall stand 114:21
R., though her eagle 558:2
R. thy Virgil's name 160:24
second at R. 24:29
strangers of R. 64:26
time will doubt of R. 116:12
varietry of censuring R. 425:34
voice of R. 279:26
when R. falls—the World 114:21
you cruel men of R. 448:8
Romeo: give me my R. 478:20
R., R.! wherefore art thou R.? 477:15
R.'s a dishclout to him 478:31
Romps: je plie et ne r. pas 209:11
Romuli: in R. faece 145:1
Ronald: Lord R. . .rode madly off 311:1
Ronsard me célébrait 408:18
Ronyon: rump-fed r. 456:10
Rood: every r. of ground 224:14
half a r. of land 521:7
Roof: arch'd and pond'rous r. 155:19
its r. may shake 379:11
living, had no r. 248:4
my tent's thin r. 492:29

Roof (cont.)
my tongue cleave to the r. of my
mouth 400:5
r. of blue Italian weather 495:8
r. of the world 227:35
this majestical r. 433:15
thou. .come under my r. 58:30
through its gorgeous r. 92:30
through the arched r. 343:21
whose humble r. 247:16
Roofs : masons building r. of gold 443:10
over the r. of the world 568:2
Roof-tree: heavens my wide r. 24:10
your ain r. stand the faster 419:29
Rookery: leads the clanging r. 534:20
Rook-racked, river-rounded 254:22
Rooks : choughs and r. 459:24
r. are blown about the skies 532:12
r. came home in scramble sort 249:13
r. in families homeward go 236:33
Rooky wood 459:8
Room: although the r. grows chilly 228:11
always r. at the top 563:1
ample r. and verge enough 229:22
bridegroom from his r. 24:6
coming to that holy r. 185:25
from my lonely r. 23:16
from r. to r. I stray 561:18
glowing embers through the r. 341:16
how little r. do we take up 501:8
infinite riches in a little r. 330:15
is there r. for Mary? 415:7
large upper r. furnished 62:43
leave r. for the mouse 414:18
man in jail has more r. 270:32
moonlight in his r. 265:16
nae r. at my head, Marg'ret 30:16
no r. for them in the inn 61:17
ocean sea. .not sufficient r. 35:23
paces about her r. again 197:32
ran about the r. and roared 140:5
Rome indeed and r. enough 448:24
r. for the bonnets 416:8
r. in the beautiful heavenly land 415:7
r. my heart keeps empty 292:19
R. of One's Own 572:22
r. to deny ourselves 291:7
sweeps a r. as for Thy laws 244:16
taper to the outward r. 186:12
to make thee a r. 281:11
two paces. .r. enough 440:38
wasn't r. to swing a cat 175:1
willing foe and sea r. 5:18
worst inn's worst r. 385:1
yes, there's r. 415:7
you shall keep your r. 516:2
Rooms : most of the r. of thy. .
country 212:11
your r. at college was beastly 299:18
Roost: curses. .come home to r. 507:13
Rooster: hungry r. don't cackle 238:22
Roosts: on the perched r. 351:2
Root: axe is laid unto the r. 57:31
eaten on the insane r. 456:19
fruit-tree's mossy r. 332:20
get with child a mandrake r. 186:16
gold. .at the r. of wisdom 111:39
nips his r. 446:24
perced to the r. 136:21
r. and father of many kings 458:30
r. and the offspring of David 72:10
r. of all evil 68:52
r. of all sins 267:29
r. of the matter is found in me 49:7
sleep at the r. of my tree 310:21
they had no r. 59:22
thy r. is ever in its grave 245:13
what you are, r. and all 529:24
wisdom's r. 104:21
Roots: broad on the r. of things 89:7
duty, faith, love, are r. 377:4
poison England at her r. 79:3
r. of sin are there 302:33
r. of the earth. .rotten 289:31
r. that can be builded up 196:19
send my r. rain 255:9
stirring dull r. with spring rain 197:27

Rope (cont.)
r. that hangs my dear 214:21
sin as it were with a cart r. 53:5
Rorum, corum, sunt Divorum l 370:5
Rosa quo locorum era 258:30
Rosaleen: my Dark R.! 329:1
Rosalind: no jewel is like R. 427:28
Rosalys: Margaret and R. 410:12
Rosaries: pictures, r., and pixes 111:12
Rosary: my r. 408:5
Rose: against the blown r. 424:29
as a dream the fabric r. 163:40
as the canker to the r. 342:15
as though a r. should shut 285:23
at last he r. 343:7
awful r. of dawn 541:10
beauty's r. might never die 486:9
blossom as the r. 54:1
breast that gives the r. 336:41
budding r. above the r. full
blown 575:3
but it r. afar 97:21
day r. with delight 292:21
deep as a r.'s 523:1
die of a r. in aromatic pain 383:16
English unofficial r. 84:9
expectancy and r. 434:14
fair as is the r. in May 138:21
gather therefore the R. 509:33
ghost of a r. 85:20
go, lovely R.! 558:4
gone with all his R. 205:10
gone with all its R. 205:9
hath not thy r. a canker? 445:23
he r. like a rocket 373:2
him that loved the r. 543:24
His blood upon the r. 380:6
his supplication to the r. 208:11
home, R., and home 146:33
I am the r. of Sharon 51:43
I bound the r. in sheaves 93:42
if love were what the r. is 524:28
if this pale r. offend 506:15
inimitable r. 571:18
I no more desire a r. 454:33
I r. politely in the club 140:5
I r. the wrong way 40:13
it wavers to a r. 183:11
lap of the crimson r. 466:37
last r. of summer 356:36
like a red red r. 107:14
long carpets r. 285:27
lovely is the r. 576:2
mast burst open with a r. 208:16
mighty lak' a r. 511:14
month that brings the R. 205:18
more labyrinthine buds the r. 96:32
musk of the r. is blown 536:9
never blows so red the R. 206:3
Nightingale cries to the R. 205:12
One who r. 493:27
on thy cheek a fading r. 286:29
or summer's r. 346:20
pluck a red r. 445:22
pluck a white r. 445:21
pretty girl—under the r. 72:17
queen r. of the rosebud garden 536:14
ravage with impunity a r. 96:34
red as any r. 29:24
red as a r. is she 148:23
reddens to a r. 561:6
red r. cries 536:15
Red R., Proud R., sad R. 586:17
Richard, that sweet lovely r. 438:36
r. by any other name 477:16
R. crossed the road 183:16
r. distill'd 466:17
r. growing on's cheek 321:14
r. her mouth 536:6
r. in the deeps of my heart 585:17
R. is Beauty 183:3
r. just newly born 268:30
R. kissed me to-day 183:17
r. leaves when the r. is dead 499:1
r. like an exhalation 345:11
R. of all Roses, R. of all the
World! 585:21
r. o' the wrong side 82:25
r. pink and dirty drab 337:9
r.'s scent is bitterness 543:24
R. that cannot wither 552:2
Rope: escape from r. and gun 214:34
his throat in a r. 525:21
pulled at one r. 149:33
refuse to set his hand to a r. 189:1

Rose (cont.)
r. the. .pine-trees 317:22
r. to touch the spheres 89:6
r. upon Truth's lips 561:11
r. up to play 46:3
r. was awake all night 536:13
r. was heaven to smell 249:10
r. with all its sweetest leaves 117:2
r. without the thorn 247:20
roves back the r. 170:26
same look. .when he r. 356:13
secret, and inviolate R. 586:2
set thick with lily and red r. 359:5
stole my r. 108:39
strew on thee r. or rue? 522:11
sweet r., whose hue 245:13
that dismal cry r. slowly 88:4
their only thornless r. 525:33
then up he r. 436:23
unceremoniously the r. 561:9
up r. the sonne, and up r.
  Emelye 137:33
vanish with the R. 207:24, 25
wears the r. of youth 424:27
we r. both at an instant 441:4
when I have pluck'd the r. 473:11
where Jove bestows. .the fading
  r. 125:9
where leaves the R. of Yesterday? 205:18
white r. weeps, 'She is late;' 536:15
wiser man he r. 150:17
within the bosom of the r. 529:1
without thorn the r. 347:6
yet a r. full-blown 247:21
Roseate hues of early dawn 4:6
Roseau: un r. pensant 374:5
Rosebery: Lord R. and Comyns
  Carr 141:31
Rose-blossoms: when the r. wither 523:15
Rosebud: r. garden of girls 536:14
r. set with. .thorns 538:8
without the fragrant r. 247:20
Rosebuds: gather ye r. 247:10
r. fill'd with snow 124:5
Rose-cheeked Laura 123:16
Rose-crowned into the darkness 84:3
Rose-in-hand 207:21
Roseleaf: only a r. down 38:28
Rose-lipped: many a r. maiden 263:21
young and r. cherubin 472:34
Rosemary: there's r. and rue 485:22
there's r. . .for remembrance 436:31
Rose-red city 100:3
Roses: all night have the r. heard 536:11
brows with r. .bound 190:34
do r. stick? 97:11
each morn a thousand R. 205:18
flung r., r., riotously 187:10
I would like my r. to see you 501:3
lilies and r. were all awake 536:13
make thee beds of r. 330:19
marriage. .not a bed of r. 514:29
morning r. newly wash'd 479:4
my own red r. 545:2
no r. at my head 409:29
on thy turf shall r. rear 118:23
raptures and r. of vice 522:23
red r. crest the caps 545:2
rod of criticism with r. 182:48
r. and lilies and violets meet 36:26
r. and white lilies 124:4
r. are her cheeks 536:6
r. at first were white 246:8
r. for the flush of youth 409:28
r. have thorns 486:31
r., red and white 253:1
r., r., all the way 94:28
r. within 333:3
scent of the r. 356:18
seek r. in December 117:13
she wore a wreath of r. 37:1
soft as the r. they twine 113:2
strew no more red r. 17:2
strew on her r., r. 17:15
sweet days and r. 245:13
time of r. 252:11
two red r. across the moon 359:17
wild r., and ivy serpentine 497:22
with r. overgrown 333:2
Rose-water: pour r. over a toad 269:17

Ross: read Alexander R. over 110:27
sing the Man of R. 384:44
Rosy: another's r. are 572:2
imbibing the r. 146:23
left the daisies r. 536:4
not grey but r. 93:26
old plain men have r. faces 516:5
r. garland and a weary head 501:27
r. is the West 536:6
r. Man, right plump to see 578:29
r. wreath 280:21(-281)
Rot: fools! 'od r. 'em! 504:10
in cold obstruction and to r. 383:24
propagate, and r. 383:24
r. high on Temple Bar 142:11
r. in hospitals 507:2
r. inwardly 342:29
r. itself with motion 423:39
very deep did r. 149:6
we r. and r. 427:14
Rota: currente r. cur urceus exit? 255:17
Rote: conn'd by r. 451:24
judge by r. 371:11
wrote it all by r. 248:12
Rots: r. itself in ease 432:12
sort of r. away 560:14
Rotted old oak stump 150:8
Rotten: choice in r. apples 478:48
fresh eggs to r. boroughs 324:29
r. at the heart 463:19
r., cold, and drenched 289:31
something is r. in the state 432:5
thought it rather r. 141:29
your navy. .r. timber 101:13
Rottenness: pillared firmament is
  r. 340:31
r. begins in his conduct 268:24
r. of eighty years in gold 119:18
Rotten-runged, rat-riddled stairs 93:19
Rotting: Dungeon that I'm r. in 124:17
mean and mighty r. together 429:39
Rotunda: or Opulent R. 514:4
Rotundity o' the world 453:5
Rotundus: teres, atque r. 262:1
Rough: hoarse, r. verse 382:32
I am r. and lecherous 452:20
more of r. than polished diamond 139:24
r. and ready man that write 89:34
r. he may be 176:24
r. is the road 124:7
r. old Martin Luther 97:11
r. places plain 54:9
straight, r., dense, or rare 346:14
turns earth's smoothness r. 95:15
Rougher: I beneath a r. sea 159:3
Rough-hew them how we will 437:27
Roughly: pass'd with me but r. 160:25
speak r. to your little boy 129:1
Roughness breedeth hate 26:26
Roughnesses: remark all these r. 167:7
Roughs: among his fellow r. 188:29
Round: golden r. 457:2
go r. about her 394:35
her diurnal r. 575:26
he turn'd him r. and r. 30:17
in the heaven, a perfect r. 89:8
life's dull r. 499:13
light fantastic r. 340:7
made the r. world so sure 397:22
makes the world
  go r. 7:23; 129:15; 219:14
or else goes r. and r. 135:1
right and r. about 106:18
r. and r. it flew 148:27
r. and r. the sand 293:23
r. and r. the spicy downs 535:18
r. and top of sovereignty 460:8
r. earth's imagined corners 185:13
r., fat, oily man of God 546:6
r. numbers are always false 273:26
r. of strenuous idleness 579:23
R. or two before 206:6
r. she turned 92:44
r. the world away 293:19
r. the world for ever and aye 15:24
r. unvarnish'd tale deliver 469:45
so beset him r. 99:36
something of a r. belly 441:21
square person. .r. hole 505:24
time is come r. 451:39

Round (cont.)
to trot the r. 189:16
walk'd their narrow r. 275:3
Roundabouts: what's lost upon
  the r. 135:2
Rounded: r. Peter's dome 199:23
r. with a sleep 480:8
Roundelay: synge untoe mie r. 136:17
Rounder 'twixt the cypresses 94:8
Round-faced man in black 239:15
Roundhead: far below the R. rode 540:19
Roundheads and Wooden-shoes 1:27
Round-hoofed, short-jointed 488:27
Rounds: R.! What R.? 301:14
unto their r. their music's aid 319:1
Rouse: at a dismal treatise r. 461:3
give a r. 90:17
no more shall r. them 229:31
r. and bestir themselves 344:27
r. him at the name of Crispian 444:28
their God will r. them 302:2
Roused in many an ancient hall 137:33
Rousing: puissant nation r. herself 352:15
r. whid at times to vend 105:6
Rousseau: ask Jean Jacques R. 161:22
mock on, Voltaire, R. 75:15
wild R. 113:48
Rout: after all their r. 142:30
in reel and r. 149:6
pleasures of having a r. 253:9
r. on r. 346:16
your r. send forth a joyous shout 322:25
Routed: thrice he r. all his foes 191:6
Rove: where'er we r. 356:35
Rover: whither away, fair r. 81:26
Roves back the rose 170:26
Roving: we'll go no more a-r. 119:4, 6
where are you r.? 262:7
Row: Devil knows how to r. 150:11
I'll r. ye so quick 333:16
long r. to hoe 319:15
r., brothers, r. 357:16
r., my knights 124:22
r. one way and look another 109:6
r. on r. burn upward 96:45
r. us o'er the ferry 122:23
Seraphim in burning r. 351:10
waited in a r. 130:15
Rowed: all r. fast 148:1
as he r. along 173:13
Cnut, King, r. thereby 124:22
Rowing: r. against the stream 419:22
r. another 99:17
r. home to haven 333:20
Rowland: Warren's blackin' or
  R.'s oil 179:5
Rowley: 'Heigh ho!' says R. 366:21
Royal: calling a crowned man r. 523:25
daughter of a r. line 118:3
men of r. siege 469:37
no 'r. road' to geometry 202:8
regular R. Queen 218:21
r. banner 472:3
r. captain of this ruin'd band 444:7
r. Dane 431:32
thus the r. mandate ran 105:25
Royal Exchange: love to frequent
  . .the R. 2:9
Royal George: down went the R. 162:10
Royaliste: plus r. que le roi 12:14
Royally: prov'd most r. 438:10
sorrow so r. in you appears 442:32
Royalty: R. . .appeals to diffused
  feeling 28:29
when you come to R. . .lay it on 181:22
Ruant: et r. coeli 561:2
Rub: r. not clean their benches 281:6
there's the r. 434:4
Rubbing the poor itch 429:4
Rubbish: cast as r. to the void 532:32
r. of an Adam 507:1
write such hopeless r. 512:7
Rubies: her price is above r. 50:57
r., fairy favours 466:34
thou. .shouldst r. find 333:8
wisdom is above r. 49:8
wisdom is better than r. 49:15
Rubious: not more smooth and r. 482:10
Rubs: fog that r. its back 197:17
no r. nor botches 459:1
Ruby: still a R. kindles 205:11

Ruby (cont.)
that r. which you wear 247:7
Vine her ancient R. yields 205:9
Rudder: bowsprit got mixed with the r. 128:8
rhyme the r. is of verses 110:22
snatch'd his r. 18:16
their tail the r. 191:29
Ruddier than the cherry 214:8
Ruddy: he was r. 47:19
lean was so r. 225:10
my beloved is white and r. 52:13
Rude: although thy breath be r. 427:22
however r. the sound 217:17
how r. are the boys 562:5
loose, plain, r. writer 109:9
manner r. and wild 40:21
poor, reckless, r. 188:31
rather r. and wild 41:14
r. am I in my speech 469:45
r. forefathers of the hamlet 229:30
r. to the Lord her Guest 302:1
savage, extreme, r. 488:11
society is all but r. 332:15
so r. to the good 572:23
very r. of him 130:10
who is here so r. 450:16
Rudely: al speke he never so r. 137:23
not r. be dismist 152:21
r. great 383:22
Rudest work that tells a story 413:11
Rudiments: first r. of education 511:29
r. of Paradise 507:1
Rudyards cease from kipling 512:8
Rue: I'll set a bank of r. 475:14
nought shall make us r. 448:2
press the r. for wine 419:8
r., even for ruth 475:14
sold for endless r. 262:17
there's rosemary and r. 485:22
wear your r. with a difference 436:32
Ruff: antique r. and bonnet 276:14
Ruffian: menaces of a r. 272:20
r. billows 442:1
that father r. 439:35
Ruffians, pitiless as proud 158:33
Ruffle up your spirits 450:34
Ruff'd: all to r. 340:20
Ruffles her pure cold plume 531:38
Rugged: antiquarian is a r. being 273:35
harsh cadence of a r. line 193:11
r. individualism 254:3
r. Pyrrhus 433:26
r. the breast 33:3
those r. names 351:17
Ruh': meine R.' ist hin 223:20
über allen Gipfeln ist R.' 224:5
Ruhm: nicht der R. 223:21
Ruhnken: more learn'd professor, R. 387:7
Ruin: around the dear r. 356:12
back, ere the r. fall! 323:24
bears the seed of r. 16:27
betwixt that smile..and their r. 446:24
formed for the r. of our sex 506:5
formless r. of oblivion 481:27
hideous r. and combustion 344:7
in r. and confusion hurled 3:2
its r. didst not share 183:22
last of a race in r. 140:14
majestic though in r. 345:24
man marks the earth with r. 114:27
red r. 530:12
resolved to r. or to rule 190:16
r., and desperation, and dismay 350:17
r. kings 190:11
r. no more lives 188:7
r. of all happiness 103:36
r...of body and soul 109:22
r. seize thee, ruthlessKing! 229:20
r. that it feeds upon 161:30
r. that's romantic 220:20
r. upon r. 346:16
r.—yet what r.! 114:20
shame and r. wait for you 158:33
speaks to a r. here 141:2
spreading r. 88:11
stern R'.s ploughshare drives 107:8
systems into r. hurled 383:10
tastes woman, r. meets 214:34
threats of pain and r. 230:5
whom God to r. has design'd 192:33

Ruinae: impavidum ferient r. 259:22
Ruined: archangel r. 345:5
no nation..r. by trade 211:6
r. at our own request 357:27
r. by buying good pennyworths 211:16
r. by Chinese cheap labour 238:36
r. on..their natural propensities 103:14
r. Mr. Hampden's fortune 100:5
Ruining along the..inane 535:24
Ruinous: hinder parts..r. and old 509:22
Ruins: flout the r. grey 417:12
human mind in r. 169:20
I'm one of the r. 315:2
mean reparations upon mighty r. 101:30
musing amidst the r. of the Capitol 217:1
r. of St. Paul's 324:31, 558:25
r. of the noblest man 450:11
Ruin-trace: print no r. 355:15
Ruksh, the horse 17:26
Rule: absolute r. 347:11
all be done by r. 424:10
arbiter and r. of right 511:23
bear r. in their kingdoms 57:15
by a r. in nature teach 443:10
cut-purse of..the r. 435:49
damn by r. 371:11
each man's r. 529:30
errors of a wise man..your r. 73:15
golden r...no golden rules 490:28
levell'd r. of streaming light 340:18
little r., a little sway 195:14
no charge of r. 518:1
not a regular r. 129:32
observ'd the golden r. 74:7
oldest r. in the book 129:32
one who can r. 535:43
priests bear r. 55:13
resolv'd to ruin or to r. 190:16
reason to r. 192:24
rhyme or reason, r. or check 381:21
r. applies to everyone 222:7
r. Britannia, Britannia, r. 8:24
r., Britannia, r. the waves 545:18
R. of three doth puzzle me 8:12
r. our spirits from their urns 118:10
r. over the day and..night 413:21
shouted, 'R. Britannia' 294:17
souls of those they r. 16:28
sure the monarch's r. 402:2
taught out of the r. of Plato 352:28
teach eternal wisdom how to r. 383:23
they that r. in England 140:24
they who r. the land 578:5
too fond to r. alone 385:29
to r. o'er freemen 83:16
Ruler: little Benjamin their r. 396:13
r. of th' inverted year 163:24
R. of the Queen's Navee 221:15
to be r. in Israel 56:7
Rulers: r. are not a terror 66:10
r. clothed most gorgeously 55:32
r. of the darkness 68:11
Rules: all a rhetorician's r. 110:8
hand that r. the world 557:19
if she r. him, never shows she r. 384:38
no golden r. 490:28
obtruding false r. 341:1
only r. by terror 528:10
pretences to break known r. 167:11
r. and models destroy genius 240:4
r. e'en the wisest and in learning r. 164:38
r...the laws of Nature 266:20
simple little r. and few 41:34
truth from r. 110:36
twelve good r. 225:4
who r. o'er freemen 275:23
with old r. jump right 110:36
woman r. us still 357:12
Ruleth: he that r. his spirit 50:17
made the world and r. it 585:9
thee r. prudently 195:7
Ruling: r. himself after thy word 399:13
r. passion! 173:31
r. passion conquers reason 384:43
r. them like slaves 497:12
various r. passions 384:35
your r. passion strong 384:27
Rum: bottle of r. 514:18

Rum (cont.)
r. and true religion 115:28
R. on the port 516:8
r., Romanism, and rebellion 99:42
what a R. Go everything is 564:28
Rumble: grumble and r. and roar 406:3
r. of a distant Drum 205:26
they roll and r. 358:10
Rumbled: under the water it r. on 150:10
Rumbling: amid their r. terrors 180:22
Ruminating: I am r. 178:25
Rumming: Tunning of Elynour R. 502:21
Rumoresque senum severiorum 132:15
Rumour: distillation of r. 126:16
r. is a pipe 441:8
r. of oppression and deceit 162:40
r. of thee there 545:1
Rumours of wars 60:21
Rump-fed ronyon 456:10
Rum-ti-Foo: balmy isle of R. 217:25
Run: all the wheels r. down 293:19
although I r. and r. 142:7
applaud us when we r. 100:15
as they r. they look behind 230:25
away he r. 369:11
considering how to r. 166:23
gay they r. and leap 338:9
giant to r. his course 392:32
grin like a dog, and r. about 395:22
half r. before 524:20
hasting day has r. 246:2
if they r., why, we follow 213:11
in any cell you r., dear 265:24
I r., I r. 338:7
I therefore so r. 66:37
many shall r. to and fro 55:45
North you may r. 298:28
not choose to r. for President 156:23
or r. it down 521:20
r. about the braes 104:13
r., and not be weary 54:14
r. at least twice as fast as that 130:4
r. because we like it 506:21
r. by one and one 302:23
r. in a race r. all 66:36
r. into't as to a lover's bed 425:24
r., rise, rest with Thee 245:9
r., r., Orlando 427:23
r., tailors, r. 366:19
r. that readeth it 56:9
r. them into verse 194:12
r. the straight race 354:11
r. to and fro like sparks 56:24
r. to meet..most avoid 340:19
r. with patience the race 69:18
see how they r.! 369:8
several ways they r. 172:9
sin through which I r. 185:24
stay, and r. again, and stay 333:1
sweet Thames, r. softly 510:20
till I end my r. 301:6
till thou r. out thy race 351:31
time will r. back 343:18
to my dead heart r. them in 510:16
to ride, to r. 510:16
to r., though not to soar 326:4
to thy motions lover's seasons r. 186:19
until it doth r. over 5:24
we do not r. for prize 506:20
wit enough to r. away 111:15
you would r. away 363:21
Runagates continue in scarceness 396:5
Runaway: curb a r. young star 119:15
Runcible: r. Cat 312:9
r. hat 311:11
r. spoon 312:3
Rune: read her r. 410:19
Rung: down the ladder r. by r. 296:28
r. the battle shout 251:5
r. the bell to him 103:29
their knell is r. 153:30
Runic: some fallen R. stone 16:6
sort of R. rhyme 380:12
Runnable stag 169:15
Runnels: meadows r., r. pebble-stones 285:1
Runneth about unto the end 392:32
Running: all the r. you can do 130:4
first sprightly r. 191:34
good measure..r. over 61:31

INDEX

Running (cont.)
hindered in r. the race   389:25
r. a man down   519:35
r. it never runs..away   184:6
r. of the deer   10:14
r. over with any little knowledge   290:14
r. stream of sparkling joy   173:34
r. the way of thy commandments   389:44
Runs: blood..r. through the springs   32:11
fights and r. away   6:25, 224:9
he that r. may read   529:23
if you fights or you r.   301:8
never r. from us away   184:6
r. not a river by my palace wall?   542:26
r. through the town   339:9
r. under water   281:19
r. with a letter   301:13
so r. the world away   435:19
there r. a road   299:23
who r. may read   291:12
Run-stealers flicker to and fro   545:2
Rupee: chapter on the Fall of the R.   569:26
Rupert: R. of Debate   322:9
R. of Parliamentary discussion   180:15
R. of the Rhine   323:1, 2
Rural: lovely woman in a r. spot   266:4
made a r. pen   76:9
nor r. sights alone, but r. sounds   162:36
retirement, r. quiet   546:13
vale of r. life   387:8
Rural Dean: shade of a R.   84:11
Rus: r. in urbe   331:28
r., quando ego te aspiciam?   261:25
Rush: as we r. in the train   546:30
fools r. in   383:5
r. into the skies   383:13
stars r. out   149:14
that blue is all in a r.   255:4
Rushed: our spirits r. together   534:17
Rushes: among the reeds and r.   317:20
green grow the r. O   105:37
Rushing: like the r. river   329:4
Rushingly: passed on, r.   236:29
Rushy: down the r. glen   4:18
matted r. isles   17:28(–18)
Ruskin: squeamish R.   293:10
Russel: Daun R. the fox   137:41
Russell: as you did my Lord R.   354:10
Russet: homely r. brown   578:31
in r. mantle clad   430:21
r. yeas   455:30
Russet-coated captain   167:3
Russet-pated choughs   467:7
Russia: last out a night in R.   461:25
Russian: Fall-Off-The-R. Empire   178:5
it is R.; ain't it, Wegg?   178:8
might have been a R.   221:25
R. is a delightful person   304:28
Russians: R. shall not have Constantinople   265:15
some..may be R.   176:17
Rust: dew will r. them   469:40
eaten to death with r.   441:25
his good sword r.   151:31
less than the r.   254:16
moth and r. doth corrupt   58:5
never taketh r.   502:5
now r. disus'd   160:22
r. in peace   507:2
r. of the Barons' Wars   558:14
r. unburnish'd   540:32(–541)
tarnished with r.   569:15
wear out than r. out   566:17
wear out than to r. out   167:19
Rustic moralist   230:8
Rusticantur: peregrinantur, r.   145:16
Rusticity: refined r.   578:13
Rustics: amazed the gazing r.   225:2
Rusticus: Ofellus r.   261:22
Rustling: r. of the grass   573:1
r. to her knees   285:21
Rustum: let R. lay about him   205:19
Zal and R. bluster   205:20
Rusty: for want of fighting..r.   110:21
his keys were r.   119:14
r. curb of old father antick   438:19
Ruth: melt with r.   343:2
rue, even for r.   475:14
sad heart of R.   288:1

Ruthless King!   229:20
Rutted: the ancient way r.   333:17
Rye: before the Roman came to R.   141:21
between the acres of the r.   428:31
coming through the r.   104:31
pocket full of r.   368:20
rob the blighted r.   165:17

S

Saba: kings of Arabia and S.   396:25
Sabachthani: Eli, Eli, lama s.?   60:52
Sabaean odours   347:1
Sabbata: illa s.   1:1
Sabbath: born on the S. day   368:1
eternal S. of his rest   193:37
hail, S.!   228:14
hallow thus the S.-day   151:27
keep holy the S.-day   390:9
Lord God of S.   388:15
one s. deep and wide   540:7
s. of the year   315:19
S. song   380:20
s. was made for man   60:53
seventh day is the S.   390:9
that great S. God..that S.'s sight   510:11
twice holy was the S.-bell   285:30
upon a S.-day it fell   285:30
when a s. appeared   164:25
Sabbath-breaking: drinking and s.   172:23
Sabbath-drawler of these old saws   540:15
Sabbaths: new moons and s.   52:29
s. of Eternity   540:7
those endless S.   1:1, 362:9
Sabina: cur valle permutem S.   259:17
Sable: of s. hue   332:23
paint the s. skies   190:4
s. silver'd   431:15
Sable-vested Night   346:15
Sabre: with his s. drawn   6:16
Sabrina fair   341:3
Sacco's name will live   551:13
Sacerdos: Musarum s.   259:14
Sack: if s. and sugar be a fault   439:36
intolerable deal of s.   439:39
nothing without s.   442:21
purge, and leave s.   441:6
s. the lot!   205:1
till s. commences it   442:21
Sackbut: harp, s., psaltery   55:36
Sacks: s. to sew up wives   542:26
seven s.   366:8
Sacrament: yon orbed s.   545:6
Sacramental: break the s. cake   287:5
Sacred: facts are s.   416:4
for s. rites unfit   502:2
s. be the flesh and blood   532:24
s. river   151:32, 33
s. to the household gods   546:26
through the S. Town   41:32
two most s. names   158:3
Sacred Heart: Convent of the S.   197:26
Sacrifice: better than s.   47:16
blood of human s.   344:28
coming to the s.   287:12
evening s.   400:13
great pinnacle of s.   216:7
perfect, and sufficient s.   390:42
provide for s.   291:5
s. of God   395:10
s...of the devil's leavings   387:1, 520:48
s. to the Graces   139:19
Thine ancient s.   300:24
thou desirest no s.   395:10
thy morning s.   292:1
turn delight into a s.   243:25
unpitied s.   101:36
your bodies a living s.   65:62
your prayers one sweet s.   446:13
Sacrificed: Christ our passover is s.   66:28
more than all that she has s.   21:6
slain and spent and s.   522:20
Sacrificers, but not butchers   449:9
Sacrifices: upon such s.   454:20
Sacrilege: consecrated s.   180:39
Sad: all their songs are s.   140:15
bring s. thoughts to the mind   581:7
conceive a thing so s. and soft   585:10

Sad (cont.)
deliciously aged and s.   489:34
his face was s.   504:3
how s. and bad and mad   90:38
how very s. thy fate!   288:20
if you find him s.   423:29
last s. squires ride slowly   141:27
make a man look s.   467:33
mine a s. one   462:31
nobody should be s. but I   447:37
not to be s. she tries   171:24
remember and be s.   409:25
s. as angels   122:39
s. bad glad mad brother   522:18
s. embroidery   342:31(–343)
s. obscure sequestered   96:16
s. or singing weather   524:28
s. sincerity   199:23
s. variety of woe   217:18
s. vicissitude of things   217:17, 513:25
say I'm s.   265:25(–266)
shrill and s. accent   145:27
so s., so fresh   538:18
so s. thou canst not sadder   545:1
thou art s., art thou kind?   359:17
when thou art absent I am s.   365:22
whose soul was s.   222:27
why I am so s.   462:28
why my soul was s.   544:1
young are s. and bewildered   504:17
young gentlemen would be as s.   447:37
your s. tires   485:21
Sad-coloured sect   253:32
Sadden after none, or bitter, Fruit   206:12
Saddens while it soothes   94:31
Sadder: s. and a wiser man   150:17
s. than owl-songs   116:50
s. than the Niobean womb   522:14
Saddest: s. of all Kings   269:27
s. when I sing   36:27, 560:18
tell of s. thought   408:9
Saddle: boot, s., to horse   90:19
come s. my horses   420:17
come s. your horses   416:8
my s. and my bow   29:24(–30)
struck in the s.   141:26
things are in the s.   199:19
Sadly I roam   210:16
Sadness: all the s. in the sweet   544:1
diverter of s.   559:15
feeleth for our s.   4:3
feeling of s. and longing   316:8
most humorous s.   428:16
no s. of farewell   528:22
s. of her might   287:21
s. of her s.   36:12
sweet though in s.   496:11
Saecla: mutantur s. animantum   321:1
Saeclo: plus uno maneat perenne s.   132:11
Saeclorum nascitur ordo   555:30
Saeclum: solvet s. in favella   34:4
Saeculi: antiquitas s.   25:7
Saepibus in nostris   556:4
Saeva: ubi s. indignatio..lacerare nequit   521:27
Saevior: calamus s. ense   109:13
Safe: bring him s. to shore   323:30
man's perdition to be s.   199:27
more s. I sing   348:23
Pobble's toes are s.   312:7
quartered s. out 'ere   297:1
s. bind, s. find   550:6
s. for democracy   571:14
s. home in port!   362:17
s. shall be my going   84:19
s. though all safety's lost   84:19
s. to the landing place   323:29
s. under every..government   272:10
s. under his feathers   397:18
s. where men fall   84:19
s. within the lifeboat   415:6
somewhere s. to sea   523:23
then..you're perfectly s.   566:9
to be direct..not s.   472:6
to fly is s.   163:19
wish him s. at home   282:10
Safeguard of the West   582:5
Safe-left: my heart, s.   502:3
Safely: s., s. gathered in   183:2
to be s. thus   458:32
we s. go   73:24

Safer: s. being meek than fierce 89:22
s. than a known way 239:4
s. to be that .. we destroy 459:3
Safest: s. of all 84:19
when we're s. 89:31
Safety: eat in s. 447:14
in the multitude of counsellors
.. s. 49:56
my s. cometh from the Lord 421:4
our s. is in our speed 200:35
pot of ale, and s. 443:28
s., honour, and welfare 389:14
s. .. of the whole state 431:21
this flower, s. 439:9
though all s.'s lost 84:19
under the smile of s. 441:7
Sagacious: s., bold 190:13
s. reader of the works of God 163:13
vigilant, resolute, s. 324:35
Sagacity: infinite-resource-and-s. 304:12
Sage: by savage, and by s. 386:29
childlike s. 163:13
hoary S. reply'd 276:15
I don't think it s. 34:34
neither saint nor s. 303:15
s. and serious poet Spenser 352:10
s. beneath a spreading oak 158:29
s. in meditation found 498:24
s.'s pride 386:24
sainted s. 231:3
without hardness will be s. 16:9
Sager sort our deeds reprove 123:19
Sages: charms that s. have seen 164:22
dozing s. 159:17
holy s. once did sing 343:9
if the s. ask thee why 199:26
than all the s. can 581:16
Said: as well s., as if I had s. it 520:18
best that has been known and s. 20:8
by and by is easily s. 435:28
cannot wisely be s. 376:19
contradict everything you s. 200:40
finer .. than anything which he s. 200:6
great deal to be s. 42:25
he himself has s. it 221:24
he s. nought to me 149:33
if I s. so 226:24
I s. the thing which was not 519:19
much .. s. on both sides 2:12
never s. in rhyme 289:8
no more to be s. 6:20
nothing is s. .. not s. before 184:3
nothing s. 342:29
s. anything that was remembered 182:25
s. before reading the Faerie
Queene 306:8
s. I to myself, said I 219:3
s. it that knew it best 25:31
s. it three thousand years ago 208:17
s. whot a owt to 'a s. 537:9
so very little s. 143:21
thing well s. 194:5
we s. nothing, all the day 184:31
what's s. or done 245:22
Sail: argosies with portly s. 462:29
attendant s. 384:16
cried, A s.! a s.! 149:9
full s., with her fan spread 156:1
in a sieve I'll thither s. 456:10
never strike s. to a fear 200:18
never weather-beaten s. 124:1
s. and s., with unshut eye 15:24
s. beyond the sunset 541:3
s. for evermore 541:16
s. in amply billowing gown 41:32
s. of his great verse 487:20
s. on, O Ship of State! 316:1
s. on the salt sea 31:8
s. the wet sea roun' 298:25
s. this hooker 303:9
s. with God the seas 200:18
sea-mark of my utmost s. 473:31
shook out more s. 18:16
silver s. of dawn 264:1
so fast for fear did he s. 508:1
take in s. 199:30
two towers of s. at dawn 147:6
when we set s. 9:3
when ye s. to meet the foe 363:3
white and rustling s. 167:20
white s.'s shaking 334:10

Sailed: hadna s. a league, a league 30:18
I've never s. the Amazon 297:23
merry of soul he s. 516:7
never s. with me before 267:26
s. away for a year and a day 312:1
s. off in a wooden shoe 204:5
s. on a river of crystal light 204:5
s. the wintry sea 318:14
they s. in to Bethlehem 7:14
Sailing: come s. to the strand 32:2
occurred in the s. 128:9
s. o'er life's .. main 317:8
s. o'er sea 114:39
this way s. 350:31
three fishers went s. 293:25
Sailor: before Noah was a s. 483:30
drunken s. 11:16
ever s. free to choose 303:14
give ear unto the s. 373:11
happiest hour a s. sees 219:17
home is the s. 516:15
light in the darkness, s. 415:6
loves a s. 173:8
never more, S. 171:19
no man will be a s. 270:32
s.'s wife had chestnuts 456:10
shrine of the s.'s devotion 489:1
soldier an' s. too 301:19
there was once an old s. 339:13
well for the s. lad 528:3
Sailor-boys: we jolly s. 9:3
Sailor-folk: silly s. 298:17
Sailor-men .. talk so very queer 34:28
Sailors: guard the s. tossing 34:37
s. but men 463:15
sorrows s. find 113:16
three s. of Bristol city 543:7
Sails: his s. fill'd 135:19
not full s. hasting 332:10
purple s. 424:6
s. by the Low-lands low 30:23
s. o' cramoisie 31:8
s. ript 160:35
still the s. made on 149:35
swallows .. in Cleopatra's s. 425:16
tackle trim, s. fill'd 350:31
torn s. 362:11
when we our s. advance 189:6
white dipping s. 334:8
white s. crowding 81:26
Sail-yards: till his s. tremble 135:19
Saint: able to corrupt a s. 438:22
accents of an expiring s. 513:21
by s., by savage 386:29
each lost day .. patron s. 238:29
follow your S. 123:22
frequent Doctor and S. 206:10
his s. is sure 377:4
in vain the s. adore 189:14
little s. best fits 245:18
make of me a s. 155:38
Miracles of S. Somebody 95:28
my late espousèd S. 351:24
neither s. nor sage 303:15
neither s. nor sophist 15:10
never a s. took pity 149:20
Poet and S.! 158:3
reel out a s. 143:13
s. in crape 384:24
s. or sinner 387:21
s. provoke 384:25
s. run mad 386:10
s. sustain'd it 382:13
seem a s. 476:12
shrine of my dead S. 292:18
to catch a s. 462:1
weakest s. upon his knees 161:15
which the S. had printed 361:24
Saint: ni s., ni romain 557:8
St. Agnes' Eve 285:12
St. Clement's: bells of S. 368:7
Sainted: ensky'd and s. 461:19
St. Ives: going to S. 366:8
Saint James: in Galice at S. 137:15
Saint James's: ladies of S. 183:11
St. John: awake, my S.! 383:7
S. .. scarce forbear 521:2
there S. mingles 386:5
Saint John's Wood: Primrose Hill
and S. 75:4
Saint-like: not too s. 316:36

Saint Loy: but by S. 136:28
Saint Mary Axe: seventy, S. 222:17
St. Paul's: description of the ruins
of S. 558:25
say I am designing S. 43:3
sketch the ruins of S. 324:31
St. Paul's Churchyard, the Strand 307:2
Saints: all s. else be defaced 232:11
all the S. adore Thee 240:19
bards, s., heroes 15:9
blood of the s. 71:32
calls His s. around 81:4
for all the S. 264:8
ghastly glories of s. 525:10
greatest s. and sinners 111:23
grow into plaster s. 303:4
his soul is with the s. 151:31
it frets the s. 87:31
jest with s. 461:32
my lost s. 88:24
never be S. in Heaven 86:16
pair of carved s. 475:10
prayers of s. 70:42
s. above 417:16
s. engage in fierce contests 111:13
s. immortal reign 562:13
s. in your injuries 470:25
s. may do the same things 111:1
s. on earth in concert sing 565:15
S. their watch are keeping 517:2
s. will aid 150:23
self-constituted s. 253:14
thy s. have dwelt secure 502:9
thy slaughtered s. 351:20
twilight s. 285:19
where S. in glory stand 586:22
with s. dost bait thy hook 462:1
with the race of S. 245:22
with s. at the river 415:8
with thy quire of S. 185:25
ye fearful s. 161:18
ye that are his s. 393:38
Saint-seducing gold 476:48
St. Vincent: Cape S. 92:17
Sairly: protects you s. 106:32
Sais: que s.-je? 355:5
Sake: for love's s. only 88:18
for old sakes' s. 293:18
for the s. of those few 200:46
for whose dear s. 295:8
truth, for its own s. 294:4
Sakes: for old s.' sake 293:18
Saki: like her, O S. 207:31
Sal Atticum 380:3
Salad: cheap but wholesome s. 164:1
Garrick's s. 225:25
my s. days 424:2
primroses make a capital s. 182:13
s. .. special receipt 335:9
Salade: into a round s. 359:9
Salamis: looks o'er sea-born S. 115:45
Salaputium disertum! 133:4
Salary to receive 216:23
Sale: all for s. 142:4
s. of chapmen's tongues 455:2
Sale lo pane altrui 169:1
Saleroom and varnishing auc-
tioneer 126:10
Salices: fugit ad s. 555:26
Salire alle stelle 168:25
Salisbury: blank cheque to Lord S. 227:37
Lord S. .. a lath of wood 73:1
S. and Gloucester 444:28
when Lord S. makes a .. speech 358:15
Salisbury Plain: crossing S. on a
bicycle 219:12
Salley: down by the s. gardens 584:11
Sallies: never s. out 352:9
s. of his mother's kisses 576:10
Sallows: among the river s. 284:14
mealed-with-yellow s. 255:6
Sally: make a sudden s. 528:5
none like pretty S. 125:17
S. is gone 41:29
Sally Lunn: gay S. 222:18
Salmon: first s. 317:1
for the s.'s tail 470:29
it was the s. 178:29
white as snow in S. 396:7
Salmons in both 445:4
Saloons: Solomon of s. 93:29

Salsa: la mejor s...hambre 134:9
Salt: cast s. on a woman's tail 110:40
drowned already..with s. water 482:25
eaten your bread and s. 297:13
eating an egg without s. 304:41
if the s. have lost his savour 57:40
pillar of s. 44:53
s., estranging sea 16:16
s. of the earth 57:40, 495:10
s. tears fell from her 473:6
s. water unbounded 301:9
seasoned with s. 68:33
verge of the s. flood 480:32
when a little s. 178:7
Salteena: Mr. S... elderly man 20:26
Saltness: s. of time 441:13
sugar and s. agree 225:25
Saltpetre: villainous s. 438:35
Salus: s. extra ecclesiam non est 22:1
s. populi suprema est lex 145:5
s. populi suprema lex esto 422:8
una s. victis 554:9
Salutant: morituri te s. 13:4, 517:22
Salutary: wise and s. neglect 100:25
Salutations: full of gentle s. 513:21
Salute: about to die s. thee 13:4, 517:22
dear earth, I do s. thee 474:34
I s. thee, Mantovano 541:8
s. me to my lord 328:13
s. the happy morn 112:24
s...with an holy kiss 66:18
Saluted: long inveterate foes s. 193:41
Salvation: bottle of s. 405:9
brought s. down 303:6
my light, and my s. 393:20
necessary to s. 391:12, 401:3
none of us should see s. 464:33
now is our s. nearer 66:13
publisheth s. 54:22
s. joins issue with death 96:24
seeks her own s. 437:3
what prawce S. nah? 490:5
working out s. 111:12
work out your own s. 68:19
Salve, magna parens frugum 556:14
Samaritan: ready..to do the S. 504:30
Samarkand: from silken S. 285:25
Golden Road to S. 208:14
Same: all comes to the same thing 89:18
all day the s. our postures 184:3
all of the s. religion 182:5
all say the s. 335:17
all the s. a hundred years hence 177:6
another, yet the s. 381:17
both in the s. minute 290:22
dies the s. 587:6
he is much the s. 23:14
just the s. as you an' me 298:25
memory of the s. 92:31
never breed the s. 288:8
never the s. again 326:20
not look the s. by day 88:9
s. as if he had not been 535:21
s., bright, patient stars 286:14
s. in thine own act 457:11
s. the whole world over 9:20
s. to-day and for ever 549:20
s. yesterday, and to day 69:23
this is the s. voice 95:36
this will go onward the s. 236:14
thou art the s. 398:2
to endless years the s. 562:9
what reason I should be the s.? 23:15
woman does the s. 161:28
Samela: fair S. 232:1
Samian wine 116:1, 3
Samite: clothed in white s. 529:42
Samminiato: lamping S. 94:8
Samphire: one that gathers s. 454:3
Sampler: ply the s. 340:38
Samson: carry the buckler unto S. 86:13
S. hath quit himself like S. 351:5
Samuel: the Lord called S. 47:4
Sana: mens s. in corpore sano 283:24
Sancta simplicitas! 266:9
Sanctified by reason 579:38
Sanctifies while it enhances 174:37
Sanctimonious pirate 461:17
Sanctities: day's dead s. 544:21
Sanctuaried: in the s. East 545:6
Sanctuarize: murder s. 436:43

Sanctuary: help from the s. 392:35
raze the s. 461:35
s. within the holier blue 95:35
went into the s. of God 396:27
Sand: abstinence sows s. 74:25
all 'ot s. an' ginger 296:24
always play with s. 40:34
crept up along the s. 293:23
die upon the s. 17:26
grain of s. 567:19
in a Grain of S. 73:18
I on the s. 419:33
its speed i' the slushy s. 93:20
length of burning s. 165:17
little grains of s. 127:33
on the edge of the s. 312:3
plain to be seen in the s. 170:7
roll down their golden s. 240:17
s. against the wind 75:17
s. and ruin and gold 525:31
s. of granite 516:19
such quantities of s. 130:12
Sandal: bright and battering s. 254:23
his s. shoon 436:19
Sandal-buds and stripes of labdanum 94:18
Sandals: bind on thy s. 521:30
s. were for Clementine 355:23
Sandalwood, cedarwood 333:20
Sanded: nicely s. floor 225:3
so flew'd, so s. 467:20
Sandford: down by S. 18:29
Sands: circled by the s. 335:27
footprints on the s. 317:8
golden s. 184:8
here are s. 37:13
lone and level s. 496:15
on s. and shores 340:10
ran itself in golden s. 534:16
s. begin to hem his..march 17:28
s. of Dee 293:22
these yellow s. 479:28
too nigh the s. 190:13
Sand-strewn caverns 15:24
Sandwich in her hand 178:24
Sandwich-men of the Daily Mail 142:4
Sandy: she was dry and s. 175:6
Sane: fitter being s. than mad 89:22
Sang: company that s. 586:14
Love s. to us 525:2
morning stars s. together 49:20
s. a kindred soul out 95:35
s. full sweet 196:2
s. it all day long 81:10
s. long years ago 35:11
s. themselves to sleep 249:13
s. the uncouth swain 343:5
s. to a small guitar 311:24
s. within the bloody wood 197:26
worked and s. 72:15
Sanglant: le dernier acte est s. 374:2
Sangreal: endeth the story of the
S. 328:14
Sanguelac: S.I the arrow! the
arrow! 529:37
S., the lake of Blood! 529:36
Sanguine and subtle Dolores 522:26
Sanguis: semen est s. Christianorum 542:3
Sank: at times her spirit s. 535:5
s. by the Lowlands low 31:1
s. her in the sea 39:19
s. him back 170:25
Sanno: il Maestro di color che s. 168:21
Sans: s. teeth, s. eyes 427:21
s. Wine, s. Song 206:8
Sansculotte: bon S. Jésus 172:28
Sap: disbranch from her material
s. 453:42
full of s. 398:9
s. and sawdust 130:5
world's whole s. 186:3
Sapiens: abnormis s. 261:22
Sapient: s. sutlers of the Lord 197:24
shake his s. head 19:5
Sapientia: de S. Veterum 28:11
quid virtus et quid s. possit 256:23
s. prima stultitia caruisse 256:17
Sapientibus: etiam s. cupido gloria 526:16
Sapphire: purer s. melts 536:8
second s. 72:1, 87:36
Sapphire-blaze 231:13

Sapphires: ivory overlaid with s. 52:14
living s. 347:19
Sappho: call me S. 152:6
my S.'s breast 246:8
S. lay her burning brows 545:7
where burning S. loved 115:43
Sapping a solemn creed 113:49
Saracens to the confines of Poland 217:12
Sarah: wherefore did S. laugh? 44:51
Sarcastical: this is rote s. 560:4
Sardine stone 70:36
Sardius: sixth, s. 72:1
Sardonyx: fifth, s. 72:1
Sash: 'oldin' on by the Sergeant's
s. 301:14
Sashes: nice new s. 228:11
Sassy: sickly but s. 238:14
Sat: came and s. down here 359:14
he that s. 70:36
horror heavy s. 193:38
kings have s...upon the ground 56:41
people s. down to eat 46:3
s. at any good man's feast 427:19
s. by a pillar alone 535:41
s. by the flesh pots 45:52
s. him down in a lonely place 538:1
s. like a cormorant 347:3
s. we two 184:29
simply s. and snored 140:5
Satan: beat down S. 389:1
Devil, and S. 71:39
ev'n S. glowr'd 108:13
messenger of S. to buffet me 67:37
St. S.'s fold 531:19
S. as lightning fall 61:36
S. came also among them 48:38
S. exalted sat 345:14
S. met his ancient friend 119:24
S., Nick, or Clootie 104:4
S., so call him now 348:17
S. trembles 161:15
truly, my S. 74:22
Satanic: dark S. mills 75:16
S. School 508:17
Satchel: schoolboy, with his s. 427:21
'Satiable curtiosity 304:16
Satiate of applause 386:7
Satiety: love's sad s. 498:9
occasion of s. 25:38
Satin: coats o' green s. 9:16
goes mad...in white s. 500:6
her petticoat was s. 298:29
Satins: cloth of gold and s. rare 218:29
Satire: alive after all this s. 274:22
s., being levelled at all 520:35
s. be my song 117:9
s. is a sort of glass 519:4
s. or sense 385:30
without a disposition to s. 223:9
Satiric: one s. touch 521:4
Satirist: second English s. 234:9
Satisfaction: sacrifice, oblation,
and s. 390:42
s.—if you think there is any 215:1
Satisfied: eye is not s. 50:61
having it, is s. 542:40
three things..never s. 50:55
well paid that is well s. 465:15
Satisfies: where most she s. 424:9
Satisfieth: s. the empty soul 398:15
s. thy mouth 398:4
that which s. not 54:29
Satisfy: poorly s. our eyes 583:14
Satura..tota nostra est 404:25
Saturday: betwixt a S. and Mon-
day 125:19
died on S. 368:21(–369)
jolly old S. 243:5
S. night! 243:4
S.'s child works hard 368:1
Saturn: S. and Love their long
repose 493:27
while S. whirls 537:35
Saturnia: redeunt S. regna 555:30
S. tellus 556:14
Saturnine: more s., dark, and
melancholic 154:26
Saturno: Pudicitiam S. rege 283:7
Satyr: hoofed heel of a s. 522:1
Hyperion to a s. 430:33(–431)
Satyrs: my men, like s. 329:20

Sauce: best s...hunger | 134:9
  chops and Tomata s. | 179:12
  make hunger thy s. | 549:22
  only one s. | 124:23
Sauce: une seule s. | 124:23
Saucer: I sing the s. | 372:16
Saucy: how many s. airs we meet | 215:27
  s. Arethusa | 248:16
  s. look of an assured man | 156:11
Saul: S. also among the prophets? | 47:11
  S. and Jonathan were lovely | 47:30
  S. hath slain his thousands | 47:25
  S., it shall be | 96:25
  S., S., why persecutest | 64:41
  S. was consenting | 64:35
  weep over S. | 47:30
  young man..whose name was S. | 64:34
Saunders: Clerk S. and may Margaret | 30:15
Savage: by saint, by s. | 386:29
  laws unto a s. race | 540:31
  noble s. | 191:41
  s. and Tartarly | 118:2
  s. anti-everythings | 250:28
  s. as a bear | 331:17
  s., extreme, rude, cruel | 488:11
  s. in his blindness | 240:18
  s. place! | 151:32
  some s. woman | 534:33
  sooth a s. breast | 155:18
  stories of s. men | 100:22
  with s.-pictures fill their gaps | 521:18
Savageness: sing the s. out | 472:27
Savages: don't cant in defence of s. | 275:22
Savage-wild: my intents are s. | 478:39
Savait: si jeunesse s. | 201:30
Savant: un sot s. | 353:18
Save: brother whom someone should s. | 550:33
  can but will not s. me | 180:14
  conquer but to s. | 122:6
  died to s. their country | 41:22
  dust thou wouldst not s. | 528:21
  God s. great George | 6:13
  God s. our gracious king! | 125:15
  God s. thee, ancient Mariner! | 149:1
  God s. the king! | 47:12, 125:15, 250:14
  God s. the king!..amen | 475:18
  himself he cannot s. | 60:51
  if I can s., so | 440:35
  many to s. with thyself | 17:19
  matter enough to s. one's own | 92:45
  one drop would s. my soul | 330:7
  repent and s. his soul | 330:7
  s. a sinking land | 384:11
  s. his soul alive | 55:30
  s. me from the lion's mouth | 393:7
  s. none of me | 185:5
  s. them from false Sextus | 323:18
  s. those that have no imagination | 491:5
  to choose time is to s. time | 26:8
  vain thing to s. a man | 393:37
  when wilt thou s. the people? | 198:22
Saved: England has s. herself | 379:16
  he s. others | 60:51
  he that endureth..s. | 58:50
  mine I s. | 93:25
  not yet s. | 116:27
  only s. by being dammed | 253:34
  only s. the world | 41:22
  s. a world | 357:9
  s. before the ancient | 471:14
  s. by the multitude of an host | 393:37
  s. the sum of things for pay | 264:4
  there be souls must be s. | 471:13
  we are not s. | 55:16
  what shall we do to be s. | 234:6
  whosoever will be s. | 388:37
Savent: les gens de qualité s. tout | 354:5
Saves: curtsey..it s. time | 130:1
  s. a description of the rising sun | 499:29
Savest: because Thou s. such | 99:31
Saveth in time of affliction | 56:30
Saviour: around the S.'s throne | 240:21
  her sins to her S. | 252:22
  on earth our S. Holy | 4:1
  our S.'s birth..celebrated | 430:20
  S. comes, the S. promised | 183:19
  S. of 'is country | 303:2
  S. of the Nations | 116:27

Saviour (cont.)
  S. of the world | 112:24
  speak low to me, my S. | 87:37
  thou S. dear | 291:9
  'tis thy S. | 161:9
Savoir: de s. quelque chose | 353:13
Savonarola: S. love-sick! | 39:21
  the less S. he | 39:22
Savory: mints, s., marjoram | 485:25
Savour: filths s. but themselves keep seeming and s. | 454:1
  salt..lost his s. | 485:22
  s. of poisonous brass | 57:40
  s. of sorrow | 286:11
  stinking s. | 183:17
Savours: live their s. | 51:23
Saw: came, s., and overcame | 466:34
     428:25, 442:19
  could resist till I s. you | 290:28
  do not s. the air | 434:15
  drowns the parson's s. | 456:1
  folk he ne'er s. in his life | 13:17
  God s. that it was good | 44:4
  he s., he sigh'd, he lov'd | 215:12
  I came, I s., I conquered | 120:13
  I never s. a Purple Cow | 100:1
  I s. and loved | 216:25
  I s. it! | 93:37
  I stumbled when I s. | 453:38
  no man ever s. | 478:46
  no sound of hammer or of s. | 163:40
  nothing else s. | 286:31
  one man s. you | 95:1
  s. thee by thine own sweet light | 166:5
  s. the face of God | 330:2
  s. what she had done | 8:7
  s. ye bonnie Lesley? | 104:25
  s. ye not fair Inez? | 252:28
  tell us what he heard and s. | 231:23
  who s. him die? | 369:19
Sawdust: sap and s. | 130:5
Saws: all s. of books | 432:20
  full of wise s. | 427:21
  sabbath-drawler of old s. | 540:15
Saxon: leave the S. alone | 300:7
  Roman-S.-Danish-Norman | 170:13
  S. and Norman and Dane | 541:18
  S. is not like us Normans | 300:7
Say: all s. the same | 335:17
  content to s. nothing | 274:20
  do as I s., not as I do | 422:11
  father used to s. | 243:2
  fear not what men s. | 99:37
  good deed to s. well | 446:21
  has her s. out | 196:10
  have to s. something | 565:25
  hear, know and s. | 84:6
  how s. ye then to my soul? | 392:17
  if y' can s. | 310:13
  I s. to thee, do thou repeat | 549:6
  knew not what to s., he swore | 118:1
  let us not always s. | 95:17
  many things to s. unto you | 63:61
  Master, s. on | 61:33
  Name which none can s. | 165:33
  Nature s. one thing | 103:16
  nothing to s., s. nothing | 154:20
  nothing to what I could s. | 129:18
  not what we ought to s. | 454:28
  s. I'm weary | 265:25(-266)
  s. little more than I have studied | 482:19
  s. naught, but suffer and die | 553:2
  s. nothing but what has been said | 109:4
  s. not, the struggle | 147:8
  s., poor sinner | 161:9
  s.! that should not s.'t | 38:12
  s.! what is that thing | 144:21
  s. what it is not | 273:13
  s. what thou seest yond | 479:31
  s. what you mean | 129:6
  she said, S. | 47:40
  somewhat to s. unto thee | 47:40, 61:33
  they are to s. what they please | 211:22
  thinking what to s. | 130:1
  thou canst not s. I did it | 459:15
  till I see what I s. | 557:20
  to neither a word will I s. | 215:4
  we men may s. more | 483:10
  what we s. here | 314:12

Say (cont.)
  what you s., or what you do | 8:17
  when he has nothing to s. | 274:20
  when I s. or I sing | 220:16
  your right to s. it | 557:15
Saying: for s. so | 186:21
  rage for s. something | 270:31
  s. anything two or three times | 22:12
  s. learnt in days far-off | 540:22
  Tar-baby ain't s. nuthin' | 238:17
  what are the wild waves s.? | 128:2
Sayings of philosophers | 110:33
Says little, thinks less | 203:7
Scabbard: sword, glued to my s. | 334:26
  threw away the s. | 145:25
Scabbards: leaped from their s. | 102:11
Scabs: make yourselves s. | 429:4
Scaffold: in the brothel or on the s. | 513:32
  s. and the doom | 24:6
  Truth forever on the s. | 320:10
Scaffoldage: 'twixt his stretch'd footing and the s. | 481:6
Scaith: he could na s. thee | 104:26
Scalam: de vitiis nostris s. | 22:6
Scald: mine own tears do s. | 454:14
Scale: by geometric s. | 110:10
  every golden s. | 128:23
  free-livers on a small s. | 267:22
  hurl'd himself into the s. | 357:9
  in equal s. | 430:24
  not sink i' the s. | 95:16
  with her lifted s. | 381:11
Scale: per l'altrui s. | 169:1
Scaled eyeball | 96:33
Scales: Sussex s. the sky | 41:21
Scallop-shell of quiet | 405:9
Scalp: hairy s. of such a one | 396:10
Scalped: red men s. each other | 324:34
Scan: presume not God to s. | 383:22
  s. his work in vain | 161:20
  s. your brother man | 104:7
Scandal: in s., as in robbery | 139:6
  love and s. | 204:21
  no s. like rags | 203:8
  no s. while you dine | 540:30
  O the disgrace of it!—The s. | 39:25
  s. about Queen Elizabeth | 499:28
  tea and s. | 154:30
Scandalous and poor | 407:20
Scanter of your maiden presence | 431:28
Scape: to s. stormy days | 185:23
Scapegoat into the wilderness | 46:8
'Scapes: hair-breadth 's. | 470:2
Scar: from cliff and s. | 538:15
  s. that whiter skin of hers | 473:11
  there is oft a s. | 90:10
Scarce: good people's wery s. | 174:7
  rhymes are so s. | 121:15
Scarce-bearded Caesar | 423:13
Scarcely tell to ony | 105:18
Scarceness: runagates continue in s. | 396:5
Scarcity: on the very first s. | 102:36
Scare me with thy tears | 540:22
Scarecrow: make a s. of the law | 461:22
  theatrical s. | 172:16
Scarecrows of fools | 266:22
Scared away the meek ethereal hours | 285:36
Scarers in Print | 178:9
Scarf: beauteous s. | 464:15
  s. up the tender eye | 459:8
Scarfs, garters, gold | 383:30
Scarlet: bird with s. breast | 580:1
  clothed you in s. | 47:30
  cowards in s. | 229:11
  his sins were s. | 41:23
  in S. town | 30:1
  like a thread of s. | 52:5
  line of s. thread | 46:38
  loves a s. coat | 252:31
  not wear his s. coat | 569:1
  s. line was slender | 293:2
  s. mantle warm | 160:30
  though clothed in s. | 281:4
  though your sins be as s. | 52:30
Scars: deep s. of thunder | 345:7
  jests at s. | 477:13
  s. remaining | 150:27
  seamed with the s. of disease | 325:28

Scars (cont.)
show his s. 444:28
Time's wrecks and s. 141:2
Scatter: s...my words among mankind 496:11
s. the good seed 121:27
s. their snow around 82:7
Scattered: all Israel s. 48:13
let his enemies be s. 396:4
s. at the feet of man 574:28
s. his Maker's image 190:8
s. into flight the Stars 205:5
s. the people that..war 396:14
s. the proud 61:14
some s. notions 519:3
thousand s. into Clay 205:17
when the Almighty s. kings 396:7
when the cloud is s. 494:20
whose bones lie s. 351:20
Scatterest: as soon as thou s. them 397:15
Scattering of all shadows 35:6
Scatteringly doth shine 332:8
Scatters the rear of darkness 341:32
Scelerisque purus 258:22
Scelestum: antecedentem s. 259:20
Scene: breath, a little s. 475:7
cunning of the s. 433:36
each dreadful s. 37:6
each lonely s. 153:22
every day speaks a new s. 404:10
gay and festive s. 178:12
highly impossible s. 218:7
I..fled the S. 560:5
in life's last s. 279:10
live o'er each s. 381:6
love gilds the s. 500:31
of what s. the actors 491:25
proud s. was o'er 381:12
s...laid in a Brothel 306:33
s. of changes 158:11
see the distant s. 304:10
sweet is the s. 250:29
that memorable s. 332:24
there I laid the s. 163:35
this our lofty s. 450:1
Scenery: s. is fine 289:30
s.'s divine 121:9
Scenes: all the changing s. 527:2
from s. like these 105:5
gay gilded s. 2:2
lent out my heart..to such s. 307:5
s. of crowded life 279:2
s. sung by him 417:29
sicken at the shifting s. 537:39
Sceneshifter: playwright, s. 237:25
Scent: not I s. the morning air 432:15
join not s. to hue 494:10
rose's s. is bitterness 543:24
s. of the roses 356:18
s. the air perfuming 147:24
sweetest flower for s. 497:27
their s. survives their close 543:24
whose s. the fair annoys 159:18
Scents: s. of the infinite Sea 16:4
sweet unmemorial s. 81:7
Sceptic: for the s. side 383:22
whatever s. could inquire for 110:12
Scepticism: all-dissolving s. 363:24
wise s. 320:19
Sceptra: mox s. tyrannis 329:6
Sceptre: his s. shows the force 404:33
my s. for a..staff 475:10
not the balm, the s. 444:23
s. and crown 501:5
s., learning, physic 430:1
stretches forth her leaden s. 587:1
Sceptred: dead but s. sovereigns 118:10
· this s. isle 474:22
Sceptreless, free, uncircumscribed 497:12
Sceptres: kings in s. 548:13
Schärf: bringt mit S. 'Er alles ein 315:22
Scheldt: by the lazy S. 226:3
Scheme: she'll project a s. 586:26
sorry S. of Things 207:26
Schemes: best-laid s. 107:11
most s. of political improvement 271:34
so many s. 17:22
Scherzando ma non troppo 218:11
Schiller has the material sublime 153:3
Schlag: zwei Herzen und ein S. 234:17
Schoenobates: augur s. 283:3

Scholar: courtier's, soldier's, s.'s 434:14
gentleman and s. 108:18
he was a s. 447:9
our S. travels yet 19:1
s. all..volumes carry 135:26
s.'s life assail 279:4
Scholars: all the lore its s. need 291:12
land of s. 226:15
nor its great s. great men 251:18
rake among s. 325:31
s. and gentlemen 579:28
School: at the head of a s. 558:9
drew me to s. 160:30
either s. or college 106:12
Fleshly S. of Poetry 98:5
microcosm of a public s. 182:38
put his heart to s. 573:5
reason for hating s. 39:13
Satanic S. 508:12
s. of mankind 103:15
s. of Stratford atte Bowe 136:29
Stealthy S. of Criticism 411:39
till her children came from s. 109:26
three little maids from s. 219:27
to s. and not to travel 27:27
toward s. with heavy looks 477:25
unwillingly to s. 427:21
vicious till he's been to a good s. 414:17
whipt at s. 194:26
Schoolboy: every s. knows it 527:14
every s. knows who 324:28
not the s. heat 533:22
s.'s tale 113:11
s.'s tip 542:17
voice of the s. 363:5
what every s. knows 520:53
what s...is ignorant? 325:20
whining s. 427:21
Schoolboys from their books 477:25
School-bred: though s. 164:13
School-days: my joyful s. 308:1
School-divine: God..turns a s. 386:15
Schoolgirl: pert as a s. 219:27
s. complexion 10:4
Schoolman: no s.'s subtle art 386:4
Schoolmaster is abroad 85:2
Schoolmastering: continue s. 127:26
Schoolmasters: injuries..their s. 453:2
let s. puzzle 226:2
then s. 245:5
School-men: searching S.'s vein 308:4
Schoolrooms for 'the boy' 156:22
Schools: cobwebs of the s. 163:36
fill the public s. with silk 329:24
in learned s. 4:10
jargon of the s. 401:30
jargon o' your s. 105:23
less flogging in our great s. 272:36
lumber of the s. 521:13
maze of s. 382:21
public s...nurseries of all vice 204:19
public s...public folly 164:6
Schooner Hesperus 318:14
Schumann's our music-maker 91:8
Schweigen ist golden 127:22
Science: at this newe s. 138:23
Art and S. cannot exist but 75:7
cookery..a noble s. 109:10
countenance of all s. 583:3
detection..an exact s. 188:18
Dismal S. 126:34
enough of s. 581:16
fairytales of s. 534:14
of s. and logic he chatters 387:20
only s. it hath pleased God 248:17
politics are not an exact s. 72:29
pretend to despise Art and S. 75:9
proud s. never taught 383:11
s. falsely so called 68:55
S. frown'd not 230:13
s. is his forte 506:2
s. is..organized common sense 266:18
s. is organized knowledge 508:21
s. moves, but slowly 534:28
to patient s. dear 573:14
Sciences: books must follow s. 24:35
great mother of the s. 28:8
Scientia potestas est 28:10
Scientiae: fraudatrix s. 414:21
Scientiarum mater 28:8

Scientific: as if they were s. terms 20:9
broken open on..s. principles 376:14
educated literary and s. opinion 19:16
s. faith's absurd 91:16
Scinde: peccavi—I've S. 403:11
Scintillations of your wit 228:2
Scio's rocky isle 113:3
Scire: nos paucula s. permittunt 414:21
s. nefas 258:16
Scissor-man: red-legged s. 250:4
Scoff: came to s. 24:1, 224:22
Scoffing his state 475:7
Scold men 302:5
Scooped the brimming stream 347:14
Scope: that man's s. 486:24
Scorched foretop 325:28
Score: from seventy springs a s. 262:10
no other books but the s. 445:40
to that kiss a s. 246:28
wallowed in a s. 185:24
Scorer: One Great S. 406:20
Scores: wipers of s. out 94:38
Scorn: dangers thou canst make us s. 108:10
disdain and s. ride sparkling 468:25
dull eye of s. 82:1
fools may our s., not envy raise 215:28
for the time of s. 472:34
had many a s. 29:24
haughty s. which mock'd 16:8
held the human race in s. 40:35
in s. of eyes 476:14
in the s. of consequence 537:33
laugh a siege to s. 461:2
laugh'd his word to s. 162:4
love he laugh'd to s. 488:25
not a thing to laugh to s. 428:25
of her s. the maid repented 33:13
s. delights 342:20
s. not one 573:18
s. not the Sonnet 580:16
s. of s. 537:40
s. the spear 491:25
s. to change my state 486:24
s. to give aught other reason 234:14
sound of public s. 349:20
think foul s. 198:11
virtuous s. 219:1
wail their s. 168:12
we s. her most 424:25
what a deal of scorn 483:28
Scorned: not s. in heaven 160:33
s. his spirit 448:27
was s. and died 215:12
woman s. 155:20
Scorner of the ground 498:10
Scornful: in the seat of the s. 391:45
s. jest 278:32
s., yet with jealous eyes 385:29
Scorning: s. the base degrees 449:3
time and nonsense s. 98:15
Scorns: he that s. and struggles 142:11
how Stanley s. the glance 322:9
whips and s. of time 434:4
Scorpion and asp 349:21
Scorpions: chastise you with s. 47:47
Scot: had Cain been S. 146:4
some be S. 301:4
Unspeakable S. 167:15
Scotch: as a S. jig 468:9
bleak S. firs 127:4
get a joke well into..S. 504:20
little..inferior to the S. 365:9
S. have found it 273:18
S. terrier..so covered with hair 82:21
Scotch'd the snake 459:4
Scotchman: half-a-crown to a beggarly S. 270:22
makes a S. happy 276:11
noblest prospect..a S...sees 271:8
S., if he be caught young 272:14
S...man of sense 315:15
Scotchmen: trying..to like S. 306:11
Scotia: chief of S.'s food 105:2
old S.'s grandeur 105:5
Scotland: come from S...cannot help it 270:34
fair S.'s spear 418:15
for poor auld S.'s sake 106:3
grave livers..in S. 580:12
I'll be in S. afore ye 9:7

INDEX

Scotland (cont.)

inferior sort of S.	505:31
in S., at the Orcades	383:27
in S. supports the people	277:29
left fair S.'s strand	106:16
love S. better than truth	277:37
Saracens to . . S.	217:12
S. counts for something	360:4
S. led in luve and le	583:26
seeing S., Madam	273:32
stands S. where it did?	460:19
succour S.	583:26

Scots: brither S. | 107:20

queen of S. . . a fair son	197:36
S. lords at his feet	32:2
S., wha hae wi' Wallace bled	107:32
six or seven dozen of S.	439:13

Scotsman: grandest moral attribute of a S. | 36:17

S. on the make	36:18
young S. of your ability	36:16

Scott: flat as Walter S. | 9:5

Liddell and S.	11:7
sick heart of a Sir Walter S.	127:4
think it was Sir Walter S.	518:13

Scottish: brave old S. Cavalier | 24:8

Scoundrel: every man over forty is a s. | 490:37

given them to such a s.	519:33
last refuge of the s.	272:29
plea of the s.	75:7
s. and a coward	270:22

Scoundrels: hatred of s. | 126:36

Scour a narrow chamber	336:15
Scoured to nothing	441:25
Scouring faults	443:6

Scourge: iron s. | 230:15

made a s. of small cords	63:6
s. . . calls us to penance	345:17
Tamburlaine, the S. of God	331:8

Scourged: s. to his dungeon | 98:3

s. us to an elevation	216:7

Scout: blabbing eastern s. | 340:6

flout 'em and s. 'em	480:3

Scowl: anxious s. | 24:7

Thunderer's s.	266:14
what a s. of cloud	97:13

Scowls the far-famed hold | 323:11

Scramble: in s. sort | 249:13

s. at the shearers' feast	342:27
Scrannel pipes	342:29
Scrap of paper	43:22

Scrape: potsherd to s. himself | 48:42

Scraped one out of the table	461:17
Scraper brave man	243:31

Scrappy: when work was s. | 142:2

Scraps: stolen the s.	455:26
those s. are good deeds past	481:17

Scratch: quick sharp s. | 93:22

s. his name	92:38
s. my head with the lightning	550:20
s. the Christian	587:17
s. the nurse	484:31

Scratched: of purpose to be s. | 110:15

Priscian a little s.	455:25
s. with a stick	205:16

Scratching of a pen | 319:11

Screaming: I am s. out loud | 177:11

Screams: strange s. of death	458:21

Screen: s. from seeing | 522:2

s. them in those looks	497:9
this pallid s.	237:8

Screw your courage | 457:13

Screw-guns: you all love the S. | 301:8

Scribblative: babblative and s.	508:6

Scribble: s., s., s.! Eh! Mr. Gibbon? | 223:5

vindictive s. of red	91:17

Scribbled: with centric. . s. o'er | 348:30

Scribbling: itch of s.	217:19, 283:12

Scribendi: nullum fere s. genus | 273:19

s. cacoethes	283:12

Scribens: aut legens, aut s. | 291:25

Scribes: not as the s.	58:29
righteousness of the s.	57:44

Scrimped and iced | 370:14

Scrip: my s. of joy | 405:9

s. and scrippage	428:2

Scriptores: cedite Romani s. | 402:17

Scripturas: scrutamini s.	422:1

Scripture: better it in S. | 371:16

devil can cite S.	463:18

Scripture (cont.)

nail't wi' S.	105:6
rock of Holy S.	223:2
S. moveth us	388:6

Scriptured petals | 411:22

Scriptures: abjure the S. | 329:25

known the holy s.	68:58
mighty in the s.	65:4
search the s.	63:19
storehouse . . holy S.	243:19

Scrisse: il libro e chi lo s. | 168:23

Scrivener: notched and cropt s.	306:18
Scrofulous French novel	96:41

Scroll: charged with punishments the s. | 241:19

long-cramped s.	92:34
s. of crystal	493:18

Scruple: not s. to pick a pocket | 172:14

some craven s.	436:16
Scruples dark and nice	110:15
Scrupulosity: oriental s.	278:11

Scrutamini Scripturas | 422:1

Scud: over the s. and the palm-trees | 296:5

white clouds s. between	80:14
Scullion: away, you s.!	441:29
Sculptor: not a great s.	412:23

Sculpture: ancient s. is the true school | 376:11

shapeless s.	230:7
Scum of the earth	564:18
Scurvy: some right s.	336:5

Scutcheon: honour is a mere s. | 440:30

my s. plain declares	455:31
shielded s. blush'd	285:19

Scuttled: ever s. ship | 115:41

Scuttling across the floors	197:19

Scylla and Charybdis: S. of anarchy and despotism | 499:11

S. of Aye and No	363:19

Scythe: poor crooked s. and spade | 501:5

whets his s.	341:34

Scythian: S., bond nor free | 68:31

snow on S. hills	330:21

Se: of townes *A per s.* | 195:3

Sea: all round to the s. | 164:22

all the s. were ink	321:19
alone on a wide wide s.	149:20, 150:14
around the glassy s.	240:19
as near to heaven by s.	217:24
as seamen use at s.	298:14
as stars look on the s.	322:8
as the waters cover the s.	3:8, 53:19
as thou by s.	537:17
beneath the bosom of the s.	75:18
best thing . . between . . the s.	269:12
blow the earth into the s.	453:3
blue days at s.	516:2
Bohemia . . near the s.	485:13
born, across the s.	264:18
bottom of the deep blue s.	8:24
breaks down in cliff to the s.	15:15
bred to the s.	331:20
broods o'er the S.	577:1
by the deep s.	114:26
by the Northern S.	309:23
by the s. shut bank	208:10
by the winter s.	531:29
call him on the deep s.	363:3
called the good s. up to Him	298:16
cold glass stones, O S.!	528:3
compass'd by the inviolate s.	539:13
cross the narrow s.	562:16
crown'd with summer s.	531:37
dance like a wave of the s.	585:2
death, like a narrow s.	562:14
deep wide s. of misery	494:21
desert of the s.	53:25
dolorous midland s.	525:31
down a steep place into the s.	58:36
down to a sunless s.	151:32
down to the s. in ships	398:17
dreary s. now flows between	150:27
drowned in the depth of the s.	59:49
English that of the s.	125:23, 407:1
espouse the everlasting S.	582:7
far over the summer s.	539:21
fearest nor s. rising	81:26
fill the s. and air	149:34
flowing s.	167:20
for the s.'s worth	469:38

Sea (cont.)

forty freighters at s.	299:16
Friend, over the s.	97:5
from Atlanta to the s.	583:7
from s. to Shining s.	36:23
gave them back their s.	298:17
goes to s. for nothing	184:20
golden s. of Wales	208:6
great and wide s.	398:11
great Voices roll in from S.	549:2
grey mist on the s.'s face	334:10
gurly grew the s.	30:18
he cast into the s.	62:27
he that commands the s.	27:26
his footsteps in the s.	161:18
home from the s.	516:15
hungry as the s.	483:9
I beneath a rougher s.	159:3
I call to the earth and s.	567:16
if we gang to s., master	31:25
in a s. of glory	446:24
in peril on the s.	566:20
in perils in the s.	67:35
in the flat s. sunk	340:20
into that silent s.	149:3
into the bosom of the s.	445:33
into the midst of the s.	394:27
into the springs of the s.	49:22
I ought to ha' sent you to s.	299:17
iron-bosomed s.	411:31
Jesus . . walking on the s.	59:35
kingdom by the s.	380:8
kings of the s.	16:1, 362:30
leaped headlong into the s.	290:7
let nae the s. come in	31:25(–32)
life's unresting s.	251:15
life's wild restless s.	3:19
light upon the shining s.	549:7
like a green s.	495:1
like stars on the s.	118:37
like sunrise from the s.	493:24
like to the Pontick s.	472:12
little cloud out of the s.	48:5
London, that great s.	495:9
lonely s. and the sky	334:10
looked across the s.	293:8
lover of men, the s.	525:29
made heaven and earth, the s.	390:11
made of earth and s.	263:36
Marathon looks on the s.	115:44
masters of the s.	208:15
mirror'd on her s.	249:11
mirrors of the s.	208:19
moon may draw the s.	539:1
more s.	411:8
more steady than the ebbing s.	210:3
most dangerous s.	404:15
mount, and stream, and s.	241:8
my bark is on the s.	118:14
nearer the crystal s.	131:32
never go to s.	221:18
never was, on s. or land	578:14
never was s. so lone	296:5
no more s.	71:44
nor earth, nor boundless s.	487:13
not having been at s.	273:34
ocean s. was not sufficient room	35:23
o'er a perfumed s.	380:17
o'er Egypt's dark s.	357:17
o'erlace the s.	90:34
of a sudden came the s.	94:27
one foot in s.	468:20
one is of the s.	581:13
on such a full s.	451:29
on the deep blue s.	34:37
on the purple s.	322:18
on this life's rough s.	135:19
ooze and bottom of the s.	443:9
open s. of the world's praise	577:2
our heritage the s.	167:21
out of the s. came he	148:21
over the s.	262:7
over the s. our galleys went	94:20
over the s. she flies	42:4
over the s. to Skye	516:7
paddles in a halcyon s.	409:14
pageants of the s.	462:29
permanence . . the s. cannot claim	237:10
Pussy-Cat went to s.	311:24
Queen of land and s.	184:2

INDEX

Sea (*cont.*)

quiver and beat of the s. 525:19
receiveth as the s. 481:30
remain in the broad s. 395:28
ride slowly towards the s. 141:27
rough rude s. 475:1
rude s. grew civil 466:38
run into the s. 50:60
sail on the salt s. 31:8
sailed the wintry s. 318:14
salt, estranging s. 10:16
say of a particular s...old 237:10
scents of the infinite S. 161:4
s. being smooth 481:1
s. beneath my feet 80:15
s. gave up the dead 71:43
S...give up her dead 400:30
s. grows stormy 15:26
s. hath no king but God alone 411:36
s. is his, and he made it 397:26
s. is not full 50:60
s. itself floweth in your veins 548:13
s. of dew 204:5
S. of Faith 15:7
s. of glass 70:37, 71:28
s. of glory streams 114:6
s. of Life and Agony 495:5
s. of troubles 434:4
s. rises higher 140:13
s. saw that, and fled 399:2
s.'s azure floor 493:12
s. that bares her bosom 582:18
s.! the s.! the open s.! 157:12
s. was made his tomb 35:23
s. where it goes 15:6
s., with such a storm 453:34
secret of the s. 317:15
see nothing but s. 24:19
sepulchre there by the s. 380:10
serpent-haunted s. 208:8
serve Him on the S. 298:16
set in the silver s. 474:22
settle somewhere near the s. 303:14
shine upon the Aral S. 17:28(-18)
shining on the s. 130:9
ship in the midst of the S. 50:56
slopes down to the s. 150:8
something of the s. 421:12
Southward dreams the s. 543:22
spouts out a s. 348:26
stilleth the raging of the s. 395:28
stillness of the central s. 533:27
stone..cast it into the s. 71:33
Sussex by the s. 302:13
swing of the s. 254:29
Sword went out to s. 359:11
take away the s. 208:11
that immortal s. 576:19
there's a s. 116:24
thousand furlongs of s. 479:17
Thracian s. 524:16
tigers or the roaring s. 478:39
trader, from the s. 18:16
tremendous s. of cloud 94:26
triumphant s. 474:23
troubled s. of the mind 284:24
under the deep deep s. 253:28
union with its native s. 574:20
upon the slimy s. 149:6
uttermost parts of the s. 400:9
vext the dim s. 540:32
waters of the dark blue s. 114:42
we'll o'er the s. 250:15
we men, at s., indite 187:2
went down into the s. 148:21
went to s. in a bowl 369:9
went to s. in a Sieve 311:21
what thing of s. or land? 350:31
when I put out to s. 528:22
whether in s. or fire 430:19
who hath desired the S.? 301:9
whose sound was like the s. 577:15
why the s. is boiling hot 130:15
willing foe and s. room 5:18
wind-ridden restless s. 171:19
wish you a wave o' the s. 485:27
with far-heard whisper, o'er
  the s. 149:14
within a walk of the s. 42:7
with Ships the s. was sprinkled 582:16
wrinkled s. beneath him 529:10

Sea (*cont.*)

world-embracing s. 374:21
world's tempestuous s. 195:23
yonder is the s. 92:3
Sea-banks: upon the wild s. 465:17
Sea-beast: like a s. crawled forth 580:10
Sea-beasts rang'd all round 15:24
Sea-blooms: far below, the s. 496:9
Sea-blue bird of March 533:12
Sea-breakers: by lone s. 370:19
Sea-breeze: with the s. hand in
  hand 543:22
Sea-change: suffer a s. 479:30
Sea-coal: by a s. fire 441:31
Sea-daisies: strong s. feast 525:24
Sea-description: nothing in s. 412:24
Sea-down's edge 523:13
Sea-faring: land travel of s. 97:20
Sea-fight: his last s. is fought 162:11
Sea-flower: quiet s. 522:11
Sea-fogs lap and cling 302:10
Sea-girt: winged s. citadel 113:16
Seagreen Incorruptible 126:19
Sea-gulfs: among s. hollow 524:16
Sea-hall: round his long s. 531:9
Sea-King's daughter 541:18
Seal: have not the s. of God 71:11
  no night s. thy sense 171:7
  S., and Maces 230:19
  s. her sweet eyes 409:26
  s. then, and all is done 425:22
  s. then this bill 185:22
  s. upon thine heart..s. upon
    thine arm 52:22
  s. up the avenues of ill 199:29
  s. with a righteous kiss 478:44
  this kingly s. 425:4
Sealed: s. in vain 462:16
  s. it with his hand 31:24
  s. thee for herself 434:25
  s. thee His 165:31
  s. to the holy book 15:27
  something s. the lips 532:22
Sea-life: come to like a s. 272:37
Sea-line: where the s. meets 366:4
Sealing-wax: gunpowder and s. 131:21
  like sticks of s. 174:11
  ships and s. 130:15
Seals: loose the s. thereof 70:40
  s. of love 462:16
  s. up all in rest 487:16
Seam: sew a fine s. 366:16
Sea-maid: hear the s.'s music 466:38
Seaman: mighty S. 537:17
Sea-mark: like a great s. 429:21
  s. of my utmost sail 473:31
Seamed with the scars of disease 325:28
Seamen: all her s. know 147:13
  as s. use at sea 298:14
  s. were not gentlemen 326:2
Sea-monster: more hideous..
  than the s. 452:28
Seams op'ning wide 160:35
Sea-nymphs hourly ring 479:30
Search: after a s. so painful 407:22
  in the s. of the depth 49:22
  not worth the s. 463:1
  s. the grassy knolls 131:24
  s. the land of living men 418:6
  s. the scriptures 63:19, 422:1
  s. will find it out 246:19
Searched: thou hast s. me out 400:7
Searching: by s. find out God 48:56
  I am s. everywhere! 512:13
Seas: all the s. of God 567:3
  dangers..incident o' th' s. 373:11
  dangers of the s. 373:12
  dear hearts across the s. 297:14
  down to the s. again 334:10
  floors of silent s. 197:19
  from the s. and the streams 492:25
  gemlike plains and s. 561:17
  gloom the dark broad s. 541:3
  guard our native s. 123:10
  half s. over 520:13
  his Briton in blown s. 537:21
  hollow s. that roar 332:3
  ice on summer s. 529:41
  isle in the far s. 94:42
  launch out on trackless s. 567:2
  multitudinous s. incarnadine 458:15

Seas (*cont.*)

newly come from the s. 406:2
no less than labouring s. 249:12
on desperate s. 380:17
on what s. shall be thy fate 264:7
O rushing s.! 147:7
paths of the s. 392:12
perilous s., in faery lands 288:1
port after stormy s. 509:28
raging s. did roar 9:3
sail with God the s. 200:18
s. are quiet 557:24
s. are too long 28:3
s. colder than the Hebrides 208:7
s. do laugh 563:35
s. of life, like wine 548:18
s. of treacle and..butter 326:7
silence of the s. 581:1
Severn into the narrow s. 212:8
strange s. of thought 579:19
such as pass upon the s. 400:29
up and down the salt s. 294:34
volume of all the s. 489:20
waste of s. 420:31
when the s. were roaring 216:5
winds and s. are troublesome 168:13
Sea-sand: ribbed s. 149:19
  your name upon the soft s. 309:7
Sea-scented beach 93:21
Sea-shore: on the warm s. 15:14
  playing on the s. 364:13
Seasickness: universal as s. 490:22
Seaside: Like to be Beside the S. 223:6
Season: but for a s. 263:16
  by s. season'd 465:22
  comet of a s. 114:37
  disturb your s. due 342:10
  each thing that in s. grows 454:33
  ever 'gainst that s. comes 430:20
  for every s...dressings 8:14
  hope of a s.'s fame 363:4
  in a somer s. 310:3
  in s., out of s. 68:59
  in the s. of the year 8:23
  love..no s. knows 186:20
  my blessing, this in theel 431:25
  proportion, s., form 481:2
  s. made for joys 214:32
  s. my fireside 578:18
  s. of all natures, sleep 459:26
  s. of calm weather 576:19
  s. of clear shining 161:21
  s. of mists 284:10
  s. of snows and sins 521:30(-522)
  s. your admiration 431:7
  soote s. 518:3
  spoken in due s. 50:14
  to every thing there is a s. 51:3
Seasoned: by season s. 465:22
  s. with a gracious voice 464:14
  s. with salt 68:33
Seasons: all s. shall be sweet 151:26
  as the swift s. roll 251:15
  envious s. roll 251:11
  few more s. come 78:16
  four s. fill the measure 288:27
  in process of the s. 487:29
  I play for S.; not Eternities! 336:23
  moon for certain s. 398:10
  of all the S...Winter 375:11
  s.' difference 426:29
  s. such as these 453:14
  s. when to take Occasion 539:12
  seen the s. through 298:12
  thou hast all s. 241:14
  to thy motions lovers' s. run 186:19
  we see the s. alter 466:37
  with the year s. return 346:20
Seat: fell from off the s. backward 47:9
  grew into his s. 436:42
  her s. is the bosom of God 253:26
  not a s. but a springboard 144:13
  panting for a happier s. 279:12
  s. of desolation 344:18
  s. of Mars 474:22
  s. of pleasures 192:44
  s. of the scornful 391:45
  s. where love is enthron'd 483:2
  so late their happy s. 349:31
  this castle hath a pleasant s. 457:7
  this the s. 344:21

Seat (cont.)
thy s. is up on high 476:1
wild sequester'd s. 154:1
Seated: all s. on the ground 527:4
s. in thy silver chair 279:31
s. one day at the organ 402:11
Seaton: Marie S. and Marie
Beaton 31:18
Seats: blissful s. 562:10
chief s. in the synagogues 60:15
Seaward: light woods go s. 266:2
looks s. 92:27
salt tides s. flow 15:23
Seawards: my road leads me s. 334:8
Sea-water: salt s. passes by 532:15
Sea-wind: no life but the s.'s 523:14
Secandi: exsors ipsa s. 256:7
Secesher: agin the S.'s fist 560:11
Second: against s. marriages 204:8
Death's s. self 487:16
each s...heir to the first 469:24
everybody allows the s. place 520:33
for my s. race 552:3
my s. leg 252:30
nature's s. course 458:11
no s. knows nor third 351:3
no s. life? 15:4
no s. stroke intend 346:7
s. and sober thoughts 242:7
s. at Rome 24:29
s. eleven sort of chap 36:2
s. of our reign 184:7
S. Mrs. Tanqueray 41:13
s. yoke 241:9
smiles upon a s. leave 431:24
some s. guest to entertain 186:8
Tom the S. 192:11
viler George the S. 309:11
walks round..the s. time 376:17
Second best bed 488:30
Second class: very small s. carriage 219:10
Seconds: sixty s.' worth 297:12
smile on you—for s. 183:12
Secrecy: for s., no lady closer 439:11
Nature's..book of s. 423:16
S. the human dress 77:4
Secret: better than s. love 50:44
bread eaten in s. 49:53
ceases to be a s. 40:5
every s. thing 51:36
her s. none can utter 404:20
in s. sin 143:12
joys of parents are s. 26:44
many a s. place 581:22
method and s. 20:18
most s. and inviolate Rose 585:23
my s. faults 392:34
no s. so close 518:42
read in s. 78:20
s., black, and midnight hags 460:2
s. ministry 151:23, 25
s. of the bull and lamb 336:25
s. of the sea 317:15
s. of the shrouded death 335:28
s. parts of Fortune 433:10
s. things belong unto..God 46:29
s. was the garden 545:3
three may keep a s. 211:13
told my s. out 81:10
Secret: Vigny plus s. 414:7
Secretary: great S. of Nature 559:29
Secreted: thought..s. by the brain 125:30
Secretest man of blood 459:24
Secrets: from whom no s. 390:4
learned the s. of the grave 374:11
s. are edged tools 193:6
s. in all families 203:15
s. of my prison-house 432:9
s. of th' abyss to spy 231:13
s. with girls 165:13
Sect: found them a s. 325:35
loving his own s. 152:22
paradise for a s. 285:32
sad-coloured s. 253:32
slave to no s. 384:14
Sectaries: jarring s. 160:41
nation of s. 181:41
Sectes: soixante s. religieuses 124:23
Sects: diversity of s. 510:15
Two-and-Seventy jarring S. 206:25
Secular bird, ages of lives 351:4

Secundas res ornant 145:16
Secundis: vosmet rebus servate s. 553:15
Secure: he is s. 492:7
here we may reign s. 344:23
love is not s. 140:16
none can thee s. 552:2
saints have dwelt s. 562:9
s. of private right 190:28
s. within 194:20
s. without a formidable Opposition 181:30
surety s. 481:11
Securely plac'd between 164:12
Securing the Church of England 2:16
Securis: nec sumit aut ponit s. 259:19
Security: our watchword is s. 379:12
put to hazard his ease, his s. 101:21
s. is mortals' chiefest enemy 459:28
s. of a God 25:17
s. to persons who are accused 172:12
Sedan chair: flood of tears and a S. 179:18
Sedate: majestic yet s. 401:22
s., sober, silent 253:32
Sedately: took the kiss s. 536:3
try to walk s. 515:23
Sedens adversus identidem te 133:2
Sedes: Dei s. nisi terra 320:26
Sedge: kiss to every s. 484:35
s. is wither'd 286:28
Seditione: de s. querentis 282:26
Seditions: way to prevent s. 27:9
Seduce: she did not s. 337:11
Seduced: so firm that cannot be s. 448:31
Seducer: strong s., opportunity! 192:1
Seduction of martial music 104:1
Seductive Waltz! 119:27
Sedulous: played the s. ape 514:9
See: alive..delighted to s. him 250:24
all that we s. or seem 380:16
as God gives us to s. 314:13
believe, and thou shalt s. 354:12
but s. her passing by 10:20, 210:5
come up and s. me sometime 565:22
damned if I s. it 362:12
day by day is nought to s. 82:2
dead..like to s. me 250:24
dost thou s. them? 361:13
ere she s. the Earl of Murray 30:10
every eye shall s. him 70:22
eyes have they, and s. not 399:4
for one short hour to s. 536:18
for to admire an' for to s. 296:22
for to s. and..to be seye 138:7
full plain I s. 150:11
Gods s. everywhere 315:28
gold that I never s. 263:13
have him s. me woman'd 472:19
here shall he s. no enemy 427:7
His own face to s. 249:10
I cannot s. what flowers 287:30
I cannot s. you 314:16
I do not ask to s. 364:10
I do not s. them here 411:14
I don't s. any wine 129:5
'I don't s.', said the Caterpillar 128:27
if I no more should s. thyself 410:24
in all things Thee to s. 244:15
in my flesh shall I s. God 49:6
into the wilderness to s. 59:6
I really do not s. the signal 362:21
I s. a hand you cannot s. 547:21
I s., not feel 151:2
I s. thee still 457:20
I s. the sights that dazzle 78:3
I s. what I eat 129:6
I would s. him 210:1
lest men s. too much at once 95:31
lest they s. with their eyes 53:10
like my roses to s. you 501:3
lookers-on...s. more 26:12
lovers' eyes are sharp to s. 417:34
may I be there to s.l 160:11
more people s. than weigh 139:27
more we s. of you 41:28
my Holy S. of love 287:5
never s. a poem lovely 292:12
never s. me more 328:18
never s. so much 454:28
no man s. me. and live 46:7
noo mwore do s. your feäce 35:16
not s. the sun 395:21

See (cont.)
now can s. no more 576:1
now I s. 63:35
plainly s. this busy world 158:12
play 'Can you s. me?' 544:6
rather s. than be one 100:1
s. and learn the noble acts 328:1
s. and to be seen 138:7, 194:24
s. anybody coming? 377:32(-378)
s. at the Zoo 297:26
s. eye to eye 54:23
s. how our works endure! 295:10
s. how you would do 74:24
s. into the life of things 581:25
s. it, and be ashamed 397:12
s., no longer blinded 84:6
s. not all clear 551:21
s. o'er the foaming billows 415:6
s. oursel as others s. us 106:33
s. the Christ stand! 96:25
s. thee at Philippi 451:32
s. the front o' battle lour 107:32
s. the goodness of the Lord 393:22
s. their foes 418:29
s. them on the street 411:13
s. the stuff again 243:6
s. the things thou dost not 454:11
s. those things which you s. 61:38
s. thou do it not 71:35
s. through a flight o' stairs 179:10
s. to thine own house, David 47:48
s. what I s. 434:14
s., where it flies! 330:5
s. ye to it 60:49
shall he not s.? 397:24
so long as..eyes can s. 486:18
sort that say they can s. it 299:20
Spanish fleet thou canst not s. 500:1
them they'll s. nae mair 32:2
they never s. us but 213:11
they shall s. God 57:39
they shall s. our God 291:13
they that won't s. 520:27
those craven ranks to s. 323:26
till I s. what I say 557:20
to s. God only 185:13
to s. her is to love her 104:25
to s. her was to love her 104:31
until we hardly s. 498:5
veil.. I could not s. 206:16, 17
Venus, let me never s. 401:36
virtue could s. 340:20
wait and s. 21:5, 324:18
weep, but never s. 308:14
we would s. Jesus 63:45
what do I s. and hear? 6:17
what you may expect to s. 188:12
when do I s. thee most? 410:23
when I s. you in the light 304:7
whom I wished to s. 292:5
ye shall not s. me 63:62
you s. me here, you gods 452:42
you should s. me on Sunday 12:8
See-saw, Margery Daw 368:18
Seed: all have got the s. 529:23
beareth forth good s. 399:34
groweth s. and bloweth med 9:26
grows to s. 430:33(-431)
his s. begging their bread 394:5
not one light s. 286:3
of the Last Harvest sow'd the S. 207:6
scatter the good s. 121:27
s. in secret slept 79:6
s. its harvest 285:1
s. of Abraham? so am I 67:33
s. of knowledge 24:11
s. of ruin in himself 16:27
s. of the Church 542:3
what sunny s. 551:16
with them the S. of Wisdom 206:12
Seeds: look into the s. of time 456:15
s. and weak beginnings 442:6
s. of godlike power 15:9
some s. fell by the wayside 59:21
winged s. 496:4
Seed-time: fair s. had my soul 579:5
s. and harvest 44:41
Seeing: adds a precious s. 455:25
delight in s. thee 109:16
if eyes were made for s. 199:26
master-light of all our s. 576:18

Seeing (*cont.*)

not satisfied with s. 50:61
only one way of s. them 413:17
s. eye 50:26
s. Scotland, Madam 273:32
s., shall take heart again 317:8
those s. tears 332:11
worth s.? yes 274:15

Seek: beds for me and all who s. 410:4
happiest if ye s. no happier 347:27
I s. and adore them 81:9
I s. thee in vain 314:20
peace is what I s. 16:25
possess the things I s. 408:15
s. all day ere you find them 463:1
s., and ye shall find 58:19
s. farther store 421:17
s. His Face 354:11
s. it in My arms 544:30
s. no more 195:13
s. not yet repose 198:19
s. out—less often sought 118:27
s. peace, and ensue it 394:2
s. power and to lose liberty 26:23
s. through the world 376:10
s. to be good 322:4
s. to do thee good 399:31
s. to mend 185:18
s. with care, difficulty 309:16
s. ye first the kingdom 58:14
s. ye the Lord while he may be found 54:30
s. your job with thankfulness 296:33
sometime did me s. 583:20
they who s. the Lord 393:38
to strive, to s., to find 541:3
treachery! s. it out 437:39
we s. him here 370:13
we s. one to come 69:24
where s. is find 503:5
why s. ye the living? 62:53
within us the wonders we s. 86:11
world was not to s. me 275:6

Seekest: He whom thou s. 544:31
s. thou great things for thyself? 55:22
whom thou s. to find him 524:2

Seeketh: he that s. findeth 58:20
Love s...self to please 76:2, 3
s. not her own 66:45

Seeking: s. after that..clime 76:7
s. help from none 227:34
s. shall find Him 91:41
s. the bubble reputation 427:21
s. the food he eats 427:9
s. whom he may devour 70:6
still be s. 574:30

Seeks: neither s., nor shuns his foe 191:28
s. her own salvation 437:3
whoever s. abroad 284:12

Seel: wise gods s. our eyes 425:2

Seelen: zwei S. und ein Gedanke 234:17
zwei S. wohnen 223:16

Seem: all that we see or s. 380:16
but s. to be so 470:22
grow to what they s. 226:12
men should be what they s. 471:29
s. to see the things 454:11
seldom what they s. 221:21
things are not what they s. 317:5
things, that only s. 510:12
wiser than they s. 27:12
would they might s. none! 471:29

Seemed: all s. well pleased 348:15
s. unto him but a few days 45:6
what s. his head 346:4

Seeming: by s. otherwise 470:27
keep s. and savour 485:22
mild as she is s. so 231:37
Seeming-virtuous eye 118:9
Seemly so to do 292:8
Seems: how sweet and fair she s. 558:4
s., madam!..I know not 's.' 430:30
so good as it s. beforehand 196:32
what England's 301:2
what s. to say her rosy mouth? 375:2
Seen: anybody here s. Kelly? 360:2
because thou art not s. 427:22
because thou hast s. me 64:11
be no more s. 394:11
daur na weel be s. 107:29
ere I had ever s. that day 431:4

Seen (*cont.*)

ever s. Brentford 275:9
evidence of things not s. 69:13
fine things to be s. 141:24
gay Robin is s. no more 80:20
God whom he hath not s. 70:15
his brother whom he hath s. 70:15
I..fled the S. 560:5
much have I s. and known 540:32
much more had s. 14:24
needs but to be s. 383:27
needs only to be s. 159:30, 192:22
never s. before 323:30
no man hath s. God 63:1, 70:13
not s. and yet have believed 64:11
people whom he has never s. 101:21
persons whom one has never s. 363:10
see, and eek for to be s. 138:7
see and to be s. 194:24
s. but an eel 173:37
s. in either of our brows 189:20
s. no more 312:24
s. of me also 67:5
s. sae mony changefu' years 106:27
s. what she could not declare 250:23
so far cannot be s. or heard 454:4
thank God..of that I have s. 328:12
that you and I have s. 32:14
things 'a didn't wish s. 237:5
things which I have s. 576:1
Thomas on earth was never s. 32:12
to have s. what I have s. 434:14
we have s. thee, O love 522:8
whom having not s., ye love 69:45
would you had never s. him 473:5

Seer: as the S. saw and said 410:34
sight of Judah's s. 329:12
some bold s. in a trance 534:8

Sees: doubts from what he s. 73:28
draw the Thing as he s. It 303:21
eye s. in it what the eye brings 126:13
neither hears nor s. 573:6
s., across the table 304:36
s...better in a cloudy day 200:3
s. it and does it 91:41
s. no more 408:7
s. what he foresaw 575:10
think the king s. thee still 243:30
what he s. in her 242:27
Seest: say what thou s. yond 479:31
what thou s., write 70:24
Seeth: now mine eye s. thee 49:33
the Lord s. not as man s. 47:18
Seethe: not s. a kid 46:1
Seething: with ceaseless turmoil s. 151:32
Segashuate: your symptoms s.? 238:16
Seges: iam s. est ubi Troia fuit 371:25
Seigneur: parce que vous êtes un grand s. 37:11
Seigneurs: les grands s. ont des plaisirs 355:7
Seine: fool-fury of the S. 533:29
parallels of latitude for a s. 550:20
Seize: cousin, s. the crown 475:19
ruin s. thee 229:20
s. and clutch and penetrate 197:34
you s. the flow'r 108:7
Seized thy parting soul 165:31
Seizes: imagination s. as beauty 289:17
Seizure: soft s. 480:39
Seldom: s. what they seem 221:21
when they s. come 438:31
Seldomer: read somewhat s. 89:34
Select: most s. and generous 431:25
not a s. party 290:27
s. out of the crowd a mistress 493:9
Selection: Natural S. 169:6
Self: arch-flatterer..a man's s. 26:33
Caesar's s. is God's 166:14
censure of a man's s. 274:5
concentred all in s. 417:22
dearer than s. 113:15
death's s. is sorry 280:10
each one a murdered s. 411:14
greater to one than one's s. 567:23
hounds lost, s. lost 518:16
infusing him with s. 475:7
it has no s. 290:9
on her sweet s...price 374:20
seeketh only S. to please 76:3
Sidney's s. 96:30

Self (*cont.*)

smote the chord of S. 534:16
swear by thy gracious s. 477:23
to my sole s. 288:2
to thine own s. be true 431:25
Self-begotten bird 351:3
Self-constituted saints 253:14
Self-control: cautious s. 104:21
self-knowledge, s. 537:32
Self-esteem: nothing profits more than s. 349:3
Self-evident: s. beings 363:14
these truths to be s. 11:11
Self-honoured, self-secure 17:24
Selfish: hard, the s. and the proud 164:34
in marriage..slack and s. 514:22
s. being all my life 23:6
Self-knowledge: more skilful in s. 575:7
self-reverence, s. 537:32
Selfless man 531:20
Self-love: golden-calf of S. 125:25
mirror of s. 334:27
s. and social 384:18
sick of s. 482:15
sin of s. 487:10
Self-lovers: extreme s. 27:39
Self-protection: sole end..s. 338:25
Self-revelation: *fluidity* of s. 268:5
Self-reverence, self-knowledge 537:32
Self-sacrifice: spirit of s. 574:1
Self-same artillery 318:24
Self-schooled, self-scann'd 17:24
Self-secure: self-honour'd, s. 17:24
Self-seeking: free from s. 308:2
Self-slaughter: his canon 'gainst s. 430:33
Self-sufficing: reasoning, s. thing 578:30
s. power of Solitude 579:15
Self-torturing sophist 113:48
Sell: buy with you, s. with you 463:16
have you buy and s. so 485:27
not s. for gold 131:24
s. that thou hast 60:1
s. them in the street 131:22
s. your heart's desire 296:15
Seller of purple 64:54
Selling: lives by s. something 513:29
Selves: let our s. benight 184:28
their dead s. 532:1
Selwyn: if Mr. S. calls again 250:24
Semblance: delights to trace its s. 159:2
outward s. of a man 179:11
thy native s. on 449:7
whose exterior s. doth belie 576:12
Semblances: outface it with their 426:28
Semblative a woman's part 482:10
Semele: appeared to hapless S. 330:6
Semen est sanguis Christianorum 542:3
Semihiante labello 133:6
Seminary: from a ladies' s. 219:29
Seminibus: caelestis origo s. 554:31
Semita: fallentis s. vitae 257:10
Semper: quod s., quod ubique 553:4
S. eadem 198:9
Sempronius: we'll do more, S. 1:14
Senate: give his little s. laws 385:29
gives his little s. laws 381:7
s. at his heels 384:10
shake alike the s. 386:21
Senates: applause of list'ning s. 230:5
cashiering most Kings and S. 127:6
flings the gauntlet down to s. 123:7
while listening s. hang 546:18
Senators of mighty woods 286:8
Send: dares s. a challenge 166:19
s. forth the best ye breed 303:24
s. me 53:9
s. me back my heart 517:16
whom shall I s.? 53:9
Seneca: S. cannot be too heavy 433:22
S. thinks he takes delight 109:16
Senectus: Morbi tristisque S. 554:27, 556:20
Senectutem: post molestam s. 13:8
s. *oblectant* 145:16
Senior-junior: this s. 455:8
Seniors: advice from my s. 546:34
Senlac Sanguelac 529:36
Se'nnights nine times nine 456:11
Sens: le bon s. et le bon goût 97:3
le bon s...la mieux partagée 172:27

INDEX

Sensation: awaiting the s. 219:31
devote myself to another s. 290:26
Permanent Possibility of S. 515:4
s is s. 276:1
uncomfortable s. 173:25
Sensational: too s. 569:26
Sensations: O for a life of s. 289:19
s. sweet 581:23
Sense: accounting for the moral s. 126:8
all my s. confined 386:29
as keen a s. of duty 221:28
batteries of alluring s. 332:7
bind the wand'ring s. 155:1
bottom of good s. 274:30
by feeble s. 161:18
can't be Nature..not s. 142:33
creeps after s. 193:43
deeper s. of her loss 214:1
devoid of s. and motion 345:19
echo in the s. 282:3
echo to the s. 382:32
fountain of good s. 194:15
gather beauty from their s. 80:23
good s. without vanity 223:9
if all want s. 244:7
in its Pickwickian s. 178:23
inlet of each s. 341:2
learn'd without s. 143:22
man of s. only trifles with them 139:23
masterly good s. 200:37
men of s. approve 382:33
men of s. never tell 423:1
Metaphysic calls for aid on S. 381:27
motions of the s. 461:20
never deviates into s. 193:2
no night seal thy s. 171:9
no s. have they of ills 230:26
no s. in gittin' riled 238:28
no substitute for s. 197:34
nothing goes for s. 110:36
not when the s. is dim 39:6
numbed s. to steel it 289:8
numbness pains my s. 287:22
of s. forlorn 150:17
palter with us in a double s. 461:12
poetry..must be good s. 153:9
polish'd manners and fine s. 164:3
read..after your own s. 469:44
retains an obscure s. 579:18
satire or s. 385:30
Scotchman..man of s. 315:15
s. aches at thee 472:35
s. and outward things 576:18
s and wit with poesy 117:15
s. faints picturing 496:8
s. may reach 185:2
s. of being well-dressed 201:7
s. of injured merit 344:13
s. of the luxurious 289:33
s. sublime 582:1
shall my s. pierce love 410:31
some nonsense about s. 514:4
song charms the s. 345:29
spirit of s. hard 480:39
take care of the s. 129:17
their s. is shut 460:23
their s...with their senses 336:33
thrive without one grain of s. 193:21
through s. and nonsense 190:32
too much s. to pray 384:31
untutor'd s. 164:33
want of s. 180:9
who all s. doth eat 436:5
whose soul is s. 186:25
within the s. they quicken 499:1
work upon the vulgar with fine s. 386:38
Senses: if Parson lost his s. 249:5
ill customs influence my very s. 201:31
my s. would have cool'd 461:3
our s. taken be 281:1
power of our s. 277:39
power to touch our s. so 343:17
soul and the s. 96:21
steep my s. in forgetfulness 441:41
Sensible: moral, s. and well-bred 159:15
more soft and s. 455:22
s. men never tell 182:5
s., temperate, sober 363:19
s. to feeling as to sight 457:20
this s. warm motion 462:9

Sensibility: dear s.! 512:29
experience..an immense s. 268:12
that s. of principle 102:13
wanting s. 164:3
Sensitive: Frog is justly s. 40:26
mind and heart, though s. 575:15
s. being, a creative soul 579:33
S. Plant 497:25
Senseless: else s. and shapeless 497:14
most s. and fit man 468:35
s. tranced thing 284:17
worse than s. things 448:8
Sensual: earthly, s., devilish 69:39
not to the s. ear 287:8
only s. pleasure without vice 277:7
s. whirlpools 337:17
throughout the s. world 357:22
Sensualism: strings of s. 337:8
Sensualist: lover and s. 241:29
Sensuous: simple, s. and passion-ate 352:28
Sensus: omnis eripit s. mihi 133:2
vita brevis, s. hebes 414:21
Sent: haughty Rome s. forth 281:15
man s. from God 62:61
s. from Heaven above 121:27
to hell; and say I s. thee 446:8
Sentence: every s. raise 385:29
half a s. at a time 159:17
mouths a s. 143:19
my s. is for open war 345:16
normal British s. 144:16
originator of a good s. 201:6
s. first—verdict afterwards 129:35
soon the s. sign 385:15
speak after s.? 269:30
Sentences without commencements 337:2
Sententiae: tot s. 542:1
Sentest it back to me 280:21(-281)
Sentiat: ita feri ut se mori s. 517:20
Sentiment: frantic s. 29:6
nurse of manly s. 102:12
religion, as a mere s. 363:18
s...not acquainted with 208:27
truth of the..s. 420:28
Sentimental: are you in s. mood? 219:16
pet-lamb in a s. farce 287:16
s. passion 220:28
s. people 337:8
S. Traveller 512:18
Sentimentally I am disposed to harmony 306:4
Sentiments: conflict of opinions and s. 277:5
imaginative s. 28:21
plague of his s.! 500:38
quiet interchange of s. 272:30
them's my s. 542:36
Sentinel: his s., the wolf 458:1
scarcely worth the s. 227:19
s. on Whitehall gate 322:20
s. stars set their watch 123:3
Sentinels: fix'd s. 444:6
walk the angels..as s. 331:3
Sentire quae velis 526:14
Sentries: like s. 193:30
s. of the shadowy night 355:10
Sentry: s., shut your eye 301:14
stands a winged s. 552:1
Senum: rumoresque s. severiorum 132:15
Separate: s. us from the love of God 65:58
two s. sides to my head 303:10
Separately: hang s. 211:18
Separateth very friends 50:18
Separation: eternal s. 513:23
prepare for a s. 404:24
September: April, June and S. 228:4
cool S. morn 568:11
thirty days hath S. 369:5
Sepulchral: like s. statues lay 184:31
old s. urns 159:21
Sepulchre: came first to the s. 64:5
cometh Mary.. unto the s. 64:4
dome of a vast s. 496:7
knoweth of his s. 46:35
new s. 64:3
s. in stubborn Jewry 474:22
s. there by the sea 380:10
s. wherein we saw thee 431:32
soldier's s. 122:20
their throat is an open s. 392:5

Sepulchred below 113:24
Sepulchres: whited s. 60:19
Sepulcri mitte supervacuous honores 259:13
Sepulcris: si quicquam mutis..s. 133:19
Sepultas: in electro, monumento plus quam regio, s. 27:47
Sequatur: quid autem s. 38:31
Sequel: what s.? 535:21
Sequentes: laudet diversa s. 261:6
Sequestered: obscure s. state 96:16
s. vale of life 230:7
wild s. seat 154:1
Sequitur: no more a s. 204:28
Sequor: deteriora s. 371:30
Sera nimis vita est crastina 331:22
Seraglio: rounded S. Point 337:7
Seram: pone s., prohibe 283:11
Seraph: rapt S. that adores 383:20
Seraph-band: this s. 150:6
Seraphim: bright S. 351:10
sister of the S. 165:31
sworded S. 343:16
Seraphims: above it stood the s. 53:8
obsequious S. 166:4
Seraph-man on every corse 150:6
Seraphs: wingèd s. of heaven 380:8
Seraph-wings of ecstasy 231:13
Serbonian bog 345:31
Sere: dry, bald, and s. 282:1
instead of plain and s. 80:23
ivy never s. 342:10
s., the yellow leaf 460:36
tickle o' the s. 433:18
Serene: breaks the s. of heaven 508:2
breathe its pure s. 288:19
drop s. 346:19
old age, s. and bright 583:2
purest ray s. 230:5
s. for contemplation 215:31
s. yet strong 401:22
that unhoped s. 83:19
Serenitas maris..prosequetur 39:1
Serfs: vassals and s. 98:21
Sergeant: might have been a s. 226:25
S.'s weddin' 301:11
S. Whatsisname 300:17
this fell s., death 438:1
Sergeants: two-an'-thirty S. 301:16
Sericana, where Chineses drive 346:23
Series of new time began 190:31
Serious: damned s. business 564:2
his s. swelling into bombast 194:6
in a s. humour 2:6
joke's a very s. thing 143:7
never means anything s. till 300:7
nothing s. in mortality 458:24
one of the most s. things 130:24
sage and s. poet Spenser 352:10
s. and the smirk 177:7
s. subject 20:5
sober, silent, s. 253:32
there is no s. conversation 277:17
trusts them with s. matters 139:23
war is much too s. 526:20
Seriously: Desdemona s. incline 470:2
Sermon: her funeral s. 41:15
honest and painful s. 377:16
liked the 'S. on the Mount' 183:4
perhaps turn out a s. 105:17
preach a better S. 201:22
s.'s dull defile 336:40
who a s. flies 243:25
Sermonem deficiente die 372:7
Sermons: s. and soda-water 115:33
s. from mystical Germans 220:4
s. in stones 426:30
write better s. now than I did 565:17
Sero te amavi 21:22
Serpent: as a s.'s egg 449:4
be the s. under't 457:5
biteth like a s. 50:32
gold and flowing s. 310:21
infernal s. 344:6
like Aaron's s. 383:25
my s. of old Nile 423:43
s. beguiled me 44:24
s. subtlest beast 349:7
s. was more subtil 44:19
sharper than a s.'s tooth 178:19, 452:30
strange s. 424:17
that old s. 71:39

INDEX

Serpent (*cont.*)
trail of the S.   357:8
way of a s.   50:56
winds into a subject like a s.   227:31
Serpent-haunted sea   208:8
Serpentine: dignify the S.   183:14
Serpents: obscene small s.   523:11
wise as s.   58:49
Serpit: dono divum gratissima s.   554:5
Servant: for master and s., oft
changing is loss   550:5
good and faithful s.   60:29
good s. does not all commands   430:2
him who was thy s.   246:26
how hard a life her s. lives   586:13
is thy s. a dog?   48:25
ken when ye hae a gude s.   420:16
ken when you have a good s.   419:25
lettest thou thy s. depart   61:20
s. above his lord   58:51
s. of God, well done   348:20
s. of the high God   359:15
s.'s . . a negligent elf   34:7
S. to Queen Elizabeth   232:16
s. with this clause   244:16
small s.   177:34
sword was s. unto right   509:35
sworn s. unto love   168:11
that s. stands you picked   516:1
this thy s.   391:20
took . . the form of a s.   68:17
thy fellow-s.   71:35
thy neighbour's wife, nor his s.   390:17
thy s. heareth   47:6
Thy s. sleeping   198:15
your s.'s cut in half   228:9
Servants: as one of thy hired s.   62:14
both good s.   232:12
equality in the s.'s hall   36:1
hired s. of my father's   62:14
his s. he with new acquist   351:7
passions . . good s.   313:19
reveal himself to His s.   352:12
S. of Light   14:30
s. of the sovereign or state   26:22
thine anxious s.   547:7
thrice s.   26:22
to s. kind   125:4
unless . . good many s.   518:20
unprofitable s.   62:28
ye s. of the Lord   183:21
Servavit: sic me s. Apollo   261:19
Serve: ere 'e's fit for to s.   304:3
freely we s.   348:12
Him s. with fear   292:7
hope they s. God   469:7
if thou come to s. the Lord   56:29
know we s. the Lord   301:26
nor s. him in a dish   40:30
not known shall s. me   392:31
not s. God if the devil bid   469:30
now will s. more strictly   573:29
s. God and mammon   58:10
s. God and the king   363:8
s. Him on the Sea   298:16
s. in heav'n   344:23
s. it right   177:2
s. my turn upon him   469:25
s. our private ends   143:6
s. thee with a quiet mind   389:48
s. the future hour   573:27
s. therewith my Maker   351:21
s. your captives' need   303:24
suit and s. his need   244:10
they also s.   351:21
they s. him best   351:21
time to s. and to sin   522:7
'tis enough, 'twill s.   478:14
Served: despised as well as s. it   112:8
had I but s. God as diligently   572:18
had I but s. my God   447:1
Jacob s. seven years   45:6
s. no private end   385:6
youth will be s.   78:29
Serves: s. and fears the . . multitude   335:3
To What S. Mortal Beauty?   255:10
Serveth: as he that s.   62:44
s. not another's will   583:9
Service: all nations . . do him s.   396:25
all s. ranks the same with God   94:46

Service (*cont.*)
before the s. begins   200:43
choke their s. up   426:38
Christian s.   474:22
creep in s.   484:39
curse of the s.   469:24
desert in s.   481:21
done the state some s.   474:2
hewn with constant s.   507:2
I lack iniquity . . to do me s.   469:36
in thee't had been good s.   424:18
made of faith and s.   428:28
our bounden duty and s.   390:44
profane the s. of the dead   437:19
see you in the vestry after s.   504:27
s. greater than the god   481:12
s. high   341:24
s. of a mind and heart   575:15
s. of my love   511:4
s. of the antique world   426:38
s. sweat for duty   426:38
small s. is true s.   573:18
solemn s. of music   306:28
song for s. divyne   136:29
strong for s. still   163:5
weary and old with s.   446:24
whose s. is perfect freedom   388:25
yeoman's s.   437:28
Serviceable: in order s.   343:25
lowly and s.   136:27
Services: goods and s.   365:3
nor s. to do   487:7
s. of Angels and men   389:54
two s. . . had fair play   310:25
Servile: labours of a s. state   117:24
not a s. band   578:5
s. ministers   453:6
s. to all the skyey influences   462:3
Serving: cumbered about much s.   61:44
s. either calamity or tyranny   56:28
s. the Lord   66:2
Serving-man: iron-bound s.   184:14
s., proud in heart   453:19
Servitors: airy s.   352:3
Servitude: base laws of s.   191:41
freedom and not s.   101:7
impatient of s.   101:4
s. is at once the consequence   167:26
s. that hugs her chain   231:2
Sesame: open S.!   14:3
Sesquipedalia verba   255:22
Sesquipedalian blackguard   146:21
Sessions of sweet silent thought   486:25
Sestos: by S. town   264:5
S. and Abydos of her breasts   184:21
Set: all, except their sun, is s.   115:43
best plain s.   25:27
by God's grace, play a s.   443:11
ere the s. of sun   456:3
have it thus s. down   433:5
in good s. terms   427:12
meet it is I s. it down   432:21
never be s.   559:5
not rise nor s.   410:1
Percy! and s. on   440:33
place I s. out for   512:27
s. before you life and death   46:30
s. down aught in malice   474:2
s. himself doggedly to it   270:11
s. not your heart upon them   395:24
s. . . our little light   123:19
s. out for Lyonnesse   236:34
s. thee right   161:10
s. thou in my breast   231:38
s. up any of their own   102:37
s. up her houses   394:36
s. up thyself, O God   395:18
s. you down this   474:2
s. your faces like a flint   99:13
she s. out one day   98:19
splendid orb . . entirely s.   100:9
sun does not s.   415:22
suns, that s.   282:6
ye Stygian s.   308:22
Setebos: S., S., and S.!   90:13
Sets: flower that never s.   497:21
on which the sun never s.   365:10
Setter up and puller down   446:4
Setteth not by himself   392:24
Setting: against a s. sun   480:23
elsewhere its s.   576:9

Setting (*cont.*)
nearer he's to s.   247:10
s. of imagery   289:27
s. of that . . *Occidental Star*   43:24
Stars are s.   206:20
with the s. sun dropt   345:12
Settle: less will you s. to one   298:3
liv'd in S.'s numbers   381:12
s. . . into a . . smiling age   514:38
s. somewhere near the sea   303:14
Settled: in authority s. and calm   26:27
people wish to be s.   200:8
s. business   27:41
s. *Hoti's* business   91:42
s. now-a-days   116:23
s. on the lee   111:24
Settlement: Act of S.   406:21
parent of s.   102:7
Settles back the blade   141:9
Set-to: can honour s. a leg?   440:30
Seul: doit se tenir tout s.   12:15
on mourra s.   374:3
Seven: heat the furnace one s.
times   55:39
his gas-lamps s.   293:10
lie till s.   145:31
morning's at s.   94:40
once in s. years I burn all my
sermons   565:17
poor Miss 7   171:24
proposed s. times   175:37
s. days and nights?   472:18
s. fat kine   45:17
s. hours to law   279:21
s. maids with s. mops   130:12
s. men that can render a reason   50:42
s. of my goldenest years   306:15
s. other spirits more wicked   59:19
7 times 7 . . cant endure   208:22
seventy times s.   59:53
s. up and six to play   228:10
s. wealthy towns   9:15
s. whole days, not one in s.   244:26
s. wives   366:8
s. women . . one man   52:36
s. years for Rachel   45:6
s. years' heat   481:32
s. years' pith   469:45
till s. years were gane   32:12
to soothing slumber s.   279:21
we are s.   582:13
Seven Dials: lowly air of S.   219:2
Seven-fold: thy s. gifts impart   400:31
**Seven hundred years and fifty-
three**   184:2
Seven-ringed: Jamshyd's S. Cup   205:9
Seventeen: Maud is not s.   536:3
Sweet S.   528:8
Seventh: rested the s. day   390:11
s. day is the sabbath   390:9
Seven thousand: Yesterday's S.
Years   206:5
Seventies: gets well into the s.   515:2
Seventy: from s. springs a score   262:10
s., Simmery Axe   222:17
s. times seven   59:53
s. years ago   303:10
s. years young   251:12
Seventy-five: eighteenth of April
in S.   317:3
Seventy-seven: at s. . . in earnest   277:38
Sever: choughs . . s. themselves   467:7
how soon we must s.   166:24
then we s.   104:21
Severae: procul este, s.   371:21
Several: for s. virtues . . lik'd s.
women   479:44
Severe: be not s.   214:21
eyes s.   427:21
from lively to s.   384:15
from pleasant to s.   193:19
if s. in aught   225:1
man s. he was   225:1
not s.   14:23
to nothing but herself s.   125:4
Truth s.   229:26
Severed: our state cannot be s.   349:19
Severely: bangs me most s.   125:18
do the thing yet more s.   194:17
talked to him s.   298:21
Severing of our loves   576:21

Severity: play with the s. of fate 209:23
  s. breedeth fear 26:26
  s. of perfect light 530:18
  with its usual s. 152:31
  with simplicity or with s. 20:5
Severn: Avon into S. 212:8
  from the S. to the Tyne 294:22
  out to S. strode 141:21
  S. fills 532:15
  where S. seeks the sunset 41:21
Severs: s. those it should unite 493:21
  sword that s. all 336:18
Seville: dogs of S. 539:20
Sew: teach the orphan-girl to s. 533:39
Sewell and Cross young man 221:8
Sewers: reign o'er s. and sinks 150:28
  s. annoy the air 349:11
Sewing: as long as her eyes 262:8
  s. at once..a shroud 253:24
Sex: all..I claim for my own s. 22:27
  either s. assume 344:29
  fair s. is your department 188:8
  female of s. it seems 350:31
  formed for the ruin of our s. 506:5
  here's the S.l 106:23
  how unseemly is it for my s. 331:2
  no stronger than my s. 449:18
  s. by themselves 39:20
  s. to the last 192:6
  s. whose presence civilizes 159:18
  soft, unhappy s. 40:14
  tyrants of thy s. 155:27
  weaker s., to piety more prone 4:9
  your s.'s earliest..care 322:3
Sexes: cleanliness of the s. 567:8
  in the name of both s. 101:27
  old women (of both s.) 513:18
Sexton: bald s., Time 447:30
  no s...toll the bell 237:7
  our honest s. tells 164:29
  told the s. 252:32
Sextus: Herminius glared on S. 324:4
  save them from false S. 323:18
  to S. nought spake he 323:26
Shabby tigers 249:5
Shackles: s. accidents 425:33
  s. of an old love 530:37
  their s. fall 162:42
Shade: after the night's s. 467:19
  along the moon-light s. 381:30
  betwixt the shine and s. 527:12
  blessèd be her s.l 297:20
  chequered s. 342:3
  contiguity of s. 162:40
  crowd into a s. 385:7
  elder brother ev'n to s. 407:19
  ever mark'd with s. 308:31
  farewell to the s. 161:23
  gentlemen of the s. 438:16
  green s. 332:19
  grow to fruit or s. 243:20
  his stedfast s. sleeps 537:35
  I bear light s. 492:25
  image of a s. 499:7
  in s. of Tempe sit 502:2
  into the s. and loneliness 84:7
  inviolable s. 18:15
  let it sleep in the s. 356:29
  lone Glenartney's hazel s. 416:11
  narrow vergèd s. 332:13
  no s., no shine 253:12
  s. it casts 94:17
  s. of an old apple tree 571:22
  s. of a Rural Dean 84:11
  s. of His hand 544:31
  s. of melancholy boughs 427:19
  s. of that which once was great 582:8
  she a s. 308:22
  sitting in a pleasant s. 35:17
  sitting in the s. 206:32
  sit under the s. of it 175:10
  sleeping in the s. 336:7
  song, or fleeting s. 246:1
  sweeter s. to shepherds 446:2
  with Amaryllis in the s. 342:20
  with vois memorial in the s. 136:19
Shaded: my grottoes are s. 499:14
  sorrow thy young days s. 356:22
Shades: chase the trembling s. 166:5
  dens and s. of death 346:12
  describe the different s. 278:15

Shades (cont.)
  doleful s. 344:9
  Etrurian s. 344:25
  evening s. prevail 2:26
  fairest s. did hide her 359:27
  field is full of s. 545:2
  fled the s. of night 347:36
  happy s.—to me unblest! 162:14
  home to s. of under ground 123:27
  lived with S. so long 236:25
  mingle s. of joy and woe 419:28
  revellers, and s. of night 466:15
  s. like these 224:15
  s. of Arabia 171:2
  s. of darkness 171:7
  s. of night were falling fast 316:17
  s. of the prison-house 576:9
  studious walks and s. 350:11
  till the s. lengthen 364:4
Shadiest: in s. covert hid 346:20
Shadow: below the s. of a dream 299:3
  between..falls the S. 197:11
  but a s.'s bliss 464:3
  but a s.'s s. 433:13
  but the s. of death 85:16
  but the s. of Heaven 348:13
  Death's s. at the door 77:27
  dream itself..but a s. 433:13
  flits as. and a sigh 301:27
  follow a s. 280:20
  God within the s. 320:11
  hence, horrible s.l 459:21
  in the s. of death 61:15, 398:15
  in the s. of the earth 85:23
  in the s. of the hill 118:8
  life's but a walking s. 461:4
  Life, the s. of death 522:5
  like a vast s. mov'd 552:13
  night, the s. of light 522:5
  possible as. of doubt 218:18
  saw the lion's s. 465:17
  S. cloak'd from head to foot 532:17
  s. of a dream 299:3, 433:13
  s. of a great rock 53:43
  s. of annoyance 498:9
  s. of death 48:54, 53:14
  s. of felicity 558:6
  s. of God 85:16
  s. of her even brows 509:31
  s. of his foe 148:24
  s. of our night 492:7
  S. of Shadows 584:9
  s. of some unseen Power 494:3
  s. of surmise 199:13
  s. of the dome of pleasure 151:33(–152)
  s. of thee 410:24
  s. of the Valois 141:4
  s. of Thy Throne 562:9
  s. of Thy wing 565:7
  s. seem'd 346:4
  s. that it casts 573:18
  s. to s., well persuaded 295:10
  ship's huge s. 149:25
  swan and s. 582:19
  swift as a s. 466:20
  Time the S. 582:22
  trees in whose dim s. 324:3
  under the s. of thy wings 392:28, 395:17
  unhappy s. 123:20
  walketh in a vain s. 394:9
  your s. at morning 197:28
Shadowing: not to employ any depth of s. 194:17
Shadowless like Silence 253:13
Shadows: beckoning s. dire 340:10
  best in this kind are but s. 467:30
  cast their s. before 122:22
  come like s. 460:10
  Earth's s. fly 492:15
  earth's vain s. flee 322:2
  fills the s. and windy places 521:30
  half sick of s. 534:3
  individuals pass like s. 101:18
  little s. come about her eyes 585:3
  millions of strange s. 487:2
  no s. great appear 247:5
  our fatal s. 37:23
  quiet s. falling 370:15
  scattering of all s. 35:6
  s. flee away 52:3

Shadows (cont.)
  s. kiss 464:3
  s., not substantial things 501:5
  s. numberless 287:23
  s. of eternity 552:4
  s. of hates 15:3
  s. of the clouds 573:1
  s. of the evening 34:35
  s. of the living 85:16
  s. of us men 280:20
  s., that showed at noon 312:26
  s. to-night 476:38
  splendour among s. 498:20
  titles are s. 170:17
  what s. we are and..pursue 100:17
Shadowy: keeps the s. kine 183:1
  s. exultation 579:17
Shadrach, Meshach, and Abed-nego 55:41
Shadwell: S. never deviates 193:2
  S.'s genuine night 193:2
Shady: s. leaves of destiny 166:17
  s. side of Pall Mall 358:19
  s. with birch 82:9
Shaft: Cupid's fiery s. 466:39
  lie like a s. of light 529:30
  many a s., at random sent 417:30
  s. of slander shot 375:23
  wing'd the s. 117:25
  with a S. of Light 205:5
Shaggy white great-coat 175:12
Shake: Brutus, will I s. with you 450:6
  by that s. of the head 500:3
  earth was feverous and did s. 458:21
  Hand..of the Potter s. 207:15
  his bridle-reins a s. 106:18
  never s. thy gory locks 459:15
  power to s. me 573:1
  seems to s. the spheres 191:1
  s. against the cold 487:16
  s. alike the senate 386:21
  s. hands for ever 189:20
  s. hands with a king 234:14
  s. off dull sloth 292:1
  s. off the bur o' the world 543:16
  s. off the dust of your feet 58:48
  s. off this downy sleep 458:23
  s. off his poor little head 220:18
  s. our disposition 431:32(–432)
  s. their heads, saying 393:3
  s. their wicked sides 584:26
  s. the massive paws 40:20
  s. the yoke of inauspicious stars 478:44
  s. thou to look on't 425:5
  s. us nightly 459:4
  slender acacia would not s. 536:13
  very earth did s. 189:7
Shaked: earth s. like a coward 439:40
  when degree is s. 481:3
Shaken: every moment, lightly s. 534:16
  is never s. 488:7
  pressed down and s. together 61:31
  reed s. with the wind? 59:6
  s. of a mighty wind 71:1
  s. with earth's old and weary cry 586:8
  so s. as we are 438:11
  well s. 154:19
Shakes: s. his dewy wings 169:13
  s. his head, and exit 500:3
  s. so my single state of man 456:24
  s. the wings 194:22
  s. this fragile frame at eve 236:12
  slightly s. his parting guest 481:20
Shake-scene: only S. in a country 232:6
Shakespeare: better done in S. 194:7
  fed with S.'s flame 141:30
  fancy S. this Presider 289:13
  for gentle S. cut 281:9
  grace before S. 306:8
  I despise S. 489:22
  immortal S. rose 278:34
  I was S.'s countryman 561:15
  less S. he 92:19
  lo, S., since thy time 80:29
  make room for S. 36:21
  mighty S. 80:24
  my being like S. 420:30
  myriad-minded S. 152:27
  my S., rise 281:11
  one wild S. 357:19
  pictures, taste, S. 227:23

Shakespeare (cont.)
quibble is to S. 278:23
read and perhaps understand S. 289:29
reading S. by flashes 153:5
S...for gain not glory 386:12
S. is not our poet 308:16
S. led a life of allegory 290:18
S. made use of it first 500:2
S. never had six lines 271:31
S...not a whit more intelligible 153:14
S. of divines 199:24
S., on whose forehead climb 89:2
S...quite forgotten 141:29
S.'s genius..cultivated 139:21
S.'s strain 199:2
S. was of us 93:4
stood with S. at the top 297:19
stuff..great part of S. 216:14
sweetest S., Fancy's child 342:7
this is the Jew that S. drew 386:34
tongue that S. spake 577:3
to S. gave as much 192:12
to the memory of S. 226:28
what needs my S. 351:8
Shaking: bright dew is s. 166:24
fall without s. 354:14
s. her invincible locks 352:15
white sail 's s. 334:10
Shalimar: beside the S. 254:14
Shall: his absolute 's.' 429:12
nor ever ever s. 369:13
that which s. be 50:61
you s. and you shan't 187:7
Shallow: idle s. things 484:9
s. brooks murmur most 501:17
s. in himself 350:13
Shallows: his depths and his s. 107:36
in s. and in miseries 451:29
Shalott: Lady of S. 534:2, 3, 7, 10
Shame: ain't it all a bloomin' s. 9:20
awkward s. 386:20
be mine the s.! 192:23
by certain s. attended 300:23
each deed of s. 316:30
erring sister's s. 117:40
foaming out their own s. 70:20
heart-sick of his country's s. 163:2
her dead and her s. 539:21(-540)
hide her s. 226:18
in a waste of s. 488:11
I see the s. they cannot see 375:23
let s. come when it will 452:40
let s. say what it will 437:2
London's lasting s. 229:24
man's best dreams to s. 88:21
may coward s. distain 106:35
neither sin nor s. 512:17
noble s. 294:3
not born to s. 478:21
not serving s. or lust 183:10
put him to an open s. 69:9
quit, quit, for s. 517:11
race of s. 350:30
say nay, for s. 583:18
secret House of S. 569:8
s. and ruin wait for you 158:33
s. for women to speak 67:3
s. is ashamed to sit 478:21
s. it is to see 293:12
s. of age 141:23
s. on us, Christian brethren 264:13
s. the devil 281:21, 439:43
s. the fools 385:22
s. to men! 345:28
so much s. 325:25
soon brought to s. 396:20
speak it to my s. 440:28
throughout the life the s. 233:3
thy father's s. 80:8
to a perpetual s. 397:1
wash for s. 11:5
whose glory is in their s. 68:24
without great s...never go back 358:2
with s. and grief I yield 292:20
with s. to take the lowest room 62:2
wrought the deed of s. 323:18
Shamed: s. life a hateful 462:9
s. thro' all my nature 534:31
's., you sleepy-head? 515:25

Shameful: s. conquest of itself 474:24
'tis a s. sight 561:27
Shameless: most s. thing in the world 102:23
Shames: all kinds of sores and s. 472:34
hold a candle to my s. 463:38
s. silliness out of me 567:14
Shamest thou to show thy..brow 449:6
Shamming: s. when 'e's dead 296:24
whate'er their gentle s. 357:20
Shamrock is by law forbid 9:6
Shandon: those S. bells 402:20
Shank: his shrunk s. 427:21
his spindle s. 106:5
Shannon: green banks of S. 122:16
Sha'n't! Won't! 300:16
Shape: any s. but that 459:20
Attic s.! Fair attitude! 287:13
dancing s., an image gay 580:19
execrable s. 346:5
gave them s. and speech 524:22
grim s. towered up 579:10
harmony of s. 401:32
if s...call'd that s. had none 346:4
imagination to give them s. 434:9
in s. and gesture..eminent 345:5
I s. me—ever removed! 92:43
let it keep one s. 461:22
mystic s. did move 88:16
not force to s. it 531:27
s. from that thy work of art 316:24
s. of a woman 290:5
S. of Things to Come 565:1
she was a gordian s. 286:37
such a questionable s. 431:32
that strange s. 149:11
two of far nobler s. 347:10
virtue in her s. how lovely 347:31
wrought me into S. 207:17
you might be any s. almost 131:4
Shaped: bore, s., made aware 84:21
s., sir, like itself 424:17
Shapeless: else senseless and s. 497:14
s. sculpture 230:7
so in a s. flame 184:4
Shapen in wickedness 395:8
Shapes: calling s. 340:10
fiery and delectable s. 442:21
full of fiery s. 439:40
horrid s. and shrieks 341:26
its s. the..thoughts outnumber 495:18
s. of foul disease 533:20
s. of sky or plain 498:8
s. our ends 437:27
s. that haunt thought 497:2
so full of s. is fancy 481:30
sublime and beauteous s. 496:19
turns them to s. 467:24
Shard: iron s. 301:1
shatter'd in s. on s. 544:28
Share: Adam shall s. with me 349:16
greater s. of honour 444:26
its ruin didst not s. 183:22
no one so true did s. it 483:6
not for having s. in Government 135:28
s. her wretched crust 320:12
s. my harvest 253:21
s. with Berkeley Square 302:26
they only ask to s. 511:10
to s. it a' 107:25
utmost s. of my desire 247:8
we'll thole our s. 360:4
Shared in the plunder 161:37
Shareth in our gladness 4:3
Sharks: among the s. and whales 8:24
Sharon: rose of S. 51:43
Sharp: billiard s. 220:6
God answers s. and sudden 87:29
s. and sided hail 254:29
s. as a pen 443:19
s. as a two-edged sword 49:44
s. remedy 405:14
s. tongue..grows keener 267:19
short, s. shock 219:31
somebody's s. 174:12
thy sting is not so s. 427:22
without s. North 185:8
Sharpeneth: iron s. iron 50:47
s. the countenance 50:47
Sharpens our skill 102:27

Sharper: s. than any two-edged sword 69:8
s. than a serpent's tooth 178:19, 452:30
s. than I received it 546:38
Sharpest you still have survived 199:25
Sharp-looking wretch 429:1
Sharpness of death 388:17
Sharps: different s. and flats 94:33
Shatter: s. would we not s. it to bits 207:26
you may s. the vase 356:18
Shattered: many were s. 539:21(-540)
s. in shard on shard 544:28
when the lamp is 494:20
Shattering all evil customs 530:30
Shave: half the s. 252:8
Shaved with a shell 309:28
Shaving: when I am s. 264:6
Shaw: Oh, Captain S.! 219:8
Shawms: trumpets also, and s. 397:32
Shay: one-hoss s. 251:6
She: any been but s. 517:19
any s. belied 488:14
cruell'st s. alive 482:20
every he has got him a s. 5:25
fresshe folkes, he or s. 138:42
innocence and s. 543:22
not impossible to s. 166:17
s., and comparisons 184:15
s., even s. 430:33(-431)
s. for God in him 347:11
s., s. is dead 185:3
that s. belov'd knows nought 480:41
this only happy S. 375:26
'tis s. 166:12
unexpressive s. 427:23
yet s. will be false, ere I come 186:18
you are s., my dearest dear 159:34
Sheaf: brushwood s. 92:14
lay thy s. adown and come 253:21
Shear: known the barber's s. 543:3
Shearers: at the s.' feast 342:20
Shears: abhorred s. 342:20
her needle an' her s. 104:34
Sheath: outwears its s. 119:5
put up thy sword into the s. 63:66
sword back in the s. 141:8
Sheathe: never s. the sword 21:6
Sheathed their swords 443:25
Sheaves: bound the rose in s. 93:42
bring his s. with him 399:34
girded up in s. 486:15
your s. stood round about 45:13
Sheba: another S. queen 572:3
queen of S. had seen all 47:42
She-bear: great s. 209:18
s. thus accosted 296:13
Shed: all his beauty s. 342:31(-343)
a' the blude that's s. 32:11
bitter tears to s. 157:15
I'll not s. her blood 473:11
its bloom is s. 108:7
lowly cattle s. 3:20
monarch of a s. 226:11
prepare to s. them now 450:27
s. innocent blood 54:38
s. one English tear 323:9
straw-built s. 229:31
tear be duly s. 153:22
Thy blood was s. for me 198:20
with that man beneath a s. 276:24
Sheddeth: whoso s. man's blood 44:43
Shedding: s. my song upon height 524:13
without s. of blood 69:10
Sheds: found in lowly s. 340:17
Sheelagh: when S. was nigh 122:16
Sheen: deck'd in glorious s. 362:3
most s. is the sonne 310:7
s. of their spears 118:37
Sheep: baa, baa, black s. 366:9
beat their love o' s. 320:1
better than s. or goats 531:36
bleating of the s. 47:15
boy that looks after the s. 367:15
bringing thy s. in thy hand 17:19
careth not for the s. 63:38
feed my s. 55:36
folds shall be full of s. 395:30(-396)
his silly s. 161:26
hungry s. look up 342:29
in s.'s clothing 58:25

Sheep (cont.)
like a flock of s. 52:5
like lost s. 388:10
like s. have gone astray 54:26
little hills like young s. 399:3
looking on their silly s. 446:2
lost her s. 367:14
lost s. of the house of Israel 58:46
mountain s...valley s. 376:23
noble ensample to his s. 137:17
old half-witted s. 512:6
one sickly s. 561:30
or else their s. 343:15
other s. I have 63:39
plunge the struggling s. 323:12
s. before her shearers 54:26
s. of his hand 397:28
s.'s guts..hale souls 468:19
s.'s in the meadow 367:15
s. that have not a shepherd 48:13
s. which was lost 62:11
when the s. are in the fauld 35:7
white over with s. 499:14
who were thy s. 351:20
with His s. securely fold you 406:1
your s...wont to be so meek 358:12
Sheep-bells and the ship-bells 302:10
Sheep-hook: how to hold a s. 342:28
Sheep-worry of Europe 82:14
Sheer: bare, s., penetrating power 19:19
down a furlong s. 301:27
Sheet: float that standard s. 234:13
great s. knit 64:46
s. were big enough 483:34
wet s. and a flowing sea 167:20
white s. bleaching 485:16
Sheets: cool kindliness of s. 83:21
fumble with the s. 443:19
whitest of s. of snow 166:3
Sheffield: Brooks of S. 174:12
Shelf: from a s. the..diadem 435:49
occupy one s. 89:29
on a s. of rock or sand 580:10
upper s. 325:1
Shell: kill him in the s. 449:4
like a rainbow s. 409:14
shaved with a s. 309:28
smooth-lipped s. 574:20
thine outgrown s. 251:15
within thy airy s. 340:13
Shelley: Burns, were with us 93:4
peace in S.'s mind 494:12
see S. plain 93:23
S., whom envy never touched 309:20
sphere for S.'s genius 19:13
there S. dream'd 269:24
to us arose S. 80:24
Shellover: 'Come!' said old S. 171:23
Shells: silver bells and cockle s. 367:21
sinuous s., of pearly hue 308:26
Shelly horns 336:38
Shelter: I'd s. thee 107:24
our s. from the stormy blast 562:9
s. me from the cold 42:7
what s. to grow ripe is ours? 17:4
Sheltered: in youth it s. me 358:21
s. about the Mahogany Tree 543:11
Shelters: naught s. thee 544:19
Shelves: spoilers of the symmetry of s. 306:21
Shem: it might be S. 303:9
S., Ham and Japheth 44:36
Tents of S. 298:27
Shenandoah, I long to hear you 8:21
Shepherd: calls up the s. 462:22
dead s. 428:15
Dick the s. 456:1
equals the s. with the king 134:18
every s.'s tongue 405:8
every s. tells his tale 341:34
fairest s. on our green 377:2
faithful s.! to come 17:19
feed his flock like a s. 54:11
gentle S., tell me where 264:14
God of love my S. is 245:10
good s. giveth his life 63:37
King of Love my S. is 29:12
lark to s.'s ear 466:21
Love tunes the s.'s reed 417:16
not love a s. swain 232:5
philosophy in thee, s.? 427:24

Shepherd (cont.)
sheep that have not a s. 48:13
S. and Bishop of your souls 69:52
s., blowing of his nails 445:44
s. in Virgil 270:17
s., I take thy word 340:17
s.—of his love 33:13
s. of the Hebrid Isles 546:3
s. of the Ocean 509:9
S.'s care 2:21
S.'s sweet lot 76:11
slighted, s.'s trade 342:20
sweet unto a s. 232:5
the Lord is my s. 393:10
the Lord's my s. 421:1
they call you, S. 18:5
weather the s. shuns 236:32
Shepherd-boy: happy S. 576:6
Shepherdess of sheep 338:8
Shepherdesses: ancient s. I have read of 370:17
Shepherding her bright fountains 492:20
Shepherds: British s. 574:2
liberal s. give a grosser name 437:1
s., looking on their silly sheep 446:2
warmth of s.' flames 331:2
while s. watch'd 527:4
Sheridan: S. twenty miles away 406:3
S. was listened to 408:11
Sheriffmuir: at S. 327:1
Sherris: this valour comes of s. 442:21
Sherris-sack: good s. 442:21
Sherry: S. is dull 271:14
with ham and s. 84:5
Sherwood: in S., in S. 366:5
S. in the red dawn 366:6
Sheugh: nor yet in any s. 33:2
She-wolf: eats the s.'s young 150:9
Shield: broken s. was hung 140:18
broken was her s.! 418:35
courteoust knight that ever bare s. 328:24
left the s. 418:11
s. of faith 68:13
s. of the mighty..cast away 47:29
sword, a horse, a s. 319:10
thy s. and buckler 397:18
wisdom the mirrored s. 491:27
Shielding men from the effects of folly 508:23
Shields: s. in Branksome Hall 417:3
s. of mighty men 52:5
Shieling: from the lone s. 420:31
Shift: coming down..s. for myself 358:6
s. one's position 267:24
we'll s. our ground 432:26
we s. and bedeck 522:22
Shifted his trumpet 225:35
Shifting his side 161:38
Shifts her passions 215:14
Shilling: Philip and Mary on a s. 111:8
raise the volume's price a s. 521:19
sell for one s. your ring 312:2
s. a day 301:12
Splendid S. 378:17
Shillings: payment of half twenty s. 100:5
reduced the answer to s. and pence 129:28
Shimmered: Jeeves s. out 572:9
Shine: afar off s. bright 563:15
anxious for to s. 220:25
arise, s. 54:39
betwixt the s. and shade 527:12
coin of silvery s. 131:24
every one doth s. 449:30
fair days will s. 221:30
few are qualified to s. 520:41
his face s. upon thee 46:10
if the moon s. at full or no 111:4
I'll s. on ye yet 167:24
let your light so s. before men 57:42
no shade, no s. 253:12
nothing does but s. 545:11
not to s. in use 540:32(–541)
scatteringly doth s. 332:8
see him s. so brisk 438:35
s., and seek to mend 185:18
s. as it shines now 185:14
s. forth upon our clouded hills 75:16
s. in my arms 231:38

Shine (cont.)
s. inward 346:20
s. no more 160:22
s. on all alike 385:11
s. the traffic of Jacob's ladder 545:1
s. through the gloom 322:2
s. upon the road 161:1
s. with Pye 117:14
singing as they s. 2:28
that sun..shall s. on me 474:13
they shall s...like sparks 56:24
wit will s. 193:11
Shined: how Bacon s. 384:12
in her person s. 351:25
s. at Lugwardin 548:17
s. in my angel-infancy 552:3
Shines: how s. your tower 77:30
more it's shook it s. 235:3
she s. sae bright 108:31
s. brightly as a king 465:21
s. over city and river 537:16
Shinest: wheresoe'er thou s. 497:9
Shineth: light s. in darkness 62:60
s. more and more 49:43
Shingles: naked s. of the world 15:7
Shining: calculation s. out of the other 176:10
I see it s. plain 263:14
once a s. store 160:22
profit of their s. nights 454:32
quietly s. to the quiet moon 151:25
season of clear s. 161:21
s. morning face 427:21
s. nowhere but in the dark 552:10
s. still 19:1
s. with all his might 130:9
somewhere the sun is s. 238:6
through the dark cloud s. 210:4
transient, s. trouble 228:18
Shins: break my s. against it 427:5
Ship: all I ask is a tall s. 334:10
brake that gallant s. 30:19
carcasses of many a tall s. 464:6
ever scuttled s. 115:41
gart build a bonny s. 31:8
he was born in a s. 16:3
idle as a painted s. 149:5
in a s...in a jail 270:32
into our s.'s side 31:25(–32)
it reached the s. 150:10
land to which the s. would go 147:13
like a stately s. 350:31
one leak will sink a s. 99:28
O S. of State! 316:1
our s. hath touch'd..Bohemia 485:14
our s. not far from land 9:3
rapt s. run on her side 135:19
s. after s., the whole night long 539:21
s., an isle, a sickle moon 208:19
s. has weather'd every rack 566:27
s. I have got 30:23
s. in a black storm 563:34
s. is anchor'd 566:28
s. is clear at last, she leaps 566:25
s. is floating in the harbour 493:12
s. me somewheres east of Suez 299:15
s.'s huge shadow 149:25
s. that goes 173:8
s. was cheered 148:21
s. was still 507:24
s. went down like lead 150:10
s. would not travel due West! 128:9
sink me the s. 540:1
so old a s. 208:16
stately s. is seen no more 312:24
there was a s. 148:20
to which yon S. must go 582:16
undergirding the s. 65:28
victor s. comes in 566:28
way of a s. 50:56
we too take s. O soul 567:2
what is a s. but a prison? 109:19
when you go on board s. 39:1
whither, O splendid s. 81:26
Ship-bells: sheep-bells and the s. 302:10
Ship-boy: seel up the s.'s eyes 442:1
Shipman: a S. was ther 137:11
Shipmate: joy, s., joy! 566:25
Shipping: fishes first to s. 191:29
sink all the s. there 281:19
Ships: break the s. of the sea 394:34

Ships (cont.)

down to the sea in s.	398:17
drew a thousand s. to Tenedos	331:5
heart of oak are our s.	213:10
howl, ye s. of Tarshish	53:30
I saw three s. a-sailing	7:14
I spied three s.	5:14
labouring s.	586:7
launch'd a thousand s.	330:5
like two doomed s.	569:6
little s. of England	233:13
mighty s. ten thousand ton	249:15
my s. are out of gear	539:17
move with the moving s.	525:30
our s. were British oak	20:20
she 'as s. on the foam	303:27
s. are but boards	463:15
s., becalm'd at eve	147:6
s., by thousands, lay below	115:45
s., dim-discovered	546:15
s. of England	295:12
s. shall go abroad	208:17
s. that pass in the night	318:10
s., towers, domes, theatres	582:14
shoes—and s.	130:15
something wrong with our bloody s.	37:7
Spanish s. of war at sea l	539:16
stately s. are twirled	249:15
stately s. go on	528:3
storm-beaten s.	327:11
tales of s. and stars	208:9
there go the s.	398:11
Thracian s.	521:30
weak s. and spirits steer	523:19
we've got the s.	265:15
with S. the sea was sprinkled	582:17

Shipwreck: s. of my..youth | 168:12
s. of time | 24:15
Shipwrecked brother | 317:8
Shire: s. for men who understand | 84:12
that s...the heart of England | 189:17
through all the s. | 262:13
Shires: round both the s. | 262:21
s. and towns from Airly | 293:3
Shirt: in your s. and your socks | 219:12
martyr in his s. of fire | 503:12
merits of a spotless s. | 537:5
s. which ought to be at wash | 325:32
shroud as well as a s. | 253:24
till he tucks in his s. | 304:28
Shirtless others | 381:19
Shirts: no s. to wear | 218:13
Shirt-sleeves: from s. to s. | 110:1
Shive: steal a s. | 480:33
Shivered was..Scotland's spear | 418:35
Shivering on the brink | 562:16
Shivers: first star s. | 208:6
Shoal: bank and s. of time | 457:7
s. of fools for tenders | 156:1
Shock: no tempest gave the s. | 162:11
s. them and keep them up to date | 489:24
short, sharp s. | 219:31
we shall s. them | 448:2
Shock-headed Peter | 250:10
Shocking: s. bad hats | 564:5
s., s.! | 178:24
Shocks: s. of young love-liking | 579:21
thousand natural s. | 434:4
twelve great s. of sound | 529:28
withindoors house the s. | 255:6
Shoddy: up goes the price of s. | 218:29
Shoe: cast out my s. | 395:23
for want of a s. | 211:10
in a s. she drops a tester | 281:7
in a wooden s. | 204:5
into a left-hand s. | 131:25
lived in a s. | 369:4
my dame has lost her s. | 366:12
s. was lost | 211:10
sixpence in her s. | 157:4
whether a s. be Spanish | 110:39
whose s.'s latchet | 63:2
Shoemaker: my shoes from the s. | 227:28
Shoes: beautiful..thy feet with s. | 52:17
boil eggs in your s. | 312:21
call for his old s. | 422:2
ere those s. were old | 430:33(-431)
her s. were number nine | 355:23
him that makes s. | 109:7

Shoes (cont.)

his s. were far too tight	311:19
my s. from the shoemaker	227:28
over s. in love	484:29
put off thy s.	45:34
s. and ships	130:15
takes off his s.	87:35
their s. were clean and neat	130:13
their s. were on their feet	504:6
thinking..most of the s.	29:6
wear wooden s.	226:29
your s. on your feet	45:47

Shoe-string: careless s. | 246:4
Shoe-tie: glist'ring s. | 166:18
Shone: armour on armour s. | 189:7
far off his coming s. | 348:21
glory of the Lord s. | 61:18
proudly s. | 122:3
s. like a meteor | 344:36
star, that once had s. | 208:10
Shook: monk who s. the world | 355:13
more it's s. it shines | 235:3
s. a dreadful dart | 346:4
s. from the tangled boughs | 496:5
s. out more sail | 18:16
Shoon: clouted s. | 340:32
cork-heel'd s. | 32:1
in her silver s. | 172:2
takes her buckled s. | 183:10
Shoot: and can s. | 244:13
do not hesitate to s. | 29:18
do not s. the pianist | 569:29
he shall s. higher | 501:18
in a watered s. | 409:14
I will s. you! | 31:1
privily s. at them | 392:18
s., if you must | 568:14
s. into the dark arrows | 540:16
s. out their lips | 393:3
teach the young idea how to s. | 546:12
up and s. themselves | 84:14
when the guns begin to s. | 303:2
Shooting: falling stars are s. | 118:8
Shooting-stars attend thee | 246:23
Shoots: s. at the mid-day sun | 501:18
s. higher much than he | 244:3
s. of everlastingness | 552:5
Shop: beggar's s. is shut | 478:36
pops its head into the s. | 209:18
s. to mind | 96:26
shun the awful s. | 141:32
talked s. like a tenth muse | 6:24
Shopkeepers: nation of s. | 1:6, 360:22, 503:11
Shopocracy: abuse the s. | 365:14
Shore: after-silence on the s | 118:24
beat on the rocky s. | 311:15
beats upon the high s. | 444:23
by river or sea s. | 287:12
control stops with the s. | 114:27
courses from the s. | 566:23
echo'd along the s. | 406:19
false impossible s. | 18:20
fast by their native s. | 162:9
for his native s. | 493:25
from s. to s. | 562:8
from the nightly s. | 380:25
guiled s. | 464:15
his own native s. | 380:17
kingdom of the s. | 487:12
lash the sounding s. | 382:32
lone Chorasmian s. | 492:17
more willing bent to s. | 124:1
my boat is on the s. | 118:14
my native s. fades | 113:6
Night's Plutonian s. | 380:25
ocean's wave-beat s. | 202:23
one on s. | 468:20
on s., and when.. | 540:32
on that beautiful s. | 415:9
on the farther s. | 323:25
on the s. of the wide world | 289:6
on thy s. | 405:19
perish on the s. | 185:24
pull for the s. | 415:6
rapture on the lonely s. | 114:26
round earth's s. lay | 15:7
s. of Gitche Gumee | 317:22
s. than labour | 535:20
spicy s. of Araby the blest | 347:1
sport upon the s. | 576:19

Shore (cont.)

stayed upon the green s.	290:7
to the Aetolian s.	16:8
to the Lesbian s.	342:19
towards the pebbled s.	487:8
unknown and silent s.	307:32
upon the farther s.	198:14
upon the Irish s.	106:18
wave along the s.	33:10
wide-watered s.	341:15
wild on this world's s.	365:23
yearning for the farther s.	554:28

Shoreditch: bells of S. | 368:8
Shores: around desolate s. | 288:30
exult, O s. | 566:28(-567)
her concave s. | 448:9
India's spicy s. | 159:7
on sands, and s. | 340:10
possess these s. with me | 168:13
round earth's human s. | 288:17
s. of old romance | 573:2
to what strange s. | 168:9
Shoreward: great winds s. blow | 15:23
Shorn: sheep that are even s. | 52:5
s. and parcell'd Oxus | 17:28(-18)
went home s. | 93:28
Short: all too s. a date | 486:18
Art stopped s. | 220:27
as s. a Spring | 246:3
at that s. space | 552:3
but a s. time to live | 391:41
Codlin's the friend, not S. | 177:30
come s. of the glory | 65:38
Eternity's too s. | 2:23
find it wond'rous s. | 225:17
from long to s. | 152:4
from s. to long | 152:5
hath but a s. time | 71:18
his legs have grown too s. | 311:14
how long or s. permit | 349:25
how s. is the longest life | 290:30
in s. measures | 282:1
joy of love is too s. | 328:9
let thy speech be s. | 57:7
life of the historian must be s. | 217:3
life so s. | 138:22, 248:13
life's too s. for chess | 120:2
long while to make it s. | 547:5
my neck is very s. | 358:7
nasty, brutish, and s. | 248:21
one cut s. and red | 358:24
one s. sleep past | 185:16
s. and bright | 365:8
s. and far between | 73:13
s. and narrow vergèd shade | 332:13
s. and simple annals | 230:1
s. and stout | 141:17
s. and the long of it | 466:1
s. as any dream | 466:20
s. as the watch | 562:9
s., bright, resistless course | 418:2
s. of the mark..Mr. Brougham | 240:7
s., sharp, shock | 219:31
s. uneasy motion | 149:36
take s. views | 504:23
time of life is s. | 440:32
we have s. time to stay | 246:3
where he falls s. | 143:26
Shorten: envy and wrath s. the life | 57:5
so s. I the stature of my soul | 336:22
Shortening: bright breast s. | 522:3
Shorter: constancy of Clement S. | 141:31
s. a prize poem is, the better | 325:17
s. by the head | 198:4
Shorter-Catechist: something of the S. | 241:29
Shortest: s. of men | 34:4
s. way..the foulest | 24:32
s. way to do many things | 503:9
Short-jointed | 488:27
Short-lived care | 361:12
Shortly be with them that rest | 350:30
Shortness: spend that s. basely | 440:32
Shot: go and get s. | 299:2
hand that fired the s. | 31:3
I s. an arrow into the air | 315:24
I. s. the Albatross | 149:1
long s., Watson | 188:4
Noll's damned troopers s. him | 90:18
off s. the spectre-bark | 149:14
s. and steel | 23:21

Shot (*cont.*)
s. at for sixpence a day 173:4
s. heard round the world 199:7
s. madly from their spheres 466:38
s. mine arrow o'er the house 437:35
s. my fawn 332:28
s. of accident 472:32
s. so trim 477:12
s. with the self-same 318:24
young Sahib s. divinely 11:12
Should: men s. be what they seem 471:29
nae better than he s. be 105:9
what s. not be known 208:14
Shoulder: and what s. 75:24(−76)
any s. that I see 452:35
Cupid hath clapped him o' the s. 428:18
giant's s. to mount on 152:29
on his s. smote 363:4
on my leaning s. 584:11
s. the sky, my lad 263:32
upon his s. 53:15
Shoulder-blade: I have a left s. 220:11
Shoulder'd his crutch 224:20
Shoulders: about the s. thrown 246:4
borne on our s. 91:38
heads..beneath their s. 470:2
his sides and his s. 562:3
on s. immense 16:11
their s. held the sky 264:4
Shout: at the s. of praise 35:2
inhuman s. 114:18
send forth a joyous s. 322:25
s. about my ears 140:22
s. and bang and roar 41:32
shouted with a great s. 46:40
s. of them that triumph 362:4
s. round me 576:6
s. that tore hell's concave 345:1
s. with the largest 178:31
universal s. 448:9
waters s. to him 337:35
with psalms must s. 243:24
you needn't s. so loud 131:12
Shouted: for joy
s., 'Rule Britannia' 294:17
s. with a great shout 46:40
went and s. in his ear 131:12
Shouting: captains, and the s. 49:27
heavens fill with s. 534:26
s. in proportion 518:30
s. their emulation 429:5
tumult and the s. dies 300:24
Shouts: not in the s. and plaudits 317:4
s. to scare the monster 296:13
s. with his sister at play 528:3
Shove: s. away the worthy..guest 342:27
that's all s. be'ind me 299:13
Shoved him into politics 41:7
Shovel: hoe and a s. also 297:28
Shoves Jesus and Judas..aside 200:42
Show: choose by s. 463:43
driv'ler and a s. 279:10
fairest s. 457:16
gentleness and s. of love 448:14
heart, that makes no s. 184:9
let him s. himself 468:40
let me a little s. it 449:30
makes no s. to move 186:25
merely to s. that you have one 139:1
Mrs. Jarley's waxwork s. 177:31
not anything to s. more fair 582:14
obscures the s. of evil 464:14
s. all, that might be in man 189:3
s. and gaze o' the time 461:13
s., contain, and nourish 455:23
s. him up 250:24
s. me so divine a thing 332:5
s. me the path of life 392:27
s. me to the shouting varlety 425:34
s. of violence 430:17
s. ourselves glad in him 397:25
s. that one's alive 104:2
s...things that are not 451:40
s. us the Father 63:54
s. vilely in me 441:32
s. yourselves joyful 397:32
s. you something different 197:28
terrible s.! 215:6
that within which passeth s. 430:30
thing they most do s. 487:24
who will s. us any good? 392:1

Show (*cont.*)
world can s. a fitter love 186:15
Showed: more things are s. unto
thee 56:32
s. she that hir was doon offence 137:24
Shower: after a s. 34:14
arrowy s. 230:14
coming s. your..corns presage 521:5
drainless s. of light is poesy 288:14
falling s. 492:2
pierced with softest s. 305:12
very s. of beauty 575:16
will not s. on me 263:13
Showers: after sharpest s. 310:7
April s. 8:9, 549:31
Aprille with his s. sote 136:21
blown seas and storming s. 537:21
I bring fresh s. 492:25
s. on her kings 345:14
small s. last long 474:21
suck the honied s. 342:31
Sydnaean s. 166:20
true-love s. 436:22
what s. arise 446:3
with s. and dewdrops wet 409:29
Showery, Flowery, Bowery 213:5
Showest: have more than thou s. 452:13
when thou s. thee in a child 452:28
Showing: men of little s. 302:4
Shown: must be s. in courts 340:38
Shows: childhood s. the man 350:10
fair seeming s. 510:14
forgets the s. of love 448:15
our s. are more than will 483:10
outward s. be least themselves 464:14
s. his honest face 191:3
submitting the s. of things 24:16
Shreds: king of s. and patches 435:50
thing of s. and patches 219:15
Shrewd: his remark was s. 162:6
lift s. steel 475:1
Shrewdly: air bites s. 431:30
Shrewishly: speaks very s. 482:17
Shrewsbury: in S. jail 262:11
long hour by S. clock 441:4
wanton S. 385:1
Shriek: short shrill s. 153:24
solitary s. 115:30
with hollow s. 343:21
Shrieked: Pilot s. 150:11
Shrieking: hooting and s. 448:33
s. and squeaking 94:33
Shrieks: horrid shapes and s. 341:26
Shrill: as the maiden's organ, s. 482:10
hear the s. sweet treble 77:31
s. and sad accent 145:27
Shriller throat 319:7
Shrill-gorg'd lark 454:4
Shrimp of an author 231:24
Shrine: Apollo from his s. 343:21
fits a little s. 245:18
her sovran s. 287:21
honour the s. 232:11
s. of my dead Saint 292:18
s. of the sailor's devotion 489:1
temple's inner s. 577:1
that pure virgin s. 551:18
this Temple keeps its s. 375:5
thy s., thy grove 288:6
within this peaceful s. 270:6
Shrines: like vapour over s. 89:5
Shrink: all the boards did s. 149:6
never make thee s. 31:13
till I s. with cold 426:29
Shrinks: s. from Principle 181:32
why s. the soul back 1:22
Shrivell'd: s. in a fruitless fire 532:33
s., meagre, hopping 102:20
Shroud: in a s. of thoughts 113:51
my sable s. 342:11
my s. of white 483:6
s. as well as a shirt 253:24
split the s. 97:13
white his s. 436:21
who ever comes to s. me 185:4
Shrouds: atmosphere divinest s.
thee 497:9
shook the s. 162:10
Shrubberies: borders, beds, and s. 296:30
Shrug: rest will give a s. 521:2
Shrunk: how much art thou s.! 440:38

Shrunk (*cont.*)
s. thy streams 344:30
s. to this little measure 450:2
swiftly s. away 508:15
Shuddering: s., also, and tears 561:12
with s. fall 336:41
Shuffle the cards 134:15
Shuffled off this mortal coil 434:4
Shuffling: s. of feet 359:7
there is no s. 435:35
Shuh-shuh-gah: heron, the S. 317:20
Shulamite: return, O S. 52:16
Shun: dews..most carefully s. 139:3
I s. the thought that lurks 338:6
I thought he would s. me 37:3
let me s. that 453:13
never s. the man of sorrow 164:34
s. a year or two 185:24
s. the fault I fell in 30:4
s. the frumious Bandersnatch 129:39
s. the heaven that leads 488:12
s. what I follow 95:20
Shunnest the noise of folly 341:13
Shunning civil rage 192:13
Shuns: neither seeks nor s. his foe 191:28
s. to know 279:7
Shut: as though a rose should s. 285:23
by the sea s. fast 208:10
conclude and s. up all 87:13
eternity s. in a span 166:6
let the doors be s. upon him 434:10
men s. their doors 480:23
men s. their gates 484:27
my eyes..when they are s. 150:29
sentry, s. your eye 301:14
s. from heaven 91:18
s. her wild, wild eyes 286:34
s. not thy heart..against S.T.C. 306:24
s. not up my soul 393:19
s., s. the door, good John! 385:20
s. stands the door 15:27
s. the door after you 195:20
s. thee from heaven 251:15
s. the gates of mercy 230:6
s. their eyes 53:10
s. the road through the woods 303:16
s. up in..content 457:19
their sense is s. 460:23
wisdom..quite s. out 346:20
would s. the book 442:5
Shuts: s. up all the passages 279:7
s. up the story of our days 405:12
Shutter: borne before her on a s. 543:12
Shuttered my doors with flame 206:4
Shutters: close the s. fast 163:21
through my back-parlour s. 376:14
Shutteth up his bowels of compassion 70:11
Shuttle: man is the s. 551:15
musical s. 567:1
swifter than the weaver's s. 48:52
Shy: birch, most s. 320:7
Jesus, wast Thou s. 544:5
we are not s. 219:34
Shyness: diffidence or s. 219:33
Siam: King of S. sent ambassadors 274:9
Sibyl: contortions of the S. 103:30
I saw the S. at Cumae 410:14
s...sew'd the work 472:16
what wouldst thou, S.? 410:19
Sibylla: teste David, cum S. 134:4
Sicco: anima Rabelaisii habitans in 153:10
Sicelides Musae 555:30
Sichem: rejoice and divide S. 395:23
Sicilian: return, S. Muse 342:30
Sicily: dost thou remember S.? 569:16
Syrtes and soft S. 18:16
Sick: all s. persons 389:3
are you s. or are you sullen? 275:31
as s. that surfeit 463:5
bore in hand all his s. men 539:19
but the daylight s. 465:23
but to make him s. 184:20
can s. men play so nicely 474:25
devil was s. 359:25
enterprise is s. 481:3
first pace that is s. 481:5
half my men are s. 539:17
half s. of shadows 534:4
hir'd to watch the s. 162:35

Sick (cont.)
I am s. at heart 430:8
I am s., I must die 361:5
I am s. of both 273:16
I am s. of love 51:45, 52:12
I am s. of many griefs 451:26
I am s. of singing 525:5
I'm s. of the hired women 299:21
I'm s. o' wastin' leather 299:14
is Brutus s.? 449:15
kill s. people 330:16
leave the s. hearts 84:17
lover, s. to death 455:17
lying s. ashore 539:18
made one s. of it 412:21
make any man s. to hear her 377:22
maketh the heart s. 50:3
Meg grew s. 105:15
metal s. 286:11
more than a little s. 295:3
never s. at sea 221:11
perhaps was s., in love 384:23
report that I am sudden s. 423:29
say I'm s., I'm dead 385:20
see me and be s. 263:11
s. almost to doomsday 430:15
s., and ye visited me 60:33
s. for home 288:1
s. in soul and body both 249:6
s. man of Europe 364:17
s. of an old passion 187:8
s. of self-love, Malvolio 482:15
s., O Lord, around thee lay 550:32
they do not make me s. 567:20
they that are s. 58:39
whole head is s. 52:27
you must not fancy I am s. 515:9
Sicken: appetite may s. 481:30
s. at the shifting scenes 537:39
s. soon and die 343:19
when love begins to s. 451:9
Sickened at all triumphs 143:16
Sickening cry 140:21
Sickens at another's praise 143:4
Sickle: his bending s.'s compass 488:7
s. in his hand 317:16
isle, a s. moon 208:19
make the s. yield 74:26
s. in the fruitful field 74:26
with his s. keen 317:9
Sicklemen: sun-burn'd s. 480:7
Sicklied: resolution is s. o'er 434:4
Sickly: kind of s. smile 239:2
s. blade 165:17
s. but sassy 238:14
Sickness: age, or grief, or s. 292:19
by His health, s. 77:2
he hath the falling s. 448:28
in health, in s. 279:7
in s. and in health 391:30
love is a s. 168:7
medicine to heal their s. 400:21
my long s. of health 480:30
s. that destroyeth 397:18
sorrow, need, s. 390:29
thy s. shall depart 295:5
warms the very s. 436:40
when your s. is your soul 263:15
with anger, with s. 48:4
Side: blind s. of the heart 140:16
grew in beauty, s. by s. 241:8
his better angel from his s. 473:25
hunter's javelin in his s. 17:26
old fool's s. 90:18
on our s. to-day 324:14
on the s. of the angels 180:35
passed by on the other s. 61:40
rose o' the wrong s. 82:25
serfs at my s. 98:21
set forth at our s. 17:18
shady s. of Pall Mall 358:19
shifting his s. 161:38
s. by s. in the ebbing tide 504:13
s. by s. those chiefs of pride 324:9
s. by s. were laid 347:25
s. that's next the sun 517:13
sounded for him on the other s. 99:41
success..on Israel's s. 161:16
this s. idolatry 280:1
the heart against thy s. 301:28
time is on our s. 222:34

Side (cont.)
to s. with Truth is noble 320:12
where we sat, s. by s. 73:10
who is on my s.? 48:30
wrong s. of the door 140:16
Side-arms: keeps 'is s. awful 295:21
Side-long looks of love 224:13
Sidera: polus dum s. pascet 553:21
suadentque cadentia s. somnos 553:26
sublimi feriam s. vertice 258:2
Sides: holding both his s. 341:29
much..said on both s. 2:12
no woman's s. 483:9
prick the s. of my intent 457:9
shake their wicked s. 584:26
s. of nature 423:32
turns his s. 562:3
two separate s. to my head 303:10
unfed s. 453:14
Sideways: looked s. up 149:15
s. would she lean 286:31
Sidnaean showers 166:20
Sidney: Friend to Sir Philip S. 232:16
miracle of our age, Sir Philip S. 124:24
S.'s self 96:30
S.'s sister 87:24
S., warbler of poetic prose 163:34
S., whom we yet admire 147:26
Siècles: du haut de ces pyramides
quarante s. 361:1
Siege: laugh a s. to scorn 461:2
lay s. to it 466:20
march to the s. of the city 31:14
men of royal s. 469:37
Sieges: battles, s., fortunes 470:2
Siesta: Englishmen detest a s. 157:25
Sieve: draws nectar in a s. 152:18
in a s. I'll thither sail 456:10
water through a s. 131:22
went to sea in a S. 311:21
Sifted three kingdoms 316:6
Sigh: beadle to a humorous s. 455:7
cheat thee of a s. 571:6
he gave a deep s. 512:26
he took her with a s. 75:22
I'll s. with you 219:16
I read and s. 243:20
kiss, a s., and so away 166:15
passing tribute of a s. 230:7
prompts th' eternal s. 384:2
regain'd my freedom with a s. 114:36
shadow and a s. 301:27
shall I ever s. and pine? 244:9
s. and wish to die 217:23
s. for the toothache? 468:29
s., heart, again 584:19
s. is the sword 75:6
s. like Tom o' Bedlam 452:21
s. much, drink little 155:27
s. no more, ladies 468:20
s. of such as bring 246:5
s. that one thing only 19:7
s. that rends thy constant heart 225:14
s. that silence heaves 286:20
s. the lack of many a thing 486:25
s. too much 326:20
s. to think 499:13
s. to those who love me 118:15
some a light s. 38:28
then s. not so 468:20
'twill cost a s. 33:14
word, or s., or tear 150:31
Sighed: Deist s. 387:24
Duncan s. 105:14
he saw, he s., he lov'd 215:12
he s. no more 222:28
he sobbed and he s. 220:19
I s., and said amang them a' 107:6
I s. as a lover 216:26
no sooner loved but they s. 428:26
she s. sore 196:2
s. and look'd and s. again 191:10
s. at the sound of a knell 164:25
s. for the dawn and the thee 536:13
s. for the love of a ladye 222:27
s. from all her caves 346:8
s. his soul toward 465:17
s...unutterable things 546:16
s. upon a midnight pillow 427:1
so he s. and pined 543:12
speaking s. 276:15

Sighed (cont.)
we have not s. deep 97:28
wept not greatly, but s. 328:21
Sighing: a-s. and a-sobbing 369:18
farewell goes out s. 481:20
it s. cries 168:7
lovers are round her, s. 356:31
my soul that lingers s. 263:20
Nature from her seat s. 349:15
plague of s. and grief! 439:30
poor soul sat s. 473:6
s., cantin', grace-proud faces 106:34
s. like furnace 427:21
s. of a contrite heart 389:8
s. sound 411:34
sorrow and s. shall flee away 54:5
with s. sent 343:22
Sighs: for my pains a world of s. 470:3
her family of S. 491:21
her winds..s. 423:26
listenest to the s. of orphans 172:18
made of s. and tears 428:28
many heartfelt s. 573:12
my s. did dry it 244:9
night of memories and of s. 308:14
on the Bridge of S. 114:1
paid with s. a plenty 262:17
shortening into s. 522:3
s. are the natural language 422:27
sobs, fiery s. 109:27
sovereign of s. and groans 455:8
temper'd with Love's s. 455:22
that s. for thee 483:19
thousand thousand s. 483:6
with her s. the strings do break 123:21
Sight: acceptable people in thy s. 389:24
all wonders in one s. 166:6
angelic in the s. of God 316:36
at s. of thee was glad 573:17
bury sorrow out of s. 97:26
by faith, not by s. 67:25
charms or ear or s. 151:6
charms strike the s. 385:19
downward bend their s. 194:25
dulness of our blinded s. 400:32
end in s. was a vice 96:46
feeling out of s. 88:24
from my aching s. 23:16
here in the s. of God 391:22
I go out of s. 185:23
in the s. of any bird 49:38
little thoughts in s. 338:9
loses s. of the loaves and fishes 376:16
loved not at first s. 330:13, 428:15
many a vanish'd s. 486:25
my aching s. 155:19, 229:25
new-appearing s. 486:12
nor any sound or s. 523:24
nor s. nor sound 522:15
not yet in s. 500:1
out of s. is out of mind 147:12
pleasant s. to see 293:3
possession of this heavenly s. 473:32
prepost'rous s.! 163:38
sensible to feeling as to s. 457:20
s. of Judah's seer 329:12
s. of lidless eyes in Hell 411:2
s. of means to do ill deeds 447:43
s. of vernal bloom 346:20
s. so touching 582:10
s. to dream of, not to tell! 150:22
so brave a s. 332:7
tho' lost to s. 314:21
thousand years in thy s. 397:15
to s. or thought be form'd 349:17
we blest the s. 166:5
where I shall live by s. 99:40
Sigh-tempests move 186:24
Sightless: to his s. eye 362:16
Sights: all s. from pole to pole 18:18
discover s. of woe 344:9
few more impressive s. 36:18
her s. and sounds 84:21
not rural s. alone 162:36
see new s. 217:16
s. of what is to be borne 578:17
s. that dazzle 78:3
s. unholy 341:26
so full of ugly s. 476:13
such s. as..poets dream 342:7
such s., or worse 578:17

Sign: creaking of a country s.   159:11
   for a mystery and a s.   141:32
   his Name and s. who bear   264:13
   I have a s.   85:13
   makes no s.   445:31
   outward and visible s.   391:13
   seeketh after a s.   59:16
   s. of love..indeed but s.   469:35
   s. you must not touch   185:4
   we made no s.   569:6
Signal: do not see the signal   362:21
   Nature's s. of retreat   279:14
   only a s. shown   318:10
   s. to a maid   338:4
Signal-elm, that looks on Ilsley   18:21
Signals: as s. to the land   150:6
Signed: s. by God's name   567:24
   s. in thy spoil   450:9
   s. with their honour   509:1
Signifies: what s. the life o' man   105:31
Signify whom one marries   408:12
Signifying nothing   461:4
Signiors: grave and reverend s.   469:45
   s...on the flood   462:29
Signo: in hoc s. vinces   156:20
Sign-post: His Majesty's head on
   a s.   325:16
Signs: not..proofs but s.   375:2
   s. and..wonders in..Egypt   45:41
   s. of the times   59:42
Sikes, housebreaker   120:26
Silbern: sprechen ist s.   127:22
Silence: acquiesce with s.   277:24
   all s.. an' all glisten   319:23
   answered best with s.   282:4
   awful darkness and s.   311:15
   bless myself with s.   94:11
   breaking the s. of the seas   581:1
   bright towers of s.   171:5
   darkness again and a s.   318:10
   elected S., sing to me   254:26
   eternal S.   540:32(–541), 576:19
   expressive S.   546:8
   fish monastic s. keep   184:24
   foster-child of s.   287:6
   God strikes a s.   88:26
   golden Gospel of S.   358:18
   his s. will sit drooping   437:25
   icy s. of the tomb   287:3
   I kept s.   394:8
   in s. and in gloom   24:2
   in s. sad   467:19
   in that s. we the tempest fear   191:31
   lies..often told in s.   514:33
   listening to s.   253:13
   mourn'd in s.   387:3
   my gracious s., hail!   429:7
   night in her s.   15:17
   occasional flashes of s.   505:2
   punishment is to s.   278:21
   rest is s.   438:6
   round his long sea-hall in s.   531:9
   shadowless like S.   253:13
   sigh that s. heaves   286:26
   s. accompanied   347:19
   S.! and Desolation!   380:14
   S. and Foresight   582:22
   s. and sleep like fields   171:1
   s. and tears   119:29, 30
   s. augmenteth grief   232:15
   s. deep as death   122:4
   s. envious tongues   446:31
   s. fell with the waking bird   536:11
   s...his mother tongue   226:38
   s. in heaven   71:9
   s. in the hills   532:15
   S. is deep as Eternity   126:1
   s. is divine   126:33
   S. is golden   127:22
   s. is most noble   522:9
   S. is of Eternity   127:22
   s. is only commendable   462:36
   s. is the perfectest herald   468:14
   s. is the virtue of fools   25:11
   s., like a poultice   251:10
   s. more musical   409:27
   s. of the many villagers   310:24
   s. of the sleep-time   97:2
   s. of the upper shelf   325:1
   s. sank like music   150:7
   s. surged softly backward   171:16

Silence (*cont.*)
   s. that dreadful bell!   471:16
   s. that is better   126:1
   s. that is in the starry sky   573:8
   s. their mourning   526:23
   s. was pleas'd   347:19
   s. when they brawl   527:20
   s...wonderful to listen to   237:17
   slowly s. all   531:11
   small change of s.   337:37
   sorrow and s. are strong   316:15
   still-born S.!   208:20
   study a long s.   563:32
   there is a s.   253:28
   thunders of white s.   88:8
   twofold s.   410:30
   upon the wings of s.   340:15
   visible s.   410:29
   your women keep s.   67:2
Silence: le s. éternel de ces espaces   374:1
   seul le s. est grand   553:2
   talent pour le s.   126:31
Silencing: justified in s. that one   338:26
Silent: all s. and all damned   578:27
   calm and s. night   184:2
   chew the cud and are s.   102:20
   deep s. slide away   501:17
   face to face, s.   88:19
   fades into dimness apace, s.   17:16
   great joys..s.   331:11
   impossible to be s.   101:24
   into the s. land   409:24
   now a s. soul, my brother   522:14
   sedate, sober, s.   253:32
   s. and amazed   566:21
   s. as the moon   350:23
   s. as the turf they trod   579:6
   s., bare   582:14
   s., flooding in, the main   147:8
   s. halls of death   98:3
   s. hours of night   311:19
   s. in seven languages   29:6
   s. in the grave   161:8
   s. joy at their arrival   149:24
   s., let thy morals tell thy mind   382:14
   s. on his horse   42:11
   s. over Africa   92:18
   s., sullen peoples   303:25
   s. touches of time   103:26
   s., upon a peak in Darien   288:19
   s. was the flock   285:12
   s. woman   280:8
   that s. sea   149:3
   thou, s. form   287:14
   'tis s.   264:2
   unknown and s. shore   307:32
   why art thou s.?   166:24
Silently: crept s. to Rest   206:6
   how s. and with how wan   501:24
   s. as a dream   163:40
   s., invisibly   75:22
   s. steal away   310:10
   slowly, s., now the moon   172:2
Silk: black s. with gold clocks   219:12
   fill the public schools with s.   329:24
   hallow'd that did breed the s.   472:16
   make his couche of s.   137:36
   s. stockings..of your actresses   270:10
   soft as s. remains   248:10
   spoil'd s. stocking   244:5
   that thing of s.   385:30
   walk in s. attire   77:22
   with a s. thread plucks   477:28
Silken: fetch a web o' the s.
   claith   31:25(–32)
   from s. Samarcand   285:25
   in s. or in leathern purse   378:17
   s. dalliance   443:12
   s. lines, and silver hooks   184:8
   s. terms precise   455:29
Silks: in fading s. compose   571:18
   whenas in s. my Julia goes   247:13
Silliest: prettiest, s., most affected   353:6
   s. woman can manage   304:38
Silliness: shames s. out of me   567:14
   s. to live   470:14
Silly: heard a lot of s. things   243:6
   it is s. sooth   483:5
   s. buckets on the deck   149:28
   s. game where nobody wins   212:9
   s. little Johnny, look   250:3

Silly (*cont.*)
   s. old angel   307:24
   s. sailor-folk   298:17
   s. 'to gild refined gold'   115:42
   undrest at Church looks s.   203:30
Siloa's brook   344:2
Siloam's shady rill   240:16
Silvae: nunc frondent s.   555:24
   paulum s.   261:24
Silvas: habitarunt di quoque s.   555:22
   resonare doces..s.   555:15
   si canimus s.   555:30
Silver: breathe thro' s.   94:5
   covered with s. wings   396:7
   for a handful of s.   93:2
   gold air and the s.   411:4
   I'll give thee a s. pound   122:23
   in a s. tassie   105:36
   in her s. shoon   172:2
   in s. nor in gold   5:16
   like as s. is tried   396:1
   little s. feet   333:1
   oars were s.   424:6
   of s. or of gold   218:29
   or ever the s. cord be loosed   51:33
   pictures of s.   50:34
   pinn'd it wi' a s. pin   32:19
   set in the s. sea   474:22
   silent s. lights   94:11
   s. and gold have I none   64:27
   S. Churn   221:1
   s. for the maid   295:14
   s. ha'e to spare   77:22
   s. hooks   184:8
   s. lining   210:4
   s. threads among the gold   406:8
   thirty pieces of s.   60:37
   tips with s.   477:22
   to s. turn'd   377:4
   Wisdom..in a s. rod   74:2
Silvered: completely s. o'er   163:5
   sable s.   431:15
   s. the walls   338:13
Silvern: Speech is s.   127:22
Silver-pointed: with the s. pencil   93:45
Silversmith: Demetrius, a s.   65:6
Silver-sweet..lovers' tongues   477:27
Silver-white: blue, s.   288:3
   lady-smocks all s.   455:35
Silvery: coin of s. shine   131:24
   fountain's s. column   152:8
   its s. splendour pant   286:18
   so s. is thy voice   247:14
Silvia: except I be by S.   484:36
   to S. let us sing that S. is excel-
     ling   484:40(–485)
   unless I look on S.   484:36
   who is S.?   484:40
Simile go on all fours   326:5
Similes: most unsavoury s.   438:20
   play with s.   573:23
Similitude: from the first s.   87:35
   worst s. in the world   325:12
Similitudes: used s.   55:49
Simmery Axe: seventy, S.   222:17
Simon: real S. Pure   134:5
   S. a tanner   64:45
   S. the Cellarer   40:15
   simple S.   368:19
Simple: as s. he looks   107:36
   delight in s. things   295:8
   ever thus with s. folk   222:30
   I sought the s. life   165:18
   mind that is grandly s.   200:28
   natural, s., affecting   225:32
   rarely pure, and never s.   569:20
   short and s. annals   230:1
   s. cases..so extremely difficult   187:13
   s. great ones gone   535:43
   s. racel   417:19
   s., sensuous and passionate   352:28
   s. Simon   368:19
   s. with the wise   134:18
   that women are so s.   479:14
   too s. and too sweet for words   374:17
   very s. gentleman   485:34
Simple: al s. con el discreto   134:18
Simpleness: knowest my s.   396:16
   s. and duty   467:27
Simples: compounded of many s.   428:16
Simplex munditiis   258:10

Simplicitas: nudaque s. 371:17
sancta s.l 266:9
Simplicity: cultivate s. Coleridge 306:31
his s. sublime 537:14
in low s. 463:17
Jeffersonian s. 387:13
makes s. a grace 280:7
meek *S.l* 152:12
pity my s. 565:9
s., a child 382:15
s. of the three per cents 182:6, 420:32
truth miscall'd s. 487:14
with s. or with severity 20:5
Simplify, simplify 546:42
Simulacrum: but the dark *s.* 85:16
Sin: banish all s. 223:10
bare the s. of many 54:28
before polygamy..a s. 190:7
be ye angry, and s. not 68:1
blossoms of my s. 432:17
branch of the s. of drunkenness 267:29
but patched with s. 482:13
by that s. fell the angels 446:30
convinceth me of s. 63:32
dead unto s. 390:59
died unto s. once 65:45
disproportion'd s. 351:11
each thing of s. and guilt 340:23
emboldens s...as mercy 480:24
England, full of s. 243:29
ere s. could blight 151:18
excepting Original S. 123:13
far from s. 183:2
folly, noise, and s. 93:11
go, and s. no more 63:27
go away and s. no more 8:11
good man's s. 122:39
guilty of dust and s. 244:21
hate, virtue, and s. 328:2
he that is without s. 63:26
his darling s. 151:11
his favourite s. 507:21
I have a s. of fear 185:24
I'm living in s. 242:26
impute my Fall to S. 207:11
in s...conceived 395:8
is the law a s.? 65:47
killing s. 516:16
laden with my s. 517:4
let His eye see s. 209:4
lukewarmness I account a s. 158:20
made almost a s. of abstinence 191:40
made my s. their door 185:24
Milton, Death, and S. 587:16
more dreadful record of s. 187:17
my s. is ever before me 395:7
neither s. nor shame 512:17
no s. but ignorance 330:14
no s. but thine 82:1
no s. but to be rich 447:26
no s. except stupidity 569:34
not innocence but s. 92:25
not known s., but by the law 65:47
one cunning bosom s. 245:6
one single venial s. 364:1
one s. will destroy a sinner 99:28
palace of sweet s. 286:40
plays with S. 569:8
pleasure's a s. 115:24
quantum o' the s. 105:19
read of that s. 302:31
remedy against s. 391:25
roots of s. are there 302:33
say that we have no s. 70:10
shall we continue in s.? 65:43
she knew no s. 192:20
s. as it were with a cart rope 53:5
s. if thou wilt..in secret s. 143:12
s. I impute 96:46
s. in loving virtue 462:1
sinned one s. 302:30
s. of self-love 487:10
s. of witchcraft 47:16
s. that amends 482:13
s. that dwelleth in me 65:48
s. that was sweet 372:18
s. the deadly s. 302:31
s. to covet honour 444:27
s...to keep in 245:26
s. wherewith the Face of Man 207:12
s. which doth so easily beset us 69:18

Sin (cont.)
s. ye do by two and two 302:28
some rise by s. 461:24
sorrow dogging s. 245:5
stand in awe, and s. not 391:52
taught Original S. 91:34
they s. who tell us 507:17
this dark world of s. 72:19
thy s.'s not accidental 462:11
triumph over death and s. 509:4
ugly, ay, as s. 315:10
wages of s. is death 65:46
wallow in our s. 12:7
want of power to s. 193:16
want, the care, the s. 533:20
weeps incessantly for my s. 75:19
when s. shall be no more 202:23
where s. abounded 65:42
which is my s. 185:24
wilt thou forgive that s. 185:24
won others to s. 185:24
your s. will find you out 46:21
Since: cease..nor has he s. 239:15
s. Cleopatra died 425:23
s. there's no help 189:20
s. 'tis so 92:31
Sincere: boast s. felicity 193:17
friend s. enough 322:14
officious, innocent, s. 275:1
of soul s. 385:6
s. in good principles 276:11
Sincerely: I love her so s. 125:18
Sincerity: bread of s. and truth 66:28
little s...dangerous 569:31
sad s. 199:23
Sinews: neither is money the s. 27:24
s. of concord 209:25
s. of love 203:24
s. of thy heart 75:24(-76)
s. of virtue 559:17
stiffen the s. 443:24
Sinful: affections of s. men 389:37
do no s. action 3:17
ma says it's s. 177:14
s. man beneath the sky 291:6
truest lover of a s. man 328:24
Sing: all small fowlys s. 187:5
arms and the man I s. 194:29
at her flowery work doth s. 341:22
birds began to s. 368:20
blind Homer s. to me 330:4
charmingly sweet you s. 312:1
cherubim does cease to s. 73:20
come s. now, s. 38:11
die before they s. 151:15
elected Silence, s. to me 254:26
heart and soul do s. in me 502:7
hear the foules s. 138:16
hearts unwounded s. again 299:24
he didn't s. to me 512:10
he'd whistle and s. 173:9
how shall we s. the Lord's song 400:5
how shall we s. to her? 521:30(-522)
how they s.l 485:16
I cannot s. the old songs 120:25
I can't s. 560:18
I do not think that they will s. 197:22
I heard a maid s. 6:2
in ev'ry corner s. 243:24
I s. the Name 165:33
I s. the progress 186:4
I s. the Sofa 162:31
knew himself to s. 342:10
let me s. and die 116:3
let's s. a dirge 170:24
lytle byrdes swetely dyd s. 239:5
Mary did s. 7:14
men s. by land and sea 303:22
nor build, nor s. 152:17
not s. so wildly well 380:18
of Agib..I s. 218:9
of thee I s. 504:19
other cannot s. a song 311:14
Places where they s. 388:27
pray, and s. 454:19
preach, and drink, and s. 76:4
reminiscence s. 567:1
saddest when I s. 36:27, 560:18
second best to s. them 42:13
s. alang wi' me 502:22(-503)
s. a merry madrigal 219:36

Sing (cont.)
s. among the branches 398:8
s. and..delight in God 548:13
s. a sang at least 106:3
s. because I must 532:16
s. both high and low 482:28
s., boys, in joyful chorus 168:14
s. cuccu 9:26, 10:1
s. in the summer day 249:14
s. in the water 176:5
s. it as we used to s. it 583:6
s. it with a spirit 583:6
s. like birds i' the cage 454:19
s.—Long live the King 160:11
s. lullaby 80:8
s. me a song of a lad 516:7
s. me your song O 222:26
s. myself 567:9
s. no more ditties 468:20
s. of her with falls 88:13
s., that I may seem valiant 191:24
s. thee a song in thy praise 105:29
s. the glorious day's renown 122:3
s. the Man of Ross l 384:44
s. them loud 482:22
s. them too 485:27
s. the savageness out 472:27
s. thou smoothly 123:16
s. thy songs 76:9
s. to find your hearts 208:9
s. together, ye waste places 54:23
s. to the Lord 292:7
s. unto God, and s. praises 396:5
s. unto mie roundelaie 136:17
s. unto the Lord a new song 393:35
s. us one of the songs of Sion 400:5
s., while the hours 524:13
s., ye gentle maidens 168:14
s. ye praises with understanding 394:32
small fowlys s. 187:5
so did she s. 319:1
soul of Orpheus s. 341:19
stayed to hear him s. 81:8
still wouldst thou s. 287:32
suppose I shall s. it again 526:7
swans s. before they die 151:13
they began to s. 218:11
tongue of the dumb s. 54:3
to Silvia let us s. 484:40(-485)
to s. the dawn 337:14
valleys..laugh and s. 395:30(-396)
we'll s. another song 583:6
we will s. one song 210:15
when he did s. 446:18
when I say or I s. 220:16
when she biginneth s. 138:34
when you s. 485:27
whilst thus I s. 144:22
who would not s. for Lycidas? 342:10
with shriller throat shall s. 319:7
wrong to s. so wildly 532:39
Singe: s. my white head 453:5
s. yourself 446:10
Singe: Ich s., wie der Vogel 224:2
Singed the beard of the Bishop 508:1
Singeing of..Spain's Beard 188:36
Singer: after the s. is dead 516:3
forget not, brother s. 561:11
he, the s., passes 336:45
idle s. of an empty day 358:25
low as the s. lies 516:4
music-hall s. 220:5
none hear beside the s. 308:13
sans Song, sans S. 206:8
S. of Persephone l 569:16
s. of sweet Colonus 16:2
stop thine ear against the s. 419:16
there lived a s. in France 525:31
thou the s. 218:33
when the s. sings them 516:3
youngest to the oldest s. 524:20
Singers: s. also 397:14
s. go before 396:12
sweetest of all s. 318:2
Singest: s. of summer 287:23
s. with vois memorial 136:19
soaring ever s. 498:2
Singeth: confirm him who s. 92:5
s...against a thorn 253:17
s. all night long 430:20
s. a quiet tune 149:35

INDEX

Singing: deathless s. 87:38
delight in s. 308:15
I am sick of s. 525:5
I was s. all the time 512:11
like a s. bird 409:14
lost it with..s. of anthems 441:21
love a woman for s. 452:23
Master of all s. 318:2
new Memnons s. 88:14
nightingales are s. 197:26,293:1
s. as they shine 2:28
s. by the weye 137:44
s. in the Wilderness 205:23
s. masons building roofs 443:10
s. of Mount Abora 151:33(-152)
s. of the nightingale 285:11
s.—'Oh, how beautiful!' 296:32
s. robes about him 352:20
s. song for song 308:17
s. so rarely 420:2
s. still dost soar 498:2
s. sweetly on a tree 512:10
s. to Father, Son 264:10
s. together 91:36
s. will never be done 415:15
suddenly burst out s. 415:14
sweet s. in the choir 10:14
those who are s. today 79:9
time of s. 334:16
time of the s. of birds 52:1
waves of thy sweet s. 493:20, 497:10
ye have a s. face 38:11
Singing-boys: six little S. 34:9
Singis: fowls s. on the spray 187:5
Singist: as a s. 560:18
Single: he who continued s. 227:15
I wish I were s. again 8:1
married to a s. life 165:32
my s. state of man 456:24
not given a s. dam 208:21
nothing in the world is s. 495:7
s. blessedness 466:17
s. in the field 580:28
s. life doth well with churchmen 26:36
s. man in possession of a good
    fortune 22:28
s. men in barricks 303:4
s. thraldom 28:18
two s. gentlemen roll'd into one 154:18
with a s. hair 194:28
with the same s. lady 116:39
Single-hearted: grown s. 492:21
Single stick (if required) 176:38
Sings: bird wings and s. 95:17
Christian while he s. 161:21
grove he s. in now 552:11
he s. and he s. 150:18
him who s. no more 417:29
hymn the Brahmin s. 199:5
immortalizes whom it s. 164:21
it sits and s. 332:20
like an angel s. 465:18
lover lingers and s. 516:4
no..pang the while she s. 217:17
not waking till she s. 321:16
s. a solitary song 577:19
s. darkling 346:20
s. for his supper 367:18
s. in his boat 528:3
tell her..she s. as sweetly 479:4
tell me what she s. 581:2
to implore your light, he s. 169:13
woe..when she s. 279:28
Singular: so s. in each particular 485:27
Singularity: not by s. 289:27
s..invariably a clue 187:13
trick of s. 483:19
Sinister: strange and s. 268:4
Sink: heave or s. it 298:15
I pant, I s., I tremble 493:15
I, who thought to s. 88:17
not s. i' the scale 95:16
one leak will s. a ship 99:28
or s. or swim 438:37
raft which will never s. 4:21
s. all the shipping there 281:19
s. heart and voice 362:1
s. me the shore 540:1
s. to rest 153:29
s. with Lamplough 514:2
they rise or s. together 539:6

Sinkest in thine own tears? 170:22
Sinketh: lie that s. in 27:31
Sinking: alacrity in s. 466:9
s. as the light wind lives 284:14
s. down in its tranquillity 577:1
s. in Poetry 386:25
s. in thy last long sleep 279:19
someone is s. today 550:33
that s. feeling 5:22
Sinks: it s., and I am ready 308:25
now s. the storm 215:14
poetry s. and swoons 309:15
point of view then s. 235:22
reign o'er sewers and s. 150:28
s. into thy depths 114:28
s. it straight 281:19
so s. the day-star 343:3
swims or s. or wades 340:14
Sinn: kommt mir nicht aus dem S. 240:25
Sinned: against thee only have I s. 395:7
all have s. 65:38
father, I have s. 62:14
more s. against than sinning 453:10
not to know we s. 169:10
s. one sin 302:30
Sinner: be merciful to me a s. 62:34
of her a s. 155:38
one s. that repenteth 62:12
one sin will destroy a s. 99:28
saint or s. 387:21
say, poor s., lov'st thou me? 161:9
Sinners: eateth..with publicans
    and s. 58:38
God and s. reconciled 565:12
greatest saints and s. 111:23
if s. entice thee 49:37
miserable s. 388:43
my soul with the s. 393:19
s...kotched out late 238:24
s. must with devils dwell 561:22
s.; of whom I am chief 68:43
s. shall be converted 395:9
s. to repentance 58:40
s.' ways prosper 255:5
we are s. all 445:32
Sinning: else s. greatly 579:22
more sinned against than s. 453:10
Sins: all my s. remember'd 434:5
chain of our s. 389:12
confess our manifold s. 388:6
cover the multitude of s. 70:5
for the Lord..forgiveth s. 56:30
from presumptuous s. 392:34
her s. to her Saviour 252:22
her s. were on her head 298:30
his s. were scarlet 41:23
oldest s. 442:28
our s. lay on the king 444:21
repent you of your s. 390:34
root of all s. 267:29
set our s. from us 398:6
s. and offences of my youth 393:14
s., negligences and ignorances 389:7
s. they are inclin'd to 110:20
s. they love to act 474:6
s. through which I run 185:24
thinkin' on their s. 106:11
though your s. be as scarlet 52:30
vengeance of our s. 388:44
visit the s. of the fathers 390:7
weep for their s. 567:20
Sinuous: s. rills 151:32
s. shells 308:26
Sion: at ease in S. 56:2
gracious unto S. 395:10
loveth the gates of S. 397:13
one of the songs of S. 400:5
remembered thee, O S. 400:5
S., city of our God 364:10
S. hill delight thee 344:2
strengthen the out of S. 392:35
the Lord shall bring again S. 54:23
walk about S. 394:35
Sip: can't be tasted in a s. 177:34
Sipped: I s. each flower 214:25
who s. no sup 222:27
Sips: in three s. 96:39
Sir: s., so what I plead is just 255:8
that s. which serves 452:38
Sire: bleeding S. to Son 117:38
from the s. to the son 418:35

Sire (cont.)
left by his s. 118:4
lisp their s.'s return 229:31
make their s. stoop 475:12
S. of an immortal strain 491:15
Sybil Kindred's s. 165:6
their s. butchered 114:19
thy s. was a knight 417:32
Siren: S. tears 488:8
S. waits thee 308:17
Sirens: blest pair of S. 351:9
S., of course 176:5
what song the S. sang 87:12
Sires: count the s. and sons 183:4
land of my s.l 417:22
whose s. have marched 323:12
Sirius: kingly brilliance of S. 236:38
Sirmio: salve O venusta S. 132:21
Sisera: mother of S. 46:51
stars..fought against S. 46:48
Sister: azure s. of the spring 496:4
erring s.'s shame 117:40
gentler s. woman 104:7
had it been his s. 6:20
his s.'s husband's niece 128:16
Innocence thy S. dear 332:14
kissed her little s. 355:24
leave thou thy s. 532:24
live a barren s. all your life 466:16
ministering angel shall my s. be 437:20
moon is my s. 41:20
my dear, dear S.l 582:3
my s. and my s.'s child 159:33
my s., my spouse 52:7
my s.l my sweet s.l 117:32
no friend like a s. 409:19
open to me, my s. 52:9
our S. the Spring 42:4
our sometime s. 430:23
Sidney's s. 87:24
S. and Auntie 303:18
S. and the Brother 35:19
s. of the Seraphim 165:31
swallow, my s., O s. swallow 524:11
we have a little s. 52:24
with his s. at play 528:3
your s. is given to government 175:21
Sisterly animosity 518:23
Sisters: all the S. virtuous 363:9
brothers and s. hate each other 269:33
men with s. dear 253:23
s. under their skins 298:6
so do his s., and his cousins 221:14
sphere-born harmonious s. 351:9
they were s. 228:5
twa s. sat in a bour 30:7
weird s. 460:13
Sit: at last s. down by thee 292:20
bids nor s. nor stand but go! 95:15
by whose living coal I s. 247:17
cannot s. on it 267:8
cannot s. upright 159:41
good thing to s. by 274:18
here will we s. 465:18
he won't s. still 249:24
I and sorrows s. 447:27
I cannot s. and think 306:25
I did s. and eat 244:22
I shall s. here..on and off 128:30
let us s. upon the ground 475:7
not fit that you should s. here 167:9
not to s. still 297:28
reluctance to s. for a picture 274:17
s. and hear each other groan 287:25
s., and play with similes 573:23
s. and read all day 290:16
s. beside the fire 41:18
s. by the fire and spin 366:14
s. down quickly 62:19
s. down to write 290:25, 521:16
s. every man under his vine 56:6
s. him down and die 442:5
s. in darkness 398:15
s. in darkness here 345:25
s. in the bar 308:5
s. i' th' centre 340:20
s. like thy grandsire 462:32
s. still for once at table 249:25
s. thee down and write 76:9
s. thou on my right hand 398:23
s. thou still when kings.. 419:16

Sit (cont.)
s. upon a stool 176:2
s. upon the curate's knee 141:17
so must he continue to s. 304:36
that I now could s. 421:11
their strength is to s. still 53:36
we'll s. contentedly 336:26
we would s. down 333:8
when..old s. under the shade 175:10
why do you s.? 220:17
you must s. down 244:22
Site: that especial s. and stone 77:30
Sits: e'er since s. on his horse 447:23
he s. high 449:1
like a bird it s., and sings 332:20
Mrs. Boffkin s. 300:21
s. our sulky..dame 108:2
s. upon my arm 334:26
Thais s. beside thee 191:9
Sitteth: s. above the water-flood 393:24
s. alone upon the house-top 398:1
s. between the cherubims 397:33
s. upon many waters 71:31
Sitting: as cheap s. as standing 520:11
a-s. on a gate 131:22
end of it's s. an' thinkin' 298:3
fire-folk s. in the air 255:5
listen where thou art s. 341:3
low s. on the ground 509:27
privilege o' s. down 196:27
s. at the receipt of custom 58:37
s. careless 284:12
s. crowned upon the grave 248:23
s. in the shade 296:32
s. in the sun 507:3
s. on the stile, Mary 73:10
soul s. in thine eyes 341:9
where he is s. now 492:5
Situation: s. at the lighthouse 179:28
Situation excellente. J'attaque! 209:9
Situm: sic melius s. 259:23
Situs: nunc s. informis 257:20
Six: all's set at s. and seven 12:7
as content with s. foot 87:21
each one had s. wings 53:8
his s. days' work 348:28
in s. days the Lord made 390:11
let's fight till s. 130:23
my s. lustres 186:6
seven up and s. to play 228:10
s. days shalt thou labour 390:9
s. feet high and look'd s. inches
  higher 165:6
s. hours ago I came 359:14
s. hours in sleep 148:8
s. impossible things 131:2
s. lines together without a fault 271:31
s. of one 331:18
s. Richmonds in the field 476:43
s. ships of the line 539:17
s. years' darling 576:10
working..s. weeks in a year 546:39
world on s. and sevene 138:37
Six-foot column of fop 253:8
Six hundred: rode the s. 528:16
s. pounds a-year 521:7
Six hundred and eighty-five ways 356:8
Six hundred threescore and six 71:22
Sixpence: bang—went s.! 403:15
found a crooked s. 369:3
I give thee s.! 124:9
I only got s. 403:24
precious little for s. 403:17
shot at for s. a-day 173:4
sing a song of s. 368:20
s. all too dear 471:11
s. at a bookstall 196:24
s. in her shoe 157:4
sovereign (to the length of s.) 127:8
Sixpences: his pockets..full of s. 182:18
two-and-forty s. 276:22
Sixteen-string Jack 273:12
Sixth: in th' S. Ward 195:9
s. age shifts 427:21
Six thousand years' traditions 374:19
Sixty: men above s. 371:3
s. seconds' worth 297:12
Sixtyfold: some s. 59:23
Size of pots of ale 110:10
Sizes: anguish of all s. 245:5
Sizzling: turned to his s. 170:25

Skater: like the s. on ice 529:20
Skating over thin ice 200:35
Skeigh: look'd..unco s. 105:13
Skeleton: Death the S. 582:22
Hiding the S. 336:24
Skeletons: brown s. of leaves 150:9
Sketch: first rude s. 295:16
s. the ruins of St. Paul's 324:31
Skid: you can s. up the trees 301:8
Skiddaw: red glare on S. 322:23
till S. saw the fire 322:23
Skies: air and s. 231:5
air, earth and s. 582:4
as long as s. are blue 491:26
common people of the s. 583:13
deep indigo transparent s. 127:4
exchange thy sullen s. 162:44
hereditary s. 194:25
in summer s. to mourn 285:11
kindled in the upper s. 199:10
looks commercing with the s. 341:9
look up at the s.! 255:5
look upward to the s. 362:8
mansions in the s. 562:12
morning s., books 516:16
new-fledg'd offspring to the s. 224:21
only matched in the s. 80:19
point me to the s. 322:2
points her to the s. 195:15
raging of the s. 122:26
rais'd a mortal to the s. 191:13
rush into the s. 383:13
s. are not cloudy all day 248:9
s. are painted 449:30
s. so dull and grey 293:6
s. they were ashen 381:1
soaring claim the s. 211:26
some watcher of the s. 288:19
sparkle in their s. 247:6
Stamper of the S. 585:10
starry s. 119:1
terrors of the s. 123:24
twitters from the quiet s. 241:21
under Ionian s. 493:13
when stars are in the quiet s. 322:8
Skiff: fragile s. attains the shore 312:24
Skiffins: here's Miss S.! 175:27
Skilful: more s. in self-knowledge 575:7
mummy..the s. conserv'd 472:16
s. in the wars 552:1
Skilfully and magnanimously 352:25
Skill: brings all s. to naught 299:5
doing nothing with a deal of s. 162:19
folly..controlling s. 487:14
foresight, strength and s. 580:21
God gives s. 197:1
his s. runs on the lees 247:18
his utmost s. 583:9
honour..no s. in surgery? 440:30
little s. in antiquity 212:12
my courage and s. 99:39
my s. goes beyond 373:14
never failing s. 161:18
none, or little s. 247:18
sharpens our s. 102:27
s. comes so slow 169:16
s. in the weapon is nothing 442:21
s. not spent amiss 80:18
such s. and dexterity 173:12
through her s. 155:36
thy s. to poet were 426:11
works of labour, or of s. 561:29
Skilled: s. in analytic 110:5
s. to sing of Time 529:17
Skim milk masquerades 221:21
Skimble-skamble stuff 440:1
Skimpole: deny to Harold S. 173:26
Skims along the main 382:32
Skin: after my s. worms destroy 49:6
Ethopian change his s. 55:18
her enamell'd s. 466:41
her s. was white as leprosy 149:13
I stuff my s. so full 516:21(-517)
my s. bristles 264:6
nothing of the bear but his s. 227:32
s. of an innocent lamb 445:38
s. of my teeth 49:4
that whiter s. of hers 473:11
through his apostolic s. 119:21
thy s. is ivory 215:42
Skin-deep: colours..but s. 242:5

Skinny: fear thy s. hand 149:19
his s. hand 148:20
Skins: sisters under their s. 298:6
Skip: made them s. 454:25
s. judiciously 234:19
Skipped: mountains s. 399:3
Skipper had taken his..daughter 318:14
Skipping: pretty s. grace 333:1
Skirts: caught at God's s. 92:26
gather my s. up 80:16
s. of happy chance 533:1
to the s. of his clothing 400:3
whose cloudy s. 153:24
Skittish: unstaid and s. 483:2
Skittles: all beer and s. 121:7, 335:8
all porter and s. 179:26
loore him on to s. 120:3
Sklaven-Moral 364:21
Skull: no more of her than the s. 48:32
not such a s. 523:9
Skulls: in dead men's s. 476:14
Skuttle Fish: put me in mind of
  the S. 2:30
Sky: about us in the s. 262:21(-263)
above the bright blue s. 338:19
admitted to that equal s. 383:12
all the milky s. 586:7
banners flout the s. 456:8
bears the falling s. 263:18
beneath what s. 264:7
blue ethereal s. 2:25
blue s. belongs to them 149:24
blue s. bends over all 150:23
blue s. bounds the ocean 80:14
blue s. of spring 4:19
blue s. over my head 240:9
Bowl..call the S. 207:3, 4
bridal of the earth and s. 245:13
broad as the blue s. above 549:6
close against the s. 253:2
crimson of the sunset s. 4:6
darkening the s. 407:8
Dawn's Left Hand..in the S. 205:6
die in yon rich s. 538:16
divides the s. with her 114:6
English earth and s. 241:26
evening s. pavilions it 495:27
first our s. was overcast 160:21
four corners of the s. 192:40
freeze thou bitter s. 427:22
he almost touch'd the s. 250:1
held the s. suspended 264:4
hot and copper s. 149:4
in the breezy s. 82:13
in the starry s. 573:8
like strips of the s. 492:29(-493)
living air and the blue s. 582:1
lonely sea and the s. 334:10
lose itself in the s. 89:10
lustre in its s. 494:6
monarch of the s. 330:6
night involv'd the s. 159:1
no cloud was in the s. 130:11
nor s. clouding 81:26
November's s. is chill 418:1
nursling of the S. 493:1
open..to the s. 582:14
out of the s. 326:18
pealing up to the sunny s. 535:39
pilgrim of the s.! 580:26
regardful of the embroiling s. 546:26
rides down the s. 204:37
sent him down the s. 157:10
shapes of s. or plain 498:8
shoulder the s., my lad 263:32
sinful man beneath the s. 291:6
s.—and what a scowl of cloud 97:13
s. changes when..wives 428:22
s. grows darker 140:12
s. imbrued with colour 94:8
s. is ever clear 97:30, 315:21
s. is red 59:41
s. resum'd her light 193:38
s. seemed not a s. 579:8
somewhere sings about the s. 116:13
spread out against the s. 197:15
stared into the s. 249:16
steal across the s. 34:35
swallows gathering in the s. 336:31
tears of the s. 139:3
their watch in the s. 123:15

INDEX

Sky (cont.)

tiger s.   336:14
to the wild s.   533:17
to the wind-swept s.   206:29
true as the s.   298:19
under the s. lie friended   403:1
untune the s.   191:39
upon the starry s.   75:5
wasted on the earth and s.   199:26
whatever s.'s above me   118:15
wheeling out on a windy s.   568:23
when all the s. is clear   515:14
who aimeth at the s.   244:3
wide and starry s.   516:15
with the earth and the s.   585:17
Skye: beyond the Isle of S.   30:13
over the sea to S.   516:7
Skyey influences   462:3
Skylark: despise the s.'s song   83:4
s. wounded in the wing   73:20
Skylight: Gothic s.   119:25
Sky-pointing tree   18:31
Slab: gruel thick and s.   459:33
Slack: in marriage..becomes s.   514:22
observing me grow s.   244:21
s. they may be   254:19
Slacken: Luke began to s.   577:22
Slain: above the noble s.   241:9
crippled and palsied and s.   422:20
deep-brooding o'er the s.   417:6
ere thou hast s. another   87:24
ever he is. should be   30:14
fight and no be s.   108:16
I have s. men   469:36
in battle   224:9
Lamb as it had been s.   70:41
law, chance, hath s.   185:14
my most noble lord s.   328:17
never do that's s.   111:17
see him s.   359:4
shall himself be s.   324:3
s. and spent and sacrificed   522:20
s. at Carrow   502:20
s. by a fair cruel maid   483:6
s. by the bloody Piedmontese   351:20
s. his thousands   47:25
s. in thine high places   47:30
s. the Earl of Murray   30:8
s. the Jabberwock   129:39(–130)
s. the Red Comyn   420:21
s. think he is s.   199:3
s. upon thy high places   47:29
s. with spears   538:26
some s. in war   475:7
thrice he slew the s.   191:6
Slander: civic s.   533:20
devis'd this s.   473:1
fear not s.   430:1
shaft of s. shot   375:23
s. any moment's leisure   431:29
s., meanest spawn of Hell   534:11
to speak no s.   530:13
who's angry at s.   279:27
Slandered: not s. his neighbour   392:24
Slanderers: persecutors and s.   389:5
Slandering: my tongue from..s.   391:8
Slang: all s. is metaphor   142:16
Slanting: rain..in s. lines   503:13
Slap-dash down in the mouth   155:30
Slap-up gal   178:16
Slashing: for a s. article   542:22
Slate: clean your s.   409:11
wiping something off a s.   294:18
Slates: all three dates on their s.   129:28
all wrote down on their s.   129:34
Slaughter: arrayed for mutual s.   578:9
as a lamb to the s.   54:26
as an ox goeth to the s.   49:51
no flocks..to s. I condemn   225:12
s. will ensue   155:26
threatenings and s.   64:40
wade through s.   230:6
when it comes to s.   207:1
Slaughtered: thy s. saints   351:20
ye have s.   363:7
Slaughterous: my s. thoughts   461:3
Slav, Teuton, Kelt   528:11
Slave: base is the s. that pays   443:16
being your s.   487:7
cogging, cozening s.   473:1
cursed, cursed s.   473:32

Slave (cont.)

fingering s.   578:30
freedom to the s.   314:11
half s. and half free   314:6
like a sad s.   487:7
made him a s.   100:5
master o'er a s.   576:14
meant them for a s.   116:2
no more s. States; no s. Territories   136:14
not passion's s.   434:26
priest, the s.   491:15
rogue and peasant s.   433:31
s. of circumstance   118:36
s. of crime   579:31
s. of pomp   415:17
s. to no sect   384:14
s. to thousands   471:30
this s.'s offal   433:35
thought's the s. of life   440:37
what a s. art thou   439:26
you were a Christian S.   241:24
Slavery: cannot..be classified as
  s.   143:36
chains and s.   107:32
s. of the tea and coffee   147:16
s. they can have anywhere   101:11
sold to s.   470:2
Slaves: army of s.   117:46
at the mill with s.   350:21
Britons never will be s.   545:18
creed of s.   379:14
ennoble sots, or s.   384:8
French..all s.   226:29
intercourse between tyrants and
  s.   226:34
land of s.   116:3
make s. of the rest   379:3
morality of s.   364:21
not press you like s.   213:10
ruling them like s.   497:12
s. cannot breathe   162:42
s., howe'er contented   162:22
S. of the Lamp   14:30
s. that take their humours   447:42
s. who fear to speak   320:14
submit to be s.   379:3
too pure for s. to breathe in   237:27
we..are the only s.   334:20
wholly s. or wholly free   192:26
Slay: s. and s. and s.   324:14
to s. their foes   326:21
Slayer: if the red s.   199:3
priest whom slew the s.   324:3
Slaying: s. of a beautiful hypothesis   266:19
s. of Itylus   524:16
Slays: moves, and checks, and s.   206:29
moves, and mates, and s.   206:28
thinks he s.   199:3
Sleary: S. babies to develop S.'s
  fits   300:21
Sleave: ravell'd s. of care   458:11
Sleek: to our like mouths grow s.   351:17
Sleek-headed men   448:26
Sleekit: wee, s., cow'rin   107:9
Sleep: afford much comfort in s.   85:20
after battle, s. is best   365:4
after-dinner's s.   462:5
always s. upon ale   203:5
as in their causes s.   125:9
awaked as one out of s.   397:1
azure-lidded s.   285:24
between s. and a s.   522:7
but to s. and feed   436:15
by a s. to say we end   434:4
call..when man doth s.   552:12
cannot break his S.   206:2
care-charmer s.   168:12
care-charming S.   38:9
come, S.! O S.   501:26
comes with the first s.   338:7
curtain'd s.   458:1
Death and his brother S.   493:2, 497:18
death..as a drunken s.   462:21
death like s.   498:25
deep and dreamless s.   84:24
deep s...upon Adam   44:16
dewy-feather'd s.   341:22
do I wake or s.?   288:2
dovecote doors of s.   338:3

Sleep (cont.)

drowsy approaches of s.   85:21
each day dies with s.   255:1
even as a s.   397:15
everything but s.   523:18
exposition of s.   467:16
first sweet s. of night   494:7
folding of the hands to s.   49:46
freed us from everlasting s.   85:21
from the City of S.   295:11
from the fields of s.   576:5
full of s.   586:21
gentle s. from Heaven   149:27
giveth His beloved s.   88:25, 399:35
Glamis hath murder'd s.   458:12
goes to s. at a bank   269:2
go s. with Turks   475:17
great gift of s.   241:22
he that keepeth thee will not s.   399:27
him who invented s.   134:18
his first s.   11:23
his s. was aery light   347:37
how s. the brave   153:29
I am fayn to s.   30:6
illumined the Land of S.   317:17
innocent s., s. that knits up   458:11
in s. a king   487:22
in that s. of death   434:4
in thy last long s.   279:19
I shall s., and move   525:30
I s., but my heart waketh   52:9
I s. on the coals   174:19
I s. well   359:21
ladies that do s.   123:26
let it s. in the shade   356:29
let it s. with death   280:11
like unwilling s.   288:21
little s., a little slumber   49:46
Macbeth does murder s.   458:11
Macbeth shall s. no more   458:12
make anyone go to s.   179:25
most that s. outside   262:11
nights with s.   444:23
no s. till morn   113:20
now I lay me down to s.   8:18
O magic s.!   284:24
one short s. past   185:16
only s.!   97:23
only the s. eternal   523:24
or let me s. alway   150:5
O s.! O gentle s.!   441:41
past their first s. in Persia   85:21
quiet s. and a sweet dream   334:12
reader's threatened..with 's.'   382:31
rounded with a s.   480:8
sang themselves to s.   249:13
season of all natures, s.   459:26
shake off this downy s.   458:23
silence and s. like fields   171:1
six hours in s.   148:8
s. after toil   509:28
S., again deceive me   155:35
s. al the night with open yĕ   136:22
s. among the wheat   131:22
s. an act or two   447:19
s. and a forgetting   576:9
s., and if life was bitter   522:13
s. and it is lifted   497:11
s. at the root of my tree   310:21
s., dear, s.   38:22
s. deeply above   84:8
s. dwell upon thine eyes   478:1
s. firmly from twelve to one   157:25
s. full of sweet dreams   284:19
s. I can get nane   104:19
s. in old England's heart   562:21
s. in one another's arms   493:14
s. in spite of thunder   460:7
s. in the arms of the blast   492:27
s. in the night   522:7
s. in..these terrible dreams   459:4
s. is a death   87:1
s. is sweet to the labouring man   99:23
S.! it is a gentle thing   149:27
s. itself must end   85:21
s. like a top   169:11
s. no more!   458:11
s. not so sound as sweet   245:16
s. of a labouring man   51:8
s. on, blest pair   347:27
s. one ever-during night   123:19

[917]

Sleep (*cont.*)
S. on, my Love 292:19
s. out the thought of it 485:19
s. out this great gap of time 423:41
s., pretty wantons 170:23
s. rock thy brain 435:14
s. shall neither night nor day 456:11
S. shall obey me 507:15
s.'s no softer 94:24
[s.]. .so like death 86:38
s. so soundly as the. .slave 444:23
s. that is among the. .hills 573:8
S., the filmy-eyed 495:23
S.l the friend of Woe 507:18
s. thegither at the foot 106:20
s. the s. of death 75:11
s. the s. that knows not breaking 416:19
S.l thou flatterer 154:39
s. to wake 97:4
s., undisturb'd 270:6
s. upon a golden bed 584:23
S., why dost thou leave me? 155:35
s. will come 495:24
s. with it now! 442:25
S., with thy rod 215:37
snuff, tobacker, and s. 174:29
sooner to s. 294:2
spend the night in s. 168:13
such as s. o' nights 448:26
suffer nobody to s. in it 2:11
sun is laid to s. 279:31
sweet restorer, balmy s. 586:29
that sweet s. 471:43
therefore s. you 170:23
think of them that s. 122:7
this peace is with her 447:16
this s. is sound. .s. that. .hath divorc'd 442:26
thy ignominy s. with thee 441:1
time to awake out of s. 66:13
to die, to s.; to s.: perchance to dream 434:4
to give their readers s. 381:13
to haunt thy s. 171:20
two gates of S. 555:2
uncanopied s. 80:12
visit the soul in s. 495:18
we must s. 425:21
we shall not all s. 67:16
we shall not s. 326:15
what hath night to do with s.? 340:5
what's to s.? 215:37
when I should s. 155:27
when shall I s. again? 263:17
whom they s. beside 262:14
would I were s. and peace 478:1
wrapp'd in guileless s. 547:7
Sleeper: me, the s. 545:9
never a quiet s. 536:20
sun-flushed s. 545:9
sun-hazed s. 545:9
Sleepers in that quiet earth 83:15
Sleepest by the fable 343:2
Sleepeth: not dead, but s. 58:43
peradventure he s. 48:3
Sleep-flower sways 545:9
Sleeping: by s. what it is to die 87:1
Capten, art tha s.? 363:3
clover and corn lay s. 293:20
growing. .when ye're s. 420:1
s. and the dead 458:14
s. found 344:27
s. hound to wake 138:31
s. in the blood 441:14
s., waking, still at ease 378:16
some s. kill'd 475:7
Thy servant s. 198:15
wakened us from s. 84:16
Sleepless: s. soul 580:7
s. . .to give their readers sleep 381:13
s. with cold. .eyes 411:18
Sleeps: heaven-eyed creature s. 575:17
he s. as sound 402:24
he s. well 459:4
his stedfast shade s. 537:35
Homer sometimes s. 116:6
in their s. will mutter 472:8
moon s. with Endymion 465:22
my lady s. 318:4
now s. the crimson petal 539:2
nurse s. sweetly 162:35

Sleeps (*cont.*)
one s. where 241:9
she s.l 318:4
s. and never palates more 425:33
s. feels not the toothache 430:3
s. in a foolish ear 436:10
s. in Elysium 444:23
s. the calm Ideal 176:26
s. with the primeval giants 125:34
so s. the pride 356:20
such s. as may beguile 518:2
swears a prayer. .and s. again 477:7
sweet the moonlight s. 465:18
there's. Titania 466:41
till tired he s. 383:30
where her young hero s. 356:31
where the M.F.H. dines he s. 518:11
while my pretty one s. 538:12
Sleep-time: silence of the s. 97:2
Sleepy: contentment is a s. thing 548:16
Sleepy-head: ain't you 'shamed, you s.? 515:25
to bed, says S. 366:13
Sleet: s. or stifling snow 94:13
whistling s. and snow 318:16
Sleeve: ace. .up his s. 305:20
me heart is on me s. 141:10
my heart upon my s. 469:28
ravelled s. of care 458:11
strip his s. 444:28
Sleeveless some 381:19
Sleeves: lawn s. and rochets 404:17
tie up my s. 266:8
Sleight: admire his s. of hand 111:3
perceive a juggler's s. 111:3
tricks by s. of hand 155:15
Slender: scarlet line was s. 293:2
Slenderly: fashion'd so s. 252:12
Slept: hath it s. since? 457:11
I s., and dreamed 7:18, 254:2
never s. an hour less 275:12
not s. one wink 429:33
seed in secret s. 79:6
s. among his ashes cold 285:29
s. in peace 447:4
s. in the contriving of lust 453:19
s. with his fathers 47:49
thought her dying when she s. 252:23
thought he thought I s. 375:3
touch'd him, and he s. 533:8
while their companions s. 316:31
whilst Adam s. 11:23
would have s. 196:2
Slew: ambitious, I s. him 450:15
priest who s. the slayer 324:3
s. his master 48:29
s. the Snapping Turtle 24:9
thrice he s. the slain 191:6
Slice: Royal s. of bread 339:17
s. him where you like 572:6
Slices of quince 312:3
Slid: s. into my soul 149:27
talk s. north 294:29
Slide: let the world s. 38:14
Slight: away, s. man! 451:14
loved so s. a thing 534:31
love is s. 330:13
s. all that do 203:19
s. little, light little 222:8
s. not the songsmith 561:5
s. what I receive 95:20
Slighted: Doctor s. 372:12
graces s. blossom 164:30
our soldiers s. 404:9
s. shepherd's trade 342:20
Slights: love s. it 26:2
Slime: daubed it with s. 45:30
slimier s. 83:25
tare each other in their s. 532:38
Slimy: s. things did crawl. .upon the s. sea 149:6
thousand s. things 149:21
woo'd the s. bottom 476:14
Slings: suffer the s. and arrows 434:4
Slingsby of the manly chest 24:9
Slinks out of the race 352:9
Slip: gave us all the s. 97:16
giving his enemies the s. for ever 513:3
if I s., Thou dost not fall 147:14
let s. the dogs of war 450:12
lets s. Fortune 158:19

Slip (*cont.*)
our feet to s. 396:1
s. and ripple idly 336:7
s. into my bosom 539:2
s. out of the world 193:4
Slipped: s. through the straw 11:1
s. up somehow 238:27
Slipper and subtle knave 471:1
Slippered: s. Hesper 84:10
s. pantaloon 427:21
Slippery: standing is s. 26:24
such s. ground 450:8
Slips: all s. of hers 252:16
greyhounds in the s. 443:27
keep from s. 7:5
s. into the bosom of the lake 539:2
s. of yew 459:12
Slithy toves 129:39
Slits the thin-spun life 342:20
Sliver: envious s. broke 437:1
s. and disbranch 453:42
Slivered in the moon's eclipse 459:32
Sloane Square: came aboard at S. 219:11
Slobbered: James I s. 422:14
Slog: foot-s.-s.-s.-sloggin' 294:37
Slogan: cry the s. 23:18
s. of Macdonald 23:20
Slope: life's darkening s. 410:22
obscure waters s. 96:31
s. of faces 163:28
s. thro' darkness up to God 532:36
solemn s. of mighty limbs 522:12
Slopes: gently s. the way 224:16
orchard s. 146:13
s. down to the sea 150:8
Slop-kettle 147:16
Sloth: most of s. 243:19
much time in studies. .s. 27:14
my love, which s. maligns 375:2
peaceful s. 345:22
resty s. 429:36
shake off dull s. 292:1
Slothful: not s. in business 66:2
s. man saith 50:41
Slough: old person of S. 312:14
s. was Despond 99:5
Slovenliness is no part of religion 565:20
Slovenly: s. unhandsome corpse 438:33
s. will spit 135:20
Slow: ain't it s.? 242:28
comfort. .comes ever s. 189:2
drops, soft and s. 166:3
good creatures: but so s.l 93:16
march of the human mind is s. 101:6
melancholy, s. 226:3
more s. 333:8
skill comes so s. 169:16
s. and moving finger 472:34
s. and steady wins 315:4
s. howe'er my marches 292:20
s. in pursuit 467:20
s. of speech and of a s. tongue 45:39
s. of study 466:28
s. rises worth 278:33
s. sinks, more lovely 115:8
s., s., fresh fount 279:28
s. to anger 50:17
s. to begin 578:11
s. to speak, s. to wrath 69:30
solid but s. 212:17
some cry 'S.' 538:3
sun climbs s. 147:8
swift, s. 255:3
swinging s. with sullen roar 341:15
tardy as too s. 478:9
tarry a while, says S. 366:13
very carefully and s. 539:19
wandering steps and s. 349:31
were he reckon'd s. 81:13
wisely and s. 478:2
words move s. 382:32
Slow-consuming Age 230:20
Slowly: experience teaches s. 212:6
grind s. 315:22, 317:13
hasten s. 517:21
nations s. wise 279:4
science moves, but s. 534:28
s., silently, now the moon 172:2
s., s. rase she up 30:2
Spring comes s. up this way 150:19
toll s. 88:5

Slow-worm bite thee 246:23
Slug-a-bed: s. snail 544:9
  sweet S. 245:25
Sluggard: foul s.'s comfort 125:33
  go to the ant, thou s. 49:45
  s. is wiser 50:42
  s.'s cradle 135:20
  voice of the s. 562:3
Slug-horn to my lips I set 90:23
Slugs: killing s. on borders 296:33
  s. leave their lair 152:17
  s. that come crawling 34:14
Sluicing: browsing and s. 572:8
Slum: swear-word in a rustic s. 39:12
Slumber: affected s. more 124:1
  death is s. 495:18
  honey-heavy dew of s. 449:13
  I must s. again 562:3
  in deathly s. 171:9
  lie still and s. 562:1
  little sleep, a little s. 49:46
  love itself shall s. on 499:1
  ports of s. 442:25
  s. did my spirit seal 573:6
  s. is more sweet than toil 535:20
  s. out their immortality 164:37
  S.'s chain 357:13
  start from her s. 16:1
  to soothing s. seven 279:21
Slumbering: dictates to me s. 349:5
  might half s. 288:14
  s. in the open air 152:17
  s. still? 166:24
  s. thoughts 85:21
Slumbers: golden s. 170:23
  hast thou golden s.? 170:21
  imagine unquiet s. 83:15
  indolent s. 156:12
  like infant s. 291:11
  s. light 318:5, 418:36
  soul is dead that s. 317:5
  visit'st my s. nightly 348:23
Slung: harp s. behind him 356:27
  s. atween the round shot 363:3
Slunk: to their nests were s. 347:19
Slut: I am not a s. 428:12
  Polly is a sad s. 214:12
Sluts indeed 11:5
Sly: dumb's a s. dog 144:24
  Stephen S. 478:46
  tough, and devilish s. 175:5
Smack: does s. sweet 93:25
  my father did something s. 463:27
  pledging with contented s. 287:2
  some s. of age in you 441:13
  they s. of honour both 456:7
Small: at noon but s. 312:26
  between the s. and great 164:12
  both great and s. 150:16
  contemneth s. things 56:47
  creatures great and s. 3:14
  day of s. nations 135:6
  day of s. things 56:11
  desire s. beer 441:32
  dull unletter'd s. 164:17
  frail, gaunt and s. 235:17
  free-livers on a s. scale 267:22
  great matter or a s. 56:35
  great ones devour'd the s. 501:14
  great things with s. 346:13
  great vulgar and the s. 158:24
  grind exceeding s. 315:22, 317:13
  how s. the world is 233:5
  how very s. the very great 543:13
  I have no s. talk 564:14
  in life's s. things 320:2
  in s. proportions 282:1
  in your arms to feel so s. 375:13
  is it s.? 311:7
  just so s. as I 544:5
  kingdom..too s. 440:38
  lovesome, white and s. 195:6
  no great and no s. 199:1
  one s. head 225:2
  one that was s. 305:9
  poor creature, s. beer 441:33
  since man's heart is s. 302:13
  s. and great beasts 398:11
  s. beginnings 191:29
  s. but sullen horn 153:24
  s. hot bird 204:2

Small (cont.)
  s. is the worth of beauty 558:5
  s. Latin and less Greek 281:13
  s. matters win great commenda-
    tion 25:37
  s. old-fashioned book 196:24
  s. one a strong nation 55:1
  s. potatoes and few 304:29
  s. servant 177:34
  s. states 267:9
  so s. a thing 15:13
  speaks s. like a woman 465:27
  still s. voice 48:8
  too s. for sight 454:3
  with s. men no great thing 339:1
Smaller: not a s. soul 530:16
  rights of the s. nationalities 21:6
Smallest: one of the s. people 29:5
Small-sword: very pretty s. light 500:27
Smart: as lief pray with Kit S. 271:3
  love and all its s. 38:22
  mock'd the s. 16:8
  of all the girls that are so s. 125:17
  s. for it 49:57
  such a s. little craft 222:8
  to feel all s. 244:11
  too s. to live 560:7
Smarts so little as a fool 385:23
Smatch: some s. of honour 452:6
Smattering of everything 174:6
Smell: ancient and fish-like s. 479:38
  cheer'd with the grateful s. 347:2
  chill the wintry s. 522:14
  flower of sweetest s. 578:3
  I'll s. it on the tree 473:11
  I s. a rat 110:25, 407:8
  I s. the blood 453:27
  noses have they, and s. not 399:4
  once more s. the dew 244:18
  rose was heaven to s. 249:10
  s. and hideous hum 223:8
  s. as sweet 477:16
  s. like what it is—a tomb 495:10
  s. my remnant out 244:20
  s. of bread and butter 112:36
  s. of burning 41:36
  s. so sweet 438:35
  s. sweet, and blossom 501:6
  s. too strong of the lamp 513:9
  sweet keen s. 411:34
Smellest so sweet 472:35
Smelleth: he s. the battle 49:27
Smelling out a suit 477:7
Smell-less: daisies s. 38:8
Smells: it s. to heaven 435:31
  s. April and May 466:5
  s., I swear, not of itself 280:21(–281)
  s. of cheese 518:25
  violet s. to him 444:18
Smile: blush and gently s. 245:20
  calm thou may'st s. 279:19
  follow'd perhaps by a s. 162:8
  forget and s. 409:25
  hear with a disdainful s. 230:1
  Heaven's blue s. 492:28
  her own dying s. 491:21
  her s., it seems half holy 88:13
  his s. it was pensive 238:33
  I dare not beg a s. 247:8
  I hear a s. 167:16
  immeasurable s. 375:10
  jest without the s. 152:21
  kind of sickly s. 239:2
  meet again..we shall s. 451:37
  mov'd to s. at anything 448:27
  one vast substantial s. 174:9
  rarely s., being urban.. 84:13
  share the good man's s. 224:23
  show their teeth in way of s. 462:30
  s., and s., and be a villain 432:21
  s. at the claims of long descent 533:38
  s. at us, pay us 141:28
  s. dwells a little longer 135:13
  s., for your lover comes 567:18
  s. his work to see 75:24(–76)
  s. in thine eyes 356:17
  s. of the brown old earth 92:28
  s. on her lips 418:20
  s. on the face of the tiger 11:2
  s. on you—for seconds 183:12
  s., s., s. 20:23

Smile (cont.)
  s. that glowed 349:4
  s. that was childlike 238:34
  s. to those who hate 118:15
  s. upon his fingers' ends 443:19
  s. upon my knee 232:2
  s. we would aspire to 446:24
  s. with the wise 271:27
  social s. 229:18
  some that s. 451:7
  thrifty wifie's s. 104:33
  tired s. 20:30
  under the s. of safety 441:7
  vain tribute of a s. 417:19
  when you gave her a s. 201:24
  where my Julia's lips do s. 245:21
  with his watery s. 529:14
  with s. so sweet 551:5
  you s., Madonna 309:18
Smiled: all around thee s. 279:19
  at me you s. 533:35
  Devil s. 151:10
  he s. as he sat 238:34
  Never S. Again 241:11
  on her it s. 196:2
  remember how you s. 309:6
  s. and said 'Good-Night' 41:24
  s. Spain's chivalry away 116:45
  s. to think God's greatness 88:5
  s. well content 516:19
  s. when a sabbath appear'd 164:25
  stretched..his little arms, and s. 231:11
  till it s. 340:15
  until she s. on me 148:12
  wanton s. 232:3
Smiler with the knyf 137:32
Smiles: Aryan s. 300:6
  Banquo s. upon me 460:12
  breath, s., tears 88:24
  daggers in men's s. 458:27
  eternal s...emptiness betray 385:32
  every time a man s. 512:32
  flower that s. to-day 247:10
  kisses, tears, and s. 580:20
  old Ocean s. 347:2
  Peace is crown'd with s. 552:1
  read in their s. 493:14
  robb'd that s. 470:6
  seldom he s., and s. in such a sort 448:27
  s. and soap 128:11
  s. awake you 170:23
  s. beneath her cow 11:20
  s., but not as Sultans smile 141:9
  s. by his cheerful fire 226:11
  s. of other maidens 148:13
  s. sae sweetly 106:28
  s. so sweet 327:5
  s. that win 119:2
  s., the tears, of boyhood 357:13
  s., wan as primroses 285:7
  sobs, sniffles, and s. 242:12
  sweet strains, or pensive s. 199:21
  tears and s. 4:3
  thy own sweet s. 160:25
  thy s. before they dwindle 497:9
  Venus when she s. 281:25
  welcome ever s. 481:20
  win their nursling with their s. 309:5
  wreathed s. 341:28
Smilest: Thou s. and art still 17:23
Smiling: by your s...say so 433:15
  died while ye were s. 87:38
  hides a s. face 161:18
  s. as they run 141:3
  s. at grief 483:10
  s., damned villain 432:21
  s., destructive man 312:27
  s. from the world's..snare 425:13
  s. of Fortune beguiling 147:23
  s., put the question by 528:27
  s. the boy fell dead 92:24
Smilingly: burst s. 454:23
Smirk: serious and the s. 177:7
Smite: God shall s. thee 65:15
  let the righteous..s. me 400:14
  s. all the firstborn 45:47
  s. once, and s. no more 342:29
  s. thee on thy right cheek 57:50
  s. them by the merit 361:13
  s. the sounding furrows 541:3
  up and s. them 361:13

Smiteth: cheek to him that s. him 55:26
Smith: chuck it, S. 140:2
  combined in Horace S. 495:14
  conceal him by naming him S. 251:21
  first s..murd'rer's son 163:43
  s., a mighty man 318:11
  S., take a fresh cigar 121:22
Smithy: sparks..out of a s. 586:2
  village s. stands 318:11
Smitten: Memnon s. 538:13
  s. me to my knee 544:22
  s. to the heart 503:3
Smock: pale as thy s. 473:32
Smock-frock: embroidery of a s. 236:42
Smoke: above the s. and stir 339:28
  and s. it! 34:22
  as the s. vanisheth 396:4
  bottle in the s. 399:18
  corrupted by this stinking s. 267:31
  counties overhung with s. 359:2
  daub his Visage with the S. 207:19
  do wid de s.? 238:23
  dunnest s. of hell 457:3
  emit so much s. 307:6
  fill him full of s. 280:14
  from the s. into the smother 426:26
  good cigar is a S. 294:32
  her beloved s. 307:5
  house was filled with s. 53:8
  in yon s. concealed 147:8
  its little s...died 285:18
  man who does not s. 514:27
  salt-caked s. stack 333:21
  s. of their torment 71:26
  s. of the pit 267:30
  thin s. without flame 236:14
Smoked: s. like a chimney 34:21
  s. with bloody execution 456:5
Smokes: nigh thatch s. 151:25
Smoking: a-s. of a whackin' white
    cheroot 299:11
  what a blessing this s. 241:2
Smoky: liest thou in s. cribs 441:41
  worse than a s. house 440:2
Smooth: billows s. and bright 130:9
  I am a s. man 44:59
  never did run s. 466:18
  pleasant s. wit 21:13
  sea being s. 481:1
  s. as monumental alabaster 473:11
  s., fair and lonely 80:19
  s. stream 382:32
  s. the ice 447:39
  so large, and s., and round 507:4
  so s., so green 352:26
  so s., so sweet 247:14
  speak unto us s. things 53:38
  supple and s. 249:8
  that s. tongue 123:27
  Waller was s. 386:17
Smoothed: my soul s. itself 92:34
  s. her work 262:8
Smoother: her mouth is s. than oil 49:44
  his words were s. than oil 395:13
Smoothes: she s. her hair 197:32
  so s. her charming tones 348:16
Smooth-faced: s. gentleman 447:25
  s...rogue 535:34
Smoothing the raven down 340:15
Smoothly: sing thou s. 123:16
Smoothness: give it s. 434:15
  turns earth's s. rough 95:15
Smooth-shaven green 341:14
Smote: s. for us a pathway 301:25
  s. him thus 474:2
  s. him under the fifth rib 47:31
  s. him with the edge 46:16
  s. itself into the bread 530:29
  s. on all the chords 534:16
  s. them hip and thigh 46:57
  s. the nail into his temples 46:46
  they s. me 52:12
Smother: from the smoke into
    the s. 426:26
Smother'd in surmise 456:24
Smouldering: five eyes s. 171:10
Smutch'd: before the soil hath s.
  it 281:24
Snagsby: favourite apology..with
  Mr. S. 173:27
Snail: beloved s. 129:24

Snail (cont.)
  consume away like a s. 395:21
  creeping like s. 427:21
  slug-abed s. 544:9
  s.'s on the thorn 94:40
  went to kill a s. 366:19
  whiting to a s. 129:22
  worm nor s. 467:1
Snails: frogs and s. 369:12
  horns of cockled s. 455:22
  pretty feet like s. 247:12
Snake: devise the S. 207:12, 13
  like a s. renew 493:25
  like a wounded s. 382:31
  nor s., or slow-worm 246:23
  scotch'd the s. 459:4
  s...in the grass 555:27
  S. is living yet 41:34
  s. slipt under a spray 538:2
  there the s. throws her..skin 466:41
Snakes: cloud of winged s. 496:25
  no s. to be met with 274:1
  two bright and aged s. 15:14
  you spotted s. 466:44
Snapdragon: gold-dusted s. 18:26
  s. growing on the walls 363:22
Snapped 'em off short 174:11
Snapper-up of..trifles 485:18
Snapping Turtle 24:9
Snare: I saw the s. 533:35
  mockery, and a s. 172:12
  s. is broken 399:32
  s. of the fowler 399:32
  s. of the hunter 397:18
  world's great s. 425:13
Snares of death 399:5
Snark: if your S. be a Boojum 128:10
  S. was a Boojum 128:14
Snarling: silver, s. trumpets 285:14
Snarls: we s. 176:23
Snatch: fiends will s. at it 473:32
  s. a fearful joy 230:25
  s. them straight away 474:7
Snatched: s. away in beauty's
    bloom 118:23
  s. from out his chariot 411:15
  worthy gentleman..s. from us 100:17
Snatches: ballads, songs and s. 219:15
  s. of old tunes 437:1
Sneaking: my valour..s. off 500:29
Sneer: laughing devil in his s. 115:2
  refute a s. 373:6
  solemn s. 113:49
  teach the rest to s. 385:29
  they s. at me 207:15
  tho' witlings s. 278:27
Sneering: I was born s. 219:19
  without s. 385:29
Sneers of selfish men 582:3
Sneery: looked very s. 21:2
Sneeze: if you s. 312:14
Sneezed: not to be s. at 154:10
Sneezes: beat him when he s. 129:1
Sneezy: Breezy, S., Freezy 213:5
Snicker: hold my coat and s. 197:20
Snicker-snack 129:39(–130)
Snickersnee: my s. 220:8
Sniffles predominating 242:12
Snivelling: what argufies s. 173:6
Snob: meanly admires mean
    things..S. 542:7
  not to be sometimes a S. 542:8
Snore: fit to s. his head off 130:22
  s. upon the flint 429:36
Snored: sat and s. 140:5
Snorer can't hear himself snore 550:26
Snores: heavy ploughman s. 467:35
  s. out the watch 442:25
Snoring: whom, s., she disturbs 162:35
Snow: architecture of the s. 199:28
  chaste as unsunn'd s. 429:27
  cherry hung with s. 262:10
  diadem of s. 118:7
  fairer than whitest s. 330:21
  fleece..white as s. 233:23
  from purest s. 429:20
  garment of unsullied s. 507:37
  giveth s. like wool 400:23
  gone with the s. 80:20
  half-buried in the s. 316:22
  heavy with s. 150:9

Snow (cont.)
  if s. be white 488:13
  I love s. 498:13
  I sift the s. 492:27
  land of mist and s. 149:7
  last long streak of s. 533:24
  little hunchback of the s. 169:23
  mark'd but the fall o' the s. 281:24
  melted like s. 118:39
  'mid s. and ice 316:17
  mockery king of s. 475:24
  moonshine an' s. 319:23
  naked in December s. 474:20
  never love the s. again 81:11
  rain, or any s. 531:37
  rosebuds fill'd with s. 124:5
  scatter their s. around 82:7
  sends the s. in winter 121:27
  shivering in the s. 508:14
  sleet or stifling s. 94:13
  s. and vapours 400:24
  s. came flying 81:15
  s. falls in the river 108:7
  s. had fallen, s. on s. 409:20
  s. hath retreated 577:21
  s. in harvest 476:17
  s. lay round about 361:19
  s. of ferne yere 138:39
  s. on a raven's back 478:19
  s...their winding-sheet 122:20
  S...top of Pindus strew 510:20
  S. upon the Desert's..Face 205:27
  tufts of s. 151:25
  under s. or rain 142:12
  untrodden s. 122:17
  Virgin shrouded in s. 76:7
  we shall have s. 368:3
  where the s. lay dinted 361:24
  white as driven s. 485:29
  white as s. in Salmon 396:7
  white..as the mountain s. 436:21
  whiter skin of hers than s. 473:11
  whiter than s. 395:8
  whitest sheets of s. 166:3
  wish a s. in May 454:33
  your sins..white as s. 52:32
Snow-broth 461:20
Snowdon: stones of S. 293:10
Snowdonian antelope 495:12
Snowdrifts: high s. in the hedge 263:13
Snowdrop: first s. 540:6
Snowed in his hous of mete and
    drinke 137:10
Snows: buds that s. have shaken 523:21
  Cecilia's lap of s. 545:7
  her couch of s. 492:20
  our Lady of the S. 300:17
  s. of yesteryear 553:3
  thro' a waste of s. 381:18
Snow-spotted heath 127:4
Snow-white: her s. hand 584:11
  little s. feet 584:11
Snowy, Flowy, Blowy 213:5
Snowy-banded, dilettante 535:42
Snub: mine has a s. nose 74:10
Snubnosed rogue 535:34
Snuff: only took s. 225:35
  s. the approach of tyranny 100:30
  s., tobacker, and sleep 174:29
  you abuse s.! 153:4
Snuff-box: amber s. 385:18
Snuffed: s. out by an article 116:25
  s. the tainted gale 416:12
Snuffle: with s. and sniff 84:5
Snug: his s. little farm 151:7, 507:19
  little s. property 195:17
  parlour s. and small 161:41
  s. little Island 173:15
  with a s. nose 281:19
So: Amen, S. be it 391:11
  even we, even s. 335:25
  if I can save, s. 440:35
  if I said s., it was s. 226:24
  if it was s. 130:8
  I told you s. 116:50
  meet and right s. to do 390:38
  persuasion that a thing is s. 77:21
  s. am I 160:3
  s. and no otherwise 301:10
  s. can I, or s. can any man 439:42
  s. did I 149:42

So (cont.)
s. do I — 236:30, 32
s. in a voice — 184:4
s. it would have done — 439:40
s. to bed — 377:11
Soap: have you used Pears' S.? — 6:15
invisible s. — 253:7
smiles and s. — 128:11
s. and education — 550:13
used your s. two years ago — 403:30
what! no s.? — 209:18
Soap-boiler: make a s. costive — 563:13
Soar: angels alone, that s. above — 319:7
creep as well as s. — 103:17
singing still dost s. — 498:2
s., but never roam — 580:27
s. not too high to fall — 334:19
s. with Eno — 514:2
spur you to s. — 524:33
thou canst not s. — 492:5
through..clouds to s. again — 117:25
to run, though not to s. — 326:4
Soaring: poet s. in the high region — 352:20
s. claim the skies — 211:26
s. ever singest — 498:2
s. human boy — 173:34
tired with s. — 191:16
Soars: lark s. — 87:30
s. on golden wing — 341:12
Sob: throb and mutual s. — 123:2
Sobbed: he s. and he sighed — 220:19
Sobbing: a-sighing and a-s. — 369:18
Sober: at least not s. — 276:3
be s., be vigilant — 70:6
compulsorily s. — 327:8
godly, righteous, and s. — 388:12
half as s. as a judge — 307:27
if she is chaste, and s. — 363:26
in her s. livery — 347:19
men at whiles are s. — 263:34
Philip drunk to Philip S. — 5:12
second and s. thoughts — 242:7
sedate, s., silent — 253:32
sensible, temperate, s. — 363:19
s. as a Judge — 204:12
s. certainty of waking bliss — 340:16
s. man, among his boys — 532:29
take a s. colouring — 576:22
to bed go s. — 37:15
to-morrow we'll be s. — 5:24
was I s. when I swore? — 207:21
Soberbia: la última camisa..s. — 329:17
Soberness: words of truth and s. — 65:24
Sobers: drinking largely s. us — 382:22
Sober-suited: s. matron — 478:18
s. songstress — 546:14
Sobs: add s., fiery sighs — 109:27
s., sniffles, and smiles — 242:12
with s. and tears — 130:20
Social: fellowship and s. comfort — 87:31
Nature's s. union — 107:10
self-love and s. are the same — 384:18
s. and economic experiment — 254:4
s., friendly, honest — 105:25
s. smile — 229:18
whole s. system — 174:33
Socialists: all S. now-a-days — 195:25
Societies: there are s. — 343:4
Society: cling together in one s. — 579:9
Corinthian capital of polished s. — 102:25
curing the maladies of S. — 126:45
desperate oddfellow s. — 546:44
equal s. with them — 158:4
four hundred people in New York s. — 322:15
gain to s. at large — 219:23
Heaven and Hell Amalgamation S. — 127:31
imposed on s. from without — 214:2
man's chief pleasure is s. — 169:18
man seeketh in s. comfort — 24:27
man was formed for s. — 73:3
mingle with s. — 459:11
no letters; no s. — 248:21
one great s. — 579:32
our noble s. — 178:43
pests of s. — 78:10
s., friendship, and love — 164:24
s...in conspiracy — 200:38
s. is all but rude — 332:15

Society (cont.)
s...my glittering bride — 574:16
s. offenders — 219:24
s...one polish'd horde — 116:48
s.'s chief joys — 159:18
s. than solitude is worse — 33:15
s...to be in it..a bore — 570:19
s., where none intrudes — 114:26
solitude.. best s. — 349:9
such s. as is quiet — 498:15
when s. requires to be rebuilt — 338:23
Sock: Jonson's learnèd s. — 342:7
Socked it them hard — 295:4
Socket: burn to the s. — 574:14
Sockets: candles burn their s. — 264:1
s. of fine gold — 52:14
Socks: in your shirt and your s. — 219:12
when thy s. were on — 281:15
Socrates: misunderstood, and S. — 200:41
Socratic manner — 39:31
Sod: hard and trampled s. — 23:24
heat was in the very s. — 361:24
thy cold pavement..a s. — 114:34
to thy high requiem..a s. — 287:32
under my head a s. — 31:22
Soda-water: sermons and s. — 115:33
their feet in s. — 197:31
Sodden: nor s. at all with water — 45:46
s. and unkind — 42:3
Sods: s. with our bayonets — 572:11
under green s. lay — 584:6
Sofa: accomplish'd S. last — 162:34
I sing the S. — 162:31
wheel the s. round — 163:21
Soft: drops, s. and slow — 166:3
fair, and s., and sweet — 332:8
heart as s. — 247:1
her voice was ever s. — 454:24
lie both s. and dry — 247:16
make it s. and narrow — 30:3
more s. and sensible — 455:22
O so s.! — 281:24
s. and chilly nest — 285:22
s. answer turneth away wrath — 50:10
s. as silk remains — 248:10
s. as the breath of even — 21:9
s. as young! — 587:8
s. complaining lute — 191:38
s. impeachment — 500:30
s. in the level races — 80:19
s. is the music — 578:3
s. is the strain — 382:32
s., meek, patient — 170:18
s. philosopher of love — 192:45
s. the zephyr blows — 229:23
s., unhappy sex — 40:14
s.! what light.. breaks? — 477:13
s. with the drops of rain — 395:30
so s. a mould — 191:19
so s. and uncompounded — 344:29
so s., so calm — 119:2
virgins are s. — 113:2
whan s. was the sonne — 310:3
Soften'd the stones — 473:6
Softer: sleep's no s. — 94:24
Softly: go s. all my years — 54:7
s. and suddenly vanish — 128:10
s., gently, kindly — 214:9
s. she was going up — 149:23
s. sweet, in Lydian measures — 191:9
speak s...carry a big stick — 408:27
step s., under snow — 142:13
Thames, run s. — 510:20
Softness: for s. she — 347:11
Sohne: zu weit dem S. — 208:30
Soi: Savoir être à s. — 354:24
Soil: before the s. hath smutch'd — 281:24
Freedom's s. — 234:13
grows on mortal s. — 342:22
high-cultured as her s. — 123:7
most subject is the fattest s. — 442:23
my carcase back to your s. — 119:33
that s...best deserve — 345:10
this the s., the clime — 344:21
weed that grows in every s. — 101:11
Soiled: cheer our s. face — 400:33
s. with all ignoble use — 533:23
Soirée: friendly s. — 179:19
Sojourner, as all my fathers — 394:11
Sol: firmat s., educat imber — 133:9
inferebatur s. et luna — 21:18

Solace: our s. is — 375:21
s. in the midst of woe — 132:2
s. ourselves with loves — 49:50
with s. and gladness — 502:18
Solaced: in childhood s. me — 160:25
Solaces: with tea s. the midnight — 278:1
Solar: far as the s. walk — 383:11
hub of the s. system — 251:16
Sold: March dust to be s. — 549:30
never s. the truth — 537:23
not have s. her for it — 473:21
sees us s. — 303:11
s. his birthright — 44:58
s., my Arab steed — 365:16
spoils were fairly s. — 323:21
Soldan of Byzantium — 141:3
Soldest him on Good Friday — 438:26
Soldier: arm our s. — 429:3
as a s. of the king — 305:1
as the s. said — 179:15
British s. fights — 360:21
British s... stand up to anything — 489:18
broken s...bade to stay — 224:20
come you back, you British s. — 299:10
courtier's, s.'s, scholar's, eye — 434:14
driveth o'er a s.'s neck — 477:7
for a s. I listed — 173:4
for her..the s. fights — 35:22
God's s. be he — 461:15
go to your Gawd like a s. — 304:4
in a s...blasphemy — 461:33
let a s. drink — 471:9
mourn'd her s. slain — 310:2
never expect a s. to think — 489:17
not having been a s. — 273:34
old S. of the Queen's — 5:9
serve as a s. — 304:3
s., and afeard? — 460:24
s. an' sailor too — 301:20
s. bold — 252:29
s., full of strange oaths — 427:21
s. is better accommodated — 442:9
s...not a romantic animal — 29:6
s. of the Legion — 365:21
s., rest — 416:19
s.'s a man — 471:9
s.'s grave — 118:27
s.'s pleasure — 191:4
s.'s pole is fall'n — 425:29
s.'s sepulchre — 122:20
s.'s virtue — 424:20
summer s. — 372:23
tell an old s. — 489:6
ten-year s. tells — 299:13
that s. a mere recreant — 481:7
tried and valiant s. — 451:6
what the s...said — 179:15
would himself have been a s. — 438:35
Soldiers: amongst a thousand s. — 38:24
Ireland gives England her s. — 337:10
men like s. may not quit — 535:25
mustered their s. — 31:14
old s. never die — 9:2
old s...surest — 563:22
others, like s. — 443:10
our God and s. — 404:9
our s. slighted — 404:9
s. of Christ, arise — 565:10
s. of the ploughshare — 413:26
steel my s.' hearts — 444:24
substance of ten thousand s. — 476:38
Soldier-saint — 96:9
Soldier-saints — 96:45
Soldiery: brutal and insolent s. — 201:28
licentious s. — 101:20
Sole: absolute s. Lord — 166:11
English subject's s. prerogative — 193:42
no rest for the s. of her foot — 44:39
s. death — 90:44
s. unbusy thing — 152:17
s. work of a lifetime — 90:39
that apparition, s. of men — 496:18
to my s. self — 288:2
you break that s. bond — 101:12
Sole: l'amor che muove il s. — 169:2
Sole: vel s. puro — 260:14
Solecism: of eternity without a s. — 86:9
Soleil: le s. d'Austerlitz — 361:3
le s. qui poudroye — 377:32

INDEX

Solemn: day becomes more s. 494:6
her s. bird 347:23
in the s. midnight 184:2
sapping a s. creed with s. sneer 113:49
s. peaks 16:14
s. troops 343:4
too s. sad 509:19
Solemnities: high s. 340:38
Solemnly: up to God so s. 380:20
Soles: bonosque s. effugere 331:26
s. occidere et redire 132:15
Sole-sitting by the shores 573:2
Solicit for it straight 473:12
Soliciting: person or persons..s.
him 268:8
supernatural s. 456:24
Solicitor: bachelor, a s., a Freemason 188:1
Protestant..only go to his s. 182:14
wound in the s. 111:29
Solid: drowns things weighty and
s. 27:1
for s., reasoning good-sense 139:22
s., but slow 212:18
s. man of Boston 317:1
too too s. flesh 430:33
toward s. good 351:23
Solitary: be not s. 109:33, 274:16
s., and cannot impart it 270:18
s. child 577:17
s. hidden anguish 106:24
s. Highland lass 580:28
s. place shall be glad 54:1
s., poor, nasty, brutish 248:21
s. song that whistles 577:19
s. sorrow 286:17
s. thinkings 284:23
their s. way 349:31
under the s. moon 17:28
wander s. there 332:22
waste and s. places 494:13
Solitude: bird in the s. singing 119:10
bliss of s. 577:7
come to him in s. 578:33
court s. 155:27
delighted in s. 26:15
disturbed its s. 29:19
how sweet..is s. 162:6
I love tranquil s. 498:15
in s. what happiness? 348:34
Islington..grow a..s. almost 158:22
life the s. 587:14
musing in s. 574:5
my faithful s. 156:12
no chasm, no s. 574:26
o'er his..desk in s. 80:28
O still s. 80:19
self-sufficing power of S. 579:15
society than s. is worse 33:15
soft like S.'s 498:21
s...best society 349:9
s...calls it—peace 113:4
s.! where are the charms? 164:22
sweet retired s. 340:20
this delicious s. 332:15
this peopled earth a s. 497:3
thoughtful Soul to S. 205:8
with dangers compass'd..and s. 348:23
worst s...destitute of..friend-
ship 25:12
Solitudes: misty s. 303:17
Solitudinem: ubi s. faciunt 526:9
Solomon: all S.'s wisdom 47:42
curtains of S. 51:39
felicities of S. 25:19
greater than S. 59:17
King David and King S. 361:7
King S. loved many..women 47:45
S. in all his glory 58:13
S. of saloons 93:29
song..which is S.'s 51:37
Solomon Grundy 368:21
Solum: nec minus s. quam cum solus 145:9
nescioqua natale s...ducit 372:8
Soluturos: ad Graecas Kalendas s. 120:9
Solve: s. 'em in a trice 110:15
s. the problem of the age 200:20
Solved: who s. it not devoured 350:17
Sombre songs and sweet 522:12
Some: I bury s. of you 185:5
s. hae meat 107:34

Some (cont.)
s. have too much 195:13
s. men must love my lady 455:10
s. say that we wan 327:1
s. to undo..s. to be undone 194:24
what s. have found so sweet 536:1
Somebody: brisk little s. 89:25
everyone is s. 218:30
let's stop s. 242:30
mine ain dear s. 526:21
Miracles of Saint S. 95:28
played by s. I do not know 290:24
s. bet on de bay 210:13
s. must 254:6
sore for S. 105:34
Someone: as s. somewhere sings 116:13
next morning..s. else 408:12
s. had blunder'd 528:15
s. is sinking today 550:33
Something: can s. 254:19
do nothing and get s. 182:26
from doing s. 242:30
good for s. 193:36
have s. to say 565:25
I too will s. make 81:9
man's worth s. 89:38
original s...Original Sin 123:13
pardon s. to the spirit of liberty 100:25
rage for saying s. 270:31
s. attempted, s. done 318:13
s. childish 152:11
s...doesn't love a wall 212:2
s. ere the end 541:3
s. far more deeply interfused 582:1
s. given that way 37:28
s. lost behind the Ranges 296:9
s., nothing 471:30
s. of a round belly 441:21
s. of the Shorter-Catechist 241:29
s., s. that replies 544:20
s. that is gone 576:8
s. there is moves me 82:23
s. too much of this 434:26
s. very like Him 140:32
that s. still 384:2
there's s. greater 128:3
there was s. in it 93:30
time for a little s. 339:22
Something-arola 39:23
Sometime: our s. sister 430:23
Sometimes: s. in the right 194:9
s. this, and s. that 246:13
Somewhat: s. against thee 70:29
s. to say unto thee 47:40
Somewhere: as some one s. sings 116:13
gives us back the thoughts 84:21
morning s. in the world 262:2
s., beyond space and time 83:25
s. safe to sea 523:23
s., surely, afar 17:17
s. the sun is shining 238:6
truth lies s. 160:18
Somewheres east of Suez 299:15
Sommeils du matin 156:12
Somni portae 555:2
Somno: nunc s. et inertibus horis 261:25
Somnus: though S. in Homer 85:21
Son: Absalom, my s. 47:37
Athena's wisest s. 113:13
beggarly s. of a gun 121:3
behold thy s. 63:72
bleeding Sire to S. 117:38
blessed Mary's S. 474:22
by meekness, call'd thy S. 503:6
damned for never a king's s. 438:24
dear s. of memory 351:8
did bear our s. 305:18
die soon, O fairy's s. 509:29
Duke's s.—cook's s. 294:19
England's greatest s. 537:18
Epicurus owne s. 137:9
every wise man's s. 482:28
first murd'rer's s. 163:43
Fitzdotterel's eldest s. 84:27(-85)
from the sire the s. shall hear 418:35
gave his only begotten S. 63:9
good man teach his s. 444:28
hateth his s. 50:6
his s. has done nearly as well 112:2
I obeyed as a s. 216:26
Joshua the s. of Nun 46:6

Son (cont.)
king of all kings to her s. 7:15
kiss the S. 391:51
left a s. who proved 297:18
little s. into his bosom 209:2
Lucifer, s. of the morning 53:22
Monk my s. 507:36
my brother's s. 149:33
my little S. 375:16
my s.—and what's a s.? 305:17
my s. in tears 219:4
my s., mine own Telemachus 541:2
my s.'s wife, Elizabeth 267:14
mystical body of thy S. 390:46
only s. of his mother 61:32
only s., sir 226:36
Pherson had a s. 23:27
Philip's peerless s. 19:3
queen of Scots..a fair s. 197:36
s. of Adam and of Eve 401:28
s. of a hundred Kings 294:19
s. of a livery stable keeper 584:14
s. of Belial 47:36
s. of consolation 64:30
S. of God goes forth 240:20
s. of Heav'n and Earth 348:10
s. of his old age 45:12
S. of man hath not where 58:30
s. of man..thou visitest 392:10
S. of Morn in..Night's decline 74:22
s. of perdition 63:65
s. of the old moon-mountains 288:29
s. of the sable Night 168:12
this is my beloved S. 57:33
this my s. was dead 62:16
this the carpenter's s.? 59:32
thy righteousness unto the
King's 396:22
thy s., thine only s. Isaac 44:54
Tom he was a piper's s. 369:10
Tom, the piper's s. 369:11
two-legg'd thing, a s. 190:15
unto us a s. is given 53:15
virgin shall..bear a s. 53:12
when the s. swore 109:28
where art thou, my beloved S.? 572:24
wise s...foolish s. 49:54
wonderful s...astonish a mother 435:21
worthy to be called thy s. 62:14
your tardy s. to chide 435:51
Song: acquaints his soul with s. 96:27
all this for a s.? 103:31
best taught s. 95:37
brotherhood in s. 285:8
burden of my s. 8:8
commence my s. 95:37
cuckoo's s. 169:21
dance, and Provençal s. 287:24
despise the skylark's s. 83:4
fable, s., or fleeting shade 246:1
Fair commands the s. 162:32
followed by a sacred s. 41:15
full lasting is the s. 336:45
give ear unto my s. 225:17
glorious s. of old 421:10
glorious the s. 503:6
goodly manor for a s. 423:6
govern thou my s. 348:23
great Venite change the s. 186:11
hallow!s. 113:13
her symphony and s. 151:33(-152)
his s. of love 81:8
hopped with his s. 171:2
hums a cheerful s. 372:16
I made another s. 81:10
in England's s. for ever 363:6
in you my s. begins 501:20
I the s. 218:33
joyful S. I'll raise 2:23
lightnings of his s. 492:1
main region of my s. 574:7
mavis' evening s. 104:29
metre of an antique s. 486:17
middle of my s. 160:2
mighty orb of s. 574:13
moralised his s. 386:1
moralize my s. 509:16
more musical than any s. 409:27
morn of s. 517:2
my echoing s. 333:9
my Reputation for a S. 207:20

Song (*cont.*)

my s. comes native	289:9
my S., I fear	493:3
my s. would have been longer	369:9
my vision with the s.	336:2
never go beyond a s.	202:3
new s...no man could learn	71:23
new s.'s measure	371:1
no man could learn that s.	71:23
no s. to give you	293:6
no sorrow in thy s.	97:30, 315:21
old and antique s.	483:1
old s. made by an aged old pate	5:10
old s. of Percy and Douglas	502:9
one grand sweet s.	293:7
one s. increase	410:16
our s. is the voice of desire	81:19
our s. shall rise	240:19
penny for a s.	584:4
perpetual Orphic s.	497:14
pipe a simple s.	575:12
pipe that s. again	76:9
rapid plumes of s.	495:26
required of us then a s.	400:5
roll forth, my s.	329:4
Sabbath s. go up to God	380:20
sang a most topical s.	10:24
sans Wine, sans S.	206:8
satire be my s.	117:9
self-same s.	288:1
shedding my s. upon height	524:13
sightless s.	533:25
sing a faery's s.	286:31
sing a s. at least	106:3
sing a s. of sixpence	368:20
singing our s. of God	567:2
singing this s.	90:16
sing me a bawdy s.	440:13
sing me a s. of a lad	516:7
sing the Lord's s.	400:5
sing unto the Lord a new s.	393:35
solitary s.	577:19
s. about a Lamb	76:9
s. and blood are pure	336:37
s. charms the sense	345:29
s. for s.	308:17
s...I found again	315:25
s. in thy praise	105:29
s. is not Truth	561:11
s. made in lieu	509:15
s. of a merryman	222:27
s. of Harvest-home	4:11
s. of love	410:30
s. of night's sweet bird	492:9
s. of songs	51:37
s. of thanks and praise	576:18
s. of the birds	233:17
s. of them that feast	362:4
s. of woe..an earthly s.	532:39
S. on your bugles blown	241:26
s. that echoes cheerly	534:1
s. that nerves a nation's heart	528:12
s. that should spur you	524:33
s. too daring	401:23
s. to sing O!	222:26
s. was wordless	415:15
spacious s.	165:35
swallow-flights of s.	532:26
swear to the truth of a s.	401:20
sweetest passage of a s.	338:6
swift stream of s.	495:3
Take up thy S.	375:19
that was the s.,—the s. for me	578:11
their low lone song	128:2
there's an end of ane old s.	370:4
these monks' s.	124:22
thinks two notes a s.	169:22
this s. is consider'd a..gem	120:22
till I end my S.	510:20
Time an endless s.	585:16
time is our tedious s.	343:25
to my s. victory and praise	494:1
to you, all s. of praise	501:20
turn out a s.	105:17
wanted one immortal s.	190:17
weigh this s.	584:16
what s. the Syrens sang	87:12
what they teach in s.	494:17
when this s. is sung	583:21
wherefrom ye learn your s.	81:18

Song (*cont.*)

wind's s.	334:10
wine, woman and s.	321:5, 543:5
with the breeze of s.	533:5
wrote one s.	94:12
you have heard the s.	298:27
Songe: la vie est un s.	355:4
Songs: after the s. of Apollo	456:2
all their s. are sad	140:15
angelic s. are swelling	202:23
ballads, s. and snatches	219:15
best of all trades, to make s.	42:13
dirty s. and dreary	84:17
drunkards make s.	396:18
fair the fall of s.	516:3
fruit for their s.	2:31
go, s...some are sung	544:4
he coude s. make	136:26
Heine for s.	91:10
her matchless s.	332:27
I cannot sing the old s.	35:11, 120:25
lean and flashy s.	342:29
let us go hence, my s.	524:25
merry s. of peace	447:14
my Book of S. and Sonnets	465:30
no sad s. for me	409:29
nothing but his S.	154:38
not make new s.	158:4
one of the s. of Sion	400:5
our sweetest s. are..saddest	498:9
piping s. of pleasant glee	76:9
s. consecrate to truth	499:9
s. may inspirit us	93:5
s. of Araby	571:6
s. of deliverance	393:33
s. of expectation	35:4
s. of his fashion	516:4
s. of the harp-player	521:30(–522)
s. that I made for thee	82:11
spiritual s.	68:5
summer s. for me	485:16
Sussex s.	42:7
we who with s. beguile	208:9
where are the s. of Spring?	284:13
your gambols? your s.?	437:15
Songsmith: slight not the s.	561:5
Songstress: sober-suited s.	546:14
Sonne: die S. geht..nicht unter	415:22
Sonnet: ode, and elegy and s.	276:14
scorn not the S.	580:16
s. is a moment's monument	410:21
turned to a S.	183:17
Sonneteer: starved hackney s.	382:34
Sonnets: century of s.	93:45
lovers' s. turn'd to holy psalms	377:4
my Book of Songs and S.	465:30
written s. all his life	115:39
Sonorous metal	345:1
Sons: all her s. at play	15:12
all the s. of God	49:20
as many s. as..hairs	461:15
bears all its s. away	562:9
bind your s. to exile	303:24
carline wife's three s.	33:2
chose their s. by name	80:24
count the sires and s.	183:4
fallen s. of Eve	142:5
giants, the s. of Anak	46:14
give them to your s.	368:5
God's s. are things	327:6
her patient s.	226:13
her S. must wait upon Mary's S.	302:1
horny-handed s. of toil	284:9
Jacob's s. and daughters	361:15
lays it on Martha's S.	302:3
mothers that lack s.	429:8
not always true s.	110:26
our s...grow up as the young plants	400:16
queens to your..s.	413:9
seldom see we s. succeed	234:8
since born his s.	347:13
s. of ale and brede	583:26
s. of Belial	190:25, 344:35
s. of Edward sleep	476:25
s. of glory	324:18
s. of God came	48:38
S. of Mary	302:1
s. of men and angels	565:4
s. of the morning	240:15

Sons (*cont.*)

s. of the waves	213:10
strong heart of her s.	188:32
their s., they gave	83:19
things are the s. of heaven	277:21
third among the s. of light	491:15
we arraign her, her s.	16:11
your s. and your daughters.. prophesy	55:52
Sonsie: honest s. face	106:4
Soon: Death..call too s.	222:25
haste away so s.	246:2
late and s.	582:18
s. he sooth'd his soul	191:9
s...high Midsummer pomps	18:26
s...the great awaking	35:6
s., too s...come s., s.l	495:24
think it s.	88:23
to Eve: Be s.	544:17
Sooner: end the s.	26:7
no s. the old hope	92:43
s. it's over..s. to sleep	294:2
s. than he wished to rise	271:36
s. will his race be run	247:10
we no s. see	281:1
Soot: in s. I sleep	76:17
Sooth: it is silly s.	483:5
Soothe: s. the grieved	164:34
what charm can s.	226:18
Soothed: soon he s. his soul	191:9
s. the griefs of..Christians	325:36
s. twenty years	277:42
sustained and s.	98:3
Soothes: saddens while it s.	94:31
Soothfastness: dwelle with s.	136:20
Sooty bosom	469:42
Sop: body gets its s.	89:28
give that Cerberus a s.	155:7
Sophist: dark-brow'd s.	537:43
neither saint nor s.-led	15:10
self-torturing s.	113:48
swift to scent the s.	4:13
Sophisters, economists, and calculators	102:11
Sophistical rhetorician	181:12
Sophistry: destroy his fib or s.	385:24
s. and affectation	28:13
Sophocles: in my declining years ..S.	153:12
Sophonisba: oh! S.l S.l oh!	546:28
Sops in wine: Coronation and S.	510:23
Sordello's story told	96:29, 35
Sordid: s., home-bred cares	101:30
s., unfeeling	124:9
Sore: bear with a s. head	331:17
critics, who themselves are s.	117:13
good for s. eyes	520:10
my heart is s.	105:34
my s. throats..always worse	22:26
s. with loving her	175:16
Sores: rain'd all kinds of s.	472:34
Sorrento: beyond S. and Amalfi	308:17
Sorrow: any s. like unto my s.	55:23
ate his bread in s.	127:30
beguile thy s.	480:34
brief s.	361:12
but labour and s.	397:16
certain of s. in store	300:22
climbing s.	452:37
ere the s. comes	88:1
far from s.	183:2
father's s.	232:3
give s. words	460:20
hang s.	280:12
I must bury s.	97:26
in s... bring forth	44:26
in spite of s.	341:31
knowledge increaseth s.	50:63
labour without s. is base	413:20
last his s., first his joy	232:2
like this s. 'twill come	82:10
Lord Lovel he died out of s.	31:9
Lycidas your s.	343:3
more in s.	431:13
my heart hath 'scap'd this s.	487:23
my old s. wakes	267:11
nature could not s. hide	232:3
neither s., nor crying	71:45
never..s. but its own	122:32
night of doubt and s.	35:4
no s. in thy song	97:30, 315:21

Sorrow (*cont.*)

no s. there, John 360:20
not a word of s. 572:13
not be in s. too 77:3
not sure of s. 523:22
no wisdom in..hopeless s. 277:41
now melt into s. 113:1
pine with fear and s. 510:16
pure and complete s. 548:8
regions of s. 344:9
resembles s. only 316:8
rooted s. 460:37
savour of s. 183:17
shun the man of s. 164:34
sighed with saving s. 387:24
sit by the fireside with S. 494:9
solitary s. 286:17
some natural s. 581:3
s. and sighing shall flee 54:5
s. and silence are strong 316:15
s. breeds 189:9
s. dogging sin 245:5
s...dureth over long 328:9
s. enough in the natural way 300:22
s. fade 151:18
s. for angels 93:6
s. for his lost Lenore 380:23
s...made s. more beautiful 286:5
s. makes us wise 533:21
s. never comes too late 230:30
s. of the meanest thing 575:14
S. proud to be exalted 7:13
s.'s crown of sorrow 534:21
s. so royally in you 442:32
s., that is not s. 579:36
s. thy young days shaded 356:22
S., why dost borrow 285:3
S., wilt thou live with me 532:41
S., with her family 491:21
sphere of our s. 499:4
such sweet s. 478:1
tales of s. done 224:20
this s.'s heavenly 473:11
thrall to s. 524:29
to his s. 50:19
to match the s. 335:10
to S. I bade good morrow 285:4
to think is to be full of s. 287:27
trouble, s., need, sickness 390:29
veiling..his song in s. 492:1
water this s. 423:28
wear a golden s. 446:16
what s. was..bad'st her know 230:16
when in s., when in danger 512:15
with night we banish s. 248:5
with s. to the grave 45:21
write s. on the ..earth 475:6
year wake year to s. 491:26
Sorrowful: fiery sighs, and s. countenance 109:27
Knight of the S. Countenance 134:8
s. birth 328:7
s.: for he had great possessions 60:2
Sorrowing: borrowing goeth a s. rejoicing,—s. 549:25 / 318:13
Sorrows: carried our s. 54:25
costly in our s. 512:29
disease, or s. strike him 146:32
few s...good income..of no avail 504:15
I and s. sit 447:27
man of s. 54:25
my s. are at an end 214:17
my s. have an end 6:28
soothes his s. 364:15
s. breed 292:19
s. end 486:25
s. of my heart 393:15
s. of thy line 183:1
s. of your changing face 586:21
s. sailors find 113:16
suffer noble s. 406:4
swallows other s. 469:43
transient s. 580:20
when s. come 436:25
Sorry: death's self is s. 280:10
dreadful s., Clementine 355:22
s.—but we all must die 521:2
s. for their childishness 375:17
s., now, I wrote it 100:2
that I shall be s. for 451:18

Sorry (*cont.*)

this s. Scheme of Things 207:26
though I'm in a s. case 218:12
Sort: like this s. of thing.. 314:17
Sorted: with..tears he s. out 130:20
Sortem seu ratio dederit 261:6
Sorts: all s. and conditions 389:15
all s. of things and weather 199:18
Sot: you drunken s. 369:17
Sot: un s. savant 353:18
Sots: what can ennoble s.? 384:8
Soudan: into the S.'s realm 19:3
your 'ome in the S. 296:23
Souffrances: majesté des s. humaines 553:1
Souffre et meurs sans parler 553:2
Souffrons sur les cimes 265:3
Sought: come, long-s. 495:22
far may be s. 502:17
he s...things to love 498:20
I never have s. the world 275:6
I s. him, but.. 394:6
I s. no more 544:20
less often s. than found 118:27
light we s...shining still 19:1
love s. is good 483:29
never s. in vain 104:35
on my bed I s. him 52:4
s. after my soul 397:11
s. it carefully with tears 69:20
s. out many inventions 51:16
s. thee wand'ring 161:10
s. the Lord aright 104:35
they s. it with thimbles 128:11
to those men that s. him 447:9
unknowing what he s. 192:5
Soul: acquaints his s. with song 96:27
adieu 'twixt s. and body 412:15
affirmations of the s. 201:12
all that a s. can do 185:5
all the heart and the s. 96:21
as active as that s. was 352:5
as angels..call to the s. 552:12
as in a s. remembering 474:28
assault and hurt the s. 389:32
as well for the body as the s. 388:9
awake my s. 292:1
bear my s. away 3:3
because his s. was great 188:33
become a living s. 581:25
belie thy s.'s immensity 576:12
be still, my s. 263:16
build..O my s. 251:15
built my s. a..pleasure-house 537:34
calm of all things 16:17
captain of my s. 241:19
careful s. 302:1
catch my flying s. 382:7
Christe receive thy s. 31:13
city of the s.! 114:12
clothing for the s. divine 73:24
come silly s. 80:8
composed in the s. 19:20
condense within thy s. 364:9
crowd not on my s. from death 229:25
delivered my s. from death 395:16, 399:6
devil and thee about thy s. 438:26
dim s. of a star 525:14
dividing asunder of s. and spirit 69:8
eloquence the s. 345:29
ensnar'd my s. and body 474:1
enters into one's s. 289:25
eternal summer in his s. 251:11
every s., it passed me by 149:18
every subject's s. 444:20
fair seed-time had my s. 579:5
felt my s. in a kiss 524:32
FIAT in my s. 38:25
fiery s. 190:13
fine point of his s. taken off 289:16
fire of s. is kindled 177:28
five windows of the s. 74:12
flattering unction to your s. 436:1
flow of s. 386:5
footsteps of thy s. 88:17
force his s. 433:31
for my s., what can it do 432:2
for that sweet s.'s sake 502:20
forth John's s. flared 92:6
freed his s. the nearest way 275:4
fret thy s. with crosses 510:16

Soul (*cont.*)

from the S.'s eternity 410:21
genial current of the s. 230:5
get his glorious s. 329:25
give his s. good reste 321:10
give me my s. again 330:5
given my s. for this 524:32
give not thy s. unto a woman 56:39
God the s. 383:18
go, S., the body's guest 405:7
grants the s. again 161:21
grapple them to thy s. 431:25
grave unto a s. 447:33
great Marlbro's mighty s. 1:9
had a little S. 357:18
half conceal the S. 532:3
half the little s. is dirt 537:5
hangs my helpless s. 565:6
happy s., she shall discover 166:9
hark! hark! my s. 202:23
harpit your midmost s. 298:18
heard them call my s. 537:1
heart, and s., and voice 361:18
heart and s. do sing in me 502:1
heaven of his high s. 544:11
height my s. can reach 88:24
her aged s. to damn 141:33
her body from her s. 411:26
her lips suck forth my s. 330:5
her love-laden s. 498:6
her pensive s. 154:1
her s. to keep 338:9
hidden s. of harmony 342:8
hides a dark s. 340:20
his angry s. ascended 23:24
his eager s., biting for anger 212:16
his own s. was like that 374:9
his pure s. unto his captain 475:16
his s. is marching on 234:7
his s. is with the saints 151:31
his s. proud science never taught 383:11
his s. shall taste the sadness 287:21
his s. sincere 230:13
his s. well-knit 16:13
his very s. listened 574:20
holdeth our s. in life 396:1
house of a brute to the s. 528:9
how prodigal the s. 431:27
how say ye then to my s. 392:17
humanized my s. 578:15
hurl my s. from heaven 473:32
I am the s. 524:1
I gave you your own s. 489:28
in body and in s. 417:21
in his altered s. 191:8
in my s. am free 319:7
in mystery our s. abides 16:29
in some part of my s. 472:34
in the bitterness of his s. 56:33
in the bitterness of s. 54:7
into which the s...has passed 374:10
invite my s. 567:10
in whose rich s. 189:3
I refrain my s. 400:1
iron entered into his s. 398:12
iron enter into his s. 512:26
I think nobly of the s. 484:22
joy's s. lies in the doing 480:41
leave my s. in hell 392:27
leaves s. free a little 89:6
let every s. be subject 66:8
lie in the s. 282:12
lift my s. to heaven 446:19
like fruit, my s. 430:5
little s. for a little bears up 525:15
little s., wandering, pleasant 233:19
lose his own s. 59:45, 61:3
man became a living s. 44:11
measured by my s. 562:2
meeting s. may pierce 342:7
merit wins the s. 385:19
merry of s. he sailed 516:7
merry old s. 368:3
might create a s. 340:28
mine eyes into my very s. 435:48
mine has opened its s. 93:35
most comprehensive s. 194:6
most offending s. alive 444:27
mount, my s.! 476:1
my dear s...mistress 434:25
my outward s. 185:4

Soul (*cont.*)

my own s...to itself decreed 288:11
my perfect s. 469:39
my prophetic s. 432:13
my rising S. surveys 2:22
my s. doth magnify the Lord 61:13
my s. drew back 244:21
my s. fleeth 399:40
my s. from the sword 393:7
my s. hath her content 470:31
my s. he doth restore 421:1
my s. in agony 149:20
my s. into the boughs 332:20
my s. is among lions 395:18
my s. is an enchanted boat 497:10
my s., like to a ship 563:34
my s. more bent to serve 351:21
my S., my daughter 545:1
my s., my life, my all 562:19
my s. once more made trial 579:1
my s.'s birth-partner 410:27
my s.'s calm retreat 551:20
my s.'s in arms 144:28
my s., sit thou 404:10
my s. smoothed itself 92:34
my s. spurned the chains 495:26
my s. that calls 477:27
my s. that lingers sighing 263:20
my s., there is a country 552:1
my s. thirsteth for thee 395:25
my s. to heaven 8:13
my s. to keep 8:18
my s. to take 8:18
my s. within the house 482:22
my unconquerable s. 241:18
neither a s. to lose 505:5
never once possess our s. 18:18
no passion in the human s. 314:1
no s. that lived, loved 522:21
no s. to be damned 547:15
not a s. knew which 313:8
not blind his s. with clay 539:8
not spoken of the s. 317:5
of a reasonable s. 388:41
offends me to the s. 434:15
of s. sincere 385:6
of the s. the body form..take 510:13
O my brave s. 567:3
one drop would save my s. 330:7
one impulse of your s. 489:27
one s...commit one..sin 364:1
our s. is escaped 399:32
overthrow of body and s. 109:22
palace of the S. 113:12
parting s. relies 230:9
peace to the s. of the man 16:4
perdition catch my s. 471:27
perplexed, labyrinthical s. 186:30
plucks the mortal s. 535:26
poor s. sat sighing 473:6
poor s. that thinks no..harm 80:8
poor s., the centre 488:20
pouring forth thy s. abroad 287:32
praise the Lord, O my s. 398:3
prepare thy s. for temptation 56:29
pressed down my s. 395:18
progress of a deathless s. 186:4
prophetic s. of the wide world 488:2
prophet of the s. 199:21
prospect of his s. 469:6
purest essence of a human s. 127:28
purest s. 125:6
roamed with my S. 381:2
roll from s. to s. 538:16
sang a kindred s. out 95:35
satisfieth the empty s. 398:15
save his s. alive 55:30
save my s., if I have a s. 8:20
scarce the s. of a louse 302:33
seized thy parting s. 165:31
shake our s. 506:19
shut not up my s. 393:19
sick in s. and body 249:6
sigh'd his s. 465:17
single s. does fence 332:7
slid into my s. 149:27
so full of care, my s. 80:17
so full of heaviness, O my s. 394:17
so longeth my s. 394:16
sooth'd his s. to pleasures 191:9
sought after my s. 397:11

Soul (*cont.*)

s. above buttons 154:14
s. and body part 166:15
s. and body rive not more 425:18
s. aspiring pants 355:17
s., be patient 80:18
s. had broken 317:17
s. helps flesh more 95:17
s...her generous aspirings 307:12
s. is dead that slumbers 317:5
s. is form 510:13
s. is in a ferment 284:18
s. is not more than the body 567:23
s. may not profit by 337:19
s. of Adonais 492:16
S. of all the worlds 574:26
s. of fire 279:5
s. of her beauty and love 497:26
s. of man is fed 334:3
s. of man is touched 331:2
s. of my s. 95:12
s. of Orpheus 341:19
s. of our grandam 484:22
s. of Rabelais 153:10
s. of Sir John Cheke 351:17
s. of the Age! 281:11
s. of the Angel 298:10
s. of the stout Apostle Paul 298:12
s. of the whole Past Time 126:27
s. of thy turtle-dove 396:28
s., remembering how 579:18
s.'s dark cottage 557:25
s.'s sincere desire 355:11
s. stands fast 524:22
S. that art the Eternity 575:21
S. that maketh all 199:1
S. that rises with us 576:9
s., thou hast much goods 61:52
s. to dare 416:17
s. to feel the flesh 83:13
s., uneasy, and confined 383:11
s. wears out the breast 119:5
stolen his s. away 549:21
strong is the s. 15:9
stumbling through my s. 227:36
sun of my s. 291:9
sweet and virtuous s. 245:14
swell the s. to rage 191:12
taught my s. to fancy aught 552:3
terror to the s. of Richard 476:38
that my s. may but ascend 330:9
their s. fainted 398:15
think then, my s. 186:12
thirst for that from the s. 280:21(-281)
this s. hath been alone 150:14
this s. to whom Luther 186:7
thou art a s. in bliss 454:14
thou free my s. 185:21
thoughtful S. to Solitude 205:8
though thy s. sail leagues 411:8
three books on the s. 90:35
thy rapt s. 341:9
thy s. and God 95:22
thy s. full in her hands 413:31
thy s. I know not from thy body 410:25
thy s. know change 95:36
thy s.'s flight 459:2
thy s. shall be required 61:53
thy s. the fixt foot 186:25
thy s. was like a star 577:15
tocsin of the s. 116:18
Tommy, 'ow's yer s.? 303:3
to remake the s. 96:16
to the lowly s. 291:14
try the s.'s strength 89:27
veil of the s. 522:7
visit the s. in sleep 495:18
wake the s. 381:6
wan s. in that golden air 411:21
war against the s. 69:49
what of s. was left 97:8
what s. was his 574:11
when your sickness is your s. 263:15
whiter s. than thine 308:2
whom my s. loveth 52:4
whom shall my s. believe? 95:20
whose s. is sense 186:25
whose s. was sad 222:27
why my s. was sad 544:1
why shrinks the s.? 1:22
windows to my s. 559:35

Soul (*cont.*)

wings the s...to the skies 195:15
with an old s. 119:20
with one long kiss my whole s. 529:22
with Psyche, my S. 381:2
wit its s. 151:14
wronged great s. 93:39
Soul-animating strains 580:17
Soul-making: vale of S. 290:20
Souls: all poor s. lost 92:7
all s. in trouble 329:5
all the s. that were were forfeit 461:29
amid men's s. 585:22
as we wish our s. to be 494:13
bane of the most generous s. 229:9
beyond the reaches of our s. 431:32(-432)
contented your s. 297:16
damp s. of housemaids 197:23
discharge their s. 193:30
drink to poor damned s. 297:5
for all sparrows' s. 502:20
hale s. out of men's bodies 468:19
harmony..in immortal s. 465:18
in..patience possess ye your s. 62:42
in s. a sympathy 163:48
instinct of all great s. 100:11
in the cure of s. 253:14
jealous s...not be answer'd 472:17
knead two virtuous s. 116:20
left your s. on earth 284:16
loud sang the s. 298:14
love and save their s. 89:33
men's defiled s. 508:15
mercy upon one of our s. 484:13
our lives, our s. 444:21
our s. as free 114:42
our s. exult 75:12
our s. have sight 576:19
our s. inspire 400:31
our s. were in our names 336:16
our s., whose faculties 330:28
our two s. stand up 88:19
our two s. therefore 186:25
our waking s. 185:7
play with s. 92:45
poor jewel of their s. 513:32
poor misguided s. 309:27
pure lovers' s. descend 536:2
see the s. we loved 536:18
Shepherd and Bishop of your s. 69:52
s. departed but the shadows 85:16
s. in heaven too? 284:16
S. in their degree 298:9
s. most fed with Shakespeare 141:30
s. mounting up to God 410:11
s. not lent in usury 336:45
s. of Christian peoples 140:2
s. of poets 287:1
s. of the brave 146:14
s. of the righteous 56:23
s. of those that die 316:27
s. of women 111:25
s. that have toil'd 541:3
such dear s. 474:22
sucks two s. 184:28
there be s. must be saved 471:13
they have no s. 148:10
thou lover of s. 56:27
through such s. alone 96:10
try men's s. 372:22
two s...in my breast 223:16
unto s. afar 88:25
vigorous s., high-cultured 123:7
warn th' immortal s. 331:3
where s. do couch 425:22
whilst our s. negotiate 184:31
Soul-sides: two s. 94:10
Sound: alien s. of melancholy 575:24
all is not s. 280:7
all the s. I heard 262:9
as the s. of lyres and flutes 374:11
born of murmuring s. 581:22
call him up the S. 363:3
deep s. strikes 113:25
doleful s. 562:11
full of s. and fury 461:4
hark, the glad s. 183:19
heal the blows of s. 251:10
hearest the s. thereof 63:7
heart as s. and free 247:1

Sound (cont.)
heart as s. as a bell 468:28
hear the lowest s. 455:22
he must s. of this and that 583:17
he sleeps as s. 402:24
however rude the s. 217:17
it may be a s. 114:5
measures of delightful s. 498:10
momentary as a s. 466:20
nor any s. or sight 523:24
nor sight nor s. 522:15
no s...of clashing wars 184:2
no s. of hammer 163:40
no s. unto the ear 86:32
not so s., and..sweet 442:25
o'er my ear like the sweet s. 481:30
other not very s. 506:4
same s. is in my ears 574:33
sighing s. 411:34
sleep not so s., as sweet 245:16
something direful in the s. 22:19
s. Conservative government 181:33
s. is forc'd 75:18
s. must seem an echo 382:32
s. of abundance of rain 48:4
s. of a trump 394:31
s. of a voice that is still 528:3
s. of his horn 229:16
s. of iron on stone 171:16
s. of Jesus' breath 74:13
s. of public scorn 349:20
s. of revelry by night 113:25
s. of the church-going bell 164:25
s. of the grinding 51:33
s. of those he wrought for 537:12
s., s. the clarion 357:22
s. the loud timbrel 357:17
s. the trumpets 191:3, 358:13
s. upon life's..slope 410:22
s. upon the bugle-horn 534:13
their s. is gone out 392:32
though the s. were parted 282:3
too full for s. 528:22
to whom no s. is dissonant 152:2
troubled s. of storms 18:24
where hath been no s. 253:28
whispering s. of the..colonnade 161:23
you would s. me 435:24
Sounded: all the trumpets s. 99:41
forward to be s. 434:2
Sounder: no s. piece of British manhood 126:3
Soundest: old lovers are s. 563:22
Sounding: as s. brass 66:44
no word however s. 514:5
s. generalities 142:25
s. labour-house 17:17
s. through the town 30:10
went s. on 574:15
Soundings: acquainted with the s. 290:7
Soundless-clapping host 545:2
Sounds: all your s. of woe 468:20
concord of sweet s. 465:20
her sights and s. 84:21
rural s...restore the tone 162:36
s. and sweet airs 480:5
s. of joyance 236:6
s...take care of themselves 129:17
s. will gather beauty 80:23
strange s. along the chancel 417:13
tempting s. I hear 78:3
well-tuned s. 486:14
Soup: let his s. get cold 249:18
s. he swallows 249:22
S. of the evening, beautiful S. 129:26
take the nasty s. away 249:18
Soup-and-fish: donning the s. 572:7
Soupe: je vis de bonne s. 353:16
Sour: in digestion s. 474:17
my life will be s. grapes 21:3
s. to them that lov'd him not sweet, s. 447:9
sweet, s. 255:3
Source: forget the s. 336:9
mighty s. of all things 503:2
pants its s. to mount 355:17
s. of all my bliss 225:9
s. of all our store 132:1
s...of all that's precious 512:29
s. of innocent merriment 220:3
s. of sympathetic tears 231:12
true s. of human offspring 347:26

Source (cont.)
variety's the s. of joy 215:19
Sour'd themselves to death 485:5
Sourest and most deadly hate 475:5
South: between the North and the S. 213:19
come, thou s. 52:8
fierce and fickle is the S. 538:20
full of the warm S. 287:24
good s. wind 148:28
hills look over on the S. 543:22
hills of the S. Country 42:3
I do but wanton in the S. 538:21
moon of beauty in the S. 538:21
Queen of the Sovereign S. 304:5
rosy is the S. 536:6
S. to the blind Horn's hate 298:28
Swallow, flying, flying S. 538:20
when the wind is in the s. 11:21
South Africa: trusting native races of S. 143:31
Southampton: weekly from S. 297:24
Southerly: when the wind is s. 433:20
Southern: bore me in the s. wild 76:13
on the s. side 94:32
to a boon s. country 18:31(-19)
wasps upon a s. wall 161:41
where S. vines are drest 241:9
South Kensington: Sloane Square and S. 219:11
Southron: matches of the S. folk 545:2
Southward dreams the sea 543:22
Southward-facing brow 18:16
Southwest-wind and the west-wind 521:30(-522)
Sovereign: bandy civilities with my S. 271:24
crosses from his s. hand 248:1
Magna Carta..will have no s. 148:2
most s. reason 434:14
Queen of the S. South 304:5
servants of the s. 26:22
s. cruelty 483:8
s. good of human nature 27:32
s. of sighs and groans 455:8
s. remedy to all diseases 109:22
s. sway..dissolv'd 190:28
s. (to the length of sixpence) 127:8
Subject and a S...different 135:28
trample on their s.'s head 475:10
welfare of our S. 389:14
what to be a s. 198:10
Sovereign'st thing on earth 438:35
Sovereigns: dead but sceptred s. 118:10
Sovereignty: to one..s. impute 189:3
top of s. 286:16, 460:8
wommen desyren to have s. 138:11
Sow: as you s...like to reap 111:2
in the morning s. thy seed 51:30
men that s. and reap 523:18
observeth the wind..not s. 51:29
right s. by the ear 242:23
s. an act 406:6
s. for him 580:6
s. som difficultee 138:3
still s. eats up all 281:22
they s. not 58:11
they that s. in tears 399:34
walk before thee like a s. 441:11
Sower went forth 79:6
Soweth: whatsoever a man s. 67:47
Sowing: reap our s. 335:10
Sown: nor was ever s. 548:14
reap where he hath s. 301:20
s. in corruption 67:14
a wonder wyde 138:15
they have s. the wind 55:46
where thou hast not s. 60:31
Sows: he s. hurry 515:1
Hope s...Love..never reap 410:33
s., and he shall not reap 522:7
s. and reaps a thousand kisses 158:1
Space: annihilate but s. and time 381:8
beyond s. and time 83:25
here is my s. 423:14
in a hollow rounded s. 311:17
king of infinite s. 433:12
nought the lettres s. 138:40
pathless realms of S. 218:12
s. for delight 522:7
Spaces: great open s. 331:13

Spacious: s. firmament 2:25
s. song 165:35
s. times of great Elizabeth 529:7
Spade: don't call me s. 520:22
entirely by the s. 339:2
fiddle, sir, and s. 419:18
loom—anvil—s. 307:17
nominate a s. a s. 281:3
poor crooked scythe and s. 501:5
S.! with which Wilkinson 581:5
truth calls a s. a 89:23
Spades: let s. be trumps! 385:16
s., the emblem 163:29
Spain: blood-red field of S. 241:9
devildoms of S. 539:18
galleons of S. 183:6
King of S. is dead 203:32
King of S.'s Beard 188:36
make castels than in S. 138:24
not into the hands of S. 540:1
not left to S. 539:19
Parma or S...dare to invade 198:11
slow old tunes of S. 333:18
smiled S.'s chivalry away 116:45
S. forming a head 235:22
Spake: at the last I s. 394:8
God s. once 395:24
God the word that s. it 197:35
if they s. worse 279:29
I s. as a child 66:46
I...s. nothing 394:8
never man s. like this 63:24
nought s. he to Lars Porsena 323:26
s. by the Prophets 390:21
s. on that ancient man 148:20
s. oo thing..thoghte another 137:27
upon this hint I s. 470:3
Spalpeen: ye s. 298:21
Span: eternity shut in a s. 166:6
Eve s. 11:18, 235:7
less than a s. 28:16
life's but a s. 471:9
Spangled: new s. ore 343:3
Spaniard: nor..behold with prejudice the..S. 86:27
Spaniards: S. seem wiser 27:12
thrash the S. too 188:35
Spaniel: hound or s. 453:30
s. fawning 449:29
Spaniel'd me at heels 425:17
Spaniels: well-bred s. 385:32
Spanish: hear a S. lady 12:1
I must learn S. 91:29
some are fond of S. wine 333:22
S. blades 477:7
S. or neats-leather 110:39
S. ships of war at sea 539:16
taken by a S. Ga-la-lee 30:23
tell her in S. 91:30
to God I speak S. 136:13
Spanking Jack 173:9
Span-new: spick and s. 110:32
Spare: advance! s. not! 262:3
not a friend to s. 201:23
original, s., strange 255:3
show how much he can s. 274:5
s. all I have 203:18
s. bed for my friends 377:29
s. me a little 394:11
s. my aching sight 229:25
s. that tree 358:21
s. the house of Pindarus 351:15
s. the poet 159:9
s. the rod 110:42
s., woodman, s. the beechen tree 122:8
that s. Cassius 448:27
Spared: author ever s. a brother 215:23
better s. a better man 441:1
s. and blest by time 114:22
Spares: fortune..s. neither man 217:13
never s. the child 253:3
thy hook s. the next swath 284:12
Spareth his rod 50:6
Spark: illustrious s. 160:38
nor human s. is left 381:27
shows a hasty s. 451:25
s. from Heaven 18:10, 12
s. of celestial fire 560:30
s. o' Nature's fire 105:24
vital s. of heav'nly flame 381:28
Sparkle: s. for ever 538:11

Sparkle (cont.)
s. in their skies 247:6
s. out among the fern 528:5
s. still..Promethean fire 455:23
Sparkled on the yellow field 534:4
Sparkles: anon it s. 311:16
new s. of her own 192:23
s. near the brim 113:23
Sparkling: disdain and scorn ride
s. 468:25
pair of his. eyes 218:25
stream of s. joy 173:34
Sparks: as the s. fly upward 48:50
like the s. of fire 246:23
s. among the stubble 56:24
s. blown out of a smithy 586:2
unnumber'd s. 449:30
Sparrer-grass: look like s. 238:11
Sparrow: brawling of a s. 586:7
fall of a s. 437:34
'I,' said the S. 369:18
my lady's s. 132:12
Philip S. 502:20
s. alight upon my shoulder 547:2
s...an house 397:5
s. fall 383:10
s...fly..into the hall 38:31(-39)
s.: that sitteth alone 398:1
Sparrows: five s. sold for two farthings 61:51
for all s.' souls 502:20
more value than many s. 58:54
team of s. 321:14
two s. sold for a farthing 58:52
when s. build 267:11
Spars: under the s. of which 247:16
Sparta: firm as S.'s king 188:33
Helen, S.'s queen 411:35
hounds of S. 467:20
Spartam nactus es 145:2
Spartan: out of the S. kind 467:20
remnant of our S. dead 115:46
Spartans: tell the S. 502:14
Spatter'd boots 163:20
Spattering: with s. noise rejected 349:22
Spawn: meanest s. of Hell 534:11
Spe: dubiae s. pendulus horae 257:11
Speak: all men..s. well of you 61:29
at midnight s. with the Sun 551:19
bondage..may not s. aloud 477:26
both of them s. of something 576:8
constantly s. the truth 389:53
could he s...not check 309:1
couldst thou s. 426:13
did he stop and s.? 93:23
difficult to s. 101:24
even whilst we s. 492:2
fear to s. for the fallen 320:14
grief that does not s. 460:20
heard Chapman s. out 288:19
hear them s. in our tongues 64:26
he could not s. to you 302:23
if any, s. 450:16
if they s. first 155:3
I never will s. word 474:1
I only s. right on 450:33
I s. as a fool 67:33
I will s. to thee 431:32
let him now s. 391:27
let not God s. with us 45:53
little..can I s. 469:45
live pure, s. true 530:4
losers..have leave to s. 144:30
might have been supposed to s. 116:35
mine to s...yours to hear 504:8
mouths, and s. not 399:4
murder..will s. 433:36
never s. well of one another 272:21
not as their friend..I s. 16:6
not care to s. ill of any man 276:25
not cease to s. 165:9
not permitted unto them to s. 67:2
one that can s. so well 334:28
one to s., and another to hear 547:3
only s. one language 182:19
province of knowledge to s. 251:22
ride, and s. the truth 117:3
slow to s. 69:30
s. after sentence? 269:30
s., and pause again 159:17
s. but one word 359:16

Speak (cont.)
s.; Caesar is turn'd 448:10
s., cousin 468:15
s. daggers to her 435:30
s. disrespectfully of the Equator 504:21
s. each other in passing 318:10
s. for himself 63:34
s. for yourself, John 316:5
s.; I'll go no further 432:6
s. in French 130:2
s. in public on the stage 202:16
s. less than thou knowest 452:25
s., Lord 47:6
s. low, if you s. love 468:11
s. low to me 87:37
s. more in a minute 478:6
s. no more 435:48
s. not when the people 419:16
s. of me as I am 474:2
s. one's mind..a pleasure 569:28
s., or die! 442:35
s. roughly 129:1
s. softly..carry a big stick 408:27
s. they through their throat 399:4
s. to Him thou 529:38
s. unto us smooth things 53:38
s. very well in the..Commons 182:47
s. what we feel 454:28
s. what you think to-day 200:40
s. when he is spoken to 515:16
s. when you're spoken to 131:26
s. ye comfortably to Jerusalem 54:8
that he can s. and flee 30:20
that it cannot s. 128:17
then, must you s. of one 474:2
thereof nedeth nat to s. 137:15
they..in the gate s. against me 396:18
those that are asleep to s. 52:20
though I s. with the tongues 66:44
to s., and to s. well 280:5
to whom you s., of whom you s. 7:5
trees to s. 459:24
we must s. by the card 437:12
we shal s. of thee 138:30
what should we s. of 429:31
when I s. unto them thereof 399:25
when I think, I must s. 428:5
when you s., sweet 485:27
women to s. in the church 67:3
Speaker: dull s...credited with..
virtues 243:17
no other s. of my..actions 447:11
Speakers: you imperfect s. 456:16
Speakest wiser than thou art ware 427:4
Speaking: and in my s. 6:10
heard for their much s. 58:3
in s. for myself 460:45
one way possible of s. truths 96:18
s. things which they ought not 68:49
s. trade 143:3
things for ever s. 574:30
thought him still s. 348:29
Speaks: Jesus s., and s. to thee 161:9
knows that he s. adequately 200:33
never s. well of me 155:22
s. all his words distinctly 204:33
s. small like a woman 465:27
when he s. the air..is still 443:7
when Love s. 455:22
Spear: bring me my s.! 75:16
ever put s. in the rest 328:24
fair Scotland's s. 418:35
his s., to equal which 344:24
idle s. and shield 343:12
Ithuriel with his s. 347:29
knappeth the s. in sunder 394:29
nor sword nor s. 161:4
scorn the s. 491:27
snatch'd the s. 418:11
unsteadfast footing of a s. 438:37
will like a dividing s. 15:21
with a burning s. 12:2
Spear-men: stubborn s. 418:34
Spears: sheen of their s. 118:37
slain with s. 538:26
s. into pruninghooks 52:31
threw down their s. 75:24(-76)
whose teeth are s. 395:18
Special: thy s. grace 389:34
Specialism: his s. is omniscience 188:10
Species: done in any one s. 154:38

Species (cont.)
female of the s. 296:13
not an individual, but a s. 204:17
not the individual, but the s. 278:15
Specimen: give a s. of both 182:47
only s. of Burke 239:11
Speckled Vanity 343:19
Spectacle: checkered s. 325:25
great s. of human happiness 505:19
s. unto the world 66:25
Spectacles: her s. lay on her..
knees 120:20
s. of books 194:6
s. on nose 427:21
without a pair of s. 250:6
Spectator of mankind 2:5
Spectators: actors or s. 491:25
pleasure to the s. 326:1
Spectatress of the mischief 412:10
Spectem: te s. 547:18
Spectre: my S. around me 75:19
off shot the s.-bark 149:14
what a dancing s. 336:29
Spectre-thin: pale, and s. 287:26
Speculation: no s. in those eyes 459:19
Specus: Idola S. 28:6
Speech: better to deal by s. 26:40
blossom into s. 90:12
cast away my s. 482:18
Consul's s. was low 323:16
eyesight and s. they wrought 522:7
freedom of s. 408:25
gave man s. and s. created
thought 497:5
gave them shape and s. 524:22
his ready s. 416:18
his s. is a burning fire 522:7
his s. was coarse 300:18
horrid s. 433:32
I am slow of s. 45:39
in the seventh s. 56:45
killed a calf..make a s. 21:12
knavish s. 436:10
let thy s. be short 57:7
measured s. 24:21
mighty likely s. 214:17
my s. distorting 81:8
neither s. nor language 392:32
neither s. nor word 81:2
nor power of s. 450:33
on him no s. 308:16
perfect plainness of s. 20:4
rude am I in my s. 469:45
speak the s...trippingly 434:15
s. is human 126:33
S. is of Time 127:22
s. is shallow as Time 126:1
S. is silvern 127:22
s. is the small change 337:37
spoke the s. of the Gaels 140:14
stately s. 580:12
strange powers of s. 150:12
sweet music of s. 164:23
their sole s. 17:24
thy s. bewrayeth thee 60:47
thy s. is comely 52:5
true use of s. 226:26
under all s...a silence 126:1
wed itself with S. 532:18
whose s...from her thought 411:26
your s. be alway with grace 68:33
Speeches: easy s. 141:18
gets his s. by it 408:13
Mr. Brougham's s. 240:7
to men's charitable s. 28:15
Speechless: Passion s. lies 189:20
Speed: all the s. desire can make 292:19
all thy winged s. 365:16
at his bidding s. 351:21
be wise with s. 586:23
courage, breath, and s. 416:13
deliberate s. 544:14
forgetting the bright s. 17:28(-18)
our good s. 170:24
our safety is in our s. 200:35
outstrip thy skiey s. 496:10
quench its s. 93:20
so spire if thou may s. 235:7
s. glum heroes 415:12
s. his plough 135:16
s. the going guest 386:6

Speed (cont.)
teach me s. 447:40
to s. today 510:16
Speeds: your wit..s. too fast 455:4
Speir nae mair 108:29
Spell: breathèd s. 343:21
first s. Man 404:14
s. better than they pronounce 550:14
s. it with a 'V' or a 'W'? 179:13
s. of far Arabia 171:3
went thy s. through him 411:11
who lies beneath your s.? 254:14
Speller: fancy of the s. 179:13
wuss s. I know of 560:15
Spells: books..talismans and s. 163:51
dealer in magic and s. 222:16
Spem nos vetat incohare longam 258:9
Spend: how they will s. half of it 23:9
lightly..so wol we s. 137:43
s. a little less 513:35
s. on our horses 413:5
s...on our libraries 413:5
s. that shortness basely 440:32
to s., and to lend 82:27
to s., to give 510:16
whatever you have, s. less 275:5
what we yet may s. 206:8
Spendest: whatsoever thou s. more 61:42
Spending: getting and s. 582:18
riches are for s. 26:10
Spenlow: Mr. S...Mr. Jorkins 174:34
Spens: ballad of Sir Patrick S. 150:30
to Sir Patrick S. 31:24
Spenser: gentle S. fondly led 309:10
little nearer S. 36:21
lodge thee by Chaucer, or S. 281:11
renowned S. 36:21
sage and serious poet S. 352:10
sweet S. 579:20
Spent: all passion s. 351:7
all's s. 459:3
being s...worst times..succeed 247:10
feels himself s. 162:25
house and land..s. 209:19
might be better s. 510:16
night is far s. 66:13
s. all that she had 60:60
s. all the money 274:33
s. lights quiver 15:24
s. with due..thrift 374:20
that we s., we had 10:5
what wee s., wee had 11:17
Sperabitur: quae non s. hora 256:27
Speranza: lasciate ogni s. 168:17
Sperat infestis 259:7
Spes: occidit s. omnis 260:23
Spet: you s. on me 463:22
Spewed up a good lump 194:18
Sphere: all quit their s. 383:13
cheering the elevated s. 102:11
gird the s. 348:30
I am the owner of the s. 199:2
my heaven's extremest s. 558:1
s. for Shelley's genius 19:13
s. of our sorrow 499:4
storm-troubled s. 83:7
that silver s. 498:5
their motion in one s. 440:36
they the s. 185:1
year and a s. 199:18
Sphere-born harmonious sisters 351:9
Sphere-descended maid 154:3
Spheres: abject from the s. 561:12
all the tuned s. 426:1
driv'n by the s. 552:13
like the harmonious s. 319:1
maintain the music of the s. 86:32
moving as the restless S. 330:28
rose to touch the s. 89:6
seems to shake the s. 191:1
s. of action 9:25, 313:21
s. of influence 9:25
start from their s. 432:9
through all s. 410:16
ye crystal s. 343:17
you ever-moving s. 330:7
Spherical: his body is perfectly s. 311:11
Sphery: higher than the s. chime 341:5
Sphinx: Minx, or a S. 178:15
subtle as S. 455:22

Spice: s. of life 163:4
s. of wit 516:12
Spiced: dish more sharply s. 375:6
s. dainties 285:25
Spices: mountain of s. 52:25
no S. wanting 246:27
s. thereof may flow out 52:8
woodbine s. 536:9
Spick and span-new 110:32
Spicy: her s. nest 125:11
India's s. shores 159:7
s. nut-brown ale 342:4
s. shore of Araby 347:1
Spider: sheet of s.'s web 237:15
smallest s.'s web 477:7
s.'s touch 383:17
s. to a fly 264:23
Spiders: s., flies, or ants..in amber 27:47
weaving s. 467:1
Spider-web: experience..huge s. 268:12
Spies: God's s. 454:19
they come not single s. 436:25
ye are s. 45:20
Spill: all germens s. 453:5
Spills itself 436:18
Spilt: as water s. 47:35
blood that she has s. 158:30
fearing to be s. 436:18
Spin: go s., you jade 420:26
great world s. for ever 534:36
neither do they s. 58:13
passions s. the plot 336:30
sit by the fire and s. 366:14
Spinach: world of gammon and s. 174:32
Spindle: his s. shank 106:5
Spindle-guide: coupler-flange to s. 299:3
Spinis de pluribus una 257:21
Spinners: long-legg'd s. 467:1
long s.' legs 477:7
Spins: s. like a fretful midge 410:10
s. the heavy world 263:18
Spinsters and the knitters 483:5
Spire: so s. if thou may spede 235:7
Spires: all her reeling s. 322:21
clustered s. of Frederick 568:11
dim-discover'd s. 153:25
dreaming s. 18:22
hundred s. 528:24
Oxford..excepting its s. 363:22
s. whose 'silent fingers' 574:21
through all the s. of form 199:17
what s., what farms? 263:14
ye distant s. 230:23
Spirit: after the S. the things of the S. 65:52
all, save the s. of man 113:2
at times her s. sank 535:5
before that s. die 516:16
be thou a s. of health 431:32
be thou, S. fierce, my s. 496:11
better lodging for his S. 375:26
blessed are the poor in s. 57:39
blithe s. 498:1
bound in the s. 65:10
'Brutus' will start a s. 448:23
Caesar's s., ranging 450:12
clear s. doth raise 342:20
come, Thou Holy S. 132:1
constrain thy unbound s. 160:34
curbing his lavish s. 456:9
dedicated s. 579:22
delighted s...in fiery floods 462:9
do the same things by the S. 111:1
every pure and wise s. 200:41
eviller s. than you 506:19
expense of s. 488:11
extravagant and erring s. 430:19
fervent in s. 66:2
fiercest S. that fought 345:15
finer s. of all knowledge 583:3
flesh lusteth against the S. 67:45
follow your s. 443:27
fruit of the S. 67:46
fruits of the S. 388:54
gentlier on the s. lies 535:14
genuine s. of localism 78:22
give me a s. 135:19
God is a S. 63:13
gray s. yearning 541:1
healthful S. of thy grace 388:30
her cabin'd ample S. 17:15

Spirit (cont.)
her s.'s vestal grace 375:4
his s. died 251:29
history of the human s. 20:8
holding the eternal s. 447:33
holy-day rejoicing s. 307:17
holy s. of discipline 56:20
holy s. of man 522:6
hope divine, informs my s. 574:2
humble, tranquil s. 170:18
I am thy father's s. 432:8
I commend my s. 62:51, 393:27
immortal s. grows 579:9
increase in thy holy S. 391:20
in s. and in truth 63:13
in the S. on the Lord's day 70:23
in the strength of thy s. 524:3
invisible s. of wine 471:21
least erected S. 345:9
lost in the same s. 567:15
make thou my s. pure 540:6
meek and quiet s. 70:1
motions of his s. 465:20
my s. can cheer 314:18
my s. hath rejoiced 61:13
my s. is too deeply laden 499:2
my s. like a charmed bark 493:20
my s. seal 573:6
my s. upon all flesh 55:52
my s. which so long darkened 495:3
needs s. lack all life 96:26
nimble, stirring, s. 455:28
no more s. in her 47:42
no s. can walk abroad 430:20
not given us the s. of fear 68:56
not of the letter, but..s. 67:22
not received the s. of bondage 65:53
of kin to God by his s. 25:26
of s. so still 470:1
one fair s. 114:25
O s. of love! 481:30
pard-like S. 492:2
pipe to the s. 287:8
present in s. 66:26
pure s. shall flow 492:5
rarer s. never 425:32
renew a right s. 395:9
rest, perturbed s. 432:31
same S. 66:43
shy s. in my heart 582:10
sing it with a s. 583:6
something to the s. of liberty 100:25
so much the s. calms 115:28
speaks to my s. of thee 119:10
s. all compact of fire 488:26
S. and the bride 72:10
s., antithetically mixt 113:40
s. bloweth 16:29
s. from on high 149:22
s. giveth life 67:22
s., I love thee 498:16
s. indeed is willing 60:43
s. in my feet 494:7
s. in the woods 578:8
S. of adoption 65:53
S. of Beauty 494:4
S. of Delight 498:11
s. of divination 64:55
s. of divinest Liberty 151:21
s. of Elijah..on Elisha 48:17
S. of God moved 44:1
s. of heaviness 55:4
s. of my dream 117:12
S. of Night 495:21
s. of romance is dead 294:16
s. of self-sacrifice 574:1
s. of the chainless mind 114:33
s. of the Graeme 23:21
s. of the Lord bloweth 54:10
S. of the Lord God is upon me 55:2
s. of the Lord shall rest 53:17
s. of the time 447:40
S. of the Universe 575:21
s. of truth, unity 390:25
s. of wisdom 53:17
s. of youth in everything 487:28
s. passed before my face 48:48
s. shall return unto God 51:33
s. that always denies 223:17
s. that knows no..solitude 574:26
s. that quickeneth 63:23

INDEX

Spirit (*cont.*)
S. that strove for truth 498:20
s. when her s. looked through 410:26
s. within me constraineth me 49:13
S. without spot 492:12
S. with S. can meet 529:38
s., yet a woman 580:20
strengthened..by his S. 67:53
strength of s. 448:36
strike with our s.'s knife 492:6
sweet S., comfort me 247:18
take not thy holy S. from me 395:9
that quick s...in Antony 448:13
there's a wicked s. 3:18
thou the anointing S. 400:31
thy free S. 395:9
thy s. walks abroad 452:1
too much s. to be..at ease 384:32
troubled s. 395:10
unsphere the s. of Plato 341:17
vexation of s. 50:62
whence th' enlighten'd s. sees 552:6
when..this body did contain a s. 440:38
wild S., which art moving 496:4
wounded s. who can bear? 50:21
yet a s. still 580:21
Spiriting: do my s. gently 479:25
Spiritless: so faint, so s. 441:9
s. outcast 124:9
Spirits: all s. are enslaved which 497:6
beauteous s. 123:27
black s. and white 338:18, 459:34
by our own s...deified 580:7
cheerer of his s. 559:15
day of s. 551:20
drooping s. can raise 158:18
flat unraised s. 443:3
her wanton s. 481:26
how bright these glorious s. 562:10
I can call s. from the..deep 439:42
inland petty s. muster 442:21
isolate pure s. 88:20
keeps up a wife's s. 214:20
like two s...suggest me still 488:18
looked the s. up and down 298:30
maketh his angels s. 398:8
master s. of this age 450:5
no revenue..but thy good s. 434:24
other s. there are 288:22
our s. rush'd together 534:17
red s. and gray 338:18, 459:34
rule our s. from their urns 118:10
seven other s. more wicked 59:19
s. are not finely touch'd 461:16
S. masculine 349:23
s. of just men 350:36
s. of those who were homing 236:29
s. passing through the streets 496:2
s. that fell with Lucifer 330:1
s. that know all..consequences 460:34
s. that tend on mortal thoughts 457:3
s. when they please 344:29
stories from the land of s. 151:26
their s. are in Heaven 582:13
weak ships and a s. steer 523:19
where'er your s. dwell 81:21
wonders at our quaint s. 466:43
Spirit-small hand 90:7
Spirit-stirring drum 472:3
Spiritual: Germany .. my 's. home' 233:21
grand and s. passage 289:26
inward and s. grace 391:13
millions of s. creatures 347:24
s. is stronger than..material 201:4
s. pastors and masters 391:7
s. repasts..before Milton 306:8
s. wickedness in high places 68:11
Spirituality about the face 188:9
Spiritualized by a Methodist preacher 558:17
Spiritus: *dum s. hos regit artus* 554:19
s. intus alit 554:30
veni, Sancte S. 310:19
Spiro: *quod s. et placeo* 260:19
Spit: slovenly will s. 135:20
s. in my face 439:20
s. out thy phlegm 243:29
s. upon him 475:15

Spit (*cont.*)
s. upon my curious floor 245:12
to s. there glorifies 91:26
Spite: civic slander and the s. 533:20
cursed s. 432:32
fortune's dearest s. 486:32
grow wise for s. 520:55
in s. of sorrow 341:31
what I do to s. the world 458:36
Splash: s. at a ten-league canvas 303:20
s.l s.l along the sea 419:10
Splashing: s. and paddling 88:11
s. the wintry mould 585:17
Spleen: excite your languid s. 220:28
in a s., unfolds..heaven 466:20
so much..mirth, and s. 2:8
Spleeny Lutheran 446:20
Splendid: age of s. discontent 355:12
how s. in the morning 208:11
how s. stars 208:19
our s. isolation 227:39
s. and a happy land 225:6
s. and sterile Dolores 522:24
s., a star 97:13
s. for the day 336:11
s. in ashes 87:20
S. Shilling 378:17
s. with swords 523:2
vision s...his way attended 576:9
Splendidly: s. isolated in Europe 210:12
s. null 535:35
Splendour: children of s. and flame 561:12
faded s. wan 347:32
guilty s. 163:7
its silvery s. pant with bliss 286:18
its s., soon or late 94:26
life, and s., and joy 102:11
more-than-oriental-s. 304:15
not in lone s. 288:17
pavilioned in s. 228:20
s. among shadows 498:20
s. and speed of thy feet 521:30
s. falls on castle walls 538:14
s. in the grass 576:20
s. of a sudden thought 90:40
s. of its prime 493:27
steep in his first s. 582:14
Splendours, and Glooms 491:21
Splenetive: not s. and rash 437:23
Spliced in the humdrum way 83:6
Split: 'E won't s. on a pal 304:53
ice did s. 148:27
make all s. 466:25
s. her in twain 540:1
s. the ears of the groundlings 434:15
s. the shroud 97:13
your tongue shall be s. 369:2
Splutters as it dies 264:5
Spohr and Beethoven 220:5
Spoil: come and s. the fun 130:10
earthquake's s. 113:24
sign'd in thy s. 450:9
s. of me 440:12
s. the child 110:42
when they divide the s. 53:14
Spoiled: find the pagan—s. 587:17
happy Greek..was not s. 281:26
nearly s. ta Flood 23:27
s. the Egyptians 45:49
Spoilers: hands of the s. 46:45
s. of the symmetry of shelves 306:21
Spoils: glories, triumphs, s. 450:2
s. of time 230:5
s. that his own hand spread 523:16
s. the rod 253:3
s. were fairly sold 323:21
to the victor..the s. 329:16
treasons, stratagems, and s. 465:20
Spoke: all that's s. is marred 474:3
check'd him while he s. 309:1
less he s. 403:22
proud word you never s. 309:4
s. among your wheels 37:34
s., and loos'd our heart 16:22
s. in her cheeks 186:13
s. the speech of the Gaels 140:14
s. what she should not 460:26
words once s. 180:7
Spoken: done and not have s. on't 424:18
glorious things of thee are s. 364:16

Spoken (*cont.*)
God hath s. in his holiness 395:23
had Sav'narola s. less 39:22
never have s. yet 141:28
never s. to each other 100:8
speak when you're s. to 131:26
the Lord hath not s. by me 48:14
when the lips have s. 494:20
word fitly s. 50:34
Sponge: married to a s. 463:13
Spongy April 480:6
Sponsors: mountains are our s. 309:5
Spontaneous: s. overflow of powerful feelings 583:4
s. wisdom 581:16
Spoon: dish ran away with the s. 367:1
runcible s. 312:3
worth a silver s. 5:17
Spoonful for each man of us 372:17
Spoons: counted our s. 200:1
guard our s. 324:19
let us count our s. 271:10
locks up its s. 490:23
out again with my silver s. 376:14
Sport: all the s. is stale 293:19
animals never kill for s. 212:4
Caesar bleed in s. 450:1
detested s...another's pain 163:16
ended his s. with Tess 237:14
kill us for their s. 453:40
make s. for our neighbours 23:5
see the children s. 576:19
spend the time in s. 217:19
s. for Jove 471:6
s. of kings 169:12, 506:13, 518:7
s. of winds 346:26
s. that wrinkled Care derides 341:19
s. with Amaryllis 342:20
strays with willing s. 484:35
to s. would be as tedious 438:31
Sported on the green 507:3
Sporting: idly s. 81:8
s. the lion ramped 347:15
Sports: Christmas brought his s. 418:24
excel in athletic s. 182:19
my joy of youthful s. 114:32
play her cruel s. 510:10
s. of love 282:5
Sportsman: fit to be called a s. 518:8
Sporus: can S. feel? 385:30
let S. tremble 385:30
Spot: angry s...on Caesar's brow 448:25
Homocea touches the s. 7:1
leave this barren s. 122:8
lovely woman in a rural s. 266:4
no s. in thee 52:6
not a s. or stain 214:18
ordains for each one s. 302:13
out, damned s. 460:24
reach the S. where I made one 207:30, 32
round about the s. 543:4
Spirit without s. 492:12
s. that's always barred 220:6
this dim s. 339:28
with a s. I damn him 451:4
Spots: in their gold coats s. 466:34
leopard (change) his s. 55:18
myriad s. of light 585:11
s. and clouds in the sun 109:15
s. in your feasts 70:18
s. quadrangular 163:29
sunny s. of greenery 151:32
Spotted with foam 16:4
Spousal: sung s. 348:38
Spouse: Adam from his fair s. 347:25
Daughter of the Vine to S. 206:23
John Gilpin's s. said 159:32
my sister, my s. 52:7
show me, dear Christ, thy s. 185:20
shuts the s. Christ home 255:6
S. and Brother 543:19
s. of the worm 122:37
Spouseless Adriatic 114:3
Spout: hurricanoes, s. 453:5
Spouts: at his trunk s. out 348:26
great fish s. music 266:13
Sprang: I s. to the stirrup 92:22
Sprat: Jack S. could eat no fat 367:10
Sprawled through the ooze 504:13
Spray: fowlys singis on the s. 187:5

Spray (cont.)
on yon bloomy s. 351:12
this is a s. 93:32
toss in the s. 15:23
wet with Channel s. 296:15
wither'd s. 18:10
Spread: masters, s. yourselves 466:24
not good except it be s. 27:10
s. my dreams 584:17
when the evening is s. out 197:15
Sprechen ist silbern 127:22
Spree: out on the s. 296:27
Sprig: hardly bears a s. of bays 521:15
Sprightly: first s. running 191:34
Sprig-muslin drest 236:31
Spring: absent in the s. 487:28
all s. through till the s. be done 524:13
all the breathing S. 153:21
and then came S. 207:21
apparell'd like the s. 474:5
as short a S. 246:3
azure sister of the s. 496:4
Baby S. 375:8
bloom in the s. 220:15
blossom by blossom the s. 521:30(–522)
blue sky of s. 4:19
braver thence doth s. 186:23
bring in the S. 247:11
can S. be far behind? 496:11
chilly finger'd s. 285:7
come, gentle S. 546:10
commonly called the s. 164:27
darling of the S. 573:20
deep of the Pierian s. 189:13
direful s. of woes 384:20
dream of S. 152:17
ever-returning s. 568:8
falsehood has a perennial s. 100:7
floures ginnen for to s. 138:16
fresh s., and summer 494:19
fresh s. the herald 509:6
from haunted s. 343:22
full of the s. 524:11
gay s. leaping 80:10
happy as birds in the s. 76:4
haunt clear s. 346:19
he passed the s. 334:5
his lady in the s. 81:8
hounds of s. 521:30
if on a S. night 213:2
in any s. 410:24
in the Fire of S. 205:14, 15
in the S. a young man's fancy 534:15
in the s. time 428:30
labour's dull, Lethaean s. 16:5
lap of the new come s. 475:30
latter s. 438:12
lead the Surrey s. 299:24
less quick to s. again 18:30
liv'd light in the s. 15:13
lovers in the s. 140:16
lovers love the s. 428:30
made a lasting s. 446:18
Main S., Mogul 83:2
meadow-gale of s. 150:3
melted into s. 83:14
messenger of S. 509:3
middle summer's s. 466:36
more business in s. 550:31
murmurs of the S. 404:23
no second s. 9:8, 378:15
no S., nor Summer beauty 184:16
our Sister the S. 42:4
perennial s. of all prodigality 101:17
pilgrim steps of s. 80:25
s. and foison of the year 487:4
S. comes slowly 150:19
s. goeth all in white 82:7
s. is come home 544:8
s. of business 28:12
s. of light 148:12
s. of love 149:26, 484:33
s. rain 197:27
s. shut up 52:7
s., the sweet s. 361:6
s. Thou up within my heart 565:8
s. thy lover 524:15
s. up into beauty 313:22
summer's eve–or s. 114:5
sweet s., full of sweet days 245:13
taste not the Pierian s. 382:22

Spring (cont.)
that S. should vanish 207:24
thine health shall s. forth 54:37
this night of S. 213:2
thou wilt s. to me 530:16
thy lover the s. 524:15
waters of the crisped s. 170:22
what hast thou found in the s. 524:11
where are the songs of S.? 284:13
white foam of the S. 561:8
winds of S. 497:3
Winter..changed to S. 497:20
year's at the s. 94:40
Springboard: not a seat but a s. 144:13
Springe: woodcock to mine own s. 437:38
Springes to catch woodcocks 431:27
Springeth and flourisheth 328:15
Springs: all my fresh s. 397:14
back to their s. 316:14
faintly, gentle s. 279:28
fifty s. are little room 262:10
four wanton s. 474:16
from seventy s. a score 262:10
from the people..all s. 182:43
hope s. eternal 383:11
no bitter s. 295:8
s. into the rivers 398:8
s. of the sea 49:22
s. o' that countrie 32:11
s. renewed by flowing 123:18
strays of ruined s. 523:21
three beauteous s. 487:29
where s. not fail 254:29
Springtide: her old s. 269:25
Springtime: coming ere the S. 264:22
in s. from the Cuckoo-bird 581:1
merry S.'s Harbinger 38:8
Sprinkled: sea was s. 582:17
Sprinkles: Grace s. another's.. face 308:18
Sprinkling it with fountain water 305:18
Sprite: angelic s. 185:12
his clear S. yet reigns 491:15
that orchard s. 249:8
Sprites: one of s. and goblins 485:10
sweet s., the burden bear 479:28
Sprouting: housemaids s. de- spondently 197:23
Spruce affectation 455:29
Sprung: newly s. in June 107:14
s. of Earth's first blood 577:3
up they s. upon the wing 344:27
Sprush: cock it fu' s. 250:18
Spue thee out of my mouth 70:34
Spun: s. like whipping tops 249:15
s. my last thread 185:24
Spur: envy's a sharper s. 215:23
fame is the s. 342:20
I have no s. to prick 457:9
s. my dull revenge 436:15
s. of all great minds 135:25
s. of industry 205:4
s. you to soar 524:33
Spurgeon: haberdasher to Mr. S. 112:18
Spurn: s. her bounded reign 278:34
s. not the nobly born 219:1
Spurned: s. in vain 377:4
you s. me such a day 463:22
Spurns that patient merit..takes 434:4
Spurred boldly on 190:32
Spurring: bloody with s. 474:29
horse came s. in 322:22
Spurs: now s. the lated traveller 459:10
s. too fast betimes 474:21
win his s. 195:24
Spurt of a lighted match 93:22
Spy: ever you did s. 264:23
letters for a s. 301:18
sent to s. out the land 46:13
s. in thy face 184:19
Squad: awkward s. 108:40
Squadron: 'arf a s. swimmin' 296:21
Squadrons: to fainting s. 1:10
Squamous, omn.potent 83:26
Squander: do not s. time 211:15
Squandering wealth 190:24
Square: broke a British s. 296:23
cannot meet you on the s. 306:17
damned, thick, s. book 223:5
glimmering s. 538:19
got into a s. hole 505:24

Square (cont.)
I have not kept the s. 424:10
not work by s. or line 159:23
Regiment's in 'ollow s. 295:20
s., and above the board 234:11
s. deal 409:2, 6
s. person..round hole 505:24
s. with Genesis 89:37
Squares: about the flowering s. 533:24
Square-turn'd joints 418:8
Squash: s. is before 'tis a peascod 482:17
this s., this gentleman 485:9
Squat: s. like a toad 347:28
urban, s. 84:13
Squatting on the coals 297:5
Squeak: hear the pips s. 216:6
naturally as pigs s. 110:4
sheeted dead did s. 430:14
Squeaking: shrieking and s. 94:33
some s. Cleopatra 426:4
Squealing: s. of the wry-neck'd fife 463:36
s. out for quarter 302:14
Squeers: Mr. Wackford S.'s Aca- demy 176:38
Squeeze: s. a right-hand foot 131:25
s. her until you can hear 216:6
Squeezing: in the s. of a lemon 227:5
Squinch-owl: say ter der s. 238:14
Squire: as low as ever was S. Wid- drington 192:19
bless the s. 174:8
many a s. 34:8
S., and Lady Susan 236:8
s. seemed struck 141:26
Squires: gallant s. of Kent 322:22
last sad s. 141:27
Squirrel: joiner s. 477:7
mountain and the s. 199:18
Staat: die Sonne..in meinem S. 415:22
Stab: s. my spirit broad awake 516:16
s. our very vitals 388:2
Stabbed: feeble God has s. me 214:6
if Caesar had s. their mothers 448:29
Stability: party of order or s. 338:28
s. or enlargement of the lan- guage 277:22
Stable: all about the courtly s. 343:25
commonwealth is..s. 101:18
good horse in the s. 226:30
hard by his own s. 151:10
nothing s. in the world 289:22
son of a livery s. keeper 584:14
s. for his steed 387:21
s. his steed 419:17
s. your stirks in the shealings 419:29
Stable-place sufficed 409:21
Stables are the real centre 489:30
Stablish: s., continue our march 17:21
s. dangerous constancy 185:29
s. me according to thy word 399:22
s. me with thy free Spirit 395:9
'**Stablished** its borders 298:10
Stabs: every word s. 468:13
Stacher through 104:33
Stack: salt-caked smoke s. 333:21
to the s...stoutly struts 341:32
Stacks: ready in s. 222:17
Stad in perplexyte 583:26
Staff: my s. of faith 405:9
palmer's walking s. 475:10
stay and the s. 52:33
thou trustest upon the s. 48:33
thy rod and s. 421:1
thy rod and thy s. 393:10
very s. of my age 463:30
your s. in your hand 45:47
Stag: runnable s. 169:15
s. at eve 416:10
Stage: all the world's a s. 427:21
daily s. of duty 292:1
dies for love, but on the s. 193:22
drown the s. with tears 433:32
frets his hour upon the s. 461:4
glory of the Attic s. 16:2
he flits across the s. 182:2
last s. of all 16:10
little man there upon the s. 204:32
on the s. again 95:32
on the s. he was natural 225:32
played upon a s. now 484:10

INDEX

Stage (cont.)
quite off this s. 386:37
shake a s. 281:15
speak in public on the s. 202:16
s. but echoes back 279:1
s.'s jewel 280:10
s. so gloom'd 537:39
s. where every man must play 462:31
this green plot. .our s. 467:2
this great s. of fools 454:12
to the well-trod s. 342:7
two hours' traffic of our s. 476:45
vet'ran on the s. 279:9
we've still our s. 89:23
when learning. .first rear'd the S. 278:34
wonder of our s. 281:11
Stage-coach: faster than a s. 226:42
on the outside of a s. 239:19
Stages: where'er his s. may have been 499:13
Stagger: s. like a drunken man 398:18
s. through to meet. .Dad 104:33
Stagger'd that stout Stagirite 308:4
Staggering on to her goal 16:11
Stagirite: stagger'd that stout S. 308:4
Stagirites: filled with S. 357:19
Stagnant: fen of s. waters 577:14
Stagnated: well-nigh s. 410:17
Stain: felt a s. like a wound 102:13
free from s. 323:7
leave not a s. in thine honour 57:8
many a s., soil'd 165:7
not a spot or a s. 214:18
s. both moon and sun 486:31
suns of the world may s. 486:29
with never a s. 493:1
without fault or s. 81:22
world's slow s. 492:7
Stained: s. his name 104:20
s. the water clear 76:9
Stainless gentleman 531:20
Stains: s. and splendid dyes 285:19
s. the white radiance 492:15
such s. there are 308:18
Stair: as I was going up the s. 335:12
by a winding s. 26:28
led her up the s. 297:19
Stairs: rat-riddled s. 93:19
see through a flight o' s. 179:16
up s. and down s. 366:23
Stairway: fine broad s. at the beginning 144:20
s. which leads to a dark gulf 144:20
Stake: I am tied to the s. 453:33
parboiled head upon a s. 355:21
sense of the deep s. they have 101:13
still hae a s. 104:5
thumbscrew and the s. 539:19
tied me to a s. 461:8
we are at the s. 451:7
Stakes: barred with s. 334:5
he s. his quiver 321:14
Stale: all the sport is s. 293:19
bound in s. parchment 337:13
poor I am s. 429:32
s. her infinite variety 424:9
weary, s., flat 430:33
Staled are my thoughts 232:15
Stalk: half asleep as they s. 236:14
He hangeth on a s. 585:9
s. is wither'd dry 32:17
thou s. o' cart-hemp 104:22
wither'd to a s. 32:17
Stalked off reluctant 73:13
Stalking-horse: his folly like a s. 428:39
truth. .a s. to error 78:12
Stalky: your Uncle S. 304:46
Stall: forth, beste, out of thy s. 136:20
Stalled ox and hatred 50:12
Stamford: bullocks at S. fair 442:7
Stamford-town: Burleigh-house by S. 535:10
Stammering: lisping s. tongue 161:8
Stamp: but the guinea's s. 105:30
penny-postage-s. 128:19
poor man is Christ's s. 244:4
s. me back to common Earth 207:17
s. of his lowly origin 169:5
Stamped with the image of the king 530:21
Stamper of the Skies 585:10

Stamping: Queen. .went s. about 129:13
Stamps: s. God's own name 162:23
s. o'er his Head 206:1, 2
Stand: above the mast did s. 149:4
bids nor sit nor s. 95:15
but the time. .men s. upon 449:33
by uniting we s. 180:5
cannot always s. upright 389:30
do I s. and stare? 93:26
farewell, and s. fast 439:4
fit to s. by Caesar 471:15
having done all, to s. 68:11
here I s., your slave 453:6
his fav'rite s. 164:11
if a' will not s.? 468:37
incessantly s. on your head 128:28
in this we s. or fall 348:12
I s. alone and think 289:6
I s. and look at them 567:20
I s. at the door 70:35
I s. in pause 435:32
I will s. and mark 540:16
must s. the course 453:33
nowhere to s. but on 292:15
obliged to s. 193:30
on what he intended to s. 181:27
our two souls s. up 88:19
risen, and s. upright 392:37
scarce could s. 189:16
see the Christ s. 96:25
s. a man a cheese 142:1
s. and love in 88:20
s. at the latter day 49:6
s. beside my knee 23:29
s. by the fire and stink 452:24
s. by your side 302:18
s. close around 308:22
s. in awe, and sin not 391:52
s. not upon the order 459:23
s. on either hand 323:19
s. still, and I will read to thee 185:30
s. still, true poet 95:1
s. still you. .spheres 330:7
s. to in a month 478:6
s. up and end you 263:15
s. up and take the war 296:19
s. up for Jesus 194:31
s. up now, Tomlinson 302:21
s. upon my kingdom 474:34
strengthen such as do s. 389:1
sun, s. thou still 46:42
that house cannot s. 60:54
time to s. and stare 169:24
waters s. in the hills 308:8
we s. to bless Thee 198:16
why s. ye here all the day 60:6
Standard: float that s. sheet 234:13
mind's the s. 562:2
your glorious s. launch 123:10
Standest: place whereon thou s. 45:34
s. meekly by 365:10
Standeth: here she s. 29:24(-30)
lo! He s. 543:19
so s. the Lord round 399:33
thinketh he s. 66:38
Standfast: Mr. S. 99:38
Standing: as cheap sitting as s. 520:11
extoll'd for s. still 162:19
God were s. there 213:2
in s. water 482:17
instead of a s. revenue 101:8
Jesus, thou art s. 264:12
keep you s. at that door 410:3
s. at ease in Nature 566:26
s. for some false. .shore 18:20
s. is slippery 26:24
s. long an oak 282:1
s. on earth 348:23
s., with reluctant feet 316:34
wilderness a s. water 398:20
Stands: coward s. aside 320:12
keeper s. up 263:6
print it as it s. 268:18
s. about the woodland ride 262:10
s. ready to smite once 342:29
s. Scotland where it did? 460:19
s. the Church clock? 84:15
their eternal s. 265:22
what s. if Freedom fall? 296:20
while s. the Coliseum 114:21
who he s. still withal 428:9

Stanhope's pencil 587:15
Stank of Logic 363:20
Stanley: approbation from Sir Hubert S. 359:20
here S. meets 322:9
on, S., on! 418:32
Stans pede in uno 261:12
Stanza: who pens a s. 385:21
Staple of his argument 387:6, 455:24
Star: across the reflex of a s. 575:25
Adonais, like a s. 492:16
against the morning s. 493:25
bid haste the evening s. 348:38
bright and morning s. 72:10
bright morning s. 343:8
bright northern s. 318:25
bright Occidental s. 43:24
bright s., would I were steadfast 288:17 ← !
catch a falling s. 186:16
constant as the northern s. 449:30 ← !
curb a runaway young s. 119:15
dim soul of a s. 525:14
disposition to the charge of a s. 452:19
each, in his separate s. 303:21
Earth is but a s. 208:10
eastern s. 106:30
evening s., Love's harbinger 349:26
every wandering s. 269:28
eve's one s. 286:2
fair as a s. 580:18
first s. shivers 208:6
glittering like the morning s. 102:11
grapples with his evil s. 533:1
great s. early droop'd 568:8
guiding-s. of a whole. .nation 359:23
heav'n's youngest teemed s. 343:25
hitch your wagon to a s. 201:14
if their s. is a world 93:35
incredible s. 141:1 ?
infect to the north s. 468:13
inquisition of each s. 545:10
Johnny-the-bright-s. 402:25
knock at as s. 246:20
light of the morning s. 75:14
lights the evening s. 122:1
like a falling s. 345:12
like a sinking s. 541:1
loftiest s. of unascended heaven 497:12
love a bright particular s. 423:2
moist s. . .sick. .to doomsday 430:15
moth for the s. 499:4
named a s. 95:1
name of the s. . . .Wormwood 71:10
name to every fixed s. 454:32
never s. was lost 97:21
new Messiah by the s. 192:28
O eastern s.! 426:13
O morning s. 586:5
one bright s. 149:10
one large s. 336:9
one particular beauteous s. 286:18
one s. differeth from another s. 67:13
our life's S. 576:9
out of thy s. 432:43
Polar s. of poetry 289:15
ran against a shooting s. 508:1
right for the Polar S. 17:28
seen his s. in the east 57:23
some fostering s. 561:10
splendid, a s. 97:13
S. for every State 572:1
s. nor sun shall waken 523:24
s. of my fate 119:9
s. of peace return 123:12
s. of stars 173:36
s. or two beside 140:23
s. to every wandering bark 488:7
s. to guide the humble 327:3
s. to steer her by 334:10
stay the morning-s. 151:28
sunset and evening s. 528:22
takes the s.'s height 525:16
that s. and garter 23:16
there was a s. danced 468:16 ??
thou lingering s. 107:4
thy soul was like a s. 577:15
twinkle, little s. 527:10
unfolding s. 462:22 ~?
vague unpunctual s. 84:10 ~?
without troubling of a s. 545:5
Star-captains: young s. 208:7

INDEX

Star-Chamber matter 465:26
Star-cross'd lovers 476:44
Stare: all the world would s. 160:8
  do I stand and s.? 93:26
  made Quintilian s. 351:17
  stony British s. 536:5
  time to stand and s. 169:24
  up-on the ground I see thee s. 138:5
Stared: s. into the sky 249:16
  s., with his foot on the prey 538:2
Staring: they stand s. 393:6
Star-inwrought 495:22
Stark: or Molly S.'s a widow 511:15
  s. insensibility 270:2
Star-led wizards 343:10
Starless: stand in s. nights 193:30
Starlight: by s. and by candlelight 549:2
  came, by the s. 92:10
  into the frosty s. 17:28
  there was nae s. 32:11
Star-like: from s. eyes 124:25
  s. sparkle 247:6
Starling: 'can't get out,' said the s. 512:25
Starlit: by the s. fences 263:20
Starry: led the s. host 347:19
  s. paladin 96:30
  s. skies 119:1
  s. stranger 166:1
Stars: all Danaë to the s. 539:2
  all the s. looked down 140:20
  all the western s. 541:3
  all ye s. and light 291:27
  amid a crowd of s. 586:21
  ask of the s. in motion 545:1
  as s. look on the sea 322:8
  as the s. come out 16:4
  beauty of a thousand s. 330:6
  between me and the s. 579:10
  blesses his s. 1:15
  blind with s. 249:16
  branch-charmèd by the earnest s. 286:8
  buttoned it with s. 251:2
→   but to the s. are known 16:14
  calculate the s. 348:30
  certain s. shot madly 466:38
  close up the s. 340:9
  continuous as the s. 577:6
  crowned with the s. 548:13
  crown of twelve s. 71:16
  cut him out in little s. 478:20
  Cyclopean arches at the s. 141:2
  doubt that the s. are fire 432:42
  falling s. are shooting 118:8
  far beyond the s. 552:1
  fleet of s. 208:7
  forgetting those good s. 140:26
  give away their motion to the s. 151:1
  glows in the s. 383:19
  her eyes as s. of twilight 580:19
  how splendid s. 208:19
  inauspicious s. 478:44
  in his right hand seven s. 70:27
  in the shining of the s. 531:26
  in the s. the glory 380:6
  journey-work of the s. 567:19
  Jove and my s. be praised 483:20
  kinship with the s. 336:20
  lady, the s. are falling 140:26
  like s. on the sea 118:37
  look at the s.! 255:5
  made the s. also 44:5
  moon and the s...ordained 392:9
  moon, or the s. 51:33
  morning s. sang 49:20
  new-bathed s. 17:28(-18)
  night of the large few s. 567:16
  nor asks of God, but of her s. 384:31
  not in our s. 448:22
  not the s...s. came otherwise 90:13
  number of the s. 400:21
  one sees..s. 310:1
  opposition of the s. 332:6
  Owl looked up to the S. 311:24
  preserve the s. from wrong 573:31
  puts the S. to Flight 205:4
  quenchless s.! 355:16
  risen s. and the fallen 521:30(-522)
  same, bright, patient s. 286:14
  scatter'd into flight the S. 205:5
  sentinel s. set their watch 123:3

Stars (cont.)
  seven s. and the solar year 199:2
  she forgot the s. 286:23
  shine aloft like s. 574:28
  shooting-s. attend thee 246:23
  silent s. go by 84:24
  some. .looking at the s. 569:37
  s. and sunbeams know 17:24
  s. and the winds 521:30(-522)
  s...are my children 290:12
  s. are old 527:11
  S. are Setting 206:20
  s. are shining bright 494:7
  s. be blown about 586:2
  s. began to blink 578:28
  s. came out 539:21
  s. hide their..heads 346:29
  s. in her hair 410:7
  s. in their calm 15:17
  s. in their courses 46:48
  s. in their stations set 269:28
  s. move still 330:7
  s. of heaven fell 71:1
  s. of midnight 581:22
  s. of the summer night 318:4
  s. on Campden Hill 141:16
  s. peep behind her 492:29
  s. rush out 149:14
  s.' tennis-balls 563:20
  s. that have a different birth 495:19
  s., that in earth's firmament 316:23
  s. that round her burn 2:27
  s...the brain of heaven 336:17
  s. threw down their spears 75:24(-76)
  s. to set 241:14
  s. with deep amaze 343:14
  s. without a name 288:8
  strives to touch the s. 510:24
  sun, moon, and s., brother 78:24
  Syrian s. look down 17:9
  tales of ships and s. 208:9
  tempt not the s. 209:23
  thy two eyes, like s. 432:9
  train of s. 241:22
  troops of s. 151:29
  two s. keep not their motion 440:36
  under the passing s. 585:22
  wandering s. 70:20
  when s. are in the quiet skies 322:8
  with s. to see 515:27
  you chaste s. 473:11
  you s. that reigned 330:9
Star-scattered: Guests S. 207:30
Star-shine at night 516:2
Star-showers: light dissolved in s. 498:22
Star-spangled banner 292:11
Start: cannot once s. me 461:3
  get the s. of this. .world 448:21
  lose, and s. again 297:11
  s. and tremble under her feet 536:15
  s. awa sae hasty 107:9
  s. from their spheres 432:9
  s. not so wildly from my affair 435:20
  s. some game 240:9
  s. their working lives 296:32
  s. the world along 583:6
Started: men s. at the intelligence 508:11
  s. like a guilty thing 430:18
Starting aside like a broken bow 396:36
Starting-post: serves him as a s. 289:26
Startle: makes thee s. 107:10
  not s. or amaze 289:25
  s. the dull night 341:31
  to haunt, to s., and waylay 580:19
Startles at destruction 1:22
Starts: at which he s. and wakes 477:7
  everything by s. 190:22
  pecks and s. 546:26
  s. for the Dawn of Nothing 206:20
  think by fits and s. 263:34
  up he s. discover'd 347:29
Starve: if any one hinders our coming s. 294:36
  let his wife s. 490:15
  let not poor Nelly s. 136:8
  let the poor..s. at door 245:12
  s. abroad 192:28
  s. for want of impudence 193:21
  s. with nothing 463:5
  swear, fool, or s. 194:27
Starved: because they s. at home 192:28

Starved (cont.)
  s., feasted, despaired 97:28
  s. lips in the gloam 286:36
Star-y-pointing pyramid 351:8
State: all were for the s. 323:21
  arguments of s. 483:19
  Atlas of the S. 161:40
  because of the s. he was in 339:13
  begins his s. 341:33
  burden on the reeling s. 159:26
  by the s. licensed 73:28(-74)
  canopies of costly s. 441:41
  cipher in the s. 415:17
  complicated s. of mind 220:26
  do my duty in that s. of life 391:9
  done the s. some service 474:2
  error..rush into the s. 465:3
  falling with a falling S. 381:7
  for worldly s. 575:9
  founding a firm s. 332:12
  free church in a free s. 134:3
  from thy s. mine never. .parted 349:18
  glories of our blood and s. 501:5
  health of the whole s. 431:21
  hides from himself its s. 279:7
  his s. empties itself 465:21
  his S. is Kingly 351:21
  in a parlous s. 427:26
  in sober s. 387:8
  in that s. I came, return 552:7
  in the youth of a s. arms 27:36
  in this s. she gallops 477:7
  labours of a servile s. 117:24
  landmarks in the s. 100:10
  life's middle s. 164:12
  maintain the s. of the world 57:13
  middle s. 383:22
  mock the air with idle s. 229:20
  my glories and my s. depose 475:20
  my single s. of man 456:24
  my s. is well 482:24
  my s. like to the lark 486:24
  no assistant for a s. 432:45
  obscure sequestered s. 96:16
  O Ship of S.! 316:1
  our s. cannot be sever'd 349:19
  pillar of s. 345:24
  quit thy s. 244:5
  rose of the fair s. 434:14
  rotten in the s. of Denmark 432:5
  ruin of the S. 73:20
  scoffing his s. 475:7
  servants of the..s. 26:22
  Star for every S. 572:1
  s. in wonted manner keep 279:31
  s. of man 446:24, 449:5, 456:24
  s. of wild alarm 220:7
  S.'s mellow forms 231:30
  S.'s pattern-man 363:26
  s.'s whole thunder 386:21
  S. which dwarfs its men 339:1
  s. without the means of. .change 102:6
  strange eruption to our s. 430:12
  to ruin or to rule the s. 190:16
  traduc'd the s. 474:2
  vassal s. of Hitler's Empire 144:6
  Venice sate in s. 114:2
  whole machinery of the S. 85:1
  whole s. of Christ's church 390:24
  world of pomp and s. 37:13
  worth of a S. 338:32
State-House: Boston S. 251:16
Stateliness of the former 154:13
Stately: full of s. views 296:30
  grow great and s. 515:23
  rather tall and s. 8:17
  s. homes of England 241:12
  s. ships are twirled 249:15
  very s. palace 99:9
Statement: unmoved that s. hears 221:37
Statements: put God in his s. 566:21
  s. was interesting, but tough 550:9
States: indestructible S. 136:15
  many goodly s. 288:19
  no more s'ave S. 136:14
  s...have their growth 309:19
  s. unborn 450:1
  these United S. 508:10
  Union of these S. 568:7
Statesman: chemist, fiddler, s. 190:22
  English s. cried 251:29

[932]

Statesman (*cont.*)
s., yet friend to truth! 385:6
too nice for a s. 225:27
Statesmen: like great S...betray 215:2
s. at her council met 539:12
Station: private s. 215:31
woman's noblest s. is retreat 322:4
Stations: know our proper s. 174:8
stars in their s. set 269:28
Statistical Christ 370:14
Stato: in libero S. 134:3
Statuaries: head which s. loved 325:14
Statue: beauty she was s. cold 208:5
Pompey's s. 450:31
s. to him under the gallows 505:14
under the s. 523:4
where the s. stood of Newton 579:19
Statues: like sepulchral s. lay 184:31
s. all arow 208:5
s. on the terraces 296:30
Stature: increased in wisdom and s. 61:22
of a tall s. 332:23
one cubit unto his s. 58:12
s. of my soul 336:22
to s. of the gods 336:1
Status quo: restored the s. 511:8
Staunch and strong 315:29
Stave: Death will listen to your s. 494:9
Staves: comest to me with s. 47:24
Stay: as hard to s. 536:27
asking people to s. with him 20:26
can't s. dying here all night 500:5
can't you s.? 551:14
hearts to s. 111:15
I still will s. with thee 478:44
let us s. rather on earth 88:20
must you s.? 551:14
no longer s. with you 10:21
not making a s. 246:23
on it may s. his eye 244:15
O s., O s...youth! 29:24(–30)
says I must not s. 547:21
short time to s. as you 246:3
s. a falling empire 161:39
s. a little..end the sooner 26:7
s. and hear 482:28
s., and run again 333:1
s. and the staff 52:33
s. and think of nought 487:7
s. at home, my heart 317:18
s. for me 425:22
s. for me there 292:19
s. me with flagons 51:45
s. not for th'other pin 244:6
s., s. 246:2
's.,' the maiden said 316:20
s. the morning-star 151:28
s., you imperfect speakers 456:16
we wish 'em to s. 213:11
whole s. of bread and..water 52:33
will not s. 194:22
will you not s.? 249:17
without thee here to s. 349:30
with thee to go is to s. here 349:30
you may s. yet here a while 245:20
Stay-at-Home: sweet S. 169:25
Stayed: while he s. with us..s. in mid-passage 525:2
Stays: Dante never s. too long 325:23
enduring to us 183:5
their white it s. for ever 183:11
Time s., *we* go 183:15
wears the s. 537:4
Steadfast: by its own weight made s. 155:19
s. of thought 502:17
would I were s. as thou art 288:17
Steadfastness and careful truth 295:6
Steadied: my preudunt course is s. 319:22
Steadier: I s. step 147:14
Steadily: saw life s. 16:2
s. cantering through 303:17
Steadiness under fire 305:1
Steady: one thought more s. 210:3
slow and s. wins the race 315:4
s., boys, s. 213:10
s. of heart 417:9
s. the Buffs 304:42
Steal: cunningly did s. away 244:20
damned good to s. from 212:19
maiden..s. after it 356:23

Steal (*cont.*)
silently s. away 316:10
s. a few hours from the night 357:1
s. away their brains 471:22
'S.!' foh! 465:32
s. from all I may be 114:26
s. from the world 386:27
s. her soul away 202:4
s. my Basil-pot 286:24
s. one poor farthing 364:1
s. out of your company 468:40
s.! to be sure they may 499:23
s. us from ourselves 191:22
then s. away 33:14
they s. my thunder 172:15
thou shalt not s. 147:2, 390:15
Stealing: my hands from picking and s. 391:8
not hanged for s. horses 234:5
s. and giving odour 481:30
sullied with the crime of s. 550:27
Steals: s. a goose 10:12
s. on the ear 264:9
s. something from the thief 470:6
s. the just's umbrella 79:7
s. your whole estate 214:19
who s. my purse s. trash 471:30
Stealth: do a good action by s. 307:28
do good by s. 386:20
lusty s. of nature 452:14
Stealthily: s. and perpetually 81:15
s., like a parson's damn 237:2
Stealthy School of Criticism 411:39
Steam: exceptin' always S. 299:3
forget the snorting s. 359:2
s. of rich distill'd perfumes 340:27
s. spoils romance 299:7
Steam-engine: s. in trousers 504:33
traces the s...back 180:19
Steamer from Harwich 219:10
Steamers: all you Big S. 294:34
coffee on board s. 542:12
great s., white and gold 297:24
Steed: farewell the neighing s. 472:3
fleetest s. 324:7
he purchased a s. 311:5
he was a noble s. 118:13
his s. was the best 418:15
on her milk-white s. 32:8
on my pacing s. 286:31
our s. the leg 429:3
sell my goodly s. 29:24(–30)
soon I'll mount my s. 228:12
stable for his s. 387:21
s. that knows his rider 113:22
s. threatens s. 444:6
s. to battle driven 122:18
thou'rt sold, my Arab s.! 365:16
Steeds: brought them their s. 417:3
fiery-footed s. 478:17
fleet s. that follow 418:22
his s. to water at those springs 429:25
reinless s. 411:15
their s. were white as snow 324:12
Steel: again in complete s. 431:32(–432)
all shod with s. 575:23
clad in complete s. 340:22
foeman bares his s. 221:33
foemen worthy of their s. 416:27
girdle me with s. 329:2
give them the cold s. 14:22
gloves of s. 417:4
hoops of s. 431:25
hurricane of s. 23:20
lift shrewd s. 475:1
long divorce of s. 446:13
more than complete s. 7:7, 331:9
nor s., nor poison 459:4
numbed sense to s. it 289:8
pinion which impell'd the s. 117:25
rattle of new-drawn s. 296:1
shot and s. 23:21
s. my soldiers' hearts 444:24
though lock'd up in s. 445:30
tipped with s. 414:4
with his brandish'd s. 456:5
Steel-true and blade-straight 516:6
Steenie lecturing on the turpitude 419:26
Steep: from th'Ismenian s. 350:17
in baths to s. him 280:10
monstrous s. of Montmorenci 288:10

Steep (*cont.*)
no towers along the s. 123:11
o'er bog or s. 346:14
on th'Indian s. 340:6
perilous in s. places 80:19
s. and thorny way to heaven 431:23
s. and trifid God 543:15
s. my senses in forgetfulness 441:41
s. of Delphos leaving 343:21
Sunium's marbled s. 116:3
violently down a s. place 58:36
wild and stormy s. 122:7
Steep-down gulfs 473:32
Steeped me in poverty 472:34
Steeple: church and no s.! 521:26
on it put a s. 42:19
shadow of the s. 146:32
Steeples: drench'd our s. 453:5
in s. far and near 262:21
pews and s. 140:2
still the s. hum 263:2
Steeply the thickets 82:9
Steer: cannot s. a middle course 334:21
fancy never taught to s. 164:33
happily to s. 384:15
in his verse can gently s. 193:19
star to s. her by 334:10
s. clear of permanent alliance 560:29
s. humanity 425:32
s. their courses 110:22
s. too nigh the sands 190:13
Steered us through 148:27
Steersman: Saint Michael was the s. 7:14
Steersmen: grow good s. 336:46
Stella's feet may kiss 502:4
Stelle: muove il sole e l'altre s. 169:2
riveder le s. 168:24
salire alle s. 168:25
Stelled: quench'd the s. fires 453:34
Stellenbosch: for fear o' S. 302:5
Stem: out of the s. of Jesse 53:17
Stemmed the rude storm 117:24
Stemming it with hearts 448:19
Stenches: two and seventy s. 150:28
Step: every s. exampled by the first pace 481:5
him one s. below 481:5
if a s. should sound 523:14
light of s. and heart was she 171:6
marriage is a s. so grave 514:28
mind the music and the s. 33:6
noting my s. in bliss 81:6
now s. I forth 455:19
one s. enough for me 364:10
s., a blow 573:7
s. is short from the Sublime 228:8
s. so active 308:17
to s. aside is human 104:7
Stephen: King S. was a worthy 471:11
on the feast of S. 361:19
Stephen Sly 478:46
Stepmother: stony-hearted s. 172:18
Stepped: in blood s. in so far 459:25
she s. to him 29:24
Stepping: s. fearless 35:5
s. where his comrade stood 418:34
Stepping-stones of their dead selves 532:1
Steps: Age, with stealing s. 552:15
ask the number of the s. 269:18
beware of desp'rate s. 160:40
brushing with hasty s. 230:11
by due s. aspire 339:29
grace was in all her s. 348:36
hear not my s. 458:1
his very s. have left a trace 114:34
in his master's s. 361:24
knowledge advances by s. 324:20
on whose last s. I climb 494:18
same s. as the author 289:34
s. almost as silent 579:6
s. of the Sun 76:7
s. solemn, mournful, and slow 568:24
s. were higher 193:41
thy s. retrace 221:29
to support uneasy s. 344:24
to these dark s. 350:20
wandering s. and slow 349:31
with how sad s., O Moon 501:24
with pilgrim s. 350:15

Sterile: bugloss paints the s. soil 165:17
splendid and s. Dolores 522:24
Sterility: convey s. 452:29
Sterling: if my word be s. yet 475:25
Stern: Caledonial s. and wild 417:22
his glance was s. and high 323:4
lantern on the s. 152:24
magnificently s. array 113:35
s. to inflict 508:5
s. to view 225:1
Sterner: rather speak of s. days 144:7
s. stuff 450:20
Sternest: nature's s. painter 117:26
s. good-night 458:3
s. knight 328:24
Stern-faced: two s. men 252:26
Sternhold: hail S., then 162:30
Steward: unjust s. 62:20
Stewards: s. of their excellence 487:25
s. of the mysteries of God 66:24
Stewed: young healthy child..s. 520:3
Stewer: Bill Brewer, Jan S. 33:1
Stick: carry a big s. 408:27
do roses s. like burrs? 97:11
fell like the s. 373:2
instead of a s. 110:3
I shall s. 462:23
liftin'..on wid the s. 229:15
scratched with a s. 295:16
s. and a string 277:13
s. close to your desks 221:18
s. more close 302:17
s. on conversation's burrs 250:31
s. to your party 181:16
Stickest: thou s. a dagger in me 464:10
Sticketh closer than a brother 50:22
Sticking: ay s. in a tree 420:1
s. in a big mud hole 210:14
Sticking-place: to the s. 457:13
Stickit: a 's. minister' 419:27
Sticks: axis..s. out visibly 251:17
brittle s. of thorn 247:17
like s. of sealing-wax 174:11
pick up s. 368:6
Stiff: s. in opinions 190:22
s. twin compasses 186:25
s. upper lip 131:31
very s. and proud 131:12
Stiffen the sinews 443:24
Stiffnecked people 46:5
Stiffness: too much s. in refusing 388:3
Stifle: opinion is endeavour-
ing to s. 338:27
Stifled: s. drowsy..grief 150:31
voice of reason is s. 103:20
Stifles..domestic happiness 290:12
Stifling it..an evil still 338:27
Stile: against a crooked s. 369:3
hent the s.-a 485:21
sitting on the s., Mary 73:10
Stiles: lame dogs over s. 293:11
Still: as patient and as s. 502:17
be s., my soul, be s. 263:16
be s. then, and know 394:29
bloweth and is s. 16:29
Caesar, now be s. 452:7
calm and s. 547:7
he came all so s. 7:16
he won't sit s. 249:24
how s. we see thee lie 84:24
in your chamber, and be s. 391:52
move s., s. so 485:27
my lute, be s. 583:21
of spirit so s. and quiet 470:1
sit s. for once at table 249:23
stand s. and I will read 185:30
stand s., true poet 95:1
stand s. you..spheres 330:7
s. and awful red 149:25
s. as the hour-glass 410:29
s. glides the Stream 573:26
s., oh s., beside me 88:17
s. point of the turning world 197:6
s. small voice 48:8
s. sow eats up all the draff 281:22
s. the enemy 392:8
sun, stand thou s. 46:42
that mighty heart is lying s.! 582:14
thou smilest and art s. 17:23
Still-born Silence! 208:20
Still-discordant..multitude 441:8

Stille: ein Talent sich in der S. 224:4
Stillest streams 164:5
Stillicide: lone cave's s. 236:10
nor S. a crime 514:39
Stillness: far in the s. a cat 241:27
horrid s. 191:31
modest s. and humility 443:24
soft s. and the night 465:18
solemn s. 229:28
s. of the central sea 533:27
world in solemn s. lay 421:10
Still-soliciting eye 452:11
Still-vexed Bermoothes 479:24
Stimulate the phagocytes 489:19
Sting: death, where is thy s.? 67:18
each s. that bids nor sit 95:15
it is a s. 377:3
thy s. is not so sharp 427:22
where is death's s.? 322:2
Sting-a-ling-a-ling: thy s. 8:19
Stingeth like an adder 50:32
Stings: armed in their s. 443:10
endure the s. 158:12
nasty long s. 34:15
s. in their tails 71:13
s. you for your pains 248:10
stinks and s. 385:31
wanton s...of the sense 461:20
Stink: stand by the fire and s. 452:24
Stinking: black, s., fume thereof 267:30
s. savour 51:23
Stinks: several s. 150:28
s. and stings 385:31
Stinte: can nat s. of singing 137:44
Stinted: not to be s. in pleasure 570:30
s. and said 'Ay' 477:4
Stinteth first whan she biginneth 138:34
Stir: above the smoke and s. 339:28
dream all night without a s. 286:8
how should we s. ourselves 12:6
let me not s. you up 450:32
make the greatest s. 210:9
never the least s. 171:15
none of your people s. me 467:16
no s. in the air 507:24
no s. of air was there 286:3
now s. the fire 163:21
see the s. of the great Babel 163:23
speech to s. men's blood 450:33
s. it and stump it 222:4
s. up, we beseech thee 389:50
s. without great argument 436:17
Stirred: Cumner cowslips never s. 18:28
s. up with envy and revenge 344:6
we have not s. 95:6
Stirring: bees are s. 152:17
nimble, s., spirit 455:28
not a creature was s. 356:1
s. dull roots 197:27
s. thrills the air 236:6
s. times we live in 236:41
while Mrs. Bennet was s. the fire 22:31
Stirrup: betwixt the s. and the
ground 121:25
his foot upon the s. 171:16
I sprang to the s. 92:22
one foot already in the s. 134:20
Stirs: blood more s. 438:37
feeling s. again 15:6
never s. abroad at all 500:44
s. this mortal frame 152:3
Stitch: s.! s.! s.! 253:22
Stitching: our s. and unstitching 584:2
Stithy: foul as Vulcan's s. 435:1
Stock: his mind into the common s. 223:3
how his s. goes on 151:7
how his s. went on 507:19
I am but a barren s. 197:36
public s. of harmless pleasure 278:7
s., stone, or other homely pedigree 190:12
Stock-dove: I heard a S. 578:11
Stocking: spoil'd silk s. 244:5
s. all the day 224:11
Stockings: black worsted s. 325:28
did you change your s.? 22:18
his s. fouled 432:35
silk s...of your actresses 270:10
s. were hung by the chimney 356:1
yellow s. 483:19, 21
Stockish: nought so s., hard 465:20

Stock-jobbers: leathern ears of s. 162:20
Stocks: ascribe unto stones and s. 56:28
feet they hurt in the s. 398:12
s. in fragrant blow 18:26
s. were sold 41:8
worshipped s. and stones 351:20
Stoic: doctors of the S. fur 340:35
every S. was a S. 200:45
for the s.'s pride 383:22
Stoicism: the Romans call it s. 1:16
Stole: as they s. betwixt me 88:17
from a better man I s. 516:11
I wonder where you s. 'em 521:10
lady s. it from me 141:10
s. a piece of beef 369:1
s. in and out 517:12
s. those tarts 129:27, 368:15
they knew 'e s. 303:23
Stolen: had I s. the whole 516:11
heart of a maiden..s. 356:23
he that has s. the treasure 155:14
not wanting what is s. 472:2
receiver of s. goods 277:16
s. his wits away 171:3
s. my soul away 549:21
s. the scraps 455:26
s. sweets are always sweeter 266:1
s. sweets are best 144:31
s. waters are sweet 49:53
that horses may not be s. 234:5
Stoles: nice white s. 34:9
Stomach: healthy s...conserva-
tive 111:37
heart and s. of a king 198:11
marches on its s. 12:10
my s. is not good 516:21
no s. for such meat 183:9
no s. to this fight 444:28
proud look and a high s. 397:34
s. for them all 473:15
unbounded s. 447:6
wine for thy s.'s sake 68:50
Stomach-aches: tuned like fifty s. 174:9
Stomacher: crimson s. 246:4
her s. was gold 298:20
red s. 184:27
Stomachs: march on their s. 422:16
Stone: as a huge s. 580:9
at his heels a s. 436:20
be s. no more 485:38
blossoming in s. 316:20
bows down to wood and s. 240:18
brass, nor s., nor earth 487:13
choosing each s. 332:12
cold as any s. 443:21
conscious s. to beauty grew 199:23
fling but a s. 231:27
flung the S. 205:4
for a s. of stumbling 53:13
give him a s. 58:21
give him a white s. 70:31
Jackson standing like a s. wall 39:2
just like pieces of s. 311:23
last to be a precious s. 247:7
lay s. on s. 17:1
let him first cast a s. at her 63:26
my heart is turned to s. 472:25
never lifted up a single s. 577:23
nickname..the heaviest s. 240:3
not a s. tell where I lie 386:27
one s. the more swings 300:5
on the s. at my door 35:10
put in a heart o' s. 32:5
raise the s...find me 9:12
rests nigh this s. 8:13
sat on a s. 148:20
seeth the s. taken away 64:4
some fallen Runic s. 16:6
sound of iron on s. 171:16
stock, s., or other..pedigree 190:12
s. like a great millstone 71:33
s. that is rolling 550:5
s. the twenty-first 90:14
s. walls do not a prison make 319:7
s. where Alexander's ashes lay 33:12
s. which the builders refused 399:11
that especial stone and s. 77:30
themselves as s. 487:24
this gray s. 376:20
this precious s. 474:22
this sword of this s. 328:3

Stone (*cont.*)

thy foot against a s. 397:19
turn but a s. 545:1
two things stand like s. 227:34
underneath this s. doth lie 280:11
under this s., Reader 202:11
untroubled heart of s. 122:32
virtue is like a rich s. 25:27
water like a s. 409:20
wept over her, carved in s. 535:41
we raised not a s. 572:14
with a s. at the gate 387:2
without a s., a name 381:36
without gout or s. 387:2
writing upon s. 309:6

Stoned: she be s. to death 74:13

Stones: ascribe unto s. and stocks 56:28
croys of latoun, ful of s. 137:22
dirty s. of Venice 293:10
enamell'd s. 484:35
fang'd with murderous s. 150:28
far beyond..philosophers' s. 109:22
five smooth s. out of the brook 47:23
his name on the Abbey-s. 92:38
inestimable s. 476:14
in piled s. 351:8
move the s. of Rome 450:34
no s. in heaven? 473:27
on thy cold gray s. 528:3
over the s. 365:6
rocks and s. and trees 573:6
sermons in s. 426:30
soften'd the s. 473:6
spares these s. 488:29
s. and clouts make martyrs 87:5
s. have been known to move 459:24
s. of Law 77:15
s. of Winchester 297:20
s. of worth..thinly placed 487:1
s. Thy pillow 506:8
s. would..cry out 62:39
there in the s. was his earth 334:5
throweth them against the s. 400:6
throw s. at him 489:22
very s. prate 458:1
we've the s. of Snowdon 293:10
worshipped stocks and s. 351:20
you are not s., but men 450:26
you blocks, you s. 448:8

Stonest them which are sent 60:20
Stonewall Jackson riding ahead 568:13
Stony limits 477:17
Stood: freely they s. who s. 346:21
in uffish thought he s. 129:39(−130)
long I s. there 380:24
since he s. for England 140:25
s. against the wall 537:38
s. against the world 450:23
s. awhile in thought 129:39(−130)
s. erect..and prayed 92:26
s. from everlasting 548:14
s. that night against my fire 454:13
s. them on their heads 36:5
they s., and earth's foundations 264:4
we two s. there 90:8
where I had s. before 494:18
your sheaves s. round 45:13

Stooks: stood amid the s. 253:20
Stool: sit upon a s. 176:2
table, s. and chair 74:8
Stools: Latin names for..s. 105:23
necessity invented s. 162:34
push us from our s. 459:17
Stoop: cloud may s. 539:1
do I s.? 93:26
heaven itself would s. 341:5
if I s. 94:26
make their sire s. 475:12
sometimes s. and sigh 171:21
s. to any other law 135:19
s. to rise 334:19
therefore does not s. 575:9
Stooped: s. the tempest of the Gods 331:2
then s. the Lord 298:16
Stooping: God s. shows sufficient 96:10
s. against the wind 411:15
s. down, as needs he must 159:41
s. through a fleecy cloud 341:14
Stoops: she s. to conquer 226:41
to rise, it s. 90:41

Stoops (*cont.*)

when lovely woman s. 197:32, 226:18
Stop: Caesar..s. a hole 437:18
did he s. and speak to you? 93:23
first cries out s. thief 155:14
know when to s. raking 409:3
let no man s. to plunder 324:14
let's s. somebody 242:30
oaten s. 153:23
so plain a s. 441:8
sound what s. she please 434:26
s. and consider! 288:10
s., Christian passer-by 151:16
s. everyone from doing it 243:1
s.!—for thy tread 113:24
s. his mouth with a kiss 468:15
s.; look; listen 551:4
s. thine ear 419:16
s. to busy fools 551:20
that honourable s. 471:5
then s. 129:30
time..must have a s. 440:37
turn and s., and bound 189:16
when the kissing had to s. 97:8
Stopped: he should be s. 280:1
nor s. till where 160:10
s. him down 376:21
s. his ears in a..dog-kennel 176:31
Stoppest: wherefore s. thou me? 148:18
Stoppeth one of three 148:18
Stops: never retreats and never s. 179:37
seem to know my s. 435:24
s. of planetary music 493:5
touch'd the tender s. 343:6
Store: amid thy s. 284:12
certain of sorrow in s. 300:22
increase his s. 251:26
large as s. 244:9
once a shining s. 160:22
rich with little s. 195:13
source of all our s. 132:1
spread her wholesome s. 224:14
s. of ladies 342:6
taketh from the s. 333:7
Stored: grapes of wrath are s. 264:15
Storehouse: [knowledge is] a rich s. 24:14
s...of life and comfort 243:19
Stores: in your mind such s. 580:23
Storied: s. of old 340:25
s. urn or animated bust 230:3
s. windows richly dight 341:24
Stories: believe..my own s. 267:23
dismal s. 99:36
garret four s. high 24:38
manifold s., I know, are told 121:18
s. from the land of spirits 151:26
s. of savage men 100:22
s. of the death of kings 475:7
s. of thy finisht love 123:27
s. to rede ar delitabill 33:16
whence these s.? 317:19
Stork: dwelling for the s. 398:10
Storm: brows like gathering s. 108:2
directs the s. 1:11
fled away into the s. 285:28
leave thee in the s. 452:38
lost in the s. 17:18
not in the s. 118:24
now sinks the s. 215:14
on the wings of the s. 228:21
pelting of this pitiless s. 453:14
rides upon the s. 161:18
ship in a black s. 563:34
stemm'd the rude s. 117:24
s. at the death of Ham 412:24
S. in a Teacup 43:18
s. is coming 140:7
s. may enter 379:11
s. of battle and calamity 200:3
s. of life 565:5
such a s. as his bare head 453:34
wind and s., fulfilling 400:24
Storm-beaten ships 327:11
Storm-clouds: when S. brood 311:15
Stormcock and Golden Gain 299:25
Storms: ere the winter s. begin 4:11
he sought the s. 190:13
no loud s. annoy 278:29
no s. come 254:29
s. of prayer 540:8

Storms (*cont.*)

s. of state 447:3
s. that rage outside 18:24
struggling in the s. of fate 381:7
sudden s. are short 474:21
they are greater s. 423:26
waves and s. are gone over me 394:19
when s. are o'er 33:10
Storm-troubled sphere 83:7
Stormy: among the s. Hebrides 546:22
lost in s. visions 492:6
on a s. day 311:22
sea grows s. 15:26
s. peple! 137:25
s. winds do blow 123:10
to scape s. days 185:23
Story: another s. 304:39, 513:13
but to hear a s. 191:19
earns a place i' the s. 424:30
endeth the s. of the Sangreal 328:14
ere their s. die 236:14
Heaven's third s. 541:22
her s. 166:22
I love to hear the s. 339:8
light of thy s. 286:1
Muses' s. 232:11
name great in s. 118:32
not that the s. need be long 547:5
old, old s. 235:10
quite a different s. 515:24
read Richardson for the s. 272:13
rudest work that tells a s. 413:11
short in the s. itself 57:20
some pretty s. tell 527:8
Sordello's s. told 96:29, 35
sorrowful s. 298:20
still is the s. told 324:1
s. always old 95:39
s. for which the world 188:16
s.!..I have none to tell, Sir 124:8
s. is extant 435:17
s. of Cambuscan bold 341:20
s. of her birth 2:26
s. of my life 470:2
s. of our days 405:12
teach him how to tell my s. 470:3
this little s. 280:10
this s. shall the good man 444:28
to tell my s. 438:4
Story-dressers: our s. 109:4
Story-teller: a s. is born 511:16
Stout: bishops..with jugs of s. 243:11
short and s. 141:17
so s. a gentleman 440:38
s. of hand 417:9
Stoutness: no objection to s. 218:31
Strachan: waiting for Sir Richard S. 6:16
Straddled: Apollyon s. quite over 99:12
s. that fence-rail 238:27
Stradivari: make Antonio S.'s violins 197:1
Straggler into loving arms 308:10
Straggling: flocks that s. feed 232:1
Straight: crooked..made s. 54:9
grow s. in the strength of thy spirit 524:3
lay them s. 368:6
make his paths s. 57:28
make s. in the desert 54:9
might have grown full s. 330:12
plough deep and s. 262:3
shall be absolutely s. 566:1
s. to the self-same mark 92:43
s. was a path of gold 94:27
street which is called S. 64:43
where Beauty .. nothing .. quite s. 213:3
Straightened out for a crowbar 251:10
Straightway I was 'ware 88:16
Strain: Big Bow-Wow s. 420:28
Dorian s. 18:28
drop the drowsy s. 159:17
hold cheap the s. 95:15
Shakespeare's s. 199:2
Sire of an immortal s. 491:15
some s. of music 80:18
something like prophetic s. 341:25
s. at a gnat 60:18
s., hard s. 299:5
s. of man's bred out 480:19

INDEX

Strain (*cont.*)
s. of strutting Chanticleer 479:28
s. of the martial airs of England 563:5
s., time's eunuch 255:9
that s. again! 481:30
that s. I heard 342:24
thy happy s. 498:8
unpremeditated s. 546:5
Strained: mercy is not s. 464:33
Straining: s. his throat 225:27
s. upon the start 443:27
Strains: fall like sweet s. 199:21
mute his tuneful s. 417:29
soul-animating s. 580:17
s. as would have won the ear 342:9
s. of unpremeditated art 498:1
s. that might create a soul 340:28
those blessed s. 202:23
Strait: driven into a desperate s. 334:21
honour travels in a s. 481:19
how s. the gate 241:19
s. is the gate 58:24
s., rough, dense 346:14
Strait jacket for humanity 337:5
Straits: outside the Western S. 18:16
whitened the s. of Propontis 522:10
Strand: destined to a barren s. 279:6
down the S. 131:34
her name upon the s. 509:7
India's coral s. 240:17
I walk down the S. 238:1
knits me to thy rugged s. 417:22
Maypole in the S. 79:17
Naiad of the s. 416:15
outer Chelsea to the S. 299:14
some far northern s. 16:6
S., Exeter Change 307:2
walk'd along the S. 277:10
Strands: last s. of man 254:19
Strange: all is s., yet nothing new 276:14
all s. hours and all s. loves 522:12
figures s. and sweet 150:21
for object s. and high 332:5
how s. it seems 93:23
jeering at everything..s. 377:20
more cunning to be s. 477:21
more s. than such a murder 459:17
original, spare, s. 255:3
passing s. and wonderful 493:2
sing..in a s. land 400:5
something rich and s. 479:30
s. and fatal interview 184:18
s. and sinister 268:4
s. and terrible events 425:25
s. and well-bred 156:13
s.—but true 117:1
s. coincidence 116:23
s. cozenage! 191:34
stranger in a s. land 45:32
s., even in a dream 149:31
s. eventful history 427:21
s. that men should fear 449:22
s. to think by the way 410:15
terrible, s., sublime 496:19
that s. shape 149:11
this is wondrous s. 432:28
too s., too restless 15:20
'twas s., 'twas passing s. 470:3
Strangely: look'd on truth askance and s. 488:5
Strangeness: some s. in the proportion 25:29
Stranger: always like a s. 12:7
extravagant and wheeling s. 469:33
I am a s. with thee 394:11
on earth I am a s. grown 106:27
s. and afraid 263:35
s., and ye took me in 60:33
s. doth not intermeddle 50:7
s. fill'd the Stuarts' throne 417:2
s.! 'Eave 'arf a brick 403:9
s. hath thy bridle-rein 305:17
s. here in Gloucestershire 474:27
s. in a strange land 45:32
s., pause 175:18
s. than fiction 117:1
s. that is within thy gates 390:10
s. to one of your parents 22:33
surety for a s. 49:57
this starry s. 166:1
to-morrow a s. will say 200:37

Stranger (*cont.*)
whate'er the s.'s caste 387:21
wilful s. 515:29
Strangers: better s. 428:6
by s. honoured and by s. mourned 381:34
courteous to s. 26:21
entertain s. 69:22
s. of Rome 64:26
the Lord careth for the s. 400:20
Strangled: s. her 95:5
who s. Atahualpa 324:28
Strangling: one s. golden hair 411:11
s. in a string 262:12
Strapped waist 163:20
Stratagem: tea without a s. 586:26
Stratagems: fine nets and s. 245:5
fit for treasons, s. 465:20
Stratford atte Bowe 136:29
Strauss: leaf dot Yawcob S. 1:3
Straw: find quarrel in a s. 436:17
lion shall eat s. 53:19
pipes of wretched s. 342:29
slipped through the s. 11:1
stumbles at a s. 510:24
take a s. and throw it up 422:5
tickled with a s. 383:30
Strawberries: feed upon s. 366:16
how many s. 367:20
I saw good s. 476:21
only netting s. 296:33
Strawberry: like s. wives 24:40
Straw-built shed 229:31
Strawed: where thou hast not s. 60:31
Straws: errors, like s. 193:20
hairs, or s., or dirt 385:27
oaths are s. 443:23
Stray: all s. thoughts 96:26
fondly s. 214:26
from their own Music..s. 124:2
howsoe'er I s. 147:14
on both her lips for ever s. 158:1
s. no further 425:22
what wonder if they s.? 161:26
wishes never learn'd to s. 230:7
Strayed: s. from thy ways 388:10
thou hast surely s. 221:29
Strays of ruined springs 523:21
Streak: last long s. of snow 533:24
Streaks: number the s. of the tulip 278:15
Stream: asleep by thy murmuring s. 105:29
brings up the s. 16:4
by haunted s. 342:7
by mount, and s. 241:8
by the s. and o'er the mead 76:10
clear and gentle s.! 80:13
dark, the silent s. 494:7
flow in such a crystal s. 498:9
freezing s. below 492:24
gentle s., the which them bare 510:20
his talk was like a s. 387:23
in the glassy s. 437:11
in vain by the meadow and s. 314:20
I strove against the s. 539:1
like an ever-rolling s. 562:9
little s. best fits 245:19
meadow, grove and s. 576:1
mercy of a rude s. 446:24
mighty s. of tendency 574:27
no s. meanders..level 325:12
over the still s. 288:2
passed many a straunge s. 137:15
purling s. 2:3
red life might s. again 287:3
round the bosom of the s. 497:20
scooped the brimming s. 347:14
secret sweetness in the s. 533:2
smooth s. 382:32
steep Atlantic s. 340:4
still glides the S. 573:26
s. of sparkling joy 173:34
s. of tendency 20:13
s. of the soft Spring breeze 293:21
s. runs fast 357:16
s. that flashest white 533:32
s. will not run long 102:19
swift s. of song 495:3
they have their s. and pond 83:23
thy s. my great example 172:10
with wind and s. 471:8

Streamed: his flaming robes s. out 285:36
Streamers: fan spread and s. out 156:1
s. waving 215:39, 350:31
Streaming: before his s. eyes 130:20
rule of s. light 340:18
s. to the wind 344:36
Streams: alone spring the great s. 16:14
bright in the..valleys the s. 81:18
by desolate s. 370:19
by what eternal s. 380:21
civil laws are derived but as s. 24:33
coil of his crystalline s. 496:8
cool s. ran beside her 359:27
dam his s. 17:28(-18)
for cooling s. 527:1
fresh s. ran by her 473:6
gilding pale s. 486:27
lapse of murmuring s. 348:32
large s. from little fountains 202:16
let your s. o'erflow 332:11
more pellucid s. 577:13
shallow s. run dimpling 385:32
shrunk thy s. 342:30
spent the s. 81:19
stillest s. 164:5
s. in the countless host 264:10
s. in the desert 54:3
s. meander level 355:17
s. of dotage 279:10
s. of revenue 563:4
s. their channels deeper wear 107:5
s. 'with pleasing murmurs' 382:31
strength of the s. 521:30(-522)
those mysterious s. 89:24
where Christ's blood s. 330:7
Strebt: so lang er s. 223:15
Street: clamour of the crowded s. 317:4
craft in the s. 504:2
cry from s. to s. 73:28(-74)
foot-path of a s. 104:28
going past me in the s. 515:14
highway, or open s. 549:6
hop..through the public s. 424:8
if the s. were time 197:3
in Heaven's s. 334:1
jostling in the s. 74:23
key of the s. 179:31
long unlovely s. 532:8
Queer S. is full 178:17
rattling o'er the stony s. 113:26
ringing down the s. 23:22
roaring s. 313:5
see them on the s. 411:13
sell them in the s. 131:22
she-bear, coming up the s. 209:18
s. cries all about 571:9
s. of the city..gold 72:3
s. which is called Straight 64:43
trouble ev'ry s. 189:19
up the s. came the rebel tread 568:13
whatever brawls disturb the s. 561:26
where the long s. roars 533:27
where the s. grows straiter 541:23
Streets: gibber in the Roman s. 430:14
in Thebes's s. 504:1
in thy dark s. shineth 84:25
on the bald s. 532:9
s. broad and narrow 7:8
s. leading from St. George's 112:13
s. of Baltimore 405:19
s...paved with gold 154:9
s. were fill'd 532:22
s. where the great men go 208:5
uttereth her voice in the s. 49:39
when night darkens the s. 344:35
when Tadlow walks the s. 202:10
Street-slang: giving a hand to s. 337:2
Strength: against thy s. 262:5
as my s. wears away 387:2
as of the *Sun* in his s. 43:26
beauty, s., youth, are flowers 377:4
by his great s. 393:37
by s. drives out another 484:34
Christ is thy s. 354:11
delivered by much s. 393:37
entangles itself with a s. 425:22
excel our s. 192:10
foresight, s. and skill 580:21
from s. to s. 397:6
giant's s. 461:30
girded himself with s. 397:22

INDEX

Strength (cont.)
God-given s.
God is our hope and s. — 418:7
growing s. in the air — 394:27
his s. make stronger — 143:40
his s. the more is — 81:23
in confidence shall be your s. — 99:36
in his s. setteth fast the mountains — 53:39
in the s. of this I rode — 395:28
man's s. to comfort — 530:30
more s., and far less odium — 295:8
my s., and my redeemer — 101:34
my s. is as the s. of ten — 392:34
my s. is made perfect — 540:11
nodosities of the oak without its s. — 67:38
no pleasure in the s. — 103:30
no s. to repent — 400:22
not s. enough to prevent — 440:11
on which all s. depends — 227:25
ordained s. — 503:2
practised that s. — 392:8
promise of s. and manhood — 17:17
recover my s. — 81:22
rejoiceth in his s. — 394:11
renew their s. — 49:26
shewed s. with his arm — 54:14
so shall thy s. be — 61:14
s. and weakness of human nature — 46:33
s. by limping sway disabled — 324:35
s. in what remains — 487:14
s. of all — 576:20
s. of my head — 383:28
s. of spirit — 395:23
s. of the hills is his also — 448:36
s. of the mountains in one clasp — 397:26
s. without hands to smite — 489:27
tell of your own s. — 522:5
that God would give him s. — 358:23
that his s. might endure — 280:3
their s. is to sit still — 522:6
their s. then but labour — 53:36
the Lord is the s. of my life — 397:16
thy s. endue — 393:20
tower of s. — 81:5
trial of her s. — 476:34
true s. of guilty kings — 579:1
try the soul's s. on — 16:28
unbend your noble s. — 89:27
vex'd his immortal s. — 458:13
we are not now that s. — 80:31
with s. and nature — 541:3
with what a s. and majesty — 412:13
Strengthen: s. man's heart — 360:21
s. such as do stand — 398:9
s. thee out of Sion — 389:1
s. whilst one stands — 392:35
s. ye the weak hands — 409:19
Strengthened with might — 54:2
Strengtheneth: Christ which s. me — 67:53
Strengthening: means of s. one's intellect — 68:28
Strengthens: s. our nerves — 290:27
s. with his strength — 102:27
Strenuous: s. life — 383:26
s. tongue — 408:26
Strepere: inter s. anser olores — 287:21
Strepitum: s.que Acherontis — 556:7
s.que Romae — 556:17
Stretch: extent and s. of grace — 260:13
s. him out longer — 190:10
s. the folly of your youth — 454:27
thou shalt s. forth thy hands — 141:23
will the line s. out — 64:18
Stretched: his hand is s. out still — 460:11
s. like a promontory — 53:7
s. metre — 348:26
s. on the rack — 486:17
s. out on the spoils — 381:25
things which he s. — 523:16
with s. forth necks — 550:8
Stretching of the hands — 52:35
Strew: shall I s. on thee rose — 372:19
s. no more red roses — 522:11
s. on her roses, roses — 17:2
Strewed: not have s. thy grave — 17:15
s. with husks — 437:22
Strewn: mirrors of the sea are s. — 481:27
'Strewth, but I socked it — 208:19
295:4

Stricken: s. at Waterloo — 141:26
s. deer — 163:8
well s. in age — 44:50
Strict in his arrest — 438:1
Stricture of these bonds — 514:5
Stride: at one s. comes the dark — 149:14
s. o' yon connectin'-rod — 299:3
Strides: s. about their lands — 533:11
Tarquin's ravishing s. — 458:1
Striding: shadow...s. behind you — 197:28
s. the blast — 457:7
Strife: at the waters of s. — 397:3
clubs typical of s. — 163:29
coupled.. for the sake of s. — 143:25
curse to party s. — 574:3
double s. — 28:18
dread s. — 574:23
dreaming on the verge of s. — 157:8
dull and endless s. — 581:15
each eager s. — 279:2
hear of the stern s. — 418:35
heavens free from s. — 157:18
I am worn with s. — 527:12
ignoble s. — 230:7
in ceaseless s. — 365:23
in the storm nor in the s. — 118:24
is it s.? — 173:32
man of s. — 55:19
no grudge, no s. — 518:1
none was worth my s. — 308:25
no s., I pray thee — 44:46
O s., O curse — 88:26
revolving hopeless s. — 80:17
shed round him in the common s. — 575:10
s. comes with manhood — 417:33
s. is o'er — 387:12
s. too humble — 579:14
s. with the palm — 15:17
that Titanic s. — 16:21
till his s. is over — 223:15
unprofitable s. — 492:6
void of s. — 192:13
when the s. is fierce — 264:9
Strike: afraid to s. — 385:29
Britons, s. home — 551:9
I s. it and it hurts my hand — 472:25
never s. sail to a fear — 200:18
particularly fine, s. it out — 272:17
pull it out and s. it — 139:18
seems to s. at me — 563:21
she will s. and sink — 489:31
s. not awry — 358:7
while you s. him down — 362:33
Strikes: how it s. a Contemporary — 92:20
noon s. on England — 208:5
s. for a Kingdom — 517:9
s. him dead for thine and thee — 538:22
s. where it doth love — 473:11
Striking: clocks were s. — 315:27
his pencil was s. — 225:34
s. sometimes a friend — 243:32
String: chewing little bits of s. — 41:1
concertina's melancholy s. — 218:9
end of a golden s. — 75:8
harp not on that s. — 476:29
one long yellow s. — 95:5
only provided the s. — 355:6
on Time's s. — 245:8
sing in a hempen s. — 37:16
stick and a s. — 277:13
strangling in a s. — 262:12
s. the pearls were strung on — 268:15
untune that s. — 481:4
warbled to the s. — 341:19
Stringent: their s. execution — 228:23
Strings: languid s. — 75:18
lyre with other s. — 164:20
revives the leaden s. — 123:21
s...in the human heart — 173:20
s. of sensualism — 337:8
two s. to my bow — 204:22
with her sighs the s. do break — 123:21
Strip his sleeve — 444:28
Stripe: s. for s. — 45:54
Striped like a zebra — 286:37
Stripes: cut 'is s. away — 295:20
forty s. save one — 67:34
s. of labdanum — 94:18
with his s. we are healed — 54:26
worthy of s...beaten with few s. — 61:55

Stripling: nor spear the s. took — 161:4
s. Thames — 18:9
Stripped: s. of its lettering — 211:21
when two are s. — 330:13
Strips: like s. of the sky — 492:29(–493)
Strive: in vain I s. — 202:4
need't not s. — 146:35
s. afresh — 364:8
s., and hold cheap the strain — 95:15
s. nor weep — 97:23
s. to be a man — 159:10
s. to wind ourselves too high — 291:6
to s., to seek, to find — 541:3
what s. for? — 81:1
with Kings to s. — 118:19
Striven: I would ne'er have s. — 496:10
Strives: s. in his little world of man — 453:4
s. to touch the stars — 510:24
Striving: s. to be man — 199:17
s. to better — 452:31
Strode after me — 579:10
Stroke: no second s. intend — 346:7
only the s. of death — 27:43
some distressful s. — 470:3
s. most dolorous — 328:5
s. of the tongue — 57:3
Stroked: hope-hour s. its sum — 235:15
Strokes: tender s. of art — 381:6
Stroking me gently — 519:14
Stroll alone through fields — 151:27
Strom: ein Charakter in dem S. — 224:4
Strong: and arms are s. — 264:9
battle to the s. — 51:22
come s. — 165:35
do not make it s. — 372:16
drank s. waters — 300:18
fifty-score s. — 90:16
fresh and s. — 573:31
God is..s. and patient — 392:7
I again am s. — 576:4
keep the s. in awe — 476:41
love is s. as death — 52:22
made us s. or weak — 585:8
make s. themselves by ill — 459:9
more s. than all poetic thought — 532:25
one still s. man — 535:43
only the S. shall thrive — 422:20
our oxen..s. to labour — 400:17
out of the s...sweetness — 46:55
quit you like men, be s. — 67:19
rousing herself like a s. man — 352:15
serene yet s. — 401:22
sorrow and silence are s. — 316:15
stand up erect and s. — 88:19
still going s. — 5:21
straight legs and passing s. — 488:27
s. and long-liv'd death — 184:25
s. and of a good courage — 46:37
s. as death — 52:22, 161:12
s. as iron bands — 318:11
s., dogged, unenlightened — 19:14
s. for service still — 163:5
s. gongs groaning — 141:5
s. in will — 541:3
s. is the horse — 503:5
s. is the soul — 15:9
s. man armed keepeth his palace — 61:46
s. men shall bow themselves — 51:33
s. persevering man — 518:35
s., thick, stupefying — 89:45
s. within us — 293:16
s. without rage — 172:10
their feelings are s. — 182:10
though men be so s. — 397:16
tired yet s. — 338:6
too s. for fantasy — 184:12
to suffer and be s. — 316:33
wall is s. — 569:11
wants that little s. — 251:1
we then that are s. — 66:17
wine the sagely s. — 42:1
yet I am s. and lusty — 426:36
Stronger: handclasp's a little s. — 135:13
if the bowl had been s. — 369:9
no s. than my sex — 449:18
s. by weakness — 557:25
s. than all the hosts of error — 98:1
s. than lions — 47:30
Strongest: s. and the fiercest Spirit — 345:15
wine is the s. — 56:16

[937]

Strong hold: turn ye to the s. 56:12
Strove: in mastery while I s. 88:16
I s. against the stream 539:1
I s., made head 95:17
I s. with none 308:25
little still she is 115:21
men that s. with gods 541:3
Spirit that s. for truth 498:20
s. against her weakness 535:5
Strow: leaves that s. the brooks 344:25
Strown: gifts of God are s. 240:18
on my black coffin..s. 483:6
Struck: each thing that he s. 238:27
immediately s. out of the question 126:42
so s. with dread and anguish 350:17
s. all of a heap 500:11
s. him and dismiss'd 375:16
s. in the saddle 141:26
s. so to the soul 433:36
Struggle: alarms of s. and flight 15:8
Manhood a s. 181:37
sacrifice in a contemptible s. 101:36
s. for existence 169:7
s. naught availeth 147:8
s. through such a raging flood 323:29
s., trust and triumph 196:24
what s. to escape? 287:7
Struggles: he that scorns and s. 142:11
s. and howls at fits 492:27
s. with and conquers Time 309:9
Struggling: brave man s. 381:7
s. for life in the water 270:18
s. in vain with..destiny 574:23
Strumpet: half some sturdy s. 236:17
she is a s. 433:10
s.'s fool 423:11
Strumpeted: virtue rudely s. 487:14
Strung with his hair 455:22
Strunt: ye s. rarely 106:32
Strut to our confusion 425:2
Struts: s. and frets his hour 461:4
s. his dames before 341:32
Strutting Chanticleer 479:28
Stuarts: fill'd the S.' throne 417:2
went out..with the S. 182:7
Stubble: earth's base built on s. 340:31
sparks among the s. 56:24
Stubble-land: like a s. 438:32
Stubborn: faithless and s. generation 396:33
s. they chastise 164:34
s. to endure 508:5
too s. and too strange a hand 448:14
very s. things 548:3
Stubbornness: impious s. 430:31
Stubbs: footman to Justinian S. 504:12
S. butters Freeman 408:4
Stuck: 'Amen' s. in my throat 458:9
big hippopotamus s. 10:8
how I'm s. on it all 422:22
s. all with yew 483:6
s. fast in Yesterday 171:12
s. full of eyes 440:31
Students shall be bravely clad 329:24
Studia: haec s. adulescentiam acuunt 145:16
Studied: he s. from the life 14:24
not s. as an oration 370:18
rather s. books than men 28:14
say little more than I have s. 482:19
s. in his death 456:27
s. men from my topsy-turvy 336:5
Studies: air of delightful s. 352:23
s. serve for delight 27:13
too much time in s. 27:14
Studious: s. cloister's pale 341:23
s. let me sit 546:27
s. of elegance and ease 215:32
s. of laborious ease 163:17
s. to please 278:27
Studiously neutral 571:11
Study: by labour and intent s. 352:21
his s. of imagination 469:6
I am slow of s. 466:28
live to s. 28:4
much s. is a weariness 51:35
my only s. is man 78:21
periphrastic s. 197:8
proper s. of mankind 383:22
s. a long silence 563:32
s...cultivated by narrow minds 338:22

Study (cont.)
s. evermore is overshot 454:34
s. first propriety 121:16
s. had made him very lean 252:24
s. household good 349:8
s. is like the..sun 454:32
s. of revenge 344:14
s. to be quiet 68:36
s. what you most affect 478:47
thy testimonies are my s. 399:20
we that did nothing s. 292:21
with s. faint 143:13
Studying: I have been s. 475:33
s. all the summer night 332:27
s. peace 192:13
Stuff: listen all day to such s. 128:29
no such s. in my thoughts 433:16
of slighter s. 141:31
of s. so fat and dull 436:39
precious as the s. they sell 207:23
see the s. again 243:6
s...great part of Shakespeare..
sad s. 216:14
s. life is made of 211:15
s. to try the soul's strength 89:27
s. will not endure 482:28
such s. as dreams 480:8
such volumes of s. 311:9
that perilous s. 460:37
very s. o' the conscience 469:36
what s. 'tis made of 462:28
write such s. for ever 275:8
Stuffed: already s. tennis-balls 468:32
s. men 197:10
s. with epithets of war 469:20
Stuffs out his vacant garments 447:34
Stultitia caruisse 256:17
Stultitiam: misce s. consiliis 261:5
Stumble: do not s. 327:3
s. that run fast 478:2
Stumbled when I saw 453:38
Stumbles: horse that s. and nods 236:14
s. at a straw 510:24
Stumbling: for a stone of s. 53:13
s. on melons 332:17
s. through my soul 227:36
Stump: stir it and s. it 222:4
Stumps: fought upon his s. 491:11
roller, pitch, and s., and all 309:27
Stung by the splendour 90:40
Stunned: one that hath been s. 150:17
Stupefying incense-smoke 89:45
Stupid: what s. age or nation 111:9
Stupidity: man's immense s. 90:25
no sin except s. 569:34
such an excess of s. 271:14
want of tenderness..proof of s. 272:2
with s. the gods..struggle 415:23
Sturm und Drang 305:2
Sty: no better than a s. 425:29
Stygian: S. cave forlorn 341:26
ye S. set 308:22
Style: any s. of writing untouched 273:19
attain an English s. 278:9
do it in a high s. 21:12
grand s. 20:5
his own towering s. 142:20
honourable s. of a Christian 86:1
how the s. refines 382:34
in so strange a s. 382:28
Johnson's s. was grand 154:13
just the proper s. 408:17
light agreeable polished s. 240:6
nothing to assert..no s. 490:11
s. is the dress of thought 565:21
s. resembling..early architecture 337:2
theirs for their s. 486:26
true definition of a s. 520:1
with his eye on his s. 20:3
Style: le s. est l'homme 98:17
le s. naturel 373:21
Styles: two distinct s. 182:47
two s. of portrait painting 177:7
Stylish: won't be a s. marriage 168:2
Subdue: chasten and s. 582:1
must s. at length 383:26
replenish the earth and s. it 44:9
s. for a moment 100:26
s. the people under us 394:30
s. your appetites 177:3

Subdued: both parties nobly are s. 442:18
my heart's s. 470:9
my nature is s. 488:6
whose s. eyes 474:2
Subdues: controls them and s. 575:6
Subduing: conceiving and s. both 331:2
necessity of s. again 100:26
Subiectione: tutius est stare in s. 291:23
Subject: as the s. owes the prince 479:13
English s.'s sole prerogative 193:42
every s.'s duty..every s.'s soul 444:20
know a s. ourselves 272:32
most s...to weeds 442:23
proper s. of conversation 139:33
serious s. 20:5
spare..for his s.'s sake 159:9
S. and a Sovereign 135:28
s. for heroic song 349:5
s. is not truth 135:24
s. made to your hand 92:46
s. of all verse 87:24
s. of almost equal importance 503:18
s. to decay 193:1
s. to his birth 431:21
s. to the same diseases 464:8
s. unto the higher powers 66:8
to these all things are s. 497:7
unlike my s. 139:4
what it is to be a s. 198:10
winds into a s. 227:31
Subjection: bring it into s. 66:37
implied s. 347:12
Subject-matter: part of the s. 570:4
Subjects: good of s. 170:17
king and his faithful s. 103:9
kings seek their s.' good 246:9
my s. for a pair of..saints 475:21
on her s.' love 402:2
paid his s. 83:20
pray to several s. 462:2
show to s. 164:34
s. all to..time 481:21
s. still loathe..Government 246:17
were their s. wise 163:42
when s. are rebels 102:17
Sublime: bards s. 316:9
boundless, endless and s. 114:31
howls the s. 176:26
how s. a thing 316:33
large front and eye s. 347:11
make our lives s. 317:8
material s. 153:3
my object all s. 220:2
never tender nor s. 309:9
one of the..most s. poems 194:11
rode s. 231:13
s. and the ridiculous 372:21
s. dashed to pieces 153:13
s. on the towers 492:27
S. to the Ridiculous 228:8; 361:2
terrible, strange, s. 496:19
true pathos and s. 104:23
Wordsworthian or egotistical s. 290:9
Sublime: du s. au ridicule 361:2
Sublimity: possible s. 579:18
Sublunary lovers' love 186:25
Submerged Tenth 78:19
Submission: make s. meet 122:6
yielded with coy s. 347:12
Submit: must he s.? 475:10
never to s. or yield 344:14
s. to be slaves 379:3
wives, s. yourselves 68:6
Submitting: by s., sways 384:38
s. the shows of things 24:16
Subscribe: though it does not s. 128:13
Subscribers: for s. baits 143:6
not printing any list of s. 274:33
Subscription: amount of his s. 518:30
S. no Bondage 335:7
you owe me no s. 453:6
Subsequent: poetry would be made s. 352:28
s. proceedings 239:2
Subsist: mine shall s. by me 232:13
Subsistence: any s. without a mind 43:12
s...in arithmetical ratio 328:25
Substance: all the s. of his house 52:23
gets at the s. of a book 305:4
material s. of it..vanished 126:27
my S. from the common Earth 207:17

Substance (*cont.*)
nor dividing the S. 388:38
persons of some s. 571:20
s. might be call'd 346:4
s. of men which is man 524:26
s. of ten thousand soldiers 476:38
s..of things hoped for 69:13
sucks his s. 306:18
very s. of the ambitious 433:13
wasted his s. 62:13
what is your s.? 487:2
Substances: sightless s. 457:3
Substantial: shadows, not s. things 501:5
s. world 578:20
Substitute: no s. for sense 197:34
s. shines brightly 465:21
Substratum: basis or s. 120:29
Subterranean: s. dark 264:2
s. fields 579:30
Subtle: less s. and fine 352:28
mathematics, s. 27:19
sanguine and s. Dolores 522:26
serpent was more s. 44:19
slipper and s. knave 471:1
s., and mighty opium 172:19
s. as Sphinx 455:22
s. ways 199:3
s. wreath of hair 185:4
Subtle-coloured hair 522:19
Subtlest: serpent s. beast 349:7
Subtleties: airy s. in religion 86:7
destroyed by s. 336:33
s. of the American joke 550:17
Subtlety: craft and s. of the devil 389:9
thy brother came with s. 45:2
Suburb of the life elysian 317:12
Suburban: city or s. 350:11
Suburbs: in the south s. 484:5
s. of your good pleasure 449:17
Subverts..his understanding 265:10
Succeed: him that shall s. me 99:39
if at first you don't s. 248:8
seldom see we sons s. 234:8
s. in that it seems to fail 95:16
s. the former 247:10
Succeeded: bores have s. 182:46
Succeeding: their s. race 183:20
Succeeds: one s. 528:26
s. in unknown fate 470:31
where he s. 143:26
Success: as a singist..not a s. 560:18
bounds of low s. 358:22
confident of s. 156:11
criterion of wisdom..s. 103:2
earnest of s. 456:24
field from which s. is banished 513:31
minute's s. 89:20
no one can guarantee s. in war 144:18
no very lively hope of s. 505:16
no way to s. in our art 199:33
often, but without s. 143:14
s. and miscarriage..empty 270:28
s. in life 374:14
s. of the British..in political life 181:6
s. perhaps may crown us 163:19
s. was found on Israel's side 161:10
to command s. 1:14
true s. is to labour 515:6
what good s. soever 404:16
with his surcease s. 457:7
Successful: s. crimes alone 193:8
s. experiment 268:20
unsuccessful or s. war 162:40
Successor: crown to its hereditary
s. 272:27
raree-show of Peter's s. 90:32
Successus: hos s. alit 554:22
Succinct: judicious, clear, s. 159:16
Succoth: mete out the valley of S. 395:23
Succour: died to s. me 31:3
so Jupiter me s. 502:19
s. Scotland, and remede 583:26
Such: of s. is the kingdom of God 61:6
s. is life! 175:23, 176:22
s. was I, s. by nature still 192:23
s. wilt thou be to me 186:25
Suck: her lips s. forth my soul 330:5
I have given s. 457:13
s. his sweet 231:39, 315:17
s. melancholy 427:8
s. my last breath 382:8

Suck (*cont.*)
s. the honied showers 342:31
s. they no small advantage 396:26
there s. I 480:14
Suck-a-Thumb: naughty little S. 250:5
Sucked: I s. the blood 149:9
s. on country pleasures 185:6
s. the breasts of my mother 52:21
s. the honey of his..vows 434:14
Sucker born every minute 35:24
Sucking: in s. at her breast 196:2
s. child shall play 53:19
Suckle fools 470:29
Sucklings: very babes and s. 392:8
Sucks: as a weasel s. eggs 427:8
s. his substance 306:18
s. the nurse asleep 426:13
s. two souls 184:28
where the bee s. 480:14
Sudden: God answers..s. 87:29
not as s. as a massacre 550:13
rather a s. pull up 179:7
s. and quick in quarrel 427:21
s. as sweet 338:10
s. death 388:48
s. thought strikes me 124:16
to Dawn: Be s. 544:17
too unadvis'd, too s. 477:24
Suddenly: repent and that s. 440:11
softly and s. vanish 128:10
s., as rare things will 93:46
Sue: charm of lovely S. 215:42
less used to s. 416:18
not born to s. 474:11
Sueño: el que inventó el s. 134:18
Suenos: hacer bien, aun en s. 120:17
Suez: somewheres east of S. 299:15
Suffer: better one s. 190:20
both the worlds s. 459:4
cannot s. wrong..will not s.
long 541:19
do well and s. for it 69:51
Hell I s. seems a Heaven 346:32
I will not s. him 397:34
make your readers s. so much 277:15
nobler in the mind to s. 434:4
not s. a witch to live 45:55
not without hope we s. 578:17
s. all alike 424:28
s. and be strong 310:33
s. and die 553:2
s. a sea-change 479:30
s. for the truth's sake 389:53
s. it to be so now 57:32
s. me to come to thee 565:9
s. noble sorrows 406:4
s. the little children 61:6
s. thy foot to be moved 399:27
s. thy Holy One to see corruption 392:27
s. to redeem our loss 8:2
s. us not..to fall from thee 391:43
those that I saw s. 479:19
ye s. fools gladly 67:32
Sufferance: in corporal s. 462:7
s. is the badge 463:21
Suffered: s. greatly 540:32
s. herself to be desir'd 558:5
s. in exile 332:23
s. many things of..physicians 60:60
s. with those that I saw suffer 479:19
Sufferer: best..was a s. 170:18
Suffereth: charity s. long 66:45
Suffering: doing or s. 344:10
knowledge by s. entereth 89:4
learn in s. 494:17
lounjun' 'roun' en s. 238:19
majesty of human s. 553:1
more exposed to s. 575:7
out of human s. 576:20
s. is permanent 573:7
s. is the lover's part 214:9
while actual s. was yet afar off 563:5
Sufferings: saith my s. 331:2
to each his s. 230:30
Suffers: does, not s. wrong 496:20
he s., but 541:19
nothing the body s. 337:19
Suffice: he shall s. me 360:11
s. for those who belong to them 568:4
Sufficed: stable-place s. 409:21

Sufficeth: it s. me 328:12
it s. us 63:54
it s. that the day will end 451:38
Sufficiency: elegant s. 546:13
Sufficient: s. conclusions 111:33
s. is Thine Arm alone 562:9
s. of His light 96:10
s. unto the day 58:15
Sufflaminandus erat 280:1
Suffolk his axe did ply 189:8
Suffusion: all colours a s. 151:6
dim s. veiled 346:19
Sugar: if sack and s. be a fault 439:36
oil, vinegar, s. 225:25
s. and spice 369:12
s. my hair 129:25
s. o'er the devil himself 434:3
Sugared about by the old men 302:5
Sugar-plum: rather give a s. 290:12
Suggestion: s...of noble grounds 412:25
take s. as a cat laps milk 479:36
yield to that s. 456:24
Suggest me still 488:18
Suicide: not even s. 514:31
s.'s grave 220:19
Suing: in s. long to bide 510:16
Suis: j'y s., j'y reste 327:4
Suisse: point de S. 405:4
Suit: certainly not s. me 220:28
fatal to my s. before 213:15
Hearts was her favourite s. 306:13
honour, or gay s. 245:2
silk s., which cost me much 377:12
smelling out a s. 477:7
still in s. 244:9
s. and serve his need 244:10
s. full well my constitution 7:10
s. her notion 219:38
s. the action to the word 434:16
Suitors: see s. following 470:29
Suits: lisp and wear strange s. 428:17
now s. with it 458:1
out of s. with fortune 426:22
s. of solemn black 430:30
s. of woe 430:30
Sulky, sullen dame 108:2
Sullen: are you sick or..s.? 275:31
as a s. bell 441:10
exchange thy s. skies 162:44
from s. earth 486:24
full sadly in his s. mind 509:27
Plato is never s. 325:23
silent, s. peoples 303:25
small but s. horn 153:24
sulky, s. dame 108:2
s. and sad 546:24
s. from the suppliant crowd 164:34
these s. fits 426:34
Sullenness against Nature 352:29
Sulphur: Calvin, oat-cakes, and s. 504:22
roast me in s.l 473:32
windy nitre and quick s. 509:25
Sulphurous and thought-executing fires 453:5
Sultan: pity S. Mahmud 205:21
S. after S. 205:29, 30
S.'s turret 205:4, 5
Sultans: not as S. smile 141:19
Sultry: where the climate's s. 115:19
Sum: giving thy s. of more 426:32
hope-hour stroked its s. 235:15
make up my s. 437:24
mighty s. of things 574:30
saved the s. of things 264:4
s. of earthly bliss 348:39
s. of human wretchedness 118:30
with a great s...this freedom 65:14
Sum: cogito, ergo s. 172:26
Sumatra: giant rat of S. 188:16
Summa: sic rerum s. novatur 321:1
Summam materiae..manere 25:13
Summas: ad s. emergere 320:30(–321)
Summed: can it be s. up so? 81:12
Summer: after many a s. 540:20
after s. merrily 480:14
All-hallown s. 438:28
all on a s. day 129:27
all on a s.'s day 368:15
all the wild s. 585:4
amorous ditties all a s.'s day 344:32
beauty's s. dead 487:29(–488)

Summer (*cont.*)
branding s. suns 532:2
brief the sun of s. 538:21
chestnuts, s. through 84:8
compare thee to a s.'s day? 486:18
coruscations of s. lightning 228:2
dark s. dawns 538:19
dew of s. nights 288:13
dews of s. night did fall 338:13
Diana in her s. weed 232:1
discontent made glorious s. 476:2
eternal s. gilds them 115:43
eternal s. in his soul 251:11
fantastic s.'s heat 474:20
fresh spring, and s. 494:19
goodbye, S. 568:23
heat of the s.'s beginning 372:18
he fell..a s.'s day 345:12
if it takes all s. 229:1
in a s.'s bower 440:4
in a s. seson 310:3
Indian S. of the heart 568:18
in s., quite the other way 515:14
in s. skies to mourn 285:11
in s.'s wonderland 365:25
last rose of s. 356:36
like s. tempest 538:27
mad naked s. night 567:16
mery s.'s day 138:32
middle s.'s spring 466:36
murmur of a s.'s day 18:6
my food, and s. rain 516:16
no Spring, nor S. beauty 184:16
not so much life as on a s.'s day 286:3
O s. swallow 524:18
Saint Martin's s. 445:18
see in a s.'s day 466:31
since s. first was leavy 468:20
singest of s. 287:23
sing in the s. day 249:14
so fades a s. cloud away 33:10
stars of the s. night 318:4
studying all the s. night 332:27
s. and winter..not cease 44:41
s. comes with flower and bee 241:7
S. has o'erbrimmed 284:11
S. has set in 152:31
s. is ended 55:16
s. is good to follow 524:15
s. is icumen in 9:26
s.—no sweeter was ever 422:22
s. redundant 97:15
s. set lip to earth's bosom 545:8
s.'s flower is to the s. sweet 487:25
s.'s joys are spoilt by use 285:38
s.'s lease 486:18
s. soldier 372:23
s. songs for me 485:16
s.'s ripening breath 477:24
s.'s rose 346:20
s. with flowers that fell 522:5
sweet as s. 447:9
this guest of s. 457:6
thou art a s. bird 442:24
through the s. is not heard 494:6
thy eternal s. shall not fade 486:18
trancèd s.-night 286:8
trills..the s. long 350:11
way to ensure s. 558:24
when the s. is shed 524:11
whether the s. clothe 151:25
your English s.'s done 298:26
Summer-friends 243:23
Summer-house: any s. in Christendom 440:2
Summers: this many s. in a sea 446:24
thousand s. are over and dead 524:11
three s.' pride' 487:29
Summerset: seen him do the s. 519:12
Summertime: in s. on Bredon 262:21
Summits: nations touch at their s. 29:2
snowy s. old in story 538:14
Summon: s. Clan-Conuil 419:2
s. his array 323:10
s. up the blood 443:24
Summoners: these dreadful s. 453:10
Summons: at the s. of the rock
gun 77:31
hark to the s. 419:2
s. thee to heaven or to hell 458:1
upon a fearful s. 430:18

Summons (*cont.*)
when fate s. 193:1
when thy s. comes 98:3
Summum bonum 145:7
Sumptuous: it was a s. spot 20:31
Sumptuously: fared s. every day 62:23
Sums: no pains with its s. 128:12
s. his years 292:17
Sun: against a setting s. 480:23
all, except their s. 115:43
all the rest the s. goes round 558:1
alone the s. arises 16:14
along Morea's hills the setting s. 115:8
as s. and showers 446:18
as the dial to the s. 78:18
as the s. breaks through 479:9
as the s. shineth in his strength 70:27
as the s. went down 293:25
at even ere the s. was set 550:32
at midnight speak with the S. 551:19
at my death thy S. 185:24
at the going down of the s. 72:23
aweary of the s. 461:6
before the rising s. 562:9
beheld the s. rise up 574:11
beneath another s. 546:23
beneath the making s. 81:5
beneath the s. 115:1, 303:5
benighted..under the midday s. 340:20
best s...Newcastle coal 558:21
better for the s...to drop 364:1
betwixt us and the S. 149:11
blessed s...fair hot wench 438:13
blessed s...prove a micher 439:33
bloody S., at noon 149:4
blushing discontented s. 475:8
born of the s. 509:2
brief the s. of summer 538:21
bright-haired s. 153:24
broad s. is sinking down 577:1
by s. and candle lit 88:24
candle in the s. 109:25
candle to the s. 501:15, 586:28
chambers of the s. 75:18
Christian charity under the s. 252:18
clear as the s. 52:15
close to the s. 529:10
command the s. 479:10
common s. 231:5
courts of the s. 141:3
distilled by the s. 237:10
doubt that the s. doth move 432:42
drum-beat, following the s. 563:5
dry s., dry wind 550:6
early-rising s. 246:2
ere the set of s. 456:3
ever braved the s. 95:35
fail, S. and Breath! 413:31
faint with the hot s. 288:22
farthing candle to the s. 586:28
feast on the s. 525:24
follow and find the s. 524:13
follow thy fair s. 123:20
forgot the stars..the s. 286:23
for the eyes to behold the s. 51:31
gather round the setting s. 576:22
God-curst s. 236:19
God himself is moon and s. 537:27
goes to bed wi' the s. 485:25
great S. begins his state 341:33
had not the great s. seen 81:13
hath Britain all the s.? 429:34
heat o' the s. 430:1
hills the s. shines sweetly on 30:18
his s. to rise on the evil 57:52
hold their..tapers to the s. 165:2
hooting at the glorious s. 151:19
if the S...should doubt 73:28
I gave you the whole s. 489:27
insultin the s. 365:10
Juliet is the s. 477:13
just as the s. was rising 6:2
kiss of the s. for pardon 233:17
lake-reflected s. 497:2
lamp of Heaven, the s. 247:10
late eclipses in the s. 452:15
leave the blessed s. 536:27
let not the s. go down 68:1
lie a-basking in the s. 221:36
like the s., come natural 289:27
like the s...shine on all 385:11

Sun (*cont.*)
live i' the s. 427:9
livery of the burnished s. 463:26
loss of the s. 139:3
make guilty of our disasters the
s. 452:18
makes a goblin of the s. 411:24
March s. feels like May 93:13
maturing s. 284:10
meet the s. 230:11
memorials catch the dying s. 516:19
Meredith climbed towards the
s. 142:19
most sheene is the s. 310:7
my s. his beams display 158:17
my s. sets to rise again 93:25
neither shall the s. light on them 71:7
never assisted the s. materially 546:36
never did s. more beautifully 582:14
never saw the s. 94:25
no homage unto the s. 86:37
none beneath the S. 303:5
no need of the s. 72:5
no new thing under the s. 50:61
no s.—no moon! 253:11
nothing like the s. 488:13
not quickened by the s. 574:2
not see the s. 395:21
no worship to the garish s. 478:20
now the s. is laid to sleep 279:31
o'er thee the s. doth pine 82:1
O glorious s. 231:38
on which the s. never sets 365:10
out in the mid-day s. 157:25
quiet as the s. 522:15
ricks stand grey to the s. 298:26
rime-ringed s. 298:28
rising of the s. 10:14
saves a description of the rising s. 499:29
scarce could see the s. 410:9
self-same s. 485:31
shoots at the mid-day s. 501:13
side that's next the s. 517:13
smitten with the morning S. 538:14
somewhere the s. is shining 238:6
splendid silent s. 566:22
spots and clouds in the s. 109:15
steps of the S. 76:7
study is like the..s. 454:32
s. and moon of the heart's desire 411:35
s. and moon, rejoice 291:27
s. and moon..sunk 340:20
s. and the rain are flying 516:9
s. ariseth 398:10
s...but the dark *simulacrum* 85:16
s. came dazzling 534:4
s. came peeping in at morn 252:33
S. came up 148:21
s. climbs slow 147:8
s. does not set 415:22
s. going down 333:16
s. had risen to hear him crow 196:13
s. has left the lea 420:9
S. himself cannot forget 11:3
s...in dim eclipse 345:6
S. in his strength 43:26
s. in mid-career 503:6
s. is coming down 337:35
s. is hot above us 295:29
s. is mounted 264:2
s. knoweth his going down 398:10
s. looked over 94:27
s., moon, and stars, brother 78:34
s., moon, and thou vain world 124:18
s. my self in Huncamunca's eyes 204:35
s. of my soul! 291:9
S. of righteousness 56:15
s. of suns 173:29
s., or the light 51:33
S.'s and moon's..at once 92:33
s. shall not burn thee 399:28
s. shines always 73:12
S.'s rim dips 149:14
s., stand thou still 46:42
s...taken out his nap 110:43
s. that warms you here 474:13
s. through the mirk 167:24
s. to course two hundred 472:16
s. to me is dark 350:23
s. was droppin' slow 299:12
S. was flecked with bars 149:12

INDEX

Sun (cont.)
s. was laughing sweetly 585:6
s. was shining on the sea 130:9
s. went down 539:21
S., who scatter'd into flight 205:5
s. will be dimmed 29:19
s. will pierce 89:22
s. with ardent frown 416:16
swear to a touch o' s. 301:16
sweetheart of the s. 253:19
sweet tale of the s. 439:14
tabernacle for the s. 392:32
thank heavens, the s. has gone in 504:18
that s., thine eye 486:33
this s. of York 476:2
till the s. grows cold 527:11
tired the s. with talking 157:16
to feel the s. 87:39
to have enjoy'd the s. 15:13
too much i' the s. 430:27
to s. itself 580:10
to the s. my little taper 116:38
unregulated s. 84:10
unruly S. 186:19
up roos the s. 137:33
warmed by the s. 204:3
warms in the s. 383:19
way is long to the s. 524:13
whan soft was the s. 310:3
when the s. in bed 343:24
when the s. is hot 339:24
when the s. rises 74:6
when the s. set 115:45
when the s. sets 312:26
where e'er the s. 562:8
white as the s. 156:19
wind up the s. and moon 119:15
with the dying s. 79:5
with the setting s. dropt 345:12
with the s. 292:1
with the s. to match 90:13
woman clothed with the s. 71:16
yet I saw no s. 547:20
Sunbeam: bathe in the fresh s. 497:8
his own pure s. 308:31
s. in a winter's day 195:14
thikke as motes in the s. 138:10
Sunbeams: stars and s. know 17:24
s. lifted higher 316:27
s. out of cucumbers 519:18
winds and s. 493:1
Sun-burned sicklemen 480:7
Sunburnt mirth 287:24
Sunday: all that calm S. 208:10
buried on S. 368:21(–369)
chicken in his pot every S. 242:1
here of a S. morning 262:21(–263)
killing of a mouse on S. 79:18
on Christ's S. at morn 7:14
on S. heaven's gate 245:8
to Hyde Park..the first S. 156:13
you should see me on S. 12:8
Sundays: begin a journey on S. 520:24
pulpits and S. 245:5
S. of man's life 245:8
Sunder: unskilled to s. 147:9
Sundered in the night of fear 533:28
Sundown: each s. makes them mournful 77:27
s. splendid and serene 241:23
Sundry: at s. times 69:6
s. and manifold changes 389:38
Sun-flower: S.l weary of time 76:7
s. turns on her god 356:13
Sung: ever she s. 359:17
ever s. 38:10
ever were s. or said 316:2
her amorous descant s. 347:19
I've only s. it once 526:7
loved and s. 115:43
Olympian bards who s. 199:20
some are s. 544:4
s. by a fair queen 440:4
s. the service divyne 136:29
their dirge is s. 153:30
war, he s. 191:9
when she is s. and heard 157:5
Sun-girt city 495:2
Sunium: S.'s height 308:24
S.'s marbled steep 116:3
Sunk: armies whole have s. 345:31

Sunk (cont.)
in the flat sea s. 340:20
so Lycidas s. low 343:3
some were s. 539:21(–540)
s. at Charing Cross 558:20
s. beneath the wave 162:9
s. so low that sacred head 342:25
s. though he be 343:3
world's whole sap is s. 186:3
Sunless: down to a s. sea 151:32
from sunshine to the s. land 575:18
s. day went down 115:29
Sunlight: as moonlight into s. 534:32
as s. drinketh dew 529:22
s. and the sward 302:9
s. clasps the earth 495:7
Sunlit heights 569:13
Sunnier side of doubt 527:22
Sunny: s. pleasure-dome 151:33(–152)
s. spots of greenery 151:32
that s. dome! 151:33(–152)
Sunny Jim 235:9
Sunrise: at s. an emerging prow 18:16
between S. and Sunset 329:9
each s. brings back 77:27
in Eternity's s. 74:27
like s. from the sea 493:24
seen their s. pass 140:11
see s. in town and country 514:35
s. blooms 411:1
that august s. 537:41
Suns: blest by s. of home 84:21
branding summer s. 532:2
light of setting s. 582:1
million million of s. 541:4
process of the s. 534:29
s. and universes ceased to be 83:11
s. of the world may stain 486:29
s., that set, may rise again 282:6
what s...make us 309:5
Sun-searched growths 410:30
Sunset: after s. fadeth 487:16
between Sunrise and S. 329:9
like s. to the skies 493:27
sail beyond the s. 541:3
seeks the s. isles 41:21
s. and evening star 528:22
s. breezes shiver 363:6
s. divides the sky 114:6
s. of life 122:22
s. ran..reeking 92:17
s...through a Gothic skylight 119:25
turns toward s. 525:1
Sunsets exquisitely dying 266:16
Sunset-seas: cloud-continents of s. 3:12
Sunset-touch 89:31
Sunshine: breezes and the s. 121:27
broad s. of life 274:11
digressions..are the s. 513:8
flies of estates and s. 243:22
from s. to the sunless land 575:18
made a s. 509:21
s. holiday 342:3
s. is a glorious birth 576:2
s. patriot 372:23
thunder and the s. 541:3
Sunshot palaces high 82:13
Sun-thaw: smokes in the s. 151:25
Sun-treader, life and light 94:30
Sup: s. before we go 366:13
s. by s. 249:22
who sipped no s. 222:27
Supellex: quam sit tibi curta s. 378:6
Superb against the dawn 42:12
Superbos: debellare s. 555:1
Supererogation: Works of S. 401:6
Superest: quod s. aevi 257:11
Superexcellent tobacco 109:22
Superficial, ignorant, unweighing 462:15
Superflu: le s...nécessaire 557:11
Superfluities: must have s. 215:33
s. of mankind 214:28
Superfluity: s. comes sooner by white hairs 463:6
s. of naughtiness 69:31
s. of words 213:21
Superfluous: in the poorest thing s. 452:41
so s. to demand the time 438:14
s. in me to point out 1:4

Superfluous (cont.)
s. kings 424:26
s. lags the vet'ran 279:9
thy s. praise 189:19
with s. burden 351:23
Superflux of pain 521:28
Superior: most s. person 8:15
notions about a s. power 519:3
sick of his s. 481:5
s. only gives us an assurance 265:7
s. toils 1:18
Superiority: one shall acquire an evident s. 277:19
s. soliciting 364:22
Supernatural: not from a s. power 363:26
s. soliciting 456:24
Superos quid quaerimus ultra? 320:26
Superscription: this image and s. 60:11
Supersede the last fashionable novel 326:11
Superstition: fabric of s. 102:38
one species of s. 265:13
remedy for s. 101:7
s. in avoiding s. 27:21
s...religion of feeble minds 102:26
Superstitions: end as s. 266:24
traditional s. of the place 239:17
Superstitious: he is s. grown 449:11
more s., more bigoted 363:17
scarecrow for s. terrors 172:16
s. reluctance to sit 274:17
ye are too s. 64:60
Supinely enjoyed 216:21
Supped full with horrors 461:3
Supper: consider s. as a turnpike 196:5
eat my s. there 582:12
Hatim call to S. 205:20
Hatim Tai cry S. 205:19
heard him speak at s. 201:32
hope..bad s. 24:39
if ever I ate a good s. 13:16
last sad s. 530:22
marriage s. of the Lamb 71:34
sings for his s. 367:18
S. of the Lord 391:12
s...to my taste 512:30
to s. with a flood of tears 174:22
Supple and smooth 249:8
Suppliance of a minute 431:20
Suppliant: sullen from the s. crowd 164:34
S. for his own 118:20
thus the s. prays 279:7
Supplicating voice 279:12
Supplication: his s. to the rose 208:11
Supplications: our common s. 388:32
Supplied: never be s. 224:14
Supply: see that the s. is not tainted 416:4
Support: I s. it from the outside 335:21
may He s. us all the day long 364:4
s. him after 480:17
to s. uneasy steps 344:24
Supporter les maux d'autrui 407:9
Supports with insolence 277:30
Suppose: 'do you s.,' the Walrus said 130:12
I s. I never will 297:25
Supposed: by some s. true paradise 347:9
might have been s. to speak 116:35
s. the Holy Land 442:29
Supposes: if the law s. that 178:1
Supposing him to be the gardener 64:6
Suppressed: not wholly s...religion 103:4
one of the guinea-pigs..s. 129:29
Supremacy: to art her fair s. 80:29
Supreme: Disposer S. 571:4
fear of..s. powers 109:31
force hath made s. 344:22
in none s. 18:1
s. of power 288:14
two only s...beings 363:14
Supremum: omnem crede diem...s. 256:27
Surcease: with his s. success 457:7
Sure: as a nail in a s. place 53:28
as s. as death 280:13
be s. of it 472:4
I'm s.—s.—s. 172:3
joy was never s. 523:22
made believe you were not s. 91:35

Sure (*cont.*)
most s. in all His ways 364:6
not s. of sorrow 523:22
one s., if another fails 96:40
perfectly s. I have none 128:28
round world so s. 397:22
sharp remedy, but a s. one 405:14
s. and firm-set earth 458:1
s. and safe one 446:29
s. she felt no pain 95:5
s. to each his own 301:26
s. you shall out-live this day? 202:1
too s. of the amour 543:20
Surest: old soldiers..s. 563:22
wound of peace is s., s. secure 481:11
Surface: errors..upon the s. flow 193:20
not for a fine glossy s. 227:16
s. of the perturbed countries 235:22
s. of Time's fleeting river 496:1
s. so unattractive 243:17
Surfeit: as sick that s. 463:5
no crude s. reigns 340:24
s., cloyment and revolt 483:9
Surfeited with honey 440:9
Surfeiting the appetite may sicken 481:30
Surfeit-swelled: so s. 442:37
Surge: Atlantic s. pours in 546:22
murmuring s. 454:3
rude imperious s. 442:1
s. and thunder of the Odyssey 309:24
turbulent s...cover 480:32
Surgeon to old shoes 448:5
Surgery: honour hath no skill in
s., then? 440:30
Surges: all the labouring s. 545:11
when loud s. lash 382:32
Surly: s. republican 278:4
went s. by 448:32
Surmise: daily with false s. 343:1
smother'd in s. 456:24
vague shadow of s. 199:13
we all s. 95:20
wild s. 288:19
Surmises: blown by s. 441:8
Surname: out of his s. 325:6
Surpass her 115:15
Surpassed: man is something to
be s. 364:22
Surplice-peg: shape of a s. 295:15
Surplice-question: view of the s. 90:29
Surplices: candle-flame beside the
s. 310:24
scarlet cloaks and s. 310:23
Surprend: la mort ne s. point le sage 209:15
Surprise: blesses us with s. 42:4
death took him mellow by s. 376:21
mingled with s. 416:27
poetry should s. 289:27
what a s.! 147:22
when the s. 199:13
Surprised: discovered and s. 347:29
guilty thing s. 576:18
Jemmy Twitcher..I own s. me 215:7
s. at Waterloo, Duke? 564:13
s. by unjust force 340:30
s. to find it done at all 271:16
you don't feel s. 219:11
Surprises: light s. 161:21
millions of s. 245:5
Surrender: send in your Chief an'
s. 301:8
unconditional and immediate s. 229:4
we shall never s. 143:40
yet be forced to s. 86:5
Surrey: I dare meet S. 475:15
Kent and S. may 296:15
lead the S. spring again 299:24
Surrounded with His protection 352:13
Survey: monarch of all I s. 164:22
s. mankind from China to Peru 279:2
s. of all the world 440:37
s. the wondrous Cross 562:18
Surveys his children's looks 226:11
Survival: S. of the Fittest 169:8, 508:26
without victory..no s. 143:39
Survive: never s. the blow 242:26
Survived: sharpest you still have
s. 199:25
s. her own wake 325:29
Survivor: *I* may be the s. 23:2

Susan: black-ey'd S. 215:39
Squire and Lady S. 236:8
Susceptible: peculiarly s. to
draughts 569:27
s. Chancellor 218:37
Suspect: s. everybody 177:35
s. much..know little 27:23
s. the thoughts of others 463:24
Suspected: new opinions are always s. 315:5
scarce-s., animate the whole 505:3
Suspects, yet soundly loves 471:32
Suspend: s. their fate 170:2
s. your mad career 162:24
Suspended: held the sky s. 264:4
laws of God will be s. 489:31
only s...religion 103:4
our human blood almost s. 581:25
s. my religious inquiries 216:24
Suspenders: *not* forget the S. 304:11
Suspense: inconvenience of s. 200:23
Suspension of disbelief 152:26
Suspicion: above s. 120:15
coachman may go vithout s. 179:34
s...haunts the guilty 446:7
s...stuck full of eyes 440:31
Suspicions: fresh s. 471:34
s. amongst thoughts 27:22
Suspicious: men are s. 246:17
s. friend 385:29
Suspiration of forc'd breath 430:30
Suspires: Jesus from the Ground
s. 205:8
Sussex: from S. Downs, a S. moon 141:13
no more than S. weed 302:12
smell the S. air 42:5
story of S. told 42:7
S. by the sea! 302:13
S. men are noted fools 74:20
S. scales the sky 41:21
S. songs be sung 42:7
Sustain: if travail you s. 233:3
sides...not s. it 423:32
s. to-morrow's road 77:30
Sustained: saint is. it 382:13
s. and soothed 98:3
Sutlers: sapient s. of the Lord 197:24
*Sutor: ne supra crepidam s. iudi-
caret* 380:5
Swab: only have to s. a plank 173:30
Swaddling-clouts: not yet out of
his s. 433:21
Swaggering: by s...never thrive 484:27
home-spuns..s. here 467:4
Swagman: jolly s. 374:15
Swain: better than a homely s. 446:1
dull s. 340:32
frugal s. 251:26
I the happy country s. 106:29
sang the uncouth s. 343:5
s. did woo 232:4
Swains: all our s. commend her 484:40
bring the s. together 516:4
Swallow: as the s. by flying 50:37
before the s. dares 485:26
chaffering s. 87:28
flies with s.'s wings 476:33
O summer s. 524:18
our principles s. 319:18
revenge s. them up 472:12
s. a camel 60:18
s. a nest 397:5
s. down the very men 358:12
s. gudgeons ere th'are catch'd 111:6
s. has set her six young 92:27
s., my sister, O sister s. 524:11
S., S., flying, flying South 538:20
s. stopt 538:2
s. twitt'ring 229:31
to lap and to s. 568:22
Swallowed: daily s. by men's eyes 440:9
easier s. than a flap-dragon 455:26
last s. 436:9
others to be s. 27:17
s. up and lost 345:19
s. what came 225:33
Swalloweth: he s. the ground 49:27
Swallow-flights of song 532:26
Swallowing his tea in oceans 325:32
Swallows: gathering s. twitter 284:15
saw the s. gathering 336:31

Swallows (*cont.*)
s. are making them ready 568:23
s...in Cleopatra's sails 425:16
s. other sorrows 469:43
Swam: she s. to the bell-rope 39:11
s. in a gondola 428:17
Swamp: botanize in the s. 142:19
Swan: dies the s. 540:20
every goose a s. 293:19
I will play the s. 473:29
like a sleeping s. 497:10
made the wild-s. pause 538:1
Mantuan s. 162:26
some full-breasted s. 531:38
stately-sailing s. 546:11
s...floats double, s. and shadow 582:19
s. her downy cygnets save 445:26
s.'s down-feather 424:21
sweet S. of Avon! 281:18
when he a S. would be 510:20
Swanee Ribber 210:16
Swan-like: s. end 464:12
s., let me sing 116:3
Swans: all his own geese are s. 558:29
geese are s. 16:19
not s...Very like s. too 176:5
s. sing before they die 151:15
two S. of goodly hue 510:20
Swap horses while crossing 314:15
Sward: died content on pleasant
s. 287:17
sunlight and the s. 302:9
Sware: the Lord s. 398:24
Swarm of bees in May 5:17
Swarming: his cassock was s. 34:17
Swarry: friendly s. 179:19
Swarthy: queen, with s. cheeks 529:9
Swashing: remember thy s. blow 476:47
s. and a martial outside 426:28
Swat: Akond of S. 312:13
Swath: spares the next s. 284:12
Sway: above this sceptred s. 464:33
govern'd by no other s. 355:18
little s. 195:14
love of s. 384:35
required with gentle s. 347:12
sovereign s...dissolv'd 190:28
sweeping whirlwind's s. 229:23
with an absolute s. 387:2
your more habitual s. 576:21
Swayed: rod of empire might have
s. 230:4
s. about upon a rocking horse 288:12
would she be s. 221:28
Sways: by submitting, s. 384:38
salt weed s. 15:24
so s. she level 483:3
Swear: by yonder blessed moon
I s. 477:22
do not s. at all 477:23
first time I ever heard you s. 203:35
say more, s. more 483:10
s. an eternal friendship 124:16
s. by thy gracious self 477:23
s. by thy self 185:24
s. eternal friendship 504:26
s., fool, or starve 194:27
s. like a comfit-maker's wife 440:6
s. me, Kate 440:7
s. not at all 57:48
s. not by the moon 477:22
s. no where 186:17
s. to a touch o' sun 301:15
s. to never kiss the girls 91:32
s. to the truth of a song 401:20
s...upon a parcel-gilt goblet 441:31
when you rant and s. 194:28
Sweareth unto his neighbour 392:24
Swearing: let me alone for s. 484:14
Swears: s. a prayer or two 477:7
s. with so much grace 312:28
Swear-word in a rustic slum 39:12
Sweat: Agony and bloody S. 388:50
all of a muck of s. 227:22
blood, s., and tear-wrung millions 112:28
blood, toil, tears and s. 143:38
die of a s. 443:1
grunt and s. 434:4
in the s. of thy face 44:27
our midday s. 404:5

Sweat (*cont.*)
s. but for promotion 426:38
they do not s. and whine 567:20
when service s. for duty 426:38
Sweated through his apostolic skin 119:21
Sweating: s. palm to palm 266:12
s. thrust-block 299:9
young and s. devil 472:13
Sweats: bloody s. 569:10
Falstaff s. to death 439:8
s. in the eye of Phoebus 444:23
Sweep: madly s. the sky 467:7
s. away the morning dew 467:20
s. it with the besom of destruction 53:23
s. on. . citizens 426:33
s. through the deep 123:10
your chimneys I s. 76:17
Sweeping: come s. by 341:18
s. them behind him 178:10
s. whirlwind's sway 229:23
Sweeps: who s. a room 244:16
Sweet: all her task to be s. 561:7
all is not s. 280:7
as s. and musical 455:22
as s. unto a shepherd 232:5
beautiful as s.! 587:8
born to love you, s. 90:11
both s. things 78:24
buried in so s. a place 491:13
by distance. .more s. 154:1, 578:19
can must be so s. 254:27
comes in the s. o' the year 485:16
custom made this life more s. 426:29
desire accomplished is s. 50:5
does smack s. 93:25
fair, and soft, and s. 332:8
fierce hour and s. 140:22
figures strange and s. 150:21
good, amiable or s. 349:17
heard melodies are s. 287:8
his mouth is most s. 52:14
how it was s. 90:38
how s. and fair she seems 558:4
how s., how passing s. 162:6
how s. is the shepherd's s. lot 76:11
how s. the lily grows 240:16
if s., give thanks 522:13
if To-day be s. 206:19
imaginary relish is so s. 481:15
in the s. by-and-by 415:9
is she not s.? 413:31
lady s. and kind 10:20, 210:5
life is very s., brother 78:24
life lay waiting, so s., so s. 334:5
little s. 286:20
make his English s. 137:4
makes Welsh as s. 440:4
my own, my s. 536:15
nothing's so dainty s. 38:1
not so sound, as s. 245:16
not so s. now 481:30
not s. with nimble feet 569:5
O fair! O s.! 502:7
O so s. is she 281:24
pray, S., for me 248:7
ravishment its s. 285:1
smell as s. 477:16
smellest so s. 472:35
smell so s. 438:35
smell s., and blossom 501:6
smile so s. 551:5
smiles so s. 327:5
so deeply s. 442:25
softly s., in Lydian measures 191:9
so smooth, so s. 247:14
so strangely s. 82:2
so s. love seemed 82:2
so s., the sense faints 496:8
so s. to rest 478:1
so s. was ne'er so fatal 473:11
so young could be so s. 82:3
stolen waters are s. 49:53
suck his s. 231:39, 315:17
sudden as s. 338:10
s. and far from cliff and scar 538:15
s. and low 538:12
s. and twenty 482:28
s. and virtuous soul 245:14
s. Anne Page! 466:3
s. are the pleasures 285:8

Sweet (*cont.*)
s. are the uses of adversity 426:30
s. as English air 538:8
s. as my revenge 429:19
s. as stops of planetary music 493:5
s. as summer 447:9
s. as the rind was 522:26
s. as those. .feigned 538:19
s. Auburn! 224:12
s., be not proud 247:6
s. bird! 97:30, 315:21, 341:13
s., good-night! 477:24
s. is death 530:38
s. is every sound 539:5
s. is pleasure after pain 191:5
s. is revenge 115:23
s. is the breath of morn 347:22
s. is true love 530:38
s. Jack Falstaff 439:37
s. morsel 242:8
s., not lasting 431:20
s. post-prandial cigar 98:7
s. reasonableness 20:18
s. season 518:3
s. simplicity of the three per
cents 182:6
s. societies 343:4
s., sour 255:3
sweets to the s. 437:21
s., s., s. poison 447:20
s. the coming on of. .evening 347:23
s. though in sadness 496:11
s. to him who all the week 151:27
s. to myself. .so s. to you 375:13
s. to the labouring man 99:23
s. water and bitter 69:38
s. wee wife 107:16
s., when the morn is grey 121:18
s. will be the flow'r 161:19
swore my lips were s. 309:3
tell me not (S.) 319:10
things s. to taste 474:17
Thy day, s.! 165:36
too s. for words 374:17
what some have found so s. 536:1
when lovers' vows seem s. 118:28
wit enough to keep it s. 275:27
you'll look s. upon the seat 168:2
Sweeten: not s. this little hand 460:27
s. Ireland's wrong 586:14
s. my imagination 454:9
Sweeteners: best s. of tea 204:21
Sweeter: anything to me is s. 250:10
life shall thereby be the s. 462:3
neater, s. maiden 299:14
not a s. creature 472:26
often chang'd the s. 209:5
pains of love be s. 194:2
s. also than honey 392:33
s. no girl ever gave 570:30
s. than the berry 214:8
s. than the lids 485:26
s. than the marriage-feast 150:15
s. thy voice 539:5
s. too 232:5
s. woman ne'er 267:14
Sweetest: Love's s. part 185:28
passing of the s. soul 532:40
possibly s. 121:18
s. flower for scent 497:27
s. girl I know 571:1
s. hours 105:37
s. love, I do not go 186:15
s. of all singers 318:2
s. thing that ever grew 577:18
Sweetheart: dead man's s. 263:7
s. of the sun 253:19
Tray, Blanch, and S. 453:29
Sweeting: pretty s. 482:28
Sweetly: goeth down s. 52:20
make a malefactor die s. 194:19
so s. were forsworn 462:19
s. as a nightingale 479:4
s. as the lark 465:22
s. play'd in tune 107:14
Sweetmeats: breaths with s.
tainted 477:7
pyramids of s. 194:16
Sweetness: every s. that inspired 331:2
folds the lily all her s. up 539:2
linked s. 342:7

Sweetness (*cont.*)
loathe the taste of s. 440:9
love, s., goodness 351:25
may, with s. 341:24
out of the strong. .s. 46:55
secret s. in the stream 533:2
s. and light 19:25, 519:5
s. in the sad 544:1
s., mercy, majesty 319:7
s. of man's breath 267:31
thoughts whose very s. 577:10
want words, and s. 281:27
waste its s. 230:5
with s. fills the breast 132:6
Sweet peas, on tiptoe 286:27
Sweets: all its s. are gone 289:1
brought'st Thy s. 244:14
feast of nectared s. 340:24
get s. into your list 265:25
instead of s. 286:11
lost in the s. 214:34
melt their s. 425:17
stolen s. are always sweeter 266:1
stolen s. are best 144:31
s. compacted lie 245:13
s. that you suck 294:36
s. to the sweet 437:21
s. with s. war not 486:13
tasted the s. and the bitters 117:44
wilderness of s. 348:6
Sweet-springing meads 81:20
Sweet-William with his. .cottage-
smell 18:26
Swell: green s.. .dumb 254:29
his weak ankles s. 580:22
o'er thee s. and throng 364:9
stands upon the s. 424:21
s., bosom 472:10
s. the curled waters 453:3
s. the soul to rage 191:12
that green fruit would s. 285:1
voluptuous s. 113:25
with its mighty s. 288:30
Swelled: pregnant bank s. up 184:29
Swelling: angelic songs are s. 202:23
s. into bombast 194:6
s. wisibly 179:9
Swept: empty, s., and garnished 59:18
I s. the floor 221:15
s. it for half a year 130:12
s. with confused alarms 15:8
Swift: as s. to scent the sophist 4:13
beautiful and s. 492:2
be s., my soul 204:17
be s. to hear 69:30
courses as s. 455:22
ousin S. . .never be a poet 194:30
dividing the s. mind 531:28
look as s. as yours 464:21
Love is s. of foot 244:13
race is not to the s. 51:22
s. as a shadow 466:20
s. be thy flight 495:21
S. expires a driv'ler 279:10
s. in all obedience 301:26
s., slow 255:3
s. to be hurl'd 252:20
s. to its close 322:1
S. was *anima Rabelaisii* 153:10
s. without violence 401:22
time too s. 377:4
to all s. things 544:18
too s. arrives as tardy 478:9
when s. Camilla 382:32
Swifter: s. than a weaver's shuttle 48:52
s. than eagles 47:30
s. than the wandering moon 467:19
Swiftly walk over the western
wave 495:21
Swiftness never ceasing 377:4
Swig: I'll get a s. in Hell 297:5
Swike: ne s. thu never nu 10:1
Swim: I can s. 527:19
naughty night to s. in 453:22
on the undulating air they s.! 253:15
said I could not s. 129:33
s. the haven at Dunkirk 281:19
s. to thee, my Maker 355:21
s. to yonder point 448:18
temples s. before my sight 382:6
Swimmer: never a s. shall cross 525:25

INDEX

Swimmer (*cont.*)
never, I ween, did s.	323:29
not to be crossed by any s.	515:3
strong s. in his agony	115:30

Swimmest thou in wealth — 170:22

Swimming: 'arf a squadron s. — 296:21
| s. down along the Lee | 510:20 |

Swims: arena s. around him — 114:18
s. into his ken	288:19
s. or sinks or wades	346:14
who s. in sight	525:25

Swine: gr-r-r—you s.! — 96:42
husks that the s. did eat	62:14
jewel of gold in a s.'s snout	49:58
nor yet feed the s.	366:16
pearls before s.	58:18
the Gadarene S.	304:48
whole herd of s. ran..down	58:36

Swing: crop-headed Parliament s. — 90:16
don't want to s. a cat	175:1
no v'ice hed sech a s.	319:25
s. low, sweet chariot	10:2
s. me suddenly	84:7
s. of the sea	254:29
that fellow's got to s.	569:3
we s. ungirded hips	506:20

Swinged the dragon — 447:23
Swinges the scaly horror — 343:20
Swinging: s. round the circle — 269:23
| s. slow with sullen roar | 341:15 |

Swings: one stone..s. into place — 300:5
slow punt s. round	18:9
s. backwards and forwards	249:24
this and that way s.	19:4
we pulls up on the s.	135:2

Swinish: hoofs of a s. multitude — 102:18
Swipes: finish up your s. — 296:17
| s. they take in | 42:12 |
Switched his long tail — 151:8
Switzerland..an inferior..Scotland — 505:31
Swollen: beareth up things light and s. — 27:1
| s. with wind | 342:29 |
Swoon: else s. to death — 288:18
Swooned: nor s., nor utter'd cry — 538:25
Swoons: poetry sinks and s. — 309:15
Swoop: all at one s. — 563:24
| one fell s. | 460:21 |
Swoops down a furlong sheer — 301:27
Swop for my dear old Dutch — 142:22
Sword: bear my trusty s. — 159:39
brave man with a s.	569:4
chase..with a naked s.	243:28
children..s. and fire	530:12
deputed s.	461:28
die on mine own s.	461:9
escapeth the s. of Hazael	48:9
ever struck with s.	328:24
every..whipster gets my s.	473:28
eye, tongue, s.	434:14
fallen by the edge of the s.	57:3
famous by my s.	355:20
flesh'd thy maiden s.	441:3
gird on thy s.	81:5
had a s. upstairs	584:4
hides a s.	443:12
his father's s.	356:27
his good s. rust	151:31
his s. was in the sheath	162:11
in which the s. was servant	509:35
is the s. unsway'd?	476:31
I with s. will open	465:37
justice to break her s.	473:11
Laws chang'd according to..the S.	135:28
lift up s. against nation	52:31
lightnings Thy s.	142:26
man for the s.	538:24
mightier than the s.	322:11
more splendid than the s.	517:9
my soul from the s.	393:7
my s., I give to him	99:39
never sheathe the s.	21:6
no flourishing with his s.	406:14
nor a good s.	245:2
nor shall my S. sleep	75:16
nor s. nor spear	161:4
not..peace, but a s.	59:1
not since put up my s.	448:32
pen is worse than the s.	109:13

Sword (*cont.*)
perish with the s.	60:46
put up thy s.	63:66
rebellion broached on his s.	445:6
rust that never stained thy s.	254:16
sets the s. back	141:8
sharp as a two-edged s.	49:44
sharper than any two edged s.	69:8
sharp two edged s.	70:27
s., a horse, a shield	319:10
s. in hand upon Afric's passes	142:3
s., glued to my scabbard	334:26
s. of an Angel King	75:6
s. of Common Sense	335:24
s. of justice..lay down	170:17
s. outwears its sheath	119:5
s. sung on the barren heath	74:26
s. that severs all	336:18
s., the mace	444:23
S. went out to sea	359:11
their tongue a sharp s.	395:18
they that take the s.	60:46
thy s. upon thy thigh	394:22
to hack thy s.	439:26
two-edged s.	400:26
unsmote by the s.	118:39
vorpal s.	129:39(−130)
when he first drew the s.	145:25
who pulleth out this s.	328:3
with s. of justice	195:7
with the edge of the s.	46:16

Swords: his words..very s. — 395:13
keep up your bright s.	469:40
our s. shall play the orators	330:22
sheath'd their s.	443:25
splendid with s.	523:2
stout hearts and sharp s.	72:25
s. into ploughshares	52:31
s. must have leapt	102:11
turns our s.	452:1
your s., made rich	459:3

Sword-sway — 418:29
Swore: by the nine gods he s. — 323:10
habitually s.	120:26
jested, quaff'd and s.	188:29
knew not what to say..s.	118:1
she s., in faith, 'twas strange	470:3
s. not at all	42:24
s. terribly in Flanders	513:14
was I sober when I s.?	207:21
when the son s.	109:28

Sworn: had I so s. as you — 457:13
I have s.	399:21
I have s. thee fair	488:22
s. brother..to..Necessity	475:27

Swosser: maxim of Captain S.'s — 173:30
Swound: noises in a s. — 148:26
Sycamore: nightingale in the s. — 516:12
| sighing by a s. tree | 473:6 |

Syllabes: still may s. jar — 281:27
Syllable: chase a panting s. — 162:2
| last s. of recorded time | 461:4 |
| s. men's names | 340:10 |

Syllables: equal s...require — 382:30
| heroic s. | 116:26 |
| s. govern the world | 148:6 |

Syllogisms hang not on my tongue — 159:12
Sylph: only s. I ever saw — 177:19
Symbols: huge cloudy s. — 289:5
| s., and inhabit s. | 200:31 |

Symmetry: its s...as of thunder — 412:29
| spoilers of the s. of shelves | 306:21 |
| thy fearful s. | 75:24(−76) |

Sympathetic: source of s. tears — 231:12
| s. gunpowder | 111:5 |
| s. tear | 229:18 |

Sympathies: vain s.! — 573:26
Sympathize: I deeply s. — 130:20
| so to s. | 343:11 |
Sympathizeth with all things — 86:25
Sympathy: by admiration, by s. — 201:3
in souls a s. with sounds	163:48
our heartfelt s.	221:3
primal s.	576:20
secret s.	417:21
s. in choice	466:20
world is wrought to s.	498:6

Symphonies: five sweet s. — 410:12
Symphony: Beethoven's Fifth S. — 210:7
| consort to th' angelic s. | 343:17 |
| her s. and song | 151:33(−152) |

Symplegades: narrowing S.	5±2:10
Symptom of constitutional liberty	217:10
Symptoms: how does your s. segashuate?	238:16
Syne: for auld land s.	104:14
Synod: s. in thy heart	355:18
S. of Cooks	271:19
Syntax: in his s. and in his words	20:2
Syrian: allur'd her S. damsels	344:32
lorn S. town..S. stars look down	17:9
Syrinx: after S. speed	332:16
Syrtes and soft Sicily	18:16
Syrups: drowsy s.	471:43
lucent s.	285:25
System: disturb the s. of life	271:33
educated by a s.	337:34
energies of our s.	29:19
erected into a s. of Government	223:1
how s. into s. runs	383:9
I must Create a S.	75:2
oppose every s.	102:37
s...last her time	414:9
s. of Prince's nails	174:33
Systems: away with S.!	337:35
our little s.	531:41
wheeling s. darken	545:1

T

T: answered..to a T.	203:26
whatever Miss T. eats	171:17
Tabac: qui vit sans t.	353:20
Tabbies: we're not as t. are	121:22
Taberna: in t. mori	13:9
Tabernacle: dwell in thy t.	392:24
from out its Orient t.	545:6
set a t. for the sun	392:32
Tabernacles of thy grace	421:3
Tabernas: pauperum t. regumque turris	258:8
Table: about my t. to and fro	586:15
etherized upon a t.	197:15
fall from their masters' t.	59:40
fell from the rich man's t.	62:24
from the t. of my memory	432:20
joy of the whole t.	459:18
made you a bad t.	271:5
more wondrous still the t.	74:8
my t. thou hast furnished	421:1
not a t. fish	40:30
repairs of a t.	277:3
round about thy t.	399:36
set the t. on a roar	437:15
sit still for once at t.	249:23
t. of green fields	443:19
T. of Kindred and Affinity	401:15
t. of the Moveable Feasts	388:5
thou shalt prepare a t.	393:10
write it before them in a t.	53:37
Table Bay: going to T.	294:19
Table-lands: shining t.	537:27
Table Mountain: I reside at T.	239:1
Tables: creatures set upon t.	272:34
fleshy t. of the heart	67:21
furnish forth the marriage t.	431:4
my t., meet it is	432:21
near a thousand t. pined	575:4
not your trade to make t.	271:5
on the t. of young ladies	326:11
plain upon t.	56:9
serve t.	64:33
Tablets: thy t., Memory!	16:24
Taboo'd: repose is t. by anxiety	219:9
Tabor: to the t.'s sound	576:3
Tabulae: solventur risu t.	261:21
Tabulis: cum t. animum censoris.. honesti	257:19
Tace..Latin for a candle	204:6
Tâche: ta longue et lourde t.	553:2
Tack about	212:18
Tackle: bravery on and t. trim	350:31
mariners, besides..t.	280:4
silken t.	424:7
try and t. him	173:17
Tactics: master of the art of t.	29:6
Tadlow: when T. walks the streets	202:10
Tadpole: T. and Taper	181:29
when you were a t.	504:13
Taffeta: changeable t.	483:7

Taffeta (cont.)
flame-colour'd t. 438:13
t. phrases 455:29
Taffy: T. dancing through the fern 299:24
T. was a Welshman 369:1
Tag, rag, merry derry 370:5
Tail: against a comet's t. 508:1
beginning with the end of the t. 129:4
Chittabob's t. was the finest 34:33
corking-pin..through his t. 33:18
durst not touch her t. 366:19
for counsel to thee t. 319:27
for the salmon's t. 470:29
guinea-pig up by the t. 315:13
has a nimble t. 281:19
her t. came out 34:20
he wagged his t. 249:20
His languid t. 585:11
horror of his folded t. 343:20
I'll not pull her t. 367:8
improve his shining t. 128:23
like a polly-wog's t. 560:14
like a rat without a t. 456:10
salt on a woman's t. 110:40
sensations of its 't.' 29:3
such a little t. behind 40:25
switched his long t. 151:8
t. must wag the dog 295:15
their t. the rudder 191:29
thereby hangs a t.
                427:14, 471:25, 479:5
thin mane, thick t. 488:27
thy t. hangs down 301:7
treading on my t. 129:22
where his t. came through 507:20
where the t. came through 151:9
with his t. awey the flye smyteth 138:20
Tailor: call'd the t. lown 471:11
my coat from the t. 227:28
ninth part..of a t. 126:7
Tailors: four and twenty t. 366:19
run, t., run 366:19
Tails: bring their t. behind them 367:14
cut off their t. 369:8
holding their neighbours' t. 298:20
nasty long t. 34:15
stings in their t. 71:13
t. of both hung down 504:6
t. you lose 167:1
up-t. all 280:12
Taint: I cannot t. with fear 460:33
never t. my love 473:3
Tainted: every t. breeze 100:30
our t. nature 582:9
see that the supply is not t. 416:4
what plea so t. 464:14
Taisez-vous! 12:19
Take: all earth can t. 493:27
believe and t. for granted 27:16
I prays der Lord, 'T. anyding'
Man's Forgiveness give—and t. 207:12
not to t. away 493:11
t. all the rest 558:1
t. and break us 241:26
t. any heart 221:30
t. a pair of sparkling eyes 218:25
t. a thought an' men' 104:5
t. away all at one swoop 563:24
t. away that star and garter 23:16
t. away the grief of a wound? 440:30
t. away these baubles 167:8
t. back the hope you gave 92:31
t. her up tenderly 252:12
t. him and cut him out 478:20
t. him as we find him 294:18
t. him for all in all 431:6
t. hold of one man 52:36
t. hold o' the Wings o' the Mornin' 304:1
t. in God 319:13
t. in sail 199:30
t. it away! 372:18
t. me back to the Gaierty hotel 21:4
t. me to you 185:19
t. my life 203:18
t. not thy holy Spirit 395:9
t. now thy son 44:54
t., O t. those lips away 462:16
t. that, you hound 188:7
t. thee with her eyelids 49:48

Take (cont.)
t. the flower 296:16
t. the Golden Road 208:14
t. the good the gods provide 191:9
t. the Name of..God in vain 390:8
t. the nasty soup away 249:18
t. the tone of the company 139:13
t. the war 296:19
t. the winds of March 485:26
t. under my wing 220:16
t. up the White Man's burden 303:24
t. up thy Song 375:19
t. what this sweet hour yields 494:9
t. what thou wilt away 163:47
t., who have the power 580:15
t. with shame our own opinion 200:37
t. your own part 78:30
that I believe, and t. it 197:35
them as t. advantage 196:11
these thou shalt not t. 525:6
this cannot t. her 517:11
whose wife shall I t.? 357:11
wilt thou yet t. all, Galilean? 525:6
Taken: all things are t. from us 535:17
have t. nothing 61:27
not be t. away from her 61:45
one shall be t. 60:27
only t. from the French 499:22
t. at the flood 451:29
t. away even that which he hath 60:32
t. away the key of knowledge 61:50
t. away this old man's daughter 469:45
t. away thy blessing 45:2
t. in and done for 292:16
t. in together 199:18
the Lord hath t. away 48:40
they've t. me in 106:23
thoughtfully t. 121:22
when t...shaken 154:19
Takes: him that t. 464:33
like that it t. away 118:18
whoever gives, t. liberty 185:21
Taketh: he that t. a city 50:17
how that glittering t. me! 247:13
the Lord t. me up 393:21
Taking: in the t. of it breathe 295:5
know what a's doing a-t. o' meä? 537:10
not worth our t. 412:11
t. in one another's washing 6:3
t. me for him 313:7
t. of the Manhood into God 388:42
Taking-off: damnation of his t. 457:9
Talbot: Warwick and T. 444:28
Tale: adorn a t. 279:6
as it were a t. that is told 397:16
cometh unto you, with a t. 502:8
debonair and gentle t. 289:3
every shepherd tells his t. 341:34
every t. condemns me 476:36
her terrible t. 220:9
his homely t. 578:11
honest t. speeds best 476:28
how many a t. 357:15
I could a t. unfold 432:9
I say the t. as 'twas said 417:15
I should have had a t. to tell 416:7
I tell this t. 303:7
listen to my t. of woe 204:4
long preamble of a t. 138:9
many a broken t. 378:16
ower true t. 419:20
plain t...put you down 439:25
sad t.'s best for winter 485:10
same t. repeat 576:8
schoolboy's t. 113:11
sweet t. of the sun 439:14
takes up the wondrous t. 2:26
t. in everything 580:23
t. is yet to run 302:24
t. not too importunate 359:1
t. of a tub 358:11, 563:26
t. of Troy divine 341:18
t. should be judicious 159:16
t. told by an idiot 461:4
t. was undoubtedly true 309:26
tell his t. untrewe 137:23
tell t., tit! 369:2
thereby hangs a t.
                427:14, 471:25, 479:5
to him my t. I teach 150:12

Tale (cont.)
told the merriest t. 418:24
twice-told t. 117:42, 447:35
unvarnish'd t. 469:45
who-so shal telle a t. 137:23
with a t. forsooth he cometh 502:8
your t., sir, would cure deafness 479:21
Tale-bearers are as bad 500:32
Talent: blest with each t. 385:29
his single t. 275:3
t. alone cannot make a writer 201:10
T. does what it can 337:43
t. instantly recognizes genius 188:28
t. of our English nation 193:23
that one T. 351:21
Talent pour le silence 126:31
Talent: es bildet ein T. 224:4
Talented: sure he's a t. man 387:20
Talents: if you have great t. 406:10
ministry of all the t. 10:16
they have tried their t. 152:30
unto one he gave five t. 60:28
Talents: ouverte aux t. 126:2, 360:26
Tales: increased with t. 26:1
mine eyes will tell t. 482:26
our dreams are t. 171:1
seemed to them as idle t. 62:54
t., marvellous 208:9
t. of wild Cashmere 571:6
t. to cheat thee of a sigh 571:6
tell old t. 454:19
tell t...to..Jove 452:40
their t. of Iove 98:22
wish the Arabian T. were true 363:13
wrapt Truth in t. 125:2
Talismans: books are not seldom t. 163:51
Talk: always t. who never think 401:39
as the Pelagians do vainly t. 401:4
beginning to t. 239:15
difference of men's t. 377:19
feed on cates and have him t. 440:2
have out his t. 273:29
high t. with the..dead 494:5
his t. was like a stream 387:23
honest t. and wholesome wine 540:30
how he will t. 312:30
if you can t. with crowds 297:12
in after-dinner t. 537:3
it would t. 38:7
leave the Wise to t. 206:9
let's t. of graves 475:6
loves to hear himself t. 478:6
made ignoble t. 530:39
mair they t. 107:28
night is crept upon our t. 451:30
nor to find t. and discourse 27:16
nothing but t. of his horse 463:9
no use to t. to me 262:16
personal t. 578:18
some little T. 206:16
t. about the pews 140:2
t. about the rest of us 249:4
t. a little wild 446:11
t., and not the intrigue 229:10
t. a word with this..Theban 453:26
t. but a tinkling cymbal 26:16
t. him out of patience 471:26
t. like whales 227:29
t. not to me of a name 118:32
t. of many things 130:15
t. six times with the same 116:39
t. slid north 294:29
t. so very queer 34:28
t. too wise 297:10
t. with marineres 150:8
t. with some old lover's ghost 185:34
t. with you, walk with you 463:16
vulgar t. like a dentist 569:19
walk..and t. with you 208:18
whose t. is of bullocks 57:12
who t. too much 190:21
winter t. by the fireside 27:2
you may t. o' gin 297:1
Talked: being t. about..not being t. about 570:5
England t. of ale 141:25
few men t. of freedom 141:25
he t. on for ever 239:21
I believe they t. of me 203:11
louder he t. of his honour 200:1

INDEX

Talked (cont.)
so much they t. 143:21
t. like poor Poll 213:12
t. the night away 224:20
t. to him sevairely 298:21
t. with him in his retirement 175:8
while he t. with us 62:55
Talkers: most fluent t. 239:28
Talking: empty heads and tongues a-t. 263:18
Frenchman must be always t. 274:20
go on t. 490:17
he is t., or he is pursuing 48:3
he will be t. 469:2
I wonder that you will still be t. 468:2
nor foolish t., nor jesting 68:2
t. about being a gentleman 518:5
t. and eloquence 280:5
t. blockhead 203:9
t. of Michelangelo 197:16
t. politics after dinner 181:6
tired the sun with t. 157:16
Talking-machine 126:35
Talks: female atheist t. you dead 278:30
fish that t. 170:25
if a man t. of his misfortunes 274:24
liked the way it t. 405:10
liquor t. mighty loud 238:21
Minerva when she t. 281:25
only t. about her hair 545:14
t. about justice and right 300:7
t. as familiary of John a Gaunt 442:16
t. it so very fast 203:14
t. loudly against religion 513:11
t. of darkness at noon-day 161:32
Tall: adequately t. 140:8
as t. a man as any 482:4
divinely t. 529:8
her stature t. 115:18
many a good t. fellow 438:35
rather t. and stately 8:17
she is t. and stately 536:3
so t., he almost touch'd 250:1
t. as Amazon 287:4
t. building 164:29
t. fellow of thy hands 485:37
t. men..empty heads 24:38
t. ship 334:10
were I so t. 562:2
where your t. young men 141:14
Taller by..the breadth of my nail 519:9
Tallest of boys 34:4
Tally: no other books but the..t. 445:40
Talmud: rather believe..the T. 25:23
Tam: T. kent what was what 108:12
T. lo'ed him 108:5
T.! thou'll get thy fairin' 108:14
T. was glorious 108:6
Tamariks: high noon behind the t. 295:9
Tambourine on her other knee 177:19
Tamburlaine, the Scourge of God 331:8
Tame: be not too t. neither 434:16
canst not t. 243:26
hey-day in the blood is t. 435:47
ne'er so t., so cherished 440:31
t. villatic fowl 351:2
that beauty cannot t. 33:3
tongue can no man t. 69:37
wholly t. 302:8
Tamed: in one year t. 332:26
Tamer of the human breast 230:15
Taming my wild heart 468:27
Tanais: hardly flows the freezing T. 381:18
Tandy: I met wid Napper T. 9:6
Tang: thy tongue t. arguments 483:19
tongue with a t. 479:42
Tangled: t. in amorous nets 350:1
t. in her hair 319:4
t. Trinities 300:19
Tangles of Neæra's hair 342:20
Tannenbaum: O T., O T. 416:3
Tanner: one Simon a t. 64:45
Tanqueray: The Second Mrs. T. 41:13
Tantallan: Time may gnaw T. 107:27
Tap at the pane 93:22
Taper: his nails, which were t. 238:37
like the gleaming t.'s light 224:10
out went the t. 285:18
saw the t. burning 417:35

Taper (cont.)
Tadpole and T. 181:29
t. of conviviality 177:28
t. to the outward room 186:12
to the sun my little t. 116:38
where yon t. cheers 225:11
with t. light 447:39
Tapers: frequent in t. 238:37
glimmering t. to the sun 165:2
lit her glimmering t. 544:21
priests, t., temples 382:6
Tapestry: in t. halls 340:17
wrong side of a Turkey t. 264:19
Tapping: suddenly there came a t. 380:22
Tapsalteerie: a' gae t. O! 105:38
Tapster: of a surly T. tell 207:19
Tar: merry maiden and the t. 221:22
Tara: once through T.'s halls 356:20
Taradiddles: for telling t. 313:10
Tarantara: t., t. 221:33
Ta-ra-ra-boom-de-ay! 415:19
Tar-Baby: T. aint sayin' nuthin' 238:17
what he call a T. 238:15
Tar-barrel: black as a t. 130:6
Tard: *l'on vient trop t.* 97:32
Tardy: as t. as too slow 478:9
t. bust 279:4
Tare each other in their slime 532:38
Tares: clasping t. cling round 165:17
his enemy..sowed t. 59:25
t. of mine own brain 86:17
Tarn: dark t. dry 172:1
Tarnish late on Wenlock Edge 263:13
Tarnished with rust 569:15
Tarnishing eye 337:6
Tarpaulin: in my t. jacket 568:24
Tarquin: great house of T. 323:10
T.'s ravishing strides 458:1
Tarried: have I not t.? 480:38
too long we have t. 312:1
Tarrieth: guest that t. but a day 56:26
Tarry: boatman, do not t.! 122:23
for ever t. 247:10
longer will t. 189:6
t. a while, says Slow 366:13
t. the grinding 480:38
t. till they push us 452:5
that he t. till I come 64:20
why t. the wheels 46:51
Tarrying: make no long t., O my God 394:14
Tarshish: howl, ye ships of T. 53:30
Tarsus: stately ship of T. 350:31
Tart: t., cathartic virtue 200:17
t. temper never mellows 267:19
Tartan: beneath the t. plaid 23:17
Tartarly: so savage and T. 118:2
Tartary: Agib, Prince of T. 218:9
Tarts: made some t. 129:27, 368:15
stole the t. 368:15
stole those t. 129:27
Task: common t. 291:7
delightful t.! 546:12
gets his t. 269:33
labourer's t. is o'er 198:14
long day's t. is done 425:21
my t. accomplished 241:23
one t. for all 296:20
sees some t. begin 318:13
sets love a t. like that 265:20
thy worldly t. hast done 430:1
to this childish t. 516:19
what he reads as a t. 271:9
with weary t. fordone 467:35
Task-master: in my great T.'s eye 351:13
Tasks: t. in hours of insight 16:29
t. of real life 575:5
Tassel-gentle: lure this t. back 477:26
Tassie: in a silver t. 105:36
Taste: bud may have a bitter t. 161:19
common sense and good t. 489:11
difference of t. in jokes 196:17
forgot the t. of fears 461:3
give us a t. of your quality 433:24
he had a kind of t. 463:27
her t. exact 220:9
himself create the t. 583:5
I did but t. a little honey 47:14
I t. no politics in boil'd 505:32
killibeate t. 179:20

Taste (cont.)
let me t. the whole of it 95:11
let me t. your ware 368:19
loathe the t. of sweetness 440:9
man's hand is not able to t. 467:23
matter o' t. 178:42
momentary t. of BEING 206:21
never t. who always drink 401:39
no t. when you married me 500:34
offended t... rejected 349:22
pictures, t., Shakespeare 227:23
sans t. 427:21
Shakespeare..wanted t. 558:16
t. and fancy of the speller 179:13
t. and see 393:38
t. any drink once 120:4
t. for drink 218:20
t. for marriages 182:23
t. for tippling 218:19
t. is the feminine of genius 207:34
t. my *Anno Domini* 203:4
t. My meat 244:22
t. not when the wine-cup 419:16
t. your legs, sir 483:25
things sweet to t. 474:17
tho' t., tho' genius bless 153:28
touch not; t. not 68:29
tree, whose mortal t. 344:1
wild vicissitudes of t. 278:36
Tasted: can't be t. in a sip 177:34
had Horace or Anacreon t. 280:9
some books are to be t. 27:17
t. her sweet body 472:3
t. two worms 511:3
Tastes: our t. greatly alter 271:23
so various are the t. of men 3:9
their t. may not be the same 490:27
Tasting of Flora 287:24
Tasty: hutch of t. lust 254:27
Tat: die T. ist alles 223:21
Tattered and torn 369:6
Tatters: tear a passion to t. 434:15
Tattle: entertaining t. 139:22
Tattlers also and busybodies 68:49
Tattling many a broken tale 378:16
Tatty-coram: count five-and-twenty, T. 175:34
Taught: afterward he t. 137:17
all they've t. me 356:33
Cristes lore..he t. 137:18
ever to be t. 384:32
happy is he born and t. 583:9
he t. us little 16:21
I was t. in Paradise 285:31
mind what I am t. 527:6
of right and wrong he t. 14:26
plainest t. and easiest learnt 350:14
t. as if you t. them not 383:3
t...as one having authority 58:29
t. by the Power 225:12
t. by time 299:3
t. me first to beg 465:16
Taunting: grave, and not t. 26:26
Tauris: de t. narrat arator 402:15
Tavern: choicer than the Mermaid T. 287:1
couplets in a t. hall 117:8
happiness .. produced .. by a good t. 272:39
t. chair 277:4
t. in the town 10:21
Voice within the T. 205:6
vulgar and t. music 86:33
within the T. caught 207:8, 9
Taverns: knew the t. wel 137:2
sat in t. 263:31
Tawny: t. body 524:13
t. weed tobacco 279:24
Tawny-throated 17:11
Tax: *Excise.* A hateful t. 277:27
I t. not you, you elements 453:6
no right to t. the Americans 388:2
to t. and to please 100:12
Taxation: t. and representation 388:2
t. without representation 371:6
Taxed: all the world should be t. 61:16
whips his t. top 505:28
Taxes: all t...fall upon agriculture 217:9
as true..as t. is 174:31
death and t. 211:9
people overlaid with t. 27:25

[946]

INDEX

Taxes (cont.)
t. upon every article 505:27
whoever pays the t. 298:8
Taylor, the Shakespeare of divines 199:24
T.C.: Picture of little T. 333:4
Te Deum laudamus 13:14
Tea: arg'd the thing at t. 125:21
best sweeteners of t. 204:21
breakfast, dinner, lunch, and t. 41:3
coffee, t., chocolate 13:17
if this is coffee, I want t. 403:39
is there honey still for t.? 84:15
nothing on it but t. 129:5
slavery of the t. and coffee 147:16
some'll swallow t. 333:22
some sipping t. 578:27
sometimes t. 385:14
swallowing his t. in oceans 325:32
take her t. without a stratagem 586:26
take some more t. 129:9
t., although an Oriental 142:9
t. and scandal 154:30
t. is not my diversion 304:23
t. of our host 222:18
t...taste of boiled boots 542:12
took t. and comfortable advice 290:7
want my cup of t. 372:20
we'll all have t. 173:19
with t. amuses the evening 278:1
Teach: easier t. twenty what were good 463:8
gladly t. 137:7
let such t. others 382:20
no matter what you t. them first 271:12
she doth t. the torches 477:9
still pleased to t. 383:6
t. him how to live 387:11
t. him how to tell my story 470:3
t. me at once 382:8
t. me half the gladness 498:10
t. me how a beggar..answer'd 465:16
t. me more than hell to shun 386:30
t. me, my God and King 244:15
t. me to feel another's woe 386:31
t. me to live 292:2
t. me yet somewhat 540:17
t. ourselves that honourable stop 471:5
t. the rustic moralist to die 230:8
t. thy ways unto the wicked 395:9
t. us delight 295:8
t. us how to live 164:34
t. us to bear the yoke 295:6
t. ye how to climb 341:5
to him my tale I t. 150:12
years t. much 200:14
Teacher: for the t.'s sake 170:3, 203:21, 250:30
let Nature be your t. 581:15
t. did reply 233:23(-234)
tenderest t. 229:14
Teachers: governors, t., spiritual pastors 391:7
his daily t. had been woods 573:8
more understanding than my t. 399:20
Teaches: he who cannot, t. 490:31
Teaching: follow my own t. 463:8
t. nations how to live 352:24
Teacup: in t. times 540:18
Storm in a T. 43:18
Tea-drinker: hardened and shameless t. 278:1
Tea-kettle: back to the t. 180:19
Team: is my t. ploughing? 263:4
t. of little atomies 477:7
Teapot: fill the t. up 372:16
Tear: all he had, a t. 230:13
aye the t. comes 104:24
charm thee to a t. 571:6
drop a t. 521:2
dropped a t. upon the word 513:20
droppe the brynie t. 136:17
dry the starting t. 218:1
Erin, the t. and the smile 356:17
every t. from every eye 73:25
every woe a t. can claim 117:40
fallen a splendid t. 536:15
forbade the rising t. 417:6
from your eyelids wip'd a t. 427:19
hast *thou* no t.? 380:19
here did she fall a t. 475:14
homage of a t. 113:15

Tear (cont.)
I did not think to shed a t. 446:28
King dropped a t. 73:16
language of a t. 143:28
many a t. 375:21
meed of some melodious t. 342:10
no longer t. his heart 521:27
not a t. must o'er her fall 89:1
part to t. a cat in 466:25
perhaps a t. 160:28
rain'd many a t. 436:30
repress'd the starting t. 276:15
shed a bitter t. 130:12
shed one English t. 323:9
sympathetic t. 229:18
t. a passion to tatters 434:15
t. be duly shed 153:22
t. blinded his e'e 30:17, 31:24
t. each other's eyes 561:25
t. her tattered ensign down 251:5
t. him for his bad verses 451:3
t. in her eye 418:20
t. is an intellectual thing 75:6
t. it from thy Throne 161:3
t. out your 'eart 299:22
t. that is wip'd 162:8
t. the cave where Echo lies 477:26
t. was in his eye 323:4
toning of a t. 246:5
'twill cost a sigh, a t. 33:14
unanswerable t. 115:5
upon Fox's grave the t. 418:5
without a t. 193:40
word, or sigh, or t. 150:31
Tear-floods: no t. 186:24
Tearing his meat 325:32
Tears: all thy T. wash out 207:2
baptiz'd in t. 310:2
Beauty, in a mist of t. 584:5
before my t. did drown it 244:9
beguile her of her t. 470:3
big round t. 426:31, 546:21
bitter t. to shed 157:15
blood, toil, t. and sweat 143:38
brings t. into his eyes 127:4
came her t. 538:27
crocodile's t. 109:27
dashed with light quick t. 522:17
dearth of woman's t. 365:21
dim with childish t. 574:33
dip their wings in t. 532:26
down and full of t. 475:19
drinkest the t. of children 172:18
drop, drop, slow t. 209:3
droppings of warm t. 89:6
drop t. as fast 474:2
drop thy foolish t. 528:21
drown the stage with t. 433:32
eyes and t...the same 332:11
falling t. which dim 497:3
fight back..the t. 551:13
foolish t. would flow 35:11
fountain of sweet t. 581:6
fountains fraught with t. 305:14
gave me up to t. 445:3
God shall wipe away all t. 71:8
greatness of the world in t. 586:7
her salt t. fell from her 473:6
her t. fell with the dews 535:31
her winds and waters sighs and t. 423:26
I forbid my t. 437:2
if you have t. 450:27
I heard her t. 410:14
in a flood of t. and a Sedan chair 179:18
in silence and t. 119:29
in t. amid the alien corn 288:1
in the mist of t. 544:13
I owe more t. to this dead man 452:2
keep time with my salt t. 279:28
kiss again with t. 538:9
kisses, t., and smiles 580:20
like Niobe, all t. 430:33(-431)
long drip of human t. 236:15
loos'd our heart in t. 16:22
made of sighs and t. 428:28
mine eyes from t. 399:6
mine own t. do scald 454:14
move the muse to t. 159:24
my son in t. 219:4
my t. into thy bottle 395:15

Tears (cont.)
my t. must stop 253:27
no arithmetic but t. 292:17
nothing is here for t. 351:6
now am full of t. 584:11
our bitter t. o'erflow 339:11
parents' t. 344:28
Pleasure, blind with t. 491:21
quite melted into t. 292:18
recollecting with t. 128:12
remember with t. 4:19
rich flames, and hired t. 87:3
scare me with thy t. 540:22
shed t. when they would devour 27:40
shuddering, also, and t. 561:12
sink'st in thine own t. 170:22
Siren t. 488:8
smiles, t., of all my life 88:24
smiles, the t. 357:13
some natural t. they dropped 349:31
sooner dry than women's t. 563:29
sought it carefully with t. 69:20
source of sympathetic t. 231:12
t. and laughters 89:2
t. and smiles like us He knew 4:3
t. are in my eyes 334:15
t. for all souls in trouble 329:5
t. from the depth 538:17
t., idle t. 538:17
t. in his eyes 433:31
t. live in an onion 423:28
t. no bitterness 322:2
t. no longer flow 83:3
t. of gold 77:2
t. of it are wet 424:17
t. of the sky 139:3
t. out the heart of it 305:4
t. shall drown the wind 457:9
t. that overflow thy urn 308:19
their t., their angry t. 584:22
their t., their little triumphs 231:4
they are cruel t. 473:11
they that sow in t. 399:34
those seeing t. 332:11
though our t. thaw not 491:14
through my t. 209:4, 545:2
Time with a gift of t. 522:5
tired of t. and laughter 523:18
too deep for t. 576:22(-577)
too freely moved to t. 41:5
to supper with a flood of t. 174:22
vale of t.? 90:36
votive t. 493:27
water'd heaven with their t. 75:24(-76)
weep barren t. 496:24
weep thy girlish t. 561:3
wipe another's t. 109:1
with mine own t. 475:22
with silence and t. 119:30
with the bread of t. 397:2
wrong'd orphans' t. 334:26
Tear-wrung millions 112:28
Teas: treat housemaids to his t. 142:1
Tease: fleas that t. 42:9
t. her with our plaint 18:28
t. the huswife's wool 340:38
t. us out of thought 287:14
thus t. me together 215:4
Teases: he knows it t. 129:1
Tea-shops: low-class t. 503:15
Tea-time: expire before t. 505:8
Teatray: like a t. in the sky 129:5
Teazle: Lady T., by all that's wonderful! 500:42
Tecum habita 378:6
Teddington: which is T. 301:6
Tedious: more t. than the dial 472:18
t. as a king 469:1
t. as a tired horse 440:2
t. as a twice-told tale 447:35
t. as go o'er 459:25
t. as to work 438:31
these t. old fools? 433:8
thinking his prattle..t. 475:29
time is our t. song 343:25
twice ten t. years 159:32
Teeming: Cynthia t. 332:10
t. mistress 384:30
Teems with hidden meaning 222:11
Tees: by Arno for my lovelier T. 323:8
Teeth: cast into my t. 451:24

Teeth (cont.)
cast me in the t. 394:20
children's t. are set on edge 55:29
gnashing of t. 58:33
makes my t. watter 208:24
not show their t. 462:30
out of the t. of emulation 449:26
sans t., sans eyes 427:21
taking out his false t. 187:15
t. and forehead of our faults 435:35
t. o' Time 107:27
thy t. are like a flock of sheep 52:5
whose t. are spears 395:18
with thy sharp t. 426:13
Teeth-chattering Month 153:15
Teetotaller: husband was a t. 187:15
no woman should marry a t. 514:27
only a beer t. 489:15
Tekel: mene, mene, t., upharsin 55:42
Tela: fidus quae t. gerebat Achates 553:12
Telemachus: mine own T. 541:2
Tell: but I can t. 82:2
canst not t. whence 63:7
canst thou t. me 29:24(-30)
can't t. where to find them 367:14
don't t. me she's a Paedobaptist? 228:1
give me leave to t. ye 245:19
I can t. you, anyhow 100:1
I can't t. how 11:20
I could never t. why 221:9
I could t. you no more 318:9
I fain would t. 410:25
I'll t. thee everything I can 131:22
I..t. thee what is to be fear'd 448:27
I t. you that..you..know 450:33
kiss and t. 155:13
let ill tidings t. themselves 424:15
little Lamb, I'll t. thee 76:10
men of sense never t. it 423:1
merry and sad to t. 38:28
needs no ghost..to t. us this 432:22
not easy to t. what it is 273:13
scarcely t. to ony 105:18
sensible men never t. 182:5
t. her in Spanish 91:30
t. her, t. her, what I t. to thee 538:19
t. him to his teeth 436:40
t. it not in Gath 47:29
t. me if that any is 88:25
t. me, my heart 322:6
t. me, my soul 381:29
t. me not, in mournful numbers 317:5
t. me not (Sweet) 319:10
t. me where 264:14
t. me, where all past years are 186:16
t. me whom you live with 139:12
t. not as new 159:16
t. tale, tit! 369:2
t. them, dear 199:26
t. the most heart-easing 288:16
t. them that come after 394:35
t. them, they are men 230:27
t. us what and where they be 536:18
t. us what he heard 231:23
t. you who Time ambles withal 428:9
that I cannot t. 507:9
that which hath wings shall t. 51:26
they cannot t. 425:16
they didn't t. 303:23
to dream of, not to t. 150:22
what I t. you three times 128:4
whereby I can t. 373:14
why I cannot t. 85:10
woman who would t. one that 570:16
you must not t. us 179:15
you must somehow t. 358:23
you never can t. 491:7
Teller: bad news infects the t. 423:23
truth never hurts the t. 91:24
Telleth: one day t. another 392:32
Telling: I am t. you 566:2
t. a man he was wrong 147:22
Tells: Bible t. me so 560:26
every shepherd t. his tale 341:34
nobody t. me anything 213:4
Tell-tale: these t. women 476:26
Tellus: cost..T. keener pangs 286:15
Tellus: fundit .. facilem victum iustissima t. 556:15
magna parens frugum, Saturnia t. 556:14
Téméraire: Fighting T. 363:6

Tempe: in shade of T. sit 502:2
Temper: because she lost her t. 302:1
equal t. of heroic hearts 541:3
man of such a feeble t. 448:21
of a t. was so absolute 189:3
only keep your t. 513:2
tart t. never mellows 267:19
t. is nine-tenths 240:28
to t. man 371:12
touch of celestial t. 347:29
Temperance: acquire and beget
a t. 434:15
as t. would be difficult 277:6
healthy by t. 386:4
meekness, t. 67:46
Temperate: more lovely and more t. 486:18
sensible, t., sober 363:19
t. affords me none 125:7
t. and furious 458:25
Tempered: despotism t. by epigrams 126:12
t. with Love's sighs 455:22
Temperent ut bene utantur 22:4
Tempers: God t. the wind 512:28
my Muse..t. her words 502:3
Tempes: fairer T. bloom 493:25
Tempest: covert from the t. 53:43
dark lowers the t. 316:19
fierce raged the t. 547:7
in the very torrent, t. 434:15
like summer t. 538:27
no t. gave the shock 162:11
stoopt the t. of the Gods 331:2
t. down the ridges 23:20
t. toss'd, sails ript 160:35
we the t. fear 191:31
while the t. hurled 263:31
while the t. still is high 565:5
windy t. of my heart 446:3
Tempestas: quo me cumque rapit t. 256:16
t. vobis..superveniet 39:1
Tempests: glasses itself in t. 114:30
looks on t. 488:7
Thy t. fell all night 244:18
Tempest-tost: it shall be t. 456:11
t., sails ript 160:35
Tempestuous: t. petticoat 246:4
with a t. wind 229:6
Templa serena 320:30
Templar Knights: wont the T. to
bide 510:21
Templars: wits and T. 385:29
Temple: dread T. of Thy worth 300:5
drove them all out of the t. 63:6
dwell in such a t. 479:33
each new t. 251:15
hangs on Dian's t. 429:20
his torch is at thy t. door 405:19
his train filled the t. 53:8
in the T. lost outright 207:8
I saw no t. therein 72:4
metropolitan t. in the hearts 574:9
open the t. gates 509:12
polished corners of the t. 400:16
second t. 192:10
some old t. 384:5
t. and tower went to the ground 351:15
t. half as old as Time 408:8
t. of fame..upon the grave 239:20
t. of the Holy Ghost 66:29
their peaceful t. 164:35
the Lord's anointed t. 458:22
this T. keeps its shrine 375:5
very t. of delight 287:21
vespers in the T. of Jupiter 217:1
when all the T. is prepared 205:7
Temple Bar: over roaring T. 541:22
rot high on T. 142:11
T. to Aldgate-street 215:27
Temple-bells: t. are callin' 299:15
t. they say 299:10
Temple-haunting martlet 457:6
Temples: domes, theatres, and t. 582:14
forsake their t. dim 343:23
mortal t. of a king 475:7
my joyful t. bind 558:1
priests, tapers, t. 382:6
smote the nail into his t. 46:46
solemn t. 480:8
t. of his Gods 323:17
thy t. are like..pomegranate 52:5

Tempora: O t., O mores! 145:12
t. mutantur 13:15, 372:13
Temporal: pass through things t. 389:41
Temporary: use of force alone..t. 100:26
Temporis: nobis incertum..t. 38:31
Temps: n'ont pas le t. d'être polis 355:8
Tempt: bad for me do not t. me 489:5
he tries to t. you 3:18
not t. the Lord thy God 57:35
so proudly t. the Son of God 350:17
t. its new-fledg'd offspring 224:21
t. me from my lonely room 23:16
t. my Lady Poltagrue 41:27
t. not a desperate man 478:40
t. the frailty of our powers 481:25
t. with wand'ring feet 345:26
Temptation: butter..makes the t. 269:7
day of t. in the wilderness 397:29
last t. 197:25
lead us not into t. 58:4
man that endureth t. 69:28
many a dangerous t. 242:5
maximum of t. 490:32
most dangerous is that t. 462:1
most men..under t. 315:9
no t..but such as is common 66:38
not over-fond of resisting t. 38:20
prepare thy soul for t. 56:29
resist everything except t. 569:35
that way going to t. 461:34
to t. slow 487:24
way to get rid of a t. 570:7
why comes t. but.. 96:13
with the t...way to escape 66:38
ye're aiblins nae t. 104:6
you oughtn't to yield to t. 254:6
Temptations: in spite of all t. 221:25
t. both in wine and women 305:1
Tempted: more pure, as t. more 575:7
one thing to be t. 401:23
other men are t. to 111:1
t. above that ye are able 66:38
t., and yet undefiled 506:7
t. by a private whim 41:27
they t. me, my beautiful! 365:19
when your fathers t. me 397:30
Tempts: not all that t. 230:22
Tempus: fugit irreparabile t. 556:12
nec defensoribus istis t. eget 554:11
t. abire tibi est 257:21
t. edax rerum 371:31
Ten: as the strength of t. 540:11
authority over t. cities 62:36
instrument of t. strings 393:35
it is t. o'clock 427:13
it's now t. o'clock 339:9
I would gladly give t. shillings 233:11
not be wanted these t. years 379:17
O for t. years 288:11
preach from t. till four 220:4
t. low words 382:30
t. men love what I hate 95:20
t. to make 363:4
t. to the world allot 279:21
t., who in ears and eyes match
me 95:20
t. years before the Flood 333:8
were there not t. cleansed? 62:29
Tenacem: iustum et t. propositi
virum 259:24
Tenant: house and t. go to ground 199:31
Tenants: nobler t. of the flood 161:34
t. of life's middle state 164:12
Tend: strange shadows on you t. 487:2
t. on mortal thoughts 457:3
t. the..shepherd's trade 342:20
what should I do but t. 487:7
Tendance: his life in so long t. 510:16
Tended her i' the eyes 424:7
Tendency: stream of t. 20:13, 574:27
Tender: coy and t. to offend 245:11
dark and true and t. 538:20
Douglas, t. and true 165:22, 250:26
how t. 'tis to love the babe 457:12
mellow'd to that t. light 119:1
never t. nor sublime 309:9
t. and unpleasing 25:42
t., bow'd locks of the corn 359:16
t. for another's pain 230:30
to-fro t. trambeams 254:18
witty and the t. Hood 308:20

INDEX

Tenderest teacher 229:14
Tender-handed stroke a nettle 248:10
Tender-hearted: no t. garden 302:7
Tenderly: take her up t. 252:12
Tenderness: more alive to t. 575:7
  no bowels, no t. 214:35
  thanks to its t. 576:22(−577)
  want of t. 272:2
Tenders: shoal of fools for t. 156:1
Tender-taken breath 288:18
Tendis: quo, Musa, t.? 259:24
Tendrils strong as flesh and blood 578:20
Tenebricosum: iter t. 132:13
Tenedos: thousand ships to T. 331:5
Tenement: clayey t. 125:6
  o'er informed the t. 190:13
  threshold of the ruined t. 379:11
Tenents: in some nice t...wrong 158:5
Teneriff: like T. or Atlas 347:35
Ten-foot: wid a t. pole 210:14
Tenir: el t. y el no t. 134:14
Tennis-balls: stars' t. 563:20
  stuffed t. 468:32
Tennyson: hoped T. was writing his 112:2
  T. was not Tennysonian 268:17
  Wordsworth, T., and Browning 29:8
Tenor: held the t. of his way 387:8
  noiseless t. of their way 230:7
1066 and all that 422:12
Tent: in his t. 450:27
  I rede you t. it 107:21
  little t. of blue 569:2
  my t.'s thin roof 492:29
  my wind-built t. 492:29(−493)
  pitch His t. 243:22
  pitch my moving t. 355:10
  yon western t. 153:24
Tenth: Submerged T. 78:19
  t. Muse 549:18
  t. transmitter of a foolish face 415:16
Ten-thirty: I rise at t. 237:28
Ten thousand: chiefest among t. 52:13
  had here but one t. 444:25
  he had t. men 10:19
  one man..out of t. 433:2
  one poor word t. ways 193:3
  t. at thy right hand 397:18
  t. fleets 114:27
  t. men on the pay-roll 299:16
  t. times t. 4:12
  upper t. 571:5
Ten thousands: David his t. 47:25
  Peace its t. 387:10
Ten-times-barr'd-up chest 474:10
Tent-royal of their emperor 443:10
Tents: among the t. of Kedar 399:24
  as the t. of Kedar 51:39
  dwelling in t. 44:57
  fold their t. like the Arabs 316:10
  ha' done with the T. of Shem 298:27
  in the t. of ungodliness 397:7
  such as dwell in t. 44:34
  thy tribe's black t. 543:17
  to your t., O Israel 47:48
  within whose magic t. 81:7
Tepores: ver..refert t. 132:24
Teres, atque rotundus 262:1
Tereu: jug, jug, jug, jug, t. 321:15
  T., T. 35:17
Terewth: it is the light of T. 173:36
Term: doom'd for a certain t. 432:8
  I served a t. 221:15
Termagant: o'erdoing T. 434:15
Terminates: effect which t. in itself 269:33
Terminations: as terrible as her t. 468:13
Terminological inexactitude 143:36
Terminus: nunc t. Britanniae patet 526:8
Terms: fair t. and a villain's mind 463:25
  gild it with the happiest t. 441:5
  good man, upon easier t. 275:15
  holiday and lady t. 438:33
  in good set t. 427:12
  no t. of moderation 25:10
  on the wery amicablest t. 179:34
  recollected t. 483:1
  silken t. precise 455:29
  t. too deep for *me* 220:26
  till I come on perfect t. 567:22
  without using..opprobrious t. 194:17

Terra: estne Dei sedes nisi t., et pontus 320:26
  e t...alterius spectare laborem 320:30
Terrace walk 521:7
Terraces: Belvoir's lordly t. 322:23
  statues on the t. 206:30
Terrent: di me t. 555:13
Terrestrial: written on t. things 235:18
Terrible: appear most long and t. 312:26
  far darker and far more t. 326:8
  if her breath were as t. 468:13
  I the elder and more t. 449:23
  it would *not* be t. 271:20
  just the t. choice 96:14
  my name were not so t. 441:25
  teach thee t. things 394:22
  t. and dear 495:21
  t. as an army with banners 52:15
  t. as hell 346:4
  t., strange, sublime 496:19
  toiling up the t. way 140:10
Terribles: les enfants t. 214:5
Terrier: Scotch t...so covered with hair 82:21
Terrify: they t. me 564:21
Territorial: last t. claim 248:15
Terror: any t. by night 397:18
  not a t. to good works 66:10
  no t., Cassius 451:19
  only rules by t. 528:10
  so full of dismal t. 476:13
  strikes an awe and t. 155:19
  struck more t. to the soul 476:38
  t. of darkness 135:18
  t. of my name 331:2
  t..of the heathen past 310:20
  T. the human form 77:4
  their perch and not their t. 461:22
  without t. great 401:22
Terrors: amid their rumbling t. 180:22
  its deadly t. clasp 75:24(−76)
  king of t. 49:3
  new t. of death 14:8
  scarecrow for superstitious t. 172:16
  t. of the earth 453:1
  t. of the skies 123:24
Terse: nervous and t., but limited 188:27
Tertium Quid: and a T. 304:52
Tess: ended his sport with T. 237:14
Test: bears Thy t. 90:28
  bring me to the t. 436:1
  ridicule..best t. of truth 139:29
  there lies the t. 143:12
  this t. for love 411:1
Testa: pia t. 260:10
Testament: commons hear this t. 450:24
  thou mak'st a t. 426:32
Tested his first plough 89:41
Tester: drops a t. 281:7
Testimonies: thy t. are my study 399:20
Testimonium animae naturaliter Christianae 542:2
Testimony: for the t. of Jesus Christ 70:23
  no t. is sufficient 265:7
Testing: some strict T. of us 207:19
Testy: touchy, t., pleasant fellow 2:8
Tetchy and wayward 476:27
Tête d'Armée 361:4
Tetigit: nullum quod t. non ornavit 273:19
Teucro: nil desperandum T. duce 258:11
Teucrorum: ingens gloria T. 554:8
Teufel: so viel T. auf mich gezielet hätten 321:7
Teuton: Slav, T., Kelt 528:11
Teviotdale: Ettrick and T. 420:8
Text: approve it with a t. 464:14
  God takes a t. 244:7
  great t. in Galatians 96:40
  holy t. of pike and gun 110:17
  many a holy t. 230:8
  neat rivulet of t. 500:33
  none can read the t. 531:18
  of that t. a pulled hen 136:31
  read ev'ry t. and gloss over 110:11
  square of t. 531:17
  to your t., Mr. Dean! 198:2
Texts: difference of t. 510:15
  great men are the inspired t. 127:16

Texture: her woof, her t. 286:42
Thackeray settled like a meat-fly 412:21
Thairm: painch, tripe, or t. 106:4
Thais: lovely T. by his side 190:34
  lovely T. sits beside thee 191:9
Thames: Arabian fleet..into..the T. 217:12
  clear T. bordered 359:2
  every drop of the T. 104:3
  flights upon the banks of T. 281:18
  hill beside the silver T. 82:9
  no allaying T. 319:5
  not of Gennesareth, but T. 545:1
  of our poor T. she never heard 18:28
  River T., attended 167:17
  stripling T. 18:9
  sweet T., run softly 510:20
  T.' broad aged back 510:21
  T. is between me and.. 558:12
  T...noblest river in Europe 2:19
  T.'s tributaries 18:29
  youthful T. 18:21
Thammuz came next 344:32
Thamyris: blind T. 346:20
Thane: I am T. of Cawdor 456:24
  T. of Cawdor lives 456:17
  T. of Fife had a wife 460:25
Thank: howsoever, I t. you 198:6
  I t. my God upon every remembrance 68:14
  I t. thee, Jew 465:13
  I t. thee, that I am not as other men 62:33
  I t. the goodness 527:5
  I t. whatever gods 241:18
  make the Moor t. me 471:4
  now t. we all our God 167:18, 571:21
  t. God from whom 376:3
  t. God of all! 136:20
  t. God you are rid of a knave 468:37
  t. heaven, fasting 428:14
  t. me no thankings 478:29
  t. the Lord, O t. the Lord 121:27
  t. you, Mister Atkins 303:1
Thanked: nobody t. him 273:24
  not t. at all..t. enough 204:30
  now, God be t. 84:16
  she t. me 470:3
  the Lord be t. 107:34
Thankful: becometh well the just to be t. 393:35
  joyful and pleasant..to be t. 400:21
  t. for illusion 146:32
Thankfulness: in pride and t. 92:31
  seek your job with t. 296:33
Thankings: thank me no t. 478:29
Thankless: t. child 452:30
  meditate the t. Muse 342:10
Thanks: give God t. 468:35
  give t. unto him for a remembrance 393:25
  if sweet, give t. 522:13
  I will give t. unto thee 400:10
  poor even in t. 433:14
  shall the dust give t.? 393:26
  some give t. 374:23
  song of t. and praise 576:18
  ta'en with equal t. 434:26
  take the t. of a boy 39:6
  t. as fits a king's remembrance 432:36
  t. be to the Lord 393:30
  t. for mercies past receive 98:14
  t. God for anything 270:23
  to give t. is good 522:13
Thanksgiving: brief t. 523:23
  received with t. 68:46
  with proud t. 72:22
Tharsis: kings of T. 396:25
That: I, t. 95:20
  take t..., you hound, and t.! 188:7
Thatch: house with deep t. 42:7
  riven the t. off seven cottar houses 419:29
  while the nigh t. smokes 151:25
Thatch-eaves: round the t. run 284:10
Thaw, and resolve itself 430:33
Thawing cold fear 444:8
Theatre: as in a t. 475:29
  everybody has his own t. 237:25
  Idols of the T. 28:6
  off to the T. 41:13

Theatre (*cont.*)
t. is irresistible; organise the t. 20:6
this t. of man's life 24:22
wait all day long in the t. 514:35
Theatres: domes, t., and temples 582:14
Theatri: Idola T. 28:6
Theatrical scarecrow 172:16
Theban: that T. monster 350:17
this same learned T. 453:26
Thebes: in T.'s streets 504:1
presenting T. 341:18
riddles. . T. never knew 493:26
T. did his. .youth engage 193:25
Thee: all of Him we have in t. 165:31
between t. and me what difference? 498:15
do it as for T. 244:15
doubled. .making t. 80:29
exist in T. 83:11
faithful to God and t. 248:7
have power in T. 83:8
if it hadna been for t. 30:17
minister of t. to me 80:21
noble world of t. 355:18
nothing less than t. 184:12
of Me and T. 206:17
speaks to my spirit of t. 119:10
t. from myself 410:25
to t. was it given 17:19
worship only t. 161:3
Theft: forgave the t. 96:5
property is t. 402:19
suspicious head of t. 455:22
t. in other poets 194:8
Theme: as it is my t. 172:10
fools are my t. 117:9
glad diviner's t. 190:18
imperial t. 456:23
t. for reason 184:12
t. too great 401:23
when God's the t. 503:6
Themes: muses on admired t. 331:2
transcend our wonted t. 552:12
Themselves: but t. confound 99:36
prayer both for t. 531:36
up and shoot t. 84:14
vilest things become t. 424:9
violent hands upon t. 391:40
Theocrite: sang T. 90:3
Theologians have employed 20:9
Theology: better than this t. 200:10
objected to his t. 503:10
Theophilus: former treatise. .O T. 64:21
most excellent T. 61:10
Theoric: bookish T. 469:22
Theorie: grau. . ist alle T. 223:19
Theorize before one has data 187:22
Theory: all t. . .is grey 223:19
life without t. 181:44
There: because he was not t. 34:20
cry over me, T., t. 396:20
I answer, t. 245:21
if I had not been t. 564:2
if thou wert t. 107:26
I have been t. 561:32
I shall not be t. 525:28
man who wasn't t. 335:12
may I be t. to see 160:11
not t., not t., my child 241:4
t. a little 53:33
t., where I have garnered 472:34
Thermopylae: new T. 115:46
old man of T. 312:21
Thersites' body 429:40
Thessalian: dew-lapp'd like T.
bulls 467:20
Thetis: in the lap of T. 110:43
Thew: men of pith and t. 77:28
They: everyone else is T. 303:18
God is, t. are 91:1
Thick: blood is t. 219:14
butter's spread too t. 130:19
damned t. square book 223:5
dash'd through t. and thin 190:32
dash through t. and thin 159:36
gruel t. and slab 459:33
make t. my blood 457:3
one can lay it on so t. 112:14
so t. a drop serene 346:19
so t. on every place 192:17
stand so t. with corn 395:30(—396)

Thick (*cont.*)
strong, t., stupefying 89:45
t. and fast they came at last 130:14
t. as autumnal leaves 344:25
t. as motes 138:10
t., bereft of beauty 479:12
through t. and thin she follow'd 110:28
Thick-coming fancies 460:37
Thickens: plot t. 98:10
Thicker: Blood. .than water's t. 266:17
pilots are t. than pilchards 294:35
t. than my father's loins 47:46
Thicket: beside a leafy t. 311:19
ram caught in a t. 44:56
t. closed 531:24
Thickets: steeply the t. 82:9
thorny t. 546:26
Thick-ribbèd ice 462:9
Thicks man's blood with cold 149:13
Thickset: bent with t. fruit 409:14
Thicksides and *hairy* Aldrich 146:22
Thick-sighted: ambition 284:18
Thick-warbled notes 350:11
Thief: as bad as the t. 139:6
embrace the impenitent t. 514:3
Eugene Aram, though a t. 121:17
first cries out stop t. 155:14
fits your t. 462:19
I come as a t. 71:29
if you do take a t. 468:40
in the sworn twelve. .a t. 461:23
opportunity makes a t. 28:2
rails upon yond simple t. 454:10
steals something from the t. 470:6
Taffy was a t. 369:1
t. doth fear each bush 446:7
t. of time 587:4
t. said the last kind word 96:5
this first grand t. 347:3
time, you t. 265:25
Translation's t. 333:7
upon a dwarfish t. 460:31
when thou sawest a t. 395:5
which is the t.? 454:10
Thieves: boldest t. 301:4
Den of T. 147:17
fell among t. 61:39
land-t. and water-t. 463:15
made it a den of t. 60:9
sharp after t. 523:4
thou best of t. 191:22
where t. break through 58:5
Thigh: honied t. 341:22
on his vesture and on his t. 71:31
smote them hip and t. 46:57
thy sword upon thy t. 394:22
touched the hollow of his t. 45:9
Thighs: his cushes on his t. 440:18
Thimbles: sought it with t. 128:11
Thin: forswear t. potations 442:22
gruel, t., but not too t. 22:9
incredibly fat or incredibly t. 36:14
one was t. 517:14
so t., so pale 165:21
so uncommonly t. 11:1
t. ears devoured 45:18
t. red line 303:3, 414:4
water's t. 219:14
witty, profligate, and t. 587:16
Thine: all were t. 308:14
continue t. for ever 391:20
for t. and thee 538:22
only call me t. 152:6
she be only t. 332:8
t. has a great hook nose 74:10
which before was t. 185:11
why not I with t.? 495:7
Thing: all comes to the same t. 89:18
any English t. 140:12
any good t. therefore 232:10
beguile the t. I am 470:27
blame the t. that's not 375:23
bonnie wee t. 104:27
converted from the t. it was 486:33
do that t. that ends all 425:33
every blessed t. you hold 218:29
far, far better t. that I do 180:2
Good T. 422:13, 15
has this t. appear'd again 430:10
have so much of the t. 19:15
holiest t. alive 152:14

Thing (*cont.*)
I know a t. or two 221:40
ill-favoured t., sir 428:35
in awe of such a t. 448:17
intellectual t. 75:6
I wove the t. 183:3
learning, what a t. it is 479:2
most dejected t. of fortune 453:36
most unattractive old t. 220:16
my wee wee t. 213:1
nameless t. 118:19
not quite the t. 22:14
one damned t. after another 264:25
play's the t. 434:1
poor t.! 368:2
Real Right T. 268:10
said the t. which was not 519:19
sole unbusy t. 152:17
so small a t. 15:13
such a t. as thou 469:42
that extremely lovely t. 218:11
that I am the t. I was 442:39
that is not the t. 290:15
that t. called Light 144:21
t. arm'd with a rake 563:21
T. as he sees It 303:21
t., a tool, a Jesuit 294:14
T. became a trumpet 580:17
t. devised by the enemy 476:40
t. of beauty 221:28, 284:17
t. on the blind side 140:16
t. that I was born to do 168:8
t. they most do show 487:24
this abject t. no more 229:5
those that fit the t. 309:16
thou art the t. itself 453:21
very Good T. 422:15
very odd t. 171:17
very t. he'll set you to 74:18
what t. is love 377:3
what t. of sea or land 350:31
winsome wee t. 107:16
Things: all four-footed t. 140:21
all good t. are ours 95:17
all sorts of t. and weather 199:18
all t. are taken from us 535:17
all t. both great and small 150:16
as t. have been, t. remain 147:8
both sweet t. 78:24
bow the mind unto the nature of
t. 24:16
can such t. be 459:22
cognizance of men and t. 92:21
desired to see those t. which you
see 61:38
dreaming on t. to come 488:2
everlasting t. that matter 216:7
fair and flagrant t. 165:26
feud 'twixt t. and me 80:22
flux of mortal t. 19:4
forms of t. unknowr 467:24
God's sons are t. 327:0
good t. which belong to prosperity 25:16
great t. are done 74:23
great ugly t. 34:15
how can these t. be? 63:8
I find. . t. very much 135:1
I love all beauteous t. 81:9
in impossible t. 141:1
I will do such t. 453:1
little t. affect little minds 182:27
man must think o' t. 299:5
old, unhappy, far-off t. 581:2
on the roots of t. 89:7
purpose of the t. themselves 448:34
said true t. 89:40
Shape of T. to Come 565:1
show. . t. that are not 451:40
so many t. which he wanted to
do 339:13
such t. to be 533:3
thank'd my God for worldly t. 74:29
these t. shall be! 526:11
t. and actions are what they are 109:37
t. are in the saddle 199:19
t. are seldom what they seem 221:21
t. are the sons of heaven 277:21
T. as They are 303:21
t. in boards 307:23
t. in books' clothing 306:27

Things (cont.)
t. like that, you know, must be 507:7
t. present, not t. to come 65:58
t. that are more excellent 561:14
t. that didn't occur 210:9
t. that do attain 518:1
t. that don't have anything to do 560:17
t. whereof our conscience is
  afraid 389:45
t. which are Caesar's 60:12
t. which belong unto thy peace 62:40
t. which elemented it 186:25
t. which I have seen 576:1
t. which may fairly be done 363:11
thousand thousand slimy t. 149:21
to bring in fine t. 98:9
to 'ide the t. 'e said 301:15
were such t. here? 456:19
whatsoever t. are true 68:27
what t. have we seen 37:12
what t. they be 497:2
what t. they ought to do 389:28
Thingummy: no What's-his-name
  but T. 175:15
Think: above all that we ask or t. 67:55
afraid to t. what I have done 458:14
always t. what is true 266:21
attains to t. right 278:8
books t. for me 306:25
cease to t. about the manner 240:1
comedy to those that t. 558:27
could not t. up to . .his. .style 142:20
haply I t. on thee 486:24
how can I know what I t. 557:20
I am inclined to t. 188:26
if the while I t. on thee 486:25
if you can t. 297:10
I must not t. of thee 338:6
I never expect a soldier to t. 489:17
I never t. about them 307:10
I stand alone, and t. 289:6
I t. and t. 193:27
I t. my wife be honest 472:7
I t., therefore I am 172:26
knew not what to t. 160:39
learn to t. Imperially 135:5
let me not t. on't 430:33(-431)
man must t. o' things 299:5
no matter what they t. 194:9
not paid to t. 299:6
not t. lang 107:35
not thoughts enough to t. 209:26
now—I t. it 512:9
picture it, t. of it 252:21
qualified my mind to t. justly 406:15
she could not t. 165:9
she that could t. 470:29
should not t. of God 443:20
speak what you t. to-day 200:40
stay and t. of nought 487:7
sure I t., that I can drink 516:21
they always talk, who never t. 401:39
t. beer 267:20
t. by fits and starts 263:34
t. for himself?. .t. like other
  people 491:12
t. for two minutes together 505:25
t. here before 185:25
t. him so because I t. him so 484:30
t., in this. .Caravanserai 205:29, 30
t. it possible you may be mistaken 167:4
t. no more, lad 263:18
t. not God at all 350:27
t. not much of my delay 292:19
t. not, thou noble Roman 451:37
t. of things that would astonish
  you 219:6
t. of your forefathers! t. of your
  posterity! 1:5
t., oh t. it worth enjoying 191:9
t. on him that's far awa 104:24
t. only this of me 84:21
t. only what concerns thee 348:31
t. on these things 68:27
t. on't now 245:23
t. o' something different 295:1
t., perhaps even less 89:34
t., this heart 84:21
t. thou and act 411:7
t. what 'e's been 301:13

Think (cont.)
t. which way to walk 333:8
those who greatly t. 381:32
we t. so because.. 501:12
we t. so then 312:4
what kind of people do they t.
  we are? 144:8
what you. .t. of this life 448:17
when I t. I must speak 428:5
when I would pray and t. 462:2
where but to t. is. .sorrow 287:27
who t. too little 190:21
Thinker: God lets loose a t. 200:7
Thinkers not always the justest t. 239:28
Thinketh no evil 66:45
Thinking: art of t. 182:49
could na preach for t. o't 107:15
dignity of t. beings 277:39
hardly seem worth t. of 584:24
hearing, t., writing on 240:13
hour of t., feeling, loving 573:21
I'm a fool for t. 387:16
in my t. 6:10
it ain't t. about it 549:16
much drinking, little t. 519:29
naked t. heart 184:9
plain living and high t. 577:16
sittin' an' t. 298:3
song for t. hearts 575:12
their modes of t. are different 274:35
then to t.! 240:9
t. for myself 221:17
t. is to me the greatest fatigue 551:10
t. lays underground 263:18
t. makes it so 433:11
t. of the old 'un 174:16
t. on the frosty Caucasus 474:20
t. on their sins 106:11
t. too precisely 436:16
t. . .waste of thought 504:9
too much t. 384:32
while you're t. what to say 130:1
Thinkings: solitary t. 284:23
Thinks: he t. too much 448:26
I know she t. o' me 299:10
most lives who t. most 29:9
never, never t. of me 10:21
on which the public t. long 278:8
says little, t. less 203:7
she t. not on what's said 245:22
then he t. he knows 15:6
t. he was not made to die 531:40
t. men honest 470:22
t. too little or too much 383:22
what to-morrow t. 200:40
whene'er she t. at all 143:10
Thinly: stones of worth. .t.
  placed 487:1
Thinner: doesn't get t. 221:5
t., clearer, farther 538:15
Thinness: gold to airy t. beat 186:25
Thin-spun: slits the t. life 342:20
Third: any good of George the T. 309:11
drink not the t. glass 243:26
every t. thought 480:16
George the T. ought never 43:4
great t. wave 525:25
in Heaven's t. story 541:22
never a t. 90:8
no t. 127:23
one—t. of a nation ill-housed 408:22
Passing of the T. Floor Back 269:6
shadowy t. 90:10
then he gave a t. 578:26
t. in your bosom 478:3
t. part of our lives 85:23
this is the t. time 466:14
to make a t. 193:9
unto the t. and fourth generation 390:7
Thirst: I t. 64:1
man can raise a t. 299:15
neither t. any more 71:7
t. after righteousness 57:39
t. of praise 162:27
t. that from the soul 280:21(-281)
t. to know 561:14
wild asses quench their t. 398:8
without the provocation of t. 519:20
Thirsteth: every one that t. 54:29
my soul. for thee 395:25

Thirsty: cold waters to a t. soul 50:36
my t. soul 421:3
t. earth 158:7
t. fly 370:11
when I was t. . .vinegar 396:19
Thirteen: t. rank 296:18
years. .scarce t. 280:10
Thirty: at t. man suspects 587:6
at t. the wit 211:14
kings t. feet high 326:7
t. days hath November 228:4
t. days hath September 369:5
t. pieces of silver 60:37
wrong side of t. 520:15
Thirty-five: compressed in t. volumes 358:18
die at t. in Babylon 19:3
Thirtyfold: some t. 59:23
Thirty-one: rest have t. 228:4, 369:5
Thirty-three: nothing—except t. 115:11
This: all t. and heaven too 242:11
no day. .like t. 81:6
pursuit of T. and That 206:22
sound of t. and that 583:17
they, t. thing 95:20
Thisbe: death of Pyramus and T. 466:23
T. fearfully o'ertrip 465:17
Thistle: stubborn t. bursting 537:26
T. across my way 74:5
t. and darnel 171:21
Thistles: figs of t. 58:26
he munched the t. 171:21
rough t., kecksies 445:11
t. stretch their prickly arms 165:17
Thomas: pop Sir T. again in 34:16
T., because thou hast seen me 64:11
T., here's my best respects 302:16
T.' ideal John
true T. 32:6, 7, 8, 12
Thomases: three T. 251:14
Thorn: brittle sticks of t. 247:17
figs grew upon t. 140:21
hath not thy rose a t.? 445:23
her breast against a t. 253:17
her breast up-till a t. 35:17
instead of the t. 54:32
kissed beside the t. 82:2
left the t. wi' me 108:39
no harvest but a t. 244:9
Oak, and Ash, and T. 303:5, 6
Oak, Elder, Elm and T. 172:6
peeps beneath the t. 225:7
pull the t. 419:8
redder berry on the t. 248:7
rose without the t. 247:20
snail's on the t. 94:40
then was the t. 247:20
this t., this canker, Bolingbroke 438:36
t. in the flesh 67:37
withering on the virgin t. 466:17
without t. the rose 347:6
writhen t. 302:7
Thorn-crown'd Man 17:9
Thorns: amid bare t. 525:33
crackling of t. under a pot 51:10
gather grapes of t. 58:26
I fall upon the t. of life 496:10
little wilful t. 538:1
made hot with t. 395:21
no t. go as deep 523:1
once was crowned with t. 291:18
roses have t. 486:31
this crown of t. 98:2
T. in the Cushion 542:29
t. that in her bosom lodge 432:18
Thorny: life is t. 150:26
t. way to heaven 431:23
Thorough: t. bush, t. brier 466:33
Thoroughfare for all thoughts 290:27
Thou: I am t. . .t. art I 524:2
if t. wert there 107:26
not only t., but. .all that hear me 65:27
poor, and T. within them 245:12
t. and I this night 32:10
T. art Being and Breath 83:12
T. beside me singing 205:23, 24
T.! if t. wast He 92:10
t., Lord, and I 172:1
t.'s for ever 107:27
t. the singer 218:33
t. to me art all things 349:30

Thou (cont.)
T. wert left alone   83:11
waken t. with me   539:2
what t. and I did   185:6
what T. art   83:12
Thought: action, and not a t.   127:12
adds to the t.   80:1, 139:5
any unproportion'd t.   431:25
as in uffish t.   129:39(-130)
as silent t. can bring   580:23
believe your own t.   200:36
best that is known and t.   19:12
beyond mortal t.   492:11
bitterly t. of the morrow   572:13
by taking t...add one cubit   58:12
by t. supplied   581:26
change of t. to find   164:35
chaos of t. and passion   383:22
curst be the heart that t. the t.   31:3
device for avoiding t.   241:17
divine his real t.   115:41
dome of T.   113:12
dress of t.   278:3, 565:21
ears, and ev'ry t.   412:19
elevation of our t.   574:27
Experience is the child of T.   182:41
fair t. to lie between   435:4
father..to that t.   442:27
flesh-garment, the body, of t.   127:10
for want of t.   192:5
garment of t.   127:10
gave that t. relief   576:4
go near to be t. so shortly   469:7
great change..in..their modes
  of t.   338:21
green t. in a green shade   332:19
haunt t.'s wildernesses   497:2
her body t.   186:13
he t. another   137:27
he t. he saw ..   128:15, 16, 17, 18, 19
he t. I t. he t. I slept   375:2
his honest t.   583:9
hit on the same t.   500:2
holy and good t.   57:22
honest without a t. of Heaven   86:21
human t. or form   494:4
if I t. that I'd beat him   482:33
in a general honest t.   452:9
in loftiness of t.   193:9
in peaceful t. the field of death
  survey'd   1:10
in the light of t.   408:6
I t. so once   215:20
keep ye t. of us?   81:1
lean upon the t.   15:11
let one's t. wander   586:4
lived with no other t.   380:7
love, and t., and joy   581:6
magnanimity of t.   587:6
man of yearning t.   411:33
mighty t. threading a dream   265:22
Ministers of t.   491:19
more strong than all poetic t. ·   532:25
much that well may be t.   376:19
my t., whose murder yet   456:24
never a man's t.   441:35
never t. of thinking   221:17
never t. upon the subject   271:30
not be t. after these ways   458:10
no t. for the morrow   58:15
nought is worth a t.   387:16
offend from want of t.   519:2
often t. upon death   27:42
oh! idle t.!   152:7
one that was never t. of   56:41
one t. of thee   382:6
one t., one grace   331:2
pale cast of t.   434:4
perish the t.!   144:29
pleased his childish t.   575:5
pleasing, dreadful t.!   1:22
plunged in t. again   17:8
possess'd a t.   113:15
precisely what we have t. and
  felt   200:37
reach on with thy t.   411:8
rear the tender t.   546:12
Roman t.   423:22
she pin'd in t.   483:10
sleep out the t. of it   485:19
some sudden t.   312:24

Thought (cont.)
speech created t.   497:5
splendour of a sudden t.   90:40
steadfast of t.   502:17
stood awhile in t.   129:39(-130)
style is the dress of t.   565:21
sudden t. strikes me   124:16
sweet silent t.   486:25
tak a t. an' men'   104:5
tease us out of t.   287:14
thing they call a t.   382:31
t. about Tom Thumb   276:17
t. again   160:39
t. as a child   66:46
t. 'e might require   303:22
t. is free   480:3
T. is the child of Action   182:41
T. leapt out to wed with T.   532:18
t. of thee   338:6
t...secreted by the brain   125:30
t.'s the slave of life   440:37
t. to leave her   285:4
t. upon thee when I was waking   395:26
t. which saddens   94:31
t. would destroy   230:30
through strange seas of t.   579:19
tire the night in t.   404:5
to have common t.   384:32
to have t., to have done   15:13
to sight or t. be form'd   349:17
Truth knows not from her t.   411:26
utmost bound of human t.   541:1
vacuity of t.   103:30
vain or shallow t.   199:22
very t. of Thee   132:6
we t. so still   312:4
what he t. he uttered   241:16
what oft was t.   382:27
white, celestial t.   552:3
white flowers of thy t.   524:4
whom Aristotle t. unfit   481:13
with eager t.   343:6
working-house of t.   445:5
wrought, and t. with me   541:3
wrought by want of t.   253:4
ye have heard, ye have t.   302:24
ye t.?   299:6
Thought-executing fires   453:5
Thoughtful: breathing t. breath   580:21
purest and most t. minds   413:14
Thoughtless: that young man..t.   22:14
Thoughts: above my t.   167:5
absent t. o' ither   108:22
all evil t.   389:32
all his t. perish   400:19
all his t. will perish   29:19
all stray t.   96:26
all the t. of God   88:25
all t., all passions   152:3
apt t. of men   451:40
begin to have bloody t.   480:9
branched t.   288:7
busy t. outnumber   495:18
covers all human t.   134:18
dark soul and foul t.   340:20
drawn from t. more far   88:13
drive my dead t.   496:11
feed on t.   346:20
feed with lofty t.   582:3
feeling of their masters' t.   331:2
fond and wayward t.   581:12
give thy t. no tongue   431:25
good t. his only friends   123:25
gor'd mine own t.   488:5
harbour t. effeminate   331:2
high erected t.   501:16
in a shroud of t.   113:51
in these t.   486:24
in t., not breaths   29:9
lift the t. of man   288:15
man's own t.   563:33
my bloody t.   472:12
my morning t.   156:12
my ripe t.   487:20
my sad t. doth clear   552:8
my slaughterous t.   461:3
my t. are not your t.   54:31
my wanton t.   359:27
not make t. your aim   297:10
not t. enough to think   209:26
one whose t. half linger   524:20

Thoughts (cont.)
on hospitable t. intent   348:8
our frail t.   343:1
our t. as boundless   114:42
pansies, that's for t.   436:31
restrain in me the cursed t.   457:18
second and sober t.   242:7
sensations rather than of t.   289:19
she holds her little t.   338:9
soothing t. that spring   576:20
stal'd are my t.   232:15
suspect the t. of others   463:24
suspicions amongst t.   27:22
sweet t. in a dream   494:7
tell me how many t.   38:30
tend on mortal t.   457:3
than I have t. to put them in   434:9
their silly t. so busy   343:15
these t. may startle   340:10
thoroughfare for all t.   290:27
t. beyond the reaches   431:32(-432)
t. by England given   84:21
t. control that o'er thee swell   364:9
t. go blowing through them   84:22
t. of heroes   337:3
t. of men accurst   441:29
t. of men are widen'd   534:29
t. of other men   163:49
t. of youth are long, long t.   316:38
t. rule the world   201:4
t. secret .. countenance open   583:14
t., such as they are   194:12
t. that arise in me   528:3
t., that breathe   231:15
t. that wander through eternity   345:19
t. to memory dear   419:5
t...too deep for tears   576:22(-577)
t. which were not their t.   113:51
t. whose very sweetness   577:10
thou understandest my t.   400:7
throng of t. and forms   497:14
thy t. in me   539:2
thy t., when thou art gone   499:1
trouble himself with any such t.   443:20
undying t. I bear   338:5
united t. and counsels   344:12
when pleasant t. bring sad t.   581:7
whose t. are legible   412:18
wording of his own highest t.   289:27
Thousand: better than a t.   397:7
braved, a t. years   123:10
draw for a t. pounds   2:3
for a t. pound!   160:2
he who has a t. friends   201:23
I owe you a t. pound   442:40
laugh broke into a t. pieces   36:7
little one shall become a t.   55:1
minute into a t. parts   428:18
one among a t.   49:14
one man among a t.   51:15
one t. shall flee   53:40
reaps a t. kisses   158:1
ring out the t. wars   533:20
t. ages in Thy sight   562:9
t. Blossoms   205:17
t. eyes   79:5
t. hearts beat happily   113:25
t. scatter'd into Clay   205:17
t. shall fall beside thee   397:18
t. t. sighs   483:29
t. t. slimy things   149:21
t. to that hundred   246:28
t. years in thy sight   397:15
t. years of gloom   532:2
t. years of peace   533:20
worth a t. men   416:28
would he had blotted a t.   280:1
Thousands: among the t. of Judah   56:7
by t. on her plains   241:13
countless t. mourn   107:2
each day too slew its t.   119:16
even t. of angels   396:8
Saul hath slain his t.   47:25
t. at his bidding speed   351:21
t. counted every groan   16:8
t. die, without or this or that   384:42
t. equally were meant   521:3
t. He hath freed   135:12
t. of gold and silver   399:17
t. of years   584:15
to murder t.   586:27

Thousands (cont.)
War its t. slays 387:10
when they die by t. 141:34
Thousandth: T. Man 302:18
t. part of a minute 428:18
Thracian sea 524:16
Thraldom: single t. 28:18
Thrall: hath thee in t. 286:35
if you were t. to sorrow 524:29
t. to the fair hair 306:15
Thrash the Spaniards too 188:35
Thrasonical: Caesar's t. brag 428:25
Thread: feels at each t. 383:17
hinders needle and t. 253:27
like a blue t. 410:30
line of scarlet t. 46:38
on an English t. 320:6
spun my last t. 185:24
t. of his verbosity 387:6, 455:24
t. of human life 419:28
thy lips are like a t. of scarlet 52:5
weave their t. with bones 483:5
with a double t. 253:24
with a silk t. 477:28
Threaded together on Time's string 245:8
Threadneedle Street: Old Lady of T. 222:32
Threat: whiles I t. he lives 458:1
Threatened: they t. its life 128:11
t., a lion 135:14
Threatening: still t. to devour us 346:32
Threatenings and slaughter 64:40
Threats: no terror, Cassius, in your t. 451:19
t. of Hell 206:26
t. of pain and ruin 230:5
Three: all the t. sweet Graces 308:13
born about t. of the clock 441:21
carrying T. Insides 124:10
Cerberus, t. gentlemen at once 500:25
clock at ten to t. 84:15
come the t. corners of the world 448:2
dauntless T. 323:20
dukes were t. a penny 218:28
ever T. and ever One 361:14
Gaul..is divided into t. parts 120:10
God in T. Persons 240:19
God is T. 364:5
grant but t. 115:46
happy in t. wives 308:8
in t. sips 96:39
league but barely t. 30:18
night she'll hae but t. 31:18
not t. Gods 388:40
not t. good men unhanged 439:15
not t. incomprehensibles 388:39
not t. of my hundred and fifty 440:34
now abideth..these t. 66:46(-67)
refused about the age of t. 141:17
Rule of t. doth puzzle me 8:12
she made t. paces 534:7
stoppeth one of t. 148:18
though he was only t. 339:15
t. acres and a cow 153:17
t. crabbed months 485:5
t. days to-day 411:32
t. feet long 581:20
t. fishers went sailing 293:25
t. great elements of..civilization 125:24
t. hours a day 549:12
t. hours' march to dinner 240:9
T. in One 300:19
t. is company 569:21
t. Johns 251:14
t. jolly Farmers 171:22
t. little maids 219:27
t. may keep a secret 211:13
t. men hold together 525:19
t. merry boys 37:16
t. misbegotten knaves 439:22
t. paynims, t. Jews 327:15
t. poets at an age 521:15
t. poets, in t. distant ages 193:9
t. rounds blank 296:18
t. things..never satisfied 50:55
t. things..the public..clamour for 253:31
t. times her little throat around 95:5
t. times to the child 573:3

Three (cont.)
t. useful things 117:3
t. whole days together 517:18
we t. meet again 456:3
what I tell you t. times is true 128:4
what more..than T. in One? 192:23
where two or t. are gathered 59:52
whom t. realms obey 385:14
wise men t. 377:1
without t. good friends 427:25
Three and thirty: dragged to t. 115:11
Three Castles: no better..than the T. 542:41
Three-corners and Banburies 219:13
Three-fifths of him genius 320:4
Threefold: t. cord 51:5
t., fourfold tomb 36:21
Three-fourths of life 20:10, 12
Three-hooped pot 445:36
Three hundred: handsome in t. pounds 466:6
long an oak, t. year 282:1
of the t. grant but three 115:46
those t. fought with Beit 42:10
Three hundred and fifty lashes 179:15
Three-mile prayers 106:34
Three millions of people, so dead 379:3
Three-months-old: corpses t. 537:38
Three-o'-clock in the morning courage 546:43
Three-parts pain 95:15
Three per Cents: money in the T. 91:12
simplicity of the t. 182:6, 420:32
Three person'd God 185:18
Three-pil'd hyperboles 455:29
Three-pipe problem 187:19
Threescore: attain to write t. 184:7
bachelor of t. 468:3
of my t. years and ten 262:10
t. miles and ten 367:4
t. years and ten 397:16
Three thousand: said it t. years ago 208:17
Thresh: t. his old jacket 164:10
t. of the deep-sea rain 298:27
Threshold: across my t. 374:24
before thou goest over the t. 212:11
by the happy t. 539:4
dares not cross the t. 379:11
t. of Jove's court 339:27
upon the t. of the new 557:25(-558)
Threw: t. him down the stairs 366:23
t. them back again 9:10
Thrice: circle round him t. 151:33(-152)
for thee t. wider 442:38
t. came on in fury 323:23
t. he routed all..t. he slew the slain 191:6
t. is he arm'd 445:30, 491:9
t. looked he at the city 323:23
t. their weight in gold 203:39
twice or t. had I loved thee 184:4
Thrice-driven bed of down 470:8
Thrice-gorgeous ceremony 444:23
Thrice-transfigured 94:8
Thrift: due, respective t. 374:20
large example of wise t. 319:3
my well-won t. 463:17
t., t., Horatio! 431:4
Thrifty: housewife that's t. 500:39
t. wife's smile 104:33
Thrill: glory's t. is o'er 356:20
t. through those roofless halls 496:2
Thrilling: some t. view 90:29
t. moment 176:25
t. voice is sounding 132:5
voice so t. 581:1
Thrills: stirring t. the air 236:6
Thrive: bold knaves t. 193:21
child that so did t. 280:10
could I never t. 484:27
he that would t. 145:31
in no other land will t. 193:42
Thriven: he that hath t. 145:31
Throat: brazen t. of war 349:27
down the t. of Old Time 175:19
each t. was parched 149:8
feel the fog in my t. 95:8
her little t. around 95:5
his t. they cut 562:24
I took by the t. 474:2
marching down your t. 371:5

Throat (cont.)
mocking-bird's t. 567:1
pours her t. 231:6
rather felt you round my t. 254:15
scuttled ship or cut a t. 115:41
speak they through their t. 399:4
straining his t. 225:27
sweet bird's t. 427:7
their t. is an open sepulchre 392:5
thy t. is shut and dried 301:28
undulating t. 41:33
your sweet dividing t. 125:10
Throats: all the singing t. 336:13
cut each other's t. 225:24
cutting foreign t. 477:7
mortal engines, whose rude t. 472:3
my sore t. 22:26
repress their patriot t. 279:3
soft stretching t. 523:11
Throb: only t. she gives 356:21
t. and mutual sob 123:2
Throbbings of noontide 236:12
Throbs of fiery pain 275:4
Throe: never grudge the t. 95:15
t. of the heart 81:19
Throne: around the Saviour's t. 240:21
around the t. of God 361:9
before the t...a sea of glass 70:37
Bust outlasts the t. 183:5
doubtful t. 529:41
fiery-wheeled t. 341:12
fill'd the Stuarts' t. 417:2
flows by the t. of God 415:8
from her ebon t. 587:1
here is my t. 447:27
high on a t. of royal state 345:14
His cradle and His t. 291:14
honour'd for his burning t. 462:25
in mercy..the t. be established 53:24
in prayer before Thy t. 233:18
I saw a great white t. 71:41
it is God's t. 57:48
King George upon the t. 282:10
light which beats upon a t. 529:39
like a burnish'd t. 424:6
living t. 231:13
love's t. 410:22
Mahmud on his golden T. 205:22
Mahmud on his T. 205:21
on a t. of rocks 118:7
on his imperial t. 190:34
Persian on his t. 119:13
proceeding out of the t. 72:6
Reason still keeps its t. 203:29
sable T. behold 381:26
seek such t. as this 413:8
shadow of Thy T. 562:9
sits lightly in his t. 478:34
something behind the t. 379:6
tear it from thy T. 161:3
this royal t. of kings 474:22
thou from a t. 540:16
t. he sits on 444:22
t. of bayonets 267:8
t. of human felicity 277:4
T. sent word to a T. 300:11
t. we honour 500:13
through slaughter to a t. 230:6
two kings..on one t. 162:33
up to the T. 304:2
up to the T. o' God 298:18
when we owed the T. 92:11
Wrong forever on the t. 320:10
Throned: t. on her hundred isles 114:2
t. on ocean's wave 493:2
Thrones: not t. and crowns 198:22
rose from their t. 492:11
they claim no t. 511:10
T., Dominations 348:14
Throng: plaudits of the t. 317:4
swift Anapaests t. 152:5
Thronged: with dreadful faces t. 349:31
Throstle: how blithe the t. sings 581:15
t. with his note so true 467:6
Throstlecock: ousel and the t. 189:18
Throstles too 529:11
Through: chance will bring us t. 15:11
do you read books t.? 272:16
t. and t. the vorpal blade 129:39(-130)
t. bush, t. brier 466:33
t. the night of doubt 35:4

INDEX

Through (cont.)
t. your body in an instant 406:14
who ever read him t.? 102:21
Throw: do not t. this book about now t. me again 40:19
t. away the dearest thing 430:5
t. away the worser part 456:27
t. away Thy rod 436:4
t. her down 244:12
t. his mind into the common stock 48:31
t. hither all your..eyes 223:3
t. myself down in my chamber 342:31
t. open the gates of new life 186:32
t. your wedded lady 96:25
Throweth them against the stones 430:5
Thrown: about the shoulders t. 400:6
Babylon, and t. 246:4
broken and t. away 71:33
t. aside to rust in peace 317:17
t. on her with a pitchfork 507:2
t. out as good for nothing 520:17
Throws: down he t. the coral of his lip 276:9
Thrush: aged t. 321:14
pipes the mounted t. 235:17
that's the wise t. 533:12
t. and the jay 92:15
Thrust: greatness t. upon them 485:16
t. my hand into his side 483:18
Thrust-block: sweatin' t. 64:9
Thrusts the thing we have prayed for 299:9
Thucydides: *The Times*..T. 87:29
T. at Boston 147:21
Thug and the Druse 558:25
Thule: ultima T. 140:28
Thumb: bite your t. at us, sir? 556:10
he put in his t. 476:46
t. each other's books 367:16
Thumbs: our t. are rough 413:7
pricking of my t. 298:14
Thumbscrew and the stake 460:1
Thummim: Urim and the T. 539:19
Thumped him on the head 46:2
Thumps upon your back 131:23
Thunder: all-shaking t. 159:31
amidst the battle's t. 453:5
at the voice of thy t. 23:21
burst of t. sound 398:8
dawn comes up like t. 241:6
deep scars of t. 299:10
deep t. peal on peal 345:7
felt him like the t.'s roll 113:31
fettered the t. 16:21
from the moan of t. 492:27
glorious the t.'s roar 492:9
God made the t. 503:6
he was as rattling t. 325:13
hills with t. riven 426:1
in t., lightning, or in rain? 122:18
its symmetry be as of t. 456:3
Jove for 's power to t. 412:29
laugh as I pass in t. 429:13
legions t. past 492:26
loud roar'd the dreadful t. 17:8
necks in t. clothed 139:1
on their hinges grate harsh t. 231:14
purr myself to sleep with the t. 346:9
sleep in spite of t. 550:20
sound like t. 460:7
state's whole t. 577:1
such sweet t. 386:21
they steal my t. 467:20
t. and the sunshine 172:15
t. of the captains 541:3
t. of the Odyssey 49:27
t. to t. 309:24
what serve for the t. 189:7
Thunder-bearer: bid the t. shoot 473:27
Thunderbolt: like a t. he falls 452:40
Thunderbolts: oak-cleaving t. 529:10
ready..with all your t. 453:5
Thunderclouds: deep t. form 451:21
Thundered: t. on to die 228:21
volley'd and t. 19:3
Thunderer's scowl 528:17
Thunder-fit: split with a t. 266:14
Thunder-harp of pines 148:27
Thundering: t. Aeschylus 503:13
words of..t. sound 281:14
225:2

Thunders: Jehovah of the T. 297:8
t. in the index 435:44
t. of white silence 88:8
Thunder-stone: all-dreaded t. 430:1
Thunder-storm: streams like the t. 114:14
Thunderstruck: stood like one t. 170:7
Thurlow: T. is a fine fellow 275:7
wise as T. looked 211:1
Thursday: on a Holy T. 76:15
T.'s child 368:1
took ill on T. 368:21
Thus: be t. when thou art dead 473:11
that we are t., or t. 470:15
t. thou must do 457:1
to be safely t. 458:32
Thusness: this t. 560:20
Thwackum was for doing justice 204:25
Thyatira: of the city of T. 64:54
Thyme: among the springing t. 263:1
sweet t. true 38:8
wild t. blows 466:41
Thyrsis: hear it, O T. 18:31
T. of his own will went away 18:23
Thyself: find thou but t. 524:2
I am t. 411:14
know then t. 383:22
know t. 12:23, 127:14
resolve to be t. 18:17
so true to t. 27:37
swear by t. 185:24
thou t. to all eternity 411:14
t. how wondrous 348:4
t. thou gav'st 487:22
Tiber: let Rome in T. melt 423:14
that T. trembled 448:9
T.l father T.l 323:27
Tiberius: Coin, T. 183:5
so T. might have sat 17:13
Tibur is beautiful too 146:13
Tickle: if you t. us 464:8
I'll t. your catastrophe 441:29
t. her with a hoe 269:15
t. o' the sere 433:18
Tickled: t. with a straw 383:30
trouts are t. best 111:27
Tickling: caught with t. 483:13
t. Commodity 447:25
Tiddle-taddle: no t. 444:16
Tide: all this tinkling t. 585:9
at full of t. 424:21
bide till Judgement T. 303:6
call of the running t. 334:11
came the t. 509:7
drifting with the t. 31:1
full t. of human existence 272:25
full t. of successful experiment 268:20
going out with the t. 174:39
lackeying the varying t. 423:39
lived in the t. of times 450:11
no t. shall ever wash away 309:6
not this t. 300:2
such a t. 528:22
tether time or t. 108:8
t. in the affairs of men 451:29
t. in the affairs of women 116:21
t. of pomp 444:23
turning o' the t. 443:19
under the whelming t. 343:2
veer in the t. 525:30
western t. crept up 293:23
when the t.'s pretty nigh out 174:39
Tide-end-town 301:6
Tideless and inert 29:19
Tides: impelled of invisible t. 525:11
salt t. seaward flow 15:23
t. of grass 524:23
Tidings: confirm the t. 2:27
convey'd the dismal t. 225:1
glad t. of great joy 527:4
him that bringeth good t. 54:22
t. of comfort and joy 6:12
Tidy Pachyderm 304:20
Tie: all the chains that t. 342:8
in whose t. I see 246:4
love endures no t. 193:13
not fit to t. his brogues 420:30
silken t. 417:21
t. my girdle for me 492:23
t. my life within this band 244:20
t. up my sleeves 266:8
t. up the knocker 385:20

Tie (cont.)
t. up thy fears 244:10
Tied: I am t. to the stake 453:33
t. and bound with..our sins 389:12
t. me to a stake 461:8
t. the world in a tether 525:20
Tienne..le théâtre rempli 78:6
Ties..strong as links of iron 101:10
Tiger: find a T. well repay 40:29
German t. 144:6
Hyrcan t. 459:20
imitate the action of the t. 443:24
master o' the T. 456:10
poor t...hadn't *got* a Christian 403:21
smile on the face of the t. 11:2
tearing his meat like a t. 325:32
t.'s heart wrapped in a player's hide 232:6
t.'s heart wrapped in a woman's hide 445:43
t. sky 336:14
Tiger-moth's..wings 285:19
Tigers: bears, t., ounces 347:15
empty t. 478:39
shabby t. 249:5
t. are getting hungry 144:19
t. of wrath 77:17
Tiger Tim, come tell me 34:5
Tight: bo'sun t. 218:14
bright little, t. little 222:8
his shoes were far too t. 311:19
t. little Island 173:15
Tight-rooted: wolf's-bane, t. 287:19
Tights: played it in t. 39:18
Tile: where did you get that t.? 408:17
Tills: man comes and t. the field 540:20
t. this lonely field 100:8
Tillyvally, lady! 482:29
Tilts up his chair 249:24
Timber: like season'd t. 245:14
your navy..rotten t. 101:13
Timbrel: sound the loud t. 357:17
Timbrels: damsels playing with the t. 396:12
what pipes and t.? 287:7
Timbuctoo: on the plains of T. 568:25
Time: above the wrecks of T. 312:24
abysm of T. 479:20
achieve in t. 220:2
act of t. 26:42
against that t. 486:33
age and body of the t. 434:18
all of the olden t. 24:8
all the people all of the t. 314:14
almost mythic t. 375:19
balance of proud t. 231:35
bald cheater, T. 281:2
bald sexton, T. 447:30
bank and shoal of t. 457:7
beyond space and t. 83:25
bid t. return 475:2
Bird of T. 205:14, 15
births of t. 26:29
books of all t. 413:2
born out of my due t. 359:1
bounds of place and t. 231:13
bourne of T. and Place 528:22
breaks t., as dancers 124:2
brief chronicles of the t. 433:29
by this t. he has tested 89:41
by t. completely silver'd 163:5
child of T. 234:10
choose thine own t. 33:14
circumscribed in t. and place 581:18
common arbitrator, T. 481:28
conspiracy his t. doth take 479:37
cormorant devouring T. 454:30
corridors of T. 316:9
count t. by heart-throbs 29:9
delightful way of wasting t. 358:17
demand the t. of day 438:14
do not squander t. 211:15
dovetailed with regard to place and t. 177:18
dust on antique t. 429:9
eighteenth century of T. 126:3
envious and calumniating t. 481:21
escaped the shipwreck of t. 24:15
even such is t. 405:12
events in the womb of t. 470:18

Time (*cont.*)

every t. she gife a shoomp	313:13
Fate, T., Occasion	497:7
figure for the t. of scorn	472:34
fly, envious T.	351:31
footprints on the sands of t.	317:8
for all t.	281:16
forefinger of all T.	538:11
friendship..master'd T.	533:9
from his Vintage rolling T.	206:7
from this t. forth	474:1
'gainst the tooth of t.	462:24
Gardener, T.	183:3
good t. coming, boys	326:23
grand Instructor, T.	103:13
had a glorious t.	190:25
half as old as T.	100:3, 408:8
Heaven a t. ordains	351:23
held his breath for a t.	122:4
his youth 'gainst t. and age	377:4
how long a t.	474:16
how T. is slipping	206:19
if I had had t.	290:29
I forget all t.	347:21
if the street were t.	197:3
if you want to know the t.	408:1
in a t. outworn	584:19
in continuance of t.	388:4
in eternal lines to t. thou grow'st	486:18
in His good t.	94:13
inseparable propriety of t.	24:34
in some t., his good t.	94:13
in thee t.'s furrows	486:19
in the Palaeozoic t.	504:13
in t. the savage bull	305:12, 468:5
I shall find t., Cassius	452:2
it also marks the t.	499:29
it saves t.	130:1
it will last my t.	125:33
keeping t., t., t.	380:12
keep t. with my salt tears	279:28
last syllable of recorded t.	461:4
laughters for all t.	89:2
life t.'s fool	440:37
little t. when it is new	32:18
liv'd a blessed t.	458:24
long result of T.	534:14
look into the seeds of t.	456:15
loss of t.	159:38
Love's not T.'s fool	488:7
Miss Jenkyns beat t., out of t.	213:23
mock the t.	457:16
move in melodious t.	343:17
my t. has been properly spent	527:9
new-hatch'd to the woeful t.	458:21
night of t.	87:18
no precious t. at all to spend	487:7
no proper t. of day	253:11
no respect of place,..nor t.	482:31
not enough t...all there is	201:20
nothing puzzles me more than t. and space	307:10
no t. like the present	329:7
no t. to read play-bills	104:2
no t. to stand and stare	169:24
not to be changed by place or t.	344:22
O aching t.!	286:7
old T. is still a-flying	247:10
old T. makes these decay	124:25
only fault's with t.	93:16
only t. for grief	253:26
on T.'s string	245:8
O t. too swift	377:4
O world! O life! O t.!	494:18
panting T.	278:34
peace for our t.	135:9
peace in our t.	388:24
phrase that t. hath flung away	276:14
prevent the t. of life	451:36
productions of t.	77:12
rags of t.	186:20
redeeming the t.	68:4
relish of the saltness of t.	441:13
remoter t.	493:27
rich with the spoils of t.	230:5
river of T.	16:3
round beneath it, T.	552:13
seen the best of our t.	452:16
series of new t. began	190:31
serve his t. to every trade	117:11
shook hands with t.	209:27

Time (*cont.*)

shop to mind in t. and place	96:26
show and gaze o' the t.	461:13
silence and slow t.	287:6
silent touches of t.	103:26
sing of T. or Eternity	529:17
so shall T. be	411:15
soul of the whole Past T.	126:27
spared and blest by t.	114:22
Speech is of T.	127:22
speech is shallow as T.	126:1
spend their t. and wits on	110:44
spirit of the t.	447:40
strain, T.'s eunuch	255:9
struggles with and conquers T.	309:9
syllabes jar with t.	281:27
syllable through t. and space	162:2
take a little t.	175:34
taught by t.	299:3
teeth o' T. may gnaw	107:27
tether t. or tide	108:8
that sweet t.	357:15
that t. may cease	330:7
that t. of year	487:16
there is a t. of life, Sir	277:3
there passed a weary t.	149:8
there was a t. when meadow	576:1
thief of t.	587:4
those feet in ancient t.	75:16
throat of Old T.	175:19
till t. and times are done	586:6
T., a maniac	532:27
T. and Fate of all their Vintage	206:6
t. and my intents are savage-wild	478:39
t. and nonsense scorning	98:15
t. and place are lost	346:10
t. and the hour	456:26
t., and the ocean	561:10
t. and the place	93:38
t. and the world	584:20
t., and times, and half a t.	71:19
T. an endless song	585:16
t...author of authors	24:12
t. but the impression deeper	107:5
t. can but make her beauty over	585:4
T. did beckon to the flow'rs	244:20
t. doth settle	262:5
t. doth transfix	487:9
t. draws near the birth of Christ	532:21
t. driveth onward fast	535:17
t. enough to mourn	168:12
t. for a little something	339:22
t. for labour and thought	522:7
t. for such a word	461:4
T., goes, you say?	183:15
t. has come	130:15
t. hath my lord, a wallet	481:17
t. hath to silver turn'd	377:4
t. hovers o'er	279:7
t. is come round	451:39
t. is drawing near	3:8
T. is fleeting	317:6
t. is like a fashionable host	481:20
t. is money	211:5
t. is on our side	222:34
t. is our tedious song	343:25
t. is out of joint	432:32
t. is the greatest innovator	26:30
t. is the great physician	182:9
t., like an ever-rolling stream	562:9
T. makes ancient good uncouth	320:13
t...man is always trying to kill	508:20
t. may restore us	16:23
t...must have a stop	440:37
T., not Corydon	18:27
t. of life is short	440:32
t. of this mortal life	389:22
T. plays the fiddle	183:7
t. present and t. past	197:4
t. remembered	521:30(-522)
t. returns again	75:12
t. runs	330:7
T.'s devouring hand	79:17
t.'s eternal motion	210:3
T.'s fell hand	487:11
T.'s fleeting river	496:1
t.'s flies	480:26
t.'s glory is to calm	486:7
T.'s iron feet	355:15
t. shall moult away his wings	517:18

Time (*cont.*)

T. shall reap	545:9
t. shall throw a dart at thee	87:24
t.'s noblest offspring	43:13
T.'s printless torrent	493:18
T.'s slow finger	33:12
T., stays, we go	183:15
T.'s wheel runs back	95:23
T.'s winged chariot	333:9
T.'s wrecks and scars	141:2
t. that cut'st down all	246:7
T., that is o'er-kind	295:10
t. that shall surely be	3:8
t., the avenger	114:17
T., the clock-setter	447:30
t. the devourer	371:31
T. the reaper	545:9
T. the Shadow	582:22
T. to act them in	434:9
t. to be born, and a t. to die	51:3
t. to be in earnest	277:38
t. to be old	199:30
t. to every purpose	51:3
t. to serve	522:7
t. to win this game	188:35
T., transported	5:8
t. travels in divers paces	428:9
t. turns the old days	523:1
t. was when Love and I	222:13
t. we may comprehend	86:9
t. whereof the memory of man	73:7, 314:22
t., which antiquates antiquities	87:9
t. which to us is uncertain	38:31
t. will come	180:13, 181:26
t. will doubt of Rome	116:12
t. will run back	343:18
t. with a gift of tears	522:5
t. writes no wrinkle	114:29
t. y-lost	138:38
t., you old gypsy man	249:17
'tis but the t.	449:33
'tis t.; descend	485:38
'tis t. to do't	460:24
to beguile the t., look like the t.	457:5
to choose t. is to save t.	26:8
took up the glass of T.	534:16
too much t. in studies	27:14
to the end of t.	269:30
turn backward, O T.	4:16
unconscionable t. dying	136:11
unimaginable touch of t.	578:2
unthinking t.	193:31
use your t.	247:10
waiting t.	187:3
weary of t.	76:7
weight of this sad t.	454:28
we take no note of T.	587:2
what's t.?	91:40
what t., what circuit first	94:13
when t. is broke	475:34
when T. shall turn	180:10
while t. serves	246:1
whips and scorns of t.	434:4
who T. ambles withal	428:9
with leaden foot t. creeps	267:28
world enough, and t.	333:8
Time-honour'd Lancaster	474:8
Time-killer	406:9
Timelessly: fading t.	341:6
Timely: by a t. compliance	204:14
Time-Machine	505:2
Timeo Danaos et dona ferentis	553:27
Times: all the t. you can	565:19
all t. I have enjoy'd	540:32
all t. when old are good	112:26
at sundry t.	69:6
epitome of our t.	200:2
ever lived in the tide of t.	450:11
giddy-paced t.	483:1
her coughs..she t. them ill	22:29
how many t. do I love thee?	38:30
in pious t.	190:7
my t. be in Thy hand!	95:26
nature of the t. deceas'd	442:6
old friends, old t.	220:43
old t. unqueen thee	148:14
one copy of The T.	147:21
our t. are in His hand	95:13
signs of the t.	59:42
stirring t. we live in	236:41

INDEX

Times (cont.)

these pursy t. 436:3
the T...many ministries 28:24
time, and t. 71:19
t. and things 265:22
t. are changed with him who
  marries 514:30
t. go by turns 508:19
t. that try men's souls 372:22
t. will not mend 373:13
wail my dear t.' waste 486:25
what I tell you three t. 128:4
Time-Spirit 20:15
Timid: Mr. Harris..dreadful t. 176:31
Timon hath made his..mansion 480:32
Timor mortis conturbat me 195:2
Timorous: cow'rin', t. beastie 107:9
t. foe 385:29
Timotheus: old T. yield 191:13
Tin: pocket full of t. 210:13
Tinct with cinnamon 285:25
Tincture: this t. in the blood 170:4
Tine: lest my jewel it should t. 104:27
Ting-a-ling-a-ling 8:19
Tinged: just t. with blue 567:17
t. her cheek with brown 416:16
t. with pink 312:6
Tingle: ears..shall t. 47:7
Tingling: whoreson t. 441:14
Tinkers: as t. do ale 109:22
Tinkle: grasped it for a t. 39:11
Tinkled like iron 575:24
Tinkling: t. cymbal 26:16, 66:44
t. with their feet 52:35
Tinklings: drowsy t. lull 229:28
Tinsel: flapt its t. wing 332:5
Tintinabulation..from the bells 380:12
Tints that glow 119:2
Tiny and cheerful 171:17
Tiny Tim 174:10
Tip: schoolboy's t. 542:17
t. me the black spot 514:19
t. of your soft ear 247:7
t. them Long Melford 78:31
within the nether t. 149:16
Tipped with steel 414:4
Tippeny: wi' t., we fear nae evil 108:10
Tipperary: long way to T. 571:1
Tipple in the deep 319:6
Tippled drink more fine 287:1
Tippling: taste for t. 218:19
Tips with silver 477:22
Tipsy: never gets t. at all 311:10
Tip-tilted: her slender nose t. 530:6
Tiptoe: day stands t. 478:27
on t. for a flight 286:27
stand a t...this day is nam'd 444:28
t. upon a little hill 286:25
Tire: gaudy t. 166:18
long before I t. 84:7
look not back nor t. 81:24
no labours t. 279:5
speeds too fast, 'twill t. 455:4
t. of all creation straightened out 251:16
Tired: not be t. by waiting 297:10
process of getting t. 111:32
tedious as a t. horse 440:2
till t. he sleeps 383:30
t. her head 48:28
t. metaphor 116:46
t. of his dark dominion 336:17
t. of London..t. of life 273:23
t. of tears and laughter 523:18
t. the sun with talking 157:10
t. with all these 487:14
t. with soaring 191:16
t. yet strong 338:5
we are t.: said Gilpin.. 160:3
what can a t. heart say 171:4
Tires: he t. betimes 474:21
in Grecian t. 487:3
t. as much 161:36
your sad t. in a mile-a 485:21
Tiresias and Phineus 346:20
Tirez: messieurs..t. 239:9
t. le rideau 404:29
Tiring-house: **this** hawthorn-
  brake our t. 467:2
Tirling at the window 339:9
Tirra-lirra: lark, that t. chants 485:13
'T.', by the river 534:6

Tit: tell tale, t.! 369:2
Titan: like thy glory, T. 497:17
she, the weary T. 16:11
T. kiss..butter—pitiful-hearted
  T. 439:14
Titania: there sleeps T. 466:41
Titanic: that T. strife 16:21
through an alley T. 381:2
Titan-woman: some pale T. 522:12
Tithe: t. or toll in our dominions 447:29
ye pay t. of mint 60:17
Tithe-pig: with a t.'s tail 477:7
Titian: nobody cares..about T. 413:18
Title: farced t. 444:23
gained no t. 385:6
his t. hang loose about him 460:31
honery t. of T.K. 559:34
like my t...it is not mine 516:11
my courage prove my t. 426:10
read my t. clear 562:12
that t. from a better man 516:11
whatever t. suit thee 104:4
Titled: feed the t. knave, man 108:17
Titles: all thy other t...given away 452:26
as due by many t. 185:11
beauty, t., wealth 381:36
despite those t. 417:22
high though his t. 417:22
t. are shadows 170:17
t. manifold 577:3
Titus Antoninus Pius..his reign 217:7
Tityre, tu patulae recubans 555:14
T.K.: honery title of T. 559:34
To: *from* something, or *t.* something 273:4
Toad: I had rather be a t. 471:40
intelligent Mr. T. 228:17
like the t...wears..a..jewel 426:30
rose-water over a t. 269:17
squat like a t. 347:28
t. beneath the harrow 300:13
worse than t. or asp 351:17
Toads: cistern for foul t. 472:34
To and fro: flicker t. 545:2
his eyes went t. 150:11
t. conflicting wind 453:4
Toast: bring me some t.! 403:8
chocolate, butter, and t. 13:17
let the t. pass 500:39
muffin and t. 222:18
never had a piece of t. 376:9
refus'd to pledge my t. 402:7
t. of the parish 409:13
t. our wants 384:31
t. that pleased the most 173:8
Toasted-cheese 128:7
Tobacco: divine t. 510:1
for thy sake, T. 307:31
leave off T. 307:8, 12
monograph on the ashes of..t. 187:14
no sweeter t...Three Castles 542:41
roguish t. 280:14
snuff, t., and sleep 174:29
superexcellent t...damned t. 109:22
tawney weed t. 279:24
Tobacco-jar: Jones, the t. 121:22
Tobacco-juice: cooked by t. 121:22
Tobias: Henry and T. 297:19
Toby: provide our little T. meat 508:16
Tocher: lass wi' a t. 106:8
Tochter aus Elysium 415:21
Tocsin of the soul 116:18
Tod: ein früher T. 224:1
To-day: call t. his own 194:20
care beyond t. 230:26
day will be t. 82:10
grassy track t. it is 299:23
here t...gone tomorrow 40:6
he t. that sheds his blood 444:28(–445)
if T. be sweet 206:19
I have lived t. 158:17, 194:20
I'm to be married t. 218:32
I shall die t. 358:3
never do t. 403:7
never jam t. 130:27
not hang myself t. 140:9
on our side t. 324:14
Rome of t. 200:2
Rose kissed me t. 183:17
same yesterday, and t. 69:23
speak what you think t. 200:40

To-day (cont.)

stern T. 402:14
such a day to-morrow as t. 485:3
t., all day, I rode 78:1
t., beneath the foeman's frown 188:30
t. I happen to have a headache 130:25
t. shalt thou be with me 62:50
t. your royal head may fall 140:10
wiser t. than he was yesterday 520:46
Toddle: I'd t. safely home 415:13
Todgers' could do it 176:11
Toe: clerical printless t. 84:11
from the crown to the t. 457:3
light fantastic t. 341:29
taken him in t. 253:5
t. of frog 459:31
t. of the peasant 437:13
with forward t. 336:21
Toes: happier without their t. 312:10
no harm can come to his t. 312:7
Pobble's t. are safe 312:7
Pobble who has no t. 312:5
so good for a Pobble's t. 312:6
warming her pretty little t. 367:17
when our t. are turned up 33:19
To-fro tender trambeams 254:18
Toga: nocitura t. 283:16
Togae: cedant arma t. 145:8
Together: let us remain t. still 493:21
never be seen there t. again 156:13
never come t. again 169:21
our lives would grow t. 524:28
pigging t., heads and points 100:8
ride, ride t. 92:40
singing t. 91:36
sleep t. at the foot 106:20
taken in t. 199:18
thus tease me t. 215:4
t. now for forty years 142:22
we've been long t. 33:14
work t. for good 65:56
Toil: blood, t., tears and sweat 143:38
day in t. 404:5
end of t. and gloom 35:6
forget his labour an' his t. 104:33
her men robust for t. 123:7
her strong t. of grace 426:16
his honour and his t. 541:3
horny-handed sons of t. 284:9
horny hands of t. 320:5
'mid t. and tribulation 517:3
mock the hope of t. 165:17
mock their useful t. 230:1
our love and t. 295:6
peril, t. and pain 240:22
remark each anxious t. 279:2
slumber is more sweet than t. 535:20
they t. not 58:13
they waste their t. 417:19
thy t. o'er books 215:21
t. and trouble 459:30
t., envy, want 279:4
t. in other men's extremes 305:15
t. of dropping buckets 163:11
verse softens t. 217:17
view their t. 168:13
war..is t. and trouble 191:9
weary t. 486:23
what with his t. he won 190:15
who climbs with t. 39:4
why all this t. and trouble? 581:14
winding up days with t. 444:23
with great t. all that I can 4:10
with much t. attain 147:9
Toiled: souls that have t. 541:3
Time t. after him 278:34
t. after it as other men after virtue 307:6
we have t. all the night 61:27
Toiling: t., rejoicing, sorrowing 318:13
t. upward in the night 316:31
Toils: distinguished from you but
  by t.? 1:18
superior t., and heavier..cares 1:18
their t. upbraid 332:13
t. much to earn 162:37
Token: shew some t. upon me 397:12
Tokens: words are the t. current 24:20
Tolbooth-gate 419:37
Told: bade me fight..t. me so 202:18
bloom as they are t. 84:9

[956]

Told (*cont.*)
half was not t. me 47:43
hath it not been t. you 54:13
he never t. anybody 304:22
I t. my wrath 76:5
I t. you so 116:50, 318:8
left half t. the story 341:20
never t. her love 483:10
they t. me, Heraclitus 157:15
they t. me I was every thing 454:6
they t. me you had been to her 129:33
t. in dim Eden 171:1
t. the sexton 252:32
Toledo: blade, T. trusty 110:21
Tolerable: most t. and not to be endured 468:38
t. were it not for its amusements 313:25
Tolerant: to know all makes one t. 511:9
Toll: tithe or t. in our dominions 447:29
t. for the brave 162:11
t. me back from thee 288:2
t. *slowly* 88:5
Tolle: t. lege, t. lege 21:21
Tolled: sexton t. the bell 252:32
t. the one bell 263:2
Tolls: faintly as t. 357:16
for whom the *bell* t. 186:28
Tom: hails you T. or Jack 159:31
T. bears logs 456:1
T. he was a piper's son 369:10
T.'s a-cold 453:16
T.'s food 453:24
T.'s no more 116:31
T. the Second. . like T. the First 192:11
T., T., the piper's son 369:11
T. was beat 369:11
Tomato: chops and T. sauce 179:12
Tomb: asleep within the t. 78:16
blossom on the t. 164:30
empty in thy t. 292:19
ev'n from the t. 230:9
Fidele's grassy t. 153:20
her t. by the sounding sea 380:10
hollow of her breasts a t. 522:14
icy silence of the t. 287:3
I've stood upon Achilles' t. 116:12
like a ghost from the t. 493:1
longing for the t. 586:10
making their t. the womb 487:20
monument, without a t. 281:11
more than royal t. 27:47
press no ponderous t. 118:23
rending of the t. 35:6
smell like what it is—a t. 495:10
the sea was made his t. 35:23
this side the t. 169:21
threefold, fourfold t. 36:21
toward the silent t. 573:27
Tombs: from the t. a doleful sound 562:11
honoured t. 196:36
register'd upon our brazen t. 454:29
towers and t. and statues 208:5
when. . t. of brass are spent 488:3
Tombstone: carve it on his t. 302:6
t. where he lies 317:2
t. white 300:6
Tom Jones: more knowledge. . than in all *T.* 272:12
T., that exquisite picture 216:17
Tomlinson: stand up now, T. 302:21
Tom Moore: before I go, T. 118:14
Tommy: T. and Jack and Joe 305:3
T. this, an' T. that 303:1
Tommy Townshend: persuade T. 225:27
Tomnoddy: my Lord T. 34:6, 84:27
Tom o' Bedlam: sigh like T. 452:21
To-morrow: altho' t. it seem 81:9
boast not thyself of t. 50:43
gone t. 40:6
I shall die to-day, and you t. 358:3
jam t. 130:27
live till t. 160:40
lose t. the ground won to-day 18:12
not too late t. 14:27
such a day t. as to-day 485:3
sustain t.'s road 77:30
that may be t. 544:4
that shall be t. 97:26
think t. will repay 191:34
this, no t. hath 184:0

To-morrow (*cont.*)
till t. eve 375:13
t., and t., and t. 461:4
t. a stranger will say 200:37
t. do thy worst 194:20
t. 'ill be the happiest time 536:26
t. is our wedding-day 159:33
t. is Saint Crispian 444:28
t. let my sun 158:17
t. let us do or die 122:14
t.'s falser 191:34
t. shall not drive it out 186:31
t. speak what t. thinks 200:40
t.'s uprising to deeds 359:7
t. the last of many battles 425:8
t. thou shalt die 411:5, 7
t. to fresh woods 343:7
t. we die 67:11
t. we shall die 53:27
T.!—why, T. I may be 206:5
t. will be dying 247:10
what you can put off till t. 403:7
will she kiss me t.? 183:17
Tom Pearse 33:1
Tom Thumb: thought about T. 276:17
Tom-tit: a little t. 220:17
Tone: ditties of no t. 287:8
look at me. . in that t. of voice 403:32
restore the t. of. . Nature 162:36
Robert Emmet and Wolfe T. 584:27
take the t. of the company 139:13
that mighty t. 128:3
that t., and gesture bland 416:18
Tones: lute its t., t. ravishment 285:1
sweet t. are remembered not 494:20
Tongs and the bones 467:14
Tongue: all. . words of t. and pen 238:31, 568:17
become his mother t. 226:38
bridleth not his t. 69:34
Chatham's. . his mother t. 163:1
every t. . . a several tale 476:36
eye, t., sword 434:14
fallen by the t. 57:3
fellows of infinite t. 445:13
flatter with their t. 392:5
for God's sake hold your t. 184:11
found her t. 280:8
from a maniac's t. 87:38
give thy thoughts no t. 431:25
had t. at will 470:29
hear that t. 412:19
her t. unbound 155:5
his t. dropt manna 345:18
his t. is the clapper 468:28
his t. sounds ever after 441:10
his t. to conceive 467:23
I held my t. 394:8
I must hold my t. 431:1
in their Mother T. 391:14
in the vulgar t. 390:55
iron t. of midnight 467:34
its all obliterated T. 206:18
lends the t. vows 431:27
let my t. cleave 400:5
lisping stammering t. 161:8
love's t. is in the eyes 209:7
love's t. proves. . Bacchus gross 455:22
murder, though it have no t. 433:36
my t. from evil-speaking 391:8
my t. is the pen 394:21
my t.'s use 474:14
nor t. to speak here 313:15
of a slow t. 45:39
on every infant's t. 120:23
persuasion tips his t. 144:33
rank t. blossom into speech 90:12
Roger's false flattering t. 306:34
rolls it under his t. 242:8
senates lending upon thy t. 546:18
sharp t. . . only edged tool 267:19
snakes with double t. 466:44
stopped his tuneful t. 385:5
strenuous t. 287:21
stroke of the t. breaketh 57:3
that his t. must vent 429:13
that my t. could utter 528:3
that smooth t. 123:27
their t. a sharp sword 395:18
thou false t. 399:24
thy t. tang arguments 483:19

Tongue (*cont.*)
t. can no man tame 69:37
t. in every wound 450:34
t. like a button-stick 295:3
t. of dog 459:31
t. of him that makes it 455:34
t. of neither maid nor wife 527:12
t. of the dumb sing 54:3
t. of thy dogs may be red 396:11
t. our trumpeter 429:3
t. so varied 308:17
t. that Shakespeare spake 577:3
t. to persuade 145:26
t. . . when it an't a woman's 178:34
t. with a tang 479:42
'tween my heart and t. 449:27
understanding, but no t. 431:16
use of my oracular t. 500:20
vent the treasure of our t. 168:9
what his heart thinks his t. speaks 468:28
while I held my t. 393:31
yet my t. could scarcely cry 76:17
your t. shall be split 369:2
your t.'s sweet air 466:21
Tongues: airy t. 340:10
aspics' t. 472:10
bestowed that time in the t. 482:7
chapmen's t. 455:2
cloven t. . . as of fire 64:25
evil t. 348:23, 582:3
from innumer ble t. 349:20
hear them speak in our t. 64:26
host of t. 424:15
kindreds, and people, and t. 71:3
lovers' t. by night 477:27
queen of t. 281:26
silence envious t. 446:31
slanderous t. 469:18
thousand several t. 476:36
t. a-talking 263:18
t. in trees 426:30
t. of men and of angels 66:44
t., they shall cease 66:45
walls have t. 521:14
we loose wild t. 300:26
whispering t. can poison truth 150:25
Tongue-tied: art made t. 487:14
To-night: find it out t. 459:2
just for t. 4:16
met in thee t. 84:25
rain set early in t. 95:4
tomorrow not t. 97:26
t. it doth inherit 17:15
t. so full of care 80:17
world may end t. 92:32
Toning of a tear 246:5
Too: this is t. bad! 203:36
when others cry, 'T. late' 88:23
Took: all which I t. from thee 544:30
God t. him 44:35
he t. her with a sigh 75:22
I t. you for that. . whore 472:37
not the men you t. them for 468:39
things that I never t. 396:16
t. them clean away 368:15
t. them quite away 129:27
went an' t.—the same as me! 303:22
ye t. me in 60:33
Tool: only edged t. 267:19
thing, a t., a Jesuit 294:14
Too-late: No-more, T., Farewell 411:17
Tool-making animal 211:20
Tools: give us the t. 144:5
nothing but to name his t. 110:8
secrets are edged t. 193:6
their working t. 549:25
t. of working out salvation 111:12
t. to him that can handle them 126:2
t. to work withal 320:5
without t. . . nothing 127:7
Tool-using animal 127:7
Too-quick: down hill 'T.' 538:3
'Too-slow' will need the whip 538:3
Tooth: alwey a coltes t. 138:8
'gainst the t. of time 462:24
in danger of her former t. 459:4
keen and angry t. 80:27
my pugging t. on edge 485:16
poison for the age's t. 447:20
red in t. and claw 532:37

INDEX

Tooth (cont.)
sharper than a serpent's t. 178:19, 452:30
thy t. is not so keen 427:22
t. for t. 45:54
Toothache: endure the t. 469:13
feels not the t. 430:3
sigh for the t.? 408:29
suffer t.'s ills 218:12
Tooth-brush: my t...haunts me 269:4
Tooth-picks: supply of t. 269:10
Tooth-point: where each t. goes 300:13
Tooth-powder: no t. 119:32
Tootle-te-tootle the fife 97:14
Toots: knocked Mr. T. about the head 175:12
Top: always room at the t. 563:1
America..clearly t. nation 422:17
below the lighthouse t. 148:21
crooked at the t. 28:12
I shall die at the t. 520:51
lighthouse t. I see 150:4
little bit off the t. 360:5
on de t. of his head 210:18
sleep like a t. 169:11
t. of it reached to heaven 45:3
t. of some bold headland 574:11
t. of sovereignty 286:16, 460:8
t. thing in the world 290:23
to the t. of every tree 218:27
to the t. of my bent 435:27
to the t. of my compass 435:24
Topaz: ninth, a t. 72:1
Toper: poor t. 164:33
Tophet-flare: by T. to Judgement Day 295:2
Topics: other fashionable t. 227:23
t. of amusement 519:3
you have but two t. 273:16
Top-mast: strack the t. wi' his hand 30:19
Top-most: on the t. twig 410:6
Tops: fruit-tree t. 477:22
their slender t. 253:2
t. cleaned with champagne 518:19
Topsails: then her t. went 237:15
Topses: herring boxes without t. 355:23
Topsy-Turveydom 218:6
Topsy-turvy: from my t. 336:5
Torch: bright t., and a casement 288:9
his t. is at thy temple door 405:19
signal t. has burned his hour 264:5
since the t. is out 425:22
t. that lighted mine 199:10
truth, like a t. 235:3
Torches: our little t. at his fire 147:26
she doth teach the t. 477:9
Torchlight procession 371:5
Tore his hair 507:27
Tories: stern and unbending T. 324:27
T. own no argument 87:26
Torment: measure of our t. 296:28
more grievous t. 286:39
no t. touch them 56:23
smoke of their t. ascendeth 71:26
there's the t. 305:16
t. of the night's untruth 168:12
when to live is t. 470:14
Tormented: his joints t. be 281:27
t. with ten thousand hells 330:2
Torments: anybody's t. in this world 139:32
how many t. lie 144:23
of all the t. 559:6
our t...become our elements 345:23
what t. of grief 199:25
Torpedo: pen..becomes a t. 270:8
Torpid: all t. inanity 147:18
Torpor: negligentiae t. 414:21
Torquatus volo parvulus 133:6
Torrent: amber t. descended 146:17
in the very t., tempest 434:15
time's printless t. 493:18
t. of a woman's will 11:22
t. of darkness 366:1
Torrid or the frozen zone 125:7
Tort: les absents ont toujours t. 172:29
quand tout le monde a t. 138:44
Tortoise: this 'ere 'T.' is a insect 403:16
Torture: all length is t. 425:22
hum of human cities t. 113:47

Torture (cont.)
those they t. not 496:25
t. and death..amusing 212:4
t. not again 492:7
t. of a lingring..passion 202:2
t. of the mind 459:4
t. one poor word 193:3
t. to her mediumistic soul 310:20
Tortures: by t. tried 382:13
Torturing: iron scourge and t. hour 230:15
To-ruffled: all t. 340:20
Tory: T. and Whig in turns 505:32
T. men and Whig measures 181:33
what is called the T...party 166:26
whether I were a Whig or a T. 519:14
Whig and T. a' agree 502:22
Toss: Book, I t. i' the air 95:27
good enough to t. 440:23
t. him to My breast 245:1
t. in the spray 15:23
t. of the parish 409:13
Tossed: He that t. you down 207:1
t. and gored several persons 271:26
t. on the wind-ridden..sea 171:19
Tossing about in a steamer 219:10
Toss-pots still had drunken heads 484:27
Total: t. abstinence is easier 22:4
t. eclipse 350:22
Totter: t. into vogue 558:19
we maun t. down, John 106:20
Totters: lift one if one t. down 409:19
t. forth..in a gauzy veil 499:5
Totus: in se ipso t. 262:1
Touch: at a t. I yield 539:1
can't t. de bottom 210:14
child beneath her t. 410:26
exquisite t...denied to me 420:28
fear not to the best 405:7
her voice, her t. 566:19
he wants the natural t. 460:17
little t. of Harry 444:9
Nelson t. 362:14, 363:8
nor lose the common t. 297:12
nothing, can t. him further 459:4
of Nelson only a t. 93:36
one t. of nature 481:21
puts it not unto the t. 355:19
sign you must not t. 185:4
so delicate his t. 162:28
some far-off t. of greatness 530:35
spider's t. 383:17
t. divine 96:33
t. him not 492:7
t. me not 64:8
t. not a single bough 358:21
t. not; taste not 68:29
t. of a vanish'd hand 528:3
t. of celestial temper 347:29
t. of cold philosophy 286:42
t. of earth 530:34
t. of earthly years 573:6
t. the Happy Isles 541:3
t. the Lord's Anointed 7:9
t. you, a passer-by 404:21
unimaginable t. of time 578:2
what is natural cannot t. me 201:31
world intangible, we t. thee 545:1
Touched: almost t. the sky 250:1
finely t. but to fine issues 461:16
t. my trembling ears 342:21
t. nothing that he did not adorn 273:19
t. the hollow of his thigh 45:9
t. with an interior touch 165:33
with his spear t. lightly 347:29
Touches: its t. of beauty..never be half-way 289:27
it t. us not 435:16
silent t. of time 103:26
such heavenly t. 486:16
t. of sweet harmony 465:18
t. of things common 89:6
t. of those flower-soft hands 424:7
who t. this t. a man 567:6
Touching: at the t. of the lips 534:17
t. all with thine opiate wand 495:22
t. in its majesty 582:14
Touchy, testy, pleasant fellow 2:8
Tough: interesting, but t. 550:9
rack of this t. world 454:27
t., and devilish sly 175:5
t. customer in argeyment 173:17

Toujours: t. gai, archy 331:12
t. perdrix! 12:20
Tour: en sa t. d'ivoire 414:7
Tous pour un 194:33
Tout for flattery 153:18
Tout: secret d'ennuyer..t. dire 557:13
t. est dit 97:32
t. passe.—L'art..seul..survit 214:3
Toves: slithy t. 129:39
Toward: with a t. or untoward lot 575:11
Towards: I hold it t. you 287:3
Tower: as a t. of ivory 52:19
as the t. of Lebanon 52:19
Caesar's ill-erected t. 475:26
Giotto's t. 316:25
how shines your t. 77:30
in Hero's t. 264:5
like the t. of David 52:5
my head on yonder t. 24:5
nor stony t. 448:36
stood like a t. 345:5
temple and t. went to the ground 351:15
to the Dark T. 90:23, 453:27
t. of strength 476:34, 537:15
with a t. and bells 164:29
yonder ivy-mantled t. 229:29
Towered: down to t. Camelot 534:1
grim shape t. up 579:10
t. above the common mark 273:12
Towering: high t. to descry 350:3
his own t. style 142:20
t. in her pride of place 458:28
Towers: branchy between t. 254:21
bricky t. 510:21
bright t. of silence 171:5
cloud-capp'd t. 480:8
down from her t. a ray 404:21
elephants endorsed with t. 350:8
from the high t. and terraces 493:14
hammer'd from a hundred t. 529:28
her t. and tombs 208:5
no t. along the steep 123:11
rolls by the t. of Rome 323:26
ships, t., domes 582:14
sublime on the t. 492:27
tell the t. thereof 394:35
topless t. of Ilium 330:5
t., and battlements 342:1
t. to a lily 561:6
two t. of sail 147:6
whispering from her t. 19:10
with walls and t. 151:32
ye antique t. 230:23
ye t. of Julius 229:24
Towery city 254:21
Town: all round the t. 367:13
Art is upon the T. 566:3
as men callen daysies in our t. 138:17
Ayr, wham ne'er a t. surpasses 108:3
Charlie came to our t. 250:17
come after me to t. 548:17
directions to the t. 521:20
down at an inland t. 219:17
down to the end of the t. 339:16
follies of the t. 226:42
give every t. a limb 24:5
leave Oxford by the t. drain 511:3
little t. of Bethlehem 84:24
London is a fine t. 154:9
lorn Syrian t. 17:9
man made the t. 162:38
moon that was the t.'s 141:13
one-horse t. 550:29
runs through the t. 339:9
seaward from the t. 266:2
sent them out of t. 367:13
spreading of the hideous t. 359:2
they are for the t.'s end 440:34
through the Sacred T. 41:32
t...lighter than vanity 99:14
t. of monks and bones 150:28
watching them out of the t. 293:25
what little t. by river or sea 287:12
what's this dull t. to me? 292:5
when he studies it in t. 162:1
Town-crier spoke my lines 434:15
Townland: riding to the t. 585:6
Towns: her t...independence flings 123:7
of t. A per se 195:3

[958]

INDEX

Towns (cont.)
 remote from t. 224:18
 see shires and t. 293:3
Townshend: persuade Tommy T. 225:27
Tow, row, row: with a t. 9:24
Toy: foolish thing was but a t. 484:27
 religion but a childish t. 330:14
 sells eternity to get a t. 486:6
Toyed: you might have t. and kist 214:15
Toys: all is but t. 458:24
 cast their t. away 160:15
 not to meddle with my t. 515:18
 t. and things to eat 515:20
 t. for your delight 516:2
 t. of age 383:30
Toy-shops: print-shops, t. 307:2
Trace: delights to t. its semblance 159:2
 his very steps have left a t. 114:34
 in my lineaments they t. 118:29
 not a t. upon her face 219:33
Traces: he t. the steam-engine 180:19
 on winter's t. 521:30
 t. of..spider's web 477:7
Track: around the ancient t. 336:17
 flying on our t. 546:30
 grassy t. to-day 299:23
 tread again that ancient t. 552:6
Tract: left a little t. 569:7
 send his penny t. to me 307:26
Trade: adepts in the speaking t. 143:3
 all nations' t. 43:11
 altered in the building t. 303:7
 cunning at his t. 295:14
 dreadful t. 454:3
 except what t. can give 96:26
 half a t...half an art 267:7
 in London only is a t. 193:24
 in the way of t. 162:23
 knows his art, but not the t. 521:8
 losing t., I assure you 78:27
 moving accident is not my t. 575:12
 not accidental, but a t. 462:11
 not your t. to make tables 271:5
 now there isn't any t. 243:3
 old t.'s plyin' 363:3
 proselytes of one another's t. 111:23
 ruined by t. 211:6
 serve his time to every t. 117:11
 some way of common t. 475:10
 this t. of mine 93:30
 though a pretty t. 87:27
 t...with the living and the dead 194:4
 transitions of t. 200:3
 us that t. in love 424:11
 venture t. abroad 443:10
 war is the t. of kings 192:43
 what t., thou knave? 448:4
Trader: some grave Tyrian t. 18:16
Tradesman..go to heaven? 194:27
Tradesmen: bow, ye t. 218:34
Trade Unionism of the married 490:24
Tradition: t. approves..competition 147:3
 youth..their oldest t. 570:14
Traditions: these legends and t. 317:19
 t. of civility 374:19
Traduced the state 474:2
Traffic: t. of Jacob's ladder 545:1
 two hours' t. of our stage 476:45
 warn all t. 299:25
Trafficked for strange webs 374:11
Traffickers: overpeer the petty t. 462:29
 shy t. 18:16
Tragedies: two t. in life 490:26
Tragedy: go litel myn t. 138:41
 gorgeous T. 341:18
 greatest t. in the world, Madam 564:10
 perfect t...noblest production 2:7
 that is their t. 569:24
 to be out of it..at t. 570:19
 t., 'Man' 380:15
 t. to those that feel 558:27
 wrote her a most tremendous t. 39:18
Tragic: for this the T. Muse 381:6
 in t. life, God wot 336:30
Tragical: very t. mirth 467:26
Trahison des clercs 42:15
Trahit sua quemque voluptas 555:23
Trail: long, long t. 293:1
 Long T. 298:27
 old t., our own t., the out t. 298:27

Trail (cont.)
 out on the t. again 298:27
 t. of the Serpent 357:8
 t. that is always new 298:27
Trail'd the hunter's javelin 17:26
Trailing: t. clouds of glory 576:9
 t. in the cool stream 18:9
 t. wing 16:5
Trails all about the written page 586:14
Train: as we rush in the t. 546:30
 descending from the t. 313:14
 follow in their t. 240:22
 glorious the comet's t. 503:6
 her starry t. 347:23
 his t. filled the temple 53:8
 knitting the loose t. 341:3
 left my glorious t. 552:6
 next t. has gone 403:18
 night with her t. of stars 241:22
 pack, and take a t. 84:12
 t. up a child 50:30
 t. up a fig-tree 175:10
 who follows in His t.? 240:20
 world and all her t. 552:13
Train-band captain 159:32
Traitable: une vertu t. 353:25
Traitor: hate the t. 168:4
 thou art a t. 476:22
 t. hate 170:20
Traitors: hate t. and the treason love 192:32
 he looked upon the t. 323:4
 more strong than t.' arms 450:31
 our doubts are t. 461:21
 our fears do make us t. 460:16
Tra la: bloom in the spring, t. 220:15
Tram: I'm a t. 237:26
Trambeams: to-fro tender t. 254:18
Trammel up the consequence 457:7
Tramp: t. of the twenty-two 79:10
 t.! t.! along the land 419:10
Trample: horses t. 263:5
 t. on my days 552:9
 t. on their sovereign's head 475:10
 t. round my fallen head 528:21
Trampled: piece of English grass t. 234:4
 t. and mocked 491:15
Trampling out the vintage 264:15
Tramplings of three conquests 87:8
Trance: bold seer in a t. 534:8
 in mad t. 492:6
 music heard in t. 493:5
 no nightly t. 343:21
Tranced: senseless, t. thing 284:17
 t. summer-night 286:8
Trances: all my days are t. 380:21
 t. of the blast 151:25
Tranquil: bright and t. 17:28(-18)
 farewell the t. mind 472:3
 humble, t. spirit 170:18
 I love t. solitude 498:15
Tranquillity: after noise, t. 365:4
 cold t. 492:19
 divine T. 535:27
 feeling of inward t. 201:7
 I am restoring t. 101:5
 looking t. 114:22, 155:19
 recollected in t. 583:4
 sinking down in its t. 577:1
Transatlantic Liberty 122:13
Transcend: t. our wonted themes 552:12
 t. the..School-men's vein 308:4
Transcendental: chatter of a t. kind 220:26
 t. moonshine 126:43
Transcending: all human thought t. 233:18
Transfigures you and me 264:18
Transform: t. men into monsters 209:29
 t. ourselves into beasts 471:22
Transgresses: virtue that t. 482:13
Transgression: no law..no t. 65:39
 t. of a law of nature 265:6
Transgressions: wounded for our t. 54:26
Transgressors: intercession for the t. 54:28
 numbered with the t. 54:28
 way of t. 50:4
Transient: t. and embarrassed phantom 182:2
 t., shining trouble 228:18

Transit: sic t. gloria mundi 291:21
Transition: what seems so is t. 317:12
Transitions of trade 200:3
Transitory: action is t. 573:7
 in this t. life 390:29
Translate: make a pudding..t. Epictetus 270:5
Translated: thou art t. 467:5
Translation: mistake in the t. 551:8
 T.'s thief 333:7
Translations not unlike to be 264:19
Translator of Homer 20:2
Translucent: glassy, cool, t. wave 341:3
Translunary: brave t. things 189:11
Transmigrates: it t. 424:17
Transmission: art is..t. of feeling 548:9
Transmitter: no tenth t. 415:16
Transmutes: subdues, t., bereaves 575:6
Transported: t. with celestial desire 510:14
 t. with the View 2:22
Tranter Reuben 236:8
Trap: mous caught in a t. 136:30
Trappings: these but the t. 430:30
Trash: poor t. of Venice 471:3
 steals my purse steals t. 471:30
 wring from..peasants their vile t. 451:20
Traurig: dass ich so t. bin 240:25
Travail: after all our t. 12:7
 if t. you sustain 233:3
 my great t. so gladly spent 583:19
 my labour for my t. 480:40
 t. and heavy sorrow 522:6
 t. on the deep 168:13
Travaileth: whole creation..t. 65:55
Travel: all that t. by land 389:3
 discredited your t. 423:27
 farther from the east must t. 576:9
 I long to t. back 552:6
 in a moment t. thither 576:19
 I t. for t.'s sake 514:14
 let it t. down the years 109:1
 our deeds still t. with us 196:21
 portance in my t.'s history 470:2
 thought the t. long 412:19
 though we t. the world over 200:5
 to discover we must t. too 206:27
 to school, and not to t. 27:27
 t. hopefully 515:6
 t. forth without my cloak 486:30
 t., in the younger sort 27:27
 t. on life's common way 577:15
 t. to their home 493:10
Travelled: t. among unknown men 577:4
 t. a short while towards the sun 509:2
 t. in the realms of gold 288:19
 t. life's dull round 499:13
Traveller: 'anybody there?' said the t. 171:13
 farewell, Monsieur T. 428:17
 forget his fellow t. 11:3
 lost t.'s dream 74:22
 luminous vapours..to the t. 278:23
 misled and lonely t. 340:9
 no t. returns 434:4
 Sentimental T. 512:18
 spurs the lated t. 459:10
 t. betwixt life and death 580:21
 t., by the faithful hound 316:22
 t. came by 75:22
 t. from an antique land 496:13
 t. from New Zealand 324:31
 t. from the cradle 497:16
 t.'s journey is done 76:7
 t. was to blame 387:22
Travellers must be content 426:39
Travelleth: as one that t. 49:47
 he that t. into a country 27:27
Travelling: good t. name 203:13
 in t... carry knowledge 274:4
 reputation by t. abroad 272:1
 t...ruin of all happiness 103:36
 unprofitably t. 579:3
 worth the t. to 516:14
Travels: contemplation of my t. 428:16
 go again to my t. 136:9
 Time t. in divers paces 428:9
 t. the fastest who t. alone 304:2
Tray: faithful T. 249:20

Tray (cont.)
my poor dog T. 122:16
T., Blanch and Sweet-heart 453:29
Trays: cheap tin t. 333:21
Treachery: fear their subjects' t. 446:2
kill'd with my own t. 437:38
machinations, hollowness, t. 452:16
t.I seek it out 437:39
Treacle: fly that sips t. 214:34
seas of t. 326:7
Tread: around these silent walks
I t. 164:35
beetle, that we t. upon 462:7
bends not as I t. 341:4
close behind him t. 150:2
endless road you t. 263:23
ever so airy a t. 536:15
face with an undaunted t. 515:26
feet of thine high priests t. 525:13
Freedom hallows with her t. 119:11
now t. we a measure 418:21
on my heart they t. 475:10
that I may t. safely 239:4
thy t. is on an Empire's dust 113:24
t. beneath our feet 316:30
t. on classic ground 2:2
t. softly..t. on my dreams 584:17
t. thee down 288:1
t. the Narrow Way 295:2
t. thou in them boldly 361:23
we live to t. on kings 440:32
where angels fear to t. 383:5
where'er we t...holy ground 113:19
where'er you t. 385:7
with unreluctant t. 84:3
Treadeth: when he t. out the corn 46:26
Treads: dull swain t. on it 340:32
Treason: bloody t. flourish'd 450:31
condoned high t. 180:39
greatest t. 197:25
Gunpowder T. and Plot 9:11, 368:13
if this be t. 242:16
in trust I have found t. 198:10
kings may love t. 170:20
love the t. 168:4
moderation..a sort of t. 103:19
pay..for t. to his country 277:31
such popular humanity is t. 1:20
they cannot commit t. 148:10
t. can but peep 436:27
t. doth never prosper 238:3
t. has done his worst 459:4
t. is but trusted like the fox 440:31
t. is not own'd 193:8
t. love 192:32
t. was no crime 190:25
Treasonous parles 90:16
Treasons: fit for t., stratagems 465:20
Treasure: as our t. 244:23
bringeth forth out of his t. 59:31
buried t. 268:15
earthen vessel, holding t. 90:33
heaps of miser's t. 340:21
he that has stoln the t. 155:14
justice, counsel, and t. 27:8
purest t. mortal times afford 474:10
rich the t. 191:5
she is your t. 479:3
to secure his t. 401:38
t. beyond measure 218:23
t. in earthen vessels 67:23
t. in heaven 60:1
vent the t. of our tongue 168:9
what trusty t. 233:2
where your t. is 58:7
your chiefest t. 40:19
Treasured: embalmed and t. up 352:7
Treasures: better than all t. 498:10
greater..than the t. in Egypt 69:16
new t. still 291:5
t. from an earthen pot 244:7
t. in heaven 58:6
t. up his bright designs 161:18
t. upon earth 58:5
Treasuries: sumless t. 443:9
Treasury: opposite the T. Bench 181:2
T...spring of business 28:22
treble of the T. Bench 180:22
Treat: all eager for the t. 130:13
gives a child a t. 334:1
that you should t. me thus 203:36

Treat (cont.)
t. housemaids to his teas 142:1
t. my friends 327:14
t. unmoneyed men 142:1
you're giving a t. 219:11
Treatise: at a dismal t. rouse 461:3
my T. of Human Nature 265:12
the former t. have I made 64:21
Trebisond: Marocco, or T. 345:4
Treble: hear the shrill sweet t. 77:31
t. of the Treasury Bench 180:22
t. that million 246:28
turning again towards childish t. 427:21
Tree: Adam sat under the T. 295:16
boughs off many a t. 244:14
break the infant t. 93:15
by the Eildon T. 32:6
by the Tumtum t. 129:39(-130)
carve on every t. 427:23
choose our t. 336:43
Clement Shorter, Herbert T. 141:31
dark t., still sad 117:39
do these things in a green t. 62:47
from a t.'s summit 288:10
from field and t. 80:12
from the greengrocer t. 219:13
fruit of that forbidden t. 344:1
garden of Liberty's t. 123:6
God-curst sun, and a t. 236:19
hang there.. till the t. die 430:5
he that means a t. 244:3
highly impossible t. 218:7
I'll smell it on the t. 473:11
in a t. did end their race 332:16
I shall be like that t. 520:51
leaves of the t...healing 72:7
many an incense-bearing t. 151:32
middle t. and highest 347:3
more to my taste than a t. 358:20
never loved a t. or flower 121:8
not growing like a t. 282:1
Old Man in a t. 311:3
on a t. by a river 220:17
only God can make a t. 292:13
on the t. top 73:14
our T. yet crowns the hill 19:1
pledges of a fruitful t. 245:20
poem lovely as a t. 292:12
sat under a t. 262:8
sees not the same t. 77:11
shade of the old apple t. 571:2
she gave me of the t. 44:22
sky-pointing t. 18:31
sleep at the root of my t. 310:21
some single herb or t. 332:13
spare the beechen t. 122:8
sticking in a t. 420:1
still our T. is there 18:31
there's a t., of many, one 576:8
there still is a t. 119:10
this t. continues to be 305:10
thocht it was a trustie t. 32:18
too happy, happy t. 289:7
to the top of every t. 218:27
t. is known by his fruit 59:13
t. is living yet 253:1
t. of diabolical knowledge 500:16
t. of liberty 268:23
t. of life 44:12, 347:3
t. of man was never quiet 263:8
t. of the knowledge of good and
evil 44:13
t. planted by the water-side 391:46
t. will wither 113:38
under the greenwood t. 427:7
was there a t. about 158:10
where the t. falleth 51:28
whittle the Eden T. 295:15
why the t. will continue to be 5:27
wish I were a t. 243:20
woodman, spare that t. 358:21
Treen chalices 269:22
Trees: all flowers and all t. 332:13
among the gusty t. 366:1
as fast as the Arabian t. 474:2
as herbs and t...in May 328:15
beneath the t. 577:5
between the t. in Ivywood 140:12
blossoms in the t. 383:19
blue above the t. 286:23
brotherhood of venerable t. 573:25

Trees (cont.)
climbing t. in the Hesperides 455:12
Dryad of the t. 287:23
filled the t. 249:13
gloomy, friendly T. 549:4
hide in cooling t. 288:22
high in tufted t. 342:11
leafless t. and every icy crag 575:24
look at the t.I 81:16
loveliest of t. 262:10
lover of t. 91:3
men as t., walking 61:2
might damage the t. 312:14
music of its t. at dawn 17:10
of all the t. in England 172:6
of all the t...in the wood 10:14
of all the t...so fair 303:5
Orpheus drew t. 465:20
Orpheus with his lute made t. 446:18
procreate like t. 86:34
promontory with t. upon't 425:19
rocks, and stones, and t. 573:6
shade of the whispering t. 293:21
tall ancestral t. 241:12
this lady by the t. 584:12
tongues in t. 426:30
t. and the houses..wheeling 546:30
t. at spring..yield forth 549:24
t. began to whisper 537:1
t. did grow 35:17
t. in whose dim shadow 324:3
t. of the Lord 398:9
t. they are so high 32:14
t. to speak 459:20
t., where you sit 385:7
under the t. 249:7
upon the t. of Paradise 516:18
when lofty t. I see 486:15
whispers through the t. 382:31
whose rich t. wept 347:5
you can skid up the t. 301:8
Tree toad is a chef-d'oeuvre 567:19
Trelawny: shall T. die? 239:7
Tremble: I t. for my country 268:27
I t., I expire 493:13
keepers of the house shall t. 51:33
let Sporus t. 385:30
make me t. lest a saying 540:22
my firm nerves shall never t. 459:20
poplars stand and t. 263:19
t. for this lovely frame 566:12
t. like a guilty thing 576:18
t., thou wretch 453:9
t. under her feet 530:15
t. with tenderer breath 525:6
Trembled: all who saw them t. 324:13
all you t. at before 161:35
Hell t. 346:8
Tiber t. 448:9
t. kissing 424:13
t. through his..good-night air 235:18
t. with fear at your frown 201:24
Trembler: no t. in the world 83:7
Tremblers: boding t. learn'd 225:1
Trembles: for ever it t. 496:1
Satan t. 161:15
touched needle t. 386:28
t. in the breast 355:11
t. to a lily 183:11
Trembling: fear and t. 68:19
t. at that..I had stood before 494:18
t., hoping 381:28
t. in the blue heavens 586:5
Trembulation: all over t. and fear 518:16
Tremendous: white t. daybreak 84:20
Trenchant: long'd for t. force 15:21
Trencher: dead Caesar's t. 425:3
Trencher-friends 480:26
Trencher-man: valiant t. 467:29
Trenches in thy beauty's field 486:10
Trent: Burton built on T. 263:24
wide vale of T. 322:23
Trépas: attend..le t. de quelqu'un 353:23
Tres: divisa in partes t. 120:10
Trespass against us 388:13
Trespasser: foreign T. 234:4
Trespasses: dead in t. 67:50
forgive us our t. 388:3
Tress: threshed corn..by a t. 586:1
Tresses: bathe thy breathing 153:26
fair t...insnare 385:13

Tresses (cont.)
knees and t. folded 336:7
t. like the morn 340:38
wither'd cheek and t. grey 416:29
Trial: all purity, all t. 428:28
democracy is on t. 184:1
made t. of her strength 579:1
that which purifies us is t., and
t. is by what is contrary 352:9
t. by jury..will be a delusion 172:12
t. of which..no conception 489:35
Triangle: eternal t. 10:11
Triangular person 505:24
Tribal: constructing t. lays 297:9
Tribe: creating a whole t. of fops 452:14
his t...God Almighty's gentle-
men 190:26
Idols of the T. 28:6
may his t. increase 265:16
richer than all his t. 474:2
thy t.'s black tents 543:17
Tribeless: equal, unclassed, t. 497:12
Tribes: our supple t. 279:3
two mighty t. 116:48
Tribuens: voluntas jus suum cuique t. 282:22
Tribulation: came out of great t. 71:6
companion in t. 70:23
danger, necessity, and t. 389:2
'mid toil and t. 517:3
ye shall have t. 63:64
Tribunal: its highest T. will accomplish 101:22
new t. now 96:15
Tribus: Idola T. 28:6
Tributaries: Thames's t. 18:29
Tribute: not a cent for t. 238:4
passing t. of a sigh 230:7
t. to whom t. is due 66:11
vain t. of a smile 417:19
Trice: solve 'em in a t. 110:15
Trick: served such another t. 466:8
t. of our English nation 441:24
t. of singularity 483:19
t. worth two of that 438:40
when in doubt, win the t. 264:24
when the long t.'s over 334:12
wild t. of his ancestors 440:31
yet it is our t. 437:2
Tricked: t. by the British into..war 38:16
t. in antique ruff 276:14
Trickle to his rival's bier 418:5
Trickled: .his answer t. through 131:22
Trickling nonsense 155:5
Tricks: all t...knavish or childish 274:14
frustrate their knavish t. 125:16
I know their t. 178:13
no t. in plain..faith 451:9
plays such fantastic t. 461:31
such t. hath strong imagination 467:24
their t. an' craft 106:23
t. and all 93:30
t. his beams 343:3
t. of that old bald cheater 281:2
t. that are vain 238:32
Trident: flatter Neptune for his t. 429:13
Trieb: immer regen T. nach Wahrheit 313:18
Tried: adherence to the old and t. 314:7
can't drop it if I t. 296:22
fire seven times t. 464:3
she for a little t. 583:12
thou that hast not t. 510:16
too much are t. 17:5
t...once a week 273:6
t. us..as silver is t. 396:1
when he is t...receive the crown 69:28
Trifid: steep and t. God 543:15
Trifle: as 'twere a careless t. 456:27
Trifled: away the rest have t. 90:39
Trifler: busy t. 159:27
Trifles: only t. with them 139:23
t. light as air 471:42
t. with all..t. with one 215:10
unconsidered t. 485:18
win us with honest t. 456:22
write t. with dignity 274:25
Trifling: my mother's deafness is
very t. 22:12
no circumstance, however t. 226:23
pretty, t., childish 165:9
t. foolish banquet 477:10

Trigger: draw the t. after his death 270:22
Triggers: dror resolves an' t. 319:19
Trills her thick-warbled notes 350:11
Trim: bowl goes t. 376:24
doff'd her gaudy t. 343:11
dress'd in all his t. 487:28
gallant t. 229:23
he that shot so t. 477:12
t. little, prim little craft 222:8
t. reckoning 440:30
Trimmer: innocent word 'T.' 234:3
Trimmings: usual t. 179:19
Trinities: tangled T. 300:19
Trinity: Blessed T. 240:19
I the T. illustrate 96:39
old Fellow of T. 10:23
T. had never been unkind 363:22
Trinity Church: at T. I met my
doom 217:21
Trinity College: Harrer an' T. 299:17
Trinket: earth a t. at my wrist 544:23
joy's a t. 512:9
Trinkets: returned to your t. 297:16
Triomphe: on t. sans gloire 157:6
Trip: 566:27, 28
his words..t. about him 352:3
once you t. on it 96:40
tho' he t. and fall 539:8
t. it as ye go 341:29
t. it up and down 5:25
t. no further 482:28
t. we after the night's shade 467:19
Tripe: painch, t., or thairm 106:4
Triple cord 103:9
Triple-arched: high and t. 285:19
Tripled: the Book, the t. Crown 404:20
Trippingly on the tongue 434:15
Trips: trochee t. 152:4
Trisagion: raise the 'T.' 362:16
Trissotin: half T. 324:35
Triste: Caballero de la T. Figura 134:8
Tristement: les anglais s'amusent t. 517:23
Tristes: oderunt hilarem t. 257:9
Tristram: let call him T. 328:7
Tristram Shandy..going back-
wards 558:15
Trite: Lamplough was t. 514:2
Triton: T. blow his wreathed horn 582:18
T. blowing..his wreathed horn 509:8
T. of the minnows 429:12
Triumph: daughters of the uncircumcised 47:29
in ourselves, are t. and defeat 317:4
in their t. die 478:8
in t. advances 416:21
in t. from the north 322:25
I t. still 322:2
let his foes t. 231:32
meet with T. and Disaster 297:10
one more devils'-t. 93:6
pedestalled in t. 96:13
poor is the t. o'er the..hare 546:20
pursue the t. 384:16
ride in t. through Persepolis 330:27
shout of them that t. 362:4
struggle, trust and t. 196:24
t. of hope over experience 272:4
t. over death and sin 509:4
Victor's t. 387:12
we shall not see the t. 179:38
what t.! hark 17:11
wrong would t. 97:4
yelps..even of t. 144:6
Triumphals: joyless t. 350:17
Triumphant: hail, Bard t. 158:6
joyful and t. 369:20
t. sea 474:23
Triumphed: Antony's hath t. on
itself 425:26
Jehovah has t. 357:17
t. over fate 117:24
Triumphing: ride on the pants t. 425:12
Triumphiren: leiden oder t. 223:23
Triumphs: all t. but his own 143:16
glories, t., spoils 450:2
revenge t. over death 26:2
their little t. o'er 231:4
t. of Love 526:22
Triumph-song: distant t. 264:9
Trivial: rise from t. things 385:8
t. and vulgar way of coition 86:34

Trivial (cont.)
t. round 291:7
Trochee trips 152:4
Trod: by man as godlike t. 524:7
sad floor..'twas t. 114:34
t., as on the four winds 333:1
t. my nursery floor 160:30
t. the ways of glory 446:29
Trodden: quickly t. out 446:5
t. down under the hoofs 102:18
t. the winepress alone 55:6
Troes: fuimus T. 554:8
Troia: iam seges est ubi T. fuit 371:25
Troiae: captae post tempora T.
T. qui primus ab oris 553:5
Troilus: in such a night T. 465:17
Trojan: mounted the T. walls 465:17
T. gestes 138:25
Tromper le trompeur 209:12
Troop: farewell the plumed t. 472:3
foreign t...landed in my country 379:8
pressing a t. unable to stoop 90:16
to Oxford sent a t. 548:20
t. cometh..his name Gad 45:7
t. home to churchyards 467:10
Troopers: Noll's damned t. 90:18
wanton t. 332:28
Troops: Æneas shall want t. 425:22
solemn t. 343:4
t. of error 86:4
t. of Midian 361:13
Troop-Sergeant-Major: late T. 301:13
Trope: out there flew a t. 110:7
Tropes: rang'd his t. 402:1
Trophies: all their t. pass away 312:24
among her cloudy t. hung 287:21
her weedy t. 437:1
t. unto the enemies of truth 86:4
Trophy: no t., sword 436:37
Tropic: our t. youth 238:29
under the t. is our language 558:8
Troppo: scherzandol ma non t. 218:11
Trot: does it t.? 312:18
to t. the round 189:16
Troth: I plight thee my t. 391:30
I wonder by my t. 185:6
noblest t. dies here 411:1
Trots: muse on dromedary t. 151:13
who Time t. withal 428:9
Trotting: t. out the Gorgonzola 304:43
t. through the dark 301:18
Troubadour: gaily the T. 37:2
Trouble: all but a t. of ants 541:4
capacity for taking t. 111:40
capacity of taking t. 126:9
cried unto the Lord in their t. 398:15
forge a lifelong t. 530:8
full of t. 49:1
getting its possessors into t. 111:40
hear thee in the day of t. 392:35
in t. to be troubled 170:9
kindness in another's t. 227:34
man is born unto t. 48:50
man w'at kin show you t. 238:9
my little t. is ended 543:16
remember David: and all his t. 400:2
Roman and his t. 263:9
smooth away t. 83:21
tears for all souls in t. 329:5
through any plague, or t. 398:21
toil and t. 459:30
transient, shining t. 228:18
t. and care 318:9
t. brewing 305:3
t. deaf heaven 486:24
t. enough of its own 568:26
t. him much more 159:38
t. out of King Charles's head 174:27
t., sorrow, need 390:29
t. to my dreams 579:12
t. weigh'd upon her 535:7
useful t. of the rain 530:9
very present help in t. 394:27
very present help in..t. 5:6
war..is toil and t. 191:9
where all t. seems 523:17
women and care and t. 560:25
you ain't seen no t. yit 238:9
your fellowship a t. 169:18
Troubled: in trouble to be t. 170:9
let not your heart be t. 63:50

Troubled (cont.)
like a fountain t.   479:12
no more was by it t.   543:12
t. heart   302:1
t. mind   155:1
t. spirit   395:10
t. with religious doubt   141:17
t. with thick-coming fancies   460:37
Troubles: I have had t. enough   93:41
little t. pass   308:30
nothing t. me less   307:10
out of all his t.   393:16
pack up your t.   20:23
sea of t.   434:4
t. of our..dust   263:32
written t. of the brain   460:37
Troublesome: somewhat t. days   210:12
t. *insects* of the hour   102:20
t. to everybody else   155:27
winds and seas are t.   168:13
women..t. cattle   319:12
Troubling: wicked cease from t.   48:46
without t. of a star   545:5
Troublous: not any t. thing   522:15
Trough was full   249:20
Trousers: bottoms of my t. rolled   197:21
hitched his t. up   34:28
put on one's best t.   267:2
steam-engine in t.   504:33
Trout: here and there a lusty t.   528:7
t. in the milk   547:4
t. not stale   119:25
t. that must be caught   483:13
Trouts are tickled best   111:27
Trouve: reprendre mon bien où je le t.   354:9
Trouvé: si tu ne m'avais t   374:7
Trovato: è molto ben t.   13:1
Trowel: laid on with a t.   426:20
lay it on with a t.   181:22
lays it on with a t.   154:33
Trowl: t. the bowl   170:24
t. the brown bowl   420:3
Troy: another T. for her to burn?   584:25
fir'd another T.   191:11
half his T. was burned   441:9
heard T. doubted   116:12
night when T. was sack'd   412:10
O TT. own!   411:35
plains of windy T.   540:32
tale of T. divine   341:18
T. passed away   585:22
where's T.?   79:17
Troynovaunt: lusty T.   195:4
Truant: every t. knew   225:1
t. been to chivalry   440:28
t. disposition   431:2
Truce: by formal t.   375:27
one day's t.   102:5
our new t.   80:22
Trucidet: ne pueros coram populo Medea t.   256:3
Truckle at the eye   254:18
Truckle-bed: in the same t.   100:8
Trudg'd along unknowing   192:5
True: always say what's t.   515:16
always think what is t.   266:21
angry at a slander makes it t.   279:27
books of the t. sort   307:23
both t., both wise   158:13
by the people as equally t.   217:5
called Faithful and T.   71:36
can the devil speak t.?   456:21
dare to be t.   243:27
dark and t. and tender   538:20
doubt him t.   309:3
Douglas, tender and t.   165:22, 250:26
easy to be t.   421:17
England to itself..but t.   448:2
every t. man's apparel   462:19
first t. gentleman   170:18
good men and t.?   468:33
good to be honest and t.   7:22, 106:6
had rather were t.   28:7
had she been t.   473:21
he said t. things   89:40
his heart *was* t. to Poll   103:32
if all be t. that I do think   3:11
if it is not...happy invention   13:1
if t., here only   347:5
I reckon, rather t.   336:5

True (cont.)
is it t. or is it **not**   339:24
it is most t.   469:45
kept him falsely t.   530:37
let God be t.   65:36
lips as soft, but t.   83:18
marriage of t. minds   488:7
no one so t. did share it   483:6
not necessarily t...dies for it   570:21
one religion is as t. as another   109:32
ower t. tale   419:20
people's judgement always t.   190:28
pity 'tis 'tis t.   432:40
Presbyterian t. blue   110:16
prithee, tell me t.   220:29
prov'd t. before..false   111:11
ring in the t.   533:18
some t., some light   530:21
so young, my lord, and t.   452:10
speak the thing that's t.   561:23
strange—but t.   117:1
strictly t.   303:7
sure they are t.   485:30
swore to be t.   6:8
taking t. for false   530:8
tale was undoubtedly t.   309:26
that I shall die, is t.   445:12
that thou wast t.   15:18
these words are t. and faithful   71:45
things more t. and deep   498:9
thing that they know isn't t.   42:18
'tis t., 'tis t.   262:17
to thine own self be t.   431:25
t. Amphitryon   191:27
t. and lively Word   390:28
t...as taxes is   174:31
t. as the needle   78:18
t. as the sky   298:19
t., brave heart!   187:1
t. for you in your private heart   200:36
t. gods sigh   88:12
t. Jack Falstaff   439:37
t. life is only *love*   96:8
t. of heart   392:18
t. of most we leave behind   147:12
t. source of human offspring   347:26
t., the blushful Hippocrene   287:24
t. to his Molly   173:9
t. to his wife   551:11
t. to thee till death   202:27
t. to the kindred points   580:27
t. to thyself   27:37
t. to your animal instincts   310:22
t., when you met her   186:18
trusty, dusky, vivid, t.   516:6
well to be honest and t.   335:4
what I tell you three times is t.   128:4
whatsoever things are t.   68:27
while Britons shall be t.   265:15
wish the Arabian Tales..t.   363:13
woman t. and fair   186:17
your heart be only t.   103:32
True-begotten: my t. father   463:28
True-fix'd and resting quality   449:30
True-love: do as much for my t.   32:16
my t. hath my heart   501:19
t. knots   151:13
t. showers   436:22
True-penny: art thou there, t.?   432:25
Truer: nothing's t. than them   174:31
Truest: one of the t. and the holiest   328:14
t. friend to thy lover   328:24
True Thomas   32:6, 7, 8, 12
Truly: he play'd so t.   280:10
t. and indifferently   390:27
t. keeps his first, last..day   184:6
t. the light is sweet   51:31
Trump: at the last t.   67:16
shrill t.   472:3
sound of the t.   394:31
speaking t. of future fame   117:19
Trumpery: with all their t.   346:24
Trumpet: blow t.   530:3
blow your own t.   222:4
dreads the final T.   236:17
First Blast of the T.   305:6
glorious the t.   503:6
great voice, as of a t.   70:23
heard the sound of the t.   46:40
hear the t. of Germinal   140:10

Trumpet (cont.)
his t. shrill   509:3
moved more than with a t.   502:9
shifted his t.   225:35
shrill t. sounds   144:28
that it is the sound of the t.   49:27
Thing became a t.   580:17
t. give an uncertain sound   67:1
t. of a prophecy   496:11
t. of his own virtues   469:17
t. shall be heard   191:39
t.'s loud clangour   191:37
t. sounds from..battlements   544:26
t.'s silver sound   418:4
t. to t. spake   189:7
Trumpeter: tongue our t.   429:3
Trumpeters shall he rehearse   397:14
Trumpets: all the t. sounded for him   99:41
blowin' er de t.   238:24
blow your t., Angels   185:13
foie gras to the sound of t.   505:10
our t. waken the Wall   301:29
saith among the t., Ha, ha   49:27
silver, snarling t.   285:14
sound the t.   191:3, 358:13
to kettle-drums and t.   154:13
t. bray   219:22
t. of the night   524:24
up-lifted Angel t.   351:10
while the t. blow   538:22
with t. also, and shawms   397:32
Trumpet-tongued: plead like angels t.   457:9
Trumps: ace of t. up his sleeve   305:20
if dirt were t.   308:6
let spades be t.!   385:16
Truncheon: marshal's t.   461:28
Trundle-tail   453:30
Trunk: at his t. spouts out   348:26
so large a t.   40:25
Trunkless: though t., yet   220:10
t. legs of stone   496:13
Trust: all power is a t.   182:43
cruel, not to t.   488:11
dare t. in His providence   559:27
held his pen in t. to Art   183:10
if you can t. yourself   297:10
in the Lord put I my t.   392:17
in t. I have found treason   198:10
little t. that when we die   335:10
not property, but a t.   210:21
on whom I built an absolute t.   456:27(–457)
put not your t. in princes   400:19
puts her t. in reeking tube   301:1
put their t. in chariots   392:37
put their t. in him   391:51
put your t. in God   73:2
slew the t.   375:19
some bird..t. her household   243:20
struggle, t. and triumph   196:24
time, which takes in t.   405:12
to frail mortality shall t.   28:17
t. God: see all   95:13
t. her not   315:26
t. him for his grace   161:18
T. his sworn brother   485:34
t. in all things high   539:8
t. in God   327:3, 504:23
t. me not at all   531:12
t. no Future   317:7
t. not in wrong and robbery   395:24
t. on..tomorrow will repay   191:34
t. themselves with men   480:20
t. thou thy Love   413:31
unfaltering t.   98:3
woman's t.   419:15
yet we t. that somehow good   532:31
Trusted: armour wherein he t.   61:47
he t. in God   393:3
in thee have I t.   388:19
no such man be t.   465:20
t. like the fox   440:31
t. with our selves   154:26
Trustees of Posterity   182:31
Trustest: t. upon the staff   48:33
Trusteth: man that t. in him   393:38
Trustier human ways   402:23
Trusting: chips to the t. native   143:31
no t. appearances   500:45

Trusts: convartin' public t. 319:20
t. them with, serious matters 139:23
Trusty, dusky 516:6
Truth: absolute T. belongs to
Thee alone 313:18
any good..of telling t. 191:26
beauty is t., t. beauty 287:15
Beauty, T., and Love 81:5
because of the word of t. 394:22
between t. and repose 200:22
bread of sincerity and t. 66:28
bright countenance of t. 352:23
brightness, purity, and t. 371:12
bring t. to light 486:7
candidate for t. 200:23
carp of t. 432:33
cause of t., in word mightier 348:20
Christianity better than T. 152:22
closing up t. to t. 352:11
commencing in a t. 456:24
consecrate to t. and liberty 499:9
constantly speak the t. 389:53
dearer still is t. 14:19
derived from t., but t. from rules 110:36
disclose t. 24:34
divine melodious t. 284:17
doubt t. to light 432:42
fiction lags after t. 100:23
find where t. is hid 432:44
for the t. he ought to die 199:27
friend to t. 385:6
full of grace and t. 62:64
full round of t. 528:20
great is t. and it prevails 56:19
great is T., and mighty 56:17
great is t., and shall prevail 84:26
great ocean of t. 364:13
heavenly t. imparts 291:12
his t. is marching on 264:16
how sweet the t. 202:23
image of t. new-born 76:6
in as just possession of t. 86:5
in possession of t. 315:8
inquiry of t. 27:32
in spirit and in t. 63:13
in the light of t. 574:1
it is the light of T. 173:36
keep abreast of T. 320:13
kept thy t. so pure of old 351:20
knowledge of t. 27:32
known for t. by..reasoning 289:18
lamp of t. 81:4
laws of poetic t. 19:22
let t. be told 82:2
lie which is part a t. 529:32
links a t. divine 532:24
look'd on t. askance 488:5
lost to love and t. 105:1
loved chivalrye, t. and honour 136:23
love of t. predominates 200:23
love Scotland better than t. 277:37
mainly he told the t. 550:8
mercy and t. are met 397:9
never..certain of any t. 290:13
never sold the t. 537:23
no mask like open t. 154:36
no other t. 182:35
not t. in him 63:30
not t., but things like t. 135:24
object of oratory..not t. 326:6
on a huge hill..T. stands 186:10
ornament which t. doth give 487:5
pain of t. 286:16
parsons do not care for t. 517:8
rejoiceth in the t. 66:45
relationship with beauty and t. 289:20
ridicule..best test of t. 139:29
ring in the love of t. 533:20
rose upon T.'s lips 561:11
seeming t...times put on 464:15
see skulking T. 381:27
seizes as beauty must be t. 289:17
send forth his mercy and t. 395:18
shall it declare thy t.? 393:26
sole judge of t. 383:22
Song is not t. 561:11
so T. be in the field 352:17
speaketh the t. from his heart 392:24
Spirit that strove for t. 498:20
spoke this mighty t. 40:4
spread the t. 2:27

Truth (cont.)
steadfastness and careful t. 295:6
stooped to t. 386:1
Strict Regard for T. 41:9
strife of T. with Falsehood 320:9
such a t. as I have meant 583:19
suffer for the t.'s sake 389:53
swears that she is made of t. 488:16
swear to t. of a song 401:20
teach..love of t. 530:14
tell how the t. may be 417:15
tell t., and shame the devil 281:21, 439:43
that stupendous t. believ'd 503:6
they worship T. 84:14
this t.—to prove 16:15
this t. within thy mind rehearse 540:25
though I perish, T. is so 147:14
thy God's, and t.'s 446:31
tongues can poison t. 150:25
to ride, and speak the t. 117:3
to side with T. 320:12
to T. aspire 81:24
to T. its state is dedicate 496:23
trophies unto the enemies of t. 86:4
trusted to speak the t. 29:20
T. beareth away the victory 56:16
t. be veiled..it burneth 493:23
t. breathed by cheerfulness 581:16
t. calls spade a spade 89:23
t. can never be told 77:20
t. discourtesy 244:1
t., ever lovely 122:38
T. forever on the scaffold 320:10
t., for its own sake 204:4
t. from his lips prevail'd 224:22
t. has such a face 192:22
t. his utmost skill 583:9
t. in action 180:21
t. in every shepherd's tongue 405:8
t. in masquerade 116:32
t. in the inward parts 395:8
t. is always strange 117:1
t. is great, and shall prevail 375:14
t. is not in us 70:10
t. is rarely pure 569:20
t. is the cry of all 43:15
t. is the golden girdle 159:4
t. is the hyeste thing 137:26
t. is well paid 157:5
t. is within ourselves 94:14
t. lies somewhere 160:18
t. lies within a little..compass 78:11
t., like a torch 235:3
t. miscall'd simplicity 487:14
t. never hurts the teller 91:24
t. of imagination 289:17
t. of the description 420:28
t. or joke? 97:20
T. put to the worse 352:17
t. serve as a stalking-horse 78:12
T. severe, by..Fiction drest 229:26
t. shall be thy warrant 405:7
t. shal delivere 136:20
t. shall flourish 397:9
t. shall make you free 63:28
t., Sir, is a cow 271:11
t. sits upon the lips 17:27
T. sometimes will lend 117:26
T.'s sacred Fort 85:4
t. that peeps 89:28
t. the..Frenchman never knew 164:16
T. the masculine of Honour 237:23
t. the poet sings 534:21
t...told with bad intent 73:24
t. to o'erpeer 429:9
t., unity, and concord 390:25
t. universally acknowledged 22:28
t., when witty 237:20
t. whereby the nations live 295:6
t. will come to light 463:32
t. with gold she weighs 381:11
turn upon the poles of t. 27:33
two to speak the t. 547:3
unclouded face of t. suffer
wrong 416:4
Valiant-for-T. 99:34
way, the t., and the life 63:53
whatever remains..must be the
t. 188:20

Truth (cont.)
what is it? 27:29, 63:68
where deviation from t. will end 273:27
whom the t. makes free 163:46
whose speech T. knows not 411:26
why..ask if t. be there 15:18
with t. it quite agrees 220:9
words of t. and soberness 65:24
wrapt T. in tales 125:2
Truthful: too t. or too wise 561:11
T. James 239:1
Truths: defends her sacred t. 164:31
fate of new t. 266:24
flat and flexible t. 85:17
for half the t. they hold 196:36
in heav'nly t. attir'd 159:30
instruments of darkness tell us t. 456:22
irrationally held t. 266:23
mighty paramount of t. 574:22
one way possible of speaking t. 96:18
some random t. 578:34
tell him disagreeable t. 322:14
these t. to be self-evident 11:11
these t. to be..undeniable 268:19
to bear all naked t. 286:19
t. as refin'd..Athens heard 14:26
t. begin as blasphemies 489:2
t. that wake 576:19
t., which transcend 308:4
t. would you teach 384:11
two t. are told 456:23
Truth-teller..Alfred 537:24
Try: ah! let us t. 15:4
end t. the man 441:34
guiltier than him they t. 461:23
I'll t. the whole cause 128:25
little Soul, let us t., t., t. 357:18
make me t., by sleeping 87:1
my wit to t. 172:1
then worms shall t. 333:9
t. again; draw a long breath 131:2
t. him afterward 550:19
t. him afterwards 354:4
t. men's souls 372:22
t. not the Pass 316:19
t. out my reins 393:17
t., t. again 248:8
t.—t.—t.—t.—to think 295:1
t. with all my might 527:6
Trying: she's t. all she can 250:7
Trysting: named a t. day 323:10
upon the t. day 323:13
Tu: et t., Brute 120:12, 449:51
t. quoque 372:4
Tub: tale of a t. 358:11, 563:26
Tubal Cain: old T. 326:24
Tube: reeking t. 301:1
Tuberose: sweet t. 497:27
Tubes are twisted 303:19
Tubes: butter from alternate t. 408:4
Tucker: little Tommy T. 367:18
Tucks: till he t. in his shirt 304:28
Tuer de temps en temps un amiral 557:1
Tuesday: christened on T. 368:21
T.'s child 368:1
Tufted crow-toe 342:31(–343)
Tufts: betwixt the t. of snow 151:25
like t. of primroses 181:35
Tugela: on T. side 42:10
Tugg'd with fortune 458:36(–459)
Tug of war: then was the t. 313:1
Tugs: each t. it a different way 117:31
Tulgey: through the t. wood 129:39(–130)
Tulip: number the streaks of the t. 278:15
Tulips: here t. bloom 84:9
Tullochgorum: reel o' T. 502:22(–503)
Tullus: quo T. dives et Ancus 260:26
Tully: no T., said I 90:1
Tumble: must t. down 501:5
they turn and t. 358:10
Tumbled off a bus 228:8
Tumble-down: only a t. nest 571:7
Tumbler: clean t., and a corkscrew 177:23
Tumbling: boys and girls t. in the
street 548:15
Jill came t. after 367:9
t. in the hay 485:16
t. into some men's laps 24:30
Tumbrils toiling up 140:10
Tumtum: by the T. tree 129:39(–130)
Tumult: depth, and not the t. 577:12

INDEX

Tumult (cont.)
into the t...alien sound 575:24
'mid this t. Kubla heard 151:33(-152)
o'er the t. 3:19
sank in t. 151:33
t. and the shouting dies 300:24
t. in the clouds 584:21
t. of her war 517:3
t. of thy mighty harmonies 496:11
when the t. dwindled 119:26
Tumultuous: t. body 84:6
t. joy 508:3
Tun of man 439:34
Tune: all the t. that he could play 369:10
good t...on an old fiddle 112:15
his t. by heart 162:28
incapable of a t. 306:4
I t. the instrument here 185:25
murder's out of t. 473:17
out of t. and harsh 434:14
singeth a quiet t. 149:35
singing out of t. 119:15
sweetly play'd in t. 107:14
tries earth if it be in t. 320:17
t. is something hard 298:14
t. that they play 304:1
we are out of t. 582:18
Tuneable: more t. than lark 466:21
Tuned like fifty stomach-aches 174:9
Tuneful: his t. brethren 416:29
soon mute, however t. 309:13
Tunes: as well as all the good t. 490:16
devil..all the good t. 248:11
found out musical t. 57:16
little list of t. 175:7
slow old t. of Spain 333:18
snatches of old t. 437:1
Tunic: all-concealing t. 496:17
Tunnel of green gloom 84:8
Tunnies steep'd in brine 18:16
Tunning of Elynour Rumming 502:21
Tupping your white ewe 469:29
Turbaned: malignant and a t. Turk 474:2
Turbans: white silken t. 350:9
Turbid look the most profound 309:21
Turbot: (by way of t.) an arch-deacon 505:36
price of a large t. 413:6
t., sir..two eyeballs 563:37
Turbulent: free me from this t. priest 242:20
t. of wit 190:13
t. surge 480:32
Turf: at his head a grass-green t. 436:20
blue ribbon of the t. 182:11
every t. beneath their feet 122:20
green be the t. 234:15
green t. beneath my feet 240:9
green t. lie lightly 381:35
lends the light t. 165:17
on the dappled t. at ease 573:23
on the green t. suck 342:31
on thy t...roses rear 118:23
shelving bank of t. 497:20
silent as the t. they trod 579:6
t. that wraps their clay 153:30
wise t. cloaks 302:8
Turgenieff: from the lips of Ivan T. 268:8
Turk: bear, like the T., no brother 385:29
comes like any T. 125:18
French, or T., or Proosian 221:25
Man is the T. 140:28
take the T. by the beard 445:14
turban'd T. 474:2
unspeakable T. 126:42
Turkey: it was a t.! 174:11
wrong side of a T. tapestry 264:19
Turkey-cock: makes a rare t. of him 483:14
Turks: Jews, T., Infidels 389:33
sleep with T. and infidels 475:17
Turmoil: ceaseless t. seething 151:32
Turmoiled in the court 445:42
Turn: alter the t. of a single phrase 236:42
as he passes t. 342:11
each gay t. 382:33
I do not hope to t. again 197:2
I t. to thee 525:1

Turn (cont.)
made him t. and stop 189:16
my t. now 362:15
nor t. my face 97:27
one t. of pitch-and-toss 297:11
pass, and t. again 199:3
says he will t. it over in.. 43:21
serve my t. upon him 469:25
they t. and tumble 358:10
to t. you out 295:19
t. again to cover the earth 398:8
t. again to his earth 400:19
t. and live with animals 567:20
t. and wind a fiery Pegasus 440:18
t. away mine eyes 399:15
t. but a stone 545:1
t. down an empty Glass 207:30
t. from us all those evils 389:11
t., gentle Hermit 225:11
t. his merry note 427:7
t. of eye 96:24
t. our captivity, O Lord 399:34
t. over a new life 208:24
t. over half a library 272:28
t. thee behind me 48:26
t. the hour 296:16
t. thou ghost that way 184:28
t. thy back on heaven 199:6
t. thy complexion there 472:34
t. to God to praise 92:18
t. to him the other 57:50
t. to nod good-bye 197:3
t. up the lights 242:15
t. us out to play 293:13
t. wheresoe'er I may 576:1
t. with all the tides 212:18
t. you to the strong hold 56:12
will often t. aside 296:13
Turned: cried, and t. away 84:4
having once t. round 150:2
he t. him right and round 106:18
his anger is not t. away 53:7
how all t. to him 97:20
in case anything t. up 174:22
I t. me to them 544:20
nor t...Adam from..Eve 347:25
round she t. 92:44
round t. he 323:26
she t. herself 64:7
thrice t. back in dread 323:23
t. aside and wept 24:1
t. away the captivity of Jacob 397:8
t. every one to his own way 54:26
t. it in his glowing hands 534:16
t. out of the Realm in my petti-coat 198:3
t. themselves back in the day of battle 396:34
t. to a Sonnet 183:16
when they t. their faces 323:25
Turneth: t. away from his wicked-ness 55:30
t. away wrath 50:10
Turning: neither shadow of t. 69:29
never t. back 409:17
no t. back 409:18
t. an immense..Mangle 179:35
t. o' the tide 443:19
wears the t. globe 263:36
Turnip: blood out of a t. 331:14
rather have a t. 276:16
Turnips cries 276:16
Turnpike: consider supper as a t. 196:5
Turns: never t. him to the bride 262:14
thy poor head almost t. 17:22
t. again home 528:22
t. in her sleep 404:23
t. into Miss T. 171:17
t. my face 411:12
t. no more his head 150:2
various t. of chance 191:8
whoso t. as I 92:18
Turpe: quid sit pulchrum, quid t. siquid t. paras 256:21 284:3
Turpissimus: nemo repente fuit t. 283:2
Turpitude of incontinence 419:26
Turret: Sultan's T. 205:4, 5
t. to foundation-stone 418:26
Turrets: half-glimpsèd t. 544:26
Turris: pauperum tabernas regum-que t. 258:8

Turtle: love of the t. 113:1
plate of t. 94:34
Snapping T. 24:9
voice of the t. 52:1
Turtle-dove: bay horse, and a t. 546:35
soul of thy t. 396:28
t. is heard 334:16
Tuscany: even the ranks of T. 323:28
Tusculan Mamilius 323:14
Tusculum: beautiful T. 175:8
lay on for T. 324:8
Tush, say they 396:26
Tutius: multo t. est stare in sub-iectione 291:23
Tutor: irreverent to my t. 270:2
Tutus: res age, t. eris 372:3
Tuum: meum and t. 306:20
Tu-who: t.; tu-whit, t. 456:1
Twain: go with him t. 57:51
metals t. 342:26
one grief brings forth t. 189:9
such a t. can do't. 423:14
t. were casting dice 149:13
with t. he covered his face 53:8
Tweed: at York, 'tis on the T. 383:27
Tweedledum and Tweedledee agreed 130:6
'twixt T. 112:12
Twelve: clock struck t. 334:6
in the sworn t...a thief 461:23
short hour ayont the t. 105:8
t. good men into a box 85:1
t. honest men 403:2
t. months in all the year 31:21
t. of the clock 236:12
'twixt eleven and t. 431:17
Twelvemonth and a day 32:12
Twelvepenny: plaguy t. weather 519:21
Twelve-Pound Look 36:13
Twenty: annual income t. pounds 174:24
at t. years of age, the will reigns 211:14
but t. miles a day 331:7
first t. years..longest half 508:10
let t. pass 90:14
long as t. days are now 573:11
marry t. husbands 463:11
on Dutch bottoms..t. per cent. 124:6
payment of half t. shillings 100:5
Sheridan t. miles away 406:3
sweet and t. 482:22
teach t...be one of the t. 463:8
to that t. add a hundred 246:18
t. love-sick maidens 220:22
t. times was Peter feared 578:21
t. will not come again 262:10
Twenty-eight: February..has t. February hath t. 369:5 228:4
Twenty-first: stone the t. 90:14
Twenty-four: then we shall be t. 263:30
Twenty-nine distinct damnations 96:14
Twenty-seven millions mostly fools 126:39
Twenty-six: towards the age of t. 41:7
Twenty thousand: chariots of God are t. 396:8
king's name t. names 475:3
t. Cornish men 239:7
Twenty-three: chaste, and t. 115:17
Twenty-two men 79:10
Twice: dipping into the water t. as often 148:1
each song t. over 92:15
nayed him t. 232:4
no man..lives t. 525:7
run at least t. as fast 130:4
t. as natural 131:18
t. five miles 151:32
t. I have also heard the same 395:24
t. or thrice had I loved 184:4
Twice-told tale 117:42, 447:35
Twickenham: a penny to T. Town 333:16
Twig: on the topmost t. 410:6
Twilight: again in the grey t. 584:19
as the t. fails 298:20
disastrous t. 345:6
dreaming through the t. 410:1
fly by t. 27:22
in me thou see'st the t. 487:16
less kind than the grey t. 584:20
like Italian t. 119:26
like t.'s, too, her..hair 580:19

Twilight (*cont.*)
'midst the't. path 153:24
over Fiesole by t. 94:8
stars of t. fair 580:19
'twas t…day went down 115:29
t. and evening bell 528:22
t. gray 347:19
t. saints 285:19
when t. was falling 536:2
Twilights: gracious t. 96:31
whose t. were more clear 186:14
Twin: don't tell my t. 242:26
great T. Brethren 324:16
one of us was born a t. 313:8
stiff t. compasses 186:25
t. halves of one..event 235:16
Twine: another o' the t. 31:25(–32)
twist ye, t. ye 419:28
Twined my love and me 31:11
Twinkle: lights begin to t. 541:3
t. on the milky way 577:6
t., t., little bat 129:8
t., t., little star 527:10
Twinkled: benefices t. from afar 192:28
Twinkles: livelier emerald t. 536:8
Twinkling: t. of a bed-staff 422:33
t. of an eye 67:16, 393:25
t. cue 220:6
Twins: Clara threw the t. 228:7
every one bear t. 52:5
good and evil as two t. 352:8
t. of learning 447:10
Twirl down the middle 183:7
Twirled: stately ships are t. 249:15
Twirling in thy hand 18:10
Twist: blossomy t. 544:23
neither t. wolf's-bane 287:19
Oliver T. has asked for more! 177:36
t. the sinews 75:24(–76)
t., ye, twine ye 419:28
Twisted: t. and dried 303:19
Twitch'd his mantle blue 343:7
Twitcher: Jemmy T…peach me 215:7
Twitter: gathering swallows t. 284:15
Twittering: swallow t. 229:31
Twitters: late lark t. 241:21
Two: at the expense of t. 146:34
bicycle made for t. 168:2
but t. days old 76:12
but t. months dead 430:33(–431)
can t. walk together 55:54
children walking t. and t. 76:15
conflux of t. eternities 126:14
dash between the t. 336:5
deemed it t. 121:10
die t. months ago 435:5
do by t. and t. 302:28
false..to t., or three 186:18
fault..grows t. thereby 243:27
for t. days' labour, you ask 566:8
game at which t. can play 39:31
I don't want t. 335:22
if they be t…t. so as..com-
passes are t. 186:25
if t. of them are dead 211:13
I must have t. you know 131:15
in favour of t. 177:1
in the right with t. or three 320:15
in t. words: im-possible 227:33
join'd the former t. 193:9
love betwixt us t. 158:10
lovers lying t. and t. 262:14
never by t. and t. 302:23
no man can serve t. masters 58:9
no t. men..half an hour together 277:19
one that hath t. gowns 469:11
one; t.: why then, 'tis time 460:24
put him outside at t. 269:2
still t. fools 154:32
that we t. were Maying 293:21
think for t. minutes together 505:25
thinks t. notes a song 169:22
this party of t. 82:21
trick worth t. of that 438:40
t. and t. only..beings 363:14
t. are walking apart 267:10
t. at a time 215:5
t. bright birds 309:26
t. ears of corn..one grew before 519:17
t. feet wide 581:20

Two (*cont.*)
t. hit it off 572:23
t. hours since hath died 540:26
t. little girls in blue 228:5
t. lovely black eyes 147:22
t. may keep counsel 478:7
t. men I honour 127:23
t. men look out 310:1
t. most sacred names 158:3
t. must discept 93:18
t. o'clock in the morning courage 360:25
t. of a frosty night 301:14
t. of far nobler shape 347:10
t. only..necessary to salvation 391:12
t. paces of the vilest earth 440:38
t. painters in the world 566:6
t. people..same thought 500:2
t. red roses 359:17
t. separate sides 303:10
t. stars keep not their motion 440:36
t. strong men 294:27
t. things stand like stone 227:34
t. to speak the truth 547:3
t. went to pray? 166:13
t. words to that bargain 520:32
we t. hae run about 104:13
we t. may meet 530:10
we t. stood there 90:8
when t. are stripped 330:13
when t. or three are gathered 388:33
when we t. parted 119:29
where t. or three are gathered 59:52
yet t. Romans living 452:2
you have but t. topics 273:16
Two-and-forty sixpences 276:22
Two and seventy: T. jarring sects 206:25
t. stenches 150:28
Two-and-thirty: t. palaces 289:26
t. Sergeants 301:16
Two-and-twenty: I am t. 262:17
sweet t. 118:32
Two-edged: out of his mouth..t.
sword 70:27
sharp as a t. sword 49:44
sharper than any t. sword 69:8
t. sword in their hands 400:26
Two-handed: that t. engine 342:29
Two hundred: t. more 111:11
t. pounds a year 111:11
you ask. t. guineas? 566:8
Two-legged: t. animals 127:5
unfeather'd t. thing 190:15
Two millions: govern t. of men 101:4
Twopence: I care not t. 37:19
t. a week 130:26
t. coloured 514:15
t…gave them to the host 61:41
without the oil and t. 504:30
Tyburn-face 155:10
Tyger! T.! burning bright 75:24
Tyne: cargo of T. coal 333:21
Severn to the T. 294:22
Type: blunt t. [ing 96:41
highest t…t. nowhere..exist- 508:24
noble t…heroic womanhood 317:14
so careful of the t. 532:35
that funny t…at Leipsic 89:30
t. as long as yourself 515:10
t. of all her race 188:30
t. of the normal 268:4
t. of the wise who soar 580:27
t. of true love 219:8
Types: loose t. of things 573:23
Movable T. 127:6
t. and symbols of Eternity 580:25
Typewriter: spirituality..t. does
not generate 188:9
Tyranni: non vultus instantis t. 259:21
Tyrannical duncery 352:22
Tyrannies: age, agues, t. 185:14
Tyrannous to use it 461:30
Tyranny: bad laws are the worst
..t. 100:16
ecclesiastic t. 170:16
from t. to God 114:34
remedy..against t. 272:10
serving either calamity or t. 56:28
snuff the approach of t. 100:30
until this t. be over-past 395:17
Tyrant: little t. of his fields 230:5

Tyrant (*cont.*)
necessity the t.'s plea 347:16
past the t.'s stroke 430:1
planet's t. 38:29
t. duke unto a t. brothe. 426:26
t. kings, or t. laws restrain 226:17
t. of the mind 192:46
t. rhyme 281:27
t., t. Jealousy 192:46
Tyrants: all men would be t. 170:4
argument of t. 379:14
barbarity of t. 505:20
bid the t. defiance 123:6
blood of patriots and t. 268:23
foe of t. 122:38
intercourse between t. and
slaves 226:34
kings..t. from policy 102:17
rebellion to t. 79:14
'twixt kings and t. 246:9
t. of thy sex 155:27
t. seldom want pretexts 103:5
t. their own 246:9
when t.' crests..are spent 488:3
Tyrawley and I have been dead 139:35
Tyre: daughter of T. 394:24
one with Nineveh and T. 300:25
Tyrian: budded T. 288:3
grave T. trader 18:16

U

Über: Deutschland ü. alles 203:3
*Übermenschen: ich lehre euch den
Ü.* 364:22
Überwunden: der Mensch..ü 364:22
Ubique: quod semper, quod u. 553:4
Ubiquities: blazing u. 201:21
Ucelagon: iam proximus ardet U. 554:7
Uffish thought 129:39(–130)
Uglier yet is the Hump 297:26
Uglification, and Derision 129:20
Ugliness: who can have made its
u.? 266:14
Ugly: as u., ay, as sin 315:10
better to be good than..u. 570:9
born old and u. 173:21
come hup, you u. beast! 518:10
elderly u. daughter 222:19
makes me u. 473:9
one's old and u. 156:4
toad, u. and venomous 426:30
you are an u. beast 40:28
Ulciscitur: victumque u. orbem 283:10
Ulixen: proposuit nobis exemplar U. 256:23
Ullin: Lord U.'s daughter 122:24
Ulpian at the best 90:1
Ulster: U. will fight; U. will be
right 143:29
Ultima Thule 556:10
Ultimate: u. conclusion in..act 296:14
u. decency of things 515:13
Ultimum: Romanorum u. 526:12
Ultio: animi exiguique voluptas u. 284:2
Ultor: ex ossibus u. 554:21
Ultra: nil u. to my proudest hopes 334:24
Ululatus: long u. of No Bastille! 119:32
Ulva: chief of U.'s isle 122:24
Ulysse: heureux qui comme U. 40:17
Ulysses: new U. 493:25
U. come 168:13
Umbered: other's u. face 444:6
Umbra: magni nominis u. 320:23
pulvis et u. sumus 260:26
Umbrae: dum montibus u. 553:21
Umbrage: Americans have taken
u. 403:19
Umbrella: just's u. 79:7
*Umbris: ex u. and imaginibus
qua veris facilis datur exitus u.* 364:2
555:2
Umbro: young boys in U. 323:12
Umpire: chaos u. sits 346:11
u., the pavilion cat 309:27
'**Umps**', said Mr. Grewgious 175:20
Un: tous pour u. 194:33
Una: heavenly U. 578:21
Unaccommodated man 453:21
Unaccountable: for some u. pur-
pose 176:2

Unaccustom'd to the yoke 161:6
Unacknowledged legislators 499:10
Unacquainted with the A.B.C. 512:7
Unadorned: beauty u. 40:12
  when u. adorned the most 546:19
Unadvised: too rash, too u. 477:24
Unaffected: affecting to seem u. 154:27
  meek and u. grace 224:22
  rational and u. 22:10
Unafraid: gentlemen u. 294:33
Unalienable: certain u. rights 11:11
  rights inherent and [u.] 268:19
Unalterable mien 114:10
Unamiable: make virtue u. 512:3
Unaneled: disappointed, u. 432:17
Unanimity: their u. is wonderful 499:30
Unannounced: they enter u. 149:24
Unapparent: far in the U. 492:11
Unapproached: in u. light dwelt 346:18
Unarm, Eros 425:21
Unarmed amongst a thousand 38:24
Unashamed: brawling judgments, u. 531:16
Unassailable holds on 449:30
Unattempted yet in prose or
  rhyme 344:3
Unattractive: most u. old thing 220:16
Unaware: he knew and I was u. 235:18
  some morning, u. 92:14
Unawares: entertained angels u. 69:22
  on some virtue u. 143:17
Unbecoming: more u. a man of
  quality 154:31
  not u. men that strove 541:3
  so u. to a woman 569:38
Unbelief: gained..by our u. 89:32
  help thou mine u. 61:4
  I did it ignorantly in u. 68:42
  land of u. and fear 75:14
  one is u. 27:20
  U., in denying them 201:12
  u. is blind 340:25
  u. is sure to err 161:20
Unbelieving husband 66:31
Unbend your noble strength 458:13
Unbends: nothing u. the mind like
  them 214:31
Unbent her mind afterwards 306:14
Unbewailed: hold u. their way 424:23
Un-birthday present 131:5
Unblamed: express thee u.? 346:18
Unblessed: every inordinate cup
  is u. 471:23
Unblest: to me u. 162:14
Unbodied joy 498:3
Unborn: child may rue that is u. 30:12
  every u. age 231:3
  states u. 450:1
  u. TOMORROW 206:19
  what men u. shall read 309:6
  ye u. ages 229:25
Unborrowed from the eye 581:26
Unbottomed infinite abyss 345:26
Unbought: health u. 192:15
  u. grace of life 102:12
Unbound: constrain thy u. spirit 160:34
  her tongue u. 155:5
Unbounded: salt water u. 301:9
  u. stomach 447:6
Unbowed: bloody, but u. 241:18
Unbraced: his doublet all u. 432:35
  melancholy as an u. drum 134:7
Unbreathed: unexercised and u. 352:9
Unbroken: old u. Pickwick 142:10
Unbuild: arise and u. it again 493:1
  build, u., contrive 348:30
Unburied: bodies of u. men 563:30
  carcases of u. men 429:14
Unbusy: sole u. thing 152:17
Unbutton'd, glowing hot 164:8
Uncanopied sleep 80:12
Unceremoniously the rose 561:9
Uncertain: climate more u. 154:26
  life's u. voyage 480:31
  time which to us is u. 38:31
  trumpet give an u. sound 67:1
  u. balance of proud time 231:35
  u., coy 418:31
  u. glory of an April day 484:33
Uncertainly: run, not as u. 66:37
Uncertainties: capable of being in
  u. 289:21

Uncertainty: quit a certainty for
  an u. 277:36
Unchanged: still remain u. 579:38
Unchanging love 161:12
Uncharitableness: all u. 388:46
Unchipt, unflead 247:17
Uncircumcised: daughters of the
  u. 47:29
Uncircumcision: circumcision nor
  u. 68:31
Uncircumscribed: sceptreless, free,
  u. 497:12
Unclassed: equal, u., tribeless 497:12
Uncle: married with mine u.
      430:33(-431)
  my prophetic soul! my u.! 432:13
  u. me no u. 474:30
Unclean: man of u. lips 53:8
Uncle Arly: my agèd U. 311:19
Uncle George: when your U. was
  living 175:36
  your U.'s workshops 175:32
Uncle Stalky: your U. 304:46
Uncle Tom Cobbleigh 33:1
Unclothe: I u. and clear 166:21
Unclouded: blue u. weather 534:5
  one u. blaze 115:8
Unclubable man 271:22
Uncoffined: unknell'd, u., and un-
  known 114:28
Uncomely: all things u. 585:17
Uncomfortable: moral when he is
  only u. 490:21
  u. sensation 173:25
  we u. feel 221:33
Uncomfortableness of it all 96:7
Uncommon: u. pretty young
  woman 196:6
  very u. cook 414:8
Uncompounded: so soft and u. 344:29
Unconcerned: sit as u. 421:11
  u...hear the mighty crack 3:2, 385:23
Unconditional: surrender 229:4
Unconfined: all her ways be u. 401:26
  let joy be u. 113:26
  Love with u. wings 319:4
  u. obey'd the dictates 371:8
Unconning: litel book..so u. 138:14
Unconquerable: man's u. mind 582:4
  my u. soul 241:18
  nursing the u. hope 18:15
  u. purpose 307:12
  u. will 344:14
Unconquered in a ring 141:30
Unconscionable time dying 136:11
Unconscious: most perfect
  humour..u. 111:31
  u. humour 112:1
  well of u. cerebration 268:6
Unconsciously: it works u. 235:20
Unconsidered trifles 485:18
Unconsoled: perish u. 309:27
Uncontrollable: O u.! 496:10
Unconvincing: bald and u. narra-
  tive 220:13
  u. possibility 14:18
Uncorrupt: leadeth an u. life 392:24
Uncorrupted with literary pre-
  judices 278:10
Uncouth: find out his u. way 345:26
  makes ancient good u. 320:13
  not unkind because u. 80:27
  sang the u. swain 343:5
  savage men, and u. manners 100:22
  u. unkist 510:26
Uncouther: the better the u. 97:11
Uncover, dogs, and lap 480:25
Uncowed: walk u. by fear 295:7
Uncreated: nor three u.: but one
  u. 388:39
  womb of u. night 345:19
Uncreating: thy u. word 381:27
Unction: not that flattering u. 436:1
Uncumber'd with a wife 192:14
Uncursed by doubt 250:30
Undaunted daughter of desires 165:28
Undecided: the character u. 284:18
Undecimo: alter ab u...annus 556:4
Undefiled: keep whole and u. 388:37
  my dove, my u. 52:9
  so shall I be u. 392:34

Undefiled (cont.)
  tempted, and yet u. 506:7
  u. heritage 295:6
  well of English u. 510:5
Under: true love kept u. 219:8
  u. the blossom 480:14
Under-belly of the Axis 144:12
Undercliff: violets of the U. 296:15
Undercurrent of...murmur about
  his name 413:18
Underfoot: brilliant u. 82:9
Undergirding the ship 65:28
Undergraduates: a twelvemonth
  with the u. 239:19
Underground: Johnny u. 402:24
  lays lads u. 263:18
  nations u. 545:4
  till she sunk u. 311:6
Underlings: that we are u. 448:22
Underneath: u. are the everlasting
  arms 46:34
  u. this sable hearse 87:24
Underrated: cultivated, u. nobleman 218:17
Undersized: he's a bit u. 219:11
Understand: cannot u. what is
  happening 135:7
  do our duty as we u. it 314:8
  few u. 384:11
  fool doth not u. it 397:20
  honour which they do not u. 578:5
  if I could u. 529:24
  I may not u. 254:11
  I u. thy kisses 440:3
  less they u. 111:3
  make him u. 407:22
  mass..u. it 28:26
  men who u. 84:12
  more things..than men u. 56:32
  not be learned nor u. 397:4
  pretend to u. the Universe 127:24
  read and perhaps u. Shakespeare 289:29
  remember, and u. 91:22
  some who did not u. them 388:1
  things which others u. 578:34
  thirst to know and u. 561:14
  thought I to u. this 396:27
  to admire, we should not u. 155:15
  u. a writer's ignorance 152:25
  u. wisdom secretly 395:8
  u. with their heart 53:10
  women don't u. 299:20
  wot do they u.? 299:14
Understanded of the people 401:8
Understandest thou what thou
  readest? 64:39
Understandeth: who u. thee not 455:13
Understanding: beasts that have
  no u. 391:23
  candle of u. 56:18
  declare, if thou hast u. 49:19
  find you an u. 275:24
  for thy more sweet u. 454:36
  get u. 49:42
  give it an u., but no tongue 431:16
  good u. have all they 398:25
  horse and mule..no u. 393:34
  ignorant of his u. 152:25
  in length of days u. 48:58
  in my u. 6:10
  in the sixth place..u. 56:45
  likely to propagate u. 276:20
  man..hath no u. 395:2
  more u. than my teachers 399:20
  pass all u. 267:32
  passeth all u. 68:26, 390:48
  pass man's u. 389:42
  praises with u. 394:32
  Republics..appeal to the u. 28:29
  spirit of wisdom and u. 53:17
  subverts all the principles of his
  u. 265:10
  to the u...strike a note 86:32
  u. to direct 282:20
  u. what metre is 153:11
Understandings: cold hearts and
  muddy u. 102:15
Understands: always u. what you
  say 274:14
  reads verse and thinks she u. 91:7

INDEX

Understood: all who u. admired 388:1
before I u. this place 552:3
by her that bore her u. 531:7
interpreter..hardest to be u. 499:26
least u. 386:29
u., and not be believ'd 77:20
u. as a child 66:46
u. I the end of these men 396:27
Undertakers: become of the u. 179:33
prologues..as u. 213:8
Underwood: in green u. 521:30(-522)
Undescribable: describe the u. 114:9
Undid: what they u. did 424:6
Undiscovered: u. clime 231:3
u. country [cies 434:4
Undisgraced by those extravagan- 139:21
Undisturbed their ancient reign` 184:2
Undo: how I will u. myself 475:21
parchment..u. a man 445:38
some to u. 172:9, 194:24
u. the heavy burdens 54:36
u. this button 454:26
Undoing: my heart's u. 356:32
Undone: by victories u. 192:16
estate o' the world..u. 461:6
I am u. 53:8
if thou lookest..thou art u. 513:22
John Donne, Anne Donne, u. 186:29
must be u. 214:34
not to leave 't u. 471:35
some to be u. 172:9, 194:24
to want, to be u. 510:16
two words..u. the world 422:1
u. vast 92:36
we have left u. 388:11
wishest should be u. 457:1
wretch u. 164:34
Undress: when I u. me 204:1
Undrest: lady, if u. at Church 203:30
Undulate round the world 568:9
Undulating: u. air 253:15
u. throat 41:33
Undying thoughts I bear 338:5
Unearned increment 338:24
Unearthly ballet of bloodless
categories 79:13
Uneasy: coaxin' u. ones 229:15
no u. feeling 270:35
short u. motion 149:36
soul, u., and confined 383:11
u. lies the head 442:3
you are u. 267:26
Uneatable: full pursuit of the u. 570:15
Uneducated: Chawcer..so u. 560:15
Uneffectual: pale his u. fire 432:19
Unenlightened: strong, dogged, u. 19:14
Unequal earnings 198:21
Unerring: Lord of the u. bow 114:23
Unespied: in th' ocean's bosom u. 332:1
Uneven: they are so u. 170:15
Unexercised and unbreathed 352:9
Unexpectedness: character, which
I call u. 376:17
Unexpert: of wiles more or u. 345:16
Unexpressed: uttered or u. 355:11
Unexpressive she 427:23
Unextinguishable laugh in heaven 85:15
Unextinguished: from an u. hearth 496:11
Unfaith in aught 531:10
Unfaltering trust 98:3
Unfathomable mines 161:18
Unfeather'd two-legg'd thing 190:15
Unfed sides 453:14
Unfeeling: sordid, u., reprobate 124:9
u. for his own 230:30
Unfix my hair 456:24
Unfixed in principles 190:13
Unfit: for a calm u. 190:13
for all things u. 225:27
u. to be alone 154:26
Unflead: unchipt, u. 247:17
Unfledg'd: new-hatch'd, u. com-
rade [u. 431:25
Unfold: such companions thou'dst 473:2
Unforgetful: teach the u. to forget 411:20
Unforgiving: fill the u. minute 297:12
Unforgotten brave 117:37
Unformed: yet u. Occident 168:9
Unfortified: heart u. 430:31
Unfortunate: never literary at-
tempt..more u. 265:12

Unfortunate (cont.)
one more U. 252:12
u. Miss Bailey! 154:11
Unfriended: remote, u., melan-
choly 226:3
Unfriendly: u. to society's..joys 159:18
u. to the nose 516:18
Unfrowning caryatides 516:17
Unfruitful: invention is u. 100:23
Unfurnished: head..to be let u. 110:14
Ungained: men prize the thing u. 480:41
Ungainly: Vessel of a more u.
Make 207:15
Ungarter'd, and down-gyved 432:35
Ungentlemanly: how u. he can
look 518:34
Ungirt loin 96:46
Ungodliness: tents of u. 397:7
Ungodly: because of the u. 394:3
let the u. fall 400:15
let the u. perish 396:4
rod of the u. 399:33
seen the u. in great power 394:6
way of the u. 400:20
Ungrateful: one u. person 318:22
Ungratefulness: call virtue there
u.? 501:25
Unguem: ad u. factus homo 261:16
Unguessed: on Earth u. at 17:24
Ungula putrem sonitu quatit u.
campum 555:6
Unhabitable: o'er u. downs 521:18
Unhand: u. it, sir! 549:15
u. me, gentlemen 432:4
u. me, grey-beard loon! 148:20
Unhandily: they plucked us 298:14
Unhanged: not three good men u. 439:15
Unhappiness: man's u...comes of
his greatness 127:18
Unhappy: better that some should
be u. 273:9
dare to be u. 412:16
each u. family is u. in its own
way 548:7
extinction of u. hates 16:25
I for an u. poet 401:24
instinct for being u. 414:11
never be very u. 215:36
not one is respectable or u. 567:20
old, u., far-off things 581:2
soft, u. sex 40:14
u. cross-breed 181:38
u. Old Man in a boat 311:4
u. wight 510:16
Unhatched rapier 484:15
Unheard: u. are sweeter 287:8
u. was her complaining 508:4
Unheard-of: beautiful, u. kind 586:3
u. as thou art 573:17
Unheeding: through the u. many 498:20
Unhinged the brains of better heads 86:7
Unholy: eyes of most u. blue 356:14
not u. names 176:12
sights u. 341:26
Unhonoured: cold and u. 356:29
mindful of th' u. dead 230:10
unwept, u., and unsung 417:22
Unhoped: that u. serene 83:19
Unhouse and house the Lord 254:28
Unhoused: my u. free condition 469:38
Unhousel'd, disappointed 432:17
Unhurt amidst the wars of ele-
ments 1:24
Unicorn: lion beat the u. 367:13
Unicorns: from the horns of the u. 393:7
Un-idea'd girls 270:15
Uniform: good u...work its way 179:22
should be more u. 252:31
u. 'e wore 297:2
when I first put this u. on 220:23
Uniformity: use..before u. 25:35
Unimaginable: u. lodge 284:23
u. touch of time 578:2
Unimpaired: strong for service..
and u. 163:5
Unimpassioned grief 150:31
Unimplored: nightly visitation u. 349:5
Unimportant: important—u. 129:31
Unintelligent: anything so u. 19:27
Unintelligible: u. patter 222:12
u. world 581:25

Uninteresting: doing u. actions 28:29
Union: best through the whole U. 268:25
indestructible U. 136:15
Nature's social u. 107:10
our Federal U. 267:27
our u. is perfect 180:4
sail on, O U. 316:1
swell the chorus of the U. 314:10
u. in partition 467:9
u. of hands and hearts 527:15
U. of these States 568:7
u. of this ever diverse pair 336:35
u. of total dissent 320:3
u. with its native sea 574:20
Unison: some chord in u. 163:48
Unit: misses an u. 91:41
Unitarian: became a U. 200:11
Unitarianism: convert me to U. 307:26
Unite: severs those it should u. 493:21
u. them there 147:7
workers of the world, u.! 12:4, 333:11
United: ev'ry flower is u. 214:25
U. Metropolitan .. Muffin ..
Company 176:37
u. thoughts and counsels 344:12
United States: British Empire and
the U. 144:2
Government of the U. helpless 571:13
these U. 568:10
Unities: preserved the u.? 177:18
Uniting: by u. we stand 180:5
Unity; dwell together in u. 400:3
in necessary things, u. 36:25
in u. and godly love 390:26
preserve the u. of the empire 101:12
send up U., Claribel 299:25
truth, u., and concord 390:25
u., peace, and concord 388:53
Univers: il connaît l'u. 209:13
Universal: largess u. 444:8
this u. frame began 191:35
this u. frame..without a mind 25:23
u. darkness buries all 381:27
u. dovetailedness 177:18
u. grin 163:28, 204:34
Universe: born for the U. 225:27
boundless u. 540:25
fathomless u. 568:9
God's great u. 187:1
I accept the u. 127:32
into this U. 206:13
measure of the u. 497:5
mingle with the U. 114:26
my dead thoughts over the u. 496:11
my u. that feels and knows 91:14
peopling the lone u. 495:4
possessed all the u. together 489:28
pretend to understand the U. 127:24
U. beholds itself 494:1
u. is not hostile 250:27
wedded to this goodly u. 574:8
wide vessel of the u. 444:6
Wisdom and Spirit of the U.! 575:21
Universes: suns and u. ceased 83:11
Universities: state of both his u. 548:20
u. incline wits 28:13
University: his own mother U. 193:17
my..residence..in my U. 363:22
true U..books 126:28
U. as a whole 148:15
U. of Gottingen 124:17
U. should be..light..learning 181:4
we are the U. 511:5
Unjust: God u. 587:10
he that is u., let him be u. still 72:8
rain..also on the u. fella 79:7
rain on the just and on the u. 57:52
surprised by u. force 340:30
u. steward 62:20
Unkempt about those hedges 84:9
Unkind: none..deform'd but the
u. 484:19
not u. because uncouth 80:27
tell me not..I am u. 319:10
thou art not so u. 427:22
u. and the unruly 515:24
when givers prove u. 434:6
Unkindest cut of all 450:30
Unkindness: drink down all u. 465:29
tax not you..with u. 453:6
u. may do much..his u... 473:3

Unkissed: uncouth u. 510:26
unknowe, u. 138:27
with hard words and u. 375:16
Unknell'd, uncoffin'd, and unknown 114:28
Unknowable: O world u. 545:1
Unknowing: u. and unknown 106:27
u. what he sought 192:5
Unknown: accents yet u. 450:1
among u. men 577:4
argues yourself u. 347:30
behind the dim u. 320:11
forms of things u. 467:24
keep 't..u. 471:35
let me live, unseen, u. 386:27
safely into the u. 239:4
she lived u. 580:18
that is to him u. 552:11
things standing thus u. 438:4
things u...as things forgot 383:3
to the U. God 64:60
uncoffin'd, and u. 114:28
u. and silent shore 307:32
u. modes of being 579:11
u., unkist 138:27
Unlamented let me die 386:27
Unlearned: amaze th' u. 382:28
u., he knew no..art 386:4
Unleavened bread 45:46, 66:28
Unlesson'd girl 464:19
Unlettered: dull u. small 164:17
Unlimited power is apt to corrupt 379:5
Unlit lamp 96:46
Unload: help the missus u. 299:19
Unlock: he only could u. 4:5
Unlocked: Shakespeare u. his
heart 92:19, 580:16
u. to your occasions 463:2
Unlooked: honour comes u. for 440:35
Unloose: not worthy to u. 63:2
Unloved: often left u. 424:22
Unlovely as thou seem'st 163:25
Unlucky: these u. deeds relate 474:2
Unmakes: God u. but to remake 96:16
Unmanly: 'tis u. grief 430:31
Unmannerly: untaught knaves, u. 438:33
Unmarried: prime-roses, that die
u. 485:26
Unmatch'd for courage 416:13
Unmeaning: master of u. rhyme 117:27
some u. thing 382:31
Unmeritable: slight u. man 451:5
Unmindfulness: skilled u. 235:21
Unmiss'd but by his dogs 161:24
Unmitigated act 296:14
Unmoisten'd foot 361:15
Unmoneyed: treat u. men 142:1
Unmoved: no Englishman u. 221:37
u., cold 487:24
u. see thee dying 178:32
u. tho' witlings sneer 278:27
u., unshaken 348:18
Unnatural: cruel, not u. 435:30
foul, strange, and u. 432:11
poetry's u. 179:5
Unnecessary: not curious in u.
matters 56:32
thou u. letter! 452:33
Unobserved: alone, and u.? 220:24
he u. home..returned 350:18
Unobtrusive: poetry should be..
u. 289:25
Uno'erleap'd Mountains 18:2
Unoffending creatures whom he
loves 575:13
Unofficial: English u. rose 84:9
Unparalleled: diet u. 176:38
lass u. 426:14
Unparticular: nice u. man 236:39
Unpastured dragon 491:27
Unperceived by us 191:22
Unperplext seeking 91:41
Unpersuadable justice 584:13
Unpitied: u. sacrifice 101:36
unrespited, u., unreprieved 345:21
Unpleasant: moist, u. body 177:21
Unpleased: in power u. 190:13
Unpleasing: things..tender and
u. 25:42
u. to a married ear 455:35
Unplumb'd, salt..sea 16:16

Unpoetical: poet..most u...thing 290:10
Unpolicied: ass u. 426:13
Unpolished: this u. rugged verse 193:26
Unpopular: I was not u. there 39:13
power..always u. 181:40
u. names 19:10
Unpractised: u. he to fawn 224:18
unschool'd, u. 464:19
Unpremeditated: u. art 498:1
u. lay 417:1
u. strain 546:5
u. verse 349:5
Unprepared: magnificently u. 157:8
u. courage 360:25
Unpriced: food u. 334:3
Unprofaned: virginal, and u. 376:2
Unprofitable: flat, and u. 430:33
most idle and u. 216:19
u. servants 62:28
Unprofitably travelling 579:3
Unpronounceable awful names 239:3
Unproportioned: any u. thought 431:25
Unpunctual star 84:10
Unqueen: old times u. thee 148:14
Unquiet: calmer of u. thoughts 559:15
earth never so u. 397:33
for the u. heart 532:4
immovably u. 496:1
sole u. thing 151:24
Unraised: flat u. spirits 443:3
Unravaged by the fierce intellec-
tual life 19:10
Unravished: still u. bride 287:6
Unreal mockery, hence 459:21
Unreasonable: progress depends
on the u. man 490:34
some u. moment of mine 127:29
Unreconciled: crime u. as yet 473:12
Unredressed: wrong left u. 294:16
Unregulated sun 84:10
Unrelenting: Juno's u. hate 194:29
Unremembered: nameless, u. acts 581:24
Unremembering: went her u. way 544:1
Unremoved: Teneriff or Atlas u. 347:35
Unreprieved: unpitied, u. 345:21
Unreproved: conjugal attraction u. 347:17
u. pleasures free 341:31
Unrequited: what u. affection is 175:17
Unrespited, unpitied 345:21
Unrest which men miscall delight 492:7
Unresting: life's u. sea 251:15
Unrewarded: nothing went u. 190:24
Unrighteousness: mammon of u. 62:21
Unripened: pale, u. beauties of
the north 1:17
Unroll: spoils of time..ne'er u. 230:5
Unruly: unkind and the u. 515:24
u. evil 69:37
u. Sun 186:19
u. wills and affections 389:37
Unsad and ever untrewe 137:25
Unsafe: most u...with our selves 154:26
Unsatisfied: cigarette..leaves one u. 570:8
Unsavoury: most u. similes 438:20
Unscalable: rocks u. 429:29
Unscathed: thence u. to go 418:27
Unschool'd, unpractis'd 464:19
Unscrupulous: keen, u. course 15:21
Unsearchable: heart of kings is u. 50:33
u. and secret aims 80:26
u. dispose 351:7
u. riches of Christ 67:52
Unseasonably: never comes u. 325:23
Unseatest: perching, u. 121:18
Unseduced: unshaken, u., unterrified 348:18
Unseemly: doth not behave itself
u. 66:45
how u...for my sex 331:2
u. exposure of the mind 240:2
Unseen: all u. Romance 298:1
born to blush u. 230:5
greet the u. with a cheer 97:3
I walk u. 341:14
leave the world u. 287:24
left u. a wonderful piece of work 423:27
let me live, u., unknown 386:27
liv'st u. within thy..shell 340:13
thou art u., but yet 498:4
though u., a kiss 160:28
though u. among us 494:3

Unseen (cont.)
u. before by Gods 286:10
u. things above 235:10
Unselfishness of an oyster 414:12
Unsettle: don't let that u. you 218:13
Unsettled: only as far as they are
u. 200:8
Unsex me here 457:3
Unshak'd of motion 449:30
Unshaken, unseduced, unterrified 348:18
Unsham'd, though foil'd 193:15
Unshapely: wrong of u. things 585:17
Unshook: thou stand'st u. 385:23
Unshorn: god u. 245:24
Unshown: love..left u. 424:22
Unshut: sail, with u. eye 15:24
Unsifted in such perilous circum-
stance 431:26
Unskilled to sunder 147:9
Unsmote by the sword 118:39
Unsought: love..giv'n u. is better 483:29
not u. be won 348:37
Unsought-for: for aye u. 285:29
Unsoundness: certain u. of mind 325:3
Unspeakable: fulfilled of u. things 525:11
u. in..pursuit of the uneatable 570:15
U. Scot 167:15
u. Turk 126:42
Unsphere the spirit of Plato 341:17
Unspotted from the world 69:34
Unstable: remember of this u.
world 328:13
u. as water 45:26
Unstaid and skittish 483:2
Unstifled: had play u. 90:39
Unstitching: stitching and u. 584:2
Unstringed viol 474:14
Unsubdued: many u. 493:27
Unsubstantial Death 478:44
Unsuccessful: u. literary man 41:33
u. or successful war 162:40
Unsung: some u. 544:4
unhonour'd, and u. 417:22
Unsunned: chaste as u. snow 429:27
u. heaps 340:21
Unsure: what's to come..still u. 482:28
Unsuspected: some u. isle 94:42
Untainted by man's misery 498:14
Untamed: too restless, too u. 15:20
u., the strong heart 188:32
Untangled: once u...misfortune
bodes 477:7
Untaught: call'd them u. knaves 438:33
low-born, u. 188:31
u. innate philosophy 113:41
Untender: so young, and so u.? 452:10
Unterrified: Satan stood u. 346:6
unseduced, u. 348:18
u., into the gulf 491:15
Unthinkable wings 141:1
Unthinking time 193:31
Unthought: left u. of in obscurity 575:11
Unthread the rude eye 447:45
Untie the winds 460:4
Untimely: u. fruit of a woman 395:21
u. grave 125:3
u. graves 163:29
why came I so u. forth 558:6
Untouched: u. by solemn thought 577:1
u. the pages lie 164:37
Untoward fate 116:35
Untravelled: my heart u. 226:4
Sussex moon, u. still 141:13
u. world 540:32(−541)
Untried: new and u. 314:7
Untrimmed: nature's changing
course u. 486:18
Untrodden: among the u. ways 580:18
u. region of my mind −288:7
Untroubled heart of stone 122:32
Untrue: on a cloth u. 220:6
telle his tale u. 137:23
unsad and ever u. 137:25
Untruth: night's u. 168:12
Untune: Music shall u. the sky 191:39
u. that string 481:4
Untutored: toper whose u. sense 164:33
Untwist: not u...these last
strands 254:10
Untwisting all the chains 342:8
Untying: knot there's no u. 123:5

Unum est pro laboribus tantis 132:21
Unuplifted eyes 577:24
Unused: fust in us u. 436:15
u. to the melting mood 474:2
Unutterable: deep, u. woe 23:25
looked u. things 546:16
Unvalued: as u. persons do 431:21
Unvarnished: round u. tale 469:45
Unveil'd her peerless light 347:19
Unveiling, affirm 380:15
Unvex'd with anxious cares 192:13
Unwashed: lean u. artificer 447:41
u. artificer 162:17
Unwedgeable and gnarled oak 461:31
Unweeded: 'tis an u. garden 430:33
Unweighing: ignorant, u. fellow 462:15
Unwelcome: bringer of u. news 441:10
Unwept, unhonour'd, and unsung 417:22
Unwhipp'd of justice 453:9
Unwholesome: not u. 22:7
Unwilling: go hence u. 349:30
like u. sleep 288:21
Unwillingly to school 427:21
Unwise: in the sight of the u. 56:23
u. man doth not well consider 397:20
Unwithstood: 'with pomp of waters,' 577:2
Unwomanly rags 253:22
Unworthiness: for our u. we dare not 390:53
Unworthy: his family..not u. of him 182:12
his lips on that u. place 425:1
merit of the u. takes 434:4
not u. to love her 118:33
opinion..u. of him 27:20
Unwounded: hearts u. sing again 299:24
Unwritten: that u. law 169:9
Up: Christian, u. and smite them cry it u. 361:13
cry it u. 521:20
levelling u. to themselves 271:12
look not thou down but u. 95:25
mostly they goes u. and down 135:1
ne'er went u. again 367:11
nothwithstanding u. 449:25
see me safe u. 358:6
u. and doing 317:8
u. and down the City Road 328:26
u. and down the salt seas 294:34
u. betimes 482:27
u. goes the price of shoddy 218:29
u. go we 250:11, 404:17
u. Guards and at them 564:24
u. in the morning early 108:24
u., Lord 392:15
u. roos the sonne, and u. roos Emelye 137:33
u. she rises 11:16
u.-tails all 280:12
u., u. and see the great doom 458:23
u.l u.! my friend 581:14
utmost u. and on 95:38
when they were u., they were u. 10:19
where he had got u. 160:10
Upbraid: their toils u. 332:13
Upbraideth: God..that u. not 69:27
Up-gathered now like sleeping flowers 582:18
Upgrowth of all virtue 294:3
Upharsin: mene, mene, tekel, u. 55:42
Upheld: aye u. the right 324:6
Uphill: escape the u. 409:17
u. all the way? 410:2
Uphold: awhile u...your idleness 438:30
by His counsels guide, u. you 406:1
u. you, Tomlinson 302:26
Uphung: high u. 343:12
Upland: this u. dim 18:31
upon the u. lawn 230:11
Uplift: never dared u. 496:17
Uplifted: high u. beyond hope 345:14
u. from the head 496:6
Upper: Englishman of our u. class 19:27
large u. room furnished 62:43
man have the u. hand 392:15
other, u. crust 221:26
silence of the u. shelf 325:1
stiff u. lip 131:31
these men are all u. crust 234:1
u. ten thousand 571:5
Uppermost: love the u. rooms 60:15

Upraised: u. me where my mother with eyes u. 543:19
with eyes u. 154:1
Upright: cannot always stand u. 389:30
cannot sit u. 159:41
God hath made man u. 51:16
just, the u., the generous 363:26
man of life u. 123:23
these our flesh u. 184:22
wise, u., valiant 578:5
Uprising: mine u. 400:7
our wakening and u. 291:4
tomorrow's u. to deeds 359:7
u., unveiling 380:15
Uprist: glorious Sun u. 149:2
Uproar: in question for this day's u. 65:9
u. is arisen in this land 352:18
u.'s your only music 289:22
Upside-down: turned the world u. 64:57
turneth it u. 400:20
Upstairs: came u. into the world 155:11
knew any kicked u. 103:34
u. and downstairs 339:9, 366:23
Upstart crow 232:6
Upward: burn u. 96:45
look u. to the skies 362:8
they must u. still 320:13
toiling u. in the night 316:31
Upwards: meandering level.. mounting u. 325:12
Ural: hemmed by the U. mountains 235:22
Urania: govern thou my song, U. 348:23
lament anew, U.! 491:15
Uranus: perturbed moon of U. 375:25
Urban, squat 84:13
Urbanum: neque elegantem..neque u. 132:22
Urbe: rus in u. 331:28
Urbem venalem...perituram 415:4
Urbes: inter caput extulit u. 555:18
Urbis: mores .. vidit et u. 255:26
Urceus: currente rota cur u. exit? 255:17
Urge: u. and u... procreant u. 567:11
u. the flying ball 230:24
Uriah: set ye U. in the forefront 47:32
Uricon: ashes under U. 263:9
Urim and the Thummim 46:2
Urn: end by Nelson's u. 141:14
favour my destin'd u. 342:11
from her pictured u. 231:15
loud-hissing u. 163:21
not to its dregs the u. 493:27(-494)
overflow thy u. 308:19
storied u. 230:3
when his dust falls to the u. 552:7
Urna: omne capax movet u. nomen 259:15
Urns: old sepulchral u. 159:21
Urrh! Yarrh! 300:16
Urs: those dreadful u. 250:31
Ursa Major: my nativity..under U. 452:20
Usage of those antique times 509:35
Usage: pas en l'éspace..en l'u. 354:20
Usance: brings down the rate of u. 463:17
Use: against the u. of nature 456:21
all animals..for the u. of man 376:15
better done, as others u. 342:20
beyond all u. 449:21
come to deadly u. 453:42
comfort, u., and protection 24:27
how u. doth breed a habit 485:1
keener with constant u. 267:19
live, and u. it 243:31
my tongue's u. 474:14
not u. a friend as I u. Thee 245:11
people who have no u. for them 254:9
perfect u. of an imperfect medium 570:4
rather u. than fame 531:15
sets it in act and u. 442:21
Shakespeare made u. of it first 500:2
singular u. for the common people 519:3
speak daggers..but u. none 435:30
spoilt by u. 285:38
such as cannot u. them 280:19
takes away the u. of 't 334:26
too rich for u. 477:9
true u. of speech 226:26
u. all gently 434:15
u. a poor maiden so 6:2
u...before uniformity 25:35

Use (cont.)
u...but of my left hand 352:19
u. him as though you loved him 559:23
u. in measured language 532:4
u. it like a giant 461:30
u. my self in jest 186:15
u. of a mirror 325:10
when *I* use a word 131:6
why deny its u. 121:22
Used: nothing like being u. to a thing 500:28
since then I have u. no other 403:30
so u. to affectation 201:31
will be u. against you 187:25
Used-to-was: my name is U. 548:19
Useful: by the magistrate, as equally u. 217:5
historians..u. to Him 111:28
mock their u. toil 230:1
Useless: lodg'd with me u. 351:21
most beautiful..most u. 413:13
u. and hopeless sorrow 277:41
u. each without the other 317:27
u. life is an early death 224:1
Uselessness of men above sixty 371:3
Uses: all the u. of this world 430:33
for mean or no u. 315:6
keep a corner..for other's u. 471:40
to what base u. 437:16
u. of a cup 95:25
u. of adversity 426:30
u. which ye may have of him 57:9
Usher: yesterday doth not u. it in 186:31
Usherest in the day 107:4
Ushers in the morn 204:37
Using: how's the world a-u. you? 168:7
most barren with best u. 168:7
Usna's children died 585:22
Usquebae: wi' u...face the devil 108:10
Usu: consumitur annulus u. 372:10
Usual: business as u. 143:37
more than u. calm 208:21
not kind sir..quite u. 20:30
Usurp: none can u. this height 285:33
Usurpation: without u., assume the..style 86:1
Usury: given his money upon u. 392:24
lent out my heart with u. 307:5
souls not lent in u. 336:45
Usus: si volet u. 255:20
Utantur: abstinent ut non u. 22:4
Uther's son 345:4
Uti: muneribus sapienter u. 261:4
Utile: miscuit u. dulci 256:9
quid u., quid non 256:21
Utili: honestum praetulit u. 261:3
Utmost: does the u. that he can 104:22
their u. up and on 95:38
u. thou hast in thee 127:21
Utopia: not in U...our happiness 579:30
principality in U. 325:24
Utter: her secret none can u. 404:20
man cannot u. it 50:61
not u. what thou dost not know 439:11
that my tongue could u. 528:3
to know, to u. and to argue 352:10
Utterance: action, nor u. 450:33
how divine is u.! 337:15
large u. of the early Gods 286:6
timely u. 576:4
with what strange u. 579:8
Uttered: not u. by base sale 455:2
u. or unexpressed 355:11
what he thought he u. 241:16
Uttereth: fool u. all his mind 50:51
u. piercing eloquence 479:4
Utterly Absurd 301:21
Uttermost parts of the sea 400:9
Uxor: cauta est et ab illis incipit u. 283:19
domus et placens u. 259:10
Uzziah: year that king U. died 53:8

V

V: put it down a V. 179:14
'V' or a 'W'? 179:13
Vacancy: but for v., had gone to gaze 424:7
in the after-v. 573:7

Vacant: in v...mood 577:7
  mind quite v. 162:3
  one v. chair 317:11
  spoke the v. mind 224:17
  stuffs out his v. garments 447:34
  v. heart and hand 419:16
  v. interlunar cave 350:23
Vacations: no extras, no v. 176:38
Vacuity: indolent v. of thought 163:30
Vacuus: cantabit v. 283:17
Vadis: quo v.? 63:59
Vae victis 314:23
Vagabond flag 423:39
Vagrom: comprehend all v. men 468:36
Vagula: animula v. blandula 233:19
Vain: after me—in v. 207:28
  all delights are v. 454:31
  all is done in v. 106:17
  beating..his luminous wings in v. 19:21
  because I weep in v. 231:19
  call it not v. 417:20
  dreme of joye, al but in v. 138:24
  else made first in v. 96:16
  flippant, v., inconstant 289:10
  for one in v. 207:29
  for tricks that are v. 238:32
  full as v. 191:20
  generous aspirings.. in v. 307:12
  given in v., in v. 530:38
  hatching v. empires 345:25
  hence with denial v. 342:11
  how v. the ardour 231:7
  in v., said she 202:4
  in v. the envious seasons 251:11
  in v. the saint adore 189:14
  in v. with lavish kindness 240:18
  I preach in v. 165:4
  I watched in v. 208:16
  John he cried in v. 159:40
  know my knowledge..v. 4:10
  learn that all is v. 410:33
  let not only mine be v. 262:13
  mock on, 'tis all in v. 75:17
  most v., most generous 241:29
  Name of..God in v. 390:8
  never sought in v. 104:35
  no great man lives in v. 126:24
  no more v. oblations 52:29
  only know we loved in v. 117:35
  Patently Impossible and V. 301:21
  people imagine a v. thing 391:47
  profane, erroneous, and v. 110:35
  scan his work in v. 161:20
  seal'd in v. 462:16
  surely not in v. 207:17
  sweep over thee in v. 114:27
  tease her with our plaint in v. 18:28
  unutterably v. 83:9
  up to God in v. 313:3
  v. are the thousand creeds 83:9
  v. faith, and courage v. 323:7
  v., ill-natur'd thing 170:12
  v. man..that dost in v. assay 509:7
  v., mightiest fleets 188:32
  v. thing to save a man 393:37
  v., those all-shattering guns 188:32
  v. was the chief's..pride 386:24
  v. wisdom all 345:30
  void as v. 233:3
  wounds are v. 147:8
  youth is v. 150:26
Vaincre sans péril 157:6
Vainly invented 401:7
Vainness: lying, v. 484:18
Vale: end in a v. 39:4
  into the v. of years 471:39
  meet thee in that hollow v. 292:19
  river, wood, and v. 285:1
  sequester'd v. of life 230:7
  sequester'd v. of rural life 387:8
  v. in Ida 537:29
  v. in the land of Moab 3:16
  v. in whose bosom 356:26
  v. of misery 397:6
  v. of Soul-making 290:20
  V., the three lone weirs 18:21
  violet-embroidered v. 340:13
  White Horse V. 140:11
  wide v. of Trent 322:23
  world as a v. of tears 90:36

Vale: ave atque v. 133:20
Valentine: hail, Bishop V. 184:26
  Saint V. is past 467:21
Valere: non est vivere, sed v. 331:27
Valerius loathed the wrong 324:6
Vales: all the v. rejoice 76:10
  from our lovely v. 314:19
Valet: hero to his v. 157:11
  to his very v...a hero 112:34
Valet: point de héros pour son v. 157:11
Valiant: all the Brothers were V. 363:9
  all v. dust 301:1
  as he was v., I honour him 450:15
  ever become v. and martial 27:25
  indeed a v. gentleman 202:12
  more active-v. or more v.-young 440:28
  more v., being..old Jack 439:37
  O v. hearts 14:20
  reproof v. 428:37
  sing, that I may seem v. 191:24
  v., but not too venturous 321:17
  v. in velvet 241:29
  v. Jack Falstaff 439:37
  v. man and free 533:20
  v. never taste of death 449:22
  who would v. be 99:35
  wise, upright, v. 578:5
Valiant-for-Truth 99:34
Validity: of what v. and pitch 481:30
Valle: cur v. permutem Sabina 259:17
Valley: bicker down a v. 528:5
  darker grows the v. 336:9
  every v. shall be exalted 54:9
  into the v. of Death 528:16
  lies now in the little v. 89:24
  Love is of the v. 539:4
  mete out the v. of Succoth 395:23
  paweth in the v. 49:26
  v. between Buxton and Bakewell 413:1
  v. of Ajalon 46:42
  v. of decision 55:53
  v. of Humiliation 99:10
  v. of the shadow of death 393:10
  v., rock, or hill 582:14
  v. sheep are fatter 376:23
  v. so sweet 356:26
  v. which was full of bones 55:33
Valley-glades: in the next v. 288:2
Valleys: bright in the fruitful v. 81:18
  down to the v. beneath 398:8
  lily of the v. 51:43
  lovelier than all the v. 537:29
  piping down the v. 76:9
  rain into the little r. 395:30
  these v. and rocks 164:25
  v., groves, hills and fields 330:17
  v...so thick with corn 395:30(-396)
Vallombrosa: brooks in V. 344:25
Valois: shadow of the V. 141:4
Valoroso is a man again 542:24
Valorous: more childish v. 331:6
Valour: better part of v. 441:2
  birthplace of v. 107:13
  false quarrel..no true v. 469:14
  for contemplation he and v. 347:11
  for v., is not love a Hercules 455:22
  like v.'s minion 456:5
  much care and v. 444:17
  my v. is certainly going 500:29
  of v., and of victory 331:2
  same in thine own act and v. 457:11
  this v. comes of sherris 442:21
  V. and Innocence 300:23
  who would true v. see 99:35
Valuable: everything dear and v. 379:15
  most v...this world affords 157:13
  riches to be a v. thing 519:33
Value: more v. than many sparrows 58:54
  news v. 405:17
  no more v. than their dress 239:24
  then we rack the v. 469:5
  v. dwells not in particular will 481:12
  v. it next to a good conscience 559:26
  v. of nothing 570:1
  what he most doth v. 575:11
Valued: aught, but as 'tis v. 481:12
  never v. till they make a noise 165:13
Values: as moneys are for v. 24:20

Vampire: like the v...dead many times 374:11
Van: cravings in the v. of Love 337:1
  take thou the v. 104:22
  thou like the v. 292:20
Vanae: quid leges sine moribus v. proficiunt? 260:11
Vanbrugh's house of clay 202:11
Vandunck: Mynheer V. 154:17
Vandyke is of the company 212:21
Vanguard of Liberty 577:8
Vanish: far from v., rather grows 91:14
  knowledge, it shall v. away 66:45
  suddenly v. away 128:10
  v. with the Rose 207:24, 25
Vanished: altogether v. like a dream 126:27
  as rare things will, it v. 93:46
  he v. from my sight 76:9
  he v. out of sight 508:15
  v. from his lonely hearth 575:17
  v. quite slowly 129:4
Vanishes: but beauty v. 171:6
Vanishest: if thus thou v. 426:12
Vanisheth: then v. away 69:41
Vanishings: fallings from us, v. 576:18
Vanitas Vanitatum 542:40
Vanity: all others are but v. 507:17
  draw iniquity with cords of v. 53:5
  every man..altogether v. 394:9
  every man..but v. 394:10
  give not yourselves unto v. 395:24
  good sense without v. 223:9
  lest they behold v. 399:15
  lighter than v. 99:14, 395:24
  no competition, no v. 272:30
  no love..but v. 265:20
  no need of such v. 468:35
  not only a great v. 267:31
  or thought of v. 123:23
  out o' touch o' v. 299:9
  speckled V. 343:19
  that v. in years 439:35
  they are but v. 395:24
  true v...in the power of pleasing 156:4
  two passions, v. and love 139:26
  v. and vexation of spirit 50:62
  v., like murder, will out 158:26
  v. of this wicked world 391:2
  V. of vanities! 543:13
  v. of vanities..all is v. 50:59
  your partickler v. 179:30
Vanity-Fair 99:14
Vanquish: I will v...my judges 363:12
Vanquished: e'en though v. 225:2
  ingratitude..quite v. him 450:31
  Macbeth shall never v. be 460:9
  valiantly v. 425:28
  v. had no despite 509:35
Vantage: coign of v. 457:6
  might the v. best have took 461:29
Vaporous: there hangs a v. drop 459:27
Vapour: like v. over shrines 89:5
  v...like a bear 425:19
  v. of a dungeon 471:40
  your life..v. 69:41
Vapours: congregation of v. 433:15
  dull and crudy v. 442:21
  luminous v...to the traveller 278:23
  snow and v. 400:24
  v. both away 184:28
  v. weep their burthen 540:20
Variable: attracts light-headed, v. men 514:28
  thy love prove likewise v. 477:22
  v. as the shade 418:31
Variableness: no v. 69:29
Variation: admitting any v. 388:3
  each slight v...preserved 169:6
Varied: so v. in discourse 308:17
  v. year 546:24
Variety: fortune is full of fresh v. 35:20
  great source of pleasure..v. 278:5
  her infinite v. 424:9
  Love's sweetest part, V. 185:28
  of priests..a charmin' v. 229:13
  sad v. of woe 217:18, 382:1
  v. is the soul of pleasure 40:9
  v.'s the source of joy 215:19
  v.'s the very spice 163:4

Vario: neque adhuc V. videor   556:7
Variorum: life is all a v.   106:25
Various: man so v.   190:22
  so v. are the tastes of men   3:9
  to v. people v. things   164:32
Varlet: baseness' v.   281:4
Varletry: show me to the shouting
  v.   425:34
Varnishing auctioneer   126:10
Varsovie: l'ordre règne à V.   12:17
Vase: you may shatter the v.   356:18
Vassal: Italy a v. state   144:6
Vassals and serfs at my side   98:21
Vast: dead v. and middle of the
  night   431:8
  empty, v., and wandering air   476:15
  undone v.   92:36
  with a dome more v.   251:15
  world so v.   266:14
Vaster than empires   333:8
Vastness! and Age!   380:14
Vasty: spirits from the v. deep   439:42
  v. hall of death   17:15
Vate: carent quia v. sacro   261:2
Vatem: me..dicunt v. pastores   556:7
Vaters: des groszen V. Helm   208:30
Vatibus: me lyricis v. inseres   258:2
Vats: in the v. of Luna   323:12
  spirited purple of the v.   539:4
Vatum: genus irritabile v.   257:18
Vault: fretted v.   230:2
  hollow v. resound   266:13
  in the v. above the Cherubim   298:9
  in thy marble v.   333:9
  leave it buried in this v.   280:11
  left this v. to brag of   458:24
  prepare v. for funeral Monday   39:30
Vaulted with such ease   440:18
Vaulter: green little v.   265:21
Vaunt: empty v.   498:10
Vaunt-couriers   453:5
Vaunteth: charity v. not itself   66:45
Vaunting aloud   344:15
Vaward: in the v. of our youth   441:18
  take thou the v.   30:6
Veal: one of Bellamy's v. pies   379:21
Vectus: multa per aequora v.   133:20
Vécu: que vous avez assez v.   354:20
Vegetable: content with a v. love   220:28
  my v. love   333:8
  passion of a v. fashion   220:28
Vegetate: one does but v.   103:37
  v. in a village   154:22
  v. like the country   240:8
Vegetation: darkest v.   237:8
Veil: death is the v.   497:11
  fiery spangled v. of heaven   331:2
  lift not the painted v.   498:19
  that sacred v.   551:18
  took away my v. from me   52:12
  v. after v. will lift   14:28
  v. of the soul therein   522:7
  V. past which I could not see   206:16
  V. through which I could not
    see   206:17
  was the v. of thee   522:11
  wrapped in a gauzy v.   499:5
Veiled: dim suffusion v.   346:19
  she will v. walk   481:32
  truth be v.   493:23
Veiling an Indian beauty   464:15
Veillons: nous v. dormants   355:4
Veils: from the v. of the morning   585:12
  through all her v.   125:2
  v. her sacred fires   381:27
Vein: but in the v. of art   290:26
  Ercles' v.   466:26
  King Cambyses' v.   439:31
  not in the giving v.   476:24
Veines: ardeur dans mes v. cachée   405:3
Veins: harebell, like thy v.   429:37
  in my v. red life   287:3
  jigging v.   330:20
  my bluest v. to kiss   424:13
  open all my v.   355:21
  sea itself floweth in your v.   548:13
Velasquez: why drag in V.?   566:6
Velle: idem v. atque idem nolle   415:2
Velvet: branched v. gown   483:15
  cowslip's v. head   341:4
  my gude lord in the black v.   31:4

Velvet (cont.)
  summer's v. buds   443:10
  through the v. leaves   455:17
  valiant in v.   241:29
  v. capt.   160:30
Vendible: maid not v.   462:36
Venerate: a petticoat   116:49
  v. art as art   240:17
Venerabile: clarum et v. nomen   320:25
Venerable: adorn'd the v. place   224:22
  beautiful cityl so v.   19:10
Venerably dull   143:22
Veneres Cupidinesque   132:12
Venetian: beat a V.   474:2
Vengeance: day of v. of our God   55:3
  heav'n awards the v.   158:33
  just my v. complete   92:26
  rouse to v.   124:9
  v., deep-brooding   417:6
  v. is mine   66:6
  v. of Jenny's case   466:12
  v. of our sins   388:44
Vengefulness: fainted on his v.   336:19
Veni: tu tamen ipse v.   371:24
  v., vidi, vici   120:13
Venice: cunning whore of V   472:37
  dirty stones of V.   293:10
  in V. they do let heaven see   471:35
  I stood in V.   114:1
  no Lord of Parys, V.   195:7
  not for V.   465:5
  ocean's nursling, V.   495:1
  poor trash of V.   471:3
  there at V. gave his body   475:16
  V...eldest Child of Liberty   582:6
  V. in their armoury   109:21
  where V. sate in state   114:2
Veniam: hanc v. petimus   255:15
Venite: God's great V.   186:11
  v., v. in Bethlehem   13:2
Venom, to thy work   437:40
Venomous: poor v. fool   426:13
  ugly and v.   426:30
Vent: that his tongue must v.   429:13
  v. the treasure of our tongue   168:9
Vent: au feu le v.   109:34
Ventiferous ripes   251:19
Ventis: navita v.   402:15
Vento: in v. et rapida scribere   133:11
Ventricle of memory   455:12
Vents in mangled forms   427:16
Venture: damn her at a v.   308:7
  drew a bow at a v.   48:15
  each v. is a new beginning   197:9
  naught v., naught have   549:27
  nothing v., nothing win   219:14
Ventured: v...beyond my depth   446:24
  you have deeply v.   118:12
Ventures: lose our v.   451:29
Venturous: not too v.   321:17
Venus: absence of the planet V.   177:22
  as V. yokes her doves   116:14
  callin' a young 'ooman a V.   179:6
  Cotytto or V.   523:6
  o'erpicturing that V.   424:6
  upon thy V. that must die   231:36
  V. clerk, Ovyde   138:15
  V. grown fat   265:19
  V. here..her dwelling   192:44
  V., let me never see   401:36
  V., take my votive glass   401:36
  V. when she smiles   281:25
Vénus: c'est V. toute entière   405:3
Venustiorum: hominum v.   132:12
Ver: first born child of V.   38:8
Ver egelidos refert tepores   132:24
Vera: cum istis v. sentire   145:23
  dinoscere..v. bona   283:15
Veracity: convince us of its v.   265:10
  tell us what he..saw with v.   231:23
Verbosa et grandis epistula   283:18
Verbosity: exuberance of his own
  v.   181:12
  thread of his v.   387:6, 455:24
Verbs and nouns do more agree   238:30
Verbum: volat irrevocabile v.   257:7
Verdantly: entwine itself v.   356:12
Verdict afterwards   129:35
Verdure: different shades in the v.   278:15
  see no other v.   288:23
Verdurous glooms   287:29

Vere de Vere: caste of V.   533:37
Vereinigt: Proletarier..v. euchl   333:11
Vereker's secret   268:15
Verge: from the v. of Heaven   348:22
  on the very v. of her confine   452:39
  v. enough   229:22
  v. of the salt flood   480:32
Verged: narrow v. shade   332:13
Verger: erudite V.   33:23
Verify your references   412:4
Verisimilitude: fine isolated v.   289:21
  give artistic v.   220:13
Veritas: in vino v.   380:2
  magis amica v.   14:19
  magna est v. et praevalebit   84:26
  magna est v. et praevalet   56:19
Veritatem: ex umbris..in v.   364:2
Vérités: mains pleines de v.   209:16
Verlieren: dienen und v.   223:23
  nichts in ihr zu v. als ihre Ketten   333:11
Vermeil-tinctur'd lip   340:38
Vermilion-spotted   286:37
Vermin: all sorts of v.   34:17
  race of little odious v.   519:15
Vernal seasons of the year   352:29
Verneint: der Geist der stets v.   223:17
Vero: se non è v.   13:1
Verre: je bois dans mon v.   360:7
Vers: chantant mes v.   408:18
  tout ce qui n'est point prose est v.   353:12
Versailles: Dauphiness, at V.   102:11
Versate: nocturna v. manu, v.
  diurna   256:6
Verse: accomplishment of v.   574:10
  Book of V.—and Thou   205:23
  decorate the v. herself inspires   117:26
  great v. unto a little clan   287:17
  harmony of instrument or v.   494:1
  high immortal v.   340:25
  hoarse, rough v.   382:32
  I court others in v.   401:21
  in his v. can gently steer   193:19
  married to immortal v.   342:7
  Miltonic v...in the vein of art   290:26
  my unpremeditated v.   349:5
  my v. again shall gild   189:10
  my v. extoll'd thy name   125:1
  my v. is not a crown   245:2
  my v. your virtues..eternize   509:7
  ne'er a v. to thee   293:12
  not v. now, only prose   90:5
  of all my v., like not a..line   516:11
  one in v. makes..more in prose   382:19
  only with those in v.   156:3
  pleasures that to v. belong   285:8
  prologues..in mournful v.   213:8
  rare gold ring of v.   96:19
  reads v. and thinks she under-
    stands   91:7
  run them into v.   194:12
  sail of his great v.   487:20
  shows that prose is v.   117:16
  sisters, Voice and V.   351:9
  still thy v. has charms   418:14
  strew of weeping v.   292:18
  subject of all v.   87:24
  this be the v. you grave   516:15
  this unpolished rugged v.   193:26
  too humble to be named in V.   579:14
  varying v.   386:17
  v., a breeze mid blossoms   152:20
  v. is a measured speech   24:21
  v. may find him   243:25
  v. softens toil   217:17
  v., that immortalizes   164:21
  v. will seem prose   98:11
  whose v...differs in nothing
    from prose   231:21
  with ends of v.   110:33
Versed: deep v. in books   350:13
  long v. in human ills   165:20
Verser: hearken unto a V.   243:25
  V. reciter, Care   494:9
Verses: Book of V.[205:24
  false gallop of v.   428:1
  he writes v.   466:5
  quire of bad v.   324:35
  recited v. in writing   57:10
  rhyme the rudder is of v.   110:22
  some for writing v.   315:12
  tear him for his bad v.   451:3

Verses (cont.)
when he repeats his v. 307:13
write halting v. 514:35
write v. without..understanding..metre 153:11
Versing: relish v. 244:18
Versum: facit indignatio v. 282:24
Vertu: la v. refuse la facilité 355:2
que le vice rend à la v. 407:11
v. traitable 353:25
Verulam: large-brow'd V. 537:37
Verum: inter silvas Academi quaerere v. 257:16
quod enim mavult homo v. esse 28:7
ridentem dicere v. quid vetat? 261:7
Very: v. God of v. God 390:19
Vesper: black v.'s pageants 425:19
Vesper: V. adest, iuvenes 133:7
V. Olympo..lumina tollit 133:7
Vesper-bell: hark the little v. 150:13
Vespers: friars were singing V. 217:1
there's V.l 96:42
Vessel: brave v...dash'd..to pieces 479:19
gilded v. goes 229:23
goodly v. 315:29
in the earthen v. 90:33
like a potter's v. 391:50
made the V. in pure Love 207:18
one v. unto honour 65:60
some V...more ungainly 207:15
v. of the state is driven 499:11
v. puffs her sail 541:3
v. swept towards the reef 318:16
weaker v. 70:2
weigh the v. up 162:12
with his hand the V. made 207:14
wide v. of the universe 444:6
Vessels: treasure in earthen v. 67:23
Vest: burning through the v. 497:9
by port and v. 323:15
casting the body's v. aside 332:20
over the purple v. 324:9
Vestal: blameless v.'s lot 382:5
Vestals: acidulous v. 514:23
Vestibulum ante..in faucibus Orci 554:27
Vestigia: me v. terrent 256:20
Vestry: see you in the v. 504:27
Vesture: as a v. shalt thou change them 398:2
cast lots upon my v. 393:6
muddy v. of decay 465:18
on his v...a name 71:37
Veteran: superfluous lags the v. 279:9
Veterans: world its v. rewards 384:37
Veterum: de Sapientia V. 28:11
Vetitum: ruit per v. nefas 258:6
Vetustas: deserta v. 257:20
nec edax abolere v. 372:1
Vex: hoped it would v. somebody 274:19
public affairs v. no man 275:12
they die to v. me 335:18
v. not his ghost 454:27
v. not thou the poet's mind 537:42
v. the unhappy dust 528:21
Vexari: non quia v. quemquamst iucunda 320:30
Vexation: fierce v. of a dream 467:17
multiplication is v. 8:12
of so infinite v. 563:33
vanity and v. of spirit 50:62
Vexed: Hyades v. the dim sea 540:32
I was not v. 275:12
see how fools are v. 170:21
v. his immortal strength 80:31
Vexes: other v. it 285:35
v. public men 541:21
Vexilla regis prodeunt 210:8
Vexing the dull ear 447:35
Vi: non v. sed saepe cadendo 372:11
Via: temptanda v. est 556:19
Vials: golden v. full of odours 70:42
Viamque adfectat Olympo 556:26
Viator: cantabit vacuus coram latrone v. 283:17
Vibrated: better not be v. 173:20
glorious people v. again 495:25
Vibrates in the memory 499:1
Vibrating: crawling, heaving and v. 235:22
Vibration: ominous v. of a pendulum 282:18
that brave v. 247:13

Viburna: inter v. cupressi 555:18
Vicar: Vicarage, nor the V. 387:22
V. of Bray 7:9
Vice: any taint of v. 484:18
apprehend and consider v. 352:9
boldly rebuke v. 389:53
bullied out of v. 518:4
end in sight was a v. 96:46
Forgiveness of each v. 74:21
in a private man a v. 334:17
lash'd the v. 521:3
lash the v. and follies 134:6
make thine honesty a v. 472:6
my v. is in the dust 8:13
no amusements..but v. and religion 505:11
no distinction..virtue and v. 271:10
no other v. content you? 185:26
no v., but beggary 447:26
nurseries of all v. 204:19
of v. must pardon beg 436:3
old-gentlemanly v. 115:27
only sensual pleasure without v. 277:7
prosperity doth best discover v. 25:21
raptures and roses of v. 522:23
reverend v. 439:35
sanction V. 117:21
spreading V.'s snares 143:17
this v. of lying 442:14
thy body is all v. 270:13
'twixt a v. and folly 300:18
v. is a monster 383:27
v. itself lost half its evil 102:14
v. to know him 437:29
when v. prevails 1:21
where th' extreme of v. 383:27
where v. is virtue 218:6
whirl'd into folly and v. 535:37
Vice: hommage que le v. rend 407:11
Viceroy to that 185:4
Vices: dwelt upon her v. too 41:15
most v...very genteelly 272:26
of our pleasant v. 454:21
of our v...a ladder 316:30
paint the v. and follies 154:29
redeemed his v. with his virtues 280:1
Vici: veni, vidi, v. 120:13
Vicinity: had to leave the v. 10:23
Vicious: can't expect a boy to be v. 414:17
Viciousness: in our v. grow hard 425:2
Vicissitude: sad v. of things 217:17, 513:25
Vicissitudes: v. of fortune 217:13
wild v. of taste 278:36
Vicisti, Galilæe 282:15
Victa Catoni 320:22
Victim: first insults the v. 165:20
v. must be found 219:24
v. o' connubiality 178:37
v. of Parthenia's pride 215:12
Victims: little v. play 230:26
Victis: una salus v. 554:9
vae v. 314:23
Victor: out spoke the v. then 122:6
potent v. in his rage 344:13
their v. vaward wing 418:33
to the v. belong the spoils 329:16
V.'s triumph won 387:12
Victor: v. que..per populos dat iura 556:26
v. que virum volitare per ora 556:19
Victorem: Graecia capta ferum v. cepit 257:14
Victories: after a thousand v. 486:22
peace hath her v. 351:29
victors are by v. undone 192:16
Victorious: great Church v. 517:3
make him v. 250:14
o'er a' the ills..v. 108:6
Victors: v. are by victories undone 192:16
v., when they come 16:20
Victory: every famous v. 507:7
gotten hast the v. 292:20
Grave, thy v.? 8:19, 322:2
grave, where is thy v.? 67:18
honour was the meed of v. 509:35
Joy, Empire, and V. 497:17
life's v. won 373:10
of valour, and of v. 331:2
or to v. 107:32
such another v...undone 25:2
such a v. as this 564:9

Victory (cont.)
that dishonest v. 351:16
to my song v. and praise 494:1
Truth beareth away the v. 56:16
v. at all costs 143:39
v...greatest tragedy 564:10
v. in him 194:8
v. is not a name strong enough 362:19
v. is twice itself 467:37
V. was gone 237:15
Westminster Abbey or v. 362:17
without v...no survival 143:39
Victrix causa deis placuit 320:22
Victuals: difficult to please about their v. 121:7
I live on broken v. 174:19
v. and drink to me 174:29
v. and the wine 121:9
we have no v. 543:8
Victum: fundit humo facilem v. 556:15
Video meliora, proboque 371:30
Videri: se cupit ante v. 555:26
Vides: Jupiter est quodcumque v. 320:26
Vidi: ut v., ut perii 556:4
veni, v., vici 120:13
Virgilium tantum v. 372:6
Vieille: quand vous serez bien v. 408:18
Vieillesse: si v. pouvoit 201:30
View: command an uninterrupted v. 177:32
do you admire the v.? 130:18
earth's majestic v. 355:14
invisible, we v. thee 545:1
learned commentators v. 521:17
lends enchantment to the v. 122:31
not fair to outward v. 148:12
Pickwickian point of v. 178:23
rapture of the forward v. 336:45
so absurd a v. 121:10
that lovely face who v. 15:18
thrilling v. of the surplice-question 90:29
transported with the V. 2:22
v. him with scornful..eyes 385:29
v. with hollow eye 465:9
v. yourselves in..self-love 334:27
wide and luminous v. 17:5
View-hollo: Peel's v. 229:16
Viewing: by v. nature 191:29
v. him since 280:10
Viewless: v. forms of air 417:7
v. wings of Poesy 287:19
Views: full of stately v. 296:30
give new v. to life 164:34
her happy v. 532:24
take short v. 504:23
Vigil: tongueless v. 521:30
yearly on the v. 444:28
Vigilance: condition..eternal v. 167:26
Vigilant: be sober, be v. 70:6
haughty, v. resolute 324:15
v. as a cat 440:22
Vigils: mine eyes their v. keep 361:17
poets painful v. keep 381:13
Vigny plus secret 414:7
Vigor: igneus est ollis v. 554:31
Vigorous: conservatives when..least v 200:25
her v. souls 123:7
Vigour: she has a secret v. 200:3
v. from our arms 101:17
v. from the limb 113:23
v. of bone 481:21
v. of the Lord 517:9
Vikings: stir the V.' blood 293:16
Vile: be he ne'er so v. 444:28(-445)
better to be v. than v. esteem'd 488:10
fled from this v. world 487:15
George the First..v. 309:11
make v. things precious 453:11
only man is v. 240:18
O v., intolerable 479:11
to the v. seem v. 454:1
v. phrase 432:41
what of v. dust? 141:19
who is here so v.? 450:11
you are a v. Whig 272:9
Vilely: show v. in me 441:32
Vileness: no inner v. 532:28
Viler George the Second 300:11
Vilest things become themselves 424:9

Vilia miretur vulgus 371:20
Vilikins and his Dinah 10:18
Villa: if one must have a v. 358:19
Village: fast from every v. round 322:22
  first in a v. 24:29
  loveliest v. of the plain 224:12
  some v.-Hampden 230:5
  sound of v. bells 253:15
  through an Alpine v. 316:17
  vegetate in a v. 154:22
  v. atheist..over the v. idiot 142:19
  v. in the country 9:19
  v. less than Islington 158:22
Villagers: priests..the v. 310:23
Villages: among the pleasant v. 349:11
Villain: alone the v. of the earth 425:11
  call rogue and v. 194:17
  condemns me for a v. 476:36
  demd v. 177:21
  determined to prove a v. 476:6
  fair terms and a v.'s mind 463:25
  hired a v. to bereave 74:16
  lean-fac'd v. 429:1
  ne'er a v...in all Denmark 432:22
  no v. need be 336:30
  one murder made a v. 387:9
  smile, and be a v. 432:21
  some eternal v. 473:1
  v. and he..asunder 478:28
  v., v., smiling, damned v. 432:21
  wretch, a v. 105:1
Villainous: company, v. company 440:12
  that's v. 434:22
Villains by necessity 452:18
Villainton: Wellington! (or 'V.') 116:26
Villainy: clothe my naked v. 476:12
  in me 'tis v. 424:18
  O v.!..let the door be lock'd 437:39
  v. you teach me 464:9
Villatic: tame v. fowl 351:2
Villiers: great V. lies 385:1
Villon, our sad bad..brother 522:18
Vinces: in hoc signo v. 156:20
Vinci: spell it V. 550:14
Vinculum: commune v. 145:15
Vindicate the ways of God 383:8
Vindicta nemo magis gaudet quam
  femina 284:2
Vindictive scribble of red 91:17
Vine: best fits a little v. 245:18
  Daughter of the V. to Spouse 206:23
  eat..under his own v. 447:14
  every man under his v. 56:6
  foxlike in the v. 539:4
  gadding v. 342:14
  laurel, ivy, v. 336:38
  luscious clusters of the v. 332:17
  maize and v. 528:23
  mantling v. 347:7
  monarch of the v. 424:19
  Ruby kindles in the V. 205:11
  thy wife..as the fruitful v. 399:36
  V. her ancient Ruby yields 205:9
  wild v. slipping down 522:3
Vinegar: gave me v. to drink 396:19
  oil, v., sugar 225:25
  pepper and v. besides 130:17
  v. aspect 462:30
Vine-leaves in his hair 267:3
Vines: beggars, fleas, and v. 293:10
  bless with fruit the v. 284:10
  France with all her v. 162:44
  spoil the v. 52:2
  where Southern v. are drest 241:9
Vineyard: my wellbeloved hath a
  v. 52:37
  who planteth a v.? 66:34
Vino: in v. veritas 380:2
  neque dulci mala v. lavere 260:6
Vintage: better than the v. of Abi-
  ezer 46:53
  for a draught of v. 287:24
  from his V. rolling Time 206:7
  of all their V. prest 206:6
  trampling out the v. 264:15
Vintager: since Ariadne was a v. 285:2
Vintners: farewell..the V. buy 207:22
Vinum: poesy v. dæmonum 24:25
  v. sit appositum sitienti ori 13:9
Viol: unstringed v. 474:14
Violence: blown with restless v. 462:9

Violence (cont.)
  by v. constrained to do anything 198:3
  essence of war is v. 324:23
  kingdom..suffereth v. 59:7
  show of v. 430:17
  swift without v. 401:22
Violent: all v. feelings..falseness 412:26
  over v., or over civil 190:23
  put it to a v. death 202:2
  v. delights have v. ends 478:8
  v. hands upon themselves 391:40
  v. take it by force 59:7
  virtue in ambition is v. 26:27
Violently: v. if they must 404:24
  v. to their place 26:27
Violet: dew that on the v. lies 417:26
  fashioned an April v. 561:9
  glowing v. 342:31(-343)
  grave's one v. 94:45
  nodding v. grows 466:41
  perfume on the v. 447:39
  she is the v. 502:19
  v., amaracus, and asphodel 537:31
  v. by a mossy stone 580:18
  v. in the youth 431:20
  v. of his native land 532:14
  v. smells to him as..to me 444:18
Violet-embroidered vale 340:13
Violets: by ashen roots the v. 533:24
  daisies pied and v. blue 455:35
  fast fading v. 287:31
  I would give you some v. 436:32
  may v. spring 437:20
  not like to mix v. 182:13
  roses and lilies and v. 36:26
  upon a bank of v. 481:30
  v., and the lily-cups 253:1
  v. blue as your eyes 536:12
  v. dim 485:26
  v. of the Undercliff 296:15
  v' reclining head 184:29
  v. suddenly bloom 42:4
  when sweet v. sicken 499:1
  where early v. die 418:12
  who are the v. now 475:30
  wind-flowers, and v. 494:10, 497:21
  with v. playing 293:21
Violin: flute, v., bassoon 536:11
Violins: dance to v. 569:5
  make Antonio Stradivari's v. 197:1
Viper: Lawyer killing a v. 151:10
Viperous: deaf and v. murderer 492:4
Vipers: extirpate the v. 23:26
  generation of v. 57:30
Virenti: donec v. canities 258:15
Virga: simili frondescit v. metallo 554:24
Virgil: English V. 291:16
  Rome thy V.'s name 160:24
  shepherd in V. 270:17
  V...'his eye on the object' 20:3
Virgilio: or se' tu quel V.? 168:16
Virgilium vidi tantum 372:6
Virgin: bashful v.'s side-long looks 224:13
  every harlot..a v. once 74:22
  God's v. 411:27
  listening v.'s heart 202:4
  pale V. shrouded in snow 76:7
  see the V. blest 343:25
  steps of v. liberty 580:20
  though a v., yet a bride 125:5
  v. shall conceive 53:12
  wedded maid, and v. mother 343:9
  withering on the v. thorn 466:17
Virginal, and unprofaned 376:2
Virginalling upon his palm 485:7
Virgin-daughter of the skies 192:37
Virgin'd it e'er since 429:19
Virginia: no sweeter tobacco..
  from V. 542:41
Virginian: not a V., but an American 242:17
Virginians: rally behind the V. 39:2
Virginibus puerisque canto 259:14
Virginity: borne into v. 583:26
  long preserved v. 333:9
  rash oath of v. 375:8
Virgins: farewell..ye v. all 30:4
  Martyrs, Prophets, V. 361:11
  of..V. none is fairer seen 376:3
  v. are soft as the roses 113:2
  v. in their ecstasies 530:31

Virgins (cont.)
  v. love thee 51:38
  v. that be her fellows 394:25
Virgin-widow 193:18
Virgo: 'ave, V.!' Gr-r-r 96:42
  iam redit et v. 555:30
  in omne v. nobilis aevum 260:5
Viris: moribus antiquis..v. que 201:25
  v. que adquirit eundo 554:16
Virtue: adversity doth best discover v. 25:21
  along with order and v. 100:13
  as other men after v. 307:6
  assume a v. 436:5
  beggar's v. 334:25
  being rich, my v. then shall be 447:26
  blunder'd on some v. 143:17
  call v. there ungratefulness? 501:25
  change to v. and to worthiness 449:1
  every v., every grace 308:14
  flattered into v. 518:4
  forbearance ceases to be a v. 101:38
  from mere natural v. 363:26
  fugitive and cloistered v. 352:9
  gaze on v. and on me 324:17
  greatest offence against v. 239:27
  he must delight in v. 1:23
  her v., and..her worth 348:37
  if there be any v. 68:27
  if v. feeble were 341:5
  in a prince, the v. 334:17
  in beauty and v. 502:19
  in conscious v. bold 381:6
  into words no v. can digest 331:2
  in V.'s name let Crabbe attest 117:26
  keep your v. 297:12
  lean'd to V.'s side 224:21
  let that arm thy v. 412:16
  lilies and languors of v. 522:23
  link'd with one v. 115:7
  lost fight of v. 513:32
  lovers of v. 559:27
  love v., she alone is free 341:5
  make ambition v. 472:3
  make v. unamiable 512:3
  more v. than doth live 280:11
  much v. in 'if' 428:38
  murder, hate, v., and sin 328:2
  my mouse of v. 482:14
  no distinction between v. and
  vice 271:10
  no. v. like necessity 474:19
  O infinite v.! 425:13
  only amaranthine flower..v. 163:15
  patched with v. 482:13
  ready way to v. 86:23
  redeem us from v. 523:3
  sinews of v. 559:17
  sin in loving v. 462:1
  soldier's v. 424:20
  some by v. fall 461:24
  some v., v. to commend 155:4
  tart, cathartic v. 200:17
  that household v. 119:19
  thy mind all v. 270:13
  upgrowth of all v. 294:3
  v.! a fig! 470:15
  v. alone is happiness 384:13
  v. alone is true nobility 217:20
  v. and human knowledge 495:14
  v., and not birth 38:3
  v. cannot live 449:26
  v. could see to do what v. would 340:20
  v. had gone out of him 61:1
  V. he had vow'd to win 375:22
  v. in ambition is violent 26:27
  v. in her shape how lovely 347:31
  v. is bold 462:13
  v. is like a rich stone 25:27
  v. is the fount 330:29
  v. itself of vice must pardon beg 436:3
  v. may be assailed 340:30
  v. of fools 25:11
  v. of wax and parchment 101:1
  v. of weak minds 192:35
  v. rudely strumpeted 487:14
  v. she finds too painful 384:34
  V. solely is the sum of glory 331:2
  v. that possession would not
  show 469:5
  v. that transgresses 482:13

INDEX

Virtue (cont.)
v...to be ever guarded   227:19
v...Trade Unionism of the married   490:24
v. with the Roman clergy   294:4
where vice is v.   218:6
whose solid v.   472:32
without eradicating the v.   226:31
Virtues: credited with all the v.   243:17
crimes, like v...own rewards   203:22
curse on his v.l   1:20
for several v...several women   479:44
his v. walk'd their..round   275:3
his v. were his arts   101:28
his v. will plead like angels   457:9
if our v. did not go forth   461:16
in v. nothing..surpass her   115:15
in war the two cardinal v.   248:22
makes some v. impracticable   275:5
mentioned her v.   41:15
my verse your v. rare   509:7
our v. barren   513:30
our v. would be proud   423:7
Princedoms, V., Powers   348:14
redeemed his vices with his v.   280:1
their v. we write in water   447:8
to her v. very kind   401:26
trumpet of his own v.   469:17
v. neglected then   164:30
v. well did suit   189:3
v. which mine eyes had seen   579:29
world to hide v. in?   482:9
Virtuous: all the Sisters v.   363:9
because thou art v.   482:32
be..v., and you will be happy   211:7
boy be v. still   164:13
gentle and v. deeds   328:1
grow v. in their old age   387:1, 520:48
harbours v. thought   509:23
his v. couch   560:8
knead two v. souls   116:20
nor treat with v. scorn   219:1
not astound the v. mind   340:10
outrageously v.   511:22
pass for a most v. Dame   401:24
seeming-v. eye   118:9
sweet and v. soul   245:14
v. and wise he was   14:23
v. things you do   140:4
v. woman is a crown   50:1
what the truly v. crave   223:7
who can find a v. woman?   50:57
Virtuousest: wisest, v.   349:1
Virtus: et coelum, et v.   320:26
quid v. et quid sapientia possit   256:23
v. est vitium fugere   256:17
v. repulsae nescia sordidae   259:19
Virtutem videant   378:3
Virtutibus opstat res angusta domi   283:5
Virum: arma v.que cano   553:5
magna Parens..v.   556:14
Vis: v. consili expers   259:28
vivida v. animi pervicit   320:27
Vishnu-land: in V. what Avatar?   97:19
Visage: all his v. wann'd   433:31
confront the v. of offence   435:33
dejected 'haviour of the v.   430:30
hides not his v. from our cottage   485:31
never see more in the v.   328:18
of a lean body and v.   212:16
Othello's v. in his mind   470:10
Sir Launcelot saw her v.   328:21
Visages: whose v. do cream   462:33
Visible: all things v. and invisible   390:18
Arch Fear in a v. form   95:9
darkness v.   344:9
outward and v. sign   391:13
power of Armies..v.   581:18
rolled with v. motion   575:26
v. silence   410:29
Visibly: swellin' v.   179:9
v. through his garden walketh   96:33
Vision: as thy v. here solicited   522:12
baseless fabric of this v.   480:8
bright the v.   329:12
by the v. splendid   576:9
double the v.   74:5
fatal v., sensible to feeling   457:20
great V. of the guarded mount   343:2
in a v. once I saw   151:33(−152)
latest-born and loveliest v.   288:4

Vision (cont.)
more delightful v.   102:11
my v.'s greatest enemy   74:10
my v.'s limited   179:16
my v. with the song   336:2
saw the V. of the world   534:25
such as v. builds   495:27
things, as in that v. seem   265:22
v. and the faculty   574:10
v. beatific   345:9
v. glorious   517:3
V. of Christ   74:10
v. of some person   268:8
v. raised its head   265:16
was it a v.?   288:2
watch or a v.   522:7
what stately v. mocks   504:7
where there is no v.   50:52
write the v.   56:9
young men's v.   190:18
Visionary: thy v. joys remove   155:35
v. blessing   215:37
v. brain   251:11
v. power   579:17, 25
Visions: I have multiplied v.   55:49
lost in stormy v.   492:6
v. before midnight   85:22
v. of glory   229:25
what v. have I seen!   467:18
your young men..see v.   55:52
Visit: his annual v.   546:26
his ready v. pays   536:29
v. Cambridge first   28:20
v. her face too roughly   430:33(−431)
v. thee never   507:15
v. the fatherless   69:34
v. them more   526:23
v. the sins of the fathers   390:7
what thy short v. meant   307:34
Visitation: her nightly v.   349:5
in rarest v.   497:3
in the time of their v.   56:24
v. of the winds   442:1
Visitations: Aeolian v.   579:1
Visited: sick, and ye v. me   60:33
v. all night by..stars   151:29
Visitest: that thou v. him   392:10
v. my slumbers nightly   348:23
v. the bottom of the..world   343:2
Visiting: beneath the v. moon   425:29
Visitings: compunctious v. of nature   457:3
Visits: like angels' v.   365:8
v. like those of angels   73:13
Viso: I pensieri stretti ed il v. sciolto   583:14
Vista: at the end of every v.   102:16
Visum: dis aliter v.   554:10
Vita: cammin di nostra v.   168:15
Vita: v. brevis   414:21
v. hominum praesens   38:31
Vitae: da spatium v.   283:23
fallentis semita v.   257:10
integer v.   258:22
oblivia v.   261:25
viam..quaerere v.   320:30(−321)
v. summa brevis   258:9
Vital: give it v. growth again   473:11
Vitality: not v. enough to preserve it   275:27
v. in a woman   490:14
Vitals: feed thee out of my own v.   155:12
stab our very v.   388:2
Vitam: det v., det opes   257:11
propter v. vivendi perdere causas   283:14
si v. puriter egi   133:15
Vite: quand on a à mourir..le plus v.   354:3
Vitiis: de v. nostris scalam   22:6
Vitio parentum rara   258:3
Vitiosiorem: progeniem v.   260:1
Vitium: virtus est v. fugere   256:17
Vitreous: earth of the v. pour   567:17
Vitro: splendidior v.   260:7
Vitruvius: best V.   192:10
Vivam: dicere 'V.'   331:22
mihi v. quod superest aevi   257:11
Vivamus, mea Lesbia   132:15
Vive: il faut que je v.   14:11, 412:3
v. l'amour! et v. la bagatelle!   512:22
V. l'Intérieur!   422:16
Vive hodie   331:22

Vivere: illic v. vellem   257:3
non est v., sed valere   331:27
tecum v. amem   260:4
v. si recte nescis   257:21
Vivid: dusky, v., true   516:6
Vivida: ergo v. vis animi pervicit   320:27
Vividly: saw them v.   268:8
Vivified by Thee   355:14
Vivre: manger pour v.   353:10
mon art, c'est v.   355:1
Vixi: cras vel atra nube..   260:14
Vizards to our hearts   459:5
Vizor'd falsehood   340:33
V-notes are something   93:31
Vobis: vos non v. mellificatis apes   556:27
Vocabula: proferet in lucem speciosa v.   257:20
quae nunc sunt in honore v.   255:20
Vocabulary of 'Bradshaw'   188:27
Vocation: his whole v...imitation   576:11
to labour in his v.   438:25
worthy of the v.   67:56
Vogel: wie der V. singt   224:2
Vogue: totter into v.   558:19
Vogue la galère!   405:1
Voice: aggravate my v.   466:30
all with one v.   65:8
audible v. of the Past   126:27
await another v.   197:14
behind me a great v.   70:23
bird..carry the v.   51:26
bridegroom's v.   63:11
broken v.   433:31
but a wandering v.   573:19
by only raising my v.   22:17
City's v...like solitude   498:21
clear sonorous v.   574:27
daughter of the v. of God   573:28
delivered o'er to the v.   442:21
distant v. in the darkness   318:10
dread v. is past   342:30
each a mighty V.   581:13
echoes back the public v.   279:1
echoes of that v.   151:6
floods have lift up their v.   397:23
for a falconer's v.   477:25
give..few thy v.   431:25
God hath shewed his v.   394:28
happy-noted v.   285:34
healing v. of Christian charity   102:5
heard the v. of..God   44:21
heart, and soul, and v.   361:21
heart and v. would fail me   35:11
hear the v. of the Bard   75:23
her v., and her hair   333:19
her v., her touch   566:19
her v. revives the..strings   123:21
her v. the harmony of the world   253:36
her v. was ever soft   454:24
his big manly v.   427:21
his sweet v. he rears   150:8
His that gentle v.   21:9
his v. as..many waters   70:27
his v. in all her music   492:9
his v. was buried among trees   578:11
his v. was propertied   426:1
if ye will hear his v.   397:29
I have lost my v.   563:36
is, and it is not, the v. of God   386:14
I thought I knew the v.   302:14
joy is the sweet v.   151:6
know thy v.   496:9
let thy v. rise   531:36
lift up your v.   565:11
Lord, hear my v.   399:32
melting v.   342:8
methought I heard a v.   458:11
monstrous little v.   466:27
more weighty v...as by chance   25:42
Mountains' slumbrous v.   496:2
my v. ascending high   562:7
my v...lost it with hollaing   441:21
no magic of her v.   376:6
no v.; but oh!   150:7
no v. but the v. of complaining   359:6
no v. hed sech a swing   319:25
no v. or hideous hum   343:21
only a look and a v.   318:10
our song is the v. of desire   81:19
people's v. is odd   386:14
rise up at the v. of the bird   51:33

INDEX

Voice (*cont.*)

season'd with a gracious v. 464:14
send out his v...a mighty v. 396:15
singest with v. memorial 136:19
sisters, V. and Verse 351:9
so charming left his v. 348:29
so in a v...angels affect us 184:4
sole daughter of his v. 349:14
so silv'ry is thy v. 247:14
still small v. 48:8
still small v. makes answer 324:18
still small v. spake unto me 540:24
such a tender v. 76:10
supplicating v. 279:12
sweeter thy v. 539:5
sweet v., sweet lips 289:1
that V. is round me 544:28
this is the same v. 95:36
thou hadst a v...like the sea 577:15
thrilling v. is sounding 132:5
thy gentle v. my spirit..cheer 314:18
thy v. and hand shake still 411:10
thy v. did weave songs 499:9
thy v. is heard 538:22
thy v., thy lute 288:6
uttereth her v. in the streets 49:39
utter forth a glorious V. 2:28
V. above their beat 544:19
v. and the shape of a woman 290:5
V. beat more instant 544:14
I hear this passing night 288:1
v. in every wind 230:25
v. is Jacob's v. 45:1
v. less loud 93:22
v. of a god 64:49
v. of all the gods 455:22
V. of Cato is the v. of Rome 279:26
v. of him that crieth 54:9
v. of joy and health 399:8
v. of my beloved 52:9
v. of my complaint 393:1
v. of my heart 166:24
v. of one beloved 497:3
v. of one crying 57:28
v. of reason is stifled 103:20
v. of the charmer 395:20
v. of the dead was a living v. 533:33
v. of the great Creator 128:3
v. of the lobster 129:25
v. of the Lord maketh.. 393:23
v. of the people hath some divineness 25:8
v. of the people..v. of God 3:10, 406:16
v. of the schoolboy 363:5
v. of the sluggard 562:3
v. of the turtle 52:1
v. of thy brother's blood 44:31
v. said, Cry 54:10
v. said in mastery 88:16
v. so sweet 282:3
v. so thrilling 581:1
v. that breathed o'er Eden 291:15
v. that is still 528:3
v. will run from hedge to hedge 288:22
V. within the Tavern 205:6, 7
v. without reply 199:27
v. you cannot hear 547:21
wake thy wild v. anew 419:2
what v. did on my spirit fall 147:5
when I shall v. aloud 319:7
wild v. pealing up 535:39
with cheerful v. 292:7
Voiced like a great bell 208:2
Voiceless: in her v. woe 114:13
Voices: ancestral v. prophesying 151:33(–152)
beyond these v. 530:20
compare their v. and beauties 370:17
earth, with her thousand v. 151:30
great V. roll in 549:2
I hear their gentle v. 210:17
I thank you for your v...most sweet 429:10
moans round with many v. 541:3
no v...not soon mute 309:13
our v. keep tune 357:16
their v. are heard 392:32
two V. are there 512:6, 581:13
v. of children 76:14
wailing in your v. 88:26

Voices (*cont.*)

when soft v. die 499:1
which angel v. tell 339:8
with heart and hands and v. 571:21
Void: beating in the v. his..wings 19:21
cast as rubbish to the v. 532:32
conscience v. of offence 65:18
left an aching v. 161:2
nor left a v. 275:3
that his might could render v. 83:12
v. as vain 233:3
v., dark and drear 150:31
v. of cares and strife 378:17
v. of light 344:18
v. of strife 192:13
without form, and v. 44:1
Vois: ma sœur Anne, ne v.-tu rien? 377:32
Vol: la propriété c'est le v. 402:19
Volaterrae: from lordly V. 323:11
Volcanoes: range of exhausted 181:2
v. burnt out 101:31
Volitare: virum v. per ora 556:19
Volition: particular v. of the Deity 265:6
Volkes: das Opium des V. 333:13
Volley'd and thunder'd 528:17
Volleying: come with the v. rain 18:25
Volo: hoc v., sic iubeo 283:9
Volontade: e'n la sua v. è nostra pace 168:26
Volonté: il gît en votre v. 354:20
Volscians: flutter'd your V. 429:23
Voltaire: mock on, V. 75:17
that moderate man V. 236:24
Volubility: commend her v. 479:4
Voluisse: in magnis et v. sat est 402:16
Volume: destroyed this world in one v. 505:23
in the v. of the book 394:13
little v., but large book 166:8
many a quaint and curious v. 380:22
over my open v. 309:4
this fair v. 189:25
to lose a v. to C[oleridge]. 306:22
v. of all the seas 480:27
v. of nature 226:20
wrote them in a certain v. 93:45
Volumes: all Earth's v. carry 135:26
Balzac..fifty v. long 89:29
pricks to their subsequent v. 481:8
such v. of stuff 311:9
v. of Addison 278:9
v. that I prize above my dukedom 479:23
whole v. in folio 455:1
Volumnius: thou seest the world, V. 452:5
Voluntary move harmonious numbers 346:20
Voluntas: pro ratione v. 283:9
v. *jus suum cuique tribuens* 282:22
Voluptas: trahit sua quemque v. 555:23
Voluptuous: music..its v. swell 113:25
v. Waltz 119:28
Voluptuousness: misanthropy and v. 325:18
Vomit: dog returneth to his v. 50:39
dog..to his own v. 70:9
when you v. forth 330:9
Vomitam: los malos la v. 134:19
Vomits its wrecks 495:9
Vorpal sword..vorpal blade 129:39(–130)
Vortex of immensity 176:26
Votaress: imperial v. 466:39
Votarist: sad v. in palmer's weed 340:8
Votary of the desk 306:18
Vote: hunt, and v. 112:27
lives he will v. away 84:27(–85)
Townshend to lend him a v. 225:27
Voted: v. at my party's call 221:17
year after year they v. 112:28
Votes: counting v. instead of weighing 267:6
price of v. 279:3
Voti..succedere partem mente dedit 555:12
Votis: hoc erat in v. 261:24
Voudrais: fay ce que v. 404:28
Voulu: vous l'avez v. 353:22
Vovi—I've Oude 403:11
Vow: better..not v., than..v. and not pay 51:7
do not v. 202:1

Vow (*cont.*)

I v. to thee, my country 511:4
that great v. which did incorporate 449:16
v. I made to her in marriage 432:14
Vowels: open v. tire 382:30
Vows: cancel all our v. 189:20
heaven v. to keep him 280:10
honey of his music v. 434:14
keep all v. unbroke 475:23
lends the tongue v. 431:27
much in our v. 483:10
our v., our prayers 183:20
patience, alms, v. 255:6
rival amorous v. 82:4
take the tongueless v. 543:16
to our moist v. denied 343:2
v. can't change nature 95:33
v. of returning 526:23
v., to the blackest devil 436:28
v. with so much passion 312:28
when lovers' v. seem sweet 118:28
Vox: v. populi, v. dei 3:10, 406:16
Voyage: biscuit after a v. 427:16
drear was the v. 415:6
its v. closed and done 566:28
life's uncertain v. 480:31
my last v. 249:2
never thus could v. on 494:22
v. of their life 451:29
Voyage: fait un beau v. 40:17
Voyager: lands the v. at last 198:14
Voyager: besion de v. 512:18
Voyaging through strange seas 579:19
Vulcan: foul as V.'s stithy 435:1
V. and his whole forge sweat 85:17
Vulgar: all is v., all clumsy 147:18
by no means v. 431:25
cocoa is a v. beast 142:9
criterion of wisdom to v. judgments 103:2
Eno..abominably v. 514:2
father is rather v. 176:1
great v., and the small 158:24
in the v. tongue 390:55
little v. Boy 34:23
no terms of moderation..with the v. 25:10
such a v. expression 154:31
v. and tavern music 86:33
v. authors in romances 110:44
v. languages that want words 281:27
v. way of coition 86:34
war..looked upon as v. 569:33
with v. brains to dwell 502:2
work upon the v. 386:38
worse than wicked..v. 403:23
ye may ca' them v. farin' 360:14
Vulgarity: Jacksonian v. 387:13
Vulgarize the day of judgment 260:13
Vulgus: odi profanum v. 259:14
Vulnera: enumerat miles v. 402:15
Vulpes: quod v. aegroto cauta leoni 256:20
Vulture: rage of the v. 113:1
Vultus: non v. instantis tyranni 259:21

W

W: 'V' or a 'W'? 179:13
Wabe: gimble in the w. 129:39
Wacht: die W. am Rhein 416:2
Waddy is an infectious disease 304:51
Wade: should I w. no more 459:25
w. through slaughter 230:6
Waded thro' red blude 32:11
Wades: swims or sinks, or w. 346:14
Wading in bells and grass 249:7
Wafer-cakes: mens' faiths are w. 443:23
Waffen: ein gute Wehr und W. 321:6
Waft her love to Carthage 465:17
Wafted downward 316:7
Wafture of your hand 449:14
Wag: mother's w. 232:2
tail must w. the dog 295:15
when beards w. all 442:33
Wage: for which they drew the w. 303:15
royal w. 83:20
Wages: apportioning of w. to work 126:44
content with your w. 61:23

[975]

INDEX

Wages (*cont.*)
give you my scanty w.   489:28
my w. taken   241:23
ta'en thy w.   430:1
took their w. and are dead   264:4
w. beauty gives   586:13
w. of going on   541:17
w. of sin is death   65:46
Wagged his tail   249:20
Waggest: tongue..thou w.   527:12
Wagging: better a finger off, as ay w.   420:11
Waggon: hitch your w. to a star   201:14
let'st fall from Dis's w.   485:26
Waggoner: her w...grey-coated gnat   477:7
Waggons: their cany w.   346:23
Waggon-spokes: her w...spinners' legs   477:7
Wags: how the world w.   427:13
w. that judge by rote   371:11
we..are w. too   441:18
Wahrheit: die reine W. ist..für Dich allein   313:18
in seiner Rechten alle W.   313:18
Wail: all kindreds..shall w.   70:22
nothing to w.   351:6
suffice to w. their scorn   168:12
w. my dear times' waste   486:25
yet so does w.   321:15
Wailers heap   88:20
Wailing: deeply w.   565:14
w. for her demon-lover   151:32
w. in your voices   88:26
Wain: wheels of Phoebus' w.   340:8
Waist: dead from the w. down   91:42
fifteen arms went round her w.   333:23
her slender w. confin'd   558:1
his arm around her w.   219:17
round her w. she felt it   528:28
to thy slender w.   401:32
you live about her w.   433:10
Waistcoat: any w. but a yellow w.   177:16
get her a flannel w.   213:22
Waistcoat-buttons: work them into w.   131:24
Waistcoats: negroes..with flannel w.   178:43
Wait: could not w. their passing   18:24
if you can w.   297:10
is this a time to w.?   23:23
lily whispers, 'I w.'   536:15
now ye w. at Heaven's Gate   302:22
only stand and w.   351:21
on Occasion's forelock..w.   350:6
she'll w. a wee   108:31
these w. all upon thee   398:11
they that w. upon the Lord   54:14
to labour and to w.   317:8
to w., to ride, to run   510:16
w. and see   21:5
w. and see, O sons of glory   324:18
w. in heavy harness   303:24
w. many years   510:16
w. the 'pointed hour   193:30
w. the turning of the phials   411:16
w. Thy word of peace   198:16
w., till one   141:2
w. till the clouds roll by   572:20
w. upon her   247:11
w. upon Mary's Sons   302:1
w. upon the tedious shores   306:7
we can w. no longer   567:2
would not w. for me   263:2
Waited: hand that w. for the heart   196:24
w., duteous, on them all   417:3
w. in a row   130:15
w. patiently for the Lord   394:12
Waiter: if you look at the w.   178:26
Waiting: long night of w.   293:1
man's w. for a answer   174:20
w. for the Earl of Chatham   6:16
w. for the long-promised invasion   144:3
w. for the Sleary babies   300:21
w. for the spark   18:10
w. revenge   345:7
w. time   187:3
with patience He stands w.   315:22, 317:13
Waiting-gentlewoman: so like a w.   438:35

Waits: goin' ware glory w. ye   319:16
w. upon the judgment   435:47
Waive: w. the quantum o' the sin   105:19
w. the Rest   205:25
Wake: do I w. or sleep?   288:2
I'd go and w. them, if—   131:12
sleeping hound to w.   138:31
sleep to w.   97:4
survived her own w.   325:29
those who w. and live   495:18
thou wilt not w.   292:19
w. a lexicographer   277:23
w. for thee   155:27
W.! for the Sun   205:5
w. him up and put him outside   269:2
w. the soul   381:6
w. thy wild voice anew   419:2
w. up, America   213:6
w. up, England   216:15
we w. and whisper awhile   171:1
we w. eternally   185:16
will you w. him?   367:15
you will w., and remember   91:22
Waked: I w., she fled   351:26
I w. to find her   348:35
w. to do it   453:19
w. to ecstasy   230:4
you have w. me too soon   562:3
Waked'st: thou w. me wisely   184:12
Wakeful: all but the w. nightingale   347:19
Waken: w. from his summer dreams   496:8
w. the dead   229:16
w. the Wall   301:29
w. thou with me   539:2
Wakened: fairer than any w. eyes behold   497:22
w. us from sleeping   84:16
Wakening: our w. and uprising   291:4
Wakes: he haunts w.   485:20
he lives, he w.   492:8
he w. or sleeps   492:5
hock-carts, wassails, w.   245:17
love w. men   374:23
my old sorrow w.   267:11
one work that w.   255:9
or w., as may betide   262:11
w. it now?   457:11
whoever w. in England   92:14
Wordsworth sometimes w.   116:6
Waketh: my heart w.   52:9
Waking: are ye w. yet?   503:1
certainty of w. bliss   340:16
good-morrow to our w. souls   185:7
nights of w.   416:19
not w. till she sings   321:16
remembered on w.   81:9
thought upon thee when I was w.   395:26
w. dream   288:2
w., no such matter   487:22
w. or asleep   498:9
w. with day   417:33
Wakings: agreeable w.   156:12
Wales: God bless the Prince of W.   314:19
golden sea of W.   208:6
he w. a portion   105:4
one road runs to W.   334:8
Walk: as you w. your mystic way   220:26
can two w. together   55:54
doom'd..to w. the night   432:8
far as the solar w.   383:11
feet have they, and w. not   399:4
for a closer w.   161:1
I w. abroad o' nights   330:16
I w. down the Strand   238:1
I w. my beat   301:6
I w. unseen   341:14
me to w. doth make   421:1
monkeys w. together   298:20
my steps, which way they w.   458:1
my very w. should be a jig   482:8
no spirit can w. abroad   430:20
now w. the angels   331:3
slow silent w.   236:14
spiritual creatures w. the earth   347:24
take a w. down Fleet Street   414:20
take up thy bed, and w.   63:16
talk with you, w. with you   463:16
that I may w. before God   395:16
think which way to w.   333:8

Walk (*cont.*)
this is the way, w. ye in it   53:42
though I w. in death's..vale   421:11
though I w. through the valley   393:10
w. about Sion   394:35
w. along the Bois Boulong   217:23
w., and not faint   54:14
w. and wot not what they are   454:32
w. at least before they dance   386:8
w. before thee like a sow   441:11
w. in fear and dread   150:2
w. in silk attire   77:22
w. in the same all..my life   391:2
w. into my parlour   264:23
w. on still in darkness   397:4
w. that afternoon   374:24
w. together to the kirk   150:15
w. uncowed   295:7
w. upon England's mountains   75:16
w. while ye have the light   63:46
w. with Death and Morning   539:4
w. within the purlieus of the Law   201:33
w. with Kings   297:12
w. with you and talk with you   208:18
we w. by faith   67:25
where'er you w.   385:7
where we used to w.   32:17
will you w. a little faster?   129:22
within one minute's w. of   177:32
Walked: as I w. through the wilderness   99:3
Enoch w. with God   44:35
hast thou w. about   504:1
hast thou w. in the search   49:22
Him that w. the waves   343:3
him who w. in glory   580:7
no man hath w. along our roads   308:17
not w. above a mile or two   552:3
once w. down a street   304:50
one before him w. very crookedly   519:1
people that w. in darkness   53:14
w. away with their clothes   180:16
w. by himself   304:21
w. in the house of God   395:12
w. owre yon garden green   30:15
w. straight out of the ark   504:24
w. their narrow round   275:3
w. with willing foot   516:13
when she has w. before   225:15
Walkedst whither thou wouldest   64:18
Walketh: devil..w. about   70:6
man w. in a vain shadow   394:9
pestilence that w. in darkness   397:18
through his garden w. God   96:33
w. upon the wings   398:8
whatsoever w. through the paths   392:12
Walking: as Joseph was a-w.   5:15
a w. the Devil is gone   151:7, 507:19
by myself w.   307:33
craves wary w.   449:2
devil's w. parody   140:21
dog's w. on his hinder legs   271:16
easy w.   263:18
from w. up and down in it   48:38
God w. in the garden   44:21
I nauseate w.   156:10
men as trees, w.   61:2
seen us w. every day   158:10
two w. baths   166:10
w. all alane   32:15
w. and mincing   52:35
w. by his wild lone   304:22
w. close at hand   130:12
w. dictionary   135:26
w. in an air of glory   552:9
w. in thy chamber   247:14
w., like two angels   81:17
w. on the sea   59:35
w. on the strand   31:24
w. round the fold   77:2
w. so early   420:2
w. up and pacing down   535:10
when I am not w...reading   306:21
Walks: benighted w.   340:20
enjoy such quiet w.   445:42
ever w. attended   340:10
eye Nature's w.   383:8
Gibbon levelled w.   154:13
God w. in mine   85:13
I w. with fifty 'ousemaids   299:14

Walks (*cont.*)

Juno when she w.	281:25
liked the way it w.	405:16
nobody w. much faster	131:17
nothing w. with aimless feet	532:32
she w. in beauty	119:1
she w.—the lady	338:8
she w. the waters	114:43
studious w. and shades	350:11
sun. .w. the fields	337:35
take my w. abroad	561:19
thy spirit w. abroad	452:1
w. round. .a second time	376:17
w. up and down with me	447:34
w. with the tender. .night	567:16
when Tadlow w. the streets	202:10

Wall: backs to the w. 233:20

blue above lane and w.	90:37
bores through his castle w.	475:7
builds. .on the outward w.	463:44
close the w. up	443:24
darkly looked he at the w.	323:16
doesn't love a w.	212:2
Humpty Dumpty sat on a w.	367:5
icicles hang by the w.	456:1
in Jerusalem's w.	75:8
in the office of a w.	474:22
I shall leap over the w.	392:30
on the old oak w.	36:30
on the orchard w.	171:21
our trumpets waken the W.	301:29
reserve the hanging w.	384:5
stood against the w.	537:38
the Lord stood upon a w.	56:3
thou whited w.	65:15
thy body by the w.	16:20
w. all Germany with brass	329:24
w. fell down flat	46:40
w. is strong	569:11
wasps upon a southern w.	161:41
watch the w., my darling	301:18
white-wash'd w.	225:3
without a city w.	4:4

Wallace: wi' W. bled 107:32
Walled round with rocks 523:13
Waller was smooth 386:17

Wallet: his w. lay biforn him 137:21
time hath, my lord, a w. 481:17

Wallow: w. in our sin 12:7
w. naked in. .snow 474:20
Wallowed in a score 185:24

Walls: build thou the w. of Jerusalem 395:10

Devil-defended w.	375:22
flesh which w. about our life	475:7
four great w.	89:16
from thy ancient w.	75:11
grey bare w. lain guestless	523:14
groaning under w.	330:16
labyrinth of w.	495:1
mounted the Troyan w.	465:17
on the outward w.	461:2
on the w. of heaven	331:3
painting thy outward w.	488:20
silver'd the w.	338:13
stone w. do not a prison make	319:7
upon the w. of thine house	399:36
w. have tongues	521:14
w. of beaten brass	448:36
w., palaces, half-cities	114:20
washes its w.	94:32
within the spacious w.	230:19
with w. and towers	151:32
wooden w. are the best w.	157:24

Walnuts: across the w. and the wine 537:3
Walrus and the Carpenter 130:12
Walsinghame: holy land of W. 405:10
Walter: good Sir W. met her 297:19
W., be wise 141:20
Walton: Worthy Friend Mr. Izaak W. 572:21

Waltz: seductive W.! 119:27
swoons to a w. 266:12
voluptuous W.! 119:28
Waltzing Matilda 374:15
Waly: w., w., up the bank 32:18

Wan: w. as primroses 285:7
w. with care 438:11
why so pale and w.? 517:10

Wand: but a w. 344:24

Wand (*cont.*)

gold ring on her w.	356:30
my lance a w.	31:6
thine opiate w.	495:22

Wander: by himself he learned to w. 107:35

let one's thought w.	586:4
might I w. there	81:18
nor forced him w.	146:4
old man's wit may w.	530:1
Road I was to w. in	207:10
thoughts that w. through eternity	345:19
to the wilderness I w.	12:2
w. in that golden maze	193:27
w. in the ways of men	106:27
w. o'er city, and sea	495:22
w. where the Muses haunt	346:19
we will not w. more	535:20
where I would w.	359:5
whither shall I w.?	366:23
whither w. you?	426:19

Wandered: I w. by the brookside 262:9
I w. lonely 577:5
I w. till I died 19:1
w. all our ways 405:12

Wanderer: do not we, W. 18:12
foil'd circuitous w. 17:28(-18)

w. from the narrow way	161:26
w. halts and hears	263:20
w. is man	16:3
weary, wayworn w.	380:17

Wanderest: brag thou w. in his shade 486:18

Wandering: as the bird by w. 50:37

beauty w. on her way	586:18
behold the w. moon	341:14
bind the w. sense	155:1
but a w. voice	573:19
every w. bark	488:7
every w. star	269:28
forget the w. and the pain	208:4
have one with me w.	359:5
leaves, w. astray	497:22
poor w. one!	221:29
restore my w. Love	155:35
sought thee w.	161:10
that w. knight so fair	438:15
vast and w. air	476:15
w. between two worlds	16:7
w. by lone sea-breakers	370:19
w. companionless	495:19
w. in many a coral grove	75:18
w. minstrel I	219:15
w. on a foreign strand	417:22
w. on as loth to die	577:10
w. stars	70:20
w. steps and slow	349:31
w. with the great Mother's train	18:31(-19)
years I've been w. away	356:10

Wanderings: chid their w. 224:19
Wanders: slowly it w.,—pauses 311:16
Wane: know'st no w. 207:28
will she wax and w. 207:29
Waneth: youth w. by increasing 377:4
Waning: beneath a w. moon 151:32
bitter barmaid, w. fast! 541:11
though the world be a-w. 359:6

Want: eternal w. of pence 541:21

first, to get what you w.	504:14
for w. of me	375:18
for w. of thought	192:5
freedom from w.	408:25
going without something you do w.	254:5
House of W.	216:9
I didn't w. to do it	326:13
I'll not w.	421:1
I w. what I w. when I w. it	77:25
known, and do not w. it	270:18
making things which he doesn't w.	254:9
never let you w.	282:7
never w. a friend in need	175:9
never w. some fruit	244:17
not what they w.	167:6
old know what they w.	504:17
ring out the w.	533:20
saying you w. to know	175:30
some hidden w.	498:7

Want (*cont.*)

those who w. it the most	139:16
though much I w.	195:12
thy w. as an armed man	49:47
toil, envy, w.	279:4
to w., to be undone	510:16
w. of a thing. .perplexing	551:6
w. of decency is w. of sense	180:9
w. of human wisdom	310:18
w. of it the fellow	384:7
w. of power to sin	193:16
what can I w. or need?	245:10
what do you w.?	369:17
with w. of genius curst	192:10

Wanted: go where you are w. 263:10
no nation w. it so much 521:4
w. only one thing 240:13

Wanteth: w. not liquor 52:18
w. there grace of lute 92:5

Wanting: found w. 55:42

not w. what is stol'n	472:2
w. is—what?	97:15
w. that have wanted everything	240:13
world which, w. thee	558:6

Wanton: ah, w., will ye? 231:39

Gods, that w. in the air	319:4
her w. spirits look out	481:26
I do but w. in the South	538:21
my w. thoughts	359:27
no further than a w.'s bird	477:28
w. and a merye	137:1
w. eyes	52:35
w. smiled	232:3
w. with long delay	80:10
weep not, my w.	232:2
with w. Paris sleeps	480:37

Wanton'd with thy breakers 114:32

Wantonness: in clothes a w. 246:4
lipsed, for his w. 137:4
sad at night, only for w. 447:37

Wantons: sleep, pretty w. 170:23

Wants: everything that he w. 265:1

man w. but little	112:10, 225:13, 587:9
my w. supply	2:21
not so much to express our w.	226:26
provide for human w.	102:10
she w. a heart	384:33
toast our w. and wishes	384:31

Wap them into our ship's side 31:25(-32)

War: all the business of w. 564:3

all the offices. .of peace and w.	352:25
all this w. been wrought	328:17
amidst the ranks of w.	323:5
arts of w. and peace	115:43
as little of the w. as he will	27:20
as long as w. is regarded as wicked	569:33
at w. 'twixt will and will not	461:26
blood-red blossom of w.	536:24
brazen throat of w.	349:27
Brutus, with himself at w.	448:15
circumstance of glorious w.	472:3
come in your w. array	419:2
condemn recourse to w.	291:17
condition of w. of everyone	248:18
Dalhousy, the great God of W.	381:9
dastard in w.	418:17
dauntless in w.	418:16
delays are dangerous in w.	194:1
epithets of w.	469:20
essence of w. is violence	324:23
first invented w.	330:26
first in w.	312:25
garland of the w.	425:29
goes forth to w.	240:20
going to the w.	141:6
great w. from Macedon	19:3
Horses and Power and W.	294:29
if. .w. should ever come	310:18
image of w. without its guilt	506:13, 518:7
in a state of w. by nature	521:21
infection and the hand of w.	474:22
in. .peace thinks of w.	109:21
in the trade of w. . .slain men	469:36
in w., he mounts	417:16
in w. the two cardinal virtues	248:22
is it w.? No.	173:32
learn w. any more	52:31
let slip the dogs of w.	450:12
like to the morning's w.	445:44

War (*cont.*)

magnificent, but it is not w. 79:1
marching as to w. 35:1
miners poured to w. 322:19
Minstrel Boy to the w. 356:27
moderation in w. is imbecility 324:23
my sentence is for open w. 345:16
never was a good w. 211:8
no discharge in that w. 51:17
no discharge in the w. 294:37
no less renowned than w. 351:29
no less than w. to waste 349:28
nor w., nor battle's sound 343:12
not believe in inevitable w. 310:19
not w. with brother 160:41
no w. with women 507:30
offer w...kneel for peace 479:14
pass for men of w. 229:11
people that delight in w. 396:14
point out..that this is w. 1:4
prepare for w. 552:16
prophesying w. 151:33(–152)
reason w. with rhyme 281:27
sinews of love, as of w. 203:24
sinews of w. 27:24
some slain in w. 475:7
start another w. 243:6
steel couch of w. 470:8
take the w. 296:19
tell us all about the w. 507:5
the Lord is a man of w. 45:51
throughout the w. 219:7
to the ragged infant threaten w. 165:17
to w. and arms I fly 319:10
tricked by the British into..w. 38:16
tumult of her w. 517:3
unsuccessful or successful w. 162:40
used to w.'s alarms 252:29
w. against thee more 522:15
w. against the soul 69:49
w. as all glory 501:4
W. between Men and Women 547:12
w., dearth, age, agues 185:14
w., death, or sickness 466:20
w. has its laws 363:11
w., he sung, is toil 191:9
w. in heaven 71:17
w. is much too serious a thing 526:20
w. is the national industry of Prussia 353:4
w. is the trade of kings 192:43
w. its thousands slays 387:10
w. lays a burden 159:26
W. makes rattling good history 236:2
w.'s a game 163:42
w.'s annals will cloud 236:14
w.'s glorious art 586:27
W. that will end W. 565:3
w...the cry, 'W. even to the knife!' 113:10
w...utterly lost 567:5
w. with rere-mice 466:42
weapons of w. perished 47:30
we've a w., an' a debt 319:28
what can w. but endless w. 351:28
what did you do in the Great W.? 11:15
when the blast of w. blows 443:24
when the w. is done 415:13
when was a w. not a w.? 123:15
who is able to make w. with him? 71:20
Warble: w., child 455:6
w. his native wood-notes 342:7
Warbled to the string 341:19
Warbler: Attic w. 231:6
ev'ry w. has his tune 162:28
w. of poetic prose 163:34
Warbl'st at eve 351:12
Warbling his Doric lay 343:6
Warburton .. rage for saying something 270:31
Ward: American nation in th' Sixth W. 195:9
Light and Mrs. Humphry W. 140:5
thou knowest my old w. 439:20
W. has no heart 408:13
Warder: king .. thrown his w. down 474:12
W. of the brain 457:14
w. silent on the hill 418:4
w.—w.! open quickly! 23:23

Wardrobe: their gay w. wear 342:16
Wards: oiled w. 288:32
pretty young w. in Chancery 218:36
Ware: big enough for the bed of W. 483:34
find him w. an' wakin' 363:3
I should dine at W. 160:8
let me taste your w. 368:19
old person of W. 312:18
w. of mine own wit 427:5
Warehouse of my knowledge 518:18
Warfare: goeth a w...at his own charges 66:34
her w. is accomplished 54:8
legitimate w. 363:11
thy w. o'er 416:19
w. long 264:9
Warily to begin charges 26:11
Waring: what's become of W.? 97:16
when I last saw W. 97:20
Warlike: each w. Lucumo 323:15
Warly: w. cares, an' w. men 105:38
Warm: aha, I am w. 54:16
be w., but pure 117:17
breaks in a w. bay 15:14
flavour o' w. flat-irons 179:20
her coat is so w. 367:8
her heart was w. and gay 235:5
his desires were as w. 100:17
if his nose is w. 312:7
keep himself w. 368:2
keeps w. her note 125:10
let the w. Love in 288:9
mothy and w. 235:14
now w. and capable 287:3
now w. in love 382:1
nursing her wrath to keep it w. 108:2
on the w. sea-shore 15:14
O! she's w. 486:1
this w. kind world 157:19
to w. their little loves 231:18
very w. weather..in bed 519:22
w. days will never cease 284:11
w. him at his fire 244:2
w. without heating 43:14
w. work 362:20, 24
your down so w. 166:4
War-man..Billy the Norman 173:16
Warmed: with both hands 308:25
w. and cooled by the same winter 464:8
w., and fed 333:24
w. by the sun 204:3
Warmer: no weder w. 310:7
w. climes give brighter plumage 308:17
w. France 162:44
when youth and blood are w. 247:10
Warmeth: he w. himself 54:16
Warming: w. his five wits 540:14
w. of the blood 442:21
Warming-pans: good as w. 337:3
Warms: it w. the very sickness 436:40
sun that w. you here 474:13
w. in the sun 383:19
w. the neighbouring poor 165:17
Warmth: awful w. about my heart 290:6
I yearn'd for w. 530:18
little w., a little light 335:10
native with the w. 289:9
no w., no cheerfulness 253:12
w. of shepherds' flames 331:2
w. to swell the grain 121:27
Warn: to w. th' immortal souls 331:3
to w., to comfort 580:21
w. all traffic 299:25
w. you that it will be used 187:25
Warned: be w. by me 41:3
be w. by my lot 298:3
w. them thence 343:14
who hath w. you to flee? 57:30
Warning: come without w. 160:27
each w. each 302:10
give little w. 33:14
give w. to the world 487:15
horrid w. 286:36
take w. by the fall 30:4
w. to all the rest of this..kingdom 442:21
Warns me not to do 386:30
War Office: anything except the.. W. 489:18

Warp: though thou the waters w. 427:22
weave the w. 229:22
War-proof: fathers of w. 443:25
Warps: love w. the mind 165:16
Warrant: here's the w., Claudio 462:20
their humours for a w. 447:42
truth shall be thy w. 405:7
Warred on by cranes 345:3
Warren's blackin' 179:5
Warring: w. in Heav'n 346:30
w. within our breasts 330:28
Warrior: British w. queen 158:29
every w. that is rapt with love 331:2
happy W. 575:5
home they brought her w. 538:25
lay like a w. 572:12
mounts the w.'s steed 417:16
painful w. famoused for fight 486:22
Warriors: joy which w. feel 416:27
Wars: all skilful in the w. 552:1
all their w. are merry 140:15
big w. that make ambition virtue 472:3
clashing w. 184:2
cluck'd thee to the w. 429:22
fierce w. and faithful loves 509:10
he maketh w. to cease 394:29
lawful..to serve in the w. 401:13
pristine w. of the Romans 444:2
ring out the thousand w. 533:20
rust of the Barons' W. 558:14
since w. begin in the minds 9:22
w. and rumours of w. 60:21
w. are over 263:29
w. of elements 1:24
W. of Kites and Crows 352:30
w. or women 446:24
Warts: remark all these..w. 167:7
Warwick: W. and Talbot 444:28
W...proud setter up 446:4
Wary: craves w. walking 449:2
Was: because he w. a Greek 309:20
he w. not; for God took him 44:35
if it w. so, it might be 130:8
I see what w., and is 573:26
thinks what ne'er w. 382:25
what I w. once 582:3
what then I w. 581:26
which is, and which w. 70:21
which w., and is 70:38
Wash: dost thou w. my feet? 63:47
flood could not w. away 155:10
gulfs will w. us down 541:3
incessantly softly w. again 567:5
I w. away my balm 475:22
never comes out in the w. 302:5
no tide shall ever w. away 309:6
shirt which ought to be at w. 325:32
they that w. on Monday 11:5
thou shalt w. me 395:8
w. for shame 11:5
w. in need 11:5
w. me in steep-down gulfs 473:32
w. me in the water 11:8
w. me, Saviour 548:12
w. my hands in innocency 393:18
w. the balm from an..king 475:1
w. their feet in soda water 197:31
w. them in my blood 508:15
w. your city of Cologne 150:28
w. your hands and pray 296:33(–297)
Washed: roses newly w. with dew 479:4
their faces w. 130:13
w., and dressed 333:24
w. by Arethusa's fount 232:1
w. by the rivers 84:21
w. headlong from on board 159:1
w. himself with oriental scrupulosity 278:1
w. his hands before the multitude 60:49
w. their robes 71:6
Washes: w. his hands, and says 439:13
w. its walls 94:32
Washing: always w. 237:12
taking in one another's w. 6:3
w. his hands with invisible soap 253:7
Washington: at W. Inn 42:12
Government at W. lives 213:7
Washingtonian dignity 387:13
Wash-pot: Moab is my w. 395:25
Waspish: when you are w. 451:15

Wasps: bottled w.   161:41
  w. and hornets break through   519:7
Wassailing: here we come a-w.   6:22
Wassails: Hock-carts, w., wakes 245:17
Wast: stand a w. of praise   518:17
Waste: across this watery w.   147:10
  all w. and solitary places   494:13
  'hush'd Chorasmian w.   17:28
  idle w. of thought   504:9
  in Annihilation's W.   206:20
  in a w. of shame   488:11
  in the wide w...is a tree   119:10
  no less than war to w.   349:28
  our young affections run to w. 114:15
  over the w. of waters   115:29
  pale w. widens   16:4
  particular glory of the Egdon w. 237:9
  that thou and I shall w.   583:21
  to the bound of the w.   17:21
  to w. long nights   510:16
  to what purpose..this w.?   60:36
  w. ground enough   461:35
  w. his whole heart   540:13
  w. howling wilderness   46:31
  w. its sweetness   230:5
  w. not your Hour   206:22
  w. places of Jerusalem   54:23
  weary w. of waters   507:28
  we lay w. our powers   582:18
  Well amid the W.   206:21
  were I in the wildest w.   107:26
  Wind along the W.   206:13
Wasted: talk not of w. affection 316:14
  w. his substance   62:13
  w. with misery   400:6
  why this charm is w.   199:26
Wasteful: ah, w. woman   374:20
  w. and ridiculous excess   447:39
  youth of pleasure w.?   93:25
Wastel-breed: milk and w.   130:30
Wastes her time and me   558:4
Wasting: a-w. Christian kisses   299:11
  delightful way of w. time   358:17
  w. in despair   572:2
Wat: poor W.   488:28
Watch: before the morning w.   399:40
  call the rest of the w.   468:37
  constable of the w.   468:35
  for the w. to babble   468:38
  full weary of her w.   106:2
  her lover keeps w.   318:5
  his life is a w.   522:7
  if you don't w. out   407:13
  keeping w. above his own   320:11
  keep w. for the life of..Jack 173:7
  kept w. o'er man's mortality   576:22
  men wont to w. on duty   344:27
  one to w., and one to pray   3:3
  past as a w. in the night   397:15
  Saints their w. are keeping   517:2
  set a w...before my mouth   400:13
  set their w. in the sky   123:3
  she shall w. all night   479:7
  snores out the w.   442:25
  the Lord w. between me and
    thee   45:8
  w. and chain, of course   408:1
  w. and pray   198:19
  w. at that midnight hour   311:16
  w. did thine anxious servants 547:7
  w. for me by moonlight   366:3
  w. from dawn to gloom   497:2
  w. from their graves   93:4
  w. not one another out of fear 185:7
  w. on the Rhine   416:2
  w. that ends the night   562:9
  w. the clock for you   487:7
  w. the ships of England   295:12
  w. the wall, my darling   301:18
  w. with me one hour   60:42
  where none can w. her   262:6
  whispers of each other's w.   444:6
  whose howl's his w.   458:1
  winding up the w. of his wit   479:34
  your learning, like your w.   139:18
Watchdog: w.'s honest bark   115:22
  w.'s voice   224:17
Watch-dogs bark   479:28
Watched: he w. and wept   224:21
  I have w.   398:1
  I w. in vain   208:16

Watcher of the skies   288:19
Watches: our judgments as our w. 382:19
  w. and receives   581:16
  w. from his mountain walls   529:10
  w. of the dark   545:10
Watchful: many a w. night   442:25
  w. at His Gate   183:21
Watching: children stood w. them 293:25
  tire of w. you   84:7
  w. for the morrow   127:30
  w. round you still   3:18
  w., with eternal lids apart   288:17
  weary of w.   409:26
  with w...faint   143:13
Watchman: w. on the lonely tower 418:3
  w. waketh but in vain   49:36, 399:35
  w., what of the night?   53:26
Watchmen that went about   52:12
Watch-tower in the skies   341:31
Watchword: our w. is security   379:12
Water: across the stormy w.   122:28
  as ready by w. as by land   198:24
  as w. is in w.   425:20
  as w. spilt   47:35
  as w. unto wine   534:32
  before it beat the w.   317:22
  benison of hot w.   83:22
  blackens all the w. about him   2:30
  but limns the w.   28:17
  by w. and the Word   517:1
  by w. he sente hem hoom   137:13
  cast the w. of my land   461:1
  charity..hardly w. the ground 26:36
  charmed w. burned   149:25
  clouds they are without w.   70:19
  come of w. and of mud   83:24
  conscious w.   165:25
  daughter of Earth and W.   493:1
  deep in the w.   41:30
  do your work on w.   297:1
  drawers of w.   46:41
  dreadful noise of w.   476:14
  drinking up ta w.   23:27
  drink no longer w.   68:50
  drowned already..with salt w. 482:25
  drunk your w. and wine   297:13
  earth and the sky and the w. 585:17
  fish out of the w.   422:31
  fountain of the w. of life   71:46
  Garden by the W. blows   205:9
  his steeds to w.   429:25
  how does the w. come down   507:11
  I came like W.   206:12
  imperceptible w.   253:7
  in standing w.   482:17
  in the w. under the earth   390:7
  in w. writ   38:2
  King over the W.   10:15
  Laughing W.   317:26
  like w. through a sieve   131:22
  little drops of w.   127:33
  little ones a cup of cold w.   59:4
  little w. clears us   458:16
  made his mouth to w.   110:31
  made the w...follow faster   424:6
  makes my teeth w.   208:24
  more w. glideth by the mill   480:33
  never hold w.   144:32
  not all the w.   109:30, 475:1
  not filled with w.   50:55
  on one lay a great w.   531:30
  our passions as..fire and w. 313:19
  over the w. and over the sea
                         250:15, 420:13
  pools are filled with w.   397:6
  pools of w.   53:23
  ridden that wan w.   31:7
  river of w. of life   72:6
  runs under w.   281:19
  she drinks w.   135:19
  sipped brandy and w. gayly   154:17
  sound of the w.'s murmuring   497:20
  sprinkling it with fountain w. 305:18
  stain'd the w. clear   76:9
  struggling for life in the w. 270:18
  sweet w. and bitter   69:38
  take the w. of life freely   72:10
  their virtues we write in w. 447:8
  tickled best in muddy w.   111:27
  too much of w. hast thou   437:2
  under the w. it rumbled   150:10

Water (cont.)
  under w. I would scarcely kick 290:1
  unseen, and full of w.   475:19
  unstable as w.   45:26
  used to sing in the w.   176:5
  wash me in the w.   11:8
  w. and a crust   286:39
  w. but the desert   114:15
  w. fairest meadows   164:5
  w., is unsuitable   243:15
  w. like a stone   409:20
  w., like a witch's oils   149:6
  w. not so fair   510:20
  w. of affliction   48:14
  w. once a day   481:32
  w. out of this rock   46:15
  w. shall hear me   507:14
  w. springs up..ready boiled   237:1
  w. steaming hot!   372:17
  w.'s thin   219:14
  w.'s wider..than Blood   266:17
  w., w., every where   149:6
  W. willy-nilly flowing   206:13
  w. your damned flower-pots   96:38
  we'll o'er the w.   250:15
  wetter w.   83:25
  what's the w. in French   177:15
  when the w. flowed in   31:1
  where no w. is   395:25
  where the w. goes   142:12
  whole stay of w.   52:33
  whose name was writ in w.   291:3
  wilderness a standing w.   398:20
  your feet are always in the w. 4:21
Water-brooks: as the hart desireth
    the w.   394:16
Water-colour: amateur painting in
    w.   514:26
Watered: Apollos w.   66:22
  fed and w.   121:27
  in a w. shoot   409:14
  milk..likely to be w.   112:6
  w. heaven with their tears 75:24(–76)
  w. orange-pulp   96:39
  w. our horses in Helicon   135:21
  w. the whole face of the ground 44:10
Waterest her furrows   395:30
Waterfall: from the w...named 317:26
Water-flags in flower   374:24
Water-flies blow me   425:34
Water-flood: sitteth above the w. 393:24
Water-floods: in the great w. 393:32
Water-fly: dost know this w.? 437:29
Watering: a-w. the last year's crop 196:7
Water-land of Dutchmen   116:29
Water-lilies: floating w.   497:23
Water-lily: saw the w. bloom 534:7
Waterloo: crowning carnage, W. 119:16
  every man meets his W.   378:20
  not yet met our W., Watson 188:6
  stricken at W.   141:26
  W.'s ensanguined plain   9:5
  W...won in the playing fields 564:6
  world-earthquake, W.   537:20
Waterloo House young man   221:8
Waterman: great-grandfather..a
    w.   99:17
  jolly young w.   173:12
Watermen, that row one way   109:6
Water-mill: noise like that of a w. 519:11
Water-pipes: noise of the w. 394:19
Water-rats: land-rats and w. 463:15
Waters: all that move in the W. 388:22
  all the w. of Israel   48:22
  all w. as the shore   522:15
  as the w. cover the sea   3:8, 53:19
  beams of his chambers in the w. 398:8
  bitter w. into sweetness   196:24
  blue Midland w.   18:16
  by his, ye w., glide   18:19
  by the w. of Babylon   400:5, 558:26
  canst drink the w.   170:22.
  cast thy bread upon the w.   51:27
  clamour of w.   521:30
  cold w. to a thirsty soul   50:36
  come ye to the w.   54:29
  crept by me upon the w.   479:29
  deeper w. than I had thought 188:3
  dells where w. run   286:23
  drank strong w.   300:18
  drifts away like the w.   585:19

Waters (*cont.*)

fen of stagnant w. 577:14
fragrant w. on my cheek 160:32
hear the mighty w. 576:19
her winds and w. sighs 423:26
his luminous home of w. 17:28(−18)
his voice as. .many w. 70:27
in our w. yet appear 281:18
in the w. under the earth 325:9
in the wilderness. .w. break out 54:3
into the main of w. 465:21
into what great w. 515:3
in whose bosom the bright w. 356:26
its w., returning 316:14
knowledge. .as the w. 24:17
like the pale w. 585:22
many w. cannot quench love 52:23
moved upon the face of the w. 44:1
moving w. at their. .task 288:17
obscure w. slope 96:31
occupy their business in great w. 398:17
o'er the glad w. 114:42
once more upon the w. 113:22
over the rolling w. go 538:12
over the waste of w. 115:29
perished in the w. 58:36
pleasant w. of the River Lee 402:21
quiet w. by 421:1
roaring w. 429:29
she walks the w. 114:43
sitteth upon many w. 71:31
sound of w. shaken 523:24
stolen w. are sweet 49:53
swell the curled w. 453:3
those cool w. . .we used to dwell 254:15
to the w. and the wild 586:9
w. murmuring 341:22
w. of comfort 393:10
w. of strife 397:3
w. of the Nile 128:23
w. of wide Agony 494:23
w. on a starry night 576:2
w. stand in the hills 398:8
w. stilled at even 410:7
w. warp 427:22
w. were his winding sheet 35:23
w. wild went o'er 122:29
weary waste of w. 507:28
while the nearer w. roll 565:5
width of the w. 16:4
winds and w. make us 309:5
with earth's w. make accord 545:7
world of w. wild 546:1
Water-side: tree planted by the w. 391:46
Water-springs of a dry ground 398:20
Water-tower: great grey w. 141:16
Watery: across this w. waste 147:10
after w. cloudes 310:7
beneath the w. floor 343:3
leaves his w. nest 169:13
Watson: I thought I knew my W. 188:11
Watter: makes my teeth w. 208:24
Wattle: Captain W. 173:3
Wattles: of clay and made 585:12
Waught: right gude-willie w. 104:14
Wave: blind w. 531:9
blue w. rolls nightly 118:37
brooding on the charmèd w. 343:13
cool, translucent w. 341:3
dance like a w. of the sea 585:2
great third w. 525:25
great w. that echoes 531:6
his chin upon an orient w. 343:24
into the billowy w. 220:19
last w. pales 208:6
life on the ocean w. 415:11
lift me as a w. 496:10
light w. lisps 'Greece' 90:34
long may it w. 292:11
never a w. . .but marks our. .
    dead 301:23
over the western w. 495:21
plough the w. no more 162:13
seen her w. her hand 533:42
so dies a w. 33:10
sunk beneath the w. 162:9
swallowing w. 319:8
turn of eye, w. of hand 96:24
w., Munich! all thy banners 122:19
w.'s intenser day 496:8
w. to pant beneath thy power 496:10

Wave (*cont.*)

weak as is a breaking w. 578:35
when the moon is on the w. 118:8
wind and w. and oar 535:20
winning w. 246:4
wish you a w. o' the sea 485:27
with w. and whirlwind 315:29
Waved: long has it w. 251:5
w. her lily hand 216:1
w. over by that flaming brand 349:31
Waver and give place 585:22
Wavering: more longing, w. 483:3
strengthen the w. line 17:21
w. like Mr. Coleridge's. .prose 240:7
Waverley: the Owl, and. .W. pen 11:4
Wavers to a rose 183:11
Waves: all thy w. and storms 394:19
as long as w. shall break 362:31
Britannia rules the w. 122:30
Britannia rule the w. 545:18
came the w. 509:7
come as the w. come 419:4
dream of w., flowers 493:14
fields, or w., or mountains 498:8
floods lift up their w. 397:23
hear the w. roar 16:1
heed not the rolling w. 415:6
Him that walked the w. 343:3
I see the w. upon the shore 498:22
it w. you to a more removed
    ground 432:1
light-hearted Masters of the w. 18:16
like as the w. make 487:8
little w. of Breffny 227:36
long'd-for dash of w. 17:28(−18)
midway on the w. 151:33(−152)
noise of his w. 395:28
o'er the mountain w. 123:11
raging w. of the sea 70:20
same w. whitened 523:15
sons of the w. 213:10
spent w.' riot 523:17
thy proud w. be stayed 49:21
thy righteousness as the w. 54:20
wan w. and wet winds 523:19
w. and I 116:3
w. be upon you 525:12
w. bound beneath me 113:22
w. clasp one another 495:7
w. in its plumes 332:20
w. of ecstasy 567:2
w. of the sea are mighty 397:23
w. of thy sweet singing 493:20, 497:10
w. roar and whirl 16:1
w. serener far 493:25
w. that beat on Heaven's shore 73:26
when the w. went high 190:13
while the tired w. . .breaking 147:8
wild w. saying 128:2
wild w. whist 479:28
yesty w. 460:4
Waving: w. his wild tail 304:22
w. me farewell 254:15
Wavy: w. and long 358:24
w. in the dusk 336:9
Wax: as w. melteth 396:4
didn't w. his moustache 304:41
frequent in tapers. .w. 238:37
honey and w. 519:5
they all shall w. old 398:2
virtue of w. and parchment 101:1
w. to receive 112:35
will she w. and wane 207:29
wyne and w. 583:26
Waxed: Jeshurun w. fat 46:32
Waxwork: Mrs. Jarley's w. show 177:31
Waxworks: if you think we're w. 130:7
Way: along the public w. 160:30
already on the w. 292:19
also make a w. to escape 66:38
beasts about Thy w. 506:8
broad is the w. 58:23
by the w. as you came 405:10
cleave thou thy w. 335:28
departed. .another w. 57:25
dirty, dangerous w. 227:6
every one to his own w. 54:26
find out his uncouth w. 345:26
flowers to strew Thy w. 244:14
found a thee a w. 446:29
goeth his w., and. .forgetteth 69:33

Way (*cont.*)

gone some other w. 31:20
grasses of the ancient w. 333:17
heav'n's wide pathless w. 341:14
his bow-wow w. 377:5
I am the w. 63:53
if a man make w. 523:14
I have no w. 453:38
I know the w. she went 536:4
in a mysterious w. 161:18
keeps the road w. better 441:35
long is the w. and hard 345:27
looking one w. 99:17
make thy w. plain 392:4
narrow is the w. 58:24
never in the w., nor *out* of the w. 136:7
noiseless tenor of their w. 230:7
not pass this w. again 232:10
one w. possible 96:18
over the whole breadth of the w. 99:12
pleasure gives w. 183:17
plods his weary w. 229:28
prepare ye the w. of the
    Lord 54:9, 57:28
pretty Fanny's w. 373:20
public opinion. .must have her
    w. 103:10
roses, roses, all the w. 94:28
safer than a known w. 239:4
see my w. as birds their. .w. 94:13
singing by the w. 137:44
such a winning w. with you 155:31
taking a little pleasure out of the
    w. 136:3
that thy w. may be known 396:2
this is the w. 53:42
this w. and that dividing 531:28
this w., and that w. 215:5
this w. or that 573:7
thorny w. to heaven 431:23
toiling up the terrible w. 140:10
tread the Narrow W. 295:2
walk your mystic w. 220:26
w. he should go 50:30
w. is all so very plain 142:13
w. is long to the sun 524:13
w. it should go 175:10
w. of all flesh 155:39, 422:28, 563:23
w. of all the earth 46:44
w. of a man with a maid 50:56
w. of an eagle 50:56
w. of a serpent 50:56
w. of a ship 50:56
w. of life uncertain 284:18
w. of putting it 197:8
w. of thy commandments 389:44
w. of transgressors 50:4
w., the truth, and the life 63:53
w. the world ends 197:12
w. to heaven. .as ready 198:24
w. to hell, even from. .heaven 99:25
w. to love each other 292:21
w. to parish church 427:18
w. was long 416:29
w. we parted 524:9
we may lose the w. 142:13
which the w. ? 276:15
whiles thou art in the w. with
    him 57:46
woman has her w. 251:13
work its w. with the women 179:22
Wayfaring: true w. Christian 352:9
w. men. .not err therein 54:4
Waylay: startle, and w. 580:19
Ways: all the w. you can 565:19
cheerful w. of men 346:20
consider her w. 49:45
forget thy thousand w. 308:10
goodness and mysterious w. 266:13
her little wishes and w. 237:5
her w. are w. of pleasantness 40:41
her w. to roam 84:21
how many w. and days 411:10
in His w. with men 531:26
just are the w. of God 350:27
justify God's w. 263:25
justify the w. of God 344:4
keep thee in all thy w. 397:19
let me count the w. 88:24
most sure in all His w. 364:6
nine and sixty w. 297:9

INDEX

Ways (cont.)
no middle w. 82:5
not be thought after these w. 458:10
perfect w. of honour 447:15
rough uneven w. 474:27
she had not these w. 585:4
subtle w. I keep 199:3
teach thy w. unto the wicked 395:9
vindicate the w. of God 383:8
walks in our w. again 83:20
wandered all our w. 405:12
wander in the w. of men 106:27
w. be foul 456:1
w. deep and weather sharp 197:13
w. that are dark 238:32
world and its w. 96:44
your great and gracious w. 375:14
your w. my w. 54:31
Wayside: fell by the w. 59:21
Wayward: fond and w. thoughts 581:12
how w. is this foolish love 484:31
how w. the decrees of Fate 543:13
purblind, w. boy 455:8
tetchy and w. 476:27
Wayworn: weary, w. wanderer 380:17
We: even w., even so 335:25
people like us are W. 303:18
put it down a w. 179:14
still it is not w. 141:27
though they're not w. 185:1
w. authors, Ma'am 181:19
w. must eat w. 543:8
w. that had loved him so 93:3
w., w. only, are left 17:18
Weak: but he is w. 578:34
but little children w. 4:7
concessions of the w. 100:21
earth is w. 396:29
flesh is w. 60:43
for the fallen and the w. 320:14
how very w. the very wise 543:13
infirmities of the w. 66:17
little, w., and helpless 4:3
made w. by time and fate 541:3
my love is w. and faint 161:13
no passion..so w. 26:2
not dispirited, not w. 200:3
otherwise w. men 25:41
pondered, and weary 380:22
refuge of w. minds 139:25
strengthen ye the w. hands 54:2
to be w. is miserable 344:16
too w. the conflict to support 454:23
too w. to cleave 147:9
trifling, childish, w. 165:9
virtue of w. minds 192:35
w. alone repent 115:4
w. and beggarly elements 67:42
w., and despis'd old man 453:6
w. as is a breaking wave 578:35
w. brother..worst of mankind 514:36
w...confound the..mighty 66:20
w. minds led captive 350:2
w. one is singled 494:21
W. shall perish 422:20
Weaker: to the w. side inclin'd 111:19
w. sex, to piety more prone 4:9
w. vessel 70:2
Weakest: fondest, blindest, w. 544:31
w. kind of fruit 464:31
w. saint 161:15
Weak-ey'd bat 153:24
Weak-hearted: help the w. 389:1
Weakness: all w. which impairs 17:24
amiable w. 204:29, 500:43
fiddle-strings is w. 176:35
is it w. of intellect? 220:18
made perfect in w. 67:38
no w., no contempt 351:6
one man's w. 383:28
owning her w. 252:22
Power girt round with w. 492:2
strength and w. of human nature 324:35
stronger by w. 557:25
strove against her w. 535:5
too much w. for the stoic 383:22
w. is not in your word 17:20
w. of our mortal nature 389:40
Weaknesses: his w. are great 294:18
his w. with a delicate hand 226:31
Wealth: all that w. e'er gave 230:1

Wealth (cont.)
as their w. increases 330:15
boundless his w. 417:22
bring home the w. of the Indies 274:4
for all the w. of Indies 543:12
gave the little w. he had 521:4
get place and w. 386:9
his w. a well-spent age 123:25
in health and w. long to live 388:28
in squandering w. 190:24
let w. and commerce..die 329:10
nor lie in wait for w. 575:9
,no w. but life 413:29
outlive his w. 465:9
outshone the w. of Ormus 345:14
poor man's w. 501:26
promoting the w., the number 101:15
rule of w. 28:33
such w. brings 486:24
swim'st thou in w. 170:22
titles, w., and fame 381:36
w. and freedom reign 226:8
w. I seek not 515:28
w. nor blessed abode 334:13
w. or rank possessing 361:24
w. which modern progress brings 216:9
what w. to me 577:7
where w. accumulates 224:14
whole w. of thy wit 464:26
worldly w. he cared not for 212:17
Weaned: as a child that is w. 400:1
not w. till then? 185:6
w. child shall put his hand 53:19
Weans: are the w. in their bed? 339:9
w. and wife 104:23
Weapon: coward's w., poison 209:6
his w. wit 254:13
skill in the w. is nothing 442:21
with the other hand held a w. 48:35
Weaponless himself 350:25
Weapon-point: at w. they close 418:29
Weapons: get your w. ready 567:4
gie's but the w. 360:4
hurt with the same w. 464:8
lawful..to wear w. 401:13
w. of war perished 47:30
Wear: clothes you w. or do not w. 140:3
fools never w. out 156:7
get that I w. 427:27
motley's the only w. 427:15
nothing else to w. 218:29
nothing to w. but clothes 292:14
not w. them out in practice 37:8
such qualities as would w. 227:16
w. him in my heart's core 434:26
w. it on both sides 481:23
w. my heart upon my sleeve 469:28
w. out, in a wall'd prison 454:19
w. out than rust out 167:19, 566:17
w. out the everlasting flint 478:10
w. thee in my bosom 104:27
w. without corrival 438:38
w. your learning 139:18
will us to w. ourselves 330:28
Weare: Mr. William W. 562:24
Wearer: merit of the w. 464:1
Wearers of rings and chains 308:24
Weareth the Christian down 300:6
Wearied: until she be w. out 495:22
w. and forlorn 359:14
Wearies: coquetry of Death, which w. me 543:20
it w. me; you say it w. you 462:28
Weariest and most loathèd..life 462:10
Weariness: deep w. and sated lust 17:7
much study..w. of the flesh 51:35
not go, for w. of thee 186:15
pale for w. 495:19
thro' w. they fail'd 161:16
w. can snore 429:36
w. may toss him to My breast 245:1
w. not on your brow 17:20
w., the fever, and the fret 287:25
Wearing: I'm w. awa' 360:19
w. all that weight 533:30
w. his wisdom lightly 529:3
w. o' the Green 9:6
w. our own noses 429:28
w. out life's evening 276:15
worse for w. 201:29

Wearisome: make them w. 474:27
w. condition of humanity 232:14
Wears: so w. she to him 483:3
w. on his smiling face 152:17
w. out his time 469:26
w. the turning globe 263:36
Weary: art thou w.? 361:10
eyelids are a little w. 374:10
great rock in a w. land 53:43
I am very w. 83:3
I sae w. fu' o' care 108:36
let him be rich and w. 245:1
not be w. in well doing 67:48
not w. in well doing 68:40
of August w. 480:7
rosy garland and a w. head 501:27
run, and not be w. 54:14
say I'm w. 265:25(-266)
very few and very w. 325:19
w. and ill at ease 402:11
w. and kind 585:22
w. and old with service 446:24
w. be at rest 48:46
w. lot is thine 419:8
w. night and day 584:6
w. of breath 252:12
w. of days and hours 523:18
w. of earth 517:4
w. of her watch 196:2
w. of these worldly bars 448:36
w., stale, flat 430:33
w. time 149:8
w., wayworn wanderer 380:17
w. with disasters 458:36(-459)
w. with toil 486:23
world is w. of the past 493:27(-494)
Weasel: as a w. sucks eggs 427:8
it is like a w. 435:26
pop goes the w. 328:26
Weather: all sorts of things and w. 199:18
blue Italian w. 495:8
calm or stormy w. 409:19
come wind, come w. 99:35
different kinds of good w. 413:30
first talk is of the w. 277:34
french wine and fine w. 290:24
fresh fierce w. 525:19
hard grey w. 293:15
if it prove fair w. 517:18
ill is the w. 170:24
it was gorgeous w. 121:15
martlet, builds in the w. 463:44
New England w...different kinds of w. 550:31
not in fine w. 146:18
not woo foul w. 253:18
no w. warmer 310:7
plaguy twelvepenny w. 519:21
politics go by the w. 231:28
sad or singing w. 524:28
serves for the old June w. 90:37
through cloudy w. 33:14
under the w. 515:9
w. ginneth clere 138:28
w. sharp 197:13
w. the cuckoo likes 236:30
w. the shepherd shuns 236:32
when God sorts out the w. 407:4
winter and rough w. 427:7
Weather-beaten: never w. sail 124:1
Weatherby George Dupree 339:15
Weather-cock: no w. 573:4
Weathered: pilot that w. the storm 124:19
Weather-proof: humble roof..w. 247:16
Weatherwise: if the Bard was w. 150:30
some are w. 211:11
Weave: ever so will w. 235:21
few would w. 236:22
hands of mem'ry w. 157:1
w. a paradise for a sect 285:32
w. their thread with bones 483:5
w. the warp 229:22
Weaver: swifter than a w.'s shuttle 48:52
Weaves: he w., and is clothed 522:7
Web: magic in the w. of it 472:16
of the smallest spider's w. 477:7
out flew the w. 534:7
she left the w. 534:7
tangled w. we weave 418:28
w. of human things 492:19
w. of our life 423:7

INDEX

Web (cont.)
w. o' the silken claith   31:25(-32)
with as little a w.   470:30
Webs: swarthy   531:38
trafficked for strange w.   374:11
Webster: Daniel W...steam-
engine in trousers   504:33
W. was much possessed   197:33
Wed: December when they w.   428:22
think to w. it   423:2
w. with Thought   532:18
with this Ring I thee w.   391:32
wooed not w.   90:6
wore when she was w.   535:11
Wedded: Faith, once w. fast   357:10
hail w. love   347:26
though w. we have been   159:32
throw your w. lady   430:5
w. to calamity   478:22
w. to the Earlie's son   419:1
w. to this goodly universe   574:8
Wedding: bought her w. clothes   2:29
get the w. dresses ready   116:39
let's have a w.   175:27
peal upon our w.   263:1
Sergeant's w.   301:11
w. cheer to..burial feast   478:33
wooing, w., and repenting   468:9
Wedding-day: dance bare-foot on
her w.   479:3
dawns our w.   219:35
drink good wine upon the w.   31:5
it is my w.   160:8
on his w.   219:4
on their w.   219:22
to-morrow is our w.   159:33
w...fixed on   204:8
Wedding-Guest stood still   148:20
Wedding-ring: torments lie in..
a w.   144:23
Wede: a' w. away   198:18
Wedges: small w. cleave   305:12
w. of gold   476:14
Wedlock: holy w.   391:35
w.'s the devil   117:45
Wednesday: he that died o' W.   440:30
married on W.   368:21
spet on me on W. last   463:22
W. in Wheeson week   441:31
W.'s child   368:1
Wee: bonnie w. thing   104:27
my w. w. thing   213:1
sweet w. wife o' mine   107:16
this little pig cried, W., w., w.,!   369:7
w. modest..flow'r   107:7
w., sleekit, cow'rin'   107:9
winsome w. thing   107:16
Weed: basest w. that grows   561:6
Diana in her summer w.   232:1
fat w. that rots itself   432:12
fragrant w.   163:37
honey from the w.   444:13
in palmer's w.   340:8
law to w. it out   27:4
less than the w.   254:16
no more than Sussex w.   302:12
o'er a w. or a flower   34:14
O thou w.!   472:35
pernicious w.   159:18
salt w. sways   15:24
scarce w. out the fault   226:12
tawney w. tobacco   279:24
w. that grows in every soil   101:11
w. wide enough   466:41
Weeded: wither'd and w. away   147:24
Weeds: all the idle w.   454:2
buy yourself w.   215:3
cottages of strowed w.   331:2
fattest soil to w.   442:23
grubbing w. from gravel paths   296:32
her coronet w.   437:1
her winter w. outworn   493:25
long live the w.   254:30
more than mundane w.   83:27
only burning w.   141:12
put on the w. of Dominic   346:25
rank w.   165:17
smell far worse than w.   487:26
w. and tares of mine own brain   86:17
worthless as withered w.   83:9
Week: accomplished in a w.   515:5

Week (cont.)
all the w. through city-crowds   151:27
all the w. to dry   11:5
argument for a w.   439:7
keep a w. away?   472:18
Middle of Next W.   128:17
proud of one another the first w.   156:13
till the w. after next   131:27
tried..once a w.   273:6
twopence a w.   130:26
w. but only four   35:10
year, a month, a w.   330:7
Weekly from Southampton   297:24
Weeks: fou for w. thegither   108:5
frown on you—for w.   183:12
his brief hours and w.   488:7
Weep: all around thee w.   279:19
bid me to w.   247:2
daffodils, we w. to see   246:2
dew shall w. thy fall   245:13
do not w. for me   176:13
even butchers w.   214:23
Hecuba that he should w. for
her   433:31
if souls can w. in bliss   160:28
I must w...cruel tears   473:11
I saw my lady w.   7:13
I w. for Adonais   491:14
I w. for joy   474:34
I w. for you   130:20
make the angels w.   461:31
man after his deeth moot w.   137:29
milk my ewes and w.   485:32
now you w.   450:31
pity them that w.   123:26
she must w. or..die   538:25
strive nor w.   97:23
that I may not w.   116:9
these wakeful eyes may w.   308:14
to chide, to laugh, to w.   423:15
to not w. before him   551:13
to w. there   483:6
w. afresh love's..woe   486:25
w., and you w. alone   568:26
w. away the life of care   498:32
w., daughter of a royal line   118:3
w. for my pardon   425:22
w. for their sins   567:20
w., if that she sawe a mous   136:30
w. no more, my lady   210:15
w. not, my wanton   232:2
w. now or nevermore   380:19
w. over Saul   47:30
w. the more because I w. in vain   231:19
w. thy girlish tears   561:3
w. to record   122:39
w. upon your hinder parts   266:15
w. when I am low?   112:31
w. with me..you that read   280:12
w. with them that w.   66:4
w. you no more, sad fountains   11:10
who would not w.   385:29
why..sit still and w.?   266:8
women must w.   294:1
'Weep: scarcely cry, "w.! 'w.! 'w.!
'w.!'   76:17
Weeping: doth that bode me w.?   473:7
dwell a w. hermit there   153:30
goeth on his way w.   399:34
hear the children w.   88:1
in a forest, w.   328:20
my eyes are tired of w.   83:3
night of w.   517:2
Rachel w. for her children   57:26
remembrance of a w. queen   475:14
so w., how a mystic shape   88:16
these w. eyes   332:11
they are w. bitterly   88:2
two eyes swoln with w.   332:10
two w. motions   166:10
w. and gnashing of teeth   58:33
w. and the laughter   187:11
w. and watching   127:30
w. in the playtime   88:2
w. thou sat'st   279:19
w., w. late and early   535:10
wild with w.   493:19
with him rises w.   485:25
with w. and with laughter   324:1
world's more full of w.   586:9
Weeps: loves, and w., and dies   493:25

Weeps (cont.)
turns from their gaze, and w.   356:31
w. incessantly for my sin   75:19
why these w.?   560:16
Wee-things: expectant w.   104:33
Wee Willie Winkie   339:9
Wehr: ein gute W. und Waffen   321:6
Weib: Wein, W. und Gesang   321:5
Weigh: let us not w. them   123:19
more people see than w.   139:27
to w. and consider   27:16
w. it down on one side   234:3
w. mine eyelids down   441:41
w. this song   584:16
w. thy words in a balance   57:4
w. your Gods and you   303:25
Weighed in the balances   55:42
Weighing: counting votes instead
of w.   267:6
not w. our merits   390:45
Weighs: mortality w. heavily on
me   288:21
w. upon the heart   460:37
Weight: all that w. of learning   533:30
bird's w. can break..tree   93:15
bowed by the w. of centuries   329:19
by its own w...stedfast   155:19
custom lie upon thee with a w.   576:19
does nothing to relieve the w.   159:26
heavy and the weary w.   581:25
he carries w.!   160:2
ills have no w.   322:2
knowledge may give w.   139:27
lay aside every w.   69:18
moderate w. of prose   309:15
number, w., and measure   77:13
poising every w.   332:12
pull his w.   409:1
some rock's vast w.   382:32
their prodigal w.   475:12
thrice their w. in gold   203:39
w. of chance-desires   573:30
w. of the superincumbent hour   492:2
w. of this sad time   454:28
w. of too much liberty   578:7
w. that pull'd me down   446:27
Weights: deceitful upon the w.   395:24
Weighty: drowns things w.   27:1
reserve the more w. voice   25:42
Wein, Weib und Gesang   321:5
Weird sisters   460:13
Weirs: about the glimmering w.   263:23
as the grass grows on the w.   584:11
three lone w.   18:21
Welcome: advice is seldom w.   139:16
aye be w. back again   108:16
bay deep-mouth'd w.   115:22
bear w. in your eye   457:5
bid you a w. adoo   559:32
first to w., foremost to defend   118:22
frolic w.   541:3
Love bade me w.   244:21
outstay'd his w. while   152:21
passionate wind of w.   410:22
rest may hearten and w.   89:11
say 'W. Friend'   166:19
terrible events are w.   425:25
thrice w., darling of the Spring   573:20
to w. Jane   297:19
warmest w., at an inn   499:13
w., all wonders   166:6
w. each rebuff   95:15
w. ever smiles   481:20
w. for himself, and dinner   387:21
w. home again..faith   447:45
w. home mankind's..friend   42:1
w., kindred glooms   546:25
w. maids of honour   247:11
w. peaceful ev'ning   163:21
w. pure-ey'd Faith   340:11
w. the coming   386:6
w. the dawn   81:20
w. the lord of lycht   187:5
w., thou kind deceiver   191:22
w. to your gory bed   107:32
w., wild North-easter   293:12
w. you and w. all   263:29
Welcomes: he w. at once   13:17
now loud as w.   253:15
w. little fishes in   128:24
with tea w. the morning   278:1

INDEX

Welcomest when they are gone 445:19
Welfare of our Sovereign 389:14
Welkin: how all the w. rings 505:12
Well: all shall be w. 467:12
all things will be w. 373:14
are you quite w., Laetitia? 337:29
as w. said, as if I had said it 520:18
come w., come wo 250:15
continuance in w. doing 65:33
cried out—W. done! 160:2
did it very w. 219:7
do all things w. 143:11
do w., and suffer for it 69:51
drank of Aganippe W. 502:2
foolish thing w. done 272:15
how w. did I behave 262:19
if we do w. here 318:9
in the w. 129:11
is it w. with the child? 48:19
laugh and be w. 231:27
looking w. can't move her 517:10
never speaks w. of me her self 155:22
not done w. 271:16
not feeling very w. myself 403:35
nothing but w. and fair 351:6
not so deep as a w. 478:14
not..weary in w. doing 67:48, 68:40
not wisely but too w. 474:2
pretty w. for a Lord 273:10
pussy's in the w. 366:18
reward of a thing w. done 200:26
sitting down by the green w. 365:18
speak very w. in the..Commons 182:47
this..crown like a deep w. 475:19
to speak, and to speak w. 280:5
'twill all be w. 207:19
use it for a w. 397:6
very w. where they are 568:4
was she nae very w. aff 12:3
W. amid the Waste 206:21
w. done, said I 166:4
w. done, thou good and faithful 60:29
w. for him whose will is strong 541:19
w. in 129:11
w. made, w. wrought 502:17
w. of English undefiled 510:5
W. of Life 206:20
w. of love 148:12
w. of unconscious cerebration 268:6
w., 'tis very w. 492:23
w. to be merry and wise 335:4
w., very w. 472:34
what fair w. or grove 552:11
when it came to know me
  w. 177:33, 357:5
wish it w. 183:22
World W. Lost 191:14
you're doin' quite w. 7:19
Well-a-way: every youth cry W.! 30:1
Wellbeloved: my w. hath a vineyard 52:37
your w.'s hair 585:3
Well-bred: sensible, and a man 159:15
very strange and w. 156:13
Well-conducted: like a w. person 543:12
Well-connected: with virtuous
  scorn the w. 219:1
Well-content: sweet W. 169:25
Well-dressed: sense of being w. 201:7
when he's w. 176:6
Weller: Mr. W.'s knowledge of
  London 178:35
Well-favoured: he is very w. 482:17
to be a w. man 468:34
Well-govern'd and wise appetite 340:34
Wellington: thinking, as the Duke
  of W. 29:6
W.! (or 'Villainton') 116:26
Well-judging: sober, w. persons 363:19
Well-knit: his soul w. 16:13
Well-langua'd Daniel 87:23
Well-liking: fat and w. 397:21
Well-looking: one of my w. days 227:2
Well-painted passion! 472:30
Wells: buckets into empty w. 163:11
go about and poison w. 330:16
John Wellington W. 222:16
poison the w. 363:11
that so musically w. 380:12
Well-shaped: handsome, w. man 21:13
Well-spent: rare as a w. one 125:22

Well-spring: holds the bubbling
  w. 336:9
Well-stocked farms 106:7
Well-written Life 125:22
Welsh: devil understands W. 440:5
makes W. as sweet 440:4
Welshman: Taffy was a W. 369:1
valour in this W. 444:17
Welt:.eine W. zu gewinnen 333:11
Welter to the parching wind 342:10
Welt'ring in his blood 191:7
Weltgeschichte: die W. ist das Weltgericht 415:24
Wen: great w. 147:20
Wenceslas: good King W. 361:19
Wench: fair hot w. 438:13
ill-starr'd w. 473:32
most sweet w. 438:17
stuff fit only for a w. 333:22
w. who is just married 214:17
Wenches: hideous w. 150:28
pinches country w. 281:6
where..young w. keep sheep 370:17
Wenlock Edge: late on W. 263:13
Went: as cooks go she w. 414:13
but she w.! 10:25
he w.; his piping took 18:24
I w. by, and lo, 394:6
of his own will w. away 18:23
people w. up into the city 46:40
that she w. away 15:25
w. her unremembering way 544:1
w. his way 205:29, 30
w. out, like all good things 182:7
what w. ye..to see? 59:6
World w. very well then 43:19
Wentest: when thou w. forth..w.
  through the wilderness 396:5
Weomen: very pretty w. 208:29
Wept: Caesar hath w. 450:20
father w. 76:8, 232:3
he watch'd and w. 224:21
he w. not greatly 328:21
he w. to hear 76:9
Jesus w. 63:41
long before had w. 196:2
much w. for 532:13
prais'd, w.,{and honour'd 382:18
turned aside and w. 24:1
w. (I heard her tears) 410:14
w. like anything to see 130:12
w. odorous gums 347:5
w. o'er his wounds 224:20
w. over her, carved in stone 535:41
we sat down and w. 400:5
who w. with delight 201:24
'would have w. to see the dolour 328:19
Were: if it w. so, it would be 130:8
we w.? 41:19
Wernher: fair young W. died 42:10
Wertenberg: Rhine circle fair W. 329:24
Werther: W. had a love for Charlotte 543:12
moral man was W. 543:12
Weser: river W., deep and wide 94:32
Wesley: John W.'s conversation 273:29
Wessex: in these W. nooks 236:42
West: April's in the w. wind 334:15
blush from W. to East 536:7
bosom of the urgent W. 81:26
Cincinnatus of the W. 118:21
come out of the w. 418:15
comes from the w. lands 334:15
daughter of the W. 529:35
dearly love the w. 107:17
dive into their w. 123:19
foreign constellations w. 235:19
gathered to the quiet w. 241:23
go w., young man 506:22
imagine me the w. 231:38
I never hear the w. wind 334:15
in the regions of the w. 24:9
lady of the W. Country 171:6
little birds sang w. 88:5
little grey home in the w. 571:7
not travel due W. 128:9
one vast Iris of the W. 114:6
O wild West Wind 496:4
rosy is the W. 536:6
safeguard of the W. 582:5
sailing away to the w. 293:25

West (cont.)
wan w. shivers 521:30
w., east, south, and north 334:9
W. in her eyes 148:17
W. is W. 294:27
W. of these out to seas 208:7
W. to the Golden Gate 298:28
when the w. is red 516:4
when the wind is in the w. 11:21
where the W. begins 135:13
without declining W. 185:8
woning fer by w. 137:11
West Port: come open the W. 416:8
Westen: Im W. nichts Neues 406:7
Western: All Quiet on the W.
  Front 406:7
far in a w. brookland 203:19
little w. flower 466:39
outside the W. Straits 18:16
spray of W. pine 238:26
w. horizon..in a blaze 100:9
w. wind, when wilt thou blow? 11:14
wind of the w. sea 538:12
yon w. tent 153:24
Westminster Abbey: I walk by
  myself in W. 2:6
peerage, or W. 362:12
W. or victory 362:17
Weston: Mr. W.'s good wine 22:11
Westward: some w....all wrong 160:16
w., look, the land is bright 147:8
w. the course of empire 43:13
Wet: bereft of w. and of wildness 254:30
hir joly whistle wel y-w. 138:2
his wings were w. 231:33
showers and dewdrops w. 409:29
tears of it are w. 424:17
through the W. Wild Woods 304:22
w. and dirty from hunting 518:40
w. bird-haunted English lawn 17:10
w.-by the dew 204:3
w. his lip 249:20
w. sheet 167:20
w.'s the rain 170:24
w. with Channel spray 296:15
Wether: I am a tainted w. 464:31
some black w. 531:19
Wetter water 83:25
Wey: above the river W. 299:23
Whacks: gave her mother forty w. 8:7
Whale: confound the prophet with
  the w. 176:27
enormous w. emerges 503:5
like a w.'s back 289:11
or like a w.? 435:26
w.'s way 334:12
W. that wanders round the Pole 40:30
Whale-backed Downs 302:7
Whales: among the sharks and w. 8:24
drag the Atlantic..for w. 550:20
great w. come sailing 15:24
O ye W. 388:22
Wharfs: sense of the adjacent w. 424:7
What: he knew w.'s w. 110:13
she knows w.'s w. 179:21
wanting is—w.? 97:15
watchman, w. of the night? 53:26
w. and where they be 536:18
w. are they among so many? 63:20
w. could she have done? 584:25
w. do you want? 369:17
w. have I done for you? 241:25
w. ha' ye done? 302:24
w. is here? 534:10
w. is it you do? 580:14
w. is that to thee? 64:20
w. is there I would not do? 241:25
w. is this that thou hast done? 44:23
w. is truth? 27:29, 63:68
w. is which and which is w. 339:24
W. Jolly Fun! 405:16
w. make you here? 34:23
w. men or gods are these? 287:7
w.! no soap? 209:18
w. of vile dust? 141:19
w. shall I cry? 54:10
w. shall I say? 201:6
w. shall we do—or go fishing? 545:15
w. so wild as words are? 97:24
w.'s the good of Hanyfink? 142:21
w.'s the next article? 221:8

What (*cont.*)
w. thou art is mine 349:19
w. was he doing? 88:11
w., without asking 206:14
whence and w. art thou? 346:5
why, or which, or w. 312:13
Whate'er he did. .so much ease 190:9
Whatever: love thee, w. thou art 356:16
w. I had she gave 40:32
w. is, is. .just 193:10
w. is, is right 383:21
w. thou hast been 117:33
What-ho! She bumps! 131:33
What-is-it: certain w. in his voice 572:5
What's-his-name: no W. but Thingummy 175:15
Whatsisname: Sergeant W. 300:17
What-you-may-call-it is his prophet 175:15
Whaups are crying 516:9
Wheat: cake out of the w. 480:38
in a mortar among w. 50:48
like an heap of w. 52:18
measure of w. for a penny 70:44
orient and immortal w. 548:14
sleep among the w. 131:22
w. for this planting 316:6
when w. is green 466:21
Wheel: bound upon a w. of fire 454:14
breaks a butterfly upon a w. 385:30
ever-whirling w. of Change 510:10
I cannot mind my w. 309:2
noisy w. was still 262:9
rolling Ixionian w. 535:26
Time's w. runs back 95:23
turns the giddy w. 217:17
w. between the poles 528:11
w. broken at the cistern 51:33
w...in the midst of a w. 55:27
w. is come full circle 454:22
w.'s kick 334:10
w. the sofa round 163:21
your w. is new 303:9
your w. is out of order 124:7
Wheelbarrow: wheeled her w. 7:8
Wheelbarrows: twa w. tremble 104:28
Wheeled: solitary cliffs w. by me 575:26
Wheeling: extravagant and w. stranger 469:33
houses go w. back 546:30
w. out on a windy sky 568:23
Wheels: all the w. run down 293:19
call upon the w., master 142:14
hindmost w. of Phoebus' wain 340:8
spoke among your w. 37:34
tarry the w. of his chariot 46:51
w. of hansom-cabs 131:24
w. within w. 179:24
Wheeson: Wednesday in W. week 441:31
Whelks: bubukles and w. 444:3
Whelm'd in deeper gulphs 159:3
Whelp: puppy, w., and hound 225:20
When: fixed the where and w. 239:7
how, and w., and where 7:5
w. do I see thee most? 410:23
w. or how I cannot tell 411:34
w. wilt thou save the people? 198:22
Whence: hither hurried w.? 206:14
know not w. you came 207:7
w. and what art thou? 346:5
w., and whither flown again 207:24
w. are we? 491:25
w. came they? 71:5
w. comest thou, Gehazi? 48:24
w. it cometh 63:7
w. these stories? 317:19
Why not knowing nor W. 206:13
Where: Alice, w. art thou? 98:20
been she knew not w. 250:23
echo answers—'W.?' 113:5
fixed the w. and when 239:7
God knows w. 116:21
going one knows not w. 334:14
ha! w. ye gaun 106:32
how, and when, and w. 7:5
if we knew but w. 160:18
I knew not w. 315:24
I well know w. 80:16
not w. to lay his head 58:34
oh w., and oh! w. 282:10

Where (*cont.*)
tell me w. 264:14
we know not w. 191:33
what and w. they be 536:18
when the sun set w. were they? 115:45
w. and what his dwelling? 361:20
w. are the galleons? 183:6
w. are you going to? 294:34, 369:14
w. are you going with your lovelocks flowing? 409:16
w. are you now? 254:14
w. are you, Robin Crusoe? 170:6
w. art thou, my beloved Son? 572:24
w. did you come from, baby dear? 326:17
w. hae ye been? 30:8
w. is it? 151:19
w. is my child? 113:5
w. is she now? 460:25
w. ish dat barty now? 313:11
w. little girls are sent 313:10
w. they do grow? 245:21
w. was he? 241:6
w. wert thou, brother? 532:22
w. you are, how happy 487:7
Whereabout: stones prate of my w. 458:1
Whereabouts: to conceal our w. 414:15
Where'er she lie 166:17
Wherefore: for every why..a w. 110:12
knew not w. they were come 65:7
w. art thou come? 60:45
w. art thou Romeo? 477:15
w. wilt thou go? 18:26
Wheresoe'er in God's great universe 187:1
Wherever: w. I travel 41:30
w. thou may'st be 36:33
Wherry: my trim-built w. 173:14
Whets: then w., and combs 332:20
Whetted: wind's like a w. knife 334:12
Which: not a soul knew w. 313:8
what is w...w. is what? 339:24
w. is to be master 131:7
w. of you have done this? 459:14
w. will reach the bottom first? 228:7
why, or w., or what 312:13
with morning, w. is w. 459:24
Whid: rousing w. 105:6
Whiddon: Dan'l W. 33:1
Whiff of grapeshot 126:15
Whiffling through the tulgey wood 129:39(–130)
Whig: cursed W., a *bottomless* W. 275:14
Erastian W. 140:28
first W. was the Devil 274:7
he hated a w. 276:18
see a W...see a rascal 277:11
Tory and W. in turns 505:32
Tory men and W. measures 181:33
whether I were a W. or a Tory 519:14
W. and Tory a' agree 502:22
W. *Dogs*..not have the best of it 276:27
W. in a parson's gown 276:6
W...The name of a faction 277:32
wise Tory and a wise W. 274:35
you are a vile W. 272:9
Whigmigmorum: drop their W. 502:22
Whigs: caught the W. bathing 180:16
dished the W. 511:12
W. admit no force 87:26
W. *not* getting into place 116:36
While: great w. ago the world begun 484:27
great w. since 210:1
never was worth w. 20:23
Whim: strangest w. has seized me 140:9
tempted by a private w. 41:27
w., envy, or resentment 142:29
Whimper: not with a bang but a w. 197:12
Whimpering to and fro 296:3
Whims of an egotist 289:24
Whimsies: they have my w. 401:21
Whimsy, not reason 229:12
Whine about their condition 567:20
Whining: in w. Poetry 186:21
w. of a door 186:32
wimpled w., purblind 455:8
Whip: her w., of cricket's bone 477:7
in every honest hand a w. 473:2

Whip (*cont.*)
not feel the driver's w. 317:17
'Too-slow' will need the w. 538:3
to w. hypocrisy 455:19
w. me such honest knaves 469:26
w. me, ye devils 473:32
Whip-lash: guid w. 106:5
Whipped: afraid of being w. 269:33
for false quantities..w. 194:26
have such a fellow w. 434:15
he w. my grandfather 2:17
if our faults w. them not 423:7
w. her little daughter 367:17
w. them all soundly 369:4
w. the offending Adam out 443:5
Whippersnapper: critic and w. 89:25
Whipping: who should 'scape w.? 433:30
Whips: chastised you with w. 47:47
w. and scorns of time 434:4
Whipster: every puny w. 473:28
Whirl: waves roar and w. 16:1
Whirled: w. into folly and vice 535:37
w. round and round 311:6
Whirligig of time 484:26
Whirlpools: sensual w. 337:17
Whirls: expectation w. me round 481:15
Whirlwind: drink of the w.'s stream 497:8
ran like a w. 324:10
reap the w. 55:46
rides in the w. 1:11
sweeping w.'s sway 229:23
w. of passion 434:15
with wave and w. wrestle 315:29
Whisker: educated w. 529:14
w. and claw 171:10
Whiskerandos quits 500:4
Whiskers: Cat with crimson w. 312:9
individual w. 110:38
oh my fur and w. 128:26
Whisky: Freedom and W. 104:18
some w. afterwards 20:29
w.'s name in Greek 104:17
Whisper: all ye cry or w. 303:9
friend..whom I may w. 162:6
His W. came to me 296:11
wake and w. awhile 171:1
well the busy w...convey'd 225:1
w., a glance 183:7
w. at the grates 319:4
w. down the field 298:26
w. who dares 339:19
with far-heard w. 149:14
you w. 'Beatrice' 93:47
Whispered: every w. word 118:28
lips that had w. 523:15
Whispering: come w. by 236:14
death..w. low 308:23
out of your w. 563:17
w. from her towers 19:10
w. sound of the cool colonnade 161:23
Whisperings: foul w. are abroad 460:20
keeps eternal w. 288:30
Whispers: Blood of Jesus w. peace 72:19
few of us whom he w. 89:11
provoke eyes and w. 156:13
w. of each other's watch 444:6
w. of fancy 278:14
w. the o'erfraught heart 460:20
w. through the trees 382:31
Whist: loved a good game at w. 306:12
my husband from his w. 91:13
wild waves w. 479:28
Whistle: again the Cousin's w. 89:17
clear as a w. 112:23
he'd w. and sing 173:9
hir joly w. wel y-wet 138:2
I'd w. her off 471:38
Joseph did w. 7:14
let it w. as it will 418:23
pay too much for your w. 211:19
to a black-bird 'tis to w. 110:4
w., and I'll come 108:28
w. and she'll come 38:13
w. owre the lave o't 108:29
w. them back 225:33
Whistled as he went 192:5
Whistles: w. in his sound 427:21
w. in the wind 577:19
w. o'er the furrowed land 341:34
w. thrice 149:13

Whistling: w...Lillabullero 513:7
w. of a name 384:12
w. to keep myself 191:25
w. to the air 424:7
White: arrayed in w. robes 71:5
azure, w., and red 190:4
become very w. 128:28
black spirits and w. 338:18, 459:34
born..with a w. head 441:21
called the chess-board w. 89:32
clad in glittering w. 216:7
comes sooner by w. hairs 463:6
fat was so w. 225:10
fat w. woman 157:9
find itself less w. 506:15
floures w. and rede 138:17
Gardener in w. 208:13
goes into w. satin 500:6
green, and blue and w. 149:6
grew more clean and w. 88:22
help you a lot with the W. 298:5
her skin was w. as leprosy 149:13
his hairs were w. like wool 70:27
how ill w. hairs become 442:37
if snow be w. 488:13
impair their w. 88:14
its fleece was w. 233:23
ivory, so w. 215:42
keep your body w. 516:2
Leda..w. as he, yet not so w. 510:20
lovesom, w. and small 195:6
moment w.—then melts 108:7
my beloved is w. and ruddy 52:13
my hills are w. over 499:14
my shroud of w. 483:6
my soul is w. 76:13
nearer the great w. throne 131:32
nights, all w. an' still 319:23
nor grew it w. 114:35
nor w. so very w. 124:12
now the w. 539:2
O so w.! 281:24
pluck a w. rose 445:21
roses at first were w. 246:8
Sappho's breast or they more w. 246:8
seas do laugh, show w. 563:35
so old and w. as this 453:6
so red and so w., dears 293:17
spring goeth all in w. 82:7
their w. it stays 183:11
upon a w. horse 368:17
wearing w. for Eastertide 262:10
what w., what purple fritillaries 18:29
where I read w. 74:11
where w. is black 218:6
where ye see my w. plume 323:5
w. already to harvest 63:14
w. and hairless as an egg 246:16
w. as an angel 76:13
w. as driven snow 485:29
w. as snow in Salmon 396:7
w. as snow their armour 324:12
w. as the sun 156:19
w. bird..his own soul 374:9
w. birds on the foam 586:11
w., black and grey 346:24
w., celestial thought 552:3
w., clear w., inside 297:3
w. founts falling 141:3
w. his shroud 436:21
w. in the blood of the Lamb 71:6
w. in the moon 263:12
W. Man's burden 303:24
w. rose weeps 536:15
w. shall not neutralize 96:14
w. silken turbans 350:9
w. tremendous daybreak 84:20
wild w. horses play 15:23
with w. fire laden 492:29
world is w. with May 530:3
your fleece is w. 166:3
your sins..as w. as snow 52:30
Whited: thou w. wall 65:15
w. sepulchres 60:19
White-faced: lies w. and still 567:5
Whitefoot: come uppe W. 267:13
Whitehall: sentinel on W. gate 322:20
Whitehall Court: grass..up and down W. 377:26
White Horse: W. of the W. Vale 140:11
White House: Log-cabin to W. 543:14

Whiten the green plains 492:26
Whitens ere his hour 531:2
Whiter: I shall be w. than snow 395:8
not found a w. soul 308:2
scar that w. skin 473:11
w. than be the flocks 232:1
w. than new snow 478:19
w. than the whitewash 11:8
Whites: all w. are ink 480:39
see the w. of their eyes 404:1
Whitewash: whiter than the w. 11:8
Whitewash'd wall 225:3
Whither: I know not W. 206:13
I well know W. 80:16
none knows w. 39:29
w. away, fair rover 81:26
w. depart the souls 146:14
w. flown again 207:24
w. hurried hence 206:14
w. is fled the..gleam? 576:8
w. it goeth 63:7
w., O splendid ship 81:26
w. thou goest 47:1
Whithersoever thou goest 46:37
Whiting: as the w. said 253:33
w. to a snail 129:22
Whitman: daintily dressed Walt W. 142:19
Whitsun: Wednesday in W. week 441:31
Whittle the Eden Tree 295:15
Whizz of my cross-bow 149:18
Who: and w. are you? 8:17
might have hated, w. can tell! 92:35
w. are you, aged man? 131:22
w. but he? 160:2
w. can say? 91:18
w. comes here? 369:17
w. is on my side? w.? 48:30
w. is the King of glory 393:13
w. is the Potter, pray 207:16
w. is this? 534:10
w. is this that cometh 52:22, 55:5
w. knows how? 255:3
w., or why, or which 312:13
w. would true valour see 99:35
w. would wish to die? 78:24
w. you are 139:12
yonder peasant, w. is he? 361:20
Whoe'er she be 166:17
Whole: equal to the w. of that commerce 100:22
gained ground upon the w. 95:17
had I stol'n the w. 516:11
half is greater than the w. 248:2
indictment against an w. people 101:2
keep w. and undefiled 388:37
not be w. of that wound 328:5
one stupendous w. 383:18
saw it w. 16:2
seeing but w. of them 413:17
taste the w. of it 95:11
they that be w. 58:39
what a w. Oxford is 148:15
w. America 100:27
w. I planned 95:13
whose prayers would make me w. 299:27(-300)
Wholesome: cheap but w. salad 164:1
nights are w. 430:20
w. parritch 105:2
w. wold 296:29
Wholly: some few to be read w. 27:17
w. hopes to be 91:1
w. slaves or w. free 192:26
Whoop: merrily we'll w. 568:22
Whooping: out of all w. 428:3
Whoops: Devil w. 295:15
Whore: cunning w. of Venice 472:37
fortune's a right w. 563:24
judgment of the great w. 71:31
morals of a w. 270:21
more like a w.'s than a man's 299:18
Pity She's a W. 210:2
posture of a w. 426:4
rogue is married to a w. 301:11
w. and gambler 73:28(-74)
woman's a w. 272:19
young man's w. 271:23
Whoremaster man 452:19
Whores I never saw so many w. 564:7
Whoreson: thou w. zed 452:33

Whoring: a w. with their own inventions 398:14
Whorlèd: beat upon my w. ear 254:26
Whose: never ask me w. 263:7
say W.? 567:12
Why: asking not wherefore nor w. 171:21
causes w. and wherefore 445:7
fell out they knew not w. 110:2
for every w...a wherefore 110:12
for w.?..God is good 292:9
I can't think w. 221:39
know not how, nor w. 82:23
know the reason w. 239:7
never tell w. 221:9
whence you came, nor w. 207:7
who, or w., or which 312:13
w. are we? Of what scene.. 491:25
w. don't you speak for yourself 316:5
w., Edward, tell me w.! 573:3
'w.' is plain 427:18
w., man of morals, tell me w.? 158:8
W. not knowing 206:13
w. so? 168:7
w. were they proud? 286:21
w. with an M.? 129:12
w. you go, nor where 207:7
without knowing how or w. 190:32
Wicked: as long as war is regarded as w. 569:33
desperately w. 55:20
fiery darts of the w. 68:13
God help the w. 439:36
half so w. as Lord George Hell 39:14
he must be w. 90:22
horrid w. boy 249:19
I's w. 517:7
little better than one of the w. 438:23
never wonder to see men w. 520:45
'no God,' the w. saith 146:31
no peace..unto the w. 54:21
something w. this way 460:1
teach thy ways unto the w. 395:9
tender mercies of the w. 50:2
thy intents w. or charitable 431:2
thy w. men from out thee 158:22
w. and the mad 386:2
w. cease from troubling 48:46
w. flee..no man pursueth 50:49
w. man turneth away 55:30
w., w. plant 305:18
w. woman liberty to gad 57:2
worse than w...vulgar 403:23
Wickedness: all the w. of the world 176:21
all w...little to the w. of a woman 57:1
God, that he should do w. 49:15
goeth on still in his w. 396:7
hated w. that hinders loving 93:48
leaven of malice and w. 389:35
loose the bands of w. 54:36
manifold sins and w. 388:6
Path of W. 32:9
shapen in w. 395:8
spiritual w. in high places 68:11
their hand unto w. 399:33
w. proceedeth from the wicked 47:27
ye have plowed w. 55:47
Wicket: flanelled fools at the w. 297:16
Wickliff: ashes of W. 212:8
Widdicombe Fair 33:1
Widdrington: low as ever was Squire W. 192:19
Wide: alone on a w. w. sea 149:20, 150:14
hath y-sowen wonder w. 138:15
his youthful hose..too w. 427:21
how w...the east is from the west 398:6
nor so w. as a church door 478:14
we're very w. awake 219:34
Weser, deep and w. 94:32
w. as his command 190:8
w. is the gate 58:23
w. of it like Mr. Canning's wit 240:7
Widened: Creation and 566:13
thoughts of men are w. 534:29
Widening: ever w. slowly silence all 531:11
Widens: pale waste w. 16:4
Wider: for thee thrice w. 442:38

Wider (*cont.*)
water's w. . . than Blood 266:17
w. still and w. 42:20
Wide-watered shore 341:15
Widow: certain poor w. 61:8
defendeth the fatherless and w. 400:20
here's to the w. of fifty 500:39
I am a w. 508:4
my basnet a w.'s curch? 31:6
or Molly Stark's a w. 511:15
she was a w. 61:32
some undone w. 334:26
virgin-w. 193:18
W. at Windsor 303:27
w. bird sate mourning 492:24
Widowhood: comfortable estate of w. 214:20
nursling of thy w. 491:16
Widows: be wery careful o' w. 178:36
defendeth the cause of the w. 396:5
devour w.' houses 61:7
do as other w. 215:3
fatherless children, and w. 389:4
many w. were in Israel 61:26
visit the fatherless and w. 60:34
when w. exclaim 204:8
w. in Corioli 429:8
w. . .most perverse creatures 2:18
Width of the waters 16:4
Wield the mighty frame 348:30
Wielder of the stateliest measure 541:8
Wife: all the world and his wife 13:17, 520:30
as the husband is, the w. is 534:18
better accommodated than with a w. 442:9
borrowed my neighbour's w. 302:31
bracelets to adorn the w. 245:8
Brutus' harlot, not his w. 449:17
Caesar's w. must be above suspicion 120:15
cares of daughter, w., or friend 358:1
carline w.'s three sons 33:2
cleave unto his w. 44:18
come and be my w.? 311:13
could not act upon my w. 74:16
covet thy neighbour's w. 390:17
damn'd in a fair w. 469:21
debauch his friend's w. genteelly 272:26
dwindle into a w. 156:14
each w. had seven sacks 366:8
faithful w., without debate 518:2
fell out, my w. and I 538:9
Giant Despair had a w. 99:20
giving honour unto the w. 70:2
have or have no w. 28:18
here lies my w. 192:18
he that hath w. and children 26:34
his w. could eat no lean 367:10
his w. looked back 44:53
husband frae the w. despises 108:4
I chose my w. . .wear well 227:16
I'd have no w. 165:32
if Laura had been Petrarch's w. 115:39
if w. should dine at Edmonton 160:8
I hadna been his w. 35:10
I hae a w. o' my ain 106:14
I have married a w. 62:7
in every port a w. 173:5
in every port he finds a w. 72:18
in the lofty character of W. 174:37
I think my w. be honest 472:7
keeps up a w.'s spirits 214:20
kick his w. out of bed 518:8
kill a w. with kindness 479:7
kiss'd the fiddler's w. 107:15
letter from his w. 128:15
light w. . .heavy husband 465:24
like a comfit-maker's w. 440:6
like Caesar's w., all things 8:6
look out for a w. 518:38
love your neighbour's w. 325:18
Man and his W. 304:52
man and w. . .never. .hang one another 203:17
man and w. one flesh 154:32
marriage with his brother's w. 446:14
match'd with an aged w. 540:31
monstrous animal a husband and w. 204:31
moral centaur, man and w. 116:20

Wife (*cont.*)
Mother, W., and Queen 539:12
must be in want of a w. 22:28
my 'oss, my w., and my name 518:29
my sonne's w., Elizabeth 267:14
my true and honourable w. 449:17
my w. . . poor wretch 377:21
my William's w. 223:9
neighed after his neighbour's w. 55:11
neither maid nor w. 527:12
no casual mistress, but a w. 532:41
not the bond of man and w. 530:40
old w. sat at her ivied door 120:20
one w. and hardly any mistresses 414:16
one w. is too much 215:5
quarrelled with his w. 376:18
railing w. 440:2
ran after the farmer's w. 369:8
remember Lot's w. 62:31
sailor's w. had chestnuts 456:10
same face of his wedded w. 304:36
sanctified by the w. 66:31
save a wretched w. 214:21
sic a w. as Willie had 108:32
Sir, your w. 277:16
sweet wee w. o' mine 107:16
Thane of Fife had a w. 460:25
thanked God my w. was dead 91:26
that Lord Brutus took to w. 449:18
there's my w. . .she's the Broad 511:5
thy bottle, and thy w. 384:6
thy w. . .as the fruitful vine 399:36
t'other w. would take ill 215:5
to thy wedded w. 391:28
true to his w. 551:11
two extremes. .like man and w. 143:25
uncumber'd with a w. 192:14
weans and w. 104:23
when his w. talks Greek 277:1
when that the w. is May 561:1
whose w. shall I take? 357:11
widow'd w. 419:14
w. and children. .bills of charges 26:35
w. for breed 216:2
w. of thy bosom 46:25
w. sing to her child 196:2
w. smiles, and lets it go 36:19
w. was pretty, trifling 165:9
w. who preaches in her gown 253:29
wind is my w. 290:12
without a w. 367:18
Wifely: flour of w. pacience 137:24
Wifie: thrifty w.'s smile 104:33
Wig: away went hat and w. 160:1
lady in the w. 176:26
my hat and w. will soon be here 160:5
thy own hare, or a w.? 306:30
w. with the scorched foretop 325:28
Wight: maid and her w. 236:14
strange and wayward w. 37:6
w., if ever such w. were 470:29
w. of high renown 6:26
Wights: with worthy w. to reign 233:3
Wigwam: lights the w. 317:23
w. of Nokomis 317:22
Wild: avoid the w. and new 141:20
beat w. on this world 365:23
brought forth w. grapes 53:1
Call of the W. 315:23
den of w. things 249:9
fluttered folk and w. 303:24
grew more fierce and w. 244:10
half-w. and wholly tame 302:8
her eyes were w. 286:30
his w. tail. .his w. lone 304:22
nobly w., not mad 246:14
pray, Mr. W., why bitch? 204:15
rather rude and w. 41:14
state of w. alarm 220:7
talk a little w. 446:11
through what w. centuries 170:26
Wet W. Woods 304:22
what so w. as words? 97:24
w. air, world-mothering air 254:17
w. and dank with foam 293:22
w. animals never kill for sport 212:4
W. Ass stamps 206:1
w. beast, or a god 26:15
w. civility 246:4
w. he may be 176:24
w. in their attire 456:13

Wild (*cont.*)
w. in woods the noble savage 191:41
w. justice 27:4
w. trick of his ancestors 440:31
w. vicissitudes of taste 278:36
w. with all regret 538:19
w. with weeping 493:19
Wilderness: cometh up from the w. 52:22
crieth in the w. 54:9
crying in the w. 57:28
day of temptation in the w. 397:29
dwellings of the w. 395:30
Heaven's constellated w. 497:15
in perils in the w. 67:35
in the w. . .waters break out 54:3
into the w. to see? 59:6
like a pelican in the w. 398:1
little w. 333:2
long live the weeds and the w. 254:30
maketh the w. a standing water 398:20
man in the w. 367:20
meet Surrey in a w. 475:15
ninety and nine in the w. 62:10
savage w. into a glorious empire 101:15
scapegoat into the w. 46:8
singing in the W. 205:23, 24
some vast w. 162:40
to the w. I wander 12:2
waste howling w. 46:31
wentest through the w. 396:5
w. and the solitary place 54:1
w. of monkeys 464:11
w. of sweets 348:6
w. of this world 99:3
W. . .Paradise enow 205:23, 24
Wildernesses: desert w. 340:10
haunt thought's w. 497:2
Wildest peal for years 249:5
Wild-fowl: fetch the w. hame 32:15
more fearful w. 467:3
Pythagoras concerning w. 484:22
Wild-geese: if the w. fly that way 452:36
Wildly: not sing so w. well 380:18
speaks somewhat w. 200:33
start not so w. 435:20
Wildness: bereft of wet and of w. 254:30
Wilds where the caribou call 422:22
Wile: follow'd with endearing w. 224:23
Wiles: of w. more unexpert 345:16
simple w. 580:20
wanton w. 341:28
Wilful: little group of w. men 571:13
to w. men 453:2
Wilfull will do't 156:16
Wilfully seeks her own salvation 437:3
Wilhelmine: little grandchild W. 507:3
Wilkes: dine with Jack W., Sir! 273:17
Wilkins and his Dinah 10:18
Wilkinson: Mr. W., a clergyman 208:1
spade! with which W. 581:5
Will: aforementioned my last w. 8:4
all-urging W. 236:5
boy's w. is the wind's w. 316:38
by a mighty effort of w. 43:2
cause is in my w.: I w. not come 449:24
complies against his w. 111:18
consciousness the W. informing 236:6
disease of the w. 200:44
eternal spirit, against her w. 447:33
fix'd fate, free w. 345:23
foreknowledge, w., and fate 345:29
forge his own w. 222:9
heroes, if we w. 15:9
his stubborn w. 521:23
his w. his law 164:19
his w. is not his own 431:21
his w. made or suffered them 497:12
humanity's afflicted w. 574:23
if she w., she w.' 11:22
in our w. to love or not 348:12
I thowt 'twur the w. o' the Lord 541:6
it is my duty, and I w. 217:26
I w. . .because I w. do it 108:41
keep God's holy w. 391:2
laid me down with a w. 516:15
let what w. be o'er me 515:28
love-sick all against our w. 220:22
man has his w. 251:15
Mariner hath his w. 148:20
Michael Henchard's W. 237:7

Will (cont.)

minister of her w.	425:33
not because we w.	15:2
not in particular w.	481:12
not my w., but thine	62:45
puzzles the w.	434:4
reason and the w. of God	19:25
Rechabite poor W. must live	402:8
said the Piggy, 'I w.'	312:2
serveth not another's w.	583:9
shows a w. most incorrect	430:31
strong in w. to strive	541:3
s'pose I never w.	297:25
take the w. for the deed	520:19
temperate w.	580:21
that I should fulfil thy w.	394:13
thou hast thy W., and W. to boot	488:15
thy poverty, and not thy w.	478:38
Thyrsis of his own w.	18:23
thy w. be done in earth	58:4
torrent of a woman's w.	11:22
'twixt w. and w. not	461:26
unconquerable w.	344:14
upon her people's w.	539:13
wanton, w. ye?	231:39
we *know* our w. is free	271:28
we've the w.	360:4
we w. hear Caesar's w.	450:25
what I w. is fate	348:25
what of the Immanent W.?	235:20
whose w. is strong	541:19
who w., may hear Sordello	96:29
W. has woven	235:21
W. in over-plus	488:15
w. in us is over-rul'd	330:13
w. is free	15:9
w. like a..spear	15:21
W. of the Yukon	422:20
w. reigns	211:14
w. to do..soul to dare	416:17
w. you, won't you?	129:23
with all my w.	375:21
with half so good a w.	452:7
won my right good-w.	327:5, 551:5
works his sovereign w.	161:18
yet His w. be done	536:27
your Majesty's w. is law	220:21
you w. and you won't	187:7
you w., Oscar, you w.	566:10
Willed: all we have w. or hoped	89:9
if forgetting could be w.	336:9
William: my W.'s wife	223:9
tell W. cook	442:30
you are old, Father W.	128:28, 507:33
William Dewy	236:8
Williams: Dr. W.' pink pills	6:1
Willie: O love my W.!	121:15
sic a wife as W. had	108:32
so, W., let you and me. .	94:38
W. shall dance with Jane	5:25
Willing: Barkis is w.	174:17
dear Pig, are you w.	312:2
spirit indeed is w.	60:43
when a man says he's w.	174:20
w. nations knew	190:31
w. suspension of disbelief	152:26
w. to wound	385:29
Willingly: not w. let it die	352:21
Willingness: doer's w.	246:18
Will-o'-th'-Wisp: no W. mislight	246:23
Willoughby: Beaumont and W.	189:8
Willow: all a green w.	248:3, 473:6
Dido make a w.	465:17
make me a w. cabin	482:22
there is a w.	437:1
under the w.	418:12
w., titwillow, titwillow	220:17
w., w., waly!	220:31
Willows whiten	533:41
Willow-tree: al under the w.	136:17
on a weeping w.	10:21
wand of the w.	31:6
Wills: make our w. and do our duty	227:38
mention it within their w.	450:24
our w. and fates	435:13
our w. are gardeners	470:15
such a lot of people's W.	140:7
talk of w.	475:6
unruly w. and affections	389:37

Wills (cont.)

what she w. to do or say	349:1
w. above be done	479:18
w. of thy faithful people	389:50
Willy-nilly: Water w. flowing	206:13
w. blowing	206:13
Wilt: if thou w., remember	409:29
'w. thou?' said the. .minute	337:4
Wimpled, whining..boy	455:8
Win: eternal glory shalt thou w.	99:8
heads I w.	167:1
he does not w.	569:8
hopes to w. her	155:38
if you want to w. her hand	79:16
let the boy w. his spurs	195:24
nothing venture, nothing w.	219:14
one should lose, the other w.	330:13
they laugh that w.	472:23
time to w. this game	188:35
us to w.	509:4
Virtue he had vow'd to w.	375:22
when in doubt, w. the trick	264:24
who would greatly w.	118:12
w. or lose it all	355:19
w. us with honest trifles	456:22
yet wouldst wrongly w.	457:1
you to w. again	140:17
Winced nor cried aloud	241:18
Winchester: Jane lies in W.	297:20
while the stones of W.	297:20
Wind: after the w. an earthquake	48:8
against the w.	114:14
air goes by in a w.	39:3
all aloud the w. doth blow	456:1
all day the w. breathes	535:18
all the airts the w. can blaw	107:17
Angel of the Off-shore W.	298:10
as a w. shall go by	525:12
as cauld a w. as ever blew	106:26
as large a charter as the w.	427:17
as piffle before the w.	21:1
as soon as the w. goeth over it	398:7
as the light w. lives or dies	284:14
bay'd the whisp'ring w.	224:17
beat of the off-shore w.	298:27
betwixt the w. and his nobility	438:33
bids the w. blow the earth	453:3
blows the w. to-day	516:9
both with w. and stream	471:8
brought forth w.	53:32
chiding of the winter's w.	426:29
clear as w.	537:42
cold's the w.	170:24
come w., come weather	99:35
conflicting w. and rain	453:4
dry sun, dry w.	550:6
east w. made flesh	13:19
endure w. and weather	482:20
every w. of criticism	275:26
every w. of doctrine	67:57
except w. stands	549:24
fair stood the w. for France	189:6
fans, whose w. did seem to glow	424:6
fill'd with a lusty w.	135:19
flower—the w...shall wound	114:5
fluttering in the w.	92:34
forgot to w. up the clock?	513:1
frosty w. made moan	409:20
frozen w. crept on	492:24
gentle w. does move	75:21
God tempers the w.	512:28
gone with the w.	187:10
good south w.	148:28
hiding place from the w.	53:43
his hammer of w.	545:13
hollow blasts of w.	216:5
hope constancy in w.	117:13
how e'er the w. doth blow	373:11
into the w. shall lightly pass	233:3
is the w. in that door?	328:6
jovial w. of winter	293:13
keep the w. away	437:18
let her down the w.	471:38
like th'inconstant w.	215:14
like the Pentecost W.	236:29
like W. I go	206:12
loose as the w.	244:9
loud blew the w.	508:4
loud dry w.	579:8
man control the w.	15:12
murmur in the w.	288:7

Wind (cont.)

nor ever w. blows loudly	531:37
not a breathing of the common w.	582:4
not with this w. blowing	300:2
observeth the w.	51:29
O wild West W.	496:4
O w., O w., the weder	138:28
pass by me as the idle w.	451:19
passionate w. of welcome	410:22
paths that w. and w.	568:27
perils both of w. and limb	110:28
pity from blust'ring w.	319:8
prevent the w. from blowing it out	311:17
rain and w. beat dark December	429:31
reed shaken with the w.	59:6
roaring in the w. all night	580:4
rude w. blows in your face	453:41
rushing mighty w.	64:24
same w. sang	523:15
shaken of a mighty w.	71:1
sits the w. in that corner?	468:21
soft-lifted by the winnowing w.	284:12
southwest-w. and the west-w.	521:30(–522)
sown the w.	55:46
stooping against the w.	411:15
storm and contrary w.	39:1
streaming to the w.	344:36
strive to w. ourselves too high	291:6
swoln with w.	342:29
tears shall drown the w.	457:9
the Lord was not in the w.	48:8
thou winter w.	427:22
throw the sand against the w.	75:17
thy great w. blows	586:2
'twas but the w.	113:26
unhelped by any w.	151:23
voice in every w.	230:25
walketh upon the wings of the w.	398:8
warm w., the west w.	334:15
welter to the parching w.	342:10
western w. was wild	293:22
western w., when wilt thou blow?	11:14
when she dances in the w.	194:22
when the w. blew due East	128:9
when the w. blows	73:14
when the w. is in the east	11:21
when the w. is..in the east	173:25
when the w. is southerly	433:20
where the w.'s feet shine	524:23
which way the w. is	422:5
whistling mane of every w.	544:18
w. a fiery Pegasus	440:18
w., all unseen	455:17
W. along the Waste	206:13
w. and storm	400:24
w. and the rain	484:27
w. and wave and oar	535:20
w. began to roll	537:1
w. bloweth where it listeth	63:7
w. blows it back	75:17
w. blows out of the gates	585:13
w. blows stronger	361:23
w. doth blow to-day	32:16
w. is chill	418:23
w. is hovering	493:12
w. is in the palm-tree	299:10
w. is my wife	290:12
w. it into a ball	75:8
w. may blow through it	379:11
w. of Death's..wing	410:24
w. of God	293:16
w. of the western sea	538:12
w. on the heath	78:24, 25
w.'s like a whetted knife	334:12
w. slowly o'er the lea	229:28
w.'s song	334:10
w. sweep man away	15:12
w.'s will	316:38
w. that blows	173:8
w. that follows fast	167:20
W., that grand old harper	503:13
w. up the sun and moon	119:15
w. was a torrent	366:1
w. was cold	416:29
w. was fair	192:31
w. was on the lea	512:10

Wind (*cont.*)
w., w.! thou art sad 359:18
with a tempestuous w. 229:6
with the w. doth go 189:2
woord is but w. 321:8
words but w. 110:46
Wind: ein sanfter W. 224:7
Windes: wie des W. Sausen 415:25
Wind-besomed chambers 544:7
Wind-flowers: pied w. 497:21
w., and violets 494:10
Wind-grieved Apennine 91:5
Winding: long, long trail a-w. 293:1
slow w. Ouse 162:7
to whose w. quest 551:15
w. His lonely horn 584:20
w. mossy ways 287:29
w. stair 26:28
w. up days with toil 444:23
w. up every meal by.. 187:15
w. up the watch of his wit 479:34
Winding-sheet: England's w. 73:28(–74)
her w...high as her throat 419:19
snow shall be their w. 122:20
waters were his w. 35:23
well wrapped in their w. 189:19
w. of Edward's race 229:22
Wind-in-the-orchard style 337:2
Windless: Elysian, w. 497:15
Windlestraw: naked Duke of W. 127:9
Windmill: cheese and garlic in a w. 440:2
Window: against the w. beats 546:26
at my w. bid good-morrow 341:31
if a thing happened at one w. 273:27
little w. where the sun 252:33
out at the w. the next 178:25
this w. for the east 169:13
through yonder w. 477:13
tirling at the w. 339:9
to thy chamber w., Sweet! 494:7
where there is no w. 336:15
w. to open onto the Lake 290:16
Windowed: w. raggedness 453:14
within a w. niche 113:28
Window-glass to shivers 419:33
Window-panes: its back upon the w. 197:17
Windows: breaking of w. 357:23
by eastern w. only 147:8
crimson-blank the w. flare 300:3
five w. of the soul 74:12
I cleaned the w. 221:15
make der w. sound 313:13
opening the w. at Randalls 22:15
rich w. that exclude 230:18
storied w. richly dight 341:24
those that look out of the w. 51:33
through w. and through curtains 186:19
up flew the w. all 160:2
wish thar was w. to my Sole 559:35
Window-sill: hopped upon the w. 515:25
Wind-ridden restless sea 171:19
Winds: all the w. of doctrine 352:17
amid the wafting in 567:2
as on the four w. 333:1
blow me about in w. 473:32
blow w., and crack your cheeks 453:5
carried about of w. 70:19
change, as ye list, ye w. 215:40
come as the w. come 419:4
courted by all the w. 350:31
dead w.' and spent waves' riot 523:17
enlarged w...no such liberty 319:7
faithless as the w. or seas 421:13
for us the w. do blow 244:23
for whom all w. are quiet 522:15
gathering w. will call 498:26
great w. shoreward blow 15:23
great w. Thy clarions 142:26
heareth not the loud w. 580:11
hear the w. howling 16:1
her w. and waters 423:26
imprisoned in the viewless w. 462:9
leaves that w. have taken 523:21
March w., and April showers 8:9
me howling w. drive devious 160:35
melodious w. have birth 75:18
motions of the viewless w. 579:25
night of south w. 567:16
north-east w. blow..odours 347:1

Winds (*cont.*)
rough w. do shake 486:18
sport of w. 346:26
stars and the w. 521:30(–522)
stormy w. did blow 9:3
stormy w. do blow 123:10
summer w. that creep 494:3
take advantage of all w. 212:18
take the w. of March 485:26
though w. blew great guns 173:9
thunder-zoned w. 495:27
untie the w. 460:4
visitation of the w. 442:1
wan waves and wet w. 523:19
what suns and w...make us 309:5
when the w. give o'er 557:24
when the w. of Spring 497:3
where the beetle w. 153:24
w. and seas are troublesome 168:13
w. and sunbeams 493:1
w. are all asleep 15:24
w. are breathing low 494:7
w. blew calm 359:27
w. come to me 576:5
w. into a subject 227:31
w. of heaven mix for ever 495:7
w. of heaven visit her face too roughly 430:33(–431)
w. of the World 296:3
w. somewhere safe to sea 523:23
w. that will be howling 582:18
w. were love-sick 424:6
w. whistle shrill 543:11
with a noise of w. 521:30
Windsor: Widow at W. 303:27
Wind-swept: hawk to the w. sky 296:29
Windward: between w. and lee 523:13
w. of the law 143:5
Windy: shadows and w. places 521:30
w. night a rainy morrow 487:23
w. side of the law 484:12
w. ways of men 541:14
Wine: across the walnuts and the w. 537:3
aged and a great w. 337:26
best fits my little w. 245:18
bin of w. 516:12
blood and w. are red 569:1
books, fruit, french w. 290:24
bored with good w. 182:24
Botticelli isn't a w. 403:36
buy w. and milk without money 54:29
can with w. dispense 164:33
Chian w. 18:16
come ye here to drink good w. 31:5
Constitutions o'er your w. 123:1
conversations over the w. 546:41
crush their w. 332:17
deep in anything but—W. 206:24
drank death like w. 141:14
drank the red w. through the helmet 417:4
drinken strong w., reed as blood 137:20
drinking the blude-red w. 31:23
drink one cup of w. 418:19
drinks his w. 'mid laughter free 10:21
drink thy w. with a merry heart 51:20
drunken, but not with w. 53:35
drunk your water and w. 297:13
fetch to me a pint o' w. 105:36
Flask of W. 205:23
flown with insolence and w. 344:35
fond of Spanish w. 333:22
forbidden W. 206:15
full of dewy w. 287:31
gave her cocktails and w. 10:25
giant refreshed with w. 397:1
good w.—a friend 3:11
good w...good familiar creature 471:23
good w. needs no bush 428:40
have some w. 129:5
having drunk old w. 61:28
he drinks no w. 442:20
honest talk and wholesome w. 540:30
hurt not the oil and the w. 70:44
I don't see any w. 129:5
if it doesn't get into the w. 142:12
I'll not look for w. 280:21
invisible spirit of w. 471:21
I rather like bad w. 182:24

Wine (*cont.*)
it wasn't the w. 178:29
Jug of W. 205:24
last Companion: W. 42:2
like generous w. 111:24
like the best w. 52:20
little w. for thy stomach 68:50
live upon w. 41:30
lordliest in their w. 350:38
loves not woman, w. 321:5, 543:5
mellow, like good w. 378:18
Mr. Weston's good w. 22:11
new friend is as new w. 56:40
new w. into old bottles 58:42
of w. and wax 583:26
old w. wholesomest 563:22
our ballast is old w. 376:24
out-did the frolic w. 246:15
pass the rosy w. 177:29
poisonous w. 287:19
press the rue for w. 419:8
red sweet w. of youth 83:19
rich Canary w. 280:9
rinsed with w. 254:27
Samian w. 116:1, 3
sans W., sans Song 206:8
seas of fire, like w. 548:18
spill'd the w. 374:20
sweet white w. 333:20
temptations both in w. and women 305:1
there was w. before 244:9
thirsty grief in w. we steep 319:6
this the W. 75:20
thy love is better than w. 51:37
victuals and the w. 121:9
when the w. is in 38:21
whose w. was the bright dew 497:22
w. and women 109:12, 115:33
w. from the royal Pope 329:1
W. has play'd the Infidel 207:22
w. in rivers 419:33
w. inspires us 214:29
w. is a mocker 50:23
w. is red 396:31
w. is the strongest 56:16
w. maketh merry 51:25
w. of life is drawn 458:24
w. that maketh glad 398:9
w., true begetter 42:1
w. when it is red 50:32
W.! W.! W.! Red W.! 205:12
women and w. 214:29
Wine-cup: when the w. glistens 419:16
Wine-lees and democracy 89:23
Wine-pots: castaway w. 146:8
Wine-press: trodden the w. alone 55:6
w. which ye tread 322:25
Wines: feast of w. on the lees 53:31
French cookery, and French w. 542:33
old books, old w. 226:43
Wing: as inconstant w. 494:3
beats with light w. 359:1
Bird is on the W. 205:14, 15
birds are on the w. 152:17
brighter plumage, stronger w. 308:17
Conquest's crimson w. 229:20
damp my intended w. 349:6
Death's imperishable w. 410:24
estridges that w. the wind 440:17
ever on the w. 350:19
flapt its tinsel w. 332:5
hide his head under his w. 368:2
lark's on the w. 94:40
longest on the w. 164:5
no world-terror's w. 140:23
on a broken w. 536:22
on leathern w. 153:24
shadow of Thy w. 565:7
soars on golden w. 341:12
spread the grey w. 584:27
start a w. 545:1
take under my w. 220:16
trailing w. 16:5
up they sprung upon the w. 344:27
white clouds on the w. 4:19
w. of friendship 177:28
w. of hippogriff 350:16
w. the midway air 454:3
wounded in the w. 73:20
Winged: Time's w. chariot 333:9

INDEX

Winged (*cont.*)
w. his roving flight 386:12
w. minute 337:4
w. sea-girt citadel 113:16
w. the shaft 117:25
w. with vain desires 192:23
Wings: all legs and w. 34:15
all the w. of the Loves 525:6
as the bird w. and sings 95:17
as the w. of a dove 396:7
bug with gilded w. 385:31
clap her broad w. 211:26
claps her w. 321:16
clip an Angel's w. 286:42
combs its silver w. 332:20
defend thee under his W. 397:18
each one had six w. 53:8
ears like errant w. 140:21
find w. waiting there 39:4
for a horse with w. 429:30
for their leathern w. 466:42
from His dripping w. 585:8
from the w. of Night 316:7
girt with golden w. 340:11
head, hands, w., or feet 346:14
healing in his w. 56:15, 161:21
hear the beating of his w. 82:17
his luminous w. 19:21
his w. were wet 231:33
ill news hath w. 189:2
imped the w. of fame 125:1
lets grow her w. 340:20
long expected healing w. 551:19
Love without his w. 117:43
Love with unconfined w. 319:4
make themselves w. 50:31
mount up with w. 54:14
my horse a thing of w. 78:2
now can spare their w. 166:4
now with his w. 231:39
on what w. dare he aspire 75:24
on w. they are carried 516:3
poor splendid w. 522:17
prisoners underneath her w. 445:26
quivering w. composed 580:26
riches have w. 163:14
sailing on obscene w. 151:19
shadow of thy w. 392:28, 395:17
shakes his dewy w. 169:13
shakes the w. 194:22
spread his w. on the blast 118:38
straight on w. I arise 80:30
that which hath w. 51:26
though he has w. 498:16
through their w. 544:6
till the little w. are stronger 540:10
unthinkable w. 141:1
upon her w. presents 245:24
upon my eagle's w. 191:16
upon the w. of night 478:19
upon the w. of silence 340:15
upon thee of the wind 398:8
viewless w. of Poesy 287:28
whether pigs have w. 130:15
while the w. aspire 580:26
w. of an ostrich 326:4
w. of grasshoppers 477:7
w. of the morning 400:9
W. o' the Mornin' 304:1
w. the soul 195:15
with ah! bright w. 254:25
with w. display'd 343:16
Wingy mysteries 86:7
Wink: never came a w. too soon 252:33
not slept one w. 429:33
w. and hold out mine iron 443:14
w. a reputation down 521:9
w. the other eye 217:23
Winked at 'Omer..he w. back 303:23
Winkie: Wee Willie W. 339:9
Winking: w. at the brim 287:24
w. Mary-buds 429:25
Winks: moon w. 472:36
w. and shuts his apprehension up 331:21
Winners: in war..no w. 135:8
Winning: glory of the w. 336:8
ne'er act the w. part 247:19
w. each heart 173:12
w. wave 246:4
w. way with you 155:31

Winning (*cont.*)
worth the wear of w. 41:17
worth thy w. 191:9
Winnings: one heap of all your w. 297:11
Wins: silly game where nobody w. 212:9
who loses, and who w. 454:19
Winsome: my w. marrow 235:1
w. wee thing 107:16
Winter: as a lusty w. 426:37
bare W. suddenly was changed 497:20
Christmas..in the middle of w. 2:15
crown old W.'s head 166:20
dark as w. was the flow 122:17
English w.—ending in July 116:47
ere the w. storms 4:11
find the w.'s rage 361:23
furious w.'s rages 430:1
her w. weeds outworn 493:25
how like a w. 487:27
if W. comes 496:11
in the haunch of w. sings 442:24
in w. I get up at night 515:14
it was not in the w. 252:11
it was the w. wild 343:11
most love W. 375:11
no w. in't 426:1
no w. in thy year 97:30, 315:21
on a w.'s morn 311:22
one cold w.'s day 249:18
on w.'s traces 521:30
our severest w. 164:27
past in the w. of love 372:18
reigns in the w.'s pale 485:16
sad tale's best for w. 485:10
same w. and summer 464:8
savour all the w. long 485:22
seem a w.'s day 407:18
summer, and w. hoar 494:19
sunbeam in a w.'s day 195:14
thou w. wind 427:22
'tis past, the w. 334:16
touched by the fury of the w. 38:31(–39)
very dead of w. 197:13
w. and rough weather 427:7
W. comes to rule the..year 546:24
w. fly-fishing 559:9
W.-garment of Repentance 205:15
W. is come and gone 491:22
w. is past 52:1
w. ling'ring chills..May 226:10
w. of our discontent 476:2
W., ruler of th'..year 163:24
W. slumbering 152:17
w.'s not gone yet 452:36
w., spring, and summer 8:14
w.'s rains and ruins 521:30(–522)
w. talk by the fireside 27:2
w. was not unkind 80:27
w., when the dismal rain 503:13
Winters: fifty w. o'er him 230:19
forty w. shall besiege 486:10
four lagging w. 474:16
in your..throat she w. 125:10
praise the w. gone 586:13
three w. cold 487:29
Wintry: long, long w. nights 311:15
Wipe: rash gazer w. his eye 245:13
w. a bloody nose 215:26
w. another's tears 109:1
w. away all tears 71:8, 45
w. my weeping eyes 562:12
Wiped: w. them soon 349:31
w. with a little address 162:8
Wipers of scores out 94:38
Wipes: cive, anheling, w. 251:19
Wiping something off a slate 294:18
Wires: across the w. 23:14
if hairs be w., black w. grow 488:13
Wisdom: all men's w. 414:3
beginning of w. 398:25
celestial W. calms 279:15
confounds its w. 251:23
contrivance of human w. 102:10
dispose of highest w. 351:7
famous then by w. 350:10
gold..at the root of w. 111:39
here is w...the royal Law 157:13
how can he get w. 57:12
if any of you lack w. 69:27
increased in w. and stature 61:22

Wisdom (*cont.*)
in w. never was so frail 470:29
knowledge, nor w., in the grave 51:21
light in W.'s eyes 561:11
love is the w. of the fool 277:12
magnanimity..truest w. 101:14
more of w. in it 581:15
no w. in useless..sorrow 277:41
only infallible criterion of w. 103:2
palace of w. 77:8
part of w. 163:19
pray for w. yet 3:6
price of w. is above rubies 49:8
privilege of w. to listen 251:22
Seed of W. did I sow 206:12
seen all Solomon's w. 47:42
song is not truth, not W. 561:11
spirit of w. and understanding 53:17
spontaneous w. 581:16
teach eternal w. 383:23
there need not be w. 411:37
thine endless w. 202:22
this w...not from above 69:39
those who love want w. 496:24
thy w., less thy certainty 12:9
understand w. secretly 395:8
vain w. all 345:30
want of human w. 310:18
wearing his w. lightly 529:3
whatever w. sleep with thee 533:21
what is better than w.? 137:37
what w. lays on evil men 163:45
w. and goodness to the vile 454:1
W. and Spirit of the Universe! 575:21
w., and wit are little seen 80:1, 139:5
w. at one entrance 346:24
W. be put in a silver rod 74:2
w. crieth without 49:39
w. excelleth folly 51:1
w. from our councils 101:17
W. goes by majorities 337:32
w. has taught us to be calm 251:4
w. in minds attentive 163:49
w. in the scorn of consequence 537:33
w. in women 84:22
w. is better than rubies 49:52
w. is humble 163:50
w. is justified of her children 59:9
w. is the principal thing..get w. 49:42
w. lingers 534:30
w. of a great minister? 282:18
w. of a learned man 57:11
w. of human contrivances 100:25
w. of our ancestors 101:35
w. of the ancients 28:11
w. of the just 61:11
W. say another 103:16
w. shall die with you 48:57
w.'s root 104:21
W.'s self oft seeks..solitude 340:20
w. the mirrored shield 491:27
w. with mirth 225:26
wise through excess of w. 200:13
with how little w...governed 372:15
with the ancient is w. 48:58
wrath of the lion..w. of God 77:16
Wise: all things w. and wonderful 3:14
beacons of w. men 266:22
being darkly w. 383:22
better to be fortunate than w. 563:31
be w. to-day 587:3
be w. with speed 586:23
both true, both w. 158:13
business of a w. man to be happy 273:20
by experience w. 386:4
confirm the w. 164:34
consider her ways, and be w. 49:45
cunning men pass for w. 25:44
either conform, or be more w. 377:24
errors of a w. man 73:15
even the w. are merry 585:15
every pure and w. spirit 200:41
every w. man's son 482:28
fair and w. and good 368:1
first be w. and good 351:19
follies of the w. 279:10
folly of the w. 277:12
folly to be w. 230:30
foolish..to confound the w. 66:20
from letters to be w. 279:4

INDEX

Wise (*cont.*)

great men are not always w.   49:12
grow w. for spite   520:55
he that hath little business..w.   57:11
he would become w.   77:14
hid these things from the w.   61:37
histories make man w.   27:19
holy, fair, and w. is she   484:40
I heard a w. man say   262:15
immediately w.   84:6
just, gentle, w.   497:12
leave the W. to talk   206:9
leisure to grow w.   17:4
lowly w.   348:31, 574:1
makes the w. man mad   93:14
merry and w.   7:22, 106:6, 335:4
more happy, if less w.   117:47
more nice than w.   160:36
more of the fool than..w.   25:30
more than woman to be w.   357:3
more..valorous than manly w.   331:6
more w. when he had   274:23
nations slowly w.   279:4
Nature..w. in every part   547:10
nor ever did a w. one   407:24
not w. in your own conceits   66:5
not worldly w.   404:6
obscurely w.   275:1
old and crafty and w.   585:14
only wretched are the w.   401:33
pretend they ne'er so w.   350:26
quiet, w., and good   498:15
reputed w., for saying nothing   462:34
simple with the w.   134:18
smile with the w.   271:27
so proud, so witty and so w.   407:22
sorrow makes us w.   533:21
so w. so young   476:19
talk too w.   297:10
teach a monarch to be w.   229:19
they are w. and honourable   450:32
those that think them w.   4:10
three w. men of Gotham   369:9
to be w. and eke to love   510:22
to be w., and love   481:16
to love and to be w.   100:12
to love is w.   82:1
to the w. man ports   474:19
tree that a w. man sees   77:11
virtuous and w. he was   14:23
Walter, be w.   141:20
well-govern'd and w. appetite   340:34
we were very, very w.   148:17
what all the w. men promised   335:14
while the great and w. decay   312:24
who are a little w.   186:22
who can be w., amazed   458:25
whoso is w. will ponder   398:22
w., and beautiful   15:9
w. and masterly inactivity   326:28
w. and salutary neglect   100:25
w. as serpents   58:49
w. as Thurlow looked   211:1
w. enough to play the fool   483:23
w., fair-spoken   447:9
w. father that knows his own   463:31
w., for cure, on exercise..   192:15
w., idle, childish   543:23
w. in his own conceit   50:40
w. in their own craftiness   48:51
W. man or a Fool   75:13
w. men from the east   57:23
w. of the world..made dumb   171:4
w. son maketh a glad father   49:54
w. through excess of wisdom   200:13
w. Tory and a w. Whig   274:35
w., upright, valiant   578:5
w. want love   496:24
w. who soar   580:27
words are w. men's counters   248:19
words of the w. are as goads   51:34
Wiseacres have seen..electric light   82:8
Wisely: not w. but too well   474:2
thou dost not enquire w.   51:12
unjust steward..done w.   62:20
w. and slow   478:2
w. worldly   404:6
Wiseman: wise-manned..by W.   95:30
Wiser: French..w. than they seem   27:12
grow w. and better   387:2
I am w. than the aged   399:20

Wiser (*cont.*)

ignorant..guided by the w.   126:5
not left a better or w.   225:34
not the w. grow   381:3
no w. than a daw   445:20
sadder and a w. man   150:17
sluggard is w. in his own conceit   50:42
Spaniards seem w.   27:12
w. being good than bad   89:22
w. than the children of light   62:20
w. than their own   84:22
w. than thou art ware   427:4
w. than we know   200:27
w. today than he was yesterday   520:46
young man will be w.   530:1
Wisest: entrap the w.   464:15
first and w. of them all   350:12
more than the w...can answer   154:21
not the w. men   138:1
w., brightest, meanest   384:12
w. fool·in Christendom   242:4
w. man the warl' saw   106:1
w. men have erred   350:26
w., virtuousest, discreetest   349:1
Wish: as women w. to be   251:25
don't you w. you may get it?   34:18
each w. of my heart   356:12
fled from her w.   470:29
god-like w., or hope divine   574:2
I never fram'd a w.   163:35
man whose w. and care   386:26
more than man to w. thee so   357:3
neither w. death   518:2
no addition nor my w.   472:19
our utmost w. possessing   215:37
she'll w. there wos more   179:7
strongly w. for what I faintly hope   193:27
thy own w. w. I thee   455:5
thy w. was father..to that thought   442:27
to his w. or not   575:11
w. him safe at home   282:10
w. it all at an end   103:37
w. it well   183:22
w. it were only mine   300:16
w. to get out   201:11
w. you all the joy that you can w.   464:20
Wished: devoutly to be w.   434:4
good things..to be w.   25:16
nor w., nor car'd   401:29
they w. for come   438:31
'twas all he w.   230:13
whom I w. to see   292:5
w. all men as rich as he   218:27
w. for the day   65:29
w. for to hear   292:5
w. himself the heaven's breath   455:17
w. she had not heard it   470:3
w. that heaven had made her   470:3
w. to be with them   416:29
Wishes: all made of w.   428:28
all their country's w.   153:29
good w. to the corpse   36:11
her little w. and ways   237:5
his nest of w.   337:18
meet you her my w.   166:18
my w.' cloudy character   166:21
so many w. feedest   17:22
their sober w.   230:7
toast our wants and w.   384:31
to whom I gave their w.   425:17
Wishest should be undone   457:1
Wishing: each w. for the sword   336:18
w. me like to one more rich   486:24
Wisp on the morass   118:8
Wissenschaft: die Politik ist keine exakte W.   72:29
Wist not that the Lord was departed   46:59
Wistful: such a w. eye   569:2
Wit: accepted w. has but to say   222:30
all thy Piety nor W.   207:2
as a w., if not first   225:31
at their w.'s end   398:18
at thirty, the w.   211:14
baiting-place of w.   501:26
beauty, w., high birth   481:21
becomes excellent w.   442:21
beef..does harm to my w.   482:6
brevity is the soul of w.   432:38

Wit (*cont.*)

cause that w. is in other men   441:11
craves a kind of w.   483:23
devise, w.!   455:1
drawn his w. as well in brass   281:9
fancy w. will come   382:9
few..plays can boast of more w.   201:32
Flavia's a w.   384:31
foolish w.   482:12
high as metaphysic w.   110:13
highest reaches of a human w.   331:2
his comic w. degenerating   194:6
his fine w...such a wound   495:13
his weapon w.   254:13
his w. in his belly   481:10
his w. invites you   159:20
his w. was in his own power   280:1
how now, w.!   426:19
how the w. brightens   382:34
I had but little w.   369:13
in her attire doth show her w.   8:14
in w. a man   382:15
let w. bear a stroke   549:26
like Mr. Canning's w.   240:7
liveliest effusions of w.   22:22
loudest w.   117:5
man of w...long time in gaol   386:36
mechanic part of w.   202:3
mingled with a little w.   192:27
miracle, instead of w.   587:15
mortify a w.   386:19
my w. to try   172:1
nature by her mother w.   510:6
neither a w. in his own eye   155:17
no more w. than a Christian   482:6
not his pointed w.   386:13
not w. enough to keep it sweet   275:27
old blind *débauchée* of w.   558:18
old man's w.   530:1
one man's w.   414:3
past the w. of man to say   467:22
pleasant smooth w.   21:13
put his whole w. in a jest   37:12
quickness of his w.   212:18
scintillations of your w.   228:2
sense and w. with poesy   117:15
shoots his w.   428:39
some beams of w.   193:2
spice of w.   516:12
tattle, and sometimes w.   139:22
the w. is out   38:21, 469:2
thy shallow w.   537:42
'tis w. in them   461:32
too nigh..to boast his w.   190:17
too proud for a w.   225:27
true w. is nature..   382:27
turbulent of w.   190:13
universal monarchy of w.   124:26
ware of mine own w.   427:5
whole wealth of thy w.   464:26
winding up the watch of his w.   479:34
Wisdom and W...little seen   80:1, 139:5
w., and mirth, and spleen   2:8
w. and sense..Horace Smith   495:14
w. enough to run away   111:15
w. in all languages   194:5
w. its soul   151:14
w., nor words   450:33
w. of fools   135:20
w.'s a feather   384:9
w.'s an unruly engine   243:32
w.'s the noblest frailty   422:29
w. that can creep   385:34
w. to persuade   169:17
w. will shine   193:11
w. with jealous eye surveys   143:4
you have a nimble w.   428:7
your w.'s too hot   455:4
Witch: aroint thee, w.!   456:10
his mother a w. maun be   31:7
like a w.'s oils   149:6
not suffer a w. to live   45:55
w. hath power to charm   430:20
w. the world with..horsemanship   440:18
Witchcraft: no w. charm thee   430:1
rebellion is as the sin of w.   47:16
w. celebrates   458:1
w. I have us'd   470:3
Witches: all the wild w.   584:22
think we're burning w.   141:12

[990]

Witching time of night 435:29
Wit-combats betwixt him and Ben Jonson 212:18
With: always w. us 284:22
be w. us yet 300:24
he that is not w. me 59:11, 61:48
I am w. them, in some ways 569:14
too much w. us 582:18
w., not thro', the eye 74:12
would I were w. him 443:18
Withal: so money comes w. 479:1
Withdraw: thou (Anthea) must w. 246:26
Withdrawing: long, w. roar 15:7
Withdrawn: as night is w. 81:20
my beloved had w. himself 52:11
Withdraws: w. into its happiness 332:18
w. us from the power of our senses 277:39
Withdrew: I w. my attention 276:17
Wither: age cannot w. her 424:9
flowers to w. 241:14
it needs must w. 473:11
names that must not w. 113:44
perforce must w. 453:42
Rose that cannot w. 552:2
w. long before it fall 113:38
Withered: could not w. be 280:21(-281)
cut down, dried up, and w. 397:15
lonely of heart is w. 585:13
no root, they w. away 9:22
so w., and so wild 456:13
waves its w. ears 165:17
w. all when my father died 436:32
w. and weeded away 147:24
w. in my hand 244:20
w. is the garland 425:29
w. to a stalk 32:17
Withereth: fast w. too 286:29
grass w. 54:10, 69:46
Withering: now w. in my bloom 382:1
w. and sere 381:1
w. on the virgin thorn 466:17
Witherington: for W. my heart was woe 30:14
for W. needs must I wail 491:11
low as ever was Squire W. 192:19
Withers: our w. are unwrung 435:16
w. on the hill 411:11
Withhold: God sometimes w. in mercy 357:27
w. not thine hand 51:30
Within: all that is w. him 460:32
equilibrium..set up from w. 214:2
he never went w. 158:1
I have that w. 430:30
I've that w...no plaisters 213:13
I w. did flow 548:18
kingdom of God is w. you 62:30
ne'er look w. 159:29
Paradise w. thee 349:29
secure w. 194:20
thou wert w. me 21:22
what is false w. 336:30
when once it is w. thee 243:26
whose fountains are w. 151:3
w. were fears 67:30
Withindoors house 255:6
Without: birds that are w. 563:25
for as much as w. Thee 305:8
w. a city wall 4:4
w. one plea 198:20
w. were fightings 67:30
Withstand: that ye may be able to w. 68:11
Withstood Christ then?..withstand Barabbas now 92:12
Witlings: tho' w. sneer 278:27
Witness: bore w. gloriously 351:7
heaven and earth to w. 46:22
not bear false w. 390:16
weak w. of thy name 351:8
Witnesses: cloud of w. 69:18
two or three w. 67:39
w. laid down their clothes 64:34
Wits: composed in their w. 19:20
dog had lost his w. 225:22
great w...to madness..alli'd 190:13
homely w. 448:28
incline w. to sophistry 28:13
Lord among w. 270:20
native to famous w. 350:11

Wits (cont.
rash bavin w. 440:8
recover his w. there 437:14
rhyming mother w. 330:20
spend their time and w. on 110:44
stolen his w. away 171:3
warming his five w. 540:14
we have w. to read 281:11
w. and Templars 385:29
w. are gamecocks 215:23
Wittiest: truth..w. of all things 237:20
Wittles: I live on broken w. 174:19
we have no w. 543:8
w. and drink to me 174:29
Witty: anger makes dull men w. 24:36
better w. fool 482:12
fancy myself mighty w. 203:29
it shall be w. 139:4
not only w. in myself 441:11
poets, w. 27:19
pretty w. Nell 377:25
so proud, so w. and so wise 407:22
so w., profligate, and thin 587:16
truth, when w. 237:20
very w. prologue 155:34
w. and the tender Hood 308:20
Wive: came, alas! to w. 484:27
Wives: beat their w. 121:20
corpses or w. 523:1
fair be their w. 195:6
husbands, love your w. 68:32
man with seven w. 366:8
many, many w. 361:7
men with mothers and w. 253:23
old w.' fables 68:47
our debts, our careful w. 444:21
sacks to sew up w. 542:26
sky changes when they are w. 428:22
so happy in three w. 308:8
some poison'd by their w. 475:7
we have children, we have w. 540:2
w. and mithers maist despairin' 360:14
w. are young men's mistresses 26:37
w. in the patriarchs' days 236:20
w., submit yourselves 68:6
Wiving: hanging and w...destiny 464:5
Wizards: star-led w. 343:10
Woa, mare! 217:22
Woe: all it yields of joy and w. 90:42
all my bliss, and all my w. 225:9
all our w. 344:1
all your sounds of w. 468:20
balm of w. 501:26
beyond this land of w. 29:13
bowed with w. 339:11
come wail, come w. 250:15
deep, unutterable w. 23:25
discover sights of w. 344:9
every w. a tear can claim 117:40
feel another's w. 386:31
from w. to w. tell o'er 486:25
groan of the martyr's w. 75:6
her face was full of w. 7:13
heritage of w. 118:4
her voiceless w. 114:13
he was glad, I was w. 232:2
hideous notes of w. 116:50
listen to my tale of w. 204:4
long since cancell'd w. 486:25
made for Joy and W. 73:24
made his w. her own 16:8
melt at others' w. 230:16
month follow month with w. 491:26
my heart is sick of w. 83:3
Norman's W. 318:16
oft in w. 566:11
old w. step on the stage 95:32
protracted w. 279:7
prov'd, a very w. 488:12
rearward of a conquer'd w. 487:23
sad variety of w. 217:18, 382:1
see a man in w. 210:10
see another's w. 77:3
share with me in bliss or w. 349:16
signs of w. that all was lost 349:15
Sleep! the friend of W. 507:18
solace in the midst of w. 132:2
song of w. 532:39
such a draught of w. 492:4
such a w...wins more hearts 7:13
suits of w. 430:30

Woe (cont.)
tried in fires of w. 269:31
Wednesday's child is full of w. 368:1
who has felt the w. 215:13
w. comforts w. again 189:9
w. is me, Alhama! 112:29
w. is me! for I am undone 53:8
w. is me for the good house 324:5
w. is me, to see.. 434:14
w. to him that is alone 56:34
w. to that man by whom the offence 59:50
w. to them that are at ease 56:2
w. to think upo' yon den 104:5
w. unto them that join 53:3
w. unto you, lawyers! 61:50
w. unto you, when..speak well 61:52
w. weeps out her division 279:28
w. worth the chase 416:14
work our w. 124:3
Woe-begone: so w. 441:9
Woeful: tho' the w. may cease 9:8
Woes: all the w. that curse 218:15
chequer'd with pleasures and w. 356:34
death is the end of w. 509:29
easer of all w. 38:9
her w. at midnight rise 321:15
Iliad of w. 172:20
in joys and w. 150:23
sickness full of w. 168:7
spring of w. unnumbered 384:20
with old w. new wail 486:25
w. that wait on age 113:20
w. which Hope thinks infinite 497:17
Woke: with the Day w. 205:17
w., and found that life 7:18, 254:2
Wold: to the wholesome w. 296:20
Wolf: belly-pinched w. 453:4
grim w. with privy paw 342:29
his sentinel, the w. 458:1
like the w. on the fold 118:37
man was w. to the man 551:13
whoops to the w. below 150:9
w. behowls the moon 467:35
w...dwell with the lamb 53:18
w. that follows 522:5
Wolfe's great name compatriot 163:1
Wolf's-bane: neither twist w. 287:19
Wollop: do you think I'd w. him? 43:23
Wolsey, that once trod 446:29
Wolves: eat like w. 444:5
hireling w. 351:30
howling of Irish w. 428:29
left the w. behind 324:10
w., bold only to pursue 491:28
w. have prey'd 469:19
w. they howled 324:10
Woman: always the w. 187:21
as far as one w. can forgive another 214:16
because a w.'s fair 572:2
believe a w. 117:13
bettre than a good w.? 137:37
bettre than wisdom? W. 137:37
body of a weak..w. 198:11
brawling w. 50:28
brief..as w.'s love 435:8
brought the trembling w. 74:13
but a w.'s might 449:27
by the influence of W. 174:37
callin' a young w. a Wenus 179:6
cheats a w. 214:33
common w. of common earth 148:16
constancy to a bad, ugly w. 119:19
constant..but yet a w. 439:11
constant w. 209:25
contentious w. 50:46
damnable, deceitful w.! 371:9
deaf man to a blind w. 152:23
dear, deluding W. 105:28
dull speaker, like a plain w. 243:17
e'en a w. and commanded 425:30
ever w. in this humour woo'd 476:8
every single w...a puzzle 542:14
every w...every sort of flattery 139:30
every w. is at heart a rake 384:36
every w. knows 36:19
excellent thing in w. 454:24
fair w...without discretion 49:58
fat white w. 157:9
for a w.'s sake 584:3

Woman (cont.)

for thy..understanding, a w.　454:36
frailty, thy name is w.　430:33(–431)
gentler sister w.　104:7
give not thy soul unto a w.　56:39
good company improves a w.　203:16
had a w. ever less?　106:31
haunted by w. wailing　151:32
here rests a w.　382:12
he that tastes w., ruin meets　214:34
how divine a thing a w.　583:1
if a w. have long hair　66:42
I grant I am a w.　449:18
in a post-chaise with a pretty w.　273:21
inconstant, w.　215:36
in that one w.　446:27
in w.'s eye　115:5
is this the silent w.?　280:8
lack of w.'s nursing..tears　365:21
large-brained w.　88:6
last of all the w. died　60:13
lays his hand upon a w.　548:5
like a w. scorn'd　155:20
lips of a strange w.　49:44
love a w. for singing　452:23
lovely w. in a rural spot　266:4
made a w. cry　326:21
made the w. for the man　529:13
man and a w. in a garden　570:17
man he must go with a w.　299:20
man's desire is for the w.　153:7
man that is born of a w.　49:1, 391:41
many a w. has a past　569:36
more than w. to be wise　357:3
most pernicious w.　432:21
nakedness of w.　77:16
never be by w. lov'd　73:22
never yet fair w.　453:7
none of w. born　460:5
no other purgatory but a w.　38:6
nor w. neither　433:15
not know I am a w.?　428:5
no w.'s heart　483:9
no w.'s sides　483:9
old w. clothed in grey　306:34
old w. who lived in a shoe　369:4
one hair of a w.　264:20
one to show a w.　94:10
only a w.'s hair　520:52
perfect w., nobly planned　580:21
play the w.　446:28
play without a w. in it　305:19
pleasant to any sort of w.　304:35
poor lone w.　441:28
rib..made he a w.　44:16
saint..but the w. died　382:13
semblative a w.'s part　482:10
shallow, changing w.　476:30
she is a w., therefore..　480:33
she was a worthy w.　137:15
silliest w...very clever w.　304:38
some tedious w.　492:22
speaks small like a w.　465:27
still be a w. to you　373:19
support of the w. I love　196:1
sweeter w. ne'er　267:14
tell a w.'s age　221:40
that princely w.　306:23
that which is eternal in W.　223:22
there shone one w.　525:31
there was no other w.　187:15
think myself a very bad w. if..　1:28
to a w., but a..ghost　184:9
torrent of a w.'s will　11:22
truest..that ever loved w.　328:24
uncommon pretty young w.　196:6
unto the man is w.　317:27
virtuous w.　50:1, 50:57
vitality in a w.　490:14
voice and shape of a w.　290:5
wasteful w.　374:20
what is w.?..agreeable blunders　158:27
what will not w., gentle w. dare?　507:31
when a w. appears　214:30
when it an't a w.'s　178:34
when lovely w. stoops　197:32, 226:18
whose heaven should be true W.　410:34
who takes a w.　214:34
who to a w. trusts　229:6
wickedness of a w.　57:1
wicked w. liberty to gad　57:2

Woman (cont.)

wilt thou have this w.　391:28
wine, w. and song　321:5, 543:5
w. among all those　51:15
w. as old as she looks　153:19
w., behold thy son　63:72
w. clothed with the sun　71:16
w. colour'd ill　488:18
w...dish for the gods　426:8
w. drunken with the blood　71:32
w. for the hearth　538:24
w. has her way　251:13
w. hath found him already　471:2
w. in her selfless mood　531:13
W.! in our hours of ease　418:31
w. is his game　538:23
w. is only a w.　294:32
w. is so hard upon the w.　538:28
w. is the lesser man　534:32
w. is the worst　229:7
W. Killed with Kindness　248:6
W...last thing civilized　337:31
w. like a dew-drop　90:2
w., lovely w.!　371:12
w., lovely w., does the same　161:28
w. must wear chains　203:9
w. mov'd..fountain troubled　479:12
w. of so shining loveliness　586:1
w. oweth to her husband　479:13
w.'s at best a contradiction　384:40
w. sat in unwomanly rags　253:22
w.'s cause is man's　539:6
W.'s cully　155:25
w.'s desire..desire of the man　153:7
w. seldom asks advice　2:29
w.'s eye　455:21
w.'s faith, and w.'s trust　419:15
w.'s friendship　215:15
w.'s happiest knowledge　347:20
w.'s looks　356:33
w.'s mind oft' shifts　215:14
w.'s noblest station　322:4
w.'s preaching　271:16
w.'s reason　108:41, 484:30
w.'s tender care　161:11
w.'s whole existence　115:25
w.'s whole life　267:21
w.'s workhouse　490:36
w. take an elder　483:3
w. that deliberates is lost　1:19
w., therefore to be won　445:27
w. to obey　538:24
w. to win　543:3
w. true and fair　180:17
w. wakes to love　531:14
w. well-reputed, Cato's daughter　449:18
w.! when I behold thee　289:10
W. who Did　4:17
w. who did not care　303:12
w. who loved him the best　293:25
w. whom thou gavest..me　44:22
w. who used to work..for my
　old aunt　233:5
w. with the heart　538:24
w. with the West in her eyes　148:17
w., w. rules us still　357:12
w. yet think him an angel　542:10
wrapp'd in a w.'s hide　445:43
yet a w. too　580:20
you was a w. and a mother　178:18
Woman-country　90:6
Womaned: see me w.　472:19
Woman-head: graves have learnt
　that w.　186:8
Womanhood: heroic w.　317:14
w. and childhood　316:34
Womankind: faith in w.　539:8
of w. but one　159:34
packs off its w.　490:23
she's the pink o' w.　107:30
think better of w.　290:3
thinks the worst..of w.　251:27
Womanly: now is pure w.　252:14
so w. her demeaning　502:18
w. discovering grace　184:19
Womb: barren w.　50:55
chaste lady's pregnant w.　332:10
cloistered in thy dear w.　185:10
events in the w. of time　470:18
foul w. of night　444:6
from his mother's w...ripp'd　461:11

Womb (cont.)

into her w...sterility　452:29
like a child from the w.　493:1
making their tomb the w.　487:20
Niobean w.　522:14
w. of nature　346:12
w. of pia mater　455:12
w. of royal kings　474:22
w. of uncreated night　345:19
Women: alas! the love of w.!　115:37
Alexander w.　313:2
all w. born..perverse　80:9
all w. labouring　389:3
among thy honourable w.　394:23
asham'd that w. are so simple　479:14
as w. wish to be　251:25
because w. have cancers　290:2
blessed art thou among w.　61:12
by bad w. been deceived　350:26
charming w...true converts　203:21
cherries, hops, and w.　178:28
dear dead w.　97:9
destroyed by subtleties these w.　336:33
devil would have him about w.　443:12
experience of w. which extends　188:19
fairest among w.　51:41
fair w. and brave men　113:25
fickleness of the w. I love　490:41
for w. to keep counsel　449:27
framed to make w. false　470:21
from w.'s eyes　455:20, 23
generality of w...as children　290:12
goes with W., and Champagne　41:26
go practise..then men and w.　96:2
happiest w...no history　196:26
her w. fair　123:7
I cannot bear men and w.　489:10
if w. could be fair　173:1
I must have w.　214:31
in w. do require　74:28
in w., two　384:35
learn about w. from me　298:3
learned about w. from 'er　298:4
Legend of Good W.　529:6
let us have wine and w.　115:33
let your w. keep silence　67:2
lik'd several w.　479:44
like w.'s letters　239:10
many men, many w.　271:1
Mary, pity w.　299:22
men that w. marry　316:37
men, w., and clergymen　504:31
men, w., and Herveys　354:13
Monstrous Regiment of W.　305:6
most w. have no characters　384:28
most w...not so young　39:7
my fifty men and w.　93:44
not denyin' the w. are foolish　196:18
nothing sooner dry than w.'s
　tears　563:29
no war with w.　507:30
old w. (of both sexes)　513:18
one of the..diseases of w.　243:12
other w. know so much　89:19
paradise for w...hell for w.　109:29
paradise of w.　209:8
passing the love of w.　47:30
passin' the love o' w.　296:18
proper function of w.　196:28
revenge—especially to w.　115:32
Solomon loved many strange w.　47:45
some w.'ll stay in a man's
　memory　304:50
souls of w. are so small　111:25
take our place, as men and w.　295:6
temptations both in wine and w.　305:1
these tell-tale w.　476:26
though w. are angels　117:45
tide in the affairs of w.　116:21
to passionate w.　584:24
to w. Italian　136:13
treating all w. with..courtesy　305:1
twixt w.'s love, and men's　184:5
two main plagues..wine and w.　109:12
War Between Men and W.　547:12
wars or w.　446:24
were w. never so fair　321:13
when I say that I know w.　542:14
when we submit to w.　124:1
wisdom in w.　84:22
with w. the heart argues　16:21

Women (cont.)
w. and care 560:25
w. and elephants never forget 414:14
w. and music..dated 227:12
w. and wine should life employ 214:29
w. are angels, wooing 480:41
w. are a sex by themselves 39:20
w. are like tricks 155:15
w. are strongest 56:16
w...as Heaven and Hell 531:22
w. become like their mothers 569:24
w...children of a larger growth 139:22
w. come and go 197:16
w. come out to cut up 304:4
w. desyren to have sovereyntee 138:11
w. do in men require 74:28
w. fair as she 238:30
w. guide the plot 500:31
w...more like each other 139:26
w. must be half-workers 429:26
w. must weep 294:1
w. never look so well 518:40
w. of good carriage 477:7
w.—one half the human race 28:28
w...shadows of us men 280:20
w. to speak in the church 67:3
w...troublesome cattle 319:12
w. walk in public processions 567:8
w. who love me 490:41
work its way with the w. 179:22
you should be w. 456:14
Won: Corinth lost and w. 114:40
field is w. 358:4
having w. her, do I woo? 375:4
I am too quickly w. 477:20
in this humour w. 476:8
I've w.! I've w.! 149:13
long lost, late w. 496:3
many a glowing kiss had w. 253:19
melancholy as a battle w. 564:4
never lost till w. 165:14
not that you w. or lost 406:20
not unsought be w. 348:37
she is w.! we are gone 418:22
some say that we w. 327:1
therefore may be w. 480:33
therefore to be w. 445:27
things w. are done 480:41
though baffled oft is ever w. 117:38
where you will never w. 30:18
w. others to sin 185:24
Wonder: all a w. 95:34
all knowledge and w. 24:11
all the w. that would be 534:25
apples of w. 189:23
great w. in heaven 71:16
how I w. what you are 311:20, 527:10
how I w. what you're at 129:8
I w. by my troth 185:6
I w. to myself a lot 339:24
I w. why he does 339:20
miles around the w. grew 262:19
no new w. may betide 585:22
no w. but the human face 285:34
'no w.,' said the lords 528:1
one w. at the least 331:2
still the w. grew 225:2
to hear, was w. 189:7
without our special w. 459:22
w. at ourselves 573:7
w. at the workmanship 340:38
w., bathed in joy 82:3
w. how the devil they got there 385:27
W., Love, and Praise 2:22
w. more and more 160:1
w. of all men 86:29
w. of an hour 113:11
w. of our age 232:15
w. of our stage 281:11
w. what she's come after 196:15
worship is transcendent w. 126:22
Wondered: all the world w. 528:19
Wonderful: all His words most w. 364:6
any thing that is w. 154:37
his name shall be called W. 53:15
how w. is Death 493:2, 497:18
Lady Teazle, by all that's w.! 500:42
left unseen a w. piece of work 423:27
my God, how w. Thou art 202:21
mystic, w. 529:42
O w. son 435:21

Wonderful (cont.)
O w., w. and most w. w. 428:3
such knowledge is too w. 400:8
thy love to me was w. 47:30
wise and w. 3:14
'W.!' I ejaculated 188:24
Wonderfully: fearfully and w. made 400:10
Wondering: stood there, w., fearing 380:24
w. for his bread 163:22
Wonderland: in summer's w. 365:25
Wonders: all w. in one sight 166:6
carry within us the w. 86:11
declare the w. that he doeth 398:15
hair on end at his own w. 163:22
his w. in the deep 398:17
his w. to perform 161:18
then I do w. 305:16
w. at our quaint spirits 466:43
w. because 'e is frequent deceased 304:3
w. in the land of Egypt 45:41
w. in the land of Ham 398:13
w. what 's to pay 264:1
w. where he is 546:26
Wondrous: moon takes up the w. tale 2:26
more w., w. still 74:8
thyself how w. 348:4
w. the gods 74:8
w. things have done 571:21
Woning fer by weste 137:11
Won't: he w.—w. he? 34:3
if she w., she w. 11:22
Sha'n't! W.! 300:16
will you, w. you? 129:23
w. go home till morning 98:15
Woo: April when they w. 428:22
Duncan Gray cam here to w. 105:13
not w. foul weather 253:18
pipe and w. her 538:21
so thou wilt w. 477:20
swain did w. 232:4
that would w. her 470:3
why, having won her, do I w.? 375:4
Wood: bows down to w. and stone 240:18
bows down to w. an' stone 295:21
brown heath and shaggy w. 417:22
cleave the w., and there am I 9:12
dark impenetrable w. 418:34
deep and gloomy w. 581:26
desk's dead w. 307:17
for a dish of w. 475:10
heap on more w.! 418:23
hewers of w. 46:41
hollow behind the little w. 535:33
impulse from a vernal w. 581:16
lath of w. painted 73:1
lives in that w. 150:8
misty border of the w. 586:5
must Thou char the w. 544:24
of true w., of yew-w. 187:12
old w. burn brightest 563:22
on the w. and the pool 172:4
river, w., and vale 285:1
rooky w. 459:8
sang within the bloody w. 197:26
set out to plant a w. 521:7
springth the w. nu 9:26
starlight w. 494:5
there in a w. a Piggy-wig stood 312:1
three in the w. 34:34
through the tulgey w. 129:39(–130)
through w. and dale 151:33
walked by the w. side 80:7
what w. a cudgel's of 110:39
w. of Crete 467:20
w. of English bows 187:12
you are not w. 450:26
Woodbine: luscious w. 466:41
well-attir'd w. 342:31(–343)
w. spices 536:9
Wood-birds: begin these w. 467:21
Woodcock: w. near the gin 483:16
w. to mine own springe 437:38
Woodcocks: springes to catch w. 431:27
Wooden: hear the w. dialogue 481:6
lies about his w. horse 208:15
off in a w. shoe 204:5
surround St. Paul's with a w. pavement 505:12

Wooden (cont.)
wear w. shoes 226:29
with a w. leg 178:2
within this w. O 443:4
w. walls are the best 157:24
Wooden-shoes: Round-heads and w. 1:27
Woodland: hear the w. linnet 581:15
stands about the w. ride 262:10
Woodlands: about the w. I will go 262:10
Woodman: w., spare that tree 358:21
w., spare the beechen tree 122:8
Wood-notes: warble his native w. 342:7
Wood-pigeons: where the w. breed 499:15
Woods: alone through fields and w. 151:27
are the w. for me? 77:29
build his house in the w. 201:22
Clouden's w. amang 104:29
clouds, w., rocks 493:14
enter these enchanted w. 336:48
flying from the golden w. 538:21
for the w. against the world 77:29
Greta w. are green 419:7
his daily teachers..w. and rills 573:8
in the Arabian w. embost 351:3
in the middle of the w. 311:12
in these wild w. forlorn 349:18
into the w. my Master went 310:10
light w. go seaward 266:2
never knew the summer w. 532:19
no bosomed w. adorn 302:7
oozy w. 496:9
pleasure in the pathless w. 114:26
road through the w. 303:16
senators of mighty w. 286:8
spirit in the w. 578:8
sunshiny w. all athrill 422:22
these hoary w. are grand 420:31
through its tall w. 288:23
through the Wet Wild W. 304:22
to-morrow to fresh w. 343:7
to the sleeping w. all night 149:35
to the w. no more 263:27
when all the w. are still 351:12
where are those starry w.? 81:18
wild in w. 191:41
w. decay and fall 540:20
w. have no voice 359:6
w. more free from peril 426:29
w. on shore look dim 357:16
w. or steepy mountain 330:17
w. shall to me answer 509:11
Woodshed: something nasty in the w. 217:15
Woodspurge has a cup of three 411:37
Wooed: how she w. an Englishman 12:1
love that he hath never w. 80:28
marri'd an' w. an' a' 409:13
pensively he w. 578:11
therefore may be w. 480:33
therefore to be w. 445:27
woman in this humour w. 476:8
w. and married and a' 12:3
w. not wed 90:6
w. the slimy bottom 476:14
would be w...not unsought 348:37
Woof: weave the w. 229:22
we know her w., her texture 286:42
w. of my tent's thin roof 492:29
Wooing: angels, w. 480:41
frog he would a-w. go 366:21
I'll go w. in my boys 5:8
who comes a-w. me? 293:9
w. of it 27:32
w. o't 105:13
w., wedding, and repenting 468:9
Wooingly: smells w. here 457:6
Wooings: at full length people's w. 115:39
Wool: clouds like w. 334:6
giveth snow like w. 400:23
have you any w.? 366:9
such as came for w., sir 93:28
tease the huswife's w. 340:38
where she w. ought to grow 210:18
w. of bat 459:31
Woollen: odious! in W.! 384:25
Woolly: softest clothing, w., bright 76:10
Woos his own end 531:2

Word: Bilbo's the w.   155:26
blessed w. Mesopotamia   213:16
but a choleric w.   461:33
by water and the W.   517:1
contempt of thy W.   388:49
dictatorial w.   221:19
doers of w.   69:32
eaten thee for a w.   455:26
even that w. alone   411:23
every fool..play upon the w.   464:25
every idle w.   59:15
every whisper'd w.   118:28
every w. be established   67:39
every w. that proceedeth   46:23, 57:34
first w. that Sir Patrick read   31:24
flowering in a lonely w.   541:7
for no w. however sounding   514:5
frantic boast and foolish w.   301:11
fulfilling his w.   400:24
God the w. that spake it   197:35
heard a discouraging w.   248:9
hear his w.   161:9
His heav'nly W.   183:21
honour his own w.   530:13
if my w. be sterling   475:25
if thou hast heard a w.   56:48
I kept my w.   171:14
ill w. may empoison liking   468:26
in one little w.   474:16
in..Patmos, for the w. of God   70:23
in the beginning was the W.   62:58
in w. mightier than they   348:20
irksome w. and task   543:6
just for a w.—'neutrality'   43:22
last kind w. to Christ   96:5
laugh'd his w. to scorn   162:4
leave the w. of God   64:33
man's w. is God in man   529:40
many a w., at random   417:30
Minister of God's W.   390:31
ne'er a w. wad..speak   30:21
neither speech nor w.   81:2
never breathe a w.   297:11
never will speak w.   474:1
not a w. of fear   308:23
not o w. wol he faille   137:39
one w. is too often profaned   499:3
perhaps we have not the w.   19:15
proud w. you never spoke   309:4
reherce..everich a w.   137:23
ruling himself after thy w.   399:13
shepherd, I take thy w.   340:17
sincere milk of the w.   69:47
so the W. had breath   532:25
speak but one w.   350:16
speak no angry w.   3:17
spoken the foremost w.   30:22
stablish me according to thy w.   399:22
suit the action to the w.   434:16
teaching me that w.   465:13
the Lord gave the w.   396:7
they hear the W.   302:3
thy uncreating w.   381:27
thy w. is a lantern   399:21
'tis a single w.   121:10
today I pronounced a w.   208:23
to neither a w. will I say   215:4
true and lively W.   390:28
two meanings..one w.   131:13
used the w. in its Pickwickian sense   178:23
wait Thy w. of peace   198:16
wash out a W. of it   207:2
weakness is not in your w.   17:20
we had no w. to say   569:6
what is honour? a w.   440:30
what the w. did make it   197:35
when I use a w.   131:6
w. and a blow   99:15, 191:23, 478:12
w. be spoken   523:14
w. fitly spoken   50:34
w. for w. without book   482:5
w. is but wynd: leff w.   321:8
w. of fear   455:35
w. of God is quick   69:8
w., or sigh, or tear   150:31
w. spoken in due season   50:14
w. that teems with..meaning   222:11
W. was God   62:58
W. was made flesh   62:64
write that w.   158:30

Word (cont.)
yesterday the w. of Caesar   450:23
Word-catching: literature looks like w.   200:28
Wording of his own highest thoughts   289:27
Wordless: song was w.   415:15
Words: abideth not in w.   296:31
actions are a kind of w.   200:29
all the Pow'r of W.   386:11
all w., and no performance   335:1
all w. forgotten   172:1
alms-basket of w.   455:26
artillery of w.   521:12
barren superfluity of w.   213:21
best w. in the best order   153:6
big w. for little matters   271:20
bright is the ring of w.   516:3
by hir w. ne hir face   137:24
choice w...measured phrases   580:12
coiner of sweet w.   17:25
deceive you with vain w.   68:3
decocted into few w.   212:10
deeds, not w. shall speak me   37:29
determination of w. to the mouth   518:43
dialect w...marks of the beast   237:6
dressing old w. new   487:18
empty w. of a dream   81:9
finde w. newe   137:23
fine w. butter no parsnips   420:7
fool and his w.   499:19
form of sound w.   68:57
gentle Muse with lucky w.   342:11
give sorrow w.   460:20
glotoun of w.   310:4
good w., I think, were best   447:44
hear what comfortable w.   390:37
Heaven hath my empty w.   462:2
he w. me, girls   426:2
his acrid w.   251:9
his w...trip about him   352:3
his w. were smoother   395:13
how he may report thy w.   350:37
I hate false w.   309:16
I have neither wit, nor w.   450:33
immodest w...no defence   180:9
in all His w.   364:6
in his syntax and..w.   20:2
instrument of w.   575:15
into w. no virtue   331:2
it wasn't the w.   10:24
kept silence..even from good w.   394:8
languages that want w.   281:27
last year's w.   197:14
let thy w. be few   51:6
little w. of love   128:1
long w. Bother me   339:21
melting melodious w.   247:14
men of few w.   443:29
mystery of w.   579:25
my w. among mankind   496:11
my w. are my own   136:4
oaths are but w., and w. but wind   110:46
perfect music unto noble w.   539:7
play 'po' w.   120:28
proper w. in proper places   520:1
rebelled against the w. of the Lord   398:15
repeats his w.   447:34
rhapsody of w.   435:43
speak great w.   406:4
speaks the kindest w.   312:28
sweet w., low-crooked curtsies   449:29
that my w. were now written!   49:5
their w. into the ends of the world   392:32
their w. seemed..idle tales   62:54
these two w...undone the world   422:1
these w...true and faithful   71:45
through w. and things   574:15
throwing w. away   582:13
thy w. are like..snakes   496:25
too sweet for w.   374:17
two w. to that bargain   520:32
uncouth w. in disarray   276:14
unpleasant'st w.   464:22
very bitter w.   441:38
weigh thy w. in a balance   57:4
well thy w. become thee   456:7

Words (cont.)
what so wild as w. are?   97:24
whose w. are of less weight   25:42
w. and deeds..indifferent   200:29
w. are..daughters of earth   277:21
w. are men's daughters   327:6
w. are no deeds   446:21
w. are quick and vain   496:21
w. are the tokens current   24:10
w. are wise men's counters   248:19
w. are w.   470:7
w. as hard as cannon-balls   200:40
w. clothed in reason's garb   345:22
w. divide and rend   522:9
w. in Mr. Montgomery's writing   325:9
w., like Nature, half reveal   532:3
w. may be false   422:27
w. move slow   382:32
w. of learned length   225:2
w. of love then spoken   357:13
w. of Mercury are harsh   456:2
w. of my mouth   392:34
w. of the wise are as goads   51:34
w. of tongue or pen   238:31, 568:17
w. of truth and soberness   65:24
w. once spoke   180:7
w. so fair   282:3
w., that burn   231:15
w. that have been so nimble   37:12
w. to the heat of deeds   458:1
w. without knowledge   49:16, 17
w., w., mere w.   481:29
w., w. or I shall burst   203:20
w., w., w.   433:4
wrestle with w. and meanings   197:8
your w...rob the Hybla bees   451:33
Wordsworth: let simple W. chime   117:28
Mr. W.'s epic poetry   240:7
out-babying W.   322:10
so W. tells you   116:25
W., both are thine   512:6
W...not prone enough to belief   239:17
W.'s eyes avert their ken   17:3
W.'s healing power   16:23
W. sometimes wakes   116:6
W.'s standard of intoxication   501:11
W.'s sweet calm   17:5
W., Tennyson, and Browning   29:8
Wordsworthian or egotistical sublime   290:9
Wore: w. enough for modesty   98:6
w. when she was wed   535:11
Work: all Nature seems at w.   152:17
all out of w.   443:8
apportioning of wages to w.   126:44
at her flowery w.   341:22
bring every w. into judgment   51:36
can't w. any faster   368:18
Creator from his w. return'd   348:28
desireth a good w.   68:44
do no w. to-day   444:25
do the hard and dirty w.   413:4
do your w. on water   297:1
every man according to his w.   395:24
every man's w...manifest   66:23
faints the cold w.   153:28
God doth not need either man's w.   351:21
God never made his w.   192:15
great, a very great w.   325:26
her noblest w. she classes   106:2
he who has found his w.   127:2
his little w. of love   4:8
his six days' w., a world   348:28
if any would not w.   68:39
if..this w. be of men   64:32
I leave my w.   125:18
I like w.   269:5
I want w.   439:13
know what thou canst w. at   127:14
left no immortal w.   290:20
life's w. well done   373:10
little w., a little play   235:10
man goeth forth to his w.   398:10
men must w.   294:11
men who did the w.   303:15
'mid w. of his own hand   570:10
Mirabeau's w., then, is done   125:32
my purpose w. on him   470:20
my w. is done   8:13

Work (cont.)
nakedness..the w. of God 77:16
night..when no man can w. 63:33
noblest w. of God 384:9
noblest w. of man 267:16
no one shall w. for money 303:21
nothing to do but w. 292:14
now let it w. 451:1
old Kaspar's w. was done 507:3
one of his hands wrought in the
  w. 48:35
one w. that wakes 255:9
our neighbour and our w. 291:6
our w. is done 364:4
plenty of w. to do 268:32
prosper..the w. of our hands 397:17
put us to w. anew 303:19
rubs nor botches in the w. 459:1
shape from that thy w. of art 316:24
smoothed her w. 262:8
sole w. of a life-time 90:39
start amid their w. 87:27
stupendous w. 504:4
tedious as to w. continueth 438:31
their w. continueth 302:4
there is no w., nor device 51:21
to make dictionaries is dull w. 277:26
tools to w. withal 320:5
to w., and back to bed 333:24
venom, to thy w. 437:40
warm w. 362:20, 24
what a piece of w. is a man 433:15
when all its w. is done 375:18
when Nature has w. to be done 201:8
when w. was scrappy 142:2
when your w. is finished 296:33(–297)
who first invented W. 307:17
whose w. is not born with him 320:5
w. apace 170:21
w. at anything but his art 490:15
w. i' the earth so fast 432:27
w. itself shall not be lost 211:21
w. its way with the women 179:22
w. like a digger on the railroad 199:33
w. like madness 150:26
w. of noble note 541:3
w. of polished idleness 326:27
w. out your own salvation 68:19
w. that 's nearest 293:11
w. the ides of March begun 451:37
w. them to their good 508:15
w. till further orders 296:33
w. together for good 65:56
w. upon the vulgar 386:38
w. without hope 152:18
years to be w. and joy 83:19
Worked: men that w. for England 140:24
w. and sang from morn 72:15
Worker: praise the honest w. 4:13
Workers: how all those w. start 87:27
men the w. 534:25
w. of the world, unite 12:4, 333:11
Workhouse: Christmas Day in the
  w. 502:15
woman's w. 490:36
Working: from her w...his visage
  wann'd 433:31
in w. well, if travail you sustain 233:3
joy of the w. 303:21
tools of w. out salvation 111:12
w. out its way 190:13
Working-class: vast portion..of
  the w. 19:29
Working-day: this w. world 426:27
Working-house of thought 445:5
Workmanship: dark inscrutable w. 579:9
wonder at the w. 340:38
Workmen: Master of All Good W. 303:19
Works: abstain you from such w. 328:19
all just w. do proceed 388:34
all our w. begun,.. 390:52
all ye W. of the Lord 388:20
cries aloud through all her w. 1:23
declare the w. of the Lord 399:10
every feature w. 22:10
faith without w. is dead 69:35
golden w. 307:24
good w. in her husband 349:8
his ordinary w. convince it 25:24
his w. are the comments 290:18
I know thy w. 70:34

Works (cont.)
look on my w., ye Mighty 496:14
move immediately upon your w. 229:4
noble w. that thou didst 389:10
pay for an edition of his w. 200:46
proudest of his w. 217:13
proved me, and saw my w. 397:30
reader of the w. of God 163:13
reward him according to his w. 69:3
see how our w. endure 295:10
see the w. of the Lord 398:17
see your good w. 57:42
subdu'd to what it w. in 488:6
their w. do follow them 71:27
thy glorious w. 348:4
universal blank of Nature's w. 346:20
vulgar w. of man 579:13
whose w. so content us 213:9
wonderful w. of God 64:26
w. hard for its living 368:1
w. of darkness 66:13, 389:22
w. of genius are the first things 289:23
w. of God..w. of men 377:9
W. of Supererogation 401:6
w. of thy fingers 392:9
Workshop of the world 180:14
Workshops: uncle George's w. 175:32
Worky-day fortune 423:21
World: abide in this dull w. 425:29
against a w. in arms 324:35
Alexander at the head of the w. 558:9
all's right with the w. 94:40
all th' inamour'd w. 319:1
all the riches of this w. 74:29
all the sad w. needs 568:27
all the uses of this w. 430:33
all the wickedness of the w. 176:21
all the w. and his wife 13:17, 520:30
all the w. and love were young 405:8
all the w. as my parish 565:16
all the w. in ev'ry corner 243:24
all the w...in love with night 478:20
all the w.'s a stage 427:21
all the w. should be taxed 61:16
all the w. would stare 160:8
all this the w. well knows 488:12
amidst a bursting w. 385:23
amidst a falling w. 3:2
anybody's torments in this w. 139:32
as good be out of the w. 144:25
attracts the envy of the w. 100:22
at which the w. grew pale 279:6
back to a w. of death 150:24
banish all the w. 439:37
beauty of the w. 433:15
be'old this w. so wide 296:22
between it and the dominion of
  the w. 327:11
between these two..moves our
  W. 19:30
bid the w. Good-night 246:6
bottom of the monstrous w. 343:2
brave new w. 480:15
brave w., Sir 40:8
Britain is a w. by itself 429:28
Britain set the w. ablaze 219:7
brought death into the w. 344:1, 550:24
burden of the w. 329:19
busy w. is hushed 364:4
came upstairs into the w. 155:11
cankers of a calm w. 440:21
care of this w. 59:24
carried them out of the w. 87:6
caught the w.'s great hands 265:23
changes the w. to-day 296:1
citizen of the w. 26:21
clearing the w. of its..problems 178:10
compare this prison..unto the
  w. 475:33
create my little w. 38:25
crowns o' the w. 89:2
daff'd the w. aside 440:16
death shall all the w. subdue 509:7
dispersed all the w. over 212:8
each a w. 578:20
ere the w. be pass'd 224:16
even so the w. 411:15
face of all the w. is changed 88:17
fact the whole w. knows 312:10
Federation of the w. 534:27
folly of the w. 251:23

World (cont.)
fool in the eye of the w. 155:17
for the woods against the w. 77:29
friendship..w. without end 91:28
from all the w. beside 167:13
from everlasting, and w. without
  end 397:15
furloughs for another w. 193:30
gain the whole w. 59:45, 61:3
gaze upon this w. no longer 586:5
get the start of the majestic w. 448:21
girdled with the gleaming w. 535:19
give the w. the lie 405:7
gladness of the w. 196:35
good deed in a naughty w. 465:21
great while ago the w. begun 484:27
had we but w. enough 333:8
hail infernal w. 344:22
half-brother of the w. 29:10
hand that rules the w. 557:19
happiness of the next w. 87:7
harmony of the w. 253:36
has the w. here 91:41
hear the w. applaud 16:10
herald of a noisy w. 163:20
here's a w. of pomp 37:13
his honours to the w. again 447:4
his rear'd arm crested the w. 426:1
history of the w...biography 126:24
hold the w. but as the w. 462:31
how dry a cinder this w. is 185:3
how small the w. is 233:5
how the w. is really going 19:27
how the w. its veterans rewards 384:37
how the w. wags 427:13
how this w. is given to lying 441:4
if their star is a w. 93:35
if there's another w. 107:18
if the w. be worth thy winning 191:9
I have not loved the w. 113:50
I have overcome the w. 63:64
I never have sought the w. 275:6
in his little w. of man 453:4
in hope the w. can show 186:15
in the morning of the w. 94:43
in the very w...w. of all of us 579:30
in the whole wide w. 517:18
in the whole w. thou canst find 247:1
in the w.'s report 424:10
in the w...tribulation 63:64
in this harsh w. 438:4
I was the w.'s commander 455:31
kind of w...born into 126:26
knew the merry w. was round 541:16
knowledge of the w...acquired
  in the w. 139:9
laid the w. away 83:9
learn the w. in 139:11
leave the w. unseen 287:24
let the great w. spin 534:36
let the w. mind him 91:41
let the w. slide 38:14
little friendship in the w. 26:13
little w. made cunningly 185:12
long prayers..in the w. 15:26
look round the habitable w. 194:23
lords of the w. besides 344:5
lost the w. for love 193:14
loved this present w. 69:1
loves His w. so much 94:41
mad w.! mad kings! 447:24
mad w., my masters 80:5, 527:16
make a hell of this w. 38:19
make me such another w. 473:21
makes the whole w. kin 481:21
makes the w. go round
  7:23, 129:15, 219:14
man is one w. 244:24
man to man the w. o'er 105:33
may the w. go well with thee 10:21
men in a w. of men 296:2
men that all the w. admires 330:25
mighty w. of eye, and ear 582:2
monster which the w. ne'er saw 98:12
month in which the w. bigan 137:40
my country is the w. 373:4
mystery to the w. 316:37
naked shingles of the w. 15:7
narrows the w. 336:39
need of a w. of men 94:27
noble w. of thee 355:18

World (*cont.*)

no longer a chaos, but a w.   127:21
not a joy the w. can give   118:18
not having hated..the w. enough   239:22
not in the w.   586:3
not our poet, but the w.'s   308:16
now a bubble..now a w.   383:10
of whom the w. was not worthy   69:17
O monstrous w.!   472:6
one half of the w.   22:8
only saved the w.   41:22
on the lunar w...pry   191:30
on the passing w...turn thine eyes   279:4
or ever..the w. were made   397:15
our country is the w.   213:18
out of the w.   252:20
over the bent w. broods   254:25
O, w., as God has made it!   92:2
O w. invisible   545:1
O w., no w.   305:14
O w.! O life!   494:18
O w.! the heart of thee   450:9
patriot of the w. alone   124:11
peace which the w. cannot give   388:35
peep at such a w.   163:23
pomp and glory of this w.   446:24
poor W. (said I)   166:1
prophetic soul of the wide w.   488:2
proud w., said I   166:2
quiet limit of the w.   540:21
rack of this tough w.   454:27
reaching to some great w.   375:25
remember of this unstable w.   328:13
ring'd with the azure w.   529:10
roll of the w. eastward   236:38
roof of the w.   227:35
roofs of the w.   568:2
round about the pendant w.   462:9
round the w. away   293:19
round the w. for ever   15:24
see how this w. goes   454:10
seek a newer w.   541:3
service of the antique w.   426:38
shakers of the w. for ever   370:19
shore of the wide w.   289:6
shot heard round the w.   199:7
six days' work, a w.   348:28
slip out of the w.   193:4
smiling from the w.'s great snare   425:13
snug farm of the W.   507:19
so runs the w. away   435:19
spectacle unto the w.   66:25
spins the heavy w.   263:18
still point of the turning w.   197:6
stood against the w.   450:23
strange to the w.   77:24
substantial w.   578:20
tell'st the w. it is not worth   426:12
ten to the w. allot   279:21
that all the w. shall—   453:1
this busy w. and I   158:12
this gewgaw w.   191:17
this little w.   474:22
this unintelligible w.   581:25
this w. is not for aye   435:11
this w. so vast   266:14
thoughts rule the w.   201:4
though we travel the w. over   200:5
Thou hast made this w.   299:3
thou seest the w.   452:5
three corners of the w.   448:2
thro' all the w. she follow'd   528:29
throughout the sensual w.   357:22
through the W. we safely go   73:24
till the w. go round   424:19
till the w. is wrought   498:6
time and the w...in flight   584:20
turned the w. upside down   64:57
unspotted from the w.   69:34
up above the w.   129:8, 527:10
very good w. we live in   82:27
very worst w.   82:27
visiting this various w.   494:3
volume which the W. we name   189:25
warm kind w.   157:19
way the w. ends   197:12
what a w. is this   78:9
whatever brute..made the w.   263:31

World (*cont.*)

what is this w.?   137:34
what would the w. be   254:30
when all the weary w.   35:7
when all the w. dissolves   330:3
when all the w. was young   140:26
when in the w. I liv'd   455:31
when Rome falls—the W.   114:21
whereon the Saviour of the w.   112:24
where the w. is quiet   523:17
whole w. in the face   318:12
whole w. is not sufficient   404:4
whole w...the minister   80:21
whole w. turn to coal   245:14
whole w. woke   141:19
whoso hath this w.'s good   70:11
wilderness of this w.   99:3
winds of the W.   296:3
wise of the w.   171:4
with the old w. to the grave   241:24
workers of the w., unite   12:4, 333:11
workshop of the w.   180:14
w...a grassy road   585:22
w. and all her train   552:13
w. and its ways   96:44
w. and they..hand and glove   162:18
w. as a vale of tears   90:36
w. be a-waning   359:6
w. before me   568:3
w. between His bill   585:8
w. can never fill   161:2
w...follow..those who have despised..it   112:8
w. forgetting, by the w. forgot   382:5
w...go round..faster   128:31
w. has little to bestow   33:11
W. in a Grain of Sand   73:18
w. I never made   263:35
w. in solemn stillness   421:10
w. is a bundle of hay   117:31
w. is a fine place   241:17
w. is charged   254:24
w. is full of meat and drink   515:15
w. is made up..fools..knaves   98:8
w. is not thy friend, nor the w.'s law   478:37
w. is so full   515:22
w. is too much with us   582:18
w. is weary   493:27(—494)
w. laughs with you   568:26
w. may end tonight   92:32
w. must be peopled   468:24
w...not an inn   86:36
w...not yet prepared   188:16
w. of vile..faults   466:6
w. of waters wild   546:1
w. on sixe and sevene   138:37
w.'s a bubble   28:16
w.'s a jest   512:9
w.'s an inn   193:17
w.'s a scene of changes   158:11
w.'s great age begins   493:25
w.'s grown honest   433:10
w. shall end when I forget   524:18
w. shall glean of me   545:9
w. should listen then   498:10
w.'s last night   185:17
w.'s mine oyster   465:37
w.'s more full of weeping   586:9
w.'s no blot for us   91:33
w.'s ransom   474:22
w.'s slow stain   492:7
w.'s tempestuous sea   195:23
w. surely is wide enough   513:10
w.'s whole sap   186:3
w., the flesh, and the devil   388:47
w. was all before them   349:31
W. Well Lost   191:14
W. went very well then   43:19
w. where all are pure   530:16
w. will give thee credit   143:12
w. will little note   314:12
w. will make a beaten path   201:22
w. without end. Amen   388:14
w. without end, reprieve   302:1
wounds the w.   441:7
your back upon the w.   316:35
World-earthquake, Waterloo   537:20
World-embracing sea   374:21
Worldkin: world, or even w.   127:21

Worldlings: mak'st a testament as w. do   426:32
w. base   442:34
World-losers and world-forsakers   370:19
Worldly: all his w. goods   311:12
breath of w. men   475:1
thank'd..for w. things   74:29
thy w. task hast done   430:1
wisely w., be not w. wise   404:6
W. Hope men set their hearts   205:27
Worldly-Wise-Man: Mr. W.   99:6
World-mothering air   254:17
Worlds: allur'd to brighter w.   224:21
best of all possible w.   120:6, 557:2
costs w. of pain   333:24
crash of w.   1:24
exhausted w.   278:34
joy for it worth w.   244:6
never-fading w.   574:22
new w. to buy   332:9
so many w.   533:3
Soul of all the w.   574:26
what w. away!   90:9
what w. in th'..Occident   168:9
w. not quickened by the sun   574:2
w. not realised   576:18
World-terror: no w.'s wing   140:23
World-wandering feet   544:8
World-wearied flesh   478:44
World-without-end: w. bargain   455:33
w. hour   487:7
Worm: cackle w'en he fine a w.   238:22
Conqueror W.   380:15
crested w.   164:4
fish with the w.   436:13
I am a w., and no man   393:2
I am but as a crushed w.   403:28
I want to be a w.   222:33
like a w. i' the bud   483:10
not a w. is cloven in vain   532:33
old Sallie W.   171:23
rather tough w.   220:18
round little w.   477:7
sets foot upon a w.   164:3
sharp-headed w.   540:17
spouse of the w.   122:37
their w. dieth not   61:5
was I a w.?   286:1
w. at one end   277:13
w. beneath the sod   493:6
w. mounts   199:17
w. nor snail, do no offence   467:1
w.'s eye point of view   404:2
w. that never dies   84:1
w., the canker   118:26
your w. is your only emperor   436:12
Worm-canker'd homily   540:15
Worms: among the hungry w. I sleep   30:16
convocation of politic w.   436:12
flies, w., and flowers   561:31
grubs, or w.   385:27
have mercy on us w.   202:20
he was eaten of w.   64:50
impaling w. to torture fish   154:16
I was one of the w.   156:18
lies here, food for w.   211:21
made the w.   585:11
made w.' meat of me   478:15
nor w. forget   176:34
talk of graves, of w.   475:6
tasted two w.   511:3
then w. shall try   333:9
though..w. destroy this body   49:6
with vilest w. to dwell   487:15
w. have eaten them   428:21
w. that are thy chambermaids   478:44
w. were hallow'd   472:16
Worms, wäre ich dennoch eingeritten   321:7
Wormwood: her end is bitter as w.   49:44
star is called W.   71:10
w. and the gall   55:24
Worn: all things w. out   585:17
ring so w.   165:21
sooner lost and w.   483:3
when we're w...with..service   507:2
w. with life's cares   165:21
w. with strife   527:12
Worn-out: all things w.   585:17
w. fetter   317:17
Worry and devour each other   160:41

INDEX

Worrying: what's the use of w.? 20:23
Worse: always w. than anyone's 22:26
  better day, the w. deed 242:6
  better, the w. 25:5
  boundless w. 540:25
  change for the w. 11:6
  confusion w. confounded 346:16
  for better for w. 391:30
  from w. to better 254:1
  good families are generally w. 254:4
  greater feeling to the w. 474:20
  kept it from being any w. 236:40
  leave the w. ones 40:20
  one penny the w. 34:11
  other things which were w. 304:30
  rather grew w. 60:60
  seeing a w. England 273:32
  Truth put to the w. 352:17
  w., and worst times..succeed 247:10
  w. appear the better reason 345:18
  w. need for them 496:24
  w. on Friday 368:21
  w. than fables 346:3
  w. than the first 59:19
  w. to me than dead 572:24
Worser: throw away the w. part 436:4
  w. spirit a woman 488:18
Worship: according to thy w. 394:22
  come to w. him 57:23
  crown him with glory and w. 392:11
  ere our w. cease 198:16
  exempt from awe, w. 497:12
  freedom..to w. God in his own way 408:25
  let us w. and fall down 397:27
  'Let us w. God!' he says 105:4
  nor w. them 390:7
  no w. to the garish sun 478:20
  simple w. of a day 287:18
  thou w. of Israel 393:1
  various modes of w. 217:5
  whom..ye ignorantly w. 64:60
  with my body I thee w. 391:32
  with what deep w. 151:21
  with which I w. thine 499:2
  w. her by years 530:14
  w. him in spirit 63:13
  w. is transcendent wonder 126:22
  w. of the great of old 118:10
  w. only thee 161:3
  w. the beast and his image 71:26
Worshipped: angels..w. be 184:4
  lifted up, or w. 401:10
  lord w. might he be 463:33
  w. by the names divine 74:22
  w. stocks and stones 351:20
Worshipper: Nature mourns her w. 417:20
  nods the drowsy W. 205:7
Worshipp'st at the..inner shrine 577:1
Worst: best is like the w. 299:15
  full look at the w. 236:13
  his w. is better 239:13
  knew the w. too young 296:28
  nor the w. of men 113:40
  say, 'This is the w.' 453:39
  so much good in the w. 249:4
  thinks the w. he can 251:27
  tomorrow do thy w. 194:20
  worse, and w. times..succeed 247:10
  w. are no worse 467:30
  w. inn's w. room 385:1
  w. is death 475:4
  w. is not 453:39
  w. is yet to come 269:32
  w. of the company 519:26
  w. of the lot..be Yank 301:4
  w. returns to laughter 453:37
  w. speaks something good 244:7
  w. that love could do 186:1
  w. time of the year 197:13
Worsted: black w. stockings 325:28
  though right were w. 97:4
Worst-humour'd muse 226:1
Worst-natur'd muse 407:17
Worth: all his worldly w. for this 540:13
  all my comfort of thy w. 486:32
  by the w. of the body 302:24
  charter of thy w. 487:22
  conscience of her w. 348:37
  country of w. 107:13

Worth (cont.)
  dread Temple of Thy w. 300:5
  early known thy wond'rous w. 412:12
  goodbye is not w. while 236:36
  in the w. and choice 279:30
  man's w. something 89:38
  much is she w. 241:28
  never was w. while 20:23
  relic of departed w. 113:17
  sixty seconds' w. 297:12
  slow rises w. 278:33
  thy own w. then not knowing 487:22
  what is the w. of anything? 121:23
  what is W. in anything 110:23
  whose w.'s unknown 488:7
  wit, nor words, nor w. 450:33
  world..a certain w. 96:44
  w. immortal 374:18
  w. makes the man 384:7
  w. more than ever I yet was 377:30
  w. of a State..w. of the individuals 338:32
  w. seeing? 274:15
Worthies: braver thing than all the W. 186:23
Worthiness: combin'd in beauty's w. 331:2
  to virtue and to w. 449:1
Worthless as withered weeds 83:9
Worthy: found them w. for himself 56:23
  how little w. of any love 544:29
  I find thee w. 320:2
  nine w. and the best 327:15
  no more w. to be called 62:14
  not w. that thou..under my roof 58:30
  not w. to unloose 63:2
  obtained w. ends 26:4
  of whom the world was not w. 69:17
  she was a w. womman 137:15
  w. fool! 427:15
  w. of his hire 61:35
  w. of stripes 61:55
  w. o' the flatterer 480:18
  w. of the vocation 67:56
  w. of your love 578:32
Worts: I went to W. 387:7
Wot: lovesome thing, God w.! 85:12
  much ado..God w. 80:7
  w. not what they are 454:32
Wotton: Sir Henry W...dear lover 559:15
Would: evil which I w. not 65:49
  if it were so, it w. be 130:8
  I w. not be..so pure 112:20
  those who w. have been 83:19
  wait upon 'I w.' 457:11
  what man w. do 96:23
  who w. has heard Sordello 96:35
  w. that I did too 17:15
Would-be: many a w. poet 80:28
Wouldst: now if thou w. 189:20
  w. thou me? 495:23
Wound: annual w. in Lebanon 344:32
  earth felt the w. 349:15
  felt a stain like a w. 102:13
  gall a new-healed w. 441:17
  heal'd thy w. 161:10
  heal me of my grievous w. 531:37
  help'd to plant the w. 117:25
  help to w. itself 448:2
  my w. is deep 30:6
  never felt a w. 477:13
  not be whole of that w. 328:5
  purple with love's w. 466:39
  see not the w. it makes 457:3
  such a w., the knife is lost 495:13
  take away the grief of a w. 440:30
  though rebels w. thee 474:34
  till thy w. be throughly heal'd 484:32
  tongue in every w. of Caesar 450:34
  trickling nonsense heal'd my w. 155:5
  what w. did ever heal 471:24
  willing to w. 385:29
  w. for w. 45:54
  w. in the solicitor 111:29
  w. of peace 481:11
  w. the head of his enemies 396:10
  w. up every morning 266:21
Wounded: tend the w. under fire 297:3

Wounded (cont.)
  they smote me, they w. me 52:12
  what a w. name 438:4
  when you're w. and left 304:4
  w. for our transgressions 54:26
  w. in the house of my friends 56:13
  w. is the wounding heart 165:27
  w. spirit who can bear? 50:21
  you're w. 92:24
Wounds: bind up my w. 476:35
  faithful are the w. of a friend 50:45
  fate never w. more deep 278:32
  guns, and drums, and w. 438:35
  heals his w. 364:15
  keeps his own w. green 27:6
  kiss dead Caesar's w. 450:24
  labour and the w. are vain 147:8
  Mizraim cures w. 87:19
  these w. I had 444:28
  thy words become thee as thy w. 456:7
  wept o'er his w. 224:20
  w. of a friend 50:45
  w. the world 441:7
Wove: I w. the thing to a..rhyme 183:3
  with brede ethereal w. 153:24
Woven: joy and woe are w. fine 73:24
  w. with an absent heed 235:21
Wrack: come, w.! 461:7
  way, out of his w. 446:29
Wracks: thousand fearful w. 476:14
Wragg is in custody 19:11
Wrangle: shall we begin to w.? 9:21
Wrap: w. a fairy in 466:41
  w. me up in my tarpaulin jacket 568:24
  w. the baby bunting in 366:11
  w. thy form in a mantle gray 495:22
Wrapped: all meanly w. 343:11
  w. in guileless sleep 547:7
  w. in purple robes 584:7
  w. in their winding-sheet 189:19
Wraps: turf that w. their clay 153:30
  w. the drapery of his couch 98:3
Wrath: chariots of w. 228:21
  cometh the w. of God 68:3
  day of w. 134:4
  devil..having great w. 71:18
  enter'd full of w. 286:12
  envy and w. shorten the life 57:5
  eternal w. burnt after them 348:22
  flee from the w. to come 57:30
  grapes of w. 264:15
  heavy w. of God 330:8
  his w. endureth but.. 393:25
  if his w. be kindled 391:51
  in after W. destroy 207:14
  infinite w., and infinite despair 346:32
  my w. did grow 76:5
  not in w., the Reaper came 317:10
  nursing her w. 108:2
  provoke not your children to w. 68:8
  slow to w. 69:30
  sun go down upon your w. 68:1
  Thou'lt leave Thy w. 375:17
  throw away Thy w. 244:12
  tigers of w. 77:17
  told my w., my w. did end 76:5
  turneth away w. 50:10
  w., by His meekness 77:2
  w. of man worketh not..righteousness 69:30
  w. of the Lamb 71:2
  w. of the lion 77:16
Wreak him on a flye 138:20
Wreath: I put on thy w. 286:1
  rides homeward with a w. 141:8
  sent these late a rosy w. 280:21(−281)
  she wore a w. of roses 37:1
  subtle w. of hair 185:4
Wreathed: w. for feasts not few 336:38
  w. his lithe proboscis 347:15
  w. the rod of criticism 182:48
Wreck: creates from its own w. 497:17
  king my brother's w. 197:30
  lit the battle's w. 241:5
  only not a w. 362:11
  rock on which thou art to w. 190:33
  sunken w. 443:10
  that colossal w. 496:15
  w. of Paradise 493:13
Wrecks: above the w. of Time 312:24
  amid Time's w. and scars 141:2

Wrecks (*cont.*)
vomits its w. 495:9
w. of a dissolving dream 493:25
w. of matter 1:24
Wren: considered Sir Christopher W. 33:23
egg off the w. 567:19
four Larks and a W. 311:2
hurt the little w. 73:22
I bore this w. 191:16
miracle..Mr. Christopher W. 202:14
no better a musician than the w. 465:22
poor w...will fight 460:17
robin redbreast and the w. 563:30
Sir Christopher W. said 43:3
w. goes to 't 454:8
w. with little quill 467:6
youngest w. of nine 484:3
Wrest once the law 465:2
Wrestle: intolerable w. with words 197:8
with..whirlwind w. 315:29
w. not against flesh and blood 68:11
Wrestled: God..w. with him 559:28
sir, you have w. well 426:24
there w. a man with him 45:9
Wrestles: he that w. with us 102:27
Wrestling: I wretch lay w. 254:20
Wretch: come, thou mortal w. 426:13
excellent w.! 471:27
for some w.'s aid 382:2
hail'd the w. who won 114:18
I w. lay wrestling 254:20
on hope the w. relies 224:10
pretty w. left crying 477:3
see thee damn'd first—w.! 124:9
sharp-looking w. 429:1
such a destin'd w. 159:1
wise w.!..too refined 384:32
w., a villain 105:1
w., concentred all in self 417:22
w. even then 160:27
w. that dares not die 106:35
w. undone 164:34
w. whom 't were gross flattery 548:5
w. who supports with insolence 277:30
yon w...famous for his falls 375:22
Wretched: life radically w. 277:42
most deject and w. 434:14
only w. are the wise 401:33
raise the w. 224:18
relieve the w. 224:21
set off w. matter 343:26
w. have no friends 191:18
w. he forsakes 586:29
w. in both 452:42
w. man outlive his wealth 465:9
w. man that I am 65:51
w. un-idea'd girls 270:15
Wretchedness: fierce w. 480:28
poverty, misery and w. 328:5
sum of human w. 118:30
Wretches: feel what w. feel 453:15
how shall w. live like us? 223:8
poor naked w. 453:14
Wriggles: he w. and giggles 249:24
with which tail she w. 281:19
Wring: soon w. their hands 558:30
w. from the hard hands 451:20
w. no more hearts 188:7
Wrinkle: stamps the w. deeper 113:20
time writes no w. 114:29
with the first w. 193:4
Wrinkled deep in time 424:1
Wrist: gyves upon his w. 252:26
Writ: ends stol'n forth of holy w. 476:12
having w. moves on 207:2
heard or w. so oft 80:24
I never w. 488:7
old Priest w. large 351:27
one w. with me 478:41
whose name was w. in water 291:3
w. in very choice Italian 435:17
Write: all the time I w. 177:11
as much as a man ought to w. 549:12
attain to w. threescore 184:7
born to w., converse 385:29
contrive to w. so even 22:30
desk to w. upon 110:41
does he w.?..fain would paint 93:49
enraged I w. 232:15
hand wherewith I w. 88:22

Write (*cont.*)
hope to w. well hereafter 352:2
I live and w. 244:18
in peers to w. at all 117:23
I sit down to w. 290:25
I will w. for Antiquity 307:22
I w. as others wrote 308:24
I w. one 181:21
I w. them 403:26
learn to w. well, or not to w. 193:28
let others w. for glory 157:5
little more I have to w. 246:6
look in thy heart, and w. 501:23
make me w. too much 168:10
man that w. apace 89:34
Nature..w. for him 19:19
not enough for me to w. 321:19
not w. himself down 239:12
not w. it right 248:12
out of the books I w. 97:5
rede hem as they w. 138:25
said unto me, W. 71:45
seemed good..to w. unto thee 61:10
sit down to w. 521:16
sit thee down and w. 76:9
so good as to w. to me 208:28
sometimes wish to w. 165:8
though an angel should w. 356:7
till you w. your letter 186:18
to w. and read..by nature 468:34
we cannot w. like Hazlitt 515:8
what thou seest, w. 70:24
win me to w. 123:13
with rainy eyes w. sorrow 475:6
w. a better book 201:22
w. fifty 62:19
w. for the sake of writing 290:14
w. God first 469:7
w. in place lyte 138:40
w. it before them in a table 53:37
w. me as one that loves 265:17
w. me down an ass 469:10
w. my name in the dust 403:38
w., pen! 455:1
w. that down 129:28
w. that word in the blood 158:30
w. the Graces' life 232:11
w. the vision 56:9
w. upon him my new name 70:33
w. your name upon the..sand 309:6
you w. with ease 501:2
Writer: loose, plain, rude w. 109:9
pen of a ready w. 394:21
understand a w.'s ignorance 152:25
whether the w...be a black man 2:4
w. of dictionaries 270:27
you w. of plays 92:46
Writers: as w. become more numerous 226:19
clear w., like fountains 300:21
thought them the best w. 24:42
w. against religion 102:37
Writes: but w. in dust 28:17
Moving Finger w. 207:2
one who w. amiss 382:19
w. as fast as they can read 239:12
W. her Mind but in her Post-script 511:18
Writest: what w. thou? 265:16
Writhed not at passing joy 289:8
Writhen thorn 302:7
Writhing, crawling, heaving 235:22
Writing: any style of w. untouched 273:19
art of w. 182:49
as I had in the w. 404:3
easy w.'s vile hard reading 501:2
fairy kind of w. 192:41
fairy way of w. 2:20
fine w. is next to fine doing 290:23
for your w. and reading 468:35
his w...same relation to poetry 325:9
medium for w. in prose 569:30
mere fine w. 552:18
much arguing, much w. 352:14
some for w. verses 315:12
true ease in w. 382:32
write for the sake of w. 290:14
w. an exact man 27:18
w. increaseth rage 232:15
w. on what pleased me 240:13

Writing (*cont.*)
w...a mechanic part of wit 202:3
w. their own reproach 480:39
Writing-book: lost your w. 250:3
Writings: I confess thy w. 281:10
Written: books..well w., or badly w. 570:3
book which thou hast w. 46:4
it is w. of me 394:13
leave something so w. 352:21
since this was w. 92:31
so many people have w. 275:34
that my words were now w. 49:5
things..w. in this book 72:12
what I have w. I have w. 63:71
who have w. well 382:20
w. down but by himself 276:7
w. in his hand 200:46
w. in the book of Jasher? 46:43
w. on terrestrial things 235:18
w. out of reputation 43:7
w. such volumes of stuff 311:9
w. what no tide..wash away 309:6
w. without effort 277:9
Wrong: all his life..in the w. 407:22
always in the w. 180:10, 190:22
avenger of sly-dealing w. 42:1
bade her w. stay 470:29
called them by w. names 89:40
career of high-handed w. 135:3
cradled into poetry by w. 494:17
cuts the w. man's head off 178:39
divinely in the w. 586:25
do a little w. 465:2
does, not suffers w. 496:20
doeth grievous w. 528:10
doing no w. 464:30
feel that I must be w. 569:32
fifty million..can't be w. 233:16
gang a kennin w. 104:7
govern w. 381:24
he done her w. 6:8
his can't be w. 384:1
how easily things go w. 326:20
how great a w. 586:4
I canna w. thee 104:26
if you w. us 464:8
I'll publish, right or w. 117:9
in some nice tenents..w. 158:5
in working w...pleasure..attain 233:3
labour to be w. 276:14
makes us right or w. 105:22
many words to prove it w. 278:25
nature is usually w. 566:5
never find an Englishman in the w. 490:38
nothing goes w. 222:1
not surely always in the w. 159:12
of right and w. he taught 14:26
one idea, and that..w. 182:28, 272:3
one w. more to man 93:6
oppressor's w. 434:4
our country, right or w. 169:28
own he has been in the w. 520:46
pardon, who have done the w. 191:42
persist in doing w. extenuates not w. 481:14
right deed for the w. reason 197:25
right of an excessive w. 96:3
rose the w. way 40:13
something w. with our bloody ships 37:7
sometimes in the w. 194:9
some westward, and all w. 160:16
suffer w. no more 323:10
sweeten Ireland's w. 586:14
telling a man he was w. 147:22
that all was w. 165:11
that the king can do no w. 73:8
trust not in w. and robbery 395:24
Valerius loathed the w. 324:6
we do him w. 532:39
we do it w. 430:17
where is the w. I did them? 93:28
where right is w. 218:6
W. forever on the throne 320:10
w. left unredressed 294:16
w. of unshapely things..w. too great to be told 585:17
w. part wrote Scott 11:7
w. side of a Turkey tapestry 264:19

Wrong (*cont.*)
w. side of the door 140:16
w. side of thirty 520:15
w. that needs resistance 33:8
w. with Plato 145:23
w. would triumph 97:4
years hath done this w. 168:10
your reasons will certainly be w. 329:11
you w. me every way 451:17
Wronging your image 585:17
Wrongs: forgive w. darker than death 497:17
free from rhyme's w. 281:26
mass of public w. 305:14
no sense of w. 124:9
people's w. his own 190:27
righting w...writing verses 315:12
Wrote: again I w. it 509:7
all that he w. 239:11
first Morning of Creation w. 207:6
I'm sorry, now, I w. it 100:2
I write as others w. 308:24
I w. the 'Purple Cow' 100:2
this is w. Sarcasticul 560:4
this they w. that another man w. 302:25
whatever he w., did it better 273:33
w., except for money 273:8
w. it all by rote 248:12
w. like an angel 213:12
w. my happy songs 76:9
w. that monarchs were divine 297:18
w. with all their might 248:12
w. with ease 386:16
Wroth with one we love 150:26
Wrought: being w. 474:2
first he w. 137:17
so distinctly w. 186:13
those he w. for 537:12
well made, well w. 502:17
with mine own hand w. 206:12
with one of his hands w. 48:35
w. about with divers colours 394:23
w., and thought with me 541:3
w. in a sad sincerity 199:23
w. the enthought 303:15
w. upon the plan 575:5
Wrung: England will have her neck w. 144:9
I had w. life dry 525:27
Wye: hushes half the babbling W. 532:15
Wynken, Blynken, and Nod 204:5

X

Xanadu: in X. did Kubla Khan 151:32
Xiphias: shoots x. to his aim 503:5

Y

Yammered, 'Let me in' 302:31
Yank: boldest thieves, be Y. 301:4
Yankee Doodle 33:6
Yard: man maketh ofte a y. 138:26
Yarely frame the office 424:7
Yarn: all I ask is a merry y. 334:12
of a mingled y. 423:7
Yarrh: Urrh! Y.! 300:16
Yarrow: flower of Y. 315:20
Yasmin: I toward thy bed, Y. 208:12
Yawning at the Mass 141:4
Yawp: my barbaric y. 568:2
Ydrad: ever was y. 509:19
Yea: everlasting Y. 127:17
let your y. be y. 69:43
Mr. Chapman's y. 42:24
Y., y.; Nay, nay 57:49
Yea-forsooth: rascally y. knave 441:12
Year: acceptable y. of the Lord 55:3
all..the golden y. 529:31
another y.!—another..blow! 578:4
as y. succeeds to y. 3:8
at the gate of the y. 239:4
a y., a month, a week 330:7
Baby Doll a y. ago 238:7
before the mellowing y. 342:10
bloom of the y. 97:1
bloom the y. long 81:18

Year (*cont.*)
dedicate all this y. to thee 550:7
dirge of the dying y. 496:7
each day is like a y. 569:11
ever-running y. 444:23
fill the measure of the y. 288:27
for a y. and a day 312:1
forget us till another y. 295:9
for half a y. 130:12
heav'n's eternal y. 192:38
if all the y. were..holidays 438:31
if the doctor does not give you a y. 515:5
in a y. of dearth 77:13
in one y. tamed 332:26
inverted y. 163:24
leading up the golden y. 529:29
May will be fine next y. 263:30
my most immemorial y. 381:1
newe corn froe y. to y. 138:23
new-fal'n y. 38:30
not a y. old 201:13
no winter in thy y. 97:30, 315:21
now the New Y. reviving 205:8
pilgrims of the y. 336:32
pleasure of the fleeting y. 487:27
rule the varied y. 546:24
sabbath of the y. 315:19
seven stars and the solar y. 199:2
shun a y. or two 185:24
snowe of ferne y. 138:39
sweet o' the y. 485:16
that night, that y. 254:20
this many and many a y. 82:24
this wonderful y. 213:10
'tis the y.'s midnight 186:2
to make up a y. 199:18
twentieth y. 160:21
two hundred pounds a y. 111:11
with the revolving y. 491:22
with the y. seasons return 346:20
y. after y. they voted 112:28
y. has shot her yield 298:26
y. is going 533:18
y. of the great crime 375:19
y. only lost to me? 244:9
y.'s at the spring 94:40
y. that King Uzziah died 53:8
y. wake y. to sorrow 491:26
Yearn: finite hearts that y. 97:12
Yearned: he y. to the flare 302:27
I y. for warmth 530:18
y. loud the iron-bosomed sea 411:31
Yearning: man of y. thought 411:33
this gray spirit y. 541:1
while your hearts are y. 210:4
with y. heart 525:16
y. like a God in pain 285:16
Yearnings for equal division 198:21
Years: after long y. 119:30
ah! happy y.! 113:14
all the long y. 356:10
arches of the y. 544:13
as the faithful y. return 299:24
braved, a thousand y. 123:10
bring our y. to an end 397:16
climate, or y. damp 349:6
fears of all the y. 84:25
few and evil. .y. of my life 45:25
few more y. shall roll 78:16
few y. to be young 519:34
for certain y...months and days 411:16
forty y. on 79:9
gave up the y. to be 83:19
golden y. return 493:25
grey, but not with y. 114:35
hopes of future y. 316:1
how, in earlier y. 128:12
how many y...man may live 446:1
hundreds of y...Stella's feet 502:4
hundred y. hence 177:6
in these y. 236:22
in the y. to be 295:6
into the vale of y. 471:39
it may be for y. 166:24
last but a few y. more 84:27
live in deeds, not y. 29:9
lost lady of the y. 97:18
moments big as y.! 286:7
new y. ruin and rend 525:9
none would live past y. 191:34

Years (*cont.*)
nor the y. condemn 72:23
nor the y. draw nigh 51:33
O for ten y. 288:11
of Riper Y. 390:61
our hope for y. to come 562:9
our noisy y. seem moments 576:19
out of me the y. roll 524:1
pays the failure of y. 89:20
provoke the y. 576:15
sang long y. ago 35:11
score of donkey's y. 171:21
seen sae mony changefu' y. 106:27
snow of ferne y. 138:39
so many y. of fearing death 449:34
sorrow comes with y. 88:1
tears of boyhood's y. 357:13
that vanity in y. 439:35
thousand y. of peace 533:20
thy y. shall not fail 398:2
to endless y. the same 562:9
too far in y. 474:15
to remember for y. 4:19
to sever for y. 119:29
touch of earthly y. 573:6
travel down the y. 109:1
what have these y. left 115:11
whose more y. might crave 292:20
y. and y. unto y. 184:7
y. glide away 34:1
y. hath done this wrong 168:10
y. he number'd scarce thirteen 280:10
y. in long procession 190:31
y. like great black oxen 584:8
y. of discretion 391:16
y. of noble deeds 530:14
y. steal fire from the mind 113:23
y. teach much 200:14
y. that are past 396:32
y. that bring the philosophic mind 576:20
y. that shall be 322:7
y. that the locust hath eaten 55:51
y. to come seemed waste 584:21
y. too many 563:18
Yesterday's Sev'n thousand Y. 206:5
Yeas: russet y. 455:30
Yell: Gêlert's dying y. 508:32
pursued with y. and blow 148:24
such a y. was there 418:29
Yellow: deeper y. on the corn 248:7
green and y. melancholy 483:10
her locks were y. as gold 149:13
in the y. leaf 118:26
learn from the Y. an' Brown 298:5
mealed-with-y. 255:6
one long y. string 95:5
sear, the y. leaf 460:36
square old y. Book 95:27
star called Capella was y. 236:38
y., and black, and pale 496:4
y. cheek, a white beard 441:19
y. like ripe corn 410:8
y. stockings 483:19, 21
y. waistcoat 177:16
Yellow-Dog Dingo 297:29
Yelps: loudest y. for liberty 278:26
Yeoman: did me y.'s service 437:28
Yeomen: nine-and-twenty y. tall 417:3
Yes: answer, Y.! 361:11
'Y.,' I answered you 88:9
Yesterday: all our pomp of y. 300:25
but as y. 397:15
but y. a King 118:19
but y. the word of Caesar 450:23
call back y. 475:2
cur'd y. of my disease 402:3
dead Y. 206:19
great families of y. 170:14
jam y. 130:27
no to-morrow hath, nor y. 184:6
Rose of Y. 205:18
same y., and today 69:23
stuck fast in Y. 171:12
that was y. 544:4
was it y.? 15:25
with Y.'s Sev'n thousand Years 206:5
y. doth not usher it in 186:31
Yesterdays: all our y. 461:4
Yester-morn our army 23:19
Yesteryear: snows of y. 553:3

INDEX

Yet: do not give it y. 21:20
Yew: dusk the hall with y. 17:2
  never a spray of y. 17:15
  of true wood, of y.-wood 187:12
  slips of y. 459:32
  solemnly to yonder y. 282:2
  stuck all with y. 483:6
  Y. alone burns lamps of peace 172:6
Yield: never to submit or y. 344:14
  not to y. 541:3
  oughtn't to y. to temptation 254:6
  why do I y. to that suggestion 456:24
  will not y. them for a day 533:11
  with shame and grief I y. 292:20
  year has shot her y. 298:26
  y., proud foe 122:6
  y. to it 570:7
Yielded: by her y. 347:12
  y. with coy submission 347:12
Yo-ho-ho, and a bottle of rum 514:18
Yoke: bear his mild y. 351:21
  bear the y. in his youth 55:25
  bear the y. in youth 295:6
  break every y. 54:36
  bring the inevitable y. 576:15
  my y. is easy 59:10
  Pharaoh's bitter y. 361:15
  receiv'd our y. 558:8
  sustains the y. 305:12
  take my y. upon you 59:10
  unaccustom'd to the y. 161:6
  unto a second y. 247:9
  y. of inauspicious stars 478:44
Yoked with a lamb 451:25
Yolk: y. of an addled egg 295:15
  y. runs down the waistcoat 177:16
Yonder: on y. lea 107:24
  y. is the moon 548:17
Yonghy-Bonghy-Bò 311:12
Yore: as it hath been of y. 576:1
Yorick: alas, poor Y. 437:15
York: at Y., 'tis on the Tweed 383:27
  I was born in..Y. 170:5
  noble Duke of Y. 10:19
  Regent and the Duke of Y. 504:4
  this sun of Y. 476:2
You: all too precious y. 487:20
  as y. or any thing 246:3
  even as y. and I 303:12
  for y. alone I ride 228:13
  for y. but not for me 8:19
  I, and y., and all of us 450:31
  is it y., y. dogs! 270:14
  really y. again? 91:25
  to y., to y.,..only in y. 501:20
  when or y. or I are made 246:1
  where y. alone are placed 232:11
  y. and I be lying 132:3
  y., who do not love her 96:28
Young: all joy is y. 338:10
  all that y. can do 489:24
  all the world and love were y. 405:8
  always find us y. 199:20
  amiably-disposed y. man 179:23
  any y. men...for Mary 23:7
  artist as a y. man 272:14
  as y. and fair 112:30
  as y. as what she was 298:29
  both were y. 117:6
  cheek of the y. person 178:11
  country of y. men 201:17
  crime of being a y. man 379:2
  death comes to y. men 25:4
  deep y. man 220:26
  eats the she-wolf's y. 150:9
  ever fair, and ever y. 191:2
  go west, y. man 506:22
  her six y. on the rail 92:27
  her y. ones in her nest 460:17
  hinds to bring forth y. 393:23
  I, being y. and foolish 584:11
  if ladies be but y. 427:16
  I have been y. 394:4
  I was very y. 76:17
  I was y. and foolish 584:11
  Je-ne-sais-quoi y. man 221:6
  knew the worst too y. 296:28
  look y. till forty 193:4
  love is too y. to know 488:23
  love so y. 82:3
  love's y. dream 356:25

Young (cont.)
  made y. with y. desires 544:8
  make an old man y. 529:26
  making thee y. and lusty 398:4
  more valiant-y. 440:28
  murderer so y. 328:7
  myself when y. 206:10
  not so y. as they are painted 39:7
  not so y., sir 452:23
  O y. fresshe folkes 138:42
  protective of his y. 546:11
  Scotchman, if he be *caught* y. 272:14
  seventy years y. 251:12
  she died y. 563:18
  she that was y. and fair 569:15
  so wise so y. 476:19
  so y. a body 464:32
  so y., and so untender? 452:10
  so y., so beautiful 115:35
  so y., so fair 114:24
  tall y. men..drank death like wine 141:14
  teach the y. idea 546:12
  that he once was y. 14:23
  that y. man..is not quite the thing 22:14
  those that are with y. 54:11
  to be y. was very heaven 575:2
  to grow y...then blest were he 410:34
  too y. such loss to know 118:4
  us that are y. 441:18
  very few years to be y. 519:34
  we that are y. 454:28
  we were y., we were merry 148:17
  when all the world is y., lad 293:19
  when all the world was y. 140:26
  when all was y. 293:19
  when a queen, long dead, was y. 94:19
  when earth was y. 326:24
  when I was y. 152:20
  when Music..was y. 153:31
  when thou wast y. 64:18
  where she may lay her y. 397:5
  whom the gods love die y. 116:10
  whose daughter was charming and y. 306:34
  yet—God guide them—y. 531:8
  y. and old come forth 342:3
  y. and rose-lipp'd cherubin 472:34
  y., and so fair 252:12
  y. and sweating devil 472:13
  y. are sad 504:17
  y. as beautiful 587:8
  y. enough for a boy 482:17
  y. for ever 263:18
  y. hearts..not so clever 263:18
  y. in limbs 463:41
  y. ladies are delicate plants 22:18
  y. lassie..wi' an auld man 108:26
  y. man cleanse his way 399:13
  y. Man crucified 338:4
  y. man feels his pockets 264:1
  y. man not yet 26:38
  y. man said 128:28
  y. man's fancy 534:15
  y. man's whore 271:23
  y. man, there is America 100:22
  y. man will be wiser 530:1
  y. men and maidens 400:25
  y. men are fitter to invent 27:41
  y. men glittering..Angels 548:15
  y. men's mistresses 26:37
  y. men's vision 190:18
  y. men taken in 292:16
  y. men, whom Aristotle thought 481:13
  y., y. children 88:2
Younger: let thy love be y. 483:4
  travel, in the y. sort 27:27
  y. generation will come 267:5
  y. than she..mothers 477:2
Youngest: not even the y. of us 545:17
  thy y., dearest one 491:16
  y. critic has died 303:19
  y. to the oldest singer 524:20
  y. wren of nine 484:3
Your Cleopatra 191:21
Yours: devoted y. 486:4
  I am mine and y. 94:6
  if from y. you will not part 517:16
  no good but y. 82:1
  we are y., England 241:26

Yours (cont.)
  what I have done is y. 486:4
  y. is the Earth 297:12
  y., Pickwick 179:12
  y. to hear 504:8
Yourself: do it y. 34:7
  go into it y. 74:24
  humph y.! 304:11
  keep something to y. 105:18
  keep y. to y. 179:2
  lord of y. 192:14
  no more a *sequitur* than y. 204:28
  two topics, y. and me 273:16
Youth: adventurous and honourable y. 514:38
  all the y. of England 443:12
  April of your y. 243:18
  as that y.'s eyes burned 411:11
  bang'd the y. into dumbness 483:31
  bear the yoke in y. 295:6
  beauty, strength, y. 377:4
  blest..with y. for evermore 410:34
  bounds of freakish y. 163:5
  brisk intemperance of y. 216:22
  caught our y. 84:16
  cheer thee in the days of thy y. 51:32
  corrupted the y. of the realm 445:40
  corrupting the y. of the city 379:24
  crabbed age and y. 486:2
  days of our y. 118:32
  do deeds of y. 486:32
  dropped from their y. and love 96:43
  everlasting y. 81:4
  everything..great..done by y. 181:36
  face to lose y. for 93:1
  fair and shining y. 573:15
  figure of blown y. 434:14
  flourish in immortal y. 1:24
  flourish set on y. 487:9
  for the flush of y. 409:28
  gave my heart another y. 488:5
  glory of y. 516:8
  had been friends in y. 150:25
  happiest y., viewing his progress 442:5
  heard in y. alone 497:3
  he has eyes of y. 466:5
  he wears the rose of y. 424:27
  his green unknowing y. 193:25
  his y. 'gainst time and age 377:4
  home-keeping y. 484:28
  hour of thoughtless y. 582:1
  in flow'r of y. 190:34
  in my y. 128:28
  in my y. I never did apply 426:36
  in the days of my y. 507:35
  in the vaward of our y. 441:18
  in the y. of a state 27:36
  in the y. of primy nature 431:20
  in y. it sheltered me 358:21
  I've done it from my y. 164:32
  laugh uproariously in y. 84:14
  let age approve of y. 95:26
  lexicon of y. 322:12
  loves the meat in his y. 468:22
  many a y., and many a maid 342:3
  measure of our y. 296:28
  mewing her mighty y. 352:15
  miracle of a y. 202:14
  my ill adventured y. 168:12
  my prime of y. 547:20
  my thoughtless y. was winged 192:23
  noble y...dress themselves 441:36
  nor y. nor age 462:5
  not clean past your y. 441:13
  not what our y. desires 19:6
  Nurseries of blooming y. 578:12
  offences of my y. 393:14
  6f y., and home 357:15
  our tropic y. 238:29
  perform the promises of y. 278:14
  rejoice..in thy y. 51:32
  remember..in the days of thy y. 51:33
  riband in the cap of y. 436:41
  shake their wicked sides at y. 584:26
  sign of an ill-spent y. 508:31
  spirit of y. in everything 487:28
  stretch the folly of our y. 141:23
  stroke that my y. suffer'd 470:3
  submit to be taught by y. 103:11
  takes in trust our y. 405:12
  things Y. needed not 573:15

Youth (cont.)

thoughts of y. 316:38
to y. and age in common 19:7
when y. and blood are warmer 247:10
when Y. and Pleasure meet 113:26
where y. grows pale 287:26
whose y...full of foolish noise 532:29
wine of y. 83:19
withouten other companye in y. 137:15
y., and a well-beloved y. 29:22
y. and observation copied 432:20
y. and thou..of one date 486:19
Y. are boarded, clothed 176:38
y., beauty, graceful action 190:27
y., I do adore thee 486:3
Y. is a blunder 181:37
y. is full of pleasance 486:2
y. is the season of credulity 379:4
y. is the time to.. 514:35
y. is vain 150:26
y. means love 95:33
y. of America 570:14
Y. of a Nation 182:31
y. of delight, come hither 76:6
y. of frolics 384:37
y. of labour 224:15
Y. on the prow 229:23
Y. pined away with desire 76:7
y. replies, I can 199:32
y.'s a stuff 482:28
y. shows but half 95:13
Y.'s sweet-scented Manuscript 207:24

Youth (cont.)

Y.'s the season made for joys 214:32
y. stone dead 415:13
y. to fortune..unknown 230:13
y. waneth by increasing 377:4
y., who daily farther 576:9
y., what man's age is like 172:11
y. whose hope is high 81:24
y. will be served 78:29
Youthful hose well sav'd 427:21
Youths: feeble and restless y. 146:15
y. and maidens gay 150:15
y. green and happy 146:32
Yucatan: aunt in Y. 41:34
Yukon: Law of the Y. 422:20
Yule-nicht: on blithe Y. 105:13
Yum-Yum: he's going to marry Y. 219:32
Yvetot: un roi d' Y. 43:9

Z

Zal and Rustum 205:20
Zauber: deine Z. binden wieder 415:21
Zeal: all z., Mr. Easy 331:16
ardour of my z. repress'd 143:10
half the z. I serv'd my king 447:1
his love, his z. 348:18
mistaken z. in politics 282:19
z. of God 65:61
z. of the Lord of hosts 53:16
z. of thine house 396:17

Zealots: graceless z. fight 384:1
Zealous: z., beneficent, firm 17:17
z. for his country's good 215:18
Zebra: striped like a z. 286:37
Zed': thou whoreson z. 452:33
Zeiten: ein Märchen aus alten Z. 240:25
Zèle: n'ayez pas de z. 526:18
Zelum putamus 291:22
Zembla: at Greenland, Z. 383:27
Zenith: dropt from the z. 345:12
Zenocrate: entertain divine Z. 331:3
fair Z., divine Z. 331:1
Z., lovelier 330:21
Zephyr: odes to every z. 293:12
soft the z. blows 229:23
when z. gently blows 382:32
Zephyrus: sweet breathing Z. 510:19
Zest: graciousness a warmer z. 80:27
Zeus: dear City of Z. 329:15
Ziehn: mit dir, o mein Geliebter, z.! 224:6
Zimri: had Z. peace? 48:29
Zitronen: wo die Z. blühn? 224:6
Zodiac: Mermaid in the Z. 287:2
Zodiacs: three fill'd Z. 280:10
Zollfrei: gedanken sind z. 416:1
Zone: torrid or the frozen z. 125:7
Zoo: see at the Z. 297:26
the Lord No Z. 176:4
Zoroaster: blank to Z. 94:9
the Magus Z. 496:18
Zuleika, on a desert island 39:27

GREEK INDEX

Α

Ἄγαν: μηδὲν ἄ.   12:22
Ἄδηλον παντὶ πλὴν ἢ τῷ θεῷ   506:9
Ἀδύνατα εἰκότα   14:18
Ἄειδε: μῆνιν ἄ., θεά, Πηληϊά-
δεω Ἀχιλῆος   251:30
Ἀκλήρῳ: θητευέμεν ἄλλῳ ἀν-
δρὶ παρ' ἄ.   252:7
Ἄλγε': ἦ μυρί' Ἀχαιοῖς ἄ.
ἔθηκε   251:30
Ἀλεκτρυόνα: τῷ Ἀσκληπιῷ
ὀφείλομεν ἄ.   506:10
Ἀλέξανδρος: εἰ μὴ Ἀ. ἤμην   3:13
Ἀμελήσητε: ἀλλὰ ἀπόδοτε
καὶ μὴ ἀ.   506:10
Ἀμύνεσθαι περὶ πάτρης   252:3
Ἄνδρες γὰρ πόλις   364:19
Ἀνδρῶν: τοίη δὲ καὶ ἀ.   251:32
Ἀνήριθμον: κυμάτων ἀ.
γέλασμα   3:4
Ἄνθρωπον: πάντων χρημά-
των ἄ. μέτρον εἶναι   402:18
Ἄνθρωπου: πολλὰ τὰ δεινὰ
κοὐδὲν ἀ. δεινότερον
πέλει   506:16
Ἀνώμοτος: ἡ δὲ φρὴν ἀ.   202:9
Ἀπαμειβόμενος: τὸν δ' ἀ.   251:31
Ἀπιέναι: ἀλλὰ γὰρ ἤδη ὥρα ἀ.   506:9
Ἀπίθανα: δυνατὰ ἀ.   14:18
Ἀπόδοτε: ἀλλὰ ἀ. καὶ μὴ
ἀμελήσητε   506:10
Ἀποθανουμένῳ: ἐμοὶ μὲν ἀ.   506:9
Ἀπόλοιτο: ὡς ἀ. καὶ ἄλλος . . .   252:6
Ἀρετῆς πέρι ἢ ψόγου ἐν τοῖς
ἄρσεσι κλέος   547:11
Ἀριστεύειν: αἰὲν ἀ. καὶ
ὑπείροχον   252:1
Ἄρσεσι: ἀρετῆς πέρι ἢ ψόγου
ἐν τοῖς ἄ. κλέος   547:11
Ἀσκληπιῷ: τῷ Ἀ. ὀφείλομεν
ἀλεκτρυόνα   506:10
Ἄστεα: πολλῶν δ' ἀνθρώπων
ἴδεν ἄ.   252:5
Ἀχαιοῖς: ἦ μυρί' Ἀ. ἄλγε'
ἔθηκε   251:30
Ἀχιλῆος: μῆνιν ἄειδε, θεά,
Πηληϊάδεω Ἀ.   251:30

Β

Βιβλίον: μέγα β. μέγα κακόν   120:19
Βίος: ὁ β. βραχύς, ἡ δὲ τέχνη
μακρή   248:13
Βίοτος: ᾧ μὴ β. πολὺς εἴη   252:7
Βιωσομένοις: ὑμῖν δὲ β.   506:9
Βραδέως: σπεῦδε β.   517:21
Βραχύς: ὁ βίος β., ἡ δὲ τέχνη
μακρή   248:13

Γ

Γελάσασα: δακρυόεν γ.   252:2
Γέλασμα: κυμάτων ἀν-
ήριθμον γ.   3:4
Γενεή: οἵη περ φύλλων γ.   251:32

Γῆ: ἀνδρῶν γὰρ ἐπιφανῶν
πᾶσα γ. τάφος   547:10
Γῆν: δός μοι ποῦ στῶ καὶ
κινῶ τὴν γ.   14:10
Γηράσκω δ' ἀεὶ πολλὰ διδα-
σκόμενος   506:11
Γλῶσσ': ἡ γ. ὀμώμοχ'   202:9
Γνῶθι σεαυτόν   12:23

Δ

Δαιμόνια: ἕτερα δὲ δ. καινά   379:24
Δακρυόεν γελάσασα   252:2
Δεινά: πολλὰ τὰ δ. κοὐδὲν
ἀνθρώπου δεινότερον
πέλει   506:16
Δημοκρατία ἐσχάτη τυραννίς   379:25
Διαφθείροντα: τούς τε νέους δ.   379:24
Διδασκόμενος: γηράσκω δ'
ἀεὶ πολλὰ δ.   506:11
Διογένης: εἰ μὴ Ἀλέξανδρος
ἤμην, Δ. ἂν ἤμην   3:13
Δόξα: ὑμῖν μεγάλη ἡ δ.   547:11
Δυνατὰ ἀπίθανα   14:18

Ε

Εἰκότα: ἀδύνατα εἰ.   14:18
Ἐλέου: δι' ἐ. καὶ φόβου   14:16
Ἐπάρουρος: βουλοίμην κ' ἐ.
ἐὼν θητευέμεν   252:7
Ἐπιφανῶν: ἀνδρῶν γὰρ ἐ.
πᾶσα γῆ τάφος   547:10
Ἑρμηνέων: ἐς δὲ τὸ πᾶν ἑ.
χατίζει   378:24
Εὔκολος: ὁ δ' εὔ. μὲν ἐνθάδ',
εὔ. δ' ἐκεῖ   14:13
Εὕρηκα   14:9
Εὐτελείας: φιλοκαλοῦμέν τε
γὰρ μετ' εὐ.   547:9
Εὐτυχέα: ἐπισχεῖν μηδὲ κα-
λέειν κω ὄλβιον, ἀλλ' εὐ.   506:12
Εὐτυχέστερος: ὦ παῖ, γένοιο
πατρὸς εὐ.   506:17

Ζ

Ζῷον: ἄνθρωπος φύσει πολιτικὸν
ζ.   14:14

Η

Ἡλίου: μικρὸν ἀπὸ τοῦ ἡ.
μετάστηθι   180:11
Ἥμισυ: πλέον ἢ. παντός   248:2

Θ

Θάλαττα θάλαττα   584:1
Θεός: ἢ θηρίον ἢ θ.   14:15
Θεοὺς οὓς ἡ πόλις νομίζει
οὐ νομίζοντα   379:24
Θηρίον: ἢ θ. ἢ θεός   14:15
Θητευέμεν ἄλλῳ ἀνδρὶ παρ'
ἀκλήρῳ   252:7

Ι

Ἱπποκλείδῃ: οὐ φροντὶς Ἱ.   245:15
Ἱστορίας: σπουδαιότερον
ποίησις ἱ. ἐστίν   14:17

Κ

Κάθαρσιν: τῶν τοιούτων
παθημάτων κ.   14:16
Κακόν: μέγα βιβλίον μέγα κ.   120:19
Καταφθιμένοισιν: ἢ πᾶσιν
νεκύεσσι κ. ἀνάσσειν   252:7
Κείμεθα: ἄγγειλον Λακεδαι-
μονίοις ὅτι τῇδε κ.   502:14
Κτῆμα ἐς ἀεί   547:8
Κυμάτων: ποντίων τε κ.
ἀνήριθμον γέλασμα   3:4

Λ

Λακεδαιμονίοις: ἄγγειλον Λ.
ὅτι τῇδε κείμεθα   502:14
Λόγον: μὴ φῦναι τὸν ἅπαντα
νικᾷ λ.   506:18

Μ

Μακρή: ὁ βίος βραχύς, ἡ δὲ
τέχνη μ.   248:13
Μαλακίας: φιλοσοφοῦμεν
ἄνευ μ.   547:9
Μένει: πάντα ῥεῖ, οὐδὲν μ.   242:24
Μετάστηθι: μικρὸν ἀπὸ τοῦ
ἡλίου μ.   180:11
Μέτρον: πάντων χρημάτων
ἄνθρωπον μ. εἶναι   402:18
Μηδὲν ἄγαν   12:22
Μῆνιν ἄειδε, θεά, Πηληϊάδεω
Ἀχιλῆος   251:30
Μίμησις πράξεως σπουδαίας
καὶ τελείας   14:16
Μυρίονους: ἀνὴρ μ.   152:27

Ν

Νεκύεσσι: ἢ πᾶσιν ν. καταφθιμένοισιν ἀνάσσειν   252:7
Νῆες: οὐ τείχη οὐδὲ ν. ἀνδρῶν κεναί   364:19
Νικῶντα: χαίρετε, ν.   378:14
Νομίζοντα: θεοὺς οὓς ἡ
πόλις νομίζει οὐ ν.   379:24
Νόον: πολλῶν δ' ἀνθρώπων
. . . ν. ἔγνω   252:5

Ο

Οἰωνός: εἷς οἰ. ἄριστος   252:3
Ὄλβιον: ἐπισχεῖν μηδὲ
καλέειν κω ὄ.   506:12
Ὀμώμοχ': ἡ γλῶσσ' ὄ.   202:9
Ὁπότεροι δὲ ἡμῶν ἔρχονται
ἐπὶ ἄμεινον πρᾶγμα   506:9
Ὀφείλομεν: τῷ Ἀσκληπιῷ
ὄ. ἀλεκτρυόνα   506:10

Π

Παντός: πλέον ἥμισυ π.   248:2
Πάτρης: ἀμύνεσθαι περὶ π.   252:3
Πατρός: ὦ παῖ, γένοιο π.
εὐτυχέστερος   506:17

[1002]

GREEK INDEX

Πειθόμενοι: τοῖς κείνων
ῥήμασι π.   502:14
Ποίησις: σπουδαιότερον π.
ἱστορίας ἐστίν   14:17
Πόλις: ἄνδρες γὰρ π.   364:19
Πολιτικόν: ἄνθρωπος φύσει
π. ζῷον   14:14
Πολύτροπον: ἄνδρα μοι ἔν-
νεπε, Μοῦσα, π.   252:4

Ρ

Ρεῖ: πάντα ῥ., οὐδὲν μένει   242:24
Ρήμασι: τοῖς κείνων ῥ.
πειθόμενοι   502:14

Σ

Σεαυτόν: γνῶθι σ.   12:23
Σπεῦδε βραδέως   517:21
Σπουδαιότερον ποίησις ἱστο-
ρίας ἐστίν   14:17
Στῶ: δός μοι ποῦ σ.   14:10
Συνετοῖσιν: φωνᾶντα σ.   378:24
Σωκράτη φησὶν ἀδικεῖν . .   379:24

Τ

Τάφος: ἀνδρῶν γὰρ ἐπι-
φανῶν πᾶσα γῆ τ.   547:10

Τείχη: οὐ τ. οὐδὲ νῆες ἀν-
δρῶν κεναί   364:19
Τελείας: μίμησις πράξεως
σπουδαίας καὶ τ.   14:16
Τελευτήσῃ: πρὶν δ᾽ ἂν τ.,
ἐπισχεῖν μηδὲ καλέειν
κω ὄλβιον   506:12
Τέχνη: ὁ βίος βραχύς, ἡ δὲ
τ. μακρή   248:13
Τοιαῦτά: ὡς ἀπόλοιτο καὶ
ἄλλος ὅτις τ. γε ῥέζοι   252:6
Τραγῳδία: ἔστιν οὖν τ. . . .   14:16
Τυραννίς: δημοκρατία ἐσχάτη
τ.   379:25

Υ

Ὕδωρ: ἄριστον μὲν ὕ.   378:23
Ὑπαρχούσης φύσεως μὴ
χείροσι γενέσθαι   547:11
Ὑπείροχον ἔμμεναι ἄλλων   252:1

Φ

Φιλοκαλοῦμέν τε γὰρ μετ᾽
εὐτελείας   547:9
Φιλοσοφοῦμεν ἄνευ μαλακίας 547:9

Φιλοσοφώτερον . . . ποίησις
ἱστορίας ἐστίν   14:17
Φόβου: δι᾽ ἐλέου καὶ φ.   14:16
Φρὴν: ἡ δὲ φ. ἀνώμοτος   202:9
Φροντὶς: οὐ φ. Ἱπποκλείδῃ   245:15
Φύλλων: οἵη περ φ. γενεή   251:32
Φῦναι: μὴ φ. τὸν ἅπαντα
νικᾷ λόγον   506:18
Φύσεως: ὑπαρχούσης φ. μὴ
χείροσι γενέσθαι   547:11
Φωνᾶντα συνετοῖσιν   378:24

Χ

Χαίρετε, νικῶμεν   378:14
Χείροσι: ὑπαρχούσης φύσεως
μὴ χ. γενέσθαι   547:11

Ψ

Ψόγου: ἀρετῆς πέρι ἢ ψ. ἐν
τοῖς ἄρσεσι κλέος   547:11

Ω

Ὥρα: ἀλλὰ γὰρ ἤδη ὥ.
ἀπιέναι   506:9